UNITY LIBRARY AND ARCHIVES
0 0051 0101403 2

Y0-BCD-846

The CONNECTED DISCOURSES *of the* BUDDHA

THE TEACHINGS OF THE BUDDHA

The Connected Discourses *of the* Buddha

A New Translation of the

Saṃyutta Nikāya

Translated from the Pāli

by

Bhikkhu Bodhi

WISDOM PUBLICATIONS • BOSTON

Wisdom Publications
199 Elm Street
Somerville MA 02144
USA

Library of Congress Cataloging-in-Publication Data

Tipiṭaka. Suttapiṭaka. Saṃyuttanikāya. English
The connected discourses of the Buddha : a new translation of the Saṃyutta Nikāya ; translated from the Pāli ; original translation by Bhikkhu Bodhi.
p. cm. — (Teachings of the Buddha)
Includes bibliographical references and index.
ISBN 0-86171-168-8 (alk. paper)
I. Bodhi, Bhikkhu. II. Title. III. Series.
BQ1332.B63 E5 2000
294.3'823—dc21 00-033417

ISBN for this single-volume edition: 9780861713318
ISBN for the eBook: 9780861719730

14 13
10 9 8 7

Set in DPalatino 10 on 12.4 point.

Wisdom Publications' books are printed on acid-free paper and meet the guidelines for permanence and durability of the Committee on Production Guidelines for Book Longevity of the Council on Library Resources.

Printed in the United States of America.

This book was produced with environmental mindfulness. We have elected to print this title on 20% PCW recycled paper. As a result, we have saved the following resources: 25 trees, 11 million BTUs of energy, 2171 lbs. of greenhouse gases, 11,780 gallons of water, and 788 lbs. of solid waste. For more information, please visit our website, www.wisdompubs.org. This paper is also FSC certified. For more information, please visit www.fscus.org.

Dedicated to
the memory of
my teacher

Venerable Abhidhajamahāraṭṭhaguru
Balangoda Ānanda Maitreya Mahānāyaka Thera
(1896–1998)

and to the
memories of my
chief kalyāṇamittas
in my life as
a Buddhist monk

Venerable Nyanaponika Mahāthera
(1901–1994)
and
Venerable Piyadassi Nāyaka Thera
(1914–1998)

General Contents

PART II: The Book of Causation (*Nidānavagga*)

PART III: The Book of the Aggregates (*Khandhavagga*)

Preface

The present work offers a complete translation of the *Saṃyutta Nikāya*, "The Connected Discourses of the Buddha," the third major collection in the Sutta Piṭaka, or "Basket of Discourses," belonging to the Pāli Canon. The collection is so named because the suttas in any given chapter are connected (*saṃyutta*) by the theme after which the chapter is named. The full Saṃyutta Nikāya has been translated previously and published in five volumes by the Pali Text Society under the title *The Book of Kindred Sayings*. The first two volumes were translated by Mrs. C.A.F. Rhys Davids, the last three by F.L. Woodward. This translation, first issued between 1917 and 1930, is dated both in style and technical terminology, and thus a fresh rendition of the Saṃyutta Nikāya into English has long been an urgent need for students of early Buddhism unable to read the texts in the original Pāli.

My own translation was undertaken in response to a request made to me in the early 1980s by then Bhikkhu Khantipālo (now Laurence Mills). This request was subsequently reinforced by an encouraging letter from Richard Gombrich, the present president of the Pali Text Society, who has been keenly aware of the need to replace the PTS translations of the Nikāyas by more contemporary versions. Although this appeal came in 1985, owing to prior literary commitments, most notably to the editing of Bhikkhu Ñāṇamoli's translation of the Majjhima Nikāya, I could not begin my translation of the Saṃyutta in earnest until the summer of 1989. Now, ten years later, after numerous interruptions and the daunting tasks of revision and annotation, it has at last reached completion.

As with *The Middle Length Discourses of the Buddha*, this translation aims to fulfil two ideals: first, fidelity to the intended meaning of the texts themselves; and second, the expression of that meaning in clear contemporary language that speaks to the nonspecialist reader whose primary interest in the Buddha's teaching is personal rather than professional. Of course, any ideas about "the intended meaning of the texts themselves" will inevitably reflect the subjective biases of the translator, but I have tried to minimize this danger to the best of my ability. To attempt to translate Pāli into a modern Western language rooted in a conceptual framework far removed from the "thought world" of the ancient suttas is also bound to involve some degree of distortion. The only remedy against this, perhaps, is to recommend to the reader the study of Pāli and the reading of the material in the original. Unlike English, or even Sanskrit, Pāli is a highly specialized language with only one major sphere of application—the Buddha's teachings—and thus its terminology is extremely precise, free from intrusive echoes from other domains of discourse. It is also rich in nuances, undertones, and conceptual interconnections that no translation can ever succeed in replicating.

My translation is a hybrid based on editions of the Saṃyutta Nikāya coming from different lines of textual transmission. In defense of this approach, as against translating exclusively from one tradition, I can do no better than quote Léon Feer in his introduction to Part I of his PTS edition of SN: "In the choice of readings, I made no preference, and I adopted always the reading which seemed the best wherever it might come from" (p. xiii). I used as my root text the Burmese-script Sixth Buddhist Council edition, but I compared this version with the Sinhala-script Buddha Jayanti edition (itself influenced by the Burmese one), and with the PTS's roman-script edition (which itself draws from older Sinhala and Burmese versions). It was not seldom that I preferred a reading from one of these other versions to that in the Burmese edition, as can be seen from my notes. I also consulted the footnotes on variants in the PTS edition, which occasionally, in my view, had a better reading than any in the printed editions. Though all versions have their flaws, as time went on I found myself increasingly leaning towards the older Sinhala transmission as in many respects the most reliable.

Because Pāli verse is generally much more difficult to translate than prose, at the outset I put aside the first volume of SN, the *Sagāthāvagga,* composed largely in verse, and began with the four prose volumes, II–V. I was apprehensive that, if I began with the Sagāthāvagga, I would have quickly lost heart and given up shortly after having made a start. This proved to be a prudent choice, for the Sagāthāvagga is indeed sometimes like a dense jungle, with the bare problem of interpreting knotty verses compounded by the multitude of variant readings. The disproportionately large number of notes attached to this volume, many dealing with the variant readings, should give the reader some idea of the difficulty.

Then in late 1998, towards the very end of this project, after I had already written, typed, proofed, and revised my translation of the Sagāthāvagga and its notes several times, the PTS issued a new edition of that volume, intended to replace Feer's pioneering edition of 1884. At that point I was hardly prepared to redo the entire translation, but I did compare the readings found in the new edition with those I had commented on in my notes. In some cases I made minor changes in the translation based on the readings of this edition; in others I stuck to my guns, mentioning the new variant in the relevant notes. This edition also introduced numbering of the verses, something not found in any previous edition of the Sagāthāvagga but an idea I had already implemented in my translation to facilitate cross-references in the notes and concordances. However, the new edition of the Sagāthāvagga numbered the verses differently than I did, and thus, to keep my translation consistent with the new Pāli text, I had to renumber all the verses—in the text, in the references to the verses in the notes, and in the concordances.

The Saṃyutta Nikāya is divided into five principal parts called *Vaggas,* which I render as books. These are in turn divided into a total of fifty-six *saṃyuttas,* the main chapters, which are further divided into *vaggas* or subchapters (the same Pāli word as used for the books; I differentiate them with capital and simple letters, an orthographic distinction not found in Oriental scripts). The vaggas finally are made up of suttas. In the text of the translation I number the saṃyuttas in two ways: as chapters within the Vagga I give them roman numbers, beginning with "I" within each Vagga; as saṃyuttas I number them in simple consecutive order through the whole collection, in arabic numerals, from 1 to 56. I number the suttas by giving first the absolute number of the sutta within the saṃyutta, and following this, in parenthesis, the number of the sutta within the vagga (except when the saṃyutta has no divisions into vaggas). In the introductions and notes I refer to the suttas by the number of the saṃyutta followed by the number of the sutta within that saṃyutta, ignoring the division into vaggas. Thus, for example, 22:95 is saṃyutta 22, sutta 95. The page numbers of the PTS edition are embedded in square brackets, with angle brackets used for the new edition of the Sagāthāvagga.

I have equipped this work with two types of introduction. At the very beginning, before Part I, there is a general introduction to the entire Saṃyutta Nikāya. Here I explain the overall structure of SN, its place in the Pāli Canon, and its particular function in relation to the Buddha's dispensation; I end with a discussion of some technical problems concerning the translation. Each of the five parts is then provided with its own introduction in which I give a survey of each saṃyutta in that part, focusing especially upon the doctrinal principles that underlie the major saṃyuttas. Those who find the General Introduction too dry for their taste should still not pass over the introductions to the parts, for in these I aim to provide the reader with a study guide to the material in the saṃyuttas. Similarly, a general table of contents precedes the entire work, dividing it only into Vaggas and saṃyuttas, while a more detailed table of contents, listing every vagga and sutta, precedes the individual parts.

To further assist the reader to make sense of the suttas, often terse and abstruse, a copious set of notes is provided. These too have been allocated to the back of each part. The purpose of the notes is to clarify difficult passages in the texts and to make explicit the reading I adopt in the face of competing variants. Though I imagine that for many readers the notes on the readings (especially to Part I) will bring on a spell of vertigo, from a scholarly point of view the discussions they contain are essential, as I must establish the text I am translating. The different recensions of SN often have different readings (especially in the verses), and a small difference in a reading can entail a big difference in the meaning. Hence, to justify my rendering for readers who know Pāli I had to explicate my understanding of the text's wording. At one point I had considered having two sets of notes for each part, one giving explanations of the suttas and other information of general interest, the other dealing with technical issues primarily aimed at specialists. But it proved too difficult to separate the notes so neatly into two classes, and therefore they are all grouped together. Though a substantial number of the notes will be of little interest to the general reader, I still encourage this type of reader to ferret out the notes concerned with meaning, for these provide helpful guidance to the interpretation of the texts.

Within the notes (as in the introductions) references to the suttas, verses, and other notes have been set in bold. When a sutta reference is followed by volume, page, and (sometimes) line numbers, without textual abbreviation, it should be understood that these are references to the PTS edition of SN. References to Part I are always to Ee1.

Many of the notes are drawn from the Pāli commentaries on SN, of which there are two. One is the authorized commentary, the *Saṃyutta Nikāya-aṭṭhakathā*, also known by its proper name, the *Sāratthappakāsinī* (abbr: Spk), "The Elucidator of the Essential Meaning." This is ascribed to the great Buddhist commentator, Ācariya Buddhaghosa, who came from South India to Sri Lanka in the fifth century C.E. and compiled the commentaries to the canonical texts on the basis of the ancient Sinhala commentaries (no longer extant) that had been preserved at the Mahāvihāra in Anuradhapura. The other commentarial work is the subcommentary, the *Saṃyutta Nikāya-ṭīkā*, also known as the *Sāratthappakāsinī-purāṇa-ṭīkā* (abbr: Spk-pṭ) and the *Līnatthappakāsanā* (Part III), "The Elucidation of the Implicit Meaning." This is ascribed to Ācariya Dhammapāla, who may have lived a century or two after Buddhaghosa and resided near Kāñcipura in South India. The main purpose of the *ṭīkā* is to clear up obscure or difficult points in the *aṭṭhakathā*, but in doing so the author often sheds additional light on the reading and meaning of the canonical text itself.

To keep the notes as concise as possible, the commentaries are generally paraphrased rather than directly quoted, but I use quotation marks to show where I am quoting directly. I have not given volume and page numbers to the citations from Spk and Spk-pṭ, for I did not have permanent access to the PTS edition of the former, while the latter is published only in Burmese script. The absence of page numbers, however, should not be a problem, for the commentaries comment on the suttas in direct sequence, and thus those using the PTS edition of Spk should be able to locate any comment easily enough simply by locating the relevant sutta. In the few cases where I cited Spk out of sequence, through inquiry I was able to find out the volume and page number of the PTS edition and I give the full reference in the note.

I should state, as a precaution, that the commentaries explain the suttas as they were understood sometime around the first century C.E. at the latest, at which time the old commentaries drawn upon by Buddhaghosa were closed to further additions. The commentaries view the suttas through the lens of the complex exegetical method that had evolved within the Theravāda school, built up from the interpretations of the ancient teachers welded to a framework constructed partly from the principles of the Abhidhamma system. This exegetical method does not necessarily correspond to the way the teachings were understood in the earliest period of Buddhist history, but it seems likely that its nucleus goes back to the first generation of monks who had gathered around the Buddha and were entrusted with the task of giving detailed, systematic explanations of his discourses. The fact that I cite the commentaries so often in the notes does not necessarily mean that I always agree with them, though where I interpret a passage differently I generally say so. I realize that the notes sometimes repeat things already explained in the introduction to the same part, but in a work of this nature such repetitions can be helpful, particularly as novel ideas briefly treated in the introduction may slip the reader's memory at the time of reading a sutta to which they pertain.

I conclude this preface by acknowledging the contributions that others have made to the completion of this project, for from an early time I was fortunate to have capable help and advice. My most assiduous helper from 1996 onward has been Ven. Bhikkhu Ñāṇatusita of the Netherlands, who read through the translation and the notes at two different stages, made numerous suggestions for improvement, and collected information and references that have been incorporated into the notes. He also kindly provided me with translations of several of the more important notes to the German translation of SN, particularly of Wilhelm Geiger's notes to the Sagāthāvagga. To Ven. Ñāṇatusita, too, belongs most of the credit for the concordances of parallel passages, an impressive undertaking which required an incredible amount of diligent work.

Ven. Vanarata Ānanda Thera read an early draft of the translation and made useful suggestions. Especially helpful were his comments on the verses, an area in which he has special expertise. A number of his perspicacious remarks, including some radical but convincing readings, are incorporated in the notes. Ayyā Nyānasirī read through the verse translations at an early stage and helped to improve the diction, as did Ven. Thanissaro Bhikkhu at a later stage. Ven. Brahmāli Bhikkhu and Ven. Sujāto Bhikkhu read through most of the prose volumes and made helpful comments, while Ven. Ajahn Brahmavaṃso, though unable to find the time to read the translation itself, made some valuable suggestions regarding terminology. I benefitted from occasional correspondence with K.R. Norman, Lambert Schmithausen, and Peter Skilling, who provided information and opinions on points that fell within their areas of expertise. I also learnt an enormous amount from Professor Norman's notes to his translations of the Thera- and Therīgāthās (*Elders' Verses*, I and II) and the Suttanipāta (*The Group of Discourses*, II). In the final stage, William Pruitt of the Pali Text Society reviewed the entire work, from start to finish, and offered suggestions drawn from his extensive experience as a scholar, translator, and editor. Besides this scholarly help, Tim McNeill of Wisdom Publications and Richard Gombrich of the Pali Text Society gave me constant encouragement. By imposing a strict deadline, Tim ensured that the work finally reached completion. I also thank Carl Yamamoto for his meticulous proofreading of the entire translation.

For all this help I am deeply grateful. For any faults that remain I am fully responsible.

This translation is dedicated to the memory of three eminent Sangha elders with whom I had the fortune to be closely associated during my life as a bhikkhu: my ordination teacher, Ven. Balangoda Ānanda Maitreya Mahānāyaka Thera (with whom I first studied the Sagāthāvagga back in 1973), and my chief *kalyāṇamittas* (spiritual friends), Ven. Nyanaponika Mahāthera and Ven. Piyadassi Nāyaka Thera. When I started this translation all three were alive and gave me their encouragement; unfortunately, none lived to see it completed.

Bhikkhu Bodhi
Forest Hermitage
Kandy, Sri Lanka

Key to the Pronunciation of Pāli

The Pāli Alphabet

Vowels: a, ā, i, ī, u, ū, e, o

Consonants:

Gutterals:	k, kh, g, gh, ṅ
Palatals	c, ch, j, jh, ñ
Cerebrals	ṭ, ṭh, ḍ, ḍh, ṇ
Dentals	t, th, d, dh, n
Labials	p, ph, b, bh, m
Other	y, r, ḷ, l, v, s, h, ṃ

Pronunciation

a as in "cut"
ā as in "father"
i as in "king"
ī as in "keen"
u as in "put"
ū as in "rule"
e as in "way"
o as in "home"

Of the vowels, *e* and *o* are long before a single consonant and short before a double consonant. Among the consonants, *g* is always pronounced as in "good," *c* as in "church," *ñ* as in "onion." The cerebrals (or retroflexes) are spoken with the tongue on the roof of the mouth; the dentals with the tongue on the upper teeth. The aspirates—*kh, gh, ch, jh, ṭh, ḍh, th, dh, ph, bh*—are single consonants pronounced with slightly more force than the nonaspirates, e.g., *th* as in "Thomas" (not as in "thin"); *ph* as in "puff" (not as in "phone"). Double consonants are always enunciated separately, e.g., *dd* as in "mad dog," *gg* as in "big gun." The pure nasal (*niggahīta*) *ṃ* is pronounced like the *ng* in "song." An *o* and an *e* always carry a stress; otherwise the stress falls on a long vowel—*ā, ī, ū*, or on a double consonant, or on *ṃ*.

General Introduction

The *Saṃyutta Nikāya* is the third great collection of the Buddha's discourses in the Sutta Piṭaka of the Pāli Canon, the compilation of texts authorized as the Word of the Buddha by the Theravāda school of Buddhism. Within the Sutta Piṭaka it follows the Dīgha Nikāya and Majjhima Nikāya, and precedes the Aṅguttara Nikāya. Like the other Pāli Nikāyas, the Saṃyutta Nikāya had counterparts in the canonical collections of the other early Buddhist schools, and one such version has been preserved in the Chinese Tripiṭaka, where it is known as the *Tsa-a-han-ching*. This was translated from the Sanskrit *Saṃyuktāgama*, which the evidence indicates belonged to the Sarvāstivāda school. Thus, while the Saṃyutta Nikāya translated in the present work has its locus within the Theravāda canon, it should never be forgotten that it belongs to a body of texts—called the Nikāyas in the Pāli tradition prevalent in southern Asia and the Āgamas in the Northern Buddhist tradition—which stands at the fountainhead of the entire Buddhist literary heritage. It was on the basis of these texts that the early Buddhist schools established their systems of doctrine and practice, and again it was to these texts that later schools also appealed when formulating their new visions of the Buddha's way.

As a source of Buddhist doctrine the Saṃyutta Nikāya is especially rich, for in this collection it is precisely doctrinal categories that serve as the primary basis for classifying the Buddha's discourses. The word *saṃyutta* means literally "yoked together," *yutta* (Skt *yukta*) being etymologically related to our English "yoked" and *saṃ* a prefix meaning "together." The word occurs in the suttas themselves with the doctrinally charged meaning of "fettered" or "bound." In this sense it is a past participle related to the technical term *saṃyojana,* "fetter," of which there are ten that bind living beings to *saṃsāra,* the round of rebirths. But the word *saṃyutta* is also used in a more ordinary sense to mean simply things that are joined or "yoked" together, as when it is said, "Suppose, friend, a black ox and a white ox were *yoked together* by a single harness or yoke" (**35:232**; S IV 163,12–13). This is the meaning relevant to the present collection of texts. They are suttas—discourses ascribed to the Buddha or to eminent disciples—yoked or connected together. And what connects them, the "harness or yoke" (*damena vā yottena vā*), are the topics that give their titles to the individual chapters, the *saṃyuttas* under which the suttas fall.

The Groundplan of the Saṃyutta Nikāya

Despite the immense dimensions of the work, the plan according to which it is constructed is fairly simple and straightforward. The Saṃyutta Nikāya that has come down in the Pāli tradition consists of five major *Vaggas,* parts or "books," each of which corresponds to a single volume in the Pali Text Society's roman-script edition of the work. Between them, these five volumes contain fifty-six *saṃyuttas,* chapters based on unifying themes.[1] The longer saṃyuttas are in turn divided into subchapters, also called *vaggas,* while the smaller saṃyuttas can be considered to consist of a single vagga identical with the saṃyutta itself. Each vagga, in this sense, ideally contains ten suttas, though in actuality the number of suttas in a vagga can range from as few as five to as many as sixty. Thus we find the word *vagga,* literally "a group," used to designate both the five major parts of the entire collection and the subordinate sections of the chapters.[2]

The two largest saṃyuttas, the Khandhasaṃyutta (22) and the Saḷāyatanasaṃyutta (35), are so massive that they employ still another unit of division to simplify organization. This is the *paññāsaka* or "set of fifty." This figure is only an approximation, since the sets usually contain slightly more than fifty suttas; indeed, the Fourth Fifty of the Saḷāyatanasaṃyutta contains ninety-three suttas, among them a vagga of sixty! Most of these suttas, however, are extremely short, being merely variations on a few simple themes.

Unlike the suttas of the first two Nikāyas, the Dīgha and the Majjhima, the suttas of SN do not have proper names unanimously agreed upon by all the textual traditions. In the old ola leaf manuscripts the suttas follow one another without a clean break, and the divisions between suttas have to be determined by certain symbolic markings. Each vagga ends with a short mnemonic verse called the *uddāna,* which sums up the contents of the vagga by means of key words representing its component suttas. In modern printed editions of SN these key words are taken to be the titles of the suttas and are placed at their head. As the *uddānas* often differ slightly between the Sinhalese and the Burmese textual traditions, with the PTS edition following now one and now the other, the names of the suttas also differ slightly between the several editions. Moreover, the most recent Burmese edition, that prepared at the Sixth Buddhist Council, sometimes assigns the suttas titles that are fuller and more meaningful than those derivable from the mnemonic verses. In this translation I have generally followed the Burmese edition.

The titles of the vaggas also occasionally differ between the traditions. Whereas the Burmese-script edition often names them simply by way of their numerical position—e.g., as "The First Subchapter" (*paṭhamo vaggo*), etc.—the Sinhala-script Buddha Jayanti edition assigns them proper names. When the titles of the vaggas differ in this way, I have placed the numerical name given in the Burmese-script edition first, followed parenthetically by the descriptive name given in the Sinhala-script edition. The titles of the vaggas are without special significance and do not imply that all the suttas within that vagga are related to the idea expressed by the title. Often these titles are assigned merely on the basis of one sutta within the vagga, often the first, occasionally a longer or weightier sutta coming later. The grouping of suttas into vaggas also appears largely arbitrary, though occasionally several successive suttas deal with a common theme or exemplify an extended pattern.

In his commentaries to the Pāli Canon, Ācariya Buddhaghosa states that SN contains 7,762 suttas, but the text that has come down to us contains, on the system of reckoning used here, only 2,904 suttas.[3] Due to minor differences in the method of distinguishing suttas, this figure differs slightly from the total of 2,889 counted by Léon Feer on the basis of his roman-script edition.

TABLE 1

A Breakdown of the Saṃyutta Nikāya by Vaggas and Suttas

(Feer's sutta counts in Ee differing from my own are shown to the far right.)

	Saṃyutta	Vaggas	Suttas	Feer
Part I: *Sagāthāvagga*	1	8	81	
	2	3	30	
	3	3	25	
	4	3	25	
	5	1	10	
	6	2	15	
	7	2	22	
	8	1	12	
	9	1	14	
	10	1	12	
	11	3	25	
	Total	28	271	
Part II: *Nidānavagga*	12	9	93	
	13	1	11	
	14	4	39	
	15	2	20	
	16	1	13	
	17	4	43	
	18	2	22	
	19	2	21	
	20	1	12	
	21	1	12	
	Total	27	286	
Part III: *Khandhavagga*	22	15	159	158
	23	4	46	
	24	4	96	114
	25	1	10	
	26	1	10	
	27	1	10	

	Saṃyutta	Vaggas	Suttas	Feer
Part III:	28	1	10	
Khandhavagga (cont'd)	29	1	50	
	30	1	46	
	31	1	112	
	32	1	57	
	33	1	55	
	34	1	55	
	Total	33	716	733
Part IV:	35	19	248	207
Saḷāyatanavagga	36	3	31	29
	37	3	34	
	38	1	16	
	39	1	16	
	40	1	11	
	41	1	10	
	42	1	13	
	43	2	44	
	44	1	11	
	Total	33	434	391
Part V:	45	16	180	
Mahāvagga	46	18	184	187
	47	10	104	103
	48	17	178	185
	49	5	54	
	50	10	108	110
	51	8	86	
	52	2	24	
	53	5	54	
	54	2	20	
	55	7	74	
	56	11	131	
	Total	111	1,197	1,208
	Grand Total	232	2,904	2,889

Table 1 shows how these figures are arrived at, with the divisions into Vaggas, saṃyuttas, and vaggas; the variant figures counted by Feer are given next to my own. The fact that our totals differ so markedly from that arrived at by Buddhaghosa should not cause alarm bells to ring at the thought that some 63% of the original Saṃyutta has been irretrievably lost since the time of the commentaries. For the *Sāratthappakāsinī,* the SN commentary, itself provides us with a check on the contents of the collection at our disposal, and from this it is evident that there are no suttas commented on by Buddhaghosa that are missing from the Saṃyutta we currently possess. The difference in totals must certainly stem merely from different ways of expanding the vaggas treated elliptically in the text, especially in Part V. However, even when the formulaic abridgements are expanded to the full, it is difficult to see how the commentator could arrive at so large a figure.

The five major Vaggas or "books" of the Saṃyutta Nikāya are constructed according to different principles. The first book, the Sagāthāvagga, is unique in being compiled on the basis of literary genre. As the name of the Vagga indicates, the suttas in this collection all contain *gāthās* or verses, though it is not the case (as Feer had assumed at an early point) that all suttas in SN containing verses are included in this Vagga. In many suttas of Part I, the prose setting is reduced to a mere framework for the verses, and in the first saṃyutta even this disappears so that the sutta becomes simply an exchange of verses, presumably between the Buddha and an interlocutor. The other four Vaggas contain major saṃyuttas concerned with the main doctrinal themes of early Buddhism, accompanied by minor saṃyuttas spanning a wide diversity of topics. Parts II, III, and IV each open with a large chapter devoted to a theme of paramount importance: respectively, the chain of causation (i.e., dependent origination, in SN 12), the five aggregates (22), and the six internal and external sense bases (35). Each of these Vaggas is named after its opening saṃyutta and also includes one other saṃyutta dealing with another important topic secondary to the main one: in Part II, the elements (14); in Part III, philosophical views (24); and in Part IV, feeling (36). The other saṃyuttas in each of these collections are generally smaller and thematically lighter, though within these we can also find texts of great depth and power.

Part V tackles themes that are all of prime importance, namely, the various groups of training factors which, in the post-canonical period, come to be called the thirty-seven aids to enlightenment (*sattatiṃsa bodhipakkhiyā dhammā*). The Vagga concludes with a saṃyutta on the original intuition around which the entire Dhamma revolves, the Four Noble Truths. Hence this book is called the Mahāvagga, the Great Book, though at one point it might have also been called the Maggavagga, the Book of the Path (and indeed the Sanskrit version translated into Chinese was so named).

The organization of SN, from Parts II to V, might be seen as corresponding roughly to the pattern established by the Four Noble Truths. The Nidānavagga, which focuses on dependent origination, lays bare the causal genesis of suffering, and is thus an amplification of the second noble truth. The Khandhavagga and the Saḷāyatanavagga highlight the first noble truth, the truth of suffering; for in the deepest sense this truth encompasses all the elements of existence comprised by the five aggregates and the six internal and external sense bases (see **56:13**, **14**). The Asaṅkhatasaṃyutta (43), coming towards the end of the Saḷāyatanavagga, discusses the unconditioned, a term for the third noble truth, Nibbāna, the cessation of suffering. Finally, the Mahāvagga, dealing with the path of practice, makes known the way to the cessation of suffering, hence the fourth noble truth. If we follow the Chinese translation of the Skt Saṃyuktāgama, the parallelism is still more obvious, for this version places the Khandhavagga first and the Saḷāyatanavagga second, followed by the Nidānavagga, thus paralleling the first and second truths in their proper sequence. But this version assigns the Asaṅkhatasaṃyutta to the end of the Mahāvagga, perhaps to show the realization of the unconditioned as the fruit of fulfilling the practice.

I said above that what makes the suttas of this collection "connected discourses" are the themes that unite them into fixed saṃyuttas. These, which we might consider the "yokes" or binding principles, constitute the groundplan of the collection, which would preserve its identity even if the saṃyuttas had been differently arranged. There are fifty-six such themes, which I have distinguished into four main categories: doctrinal topics, specific persons, classes of beings, and types of persons. Of the two saṃyuttas that do not fall neatly into this typology, the Vanasaṃyutta (9) is constructed according to a fixed scenario, generally a monk being admonished by a woodland deity to strive more strenuously for the goal; the Opammasaṃyutta (20) is characterized by the use of an extended simile to convey its message.

In Table 2 (A) I show how the different saṃyuttas can be assigned to these categories, giving the total numbers of suttas in each class and the percentage which that class occupies in the whole. The results of this tabulation should be qualified by noting that the figures given are based on a calculation for the whole Saṃyutta Nikāya. But the Sagāthāvagga is so different in character from the other Vaggas that its eleven saṃyuttas skew the final results, and thus to arrive at a more satisfactory picture of the overall nature of the work we might omit this Vagga. In Table 2 (B) I give the results when the Sagāthāvagga is not counted. Even these figures, however, can convey a misleading picture, for the classification is made by way of titles only, and these provide a very inadequate indication of the contents of the actual saṃyutta. The Rāhulasaṃyutta and the Rādhasaṃyutta, for example, are classified under "Specific Person," but they deal almost exclusively with the three characteristics and the five aggregates, respectively, and give us absolutely no personal information about these individuals; thus their content is properly doctrinal rather than biographical. Moreover, of the eleven chapters named after specific persons, nine are almost entirely doctrinal. Only saṃyuttas 16 and 41, respectively on Mahākassapa and Citta the householder, include material that might be considered of biographical interest. Since the chapters on the main doctrinal topics are invariably much longer than the other chapters, the number of *pages* dealing with doctrine would be immensely greater than those dealing with other themes.

The Saṃyutta Nikāya and the Saṃyuktāgama

The Pāli commentaries, and even the canonical Cullavagga, give an account of the First Buddhist Council which conveys the impression that the participating elders arranged the Sutta Piṭaka into essentially the form in which it has come down to us today, even with respect to the precise sequence of texts. This is extremely improbable, and it is also unlikely that the council

TABLE 2

Thematic Analysis of the Saṃyutta Nikāya

A. Including the Sagāthāvagga

Topics	Saṃyuttas	Total	Percentage
Doctrinal Topic	12 13 14 15 17 22 24 25 26 27 34 35 36 43 44 45 46 47 48 49 50 51 53 54 55 56	26	46%
Specific Person	3 4 8 11 16 18 19 23 28 33 38 39 40 41 52	15	27%
Class of Beings	1 2 6 10 29 30 31 32	8	14%
Type of Person	5 7 21 37 42	5	9%
Other	9 20	2	4%

B. Excluding the Sagāthāvagga

Topics	Saṃyuttas	Total	Percentage
Doctrinal Topic	12 13 14 15 17 22 24 25 26 27 34 35 36 43 44 45 46 47 48 49 50 51 53 54 55 56	26	58%
Specific Person	16 18 19 23 28 33 38 39 40 41 52	11	24%
Class of Beings	29 30 31 32	4	9%
Type of Person	21 37 42	3	7%
Other	20	1	2%

established a fixed and final recension of the Nikāyas. The evidence to the contrary is just too massive. This evidence includes the presence in the canon of suttas that could only have appeared after the First Council (e.g., MN Nos. 84, 108, 124); signs of extensive editing internal to the suttas themselves; and, a weighty factor, the differences in content and organization between the Pāli Nikāyas and the North Indian Āgamas preserved in the Chinese Tripiṭaka. It is much more likely that what took place at the First Council was the drafting of a comprehensive scheme for classifying the suttas (preserved only in the memory banks of the monks) and the appointment of an editorial committee (perhaps several) to review the material available and cast it into a format conducive to easy memorization and oral transmission. Possibly too the editorial committee, in compiling an authorized corpus of texts, would have closely considered the purposes their collections were intended to serve and then framed their guidelines for classification in ways designed to fulfil these purposes. This is a point I will return to below. The distribution of the texts among groups of reciters (*bhāṇakas*), charged with the task of preserving and transmitting them to posterity, would help to explain the divergences between the different recensions as well as the occurrence of the same suttas in different Nikāyas.[4]

Comparison of the Pāli SN with the Chinese Saṃyuktāgama is particularly instructive and reveals a remarkable correspondence of contents arranged in a different order. I already alluded just above to some differences in organization, but it is illuminating to examine this in more detail.[5] The Chinese version contains nine major Vaggas (following Anesaki, I use the Pāli terms and titles for consistency). The first is the Khandhavagga (our III), the second the Saḷāyatanavagga (our IV), the third the Nidānavagga (our II), which latter also contains the Saccasaṃyutta (56) and the Vedanāsaṃyutta (36), departing markedly from SN in these allocations. Then follows a fourth part named Sāvakavagga, without a counterpart in the Pāli version but which includes among others the Sāriputta- (28), Moggallāna- (40), Lakkhaṇa- (19), Anuruddha- (52), and Cittasaṃyuttas (41). The fifth part, whose Pāli title would be Maggavagga, corresponds to SN Mahāvagga (our V), but its saṃyuttas are arranged in a sequence that follows more closely the canonical order of the sets making up the thirty-seven aids to enlightenment: Satipaṭṭhāna (47), Indriya (48), Bala (50), Bojjhaṅga (46), and Magga (45); this part also includes the Ānāpānasati- (54) and Sotāpattisaṃyuttas (55), while a series of small chapters at the end includes a Jhānasaṃyutta (53) and an Asaṅkhatasaṃyutta (43). The sixth Vagga of the Saṃyuktāgama is without a Pāli parallel but contains the Opammasaṃyutta (20) and a collection of suttas on sick persons which draws together texts distributed among various chapters of SN. Then, as the seventh book, comes the Sagāthāvagga (our I), with twelve saṃyuttas—all eleven of the Pāli version but in a different order and with the addition of the Bhikkhusaṃyutta (21), which in this recension must contain only suttas with verses. Finally comes a Buddha- or Tathāgatavagga, which includes the Kassapa- (16) and Gāmanisaṃyuttas (42), and an Assasaṃyutta, "Connected Discourses on Horses." This last chapter includes suttas that in the Pāli Canon are found in the Aṅguttara Nikāya.

The Role of the Saṃyutta among the Four Nikāyas

Prevalent scholarly opinion, fostered by the texts themselves, holds that the principal basis for distinguishing the four Nikāyas is the length of their suttas. Thus the largest suttas are collected into the Dīgha Nikāya, the middle length suttas into the Majjhima Nikāya, and the shorter suttas are distributed between the Saṃyutta and the Aṅguttara Nikāyas, the former classifying its suttas thematically, the latter by way of the number of items in terms of which the exposition is framed. However, in an important groundbreaking study, Pāli scholar Joy Manné has challenged the assumption that length alone explains the differences between the Nikāyas.[6] By carefully comparing the suttas of DN with those of MN, Manné concludes that the two collections are intended to serve two different purposes within the Buddha's dispensation. In her view, DN was primarily intended for the purpose of propaganda, to attract converts to the new religion, and thus is aimed mainly at non-Buddhists favourably disposed to Buddhism; MN, in contrast, was directed inwards towards the Buddhist community and its purpose was to extol the Master (both as a real person and as an archetype) and to integrate monks into the community and the practice. Manné also proposes that "each of the first four Nikāyas came about in order to serve a distinct need and purpose in the growing and developing Buddhist community" (p. 73). Here we shall briefly address the question what purposes may have been behind the compilation of SN and AN, in contradistinction to the other two Nikāyas.

In approaching this question we might first note that the suttas of these two Nikāyas provide only minimal circumstantial background to the delivery of the Buddha's discourses. With rare exceptions, in fact, a background story is completely absent and the *nidāna* or "setting" simply states that the sutta was spoken by the Blessed One at such and such a locale. Thus, while DN and MN are replete with drama, debate, and narrative, with DN especially abounding in imaginative excursions, here this decorative framework is missing. In SN the whole setting becomes reduced to a single sentence, usually abbreviated to "At Sāvatthī, in Jeta's Grove," and by the fourth book even this disappears. Apart from the Sagāthāvagga, which is in a class of its own, the other four books of SN have little ornamentation. The suttas themselves are usually issued as direct proclamations on the doctrine by the Buddha himself; sometimes they take the form of consultations with the Master by a single monk or group of monks; occasionally they are framed as discussions between two eminent monks. Many suttas consist of little more than a few short sentences, and it is not unusual for them simply to ring the permutations on a single theme. When we reach Part V whole chains of suttas are reduced to mere single words in mnemonic verses, leaving to the reciter (or to the modern reader) the task of blowing up the outline and filling in the contents. This indicates that the suttas in SN (as also in AN) were, as a general rule, not targetted at outsiders or even at the newly converted, but were intended principally for those who had already turned for refuge to the Dhamma and were deeply immersed in its study and practice.

On the basis of its thematic arrangement, we might postulate that, in its most distinctive features as a collection (though certainly not in all particulars), SN was compiled to serve as the repository for the many short but pithy suttas disclosing the Buddha's radical insights into the nature of reality and his unique path to spiritual emancipation. This collection would have served the needs of two types of disciples within the monastic order. One were the doctrinal specialists, those monks and nuns who were capable of grasping the deepest dimensions of wisdom and took upon themselves the task of clarifying for others the subtle perspectives on reality opened up by the Buddha's teachings. Because SN brings together in its major saṃyuttas the many abstruse, profound, and delicately nuanced suttas on such weighty topics as dependent origination, the five aggregates, the six sense bases, the factors of the path, and the Four Noble Truths, it would have been perfectly suited for those disciples of intellectual bent who delighted in exploring the deep implications of the Dhamma and in explaining them to their spiritual companions. The second type of disciples for whom SN seems to have been designed were those monks and nuns who had already fulfilled the preliminary stages of meditative training and were intent on consummating their efforts with the direct realization of the ultimate truth. Because the suttas in this collection are vitally relevant to meditators bent on arriving at the undeceptive "knowledge of things as they really are," they could well have formed the main part of a study syllabus compiled for the guidance of insight meditators.

With the move from SN to AN, a shift in emphasis takes place from comprehension to personal edification. Because the shorter suttas that articulate the philosophical theory and the main structures of training have found their way into SN, what have been left for inclusion in AN are the short suttas whose primary concern is practical. To some extent, in its practical orientation, AN partly overlaps with SN Mahāvagga, which treats the various groups of path factors. To avoid unnecessary duplication the redactors of the canon did not include these topics again in AN under their numerical categories, thereby leaving AN free to focus on those aspects of the training not incorporated in the repetitive sets. AN also includes a notable proportion of suttas addressed to lay disciples, dealing with the mundane, ethical, and spiritual concerns of life within the world. This makes it especially suitable as a text for the edification of the laity.

From this way of characterizing the two Nikayas, we might see SN and AN as offering two complementary perspectives on the Dhamma, both inherent in the original teaching. SN opens up to us the profound perspective reached through contemplative insight, where the familiar consensual world of persons and things gives way to the sphere of impersonal conditioned phenomena arising and perishing in accordance with laws of conditionality. This is the perspective on reality that, in the next stage in the evolution of Buddhist thought, will culminate in the Abhidhamma. Indeed, the connection between SN and the

Abhidhamma appears to be a close one, and we might even speculate that it was the nonsubstantialist perspective so prominent in SN that directly gave rise to the type of inquiry that crystallized in the Abhidhamma philosophy. The close relationship between the two is especially evident from the second book of the Pāli Abhidhamma Piṭaka, the *Vibhaṅga,* which consists of eighteen treatises each devoted to the analysis of a particular doctrinal topic. Of these eighteen, the first twelve have their counterparts in SN.[7] Since most of these treatises include a "Suttanta Analysis" (*suttantabhājaniya*) as well as a more technical "Abhidhamma Analysis" (*abhidhammabhājaniya*), it is conceivable that the Suttanta Analyses of the *Vibhaṅga* were the primordial seeds of the Abhidhamma and that it was among the specialists in SN that the idea arose of devising a more technical expository system which eventually came to be called the Abhidhamma.

The Aṅguttara Nikāya serves to balance the abstract philosophical point of view so prominent in SN with an acceptance of the conventional world of consensual realities. In AN, persons are as a rule not reduced to mere collections of aggregates, elements, and sense bases, but are treated as real centres of living experience engaged in a heartfelt quest for happiness and freedom from suffering. The suttas of this collection typically address these needs, many dealing with the practical training of monks and a significant number with the everyday concerns of lay followers. The numerical arrangement makes it particularly convenient for use in formal instruction, and thus it could be easily drawn upon by senior monks when teaching their pupils and by preachers when preparing sermons for the lay community. AN is replete with material that serves both purposes, and even today within the living Theravāda tradition it continues to fulfil this dual function.

The preceding attempt to characterize each Nikāya in terms of a ruling purpose should not be understood to imply that their internal contents are in any way uniform. To the contrary, amidst a welter of repetition and redundancy, each displays enormous diversity, somewhat like organisms of the same genera that exhibit minute specific differences absolutely essential to their survival. Further, it remains an open question, particularly in the case of SN and AN, whether their blueprints were drawn up with a deliberate pedagogical strategy in mind or whether, instead, the method of arrangement came first and their respective tactical applications followed as a matter of course from their groundplans.

Relationship with Other Parts of the Canon

Due partly to the composition of the suttas out of blocks of standardized, transposable text called pericopes, and partly to common points of focus throughout the Sutta Piṭaka, a considerable amount of overlapping can be discovered between the contents of the four Nikāyas. In the case of SN, parallels extend not only to the other three Nikāyas but to the Vinaya Piṭaka as well. Thus we find three SN suttas of great importance also recorded in the Vinaya Mahāvagga, represented as the first three discourses given by the Buddha at the dawn of his ministry: the Dhammacakkappavattana, the Anattalakkhaṇa, and the Ādittapariyāya (**56:11**; **22:59**; **35:28**).[8] In the Vinaya, too, there are parallels to the SN suttas on the Buddha's encounters with Māra (**4:4**, **5**), on his hesitation to teach the Dhamma (**6:1**), on his first meeting with Anāthapiṇḍika (**10:8**), on the secession of Devadatta (**17:35**), and on the tormented spirits seen by Mahāmoggallāna (**19:1–21**). While it is possible that both the Vinaya and SN received this material via separate lines of oral transmission, in view of the fact that the narrative portions of the Vinaya Piṭaka appear to stem from a later period than the Nikāyas, we might conjecture that the redactors of the Vinaya drew freely upon texts preserved by the Saṃyutta reciters when composing the frameworks for the disciplinary injunctions.

SN includes as individual suttas material which, in DN, is embedded in larger suttas. The most notable instances of this are segments of the Mahāparinibbāna Sutta (e.g., at **6:15**; **47:9**; **47:12**; **51:10**), but we find as well a few snippets shared by the Mahāsatipaṭṭhāna Sutta (**47:1**, **2**; **45:8**) and a short (*cūḷa*) version of the Mahānidāna Sutta (**12:60**). The latter shares with its larger counterpart (DN No. 15) only the opening paragraph but thereafter diverges in a completely different direction. Again, any solution to the question of borrowing can only be hypothetical.

The compilers of the canon seem to have laid down stringent rules governing the allocation of texts between SN and AN, intended to avoid extensive reduplication when a doctrinal theme is also a numerical set. Still, within the bounds set by that condition, a certain amount of overlapping has taken place between the two Nikāyas. They hold in common the suttas on Rohitassa's search for the end of the world (**2:26**), on the lion's roar (**22:78**), on the ten qualities of the stream-enterer (**12:41** = **55:28**), on the death of Kokālika (**6:9–10**), on the five hindrances (**46:55**, but in AN without the section on the enlightenment factors), as well as several large blocks of text that in SN do not constitute separate suttas.

It is, however, between SN and MN that the boundary appears to have been the most permeable, for SN contains five whole suttas also found in MN (**22:82**; **35:87**, **88**, **121**; **36:19**), as well as the usual common text blocks. We cannot know whether this dual allocation of the suttas was made with the general consent of the redactors responsible for the whole Sutta Piṭaka or came about because the separate companies of reciters responsible for the two Nikāyas each thought these suttas fitted best into their own collections. But in view of the fact that in SN several suttas appear in two saṃyuttas, thus even in the same Nikāya, the first alternative is not implausible. Suttas from SN have also found their way into the smaller works of the Khuddaka Nikāya—the Suttanipāta, the Udāna, and the Itivuttaka—while the correspondence between verses is legion, as can be seen from Concordance 1 (B).

Literary Features of the Saṃyutta

Of the four Nikāyas, SN seems to be the one most heavily subjected to "literary embellishment." While it is possible that some of the variations stemmed from the Buddha himself, it also seems plausible that many of the more minute elaborations were introduced by the redactors of the canon. I wish to call attention to two distinctive features of the collection which bear testimony to this hypothesis. We might conveniently call them "template parallelism" and "auditor-setting variation." The texts that exhibit these features are collated in Concordances 3 and 4 respectively. Here I will explain the principles that lie behind these editorial devices and cite a few notable examples of each.

Template parallels are suttas constructed in accordance with the same formal pattern but which differ in the content to which this pattern is applied. The template is the formal pattern or mould; the template sutta, a text created by applying this mould to a particular subject, the "raw material" to be moulded into a sutta. Template parallels cut across the division between saṃyuttas and show how the same formula can be used to make identical statements about different categories of phenomena, for example, about the elements, aggregates, and sense bases (*dhātu, khandha, āyatana*), or about path factors, enlightenment factors, and spiritual faculties (*maggaṅga, bojjhaṅga, indriya*). The recurrence of template parallels throughout SN gives us an important insight into the structure of the Buddha's teaching. It shows that the teaching is constituted by two intersecting components: a formal component expressed by the templates themselves, and a material component provided by the entities that are organized by the templates. The application of the templates to the material components instructs us how the latter are to be treated. Thus we are made to see, from the template suttas, that the constituent factors of existence are to be understood with wisdom; that the defilements are to be abandoned; and that the path factors are to be developed.

The templates are in turn sometimes subsumed at a higher level by what we might call a paradigm, that is, a particular perspective offering us a panoramic overview of the teaching as a whole. Paradigms generate templates, and templates generate suttas. Thus all one need do to compose different suttas is to subject various types of material to the same templates generated by a single paradigm.

SN abounds in examples of this. One prevalent paradigm in the collection, central to the Dhamma, is the three characteristics of existence: impermanence (*anicca*), suffering (*dukkha*), and nonself (*anattā*). This paradigm governs whole series of suttas both in SN 22 and SN 35, the royal saṃyuttas of Parts III and IV, respectively; for it is above all the five aggregates and the six pairs of sense bases that must be seen with insight in order to win the fruits of liberation. The "three characteristics paradigm" generates four common templates: impermanent, etc., in the three times; the simple contemplation of impermanence, etc.; impermanent, etc., through causes and conditions; and, most critical in the Buddha's soteriological plan, the "what is impermanent is suffering" template, which sets the three characteristics in relation to one another.

Another major paradigm is the triad of gratification, danger, and escape (*assāda, ādīnava, nissaraṇa*), which generates three templates. At AN I 258–60 we find these templates used to generate three suttas in which the material content is the world as a whole (*loka*). SN, apparently drawing upon certain ways of understanding the concept of the world, contains twelve suttas churned out by these templates—three each in the saṃyuttas on the elements and the aggregates (**14:31–33**; **22:26–28**), and six in the saṃyutta on the sense bases (**35:13–18**; six because the internal and external sense bases are treated separately). This paradigm is in turn connected to another, on the qualities of true ascetics and brahmins, and together they give birth to three more recurrent templates on how true ascetics and brahmins understand things: by way of the gratification triad; by way of the origin pentad (the gratification triad augmented by the origin and passing away of things); and by way of the noble-truth tetrad (modelled on the Four Noble Truths: suffering, its origin, its cessation, and the way to its cessation). These templates generate suttas on the four elements, gain and honour, the five aggregates, feelings, and the faculties. The last template is also applied several times to the factors of dependent origination, but strangely they are all missing in the Saḷāyatanasaṃyutta.

The main cause of suffering, according to the Buddha, is craving (*taṇhā*), also known as desire and lust (*chanda-rāga*). In SN the task of removing craving serves as a paradigm which generates another set of templates, arrived at by splitting and then recombining the terms of the compound: abandon desire, abandon lust, abandon desire and lust. These are each connected separately to whatever is impermanent, whatever is suffering, and whatever is nonself (intersecting with the three characteristics paradigm), thereby giving rise to nine templates. These are then extended to the aggregates and to the internal and external sense bases, generating respectively nine and eighteen suttas (**22:137–45**; **35:168–85**).

Some templates must have emerged from the conversations into which the monks were drawn in their everyday lives, such as the one based on the question why the holy life is lived under the Blessed One (**35:81, 152**; **38:4**; **45:5, 41–48**). Part V, on the groups pertaining to the path, employs still new templates, though without a single dominant paradigm. Many of the templates occur in the repetition series, which are elaborated in full only in the Maggasaṃyutta and thereafter abbreviated in mnemonic verses. But more substantive templates generate suttas in the bodies of these saṃyuttas, which will be discussed at greater length in the introduction to Part V.

If we closely inspect the concordance of template parallels, we would notice that certain templates are not employed to generate suttas in domains where they seem perfectly applicable. Thus, as noted above, we do not find the "ascetics and brahmins" templates applied to the six sense bases, or the "noble and emancipating" template applied to the five spiritual faculties, or the "seven fruits and benefits" template applied to the four establishments of mindfulness. This raises the intriguing question whether these omissions were made by deliberate design, or because the applications were overlooked, or because suttas got lost in the process of oral transmission. To arrive at cogent hypotheses concerning this question we would have to compare the Pāli recension of SN with the Chinese translation of the Saṃyuktāgama, which would no doubt be a major undertaking requiring a rare combination of skills.

The second distinctive editorial technique of SN is what I call "auditor-setting variation." This refers to suttas that are identical (or nearly identical) in content but differ in regard to the person to whom they are addressed, or in the protagonist involved (in a sutta involving a "plot"), or in the circumstances under which they are spoken. The most notable example of this device is the sutta on how a bhikkhu attains or fails to attain Nibbāna, which occurs seven times (at **35:118**, **119**, **124**, **125**, **126**, **128**, **131**), in exactly the same words, but addressed to different auditors, including the deva-king Sakka and the gandhabba Pañcasikha. As the Buddha must have reiterated many suttas to different inquirers, the question arises why this one was selected for such special treatment. Could it have been a way of driving home, to the monks, what they must do to win the goal of the holy life? Or were there more mundane motives behind the redundancy, such as a desire to placate the families of important lay supporters?

Under this category fall several instances where a sutta is

spoken by the Buddha a first time in response to a question from Ānanda, a second time to Ānanda on his own initiative, a third time in response to a question from a group of bhikkhus, and a fourth time to a group of bhikkhus on his own initiative (e.g., **36:15–18**; **54:13–16**). Again, the Rādhasaṃyutta includes two vaggas of twelve suttas each identical in all respects except that in the first (**23:23–34**) Rādha asks for a teaching while in the second (**23:35–46**) the Buddha takes the initiative in speaking.

A third literary embellishment, not quite identical with auditor-setting variation, is the inclusion of chains of suttas that ring the permutations on a simple idea by using different phrasing. Thus the Diṭṭhisaṃyutta (24) contains four "trips" (*gamana*) on speculative views differing only in the framework within which the exposition of views is encased (partial exception being made of the first trip, which for some unclear reason lacks a series of views included in the other three). In the Vacchagottasaṃyutta (33), the wanderer so named approaches the Buddha five times with the same question, about the reason why the ten speculative views arise in the world, and each time the answer is given as not knowing one of the five aggregates; each question and answer makes a separate sutta. Not content with this much, the compilers of the canon seem to have felt obliged to make it clear that each answer could have been formulated using a different synonym for lack of knowledge. Thus the saṃyutta is built up out of ten variants on the first pentad, identical in all respects except for the change of synonyms. The Jhānasaṃyutta (34) exhibits still another literary flourish, the "wheel" (*cakka*) of permutations, whereby a chain of terms is taken in pairwise combinations, exhausting all possibilities.

Technical Notes

Here I will discuss a few technical matters pertaining to the translation, emphasizing particularly why my renderings here sometimes differ from those used in MLDB. For the sake of precision, I usually refer to SN by volume, page, and line numbers of Ee (Ee1 in references to Part I), and use the saṃyutta and sutta numbers only when the whole sutta is relevant.[9]

THE REPETITIONS

Readers of the Pāli suttas are invariably irked, and sometimes dismayed, by the ponderous repetitiveness of the texts. In SN these are more blatant than in the other Nikāyas, even to the extent that in whole vaggas the suttas might differ from one another only in regard to a single word or phrase. Besides this type of reiterative pattern, we also come across the liberal use of stock definitions, stereotyped formulas, and pericopes typical of the Nikāyas as a whole, stemming from the period when they were transmitted orally. It is difficult to tell how much of the repetition stems from the Buddha himself, who as an itinerant teacher must have often repeated whole discourses with only slight variations, and how much is due to zealous redactors eager to ring every conceivable change on a single idea and preserve it for posterity. It is hard, however, not to suspect that the latter have had a heavy hand in the redaction of the texts.

To avoid excessive repetitiveness in the translation I have had to make ample use of elisions. In this respect I follow the printed editions of the Pāli texts, which are also highly abridged, but a translation intended for a contemporary reader requires still more compression if it is not to risk earning the reader's wrath. On the other hand, I have been keen to see that nothing essential to the original text, including the flavour, has been lost due to the abridgement. The ideals of considerateness to the reader and fidelity to the text sometimes make contrary demands on a translator.

The treatment of repetition patterns in which the same utterance is made regarding a set of items is a perpetual problem in translating Pāli suttas. When translating a sutta about the five aggregates, for example, one is tempted to forgo the enumeration of the individual aggregates and instead turn the sutta into a general statement about the aggregates as a class. To my mind, such a method veers away from proper translation towards paraphrase and thus risks losing too much of the original text. My general policy has been to translate the full utterance in relation to the first and last members of the set, and merely to enumerate the intermediate members separated by ellipsis points. Thus, in a sutta about the five aggregates, I render the statement in full only for form and consciousness, and in between have "feeling

... perception ... volitional formations ...," implying thereby that the full statement likewise applies to them. With the bigger sets I often omit the intermediate terms, rendering the statement only for the first and last members.

This approach has required the frequent use of ellipsis points, a practice which also invites criticism. Several consulting readers thought I might improve the aesthetic appearance of the page (especially in Part IV) by rephrasing repetitive passages in a way that would eliminate the need for ellipsis points. I accepted this suggestion in regard to repetitions in the narrative framework, but in texts of straight doctrinal exposition I adhered to my original practice. The reason is that I think it an important responsibility of the translator, when translating passages of doctrinal significance, to show exactly where text is being elided, and for this ellipsis points remain the best tool at hand.

Dhamma

Rather than embark on the quest for a single English rendering that can capture all the meanings of this polyvalent Pāli word, I have settled for the more pragmatic approach of using different renderings intended to match its different applications.[10] When the word denotes the Buddha's teaching, I have retained the Pāli "Dhamma," for even "teaching" fails to convey the idea that what the Buddha teaches as the Dhamma is not a system of thought original to himself but the fundamental principles of truth, virtue, and liberation discovered and taught by all Buddhas throughout beginningless time. This is the Dhamma venerated by the Buddhas of the past, present, and future, which they look upon as their own standard and guide (see **6:2**). From an internal "emic" point of view, the Dhamma is thus more than a particular religious teaching that has appeared at a particular epoch of human history. It is the timeless law in which reality, truth, and righteousness are merged in a seamless unity, and also the conceptual expression of this law in a body of spiritual and ethical teachings leading to the highest goal, Nibbāna, which is likewise comprised by the Dhamma. The word "Dhamma," however, can also signify teachings that deviate from the truth, including the erroneous doctrines of the "outside" teachers. Thus the Jain teacher Nigaṇṭha Nātaputta is said to "teach the Dhamma to his disciples" (IV 317,25)—certainly not the Buddha's teaching.

In one passage I render Dhamma as "righteousness" (at the Se counterpart of IV 303,21). This is in the epithet *dhammarājā* used for a universal monarch, where "king of righteousness" fits better than "king of the Dhamma," the significance the epithet has relative to the Buddha. The corresponding adjective, *dhammika,* is "righteous."

When *dhamma* occurs as a general term of reference, often in the plural, I usually render it "things." As such, the word does not bear the narrow sense of concrete material objects but includes literally *every-thing,* such as qualities, practices, acts, and relationships. Thus the four factors of stream-entry are, as *dhammas,* things; so too are the twelve factors of dependent origination, the five aggregates, the six pairs of sense bases, and the diverse practices leading to enlightenment. Used in the plural, *dhammā* can also mean teachings, and so I render it at III 225,9 foll., though the exact sense there is ambiguous and the word might also mean the things that are taught rather than the teachings about them. One expression occurring in two suttas (II 58,3–4; IV 328,21–22), *iminā dhammena,* can be most satisfactorily rendered "by this principle," though here *dhamma* points to *the* Dhamma as the essential teaching. Again, at I 167,9 (= I 168,25, 173,10), we have *dhamme sati,* "when this principle exists," a rule of conduct followed by the Buddha.

When plural *dhammā* acquires a more technical nuance, in contexts with ontological overtones, I render it "phenomena." For instance, *paṭicca-samuppannā dhammā* are "dependently arisen phenomena" (II 26,7), and each of the five aggregates is *loke lokadhamma,* "a world-phenomenon in the world" that the Buddha has penetrated and taught (III 139,22 foll.). When the word takes on a more psychological hue, I render it "states." The most common example of this is in the familiar pair *kusalā dhammā,* wholesome states, and *akusalā dhammā,* unwholesome states (found, for example, in the formula for right effort; V 9,17–27). The enlightenment factor *dhammavicaya-sambojjhaṅga* is said to be nurtured by giving careful attention to pairs of contrasting mental states (among them wholesome and unwholesome states; V 66,18), and thus I render it "the enlightenment factor of discrimination of states." But since the *dhammas* investigated can also be the four objective supports of mindfulness (V 331–32), *dhammavicaya* might have been translated "discrimination of phenomena." Sometimes *dhammā* signifies traits of character more persistent than transient mental states; in this context I render it "qualities," e.g., Mahākassapa complains that the bhikkhus "have qualities which make them difficult to admonish" (II 204,3–4).

As a sense base and element, the *dhammāyatana* and *dhammadhātu* are the counterparts of the *manāyatana*, the mind base, and the *manoviññāṇadhātu*, the mind-consciousness element. The appropriate sense here would seem to be that of ideas and mental images, but the commentaries understand *dhammas* in these contexts to include not only the objects of consciousness but its concomitants as well. Thus I translate it "mental phenomena," which is wide enough to encompass both these aspects of experience. As the fourth *satipaṭṭhāna*, objective base of mindfulness, *dhammā* is often translated "mind-objects." So I rendered it in MLDB, but in retrospect this seems to me unsatisfactory. Of course, any existent can become an object of mind, and thus all *dhammas* in the fourth *satipaṭṭhāna* are necessarily mind-objects; but the latter term puts the focus in the wrong place. I now understand *dhammas* to be phenomena in general, but phenomena arranged in accordance with the categories of *the* Dhamma, the teaching, in such a way as to lead to a realization of the essential Dhamma embodied in the Four Noble Truths.

Finally, *-dhamma* as a suffix has the meaning "is subject to" or "has the nature of." Thus all dependently arisen phenomena are "subject to destruction, vanishing, fading away, and cessation" (*khayadhamma, vayadhamma, virāgadhamma, nirodhadhamma*; II 26,9 foll.). The five aggregates are "of impermanent nature, of painful nature, of selfless nature" (*aniccadhamma, dukkhadhamma, anattadhamma*; III 195–96).

Saṅkhārā

In MLDB I had changed Ven. Ñāṇamoli's experimental rendering of *saṅkhārā* as "determinations" back to his earlier choice, "formations." Aware that this word has its own drawbacks, in preparing this translation I had experimented with several alternatives. The most attractive of these was "constructions," but in the end I felt that this term too often led to obscurity. Hence, like the land-finding crow which always returns to the ship when land is not close by (see Vism 657; Ppn 21:65), I had to fall back on "formations," which is colourless enough to take on the meaning being imparted by the context. Sometimes I prefixed this with the adjective "volitional" to bring out the meaning more clearly.

Saṅkhārā is derived from the prefix *saṃ* (= con), "together," and the verb *karoti*, "to make." The noun straddles both sides of the active-passive divide. Thus *saṅkhāras* are both things which put together, construct, and compound other things, *and* the things that are put together, constructed, and compounded.

In SN the word occurs in five major doctrinal contexts:

(1) As the second factor in the formula of dependent origination, *saṅkhāras* are the kammically active volitions responsible, in conjunction with ignorance and craving, for generating rebirth and sustaining the forward movement of saṃsāra from one life to the next. *Saṅkhārā* is synonymous with *kamma*, to which it is etymologically related, both being derived from *karoti*. These *saṅkhāras* are distinguished as threefold by their channel of expression, as bodily, verbal, and mental (II 4,8–10, etc.); they are also divided by ethical quality into the meritorious, demeritorious, and imperturbable (II 82,9–13). To convey the relevant sense of *saṅkhārā* here I render the term "volitional formations." The word might also have been translated "activities," which makes explicit the connection with *kamma*, but this rendering would sever the connection with *saṅkhārā* in contexts other than dependent origination, which it seems desirable to preserve.

(2) As the fourth of the five aggregates, *saṅkhārā* is defined as the six classes of volitions (*cha cetanākāyā*, III 60,25–28), that is, volition regarding the six types of sense objects. Hence again I render it volitional formations. But the *saṅkhārakkhandha* has a wider compass than the *saṅkhārā* of the dependent origination series, comprising all instances of volition and not only those that are kammically active. In the Abhidhamma Piṭaka and the commentaries the *saṅkhārakkhandha* further serves as an umbrella category for classifying all mental concomitants of consciousness apart from feeling and perception. It thus comes to include all wholesome, unwholesome, and variable mental

factors mentioned but not formally classified among the aggregates in the Sutta Piṭaka.

(3) In the widest sense, *saṅkhārā* comprises all conditioned things, everything arisen from a combination of conditions. In this sense all five aggregates, not just the fourth, are *saṅkhāras* (see III 132,22–27), as are all external objects and situations (II 191,11–17). The term here is taken to be of passive derivation—denoting what is conditioned, constructed, compounded—hence I render it simply "formations," without the qualifying adjective. This notion of *saṅkhārā* serves as the cornerstone of a philosophical vision which sees the entire universe as constituted of conditioned phenomena. What is particularly emphasized about *saṅkhāras* in this sense is their impermanence. Recognition of their impermanence brings insight into the unreliable nature of all mundane felicity and inspires a sense of urgency directed towards liberation from saṃsāra (see **15:20**; **22:96**).

(4) A triad of *saṅkhāras* is mentioned in connection with the attainment of the cessation of perception and feeling: the bodily formation, the verbal formation, and the mental formation (IV 293,7–28). The first is in-and-out breathing (because breath is bound up with the body); the second, thought and examination (because by thinking one formulates the ideas one expresses by speech); the third, perception and feeling (because these things are bound up with the mind). Two of these terms—the bodily formation and the mental formation—are also included in the expanded instructions on mindfulness of breathing (V 311,21–22; 312,4–5).

(5) The expression *padhānasaṅkhārā* occurs in the formula for the four *iddhipādas*, the bases for spiritual power. The text explains it as the four right kinds of striving (V 268,8–19). I render it "volitional formations of striving." Though, strictly speaking, the expression signifies energy (*viriya*) and not volition (*cetanā*), the qualifier shows that these formations occur in an active rather than a passive mode.

Apart from these main contexts, the word *saṅkhāra* occurs in several compounds—*āyusaṅkhāra* (II 266,19; V 262,22–23), *jīvitasaṅkhāra* (V 152,29–153,2) *bhavasaṅkhāra* (V 263,2)—which can be understood as different aspects of the life force.

The past participle connected with *saṅkhārā* is *saṅkhata*, which I translate "conditioned." Unfortunately I could not render the two Pāli words into English in a way that preserves the vital connection between them: "formed" is too specific for *saṅkhata,* and "conditions" too wide for *saṅkhārā* (and it also encroaches on the domain of *paccaya*). If "constructions" had been used for *saṅkhārā, saṅkhata* would have become "constructed," which preserves the connection, though at the cost of too stilted a translation. Regrettably, owing to the use of different English words for the pair, a critically important dimension of meaning in the suttas is lost to view. In the Pāli we can clearly see the connection: the *saṅkhāras,* the active constructive forces instigated by volition, create and shape conditioned reality, especially the conditioned factors classified into the five aggregates and the six internal sense bases; and this conditioned reality itself consists of *saṅkhāras* in the passive sense, called in the commentaries *saṅkhata-saṅkhārā.*

Further, it is not only this connection that is lost to view, but also the connection with Nibbāna. For Nibbāna is the *asaṅkhata,* the unconditioned, which is called thus precisely because it is neither made by *saṅkhāras* nor itself a *saṅkhāra* in either the active or passive sense. So, when the texts are taken up in the Pāli, we arrive at a clear picture in fine focus: the active *saṅkhāras* generated by volition perpetually create passive *saṅkhāras,* the *saṅkhata dhammas* or conditioned phenomena of the five aggregates (and, indirectly, of the objective world); and then, through the practice of the Buddha's path, the practitioner arrives at the true knowledge of conditioned phenomena, which disables the generation of active *saṅkhāras,* putting an end to the constructing of conditioned reality and opening up the door to the Deathless, the *asaṅkhata,* the unconditioned, which is Nibbāna, final liberation from impermanence and suffering.

Nāmarūpa

In MLDB, I also had changed Ven. Ñāṇamoli's "name-and-form" back to his earlier rendering, "mentality-materiality." In some respects the latter is doctrinally more accurate, but it is also unwieldly, particularly when translating verse, and thus here I return to "name-and-form." The compound was of pre-Buddhistic origins and is used in the Upaniṣads to denote the differentiated manifestation of *brahman,* the nondual reality. For the sages of the Upaniṣads, *nāmarūpa* is the manifestation of *brahman* as multiplicity, apprehended by the senses as diversified appearances or forms, and by thought as diversified names or concepts (the assignment of names and concepts being understood as grounded in objective reality rather than as the end-product of a purely subjective process). The Buddha adopted this expression and invested it with a meaning consonant with his own system. Here it becomes the physical and cognitive sides of individual existence. In the expression *bahiddhā nāmarūpa,* "external name-and-form" (at II 24,2), we seem to find a vestige of the original meaning—the world as distinguished according to its appearances and names—but divested of the monistic implications.

In the Buddha's system, *rūpa* is defined as the four great elements and the form derived from them. Form is both internal to the person (as the body with its senses) and external (as the physical world). The Nikāyas do not explain derived form (*upādāya rūpaṃ*), but the Abhidhamma analyses it into some twenty-four kinds of secondary material phenomena which include the sensitive substances of the sense faculties and four of the five sense objects (the tactile object is identified with three of the great elements—earth, heat, and air—which each exhibit tangible properties). Though I render *nāma* as name, this should not be taken too literally. *Nāma* is the assemblage of mental factors involved in cognition: feeling, perception, volition, contact, and attention (*vedanā, saññā, cetanā, phassa, manasikāra;* II 3,34–35). These are called "name" because they contribute to the process of cognition by which objects are subsumed under conceptual designations.

It should be noted that in the Nikāyas, *nāmarūpa* does not include consciousness (*viññāṇa*). Consciousness is its condition, and the two are mutually dependent, like two sheaves of reeds leaning one against the other (II 114,17–19). Consciousness can operate only in dependence on a physical body (*rūpa*) and in conjunction with its constellation of concomitants (*nāma*); conversely, only when consciousness is present can a compound of material elements function as a sentient body and the mental concomitants participate in cognition. Occasionally the texts speak of the "descent of consciousness" (*viññāṇassa avakkanti*) serving as a condition for name-and-form (II 91,14–15); this means that the arrival of the current of consciousness from the past existence into the new one is the necessary condition for the arising of a new psychophysical organism at conception. Sometimes too the texts speak of the descent of name-and-form (*nāmarūpassa avakkanti,* II 66,12, 90,19, 101,13); this denotes the beginning of sentient life when the current of consciousness, arriving from the previous existence, becomes established under the fresh conditions.

Nibbāna, Parinibbāna

As is well known, *nibbāna* literally means the extinction of a fire. In popular works on Buddhism, *nibbāna* plain and simple is often taken to signify Nibbāna as experienced in life, *parinibbāna* Nibbāna attained at death. This is a misinterpretation. Long ago E.J. Thomas pointed out (possibly on the basis of a suggestion by E. Kuhn) that the prefix *pari-* converts a verb from the expression of a state into the expression of the achievement of an action, so that the corresponding noun *nibbāna* becomes the state of release, *parinibbāna* the attaining of that state.[11] The distinction does not really work very well for the verb, as we find both *parinibbāyati* and *nibbāyati* used to designate the act of attaining release, but it appears to be fairly tenable in regard to the nouns. (In verse, however, we do sometimes find *nibbāna* used to denote the event, for example in the line *pajjotass' eva nibbānaṃ* at v. 612c.) Words related to both *nibbāna* and *parinibbāna* designate *both* the attaining of release during life through the experience of full enlightenment, and the attaining of final release from conditioned existence through the breakup of the physical body at death. Thus, for instance, the verb *parinibbāyati* is commonly used to describe how a bhikkhu achieves release while alive (e.g., at II 82,20; III 54,3; IV 23,8–9, etc.) and also to indicate the passing away of the Buddha or an arahant (e.g., at I 158,23; V 161,25).

The past participle forms, *nibbuta* and *parinibbuta,* are from a different verbal root than the nouns *nibbāna* and *parinibbāna*. The former is from *nir + vṛ,* the latter from *nir + vā*. The noun appropriate to the participles is *nibbuti,* which occasionally occurs in the texts as a synonym for *nibbāna* but with a function that is more evocative (of tranquillity, complete rest, utter peace) than systematic. (It seems no prefixed noun *parinibbuti* is attested to in Pāli.) At an early time the two verb forms were conflated, so that the participle *parinibbuta* became the standard adjective used to denote one who has undergone *parinibbāna*. Like the verb, the participle is used in apposition to both the living Buddha or arahant (I 1,21, 187,8) and the deceased one (I 122,13, 158,24). Possibly, however, *parinibbuta* is used in relation to the living arahant only in verse, while in prose its technical use is confined to one who has expired. In sutta usage, even when the noun *parinibbāna* denotes the passing away of an arahant (particularly of the Buddha), it does not mean "Nibbāna after death." It is, rather, the *event* of passing away undergone by one who has already attained Nibbāna during life.

The suttas distinguish between two elements of Nibbāna: the Nibbāna element with residue (*sa-upādisesa-nibbānadhātu*) and the Nibbāna element without residue (*anupādisesa-nibbānadhātu*)—the residue (*upādisesa*) being the compound of the five aggregates produced by prior craving and kamma (It 38–39). The former is the extinction of lust, hatred, and delusion attained by the arahant while alive; the latter is the remainderless cessation of all conditioned existence that occurs with the arahant's death. In the commentaries the two elements of Nibbāna are respectively called *kilesaparinibbāna*, the quenching of defilements at the attainment of arahantship, and *khandha-parinibbāna*, the quenching of the continuum of aggregates with the arahant's demise. Though the commentaries treat the two Nibbāna elements and the two kinds of *parinibbāna* as interchangeable and synonymous, in sutta usage it may be preferable to see the two kinds of *parinibbāna* as the events which give access to the two corresponding Nibbāna elements. *Parinibbāna*, then, is the act of quenching; *nibbāna*, the state of quenchedness.

To explain the philology of a term is not to settle the question of its interpretation. What exactly is to be made of the various explanations of Nibbāna given in the Nikāyas has been a subject of debate since the early days of Buddhism, with the ground divided between those who regard it as the mere extinction of defilements and cessation of existence and those who understand it as a transcendental (*lokuttara*) ontological reality. In SN some suttas explain Nibbāna as the destruction of lust, hatred, and delusion, which emphasizes the experiential psychological dimension; elsewhere it is called the unconditioned, which seems to place the stress on ontological transcendence. The Theravāda commentators regard Nibbāna as an unconditioned element.[12] They hold that when Nibbāna is called the destruction of the defilements (of lust, hatred, and delusion, etc.) and the cessation of the five aggregates, this requires interpretation. Nibbāna itself, as an existent, is unborn, unmade, unbecome, unconditioned (see Ud 80–81). It is in dependence on this element (*taṃ āgamma*), by arriving at it, that there takes place the destruction of the defilements and release from conditioned existence. Nibbāna itself, however, is not reducible to these two events, which are, in their actual occurrence, conditioned events happening in time. On this interpretation, the two Nibbāna elements are seen as stages in the full actualization of the unconditioned Nibbāna, not simply as two discrete events.

In the present work I leave *nibbāna* untranslated, for the term is too rich in evocative meaning and too defiant of conceptual specification to be satisfactorily captured by any proposed English equivalent. I translate *parinibbāna* as "final Nibbāna," since the noun form usually means the passing away of an arahant (or the Buddha), final release from conditioned existence; sometimes, however, its meaning is ambiguous, as in the statement "the Dhamma [is] taught by the Blessed One for the sake of final Nibbāna without clinging (*anupādāparinibbānatthaṃ*)" (IV 48,78), which can mean either Nibbāna during life or the full cessation of existence.

The verb *parinibbāyati* perhaps could have been incorporated into English with "nibbanize," which would be truest to the Pāli, but this would be too much at variance with current conventions. Thus when the verb refers to the demise of the Buddha or an arahant, I render it "attains final Nibbāna," but when it designates the extinguishing of defilements by one who attains enlightenment, I render it simply "attains Nibbāna." We also find a personal noun form, *parinibbāyī*, which I render "an attainer of Nibbāna," as it can be construed in either sense. In prose the past participle *parinibbuta*, used as a doctrinal term, always occurs with reference to a deceased arahant and so it is translated "has attained final Nibbāna." In verse, it can take on either meaning; when it describes a living arahant (or the

Buddha) I translate it more freely as "fully quenched." The unprefixed form *nibbuta* does not always carry the same technical implications as *parinibbuta*, but can mean simply "peaceful, satisfied, at ease," without necessarily establishing that the one so described has attained Nibbāna.[13] At I 24,11 and II 279,8 it has this implication; at I 236,21 it seems to mean simply peaceful; at III 43, in the compound *tadaṅganibbuta*, it definitely does not imply Nibbāna, for the point there is that the monk has only approximated to the real attainment of the goal. Cognates of *parinibbāna* appear in colloquial speech with a nondoctrinal sense; for example, both *parinibbāyati* and *parinibbuta* are used to describe the taming of a horse (at MN I 446,8–10). But even here they seem to be used with a "loaded meaning," since the horse simile is introduced to draw a comparison with a monk who attains arahantship.

Other Changes

In MLDB I rendered *vitakka* and *vicāra* respectively as "applied thought" and "sustained thought." In this translation they become "thought" and "examination." The latter is surely closer to the actual meaning of *vicāra*. When *vitakka* is translated as "thought," however, a word of caution is necessary. In common usage, *vitakka* corresponds so closely to our "thought" that no other rendering seems feasible; for example, in *kāmavitakka*, sensual thought, or its opposite, *nekkhammavitakka*, thought of renunciation. When, however, *vitakka* and *vicāra* occur as constituents of the first jhāna, they do not exercise the function of discursive thinking characteristic of ordinary consciousness. Here, rather, *vitakka* is the mental factor with the function of applying the mind to the object, and *vicāra* the factor with the function of examining the object nondiscursively in order to anchor the mind in the object.

Bhava, in MLDB, was translated "being." In seeking an alternative, I had first experimented with "becoming," but when the shortcomings in this choice were pointed out to me I decided to return to "existence," used in my earlier translations. *Bhava*, however, is not "existence" in the sense of the most universal ontological category, that which is shared by everything from the dishes in the kitchen sink to the numbers in a mathematical equation. Existence in the latter sense is covered by the verb *atthi* and the abstract noun *atthitā*. *Bhava* is concrete sentient existence in one of the three realms of existence posited by Buddhist cosmology, a span of life beginning with conception and ending in death. In the formula of dependent origination it is understood to mean both (i) the active side of life that produces rebirth into a particular mode of sentient existence, in other words rebirth-producing kamma; and (ii) the mode of sentient existence that results from such activity.

Sakkāya is a term for the five aggregates as a collective whole (III 159,10–13). The word is derived from *sat* + *kāya*, and literally means "the existing body," the assemblage of existent phenomena that serve as the objective basis of clinging. Most translators render it "personality," a practice I followed in MLDB (departing from Ven. Ñāṇamoli, who rendered it, too literally in my view, "embodiment"). But since, under the influence of modern psychology, the word "personality" has taken on connotations quite foreign to what is implied by *sakkāya*, I now translate it as "identity" (a suggestion made to me by Ven. Thanissaro Bhikkhu). *Sakkāya-diṭṭhi* accordingly becomes "identity view," the view of a self existing either behind or among the five aggregates.

Nibbidā, in MLDB, was translated "disenchantment." However, the word or its cognates is sometimes used in ways which suggest that something stronger is intended. Hence I now translate the noun as "revulsion" and the corresponding verb *nibbindati* as "to experience revulsion." What is intended by this is not a reaction of emotional disgust, accompanied by horror and aversion, but a calm inward turning away from all conditioned existence as comprised in the five aggregates, the six sense bases, and the first noble truth. Revulsion arises from knowledge and vision of things as they really are (*yathābhūtañāṇadassana*), and naturally leads to dispassion (*virāga*) and liberation (*vimutti*; on the sequence, see **12:23**).

NOTES TO GENERAL INTRODUCTION

1 The Burmese textual tradition of SN, followed by the Pali Text Society edition, counts fifty-six saṃyuttas, but the Sinhalese tradition counts fifty-four. The difference comes about because the Sinhalese tradition treats the Abhisamayasaṃyutta (our 13) as a subchapter of the Nidānasaṃyutta (12), and the Vedanāsaṃyutta (our 36) as a subchapter of the Saḷāyatanasaṃyutta (35). Neither of these allocations seems justifiable, as these minor saṃyuttas have no explicit thematic connection with the topics of the larger saṃyuttas into which the Sinhalese tradition has incorporated them.

2 I use "Vagga" to refer to the major parts, and "vagga" to refer to the subchapters. Since the Oriental scripts in which the texts are preserved do not have distinct capital and lower case letters, they use the same word for both without orthographic differentiation.

3 Buddhaghosa's figure is given at Sp I 18,9–10, Sv I 23,16–17, and Spk I 2,25–26.

4 Norman makes this point in *Pāli Literature*, p. 31.

5 For the arrangement of the Chinese Saṃyuktāgama I rely on Anesaki, "The Four Buddhist Āgamas in Chinese."

6 "Categories of Sutta in the Pāli Nikāyas." See especially pp. 71–84.

7 The twelve chapters of the *Vibhaṅga* with counterparts in SN are as follows: (1) Khandhavibhaṅga (= SN 22); (2) Āyatana- (= 35); (3) Dhātu- (= 14); (4) Sacca- (= 56); (5) Indriya- (= 48); (6) Paṭicca-samuppāda- (= 12); (7) Satipaṭṭhāna- (= 47); (8) Sammappadhāna- (= 49); (9) Iddhipāda- (= 51); (10) Bojjhaṅga- (= 46); (11) Magga- (= 45); (12) Jhāna- (= 53).

8 My references here are all to SN (by saṃyutta and sutta). To find the parallels, use Concordance 2 (B), pp. 1984–85.

9 What follows partly overlaps with MLDB, pp. 52–58, but as my handling of certain terms differs from that of the earlier work, a full discussion is justified.

10 Norman takes a similar approach to his translation of *dhamma* in EV I. See his discussion of the word at EV I, n. to 2 (p. 118).

11 *History of Buddhist Thought*, p. 121, n. 4.

12 This is clearly maintained in the debate on Nibbāna recorded at Vism 507–9 (Ppn 16:67–74). See too the long extract from the *Paramatthamañjūsā*, Dhammapāla's commentary on Vism, translated by Ñāṇamoli at Ppn pp. 825–26, n. 18.

13 For a play on the two senses of *nibbuta*, see the Bodhisatta's reflections before his great renunciation at Ja I 60–61.

Part I

The Book with Verses

(*Sagāthāvagga*)

Contents

Chapter III
3 *Kosalasaṃyutta*
Connected Discourses with the Kosalan

Chapter V
5 *Bhikkhunīsaṃyutta*
Connected Discourses with Bhikkhunīs

Chapter VI
6 *Brahmasaṃyutta*
Connected Discourses with Brahmās

Chapter VII
7 *Brāhmaṇasaṃyutta*
Connected Discourses with Brahmins

Chapter VIII
8 *Vaṅgīsasaṃyutta*
Connected Discourses with Vaṅgīsa

Chapter IX
9 *Vanasaṃyutta*
Connected Discourses in the Woods

Chapter X
10 *Yakkhasaṃyutta*
Connected Discourses with Yakkhas

Chapter XI
11 *Sakkasaṃyutta*
Connected Discourses with Sakka

Introduction

The *Sagāthāvagga* is so called because all the suttas in this book contain verses, at least one, usually more. The Vagga is divided into eleven saṃyuttas containing a total of 271 suttas. Most of these saṃyuttas are subdivided into several vaggas, usually of ten suttas each. In four saṃyuttas (3, 4, 6, 11), the last vagga contains only five suttas, half the standard number, and these are therefore called "pentads" (*pañcaka*). Four saṃyuttas are not divided into separate vaggas (5, 8, 9, 10), and thus may be considered as made up of a single vagga. I have numbered the suttas consecutively within each saṃyutta starting from 1, with the number within the vagga given in parenthesis. The recent PTS edition of the Sagāthāvagga (Ee2) numbers the suttas consecutively through the entire collection, from 1 to 271.

The number of verses varies from edition to edition, depending on differences in readings and on alternative ways of grouping *pādas* or lines into stanzas; for a sequence of twelve pādas might be divided into either two stanzas of six lines each or three stanzas of four lines each. Ee2 is the only one that numbers the verses, and this edition has 945; of these I have not included three (**vv. 70, 138, 815**), for reasons explained in the notes (**nn. 53, 96, 573**). Many of the verses occur several times within the Saṃyutta Nikāya, usually within the Sagāthāvagga, occasionally elsewhere, as can be seen from Concordance 1 (A). The verses also have extensive parallels elsewhere in the Pāli Canon. A large number are shared by such texts as the Thera- and Therīgāthās, the Suttanipāta, the Dhammapada, and the Jātakas, as well as by the other Nikāyas. They are also quoted in paracanonical texts such as the *Milindapañha*, the *Peṭakopadesa*, and the *Nettippakaraṇa*. A significant number have parallels in the vast corpus of non-Pāli Indian Buddhist literature, such as the Patna and Gāndhārī Dharmapadas, the *Udānavarga*, the *Mahāvastu*, and even the much later *Yogācārabhūmi*. All these "external" parallels are shown in Concordance 1 (B). Doubtlessly some of the verses were not original to the suttas in our collection but belonged to the vast, free floating mass of Buddhist didactic verse which the compilers of the texts pinned down to specific contexts by providing them with narrative settings such as those found in the Sagāthāvagga.

Of the eleven saṃyuttas in this Vagga, eight revolve around encounters between the Buddha (or his disciples) and beings from other planes of existence. Since we will repeatedly run across beings from nonhuman planes in the other Vaggas too, a short summary of the Buddhist picture of the sentient universe will help us to identify them and to understand their place in early Buddhist cosmology. (See Table 3, which gives a visual representation of this cosmology.)

TABLE 3

The Thirty-One Planes of Existence according to Traditional Theravāda Cosmology (see CMA 5:3–7)

The Formless Realm (4 planes)

(31) Base of neither-perception-nor-nonperception
(30) Base of nothingness
(29) Base of infinity of consciousness
(28) Base of infinity of space

The Form Realm (16 planes)

Fourth jhāna plane: Five Pure Abodes
(27) Akaniṭṭha realm
(26) Clear-sighted realm
(25) Beautiful realm
(24) Serene realm
(23) Durable realm

Ordinary fourth jhāna plane
(22) Nonpercipient beings
(21) Devas of great fruit

Third jhāna plane
(20) Devas of steady aura
(19) Devas of measureless aura
(18) Devas of minor aura

Second jhāna plane
(17) Devas of streaming radiance
(16) Devas of measureless radiance
(15) Devas of minor radiance

First jhāna plane
(14) Mahābrahmā realm
(13) Brahmā's ministers
(12) Brahmā's assembly

The Sense-Sphere Realm (11 planes)

Seven good destinations
Six sense-sphere heavenly realms
(11) Paranimmitavasavattī devas
(10) Nimmānaratī devas
(9) Tusita devas
(8) Yāma devas
(7) Tāvatiṃsa devas
(6) Four Great Kings
Human realm
(5) Human realm

Four bad destinations
(4) Host of asuras
(3) Domain of ghosts
(2) Animal realm
(1) Hell realms

The early Buddhist texts envisage a universe with three principal tiers subdivided into numerous planes. The lowest tier is the sense-sphere realm (*kāmadhātu*), so called because the driving force within this realm is sensual desire. The sense-sphere realm (in the oldest cosmology) contains ten planes: the hells (*niraya*), planes of extreme torment; the animal realm (*tiracchānayoni*); the domain of *petas* or ghosts (*pettivisaya*), shade-like spirits subject to various kinds of misery; the human realm (*manussaloka*); and six sense-sphere heavens (*sagga*) inhabited by the *devas*, celestial beings who enjoy far greater happiness, beauty, power, and glory than we know in the human realm. Later tradition adds the *asuravisaya*, the domain of titans or antigods, to the bad destinations, though in the Nikāyas they are depicted as occupying a region adjacent to the Tāvatiṃsa heaven, from which they often launch invasions against the devas.

Above the sense-sphere realm is the form realm (*rūpadhātu*), where gross material form has vanished and only the subtler kinds of form remain. The realm is divided into four main tiers with several planes in each. The inhabitants of these planes are also devas, though to distinguish them from the gods of the sensuous heavens they are usually called *brahmās*. The life spans in the various brahmā planes increase exponentially, being far longer than those in the sensuous heavens, and sensual desire has largely abated. The prevalent mode of experience here is meditative rather than sensory, as these planes are the ontological counterparts of the four *jhānas* or meditative absorptions. They include the five "Pure Abodes" (*suddhāvāsa*), spheres of rebirth accessible only to nonreturners.

Beyond the form realm lies an even more exalted sphere of existence called the formless realm (*arūpadhātu*). The beings in this realm consist solely of mind, without a material basis, as physical form is here entirely absent. The four planes that make up this realm, successively more subtle, are the ontological counterparts of the four *āruppas* or formless meditative attainments, after which they are named: the base of the infinity of space, the base of the infinity of consciousness, the base of nothingness, and the base of neither-perception-nor-nonperception.

The suttas often compress this elaborate cosmology into a simpler scheme of five destinations (*pañcagati*): the hells, the animal realm, the domain of ghosts, the human realm, and the deva world. The last includes all the many deva planes of the three realms. The first three are called the plane of misery (*apāya-*

bhūmi), the nether world (*vinipāta*), or the bad destinations (*duggati*); the human realm and the deva planes are collectively called the good destinations (*sugati*). Rebirth into the plane of misery is the fruit of unwholesome kamma, rebirth into the good destinations the fruit of wholesome kamma. Beyond all realms and planes of existence is the unconditioned, Nibbāna, the final goal of the Buddha's teaching.

1. Devatāsaṃyutta

Devatā is an abstract noun based on *deva*, but in the Nikāyas it is invariably used to denote particular celestial beings, just as the English word "deity," originally an abstract noun meaning the divine nature, is normally used to denote the supreme God of theistic religions or an individual god or goddess of polytheistic faiths. Though the word is feminine, the gender comes from the abstract suffix *-tā* and does not necessarily mean the devatās are female. The texts rarely indicate their sex, though it seems they can be of either sex and perhaps sometimes beyond sexual differentiation.

For Buddhism the devas are not immortal gods exercising a creative role in the cosmic process. They are simply elevated beings, blissful and luminous, who had previously dwelt in the human world but had been reborn in the celestial planes as the fruit of their meritorious deeds. With rare exceptions they are just as much in bondage to delusion and desire as human beings, and they equally stand in need of guidance from the Enlightened One. The Buddha is the "teacher of devas and humans" (*satthā devamanussānaṃ*), and though squarely established in the human world he towers above the most exalted deities by reason of his supreme wisdom and perfect purity.

The devas usually come to visit the Buddha in the deep stillness of the night, while the rest of the world lies immersed in sleep. The Devatāsaṃyutta gives us a record of their conversations. Sometimes the devas come to recite verses in praise of the Master, sometimes to ask questions, sometimes to request instruction, sometimes to win approval of their views, sometimes even to challenge or taunt him. On approaching they almost always bow down to him in homage, for the Buddha is their spiritual and moral superior. Not to bow down to him, as some devas do (see **1:35**), is provocative, a deliberate withholding of due respect.

Each of the four Nikāyas opens with a sutta of deep significance. Though the first sutta of SN is very short, it is rich in implications. In this case a devatā comes to the Buddha to ask how he "crossed the flood," that is, how he attained deliverance, and in his reply the Buddha points to the "middle way" as the key to his attainment. This answer conveys the essential spirit of the Dhamma, which avoids all extremes in views, attitudes, and conduct. The commentary draws out the ramifications of the Buddha's statement with a list of seven extremes, philosophical and practical, transcended by the middle way.

The following suttas in this saṃyutta cover a wide spectrum of subjects without any particular logic in their sequence. They range from the simple to the profound, from the commonplace to the sublime, from the humorous to the stern. The exchanges discuss such ethical practices as giving, service to others, and noninjury; the difficulties of renunciation and the life of meditation; the call for earnest effort; the sorrows of human existence and the need for deliverance. There are also suttas on the bliss and equanimity of the arahant, and a few which touch on his transcendental stature. In most suttas the prose portion serves no other function than to establish a framework for the conversation, which eventually falls away leaving only an exchange of verses with the speakers' identities understood. But we occasionally find brief stories, such as that of the female devatā who tried to seduce the bhikkhu Samiddhi (**1:20**), or of the "faultfinding devas" who accused the Buddha of hypocrisy (**1:35**), or of the visit paid to the Buddha by a group of devas when his foot was injured by a stone splinter (**1:38**).

Usually the personal identity of the devatā is not revealed. An exception is the pair of suttas where the two Kokanadā sisters, daughters of the weather god Pajjunna, visit the Buddha and praise him and his Dhamma (**1:39–40**). Sometimes verses spoken by an anonymous deity recur elsewhere with the identity specified; for example, **v. 22** reappears as **v. 461**, ascribed to Māra the Evil One; **vv. 156–59** reappear as **vv. 312–15**, ascribed to Anāthapiṇḍika, the celestial reincarnation of the great philanthropist. It is also rare for the suttas to assign the devas to particular realms, but there are exceptions, such as those on the "extolling of the good" host of devas (*satullapakāyikā devā;* **1:31–34**, etc.) and the one on the devas of the Pure Abodes (*suddhāvāsakāyikā devā;* **1:37**). The commentary, cited in the notes, often provides more background information.

When the devatā does not ask a question but voices an opinion, a contrast is usually established between the viewpoint of the deity, generally valid from within his or her limited horizons, and the viewpoint of the Buddha, who sees things far beyond the ken of the devas (see, e.g., **vv. 3–6**). Sometimes a group of devas express their opinions, which the Buddha surpasses with his own more profound contribution (**vv. 78–84**, **95–101**). In several suttas the verses are not spoken in the context of a conversation but express the personal views of the deva, which the Buddha tacitly endorses (**vv. 136–40**), and two verses are simple paeans of praise to the Blessed One (**vv. 147, 148**). Beginning with **v. 183**, the suttas assume a standard format, with the devas posing a series of riddles which the Buddha answers to their satisfaction. A memorable example of this is the riddle about the type of killing that the Buddha approves of, to which the answer is the killing of anger (**vv. 223–24**). In one sutta we find a gentle touch of humour: a devatā has asked the Buddha a series of questions, apparently mundane in intent, but before the Blessed One can reply another devatā breaks in and gives his own answers, which remain at the mundane level. Then the Buddha replies, lifting the dialogue to the transcendent plane (**vv. 229–31**). Because of its varied content and the piquancy of its verses, within the Theravāda tradition, at least in Sri Lanka, the Devatāsaṃyutta is extremely popular as a source of texts to be drawn upon for sermons.

2. Devaputtasaṃyutta

The *devaputtas*, or "sons of the devas," are young devas newly arisen in their respective heavenly planes; *devaduhitās*, "daughters of the devas," are also mentioned in the commentary but none appear in this saṃyutta. The commentary says these beings are reborn spontaneously in the laps of the devas. While the devatās in the preceding saṃyutta remain mostly anonymous, the young devas are always identified by name, and it is surprising to find that several of them—or at least their verses—

have already appeared in the Devatāsaṃyutta (see **2:3**, **4**, **16**, **19**, **20**, **21**, **24**, **27**). This suggests that the dividing line between the two classes of deities is not a hard and fast one, just as the dividing line between an adult and an adolescent is not hard and fast. A relatively large proportion of the verses in this chapter focus on the monastic training, substantially more than in the Devatāsaṃyutta. The texts themselves do not drop any hints as to why this should be so; at least there are none that are readily visible.

Several suttas raise points of special interest from a doctrinal perspective. We meet, for example, the young deva Dāmali who thought that the arahant must still "strive without weariness," until the Buddha told him that the arahant had completed his task and need not strive further (**2:5**). The commentary says this sutta is almost unique in that the Buddha here does *not* speak in praise of effort. Again, we meet Tāyana, whose verses on exertion are applauded by the Blessed One and, the next morning, are commended by him to the monks (**2:8**). The two suttas on the capture of the moon god Candimā and the sun god Suriya include verses that must have functioned as charms for terminating lunar and solar eclipses (**2:9**, **10**); in Sri Lanka they are included in the *Maha Pirit Pota*, "The Great Book of Protection," made up of suttas and other chants recited for spiritual and physical protection. We also meet Subrahmā, whose single verse is one of the pithiest expressions in world literature of the anguish at the heart of the human condition (**2:17**). The story of Rohitassa, who tried to reach the end of the world by travelling, elicits from the Buddha a momentous reply about where the world and its end are ultimately to be found (**2:26**). In this saṃyutta we also meet two young devas named Veṇhu and Siva (at **2:12** and **2:21**), who may be early prototypes of the Indian gods Viṣṇu and Śiva (the Sanskrit forms of their names); our text, however, apparently dates from a period before they became the chief deities of theistic devotional Hinduism. The last sutta in the chapter (**2:30**) introduces us to a group of young devas who were formerly disciples of the Buddha's rivals on the Indian scene, Pūraṇa Kassapa, Makkhali Gosāla, and Nigaṇṭha Nātaputta, teachers whose views had been unequivocally rejected by the Buddha. It is thus perplexing that their disciples should have been reborn in heaven, especially when the first two teachers propagated such doctrines as moral anarchism and fatalism. But the conclusion reached in the sutta is that such teachers were as far from the stature of true holy men as the jackal is from the lion.

3. Kosalasaṃyutta

This chapter introduces us to King Pasenadi of Kosala. According to the Buddhist texts, Pasenadi was deeply devoted to the Buddha and often sought his counsel, though there is no record of him reaching any stage of awakening (and thus medieval Sri Lankan tradition holds that he was a bodhisatta, who does not attain enlightenment so that he might continue fulfilling the perfect virtues that culminate in Buddhahood). Pasenadi had been led to the Buddha by his wife, Queen Mallikā, whose devotion to the Master he had previously resented. The story of how Mallikā convinced him of the Buddha's wisdom is related in MN No. 87; MN No. 89 gives us a moving account of the king's last meeting with the Master when they were both in their eightieth year. The first sutta of the Kosalasaṃyutta apparently records Pasenadi's first meeting with the Blessed One, after his confidence had been aroused by Mallikā's ruse. Here the Buddha is described as young, and when the king questions the claim that such a youthful ascetic can be perfectly enlightened, the Buddha replies with a series of verses that dispels the king's doubts and inspires him to go for refuge.

Unlike the first two saṃyuttas, the present one employs substantial prose backgrounds to the verses, and often the stanzas merely restate metrically the moral of the Buddha's discourse. Though the topics discussed are not especially profound, they are almost all relevant to the busy lay person faced with the difficult challenge of living a moral life in the world. Especially noteworthy is the stress they lay on the need to adhere unflinchingly to the path of rectitude amidst the world's temptations. Several suttas (**3:4**, **5**) show how easy it is to fall away from righteous standards, especially in an age like the Buddha's when, as in our own time, stiff competition for wealth, position, and power was driving hallowed ethical values out of circulation. The remedy against temptation is diligence (*appamāda*), and when the Buddha extols diligence to the king the word does not mean, as it does in a monastic context, constant devotion to meditation, but persistence in the performance of meritorious deeds. For a man like Pasenadi, a happy rebirth rather than Nibbāna is the immediate goal.

The king's conversation with Mallikā, in which they both admit they cherish themselves more than anyone else (**3:8**), elicits from the Buddha a verse which gives an ethical slant to a metaphysical thesis found in the Bṛhadāraṇyaka Upaniṣad, also occurring in a conversation between husband and wife, that of all things the self is the most precious. This raises the interesting question whether the close correspondence between the two is sheer coincidence (not impossible) or the result of a deliberate reworking by the Buddha of the old Upaniṣad. On another occasion we see the king display lack of acumen in his assessment of ascetics (**3:11**)—perhaps a hint that his commitment to the Dhamma was not unwavering—and the Buddha's response offers astute counsel on how to judge a person's character.

In this saṃyutta we even find, from the Master's golden lips, enlightened advice for losing weight (**3:12**), while two other suttas provide an historical perspective on the conflict between Kosala and Magadha, with reflections on war and peace (**3:14–15**). Of timely interest is the Buddha's verse explaining to the king that a woman can turn out better than a man (**3:16**). Elsewhere the Buddha rejects the idea, propagated by the brahmins, that birth is an important criterion of spiritual worth, stressing instead that the true marks of spiritual nobility are ethical purity and wisdom (**3:24**).

A theme that recurs throughout this saṃyutta is the inevitability of death and the inexorable operation of the law of kamma, which ensures that good and bad actions meet with due recompense. Beings pass from bright states to dark ones and from dark states to bright ones depending on their actions (**3:21**). All that we take with us when we die are our good and bad deeds, and thus we should be sure to accumulate merits, for in the next world these are "the support for living beings" (**3:4**, **20**, **22**). Among several texts on the inevitability of death, the most memorable is the last sutta in the chapter (**3:25**), with its startling parable of the mountains advancing from all quarters, crushing everything in their way.

4. Mārasaṃyutta

Māra is the Evil One of Buddhism, the Tempter and Lord of Sensuality bent on distracting aspirants from the path to liberation and keeping them trapped in the cycle of repeated birth and death. Sometimes the texts use the word "Māra" in a metaphorical sense, as representing the inward psychological causes of bondage such as craving and lust (**22:63–65**) and the external things to which we become bound, particularly the five aggregates themselves (**23:11–12**). But it is evident that the thought world of the suttas does not conceive Māra only as a personification of humankind's moral frailty, but sees him as a real evil deity out to frustrate the efforts of those intent on winning the ultimate goal. The proof of this lies in his pursuit of the Buddha and the arahants *after* their enlightenment, which would not be credible if he were conceived of merely as a psychological projection.

The Mārasaṃyutta opens in the vicinity of the Bodhi Tree soon after the Buddha has attained the supreme enlightenment. Here Māra challenges the Blessed One's claim to have reached the goal. He taunts him for abandoning the path of self-mortification (**4:1**), tries to frighten him by assuming horrific shapes (**4:2**), and seeks to break his equanimity by displaying beautiful and hideous forms (**4:3**). For the Buddha to triumph in these contests he need only call Māra's bluff, to announce that he knows the adversary before him is none other than the Evil One. Then Māra must disappear, frustrated and mournful.

Māra also appears as the cynic who denies that mortals can attain perfect purity (**4:4, 15**). On several occasions he tries to confound the monks while they are listening to the Buddha speak, but each time the Buddha calls his number (**4:16, 17, 19**). On another occasion Māra tries to tempt the Master with the lure of worldly power, but the Buddha staunchly rejects this (**4:20**). Especially impressive is the Godhika Sutta (**4:23**), where the bhikkhu Godhika, afflicted with an illness that obstructs his meditative progress, plans to take his own life. Māra presents himself before the Buddha, pleading with him to discourage his disciple from such folly, but the Master extols devotion to the goal even at the cost of life. At the end of the sutta Māra is searching vainly for the rebirth-consciousness of Godhika, unaware that the monk had attained Nibbāna and expired "with consciousness unestablished."

The last two suttas in this saṃyutta take us back to the site of the enlightenment. Here we see first Māra and then Māra's three daughters—Taṇhā, Aratī, and Ragā (Craving, Discontent, and Lusting)—trying to find a point of vulnerability in the newly enlightened Buddha, but their efforts are in vain and they must depart disappointed (**4:24**, **25**).

5. Bhikkhunīsaṃyutta

The Bhikkhunīsaṃyutta is a compilation of ten short suttas in mixed prose and verse, undivided into vaggas. The protagonists are all bhikkhunīs, Buddhist nuns. Though several of its thirty-seven verses have parallels in the Therīgāthā (mentioned in the notes and Concordance 1 (B)), a substantial number are unique to this collection, while often the variations in roughly parallel versions are themselves of intrinsic interest. At least one nun in the Bhikkhunīsaṃyutta, Vajirā, does not appear at all in the Therīgāthā, while the case of another nun, Selā, is problematic. A comparison between the two collections also brings to light some noteworthy differences in the ascription of authorship. Since SN and the Therīgāthā were evidently transmitted by different lines of reciters, it was only too easy for verses to break off from their original narrative setting and merge with a different background story connecting them to a different author.

All the ten suttas are constructed according to the same pattern, a direct confrontation between Māra and an individual nun. This structure probably accounts for the placement of the Bhikkhunīsaṃyutta immediately after the Mārasaṃyutta. Each sutta of this collection begins with a nun going off by herself to pass the day in solitary meditation. Then Māra approaches her with a challenge—a provocative question or a taunt—intending to make her fall away from concentration. What Māra has failed to realize is that each of these nuns is an arahant who has seen so deeply into the truth of the Dhamma that she is utterly inaccessible to his wiles. Far from being flustered by Māra's challenge, the nun promptly guesses her adversary's identity and meets his challenge with a sharp retort.

In a dialogue that brings together the Lord of Sensuality with a solitary nun one might expect each of Māra's overtures to be aimed at sexual seduction. This, however, is so only in several suttas. The actual themes of the discourses vary widely and expose us to a broad range of perspectives on the attitudes and insights of the renunciant life. The contrast between the allurement and misery of sensual pleasures is the theme of **5:1**, **4**, and **5**. In all three cases the nuns sharply rebuke Māra with verses that reveal their utter indifference to his solicitations.

Māra's dialogue with Somā (**5:2**) voices the ancient Indian prejudice that women are endowed with "mere two-fingered wisdom" and thus cannot attain Nibbāna. Somā's rejoinder is a forceful reminder that enlightenment does not depend on gender but on the mind's capacity for concentration and wisdom, qualities accessible to any human being who earnestly seeks to penetrate the truth. In **5:3**, Māra approaches Kisāgotamī, the heroine of the well-known parable of the mustard seed, trying to arouse her maternal instincts to beget another son. His challenge thus touches on sensuality only indirectly, his primary appeal being aimed at the feminine desire for children.

The last two suttas are philosophical masterpieces, compressing into a few tight stanzas insights of enormous depth and wide implications. When Māra challenges Selā with a question on the origins of personal existence, she replies with a masterly poem that condenses the whole teaching of dependent origination into three four-line stanzas adorned with an illuminating simile (**5:9**). He poses a similar problem to Vajirā, who answers with a stunning exposition of the teaching of nonself, illustrating the composite nature of personal identity with the famous simile of the chariot (**5:10**).

Though set against a mythological background in an ancient world whose customs and norms seem so remote from our own, these poems of the ancient nuns still speak to us today through their sheer simplicity and uncompromising honesty. They need no ornamentation or artifice to convey their message, for they are sufficient in themselves to startle us with the clarity of unadorned truth.

6. Brahmasaṃyutta

Brahmā was the supreme deity of early Brahmanism, conceived

as the creator of the universe and venerated by the brahmins with sacrifices and rituals. Occasionally this conception of Brahmā persists in the Buddhist canon, though as a target of criticism and satire rather than as an article of faith. In such contexts the word "brahmā" is used as a proper name, often augmented to Mahābrahmā, "Brahmā the Great." The Buddha reinterpreted the idea of brahmā and transformed the single, all-powerful deity of the brahmins into a class of exalted gods dwelling in the form realm (*rūpadhātu*) far above the sense-sphere heavens. Their abode is referred to as "the brahmā world," of which there are many, of varying dimensions and degrees of hegemony. Within their realm the brahmās dwell in companies, and Mahābrahmā (or sometimes a brahmā of a more personal name) is seen as the ruler of that company, complete with ministers and assembly. Like all sentient beings, the brahmās are impermanent, still tied to the round of rebirth, though sometimes they forget this and imagine themselves immortal.

The path to rebirth in the brahmā world is mastery over the jhānas, each of which is ontologically attuned to a particular level of the form realm (see Table 3). Sometimes the Buddha mentions the four "divine abodes" (*brahmavihāra*) as the means to rebirth in the brahmā world. These are the "immeasurable" meditations on lovingkindness, compassion, altruistic joy, and equanimity (*mettā, karuṇā, muditā, upekkhā*).

The Nikāyas offer an ambivalent evaluation of the brahmās, as can be seen from the present saṃyutta. On the one hand, certain brahmās are depicted as valiant protectors of the Buddha's dispensation and devoted followers of the Master. But precisely because of their longevity and elevated stature in the cosmic hierarchy, the brahmās are prone to delusion and conceit; indeed, they sometimes imagine they are all-powerful creators and rulers of the universe. Perhaps this dual evaluation reflects the Buddha's ambivalent attitude towards the brahmins: admiration for the ancient spiritual ideals of the brahmin life (as preserved in the expressions *brahmacariya* and *brahmavihāra*) coupled with rejection of the pretensions of the contemporary brahmins to superiority based on birth and lineage.

The most eminent of the brahmās devoted to the Buddha is Brahmā Sahampati, who appears several times in SN. Soon after the enlightenment he descends from his divine abode and reappears before the Blessed One to beseech him to teach the Dhamma to the world (**6:1**). He applauds the Buddha's reverence for the Dhamma (**6:2**), extols an arahant bhikkhu on alms round (**6:3**), reproaches the evil Devadatta (**6:12**), and shows up again at the Buddha's parinibbāna, where he recites a verse of eulogy (**6:15**). He will also appear in other saṃyuttas (at **11:17**; **22:80**; **47:18**, **43**; and **48:57**).

Brahmās of the deluded type are epitomized by Brahmā Baka, who imagined himself eternal and had to be divested of this illusion by the Master (**6:4**). On another occasion, an unnamed brahmā imagined he was superior to the arahants, and the Buddha and four great disciples visited his realm to make him alter his views (**6:5**). We also witness a contest between a negligent brahmā, stiff with pride, and two colleagues of his, devotees of the Buddha, who sweep away his illusions (**6:6**). The penultimate sutta shows a disciple of the past Buddha Sikhī awing a whole assembly of proud brahmās with his display of psychic powers (**6:14**). This saṃyutta also relates the sad story of the monk Kokālika, a cohort of Devadatta, who tried to defame the chief disciples Sāriputta and Moggallāna and had to reap the kammic result as a rebirth in hell (**6:9–10**). The last sutta in this collection, included here only because of Brahmā Sahampati's single verse, is a parallel of the death scene in the long Mahāparinibbāna Sutta of the Dīgha Nikāya.

7. Brāhmaṇasaṃyutta

This saṃyutta, recording the Buddha's conversations with brahmins, contains two vaggas, each with a different unifying theme. In the first all the brahmins who come to the Buddha, often angry (**7:1–4**) or disdainful (**7:7–9**), are so deeply stirred by his words that they ask for ordination into the Saṅgha and "not long afterwards" attain arahantship. These suttas display the Buddha as the incarnation of patience and peace, capable of working, in those who would attack him, the miracle of transformation simply by his unshakable equanimity and impeccable wisdom. In this vagga we also see how the Buddha assessed the brahmin claim to superior status based on birth. He here interprets the word "brahmin" by way of its original meaning, as a holy man, and on this basis redefines the true brahmin as the arahant. The three Vedas which the brahmins revered and diligently studied are replaced by the three *vijjās* or true knowledges possessed by the arahant: knowledge of past births, of the laws of kammic retribution, and of the destruction of the taints (**7:8**). The last sutta adds a touch of humour, still recognizable today, by depicting the contrast between the oppressive cares of the household life and the untrammelled freedom of the life of renunciation (**7:10**).

In the second vagga the brahmins come to challenge the Buddha in still different ways, and again the Buddha rises to the occasion with his inexhaustible wit and wisdom. In this vagga, however, though the Buddha inspires in his antagonists a newly won faith, the brahmin converts do not become monks but declare themselves lay followers "who have gone for refuge for life."

8. Vaṅgīsasaṃyutta

The bhikkhu Vaṅgīsa was declared by the Buddha the foremost disciple of those gifted with inspirational speech (*paṭibhānavantānaṃ*, at AN I 24,21). This title accrued to him on account of his skill in composing spontaneous verse. His verses make up the longest chapter in the Theragāthā, whose seventy-one verses (Th 1209–79) closely correspond with those in the present saṃyutta but lack the prose frameworks. Another poem by Vaṅgīsa, found at Sn II, 12, is not included in the present compilation but does have a counterpart in the Theragāthā.

The verses of Vaṅgīsa are not mere metrical aphorisms (as are so many verses in this collection) but skilfully wrought poetic compositions that can well claim an honoured place in early Indian poetry. They also reveal, with unabashed honesty, the trials and temptations which their author faced in his career as a monk. Having an aesthetic bent of character and a natural appreciation of sensuous beauty, Vaṅgīsa must have gone through a difficult struggle in his early days as a monk adjusting to the strict discipline required of a bhikkhu, with its training in sense restraint and vigilant control of the mind. The early suttas in this chapter (**8:1–4**) speak of his battle against sensual lust, his susceptibility to the charms of the opposite sex, and his firm determination not to succumb but to continue bravely along the path laid down by his Master. They also tell of his proclivity to pride, no doubt based on his natural talent as a poet, and of his endeavour to subdue this flaw of character. Later in his monastic career, apparently after he gained a greater degree of self-mastery, he often extolled the Buddha in verse, and on one occasion the Blessed One requested him to compose extemporaneous verses (**8:8**). In other poems he praises the great disciples Sāriputta, Moggallāna, and Koṇḍañña (**8:6**, **9**, **10**). The last poem in the saṃyutta, partly autobiographical, concludes with a declaration that the author has become an arahant equipped with the three true knowledges and other spiritual powers (**8:12**).

9. Vanasaṃyutta

This saṃyutta consists of fourteen suttas most of which are constructed according to a stereotyped pattern. A bhikkhu is living alone in a woodland thicket, where he should be meditating ardently, but human weakness gets the better of him and causes him to swerve from his religious duties. Then a devatā dwelling in the thicket takes compassion on him and chides him in verse, seeking to reawaken his sense of urgency. Apparently these devatās are not celestial beings, like those we meet in the Devatāsaṃyutta, but dryads or fairies, and they seem to be feminine. On a few occasions the devatā errs in her assessment of the bhikkhu's behaviour. Thus in **9:2** the devatā comes to reproach the bhikkhu for taking a nap, unaware he has already attained arahantship, and in **9:8** for associating too closely with a woman, again unaware the bhikkhu is an arahant (according to the commentary). In **9:6**, a devatā from the Tāvatiṃsa heaven tries to persuade the Venerable Anuruddha to aspire for rebirth in her realm, but he declares that he has ended the process of rebirth and will never take another existence. The last sutta in the chapter (**9:14**) also occurs in the Jātakas, interestingly with the Bodhisatta in the role played here by the bhikkhu.

10. Yakkhasaṃyutta

The yakkhas are fierce spirits inhabiting remote areas such as forests, hills, and abandoned caves. They are depicted as of hideous mien and wrathful temperament, but when given offerings and shown respect they become benign and may protect people rather than harm them. Many of the shrines that dotted the North Indian countryside were built to honour the yakkhas and secure their favours. Though living in misery they have the potential for awakening and can attain the paths and fruits of the spiritual life.

The suttas in this chapter cover a wide range of topics. What unites them is not so much the content of the verses but their propagational function in showing the Buddha as the invincible sage who, by his skilful means, can tame and transform even the most violent and fearsome ogres, such as Sūciloma (**10:3**) and Āḷavaka (**10:12**). The saṃyutta also includes two charming tales of female yakkhas, famished spirits haunting the outskirts of Jeta's Grove, who are so deeply moved by the Buddha's sermons and the chanting of the monks that they turn over a new leaf and become pious lay devotees (**10:6**, **7**). In this saṃyutta too we find the story of Anāthapiṇḍika's first meeting with the Buddha, which was abetted by friendly advice from a benevolent yakkha (**10:8**). In three suttas the yakkhas speak verses in praise of bhikkhunīs (**10:9–11**).

11. Sakkasaṃyutta

In the early Buddhist pantheon, Sakka is the ruler of the devas in the Tāvatiṃsa heaven and also a follower of the Buddha. A long conversation between him and the Buddha, culminating in his attainment of stream-entry, is told in the Sakkapañha Sutta (DN No. 20). This saṃyutta does not report the Buddha's own encounters with Sakka, but gives (in the Buddha's words) accounts of Sakka's deeds and conversations. The suttas are thus presented as fables, but fables which always embody a moral message. The saṃyutta also includes the famous Dhajagga Sutta (**11:3**), in which the Buddha commends to the monks recollection of the Three Jewels—the Buddha, the Dhamma, and the Saṅgha—as an antidote to fear.

In Buddhist legend the Tāvatiṃsa devas are perpetually being attacked by the asuras, the titans, beings of great physical prowess and violent ambition who seek to conquer them and take control of their domain. The Sakkasaṃyutta repeatedly pits Sakka in struggle against the leaders of the asuras, Vepacitti and

Verocana. The two sides can be read as symbolizing alternative political philosophies. The asura leaders favour rule by force and retaliation against enemies; they rationalize aggression and extol the ethic of "might makes right." Sakka, in contrast, stands for rule by righteousness, patience towards aggressors, and the compassionate treatment of wrongdoers (**11:4**, **5**, **8**). Sakka and the devas honour sages and holy men, the asuras scorn them, and thus the sages help the devas but curse the asuras (**11:9**, **10**).

In this saṃyutta Sakka appears as the ideal lay devotee. He earned his place as ruler of the devas, while he was still a human being, by fulfilling seven vows which embody the standards of the virtuous householder (**11:11**). His understanding of the Buddha's excellence is inferior to Brahmā Sahampati's (**11:17**), but in three suttas he eloquently proclaims the reasons for his devotion to the Buddha, the Saṅgha, and even devout householders (**11:18–20**). In the last three suttas, the Buddha holds up Sakka's patience and forgiveness as a model for the bhikkhus (**11:23–25**).

[1] <1> PART I: The Book with Verses (*Sagāthāvagga*)

Homage to the Blessed One,
the Arahant, the Perfectly Enlightened One

Chapter I

1 *Devatāsaṃyutta*
Connected Discourses with Devatās

I. A REED

1 (1) Crossing the Flood

Thus have I heard. On one occasion the Blessed One was dwelling at Sāvatthī in Jeta's Grove, Anāthapiṇḍika's Park. Then, when the night had advanced, a certain devatā of stunning beauty, illuminating the entire Jeta's Grove, approached the Blessed One. Having approached, he paid homage to the Blessed One, stood to one side, and said to him:

"How, dear sir, did you cross the flood?"[1]

"By not halting, friend, and by not straining I crossed the flood."[2]

"But how is it, dear sir, that by not halting and by not straining you crossed the flood?"

"When I came to a standstill, friend, then I sank; but when I struggled, then I got swept away. It is in this way, friend, that by not halting and by not straining I crossed the flood."[3] <2>

[The devatā:]

1 "After a long time at last I see
A brahmin who is fully quenched,
Who by not halting, not straining,
Has crossed over attachment to the world."[4]

This is what that devatā said.[5] The Teacher approved. Then that devatā, thinking, "The Teacher has approved of me," paid homage to the Blessed One and, keeping him on the right, disappeared right there. [2]

2 (2) Emancipation

<3> At Sāvatthī. Then, when the night had advanced, a certain devatā of stunning beauty, illuminating the entire Jeta's Grove, approached the Blessed One. Having approached, he paid homage to the Blessed One, stood to one side, and said to him:

"Do you know, dear sir, emancipation, release, seclusion for beings?"[6]

"I know, friend, emancipation, release, seclusion for beings."

"But in what way, dear sir, do you know emancipation, release, seclusion for beings?"

[The Blessed One:]
2 "By the utter destruction of delight in existence,[7]
By the extinction of perception and consciousness,
By the cessation and appeasement of feelings: <4>
It is thus, friend, that I know for beings—
Emancipation, release, seclusion."[8]

3 (3) Reaching

At Sāvatthī. Standing to one side, that devatā recited this verse in the presence of the Blessed One:

3 "Life is swept along, short is the life span;
No shelters exist for one who has reached old age.
Seeing clearly this danger in death,
One should do deeds of merit that bring happiness."[9]

[The Blessed One:]
4 "Life is swept along, short is the life span;
No shelters exist for one who has reached old age.
Seeing clearly this danger in death,
A seeker of peace should drop the world's bait."[10] [3] <5>

4 (4) Time Flies By

At Sāvatthī. Standing to one side, that devatā recited this verse in the presence of the Blessed One:

5 "Time flies by, the nights swiftly pass;
The stages of life successively desert us.[11]
Seeing clearly this danger in death,
One should do deeds of merit that bring happiness."

[The Blessed One:]
6 "Time flies by, the nights swiftly pass;
The stages of life successively desert us.
Seeing clearly this danger in death,
A seeker of peace should drop the world's bait."

5 (5) How Many Must One Cut?

At Sāvatthī. Standing to one side, that devatā recited this verse in the presence of the Blessed One:

7 "How many must one cut, how many abandon,
And how many further must one develop?
When a bhikkhu has surmounted how many ties
Is he called a crosser of the flood?"

[The Blessed One:] <6>
8 "One must cut off five, abandon five,
And must develop a further five.
A bhikkhu who has surmounted five ties
Is called a crosser of the flood."[12]

6 (6) Awake

At Sāvatthī. Standing to one side, that devatā recited this verse in the presence of the Blessed One:

9 "How many are asleep when [others] are awake?
How many are awake when [others] sleep?

By how many does one gather dust?
By how many is one purified?"

[The Blessed One:]
10 "Five are asleep when [others] are awake;
Five are awake when [others] sleep.
By five things one gathers dust,
By five things one is purified."[13] [4] <7>

7 (7) Not Penetrated

At Sāvatthī. Standing to one side, that devatā recited this verse in the presence of the Blessed One:

11 "Those who have not penetrated things,
Who may be led into others' doctrines,
Fast asleep, they have not yet awakened:
It is time for them to awaken."[14]

[The Blessed One:]
12 "Those who have penetrated things well,
Who cannot be led into others' doctrines,
Those awakened ones, having rightly known,
Fare evenly amidst the uneven."[15]

8 (8) Utterly Muddled

At Sāvatthī. Standing to one side, that devatā recited this verse in the presence of the Blessed One:

13 "Those who are utterly muddled about things,
Who may be led into others' doctrines, <8>
Fast asleep, they have not yet awakened:
It is time for them to awaken."

[The Blessed One:]
14 "Those who aren't muddled about things,
Who cannot be led into others' doctrines,
Those awakened ones, having rightly known,
Fare evenly amidst the uneven."

9 (9) One Prone to Conceit

At Sāvatthī. Standing to one side, that devatā recited this verse in the presence of the Blessed One:

15 "There is no taming here for one fond of conceit,
Nor is there sagehood for the unconcentrated:
Though dwelling alone in the forest, heedless,
One cannot cross beyond the realm of Death."[16]

[The Blessed One:]
16 "Having abandoned conceit, well concentrated,
With lofty mind, everywhere released: <9>
While dwelling alone in the forest, diligent,
One can cross beyond the realm of Death."[17] [5]

10 (10) Forest

At Sāvatthī. Standing to one side, that devatā recited this verse in the presence of the Blessed One:

17 "Those who dwell deep in the forest,
Peaceful, leading the holy life,
Eating but a single meal a day:
Why is their complexion so serene?"[18]

[The Blessed One:]
18 "They do not sorrow over the past,
Nor do they hanker for the future.
They maintain themselves with what is present:
Hence their complexion is so serene.

19 "Through hankering for the future,
Through sorrowing over the past,
Fools dry up and wither away
Like a green reed cut down."

<10> II. Nandana

11 (1) Nandana

Thus have I heard. On one occasion the Blessed One was dwelling at Sāvatthī in Jeta's Grove, Anāthapiṇḍika's Park. There the Blessed One addressed the bhikkhus thus: "Bhikkhus!"

"Venerable sir!" those bhikkhus replied. The Blessed One said this:

"Once in the past, bhikkhus, a certain devatā of the Tāvatiṃsa host was revelling in Nandana Grove, <11> supplied and endowed with the five cords of celestial sensual pleasure, accompanied by a retinue of celestial nymphs. On that occasion he spoke this verse:

20 "'They do not know bliss
Who have not seen Nandana,
The abode of the glorious male devas
Belonging to the host of Thirty.'[19] [6]

"When this was said, bhikkhus, a certain devatā replied to that devatā in verse:

21 "'Don't you know, you fool,
That maxim of the arahants?
Impermanent are all formations;
Their nature is to arise and vanish.
Having arisen, they cease:
Their appeasement is blissful.'"[20]

12 (2) Delight

At Sāvatthī. Standing to one side, that devatā recited this verse in the presence of the Blessed One: <12>

22 "One who has sons delights in sons,
One with cattle delights in cattle.
Acquisitions truly are a man's delight;
Without acquisitions one does not delight."[21]

[The Blessed One:]

23 "One who has sons sorrows over sons,
One with cattle sorrows over cattle.
Acquisitions truly are a man's sorrows;
Without acquisitions one does not sorrow."

13 (3) None Equal to That for a Son

At Sāvatthī. Standing to one side, that devatā spoke this verse in the presence of the Blessed One:

24 "There is no affection like that for a son,
No wealth equal to cattle,
There is no light like the sun,
Among the waters the ocean is supreme."[22]

[The Blessed One:]

25 "There is no affection like that for oneself,
No wealth equal to grain,
There is no light like wisdom,
Among the waters the rain is supreme." <13>

14 (4) The Khattiya

26 "The khattiya is the best of bipeds,
The ox, the best of quadrupeds;
A maiden is the best of wives,
The first born, the best of sons."[23]

27 "The Buddha is the best of bipeds,
A steed, the best of quadrupeds;
An obedient woman is the best of wives,
A dutiful boy, the best of sons." [7]

15 (5) Murmuring

28 "When the noon hour sets in
And the birds have settled down, <14>
The mighty forest itself murmurs:
How fearful that appears to me!"[24]

29 "When the noon hour sets in
And the birds have settled down,
The mighty forest itself murmurs:
How delightful that appears to me!"

16 (6) Drowsiness and Lethargy

30 "Drowsiness, lethargy, lazy stretching, <15>
Discontent, torpor after meals:
Because of this, here among beings,
The noble path does not appear."

31 "Drowsiness, lethargy, lazy stretching,
Discontent, torpor after meals:
When one dispels this with energy,
The noble path is cleared."[25]

17 (7) Difficult to Practise

32 "The ascetic life is hard to practise
And hard for the inept to endure,
For many are the obstructions there
In which the fool founders."

33 "How many days can one practise the ascetic life
If one does not rein in one's mind?
One would founder with each step
Under the control of one's intentions.[26]

34 "Drawing in the mind's thoughts
As a tortoise draws its limbs into its shell, <16>
Independent, not harassing others, fully quenched,
A bhikkhu would not blame anyone."[27]

18 (8) A Sense of Shame

35 "Is there a person somewhere in the world
Who is restrained by a sense of shame,
One who draws back from blame
As a good horse does from the whip?"[28]

36 "Few are those restrained by a sense of shame
Who fare always mindful;
Few, having reached the end of suffering,
Fare evenly amidst the uneven." [8] <17>

19 (9) A Little Hut

37 "Don't you have a little hut?
Don't you have a little nest?
Don't you have any lines extended?
Are you free from bondage?"

38 "Surely I have no little hut,
Surely I have no little nest,
Surely I have no lines extended,
Surely I'm free from bondage."[29]

39 "What do you think I call a little hut?
What do you think I call a little nest?
What do you think I call lines extended?
What do you think I call bondage?"[30]

40 "It's a mother that you call a little hut,
A wife that you call a little nest, <18>
Sons that you call lines extended,
Craving that you tell me is bondage."

41 "It's good that you have no little hut,
Good that you have no little nest,
Good that you have no lines extended,
Good that you are free from bondage."

20 (10) Samiddhi

Thus have I heard. On one occasion the Blessed One was dwelling at Rājagaha in the Hot Springs Park. Then the Venerable Samiddhi, having risen at the first flush of dawn, went to the hot springs to bathe. Having bathed in the hot springs and come back out, he stood in one robe drying his limbs.

Then, when the night had advanced, a certain devatā of stunning beauty, illuminating the entire hot springs, approached the Venerable Samiddhi. Having approached, she stood in the air and addressed the Venerable Samiddhi in verse:[31] <19>

42 "Without having enjoyed you seek alms, bhikkhu,
You don't seek alms after you've enjoyed.
First enjoy, bhikkhu, then seek alms:
Don't let the time pass you by!" [9]

43 "I do not know what the time might be;
The time is hidden and cannot be seen.
Hence, without enjoying, I seek alms:
Don't let the time pass me by!"[32]

Then that devatā alighted on the earth and said to the Venerable Samiddhi: "You have gone forth while young, bhikkhu, a lad with black hair, endowed with the blessing of youth, in the prime of life, without having dallied with sensual pleasures. Enjoy human sensual pleasures, bhikkhu; do not abandon what is directly visible in order to pursue what takes time."

"I have not abandoned what is directly visible, friend, in order to pursue what takes time. I have abandoned what takes time in order to pursue what is directly visible. <20> For the Blessed One, friend, has stated that sensual pleasures are time-consuming, full of suffering, full of despair, and the danger in them is still greater, while this Dhamma is directly visible, immediate, inviting one to come and see, applicable, to be personally experienced by the wise."[33]

"But how is it, bhikkhu, that the Blessed One has stated that sensual pleasures are time-consuming, full of suffering, full of despair, and the danger in them is still greater? How is it that this Dhamma is directly visible, immediate, inviting one to come and see, applicable, to be personally experienced by the wise?"

"I am newly ordained, friend, not long gone forth, just recently come to this Dhamma and Discipline. I cannot explain it in detail. But that Blessed One, the Arahant, the Perfectly Enlightened One, is dwelling at Rājagaha in the Hot Springs Park. Approach that Blessed One and ask him about this matter.

As he explains it to you, so you should remember it."

"It isn't easy for us to approach that Blessed One, bhikkhu, as he is surrounded by other devatās of great influence.[34] If you would approach him <21> and ask him about this matter, we will come along too in order to hear the Dhamma."

"Very well, friend," the Venerable Samiddhi replied. Then he approached the Blessed One, paid homage to him, sat down to one side, [10] and reported his entire discussion with that devatā, [11] <22–23> (*verses 44–45, included in the report, repeat verses 42–43*) adding: "If that devatā's statement is true, venerable sir, then that devatā should be close by."

When this was said, that devatā said to the Venerable Samiddhi: "Ask, bhikkhu! Ask, bhikkhu! For I have arrived."

Then the Blessed One addressed that devatā in verse:

46 "Beings who perceive what can be expressed
Become established in what can be expressed. <24>
Not fully understanding what can be expressed,
They come under the yoke of Death.[35]

47 "But having fully understood what can be expressed,
One does not conceive 'one who expresses.'
For that does not exist for him
By which one could describe him.[36]

"If you understand, spirit, speak up."

"I do not understand in detail, venerable sir, the meaning of what was stated in brief by the Blessed One. Please, venerable sir, let the Blessed One explain it to me in such a way that I might understand in detail the meaning of what he stated in brief." [12]

[The Blessed One:]

48 "One who conceives 'I am equal, better, or worse,'
Might on that account engage in disputes.
But one not shaken in the three discriminations
Does not think, 'I am equal or better.'[37] <25>

"If you understand, spirit, speak up."

"In this case too, venerable sir, I do not understand in detail …

let the Blessed One explain it to me in such a way that I might understand in detail the meaning of what he stated in brief."

[The Blessed One:]
49 "He abandoned reckoning, did not assume conceit;[38]
He cut off craving here for name-and-form.
Though devas and humans search for him
Here and beyond, in the heavens and all abodes,
They do not find the one whose knots are cut,
The one untroubled, free of longing.

"If you understand, spirit, speak up."

"I understand in detail, venerable sir, the meaning of what was stated in brief by the Blessed One thus: <26>

50 "One should do no evil in all the world,
Not by speech, mind, or body.
Having abandoned sense pleasures,
Mindful and clearly comprehending,
One should not pursue a course
That is painful and harmful."[39]

[13] <27> III. A Sword

21 (1) A Sword

At Sāvatthī. Standing to one side, that devatā recited this verse in the presence of the Blessed One:

51 "As if smitten by a sword,
As if his head were on fire,
A bhikkhu should wander mindfully
To abandon sensual lust."

[The Blessed One:]
52 "As if smitten by a sword,
As if his head were on fire,
A bhikkhu should wander mindfully
To abandon identity view."[40]

22 (2) It Touches <28>

53 "It does not touch one who does not touch,
But then will touch the one who touches.
Therefore it touches the one who touches,
The one who wrongs an innocent man."[41]

54 "If one wrongs an innocent man,
A pure person without blemish,
The evil falls back on the fool himself
Like fine dust thrown against the wind."[42]

23 (3) Tangle

55 "A tangle inside, a tangle outside,
This generation is entangled in a tangle.
I ask you this, O Gotama,
Who can disentangle this tangle?"[43] <29>

56 "A man established on virtue, wise,
Developing the mind and wisdom,
A bhikkhu ardent and discreet:
He can disentangle this tangle.[44]

57 "Those for whom lust and hatred
Along with ignorance have been expunged,
The arahants with taints destroyed:
For them the tangle is disentangled.[45]

58 "Where name-and-form ceases,
Stops without remainder,
And also impingement and perception of form:
It is here this tangle is cut."[46] [14]

24 (4) Reining in the Mind

59 "From whatever one reins in the mind,
From that no suffering comes to one. <30>
Should one rein in the mind from everything,
One is freed from all suffering."

60 "One need not rein in the mind from everything
When the mind has come under control.
From whatever it is that evil comes,
From this one should rein in the mind."[47]

25 (5) *The Arahant*

61 "If a bhikkhu is an arahant,
Consummate, with taints destroyed,
One who bears his final body,
Would he still say, 'I speak'?
And would he say, 'They speak to me'?"[48]

62 "If a bhikkhu is an arahant, <31>
Consummate, with taints destroyed,
One who bears his final body,
He might still say, 'I speak,'
And he might say, 'They speak to me.'
Skilful, knowing the world's parlance,
He uses such terms as mere expressions."[49]

63 "When a bhikkhu is an arahant,
Consummate, with taints destroyed,
One who bears his final body,
Is it because he has come upon conceit
That he would say, 'I speak,'
That he would say, 'They speak to me'?"[50]

64 "No knots exist for one with conceit abandoned;
For him all knots of conceit are consumed.
Though the wise one has transcended the conceived, [15]
He still might say, 'I speak,' <32>
He might say too, 'They speak to me.'
Skilful, knowing the world's parlance,
He uses such terms as mere expressions."[51]

26 (6) *Sources of Light*

65 "How many sources of light are in the world
By means of which the world is illumined?

We have come to ask the Blessed One this:
How are we to understand it?"

66 "There are four sources of light in the world;
A fifth one is not found here.
The sun shines by day,
The moon glows at night,
67 And fire flares up here and there
Both by day and at night.
But the Buddha is the best of those that shine: <33>
He is the light unsurpassed."

27 (7) Streams

68 "From where do the streams turn back?
Where does the round no longer revolve?
Where does name-and-form cease,
Stop without remainder?"

69 "Where water, earth, fire, and air,
Do not gain a footing:
It is from here that the streams turn back,
Here that the round no longer revolves;
Here name-and-form ceases,
Stops without remainder."[52]

28 (8) Those of Great Wealth <34>

71[53] "Those of great wealth and property,
Even khattiyas who rule the country,
Look at each other with greedy eyes,
Insatiable in sensual pleasures.
72 Among these who have become so avid,
Flowing along in the stream of existence,
Who here have abandoned craving?
Who in the world are no longer avid?"[54]

73 "Having left their homes and gone forth,
Having left their dear sons and cattle,
Having left behind lust and hatred, <35>

Having expunged ignorance—
The arahants with taints destroyed
Are those in the world no longer avid." [16]

29 (9) Four Wheels

74 "Having four wheels and nine doors,
Filled up and bound with greed,
Born from a bog, O great hero!
How does one escape from it?"[55]

75 "Having cut the thong and the strap,
Having cut off evil desire and greed,
Having drawn out craving with its root:
Thus one escapes from it."[56]

30 (10) Antelope Calves <36>

76 "Having approached you, we ask a question
Of the slender hero with antelope calves,
Greedless, subsisting on little food,
Wandering alone like a lion or nāga,
Without concern for sensual pleasures:
How is one released from suffering?"[57]

77 "Five cords of sensual pleasure in the world,
With mind declared to be the sixth:
Having expunged desire here,
One is thus released from suffering."[58]

<37> IV. The Satullapa Host

31 (1) With the Good

Thus have I heard. On one occasion the Blessed One was dwelling at Sāvatthī in Jeta's Grove, Anāthapiṇḍika's Park. Then, when the night had advanced, a number of devatās belonging to the Satullapa host, of stunning beauty, illuminating the entire Jeta's Grove, approached the Blessed One.[59] Having approached, they paid homage to the Blessed One and stood to one side. [17]

Then one devatā, standing to one side, recited this verse in the presence of the Blessed One:

78 "One should associate only with the good; <38>
With the good one should foster intimacy.
Having learnt the true Dhamma of the good,
One becomes better, never worse."

Then five other devatās in turn recited their verses in the presence of the Blessed One:

79 "One should associate only with the good;
With the good one should foster intimacy.
Having learnt the true Dhamma of the good,
Wisdom is gained, but not from another."[60]

80 "One should associate only with the good;
With the good one should foster intimacy.
Having learnt the true Dhamma of the good, <39>
One does not sorrow in the midst of sorrow."

81 "One should associate only with the good;
With the good one should foster intimacy.
Having learnt the true Dhamma of the good,
One shines amidst one's relations."

82 "One should associate only with the good;
With the good one should foster intimacy.
Having learnt the true Dhamma of the good,
Beings fare on to a good destination."

83 "One should associate only with the good;
With the good one should foster intimacy.
Having learnt the true Dhamma of the good,
Beings abide comfortably."[61]

Then another devatā said to the Blessed One: "Which one, Blessed One, has spoken well?"

"You have all spoken well in a way.[62] But listen to me too: [18]

84 "One should associate only with the good;
With the good one should foster intimacy.
Having learnt the true Dhamma of the good,
One is released from all suffering."

This is what the Blessed One said. Elated, those devatās paid homage to the Blessed One and, keeping him on the right, they disappeared right there.

32 (2) Stinginess

On one occasion the Blessed One was dwelling at Sāvatthī in Jeta's Grove, Anāthapiṇḍika's Park. Then, when the night had advanced, a number of devatās belonging to the Satullapa host, of stunning beauty, illuminating the entire Jeta's Grove, approached the Blessed One. Having approached, they paid homage to the Blessed One and stood to one side.

Then one devatā, standing to one side, recited this verse in the presence of the Blessed One:

85 "Through stinginess and negligence
A gift is not given.
One who knows, desiring merit, <40>
Should surely give a gift."

Then another devatā recited these verses in the presence of the Blessed One:

86 "That which the miser fears when he does not give
Is the very danger that comes to the nongiver.
The hunger and thirst that the miser fears
Afflict that fool in this world and the next.

87 "Therefore, having removed stinginess,
The conqueror of the stain should give a gift.[63]
Deeds of merit are the support for living beings
[When they arise] in the other world."

Then another devatā recited these verses in the presence of the Blessed One:

88 "They do not die among the dead
Who, like fellow travellers on the road,
Provide though they have but a little:
This is an ancient principle.[64] <41>

89 "Some provide from the little they have,
Others who are affluent don't like to give.
An offering given from what little one has
Is worth a thousand times its value." [19]

Then another devatā recited these verses in the presence of the Blessed One:

90 "The bad do not emulate the good,
Who give what is hard to give
And do deeds hard to do:
The Dhamma of the good is hard to follow.

91 "Therefore their destination after death
Differs for the good and the bad:
The bad go to hell,
The good are bound for heaven."

Then another devatā said to the Blessed One: "Which one, Blessed One, has spoken well?"

"You have all spoken well in a way. But listen to me too: <42>

92 "If one practises the Dhamma
Though getting on by gleaning,
If while one supports one's wife
One gives from the little one has,
Then a hundred thousand offerings
Of those who sacrifice a thousand
Are not worth even a fraction
[Of the gift] of one like him."[65]

Then another devatā addressed the Blessed One in verse:

93 "Why does their sacrifice, vast and grand,
Not share the value of the righteous one's gift?
Why are a hundred thousand offerings
Of those who sacrifice a thousand
Not worth even a fraction
[Of the gift] of one like him?"

Then the Blessed One answered that devatā in verse:

94 "Since they give while settled in unrighteousness,
Having slain and killed, causing sorrow,
Their offering—tearful, fraught with violence—
Shares not the value of the righteous one's gift. <43>
That is why a hundred thousand offerings
Of those who sacrifice a thousand
Are not worth even a fraction
[Of the gift] of one like him." [20]

33 (3) Good

At Sāvatthī. Then, when the night had advanced, a number of devatās belonging to the Satullapa host, of stunning beauty, illuminating the entire Jeta's Grove, approached the Blessed One. Having approached, they paid homage to the Blessed One and stood to one side.

Then one devatā, standing to one side, uttered this inspired utterance in the presence of the Blessed One:

"Good is giving, dear sir!

95 "Through stinginess and negligence
A gift is not given.
One who knows, desiring merit,
Should surely give a gift."

Then another devatā uttered this inspired utterance in the presence of the Blessed One:

"Good is giving, dear sir!

And further:
Even when there's little, giving is good. <44>

96 "Some provide from what little they have,
Others who are affluent don't like to give.
An offering given from what little one has
Is worth a thousand times its value."

Then another devatā uttered this inspired utterance in the presence of the Blessed One:

"Good is giving, dear sir!
Even when there's little, giving is good.
And further:
When done with faith too, giving is good.

97 "Giving and warfare are similar, they say:
A few good ones conquer many.
If one with faith gives even a little,
He thereby becomes happy in the other world."[66]

Then another devatā uttered this inspired utterance in the presence of the Blessed One:

"Good is giving, dear sir!
Even when there's little, giving is good. [21]
When done with faith too, giving is good.
And further:
The gift of a righteous gain is also good. <45>

98 "When he gives a gift of a righteous gain
Obtained by exertion and energy,
Having passed over Yama's Vetaraṇī River,
That mortal arrives at celestial states."[67]

Then another devatā uttered this inspired utterance in the presence of the Blessed One:

"Good is giving, dear sir!
Even when there's little, giving is good.

When done with faith too, giving is good;
The gift of a righteous gain is also good.
And further:
Giving discriminately too is good.[68]

99 "Giving discriminately is praised by the Fortunate One—
To those worthy of offerings
Here in the world of the living.
What is given to them bears great fruit
Like seeds sown in a fertile field."

Then another devatā uttered this inspired utterance in the presence of the Blessed One:

"Good is giving, dear sir!
Even when there's little, giving is good.
When done with faith too, giving is good;
The gift of a righteous gain is also good.
Giving with discretion too is good. <46>
And further:
Restraint towards living beings is also good.

100 "One who fares harming no living beings
Does no evil from fear of others' censure.
In that they praise the timid, not the brave,
For out of fear the good do no evil."

Then another devatā said to the Blessed One: [22] "Which one, Blessed One, has spoken well?"

"You have all spoken well in a way. But listen to me too:

101 "Surely giving is praised in many ways,
But the path of Dhamma surpasses giving.
For in the past and even long ago,
The good and wise ones attained Nibbāna."[69]

34 (4) There Are No <47>

On one occasion the Blessed One was dwelling at Sāvatthi in Jeta's Grove, Anāthapiṇḍika's Park. Then, when the night had advanced, a number of devatās belonging to the Satullapa host, of stunning beauty, illuminating the entire Jeta's Grove, approached the Blessed One. Having approached, they paid homage to the Blessed One and stood to one side.

Then one devatā, standing to one side, recited this verse in the presence of the Blessed One:

102 "There are among humans
No permanent sensual pleasures;
Here there are just desirable things.
When a person is bound to these,
Heedless in their midst,
From Death's realm he does not reach
The state of no-more-coming-back."[70]

[Another devatā:] "Misery is born of desire; suffering is born of desire. By the removal of desire, misery is removed; by the removal of misery, suffering is removed."[71]

[The Blessed One:]
103 "They are not sense pleasures, the world's pretty things:
Man's sensuality is the intention of lust. <48>
The pretty things remain as they are in the world
But the wise remove the desire for them.[72] [23]

104 "One should discard anger, cast off conceit,
Transcend all the fetters.
No sufferings torment one who has nothing,
Who does not adhere to name-and-form.[73]

105 "He abandoned reckoning, did not assume conceit;
He cut off craving here for name-and-form.
Though devas and humans search for him
Here and beyond, in the heavens and all abodes,
They do not find the one whose knots are cut,
The one untroubled, free of longing."

106 "If devas and humans have not seen
The one thus liberated here or beyond,"
[said the Venerable Mogharāja],

"Are they to be praised who venerate him,
The best of men, faring for the good of humans?"[74] <49>

107 "Those bhikkhus too become worthy of praise,
[Mogharāja," said the Blessed One,]
"Who venerate him, the one thus liberated.
But having known Dhamma and abandoned doubt,
Those bhikkhus become even surmounters of ties."[75]

35 (5) Faultfinders

On one occasion the Blessed One was dwelling at Sāvatthī in Jeta's Grove, Anāthapiṇḍika's Park. Then, when the night had advanced, a number of "faultfinding" devatās, of stunning beauty, illuminating the entire Jeta's Grove, approached the Blessed One and stood in the air.[76] [24]

Then one devatā, standing in the air, recited this verse in the presence of the Blessed One:

108 "If one shows oneself in one way
While actually being otherwise,
What one enjoys is obtained by theft
Like the gains of a cheating gambler."[77]

[Another devatā:] <50>
109 "One should speak as one would act;
Don't speak as one wouldn't act.
The wise clearly discern the person
Who does not practise what he preaches."

[The Blessed One:]
110 "Not by mere speech nor solely by listening
Can one advance on this firm path of practice
By which the wise ones, the meditators,
Are released from the bondage of Māra.

111 "Truly, the wise do not pretend,
For they have understood the way of the world.
By final knowledge the wise are quenched:
They have crossed over attachment to the world."

Then those devatās, having alighted on the earth, prostrated themselves with their heads at the Blessed One's feet and said to the Blessed One: <51>"A transgression overcame us, venerable sir, being so foolish, so stupid, so unskilful that we imagined we could assail the Blessed One. Let the Blessed One pardon us for our transgression seen as such for the sake of restraint in the future."

Then the Blessed One displayed a smile.[78] Those devatās, finding fault to an even greater extent, then rose up into the air. One devatā recited this verse in the presence of the Blessed One:

112 "If one does not grant pardon
To those who confess transgression,
Angry at heart, intent on hate,
One strongly harbours enmity."

[The Blessed One:] <52>
113 "If there was no transgression,
If here there was no going astray,
And if enmities were appeased,
Then one would be faultless here."[79]

[A devatā:]
114 "For whom are there no transgressions?
For whom is there no going astray?
Who has not fallen into confusion?
And who is the wise one, ever mindful?" [25]

[The Blessed One:]
115 "The Tathāgata, the Enlightened One,
Full of compassion for all beings:
For him there are no transgressions,
For him there is no going astray;
He has not fallen into confusion,
And he is the wise one, ever mindful.

116 "If one does not grant pardon
To those who confess transgression, <53>
Angry at heart, intent on hate,
One strongly harbours enmity.

In that enmity I do not delight,
Thus I pardon your transgression."

36 (6) Faith

On one occasion the Blessed One was dwelling at Sāvatthī in Jeta's Grove, Anāthapiṇḍika's Park. Then, when the night had advanced, a number of devatās belonging to the Satullapa host, of stunning beauty, illuminating the entire Jeta's Grove, approached the Blessed One. Having approached, they paid homage to the Blessed One and stood to one side.

Then one devatā, standing to one side, recited this verse in the presence of the Blessed One:

117 "Faith is a person's partner;
If lack of faith does not persist,
Fame and renown thereby come to him, <54>
And he goes to heaven on leaving the body."

Then another devatā recited these verses in the presence of the Blessed One:[80]

118 "One should discard anger, cast off conceit,
Transcend all the fetters.
No ties torment one who has nothing,
Who does not adhere to name-and-form."[81]

[Another devatā:]
119 "Foolish people devoid of wisdom
Devote themselves to negligence.
But the wise man guards diligence
As his foremost treasure.

120 "Do not yield to negligence,
Don't be intimate with sensual delight.
For the diligent ones, meditating,
Attain supreme happiness." [26]

37 (7) Concourse <55>

Thus have I heard. On one occasion the Blessed One was dwelling among the Sakyans at Kapilavatthu in the Great Wood together with a great Saṅgha of bhikkhus, with five hundred bhikkhus all of whom were arahants.[82] And the devatās from ten world systems had for the most part assembled in order to see the Blessed One and the Bhikkhu Saṅgha. Then the thought occurred to four devatās of the host from the Pure Abodes:[83] "This Blessed One is dwelling among the Sakyans at Kapilavatthu in the Great Wood together with a great Saṅgha of bhikkhus, with five hundred bhikkhus all of whom are arahants. And the devatās from ten world systems have for the most part assembled in order to see the Blessed One and the Bhikkhu Saṅgha. Let us also approach the Blessed One and, in his presence, each speak our own verse."

Then, just as quickly as a strong man might extend his drawn-in arm or draw in his extended arm, those devatās disappeared from among the devas of the Pure Abodes <56> and reappeared before the Blessed One. Then those devatās paid homage to the Blessed One and stood to one side. Standing to one side, one devatā recited this verse in the presence of the Blessed One:

121 "A great concourse takes place in the woods,
The deva hosts have assembled.
We have come to this Dhamma concourse
To see the invincible Saṅgha."

Then another devatā recited this verse in the presence of the Blessed One:

122 "The bhikkhus there are concentrated;
They have straightened their own minds.
Like a charioteer who holds the reins,
The wise ones guard their faculties." [27]

Then another devatā recited this verse in the presence of the Blessed One:

123 "Having cut through barrenness, cut the cross-bar,

Having uprooted Indra's pillar, unstirred,
They wander about pure and stainless,
Young nāgas well tamed by the One with Vision."[84] <57>

Then another devatā recited this verse in the presence of the Blessed One:

124 "Those who have gone to the Buddha for refuge
Will not go to the plane of misery.
On discarding the human body,
They will fill the hosts of devas."[85]

38 (8) The Stone Splinter

Thus have I heard. On one occasion the Blessed One was dwelling at Rājagaha in the Maddakucchi Deer Park. Now on that occasion the Blessed One's foot had been cut by a stone splinter.[86] Severe pains assailed the Blessed One—bodily feelings that were painful, racking, sharp, piercing, harrowing, disagreeable. But the Blessed One endured them, mindful and clearly comprehending, without becoming distressed. Then the Blessed One had his outer robe folded in four, and he lay down on his right side in the lion posture with one leg overlapping the other, mindful and clearly comprehending. <58>

Then, when the night had advanced, seven hundred devatās belonging to the Satullapa host, of stunning beauty, illuminating the entire Maddakucchi Deer Park, approached the Blessed One. Having approached, they paid homage to the Blessed One and stood to one side.

Then one devatā, standing to one side, uttered this inspired utterance in the presence of the Blessed One: [28] "The ascetic Gotama is indeed a nāga, sir! And when bodily feelings have arisen that are painful, racking, sharp, piercing, harrowing, disagreeable, through his nāga-like manner he endures them, mindful and clearly comprehending, without becoming distressed."[87]

Then another devatā uttered this inspired utterance in the presence of the Blessed One: "The ascetic Gotama is indeed a lion, sir! And when bodily feelings have arisen that are painful, racking, sharp, piercing, harrowing, disagreeable, through his leonine manner he endures them, mindful and clearly comprehending, without becoming distressed."

Then another devatā uttered this inspired utterance in the presence of the Blessed One: "The ascetic Gotama is indeed a thoroughbred, sir! And when bodily feelings have arisen that are painful ... disagreeable, through his thoroughbred manner he endures them, mindful and clearly comprehending, without becoming distressed."

Then another devatā uttered this inspired utterance in the presence of the Blessed One: "The ascetic Gotama is indeed a chief bull, sir! <59> And when bodily feelings have arisen that are painful ... disagreeable, through his chief bull's manner he endures them, mindful and clearly comprehending, without becoming distressed."

Then another devatā uttered this inspired utterance in the presence of the Blessed One: "The ascetic Gotama is indeed a beast of burden, sir! And when bodily feelings have arisen that are painful ... disagreeable, through his beast-of-burden's manner he endures them, mindful and clearly comprehending, without becoming distressed."

Then another devatā uttered this inspired utterance in the presence of the Blessed One: "The ascetic Gotama is indeed tamed, sir! And when bodily feelings have arisen that are painful, racking, sharp, piercing, harrowing, disagreeable, through his tamed manner he endures them, mindful and clearly comprehending, without becoming distressed."

Then another devatā uttered this inspired utterance in the presence of the Blessed One: "See his concentration well developed and his mind well liberated—not bent forward and not bent back, and not blocked and checked by forceful suppression![88] If anyone would think such a one could be violated—such a nāga of a man, such a lion of a man, [29] such a thoroughbred of a man, <60> such a chief bull of a man, such a beast of burden of a man, such a tamed man—what is that due to apart from lack of vision?"

125 Though brahmins learned in the five Vedas
Practise austerities for a hundred years,
Their minds are not rightly liberated:
Those of low nature do not reach the far shore.[89]

126 They founder in craving, bound to vows and rules,
Practising rough austerity for a hundred years,
But their minds are not rightly liberated:
Those of low nature do not reach the far shore.

127 There is no taming here for one fond of conceit,
Nor is there sagehood for the unconcentrated:
Though dwelling alone in the forest, heedless, <61>
One cannot cross beyond the realm of Death.

128 Having abandoned conceit, well concentrated,
With lofty mind, everywhere released:
While dwelling alone in the forest, diligent,
One can cross beyond the realm of Death.

39 (9) Pajjunna's Daughter (1)

Thus have I heard. On one occasion the Blessed One was dwelling at Vesālī in the Great Wood in the Hall with the Peaked Roof. Then, when the night had advanced, Kokanadā, Pajjunna's daughter, of stunning beauty, illuminating the entire Great Wood, approached the Blessed One.[90] Having approached, she paid homage to the Blessed One, stood to one side, and recited these verses in the presence of the Blessed One:[91]

129 "I worship the Buddha, the best of beings,
Dwelling in the woods at Vesālī. [30] <62>
Kokanadā am I,
Kokanadā, Pajjunna's daughter.[92]

130 "Earlier I had only heard that the Dhamma
Has been realized by the One with Vision;
But now I know it as a witness
While the Sage, the Fortunate One, teaches.

131 "Those ignorant people who go about
Criticizing the noble Dhamma
Pass on to the terrible Roruva hell
And experience suffering for a long time.[93]

132 "But those who have peace and acquiescence
In regard to the noble Dhamma,
On discarding the human body,
Will fill the host of devas."[94]

40 (10) Pajjunna's Daughter (2) <63>

Thus have I heard. On one occasion the Blessed One was dwelling at Vesālī in the Great Wood, in the Hall with the Peaked Roof. Then, when the night had advanced, Cūḷakokanadā, Pajjunna's [younger] daughter, of stunning beauty, illuminating the entire Great Wood, approached the Blessed One. Having approached, she paid homage to the Blessed One, stood to one side, and recited these verses in the presence of the Blessed One:

133 "Here came Kokanadā, Pajjunna's daughter,
Beautiful as the gleam of lightning.
Venerating the Buddha and the Dhamma,
She spoke these verses full of meaning. [31]

134 "Though the Dhamma is of such a nature
That I might analyse it in many ways,
I will state its meaning briefly
To the extent I have learnt it by heart.[95]

135 "One should do no evil in all the world, <64>
Not by speech, mind, or body.
Having abandoned sense pleasures,
Mindful and clearly comprehending,
One should not pursue a course
That is painful and harmful."

V. Ablaze

41 (1) Ablaze

Thus have I heard. On one occasion the Blessed One was dwelling at Sāvatthī in Jeta's Grove, Anāthapiṇḍika's Park. Then, when the night had advanced, a certain devatā of stunning beauty, illuminating the entire Jeta's Grove, approached the Blessed One. <65> Having approached, he paid homage to the Blessed One, stood to one side, and recited these verses in the presence of the Blessed One:

136 "When one's house is ablaze
The vessel taken out
Is the one that is useful,
Not the one left burnt inside.

137 "So when the world is ablaze
With [the fires of] aging and death,
One should take out [one's wealth] by giving:
What is given is well salvaged. [32] <66>

139[96] "What is given yields pleasant fruit,
But not so what is not given.
Thieves take it away, or kings,
It gets burnt by fire or is lost.

140 "Then in the end one leaves the body
Along with one's possessions.
Having understood this, the wise person
Should enjoy himself but also give.
Having given and enjoyed as fits his means,
Blameless he goes to the heavenly state."

42 (2) Giving What?

[A devatā:]
141 "Giving what does one give strength?
Giving what does one give beauty?
Giving what does one give ease?
Giving what does one give sight?
Who is the giver of all?
Being asked, please explain to me." <67>

[The Blessed One:]
142 "Giving food, one gives strength;
Giving clothes, one gives beauty;

Giving a vehicle, one gives ease;
Giving a lamp, one gives sight.

143 "The one who gives a residence
Is the giver of all.
But the one who teaches the Dhamma
Is the giver of the Deathless."

43 (3) Food

144 "They always take delight in food,
Both devas and human beings.
So what sort of spirit could it be
That does not take delight in food?"[97]

145 "When they give out of faith
With a heart of confidence,
Food accrues to [the giver] himself
Both in this world and the next. <68>

146 "Therefore, having removed stinginess,
The conqueror of the stain should give a gift.
Merits are the support for living beings
[When they arise] in the other world."

44 (4) One Root

[A devatā:]
147 "The seer has crossed over the abyss
With its one root, two whirlpools,
Three stains, five extensions,
An ocean with twelve eddies."[98] [33]

45 (5) Perfect

[A devatā:]
148 "Behold him of perfect name,
The seer of the subtle goal,
The giver of wisdom, unattached
To the lair of sensual pleasures. <69>

Behold the wise one, all-knowing,
The great seer treading the noble path."[99]

46 (6) Nymphs

149 "Resounding with a host of nymphs,
Haunted by a host of demons!
This grove is to be called 'Deluding':
How does one escape from it?"[100]

150 "'The straight way' that path is called,
And 'fearless' is its destination.
The chariot is called 'unrattling,'
Fitted with wheels of wholesome states.

151 "The sense of shame is its leaning board,
Mindfulness its upholstery;
I call the Dhamma the charioteer,
With right view running out in front.[101] <70>

152 "One who has such a vehicle—
Whether a woman or a man—
Has, by means of this vehicle,
Drawn close to Nibbāna."[102]

47 (7) Planters of Groves

153 "For whom does merit always increase,
Both by day and by night?
Who are the people going to heaven,
Established in Dhamma, endowed with virtue?"

154 "Those who set up a park or a grove,
The people who construct a bridge,
A place to drink and a well,
Those who give a residence:[103]

155 "For them merit always increases,
Both by day and by night;

Those are the people going to heaven,
Established in Dhamma, endowed with virtue." <71>

48 (8) Jeta's Grove

[The devatā Anāthapiṇḍika:]
156 "This indeed is that Jeta's Grove,
The resort of the Order of seers,
Dwelt in by the Dhamma King,
A place that gives me joy.[104] [34]

157 "Action, knowledge, righteousness,
Virtue, an excellent life:
By this are mortals purified,
Not by clan or wealth.

158 "Therefore a person who is wise,
Out of regard for his own good,
Should carefully examine the Dhamma:
Thus he is purified in it.

159 "Sāriputta truly is endowed with wisdom,
With virtue and with inner peace.
Even a bhikkhu who has gone beyond
At best can only equal him."[105] <72>

49 (9) Stingy

[A devatā:]
160 "Those who are stingy here in the world,
Niggardly folk, revilers,
People who create obstacles
For others engaged in giving alms:
161 What kind of result do they reap?
What kind of future destiny?
We've come to ask the Blessed One this:
How are we to understand it?"

[The Blessed One:]
162 "Those who are stingy here in the world,

Niggardly folk, revilers,
People who create obstacles
For others engaged in giving alms:
They might be reborn in hell,
In the animal realm or Yama's world.[106]

163 "If they come back to the human state
They are born in a poor family <73>
Where clothes, food, pleasures, and sport
Are obtained only with difficulty.

164 "Whatever the fools may expect from others,
Even that they do not obtain.
This is the result in this very life;
And in the future a bad destination."

[A devatā:]
165 "We understand thus what you have said;
We ask, O Gotama, another question:
Those here who, on gaining the human state,
Are amiable and generous,
Confident in the Buddha and the Dhamma
And deeply respectful towards the Saṅgha:
166 What kind of result do they reap?
What kind of future destiny?
We've come to ask the Blessed One this:
How are we to understand it?" <74>

[The Blessed One:]
167 "Those here who, on gaining the human state,
Are amiable and generous,
Confident in the Buddha and the Dhamma
And deeply respectful towards the Saṅgha,
These brighten up the heavens
Where they've been reborn.[107] [35]

168 "If they come back to the human state
They are reborn in a rich family
Where clothes, food, pleasures, and sport
Are obtained without difficulty.

169 "They rejoice like the devas who control
The goods amassed by others.[108]
This is the result in this very life;
And in the future a good destination." <75>

50 (10) Ghaṭīkāra

[The devatā Ghaṭīkāra:]
170 "Seven bhikkhus reborn in Avihā
Have been fully liberated.
With lust and hatred utterly destroyed,
They have crossed over attachment to the world."[109]

[The Blessed One:]
171 "And who are those who crossed the swamp,
The realm of Death so hard to cross?
Who, having left the human body,
Have overcome the celestial bond?"[110]

[Ghaṭīkāra:]
172 "Upaka and Palagaṇḍa,
With Pukkusāti—these are three.
Then Bhaddiya and Bhaddadeva,
And Bāhudantī and Piṅgiya.
These, having left the human body,
Have overcome the celestial bond."[111]

[The Blessed One:] <76>
173 "Good is the word you speak of them,
Of those who have abandoned Māra's snares.
Whose Dhamma was it that they understood
Whereby they cut through the bondage of existence?"[112]

[Ghaṭīkāra:]
174 "It was not apart from the Blessed One!
It was not apart from your Teaching!
By having understood your Dhamma
They cut through the bondage of existence.

175 "Where name-and-form ceases,
Stops without remainder:
By understanding that Dhamma here
They cut through the bondage of existence."[113]

[The Blessed One:]
176 "Deep is the speech you utter,
Hard to understand, very hard to grasp.
Having understood whose Dhamma
Do you utter such speech?" <77>

[Ghaṭīkāra:]
177 "In the past I was the potter,
Ghaṭīkāra in Vehaḷiṅga.
I supported my mother and father then
As a lay follower of the Buddha Kassapa. [36]

178 "I abstained from sexual intercourse,
I was celibate, free from carnal ties.
I was your fellow villager,
In the past I was your friend.

179 "I am the one who knows
These seven liberated bhikkhus,
Who with lust and hatred utterly destroyed
Have crossed over attachment to the world."

[The Blessed One:]
180 "Just so it was at that time,
As you say, O Bhaggava:[114]
In the past you were the potter, <78>
Ghaṭikara in Vehaḷiṅga.
You supported your mother and father then
As a lay follower of the Buddha Kassapa.

181 "You abstained from sexual intercourse,
You were celibate, free from carnal ties.
You were my fellow villager,
In the past you were my friend."

182 Such was the meeting that took place
Between those friends from the past,
Both now inwardly developed,
Bearers of their final bodies.[115]

<79>

VI. Old Age

51 (1) Old Age

[A devatā:]
183 "What is good until old age?
What is good when established?
What is the precious gem of humans?
What is hard for thieves to steal?"

[The Blessed One:]
184 "Virtue is good until old age;
Faith is good when established;
Wisdom is the precious gem of humans;
Merit is hard for thieves to steal."

52 (2) Undecaying <80>

185 "What is good by not decaying?
What is good when made secure?
What is the precious gem of humans?
What cannot be stolen by thieves?"[116] [37]

186 "Virtue is good by not decaying;
Faith is good when made secure;
Wisdom is the precious gem of humans;
Merit cannot be stolen by thieves."

53 (3) The Friend

187 "What is the friend of one on a journey?
What is the friend in one's own home?
What is the friend of one in need?
What is the friend in the future life?"[117]

188 "A caravan is the friend of one on a journey; <81>
A mother is the friend in one's own home;
A comrade when the need arises
Is one's friend again and again.
The deeds of merit one has done—
That is the friend in the future life."

54 (4) Support

189 "What is the support of human beings?
What is the best companion here?
The creatures who dwell on the earth—
By what do they sustain their life?"

190 "Sons are the support of human beings,
A wife the best companion;
The creatures who dwell on the earth
Sustain their life by rain."[118] <82>

55 (5) Produces (1)

191 "What is it that produces a person?
What does he have that runs around?
What enters upon saṃsāra?
What is his greatest fear?" <83>

192 "It is craving that produces a person;
His mind is what runs around;
A being enters upon saṃsāra;
Suffering is his greatest fear."

56 (6) Produces (2)

193 "What is it that produces a person?
What does he have that runs around?
What enters upon saṃsāra?
From what is he not yet freed?"

194 "Craving is what produces a person;
His mind is what runs around;

A being enters upon saṃsāra;
He is not freed from suffering." [38]

57 (7) Produces (3)

195 "What is it that produces a person?
What does he have that runs around?
What enters upon saṃsāra?
What determines his destiny?"

196 "Craving is what produces a person;
His mind is what runs around;
A being enters upon saṃsāra;
Kamma determines his destiny."

58 (8) The Deviant Path

197 "What is declared the deviant path?
What undergoes destruction night and day? <84>
What is the stain of the holy life?
What is the bath without water?"

198 "Lust is declared the deviant path;
Life undergoes destruction night and day;
Women are the stain of the holy life:
Here menfolk are enmeshed.
Austerity and the holy life—
That is the bath without water."[119]

59 (9) Partner

199 "What is a person's partner?
What is it that instructs him?
Taking delight in what is a mortal
Released from all suffering?"

200 "Faith is a person's partner,
And wisdom is what instructs him. <85>
Taking delight in Nibbāna, a mortal
Is released from all suffering."

60 (10) Poetry

201 "What is the scaffolding of verses?
What constitutes their phrasing?
On what base do verses rest?
What is the abode of verses?"

202 "Metre is the scaffolding of verses;
Syllables constitute their phrasing;
Verses rest on a base of names;
The poet is the abode of verses."[120]

[39] <86> VII. Weighed Down

61 (1) Name

203 "What has weighed down everything?
What is most extensive?
What is the one thing that has
All under its control?"

204 "Name has weighed down everything;
Nothing is more extensive than name. <87>
Name is the one thing that has
All under its control."[121]

62 (2) Mind

205 "By what is the world led around?
By what is it dragged here and there?
What is the one thing that has
All under its control?"

206 "The world is led around by mind;
By mind it's dragged here and there.
Mind is the one thing that has
All under its control."[122]

63 (3) Craving

207 "By what is the world led around?
By what is it dragged here and there? <88>
What is the one thing that has
All under its control?"

208 "The world is led around by craving;
By craving it is dragged here and there.
Craving is the one thing that has
All under its control."

64 (4) Fetter

209 "By what is the world tightly fettered?
What is its means of travelling about?
What is it that one must forsake
In order to say, 'Nibbāna'?"

210 "The world is tightly fettered by delight;
Thought is its means of travelling about.
Craving is what one must forsake
In order to say, 'Nibbāna.'"[123] <89>

65 (5) Bondage

211 "By what is the world held in bondage?
What is its means of travelling about?
What is it that one must forsake
To cut off all bondage?" [40]

212 "The world is held in bondage by delight;
Thought is its means of travelling about.
Craving is what one must forsake
To cut off all bondage."

66 (6) Afflicted

213 "By what is the world afflicted?
By what is it enveloped?

By what dart has it been wounded?
With what is it always burning?"[124] <90>

214 "The world is afflicted with death,
Enveloped by old age;
Wounded by the dart of craving,
It is always burning with desire."

67 (7) Ensnared

215 "By what is the world ensnared?
By what is it enveloped?
By what is the world shut in?
On what is the world established?"

216 "The world is ensnared by craving;
It is enveloped by old age;
The world is shut in by death;
The world is established on suffering."[125] <91>

68 (8) Shut In

217 "By what is the world shut in?
On what is the world established?
By what is the world ensnared?
By what is it enveloped?"

218 "The world is shut in by death;
The world is established on suffering;
The world is ensnared by craving;
It is enveloped by old age."

69 (9) Desire

219 "By what is the world bound?
By the removal of what is it freed?
What is it that one must forsake
To cut off all bondage?"

220 "By desire is the world bound;

By the removal of desire it is freed.
Desire is what one must forsake <92>
To cut off all bondage." [41]

70 (10) World

221 "In what has the world arisen?
In what does it form intimacy?
By clinging to what is the world
Harassed in regard to what?"

222 "In six has the world arisen;
In six it forms intimacy;
By clinging to six the world
Is harassed in regard to six."[126]

<93> VIII. HAVING SLAIN

71 (1) Having Slain

At Sāvatthī. Standing to one side, that devatā addressed the Blessed One in verse:

223 "Having slain what does one sleep soundly?
Having slain what does one not sorrow?
What is the one thing, O Gotama,
Whose killing you approve?"[127]

[The Blessed One:]
224 "Having slain anger, one sleeps soundly;
Having slain anger, one does not sorrow;
The killing of anger, O devatā,
With its poisoned root and honeyed tip:
This is the killing the noble ones praise,
For having slain that, one does not sorrow."[128]

72 (2) Chariot

225 "What is the token of a chariot?
What, the token of a fire?

What is the token of a country?
What, the token of a woman?"[129] [42] <94>

226 "A standard is the token of a chariot;
Smoke, the token of a fire;
The king is a country's token;
A husband, the token of a woman."

73 (3) Treasure

227 "What here is a man's best treasure?
What practised well brings happiness?
What is really the sweetest of tastes?
How lives the one whom they say lives best?"

228 "Faith is here a man's best treasure;
Dhamma practised well brings happiness;
Truth is really the sweetest of tastes; <95>
One living by wisdom they say lives best."[130]

74 (4) Rain

[A devatā:]
229 "What is the best of things that rise up?
What excels among things that fall down?
What is the best of things that go forth?
Who is the most excellent of speakers?"

[Another devatā:]
230 "A seed is the best of things that rise up;
Rain excels among things that fall down;
Cattle are the best of things that go forth;
A son is the most excellent of speakers."[131]

[The Blessed One:]
231 "Knowledge is the best of things that rise up;
Ignorance excels among things that fall down;
The Saṅgha is the best of things that go forth;
The most excellent of speakers is the Buddha."[132]

75 (5) Afraid <96>

232 "Why are so many people here afraid
When the path has been taught with many bases?[133]
I ask you, O Gotama, broad of wisdom:
On what should one take a stand
To have no fear of the other world?"

233 "Having directed speech and mind rightly,
Doing no evil deeds with the body,
Dwelling at home with ample food and drink, [43]
Faithful, gentle, generous, amiable:
When one stands on these four things,
Standing firmly on the Dhamma,
One need not fear the other world."[134]

76 (6) Does Not Decay

234 "What decays, what does not decay?
What is declared the deviant path? <97>
What is the impediment to [wholesome] states?
What undergoes destruction night and day?
What is the stain of the holy life?
What is the bath without water?

235 "How many fissures are there in the world
Wherein the mind does not stand firm?
We've come to ask the Blessed One this:
How are we to understand it?"

236 "The physical form of mortals decays,
Their name and clan does not decay.
Lust is declared the deviant path,
Greed the impediment to [wholesome] states.

237 "Life undergoes destruction night and day;
Women are the stain of the holy life:
Here's where menfolk are enmeshed.
Austerity and the holy life—
That is the bath without water. <98>

238 "There are six fissures in the world
Wherein the mind does not stand firm:
Laziness and negligence,
Indolence, lack of self-control,
Drowsiness and lethargy—
Avoid these fissures completely."[135]

77 (7) Sovereignty

239 "What is sovereignty in the world?
What ranks as the best of goods?
What in the world is a rusty sword?
What in the world is considered a plague?

240 "Whom do they arrest when he takes away?
And who, when he takes away, is dear?
In whom do the wise take delight
When he returns again and again?" <99>

241 "Mastery is sovereignty in the world;[136]
A woman ranks as the best of goods;
In the world anger is a rusty sword;
Thieves in the world are considered a plague.[137]

242 "They arrest a thief when he takes away,
But an ascetic who takes away is dear.
The wise take delight in an ascetic
When he returns again and again." [44]

78 (8) Love

243 "What should he not give who loves the good?
What should a mortal not relinquish?
What should one release when it's good,
But not release when it's bad?"

244 "A person should not give himself away; <100>
He should not relinquish himself.[138]
One should release speech that is good,
But not speech that is bad."

79 (9) Provisions for a Journey

245 "What secures provisions for a journey?
What is the abode of wealth?
What drags a person around?
What in the world is hard to discard?
By what are many beings bound
Like birds caught in a snare?"

246 "Faith secures provisions for a journey;
Fortune is the abode of wealth;
Desire drags a person around;
Desire is hard to discard in the world.
By desire many beings are bound <101>
Like birds caught in a snare."

80 (10) Source of Light

247 "What is the source of light in the world?
What in the world is the wakeful one?
What are [the colleagues] of those living by work?
What is one's course of movement?

248 "What nurtures both the slack and active
Just as a mother nurtures her child?
The creatures who dwell on the earth—
By what do they sustain their life?"

249 "Wisdom is the source of light in the world;
Mindfulness, in the world, is the wakeful one;
Cattle are [the colleagues] of those living by work; <102>
One's course of movement is the furrow.[139]

250 "Rain nurtures both the slack and active
Just as a mother nurtures her child.
Those creatures who dwell on the earth
Sustain their life by rain."

81 (11) Without Conflict

251 "Who here in the world are placid?
Whose mode of life is not squandered?
Who here fully understand desire?
Who enjoy perpetual freedom? [45]

252 "Whom do parents and brothers worship
When he stands firmly established?
Who is the one of humble birth
That even khattiyas here salute?" <103>

253 "Ascetics are placid in the world;
The ascetic life is not squandered;
Ascetics fully understand desire;
They enjoy perpetual freedom.

254 "Parents and brothers worship an ascetic
When he stands firmly established.[140]
Though an ascetic be of humble birth
Even khattiyas here salute him."

[46] <104>

Chapter II

2 *Devaputtasaṃyutta*
Connected Discourses with Young Devas

I. The First Subchapter (Suriya)

1 (1) Kassapa (1)

Thus have I heard. On one occasion the Blessed One was dwelling at Sāvatthī in Jeta's Grove, Anāthapiṇḍika's Park. Then, when the night had advanced, the young deva Kassapa, of stunning beauty, illuminating the entire Jeta's Grove, approached the Blessed One.[141] Having approached, he paid homage to the Blessed One, stood to one side, and said to the Blessed One:

"The Blessed One has revealed the bhikkhu but not the instruction to the bhikkhu."[142]

"Well then, Kassapa, clear up this point yourself."[143]

255 "He should train in well-spoken counsel,
And in the exercise of an ascetic,
In a solitary seat, alone,
And in the calming of the mind."[144] <105>

This is what the young deva Kassapa said. The Teacher approved. Then the young deva Kassapa, thinking, "The Teacher has approved of me," paid homage to the Blessed One and, keeping him on the right, he disappeared right there.

2 (2) Kassapa (2)

At Sāvatthī. Standing to one side, the young deva Kassapa recited this verse in the presence of the Blessed One:

256 "A bhikkhu should be a meditator,
One who is liberated in mind,
If he desires the heart's attainment,
Bent on that as his advantage.
Having known the world's rise and fall,
Let him be lofty in mind and unattached."[145] [47]

3 (3) Māgha

At Sāvatthī. Then, when the night had advanced, the young deva Māgha, of stunning beauty, illuminating the entire Jeta's Grove, approached the Blessed One. Having approached, he paid homage to the Blessed One, stood to one side, <106> and addressed the Blessed One in verse:[146]

257 "Having slain what does one sleep soundly?
Having slain what does one not sorrow?
What is the one thing, O Gotama,
Whose killing you approve?"

258 "Having slain anger, one sleeps soundly;
Having slain anger, one does not sorrow;
The killing of anger, O Vatrabhū,
With its poisoned root and honeyed tip:
This is the killing the noble ones praise,
For having slain that, one does not sorrow."

4 (4) Māgadha

At Sāvatthī. Standing to one side, the young deva Māgadha addressed the Blessed One in verse:

259 "How many sources of light are in the world
By means of which the world is illumined? <107>

We've come to ask the Blessed One this:
How are we to understand it?"

260 "There are four sources of light in the world;
A fifth one is not found here.
The sun shines by day,
The moon glows at night,
261 And fire flares up here and there
Both by day and at night.
But the Buddha is the best of those that shine:
He is the light unsurpassed."

5 (5) Dāmali

At Sāvatthī. Then, when the night had advanced, the young deva Dāmali, of stunning beauty, illuminating the entire Jeta's Grove, approached the Blessed One. Having approached, he paid homage to the Blessed One, stood to one side, and recited this verse in the presence of the Blessed One:

262 "This should be done by the brahmin:
Striving without weariness, <108>
That by his abandoning of sensual desires
He does not yearn for existence."[147]

263 "For the brahmin there is no task to be done,
[O Dāmali," said the Blessed One],
"For the brahmin has done what should be done.
While he has not gained a footing in the river, [48]
A man will strain with all his limbs;
But a footing gained, standing on the ground,
He need not strain for he has gone beyond.

264 "This is a simile for the brahmin, O Dāmali,
For the taintless one, the discreet meditator.
Having reached the end of birth and death,
He need not strain for he has gone beyond."[148] <109>

6 (6) Kāmada

At Sāvatthī. Standing to one side, the young deva Kāmada said to the Blessed One:

"Hard to do, Blessed One! Very hard to do, Blessed One!"[149]

265 "They do even what is hard to do,
[O Kāmada," said the Blessed One,]
"The trainees endowed with virtue, steadfast.
For one who has entered the homeless life
Contentment brings along happiness."

"That is hard to gain, Blessed One, namely, contentment."

266 "They gain even what is hard to gain,
[O Kāmada," said the Blessed One,]
"Who delight in calming the mind,
Whose minds, day and night,
Take delight in development."

"That is hard to concentrate, Blessed One, namely, the mind."

267 "They concentrate even what is hard to concentrate,
[O Kāmada," said the Blessed One,]
"Who delight in calming the faculties.
Having cut through the net of Death,
The noble ones, O Kāmada, go their way."

"The path is impassable and uneven, Blessed One."[150] <110>

268 "Though the path is impassable and uneven,
The noble ones walk it, Kāmada.
The ignoble ones fall down head first,
Right there on the uneven path,
But the path of the noble ones is even,
For the noble are even amidst the uneven."

7 (7) Pañcālacaṇḍa

At Sāvatthī. Standing to one side, the young deva Pañcālacaṇḍa recited this verse in the presence of the Blessed One:

269 "The one of broad wisdom has indeed found
The opening in the midst of confinement,
The Buddha who discovered jhāna,
The withdrawn chief bull, the sage."[151]

270 "Even in the midst of confinement they find it,
[O Pañcālacaṇḍa," said the Blessed One,] <111>
"The Dhamma for the attainment of Nibbāna—
Those who have acquired mindfulness,
Those perfectly well concentrated."[152] [49]

8 (8) Tāyana

At Sāvatthī. Then, when the night had advanced, the young deva Tāyana, formerly the founder of a religious sect, of stunning beauty, illuminating the entire Jeta's Grove, approached the Blessed One.[153] Having approached, he paid homage to the Blessed One, stood to one side, and recited these verses in the presence of the Blessed One:

271 "Having exerted oneself, cut the stream!
Dispel sensual desires, O brahmin!
Without having abandoned sensual desires,
A sage does not reach unity.[154]

272 "If one would do what should be done,
One should firmly exert oneself. <112>
For a slack wanderer's life
Only scatters more dust.

273 "Better left undone is the misdeed,
A deed that later brings repentance.
Better done is the good deed
Which when done is not repented.

274 "As *kusa*-grass, wrongly grasped,
Only cuts one's hand,
So the ascetic life, wrongly taken up,
Drags one down to hell.

275 "Any deed that is slackly done,
Any corrupted vow,
A holy life that breeds suspicion,
Does not yield great fruit."[155]

This is what the young deva Tāyana said. Having said this, he paid homage to the Blessed One and, keeping him on the right, he disappeared right there.

Then, when the night had passed, the Blessed One addressed the bhikkhus thus: "Bhikkhus, last night, when the night had advanced, the young deva Tāyana, formerly the founder of a religious sect … <113> … approached me … and in my presence recited these verses:

276–80 "'Having exerted oneself, cut the stream!… [50] …
Does not yield great fruit.'

"This is what the young deva Tāyana said. Having said this, he paid homage to me and, keeping me on the right, he disappeared right there. Learn Tāyana's verses, bhikkhus. Master <114> Tāyana's verses, bhikkhus. Remember Tāyana's verses, bhikkhus. Tāyana's verses are beneficial, bhikkhus, they pertain to the fundamentals of the holy life."

9 (9) Candimā

At Sāvatthī. Now on that occasion the young deva Candimā had been seized by Rāhu, lord of the asuras.[156] Then, recollecting the Blessed One, the young deva Candimā on that occasion recited this verse:

281 "Let homage be to you, the Buddha!
O hero, you are everywhere released.
I have fallen into captivity,
So please be my refuge."

Then, referring to the young deva Candimā, the Blessed One addressed Rāhu, lord of the asuras, in verse:

282 "Candimā has gone for refuge
To the Tathāgata, the Arahant.
Release Candimā, O Rāhu,
Buddhas have compassion for the world."

Then Rāhu, lord of the asuras, released the young deva Candimā and hurriedly approached Vepacitti, lord of the asuras.[157] Having approached, shocked and terrified, he stood to one side. <115> Then, as he stood there, Vepacitti, lord of the asuras, addressed him in verse:

283 "Why, Rāhu, did you come in a hurry?
Why did you release Candimā?
Having come as if in shock,
Why do you stand there frightened?"

284 "My head would have split in seven parts,
While living I would have found no ease,
If, when chanted over by the Buddha's verse,
I had not let go of Candimā." [51]

10 (10) Suriya

At Sāvatthī. Now on that occasion the young deva Suriya had been seized by Rāhu, lord of the asuras.[158] Then, recollecting the Blessed One, the young deva Suriya on that occasion recited this verse:

285 "Let homage be to you, the Buddha!
O hero, you are everywhere released.
I have fallen into captivity,
So please be my refuge." <116>

Then, referring to the young deva Suriya, the Blessed One addressed Rāhu, lord of the asuras, in verse:

286 "Suriya has gone for refuge
To the Tathāgata, the Arahant.
Release Suriya, O Rāhu,
Buddhas have compassion for the world.

287 "While moving across the sky, O Rāhu,
Do not swallow the radiant one,
The maker of light in darkness,
The disk of fiery might in the gloom.
Rāhu, release my child Suriya."[159]

Then Rāhu, lord of the asuras, released the young deva Suriya and hurriedly approached Vepacitti, lord of the asuras. Having approached, shocked and terrified, he stood to one side. Then, as he stood there, Vepacitti, lord of the asuras, addressed him in verse:

288 "Why, Rāhu, did you come in a hurry?
Why did you release Suriya?
Having come as if in shock, <117>
Why do you stand there frightened?"

289 "My head would have split in seven parts,
While living I would have found no ease,
If, when chanted over by the Buddha's verses,
I had not let go of Suriya."

II. Anāthapiṇḍika

11 (1) Candimasa

At Sāvatthī. Then, when the night had advanced, the young deva Candimasa, of stunning beauty, illuminating the entire Jeta's Grove, [52] approached the Blessed One. Having approached, he paid homage to the Blessed One, stood to one side, <118> and recited this verse in the presence of the Blessed One:

290 "They will surely reach to safety
Like deer in a mosquito-free marsh,
Who, having attained the jhānas,
Are unified, discreet, mindful."[160]

[The Blessed One:]
291 "They will surely reach the far shore
Like a fish when the net is cut,

Who, having attained the jhānas,
Are diligent, with flaws discarded."[161]

12 (2) Veṇhu

At Sāvatthī. Standing to one side, the young deva Veṇhu recited this verse in the presence of the Blessed One:[162]

292 "Happy indeed are those human beings
Attending on the Fortunate One,
Applying themselves to Gotama's Teaching,
Who train in it with diligence."[163] <119>

293 "When the course of teaching is proclaimed by me,
[O Veṇhu," said the Blessed One,]
"Those meditators who train therein,
Being diligent at the proper time,
Will not come under Death's control."

13 (3) Dīghalaṭṭhi

Thus have I heard. On one occasion the Blessed One was dwelling at Rājagaha in the Bamboo Grove, the Squirrel Sanctuary. Then, when the night had advanced, the young deva Dīghalaṭṭhi, of stunning beauty, illuminating the entire Bamboo Grove, approached the Blessed One. Having approached, he paid homage to the Blessed One, stood to one side, and recited this verse in the presence of the Blessed One:

294 "A bhikkhu should be a meditator,
One who is liberated in mind,
If he desires the heart's attainment,
Bent on that as his advantage.
Having known the world's rise and fall, <120>
Let him be lofty in mind and unattached."

14 (4) Nandana

Standing to one side, the young deva Nandana addressed the Blessed One in verse:

295 "I ask you, Gotama, broad of wisdom—
Unobstructed is the Blessed One's knowledge and vision: [53]
What is he like whom they call virtuous?
What is he like whom they call wise?
What is he like who has passed beyond suffering?
What is he like whom the devatās worship?"

296 "One virtuous, wise, of developed mind,
Concentrated, mindful, enjoying jhāna,
For whom all sorrows are gone, abandoned,
A taint-destroyer bearing his final body:

297 It is such a one that they call virtuous, <121>
Such a one that they call wise,
Such a one has passed beyond suffering,
Such a one the devatās worship."

15 (5) Candana

Standing to one side, the young deva Candana addressed the Blessed One in verse:

298 "Who here crosses over the flood,
Unwearying by day and night?
Who does not sink in the deep,
Without support, without a hold?"[164]

299 "One always perfect in virtue,
Endowed with wisdom, well concentrated,
One energetic and resolute
Crosses the flood so hard to cross.

300 "One who desists from sensual perception,
Who has overcome the fetter of form, <122>
Who has destroyed delight in existence—
He does not sink in the deep."[165]

16 (6) Vasudatta

Standing to one side, the young deva Vasudatta recited this verse in the presence of the Blessed One:

301 "As if smitten by a sword,
As if his head were on fire,
A bhikkhu should wander mindfully
To abandon sensual lust."

302 "As if smitten by a sword,
As if his head were on fire,
A bhikkhu should wander mindfully
To abandon identity view."

17 (7) Subrahmā

<123> Standing to one side, the young deva Subrahmā addressed the Blessed One in verse:[166]

303 "Always frightened is this mind,
The mind is always agitated [54]
About unarisen problems
And about arisen ones.
If there exists release from fear,
Being asked, please declare it to me."[167]

304 "Not apart from enlightenment and austerity,
Not apart from restraint of the sense faculties,
Not apart from relinquishing all,
Do I see any safety for living beings."[168]

This is what the Blessed One said.... He [the young deva] disappeared right there.

18 (8) Kakudha

Thus have I heard. On one occasion the Blessed One was dwelling at Sāketa in the Añjana Grove, the Deer Park. Then, when the night had advanced, the young deva Kakudha, <124>

of stunning beauty, illuminating the entire Añjana Grove, approached the Blessed One. Having approached, he paid homage to the Blessed One, stood to one side, and said to him:

"Do you delight, ascetic?"

"Having gained what, friend?"

"Then, ascetic, do you sorrow?"

"What has been lost, friend?"

"Then, ascetic, do you neither delight nor sorrow?"

"Yes, friend."

305 "I hope that you're untroubled, bhikkhu.
I hope no delight is found in you.
I hope that when you sit all alone
Discontent doesn't spread over you."[169]

306 "Truly, I'm untroubled, spirit,
Yet no delight is found in me.
And when I'm sitting all alone <125>
Discontent doesn't spread over me."

307 "How are you untroubled, bhikkhu?
How is no delight found in you?
How come, when you sit all alone,
Discontent doesn't spread over you?"

308 "Delight comes to one who is miserable,
Misery to one filled with delight.
As a bhikkhu undelighted, untroubled:
That's how you should know me, friend."

309 "After a long time at last I see
A brahmin who is fully quenched,
A bhikkhu undelighted, untroubled,
Who has crossed over attachment to the world."[170]

19 (9) Uttara

Setting at Rājagaha. Standing to one side, the young deva Uttara recited this verse in the presence of the Blessed One: [55] <126>

310 "Life is swept along, short is the life span;
No shelters exist for one who has reached old age.
Seeing clearly this danger in death,
One should do deeds of merit that bring happiness."

311 "Life is swept along, short is the life span;
No shelters exist for one who has reached old age.
Seeing clearly this danger in death,
A seeker of peace should drop the world's bait."

20 (10) Anāthapiṇḍika

Standing to one side, the young deva Anāthapiṇḍika recited these verses in the presence of the Blessed One:

312 "This indeed is that Jeta's Grove,
The resort of the Order of seers,
Dwelt in by the Dhamma King,
A place that gives me joy.

313 "Action, knowledge, righteousness,
Virtue, an excellent life:
By this are mortals purified, <127>
Not by clan or wealth.

314 "Therefore a person who is wise,
Out of regard for his own good, [56]
Should carefully examine the Dhamma:
Thus he is purified in it.

315 "Sāriputta truly is endowed with wisdom,
With virtue and with inner peace.
Even a bhikkhu who has gone beyond
At best can only equal him."

This is what the young deva Anāthapiṇḍika said. Having said this, he paid homage to the Blessed One and, keeping him on the right, he disappeared right there.

Then, when the night had passed, the Blessed One addressed the bhikkhus thus: "Bhikkhus, last night, when the night had advanced, a certain young deva … approached me … and in my presence recited these verses:

316–19 "'This indeed is that Jeta's Grove, … <128>
At best can only equal him.'

"This is what that young deva said. Having said this, he paid homage to me and, keeping me on the right, he disappeared right there."

When this was said, the Venerable Ānanda said to the Blessed One: "Venerable sir, that young deva must surely have been Anāthapiṇḍika. For Anāthapiṇḍika the householder had full confidence in the Venerable Sāriputta."

"Good, good, Ānanda! You have drawn the right inference by reasoning.[171] For that young deva, Ānanda, was Anāthapiṇḍika."

<129>

III. Various Sectarians

21 (1) Siva

Thus have I heard. On one occasion the Blessed One was dwelling at Sāvatthī in Jeta's Grove, Anāthapiṇḍika's Park. Then, when the night had advanced, the young deva Siva, of stunning beauty, illuminating the entire Jeta's Grove, approached the Blessed One. Having approached, he paid homage to the Blessed One, stood to one side, and recited these verses in the presence of the Blessed One:[172]

320 "One should associate only with the good;
With the good one should foster intimacy.
Having learnt the true Dhamma of the good,
One becomes better, never worse. <130>

321 "One should associate only with the good;
With the good one should foster intimacy.
Having learnt the true Dhamma of the good,
Wisdom is gained, but not from another.

322 "One should associate only with the good;
With the good one should foster intimacy.

Having learnt the true Dhamma of the good,
One does not sorrow in the midst of sorrow.

323 "One should associate only with the good;
With the good one should foster intimacy. [57]
Having learnt the true Dhamma of the good,
One shines amidst one's relations.

324 "One should associate only with the good;
With the good one should foster intimacy.
Having learnt the true Dhamma of the good,
Beings fare on to a good destination.

325 "One should associate only with the good;
With the good one should foster intimacy.
Having learnt the true Dhamma of the good,
Beings abide comfortably." <131>

Then the Blessed One replied to the young deva Siva in verse:

326 "One should associate only with the good;
With the good one should foster intimacy.
Having learnt the true Dhamma of the good,
One is released from all suffering."

22 (2) *Khema*

Standing to one side, the young deva Khema recited these verses in the presence of the Blessed One:

327 "Foolish people devoid of wisdom
Behave like enemies towards themselves.
They go about doing evil deeds
Which yield only bitter fruit.

328 "That deed is not well performed
Which, having been done, is then repented,
The result of which one experiences
Weeping with a tearful face.

329 "But that deed is well performed
Which, having been done, is not repented,
The result of which one experiences
Joyfully with a happy mind."[173] <132>

[The Blessed One:]
330 "One should promptly do the deed
One knows leads to one's own welfare;
The thinker, the wise one, should not advance
With the reflection of the carter.

331 "As the carter who left the highway,
A road with an even surface,
And entered upon a rugged bypath
Broods mournfully with a broken axle—

332 "So the fool, having left the Dhamma
To follow a way opposed to Dhamma,
When he falls into the mouth of Death
Broods like the carter with a broken axle."[174]

23 (3) Serī

Standing to one side, the young deva Serī addressed the Blessed One in verse: <133>

333 "They always take delight in food,
Both devas and human beings.
So what sort of spirit could it be
That does not take delight in food?"

334 "When they give out of faith
With a heart of confidence,
Food accrues to [the giver] himself
Both in this world and the next.

335 "Therefore, having removed stinginess,
The conqueror of the stain should give a gift.
Merits are the support for living beings
[When they arise] in the other world." [58]

"It is wonderful, venerable sir! It is amazing, venerable sir! How well this was stated by the Blessed One:

336–37 "'When they give out of faith ... <134>
[When they arise] in the other world.'

"Once in the past, venerable sir, I was a king named Serī, a donor, a philanthropist, one who spoke in praise of giving. At the four gates I had gifts given to ascetics, brahmins, paupers, wayfarers, mendicants, and beggars. Then, venerable sir, the harem women came to me and said: 'Your majesty gives gifts, but we do not give gifts. It would be good if, with your majesty's assistance, we too might give gifts and do meritorious deeds.' It occurred to me: 'I am a donor, a philanthropist, one who speaks in praise of giving. So when they say, "Let us give gifts," what am I to say to them?' So, venerable sir, I gave the first gate to the harem women. There the harem women gave gifts, and my gifts returned to me. <135>

"Then, venerable sir, my khattiya vassals came to me and said: 'Your majesty gives gifts, the harem women give gifts, but we do not give gifts. It would be good if, with your majesty's assistance, we too might give gifts and do meritorious deeds.' It occurred to me: 'I am a donor....' So, venerable sir, I gave the second gate to the khattiya vassals. There the khattiya vassals gave gifts, and my gifts returned to me.

"Then, venerable sir, my troops came to me ... [59] ... So, venerable sir, I gave the third gate to the troops. There the troops gave gifts, and my gifts returned to me. <136>

"Then, venerable sir, the brahmins and householders came to me ... So, venerable sir, I gave the fourth gate to the brahmins and householders. There the brahmins and householders gave gifts, and my gifts returned to me.

"Then, venerable sir, my men came to me and said: 'Now your majesty is not giving gifts anywhere.'[175] When this was said, I told those men: 'Well then, I say, send half of the revenue generated in the outlying provinces from there to the palace. There itself give half as gifts to ascetics, brahmins, paupers, wayfarers, mendicants, and beggars.'

"I did not reach any limit, venerable sir, to the meritorious deeds that I did for such a long time, to the wholesome deeds that I did for such a long time, <137> such that I could say: 'There is just so much merit,' or 'There is just so much result of merit,' or 'For just so long am I to dwell in heaven.' It is wonderful, venerable sir! It is amazing, venerable sir! How well this was stated by the Blessed One:

338 "'When they give out of faith
With a heart of confidence,
Food accrues to [the giver] himself
Both in this world and the next.

339 "'Therefore, having removed stinginess,
The conqueror of the stain should give a gift.
Deeds of merit are the support for living beings
[When they arise] in the other world.'" [60]

24 (4) Ghaṭikāra

Standing to one side, the young deva Ghaṭikāra recited this verse in the presence of the Blessed One:...

340–52 "Seven bhikkhus reborn in Avihā
Have been fully liberated...."
... (*verses 340–52 = verses 170–82, in 1:50*) <138–41>...
Both now inwardly developed,
Bearers of their final bodies. [61]

25 (5) Jantu

Thus have I heard. On one occasion a number of bhikkhus were dwelling among the Kosalans in a little forest hut on a slope of the Himalayas—restless, puffed up, personally vain, rough-tongued, rambling in their talk, muddle-minded, without clear comprehension, unconcentrated, scatter-brained, loose in their sense faculties.[176]

Then, on the Uposatha day of the fifteenth, the young deva Jantu approached those bhikkhus and addressed them in verses:[177]

353 "In the past the bhikkhus lived happily,
The disciples of Gotama.

Without wishes they sought their alms,
Without wishes they used their lodgings.
Having known the world's impermanence,
They made an end to suffering.

354 "But now like headmen in a village
They make themselves hard to maintain.
They eat and eat and then lie down, <142>
Infatuated in others' homes.[178]

355 "Having reverently saluted the Saṅgha,
I here speak only about some:
They are rejected, without protector,
Become just like the dead.[179]

356 "My statement is made with reference
To those who dwell in negligence.
As for those who dwell in diligence,
To them I humbly pay homage."

26 (6) Rohitassa

At Sāvatthī. Standing to one side, the young deva Rohitassa said to the Blessed One:

"Is it possible, venerable sir, by travelling to know or to see or to reach the end of the world, where one is not born, does not age, does not die, does not pass away, and is not reborn?" <143>

"As to that end of the world, friend, where one is not born, does not age, does not die, does not pass away, and is not reborn—I say that it cannot be known, seen, or reached by travelling."[180]

"It is wonderful, venerable sir! It is amazing, venerable sir! How well this was stated by the Blessed One: 'As to that end of the world, friend, ... I say that it cannot be known, seen, or reached by travelling.'

"Once in the past, venerable sir, I was a seer named Rohitassa, son of Bhoja, possessed of spiritual power, able to travel through the sky. [62] My speed was such, venerable sir, that I could move just as swiftly as a firm-bowed archer—trained, skilful, practised, experienced—could easily shoot past the shadow of a palmyra tree with a light arrow.[181] My stride was such, venerable sir, that it seemed to reach from the eastern ocean to the western ocean. Then, venerable sir, the wish arose in me: 'I will reach the end of the world by travelling.' <144> Possessing such speed and such a stride, and having a life span of a hundred years, living for a hundred years, I travelled for a hundred years, without pausing except to eat, drink, take meals and snacks, to defecate and urinate, to sleep and dispel fatigue; yet I died along the way without having reached the end of the world.

"It is wonderful, venerable sir! It is amazing, venerable sir! How well this was stated by the Blessed One: 'As to that end of the world, friend, where one is not born, does not age, does not die, does not pass away, and is not reborn—I say that it cannot be known, seen, or reached by travelling.'"

"However, friend, I say that without having reached the end of the world there is no making an end to suffering. It is, friend, in just this <145> fathom-high carcass endowed with perception and mind that I make known the world, the origin of the world, the cessation of the world, and the way leading to the cessation of the world.[182]

357 "The world's end can never be reached
By means of travelling [through the world],
Yet without reaching the world's end
There is no release from suffering.

358 "Therefore, truly, the world-knower, the wise one,
Gone to the world's end, fulfiller of the holy life,
Having known the world's end, at peace,
Longs not for this world or another."

27 (7) Nanda

Standing to one side, the young deva Nanda recited this verse in the presence of the Blessed One:

359 "Time flies by, the nights swiftly pass;
The stages of life successively desert us.

Seeing clearly this danger in death,
One should do deeds of merit that bring happiness."

360 "Time flies by, the nights swiftly pass;
The stages of life successively desert us. [63]
Seeing clearly this danger in death,
A seeker of peace should drop the world's bait." <146>

28 (8) Nandivisāla

Standing to one side, the young deva Nandivisāla addressed the Blessed One in verse:

361 "Having four wheels and nine doors,
Filled up and bound with greed,
Born from a bog, O great hero!
How does one escape from it?"

362 "Having cut the thong and the strap,
Having cut off evil desire and greed,
Having drawn out craving with its root:
Thus one escapes from it."

29 (9) Susīma

<147> At Sāvatthī. Then the Venerable Ānanda approached the Blessed One, paid homage to him, and sat down to one side. The Blessed One then said to him: "Do you too, Ānanda, approve of Sāriputta?"[183]

"Indeed, venerable sir, who would not approve of the Venerable Sāriputta, unless he were foolish, full of hatred, deluded, or mentally deranged? The Venerable Sāriputta, venerable sir, is wise, one of great wisdom, of wide wisdom, of joyous wisdom, of swift wisdom, of sharp wisdom, of penetrative wisdom.[184] The Venerable Sāriputta, venerable sir, has few wishes; he is content, secluded, aloof, energetic. The Venerable Sāriputta, venerable sir, is one who gives advice, one who accepts advice, a reprover, one who censures evil. Indeed, venerable sir, who would not approve of the Venerable Sāriputta, unless he were foolish, full of hatred, deluded, or mentally deranged?" [64]

"So it is, Ānanda, so it is! Indeed, Ānanda, who would not approve of Sāriputta, unless he were foolish, full of hatred, deluded, or mentally deranged? Sāriputta, Ānanda, is wise ... (*as above*) <148>... unless he were mentally deranged?"

Then, while this praise of the Venerable Sāriputta was being spoken, the young deva Susīma, accompanied by a great assembly of young devas, approached the Blessed One.[185] Having approached, he paid homage to the Blessed One, stood to one side, and said to him: "So it is, Blessed One! So it is, Fortunate One! Indeed, venerable sir, who would not approve of the Venerable Sāriputta ... (*all as above*) <149>... unless he were mentally deranged? In my case too, venerable sir, no matter what assembly of young devas I have approached, I have often heard this same report: 'The Venerable Sāriputta is wise ... one who censures evil. Indeed, who would not approve of the Venerable Sāriputta, unless he were foolish, full of hatred, deluded, or mentally deranged?'"

Then, while this praise of the Venerable Sāriputta was being spoken, the young devas in Susīma's assembly—elated, gladdened, full of rapture and joy—displayed diverse lustrous colours.[186] Just as a beryl gem—beautiful, of fine quality, eight-faceted, of excellent workmanship—when placed on a brocade cloth, shines and beams and radiates, <150> so too the young devas in Susīma's assembly [65] ... displayed diverse lustrous colours.

And just as an ornament of finest gold—very skilfully burnished in a furnace by an adroit goldsmith—when placed on a brocade cloth, shines and beams and radiates, so too the young devas in Susīma's assembly ... displayed diverse lustrous colours.

And just as, when the night is fading, the morning star shines and beams and radiates, so too the young devas in Susīma's assembly ... displayed diverse lustrous colours.[187]

And just as in the autumn, when the sky is clear and cloudless, the sun, ascending in the sky, <151> dispels all darkness from space as it shines and beams and radiates,[188] so too the young devas in Susīma's assembly—elated, gladdened, full of rapture and joy—displayed diverse lustrous colours.

Then, with reference to the Venerable Sāriputta, the young deva Susīma recited this verse in the presence of the Blessed One:

363 "He is widely known to be a wise man,
Sāriputta, who is free of anger;
Of few wishes, gentle, tamed,
The seer adorned by the Teacher's praise."

Then the Blessed One, with reference to the Venerable Sāriputta, replied to the young deva Susīma in verse:

364 "He is widely known to be a wise man,
Sāriputta, who is free of anger;
Of few wishes, gentle, tamed,
Developed, well tamed, he awaits the time."[189]

30 (10) Various Sectarians

Thus have I heard. On one occasion the Blessed One was dwelling at Rājagaha in the Bamboo Grove, the Squirrel Sanctuary. Then, when the night had advanced, a number <152> of young devas, disciples of various sectarian teachers—Asama and Sahalī and Niṅka and Ākoṭaka and Vetambarī and Māṇavagāmiya—of stunning beauty, [66] illuminating the entire Bamboo Grove, approached the Blessed One. Having approached, they paid homage to the Blessed One and stood to one side.[190]

Then, standing to one side, the young deva Asama spoke this verse referring to Pūraṇa Kassapa in the presence of the Blessed One:

365 "In injuring and killing here,
In beating and extortion,
Kassapa did not recognize evil
Nor see any merit for oneself.
He indeed taught what is worthy of trust:
That teacher deserves esteem."[191]

Then the young deva Sahalī spoke this verse referring to Makkhali Gosāla in the presence of the Blessed One:[192]

366 "By austerity and scrupulousness <153>
He attained complete self-restraint.

He abandoned contentious talk with people,
Refrained from falsehood, a speaker of truth.
Surely such a one does no evil."[193]

Then the young deva Niṅka spoke this verse referring to Nigaṇṭha Nātaputta in the presence of the Blessed One:

367 "A scrupulous discerning bhikkhu,
Well restrained by the four controls,
Explaining what is seen and heard:
Surely, he could not be a sinner."[194]

Then the young deva Ākoṭaka spoke this verse referring to various sectarian teachers in the presence of the Blessed One:

368 "Pakudhaka Kātiyāna and the Nigaṇṭha,
Along with Makkhali and Pūraṇa:
Teachers of companies, attained to ascetic stature:
They were surely not far from superior men."[195] <154>

Then the young deva Vetambarī replied to the young deva Ākoṭaka in verse:

369 "Even by howling along the wretched jackal
Remains a vile beast, never the lion's peer.
So though he be the teacher of a group,
The naked ascetic, speaker of falsehood,
Arousing suspicion by his conduct,
Bears no resemblance to superior men."[196] [67]

Then Māra the Evil One took possession of the young deva Vetambarī and recited this verse in the presence of the Blessed One:[197]

370 "Those engaged in austerity and scrupulousness,
Those protecting their solitude,
And those who have settled on form,
Delighting in the world of devas: <155>
Indeed, these mortals instruct rightly
In regard to the other world."

Then the Blessed One, having understood, "This is Māra the Evil One," replied to Māra the Evil One in verse:

371 "Whatever forms exist here or beyond,
And those of luminous beauty in the sky,
All these, indeed, you praise, Namuci,
Like bait thrown out for catching fish."[198]

Then, in the Blessed One's presence, the young deva Māṇavagāmiya recited these verses referring to the Blessed One:

372 "Vipula is called the best of mountains
Among the hills of Rājagaha,
Seta, the best of snow-clad mountains,
The sun, the best of travellers in the sky.

373 "The ocean is the best body of water,
The moon, the best of nocturnal lights, <156>
But in this world together with its devas
The Buddha is declared supreme."

[68] <157> Chapter III

3 *Kosalasaṃyutta*

Connected Discourses with the Kosalan

I. The First Subchapter
(Bondage)

1 (1) Young

Thus have I heard. On one occasion the Blessed One was dwelling at Sāvatthī in Jeta's Grove, Anāthapiṇḍika's Park. Then King Pasenadi of Kosala approached the Blessed One and exchanged greetings with him. When they had concluded their greetings and cordial talk, he sat down to one side and said to the Blessed One: "Does Master Gotama too claim, 'I have awakened to the unsurpassed perfect enlightenment'?"[199]

"If, great king, one speaking rightly could say of anyone, 'He has awakened to the unsurpassed perfect enlightenment,' it is of me that one might rightly say this. For I, great king, have awakened to the unsurpassed perfect enlightenment."

"Master Gotama, even those ascetics and brahmins who are the heads of orders and companies, the teachers of companies, well known and famous founders of sects considered by the multitude to be holy men—that is, Pūraṇa Kassapa, Makkhali Gosāla, <158> Nigaṇṭha Nātaputta, Sañjaya Belaṭṭhiputta, Pakudha Kaccāyana, Ajita Kesakambalī—even these, when I asked them whether they had awakened to the unsurpassed perfect enlightenment, did not claim to have done so.[200] So why then should Master Gotama [make such a claim] when he is so young in years and has newly gone forth?" [69]

"There are four things, great king, that should not be despised and disparaged as 'young.'[201] What four? A khattiya, great king, should not be despised and disparaged as 'young'; a snake should not be despised and disparaged as 'young'; a fire should not be despised and disparaged as 'young'; and a bhikkhu should not be despised and disparaged as 'young.' These are the four." <159>

This is what the Blessed One said. Having said this, the Fortunate One, the Teacher, further said this:

374 "One should not despise as 'young'
A khattiya of noble birth,
A high-born prince of glorious fame:
A man should not disparage him.
375 For it may happen that this lord of men,
This khattiya, shall gain the throne,
And in his anger thrash one harshly
With a royal punishment.
Therefore guarding one's own life,
One should avoid him.

376 "One should not despise as 'young'
A serpent one may see by chance
In the village or a forest:
A man should not disparage it.
377 For as that fierce snake glides along,
Manifesting in diverse shapes,[202]
It may attack and bite the fool, <160>
Whether a man or a woman.
Therefore guarding one's own life,
One should avoid it.

378 "One should not despise as 'young'
A blazing fire that devours much,
A conflagration with blackened trail:
A man should not disparage it.
379 For if it gains a stock of fuel,
Having become a conflagration,
It may attack and burn the fool,
Whether a man or a woman.
Therefore guarding one's own life,
One should avoid it.

380 "When a fire burns down a forest—
That conflagration with blackened trail—
The shoots there spring to life once more
As the days and nights pass by.
381 But if a bhikkhu of perfect virtue <161>
Burns one with [his virtue's] fire,
One does not gain sons and cattle,
Nor do one's heirs acquire wealth.
Childless and heirless they become,
Like stumps of palmyra trees.[203] [70]

382 "Therefore a person who is wise,
Out of regard for his own good,
Should always treat these properly:
A fierce serpent and a blazing fire,
A famous khattiya,
And a bhikkhu of perfect virtue."

When this was said, King Pasenadi of Kosala said to the Blessed One: "Magnificent, venerable sir! Magnificent, venerable sir! The Dhamma has been made clear in many ways by the Blessed One, as though he were turning upright what had been turned upside down, revealing what was hidden, showing the way to one who was lost, or holding up a lamp in the dark for those with eyesight to see forms. I go for refuge to the Blessed One, and to the Dhamma, and to the Bhikkhu Saṅgha. From today let the Blessed One remember me as a lay follower who has gone for refuge for life." <162>

2 (2) A Person

At Sāvatthī. Then King Pasenadi of Kosala approached the Blessed One, paid homage to him, sat down to one side, and said to him:

"Venerable sir, how many things are there which, when they arise within a person, arise for his harm, suffering, and discomfort?"

"There are, great king, three things which, when they arise within a person, arise for his harm, suffering, and discomfort. What are the three? Greed, hatred, and delusion. These are the three things which, when they arise within a person, arise for his harm, suffering, and discomfort.

383 "Greed, hatred, and delusion,
Arisen from within oneself,
Injure the person of evil mind <163>
As its own fruit destroys the reed."[204] [71]

3 (3) Aging and Death

At Sāvatthī. Sitting to one side, King Pasenadi of Kosala said to the Blessed One: "Venerable sir, for one who has taken birth, is there anything other [to expect] than aging and death?"[205]

"For one who has taken birth, great king, there is nothing other [to expect] than aging and death. Even in the case of those affluent khattiyas—rich, with great wealth and property, with abundant gold and silver, abundant treasures and commodities, abundant wealth and grain—because they have taken birth, there is nothing other [to expect] than aging and death. Even in the case of those affluent brahmins ... affluent householders—rich ... with abundant wealth and grain—because they have taken birth, there is nothing other [to expect] than aging and death. Even in the case of those bhikkhus who are arahants, whose taints are destroyed, who have lived the holy life, done what had to be done, laid down the burden, <164> reached their own goal, utterly destroyed the fetters of existence, and are completely liberated through final knowledge: even for them this body is subject to breaking up, subject to being laid down.[206]

384 "The beautiful chariots of kings wear out,
This body too undergoes decay.
But the Dhamma of the good does not decay:
So the good proclaim along with the good."[207]

4 (4) Dear

At Sāvatthī. Sitting to one side, King Pasenadi of Kosala said to the Blessed One: "Here, venerable sir, while I was alone in seclusion, a reflection arose in my mind thus: 'Who now treat themselves as dear, and who treat themselves as a foe?' Then, venerable sir, it occurred to me: 'Those who engage in misconduct of body, speech, and mind treat themselves as a foe. Even though they may say, "We regard ourselves as dear," still they treat themselves as a foe. For what reason? [72] Because of their own accord they act towards themselves in the same way that a foe might act towards a foe; therefore they treat themselves as a foe. <165> But those who engage in good conduct of body, speech, and mind treat themselves as dear. Even though they may say, "We regard ourselves as a foe," still they treat themselves as dear. For what reason? Because of their own accord they act towards themselves in the same way that a dear person might act towards one who is dear; therefore they treat themselves as dear.'"

"So it is, great king! So it is, great king!"

(*The Buddha then repeats the entire statement of King Pasenadi and adds the following verses:*)

385 "If one regards oneself as dear
One should not yoke oneself to evil,
For happiness is not easily gained
By one who does a wrongful deed. <166>

386 "When one is seized by the End-maker
As one discards the human state,
What can one call truly one's own?
What does one take when one goes?
What follows one along
Like a shadow that never departs?[208]

387 "Both the merits and the evil
That a mortal does right here:
This is what is truly one's own,
This one takes when one goes;
This is what follows one along
Like a shadow that never departs.

388 "Therefore one should do what is good
As a collection for the future life.
Merits are the support for living beings
[When they arise] in the other world."

5 (5) Self-Protected

<167> At Sāvatthī. Sitting to one side, King Pasenadi of Kosala said to the Blessed One: "Here, venerable sir, while I was alone in seclusion, a reflection arose in my mind thus: 'Who now protect themselves and who leave themselves unprotected?' Then, venerable sir, it occurred to me: 'Those who engage in misconduct of body, speech, and mind leave themselves unprotected. Even though a company of elephant troops may protect them, or a company of cavalry, or a company of chariot troops, [73] or a company of infantry, still they leave themselves unprotected. For what reason? Because that protection is external, not internal; therefore they leave themselves unprotected. But those who engage in good conduct of body, speech, and mind protect themselves. Even though no company of elephant troops protects them, nor a company of cavalry, nor a company of charioteers, nor a company of infantry, still they protect themselves. For what reason? Because that protection is internal, not external; therefore they protect themselves.'"

"So it is, great king! So it is, great king!"

(*The Buddha then repeats the entire statement of King Pasenadi and adds the following verse:*) <168>

389 "Good is restraint with the body,
Restraint by speech is also good;
Good is restraint with the mind,
Restraint everywhere is good.
Conscientious, everywhere restrained,
One is said to be protected."

6 (6) Few

At Sāvatthī. Sitting to one side, King Pasenadi of Kosala said to the Blessed One: "Here, venerable sir, while I was alone in seclusion, a reflection arose in my mind thus: 'Few are those people in the world who, <169> when they obtain superior possessions, do not become intoxicated and negligent, yield to greed for sensual pleasures, and mistreat other beings. Far more numerous are those people in the world who, when they obtain superior possessions, become intoxicated and negligent, [74] yield to greed for sensual pleasures, and mistreat other beings.'"

"So it is, great king! So it is, great king!"

(The Buddha then repeats the entire statement of King Pasenadi and adds the following verse:)

390 "Enamoured with their pleasures and wealth,
Greedy, dazed by sensual pleasures,
They do not realize they have gone too far
Like deer that enter the trap laid out.
Afterwards the bitter fruit is theirs,
For bad indeed is the result."[209] <170>

7 (7) The Judgement Hall

At Sāvatthī. Sitting to one side, King Pasenadi of Kosala said to the Blessed One: "Here, venerable sir, when I am sitting in the judgement hall,[210] I see even affluent khattiyas, affluent brahmins, and affluent householders—rich, with great wealth and property, with abundant gold and silver, abundant treasures and commodities, abundant wealth and grain—speaking deliberate lies for the sake of sensual pleasures, with sensual pleasures as the cause, on account of sensual pleasures. Then, venerable sir, it occurs to me: 'I've had enough now with the judgement hall! Now it is Good Face who will be known by his judgements.'"[211]

"So it is, great king! So it is, great king! Even affluent khattiyas, affluent brahmins, and affluent householders ... speak deliberate lies for the sake of sensual pleasures, with sensual pleasures as the cause, on account of sensual pleasures. That will lead to their harm and suffering for a long time to come.

391 "Enamoured with their pleasures and wealth,
Greedy, dazed by sensual pleasures,
They do not realize they have gone too far
Like fish that enter the net spread out.
Afterwards the bitter fruit is theirs, <171>
For bad indeed is the result." [75]

8 (8) Mallikā

At Sāvatthī. Now on that occasion King Pasenadi of Kosala had gone together with Queen Mallikā to the upper terrace of the palace. Then King Pasenadi of Kosala said to Queen Mallikā: "Is there, Mallikā, anyone more dear to you than yourself?"[212]

"There is no one, great king, more dear to me than myself. But is there anyone, great king, more dear to you than yourself?"

"For me too, Mallikā, there is no one more dear than myself."

Then King Pasenadi of Kosala descended from the palace and approached the Blessed One. Having approached, he paid homage to the Blessed One, sat down to one side, and related to the Blessed One his conversation with Queen Mallikā. Then the Blessed One, having understood the meaning of this, on that occasion recited this verse: <172>

392 "Having traversed all quarters with the mind,
One finds none anywhere dearer than oneself.
Likewise, each person holds himself most dear;
Hence one who loves himself should not harm others."

9 (9) Sacrifice

At Sāvatthī. Now on that occasion a great sacrifice had been set up for King Pasenadi of Kosala. Five hundred bulls, five hundred bullocks, five hundred heifers, [76] five hundred goats, and five hundred rams had been led to the pillar for the sacrifice. And his slaves, servants, and workers, spurred on by punishment and fear, were busy making the preparations, wailing with tearful faces.[213]

Then, in the morning, a number of bhikkhus dressed and, taking their bowls and robes, entered Sāvatthī for alms. When they had walked for alms in Sāvatthī and had returned from their alms round, after the meal they approached the Blessed One, <173> paid homage to him, sat down to one side, and said: "Here, venerable sir, a great sacrifice has been set up for King Pasenadi of Kosala. Five hundred bulls ... have been led to the pillar for the sacrifice. And his slaves ... are busy making preparations, wailing with tearful faces."

Then the Blessed One, having understood the meaning of this, on that occasion recited these verses:

393 "The horse sacrifice, human sacrifice,
Sammāpāsa, vājapeyya, niraggaḷa:

These great sacrifices, fraught with violence,
Do not bring great fruit.[214]

394 "The great seers of right conduct
Do not attend that sacrifice
Where goats, sheep, and cattle
Of various kinds are slain. <174>

395 "But when sacrifices free from violence
Are always offered by family custom,[215]
Where no goats, sheep, or cattle
Of various kinds are slain:
The great seers of right conduct
Attend a sacrifice like this.

396 "The wise person should offer this,
A sacrifice bringing great fruit.
For one who makes such sacrifice
It is indeed better, never worse.
Such a sacrifice is truly vast
And the devatās too are pleased."

10 (10) Bondage

Now on that occasion a great mass of people had been put in bondage by King Pasenadi of Kosala—some with ropes, some with clogs, some with chains.[216] [77] <175> Then, in the morning, a number of bhikkhus dressed ... and said to the Blessed One: "Here, venerable sir, a great mass of people have been put in bondage by King Pasenadi of Kosala, some with ropes, some with clogs, some with chains."

Then the Blessed One, having understood the meaning of this, on that occasion recited these verses:

397 "That bond, the wise say, is not strong
Made of iron, wood, or rope;
But infatuation with jewellery and earrings,
Anxious concern for wives and children—
398 This, the wise say, is the strong bond,
Degrading, supple, hard to escape.

But even this they cut and wander forth, <176>
Unconcerned, having abandoned sensual pleasures."[217]

II. The Second Subchapter (Childless)

11 (1) Seven Jaṭilas

On one occasion the Blessed One was dwelling at Sāvatthī in the Eastern Park in the Mansion of Migāra's Mother.[218] Now on that occasion, in the evening, the Blessed One had emerged from seclusion and was sitting by the outer gateway. Then King Pasenadi of Kosala approached the Blessed One, paid homage to him, and sat down to one side. [78] <177>

Now on that occasion seven jaṭilas, seven nigaṇṭhas, seven naked ascetics, seven one-robed ascetics, and seven wanderers—with hairy armpits, long fingernails and long body hairs, carrying their bundles of requisites—passed by not far from the Blessed One.[219] Then King Pasenadi of Kosala rose from his seat, arranged his upper robe over one shoulder, knelt down with his right knee on the ground, and, raising his joined hands in reverential salutation towards the seven jaṭilas, seven nigaṇṭhas, seven naked ascetics, seven one-robed ascetics, and seven wanderers, he announced his name three times: "I am the king, venerable sirs, Pasenadi of Kosala!... I am the king, venerable sirs, Pasenadi of Kosala!"

Then, not long after those seven jaṭilas ... <178> ... and seven wanderers had departed, King Pasenadi of Kosala approached the Blessed One, paid homage to him, sat down to one side, and said to the Blessed One: "Those, venerable sir, are to be included among the men in the world who are arahants or who have entered upon the path to arahantship."[220]

"Great king, being a layman who enjoys sensual pleasures, dwelling in a home crowded with children, enjoying the use of Kāsian sandalwood, wearing garlands, scents, and unguents, receiving gold and silver, it is difficult for you to know: 'These are arahants or these have entered upon the path to arahantship.'

"It is by living together with someone, great king, that his virtue is to be known, and that after a long time, not after a short time; by one who is attentive, not by one who is inattentive; by one who is wise, not by a dullard.

"It is by dealing with someone, great king, that his honesty is to be known, and that after a long time, not after a short time; by one who is attentive, not by one who is inattentive; by one who is wise, not by a dullard. <179>

"It is in adversities, great king, that a person's fortitude is to be known, and that after a long time, not after a short time; by one who is attentive, not by one who is inattentive; by one who is wise, not by a dullard. [79]

"It is by discussion with someone, great king, that his wisdom is to be known, and that after a long time, not after a short time; by one who is attentive, not by one who is inattentive; by one who is wise, not by a dullard."[221]

"It is wonderful, venerable sir! It is amazing, venerable sir! How well this has been stated by the Blessed One: 'Great king, being a layman … it is difficult for you to know … (*as above*) <180> … by one who is wise, not by a dullard.'

"These, venerable sir, are my spies, undercover agents, coming back after spying out the country.[222] First information is gathered by them and afterwards I will make them disclose it.[223] Now, venerable sir, when they have washed off the dust and dirt and are freshly bathed and groomed, with their hair and beards trimmed, clad in white garments, they will enjoy themselves supplied and endowed with the five cords of sensual pleasure."

Then the Blessed One, having understood the meaning of this, on that occasion recited these verses: <181>

399 "A man is not easily known by outward form
Nor should one trust a quick appraisal,
For in the guise of the well controlled
Uncontrolled men move in this world.

400 "Like a counterfeit earring made of clay,
Like a bronze half-pence coated with gold,
Some move about in disguise:
Inwardly impure, outwardly beautiful."

12 (2) Five Kings

At Sāvatthī. Now on that occasion five kings headed by King Pasenadi were enjoying themselves supplied and endowed with the five cords of sensual pleasure when this conversation arose among them: "What is the chief of sensual pleasures?"[224]

Some among them said: "Forms are the chief of sensual pleasures." Some said: "Sounds are the chief." Some: "Odours are the chief." Some: "Tastes are the chief." Some: [80] "Tactile objects are the chief."[225] <182>

Since those kings were unable to convince one another, King Pasenadi of Kosala said to them: "Come, dear sirs, let us approach the Blessed One and question him about this matter. As the Blessed One answers us, so we should remember it."

"All right, dear sir," those kings replied. Then those five kings, headed by King Pasenadi, approached the Blessed One, paid homage to him, and sat down to one side. King Pasenadi then reported their entire discussion to the Blessed One, asking: "What now, venerable sir, is the chief of sensual pleasures?" <183>

"Great king, I say that what is chief among the five cords of sensual pleasure is determined by whatever is most agreeable.[226] Those same forms that are agreeable to one person, great king, are disagreeable to another. When one is pleased and completely satisfied with certain forms, then one does not yearn for any other form higher or more sublime that those forms. For him those forms are then supreme; for him those forms are unsurpassed.

"Those same sounds ... Those same odours ... Those same tastes ... <184> ... Those same tactile objects that are agreeable to one person, great king, are disagreeable to another. [81] When one is pleased and completely satisfied with certain tactile objects, then one does not yearn for any other tactile object higher or more sublime that those tactile objects. For him those tactile objects are then supreme; for him those tactile objects are unsurpassed."

Now on that occasion the lay follower Candanaṅgalika was sitting in that assembly. Then the lay follower Candanaṅgalika rose from his seat, arranged his upper robe over one shoulder, and, raising his joined hands in reverential salutation towards the Blessed One, said to him: "An inspiration has come to me, Blessed One! An inspiration has come to me, Fortunate One!"

"Then express your inspiration, Candanaṅgalika," the Blessed One said.[227]

Then the lay follower Candanaṅgalika, in the presence of the Blessed One, extolled him with an appropriate verse:

401 "As the fragrant red lotus Kokanada
Blooms in the morning, its fragrance unspent,
Behold Aṅgīrasa, the Radiant One,
Like the sun beaming in the sky."[228]

Then those five kings bestowed five upper robes upon the lay follower Candanaṅgalika. But the lay follower Candanaṅgalika <185> bestowed those five upper robes upon the Blessed One.

13 (3) A Bucket Measure of Food

At Sāvatthī. Now on that occasion King Pasenadi of Kosala had eaten a bucket measure of rice and curries.[229] Then, while still full, huffing and puffing, the king approached the Blessed One, paid homage to him, and sat down to one side.

Then the Blessed One, having understood that King Pasenadi was full and was huffing and puffing, on that occasion recited this verse:

402 "When a man is always mindful,
Knowing moderation in the food he eats,
His ailments then diminish:
He ages slowly, guarding his life." [82] <186>

Now on that occasion the brahmin youth Sudassana was standing behind King Pasenadi of Kosala. The king then addressed him thus: "Come now, dear Sudassana, learn this verse from the Blessed One and recite it to me whenever I am taking my meal. I will then present you daily with a hundred *kahāpaṇas* as a perpetual grant."[230]

"Yes, sire," the brahmin youth Sudassana replied. Having learned this verse from the Blessed One, whenever King Pasenadi was taking his meal the brahmin youth Sudassana recited:

403 "When a man is always mindful … <187>
He ages slowly, guarding his life."

Then King Pasenadi of Kosala gradually reduced his intake of food to at most a pint-pot measure of boiled rice.[231] At a later time, when his body had become quite slim, King Pasenadi of Kosala stroked his limbs with his hand and on that occasion uttered this inspired utterance: "The Blessed One showed compassion towards me in regard to both kinds of good—the good pertaining to the present life and that pertaining to the future life."[232]

14 (4) Battle (1)

At Sāvatthī. Then King Ajātasattu of Magadha, the Videhan son, mobilized a four-division army and marched in the direction of Kāsi against King Pasenadi of Kosala.[233] King Pasenadi heard this report, mobilized a four-division army, and launched a counter-march in the direction of Kāsi against King Ajātasattu. [83] Then King Ajātasattu of Magadha and King Pasenadi of Kosala fought a battle. In that <188> battle King Ajātasattu defeated King Pasenadi, and King Pasenadi, defeated, retreated to his own capital of Sāvatthī.

Then, in the morning, a number of bhikkhus dressed and, taking their bowls and robes, entered Sāvatthī for alms. When they had walked for alms in Sāvatthī and had returned from their alms round, after the meal they approached the Blessed One, paid homage to him, sat down to one side, and reported what had happened. <189> [The Blessed One said:]

"Bhikkhus, King Ajātasattu of Magadha has evil friends, evil companions, evil comrades. King Pasenadi of Kosala has good friends, good companions, good comrades. Yet for this day, bhikkhus, King Pasenadi, having been defeated, will sleep badly tonight.[234]

404 "Victory breeds enmity,
The defeated one sleeps badly.
The peaceful one sleeps at ease,
Having abandoned victory and defeat."[235] <190>

15 (5) Battle (2)

[84] (*Opening as in §14:*)
In that battle King Pasenadi defeated King Ajātasattu and captured him alive. Then it occurred to King Pasenadi: "Although this King Ajātasattu of Magadha has transgressed against me while I have not transgressed against him, still, he is my nephew. Let me now confiscate all his elephant troops, all his cavalry, all his chariot troops, <191> and all his infantry, and let him go with nothing but his life."

Then King Pasenadi confiscated all King Ajātasattu's elephant troops, all his cavalry, all his chariot troops, and all his infantry, and let him go with nothing but his life.

Then, in the morning, a number of bhikkhus dressed and, taking their bowls and robes, entered Sāvatthī for alms. When they had walked for alms in Sāvatthī and had returned from their alms round, after the meal they approached the Blessed One, paid homage to him, sat down to one side, and reported what had happened. [85] <192>

Then the Blessed One, having understood the meaning of this, on that occasion recited these verses:

405 "A man will go on plundering
So long as it serves his ends, <193>
But when others plunder him,
The plunderer is plundered.[236]

406 "The fool thinks fortune is on his side
So long as his evil does not ripen,
But when the evil ripens
The fool incurs suffering.

407 "The killer begets a killer,
One who conquers, a conqueror.
The abuser begets abuse,
The reviler, one who reviles.
Thus by the unfolding of kamma
The plunderer is plundered."[237] [86]

16 (6) Daughter

At Sāvatthī. Then King Pasenadi of Kosala approached the Blessed One, paid homage to him, and sat down to one side. Then a certain man approached King Pasenadi <194> and informed him in a whisper: "Sire, Queen Mallikā has given birth to a daughter." When this was said, King Pasenadi was displeased.[238] Then the Blessed One, having understood that King Pasenadi was displeased, on that occasion recited these verses:

408 "A woman, O lord of the people,
May turn out better than a man:
She may be wise and virtuous,
A devoted wife, revering her mother-in-law.[239]

409 "The son to whom she gives birth
May become a hero, O lord of the land.
The son of such a blessed woman
May even rule the realm."[240] <195>

17 (7) Diligence (1)

At Sāvatthī. Sitting to one side, King Pasenadi of Kosala said to the Blessed One: "Is there, venerable sir, one thing which secures both kinds of good, the good pertaining to the present life and that pertaining to the future life?"

"There is one thing, great king, which secures both kinds of good, the good pertaining to the present life and that pertaining to the future life."

"But what, venerable sir, is that one thing?"

"Diligence, great king. Just as the footprints of all living beings that walk fit into the footprint of the elephant, and the elephant's footprint is declared to be their chief by reason of its size, so diligence is the one <196> thing which secures both kinds of good, [87] the good pertaining to the present life and that pertaining to the future life.[241]

410 "For one who desires long life and health,
Beauty, heaven, and noble birth,
[A variety of] lofty delights

Following in succession,
The wise praise diligence
In doing deeds of merit.

411 "The wise person who is diligent
Secures both kinds of good:
The good visible in this very life
And the good of the future life.
The steadfast one, by attaining the good,
Is called a person of wisdom."[242]

18 (8) Diligence (2)

At Sāvatthī. Sitting to one side, King Pasenadi of Kosala said to the Blessed One: <197> "Here, venerable sir, while I was alone in seclusion, the following reflection arose in my mind: 'The Dhamma has been well expounded by the Blessed One, and that is for one with good friends, good companions, good comrades, not for one with bad friends, bad companions, bad comrades.'"[243]

"So it is, great king! So it is, great king! The Dhamma has been well expounded by me, and that is for one with good friends, good companions, good comrades, not for one with bad friends, bad companions, bad comrades.

"On one occasion, great king, I was living among the Sakyans, where there is a town of the Sakyans named Nāgaraka.[244] Then the bhikkhu Ānanda approached me, paid homage to me, sat down to one side, and said: 'Venerable sir, this is half of the holy life, that is, good friendship, good companionship, good comradeship.'

"When this was said, great king, I told the bhikkhu Ānanda: 'Not so, Ānanda! Not so, Ānanda! <198> This is the entire holy life, Ānanda, that is, good friendship, [88] good companionship, good comradeship. When a bhikkhu has a good friend, a good companion, a good comrade, it is to be expected that he will develop and cultivate the Noble Eightfold Path. And how, Ānanda, does a bhikkhu who has a good friend, a good companion, a good comrade, develop and cultivate the Noble Eightfold Path? Here, Ānanda, a bhikkhu develops right view, which is based upon seclusion, dispassion, and cessation, maturing in release. He develops right intention ... right speech

... right action ... right livelihood ... right effort ... right mindfulness ... right concentration, which is based upon seclusion, dispassion, and cessation, maturing in release. It is in this way, Ānanda, that a bhikkhu who has a good friend, a good companion, a good comrade, develops and cultivates the Noble Eightfold Path.

"'By the following method too, Ānanda, it may be understood how the entire holy life is good friendship, good companionship, good comradeship: <199> by relying upon me as a good friend, Ānanda, beings subject to birth are freed from birth; beings subject to aging are freed from aging; beings subject to illness are freed from illness; beings subject to death are freed from death; beings subject to sorrow, lamentation, pain, displeasure, and despair are freed from sorrow, lamentation, pain, displeasure, and despair. By this method, Ānanda, it may be understood how the entire holy life is good friendship, good companionship, good comradeship.'

"Therefore, great king, you should train yourself thus: 'I will be one who has good friends, good companions, good comrades.' It is in such a way that you should train yourself.

"When, great king, you have good friends, good companions, good comrades, [89] you should dwell with one thing for support: diligence in wholesome states.

"When, great king, you are dwelling diligently, with diligence for support, your retinue of harem women will think thus: 'The king dwells diligently, with diligence for support. Come now, let us also dwell diligently, with diligence for support.' <200>

"When, great king, you are dwelling diligently, with diligence for support, your retinue of khattiya vassals will think thus ... your troops will think thus ... your subjects in town and countryside will think thus: 'The king dwells diligently, with diligence for support. Come now, let us also dwell diligently, with diligence for support.'

"When, great king, you are dwelling diligently, with diligence for support, you yourself will be guarded and protected, your retinue of harem women will be guarded and protected, your treasury and storehouse will be guarded and protected.

412 "For one who desires lofty riches
Following in succession,

The wise praise diligence
In doing deeds of merit.

413 "The wise person who is diligent <201>
Secures both kinds of good:
The good visible in this very life
And the good of the future life.
The steadfast one, by attaining the good,
Is called a person of wisdom."

19 (9) Childless (1)

At Sāvatthī. Then King Pasenadi of Kosala approached the Blessed One, paid homage to him, and sat down to one side. The Blessed One then said to him: "Where are you coming from, great king, in the middle of the day?"

"Here, venerable sir, a financier householder in Sāvatthī has died. I have come after conveying his heirless fortune to the palace, as he died intestate.[245] There were eighty lakhs of gold, [90] not to speak of silver, and yet, venerable sir, that financier householder's meals were like this: he ate red rice along with sour gruel. His clothes were like this: he wore a three-piece hempen garment. His vehicle was like this: <202> he went about in a dilapidated little cart with a leaf awning."[246]

"So it is, great king! So it is, great king! When an inferior man gains abundant wealth, he does not make himself happy and pleased, nor does he make his mother and father happy and pleased, nor his wife and children, nor his slaves, workers, and servants, nor his friends and colleagues; nor does he establish an offering for ascetics and brahmins, one leading upwards, of heavenly fruit, resulting in happiness, conducive to heaven. Because his wealth is not being used properly, kings take it away, or thieves take it away, or fire burns it, or water carries it away, or unloved heirs take it. Such being the case, great king, that wealth, not being used properly, goes to waste, not to utilization.

"Suppose, great king, in a place uninhabited by human beings, there was a lotus pond with clear, cool, sweet, clean water, with good fords, <203> delightful; but no people would take that water, or drink it, or bathe in it, or use it for any purpose. In such a case, great king, that water, not being used properly, would go to waste, not to utilization. So too, great king, when an inferior man gains abundant wealth ... that wealth, not being used properly, goes to waste, not to utilization.

"But, great king, when a superior man gains abundant wealth, he makes himself happy and pleased, and he makes his mother and father happy and pleased, and his wife and children, and his slaves, workers, and servants, and his friends and colleagues; <204> and he establishes an offering for ascetics and brahmins, one leading upwards, of heavenly fruit, resulting in happiness, conducive to heaven. Because his wealth is being used properly, [91] kings do not take it away, thieves do not take it away, fire does not burn it, water does not carry it away, and unloved heirs do not take it. Such being the case, great king, that wealth, being used properly, goes to utilization, not to waste.

"Suppose, great king, not far from a village or a town, there was a lotus pond with clear, cool, sweet, clean water, with good fords, delightful; and people would take that water, and drink it, and bathe in it, and use it for their purposes. In such a case, great king, that water, being used properly, would go to utilization, not to waste. So too, great king, when a superior man gains abundant wealth ... <205> that wealth, being used properly, goes to utilization, not to waste.

414 "As cool water in a desolate place
Evaporates without being drunk,
So when a scoundrel acquires wealth
He neither enjoys himself nor gives.

415 "But when the wise man obtains wealth
He enjoys himself and does his duty.
Having supported his kin, free from blame,
That noble man goes to a heavenly state."

20 (10) Childless (2)

(*As above, except that the amount is a hundred lakhs of gold, a lakh being equal to a hundred thousand:*) [92] <206>

"So it is, great king! So it is, great king! Once in the past, great king, that financier householder provided a paccekabuddha named Tagarasikhī with almsfood. Having said, 'Give alms to the ascetic,' he rose from his seat and departed. But after giving, he later felt regret and thought: 'It would have been better if the slaves or workers had eaten that almsfood!' Moreover, he murdered his brother's only son for the sake of his fortune.[247]

"Because that financier householder provided the paccekabuddha Tagarasikhī with almsfood, <207> as a result of that kamma he was reborn seven times in a good destination, in the heavenly world. As a residual result of that same kamma, he obtained the position of financier seven times in this same city of Sāvatthī. But because that financier householder later felt regret about giving, as a result of that kamma his mind did not incline to the enjoyment of excellent food, excellent clothing, and excellent vehicles, nor to the enjoyment of excellent items among the five cords of sensual pleasure. And because that financier householder murdered his brother's only son for the sake of his fortune, as a result of that kamma he was tormented in hell for many years, for many hundreds of years, for many thousands of years, for many hundreds of thousands of years. As a residual result of that same kamma, he has furnished the royal treasury with this seventh heirless fortune.

"The old merit of that financier householder has been utterly exhausted, <208> and he had not accumulated any fresh merit. But today, great king, the financier householder is being roasted in the Great Roruva Hell."[248]

"So, venerable sir, that financier householder has been reborn in the Great Roruva Hell?" [93]

"Yes, great king, that financier householder has been reborn in the Great Roruva Hell.

416 "Grain, wealth, silver, gold,
Or whatever other possessions there are,
Slaves, workers, messengers,
And those who live as one's dependants:
Without taking anything one must go,
Everything must be left behind.

417 "But what one has done by body,
Or by speech or mind:
This is what is truly one's own,
This one takes when one goes;

This is what follows one along
Like a shadow that never departs.

418 "Therefore one should do what is good <209>
As a collection for the future life.
Merits are the support for living beings
[When they arise] in the other world."

III. The Third Subchapter
(The Kosalan Pentad)

21 (1) Persons

At Sāvatthī. Then King Pasenadi of Kosala approached the Blessed One, paid homage to him, and sat down to one side. The Blessed One then said to him: <210>

"Great king, there are these four kinds of persons found existing in the world. What four? The one heading from darkness to darkness, the one heading from darkness to light, the one heading from light to darkness, the one heading from light to light.[249]

"And how, great king, is a person one heading from darkness to darkness? Here some person has been reborn in a low family—a family of caṇḍālas, bamboo workers, hunters, cartwrights, or flower-scavengers—a poor family in which there is little food and drink and which subsists with difficulty, [94] one where food and clothing are obtained with difficulty; and he is ugly, unsightly, deformed, chronically ill—purblind or cripple-handed or lame or paralyzed.[250] He is not one who gains food, drink, clothing, and vehicles; garlands, scents, and unguents; bedding, housing, and lighting. He engages in misconduct of body, speech, and mind. Having done so, with the breakup of the body, <211> after death, he is reborn in the plane of misery, in a bad destination, in the nether world, in hell.

"Suppose, great king, a man would go from darkness to darkness, or from gloom to gloom, or from stain to stain: this person, I say, is exactly similar. It is in this way, great king, that a person is one heading from darkness to darkness.

"And how, great king, is a person one heading from darkness to light? Here some person has been reborn in a low family … one where food and clothing are obtained with difficulty; and he is ugly ... or paralyzed. He is not one who gains food ... and lighting. He engages in good conduct of body, speech, and mind. Having done so, with the breakup of the body, after death, he is reborn in a good destination, in a heavenly world.

"Suppose, great king, a man would climb from the ground on to a palanquin, or from a palanquin on to horseback, <212> or from horseback to an elephant mount, or from an elephant mount to a mansion: this person, I say, is exactly similar. It is in this way, great king, that a person is one heading from darkness to light.

"And how, great king, is a person one heading from light to darkness? Here some person has been reborn in a high family—an affluent khattiya family, an affluent brahmin family, or an affluent householder family—one which is rich, with great wealth and property, [95] with abundant gold and silver, abundant treasures and commodities, abundant wealth and grain; and he is handsome, attractive, graceful, possessing supreme beauty of complexion. He is one who gains food, drink, clothing, and vehicles; garlands, scents, and unguents; bedding, housing, and lighting. He engages in misconduct of body, speech, and mind. Having done so, with the breakup of the body, after death, he is reborn in the plane of misery, in a bad destination, in the nether world, in hell.

"Suppose, great king, a man would descend from a mansion to an elephant mount, or from an elephant mount to horseback, or from horseback to a palanquin, or from a palanquin to the ground, or from the ground to underground darkness: this person, I say, is exactly similar. It is in this way, great king, that a person is one heading from light to darkness. <213>

"And how, great king, is a person one heading from light to light? Here some person has been reborn in a high family ... with abundant wealth and grain; and he is handsome, attractive, graceful, possessing supreme beauty of complexion. He is one who gains food ... and lighting. He engages in good conduct of body, speech, and mind. Having done so, with the breakup of the body, after death, he is reborn in a good destination, in a heavenly world.

"Suppose, great king, a man would cross over from palanquin to palanquin, or from horseback to horseback, or from elephant mount to elephant mount, or from mansion to mansion: this person, I say, is exactly similar. It is in this way, great king, that a person is one heading from light to light. [96]

"These, great king, are the four kinds of persons found existing in the world.

(i)

419 "The person, O king, who is poor,
Lacking in faith, stingy,
Niggardly, with bad intentions,
Wrong in views, disrespectful, <214>
420 Who abuses and reviles ascetics,
Brahmins, and other mendicants;
A nihilist, a scoffer, who hinders
Another giving food to beggars:
421 When such a person dies, O king,
He goes, lord of the people,
To the terrible hell,
Heading from darkness to darkness.

(ii)

422 "The person, O king, who is poor,
Endowed with faith, generous,
One who gives, with best intentions,
A person with unscattered mind
423 Who rises up and venerates ascetics,
Brahmins, and other mendicants;
One who trains in righteous conduct,
Who hinders none giving food to beggars:
424 When such a person dies, O king, <215>
He goes, lord of the people,
To the triple heaven,
Heading from darkness to light.

(iii)

425 "The person, O king, who is rich,
Lacking in faith, stingy,
Niggardly, with bad intentions,
Wrong in views, disrespectful,
426 Who abuses and reviles ascetics,
Brahmins, and other mendicants;

A nihilist, a scoffer, who hinders
Another giving food to beggars:
427 When such a person dies, O king,
He goes, lord of the people,
To the terrible hell,
Heading from light to darkness.

(iv)

428 "The person, O king, who is rich,
Endowed with faith, generous,
One who gives, with best intentions, <216>
A person with unscattered mind
429 Who rises up and venerates ascetics,
Brahmins, and other mendicants;
One who trains in righteous conduct,
Who hinders none giving food to beggars:
430 When such a person dies, O king,
He goes, lord of the people,
To the triple heaven,
Heading from light to light."

22 (2) Grandmother

At Sāvatthī. Then, in the middle of the day, King Pasenadi of Kosala approached the Blessed One.... The Blessed One said to him as he was sitting to one side: [97] "Where are you coming from, great king, in the middle of the day?" <217>

"Venerable sir, my grandmother has died. She was old, aged, burdened with years, advanced in life, come to the last stage, 120 years from birth. Venerable sir, my grandmother was dear and beloved to me. If, venerable sir, by means of the elephant-gem I could have redeemed her from death, I would have given away even the elephant-gem so that she would not have died.[251] If by means of the horse-gem I could have redeemed her from death ... If by a prize village I could have redeemed her from death ... If by means of the country I could have redeemed her from death, I would have given away even the country so that she would not have died."

"All beings, great king, are subject to death, terminate in death, and cannot escape death."

"It is wonderful, venerable sir! It is amazing, venerable sir! How well this has been stated by the Blessed One: 'All beings, great king, are subject to death, terminate in death, and cannot escape death.'"

"So it is, great king! So it is, great king! All beings, great king, are subject to death, terminate in death, and cannot escape death. <218> Just as all the potter's vessels, whether unbaked or baked, are subject to a breakup, terminate in their breakup, and cannot escape their breakup, so all beings are subject to death, terminate in death, and cannot escape death.

431 "All beings will die,
For life ends in death.
They will fare according to their deeds,
Reaping the fruits of their merit and evil:
The doers of evil go to hell,
The doers of merit to a happy realm.

432 "Therefore one should do what is good
As a collection for the future life.
Merits are the support for living beings
[When they arise] in the other world." [98]

23 (3) World

At Sāvatthī. Sitting to one side, King Pasenadi of Kosala said to the Blessed One: "Venerable sir, how many things are there in the world which, when they arise, arise for one's harm, suffering, and discomfort?"[252] <219>

"There are, great king, three things in the world which, when they arise, arise for one's harm, suffering, and discomfort. What are the three? Greed, hatred, and delusion. These are the three things in the world which, when they arise, arise for one's harm, suffering, and discomfort.

433 "Greed, hatred, and delusion,
Arisen from within oneself,
Injure the person of evil mind
As its own fruit destroys the reed."

24 (4) Archery

At Sāvatthī. Sitting to one side, King Pasenadi of Kosala said to the Blessed One:

"Venerable sir, where should a gift be given?"[253]

"Wherever one's mind has confidence, great king."[254]

"But, venerable sir, where does what is given become of great fruit?" <220>

"This is one question, great king, 'Where should a gift be given?' and this another, 'Where does what is given become of great fruit?' What is given to one who is virtuous, great king, is of great fruit, not so what is given to an immoral person. Now then, great king, I will question you about this same point. Answer as you see fit. What do you think, great king? Suppose you are at war and a battle is about to take place. Then a khattiya youth would arrive, one who is untrained, unskilful, unpractised, [99] inexperienced, timid, petrified, frightened, quick to flee. Would you employ that man, and would you have any use for such a man?"

"Surely not, venerable sir." <221>

"Then a brahmin youth would arrive ... a vessa youth ... a sudda youth ... who is untrained ... quick to flee. Would you employ that man, and would you have any use for such a man?"

"Surely not, venerable sir."

"What do you think, great king? Suppose you are at war and a battle is about to take place. Then a khattiya youth would arrive, one who is trained, skilful, practised, experienced, brave, courageous, bold, ready to stand his place. Would you employ that man, and would you have any use for such a man?"

"Surely I would, venerable sir."

"Then a brahmin youth would arrive ... a vessa youth ... a sudda youth ... who is trained ... ready to stand his place. Would you employ that man, and would you have any use for such a man?" <222>

"Surely I would, venerable sir."

"So too, great king, when a person has gone forth from the household life into homelessness, no matter from what clan, if he has abandoned five factors and possesses five factors, then what is given to him is of great fruit. What five factors have been abandoned? Sensual desire has been abandoned; ill will has been abandoned; sloth and torpor have been abandoned; restlessness and remorse have been abandoned; doubt has been abandoned. What five factors does he possess? He possesses the aggregate of virtue of one beyond training, the aggregate of concentration of one beyond training, the aggregate of wisdom of one beyond training, [100] the aggregate of liberation of one beyond training, the aggregate of the knowledge and vision of liberation of one beyond training. He possesses these five factors. Thus what is given to one who has abandoned five factors and who possesses five factors is of great fruit.[255] <223>

434 "As a king intent on waging war
Would employ a youth skilled with the bow,
One endowed with strength and vigour,
But not the coward on account of his birth—
435 So even though he be of low birth,
One should honour the person of noble conduct,
The sagely man in whom are established
The virtues of patience and gentleness.[256]

436 "One should build delightful hermitages
And invite the learned to dwell in them;
One should build water tanks in the forest
And causeways over rough terrain.

437 "With a confident heart one should give
To those of upright character:
Give food and drink and things to eat,
Clothing to wear and beds and seats.

438 "For as the rain-cloud, thundering, <224>
Wreathed in lightning, with a hundred crests,
Pours down its rain upon the earth,
Flooding both the plain and valley—
439 So the wise man, faithful, learned,
Having had a meal prepared,
Satisfies with food and drink
The mendicants who live on alms.
Rejoicing, he distributes gifts,
And proclaims, 'Give, give.'

440 "For that is his thundering
Like the sky when it rains.
That shower of merit, so vast,
Will pour down on the giver."

25 (5) The Simile of the Mountain

At Sāvatthī. Then, in the middle of the day, King Pasenadi of Kosala approached the Blessed One.... <225> The Blessed One said to him as he was sitting to one side: "Now where are you coming from, great king, in the middle of the day?"

"Just now, venerable sir, I have been engaged in those affairs of kingship typical for head-anointed khattiya kings, who are intoxicated with the intoxication of sovereignty, who are obsessed by greed for sensual pleasures, who have attained stable control in their country, and who rule having conquered a great sphere of territory on earth."[257]

"What do you think, great king? [101] Here, a man would come to you from the east, one who is trustworthy and reliable; having approached, he would tell you: 'For sure, great king, you should know this: I am coming from the east, and there I saw a great mountain high as the clouds coming this way, crushing all living beings. Do whatever you think should be done, great king.' Then a second man would come to you from the west ... Then a third man would come to you from the north ... <226> ... Then a fourth man would come to you from the south, one who is trustworthy and reliable; having approached, he would tell you: 'For sure, great king, you should know this: I am coming from the south, and there I saw a great mountain high as the clouds coming this way, crushing all living beings. Do whatever you think should be done, great king.' If, great king, such a great peril should arise, such a terrible destruction of human life, the human state being so difficult to obtain, what should be done?"

"If, venerable sir, such a great peril should arise, such a terrible destruction of human life, the human state being so difficult to obtain, what else should be done but to live by the Dhamma, to live righteously, and to do wholesome and meritorious deeds?"[258]

"I inform you, great king, I announce to you, great king: aging and death are rolling in on you. When aging and death are rolling in on you, great king, what should be done?"

"As aging and death are rolling in on me, venerable sir, what else should be done but to live by the Dhamma, to live righteously, and to do wholesome and meritorious deeds? <227>

"There are, venerable sir, elephant battles [fought by] head-anointed khattiya kings, who are intoxicated with the intoxication of sovereignty, who are obsessed by greed for sensual pleasures, who have attained stable control in their country, and who rule having conquered a great sphere of territory on earth; but there is no place for those elephant battles, no scope for them, when aging and death are rolling in.[259] There are, venerable sir, cavalry battles [fought by] head-anointed khattiya kings ... There are chariot battles ... infantry battles ... [102] but there is no place for those infantry battles, no scope for them, when aging and death are rolling in. In this royal court, venerable sir, there are counsellors who, when the enemies arrive, are capable of dividing them by subterfuge; but there is no place for those battles of subterfuge, no scope for them, when aging and death are rolling in. In this royal court, venerable sir, there exists abundant bullion and gold stored in vaults and depositories, and with such wealth we are capable of mollifying the enemies when they come; but there is no place for those battles of wealth, no scope for them, when aging and death are rolling in. As aging and death are rolling in on me, venerable sir, what else should be done but to live by the Dhamma, to live righteously, and to do wholesome and meritorious deeds?" <228>

"So it is, great king! So it is, great king! As aging and death are rolling in on you, what else should be done but to live by the Dhamma, to live righteously, and to do wholesome and meritorious deeds?"

This is what the Blessed One said. Having said this, the Fortunate One, the Teacher, further said this:

441 "Just as mountains of solid rock,
Massive, reaching to the sky,
Might draw together from all sides,
Crushing all in the four quarters—
So aging and death come
Rolling over living beings—
442 Khattiyas, brahmins, vessas, suddas,
Caṇḍālas and scavengers:

They spare none along the way
But come crushing everything.

443 "There's no ground there for elephant troops,
For chariot troops and infantry.
One can't defeat them by subterfuge,
Or buy them off by means of wealth. <229>

444 "Therefore a person of wisdom here,
Out of regard for his own good,
Steadfast, should settle faith
In the Buddha, Dhamma, and Saṅgha.

445 "When one conducts oneself by Dhamma
With body, speech, and mind,
They praise one here in the present life,
And after death one rejoices in heaven." <230>

[103] <231> Chapter IV

4 *Mārasaṃyutta*
Connected Discourses with Māra

I. The First Subchapter (Life Span)

1 (1) Austere Practice

Thus have I heard. On one occasion the Blessed One was dwelling at Uruvelā on the bank of the river Nerañjarā at the foot of the Goatherd's Banyan Tree just after he had become fully enlightened.[260] Then, while the Blessed One was alone in seclusion, a reflection arose in his mind thus: "I am indeed freed from that gruelling asceticism! It is good indeed that I am freed from that useless gruelling asceticism! It is good that, steady and mindful, I have attained enlightenment!"[261]

Then Māra the Evil One, having known with his own mind the reflection in the Blessed One's mind, approached the Blessed One and addressed him in verse:

446 "Having deviated from the austere practice
By which men purify themselves,
Being impure, you think you're pure: <232>
You have missed the path to purity."[262]

Then the Blessed One, having understood, "This is Māra the Evil One," replied to him in verses:

447 "Having known as useless any austerity
Aimed at the immortal state,[263]
That all such penances are futile
Like oars and rudder on dry land,[264]

448 By developing the path to enlightenment—
Virtue, concentration, and wisdom—
I have attained supreme purity:
You're defeated, End-maker!"[265]

Then Māra the Evil One, realizing, "The Blessed One knows me, the Fortunate One knows me," sad and disappointed, disappeared right there.

2 (2) The King Elephant

Thus have I heard. On one occasion the Blessed One was dwelling at Uruvelā on the bank of the river Nerañjarā at the foot of the Goatherd's Banyan Tree just after he had become fully enlightened. [104] <233> Now on that occasion the Blessed One was sitting out in the open air in the thick darkness of the night while it was drizzling.[266]

Then Māra the Evil One, wishing to arouse fear, trepidation, and terror in the Blessed One, manifested himself in the form of a giant king elephant and approached the Blessed One. His head was like a huge block of steatite; his tusks were like pure silver; his trunk was like a huge plough pole.

Then the Blessed One, having understood, "This is Māra the Evil One," addressed him in verse:

449 "You've wandered through the long course
Creating beautiful and hideous shapes.
Enough, Evil One, with that trick of yours:
You're defeated, End-maker!"[267]

Then Māra the Evil One, realizing, "The Blessed One knows me, the Fortunate One knows me," sad and disappointed, disappeared right there.

3 (3) Beautiful

<234> While dwelling at Uruvelā. Now on that occasion the Blessed One was sitting out in the open air in the thick darkness of the night while it was drizzling. Then Māra the Evil One, wishing to arouse fear, trepidation, and terror in the Blessed

One, approached the Blessed One and, not far from him, displayed diverse lustrous shapes, both beautiful and hideous. Then the Blessed One, having understood, "This is Māra the Evil One," addressed him in verses:

450 "You've wandered on through the long course
Creating beautiful and hideous shapes.
Enough, Evil One, with that trick of yours:
You're defeated, End-maker!

451 "Those who are well restrained
In body, speech, and mind,
Do not come under Māra's control
Nor become Māra's henchmen."[268]

Then Māra the Evil One ... disappeared right there. [105]

4 (4) Māra's Snare (1)

<235> Thus have I heard. On one occasion the Blessed One was dwelling at Bārāṇasī in the Deer Park at Isipatana. There the Blessed One addressed the bhikkhus thus: "Bhikkhus!"[269]

"Venerable sir!" those bhikkhus replied. The Blessed One said this:

"Bhikkhus, by careful attention, by careful right striving, I have arrived at unsurpassed liberation, I have realized unsurpassed liberation. You too, bhikkhus, by careful attention, by careful right striving, must arrive at unsurpassed liberation, must realize unsurpassed liberation."[270]

Then Māra the Evil One approached the Blessed One and addressed him in verse:[271]

452 "You are bound by Māra's snare
Both celestial and human;
You are bound by Māra's bondage:
You won't escape me, ascetic!"[272]

[The Blessed One:]
453 "I am freed from Māra's snare
Both celestial and human;

I am freed from Māra's bondage: <236>
You're defeated, End-maker!"

Then Māra the Evil One ... disappeared right there.

5 (5) Māra's Snare (2)

Thus have I heard. On one occasion the Blessed One was dwelling at Bārāṇasī in the Deer Park at Isipatana. There the Blessed One addressed the bhikkhus thus: "Bhikkhus!"

"Venerable sir!" those bhikkhus replied. The Blessed One said this:

"Bhikkhus, I am freed from all snares, both celestial and human. You too, bhikkhus, are freed from all snares, both celestial and human. Wander forth, O bhikkhus, for the welfare of the multitude, for the happiness of the multitude, out of compassion for the world, for the good, welfare, and happiness of devas and humans. Let not two go the same way. Teach, O bhikkhus, the Dhamma that is good in the beginning, good in the middle, good in the end, with the right meaning and phrasing. Reveal the perfectly complete and purified holy life. There are beings with little dust in their eyes who are falling away because they do not hear the Dhamma. [106] There will be those who will understand the Dhamma. I too, bhikkhus, will go to Senānigama in Uruvelā in order to teach the Dhamma."[273] <237>

Then Māra the Evil One approached the Blessed One and addressed him in verse:[274]

454 "You are bound by all the snares
Both celestial and human;
You are bound by the great bondage:
You won't escape me, ascetic!"

[The Blessed One:]
455 "I am freed from all the snares
Both celestial and human;
I am freed from the great bondage:
You're defeated, End-maker!"

6 (6) Serpent

Thus have I heard. On one occasion the Blessed One was dwelling at Rājagaha in the Bamboo Grove, the Squirrel Sanctuary. Now on that occasion the Blessed One was sitting out in the open in the thick darkness of the night while it was drizzling. Then Māra the Evil One … manifested himself in the form of a giant king serpent and approached the Blessed One. <238> Its body was like a huge boat made from a single tree trunk; its hood, like a large brewer's sieve; its eyes, like the large bronze dishes of Kosala; its tongue darting out from its mouth, like flashes of lightning emitted when the sky thunders; the sound of its breathing in and out, like the sound of a smith's bellows filling with air.

Then the Blessed One, having understood, "This is Māra the Evil One," addressed Māra the Evil One in verses:

456 "He who resorts to empty huts for lodging—
He is the sage, self-controlled.
He should live there, having relinquished all:
That is proper for one like him.[275]

457 "Though many creatures crawl about,
Many terrors, flies, serpents, [107] <239>
The great sage gone to his empty hut
Stirs not a hair because of them.

458 "Though the sky might split, the earth quake,
And all creatures be stricken with terror,
Though men brandish a dart at their breast,
The enlightened take no shelter in acquisitions."[276]

Then Māra the Evil One … disappeared right there.

7 (7) Sleep

On one occasion the Blessed One was dwelling at Rājagaha in the Bamboo Grove, the Squirrel Sanctuary. Then, when the night was fading, the Blessed One, having spent much of the night walking back and forth in the open, washed his feet, entered his dwelling, and lay down on his right side in the lion's posture, with one leg overlapping the other, mindful and clearly comprehending, having attended to the idea of rising.

Then Māra the Evil One approached the Blessed One and addressed him in verse: <240>

459 "What, you sleep? Why do you sleep?
What's this, you sleep like a wretch?[277]
Thinking 'The hut's empty' you sleep:
What's this, you sleep when the sun has risen?"

[The Blessed One:]
460 "Within him craving no longer lurks,
Entangling and binding, to lead him anywhere;
With the destruction of all acquisitions
The Awakened One sleeps:
Why should this concern you, Māra?"[278]

Then Māra the Evil One … disappeared right there.

8 (8) He Delights

Thus have I heard. On one occasion the Blessed One was dwelling at Sāvatthī in Jeta's Grove, Anāthapiṇḍika's Park.

Then Māra the Evil One approached the Blessed One and recited this verse in the presence of the Blessed One:

461 "One who has sons delights in sons,
One with cattle delights in cattle. [108] <241>
Acquisitions truly are a man's delight;
Without acquisitions one does not delight."

[The Blessed One:]
462 "One who has sons sorrows over sons,
One with cattle sorrows over cattle.
Acquisitions truly are a man's sorrow;
Without acquisitions one does not sorrow."

Then Māra the Evil One … disappeared right there.

9 (9) Life Span (1)

Thus have I heard. On one occasion the Blessed One was dwelling at Rājagaha in the Bamboo Grove, the Squirrel Sanctuary. There the Blessed One addressed the bhikkhus thus: "Bhikkhus!"

"Venerable sir!" those bhikkhus replied. The Blessed One said this:

"Bhikkhus, this life span of human beings is short. One has to go on to the future life. One should do what is wholesome and lead the holy life; for one who has taken birth there is no avoiding death. One who lives long, bhikkhus, lives a hundred years or a little longer."

Then Māra the Evil One approached the Blessed One and addressed him in verse:

463 "Long is the life span of human beings,
The good man should not disdain it.
One should live like a milk-sucking baby:
Death has not made its arrival."[279] <242>

[The Blessed One:]
464 "Short is the life span of human beings,
The good man should disdain it.
One should live like one with head aflame:
There is no avoiding Death's arrival."

Then Māra the Evil One ... disappeared right there.

10 (10) Life Span (2)

(*Opening as in preceding sutta:*)
Then Māra the Evil One approached the Blessed One and addressed him in verse: [109]

465 "The days and nights do not fly by,
Life does not come to a stop.
The life span of mortals rolls along
Like the chariot's felly round the hub."[280] <243>

[The Blessed One:]
466 "The days and nights go flying by,
Life comes to a stop.
The life span of mortals is depleted
Like the water in rivulets."

Then Māra the Evil One ... disappeared right there.

II. The Second Subchapter (Rulership)

11 (1) The Boulder

On one occasion the Blessed One was dwelling at Rājagaha on Mount Vulture Peak. Now on that occasion the Blessed One was sitting out in the open in the thick darkness of the night while it was drizzling. <244> Then Māra the Evil One, wishing to arouse fear, trepidation, and terror in the Blessed One, shattered a number of huge boulders not far away from him.

Then the Blessed One, having understood, "This is Māra the Evil One," addressed Māra the Evil One in verse:

467 "Even if you make this Vulture Peak
Quake all over in its entirety,
The enlightened are not perturbed,
For they are are fully liberated."

Then Māra the Evil One, realizing, "The Blessed One knows me, the Fortunate One knows me," sad and disappointed, disappeared right there.

12 (2) Lion

On one occasion the Blessed One was dwelling at Sāvatthī in Jeta's Grove, Anāthapiṇḍika's Park. Now on that occasion the Blessed One was teaching the Dhamma while surrounded by a large assembly. [110]

Then it occurred to Māra the Evil One: "This ascetic Gotama is teaching the Dhamma while surrounded by a large assembly. <245> Let me approach the ascetic Gotama in order to confound them."[281]

Then Māra the Evil One approached the Blessed One and addressed him in verse:

468 "Why now do you roar like a lion,
Confident in the assembly?
For there is one who's a match for you,
So why think yourself the victor?"

[The Blessed One:]
469 "The great heroes roar their lion's roar
Confident in the assemblies—
The Tathāgatas endowed with the powers
Have crossed over attachment to the world."[282]

Then Māra the Evil One ... disappeared right there.

13 (3) The Splinter

Thus have I heard. On one occasion the Blessed One was dwelling at Rājagaha in the Maddakucchi Deer Park. Now on that occasion the Blessed One's foot had been cut by a stone splinter. Severe pains assailed the Blessed One—bodily feelings that were painful, racking, <246> sharp, piercing, harrowing, disagreeable. But the Blessed One endured them, mindful and clearly comprehending, without becoming distressed. Then the Blessed One had his outer robe folded in four, and he lay down on his right side in the lion posture with one leg overlapping the other, mindful and clearly comprehending.[283]

Then Māra the Evil One approached the Blessed One and addressed him in verse:

470 "Do you lie down in a daze or drunk on poetry?
Don't you have sufficient goals to meet?
Alone in a secluded lodging
Why do you sleep with a drowsy face?"[284]

[The Blessed One:]
471 "I do not lie in a daze or drunk on poetry;
Having reached the goal, I am rid of sorrow.
Alone in a secluded lodging
I lie down full of compassion for all beings.

472 "Even those with a dart stuck in the breast <247>
Piercing their heart moment by moment—
Even these here, stricken, get to sleep; [111]
So why should I not get to sleep
When my dart has been drawn out?[285]

473 "I do not lie awake in dread,
Nor am I afraid to sleep.
The nights and days do not afflict me,
I see for myself no decline in the world.
Therefore I can sleep in peace,
Full of compassion for all beings."

Then Māra the Evil One … disappeared right there.

14 (4) Suitable

On one occasion the Blessed One was dwelling among the Kosalans at the brahmin village of Ekasālā. Now on that occasion the Blessed One was teaching the Dhamma surrounded by a large assembly of laypeople.

Then it occurred to Māra the Evil One: "This ascetic Gotama is teaching the Dhamma while surrounded by a large assembly of laypeople. <248> Let me approach the ascetic Gotama in order to confound them."

Then Māra the Evil One approached the Blessed One and addressed him in verse:

474 "This is not suitable for you,
That you instruct others.
When so engaged don't get caught
In attraction and repulsion."[286]

[The Blessed One:]
475 "Compassionate for their welfare,
The Buddha instructs others.
The Tathāgata is fully released
From attraction and repulsion."

Then Māra the Evil One … disappeared right there.

15 (5) Mental

Thus have I heard. On one occasion the Blessed One was dwelling at Sāvatthī in Jeta's Grove, Anāthapiṇḍika's Park. Then Māra the Evil One approached the Blessed One and addressed him in verse:[287]

476 "There is a snare moving in the sky, <249>
Something mental which moves about[288]
By means of which I'll catch you yet:
You won't escape me, ascetic!"

[The Blessed One:]
477 "Forms, sounds, tastes, odours,
And delightful tactile objects—
Desire for these has vanished in me:
You're defeated, End-maker!"

Then Māra the Evil One … disappeared right there. [112]

16 (6) Almsbowls

At Sāvatthī. Now on that occasion the Blessed One was instructing, exhorting, inspiring, and gladdening the bhikkhus with a Dhamma talk concerning the five aggregates subject to clinging. And those bhikkhus were listening to the Dhamma with eager ears, attending to it as a matter of vital concern, applying their whole minds to it.

Then it occurred to Māra the Evil One: "This ascetic Gotama is instructing, exhorting, inspiring, and gladdening the bhikkhus … <250> who are applying their whole minds to it. Let me approach the ascetic Gotama in order to confound them."

Now on that occasion a number of almsbowls had been put out in the open. Then Māra the Evil One manifested himself in the form of an ox and approached those almsbowls. Then one bhikkhu said to another: "Bhikkhu, bhikkhu! That ox may break the almsbowls." When this was said, the Blessed One said to that bhikkhu: "That is not an ox, bhikkhu. That is Māra the Evil One, who has come here in order to confound you."

Then the Blessed One, having understood, "This is Māra the Evil One," addressed Māra the Evil One in verses:

478 "Form, feeling, and perception,
Consciousness, and formations—
'I am not this, this isn't mine,'
Thus one is detached from it.[289]

479 "Though they seek him everywhere,
Māra and his army do not find him:
The one thus detached, secure,
Who has gone beyond all fetters."[290] <251>

Then Māra the Evil One … disappeared right there.

17 (7) Six Bases for Contact

On one occasion the Blessed One was dwelling at Vesālī in the Great Wood in the Hall with the Peaked Roof. [113] Now on that occasion the Blessed One was instructing, exhorting, inspiring, and gladdening the bhikkhus with a Dhamma talk concerning the six bases for contact. And those bhikkhus were listening to the Dhamma with eager ears, attending to it as a matter of vital concern, applying their whole minds to it.

Then it occurred to Māra the Evil One: "This ascetic Gotama is instructing, exhorting, inspiring, and gladdening the bhikkhus … who are applying their whole minds to it. Let me approach the ascetic Gotama in order to confound them."

Then Māra the Evil One approached the Blessed One and, not far from him, made a loud noise, frightful and terrifying, as though the earth were splitting open.[291] Then one bhikkhu said to another: "Bhikkhu, bhikkhu! It seems as though the earth is splitting open." When this was said, the Blessed One said to that bhikkhu: <252> "The earth is not splitting open, bhikkhu. That is Māra the Evil One, who has come here in order to confound you."

Then the Blessed One, having understood, "This is Māra the Evil One," addressed Māra the Evil One in verses:

480 "Forms, sounds, tastes, odours,
Tactiles, and all mental objects:
This is the terrible bait of the world
With which the world is infatuated.

481 "But when he has transcended this,
The mindful disciple of the Buddha
Shines radiantly like the sun,
Having surmounted Māra's realm."[292]

Then Māra the Evil One … disappeared right there.

18 (8) Alms

On one occasion the Blessed One was dwelling among the Magadhans at the brahmin village of Pañcasālā. [114] Now on that occasion the gift-festival of the young people was being held at the brahmin village of Pañcasālā.[293] <253> Then, in the morning, the Blessed One dressed and, taking bowl and robe, entered Pañcasālā for alms. Now on that occasion Māra the Evil One had taken possession of the brahmin householders of Pañcasālā, [inciting in them the thought,] "Don't let the ascetic Gotama get alms."

Then the Blessed One left Pañcasālā with his bowl just as cleanly washed as it was when he entered it for alms. Then Māra the Evil One approached the Blessed One and said to him: "Maybe you got alms, ascetic?"

"Was it you, Evil One, who saw to it that I didn't get alms?"

"Then, venerable sir, let the Blessed One enter Pañcasālā a second time for alms. I will see to it that the Blessed One gets alms."[294]

[The Blessed One:]
482 "You have produced demerit, Māra,
Having assailed the Tathāgata.
Do you really think, O Evil One, <254>
'My evil does not ripen'?

483 "Happily indeed we live,
We who own nothing at all.

We shall dwell feeding on rapture
Like the devas of Streaming Radiance."[295]

Then Māra the Evil One … disappeared right there.

19 (9) The Farmer

At Sāvatthī. Now on that occasion the Blessed One was instructing, exhorting, inspiring, and gladdening the bhikkhus with a Dhamma talk concerning Nibbāna. And those bhikkhus were listening to the Dhamma with eager ears, attending to it as a matter of vital concern, applying their whole minds to it. [115]

Then it occurred to Māra the Evil One: "This ascetic Gotama is instructing, exhorting, inspiring, and gladdening the bhikkhus … who are applying their whole minds to it. Let me approach the ascetic Gotama in order to confound them." Then Māra the Evil One manifested himself in the form of a farmer, carrying a large plough on his shoulder, <255> holding a long goad stick, his hair dishevelled, wearing hempen garments, his feet smeared with mud. He approached the Blessed One and said to him: "Maybe you've seen oxen, ascetic?"

"What are oxen to you, Evil One?"

"The eye is mine, ascetic, forms are mine, eye-contact and its base of consciousness are mine.[296] Where can you go, ascetic, to escape from me? The ear is mine, ascetic, sounds are mine … The nose is mine, ascetic, odours are mine … The tongue is mine, ascetic, tastes are mine … The body is mine, ascetic, tactile objects are mine … The mind is mine, ascetic, mental phenomena are mine, mind-contact and its base of consciousness are mine. Where can you go, ascetic, to escape from me?"

"The eye is yours, Evil One, forms are yours, eye-contact and its base of consciousness are yours; but, Evil One, where there is no eye, no forms, no eye-contact <256> and its base of consciousness—there is no place for you there, Evil One.[297] The ear is yours, Evil One, sounds are yours, ear-contact and its base of consciousness are yours; but, Evil One, where there is no ear, no sounds, no ear-contact and its base of consciousness—there is no place for you there, Evil One. The nose is yours, Evil One, odours are yours, nose-contact and its base of consciousness are yours; but, Evil One, where there is no nose, no odours, no nose-contact and its base of consciousness—there is no place for you there, Evil One. [116] The tongue is yours, Evil One, tastes are yours, tongue-contact and its base of consciousness are yours; but, Evil One, where there is no tongue, no tastes, no tongue-contact and its base of consciousness—there is no place for you there, Evil One. The body is yours, Evil One, tactile objects are yours, body-contact and its base of consciousness are yours; but, Evil One, where there is no body, no tactile objects, no body-contact and its base of consciousness—there is no place for you there, Evil One. The mind is yours, Evil One, mental phenomena are yours, mind-contact and its base of consciousness are yours; but, Evil One, where there is no mind, no mental phenomena, no mind-contact and its base of consciousness—there is no place for you there, Evil One."

[Māra:]
484 "That of which they say 'It's mine,'
And those who speak in terms of 'mine'—
If your mind exists among these,
You won't escape me, ascetic."

[The Blessed One:]
485 "That which they speak of is not mine,
I'm not one of those who speak [of mine].
You should know thus, O Evil One:
Even my path you will not see."

Then Māra the Evil One … disappeared right there. <257>

20 (10) Rulership

On one occasion the Blessed One was dwelling among the Kosalans in a small forest hut in the Himalayan region. Then, when the Blessed One was alone in seclusion, a reflection arose in his mind thus: "Is it possible to exercise rulership righteously: without killing and without instigating others to kill, without confiscating and without instigating others to confiscate, without sorrowing and without causing sorrow?"[298]

Then Māra the Evil One, having known with his own mind the reflection in the Blessed One's mind, approached the Blessed

One and said to him: "Venerable sir, let the Blessed One exercise rulership righteously: without killing and without instigating others to kill, without confiscating and without instigating others to confiscate, without sorrowing and without instigating others to cause sorrow."

"But what do you see, Evil One, that you speak thus to me?" <258>

"Venerable sir, the Blessed One has developed and cultivated the four bases for spiritual power, made them a vehicle, made them a basis, stabilized them, exercised himself in them, and fully perfected them. And, venerable sir, if the Blessed One wishes, he need only resolve that the Himalayas, the king of mountains, should become gold, and it would turn to gold."[299] [117]

[The Blessed One:]

486 "If there were a mountain made of gold,
Made entirely of solid gold,
Not double this would suffice for one:
Having known this, fare evenly.[300]

487 "How could a person incline to sensual pleasures
Who has seen the source whence suffering springs?
Having known acquisition as a tie in the world,
A person should train for its removal."[301]

Then Māra the Evil One, realizing, "The Blessed One knows me, the Fortunate One knows me," sad and disappointed, disappeared right there.

<259>

III. The Third Subchapter (The Māra Pentad)

21 (1) A Number

Thus have I heard. On one occasion the Blessed One was dwelling among the Sakyans at Silāvatī. Now on that occasion a number of bhikkhus were dwelling not far from the Blessed One—diligent, ardent, and resolute. Then Māra the Evil One manifested himself in the form of a brahmin, with a large matted topknot, clad in an antelope hide, old, crooked like a roof bracket, wheezing, holding a staff of *udumbara* wood.[302] He approached those bhikkhus <260> and said to them: "You, sirs, have gone forth while young, lads with black hair, endowed with the blessing of youth, in the prime of life, without having dallied with sensual pleasures. Enjoy human sensual pleasures, sirs; do not abandon what is directly visible in order to pursue what takes time."[303]

"We have not abandoned what is directly visible, brahmin, in order to pursue what takes time. We have abandoned what takes time in order to pursue what is directly visible. For the Blessed One, brahmin, has stated that sensual pleasures are time-consuming, full of suffering, full of despair, and the danger in them is still greater, while this Dhamma is directly visible, immediate, inviting one to come and see, applicable, to be personally experienced by the wise." [118]

When this was said, Māra the Evil One shook his head, lolled his tongue, knit his brow into three furrows, and departed leaning on his staff.[304]

Then those bhikkhus approached the Blessed One, paid homage to him, sat down to one side, and reported everything in full. <261> [The Blessed One said:] "That was not a brahmin, bhikkhus. That was Māra the Evil One, who had come in order to confound you."

Then the Blessed One, having understood the meaning of this, on that occasion recited this verse: <262>

488 "How could a person incline to sensual pleasures
Who has seen the source whence suffering springs?
Having known acquisition as a tie in the world,
A person should train for its removal." [119]

22 (2) Samiddhi

On one occasion the Blessed One was dwelling among the Sakyans at Silāvatī. Now on that occasion the Venerable Samiddhi was dwelling not far from the Blessed One—diligent, ardent, and resolute.[305] Then, while the Venerable Samiddhi was alone in seclusion, a reflection arose in his mind thus: "It is indeed a gain for me, it is well gained by me, that my teacher is the Arahant, the Perfectly Enlightened One! It is indeed a gain for me, it is well gained by me, that I have gone forth in this well-expounded Dhamma and Discipline! It is indeed a gain for me, it is well gained by me, that my companions in the holy life are virtuous, of good character!"

Then Māra the Evil One, having known with his own mind the reflection in the mind of the Venerable Samiddhi, approached him and, not far from him, made a loud noise, frightful and terrifying, <263> as though the earth were splitting open.[306]

Then the Venerable Samiddhi approached the Blessed One, paid homage to him, sat down to one side, and reported what had happened. [The Blessed One said:] "That was not the earth splitting open, Samiddhi. That was Māra the Evil One, who had come in order to confound you. Go back, Samiddhi, and dwell diligent, ardent, and resolute."

"Yes, venerable sir," the Venerable Samiddhi replied. [120] Then he rose from his seat, paid homage to the Blessed One, and departed, keeping him on the right.

A second time, while the Venerable Samiddhi was alone in seclusion, a reflection arose in his mind ... And a second time Māra the Evil One ... <264> ... made a loud noise, frightful and terrifying, as though the earth were splitting open.

Then the Venerable Samiddhi, having understood, "This is Māra the Evil One," addressed him in verse:

489 "I have gone forth out of faith
From the home to the homeless life.
My mindfulness and wisdom are mature,
And my mind well concentrated.
Conjure up whatever forms you wish,
But you will never make me tremble."[307]

Then Māra the Evil One, realizing, "The bhikkhu Samiddhi knows me," sad and disappointed, disappeared right there.

23 (3) Godhika

Thus have I heard. On one occasion the Blessed One was dwelling at Rājagaha in the Bamboo Grove, the Squirrel Sanctuary.

Now on that occasion the Venerable Godhika was dwelling on the Black Rock on the Isigili Slope. Then, while the Venerable Godhika was dwelling diligent, ardent, and resolute, <265> he reached temporary liberation of mind, but he fell away from that temporary liberation of mind.[308] A second time, while the Venerable Godhika was dwelling diligent, ardent, and resolute, he reached temporary liberation of mind, but he fell away from that temporary liberation of mind. A third time … A fourth time … [121] A fifth time … A sixth time, while the Venerable Godhika was dwelling diligent, ardent, and resolute, he reached temporary liberation of mind, but he fell away from that temporary liberation of mind. A seventh time, while the Venerable Godhika was dwelling diligent, ardent, and resolute, he reached temporary liberation of mind.

Then it occurred to the Venerable Godhika: "Six times already I have fallen away from temporary liberation of mind. Let me use the knife."[309] <266>

Then Māra the Evil One, having known with his own mind the reflection in the Venerable Godhika's mind, approached the Blessed One and addressed him with these verses:[310]

490 "O great hero, great in wisdom,
Blazing forth with power and glory!
I worship your feet, One with Vision,
Who has overcome all enmity and fear.

491 "O great hero who has vanquished death,
Your disciple is longing for death.
He intends [to take his own life]:
Restrain him from this, O luminous one!

492 "How, O Blessed One, can your disciple—
One delighting in the Teaching,
A trainee seeking his mind's ideal—
Take his own life, O widely famed?"[311]

Now on that occasion the Venerable Godhika had just used the knife.[312] Then the Blessed One, having understood, "This is Māra the Evil One," addressed him in verse:

493 "Such indeed is how the steadfast act:
They are not attached to life. <267>
Having drawn out craving with its root,
Godhika has attained final Nibbāna."

Then the Blessed One addressed the bhikkhus thus: "Come, bhikkhus, let us go to the Black Rock on the Isigili Slope, where the clansman Godhika has used the knife."

"Yes, venerable sir," those bhikkhus replied. Then the Blessed One, together with a number of bhikkhus, went to the Black Rock on the Isigili Slope. The Blessed One saw in the distance the Venerable Godhika lying on the bed with his shoulder turned.[313] [122]

Now on that occasion a cloud of smoke, a swirl of darkness, was moving to the east, then to the west, to the north, to the south, upwards, downwards, and to the intermediate quarters. The Blessed One then addressed the bhikkhus thus: "Do you see, bhikkhus, that cloud of smoke, that swirl of darkness, moving to the east, then to the west, to the north, to the south, upwards, downwards, and to the intermediate quarters?"

"Yes, venerable sir."

"That, bhikkhus, is Māra the Evil One searching for the consciousness of the clansman Godhika, wondering: 'Where now <268> has the consciousness of the clansman Godhika been established?' However, bhikkhus, with consciousness unestablished, the clansman Godhika has attained final Nibbāna."[314]

Then Māra the Evil One, taking a lute of yellow *vilva*-wood, approached the Blessed One and addressed him in verse:

494 "Above, below, and across,
In the four quarters and in between,
I have been searching but do not find
Where Godhika has gone."

[The Blessed One:]
495 "That steadfast man was resolute,
A meditator always rejoicing in meditation,
Applying himself day and night
Without attachment even to life.

496 "Having conquered the army of Death,
Not returning to renewed existence,
Having drawn out craving with its root,
Godhika has attained final Nibbāna." <269>

497 So much was he stricken with sorrow
That his lute dropped from his armpit.
Thereupon that disappointed spirit
Disappeared right on the spot.[315]

24 (4) Seven Years of Pursuit

Thus have I heard. On one occasion the Blessed One was dwelling at Uruvelā on the bank of the river Nerañjarā at the foot of the Goatherd's Banyan Tree. Now on that occasion Māra the Evil One had been following the Blessed One for seven years, seeking to gain access to him but without success.[316] Then Māra the Evil One approached the Blessed One and addressed him in verse: [123]

498 "Is it because you are sunk in sorrow
That you meditate in the woods?
Because you've lost wealth or pine for it,
Or committed some crime in the village?
Why don't you make friends with people? <270>
Why don't you form any intimate ties?"

[The Blessed One:]
499 "Having dug up entirely the root of sorrow,
Guiltless, I meditate free from sorrow.
Having cut off all greedy urge for existence,[317]
I meditate taintless, O kinsman of the negligent!"

[Māra:]
500 "That of which they say 'It's mine,'
And those who speak in terms of 'mine'—
If your mind exists among these,
You won't escape me, ascetic."

[The Blessed One:]
501 "That which they speak of is not mine,

I'm not one of those who speak [of mine].
You should know thus, O Evil One:
Even my path you will not see."

[Māra:]
502 "If you have discovered the path,
The secure way leading to the Deathless, <271>
Be off and walk that path alone;
What's the point of instructing others?"

[The Blessed One:]
503 "Those people going to the far shore
Ask what lies beyond Death's realm.
When asked, I explain to them
The truth without acquisitions."[318]

[Māra:] "Suppose, venerable sir, not far from a village or a town there was a lotus pond in which a crab was living.[319] Then a group of boys and girls would leave the village or town and go to the pond. They would pull the crab out from the water and set it down on high ground. Then, whenever that crab would extend one of its claws, those boys and girls would cut it off, break it, and smash it to bits with sticks and stones. Thus, when all its claws have been cut off, broken, and smashed to bits, that crab would be unable to return to that pond. <272> So too, venerable sir, all those distortions, manoeuvres, and contortions of mine have been cut off, [124] broken, and smashed to bits by the Blessed One. Now, venerable sir, I am unable to approach the Blessed One again seeking to gain access to him."

Then Māra the Evil One, in the presence of the Blessed One, recited these verses of disappointment:[320]

504 "There was a crow that walked around
A stone that looked like a lump of fat.
'Let's find something tender here,' [he thought,]
'Perhaps there's something nice and tasty.'

505 But because he found nothing tasty there,
The crow departed from that spot.

Just like the crow that attacked the stone,
We leave Gotama disappointed." <273>

25 (5) Māra's Daughters

Then Māra the Evil One, having spoken these verses of disappointment in the presence of the Blessed One, went away from that spot and sat down cross-legged on the ground not far from the Blessed One, silent, dismayed, with his shoulders drooping, downcast, brooding, unable to speak, scratching the ground with a stick.[321]

Then Māra's daughters—Taṇhā, Aratī, and Ragā—approached Māra the Evil One and addressed him in verse:[322]

506 "Why are you despondent, father?
Who's the man for whom you grieve?
We'll catch him with the snare of lust
As they catch the forest elephant.
We'll bind him tightly and bring him back,
And he'll be under your control."[323]

[Māra:]
507 "The Arahant, the Fortunate One in the world,
Is not easily drawn by means of lust.
He has gone beyond Māra's realm:
Therefore I sorrow so bitterly." <274>

Then Māra's daughters—Taṇhā, Aratī, and Ragā—approached the Blessed One and said to him: "We serve at your feet, ascetic." But the Blessed One paid no attention, as he was liberated in the unsurpassed extinction of acquisitions.[324]

Then Māra's daughters—Taṇhā, Aratī, and Ragā—went off to the side and took counsel: "Men's tastes are diverse. Suppose we each manifest ourselves in the form of a hundred maidens." [125] Then Māra's three daughters, each manifesting herself in the form of a hundred maidens, approached the Blessed One and said to him: "We serve at your feet, ascetic." But the Blessed One paid no attention, as he was liberated in the unsurpassed extinction of acquisitions.

Then Māra's daughters went off to the side and again took

counsel: "Men's tastes are diverse. Suppose we each manifest ourselves in the form of a hundred women who have never given birth." Then Māra's three daughters, each manifesting herself in the form of a hundred women who have never given birth ... in the form of a hundred women who have given birth once ... <275> ... in the form of a hundred women who have given birth twice ... in the form of a hundred women of middle age ... in the form of a hundred old women, approached the Blessed One and said to him: "We serve at your feet, ascetic." But the Blessed One paid no attention, as he was liberated in the unsurpassed extinction of acquisitions.

Then Māra's daughters—Taṇhā, Aratī, and Ragā—went off to the side and said: "What our father told us is true:

508 "'The Arahant, the Fortunate One in the world ...
Therefore I sorrow so bitterly.'

"If we had assailed with such tactics any ascetic or brahmin who was not devoid of lust, either his heart would have burst, or he would have vomited hot blood from his mouth, [126] or he would have gone mad or become mentally deranged; or else he would have dried up and withered away and become shrivelled, just as a green reed that has been mowed down would dry up and wither away and become shrivelled."

Then Māra's daughters—Taṇhā, Aratī, and Ragā—approached the Blessed One and stood to one side. <276> Standing to one side, Māra's daughter Taṇhā addressed the Blessed One in verse:

509 "Is it because you are sunk in sorrow
That you meditate in the woods?
Because you have lost wealth or pine for it,
Or committed some crime in the village?
Why don't you make friends with people?
Why don't you form any intimate ties?"

[The Blessed One:]
510 "Having conquered the army of the pleasant and agreeable,
Meditating alone, I discovered bliss,
The attainment of the goal, the peace of the heart.[325]

Therefore I don't make friends with people,
Nor will I form any intimate ties."

Then Māra's daughter Aratī addressed the Blessed One in verse: <277>

511 "How does a bhikkhu here often dwell
That, five floods crossed, he here has crossed the sixth?
How does he meditate so sensual perceptions
Are kept at bay and fail to grip him?"[326]

[The Blessed One:]
512 "Tranquil in body, in mind well liberated,
Not generating, mindful, homeless,
Knowing Dhamma, meditating thought-free,
He does not erupt, or drift, or stiffen.[327]

513 "When a bhikkhu here often dwells thus,
With five floods crossed, he here has crossed the sixth.
When he meditates thus, sensual perceptions
Are kept at bay and fail to grip him." [127]

Then Māra's daughter Ragā addressed the Blessed One in verse: <278>

514 "He has cut off craving, faring with his group and order;
Surely many other beings will cross.
Alas, this homeless one will snatch many people
And lead them away beyond the King of Death."[328]

[The Blessed One:]
515 "Truly the Tathāgatas, the great heroes,
Lead by means of the true Dhamma.
When they are leading by means of the Dhamma,
What envy can there be in those who understand?"[329]

Then Māra's daughters—Taṇhā, Aratī, and Ragā—approached Māra the Evil One. Māra saw them coming in the distance and addressed them in verses:[330]

516 "Fools! You tried to batter a mountain
With the stalks of lotus flowers,
To dig up a mountain with your nails,
To chew iron with your teeth. <279>

517 "As if, having lifted a rock with your head,
You sought a foothold in the abyss;
As if you struck a stump with your breast,
You part from Gotama disappointed."

518 They had come to him glittering with beauty—
Taṇhā, Aratī, and Ragā—
But the Teacher swept them away right there
As the wind, a fallen cotton tuft. <280>

[128] <281> Chapter V

5 *Bhikkhunīsaṃyutta*

Connected Discourses with Bhikkhunīs

1 Āḷavikā

Thus have I heard. On one occasion the Blessed One was dwelling at Sāvatthī in Jeta's Grove, Anāthapiṇḍika's Park.

Then, in the morning, the bhikkhunī Āḷavikā dressed and, taking bowl and robe, entered Sāvatthī for alms.[331] When she had walked for alms in Sāvatthī and had returned from her alms round, after her meal she went to the Blind Men's Grove seeking seclusion.[332]

Then Māra the Evil One, desiring to arouse fear, trepidation, and terror in the bhikkhunī Āḷavikā, desiring to make her fall away from seclusion, approached her and addressed her in verse:

519 "There is no escape in the world,
So what will you do with seclusion?
Enjoy the delights of sensual pleasure:
Don't be remorseful later!"

Then it occurred to the bhikkhunī Āḷavikā: "Now who is it that recited the verse—a human being or a nonhuman being?" Then <282> it occurred to her: "This is Māra the Evil One, who has recited the verse desiring to arouse fear, trepidation, and terror in me, desiring to make me fall away from seclusion."

Then the bhikkhunī Āḷavikā, having understood, "This is Māra the Evil One," replied to him in verses:

520 "There is an escape in the world
Which I have closely touched with wisdom.

O Evil One, kinsman of the negligent,
You do not know that state.[333]

521 "Sensual pleasures are like swords and stakes;
The aggregates like their chopping block.
What you call sensual delight
Has become for me nondelight."[334] [129]

Then Māra the Evil One, realizing, "The bhikkhunī Āḷavikā knows me," sad and disappointed, disappeared right there. <283>

2 Somā

At Sāvatthī. Then, in the morning, the bhikkhunī Somā dressed and, taking bowl and robe, entered Sāvatthī for alms.[335] When she had walked for alms in Sāvatthī and had returned from her alms round, after her meal she went to the Blind Men's Grove for the day's abiding. Having plunged into the Blind Men's Grove, she sat down at the foot of a tree for the day's abiding.

Then Māra the Evil One, desiring to arouse fear, trepidation, and terror in the bhikkhunī Somā, desiring to make her fall away from concentration, approached her and addressed her in verse:

522 "That state so hard to achieve
Which is to be attained by the seers,
Can't be attained by a woman
With her two-fingered wisdom."[336]

Then it occurred to the bhikkhunī Somā: "Now who is this that recited the verse—a human being or a nonhuman being?" Then it occurred to her: "This is Māra the Evil One, who has recited the verse desiring to arouse fear, trepidation, and terror in me, desiring to make me fall away from concentration."

Then the bhikkhunī Somā, having understood, "This is Māra the Evil One," replied to him in verses: <284>

523 "What does womanhood matter at all
When the mind is concentrated well,

When knowledge flows on steadily
As one sees correctly into Dhamma.[337]

524 "One to whom it might occur,
'I'm a woman' or 'I'm a man'
Or 'I'm anything at all'—
Is fit for Māra to address."[338]

Then Māra the Evil One, realizing, "The bhikkhunī Somā knows me," sad and disappointed, disappeared right there.

3 Gotamī

At Sāvatthī. Then, in the morning, the bhikkhunī Kisāgotamī dressed and, taking bowl and robe, entered Sāvatthī for alms.[339] When she had walked for alms in Sāvatthī and had returned from her alms round, [130] after her meal she went to the Blind Men's Grove for the day's abiding. Having plunged into the Blind Men's Grove, she sat down at the foot of a tree for the day's abiding. <285>

Then Māra the Evil One, desiring to arouse fear, trepidation, and terror in the bhikkhunī Kisāgotamī, desiring to make her fall away from concentration, approached her and addressed her in verse:

525 "Why now, when your son is dead,
Do you sit alone with tearful face?
Having entered the woods all alone,
Are you on the lookout for a man?"

Then it occurred to the bhikkhunī Kisāgotamī: "Now who is this that recited the verse—a human being or a nonhuman being?" Then it occurred to her: "This is Māra the Evil One, who has recited the verse desiring to arouse fear, trepidation, and terror in me, desiring to make me fall away from concentration."

Then the bhikkhunī Kisāgotamī, having understood, "This is Māra the Evil One," replied to him in verses:

526 "I've gotten past the death of sons;
With this, the search for men has ended.

I do not sorrow, I do not weep,
Nor do I fear you, friend.[340]

527 "Delight everywhere has been destroyed,
The mass of darkness has been sundered. <286>
Having conquered the army of Death,
I dwell without defiling taints."[341]

Then Māra the Evil One, realizing, "The bhikkhunī Kisāgotamī knows me," sad and disappointed, disappeared right there.

4 Vijayā

At Sāvatthī. Then, in the morning, the bhikkhunī Vijayā dressed … she sat down at the foot of a tree for the day's abiding.[342]

Then Māra the Evil One, desiring to arouse fear, trepidation, and terror in the bhikkhunī Vijayā, desiring to make her fall away from concentration, approached her and addressed her in verse: [131]

528 "You are so young and beautiful,
And I too am a youth in my prime.
Come, noble lady, let us rejoice
With the music of a fivefold ensemble."[343]

Then it occurred to the bhikkhunī Vijayā: "Now who is this…? This is Māra the Evil One … desiring to make me fall away from concentration." <287>

Then the bhikkhunī Vijayā, having understood, "This is Māra the Evil One," replied to him in verses:

529 "Forms, sounds, tastes, odours,
And delightful tactile objects—
I offer them right back to you,
For I, O Māra, do not need them.

530 "I am repelled and humiliated
By this foul, putrid body,
Subject to break up, fragile:
I've uprooted sensual craving.[344]

531 "As to those beings who fare amidst form,
And those who abide in the formless,
And those peaceful attainments too:
Everywhere darkness has been destroyed."[345]

Then Māra the Evil One, realizing "The bhikkhunī Vijayā knows me," sad and disappointed, disappeared right there.

5 Uppalavaṇṇā

<288> At Sāvatthī. Then, in the morning, the bhikkhunī Uppalavaṇṇā dressed … she stood at the foot of a sal tree in full flower.[346]

Then Māra the Evil One, desiring to arouse fear, trepidation, and terror in the bhikkhunī Uppalavaṇṇā, desiring to make her fall away from concentration, approached her and addressed her in verse:

532 "Having gone to a sal tree with flowering top,
You stand at its foot all alone, bhikkhunī.
There is none whose beauty rivals yours:
Foolish girl, aren't you afraid of rogues?"[347]

Then it occurred to the bhikkhunī Uppalavaṇṇā: [132] "Now who is this…? This is Māra the Evil One … desiring to make me fall away from concentration." <289>

Then the bhikkhunī Uppalavaṇṇā, having understood, "This is Māra the Evil One," replied to him in verses:

533 "Though a hundred thousand rogues
Just like you might come here,
I stir not a hair, I feel no terror;
Even alone, Māra, I don't fear you.[348]

534 "I can make myself disappear
Or I can enter inside your belly.
I can stand between your eyebrows
Yet you won't catch a glimpse of me.

535 "I am the master of my mind,
The bases of power are well developed;
I am freed from all bondage,
Therefore I don't fear you, friend."[349] <290>

Then Māra the Evil One, realizing, "The bhikkhunī Uppalavaṇṇā knows me," sad and disappointed, disappeared right there.

6 Cālā

At Sāvatthī. Then, in the morning, the bhikkhunī Cālā dressed ... she sat down at the foot of a tree for the day's abiding.[350]

Then Māra the Evil One approached the bhikkhunī Cālā and said to her: "What don't you approve of, bhikkhunī?"

"I don't approve of birth, friend."

536 "Why don't you approve of birth?
Once born, one enjoys sensual pleasures.
Who now has persuaded you of this:
'Bhikkhunī, don't approve of birth'?"

[The bhikkhunī Cālā:]
537 "For one who is born there is death;
Once born, one encounters sufferings—
Bondage, murder, affliction—
Hence one shouldn't approve of birth.[351]

538 "The Buddha has taught the Dhamma, <291>
The transcendence of birth;
For the abandoning of all suffering
He has settled me in the truth. [133]

539 "As to those beings who fare amidst form,
And those who abide in the formless—
Not having understood cessation,
They come again to renewed existence."[352]

Then Māra the Evil One, realizing, "The bhikkhunī Cālā knows me," sad and disappointed, disappeared right there.

7 Upacālā

At Sāvatthī. Then, in the morning, the bhikkhunī Upacālā dressed ... she sat down at the foot of a tree for the day's abiding.

Then Māra the Evil One approached the bhikkhunī Upacālā and said to her: "Where do you wish to be reborn, bhikkhunī?"

"I do not wish to be reborn anywhere, friend."

540 "There are Tāvatiṃsa and Yāma devas,
And devatās of the Tusita realm,
Devas who take delight in creating, <292>
And devas who exercise control.
Direct your mind there [to those realms]
And you'll experience delight."[353]

[The bhikkhunī Upacālā:]
541 "There are Tāvatiṃsa and Yāma devas,
And devatās of the Tusita realm,
Devas who take delight in creating,
And devas who exercise control.
They are still bound by sensual bondage,
They come again under Māra's control.

542 "All the world is on fire,
All the world is burning,
All the world is ablaze,
All the world is quaking.

543 "That which does not quake or blaze,
That to which worldlings do not resort,
Where there is no place for Māra:
That is where my mind delights."[354]

Then Māra the Evil One, realizing, "The bhikkhunī Upacālā knows me," sad and disappointed, disappeared right there.

8 Sīsupacālā

<293> At Sāvatthī. Then, in the morning, the bhikkhunī Sīsupacālā dressed ... she sat down at the foot of a tree for the day's abiding.

Then Māra the Evil One approached the bhikkhunī Sīsupacālā and said to her: "Whose creed do you approve of, bhikkhunī?"
"I don't approve of anyone's creed, friend."

544 "Under whom have you shaved your head?
You do appear to be an ascetic,
Yet you don't approve of any creed,
So why wander as if bewildered?"[355]

[The bhikkhunī Sīsupacālā:]
545 "Outside here the followers of creeds
Place their confidence in views.
I don't approve of their teachings;
They are not skilled in the Dhamma. [134]

546 "But there's one born in the Sakyan clan,
The Enlightened One, without an equal, <294>
Conqueror of all, Māra's subduer,
Who everywhere is undefeated,
Everywhere freed and unattached,
The One with Vision who sees all.

547 "Attained to the end of all kamma,
Liberated in the extinction of acquisitions,
That Blessed One is my Teacher:
His is the teaching I approve."[356]

Then Māra the Evil One, realizing, "The bhikkhunī Sīsupacālā knows me," sad and disappointed, disappeared right there.

9 Selā

At Sāvatthī. Then, in the morning, the bhikkhunī Selā dressed … she sat down at the foot of a tree for the day's abiding.[357]

Then Māra the Evil One, desiring to arouse fear, trepidation, and terror in the bhikkhunī Selā, desiring to make her fall away from concentration, approached her and addressed her in verse:

548 "By whom has this puppet been created?
Where is the maker of the puppet?

Where has the puppet arisen?
Where does the puppet cease?"[358] <295>

Then it occurred to the bhikkhunī Selā: "Now who is this...? This is Māra the Evil One ... desiring to make me fall away from concentration."

Then the bhikkhunī Selā, having understood, "This is Māra the Evil One," replied to him in verses:

549 "This puppet is not made by itself,
Nor is this misery made by another.
It has come to be dependent on a cause;
With the cause's breakup it will cease.

550 "As when a seed is sown in a field
It grows depending on a pair of factors:
It requires both the soil's nutrients
And a steady supply of moisture:

551 "Just so the aggregates and elements,
And these six bases of sensory contact,
Have come to be dependent on a cause;
With the cause's breakup they will cease."[359]

Then Māra the Evil One, realizing, "The bhikkhunī Selā knows me," sad and disappointed, disappeared right there.

10 Vajirā

<296> At Sāvatthī. Then, in the morning, the bhikkhunī Vajirā dressed and, taking bowl and robe, entered Sāvatthī for alms.[360] When she had walked for alms in Sāvatthī [135] and had returned from her alms round, after her meal she went to the Blind Men's Grove for the day's abiding. Having plunged into the Blind Men's Grove, she sat down at the foot of a tree for the day's abiding.

Then Māra the Evil One, desiring to arouse fear, trepidation, and terror in the bhikkhunī Vajirā, desiring to make her fall away from concentration, approached her and addressed her in verse:

552 "By whom has this being been created?
Where is the maker of the being?
Where has the being arisen?
Where does the being cease?"

Then it occurred to the bhikkhunī Vajirā: "Now who is this that recited the verse—a human being or a nonhuman being?" Then it occurred to her: "This is Māra the Evil One, who has recited the verse desiring to arouse fear, trepidation, and terror in me, desiring to make me fall away from concentration."

Then the bhikkhunī Vajirā, having understood, "This is Māra the Evil One," replied to him in verses:

553 "Why now do you assume 'a being'?
Māra, is that your speculative view? <297>
This is a heap of sheer formations:
Here no being is found.

554 "Just as, with an assemblage of parts,
The word 'chariot' is used,
So, when the aggregates exist,
There is the convention 'a being.'

555 "It's only suffering that comes to be,
Suffering that stands and falls away.
Nothing but suffering comes to be,
Nothing but suffering ceases."[361]

Then Māra the Evil One, realizing, "The bhikkhunī Vajirā knows me," sad and disappointed, disappeared right there.

[136] <298> Chapter VI

6 *Brahmasaṃyutta*

Connected Discourses with Brahmās

I. The First Subchapter (The Request)

1 (1) Brahmā's Request

Thus have I heard.[362] On one occasion the Blessed One was dwelling at Uruvelā on the bank of the river Nerañjarā at the foot of the Goatherd's Banyan Tree just after he had become fully enlightened. Then, while the Blessed One was alone in seclusion, a reflection arose in his mind thus: "This Dhamma that I have discovered is deep, hard to see, hard to understand, peaceful and sublime, not within the sphere of reasoning, subtle, to be experienced by the wise. But this generation delights in adhesion, takes delight in adhesion, rejoices in adhesion.[363] For such a generation this state is hard to see, that is, specific conditionality, dependent origination. And this state too is hard to see, that is, the stilling of all formations, <299> the relinquishment of all acquisitions, the destruction of craving, dispassion, cessation, Nibbāna.[364] If I were to teach the Dhamma and if others would not understand me, that would be wearisome for me, that would be troublesome."

Thereupon these astounding verses, not heard before in the past, occurred to the Blessed One:[365]

556 "Enough now with trying to teach
What I found with so much hardship;
This Dhamma is not easily understood
By those oppressed by lust and hate.

557 "Those fired by lust, obscured by darkness,
Will never see this abstruse Dhamma,
Deep, hard to see, subtle,
Going against the stream." [137]

As the Blessed One reflected thus, his mind inclined to living at ease, not to teaching the Dhamma.[366] <300>

Then Brahmā Sahampati, having known with his own mind the reflection in the Blessed One's mind, thought: "Alas, the world is lost! Alas, the world is to perish, in that the mind of the Tathāgata, the Arahant, the Perfectly Enlightened One, inclines to living at ease, not to teaching the Dhamma."[367] Then, just as quickly as a strong man might extend his drawn-in arm or draw in his extended arm, Brahmā Sahampati disappeared from the brahmā world and reappeared before the Blessed One. He arranged his upper robe over one shoulder, knelt down with his right knee on the ground, raised his joined hands in reverential salutation towards the Blessed One, and said to him: "Venerable sir, let the Blessed One teach the Dhamma; let the Fortunate One teach the Dhamma. There are beings with little dust in their eyes who are falling away because they do not hear the Dhamma. There will be those who will understand the Dhamma."

This is what Brahmā Sahampati said. Having said this, he further said this:

558 "In the past there appeared among the Magadhans
An impure Dhamma devised by those still stained.
Throw open this door to the Deathless! Let them hear
<301>
The Dhamma that the Stainless One discovered.[368]

559 "Just as one standing on a mountain peak
Might see below the people all around,
So, O wise one, universal eye,
Ascend the palace made of the Dhamma.
Being yourself free from sorrow, behold the people
Submerged in sorrow, oppressed by birth and decay.

560 "Rise up, O hero, victor in battle!
O caravan leader, debt-free one, wander in the world.

> Teach the Dhamma, O Blessed One:
> There will be those who will understand."[369] [138]

Then the Blessed One, having understood Brahmā's request, out of compassion for beings surveyed the world with the eye of a Buddha.[370] As he did so, the Blessed One saw beings with little dust in their eyes and with much dust in their eyes, with keen faculties and with dull faculties, with good qualities and with bad qualities, easy to teach and difficult to teach, <302> and a few who dwelt seeing blame and fear in the other world.[371] Just as in a pond of blue or red or white lotuses, some lotuses might be born in the water, grow up in the water, and thrive while submerged in the water, without rising up from the water; some lotuses might be born in the water, grow up in the water, and stand at an even level with the water; some lotuses might be born in the water and grow up in the water, but would rise up from the water and stand without being soiled by the water—so too, surveying the world with the eye of a Buddha, the Blessed One saw beings with little dust in their eyes and with much dust in their eyes, with keen faculties and with dull faculties, with good qualities and with bad qualities, easy to teach and hard to teach, and a few who dwelt seeing blame and fear in the other world.

Having seen this, he answered Brahmā Sahampati in verse: <303>

561 "Open to them are the doors to the Deathless:
Let those who have ears release faith.
Foreseeing trouble, O Brahmā, I did not speak
The refined, sublime Dhamma among human beings."

Then Brahmā Sahampati, thinking, "The Blessed One has given his consent [to my request] regarding the teaching of the Dhamma," paid homage to the Blessed One and disappeared right there.[372]

2 (2) Reverence

Thus have I heard.[373] On one occasion the Blessed One was dwelling at Uruvelā on the bank of the river Nerañjarā at the foot of the Goatherd's Banyan Tree just after he had become fully enlightened. [139] Then, while the Blessed One was alone in seclusion, a reflection arose in his mind thus: "One dwells in suffering if one is without reverence and deference. Now what ascetic or brahmin can I honour and respect and dwell in dependence on?"

Then it occurred to the Blessed One: "It would be for the sake of fulfilling an unfulfilled aggregate of virtue that I would honour, respect, and dwell in dependence on another ascetic or brahmin. However, in this world with its devas, Māra, and Brahmā, <304> in this generation with its ascetics and brahmins, its devas and humans, I do not see another ascetic or brahmin more perfect in virtue than myself, whom I could honour and respect and dwell in dependence on.

"It would be for the sake of fulfilling an unfulfilled aggregate of concentration that I would honour, respect, and dwell in dependence on another ascetic or brahmin. However ... I do not see another ascetic or brahmin more perfect in concentration than myself....

"It would be for the sake of fulfilling an unfulfilled aggregate of wisdom that I would honour, respect, and dwell in dependence on another ascetic or brahmin. However ... I do not see another ascetic or brahmin more perfect in wisdom than myself....

"It would be for the sake of fulfilling an unfulfilled aggregate of liberation that I would honour, respect, and dwell in dependence on another ascetic or brahmin. However ... I do not see another ascetic or brahmin more perfect in liberation than myself....

"It would be for the sake of fulfilling an unfulfilled aggregate of the knowledge and vision of liberation that I would honour, respect, and dwell in dependence on another ascetic or brahmin. However ... I do not see another ascetic or brahmin more perfect in the knowledge and vision of liberation than myself, whom I could honour and respect, and on whom I could dwell in dependence.[374] <305>

"Let me then honour, respect, and dwell in dependence on this very Dhamma to which I have fully awakened."

Then, having known with his own mind the reflection in the Blessed One's mind, just as quickly as a strong man might extend his drawn-in arm or draw in his extended arm, Brahmā

Sahampati disappeared from the brahmā world and reappeared before the Blessed One. He arranged his upper robe over one shoulder, raised his joined hands in reverential salutation towards the Blessed One, and said to him: [140] "So it is, Blessed One! So it is, Fortunate One! Venerable sir, those who were the Arahants, the Perfectly Enlightened Ones in the past—those Blessed Ones too honoured, respected, and dwelt in dependence just on the Dhamma itself. Those who will be the Arahants, the Perfectly Enlightened Ones in the future—those Blessed Ones too will honour, respect, and dwell in dependence just on the Dhamma itself. Let the Blessed One too, who is at present the Arahant, the Perfectly Enlightened One, honour, respect, and dwell in dependence just on the Dhamma itself."

This is what Brahmā Sahampati said. Having said this, he further said this: <306>

562 "The Buddhas of the past,
The future Buddhas,
And he who is the Buddha now,
Removing the sorrow of many—

563 "All have dwelt, will dwell, and dwell,
Deeply revering the true Dhamma:
For the Buddhas
This is a natural law.

564 "Therefore one desiring his own good,
Aspiring for spiritual greatness,
Should deeply revere the true Dhamma,
Recollecting the Buddhas' Teaching."[375]

3 (3) Brahmadeva

Thus have I heard. On one occasion the Blessed One was dwelling at Sāvatthī in Jeta's Grove, Anāthapiṇḍika's Park. Now on that occasion a certain brahmin lady had a son named Brahmadeva <307> who had gone forth from the household life into homelessness under the Blessed One.

Then, dwelling alone, withdrawn, diligent, ardent, and resolute, the Venerable Brahmadeva, by realizing it for himself with direct knowledge, in this very life entered and dwelt in that unsurpassed goal of the holy life for the sake of which clansmen rightly go forth from the household life into homelessness. He directly knew: "Destroyed is birth, the holy life has been lived, what had to be done has been done, there is no more for this state of being." And the Venerable Brahmadeva became one of the arahants.[376]

Then, in the morning, the Venerable Brahmadeva dressed and, taking bowl and robe, entered Sāvatthī for alms. Walking on continuous alms round in Sāvatthī, he came to his own mother's residence.[377] [141] Now on that occasion the brahmin lady, the Venerable Brahmadeva's mother, had been offering a constant oblation to Brahmā.[378] Then it occurred to Brahmā Sahampati: "This brahmin lady, the Venerable Brahmadeva's mother, has been offering a constant oblation to Brahmā. Let me approach her and stir up a sense of urgency in her."

Then, <308> just as quickly as a strong man might extend his drawn-in arm or draw in his extended arm, Brahmā Sahampati disappeared from the brahmā world and reappeared in the residence of the Venerable Brahmadeva's mother. Then, standing in the air, Brahmā Sahampati addressed the brahmin lady in verse:

565 "Far from here, madam, is the brahmā world
To which you offer a constant oblation.
Brahmā does not eat such food, lady:
So why mumble, not knowing the path to Brahmā?[379]

566 "This Brahmadeva, madam,
Without acquisitions, has surpassed the devas.
Owning nothing, nourishing no other,
The bhikkhu has entered your house for alms.[380]

567 "Gift-worthy, knowledge-master, inwardly developed, <309>
He deserves offerings from humans and devas.
Having expelled all evil, unsullied,
Cooled at heart, he comes seeking alms.

568 "For him there is nothing behind or in front—
Peaceful, smokeless, untroubled, wishless;

He has laid down the rod towards frail and firm:
Let him eat your oblation, the choicest alms.[381]

569 "Aloof from the crowd, with peaceful mind,
Like a nāga he fares, tamed, unstirred.
A bhikkhu of pure virtue, well liberated in mind:
Let him eat your oblation, the choicest alms.[382]

570 "With confidence in him, free from wavering, [142]
Present your offering to one who deserves it.
Having seen a sage who has crossed the flood,
O madam, make merit leading to future bliss."[383] <310>

571 With confidence in him, free from wavering,
She presented her offering to one who deserved it.
Having seen a sage who has crossed the flood,
The lady made merit leading to future bliss.[384]

4 (4) Brahmā Baka

Thus have I heard.[385] On one occasion the Blessed One was dwelling at Sāvatthī in Jeta's Grove, Anāthapiṇḍika's Park. Now on that occasion the following evil speculative view had arisen in Brahmā Baka: "This is permanent, this is stable, this is eternal, this is complete, this is imperishable. Indeed, this is where one is not born, does not age, does not die, does not pass away, and is not reborn; and there is no other escape superior to this."[386]

Then, having known with his own mind the reflection in Brahmā Baka's mind, just as quickly as a strong man might extend his drawn-in arm or draw in his extended arm, the Blessed One disappeared from Jeta's Grove and reappeared in that brahmā world. <311> Brahmā Baka saw the Blessed One coming in the distance and said to him: "Come, dear sir! Welcome, dear sir! It has been a long time, dear sir, since you took the opportunity of coming here. Indeed, dear sir, this is permanent, this is stable, this is eternal, this is complete, this is imperishable. Indeed, this is where one is not born, does not age, does not die, does not pass away, and is not reborn; and there is no other escape superior to this."

When this was said, the Blessed One said to Brahmā Baka:

"Alas, sir, Brahmā Baka is immersed in ignorance! Alas, sir, Brahmā Baka is immersed in ignorance, in so far as he will say of what is actually impermanent that it is permanent; and will say of what is actually unstable that it is stable; and will say of what is actually noneternal that it is eternal; [143] and will say of what is actually incomplete that it is complete; and will say of what is actually perishable that it is imperishable; and with reference to [a realm] where one is born, ages, dies, passes away, and is reborn, will say thus: 'Indeed, this is where one is not born, does not age, does not die, does not pass away, and is not reborn'; and when there is another escape superior to this, will say, 'There is no other escape superior to this.'"

[Brahmā Baka:]

572 "We seventy-two, Gotama, were merit-makers; <312>
Now we wield power, beyond birth and aging.
This, knowledge-master, is our final attainment of Brahmā.
Many are the people who yearn for us."[387]

[The Blessed One:]

573 "The life span here is short, not long,
Though you, Baka, imagine it is long.
I know, O Brahmā, your life span to be
A hundred thousand *nirabbudas*."[388]

[Brahmā Baka:]

574 "O Blessed One, [you say]:
'I am the one of infinite vision
Who has overcome birth, aging, and sorrow.'
What was my ancient practice of vow and virtue?
Tell me this so I might understand."[389]

[The Blessed One:]

575 "You gave drink to many people
Who were thirsty, afflicted by heat:
That was your ancient practice of vow and virtue, <313>
Which I recollect as if just waking up.[390]

576 "When people were abducted at Antelope Bank,
You released the captives being led away.

That was your ancient practice of vow and virtue,
Which I recollect as if just waking up.

577 "When a ship was seized on the river Ganges
By a fierce nāga longing for human flesh,
You freed it forcefully by a valiant act:
That was your ancient practice of vow and virtue,
Which I recollect as if just waking up. [144]

578 "I was your apprentice named Kappa;
You thought him intelligent and devout:
That was your ancient practice of vow and virtue,
Which I recollect as if just waking up."[391]

[Brahmā Baka:] <314>
579 "Surely you know this life span of mine;
The others too you know, thus you're the Buddha.
Thus this blazing majesty of yours
Illumines even the brahmā world."

5 (5) A Certain Brahmā (Another View)

At Sāvatthī. Now on that occasion the following evil speculative view had arisen in a certain brahmā: "There is no ascetic or brahmin who can come here." Then, having known with his own mind the reflection in that brahmā's mind, just as quickly as a strong man might extend his drawn-in arm or draw in his extended arm, the Blessed One disappeared from Jeta's Grove and reappeared in that brahmā world. The Blessed One sat cross-legged in the air above that brahmā, having entered into meditation on the fire element.[392]

Then it occurred to the Venerable Mahāmoggallāna: "Where now is the Blessed One dwelling at present?" With the divine eye, which is purified and surpasses the human, the Venerable Mahāmoggallāna saw the Blessed One sitting cross-legged in the air above that brahmā, having entered into meditation on the fire element. Having seen this, <315> just as quickly as a strong man might extend his drawn-in arm or draw in his extended arm, the Venerable Mahāmoggallāna disappeared from Jeta's Grove and reappeared in that brahmā world. Then the Venerable Mahāmoggallāna stationed himself in the eastern quarter and sat cross-legged in the air above that brahmā—though lower than the Blessed One—having entered into meditation on the fire element.

Then it occurred to the Venerable Mahākassapa: "Where now is the Blessed One dwelling at present?" With the divine eye ... the Venerable Mahākassapa saw the Blessed One sitting cross-legged in the air above that brahmā.... Having seen this, ... [145] the Venerable Mahākassapa disappeared from Jeta's Grove and reappeared in that brahmā world. Then the Venerable Mahākassapa stationed himself in the southern quarter and sat cross-legged in the air above that brahmā—though lower than the Blessed One—having entered into meditation on the fire element.

Then it occurred to the Venerable Mahākappina: "Where now is the Blessed One dwelling at present?" With the divine eye ... the Venerable Mahākappina saw the Blessed One sitting cross-legged in the air above that brahmā.... Having seen this, ... the Venerable Mahākappina disappeared from Jeta's Grove and reappeared in that brahmā world. Then the Venerable Mahākappina stationed himself in the western quarter <316> and sat cross-legged in the air above that brahmā—though lower than the Blessed One—having entered into meditation on the fire element.

Then it occurred to the Venerable Anuruddha: "Where now is the Blessed One dwelling at present?" With the divine eye ... the Venerable Anuruddha saw the Blessed One sitting cross-legged in the air above that brahmā.... Having seen this, ... the Venerable Anuruddha disappeared from Jeta's Grove and reappeared in that brahmā world. Then the Venerable Anuruddha stationed himself in the northern quarter and sat cross-legged in the air above that brahmā—though lower than the Blessed One—having entered into meditation on the fire element.

Then the Venerable Mahāmoggallāna addressed that brahmā in verse:

580 "Today, friend, do you still hold that view,
The view that you formerly held?
Do you see the radiance
Surpassing that in the brahmā world?"[393] <317>

581 "I no longer hold that view, dear sir,
The view that I formerly held.
Indeed I see the radiance
Surpassing that in the brahmā world.
Today how could I maintain,
'I am permanent and eternal'?"[394]

Then, having stirred up a sense of urgency in that brahmā, just as quickly as a strong man might extend his drawn-in arm or draw in his extended arm, the Blessed One disappeared from that brahmā world and reappeared in Jeta's Grove.

Then that brahmā addressed one member of his assembly thus: "Come now, dear sir, approach the Venerable Mahāmoggallāna and say to him: 'Sir Moggallāna, are there any other disciples of the Blessed One that are as powerful [146] and mighty as Masters Moggallāna, Kassapa, Kappina, and Anuruddha?'"

"Yes, dear sir," that member of Brahmā's assembly replied. Then he approached the Venerable Mahāmoggallāna and asked him: "Sir Moggallāna, are there any other disciples of the Blessed One that are as powerful and mighty as Masters Moggallāna, Kassapa, Kappina, and Anuruddha?"

Then the Venerable Mahāmoggallāna addressed that member of Brahmā's assembly in verse:

582 "Many are the disciples of the Buddha
Who are arahants with taints destroyed,
Triple-knowledge bearers with spiritual powers,
Skilled in the course of others' minds."[395] <318>

Then that member of Brahmā's assembly, having delighted and rejoiced in the Venerable Mahāmoggallāna's statement, approached that brahmā and told him: "Dear sir, the Venerable Mahāmoggallāna speaks thus:

583 "'Many are the disciples of the Buddha …
Skilled in the course of others' minds.'"

This is what that member of Brahmā's assembly said. Elated, that brahmā delighted in his statement.

6 (6) A Brahmā World (Negligence)

At Sāvatthī. Now on that occasion the Blessed One had gone for his day's abiding and was in seclusion. Then the independent brahmās Subrahmā and Suddhāvāsa approached the Blessed One and stood one at each doorpost.[396] Then the independent brahmā Subrahmā said to the independent brahmā Suddhāvāsa: <319> "It is not the right time, dear sir, to visit the Blessed One. The Blessed One has gone for his day's abiding and is in seclusion. Such and such a brahmā world is rich and prosperous, and the brahmā there is dwelling in negligence. Come, dear sir, let us go to that brahmā world and stir up a sense of urgency in that brahmā." [147]

"Yes, dear sir," the independent brahmā Suddhāvāsa replied.

Then, just as quickly as a strong man might extend his drawn-in arm or draw in his extended arm, the independent brahmās Subrahmā and Suddhāvāsa disappeared in front of the Blessed One and reappeared in that brahmā world. That brahmā saw those brahmās coming in the distance and said to them: "Now where are you coming from, dear sirs?" <320>

"We have come, dear sir, from the presence of the Blessed One, the Arahant, the Perfectly Enlightened One. Dear sir, you should go to attend upon that Blessed One, the Arahant, the Perfectly Enlightened One."

When this was said, that brahmā refused to accept their advice. Having created a thousand transformations of himself, he said to the independent brahmā Subrahmā: <321> "Do you see, dear sir, how much power and might I have?"

"I see, dear sir, that you have so much power and might."

"But, dear sir, when I am so powerful and mighty, what other ascetic or brahmin should I go to attend upon?"

Then the independent brahmā Subrahmā, having created two thousand transformations of himself, said to that brahmā: "Do you see, dear sir, how much power and might I have?"

"I see, dear sir, that you have so much power and might."

"That Blessed One, dear sir, is still more powerful and mighty than both you and I. You should go, dear sir, to attend upon that Blessed One, the Arahant, the Perfectly Enlightened One."

Then that brahmā addressed the independent brahmā Subrahmā in verse: [148]

584 "Three [hundred] supaṇṇas, four [hundred] geese,
And five hundred falcons:
This palace, O Brahmā, of the meditator shines
Illuminating the northern quarter."[397]

[The independent brahmā Subrahmā:]
585 "Even though that palace of yours shines
Illuminating the northern quarter, <322>
Having seen form's flaw, its chronic trembling,
The wise one takes no delight in form."[398]

Then the independent brahmās Subrahmā and Suddhāvāsa, having stirred up a sense of urgency in that brahmā, disappeared right there. And on a later occasion that brahmā went to attend upon the Blessed One, the Arahant, the Perfectly Enlightened One.

7 (7) Kokālika (1)

At Sāvatthī. Now on that occasion the Blessed One had gone for his day's abiding and was in seclusion. Then the independent brahmās Subrahmā and Suddhāvāsa approached the Blessed One and stood one at each doorpost. Then, referring to the bhikkhu Kokālika, the independent brahmā Subrahmā recited this verse in the presence of the Blessed One:[399]

586 "What wise man here would seek to define
An immeasurable one by taking his measure? <323>
He who would measure an immeasurable one
Must be, I think, an obstructed worldling."[400]

8 (8) Tissaka

At Sāvatthī.... (*as above*) ... Then, referring to the bhikkhu Katamorakatissaka, the independent brahmā Suddhāvāsa recited this verse in the presence of the Blessed One:[401] [149]

587 "What wise man here would seek to define
An immeasurable one by taking his measure?

He who would measure an immeasurable one
Must be, I think, an obstructed moron."

9 (9) Brahmā Tudu

<324> At Sāvatthī. Now on that occasion the bhikkhu Kokālika was sick, afflicted, gravely ill. Then, when the night had advanced, the independent brahmā Tudu, of stunning beauty, illuminating the entire Jeta's Grove, approached the bhikkhu Kokālika.[402] Having approached, he stood in the air and said to the bhikkhu Kokālika: "Place confidence in Sāriputta and Moggallāna, Kokālika. Sāriputta and Moggallāna are well behaved."

"Who are you, friend?"

"I am the independent brahmā Tudu."

"Didn't the Blessed One declare you to be a nonreturner, friend? Then why have you come back here? See how far you have transgressed."[403]

[Brahmā Tudu:]

588 "When a person has taken birth
An axe is born inside his mouth
With which the fool cuts himself
Uttering defamatory speech. <325>

589 "He who praises one deserving blame,
Or blames one deserving praise,
Casts with his mouth an unlucky throw
By which he finds no happiness.[404]

590 "Trifling is the unlucky throw
That brings the loss of wealth at dice,
[The loss] of all, oneself included;
Worse by far—this unlucky throw
Of harbouring hate against the fortunate ones.[405]

591 "For a hundred thousand nirabbudas
And thirty-six more, and five *abbudas*,
The maligner of noble ones goes to hell,
Having set evil speech and mind against them."[406]

10 (10) Kokālika (2)

At Sāvatthī.[407] Then the bhikkhu Kokālika approached the Blessed One, [150] <326> paid homage to him, sat down to one side, and said: "Venerable sir, Sāriputta and Moggallāna have evil wishes; they have come under the control of evil wishes."

When this was said, the Blessed One said to the bhikkhu Kokālika: "Do not speak thus, Kokālika! Do not speak thus, Kokālika! Place confidence in Sāriputta and Moggallāna, Kokālika. Sāriputta and Moggallāna are well behaved."

A second time the bhikkhu Kokālika said to the Blessed One: "Venerable sir, although the Blessed One has my faith and trust, all the same I say that Sāriputta and Moggallāna have evil wishes; they have come under the control of evil wishes." And a second time the Blessed One said to the bhikkhu Kokālika: "Do not speak thus, Kokālika!... Sāriputta and Moggallāna are well behaved."

A third time the bhikkhu Kokālika said to the Blessed One: "Venerable sir, although the Blessed One has my faith and trust, all the same I say that Sāriputta and Moggallāna have evil wishes; they have come under the control of evil wishes." And a third time the Blessed One said to the bhikkhu Kokālika: "Do not speak thus, Kokālika!... Sāriputta and Moggallāna are well behaved."

Then the bhikkhu Kokālika rose from his seat, paid homage to the Blessed One, and departed, keeping him on his right. Not long after the bhikkhu Kokālika had left, his entire body became covered with boils the size of mustard seeds. <327> These then grew to the size of mung beans; then to the size of chickpeas; then to the size of jujube stones; then to the size of jujube fruits; then to the size of myrobalans; then to the size of unripe *beluva* fruits; then to the size of ripe *beluva* fruits. When they had grown to the size of ripe *beluva* fruits, they burst open, exuding pus and blood. Then, on account of that illness, the bhikkhu Kokālika died, [151] and because he had harboured animosity towards Sāriputta and Moggallāna, after his death he was reborn in the Paduma hell.[408]

Then, when the night had advanced, Brahmā Sahampati, of stunning beauty, illuminating the entire Jeta's Grove, approached the Blessed One, paid homage to him, stood to one side, <328>

and said to him: "Venerable sir, the bhikkhu Kokālika has died, and because he harboured animosity towards Sāriputta and Moggallāna, after his death he has been reborn in the Paduma hell." This is what Brahmā Sahampati said. Having said this, he paid homage to the Blessed One and, keeping him on his right, he disappeared right there.

Then, when the night had passed, the Blessed One addressed the bhikkhus thus: "Bhikkhus, last night, when the night had advanced, Brahmā Sahampati approached me and said to me:... (*as above*) ... Having said this, he paid homage to me and, keeping me on his right, he disappeared right there."

When this was said, a certain bhikkhu said to the Blessed One: "Venerable sir, how long is the life span in the Paduma hell?"

"The life span in the Paduma hell is long, bhikkhu. It is not easy to count it and say it is so many years, or so many hundreds of years, or so many thousands of years, or so many hundreds of thousands of years." <329>

"Then is it possible to give a simile, venerable sir?" [152]

"It is possible, bhikkhu. Suppose, bhikkhu, there was a Kosalan cartload of twenty measures of sesamum seed. At the end of every hundred years a man would remove one seed from there. That Kosalan cartload of twenty measures of sesamum seed might by this effort be depleted and eliminated more quickly than a single Abbuda hell would go by. Twenty Abbuda hells are the equivalent of one Nirabbuda hell; twenty Nirabbuda hells are the equivalent of one Ababa hell; twenty Ababa hells are the equivalent of one Aṭaṭa hell; twenty Aṭaṭa hells are the equivalent of one Ahaha hell; twenty Ahaha hells are the equivalent of one Kumuda hell; twenty Kumuda hells are the equivalent of one Sogandhika hell; twenty Sogandhika hells are the equivalent of one Uppala hell; twenty Uppala hells are the equivalent of one Puṇḍarīka hell; and twenty Puṇḍarīka hells are the equivalent of one Paduma hell. Now, bhikkhu, the bhikkhu Kokālika has been reborn in the Paduma hell because he harboured animosity towards Sāriputta and Moggallāna."[409] <330>

This is what the Blessed One said. Having said this, the Fortunate One, the Teacher, further said this:

592–95 "When a person has taken birth
... (*verses = 588–91*) ... [153] <331>
Having set evil speech and mind against them."

II. The Second Subchapter
(Brahmā Pentad)

11 (1) Sanaṅkumāra

Thus have I heard. On one occasion the Blessed One was dwelling at Rājagaha on the bank of the river Sappinī. Then, when the night had advanced, Brahmā Sanaṅkumāra, of stunning beauty, illuminating the entire bank of the river Sappinī, approached the Blessed One, paid homage to him, and stood to one side.[410] Standing to one side, he recited this verse in the presence of the Blessed One: <332>

596 "The khattiya is the best among people
For those whose standard is the clan,
But one accomplished in knowledge and conduct
Is best among devas and humans."

This is what Brahmā Sanaṅkumāra said. The Teacher approved. Then Brahmā Sanaṅkumāra, thinking, "The Teacher has approved of me," paid homage to the Blessed One and, keeping him on his right, he disappeared right there.

12 (2) Devadatta

Thus have I heard. On one occasion the Blessed One was dwelling at Rājagaha on Mount Vulture Peak not long after Devadatta had left.[411] Then, when the night had advanced, Brahmā Sahampati, of stunning beauty, illuminating the entire Mount Vulture Peak, approached the Blessed One, paid homage to him, and stood to one side. [154] Standing to one side, referring to Devadatta, he recited this verse in the presence of the Blessed One:

597 "As its own fruit brings destruction
To the plantain, bamboo, and reed,
As its embryo destroys the mule, <333>
So do honours destroy the scoundrel."[412]

13 (3) Andhakavinda

On one occasion the Blessed One was dwelling among the Magadhans at Andhakavinda. Now on that occasion the Blessed One was sitting out in the open in the thick darkness of the night while it was drizzling. Then, when the night had advanced, Brahmā Sahampati ... approached the Blessed One, paid homage to him, and stood to one side. Standing to one side, he recited these verses in the presence of the Blessed One:

598 "One should resort to remote lodgings,
Practise for release from the fetters.
But if one does not find delight there,
Guarded and mindful, dwell in the Saṅgha.[413] <334>

599 "Walking for alms from family to family,
Faculties guarded, discreet, mindful,
One should resort to remote lodgings,
Freed from fear, liberated in the fearless.[414]

600 "Where terrible serpents glide,
Where lightning flashes and the sky thunders,
In the thick darkness of the night
There sits a bhikkhu devoid of terror.[415]

601 "For this has actually been seen by me,
It is not merely hearsay:
Within a single holy life
A thousand have left Death behind.[416]

602 "There are five hundred more trainees,
And ten times a tenfold ten:
All have entered the stream,
Never returning to the animal realm.

603 "As for the other people who remain— <335>
Who, to my mind, partake of merit—
I cannot even number them
From dread of speaking falsely."[417] [155]

14 (4) Aruṇavatī

Thus have I heard. On one occasion the Blessed One was dwelling at Sāvatthī.... There the Blessed One addressed the bhikkhus thus: "Bhikkhus!"

"Venerable sir!" those bhikkhus replied. The Blessed One said this:

"Bhikkhus, once in the past there was a king named Aruṇavā whose capital was named Aruṇavatī. The Blessed One Sikhī, the Arahant, the Perfectly Enlightened One, dwelt in dependence on the capital Aruṇavatī.[418] The chief pair of disciples of the Blessed One Sikhī were named Abhibhū and Sambhava, an excellent pair. Then the Blessed One Sikhī addressed the bhikkhu Abhibhū: 'Come, <336> brahmin, let us go to a certain brahmā world until it is time for our meal.' – 'Yes, venerable sir,' the bhikkhu Abhibhū replied.

"Then, bhikkhus, just as quickly as a strong man might extend his drawn-in arm or draw in his extended arm, so the Blessed One Sikhī, the Arahant, the Perfectly Enlightened One, and the bhikkhu Abhibhū disappeared from the capital Aruṇavatī and reappeared in that brahmā world. Then the Blessed One Sikhī addressed the bhikkhu Abhibhū thus: 'Give a Dhamma talk, brahmin, to Brahmā and to Brahmā's retinue and to Brahmā's assembly.' – 'Yes, venerable sir,' the bhikkhu Abhibhū replied. Then, by means of a Dhamma talk, he instructed, exhorted, inspired, and gladdened Brahmā and Brahmā's retinue and Brahmā's assembly. Thereupon Brahmā and Brahmā's retinue and [156] Brahmā's assembly found fault with this, grumbled, and complained about it, saying: 'It is wonderful indeed, sir! It is amazing indeed, sir! How <337> can a disciple teach the Dhamma in the very presence of the Teacher?'

"Then, bhikkhus, the Blessed One Sikhī addressed the bhikkhu Abhibhū thus: 'Brahmin, Brahmā and Brahmā's retinue and Brahmā's assembly deplore this, saying, "It is wonderful indeed, sir! It is amazing indeed, sir! How can a disciple teach the Dhamma in the very presence of the Teacher?" Well then, brahmin, stir up an even greater sense of urgency in Brahmā and in Brahmā's retinue and in Brahmā's assembly.' – 'Yes, venerable sir,' the bhikkhu Abhibhū replied. Then he taught the Dhamma with his body visible, and with his body invisible, and with the lower half of his body visible and the upper half invisible, and with the upper half of his body visible and the lower half invisible.[419] Thereupon, bhikkhus, Brahmā and Brahmā's retinue and Brahmā's assembly were struck with wonder and amazement, saying: 'It is wonderful indeed, sir! It is amazing indeed, sir! How the ascetic has such great power and might!'

"Then, bhikkhus, the bhikkhu Abhibhū said to the Blessed One Sikhī, the Arahant, the Perfectly Enlightened One: 'I recall, venerable sir, having made such a statement as this in the midst of the Bhikkhu Saṅgha: <338> "Friends, while standing in the brahmā world I can make my voice heard throughout the thousandfold world system."' – 'Now is the time for that, brahmin! Now is the time for that, brahmin! While standing in the brahmā world you should make your voice heard throughout the thousandfold world system.' – 'Yes, venerable sir,' the bhikkhu Abhibhū replied. Then, while standing in the brahmā world, he recited these verses:[420]

604 "'Arouse your energy, strive on!
Exert yourself in the Buddha's Teaching.
Sweep away the army of Death
As an elephant does a hut of reeds. [157]

605 "'One who dwells diligently
In this Dhamma and Discipline,
Having abandoned the wandering on in birth,
Will make an end to suffering.'

"Then, bhikkhus, having stirred up a sense of urgency in Brahmā and in Brahmā's retinue and in Brahmā's assembly, just as quickly as a strong man might extend his drawn-in arm or draw in his extended arm, the Blessed One Sikhī, the Arahant, the Perfectly Enlightened One, and the bhikkhu Abhibhū disappeared from that brahmā world and reappeared in the capital Aruṇavatī. <339> Then the Blessed One Sikhī addressed the bhikkhus thus: 'Bhikkhus, did you hear the verses that the bhikkhu Abhibhū recited while he was standing in the brahmā world?' – 'We did, venerable sir.' – 'What were the verses that you heard, bhikkhus?' – 'We heard the verses of the bhikkhu Abhibhū thus:

606–7 "Arouse your energy, strive on!...
Will make an end to suffering."

Such were the verses that we heard the bhikkhu Abhibhū recite while he was standing in the brahmā world.' – 'Good, good, bhikkhus! It is good that you heard the verses that the bhikkhu Abhibhū recited while he was standing in the brahmā world.'" <340>

This is what the Blessed One said. Elated, those bhikkhus delighted in the Blessed One's statement.

15 (5) Final Nibbāna

On one occasion the Blessed One was dwelling at Kusinārā in Upavattana, the sal tree grove of the Mallans, between the twin sal trees, on the occasion of his final Nibbāna.[421] Then the Blessed One addressed the bhikkhus thus: "Now [158] I address you, bhikkhus: Formations are bound to vanish. Strive to attain the goal by diligence." This was the last utterance of the Tathāgata.

Then the Blessed One attained the first jhāna. Having emerged from the first jhāna, he attained the second jhāna. Having emerged from the second jhāna, he attained the third jhāna. Having emerged from the third jhāna, he attained the fourth jhāna. Having emerged from the fourth jhāna, he attained the base of the infinity of space. Having emerged from the base of the infinity of space, he attained the base of the infinity of consciousness. Having emerged from the base of the infinity of consciousness, he attained the base of nothingness. Having emerged from the base of nothingness, he attained the base of neither-perception-nor-nonperception. Having emerged from the base of neither-perception-nor-nonperception, he attained the cessation of perception and feeling. <341>

Having emerged from the cessation of perception and feeling, he attained the base of neither-perception-nor-nonperception. Having emerged from the base of neither-perception-nor-nonperception, he attained the base of nothingness. Having emerged from the base of nothingness, he attained the base of the infinity of consciousness. Having emerged from the base of the infinity of consciousness, he attained the base of the infinity of space. Having emerged from the base of the infinity of space, he attained the fourth jhāna. Having emerged from the fourth jhāna, he attained the third jhāna. Having emerged from the third jhāna, he attained the second jhāna. Having emerged from the second jhāna, he attained the first jhāna.

Having emerged from the first jhāna, he attained the second jhāna. Having emerged from the second jhāna, he attained the third jhāna. Having emerged from the third jhāna, he attained the fourth jhāna. Having emerged from the fourth jhāna, immediately after this the Blessed One attained final Nibbāna.[422]

When the Blessed One attained final Nibbāna, simultaneously with his final Nibbāna Brahmā Sahampati recited this verse:

608 "All beings in the world
Will finally lay the body down,
Since such a one as the Teacher,
The peerless person in the world,
The Tathāgata endowed with the powers,
The Buddha, has attained final Nibbāna."[423] <342>

When the Blessed One attained final Nibbāna, simultaneously with his final Nibbāna Sakka, lord of the devas, recited this verse:

609 "Impermanent indeed are formations;
Their nature is to arise and vanish.
Having arisen, they cease:
Their appeasement is blissful."[424]

When the Blessed One attained final Nibbāna, simultaneously with his final Nibbāna the Venerable Ānanda recited this verse:[425]

610 "Then there was terror,
Then there was trepidation,
When the one perfect in all excellent qualities,
The Buddha, attained final Nibbāna." [159]

When the Blessed One attained final Nibbāna, simultaneously with his final Nibbāna the Venerable Anuruddha recited these verses:

611 "There was no more in-and-out breathing
In the Stable One of steady mind
When unstirred, bent on peace,
The One with Vision attained final Nibbāna.[426]

612 "With unshrinking mind
He endured the pain;
Like the quenching of a lamp
Was the deliverance of the mind."[427] <343>

[160] <344> Chapter VII

7 *Brāhmaṇasaṃyutta*
Connected Discourses with Brahmins

I. The Arahants

1 (1) Dhanañjanī

Thus have I heard. On one occasion the Blessed One was dwelling at Rājagaha in the Bamboo Grove, the Squirrel Sanctuary. Now on that occasion the wife of a certain brahmin of the Bhāradvāja clan, a brahmin lady named Dhanañjānī, had full confidence in the Buddha, the Dhamma, and the Saṅgha.[428] Once, while the brahmin lady Dhanañjānī was bringing the brahmin his meal, she stumbled, whereupon she uttered three times this inspired utterance: "Homage to the Blessed One, the Arahant, the Perfectly Enlightened One! Homage to the Blessed One, the Arahant, the Perfectly Enlightened One! Homage to the Blessed One, the Arahant, the Perfectly Enlightened One!"[429]

When this was said, the brahmin of the Bhāradvāja clan said to her: "For the slightest thing this wretched woman <345> spouts out praise of that shaveling ascetic! Now, wretched woman, I am going to refute the doctrine of that teacher of yours."[430]

"I do not see anyone, brahmin, in this world with its devas, Māra, and Brahmā, in this generation with its ascetics and brahmins, its devas and humans, who could refute the doctrine of the Blessed One, the Arahant, the Perfectly Enlightened One. But go, brahmin. When you have gone, you will understand."

Then the brahmin of the Bhāradvāja clan, angry and displeased, approached the Blessed One and exchanged greetings with him. When they had concluded their greetings and cordial talk, he sat down to one side [161] and addressed the Blessed One in verse:[431]

613 "Having slain what does one sleep soundly?
Having slain what does one not sorrow? <346>
What is the one thing, O Gotama,
Whose killing you approve?"

[The Blessed One:]
614 "Having slain anger, one sleeps soundly;
Having slain anger, one does not sorrow;
The killing of anger, O brahmin,
With its poisoned root and honeyed tip:
This is the killing the noble ones praise,
For having slain that, one does not sorrow."

When this was said, the brahmin of the Bhāradvāja clan said to the Blessed One: "Magnificent, Master Gotama! Magnificent, Master Gotama! The Dhamma has been made clear in many ways by Master Gotama, as though he were turning upright what had been turned upside down, revealing what was hidden, showing the way to one who was lost, or holding up a lamp in the dark for those with eyesight to see forms. I go for refuge to Master Gotama, and to the Dhamma, and to the Bhikkhu Saṅgha. May I receive the going forth under Master Gotama, may I receive the higher ordination?"

Then the brahmin of the Bhāradvāja clan received the going forth under the Blessed One, he received the higher ordination. And soon, not long after his higher ordination, dwelling alone, withdrawn, diligent, ardent, and resolute, the Venerable Bhāradvāja, by realizing it for himself with direct knowledge, in this very life entered and dwelt in that unsurpassed goal of the holy life for the sake of which clansmen rightly go forth from the household life into homelessness. <347> He directly knew: "Destroyed is birth, the holy life has been lived, what had to be done has been done, there is no more for this state of being."[432] And the Venerable Bhāradvāja became one of the arahants.

2 (2) Abuse

On one occasion the Blessed One was dwelling at Rājagaha in the Bamboo Grove, the Squirrel Sanctuary. The brahmin

Akkosaka Bhāradvāja, Bhāradvāja the Abusive, heard:[433] "It is said that the brahmin of the Bhāradvāja clan has gone forth from the household life into homelessness under the ascetic Gotama." Angry and displeased, he approached the Blessed One and [162] abused and reviled him with rude, harsh words.

When he had finished speaking, the Blessed One said to him: "What do you think, brahmin? Do your friends and colleagues, kinsmen and relatives, as well as guests come to visit you?"

"Sometimes they come to visit, Master Gotama."

"Do you then offer them some food or a meal or a snack?" <348>

"Sometimes I do, Master Gotama."

"But if they do not accept it from you, then to whom does the food belong?"

"If they do not accept it from me, then the food still belongs to us."

"So too, brahmin, we—who do not abuse anyone, who do not scold anyone, who do not rail against anyone—refuse to accept from you the abuse and scolding and tirade you let loose at us. It still belongs to you, brahmin! It still belongs to you, brahmin!

"Brahmin, one who abuses his own abuser, who scolds the one who scolds him, who rails against the one who rails at him—he is said to partake of the meal, to enter upon an exchange. But we do not partake of your meal; we do not enter upon an exchange. It still belongs to you, brahmin! It still belongs to you, brahmin!"

"The king and his retinue understand the ascetic Gotama to be an arahant, yet Master Gotama still gets angry."[434]

[The Blessed One:]

615 "How can anger arise in one who is angerless,
In the tamed one of righteous living, <349>
In one liberated by perfect knowledge,
In the Stable One who abides in peace?[435]

616 "One who repays an angry man with anger
Thereby makes things worse for himself.
Not repaying an angry man with anger,
One wins a battle hard to win.

617 "He practises for the welfare of both—
His own and the other's—
When, knowing that his foe is angry,
He mindfully maintains his peace.

618 "When he achieves the cure of both—
His own and the other's—
The people who consider him a fool
Are unskilled in the Dhamma."[436] [163]

When this was said, the brahmin Akkosaka Bhāradvāja said to the Blessed One: "Magnificent, Master Gotama!... I go for refuge to Master Gotama, and to the Dhamma, and to the Bhikkhu Saṅgha. May I receive the going forth under Master Gotama, may I receive the higher ordination?"

Then the brahmin of the Bhāradvāja clan received the going forth under the Blessed One, he received the higher ordination. And soon, not long after his higher ordination, dwelling alone ... <350> ... the Venerable Bhāradvāja became one of the arahants.

3 (3) *Asurindaka*

On one occasion the Blessed One was dwelling at Rājagaha in the Bamboo Grove, the Squirrel Sanctuary. The brahmin Asurindaka Bhāradvāja heard:[437] "It is said that the brahmin of the Bhāradvāja clan has gone forth from the household life into homelessness under the ascetic Gotama." Angry and displeased, he approached the Blessed One and abused and reviled him with rude, harsh words.

When he had finished speaking, the Blessed One remained silent. Then the brahmin Asurindaka Bhāradvāja said to the Blessed One: "You're beaten, ascetic! You're beaten, ascetic!"

[The Blessed One:]
619 "The fool thinks victory is won
When, by speech, he bellows harshly;
But for one who understands,
Patient endurance is the true victory.[438]

620–22 "One who repays an angry man with anger
… (*verses = 616–18*) … <351>
Are unskilled in the Dhamma." [164]

When this was said, the brahmin Asurindaka Bhāradvāja said to the Blessed One: "Magnificent, Master Gotama!…" And the Venerable Bhāradvāja became one of the arahants.

4 (4) Bilaṅgika

On one occasion the Blessed One was dwelling at Rājagaha in the Bamboo Grove, the Squirrel Sanctuary. The brahmin Bilaṅgika Bhāradvāja heard:[439] "It is said that the brahmin of the Bhāradvāja clan has gone forth from the household life into homelessness under the ascetic Gotama." Angry and displeased, he approached the Blessed One and silently stood to one side.[440] <352>

Then the Blessed One, having known with his own mind the reflection in the brahmin Bilaṅgika Bhāradvāja's mind, addressed him in verse:

623 "If one wrongs an innocent man,
A pure person without blemish,
The evil falls back on the fool himself
Like fine dust thrown against the wind."

When this was said, the brahmin Bilaṅgika Bhāradvāja said to the Blessed One: "Magnificent, Master Gotama!…" And the Venerable Bhāradvāja became one of the arahants.

5 (5) Ahiṃsaka

At Sāvatthī. Then the brahmin Ahiṃsaka Bhāradvāja, Bhāradvāja the Harmless, approached the Blessed One and exchanged greetings with him.[441] When they had concluded their greetings and cordial talk, he sat down to one side [165] and said to the Blessed One: "I am Ahiṃsaka the Harmless, Master Gotama. I am Ahiṃsaka the Harmless, Master Gotama."

[The Blessed One:] <353>

624 "If one were as one's name implies
You would be a harmless one.
But it is one who does no harm at all
By body, speech, or mind,
Who really is a harmless one
As he does not harm others."

When this was said, the brahmin Ahiṃsaka Bhāradvāja said to the Blessed One: "Magnificent, Master Gotama!..." And the Venerable Ahiṃsaka Bhāradvāja became one of the arahants.

6 (6) Tangle

At Sāvatthī. Then the brahmin Jaṭā Bhāradvāja, Bhāradvāja of the Tangle, approached the Blessed One and exchanged greetings with him. When they had concluded their greetings and cordial talk, he sat down to one side and addressed the Blessed One in verse:

625 "A tangle inside, a tangle outside,
This generation is entangled in a tangle.
I ask you this, O Gotama,
Who can disentangle this tangle?" <354>

[The Blessed One:]

626 "A man established on virtue, wise,
Developing the mind and wisdom,
A bhikkhu ardent and discreet:
He can disentangle this tangle.

627 "Those for whom lust and hatred
Along with ignorance have been expunged,
The arahants with taints destroyed:
For them the tangle is disentangled.

628 "Where name-and-form ceases,
Stops without remainder,
And also impingement and perception of form:
It is here this tangle is cut."

When this was said, the brahmin Jaṭā Bhāradvāja said to the Blessed One: "Magnificent, Master Gotama!..." And the Venerable Bhāradvāja became one of the arahants.

7 (7) Suddhika

At Sāvatthī. Then the brahmin Suddhika Bhāradvāja approached the Blessed One <355> and exchanged greetings with him. When they had concluded their greetings and cordial talk, he sat down to one side [166] and recited this verse in the presence of the Blessed One:

629 "In the world no brahmin is ever purified
Though he be virtuous and austere in practice;
One accomplished in knowledge and conduct is purified,
Not the others, the common folk."[442]

[The Blessed One:]
630 "Even though one mutters many chants,
One does not become a brahmin by birth
If one is rotten within and defiled,
Supporting oneself by fraudulent means.

631 "Whether khattiya, brahmin, vessa, sudda,
Caṇḍāla or scavenger,
If one is energetic and resolute,
Always firm in exertion,
One attains the supreme purity:
Know, O brahmin, that this is so." <356>

When this was said, the brahmin Suddhika Bhāradvāja said to the Blessed One: "Magnificent, Master Gotama!"... And the Venerable Bhāradvāja became one of the arahants.

8 (8) Aggika

On one occasion the Blessed One was dwelling at Rājagaha in the Bamboo Grove, the Squirrel Sanctuary. Now on that occasion milk-rice with ghee had been set out for the brahmin Aggika Bhāradvāja, who had thought: "I will offer a fire sacrifice, I will perform the fire oblation."[443]

Then, in the morning, the Blessed One dressed and, taking bowl and robe, entered Rājagaha for alms. Walking for alms on uninterrupted alms round in Rājagaha, the Blessed One approached the residence of the brahmin Aggika Bhāradvāja and stood to one side. The brahmin Aggika Bhāradvāja saw the Blessed One standing for alms and addressed him in verse: <357>

632 "One endowed with the triple knowledge,
Of proper birth, of ample learning,
Accomplished in knowledge and conduct,
Might partake of this milk-rice meal."[444]

[The Blessed One:]
633 "Even though one mutters many chants,
One does not become a brahmin by birth
If one is rotten within and defiled,
With followers gained by fraudulent means. [167]

634 "One who has known his past abodes,
Who sees heaven and the plane of woe,
Who has reached the destruction of birth,
A sage consummate in direct knowledge:[445]

635 "By means of these three kinds of knowledge
One is a triple-knowledge brahmin.
This one accomplished in knowledge and conduct
Might partake of this milk-rice meal." <358>

[The brahmin Aggika Bhāradvāja:] "Let Master Gotama eat. The worthy is a brahmin."

[The Blessed One:]
636 "Food over which verses have been sung
Is not fit to be eaten by me.
This, brahmin, is not the principle
Observed by those who see.
The Enlightened Ones reject such food
Over which verses have been sung.
As such a principle exists, O brahmin,
This is their rule of conduct.

637 "Serve with other food and drink
The consummate one, the great seer
With taints destroyed and remorse stilled,
For he is the field for one seeking merit."[446]

When this was said, the brahmin Aggika Bhāradvāja said to the Blessed One: "Magnificent, Master Gotama!"... And the Venerable Aggika Bhāradvāja became one of the arahants.

9 (9) Sundarika

On one occasion the Blessed One was dwelling among the Kosalans on the bank of the river Sundarika. Now on that occasion <359> the brahmin Sundarika Bhāradvāja was offering a fire sacrifice and performing the fire oblation on the bank of the river Sundarika. Then the brahmin Sundarika Bhāradvāja, having offered the fire sacrifice and performed the fire oblation, rose from his seat and surveyed the four quarters all around, wondering: "Who now might eat this sacrificial cake?"[447]

The brahmin Sundarika Bhāradvāja saw the Blessed One sitting at the foot of a tree with his head covered. Having seen him, he took the sacrificial cake in his left hand and the waterpot in his right hand and approached the Blessed One. When the Blessed One heard the sound of the brahmin's footsteps, he uncovered his head. Then the brahmin Sundarika Bhāradvāja, thinking, "This worthy is shaven-headed, [168] this worthy is a shaveling," wanted to turn back; <360> but it occurred to him: "Some brahmins here are also shaven-headed. Let me approach him and inquire about his birth."

Then the brahmin Sundarika Bhāradvāja approached the Blessed One and said to him: "What is the worthy one's birth?"

[The Blessed One:]
638 "Ask not of birth but ask of conduct:
Fire is indeed produced from any wood.
A resolute sage, though from low family,
Is a thoroughbred restrained by a sense of shame.[448]

639 "The sacrificer should invoke this one:
One tamed by truth, perfect by taming,

Who has reached the end of knowledge,
A fulfiller of the holy life.
Then he makes a timely oblation
To one worthy of offerings."[449] <361>

[The brahmin Sundarika Bhāradvāja:]
640 "Surely my sacrifice is well performed
As I have seen such a knowledge-master.
Because I had not seen those like yourself
Other people ate the sacrificial cake.

"Let Master Gotama eat. The worthy is a brahmin."

[The Blessed One:]
641–42 "Food over which verses have been sung
... (*verses = 636–37*) ...
For he is the field for one seeking merit." <362>

"Then, Master Gotama, should I give this sacrificial cake to someone else?"

"I do not see anyone, brahmin, in this world with its devas, Māra, and Brahmā, in this generation with its ascetics and brahmins, its devas and humans, who could eat and properly digest this sacrificial cake [169] except the Tathāgata or a disciple of the Tathāgata.[450] Therefore, brahmin, throw away the sacrificial cake in a place where there is sparse vegetation or dispose of it in water where there are no living beings."

Then the brahmin Sundarika Bhāradvāja disposed of that sacrificial cake in water where there were no living beings. When it was disposed of in the water, that sacrificial cake sizzled and hissed and gave off steam and smoke.[451] Just as a ploughshare, heated all day, sizzles and hisses and gives off steam and smoke if placed in water, so too that sacrificial cake, <363> when disposed of in the water, sizzled and hissed and gave off steam and smoke.

Then the brahmin Sundarika Bhāradvāja, shocked and terrified, approached the Blessed One and stood to one side. The Blessed One then addressed him with verses:

643 "When kindling wood, brahmin, do not imagine
This external deed brings purity;

For experts say no purity is gained
By one who seeks it outwardly.

644 "Having given up the fire made from wood,
I kindle, O brahmin, the inner light alone.
Always ablaze, my mind always concentrated,
I am an arahant living the holy life.

645 "Conceit, O brahmin, is your shoulder-load, <364>
Anger the smoke, false speech the ashes;
The tongue is the ladle, the heart the altar,
A well-tamed self is the light of a man.[452]

646 "The Dhamma is a lake with fords of virtue—
Limpid, praised by the good to the good—
Where the knowledge-masters go to bathe,
And, dry-limbed, cross to the far shore.[453]

647 "Truth, Dhamma, restraint, the holy life,
Attainment of Brahmā based on the middle: [170]
Pay homage, O brahmin, to the upright ones;
I call that person one impelled by Dhamma."[454]

When this was said, the brahmin Sundarika Bhāradvāja said to the Blessed One: "Magnificent, Master Gotama!"... And the Venerable Sundarika Bhāradvāja became one of the arahants. <365>

10 (10) Many Daughters

On one occasion the Blessed One was dwelling among the Kosalans in a certain woodland thicket. Now on that occasion fourteen oxen belonging to a certain brahmin of the Bhāradvāja clan had gotten lost. Then the brahmin of the Bhāradvāja clan, while searching for those oxen, went to the woodland thicket where the Blessed One was staying. There he saw the Blessed One sitting with his legs folded crosswise, holding his body erect, having set up mindfulness in front of him. Having seen him, he approached the Blessed One and recited these verses in the presence of the Blessed One:

648 "Surely this ascetic does not have
Fourteen oxen [that have gotten lost],
Not seen now for the past six days:
Hence this ascetic is happy.[455]

649 "Surely this ascetic does not have
A field of blighted sesamum plants,
Some with one leaf, some with two:
Hence this ascetic is happy. <366>

650 "Surely this ascetic does not have
Rats inside an empty barn
Dancing around merrily:
Hence this ascetic is happy.

651 "Surely this ascetic does not have
A blanket that for seven months
Has been covered with swarms of vermin:
Hence this ascetic is happy.

652 "Surely this ascetic does not have
Seven daughters left for widows,
Some with one son, some with two:
Hence this ascetic is happy.[456]

653 "Surely this ascetic does not have
A tawny wife with pockmarked face
Who wakes him up with a kick:
Hence this ascetic is happy.

654 "Surely this ascetic does not have
Creditors who call at dawn,
Chiding him, 'Pay up! Pay up!': <367>
Hence this ascetic is happy."

[The Blessed One:]

655 "Surely, brahmin, I do not have
Fourteen oxen [that have gotten lost],
Not seen now for the past six days:
Hence, O brahmin, I am happy. [171]

656 "Surely, brahmin, I do not have
A field of blighted sesamum plants,
Some with one leaf, some with two:
Hence, O brahmin, I am happy.

657 "Surely, brahmin, I do not have
Rats inside an empty barn
Dancing around merrily:
Hence, O brahmin, I am happy.

658 "Surely, brahmin, I do not have
A blanket that for seven months
Has been covered with swarms of vermin:
Hence, O brahmin, I am happy.

659 "Surely, brahmin, I do not have
Seven daughters left for widows,
Some with one son, some with two:
Hence, O brahmin, I am happy. <368>

660 "Surely, brahmin, I do not have
A tawny wife with pockmarked face
Who wakes me up with a kick:
Hence, O brahmin, I am happy.

661 "Surely, brahmin, I do not have
Creditors who call at dawn,
Chiding me, 'Pay up! Pay up!':
Hence, O brahmin, I am happy."

When this was said, the brahmin of the Bhāradvāja clan said to the Blessed One: "Magnificent, Master Gotama!"... And the Venerable Bhāradvāja became one of the arahants.[457] <369>

[172] II. The Lay Followers

11 (1) Kasi Bhāradvāja

Thus have I heard.[458] On one occasion the Blessed One was dwelling among the Magadhans at Dakkhiṇāgiri near the brahmin village of Ekanāḷa. Now on that occasion the brahmin Kasi Bhāradvāja, Bhāradvāja the Ploughman, had five hundred ploughs fastened to their yokes at the time of sowing.[459] Then, in the morning, the Blessed One dressed and, taking bowl and robe, went to the place where the brahmin Kasi Bhāradvāja was at work.

Now on that occasion the brahmin Kasi Bhāradvāja's food distribution was taking place.[460] Then the Blessed One approached the place of the food distribution <370> and stood to one side. The brahmin Kasi Bhāradvāja saw the Blessed One standing for alms and said to him:

"Recluse, I plough and sow, and when I have ploughed and sown I eat. You too, ascetic, ought to plough and sow; then, when you have ploughed and sown, you will eat."

"I too, brahmin, plough and sow, and when I have ploughed and sown I eat."

"But we do not see Master Gotama's yoke or plough or ploughshare or goad or oxen; yet Master Gotama says, 'I too, brahmin, plough and sow, and when I have ploughed and sown I eat.'"

Then the brahmin Kasi Bhāradvāja addressed the Blessed One in verse: <371>

662 "You claim to be a man who works the plough,
But I do not see your ploughing.
If you're a ploughman, answer me:
How should we understand your ploughing?"

[The Blessed One:]
663 "Faith is the seed, austerity the rain,
Wisdom my yoke and plough;
Shame is the pole, mind the yoke-tie,
Mindfulness my ploughshare and goad.[461]

664 "Guarded in body, guarded in speech,
Controlled in my appetite for food,
I use truth as my weeding-hook,
And gentleness as my unyoking.[462] [173]

665 "Energy is my beast of burden,
Carrying me to security from bondage.

It goes ahead without stopping
To where, having gone, one does not sorrow.[463]

666 "In such a way this ploughing is done
Which has the Deathless as its fruit.
Having finished this work of ploughing, <372>
One is released from all suffering."

"Let Master Gotama eat! The worthy is a ploughman, since Master Gotama does ploughing that has even the Deathless as its fruit."

667–68 "Food over which verses have been sung
… (*verses = 636–37*) …
For he is the field for one seeking merit."

When this was said, the brahmin Kasi Bhāradvāja said to the Blessed One: "Magnificent, Master Gotama! Magnificent, Master Gotama! The Dhamma has been made clear in many ways by Master Gotama, as though he were turning upright what had been turned upside down, revealing what was hidden, showing the way to one who was lost, or holding up a lamp in the dark for those with eyesight to see forms. <373> I go for refuge to Master Gotama, and to the Dhamma, and to the Bhikkhu Saṅgha. Let Master Gotama remember me as a lay follower who from today has gone for refuge for life."

12 (2) Udaya

At Sāvatthī. Then, in the morning, the Blessed One dressed and, taking bowl and robe, approached the residence of the brahmin Udaya. Then the brahmin Udaya filled the Blessed One's bowl with rice. A second time in the morning the Blessed One dressed and, taking bowl and robe, approached the residence of the brahmin Udaya…. A third time in the morning the Blessed One dressed and, taking bowl and robe, approached the residence of the brahmin Udaya.[464] Then a third time the brahmin Udaya filled the Blessed One's bowl with rice, [174] after which he said to the Blessed One: "This pesky ascetic Gotama keeps coming again and again."[465]

[The Blessed One:]

669 "Again and again, they sow the seed;
Again and again, the sky-god sends down rain; <374>
Again and again, ploughmen plough the field;
Again and again, grain comes to the realm.

670 "Again and again, the mendicants beg;
Again and again, the donors give;
When donors have given again and again,
Again and again they go to heaven.

671 "Again and again, the dairy folk draw milk;
Again and again, the calf goes to its mother;
Again and again, one wearies and trembles;
Again and again, the dolt enters the womb;
Again and again, one is born and dies;
Again and again, they take one to the cemetery.

672 "But when one has obtained the path
That leads to no more renewed existence,
Having become broad in wisdom,
One is not born again and again!"

When this was said, the brahmin Udaya said to the Blessed One: "Magnificent, Master Gotama! Magnificent, Master Gotama!... Let Master Gotama remember me as a lay follower who from today has gone for refuge for life." <375>

13 (3) Devahita

At Sāvatthī. Now on that occasion the Blessed One was afflicted by winds and the Venerable Upavāṇa was his attendant.[466] Then the Blessed One addressed the Venerable Upavāṇa thus: "Come now, Upavāṇa, find some hot water for me."

"Yes, venerable sir," the Venerable Upavāṇa replied. Then he dressed and, taking bowl and robe, went to the residence of the brahmin Devahita, where he stood silently to one side. The brahmin Devahita saw the Venerable Upavāṇa standing silently to one side and addressed him in verse: [175]

673 "Silent, the worthy one stands,
Shaven-headed, clad in a stitched robe.
What do you want, what do you seek,
What have you come here to beg?"

[The Venerable Upavāṇa:]
674 "The Arahant, the Fortunate One in the world,
The Sage, is afflicted with winds. <376>
If there is any hot water, brahmin,
Please give it for the Sage.

675 "He is worshipped by those worthy of worship,
Honoured by those worthy of honour,
Respected by those worthy of respect:
It is to him that I wish to take it."

Then the brahmin Devahita ordered a man to bring a carrying pole with hot water and presented a bag of molasses to the Venerable Upavāṇa. Then the Venerable Upavāṇa approached the Blessed One. He had the Blessed One bathed with the hot water, and he mixed the molasses with hot water and offered it to him. Then the Blessed One's ailment subsided.

Then the brahmin Devahita approached the Blessed One and exchanged greetings with him, after which he sat down to one side and addressed the Blessed One in verse:

676 "Where should one give a proper gift? <377>
Where does a gift bear great fruit?
How, for one bestowing alms,
Does an offering bring success—just how?"[467]

[The Blessed One:]
677 "One who has known his past abodes,
Who sees heaven and the plane of woe,
Who has reached the destruction of birth,
A sage consummate in direct knowledge:
678 Here one should give a proper gift,
Here a gift bears great fruit.
That's how, for one bestowing alms,
An offering brings success—just so!"

When this was said, the brahmin Devahita said to the Blessed One: "Magnificent, Master Gotama! Magnificent, Master Gotama!... Let Master Gotama remember me as a lay follower who from today has gone for refuge for life."

14 (4) *The Affluent One*

At Sāvatthī.[468] Then a certain affluent brahmin, shabby, clad in a shabby cloak, [176] approached the Blessed One <378> and exchanged greetings with him. When they had concluded their greetings and cordial talk, he sat down to one side, and the Blessed One then said to him: "Why now, brahmin, are you so shabby, clad in a shabby cloak?"

"Here, Master Gotama, my four sons, instigated by their wives, have expelled me from the house."

"Well then, brahmin, learn these verses and recite them when the multitude has assembled in the meeting hall with your sons sitting together there:

679 "Those at whose birth I took delight
And whose success I much desired,
Being instigated by their wives,
Chase me out as dogs chase swine.

680 "These evil fellows are indeed mean,
Although they call me, 'Dad, dear Dad.'
They're demons in the guise of sons <379>
To abandon me when I've grown old.

681 "As an old horse of no more use
Is led away from its fodder,
So the old father of those boys
Begs for alms at others' homes.

682 "Better for me is the staff I use
Than those disobedient sons;
For the staff drives off the wild bull
And drives away the wild dog.

683 "In the dark it goes before me,

In the deep it gives me support.
By the gracious power of the staff,
If I stumble I still stand firm."

Then that affluent brahmin, having learned these verses in the presence of the Blessed One, recited them when the multitude had assembled in the meeting hall with his sons sitting together there:

684–88 "Those at whose birth I took delight … <380>
If I stumble I still stand firm." [177]

Then the sons led that affluent brahmin to their house, bathed him, and each gave him a pair of clothes. Then that affluent brahmin, having taken one pair of clothes, approached the Blessed One and exchanged greetings with him. <381> Then he sat down to one side and said to the Blessed One: "Master Gotama, we brahmins seek a teacher's fee for our teacher. Let Master Gotama accept a teacher's fee from me." The Blessed One accepted out of compassion.

Then that affluent brahmin said to the Blessed One: "Magnificent, Master Gotama! Magnificent, Master Gotama!… Let Master Gotama remember me as a lay follower who from today has gone for refuge for life."

15 (5) Mānatthaddha

At Sāvatthī. Now on that occasion a brahmin named Mānatthaddha, Stiff with Conceit, was residing at Sāvatthī.[469] He did not pay homage to his mother or father, nor to his teacher or eldest brother. Now on that occasion the Blessed One was teaching the Dhamma surrounded by a large assembly. <382> Then it occurred to the brahmin Mānatthaddha: "This ascetic Gotama is teaching the Dhamma surrounded by a large assembly. Let me approach him. If the ascetic Gotama addresses me, then I will address him in turn. But if he does not address me, neither will I address him."

Then the brahmin Mānatthaddha approached the Blessed One and stood silently to one side, but the Blessed One did not address him. Then the brahmin Mānatthaddha, thinking, "This ascetic Gotama doesn't know anything,"[470] wanted to turn back, [178] but the Blessed One, having known with his own mind the reflection in the brahmin's mind, addressed the brahmin Mānatthaddha in verse:

689 "The fostering of conceit is never good
For one keen on his welfare, brahmin.
You should instead foster that purpose
Because of which you've come here."[471] <383>

Then the brahmin Mānatthaddha, thinking, "The ascetic Gotama knows my mind," prostrated himself right there with his head at the Blessed One's feet. He kissed the Blessed One's feet, stroked them with his hands, and announced his name thus: "I am Mānatthaddha, Master Gotama! I am Mānatthaddha, Master Gotama!"

Then that assembly was struck with amazement and the people said: "It is wonderful indeed, sir! It is amazing indeed, sir! This brahmin Mānatthaddha does not pay homage to his mother and father, nor to his teacher or eldest brother, yet he shows such supreme honour towards the ascetic Gotama."[472]

Then the Blessed One said to the brahmin Mānatthaddha: "Enough, brahmin! Get up and sit in your own seat, as your mind has confidence in me."

Then the brahmin Mānatthaddha sat down in his own seat and addressed the Blessed One in verse:

690 "Towards whom should one avoid conceit?
Towards whom should one show reverence?
To whom should one be ever respectful? <384>
Whom is it proper to venerate deeply?"

[The Blessed One:]
691 "First one's own mother and father,
Then one's eldest family brother,
Then one's teacher as the fourth:
Towards these one should avoid conceit;
Towards these one should be reverential;
These should be well respected;
These it is good to venerate deeply.

692 "Having struck down conceit, humble,
One should pay homage to the arahants,
Those cool of heart, their tasks done,
The taintless ones, unsurpassed."

When this was said, the brahmin Mānatthaddha said to the Blessed One: "Magnificent, Master Gotama! Magnificent, Master Gotama!… <385> Let Master Gotama remember me as a lay follower who from today has gone for refuge for life." [179]

16 (6) Paccanīka

At Sāvatthī. Now on that occasion a brahmin named Paccanīkasāta, Relisher of Contradiction, was residing at Sāvatthī. Then it occurred to the brahmin Paccanīkasāta: "Let me approach the ascetic Gotama and contradict whatever he says."

Now on that occasion the Blessed One was walking back and forth in the open. Then the brahmin Paccanīkasāta approached the Blessed One and said to him while he was walking back and forth: "Speak Dhamma, ascetic!"

[The Blessed One:]
693 "Well-spoken counsel is hard to understand
By one who relishes contradiction,
By one with a corrupt mind <386>
Who is engrossed in aggression.

694 "But if one has removed aggression
And the distrust of one's heart,
If one has cast away aversion,
One can understand well-spoken counsel."

When this was said, the brahmin Paccanīkasāta said to the Blessed One: "Magnificent, Master Gotama! Magnificent, Master Gotama!… Let Master Gotama remember me as a lay follower who from today has gone for refuge for life."

17 (7) Navakammika

On one occasion the Blessed One was dwelling among the

Kosalans in a certain woodland thicket. Now on that occasion the brahmin Navakammika Bhāradvāja was getting some work done in that woodland thicket.[473] The brahmin Navakammika Bhāradvāja saw the Blessed One sitting at the foot of a certain sal tree with his legs folded crosswise, holding his body erect, having set up mindfulness in front of him. Having seen him, he thought: <387> "I take delight in getting work done in this woodland thicket. What does this ascetic Gotama take delight in getting done?"

Then the brahmin Navakammika Bhāradvāja approached the Blessed One [180] and addressed him in verse:

695 "With what kind of work are you engaged
Here in this sal woods, bhikkhu,
By reason of which you find delight
Alone in the forest, Gotama?"

[The Blessed One:]
696 "There is nothing in the woods I need to do;
Cut down at the root, my woods is dried up.
Woodless and dartless, discontent cast off,
I find delight alone in the woods."[474] <388>

When this was said, the brahmin Navakammika Bhāradvāja said to the Blessed One: "Magnificent, Master Gotama! Magnificent, Master Gotama!... Let Master Gotama remember me as a lay follower who from today has gone for refuge for life."

18 (8) The Wood Gatherers

On one occasion the Blessed One was dwelling among the Kosalans in a certain woodland thicket. Now on that occasion a number of brahmin boys, students of a certain brahmin of the Bhāradvāja clan, approached that woodland thicket while collecting firewood. Having approached, they saw the Blessed One sitting in that woodland thicket with his legs folded crosswise, holding his body erect, having set up mindfulness in front of him. Having seen him, they approached the brahmin of the Bhāradvāja clan and said to him: "See now, master, you should know that in such and such a woodland thicket an ascetic is sitting with his legs folded crosswise, holding his body erect, having set up mindfulness in front of him."

Then the brahmin of the Bhāradvāja clan, together with those brahmin boys, went to that woodland thicket. He saw the Blessed One sitting there ... <389> ... having set up mindfulness in front of him. He then approached the Blessed One and addressed him in verse:

697 "Having entered the empty, desolate forest,
Deep in the woods where many terrors lurk, [181]
With a motionless body, steady, lovely,
How you meditate, bhikkhu, so beautifully![475]

698 "In the forest where no song or music sounds,
A solitary sage has resorted to the woods!
This strikes me as a wonder—that you dwell
With joyful mind alone in the woods.

699 "I suppose you desire the supreme triple heaven,
The company of the world's divine lord. <390>
Therefore you resort to the desolate forest:
You practise penance here for attaining Brahmā."[476]

[The Blessed One:]
700 "Whatever be the many desires and delights
That are always attached to the manifold elements,
The longings sprung from the root of unknowing:
All I have demolished along with their root.[477]

701 "I am desireless, unattached, disengaged;
My vision of all things has been purified.
Having attained the auspicious—supreme enlightenment—
Self-confident, brahmin, I meditate alone."[478]

When this was said, the brahmin of the Bhāradvāja clan said to the Blessed One: "Magnificent, Master Gotama! Magnificent, Master Gotama!... Let Master Gotama remember me as a lay follower who from today has gone for refuge for life."

19 (9) The Mother Supporter

<391> At Sāvatthī. Then a brahmin who supported his mother approached the Blessed One ... and said to him: "Master Gotama, I seek almsfood righteously and thereby support my mother and father. In doing so, am I doing my duty?"

"For sure, brahmin, in doing so you are doing your duty. One who seeks almsfood righteously [182] and thereby supports his mother and father generates much merit.

702 "When a mortal righteously supports his parents,
Because of this service to them
The wise praise him here in this world,
And after death he rejoices in heaven." <392>

When this was said, the brahmin who supported his mother said to the Blessed One: "Magnificent, Master Gotama! Magnificent, Master Gotama!... Let Master Gotama remember me as a lay follower who from today has gone for refuge for life."

20 (10) The Mendicant

At Sāvatthī. Then a mendicant brahmin approached the Blessed One ... and said to him: "Master Gotama, I am a mendicant and you are a mendicant. What is the difference between us in this respect?"[479]

[The Blessed One:]
703 "It is not thus that one becomes a mendicant,
Just because one begs others for alms.
If one has taken up a domestic practice,
One still has not become a bhikkhu.[480]

704 "But one here who leads the holy life,
Having expelled merit and evil, <393>
Who fares in the world with comprehension:
He is truly called a bhikkhu."

When this was said, the mendicant brahmin said to the Blessed One: "Magnificent, Master Gotama! Magnificent, Master

Gotama!... Let Master Gotama remember me as a lay follower who from today has gone for refuge for life."

21 (11) Saṅgārava

At Sāvatthī. Now on that occasion a brahmin named Saṅgārava was residing at Sāvatthī. He was a practitioner of water-purification, one who believed in purification by water, who dwelt devoted to the practice of immersing himself in water at dusk and at dawn.

Then, in the morning, the Venerable Ānanda dressed and, taking bowl and robe, entered Sāvatthī for alms. Having walked for alms in Sāvatthī, when he had returned from his alms round, after his meal he approached the Blessed One, paid homage to him, sat down to one side, [183] and said to him:

"Here, venerable sir, a brahmin named Saṅgārava is residing at Sāvatthī. He is a practitioner of water-purification ... devoted to the practice of immersing himself in water at dusk and at dawn. It would be good, venerable sir, if the Blessed One would approach the residence of the brahmin Saṅgārava <394> out of compassion." The Blessed One consented by silence.

Then, in the morning, the Blessed One dressed and, taking bowl and robe, approached the brahmin Saṅgārava's residence, where he sat down in the appointed seat. Then the brahmin Saṅgārava approached the Blessed One and exchanged greetings with him, after which he sat down to one side. The Blessed One then said to him: "Is it true, brahmin, that you are a practitioner of water-purification, one who believes in purification by water, devoted to the practice of immersing yourself in water at dusk and at dawn?"

"Yes, Master Gotama."

"Considering what benefit do you do this, brahmin?"

"Here, Master Gotama, whatever evil deed I have done during the day I wash away by bathing at dusk. Whatever evil deed I have done at night I wash away by bathing at dawn." <395>

[The Blessed One:]

705 "The Dhamma, brahmin, is a lake with fords of virtue—
A limpid lake the good praise to the good—

Where the knowledge-masters go to bathe,
And, dry-limbed, cross to the far shore."[481]

When this was said, the brahmin Saṅgārava said to the Blessed One: "Magnificent, Master Gotama! Magnificent, Master Gotama!... Let Master Gotama remember me as a lay follower who from today has gone for refuge for life." [184]

22 (12) Khomadussa

Thus have I heard. On one occasion the Blessed One was dwelling among the Sakyans where there was a town of the Sakyans named Khomadussa.[482] Then the Blessed One dressed and, taking bowl and robe, entered Khomadussa for alms.

Now on that occasion the brahmin householders of Khomadussa had assembled in council on some business matter while it was drizzling. <396> Then the Blessed One approached the council. The brahmin householders of Khomadussa saw the Blessed One coming in the distance and said: "Who are these shaveling ascetics? Don't they know the rule of order?"[483]

Then the Blessed One addressed the brahmin householders of Khomadussa in verse:

706 "That is no council where the good are absent;
They are not the good who don't speak Dhamma.
But having abandoned lust, hate, and delusion,
Those speaking on Dhamma are alone the good."

When this was said, the brahmin householders of Khomadussa said to the Blessed One: "Magnificent, Master Gotama! Magnificent, Master Gotama! The Dhamma has been made clear in many ways by Master Gotama, as though he were turning upright what had been turned upside down, revealing what was hidden, showing the way to one who was lost, or holding up a lamp in the dark for those with eyesight to see forms. We go for refuge to Master Gotama, and to the Dhamma, and to the Bhikkhu Saṅgha. Let Master Gotama remember us as lay followers who from today have gone for refuge for life." <397>

[185] <398> Chapter VIII

8 *Vaṅgīsasaṃyutta*
Connected Discourses with Vaṅgīsa

1 Renounced

Thus have I heard.[484] On one occasion the Venerable Vaṅgīsa was dwelling at Āḷavī at the Aggāḷava Shrine together with his preceptor, the Venerable Nigrodhakappa.[485] Now on that occasion the Venerable Vaṅgīsa, newly ordained, not long gone forth, had been left behind as a caretaker of the dwelling.

Then a number of women, beautifully adorned, approached the Aggāḷavaka Park in order to see the dwelling. When the Venerable Vaṅgīsa saw those women, dissatisfaction arose in him; lust infested his mind.[486] Then it occurred to him: "It is a loss for me indeed, it is no gain for me! It is a mishap for me indeed, it is not well gained by me, that dissatisfaction has arisen in me, that lust has infested my mind. How could anyone else dispel my dissatisfaction and arouse delight? <399> Let me dispel my own dissatisfaction and arouse delight by myself."

Then the Venerable Vaṅgīsa, having dispelled his own dissatisfaction and aroused delight by himself, on that occasion recited these verses:

707 "Alas, though I am one who has renounced,
Gone from home into homelessness,
These thoughts still run over me,
Impudent thoughts from the Dark One.[487]

708 "Even if mighty youths, great archers,
Trained men, masters of the bow,
A thousand such men who do not flee
Should surround me on all sides,[488]

709 And if women were to come here
Still more numerous than this,
They would never make me tremble
For I stand firmly in the Dhamma.[489] [186]

710 "I have heard this as a witness <400>
From the Buddha, Kinsman of the Sun:
The path leading to Nibbāna—
That is where my mind delights.[490]

711 "If, while I am dwelling thus,
You approach me, Evil One,
I will act in such a way, O Death,
That you won't even see my path."[491]

2 Discontent

On one occasion the Venerable Vaṅgīsa was dwelling at Āḷavī at the Aggāḷava Shrine together with his preceptor, the Venerable Nigrodhakappa. Now on that occasion, when the Venerable Nigrodhakappa returned from his alms round, after his meal he would enter the dwelling and would come out either in the evening or on the following day.

Now on that occasion dissatisfaction had arisen in the Venerable Vaṅgīsa; lust had infested his mind. Then it occurred to the Venerable Vaṅgīsa: "It is a loss for me indeed, it is no gain for me! It is a mishap for me indeed, it is not well gained by me, that dissatisfaction has arisen in me, that lust has infested my mind. <401> How could anyone else dispel my dissatisfaction and arouse delight? Let me dispel my own dissatisfaction and arouse delight."

Then the Venerable Vaṅgīsa, having dispelled his own dissatisfaction and aroused delight, on that occasion recited these verses:

712 "Having abandoned discontent and delight
And household thoughts entirely,
One should not nurture lust towards anything;
The lustless one, without delight—
He is indeed a bhikkhu.[492]

713 "Whatever exists here on earth and in space,
Comprised by form, included in the world—
Everything impermanent decays;
The sages fare having pierced this truth.[493] <402>

714 "People are tied to their acquisitions,
To what is seen, heard, sensed, and felt;
Dispel desire for this, be unstirred:
They call him a sage
Who clings to nothing here.[494] [187]

715 "Then those caught in the sixty,
Led by their own thoughts—
There are many such among the people
Who have settled on wrong doctrine:
One who would not join their faction anywhere,
Nor utter corrupt speech—he is a bhikkhu.[495]

716 "Proficient, long trained in concentration,
Honest, discreet, without longing,
The sage has attained the peaceful state,
Depending on which he bides his time
Fully quenched within himself."[496] <403>

3 Well Behaved

On one occasion the Venerable Vaṅgīsa was living at Āḷavī at the Aggāḷava Shrine together with his preceptor, the Venerable Nigrodhakappa. Now on that occasion, the Venerable Vaṅgīsa, because of his own ingenuity, had been looking down at other well-behaved bhikkhus.[497] Then the thought occurred to the Venerable Vaṅgīsa: "It is a loss for me indeed, it is no gain for me! It is a mishap for me indeed, it is not well gained by me, that because of my ingenuity I look down upon other well-behaved bhikkhus."

Then the Venerable Vaṅgīsa, having aroused remorse in himself, on that occasion recited these verses:

717 "Abandon conceit, O Gotama,
And leave the pathway of conceit entirely.

Infatuated with the pathway of conceit,
For a long time you've been remorseful.[498] <404>

718 "People smeared by denigration,
Slain by conceit, fall into hell.
People sorrow for a long time,
Slain by conceit, reborn in hell.

719 "But a bhikkhu never sorrows at all,
A path-knower practising rightly.
He experiences acclaim and happiness;
Truly they call him a seer of Dhamma.[499] [188]

720 "Therefore be pliant here and strenuous;
Having abandoned the hindrances, be pure.
Having entirely abandoned conceit,
Be an end-maker by knowledge, peaceful."[500]

4 Ānanda

On one occasion the Venerable Ānanda was dwelling at Sāvatthī in Jeta's Grove, Anāthapiṇḍika's Park. Then, in the morning, the Venerable Ānanda <405> dressed and, taking bowl and robe, entered Sāvatthī for alms with the Venerable Vaṅgīsa as his companion. Now on that occasion dissatisfaction had arisen in the Venerable Vaṅgīsa; lust had infested his mind.[501] Then the Venerable Vaṅgīsa addressed the Venerable Ānanda in verse:

721 "I am burning with sensual lust,
My mind is engulfed by fire.
Please tell me how to extinguish it,
Out of compassion, O Gotama."[502]

[The Venerable Ānanda:]
722 "It is through an inversion of perception
That your mind is engulfed by fire.
Turn away from the sign of beauty
Provocative of sensual lust.[503]

723 "See formations as alien,
As suffering, not as self.
Extinguish the great fire of lust;
Don't burn up again and again.[504]

724 "Develop the mind on foulness,
One-pointed, well concentrated; <406>
Apply your mindfulness to the body,
Be engrossed in revulsion.[505]

725 "Develop meditation on the signless,
And discard the tendency to conceit.
Then, by breaking through conceit,
You will be one who fares at peace."[506]

5 Well Spoken

At Sāvatthī.[507] There the Blessed One addressed the bhikkhus thus: "Bhikkhus!"

"Venerable sir!" those bhikkhus replied. The Blessed One said this:

"Bhikkhus, when speech possesses four factors, then it is well spoken, not badly spoken, and it is blameless, not blameworthy among the wise. What four? Here, bhikkhus, a bhikkhu speaks only what is well spoken, not what is badly spoken. He speaks only on the Dhamma, not on non-Dhamma. [189] He speaks only what is pleasant, not what is unpleasant. He speaks only what is true, not what is false. <407> When speech possesses these four factors, it is well spoken, not badly spoken, and it is blameless, not blameworthy among the wise."[508]

This is what the Blessed One said. Having said this, the Fortunate One, the Teacher, further said this:

726 "What is well spoken, the good say, is foremost;
Second, speak Dhamma, not non-Dhamma;
Third, speak what is pleasant, not unpleasant;
Fourth, speak the truth, not falsehood."

Then the Venerable Vaṅgīsa rose from his seat, arranged his upper robe over one shoulder, and, raising his joined hands in reverential salutation towards the Blessed One, said to him: "An inspiration has come to me, Blessed One! An inspiration has come to me, Fortunate One!"[509]

The Blessed One said: "Then express your inspiration, Vaṅgīsa."

Then the Venerable Vaṅgīsa extolled the Blessed One to his face with suitable verses:

727 "One should utter only such speech
By which one does not afflict oneself
Nor cause harm to others:
Such speech is truly well spoken. <408>

728 "One should utter only pleasant speech,
Speech that is gladly welcomed.
When it brings them nothing evil
What one speaks is pleasant to others.

729 "Truth, indeed, is deathless speech:
This is an ancient principle.
The goal and the Dhamma, the good say,
Are established upon truth.[510]

730 "The secure speech which the Buddha utters
For the attainment of Nibbāna,
For making an end to suffering
Is truly the foremost speech."[511]

6 Sāriputta

On one occasion the Venerable Sāriputta was dwelling at Sāvatthī in Jeta's Grove, Anāthapiṇḍika's Park. Now on that occasion the Venerable Sāriputta was instructing, exhorting, inspiring, and gladdening the bhikkhus with a Dhamma talk, <409> [spoken] with speech that was polished, fluent, articulate, expressing well the meaning. And those bhikkhus were listening to the Dhamma with eager ears, attending to it as a matter of vital concern, directing their whole mind to it.

Then it occurred to the Venerable Vaṅgīsa: [190] "This Venerable Sāriputta is instructing the bhikkhus with a Dhamma talk, [spoken] with speech that is polished, clear, articulate, expressing well the meaning. And those bhikkhus are listening to the Dhamma with eager ears.... Let me extol the Venerable Sāriputta to his face with suitable verses."

Then the Venerable Vaṅgīsa rose from his seat, arranged his upper robe over one shoulder, and, raising his joined hands in reverential salutation towards the Venerable Sāriputta, said to him: "An inspiration has come to me, friend Sāriputta! An inspiration has come to me, friend Sāriputta!"

"Then express your inspiration, friend Vaṅgīsa."

Then the Venerable Vaṅgīsa extolled the Venerable Sāriputta to his face with suitable verses:

731 "Deep in wisdom, intelligent,
Skilled in the true path and the false,
Sāriputta, of great wisdom,
Teaches the Dhamma to the bhikkhus.

732 "He teaches briefly, <410>
He speaks in detail.
His voice, like that of a myna bird,
Pours forth inspired discourse.[512]

733 "As he teaches them, they listen
To his sweet utterance.
Uplifted in mind, made joyful
By his delightful voice,
Sonorous and lovely,
The bhikkhus incline their ears."

7 Pavāraṇā

On one occasion the Blessed One was dwelling at Sāvatthī in the Eastern Park in the Mansion of Migāra's Mother together with a great Saṅgha of bhikkhus, with five hundred bhikkhus, all of them arahants. Now on that occasion—the Uposatha day of the fifteenth—the Blessed One was sitting in the open surrounded by the Bhikkhu Saṅgha in order to hold the Pavāraṇā.[513] Then, having surveyed the silent Bhikkhu Saṅgha, the Blessed One addressed the bhikkhus thus: "Come now, <411> bhikkhus, let me invite you: Is there any deed of mine, either bodily or verbal, which you would censure?"

When this was said, the Venerable Sāriputta rose from his seat, arranged his upper robe over one shoulder, and, raising his joined hands in reverential salutation towards the Blessed One, said to him: "Venerable sir, there is no deed of the Blessed One, either bodily or verbal, that we censure. [191] For, venerable sir, the Blessed One is the originator of the path unarisen before, the producer of the path unproduced before, the declarer of the path undeclared before. He is the knower of the path, the discoverer of the path, the one skilled in the path. And his disciples now dwell following that path and become possessed of it afterwards.[514] And I, venerable sir, invite the Blessed One: Is there any deed of mine, either bodily or verbal, which the Blessed One would censure?"

"There is no deed of yours, Sāriputta, either bodily or verbal, that I censure. For you, Sāriputta, are wise, one of great wisdom, of wide wisdom, of joyous wisdom, of swift wisdom, <412> of sharp wisdom, of penetrative wisdom. Just as the eldest son of a wheel-turning monarch properly keeps in motion the wheel [of sovereignty] set in motion by his father, so do you, Sāriputta, properly keep in motion the Wheel of Dhamma set in motion by me."[515]

"If, venerable sir, the Blessed One does not censure any deed of mine, bodily or verbal, does he censure any deed, bodily or verbal, of these five hundred bhikkhus?"

"There is no deed, Sāriputta, bodily or verbal, of these five hundred bhikkhus that I censure. For of these five hundred bhikkhus, Sāriputta, sixty bhikkhus are triple-knowledge bearers, sixty bhikkhus are bearers of the six direct knowledges, sixty bhikkhus are liberated in both ways, while the rest are liberated by wisdom."[516]

Then the Venerable Vaṅgīsa rose from his seat, arranged his upper robe over one shoulder, and, raising his joined hands in reverential salutation towards the Blessed One, said to him: "An inspiration has come to me, Blessed One! An inspiration has come to me, Fortunate One!"

The Blessed One said: "Then express your inspiration, Vaṅgīsa." <413>

Then the Venerable Vaṅgīsa extolled the Blessed One to his face with suitable verses:

734 "Five hundred bhikkhus have gathered today,
The fifteenth day, for purification—
Untroubled seers who have ended renewed existence,
Who have cut off all fetters and bonds. [192]

735 "Just as a king, a wheel-turning monarch,
Accompanied by his ministers,
Travels all over this mighty earth
Bounded by the deep dark ocean—
736 So they attend on the victor in battle,
The unsurpassed caravan leader—
The disciples bearing the triple knowledge,
Who have left Death far behind.[517]

737 "All are true sons of the Blessed One,
Here no worthless chaff is found.
I worship the Kinsman of the Sun, <414>
Destroyer of the dart of craving."

8 Over a Thousand

On one occasion the Blessed One was dwelling at Sāvatthī in Jeta's Grove, Anāthapiṇḍika's Park, together with a great Saṅgha of bhikkhus, with 1,250 bhikkhus. Now on that occasion the Blessed One was instructing, exhorting, inspiring, and encouraging the bhikkhus with a Dhamma talk concerning Nibbāna. And those bhikkhus were listening to the Dhamma with eager ears, attending to it as a matter of vital concern, directing their whole mind to it.

Then it occurred to the Venerable Vaṅgīsa: "This Blessed One is instructing the bhikkhus with a Dhamma talk concerning Nibbāna. And those bhikkhus are listening to the Dhamma with eager ears.... Let me extol the Blessed One to his face with suitable verses."

Then the Venerable Vaṅgīsa rose from his seat, arranged his upper robe over one shoulder, and, raising his joined hands in reverential salutation towards the Blessed One, said to him: "An inspiration has come to me, Blessed One! An inspiration has come to me, Fortunate One!"

"Then express your inspiration, Vaṅgīsa."

Then the Venerable Vaṅgīsa extolled the Blessed One to his face with suitable verses: <415>

738 "Over a thousand bhikkhus here
Attend upon the Fortunate One
As he teaches the dust-free Dhamma,
Nibbāna inaccessible to fear.[518]

739 "They listen to the stainless Dhamma
Taught by the Perfectly Enlightened One.
The Enlightened One indeed shines
Honoured by the Bhikkhu Saṅgha.

740 "O Blessed One, your name is 'Nāga,'
The best seer of the seers.
Like a great cloud bearing rain
You pour down on the disciples.[519] [193]

741 "Having emerged from his daytime abode
From a desire to behold the Teacher,
Your disciple Vaṅgīsa, O great hero,
Bows down in worship at your feet."

"Had you already thought out these verses, Vaṅgīsa, or did they occur to you spontaneously?"[520] <416>

"I had not already thought out these verses, venerable sir; they occurred to me spontaneously."

"In that case, Vaṅgīsa, let some more verses, not already thought out, occur to you."

"Yes, venerable sir," the Venerable Vaṅgīsa replied. Then he extolled the Blessed One with some more verses that had not been previously thought out:

742 "Having overcome the deviant course of Māra's path,
You fare having demolished barrenness of mind.
Behold him, the releaser from bondage,
Unattached, dissecting into parts.[521]

743 "For the sake of leading us across the flood
You declared the path with its many aspects.

The seers of Dhamma stand immovable
In that Deathless declared by you.[522] <417>

744 "The light-maker, having pierced right through,
Saw the transcendence of all stations;
Having known and realized it himself,
He taught the chief matter to the five.[523]

745 "When the Dhamma has been so well taught,
What negligence is there for those who understand it?
Therefore, living diligent in the Blessed One's Teaching,
One should always reverently train in it."

9 Koṇḍañña

On one occasion the Blessed One was dwelling at Rājagaha in the Bamboo Grove, the Squirrel Sanctuary. Then the Venerable Aññā Koṇḍañña, after a very long absence, approached the Blessed One, prostrated himself with his head at the Blessed One's feet, kissed the Blessed One's feet, [194] stroked them with his hands, <418> and announced his name thus: "I am Koṇḍañña, Blessed One! I am Koṇḍañña, Fortunate One!"[524]

Then it occurred to the Venerable Vaṅgīsa: "This Venerable Aññā Koṇḍañña, after a very long absence, has approached the Blessed One … kisses the Blessed One's feet, strokes them with his hands, and announces his name…. Let me extol the Venerable Aññā Koṇḍañña in the Blessed One's presence with suitable verses."

Then the Venerable Vaṅgīsa rose from his seat, arranged his upper robe over one shoulder, and, raising his joined hands in reverential salutation towards the Blessed One, said to him: "An inspiration has come to me, Blessed One! An inspiration has come to me, Fortunate One!"

"Then express your inspiration, Vaṅgīsa."

Then the Venerable Vaṅgīsa extolled the Venerable Aññā Koṇḍañña in the Blessed One's presence with suitable verses:

746 "Enlightened in succession to the Buddha,
The elder Koṇḍañña, of strong endeavour,

Is one who gains pleasant dwellings,
One who often gains the seclusions.[525]

747 "Whatever may be attained by a disciple
Who practises the Master's Teaching,
All that has been attained by him, <419>
One who trained diligently.

748 "Of great might, a triple-knowledge man,
Skilled in the course of others' minds—
Koṇḍañña, a true heir of the Buddha,
Pays homage at the Teacher's feet."[526]

10 Moggallāna

On one occasion the Blessed One was dwelling at Rājagaha on the Black Rock on the Isigili Slope, together with a great Saṅgha of bhikkhus, with five hundred bhikkhus all of whom were arahants. Thereupon the Venerable Mahāmoggallāna searched their minds with his own mind [and saw that they were] released, without acquisitions.

Then it occurred to the Venerable Vaṅgīsa: "The Blessed One is dwelling at Rājagaha on the Black Rock on the Isigili Slope.... Thereupon the Venerable Mahāmoggallāna has searched their minds with his own mind [and seen that they are] released, without acquisitions. Let me extol the Venerable Mahāmoggallāna in the Blessed One's presence with suitable verses." [195]

Then the Venerable Vaṅgīsa rose from his seat, arranged his upper robe over one shoulder, and, raising his joined hands in reverential salutation towards the Blessed One, said to him: <420> "An inspiration has come to me, Blessed One! An inspiration has come to me, Fortunate One!"

"Then express your inspiration, Vaṅgīsa."

Then the Venerable Vaṅgīsa extolled the Venerable Mahāmoggallāna in the Blessed One's presence with suitable verses:

749 "While the sage is seated on the mountain slope,
Gone to the far shore of suffering,
His disciples sit in attendance on him,
Triple-knowledge men who have left Death behind.

750 "Moggallāna, great in spiritual power,
Encompassed their minds with his own,
And searching [he came to see] their minds:
Fully released, without acquisitions!

751 "Thus those perfect in many qualities
Attend upon Gotama,
The sage perfect in all respects,
Gone to the far shore of suffering."[527]

11 Gaggarā

On one occasion the Blessed One was dwelling at Campā on the bank of the Gaggarā Lotus Pond together with a great Saṅgha of bhikkhus, with five hundred bhikkhus, seven hundred male lay followers, <421> seven hundred female lay followers, and many thousands of devatās. The Blessed One outshone them in beauty and glory.

Then it occurred to the Venerable Vaṅgīsa: "This Blessed One is dwelling at Campā … and many thousands of devatās. The Blessed One outshines them in beauty and glory. Let me extol the Blessed One to his face with suitable verses."

Then the Venerable Vaṅgīsa rose from his seat, arranged his upper robe over one shoulder, and, raising his joined hands in reverential salutation towards the Blessed One, said to him: "An inspiration has come to me, Blessed One! An inspiration has come to me, Fortunate One!"

"Then express your inspiration, Vaṅgīsa."

Then the Venerable Vaṅgīsa extolled the Blessed One to his face with a suitable verse: [196]

752 "As the moon shines in a cloudless sky,
As the sun shines devoid of stain,
So you, Aṅgīrasa, O great sage,
Outshine the whole world with your glory."

12 Vaṅgīsa

<422> On one occasion the Venerable Vaṅgīsa was dwelling at Sāvatthī in Jeta's Grove, Anāthapiṇḍika's Park. Now on that

occasion the Venerable Vaṅgīsa had only recently attained arahantship and, while experiencing the happiness of liberation, on that occasion he recited these verses:[528]

753 "Drunk on poetry, I used to wander
From village to village, town to town.
Then I saw the Enlightened One
And faith arose within me.[529]

754 "He then taught me the Dhamma:
Aggregates, sense bases, and elements.
Having heard the Dhamma from him,
I went forth into homelessness.

755 "Indeed, for the good of many,
The sage attained enlightenment,
For the bhikkhus and bhikkhunīs <423>
Who have reached and seen the fixed course.[530]

756 "Welcome indeed has it been for me,
My coming into the Buddha's presence.
The three knowledges have been obtained,
The Buddha's Teaching has been done.

757 "I know now my past abodes,
The divine eye is purified.
A triple knowledge man, attained to spiritual powers,
I am skilled in the course of others' minds."[531]

[197] <424>

Chapter IX

9 *Vanasaṃyutta*

Connected Discourses in the Woods

1 Seclusion

Thus have I heard. On one occasion a certain bhikkhu was dwelling among the Kosalans in a certain woodland thicket. Now on that occasion, while that bhikkhu had gone for his day's abiding, he kept on thinking evil unwholesome thoughts connected with the household life.

Then the devatā that inhabited that woodland thicket, having compassion for that bhikkhu, desiring his good, desiring to stir up a sense of urgency in him, approached him and addressed him in verses:

758 "Desiring seclusion you entered the woods,
Yet your mind gushes outwardly.
Remove, man, the desire for people;
Then you'll be happy, devoid of lust.[532]

759 "You must abandon discontent, be mindful—
Let us remind [you] of that [way] of the good. <425>
Hard to cross, indeed, is the dusty abyss;
Don't let sensual dust drag you down.[533]

760 "Just as a bird littered with soil
With a shake flicks off the sticky dust,
So a bhikkhu, strenuous and mindful,
With a shake flicks off the sticky dust."

Then that bhikkhu, stirred up by that devatā, acquired a sense of urgency.

2 Rousing

On one occasion a certain bhikkhu was dwelling among the Kosalans in a certain woodland thicket. [198] Now on that occasion when that bhikkhu had gone for his day's abiding he fell asleep.[534] Then the devatā that inhabited that woodland thicket, having compassion for that bhikkhu, desiring his good, desiring to stir up a sense of urgency in him, approached him and addressed him in verses:

761 "Get up, bhikkhu, why lie down? <426>
What need do you have for sleep?
What slumber [can there be] for one afflicted,
Stricken, pierced by the dart?

762 "Nurture in yourself that faith
With which you left behind the home life
And went forth into homelessness:
Don't come under sloth's control."

[The bhikkhu:][535]
763 "Sensual pleasures are impermanent, unstable,
Though the dullard is enthralled with them.
When he's free, detached among those bound,
Why trouble one gone forth?

764 "When, by the removal of desire and lust
And the transcendence of ignorance,
That knowledge has been cleansed,
Why trouble one gone forth?[536] <427>

765 "When, by breaking ignorance with knowledge
And by destruction of the taints,
He is sorrowless, beyond despair,
Why trouble one gone forth?

766 "When he is energetic and resolute,
Always firm in his exertion,
Aspiring to attain Nibbāna,
Why trouble one gone forth?"[537]

3 Kassapagotta

On one occasion the Venerable Kassapagotta was dwelling among the Kosalans in a certain woodland thicket. Now on that occasion, when he had gone for his day's abiding, the Venerable Kassapagotta exhorted a certain hunter.[538] Then the devatā that inhabited that woodland thicket, having compassion for the Venerable Kassapagotta, desiring his good, desiring to stir up a sense of urgency in him, approached him and addressed him in verses:

767 "The bhikkhu strikes me as a dolt <428>
Who out of season exhorts a hunter
Roaming in the rugged mountains
With little wisdom, devoid of sense.

768 "He listens but does not understand,
He looks but does not see;
Though the Dhamma is being spoken,
The fool does not grasp the meaning. [199]

769 "Even if you would bring ten lamps
[Into his presence], Kassapa,
Still he would not see forms,
For he does not have eyes to see."

Then the Venerable Kassapagotta, stirred up by that devatā, acquired a sense of urgency.

4 A Number

On one occasion a number of bhikkhus were dwelling among the Kosalans in a certain woodland thicket. Then, when they had spent the rains there, after the three months had passed those bhikkhus set out on tour. <429> Then the devatā that inhabited that woodland thicket, not seeing those bhikkhus, lamenting, on that occasion recited this verse:

770 "Today discontent appears to me
When I see here so many vacant seats.

Where have they gone, Gotama's disciples,
Those splendid speakers rich in learning?"[539]

When this was said, another devatā replied in verse:

771 "They've gone to Magadha, gone to Kosala,
And some are in the Vajjian land.
Like deer that roam free from ties,
The bhikkhus dwell without abode."[540]

5 Ānanda

On one occasion the Venerable Ānanda was dwelling among the Kosalans in a certain woodland thicket. Now on that occasion the Venerable Ānanda was excessively involved instructing lay people.[541] <430> Then the devatā that inhabited that woodland thicket, having compassion for the Venerable Ānanda, desiring his good, desiring to stir up a sense of urgency in him, approached him and addressed him in verse:

772 "Having entered the thicket at the foot of a tree,
Having placed Nibbāna in your heart, [200]
Meditate, Gotama, and don't be negligent!
What will this hullabaloo do for you?"[542]

Then the Venerable Ānanda, stirred up by that deity, acquired a sense of urgency.

6 Anuruddha

On one occasion the Venerable Anuruddha was dwelling among the Kosalans in a certain woodland thicket. Then a certain devatā of the Tāvatiṃsa host named Jālinī, a former consort of the Venerable Anuruddha, approached him and addressed him in verse:[543]

773 "Direct your mind there [to that realm]
Where you dwelt in the past
Among the Tāvatiṃsa devas <431>
For whom all desires are fulfilled.

You will shine forth highly honoured,
Surrounded by celestial maidens."

[Anuruddha:]
774 "Miserable are celestial maidens
Established in identity,
And miserable too are those beings
Attached to celestial maidens."[544]

[Jālinī:]
775 "They do not know bliss
Who have not seen Nandana,
The abode of the glorious male devas
Belonging to the host of Thirty."

[Anuruddha:]
776 "Don't you know, you fool,
That maxim of the arahants?
Impermanent are all formations;
Their nature is to arise and vanish.
Having arisen, they cease:
Their appeasement is blissful.

777 "Now I will never again dwell <432>
Among the deva host, Jālinī!
The wandering on in birth is ended:
Now there is no more renewed existence."

7 Nāgadatta

On one occasion the Venerable Nāgadatta was dwelling among the Kosalans in a certain woodland thicket.[545] Now on that occasion the Venerable Nāgadatta had been entering the village too early and returning too late in the day. Then the devatā that inhabited that woodland thicket, having compassion for the Venerable Nāgadatta, desiring his good, desiring to stir up a sense of urgency in him, [201] approached him and addressed him in verses:

778 "Entering the village early,
Returning late in the day,
Nāgadatta associates too closely with lay folk,
Sharing their happiness and suffering.[546]

779 "I am afraid for Nāgadatta,
So impudent, bound to families.
Do not come under the End-maker's control, <433>
[In the grip] of the powerful King of Death."

Then the Venerable Nāgadatta, stirred up by that deity, acquired a sense of urgency.

8 Family Mistress

On one occasion a certain bhikkhu was dwelling among the Kosalans in a certain woodland thicket. Now on that occasion that bhikkhu had become excessively intimate with a certain family. Then the devatā that inhabited that woodland thicket, having compassion for that bhikkhu, desiring his good, desiring to stir up a sense of urgency in him, manifested herself in the form of the mistress of that family. Having approached that bhikkhu, she addressed him in verse:[547]

780 "By the riverbanks and in the rest house,
In the meeting halls and along the roads,
People meet and gossip about this:
What's going on between you and me?"

[The bhikkhu:]
781 "There are many disagreeable sounds <434>
That an ascetic must patiently endure.
One should not be dismayed because of that,
For it is not by this one is defiled.

782 "If one is frightened by random sounds
Like an antelope dwelling in the woods,
They call him 'one with a fickle mind':
His practice does not succeed."[548]

9 Vajjian Prince (or Vesālī)

On one occasion a certain bhikkhu, a Vajjian prince, was dwelling at Vesālī in a certain woodland thicket. Now on that occasion an all-night festival was being held in Vesālī. [202] Then that bhikkhu, lamenting as he heard the clamour of instruments, gongs, and music coming from Vesālī,[549] on that occasion recited this verse:

783 "We dwell in the forest all alone
Like a log rejected in the woods.
On such a splendid night as this <435>
Who is there worse off than us?"

Then the devatā that inhabited that woodland thicket, having compassion for that bhikkhu, desiring his good, desiring to stir up a sense of urgency in him, approached him and addressed him in verse:

784 "As you dwell in the forest all alone
Like a log rejected in the woods,
Many are those who envy you,
As hell-beings envy those going to heaven."[550]

Then that bhikkhu, stirred up by that devatā, acquired a sense of urgency.

10 Reciting

On one occasion a certain bhikkhu was dwelling among the Kosalans in a certain woodland thicket. Now on that occasion that bhikkhu had been excessively engrossed in recitation, but on a later occasion he passed the time living at ease and keeping silent.[551] Then the devatā that inhabited that woodland thicket, no longer hearing that bhikkhu recite the Dhamma, <436> approached him and addressed him in verse:

785 "Bhikkhu, why don't you recite Dhamma-stanzas,
Living in communion with other bhikkhus?

Hearing the Dhamma, one gains confidence;
In this very life [the reciter] gains praise."

[The bhikkhu:]
786 "In the past I was fond of Dhamma-stanzas
So long as I had not achieved dispassion. [203]
But from the time I achieved dispassion
[I dwell in what] the good men call
'The laying down by final knowledge
Of whatever is seen, heard, or sensed.'"[552]

11 Unwholesome Thoughts

On one occasion a certain bhikkhu was dwelling among the Kosalans in a certain woodland thicket. Now on that occasion, when that bhikkhu had gone for the day's abiding, he kept on thinking evil unwholesome thoughts, that is, thoughts of sensuality, ill will, and harming. <437> Then the devatā that inhabited that woodland thicket, having compassion for that bhikkhu, desiring his good, desiring to stir up a sense of urgency in him, approached him and addressed him in verses:

787 "Because of attending carelessly,
You, sir, are eaten by your thoughts.
Having relinquished the careless way,
You should reflect carefully.[553]

788 "By basing your thoughts on the Teacher,
On Dhamma, Saṅgha, and your own virtues,
You will surely attain to gladness,
And rapture and happiness as well.
Then when you are suffused with gladness,
You'll make an end to suffering."

Then that bhikkhu, stirred up by that devatā, acquired a sense of urgency.

12 Noon

On one occasion a certain bhikkhu was dwelling among the

Kosalans in a certain woodland thicket. Then the devatā that inhabited that woodland thicket <438> approached that bhikkhu and recited this verse in his presence:

789 "When the noon hour sets in
And the birds have settled down,
The mighty forest itself murmurs:
How fearful that appears to me!"

[The bhikkhu:]
790 "When the noon hour sets in
And the birds have settled down,
The mighty forest itself murmurs:
How delightful that appears to me!"

13 Loose in Sense Faculties

On one occasion a number of bhikkhus were dwelling among the Kosalans in a certain woodland thicket. They were restless, puffed up, personally vain, rough-tongued, [204] rambling in their talk, muddle-minded, without clear comprehension, unconcentrated, scatter-brained, loose in their sense faculties. Then the devatā that inhabited that woodland thicket, having compassion for those bhikkhus, desiring their good, <439> desiring to stir up a sense of urgency in them, approached them and addressed them with verses:

791 "In the past the bhikkhus lived happily,
The disciples of Gotama.
Without wishes they sought their alms,
Without wishes they used their lodgings.
Having known the world's impermanence,
They made an end to suffering.

792 "But now like headmen in a village
They make themselves hard to maintain.
They eat and eat and then lie down,
Infatuated in others' homes.

793 "Having reverently saluted the Saṅgha,
I here speak only about some:
They are rejected, without protector,
Become just like the dead.

794 "My statement is made with reference
To those who dwell in negligence.
As for those who dwell in diligence,
To them I humbly pay homage."

Then those bhikkhus, stirred up by that devatā, acquired a sense of urgency. <440>

14 The Thief of Scent

On one occasion a certain bhikkhu was dwelling among the Kosalans in a certain woodland thicket. Now on that occasion, when he had returned from his alms round, after his meal that bhikkhu used to descend into a pond and sniff a red lotus. Then the devatā that inhabited that woodland thicket, having compassion for that bhikkhu, desiring his good, desiring to stir up a sense of urgency in him, approached him and addressed him in verse:[554]

795 "When you sniff this lotus flower,
An item that has not been given,
This is one factor of theft:
You, dear sir, are a thief of scent."

[The bhikkhu:]
796 "I do not take, I do not damage,
I sniff the lotus from afar;
So for what reason do you say
That I am a thief of scent?[555]

797 "One who digs up the lotus stalks,
One who damages the flowers,
One of such rough behaviour: <441>
Why is he not spoken to?"[556] [205]

[The devatā:]
798 "When a person is rough and fierce,
Badly soiled like a nursing cloth,
I have nothing to say to him;
But it's to you that I ought to speak.

799 "For a person without blemish,
Always in quest of purity,
Even a mere hair's tip of evil
Appears as big as a cloud."

[The bhikkhu:]
800 "Surely, spirit, you understand me,
And you have compassion for me.
Please, O spirit, speak to me again,
Whenever you see such a deed."

[The devatā:]
801 "We don't live with your support,
Nor are we your hired servant.
You, bhikkhu, should know for yourself <442>
The way to a good destination."[557]

Then that bhikkhu, stirred by that devatā, acquired a sense of urgency.

[206] <443> Chapter X

10 *Yakkhasaṃyutta*

Connected Discourses with Yakkhas

1 Indaka

Thus have I heard. On one occasion the Blessed One was dwelling at Rājagaha on Mount Inda's Peak, the haunt of the yakkha Indaka.[558] Then the yakkha Indaka approached the Blessed One and addressed him in verse:

802 "As the Buddhas say that form is not the soul,
How then does one obtain this body?
From where do one's bones and liver come?
How is one begotten in the womb?"[559]

[The Blessed One:]
803 "First there is the *kalala*;
From the *kalala* comes the *abbuda*;
From the *abbuda* the *pesī* is produced;
From the *pesī* the *ghana* arises;
From the *ghana* emerge the limbs,
The head-hair, body-hair, and nails. <444>
804 And whatever food the mother eats—
The meals and drink that she consumes—
By this the being there is maintained,
The person inside the mother's womb."[560]

2 Sakkanāmaka

On one occasion the Blessed One was dwelling at Rājagaha on Mount Vulture Peak. Then the yakkha Sakkanāmaka approached the Blessed One and addressed him in verse:

805 "Having abandoned all the knots
As one fully released,
It isn't good for you, an ascetic,
To be instructing others."[561]

[The Blessed One:]
806 "If, O Sakka, for some reason
Intimacy with anyone should arise,
The wise man ought not to stir his mind
With compassion towards such a person.

807 "But if with a mind clear and pure
He gives instructions to others,
He does not become fettered <445>
By his compassion and sympathy."[562] [207]

3 Sūciloma

On one occasion the Blessed One was dwelling at Gayā at the Ṭaṅkita Bed, the haunt of the yakkha Sūciloma.[563] Now on that occasion the yakkha Khara and the yakkha Sūciloma were passing by not far from the Blessed One. Then the yakkha Khara said to the yakkha Sūciloma: "That is an ascetic."

"That is not an ascetic; that is a sham ascetic.[564] I'll soon find out whether he is an ascetic or a sham ascetic."

Then the yakkha Sūciloma approached the Blessed One and bent over the Blessed One. The Blessed One drew back. Then the yakkha Sūciloma said to the Blessed One: "Are you afraid of me, ascetic?"

"I'm not afraid of you, friend. It is just that your touch is evil."[565] <446>

"I'll ask you a question, ascetic. If you won't answer me, I'll drive you insane or I'll split your heart or I'll grab you by the feet and hurl you across the Ganges."

"I do not see anyone in this world, friend, with its devas, Māra, and Brahmā, in this generation with its ascetics and brahmins, its devas and humans, who could drive me insane or split my heart or grab me by the feet and hurl me across the Ganges. But ask whatever you want, friend."

808 "What is the source of lust and hatred?
Whence spring discontent, delight, and terror?
Having arisen from what do the mind's thoughts
[Toss one around] as boys toss up a crow?"[566] <447>

[The Blessed One:]
809 "Lust and hatred have their source here;
From this spring discontent, delight, and terror;
Having arisen from this, the mind's thoughts
[Toss one around] as boys toss up a crow.[567]

810 "Sprung from affection, arisen from oneself,
Like the trunk-born shoots of the banyan tree;
Manifold, clinging to sensual pleasures,
Like a *māluvā* creeper stretched across the woods. [568] [208]

811 "Those who understand their source,
They dispel it—listen, O yakkha!—
They cross this flood so hard to cross,
Uncrossed before, for no renewed existence."[569]

4 Maṇibhadda

On one occasion the Blessed One was dwelling among the Magadhans at the Maṇimālaka Shrine, the haunt of the yakkha Maṇibhadda. Then the yakkha Maṇibhadda approached the Blessed One and in the Blessed One's presence recited this verse:

812 "It is always good for the mindful one,
The mindful one thrives in happiness.
It is better each day for the mindful one,
And he is freed from enmity."[570]

[The Blessed One:] <448>
813 "It is always good for the mindful one,
The mindful one thrives in happiness.
It is better each day for the mindful one,
But he is not freed from enmity.

814 "One whose mind all day and night
Takes delight in harmlessness,
Who has lovingkindness for all beings—
For him there is enmity with none."[571]

5 Sānu

On one occasion the Blessed One was dwelling at Sāvatthī in Jeta's Grove, Anāthapiṇḍika's Park. Now on that occasion a certain female lay follower had a son named Sānu who had been possessed by a yakkha.[572] Then that female lay follower, lamenting, on that occasion recited these verses:

816 "With those who lead the holy life,[573]
Who observe the Uposatha days
Complete in eight factors
On the fourteenth or fifteenth,
817 And on the eighths of the fortnight, <449>
And during special periods,
The yakkhas do not sport around:
So I have heard from the arahants.
But now today I see for myself
The yakkhas sporting with Sānu."

[The yakkha that has entered Sānu:] [209]
818 "With those who lead the holy life,
Who observe the Uposatha days
Complete in eight factors
On the fourteenth or fifteenth,
819 And on the eighths of the fortnight,
And during special periods,
The yakkhas do not sport around:
What you heard from the arahants is good.

820 "When Sānu has awakened tell him
This injunction of the yakkhas: <450>
Do not do an evil deed
Either openly or in secret.
821 If you should do an evil deed,
Or if you are doing one now,

You won't be free from suffering
Though you fly up and flee."[574]

[Sānu:][575]
822 "They weep, mother, for the dead
Or for one living who isn't seen.
When you see, mother, that I'm alive,
Why, O mother, do you weep for me?"

[Sānu's mother:]
823 "They weep, O son, for the dead
Or for one living who isn't seen;
But when one returns to the home life
After renouncing sensual pleasures,
They weep for this one too, my son,
For though alive he's really dead.[576]

824 "Drawn out, my dear, from hot embers, <451>
You wish to plunge into hot embers;
Drawn out, my dear, from an inferno,
You wish to plunge into an inferno.[577]

825 "Run forward, good luck be with you!
To whom could we voice our grief?
Being an item rescued from the fire,
You wish to be burnt again."[578]

6 Piyaṅkara

On one occasion the Venerable Anuruddha was dwelling at Sāvatthī in Jeta's Grove, Anāthapiṇḍika's Park. Now on that occasion the Venerable Anuruddha, having risen at the first flush of dawn, was reciting stanzas of Dhamma. Then the female yakkha Piyaṅkara's Mother hushed her little child thus:[579]

826 "Do not make a sound, Piyaṅkara,
A bhikkhu recites Dhamma-stanzas. <452>
Having understood a Dhamma-stanza,
We might practise for our welfare.

827 "Let us refrain from harming living beings,
Let us not speak a deliberate lie,
We should train ourselves in virtue:
Perhaps we'll be freed from the goblin realm."

7 Punabbasu

On one occasion the Blessed One was dwelling at Sāvatthī in Jeta's Grove, Anāthapiṇḍika's Park. [210] Now on that occasion the Blessed One was instructing, exhorting, inspiring, and gladdening the bhikkhus with a Dhamma talk concerning Nibbāna. And those bhikkhus were listening to the Dhamma with eager ears, attending to it as a matter of vital concern, applying their whole mind to it. Then the female yakkha Punabbasu's Mother hushed her little children thus:[580]

828 "Be quiet, Uttarikā,
Be quiet, Punabbasu! <453>
I wish to listen to the Dhamma
Of the Teacher, the Supreme Buddha.

829 "When the Blessed One speaks of Nibbāna,
Release from all the knots,
There has arisen within me
Deep affection for this Dhamma.

830 "In the world one's own son is dear,
In the world one's own husband is dear;
But for me the quest for this Dhamma
Has become even dearer than them.

831 "For neither one's own son nor husband,
Though dear, can release one from suffering
As listening to true Dhamma frees one
From the suffering of living beings.[581]

832 "In this world steeped in suffering,
Fettered by aging and death,
I wish to listen to the Dhamma
That he—the Buddha—fully awakened to,

For freedom from aging and death.
So be quiet, Punabbasu!"[582] <454>

[Punabbasu:]
833 "Mother dear, I am not talking;
This Uttarā is silent, too.
Pay attention only to the Dhamma,
For listening to true Dhamma is pleasant.
Because we have not known true Dhamma
We've been living miserably, mother.

834 "He is the maker of light
For bewildered devas and humans;
Enlightened, bearing his final body,
The One with Vision teaches the Dhamma."

[Punabbasu's mother:]
835 "It is good that my son has become so wise,
He whom I bore and nursed at my breast.
My son loves the pure Dhamma
Of the Supremely Enlightened One.

836 "Punabbasu, be happy!
Today I have emerged at last. <455>
Hear me too, O Uttarā:
The noble truths are seen!"[583]

8 Sudatta

On one occasion the Blessed One was dwelling at Rājagaha in the Cool Grove. Now on that occasion the householder Anāthapiṇḍika had arrived in Rājagaha on some business.[584] He heard: "A Buddha, it is said, has arisen in the world!" He wanted to go and see the Blessed One immediately, [211] but it occurred to him: "It is not the right time to go and see the Blessed One today. I will go and see the Blessed One early tomorrow morning."

He lay down with his mindfulness directed to the Buddha, and during the night he got up three times thinking it was morning. Then the householder Anāthapiṇḍika approached the gate of the charnel ground. Nonhuman beings opened the gate.

<456> Then, as the householder Anāthapiṇḍika was leaving the city, the light disappeared and darkness appeared. Fear, trepidation, and terror arose in him and he wanted to turn back. But the yakkha Sīvaka, invisible, made the proclamation:[585]

837 "A hundred [thousand] elephants,
A hundred [thousand] horses,
A hundred [thousand] mule-drawn chariots,
A hundred thousand maidens
Adorned with jewellery and earrings,
Are not worth a sixteenth part
Of a single step forward.[586]

"Go forward, householder! Go forward, householder! Going forward is better for you, not turning back again."

Then the darkness disappeared and light appeared to the householder Anāthapiṇḍika, and the fear, trepidation, and terror that had arisen in him subsided.

A second time ... (*verse 838 is included in this repetition*) <457> ... A third time the light disappeared and darkness appeared before the householder Anāthapiṇḍika. Fear, trepidation, and terror arose in him and he wanted to turn back. But a third time the yakkha Sīvaka, invisible, made the proclamation:

839 "A hundred [thousand] elephants ...
Of a single step forward.

"Go forward, householder! Go forward, householder! Going forward is better for you, not turning back again."

Then the darkness [212] disappeared and light appeared to the householder Anāthapiṇḍika, and the fear, trepidation, and terror that had arisen in him subsided.

Then the householder Anāthapiṇḍika approached the Blessed One in the Cool Grove. Now on that occasion the Blessed One, having risen at the first flush of dawn, was walking back and forth in the open. The Blessed One saw the householder Anāthapiṇḍika coming in the distance. He descended from the walkway, sat down in the seat that was prepared, and said to the householder Anāthapiṇḍika: "Come, Sudatta."[587]

Then the householder Anāthapiṇḍika, thinking, "The Blessed

One has addressed me by my name," [thrilled and elated],[588] prostrated himself right on the spot with his head at the Blessed One's feet <458> and said to him: "I hope, venerable sir, that the Blessed One slept well."

[The Blessed One:]
840 "Always indeed he sleeps well,
The brahmin who is fully quenched,
Who does not cling to sensual pleasures,
Cool at heart, without acquisitions.

841 "Having cut off all attachments,
Having removed care from the heart,
The peaceful one sleeps well,
Having attained peace of mind."[589]

9 Sukkā (1)

On one occasion the Blessed One was dwelling at Rājagaha in the Bamboo Grove, the Squirrel Sanctuary. Now on that occasion the bhikkhunī Sukkā, surrounded by a large assembly, was teaching the Dhamma. Then a yakkha who had full confidence in the bhikkhunī Sukkā, going from street to street and from square to square in Rājagaha, on that occasion recited these verses:

842 "What has happened to these people in Rājagaha? <459>
They sleep as if they've been drinking mead.
Why don't they attend on Sukkā
As she teaches the deathless state?[590]

843 "But the wise, as it were, drink it up—
That [Dhamma] irresistible,
Ambrosial, nutritious—
As travellers do a cloud."[591]

10 Sukkā (2)

On one occasion the Blessed One was dwelling at Rājagaha in the Bamboo Grove, the Squirrel Sanctuary. [213] Now on that occasion a certain lay follower gave food to the bhikkhunī

Sukkā. Then a yakkha who had full confidence in the bhikkhunī Sukkā, going from street to street and from square to square in Rājagaha, on that occasion recited this verse:

844 "He has engendered much merit—
Wise indeed is this lay follower,
Who just gave food to Sukkā, <460>
One released from all the knots."[592]

11 Cīrā

On one occasion the Blessed One was dwelling at Rājagaha in the Bamboo Grove, the Squirrel Sanctuary. Now on that occasion a certain lay follower gave a robe to the bhikkhunī Cīrā. Then a yakkha who had full confidence in the bhikkhunī Cīrā, going from street to street and from square to square in Rājagaha, on that occasion recited this verse:

845 "He has engendered much merit—
Wise indeed is this lay follower,
Who just gave a robe to Cīrā,
One released from all the bonds."

12 Āḷavaka

Thus have I heard. On one occasion the Blessed One was dwelling at Āḷavī, the haunt of the yakkha Āḷavaka.[593] Then the yakkha Āḷavaka approached the Blessed One and said to him: "Get out, ascetic!" <461>

"All right, friend," the Blessed One said, and he went out.[594]

"Come in, ascetic."

"All right, friend," the Blessed One said, and he went in.

A second time ... [214] A third time the yakkha Āḷavaka said to the Blessed One: "Get out, ascetic!"

"All right, friend," the Blessed One said, and he went out.

"Come in, ascetic."

"All right, friend," the Blessed One said, and he went in.

A fourth time the yakkha Āḷavaka said to the Blessed One: "Get out, ascetic."

"I won't go out, friend. Do whatever you have to do."

"I'll ask you a question, ascetic. If you won't answer me, I'll drive you insane or I'll split your heart or I'll grab you by the feet and hurl you across the Ganges."[595]

"I do not see anyone in this world, friend, with its devas, Māra, and Brahmā, in this generation with its ascetics and brahmins, its devas and humans, who could drive me insane or split my heart or grab me by the feet and hurl me across the Ganges. But ask whatever you want, friend."[596]

[Āḷavaka:] <462>

846 "What here is a man's best treasure?
What practised well brings happiness?
What is really the sweetest of tastes?
How lives the one who they say lives best?"

[The Blessed One:]

847 "Faith is here a man's best treasure;
Dhamma practised well brings happiness;
Truth is really the sweetest of tastes;
One living by wisdom they say lives best."[597]

[Āḷavaka:]

848 "How does one cross over the flood?
How does one cross the rugged sea?
How does one overcome suffering?
How is one purified?"

[The Blessed One:]

849 "By faith one crosses over the flood,
By diligence, the rugged sea.
By energy one overcomes suffering,
By wisdom one is purified."[598]

[Āḷavaka:]

850 "How does one gain wisdom?[599]
How does one find wealth? <463>
How does one achieve acclaim?
How bind friends to oneself?
When passing from this world to the next,
How does one not sorrow?"

[The Blessed One:]

851 "Placing faith in the Dhamma of the arahants
For the attainment of Nibbāna,
From desire to learn one gains wisdom
If one is diligent and astute.[600]

852 "Doing what is proper, dutiful,
One with initiative finds wealth. [215]
By truthfulness one wins acclaim;
Giving, one binds friends.
That is how one does not sorrow
When passing from this world to the next.[601]

853 "The faithful seeker of the household life
In whom dwell these four qualities—
Truth, Dhamma, steadfastness, generosity—
Does not sorrow when he passes on. <464>

854 "Come now, ask others as well,
The many ascetics and brahmins,
Whether there is found here anything better
Than truth, self-control, generosity, and patience."[602]

[Āḷavaka:]

855 "Why now should I ask this question
Of the many ascetics and brahmins?
Today I have understood
The good pertaining to the future life.[603]

856 "Indeed, for my sake the Buddha came
To reside at Āḷavī.
Today I have understood
Where a gift bears great fruit.

857 "I myself will travel about
From village to village, town to town,
Paying homage to the Enlightened One
And to the excellence of the Dhamma."[604] <465>

[216] <466>

Chapter XI

11 *Sakkasaṃyutta*

Connected Discourses with Sakka

I. The First Subchapter (Suvīra)

1 (1) Suvīra

Thus have I heard. On one occasion the Blessed One was dwelling at Sāvatthī in Jeta's Grove, Anāthapiṇḍika's Park. There the Blessed One addressed the bhikkhus thus: "Bhikkhus!"

"Venerable sir!" those bhikkhus replied. The Blessed One said this:

"Bhikkhus, once in the past the asuras marched against the devas.[605] Then Sakka, lord of the devas, addressed Suvīra, a young deva, thus: 'Dear Suvīra, these asuras are marching against the devas. Go, dear Suvīra, launch a counter-march against the asuras.' – 'Yes, your lordship,' Suvīra replied, but he became negligent.[606] A second time Sakka addressed Suvīra … <467> … but a second time Suvīra became negligent. A third time Sakka addressed Suvīra … but a third time Suvīra became negligent. [217] Then, bhikkhus, Sakka addressed Suvīra in verse:

858 "'Where one need not toil and strive
Yet still may attain to bliss:
Go there, Suvīra,
And take me along with you.'

[Suvīra:]
859 "'That a lazy man who does not toil
Nor attend to his duties

Might still have all desires fulfilled:
Grant me that, Sakka, as a boon.'[607] <468>

[Sakka:]
860 "'Where a lazy man who does not toil
Might achieve unending bliss:
Go there, Suvīra,
And take me along with you.'

[Suvīra:]
861 "'The bliss, supreme deva, we might find
Without doing work, O Sakka,
The sorrowless state without despair:
Grant me that, Sakka, as a boon.'

[Sakka:]
862 "'If there exists any place anywhere
Where without work one won't decline,
That is indeed Nibbāna's path:
Go there, Suvīra,
And take me along with you.'[608]

"So, bhikkhus, if Sakka, lord of the devas, subsisting on the fruit of his own merit, <469> exercising supreme sovereignty and rulership over the Tāvatiṃsa devas, will be one who speaks in praise of initiative and energy, then how much more would it be fitting here for you,[609] who have gone forth in such a well-expounded Dhamma and Discipline, to toil, struggle, and strive for the attainment of the as-yet-unattained, for the achievement of the as-yet-unachieved, for the realization of the as-yet-unrealized."

2 (2) Susīma

(This sutta is identical with the preceding one, except that a young deva is named Susīma. Verses 863–67 = 858–62.) [218] <470–72>

3 (3) The Crest of the Standard

At Sāvatthī. There the Blessed One addressed the bhikkhus thus: "Bhikkhus!"[610]

"Venerable sir!" those bhikkhus replied. The Blessed One said this:

"Bhikkhus, once in the past the devas and the asuras were arrayed for battle. Then Sakka, lord of the devas, addressed the Tāvatiṃsa devas thus: 'Dear sirs, when the devas are engaged in battle, [219] if fear or trepidation or terror should arise, on that occasion you should look up at the crest of my standard. For when you look up at the crest of my standard, whatever fear or trepidation or terror you may have will be abandoned.[611]

"'If you cannot look up at the crest of my standard, then you should look up at the crest of the deva-king Pajāpati's standard. For when you look up at the crest of his standard, whatever fear or trepidation or terror you may have will be abandoned.

"'If you cannot look up at the crest of the deva-king Pajāpati's standard, then you should look up at the crest of the deva-king Varuṇa's standard.... If you cannot look up at the crest of the deva-king Varuṇa's standard, then you should look up at the crest of the deva-king Īsāna's standard.... For when you look up at the crest of his standard, whatever fear or trepidation or terror you may have will be abandoned.'[612] <473>

"Bhikkhus, for those who look up at the crest of the standard of Sakka, lord of the devas; or of Pajāpati, the deva-king; or of Varuṇa, the deva-king; or of Īsāna, the deva-king, whatever fear or trepidation or terror they may have may or may not be abandoned. For what reason? Because Sakka, lord of the devas, is not devoid of lust, not devoid of hatred, not devoid of delusion; he can be timid, petrified, frightened, quick to flee.

"But, bhikkhus, I say this: If you have gone to a forest or to the foot of a tree or to an empty hut, and fear or trepidation or terror should arise in you, on that occasion you should recollect me thus: 'The Blessed One is an arahant, perfectly enlightened, accomplished in true knowledge and conduct, fortunate, knower of the world, unsurpassed leader of persons to be tamed, teacher of devas and humans, the Enlightened One, the Blessed One.' For when you recollect me, bhikkhus, whatever fear or trepidation or terror you may have will be abandoned. [220]

"If you cannot recollect me, then you should recollect the Dhamma thus: 'The Dhamma is well expounded by the Blessed One, directly visible, immediate, inviting one to come and see, applicable, to be personally experienced by the wise.' For when you recollect the Dhamma, bhikkhus, whatever fear or trepidation or terror you may have will be abandoned.

"If you cannot recollect the Dhamma, then you should recollect the Saṅgha thus: 'The Saṅgha of the Blessed One's disciples is practising the good way, <474> practising the straight way, practising the true way, practising the proper way; that is, the four pairs of persons, the eight types of individuals—this Saṅgha of the Blessed One's disciples is worthy of gifts, worthy of hospitality, worthy of offerings, worthy of reverential salutation, the unsurpassed field of merit for the world.' For when you recollect the Saṅgha, bhikkhus, whatever fear or trepidation or terror you may have will be abandoned.

"For what reason? Because, bhikkhus, the Tathāgata, the Arahant, the Perfectly Enlightened One is devoid of lust, devoid of hatred, devoid of delusion; he is brave, courageous, bold, ready to stand his place."

This is what the Blessed One said. Having said this, the Fortunate One, the Teacher, further said this:

868 "In a forest, at the foot of a tree,
Or in an empty hut, O bhikkhus,
You should recollect the Buddha:
No fear will then arise in you.

869 "But if you cannot recall the Buddha,
Best in the world, the bull of men,
Then you should recall the Dhamma,
Emancipating, well expounded.

870 "But if you cannot recall the Dhamma,
Emancipating, well expounded,
Then you should recall the Saṅgha,
The unsurpassed field of merit. <475>

871 "For those who thus recall the Buddha,
The Dhamma, and the Saṅgha, bhikkhus,

No fear or trepidation will arise,
Nor any grisly terror."

4 (4) Vepacitti (or Patience)

At Sāvatthī. The Blessed One said this: [221]

"Once in the past, bhikkhus, the devas and the asuras were arrayed for battle. Then Vepacitti, lord of the asuras, addressed the asuras thus:[613] 'Dear sirs, in the impending battle between the devas and the asuras, <476> if the asuras win and the devas are defeated, bind Sakka, lord of the devas, by his four limbs and neck and bring him to me in the city of the asuras.' And Sakka, lord of the devas, addressed the Tāvatiṃsa devas thus: 'Dear sirs, in the impending battle between the devas and the asuras, if the devas win and the asuras are defeated, bind Vepacitti, lord of the asuras, by his four limbs and neck and bring him to me in the Sudhamma assembly hall.'

"In that battle, bhikkhus, the devas won and the asuras were defeated. Then the Tāvatiṃsa devas bound Vepacitti by his four limbs and neck and brought him to Sakka in the Sudhamma assembly hall.[614] When Sakka was entering and leaving the Sudhamma assembly hall, Vepacitti, bound by his four limbs and neck, abused and reviled him with rude, harsh words. Then, bhikkhus, Mātali the charioteer addressed Sakka, lord of the devas, in verse:

872 "'When face to face with Vepacitti
Is it, Maghavā, from fear or weakness <477>
That you endure him so patiently,
Listening to his harsh words?'

[Sakka:]
873 "'It is neither through fear nor weakness
That I am patient with Vepacitti.
How can a wise person like me
Engage in combat with a fool?'

[Mātali:]
874 "'Fools would vent their anger even more
If no one would keep them in check.

Hence with drastic punishment
The wise man should restrain the fool.'[615]

[Sakka:]
875 "'I myself think this alone
Is the way to check the fool:
When one knows one's foe is angry
One mindfully maintains one's peace.'

[Mātali:]
876 "'I see this fault, O Vāsava,
In practising patient endurance:
When the fool thinks of you thus,
"He endures me out of fear," <478>
The dolt will chase you even more
As a bull does one who flees.' [222]

[Sakka:]
877 "'Let it be whether or not he thinks,
"He endures me out of fear,"
Of goals that culminate in one's own good
None is found better than patience.[616]

878 "'When a person endowed with strength
Patiently endures a weakling,
They call that the supreme patience;
The weakling must be patient always.[617]

879 "'They call that strength no strength at all—
The strength that is the strength of folly—
But no one can reproach a person
Who is strong because guarded by Dhamma.[618]

880 "'One who repays an angry man with anger
Thereby makes things worse for himself.
Not repaying an angry man with anger, <479>
One wins a battle hard to win.

881 "'He practises for the welfare of both,
His own and the other's,

When, knowing that his foe is angry,
He mindfully maintains his peace.

882 "'When he achieves the cure of both—
His own and the other's—
The people who consider him a fool
Are unskilled in the Dhamma.'

"So, bhikkhus, if Sakka, lord of the devas, subsisting on the fruit of his own merit, exercising supreme sovereignty and rulership over the Tāvatiṃsa devas, will be one who speaks in praise of patience and gentleness, then how much more would it be fitting here for you, who have gone forth in such a well-expounded Dhamma and Discipline, to be patient and gentle."

5 (5) Victory by Well-Spoken Counsel

<480> At Sāvatthī. "Bhikkhus, once in the past the devas and the asuras were arrayed for battle. Then Vepacitti, lord of the asuras, said to Sakka, lord of the devas: 'Lord of the devas, let there be victory by well-spoken counsel.' [And Sakka replied:] 'Vepacitti, let there be victory by well-spoken counsel.'

"Then, bhikkhus, the devas and the asuras appointed a panel of judges, saying: 'These will ascertain what has been well spoken and badly spoken by us.'

"Then Vepacitti, lord of the asuras, said to Sakka, lord of the devas: 'Speak a verse, lord of the devas.' When this was said, Sakka said to Vepacitti: 'You, Vepacitti, being the senior deva here, speak a verse.'[619] [223] When this was said, Vepacitti, lord of the asuras, recited this verse:[620]

883 "'Fools would vent their anger even more
If no one would keep them in check.
Hence with drastic punishment
The wise man should restrain the fool.'

"When, bhikkhus, Vepacitti, lord of the asuras, spoke this verse, the asuras applauded but the devas were silent. Then Vepacitti said to Sakka: 'Speak a verse, lord of the devas.' When this was said, Sakka, lord of the devas, recited this verse:

884 "'I myself think this alone <481>
Is the way to check the fool:
When one knows one's foe is angry
One mindfully maintains one's peace.'

"When, bhikkhus, Sakka, lord of the devas, spoke this verse, the devas applauded but the asuras were silent. Then Sakka said to Vepacitti: 'Speak a verse, Vepacitti.' When this was said, Vepacitti, lord of the asuras, recited this verse:

885 "'I see this fault, O Vāsava,
In practising patient endurance:
When the fool thinks of you thus,
"He endures me out of fear,"
The dolt will chase you even more
As a bull does one who flees.'

"When, bhikkhus, Vepacitti, lord of the asuras, spoke this verse, the asuras applauded but the devas were silent. Then Vepacitti said to Sakka: 'Speak a verse, lord of the devas.' When this was said, Sakka, lord of the devas, recited these verses:

886–891 "'Let it be whether or not he thinks,
... (*verses = 877–82*) ... [224] <482>
Are unskilled in the Dhamma.'

"When, bhikkhus, these verses were spoken by Sakka, lord of the devas, the devas applauded but the asuras were silent. Then the panel of judges appointed by the devas and the asuras said this: 'The verses spoken by Vepacitti, lord of the asuras, are in the sphere of punishment and violence; hence [they entail] conflict, contention, and strife. But the verses spoken by Sakka, lord of the devas, <483> are in the sphere of nonpunishment and nonviolence; hence [they entail] freedom from conflict, freedom from contention, and freedom from strife. Sakka, lord of the devas, has won the victory by well-spoken counsel.'

"In this way, bhikkhus, Sakka, lord of the devas, won the victory by well-spoken counsel."

6 (6) The Bird Nests

At Sāvatthī. "Bhikkhus, once in the past the devas and the asuras were arrayed for battle. In that battle the asuras won and the devas were defeated. In defeat the devas withdrew towards the north while the asuras pursued them. Then Sakka, lord of the devas, addressed his charioteer Mātali in verse:

892 "'Avoid, O Mātali, with your chariot pole
The bird nests in the silk-cotton woods;
Let's surrender our lives to the asuras <484>
Rather than make these birds nestless.'[621]

"'Yes, your lordship,' Mātali the charioteer replied, and he turned back the chariot with its team of a thousand thoroughbreds.

"Then, bhikkhus, it occurred to the asuras: 'Now Sakka's chariot with its team of a thousand thoroughbreds has turned back. [225] The devas will engage in battle with the asuras for a second time.' Stricken by fear, they entered the city of the asuras. In this way, bhikkhus, Sakka, lord of the devas, won a victory by means of righteousness itself."

7 (7) One Should Not Transgress

At Sāvatthī. "Bhikkhus, once in the past, when Sakka, lord of the devas, was alone in seclusion, the following reflection arose in his mind: 'Though someone may be my sworn enemy, I should not transgress even against him.'

"Then, bhikkhus, Vepacitti, lord of the asuras, <485> having known with his own mind the reflection in Sakka's mind, approached Sakka, lord of the devas. Sakka saw Vepacitti coming in the distance and said to him: 'Stop, Vepacitti, you're caught!'[622] – 'Dear sir, do not abandon the idea that just occurred to you.'[623] – 'Swear, Vepacitti, that you won't transgress against me.'

[Vepacitti:]
893 "'Whatever evil comes to a liar,
Whatever evil to a reviler of noble ones,

Whatever evil to a betrayer of friends,
Whatever evil to one without gratitude:
That same evil touches the one
Who transgresses against you, Sujā's husband.'"[624]

8 (8) Verocana, Lord of the Asuras

At Sāvatthī in Jeta's Grove. Now on that occasion the Blessed One had gone for his day's abiding and was in seclusion. Then Sakka, <486> lord of the devas, and Verocana, lord of the asuras, approached the Blessed One and stood one at each door post. Then Verocana, lord of the asuras, recited this verse in the presence of the Blessed One:[625]

894 "A man should make an effort
Until his goal has been achieved.
Goals shine when achieved:
This is the word of Verocana." [226]

[Sakka:]
895 "A man should make an effort
Until his goal has been achieved.
Of goals that shine when achieved,
None is found better than patience."[626]

[Verocana:]
896 "All beings are bent on a goal
Here or there as fits the case,
But for all creatures association
Is supreme among enjoyments.
Goals shine when achieved:
This is the word of Verocana."[627] <487>

[Sakka:]
897 "All beings are bent upon a goal
Here or there as fits the case,
But for all creatures association
Is supreme among enjoyments.
Of goals that shine when achieved,
None is found better than patience."

9 (9) Seers in a Forest

At Sāvatthī. "Bhikkhus, once in the past a number of seers who were virtuous and of good character had settled down in leaf huts in a tract of forest. Then Sakka, lord of the devas, and Vepacitti, lord of the asuras, approached those seers.

"Vepacitti, lord of the asuras, put on his boots, bound his sword on tightly, and, with a parasol borne aloft, entered the hermitage through the main gate; then, having turned his left side towards them,[628] he walked past those seers who were virtuous and of good character. But Sakka, lord of the devas, took off his boots, handed over his sword to others, <488> lowered his parasol, and entered the hermitage through an [ordinary] gate; then he stood on the lee side, raising his joined hands in reverential salutation, paying homage to those seers who were virtuous and of good character.

"Then, bhikkhus, those seers addressed Sakka in verse:

898 "'The odour of the seers long bound by their vows,
Emitted from their bodies, goes with the wind.
Turn away from here, O thousand-eyed god,
For the seers' odour is foul, O deva-king.'[629]

[Sakka:]
899 "'Let the odour of the seers long bound by their vows,
Emitted from their bodies, go with the wind;
We yearn for this odour, O venerable sirs,
As for a garland of flowers on the head. [227]
The devas do not perceive it as repulsive.'"[630] <489>

10 (10) Seers by the Ocean

At Sāvatthī. "Bhikkhus, once in the past a number of seers who were virtuous and of good character had settled down in leaf huts along the shore of the ocean. Now on that occasion the devas and the asuras were arrayed for a battle. Then it occurred to those seers who were virtuous and of good character: 'The devas are righteous, the asuras unrighteous. There may be danger to us from the asuras. Let us approach Sambara, lord of the asuras, and ask him for a guarantee of safety.'[631]

"Then, bhikkhus, just as quickly as a strong man might extend his drawn-in arm or draw in his extended arm, those seers who were virtuous and of good character disappeared from their leaf huts along the shore of the ocean and reappeared in the presence of Sambara, lord of the asuras. Then those seers addressed Sambara in verse:

900 "'The seers who have come to Sambara
Ask him for a guarantee of safety. <490>
For you can give them what you wish,
Whether it be danger or safety.'[632]

[Sambara:]
901 "'I'll grant no safety to the seers,
For they are hated devotees of Sakka;
Though you appeal to me for safety,
I'll give you only danger.'

[The seers:]
902 "'Though we have asked for safety,
You give us only danger.
We receive this at your hands:
May ceaseless danger come to you!

903 "'Whatever sort of seed is sown,
That is the sort of fruit one reaps:
The doer of good reaps good;
The door of evil reaps evil.
By you, dear, has the seed been sown;
Thus you will experience the fruit.'

"Then, bhikkhus, having put a curse on Sambara, lord of the asuras, just as quickly as a strong man might extend his drawn-in arm <491> or draw in his extended arm, those seers who were virtuous and of good character disappeared from the presence of Sambara and reappeared in their leaf huts on the shore of the ocean. [228] But after being cursed by those seers who were virtuous and of good character, Sambara, lord of the asuras, was gripped by alarm three times in the course of the night."[633] <492>

II. The Second Subchapter (The Seven Vows)

11 (1) Vows

At Sāvatthī. "Bhikkhus, in the past, when Sakka, lord of the devas, was a human being, he adopted and undertook seven vows by the undertaking of which he achieved the status of Sakka.[634] What were the seven vows?

(1) "'As long as I live may I support my parents.'

(2) "'As long as I live may I respect the family elders.'

(3) "'As long as I live may I speak gently.'

(4) "'As long as I live may I not speak divisively.'

(5) "'As long as I live may I dwell at home with a mind devoid of the stain of stinginess, freely generous, open-handed, delighting in relinquishment, devoted to charity,[635] delighting in giving and sharing.'

(6) "'As long as I live may I speak the truth.'

(7) "'As long as I live may I be free from anger, and if anger should arise in me may I dispel it quickly.'

"In the past, bhikkhus, when Sakka, lord of the devas, was a human being, he adopted and undertook these seven vows by the undertaking of which he achieved the status of Sakka. <493>

904 "When a person supports his parents,
And respects the family elders;
When his speech is gentle and courteous,
And he refrains from divisive words;
905 When he strives to remove meanness,
Is truthful, and vanquishes anger,
The Tāvatiṃsa devas call him
Truly a superior person." [229]

12 (2) Sakka's Names

At Sāvatthī in Jeta's Grove. There the Blessed One said to the bhikkhus:

"Bhikkhus, in the past, when Sakka, lord of the devas, was a human being, he was a brahmin youth named Magha; therefore he is called Maghavā.[636]

"Bhikkhus, in the past, when Sakka, lord of the devas, was a human being, he gave gifts in city after city; therefore he is called Purindada, the Urban Giver.[637]

"Bhikkhus, in the past, when Sakka, lord of the devas, was a human being, he gave gifts considerately; therefore he is called Sakka.[638]

"Bhikkhus, in the past, when Sakka, lord of the devas, was a human being, <494> he gave a rest house; therefore he is called Vāsava.[639]

"Bhikkhus, Sakka, lord of the devas, thinks of a thousand matters in a moment; therefore he is called Sahassakkha, Thousand-eyed.[640]

"Bhikkhus, Sakka's wife is the asura maiden named Sujā; therefore he is called Sujampati, Sujā's husband.[641]

"Bhikkhus, Sakka, lord of the devas, exercises supreme sovereignty and rulership over the Tāvatiṃsa devas; therefore he is called lord of the devas.

"Bhikkhus, in the past, when Sakka, lord of the devas, was a human being, he adopted and undertook seven vows by the undertaking of which he achieved the status of Sakka…."

(*The remainder of this sutta is identical with the preceding one. Verses 906–7 = 904–5.*) [230] <495>

13 (3) Mahāli

Thus have I heard. On one occasion the Blessed One was dwelling at Vesālī in the Great Wood in the Hall with the Peaked Roof. Then Mahāli the Licchavi approached the Blessed One, paid homage to him, sat down to one side, and said to him:

"Venerable sir, has the Blessed One seen Sakka, lord of the devas?"

"I have, Mahāli."

"Surely, venerable sir, that must have been one who looked like Sakka, lord of the devas; for Sakka, lord of the devas, is difficult to see."

"I know Sakka, Mahāli, and I know the qualities that make for Sakka, by the undertaking of which Sakka achieved the status of Sakka. <496>

"In the past, Mahāli, when Sakka, lord of the devas, was a human being, he was a brahmin youth named Magha. Therefore he is called Maghavā…."

(*Here follows the names of Sakka as in 11:12 and the seven vows as in 11:11, followed by verses 908–9 = 904–5.*) [231] <497>

14 (4) Poor

On one occasion the Blessed One was dwelling at Rājagaha in the Bamboo Grove, the Squirrel Sanctuary. There the Blessed One addressed the bhikkhus thus: "Bhikkhus!"

"Venerable sir!" those bhikkhus replied. The Blessed One said this:

"Bhikkhus, once in the past in this same Rājagaha there was a poor man, a pauper, an indigent. He undertook faith, virtue, learning, generosity, and wisdom in the Dhamma and Discipline proclaimed by the Tathāgata. Having done so, with the breakup of the body, after death, [232] <498> he was reborn in a good destination, in a heavenly world, in the company of the Tāvatiṃsa devas, where he outshone the other devas in regard to beauty and glory.[642]

"Thereupon the Tāvatiṃsa devas found fault with this, grumbled, and complained about it, saying: 'It is wonderful indeed, sir! It is amazing indeed, sir! For formerly, when this young deva was a human being, he was a poor man, a pauper, an indigent. Yet with the breakup of the body, after death, he has been reborn in a good destination, in a heavenly world, in the company of the Tāvatiṃsa devas, where he outshines the other devas in regard to beauty and glory.'

"Then, bhikkhus, Sakka, lord of the devas, addressed the Tāvatiṃsa devas thus: 'Dear sirs, do not find fault with this young deva. Formerly, when this young deva was a human being, he undertook faith, virtue, learning, generosity, and wisdom in the Dhamma and Discipline proclaimed by the Tathāgata. Having done so, with the breakup of the body, after death, he has been reborn in a good destination, in a heavenly world, in the company of the Tāvatiṃsa devas, where he outshines the other devas in regard to beauty and glory.'

"Then, bhikkhus, instructing the Tāvatiṃsa devas,[643] Sakka, lord of the devas, on that occasion recited these verses: <499>

910 "'When one has faith in the Tathāgata,
Unshakable and well established,

And good conduct built on virtue,
Dear to the noble ones and praised;[644]

911 "'When one has confidence in the Saṅgha
And one's view is straightened out,
They say that one isn't poor;
One's life is not lived in vain.

912 "'Therefore the person of intelligence,
Remembering the Buddha's Teaching,
Should be devoted to faith and virtue,
To confidence and vision of the Dhamma.'"

15 (5) A Delightful Place

At Sāvatthī in Jeta's Grove. Then Sakka, lord of the devas, approached the Blessed One, paid homage to him, stood to one side, and said to him: "Venerable sir, what is a delightful place?" [233]

[The Blessed One:] <500>
913 "Shrines in parks and woodland shrines,
Well-constructed lotus ponds:
These are not worth a sixteenth part
Of a delightful human being.

914 "Whether in a village or forest,
In a valley or on the plain—
Wherever the arahants dwell
Is truly a delightful place."

16 (6) Bestowing Alms

On one occasion the Blessed One was dwelling at Rājagaha on Mount Vulture Peak. Then Sakka, lord of the devas, approached the Blessed One, paid homage to him, and stood to one side. Standing to one side, he addressed the Blessed One in verse:[645]

915 "For those people who bestow alms,
For living beings in quest of merit,

Performing merit of the mundane type,
Where does a gift bear great fruit?"[646]

[The Blessed One:] <501>
916 "The four practising the way
And the four established in the fruit:
This is the Saṅgha of upright conduct
Endowed with wisdom and virtue.[647]

917 "For those people who bestow alms,
For living beings in quest of merit,
Performing merit of the mundane type,
A gift to the Saṅgha bears great fruit."

17 (7) Veneration of the Buddha

At Sāvatthī in Jeta's Grove. Now on that occasion the Blessed One had gone for his day's abiding and was in seclusion. Then Sakka, lord of the devas, and Brahmā Sahampati approached the Blessed One and stood one at each doorpost. Then Sakka, lord of the devas, recited this verse in the presence of the Blessed One:

918 "Rise up, O hero, victor in battle!
Your burden lowered, debt-free one, wander in the world.
Your mind is fully liberated
Like the moon on the fifteenth night."[648] [234]

[Brahmā Sahampati:] "It is not in such a way that the Tathāgatas are to be venerated, lord of the devas. The Tathāgatas are to be venerated thus:

919 "Rise up, O hero, victor in battle! <502>
O caravan leader, debt-free one, wander in the world.
Teach the Dhamma, O Blessed One:
There will be those who will understand."[649]

18 (8) The Worship of Householders (or Sakka's Worship (1))

At Sāvatthī. There the Blessed One said this: "Bhikkhus, once in the past Sakka, lord of the devas, addressed his charioteer

Mātali thus: 'Harness the chariot with its team of a thousand thoroughbreds, friend Mātali. Let us go to the park grounds to see the beautiful scenery.' – 'Yes, your lordship,' Mātali the charioteer replied. Then he harnessed the chariot with its team of a thousand thoroughbreds and announced to Sakka, lord of the devas: 'The chariot has been harnessed, dear sir. You may come at your own convenience.'[650]

"Then, bhikkhus, Sakka, lord of the devas, descending from the Vejayanta Palace, raised his joined hands in reverential salutation, and worshipped the different quarters. Then Mātali the charioteer addressed Sakka in verse:

920 "'These all humbly worship you—
Those versed in the Triple Veda,
All the khattiyas reigning on earth,
The Four Great Kings and the glorious Thirty— <503>
So who, O Sakka, is that spirit
To whom you bow in worship?'[651]

[Sakka:]
921 "'These all humbly worship me—
Those versed in the Triple Veda,
All the khattiyas reigning on earth,
The Four Great Kings and the glorious Thirty—
922 But I worship those endowed with virtue,
Those long trained in concentration,
Those who have properly gone forth
With the holy life their destination.[652]

923 "'I worship as well, O Mātali,
Those householders making merit,
The lay followers possessed of virtue
Who righteously maintain a wife.'

[Mātali:]
924 "'Those whom you worship, my lord Sakka,
Are indeed the best in the world.
I too will worship them—
Those whom you worship, Vāsava.' <504>

[The Blessed One:]

925 "Having given this explanation,
Having worshipped the different quarters,
The deva-king Maghavā, Sujā's husband,
The chief, climbed into his chariot." [235]

19 (9) The Worship of the Teacher (or Sakka's Worship (2))

(*As above down to:*)

"Then, bhikkhus, Sakka, lord of the devas, descending from the Vejayanta Palace, raised his joined hands in reverential salutation and worshipped the Blessed One. Then Mātali the charioteer addressed Sakka, lord of the devas, in verse:

926 "'Both devas and human beings
Humbly worship you, Vāsava.
So who, O Sakka, is that spirit
To whom you bow in worship?'

[Sakka:] <505>

927 "'The Perfectly Enlightened One here
In this world with its devas,
The Teacher of perfect name:
He is the one whom I worship, Mātali.[653]

928 "'Those for whom lust and hatred
And ignorance have been expunged,
The arahants with taints destroyed:
These are the ones whom I worship, Mātali.

929 "'The trainees who delight in dismantling,
Who diligently pursue the training
For the removal of lust and hatred,
For transcending ignorance:
These are the ones whom I worship, Mātali.'[654]

[Mātali:]

930 "'Those whom you worship, my lord Sakka,
Are indeed the best in the world.

I too will worship them—
Those whom you worship, Vāsava.'

[The Blessed One:]
931 "Having given this explanation,
Having worshipped the Blessed One,
The deva-king Maghavā, Sujā's husband,
The chief, climbed into his chariot." <506>

20 (10) The Worship of the Saṅgha (or Sakka's Worship (3))

(*As above down to:*) [236]
"Then, bhikkhus, Sakka, lord of the devas, descending from the Vejayanta Palace, raised his joined hands in reverential salutation and worshipped the Saṅgha of bhikkhus. Then Mātali the charioteer addressed Sakka, lord of the devas, in verse:

932 "'It is these that should worship you—
The humans stuck in a putrid body,
Those submerged inside a corpse,
Afflicted with hunger and thirst.[655]
933 Why then do you envy them,
These who dwell homeless, Vāsava?
Tell us about the seers' conduct;
Let us hear what you have to say.'

[Sakka:] <507>
934 "'This is why I envy them,[656]
Those who dwell homeless, Mātali:
Whatever village they depart from,
They leave it without concern.

935 "'They do not keep their goods in storage,
Neither in a pot nor in a box.
Seeking what has been prepared by others,
By this they live, firm in vows:
Those wise ones who give good counsel,
Maintaining silence, of even faring.[657]

936 "'While devas fight with asuras

And people fight with one another,
Among those who fight, they do not fight;
Among the violent, they are quenched;
Among those who grasp, they do not grasp:
These are the ones whom I worship, Mātali.'

[Mātali:]
937 "'Those whom you worship, my lord Sakka,
Are indeed the best in the world.
I too will worship them—
Those whom you worship, Vāsava.' <508>

[The Blessed One:]
938 "Having given this explanation,
Having worshipped the Bhikkhu Saṅgha,
The deva-king Maghavā, Sujā's husband,
The chief, climbed into his chariot."

[237]

III. The Third Subchapter (Sakka Pentad)

21 (1) Having Slain

At Sāvatthī in Jeta's Grove. Then Sakka, lord of the devas, approached the Blessed One, paid homage to him, and stood to one side. Standing to one side, Sakka, lord of the devas, addressed the Blessed One in verse:

939 "Having slain what does one sleep soundly?
Having slain what does one not sorrow? <509>
What is the one thing, O Gotama,
Whose killing you approve?"

[The Blessed One:]
940 "Having slain anger, one sleeps soundly;
Having slain anger, one does not sorrow;
The killing of anger, O Vāsava,
With its poisoned root and honeyed tip:
This is the killing the noble ones praise,
For having slain that, one does not sorrow."

22 (2) Ugly

At Sāvatthī in Jeta's Grove. There the Blessed One said this: "Bhikkhus, once in the past a certain ugly deformed yakkha sat down on the seat of Sakka, lord of the devas.[658] Thereupon the Tāvatiṃsa devas found fault with this, grumbled, and complained about it, saying: 'It is wonderful indeed, sir! It is amazing indeed, sir! This ugly deformed yakkha has sat down on the seat of Sakka, lord of the devas!' <510> But to whatever extent the Tāvatiṃsa devas found fault with this, grumbled, and complained about it, to the same extent that yakkha became more and more handsome, more and more comely, more and more graceful.

"Then, bhikkhus, the Tāvatiṃsa devas approached Sakka and said to him: 'Here, dear sir, an ugly deformed yakkha has sat down on your seat.... But to whatever extent the devas found fault with this ... [238] that yakkha became more and more handsome, more and more comely, more and more graceful.' – 'That must be the anger-eating yakkha.'

"Then, bhikkhus, Sakka, lord of the devas, approached that anger-eating yakkha.[659] Having approached, he arranged his upper robe over one shoulder, knelt down with his right knee on the ground, and, raising his joined hands in reverential salutation towards that yakkha, <511> he announced his name three times: 'I, dear sir, am Sakka, lord of the devas! I, dear sir, am Sakka, lord of the devas!' To whatever extent Sakka announced his name, to the same extent that yakkha became uglier and uglier and more and more deformed until he disappeared right there.

"Then, bhikkhus, having sat down on his own seat, instructing the Tāvatiṃsa devas, Sakka, lord of the devas, on that occasion recited these verses:

941 "'I am not one afflicted in mind,
Nor easily drawn by anger's whirl.
I never become angry for long,
Nor does anger persist in me.[660]

942 "'When I'm angry I don't speak harshly
And I don't praise my virtues.

I keep myself well restrained <512>
Out of regard for my own good.'"[661]

23 (3) Magic

At Sāvatthī. The Blessed One said this: "Bhikkhus, once in the past Vepacitti, lord of the asuras, was sick, afflicted, gravely ill.[662] Then Sakka, lord of the devas, approached Vepacitti to inquire about his illness. Vepacitti saw Sakka coming in the distance and said to him: 'Cure me, lord of the devas.' – [239] 'Teach me, Vepacitti, the Sambari magic.'[663] – 'I won't teach it, dear sir, until I have asked the asuras for permission.'

"Then, bhikkhus, Vepacitti, lord of the asuras, asked the asuras: 'May I teach the Sambari magic to Sakka, lord of the devas?' – 'Do not teach him the Sambari magic, dear sir.'[664]

"Then, bhikkhus, Vepacitti, lord of the asuras, addressed Sakka, lord of the devas, in verse: <513>

943 "'A magician—O Maghavā, Sakka,
King of devas, Sujā's husband—
Goes to the terrible hell,
Like Sambara, for a hundred years.'"[665]

24 (4) Transgression

At Sāvatthī. Now on that occasion two bhikkhus had a quarrel and one bhikkhu had transgressed against the other. Then the former bhikkhu confessed his transgression to the other bhikkhu, but the latter would not pardon him.[666]

Then a number of bhikkhus approached the Blessed One, paid homage to him, sat down to one side, and reported to him what had happened. <514> [The Blessed One said:]

"Bhikkhus, there are two kinds of fools: one who does not see a transgression as a transgression; and one who, when another is confessing a transgression, does not pardon him in accordance with the Dhamma. These are the two kinds of fools.

"There are, bhikkhus, two kinds of wise people: one who sees a transgression as a transgression; and one who, when another is confessing a transgression, pardons him in accordance with the Dhamma. These are the two kinds of wise people.

"Once in the past, bhikkhus, Sakka, lord of the devas, instructing the Tāvatiṃsa devas in the Sudhamma assembly hall, on that occasion recited this verse: [240]

944 "'Bring anger under your control;
Do not let your friendships decay.
Do not blame one who is blameless;
Do not utter divisive speech.
Like a mountain avalanche
Anger crushes evil people.'"[667]

25 (5) Nonanger

Thus have I heard. On one occasion the Blessed One was dwelling at Sāvatthī in Jeta's Grove, Anāthapiṇḍika's Park. There the Blessed One said this:

"Bhikkhus, once in the past Sakka, lord of the devas, instructing the Tāvatiṃsa devas in the Sudhamma assembly hall, on that occasion recited this verse: <515>

945 "'Do not let anger overpower you;
Do not become angry at those who are angry.
Nonanger and harmlessness always dwell
Within [the hearts of] the noble ones.
Like a mountain avalanche
Anger crushes evil people.'"[668]

<516>

The Book with Verses is finished.

Notes

1. Devatāsaṃyutta

1 *Mārisa*, "dear sir," is the term which the devas generally use to address the Buddha, eminent bhikkhus (see, e.g., **40:10**; IV 270,16), and members of their own community (**11:3**; I 218,34); kings also use it to address one another (**3:12**; I 80,4). Spk explains it as a term of affection meaning "one without suffering" (*niddukkha*), but it is probably a Middle Indic form of Skt *madṛsa*.

The word "flood" (*ogha*) is used metaphorically, but here with technical overtones, to designate a doctrinal set of four floods (see **45:171**), so called, according to Spk, "because they keep beings submerged within the round of existence and do not allow them to rise up to higher states and to Nibbāna." The four (with definitions from Spk) are: (i) the flood of sensuality (*kāmogha*) = desire and lust for the five cords of sensual pleasure (agreeable forms, sounds, etc.—see **45:176**); (ii) the flood of existence (*bhavogha*) = desire and lust for form-sphere existence and formless-sphere existence and attachment to jhāna; (iii) the flood of views (*diṭṭhogha*) = the sixty-two views (DN I 12–38); and (iv) the flood of ignorance (*avijjogha*) = lack of knowledge regarding the Four Noble Truths. Flood imagery is also used at **vv. 298–300, 511–13**, and **848–49.**

2 *Appatiṭṭhaṃ khvāhaṃ āvuso anāyūhaṃ ogham atariṃ.* Spk: The Buddha's reply is intended to be paradoxical, for one normally crosses a flood by halting in places that offer a foothold and by straining in places that must be crossed.

Spk glosses *appatiṭṭhaṃ* only with *appatiṭṭhahanto* (an alternative form of the present participle), but Spk-pṭ elaborates: "*Not halting*: not coming to a standstill on account of the defilements and so forth; the meaning is 'not sinking' (*appatiṭṭhahanto ti kilesādīnaṃ vasena asantiṭṭhanto, asaṃsīdanto ti attho*)." The verb *patitiṭṭhati* usually means "to become established," i.e., attached, principally on account of craving and other defilements: see below **v. 46** and **n. 35**. Consciousness driven by craving is "established" (see **12:38–40**, **12:64**, **22:53–54**), and when craving is removed it becomes "unestablished, unsupported." The arahant expires "with consciousness unestablished" (*appatiṭṭhitena viññāṇena ... parinibbuto*; see **4:23** (I 122,12–13)). All these nuances resonate in the Buddha's reply.

The verb *āyūhati* is rare in the Nikāyas, but see below **v. 263**df, **v. 264**d, and Sn 210d. It is an intensification of *ūhati* (augmented by *ā-* with *-y-* as liaison); the simple verb occurs at MN I 116,13–14, where it might be rendered "to be strained." Its occurrence there ties up with the present context: a strained mind is far from concentration. In the later literature the noun form *āyūhana* acquires the technical sense of "accumulation," with specific reference to kamma; in the formula of dependent origination (*paṭiccasamuppāda*), volitional formations (*saṅkhārā*) are said to have the function of *āyūhana*; see Paṭis I 52,14, 26; Vism 528,12 (Ppn 17:51), 579,31–580,4 (Ppn 17:292–93).

Spk: The Blessed One deliberately gave an obscure reply to the deva in order to humble him, for he was stiff with conceit yet imagined himself wise. Realizing that the deva would not be able to penetrate the teaching unless he first changed his attitude, the Buddha intended to perplex him and thereby curb his pride. At that point, humbled, the deva would ask for clarification and the Buddha would explain in such a way that he could understand.

3 The Buddha's brief reply points to the middle way (*majjhimā paṭipadā*) in its most comprehensive range, both practical and philosophical. To make this implication clear Spk enumerates seven dyads: (i) "halting" by way of defilements, one sinks; "straining" by way of volitional formations, one gets swept away; (ii) by way of craving

and views, one sinks; by way of the other defilements, one gets swept away; (iii) by way of craving, one sinks; by way of views, one gets swept away; (iv) by way of the eternalist view, one sinks; by way of the annihilationist view, one gets swept away (see It 43,12–44,4); (v) by way of slackness one sinks, by way of restlessness one gets swept away; (vi) by way of devotion to sensual pleasures one sinks, by way of devotion to self-mortification one gets swept away; (vii) by way of all unwholesome volitional formations one sinks, by way of all mundane wholesome volitional formations one gets swept away. Ñāṇananda suggests connecting the principle of "not halting, not straining" with each of the four floods: see SN-Anth 2:56–58.

4 Spk: The Buddha is called a *brahmin* in the sense of arahant (see Dhp 388, 396–423). He is *fully quenched* (*parinibbuto*) in that he is quenched through the quenching of defilements (*kilesanibbānena nibbutaṃ*). Craving is designated *attachment* (*visattikā*) because it clings and adheres to a variety of sense objects.

5 Spk: When the deva heard the Buddha's reply he was established in the fruit of stream-entry.

6 *Sattānaṃ nimokkhaṃ pamokkhaṃ vivekaṃ.* Spk: "Emancipation (*nimokkha*) is the path, for beings are emancipated from the bondage of defilements by the path; release (*pamokkha*) is the fruit, for at the moment of the fruit beings have been released from the bondage of defilements; seclusion (*viveka*) is Nibbāna, for when they attain Nibbāna beings are separated from all suffering. Or, alternatively, all three are designations for Nibbāna: for having attained Nibbāna, beings are emancipated, released, separated from all suffering." The actual wording of the verse seems to confirm the second alternative.

7 Spk glosses: *Nandībhavaparikkhayā ti nandīmūlakassa kammabhavassa parikkhayena; nandiyā ca bhavassa cā ti pi vaṭṭati; "By delight-existence-destruction*: by the utter destruction of kamma-process existence rooted in delight; it is also proper to understand it as meaning '(the destruction) of delight and of existence.'" It would be more plausible, however, to construe this three-term *tappurisa* as an

inverted compound placed in irregular order probably owing to the exigencies of verse. This interpretation is confirmed by Pj II 469,14 and Dhp-a IV 192,7–8 in their gloss on the related *bahubbīhi* compound *nandībhava-parikkhīṇaṃ* as *tīsu bhavesu parikkhīṇataṇhaṃ*; "one who has destroyed craving for the three realms of existence." See too below **v. 300**c and **n. 165**.

8 In this verse only the first two pādas conform to a recognizable metre (Vatta), which indicates that the verse is corrupt. Ee2 amends the third pāda and adds a line found only in a Lanna ms to arrive at a novel reading: *vedanānaṃ nirodhā ca/ upasanto carissatī ti*. It then treats the last three pādas of the other editions as prose. This, however, alters the meaning of the verse in such a way that it no longer directly answers the question.

Spk: By the first method of explanation, *delight in existence* (*nandībhava*, or, following the gloss: "existence rooted in delight"), being the threefold activity of kammic formation (*tividhakammābhisaṅkhāra*—see **12:51**), implies the aggregate of volitional formations (*saṅkhārakkhandha*); *perception and consciousness* implies the two aggregates associated therewith; and by mentioning this, the feeling associated with those three aggregates is included. Thus, by way of the nonoccurrence of the four kammically active mental aggregates (*anupādiṇṇaka-arūpakkhandhā*), "Nibbāna with residue" (*sa-upādisesa-nibbāna*) is indicated. By the phrase *by the cessation and appeasement of feelings* (*vedanānaṃ nirodhā upasamā*), the kammically acquired (*upādiṇṇaka*) feeling is referred to, and by mentioning this the other three associated aggregates are implied; the aggregate of form is included as their physical basis and object. Thus, by way of the nonoccurrence of the five kammically acquired aggregates, "Nibbāna without residue" (*anupādisesa-nibbāna*) is indicated. By the second method (taking "delight" and "existence" as parallel terms), *delight* implies the aggregate of volitional formations; *existence*, the aggregate of form; and the other three aggregates are shown under their own names. Nibbāna is indicated as the nonoccurrence of these five aggregates. Thus the Blessed One concludes the teaching with Nibbāna itself.

On the two elements of Nibbāna, see the General Introduction, p. 50.

9 Spk: "Life is swept along" (*upanīyati jīvitaṃ*) means: "(Life) is destroyed, it ceases; or it moves towards, i.e., gradually approaches, death" (*upanīyatī ti parikkhīyati nirujjhati; upagacchati vā; anupubbena maraṇaṃ upetī ti attho*). "Short is the life span" (*appam āyu*): "The life span is limited in two ways: first, because it is said, 'One who lives long lives for a hundred years or a little longer' (see **4:9**); and second, because in the ultimate sense the life-moment of beings is extremely limited, enduring for a mere act of consciousness." Spk continues as at Vism 238 (Ppn 8:39).

10 Spk: This deva had been reborn into one of the brahmā worlds with a long life span. When he saw beings passing away and taking rebirth in realms with a short life span, he was moved to pity and urged them to do "deeds of merit" (*puññāni*)—to develop the form-sphere and formless-sphere jhānas—so that they would be reborn into the form and formless realms with a long life span. The Buddha's verse is a rejoinder intended to show that the deva's advice is still tied to the round of existence and does not lead to emancipation. The *peace* (*santi*) which the Buddha commends is Nibbāna.

Spk explains two denotations of *lokāmisa*, literally "carnal things": (i) figuratively (*pariyāyena*), it denotes the entire round of existence with its three planes, the objective sphere of attachment, "the bait of the world"; (ii) literally (*nippariyāyena*), it signifies the four requisites (clothing, food, dwelling, and medicines), the material basis for survival. For the figurative use of *āmisa*, see **v. 371**d, **v. 480,** and **35:230**; in the last text, however, the six sense objects are compared to baited hooks rather than to the bait itself.

11 *Vayoguṇā anupubbaṃ jahanti.* Spk: Youth deserts one who reaches middle age; both youth and middle age desert one who reaches old age; and at the time of death, all three stages desert us.

12 Spk: One must *cut off* (*chinde*) the five lower fetters (identity view, doubt, the distorted grasp of rules and vows, sensual desire, ill will). One must *abandon* (*jahe*) the five higher

fetters (lust for form, lust for the formless, conceit, restlessness, ignorance). In order to cut off and abandon these fetters one must *develop a further five* (*pañca cuttari bhāvaye*), namely, the five spiritual faculties (faith, energy, mindfulness, concentration, wisdom). The *five ties* (*pañcasaṅgā*) are: lust, hatred, delusion, conceit, and views. A bhikkhu who has surmounted these five ties is called *a crosser of the flood* (*oghatiṇṇo*), that is, a crosser of the fourfold flood (see **n. 1**).

Strangely, although the verses refer to the five ties as if they are a standard doctrinal set, no pentad of *saṅgas* can be found as such in the Nikāyas; the five *saṅgas* are mentioned at Vibh 377,16–18.

13 Spk says, "When the five faculties are awake the five hindrances are asleep, and when the five hindrances are asleep the five faculties are awake," but this seems redundant; the explanation would be more satisfactory if we take the first phrase to be stating that when the five faculties are asleep the five hindrances are awake, thus making more explicit the relationship of diametric opposition and mutual exclusion between the two pentads. Spk continues: "It is by the same five hindrances that *one gathers dust*, i.e., the dust of the defilements; and it is by the five faculties that *one is purified*."

14 Spk identifies the *dhammā* of pāda a as the *catusacca-dhammā*, "the things (or teachings) of the four (noble) truths." *Who may be led into others' doctrines*: Spk: The doctrines of the other spiritual sects apart from the Buddha's Teaching are called "others' doctrines" (*paravādā*); specifically, the doctrines of the sixty-two views (DN I 12–38). Some tend to these doctrines of their own accord, some are led into them and adopt them through the influence of others.

15 *Those awakened ones* (*sambuddhā*). Spk: There are four kinds of awakened ones: omniscient Buddhas, paccekabuddhas, "four-truth awakened ones" (i.e., arahant disciples), and those awakened through learning. The first three types are indicated in the present context. They *fare evenly amidst the uneven*: they fare evenly amidst the uneven common domain of the world, or amidst the uneven community of sentient beings, or amidst the uneven multitude of defilements.

16 Spk: Here *taming* (*dama*) signifies the qualities pertaining to concentration. *Sagehood* (*mona*) is the knowledge of the four supramundane paths, so called because it experiences (*munāti ti monaṃ*); that is, it knows the four truths. The *realm of Death* (*maccudheyya*) is the round with its three planes, so called because it is the domain of Death; its *beyond* or *far shore* (*pāra*) is Nibbāna.

17 Spk sees this couplet as an implicit formulation of the threefold training: by the abandoning of conceit the higher virtue (*adhisīla*) is implied; by *well concentrated* (*susamāhitatto*), the training in concentration or the higher mind (*adhicitta*); and by *lofty mind* (*sucetaso*), denoting a mind endowed with wisdom, the training in the higher wisdom (*adhipaññā*). To this we might add that the last phrase, *everywhere released* (*sabbadhi vippamutto*), points to the culmination of the threefold training in liberation (*vimutti*). See DN II 122,15–123,12.

18 Spk: This verse was spoken by an earth-bound deva who dwelt in that forest. Each day he would see the bhikkhus who inhabited the forest sitting in meditation after their meal. As they sat, their minds would become unified and serene, and the serenity of their minds would become manifest in their complexion (*vaṇṇa*). Puzzled that they could have such serene faces while living under these austere conditions, the deva came to the Buddha to inquire into the cause. The facial complexion (*mukhavaṇṇa*) or complexion of the skin (*chavivaṇṇa*) is understood to indicate success in meditation; see **21:3** (II 275,20–21), **28:1** (III 235,22); and Vin I 40,14, and 41,2.

19 *Tāvatiṃsa*, "the realm of the thirty-three," is the third sense-sphere heaven. It is so named because thirty-three youths, headed by the youth Magha, had been reborn here as a result of their meritorious deeds. Magha himself became Sakka, ruler of the devas. Nandana is the Garden of Delight in Tāvatiṃsa, so called because it gives delight and joy to anyone who enters it. According to Spk, this deva had just taken rebirth into this heaven and, while wandering through the Nandana Grove, he spoke the verse as a spontaneous paean of joy over his celestial glory. Spk glosses *naradevānaṃ* with *devapurisānaṃ*, "deva-

males"; it is clearly not a *dvanda* compound. *Tidasa*, "the Thirty" (lit. "triple ten"), is a poetic epithet for Tāvatiṃsa.

20 Spk ascribes this rejoinder to a female deva who was a noble disciple (*ariyasāvikā*). Thinking, "This foolish deva imagines his glory to be permanent and unchanging, unaware that it is subject to cutting off, perishing, and dissolution," she spoke her stanza in order to dispel his delusion. The "maxim of the arahants" is pronounced by the Buddha at **15:20** (II 193, also at DN II 199,6–7); the deva-king Sakka repeats it on the occasion of the Buddha's parinibbāna (see **v. 609**). The first line usually reads *aniccā vata saṅkhārā* rather than, as here, *aniccā sabbasaṅkhārā*. An identical exchange of verses occurs below at **9:6**, with the goddess Jālinī and the Venerable Anuruddha as speakers. The feminine vocative *bāle* in pāda b implies that the latter dialogue was the original provenance of the verse, or in any case that the first devatā is female.

Spk: *Formations* here are all formations of the three planes of existence (*sabbe tebhūmakasaṅkhārā*), which are impermanent in the sense that they become nonexistent after having come to be (*hutvā abhāvaṭṭhena aniccā*). *Their appeasement is blissful* (*tesaṃ vūpasamo sukho*): Nibbāna itself, called the appeasement of those formations, is blissful.

21 *Upadhi*, "acquisitions" (from *upa* + *dhā*, "to rest upon") means literally "that upon which something rests," i.e., the "foundations" or "paraphernalia" of existence. The word has both objective and subjective extensions. Objectively, it refers to the things acquired, i.e., one's assets and possessions; subjectively, to the act of appropriation rooted in craving. In many instances the two senses merge, and often both are intended. The word functions as a close counterpart of *upādāna*, "clinging," to which, however, it is not etymologically related. See in this connection **12:66** and **II, n. 187**, and Sn p. 141.

Spk (along with other commentaries) offers a fourfold classification of *upadhi*: (i) *kāmūpadhi*, acquisitions as sensual pleasures and material possessions; (ii) *khandhūpadhi*, the five aggregates; (iii) *kilesūpadhi*, defilements, which are the foundation for suffering in the realm of misery; and

(iv) *abhisaṅkhārūpadhi,* volitional formations, accumulations of kamma, which are the foundation for all suffering in saṃsāra. In the deva's verse *upadhi* is used in the first sense.

In his reply the Buddha turns the devatā's expression "one without acquisitions" (*nirupadhi*) on its head by using the term as a designation for the arahant, who is free from all four kinds of *upadhi* and thus completely free from suffering. The pair of verses recurs below at **4:8**, with Māra as the interlocutor.

22 Spk: *There is no affection like that for oneself* because people, even if they discard their parents and neglect to care for their children, still care for themselves (see **v. 392**). There is *no wealth equal to grain* because people, when famished, will give away gold and silver and other assets in order to obtain grain. *There is no light like wisdom* because wisdom can illumine the ten-thousandfold world system and dispel the darkness concealing the three periods of time, which even the sun cannot do (see AN II 139–40). *Among the waters the rain is supreme* because if the rainfall were to be cut off even the great ocean would dry up, but when the rain continues to pour down the world becomes one mass of water even up to the Ābhassara deva world.

23 From this point on, wherever the text does not specify the identity of the speakers, it is implied that the first verse is spoken by a devatā and the reply by the Buddha.

24 In pāda b, Be and Se read *sannisīvesu,* a word not encountered elsewhere, while Ee1 & 2, following SS, read *sannisinnesu,* which may be a "correction" of the original reading; the text available to the subcommentator evidently read *sannisīvesu.* Spk glosses: *yathā phāsukaṭṭhānaṃ upagantvā sannisinnesu vissamānesu.* [Spk-pṭ: *parissamavinodanatthaṃ sabbaso sannisīdantesu; d-kārassa hi v-kāraṃ katvā niddeso.*] The gist of this explanation is that at noon all the birds (and other animals), exhausted by the heat, are quietly resting in order to dispel their fatigue.

In pāda c the resolution of *saṇateva* is problematic. Spk glosses: *saṇati viya mahāviravaṃ viya muccati,* "it seems to make a sound, it seems as if it releases a great roar." This implies that Spk divides the *sandhi* into *saṇate iva.* Ee2 apparently accepts this with its reading *saṇate va*. Following a suggestion of VĀT, I resolve it *saṇati eva*, taking the sense to be that the forest itself is emitting the sound. The verb *saṇati* means merely to make a sound, and is elsewhere used to describe a noisy creek (Sn 720–21), so here the sound might be more appropriately described as a murmur than as a roar. In pāda d the verb is *paṭibhāti*, glossed by Spk as *upaṭṭhāti*.

Spk: In the dry season, at high noon, when the animals and birds are all sitting quietly, a great sound arises from the depths of the forest as the wind blows through the trees, bamboo clusters, and hollows. At that moment an obtuse deva, unable to find a companion with whom to sit and converse amiably, uttered the first stanza. But when a bhikkhu has returned from his alms round and is sitting alone in a secluded forest abode attending to his meditation subject, abundant happiness arises (as is expressed in the rejoinder).

25 *Arati, tandi, vijambhikā*, and *bhattasammada* recur at **46:2** (V 64,31–32) and **46:51** (V 103,13–14). Formal definitions are at Vibh 352. Spk: The *noble path* (*ariyamagga*) is both the mundane and supramundane path. The clearing of the path comes about when one expels the mental corruptions by means of the path itself, with the energy (*viriya*) conascent with the path.

On the distinction between the mundane and supramundane paths, see the Introduction to Part V, pp.1490–92.

26 Spk explains *pade pade*, in pāda c, thus: "In each object (*ārammaṇe ārammaṇe*); for whenever a defilement arises in relation to any object, it is just there that one founders (*visīdati*). But the phrase can also be interpreted by way of the modes of deportment (*iriyāpatha*); if a defilement arises while one is walking, (standing, sitting, or lying down), it is just there that one founders. *Intentions* (*saṅkappa*) should be understood here by way of the three wrong intentions, i.e., of sensuality, ill will, and harming."

27 The simile of the tortoise is elaborated at **35:240**, followed by the same verse. Spk: One is *independent* (*anissito*) of the dependencies of craving and views, and *fully quenched* by

the quenching of defilements (*kilesaparinibbāna*). He would not reprove another person for defects in conduct, etc., from a desire to humiliate him, but he would speak out of compassion, with the idea of rehabilitating him, having set up in himself the five qualities (speaking at the right time, about a true matter, gently, in a beneficial way, with a mind of lovingkindness; see AN III 244,1–3).

28 Be and Se read the verb in pāda c as *apabodhati,* Ee1 as *appabodhati,* Ee2 as *appabodheti.* Apparently the latter readings arose on the supposition that the word is formed from *a* + *pabodh.* Spk's gloss—*apaharanto bujjhati,* "who, pulling back, knows"—supports *apabodhati* (*apa* + *bodh*). The Skt parallel at Uv 19:5 has a different pāda altogether, *sarvapāpaṃ jahāty eṣa.* Though the verse includes no ostensible interrogative, Spk interprets it as posing a question. I take *koci* to be equivalent to *kvaci,* though Spk glosses it as a personal pronoun.

Spk: As a good thoroughbred who knows to pull back from the whip does not let it strike him, so a bhikkhu who is keen to avoid blame—who knows to pull back from it—does not let any genuine ground for abuse strike him. The deva asks: "Is there any such arahant?" But no one is wholly free from abuse on false grounds. The Buddha answers that such arahants, who avoid unwholesome states from a sense of shame, are few.

29 Spk: The deva refers to one's mother as a "little hut" because one dwells in her womb for ten months; to a wife as a "little nest" because, after a hard day's work, men resort to the company of women in the way that birds, after searching for food during the day, resort to their nests at night; to sons as "lines extended" (*santānakā*) because they extend the family lineage; and to craving as bondage. The Buddha replies as he does because he will never again dwell within a mother's womb, or support a wife, or beget sons.

30 Spk: The deva asked these additional questions because he was astonished by the Buddha's quick replies and wanted to find out if he had really grasped the meaning.

Although three eds. employ the singular *santānakaṃ* in

pāda c of this verse, SS and Ee2 have the plural *santānake*, which seems preferable for maintaining consistency with the other verses. *Kintāham* should be resolved *kin te ahaṃ*.

31 The opening portion of this sutta appears, with elaboration, in the prologue to the Samiddhi Jātaka (Ja No. 167), which includes the first pair of verses as well. MN No. 133 opens in a similar way, with Samiddhi as the protagonist. The bhikkhu Samiddhi was so named because his body was splendid (*samiddha*), handsome and lovely. Spk makes it clear that this is a female devatā (called a *devadhītā* in the Jātaka), an earth-deity (*bhummadevatā*) who resided in the grove. When she saw Samiddhi in the light of the early dawn, she fell in love with him and planned to seduce him. Samiddhi appears below at **4:22** and **35:65–68**.

32 The verses revolve around a pun on the double meaning of *bhuñjati*, to eat food and to enjoy sense pleasures. The devatā is ostensibly telling Samiddhi to eat before going on alms round (i.e., to get his fill of sensual pleasures before taking to the monk's life), but Samiddhi insists he will not abandon the monk's life for the sake of sensual enjoyment.

Spk: The devatā had spoken of *time* with reference to the time of youth, when one is able to enjoy sensual pleasures. In pādas ab of his reply Samiddhi speaks with reference to the time of death (*maraṇakāla*), which is *hidden* (*channa*) in that one never knows when it will arrive. In pāda d he refers to the time for practising the duty of an ascetic (*samaṇadhammakaraṇakāla*), as it is difficult for an old person to learn the Dhamma, practise austerities, dwell in the forest, and develop the meditative attainments. The *vo* in pāda a is a mere indeclinable (*nipātamatta*).

33 At **4:21** Māra offers the same advice to a group of young bhikkhus, who reply in words identical with those of Samiddhi. The Buddha's exposition of the dangers in sensual pleasures may be found at MN I 85–87, 364–67, 506–8, and elsewhere. Samiddhi's answer reiterates the standard verse of homage to the Dhamma, omitting only the first term ("well expounded"), which is not relevant here. Spk interprets the "immediate" or "timeless" (*akālika*) character of the Dhamma by way of the Abhidhamma doctrine

that the fruit (*phala*) arises in immediate succession to its respective path (*magga*), but this idea certainly seems too narrow for the present context, where the contrast is simply between the immediately beneficial Dhamma and "time-consuming" sensual pleasures. For more on *akālika*, see **II, n. 103**.

A few words are called for in explanation of my translation of *opanayika* as "applicable," which departs from the prevalent practice of rendering it "leading onward." CPD points out that "the context in which [the word] occurs shows clearly that it cannot have the active sense of 'leading to' ... but must rather be interpreted in a passive sense (gerundive) in accordance with the commentaries." To be sure, Vism 217,10–12 (Ppn 7:84) does allow for an active sense with its alternative derivation: *nibbānaṃ upanetī ti ariyamaggo upaneyyo ... opanayiko*, "it leads on to Nibbāna, thus the noble path is onward-leading ... so it is leading onwards"; this derivation, however, is almost surely proposed with "edifying" intent. Earlier in the same passage the word is glossed by the gerundive *upanetabba*, "to be brought near, to be applied," so I follow the derivation at Vism 217,3–9 (Ppn 7:83), which is probably correct etymologically: *bhāvanāvasena attano citte upanayanaṃ arahatī ti opanayiko ... asaṅkhato pana attano cittena upanayanaṃ arahatī ti opanayiko; sacchikiriyāvasena allīyanaṃ arahatī ti attho*; "The Dhamma (as noble path) is applicable because it deserves application within one's own mind by way of meditative development.... But the unconditioned Dhamma (i.e., Nibbāna) is applicable because it deserves application with one's own mind; that is, it deserves being resorted to by way of realization." While the word *opanayika* does not occur in any other context that allows us to draw inferences about its meaning, the cognate expression *att' ūpanāyiko* (at **55:7** (V 353,21, 26) and Vin III 91,33–34) clearly means "applicable to oneself." On the other hand, to indicate that the Dhamma conduces to Nibbāna the texts use another expression, *niyyānika upasamasaṃvattanika* (see, e.g., **55:25** (V 380,11) and MN I 67,13), which would not fit the contexts where the above formula appears.

34 Spk: "Each of the deva-kings has a retinue of a hundred or a thousand *koṭis* of devas. Placing themselves in grand positions, they see the Tathāgata. How can powerless female devas like us get a chance to see him?" A *koṭi* = 10,000,000.

35 Spk: *What can be expressed* (*akkheyya*) are the five aggregates, the objective sphere of linguistic reference (*not* the terms of expression themselves). *Beings who perceive what can be expressed* (*akkheyyasaññino sattā*): When ordinary beings perceive the five aggregates, their perceptions are affected by the ideas of permanence, pleasure, and self, elsewhere called "distortions" (*vipallāsa*, AN II 52,4–8). These distorted perceptions then provoke the defilements, on account of which beings *become established in what can be expressed* (*akkheyyasmiṃ patiṭṭhitā*). Beings "become established in" the five aggregates in eight ways: by way of lust, hatred, delusion, views, the underlying tendencies, conceit, doubt, and restlessness (see **n. 2**).

It-a II 31–32, commenting on the same couplet at It 53, says that "beings who perceive what can be expressed" are those who perceive the five aggregates by way of a percept occurring in the mode of "I," "mine," "deva," "human," "woman," or "man," etc. That is, they perceive the five aggregates as a being or person, etc.

Spk suggests that this verse is stated in order to show how sensual pleasures are "time-consuming." [Spk-pṭ: *Kāmā* here denotes all phenomena of the three planes, called sensual pleasures because they are pleasurable (*kamanīyā*).] This suggestion seems confirmed by the last line: those who do not understand the five aggregates correctly "come under the yoke of Death"; they undergo repeated birth and death and hence remain caught in saṃsāra, the net of time.

36 Spk: One "fully understands what can be expressed" by way of the three kinds of full understanding: (i) by full understanding of the known (*ñātapariññā*) one understands the five aggregates in terms of their individual characteristics, etc.; (ii) by full understanding by scrutinization (*tīraṇapariññā*) one scrutinizes them in forty-two modes as impermanent, suffering, etc.; (iii) by full understanding as abandonment (*pahānapariññā*) one abandons

desire and lust for the aggregates by means of the supreme path. For a fuller discussion, see Vism 606–7 (Ppn 20:3–4) and Vism 611–13 (Ppn 20:18–19), based on Paṭis II 238–42, where, however, only forty modes are enumerated under (ii). The forty-two modes are at Vism 655,15–30 (Ppn 21:59), in connection with "discerning formations as void."

One does not conceive "one who expresses" (*akkhātaraṃ na maññati*). Spk: The arahant does not conceive the speaker as an individual (*puggala*); that is, he no longer takes the five aggregates to be "mine," "I," and "my self."

That does not exist for him (*taṃ hi tassa na hotī ti*): In this couplet I follow SS in omitting, as an interpolation, the words *na tassa atthi*, included in all the printed eds. The Skt version too, cited at Ybhūś 2:2 (Enomoto, CSCS, p. 23), does not include such a phrase, but reads: *tad vai na vidyate tasya, vadeyur yena tam pare*, "That does not exist for him by which others might speak of him."

Spk explains that there exist no grounds for speaking of the arahant as lustful, or as hating, or as deluded. It would be more fitting, perhaps, to see this second couplet as referring to the arahant after his parinibbāna, when by casting off the five aggregates ("what can be expressed") he goes beyond the range of verbal expression (see Sn 1076). It should be noted that thematically these two verses closely correspond to the Mūlapariyāya Sutta (MN No. 1). Spk states that this verse discusses the "directly visible" ninefold supramundane Dhamma, i.e., the four paths, their fruits, and Nibbāna.

37 The "three discriminations" (*tayo vidhā*) are the three modes of conceit: the conceit "I am better" (*seyyo 'ham asmimāna*), the conceit "I am equal" (*sadiso 'ham asmimāna*), and the conceit "I am worse" (*hīno 'ham asmimāna*). See **22:49** (III 48–49), **45:162**, **46:41**. At Vibh 389–90 it is shown that these three become ninefold in so far as each triad may be entertained by one who is truly better, truly equal, or truly worse. One "not shaken in the three discriminations" is the arahant, who alone has completely eradicated the fetter of conceit. Spk points out that the first couplet shows how sensual pleasures are time-consuming, while

the second couplet discusses the supramundane Dhamma.

38 The most common reading of this pāda is *pahāsi saṅkhaṃ na vimānam ajjhagā*, found in Be, Se, and Ee1 of **v. 49**, in Be and Ee1 of the parallel **v. 105**, and in the lemma in Spk (Be, Se) to **v. 49**. From his comments it is clear the commentator had a text with *vimāna*, which he explains as equivalent to *vividhamāna*: "He does not assume the threefold conceit with its nine divisions" (*navabhedaṃ tividhamānaṃ na upagato*). Spk's alternative explanation, which takes *vimānaṃ* to be the mother's womb, the destination of the rebirth process, seems too fanciful to be taken seriously. *Vimānadassī* occurs at Sn 887b in the sense of "contemptuous," but this meaning of *vimāna* may be too narrow for the present context.

The verse may have originally read *na ca mānam* and this reading may have already been corrupted before the age of the commentaries, *c/v* confusion being not uncommon in Sinhala-script texts. The corruption would then have been preserved and perpetuated by the commentators. Despite the dominance of *na vimānam*, the reading *na ca mānam* is found in **v. 105** of Se, in the lemma to **v. 49** in four Sinhala mss of Spk (referred to in the notes to Spk (Se)), and in Thai eds. of SN and Spk. The Skt counterpart (quoted at Ybhūś 2:4; Enomoto, CSCS, p. 23) has *prahāya mānaṃ ca na saṅgam eti*, which corresponds more closely to the alternative reading of the Pāli. The original finite verb may have been the rare reduplicative perfect *ājā* (as in SS) or *āgā* (as in Ee2 and Thai eds.). See von Hinüber, "On the Perfect in Pāli," *Selected Papers*, pp. 174–76.

Spk understands *pahāsi saṅkhaṃ* to mean that the arahant can no longer be described by such concepts as lustful, hating, or deluded, but the point is more likely to be that he has stopped forming *papañcasaññāsaṅkhā*, "ideas and notions arisen from mental proliferation" (see MN I 112,2–3). The Skt reading *saṅgam* may actually make better sense in this context. It seems that this phrase refers back to **v. 47** and *na vimānam ajjhagā* back to **v. 48**. It is possible, too, that the lines describe the arahant after his parinibbāna, when he can no longer be reckoned by way of the five aggregates (see **44:1**). Pādas cf seem to be describing the arahant after his parinibbāna, though elsewhere he is also said to be unfindable here and now (e.g., at **22:86**; III 118,35–36).

39 Spk explains the avoidance of evil in body, speech, and mind by way of the ten courses of wholesome kamma (see MN I 47,12–17, 287–288, etc.). The phrase *having abandoned sense pleasures* rejects the extreme of indulgence in sensual pleasures; *one should not pursue a course that is painful and harmful* rejects the extreme of self-mortification. Thus, Spk says, the verse points to the middle way that avoids the two extremes. The whole verse can also be construed positively in terms of the Noble Eightfold Path: doing no evil by body and speech implies right speech, right action, and right livelihood; "mindful" implies right effort, right mindfulness, and right concentration; "clearly comprehending" implies right view and right intention. Spk says that at the end of the Buddha's discourse the devatā was established in the fruit of stream-entry and spoke this verse, "a great Dhamma teaching," in order to show the eightfold path by which she had attained the fruit.

40 In pāda b, I read *ḍayhamāne va,* with Ee1 and SS, as against *ḍayhamāno va* in Be, Se, and Ee2. With *bhavarāga* in pāda c, these verses also appear as Th 39–40 and 1162–63. In the present form the pair of verses sets a problem in interpretation, for *kāmarāga*, sensual lust, is abandoned by the third path, while *sakkāyadiṭṭhi*, identity view, is abandoned by the first path, so the devatā appears to be advocating a higher attainment than the Buddha. This problem does not arise in the Th version, since *bhavarāga*, lust for existence, is abandoned by the fourth path, that of arahantship. Spk gives an ingenious solution: The deva spoke his verse with reference to the abandoning of sensual lust by way of suppression only (*vikkhambhanappahānam eva*), i.e., temporarily through the attainment of jhāna, while the Buddha recommended the attainment of stream-entry, which eliminates identity view by way of eradication (*samuccheda*) so that not even the subtle underlying tendency (*anusaya*) remains, thus ensuring full liberation in a maximum of seven more lives.

41 The verse poses a riddle which hinges on two connota-

tions of *phusati*, "to touch": (i) to acquire a particular kamma, here the grave kamma of wronging an innocent person; and (ii) to reap the result of that kamma when it comes to maturity.

42 At Sn 662 this verse refers to Kokāliya's calumny of Sāriputta and Moggallāna (see **6:10**, which includes the story but not this verse). A different, and less credible, background story is told at Dhp-a III 31–33, commenting on Dhp 125; see BL 2:282–84. On the kammic result of harming innocents, see Dhp 137–40.

43 This verse and the next form the opening theme of Vism and are commented on at Vism 1–4 (Ppn 1:1–8); the explanation is incorporated into Spk. VĀT suggests that the words *antojaṭā bahijaṭā* should be taken as *bahubbīhi* compounds in apposition to *pajā* ("having a tangle inside, having a tangle outside"), but I translate in accordance with Spk, which treats them as *tappurisa*.

Spk: *Tangle* (*jaṭā*) is a term for the network of craving, in the sense that it "laces together," for it arises repeatedly up and down among the sense objects such as forms. There is *a tangle inside, a tangle outside*, because craving arises with respect to one's own possessions and those of others; with respect to one's own body and the bodies of others; and with respect to the internal and external sense bases.

44 The Buddha's reply is a succinct statement of the threefold training, with *samādhi* referred to by the word *citta*. Spk says wisdom is mentioned three times in the verse: first as innate intelligence ("wise"); second, as insight-wisdom (*vipassanā-paññā*), the wisdom to be developed; and third, as "discretion," the pragmatic wisdom that takes the lead in all tasks (*sabbakiccaparināyikā parihāriyapaññā*).

Spk: "Just as a man standing on the ground and taking up a well-sharpened knife might disentangle a great tangle of bamboos, so this bhikkhu ... standing on the ground of virtue and taking up, with the hand of practical intelligence exerted by the power of energy, the knife of insight-wisdom well sharpened on the stone of concentration, might disentangle, cut away, and demolish the entire tangle of craving that had overgrown his own mental continuum" (adapted from Ppn 1:7).

45 While the previous verse shows the trainee (*sekha*), who is capable of disentangling the tangle, this verse shows the arahant, the one beyond training (*asekha*), who has finished disentangling the tangle.

46 Spk says this verse is stated to show the opportunity (or region) for the disentangling of the tangle (*jaṭāya vijaṭanokāsa*). Here *name* (*nāma*) represents the four mental aggregates. Spk treats *impingement* (*paṭigha*) as metrical shorthand for perception of impingement (*paṭighasaññā*). According to Spk-pṭ, in pāda c we should read a compressed *dvanda* compound, *paṭigharūpasaññā* ("perceptions of impingement and of form"), the first part of which has been truncated, split off, and nasalized to fit the metre. Impingement being the impact of the five sense objects on the five sense bases, "perception of impingement" (*paṭighasaññā*) is defined as the fivefold sense perception (see Vibh 261,31–34 and Vism 329,22–24; Ppn 10:16). Perception of form (*rūpasaññā*) has a wider range, comprising as well the perceptions of form visualized in the jhānas [Spk-pṭ: perception of the form of the earth-*kasiṇa*, etc.]. Spk explains that the former implies sense-sphere existence, the latter form-sphere existence, and the two jointly imply formless-sphere existence, thus completing the three realms of existence.

It is here that this tangle is cut. Spk: The tangle is cut, in the sense that the round with its three planes is terminated; it is cut and ceases in dependence on Nibbāna.

47 Readings of pāda b differ. I follow Se and Ee2, *mano yatattam āgataṃ*, as against Be *na mano saṃyatattam āgataṃ*.

Spk: This deva held the view that one should rein in every state of mind; whether wholesome or not, whether mundane or supramundane, the mind should be reined in, not aroused. [Spk-pṭ: He believed that every state of mind brings suffering and that the unconscious state is better.] The Buddha spoke the rejoinder to show that a distinction should be made between the mind to be reined in and the mind to be developed. See **35:205** (IV 195,15–30), where the Buddha advises reining in the mind (*tato cittaṃ nivāraye*) from objects that arouse the defilements.

48 Spk: This deva, who dwelt in a forest grove, heard the

forest bhikkhus using such expressions as "I eat, I sit, my bowl, my robe," etc. Thinking, "I had imagined these bhikkhus to be arahants, but can arahants speak in ways that imply belief in a self?" he approached the Buddha and posed his question.

49 *Vohāramattena so vohareyya*. Spk: "Although arahants have abandoned talk that implies belief in a self, they do not violate conventional discourse by saying, 'The aggregates eat, the aggregates sit, the aggregates' bowl, the aggregates' robe'; for no one would understand them." See in this connection DN I 202,7–9: "Thus, Citta, there are these worldly expressions, worldly terms, worldly conventions, worldly concepts, which the Tathāgata uses without grasping them."

50 Spk: At this point the deva thought that while arahants may not speak thus because they hold a view (of self), they might do so because they still have conceit (i.e., *asmimāna*, the conceit "I am"). Hence he asked the second question, and the Buddha's reply indicates arahants have abandoned the ninefold conceit (see **n. 37**).

51 Spk resolves *mānaganthassa* in pāda b as *māno ca ganthā assa*, "for him conceit and knots," in order to conform to the doctrinal tetrad of *gantha*, which does not include *māna*; see **45:174**. It seems, however, that here *mānaganthā* should be understood in a looser sense, as *mānassa ganthā*. At It 4,16, in a sutta solely about *māna*, we find *mānaganthā* used as a *bahubbīhi* compound qualifying *pajā* ("a generation knotted by conceit") and arahants described as *mānaganthābhibhuno* ("those who have overcome the knots of conceit"), which supports my rendering here. The readings of pāda c vary: Be has *maññataṃ*, Se *maññanaṃ* (which is the gloss in Spk (Be)), Ee1 *yamataṃ*, Ee2 *ya mataṃ* (= *yam mataṃ*?). Spk explains that he has transcended the threefold conceiving due to craving, views, and conceit.

52 Spk: The question refers to the "streams" of saṃsāra, the answer to Nibbāna. Portions of the reply can be found at DN I 223,13–15 and Ud 9,4. On the stopping of the streams, see Sn 1034–37, and on the round not revolving see the expression *vaṭṭaṃ … natthi paññāpanāya* at **22:56–57** and **44:6** (IV 391,9).

53 Ee2 precedes this verse with another (**v. 70**) found only in two Lanna mss from northern Thailand. As that verse is not included in any other edition or known ms of SN, and hardly relates to the subject matter of the dialogue between the Buddha and the devatā, it clearly does not belong here; thus I have not translated it. My decision is further supported by the absence of any gloss on the verse in Spk and Spk-pṭ, which indicates it was not found in the texts available to the commentators. At Ee2, p. xvii, the editor argues that this verse must be "restored" to provide a question put by the deity, but he assumes that the sutta originally read the first word of **v. 72**d as *te* which was then changed to *ko* or *ke* by the textual tradition in order to supply a question. But since *ke* as a question makes perfectly good sense, both syntactically and semantically, there is no reason to suppose the original reading was *te* and thus no need to interpolate a new verse to supply the question.

54 Spk: "*Among those who have become so avid* (*ussukkajātesu*): Among those who are engaged in various tasks, avid to produce unarisen forms, etc., and to enjoy those that have arisen." In pāda c of the second verse I read *ke 'dha taṇhaṃ* with Be and Se, as against *gedhataṇhaṃ* ("greed and craving") in Ee1 & 2, and *kodhataṇhaṃ* ("anger and craving") in SS. In pāda d, Ee2 reads *te lokasmiṃ* as against *ke lokasmiṃ* in the other eds.

Ussuka (Skt *utsuka*) means anxiously desirous, zealous, or busily engaged in some pursuit. The corresponding noun is *ussukka*, which is sometimes found where the adjective would have been more appropriate. *Ussuka* is used in both a laudatory and reprobative sense. At **41:3** (IV 288,12 = 291,4, 302,7), it occurs in the commendatory sense, which I render "zealous." See too MN I 324,27 and Vin I 49,19–50,8. The negative sense—of being greedy, ambitious, or "avid" (my preferred rendering)—is found here and at Dhp 199. The expression *appossukka*, lit. "having little zeal," is used to describe one who refrains from busy activity. In SN we find this expression—which I generally render, loosely, "(living) at ease"—at **9:10** (I 202,22), **21:4** (II 277,12), **35:240** (IV 178,1, here "keeping still"), and

51:10 (V 262,18). The abstract noun *appossukkatā,* at **6:1** (I 137,1, 6), characterizes the Buddha's original inclination, just after his enlightenment, towards a life of quietude rather than towards the "busy work" of preaching the Dhamma. See too below **n. 366** and **n. 551**.

55 Spk: The *four wheels* are the four modes of deportment (walking, standing, sitting, lying down). The *nine doors* are the nine "wound openings" (eyes, ears, nostrils, mouth, genitals, anus). It is *filled up* with impure body parts (head-hairs, etc.), and *bound with greed,* i.e., with craving. *How does one escape from it?*: How can there be emergence from such a body? How can there be freedom, release, a transcendence of it? Spk-pṭ adds: It is *born from a bog* (*paṅkajāta*) because it is produced in the foul bog of the mother's womb. The Pāli expression could also have been rendered, "It *is* a bog," but I follow Spk-pṭ. This stark perspective on the body is elaborated at Sn I, 11, pp. 34–35.

56 In pāda a (= Dhp 398a), Ee1 *nandiṃ* should be amended to *naddhiṃ*. Spk explains that in the Dhp verse *varattā* is craving (*taṇhā*), but as craving is mentioned separately in our verse, *varattā* is glossed differently here.

Spk: The *thong* (*naddhi*) is hostility (*upanāha*), i.e., strong anger; the *strap* (*varattā*) is the remaining defilements. *Desire and greed* refer to the same mental state spoken of in two senses: desire (*icchā*) is the preliminary weak stage, or the desire for what has not been obtained; greed (*lobha*) is the subsequent strong stage, or the holding to an acquired object. *Craving with its root*: with its root of ignorance.

57 This verse of inquiry occurs at Sn 165–66, though with an additional couplet and with a variant line in place of the actual question. The inquirers there are the two yakkhas, Hemavata and Sātāgira. The question (or rather, string of questions) is posed only at Sn 168 and the reply given at Sn 169; they are identical with the question and reply at **vv. 221–22**. It is only after receiving this reply that the yakkhas pose the present question, *kathaṃ dukkhā pamuccati?*, and the answer given is identical. Having antelope calves (*eṇijaṅgha*) is one of the thirty-two marks of a great man (see DN III 156,5–12; MN II 136,14). On nāga, see below **n. 84**.

58 Spk: *Here*: in this name-and-form (*nāmarūpa*). By mentioning the five cords of sensual pleasure, form is indicated [Spk-pṭ: because they have the nature of form]. By mind (*mano*), name (*nāma*), i.e., the four mental aggregates, is indicated. Thus the basis (of desire) here can be interpreted by way of the five aggregates, etc.

59 Spk explains that these devas were called *satullapakāyikā* ("belonging to the extolling-of-the-good group") because they had been reborn in heaven as a result of extolling the Dhamma of the good by way of undertaking it [Spk-pṭ: that is, the Dhamma of the good which consists of going for refuge, taking the precepts, etc.].

The background story is as follows: Once a merchant ship with a crew of seven hundred men, while crossing the sea, was beset by a terrible storm. As the ship sank, the crew members, praying frantically to their gods, noticed one of their number sitting calmly, cross-legged "like a yogi," free from fear. They asked him how he could remain so calm, and he explained that as he had undertaken the Three Refuges and Five Precepts he had no reason for fear. They requested the same from him, and after dividing them into seven groups of a hundred each he gave each group in turn the refuges and precepts, completing the procedure just as the ship was swallowed up by the sea. As the fruit of this final deed of merit, all the men were immediately reborn in the Tāvatiṃsa heaven in a single group with their leader at the head. Recognizing that they had attained such fortune through their leader's kindness, they came to the Blessed One's presence to speak praise of him.

60 Spk: Just as oil is not to be obtained from sand, so wisdom is not gained *from another*, from the blind fool; but just as oil is obtained from sesamum seeds, so one gains wisdom by learning the Dhamma of the good and by following a wise person.

61 I take *sātataṃ* to be an accusative adverb from the abstract noun of *sāta*. Spk, however, takes it as an adverb from *satata*, "continually," which seems less satisfactory.

62 *Pariyāyena*. Spk glosses *kāraṇena*, "for a reason," which does not help much. I understand the purport to be that

their verses are only provisionally correct, acceptable from a mundane point of view. The Buddha's verse is definitive (*nippariyāyena*) because it points to the ultimate goal. See the contrast of *pariyāyena* and *nippariyāyena* at AN IV 449–54.

63 The stain (*mala*) is stinginess itself; see the stock description of the generous lay follower as one who "dwells at home with a mind rid of the stain of stinginess" (*vigatamalamaccherena cetasā agāraṃ ajjhāvasati*).

64 Spk: *Those do not die among the dead*: They do not die among those who are "dead" by the death consisting in miserliness. The goods of the miser are just like those of the dead, for neither distribute their belongings.

65 Spk: *If one practises the Dhamma*: if one practises the Dhamma by way of the ten courses of wholesome kamma. *Though getting on by gleaning* (*samuñjakaṃ care*): one gets on "by gleaning" by cleaning up the threshing floor, etc., beating the straw, etc. *Of those who sacrifice a thousand*: Of those who sacrifice (offer alms) to a thousand bhikkhus or who offer alms purchased with a thousand pieces of money. This done a hundred thousand times is equivalent to alms given to ten *koṭis* of bhikkhus or worth ten *koṭis* of money (a *koṭi* = 10,000,000). *Are not worth even a fraction*: the word "fraction" (*kala*) can mean a sixteenth part, or a hundredth part, or a thousandth part; here a hundredth part is intended. If one divides into a hundred parts (the value of) a gift given by him, the gift of 10,000 *koṭis* given by the others is not worth one portion of that.

Though Spk speaks of alms offerings to bhikkhus, **v. 94** just below implies that the animal sacrifices of the brahmins are what is being rejected.

66 Spk: "Faith" here means faith in kamma and its fruit. Just as in war a few heroic men conquer even many cowards, so one endowed with faith, etc., in giving even a small gift, crushes much stinginess and achieves abundant fruit.

67 Spk explains *dhammaladdhassa* as either wealth righteously gained, or a person who has gained righteousness, i.e., a noble disciple. The former alternative makes better sense; see AN II 68,13–20. Yama is the god of the nether world; Vetaraṇī is the Buddhist equivalent of the river Styx (see

Sn 674 and Pj II 482,4–6). Spk says that Vetaraṇī is mentioned only as "the heading of the teaching," i.e., as an example; he has actually passed over all thirty-one great hells.

68 *Viceyyadānaṃ.* The expression is an absolutive syntactical compound; see Norman, "Syntactical Compounds in Middle Indo-Aryan," in *Collected Papers,* 4:218–19.

Spk: A gift given after making discrimination. There are two kinds of discrimination: (i) regarding the offering, i.e., one puts aside inferior items and gives only superior items; and (ii) regarding the recipient, i.e., one leaves aside those defective in morality or the followers of the ninety-five heretical creeds (*pāsaṇḍa,* the non-Buddhist sects; see **n. 355**) and gives to those endowed with such qualities as virtue, etc., who have gone forth in the Buddha's dispensation.

69 In pāda a, I read *addhā hi* with Ee2 and SS (also at Ja III 472,29), as against *saddhā hi* in Be and Ee1 and *saddhābhi* in Se. Spk glosses *dhammapadaṃ va* in pāda b thus: *nibbānasaṅkhātaṃ dhammapadam eva,* "just the state of Dhamma known as Nibbāna." Usually *dhammapada* is a stanza or saying of Dhamma (as at **vv. 785–86, 826**), which is also plausible in this context, but I prefer to take it as a metrical contraction of *dhammapaṭipadā,* the practice-path of Dhamma, a sense attested to at Sn 88, which explicitly equates *dhammapada* with *magga.* The point the Buddha is then making is that the practice of Dhamma (by the Noble Eightfold Path aimed at Nibbāna) is better than the practice of giving aimed at a heavenly rebirth.

The fuller gloss on the verse at Ja III 474 supports the above interpretation: "Although giving is definitely (*ekaṃsen' eva,* apparently the gloss on *addhā hi*) praised in many ways, a *dhammapada*—a portion of Dhamma (*dhammakoṭṭhāsa*) consisting in serenity and insight and in Nibbāna—is even better than giving. Why so? Because in the past (*pubb' eva*)—that is, in this aeon, Kassapa Buddha and so on—and even earlier (*pubbatar' eva*), that is, Vessabhū Buddha and so on (in earlier aeons), the good, the superior persons (*sappurisā*), endowed with wisdom, developed serenity and insight and attained Nibbāna."

70 In pāda d, we should adopt the reading of the agent noun

āgantā in Be, Se, and Ee2, as against *āgantvā* in Ee1, which leaves the sentence with an unresolved absolutive clause. We find *āgantā* used in the sense of *āgāmī*, and *anāgantā* used synonymously with *anāgāmī* (in relation to *itthattaṃ*, "this state of being") at AN I 63,30–64,18.

Spk: They do not come from *Death's realm*, that is, from the round of existence with its three planes, to Nibbāna, which is *the state of no-more-coming-back* (*apunāgamana*), so called because beings do not return from Nibbāna. One who is heedless and bound to sensual pleasures cannot attain that.

71 The identity of the speaker of this passage is difficult to determine from the text. I follow Ee2 in taking it to be another devatā. Though most editions break the lines up as if they were verse, there is no recognizable metre and it seems likely they are intended as prose. Ee2 does not number it as a verse.

Spk says that misery (*agha*) in the first line is the suffering of the five aggregates, and suffering (*dukkha*) in the second line is synonymous with it. The fourth line is paraphrased: "By the removal of the five aggregates the suffering of the round is removed."

72 In pāda b the unusual compound *saṅkapparāga* is glossed by Spk as *saṅkappitarāga*, "intended lust." Mp III 407,5 glosses: *saṅkappavasena uppannarāgo*, "lust arisen by way of intention (or thought)." Spk-pṭ adds: *subhādivasena saṅkappitavatthumhi rāgo*, "lust in regard to an object thought about as beautiful, etc." The key to the expression, however, is probably Dhp 339d (= Th 760d), where we find *saṅkappā rāganissitā*, "intentions based on lust." Spk sums up the purport of the verse thus: "Here the identification of sensuality with the sensual object is rejected; it is the sensual defilement that is called sensuality."

Dhīra allows of two derivations, one meaning "wise," the other "firm, steadfast"; see PED and MW, s.v. *dhīra*. I have usually translated it as "wise," following the commentarial gloss *paṇḍita*, but elsewhere (e.g., at **vv. 411**e, **413**e, **493**a, **495**a) I have taken advantage of the word's ambivalence to render it "steadfast." The word has elevated overtones and seems to be used solely in verse.

73 *Akiñcana* in pāda c is a common epithet of the arahant. Spk explains it as devoid of the "something" (or impediments) of lust, hatred, and delusion (see **41:7**; IV 297,18–19 = MN I 298,14–15).

74 Spk: Mogharāja was an elder skilled in the sequential structure of discourses (*anusandhikusala*). [Spk-pṭ: He was one of the sixteen pupils of the brahmin Bāvari; see Sn 1116–19.] Having observed that the meaning of the last verse had not gone in sequence, he spoke thus to connect it in sequence (perhaps by drawing out its implications?). Spk points out that although all arahants can be described as "the best of men, faring for the good of humans" (*naruttamaṃ atthacaraṃ narānaṃ*), the elder used this expression with specific reference to the Buddha (*dasabalaṃ sandhāy' eva*). Spk paraphrases his statement as an interrogative (*te kiṃ pasaṃsiyā udāhu apasaṃsiyā*), which I follow, but it might also be read as a simple declaration which is first confirmed and then improved upon by the Buddha.

75 Spk explains *bhikkhū* in pāda a (and presumably in pāda d too) as a vocative addressed to Mogharāja; but as the latter is also addressed by name it seems preferable to take the word in both instances as a nominative plural. In both Be and Se the word is clearly plural. The Buddha thus confirms that those who venerate him are praiseworthy, but steers the inquirer beyond mere devotion by adding that those who understand the truth and abandon doubt (by attaining the path of stream-entry) are even more praiseworthy; for they will eventually become "surmounters of ties" (*saṅgātigā*), i.e., arahants.

76 Spk: There is no separate deva world named "the faultfinders" (*ujjhānasaññino*). This name was given to these devas by the redactors of the texts because they arrived in order to find fault with the Tathāgata for his "misuse" of the four requisites. They had thought: "The ascetic Gotama praises contentment with simple requisites to the bhikkhus, but he himself lives luxuriously. Daily he teaches the Dhamma to the multitude. His speech goes in one direction, his deeds in another." The fact that they address the Buddha while they are still hovering in the air is already indicative of disrespect.

77 Spk defines *kitavā* as a fowler (*sākuṇika*) and explains: "As a fowler conceals himself behind branches and foliage and kills the fowl that come near, thereby supporting his wife, so the swindler conceals himself behind a rag-robe and cheats the multitude with clever talk. All the use he makes of the four requisites (robes, food, lodging, and medicines) is use by theft. The deva utters this verse with reference to the Blessed One." The same explanation of *kitavā* is given at Dhp-a III 375 (to Dhp 252). However, at Ja VI 228,19 the word occurs in a context that clearly shows it means a gambler; it is glossed by *akkhadhutta*, a dice-gambler, and I translate accordingly here. See Palihawadana, "From Gambler to Camouflage: The Strange Semantic Metamorphosis of Pāli *Kitavā*."

78 Spk: Why did the Buddha display a smile? It is said that those devas did not apologize in a way that accorded with the Buddha's true nature (*sabhāvena*); they acted as if there were no difference between the Tathāgata, the supreme person in the world, and ordinary worldly people. The Blessed One smiled with the intention: "When discussion arises from this, I will show the power of a Buddha and thereafter I will pardon them."

79 In pāda d, I follow Se in reading *tenīdha*, as against *kenīdha* in Be and Ee1 and *ko nīdha* in Ee2. Neither Spk nor Spk-pṭ offers any help with the meaning of the verse. I translate *kusala* here in accordance with Spk-pṭ's gloss, *anavajja*. At KS 1:35 this verse has been overlooked.

80 This line is missing only in Ee1, which gives the impression that the following verses are spoken by the same deva (and so C.Rh.D has translated them).

81 This verse is identical with **v. 104** except that in pāda d *saṅgā* replaces *dukkhā*. On the five ties, see **n. 12**.

82 This sutta reproduces the opening of the Mahāsamaya Sutta (DN No. 20). The background story, related in detail in Spk (as well as in Sv II 672–77 on DN No. 20), begins when the Buddha intervened to prevent a war between the Sakyans and Koliyans, his paternal and maternal kinsmen, over the waters of the river Rohiṇī. After he mediated a peaceful resolution of their conflict, 250 youths from each community went forth under him as monks. After a

period of exertion, they all attained arahantship on the same day, the full-moon day of the month of Jeṭṭhamūla (May-June). When the sutta opens, on the same night, they have all assembled in the Master's presence in order to announce their attainments. The word *samaya* in the title means, not "occasion," but meeting or "concourse"; Spk glosses *mahāsamaya* in **v. 121** as *mahāsamūha*, "great assembly."

83 The Pure Abodes (*suddhāvāsā*) are five planes in the form realm into which only nonreturners can be reborn: Aviha, Atappa, Sudassa, Sudassī, and Akaniṭṭha. Here they attain final deliverance without ever returning from that realm. All the inhabitants are thus either nonreturners or arahants.

84 In pāda a, I read *khilaṃ* with Se and Ee1 & 2, as against *khīlaṃ* in Be. As *indakhīlaṃ* appears in pāda b, *khīlaṃ* would be redundant in pāda a. The two words are unrelated: *khila* is a wasteland, both literally and figuratively; *khīla*, a stake or pillar, of which a particular kind, the *indakhīla*, is planted in front of a city gate or at the entrance to a house as an auspicious symbol. Spk defines all three terms—*khila*, *paligha*, and *indakhīla*—in the same way, as lust, hatred, and delusion. At **45:166** these three are called *khila*, but at MN I 139,19–22 *paligha* is identified with ignorance (*avijjā*). A set of five *cetokhila* is mentioned at MN I 101,9–27.

These bhikkhus are *unstirred* (*anejā*) by the stirring (or commotion, *ejā*) of craving (see **35:90**). *Nāga* is a word used to designate various types of powerful beings, particularly a class of semi-divine dragons, but it also can denote cobras and bull elephants and is used as a metaphor for the arahant; see MN I 145,5–7. In relation to the arahant the dominant sense is that of the bull elephant (see Dhp chap. 23), but because the latter expression would, in English, seem demeaning rather than complimentary I have left *nāga* untranslated. Spk explains the word by way of "edifying etymology" thus: *chandādīhi* ***na ga****cchantī ti* ***nāgā****; tena tena maggena pahīne kilese* ***na āga****cchantī ti* ***nāgā****;* ***nā****nappakāraṃ* ***āguṃ*** *na karontī ti* ***nāgā***; "nāgas, because they do not go along by way of desire and so forth; nāgas, because they do not return to the defilements abandoned by the successive paths; nāgas, because they do not commit the various kinds of crime." Spk calls this a brief account and refers the reader to Nidd I 201–2 for a full explanation. See too Sn 522, which offers a similar etymology.

The "One with Vision" (*cakkhumā*) is the Buddha, so called because he possesses the "five eyes" (see **n. 370**).

85 Spk: This verse refers to those who have gone for refuge by the definitive going for refuge (*nibbematika-saraṇagamana*). Spk-pṭ: By this the supramundane going for refuge is meant (i.e., by the minimal attainment of stream-entry). But those who go for refuge to the Buddha by the mundane going for refuge (i.e., without a noble attainment) will not go to the plane of misery; and if there are other suitable conditions, on leaving the human body they will fill up the hosts of devas.

86 The Buddha's foot had been injured when his evil cousin Devadatta tried to murder him by hurling a boulder at him on Mount Vulture Peak. The boulder was deflected, but a splinter that broke off from it cut the Buddha's foot and drew blood. The full story of Devadatta's evil schemes is related at Vin II 184–203; see too Ñāṇamoli, *Life of the Buddha*, chap. 13. This same incident forms the background to **4:13** below. According to Spk, the seven hundred devas who came to see the Blessed One included all the devas of the Satullapa host.

87 Spk: He is called a *nāga* on account of his strength (see **n. 84**); a *lion* (*sīha*) on account of his fearlessness; a *thoroughbred* (*ājānīya*) on account of his familiarity with what he has learned (?*byattaparicayaṭṭhena*), or because he knows what is the right means and the wrong means; a *chief bull* (*nisabha*) because he is without a rival; a *beast of burden* (*dhorayha*) because of bearing the burden; *tamed* (*danta*) because he is free from deviant conduct.

Spk glosses *nāgavatā* as *nāgabhāvena*. Geiger takes *nāgavatā* as the instrumental of the adjective *nāgavant* used adverbially in the sense of a comparison (GermTr, p. 93). However, I follow Norman's suggestion (in a personal communication) that *-vata* here may be the Pāli equivalent of Skt *-vrata*, in the sense of "sphere of action, function, mode or manner of life, vow" (MW). Ee2, based on a Lanna commentary, emends the text to read *nāgo va tā ca pan' uppannā sārīrikā vedanā* (and similarly in the parallel passages that follow); see Ee2, p. xviii. But I am doubtful that the text would switch so suddenly from metaphor (in the previous sentence) to simile, and then back to metaphor below.

88 I read with Se: *Passa samādhiṃ subhāvitaṃ cittañ ca suvimuttaṃ na cābhinataṃ na cāpanataṃ na ca sasaṅkhāraniggayhavāritavataṃ.* Be is identical except that the final word in the compound is read as *-gataṃ*; Ee1 *-cāritavataṃ* is clearly an error, rectified in PED, s.v. *vāritavata.* Ee2 reads as in Se, but with *niggayha* taken as uncompounded, which leaves *sasaṅkhāra* dangling. The same expression occurs elsewhere: at AN IV 428,9–10 the full formula is used to describe a *samādhi* called *aññāphala,* the fruit of final knowledge (or perhaps, "having final knowledge as its fruit"); *sasaṅkhāraniggayhavāritavata,* at AN I 254,34, describes a *samādhi* developed as the basis for the six *abhiññā* (probably the fourth jhāna); and at AN III 24,9, DN III 279,4, and Vibh 334,15, it characterizes a "right concentration of fivefold knowledge" (*pañcañāṇika sammā samādhi*). In the present context, it seems, the expression qualifies *cittaṃ,* mind, though the mind has these qualities by virtue of the *samādhi* in which it is absorbed. At AN IV 428,9–10 and elsewhere the phrase clearly qualifies the *samādhi.*

Spk (Se): The concentration is that of the fruit of arahantship (*arahattaphalasamādhi*). The mind is said to be *well liberated* (*suvimuttaṃ*) because it is liberated by the fruit. *Not bent forward and not bent back*: the mind accompanied by lust is said to be "bent forward" (*abhinataṃ*), that accompanied by hate to be "bent back" (*apanataṃ*). Rejecting both, he speaks thus. *Not blocked and checked by forceful suppression*: It is not blocked and checked, having suppressed the defilements forcefully, with effort; rather, it is checked because the defilements have been cut off. The meaning is that it is concentrated by the concentration of fruition (*na ca sasaṅkhāraniggayhavāritavatan ti na sasaṅkhārena sappayogena kilese niggahetvā vāritavataṃ;*

kilesānaṃ pana chinnattā vataṃ, phalasamādhinā samāhitan ti attho). (N.B. While Spk (Be) reads *-gataṃ* in the lemma, it reads *-vataṃ* twice in the explanation.)

Spk-pṭ: This is not achieved, not fixed, forcefully, with effort, by way of abandoning in a particular respect or by way of abandoning through suppression as is the mundane-jhāna mind or insight; but rather (it is achieved) because the defilements have been completely cut off (*lokiyajjhānacittaṃ viya vipassanā viya ca sasaṅkhārena sappayogena tadaṅgappahāna-vikkhambhanappahānavasena ca vikkhambhetvā na adhigataṃ na ṭhapitaṃ, kiñcarahi kilesānaṃ sabbaso chinnatāya*).

The Pāli phrase is extremely difficult and the exact reading uncertain. Indeed, in the Central Asian Skt ms corresponding to DN III 279,4 (Waldschmidt, *Sanskrittexte aus den Turfanfunden* IV, p. 70, V.8 (3)), it is conspicuously absent. A Skt version in Śrāv-bh (p. 444,19–21) reads *vārivad dhṛtaṃ*, "maintained like water," which seems to me unlikely to correspond to the original reading.

Ee1 puts a hiatus after *niggayha*, and Ee2 separates it off entirely; the other eds. integrate *niggayha* into the long compound. There is no way to determine, on the basis of grammar alone, which is correct. Each attempt to resolve the expression into its elements gives rise to its own special problems, and even the *aṭṭhakathās* and *ṭīkās* offer conflicting explanations, e.g., Sv III 1060,11–13 and Vibh-a 421,13–15 take *niggayha* to be absolutive (as does Spk) and turn *vārita* into the absolutive *vāretvā*; their respective *ṭīkās*, Sv-pṭ III 284,24–27 (Be) and Vibh-mṭ 205,16–18 (Be), take *niggayha* as the gerundive *niggahetabba* and *vārita* as the gerundive *vāretabba*. Since *niggayha* occurs elsewhere unambiguously as an absolutive (e.g., at MN III 118,4, interestingly, as here, without a direct object), while there seem to be no instances in canonical Pāli of the word occurring as a gerundive, the *aṭṭhakathās* are more likely to be right. Norman questions this interpretation on the ground that there is no other known instance in Pāli of an absolutive occurring as the second member of a compound (personal communication), but perhaps we should not rule out the possibility that we have such a construction here. I translate, however, in compliance with natural English idiom rather than in strict conformity with the syntax of the Pāli.

Readings of the last part of the compound vary among the different traditions: in general *vāritavata* prevails in the Sinhalese tradition, *vāritagata* in the Burmese, with Burmese vv.ll. *vārivāvata* and *vārivāvaṭa* also recorded. *Vārita* here is a past participle of the causative *vāreti*, to block, to restrain. The terminal member of the compound could then be either *vata* or *gata*. *Gata* is clearly a past participle. *Vata* is more problematic. At KS 1:39, *vāritavataṃ* is rendered "having the habit of self-denial." Apparently C.Rh.D understands *vata* as equivalent to Skt *vrata*. However, Spk's gloss, *chinnattā vataṃ phalasamādhinā samāhitaṃ*, suggests that we have a past participle here, and I would propose that *vata* represents Skt *vṛta*, which according to MW can mean "stopped, checked, held back." I cannot cite other occurrences of the simple participle *vata* in Pāli, but prefixed forms are common enough: *saṃvuta, nibbuta, vivaṭa, āvaṭa*, etc. Thus we would have here two past participles from the same root, one causative, the other simple, so that the compound *vāritavata* would mean "blocked and checked" (unfortunately two distinct English verbs are needed to capture the nuances). Although this construction is certainly unusual, it need not be rejected out of hand, as it may have been used for special emphasis. If the reading *gata* is accepted, *vāritagata* could mean "gone to (attained to) control," with *varita* taken as a noun of state. This certainly sounds more natural than *vāritavata*, but the prevalence of *vata* in the textual tradition lends strong support to its authenticity.

89 It is not clear who is speaking these stanzas, and the verses themselves have no evident connection to the preceding prose portion of the sutta. It is possible they were annexed to the prose text by the redactors of the canon.

I read pāda a as in Be, Se, and Ee2 thus: *pañcavedā sataṃ samaṃ*. The mention of five Vedas is strange but Spk explains: *itihāsapañcamānaṃ vedānaṃ*, "the Vedas with the histories as a fifth." Spk glosses *sataṃ samaṃ* as *vassasataṃ*; Geiger is certainly wrong in rejecting this explanation (GermTr, p. 41, n. 3). Spk also glosses *hīnattarūpā* as *hīnatta-*

sabhāvā and mentions a variant, *hīnattharūpā*, glossed by Spk-pṭ as *hīnatthajātikā parihīnatthā*, "those of low goals, those who have fallen away from the goal."

90 Pajjunna (Skt Parjanya) is the deva-king of rain clouds; originally a Vedic deity, Spk assigns him to the heaven of the Four Great Kings. He is mentioned at DN III 205,6. Nothing else is known about his two daughters, named after the red lotus (see **v. 401**a).

91 These four verses, in the old Āryā metre, have been reconstructed by Alsdorf, *Die Āryā-Strophen des Pali-Kanons*, p. 321.

92 Neither Spk nor Spk-pṭ offers help with the singular *sattassa* in pāda a, but I take this simply as a metrical adaptation of *sattānaṃ*. The line then expresses the same idea as **45:139** (V 41,23–42,2).

93 Spk: There are two Roruva hells: the Smokey Roruva (*dhūmaroruva*) and the Flaming Roruva (*jālaroruva*). The Smokey Roruva is a separate hell, but the Flaming Roruva is a name for the great hell Avīci, called Roruva because when beings are roasted there they cry out again and again (*punappunaṃ ravaṃ ravanti*). At **3:20** the Flaming Roruva is spoken of as the Great Roruva (*mahāroruva*).

94 Spk-pṭ glosses *khantiyā* in pāda b as *ñāṇakhantiyā*, which implies that here the word does not bear its usual meaning of patience, but the special sense of "acquiescence" (in the Teaching). See the expression *dhammanijjhānakkhanti* at MN II 173,21–22.

95 *The Dhamma is of such a nature* (*tādiso dhammo*). Spk: "For such is the nature of the Dhamma, O Blessed One, it has such a structure, such divisions, that it lends itself to analysis in many ways." Spk-pṭ: "It is such that one who has penetrated the truths as they are, skilled in the meaning and the doctrine, might explain, teach, proclaim, establish, disclose, analyse, and elucidate it, bringing forth examples, reasons, and conclusions."

96 Ee2, again on the testimony of the Lanna mss, precedes this verse with another one (**v. 138**) on the unpredictability of death, found also at Ja II 58. But if the verse were originally part of the text, Spk would surely have incorporated here the commentary on it found, with the verse itself, at

Vism 236–37 (Ppn 8:29–34). Since there are strong reasons against the inclusion of the verse, I have passed over it in this translation.

97 *Yakkha* in pāda c is glossed by Spk-pṭ as *satta*. Although *ko* is an interrogative, it seems that the sentence is declarative in force. The verse may be echoing the Taittirīyaka Upaniṣad, II.2, III.2, 7–10.

98 Spk explains the riddle thus: The ocean (*samudda*) or abyss (*pātāla*) is craving, called an ocean because it is unfillable and an abyss because it gives no foothold. Its one root (*ekamūla*) is ignorance; the two whirlpools (*dvirāvaṭṭa*) are the views of eternalism and annihilationism. [Spk-pṭ: Craving for existence revolves by way of the eternalist view; craving for extermination by way of the annihilationist view.] The three stains (*timala*) are lust, hatred, and delusion; the five extensions (*pañcapatthara*), the five cords of sensual pleasure; and the twelve eddies (*dvādasāvaṭṭa*), the six internal and external sense bases.

Ñāṇananda proposes an alternative interpretation of some of these terms: with reference to **36:4**, he takes the abyss to be painful feeling, and with reference to **35:228**, the ocean to be the six sense faculties. The two whirlpools are pleasant and painful feeling; the one root, contact. For details see SN-Anth 2:63–66.

99 Spk: *Of perfect name* (*anomanāma*): of undefective name, of complete name, because he (the Buddha) possesses all excellent qualities (see too **v. 927**c and **n. 653**). *The seer of the subtle goal* (or "meanings": *nipuṇatthadassiṃ*): because he sees the fine, recondite meanings such as the diversity of aggregates, etc. He is *the giver of wisdom* (*paññādadaṃ*) by teaching the path of practice for the achievement of wisdom. *Treading the noble path* (*ariye pathe kamamānaṃ*): the present tense is used with reference to the past, for the Blessed One *had gone* along the noble path on the site of the great enlightenment; he is not going along it now.

I question Spk's explanation of *nipuṇattha*, which seems to refer to *attha* in the sense of the goal, i.e., Nibbāna.

100 Spk relates the background story: In his previous life this deva had been an overzealous bhikkhu who had neglected sleep and food in order to attend to his meditation subject.

Because of his excessive zeal, he died of a wind ailment and was immediately reborn in the Tāvatiṃsa heaven amidst a retinue of celestial nymphs (*accharā*). The change occurred so quickly that he did not even know he had expired and thought he was still a bhikkhu. The nymphs tried to seduce him, but he rejected their amorous advances and tried to resume his meditation practice. Finally, when the nymphs brought him a mirror, he realized he had been reborn as a deva, but he thought: "I did not practise the work of an ascetic in order to take rebirth here, but to attain the supreme goal of arahantship." Then, with his virtue still intact, surrounded by the retinue of nymphs, he went to the Buddha and spoke the first verse.

The verse revolves around a word play between Nandana, the garden of delight, and Mohana, the garden of delusion. The garden was "resounding with a host of nymphs" because the nymphs were singing and playing musical instruments. Spk paraphrases the question by way of its intent: "Teach me insight meditation, which is the basis for arahantship."

101 Spk: The eightfold path is called *the straight way* (*ujuko maggo*) because it is devoid of crookedness of bodily conduct, etc. The destination, Nibbāna, is said to be *fearless* (*abhaya*) because there is nothing to fear in that and because there is no fear for one who has attained it. Unlike an actual chariot, which rattles or whines when its axle is not lubricated or when it is mounted by too many people, the eightfold path does not rattle or whine (*na kūjati na viravati*) even when mounted simultaneously by 84,000 beings. The chariot itself is also the eightfold path, and its *wheels of wholesome states* (*dhammacakka*) are bodily and mental energy. The "Dhamma" that is called *the charioteer* is the supramundane path, with the *right view* of insight (*vipassanā-sammādiṭṭhi*) *running out in front* (*purejava*). For just as the king's servants first clear the path before the king comes out, so the right view of insight clears the way by contemplating the aggregates, etc., as impermanent, etc., and then the right view of the path (*magga-sammādiṭṭhi*) arises fully understanding the round of existence.

In **v. 150**c I read *akūjano* with Be and Ee2, as against *aku-*

jano in Se and Ee1. Geiger derives *akujano* from *kujati*, "to be crooked" (GermTr, p. 51, n. 3), but see Ja VI 252,20, where the "chariot of the body" is described as *vācāsaññamakūjano*, "not rattling by restraint of speech," which supports the reading and rendering adopted here. The extended simile should be compared with that of the *brahmayāna*, the divine vehicle, at **45:4**; see too the extended chariot simile at Ja VI 252–53.

102 Spk: Having completed the discourse (the verse), the Buddha taught the Four Noble Truths, and at the end of that discourse the deva was established in the fruit of stream-entry; the other beings present attained the fruits that accorded with their own supporting conditions.

103 Spk explains all these as gifts to the Saṅgha. Parks (*ārāma*) are distinguished by planted flowering trees and fruit trees, while groves (*vana*) are clusters of wild trees. *Papa* is glossed as a shed for giving drinking water.

104 These verses were spoken by Anāthapiṇḍika, chief patron of the Buddha, after he was reborn in the Tusita heaven. They recur below, with prose text, at **2:20**.

105 Anāthapiṇḍika had been especially devoted to Sāriputta, who delivered a moving sermon to him while he was on his deathbed: see MN No. 143, which also includes the same account of the great patron's posthumous visit to Jeta's Grove.

Spk: *At best can only equal him* (*etāvaparamo siyā*): There is no bhikkhu, not even one who has attained Nibbāna, who surpasses the Elder Sāriputta (*na therena uttaritaro nāma atthi*).

106 "Yama's world" (*yamaloka*) here evidently refers to the *pettivisaya*, the domain of ghosts. Yama is the Lord of Death; see MN III 179–86, AN I 138–42.

107 I read with Se and Ee1 *ete sagge pakāsenti*, as against Be *ete saggā pakāsanti*, "these heavens shine," and Ee2 *ete sagge pakāsanti*, "these shine in heaven." I take *sagge* as accusative plural rather than locative singular, which is also plausible.

108 Spk-pṭ: Because they are endowed with happiness they are like the devas who exercise control over the goods created by others. The comparison is with the devas of the *paranimmitavasavattī* realm, the sixth sense-sphere heaven.

109 The deva Ghaṭīkāra had been a potter during the dispen-

sation of the Buddha Kassapa, who had a monastic seat at Vehaliṅga, the potter's home town. At that time the future Buddha Gotama was his closest friend, the brahmin youth Jotipāla. Although Jotipāla went forth as a bhikkhu under the Buddha Kassapa, Ghaṭikāra had to remain in the household life to support his blind, aged parents. He was the Buddha's chief supporter and had attained the stage of nonreturner. Highlights from the story, related in MN No. 81, appear in the verses to follow here.

Avihā is one of the Pure Abodes (see **n. 83**). Spk says that the seven bhikkhus were liberated by the liberation of the fruit of arahantship, which they attained immediately after taking rebirth into the Avihā brahmā world.

110 In pāda a, I read *paṅkaṃ* with Be and Ee1 as against *saṅgaṃ* ("tie") in Se and Ee2. Spk states that the abandoning of the human body implies the eradication of the five lower fetters and the celestial bond (*dibbayoga*) signifies the five higher fetters.

111 I follow the spelling of the names in Se. Upaka is the former Ājīvaka ascetic whom the newly enlightened Buddha met while en route to Isipatana (MN I 170,33–171,20). Later, after an unhappy marriage, he entered the Saṅgha: see DPPN 1:386. The story of Pukkusāti is related in MN No. 140 and Ps V 33–63; see too DPPN 2:214–16. Piṅgiya here may be identical with the pupil of Bāvarī whose verses occur at Sn 1131–49, though this remains uncertain. The identity of the other bhikkhus cannot be established.

112 I read pāda a with Be and Se *kusalī bhāsasi tesaṃ*. Spk: *Kusalan ti idaṃ vacanaṃ imassa atthī ti kusalī; tesaṃ therānaṃ tvaṃ kusalaṃ anavajjaṃ bhāsasi.*

113 On "where name-and-form ceases" see above **n. 46**. Spk paraphrases the next to last line: "Those elders (did so) having understood that Dhamma here in your dispensation."

114 Bhaggava was the potter's name, possibly a clan name.

115 Spk says that the concluding verse was added by the redactors of the texts. The statement that both were inwardly developed (*bhāvitattānaṃ*) and were bearing their final bodies (*sarīrantimadhārinaṃ*) implies that after his rebirth in the Pure Abodes, Ghaṭikāra too had become an arahant.

116 Se and Ee2 read *corehi 'hāriyaṃ*, Be *corehyahāriyaṃ*. Both are orthographical attempts to salvage a text that appears to assert the exact opposite of the meaning required. Without such editorial moulding *corehi hāriyaṃ* (the reading of Ee1) would mean, "What is it that thieves should bear away?" —the rendering used at KS 1:51. Spk offers no help.

117 Reading in pāda a (in the next verse too) *pavasato* with Be, Se, and Ee2, as against *pathavato* in Ee1.

118 Spk: Sons are the support (*vatthu*) of human beings because they care for their parents in old age. A wife is the best companion because one can confide to her one's most personal secrets.

119 Spk: *The deviant path* (*uppatha*) is a nonpath (*amagga*) for going to heaven and Nibbāna. *Undergoes destruction day and night* (*rattindivakkhaya*): it is destroyed *by* the days and nights or *during* the days and nights. *Women are the stain of the holy life*: by washing off an external stain one can become clean, but if one is defiled by the stain of women it is not possible to make oneself pure. *Austerity* (*tapa*) is a name for restraint, the ascetic practices (*dhutaṅgaguṇa*), energy, and extreme asceticism (*dukkarakārika*); all these except extreme asceticism (i.e., self-mortification) are practices that burn up the defilements. *The holy life* (*brahmacariya*) is abstinence from sexual intercourse.

On "the bath without water" see **vv. 646, 705**. To appreciate this expression one must remember that for the brahmins in the Buddha's time (as for many Hindus today) ritual bathing was a way to wash away one's sins. The Buddha replaced this with the "internal bath" of the mind; see **7:21** below and MN I 39,1–2, 280,18–20.

120 Spk: *Metre is the scaffolding of verses* (*chando nidānaṃ gāthānaṃ*): Metres, beginning with the *gāyatti*, are the scaffolding of verses; for one beginning the preliminary verses first considers, "In which metre should it be?" *Syllables constitute their phrasing* (*akkharā tāsaṃ viyañjanaṃ*): For syllables make up words, and words make up a verse, and a verse reveals the meaning. *Verses rest on a base of names*: One composing a verse composes it by relying on some name such as "the ocean" or "the earth." *The poet is the abode where verses dwell*: The *abode* (*āsaya*) of verses is their

support (*patiṭṭhā*); verses come forth from the poet, and thus he is their support.

121 In pāda a, I read *addhabhavi* with Be and Ee1 & 2, as against *anvabhavi* in Se. *Addhabhavi* is aorist of *adhibhavati*, to overcome, to overpower; see CPD, s.v. *addhabhavati*. Spk: There is no living being or entity that is free from a name, whether the name be natural or fabricated. Even a tree or stone with no known name is still called "the nameless one."

122 The verb in pāda b is passive. Spk to **v. 246** glosses the active *parikassati* as *parikaḍḍhati*, to drag around. Spk: Those who come under the control of the mind are subjected to total obsession. Spk-pṭ: The sutta speaks of those who have not fully understood reality. But those who have fully understood the aggregates and abandoned the defilements do not come under control of the mind; rather, it is the mind that comes under their control.

123 Spk glosses *vicāraṇa* in pāda b by *pādāni*, feet, explaining that the singular should be understood as a plural. In doctrinal contexts the cognate *vicāra* means examination, and is regularly coupled with *vitakka* to describe the thought process, e.g., in the formula for the first jhāna. Here, however, the point seems to be that thought can travel over vast distances without physical locomotion.

124 I read with Be, Se, Ee1, and Spk (Be) *kissa dhūpāyito*, as against *kissā dhūmāyito* in Ee2, SS, and Spk (Se). The verse is also at Th 448 with *dhūpāyito*. Norman (at EV I, n. to 448) contends this word means "perfumed" or "obscured (by smoke)," but Spk glosses as *āditto*; see too **v. 542**, where *padhūpito* must mean "burning."

125 Spk: The world is *ensnared by craving* (*taṇhāya uḍḍito*) because the eye, caught with the rope of craving, is ensnared on the peg of forms; so too with the ear and sounds, etc. *The world is shut in by death* (*maccunā pihito*): Even though the kamma done in the last life is only one mind-moment away, beings do not know it because they are shut off from it, as if by a mountain, by the strong pains occurring at the time of death.

126 See above **n. 57**. Following a suggestion of VĀT, I take *upādāya* in pāda c to be an absolutive with the literal

meaning "clinging," completed by the finite verb *vihaññati* in pāda d; *loko* in **v. 221**c thus becomes a mere metrical filler. Spk, however, has adopted an alternative solution, supplying a suppressed finite verb and interpreting *upādāya* in the extended sense of "depending on" thus: *tāni yeva ca upādāya āgamma paṭicca pavattati;* "It occurs dependent on, contingent on, in dependence on them." Pj II 210,27–28, commenting on Sn 168, takes a similar approach, though with a different finite verb.

The Hemavata Sutta itself, however, suggests that *upādāya* should be taken in the literal sense of "clinging to." For after the Buddha has replied at Sn 169 with an answer identical to that in the present sutta, at Sn 170 the yakkha asks: *Katamaṃ taṃ upādānaṃ yattha loko vihaññati?,* "What is that clinging wherein the world is harassed?"—a question which surely refers back to that same *upādāya.*

Spk: The "six" in the question should be understood by way of the six internal sense bases, but it may also be interpreted by way of the six internal and external bases. For the world *has arisen* in the six internal bases, *forms intimacy* with the six external bases, and *by clinging to* (or depending on) the six internal bases, *it is harassed* in the six external bases.

The verse offers a solution to the problem posed below at **2:26**, on how the world exists and arises in this very body endowed with perception and mind. On the origination of the world in the six internal bases, see **12:44** (= **35:107**). Norman discusses the verses from a philological angle at GD, pp. 181–82, n. to 168.

127 Se, Ee2 *jhatvā* is certainly the correct reading, *chetvā* in Be and Ee1 a normalization. The gloss in Spk, *vadhitvā*, supports *jhatvā*, and G-Dhp 288–89 has *jatva*, the Gāndhārī Prakrit counterpart. See Brough, *Gāndhārī Dharmapada*, pp. 164, 265–66. *Jhatvā* is also found in the SS reading of **v. 94**b.

128 Spk: Anger has a *poisoned root* (*visamūla*) because it results in suffering. It has a *honeyed tip* (*madhuragga*) because pleasure arises when one returns anger with anger, abuse with abuse, or a blow with a blow.

129 Spk: A token is that by which something is discerned

(*paññāyati etenā ti paññāṇaṃ*). *A standard is the token of a chariot* because a chariot, seen from a distance, is identified by its standard as belonging to such and such a kind. A married woman, even the daughter of a universal monarch, is identified as Mrs. So-and-So; hence *a husband is the token of a woman*. On the standard (*dhaja*) as the token of a chariot, see **11:2** and **n. 611**.

130 SS record a v.l. *sādhutaraṃ* in pāda c, but Spk's gloss *madhutaraṃ* indicates that the reading available to the commentator here was *sādutaraṃ*. However, Spk recognizes the same v.l. in connection with the identical **vv. 846–47**. See **n. 597**.

Spk: A householder who lives by wisdom (*paññājīvī*) is one who becomes established in the Five Precepts and offers regular almsfood, etc.; one gone forth who lives by wisdom uses his requisites with proper reflection, takes up a meditation subject, sets up insight, and attains the noble paths and fruits.

131 Spk: The former deva had asked the Buddha these questions, but the second deva interrupted, saying, "Why ask the Buddha? I'll answer you," and then offered his own ideas. But the first deva rebuked him for intruding and again addressed the questions to the Buddha.

Spk: Seed of the seven kinds of grain is *the best of things that rise up* because, when seed rises, food becomes plentiful and the country is secure. Rain from a rain cloud *excels among things that fall down* for this ensures a plentiful crop. *Cattle are the best of things that go forth*, that walk about on foot, because they produce the five kinds of dairy products (milk, curd, butter, ghee, and cream-of-ghee) by which people sustain their health. *A son is the most excellent of speakers* because he does not say anything harmful to his parents in the royal court, etc.

It should be noted that *pavajamānānaṃ* in pāda c is the present participle of *pavajati* or *pabbajati*, which, in a religious context, signifies the act of leaving the household life to become a monk (*pabbajjā*). Hence the Buddha's reply in the next verse.

132 Spk: *Knowledge* (*vijjā*) is the knowledge of the four paths; *ignorance* (*avijjā*) is the great ignorance at the root of the

round. *The Saṅgha* is the best of things that go forth because it is a rich field of merit. *The Buddha* is the best of speakers because his teaching of the Dhamma helps release many hundred thousands of beings from bondage.

133 *Maggo c' anekāyatanappavutto.* Spk: He says, "The path is explained by many methods (*kāraṇehi*), by way of the thirty-eight meditation objects. Such being the case, why have these people become frightened and grasped hold of the sixty-two views?" The thirty-eight meditation objects (*aṭṭhatiṃsārammaṇa*) are identical with the classical forty *kammaṭṭhāna* (e.g., in Vism) except that the list of *kasiṇas* is drawn from the Nikāyas (e.g., MN II 14,29–15,2), in which the last two (the space *kasiṇa* and the consciousness *kasiṇa*) are the same as the first two formless attainments (*āruppa*) and hence are not reckoned twice. In the Vism system these two are replaced by the limited space *kasiṇa* and the light *kasiṇa*, which brings the number up to forty.

134 The last line should be read with Be, Se, and Ee2 as *dhamme ṭhito paralokaṃ na bhāye.* Ee1 omits *dhamme ṭhito*, apparently by oversight. Spk interprets "rightly directed speech and mind" and "doing no evil deeds with the body" as the preliminary factors of purification, and takes the four qualities mentioned in pāda d to be the "four things" on which one should stand. But it also suggests another interpretation: right bodily, verbal, and mental conduct are the first three things, and the four qualities in pāda d taken together are the fourth. The first alternative sounds more plausible.

135 The Pāli terms for the six fissures (*chiddāni*) are: *ālassa, pamāda, anuṭṭhāna, asaṃyama, niddā, tandi.* Spk-pṭ: These six things are called fissures because they do not give an opportunity for wholesome states of mind to occur.

136 Spk: A woman is called *the best of goods* because a woman is an article that should not be given away (*avissajjanīya-baṇḍattā*); or else she is so called because all bodhisattas and wheel-turning monarchs are conceived in a mother's womb. Spk-pṭ: Even the most precious jewel is not called "the best of goods" because it still falls into the category of things that might be given away; but a woman who has not abandoned the family customs should not be relin-

quished to anyone, and hence she is called the best of goods. Further, a woman is the best of goods because she is a mine for the best of gems, that is, because (her body) is the place for the birth of the human thoroughbreds (i.e., Buddhas and arahants).

137 *Abbuda* ("plague") is glossed by Spk as *vināsakāraṇa*, a cause of destruction. The word also occurs in **v. 591** as an extremely high number, in **6:10** as the name of a hell, and at **v. 803** as a stage in the development of the fetus.

138 Spk: One should not give oneself away by becoming the slave of another, but an exception is made of all bodhisattas. So too, except for all bodhisattas, one should not relinquish oneself to lions and tigers, etc.

139 I interpret pāda c, in both the question and the reply, with the aid of Spk, which paraphrases only the reply: *Gāvo kamme sajīvānan ti kammena saha jīvantānaṃ gāvo va kamme kammasahāyā kammadutiyakā nāma honti*; "For those who live together with work, cattle are called the work-companions, the work-partners, in work; for the work of ploughing, etc., is accomplished along with a team of cattle."

In pāda d, *sītassa* (Ee2: *sīta 'ssa*) should be resolved *sītaṃ assa*. Spk takes *assa* to refer to "the mass of beings" (or of people: *sattakāyassa*) and explains *iriyāpatha*, "the course of movement" (or "mode of deportment"), as the means of livelihood (*jīvitavutti*); it glosses *sīta* (furrow) with *naṅgala* (plough). The purport is that the activity of ploughing is the essential means for sustaining human life.

140 Spk: Firmly established in virtue.

2. *Devaputtasaṃyutta*

141 *Devaputta* means literally "son of the devas," but since devas are depicted as arising in their celestial abodes by way of spontaneous birth, I translate the compound simply as "young deva."

Spk: They are reborn in the laps (*aṅka*) of devas. The males are called sons of the devas (*devaputtā*); the females, daughters of the devas (*devadhītaro*). When they are not known by name it is said, "a certain devatā" (as in the preceding saṃyutta); but those who are known by name are referred to as "a son of the devas named So-and-So" (as here). Spk-pṭ: This last statement is made only as a generalization, for the identity of several devatās is known.

142 Spk: When the Buddha taught the Abhidhamma in the Tāvatiṃsa heaven during the seventh rains retreat after his enlightenment, this young deva heard him give a description of the bhikkhu (as at Vibh 245–46), but did not hear his instruction to the bhikkhu, his exhortation to the bhikkhu, "Think in this way, not in that way; attend in this way, not in that way; abandon this, enter and dwell in that" (as at DN I 214,18–21). He speaks with reference to this.

143 *Taññev' ettha paṭibhātu*. Lit. "Let it occur to you yourself in regard to this." Throughout this work I have rendered this peculiar Pāli idiom, and its variants, in ways that best accord with natural English diction.

144 *Well-spoken counsel* (*subhāsitassa*). Spk interprets this to mean that one should train oneself in just the fourfold good conduct of speech (see below **8:5**; also MN I 288,1–22), (and in talk) concerning the Four Noble Truths, the ten suitable topics of discussion (see MN III 113,25–31), and the thirty-seven aids to enlightenment. It seems to me more likely the purport is that one should train *in accordance with* good counsel.

Spk offers two interpretations of *samaṇupāsana* in pāda b: (i) that which is to be attended to by an ascetic, namely, one of the thirty-eight meditation subjects (see **n. 133**); and (ii) attending upon an ascetic, i.e., serving learned bhikkhus in order to increase one's wisdom. The first seems more plausible. The *calming of the mind* (*cittūpasama*) is the training by way of the eight meditative attainments (*aṭṭhasamāpatti*).

145 In pāda b, I read *ce* with Be, Se, and Ee2, as against *ca* in Ee1. I construe the convoluted syntax of this verse in accordance with Spk. Spk explains that he should be *liberated in mind* (*vimuttacitto*) through (temporary) liberation by devotion to the meditation subject [Spk-pṭ: liberation by insight and jhāna, which are temporary types of liberation, since at this point he has not yet attained arahantship, the final liberation of mind]. *The heart's attain-*

ment (*hadayassānupatti*) is arahantship, which is also the *advantage* (*ānisaṃsa*) on which he should be bent.

146 Spk: Māgha is a name for Sakka, who asks the same set of questions below and receives the same reply (at **vv. 939–40**). It is a derivative of the name Magha, by which he was known during his life as a human being. He is called Vatrabhū because he attained rulership among the devas by overcoming others with his conduct (*vattena aññe abhibhavati*), or because he overcame the asura named Vatra. Neither of these names is mentioned among Sakka's names at **11:12**.

147 By "brahmin" he refers to the arahant. Spk: This young deva believed that there was no end to the arahant's duties and that the arahant must continue striving even after reaching arahantship. The Buddha spoke the rejoinder to correct him. The Buddha's verse is unique (*asaṅkiṇṇā*) in the Tipiṭaka, for nowhere else does the Buddha criticize the arousing of energy, but here he speaks thus to show that there is a conclusion to the arahant's duty.

148 On the verb *āyūhati*, encountered in **1:1**, see **n. 2**. To have *gone beyond* (*pāragata*) is to have attained Nibbāna.

149 Spk: This young deva, it is said, had been a meditator in a previous life, but he had thick defilements and thus could suppress them only with much effort. Though he did the work of an ascetic, because his supporting conditions were weak he passed away and took rebirth in the deva world without having reached the plane of the noble ones. He came to the Blessed One's presence to proclaim the difficulty of the ascetic life.

150 Spk: Although the noble path is neither impassable nor uneven (*duggamo visamo*), this is said because there are many impediments in the preliminary portion of the path.

151 At AN IV 449–51 the Venerable Ānanda gives a detailed explanation of the verse. Readings of the aorists in pādas b and c differ among the various eds., but without affecting the meaning. Spk explains that there are two kinds of *confinement* (*sambādha*): confinement by the five hindrances and confinement by the five cords of sensual pleasure, the former being intended here. The *opening*

(*okāsa*) is a name for jhāna. In the analysis given by Ānanda, however, confinement and the opening are explained sequentially: first the five cords of sensual pleasure are called confinement and the first jhāna the opening; then *vitakka-vicāra* are confinement and the second jhāna the opening; and so on, culminating in the destruction of the *āsavas* as the final opening.

The withdrawn chief bull (*paṭilīnanisabho*): The Buddha was called a chief bull at **1:38**. At AN II 41,29–32 a bhikkhu is said to be *paṭilīna*, "withdrawn," when he has abandoned the conceit "I am."

152 The "Dhamma for the attainment of Nibbāna" (*dhammaṃ nibbānapattiyā*) is presumably the Noble Eightfold Path. Spk-pṭ: This young deva had been an obtainer of the first jhāna in a previous existence. He spoke his verse to extol the Blessed One for obtaining the bliss of jhāna. The Buddha's reply is intended to show that the first form-sphere jhāna is a mere fragment of the infinite and immeasurable qualities of a Buddha. By *mindfulness* (*sati*) he refers to the mindfulness of insight and of the noble path. *Well concentrated* (*susamāhita*) signifies both mundane and supramundane concentration.

153 Spk explains "religious sect" (*tittha*) as the sixty-two views (of the Brahmajāla Sutta, DN No. 1). If he founded a sect based on one of these views, how could he have been reborn in heaven? Because he affirmed the doctrine of kamma and did many virtuous deeds. When he was reborn in heaven, he recognized the emancipating quality of the Buddha's dispensation and came into the Master's presence in order to recite verses in praise of energy conformable with the dispensation.

154 In pāda a, *parakkamma* is an absolutive, not an imperative, and hence in sense should precede *chinda sotaṃ*. *Parakkama,* the corresponding noun, is the third member of a set of three terms denoting successive stages in the development of energy: *ārambhadhātu, nikkamadhātu, parakkamadhātu;* at **46:2**, **46:51** they have been translated "the element of arousal, the element of endeavour, the element of exertion."

155 Spk explains *saṅkassaraṃ* in pāda c as *saṅkāya saritaṃ,*

"remembered with suspicion": "It is subject to such doubt and suspicion, 'He must have done this, he must have done that.'"

156 Candimā is a deva dwelling in the mansion of the moon; the word itself usually simply means the moon. Obviously his seizure by Rāhu represents the lunar eclipse.

157 Although both Rāhu and Vepacitti are described as "lords of the asuras" (*asurinda*), it seems that Vepacitti is the overlord and Rāhu a subordinate. Vepacitti is the perennial antagonist of Sakka, lord of the devas, as seen at **11:4**, **11:5**, **11:23**, and **35:248**.

158 Suriya (usually meaning simply the sun) is the deva dwelling in the mansion of the sun. Here the solar eclipse is being represented. Spk, after impressing us with Rāhu's physical dimensions, offers some interesting insights into ancient Buddhist views about eclipses: When Rāhu sees the sun and moon shining brightly, he becomes jealous and enters their orbital paths, where he stands with mouth agape. It then seems as if the lunar and solar mansions have been plunged into the great hell, and the devas in those mansions all cry out simultaneously in terror. While Rāhu can cover the mansions with his hands, jaw, and tongue, and can even stuff his cheeks with them, he is unable to obstruct their motion. If he did make such an attempt they would split his head and come through the other side or pull him along and push him down [Spk-pṭ: because their motion is determined by the law of kamma and is extremely hard for anyone to stop directly].

159 *Pajaṃ mama*. Spk: It is said that on the day the Buddha spoke the Mahāsamaya Sutta (DN No. 20) the two young devas Candimā and Suriya attained the fruit of stream-entry. Hence the Blessed One says "my child," meaning "he is my (spiritual) son." C.Rh.D's conjecture (at KS 1:72, n. 2) that the Buddha speaks thus with reference to his own (legendary) solar descent seems unlikely.

160 Spk glosses *kacche va* in pāda b by *kacche viya*, "like an armpit" [Spk-pṭ: in the sense of a cramped place]. Spk: *Kaccha* (used metaphorically) means either a cramped mountain pass (*pabbatakaccha*) or a constriction in a river (*nadīkaccha*).

161 Spk: *With flaws discarded* (*raṇañjahā*): with defilements discarded (*kilesañjahā*). In MLDB, in the translation of MN No. 139, *araṇa* is rendered "nonconflict" or "without conflict," and *sa-raṇa* "with conflict." However, while in both Pāli and Sanskrit *raṇa* can mean battle or conflict, the Pāli commentators consistently gloss it with *raja-kilesa*, "dust, defilement." Thus Ps V 32 has *sa-raṇo ti sarajo sakileso, araṇo ti arajo nikkileso*. See too **v. 585**c and **n. 398**.

162 I adopt Se and Ee2 *Veṇhu* over Be and Ee1 *Veṇḍu*; the reading *Veṇṇu* in SS may, however, be the historical form. The name is the Pāli equivalent of Skt Viṣṇu; perhaps this young deva is a prototype of the Hindu deity.

163 The reading of pāda c is uncertain: Be and Se read *yuñjaṃ* (a modified plural participle?), Ee1 & 2 *yuñja*, and SS *yajja*. VĀT suggests an absolutive *yujja*.

164 The question and the reply are found, with several differences, at Sn 173–75. I read pāda a with Se, Ee2, and Sn 173 *ko sū 'dha*, as against *kathaṃ su* in Be and Ee1; the Skt cited at Ybhūś 10:1 has *ka etam oghaṃ tarati* (Enomoto, CSCS, p. 52). Spk explains pāda c of the question: below it is *without support* (*appatiṭṭhe*), above it is *without a hold* (*anālambe* in text, *anālambane* in gloss). The Pāli words *patiṭṭhā* and *ālambana* (or *ārammaṇa*) have doctrinally important nuances; see **n. 2** above and **12:38–40** and **22:53–54**.

165 In pāda c, I read with Ee1 and SS *nandībhavaparikkhīṇo*, as against Be, Se, and Ee2 *nandīrāgaparikkhīṇo* (in both text and Spk). Spk's gloss on *nandīrāga* here (*tayo kammābhisaṅkhārā*) corresponds so closely to its gloss on *nandībhava* in **v. 2** (see **n. 8**) that we might well suppose the original text available to the commentator read *-bhava-* rather than *-rāga-*. Sn 175 also reads *-bhava-*, as does the version of the verse cited at Nett 146,22.

Spk: By the mention of *sensual perception* (*kāmasaññā*) the five lower fetters are implied; by *the fetter of form* (*rūpasaṃyojana*), the five higher fetters; by *delight in existence*, the three kinds of kammic volitional formations (demeritorious, meritorious, imperturbable—see **12:51**). Thus one who has abandoned the ten fetters and the three kinds of kammic formations *does not sink in the deep*, in the great flood. Or else: *sensual perception* implies sense-sphere existence; *the fetter of form*, form-sphere existence; and formless-sphere existence is implied by the former two. *Delight in existence* denotes the three kinds of kammic formations. Thus one who does not generate the three kinds of volitional formations regarding the three realms of existence *does not sink in the deep*.

166 Spk: This young deva had been playing in the Nandana Grove together with his retinue of a thousand nymphs. Five hundred nymphs had climbed up a tree and were singing and throwing down flowers when they suddenly expired and were immediately reborn in the Avīci hell. When the young deva realized they were missing and discovered they had been reborn in hell, he examined his own vital force and saw that he himself and the other five hundred nymphs were due to die in seven days and to take rebirth in hell. Hence, in utter fear, he came to the Buddha seeking consolation.

The story (along with the verses) is also related in the two commentaries to the Satipaṭṭhāna Sutta (Sv III 750,3–27; Ps I 235,16–236,3). Despite the commentaries, however, I prefer to regard the young deva's question as an expression of the deep anxiety perpetually at the core of the human (and celestial) situation.

167 In pāda c, I read *kicchesu* with Be, Se, and Ee2, as against *kiccesu* (duties) in Ee1 and certain SS. *Kicchesu* is better supported by the comment in Spk: *imesu uppannānuppannesu dukkhesu*, "these sufferings both arisen and unarisen."

168 I read pāda a with Be: *nāññatra bojjhā tapasā*. The reading *bojjhaṅga-tapasā*, in Se and Ee1 & 2, may have crept into the text from the commentarial paraphrase in Spk, which is most intelligible in the Be reading: *Nāññatra bojjhā tapasā ti bojjhaṅgabhāvanañ ca tapoguṇañ ca aññatra muñcitvā sotthiṃ na passāmi*. Spk-pṭ lends further support to this reading by glossing *bojjhā* with *bodhito* and explaining it as an ablative. The Skt version cited at Ybhūś 5:2 has *jñānatapaso* (Enomoto, CSCS, p. 8).

Spk: Even though the development of the enlightenment factors is mentioned first and restraint of the sense faculties afterwards, sense restraint should be understood first. For when this is mentioned, the fourfold purification of virtue is implied (see Vism 15,29–16,16; Ppn 1:42). Established on this, a bhikkhu undertakes the ascetic practices, here called austerity (*tapa*), enters a forest, and by developing a meditation subject he develops the enlightenment factors together with insight. Then the noble path arises in him with Nibbāna as its object; the latter is what is meant by *relinquishing all* (*sabbanissagga*). [Spk-pṭ: For here everything comprised in formations is relinquished.] Thus the Blessed One turned the discourse into one on the Four Noble Truths, at the end of which the young deva was established in the fruit of stream-entry.

Spk-pṭ: Though here only his own attainment of distinction is mentioned, it should be understood that the five hundred nymphs were also established in the fruit of stream-entry; for that is said in the commentary to the Mahāsatipaṭṭhāna Sutta.

Neither Spk nor Spk-pṭ comments on the single prose line that follows the verse (in Be: *idam avoca, pa, tatth' eva antaradhāyī ti*). Perhaps the young deva had acquired such a compelling sense of urgency that he quickly returned to the deva world to practise in accordance with the Buddha's instructions. The Skt version has an additional verse, which reads in translation:

> After a long time at last I see
> A brahmin who is fully quenched,
> Who has gone beyond all enmity and fear
> (*sarvavairabhayātītaṃ*),
> Who has crossed over attachment to the world.
> (Ybhūś 5:3; Enomoto, CSCS, p. 8)

169 The texts show variations between *anagho*, *anigho*, and *anīgho* in pāda a of **vv. 305–7**. Ee2 uses *anigho* throughout.

170 The verse differs from **v. 1** in pāda c only.

171 *Yāvatakaṃ kho Ānanda takkāya pattabbaṃ anuppattaṃ taṃ tayā*. Lit., "Whatever can be reached by reasoning, Ānanda, that you have arrived at." Spk: The Buddha had spoken about the visit of the young deva without disclosing his name in order to show the great might of the Elder Ānanda's inferential intelligence.

172 Spk does not comment on the name of this young deva, who may be an early prototype of the Hindu god Śiva.

173 I follow Se, which adds a terminal *ti* after the third verse and ascribes the next three verses to the Buddha. No change of speaker is indicated in Be or Ee1.

174 **Vv. 330–31** are quoted at Mil 66–67. In **v. 330**c I read with Be, Se, and Ee2 *sākaṭikacintāya; mantā* in pāda d must be the nominative of the agent noun *mantar*. In **v. 331**a I follow Se and Ee1 & 2, which read *panthaṃ*, as against Be *maṭṭhaṃ*; Mil (Ee and Se) reads *nāma* (a corruption?). Spk glosses pāda d: *akkhachinno va jhāyatī ti akkhachinno avajhāyati*, which suggests that *va* is not the emphatic indeclinable but a verbal prefix. Spk, however, takes the *va* in **v. 332**d to represent *viya*. On *maccumukha* (in **v. 332**c) as "the mouth of Death" rather than "the face of Death," see Ja IV 271,7, Ja V 479,29, and Vism 233,21–22 (Ppn 8:20).

175 Spk: *koci = katthaci. Koci* in this sense is probably a contraction of *kvaci*.

176 Spk: *Restless* (*uddhatā*): of a restless temperament because of perceiving what is unallowable and blameworthy as allowable and blameless (according to the Vinaya), and the converse. *Puffed up* (*unnaḷā*): full of hollow conceit like an erect (pithless) reed. *Personally vain* (*capalā*): by adorning their bowls and robes, etc. *Mukharā = mukhakharā* ("mouth-rough"): of rough speech. *Rambling in their talk* (*vikiṇṇavācā*): of uncontrolled speech, chattering away pointlessly all day long. *Muddle-minded* (*muṭṭhassatino*): with lost mindfulness, devoid of mindfulness, forgetful of whatever they have done. *Without clear comprehension* (*asampajānā*): without wisdom. *Unconcentrated* (*asamāhitā*): devoid of access and absorption concentration, like a ship cast about by a fierce current. *Scatter-brained* (*vibbhantacittā*, lit. "with wandering minds"): like foolish deer on a road. *Loose in their sense faculties* (*pākatindriyā*): with open faculties due to lack of restraint, just as when they were laymen.

177 Spk: The young deva realized that his exhortation would not be effective if he approached each monk individually, and thus he approached them when they had assembled for the Uposatha day observance (see **n. 513**).

178 Spk: Through infatuation by defilements [Spk-pṭ: by craving], they are infatuated with the daughters-in-law, etc., in the homes of others.

179 In pāda b, I read *vadāmahaṃ*, with Be, Se, and Ee2, as against Ee1 *vandāmahaṃ*. Ee1 has the former reading in the parallel **v. 794b**.

Spk: As dead bodies, thrown into the charnel ground, are eaten by various predators and even their relatives do not protect them or guard them, so such men are *rejected, without protector,* in that they do not get any instruction or advice from their preceptors and teachers. They are just like the dead.

180 Spk: Rohitassa posed his question about the end of the world with reference to the stellar world-sphere (*cakkavāḷa-loka*), but the Blessed One answered with reference to the world of formations (*saṅkhāra-loka*).

181 This stock description of the archer is also at **20:6** (II 265,27–266,2). Spk: *Daḷhadhammo* = *daḷhadhanu*; possessed of a bow of the maximum size (*uttamappamāṇena dhanunā samannāgato*). A plural *daḷhadhammino* occurs below at **v. 708**b. At EV I, n. to 1210, Norman proposes that this form must have been borrowed from a dialect where *-nv-* > *-mm-* instead of *-nn-*. MW lists two Skt words meaning "with firm bows," *dṛḍhadhanvan* and *dṛḍhadhanvin*. We might assume it is the former that appears in Pāli as *daḷhadhamma,* the latter as *daḷhadhammin*; see too **n. 488**. A similar development affected the homonym *dhanvan* (= desert); see **n. 264**.

182 Spk glosses *loka* with *dukkhasacca* and each of the other terms by way of the other three noble truths. Thus the Buddha shows: "I do not make known these four truths in external things like grass and wood, but right here in this body composed of the four great elements."

This pithy utterance of the Buddha, which may well be the most profound proposition in the history of human thought, is elucidated at **35:116** by the Venerable Ānanda, who explains that in the Noble One's Discipline "the world" is "that in the world by which one is a perceiver and conceiver of the world," i.e., the six sense bases. From Ānanda's explanation we can draw out the following implications: The world with which the Buddha's teaching is principally concerned is "the world of experience," and even the objective world is of interest only to the extent that it serves as the necessary external condition for experience. The world is identified with the six sense bases because the latter are the necessary internal condition for experience and thus for the presence of a world. As long as the six sense bases persist, a world will always be spread out before us as the objective range of perception and cognition. Thus one cannot reach the end of the world by travelling, for wherever one goes one inevitably brings along the six sense bases, which necessarily disclose a world extended on all sides. Nevertheless, by reversing the direction of the search it is possible to reach the end of the world. For if the world ultimately stems from the six sense bases, then by bringing an end to the sense bases it is possible to arrive at the end of the world.

Now the six sense bases are themselves conditioned, having arisen from a chain of conditions rooted in one's own ignorance and craving (see **12:44** = **35:107**). Thus by removing ignorance and craving the re-arising of the six sense bases can be prevented, and therewith the manifestation of the world is terminated. This end of the world cannot be reached by travelling, but it can be arrived at by cultivating the Noble Eightfold Path. Perfect development of the path brings about the eradication of ignorance and craving, and with their removal the underlying ground is removed for the renewed emergence of the six senses, and therewith for the reappearance of a world. For a long philosophical commentary on this sutta by Ñāṇananda, see SN-Anth 2:70–85.

183 Spk: The Buddha asked this question because he wanted to speak praise of the Elder Sāriputta. He chose to address Ānanda because the two monks were close friends and had deep admiration for each other's virtues, and he knew Ānanda would answer in an appropriate way.

184 These words of praise are spoken by the Buddha himself of Sāriputta at MN III 25,6–10. Spk explains: *Wise* (*paṇḍita*) designates one who possesses the four kinds of skilfulness (*kosalla*)—in the elements, in the sense bases, in dependent

origination, and in what is possible and impossible (MN III 62,4–6).

The next series of definitions, which continues for several pages, is drawn from Paṭis II 190–202. Here I give only extracts: One is *of great wisdom* (*mahāpañña*) when one has great virtue, concentration, wisdom, liberation, etc., great dwellings and meditative attainments, great development of the thirty-seven aids to enlightenment, great paths and fruits, great direct knowledges, and attainment of Nibbāna, the great ultimate goal. One is *of wide wisdom* (*puthupañña*) when one's knowledge occurs regarding the diverse aggregates, elements, sense bases, etc. (Apparently Paṭis takes Pāli *puthu* to be from Vedic *pṛthak,* "distinct," but *pṛthu,* "wide," is more likely the original sense.) One is *of joyous wisdom* (*hāsapañña*) when one fulfils all the steps of training full of joy, inspiration, delight, and gladness. One is *of swift wisdom* (*javanapañña*) when one swiftly understands all the five aggregates as impermanent, suffering, and nonself. One is *of sharp wisdom* (*tikkhapañña*) when one quickly cuts off all defilements and realizes the four paths and fruits in one sitting. One is *of penetrative wisdom* (*nibbedhikapañña*) when, full of disgust and revulsion towards all formations, one penetrates and splits apart the mass of greed, hatred, and delusion that had not been penetrated earlier. These terms, and other types of wisdom, are enumerated at **55:62–74**.

185 Spk: When the Tathāgata and the Elder Ānanda had praised the Elder Sāriputta thus, the devas in 10,000 world systems rose up and praised him with the same sixteen terms. Then the young deva Susīma, who had formerly (as a human being) been a pupil of Sāriputta, decided to approach the Blessed One with his own retinue and recite the same praise of his preceptor.

Spk does not say whether this Susīma is identical with the protagonist of **12:70**. A young deva of this name is also mentioned at **11:2** as a subordinate of Sakka.

186 Spk: Elsewhere *uccāvaca* means: *ucca* = excellent (*paṇīta*) + *avaca* = inferior (*hīna*). But here it means diverse (*nānāvidhā*), in apposition to *vaṇṇanibhā*. For the blue young devas in the assembly became exceptionally blue, and so

too the yellow, red, and white young devas became exceptionally yellow, red, and white. To illustrate this the four similes are given.

187 Be and Ee2 include here the phrase *saradasamaye viddhe vigatavalāhake deve*, but as this seems to be an interpolation based on the following paragraph I have followed Se and Ee1, which omit it.

188 The simile recurs at **22:102** and **45:147**. Spk glosses *nabhaṃ abbhussakkamāno* (as in Be) with *ākāsaṃ abhilaṅghanto* and says this shows the "tender time of the sun" [Spk-pṭ: the time when it is neither too low nor too high]. The verb *abbhussakkati* comes from the root *sakk*, and has no relation to the adjective *sukka* as Geiger supposes.

189 I read pāda d with SS thus: *kālaṃ kaṅkhati bhāvito sudanto*. This reading is suggested by VĀT, who writes: "The third word has been removed by Be and Se, no doubt in the belief that it is a Śloka pāda (failing, however, to regularize the cadence). But if one takes it as an Aupacchandasaka pāda there is no need to remove anything. Confirmation is got from Sn 516, the alteration of *sa danto* to *sudanto* being appropriate for the different contexts."

Spk does not offer help with the reading but explains the sense: "He awaits the time of his parinibbāna. For the arahant does not delight in death or yearn for life; he yearns for the time like a worker standing awaiting his day's wage." Spk then quotes Th 1003, which may account for the replacement of *bhāvito* by *bhatiko* in Ee1. To obtain a Śloka line, Ee2 retains *bhāvito* but deletes *sudanto*.

190 Spk: "These young devas were proponents of kamma; therefore they performed meritorious deeds and were reborn in heaven. Thinking that they had been reborn there on account of their confidence in their respective teachers, they came to the Buddha in order to recite verses in praise of those teachers." Both Pūraṇa Kassapa and Makkhali Gosāla advocated doctrines that were opposed to the Buddhist teaching on kamma; their teachings are classified among the views that normally lead to a bad rebirth.

191 The verse is a concise statement of Pūraṇa Kassapa's doctrine of nonaction (*akiriyavāda*), for which see DN I 52,22–53,4

and **24:6** (in the latter source no ascription of the view to a teacher is made). A detailed account of the teachings of the six "heretical teachers" (of whom four are mentioned here and all six just below at **3:1**) can be found in the Sāmaññaphala Sutta, DN No. 2; for a translation with commentary, see Bodhi, *The Discourse on the Fruits of Recluseship*, esp. pp. 6–9, 19–26, 69–86. Spk paraphrases: "In declaring that there is no result of evil or merit, he taught to beings what is trustworthy as the foundation, the support; therefore he deserves esteem, veneration, worship."

192 Makkhali Gosāla was the founder and leader of the sect of ascetics known as the Ājīvikas. For his doctrine of non-causality (*ahetukavāda*), also called "purification by wandering on" (*saṃsārasuddhi*), see DN I 53,25–54,21 and **24:7**. A full account of his life and teachings can be found in Basham, *History and Doctrines of the Ājīvikas*.

193 The verse alludes to Makkhali's style of ascetic practice but, strangely, makes no mention of his doctrines. Spk explains his austerity (*tapa*) as bodily mortification and his scrupulousness (*jigucchā*) as the loathing of evil [Spk-pṭ: the undertaking of the vow of nudity, etc., in the belief that this is the way to eliminate evil]. This explanation shows that Spk regards *tapojigucchā* here as a collective *dvanda* compound, "austerity *and* scrupulousness," and so I have rendered it. Sv III 834,37, however, commenting on DN III 40,13–52,22 (where the Buddha gives a long disquisition on how *tapojigucchā* is imperfect and perfect (*aparipuṇṇā, paripuṇṇā*)), explains the compound as a *tappurisa* meaning "scrupulousness by austerity": *Tapojigucchā ti viriyena pāpajigucchā pāpavivajjanā*; "*Austerity-scrupulousness*: scrupulousness in regard to evil, the avoidance of evil, by means of energy." *Tapassī* and *jegucchī* (the corresponding nouns of personal reference) are used to designate *separate* factors of the Bodhisatta's "fourfold holy life" practised before his enlightenment at MN I 77,23–27 and 78,32–36. See too Basham, pp. 109–15, for a description of Ājīvika asceticism.

194 Nigaṇṭha Nātaputta is identical with Mahāvīra, the historical progenitor of Jainism. His discipline of restraint by the

four controls (*cātuyāmasaṃvara*) is described at DN I 57,25–27 and MN I 377,1–2. At MLDB, p. 482, the formula is translated: "(he is) curbed by all curbs, clamped by all curbs, cleansed by all curbs, and claimed by all curbs." It is questionable whether either the text or its commentary (Sv I 168–69, Ps III 58–59) represents a genuine Jaina tradition.

195 Pakudhaka Kātiyāna is an alternative spelling of Pakudha Kaccāyana, whose doctrine of the seven bodies (*sattakāya*) is described at DN I 56,21–57,34 and at **24:8**. Spk says that the statement that "they were not far from superior men" means, in effect, that they were superior men (*sappurisa*), i.e., ariyans or noble ones.

196 In pāda a, Be and Se read *sahācaritena;* Ee1 reads *sagāravena,* corrected in Ee2 to *sahāravena,* "along with (his) howling." Spk-pṭ supports this: "By merely making a howl along with the roar of the lion; that is, the jackal (is not the lion's equal) merely by making a jackal's howl at the same time that the lion makes its lion's roar." The jackal and the lion form a classical pair of opposites in ancient Indian literature; see Ja Nos. 143 and 335, where a jackal does himself to death trying to emulate the lion's prowess in hunting, and especially Ja No. 172, where a jackal shames a group of young lions to silence by trying to imitate their roar.

197 Spk: Māra thought, "He has spoken dispraise of the other teachers. I will make him speak praise of them through his own mouth."

198 *Namuci* is a name of Māra, which Spk-pṭ (to **4:1**) explains as meaning "he does not free" (*na muci*): *vaṭṭadukkhato aparimuttapaccayattā namuci;* "He is called Namuci because he does not let one get free from the suffering of the round." Spk paraphrases the Buddha's remark: "Just as a fisherman throws out bait at the end of a hook for the purpose of catching fish, so, by praising these forms, you throw them out in order to catch living beings." See **35:230**.

3. Kosalasaṃyutta

199 King Pasenadi was to become one of the Buddha's most

devoted lay followers, though the texts never say that he attained any of the stages of sanctity. This sutta, it seems, records his first personal encounter with the Buddha. His cordial (as distinct from reverential) manner of greeting the Blessed One indicates that he has not yet acknowledged the Buddha as his master.

200 These are the six sectarian teachers (*cha satthāro*) or "ford makers" (*titthakārā*), of whom four are mentioned in **2:30**. Of the two not mentioned above, Sañjaya Belaṭṭhiputta was a sceptic (DN I 58,23–59,7) and Ajita Kesakambalī a materialist (DN I 55,15–56,31).

201 Spk: *Na uññātabbā = na avajānitabbā; na paribhotabbā = na paribhavitabbā*. Spk distinguishes between "to despise" and "to disparage" with respect to each of the four things mentioned by the Buddha. For example: One *despises* a young prince if, when one meets him, one does not yield way or remove one's cloak or rise up from one's seat, etc. One *disparages* him if one says such things as, "This prince has a big neck (Se: big ears) and a big belly. How will he be able to exercise rulership?"

202 *Uccāvacehi vaṇṇehi*. This line reflects the belief, widespread in Indian mythology, that serpents can change their appearance at will. As Spk testifies: "A serpent glides along in whatever form it finds prey, even in the form of a squirrel." See Vin I 86–87, where a nāga serpent assumes the form of a young man in order to receive ordination as a monk.

203 The grim consequences of despising and disparaging a virtuous bhikkhu do not come to pass because he harbours vindictive intentions, but as natural fruits of the offensive deeds. Spk explains that a bhikkhu who retaliates when provoked is incapable of harming anyone with "(his virtue's) fire" (*tejasā*); the transgressor is burned only when the bhikkhu bears up patiently. In this respect the bhikkhu contrasts with the archetypal Indian figure of the maligned holy man who deliberately inflicts a curse on his enemies (see below **11:10**).

204 *Tacasāraṃ va sam phalaṃ*. Spk: As its own fruit injures, destroys, the bamboo or reed, so do they injure, destroy, him.

The reed family is called *tacasāra* because its bark is hard like heartwood. *Sam* here is the reflexive pronominal adjective, glossed *attano*. See EV I, n. to 659, EV II, n. to 136, and **n. 657** below. Compare the present verse with **v. 597**.

205 *Atthi nu kho bhante jātassa aññatra jarāmaraṇā*. Spk: He asks, "Is there anyone who is free from aging and death?"

206 When speaking of the arahant, the Buddha does not describe his destiny as viewed from the outside, i.e., as aging and death, but in terms of the arahant's own experience, as a mere breaking up and discarding of the body.

207 *Santo have sabbhi pavedayanti*. Spk offers three interpretations, of which only the first, which I follow, sounds plausible: "The good, together with the good, declare: 'The Dhamma of the good does not decay.' The Dhamma of the good is Nibbāna; since that does not decay they call it unaging, deathless." The verse = Dhp 151, on which Dhp-a III 123,2–5 comments: "*The* ninefold *Dhamma of the good*—of the Buddhas, etc.—*does not decay*, does not undergo destruction. *So the good*—the Buddhas, etc.—*proclaim* this, declare it, *along with the good*, with the wise." The ninefold supramundane Dhamma is the four paths, their fruits, and Nibbāna. Brough argues that *sabbhi* here must be understood to bear the sense of a dative, and he takes the point to be that "the doctrine does not wear out 'because good men teach it to other good men,' their disciples and successors" (p. 228, n. 160). I do not find his interpretation convincing, for the Dhamma-as-teaching must certainly decay, and only the supramundane Dhamma remains immune to aging and death.

208 "The End-maker" (*antaka*), in pāda a, is a personification of death; elsewhere (e.g., at **v. 448**) the word refers expressly to Māra.

209 Spk resolves *pacchāsaṃ*, in pāda c, into *pacchā tesaṃ*. *Saṃ* is from *esaṃ*, a genitive plural form of the third person pronoun; see Geiger, *Pāli Grammar*, §108.1. In pāda f, *hissa* = *hi ssa* < Skt *hi sma*. See EV I, nn. to 225, 705.

210 Be: *aṭṭakaraṇa*; Se and Ee1 & 2: *atthakaraṇa*. See CPD, s.v. *aṭṭa*, for hypotheses concerning the derivation. Spk-pṭ explains *aṭṭakaraṇa* as *vinicchayaṭṭhāna*, a place for making judgements (regarding litigation).

211 Spk: One day, when the king was sitting in the judgement hall, he saw his ministers accepting bribes and deciding cases in favour of their benefactors. He thought, "When they do such things right in front of me, the sovereign, what won't they do behind my back? Now it is General Viḍūḍabha who will be known through his own reign. Why should I sit in the same place with these bribe-eating liars?" The exact purport of this last sentence is obscure, and neither Spk nor Spk-pṭ sheds much light on it. *Bhadramukha,* "Good Face," is a term of affection (see MN II 53,27, 210,11 foll.; Ja II 261,14; Vism 92,21), which according to Spk and Spk-pṭ here refers to Viḍūḍabha, the king's son and commander-in-chief. However, the prologue to Ja No. 465 (Ja IV 148–50) relates that King Pasenadi's earlier commander-in-chief was a warrior named Bandhula, who assumed the role of judge when he learned that the official judges had become corrupt. Thus, despite the gloss, it is possible the king here uses the term with reference to Bandhula rather than his son.

212 Mallikā had been a poor flower girl whom King Pasenadi met by chance after a military defeat. He fell in love with her, married her, and appointed her his chief queen (see prologue to Ja No. 415).

Spk: The king had asked her this question expecting her to say, "You are dearer to me than myself," and then to ask him the same question, to which he would have given the same reply, so that they would have strengthened their mutual love. But Mallikā, being wise and learned, answered with complete honesty (*sarasen' eva*) and the king too had to reply in the same way. The translation of *attā* as soul at KS 1:101 is misleading, despite the attempt at justification in the accompanying footnote. The sutta (inclusive of the verse) is at Ud 47, with the verse described as an "inspired utterance" (*udāna*).

The conversation between King Pasenadi and Mallikā is strikingly reminiscent of the discussion between the sage Yājñavalkya and his wife Maitreyi recorded at Bṛhadāraṇyaka Upaniṣad II.4.5 (also at IV.5.6): "Verily, a husband is not dear, that you may love the husband; but that you may love the Self, therefore a husband is dear.

Verily, a wife is not dear, that you may love the wife; but that you may love the Self, therefore a wife is dear" (Muller, *The Upanishads*, 2:109–10, 182–83). It is conceivable that the Buddhist conversation is modelled after the Upaniṣad but with a different message. Whereas Yājñavalkya affirms a transcendent Self—the Ātman—which is "to be seen, to be heard, to be perceived, to be marked," the Buddha extracts an ethical maxim: since one loves oneself above all others, one should realize the same is true of others and treat them with kindness and respect.

213 Spk relates the background story, also found (in greater detail) at Dhp-a II 1–12; see BL 2:100–7 and Ja No. 314. In brief: The king had become infatuated with a married woman and planned to have her husband killed so that he could take his wife. One night, unable to sleep, he heard eerie cries of inexplicable origin. The next day, when he anxiously asked his brahmin chaplain to explain the meaning, the priest told him that the voices portended his imminent death, which he could avert only by performing a great sacrifice. When the king later inquired from the Buddha about the voices, the Buddha told him these were the cries of adulterers boiling in a cauldron in the great hell.

214 The sacrifices are also referred to at It 21,12–17, and their origin related at Sn 299–305. Spk explains that in the times of the ancient kings the first four sacrifices were actually the four bases of beneficence (*saṅgahavatthu*)—giving, pleasant speech, beneficent conduct, and equality of treatment—by means of which the kings conferred benefits on the world. But during the time of King Okkāka the brahmins reinterpreted the bases of beneficence (which they augmented to five) as bloody sacrifices involving slaughter and violence.

In pāda c, I include *mahāyaññā*, found in Se and Ee2 but absent from Be and Ee1. Spk explains *mahārambhā* as *mahākiccā mahākaraṇīyā*, "great activities, great duties," which Spk-pṭ clarifies: *bahupasughātakammā*, "the action of slaughtering many animals."

215 *Yajanti anukulaṃ sadā*. Spk-pṭ explains *anukulaṃ* as *kulānugataṃ*, "what has come down in the family (as family tradition)." Spk: The regular meal offering that was

started by people earlier—this the people give in uninterrupted succession through the generations.

216 Spk relates, as the background story, an abridged version of the prologue to Ja No. 92. The verses appear, however, also at Dhp 345–46, the commentarial background story to which states merely that the king had ordered the criminals brought before him to be bound with fetters, ropes, and chains. See Dhp-a IV 53–55; BL 3:223–24. The same story is in the prologue to Ja No. 201.

217 Spk: It is *degrading* (*ohārina*) because it drags one down to the four realms of misery; *supple* (*sithila*), because unlike iron bonds it does not constrict one's physical movement but holds one in bondage wherever one goes; *hard to escape* (*duppamuñca*), because one cannot break free from it except by supramundane knowledge.

218 The sutta is also at Ud 64–66, but with a different verse attached. The Eastern Park is the monastery built by Visākhā, the Buddha's chief female patron, who was called "Mother" by her father-in-law Migāra because she skilfully led him to the Dhamma.

219 The jaṭilas were matted hair ascetics; the nigaṇṭhas, the Jains, followers of Nātaputta.

220 All eds. of SN read this sentence as a declarative (*ye te bhante loke arahanto*), but Ud 65,22–23 (Ee) reads it as an interrogative (*ye nu keci kho bhante loke arahanto*).

221 This condensed fourfold statement is expanded upon at AN II 187–90.

222 *Ete bhante mama purisā carā* (Se: *cārā*) *ocarakā janapadaṃ ocaritvā āgacchanti.* Some SS read *corā* (= thieves) in place of *carā*, and the same v.l. appears in many eds. of Ud. Ud-a 333,18–24, commenting on the passage, explains why the king's spies can be considered thieves, which indicates that even Dhammapāla had accepted the Ud reading *corā*. Spk, however, treats *ocarakā* and *carā* as synonyms, glossing both as *heṭṭhacarakā*, "undercover agents," those who move below the surface (for the purpose of gathering intelligence). Spk-pṭ says: "The expression 'undercover agents'—which is what is meant by *carā*—refers to those who enter amidst (other groups) in order to investigate the secrets of others." The expression *carapurisā* occurs too

at Dhp-a I 193,1, Ja II 404,9–18, and Ja VI 469,12, in contexts where it can only mean spies.

223 Be and Ee1 & 2 read *osāpayissāmi*, Se *oyāyissāmi*. Texts of Ud and Ud-a record still more vv.ll., even up to nine; see Masefield, *The Udāna Commentary*, 2:918, n. 195. Neither Spk nor Spk-pṭ offers any help. Ud-a 333,25 glosses *paṭipajjissāmi karissāmi*, "I will enter upon it, I will act," which seems a learned way of admitting uncertainty. If we accept Norman's reasonable suggestion (at EV I, n. to 119) that we should recognize in Pāli a verb *oseti*, "to deposit" (< Skt **avaśrayati*), *osāpeti* can then be understood as the causative form of this verb (< Skt **avaśrāyati*, as pointed out by Norman in the same note). Here it is the first person future used metaphorically to mean "I will make them deposit the information with me." See too **n. 542** and **n. 657**. Its absolutive, *osāpetvā*, occurs at Spk III 92,2, meaning "having put away."

224 Spk does not identify the other four kings. The fact that they are designated *rājā* does not necessarily imply they were rulers of independent states on a par with Pasenadi, though the mutual use of the address *mārisa* suggests they enjoyed parity of status with him.

225 The Pāli uses the plural *ekacce* with each assertion, but it is evident from the context that each assertion was made by only one king.

226 *Manāpapariyantaṃ khvāhaṃ mahārāja pañcasu kāmaguṇesu aggan ti vadāmi*. My rendering expands slightly on the compressed Pāli idiom. Spk glosses *manāpapariyantaṃ* by *manāpanipphattiṃ manāpakoṭikaṃ*. Spk-pṭ: Whatever a person cherishes, being in his view the chief, is presented by him as the culmination, as the ultimate.

227 *Paṭibhāti maṃ bhagavā, paṭibhāti maṃ sugata*. The same verb *paṭibhāti* is used by both the interlocutor and the Buddha (by the latter, as the imperative *paṭibhātu*), but I have varied the rendering slightly in each case as befits the speaker's situation. This type of exchange occurs repeatedly at **8:5–11** below; **8:8** (I 193,3–4), which contrasts *ṭhānaso paṭibhanti* with *pubbe parivitakkita*, "premeditated," indicates the exact nuance of the verb in such a context; see too **n. 143**. The lay follower Candanaṅgalika is not met

elsewhere in the canon. Apparently he had been inspired because he had seen how the Buddha's glory surpassed that of the five kings.

228 Spk: *Kokanada* is a synonym for the red lotus (*paduma*). The Buddha is called *Aṅgīrasa* because rays issue from his body (*aṅgato rasmiyo nikkhamanti*). A parallel including the verse is at AN III 239–40. See too Vism 388,1–4 (Ppn 12:60) and Dhp-a I 244 (BL 1:302), and cp. **v. 752**.

On *Aṅgīrasa* Malalasekera remarks (DPPN 1:20): "It is, however, well known that, according to Vedic tradition, the Gautamas belong to the Aṅgīrasa tribe; the word, as applied to the Buddha, therefore is probably a patronymic."

229 Be: *doṇapākakuraṃ*; Se and Ee1: *doṇapākasudaṃ*; Ee2: *doṇapākaṃ sudaṃ*. Spk: He ate rice cooked from a *doṇa* of rice grains along with suitable soups and curries.

The *doṇa* is a measure of volume, perhaps a "bucket," obviously far more than the capacity of an ordinary person's stomach.

230 The *kahāpaṇa* was the standard currency unit of the period. See Singh, *Life in North-Eastern India*, pp. 255–57.

231 Spk says that the *nāḷika*, which I render pint-pot (after Burlingame), is the proper portion for a man; I could not find any source specifying the relation between *doṇa* and *nāḷika*. Spk explains that the Buddha had instructed Sudassana to recite the verse, not when the king began his meal, but when he approached the end. In this way each day the king gradually left aside the last portion of food until he reached the proper measure.

A more elaborate version of the story is at Dhp-a III 264–66, where it serves as the background to Dhp 325; see BL 3:76–77. In this version the king's advisor is Prince Uttara rather than the brahmin youth Sudassana.

232 Spk: The good pertaining to the present life was the slimming of the body; the good pertaining to the future was virtue (*sīla*), one aspect of which is moderation in eating. See **3:17** below.

233 Ajātasattu was Pasenadi's nephew, son of his sister and King Bimbisāra, ruler of Magadha. While still a prince Ajātasattu was incited by Devadatta to usurp the throne

and have his father executed; soon afterwards his mother died of grief. War broke out when Pasenadi and Ajātasattu both laid claim to the prosperous village of Kāsī, situated between the two kingdoms, which Pasenadi's father, King Mahākosala, had given to his daughter when she married Bimbisāra (see prologue to Ja No. 239). The four divisions of the army are elephant troops, cavalry, chariot troops, and infantry, enumerated in the next sutta.

Spk explains the epithet *Vedehiputta*: "*Vedehi* means wise; he was so called because he was the son of a wise woman." This is almost certainly a fabrication. Videha was a country in north India, and the epithet suggests his ancestry was from that land. Since Ajātasattu's mother was from Kosala, Geiger surmises that it must have been his maternal grandmother who came from Videha (GermTr, p. 131, n. 3). See too **II, n. 288**.

234 Spk says Ajātasattu has evil friends such as Devadatta, Pasenadi has good friends such as Sāriputta. *Pāpamitta* and *kalyāṇamitta* are *bahubbīhi* compounds meaning respectively "one with an evil friend" and "one with a good friend." They do not mean, as C.Rh.D translates at KS 1:112, "a friend of that which is wicked" and "a friend of that which is righteous"; nor do they mean "a friend of evil people" and "a friend of good people" (though this is entailed). The rare word *ajjatañ* (as in Se and Ee1; Be has normalized the difficult reading to *ajj' eva*) seems to mean "for today, for this day," with the implication that the situation will soon change.

235 Spk: *Jayaṃ veraṃ pasavatī ti jinanto veraṃ pasavati, veripuggalaṃ labhati*; "*The victorious one breeds enmity*: one conquering breeds enmity, begets an inimical person." Spk thus interprets *jayaṃ* in pāda a as a nominative present participle functioning as subject. At EV II, n. to 26, Norman suggests it might be a *ṇamul* absolutive, i.e., a rare type of absolutive formed from the *-aṃ* termination (see too EV I, n. to 22). While at **v. 407** we do find *jayaṃ* as a participle, the word also occurs as a neuter nominative at **v. 619**c, and thus there should be no reason not to interpret it in the same way here. See the discussion in Brough, *Gāndhārī Dharmapada*, pp. 238–39, n. to 180.

236 I read pāda d with Be and Se: *so vilutto viluppati,* as against Ee1 & 2 *vilumpati.* Spk glosses the line, in its occurrence at **v. 407**f, with a passive verb: *so vilumpako vilumpiyati.* To preserve the logic of the verse it is really necessary to accept the passive verb and to understand the passive past participle as active in sense. The BHS version at Uv 9:9 is more intelligible, with an agent noun in place of the past participle: *so viloptā vilupyate.*

237 Spk glosses *kammavivaṭṭena*: "By the maturation of kamma, when the kamma of plundering yields its result." Spk-pṭ adds: "The kamma which has vanished matures when it gains an opportunity (to ripen) by meeting a condition (conducive to its ripening)."

238 Spk: He was displeased thinking, "I elevated Queen Mallikā from a poor family to the rank of queen. If she had given birth to a son she would have won great honour, but now she has lost that opportunity."

This daughter was almost certainly the Princess Vajīrī (see MN II 110,10–18), who was later married to King Ajātasattu of Magadha after the two kings were reconciled. Prince Viḍūḍabha, the heir to the throne, was begotten from another wife of Pasenadi, Vāsabhā-khattiyā, a Sakyan lady of mixed descent who was passed off to Pasenadi as a pure-bred Sakyan princess. Viḍūḍabha later usurped the throne and left his father to die in exile. When he learned that the Sakyans had deceived his father he massacred them and almost decimated the entire Sakyan clan.

239 In pāda b, I follow Ee1 & 2 in reading *posā,* "than a man," though Be and Se, as well as Spk, read *posa,* which Spk glosses as the imperative *posehi,* "nourish (her)." Spk sees the comparison with a son implicit in *seyyā*: "Even a woman may be better than a dull, stupid son." In pāda d, *sassudevā* literally means "having (her) mother-in-law as a deva"; Spk adds father-in-law in the gloss.

240 In pāda b, it is uncertain from the text whether *disampati* is nominative or vocative, but I follow Spk, which glosses it with the vocative *disājeṭṭhaka.* With Be, Se, and Ee2, I read pāda c as *tādisā subhagiyā putto* and comply with Spk by translating *tādisā* as if it were a truncated genitive qualifying the woman. Ee1 reads *tādiso* in apposition to *putto.*

241 Spk explains *appamāda* as *kārāpaka-appamāda*, "activating diligence," which Spk-pṭ says is diligence that motivates one to engage in the three bases of meritorious deeds (giving, virtue, and meditation). Spk: Diligence, though mundane, is still the chief even among the exalted and supramundane states (i.e., the jhānas, paths, and fruits) because it is the cause for their attainment.

242 In pāda e, *atthābhisamayā* is glossed by Spk with *atthapaṭilābhā*. The couplet is often quoted by the commentaries, when commenting on the *ekaṃ samayaṃ* formula, to illustrate *samaya* as meaning *paṭilābha*. I have tried to avoid the tautology of translating *dhīro paṇḍito ti vuccati* "the wise one is called a person of wisdom" by rendering *dhīra* with its homonym, "steadfast"; see **n. 72**.

243 Spk: Although the Dhamma is well expounded for all, just as medicine is effective only for one who takes it so the Dhamma fulfils its purpose only for a compliant and faithful person having good friends, not for the other type.

244 The incident reported here, including the discourse on good friendship, is related at **45:2**. The later version, however, does not include the line "beings subject to illness are freed from illness" (*vyādhidhammā sattā vyādhiyā parimuccanti*), found at I 88,23. Explanatory notes to the embedded discourse will be found below **V, nn. 5–7**.

245 The *seṭṭhi* were the wealthy money lenders in the large towns and cities of northern India. Originally guild masters, in time they came to function as private bankers and often played decisive roles in political affairs. Anāthapiṇḍika was said to be a *seṭṭhi*. See Singh, *Life in North-Eastern India*, pp. 249–51. Apparently when a wealthy man died intestate, the king was entitled to his fortune.

246 A lakh is a hundred thousand. Spk explains *kaṇājaka* as rice with the red powder from the husk (*sakuṇḍakabhatta*); *tipakkhavasana*, as a garment made by sewing together three pieces of cloth.

247 A paccekabuddha is one who attains enlightenment independently of a perfectly enlightened Buddha (*sammā sambuddha*), but unlike a perfectly enlightened Buddha does not establish a *sāsana*, a religious "dispensation." They are said to arise only at times when a Buddha's dispensation

does not exist in the world. The story is elaborated in Spk and at Dhp-a IV 77–78; see BL 3:240. A version at Ja No. 390 does not mention the murder of the nephew or the rebirth in hell. A partly parallel story of abuse towards the paccekabuddha Tagarasikhī is related at Ud 50,14–19.

248 See **n. 93**.

249 The sutta without the similes and verses is at AN II 85–86; see too Pp 51,21–52,23. Spk: One is *in darkness* (*tamo*) because one is conjoined with darkness by being reborn in a low family, and one is *heading towards darkness* (*tamoparāyaṇa*) because one is approaching the darkness of hell. One is *in light* (*joti*) because one is conjoined with light by being reborn in a high family, and one is *heading towards light* (*jotiparāyaṇa*) because one is approaching the light of a heavenly rebirth.

250 The caṇḍālas were the most despised of the outcasts; see Singh, *Life in North-Eastern India*, pp. 16–20. Spk glosses *venakula* as *vilīvakārakula*, family of basket weavers; the two occupations are listed separately at Mil 331. *Rathakārakula* is glossed as *cammakārakula*, family of leather workers [Spk-pṭ: because the straps of carts are made of leather]; and *pukkusakula* as *pupphachaḍḍakakula*, family of those who throw away wilted flowers. Perhaps the latter more generally included all sweepers and refuse removers.

251 Lit., "If by means of the elephant-gem I could have it, 'Let my grandmother not die,' I would have given away the elephant-gem, (thinking), 'Let my grandmother not die.'"

Spk: When his mother died his grandmother filled her place in bringing him up; hence he had such strong affection for her. The elephant-gem was an elephant worth 100,000 *kahāpaṇa*, decked with ornaments worth the same amount. The same explanation applies to the horse-gem and the prize village.

252 Cp. with **3:2**. The verses are identical.

253 *Kattha nu kho bhante dānaṃ dātabbaṃ*. I have translated in accordance with the Pāli idiom, though in English we would normally say, "To whom should a gift be given?" Spk relates the background story: When the Buddha began his ministry, great gains and honour accrued to him and the Bhikkhu Saṅgha, and thus the fortunes of the rival

sects declined. The rival teachers, intent on besmirching his reputation, told the householders that the ascetic Gotama was proclaiming that gifts should be given only to him and his disciples, not to other teachers and their disciples. When the king heard this he realized it was a malicious falsehood, and to convince the multitude of this he assembled the entire populace on a festival day and questioned the Buddha about the matter before the whole assembly.

254 Spk paraphrases: "One should give to whichever person one's mind has confidence in." When the Buddha spoke thus, the king announced to the crowd: "With one statement the sectarian teachers have been crushed." To clear up the ambiguity he next asked: "Lord, the mind may have confidence in anyone—in the Jains, the naked ascetics, the wanderers, etc.—but where does a gift produce great fruit?" What underlies the question is a basic premise of Indian ascetic spirituality, namely, that gifts given to renunciants generate "merit" (*puñña*), which in turn yields fruits (*phala*)—mundane and spiritual benefits—in proportion to the spiritual purity of the recipients. The mechanism that governs the relationship between giving and its fruits is the law of kamma. For a full disquisition on giving and its rewards, see MN No. 142.

255 The five factors abandoned are the five hindrances (*pañca nīvaraṇā*); the five factors possessed are the five aggregates of one beyond training (*pañca asekhakkhandhā*), the *asekha* being the arahant.

256 Spk equates patience (*khanti*) with forbearance (*adhivāsana*) and gentleness (*soracca*) with arahantship [Spk-pṭ: because only the arahant is exclusively gentle (*sorata*)]. Dhs §1342 defines *soracca* as nontransgression by body, speech, and mind, and as complete restraint by virtue; but see **n. 462**.

257 Spk says that Pasenadi arrived after he had just finished impaling a band of criminals that he had arrested when they tried to ambush him and usurp the kingdom. The Buddha thought, "If I reprimand him for such a terrible deed, he will feel too dismayed to associate closely with me. Instead I will instruct him by an indirect method." I agree with C.Rh.D that the story does not fit well, and I

would add that it even detracts from the solemn dignity of the Buddha's discourse.

258 Spk explains *dhammacariyā* as the ten wholesome courses of kamma and says that *samacariyā*, righteous conduct, means the same.

259 *Natthi gati natthi visayo adhivattamāne jarāmaraṇe*. Spk glosses *gati* (= place of motion, "room") as *nipphatti*, success [Spk-pṭ: "The point is that there is no success to be achieved by battle"]; *visaya* ("scope"), as *okāsa*, opportunity, or *samatthabhāva*, capability; "for it is not possible to ward off aging and death by these battles."

4. Mārasaṃyutta

260 Spk assigns this sutta to the first week after the Buddha's enlightenment.

261 I translate the last sentence in accordance with the reading of Se and Ee1 & 2: *sādhu ṭhito sato bodhiṃ samajjhagaṃ*. Be reads: *sādhu vatamhi mutto bodhiṃ samajjhagaṃ*. By *gruelling asceticism* (*dukkarakārikā*) the Buddha refers to the rigorous austerities he practised for six years before he discovered the "middle way" to enlightenment.

262 There is a delicate irony here in Māra the Tempter, usually the suave proponent of sensual indulgence, now recommending strict asceticism. This confirms the old maxim that the extremes are actually closer to each other than either is to the mean. I read pāda d with Se and Ee1 as *suddhimaggam aparaddho* as against Be and Ee2 *suddhimaggā aparaddho*.

263 I read with Be and Se *amaraṃ tapaṃ*, as against Ee1 & 2 *aparaṃ tapaṃ*. The expression, a split compound, occurs also at Th 219d. See CPD, s.v. *amaratapa*. Spk: Low austerity practised for the sake of immortality (*amarabhāvatthāya kataṃ lukhatapaṃ*); that is, devotion to self-mortification (*attakilamathānuyogo*). Spk-pṭ: For the most part one is devoted to the practice of bodily mortification for the sake of immortality, and when that is pursued by those who accept kamma it may be for the sake of becoming a deva (believed to be immortal). See too Sn 249d.

264 *Piyārittaṃ va dhammani*. Spk: *Araññe thale piyārittaṃ viya*;

"like oars and rudder on high forest ground." Spk-pṭ: *Dhammaṃ vuccati vaṇṇu; so idha dhamman ti vuttaṃ. Dhammani vaṇṇupadese ti attho*; "It is sand that is called '*dhammaṃ*'; that is what is meant here by '*dhammaṃ*.' The meaning is: in a sandy place." PED lists *dhammani* but does not explain the derivation; but see MW, s.v. *dhanvan*, where the meanings given include dry soil, shore, desert.

Spk: "This is meant: If a ship were placed on high ground, and were loaded with merchandise, and the crew would board it, take hold of the oars and rudder, and pull and push with all their might, for all their effort they would not be able to advance the ship even one or two inches; the effort would be useless, futile. So, having known austerities thus, I rejected them as futile."

265 Virtue, concentration, and wisdom are the three divisions of the Noble Eightfold Path: virtue (*sīla*) includes right speech, action, and livelihood; concentration (*samādhi*), right effort, mindfulness, and concentration; and wisdom (*paññā*), right view and right intention. Māra is called the End-maker (*antaka*) because he binds beings to death.

266 *Devo ca ekam ekaṃ phusāyati*. I understand this idiom (which recurs at **6:13** and **7:22**) to mean that rain was falling drop by drop, not that it was falling continuously (the meaning ascribed to it by CPD). It would hardly seem sensible for the Buddha to sit out in the open if rain was falling heavily.

Spk: He was sitting there reviewing his practice of striving in order to provide a model for clansmen in the future, who would strive in emulation of the Teacher.

267 In pāda a we should read with Be, Se, and Ee2 *saṃsaraṃ* rather than Ee1 *saṃsāraṃ*. The "long course" (*dīgham addhānaṃ*) is saṃsāra. Spk: It is said that there is no form that Māra had not previously assumed in order to frighten the Blessed One.

268 *Na te mārassa paddhagū*. The last word is read here as in Ee2 and Sn 1095. Be and Se have *baddhagū*, Ee1 *paccagū*. PED conjectures that *paddhagu* may represent Skt **prādhva-ga*, "those who accompany one on a journey," that is, one's servants. Spk glosses: "They do not become your disciples, pupils, apprentices" (*baddhacarā sissā antevāsikā*

na honti). The word *baddhacara* [Spk-pṭ: = *paṭibaddhacariya*] occurs at **v. 578**a.

269 This discourse is also at Vin I 22,24–36, set soon after the Buddha's first rains residence at the Deer Park in Isipatana. The Buddha had already sent out his first sixty arahant disciples to spread the Dhamma. The present admonition, it seems, is addressed to the newly ordained bhikkhus who had come to the Buddha in response to the missionary work of the first disciples.

270 Spk: *Careful attention* (*yoniso manasikāra*) is attention that is the right means (*upāyamanasikāra*). *Careful right striving* (*yoniso sammappadhāna*) is energy that is the right means, energy that is the causal basis (*upāyaviriya kāraṇaviriya*). *Unsurpassed liberation* (*anuttaravimutti*) is liberation of the fruit of arahantship. On the role of careful attention, see **46:51**. Right striving is the fourfold right effort; see **45:8**, **49:1**.

271 Spk: Māra approached and spoke, thinking: "He won't be satisfied that he himself put forth energy and attained arahantship. Now he is eager to get others to attain it. Let me stop him!"

272 Spk: Māra's snare (*mārapāsa*) is the snare of the defilements, that is, the celestial and human cords of sensual pleasure.

273 This is the Buddha's famous injunction to his first sixty arahant disciples to go forth and spread the Dhamma. The passage also occurs at Vin I 20,36–21,16, in correct temporal sequence, preceding **4:4**. **Vv. 476–77** follow immediately, though here they are separated and assigned to an encounter in Sāvatthī. A BHS parallel, including the verses, is at Mvu III 415–16; see Jones, 3:416–17.

Spk explains the threefold goodness of the Dhamma in various ways pertaining both to practice and doctrine. For example, virtue is the beginning; serenity, insight, and the path are the middle; the fruits and Nibbāna are the end; or the opening of a sutta is good, and so too the middle portion and the conclusion. When the Buddha went to Uruvelā he converted the thousand jaṭila ascetics, which culminated in the Fire Sermon (**35:28**).

274 Spk: Māra approached and spoke, thinking: "Like one directing a great war, the ascetic Gotama enjoins the sixty

men to teach the Dhamma. I am not pleased even if one should teach, let alone sixty. Let me stop him!"

275 I follow Spk in dividing *seyyā* and *so* and in taking *seyyā* to be dative in sense (Spk = *seyyatthāya*), and *so* a pronoun used in apposition to *muni* (Spk: *so buddhamuni*). I also follow Spk in taking *seyyā* to mean "lodging," though both C.Rh.D and Geiger interpret it as well-being. Spk explains *vossajja careyya tattha so* thus: "He should live having relinquished—that is, having abandoned—desire for and attachment to his individual existence (i.e., his body and life)."

276 Spk: *Upadhi* here is *khandhūpadhi*, "acquisitions as the aggregates"; see **n. 21**. In the last line the change of the subject from the singular to the plural is in the text. Spk: The enlightened do not resort to such a shelter because they have eradicated all fear.

277 Be, Se, and Ee2 read *dubbhago*; Ee1 *dubbhayo* (which may be a misprint); SS *dubbhato*. Spk: Like one dead and unconscious (*mato viya visaññī viya ca*). Spk-pṭ: A wretch is one who is luckless, whose fortune has been broken; he is similar to the dead and the unconscious.

278 Spk: Craving is said to be *entangling* (*jālinī*) because it spreads net-like over the three realms of existence. It is called *binding* (*visattikā*) because it latches on to sense objects such as forms. It *leads anywhere* [Spk-pṭ: within the three realms of existence]. The *acquisitions* that are all destroyed are the aggregates, defilements, volitional formations, and cords of sensual pleasure (see **n. 21**). *Why should this concern you, Māra?*: "Māra, why do you go about finding fault with this and that like small flies unable to settle on hot porridge?"

This sutta might be compared with **4:13** and **9:2**, which have a similar theme. I have translated Buddha here as "Awakened One" to highlight the contrast with sleep, but it is uncertain whether such a tension of ideas was intended in the original. On the description of craving as "entangling and binding," see AN II 211–13.

279 Spk paraphrases: "The good man should live like a baby who, after drinking milk, might lie down on a blanket and fall asleep, unconcerned whether life is long or short."

280 The point may be that as the felly revolves around the stable hub, so the changing forms of life revolve around the stable soul or life-principle. The verse seems to be alluding to a simile in the Bṛhadāraṇyaka Upaniṣad II.5.15: "And as all spokes are contained in the axle and in the felly of a wheel, all beings, and all those selves (of the earth, water, etc.), are contained in that Self" (Muller, *The Upanishads,* 2:116). See too Chāndogya Upaniṣad VII.15.1 (*The Upanishads,* 1:120).

281 *Vicakkhukammāya,* lit. "for making eyeless." Spk: Out of a desire to destroy the wisdom-eye of the people in the assembly. He is unable to destroy the Buddha's wisdom-eye, but he could do so for the people in the assembly by manifesting a frightening sight or noise.

282 Spk: *In the assemblies*: in the eight assemblies (see MN I 72,18–20). *Endowed with the powers*: endowed with the ten powers of a Tathāgata (see MN I 69–71). At MN I 69,31–34, the Buddha says that, endowed with the ten Tathāgata powers, he roars his lion's roar in the assemblies.

283 See **1:38** and **n. 86**.

284 Spk paraphrases *kāveyyamatto* in pāda a thus: "Do you lie down thinking up a poem like a poet, who lies down intoxicated with the composing of poetry?" The expression recurs at **v. 753**a. *Sampacurā,* glossed by *bahuvo,* is at AN II 59,12 and 61,10, also in apposition to *atthā.*

285 *Muhuṃ muhuṃ,* in pāda b, is not in PED, and Spk and Spk-pṭ are silent, but see MW, s.v. *muhur.* The expression occurs at Th 125d, glossed by Th-a II 7,13–14 as *abhikkhaṇaṃ,* and at Th 1129b, glossed by Th-a III 158,8–9 as *abhiṇhato.* Both glosses mean "often," but here it seems the more literal sense of "moment by moment" or "constantly" is implied. The dart (*salla*) is elsewhere identified with craving; see **vv. 214**c, **737**c. At **35:90** (IV 64,33–34) it is said that the dart is the state of being stirred (*ejā sallaṃ*), *ejā* being a synonym for *taṇhā;* and the Tathāgata, who is unstirred by craving, dwells with the dart removed (*vītasallo*). See too MN II 260,17: *Sallan ti kho Sunakkhatta taṇhāy' etaṃ adhivacanaṃ.*

286 Spk: *Attraction and repulsion* (*anurodha-virodha*): attachment and aversion (*rāga-paṭigha*). For when someone gives a

Dhamma talk, some people express appreciation, and towards them attachment arises; but others listen disrespectfully, and towards them aversion arises. Thus a speaker on the Dhamma becomes caught in attraction and repulsion. But because the Tathāgata is compassionate for others, he is free from attraction and repulsion.

287 At Vin I 21 this exchange of verses is set in the Deer Park at Isipatana and immediately follows the pair of verses at **4:5**. A BHS parallel is at Mvu III 416–17, but the first couplet is equivalent to **v. 77**ab.

288 *Antalikkhacaro pāso yo yaṃ carati mānaso*. Spk states: "The snare is the snare of lust (*rāgapāsa*), which binds even those who move in the sky (i.e., by psychic power)." It is more likely *antalikkhacaro* is intended to suggest the incorporeal nature of lust, which can propel the mind across vast distances; see **vv. 210**b, **211**b.

289 *Vedayitaṃ* in pāda a and *saṅkhataṃ* in pāda b are merely metrical adaptations of *vedanā* and *saṅkhārā*, the second and fourth aggregates.

290 Spk: *Though they seek him everywhere*—in all realms of existence, modes of origin, destinations, stations of consciousness, and abodes of beings—*they do not find him*, do not see him. See **v. 49** (= **v. 105**), **4:23** (I 122,1–13), **22:87** (III 124,1–13), and MN I 140,3–7. It seems that both the living arahant and the arahant after his parinibbāna are intended.

291 Se and Ee1 & 2: *udrīyati*; Be: *undrīyati*. PED explains as a passive form from *ud* + *dṛṇoti*. See MW, s.v. *dṛī* > pass. *dīryate*. Spk: *Ayaṃ mahāpaṭhavī paṭapaṭasaddaṃ kurumānā viya ahosi*; "This great earth seemed to be making a crackling sound." Spk-pṭ: *Undrīyati ti viparivattati*; "'Is splitting open' means: is turning over." The word recurs at **4:22** (I 119,17 foll.). On the evolution of the word in Pāli, see von Hinüber, "Remarks on the Critical Pāli Dictionary (II)," in *Selected Papers*, pp. 152–55.

292 On *lokāmisa*, "the bait of the world," see **n. 10**. Spk explains *māradheyya*, "Māra's realm," as the round of existence with its three realms, which is the place for Māra to stand. The more usual expression is *maccudheyya*, "the realm of Death," as at **v. 16**d; the two are effectively synonymous. See too **v. 102**d and **n. 70**.

293 Se and Ee1 & 2 have *kumārakānaṃ* as against Be *kumārikānaṃ*, "of the young girls." Spk explains that on this day—"a kind of St. Valentine's Day" (KS 1:143, n. 1)—the young girls send presents to their sweethearts among the boys, and the boys send ornaments to the girls, even a garland of flowers if they can give nothing else.

294 Spk: Five hundred maidens were about to offer festival cakes to the Buddha, and the Buddha would have given them a discourse at the conclusion of which they would have been established in the fruit of stream-entry; but Māra, wishing to prevent this outcome, took possession of the girls. The expression *yathā dhotena pattena*, "with a bowl just as cleanly washed as when he entered," is a euphemistic way of saying that the bowl was empty.

Spk: Māra made a false promise when he offered "to see to it" that the Buddha would get alms. He actually wanted the Buddha to expose himself to ridicule by the village boys (for coming for alms a second time after leaving with an empty bowl).

295 Spk explains *kiñcana*, in pāda b, as "the various kinds of defilements such as the 'something' (called) lust, etc." On the use of *kiñcana* to denote defilements, see **41:7** (IV 297,18–19). The devas of Streaming Radiance (*devā ābhassarā*) inhabit the highest plane corresponding to the second jhāna, located in the form realm. They are said to subsist on rapture (*pītibhakkhā*) because they are sustained by the nourishment of the jhāna. The verse occurs at Dhp 200, the story at Dhp-a 257–58; see BL 3:72–73. In the sequel to the verse, omitted in BL, the five hundred girls hear the Buddha's verse and become established in the fruit of stream-entry.

296 I follow Spk, which resolves *cakkhusamphassaviññāṇāyatana* thus: *cakkhuviññāṇena sampayutto cakkhusamphasso pi viññāṇāyatanam pi*; "eye-contact associated with eye-consciousness and also the base of consciousness." Spk says that "eye-contact" implies all the mental phenomena associated with consciousness; "the base of consciousness," all types of consciousness that have arisen in the eye door beginning with the adverting consciousness (*āvajjanacitta*). The same method applies to the ear door, etc. But in the

mind door, "mind" (*mano*) is the *bhavaṅgacitta* together with adverting; "mental phenomena" are the mental objects (*ārammaṇadhammā*); "mind-contact," the contact associated with *bhavaṅga* and adverting; and "the base of consciousness," the *javanacitta* and *tadārammaṇacitta*, i.e., the "impulsion" and "registration" consciousness. For an account of these types of consciousness (fundamental to the Pāli Abhidhamma), see CMA 3:8.

Māra's reply, and the Buddha's rejoinder, hinge on the practice of using Pāli words for cattle metaphorically to signify the sense faculties. See GD, pp. 141–42, n. to 26–27.

297 Here the Buddha is obviously referring to Nibbāna. Cp. **35:117** on the cessation of the six sense bases.

298 A slightly more elaborate version of the incident, including the verses, is recorded at Dhp-a IV 31–33; see BL 3:213–14. Spk: "The Buddha reflected thus with compassion, having seen people afflicted with punishments in realms ruled by unrighteous kings."

299 At **51:10** (V 259,18–20 = DN II 103,23–26) it is said that one who has mastery over the four bases for spiritual power could, if he so desired, live on for an aeon or for the remainder of an aeon. Māra has made this appeal to the Buddha, not out of respect for his leadership ability, but because he wants to tempt him with lust for power and thereby keep him under his own control. It is interesting that the sutta does not offer an answer to the question whether righteous governance is possible, and this ambiguity pervades the Pāli Canon as a whole. While some texts admit that righteous rulers do arise (the "wheel-turning monarchs"), the general consensus is that the exercise of rulership usually involves the use of violence and thus is hard to reconcile with perfect observance of the precepts. For an insightful discussion of the ambiguity, see Collins, *Nirvana and Other Buddhist Felicities*, pp. 419–36, 448–70.

300 In pāda c, Be and Se read *dvittāva*, though the orthography in Ee1 & 2, *dvittā va*, is preferable. Spk: "Let alone one mountain, even as much as double (*dvikkhattum pi tāva*) a large golden mountain would not suffice for one person." BHS parallels to this verse read *vittaṃ*, treasure, in place of *dvittā* (see Concordance 1 (B)).

301 Spk: "Suffering has its source in the five cords of sensual pleasure; that is 'the source whence it springs' (*yato-nidānaṃ*). When a person has seen this thus, for what reason should he incline to those sensual pleasures which are the source of suffering?" *Upadhi* in pāda c is glossed by Spk as *kāmaguṇa-upadhi*; see **n. 21**. In place of *saṅgo*, tie, the BHS versions read *śalyam* (Pāli: *sallam*), dart.

Spk-pṭ: The source of suffering is craving, and the source of craving is the five cords of sensual pleasure. Therefore it is said that the five cords of sensual pleasure—the condition for craving—are the source of suffering. When one who has fully understood reality has seen suffering as it really is with the eye of wisdom, and seen the cords of sensual pleasure to be its source, there is no reason for him to incline to sensual pleasures.

302 Spk: "The staff of *udumbara* wood, slightly crooked, was for the sake of showing that he was of few wishes (*appiccha-bhāva*, an ascetic virtue)." In the Vedic sacrifices, *udumbara* wood was used for all kinds of ritual purposes; the sacrificial post, ladle, and amulets were made of this wood (Macdonell and Keith, *Vedic Index*, s.v. *udumbara*).

303 See **1:20**. Here Māra appears as a proponent of the brahmanical idea that renunciation (*sannyāsa*) must be postponed until after one has enjoyed a full married life. On how young bhikkhus, lads "in the prime of life, who have not dallied with sensual pleasures," can live the holy life without being overcome by sensual desire, see **35:127**.

304 This is a gesture of frustration. Daṇḍapāṇi the Sakyan is described in the same terms at MN I 109,1–2.

305 Samiddhi has already appeared at **1:20.**

306 As at **4:17**; see **n. 291**.

307 The verse = Th 46, Samiddhi's sole stanza. I understand *buddhā* in pāda b to be simply a variant spelling of *vuḍḍhā* (the reading at Th 46), though Spk glosses *buddhā* here as *ñātā*, to which Spk-pṭ adds: *Tā ariyamaggena jānanasamatthanabhāvena avabuddhā*; "They have been comprehended by the noble path through its capacity for knowledge."

308 The story of Godhika is told at Dhp-a I 431–33; see BL 2:90–91. Spk explains *sāmayikā cetovimutti*, "temporary liberation of mind," as the mundane meditative attain-

ments (*lokiya-samāpatti*), i.e., the jhānas and formless attainments, so called because at the moments of absorption the mind is liberated from the opposing states and is resolved upon its object. He fell away from this liberation of mind on account of illness. Being disposed to chronic illness due to winds, bile, and phlegm (the "three humours" of traditional Indian medicine), he could not fulfil the states conducive to concentration. Each time he entered upon an attainment, he soon fell away from it.

309 *Sattham āhareyyam*. A euphemistic expression for suicide; see **22:87** (III 123,10,26), **35:87** (IV 57,6), and **54:9** (V 320,24–25). Spk: He reflected thus: "Since the destination after death of one who has fallen away from jhāna is uncertain, while one who has not fallen away is certain of rebirth in the brahmā world, let me use the knife." On the Buddha's own attitude towards suicide, see **35:87** (IV 60,1–5).

310 Spk: Māra thought: "This ascetic desires to use the knife. This indicates that he is unconcerned with body and life, and such a one is capable of attaining arahantship. If I try to forbid him he will not desist, but if the Teacher forbids him he will." Therefore, pretending to be concerned for the elder's welfare, he approached the Blessed One.

311 Spk: *Jane sutā ti jane vissuta*; lit. "heard among the people = famed among the people," i.e., widely famed. There is a delicious irony, in the above three verses, in the way Māra—who usually addresses the Buddha discourteously as "ascetic"—here showers him with glowing epithets.

312 Spk: The elder, thinking, "What is the use of living?" lay down and slit his jugular vein with a knife. Painful feelings arose. He suppressed them, comprehended the pains (with insight), set up mindfulness, explored his meditation subject, and attained arahantship as a "same-header" (*samasīsī*; see Pp 13,25–27, commented on at Pp-a 186–87). He was a *jīvitasamasīsī*, one who attains the destruction of defilements and the end of life simultaneously. (Another kind of *samasīsī* recovers from a grave illness at the same time that he attains arahantship.)

313 Spk: *Vivattakkhandhan ti parivattakkhandham*; "with his

shoulder turned" means with twisted shoulder. He had been lying on his back when he took the knife, but because he was accustomed to lying on his right side, he had turned his head towards the right and had so remained.

314 *Appatiṭṭhena ca bhikkhave viññāṇena Godhiko kulaputto parinibbuto.* Spk: Māra was searching for his rebirth-consciousness (*paṭisandhicitta*), but Godhika had passed away with rebirth-consciousness unestablished; the meaning is: because it was unestablished (*appatiṭṭhitakāraṇā*: or, with unestablished cause).

Spk-pṭ: *Appatiṭṭhena* is an instrumental used as an indication of modality (*itthambhūtalakkhaṇa*). The meaning is: with (consciousness) not subject to arising (*anuppattidhammena*); for if there were an arising, consciousness would be called "established." But when the commentator says, "because it was unestablished," what is meant is that the cause for the nonestablishment of consciousness was precisely the cause for his parinibbāna (*yadeva tassa viññāṇassa appatiṭṭhānakāraṇaṃ tadeva parinibbānakāraṇaṃ*).

A similar case of suicide is reported of the bhikkhu Vakkali at **22:87**. When the monk is said to attain final Nibbāna with consciousness unestablished, this should not be understood to mean that after death consciousness survives in an "unestablished" condition (a thesis argued by Harvey, *The Selfless Mind*, pp. 208–210); for enough texts make it plain that with the passing away of the arahant consciousness too ceases and no longer exists (see, e.g., **12:51**).

315 The verse (which must have been added by the redactors) occurs at Sn 449, where, however, it follows the verses that correspond to **vv. 504–5**. In the verse Māra is spoken of as *yakkha*.

316 Spk explains the seven years of pursuit as the Buddha's six years (of striving) before the enlightenment and the first year after. However, the next sutta, which apparently follows in immediate temporal sequence, is the temptation by Māra's daughters, which other sources clearly place right after the enlightenment (see **n. 322**). The present sutta seems to confirm this by locating the dialogue

with Māra at the foot of the Goatherd's Banyan Tree, in the vicinity of the Bodhi Tree. The commentaries generally assign the Buddha's stay under this tree to the fifth week after the enlightenment (see Ja I 78,9–11).

Seeking to gain access (*otārāpekkho*). Spk: He thought: "If I see anything improper (*ananucchavikaṃ*) in the ascetic Gotama's conduct through the body door, etc., I will reprove him." But he could not find even a dust mote (of misconduct) to be washed away. On *otāra* (= *vivara*, Spk) see **35:240** (IV 178,13–16, 33), **35:243** (IV 185,11–15; 186,27–30), **47:6** (V 147,17–18, 27–28), **47:7** (V 149,7, 16).

317 Spk: *Bhavalobhajappan ti bhavalobhasaṅkhātaṃ taṇhaṃ*; "The greedy urge for existence is craving consisting in greed for existence."

318 I read pāda d with Be, Se, and Ee2: *yaṃ saccaṃ taṃ nirūpadhiṃ* (Ee1: *yaṃ sabbantaṃ nirūpadhiṃ*). Nibbāna, the supreme truth (*paramasacca*), is often described as *sabbupadhipaṭinissagga*, "the relinquishing of all acquisitions," and here as *nirūpadhi*. See **n. 21**.

319 The same simile occurs in a very different context at MN I 234,7–18.

320 *Nibbejanīyā gāthā*. Spk glosses *nibbejanīyā* as *ukkaṇṭhanīyā* (dissatisfaction) but does not explain the derivation. It is likely the word is related to *nibbidā*, though employed in a different sense; see MW, s.v. *nirvid*.

321 This passage, as far as "unable to speak," is the stock description of the defeated contestant; also at MN I 132,28–30, 234,1–2, 258,28–30. Se and Ee1 make this paragraph the last of the preceding sutta, but I follow Be and Ee2. As the two suttas form a single narrative, the division between them is arbitrary.

322 Their names mean craving, discontent, and lusting. Spk explains that they saw their father in a despondent mood and approached to find out the reason. The story of the Buddha's encounter with Māra's daughters is also recorded at Ja I 78–79 and Dhp-a III 195–98; see BL 3:33–34. There it is clearly set in the fifth week after the enlightenment. The BHS parallel at Mvu III 281–86 is also assigned to this period; see Jones, 3:269–74.

323 Spk's explanation shows that there is more to the simile

than meets the eye: "They capture an elephant and lead him out of the forest by sending a female decoy, who entices him by displaying her feminine wiles."

324 On the idiom *pāde te samaṇa paricārema*, Geiger remarks: "In courteous speech one uses *pādā*, feet, for the person. The meaning is: 'We want to be at your command like slave-women'" (GermTr, p. 193, n. 5). A sexual innuendo is unmistakable. Spk, strangely, does not offer any explanation here of *anuttare upadhisaṅkhaye vimutto*, but see **n. 356**.

325 Spk glosses *senaṃ* as *kilesasenaṃ*, "the army of defilements," and paraphrases: "Having conquered the army of the pleasant and agreeable, meditating alone, I discovered the bliss of arahantship, which is called 'the attainment of the goal, the peace of the heart' (*atthassa pattiṃ hadayassa santiṃ*)." Mahākaccāna provides a long commentary on this verse at AN V 47,3–48,4. On *piyarūpaṃ sātarūpaṃ*, "the pleasant and agreeable," see **12:66** (II 109–12), DN II 308–11.

326 Both the BHS version of these verses (at Mvu III 283–84) and the Skt (cited at Ybhūś 4:1–3; Enomoto, CSCS, pp. 25–26) have the present tense *tarati* in pāda b, as against the aorist *atari* in the Pāli; while the present makes better sense, I translate following the Pāli.

Spk: *Five floods crossed* (*pañcoghatiṇṇo*): one who has crossed the flood of defilements in the five sense doors. *The sixth*: he has crossed the sixth flood of defilements, that pertaining to the mind door. Or alternatively: by the mention of five floods, the five lower fetters are meant; by the sixth, the five higher fetters.

327 Spk: *Tranquil in body* (*passaddhikāyo*): this comes about with the tranquillizing of the in-and-out breathing by the fourth jhāna (see AN II 41,21–28). *In mind well liberated* (*suvimuttacitto*): well liberated by the liberation of the fruit of arahantship. *Not generating* (*asaṅkharāno*): not generating the three types of volitional formations (see **12:51**; also **n. 165**). *Meditating thought-free* in the fourth jhāna. *He does not erupt, etc.*: He does not erupt (*na kuppati*) because of hatred, or drift (*sarati*) because of lust, or stiffen (*na thīno*) because of delusion. Or alternatively: by the first term the

hindrance of ill will is intended; by the second, the hindrance of sensual desire; by the third, the remaining hindrances (see **46:2**).

328 In pāda a, I read *acchejji* with Se, an aorist of *chindati,* to cut. The finite verb seems to me preferable to the absolutive *acchejja* of Be and Ee1 & 2; the variant *acchecchi* suggested by PED may also be acceptable. This verb should be distinguished from *acchejja* (or *acchijja,* Ee1) in pāda d, an absolutive of *acchindati,* to rob, to snatch away. The Be and Ee1 reading of pāda a may have arisen through a confusion of the two forms.

I read pāda b: *addhā tarissanti bahū ca sattā*. Be, Ee2, and SS read the last word as *saddhā*, but the gloss in Spk supports *sattā*: *addhā aññe pi bahujanā ekaṃsena tarissanti.* The BHT version of Mvu is too different to be of help and may be corrupt, but Jones (at 3:273, n. 4) suggests replacing *raktā* with *sattvā*, which would then support the reading I have adopted. *Tarissanti* is certainly preferable to the v.l. *carissanti*, found in Be, Se, and Ee1.

329 The verse occurs in a different context at Vin I 43,27–28. I follow Be and Se in reading, in pāda c, the active *nayamānānaṃ*, the prevalent reading of Vin. Ee1 & 2, on the basis of SS, read the passive *nīyamānānaṃ/niyyamānānaṃ*. BHS versions at Uv 21:8 and Mvu III 90 also have the active form, while the Prakrit at G-Dhp 267 is ambiguous.

330 In the BHS version **vv. 516–17** are ascribed to the Buddha. The concluding verse was apparently added by the redactors.

5. Bhikkhunīsaṃyutta

331 Thī does not ascribe any verses to a bhikkhunī named Āḷavikā, but two of the verses in this sutta are to be found among Selā's verses: **v. 519** = Thī 57 and **v. 521** = Thī 58. Thī-a 60 confirms the identity of the two bhikkhunīs, explaining that Selā was called Āḷavikā because she was the daughter of the king of Āḷavaka. She heard the Buddha preach and became a lay follower. Later she took ordination as a nun and attained arahantship. See Pruitt, *Commentary on the Verses of the Therīs*, pp. 83–87.

332 Spk explains the origin of the name: After the parinibbāna of the Buddha Kassapa a lay disciple named Yasodhara, while bringing money to build the cetiya for the relics, was ambushed there and blinded by five hundred thieves. Because Yasodhara was a noble disciple, the thieves straightaway lost their own vision as an immediate kammic result. They continued to dwell there and thus it became known as the Blind Men's Grove. Bhikkhus and bhikkhunīs went there for seclusion. It was about three kilometres south of Sāvatthī and was protected by royal guards.

333 Strangely, this verse, the appropriate response to Māra's taunt, is not found in Thī. Spk: The *escape* (*nissaraṇa*) is Nibbāna. *With wisdom* (*paññā*): with reviewing knowledge. Spk-pṭ: The intention is: "How much more, then, with the knowledge of the path and fruit?"

334 In pāda b, *khandhāsaṃ* should be resolved *khandhā esaṃ*. Spk glosses *khandhā tesaṃ*. See above **n. 209** and EV II, n. to 58.

335 Thī-a 64 identifies her as the daughter of King Bimbisāra's chaplain. Two verses here = Thī 60–61, also ascribed to Somā, but the third verse differs in the two sources. For the background, see *Commentary on the Verses*, pp. 87–90.

336 Spk: *That state* (*ṭhāna*): arahantship. *With her two-fingered wisdom* (*dvaṅgulapaññāya*): with limited wisdom (*paritta-paññāya*); or else this is said of women because they cut the thread while holding the cotton ball between two fingers. Spk-pṭ and Thī-a 65 offer a different explanation: "From the age of seven on they are always testing whether the rice is cooked by taking grains out from the pot and pressing them between two fingers. Therefore they are said to have 'two-fingered wisdom.'" It should be noted that it is Māra who voices this ancient bias. See too Mvu III 391,19, where we find *dvaṅgulaprajñāye strīmātrāye*.

337 Spk: *When knowledge flows on steadily* (*ñāṇamhi vattamānamhi*): while the knowledge of the attainment of fruition is occurring (*phalasamāpattiñāṇe pavattamāne*). *As one sees correctly into Dhamma* (*sammā dhammaṃ vipassato*): seeing into the Dhamma of the four truths, or into the five aggregates that form the object of insight in the preliminary phase of practice.

Spk-pṭ: By mentioning the occurrence of the knowledge of fruition attainment, the commentator shows that she has been dwelling in nondelusion regarding the four truths (*catūsu saccesu asammohavihāro*). *Seeing into* (*vipassantassa*; or, "seeing with insight"): for one seeing distinctly by the penetration of nondelusion; for one seeing into the five aggregates themselves in the preliminary portion (of the practice) prior to the breakthrough to the truths (*asammohapaṭivedhato visesena passantassa khandhapañcakam eva saccābhisamayato pubbabhāge vipassantassa*).

Spk explains in terms of the knowledge of fruition attainment because Somā, being already an arahant, would have been dwelling in the concentration of fruition. In elucidating *vipassantassa*, Spk-pṭ, in the first clause, connects the word with the realization of the Four Noble Truths on the occasion of the supramundane path; in the second, it takes the word as signifying *vipassanā* in the technical sense of the preparatory work of insight meditation that leads to the path and fruition.

338 Spk says one entertains such thoughts on account of craving, conceit, and views. In pāda c, I read with Ee1 & 2 *asmī ti*, as against Be and Se *aññasmiṃ*. Strangely, though it delivers the coup de grace to Māra, this verse is without a parallel in Thī.

339 Spk recapitulates the popular story of her search for the mustard seeds to bring her dead son back to life, told in greater detail at Dhp-a II 270–75; see BL 2:257–60 and *Commentary on the Verses*, pp. 222–24. Her verses at Thī 213–23 do not correspond to the verses here.

340 Pādas ab read: *Accantaṃ mataputtāmhi/Purisā etadantikā*. A pun seems to be intended between two senses of being "past the death of sons." I translate in accordance with the paraphrase of Spk: "I have 'gotten past the death of sons' as one for whom the death of a son is over and done with. Now I will never again undergo the death of a son.... The ending of the death of sons is itself the ending of men. Now it is impossible for me to seek a man." *Etadantikā* occurs too at Thī 138b.

341 The first couplet is common in Thī, found at vv. 59, 142, 195, 203, 235, etc. Spk elaborates: "The delight of craving

has been destroyed for me in regard to all the aggregates, sense bases, elements, kinds of existence, modes of origin, destinations, stations, and abodes. The mass of ignorance has been broken up by knowledge."

342 Thī-a 156 says that in lay life she had been a friend of Khemā, the chief consort of King Bimbisāra. When she heard that Khemā had gone forth under the Buddha, she visited her and was so inspired by their conversation that she too decided to take ordination. Khemā became her preceptor. See *Commentary on the Verses*, pp. 204–6. Her verses are at Thī 169–74. While the verses here are not among them, interestingly **vv. 528** and **530** (with minor differences) are found among *Khemā's* verses, Thī 139 and 140.

343 Spk enumerates the five instruments: *ātata, vitata, ātata-vitata, susira, ghana*. Spk-pṭ explains *ātata* as an instrument with one surface covered by skin, such as a kettle drum (*kumbha*); *vitata*, an instrument with two surfaces covered with skins, such as the *bheri* and *mudiṅga* drums; *ātata-vitata*, an instrument with a head covered with skin and bound with strings, such as a lute (*vīṇā*); *susira*, wind instruments, include flutes, conches, and horns; and *ghana* is the class of percussion instruments (excluding drums), such as cymbals, tambourines, and gongs.

344 Though three eds. read in pāda c *bhindanena*, Ee2 and SS have *bhindarena*, which perhaps points to an historical reading *bhidurena*. The Thī counterpart, v. 140, has *āturena*, but Thī 35a contains the phrase *bhiduro kāyo*. Both *bhindana* and *bhidura* are glossed identically in their respective commentaries as *bhijjanasabhāva*, "subject to breaking up."

345 Spk: Pāda a refers to the form realm, pāda b to the formless realm, and pāda c to the eight mundane meditative attainments. By the mention of the two higher realms, the sensory realm is also implied. Hence she says, "everywhere the darkness of ignorance has been dispelled."

346 She was the foremost among the bhikkhunīs in the exercise of supernormal powers (*iddhi*), to which she testifies in **vv. 534–35**. Her verses are at Thī 224-35. **Vv. 532–35** correspond to Thī 230–33, but with significant differences. Thī 234 is identical with **v. 521** here ascribed to Āḷavikā.

347 Pāda c: *Na c' atthi te dutiyā vaṇṇadhātu*. I translate freely in accordance with the gloss of Spk: "There is no second beauty element like your beauty element; there is no other bhikkhunī similar to you." A pun on the bhikkhunī's name is probably intended. Se and Ee1 & 2 include an additional pāda between pādas c and d, *idh' āgatā tādisikā bhaveyyuṃ*, absent in Be and Thī 230. This seems to me a scribal error, as it is identical with pāda b of the next verse, where it fits.

348 Spk explains pādas ab as if they meant: "Though a hundred thousand rogues might come here, they would be treated just like you in that they would get no intimacy or affection." I translate, however, in accordance with the apparent sense, which also can claim support from the gloss of Thī-a on Thī 231.

349 The *iddhipādā*, "bases for spiritual power," are the supporting conditions for the exercise of the *iddhi* or supernormal powers described in the previous verse. See **51:11**.

350 Cālā, Upacālā, and Sīsupacālā—whose verses appear in **5:6–8** respectively—were the younger sisters of Sāriputta, in descending order of age. Their verses are at Thī 182–88, 189–95, and 196–203. However, not only is the correspondence between the two collections fragmentary, but the ascriptions of authorship also differ. Cālā's **v. 537** corresponds to Thī 191, and **v. 538** is reflected obscurely in Thī 192, both of which are there ascribed to Upacālā. Upacālā's **vv. 540–43** correspond to Thī 197, 198, 200, and 201, there ascribed to Sīsupacālā. And Sīsupacālā's **vv. 544–46** correspond to Thī 183–85, but there are ascribed to Cālā.

351 In pāda b I read *phussati* with Be, Se, and Ee2, as against Ee1 *passati*.

352 On pādas ab, see **n. 345**.

353 This verse alludes to five of the six sense-sphere heavens. Only the lowest plane, the heaven of the Four Great Kings, is not mentioned.

354 In pāda a, I read *ajalitaṃ* with Se. Be *apajjalitaṃ*, though hypermetrical, gives the same sense. Ee1 & 2 *acalitaṃ*, apparently derived from SS, would mean "unshaken."

355 *Pāsaṇḍa*, in pāda c, refers to the "heretical" systems out-

side the Buddha's dispensation. I render it, inadequately, as "creed." Spk explains the word derivation by way of "folk etymology": "They are called *pāsaṇḍas* because they lay out a snare (Be: *pāsaṃ ḍenti*; Se: *pāsaṃ oḍḍenti*); the meaning is that they throw out the snare of views among the minds of beings. But the Buddha's dispensation frees one from the snare, so it is not called a *pāsaṇḍa*; the *pāsaṇḍas* are found only outside the dispensation." MW defines *pāṣaṇḍa* as "a heretic ... anyone who falsely assumes the characteristics of an orthodox Hindu, a Jaina, a Buddhist, etc.; a false doctrine, heresy."

356 Spk explains *vimutto upadhisaṅkhaye* in pāda d thus: "He is liberated into Nibbāna, known as the extinction of acquisitions, as object." The expression is also at MN I 454,3–4 and II 260,22–23. Spk-pṭ defines "the end of all kamma" (*sabbakammakkhaya*) as arahantship and "the extinction of acquisitions" as Nibbāna. See too **4:25** and **n. 324**.

357 There is no way to determine whether this bhikkhunī is identical with Āḷavikā; see **n. 331**. The verses do not appear in Thī.

358 Spk: Both *puppet* (*bimba*) here, and *misery* (*agha*) at **v. 549**b, refer to individual existence (*attabhāva*), in the latter case because individual existence is a foundation for suffering.

The philosophers of the Buddha's time were divided on the question whether suffering is created by oneself (*attakata*) or by another (*parakata*). The former was the position of the eternalists, who held there is a permanent self which transmigrates from life to life reaping the fruits of its own deeds. The latter was the position of the annihilationists, who held that a being is annihilated at death and nothing survives, so that one's share of suffering and happiness is due entirely to external conditions. See the debates recorded at **12:17**, **18**, **24**, **25**.

359 One key to the interpretation of Selā's reply is AN I 223–24, where it is said that kamma is the field, consciousness the seed, and craving the moisture, for the production of future renewed existence. The cause (*hetu*), then, is the kammically formative consciousness accompanied by ignorance and craving. When that dissolves through the elimination of ignorance and craving there is no production

of aggregates, elements, and sense bases in a future life. The imagery of seeds and vegetation recurs at **22:54**, which also helps to illuminate these verses.

360 Spk provides no personal identification, and no verses in her name have come down in Thī.

361 The simile of the chariot is elaborated at Mil 27–28, which quotes the previous verse. Vism 593,18–19 (Ppn 18:28) also quotes these two verses to confirm that "there is no being apart from name-and-form." **Vv. 553–54** are quoted at Abhidh-k-bh pp. 465–66, ascribed to the arahant nun Śailā (= Selā); see Enomoto, CSCS, p. 42.

In **v. 555** *suffering* signifies the inherent unsatisfactoriness of the five aggregates (*pañcakkhandhadukkha*), which is identical with the *heap of sheer formations* (*suddhasaṅkhārapuñja*) in **v. 553**c. See too **12:15**: "What arises is only suffering arising, what ceases is only suffering ceasing."

6. Brahmasaṃyutta

362 The incident is also recorded at Vin I 4–7 and MN I 167–169, and at DN II 36–40 with the Buddha Vipassī and Mahābrahmā as the speakers. Spk assigns the incident to the eighth week after the enlightenment. A BHS parallel at Mvu III 314–19, considerably more ornate, records several variant traditions of the encounter, more or less corresponding with the Pāli version; see Jones, 3:302–9.

363 Spk explains *ālaya* objectively as the five cords of sensual pleasure, called "adhesions" because it is these to which beings adhere; and again, subjectively, as the 108 mental examinations driven by craving (*taṇhāvicaritāni*; see AN II 212,8–213,2), since it is these that adhere to their objects.

364 Spk: All these terms are synonyms for Nibbāna. For contingent upon that (*taṃ āgamma*), all the vacillations of formations become still and calm down; all acquisitions are relinquished; all cravings are destroyed; all lustful defilements fade away; and all suffering ceases. Spk-pṭ: *Contingent upon that*: in dependence upon that, because it is the object condition for the noble path.

365 The exact meaning of *anacchariyā* is uncertain. Spk (along with other commentaries) offers only a verbal resolution, which is hardly a semantic solution: *Anacchariyā ti anu-acchariyā* ("repeatedly (or according to) *acchariyā*"). Most translators render it "spontaneously," apparently taking the stem to be *acchara* = "moment"; but the commentators seem to understand the stem to be *acchariya* = "wonderful."

Spk-pṭ proposes an additional etymology which entails the same meaning: *Vuddhippattā vā acchariyā anacchariyā; vuddhi-attho pi hi a-kāro hoti yathā asekkhā dhammā ti*; "Or non-wonderful is the wonderful that has increased, for the syllable *a* (the negative prefix) also signifies what has increased, as in 'qualities of a non-trainee' (i.e., of an arahant, 'one beyond training')." Though the derivation is problematic, from lack of an alternative I conform to current practice and use "astounding" as the intensification.

Spk-pṭ says: "The verses have the quality of 'astoundingness' because they indicate that after having fulfilled the perfections (*pāramī*) for four incalculables and 100,000 aeons for the sake of sharing the Dhamma with the world and its devas, now that he has achieved kingship of the Dhamma he wishes to live at ease. It is this 'astoundingness' that is intensified [by the negative prefix *an-*]."

Von Hinüber contends that *anacchariyā* represents Skt **an-akṣar-ikā* (see "*Anacchariyā pubbe assutapubbā*," in *Selected Papers*, pp. 17–24), but his argument rests on the assumption that *pubbe assutapubbā* would be a redundancy and therefore *pubbe* must be taken in apposition to the preceding *anacchariyā*. This assumption, however, is contradicted by DN I 184,27–29, where we find *pubbe ... suta-pubbā* as one block. Interestingly, no corresponding word is to be found in the Mvu and Lalitavistara versions of the same incident.

366 Spk: *Living at ease* (*appossukkatā*, lit. "little zeal") means lack of desire to teach. But why did his mind so incline after he had made the aspiration to Buddhahood, fulfilled the perfections, and attained omniscience? Because as he reflected, the density of the defilements of beings and the profundity of the Dhamma became manifest to him. Also,

he knew that if he inclined to living at ease, Brahmā would request him to teach, and since beings esteem Brahmā, this would instill in them a desire to hear the Dhamma. On *ussukka*, see **n. 54**.

367 Brahmā Sahampati appears in dramatic roles at key points in the Buddha's ministry and also utters the first verse at his parinibbāna (**v. 608** below). See **48:57** for his own account of how he become a prominent deity in the brahmā world. His other appearances in SN are at: **6:2, 3, 10, 12, 13**; **11:17**; **22:80**; **47:18, 43**. In the Mvu version the deity who arrives is referred to simply as Mahābrahmā, without a personal name. He comes accompanied by many other gods including Sakka.

In this chapter (and elsewhere in this translation), I use "Brahmā" when the word is part of a proper name and "brahmā" when it refers more generally to a being or class of beings. Sometimes there is no hard and fast boundary between the two.

368 Spk identifies the door to the Deathless (*amatassa dvāra*) with the noble path, "the door to the deathless Nibbāna." Although the text here uses the singular *dvāra*, just below it has the plural *dvārā*.

369 I translate pāda c in accordance with the reading in Be, Se, and Ee2, *desassu bhagavā dhammaṃ*, found consistently in the Sinhalese texts. Ee1 *desetu* (found also in the DN and Vin parallels) seems to be a normalization influenced by the preceding prose passage. The verse is recited again by Brahmā Sahampati at **v. 919**. The Buddha is called the "unsurpassed caravan leader" at **v. 736**b; see **n. 517**.

370 Spk: The eye of a Buddha (*buddhacakkhu*) is a name for the knowledge of the degrees of maturity in the faculties of beings (*indriyaparopariyattañāṇa*) and the knowledge of the dispositions and underlying tendencies of beings (*āsayānusayañāṇa*). The knowledge of omniscience is called the universal eye (*samantacakkhu*, at **v. 559**d). The knowledge of the three lower paths is called the Dhamma eye (or "vision of Dhamma," *dhammacakkhu*). Together with the divine eye (*dibbacakkhu*: see **6:5**, **12:70**) and the fleshly eye (*maṃsacakkhu*), these make up the "five eyes" of a Buddha.

371 *Paralokavajjabhayadassāvino.* At MLDB, p. 261, the ambiguous compound is rendered "seeing fear in blame and in the other world." This agrees well enough with the commentaries, which resolve it: *paralokañ c' eva vajjañ ca bhayato passanti.* At Dhp 317–18, however, *bhaya* and *vajja* are treated as parallel terms, which suggests that the compound should be resolved: *paraloke vajjañ c' eva bhayañ ca passanti.*

372 *Katāvakāso kho 'mhi bhagavatā dhammadesanāya.* Ee1 *bhagavato* here must be an error. At MLDB, p. 262, in accordance with prevalent practice this phrase was rendered, "I have created the opportunity for the Blessed One to teach the Dhamma." CPD (s.v. *katāvakāsa*) remarks that this construal "is both grammatically impossible and contextually unlikely." The rendering here, based on a suggestion of VĀT, uses the active voice in place of an awkward passive construction imitative of the Pāli.

373 Spk assigns this sutta to the fifth week after the enlightenment. The sutta is also at AN II 20–21 with an additional paragraph.

374 Spk: The first four qualities—virtue, etc.—are both mundane and supramundane. The knowledge and vision of liberation is mundane only, for this is reviewing knowledge (*paccavekkhaṇañāṇa*). On this last term, see **n. 376** just below.

375 In pāda a, Se and Ee1 read *atthakāmena,* also at AN II 21,23, as against Be and Ee2 *attakāmena,* also at AN IV 91,1. Spk glosses *abhikaṅkhatā* in pāda c as *patthayamānena. Saraṃ* in pāda d is probably a truncated instrumental, glossed by Spk as *sarantena;* Norman, however, suggests it could be a *ṇamul* absolutive (see **n. 235** above and EV II, n. to 26).

376 This is the stock canonical description of the attainment of arahantship. The sentence beginning "He directly knew," according to Spk, shows "the plane of reviewing" (*paccavekkhaṇabhūmi*).

The commentaries propose two ways of interpreting *nāparaṃ itthattāya,* depending on whether the last word is taken as dative or ablative. Spk: "Now there is no development of the path again done '*for* this state' (*itthabhāvāya* = *itthattāya* as dative), that is, for the state of the sixteen tasks or for the destruction of the defilements. (The 'sixteen tasks' are the four tasks of the path—full understanding, abandonment, realization, and development (as at **56:11**; V 422,3–30)—taken in conjunction with each of the four supramundane paths.) Or alternatively: *itthattāya* = *itthabhāvato* (the ablative, 'beyond thisness'). Now there is no further continuum of aggregates beyond this present continuum of aggregates. These five aggregates stand fully understood like a tree cut down at the root."

I take *itthattāya* as a dative meaning "for this state of being," i.e., for existence in *any* state of being, so that the phrase conveys the same sense as the alternative "roar of liberation," *natthi dāni punabbhavo*, "Now there is no renewed existence" (see **22:27** (III 29,30), etc.). Elsewhere (e.g., at DN I 17,33; MN II 130,16 foll.; AN I 63,30–64,18) *itthatta* signifies the human state (or perhaps the entire sensory realm) as contrasted with higher states of being. As the stem form *itthatta* is clearly neuter, it is difficult to accept the commentarial explanation of *itthattāya* as an ablative.

377 Walking on continuous alms round (*sapadānaṃ piṇḍāya caramāno*) is the ascetic practice of going for alms to each house along the route, without discriminating between those who regularly give and those who do not; see Vism 60,19–24 (Ppn 2:6), 67–68 (Ppn 2:31).

378 *Āhutiṃ niccaṃ paggaṇhāti.* From the detailed description in Spk, this seems to have been an elaborate ceremony in which sweetened milk-rice was offered to Brahmā with accompanying invocations.

379 Spk: "*The path to Brahmā* (*brahmapatha*) is a name for the four wholesome jhānas; the resultant jhānas are called their path of living (*jīvitapatha*). Ignorant of this path, why do you mumble and mutter? For the brahmās subsist on the rapturous jhānas; they do not eat curdled milk flavoured with herbs and seeds." Usually the four *brahmavihāras* are called the path to the company of Brahmā, as at DN I 250,32–251,21 and MN II 207,14–208,8.

380 Spk explains *nirūpadhika* in pāda b as one devoid of the *upadhi* of defilements, volitional formations, and sensual pleasures. Spk-pṭ: The *upadhi* of the aggregates is not mentioned because the aggregates still exist. *Has surpassed the*

devas (*atidevapatto*). Spk: He has attained the state of a deva beyond the devas, the state of a brahmā beyond the brahmās. (There is an evident pun here on the bhikkhu's name.) On *akiñcana*, "owning nothing," see **n. 73**. *Nourishing no other* (*anaññaposī*). Spk: This is said because he does not maintain a wife and children, or because he will not maintain another body after the present one.

381 Spk: What is *behind* (*pacchā*) is the past, what is *in front* (*purattham*) is the future. He has nothing behind or in front because he is devoid of desire and lust for past and future aggregates. He is *smokeless* (*vidhūmo*) with the vanishing of the smoke of anger. On the "front-behind" dichotomy, see Dhp 348, 421; Sn 949; Th 537.

382 Spk explains *visenibhūto* in pāda a as "disarmed, without the army of defilements" (*kilesasenāya viseno jāto*). Here, however, I follow Norman's suggestion (at GD, pp. 307–8, n. to 793) that *viseni* corresponds to BHS *viśreṇi*, meaning "without association." At Uv 11:12, we find *viseṇikṛtvā* (translated into Tibetan by an expression meaning "free from the crowd").

383 On *oghatiṇṇaṃ* see **n. 2**.

384 Spk: This verse was added by the redactors.

385 The prose opening of this sutta is identical with that of MN No. 49, except that the latter is set at Ukkaṭṭha. The episode and verses make up the Brahmā Baka Jātaka (Ja No. 405). This brahmā's name means "crane," in Indian tradition regarded as a bird of cunning and deceit.

386 Spk glosses *kevalaṃ* as *akaṇḍaṃ sakalaṃ*, "unbroken, whole," and explains the background thus: In an earlier human birth this brahmā had developed the jhānas and was reborn in the Vehapphala brahmā world, a fourth jhāna plane with a life span of five hundred aeons. Thereafter he was reborn in the Subhakiṇha brahmā world, a third jhāna plane with a life span of sixty-four aeons. Next he was reborn in the Ābhassara brahmā world, a second jhāna plane with a life span of eight aeons. Then he was reborn in the first jhāna plane with a life span of one aeon. At first he knew his own past kamma and planes of rebirth, but as time passed he forgot both and adopted an eternalist view.

387 Pāda a reads: *Dvāsattati Gotama puññakammā*. I translate in accordance with the paraphrase of Spk: "Master Gotama, we seventy-two men of meritorious kamma [Spk-pṭ: i.e., doers of meritorious deeds] have been reborn here through that meritorious kamma (*bho Gotama mayaṃ dvāsattati janā puññakammā* [Spk-pṭ: *puññakārino*] *tena puññakammena idha nibbattā*)." Neither Spk nor Spk-pṭ offers any further clue as to what the seventy-two refers to. I read pāda c with Ee2 as having *brahmapatti* rather than *brahmuppatti* or *brahmupapatti* as in the other eds.

Spk glosses *abhijappanti* in pāda d with *patthenti pihenti*, "yearn for, desire." Ja III 359,25-29 employs three verbs: "Many people, with their hands joined in reverence, worship us, yearn for us, desire us (*namassanti patthenti pihayanti*), saying, 'He is the Lord Brahmā, Mahābrahmā,' and so forth. They wish, 'Oh, that we too might become thus.'"

388 For *nirabbuda*, see **n. 409**. Spk says that this is the extent of the life span that remains.

389 I follow Spk in ascribing the statement "I am the one of infinite vision ..." to the Buddha. If the text is read without the commentary, the words would have to be attributed to Baka. The request that follows, however, seems to confirm Spk's interpretation.

Spk glosses: *Vatasīlavattan ti vuccati sīlam eva* ("It is virtue alone that is referred to as 'practice of vow and virtue'"). Spk-pṭ: "It is a vow (*vatabhūtaṃ*) because it is formally undertaken, and a practice of virtue (*sīlavattaṃ*) because it is practised by way of virtuous conduct, but the two terms actually refer to one thing; thus the commentary says, 'It is virtue alone.'"

390 Spk relates detailed stories behind each of the incidents referred to in **vv. 575–77**. See too DPPN, 2:259–60. Malalasekera errs, however, in stating that all the incidents occurred during his incarnation as Kesava. It seems Spk ascribes **v. 578** alone to the life as Kesava.

391 This verse refers to the Kesava Jātaka (Ja No. 346; see too Dhp-a I 342–44). In pāda a, *baddhacara* is glossed by Spk as *antevāsika*; see **n. 268**. I read the verb in pāda b with Be as *amaññi* (or *amañña* in Ee2) as against *amaññiṃ* = "I

thought" in Se and Ee1. Though Spk takes the line to mean that Kappa thought thus of his teacher, I follow the Jātaka, in which the teacher Kesava esteems his pupil Kappa as intelligent and devout while Kesava himself appears almost maudlin.

392 Spk: He did the preparatory work on the fire-*kasiṇa*, emerged from the basic jhāna, and made a determination: "Let flames come forth from my body." By the power of his determination, flames came out from his entire body.

393 I translate pādas cd in accordance with Spk's paraphrase: "Do you see the radiance, the aura, of the Buddha, the Blessed One, surpassing the other auras of the brahmā's bodies, mansions, and ornaments in this brahmā world?"

394 According to Spk, this brahmā had held two views: first, the view that no ascetics could come to his world; and second, an eternalist view. The first was abandoned when he saw the Buddha and his disciples arrive in his realm. Thereafter the Buddha gave him a discourse at the conclusion of which he was established in the fruit of stream-entry, and thus, through the path of stream-entry, he abandoned his eternalist view.

395 The three knowledges implied by "triple-knowledge bearers" (*tevijjā*) are: the knowledge of the recollection of past abodes, the divine eye (also called the knowledge of the passing away and rebirth of beings), and the knowledge of the destruction of the taints. Together with spiritual powers (*iddhi*) and the capacity for reading others' minds, these make five of the six *abhiññās* or direct knowledges. Spk says that the sixth, the divine ear, is also implied.

396 Spk-pṭ: A *paccekabrahmā* is a brahmā who moves about alone, without a retinue. Spk: They stood outside the door like sentries.

397 Spk says that *satā* in pāda b should also be connected with *tayo* and *caturo* in pāda a; the numbers can be interpreted by way of either individual figures (*rūpa*) or rows (*panti*). The *supaṇṇa* is identical with the *garuḍa*, the giant eagle of Indian mythology; see **30:1**. Spk explains *byagghīnisā* as beasts similar to tigers (*byagghasadisā*), but the word occurs at Ja VI 538,9 in a list of birds; it is there glossed as *sena*, a hawk or falcon. It seems that all these figures are

illusory creations of the brahmā's meditative power. Spk: "He shows, 'This is the splendour of the palace belonging to me, the meditator.'"

398 Pāda c reads: *rūpe raṇaṃ disvā sadā pavedhitaṃ*. Spk: *Having seen form's flaw*—the fault (*dosa*) consisting in birth, aging, and dissolution; having seen *its chronic trembling*—that form is always trembling, shaken, stricken by cold, etc. *The wise one* is the Teacher (the Buddha).

While the deity is proud of the forms—the figures that ornament his palace—Subrahmā reproves him by taking up "form" in its technical sense, as the first of the five aggregates, and then exposing its dangers.

399 The story of Kokālika is related below at **6:10**.

400 Spk: The *immeasurable one* (*appameyyaṃ*) is the arahant; one takes his measure by determining, "He has this much virtue, this much concentration, this much wisdom." Spk-pṭ: The states that make for measurement (*pamāṇakara*) are lust, hatred, and delusion, and with their removal it is impossible "to measure" the arahant by way of lust, etc. In this connection see **41:7** (IV 297,11–14 = MN I 298,8–11).

401 In Be and Ee1 & 2 the monk's name is spelt "-modaka-." He was one of the renegades who joined Devadatta in his plot to create a schism in the Saṅgha. Spk explains *akissava*, in pāda d, as *nippañña*, *kissava* being equivalent to *paññā*. Spk-pṭ derives *kissava*, perhaps by "folk etymology," from "that by which one hears what" (*kinti suṇāti etāyā ti*), i.e., learns what is wholesome and unwholesome, etc.

402 In Be the deity's name is Turu. Spk explains that in his previous birth he had been Kokālika's preceptor; he passed away as a nonreturner and had been reborn in the brahmā world. He heard about Kokālika's attempt to malign Sāriputta and Moggallāna and came to advise him to abandon this misguided behaviour.

403 Since the Buddha had declared Tudu a nonreturner, Kokālika reproves him for reappearing in the human world. A nonreturning brahmā does not, of course, take rebirth into the human world, but he may manifest himself to humans. Spk paraphrases: "He does not see the boil on his own forehead, yet he thinks he should reproach me for a pimple the size of a mustard seed." Tudu then real-

ized the wretch was incorrigible and spoke the following verses.

404 In **v. 589** I have translated pāda c a little freely in order to make more apparent the connection with **v. 590**. Literally it should be rendered: "The fool collects a disaster with his mouth." *Kali* means both the losing throw at dice and a disaster.

405 Spk paraphrases pādas a–c: "This misfortune is trifling, that is, the loss of wealth at dice along with all that one owns too, including oneself." Spk glosses *sugatesu*, "fortunate ones," in pāda e as *sammaggatesu puggalesu*, "persons who have rightly attained"; thus here the term refers more widely to all arahants, not only to the Buddha. The verse is also at Uv 8:4, minus pāda c (which Norman considers a later addition), and at P-Dhp 301, which includes pāda c but with *saddhammam pi* in place of SN's *sabbassā pi*. For a theory regarding the historical evolution of the verse, see GD, p. 268, n. to 659.

406 The relationship of the figures here will be clarified in **n. 409**.

407 This sutta is also at Sn III, 10 (pp. 123–31), with the name spelt Kokāliya. The prose portions are identical, but Sn 661–78 gives detailed descriptions of the torments in hell not included here. AN V 170–74 combines **6:9** and **6:10**. The background to Kokālika's animosity towards the two chief disciples is related in the prologue to Ja No. 480; see too Dhp-a IV 90–93; BL 3:247–49.

408 Spk: The Paduma hell is not a separate hell realm but a particular place in the great Avīci hell where the duration of the torment is measured by *paduma* units. The same applies to the Abbuda hell, etc., mentioned below.

409 Spk explains the scale for measuring time as follows: one *koṭi* = ten million years; a koṭi of koṭis = one *pakoṭi;* a koṭi of pakoṭis = one *koṭipakoṭi;* a koṭi of koṭipakoṭis = one *nahuta;* a koṭi of nahutas = one *ninnahuta;* a koṭi of ninnahutas = one *abbuda;* twenty abbudas = one *nirabbuda.*

410 Spk: When he was the youth Pañcasikha he developed jhāna and was reborn in the brahmā world. Because he retained the appearance of a youth they knew him as Kumāra, but because of his great age he was called

Sanaṅkumāra, "Forever Youthful." He makes a dramatic appearance at DN II 210–19. At MN I 358,28–29 Ānanda utters the verse after he has given a detailed analysis of the two terms knowledge (*vijjā*) and conduct (*caraṇa*).

411 Spk says this took place not long after Devadatta had created a schism and had gone from the Bamboo Grove to Gayā's Head; see Vin II 199. In the Vin version, however, the Buddha pronounces this verse, not after Devadatta creates a schism, but when he wins the patronage of the parricide King Ajātasattu; see Vin II 188.

412 The similes are elaborated at **17:35**, followed by the same verse. Cp. **v. 383**.

413 In pāda b, *-vippamokkhā* can be understood as a truncated dative (Spk = *-vippamokkhatthāya*).

414 Spk: Though one has entered into the midst of the Saṅgha, one should not dwell there socializing with one's lay supporters. Having made the mind proficient, having suffused it with joy and contentment, one should again resort to a remote lodging. Pāda d is explained: "Freed from the fear of saṃsāra, one should dwell liberated in (*vimutto*)—that is, resolved upon (*adhimutto hutvā*)—the fearless, Nibbāna."

415 Spk: By this he explains: "Blessed One, just as you are now sitting without attending to the fearful objects situated there, or to the serpents, or to the lightning and thunder, just so do bhikkhus sit when they are intent on striving."

416 Spk explains *itihītaṃ* in pāda b as if it meant deduced by reasoning or logic or inferred from scripture (*idaṃ itiha itihā ti na takkahetu vā nayahetu vā piṭakasampadānena vā ahaṃ vadāmi*). The use of the expression elsewhere, however, indicates that it is specifically connected with oral tradition, e.g., at MN I 520,4: *so anussavena itihītihaparamparāya piṭakasampadāya dhammaṃ deseti*; "he teaches a doctrine by oral tradition, by transmission of hearsay, by what has come down in scriptures." See too MN II 169,12.

In pāda d, the *thousand who have left Death behind* (*sahassaṃ maccuhāyinaṃ*) are the arahants.

417 I interpret the numbers in **v. 602** with the aid of Spk, even though this leads to the unlikely conclusion that the number of stream-enterers is not significantly higher than the

number of arahants (cp. **55:5**, V 406,11–30). I read pāda b with Be, Se, and Ee2 as *dasā ca dasadhā dasa* rather than with Ee1 *dasā ca dasadhā sataṃ*. Though the latter gives a ten times higher figure, it does not agree with the commentary, which glosses: *dasadhā dasā ti sataṃ*. It is not clear to me whether the "five hundred more trainees" (*bhiyyo pañcasatā sekkhā*) means that there are fifteen hundred trainees between the arahant and stream-enterer stages plus an additional thousand stream-enterers, or fifteen hundred trainees who are stream-enterers. **V. 603** is also at DN II 218,6–9, uttered by Brahmā Sanaṅkumāra after he has said that twenty-four hundred thousand (*not* twenty-four hundred, as Walshe has it at LDB, p. 299) Magadhan followers had passed away as stream-enterers and once-returners. According to Spk-pṭ, "the other people who partake of merit" (*itarā pajā puññabhāgā*) are those who have partaken of merit aimed at the ending of the round (but who, presumably, have not yet reached any path or fruit).

418 Sikhī was the fifth Buddha of antiquity counting back from Gotama. He arose thirty-one aeons ago (see DN II 2,14–16).

419 For a more detailed account of Abhibhū's power of transformation (*vikubbanā-iddhi*) see Paṭis II 210,14–30.

420 This incident is referred to elsewhere by Ānanda, and in response the Buddha describes the structure of the world system (AN I 227–28). There the Buddha claims that he himself is capable of making his voice heard throughout a three-thousand great thousandfold world system.

Spk: The elder first asked himself what kind of Dhamma discourse would be pleasing and agreeable to everyone, and he then realized that all devas and humans praise manly effort. Thus he taught a discourse concerning energy (*viriya-paṭisaṃyutta*). The two verses are ascribed to an Abhibhūta Thera at Th 256–57; perhaps the similarity of names has resulted from a garbled transmission. See Horner's trans. of Mil, *Milinda's Questions*, 2:51, n. 5, for ascriptions of the first verse in Pāli and Skt Buddhist literature.

421 This sutta corresponds to the portion of the Mahāpari-

nibbāna Sutta that reports the actual passing away of the Buddha (DN II 156,1–157,19). A few discrepancies between the two versions are noticeable. The omission of the attainment of cessation of perception and feeling, noted by C.Rh.D, seems to be peculiar to Ee1; the passage is in Be, Se, and Ee2 as well as in the lemma of Spk. All four eds., however, omit Ānanda's assertion that the Blessed One (while still in cessation) has attained parinibbāna and Anuruddha's correction. The SN version also omits the earthquake and thundering, mentioned at DN II 156,35–37.

422 Spk: Here there are two kinds of "immediately after" (*samanantarā*): immediately after jhāna and immediately after reviewing. In the former case one emerges from the fourth jhāna, descends into the *bhavaṅga*, and attains parinibbāna. In the latter case, one emerges from the fourth jhāna, reviews the jhāna factors again, then descends into the *bhavaṅga*, and attains parinibbāna. In the case of the Blessed One, the parinibbāna occurred in the second way. But all beings whatsoever, from Buddhas down to ants and termites, pass away with a kammically indeterminate *bhavaṅga* consciousness.

423 On Brahmā Sahampati, see **n. 367**. The *powers* (*bala*) are the ten Tathāgata's powers, enumerated at MN I 69–71.

424 At **v. 21**, we have the same verse with a reading *sabba-saṅkhārā* in place of *vata saṅkhārā* in pāda a. See **n. 20**.

425 In the DN version Anuruddha's verses precede Ānanda's.

426 VĀT remarks: "The absence of in-and-out breathing (in pāda a) refers to the state in the fourth jhāna, where breathing ceases, from which the Buddha passed away. This is not the ordinary cessation of breathing that sets in when anyone dies. The verse states something remarkable: that already *before* 'dying' there was no breathing." On "the Stable One" (*tādī*), see below **n. 435**. On the ceasing of the breath in the fourth jhāna, see **36:11** (IV 217,8–9).

Spk: *Bent on peace* (*santiṃ ārabbha*): bent upon, depending upon, leaning towards Nibbāna without residue. *The One with Vision*—he with the five eyes—*attained final Nibbāna* through the full quenching of the aggregates (*khandhaparinibbāna*). On the five eyes, see **n. 370**; on the two kinds of parinibbāna, see General Introduction, p. 50.

At DN II 157,13 this pāda reads: *yaṃ kālam akarī munī*; "when the Sage passed away."

427 Pādas cd read: *Pajjotasseva nibbānaṃ/Vimokkho cetaso ahū*. The word *nibbāna* is used here in its literal sense but with doctrinal overtones that fit the context. Spk: His deliverance, not obstructed by anything, his approaching the completely indescribable state (*sabbaso apaññattibhāvūpagamo*), resembled the quenching of a lamp. Anuruddha's verses on the Buddha's parinibbāna in Th include an additional verse, Th 907.

7. Brāhmaṇasaṃyutta

428 The story related here is also at Dhp-a IV,161–63; see BL 3:288–89. The opening is similar to that of MN No. 100 (II 209,21 foll.), which concerns a brahmin lady of the same name, there spelt Dhānañjānī.

Spk: The Dhanañjāni clan was reputed to be the highest clan of brahmins. They believed that while other brahmins had been born from Brahmā's mouth, they themselves had issued from the top of his head. This woman was a noble disciple, a stream-enterer, but her husband was staunchly opposed to the Buddha's dispensation and would block his ears whenever she spoke in praise of the Triple Gem.

429 Spk: The brahmin had invited five hundred fellow brahmins to a banquet. The previous day he had pleaded with his wife not to disgrace him by praising the Buddha before his peers. When she stumbled over a stack of firewood while serving food to the brahmins, she knelt down and paid homage to the Buddha. Scandalized by this, the brahmins reviled her husband and walked out without even finishing their meal.

430 *Vasalī*, here rendered "wretched woman," is a term of severe contempt, used by the brahmins to address outcasts.

431 The verses have already appeared at **1:71** and **2:3**, with different narrative settings. This illustrates once again how the "floating mass" of didactic verses could be freely drawn upon to suit different pedagogical requirements.

Spk: He formulated his question with the following

intent: "If he says, 'I approve of the killing of such and such,' then I'll call him a killer and challenge his claim to be an ascetic; but if he says he doesn't approve of any killing, I'll say, 'Then you don't desire the killing of lust, etc., so why do you wander about as an ascetic?' Thus the ascetic Gotama will be caught on the horns of this dilemma, unable either to swallow it or to cough it up." He greeted the Buddha cordially in order to hide his anger.

432 See **n. 376**.

433 I give the sobriquet both in Pāli and in English. Spk, which identifies him as the younger brother of the first Bhāradvāja brahmin, says that the epithet was added by the redactors of the canon because he came abusing (*akkosanto*) the Tathāgata with five hundred verses.

434 Spk: He had heard that seers (*isi*) inflict a curse when they become angry, so when the Buddha said, "It still belongs to you, brahmin!" he was frightened, thinking, "The ascetic Gotama, it seems, is putting a curse on me." Therefore he spoke thus.

435 I have translated *tādī* as "the Stable One" in accordance with the commentarial gloss, *tādilakkhaṇaṃ pattassa*, which alludes to the explanation of *tādī* at Nidd I 114–16: "The arahant is *tādī* because he is 'stable' (*tādī*) in the face of gain and loss, etc.; he is *tādī* because he has given up all defilements, etc.; he is *tādī* because he has crossed the four floods, etc.; he is *tādī* because his mind is free from all defilements; and he is *tādī* as a description of him in terms of his qualities" (condensed). A similar but slightly different definition of *tādī* in relation to the Buddha occurs at Nidd I 459–61.

436 Be and Ee1 & 2 read pāda a: *ubhinnaṃ tikicchantānaṃ*, which Spk (Be) includes in the lemma and glosses *ubhinnaṃ tikicchantaṃ*, adding: "Or the latter is itself the reading." In Se and Spk (Se) the readings are exactly the reverse. As the sense requires an accusative singular, the reading *ubhinnaṃ tikicchantaṃ taṃ*, found at Th 444a, offends against neither grammar nor metre. Ee2 has adopted this reading for the exact parallel **v. 882** below, but strangely reverts to *ubhinnaṃ tikicchantānaṃ* in the third parallel, **v. 891**.

437 He was the youngest of the Bhāradvāja brothers.

438 Spk: "For one who understands the excellence of endurance, this victory—patient endurance—is his alone (*yā titikkhā vijānato adhivāsanāya guṇaṃ vijānantassa titikkhā adhivāsanā, ayaṃ tassa vijānato va jayo*)." Note that neuter *jayaṃ* is here nominative.

439 Spk: He was another of the Bhāradvāja brothers. The name Bilaṅgika was assigned to him by the redactors because he became rich by selling delicious conjee (*kañjika*, a synonym for *bilaṅga*).

440 Spk: He was so angry his three brothers had been ordained as monks that he could not speak.

441 Spk says that the name Ahiṃsaka may have been assigned to him by the redactors because he "asked a question" (i.e., made an assertion) about harmlessness; or, alternatively, Ahiṃsaka may have been his given name. From his opening statement and the Buddha's reply the second alternative seems more likely.

442 Spk-pṭ explains the *sīla* referred to in pāda b as *pañcavidha-niyama*, an obvious allusion to the second limb of Patañjali's Yoga system.

Spk: By knowledge (*vijjā*) he means the Three Vedas, by conduct (*caraṇa*) the conduct of one's clan (*gottacaraṇa*; Spk-pṭ: the clan itself, called conduct).

As *vijjācaraṇasampanna* is one of the nine chief epithets of the Buddha and is also used to describe the arahant (see **v. 596**), the second couplet, if read apart from the commentarial explanation, expresses the Buddhistic rather than the brahmanical point of view. See too the Buddha's argument with the brahmin youth Ambaṭṭha at DN I 99,19–100,16.

443 A brahmin of this name is encountered in the Vasala Sutta (Sn I, 7; p. 21), but he seems to be a different person. According to Spk, this brahmin was given the soubriquet "Aggika" because he tended the sacred fire.

444 Spk: He speaks of one endowed "with the triple knowledge" (*tīhi vijjāhi*) with reference to the Three Vedas. By "proper birth" (*jātimā*) he means one of pure birth through seven generations.

445 The Buddha's reply refers to the *tevijjā* of his own system

of training: pāda a, to knowledge of the recollection of past abodes; pāda b, to the divine eye, i.e., the knowledge of the passing away and rebirth of beings; and pāda c, to the knowledge of the destruction of the taints.

446 Spk paraphrases the idea behind **vv. 636–37** thus: "Though I stood for such a long time waiting for alms, you would not give me even a spoonful; but now, after I have revealed all the Buddha-qualities to you as though spreading out sesamum seeds on a mat, (you wish to give). This food has been gained, as it were, by chanting a song; therefore, because it has been 'chanted over with verses' (*gāthābhigīta*) it is not fit to be eaten by me. As such a principle exists (*dhamme sati*), out of regard for the Dhamma, established on the Dhamma, the Buddhas sustain their life. This is their rule of conduct; this is their way of livelihood (*esā vutti ayaṃ ājīvo*). Such food is to be discarded and only what is righteously gained is to be eaten."

The Buddha's practice is discussed at Mil 228–32. CPD (s.v. *abhigīta*) suggests that the reason the Buddha rejects such food is because it has been "spoken over with mantras"—by the brahmin while chanting the sacrificial hymns—but to me it is doubtful the Buddha would reject food for such a reason. Further, according to MW, *gāthā* is not used with reference to the verses of the Vedas, and thus here the word more likely refers to the Buddha's own verses.

Spk does not comment on *kevalinaṃ*, "the consummate one," in pāda a, but Pj II 153,9–10 (to Sn 82) says: *Kevalinan ti sabbaguṇaparipuṇṇaṃ sabbayogavisaṃyuttaṃ vā*; "a consummate one is one complete in all excellent qualities or one detached from all bonds." Spk II 276,32–277,1 (to SN III 59,34) explains: *Kevalino ti sakalino katasabbakiccā*; "the consummate ones are entire, they have completed all their tasks." For a further selection of relevant passages, see GD, p. 161, n. to 82. For reflections on the implications of the term, see Ñāṇananda, SN-Anth 2:100–1.

Spk explains *kukkuccavūpasantaṃ* thus: *hatthakukkuccādīnaṃ vasena vūpasantakukkuccaṃ*; "one in whom remorse has been stilled by the stilling of fidgety behaviour with the hands, etc." Here *kukkucca* is understood in the literal sense of "bad activity" or "fidgety behaviour" rather than in the extended sense of remorse or worry, one of the five hindrances.

447 Spk: This was his thought: "The portion of milk-rice placed in the fire has been eaten by Mahābrahmā. If this remainder is given to a brahmin, one born from the mouth of Brahmā, my father and son would be pleased and I will clear the path to the brahmā world." See Deussen, *Sixty Upaniṣads of the Veda*, 1:148: "The residue (*ucchiṣṭaṃ*) of the offering, i.e., what remains in the ladle, in the saucepan, or vessel, is to be eaten only by a brāhmaṇa, not in his own house; no kṣatriya or vaiśya is to eat it." This explains why the brahmin, just below, is so concerned about the Buddha's caste.

448 *Fire is indeed produced from any wood* (*kaṭṭhā have jāyati jātavedo*). Spk: This is the purport: "It is not the case that only fire produced from a pure type of wood, such as sal-tree logs, can perform the work of fire, but not fire produced from the wood of a dog's trough, etc. Rather, by reason of its flame, etc., fire produced from any kind of wood can do the work of fire. So you should not think that only one born in a brahmin family is worthy of offerings, but not one born in a caṇḍāla family, etc. Whether from a low family or a high family, an arahant sage is a thoroughbred—resolute, restrained by a sense of shame." See in this connection the arguments at MN II 129–30, 151–53.

449 Spk explains *one who has reached the end of knowledge* (*vedāntagū*) in pāda b thus: "one gone to the end of the four path knowledges, or one gone to the end of defilements by the four path knowledges" (*catunnaṃ maggavedānaṃ antaṃ, catūhi vā maggavedehi kilesānaṃ antaṃ gato*). Evidently, the Buddha is here deliberately using brahmanical terminology in order to adjust the Dhamma to the mental disposition of the brahmin.

450 Spk: Why does he say this? It is said that when the brahmin presented the food to the Buddha, the devas from the four world-regions, etc., suffused the food with nutritive essence (*ojā*) produced by their celestial power. Thus it

became extremely subtle. It was too subtle for the coarse digestive systems of ordinary human beings to digest properly; yet, because the food had a base of coarse material food, it was too coarse for the devas to digest. Even dry-insight arahants could not digest it. Only arahants who obtain the eight meditative attainments could digest it by the power of their attainment, while the Blessed One could digest it by his own natural digestive power.

451 Spk: This did not occur through the power of the food itself but through the Buddha's power. The Buddha had made such a determination so that the brahmin would be favourably disposed to hear the Dhamma.

452 *Khāribhāra*, "shoulder-load," is a carrying device commonly used in South Asia, consisting of two trays at each end of a pole borne across the shoulder.

Spk: "*Conceit, O brahmin, is your shoulder-load*: When a shoulder-load is being carried, with each step the weight of the load brings the trays into contact with the ground; similarly, though conceit props one up on account of birth, clan, family, etc., it causes envy to arise and thereby pulls one down to the four realms of misery. *Anger the smoke*: because the fire of knowledge does not shine when defiled by the smoke of anger. *False speech the ashes*: because the fire of knowledge does not burn when covered by false speech. *The tongue is the ladle*: my [the Buddha's] tongue is a ladle offering the Dhamma sacrifice. *The heart the altar*: the hearts of beings are the altar, the fireplace, for my offering of the Dhamma sacrifice. *The self* (*attā*) is the mind."

453 Spk: "Just as, after you have worshipped the fire, you enter the Sundarikā River and wash the ashes, soot, and sweat from your body, so for me the Dhamma of the eightfold path is the lake where I bathe thousands of living beings. The lake is limpid (*anāvila*) because, unlike your river which becomes muddy when four or five bathe in it at the same time, the lake of the Dhamma remains limpid and clear even when hundreds of thousands enter it to bathe." On "the bath without water," see **v. 198**ef and **n. 119**.

454 Spk suggests several alternative schemes by which the

three terms in pāda a—*sacca, dhamma,* and *saṃyama*—can be correlated with the eightfold path: e.g., *sacca* = right speech; *saṃyama* = right action and right livelihood; *dhamma* = the other five factors. Spk explains *brahmacariya* as if it were equivalent to the entire eightfold path (*magga-brahmacariya*), but it seems more likely that here the term was originally intended in the specific sense of celibacy, to be understood as a fourth item alongside the preceding three and not as an umbrella term comprising them.

In pāda b, *the attainment of Brahmā* (*brahmapatti*): the attainment of the best (*seṭṭhapatti*). *Based on the middle* (*majjhesitā*): avoiding the extremes of eternalism and annihilationism. [Spk-pṭ: That is, based on the development of the middle way by avoiding all extremes such as sluggishness and restlessness, of which the pair eternalism and annihilationism is merely one instance.]

In pāda c, *the upright ones* (*ujjubhūtesu*): the arahants. Spk explains that the *sat* here represents *tvaṃ*, the *-t-* being a mere conjunct consonant (*padasandhi*). Though not as common as its use to convey a first person meaning, the third person demonstrative pronoun is occasionally used with a second person sense.

455 In pāda c, *ajjasaṭṭhiṃ na dissanti* is glossed by Spk, "they are not seen for six days from today," indicating that *saṭṭhi* here is an alternative form of *chaṭṭha*, sixth. Spk-pṭ: *Ajjasaṭṭhiṃ* is an accusative used to indicate a continuing passage of time (*accantasaṃyoge c' etaṃ upayogavacanaṃ*).

456 Spk: As long as the brahmin was affluent, even though his daughters were widows, their parents-in-law allowed them to stay in their husbands' homes. But when he became poor their parents-in-law sent them to their father's home. Then, when he would take his meals, their children would put their hands in his plate and he would not find sufficient room for his own hand.

457 Spk appends a story which relates how the Buddha took the brahmin (after his novice ordination) to King Pasenadi. The king repaid his debts, provided for the welfare of his daughters, and placed his wife in the position of his own grandmother, thereby removing the obstacles to his higher ordination as a bhikkhu.

458 This sutta is also found at Sn I, 4 (pp. 12–16), but the prose portion adds the wonder of the sizzling cake described in **7:9**. It also has the brahmin request ordination as a bhikkhu and attain arahantship. It must have been a common subject for sermons, as the commentary to it is long and elaborate. It is also included in the *Maha Pirit Pota*, "The Great Book of Protection," the standard collection of protective suttas used in Sri Lanka.

459 Spk: He was called thus because he earned his living by ploughing. This occasion was not an ordinary work day but a special festival which marked the inception of the light-soil sowing (*paṃsuvappa*). Spk gives a detailed account of the preparations and the festival activities.

460 Spk: At the food distribution (*parivesanā*) five hundred ploughmen had taken silver vessels, etc., and were sitting while the food was being distributed to them. Then the Buddha arrived and stood in a high place within range of the brahmin, close enough so that they could easily converse.

461 Spk: Why did the Blessed One begin with faith? Because this brahmin was reputed to be intelligent (*paññavā*) but was deficient in faith. Thus a talk on faith would be helpful to him. Why is faith called the seed (*saddhā bījaṃ*)? Because it is the foundation of all wholesome qualities. When a seed is planted in the ground, it becomes established by its root and sends up a sprout. Through the root it absorbs the soil's nutrients and water, and it grows through the stalk in order to yield the grain. Coming to growth and maturity, it finally produces a head bearing many rice grains. So faith becomes established with the root of virtue and sends up the sprout of serenity and insight. Absorbing the nutrients of serenity and insight through the root of virtue, it grows through the stalk of the noble path to yield the crop of the noble fruits. Finally, after coming to growth through six stages of purification, and producing the sap of purification by knowledge and vision, it culminates in the fruit of arahantship bearing many discriminating knowledges and direct knowledges (*anekapaṭisambhidābhiññā*). Therefore it is said, "Faith is the seed."

On austerity (*tapa*), see **n. 119**. Spk: Here sense restraint is intended. Wisdom (*paññā*) is insight together with path-wisdom. Just as the brahmin has a yoke and plough, so the Blessed One has the twofold insight and (path-)wisdom.

Spk devotes several pages to the analogy between path factors and ploughing implements. I adopt the renderings of ploughing terms from GD, p. 9.

462 Spk: In some places gentleness (*soracca*) denotes bodily and verbal nontransgression, but this is not intended here. Here the fruit of arahantship is intended, for that is called *soracca* (the abstract noun of *su* + *rata*) because it finds delight in the good Nibbāna (***su****ndare nibbāne* ***ratattā***). What he is saying is this: "By attaining arahantship at the foot of the Bodhi Tree, I am released, and never again must I come under the yoke."

463 Spk explains *yogakkhema* as Nibbāna "because it is secure from the bonds" (*yogehi khemattā*). The four bonds are identical with the four floods, on which see **n. 1**. For a discussion of the literary history of *yogakkhema*, see EV I, n. to 32.

To where, having gone, one does not sorrow (*yattha gantvā na socati*). Spk: It goes to the unconditioned state known as Nibbāna, which is the extraction of all the darts of sorrow.

464 Spk explains that the phrases "a second time" and "a third time" mean the next day and the day after that. Although the text itself conveys the impression that the Buddha went to the same house for alms three times on the same morning, this would be contrary to proper monastic etiquette, so Spk must be reliable on this point.

465 *Pakaṭṭhaka* < Skt *prakarṣaka*, "harasser, disquieter," from *prakṛṣ*, to trouble, to disturb (SED). Spk glosses with *rasagiddha*, "greedy for tastes." Spk-pṭ explains: "He is dragged forward by craving for tastes" (*rasataṇhāya pakaṭṭho*).

466 That is, he was afflicted by an illness arisen from the wind humour, one of the three bodily humours according to the ancient Indian system of ayurvedic medicine; on wind as one of the eight causes of illness, see **36:21**.

Spk: The Buddha was prone to occasional gastric ailments as a consequence of his six years of ascetic practices before his enlightenment.

467 For a full analysis of the two questions, see **3:24** and

nn. 253, 254. I take *kathaṃ* in pāda d here, and *evaṃ* in **v. 678**d, to be mere metrical fillers.

468 A much more elaborate version of the same encounter is found at Dhp-a IV 7–15, where it forms the background story to Dhp 324; see BL 3:201–5. The story is incorporated into Spk.

469 Th-a II 179–80 relates exactly the same story about the elder Jenta (Th 423–28), the son of the king of Kosala's chaplain. In his youth he was stiff with conceit (*mānatthaddha*, used as a description, not a name), but was humbled by the Buddha with exactly the same exchange of verses as is related here. He became a stream-enterer on hearing the Buddha's verses, went forth as a bhikkhu, and attained arahantship.

470 Spk: He thought, "When a brahmin of high birth like myself has arrived, this ascetic does not show me any special courtesy; therefore he does not know anything."

471 In pāda a, it seems better to read *mānabrūhaṇā*, with Se and Ee2, as against *mānaṃ brāhmaṇa* in Be and Ee1. The version at Th-a reads *brāhmaṇa* in all three eds. available to me.

472 *Evarūpaṃ paramanipaccākāraṃ karoti*. The expression occurs at MN II 120,6, referring to the same kind of action (shown by King Pasenadi towards the Buddha); see too **48:58**, which discusses the reason an arahant shows "supreme honour" towards the Buddha and his teaching.

473 Spk: He was called Navakammika ("New Works") because he earned his living by felling timber in the forest, seasoning the wood for construction work, and selling it in the city.

474 In pāda b, *ucchinnamūlaṃ* appears often in a stock formula describing the arahant's liberation from defilements (e.g., **12:35** (II 62,20–63,11); **22:3** (III 10,27, 33); **35:104** (IV 85,9, 14); **54:12** (V 327,26–328,6)); thus the allusion, already obvious, is made explicit by Spk: "The woods of defilements is cut down at its root." In pāda b, I follow the SS reading *visukkhaṃ*, "dried up," also adopted by Ee2, over Be and Se *visūkaṃ* and Ee1 *visukaṃ*.

Spk glosses *nibbanatho* in pāda c with *nikkilesavano*. This involves a pun difficult to reproduce in translation. Literally, *vanatha* means a woods, but the word is often used to signify, metaphorically, "the woods of defilements," particularly craving. Here I have translated *nibbanatha* as "woodless" to preserve the pun. At **v. 712**, however, where the literal meaning has little bearing on the verse as a whole, I have rendered *nibbanatha* by way of its metaphorical meaning. Analogous puns on *vana* and *vanatha* are at **14:16** (see too **II, n. 245**), and also at Dhp 283–84 and 344 (which, incidentally, answer Norman's puzzling observation at EV I, n. to 338, that the canon seems not to include any example of a pun on the double meaning of *vanatha* to match the puns upon *vana*). The Buddha is "dartless" (*visallo*) because he has extracted the dart of craving (see **v. 214**c).

475 In the third line I supply "body" in deference to Spk, which explains the instrumentals as qualifying the body (*kāyavisesanāni*). Spk glosses *sucārurūpaṃ* with *atisundaraṃ*.

476 Spk: *The world's divine lord* (*lokādhipati*) is Mahābrahmā, *the supreme triple heaven* (*tidivam anuttaraṃ*) is said with reference to the brahmā world. I translate pādas cd as an assertion based on the v.l. *tasmā* found in some SS and adopted by Ee2 rather than as a question signalled by *kasmā*, the reading in Be, Se, and Ee1.

477 Spk explains desires (*kaṅkhā*), delights (*abhinandanā*), and longings (*pajappitā*) as modes of craving (*taṇhā*). *The root of unknowing* (*aññāṇamūla*) is ignorance (*avijjā*). A parallel to this verse is at Nett 24 and Peṭ 17, but with pāda a reading *āsā pihā ca abhinandanā ca.*

478 In pāda a, I read *asito* with Be, Se, and Ee2, as against Ee1 *apiho*, "without envy." Spk takes "my purified vision of all things" to be an allusion to the knowledge of omniscience. In pāda c, it glosses *sivaṃ* with *seṭṭhaṃ*, and *sambodhim anuttaraṃ* with *arahatta*.

479 "Mendicant" is a rendering of *bhikkhaka*, which is of course related to *bhikkhu*, a fully ordained Buddhist monk.

480 Ee1 *bhikkhavo* in pāda b should be amended to *bhikkhate*. Spk explains *vissaṃ dhammaṃ* in the next pāda as *duggandhaṃ akusaladhammaṃ*, "a foul smelling unwholesome state," assuming that *vissa* < Skt *visra*, raw meat. Spk-pṭ adds: "It produces a putrid smell, thus it is *vissa*, i.e., foul smelling" (*virūpaṃ gandhaṃ pasavatī ti visso duggandho*).

Dhp-a III 393,2 (commenting on the verse at Dhp 266) says: "*Vissa* is an uneven doctrine (*visamaṃ dhammaṃ*); or else, a putrid-smelling state of bodily action, etc. (*vissagandhaṃ vā kāyakammādikaṃ dhammaṃ*), having undertaken which one is not called a bhikkhu." As Brough points out, however, the original Pāli term is probably derived from Vedic *veśman*, domestic (*Gāndhārī Dharmapada*, pp. 191–92, n. to 67). *Vesma* occurs in Pāli at Ja V 84,17. Uv 32:18, the Skt parallel to the present verse, has *veśmāṃ dharmaṃ*.

In the next verse, in pāda b, I read *brahmacariyavā*, with Se and SS, as against *brahmacariyaṃ* in the other eds. The latter does not seem to fit into the syntax, as it is neither subject nor object of the verb. Since the Buddha here defines a bhikkhu as one who has expelled both merit and evil (*puññañ ca pāpañ ca bāhitvā*), this means he is equating the real monk solely with the arahant.

481 See **n. 453**.

482 The name Khomadussa means "linen cloth." Spk says that the town was given this name because of the prevalence of linen there. From what follows it seems the town was a brahmin enclave in the predominantly khattiya Sakyan republic. In the irate reaction of the brahmins to the Buddha's arrival on the scene we can detect a note of hostility rooted in caste prejudice.

483 My rendering is not strictly literal but is intended to convey the sense of indignation. Spk: The "rule of order" (*sabhādhammaṃ*, lit. "rule of the council") was that latecomers should enter through a side entrance so as not to disturb those comfortably settled in their seats. But the Buddha entered from the front, so the brahmins spoke scornfully.

The Buddha picks up on the the word *dhamma*, in the sense of rule, and speaks with reference to the true doctrine. There is also a pun on *sabhā* as council (or meeting hall) and *santo* as the good ones. According to Spk, the Buddha had caused the rain to fall by an act of will to give himself a reason for entering the meeting hall. A clearer example of rain created by psychic power is at **41:4**.

8. Vaṅgīsasaṃyutta

484 His verses are at Th 1209–79. **Vv. 707–57** are parallel to Th 1209–62, but with variant readings and major differences especially in the verses corresponding to **vv. 753–57**. The verses are collected and translated in Ireland, *Vaṅgīsa: An Early Buddhist Poet*. For the resolution of philological problems posed by these verses I have relied largely upon Norman's notes in EV I.

485 *Cetiyas* are memorial shrines, similar to stūpas, originally made from mounds of earth.

Spk: Before the Buddhas arise the shrines such as Aggāḷava and Gotamaka are the haunts of yakkhas and nāgas, etc., but when Buddhas arise people drive the spirits away and build monasteries there.

486 I translate *anabhirati* as "dissatisfaction," and the nearly synonymous *arati* as "discontent." Although the meanings of the two words overlap, *arati* is often glossed in the commentaries as discontent with remote lodgings and with meditation (*pantasenāsanesu c' eva bhāvanāya ca ukkaṇṭhitaṃ*: Spk I 264,29–31 [to **7:17**]) or discontent with the Buddha's Teaching (*sāsane aratiṃ*: Spk I 269,23–24 [to **8:2**]). *Anabhirati* usually implies distress caused by sensual passion, often inducing a wish to give up the celibate life and return to the enjoyment of sensual pleasures. In the expression *sabbaloke anabhiratasaññā*, "the perception of nondelight in the entire world," *anabhirata* is used in a positive sense as the designation for a particular topic of insight meditation (see AN V 111,3–7). The delight (*abhirati*) that Vaṅgīsa will arouse in himself is, of course, delight in the holy life, not the unwholesome delight in the five sense objects, a mode of craving.

487 *From the Dark One* (*kaṇhato*). Spk: "From the dark faction, the faction of Māra." Māra is addressed as Kaṇha in the refrain of the verses at MN I 337–38.

488 Spk explains *uggaputtā* in pāda a as the powerful and royal sons of aristocrats (*uggatānaṃ puttā mahesakkhā rājaññabhūtā*). CPD, s.v. *ugga*, says they are members of the *ugga* caste, a mixed caste sprung from a kṣatriya father and a śūdrā mother. Members of this caste, it seems,

served as police, guards, and professional soldiers. Spk glosses *daḷhadhammino* as "those of firm bows bearing a teacher's bow of the maximum size" (*daḷhadhanuno uttama-pamāṇaṃ ācariyadhanuṃ dhārayamānā*); see **n. 181** above, **II, n. 365**, and EV I, n. to 1210. With Spk, I take *apalāyinaṃ* as a metrically shortened genitive plural used in apposition to *sahassaṃ*, not as an accusative singular. Spk paraphrases pāda d: *te samantā sarehi parikireyyuṃ*; "they might surround (me) with arrows on all sides." Although Spk-pṭ glosses *parikireyyuṃ* with *vijjheyyuṃ*, "they might shoot," the use of the expression *samantā parikiriṃsu* at Ja VI 592,11–15 clearly shows that *parikireyyuṃ* does not imply shooting. (The wrong spelling *parikaraṃsu* in Ee of Ja should be corrected to *parikiriṃsu* as in Be: Ja II 372, vv. 2431–35.) The commentary (Ja VI 589,5) glosses the word with *parivārayiṃsu*, "to accompany (as members of a retinue)."

489 I read pāda d with Ee1 as *dhamme s' amhi patiṭṭhito* and take *s' amhi* to be a conjunct of *so amhi*, with *so* functioning as the first person pronoun, a common enough form in Pāli. Ee2 supports this with its reading *dhamme sv amhi patiṭṭhito*. The whole expression *dhamme s' amhi patiṭṭhito* would then be a nominative periphrastic construction, with the word order inverted in compliance with the metre. Th 1211 can also support this interpretation if read, as Norman suggests, as *dhamme svamhi*. Be and Se, however, have the accusative *patiṭṭhitaṃ*, apparently in apposition to *maṃ* in pāda c. Commenting on the basis of this reading, Spk explains *dhamme samhi* as meaning *sake sāsanadhamme*, "in my own Dhamma teaching," with *samhi* understood as the locative singular of *sa* < Skt *sva*. While this interpretation at first sight seems strained, we do find *sehi dhammehi* at Sn 298, glossed by Pj II 319,16 as *sakehi cārittehi*. This shows that the reading accepted by Spk is feasible, though less plausible than the alternative.

Spk connects the simile with this verse thus: "If a thousand archers were to shoot arrows all around, a trained person might take a staff and knock down all the arrows in flight before they strike him, bringing them to his feet. One archer cannot shoot more than one arrow at a time, but these women each shoot five arrows at a time, by way of form and the other sense objects. If more than a thousand of these were to shoot in such a way, still they would not be able to shake me."

490 Spk explains *maggaṃ* in pāda c as a transformation of case (*liṅgavipallāsa*). Spk: "This statement refers to insight (*vipassanā*); for that is the preliminary phase of the path leading to Nibbāna. His mind delights in his own tender insight called the path leading to Nibbāna."

491 Spk: "I will so act that you will not even see the path I have gone along among the realms of existence, modes of origin, etc." See **vv. 49** (= **105**), **479**, **494**.

492 Spk: *Discontent and delight* (*aratiñ ca ratiñ ca*): discontent with the dispensation [Spk-pṭ: dissatisfaction with the fulfilment of virtue and the development of serenity and insight] and delight in the cords of sensual pleasure. *Household thoughts* (*gehasitañ ca vitakkaṃ*): having abandoned in all ways evil thoughts connected with "the household," i.e., with the five cords of sensual pleasure.

The next couplet plays upon the double meaning of *vanatha*; see **n. 474**. Spk glosses *vanathaṃ* as *kilesamahāvanaṃ*, "the great woods of defilements," and *nibbanatho* as *nikkilesavano*, "without the woods of defilements." The last word in pāda d is read *arato* in Be, Se, and Ee2, but in Ee1 as *anato*, "uninclined." Spk (both Be and Se) reads *arato* in the lemma and glosses *taṇhāratirahito*, "devoid of delight on account of craving," but *anato* and *nati* would also fit the lemma and gloss respectively, as *nati* too is a synonym for *taṇhā*. The reading at Th 1214 is *avanatho*, which expresses virtually the same idea as *nibbanatho*.

493 *Kiñci* should be brought into pāda b (as at Th 1215) and connected semantically with *yam* in pāda a. Spk explains *jagatogadhaṃ* in pāda b as what exists *within* the earth, e.g., in the realm of the nāgas, but I take the expression in a wider sense, supported by Th-a III 190,4–5, which glosses: "Whatever is mundane, conditioned, included in the three realms of existence." "Everything impermanent decays (*parijīyati sabbam aniccaṃ*)"—this, says Spk, was "the elder's great insight" (*mahāvipassanā*).

494 Spk identifies the *upadhi* in pāda a as the "acquisitions" of the aggregates, defilements, and volitional formations; see

n. 21. No explanation is given for the exclusion of "acquisitions as sensual pleasures" (*kāmūpadhi*) which the context seems to allow, indeed even to require. In commenting on pāda b, Spk says *paṭigha*, "the sensed," comprises odour and taste, while *muta*, "the felt," denotes the tactile object. Th-a III 190,15–20 inverts the explanation: *paṭigha* is glossed as *phoṭṭhabba*, and *muta* as *gandha-rasa*. The familiar tetrad is *diṭṭha*, *suta*, *muta*, and *viññāta* (see **35:95**; IV 73,4–7); the commentaries explain *muta* as comprising odour, taste, and the tactile object, and *viññāta* as mental objects. Norman translates *muta* as thought (its original sense), implying that this tetrad corresponds to the more familiar one, with *paṭigha* assuming the usual role of *muta* and the latter serving in place of *viññāta*. In deference to Spk and Th-a, I prefer to translate the present tetrad in a way that comprises only the five external sense bases and thus as signifying the five cords of sensual pleasure.

495 The readings of pāda ab vary among the different eds. I prefer that of Ee2: *Atha saṭṭhisitā savitakkā/Puthū janatāya adhammaniviṭṭhā*. The metre is irregular Vegavatī.

The verse is obscure and evidently challenged the ingenuity of the commentators. Spk paraphrases: "Then many unrighteous thoughts attached to the six sense objects have settled upon the people" (*atha cha ārammaṇanissitā puthū adhammavitakkā janatāya niviṭṭhā*). This explanation is flawed in two respects: (i) it construes the subject as *vitakkā*, thoughts, when the Pāli reads *savitakkā*, a *bahubbīhi* compound denoting persons with thoughts; if we take *sa* here to represent Skt *sva* rather than *saha*, *savitakkā* means those who are led by (or full of) their *own* thoughts; (ii) it explains *saṭṭhi* as *cha*, six, when it properly means sixty. Th-a III 190,28–31 mentions the opinion held by some commentators that *saṭṭhisitā* is an allusion to the sixty-two views of the Brahmajāla Sutta, and the verse does in fact echo the closing simile of that sutta (DN I 45,25–27): "Just as all large sea creatures are caught in the fisherman's net, so all these speculative thinkers are trapped within this net of *sixty*-two cases; here they are *caught* whenever they emerge" (*te imeh' eva dvā***saṭṭhiyā** *vatthūhi antojālikatā ettha* **sitā** *va ummujjamānā ummujjanti*).

In pāda c, *vaggagatassa* should be resolved *vaggagato assa*. Spk takes the line to mean that one should not join the faction of defilements (*kilesavagga*), but I understand it literally. In fact, at Sn 371b we find *vaggagatesu na vaggasāri dhīro*, "Among those who are factious, the wise one does not follow a faction." Pj II 365,20–24 explains this by reference to the sixty-two speculative views, thus linking it to the present verse. See in this connection GD, p. 217, n. to 371.

Pāda d reads *no pana duṭṭhullabhāṇī sa bhikkhu*, which Spk-pṭ explains as an injunction not to speak words connected with sensuality (*kāmapaṭisaṃyuttakathā*). Th 1217 reads here *duṭṭhullagāhī*, "one should not grasp what is corrupt," which Th-a explains as referring to the grasping of corrupt views.

496 Spk identifies "the peaceful state" (of pāda c) with Nibbāna and paraphrases pāda d thus: "Fully quenched by the full quenching of defilements in dependence on Nibbāna, he awaits the time of his parinibbāna [Spk-pṭ: the time of the Nibbāna element without residue]" (*nibbānaṃ paṭicca kilesaparinibbānena parinibbuto parinibbānakālaṃ [anupādisesanibbānakālaṃ] āgameti*).

497 Spk states that he prided himself on his learning; however, *paṭibhāna* is used to mean skill in verbal expression and thus probably refers here specifically to Vaṅgīsa's poetic talent.

498 *Asesaṃ* should be moved from pāda c into pāda b. Spk explains "pathway of conceit" (*mānapathaṃ*) as the object of conceit and the states coexistent with conceit, but it may be just a metaphorical expression for conduct governed by conceit. Spk says he addressed himself as "Gotama" (the Buddha's clan name) because he is a disciple of the Buddha Gotama, but this is hard to accept; see **v. 721** just below where Ānanda is so addressed because he actually was a member of the Gotama clan. I do not know of any other instance of monks addressing themselves (or others) as "Gotama" simply on the ground that they are disciples of the Buddha Gotama.

In the next verse we should twice read *mānahatā* in place of Ee1 *mānagatā*. Th-a glosses *mānena hataguṇā*, "with good qualities destroyed by conceit."

499 Spk explains *maggajino* in pāda b as a "path-conqueror," i.e., "one who has conquered defilements by the path," but I follow Norman's suggestion (at GD, p. 164, n. to 84) that the word is a variant of *maggaññu* (< Skt *mārgajña*), formed by resolution with an epenthetic (*svarabhakti*) vowel rather than by assimilation.

500 Th-a glosses *akhilo* in pāda a with *pañcacetokhilarahito*, "devoid of the five kinds of mental barrenness," with reference to MN I 101,9–27. The five are doubt and perplexity about the Buddha, Dhamma, Saṅgha, and training, and anger towards one's co-religionists. This seems preferable to interpreting the word by way of the three *khila*—greed, hatred, and delusion (see **n. 84**)—as the five *cetokhila* are said to be obstacles to "ardour, exertion, persistence, and striving" and their elimination is thus a prerequisite for strenuous effort.

In pāda d, *vijjāyantakaro* is a syntactical compound, here with the first member an instrumental or ablative; see **n. 68**. The verse lacks a finite verb, but Th-a says that the verse was spoken by way of self-admonition, and I have therefore supplied imperatives to convey this effect. The verse can be seen as describing a progression: "First be rid of the five obstacles to striving, then be strenuous. By effort abandon the five hindrances and attain purity of mind through concentration. On this basis, develop insight into nonself and abandon conceit. Thereby you will eradicate the taints by knowledge, make an end to suffering, and dwell in the peace of Nibbāna."

501 Spk: Once, when the Venerable Ānanda was invited to the royal palace to teach the Dhamma to the womenfolk, he brought along Vaṅgīsa, then newly ordained, as his companion. When Vaṅgīsa saw the women, beautifully attired in their best ornaments, lust infested his mind, and at the first opportunity he revealed his distress to Ānanda. Vism 38 (Ppn 1:103), which cites the verses (though in a different sequence), relates that Vaṅgīsa had become overpowered by lust when he caught sight of a woman on his alms round soon after going forth. A Skt version of the same story, with the verses, is cited in Enomoto, CSCS, pp. 44–45.

502 He addresses Ānanda as "Gotama" because Ānanda was a member of the Gotama clan. Here there is surely a word play on *nibbāpana* (and on *nibbāpehi* in **v. 723**c) as meaning both the extinguishing of a fire and the attainment of Nibbāna.

503 **Vv. 722** and **724–25**, though spoken by Ānanda, are included among Vaṅgīsa's verses as Th 1224–26. The "inversion of perception" (*saññāya vipariyesā*) is fourfold: perceiving permanence, happiness, selfhood, and beauty in what is actually impermanent, suffering, nonself, and foul; see AN II 52,4–7.

504 The verse is not found in Th proper, but occurs in the text of Th cited in ThA, though without comment. The idea expressed in pādas ab is at Th 1160–61, ascribed to Mahāmoggallāna.

505 At Sn II, 11 (pp. 58–59) both this verse and the next are included in the Buddha's advice to his son Rāhula. The meditation on foulness (*asubha*) is the contemplation of the parts of the body, as at **51:20** (V 278,6–14), or the cemetery meditations, as at **46:57–61**.

506 The signless (*animitta*), according to Spk, is insight (*vipassanā*), so called because it strips away the "signs" of permanence, etc.

507 The entire sutta is at Sn III, 3 (pp. 78–79).

508 The Buddha's statement seems partly redundant by making well spoken (*subhāsita*) one among four factors of well-spoken speech. Spk proposes a solution by first defining well-spoken speech in the wider sense as speech that brings benefit, and by then correlating the four factors of well-spoken speech with the four aspects of right speech—being truthful, conducive to harmony, gentle, and meaningful. Well-spoken speech in the narrower sense is identified with speech that promotes harmony. At AN III 243,27–244,6 well-spoken speech is defined by way of five different factors all external to itself: it is spoken at the proper time, is truthful, gently stated, beneficial, and spoken with a mind of lovingkindness.

509 See **n. 227**.

510 Spk: "'Truth, indeed, is deathless speech' (*saccaṃ ve amatā vācā*) means that the Buddha's speech is similar to the

Deathless because of its goodness (*sādhubhāvena*, Be; or its sweetness, if we read *sādubhāvena* with Se and Ee); or it is deathless because it is a condition for attaining Nibbāna the Deathless." The former explanation indicates that the text is playing upon the two meanings of *amata*, "deathless" (= Nibbāna) and "ambrosia," in Vedic mythology the drink of the immortal gods.

Spk remarks on pādas cd: "Being established in truth they were established in the goal (or the good) of oneself and others; being established in the goal (the good), they were established in the Dhamma. Or else, *sacca* is to be taken as an adjective (= true) qualifying the goal and the Dhamma."

Spk's explanation presupposes that the three nouns—*sacce*, *atthe*, and *dhamme*—are proper locatives and *āhu* an aorist of *honti* (= *ahū*). Based on the work of Lüders, Norman suggests (at EV I, n. to 1229) that *atthe* and *dhamme* were originally nominatives in an Eastern dialect that had the nominative singular in *-e*, and were then mistaken for locatives in the process of "translation" into Pāli. I follow Norman in my rendering of the line. In the BHS version (Uv 8:14) the translation went in the opposite direction: into *satyaṃ* as a nominative and *arthe* and *dharme* as locatives.

511 Spk-pṭ: "Since the Buddha speaks for the sake of security (*khemāya*), his speech is 'secure,' as it is the cause for the arising of security. Thus it is the foremost speech."

512 Spk paraphrases pāda c as if it contained an implicit verb *hoti* and treats pāda d as an independent sentence with *paṭibhānaṃ* as subject. It seems more fitting, however, to take *nigghoso* in pāda c as the subject of *udīrayi* and *paṭibhānaṃ* as its object, and I translate accordingly. Spk explains the simile: "The elder's sweet voice, as he teaches the Dhamma, is like the voice of a myna bird when, having tasted a sweet ripe mango, it strikes up a breeze with its wings and emits a sweet sound." Spk glosses the verb with *uṭṭhahati*, and paraphrases with an intransitive sense: "Inspired discourse rises up (from him) endlessly, like waves from the ocean." This implies that Spk reads *udiyyati*, the Be reading of Th 1232.

513 The Uposatha is the Buddhist "observance day," held in accordance with the phases of the moon. The major Uposathas occur on the full-moon and new-moon days, the fifteenth of the fortnight (except six times per year—two for each of the three seasons of the Indian calendar—when the Uposatha falls on the new-moon day of a shorter, fourteen-day fortnight). On these days the bhikkhus normally gather to recite the Pātimokkha, the code of monastic rules. At the end of the annual rains residence (*vassāvāsa*), however, the recital of the rules is replaced by a ceremony called the Pavāraṇā, the Invitation, at which each bhikkhu in order of seniority invites (*pavāreti*) the other bhikkhus in his fraternity to point out any misconduct on his part.

514 On the Buddha as the originator of the path, see **22:58**.

515 The eulogy of Sāriputta is at **2:29**; see too **n. 184**. The wheel-turning monarch (*rājā cakkavattī*) is the ideal world-ruler of Buddhist tradition; see DN III 59–63 and MN III 172–77.

516 On the triple knowledge (*tevijjā*) and the six direct knowledges (*chaḷabhiññā*), see **n. 395**. Those liberated in both ways (*ubhatobhāgavimutta*) are arahants who attain arahantship along with mastery over the formless meditative attainments. Those liberated by wisdom (*paññāvimutta*) are arahants who attain the goal without mastering the formless meditations; for formal definitions see MN I 477,25–478,1, and **12:70** (II 123,26–124,2).

517 On the wheel-turning monarch see **n. 515**. Spk explains that the Buddha is *the victor in battle* (*vijitasaṅgāmaṃ*) because he has won the battle against lust, hatred, and delusion, and because he has triumphed over the army of Māra. He is *the caravan leader* (*satthāvāha*) because he leads beings across the desert of saṃsāra on the chariot of the Noble Eightfold Path.

518 Spk: Nibbāna is called "inaccessible to fear" (*akutobhayaṃ*, lit. "no fear from anywhere") because there is no fear from any quarter *in* Nibbāna, or because there is no fear from any quarter *for one who has attained* Nibbāna. More typically, *akutobhaya* is used as a personal epithet of the Buddha or an arahant, as at Dhp 196, Th 289, and Thī 333; see EV I,

n. to 289. Even in the present case we cannot be certain that the expression is not used in apposition to the Buddha rather than to Nibbāna, as both are accusative singulars, but I follow Spk.

519 On *nāga* see **n. 84**. Spk explains the ambiguous expression *isīnaṃ isisattamo* as "the seventh seer of the seers beginning with Vipassī," referring to the lineage of the seven Buddhas. Spk-pṭ offers, besides this explanation, an alternative based on *sattama* as the superlative of *sant*: "He is the best, the highest, the supreme (*sattamo uttaro* [sic: read *uttamo*?] *seṭṭho*) of seers including paccekabuddhas, Buddhist disciples, and outside seers." I agree with Norman that this second alternative is more likely to be correct; see EV I, n. to 1240.

520 The contrast is between *pubbe parivitakkitā* and *ṭhānaso paṭibhanti*. Spk explains that the Buddha asked this question because other bhikkhus had been criticizing Vaṅgīsa, thinking that he neglected study and meditation and passed all his time composing verses. The Master wanted to make them recognize the excellence of his spontaneous ingenuity (*paṭibhānasampatti*).

521 Spk: *The deviant course of Māra's path* (*ummaggapathaṃ Mārassa*) refers to the emergence of the hundreds of defilements, called a path because they are the path into the round of existence.

On barrenness of mind (*khila*) see **n. 500**. In pāda d, I read *asitaṃ bhāgaso pavibhajjaṃ*, with Se and Ee1 & 2. Be reads *pavibhajaṃ*. Spk glosses as *vibhajantaṃ*, an accusative present participle, but Norman suggests *pavibhajjaṃ* may be an absolutive with *-ṃ* added, and Spk mentions a v.l. *pavibhajja*, a clear absolutive. Spk paraphrases: "who analyses the Dhamma by way of such groups as the establishments of mindfulness," etc. The explanation sounds contrived, but it is difficult to determine the original meaning.

522 In pāda c, Be reads *tasmiṃ ce* in text, while Ee2 has *tasmiṃ ca*, which Spk (Be) reads in the lemma (but not in the text); the latter is the reading at Th 1243. Norman, on metrical grounds, suggests amending the latter to *tamhi ca* or *tasmi*[*ṃ*] *ca*. Se and Ee1 have *tasmiṃ te*, which Spk (Se) has

in the lemma. Spk glosses with *tasmiṃ tena akkhāte amate* (Be and Se concur). Since here the aorist *akkhāsi* can be taken as either second person or third person, I translate on the supposition that the second person is intended, which is consistent with *carasi* in the previous verse. Th 1242 has *carati,* which justifies the translation of the parallel verse in that work as a third person. I also take *te* to be the enclitic for *tayā* rather than *tena.* I understand the clause to be a true locative rather than a locative absolute and take "the Deathless" here to be a contraction of "the path to the Deathless," alluded to in pāda b. This has the support of Spk-pṭ, which says: *amate akkhāte ti amatāvahe dhamme desite,* "'In that Deathless declared' means in that Dhamma taught (by you) which brings the Deathless."

523 *[He] saw the transcendence of all stations* (*sabbaṭṭhitīnam atikkamam addasa*). Spk: "He saw Nibbāna, the transcendence of all the standpoints of views and of all the stations of consciousness." Six standpoints of views (*diṭṭhiṭṭhāna*) are mentioned at MN I 135,27–136,2; eight at Paṭis I 138,14–26). Four stations of consciousness (*viññāṇaṭṭhiti*) are at DN III 228,6–13, seven at DN III 253,9–20; see too **22:54**.

Spk: *The chief matter* (*agga*) is the supreme Dhamma; or if the v.l. *agge* is adopted, the meaning is: at the beginning, first of all. *The five* (*dasaddhānaṃ,* lit. "half of ten") are the bhikkhus of the group of five (i.e., the first five disciples). Thus the meaning is: He taught the chief Dhamma to the five bhikkhus, or he taught the five bhikkhus at the beginning (of his ministry).

524 The elder's first name is spelled Aññāsi in Be and Ee1; here I follow Se and Ee2. He was one of the first five disciples and the very first to obtain comprehension of the Dhamma; it was for this reason that he was given the name "Aññā" (or "Aññāsi"), which means "understanding" (or "understood"). See **56:11** (V 424,8–11). According to Spk, the "very long absence" was twelve years, during which he dwelt on the bank of the Mandākini Lotus Pond in the Chaddanta Forest in the Himalayas, a dwelling place favoured by paccekabuddhas. He was fond of seclusion and thus rarely joined the community.

525 *Enlightened in succession to the Buddha* (*buddhānubuddho*).

Spk: First the Teacher awakened to the Four Noble Truths and after him the Elder Koṇḍañña awakened to them. The pleasant dwellings (*sukhavihārā*) are the "pleasant dwellings in this present life" (*diṭṭhadhammasukhavihārā*), i.e., the jhānas and fruition attainment; the seclusions (*vivekā*) are the three seclusions (of *body* through physical solitude, of *mind* through jhāna, and *seclusion from the acquisitions* by destruction of all defilements). *Buddhānubuddhasāvakā* is used in a more general sense in **16:5** (II 203,7) with reference to the old generation of enlightened monks.

526 In pāda c we should read *buddhadāyādo* with Be, Se, and Ee2, as against Ee1 *buddhasāvako*. Spk states that although only four *abhiññās* are mentioned, the elder possessed all six. He had come to take leave of the Buddha as he realized the time for his parinibbāna was approaching. After this meeting he returned to the Himalayas and passed away in his hut. The elephants were the first to mourn his death and honoured him by escorting his body in procession across the Himalayas. Then the devas built a casket for the body and passed it up through the various celestial realms so the devas and brahmās could pay final homage to him, after which the casket was returned to earth for the cremation. The remains were brought to the Buddha, who placed them in a cetiya, "and even today, it is said, that cetiya still stands."

527 In all eds. of SN and Th 1251 the text here reads *sabbaṅgasampannaṃ* in pāda a and *anekākārasampannaṃ* in pāda c, both accusative singulars set in apposition to the Buddha. This reading is doubtlessly ancient, for it is commented on as such by both Spk and Th-a. It is puzzling, however, that after having been described as "perfect in all respects" the Buddha should then be described as "perfect in many qualities"—almost as if his excellence is being diminished. I have accepted VĀT's ingenious solution to this problem: amending the compound in pāda c to a nominative plural, *anekākārasampannā*, which then becomes a description, altogether apt, of the triple-knowledge arahants attending on the Buddha. These are the subject of *payirūpāsanti*, while *Gotamaṃ* remains the object,

still qualified as *sabbaṅgasampannaṃ*. Note that at Th 1158c *anekākārasampanne* is used with reference to Sāriputta on the occasion of his parinibbāna; significantly, that verse mirrors **v. 610** (SN I 158 = DN II 157), recited at the Buddha's parinibbāna, extolling the Master as *sabbākāra-varūpete*, "perfect in *all* excellent qualities."

528 **Vv. 753–57** are considerably more compressed than the partly parallel verses at Th 1253–67. For a concise comparison of the two versions, see Ireland, *Vaṅgīsa*, pp. 7–8.

529 *Kāveyyamattā*, "drunk on poetry," occurs at **v. 470**a. Spk relates here the story of Vaṅgīsa's first meeting with the Buddha, also found at Dhp-a IV 226–28; see BL 3:334–36. According to this story, Vaṅgīsa had been a wandering brahmin who earned his living by tapping the skulls of dead men and declaring their place of rebirth. When he met the Buddha, the Master presented him with several skulls, including the skull of an arahant. Vaṅgīsa could guess correctly the rebirth of the deceased owners of the other skulls, but when he came to the arahant he was baffled. He entered the Saṅgha for the purpose of learning how to determine an arahant's realm of rebirth, but soon thereafter discarded this aim when he realized the holy life was lived for a nobler purpose.

530 If this verse seems narrowly monastic in focus, its counterpart Th 1256–57 corrects the imbalance by mentioning all four classes of disciples:

> Indeed, for the good of many
> The Tathāgatas arise,
> For the women and men
> Who practise their teaching.
>
> For their sake indeed
> The sage attained enlightenment,
> For the bhikkhus and bhikkhunīs
> Who have reached and seen the fixed course.

Pāda d reads: *ye niyāmagataddasā*. Spk glosses: *ye niyāmagatā c' eva niyāmadasā ca*; "who have reached the fixed course and seen the fixed course." Spk-pṭ: "The bhikkhus and bhikkhunīs who are noble disciples of the Buddha have 'reached the fixed course' by abiding in the fruit and have 'seen the fixed course' by abiding in the path." *Niyāma* here no doubt represents *sammattaniyāma*, "the fixed course of rightness," i.e., the supramundane path; see **25:1–10** and **III, n. 268**.

531 Spk: Although the divine ear is not mentioned it should be included. Thus he was a great disciple who had attained the six *abhiññās*.

9. Vanasaṃyutta

532 In pāda c, since *vinayassu* is a middle voice, second person imperative, *jano*, though nominative, may function as a vocative lengthened to fit the metre. Spk seems to support this with its gloss: *tvaṃ jano aññasmiṃ jane chandarāgaṃ vinayassu*; "you, a person, remove desire and lust for other people." The sentiment of this verse is echoed by Th 149–50.

533 I read pādas ab with Ee1: *Aratiṃ pajahāsi so sato/Bhavāsi sataṃ taṃ sārayāmase*. Norman understands the metre as irregular Vaitālīya (personal communication). Be has the same but without the *so* in pāda a. The *so* is probably a third person demonstrative used with a second person verb, a construction already encountered at **v. 647**c; see **n. 454**. VĀT prefers a reading found among SS, *Aratiṃ pajahāsi sato bhavāsi/Bhavataṃ sataṃ taṃ sārayāmase*, but since Spk and Spk-pṭ do not comment on *bhavataṃ* it seems this word was not in the texts available to the commentators; Ee2 reads as above but omits *bhavataṃ*. The verbs *pajahāsi* and *bhavāsi*, which Spk glosses with the imperatives *pajaha* and *bhava*, conform to the criteria of the subjunctive, rare and archaic in Pāli (see Geiger, *Pāli Grammar*, §123). Se reads the last verb as *sādayāmase*, but *sārayāmase* in the other eds. makes better sense as the subjunctive causative of *sarati*, to remember > to remind (see Geiger, *Pāli Grammar*, §126).

Pāda b is particularly obscure and the commentators seem to have been unsure how to handle it. Spk offers two alternative interpretations of *sataṃ taṃ sārayāmase*: "'Let us also remind you, a mindful one, a wise one [Spk-pṭ: to dispel worldly thoughts whenever they arise]'; or, 'Let us remind you of the Dhamma of the good ones [Spk-pṭ: of the Dhamma of the good persons for the removal of defilements]' (*satimantaṃ paṇḍitaṃ taṃ mayam pi [yathā-uppannaṃ vitakkaṃ vinodanāya] sārayāma, sataṃ vā dhammaṃ [sappurisānaṃ kilesavigamanadhammaṃ] mayaṃ tam sārayāma*)." I have bypassed both alternatives and adopted VĀT's suggestion that "you" is implicit and *taṃ* is "that," representing the way of the good. In pāda c we should read *duttaro* over Ee1 *duruttamo*.

534 Spk: It is said that this bhikkhu was an arahant. After returning from a distant alms round he was fatigued and lay down to rest, but he did not actually fall asleep (even though the text says he did!). Thinking that he was lethargic and was neglecting his meditation practice, the devatā came to reprove him.

535 Spk is unsure whether to ascribe the verses that follow to the devatā or to the bhikkhu and therefore proposes two alternative interpretations. All four printed eds. indicate a change of voice before this verse, and thus I translate on the assumption that the bhikkhu is the speaker. Further, Spk takes the implicit subject of *tape* to be *divāsoppaṃ*, and explains the sense, "Why should sleeping by day trouble an arahant bhikkhu?"; but as the optative *tape* can be either second or third person singular, it seems more fitting to take the implicit subject to be the devatā, addressed by the elder in the second person, "Why (should you) trouble…?"

536 Spk: "That knowledge" (*taṃ ñāṇaṃ*) is the knowledge of the Four Noble Truths. In pāda a of the next verse I read *bhetvā* with Se and Ee1 & 2, as against *chetvā* in Be.

537 It seems that while the preceding two verses describe the arahant, this verse describes the *sekha*, the trainee, who is still striving to attain Nibbāna.

538 Spk glosses *cheta* with *migaluddaka*, a deer-hunter. He had gone out that morning to hunt and was pursuing a deer when he came upon the elder meditating in the woods. The elder set about teaching him the Dhamma, but though

the hunter looked with his eyes and listened with his ears, his mind still ran in pursuit of the deer.

539 Geiger has caught the sense: "It seemed to the devatā that discontent with the monastic life had overcome the bhikkhus and they had given it up" (GermTr, p. 311, n. 2). On *arati* see **n. 486**.

540 Spk: Just as deer, wandering in the foothills or woodland thickets, wander wherever they find pleasant pastureland and dangers are absent, and have no attachment to their parents' property or a family heirloom, so the homeless bhikkhus, without fixed abode, wander wherever they can easily find suitable climate, food, companionship, lodgings, and Dhamma-teachings, and have no attachment to the property of their teacher and preceptor or to a family heirloom.

541 Spk: This sutta takes place shortly after the Buddha's parinibbāna. The Venerable Mahākassapa had enjoined Ānanda to attain arahantship before the first Buddhist council convened, scheduled to begin during the rains retreat. Ānanda had gone to the Kosala country and entered a forest abode to meditate, but when the people found out he was there they continually came to him lamenting over the demise of the Master. Thus Ānanda constantly had to instruct them in the law of impermanence. The devatā, aware that the council could succeed only if Ānanda attended as an arahant, came to incite him to resume his meditation.

542 At Th 119 the verse is ascribed to one Vajjiputtaka Thera but is not found among Ānanda's own verses in Th.

All four eds. read pāda b: *Nibbānaṃ hadayasmiṃ opiya*. At Th 119 the last word is read *osiya*, and we should adopt this reading here. I take it as absolutive of the verb *oseti* proposed by Norman at EV I, n. to 119; see too **n. 223** above. Spk supports this with its gloss *pakkhipitvā*, "having placed." Spk explains that one deposits Nibbāna in one's heart by way of function (*kiccato*) and by way of object (*ārammaṇato*): by way of function when one arouses energy with the thought, "I will attain Nibbāna"; by way of object when one sits absorbed in a meditative attainment having Nibbāna as its object (i.e., in *phalasamāpatti*, the attainment of fruition).

In pāda d, *biḷibiḷikā* is explained by Spk-pṭ as purposeless activity (*atthavirahitā pavattā kiriyā*). The devatā refers thus to Ānanda's talk with the lay people because it does not conduce to his attainment of the goal of the holy life.

543 Her name Jālinī, "Ensnarer," is used as an epithet for *taṇhā* at **v. 460**a; see too **n. 278** and AN II 211,31. According to Spk, she had been his chief consort in their immediately preceding existence in the Tāvatiṃsa heaven.

544 Spk: They are not *duggata* in the sense that they live in a miserable realm (*duggati*), for they dwell in a fortunate realm enjoying their success. They are miserable because of their conduct, for when they expire they might be reborn even in hell.

In pāda b, *sakkāya*, "identity," is the compound of the five aggregates of clinging, which are all suffering (*dukkha*) because of their impermanence. Spk explains that the celestial maidens are "established in identity" (*sakkāyasmiṃ patiṭṭhitā*) for eight reasons: because of lust, hatred, delusion, views, the underlying tendencies, conceit, doubt, and restlessness. These are the same as the eight ways beings are "established in what can be expressed"; see **n. 35**. On *sakkāya* see **22:105**, and on the devas being included in *sakkāya*, **22:78** (III 85,26–28).

In pāda d, Be, Se, and Ee2 read *devakaññāhi patthitā*, "desired by celestial maidens," and Ee1 *devakaññābhipattikā*. Since *p/s* confusion is not uncommon in the texts (see EV I, n. to 49), we can infer that the original reading is the one found in SS, *devakaññābhisattikā*, the reading also preferred by CPD. *Abhisattika* is an adjective formed from the past participle of *abhisajjati*, "to be attached to." I am thankful to VĀT for pointing this out to me.

545 He is not identified in Spk, and DPPN records nothing about him except what is found in the present sutta.

546 I follow the reading of this verse and the next proposed by Alsdorf (in *Die Āryā-Strophen des Pali-Kanons*, pp. 319–20), but with modifications suggested by VĀT (namely, changing Alsdorf's long vocative Nāgadattā to the nominative, and the four long vocatives in the second verse to accusatives, as in the printed eds.):

Kāle pavissa gāmaṃ/Nāgadatto divā ca āgantvā
ativelacārī saṃsaṭṭho/gahaṭṭhehi samānasukhadukkho.
Bhāyāmi Nāgadattaṃ/suppagabbhaṃ kulesu vinibaddhaṃ,
mā h' eva maccurañño/ balavato antakassa vasam esi!

"Entering the village too early and returning too late in the day" and "associating closely with lay people and monks in a worldly way" are two of five factors said to lead to a bhikkhu's falling away from the higher training (AN III 116,27–117,7). The meaning of the compound *samānasukhadukkha* is explained at **22:3** (III 11,5–6), though the compound itself does not occur there. The same compound is used at DN III 187,11–15 in a positive sense as a characteristic of a true friend.

547 Spk: He had received a meditation subject from the Buddha and entered a woodland thicket. The next day a family gave him alms and offered to provide him with regular support. Thereby he attained arahantship and continued to dwell in the same place enjoying the bliss of fruition attainment. The devatā (a female) was not aware of the elder's attainment and thought he had formed an intimate relationship with the mistress of the family. Therefore she came in order to reproach him. Neither Spk nor Spk-pṭ comments on the rare expression *kulagharaṇī*.

548 The antelope (*vātamiga*, lit. "wind-deer") is the subject of Ja No. 14. Spk: As an antelope in the woods becomes frightened by the sound of the wind rustling the leaves, so is it with one frightened by sounds (i.e., by rumours). The practice (*vata*) of one who is fickle-minded (*lahucitta*, lit. "light-minded") does not succeed; but this elder, being an arahant, was one with a successful practice.

549 An expanded version of this sutta is found at Dhp-a III 460–62; see BL 3:182–83.

Spk: The clamour (*nigghosasadda*) of *instruments* (*turiya*; Spk-pṭ: of drums, conch shells, cymbals, lutes, etc.); of *gongs* (*tāḷita*; Spk-pṭ: of things that are struck in rhythm); and of *music* (*vādita*; Spk-pṭ: of lutes, flutes, horns, etc.). See too **n. 343**.

550 Spk: "Many are those who yearn for your state—a forest-dwelling elder clad in rag-robes, subsisting on almsfood,

going on uninterrupted alms round, with few wishes, content, etc." Spk glosses *saggagāminaṃ* as "those going to heaven and those (already) gone there."

551 *Appossukko tuṇhībhūto saṅkasāyati.* The expression occurs also at **21:4** (II 277,12) and **35:240** (IV 178,1–2); see above **n. 54**. Spk: He attained arahantship and reflected, "I have attained the goal for the sake of which I did the recitation, so why continue with it?" Then he passed the time in the bliss of fruition attainment.

552 The five-pāda verse is unusual. The sense requires that in pāda b we read *na samāgamimha*; though the printed eds. do not include *na*, the suggested reading is found in Burmese mss referred to in the notes of Ee1 & 2. Spk explains *virāgena*, dispassion, as the noble path. In pāda d, *aññāyanikkhepanaṃ* is a syntactical compound; see **n. 68**. Spk takes *aññāya* as absolutive (= *jānitvā*), but it could also be instrumental.

553 In pāda a, I read the verb as *khajjasi* with Be, Se, and Ee2, as against Ee1 *majjasi*, "intoxicated with." Careless attention (*ayoniso manasikāra*) is traditionally explained as attending to things as permanent, pleasurable, self, and beautiful; careful attention (*yoniso manasikāra*), as attending to their true characteristics—impermanence, suffering, nonself, and foulness.

554 An identical story, including the verses, is at Ja No. 392 (III 307–10), with the Bodhisatta in the role of the bhikkhu.

Spk: When she saw the bhikkhu sniff the lotus, the devatā thought: "Having received a meditation subject from the Buddha and entered the forest to meditate, this bhikkhu is instead meditating on the scent of flowers. If his craving for scent increases it will destroy his welfare. Let me draw near and reproach him."

555 Spk: *Vaṇṇena* (in pāda c): *kāraṇena*. See PED, s.v. *vaṇṇa* (11), and **v. 806**a below.

556 All four eds. read, in pāda c, *ākiṇṇakammanto*, which Spk glosses *aparisuddhakammanto*, "of impure deed." But SS read *akhīṇa-*, *ākhīṇa-*, and *akkhīṇa-*, which is acknowledged by Spk as a v.l. and glossed *kakkhaḷakammanto*, "of rough deed." Spk (Be) reads *akhīṇakammanto*, Spk (Se) *akkhīṇakammanto*, which represents more correctly initial *ā* + *kh*.

That this reading is to be preferred to *ākiṇṇa-* is confirmed by **v. 798**a, where *ākhīṇaluddo* would certainly make much better sense than the given reading *ākiṇṇaluddho.* See Norman, "Two Pāli Etymologies," *Collected Papers,* 2:78–79.

557 In pāda b we should read *bhatakāmhase,* as in Be, Se, and Ee2. Spk: The devatā, it is said, thought: "This bhikkhu might become negligent, thinking he has a deity looking after his welfare. I won't accept his proposal."

10. Yakkhasaṃyutta

558 Spk: This was the yakkha who dwelt on Inda's Peak. Sometimes a peak is named after a yakkha, sometimes a yakkha after a peak.

559 Spk glosses *sajjati* in pāda d with *laggati tiṭṭhati,* "sticks, persists," apparently taking *sajjati* as equivalent to Skt *sajyate* (see MW, s.v. *sañj* (2)). But the word may be a passive representing Skt *sṛjyati* for which MW (s.v. *sṛj*) lists as meanings "to create, procreate, beget, produce." I translate on the assumption that this is the original derivation. See too PED, s.v. *sajati* (1).

Spk says that this yakkha was a personalist (*puggalavādī*) who held the view that a being is produced in the womb at a single stroke (*ekappahāren' eva satto mātukucchismiṃ nibbattati*). The Buddha's answer is intended to refute the yakkha's belief by showing that a being develops gradually (*anupubbena pana vaḍḍhati*).

560 The Pāli terms refer to the different stages in the formation of the embryo. Spk: The *kalala* is the size of a drop of oil placed on the tip of a thread made from three strands of wool. After a week *from the kalala comes the abbuda,* which is the colour of meat-washing water. After another week, *from the abbuda the pesī is produced,* which is similar to molten tin [Spk-pṭ: in shape, but in colour it is pink]. After still another week, *from the pesī the ghana arises,* which has the shape of a chicken egg. In the fifth week, *from the ghana emerge the limbs*: five pimples appear, the rudiments of the arms, legs, and head. But the head-hairs, body-hairs, and nails are not produced until the forty-second week.

561 Spk: This yakkha, it is said, belonged to Māra's faction

(*mārapakkhika-yakkha*). His verse parallels Māra's reproach to the Buddha at **v. 474**, and the Buddha's reply echoes **v. 475**. Spk-pṭ explains the purport to be that the wise man's compassion and sympathy are not tainted by worldly affection.

562 Spk glosses *vaṇṇena* with *kāraṇena* (as in **v. 796**c; see **n. 555**), and Spk-pṭ glosses *yena kena ci* with *gahaṭṭhena vā pabbajitena vā*, "with a householder or one gone forth," thus separating it from *vaṇṇena* and treating it as an expression of personal reference. The purport of the Buddha's verses is that a wise man should not take to instructing others if he is at risk of becoming attached, but he may do so out of compassion when his mind is purified and his sympathy is not tainted by worldly affection.

563 This sutta is also at Sn II, 5 (pp. 47–49) and commented on at Pj II 301–5. The name of this yakkha means "Needle-hair"; he was called thus because his body was covered with needle-like hairs. According to Spk, he had been a bhikkhu under the Buddha Kassapa but was unable to attain any distinction. During the time of the Buddha Gotama he was reborn as a yakkha in the rubbish dump at the entrance to Gayā village. The Buddha saw that he had the potential for attaining the path of stream-entry and went to his haunt in order to teach him. His haunt, the Ṭaṅkita Bed, was made of a stone slab mounted on four other stones.

564 Spk: He spoke thus thinking, "One who gets frightened and flees when he sees me is a sham ascetic (*samaṇaka*); one who does not get frightened and flee is an ascetic (*samaṇa*). This one, having seen me, will get frightened and flee."

565 Spk: The yakkha assumed a frightful manifestation, opened his mouth wide, and raised his needle-like hairs all over his body. His touch is "evil" (*pāpaka*) and should be avoided like excrement, fire, or a poisonous snake. When the Buddha said this, Sūciloma became angry and spoke as follows.

566 In all eds. of SN, and most eds. of Sn, as well as their respective commentaries, **vv. 808**d, **809**d read: *Kumārakā dhaṅkam iv' ossajanti*. A v.l. *vaṅkam* (in place of *dhaṅkam*) is

found in several mss of Sn (vv. 270–71) and has been incorporated into Sn (Ee1). *Dhaṅkam* (< Skt *dvāṅkṣam*) was certainly the reading known to the commentators, for both Spk and Pj II 303,22 foll. gloss the word with *kākaṃ*, crow, which they would not have done if *vaṅkam* was the reading. Spk glosses *ossajanti* with *khipanti*, and explains the simile: "Little boys bind a crow by its feet with a long cord, tie one end of the cord around their fingers, and release the crow. After the crow has gone some distance, it falls down again at their feet."

Spk paraphrases the question thus: "Whence do evil thoughts rise up and toss the mind?" (*pāpavitakkā kuto samuṭṭhāya cittaṃ ossajanti*). This seems to separate *mano* and *vitakkā* and to treat *mano* as accusative. I prefer to retain *manovitakkā* as a compound (as is clearly the case at **v. 34**b) and to see the object of *ossajanti* as merely implicit, namely, *oneself*, the very source from which the thoughts arise, as **v. 810**a asserts with the expression *attasambhūtā*.

Norman, who also accepts *dhaṅkam*, discusses the problem at GD, p. 200, n. to 270–71. For an alternative rendering based on the reading *vaṅkam*, see Ñāṇananda, SN-Anth 2:13, 89–90. The Skt version cited at Ybhūś 11.1 reads *kumārakā dhātrīm ivāśrayante*, "as little boys depend on a wet-nurse" (Enomoto, CSCS, p. 59).

567 *Itonidānā*. Spk: "This individual existence (*attabhāva*) is their source; they have sprung up from this individual existence. As boys at play toss up a crow, so do evil thoughts rise up from this individual existence and toss the mind [Spk-pṭ: by not giving an opening for wholesome states of mind to occur]."

Spk-pṭ: In the application of the simile, the evil thoughts are like the boys at play; this world of our individual existence is like the world in which the boys have arisen; the mind is like the crow; and the fetter (*saṃyojana*) which follows one to a distance is like the long thread tied around the crow's feet.

568 *Like the trunk-born shoots of the banyan tree* (*nigrodhasseva khandhajā*). The banyan tree, and other related species of fig trees, "develop from their branches aerial roots that may reach the ground and thicken into 'pillar-roots' or

subsidiary trunks. The continually expanding system of new trunks, all connected through the branches, may support a crown up to 2,000 feet in circumference" (Emeneau, "The Strangling Figs in Sanskrit Literature," p. 346). Emeneau quotes Milton's *Paradise Lost*, IX, 1100–11, "the *locus classicus* on these trees in English literature":

> The Figtree ... spreds her Armes
> Braunching so broad and long, that in the ground
> The bended Twigs take root, and Daughters grow
> About the Mother Tree, a Pillard shade
> High overarch't, and echoing Walks between....

Like a māluvā creeper stretched across the woods (*māluvā va vitatā vane*). Spk: "When the *māluvā* creeper grows by supporting itself against a particular tree, it weaves itself around that tree again and again and spreads over it from bottom to top and from top to bottom, so that it stands suspended and stretched out. In a similar way the manifold defilements of sensual desire cling to the objects of sensual desire, or the manifold beings cling to the objects of sensual desire on account of those defilements of sensual desire." The point, rather, seems to be that sensual desire spreads from object to object just as the creeper stretches itself out in the woods by spreading from tree to tree. For more on the *māluvā* creeper, see MN I 306–7, AN I 202,32–34 and 204,23–205,4, and Dhp 162, 334.

569 Spk paraphrases: "*Those who understand their source* of this individual existence *dispel it*, that is, with the truth of the path, they dispel the truth of the origin (= craving), which is the source of the truth of suffering that consists in this individual existence. By driving away the truth of the origin, *they cross this hard-to-cross flood* of defilements, *uncrossed before* in this beginningless saṃsāra even in a dream, *for no renewed existence*, for the sake of the truth of cessation (= Nibbāna), which is called 'no renewed existence' (*apunabbhavāya*). Thus with this verse the Master reveals the Four Noble Truths, bringing the discourse to its climax in arahantship. At its conclusion, Sūciloma was established in the fruit of stream-entry. And since stream-

enterers do not live on in monstrous bodies, simultaneously with his attainment his needle-hairs all fell out and he obtained the appearance of an earth-deity (*bhummadevatāparihāra*)."

570 Spk glosses *sukham edhati* in pāda a as *sukhaṃ paṭilabhati*, "obtains happiness." CPD points out (s.v. *edhati*) that this interpretation is probably a misunderstanding stemming from the supposition that *sukham* is a direct object of the verb rather than an adverbial accusative. The original meaning appears in the commentarial gloss on the expression *sukhedhito* as *sukhasaṃvaddhito*. See too EV I, n. to 475.

Spk glosses *suve seyyo* in pāda c as *suve suve seyyo, niccam eva seyyo*; "It is better morrow upon morrow, it is always better."

571 Spk: *Ahiṃsāya*, "in harmlessness," means "in compassion and in the preliminary stage of compassion" [Spk-pṭ: that is, the access to the first jhāna produced by the meditation on compassion]. *Mettaṃ so*, "who has lovingkindness," means "he (*so*) develops lovingkindness (*mettaṃ*) and the preliminary stage of lovingkindness." [Spk-pṭ: He (*so*) is the person developing meditation on compassion.]

Evidently Spk and Spk-pṭ take *so* in pāda c to be the demonstrative counterpart of *yassa* in pāda a, with an implicit transitive verb *bhāveti* understood. While the exact meaning of *mettaṃ so* (or *mettaṃso*) is problematic, I prefer to take pāda c as an additional relative clause, the relatives being resolved only in pāda d by the clearly demonstrative *tassa*. Spk offers an alternative interpretation of *mettaṃso* as a compound of *mettā* and *aṃsa*, glossed as *koṭṭhāsa*, "portion": *mettā aṃso etassā ti mettaṃso*; "one for whom lovingkindness is a portion (of his character) is *mettaṃso*." Mp IV 71,9 glosses *mettaṃso*: *mettāyamānacittakoṭṭhāso hutvā*; "having become one for whom a loving mind is a portion"; see too It-a I 95,13–15. Brough remarks that *mitrisa* (in G-Dhp 198) "appears to have been interpreted by the Prakrit translator as equivalent to [Skt] *maitrī asya*" (*Gāndhārī Dharmapada*, p. 242, n. 198).

Spk-pṭ: Because of his own hating mind someone might nurture enmity even towards an arahant who lacks meditation on lovingkindness and compassion. But no one could nurture enmity towards one who is endowed with liberation of mind through lovingkindness and compassion. So powerful is the meditation on the divine abodes (*evaṃ mahiddhikā brahmavihāra-bhāvanā*).

572 The background story, related in Spk, is also found at Dhp-a IV 18–25, which includes the verses as well; see BL 3:207–11. In brief: Sānu was a devout novice who, on reaching maturity, had become dissatisfied with the monk's life and had returned to his mother's house intending to disrobe. His mother, after pleading with him to reconsider his decision, went to prepare a meal for him, and just then a female yakkha—his mother from the previous life, who was also anxious to prevent him from disrobing—took possession of him and threw him down to the ground, where he lay quivering with rolling eyes and foaming mouth. When his present mother returned to the room, she found him in this condition.

573 I follow the reading in Be. Ee1 & Ee2 insert another verse here (**v. 815** in Ee2), but since this verse seems to be the product of a scribal error I do not translate it. The Be reading is supported by the Dhp-a version. Se reads as in Be, but with *yā va* in place of *yā ca* in the second pāda of both the exclamation and the reply. In order to translate in accordance with natural English syntax, I have had to invert lines of the Pāli in a way which crosses over the division of verses in the Pāli text.

The Uposatha complete in eight factors (*aṭṭhasusamāgataṃ uposathaṃ*): On the Uposatha, see **n. 513**. Besides the two major Uposathas falling on the full-moon and new-moon days (respectively either the fourteenth or fifteenth, and the first, of the fortnight), minor Uposathas fall on the half-moon days, the eighths of the fortnight. Lay people observe the Uposatha by taking upon themselves the Eight Precepts (*aṭṭhaṅga-sīla*), a stricter discipline than the Five Precepts of daily observance. These entail abstaining from: (1) taking life, (2) stealing, (3) all sexual activity, (4) false speech, (5) taking intoxicants, (6) eating past noon, (7) dancing, singing, listening to music, seeing improper shows, and using personal ornaments and cosmetics, and (8) using high and luxurious beds and seats. For more on the Uposatha duties for the laity, see AN IV 248–62.

And during special periods (*pātihāriyapakkhañ ca*). Spk explains this as if it meant the days proximate to the Uposatha: "This is said with reference to those who undertake the Uposatha observances on the seventh and ninth of the fortnight too (in addition to the eighth), and who also undertake the practices on the days preceding and following the Uposatha on the fourteenth or fifteenth (the full-moon and new-moon observance days). Further, following the Pavāraṇā day (see **n. 513**) they observe the Uposatha duties continuously for a fortnight [Spk-pṭ: that is, during the waning fortnight]." Different explanations of the expression *pātihāriyapakkha* are given at Mp II 234 and Pj II 378.

574 Spk glosses *uppaccā pi* as *uppatitvā pi,* and paraphrases: "Even if you fly up like a bird and flee, there will still be no freedom for you." The same verse is at Thī 247c–248b, Pv 236, Ud 51,17–18, Peṭ 44,20–21, and Nett 131,19–20. These versions (except Pv) read the absolutive as *upecca,* with a strange gloss *sañcicca* in their commentaries; Pv follows SN, but its commentary recognizes *upecca* as a v.l. A parallel is at Uv 9:4, with the absolutive *utplutya.* See von Hinüber, "On the Tradition of Pāli Texts in India, Ceylon, and Burma," pp. 51–53.

575 At this point the yakkha has released Sānu and he has regained consciousness, unaware of what had just occurred.

576 See **20:10** (II 271,13–14): "For this is death in the Noble One's Discipline: that one gives up the training and returns to the lower life."

577 Spk: She says this to show the danger in household life; for household life is called "hot embers" (*kukkuḷā*) in the sense of being hot. *Kukkuḷā* is also at **22:136**.

578 Spk paraphrases *kassa ujjhāpayāmase,* in pāda b, thus: "When you were intent on disrobing and had been possessed by the yakkha, to whom could we have voiced our grief (complained), to whom could we have appealed and reported this (*kassa mayaṃ ujjhāpayāma nijjhāpayāma ārocayāma*)?" On pāda cd: "When you went forth into the Buddha's Teaching, drawn out from the household, you were like an item rescued from a blazing house. But now

you wish to be burnt again in the household life, which is like a great conflagration." According to Spk, the yakkha's intervention proved effective. After listening to his mother, Sānu gave up his idea of disrobing, received the higher ordination, mastered the Buddha's teachings, and quickly attained arahantship. He became a great preacher who lived to the age of 120.

579 Spk: She had taken her son Piyaṅkara on her hip and was searching for food behind Jeta's Grove when she heard the sweet sound of the elder's recitation. The sound went straight to her heart and, transfixed, she stood there listening to the Dhamma, her interest in food gone. But her little son was too young to appreciate the recitation and kept complaining to his mother about his hunger.

580 Spk: She was carrying her daughter on her hip and leading her son by the hand. When she heard the Dhamma she stood transfixed, but her children clamoured for food.

581 Spk explains that *pāṇinaṃ* in pāda d may be understood as either a genitive plural or an accusative singular representing the plural (= *pāṇine*): *Pāṇinan ti yathā pāṇinaṃ dukkhā moceti. Ke moceti ti? Pāṇine ti āharitvā vattabbaṃ.*

582 I follow VĀT's perspicacious suggestion that pāda d should be read: *yaṃ dhammaṃ abhisambudhā*, taking the verb as a root aorist (see Geiger, *Pāli Grammar*, §159, 161.1). Be and Ee2 read *abhisambudhaṃ*, Se and Ee1 *abhisambuddhaṃ*, accusative past participles which seem syntactically out of place. The accusative *yaṃ dhammaṃ* requires an active transitive verb, yet the only solution Spk can propose is to turn the passive accusative participle into a nominative with active force, a role it is ill-designed to play. Since verb forms from *abhisambudh* always refer to the Buddha, I have made explicit the verb's subject, not mentioned as such in the text.

583 Spk: Having listened to the Buddha's discourse, the yakkha and her son were established in the fruit of stream-entry. Though the daughter had good supporting conditions, she was too young to understand the discourse.

584 The story of Anāthapiṇḍika's first meeting with the Buddha is told in greater detail at Vin II 154–59; see too

Ñāṇamoli, *Life of the Buddha*, pp. 87–91. His given name was Sudatta, "Anāthapiṇḍika" being a nickname meaning "(giver) of alms to the helpless"; he was so called because of his generosity.

585 Spk: After the first watch of the night had passed he woke up thinking of the Buddha, full of confidence and joy so intense that light became manifest and drove away the darkness. Hence he thought it was already dawn and set out for the monastery, realizing his error only when he went outside. The same thing happened at the end of the middle watch.

From Spk's account, it seems that the Cool Grove was located near the cremation ground (*sīvathikā*) and thus Anāthapiṇḍika had to pass through the cemetery to reach the monastery. It was for this reason that he became frightened. The fluctuation in the intensity of the light, Spk says, reflects his inward battle between faith and fear.

586 Spk: The word *sahassa* (thousand), found only in conjunction with *kaññā*, should be conjoined with each of the preceding three terms as well. All this is "not worth a sixteenth part of a single step forward" because, when he arrives at the monastery, he will be established in the fruit of stream-entry.

587 Spk: While he was approaching, Anāthapiṇḍika wondered how he could determine for himself whether or not the Teacher was a genuine Buddha. He then resolved that if the Teacher was a Buddha he would address him by his given name, Sudatta, known only to himself.

588 The words in brackets render *haṭṭho udaggo*, found in Be only.

589 I prefer Se and Ee2 *cetaso* to Be and Ee1 *cetasā*. The parallel at AN I 138,3–6 also has *cetaso*. In the Vinaya version the Buddha next delivers a graduated sermon to Anāthapiṇḍika at the conclusion of which he attains stream-entry.

590 This verse and the next are found, with several variations, at Thī 54–55. Spk glosses *kiṃ me katā*, in pāda a, with *kiṃ ime katā, kiṃ karonti*, but I think it more likely that we have here a split *bahubbīhi* compound *kiṃkatā*, and I translate accordingly.

Be reads pāda b: *madhupītā va seyare* (Se and Ee2: *seyyare;* Ee1 and Thī 54: *acchare*). Spk: They sleep as if they have been drinking sweet mead (Be: *gandhamadhupāna;* Se: *gaṇḍamadhupāna*); for it is said that one who drinks this is unable to lift up his head but just lies there unconscious. Spk-pṭ: *Gandhamadhu* is a particular type of honey that is extremely sweet and intoxicating.

Spk I 338,13–14 (to **11:1**) mentions a drink called *gandhapāna* (in Be; *gaṇḍapāna* in Se and Ee), an intoxicating beverage (*surā*) used by the older generation of devas in the Tāvatiṃsa heaven but rejected by Sakka after he assumed rulership over that world. At Dhp-a I 272,9 the drink is called *dibbapāna*. MW lists *gandhapāna,* defined as a fragrant beverage. "*Madhu* denotes anything sweet used as food and especially drink, 'mead,' a sense often found in the Rigveda" (Macdonell and Keith, *Vedic Index*, s.v. *madhu*).

591 Spk explains *appaṭivānīyaṃ* ("irresistible"), in pāda a, thus: "Whereas ordinary food, even though very delicious, fails to give pleasure when one eats it again and again and becomes something to be rejected and removed, this Dhamma is different. The wise can listen to this Dhamma for a hundred or a thousand years without becoming satiated." Spk glosses *asecanakam ojavaṃ,* in pāda b, as *anāsittakaṃ ojavantaṃ,* "unadulterated, nourishing," and explains that unlike material food, which becomes tasty by the addition of condiments, this Dhamma is sweet and nutritious by its own nature.

While Spk thus takes *asecanaka* to be derived from *siñcati,* to sprinkle, Brough maintains that the word is derived from a different root *sek,* meaning "to satiate." He renders it "never causing surfeit" (*Gāndhārī Dharmapada,* p. 193, n. to 72). See too CPD, s.v. *asecanaka,* which quotes the traditional Skt explanation from the *Amarakośa*: *tṛpter nāsty anto yasya darśanāt;* "that the sight of which gives endless satisfaction." In Pāli the word is used more in connection with the senses of smell and taste (e.g., at AN III 237,22 and 238,1). My rendering "ambrosial" is intended to suggest the same idea as the Skt definition, but more concisely so that it can also be incorporated into the description of mindfulness of breathing at **54:9** (V 321,22 and 322,1,11).

Pāda d reads: *valāhakam iva panthagū* (in Be and Ee1; Se and Thī 55 end with *addhagū*). Spk: "Like travellers (*pathikā*) oppressed by the heat (who drink) the water released from within a cloud."

592 This verse and the next resemble Thī 111, which contains features of both. In pāda d, I prefer *vippamuttāya* in Se and SS, as against *vippamuttiyā* in Be and Ee1 & 2. At EV II, n. to 111, Norman suggests, on metrical grounds, inverting pādas c and d, but the resultant meaning seems to undermine the cogency of this suggestion.

593 This sutta, also found at Sn I, 10 (pp. 31–33), is included in the Sri Lankan *Maha Pirit Pota*. Spk relates the long background story, of which I sketch only the highlights:

One day King Āḷavaka of Āḷavī, while on a hunt, was captured by the ferocious yakkha Āḷavaka, who threatened to eat him. The king could obtain release only by promising the demon that he would provide him daily with a human victim. First the king sent the criminals from the prison, but when there were no more prisoners he required every family to provide a child. All the families with children eventually fled to other lands and it became incumbent on the king to offer his own son, the Āḷavaka prince. The Buddha, aware of the impending sacrifice, went to the yakkha's haunt on the day before the offering was to take place in order to convert the demon from his evil ways. At that time the yakkha was attending a meeting in the Himalayas, but the Buddha entered his cave, sat down on the yakkha's throne, and preached the Dhamma to his harem ladies. When the yakkha heard about this, he hastened back to Āḷavī in a fury and demanded that the Blessed One leave.

594 Spk: The Buddha complied with the yakkha's demands three times because he knew that compliance was the most effective way to soften his mind. But when the yakkha thought to send the Buddha in and out all night long, the Master refused to obey.

595 Spk: It is said that when he was a child his parents had taught him eight questions and answers which they had

learnt from the Buddha Kassapa. As time passed he forgot the answers, but he had preserved the questions written in vermillion on a golden scroll, which he kept in his cave.

596 *Api ca tvaṃ āvuso puccha yad ākaṅkhasi.* Spk: With these words the Buddha extended to him the invitation of an Omniscient One (*sabbaññupavāraṇaṃ pavāresi*), which cannot be extended by any paccekabuddhas, chief disciples, or great disciples.

597 Spk: *Faith* is a man's best treasure because it brings mundane and supramundane happiness as its result; it alleviates the suffering of birth and aging; it allays poverty with respect to excellent qualities; and it is the means of obtaining the gems of the enlightenment factors, etc. *Dhamma* here is the ten wholesome qualities, or giving, virtue, and meditation. This brings human happiness, celestial happiness, and in the end the happiness of Nibbāna. By *truth* here truthful speech is intended, with Nibbāna as the ultimate truth (*paramatthasacca*) and truth as abstinence (from falsehood; *viratisacca*) comprised within that. Of the various kinds of tastes, *truth is really the sweetest of tastes*, truth alone is the sweetest (*sādutaraṃ*). Or it is the best (*sādhutaraṃ*), the supreme, the highest. For such tastes as that of roots, etc., nourish only the body and bring a defiled happiness, but the taste of truth nourishes the mind with serenity and insight and brings an undefiled happiness.

One living by wisdom (*paññājīviṃ jīvitaṃ*): A householder lives by wisdom when he works at an honourable occupation, goes for refuge, gives alms, observes the precepts, and fulfils the Uposatha duties, etc. One gone forth as a monk lives by wisdom when he undertakes pure virtue and the superior practices beginning with purification of mind.

598 Spk distributes the four "floods" (*ogha*) over the four lines of the reply and sees each line as implying a particular path and fruit; on the four floods, see **n. 1**. Since the faith faculty is the basis for the four factors of stream-entry (see **55:1**), the first line shows the stream-enterer, who has crossed the flood of views; the second line shows the once-returner, who by means of diligence has crossed the

flood of existence except for one more existence in the sense-sphere world; the third line shows the nonreturner, who has overcome the flood of sensuality, a mass of suffering; and the fourth line shows the path of arahantship, which includes the fully purified wisdom by means of which one crosses over the flood of ignorance.

This completes the eight questions that the yakkha had learnt from his parents. When the Buddha finished speaking, bringing his verse to a climax in arahantship, the yakkha was established in the fruit of stream-entry.

599 Spk: When the Buddha said, "By wisdom one is purified," the yakkha picked up on the word "wisdom" and, through his own ingenuity, asked a question of mixed mundane and supramundane significance.

600 In pāda c, I read *sussūsā* with Se and Ee1 & 2. Be reads *sussūsaṃ* as does the lemma of Spk (Be), while the corresponding lemma in Spk (Se) has *sussūsā*. From the paraphrase (see below) *sussūsā* can be understood as a truncated instrumental (= *sussūsāya*). In Be, *sussūsaṃ* seems to function as an accusative in apposition to *paññaṃ*, perhaps as the first member of a split compound, i.e., "the wisdom (consisting in) the desire to learn."

Spk: The Blessed One shows here four causes for the gaining of wisdom. First one places *faith* in the Dhamma by which the arahants—Buddhas, paccekabuddhas, and disciples—attained Nibbāna. By so doing one gains the mundane and supramundane wisdom for the attainment of Nibbāna. But that does not come to pass merely by faith. When faith is born one approaches a teacher, lends an ear, and hears the Dhamma; thus one gains *a desire to learn* (*sussūsaṃ*). When one lends an ear and listens from a desire to learn, one gains wisdom. But one must also be *diligent* (*appamatto*), in the sense of being constantly mindful, and *astute* (*vicakkhaṇa*), able to distinguish what is well spoken and badly spoken. Through *faith* one enters upon the practice that leads to gaining wisdom. Through *a desire to learn* (*sussūsāya*) one carefully listens to the means for acquiring wisdom; through *diligence* (*appamādena*) one does not forget what one has learnt; through *astuteness* (*vicakkhaṇatāya*) one expands upon what one has learnt. Or else: through a desire to learn one lends an ear and listens to the Dhamma by which one gains wisdom; through diligence one bears in mind the Dhamma heard; by astuteness one examines the meaning and then gradually one realizes the ultimate truth.

601 Spk: *Dutiful* (*dhuravā*) means not neglecting one's responsibilities and implies mental energy; *one with initiative* (*uṭṭhātā*) implies physical energy. I here follow Be; in Se the last two lines come at the end of **v. 850**; in Ee1, at the end of both **v. 849** and **v. 850**; in Sn, they are attached to neither verse.

602 The problem is to correlate the two tetrads mentioned in **vv. 853–54**. The difficulty arises not only on account of the replacement of *dhiti* by *khantyā* in the second verse but also because of the variant readings of the second term. Perhaps the best reading is that in Se, which accords with Sn (Ee1) vv. 187–88: in **v. 853**, *saccaṃ dhammo dhiti cāgo*; in **v. 854**, *saccā damā cāgā khantyā*. Spk (Be) and Spk (Se) differ over the second term: the former has *dammo* and *dammā*, the latter *dhammo* and *dhammā*. The explanations in Spk-pṭ establish beyond doubt that *dhammo* and *damā* were the respective readings known to Dhammapāla.

The four qualities mentioned at **vv. 853–54** refer back to **vv. 851–52**. *Truth* corresponds to truthfulness in **v. 852**c (*sacca* in all three instances), while *generosity* (*cāga*) clearly corresponds to giving (*dadaṃ*) in **v. 852**d. Spk (Se) explains that Dhamma is spoken of (in **v. 851**c) under the name of wisdom gained through a desire to learn, on which Spk-pṭ comments: "Wisdom is called Dhamma because of bearing up and examining (*dhāraṇato upadhāraṇato*) entities in accordance with actuality." (As the verb *dhāreti* (> *dhāraṇa*) is the stock etymological explanation of *dhamma* in the commentaries, we can infer that the author of Spk-pṭ had a text that read *dhammo*.) *Steadfastness* (*dhiti*) is spoken of under the names dutifulness and initiative (in **v. 852**ab).

In its paraphrase of **v. 854**, Spk states: "Come now, ask the many ascetics and brahmins whether there is any greater means for winning acclaim *than truthfulness*; any greater means for gaining mundane and supramundane wisdom *than self-control* (I suggest reading *damā*, following

Spk-pṭ, which explains that wisdom is so designated because it controls (*dameti*) the defilements as well as body and speech, etc.); any greater means of binding friends *than generosity;* and any greater means for finding mundane and supramundane wealth *than patience,* which is identical with activated energy, (called patience) in the sense that it endures heavy burdens, and which is referred to by the names dutifulness and initiative."

Thus the correlations can be shown schematically as follows:

(1) **852**: truthfulness = **853** & **854**: truth.
(2) **851**: wisdom = **853**: Dhamma = **854**: self-control.
(3) **852**: giving = **853** & **854**: generosity.
(4) **852**: dutifulness, initiative = **853**: steadfastness = **854**: patience.

603 Although Spk explains *attho* in pāda d as the visible benefit (*diṭṭhadhammika*) and *samparāyiko* as the benefit in a future life, there seems to be no compelling reason not to take the two words at their face value as adjective and noun bearing a single significance, namely, the good pertaining to the future life.

604 Spk continues with the background story: Just as the yakkha finished speaking this verse, the sun rose and the king's men arrived bringing the prince as a sacrificial offering. They handed the infant to the yakkha, who presented him to the Buddha. The Master recited some verses of blessing over the boy and returned him to the king's men. When the prince reached maturity, he was known as Hatthaka Āḷavaka, because he had been passed around from one person's hands (*hattha*) to another's. He attained the stage of nonreturner and was one of the Buddha's foremost lay disciples, the chief of those who win followings through the four bases of beneficence (*saṅgahavatthu*; see AN I 26,7–9). The Buddha holds him up as a model for male lay followers at **17:23** and praises his virtues at AN IV 217–20.

11. Sakkasaṃyutta

605 The texts commonly depict the Tāvatiṃsa devas and the asuras as engaged in perpetual strife, the devas representing the forces of light, peace, and harmony, the asuras or "jealous titans" the forces of violence, conflict, and dissension; see too **35:248**.

Spk explains that the devas are protected by five lines of defense: the nāgas, the supaṇṇas (**n. 397**), the kumbhaṇḍas (a kind of goblin), the yakkhas, and the Four Great Kings, the presiding deities of the lowest sense-sphere heaven. When the asuras penetrate these five lines, the Four Great Kings inform Sakka, who mounts his chariot and then either goes to the battlefront himself or commissions one of his sons to lead the devas into battle. On this occasion he wanted to send his son Suvīra.

606 Spk: Accompanied by his retinue of nymphs, he entered upon the great golden highway sixty *yojanas* wide and roamed around in the Nandana Grove playing (the game of) Constellation.

607 Spk: In pāda a, *alasassa* (in Se and Ee1; *alasvassa* in Be & Ee2) should be resolved: *alaso assa*; in pāda c, *sabbakāmasamiddhassa* should be resolved: *sabbakāmehi samiddho assa*. In pāda d, I read *disā ti* with Be, Se, and Ee2, as against *disan ti* in Ee1.

Spk paraphrases pāda d thus: "O Sakka, supreme deva, show me that blessed, supreme, state (or) region, point it out to me, describe it" (*sakka devaseṭṭha taṃ me varaṃ uttamaṃ ṭhānaṃ okāsaṃ disa ācikkha kathehi*). VĀT proposes that because pāda d includes no other noun for an adjective *varaṃ* to qualify, it would be better to take *varaṃ* itself as the noun meaning "a boon" and *disa* as meaning "to grant, to bestow." This meaning is attested to in PED, s.v. *disati*, but without references. I have followed VĀT's suggestion, though I cannot cite any other instances where *varaṃ* is used in relation to *disati*. It is usually governed by the verb *dadāti*, as at Vin I 278,23.

608 The verse is particularly obscure. Spk and Spk-pṭ offer little more than glosses, and a translator can do little better than take a shot in the dark. In pāda a, I regard *koci* as

equivalent to *kvaci* (see **n. 175**). I read the verb in pāda b with Ee1 & 2 as *jīyati*, as against *jīvati* in Be and Se; the latter may have entered the text through a misunderstanding of the commentarial gloss.

Spk: "The place of living without doing work is the path of Nibbāna (*kammaṃ akatvā jīvitaṭṭhānaṃ nāma nibbānassa maggo*)." Spk-pṭ: "The 'path of Nibbāna' is the path which serves as the means for attainment of Nibbāna." This is perplexing: since "work" (*kamma*) in the sense of exertion is certainly needed to attain Nibbāna, the purport may be that with the attainment of Nibbāna no more work is needed to attain it. The verse may also be playing upon two meanings of *kamma*, suggesting that one who attains Nibbāna does not create further *kamma*, volitional action ripening in rebirth.

609 The verb *sobhetha*, in this stock expression, has proved troublesome to previous translators. C.Rh.D renders it "do ye enhance his words" (at KS 1:281); Horner, based on PED, as "let your light shine forth" (in BD 4:249, 4:498, 5:227 = Vin I 187,23, I 349,7, II 162,15). Neither of these offerings captures the intended meaning. The verb—a middle voice, third person singular optative—always occurs in a context where the Buddha is speaking of a type of lay conduct that the bhikkhus, as renunciants, should be able to surpass. Hence the verb points to how one should act to make oneself shine, i.e., the mode of conduct that is fitting for one's station.

610 This sutta is a popular *paritta* or protective discourse, included in the *Maha Pirit Pota*. The Northern Buddhist tradition has preserved versions in Tibetan and Chinese, translated from the Skt, and Skt fragments also have been found. The various versions are discussed in detail by Skilling, *Mahā Sūtras* II, pp. 441–67.

611 Spk does not gloss the compound *dhajagga*, but it occurs at AN III 89,17 foll. and is explained at Mp III 267,18 as "the crests of standards raised up from the backs of elephants, horses, etc., or from chariots." Skilling discusses the Skt words *dhvaja* and *dhvajāgra* at length and concludes that "in its early form a *dhvaja* was a pole surmounted by an emblem, carried as a military or royal symbol" (*Mahā*

Sūtras II, p. 457). The emblem is the *dhvajāgra*, the "crest of the standard," though it seems that over time the two terms came to be used almost interchangeably. Since the standard often also bore a flag, the word *dhvaja* eventually was transferred to the flag; this understanding of the term seems to be implicit in Spk's remark (just below). *Dhaja* occurs at **v. 226**a.

Spk: "The crest of Sakka's standard is raised up from his chariot 250 *yojanas* high, and when it is struck by the wind it gives forth the sound of a five-piece orchestra. When the devas look up at it, they think, 'Our king has come and stands by his troops like a deeply planted pillar. Of whom need we be afraid?' Thus they have no fear."

612 Of these three deities, Spk says only that Pajāpati is of the same appearance and life span as Sakka and gets the second seat, while Varuṇa and Īsāna respectively get the third and fourth seats. According to MW, *Prajāpati* was originally "lord of creatures, creator, … a supreme god above the Vedic deities." *Varuṇa* "is one of the oldest Vedic gods … often regarded as the supreme deity." *Īsāna* is "one of the older names of Śiva-Rudra."

613 See **n. 157**. Spk here says that he is the oldest of all the asuras.

614 A similar incident is related at **35:248** (IV 201,18–202,4).

615 In pāda a, Be, Se, and Ee2 read *pabhijjeyyuṃ*, Ee1 *pakujjheyyuṃ*. The latter is recognized by Spk as a v.l. The dialogue represents a contest between two opposing models of political leadership, with Mātali advocating the principle of despotic rule, Sakka the principle of benevolent rule. The despotic political philosophy seems more in keeping with the character of the asuras, and indeed in the following sutta Vepacitti himself proclaims the verses here ascribed to Mātali.

616 I translate pādas cd guided by Spk's paraphrase: "Among the goals (or goods) which culminate in one's own good, there is found no other goal (or good) better than patience" (*tesu saka-atthaparamesu atthesu khantito uttaritaro añño attho na vijjati*). Because of the discrepancy between the plural *sadatthaparamā atthā* in pāda c and the singular verb *vijjati* in pāda d, it seems necessary to read the nomi-

native clause in pāda a as doing service for a locative or genitive, as Spk suggests, with a singular subject implicit. The only alternative would be to amend pāda a to read singular *sadatthaparamo attho*, but no text has this reading. Cp. **v. 854**d above and **v. 895**d below. Ñāṇamoli splits the two pādas syntactically and translates: "One's own good is the best of all, and there is none surpasses patience" (*The Guide*, p. 227), but this seems too free.

Note that Sakka speaks from the perspective of mundane ethical values rather than from the transcendent perspective of the Dhamma. From that perspective *sadattha* is identified with arahantship, which cannot be gained simply by patience.

617 C.Rh.D takes *niccaṃ khamati dubbalo* to mean that a weak person must always be tolerated (see KS 1:285), but *dubbalo*, as nominative, is clearly the subject of *khamati*, not its object. My translation conforms to Ñāṇamoli's (in *Minor Readings and Illustrator*, p. 162), but was made independently. Ñāṇamoli's note speaks for my interpretation as well: "The rendering here ... seeks to bring out that patience is a necessity rather than a virtue in the weak, but appears as a virtue in the forbearance of the strong. The verse is a difficult one."

618 Spk: *Dhammaguttassa*: to one who is protected by the Dhamma or to one who is protecting the Dhamma (*dhammena rakkhitassa dhammaṃ vā rakkhantassa*).

619 *Tumhe khvettha vepacitti pubbadevā*. Spk paraphrases: "Being the senior master long residing in the deva world, speak what has been transmitted to you." Spk-pṭ: Because he had arisen in this world earlier than Sakka and his retinue of devas, he is extolled as "the senior deva" (*pubbadevā*, lit. "former deva"). He addresses Vepacitti with plural forms as a sign of respect.

Both Spk (to **11:1**) and Dhp-a I 272–73 relate how Sakka ousted the old generation of devas and drove them out to the asura world; see BL 1:319.

620 The verses of Vepacitti are identical with those of Mātali in the preceding sutta, and Sakka's verses here are identical with his own verses above.

621 The same incident, set in a different context, is related at

Dhp-a I 279 (see BL 1:323–24) and in Ja No. 31 (I 202–3). Ja I 203 glosses *kulāvakā* as *supaṇṇapotakā*, baby supaṇṇa birds, but at **v. 37**b the word clearly means a nest and not its occupants.

Spk: As they headed towards the silk-cotton woods, the noise of the chariot, the horses, and the standard was like thunderbolts on all sides. The strong supaṇṇa birds in the forest fled, but those that were old, ill, and too young to fly were terrified and let loose a loud cry. Sakka asked, "What is that sound?" and Mātali told him. Sakka's heart was shaken by compassion and he spoke the verse.

622 Spk: As soon as Sakka said this, Vepacitti became as if bound by bonds on his four limbs and neck.

623 I read with Be: *tadeva tvaṃ mā pajahāsi*. Ee1 reads *pahāsi*, which gives the same sense, but Se and Ee2 have *mārisa pahāsi*, which yields the opposite meaning.

624 Spk: The verse refers to four great evils (*mahāpāpāni*) of the present aeon: (i) "the evil that comes to a liar": the evil of the king of Ceti, the first liar of the present aeon (see the Cetiya Jātaka, Ja No. 422); (ii) "to a reviler of noble ones": evil like that of Kokālika (see **6:10**); (iii) "to a betrayer of friends": evil like that of the betrayer of the Great Being in the Mahākapi Jātaka (Ja No. 516); (iv) "to one without gratitude": the evil of an ingrate like Devadatta.

In pāda e, I read *phusati* with Se and Ee1 & 2, as against *phusatu* in Be. "Sujā's husband" (*Sujampati*) is a name for Sakka; see **11:12** and **n. 641**.

625 Neither Spk nor Spk-pṭ offers any help in identifying Verocana. At DN II 259,11 mention is made of "a hundred sons of (the asura) Bali, all named Veroca" (*satañ ca baliputtānaṃ sabbe Verocanāmakā*), on which Sv II 689,26–27 comments: "They all bore the name of their uncle Rāhu." This might suggest that Verocana and Rāhu are identical, but there is no additional evidence for this.

626 Both C.Rh.D and Geiger translate pādas cd as if they were two independent sentences: "A purpose shines when perfected./Nothing forbearance doth excel." I go along with the paraphrase of Spk, which treats them as forming one sentence: "Among the goals (goods) that shine when achieved, there is no goal better than patience." I read

pada c here (and in **v. 894** just above) with Se and Ee2 as plural: *nipphannasobhino atthā*, as against the singular *nipphannasobhano attho* of Be and Ee1. Pāda d here is identical with **v. 854**d and **v. 877**d. See **n. 616**.

627 In pāda a, *sabbe sattā atthajātā* might also have been rendered, "All beings are beset by needs." Spk explains: "*Bent upon a goal* means engaged in a task (*atthajātā ti kiccajātā*); for there is no being at all, including dogs and jackals, that is not engaged in a task. Even walking to and fro can be called a task."

Pādas cd read: *Saṃyogaparamā tveva/Sambhogā sabbapāṇinaṃ*. The exact meaning and relevance are obscure. Spk interprets the line with an example—bland food may be made savoury when combined with various condiments—which construes *saṃyoga* as meaning combination or preparation. This seems to me unlikely. At Ja IV 127,14–15 the couplet occurs in a context which implies that the meaning is association with other people; see too AN IV 57–58, where *saṃyoga* signifies contact or association between man and woman (sexual, but not necessarily coitus). I understand the syntax as parallel to that of Dhp 203–4, that is, "enjoyments have association as supreme," rather than "through association enjoyments become supreme," the sense proposed by Spk.

628 *Apabyāmato karitvā* (or *apavyāmato karitvā*, in Ee1). CPD says *apavyāma* is a v.l. for *apasavya*. At Ud 50,18 the expression *apasabyāmato karitvā* occurs, which Ud-a 292,4 explains as turning the left side towards a holy person as a sign of disrespect.

629 Spk glosses *ciradikkhitānaṃ* in pāda a as *cirasamādiṇṇavatānaṃ*, "who have long undertaken vows." On "thousand-eyed" (*sahassanetta*) as an epithet of Sakka, see **11:12**; though there the Pāli is *sahassakkha*, the meaning is the same. The seers say this because they subscribe to the common belief that the devas find the smell of human bodies repulsive—particularly ascetics who may not bathe frequently (see Mātali's argument at **v. 932**). Sakka's reply conveys the same point as Dhp 54–56: the scent of virtue is supreme among all scents and pervades even the worlds of the devas.

630 Spk paraphrases: "The devas do not perceive anything repulsive in this odour of the virtuous ones; they perceive it as desirable, lovely, agreeable."

631 Spk: For the most part, it is said, the battles between the devas and the asuras take place behind the great ocean. Often the asuras are defeated, and when they are fleeing from the devas, as they pass the hermitages of seers, they destroy their halls and walkways, etc.; for they believe that the seers are partial to Sakka and give him the counsel that leads to their defeat. Since the seers can repair the damaged facilities only with difficulty, when they heard that a battle was about to take place they realized they needed a guarantee of safety.

The identity of Sambara is problematic. Spk identifies him with Vepacitti (see **n. 633**), but C.Rh.D points out (at KS 1:305, n. 4) that **11:23** suggests the two are distinct, Sambara having been Vepacitti's predecessor as lord of the asuras. MW states that Śambara is a demon often mentioned in the Ṛgveda; he was slain by Indra. For further discussion, see below **n. 665**.

632 Pāda c should be divided as in Be & Ee2: *Kāmaṅkaro hi te dātuṃ*. Spk glosses *kāmaṅkaro* with *icchitakaro* and paraphrases: "If you want to give safety, you are able to give safety; if you want to give danger, you are able to give danger."

633 Spk: As soon as he fell asleep, he woke up howling as though he had been struck from all sides by a hundred spears. The other asuras came to inquire about his health and were still consoling him when dawn arrived. From then on his mind became sick and trembled (*cittaṃ vepati*); hence his other name, "Vepacitti," arose. *Vepati* is not in PED, but see MW, s.v. *vip* > *vepate*. Spk-pṭ glosses *vepati* with *kampati pavedhati*.

634 Spk glosses *samattāni* with *paripuṇṇāni* and *samādinnāni* with *gahitāni*. Evidently Spk assumes that *samatta* here is equivalent to Skt *samāpta*. But the participle *samatta* can represent either Skt *samāpta* or *samātta*, and from its placement *before samādinnāni* in the present passage, I take *samattāni* in the latter sense. Both *samatta* and *samādinna* are alternative past participle formations of *sam* + *ā* + *dā*.

PED does not mention this derivation, but only that from Skt *samāpta* (and from Skt *samasta*, not relevant here). For the derivation from *samātta*, see Nidd I 289,16–18; for the derivation from *samāpta*, see Nidd I 65,9–11.

635 Although the form *yācayoga* prevails in the Pāli textual tradition, it is likely that the original compound was *yājayoga*, recognized as a v.l. at Vism 224,11–12 (Ppn 7:112). I translate on the basis of this reading, which means literally "devoted to sacrifice," a brahmanical notion reinterpreted by the Buddha to mean self-sacrifice through the practice of charity (see **vv. 395–96**). Since charity (*yāja*) is directed to supplicants (*yācaka*), the variant *yācayoga* could have arisen through substitution of object for act; see GD, p. 241, n. to p. 87,2.

636 Spk (to **11:13**) briefly relates how Sakka, in his existence as the brahmin youth Magha, went about performing deeds of merit at the head of a band of thirty-three friends. Having fulfilled his seven vows, he was reborn after death in the Tāvatiṃsa heaven along with his friends. Hence the name Tāvatiṃsa, "(heaven) of the thirty-three." See Dhp-a I 265–72; BL 1:315–19. Ja No. 31 tells the same story with the Bodhisatta—the future Buddha Gotama—in the role of Magha and reborn as Sakka.

637 I read with Se and Ee1 & 2 *pure pure dānaṃ adāsi tasmā Purindado ti vuccati.* Be has *pure* only once. MW (s.v. *pur* > *puraṃ*) gives *puraṃda* and *puraṃdara* as names of Indra; both mean "destroyer of strongholds." This explanation, and the following three, depend on puns almost impossible to reproduce in English.

638 *Sakkaccaṃ dānaṃ adāsi tasmā Sakko ti vuccati.*

639 The story of the rest house (*āvasatha*) is at Dhp-a I 269–70; BL 1:317–18.

640 *Sahassam pi atthānaṃ muhuttena cinteti tasmā Sahassakkho ti vuccati.* Spk: Standing upon a single word propounded in regard to a thousand people or a thousand statements, he decides, "This one has need of this, that one has need of that." Spk-pṭ: He has a thousand wisdom-eyes.

641 The story of how Sakka won the hand of Sujā, Vepacitti's daughter, is told at Dhp-a I 278–79 (see BL 1:323), and Ja I 206.

642 Spk says that this pauper was the leper Suppabuddha, whose story is told at Ud 48–50 and, more elaborately with several variations, in Spk. According to the Spk version, in an earlier life he had been a king of Bārāṇasī who had spitefully reviled an aged paccekabuddha. As a kammic result he was reborn in hell and then, through the residue of the evil kamma, as a poor leper in Rājagaha. One day, on his begging rounds, he heard the Buddha preach and attained stream-entry. Shortly afterwards he was killed by a wild cow and was reborn in the Tāvatiṃsa heaven.

643 *Deve tāvatiṃse anunayamāno.* Spk does not gloss *anunayamāno*, but the same expression is at AN I 143,30, where *anunayamāno* is glossed by Mp II 123,19 (Be; the Ee and Se readings are corrupt) with *anubodhayamāno*, "making understand." The participle also occurs in the form *anunentī* at Thī 514, where it is glossed by Thī-a 267,8–9 with *saññāpentī*, "convincing."

644 Spk explains *faith* as faith arrived at via the path (*maggen' āgatasaddhā*). *Good conduct built on virtue* (*sīlaṃ kalyāṇaṃ*) is the noble disciple's "virtue dear to the noble ones" (*ariyakantasīla*), one of the four factors of stream-entry (**55:1**), which the stream-enterer does not abandon even in a future existence.

645 Spk: Each year the people of Aṅga and Magadha used to assemble and offer a grand sacrifice of their best ghee, honey, molasses, etc., to Mahābrahmā. Out of compassion Sakka appeared before them in the guise of Mahābrahmā, led them to the Buddha, and asked him a question about the most fruitful type of sacrifice.

646 In pāda c, *opadhikaṃ puññaṃ*, which I render loosely as "merit of the mundane type," is explained by Spk as merit that ripens in the acquisitions (*upadhivipākaṃ puññaṃ*), that is, good kamma that leads to rebirth. See the expression *puññabhāgiyā upadhivepakkā* at MN III 72,6 foll.

647 The four practising the way are those on the four paths—of stream-entry, once-returning, nonreturning, and arahantship. The four established in the fruit are those who, by developing the respective paths, have attained the four corresponding fruits. The past participle *samāhito* in pāda d

might be understood to mean either "endowed with" or "concentrated," the latter representing the *samādhi* division of the path. I have taken it in the former sense, following **v. 265**a, where *sīlasamāhitā* is glossed by Spk: *sīlena samāhitā samupetā.*

648 Spk: *Your burden lowered* (*pannabhāro*): He has put down the burden of the aggregates, the defilements, and the volitional formations. The fifteenth of the bright lunar fortnight is the full-moon night.

649 The verse is identical with his entreaty at **v. 560**. Neither Spk nor Spk-pṭ explains why Brahmā Sahampati corrects Sakka. The reason may be that Sakka praises only those qualities of the Buddha that he shares with other arahants, while Brahmā addresses him in his role as *satthā*, the Teacher and Master of the dispensation. The same exchange of verses, between Śakra and Mahābrahmā, is recorded at Mvu III 315–16, but set at the Goatherd's Banyan Tree in the period immediately following the Buddha's enlightenment; see Jones, 3:304–5.

650 *Yassa dāni kālaṃ maññasi*. See Manné, "On a Departure Formula and its Translation." The expression also occurs at **35:88** (IV 62,31), **35:243** (IV 183,15, 30), **44:1** (IV 379,29), **54:9** (V 321,16–17), and **55:6** (V 348,27); I have varied the rendering slightly to fit the context.

651 *Those versed in the Triple Veda* are the brahmins; *the Four Great Kings* are the four divine rulers of the lowest sense-sphere heaven; *the glorious Thirty* are the presiding devas of the Tāvatiṃsa heaven. The word rendered "spirit" is *yakkha*, used in a broad sense without specific reference to the demonic spirits.

652 *Brahmacariyaparāyaṇe*. Spk does not explain the exact sense, but I interpret it as a compressed way of saying "those living the holy life that has Nibbāna as its destination." See **48:42** (V 218,21): *brahmacariyaṃ vussati nibbānaparāyaṇaṃ.*

653 Spk explains *of perfect name* (*anomanāmaṃ*) in pāda c thus: "He is of perfect name on account of names that indicate all his excellent qualities, for he is not deficient in any excellent quality." See **v. 148**a and **n. 99**.

654 The verse has five pādas. Pādas ab read: *ye rāgadosavinayā*

avijjāsamatikkamā, which Spk paraphrases: "by the transcendence of ignorance, the root of the round, which conceals the four truths" (*catusaccapaṭicchādikāya vaṭṭamūlaka-avijjāya samatikkamena*). The same lines appeared at **v. 764**ab, where, as referring to an arahant, they were appropriately translated as ablative in force. However, despite Spk's paraphrase, this would not be suitable in relation to trainees (*sekha*), who have not yet fully removed the lust for existence or transcended all ignorance. I have therefore translated them as truncated datives.

Dismantling (*apacaya*) means the undoing of the process that sustains the round of existence. At **22:79** (III 89,22–24) it is said that the noble disciple in training is dismantling the five aggregates, while the arahant (III 90,11) abides having dismantled them (*apacinitvā ṭhito*). See too MN III 288,30.

655 *Stuck in a putrid body* (*pūtidehasayā*). Spk: This is said because they stay within the putrid body of the mother (during the fetal stage) or because they are stuck within their own body.

Those submerged inside a corpse. I read this line as in Be (in both text and the lemma of Spk) as *nimuggā kuṇapamhete*, with the indirect object a locative singular. Se reads *kuṇapasmete*, using an alternative form of the locative singular. Ee1 & 2, however, and Spk (Se) in the lemma read the line with the locative plural *kuṇapesv ete*. Spk explains: "These are submerged for ten months in a corpse, namely, in the mother's womb." Despite this comment, it seems more likely that the reference is to the individual's own living body.

656 **Vv. 934–35** correspond in part to Thī 282–83. I take **vv. 935–36** to be two verses of six pādas each (as in Se and Ee2) rather than three verses of four pādas each (as in Be).

657 I read pāda a differently from the four eds., *na te saṃ koṭṭhe osenti* (the reading at Thī 283; Ee2 correctly separates *te* and *saṃ* but has *openti*). Spk explains: *na te saṃ santakaṃ dhaññaṃ koṭṭhe pakkhipanti*; "they do not place their own goods, property, grain in storage." *Saṃ* thus has the sense of "own goods"; see EV I, n. to 743 and EV II, n. to 283. The gloss on the verb, *pakkhipanti*, establishes that we

should read *osenti* rather than *openti*, the prevalent reading. Thī-a 208,21–22 glosses: *na openti na paṭisāmetvā ṭhapenti tādisassa pariggahassa abhāvato*; "they do not deposit, do not pack up and put away, owing to the absence of any such possession." The corresponding verb at Mvu III 453 is *osaranti*, which Jones suggests might be amended to *osārenti*. Jones is also aware of the Pāli form *osāpenti*. See too **nn. 223** and **542** above.

In pāda c, Thī 283 reads *pariniṭṭhitam* as does the text and lemma of Thī-a. Norman prefers the latter by comparison with a similar verse in a Jain text (see EV II, n. to 283), but the explanations in both Thī-a and Spk support *paraniṭṭhitam*, the reading in all eds. of SN. Spk: *Seeking what has been prepared by others* (*paraniṭṭhitam esānā*): seeking out, searching out, by the practice of the alms round, food prepared by others, cooked in others' homes (*paresaṃ niṭṭhitaṃ paraghare pakkaṃ bhikkhācāravattena esamānā gavesamānā*; I take the genitive *paresaṃ* here in an instrumental sense, which the context implies).

Spk explains pāda e: *Who give good counsel* (*sumantamantino*): They utter well-spoken words, saying "We will recite the Dhamma, undertake an ascetic practice, enjoy the Deathless, do the work of an ascetic." *Maintaining silence, of even faring* (*tuṇhībhūtā samañcarā*): Even though they might speak the Dhamma with a voice as loud as thunder through the three watches of the night, they are still said to be "maintaining silence, of even faring." Why so? Because they avoid all useless talk.

658 Spk: He was a dwarf the colour of a burnt stump and with a pot belly. He sat down on Sakka's Yellowstone Throne (*paṇḍukambalasilā*; see Dhp-a I 273,9–12; BL 1:320). It is said that he was actually a brahmā from the form realm. Having heard about Sakka's patience, he came in order to test him; for it is impossible for any malevolent spirit (*avaruddhaka-yakkha*) to infiltrate a place so well guarded.

659 Spk: Sakka had heard from the devas: "It is impossible to make that yakkha budge by harsh means, but if one assumes a humble manner and remains firm in patience, one can get him to leave." Thus he adopted this tactic.

660 Spk states that *su*, in pāda a, is a mere indeclinable (*nipātamattaṃ*), and thus we should resolve the compound: *su upahatacitto 'mhi*. Spk-pṭ: Sakka speaks of his own nature thus, "Because of the presence in me of patience, love, and sympathy, I am not afflicted in mind against others."

Pāda b is read in Be and Se as *nāvattena suvānayo* (Ee1: *nāvaṭṭena suvānayo*; Ee2: *n' āvaṭṭe na suvānayo*). Spk: He states: "I am not easily drawn by anger's whirl; I am not easily brought under the control of anger." Pādas cd allude to the seventh of Sakka's vows (see **11:11**). Spk explains that *vo* in pāda c is an indeclinable. *Suvānayo* is also at **v. 507**b, where lust (*rāga*) rather than anger is the lure.

661 I read pādas ab with Be and Ee1 & 2: *Kuddhāhaṃ na pharusaṃ brūmi/Na ca dhammāni kittaye*. Se omits the *na* in pāda a, apparently out of concern for the metre, but the metre can be preserved with *na* if we assume resolution of the fourth syllable. Neither Spk nor Spk-pṭ offers any help with the meaning. VĀT proposes, "And I do not speak on Dhamma matters," but at Ja V 172,23 and 221,27 we find *satañ ca dhammāni sukittitāni*, "the well-proclaimed qualities of the good," which suggests that here too the rare neuter plural *dhammāni* refers to personal virtues, not to spiritual teachings.

662 Spk: He was afflicted with the illness that arose at the time he was cursed by the group of seers; see **vv. 902–3**.

663 *Sambarimāyā*. MW has two relevant listings: *śambaramāyā* = sorcery, magic; and *śāmbarī* = jugglery, sorcery, illusion (as practised by the daitya Śambara).

664 Spk paraphrases: "Even without the Sambari magic Sakka oppresses us, but if he learns it we are lost. Don't destroy us for the sake of your own personal welfare."

665 As C.Rh.D points out (at KS 1:305, n. 4), in this verse Vepacitti makes a distinction between Sambara and himself. Even though Spk identifies the two, the commentator does not seem to be bothered by the discrepancy but paraphrases the verse: "Just as Sambara, lord of the asuras, a magician who practised magic, was tortured in hell for a hundred years, so one who applies his magic is tortured."

Spk-pṭ offers some further help with Sambara: "Sambara was the former head of the asuras, the originator (*ādi-purisa*) of the asura magic."

Spk continues: "Was Sakka able to cure him of his anger? Yes, he was able. How? At that time, it is said, the group of seers was still living. Therefore Sakka would have brought him to them and made him apologize, and he would then have become healthy. But because of his perverse nature (*vañcitattā*) he did not comply but simply left."

666 According to monastic discipline (Vin I 54), if one bhikkhu offends against another he should apologize, and the latter should accept his apology.

667 Spk offers alternative explanations of pāda b: *mā ca mittehi vo jarā*. "Here, *hi* is a mere indeclinable, and the sense is: 'Do not let decay be produced in your friendliness (*tumhākaṃ mittadhamme jarā nāma mā nibbatti*).' Or else *mittehi* is an instrumental used with a locative sense, that is: 'Do not let decay be produced among your friends (*mittesu vo jarā mā nibbatti*).' The meaning is: 'Do not let deterioration be produced in your friendships.'" It is likely that *mittehi* here is a vestigial Eastern form of the locative plural; see Geiger, *Pāli Grammar*, §80.3.

668 Spk: *Nonanger* (*akkodha*) is lovingkindness (*mettā*) and the preliminary phase of lovingkindness; *harmlessness* (*avihiṃsā*) is compassion (*karuṇā*) and the preliminary phase of compassion.

Part II
The Book of Causation
(*Nidānavagga*)

Contents

Chapter II
13 *Abhisamayasaṃyutta*
Connected Discourses on the Breakthrough

Chapter III
14 *Dhātusaṃyutta*
Connected Discourses on Elements

Chapter IV
15 *Anamataggasaṃyutta*
Connected Discourses on Without Discoverable Beginning

Chapter V
16 *Kassapasaṃyutta*
Connected Discourses with Kassapa

Chapter VI
17 *Lābhasakkārasaṃyutta*
Connected Discourses on Gains and Honour

Chapter VIII
19 *Lakkhaṇasaṃyutta*
Connected Discourses with Lakkhaṇa

Chapter IX
20 *Opammasaṃyutta*
Connected Discourses with Similes

Chapter X
21 *Bhikkhusaṃyutta*
Connected Discourses with Bhikkhus

Introduction

The *Nidānavagga,* The Book of Causation, is named after its first saṃyutta, one of the deep royal saṃyuttas setting forth the radical philosophical vision of early Buddhism. The Vagga contains ten saṃyuttas, of which the first takes up almost half the volume. The other nine deal with less weighty topics, though it is possible the Dhātusaṃyutta, which is also devoted to first principles of Buddhist phenomenology, was intentionally included in the Vagga as a "junior partner" to the Nidānasaṃyutta. While this hypothesis must remain unconfirmable, what is beyond doubt is that with this Vagga we enter upon a very different terrain from that traversed in the Sagāthāvagga, a terrain where precise philosophical exposition takes priority over literary grace, inspirational charm, and moral edification.

Having used the expression "precise philosophical exposition," however, I must at once qualify it in two respects. First, the word "philosophical" applies to the contents of these saṃyuttas only in the sense that they articulate a body of first principles which disclose the deep underlying structures of actuality, not in the sense that they set out to construct a systematic edifice of thought whose primary appeal is to the intellect. Their disclosures always take place within the framework laid out by the Four Noble Truths, which makes it clear that their primary intent is pragmatic, directed towards the cessation of suffering. They are expounded, not to delineate an intellectually satisfying system of ideas, but to make known those aspects of actuality, deep and hidden, that must be penetrated by wisdom to eradicate the ignorance at the bottom of existential suffering. The suttas are guidelines to seeing and understanding, signposts pointing to what one must see for oneself with direct insight. To regard their themes as topics for intellectual entertainment and argumentation is to miss the point.

Second, when I use the word "exposition," this should not arouse expectations that the suttas are going to provide us with thorough, systematic, logically progressive treatises of the type we find in the history of Western philosophy. Far to the contrary, what we are presented with is a virtual mosaic of reconnaissance photographs laying bare a landscape that is strange but uncannily familiar. The landscape, ultimately, is our own personal experience, seen in depth and with microscopic precision. Each sutta shows up this landscape from a distinctive angle. Like any photo, the picture given by a single sutta is necessarily limited, taken from a single standpoint and with a narrow point of focus, but in its capacity for revelation it can be stark and powerful. To make sense of the multiple shots offered by the suttas, following one another with hardly a hair's breadth of logical order, we must reshuffle them many times, ponder them deeply, and investigate them closely with wisdom. To arrive at the total picture, or at least at a fuller picture than we possess when we approach the texts in a cursory way, we must consider the suttas in a given saṃyutta in their totality, compare them with parallel discourses in other saṃyuttas, and then try to fit them together, like the pieces in a jigsaw puzzle, into a coherent whole. This is about as far from systematic exposition as one can get, for the purpose is not to gratify the intellect with a fully articulated system but to awaken insight, and such an aim requires a methodology of its own.

12. Nidānasaṃyutta

The Nidānasaṃyutta collects into one chapter of nine vaggas ninety-three short suttas concerned with dependent origination (*paṭicca-samuppāda*). This chapter might have even been named the Paṭicca-samuppādasaṃyutta, but the compilers of the canon must have considered such a title too unwieldy and settled upon a more concise designation for it. The word *nidāna* means cause or source, and is sometimes used in a chain of synonyms that includes *hetu*, *samudaya*, and *paccaya*, "cause, origin, condition" (see DN II 57,27 foll.). The word gives its name to the longest sutta in the Nikāyas on *paṭicca-samuppāda*, the Mahānidāna Sutta (DN No. 15).

Dependent origination is one of the central teachings of early Buddhism, so vital to the teaching as a whole that the Buddha is quoted elsewhere as saying, "One who sees dependent origination sees the Dhamma, and one who sees the Dhamma sees dependent origination" (MN I 190,37–191,2). The ultimate purpose of the teaching on dependent origination is to expose the conditions that sustain the round of rebirths, saṃsāra, so as to show what must be done to gain release from the round. Existence within saṃsāra is suffering and bondage (*dukkha*), and hence the ending of suffering requires deliverance from the round. To win deliverance is a matter of unravelling the causal pattern that underlies our bondage, a process that begins with understanding the causal pattern itself. It is dependent origination that defines this causal pattern.

Dependent origination is usually expounded in a sequence of twelve factors (*dvādasaṅga*) joined into a chain of eleven propositions. In the Nidānasaṃyutta this formula is cited many times. It is expounded in two orders: by way of origination (called *anuloma* or forward sequence), and by way of cessation (called *paṭiloma* or reverse sequence). Sometimes the presentation proceeds from the first factor to the last, sometimes it begins at the end and traces the chain of conditions back to the first. Other suttas pick up the chain somewhere in the middle and work either backwards or forwards. We find the bare formula at **12:1**, with formal definitions of the twelve factors in the "analysis of dependent origination" at **12:2**. The whole formula in turn exemplifies an abstract structural principle of conditionality, "When this exists, that comes to be; with the arising of this, that arises. When this does not exist, that does not come to be; with the cessation of this, that ceases" (for references, see **II, n. 14**). This structural principle can be given different applications than those found in the formula of dependent origination, and indeed underlies almost every aspect of the Buddha's teaching, from his ideas about social reformation to his outline of the path to Nibbāna.

To hope to find in the Nidānasaṃyutta a clear explanation of the sequence of conditions, as we might expect from a modern textbook on the subject, is to court disappointment. The formula preserved in the texts is stripped to the bone, perhaps serving as a mnemonic device, and it seems likely that the original expositions on the topic were fleshed out with elaborations that were not recorded in the suttas but were transmitted orally within the lineage of teachers. Because the texts lack a clearcut explanation of the formula, modern interpreters of early Buddhism have sometimes devised capricious theories about its original meaning, theories which assume that the Buddhist tradition itself has muddled up the interpretation of this most basic Buddhist doctrine. To avoid the arbitrariness and wilfulness of personal opinion, it seems more prudent to rely on the method of explanation found in the Buddhist exegetical tradition, which despite minor differences in details is largely the same across the spectrum of early Buddhist schools. Here I will give only a concise summary of the interpretation offered by the Pāli tradition.

Because of (i) ignorance (*avijjā*), lack of direct knowledge of the Four Noble Truths, a person engages in volitional actions, wholesome and unwholesome activities of body, speech, and mind; these are (ii) the volitional formations (*saṅkhārā*), in other words, kamma. The volitional formations sustain consciousness from one life to the next and determine where it re-arises; in this way volitional formations condition (iii) consciousness (*viññāṇa*). Along with consciousness, beginning with the moment of conception, comes (iv) "name-and-form" (*nāmarūpa*), the sentient organism with its physical form (*rūpa*) and its sensitive and cognitive capacities (*nāma*). The sentient organism is equipped with (v) six sense bases (*saḷāyatana*), the five physical sense faculties and the mind as organ of cognition. The sense bases allow (vi) contact (*phassa*) to occur between consciousness and its objects, and contact conditions (vii) feeling (*vedanā*). Called into play by feeling, (viii) craving (*taṇhā*) arises, and when craving intensifies it gives rise to (ix) clinging (*upādāna*), tight attachment to the objects of desire through sensuality and wrong views. Impelled by one's attachments, one again engages in volitional actions pregnant with (x) a new existence (*bhava*). At death this potential for new existence is actualized in a new life beginning with (xi) birth (*jāti*) and ending in (xii) aging-and-death (*jarāmaraṇa*).

From this we can see that the traditional interpretation regards the twelve factors as spread out over a span of three lives, with ignorance and volitional formations pertaining to the past, birth and aging-and-death to the future, and the intermediate factors to the present. The segment from consciousness through feeling is the resultant phase of the present, the phase resulting from past

TABLE 4

Dependent Origination
according to the Pāli exegetical tradition

3 Periods	12 Factors	20 Modes and 4 Groups
past	1. ignorance 2. volitional formations	5 past causes: 1, 2, 8, 9, 10
present	3. consciousness 4. name-and-form 5. six sense bases 6. contact 7. feeling	5 present effects: 3, 4, 5, 6, 7
	8. craving 9. clinging 10. existence	5 present causes: 8, 9, 10, 1, 2
future	11. birth 12. aging-and-death	5 future effects: 3, 4, 5, 6, 7

The two roots
1. Ignorance (from past to present)
2. Craving (from present to future)

The three connections
1. Past causes with present effects (between 2 & 3)
2. Present effects with present causes (between 7 & 8)
3. Present causes with future effects (between 10 & 11)

The three rounds
1. The round of defilements: 1, 8, 9
2. The round of kamma: 2, 10 (part)
3. The round of results: 3, 4, 5, 6, 7, 10 (part), 11, 12

---

ignorance and kamma; the segment from craving through active existence is the kammically creative phase of the present, leading to renewed existence in the future. Existence is distinguished into two phases: one, called kamma-existence (*kammabhava*), belongs to the causal phase of the present; the other, called rebirth-existence (*upapattibhava*), belongs to the resultant phase of the future. The twelve factors are also distributed into three "rounds": the round of defilements (*kilesavaṭṭa*) includes ignorance, craving, and clinging; the round of action (*kammavaṭṭa*) includes volitional formations and kamma-existence; all the other factors belong to the round of results (*vipākavaṭṭa*). Defilements give rise to defiled actions, actions bring forth results, and results serve as the soil for more defilements. In this way the round of rebirths revolves without discernible beginning.

This method of dividing up the factors should not be misconstrued to mean that the past, present, and future factors are mutually exclusive. The distribution into three lives is only an expository device which, for the sake of concision, has to resort to abstraction and oversimplification. As many of the suttas in the Nidānasaṃyutta show, in their dynamic operation groups of factors separated in the formula inevitably become intertwined. Thus whenever there is ignorance, then craving and clinging invariably come along; and whenever there is craving and clinging, then ignorance stands behind them. We might regard the twelve factors as composed of two parallel series defining a single process, the conditioned regeneration of saṃsāra from within itself, but doing so from complementary angles. The first series treats ignorance as the root, and shows how ignorance leads to kammic activity (i.e., the volitional formations) and thence to a new existence consisting in the interplay of consciousness and name-and-form. The second series makes craving the root, and shows how craving leads to clinging and kammic activity (i.e., active existence) and thence to the production of a new existence that begins with birth and ends in aging and death. To join the two segments, the factors within name-and-form from which craving arises must be drawn out, and thus we get the three links—the six sense bases, contact, and feeling.

The three-life interpretation of dependent origination has sometimes been branded a commentarial invention on the ground that the suttas themselves do not divide the terms up into different lifetimes. However, while it is true that we do not find in the suttas an explicit distribution of the factors into three lives, close examination of the variants on the standard formula lend strong support to the three-life interpretation. One example is

12:19, where ignorance and craving are first assigned jointly to a past life, giving rise to a new life lived in a conscious body with its six sense bases; and then, in the case of the fool (but not the wise man), ignorance and craving again function as joint causes in the present life to bring about renewed birth and suffering in the future life. A close examination of other variants in this saṃyutta would also establish that the series of terms extends over several lives.

The opening vagga calls immediate attention to the importance of dependent origination with a string of suttas showing how the seven Buddhas of the past, ending in "our" Buddha Gotama, attained perfect enlightenment by awakening to dependent origination, the eye-opening discovery that ended their long search for the light of wisdom (**12:4–10**). Later the Buddha gives a more detailed account of his own awakening to dependent origination, where he illustrates his discovery of the Noble Eightfold Path with the beautiful parable of the ancient city (**12:65**). According to **12:20**, the causal connections between the factors operate whether or not Buddhas arise: they are the persistent, stable, invariable laws of actuality. The task of a Tathāgata is to discover them, fathom them thoroughly, and then proclaim them to the world. The invariability of the causal law, and the regularity in the arising of Perfectly Enlightened Buddhas, are thus joined into a single order ultimately identical with the Dhamma itself.

Several suttas show that dependent origination served the Buddha as a "teaching by the middle" (*majjhena tathāgato dhammaṃ deseti*), enabling him to steer clear of the two extreme views about the human condition that have polarized reflective thought through the centuries. One is the metaphysical thesis of eternalism (*sassatavāda*), which posits a permanent self as the underlying ground of personal existence, a self which, in classical Indian thought, transmigrates from one life to the next while retaining its individual identity. The other extreme is annihilationism (*ucchedavāda*), which holds that the individual can be reduced to the phenomenal personality and that at death, with the dissolution of the body, the person is entirely cut off and annihilated. Both extremes pose insuperable problems, for the one encourages an obstinate clinging to the conditions out of which suffering arises while the other threatens to undermine ethics and to make suffering inexplicable except as the product of chance. Dependent origination offers a new perspective which rises above the extremes. The teaching shows individual existence to be constituted by a current of conditioned phenomena which is devoid of a metaphysical self, yet which continues from life to life as long as the causes that sustain it remain efficacious. Thereby dependent origination offers a meaningful explanation of the problem of suffering which avoids, on the one hand, the philosophical conundrums posed by the hypothesis of a permanent self, and on the other the dangers of ethical anarchy posed by annihilationism. As long as ignorance and craving remain, the round of rebirths continues on, kamma yields its pleasant and painful fruit, and the great mass of suffering accumulates. With their removal, and only with their removal, can a complete end be made to the whole round of saṃsāric suffering.

The most elegant exposition of dependent origination as the "middle teaching" is without doubt the famous Kaccānagotta Sutta (**12:15**), in which the Buddha holds up this principle as an alternative to the extremes of existence and nonexistence. Dependent origination provides the key for understanding the arising of suffering as well as pleasure and pain (**12:17, 18**; see too **12:24–26**), and again for cutting through a variety of philosophical antinomies adopted by the thinkers of his era (**12:46–48**).

Though the twelve-factored formula of dependent origination is the most common expression of the doctrine, the Nidānasaṃyutta introduces a number of little-known variants that help to illuminate the standard version. One is a ten-factored variant in which ignorance and volitional formations are omitted and consciousness and name-and-form become mutually dependent (**12:65**). This is illustrated by the simile of two sheaves of reeds which support each other and collapse when either is withdrawn (**12:67**). An interesting sequence of three texts (**12:38–40**) speaks about the conditions for "the maintenance of consciousness" (*viññāṇassa ṭhitiyā*), that is, how consciousness passes on to a new existence. The causes are said to be the underlying tendencies, i.e., ignorance and craving, and "what one intends and plans," i.e., one's volitional activities. Once consciousness becomes established, the production of a new existence begins, thus showing that we can proceed directly from consciousness (the usual third factor) to existence (the usual tenth factor).

These variants make it plain that the sequence of factors should not be regarded as a linear causal process in which each preceding factor gives rise to its successor through the simple exercise of efficient causality. The relationship among the factors is always one of complex conditionality rather than linear causation. The conditioning function can include such diverse relations as mutuality (when two factors mutually support each other), necessary antecedence (when one factor must be present for another to arise), distal efficiency (as when a remotely past volitional formation generates consciousness in a new life), etc. Moreover, by contemplating a number of variant texts side by side, we can see that at selected points in the series the links loop back in ways that reinforce the complexity of the process. Thus, while consciousness precedes the six sense bases in the usual formula, at **12:43** and **12:44** the six sense bases are shown to be conditions for consciousness. While consciousness normally precedes craving, **12:64** makes craving (with lust and delight) the condition for the continuation of consciousness and volitional formations the condition for existence.

The positive and negative sequences of dependent origination are expanded definitions of the second and third of the Four Noble Truths, as shown by the variant at **12:43**. From the six internal and external sense bases, as we just saw, consciousness arises, and this is followed by contact, feeling, and craving, which is then declared to be the origin of suffering; when craving is abandoned, suffering stops. The next sutta, **12:44**, employs a similar pattern to explain the origin and passing away of the world. This reveals dependent origination to be, not a remote and inaccessible metaphysical law, but a process perpetually underpinning our own everyday sensory experience, activated by our responses to the feelings arisen at the six sense bases. As the suttas **12:52–60** show, when attention to the objects of perception is driven by a thirst for gratification, craving is intensified, and this builds up another round of suffering. But when one learns to discern the danger in the objects of clinging, craving ceases, bringing the subsequent factors to a standstill.

In several suttas the formula for dependent origination is integrated with another doctrinal paradigm, that of the four nutriments (*āhāra*). These are the four strong supports for sentient existence, namely, edible food (for the body), contact (for feeling), mental volition (for the production of renewed existence), and consciousness (for name-and-form). The ideas of nutrition and conditionality closely correspond, both implying the contingency and insubstantiality of all phenomena of existence. Hence it is natural for the formula of the four nutriments to be grafted on to an exposition of dependent origination. In **12:12**, in relation to the nutriments, the Buddha repeatedly rejects questions that imply the presence of a substantial subject or agent behind the process of experience. The conditioning factors themselves constitute the ongoing flow of experience, with no need to posit a permanent self as the "someone" at the receiving end of feeling and perception, or at the instigating end of action. **12:63**, entirely devoted to the four nutriments with no explicit mention made of dependent origination, introduces four thought-provoking similes to expose the dangers in the four nutriments and to inspire a sense of revulsion towards the whole process of nutrition. Because at least three of the four nutriments are internal to the sentient organism itself, the teaching of the four nutriments implies, at a very deep level, that sentient existence not only requires nutriment from outside but is itself a self-sustaining process of nutrition.

One variant in this saṃyutta stands in a class of its own. This is the short but pithy Upanisā Sutta (**12:23**), which shows that the same principle of conditionality that underlies the movement of saṃsāra also undergirds the path to liberation. Each stage of the path arises with its predecessor as a condition or proximate cause, all the way from the initial act of faith to the final knowledge of deliverance. This presentation of the doctrine has sometimes been called "transcendental dependent origination."

Since the round is propelled by craving, and craving is nurtured by ignorance, to break the forward movement of the series ignorance must be replaced by knowledge. With the removal of ignorance all the factors that flow from it—craving, clinging, and kammic activity—come to a halt, bringing to an end the round of rebirths with all its attendant suffering. From one angle, as is often shown in the Nidānasaṃyutta, ignorance means not knowing the dependently arisen phenomena, their origin, their cessation, and the way to their cessation (**12:14**, **49**, etc.). Thus the ignorance at the head of the causal series, the ignorance which sustains the forward movement of dependent origination, is nothing other than ignorance about dependent origination itself. From this it follows that the knowledge needed to bring dependent origination to a stop is just knowledge of how dependent origination works.

Several important suttas in the Nidānasaṃyutta make it clear that dependent origination is not merely an explanatory principle to be accepted on trust but an essential component of the knowledge needed to reach the end of suffering. Often the Buddha states that the connections among the factors are to be directly known, both by way of origination and by way of cessation. They are thus not merely aspects of theory but the content of intuitive insight. To gain this knowledge is to acquire the right view of a noble disciple who has personally seen the truth of the Dhamma and entered the path of a trainee (*sekha*), one bound to reach the Deathless in seven more lives at most, without ever falling away. Direct knowledge of dependent origination is not the unique mark of the arahant—a widespread misconception—but an achievement already reached by the stream-enterer on making "the breakthrough to the Dhamma" (*dhammābhisamaya*). The noble disciple's knowledge of dependent origination has two aspects: one is a direct perception of the relationships between each pair of factors in the present; the other, an inferential knowledge that this fixed order of phenomena holds invariably in the past and future, so that anyone who comprehends dependent origination must comprehend it in exactly the same way that the noble disciple has comprehended it (see **12:33–34**). Once the stream-enterer gains this knowledge, attainment of the final goal is irrevocably assured, as is clear from **12:41** and from the paragraph concluding **12:27**, **28**, and **49–50**.

Towards the end of this chapter, in **12:70** we read the story of the wanderer Susīma, who entered the order as a "thief of Dhamma" intending to learn the Buddha's teaching to gain advantages for his own company of followers. On being subjected to a catechism by the Buddha on the five aggregates and dependent origination, he underwent a genuine change of heart and confessed his evil intentions. This sutta introduces a class of arahants described as "liberated by wisdom" (*paññāvimutta*), who have won the final goal by understanding the Dhamma without gaining the supernormal powers or the formless meditations. The sutta also makes it clear that knowledge of the true nature of phenomena, i.e., of the five aggregates and dependent origination, precedes knowledge of Nibbāna.

The Nidānasaṃyutta closes with two vaggas cast as repetition series. Vagga VIII applies the four-truth template of the "ascetics and brahmins" paradigm to each factor of the standard formula (excluding ignorance, implicitly included as the condition for volitional formations). Vagga IX is an "incorporated repetition series," because each sutta incorporates all eleven factors along with their conditions into an abbreviated text. It is thus implied that each sutta could be "unpacked" by taking each factor with its condition as the subject of a separate sutta, so that the total number of suttas in the vagga would increase from twelve to 132.

13. Abhisamayasaṃyutta

This saṃyutta contains only eleven suttas without division into vaggas. Strangely, the Sinhala edition of SN and its commentary do not count it as a separate saṃyutta but treat it as a vagga within the Nidānasaṃyutta. This seems difficult to justify, as the suttas make no mention of dependent origination nor do they allude to the chain of causation. Perhaps the Sinhalese redactors included it in the Nidānasaṃyutta because the disciple's breakthrough to stream-entry comes about through the realization of dependent origination. As an explanation, however, this seems inadequate when the suttas do not explicitly mention dependent origination.

The purpose of this saṃyutta is to extol the breakthrough to the Dhamma (*dhammābhisamaya*), also called the obtaining of the vision of the Dhamma (*dhammacakkhupaṭilābha*), the event that transforms a person into a noble disciple at the minimum level of stream-enterer. The stream-enterer is one who has obtained the transcendental path leading to Nibbāna and is bound to put an end to saṃsāric wandering after seven more lives at most, all lived in either the heavens or the human world. The first ten suttas are all moulded on the same pattern: the Buddha first contrasts two obviously incommensurate quantities and then compares this disparity with that between the amount of suffering the noble disciple has eliminated and the amount that still remains in the maximum span of seven lives. The last sutta differs in the terms of comparison: here the contrast is between the achievements of the non-Buddhist ascetics and the achievement of the noble disciple who has made the breakthrough, the latter being immensely greater than the former.

14. Dhātusaṃyutta

This saṃyutta consists of thirty-nine suttas, arranged into four vaggas, all concerned in some way with elements. The word "elements" (*dhātu*) is applied to several quite disparate groups of phenomena, and thus the suttas in this chapter fall into separate clusters with nothing in common but their concern with entities called elements. The four vaggas could not be neatly divided into decads each devoted to a different group of elements, for the number of suttas to be included in the middle two vaggas did not allow for this.

The first vagga deals with eighteen elements that make up one of the major models of phenomenological analysis used in the Nikāyas, often mentioned alongside the five aggregates and the six internal and external sense bases. The eighteen elements fall into six triads: sense faculties, objects, and corresponding types of consciousness. The denotations of the first five triads seem obvious enough, but unclarity surrounds the last, the triad of mind (*mano*), mental phenomena (*dhammā*), and mind-consciousness (*manoviññāṇa*). Strangely, the Nikāyas themselves do not explain the precise referents of these three elements or the nature of their relationship. This is first done in the Abhidhamma Piṭaka. In the developed systematic version of the Abhidhamma, the mind element is a simpler type of cognitive act than the mind-consciousness element, to which is assigned the more advanced cognitive operations. The mental phenomena element denotes not only objects of mind-consciousness, but also the mental factors that accompany consciousness, included in the aggregates of feeling, perception, and volitional formations (for details see **n. 224**).

This first vagga is divided into two "pentads" (*pañcaka*): an "internal pentad," which takes the sense faculties as the point of departure; and an "external pentad," which begins with the objects. The first sutta really belongs to neither set, as it merely enumerates the eighteen elements. The internal series, which starts with **14:2**, shows how successive mental functions—first contact and then feeling—arise in dependence on their predecessors in a fixed order which cannot be inverted. In the external pentad the same mode of treatment is applied to the mental functions that relate more specifically to the objects; the chain here is more complex and the internal relationships in need of explanation. The explanations offered by the commentary are intended to square apparent irregularities with patterns of relationship accepted as authoritative by the age of the commentators. It is an open question whether these explanations reflect the understanding of the elements held in the earliest phase of Buddhist thought.

The second vagga opens with three suttas on miscellaneous types of elements, not highly systematized. Then there follows a long series of suttas, **14:14–29**, in which the word "element" is used in the sense of personal disposition. With respect to numerous contrasting qualities, good and bad, the point is made that people come together because of personal affinities rooted in these qualities. One memorable sutta in this group shows each of the Buddha's leading disciples walking in the company of fellow monks who share his field of interest; even Devadatta, the miscreant in the Saṅgha, has his own entourage made up of those with evil wishes (**14:15**).

The fourth vagga focuses upon the four primary elements of physical form: earth, water, heat, and air. The suttas in this vagga are all moulded upon templates, including the gratification triad and the ascetics and brahmins series discussed in the General Introduction (see above, p. 38).

15. Anamataggasaṃyutta

The Anamataggasaṃyutta, "On Without Discoverable Beginning," is so called because its theme is the unbounded temporal extent of saṃsāra. The precise meaning of the phrase *anamatagga* is uncertain, the term itself differing in the texts of the early Buddhist schools, but the idea it is intended to suggest is conveyed well enough by the second sentence of the opening homily: that a first point of the round of rebirths cannot be discerned. The underlying purpose of this saṃyutta is to situate the Buddha's teaching of liberation against its cosmic background by underscoring the immeasurable mass of suffering we have experienced while wandering from life to life in unbounded time, "hindered by ignorance and fettered by craving."

In sutta after sutta the Buddha illustrates the vastness of saṃsāric suffering with awe-inspiring similes, always drawing the inevitable conclusion that we have experienced the suffering of repeated birth and death long enough and it is time to strive for ultimate freedom. Four suttas illustrate, by means of memorable similes, the duration of a cosmic aeon (*kappa*), of which countless numbers have elapsed (**15:5–8**). Sutta **15:10** reinforces the point with its image of the heap of bones one person leaves behind in the course of a single aeon. Particularly stirring is the discourse to the thirty bhikkhus from Pāvā, on the frightful dangers of saṃsāra, a sutta powerful enough to bring all of them to the realization of arahantship right on the spot (**15:13**). The final sutta in the chapter gives us a retrospective overview of the epochs during which three past Buddhas lived, with some information about conditions of human life during their dispensations.

16. Kassapasaṃyutta

Mahākassapa, Kassapa the Great, was named by the Buddha the most eminent disciple in the observance of the ascetic practices (AN I 23,20). Though he did not accompany the Master as regularly as many of the other close disciples did, the Buddha had the highest regard for Kassapa and often spoke in his praise. According to the Cullavagga (Vin II 284–85), after the Buddha's parinibbāna Mahākassapa became the foster father of the newly orphaned Saṅgha and took the initiative in convening a council of elders to rehearse the Dhamma and Discipline. This was a necessary measure to preserve the Buddha's dispensation for posterity.

This saṃyutta brings together thirteen suttas featuring the great disciple. Though they offer us glimpses into Mahākassapa's role in the Saṅgha and a sharply sketched portrait of his personality, their underlying purpose is not so much to preserve biographical information as it is to hold up Mahākassapa as a role model for the monks to emulate. In the first sutta the Buddha extols him for his simplicity and frugality and enjoins the monks to imitate him in this respect (**16:1**). He dwells detached and equanimous, yet is also imbued with compassion, sympathy, and tender concern for householders (**16:3, 4**). He continues to observe the ascetic practices even in old age, for his own happiness and to set an example for future generations (**16:5**). The Buddha often asked Kassapa to exhort the bhikkhus, but on three occasions he refuses because the bhikkhus are no longer open to instruction (**16:6–8**). This introduces a theme that comes to a crescendo in **16:13**: the Buddha's dispensation is already starting to decline, and the cause is not external but internal, namely, corruption within the Saṅgha. In **16:9** the Buddha applauds Kassapa for his mastery over the meditative attainments and the direct knowledges, and in **16:10–11** we are given closeup shots of Kassapa's sometimes stressful relationship with Ānanda. Though his attitude towards the gentle Ānanda seems too stern, we must remember that it was through Kassapa's prodding that Ānanda put forth the effort to win arahantship before the First Buddhist Council. In **16:11** Kassapa relates the story of his first meeting with the Buddha, which culminated in an exchange of robes with the Master. This was an honour not bestowed on any other bhikkhu, and presaged Mahākassapa's future role as a leader of the Saṅgha.

17. Lābhasakkārasaṃyutta

The life of a bhikkhu requires the renunciation of sensual pleasures and detachment from the normal round of satisfactions provided by family, livelihood, and an active role in civil society. Precisely because he has dedicated himself to a life of austerity and spiritual self-cultivation, the bhikkhu is liable to be regarded prematurely as a holy man and to be showered with gifts, honour, and praise, especially by pious but ingenuous lay devotees in quest of merit. For an unwary bhikkhu the gains and honour that may unexpectedly pour down on him can cast a spell more subtle and seductive even than the lure of the senses. The bhikkhu interprets the gain and honour as an index of his spiritual worth; the praises sung over his name can inflate his ego to dizzying heights. Thus from gain and honour there may arise conceit, self-exaltation, and contempt for others—all stumbling blocks along the path to the "unsurpassed security from bondage."

To protect the bhikkhus from losing sight of their goal, the Buddha often warned them about the dangers in gain, honour, and praise. The present saṃyutta collects forty-three suttas on this theme. The tone of the discourses is unusually grave: one attached to gain and honour is like a fish caught on a baited hook, like a turtle hit by a harpoon, like a goat caught in a thorny briar patch (**17:2–4**). Even a man who earlier would not tell a deliberate lie to save his life might later lie to win gain and honour (**17:19**), and some would even sacrifice their mother for such rewards (**17:37**). But humour is not lacking: one text compares the monk revelling in his gain and honour to a dung beetle revelling in a heap of dung (**17:5**). The last vagga exhibits Devadatta as a notorious example of one who fell away from the spiritual life owing to hunger for gain, honour, and praise.

18. Rāhulasaṃyutta

Rāhula was the Buddha's son, born shortly before he left the household life to embark on his quest for enlightenment. When the Buddha returned to his native city of Kapilavatthu in the first year after the enlightenment, he had Rāhula ordained as a novice, and thereafter often gave him instruction. Three longer suttas to Rāhula are found in the Majjhima Nikāya (MN Nos. 61, 62, and 147, the latter identical with SN **35:121**). The Rāhulasaṃyutta collects twenty-two short texts arranged in two vaggas. The first ten explain the three characteristics in relation to ten groups of phenomena: the six internal sense bases; the six external sense bases; the six classes each of consciousness, contact, feeling, perception, volition, and craving; the six elements; and the five aggregates. They are addressed to Rāhula in response to a request for instruction. The first ten suttas of the second vagga show the Buddha speaking the same ten suttas to Rāhula, but this time on his own initiative. Two additional suttas give instructions on how to eradicate the sense of "I" and "mine" and the tendency to conceit.

19. Lakkhaṇasaṃyutta

Although this saṃyutta is named after the elder Lakkhaṇa, his role is to serve as a foil for Mahāmoggallāna, the disciple who excelled in the exercise of psychic powers. Each sutta is constructed according to the same format, in which Moggallāna describes the sufferings of a *peta* or tormented spirit, whom he has seen with supernormal vision, and the Buddha confirms the truth of his vision, giving an explanation of the kammic cause that underlies such misery. Here, as in the printed editions of the Pāli text, the first sutta alone is given in full and thereafter only the variations are recorded. The last five suttas deliver a stern message to miscreant monks and nuns, perhaps reflecting modes of misbehaviour that were becoming increasingly manifest in the Saṅgha.

20. Opammasaṃyutta

This saṃyutta contains twelve suttas touching on miscellaneous topics mostly related to the training of the bhikkhus. Though the topics are diverse, each sutta incorporates an extended simile and it is on this basis that they are brought together into one saṃyutta. The themes that emerge include the rarity of human birth, the blessings of developing lovingkindness, the impermanence of life, and the need for constant diligence. In this collection we also find the Buddha's prophecy of how the Dhamma will decline when the bhikkhus neglect the deep suttas dealing with emptiness in favour of works composed by poets "with beautiful words and phrases."

21. Bhikkhusaṃyutta

This saṃyutta collects twelve miscellaneous suttas spoken by or about individual bhikkhus. It is noteworthy that, apart from the first two texts, all the others contain verses, and this arouses suspicion that the saṃyutta originally belonged to the Sagāthāvagga. Indeed, in the Chinese translation of the Saṃyuktāgama, the Bhikkhusaṃyutta is found in the Sagāthāvagga, coming just before the Bhikkhunīsaṃyutta. Perhaps at some point in the transmission of the Pāli version the redactors added two verseless suttas on Moggallāna and Sāriputta, and then, in consequence, had to transpose the whole saṃyutta from Part I to Part II. In the midst of the suttas on famous elders there is one addressed to an otherwise unknown bhikkhu named Elder (a fictitious name?) offering pithy instruction on the real meaning of solitude.

[1] PART II: The Book of Causation (*Nidānavagga*)

Homage to the Blessed One,
the Arahant, the Perfectly Enlightened One

Chapter I

12 *Nidānasaṃyutta*
Connected Discourses on Causation

I. THE BUDDHAS

1 (1) Dependent Origination

Thus have I heard. On one occasion the Blessed One was dwelling at Sāvatthī in Jeta's Grove, Anāthapiṇḍika's Park. There the Blessed One addressed the bhikkhus thus: "Bhikkhus!"

"Venerable sir!" those bhikkhus replied. The Blessed One said this:

"Bhikkhus, I will teach you dependent origination. Listen to that and attend closely, I will speak." – "Yes, venerable sir," those bhikkhus replied. The Blessed One said this:

"And what, bhikkhus, is dependent origination? With ignorance as condition, volitional formations [come to be];[1] with volitional formations as condition, consciousness; with consciousness as condition, name-and-form; with name-and-form as condition, the six sense bases; with the six sense bases as condition, contact; with contact as condition, feeling; with feeling as condition, craving; with craving as condition, clinging; with clinging as condition, existence; with existence as condition, birth; with birth as condition, aging-and-death, sorrow, lamentation, pain, displeasure, and despair come to be. Such is the origin of this whole mass of suffering. This, bhikkhus, is called dependent origination.

"But with the remainderless fading away and cessation of ignorance comes cessation of volitional formations; [2] with the cessation of volitional formations, cessation of consciousness; with the cessation of consciousness, cessation of name-and-form; with the cessation of name-and-form, cessation of the six sense bases; with the cessation of the six sense bases, cessation of contact; with the cessation of contact, cessation of feeling; with the cessation of feeling, cessation of craving; with the cessation of craving, cessation of clinging; with the cessation of clinging, cessation of existence; with the cessation of existence, cessation of birth; with the cessation of birth, aging-and-death, sorrow, lamentation, pain, displeasure, and despair cease. Such is the cessation of this whole mass of suffering."

This is what the Blessed One said. Elated, those bhikkhus delighted in the Blessed One's statement.

2 (2) *Analysis of Dependent Origination*

At Sāvatthī. "Bhikkhus, I will teach you dependent origination and I will analyse it for you. Listen to that and attend closely, I will speak."

"Yes, venerable sir," those bhikkhus replied. The Blessed One said this:

"And what, bhikkhus, is dependent origination? With ignorance as condition, volitional formations [come to be]; with volitional formations, consciousness ... (*as in preceding sutta*) ... Such is the origin of this whole mass of suffering.

"And what, bhikkhus, is aging-and-death? The aging of the various beings in the various orders of beings, their growing old, brokenness of teeth, greyness of hair, wrinkling of skin, decline of vitality, degeneration of the faculties: this is called aging. [3] The passing away of the various beings from the various orders of beings, their perishing, breakup, disappearance, mortality, death, completion of time, the breakup of the aggregates, the laying down of the carcass: this is called death.[2] Thus this aging and this death are together called aging-and-death.

"And what, bhikkhus, is birth? The birth of the various beings into the various orders of beings, their being born, descent [into the womb], production, the manifestation of the aggregates, the obtaining of the sense bases. This is called birth.[3]

"And what, bhikkhus, is existence? There are these three kinds of existence: sense-sphere existence, form-sphere existence, formless-sphere existence. This is called existence.[4]

"And what, bhikkhus, is clinging? There are these four kinds of clinging: clinging to sensual pleasures, clinging to views, clinging to rules and vows, clinging to a doctrine of self. This is called clinging.[5]

"And what, bhikkhus, is craving? There are these six classes of craving: craving for forms, craving for sounds, craving for odours, craving for tastes, craving for tactile objects, craving for mental phenomena. This is called craving.

"And what, bhikkhus, is feeling? There are these six classes of feeling: feeling born of eye-contact, feeling born of ear-contact, feeling born of nose-contact, feeling born of tongue-contact, feeling born of body-contact, feeling born of mind-contact. This is called feeling.

"And what, bhikkhus, is contact? There are these six classes of contact: eye-contact, ear-contact, nose-contact, tongue-contact, body-contact, mind-contact. This is called contact.

"And what, bhikkhus, are the six sense bases? The eye base, the ear base, the nose base, the tongue base, the body base, the mind base. These are called the six sense bases.

"And what, bhikkhus, is name-and-form? Feeling, perception, volition, contact, attention: this is called name. The four [4] great elements and the form derived from the four great elements: this is called form. Thus this name and this form are together called name-and-form.[6]

"And what, bhikkhus, is consciousness? There are these six classes of consciousness: eye-consciousness, ear-consciousness, nose-consciousness, tongue-consciousness, body-consciousness, mind-consciousness. This is called consciousness.

"And what, bhikkhus, are the volitional formations? There are these three kinds of volitional formations: the bodily volitional formation, the verbal volitional formation, the mental volitional formation. These are called the volitional formations.[7]

"And what, bhikkhus, is ignorance? Not knowing suffering, not knowing the origin of suffering, not knowing the cessation of suffering, not knowing the way leading to the cessation of suffering. This is called ignorance.[8]

"Thus, bhikkhus, with ignorance as condition, volitional formations [come to be]; with volitional formations as condition, consciousness.... Such is the origin of this whole mass of suffering. But with the remainderless fading away and cessation of ignorance comes cessation of volitional formations; with the cessation of volitional formations, cessation of consciousness.... Such is the cessation of this whole mass of suffering."[9]

3 (3) The Two Ways

At Sāvatthī. "Bhikkhus, I will teach you the wrong way and the right way. Listen to that and attend closely, I will speak."

"Yes, venerable sir," those bhikkhus replied. The Blessed One said this:

"And what, bhikkhus, is the wrong way? With ignorance as condition, volitional formations [come to be]; with volitional formations as condition, consciousness.... Such is the origin of this whole mass of suffering. This, bhikkhus, is called the wrong way. [5]

"And what, bhikkhus, is the right way? With the remainderless fading away and cessation of ignorance comes cessation of volitional formations; with the cessation of volitional formations, cessation of consciousness.... Such is the cessation of this whole mass of suffering. This, bhikkhus, is called the right way."

4 (4) Vipassī

At Sāvatthī.[10]

"Bhikkhus, before his enlightenment, while he was still a bodhisatta,[11] not yet fully enlightened, it occurred to Vipassī, the Blessed One, the Arahant, the Perfectly Enlightened One:[12] 'Alas, this world has fallen into trouble, in that it is born, ages, and dies, it passes away and is reborn, yet it does not understand the escape from this suffering [headed by] aging-and-death. When now will an escape be discerned from this suffering [headed by] aging-and-death?' ... [6–9] ...

"'Cessation, cessation'—thus, bhikkhus, in regard to things unheard before there arose in the Bodhisatta Vipassī vision, knowledge, wisdom, true knowledge, and light."

5 (5) Sikhī

6 (6) Vessabhū

7 (7) Kakusandha

8 (8) Koṇāgamana

9 (9) Kassapa

[10]

10 (10) Gotama the Great Sakyan Sage

(i. Origination)

"Bhikkhus, before my enlightenment, while I was still a bodhisatta, not yet fully enlightened, it occurred to me: 'Alas, this world has fallen into trouble, in that it is born, ages, and dies, it passes away and is reborn, yet it does not understand the escape from this suffering [headed by] aging-and-death. When now will an escape be discerned from this suffering [headed by] aging-and-death?'

"Then, bhikkhus, it occurred to me: 'When what exists does aging-and-death come to be? By what is aging-and-death conditioned?' Then, bhikkhus, through careful attention, there took place in me a breakthrough by wisdom:[13] 'When there is birth, aging-and-death comes to be; aging-and-death has birth as its condition.'[14]

"Then, bhikkhus, it occurred to me: 'When what exists does birth come to be? By what is birth conditioned?' Then, bhikkhus, through careful attention, there took place in me a breakthrough by wisdom: 'When there is existence, birth comes to be; birth has existence as its condition.'

"Then, bhikkhus, it occurred to me: 'When what exists does existence come to be? By what is existence conditioned?' Then, bhikkhus, through careful attention, there took place in me a breakthrough by wisdom: 'When there is clinging, existence comes to be; existence has clinging as its condition.'

"Then, bhikkhus, it occurred to me: 'When what exists does clinging come to be? By what is clinging conditioned?' Then, bhikkhus, through careful attention, there took place in me a breakthrough by wisdom: 'When there is craving, clinging comes to be; clinging has craving as its condition.'

"Then, bhikkhus, it occurred to me: 'When what exists does craving come to be? By what is craving conditioned?' Then, bhikkhus, through careful attention, there took place in me a breakthrough by wisdom: 'When there is feeling, craving comes to be; craving has feeling as its condition.'

"Then, bhikkhus, it occurred to me: 'When what exists does feeling come to be? By what is feeling conditioned?' Then, bhikkhus, through careful attention, there took place in me a breakthrough by wisdom: 'When there is contact, feeling comes to be; feeling has contact as its condition.'

"Then, bhikkhus, it occurred to me: 'When what exists does contact come to be? By what is contact conditioned?' Then, bhikkhus, through careful attention, there took place in me a breakthrough by wisdom: 'When there are the six sense bases, contact comes to be; contact has the six sense bases as its condition.'

"Then, bhikkhus, it occurred to me: 'When what exists do the six sense bases come to be? By what are the six sense bases conditioned?' Then, bhikkhus, through careful attention, there took place in me a breakthrough by wisdom: 'When there is name-and-form, the six sense bases come to be; the six sense bases have name-and-form as their condition.'

"Then, bhikkhus, it occurred to me: 'When what exists does name-and-form come to be? By what is name-and-form conditioned?' Then, bhikkhus, through careful attention, there took place in me a breakthrough by wisdom: 'When there is consciousness, name-and-form comes to be; name-and-form has consciousness as its condition.'

"Then, bhikkhus, it occurred to me: 'When what exists does consciousness come to be? By what is consciousness conditioned?' Then, bhikkhus, through careful attention, there took place in me a breakthrough by wisdom: 'When there are volitional formations, consciousness comes to be; consciousness has volitional formations as its condition.'[15]

"Then, bhikkhus, it occurred to me: 'When what exists do volitional formations come to be? By what are volitional formations conditioned?' Then, bhikkhus, through careful attention, there took place in me a breakthrough by wisdom: 'When there is ignorance, volitional formations come to be; volitional formations have ignorance as their condition.'

"Thus with ignorance as condition, volitional formations [come to be]; with volitional formations as condition, consciousness.... Such is the origin of this whole mass of suffering.

"'Origination, origination'—thus, bhikkhus, in regard to things unheard before there arose in me vision, knowledge, wisdom, true knowledge, and light.[16]

(ii. Cessation)

"Then, bhikkhus, it occurred to me: 'When what does not exist does aging-and-death not come to be? With the cessation of what does the cessation of aging-and-death come about?' Then, bhikkhus, through careful attention, there took place in me a breakthrough by wisdom: 'When there is no birth, aging-and-death does not come to be; with the cessation of birth comes cessation of aging-and-death.'

"Then, bhikkhus, it occurred to me: [11] 'When what does not exist does birth not come to be? By the cessation of what does the cessation of birth come about?' Then, bhikkhus, through careful attention, there took place in me a breakthrough by wisdom: 'When there is no existence, birth does not come to be; with the cessation of existence comes cessation of birth.'... 'When there is no clinging, existence does not come to be; with the cessation of clinging comes cessation of existence.'... 'When there is no craving, clinging does not come to be; with the cessation of craving comes cessation of clinging.'... 'When there is no feeling, craving does not come to be; with the cessation of feeling comes cessation of craving.'... 'When there is no contact, feeling does not come to be; with the cessation of contact comes cessation of feeling.'... 'When there are no six sense bases, contact does not come to be; with the cessation of the six sense bases comes cessation of contact.'... 'When there is no name-and-form, the six sense bases do not come to be; with the cessation of name-and-form comes cessation of the six sense bases.'... 'When there is no consciousness, name-and-form does not come to be; with the cessation of consciousness comes cessation of name-and-form.'... 'When there are no volitional formations, consciousness does not come to be; with the cessation of volitional formations comes cessation of consciousness.'... 'When there is no ignorance, volitional formations do not come to be; with the cessation of ignorance comes cessation of volitional formations.'

"Thus with the remainderless fading away and cessation of ignorance comes cessation of volitional formations; with the cessation of volitional formations, cessation of consciousness....

Such is the cessation of this whole mass of suffering.

"'Cessation, cessation'—thus, bhikkhus, in regard to things unheard before there arose in me vision, knowledge, wisdom, true knowledge, and light."

II. Nutriment

11 (1) Nutriment

Thus have I heard. On one occasion the Blessed One was dwelling at Sāvatthī in Jeta's Grove, Anāthapiṇḍika's Park....

"Bhikkhus, there are these four kinds of nutriment for the maintenance of beings that have already come to be and for the assistance of those about to come to be.[17] What four? The nutriment edible food, gross or subtle; second, contact; third, mental volition; fourth, consciousness. These are the four kinds of nutriment for the maintenance of beings that have already come to be and for the assistance of those about to come to be.[18]

"Bhikkhus, these four kinds of nutriment have what as their source, [12] what as their origin, from what are they born and produced? These four kinds of nutriment have craving as their source, craving as their origin; they are born and produced from craving.[19]

"And this craving has what as its source, what as its origin, from what is it born and produced? This craving has feeling as its source, feeling as its origin; it is born and produced from feeling.

"And this feeling has what as its source...? Feeling has contact as its source.... And this contact has what as its source...? Contact has the six sense bases as its source.... And these six sense bases have what as their source...? The six sense bases have name-and-form as their source.... And this name-and-form has what as its source...? Name-and-form has consciousness as its source.... And this consciousness has what as its source...? Consciousness has volitional formations as its source.... And these volitional formations have what as their source, what as their origin, from what are they born and produced? Volitional formations have ignorance as their source, ignorance as their origin; they are born and produced from ignorance.

"Thus, bhikkhus, with ignorance as condition, volitional formations [come to be]; with volitional formations as condition, consciousness.... Such is the origin of this whole mass of suffering. But with the remainderless fading away and cessation of ignorance comes cessation of volitional formations; with the cessation of volitional formations, cessation of consciousness.... Such is the cessation of this whole mass of suffering."

12 (2) Moḷiyaphagguna

At Sāvatthī. [13] "Bhikkhus, there are these four kinds of nutriment for the maintenance of beings that have already come to be and for the assistance of those about to come to be. What four? The nutriment edible food, gross or subtle; second, contact; third, mental volition; fourth, consciousness. These are the four kinds of nutriment for the maintenance of beings that have already come to be and for the assistance of those about to come to be."[20]

When this was said, the Venerable Moḷiyaphagguna said to the Blessed One: "Venerable sir, who consumes the nutriment consciousness?"[21]

"Not a valid question," the Blessed One replied. "I do not say, 'One consumes.'[22] If I should say, 'One consumes,' in that case this would be a valid question: 'Venerable sir, who consumes?' But I do not speak thus. Since I do not speak thus, if one should ask me, 'Venerable sir, for what is the nutriment consciousness [a condition]?'[23] this would be a valid question. To this the valid answer is: 'The nutriment consciousness is a condition for the production of future renewed existence.[24] When that which has come into being exists, the six sense bases [come to be];[25] with the six sense bases as condition, contact.'"

"Venerable sir, who makes contact?"

"Not a valid question," the Blessed One replied. "I do not say, 'One makes contact.' If I should say, 'One makes contact,' in that case this would be a valid question: 'Venerable sir, who makes contact?' But I do not speak thus. Since I do not speak thus, if one should ask me, 'Venerable sir, with what as condition does contact [come to be]?' this would be a valid question. To this the valid answer is: 'With the six sense bases as condition, contact [comes to be]; with contact as condition, feeling.'"

"Venerable sir, who feels?"

"Not a valid question," the Blessed One replied. "I do not say, 'One feels.' If I should say, 'One feels,' in that case this would be a valid question: 'Venerable sir, who feels?' But I do not speak thus. Since I do not speak thus, if one should ask me, 'Venerable sir, with what as condition does feeling [come to be]?' this would be a valid question. To this the valid answer is: 'With contact as condition, feeling [comes to be]; with feeling as condition, craving.'"

"Venerable sir, who craves?"

"Not a valid question," the Blessed One replied. "I do not say, 'One craves.' [14] If I should say, 'One craves,' in that case this would be a valid question: 'Venerable sir, who craves?' But I do not speak thus. Since I do not speak thus, if one should ask me, 'Venerable sir, with what as condition does craving [come to be]?' this would be a valid question. To this the valid answer is: 'With feeling as condition, craving [comes to be]; with craving as condition, clinging; with clinging as condition, existence....[26] Such is the origin of this whole mass of suffering.'

"But, Phagguna, with the remainderless fading away and cessation of the six bases for contact comes cessation of contact; with the cessation of contact, cessation of feeling; with the cessation of feeling, cessation of craving; with the cessation of craving, cessation of clinging; with the cessation of clinging, cessation of existence; with the cessation of existence, cessation of birth; with the cessation of birth, aging-and-death, sorrow, lamentation, pain, displeasure, and despair cease. Such is the cessation of this whole mass of suffering."

13 (3) Ascetics and Brahmins (1)

At Sāvatthī. "Bhikkhus, those ascetics or brahmins who do not understand aging-and-death, its origin, its cessation, and the way leading to its cessation;[27] who do not understand birth ... existence ... clinging ... craving ... feeling ... contact ... the six sense bases ... name-and-form ... consciousness ... volitional formations, their origin, their cessation, and the way leading to their cessation: [15] these I do not consider to be ascetics among ascetics or brahmins among brahmins, and these venerable ones do not, by realizing it for themselves with direct knowledge, in this very life enter and dwell in the goal of asceticism or the goal of brahminhood.[28]

"But, bhikkhus, those ascetics and brahmins who understand aging-and-death, its origin, its cessation, and the way leading to its cessation; who understand birth … volitional formations, their origin, their cessation, and the way leading to their cessation: these I consider to be ascetics among ascetics and brahmins among brahmins, and these venerable ones, by realizing it for themselves with direct knowledge, in this very life enter and dwell in the goal of asceticism and the goal of brahminhood."

14 (4) Ascetics and Brahmins (2)

At Sāvatthī. "Bhikkhus, as to those ascetics and brahmins who do not understand these things, the origin of these things, the cessation of these things, and the way leading to the cessation of these things: what are those things that they do not understand, whose origin they do not understand, whose cessation they do not understand, and the way leading to whose cessation they do not understand?

"They do not understand aging-and-death, its origin, its cessation, and the way leading to its cessation. They do not understand birth … existence … clinging … craving … feeling … contact … the six sense bases … name-and-form … consciousness … volitional formations, their origin, their cessation, and the way leading to their cessation. These are the things that they do not understand, whose origin they do not understand, [16] whose cessation they do not understand, and the way leading to whose cessation they do not understand.

"These I do not consider to be ascetics among ascetics or brahmins among brahmins, and these venerable ones do not, by realizing it for themselves with direct knowledge, in this very life enter and dwell in the goal of asceticism or the goal of brahminhood.

"But, bhikkhus, as to those ascetics and brahmins who understand these things, the origin of these things, the cessation of these things, and the way leading to the cessation of these things: what are those things that they understand, whose origin they understand, whose cessation they understand, and the way leading to whose cessation they understand?

"They understand aging-and-death, its origin, its cessation, and the way leading to its cessation. They understand birth … volitional formations, their origin, their cessation, and the way leading to their cessation. These are the things that they understand, whose origin they understand, whose cessation they understand, and the way leading to whose cessation they understand.

"These I consider to be ascetics among ascetics and brahmins among brahmins, and these venerable ones, by realizing it for themselves with direct knowledge, in this very life enter and dwell in the goal of asceticism and the goal of brahminhood."

15 (5) Kaccānagotta

At Sāvatthī. [17] Then the Venerable Kaccānagotta approached the Blessed One, paid homage to him, sat down to one side, and said to him: "Venerable sir, it is said, 'right view, right view.' In what way, venerable sir, is there right view?"

"This world, Kaccāna, for the most part depends upon a duality—upon the notion of existence and the notion of nonexistence.[29] But for one who sees the origin of the world as it really is with correct wisdom, there is no notion of nonexistence in regard to the world. And for one who sees the cessation of the world as it really is with correct wisdom, there is no notion of existence in regard to the world.[30]

"This world, Kaccāna, is for the most part shackled by engagement, clinging, and adherence.[31] But this one [with right view] does not become engaged and cling through that engagement and clinging, mental standpoint, adherence, underlying tendency; he does not take a stand about 'my self.'[32] He has no perplexity or doubt that what arises is only suffering arising, what ceases is only suffering ceasing. His knowledge about this is independent of others. It is in this way, Kaccāna, that there is right view.[33]

"'All exists': Kaccāna, this is one extreme. 'All does not exist': this is the second extreme. Without veering towards either of these extremes, the Tathāgata teaches the Dhamma by the middle: 'With ignorance as condition, volitional formations [come to be]; with volitional formations as condition, consciousness.... Such is the origin of this whole mass of suffering. But with the remainderless fading away and cessation of ignorance comes cessation of volitional formations; with the cessation of volitional formations, cessation of consciousness.... Such is the cessation of this whole mass of suffering." [18]

16 (6) A Speaker on the Dhamma

At Sāvatthī. Then a certain bhikkhu approached the Blessed One, paid homage to him, sat down to one side, and said to him: "Venerable sir, it is said, 'a speaker on the Dhamma, a speaker on the Dhamma.' In what way, venerable sir, is one a speaker on the Dhamma?"

"Bhikkhu, if one teaches the Dhamma for the purpose of revulsion towards aging-and-death, for its fading away and cessation, one is fit to be called a bhikkhu who is a speaker on the Dhamma. If one is practising for the purpose of revulsion towards aging-and-death, for its fading away and cessation, one is fit to be called a bhikkhu who is practising in accordance with the Dhamma.[34] If, through revulsion towards aging-and-death, through its fading away and cessation, one is liberated by nonclinging, one is fit to be called a bhikkhu who has attained Nibbāna in this very life.[35]

"Bhikkhu, if one teaches the Dhamma for the purpose of revulsion towards birth ... for the purpose of revulsion towards ignorance, for its fading away and cessation, one is fit to be called a bhikkhu who is a speaker on the Dhamma. If one is practising for the purpose of revulsion towards ignorance, for its fading away and cessation, one is fit to be called a bhikkhu who is practising in accordance with the Dhamma. If, through revulsion towards ignorance, through its fading away and cessation, one is liberated by nonclinging, one is fit to be called a bhikkhu who has attained Nibbāna in this very life."

17 (7) The Naked Ascetic Kassapa

Thus have I heard. On one occasion the Blessed One was dwelling at Rājagaha in the Bamboo Grove, the Squirrel Sanctuary. [19] Then, in the morning, the Blessed One dressed and, taking bowl and robe, entered Rājagaha for alms. The naked ascetic Kassapa saw the Blessed One coming in the distance. Having seen him, he approached the Blessed One and exchanged greetings with him. When they had concluded their greetings and cordial talk, he stood to one side and said to him: "We would like to ask Master Gotama about a certain point, if he would grant us the favour of answering our question."

"This is not the right time for a question, Kassapa. We have entered among the houses."[36]

A second time and a third time the naked ascetic Kassapa said to the Blessed One: "We would like to ask Master Gotama about a certain point, if he would grant us the favour of answering our question."

"This is not the right time for a question, Kassapa. We have entered among the houses."

Then the naked ascetic Kassapa said to the Blessed One: "We do not wish to ask Master Gotama much."

"Then ask what you want, Kassapa."

"How is it, Master Gotama: is suffering created by oneself?"

"Not so, Kassapa," the Blessed One said.

"Then, Master Gotama, is suffering created by another?"

"Not so, Kassapa," the Blessed One said.

"How is it then, Master Gotama: is suffering created both by oneself and by another?"

"Not so, Kassapa," the Blessed One said. [20]

"Then, Master Gotama, has suffering arisen fortuitously, being created neither by oneself nor by another?"[37]

"Not so, Kassapa," the Blessed One said.

"How is it then, Master Gotama: is there no suffering?"

"It is not that there is no suffering, Kassapa; there is suffering."

"Then is it that Master Gotama does not know and see suffering?"

"It is not that I do not know and see suffering, Kassapa. I know suffering, I see suffering."

"Whether you are asked: 'How is it, Master Gotama: is suffering created by oneself?' or 'Is it created by another?' or 'Is it created by both?' or 'Is it created by neither?' in each case you say: 'Not so, Kassapa.' When you are asked: 'How is it then, Master Gotama: is there no suffering?' you say: 'It is not that there is no suffering, Kassapa; there is suffering.' When asked: 'Then is it that Master Gotama does not know and see suffering?' you say: 'It is not that I do not know and see suffering, Kassapa. I know suffering, I see suffering.' Venerable sir, let the Blessed One explain suffering to me. Let the Blessed One teach me about suffering."[38]

"Kassapa, [if one thinks,] 'The one who acts is the same as the one who experiences [the result],' [then one asserts] with reference to one existing from the beginning: 'Suffering is created by oneself.' When one asserts thus, this amounts to eternalism.[39] But, Kassapa, [if one thinks,] 'The one who acts is one, the one who experiences [the result] is another,' [then one asserts] with reference to one stricken by feeling: 'Suffering is created by another.' When one asserts thus, this amounts to annihilationism.[40] Without veering towards either of these extremes, the Tathāgata teaches the Dhamma by the middle:[41] 'With ignorance as condition, volitional formations [come to be]; with volitional formations as condition, consciousness.... Such is the origin of this whole mass of suffering. [21] But with the remainderless fading away and cessation of ignorance comes cessation of volitional formations; with the cessation of volitional formations, cessation of consciousness.... Such is the cessation of this whole mass of suffering.'"

When this was said, the naked ascetic Kassapa said to the Blessed One: "Magnificent, venerable sir! Magnificent, venerable sir! The Dhamma has been made clear in many ways by the Blessed One, as though he were turning upright what had been turned upside down, revealing what was hidden, showing the way to one who was lost, or holding up a lamp in the dark for those with eyesight to see forms. I go for refuge to the Blessed One, and to the Dhamma, and to the Bhikkhu Saṅgha. May I receive the going forth under the Blessed One, may I receive the higher ordination?"[42]

"Kassapa, one formerly belonging to another sect who desires the going forth and the higher ordination in this Dhamma and Discipline lives on probation for four months. At the end of the four months, if the bhikkhus are satisfied with him, they may if they wish give him the going forth and the higher ordination to the state of a bhikkhu. But individual differences are recognized by me."[43]

"If, venerable sir, one formerly belonging to another sect who desires the going forth and the higher ordination in this Dhamma and Discipline lives on probation for four months, and if at the end of the four months the bhikkhus, being satisfied with him, may if they wish give him the going forth and the higher ordination to the state of a bhikkhu, then I will live on probation for four years. At the end of the four years, if the bhikkhus are satisfied with me, let them if they wish give me the going forth and the higher ordination to the state of a bhikkhu."

Then the naked ascetic Kassapa received the going forth under the Blessed One, and he received the higher ordination. And soon, not long after his higher ordination, dwelling alone, withdrawn, diligent, ardent, and resolute, the Venerable Kassapa, [22] by realizing it for himself with direct knowledge, in this very life entered and dwelt in that unsurpassed goal of the holy life for the sake of which clansmen rightly go forth from the household life into homelessness. He directly knew: "Destroyed is birth, the holy life has been lived, what had to be done has been done, there is no more for this state of being." And the Venerable Kassapa became one of the arahants.[44]

18 (8) Timbaruka

At Sāvatthī. Then the wanderer Timbaruka approached the Blessed One and exchanged greetings with him. When they had concluded their greetings and cordial talk, he sat down to one side and said to him: "How is it, Master Gotama: are pleasure and pain created by oneself?"[45]

"Not so, Timbaruka," the Blessed One said.

"Then, Master Gotama, are pleasure and pain created by another?"

"Not so, Timbaruka," the Blessed One said.

"How is it then, Master Gotama: are pleasure and pain created both by oneself and by another?"

"Not so, Timbaruka," the Blessed One said.

"Then, Master Gotama, have pleasure and pain arisen fortuitously, being created neither by oneself nor by another?"

"Not so, Timbaruka," the Blessed One said.

"How is it then, Master Gotama: is there no pleasure and pain?"

"It is not that there is no pleasure and pain, Timbaruka; there is pleasure and pain."

"Then is it that Master Gotama does not know and see pleasure and pain?"

"It is not that I do not know and see pleasure and pain, Timbaruka. I know pleasure and pain, I see pleasure and pain."

"Whether you are asked: 'How is it, Master Gotama: are pleasure and pain created by oneself?' or 'Are they created by another?' [23] or 'Are they created by both?' or 'Are they created by neither?' in each case you say: 'Not so, Timbaruka.' When you are asked: 'How is it then, Master Gotama: is there no pleasure and pain?' you say: 'It is not that there is no pleasure and pain, Timbaruka; there is pleasure and pain.' When asked: 'Then is it that Master Gotama does not know and see pleasure and pain?' you say: 'It is not that I do not know and see pleasure and pain, Timbaruka. I know pleasure and pain, I see pleasure and pain.' Venerable sir, let the Blessed One explain pleasure and pain to me. Let the Blessed One teach me about pleasure and pain."

"Timbaruka, [if one thinks,] 'The feeling and the one who feels it are the same,' [then one asserts] with reference to one existing from the beginning: 'Pleasure and pain are created by oneself.' I do not speak thus.[46] But, Timbaruka, [if one thinks,] 'The feeling is one, the one who feels it is another,' [then one asserts] with reference to one stricken by feeling: 'Pleasure and pain are created by another.' Neither do I speak thus.[47] Without veering towards either of these extremes, the Tathāgata teaches the Dhamma by the middle: 'With ignorance as condition, volitional formations [come to be]; with volitional formations as condition, consciousness.... Such is the origin of this whole mass of suffering. But with the remainderless fading away and cessation of ignorance comes cessation of volitional formations; with the cessation of volitional formations, cessation of consciousness.... Such is the cessation of this whole mass of suffering.'"

When this was said, the naked ascetic Timbaruka said to the Blessed One: "Magnificent, Master Gotama!... I go for refuge to Master Gotama, and to the Dhamma, and to the Bhikkhu Saṅgha. From today let Master Gotama remember me as a lay follower who has gone for refuge for life."

19 (9) The Wise Man and the Fool

At Sāvatthī. "Bhikkhus, for the fool, hindered by ignorance and fettered by craving, [24] this body has thereby originated. So there is this body and external name-and-form: thus this dyad. Dependent on the dyad there is contact. There are just six sense bases, contacted through which—or through a certain one among them—the fool experiences pleasure and pain.[48]

"Bhikkhus, for the wise man, hindered by ignorance and fettered by craving, this body has thereby originated. So there is this body and external name-and-form: thus this dyad. Dependent on the dyad there is contact. There are just six sense bases, contacted through which—or through a certain one among them—the wise man experiences pleasure and pain. What, bhikkhus, is the distinction here, what is the disparity, what is the difference between the wise man and the fool?"

"Venerable sir, our teachings are rooted in the Blessed One, guided by the Blessed One, take recourse in the Blessed One. It would be good if the Blessed One would clear up the meaning of this statement.[49] Having heard it from him, the bhikkhus will remember it."

"Then listen and attend closely, bhikkhus, I will speak."

"Yes, venerable sir," the bhikkhus replied. The Blessed One said this:

"Bhikkhus, for the fool, hindered by ignorance and fettered by craving, this body has originated. For the fool that ignorance has not been abandoned and that craving has not been utterly destroyed. For what reason? Because the fool has not lived the holy life for the complete destruction of suffering. Therefore, with the breakup of the body, the fool fares on to [another] body. Faring on to [another] body, he is not freed from birth, aging, and death; not freed from sorrow, lamentation, pain, displeasure, and despair; not freed from suffering, I say.

"Bhikkhus, for the wise man, hindered by ignorance and fettered by craving, this body has originated. For the wise man that ignorance has been abandoned and that craving has been utterly destroyed. For what reason? Because the wise man has lived the holy life [25] for the complete destruction of suffering. Therefore, with the breakup of the body, the wise man does not fare on to [another] body. Not faring on to [another] body, he is freed from birth, aging, and death; freed from sorrow, lamentation, pain, displeasure, and despair; freed from suffering, I say.

"This, bhikkhus, is the distinction, the disparity, the difference between the wise man and the fool, that is, the living of the holy life."[50]

20 (10) Conditions

At Sāvatthī. "Bhikkhus, I will teach you dependent origination and dependently arisen phenomena. Listen and attend closely, I will speak."

"Yes, venerable sir," those bhikkhus replied. The Blessed One said this:

"And what, bhikkhus, is dependent origination? 'With birth as condition, aging-and-death [comes to be]': whether there is an arising of Tathāgatas or no arising of Tathāgatas, that element still persists, the stableness of the Dhamma, the fixed course of the Dhamma, specific conditionality.[51] A Tathāgata awakens to this and breaks through to it.[52] Having done so, he explains it, teaches it, proclaims it, establishes it, discloses it, analyses it, elucidates it. And he says: 'See! With birth as condition, bhikkhus, aging-and-death.'[53]

"'With existence as condition, birth' … 'With clinging as condition, existence' … 'With craving as condition, clinging' … 'With feeling as condition, craving' … 'With contact as condition, feeling' … 'With the six sense bases as condition, contact' … 'With name-and-form as condition, the six sense bases' … 'With consciousness as condition, name-and-form' … 'With volitional formations as condition, consciousness' … 'With ignorance as condition, volitional formations': whether there is an arising of Tathāgatas or no arising of Tathāgatas, that element still persists, the stableness of the Dhamma, the fixed course of the Dhamma, specific conditionality. A Tathāgata awakens to this and [26] breaks through to it. Having done so, he explains it, teaches it, proclaims it, establishes it, discloses it, analyses it, elucidates it. And he says: 'See! With ignorance as condition, bhikkhus, volitional formations.'

"Thus, bhikkhus, the actuality in this, the inerrancy, the not-otherwiseness, specific conditionality: this is called dependent origination.[54]

"And what, bhikkhus, are the dependently arisen phenomena? Aging-and-death, bhikkhus, is impermanent, conditioned, dependently arisen, subject to destruction, vanishing, fading away, and cessation. Birth is impermanent … Existence is impermanent … Clinging is impermanent … Craving is impermanent … Feeling is impermanent … Contact is impermanent … The six sense bases are impermanent … Name-and-form is impermanent … Consciousness is impermanent … Volitional formations are impermanent … Ignorance is impermanent, conditioned, dependently arisen, subject to destruction, vanishing, fading away, and cessation. These, bhikkhus, are called the dependently arisen phenomena.

"When, bhikkhus, a noble disciple has clearly seen with correct wisdom[55] as it really is this dependent origination and these dependently arisen phenomena, it is impossible that he will run back into the past, thinking: 'Did I exist in the past? Did I not exist in the past? What was I in the past? How was I in the past? Having been what, what did I become in the past?' Or that he will run forward into the future, thinking: 'Will I exist in the future? Will I not exist [27] in the future? What will I be in the future? How will I be in the future? Having been what, what will I become in the future?' Or that he will now be inwardly confused about the present thus: 'Do I exist? Do I not exist? What am I? How am I? This being—where has it come from, and where will it go?'[56]

"For what reason [is this impossible]? Because, bhikkhus, the noble disciple has clearly seen with correct wisdom as it really is this dependent origination and these dependently arisen phenomena."

III. The Ten Powers

21 (1) The Ten Powers (1)

At Sāvatthī. "Bhikkhus, possessing the ten powers and the four grounds of self-confidence, the Tathāgata claims the place of the chief bull of the herd, roars his lion's roar in the assemblies, and sets rolling the Brahma-wheel thus:[57] [28] 'Such is form, such its origin, such its passing away; such is feeling, such its origin, such its passing away; such is perception, such its origin, such its passing away; such are volitional formations, such their origin, such their passing away; such is consciousness, such its origin, such its passing away.[58] Thus when this exists, that comes to be; with the arising of this, that arises. When this does not exist, that does not come to be; with the cessation of this, that ceases.[59] That is, with ignorance as condition, volitional formations [come to be]; with volitional formations as condition, consciousness.... Such is the origin of this whole mass of suffering. But with the remainderless fading away and cessation of ignorance comes cessation of volitional formations; with the cessation of volitional formations, cessation of consciousness.... Such is the cessation of this whole mass of suffering.'"

22 (2) The Ten Powers (2)

At Sāvatthī. "Bhikkhus, possessing the ten powers and the four grounds of self-confidence, the Tathāgata claims the place of the chief bull of the herd, roars his lion's roar in the assemblies, and sets rolling the Brahma-wheel thus: 'Such is form ... (*as in §21*) ... Such is the cessation of this whole mass of suffering.'

"Bhikkhus, the Dhamma has thus been well expounded by me, elucidated, disclosed, revealed, stripped of patchwork.[60] When, bhikkhus, the Dhamma has thus been well expounded by me, elucidated, disclosed, revealed, stripped of patchwork, this is enough for a clansman who has gone forth out of faith to arouse his energy thus: 'Willingly, let only my skin, sinews, and bones remain, and let the flesh and blood dry up in my body, but I will not relax my energy so long as I have not attained what can be attained by manly strength, by manly energy, by manly exertion.'[61] [29]

"Bhikkhus, the lazy person dwells in suffering, soiled by evil unwholesome states, and great is the personal good that he neglects.[62] But the energetic person dwells happily, secluded from evil unwholesome states, and great is the personal good that he achieves. It is not by the inferior that the supreme is attained; rather, it is by the supreme that the supreme is attained.[63] Bhikkhus, this holy life is a beverage of cream; the Teacher is present.[64] Therefore, bhikkhus, arouse your energy for the attainment of the as-yet-unattained, for the achievement of the as-yet-unachieved, for the realization of the as-yet-unrealized, [with the thought]: 'In such a way this going forth of ours will not be barren, but fruitful and fertile; and when we use the robes, almsfood, lodgings, and medicinal requisites [offered to us by others], these services they provide for us will be of great fruit and benefit to them.'[65] Thus, bhikkhus, should you train yourselves.

"Considering your own good, bhikkhus, it is enough to strive for the goal with diligence; considering the good of others, it is enough to strive for the goal with diligence; considering the good of both, it is enough to strive for the goal with diligence."[66]

23 (3) Proximate Cause

At Sāvatthī.[67] "Bhikkhus, I say that the destruction of the taints is for one who knows and sees, not for one who does not know and does not see. For one who knows what, for one who sees what, does the destruction of the taints come about? 'Such is form, such its origin, such its passing away; such is feeling ... such is perception ... such are volitional formations ... such is consciousness, such its origin, such its passing away': it is for one who knows thus, for one who sees thus, that the destruction of the taints comes about. [30]

"I say, bhikkhus, that the knowledge of destruction in regard to destruction has a proximate cause; it does not lack a proximate cause. And what is the proximate cause for the knowledge of destruction? It should be said: liberation.[68]

"I say, bhikkhus, that liberation too has a proximate cause; it does not lack a proximate cause. And what is the proximate cause for liberation? It should be said: dispassion.

"I say, bhikkhus, that dispassion too has a proximate cause; it does not lack a proximate cause. And what is the proximate cause for dispassion? It should be said: revulsion.

"I say, bhikkhus, that revulsion too has a proximate cause; it does not lack a proximate cause. And what is the proximate cause for revulsion? It should be said: the knowledge and vision of things as they really are.

"I say, bhikkhus, that the knowledge and vision of things as they really are too has a proximate cause; it does not lack a proximate cause. And what is the proximate cause for the knowledge and vision of things as they really are? It should be said: concentration.

"I say, bhikkhus, that concentration too has a proximate cause; it does not lack a proximate cause. And what is the proximate cause for concentration? It should be said: happiness.

"I say, bhikkhus, that happiness too has a proximate cause; it does not lack a proximate cause. And what is the proximate cause for happiness? It should be said: tranquillity.

"I say, bhikkhus, that tranquillity too has a proximate cause; it does not lack a proximate cause. And what is the proximate cause for tranquillity? It should be said: rapture.

"I say, bhikkhus, that rapture too has a proximate cause; it does not lack a proximate cause. And what is the proximate cause for rapture? It should be said: gladness.

"I say, bhikkhus, that gladness too has a proximate cause; it does not lack a proximate cause. And what is the proximate cause for gladness? It should be said: faith.

"I say, bhikkhus, that faith too has a proximate cause; it does not lack a proximate cause. [31] And what is the proximate cause for faith? It should be said: suffering.[69]

"I say, bhikkhus, that suffering too has a proximate cause; it does not lack a proximate cause. And what is the proximate cause for suffering? It should be said: birth.

"I say, bhikkhus, that birth too has a proximate cause; it does not lack a proximate cause. And what is the proximate cause for birth? It should be said: existence.

"I say, bhikkhus, that existence too has a proximate cause; it does not lack a proximate cause. And what is the proximate cause for existence? It should be said: clinging.

"I say, bhikkhus, that clinging too has a proximate cause; it does not lack a proximate cause. And what is the proximate cause for clinging? It should be said: craving.

"I say, bhikkhus, that craving too has a proximate cause; it does not lack a proximate cause. And what is the proximate cause for craving? It should be said: feeling.

"For feeling, it should be said: contact. For contact: the six sense bases. For the six sense bases: name-and-form. For name-and-form: consciousness. For consciousness: volitional formations.

"I say, bhikkhus, that volitional formations too have a proximate cause; they do not lack a proximate cause. And what is the proximate cause for volitional formations? It should be said: ignorance.

"Thus, bhikkhus, with ignorance as proximate cause, volitional formations [come to be]; with volitional formations as proximate cause, consciousness; with consciousness as proximate cause, name-and-form; with name-and-form as proximate cause, the six sense bases; with the six sense bases as proximate cause, contact; with contact as proximate cause, feeling; with feeling as proximate cause, craving; with craving as proximate cause, clinging; with clinging as proximate cause, existence; with existence as proximate cause, birth; with birth as proximate cause, suffering; with suffering as proximate cause, faith; with faith as proximate cause, gladness; with gladness as proximate cause, rapture; with rapture as proximate cause, tranquillity; with tranquillity as proximate cause, happiness; with happiness as proximate cause, concentration; with concentration as proximate cause, the knowledge and vision of things as they really are; [32] with the knowledge and vision of things as they really are as proximate cause, revulsion; with revulsion as proximate cause, dispassion; with dispassion as proximate cause, liberation; with liberation as proximate cause, the knowledge of destruction.

"Just as, bhikkhus, when rain pours down in thick droplets on a mountain top, the water flows down along the slope and fills the cleft, gullies, and creeks; these being full fill up the pools; these being full fill up the lakes; these being full fill up the streams; these being full fill up the rivers; and these being full fill up the great ocean;[70] so too, with ignorance as proximate cause, volitional formations [come to be]; with volitional formations as proximate cause, consciousness ... with liberation as proximate cause, the knowledge of destruction."

24 (4) Wanderers of Other Sects

At Rājagaha in the Bamboo Grove.

(i)

Then, in the morning, the Venerable Sāriputta dressed and, taking bowl and robe, entered Rājagaha for alms. Then it occurred to him: "It is still too early to walk for alms in Rājagaha. Let me go to the park of the wanderers of other sects."

Then the Venerable Sāriputta [33] went to the park of the wanderers of other sects. He exchanged greetings with those wanderers and, when they had concluded their greetings and cordial talk, he sat down to one side. The wanderers then said to him:

"Friend Sāriputta, some ascetics and brahmins, proponents of kamma, maintain that suffering is created by oneself; some ascetics and brahmins, proponents of kamma, maintain that suffering is created by another; some ascetics and brahmins, proponents of kamma, maintain that suffering is created both by oneself and by another; some ascetics and brahmins, proponents of kamma, maintain that suffering has arisen fortuitously, being created neither by oneself nor by another.[71] Now, friend Sāriputta, what does the ascetic Gotama say about this? What does he teach? How should we answer if we are to state what has been said by the ascetic Gotama and not misrepresent him with what is contrary to fact? And how should we explain in accordance with the Dhamma so that no reasonable consequence of our assertion would give ground for criticism?"[72]

"Friends, the Blessed One has said that suffering is dependently arisen. Dependent on what? Dependent on contact. If one were to speak thus one would be stating what has been said by the Blessed One and would not misrepresent him with what is contrary to fact; one would explain in accordance with the Dhamma, and no reasonable consequence of one's assertion would give ground for criticism.

"Therein, friends, in the case of those ascetics and brahmins, proponents of kamma, who maintain that suffering is created by oneself, that is conditioned by contact.[73] Also, in the case of those ascetics and brahmins, proponents of kamma, who maintain that suffering is created by another, that too is conditioned by contact. Also, in the case of those ascetics and brahmins, proponents of kamma, who maintain that suffering is created both by oneself and by another, that too is conditioned by contact. [34] Also, in the case of those ascetics and brahmins, proponents of kamma, who maintain that suffering has arisen fortuitously, being created neither by oneself nor by another, that too is conditioned by contact.

"Therein, friends, in the case of those ascetics and brahmins, proponents of kamma, who maintain that suffering is created by oneself, it is impossible that they will experience [anything] without contact. Also, in the case of those ascetics and brahmins, proponents of kamma, who maintain that suffering is created by another, it is impossible that they will experience [anything] without contact. Also, in the case of those ascetics and brahmins, proponents of kamma, who maintain that suffering is created both by oneself and by another, it is impossible that they will experience [anything] without contact. Also, in the case of those ascetics and brahmins, proponents of kamma, who maintain that suffering has arisen fortuitously, being created neither by oneself nor by another, it is impossible that they will experience [anything] without contact."

(ii)

The Venerable Ānanda heard this conversation between the Venerable Sāriputta and the wanderers of other sects. Then, when he had walked for alms in Rājagaha and had returned from the alms round, after his meal he approached the Blessed One, paid homage to him, sat down to one side, and reported to the Blessed One the entire conversation between the Venerable Sāriputta and those wanderers of other sects. [The Blessed One said:]

"Good, good, Ānanda! Anyone answering rightly would answer just as Sāriputta has done. I have said, Ānanda, that suffering is dependently arisen. Dependent on what? Dependent on contact. If one were to speak thus one would be stating what has been said by me and would not misrepresent me with what is contrary to fact; one would explain in accordance with the Dhamma, and no reasonable consequence of one's assertion would give ground for criticism.

"Therein, Ānanda, in the case of those ascetics and brahmins, proponents of kamma, who maintain that suffering is created by oneself … [35] … and those who maintain that suffering has arisen fortuitously, being created neither by oneself nor by another, that too is conditioned by contact.

"Therein, Ānanda, in the case of those ascetics and brahmins, proponents of kamma, who maintain that suffering is created by oneself … and those who maintain that suffering has arisen fortuitously, being created neither by oneself nor by another, it is impossible that they will experience [anything] without contact.

"On one occasion, Ānanda, I was dwelling right here in Rājagaha, in the Bamboo Grove, the Squirrel Sanctuary. Then, in the morning, I dressed and, taking bowl and robe, I entered Rājagaha for alms. Then it occurred to me: 'It is still too early to walk for alms in Rājagaha. Let me go to the park of the wanderers of other sects.' Then I went to the park of the wanderers of other sects. I exchanged greetings with those wanderers and, when we had concluded our greetings and cordial talk, I sat down to one side. The wanderers then said to me as I was sitting to one side: … (*the wanderers ask exactly the same question as they had asked Sāriputta and receive an identical reply*) [36] … it is impossible that they will experience [anything] without contact."

"It is wonderful, venerable sir! It is amazing, venerable sir! How the entire meaning can be stated by a single phrase! Can this same meaning be stated in detail in a way that is deep and deep in implications?"[74]

"Well then, Ānanda, clear up that same matter yourself."

"Venerable sir, if they were to ask me: 'Friend Ānanda, what is the source of aging-and-death, what is its origin, from what is it born and produced?'—being asked thus, I would answer thus: 'Friends, aging-and-death has birth as its source, birth as its origin; it is born and produced from birth.' Being asked thus, I would answer in such a way. [37]

"Venerable sir, if they were to ask me: 'Friend Ānanda, what is the source of birth, what is its origin, from what is it born and produced?'—being asked thus, I would answer thus: 'Friends, birth has existence as its source, existence as its origin; it is born and produced from existence.... Existence has clinging as its source ... Clinging has craving as its source ... Craving has feeling as its source ... Feeling has contact as its source ... Contact has the six sense bases as its source, the six sense bases as its origin; it is born and produced from the six sense bases. But with the remainderless fading away and cessation of the six bases for contact comes cessation of contact; with the cessation of contact, cessation of feeling; with the cessation of feeling, cessation of craving; with the cessation of craving, cessation of clinging; with the cessation of clinging, cessation of existence; with the cessation of existence, cessation of birth; with the cessation of birth, aging-and-death, sorrow, lamentation, pain, displeasure, and despair cease. Such is the cessation of this whole mass of suffering.' Being asked thus, venerable sir, I would answer in such a way."

25 (5) Bhūmija

At Sāvatthī.

(i)

Then, in the evening, the Venerable Bhūmija emerged from seclusion and approached the Venerable Sāriputta.[75] [38] He exchanged greetings with the Venerable Sāriputta and, when they had concluded their greetings and cordial talk, he sat down to one side and said to him:

"Friend Sāriputta, some ascetics and brahmins, proponents of kamma, maintain that pleasure and pain are created by oneself; some ascetics and brahmins, proponents of kamma, maintain that pleasure and pain are created by another; some ascetics and brahmins, proponents of kamma, maintain that pleasure and pain are created both by oneself and by another; some ascetics and brahmins, proponents of kamma, maintain that pleasure and pain have arisen fortuitously, being created neither by oneself nor by another.[76] Now, friend Sāriputta, what does the Blessed One say about this? What does he teach? How should we answer if we are to state what has been said by the Blessed One and not misrepresent him with what is contrary to fact? And how should we explain in accordance with the Dhamma so that no reasonable consequence of our assertion would give ground for criticism?"

"Friend, the Blessed One has said that pleasure and pain are dependently arisen. Dependent on what? Dependent on contact. If one were to speak thus one would be stating what has been said by the Blessed One and would not misrepresent him with what is contrary to fact; one would explain in accordance with the Dhamma, and no reasonable consequence of one's assertion would give ground for criticism.

"Therein, friend, in the case of those ascetics and brahmins, proponents of kamma, who maintain that pleasure and pain are created by oneself, and those who maintain that pleasure and pain are created by another, and those who maintain that pleasure and pain are created both by oneself and by another, and those who maintain that pleasure and pain have arisen fortuitously, being created neither by oneself nor by another—in each case that is conditioned by contact.

"Therein, friends, in the case of those ascetics and brahmins, proponents of kamma, who maintain that pleasure and pain are created by oneself, and those who maintain that pleasure and pain are created by another, and those who maintain that pleasure and pain are created both by oneself and by another, and those [39] who maintain that pleasure and pain have arisen fortuitously, being created neither by oneself nor by another—in each case it is impossible that they will experience [anything] without contact."

(ii)

The Venerable Ānanda heard this conversation between the Venerable Sāriputta and the Venerable Bhūmija. He then approached the Blessed One, paid homage to him, sat down to one side, and reported to the Blessed One the entire conversation between the Venerable Sāriputta and the Venerable Bhūmija. [The Blessed One said:]

"Good, good, Ānanda! Anyone answering rightly would answer just as Sāriputta has done. I have said, Ānanda, that pleasure and pain are dependently arisen. Dependent on what? Dependent on contact. If one were to speak thus one would be stating what has been said by me and would not misrepresent me with what is contrary to fact; one would explain in accordance with the Dhamma, and no reasonable consequence of one's assertion would give ground for criticism.

"Therein, Ānanda, in the case of those ascetics and brahmins, proponents of kamma, who maintain that pleasure and pain are created by oneself … and those who maintain that pleasure and pain have arisen fortuitously … in each case that is conditioned by contact.

"Therein, Ānanda, in the case of those ascetics and brahmins, proponents of kamma, who maintain that pleasure and pain are created by oneself … and those who maintain that pleasure and pain have arisen fortuitously … in each case it is impossible that they will experience [anything] without contact.

(iii)

"Ānanda, when there is the body, because of bodily volition pleasure and pain arise [40] internally; when there is speech, because of verbal volition pleasure and pain arise internally; when there is the mind, because of mental volition pleasure and pain arise internally—and with ignorance as condition.[77]

"Either on one's own initiative, Ānanda, one generates that bodily volitional formation conditioned by which pleasure and pain arise internally; or prompted by others one generates that bodily volitional formation conditioned by which pleasure and pain arise internally. Either deliberately, Ānanda, one generates that bodily volitional formation conditioned by which pleasure and pain arise internally; or undeliberately one generates that bodily volitional formation conditioned by which pleasure and pain arise internally.[78]

"Either on one's own initiative, Ānanda, one generates that verbal volitional formation conditioned by which pleasure and pain arise internally; or prompted by others one generates that verbal volitional formation conditioned by which pleasure and pain arise internally. Either deliberately, Ānanda, one generates that verbal volitional formation conditioned by which pleasure and pain arise internally; or undeliberately one generates that verbal volitional formation conditioned by which pleasure and pain arise internally.

"Either on one's own initiative, Ānanda, one generates that mental volitional formation[79] conditioned by which pleasure and pain arise internally; or prompted by others one generates that mental volitional formation conditioned by which pleasure and pain arise internally. Either deliberately, Ānanda, one generates that mental volitional formation conditioned by which pleasure and pain arise internally; or undeliberately one generates that mental volitional formation conditioned by which pleasure and pain arise internally.

"Ignorance is comprised within these states.[80] But with the remainderless fading away and cessation of ignorance that body does not exist conditioned by which that pleasure and pain arise internally; that speech does not exist conditioned by which that pleasure and pain arise internally; that mind does not exist conditioned by which [41] that pleasure and pain arise internally.[81] That field does not exist, that site does not exist, that base does not exist, that foundation does not exist conditioned by which that pleasure and pain arise internally."[82]

26 (6) Upavāṇa

At Sāvatthī. Then the Venerable Upavāṇa approached the Blessed One, paid homage to him, sat down to one side, and said to him:[83]

"Venerable sir, some ascetics and brahmins maintain that suffering is created by oneself; some ascetics and brahmins maintain that suffering is created by another; some ascetics and brahmins maintain that suffering is created both by oneself and by another; some ascetics and brahmins maintain that suffering has arisen fortuitously, being created neither by oneself nor by another. Now, venerable sir, what does the Blessed One say about this? What does he teach? How should we answer if we are to state what has been said by the Blessed One and not misrepresent him with what is contrary to fact? And how should we explain in accordance with the Dhamma so that no reasonable consequence of our assertion would give ground for criticism?"

"Upavāṇa, I have said that suffering is dependently arisen. Dependent on what? Dependent on contact. If one were to speak thus one would be stating what has been said by me and would not misrepresent me with what is contrary to fact; one would explain in accordance with the Dhamma, and no reasonable consequence of one's assertion would give ground for criticism.

"Therein, Upavāṇa, in the case of those ascetics and brahmins who maintain that suffering is created by oneself, and those who maintain that suffering is created by another, and those who maintain that suffering is created both by oneself and by another, and those who maintain that suffering has arisen fortuitously, being created neither by oneself nor by another—in each case that is conditioned by contact. [42]

"Therein, Upavāṇa, in the case of those ascetics and brahmins who maintain that suffering is created by oneself, and those who maintain that suffering is created by another, and those who maintain that suffering is created both by oneself and by another, and those who maintain that suffering has arisen fortuitously, being created neither by oneself nor by another—in each case it is impossible that they will experience [anything] without contact."

27 (7) Conditions

At Sāvatthī. "Bhikkhus, with ignorance as condition, volitional formations [come to be]; with volitional formations as condition, consciousness … Such is the origin of this whole mass of suffering.

"And what, bhikkhus, is aging-and-death? The aging of the various beings … (*as in* §2) … thus this aging and this death are together called aging-and-death. With the arising of birth there is the arising of aging-and-death; with the cessation of birth there is the cessation of aging-and-death. Just this Noble Eightfold Path is the way leading to the cessation of aging-and-death; that is, right view, right intention, right speech, right action, right livelihood, right effort, right mindfulness, right concentration.

"And what, bhikkhus, is birth?… existence?… clinging?… [43] … craving?… feeling?… contact?… the six sense bases?… name-and-form?… consciousness?… volitional formations? There are these three kinds of volitional formations: the bodily volitional formation, the verbal volitional formation, the mental volitional formation. With the arising of ignorance there is the arising of volitional formations. With the cessation of ignorance there is the cessation of volitional formations. Just this Noble Eightfold Path is the way leading to the cessation of volitional formations; that is, right view … right concentration.

"When, bhikkhus, a noble disciple thus understands the condition; thus understands the origin of the condition; thus understands the cessation of the condition; thus understands the way leading to the cessation of the condition,[84] he is then called a noble disciple who is accomplished in view, accomplished in vision, who has arrived at this true Dhamma, who sees this true Dhamma, who possesses a trainee's knowledge, a trainee's true knowledge, who has entered the stream of the Dhamma, a noble one with penetrative wisdom, one who stands squarely before the door to the Deathless."[85]

28 (8) Bhikkhu

At Sāvatthī. "Herein, bhikkhus, a bhikkhu understands aging-and-death, its origin, its cessation, and the way leading to its cessation. He understands birth … existence … clinging [44] … craving … feeling … contact … the six sense bases … name-and-form … consciousness … volitional formations, their origin, their cessation, and the way leading to their cessation.

"And what, bhikkhus, is aging-and-death?… (*as in preceding sutta*) … Just this Noble Eightfold Path is the way leading to the cessation of volitional formations; that is, right view … right concentration.

"When, bhikkhus, a bhikkhu thus understands aging-and-death, its origin, its cessation, and the way leading to its cessation; when he thus understands birth … existence … clinging … craving … feeling … contact … the six sense bases … name-and-form … [45] consciousness … volitional formations, their origin, their cessation, and the way leading to their cessation, he is then called a bhikkhu who is accomplished in view, accomplished in vision, who has arrived at this true Dhamma, who sees this true Dhamma, who possesses a trainee's knowledge, a trainee's true knowledge, who has entered the stream of the Dhamma, a noble one with penetrative wisdom, one who stands squarely before the door to the Deathless."

29 (9) *Ascetics and Brahmins (1)*

At Sāvatthī. "Bhikkhus, those ascetics or brahmins who do not fully understand aging-and-death, its origin, its cessation, and the way leading to its cessation;[86] who do not fully understand birth ... existence ... clinging ... craving ... feeling ... contact ... the six sense bases ... name-and-form ... consciousness ... volitional formations, their origin, their cessation, and the way leading to their cessation: these I do not consider to be ascetics among ascetics or brahmins among brahmins, and these venerable ones do not, by realizing it for themselves with direct knowledge, in this very life enter and dwell in the goal of asceticism or the goal of brahminhood.

"But, bhikkhus, those ascetics and brahmins who fully understand aging-and-death, its origin, its cessation, and the way leading to its cessation; who fully understand birth ... volitional formations, [46] their origin, their cessation, and the way leading to their cessation: these I consider to be ascetics among ascetics and brahmins among brahmins, and these venerable ones, by realizing it for themselves with direct knowledge, in this very life enter and dwell in the goal of asceticism and the goal of brahminhood."

30 (10) *Ascetics and Brahmins (2)*

At Sāvatthī. "Bhikkhus, as to those ascetics or brahmins who do not understand aging-and-death, its origin, its cessation, and the way leading to its cessation: it is impossible that they will abide having transcended aging-and-death. As to those ascetics and brahmins who do not understand birth ... existence ... clinging ... craving ... feeling ... contact ... the six sense bases ... name-and-form ... consciousness ... volitional formations, their origin, their cessation, and the way leading to their cessation: it is impossible that they will abide having transcended volitional formations.

"But, bhikkhus, as to those ascetics or brahmins who understand aging-and-death, its origin, its cessation, and the way leading to its cessation: it is possible that they will abide having transcended aging-and-death. As to those ascetics and brahmins who understand birth ... volitional formations, their origin, their cessation, and the way leading to their cessation: it is possible that they will abide having transcended volitional formations."

[47] IV. The Kaḷāra Khattiya

31 (1) What Has Come to Be

On one occasion the Blessed One was dwelling at Sāvatthī.... There the Blessed One addressed the Venerable Sāriputta thus: "Sāriputta, in 'The Questions of Ajita' of the Pārāyana it is said:[87]

> 'Those who have comprehended the Dhamma,
> And the manifold trainees here:
> Asked about their way of conduct,
> Being discreet, tell me, dear sir.'[88]

How should the meaning of this, stated in brief, be understood in detail?"

When this was said, the Venerable Sāriputta was silent. A second time and a third time the Blessed One addressed the Venerable Sāriputta thus: "Sāriputta, in 'The Questions of Ajita' in the Pārāyana it is said ... [48] How should the meaning of this, stated in brief, be understood in detail?" A second time and a third time the Venerable Sāriputta was silent.[89]

"Sāriputta, do you see: 'This has come to be'? Sāriputta, do you see: 'This has come to be'?"

"Venerable sir, one sees as it really is with correct wisdom: 'This has come to be.' Having seen as it really is with correct wisdom: 'This has come to be,' one is practising for the purpose of revulsion towards what has come to be, for its fading away and cessation.[90] One sees as it really is with correct wisdom: 'Its origination occurs with that as nutriment.'[91] Having seen as it really is with correct wisdom: 'Its origination occurs with that as nutriment,' one is practising for the purpose of revulsion towards its origination through nutriment, for its fading away and cessation. One sees as it really is with correct wisdom: 'With the cessation of that nutriment, what has come to be is subject to cessation.' Having seen as it really is with correct wisdom: 'With the cessation of that nutriment, what has come to be is subject to cessation,' one is practising for the purpose of revulsion towards what is subject to cessation, for its fading away and cessation. It is in such a way that one is a trainee.

"And how, venerable sir, has one comprehended the

Dhamma? Venerable sir, one sees as it really is with correct wisdom: 'This has come to be.' Having seen as it really is with correct wisdom: 'This has come to be,' through revulsion towards what has come to be, through its fading away and cessation, one is liberated by nonclinging. One sees as it really is with correct wisdom: 'Its origination occurs with that as nutriment.' Having seen as it really is with correct wisdom: 'Its origination occurs with that as nutriment,' through revulsion towards its origination through nutriment, through its fading away and cessation, one is liberated by nonclinging. One sees as it really is with correct wisdom: 'With the cessation of that nutriment, what has come to be is subject to cessation.' Having seen as it really is with correct wisdom: 'With the cessation of that nutriment, what has come to be is subject to cessation,' through revulsion towards what is subject to cessation, through its fading away [49] and cessation, one is liberated by nonclinging.[92] It is in such a way that one has comprehended the Dhamma.

"Thus, venerable sir, when it is said in 'The Questions of Ajita' of the Pārāyana:

'Those who have comprehended the Dhamma,
And the manifold trainees here:
Asked about their way of conduct,
Being discreet, tell me, dear sir.'—

it is in such a way that I understand in detail the meaning of this that was stated in brief."

"Good, good, Sāriputta!... (*the Buddha repeats here the entire statement of the Venerable Sāriputta*) [50] ... it is in such a way that the meaning of this, stated in brief, should be understood in detail."

32 (2) The Kaḷāra

At Sāvatthī.

(i)

Then the bhikkhu Kaḷāra the Khattiya approached the Venerable Sāriputta and exchanged greetings with him. When they had concluded their greetings and cordial talk, he sat down to one side and said to the Venerable Sāriputta: "Friend Sāriputta, the bhikkhu Moḷiyaphagguna has abandoned the training and returned to the lower life."[93]

"Then surely that venerable did not find solace in this Dhamma and Discipline."

"Well then, has the Venerable Sāriputta attained solace in this Dhamma and Discipline?"

"I have no perplexity, friend."

"But as to the future, friend?"

"I have no doubt, friend."

Then the bhikkhu Kaḷāra the Khattiya rose from his seat and approached the Blessed One. Having approached, he paid homage to the Blessed One, sat down to one side, [51] and said to him: "Venerable sir, the Venerable Sāriputta has declared final knowledge thus: 'I understand: Destroyed is birth, the holy life has been lived, what had to be done has been done, there is no more for this state of being.'"[94]

Then the Blessed One addressed a certain bhikkhu thus: "Come, bhikkhu, tell Sāriputta in my name that the Teacher calls him."

"Yes, venerable sir," that bhikkhu replied, and he went to the Venerable Sāriputta and told him: "The Teacher calls you, friend Sāriputta."

"Yes, friend," the Venerable Sāriputta replied, and he approached the Blessed One, paid homage to him, and sat down to one side. The Blessed One then said to him: "Is it true, Sāriputta, that you have declared final knowledge thus: 'I understand: Destroyed is birth, the holy life has been lived, what had to be done has been done, there is no more for this state of being'?"

"Venerable sir, I did not state the matter in those terms and phrases."

"In whatever way, Sāriputta, a clansman declares final knowledge, what he has declared should be understood as such."

"Venerable sir, didn't I too speak thus: 'Venerable sir, I did not state the matter in those terms and phrases'?"

"If, Sāriputta, they were to ask you:[95] 'Friend Sāriputta, how have you known, how have you seen, that you have declared final knowledge thus: 'I understand: Destroyed is birth, the holy life has been lived, what had to be done has been done, there is no more for this state of being'—being asked thus, how would you answer?"

"If they were to ask me this, venerable sir, [52] I would answer thus: 'With the destruction of the source from which birth originates, I have understood: "When [the cause] is destroyed, [the effect] is destroyed." Having understood this, I understand: Destroyed is birth, the holy life has been lived, what had to be done has been done, there is no more for this state of being.' Being asked thus, venerable sir, I would answer in such a way."[96]

"But, Sāriputta, if they were to ask you: 'But, friend Sāriputta, what is the source of birth, what is its origin, from what is it born and produced?'—being asked thus, how would you answer?"

"If they were to ask me this, venerable sir, I would answer thus: 'Birth, friends, has existence as its source, existence as its origin; it is born and produced from existence.' Being asked thus, venerable sir, I would answer in such a way."

"But, Sāriputta, if they were to ask you: 'But, friend Sāriputta, what is the source of existence...?'—being asked thus, how would you answer?"

"If they were to ask me this, venerable sir, I would answer thus: 'Existence, friends, has clinging as its source....'"

"But, Sāriputta, if they were to ask you: 'But, friend Sāriputta, what is the source of clinging...? What is the source of craving, what is its origin, from what is it born and produced?'—being asked thus, how would you answer?" [53]

"If they were to ask me this, venerable sir, I would answer thus: 'Craving, friends, has feeling as its source, feeling as its origin; it is born and produced from feeling.' Being asked thus, venerable sir, I would answer in such a way."

"But, Sāriputta, if they were to ask you: 'Friend Sāriputta, how have you known, how have you seen, that delight in feelings no longer remains present in you?'—being asked thus, how would you answer?"[97]

"If they were to ask me this, venerable sir, I would answer thus: 'Friends, there are these three feelings. What three? Pleasant feeling, painful feeling, neither-painful-nor-pleasant feeling. These three feelings, friends, are impermanent; whatever is impermanent is suffering. When this was understood, delight in feelings no longer remained present in me.' Being asked thus, venerable sir, I would answer in such a way."

"Good, good, Sāriputta! This is another method of explaining in brief that same point: 'Whatever is felt is included within suffering.'[98] But, Sāriputta, if they were to ask you: 'Friend Sāriputta, through what kind of deliverance have you declared final knowledge thus: "I understand: Destroyed is birth, the holy life has been lived, what had to be done has been done, there is no more for this state of being"?'—being asked thus, how would you answer?"

"If they were to ask me this, venerable sir, I would answer thus: [54] 'Friends, through an internal deliverance, through the destruction of all clinging, I dwell mindfully in such a way that the taints do not flow within me and I do not despise myself.' Being asked thus, venerable sir, I would answer in such a way."[99]

"Good, good, Sāriputta! This is another method of explaining in brief that same point: 'I have no perplexity in regard to the taints spoken of by the Ascetic; I do not doubt that they have been abandoned by me.'"

This is what the Blessed One said. Having said this, the Sublime One rose from his seat and entered his dwelling.

(ii)

Then, soon after the Blessed One had departed, the Venerable Sāriputta addressed the bhikkhus thus:

"Friends, the first question that the Blessed One asked me had not been previously considered by me:[100] thus I hesitated over it. But when the Blessed One approved of my answer, it occurred to me: 'If the Blessed One were to question me about this matter with various terms and with various methods for a whole day, for a whole day I would be able to answer him with various terms and with various methods. If he were to question me about this matter with various terms and with various methods for a whole night, for a day and night, [55] for two days and nights, for three, four, five, six, or seven days and nights—for seven days and nights I would be able to answer him with various terms and with various methods.'"

Then the bhikkhu Kaḷāra the Khattiya rose from his seat and approached the Blessed One. Having approached, he paid homage to the Blessed One, sat down to one side, and said to him: "Venerable sir, the Venerable Sāriputta has roared his lion's roar thus: 'Friends, the first question that the Blessed One asked me had not been previously considered by me: thus I hesitated over it. But when the Blessed One approved of my answer, it occurred to me: "If the Blessed One were to question me about this matter for up to seven days and nights, [56] for up to seven days and nights I would be able to answer him with various terms and with various methods."'"

"Bhikkhu, the Venerable Sāriputta has thoroughly penetrated that element of the Dhamma by the thorough penetration of which, if I were to question him about that matter with various terms and with various methods for up to seven days and nights, for up to seven days and nights he would be able to answer me with various terms and with various methods."[101]

33 (3) Cases of Knowledge (1)

At Sāvatthī. "Bhikkhus, I will teach you forty-four cases of knowledge. Listen to that and attend closely, I will speak."

"Yes, venerable sir," those bhikkhus replied. The Blessed One said this:

"Bhikkhus, what are the forty-four cases of knowledge? [57] Knowledge of aging-and-death, knowledge of its origin, knowledge of its cessation, knowledge of the way leading to its cessation. Knowledge of birth ... Knowledge of existence ... Knowledge of clinging ... Knowledge of craving ... Knowledge of feeling ... Knowledge of contact ... Knowledge of the six sense bases ... Knowledge of name-and-form ... Knowledge of consciousness ... Knowledge of volitional formations, knowledge of their origin, knowledge of their cessation, knowledge of the way leading to their cessation. These, bhikkhus, are the forty-four cases of knowledge.

"And what, bhikkhus, is aging-and-death?... (*definition as in* §2) ... Thus this aging and this death are together called aging-and-death. With the arising of birth there is the arising of aging-and-death. With the cessation of birth there is the cessation of aging-and-death. This Noble Eightfold Path is the way leading to the cessation of aging-and-death; that is, right view ... right concentration.

"When, bhikkhus, a noble disciple thus understands aging-and-death, its origin, [58] its cessation, and the way leading to its cessation, this is his knowledge of the principle.[102] By means of this principle that is seen, understood, immediately attained, fathomed,[103] he applies the method to the past and to the future thus: 'Whatever ascetics and brahmins in the past directly knew aging-and-death, its origin, its cessation, and the way leading to its cessation, all these directly knew it in the very same way that I do now. Whatever ascetics and brahmins in the future will directly know aging-and-death, its origin, its cessation, and the way leading to its cessation, all these will directly know it in the very same way that I do now.' This is his knowledge of entailment.[104]

"When, bhikkhus, a noble disciple has purified and cleansed these two kinds of knowledge—knowledge of the principle and knowledge of entailment—he is then called a noble disciple who is accomplished in view, accomplished in vision, who has arrived at this true Dhamma, who sees this true Dhamma, who possesses a trainee's knowledge, a trainee's true knowledge, who has entered the stream of the Dhamma, a noble one with penetrative wisdom, one who stands squarely before the door to the Deathless.

"And what, bhikkhus, is birth?... What are the volitional formations?... (*definitions as in §2*) [59] ... This Noble Eightfold Path is the way leading to the cessation of volitional formations; that is, right view ... right concentration.

"When, bhikkhus, a noble disciple thus understands volitional formations, their origin, their cessation, and the way leading to their cessation, this is his knowledge of the principle. By means of this principle that is seen, understood, immediately attained, fathomed, he applies the method to the past and to the future.... This is his knowledge of entailment.

"When, bhikkhus, a noble disciple has purified and cleansed these two kinds of knowledge—knowledge of the principle and knowledge of entailment—he is then called a noble disciple who is accomplished in view ... one who stands squarely before the door to the Deathless."

34 (4) Cases of Knowledge (2)

At Sāvatthī. "Bhikkhus, I will teach you seventy-seven cases of knowledge. Listen to that and attend closely, I will speak." [60]

"Yes, venerable sir," those bhikkhus replied. The Blessed One said this:

"Bhikkhus, what are the seventy-seven cases of knowledge?

The knowledge: 'Aging-and-death has birth as its condition.' The knowledge: 'When there is no birth, there is no aging-and-death.' The knowledge: 'In the past too aging-and-death had birth as its condition.' The knowledge: 'In the past too, had there been no birth, there would have been no aging-and-death.' The knowledge: 'In the future too aging-and-death will have birth as its condition.' The knowledge: 'In the future too, should there be no birth, there will be no aging-and-death.' The knowledge: 'That knowledge of the stability of the Dhamma is also subject to destruction, vanishing, fading away, and cessation.'[105]

"The knowledge: 'Birth has existence as its condition.'... The knowledge: 'Volitional formations have ignorance as their condition.' The knowledge: 'When there is no ignorance, there are no volitional formations.' The knowledge: 'In the past too volitional formations had ignorance as their condition.' The knowledge: 'In the past too, had there been no ignorance, there would have been no volitional formations.' The knowledge: 'In the future too volitional formations will have ignorance as their condition.' The knowledge: 'In the future too, should there be no ignorance, there will be no volitional formations.' The knowledge: 'That knowledge of the stability of the Dhamma is also subject to destruction, vanishing, fading away, and cessation.'

"These, bhikkhus, are called the seventy-seven cases of knowledge."

35 (5) With Ignorance as Condition (1)

At Sāvatthī. "Bhikkhus, with ignorance as condition, volitional formations [come to be]; with volitional formations as condition, consciousness.... Such is the origin of this whole mass of suffering."

When he had said this, a certain bhikkhu said to the Blessed One: "Venerable sir, what now is aging-and-death, and for whom is there this aging-and-death?"

"Not a valid question," the Blessed One replied.[106] [61] "Bhikkhu, whether one says, 'What now is aging-and-death, and for whom is there this aging-and-death?' or whether one says, 'Aging-and-death is one thing, the one for whom there is this aging-and-death is another'—both these assertions are identical in meaning; they differ only in the phrasing. If there is the view, 'The soul and the body are the same,' there is no living of the holy life; and if there is the view, 'The soul is one thing, the body is another,' there is no living of the holy life.[107] Without veering towards either of these extremes, the Tathāgata teaches the Dhamma by the middle: 'With birth as condition, aging-and-death.'"

"Venerable sir, what now is birth, and for whom is there this birth?"

"Not a valid question," the Blessed One replied. "Bhikkhu, whether one says, 'What now is birth, and for whom is there this birth?' or whether one says, 'Birth is one thing, the one for whom there is this birth is another'—both these assertions are identical in meaning; they differ only in the phrasing.... Without veering towards either of these extremes, the Tathāgata teaches the Dhamma by the middle: 'With existence as condition, birth.'"

"Venerable sir, what now is existence, and for whom is there this existence?"

"Not a valid question," the Blessed One replied. "Bhikkhu, whether one says, 'What now is existence, and for whom is there this existence?' or whether one says, 'Existence is one thing, the one for whom there is this existence is another'—both these assertions are identical in meaning; they differ only in the phrasing.... Without veering towards either of these extremes, the Tathāgata teaches the Dhamma by the middle: 'With clinging as condition, existence.... With craving as condition, clinging.... With feeling as condition, craving.... With contact as condition, feeling.... With the six sense bases as condition, contact.... With name-and-form as condition, the six sense bases.... [62] With consciousness as condition, name-and-form.... With volitional formations as condition, consciousness.'"

"Venerable sir, what now are volitional formations, and for whom are there these volitional formations?"

"Not a valid question," the Blessed One replied. "Bhikkhu, whether one says, 'What now are volitional formations, and for whom are there these volitional formations?' or whether one says, 'Volitional formations are one thing, the one for whom there are these volitional formations is another'—both these assertions are identical in meaning; they differ only in the phrasing. If there is the view, 'The soul and the body are the same,' there is no living of the holy life; and if there is the view, 'The soul is one thing, the body is another,' there is no living of the holy life. Without veering towards either of these extremes, the Tathāgata teaches the Dhamma by the middle: 'With ignorance as condition, volitional formations.'

"But with the remainderless fading away and cessation of ignorance, whatever kinds of contortions, manoeuvres, and vacillations there may be[108]—'What now is aging-and-death, and for whom is there this aging-and-death?' or 'Aging-and-death is one thing, the one for whom there is this aging-and-death is another,' or 'The soul and the body are the same,' or 'The soul is one thing, the body is another'—all these are abandoned, cut off at the root, made like a palm stump, obliterated so that they are no more subject to future arising.[109]

"With the remainderless fading away and cessation of ignorance, whatever kinds of contortions, manoeuvres, and vacillations there may be—'What now is birth, and for whom is there this birth?'... [63] ... 'What now are volitional formations, and for whom are there these volitional formations?' or 'Volitional formations are one thing, the one for whom there are these volitional formations is another,' or 'The soul and the body are the same,' or 'The soul is one thing, the body is another'—all these are abandoned, cut off at the root, made like a palm stump, obliterated so that they are no more subject to future arising."

36 (6) With Ignorance as Condition (2)

(*This sutta is identical with the preceding one, differing only in that the bhikkhus are addressed collectively throughout, and there is no interlocutor who asks inappropriate questions. The Buddha simply cites the invalid types of assertions on his own.*) [64]

37 (7) Not Yours

At Sāvatthī. "Bhikkhus, this body is not yours, nor does it belong to others.[110] [65] It is old kamma, to be seen as generated and fashioned by volition, as something to be felt.[111] Therein, bhikkhus, the instructed noble disciple attends carefully and closely to dependent origination itself thus: 'When this exists, that comes to be; with the arising of this, that arises. When this does not exist, that does not come to be; with the cessation of this, that ceases. That is, with ignorance as condition, volitional formations [come to be]; with volitional formations as condition, consciousness.... Such is the origin of this whole mass of suffering. But with the remainderless fading away and cessation of ignorance comes cessation of volitional formations; with the cessation of volitional formations, cessation of consciousness.... Such is the cessation of this whole mass of suffering."

38 (8) Volition (1)

At Sāvatthī. "Bhikkhus, what one intends, and what one plans, and whatever one has a tendency towards: this becomes a basis for the maintenance of consciousness. When there is a basis there is a support for the establishing of consciousness. When consciousness is established and has come to growth, there is the production of future renewed existence. When there is the production of future renewed existence, future birth, aging-and-death, sorrow, lamentation, pain, displeasure, and despair come to be. Such is the origin of this whole mass of suffering.[112]

"If, bhikkhus, one does not intend, and one does not plan, but one still has a tendency towards something, this becomes a basis for the maintenance of consciousness. When there is a basis, there is a support for the establishing of consciousness.... Such is the origin of this whole mass of suffering.[113]

"But, bhikkhus, when one does not intend, and one does not plan, and one does not have a tendency towards anything, no basis exists for the maintenance of consciousness. [66] When there is no basis, there is no support for the establishing of consciousness. When consciousness is unestablished and does not come to growth, there is no production of future renewed existence. When there is no production of future renewed existence, future birth, aging-and-death, sorrow, lamentation, pain, displeasure, and despair cease. Such is the cessation of this whole mass of suffering."[114]

39 (9) Volition (2)

At Sāvatthī. "Bhikkhus, what one intends, and what one plans, and whatever one has a tendency towards: this becomes a basis for the maintenance of consciousness. When there is a basis, there is a support for the establishing of consciousness. When consciousness is established and has come to growth, there is a descent of name-and-form.[115] With name-and-form as condition, the six sense bases [come to be]; with the six sense bases as condition, contact; with contact as condition, feeling … craving … clinging … existence … birth; with birth as condition, aging-and-death, sorrow, lamentation, pain, displeasure, and despair come to be. Such is the origin of this whole mass of suffering.

"If, bhikkhus, one does not intend, and one does not plan, but one still has a tendency towards something, this becomes a basis for the maintenance of consciousness. When there is a basis, there is a support for the establishing of consciousness. When consciousness is established and has come to growth, there is a descent of name-and-form. With name-and-form as condition, the six sense bases [come to be].... Such is the origin of this whole mass of suffering.

"But, bhikkhus, when one does not intend, and one does not plan, and one does not have a tendency towards anything, no basis exists for the maintenance of consciousness. When there is no basis, there is no support for the establishing of consciousness. When consciousness is unestablished and does not come to growth, there is no descent of name-and-form. With the cessation of name-and-form comes cessation of the six sense bases.... Such is the cessation of this whole mass of suffering."

40 (10) Volition (3)

At Sāvatthī. [67] "Bhikkhus, what one intends, and what one plans, and whatever one has a tendency towards: this becomes a basis for the maintenance of consciousness. When there is a basis, there is a support for the establishing of consciousness. When consciousness is established and has come to growth, there is inclination. When there is inclination, there is coming and going. When there is coming and going, there is passing away and being reborn.[116] When there is passing away and being reborn, future birth, aging-and-death, sorrow, lamentation, pain, displeasure, and despair come to be. Such is the origin of this whole mass of suffering.

"If, bhikkhus, one does not intend, and one does not plan, but one still has a tendency towards something, this becomes a basis for the maintenance of consciousness. When there is a basis, there is a support for the establishing of consciousness.... Such is the origin of this whole mass of suffering.

"But, bhikkhus, when one does not intend, and one does not plan, and one does not have a tendency towards anything, no basis exists for the maintenance of consciousness. When there is no basis, there is no support for the establishing of consciousness. When consciousness is unestablished and does not come to growth, there is no inclination. When there is no inclination, there is no coming and going. When there is no coming and going, there is no passing away and being reborn. When there is no passing away and being reborn, future birth, aging-and-death, sorrow, lamentation, pain, displeasure, and despair cease. Such is the cessation of this whole mass of suffering."[117]

[68] V. The Householder

41 (1) Five Fearful Animosities (1)

At Sāvatthī. Then the householder Anāthapiṇḍika approached the Blessed One, paid homage to him, and sat down to one side. The Blessed One then said to him:

"Householder, when five fearful animosities have subsided in a noble disciple, and he possesses the four factors of stream-entry, and he has clearly seen and thoroughly penetrated with wisdom the noble method, if he wishes he could by himself declare of himself: 'I am one finished with hell, finished with the animal realm, finished with the domain of ghosts, finished with the plane of misery, the bad destinations, the nether world. I am a stream-enterer, no longer bound to the nether world, fixed in destiny, with enlightenment as my destination.'[118]

"What are the five fearful animosities that have subsided? Householder, one who destroys life engenders, on account of such behaviour, fearful animosity pertaining to the present life and fearful animosity pertaining to the future life, and he experiences mental pain and displeasure.[119] Thus for one who abstains from destroying life, this fearful animosity has subsided.

"One who takes what is not given ... [69] ... who engages in sexual misconduct ... who speaks falsely ... who indulges in wine, liquor, and intoxicants that are a basis for negligence engenders, on account of such behaviour, fearful animosity pertaining to the present life and fearful animosity pertaining to the future life, and he experiences mental pain and displeasure. Thus for one who abstains from wine, liquor, and intoxicants that are a basis for negligence, this fearful animosity has subsided.

"These are the five fearful animosities that have subsided.

"What are the four factors of stream-entry that he possesses?[120] Here, householder, the noble disciple possesses confirmed confidence in the Buddha thus: 'The Blessed One is an arahant, perfectly enlightened, accomplished in true knowledge and conduct, fortunate, knower of the world, unsurpassed leader of persons to be tamed, teacher of devas and humans, the Enlightened One, the Blessed One.'

"He possesses confirmed confidence in the Dhamma thus: 'The Dhamma is well expounded by the Blessed One, directly visible, immediate, inviting one to come and see, applicable, to be personally experienced by the wise.'

"He possesses confirmed confidence in the Saṅgha thus: 'The Saṅgha of the Blessed One's disciples is practising the good way, practising the straight way, practising the true way, practising the proper way; that is, the four pairs of persons, the eight types of individuals—this [70] Saṅgha of the Blessed One's disciples is worthy of gifts, worthy of hospitality, worthy of offerings, worthy of reverential salutation, the unsurpassed field of merit for the world.'

"He possesses the virtues dear to the noble ones—unbroken, untorn, unblemished, unmottled, freeing, praised by the wise, ungrasped, leading to concentration.[121]

"These are the four factors of stream-entry that he possesses.

"And what is the noble method that he has clearly seen and thoroughly penetrated with wisdom?[122] Here, householder, the noble disciple attends closely and carefully to dependent origination itself thus: 'When this exists, that comes to be; with the arising of this, that arises. When this does not exist, that does not come to be; with the cessation of this, that ceases. That is, with ignorance as condition, volitional formations [come to be]; with volitional formations as condition, consciousness.... Such is the origin of this whole mass of suffering. But with the remainderless fading away and cessation of ignorance comes cessation of volitional formations; with the cessation of volitional formations, cessation of consciousness.... Such is the cessation of this whole mass of suffering.'

"This is the noble method that he has clearly seen and thoroughly penetrated with wisdom.

"When, householder, these five fearful animosities have subsided in a noble disciple, and he possesses these four factors of stream-entry, and he has clearly seen and thoroughly penetrated with wisdom this noble method, if he wishes he could by himself declare of himself: 'I am one finished with hell, finished with the animal realm, finished with the domain of ghosts, finished with the plane of misery, the bad destinations, the nether world. I am a stream-enterer, no longer bound to the nether world, fixed in destiny, with enlightenment as my destination.'"

42 (2) Five Fearful Animosities (2)

(*This sutta is identical with the preceding one except that it is addressed to "a number of bhikkhus."*) [71]

43 (3) Suffering

At Sāvatthī. [72] "Bhikkhus, I will teach you the origin and the passing away of suffering. Listen to that and attend closely, I will speak."[123]

"Yes, venerable sir," the bhikkhus replied. The Blessed One said this:

"And what, bhikkhus, is the origin of suffering? In dependence on the eye and forms, eye-consciousness arises. The meeting of the three is contact. With contact as condition, feeling [comes to be]; with feeling as condition, craving. This is the origin of suffering.

"In dependence on the ear and sounds ... In dependence on the nose and odours ... In dependence on the tongue and tastes ... In dependence on the body and tactile objects ... In dependence on the mind and mental phenomena, mind-consciousness arises. The meeting of the three is contact. With contact as condition, feeling [comes to be]; with feeling as condition, craving. This is the origin of suffering.

"And what, bhikkhus, is the passing away of suffering? In dependence on the eye and forms, eye-consciousness arises. The meeting of the three is contact. With contact as condition, feeling [comes to be]; with feeling as condition, craving. But with the remainderless fading away and cessation of that same craving comes cessation of clinging; with the cessation of clinging, cessation of existence; with the cessation of existence, cessation of birth; with the cessation of birth, aging-and-death, sorrow, lamentation, pain, displeasure, and despair cease. Such is the cessation of this whole mass of suffering. This is the passing away of suffering.

"In dependence on the ear and sounds … In dependence on the mind and mental phenomena, mind-consciousness arises. The meeting of the three is contact. With contact as condition, feeling [comes to be]; with feeling as condition, craving. But with the remainderless fading away and cessation of that same craving comes cessation of clinging … cessation of existence … cessation of birth; with the cessation of birth, aging-and-death, [73] sorrow, lamentation, pain, displeasure, and despair cease. Such is the cessation of this whole mass of suffering. This is the passing away of suffering."

44 (4) The World

At Sāvatthī. "Bhikkhus, I will teach you the origin and the passing away of the world. Listen to that and attend closely, I will speak."[124]

"Yes, venerable sir," the bhikkhus replied. The Blessed One said this:

"And what, bhikkhus, is the origin of the world? In dependence on the eye and forms, eye-consciousness arises. The meeting of the three is contact. With contact as condition, feeling [comes to be]; with feeling as condition, craving; with craving as condition, clinging; with clinging as condition, existence; with existence as condition, birth; with birth as condition, aging-and-death, sorrow, lamentation, pain, displeasure, and despair come to be. This, bhikkhus, is the origin of the world.

"In dependence on the ear and sounds … In dependence on the nose and odours … In dependence on the tongue and tastes … In dependence on the body and tactile objects … In dependence on the mind and mental phenomena, mind-consciousness arises. The meeting of the three is contact. With contact as condition, feeling [comes to be]; with feeling as condition, craving; with craving as condition, clinging … existence … birth; with birth as condition, aging-and-death, sorrow, lamentation, pain, displeasure, and despair come to be. This, bhikkhus, is the origin of the world.

"And what, bhikkhus, is the passing away of the world? In dependence on the eye and forms, eye-consciousness arises. The meeting of the three is contact. With contact as condition, feeling [comes to be]; with feeling as condition, craving. But with the remainderless fading away and cessation of that same craving comes cessation of clinging; with the cessation of clinging, cessation of existence; with the cessation of existence, cessation of birth; with the cessation of birth, aging-and-death, sorrow, lamentation, pain, displeasure, and despair cease. Such is the cessation of this whole mass of suffering. This, bhikkhus, is the passing away of the world.

"In dependence on the ear and sounds … [74] … In dependence on the mind and mental phenomena, mind-consciousness arises. The meeting of the three is contact. With contact as condition, feeling [comes to be]; with feeling as condition, craving. But with the remainderless fading away and cessation of that same craving comes cessation of clinging … cessation of existence … cessation of birth; with the cessation of birth, aging-and-death, sorrow, lamentation, pain, displeasure, and despair cease. Such is the cessation of this whole mass of suffering. This, bhikkhus, is the passing away of the world."

45 (5) At Ñātika

Thus have I heard. On one occasion the Blessed One was dwelling at Ñātika in the Brick Hall. Then, while the Blessed One was alone in seclusion, he uttered this Dhamma exposition:[125]

"In dependence on the eye and forms, eye-consciousness arises. The meeting of the three is contact. With contact as condition, feeling [comes to be]; with feeling as condition, craving; with craving as condition, clinging…. Such is the origin of this whole mass of suffering.

"In dependence on the ear and sounds … In dependence on the mind and mental phenomena, mind-consciousness arises. The meeting of the three is contact. With contact as condition, feeling [comes to be]; with feeling as condition, craving; with craving as condition, clinging…. Such is the origin of this whole mass of suffering.

"In dependence on the eye and forms, eye-consciousness arises.

The meeting of the three is contact. With contact as condition, feeling [comes to be]; with feeling as condition, craving. But with the remainderless fading away and cessation of that same craving comes cessation of clinging; with the cessation of clinging, cessation of existence.... Such is the cessation of this whole mass of suffering. [75]

"In dependence on the ear and sounds ... In dependence on the mind and mental phenomena, mind-consciousness arises. The meeting of the three is contact. With contact as condition, feeling [comes to be]; with feeling as condition, craving. But with the remainderless fading away and cessation of that same craving comes cessation of clinging; with the cessation of clinging, cessation of existence.... Such is the cessation of this whole mass of suffering."

Now on that occasion a certain bhikkhu was standing listening in on the Blessed One. The Blessed One saw him standing there listening in and said to him: "Did you hear that Dhamma exposition, bhikkhu?"

"Yes, venerable sir."

"Learn that Dhamma exposition, bhikkhu, master it and remember it. That Dhamma exposition is beneficial and relevant to the fundamentals of the holy life."

46 (6) A Certain Brahmin

At Sāvatthī. Then a certain brahmin approached the Blessed One and exchanged greetings with him. When they had concluded their greetings and cordial talk, he sat down to one side and said to him:

"How is it, Master Gotama: is the one who acts the same as the one who experiences [the result]?"[126]

"'The one who acts is the same as the one who experiences [the result]': this, brahmin, is one extreme." [76]

"Then, Master Gotama, is the one who acts one, and the one who experiences [the result] another?"

"'The one who acts is one, and the one who experiences [the result] is another': this, brahmin, is the second extreme. Without veering towards either of these extremes, the Tathāgata teaches the Dhamma by the middle: 'With ignorance as condition, volitional formations [come to be]; with volitional formations as condition, consciousness.... Such is the origin of this whole mass of suffering. But with the remainderless fading away and cessation of ignorance comes cessation of volitional formations; with the cessation of volitional formations, cessation of consciousness.... Such is the cessation of this whole mass of suffering.'"

When this was said, that brahmin said to the Blessed One: "Magnificent, Master Gotama!... I go for refuge to Master Gotama, and to the Dhamma, and to the Bhikkhu Saṅgha. From today let Master Gotama remember me as a lay follower who has gone for refuge for life."

47 (7) Jāṇussoṇi

At Sāvatthī. Then the brahmin Jāṇussoṇi approached the Blessed One and exchanged greetings with him. When they had concluded their greetings and cordial talk, he sat down to one side and said to him:[127]

"How is it, Master Gotama: does all exist?"

"'All exists': this, brahmin, is one extreme."

"Then, Master Gotama, does all not exist?"

"'All does not exist': this, brahmin, is the second extreme. Without veering towards either of these extremes, the Tathāgata teaches the Dhamma by the middle...."

When this was said, the brahmin Jāṇussoṇi said to the Blessed One: [77] "Magnificent, Master Gotama!... From today let Master Gotama remember me as a lay follower who has gone for refuge for life."

48 (8) A Cosmologist

At Sāvatthī. Then a brahmin who was a cosmologist[128] approached the Blessed One ... and said to him:

"How is it, Master Gotama: does all exist?"

"'All exists': this, brahmin, is the oldest cosmology."[129]

"Then, Master Gotama, does all not exist?"

"'All does not exist': this, brahmin, is the second cosmology."

"How is it, Master Gotama: is all a unity?"[130]

"'All is a unity': this, brahmin, is the third cosmology."

"Then, Master Gotama, is all a plurality?"[131]

"'All is a plurality': this, brahmin, is the fourth cosmology.

Without veering towards either of these extremes, the Tathāgata teaches the Dhamma by the middle…."

When this was said, that brahmin said to the Blessed One: "Magnificent, Master Gotama!… From today let Master Gotama remember me as a lay follower who has gone for refuge for life."

49 (9) The Noble Disciple (1)

At Sāvatthī. [78] "Bhikkhus, an instructed noble disciple does not think: 'When what exists does what come to be? With the arising of what does what arise? [When what exists do volitional formations come to be? When what exists does consciousness come to be?][132] When what exists does name-and-form come to be?… When what exists does aging-and-death come to be?'

"Rather, bhikkhus, the instructed noble disciple has knowledge about this that is independent of others: 'When this exists, that comes to be; with the arising of this, that arises. [When there is ignorance, volitional formations come to be. When there are volitional formations, consciousness comes to be.] When there is consciousness, name-and-form comes to be…. When there is birth, aging-and-death comes to be.' He understands thus: 'In such a way the world originates.'

"Bhikkhus, an instructed noble disciple does not think: 'When what does not exist does what not come to be? With the cessation of what does what cease? [When what does not exist do volitional formations not come to be? When what does not exist does consciousness not come to be?] When what does not exist does name-and-form not come to be?… When what does not exist does aging-and-death not come to be?'"

"Rather, bhikkhus, the instructed noble disciple has knowledge about this that is independent of others: 'When this does not exist, that does not come to be; with the cessation of this, that ceases. [When there is no ignorance, volitional formations do not come to be. When there are no volitional formations, consciousness does not come to be.] When there is no consciousness, name-and-form does not come to be…. When there is no birth, aging-and-death does not come to be.' He understands thus: 'In such a way the world ceases.' [79]

"Bhikkhus, when a noble disciple thus understands as they really are the origin and the passing away of the world, he is then called a noble disciple who is accomplished in view, accomplished in vision, who has arrived at this true Dhamma, who sees this true Dhamma, who possesses a trainee's knowledge, a trainee's true knowledge, who has entered the stream of the Dhamma, a noble one with penetrative wisdom, one who stands squarely before the door to the Deathless."

50 (10) The Noble Disciple (2)

(*This sutta is identical with the preceding one except that the passages enclosed in brackets there as absent in some editions are here clearly included in all editions.*) [80]

VI. Suffering (or The Tree)[133]

51 (1) Thorough Investigation

Thus have I heard. On one occasion the Blessed One was dwelling at Sāvatthī in Jeta's Grove, Anāthapiṇḍika's Park. There the Blessed One addressed the bhikkhus thus: "Bhikkhus!"

"Venerable sir!" those bhikkhus replied. The Blessed One said this:

"Bhikkhus, when a bhikkhu is making a thorough investigation, in what way should he thoroughly investigate for the utterly complete destruction of suffering?"[134]

"Venerable sir, our teachings are rooted in the Blessed One, guided by the Blessed One, [81] take recourse in the Blessed One. It would be good if the Blessed One would clear up the meaning of this statement. Having heard it from him, the bhikkhus will remember it."

"Then listen and attend closely, bhikkhus, I will speak."

"Yes, venerable sir," the bhikkhus replied. The Blessed One said this:

"Here, bhikkhus, when he makes a thorough investigation, a bhikkhu thoroughly investigates thus: 'The many diverse kinds of suffering that arise in the world [headed by] aging-and-death: what is the source of this suffering, what is its origin, from what is it born and produced? When what exists does aging-and-death come to be? When what does not exist does aging-and-death not come to be?'

"As he thoroughly investigates he understands thus: 'The many diverse kinds of suffering that arise in the world [headed by] aging-and-death: this suffering has birth as its source, birth as its origin; it is born and produced from birth. When there is birth, aging-and-death comes to be; when there is no birth, aging-and-death does not come to be.'

"He understands aging-and-death, its origin, its cessation, and the way leading on that is in conformity with its cessation.[135] He practises that way and conducts himself accordingly. This is called a bhikkhu who is practising for the utterly complete destruction of suffering, for the cessation of aging-and-death.

"Then, investigating further, he thoroughly investigates thus: 'What is the source of this birth, what is its origin, from what is it born and produced?... What is the source of this existence?... this clinging?... this craving?... this feeling?... this contact?... these six sense bases?... this name-and-form?... this consciousness?... What is the source of these volitional formations, what is their origin, from what are they born and produced? When what exists do volitional formations come to be? When what does not exist do volitional formations not come to be?'

"As he thoroughly investigates he understands thus: 'Volitional formations have ignorance as their source, ignorance as their origin; they are born and produced from ignorance. [82] When there is ignorance, volitional formations come to be; when there is no ignorance, volitional formations do not come to be.'

"He understands volitional formations, their origin, their cessation, and the way leading on that is in conformity with their cessation. He practises that way and conducts himself accordingly. This is called a bhikkhu who is practising for the utterly complete destruction of suffering, for the cessation of volitional formations.

"Bhikkhus, if a person immersed in ignorance generates a meritorious volitional formation, consciousness fares on to the meritorious; if he generates a demeritorious volitional formation, consciousness fares on to the demeritorious; if he generates an imperturbable volitional formation, consciousness fares on to the imperturbable.[136] But when a bhikkhu has abandoned ignorance and aroused true knowledge, then, with the fading away of ignorance and the arising of true knowledge, he does not generate a meritorious volitional formation, or a demeritorious volitional formation, or an imperturbable volitional formation. Since he does not generate or fashion volitional formations, he does not cling to anything in the world. Not clinging, he is not agitated.[137] Not being agitated, he personally attains Nibbāna. He understands: 'Destroyed is birth, the holy life has been lived, what had to be done has been done, there is no more for this state of being.'

"If he feels a pleasant feeling,[138] he understands: 'It is impermanent'; he understands: 'It is not held to'; he understands: 'It is not delighted in.' If he feels a painful feeling, he understands: 'It is impermanent'; he understands: 'It is not held to'; he understands: 'It is not delighted in.' If he feels a neither-painful-nor-pleasant feeling, he understands: 'It is impermanent'; he understands: 'It is not held to'; he understands: 'It is not delighted in.'

"If he feels a pleasant feeling, he feels it detached; if he feels a painful feeling, he feels it detached; if he feels a neither-painful-nor-pleasant feeling, he feels it detached. [83]

"When he feels a feeling terminating with the body, he understands: 'I feel a feeling terminating with the body.' When he feels a feeling terminating with life, he understands: 'I feel a feeling terminating with life.'[139] He understands: 'With the breakup of the body, following the exhaustion of life, all that is felt, not being delighted in, will become cool right here; mere bodily remains will be left.'[140]

"Suppose, bhikkhus, a man would remove a hot clay pot from a potter's kiln and set it on smooth ground: its heat would be dissipated right there and potsherds would be left. So too, when he feels a feeling terminating with the body ... terminating with life.... He understands: 'With the breakup of the body, following the exhaustion of life, all that is felt, not being delighted in, will become cool right here; mere bodily remains will be left.'[141]

"What do you think, bhikkhus, can a bhikkhu whose taints are destroyed generate a meritorious volitional formation, or a demeritorious volitional formation, or an imperturbable volitional formation?"

"No, venerable sir."

"When there are utterly no volitional formations, with the cessation of volitional formations, would consciousness be discerned?"[142]

"No, venerable sir."

"When there is utterly no consciousness, with the cessation of consciousness, would name-and-form be discerned?"

"No, venerable sir."

"When there is utterly no name-and-form … no six sense bases … [84] … no contact … no feeling … no craving … no clinging … no existence … no birth, with the cessation of birth, would aging-and-death be discerned?"

"No, venerable sir."

"Good, good, bhikkhus! It is exactly so and not otherwise! Place faith in me about this, bhikkhus, resolve on this. Be free from perplexity and doubt about this. Just this is the end of suffering."[143]

52 (2) Clinging

At Sāvatthī. "Bhikkhus, when one dwells contemplating gratification in things that can be clung to,[144] craving increases. With craving as condition, clinging [comes to be]; with clinging as condition, existence; with existence as condition, birth; with birth as condition, aging-and-death, sorrow, lamentation, pain, displeasure, and despair come to be. Such is the origin of this whole mass of suffering.

"Suppose, bhikkhus, [85] a great bonfire was burning, consuming ten, twenty, thirty, or forty loads of wood, and a man would cast dry grass, dry cowdung, and dry wood into it from time to time. Thus, sustained by that material, fuelled by it, that great bonfire would burn for a very long time. So too, when one lives contemplating gratification in things that can be clung to, craving increases…. Such is the origin of this whole mass of suffering.

"Bhikkhus, when one dwells contemplating danger in things that can be clung to, craving ceases. With the cessation of craving comes cessation of clinging; with the cessation of clinging, cessation of existence … cessation of birth … aging-and-death, sorrow, lamentation, pain, displeasure, and despair cease. Such is the cessation of this whole mass of suffering.[145]

"Suppose, bhikkhus, a great bonfire was burning, consuming ten, twenty, thirty, or forty loads of wood, and a man would not cast dry grass, dry cowdung, or dry wood into it from time to time. Thus, when the former supply of fuel is exhausted, that great bonfire, not being fed with any more fuel, lacking sustenance, would be extinguished. So too, when one lives contemplating danger in things that can be clung to, craving ceases.... Such is the cessation of this whole mass of suffering."[146] [86]

53 (3) Fetters (1)

At Sāvatthī. "Bhikkhus, when one dwells contemplating gratification in things that can fetter,[147] craving increases. With craving as condition, clinging [comes to be]; with clinging as condition, existence; with existence as condition, birth; with birth as condition, aging-and-death, sorrow, lamentation, pain, displeasure, and despair come to be. Such is the origin of this whole mass of suffering.

"Suppose, bhikkhus, an oil lamp was burning in dependence on oil and a wick, and a man would pour oil into it and adjust the wick from time to time. Thus, sustained by that oil, fuelled by it, that oil lamp would burn for a very long time. So too, when one lives contemplating gratification in things that can fetter, craving increases.... Such is the origin of this whole mass of suffering.

"Bhikkhus, when one dwells contemplating danger in things that can fetter, craving ceases. With the cessation of craving comes cessation of clinging; with the cessation of clinging, cessation of existence ... cessation of birth ... aging-and-death, sorrow, lamentation, pain, displeasure, and despair cease. Such is the cessation of this whole mass of suffering.

"Suppose, bhikkhus, an oil lamp was burning in dependence on oil and a wick, and the man would not pour oil into it or adjust the wick from time to time. Thus, when the former supply of fuel is exhausted, that oil lamp, not being fed with any more fuel, lacking sustenance, would be extinguished. So too, when one lives contemplating danger in things that can fetter, craving ceases.... Such is the cessation of this whole mass of suffering." [87]

54 (4) Fetters (2)

(This sutta is identical with the preceding one except that in both the sections on origination and cessation the similes come first and their applications only afterwards.)

55 (5) The Great Tree (1)

At Sāvatthī. "Bhikkhus, when one dwells contemplating gratification in things that can be clung to, craving increases. With craving as condition, clinging [comes to be].... Such is the origin of this whole mass of suffering.

"Suppose, bhikkhus, there was a great tree, and all its roots going downwards and across would send the sap upwards. Sustained by that sap, nourished by it, that great tree would stand for a very long time. So too, when one lives contemplating gratification in things that can be clung to, craving increases.... Such is the origin of this whole mass of suffering.[148] [88]

"When, bhikkhus, one dwells contemplating danger in things that can be clung to, craving ceases. With the cessation of craving comes cessation of clinging.... Such is the cessation of this whole mass of suffering.

"Suppose, bhikkhus, there was a great tree. Then a man would come along bringing a shovel and a basket. He would cut down the tree at its foot, dig it up, and pull out the roots, even the fine rootlets and root-fibre. He would cut the tree into pieces, split the pieces, and reduce them to slivers. Then he would dry the slivers in the wind and sun, burn them in a fire, and collect the ashes. Having done so, he would winnow the ashes in a strong wind or let them be carried away by the swift current of a river. Thus that great tree would be cut off at the root, made like a palm stump, obliterated so that it is no more subject to future arising.

"So too, bhikkhus, when one dwells contemplating danger in things that can be clung to, craving ceases.... Such is the cessation of this whole mass of suffering."[149]

56 (6) The Great Tree (2)

(*This sutta is identical with the preceding one except that in both the sections on origination and cessation the similes come first and their applications only afterwards.*) [89]

57 (7) The Sapling

At Sāvatthī. "Bhikkhus, when one dwells contemplating gratification in things that can fetter, craving increases. With craving as condition, clinging [comes to be].... Such is the origin of this whole mass of suffering.

"Suppose, bhikkhus, there was a sapling, and from time to time a man would clear the area around the roots, from time to time provide it with good soil, from time to time water it. Sustained by that care, nourished by it, that sapling would attain to growth, increase, and expansion. So too, when one dwells contemplating gratification in things that can fetter, craving increases.... Such is the origin of this whole mass of suffering.

"When, bhikkhus, one dwells contemplating danger in things that can fetter, craving ceases. With the cessation of craving comes cessation of clinging.... Such is the cessation of this whole mass of suffering. [90]

"Suppose, bhikkhus, there was a sapling. Then a man would come along bringing a shovel and a basket. He would cut down the sapling at its foot ... (*as in §55*) ... he would winnow the ashes in a strong wind or let them be carried away by the swift current of a river. Thus that sapling would be cut off at the root, made like a palm stump, obliterated so that it is no more subject to future arising.

"So too, bhikkhus, when one dwells contemplating danger in things that can fetter, craving ceases.... Such is the cessation of this whole mass of suffering."

58 (8) Name-and-Form

At Sāvatthī. "Bhikkhus, when one dwells contemplating gratification in things that can fetter, there is a descent of name-and-form.[150] With name-and-form as condition, the six sense bases [come to be].... Such is the origin of this whole mass of suffering.

"Suppose, bhikkhus, there was a great tree, and all its roots going downwards and across would send the sap upwards. Sustained by that sap, nourished by it, that great tree would stand for a very long time. So too, when one lives contemplating gratification in things that can fetter, there is a descent of name-and-form.... Such is the origin of this whole mass of suffering.

"When, bhikkhus, one dwells contemplating danger in things that can fetter, there is no descent of name-and-form. [91] With the cessation of name-and-form comes cessation of the six sense bases.... Such is the cessation of this whole mass of suffering.

"Suppose, bhikkhus, there was a great tree. Then a man would come along bringing a shovel and a basket. He would cut down the tree at its foot ... he would winnow the ashes in a strong wind or let them be carried away by the swift current of a river. Thus that great tree would be cut off at the root, made like a palm stump, obliterated so that it is no more subject to future arising.

"So too, bhikkhus, when one dwells contemplating danger in things that can fetter, there is no descent of name-and-form.... Such is the cessation of this whole mass of suffering."

59 (9) Consciousness

At Sāvatthī. "Bhikkhus, when one dwells contemplating gratification in things that can fetter, there is a descent of consciousness.[151] With consciousness as condition, name-and-form [comes to be].... Such is the origin of this whole mass of suffering.

"Suppose, bhikkhus, there was a great tree, and all its roots going downwards and across would send the sap upwards. Sustained by that sap, nourished by it, that great tree would stand for a very long time. So too, when one lives contemplating gratification in things that can fetter, there is a descent of consciousness.... Such is the origin of this whole mass of suffering.

"When, bhikkhus, one dwells contemplating danger in things that can fetter, there is no descent of consciousness. With the cessation of consciousness comes cessation of name-and-form.... Such is the cessation of this whole mass of suffering.

"Suppose, bhikkhus, there was a great tree. Then a man would come along bringing a shovel and a basket. He would cut down the tree at its foot ... he would winnow the ashes in a strong wind or let them be carried away by the swift current of a river. Thus that great tree would be cut off at the root, made like a palm stump, obliterated so that it is no more subject to future arising.

"So too, bhikkhus, when one dwells contemplating danger in things that can fetter, there is no descent of consciousness.... Such is the cessation of this whole mass of suffering." [92]

60 (10) Causation

On one occasion the Blessed One was dwelling among the Kurus, where there was a town of the Kurus named Kammāsadamma.

Then the Venerable Ānanda approached the Blessed One, paid homage to him, sat down to one side, and said to him:[152]

"It is wonderful, venerable sir! It is amazing, venerable sir! This dependent origination is so deep and so deep in implications, yet to me it seems as clear as clear can be."

"Not so, Ānanda! Not so, Ānanda! This dependent origination is deep and deep in implications. It is because of not understanding and not penetrating this Dhamma, Ānanda, that this generation has become like a tangled skein, like a knotted ball of thread, like matted reeds and rushes, and does not pass beyond the plane of misery, the bad destinations, the nether world, saṃsāra.

"Ānanda, when one dwells contemplating gratification in things that can be clung to, craving increases. With craving as condition, [93] clinging [comes to be].... Such is the origin of this whole mass of suffering.

"Suppose, Ānanda, there was a great tree, and all its roots going downwards and across would send the sap upwards. Sustained by that sap, nourished by it, that great tree would stand for a very long time. So too, when one lives contemplating gratification in things that can be clung to, craving increases.... Such is the origin of this whole mass of suffering.

"When, Ānanda, one dwells contemplating danger in things that can be clung to, craving ceases. With the cessation of craving comes cessation of clinging.... Such is the cessation of this whole mass of suffering.

"Suppose, Ānanda, there was a great tree. Then a man would come along bringing a shovel and a basket. He would cut down the tree at its foot ... he would winnow the ashes in a strong wind or let them be carried away by the swift current of a river. Thus that great tree would be cut off at the root, made like a palm stump, obliterated so that it is no more subject to future arising.

"So too, Ānanda, when one dwells contemplating danger in things that can be clung to, craving ceases. With the cessation of craving comes cessation of clinging; with the cessation of clinging, cessation of existence; with the cessation of existence, cessation of birth; with the cessation of birth, aging-and-death, sorrow, lamentation, pain, displeasure, and despair cease. Such is the cessation of this whole mass of suffering."

[94] VII. The Great Subchapter

61 (1) Uninstructed (1)

Thus have I heard. On one occasion the Blessed One was dwelling at Sāvatthī in Jeta's Grove, Anāthapiṇḍika's Park....

"Bhikkhus, the uninstructed worldling[153] might experience revulsion towards this body composed of the four great elements; he might become dispassionate towards it and be liberated from it. For what reason? Because growth and decline is seen in this body composed of the four great elements, it is seen being taken up and laid aside. Therefore the uninstructed worldling might experience revulsion towards this body composed of the four great elements; he might become dispassionate towards it and be liberated from it.

"But, bhikkhus, as to that which is called 'mind' and 'mentality' and 'consciousness'[154]—the uninstructed worldling is unable to experience revulsion towards it, unable to become dispassionate towards it and be liberated from it. For what reason? Because for a long time this has been held to by him, appropriated, and grasped thus: 'This is mine, this I am, this is my self.'[155] Therefore the uninstructed worldling is unable to experience revulsion towards it, unable to become dispassionate towards it and be liberated from it.

"It would be better, bhikkhus, for the uninstructed worldling to take as self this body composed of the four great elements rather than the mind. For what reason? Because this body composed of the four great elements is seen standing for one year, for two years, for three, four, five, or ten years, for twenty, thirty, forty, or fifty years, for a hundred years, [95] or even longer.[156] But that which is called 'mind' and 'mentality' and 'consciousness' arises as one thing and ceases as another by day and by night. Just as a monkey roaming through a forest grabs hold of one branch, lets that go and grabs another, then lets that go and grabs still another, so too that which is called 'mind' and 'mentality' and 'consciousness' arises as one thing and ceases as another by day and by night.[157]

"Therein, bhikkhus, the instructed noble disciple attends closely and carefully to dependent origination itself thus:[158] 'When this exists, that comes to be; with the arising of this, that arises.

When this does not exist, that does not come to be; with the cessation of this, that ceases. That is, with ignorance as condition, volitional formations [come to be]; with volitional formations as condition, consciousness.... Such is the origin of this whole mass of suffering. But with the remainderless fading away and cessation of ignorance comes cessation of volitional formations; with the cessation of volitional formations, cessation of consciousness.... Such is the cessation of this whole mass of suffering.

"Seeing thus, bhikkhus, the instructed noble disciple experiences revulsion towards form, revulsion towards feeling, revulsion towards perception, revulsion towards volitional formations, revulsion towards consciousness. Experiencing revulsion, he becomes dispassionate. Through dispassion [his mind] is liberated. When it is liberated there comes the knowledge: 'It's liberated.' He understands: 'Destroyed is birth, the holy life has been lived, what had to be done has been done, there is no more for this state of being.'"

62 (2) Uninstructed (2)

(*This sutta is identical with the preceding one from the opening down to the monkey simile. It then omits the monkey simile and continues as follows:*) [96]

"Therein, bhikkhus, the instructed noble disciple attends closely and carefully to dependent origination itself thus: 'When this exists, that comes to be; with the arising of this, that arises. When this does not exist, that does not come to be; with the cessation of this, that ceases.' Bhikkhus, in dependence on a contact to be experienced as pleasant, a pleasant feeling arises. With the cessation of that contact to be experienced as pleasant, the corresponding feeling—the pleasant feeling that arose in dependence on that contact to be experienced as pleasant—ceases and subsides. In dependence on a contact to be experienced as painful, a painful feeling arises. With the cessation of that contact to be experienced as painful, the corresponding feeling—the painful feeling [97] that arose in dependence on that contact to be experienced as painful—ceases and subsides. In dependence on a contact to be experienced as neither-painful-nor-pleasant, a neither-painful-nor-pleasant feeling arises. With the cessation of that contact to be experienced as neither-painful-nor-pleasant, the corresponding feeling—the neither-painful-nor-pleasant feeling that arose in dependence on that contact to be experienced as neither-painful-nor-pleasant—ceases and subsides.

"Bhikkhus, just as heat is generated and fire is produced from the conjunction and friction of two fire-sticks, but with the separation and laying aside of the sticks[159] the resultant heat ceases and subsides; so too, in dependence on a contact to be experienced as pleasant ... a contact to be experienced as painful ... a contact to be experienced as neither-painful-nor-pleasant, a neither-painful-nor-pleasant feeling arises.... With the cessation of that contact to be experienced as neither-painful-nor-pleasant, the corresponding feeling ... ceases and subsides.

"Seeing thus, bhikkhus, the instructed noble disciple experiences revulsion towards contact, revulsion towards feeling, revulsion towards perception, revulsion towards volitional formations, revulsion towards consciousness. Experiencing revulsion, he becomes dispassionate. Through dispassion [his mind] is liberated. When it is liberated there comes the knowledge: 'It's liberated.' He understands: 'Destroyed is birth, the holy life has been lived, what had to be done has been done, there is no more for this state of being.'"

63 (3) Son's Flesh

At Sāvatthī.[160] [98] "Bhikkhus, there are these four kinds of nutriment for the maintenance of beings that have already come to be and for the assistance of those about to come to be. What four? The nutriment edible food, gross or subtle; second, contact; third, mental volition; fourth, consciousness. These are the four kinds of nutriment for the maintenance of beings that have already come to be and for the assistance of those about to come to be.

"And how, bhikkhus, should the nutriment edible food be seen? Suppose a couple, husband and wife, had taken limited provisions and were travelling through a desert. They have with them their only son, dear and beloved. Then, in the middle of the desert, their limited provisions would be used up and exhausted, while the rest of the desert remains to be crossed. The husband and wife would think: 'Our limited provisions have been used up and exhausted, while the rest of this desert remains to be crossed. Let us kill our only son, dear and beloved, and prepare dried and spiced meat. By eating our son's flesh we can cross the rest of this desert. Let not all three of us perish!'

"Then, bhikkhus, the husband and wife would kill their only son, dear and beloved, prepare dried and roasted meat, and by eating their son's flesh they would cross the rest of the desert. While they are eating their son's flesh, they would beat their breasts and cry: 'Where are you, our only son? Where are you, our only son?'

"What do you think, bhikkhus? Would they eat that food for amusement or for enjoyment [99] or for the sake of physical beauty and attractiveness?"

"No, venerable sir."

"Wouldn't they eat that food only for the sake of crossing the desert?"

"Yes, venerable sir."

"It is in such a way, bhikkhus, that I say the nutriment edible food should be seen.[161] When the nutriment edible food is fully understood, lust for the five cords of sensual pleasure is fully understood.[162] When lust for the five cords of sensual pleasure is fully understood, there is no fetter bound by which a noble disciple might come back again to this world.[163]

"And how, bhikkhus, should the nutriment contact be seen? Suppose there is a flayed cow. If she stands exposed to a wall, the creatures dwelling in the wall would nibble at her. If she stands exposed to a tree, the creatures dwelling in the tree would nibble at her. If she stands exposed to water, the creatures dwelling in the water would nibble at her. If she stands exposed to the open air, the creatures dwelling in the open air would nibble at her. Whatever that flayed cow stands exposed to, the creatures dwelling there would nibble at her.

"It is in such a way, bhikkhus, that I say the nutriment contact should be seen.[164] When the nutriment contact is fully understood, the three kinds of feeling are fully understood. When the three kinds of feeling are fully understood, I say, there is nothing further that a noble disciple needs to do.[165]

"And how, bhikkhus, should the nutriment mental volition be seen? Suppose there is a charcoal pit deeper than a man's height, filled with glowing coals without flame or smoke. A man would come along wanting to live, not wanting to die, desiring happiness and averse to suffering. Then two strong men would grab him by both arms and drag him towards the charcoal pit. The man's volition would be to get far away, his longing would be to get far away, his wish would be to get far away [from the charcoal pit]. [100] For what reason? Because he knows: 'I will fall into this charcoal pit and on that account I will meet death or deadly suffering.'

"It is in such a way, bhikkhus, that I say the nutriment mental volition should be seen.[166] When the nutriment mental volition is fully understood, the three kinds of craving are fully understood. When the three kinds of craving are fully understood, I say, there is nothing further that a noble disciple needs to do.[167]

"And how, bhikkhus, should the nutriment consciousness be seen? Suppose they were to arrest a bandit, a criminal, and bring him before the king, saying: 'Sire, this man is a bandit, a criminal. Impose on him whatever punishment you wish.' The king says to them: 'Go, men, in the morning strike this man with a hundred spears.' In the morning they strike him with a hundred spears. Then at noon the king asks: 'Men, how's that man?' – 'Still alive, sire.' – 'Then go, and at noon strike him with a hundred spears.' At noon they strike him with a hundred spears. Then in the evening the king asks: 'Men, how's that man?' – 'Still alive, sire.' – 'Then go, and in the evening strike him with a hundred spears.' In the evening they strike him with a hundred spears.

"What do you think, bhikkhus? Would that man, being struck with three hundred spears, experience pain and displeasure on that account?"

"Venerable sir, even if he were struck with one spear he would experience pain and displeasure on that account, not to speak of three hundred spears."

"It is in such a way, bhikkhus, that I say the nutriment consciousness should be seen.[168] When the nutriment consciousness is fully understood, name-and-form is fully understood. When name-and-form is fully understood, I say, there is nothing further that a noble disciple needs to do."[169] [101]

64 (4) If There Is Lust

At Sāvatthī. "Bhikkhus, there are these four kinds of nutriment for the maintenance of beings that have already come to be and for the assistance of those about to come to be. What four? The nutriment edible food, gross or subtle; second, contact; third, mental volition; fourth, consciousness. These are the four kinds of nutriment for the maintenance of beings that have already come to be and for the assistance of those seeking a new existence.

"If, bhikkhus, there is lust for the nutriment edible food, if there is delight, if there is craving, consciousness becomes established there and comes to growth.[170] Wherever consciousness becomes established and comes to growth, there is a descent of name-and-form.[171] Where there is a descent of name-and-form, there is the growth of volitional formations.[172] Where there is the growth of volitional formations, there is the production of future renewed existence. Where there is the production of future renewed existence, there is future birth, aging, and death. Where there is future birth, aging, and death, I say that is accompanied by sorrow, anguish, and despair.

"If, bhikkhus, there is lust for the nutriment contact, or for the nutriment mental volition, or for the nutriment consciousness, if there is delight, if there is craving, consciousness becomes established there and comes to growth. Wherever consciousness becomes established and comes to growth ... I say that is accompanied by sorrow, anguish, and despair.

"Suppose, bhikkhus, an artist or a painter, using dye or lac or turmeric or indigo or crimson, [102] would create the figure of a man or a woman complete in all its features on a well-polished plank or wall or canvas. So too, if there is lust for the nutriment edible food, or for the nutriment contact, or for the nutriment mental volition, or for the nutriment consciousness, if there is delight, if there is craving, consciousness becomes established there and comes to growth. Wherever consciousness becomes established and comes to growth ... I say that is accompanied by sorrow, anguish, and despair.[173]

"If, bhikkhus, there is no lust for the nutriment edible food, or [103] for the nutriment contact, or for the nutriment mental volition, or for the nutriment consciousness, if there is no delight, if there is no craving, consciousness does not become established there and come to growth. Where consciousness does not become established and come to growth, there is no descent of name-and-form. Where there is no descent of name-and-form, there is no growth of volitional formations. Where there is no growth of volitional formations, there is no production of future renewed existence. Where there is no production of future renewed existence, there is no future birth, aging, and death. Where there is no future birth, aging, and death, I say that is without sorrow, anguish, and despair.

"Suppose, bhikkhus, there was a house or a hall with a peaked roof, with windows on the northern, southern, and eastern sides. When the sun rises and a beam of light enters through a window, where would it become established?"

"On the western wall, venerable sir."

"If there were no western wall, where would it become established?"

"On the earth, venerable sir."

"If there were no earth, where would it become established?"

"On the water, venerable sir."

"If there were no water, where would it become established?"

"It would not become established anywhere, venerable sir."

"So too, bhikkhus, if there is no lust for the nutriment edible food … for the nutriment contact … for the nutriment mental volition … for the nutriment consciousness … consciousness does not become established there and come to growth. Where consciousness does not become established and come to growth … [104] … I say that is without sorrow, anguish, and despair."[174]

65 (5) The City

At Sāvatthī. "Bhikkhus, before my enlightenment, while I was still a bodhisatta, not yet fully enlightened, it occurred to me: 'Alas, this world has fallen into trouble, in that it is born, ages, and dies, it passes away and is reborn, yet it does not understand the escape from this suffering [headed by] aging-and-death. When now will an escape be discerned from this suffering [headed by] aging-and-death?'[175]

"Then, bhikkhus, it occurred to me: 'When what exists does aging-and-death come to be? By what is aging-and-death conditioned?' Then, bhikkhus, through careful attention, there took place in me a breakthrough by wisdom: 'When there is birth, aging-and-death comes to be; aging-and-death has birth as its condition.'

"Then, bhikkhus, it occurred to me: 'When what exists does birth come to be?… existence?… clinging?… craving?… feeling?…

contact?... the six sense bases?... name-and-form? By what is name-and-form conditioned?' Then, bhikkhus, through careful attention, there took place in me a breakthrough by wisdom: 'When there is consciousness, name-and-form comes to be; name-and-form has consciousness as its condition.'

"Then, bhikkhus, it occurred to me: 'When what exists does consciousness come to be? By what is consciousness conditioned?' Then, bhikkhus, through careful attention, there took place in me a breakthrough by wisdom: 'When there is name-and-form, consciousness comes to be; consciousness has name-and-form as its condition.'[176]

"Then, bhikkhus, it occurred to me: 'This consciousness turns back; it does not go further than name-and-form.[177] It is to this extent that one may be born and age and die, pass away and be reborn, that is, when there is consciousness with name-and-form as its condition, and name-and-form with consciousness as its condition.[178] With name-and-form as condition, the six sense bases; with the six sense bases as condition, contact.... [105] Such is the origin of this whole mass of suffering.'

"'Origination, origination'—thus, bhikkhus, in regard to things unheard before there arose in me vision, knowledge, wisdom, true knowledge, and light.

"Then, bhikkhus, it occurred to me: 'When what does not exist does aging-and-death not come to be? With the cessation of what does the cessation of aging-and-death come about?' Then, bhikkhus, through careful attention, there took place in me a breakthrough by wisdom: 'When there is no birth, aging-and-death does not come to be; with the cessation of birth comes cessation of aging-and-death.'

"It occurred to me: 'When what does not exist does birth not come to be?... existence?... clinging?... craving?... feeling?... contact?... the six sense bases?... name-and-form? With the cessation of what does the cessation of name-and-form come about?' Then, bhikkhus, through careful attention, there took place in me a breakthrough by wisdom: 'When there is no consciousness, name-and-form does not come to be; with the cessation of consciousness comes cessation of name-and-form.'

"It occurred to me: 'When what does not exist does consciousness not come to be? With the cessation of what does the cessation of consciousness come about?' Then, bhikkhus, through careful attention, there took place in me a breakthrough by wisdom: 'When there is no name-and-form, consciousness does not come to be; with the cessation of name-and-form comes cessation of consciousness.'

"Then, bhikkhus, it occurred to me: 'I have discovered this path to enlightenment, that is, with the cessation of name-and-form comes cessation of consciousness; with the cessation of consciousness comes cessation of name-and-form; with the cessation of name-and-form, cessation of the six sense bases; with the cessation of the six sense bases, cessation of contact.... Such is the cessation of this whole mass of suffering.'[179]

"'Cessation, cessation'—thus, bhikkhus, in regard to things unheard before there arose in me vision, knowledge, wisdom, true knowledge, and light.

"Suppose, bhikkhus, a man wandering through a forest would see an ancient path, an ancient road travelled upon by people in the past. He would follow it and would see an ancient city, an ancient capital [106] that had been inhabited by people in the past, with parks, groves, ponds, and ramparts, a delightful place. Then the man would inform the king or a royal minister: 'Sire, know that while wandering through the forest I saw an ancient path, an ancient road travelled upon by people in the past. I followed it and saw an ancient city, an ancient capital that had been inhabited by people in the past, with parks, groves, ponds, and ramparts, a delightful place. Renovate that city, sire!' Then the king or the royal minister would renovate the city, and some time later that city would become successful and prosperous, well populated, filled with people, attained to growth and expansion.

"So too, bhikkhus, I saw the ancient path, the ancient road travelled by the Perfectly Enlightened Ones of the past.[180] And what is that ancient path, that ancient road? It is just this Noble Eightfold Path; that is, right view, right intention, right speech, right action, right livelihood, right effort, right mindfulness, right concentration. I followed that path and by doing so I have directly known aging-and-death, its origin, its cessation, and the way leading to its cessation. I have directly known birth … existence … clinging … craving … feeling … contact … the six sense bases … name-and-form … consciousness … volitional formations, their origin, their cessation, and the way leading to their cessation.[181] [107] Having directly known them, I have explained them to the bhikkhus, the bhikkhunīs, the male lay followers, and the female lay followers. This holy life, bhikkhus, has become successful and prosperous, extended, popular, widespread, well proclaimed among devas and humans."[182]

66 (6) Exploration

Thus have I heard. On one occasion the Blessed One was dwelling among the Kurus, where there was a town of the Kurus named Kammāsadamma. There the Blessed One addressed the bhikkhus thus: "Bhikkhus!"[183]

"Venerable sir!" those bhikkhus replied. The Blessed One said this:

"Do you engage in inward exploration, bhikkhus?"[184]

When this was said, one bhikkhu said to the Blessed One: "Venerable sir, I engage in inward exploration."

"How do you engage in inward exploration, bhikkhu?"

The bhikkhu then explained but the way he explained did not satisfy the Blessed One.[185] Then the Venerable Ānanda said: "Now is the time for this, Blessed One! Now is the time for this, Fortunate One! Let the Blessed One explain inward exploration. Having heard it from the Blessed One, the bhikkhus will remember it."

"Then listen and attend closely, Ānanda, I will speak."

"Yes, venerable sir," the bhikkhus replied. The Blessed One said this:

"Here, bhikkhus, when engaged in inward exploration, a bhikkhu explores thus: 'The many diverse kinds of suffering that arise in the world [headed by] aging-and-death: what is the source of this suffering, what is its origin, [108] from what is it born and produced? When what exists does aging-and-death come to be? When what does not exist does aging-and-death not come to be?'[186]

"As he explores he understands thus: 'The many diverse kinds of suffering that arise in the world [headed by] aging-and-death: this suffering has acquisition as its source, acquisition as its origin; it is born and produced from acquisition.[187] When there is acquisition, aging-and-death comes to be; when there is no acquisition, aging-and-death does not come to be.'

"He understands aging-and-death, its origin, its cessation, and the way leading on that is in conformity with its cessation.[188] He practises in that way and conducts himself accordingly. This is called a bhikkhu who is practising for the utterly complete destruction of suffering, for the cessation of aging-and-death.

"Then, engaging further in inward exploration, he explores thus: 'What is the source of this acquisition, what is its origin, from what is it born and produced? When what exists does acquisition come to be? When what is absent does acquisition not come to be?'

"As he explores he understands thus: 'Acquisition has craving as its source, craving as its origin; it is born and produced from craving. When there is craving, acquisition comes to be; when there is no craving, acquisition does not come to be.'

"He understands acquisition, its origin, its cessation, and the way leading on that is in conformity with its cessation. He practises in that way and conducts himself accordingly. This is called a bhikkhu who is practising for the utterly complete destruction of suffering, for the cessation of acquisition.

"Then, engaging further in inward exploration, he explores thus: 'When this craving arises, where does it arise? When it settles down, upon what does it settle?'

"As he explores he understands thus: 'Whatever in the world has a pleasant and agreeable nature: it is here that this craving arises when it arises; it is here that it settles when it settles down.'[189] And what in the world has a pleasant and agreeable nature? The eye has a pleasant and agreeable nature in the world: it is here that this craving arises when it arises; it is here that it settles when it settles down. So too the ear, [109] the nose, the tongue, the body, and the mind have a pleasant and agreeable nature: it is here that this craving arises when it arises; it is here that it settles when it settles down.

"Bhikkhus, whatever ascetics and brahmins in the past regarded that in the world with a pleasant and agreeable nature as permanent, as happiness, as self, as healthy, as secure: they nurtured craving. In nurturing craving they nurtured acquisition. In nurturing acquisition they nurtured suffering. In nurturing suffering they were not freed from birth, aging, and death; they were not freed from sorrow, lamentation, pain, displeasure, and despair; they were not freed from suffering, I say.

"Whatever ascetics and brahmins in the future will regard that in the world with a pleasant and agreeable nature as permanent, as happiness, as self, as healthy, as secure: they will nurture craving. In nurturing craving they will nurture acquisition. In nurturing acquisition they will nurture suffering. In nurturing suffering they will not be freed from birth, aging, and death; they will not be freed from sorrow, lamentation, pain, displeasure, and despair; they will not be freed from suffering, I say.

"Whatever ascetics and brahmins at present regard that in the world with a pleasant and agreeable nature as permanent, as happiness, as self, as healthy, as secure: they are nurturing craving. In nurturing craving they are nurturing acquisition. In nurturing acquisition they are nurturing suffering. In nurturing suffering they are not freed from birth, aging, and death; they are not freed from sorrow, lamentation, pain, displeasure, and despair; they are not freed from suffering, I say. [110]

"Suppose, bhikkhus, there was a bronze cup of a beverage having a fine colour, aroma, and taste, but it was mixed with poison. Then a man would come along, oppressed and afflicted by the heat, tired, parched, and thirsty. They would tell him: 'Good man, this beverage in the bronze cup has a fine colour, aroma, and taste, but it is mixed with poison. Drink it if you wish. If you drink it, it will gratify you with its colour, aroma, and taste, but by drinking it you will meet death or deadly suffering.' Suddenly, without reflecting, he would drink the beverage—he would not reject it—and thereby he would meet death or deadly suffering.[190]

"So too, bhikkhus, whatever ascetics and brahmins in the past … in the future … at present regard that in the world with a pleasant and agreeable nature as permanent, as happiness, as self, as healthy, as secure: they are nurturing craving. In nurturing craving … they are not freed from suffering, I say.[191]

"Bhikkhus, whatever ascetics and brahmins in the past regarded that in the world with a pleasant and agreeable nature as impermanent, as suffering, as nonself, as a disease, as fearful: they abandoned craving. In abandoning craving they abandoned acquisition. In abandoning acquisition they abandoned suffering. In abandoning suffering they were freed from birth, aging, and death; they were freed from sorrow, lamentation, pain, displeasure, and despair; they were freed from suffering, I say.

"Whatever ascetics and brahmins in the future [111] will

regard that in the world with a pleasant and agreeable nature as impermanent, as suffering, as nonself, as a disease, as fearful: they will abandon craving. In abandoning craving … they will be freed from suffering, I say.

"Whatever ascetics and brahmins at present regard that in the world with a pleasant and agreeable nature as impermanent, as suffering, as nonself, as a disease, as fearful: they are abandoning craving. In abandoning craving … they are freed from suffering, I say.

"Suppose, bhikkhus, there was a bronze cup of a beverage having a fine colour, aroma, and taste, but it was mixed with poison. Then a man would come along, oppressed and afflicted by the heat, tired, parched, and thirsty. They would tell him: 'Good man, this beverage in the bronze cup has a fine colour, aroma, and taste, but it is mixed with poison. Drink it if you wish. If you drink it, it will gratify you with its colour, aroma, and taste, but by drinking it you will meet death or deadly suffering.' Then the man would think: 'I can quench my thirst with water, whey, porridge, or soup, but I should not drink that beverage, since to do so would lead to my harm and suffering for a long time.' Having reflected, he would not drink the beverage but would reject it, [112] and thereby he would not meet death or deadly suffering.

"So too, bhikkhus, whatever ascetics and brahmins in the past … in the future … at present regard that in the world with a pleasant and agreeable nature as impermanent, as suffering, as nonself, as a disease, as fearful: they are abandoning craving. In abandoning craving … they are freed from suffering, I say."[192]

67 (7) The Sheaves of Reeds

On one occasion the Venerable Sāriputta and the Venerable Mahākoṭṭhita were dwelling at Bārāṇasī in the Deer Park at Isipatana.[193] Then, in the evening, the Venerable Mahākoṭṭhita emerged from seclusion and approached the Venerable Sāriputta. He exchanged greetings with the Venerable Sāriputta and, when they had concluded their greetings and cordial talk, he sat down to one side and said to him:

"How is it, friend Sāriputta: Is aging-and-death created by oneself, or is it created by another, [113] or is it created both by oneself and by another, or has it arisen fortuitously, being created neither by oneself nor by another?"[194]

"Friend Koṭṭhita, aging-and-death is not created by oneself, nor is it created by another, nor is it created both by oneself and by another, nor has it arisen fortuitously, being created neither by oneself nor by another. But rather, with birth as condition, aging-and-death [comes to be]."

"How is it, friend Sāriputta: Is birth created by oneself ... Is existence ... clinging ... craving ... feeling ... contact ... the six sense bases ... name-and-form created by oneself, or is it created by another, or is it created both by oneself and by another, or has it arisen fortuitously, being created neither by oneself nor by another?"

"Name-and-form, friend Koṭṭhita, is not created by oneself, nor is it created by another, nor is it created both by oneself and by another, nor has it arisen fortuitously, being created neither by oneself nor by another; but rather, with consciousness as condition, name-and-form [comes to be]."

"How is it, friend Sāriputta: Is consciousness created by oneself, or is it created by another, or is it created both by oneself and by another, or has it arisen fortuitously, being created neither by oneself nor by another?"

"Consciousness, friend Koṭṭhita, is not created by oneself, nor is it created by another, nor is it created both by oneself and by another, nor has it arisen fortuitously, being created neither by oneself nor by another; but rather, with name-and-form as condition, consciousness [comes to be]."[195] [114]

"Now we understand the Venerable Sāriputta's statement thus: 'Name-and-form, friend Koṭṭhita, is not created by oneself ... but rather, with consciousness as condition, name-and-form [comes to be].' Now we also understand the Venerable Sāriputta's [other] statement thus: 'Consciousness, friend Koṭṭhita, is not created by oneself ... but rather, with name-and-form as condition, consciousness [comes to be].' But how, friend Sāriputta, should the meaning of this statement be seen?"

"Well then, friend, I will make up a simile for you, for some intelligent people here understand the meaning of a statement by means of a simile. Just as two sheaves of reeds might stand leaning against each other, so too, with name-and-form as condition, consciousness [comes to be]; with consciousness as condition, name-and-form [comes to be]. With name-and-form as condition, the six sense bases [come to be]; with the six sense bases as condition, contact.... Such is the origin of this whole mass of suffering.

"If, friend, one were to remove one of those sheaves of reeds, the other would fall, and if one were to remove the other sheaf, the first would fall. So too, with the cessation of name-and-form comes cessation of consciousness; with the cessation of consciousness comes cessation of name-and-form. With the cessation of name-and-form comes cessation of the six sense bases; with the cessation of the six sense bases, cessation of contact.... Such is the cessation of this whole mass of suffering."

"It is wonderful, friend Sāriputta! It is amazing, friend Sāriputta! How well this has been stated by the Venerable Sāriputta. We rejoice in the Venerable Sāriputta's statement on these thirty-six grounds:[196] If, friend, a bhikkhu teaches the Dhamma for the purpose of revulsion towards aging-and-death, for its fading away and cessation, he can be called a bhikkhu who is a speaker on the Dhamma. [115] If a bhikkhu is practising for the purpose of revulsion towards aging-and-death, for its fading away and cessation, he can be called a bhikkhu who is practising in accordance with the Dhamma. If through revulsion towards aging-and-death, through its fading away and cessation, a bhikkhu is liberated by nonclinging, he can be called a bhikkhu who has attained Nibbāna in this very life.

"If, friend, a bhikkhu teaches the Dhamma for the purpose of revulsion towards birth ... existence ... clinging ... craving ... feeling ... contact ... the six sense bases ... name-and-form ... consciousness ... volitional formations ... ignorance, for its fading away and cessation, he can be called a bhikkhu who is a speaker on the Dhamma. If a bhikkhu is practising for the purpose of revulsion towards ignorance, for its fading away and cessation, he can be called a bhikkhu who is practising in accordance with the Dhamma. If through revulsion towards ignorance, through its fading away and cessation, a bhikkhu is liberated by nonclinging, he can be called a bhikkhu who has attained Nibbāna in this very life."

68 (8) Kosambī

On one occasion the Venerable Musīla, the Venerable Saviṭṭha, the Venerable Nārada, and the Venerable Ānanda were living at Kosambī in Ghosita's Park.[197]

Then the Venerable Saviṭṭha said to the Venerable Musīla: "Friend Musīla, apart from faith, apart from personal preference, apart from oral tradition, apart from reasoned reflection, apart from acceptance of a view after pondering it,[198] does the Venerable Musīla have personal knowledge thus: 'With birth as condition, aging-and-death [comes to be]'?"

"Friend Saviṭṭha, apart from faith, apart from personal preference, apart from oral tradition, apart from reasoned reflection, apart from acceptance of a view after pondering it, I know this, I see this: 'With birth as condition, aging-and-death [comes to be].'" [116]

"Friend Musīla, apart from faith ... apart from acceptance of a view after pondering it, does the Venerable Musīla have personal knowledge thus: 'With existence as condition, birth'?... 'With ignorance as condition, volitional formations'?"

"Friend Saviṭṭha, apart from faith ... apart from acceptance of a view after pondering it, I know this, I see this: 'With ignorance as condition, volitional formations.'"

"Friend Musīla, apart from faith ... apart from acceptance of a view after pondering it, does the Venerable Musīla have personal knowledge: 'With the cessation of birth comes cessation of aging-and-death'?... [117] ... 'With the cessation of ignorance comes cessation of volitional formations'?"

"Friend Saviṭṭha, apart from faith ... apart from acceptance of a view after pondering it, I know this, I see this: 'With the cessation of birth comes cessation of aging-and-death.'... 'With the cessation of ignorance comes cessation of volitional formations.'"

"Friend Musīla, apart from faith, apart from personal preference, apart from oral tradition, apart from reasoned reflection, apart from acceptance of a view after pondering it, does the Venerable Musīla have personal knowledge thus: 'Nibbāna is the cessation of existence'?"[199]

"Friend Saviṭṭha, apart from faith, apart from personal preference, apart from oral tradition, apart from reasoned reflection, apart from acceptance of a view after pondering it, I know this, I see this: 'Nibbāna is the cessation of existence.'"

"Then the Venerable Musīla is an arahant, one whose taints are destroyed."

When this was said, the Venerable Musīla kept silent.[200]

Then the Venerable Nārada said to the Venerable Saviṭṭha: "Friend Saviṭṭha, it would be good if I were asked that series of questions. Ask me that series of questions and I will answer you."[201]

"Then let the Venerable Nārada get to answer that series of questions. I will ask the Venerable Nārada that series of questions, and let him answer me."

(*Here the Venerable Saviṭṭha asks the Venerable Nārada the same series of questions as were addressed to the Venerable Musīla, and he answers in exactly the same way.*)

"Then the Venerable Nārada is an arahant, one whose taints are destroyed." [118]

"Friend, though I have clearly seen as it really is with correct wisdom, 'Nibbāna is the cessation of existence,' I am not an arahant, one whose taints are destroyed.[202] Suppose, friend, there was a well along a desert road, but it had neither a rope nor a bucket. Then a man would come along, oppressed and afflicted by the heat, tired, parched, and thirsty. He would look down into the well and the knowledge would occur to him, 'There is water,' but he would not be able to make bodily contact with it.[203] So too, friend, though I have clearly seen as it really is with correct wisdom, 'Nibbāna is the cessation of existence,' I am not an arahant, one whose taints are destroyed."[204]

When this was said, the Venerable Ānanda asked the Venerable Saviṭṭha: "When he speaks in such a way, friend Saviṭṭha, what would you say about the Venerable Nārada?"

"When he speaks in such a way, friend Ānanda, I would not say anything about the Venerable Nārada except what is good and favourable."[205]

69 (9) The Surge

Thus have I heard. On one occasion the Blessed One was dwelling at Sāvatthī in Jeta's Grove, Anāthapiṇḍika's Park. There the Blessed One said:

"Bhikkhus, the ocean surging causes the rivers to surge; the rivers surging cause the streams to surge; the streams surging cause the lakes to surge; the lakes surging cause the pools to surge. So too, ignorance surging causes volitional formations to surge; volitional formations surging cause consciousness to surge; consciousness surging causes name-and-form to surge; name-and-form surging causes the six sense bases to surge; the six sense bases surging cause contact to surge; contact surging causes feeling to surge; feeling surging causes craving to surge; craving surging causes clinging to surge; clinging [119] surging causes existence to surge; existence surging causes birth to surge; birth surging causes aging-and-death to surge.

"Bhikkhus, the ocean receding causes the rivers to recede; the rivers receding cause the streams to recede; the streams receding cause the lakes to recede; the lakes receding cause the pools to recede. So too, ignorance receding causes volitional formations to recede; volitional formations receding cause consciousness to recede … birth receding causes aging-and-death to recede."

70 (10) Susīma

Thus have I heard. On one occasion the Blessed One was dwelling at Rājagaha in the Bamboo Grove, the Squirrel Sanctuary.

(i)

Now on that occasion the Blessed One was honoured, respected, esteemed, venerated, and revered, and he obtained robes, almsfood, lodgings, and medicinal requisites. The Bhikkhu Saṅgha too was honoured, respected, esteemed, venerated, and revered, and the bhikkhus too obtained robes, almsfood, lodgings, and medicinal requisites. But the wanderers of other sects were not honoured, respected, esteemed, venerated, and revered, and they did not obtain robes, almsfood, lodgings, and medicinal requisites.

Now on that occasion the wanderer Susīma was residing in Rājagaha along with a large company of wanderers. [120] Then his company said to the wanderer Susīma: "Come, friend Susīma, lead the holy life under the ascetic Gotama. Master his Dhamma and teach it to us. We will master his Dhamma and preach it to the lay people. Thus we too will be honoured, respected, esteemed, venerated, and revered, and we too will obtain robes, almsfood, lodgings, and medicinal requisites."

"All right, friends," the wanderer Susīma replied. He then approached the Venerable Ānanda and exchanged greetings with him. When they had concluded their greetings and cordial talk, he sat down to one side and said to him: "Friend Ānanda, I wish to lead the holy life in this Dhamma and Discipline."

Then the Venerable Ānanda took the wanderer Susīma and approached the Blessed One. He paid homage to the Blessed One, and then he sat down to one side and said to him: "Venerable sir, this wanderer Susīma says that he wishes to lead the holy life in this Dhamma and Discipline."

"Well then, Ānanda, give him the going forth." The wanderer Susīma then received the going forth and the higher ordination under the Blessed One.[206]

(ii)

Now on that occasion a number of bhikkhus had declared final knowledge in the presence of the Blessed One, saying: "We understand: Destroyed is birth, the holy life has been lived, what had to be done has been done, there is no more for this state of being." The Venerable Susīma heard about this, [121] so he approached those bhikkhus, exchanged greetings with them, and then sat down to one side and said to them: "Is it true that you venerable ones have declared final knowledge in the presence of the Blessed One, saying: 'We understand: Destroyed is birth, the holy life has been lived, what had to be done has been done, there is no more for this state of being'?"[207]

"Yes, friend."

"Then knowing and seeing thus, do you venerable ones wield the various kinds of spiritual power, such that: having been one, you become many; having been many, you become one; you appear and vanish; you go unhindered through a wall, through a rampart, through a mountain as though through space; you dive in and out of the earth as though it were water; you walk on water without sinking as though it were earth; seated cross-legged, you travel in space like a bird; with your hand you touch and stroke the moon and sun so powerful and mighty; you exercise mastery with the body as far as the brahmā world?"

"No, friend."

"Then knowing and seeing thus, do you venerable ones, with the divine ear element, which is purified and surpasses the human, hear both kinds of sounds, the divine and human, those that are far as well as near?"

"No, friend."

"Then knowing and seeing thus, do you venerable ones understand the minds of other beings and persons, having encompassed them with your own minds? Do you understand a mind with lust as a mind with lust; a mind without lust as a mind without lust; a mind with hatred as a mind with hatred; a mind without hatred as a mind without hatred; a mind with delusion [122] as a mind with delusion; a mind without delusion as a mind without delusion; a contracted mind as contracted and a distracted mind as distracted; an exalted mind as exalted and an unexalted mind as unexalted; a surpassable mind as surpassable and an unsurpassable mind as unsurpassable; a concentrated mind as concentrated and an unconcentrated mind as unconcentrated; a liberated mind as liberated and an unliberated mind as unliberated?"

"No, friend."

"Then knowing and seeing thus, do you venerable ones recollect your manifold past abodes, that is, one birth, two births, three births, four births, five births, ten births, twenty births, thirty births, forty births, fifty births, a hundred births, a thousand births, a hundred thousand births, many aeons of world-contraction, many aeons of world-expansion, many aeons of world-contraction and expansion thus: 'There I was so named, of such a clan, with such an appearance, such was my food, such my experience of pleasure and pain, such my life span; passing away from there, I was reborn elsewhere, and there too I was so named, of such a clan, with such an appearance, such was my food, such my experience of pleasure and pain, such my life span; passing away from there, I was reborn here'? Do you thus recollect your manifold past abodes with their modes and details?"

"No, friend."

"Then knowing and seeing thus, do you venerable ones, with the divine eye, which is purified and surpasses the human, see beings passing away and being reborn, inferior and superior, beautiful and ugly, fortunate and unfortunate, and understand how beings fare on in accordance with their kamma thus: 'These beings who engaged in misconduct of body, [123] speech, and mind, who reviled the noble ones, held wrong view, and undertook actions based on wrong view, with the breakup of the body, after death, have been reborn in a state of misery, in a bad destination, in the nether world, in hell; but these beings who engaged in good conduct of body, speech, and mind, who did not revile the noble ones, who held right view, and undertook action based on right view, with the breakup of the body, after death, have been reborn in a good destination, in a heavenly world'? Thus with the divine eye, which is purified and surpasses the human, do you see beings passing away and being reborn, inferior and superior, beautiful and ugly, fortunate and unfortunate, and understand how beings fare on in accordance with their kamma?"

"No, friend."

"Then knowing and seeing thus, do you venerable ones dwell in those peaceful deliverances that transcend forms, the formless attainments, having touched them with the body?"[208]

"No, friend."

"Here now, venerable ones: this answer and the nonattainment of those states, how could this be, friends?"[209]

"We are liberated by wisdom, friend Susīma."[210]

"I do not understand in detail, friends, the meaning of what has been stated in brief by the venerable ones. It would be good if the venerable ones would explain to me in such a way that I could understand in detail what has been stated in brief." [124]

"Whether or not you understand, friend Susīma, we are liberated by wisdom."

(iii)

Then the Venerable Susīma rose from his seat and approached the Blessed One. Having approached, he paid homage to the Blessed One, sat down to one side, and reported to the Blessed One the entire conversation he had had with those bhikkhus. [The Blessed One said:]

"First, Susīma, comes knowledge of the stability of the Dhamma, afterwards knowledge of Nibbāna."[211]

"I do not understand in detail, venerable sir, the meaning of what was stated in brief by the Blessed One. It would be good if the Blessed One would explain to me in such a way that I could understand in detail what has been stated in brief."

"Whether or not you understand, Susīma, first comes knowledge of the stability of the Dhamma, afterwards knowledge of Nibbāna.[212]

"What do you think, Susīma, is form permanent or impermanent?" – "Impermanent, venerable sir."[213] – "Is what is impermanent suffering or happiness?" – "Suffering, venerable sir." – "Is what is impermanent, suffering, and subject to change fit to be regarded thus: 'This is mine, this I am, this is my self'?" – "No, venerable sir."

"Is feeling permanent or impermanent?... Is perception permanent or impermanent?... Are volitional formations permanent or impermanent?... Is consciousness permanent or impermanent?" [125] – "Impermanent, venerable sir." – "Is what is impermanent suffering or happiness?" – "Suffering, venerable sir." – "Is what is impermanent, suffering, and subject to change fit to be regarded thus: 'This is mine, this I am, this is my self'?" – "No, venerable sir."

"Therefore, Susīma, any kind of form whatsoever, whether past, future, or present, internal or external, gross or subtle, inferior or superior, far or near, all form should be seen as it really is with correct wisdom thus: 'This is not mine, this I am not, this is not my self.'

"Any kind of feeling whatsoever ... Any kind of perception whatsoever ... Any kind of volitional formations whatsoever ... Any kind of consciousness whatsoever, whether past, future, or present, internal or external, gross or subtle, inferior or superior, far or near, all consciousness should be seen as it really is with correct wisdom thus: 'This is not mine, this I am not, this is not my self.'

"Seeing thus, Susīma, the instructed noble disciple experiences revulsion towards form, revulsion towards feeling, revulsion towards perception, revulsion towards volitional formations, revulsion towards consciousness. Experiencing revulsion, he becomes dispassionate. Through dispassion [his mind] is liberated. When it is liberated there comes the knowledge: 'It's liberated.' He understands: 'Destroyed is birth, the holy life has been lived, what had to be done has been done, there is no more for this state of being.'

"Do you see, Susīma: 'With birth as condition, aging-and-death [comes to be]'?"

"Yes, venerable sir."

"Do you see, Susīma: 'With existence as condition, birth'?... 'With clinging as condition, existence'?... [126] ... 'With craving as condition, clinging'?... 'With feeling as condition, craving'?...

'With contact as condition, feeling'?... 'With the six sense bases as condition, contact'?... 'With name-and-form as condition, the six sense bases'?... 'With consciousness as condition, name-and-form'?... 'With volitional formations as condition, consciousness'?... 'With ignorance as condition, volitional formations [come to be]'?"

"Yes, venerable sir."

"Do you see, Susīma: 'With the cessation of birth comes cessation of aging-and-death'?"

"Yes, venerable sir."

"Do you see, Susīma: 'With the cessation of existence comes cessation of birth'?... 'With the cessation of clinging comes cessation of existence'?... 'With the cessation of ignorance comes cessation of volitional formations'?"

"Yes, venerable sir."

"Knowing and seeing thus, Susīma, do you wield the various kinds of spiritual power, such that: having been one, you become many ... and exercise bodily mastery as far as the brahmā world?"[214]

"No, venerable sir."

"Then knowing and seeing thus, Susīma, do you, with the divine ear element, which is purified and surpasses the human, hear both kinds of sounds, the divine and human, those that are far as well as near?" [127]

"No, venerable sir."

"Then knowing and seeing thus, Susīma, do you understand the minds of other beings and persons, having encompassed them with your own mind?"

"No, venerable sir."

"Then knowing and seeing thus, Susīma, do you recollect your manifold past abodes with their modes and details?"

"No, venerable sir."

"Then knowing and seeing thus, Susīma, do you, with the divine eye, which is purified and surpasses the human, see beings passing away and being reborn and understand how beings fare on in accordance with their kamma?"

"No, venerable sir."

"Then knowing and seeing thus, Susīma, do you dwell in those peaceful deliverances that transcend forms, the formless attainments, having touched them with the body?"

"No, venerable sir."

"Here now, Susīma: this answer and the nonattainment of those states, how could this be, Susīma?"

(iv)

Then the Venerable Susīma prostrated himself with his head at the Blessed One's feet and said: "Venerable sir, I have committed a transgression in that I was so foolish, so confused, so inept that I went forth as a thief of the Dhamma in such a well-expounded Dhamma and Discipline as this. Venerable sir, may the Blessed One pardon me for my transgression seen as a transgression for the sake of future restraint."

"Surely, Susīma, you have committed a transgression in that you were so foolish, so confused, so inept that you went forth as a thief of the Dhamma in such a well-expounded Dhamma and Discipline as this.[215] [128] Suppose, Susīma, they were to arrest a bandit, a criminal, and bring him before the king, saying: 'Sire, this man is a bandit, a criminal. Impose on him whatever punishment you wish.' The king would say to them: 'Come, men, bind this man's arms tightly behind his back with a strong rope, shave his head, and lead him around from street to street and from square to square, beating a drum. Then take him out through the southern gate and to the south of the city cut off his head.' What do you think, Susīma, would that man experience pain and displeasure on that account?"

"Yes, venerable sir."

"Although that man would experience pain and displeasure on that account, going forth as a thief of the Dhamma in such a well-expounded Dhamma and Discipline as this has results that are far more painful, far more bitter, and further, it leads to the nether world. But since you see your transgression as a transgression and make amends for it in accordance with the Dhamma, we pardon you for it. For it is growth in the Noble One's Discipline when one sees one's transgression as a transgression, makes amends for it in accordance with the Dhamma, and undertakes future restraint."

[129] VIII. ASCETICS AND BRAHMINS

71 (1) Aging-and-Death

Thus have I heard. On one occasion the Blessed One was dwelling at Sāvatthī in Jeta's Grove, Anāthapiṇḍika's Park. There the Blessed One said:

"Bhikkhus, those ascetics or brahmins who do not understand aging-and-death, its origin, its cessation, and the way leading to its cessation: these I do not consider to be ascetics among ascetics or brahmins among brahmins, and these venerable ones do not, by realizing it for themselves with direct knowledge, in this very life enter and dwell in the goal of asceticism or the goal of brahminhood.

"But, bhikkhus, those ascetics and brahmins who understand aging-and-death, its origin, its cessation, and the way leading to its cessation: these I consider to be ascetics among ascetics and brahmins among brahmins, and these venerable ones, by realizing it for themselves with direct knowledge, in this very life enter and dwell in the goal of asceticism and the goal of brahminhood."

72 (2)–81 (11) Birth, Etc.

"Bhikkhus, those ascetics or brahmins who do not understand birth … existence … clinging … craving … feeling … contact … the six sense bases … name-and-form … consciousness [130] … volitional formations, their origin, their cessation, and the way leading to their cessation: these I do not consider to be ascetics among ascetics or brahmins among brahmins, and these venerable ones do not, by realizing it for themselves with direct knowledge, in this very life enter and dwell in the goal of asceticism or the goal of brahminhood.

"But, bhikkhus, those ascetics and brahmins who understand these things: these I consider to be ascetics among ascetics and brahmins among brahmins, and these venerable ones, by realizing it for themselves with direct knowledge, in this very life enter and dwell in the goal of asceticism and the goal of brahminhood."

IX. With Incorporated Repetition Series[216]

82 (1) A Teacher

At Sāvatthī. "Bhikkhus, one who does not know and see as it really is aging-and-death, its origin, its cessation, and the way leading to its cessation, should search for a teacher in order to know this as it really is.[217] [131]

"Bhikkhus, one who does not know and see as it really is birth ... existence ... clinging ... craving ... feeling ... contact ... the six sense bases ... name-and-form ... consciousness ... volitional formations, their origin, their cessation, and the way leading to their cessation, should search for a teacher in order to know this as it really is."

83 (2) Training

"Bhikkhus, one who does not know and see as it really is aging-and-death ... volitional formations, their origin, their cessation, and the way leading to their cessation, should practise the training in order to know this as it really is."

84 (3)–93 (12) Exertion, Etc.

"Bhikkhus, one who does not know and see as it really is aging-and-death ... volitional formations, their origin, their cessation, and the way leading to their cessation, should make an exertion ... [132] arouse a desire ... arouse enthusiasm ... be unremitting ... arouse ardour ... apply energy ... practise perseverance ... practise mindfulness ... practise clear comprehension ... practise diligence in order to know this as it really is."

[133] Chapter II

13 *Abhisamayasaṃyutta* Connected Discourses on the Breakthrough

1 The Fingernail

Thus have I heard. On one occasion the Blessed One was dwelling at Sāvatthī in Jeta's Grove, Anāthapiṇḍika's Park. Then the Blessed One took up a little bit of soil in his fingernail and addressed the bhikkhus thus:

"Bhikkhus, what do you think, which is more: the little bit of soil that I have taken up in my fingernail or this great earth?"

"Venerable sir, the great earth is more. The little bit of soil that the Blessed One has taken up in his fingernail is trifling. It does not amount to a hundredth part, or a thousandth part, or a hundred thousandth part of the great earth."

"So too, bhikkhus, for a noble disciple, a person accomplished in view who has made the breakthrough, the suffering that has been destroyed and eliminated is more, while that which remains is trifling.[218] The latter does not amount to a hundredth part, [134] or a thousandth part, or a hundred thousandth part of the former mass of suffering that has been destroyed and eliminated, as there is a maximum of seven more lives. Of such great benefit, bhikkhus, is the breakthrough to the Dhamma, of such great benefit is it to obtain the vision of the Dhamma."[219]

2 The Pond

At Sāvatthī. "Bhikkhus, suppose there was a pond fifty *yojanas* long, fifty *yojanas* wide, and fifty *yojanas* deep, full of water, overflowing so that a crow could drink from it, and a man would draw out some water from it on the tip of a blade of *kusa* grass.

What do you think, bhikkhus, which is more: the water drawn out on the tip of the blade of *kusa* grass or the water in the pond?"[220]

"Venerable sir, the water in the pond is more. The water drawn out on the tip of the blade of *kusa* grass is trifling. It does not amount to a hundredth part, or a thousandth part, or a hundred thousandth part of the water in the pond."

"So too, bhikkhus, for a noble disciple, a person accomplished in view who has made the breakthrough, the suffering that has been destroyed and eliminated is more, while that which remains is trifling.... Of such great benefit, bhikkhus, is the breakthrough to the Dhamma, of such great benefit is it to obtain the vision of the Dhamma."

3 Water at the Confluence (1)

At Sāvatthī. [135] "Bhikkhus, suppose that in the place where these great rivers meet and converge—that is, the Ganges, the Yamunā, the Aciravatī, the Sarabhū, and the Mahī—a man would draw out two or three drops of water. What do you think, bhikkhus, which is more: these two or three drops of water that have been drawn out or the water at the confluence?"

"Venerable sir, the water at the confluence is more. The two or three drops of water that have been drawn out are trifling. They do not amount to a hundredth part, or a thousandth part, or a hundred thousandth part of the water at the confluence."

"So too, bhikkhus, for a noble disciple ... of such great benefit is it to obtain the vision of the Dhamma."

4 Water at the Confluence (2)

At Sāvatthī. "Bhikkhus, suppose that in the place where these great rivers meet and converge—that is, the Ganges, the Yamunā, the Aciravatī, the Sarabhū, and the Mahī—their water would be destroyed and eliminated except for two or three drops. What do you think, bhikkhus, which is more: the water at the confluence that has been destroyed and eliminated or the two or three drops of water that remain?"

"Venerable sir, the water at the confluence that has been destroyed and eliminated is more. The two or three drops of water that remain are trifling. They do not amount to a hundredth part, or a thousandth part, or a hundred thousandth part of the water that has been destroyed and eliminated."

"So too, bhikkhus, for a noble disciple ... of such great benefit is it to obtain the vision of the Dhamma."

5 The Earth (1)

At Sāvatthī. [136] "Bhikkhus, suppose that a man would place seven little balls of clay the size of jujube kernels on the great earth. What do you think, bhikkhus, which is more: those seven little balls of clay the size of jujube kernels that have been placed there or the great earth?"

"Venerable sir, the great earth is more. The seven little balls of clay the size of jujube kernels are trifling. They do not amount to a hundredth part, or a thousandth part, or a hundred thousandth part of the great earth."

"So too, bhikkhus, for a noble disciple ... of such great benefit is it to obtain the vision of the Dhamma."

6 The Earth (2)

At Sāvatthī. "Bhikkhus, suppose that the great earth would be destroyed and eliminated except for seven little balls of clay the size of jujube kernels. What do you think, bhikkhus, which is more: the great earth that has been destroyed and eliminated or the seven little balls of clay the size of jujube kernels that remain?"

"Venerable sir, the great earth that has been destroyed and eliminated is more. The seven little balls of clay the size of jujube kernels that remain are trifling. They do not amount to a hundredth part, or a thousandth part, or a hundred thousandth part of the great earth that has been destroyed and eliminated."

"So too, bhikkhus, for a noble disciple ... of such great benefit is it to obtain the vision of the Dhamma."

7 The Ocean (1)

At Sāvatthī. "Bhikkhus, suppose that a man would draw out two or three drops of water from the great ocean. What do you think, bhikkhus, which is more: the two or three drops of water that have been drawn out or the water in the great ocean?" [137]

"Venerable sir, the water in the great ocean is more. The two or three drops of water that have been drawn out are trifling. They do not amount to a hundredth part, or a thousandth part, or a hundred thousandth part of the water in the great ocean."

"So too, bhikkhus, for a noble disciple ... of such great benefit is it to obtain the vision of the Dhamma."

8 The Ocean (2)

At Sāvatthī. "Bhikkhus, suppose that the great ocean would be destroyed and eliminated except for two or three drops of water. What do you think, bhikkhus, which is more: the water in the great ocean that has been destroyed and eliminated or the two or three drops of water that remain?"

"Venerable sir, the water in the great ocean that has been destroyed and eliminated is more. The two or three drops of water that remain are trifling. They do not amount to a hundredth part, or a thousandth part, or a hundred thousandth part of the water in the great ocean that has been destroyed and eliminated."

"So too, bhikkhus, for a noble disciple ... of such great benefit is it to obtain the vision of the Dhamma."

9 The Mountain (1)

At Sāvatthī. "Bhikkhus, suppose that a man would place on the Himalayas, the king of mountains, seven grains of gravel the size of mustard seeds. What do you think, bhikkhus, which is more: the seven grains of gravel the size of mustard seeds that have been placed there or the Himalayas, the king of mountains?"

"Venerable sir, the Himalayas, the king of mountains, is more. The seven grains of gravel the size of mustard seeds are trifling. [138] They do not amount to a hundredth part, or a thousandth part, or a hundred thousandth part of the Himalayas, the king of mountains.

"So too, bhikkhus, for a noble disciple ... of such great benefit is it to obtain the vision of the Dhamma."

10 The Mountain (2)

At Sāvatthī. "Bhikkhus, suppose that the Himalayas, the king of mountains, would be destroyed and eliminated except for seven grains of gravel the size of mustard seeds. What do you think, bhikkhus, which is more: the portion of the Himalayas, the king of mountains, that has been destroyed and eliminated or the seven grains of gravel the size of mustard seeds that remain?"

"Venerable sir, the portion of the Himalayas, the king of mountains, that has been destroyed and eliminated is more. The seven grains of gravel the size of mustard seeds that remain are trifling. They do not amount to a hundredth part, or a thousandth part, or a hundred thousandth part of the portion of the Himalayas, the king of mountains, that has been destroyed and eliminated."

"So too, bhikkhus, for a noble disciple, a person accomplished in view who has made the breakthrough, the suffering that has been destroyed and eliminated is more, while that which remains is trifling. The latter does not amount to a hundredth part, or a thousandth part, or a hundred thousandth part of the former mass of suffering that has been destroyed and eliminated, as there is a maximum of seven more lives. Of such great benefit, bhikkhus, is the breakthrough to the Dhamma, of such great benefit is it to obtain the vision of the Dhamma."

11 The Mountain (3)

At Sāvatthī. [139] "Bhikkhus, suppose that a man would place on Sineru,[221] the king of mountains, seven grains of gravel the size of mung beans. What do you think, bhikkhus, which is more: the seven grains of gravel the size of mung beans that have been placed there or Sineru, the king of mountains?"

"Venerable sir, Sineru, the king of mountains, is more. The seven grains of gravel the size of mung beans are trifling. They do not amount to a hundredth part, or a thousandth part, or a hundred thousandth part of Sineru, the king of mountains."

"So too, bhikkhus, the achievements of ascetics, brahmins, and wanderers of other sects do not amount to a hundredth part, or a thousandth part, or a hundred thousandth part of the achievement of a noble disciple, a person accomplished in view who has made the breakthrough. So great in achievement, bhikkhus, is a person accomplished in view, so great in direct knowledge."[222]

[140] Chapter III

14 *Dhātusaṃyutta*
Connected Discourses on Elements

I. Diversity
(Internal Pentad)

1 (1) Diversity of Elements

At Sāvatthī. "Bhikkhus, I will teach you the diversity of elements.[223] Listen to that and attend closely, I will speak."

"Yes, venerable sir," those bhikkhus replied. The Blessed One said this:

"And what, bhikkhus, is the diversity of elements? The eye element, form element, eye-consciousness element; the ear element, sound element, ear-consciousness element; the nose element, odour element, nose-consciousness element; the tongue element, taste element, tongue-consciousness element; the body element, tactile-object element, body-consciousness element; the mind element, mental-phenomena element, mind-consciousness element. This, bhikkhus, is called the diversity of elements."[224]

2 (2) Diversity of Contacts

At Sāvatthī. "Bhikkhus, it is in dependence on the diversity of elements that there arises the diversity of contacts. And what, bhikkhus, is the diversity of elements? The eye element, the ear element, the nose element, the tongue element, the body element, the mind element. This is called the diversity of elements.

"And how is it, bhikkhus, that in dependence on the diversity of elements there arises the diversity of contacts? In dependence on the eye element there arises eye-contact; in dependence on the ear element there arises ear-contact; in dependence on the nose element there arises nose-contact; [141] in dependence on the tongue element there arises tongue-contact; in dependence on the body element there arises body-contact; in dependence on the mind element there arises mind-contact.[225] It is in this way, bhikkhus, that in dependence on the diversity of elements there arises the diversity of contacts."

3 (3) Not Diversity of Contacts

At Sāvatthī. "Bhikkhus, it is in dependence on the diversity of elements that there arises the diversity of contacts. The diversity of elements does not arise in dependence on the diversity of contacts.

"And what, bhikkhus, is the diversity of elements? The eye element ... the mind element. This is called the diversity of elements.

"And how is it, bhikkhus, that in dependence on the diversity of elements there arises the diversity of contacts; that the diversity of elements does not arise in dependence on the diversity of contacts?

"In dependence on the eye element there arises eye-contact; the eye element does not arise in dependence on eye-contact.... In dependence on the mind element there arises mind-contact; the mind element does not arise in dependence on mind-contact.[226] It is in this way, bhikkhus, that in dependence on the diversity of elements there arises the diversity of contacts; that the diversity of elements does not arise in dependence on the diversity of contacts."

4 (4) Diversity of Feelings (1)

At Sāvatthī. "Bhikkhus, it is in dependence on the diversity of elements that there arises the diversity of contacts; in dependence on the diversity of contacts that there arises the diversity of feelings.

"And what, bhikkhus, is the diversity of elements? [142] The eye element ... the mind element. This is called the diversity of elements.

"And how is it, bhikkhus, that in dependence on the diversity of elements there arises the diversity of contacts; that in dependence on the diversity of contacts there arises the diversity of feelings? In dependence on the eye element there arises eye-contact;

in dependence on eye-contact there arises feeling born of eye-contact. In dependence on the ear element there arises ear-contact; in dependence on ear-contact there arises feeling born of ear-contact. In dependence on the nose element there arises nose-contact; in dependence on nose-contact there arises feeling born of nose-contact. In dependence on the tongue element there arises tongue-contact; in dependence on tongue-contact there arises feeling born of tongue-contact. In dependence on the body element there arises body-contact; in dependence on body-contact there arises feeling born of body-contact. In dependence on the mind element there arises mind-contact; in dependence on mind-contact there arises feeling born of mind-contact.

"It is in this way, bhikkhus, that in dependence on the diversity of elements there arises the diversity of contacts; that in dependence on the diversity of contacts there arises the diversity of feelings."

5 (5) Diversity of Feelings (2)

At Sāvatthī. "Bhikkhus, it is in dependence on the diversity of elements that there arises the diversity of contacts; in dependence on the diversity of contacts that there arises the diversity of feelings. The diversity of contacts does not arise in dependence on the diversity of feelings; the diversity of elements does not arise in dependence on the diversity of contacts.

"And what, bhikkhus, is the diversity of elements? The eye element ... the mind element. This is called the diversity of elements.

"And how is it, bhikkhus, that in dependence on the diversity of elements there arises the diversity of contacts; that in dependence on the diversity of contacts there arises the diversity of feelings? That the diversity of contacts does not arise in dependence on the diversity of feelings; that the diversity of elements does not arise in dependence on the diversity of contacts?

"In dependence on the eye element there arises eye-contact; in dependence on eye-contact there arises feeling born of eye-contact. Eye-contact does not arise in dependence on feeling born of eye-contact; [143] the eye element does not arise in dependence on eye-contact.... In dependence on the mind element there arises mind-contact; in dependence on mind-contact there arises feeling born of mind-contact. Mind-contact does not arise in dependence on feeling born of mind-contact; the mind element does not arise in dependence on mind-contact.

"It is in this way, bhikkhus, that in dependence on the diversity of elements there arises the diversity of contacts ... the diversity of elements does not arise in dependence on the diversity of contacts."

(External Pentad)

6 (6) Diversity of External Elements

At Sāvatthī. "Bhikkhus, I will teach you the diversity of elements. Listen to that and attend closely, I will speak....

"And what, bhikkhus, is the diversity of elements? The form element, the sound element, the odour element, the taste element, the tactile-object element, the mental-phenomena element. This, bhikkhus, is called the diversity of elements."

7 (7) Diversity of Perceptions

At Sāvatthī. "Bhikkhus, it is in dependence on the diversity of elements that there arises the diversity of perceptions; in dependence on the diversity of perceptions that there arises the diversity of intentions; in dependence on the diversity of intentions that there arises the diversity of desires; in dependence on the diversity of desires that there arises the diversity of passions; in dependence on the diversity of passions that there arises the diversity of quests.

"And what, bhikkhus, is the diversity of elements? The form element ... the mental-phenomena element. This, bhikkhus, is called the diversity of elements. [144]

"And how is it, bhikkhus, that in dependence on the diversity of elements there arises the diversity of perceptions ... that in dependence on the diversity of passions there arises the diversity of quests?

"In dependence on the form element there arises perception of form; in dependence on perception of form there arises intention regarding form; in dependence on intention regarding form there arises desire for form; in dependence on desire for form there arises passion for form; in dependence on passion for form there arises the quest for form....[227]

"In dependence on the mental-phenomena element there arises perception of mental phenomena; in dependence on perception of mental phenomena there arises intention regarding mental phenomena; in dependence on intention regarding mental phenomena there arises desire for mental phenomena; in dependence on desire for mental phenomena there arises passion for mental phenomena; in dependence on passion for mental phenomena there arises the quest for mental phenomena.

"It is in this way, bhikkhus, that in dependence on the diversity of elements there arises the diversity of perceptions ... that in dependence on the diversity of passions there arises the diversity of quests."

8 (8) Not Diversity of Quests

At Sāvatthī. "Bhikkhus, it is in dependence on the diversity of elements that there arises the diversity of perceptions ... (*as in preceding sutta*) ... in dependence on the diversity of passions that there arises the diversity of quests. The diversity of passions does not arise in dependence on the diversity of quests; [145] the diversity of desires does not arise in dependence on the diversity of passions; the diversity of intentions does not arise in dependence on the diversity of desires; the diversity of perceptions does not arise in dependence on the diversity of intentions; the diversity of elements does not arise in dependence on the diversity of perceptions.[228]

"And what, bhikkhus, is the diversity of elements? The form element ... the mental-phenomena element. This, bhikkhus, is called the diversity of elements.

"And how is it, bhikkhus, that in dependence on the diversity of elements there arises the diversity of perceptions ... that in dependence on the diversity of passions there arises the diversity of quests? That the diversity of passions does not arise in dependence on the diversity of quests ... that the diversity of elements does not arise in dependence on the diversity of perceptions?

"In dependence on the form element there arises perception of form; [... in dependence on passion for form there arises the quest for form. Passion for form does not arise in dependence on the quest for form; desire for form does not arise in dependence on passion for form; intention regarding form does not arise in dependence on desire for form; perception of form does not arise in dependence on intention regarding form; the form element does not arise in dependence on perception of form.] ...[229]

"In dependence on the mental-phenomena element there arises perception of mental phenomena; [146] ... in dependence on passion for mental phenomena there arises the quest for mental phenomena. Passion for mental phenomena does not arise in dependence on the quest for mental phenomena ... the mental-phenomena element does not arise in dependence on perception of mental phenomena.

"It is in this way, bhikkhus, that in dependence on the diversity of elements there arises the diversity of perceptions ... that in dependence on the diversity of passions there arises the diversity of quests. That the diversity of passions does not arise in dependence on the diversity of quests ... that the diversity of elements does not arise in dependence on the diversity of perceptions."

9 (9) Diversity of External Contacts (1)

At Sāvatthī. "Bhikkhus, it is in dependence on the diversity of elements that there arises the diversity of perceptions; in dependence on the diversity of perceptions that there arises the diversity of intentions; in dependence on the diversity of intentions that there arises the diversity of contacts; in dependence on the diversity of contacts that there arises the diversity of feelings; in dependence on the diversity of feelings that there arises the diversity of desires; in dependence on the diversity of desires that there arises the diversity of passions; in dependence on the diversity of passions that there arises the diversity of quests; in dependence on the diversity of quests that there arises the diversity of gains.[230]

"And what, bhikkhus, is the diversity of elements? The form element ... the mental-phenomena element. This, bhikkhus, is called the diversity of elements.

"And how is it, bhikkhus, that in dependence on the diversity of elements [147] there arises the diversity of perceptions ... that in dependence on the diversity of quests there arises the diversity of gains?

"In dependence on the form element there arises perception of form; in dependence on perception of form there arises intention regarding form; in dependence on intention regarding form there arises contact with form; in dependence on contact with form there arises feeling born of contact with form; in dependence on feeling born of contact with form there arises desire for form; in dependence on desire for form there arises passion for form; in dependence on passion for form there arises the quest for form; in dependence on the quest for form there arises the gain of form....

"In dependence on the mental-phenomena element there arises perception of mental phenomena; in dependence on perception of mental phenomena there arises intention regarding mental phenomena ... contact with mental phenomena ... feeling born of contact with mental phenomena ... desire for mental phenomena ... passion for mental phenomena ... the quest for mental phenomena; in dependence on the quest for mental phenomena there arises the gain of mental phenomena.

"It is in this way, bhikkhus, that in dependence on the diversity of elements there arises the diversity of perceptions ... that in dependence on the diversity of quests there arises the diversity of gains."

10 (10) Diversity of External Contacts (2)

At Sāvatthī. "Bhikkhus, it is in dependence on the diversity of elements that there arises the diversity of perceptions ... [148] (*as in the preceding sutta*) ... in dependence on the diversity of quests that there arises the diversity of gains. The diversity of quests does not arise in dependence on the diversity of gains; the diversity of passions does not arise in dependence on the diversity of quests ... the diversity of elements does not arise in dependence on the diversity of perceptions.

"And what, bhikkhus, is the diversity of elements? The form element ... the mental-phenomena element. This, bhikkhus, is called the diversity of elements.

"And how is it, bhikkhus, that in dependence on the diversity of elements there arises the diversity of perceptions ... that in dependence on the diversity of quests there arises the diversity of gains? That the diversity of quests does not arise in dependence on the diversity of gains ... that the diversity of elements does not arise in dependence on the diversity of perceptions?

"In dependence on the form element there arises perception of form … in dependence on the mental-phenomena element there arises perception of mental phenomena … in dependence on the quest for mental phenomena there arises the gain of mental phenomena. The quest for mental phenomena does not arise in dependence on the gain of mental phenomena; passion for mental phenomena does not arise in dependence on the quest for mental phenomena; [149] desire for mental phenomena does not arise in dependence on passion for mental phenomena; feeling born of contact with mental phenomena does not arise in dependence on desire for mental phenomena; contact with mental phenomena does not arise in dependence on feeling born of contact with mental phenomena; intention regarding mental phenomena does not arise in dependence on contact with mental phenomena; perception of mental phenomena does not arise in dependence on intention regarding mental phenomena; the mental-phenomena element does not arise in dependence on perception of mental phenomena.

"It is in this way, bhikkhus, that in dependence on the diversity of elements there arises the diversity of perceptions … that in dependence on the diversity of quests there arises the diversity of gains; that the diversity of quests does not arise in dependence on the diversity of gains … that the diversity of elements does not arise in dependence on the diversity of perceptions."

II. The Second Subchapter
(Seven Elements)

11 (1) Seven Elements

At Sāvatthī. [150] "Bhikkhus, there are these seven elements. What seven? The light element, the beauty element, the base of the infinity of space element, the base of the infinity of consciousness element, the base of nothingness element, the base of neither-perception-nor-nonperception element, the cessation of perception and feeling element. These are the seven elements."[231]

When this was said, a certain bhikkhu asked the Blessed One: "Venerable sir, as to the light element … the cessation of perception and feeling element: in dependence on what are these elements discerned?"

"Bhikkhu, the light element is discerned in dependence on darkness. The beauty element is discerned in dependence on foulness. The base of the infinity of space element is discerned in dependence on form. The base of the infinity of consciousness element is discerned in dependence on the base of the infinity of space. The base of nothingness element is discerned in dependence on the base of the infinity of consciousness. The base of neither-perception-nor-nonperception element is discerned in dependence on the base of nothingness. The cessation of perception and feeling element is discerned in dependence on cessation."[232]

"But, venerable sir, as to the light element ... the cessation of perception and feeling element: how is the attainment of these elements to be attained?"

"The light element, the beauty element, the base of the infinity of space element, the base of the infinity of consciousness element, [151] and the base of nothingness element: these elements are to be attained as attainments with perception. The base of neither-perception-nor-nonperception element: this element is to be attained as an attainment with a residue of formations.[233] The cessation of perception and feeling element: this element is to be attained as an attainment of cessation."

12 (2) With a Source

At Sāvatthī. "Bhikkhus, sensual thought arises with a source, not without a source; thought of ill will arises with a source, not without a source; thought of harming arises with a source, not without a source. And how is this so?

"In dependence on the sensuality element there arises sensual perception;[234] in dependence on sensual perception there arises sensual intention; in dependence on sensual intention there arises sensual desire; in dependence on sensual desire there arises sensual passion; in dependence on sensual passion there arises a sensual quest. Engaged in a sensual quest, the uninstructed worldling conducts himself wrongly in three ways—with body, speech, and mind.

"In dependence on the ill will element there arises perception of ill will;[235] in dependence on perception of ill will there arises intention of ill will; in dependence on intention of ill will there arises desire [driven by] ill will; in dependence on desire [driven by] ill will there arises passion [driven by] ill will; in dependence on passion [driven by] ill will there arises a quest [driven by] ill will. Engaged in a quest [driven by] ill will, the uninstructed worldling conducts himself wrongly in three ways—with body, speech, and mind.

"In dependence on the harmfulness element there arises perception of harming;[236] in dependence on perception of harming there arises intention to harm; in dependence on intention to harm there arises desire to harm; in dependence on desire to harm there arises passion to harm; in dependence on passion to harm there arises a quest to harm. Engaged in a quest to harm, [152] the uninstructed worldling conducts himself wrongly in three ways—with body, speech, and mind.

"Suppose, bhikkhus, a man would drop a blazing grass torch into a thicket of dry grass. If he does not quickly extinguish it with his hands and feet, the creatures living in the grass and wood will meet with calamity and disaster. So too, if any ascetic or brahmin does not quickly abandon, dispel, obliterate, and annihilate the unrighteous perceptions that have arisen in him, he dwells in suffering in this very life, with vexation, despair, and fever; and with the breakup of the body, after death, a bad destination may be expected for him.

"Bhikkhus, thought of renunciation arises with a source, not without a source; thought of non-ill will arises with a source, not without a source; thought of harmlessness arises with a source, not without a source. And how is this so?

"In dependence on the renunciation element there arises perception of renunciation;[237] in dependence on perception of renunciation there arises intention of renunciation; in dependence on intention of renunciation there arises desire for renunciation; in dependence on desire for renunciation there arises passion for renunciation; in dependence on passion for renunciation there arises a quest for renunciation. Engaged in a quest for renunciation, the instructed noble disciple conducts himself rightly in three ways—with body, speech, and mind.

"In dependence on the non-ill will element there arises perception of non-ill will;[238] in dependence on perception of non-ill will there arises intention of non-ill will; in dependence on intention of non-ill will there arises desire [guided by] non-ill will; in dependence on desire [guided by] non-ill will there arises passion [guided by] non-ill will; in dependence on passion [guided by] non-ill will there arises a quest [guided by] non-ill will. Engaged in a quest [guided by] non-ill will, the instructed noble disciple conducts himself rightly in three ways—with body, speech, and mind.

"In dependence on the harmlessness element there arises perception of harmlessness;[239] [153] in dependence on perception of harmlessness there arises intention of harmlessness; in dependence on intention of harmlessness there arises desire for harmlessness; in dependence on desire for harmlessness there arises passion for harmlessness; in dependence on passion for harmlessness there arises a quest for harmlessness. Engaged in a quest for harmlessness, the instructed noble disciple conducts himself rightly in three ways—with body, speech, and mind.

"Suppose, bhikkhus, a man would drop a blazing grass torch into a thicket of dry grass. If he quickly extinguishes it with his hands and feet, the creatures living in the grass and wood will not meet with calamity and disaster. So too, if any ascetic or brahmin quickly abandons, dispels, obliterates, and annihilates the unrighteous perceptions that have arisen in him, he dwells happily in this very life, without vexation, despair, and fever; and with the breakup of the body, after death, a good destination may be expected for him."

13 (3) The Brick Hall

On one occasion the Blessed One was dwelling at Ñātika in the Brick Hall. There the Blessed One addressed the bhikkhus thus: "Bhikkhus!"

"Venerable sir!" those bhikkhus replied. The Blessed One said this:

"Bhikkhus, in dependence on an element there arises a perception, there arises a view, there arises a thought."[240]

When this was said, the Venerable Saddha Kaccāyana said to the Blessed One: "Venerable sir, when, in regard to those who are not perfectly enlightened, the view arises, 'These are Perfectly Enlightened Ones,' in dependence on what is this view discerned?"[241]

"Mighty, Kaccāyana, is this element, the element of ignorance. [154] In dependence on an inferior element, Kaccāyana, there arises an inferior perception, an inferior view, inferior thought, inferior volition, inferior longing, an inferior wish, an inferior person, inferior speech. He explains, teaches, proclaims, establishes, discloses, analyses, and elucidates the inferior. His rebirth, I say, is inferior.

"In dependence on a middling element, Kaccāyana, there arises a middling perception, a middling view, middling thought, middling volition, middling longing, a middling wish, a middling person, middling speech. He explains, teaches, proclaims, establishes, discloses, analyses, and elucidates the middling. His rebirth, I say, is middling.

"In dependence on a superior element, Kaccāyana, there arises a superior perception, a superior view, superior thought, superior volition, superior longing, a superior wish, a superior person, superior speech. He explains, teaches, proclaims, establishes, discloses, analyses, and elucidates the superior. His rebirth, I say, is superior."

14 (4) Inferior Disposition

At Sāvatthī. "Bhikkhus, it is by way of elements that beings come together and unite. Those of an inferior disposition come together and unite with those of an inferior disposition; those of a good disposition come together and unite with those of a good disposition.[242] In the past, by way of elements, beings came together and united.... In the future, too, by way of elements, beings will come together and unite.... [155] Now too, at present, by way of elements, beings come together and unite. Those of an inferior disposition come together and unite with those of an inferior disposition; those of a good disposition come together and unite with those of a good disposition."

15 (5) Walking Back and Forth

On one occasion the Blessed One was dwelling at Rājagaha on Mount Vulture Peak. Now on that occasion, not far from the Blessed One, the Venerable Sāriputta was walking back and forth with a number of bhikkhus; the Venerable Mahāmoggallāna ... the Venerable Mahākassapa ... the Venerable Anuruddha ... the Venerable Puṇṇa Mantāniputta ... the Venerable Upāli ... the

Venerable Ānanda was walking back and forth with a number of bhikkhus. And not far from the Blessed One, Devadatta too was walking back and forth with a number of bhikkhus.

Then the Blessed One addressed the bhikkhus thus: "Bhikkhus, do you see Sāriputta walking back and forth with a number of bhikkhus?"[243]

"Yes, venerable sir."

"All those bhikkhus are of great wisdom. Do you see Moggallāna walking back and forth with a number of bhikkhus?"

"Yes, venerable sir."

"All those bhikkhus have great spiritual power. Do you see Kassapa walking back and forth with a number of bhikkhus?" [156]

"Yes, venerable sir."

"All those bhikkhus are proponents of the ascetic practices. Do you see Anuruddha walking back and forth with a number of bhikkhus?"

"Yes, venerable sir."

"All those bhikkhus possess the divine eye. Do you see Puṇṇa Mantāniputta walking back and forth with a number of bhikkhus?"

"Yes, venerable sir."

"All those bhikkhus are speakers on the Dhamma. Do you see Upāli walking back and forth with a number of bhikkhus?"

"Yes, venerable sir."

"All those bhikkhus are upholders of the Discipline. Do you see Ānanda walking back and forth with a number of bhikkhus?"

"Yes, venerable sir."

"All those bhikkhus are highly learned. Do you see Devadatta walking back and forth with a number of bhikkhus?"

"Yes, venerable sir."

"All those bhikkhus have evil wishes.

"Bhikkhus, it is by way of elements that beings come together and unite. Those of an inferior disposition come together and unite with those of an inferior disposition; those of a good disposition come together and unite with those of a good disposition. In the past they did so, in the future they will do so, [157] and now at present they do so too."

16 (6) With Verses

At Sāvatthī.[244] "Bhikkhus, it is by way of elements that beings come together and unite: those of an inferior disposition come together and unite with those of an inferior disposition. In the past they did so, in the future they will do so, and now at present they do so too.

"Just as excrement comes together and unites with excrement, urine with urine, spittle with spittle, pus with pus, and blood with blood, so too, bhikkhus, it is by way of elements that beings come together and unite: those of an inferior disposition come together and unite with those of an inferior disposition. In the past they did so, in the future they will do so, and now at present they do so too. [158]

"Bhikkhus, it is by way of elements that beings come together and unite: those of a good disposition come together and unite with those of a good disposition. In the past they did so, in the future they will do so, and now at present they do so too.

"Just as milk comes together and unites with milk, oil with oil, ghee with ghee, honey with honey, and molasses with molasses, so too, bhikkhus, it is by way of elements that beings come together and unite: those of a good disposition come together and unite with those of a good disposition. In the past they did so, in the future they will do so, and now at present they do so too."

This is what the Blessed One said. Having said this, the Fortunate One, the Teacher, further said this:

"From association the woods of lust is born,[245]
By nonassociation the woods is cut.
Just as one who has mounted a wooden plank
Would sink upon the mighty sea,
So one of virtuous living sinks
By consorting with a lethargic person.

"Thus one should avoid such a person—
One lethargic, devoid of energy.
Keep company with the wise,
With resolute meditators,
With the noble ones who dwell secluded,
Their energy constantly aroused." [159]

17 (7) Lacking Faith

At Sāvatthī. "Bhikkhus, it is by way of elements that beings come together and unite. Those lacking faith come together and unite with those lacking faith, the shameless with the shameless, those unafraid of wrongdoing with those unafraid of wrongdoing, the unlearned with the unlearned, the lazy with the lazy, the muddle-minded with the muddle-minded, the unwise with the unwise. In the past it was so; in the future it will be so; [160] and now too at present it is so.

"Bhikkhus, it is by way of elements that beings come together and unite. Those having faith come together and unite with those having faith, those having a sense of shame with those having a sense of shame, those afraid of wrongdoing with those afraid of wrongdoing, the learned with the learned, the energetic with the energetic, the mindful with the mindful, the wise with the wise. In the past it was so; in the future it will be so; and now too at present it is so."

18 (8) Rooted in those Lacking Faith

(i)

"Bhikkhus, it is by way of elements that beings come together and unite. [161] Those lacking faith come together and unite with those lacking faith, the shameless with the shameless, the unwise with the unwise. Those having faith come together and unite with those having faith, those having a sense of shame with those having a sense of shame, the wise with the wise. In the past it was so; in the future it will be so; and now too at present it is so."

(*The next four parts of this sutta substitute the following in the second place, instead of "the shameless," and "those having a sense of shame"*:)

(ii) those unafraid of wrongdoing, those afraid of wrongdoing;

(iii) the unlearned, the learned; [162]

(iv) the lazy, the energetic;

(v) the muddle-minded, the mindful.

19 (9) Rooted in the Shameless

(i)

"Bhikkhus, it is by way of elements that beings come together and unite. The shameless come together and unite with the shameless, [163] those unafraid of wrongdoing with those unafraid of wrongdoing, the unwise with the unwise. Those having a sense of shame come together and unite with those having a sense of shame, those afraid of wrongdoing with those afraid of wrongdoing, the wise with the wise. [In the past it was so; in the future it will be so; and now too at present it is so.]"

(The next three parts of this sutta substitute the following in the second place, instead of "those unafraid of wrongdoing," and "those afraid of wrongdoing":)

(ii) the unlearned, the learned;
(iii) the lazy, the energetic;
(iv) the muddle-minded, the mindful.

20 (10) Rooted in those Unafraid of Wrongdoing

(i)

[164] "Bhikkhus, it is by way of elements that beings come together and unite. Those unafraid of wrongdoing come together and unite with those unafraid of wrongdoing, the unlearned with the unlearned, the unwise with the unwise. Those afraid of wrongdoing come together and unite with those afraid of wrongdoing, the learned with the learned, the wise with the wise. In the past it was so; in the future it will be so; and now too at present it is so."

(The next two parts of this sutta substitute the following in the second place, instead of "the unlearned," and "the learned":)

(ii) the lazy, the energetic;
(iii) the muddle-minded, the mindful.

21 (11) Rooted in the Unlearned

(i)

"Bhikkhus, it is by way of elements that beings come together and unite. The unlearned come together and unite with the unlearned, the lazy with the lazy, the unwise with the unwise. The learned come together and unite with the learned, the energetic [165] with the energetic, the wise with the wise. In the past it was so; in the future it will be so; and now too at present it is so."

(ii)

"The unlearned come together and unite with the unlearned, the muddle-minded with the muddle-minded, the unwise with the unwise. The learned come together and unite with the learned, the mindful with the mindful, the wise with the wise. In the past it was so; in the future it will be so; and now too at present it is so."

22 (12) *Rooted in the Lazy*

"Bhikkhus, it is by way of elements that beings come together and unite. The lazy come together and unite with the lazy, the muddle-minded with the muddle-minded, the unwise with the unwise. The energetic come together and unite with the energetic, the mindful with the mindful, the wise with the wise. In the past it was so; in the future it will be so; and now too at present it is so."

[166]

III. Courses of Kamma

23 (1) *Unconcentrated*

At Sāvatthī. "Bhikkhus, it is by way of elements that beings come together and unite. Those lacking faith come together and unite with those lacking faith, the shameless with the shameless, those unafraid of wrongdoing with those unafraid of wrongdoing, the unconcentrated with the unconcentrated, the unwise with the unwise.

"Those having faith come together and unite with those having faith, those having a sense of shame with those having a sense of shame, those afraid of wrongdoing with those afraid of wrongdoing, the concentrated with the concentrated, the wise with the wise."

24 (2) *Immoral*

(*As above, except that "the unconcentrated" and "the concentrated" are replaced by "the immoral" and "the virtuous," respectively.*) [167]

25 (3) The Five Training Rules

At Sāvatthī. "Bhikkhus, it is by way of elements that beings come together and unite. Those who destroy life come together and unite with those who destroy life; those who take what is not given ... who engage in sexual misconduct ... who speak falsehood ... who indulge in wine, liquor, and intoxicants that cause negligence come together and unite with those who so indulge.

"Those who abstain from the destruction of life come together and unite with those who abstain from the destruction of life; those who abstain from taking what is not given ... from sexual misconduct ... from false speech ... from wine, liquor, and intoxicants that cause negligence come together and unite with those who so abstain."

26 (4) Seven Courses of Kamma

At Sāvatthī. "Bhikkhus, it is by way of elements that beings come together and unite. Those who destroy life come together and unite with those who destroy life; those who take what is not given ... who engage in sexual misconduct ... who speak falsehood ... who speak divisively ... who speak harshly ... who indulge in idle chatter come together and unite with those who so indulge.

"Those who abstain from the destruction of life ... from taking what is not given ... from sexual misconduct ... from false speech ... from divisive speech ... from harsh speech ... from idle chatter come together and unite with those who so abstain."

27 (5) Ten Courses of Kamma

At Sāvatthī. [168] "Bhikkhus, it is by way of elements that beings come together and unite. Those who destroy life come together and unite with those who destroy life; those ... (*as above, continuing:*) ... who are covetous ... who bear ill will ... of wrong view come together and unite with those of wrong view.

"Those who abstain from the destruction of life ... (*as above*) ... who are uncovetous ... without ill will ... of right view come together and unite with those of right view."

28 (6) The Eightfold Path

At Sāvatthī. "Bhikkhus, it is by way of elements that beings come together and unite. Those of wrong view come together and unite with those of wrong view; those of wrong intention ... wrong speech ... wrong action ... wrong livelihood ... wrong effort ... wrong mindfulness ... wrong concentration come together and unite with those of wrong concentration.

"Those of right view come together and unite with those of right view; those of right intention ... right speech ... right action ... right livelihood ... right effort ... right mindfulness ... right concentration come together and unite with those of right concentration."

29 (7) Ten Factors

At Sāvatthī. "Bhikkhus, it is by way of elements that beings come together and unite. Those of wrong view ... (*as above*) [169] wrong concentration ... wrong knowledge ... wrong liberation come together and unite with those of wrong liberation.

"Those of right view ... (*as above*) right concentration ... right knowledge ... right liberation come together and unite with those of right liberation."[246]

IV. The Fourth Subchapter
(The Four Elements)

30 (1) Four Elements

On one occasion the Blessed One was dwelling at Sāvatthī in Jeta's Grove, Anāthapiṇḍika's Park....

"Bhikkhus, there are these four elements. What four? The earth element, the water element, the heat element, the air element. These are the four elements."[247]

31 (2) Before My Enlightenment

At Sāvatthī. [170] "Bhikkhus, before my enlightenment, while I was still a bodhisatta, not yet perfectly enlightened, it occurred to me: 'What is the gratification, what is the danger, what is the escape in the case of the earth element? What is the gratification, what is the danger, what is the escape in the case of the water element ... the heat element ... the air element?'

"Then, bhikkhus, it occurred to me: 'The pleasure and joy that arise in dependence on the earth element: this is the gratification in the earth element. That the earth element is impermanent, suffering, and subject to change: this is the danger in the earth element. The removal and abandonment of desire and lust for the earth element: this is the escape from the earth element.[248]

"'The pleasure and joy that arise in dependence on the water element ... the heat element ... the air element: this is the gratification in the air element. That the air element is impermanent, suffering, and subject to change: this is the danger in the air element. The removal and abandonment of desire and lust for the air element: this is the escape from the air element.'[249]

"So long, bhikkhus, as I did not directly know as they really are the gratification as gratification, the danger as danger, and the escape as escape in the case of these four elements, I did not claim to have awakened to the unsurpassed perfect enlightenment in this world with its devas, Māra, and Brahmā, in this generation with its ascetics and brahmins, its devas and humans. But when I directly knew all this as it really is, then I claimed to have awakened to the unsurpassed perfect enlightenment in this world with ... its devas and humans. [171]

"The knowledge and vision arose in me: 'Unshakable is my liberation of mind;[250] this is my last birth; now there is no more renewed existence.'"

32 (3) I Set Out

At Sāvatthī. "Bhikkhus, I set out seeking the gratification in the earth element. Whatever gratification there is in the earth element—that I discovered. I have clearly seen with wisdom just how far the gratification in the earth element extends.

"Bhikkhus, I set out seeking the danger in the earth element. Whatever danger there is in the earth element—that I discovered. I have clearly seen with wisdom just how far the danger in the earth element extends.

"Bhikkhus, I set out seeking the escape from the earth element. Whatever escape there is from the earth element—that I discovered. I have clearly seen with wisdom just how far the escape from the earth element extends.

"Bhikkhus, I set out seeking the gratification in … the danger in … the escape from the water element … the heat element … the air element. Whatever escape there is from the air element—that I discovered. I have clearly seen with wisdom just how far the escape from the air element extends.

"So long, bhikkhus, as I did not directly know as they really are the gratification, the danger, and the escape in the case of these four elements … (*as above*) [172] … devas and humans.

"The knowledge and vision arose in me: 'Unshakable is my liberation of mind; this is my last birth; now there is no more renewed existence.'"

33 (4) If There Were No

At Sāvatthī. "Bhikkhus, if there were no gratification in the earth element, beings would not become enamoured with it; but because there is gratification in the earth element, beings become enamoured with it. If there were no danger in the earth element, beings would not experience revulsion towards it; but because there is danger in the earth element, beings experience revulsion towards it. If there were no escape from the earth element, beings would not escape from it; but because there is an escape from the earth element, beings escape from it.

"Bhikkhus, if there were no gratification in the water element … in the heat element … in the air element, beings would not become enamoured with it … [173] … but because there is an escape from the air element, beings escape from it.

"So long, bhikkhus, as beings have not directly known as they really are the gratification as gratification, the danger as danger, and the escape as escape in the case of these four elements, they have not escaped from this world with its devas, Māra, and Brahmā, from this generation with its ascetics and brahmins, its devas and humans; they have not become detached from it, released from it, nor do they dwell with a mind rid of barriers. But when beings have directly known all this as it really is, then they have escaped from this world with its devas and humans … they have become detached from it, released from it, and they dwell with a mind rid of barriers."[251]

34 (5) Exclusively Suffering

At Sāvatthī. "Bhikkhus, if this earth element were exclusively suffering, immersed in suffering, steeped in suffering, and if it were not [also] steeped in pleasure, beings would not become enamoured with it. But because the earth element is pleasurable,[252] immersed in pleasure, steeped in pleasure, and is not steeped [only] in suffering, beings become enamoured with it. [174]

"Bhikkhus, if this water element were exclusively suffering … if this heat element were exclusively suffering … if this air element were exclusively suffering, immersed in suffering, steeped in suffering, and if it was not [also] steeped in pleasure, beings would not become enamoured with it. But because the air element is pleasurable, immersed in pleasure, steeped in pleasure, and is not steeped [only] in suffering, beings become enamoured with it.

"Bhikkhus, if this earth element were exclusively pleasurable, immersed in pleasure, steeped in pleasure, and if it were not [also] steeped in suffering, beings would not experience revulsion towards it. But because the earth element is suffering, immersed in suffering, steeped in suffering, and is not steeped [only] in pleasure, beings experience revulsion towards it.

"Bhikkhus, if this water element were exclusively pleasurable … if this heat element were exclusively pleasurable … if this air element were exclusively pleasurable, immersed in pleasure, steeped in pleasure, and if it were not [also] steeped in suffering, beings would not experience revulsion towards it. But because the air element is suffering, immersed in suffering, steeped in suffering, and is not steeped [only] in pleasure, beings experience revulsion towards it."

35 (6) Delight

At Sāvatthī. "Bhikkhus, one who seeks delight in the earth element seeks delight in suffering. One who seeks delight in suffering, I say, is not freed from suffering. One who seeks delight in the water element … in the heat element … in the air element seeks delight in suffering. One who seeks delight in suffering, I say, is not freed from suffering. [175]

"One who does not seek delight in the earth element ... in the air element does not seek delight in suffering. One who does not seek delight in suffering, I say, is freed from suffering."

36 (7) Arising

At Sāvatthī. "Bhikkhus, the arising, continuation, production, and manifestation of the earth element is the arising of suffering, the continuation of disease, the manifestation of aging-and-death.[253] The arising, continuation, production, and manifestation of the water element ... the heat element ... the air element is the arising of suffering, the continuation of disease, the manifestation of aging-and-death.

"The cessation, subsiding, and passing away of the earth element ... the air element is the cessation of suffering, the subsiding of disease, the passing away of aging-and-death."

37 (8) Ascetics and Brahmins (1)

At Sāvatthī. "Bhikkhus, there are these four elements. What four? The earth element, the water element, the heat element, the air element.

"Those ascetics or brahmins, bhikkhus, who do not understand as they really are the gratification, the danger, and the escape in the case of these four elements: [176] these I do not consider to be ascetics among ascetics or brahmins among brahmins, and these venerable ones do not, by realizing it for themselves with direct knowledge, in this very life enter and dwell in the goal of asceticism or the goal of brahminhood.

"But, bhikkhus, those ascetics and brahmins who understand as they really are the gratification, the danger, and the escape in the case of these four elements: these I consider to be ascetics among ascetics and brahmins among brahmins, and these venerable ones, by realizing it for themselves with direct knowledge, in this very life enter and dwell in the goal of asceticism and the goal of brahminhood."

38 (9) Ascetics and Brahmins (2)

At Sāvatthī. "Bhikkhus, there are these four elements. What four?

The earth element, the water element, the heat element, the air element.

"Those ascetics or brahmins, bhikkhus, who do not understand as they really are the origin and the passing away, the gratification, the danger, and the escape in the case of these four elements: these I do not consider to be ascetics among ascetics....

"But, bhikkhus, those ascetics and brahmins who understand as they really are the origin and the passing away, the gratification, the danger, and the escape in the case of these four elements: these I consider to be ascetics among ascetics and brahmins among brahmins, and these venerable ones, by realizing it for themselves with direct knowledge, in this very life enter and dwell in the goal of asceticism and the goal of brahminhood."

39 (10) Ascetics and Brahmins (3)

At Sāvatthī. "Bhikkhus, those ascetics or brahmins who do not understand the earth element, its origin, its cessation, and the way leading to its cessation; [177] who do not understand the water element ... the heat element ... the air element, its origin, its cessation, and the way leading to its cessation: these I do not consider to be ascetics among ascetics....

"But, bhikkhus, those ascetics and brahmins who understand these things: these I consider to be ascetics among ascetics and brahmins among brahmins, and these venerable ones, by realizing it for themselves with direct knowledge, in this very life enter and dwell in the goal of asceticism and the goal of brahminhood."

[178] Chapter IV

15 *Anamataggasaṃyutta*
Connected Discourses on Without Discoverable Beginning

I. The First Subchapter
(Grass and Wood)

1 (1) Grass and Wood

Thus have I heard. On one occasion the Blessed One was dwelling at Sāvatthī in Jeta's Grove, Anāthapiṇḍika's Park. There the Blessed One addressed the bhikkhus thus: "Bhikkhus!"

"Venerable sir!" those bhikkhus replied. The Blessed One said this:

"Bhikkhus, this saṃsāra is without discoverable beginning.[254] A first point is not discerned of beings roaming and wandering on hindered by ignorance and fettered by craving. Suppose, bhikkhus, a man would cut up whatever grass, sticks, branches, and foliage there are in this Jambudīpa and collect them together into a single heap. Having done so, he would put them down, saying [for each one]: 'This is my mother, this my mother's mother.' The sequence of that man's mothers and grandmothers would not come to an end, yet the grass, wood, branches, and foliage in this Jambudīpa would be used up and exhausted. For what reason? Because, bhikkhus, this saṃsāra is without discoverable beginning. A first point is not discerned of beings roaming and wandering on hindered by ignorance and fettered by craving. For such a long time, bhikkhus, you have experienced suffering, anguish, and disaster, and swelled the cemetery. It is enough to experience revulsion towards all formations, enough to become dispassionate towards them, enough to be liberated from them." [179]

2 (2) The Earth

At Sāvatthī. "Bhikkhus, this saṃsāra is without discoverable beginning. A first point is not discerned of beings roaming and wandering on hindered by ignorance and fettered by craving. Suppose, bhikkhus, a man would reduce this great earth to balls of clay the size of jujube kernels and put them down, saying [for each one]: 'This is my father, this my father's father.' The sequence of that man's fathers and grandfathers would not come to an end, yet this great earth would be used up and exhausted. For what reason? Because, bhikkhus, this saṃsāra is without discoverable beginning. A first point is not discerned of beings roaming and wandering on hindered by ignorance and fettered by craving. For such a long time, bhikkhus, you have experienced suffering, anguish, and disaster, and swelled the cemetery. It is enough to experience revulsion towards all formations, enough to become dispassionate towards them, enough to be liberated from them."

3 (3) Tears

At Sāvatthī. "Bhikkhus, this saṃsāra is without discoverable beginning. A first point is not discerned of beings roaming and wandering on hindered by ignorance and fettered by craving. What do you think, bhikkhus, which is more: the stream of tears that you have shed as you roamed and wandered on through this long course, weeping and wailing because of being united with the disagreeable and separated from the agreeable—this or the water in the four great oceans?"[255]

"As we understand the Dhamma taught by the Blessed One, venerable sir, [180] the stream of tears that we have shed as we roamed and wandered through this long course, weeping and wailing because of being united with the disagreeable and separated from the agreeable—this alone is more than the water in the four great oceans."

"Good, good, bhikkhus! It is good that you understand the Dhamma taught by me in such a way. The stream of tears that you have shed as you roamed and wandered through this long course, weeping and wailing because of being united with the disagreeable and separated from the agreeable—this alone is more than the water in the four great oceans. For a long time, bhikkhus, you have experienced the death of a mother; as you have experienced this, weeping and wailing because of being united with the disagreeable and separated from the agreeable, the stream of tears that you have shed is more than the water in the four great oceans.

"For a long time, bhikkhus, you have experienced the death of a father ... the death of a brother ... the death of a sister ... the death of a son ... the death of a daughter ... the loss of relatives ... the loss of wealth ... loss through illness; as you have experienced this, weeping and wailing because of being united with the disagreeable and separated from the agreeable, the stream of tears that you have shed is more than the water in the four great oceans. For what reason? Because, bhikkhus, this saṃsāra is without discoverable beginning.... It is enough to experience revulsion towards all formations, enough to become dispassionate towards them, enough to be liberated from them."

4 (4) Mother's Milk

At Sāvatthī. "Bhikkhus, this saṃsāra is without discoverable beginning. A first point is not discerned of beings roaming and wandering on hindered by ignorance and fettered by craving. What do you think, bhikkhus, which is more: [181] the mother's milk that you have drunk as you roamed and wandered on through this long course—this or the water in the four great oceans?"

"As we understand the Dhamma taught by the Blessed One, venerable sir, the mother's milk that we have drunk as we roamed and wandered on through this long course—this alone is more than the water in the four great oceans."

"Good, good, bhikkhus! It is good that you understand the Dhamma taught by me in such a way. The mother's milk that you have drunk as you roamed and wandered through this long course—this alone is more than the water in the four great oceans. For what reason? Because, bhikkhus, this saṃsāra is without discoverable beginning.... It is enough to be liberated from them."

5 (5) The Mountain

At Sāvatthī. Then a certain bhikkhu approached the Blessed One, paid homage to him, sat down to one side, and said to him: "Venerable sir, how long is an aeon?"[256]

"An aeon is long, bhikkhu. It is not easy to count it and say it is so many years, or so many hundreds of years, or so many thousands of years, or so many hundreds of thousands of years."

"Then is it possible to give a simile, venerable sir?"

"It is possible, bhikkhu," the Blessed One said. "Suppose, bhikkhu, there was a great stone mountain a *yojana* long, a *yojana* wide, and a *yojana* high, without holes or crevices, one solid mass of rock. At the end of every hundred years a man would stroke it once with a piece of Kāsian cloth.[257] That great stone mountain might by this effort be worn away and eliminated but the aeon would still not have come to an end. So long is an aeon, bhikkhu. [182] And of aeons of such length, we have wandered through so many aeons, so many hundreds of aeons, so many thousands of aeons, so many hundreds of thousands of aeons. For what reason? Because, bhikkhu, this saṃsāra is without discoverable beginning.... It is enough to be liberated from them."

6 (6) The Mustard Seed

At Sāvatthī. Then a certain bhikkhu approached the Blessed One, paid homage to him, sat down to one side, and said to him: "Venerable sir, how long is an aeon?"

"An aeon is long, bhikkhu. It is not easy to count it and say it is so many years, or so many hundreds of years, or so many thousands of years, or so many hundreds of thousands of years."

"Then is it possible to give a simile, venerable sir?"

"It is possible, bhikkhu," the Blessed One said. "Suppose, bhikkhu, there was a city with iron walls a *yojana* long, a *yojana* wide, and a *yojana* high, filled with mustard seeds as dense as a topknot. At the end of every hundred years a man would remove one mustard seed from there. The great heap of mustard seeds might by this effort be depleted and eliminated but the aeon would still not have come to an end. So long is an aeon, bhikkhu. And of aeons of such length, we have wandered through so many aeons, so many hundreds of aeons, so many thousands of aeons, so many hundreds of thousands of aeons. For what reason? Because, bhikkhu, this saṃsāra is without discoverable beginning.... It is enough to be liberated from them."

7 (7) Disciples

At Sāvatthī. [183] Then a number of bhikkhus approached the Blessed One, paid homage to him, sat down to one side, and said to him: "Venerable sir, how many aeons have elapsed and gone by?"

"Bhikkhus, many aeons have elapsed and gone by. It is not easy to count them and say they are so many aeons, or so many hundreds of aeons, or so many thousands of aeons, or so many hundreds of thousands of aeons."

"But is it possible to give a simile, venerable sir?"

"It is possible, bhikkhus," the Blessed One said. "Suppose, bhikkhus, there were four disciples here each with a life span of a hundred years, living a hundred years, and each day they were each to recollect a hundred thousand aeons. There would still be aeons not yet recollected by them when those four disciples each with a life span of a hundred years, living a hundred years, would pass away at the end of a hundred years.[258] It is not easy to count them and say that they are so many aeons, or so many hundreds of aeons, or so many thousands of aeons, or so many hundreds of thousands of aeons. For what reason? Because, bhikkhus, this saṃsāra is without discoverable beginning.... It is enough to be liberated from them."

8 (8) The River Ganges

On one occasion the Blessed One was dwelling at Rājagaha in the Bamboo Grove, the Squirrel Sanctuary. Then a certain brahmin approached the Blessed One and exchanged greetings with him. When they had concluded their greetings and cordial talk, he sat down to one side and said to him: "Master Gotama, how many aeons have elapsed and gone by?"

"Brahmin, many aeons have elapsed and gone by. It is not easy to count them and say they are so many aeons, or so many hundreds of aeons, or so many thousands of aeons, or so many hundreds of thousands of aeons." [184]

"But is it possible to give a simile, Master Gotama?"

"It is possible, brahmin," the Blessed One said. "Suppose, brahmin, the grains of sand between the point where the river Ganges originates and the point where it enters the great ocean: it is not easy to count these and say there are so many grains of sand, or so many hundreds of grains, or so many thousands of grains, or so many hundreds of thousands of grains. Brahmin, the aeons that have elapsed and gone by are even more numerous than that. It is not easy to count them and say that they are so many aeons, or so many hundreds of aeons, or so many thousands of aeons, or so many hundreds of thousands of aeons. For what reason? Because, brahmin, this saṃsāra is without discoverable beginning.... It is enough to be liberated from them."

When this was said, that brahmin said to the Blessed One: "Magnificent, Master Gotama! Magnificent, Master Gotama!... From today let Master Gotama remember me as a lay follower who has gone for refuge for life."

9 (9) The Stick

At Sāvatthī. "Bhikkhus, this saṃsāra is without discoverable beginning. A first point is not discerned of beings roaming and wandering on hindered by ignorance and fettered by craving. Just as a stick thrown up into the air falls now on its bottom, now on its side, and now on its top, so too [185] as beings roam and wander on hindered by ignorance and fettered by craving, now they go from this world to the other world, now they come from the other world to this world.[259] For what reason? Because, bhikkhus, this saṃsāra is without discoverable beginning.... It is enough to be liberated from them."

10 (10) Person

On one occasion the Blessed One was dwelling at Rājagaha on Mount Vulture Peak. There the Blessed One addressed the bhikkhus thus: "Bhikkhus!"[260]

"Venerable sir!" those bhikkhus replied. The Blessed One said this:

"Bhikkhus, this saṃsāra is without discoverable beginning. A first point is not discerned of beings roaming and wandering on hindered by ignorance and fettered by craving. One person, roaming and wandering on hindered by ignorance and fettered by craving, would leave behind a stack of bones, a heap of bones, a pile of bones as large as this Mount Vepulla, if there were someone to collect them and what is collected would not perish.[261] For what reason? Because, bhikkhus, this saṃsāra is without discoverable beginning.... It is enough to be liberated from them."

This is what the Blessed One said. Having said this, the Fortunate One, the Teacher, further said this:

"The heap of bones one person leaves behind
With the passing of a single aeon
Would form a heap as high as a mountain:
So said the Great Sage.
This is declared to be as massive
As the tall Vepulla Mountain
Standing north of Vulture Peak
In the Magadhan mountain range.

"But when one sees with correct wisdom
The truths of the noble ones—
Suffering and its origin,
The overcoming of suffering,
And the Noble Eightfold Path
That leads to suffering's appeasement—
Then that person, having wandered on
For seven more times at most, [186]
Makes an end to suffering
By destroying all the fetters."

II. The Second Subchapter
(Unfortunate)

11 (1) Unfortunate

On one occasion, while dwelling at Sāvatthī, the Blessed One said this: "Bhikkhus, this saṃsāra is without discoverable beginning. A first point is not discerned of beings roaming and wandering on hindered by ignorance and fettered by craving. Whenever you see anyone in misfortune, in misery, you can conclude: 'We too have experienced the same thing in this long course.' For what reason? Because, bhikkhus, this saṃsāra is without discoverable beginning.... It is enough to be liberated from them."

12 (2) Happy

At Sāvatthī. "Bhikkhus, this saṃsāra is without discoverable beginning.... Whenever you see anyone happy and fortunate, [187] you can conclude: 'We too have experienced the same thing in this long course.' For what reason? Because, bhikkhus, this saṃsāra is without discoverable beginning.... It is enough to be liberated from them."

13 (3) Thirty Bhikkhus

At Rājagaha in the Bamboo Grove. Then thirty bhikkhus from Pāvā approached the Blessed One—all forest dwellers, almsfood eaters, rag-robe wearers, triple-robe users, yet all were still with fetters.[262] Having approached, they paid homage to the Blessed One and sat down to one side. Then it occurred to the Blessed One: "These thirty bhikkhus from Pāvā are all forest dwellers, almsfood eaters, rag-robe wearers, triple-robe users, yet all are still with fetters. Let me teach them the Dhamma in such a way that while they are sitting in these very seats their minds will be liberated from the taints by nonclinging."

Then the Blessed One addressed those bhikkhus thus: "Bhikkhus!"

"Venerable sir!" those bhikkhus replied. The Blessed One said this:

"Bhikkhus, this saṃsāra is without discoverable beginning. A first point is not discerned of beings roaming and wandering on hindered by ignorance and fettered by craving. What do you think, bhikkhus, which is more: the stream of blood that you have shed when you were beheaded as you roamed and wandered on through this long course—this or the water in the four great oceans?"

"As we understand the Dhamma taught by the Blessed One, venerable sir, the stream of blood that we have shed when our heads were cut off as we roamed and wandered on through this long course—this alone [188] is more than the water in the four great oceans."

"Good, good, bhikkhus! It is good that you understand the Dhamma taught by me in such a way. The stream of blood that you have shed as you roamed and wandered on through this long course—this alone is more than the water in the four great oceans. For a long time, bhikkhus, you have been cows, and when as cows you were beheaded, the stream of blood that you shed is greater than the waters in the four great oceans. For a long time you have been buffalo, sheep, goats, deer, chickens, and pigs…. For a long time you have been arrested as burglars, highwaymen, and adulterers, and when you were beheaded, the stream of blood that you shed is greater than the water in the four great oceans. For what reason? Because, bhikkhus, this saṃsāra is without discoverable beginning…. It is enough to be liberated from them."

This is what the Blessed One said. Elated, those bhikkhus delighted in the Blessed One's statement. [189] And while this exposition was being spoken, the minds of the thirty bhikkhus from Pāvā were liberated from the taints by nonclinging.

14 (4)–19 (9) Mother, Etc.

At Sāvatthī. "Bhikkhus, this saṃsāra is without discoverable beginning…. It is not easy, bhikkhus, to find a being who in this long course has not previously been your mother … your father … your brother … your sister … [190] … your son … your daughter. For what reason? Because, bhikkhus, this saṃsāra is without discoverable beginning…. It is enough to be liberated from them."

20 (10) Mount Vepulla

On one occasion the Blessed One was dwelling at Rājagaha on Mount Vulture Peak. There the Blessed One addressed the bhikkhus thus: "Bhikkhus!"

"Venerable sir!" those bhikkhus replied. The Blessed One said this:

"Bhikkhus, this saṃsāra is without discoverable beginning. A first point is not discerned of beings roaming and wandering on hindered by ignorance and fettered by craving. In the past, bhikkhus, this Mount Vepulla was called Pācīnavaṃsa, [191] and at that time these people were called Tivaras. The life span of the Tivaras was 40,000 years.[263] They could climb Mount Pācīnavaṃsa in four days and descend in four days. At that time the Blessed One Kakusandha, an Arahant, a Perfectly Enlightened One, had arisen in the world. His two chief disciples were named Vidhura and Sañjīva, an excellent pair. See, bhikkhus! That name for this mountain has disappeared, those people have died, and that Blessed One has attained final Nibbāna. So impermanent are formations, bhikkhus, so unstable, so unreliable. It is enough, bhikkhus, to experience revulsion towards all formations, enough to become dispassionate towards them, enough to be liberated from them.

"[At another time] in the past, bhikkhus, this Mount Vepulla was called Vaṅkaka, and at that time these people were called Rohitassas. The life span of the Rohitassas was 30,000 years.[264] They could climb Mount Vaṅkaka in three days and descend in three days. At that time the Blessed One Koṇāgamana, an Arahant, a Perfectly Enlightened One, had arisen in the world. His two chief disciples were named Bhiyyosa and Uttara, an excellent pair. See, bhikkhus! That name for this mountain has disappeared, those people have died, and that Blessed One has attained final Nibbāna. [192] So impermanent are formations.... It is enough to be liberated from them.

"[At still another time] in the past, bhikkhus, this Mount Vepulla was called Supassa, and at that time these people were called Suppiyas. The life span of the Suppiyas was 20,000 years. They could climb Mount Supassa in two days and descend in two days. At that time the Blessed One Kassapa, an Arahant, a Perfectly Enlightened One, had arisen in the world. His two chief disciples were named Tissa and Bhāradvāja, an excellent pair. See, bhikkhus! That name for this mountain has disappeared, those people have died, and that Blessed One has attained final Nibbāna. So impermanent are formations.... It is enough to be liberated from them.

"At present, bhikkhus, this Mount Vepulla is called Vepulla, and at present these people are called Magadhans. The life span of the Magadhans is short, limited, fleeting; one who lives long lives a hundred years or a little more. The Magadhans climb Mount Vepulla in an hour and descend in an hour. At present I have arisen in the world, an Arahant, a Perfectly Enlightened One.

My two chief disciples are named Sāriputta and Moggallāna, an excellent pair. There will come a time, bhikkhus, [193] when the name for this mountain will have disappeared, when these people will have died, and I will have attained final Nibbāna. So impermanent are formations, bhikkhus, so unstable, so unreliable. It is enough, bhikkhus, to experience revulsion towards all formations, enough to become dispassionate towards them, enough to be liberated from them."

This is what the Blessed One said. Having said this, the Fortunate One, the Teacher, further said this:

"This was called Pācīnavaṃsa by the Tivaras,
And Vaṅkaka by the Rohitassas,
Supassa by the Suppiya people,
Vepulla by the Magadhan folk.

"Impermanent, alas, are formations,
Subject to arising and vanishing.
Having arisen, they cease:
Their appeasement is blissful."[265]

[194] Chapter V

16 *Kassapasaṃyutta*

Connected Discourses with Kassapa

1 Content

At Sāvatthī. "Bhikkhus, this Kassapa is content with any kind of robe, and he speaks in praise of contentment with any kind of robe, and he does not engage in a wrong search, in what is improper, for the sake of a robe.[266] If he does not get a robe he is not agitated, and if he gets one he uses it without being tied to it, uninfatuated with it, not blindly absorbed in it, seeing the danger in it, understanding the escape.[267]

"Bhikkhus, this Kassapa is content with any kind of almsfood ... with any kind of lodging ... with any kind of medicinal requisites ... and if he gets them he uses them without being tied to them, uninfatuated with them, not blindly absorbed in them, seeing the danger in them, understanding the escape.

"Therefore, bhikkhus, you should train yourselves thus: 'We will be content with any kind of robe, and we will speak in praise of contentment with any kind of robe, [195] and we will not engage in a wrong search, in what is improper, for the sake of a robe. If we do not get a robe we will not be agitated, and if we get one we will use it without being tied to it, uninfatuated with it, not blindly absorbed in it, seeing the danger in it, understanding the escape.

"'We will be content with any kind of almsfood ... with any kind of lodging ... with any kind of medicinal requisites ... and if we get them we will use them without being tied to them, uninfatuated with them, not blindly absorbed in them, seeing the danger in them, understanding the escape.' Thus should you train yourselves.

"Bhikkhus, I will exhort you by the example of Kassapa or one who is similar to Kassapa.[268] Being exhorted, you should practise accordingly."[269]

2 Unafraid of Wrongdoing

Thus have I heard. On one occasion the Venerable Mahākassapa and the Venerable Sāriputta were dwelling at Bārāṇasī in the Deer Park at Isipatana. Then, in the evening, the Venerable Sāriputta emerged from seclusion and approached the Venerable Mahākassapa. He exchanged greetings with the Venerable Mahākassapa and, when they had concluded their greetings and cordial talk, he sat down to one side and said to him:

"Friend, it is said that one who is not ardent and who is unafraid of wrongdoing is incapable of enlightenment, incapable of Nibbāna, incapable of achieving the unsurpassed security from bondage; but one who is ardent [196] and afraid of wrongdoing is capable of enlightenment, capable of Nibbāna, capable of achieving the unsurpassed security from bondage.[270] In what way is this so, friend?"

"Here, friend, a bhikkhu does not arouse ardour by thinking: 'If unarisen evil unwholesome states arise in me, this may lead to my harm'; nor by thinking: 'If evil unwholesome states that have arisen in me are not abandoned, this may lead to my harm'; nor by thinking: 'If unarisen wholesome states do not arise in me, this may lead to my harm'; nor by thinking: 'If wholesome states that have arisen in me cease, this may lead to my harm.' Thus he is not ardent.[271]

"And how, friend, is he unafraid of wrongdoing? Here, friend, a bhikkhu does not become afraid at the thought: 'If unarisen evil unwholesome states arise in me, this may lead to my harm' ... nor at the thought: 'If wholesome states that have arisen in me cease, this may lead to my harm.' Thus he is unafraid of wrongdoing.

"It is in this way, friend, that one who is not ardent and who is unafraid of wrongdoing is incapable of enlightenment, incapable of Nibbāna, incapable of achieving the unsurpassed security from bondage.

"And how, friend, is one ardent? Here, friend, a bhikkhu arouses ardour by thinking: 'If unarisen evil unwholesome states arise in me, this may lead to my harm' ... and by thinking: 'If wholesome states that have arisen in me cease, this may lead to my harm.' Thus he is ardent.

"And how, friend, is he afraid of wrongdoing? Here, friend, a bhikkhu becomes afraid at the thought: 'If unarisen evil unwholesome states arise in me, this may lead to my harm'; ... and at the thought: 'If wholesome states that have arisen in me cease, this may lead to my harm.' [197] Thus he is afraid of wrongdoing.

"It is in this way, friend, that one who is ardent and afraid of wrongdoing is capable of enlightenment, capable of Nibbāna, capable of achieving the unsurpassed security from bondage."

3 Like the Moon

At Sāvatthī. "Bhikkhus, you should approach families like the moon—[198] drawing back the body and mind, always acting like newcomers, without impudence towards families.[272] Just as a man looking down an old well, a precipice, or a steep riverbank would draw back the body and mind, so too, bhikkhus, should you approach families.

"Bhikkhus, Kassapa approaches families like the moon—drawing back the body and mind, always acting like a newcomer, without impudence towards families. What do you think, bhikkhus, what kind of bhikkhu is worthy to approach families?"

"Venerable sir, our teachings are rooted in the Blessed One, guided by the Blessed One, take recourse in the Blessed One. It would be good if the Blessed One would clear up the meaning of this statement. Having heard it from him, the bhikkhus will remember it."

Then the Blessed One waved his hand in space[273] and said: "Bhikkhus, just as this hand does not get caught in space, is not held fast by it, is not bound by it, so when a bhikkhu approaches families his mind does not get caught, held fast, and bound amidst families, thinking: 'May those desiring gains acquire gains, may those desiring merits make merits!'[274] He is as elated and happy over the gains of others as he is over his own gains. Such a bhikkhu is worthy to approach families.

"Bhikkhus, when Kassapa approaches families his mind does not get caught, held fast, or bound amidst families, thinking: 'May those desiring gains acquire gains, may those desiring merits make merits!' He is as elated and happy over the gains of others as he is over his own gains. [199]

"What do you think, bhikkhus, how is a bhikkhu's teaching of the Dhamma impure, and how is his teaching of the Dhamma pure?"

"Venerable sir, our teachings are rooted in the Blessed One...."

"Then listen and attend closely, bhikkhus, I will speak."

"Yes, venerable sir," those bhikkhus replied. The Blessed One said this:

"A bhikkhu teaches the Dhamma to others with the thought: 'Oh, may they listen to the Dhamma from me! Having listened, may they gain confidence in the Dhamma! Being confident, may they show their confidence to me!'[275] Such a bhikkhu's teaching of the Dhamma is impure.

"But a bhikkhu teaches the Dhamma to others with the thought: 'The Dhamma is well expounded by the Blessed One, directly visible, immediate, inviting one to come and see, applicable, to be personally experienced by the wise. Oh, may they listen to the Dhamma from me! Having listened, may they understand the Dhamma! Having understood, may they practise accordingly!' Thus he teaches the Dhamma to others because of the intrinsic excellence of the Dhamma; he teaches the Dhamma to others from compassion and sympathy, out of tender concern.[276] Such a bhikkhu's teaching of the Dhamma is pure.

"Bhikkhus, Kassapa teaches the Dhamma to others with the thought: 'The Dhamma is well expounded by the Blessed One.... Oh, [200] may they listen to the Dhamma from me! Having listened, may they understand the Dhamma! Having understood, may they practise accordingly!' He teaches the Dhamma to others because of the intrinsic excellence of the Dhamma; he teaches the Dhamma to others from compassion and sympathy, out of tender concern.

"Bhikkhus, I will exhort you by the example of Kassapa or one who is similar to Kassapa. Being exhorted, you should practise accordingly."

4 A Visitor of Families

At Sāvatthī. "Bhikkhus, what do you think, what kind of bhikkhu is worthy to be a visitor of families,[277] and what kind of bhikkhu is not worthy to be a visitor of families?"

"Venerable sir, our teachings are rooted in the Blessed One...."

The Blessed One said this: "Bhikkhus, a bhikkhu might approach families with the thought: 'May they give to me, not hold back! May they give me much, not a little! May they give me fine things, not shabby things! May they give me promptly, not slowly! May they give me considerately, not casually!' When a bhikkhu approaches families with such a thought, if they do not give, he thereby becomes hurt; on that account he experiences pain and displeasure. If they give little rather than much ... If they give shabby things rather than fine things ... If they give slowly rather than promptly ... If they give casually rather than considerately, he thereby becomes hurt; [201] on that account he experiences pain and displeasure. Such a bhikkhu is not worthy to be a visitor of families.

"Bhikkhus, a bhikkhu might approach families with the thought: 'When among others' families, how could I possibly think: "May they give to me, not hold back!... May they give me respectfully, not casually!"?' When a bhikkhu approaches families with such a thought, if they do not give ... if they give casually rather than considerately, he does not thereby become hurt; he does not on that account experience pain and displeasure. Such a bhikkhu is worthy to be a visitor of families.

"Bhikkhus, Kassapa approaches families with such a thought.... Thus if they do not give ... if they give casually rather than considerately, he does not thereby become hurt; [202] he does not on that account experience pain and displeasure.

"Bhikkhus, I will exhort you by the example of Kassapa or one who is similar to Kassapa. Being exhorted, you should practise accordingly."

5 Old

Thus have I heard. On one occasion the Blessed One was dwelling at Rājagaha in the Bamboo Grove, the Squirrel Sanctuary. Then the Venerable Mahākassapa approached the Blessed One, paid homage to him, and sat down to one side. The Blessed One then said to him: "You are old now, Kassapa, and those worn-out hempen rag-robes must be burdensome for you. Therefore you should wear robes offered by householders, Kassapa, accept meals given on invitation, and dwell close to me."[278]

"For a long time, venerable sir, I have been a forest dweller and have spoken in praise of forest dwelling; I have been an almsfood eater and have spoken in praise of eating almsfood; I have been a rag-robe wearer and have spoken in praise of wearing rag-robes; I have been a triple-robe user and have spoken in praise of using the triple robe; I have been of few wishes and have spoken in praise of fewness of wishes; I have been content and have spoken in praise of contentment; I have been secluded and have spoken in praise of solitude; I have been aloof from society and have spoken in praise of aloofness from society; I have been energetic and have spoken in praise of arousing energy."[279]

"Considering what benefit, Kassapa, have you long been a forest dweller … and spoken in praise of arousing energy?"

"Considering two benefits, venerable sir. [203] For myself I see a pleasant dwelling in this very life, and I have compassion for later generations, thinking, 'May those of later generations follow my example!'[280] For when they hear, 'The enlightened disciples of the Buddha were for a long time forest dwellers and spoke in praise of forest dwelling … were energetic and spoke in praise of arousing energy,' then they will practise accordingly, and that will lead to their welfare and happiness for a long time. Considering these two benefits, venerable sir, I have long been a forest dweller … and have spoken in praise of arousing energy."

"Good, good, Kassapa! You are practising for the welfare and happiness of the multitude, out of compassion for the world, for the good, welfare, and happiness of devas and humans. Therefore, Kassapa, wear worn-out hempen rag-robes, walk for alms, and dwell in the forest."

6 Exhortation (1)

At Rājagaha in the Bamboo Grove. Then the Venerable Mahākassapa approached the Blessed One, paid homage to him, and sat down to one side. The Blessed One then said to him: "Exhort the bhikkhus, Kassapa, give them a Dhamma talk. Either I [204] should exhort the bhikkhus, Kassapa, or you should. Either I should give them a Dhamma talk or you should."[281]

"Venerable sir, the bhikkhus are difficult to admonish now, and they have qualities which make them difficult to admonish.[282] They are impatient and do not accept instruction respectfully.

Here, venerable sir, I saw a bhikkhu named Bhaṇḍa, a pupil of Ānanda, and a bhikkhu named Abhiñjika, a pupil of Anuruddha, competing with each other in regard to their learning, saying: 'Come, bhikkhu, who can speak more? Who can speak better? Who can speak longer?'"

Then the Blessed One addressed a certain bhikkhu thus: "Come, bhikkhu, tell the bhikkhu Bhaṇḍa and the bhikkhu Abhiñjika in my name that the Teacher calls them."

"Yes, venerable sir," that bhikkhu replied, and he went to those bhikkhus and told them: "The Teacher calls the venerable ones."

"Yes, friend," those bhikkhus replied, and they approached the Blessed One, paid homage to him, and sat down to one side. The Blessed One then said to them: "Is it true, bhikkhus, that you have been competing with each other in regard to your learning, as to who can speak more, who can speak better, who can speak longer?"

"Yes, venerable sir."

"Have you ever known me to teach the Dhamma thus: 'Come, bhikkhus, compete with each other in regard to your learning, and see who can speak more, who can speak better, who can speak longer'?" [205]

"No, venerable sir."

"Then if you have never known me to teach the Dhamma thus, what do you senseless men know and see that, having gone forth in such a well-expounded Dhamma and Discipline, you compete with each other in regard to your learning, as to who can speak more, who can speak better, who can speak longer?"

Then those bhikkhus prostrated themselves with their heads at the Blessed One's feet and said: "Venerable sir, we have committed a transgression—so foolish, so confused, so inept were we—in that, having gone forth in such a well-expounded Dhamma and Discipline, we competed with each other in regard to our learning, as to who can speak more, who can speak better, who can speak longer. Venerable sir, may the Blessed One pardon us for our transgression seen as a transgression for the sake of future restraint."

"Surely, bhikkhus, you have committed a transgression—so foolish, so confused, so inept were you—in that, having gone forth in such a well-expounded Dhamma and Discipline, you competed with each other in regard to your learning.... But since you see your transgression as a transgression and make amends for it in accordance with the Dhamma, we pardon you for it. For it is growth in the Noble One's Discipline when one sees one's transgression as a transgression, makes amends for it in accordance with the Dhamma, and undertakes future restraint."

7 Exhortation (2)

At Rājagaha in the Bamboo Grove. Then the Venerable Mahākassapa approached the Blessed One, paid homage to him, and sat down to one side. The Blessed One then said to him: "Exhort the bhikkhus, Kassapa, give them a Dhamma talk. Either I should exhort the bhikkhus, Kassapa, [206] or you should. Either I should give them a Dhamma talk or you should."

"Venerable sir, the bhikkhus are difficult to admonish now, and they have qualities which make them difficult to admonish. They are impatient and do not accept instruction respectfully. Venerable sir,[283] for one who has no faith in regard to wholesome states, no sense of shame, no fear of wrongdoing, no energy, and no wisdom, whether day or night comes only decline is to be expected in regard to wholesome states, not growth. Just as, during the dark fortnight, whether day or night comes the moon declines in colour, circularity, and luminosity, in diameter and circumference, so too, venerable sir, for one who has no faith in wholesome states, no sense of shame, no fear of wrongdoing, no energy, and no wisdom, whether day or night comes only decline is to be expected in regard to wholesome states, not growth.

"A person without faith, venerable sir: this is a case of decline. A person without a sense of shame … who is unafraid of wrongdoing … who is lazy … unwise … angry … malicious: this is a case of decline. When there are no bhikkhus who are exhorters: this is a case of decline.

"Venerable sir, for one who has faith in regard to wholesome states, a sense of shame, fear of wrongdoing, energy, and wisdom, whether day or night comes only growth is to be expected in regard to wholesome states, not decline. Just as, during the bright fortnight, whether day or night comes the moon grows in colour, circularity, [207] and luminosity, in diameter and circumference, so too, venerable sir, for one who has faith in wholesome states, a sense of shame, fear of wrongdoing, energy, and wisdom, whether day or night comes only growth is to be expected in regard to wholesome states, not decline.

"A person with faith, venerable sir: this is a case of nondecline. A person with a sense of shame ... who is afraid of wrongdoing ... energetic ... wise ... without anger ... without malice: this is a case of nondecline. When there are bhikkhus who are exhorters: this is a case of nondecline."

"Good, good, Kassapa!"

(*The Buddha then repeats the entire statement of the Venerable Mahākassapa.*) [208]

8 Exhortation (3)

At Rājagaha in the Bamboo Grove. Then the Venerable Mahākassapa approached the Blessed One, paid homage to him, and sat down to one side. The Blessed One then said to him: "Exhort the bhikkhus, Kassapa, give them a Dhamma talk. Either I should exhort the bhikkhus, Kassapa, or you should. Either I should give them a Dhamma talk or you should."

"Venerable sir, the bhikkhus are difficult to admonish now, and they have qualities which make them difficult to admonish. They are impatient and do not accept instruction respectfully."

"Just so, Kassapa, in the past the elder bhikkhus were forest dwellers and spoke in praise of forest dwelling; they were almsfood eaters and spoke in praise of eating almsfood; they were rag-robe wearers and spoke in praise of wearing rag-robes; they were triple-robe users and spoke in praise of using the triple robe; they were of few wishes and spoke in praise of fewness of wishes; they were content and spoke in praise of contentment; they were secluded and spoke in praise of solitude; they were aloof from society and spoke in praise of aloofness from society; they were energetic and spoke in praise of arousing energy.

"Then, when a bhikkhu was a forest dweller and spoke in praise of forest dwelling ... [209] ... when he was energetic and spoke in praise of arousing energy, the elder bhikkhus would invite him to a seat, saying: 'Come, bhikkhu. What is this bhikkhu's name? This is an excellent bhikkhu. This bhikkhu is keen on training. Come, bhikkhu, here's a seat, sit down.' Then it would occur to the newly ordained bhikkhus: 'It seems that when a bhikkhu is a forest dweller and speaks in praise of forest dwelling ... when he is energetic and speaks in praise of arousing energy, the elder bhikkhus invite him to a seat....' They would practise accordingly, and that would lead to their welfare and happiness for a long time.

"But now, Kassapa, the elder bhikkhus are no longer forest dwellers and do not speak in praise of forest dwelling ... [210] ... they are no longer energetic and do not speak in praise of arousing energy. Now it is the bhikkhu who is well known and famous, one who gains robes, almsfood, lodgings, and medicinal requisites, that the elder bhikkhus invite to a seat, saying: 'Come, bhikkhu. What is this bhikkhu's name? This is an excellent bhikkhu. This bhikkhu is keen on the company of his brothers in the holy life. Come, bhikkhu, here's a seat, sit down.' Then it occurs to the newly ordained bhikkhus: 'It seems that when a bhikkhu is well known and famous, one who gains robes, almsfood, lodgings, and medicinal requisites, the elder bhikkhus invite him to a seat....' They practise accordingly, and that leads to their harm and suffering for a long time.

"If, Kassapa, one speaking rightly could say: 'Those leading the holy life have been ruined by the ruination of those who lead the holy life; those leading the holy life have been vanquished by the vanquishing of those who lead the holy life,'[284] it is just thus that one could rightly say this."

9 Jhānas and Direct Knowledges

At Sāvatthī. "Bhikkhus, to whatever extent I wish, secluded from sensual pleasures, secluded from unwholesome states, I enter and dwell in the first jhāna, which is accompanied by thought and examination, with rapture and happiness born of seclusion. [211] Kassapa too, to whatever extent he wishes, secluded from sensual pleasures, secluded from unwholesome states, enters and dwells in the first jhāna.

"Bhikkhus, to whatever extent I wish, with the subsiding of thought and examination, I enter and dwell in the second jhāna, which has internal confidence and unification of mind, is without thought and examination, and has rapture and happiness born of concentration. Kassapa too, to whatever extent he wishes, with the subsiding of thought and examination, enters and dwells in the second jhāna.

"Bhikkhus, to whatever extent I wish, with the fading away as well of rapture, I dwell equanimous, and mindful and clearly comprehending, I experience happiness with the body; I enter and dwell in the third jhāna of which the noble ones declare: 'He is equanimous, mindful, one who dwells happily.' Kassapa too, to whatever extent he wishes, enters and dwells in the third jhāna.

"Bhikkhus, to whatever extent I wish, with the abandoning of pleasure and pain, and with the previous passing away of joy and displeasure, I enter and dwell in the fourth jhāna, which is neither painful nor pleasant and includes the purification of mindfulness by equanimity. Kassapa too, to whatever extent he wishes, enters and dwells in the fourth jhāna.

"Bhikkhus, to whatever extent I wish, with the complete transcendence of perceptions of forms, with the passing away of perceptions of sensory impingement, with nonattention to perceptions of diversity, aware that 'space is infinite,' I enter and dwell in the base of the infinity of space. Kassapa too, to whatever extent he wishes, enters and dwells in the base of the infinity of space.

"Bhikkhus, to whatever extent I wish, by completely transcending the base of the infinity of space, aware that 'consciousness is infinite,' I enter and dwell in the base of the infinity of consciousness. [212] Kassapa too, to whatever extent he wishes, enters and dwells in the base of the infinity of consciousness.

"Bhikkhus, to whatever extent I wish, by completely transcending the base of the infinity of consciousness, aware that 'there is nothing,' I enter and dwell in the base of nothingness. Kassapa too, to whatever extent he wishes, enters and dwells in the base of nothingness.

"Bhikkhus, to whatever extent I wish, by completely transcending the base of nothingness, I enter and dwell in the base of neither-perception-nor-nonperception. Kassapa too, to whatever extent he wishes, enters and dwells in the base of neither-perception-nor-nonperception.

"Bhikkhus, to whatever extent I wish, by completely transcending the base of neither-perception-nor-nonperception, I enter and dwell in the cessation of perception and feeling. Kassapa too, to whatever extent he wishes, enters and dwells in the cessation of perception and feeling.

"Bhikkhus, to whatever extent I wish, I wield the various kinds of spiritual power: having been one, I become many; having been many, I become one; I appear and vanish; I go unhindered through a wall, through a rampart, through a mountain as though through space; I dive in and out of the earth as though it were water; I walk on water without sinking as though it were earth; seated cross-legged, I travel in space like a bird; with my hand I touch and stroke the moon and sun so powerful and mighty; I exercise mastery with the body as far as the brahmā world. Kassapa too, to whatever extent he wishes, wields the various kinds of spiritual power.

"Bhikkhus, to whatever extent I wish, with the divine ear element, which is purified and surpasses the human, I hear both kinds of sounds, the divine and human, those that are far as well as near. Kassapa too, to whatever extent he wishes, with the divine ear element, which is purified and surpasses the human, hears both kinds of sounds. [213]

"Bhikkhus, to whatever extent I wish, I understand the minds of other beings and persons, having encompassed them with my own mind. I understand a mind with lust as a mind with lust; a mind without lust as a mind without lust; a mind with hatred as a mind with hatred; a mind without hatred as a mind without hatred; a mind with delusion as a mind with delusion; a mind without delusion as a mind without delusion; a contracted mind as contracted and a distracted mind as distracted; an exalted mind as exalted and an unexalted mind as unexalted; a surpassable mind as surpassable and an unsurpassable mind as unsurpassable; a concentrated mind as concentrated and an unconcentrated mind as unconcentrated; a liberated mind as liberated and an unliberated mind as unliberated. Kassapa too, to whatever extent he wishes, understands the minds of other beings and persons, having encompassed them with his own mind.

"Bhikkhus, to whatever extent I wish, I recollect my manifold past abodes, that is, one birth, two births, three births, four births, five births, ten births, twenty births, thirty births, forty births, fifty births, a hundred births, a thousand births, a hundred thousand births, many aeons of world-contraction, many aeons of world-expansion, many aeons of world-contraction and expansion thus: 'There I was so named, of such a clan, with such an appearance, such was my food, such my experience of pleasure and pain, such my life span; passing away from there, I was reborn elsewhere, and there too I was so named, of such a clan, with such an appearance, such was my food, such my experience of pleasure and pain, such my life span; passing away from there, I was reborn here.' Thus I recollect my manifold past abodes with their modes and details. Kassapa too, to whatever extent he wishes, recollects his manifold past abodes with their modes and details.

"Bhikkhus, to whatever extent I wish, with the divine eye, which is purified and surpasses the human, I see beings [214] passing away and being reborn, inferior and superior, beautiful and ugly, fortunate and unfortunate, and I understand how beings fare on according to their kamma thus: 'These beings who engaged in misconduct of body, speech, and mind, who reviled the noble ones, held wrong view, and undertook actions based on wrong view, with the breakup of the body, after death, have been reborn in a state of misery, in a bad destination, in the nether world, in hell; but these beings who engaged in good conduct of body, speech, and mind, who did not revile the noble ones, who held right view, and undertook action based on right view, with the breakup of the body, after death, have been reborn in a good destination, in a heavenly world.' Thus with the divine eye, which is purified and surpasses the human, I see beings passing away and being reborn, inferior and superior, beautiful and ugly, fortunate and unfortunate, and I understand how beings fare on according to their kamma. Kassapa too, to whatever extent he wishes, with the divine eye, which is purified and surpasses the human, sees beings passing away and being reborn, inferior and superior, beautiful and ugly, fortunate and unfortunate, and he understands how beings fare on according to their kamma.

"Bhikkhus, by the destruction of the taints, in this very life I enter and dwell in the taintless liberation of mind, liberation by wisdom, realizing it for myself with direct knowledge.[285] Kassapa too, by the destruction of the taints, in this very life enters and dwells in the taintless liberation of mind, liberation by wisdom, realizing it for himself with direct knowledge."

10 The Bhikkhunīs' Quarters

Thus have I heard. On one occasion the Venerable Mahākassapa was dwelling at Sāvatthī in Jeta's Grove, Anāthapiṇḍika's Park.

Then, in the morning, the Venerable Ānanda dressed and, [215] taking bowl and robe, he approached the Venerable Mahākassapa and said: "Come, Venerable Kassapa, let us go to the bhikkhunīs' quarters."[286]

"You go, friend Ānanda, you're the busy one with many duties."[287]

A second time the Venerable Ānanda said to the Venerable Mahākassapa: "Come, Venerable Kassapa, let us go to the bhikkhunīs' quarters."

"You go, friend Ānanda, you're the busy one with many duties."

A third time the Venerable Ānanda said to the Venerable Mahākassapa: "Come, Venerable Kassapa, let us go to the bhikkhunīs' quarters."

Then, in the morning, the Venerable Mahākassapa dressed and, taking bowl and robe, went to the bhikkhunīs' quarters with the Venerable Ānanda as his companion. When he arrived he sat down on the appointed seat. Then a number of bhikkhunīs approached the Venerable Mahākassapa, paid homage to him, and sat down to one side. As they were sitting there, the Venerable Mahākassapa instructed, exhorted, inspired, and gladdened those bhikkhunīs with a Dhamma talk, after which he rose from his seat and departed.

Then the bhikkhunī Thullatissā, being displeased, expressed her displeasure thus: "How can Master Mahākassapa think of speaking on the Dhamma in the presence of Master Ānanda, the Videhan sage?[288] For Master Mahākassapa to think of speaking on the Dhamma in the presence of Master Ānanda, the Videhan sage—this is just as if a needle-peddler [216] would think he could sell a needle to a needle-maker!"

The Venerable Mahākassapa overheard the bhikkhunī Thullatissā making this statement and said to the Venerable Ānanda: "How is it, friend Ānanda, am I the needle-peddler and you the needle-maker, or am I the needle-maker and you the needle-peddler?"

"Be patient, Venerable Kassapa, women are foolish."[289]

"Hold it, friend Ānanda! Don't give the Saṅgha occasion to investigate you further.[290] What do you think, friend Ānanda, was it you that the Blessed One brought forward in the presence of the Bhikkhu Saṅgha, saying: 'Bhikkhus, to whatever extent I wish, secluded from sensual pleasures, secluded from unwholesome states, I enter and dwell in the first jhāna, which is accompanied by thought and examination, with rapture and happiness born of seclusion. Ānanda too, to whatever extent he wishes, secluded from sensual pleasures, secluded from unwholesome states, enters and dwells in the first jhāna'?"

"No, venerable sir."

"I was the one, friend, that the Blessed One brought forward in the presence of the Bhikkhu Saṅgha, saying: 'Bhikkhus, to whatever extent I wish, ... I enter and dwell in the first jhāna.... Kassapa too, to whatever extent he wishes, enters and dwells in the first jhāna.'

(*The same exchange is repeated for the remaining meditative attainments and the six direct knowledges, all as in the preceding sutta.*) [217]

"I was the one, friend, that the Blessed One brought forward in the presence of the Bhikkhu Saṅgha, saying: 'Bhikkhus, by the destruction of the taints, in this very life I enter and dwell in the taintless liberation of mind, liberation by wisdom, realizing it for myself with direct knowledge. Kassapa too, by the destruction of the taints, in this very life enters and dwells in the taintless liberation of mind, liberation by wisdom, realizing it for himself with direct knowledge.'

"Friend, one might just as well think that a bull elephant seven or seven and a half cubits high could be concealed by a palm leaf as think that my six direct knowledges could be concealed."[291]

But the bhikkhunī Thullatissā fell away from the holy life.[292]

11 The Robe

On one occasion the Venerable Mahākassapa was dwelling in Rājagaha in the Bamboo Grove, the Squirrel Sanctuary. Now on that occasion the Venerable Ānanda was wandering on tour in Dakkhiṇāgiri together with a large Saṅgha of bhikkhus.[293] Now on that occasion thirty bhikkhus—pupils of the Venerable Ānanda—most of them youngsters, had given up the training and had returned to the lower life. [218]

When the Venerable Ānanda had wandered on tour in Dakkhiṇāgiri as long as he wanted, he came back to Rājagaha, to the Bamboo Grove, the Squirrel Sanctuary. He approached the

Venerable Mahākassapa, paid homage to him, and sat down to one side, and the Venerable Mahākassapa said to him: "Friend Ānanda, for how many reasons did the Blessed One lay down the rule that bhikkhus should not take meals among families in groups of more than three?"[294]

"The Blessed One laid down this rule for three reasons, Venerable Kassapa: for restraining ill-behaved persons and for the comfort of well-behaved bhikkhus, [with the intention,] 'May those of evil wishes, by forming a faction, not create a schism in the Saṅgha!'; and out of sympathy towards families.[295] It is for these three reasons, Venerable Kassapa, that the Blessed One laid down this rule."

"Then why, friend Ānanda, are you wandering about with these young bhikkhus who are unguarded in their sense faculties, immoderate in eating, and not devoted to wakefulness? One would think you were wandering about trampling on crops; one would think you were wandering about destroying families. Your retinue is breaking apart, friend Ānanda, your young followers are slipping away. But still this youngster does not know his measure!"

"Grey hairs are growing on my head, Venerable Kassapa. Can't we escape being called a youngster by the Venerable Mahākassapa?"[296] [219]

"Friend Ānanda, it is just because you wander around with these young bhikkhus who are unguarded in their sense faculties.... But still this youngster does not know his measure!"

The bhikkhunī Thullanandā heard:[297] "Master Mahākassapa has disparaged Master Ānanda, the Videhan sage, by calling him a youngster." Then, being displeased at this, she expressed her displeasure thus: "How can Master Mahākassapa, who was formerly a member of another sect,[298] think to disparage Master Ānanda, the Videhan sage, by calling him a youngster?"

The Venerable Mahākassapa overheard the bhikkhunī Thullanandā making this statement and said to the Venerable Ānanda: "Surely, friend Ānanda, the bhikkhunī Thullanandā made that statement rashly, without consideration. For since I shaved off my hair and beard, put on saffron robes, and went forth from the home life into homelessness, I do not recall ever having acknowledged any other teacher except the Blessed One, the Arahant, the Perfectly Enlightened One.

"In the past, friend, when I was still a householder, it occurred to me: 'Household life is confinement, a path of dust, going forth is like the open air. It is not easy for one living at home to lead the perfectly complete, perfectly purified holy life, which is like polished conch. Let me then shave off my hair and beard, put on saffron robes, and go forth from the household life into homelessness.' Some time later [220] I had an outer robe made from patches of cloth;[299] then, acknowledging those who were arahants in the world [as models], I shaved off my hair and beard, put on saffron robes, and went forth from the household life into homelessness.

"When I had thus gone forth, I was travelling along a road when I saw the Blessed One sitting by the Bahuputta Shrine between Rājagaha and Nālandā.[300] Having seen him, I thought: 'If I should ever see the Teacher, it is the Blessed One himself that I would see. If I should ever see the Fortunate One, it is the Blessed One himself that I would see. If I should ever see the Perfectly Enlightened One, it is the Blessed One himself that I would see.' Then I prostrated myself right there at the Blessed One's feet and said to him: 'Venerable sir, the Blessed One is my teacher, I am his disciple. Venerable sir, the Blessed One is my teacher, I am his disciple.'[301]

"When I had said this, the Blessed One said to me: 'Kassapa, if one who does not know and see should say to a disciple so single-minded as yourself: "I know, I see," his head would split. But knowing, Kassapa, I say, "I know"; seeing, I say, "I see."[302]

"'Therefore, Kassapa, you should train yourself thus: "I will arouse a keen sense of shame and fear of wrongdoing towards elders, the newly ordained, and those of middle status." Thus should you train yourself.

"'Therefore, Kassapa, you should train yourself thus: "Whenever I listen to any Dhamma connected with the wholesome, I will listen to it with eager ears, attending to it as a matter of vital concern, applying my whole mind to it."[303] Thus should you train yourself.

"'Therefore, Kassapa, you should train yourself thus: "I will never relinquish mindfulness directed to the body associated with joy." Thus should you train yourself.'[304]

"Then, having given me this exhortation, the Blessed One rose from his seat and departed. [221] For seven days, friend, I ate the country's almsfood as a debtor, but on the eighth day final knowledge arose.[305]

"Then, friend, the Blessed One descended from the road and went to the foot of a tree.[306] I folded in four my outer robe of patches and said to him: 'Venerable sir, let the Blessed One sit down here. This will lead to my welfare and happiness for a long time.' The Blessed One sat down on the appointed seat and said to me: 'Your outer robe of patches is soft, Kassapa.' – 'Venerable sir, let the Blessed One accept my outer robe of patches, out of compassion.' – 'Then will you wear my worn-out hempen rag-robes?' – 'I will, venerable sir.' Thus I offered the Blessed One my outer robe of patches and received from him his worn-out hempen rag-robes.[307]

"If, friend, one speaking rightly could say of anyone: 'He is a son of the Blessed One, born of his breast, born of his mouth, born of the Dhamma, created by the Dhamma, an heir to the Dhamma, a receiver of worn-out hempen rag-robes,' it is of me that one could rightly say this.[308]

"Friend, to whatever extent I wish, secluded from sensual pleasures, secluded from unwholesome states, I enter and dwell in the first jhāna, which is accompanied by thought and examination, [222] with rapture and happiness born of seclusion.... (*As in §9, down to:*)

"Friend, by the destruction of the taints, in this very life I enter and dwell in the taintless liberation of mind, liberation by wisdom, realizing it for myself with direct knowledge.

"Friend, one might just as well think that a bull elephant seven or seven and a half cubits high could be concealed by a palm leaf as think that my six direct knowledges could be concealed."[309]

But the bhikkhunī Thullanandā fell away from the holy life.

12 After Death

On one occasion the Venerable Mahākassapa and the Venerable Sāriputta were dwelling at Bārāṇasī in the Deer Park at Isipatana. Then, in the evening, the Venerable Sāriputta emerged from seclusion and approached the Venerable Mahākassapa. He exchanged greetings with the Venerable Mahākassapa and, when they had concluded their greetings and cordial talk, he sat down to one side and said to him:

"How is it, friend Kassapa, does the Tathāgata exist after death?"[310]

"The Blessed One, friend, has not declared this: 'The Tathāgata exists after death.'"

"Then, friend, does the Tathāgata not exist after death?"

"The Blessed One, friend, has not declared this either: 'The Tathāgata does not exist after death.'" [223]

"How is it then, friend, does the Tathāgata both exist and not exist after death?"

"The Blessed One, friend, has not declared this: 'The Tathāgata both exists and does not exist after death.'"

"Then, friend, does the Tathāgata neither exist nor not exist after death?"

"The Blessed One, friend, has not declared this either: 'The Tathāgata neither exists nor does not exist after death.'"

"Why hasn't the Blessed One declared this, friend?"

"Because this is unbeneficial, irrelevant to the fundamentals of the holy life, and does not lead to revulsion, to dispassion, to cessation, to peace, to direct knowledge, to enlightenment, to Nibbāna. Therefore the Blessed One has not declared this."

"And what, friend, has the Blessed One declared?"

"The Blessed One, friend, has declared: 'This is suffering,' and 'This is the origin of suffering,' and 'This is the cessation of suffering,' and 'This is the way leading to the cessation of suffering.'"

"And why, friend, has the Blessed One declared this?"

"Because, friend, this is beneficial, relevant to the fundamentals of the holy life, and leads to revulsion, to dispassion, to cessation, to peace, to direct knowledge, to enlightenment, to Nibbāna. Therefore the Blessed One has declared this."

13 The Counterfeit of the True Dhamma

Thus have I heard. On one occasion the Blessed One was dwelling at Sāvatthī in Jeta's Grove, Anāthapiṇḍika's Park. Then the Venerable Mahākassapa approached the Blessed One, paid homage to him, sat down to one side, and said to him: [224]

"Venerable sir, what is the reason, what is the cause, why formerly there were fewer training rules but more bhikkhus were established in final knowledge, while now there are more training rules but fewer bhikkhus are established in final knowledge?"[311]

"That's the way it is, Kassapa. When beings are deteriorating and the true Dhamma is disappearing there are more training rules but fewer bhikkhus are established in final knowledge. Kassapa, the true Dhamma does not disappear so long as a counterfeit of the true Dhamma has not arisen in the world. But when a counterfeit of the true Dhamma arises in the world, then the true Dhamma disappears.[312]

"Just as, Kassapa, gold does not disappear so long as counterfeit gold has not arisen in the world, but when counterfeit gold arises then true gold disappears, so the true Dhamma does not disappear so long as a counterfeit of the true Dhamma has not arisen in the world, but when a counterfeit of the true Dhamma arises in the world, then the true Dhamma disappears.

"It is not the earth element, Kassapa, that causes the true Dhamma to disappear, nor the water element, nor the heat element, nor the air element. It is the senseless people who arise right here who cause the true Dhamma to disappear.

"The true Dhamma does not disappear all at once in the way a ship sinks.[313] There are, Kassapa, five detrimental things[314] that lead to the decay and disappearance of the true Dhamma. What are the five? Here the bhikkhus, the bhikkhunīs, the male lay followers, and the female lay followers dwell without reverence and deference towards the Teacher; they dwell without reverence and deference towards the Dhamma; they dwell without reverence and deference towards the Saṅgha; [225] they dwell without reverence and deference towards the training; they dwell without reverence and deference towards concentration.[315] These, Kassapa, are the five detrimental things that lead to the decay and disappearance of the true Dhamma.

"There are five things, Kassapa, that lead to the longevity of the true Dhamma, to its nondecay and nondisappearance. What are the five? Here the bhikkhus, the bhikkhunīs, the male lay followers, and the female lay followers dwell with reverence and deference towards the Teacher; they dwell with reverence and deference towards the Dhamma; they dwell with reverence and deference towards the Saṅgha; they dwell with reverence and deference towards the training; they dwell with reverence and deference towards concentration. These, Kassapa, are the five things that lead to the longevity of the true Dhamma, to its nondecay and nondisappearance."

Chapter VI

17 *Lābhasakkārasaṃyutta*
Connected Discourses on Gains and Honour

I. The First Subchapter
(Dreadful)

1 (1) Dreadful

Thus have I heard. On one occasion the Blessed One was dwelling at Sāvatthī in Jeta's Grove, Anāthapiṇḍika's Park. There the Blessed One addressed the bhikkhus thus: "Bhikkhus!" [226]

"Venerable sir!" those bhikkhus replied. The Blessed One said this:

"Bhikkhus, dreadful are gain, honour, and praise, bitter, vile, obstructive to achieving the unsurpassed security from bondage.[316] Therefore, bhikkhus, you should train yourselves thus: 'We will abandon the arisen gain, honour, and praise, and we will not let the arisen gain, honour, and praise persist obsessing our minds.' Thus should you train yourselves."

2 (2) The Hook

At Sāvatthī. "Bhikkhus, dreadful are gain, honour, and praise, bitter, vile, obstructive to achieving the unsurpassed security from bondage. Suppose a fisherman would cast a baited hook into a deep lake, and a fish on the lookout for food would swallow it. That fish, having swallowed the fisherman's hook, would meet with calamity and disaster, and the fisherman could do with it as he wishes.

"'Fisherman,' bhikkhus: this is a designation for Māra the Evil One. 'Baited hook': this is a designation for gain, honour, and praise. Any bhikkhu who relishes and enjoys the arisen gain, honour, and praise is called a bhikkhu who has swallowed the baited hook, who has met with calamity and disaster, and the Evil One can do with him as he wishes. So dreadful, bhikkhus, are gain, honour, and praise, so bitter, vile, obstructive to achieving the unsurpassed security from bondage. Therefore, bhikkhus, you should train yourselves thus: 'We will abandon the arisen gain, honour, and praise, and we will not let the arisen gain, honour, and praise persist obsessing our minds.' Thus should you train yourselves."

3 (3) *The Turtle*

At Sāvatthī. [227] "Bhikkhus, dreadful are gain, honour, and praise.... Once in the past there was a large family of turtles that had been living for a long time in a certain lake.[317] Then one turtle said to another: 'Dear turtle, do not go to such and such a region.' But that turtle went to that region, and a hunter struck him with a corded harpoon.[318] Then that turtle approached the first one. When the first turtle saw him coming in the distance, he said to him: 'I hope, dear turtle, that you didn't go to that region.' – 'I did go to that region, dear.' – 'I hope you haven't been hit or struck, dear.' – 'I haven't been hit or struck; but there is this cord constantly following behind me.' – 'Indeed you've been hit, dear turtle, indeed you've been struck! Your father and grandfather also met with calamity and disaster on account of such a cord. Go now, dear turtle, you are no longer one of us.'

"'Hunter,' bhikkhus: this is a designation for Māra the Evil One. 'Corded harpoon': this is a designation for gain, honour, and praise. 'Cord': this is a designation for delight and lust. Any bhikkhu who relishes and enjoys the arisen gain, honour, and praise is called a bhikkhu who has been struck with a corded harpoon,[319] who has met with calamity and disaster, and the Evil One can do with him as he wishes. So dreadful, bhikkhus, are gain, honour, and praise.... [228] Thus should you train yourselves."

4 (4) *The Long-Haired Goat*

At Sāvatthī. "Bhikkhus, dreadful are gain, honour, and praise.... Suppose a long-haired she-goat would enter a briar patch. She would get caught here and there, be held fast here and there, be bound here and there, and here and there she would meet with calamity and disaster. So too, bhikkhus, a bhikkhu here whose mind is overcome and obsessed by gain, honour, and praise dresses in the morning and, taking bowl and robe, enters a village or town for alms. He gets caught here and there, is held fast here and there, is bound here and there, and here and there he meets with calamity and disaster. So dreadful, bhikkhus, are gain, honour, and praise.... Thus should you train yourselves."

5 (5) The Dung Beetle

At Sāvatthī. "Bhikkhus, dreadful are gain, honour, and praise.... Suppose there was a beetle, a dung-eater, stuffed with dung, full of dung, and in front of her was a large dunghill. Because of this she would despise the other beetles, thinking: 'I am a dung-eater, stuffed with dung, full of dung, and in front of me there is a large dunghill.' [229] So too, bhikkhus, a bhikkhu here whose mind is overcome and obsessed by gain, honour, and praise dresses in the morning and, taking bowl and robe, enters a village or town for alms. There he would eat as much as he wants, he would be invited for the next day's meal, and his almsfood would be plentiful. When he goes back to the monastery, he boasts before a group of bhikkhus: 'I have eaten as much as I want, I have been invited for tomorrow's meal, and my almsfood is plentiful. I am one who gains robes, almsfood, lodgings, and medicinal requisites, but these other bhikkhus have little merit and influence, and they do not gain robes, almsfood, lodgings, and medicinal requisites.' Thus, because his mind is overcome and obsessed by gain, honour, and praise, he despises the other well-behaved bhikkhus. That will lead to the harm and suffering of this senseless person for a long time. So dreadful, bhikkhus, are gain, honour, and praise.... Thus should you train yourselves."

6 (6) The Thunderbolt

At Sāvatthī. "Bhikkhus, dreadful are gain, honour, and praise.... Whom should a thunderbolt strike, bhikkhus? A trainee upon whom come gain, honour, and praise while he has not yet reached his mind's ideal.[320]

"'Thunderbolt,' bhikkhus: this is a designation for gain, honour, and praise. So dreadful, bhikkhus, are gain, honour, and praise.... Thus should you train yourselves."

7 (7) The Poisoned Dart

At Sāvatthī. [230] "Bhikkhus, dreadful are gain, honour, and praise.... Whom should one pierce with a dart smeared in poison, bhikkhus? A trainee upon whom come gain, honour, and praise while he has not yet reached his mind's ideal.[321]

"'Dart,' bhikkhus: this is a designation for gain, honour, and praise. So dreadful, bhikkhus, are gain, honour, and praise.... Thus should you train yourselves."

8 (8) The Jackal

At Sāvatthī. "Bhikkhus, dreadful are gain, honour, and praise.... Did you hear an old jackal howling when the night was fading?"

"Yes, venerable sir."

"That old jackal is afflicted with a disease called mange.[322] He cannot feel at ease whether he goes into a cave, or to the foot of a tree, or into the open air. Wherever he goes, wherever he stands, wherever he sits, wherever he lies down, there he meets with calamity and disaster. So too, bhikkhus, a bhikkhu here whose mind is overcome and obsessed with gain, honour, and praise does not feel at ease whether he goes into an empty hut, or to the foot of a tree, or into the open air. Wherever he goes, wherever he stands, wherever he sits, wherever he lies down, there he meets with calamity and disaster. [231] So dreadful, bhikkhus, are gain, honour, and praise.... Thus should you train yourselves."

9 (9) The Gale Winds

At Sāvatthī. "Bhikkhus, dreadful are gain, honour, and praise.... Bhikkhus, high in the sky winds called gales are blowing.[323] If a bird goes up there, the gale winds fling it about, and as it is flung about by the gale winds, its feet go one way, its wings another way, its head still another way, and its body still another way. So too, bhikkhus, a bhikkhu here whose mind is overcome and obsessed by gain, honour, and praise dresses in the morning and, taking bowl and robe, enters a village or town for alms with body, speech, and mind unguarded, without setting up mindfulness, unrestrained in his sense faculties. He sees women there lightly clad or lightly attired and lust invades his mind. With his mind invaded by lust he gives up the training and returns to the lower life. Some take his robe, others his bowl, others his sitting cloth, and still others his needle case, as with the bird flung by the gale winds. So dreadful, bhikkhus, are gain, honour, and praise.... Thus should you train yourselves."

10 (10) With Verses

At Sāvatthī. "Bhikkhus, dreadful are gain, honour, and praise.... Bhikkhus, I see some person here [232] whose mind is overcome and obsessed by honour, with the breakup of the body, after death, reborn in a state of misery, in a bad destination, in the nether world, in hell. Then I see some person here whose mind is overcome and obsessed by lack of honour ... reborn in a state of misery.... Then I see some person here whose mind is overcome and obsessed by both honour and lack of honour, with the breakup of the body, after death, reborn in a state of misery, in a bad destination, in the nether world, in hell. So dreadful, bhikkhus, are gain, honour, and praise.... Thus should you train yourselves."

This is what the Blessed One said. Having said this, the Fortunate One, the Teacher, further said this:

"Whether he is showered with honour,
Shown dishonour, or offered both,
His concentration does not vacillate
As he dwells in the measureless state.[324]

When he meditates with perseverance,
An insight-seer of subtle view
Delighting in the destruction of clinging,
They call him truly a superior man."[325]

[233]

II. The Second Subchapter (The Bowl)

11 (1) Golden Bowl

At Sāvatthī. "Bhikkhus, dreadful are gain, honour, and praise.... Bhikkhus, I have known of a certain person here whose mind I have encompassed with my own mind: 'This venerable one would not tell a deliberate lie even for the sake of a golden bowl filled with powdered silver.' Yet some time later I see him, his mind overcome and obsessed by gain, honour, and praise, telling a deliberate lie. So dreadful, bhikkhus, are gain, honour, and praise.... Thus should you train yourselves."

12 (2) Silver Bowl

At Sāvatthī. "Bhikkhus, dreadful are gain, honour, and praise.... Bhikkhus, I have known of a certain person here whose mind I have encompassed with my own mind: 'This venerable one would not tell a deliberate lie even for the sake of a silver bowl filled with powdered gold.' Yet some time later I see him, his mind overcome and obsessed by gain, honour, and praise, telling a deliberate lie. So dreadful, bhikkhus, are gain, honour, and praise.... Thus should you train yourselves."

13 (3)–20 (10) Suvaṇṇanikkha, Etc.

At Sāvatthī. [234] "Bhikkhus, dreadful are gain, honour, and praise.... Bhikkhus, I have known of a certain person here whose mind I have encompassed with my own mind: 'This venerable one would not tell a deliberate lie even for the sake of a *suvaṇṇanikkha* ... even for the sake of a hundred *suvaṇṇanikkhas* ... even for the sake of a *siṅginikkha* ... for a hundred *siṅginikkhas*[326] ... for the earth filled with gold ... for any material reward ... for the sake of his life ... for the most beautiful girl of the land.[327] Yet some time later I see him, his mind overcome and obsessed by gain, honour, and praise, telling a deliberate lie. So dreadful, bhikkhus, are gain, honour, and praise.... Thus should you train yourselves."

III. The Third Subchapter
(A Woman)

21 (1) A Woman

At Sāvatthī. "Bhikkhus, dreadful are gain, honour, and praise.... [235] Bhikkhus, even though a woman, when one is alone with her, may not persist obsessing one's mind, still gain, honour, and praise might persist obsessing one's mind. So dreadful, bhikkhus, are gain, honour, and praise.... Thus should you train yourselves."

22 (2) The Most Beautiful Girl of the Land

At Sāvatthī. "Bhikkhus, dreadful are gain, honour, and praise.... Bhikkhus, even though the most beautiful girl of the land, when one is alone with her, may not persist obsessing one's mind, still gain, honour, and praise might persist obsessing one's mind. So dreadful, bhikkhus, are gain, honour, and praise.... Thus should you train yourselves."

23 (3) Only Son

At Sāvatthī. "Bhikkhus, dreadful are gain, honour, and praise.... A faithful female lay follower, rightly imploring her only son, dear and beloved, might implore him thus: 'Dear, you should become like Citta the householder and Hatthaka of Āḷavaka'—for this is the standard and criterion for my male disciples who are lay followers, that is, Citta the householder and Hatthaka of Āḷavaka.[328] 'But if, dear, you go forth from the household life into homelessness, you should become like Sāriputta and Moggallāna'—for this is the standard and criterion for my male disciples who are bhikkhus, that is, Sāriputta and Moggallāna. 'While, dear, you are a trainee, one who has not yet reached his mind's ideal, may gain, honour, and praise not come upon you!'

"Bhikkhus, if [236] gain, honour, and praise come upon a bhikkhu while he is a trainee, one who has not yet reached his mind's ideal, this is an obstacle for him. So dreadful, bhikkhus, are gain, honour, and praise.... Thus should you train yourselves."

24 (4) Only Daughter

At Sāvatthī. "Bhikkhus, dreadful are gain, honour, and praise.... A faithful female lay follower, rightly imploring her only daughter, dear and beloved, might implore her thus: 'Dear, you should become like Khujjuttarā the lay follower and Veḷukaṇḍakiyā, Nanda's mother'—for this is the standard and criterion for my female disciples who are lay followers, that is, Khujjuttarā the lay follower and Veḷukaṇḍakiyā, Nanda's mother.[329] 'But if, dear, you go forth from the household life into homelessness, you should become like the bhikkhunīs Khemā and Uppalavaṇṇā'—for this is the standard and criterion for my female disciples who are bhikkhunīs, that is, Khemā and Uppalavaṇṇā. 'While, dear, you are a trainee, one who has not yet reached her mind's ideal, may gain, honour, and praise not come upon you!'

"Bhikkhus, if gain, honour, and praise come upon a bhikkhunī while she is still a trainee, one who has not yet reached her mind's ideal, this is an obstacle for her. So dreadful, bhikkhus, are gain, honour, and praise.... Thus should you train yourselves."

25 (5) Ascetics and Brahmins (1)

At Sāvatthī. [237] "Bhikkhus, those ascetics or brahmins who do not understand as they really are the gratification, the danger, and the escape in the case of gain, honour, and praise:[330] these I do not consider to be ascetics among ascetics or brahmins among brahmins, and these venerable ones do not, by realizing it for themselves with direct knowledge, in this very life enter and dwell in the goal of asceticism or the goal of brahminhood.

"But, bhikkhus, those ascetics and brahmins who understand as they really are the gratification, the danger, and the escape in the case of gain, honour, and praise: these I consider to be ascetics among ascetics and brahmins among brahmins, and these venerable ones, by realizing it for themselves with direct knowledge, in this very life enter and dwell in the goal of asceticism and the goal of brahminhood."

26 (6) Ascetics and Brahmins (2)

At Sāvatthī. "Bhikkhus, those ascetics or brahmins who do not understand as they really are the origin and the passing away, the gratification, the danger, and the escape in the case of gain, honour, and praise: these I do not consider to be ascetics among ascetics....

"But, bhikkhus, those ascetics and brahmins who understand these things: these I consider to be ascetics among ascetics and brahmins among brahmins, and these venerable ones, by realizing it for themselves with direct knowledge, in this very life enter and dwell in the goal of asceticism and the goal of brahminhood."

27 (7) Ascetics and Brahmins (3)

At Sāvatthī. "Bhikkhus, those ascetics or brahmins who do not understand gain, honour, and praise, its origin, its cessation, and the way leading to its cessation: these I do not consider to be ascetics among ascetics....[331]

"But, bhikkhus, those ascetics and brahmins who understand these things: these I consider to be ascetics among ascetics and brahmins among brahmins, and these venerable ones, by realizing it for themselves with direct knowledge, in this very life enter and dwell in the goal of asceticism and the goal of brahminhood."

28 (8) Skin

At Sāvatthī. "Bhikkhus, dreadful are gain, honour, and praise.... [238] Gain, honour, and praise cut through the outer skin, then through the inner skin, then through the flesh, then through the sinews, then through the bone. Having cut through the bone, they reach right to the marrow. So dreadful, bhikkhus, are gain, honour, and praise.... Thus should you train yourselves."

29 (9) The Rope

At Sāvatthī. "Bhikkhus, dreadful are gain, honour, and praise.... Gain, honour, and praise cut through the outer skin, then through the inner skin, then through the flesh, then through the sinews, then through the bone. Having cut through the bone, they reach right to the marrow. Suppose, bhikkhus, a strong man would wrap one's leg with a taut horsehair rope and pull it tight. It would cut through the outer skin, then through the inner skin, then through the flesh, then through the sinews, then through the bone. Having cut through the bone, it would reach right to the marrow. So too, bhikkhus, gain, honour, and praise cut through the outer skin ... they reach right to the marrow. So dreadful, bhikkhus, are gain, honour, and praise.... Thus should you train yourselves."

30 (10) The Bhikkhu

At Sāvatthī. [239] "Bhikkhus, gain, honour, and praise, I say, are an obstacle even for a bhikkhu who is an arahant, one with taints destroyed."

When this was said, the Venerable Ānanda asked the Blessed One: "Why, venerable sir, are gain, honour, and praise an obstacle even for a bhikkhu with taints destroyed?"

"I do not say, Ānanda, that gain, honour, and praise are an obstacle to his unshakable liberation of mind. But I say they are an obstacle to [his attainment of] those pleasant dwellings in this very life which are achieved by one who dwells diligent, ardent, and resolute.[332] So dreadful, Ānanda, are gain, honour, and praise, so bitter, vile, obstructive to achieving the unsurpassed security from bondage. Therefore, Ānanda, you should train yourselves thus: 'We will abandon the arisen gain, honour, and praise, and we will not let the arisen gain, honour, and praise persist obsessing our minds.' Thus should you train yourselves."

IV. The Fourth Subchapter
(Schism in the Saṅgha)

31 (1) Schism

At Sāvatthī. "Bhikkhus, dreadful are gain, honour, and praise.... [240] Because his mind was overcome and obsessed by gain, honour, and praise, Devadatta provoked a schism in the Saṅgha. So dreadful, bhikkhus, are gain, honour, and praise.... Thus should you train yourselves."

32 (2) Wholesome Root

... "Because his mind was overcome and obsessed by gain, honour, and praise, Devadatta's wholesome root was cut off...."[333]

33 (3) Wholesome Nature

... "Because his mind was overcome and obsessed by gain, honour, and praise, Devadatta's wholesome nature was cut off...."

34 (4) Bright Nature

... "Because his mind was overcome and obsessed by gain, honour, and praise, Devadatta's bright nature was cut off...."

35 (5) Not Long After He Left

[241] On one occasion the Blessed One was dwelling in Rājagaha on Mount Vulture Peak not long after Devadatta had left. There, with reference to Devadatta, the Blessed One addressed the bhikkhus thus:[334]

"Bhikkhus, Devadatta's gain, honour, and praise arose to his own downfall and destruction. Just as a plantain tree, a bamboo, or a reed yields fruit to its own downfall and destruction, so Devadatta's gain, honour, and praise arose to his own downfall and destruction. Just as a mule becomes pregnant to its own downfall and destruction, so Devadatta's gain, honour, and praise arose to his own downfall and destruction. So dreadful, bhikkhus, are gain, honour, and praise.... Thus should you train yourselves."

This is what the Blessed One said. Having said this, the Fortunate One, the Teacher, further said this:

"As its own fruit brings destruction
To the plantain, bamboo, and reed,
As its embryo destroys the mule,
So do honours destroy the scoundrel." [242]

36 (6) Five Hundred Carts

While dwelling at Rājagaha in the Bamboo Grove, the Squirrel Sanctuary. Now on that occasion Prince Ajātasattu was going to attend upon Devadatta morning and evening with five hundred carts, and an offering of food was conveyed to him in five hundred pots. Then a number of bhikkhus approached the Blessed

One, paid homage to him, sat down to one side, and reported this matter to the Blessed One. [The Blessed One said:]

"Bhikkhus, do not be envious of Devadatta's gain, honour, and praise. As long as Prince Ajātasattu goes to attend upon Devadatta morning and evening with five hundred carts, and an offering of food is conveyed to him in five hundred pots, only decline can be expected of Devadatta in regard to wholesome states, not growth.

"Just as a wild dog becomes even wilder when they sprinkle bile over its nose,[335] so too, bhikkhus, so long as Prince Ajātasattu goes to attend upon Devadatta ... only decline can be expected of Devadatta in regard to wholesome states, not growth. So dreadful, bhikkhus, are gain, honour, and praise.... Thus should you train yourselves."

37 (7)–43 (13) Mother Sutta, Etc.

At Sāvatthī. "Bhikkhus, dreadful are gain, honour, and praise, bitter, vile, obstructive to achieving the unsurpassed security from bondage. [243] Bhikkhus, I have known of a certain person here, whose mind I have encompassed with my own mind: 'This venerable one would not tell a deliberate lie even for the sake of his mother ... even for the sake of his father ... even for the sake of his brother ... his sister ... his son ... his daughter ... his wife.'[336] Yet some time later I see him, his mind overcome and obsessed by gain, honour, and praise, telling a deliberate lie. So dreadful, bhikkhus, are gain, honour, and praise, so bitter, vile, obstructive to achieving the unsurpassed security from bondage. Therefore, bhikkhus, you should train yourselves thus: [244] 'We will abandon the arisen gain, honour, and praise, and we will not let the arisen gain, honour, and praise persist obsessing our minds.' Thus should you train yourselves."

Chapter VII

18 *Rāhulasaṃyutta*
Connected Discourses with Rāhula

I. The First Subchapter

1 (1) The Eye, Etc.

Thus have I heard. On one occasion the Blessed One was dwelling at Sāvatthī in Jeta's Grove, Anāthapiṇḍika's Park. Then the Venerable Rāhula approached the Blessed One, paid homage to him, sat down to one side, and said to him:[337]

"Venerable sir, it would be good if the Blessed One would teach me the Dhamma in brief, so that, having heard the Dhamma from the Blessed One, I might dwell alone, withdrawn, diligent, ardent, and resolute."

"What do you think, Rāhula, is the eye permanent or impermanent?" – "Impermanent, venerable sir." – "Is what is impermanent suffering or happiness?" – "Suffering, venerable sir." – [245] "Is what is impermanent, suffering, and subject to change fit to be regarded thus: 'This is mine, this I am, this is my self'?" – "No, venerable sir."

"Is the ear ... the nose ... the tongue ... the body ... the mind permanent or impermanent?" – "Impermanent, venerable sir." – "Is what is impermanent suffering or happiness?" – "Suffering, venerable sir." – "Is what is impermanent, suffering, and subject to change fit to be regarded thus: 'This is mine, this I am, this is my self'?" – "No, venerable sir."

"Seeing thus, Rāhula, the instructed noble disciple experiences revulsion towards the eye, revulsion towards the ear, revulsion towards the nose, revulsion towards the tongue, revulsion towards the body, revulsion towards the mind. Experiencing revulsion, he becomes dispassionate. Through dispassion [his mind] is liberated.[338] When it is liberated there comes the knowledge: 'It's liberated.' He understands: 'Destroyed is birth, the holy life has been lived, what had to be done has been done, there is no more for this state of being.'"

2 (2) Forms, Etc.

… "What do you think, Rāhula, are forms … [246] … sounds … odours … tastes … tactile objects … mental phenomena permanent or impermanent?" – "Impermanent, venerable sir."…

"Seeing thus, Rāhula, the instructed noble disciple experiences revulsion towards forms ... revulsion towards mental phenomena. Experiencing revulsion, he becomes dispassionate…. He understands: '... there is no more for this state of being.'"

3 (3) Consciousness

… "What do you think, Rāhula, is eye-consciousness … ear-consciousness … nose-consciousness … tongue-consciousness … body-consciousness … mind-consciousness permanent or impermanent?" – "Impermanent, venerable sir."…

"Seeing thus, Rāhula, the instructed noble disciple experiences revulsion towards eye-consciousness … revulsion towards mind-consciousness. Experiencing revulsion, he becomes dispassionate…. He understands: '... there is no more for this state of being.'"

4 (4) Contact

… "What do you think, Rāhula, is eye-contact … ear-contact … nose-contact … tongue-contact … body-contact … mind-contact permanent or impermanent?" – "Impermanent, venerable sir."…

"Seeing thus, Rāhula, the instructed noble disciple experiences revulsion towards eye-contact … revulsion towards mind-contact. Experiencing revulsion, he becomes dispassionate…. [247] He understands: '... there is no more for this state of being.'"

5 (5) Feeling

… "What do you think, Rāhula, is feeling born of eye-contact … feeling born of ear-contact … feeling born of nose-contact … feeling born of tongue-contact … feeling born of body-contact … feeling born of mind-contact permanent or impermanent?" – "Impermanent, venerable sir."…

"Seeing thus, Rāhula, the instructed noble disciple experiences revulsion towards feeling born of eye-contact … revulsion towards feeling born of mind-contact. Experiencing revulsion, he becomes dispassionate…. He understands: '... there is no more for this state of being.'"

6 (6) Perception

… "What do you think, Rāhula, is perception of forms … perception of sounds … perception of odours … perception of tastes … perception of tactile objects … perception of mental phenomena permanent or impermanent?" – "Impermanent, venerable sir."…

"Seeing thus, Rāhula, the instructed noble disciple experiences revulsion towards perception of forms … revulsion towards perception of mental phenomena. Experiencing revulsion, he becomes dispassionate…. He understands: '... there is no more for this state of being.'"

7 (7) Volition

… "What do you think, Rāhula, is volition regarding forms … volition regarding sounds … volition regarding odours … volition regarding tastes … [248] volition regarding tactile objects … volition regarding mental phenomena permanent or impermanent?" – "Impermanent, venerable sir."…

"Seeing thus, Rāhula, the instructed noble disciple experiences revulsion towards volition regarding forms … revulsion towards volition regarding mental phenomena. Experiencing revulsion, he becomes dispassionate…. He understands: '... there is no more for this state of being.'"

8 (8) Craving

… "What do you think, Rāhula, is craving for forms … craving for sounds … craving for odours … craving for tastes … craving for tactile objects … craving for mental phenomena permanent or impermanent?" – "Impermanent, venerable sir."…

"Seeing thus, Rāhula, the instructed noble disciple experiences revulsion towards craving for forms … revulsion towards craving for mental phenomena. Experiencing revulsion, he becomes dispassionate…. He understands: '... there is no more for this state of being.'"

9 (9) Elements

… "What do you think, Rāhula, is the earth element … the water element … the heat element … the air element … the space element … the consciousness element permanent or impermanent?"[339] – "Impermanent, venerable sir."…

"Seeing thus, Rāhula, the instructed noble disciple experiences revulsion towards the earth element … [249] … revulsion towards the water element … revulsion towards the heat element … revulsion towards the air element … revulsion towards the space element … revulsion towards the consciousness element. Experiencing revulsion, he becomes dispassionate…. He understands: '... there is no more for this state of being.'"

10 (10) Aggregates

… "What do you think, Rāhula, is form … feeling … perception … volitional formations … consciousness permanent or impermanent?" – "Impermanent, venerable sir." …

"Seeing thus, Rāhula, the instructed noble disciple experiences revulsion towards form … revulsion towards consciousness. Experiencing revulsion, he becomes dispassionate…. He understands: '... there is no more for this state of being.'"

II. The Second Subchapter

11 (1)–20 (10) The Eye, Etc.

(*These ten suttas are identical in all respects with §§1–10, except that in these suttas the Buddha interrogates Rāhula on his own initiative, without first being asked for a teaching.*) [250–52]

21 (11) Underlying Tendency

At Sāvatthī. Then the Venerable Rāhula approached the Blessed One, paid homage to him, sat down to one side, and said to him:

"Venerable sir, how should one know, how should one see so that, in regard to this body with consciousness and in regard to all external signs, I-making, mine-making, and the underlying tendency to conceit no longer occur within?"[340]

"Any kind of form whatsoever, Rāhula, whether past, future, or present, internal or external, gross or subtle, inferior or superior, far or near—one sees all form as it really is with correct wisdom thus: 'This is not mine, this I am not, this is not my self.'[341]

"Any kind of feeling whatsoever ... Any kind of perception whatsoever ... Any kind of volitional formations whatsoever ... Any kind of consciousness whatsoever, whether past, future, or present, internal or external, gross or subtle, inferior or superior, far or near—one sees all consciousness as it really is with correct wisdom thus: 'This is not mine, this I am not, this is not my self.'

"When one knows and sees thus, Rāhula, then in regard to this body with consciousness and in regard to all external signs, I-making, mine-making, and the underlying tendency to conceit no longer occur within." [253]

22 (12) Rid Of

At Sāvatthī. Then the Venerable Rāhula approached the Blessed One, paid homage to him, sat down to one side, and said to him:

"Venerable sir, how should one know, how should one see so that, in regard to this body with consciousness and in regard to all external signs, the mind is rid of I-making, mine-making, and conceit, has transcended discrimination, and is peaceful and well liberated?"[342]

"Any kind of form whatsoever, Rāhula, whether past, future, or present, internal or external, gross or subtle, inferior or superior, far or near—having seen all form as it really is with correct wisdom thus: 'This is not mine, this I am not, this is not my self,' one is liberated by nonclinging.

"Any kind of feeling whatsoever ... Any kind of perception whatsoever ... Any kind of volitional formations whatsoever ... Any kind of consciousness whatsoever, whether past, future, or present, internal or external, gross or subtle, inferior or superior, far or near—having seen all consciousness as it really is with correct wisdom thus: 'This is not mine, this I am not, this is not my self,' one is liberated by nonclinging.

"When one knows and sees thus, Rāhula, then in regard to this body with consciousness and in regard to all external signs, the mind is rid of I-making, mine-making, and conceit, has transcended discrimination, and is peaceful and well liberated."

[254] Chapter VIII

19 *Lakkhaṇasaṃyutta*
Connected Discourses with Lakkhaṇa

I. The First Subchapter

1 (1) The Skeleton

Thus have I heard. On one occasion the Blessed One was dwelling at Rājagaha, in the Bamboo Grove, the Squirrel Sanctuary. Now on that occasion the Venerable Lakkhaṇa and the Venerable Mahāmoggallāna were dwelling on Mount Vulture Peak.[343] Then, in the morning, the Venerable Mahāmoggallāna dressed and, taking bowl and robe, he approached the Venerable Lakkhaṇa and said to him: "Come, friend Lakkhaṇa, let us enter Rājagaha for alms."

"All right, friend," the Venerable Lakkhaṇa replied. Then, as he was coming down from Mount Vulture Peak, the Venerable Mahāmoggallāna displayed a smile in a certain place.[344] The Venerable Lakkhaṇa said to him: "For what reason, friend Moggallāna, did you display a smile?"

"This is not the time for that question, friend Lakkhaṇa. Ask me that question when we are in the presence of the Blessed One." [255]

Then, when the Venerable Lakkhaṇa and the Venerable Mahāmoggallāna had walked for alms in Rājagaha and returned from their alms round, after their meal they approached the Blessed One. Having paid homage to the Blessed One, they sat down to one side, and the Venerable Lakkhaṇa said to the Venerable Mahāmoggallāna: "Here, as he was coming down from Mount Vulture Peak, the Venerable Mahāmoggallāna displayed a smile in a certain place. For what reason, friend Moggallāna, did you display that smile?"

"Here, friend, as I was coming down from Mount Vulture Peak, I saw a skeleton moving through the air. Vultures, crows, and hawks, following it in hot pursuit, were pecking at it between the ribs, stabbing it, and tearing it apart while it uttered cries of pain.[345] It occurred to me: 'It is wonderful, indeed! It is amazing, indeed! That there could be such a being, that there could be such a spirit, that there could be such a form of individual existence!'"[346]

Then the Blessed One addressed the bhikkhus thus: "Bhikkhus, there are disciples who dwell having become vision, having become knowledge, in that a disciple can know, see, and witness such a sight. In the past, bhikkhus, I too saw that being, but I did not speak about it. For if I had spoken about it, others would not have believed me, and if they had not believed me that would have led to their harm and suffering for a long time.

"That being, bhikkhus, used to be a cattle butcher in this same Rājagaha. Having been tormented in hell for many years, for many hundreds of years, for many thousands of years, for many hundreds of thousands of years as a result of that kamma, [256] as a residual result of that same kamma he is experiencing such a form of individual existence."[347]

(*The remaining suttas of this subchapter follow the same pattern as the first. As in the Pāli text, so in translation here only the phrases that differ are given.*)

2 (2) *The Piece of Meat*

... "Here, friend, as I was coming down from Mount Vulture Peak, I saw a piece of meat moving through the air. Vultures, crows, and hawks, following it in hot pursuit, were stabbing at it and tearing it apart as it uttered cries of pain." ...

"That being, bhikkhus, was a cattle butcher in this same Rājagaha...."[348]

3 (3) *The Lump of Meat*

... "I saw a lump of meat...."

"That being was a poultry butcher in this same Rājagaha...."

4 (4) The Flayed Man

... "I saw a flayed man...."

"That being was a sheep butcher in this same Rājagaha...." [257]

5 (5) Sword Hairs

... "I saw a man with body-hairs of swords moving through the air. Those swords kept on rising up and striking his body while he uttered cries of pain...."

"That being was a hog butcher in this same Rājagaha...."

6 (6) Spear Hairs

... "I saw a man with body-hairs of spears moving through the air. Those spears kept on rising up and striking his body while he uttered cries of pain...."

"That being was a deer hunter in this same Rājagaha...."

7 (7) Arrow Hairs

... "I saw a man with body-hairs of arrows moving through the air. Those arrows kept on rising up and striking his body while he uttered cries of pain...."

"That being was a torturer in this same Rājagaha...."[349]

8 (8) Needle Hairs (1)[350]

... "I saw a man with body-hairs of needles moving through the air. Those needles kept on rising up and striking his body while he uttered cries of pain...."

"That being was a horse trainer in this same Rājagaha...."

9 (9) Needle Hairs (2)

... "I saw a man with body-hairs of needles moving through the air. [258] Those needles entered his head and came out from his mouth; they entered his mouth and came out from his chest; they entered his chest and came out from his belly; they entered his belly and came out from his thighs; they entered his thighs and came out from his calves; they entered his calves and came out from his feet, while he uttered cries of pain…."

"That being was a slanderer in this same Rājagaha…."[351]

10 (10) Pot Testicles

… "I saw a man whose testicles were like pots moving through the air. When he walked, he had to lift his testicles onto his shoulders, and when he sat down he sat on top of his testicles. Vultures, crows, and hawks, following him in hot pursuit, were stabbing at him and tearing him apart while he uttered cries of pain…."

"That being was a corrupt magistrate in this same Rājagaha…."[352]

[259] II. THE SECOND SUBCHAPTER

11 (1) With Head Submerged

… "I saw a man with head submerged in a pit of dung…."

"That being was an adulterer in this same Rājagaha…."[353]

12 (2) The Dung Eater

… "I saw a man submerged in a pit of dung, eating dung with both hands…."

"That being, bhikkhus, was a hostile brahmin in this same Rājagaha. In the time of the Buddha Kassapa's Dispensation, he invited the Bhikkhu Saṅgha to a meal. Having had rice pots filled with dung, he said to the bhikkhus: 'Sirs, eat as much as you want from this and take the rest away with you.'…"[354]

13 (3) The Flayed Woman

… "I saw a flayed woman moving through the air. Vultures, crows, and hawks, following her in hot pursuit, were stabbing at her and tearing her apart while she uttered cries of pain…."

"That woman was an adulteress in this same Rājagaha…."[355] [260]

14 (4) The Ugly Woman

… "I saw a woman, foul-smelling and ugly, moving through the air. Vultures, crows, and hawks, following her in hot pursuit, were stabbing at her and tearing her apart while she uttered cries of pain…."

"That woman was a fortune-teller in this same Rājagaha…."[356]

15 (5) The Sweltering Woman

… "I saw a woman, her body roasting, sweltering, sooty, moving through the air, while she uttered cries of pain…."[357]

"That woman was the chief queen of the king of Kaliṅga. Of a jealous character, she poured a brazier of coals over one of the king's consorts…."

16 (6) The Headless Trunk

… "I saw a headless trunk moving through the air; its eyes and mouth were on its chest. Vultures, crows, and hawks, following it in hot pursuit, were stabbing at it and tearing it apart while it uttered cries of pain…."

"That being was an executioner named Hārika in this same Rājagaha…."

17 (7) The Evil Bhikkhu

… "I saw a bhikkhu moving through the air. His outer robe, bowl, waistband, [261] and body were burning, blazing, and flaming while he uttered cries of pain…."

"That bhikkhu had been an evil bhikkhu in the Buddha Kassapa's Dispensation…."[358]

18 (8) The Evil Bhikkhunī

… "I saw a bhikkhunī moving through the air. Her outer robe, bowl, waistband, and body were burning, blazing, and flaming while she uttered cries of pain…."

"That bhikkhunī had been an evil bhikkhunī in the Buddha Kassapa's Dispensation…."

19 (9)–21 (11) The Evil Probationary Nun, Etc.

… "Here, friend, as I was coming down from Mount Vulture Peak, I saw a probationary nun … a novice monk … a novice nun moving through the air. Her outer robe, bowl, waistband, and body were burning, blazing, and flaming while she uttered cries of pain. It occurred to me: 'It is wonderful, indeed! It is amazing, indeed! That there could be such a being, that there could be such a spirit, that there could be such a form of individual existence!'"

Then the Blessed One addressed the bhikkhus thus: "Bhikkhus, there are disciples who dwell having become vision, having become knowledge, in that a disciple can know, see, and witness such a sight. [262] In the past, bhikkhus, I too saw that novice nun, but I did not speak about it. For if I had spoken about it, others would not have believed me, and if they had not believed me that would have led to their harm and suffering for a long time.

"That novice nun had been an evil novice nun in the Buddha Kassapa's Dispensation. Having been tormented in hell for many years, for many hundreds of years, for many thousands of years, for many hundreds of thousands of years as a result of that kamma, as a residual result of that same kamma she is experiencing such a form of individual existence."

Chapter IX

20 *Opammasaṃyutta*
Connected Discourses with Similes

1 The Roof Peak

Thus have I heard. On one occasion the Blessed One was dwelling at Sāvatthī in Jeta's Grove, Anāthapiṇḍika's Park.... [263] There the Blessed One said this:

"Bhikkhus, just as all the rafters of a peaked house lead to the roof peak and converge upon the roof peak, and all are removed when the roof peak is removed, so too all unwholesome states are rooted in ignorance and converge upon ignorance, and all are uprooted when ignorance is uprooted.[359] Therefore, bhikkhus, you should train yourselves thus: 'We will dwell diligently.' Thus should you train yourselves."

2 The Fingernail

At Sāvatthī. Then the Blessed One took up a little bit of soil in his fingernail and addressed the bhikkhus thus: "Bhikkhus, what do you think, which is more: the little bit of soil that I have taken up in my fingernail or the great earth?"

"Venerable sir, the great earth is more. The little bit of soil that the Blessed One has taken up in his fingernail is trifling. Compared to the great earth, it is not calculable, does not bear comparison, does not amount even to a fraction."

"So too, bhikkhus, those beings who are reborn among human beings are few. But those beings are more numerous who are reborn elsewhere than among human beings.[360] Therefore, bhikkhus, you should train yourselves thus: 'We will dwell diligently.' Thus should you train yourselves."

3 Families

At Sāvatthī. [264] "Bhikkhus, just as it is easy for burglars to assail those families that have many women and few men, so too it is easy for nonhuman beings to assail a bhikkhu who has not developed and cultivated the liberation of mind by lovingkindness.[361]

"Just as it is difficult for burglars to assail those families that have few women and many men, so too it is difficult for nonhuman beings to assail a bhikkhu who has developed and cultivated the liberation of mind by lovingkindness.

"Therefore, bhikkhus, you should train yourselves thus: 'We will develop and cultivate the liberation of mind by lovingkindness, make it our vehicle, make it our basis, stabilize it, exercise ourselves in it, and fully perfect it.' Thus should you train yourselves."

4 Pots of Food

At Sāvatthī. "Bhikkhus, if someone were to give away a hundred pots of food[362] as charity in the morning, a hundred pots of food as charity at noon, and a hundred pots of food as charity in the evening, and if someone else were to develop a mind of lovingkindness even for the time it takes to pull a cow's udder, either in the morning, at noon, or in the evening, this would be more fruitful than the former.[363]

"Therefore, bhikkhus, you should train yourselves thus: 'We will develop and cultivate the liberation of mind by lovingkindness, make it our vehicle, make it our basis, stabilize it, exercise ourselves in it, and fully perfect it.' Thus should you train yourselves." [265]

5 The Spear

At Sāvatthī. "Bhikkhus, suppose there was a sharp-pointed spear, and a man would come along thinking: 'I will bend back this sharp-pointed spear with my hand or fist, twist it out of shape, and twirl it around.'[364] What do you think bhikkhus, would it be possible for that man to do so?"

"No, venerable sir. For what reason? Because it is not easy to bend back that sharp-pointed spear with one's hand or fist, to twist it out of shape, or to twirl it around. That man would only experience fatigue and vexation."

"So too, bhikkhus, when a bhikkhu has developed and cultivated the liberation of mind by lovingkindness, made it a vehicle, made it a basis, stabilized it, exercised himself in it, and fully perfected it, if a nonhuman being thinks he can overthrow his mind, that nonhuman being would only experience fatigue and vexation.

"Therefore, bhikkhus, you should train yourselves thus: 'We will develop and cultivate the liberation of mind by lovingkindness, make it our vehicle, make it our basis, stabilize it, exercise ourselves in it, and fully perfect it.' Thus should you train yourselves."

6 The Archers

At Sāvatthī. "Bhikkhus, suppose there were four firm-bowed archers, [266] trained, dexterous, experienced, standing in each of the four directions.[365] Then a man would come along, thinking: 'I will catch the arrows shot by these four archers in each of the four directions before they reach the ground and then I will bring them back.' What do you think, bhikkhus, would this be enough to say: 'That man is a speedster endowed with supreme speed'?"

"Venerable sir, even if he could catch the arrow shot by one archer before it reached the ground and could bring it back, that would be enough to say: 'That man is a speedster endowed with supreme speed.' There is no need to speak about the arrows shot by all four archers!"

"Bhikkhus, as swift as that man is, still swifter are the sun and moon. As swift as that man is, and as swift as are the sun and moon, and as swift as are the deities that run before the sun and moon, the vital formations[366] perish even more swiftly than that. Therefore, bhikkhus, you should train yourselves thus: 'We will dwell diligently.' Thus should you train yourselves."

7 The Drum Peg

At Sāvatthī. "Bhikkhus, once in the past the Dasārahas had a kettle drum called the Summoner.[367] When the Summoner became cracked, the Dasārahas inserted another peg. [267] Eventually the time came when the Summoner's original drumhead had disappeared and only a collection of pegs remained.

"So too, bhikkhus, the same thing will happen with the

bhikkhus in the future. When those discourses spoken by the Tathāgata that are deep, deep in meaning, supramundane, dealing with emptiness, are being recited,[368] they will not be eager to listen to them, nor lend an ear to them, nor apply their minds to understand them; and they will not think those teachings should be studied and mastered. But when those discourses that are mere poetry composed by poets, beautiful in words and phrases, created by outsiders, spoken by [their] disciples,[369] are being recited, they will be eager to listen to them, will lend an ear to them, will apply their minds to understand them; and they will think those teachings should be studied and mastered. In this way, bhikkhus, those discourses spoken by the Tathāgata that are deep, deep in meaning, supramundane, dealing with emptiness, will disappear.

"Therefore, bhikkhus, you should train yourselves thus: 'When those discourses spoken by the Tathāgata that are deep, deep in meaning, supramundane, dealing with emptiness, are being recited, we will be eager to listen to them, will lend an ear to them, will apply our minds to understand them; and we will think those teachings should be studied and mastered.' Thus should you train yourselves."

8 Blocks of Wood

Thus have I heard. On one occasion the Blessed One was dwelling at Vesālī in the Great Wood in the Hall with the Peaked Roof. There the Blessed One addressed the bhikkhus thus: "Bhikkhus!"

"Venerable sir!" those bhikkhus replied. The Blessed One said this:

"Bhikkhus, now the Licchavis dwell using blocks of wood as cushions; [268] they are diligent and ardent in exercise. King Ajātasattu of Magadha, the Videhan son, does not gain access to them; he does not get a hold on them. But in the future the Licchavis will become delicate, with soft and tender hands and feet; they will sleep until sunrise on soft beds with pillows of cotton wool. Then King Ajātasattu of Magadha will gain access to them; then he will get a hold on them.

"Bhikkhus, now the bhikkhus dwell using blocks of wood as cushions; they are diligent and ardent in striving. Māra the Evil

One does not gain access to them; he does not get a hold on them. But in the future the bhikkhus will become delicate, with soft and tender hands and feet; they will sleep until sunrise on soft beds with pillows of cotton wool. Then Māra the Evil One will gain access to them; he will get a hold on them.

"Therefore, bhikkhus, you should train yourselves thus: 'Using blocks of wood as cushions, we will dwell diligent and ardent in striving.' Thus should you train yourselves."[370]

9 The Bull Elephant

Thus have I heard. On one occasion the Blessed One was dwelling at Sāvatthī in Jeta's Grove, Anāthapiṇḍika's Park. Now on that occasion a certain newly ordained bhikkhu was approaching families excessively. The other bhikkhus told him: "The venerable one should not approach families excessively," but when he was being admonished by them he said: "These elder bhikkhus think they can approach families, so why can't I?"

Then a number of bhikkhus approached the Blessed One, paid homage to him, sat down to one side, [269] and reported this matter to the Blessed One. [The Blessed One said:]

"Bhikkhus, once in the past there was a great lake in a forest, with bull elephants dwelling in its vicinity.[371] Those elephants would plunge into the lake, pull up lotus stalks with their trunks, and, having washed them thoroughly, would chew them and swallow them free from mud. This increased their beauty and strength, and on that account they did not meet death or deadly suffering.

"Their young offspring, emulating those great bull elephants, would plunge into the lake and pull up lotus stalks with their trunks, but without washing them thoroughly, without chewing them, they would swallow them along with the mud. This did not increase their beauty and strength, and on that account they met death or deadly suffering.

"So too, bhikkhus, here the elder bhikkhus dress in the morning and, taking bowl and robe, enter a village or town for alms. There they speak on the Dhamma, and the laypeople show their confidence to them.[372] They use their gains without being tied to them, uninfatuated with them, not blindly absorbed in them, seeing the danger in them and understanding the escape. This increases their beauty and strength, and on that account they do not meet death or deadly suffering.

"The newly ordained bhikkhus, emulating the elder bhikkhus, dress in the morning and, taking bowl and robe, enter a village or town for alms. There they speak on the Dhamma, and the laypeople show their confidence to them. [270] They use their gains while being tied to them, infatuated with them, blindly absorbed in them, not seeing the danger in them and not understanding the escape. This does not increase their beauty and strength, and on that account they meet death or deadly suffering.[373]

"Therefore, bhikkhus, you should train yourselves thus: 'We will use our gains without being tied to them, uninfatuated with them, not blindly absorbed in them, seeing the danger in them and understanding the escape.' Thus should you train yourselves."

10 The Cat

At Sāvatthī. Now on that occasion a certain bhikkhu was socializing with families excessively. The other bhikkhus told him: "The venerable one should not socialize with families excessively," but though he was admonished by them he did not desist.

Then a number of bhikkhus approached the Blessed One, paid homage to him, sat down to one side, and reported this matter to the Blessed One. [The Blessed One said:]

"Bhikkhus, once in the past a cat stood by an alley or a drain or a rubbish bin[374] watching for a little mouse, thinking: 'When this little mouse comes out for food, right there I will grab it and eat it.' Then that mouse came out for food, and the cat grabbed it and swallowed it hastily, without chewing it. Then that little mouse ate the cat's intestines and mesentery, [271] and on that account the cat met with death and deadly suffering.

"So too, bhikkhus, here some bhikkhu dresses in the morning and, taking bowl and robe, enters a village or town for alms with body, speech, and mind unguarded, without setting up mindfulness, unrestrained in his sense faculties. He sees women there lightly clad or lightly attired and lust invades his mind. With his mind invaded by lust he meets death or deadly suffering. For this, bhikkhus, is death in the Noble One's Discipline: that one gives up the training and returns to the lower life. This is deadly suffering: that one commits a certain defiled offence of a kind that allows for rehabilitation.[375]

"Therefore, bhikkhus, you should train yourselves thus: 'We will enter a village or town for alms with body, speech, and mind guarded, with mindfulness set up, restrained in our sense faculties.' Thus should you train yourselves."

11 The Jackal (1)

At Sāvatthī. "Bhikkhus, did you hear an old jackal howling at the flush of dawn?"

"Yes, venerable sir."

"That old jackal is afflicted with a disease called mange. Yet he still goes wherever he wants, stands wherever he wants, sits wherever he wants, [272] lies down wherever he wants, and a cool breeze even blows upon him. It would be good for a certain person here claiming to be a follower of the Sakyan son if he were to experience even such a form of individual existence.[376]

"Therefore, bhikkhus, you should train yourselves thus: 'We will dwell diligently.' Thus should you train yourselves."

12 The Jackal (2)

At Sāvatthī. "Bhikkhus, did you hear an old jackal howling at the flush of dawn?"

"Yes, venerable sir."

"There may be some gratitude and thankfulness in that old jackal, but there is no gratitude and thankfulness in a certain person here claiming to be a follower of the Sakyan son.[377]

"Therefore, bhikkhus, you should train yourselves thus: 'We will be grateful and thankful, and we will not overlook even the least favour done to us.' Thus should you train yourselves."

[273]

Chapter X

21 *Bhikkhusaṃyutta*

Connected Discourses with Bhikkhus

1 Kolita[378]

Thus have I heard. On one occasion the Blessed One was dwelling at Sāvatthī in Jeta's Grove, Anāthapiṇḍika's Park. There the Venerable Mahāmoggallāna addressed the bhikkhus thus: "Friends, bhikkhus!"

"Friend!" those bhikkhus replied. The Venerable Mahāmoggallāna said this:

"Here, friends, while I was alone in seclusion, a reflection arose in my mind thus: 'It is said, "noble silence, noble silence." What now is noble silence?'[379]

"Then, friends, it occurred to me: 'Here, with the subsiding of thought and examination, a bhikkhu enters and dwells in the second jhāna, which has internal confidence and unification of mind, is without thought and examination, and has rapture and happiness born of concentration. This is called noble silence.'

"Then, friends, with the subsiding of thought and examination, I entered and dwelt in the second jhāna, which … has rapture and happiness born of concentration. While I dwelt therein, perception and attention accompanied by thought assailed me.

"Then, friends, the Blessed One came to me by means of spiritual power and said this: 'Moggallāna, Moggallāna, do not be negligent regarding noble silence, brahmin. Steady your mind in noble silence, unify your mind in noble silence, concentrate your mind on noble silence.' Then, friends, on a later occasion, with the subsiding of thought and examination, I entered and dwelt in the second jhāna, which has internal confidence and unification of mind, is without thought and examination, and has rapture and happiness born of concentration.

"If, [274] friends, one speaking rightly could say of anyone: 'He is a disciple who attained to greatness of direct knowledge with the assistance of the Teacher,' it is of me that one could rightly say this."[380]

2 Upatissa[381]

At Sāvatthī. There the Venerable Sāriputta addressed the bhikkhus thus: "Friends, bhikkhus!"

"Friend!" those bhikkhus replied. The Venerable Sāriputta said this:

"Here, friends, when I was alone in seclusion, a reflection arose in my mind thus: 'Is there anything in the world through the change and alteration of which sorrow, lamentation, pain, displeasure, and despair might arise in me?' Then it occurred to me: 'There is nothing in the world through the change and alteration of which sorrow, lamentation, pain, displeasure, and despair might arise in me.'"

When this was said, the Venerable Ānanda said to the Venerable Sāriputta: "Friend Sāriputta, even if the Teacher himself were to undergo change and alteration, wouldn't sorrow, lamentation, pain, displeasure, and despair arise in you?"

"Friend,[382] even if the Teacher himself were to undergo change and alteration, still sorrow, lamentation, pain, displeasure, and despair would not arise in me. However, it would occur to me: 'The Teacher, so influential, so powerful and mighty, has passed away. If the Blessed One had lived for a long time, that would have been for the welfare and happiness of the multitude, out of compassion for the world, for the good, welfare, and happiness of devas and humans.'" [275]

"It must be because I-making, mine-making, and the underlying tendency to conceit have been thoroughly uprooted in the Venerable Sāriputta for a long time[383] that even if the Teacher himself were to undergo change and alteration, still sorrow, lamentation, pain, displeasure, and despair would not arise in him."

3 The Barrel

Thus have I heard. On one occasion the Blessed One was dwelling at Sāvatthī in Jeta's Grove, Anāthapiṇḍika's Park. Now on that occasion the Venerable Sāriputta and the Venerable Mahāmoggallāna were dwelling at Rājagaha in a single dwelling in the Bamboo Grove, the Squirrel Sanctuary. Then, in the evening, the Venerable Sāriputta emerged from seclusion and approached the Venerable Mahāmoggallāna. He exchanged greetings with the Venerable Mahāmoggallāna and, when they had concluded their greetings and cordial talk, he sat down to one side and said to him:

"Friend Moggallāna, your faculties are serene, your facial complexion is pure and bright. Has the Venerable Mahāmoggallāna spent the day in a peaceful dwelling?"

"I spent the day in a gross dwelling, friend, but I did have some Dhamma talk."[384]

"With whom did the Venerable Mahāmoggallāna have some Dhamma talk?"

"I had some Dhamma talk with the Blessed One, friend."

"But the Blessed One is far away, friend. He is now dwelling at Sāvatthī in Jeta's Grove, Anāthapiṇḍika's Park. Did the Venerable Mahāmoggallāna approach the Blessed One by means of spiritual power, or did the Blessed One approach the Venerable Mahāmoggallāna by means of spiritual power?" [276]

"I didn't approach the Blessed One by means of spiritual power, friend, nor did the Blessed One approach me by means of spiritual power. Rather, the Blessed One cleared his divine eye and divine ear element to communicate with me, and I cleared my divine eye and divine ear element to communicate with the Blessed One."[385]

"What kind of Dhamma talk did the Venerable Mahāmoggallāna have with the Blessed One?"

"Here, friend, I said to the Blessed One: 'Venerable sir, it is said, "one with energy aroused, one with energy aroused." In what way, venerable sir, does one have energy aroused?' The Blessed One then said to me: 'Here, Moggallāna, a bhikkhu with energy aroused dwells thus: "Willingly, let only my skin, sinews, and bones remain, and let the flesh and blood dry up in my body, but I will not relax my energy so long as I have not attained what can be attained by manly strength, by manly energy, by manly exertion."[386] It is in such a way, Moggallāna, that one has aroused energy.' Such, friend, is the Dhamma talk that I had with the Blessed One."

"Friend, compared to the Venerable Mahāmoggallāna we are

like a few grains of gravel compared to the Himalayas, the king of mountains. For the Venerable Mahāmoggallāna is of such great spiritual power and might that if so he wished he could live on for an aeon."[387]

"Friend, compared to the Venerable Sāriputta we are like a few grains of salt compared to a barrel of salt. [277] For the Venerable Sāriputta has been extolled, lauded, and praised in many ways by the Blessed One:

"'As Sāriputta is supreme
In wisdom, virtue, and peace,
So a bhikkhu who has gone beyond
At best can only equal him.'"

In this manner both these great nāgas rejoiced in what was well stated and well declared by the other.[388]

4 The Newly Ordained Bhikkhu

At Sāvatthī. Now on that occasion a certain newly ordained bhikkhu, after returning from the alms round, would enter his dwelling after the meal and pass the time living at ease and keeping silent. He did not render service to the bhikkhus at the time of making robes. Then a number of bhikkhus approached the Blessed One, paid homage to him, sat down to one side, and reported this matter to him. Then the Blessed One addressed a certain bhikkhu thus: "Come, bhikkhu, tell that bhikkhu in my name that the Teacher calls him."

"Yes, venerable sir," that bhikkhu replied, and he went to that bhikkhu and told him: "The Teacher calls you, friend."

"Yes, friend," that bhikkhu replied, and he approached the Blessed One, paid homage to him, and sat down to one side. [278] The Blessed One then said to him: "Is it true, bhikkhu, that after returning from the alms round you enter your dwelling after the meal and pass the time living at ease and keeping silent, and you do not render service to the bhikkhus at the time of making robes?"

"I am doing my own duty, venerable sir."

Then the Blessed One, having known with his own mind the reflection in that bhikkhu's mind, addressed the bhikkhus thus:

"Bhikkhus, do not find fault with this bhikkhu. This bhikkhu is one who gains at will, without trouble or difficulty, the four jhānas that constitute the higher mind and provide a pleasant dwelling in this very life. And he is one who, by realizing it for himself with direct knowledge, in this very life enters and dwells in that unsurpassed goal of the holy life for the sake of which clansmen rightly go forth from the household life into homelessness."

This is what the Blessed One said. Having said this, the Fortunate One, the Teacher, further said this:

"Not by means of slack endeavour,
Not by means of feeble effort,
Is this Nibbāna to be achieved,
Release from all suffering.

"This young bhikkhu [by my side]
Is a supreme man indeed:
He carries about his final body,
Having conquered Māra and his mount."[389]

5 Sujāta

At Sāvatthī. Then the Venerable Sujāta approached the Blessed One. The Blessed One saw him coming in the distance and addressed the bhikkhus thus: "Bhikkhus, this clansman is beautiful in both respects. [279] He is handsome, good-looking, pleasing to behold, possessing supreme beauty of complexion. And he is one who, by realizing it for himself with direct knowledge, in this very life enters and dwells in that unsurpassed goal of the holy life for the sake of which clansmen rightly go forth from the household life into homelessness."

This is what the Blessed One said … [who] further said this:

"This bhikkhu shines with sublime beauty,
Having a mind utterly straight.
Detached is he, free from fetters,
Attained to Nibbāna by nonclinging.
He carries about his final body,
Having conquered Māra and his mount."

6 Lakuṇṭaka Bhaddiya

At Sāvatthī. Then the Venerable Lakuṇṭaka Bhaddiya approached the Blessed One.[390] The Blessed One saw him coming in the distance and addressed the bhikkhus thus: "Bhikkhus, do you see that bhikkhu coming, ugly, unsightly, deformed, despised among the bhikkhus?"

"Yes, venerable sir."

"That bhikkhu is of great spiritual power and might. It is not easy to find an attainment which that bhikkhu has not already attained. And he is one who, by realizing it for himself with direct knowledge, in this very life enters and dwells in that unsurpassed goal of the holy life for the sake of which clansmen rightly go forth from the household life into homelessness."

This is what the Blessed One said ... [who] further said this:

"Geese, herons, and peacocks,
Elephants, and spotted deer,
All are frightened of the lion
Regardless of their bodies' size.

"In the same way among human beings
The small one endowed with wisdom—
He is the one that is truly great,
Not the fool with a well-built body." [280]

7 Visākha

Thus have I heard. On one occasion the Blessed One was dwelling at Vesālī in the Great Wood in the Hall with the Peaked Roof. Now on that occasion the Venerable Visākha Pañcāliputta was instructing, exhorting, inspiring, and gladdening the bhikkhus in the assembly hall with a Dhamma talk, [spoken] with speech that was polished, clear, articulate, expressing well the meaning, comprehensive, unattached.[391]

Then, in the evening, the Blessed One emerged from seclusion and approached the assembly hall. He sat down in the appointed seat and addressed the bhikkhus thus: "Bhikkhus, who has been instructing, exhorting, inspiring, and gladdening the bhikkhus in the assembly hall with a Dhamma talk, [spoken] with speech that is polished, clear, articulate, expressing well the meaning, comprehensive, unattached?"

"It was this Venerable Visākha Pañcāliputta, venerable sir."

Then the Blessed One addressed the Venerable Visākha Pañcāliputta thus: "Good, good, Visākha! It is good that you thus instruct the bhikkhus with a Dhamma talk."

This is what the Blessed One said … [who] further said this:

"When the wise man is in the midst of fools
They do not know him if he does not speak,[392]
But they know him when he speaks,
Pointing out the deathless state.

"He should speak and explain the Dhamma,
He should raise high the seers' banner.
Well-spoken words are the seers' banner:
For the Dhamma is the banner of seers." [281]

8 Nanda

At Sāvatthī. Then the Venerable Nanda, the Blessed One's maternal cousin, put on well-pressed and well-ironed robes, painted his eyes, took a glazed bowl, and approached the Blessed One.[393] Having paid homage to the Blessed One, he sat down to one side, and the Blessed One said to him:

"Nanda, this is not proper for you, a clansman who has gone forth out of faith from the household life into homelessness, that you wear well-pressed and well-ironed robes, paint your eyes, and carry a glazed bowl. This is proper for you, Nanda, a clansman who has gone forth out of faith from the household life into homelessness, that you be a forest dweller, an almsfood eater, a rag-robes wearer, and that you dwell indifferent to sensual pleasures."

This is what the Blessed One said … [who] further said this:

"When shall I see Nanda as a forest dweller,
Wearing robes stitched from rags,
Subsisting on the scraps of strangers,[394]
Indifferent towards sensual pleasures?"

Then, some time later, the Venerable Nanda became a forest dweller, an almsfood eater, a rag-robes wearer, and he dwelt indifferent to sensual pleasures.

9 Tissa

At Sāvatthī. [282] Then the Venerable Tissa, the Blessed One's paternal cousin,[395] approached the Blessed One, paid homage to him, and sat down to one side—miserable, sorrowful, with tears streaming down. Then the Blessed One said to him:

"Tissa, why are you sitting there, miserable, sorrowful, with tears streaming down?"

"Because, venerable sir, the bhikkhus have attacked me on all sides with sharp words."[396]

"That, Tissa, is because you admonish others but cannot bear being admonished yourself. Tissa, this is not proper for you, a clansman who has gone forth out of faith from the household life into homelessness, that you admonish others but cannot accept admonition in turn. This is proper for you, Tissa, a clansman who has gone forth out of faith from the household life into homelessness, that you admonish others and accept admonition in turn."

This is what the Blessed One said. Having said this, the Fortunate One, the Teacher, further said this:

"Why are you angry? Don't be angry!
Nonanger is better for you, Tissa.
It is to remove anger, conceit, and scorn,
That the holy life is lived, O Tissa."

10 A Bhikkhu Named Elder

On one occasion the Blessed One was dwelling at Rājagaha in the Bamboo Grove, the Squirrel Sanctuary. Now on that occasion a certain bhikkhu named Elder[397] was a lone dweller and spoke in praise of dwelling alone. He entered the village for alms alone, he returned alone, he sat alone in private, he undertook walking meditation alone.

Then a number of bhikkhus approached the Blessed One, [283] paid homage to him, sat down to one side, and said to him:

"Here, venerable sir, there is a certain bhikkhu named Elder who is a lone dweller and who speaks in praise of dwelling alone."

Then the Blessed One addressed a certain bhikkhu thus: "Come, bhikkhu, tell the bhikkhu Elder in my name that the Teacher calls him."

"Yes, venerable sir," that bhikkhu replied, and he went to the Venerable Elder and told him: "The Teacher calls you, friend Elder."

"Yes, friend," the Venerable Elder replied, and he approached the Blessed One, paid homage to him, and sat down to one side. The Blessed One then said to him: "Is it true, Elder, that you are a lone dweller and speak in praise of dwelling alone?"

"Yes, venerable sir."

"But how, Elder, are you a lone dweller and how do you speak in praise of dwelling alone?"

"Here, venerable sir, I enter the village for alms alone, I return alone, I sit alone in private, and I undertake walking meditation alone. It is in such a way that I am a lone dweller and speak in praise of dwelling alone."

"That is a way of dwelling alone, Elder, I do not deny this. But as to how dwelling alone is fulfilled in detail, listen to that and attend closely, I will speak."

"Yes, venerable sir."

"And how, Elder, is dwelling alone fulfilled in detail? Here, Elder, what lies in the past has been abandoned, what lies in the future has been relinquished, and desire and lust for present forms of individual existence has been thoroughly removed.[398] It is in such a way, Elder, that dwelling alone is fulfilled in detail." [284]

This is what the Blessed One said. Having said this, the Fortunate One, the Teacher, further said this:

"The wise one, all-conqueror, all-knower,
Among all things unsullied, with all cast off,
Liberated in the destruction of craving:
I call that person 'one who dwells alone.'"[399]

11 Mahākappina

At Sāvatthī. Then the Venerable Mahākappina approached the Blessed One.[400] The Blessed One saw him coming in the distance and addressed the bhikkhus thus: "Bhikkhus, do you see that bhikkhu coming, fair-skinned, thin, with a prominent nose?"

"Yes, venerable sir."

"That bhikkhu is of great spiritual power and might. It is not easy to find an attainment which that bhikkhu has not already attained. And he is one who, by realizing it for himself with direct knowledge, in this very life enters and dwells in that unsurpassed goal of the holy life for the sake of which clansmen rightly go forth from the household life into homelessness."

This is what the Blessed One said. Having said this, the Fortunate One, the Teacher, further said this:

"The khattiya is the best among people
For those whose standard is the clan,
But one accomplished in knowledge and conduct
Is best among devas and humans.

"The sun shines by day,
The moon glows at night,
The khattiya shines clad in armour,
The meditative brahmin shines.
But all the time, day and night,
The Buddha shines with glory." [285]

12 Companions

At Sāvatthī. Then two bhikkhus who were companions, pupils of the Venerable Mahākappina, approached the Blessed One. The Blessed One saw them coming in the distance and addressed the bhikkhus thus: "Bhikkhus, do you see those two bhikkhus who are companions coming, pupils of Kappina?"

"Yes, venerable sir."

"Those bhikkhus are of great spiritual power and might. It is not easy to find an attainment that those bhikkhus have not already attained. And they are ones who, by realizing it for themselves with direct knowledge, in this very life enter and dwell in that unsurpassed goal of the holy life for the sake of which clansmen rightly go forth from the household life into homelessness."

This is what the Blessed One said. Having said this, the Fortunate One, the Teacher, further said this:

"These [two] companion bhikkhus
Have been united for a very long time.[401]
The true Dhamma has united them
In the Dhamma proclaimed by the Buddha.

"They have been disciplined well by Kappina
In the Dhamma proclaimed by the Noble One.
They carry about their final bodies,
Having conquered Māra and his mount."

The Book of Causation is finished.

Notes

12. Nidānasaṃyutta

1 Spk: When it is said, "With ignorance as condition, volitional formations," the meaning should be understood by this method: "It is ignorance and it is a condition, hence 'ignorance-as-condition' (*avijjā ca sā paccayo cā ti avijjāpaccayo*). Through that ignorance-as-condition volitional formations come to be (*tasmā avijjāpaccayā saṅkhārā sambhavanti*)."

This explanation suggests that the verb *sambhavanti,* which in the text occurs only at the end of the whole formula, should be connected to each proposition, thus establishing that each conditioned state arises through its condition. The twelve terms of the formula are treated analytically in the next sutta.

At the end of the paragraph, Ee reads *ayaṃ vuccati bhikkhave samuppādo,* but this must be an editorial error as both Be and Se have *paṭicca-samuppādo.*

2 Se adds, at the end of the definition of death, *jīvitindriyassa upacchedo,* which (according to a note in Be) is also found in the Thai and Cambodian eds. The fact that Spk does not gloss this expression may be taken as evidence that it was not in the text available to the commentator. The expression is found, however, in the definition of death at Vibh 99,23–24 and is commented upon at Vibh-a 101,8–12.

Spk: By the terms from "passing away" through "completion of time" he expounds death in worldly conventional terminology (*lokasammutiyā*); by the expressions "breakup of the aggregates" and "the laying down of the carcass" he expounds death in the ultimate sense (*paramattha*). For in the ultimate sense it is only the aggregates that break up; there is no "being" that dies. When the aggregates are breaking up one says, "A being is dying," and when they have broken up it is said, "The being has died."

3 Spk: From "birth" through "production" the teaching is conventional (*vohāradesanā*); the last two terms are an ultimate teaching (*paramatthadesanā*). For in the ultimate sense it is only aggregates that become manifest, not a being.

4 On the meaning of *bhava*, see the General Introduction, pp. 52–53. Spk: In the exposition of existence, *sense-sphere existence* is both kamma-existence (*kammabhava*) and rebirth-existence (*upapattibhava*). Of these, *kamma-existence* is just kamma that leads to sense-sphere existence; for the kamma, being the cause for rebirth-existence in that realm, is spoken of as "existence" by assigning the name of the result to the cause. *Rebirth-existence* is the set of five kammically acquired aggregates produced by that kamma; for this is called "existence" in the sense that "it comes to be there." The same method of explanation applies to form-sphere and formless-sphere existence (except that in formless-sphere rebirth-existence only the four mental aggregates exist).

It should be noted that in interpreting the expression *upādānapaccayā bhavo*, the commentaries take *bhava* as either *kammabhava* or *upapattibhava*, since both volitional activity and rebirth are conditioned by clinging; but in the expression *bhavapaccayā jāti*, they confine *bhava* to *kammabhava*, since *upapattibhava* includes *jāti* and thus cannot be a condition for it. See Vism 572–73 (Ppn 17:258–60) and Vism 575 (Ppn 17:270).

5 Spk defines clinging as tight grasping (*upādānan ti daḷhaggahaṇaṃ vuccati*). Definitions of the four kinds of clinging are at Dhs §§1214–17. In brief, *clinging to sensual pleasures* (*kāmupādāna*) is identical with sensual desire, sensual lust, sensual delight, sensual craving, etc. *Clinging to views* (*diṭṭhupādāna*) is the adoption of any wrong view except those included in the third and fourth types of clinging; Dhs §1215 mentions as an example the nihilist view (see **24:5**). The expression *sīlabbatupādāna* is often translated "clinging to rites and rituals," but neither the canon nor commentaries supports this. I render *sīla* as rules and *vata* as vows, though the intention is actual modes of behaviour prescribed by rules and vows. The laconic definition at

Dhs §1222 reads: "Clinging to rules and vows is the view of ascetics and brahmins outside of here (i.e., outside the Buddhist fold) that purification is achieved by rules, by vows, by rules and vows" (condensed). The reference is evidently to the various types of austerities that the Buddha's contemporaries adopted in the belief that they lead to heaven or to ultimate purification. An example is the "dog rule, dog vow" (*kukkurasīla, kukkuravata*) at MN I 387,18–20; see too the common phrase, *iminā 'haṃ sīlena vā vatena vā tapena vā brahmacariyena vā devo vā bhavissāmi devaññataro vā* (e.g., at MN I 102,10–11). *Clinging to a doctrine of self* (*attavādupādāna*) is defined by way of the twenty types of identity view (*sakkāyadiṭṭhi*), on which see **22:7**, etc.

6 On the translation of *nāmarūpa,* see the General Introduction, pp. 47–49. Vism 558,23–28 (Ppn 17:187) explains that *nāma* denotes the three aggregates—of feeling, perception, and volitional formations—which are called thus because of their "bending" (*namana*) on to an object (in the act of cognizing it). Volition, contact, and attention belong to the aggregate of volitional formations and, according to Spk, have been selected to represent that aggregate here because they are operative even in the weakest classes of consciousness.

7 On the translation of *saṅkhārā,* see the General Introduction, pp. 44–47. Spk: Volitional formations have the characteristic of forming (*abhisaṅkharaṇa*). The *bodily volitional formation* is a volitional formation that occurs through the body; the term is a designation for the twenty kinds of bodily volition (*kāyasañcetanā*)—eight sense-sphere wholesome and twelve unwholesome—that motivate activity in the body door (see CMA 1:4–7, 13). The *verbal volitional formation* is a volitional formation that occurs through speech; the term is a designation for the twenty kinds of verbal volition (*vacīsañcetanā*) that motivate verbal utterances (i.e., the same twenty kinds as mentioned just above, but expressed through speech rather than bodily action). The *mental volitional formation* is a volitional formation that occurs through the mind; the term is a designation for the twenty-nine mundane wholesome and unwholesome mental volitions (*manosañcetanā*) that occur

privately in thought without motivating action in the doors of body and speech. (The additional nine volitions are the five of the form-sphere and four of the formless-sphere cittas, states of purely meditative experience; see CMA 1:18, 22.)

This triad of *saṅkhārā* should not be confused with the triad discussed at **41:6** (IV 293,14–28, also at MN I 301,17–29). I have added "volitional" to the present set to distinguish them from the other, though the Pāli terms are identical. The latter triad is always introduced in relation to the cessation of perception and feeling and is never brought into connection with dependent origination.

8 This definition shows that ignorance, as the most basic cause of saṃsāric existence, is lack of knowledge of the Four Noble Truths. Although in popular accounts ignorance is often identified with the idea of self, the definitions here show that the view of self is an aspect of clinging, which is itself conditioned by craving, while the latter is in turn conditioned by ignorance (see AN V 116,16–21).

9 Spk: By the term "cessation" in all these phrases Nibbāna is being expounded. For all those phenomena cease in dependence on Nibbāna, and therefore the latter is spoken of as their cessation. Thus in this sutta the Blessed One taught the round of existence (*vaṭṭa*) and the ending of the round (*vivaṭṭa*) by twelve phrases and brought the discourse to a climax in arahantship.

10 The next seven suttas describe, in identical terms, the enlightenment of the six past Buddhas and the present Buddha Gotama as the discovery of dependent origination and its cessation. The Pāli text is filled out only for Vipassī and Gotama; the others are drastically abridged. I have translated in full only the last sutta, where Gotama speaks of his own attainment of enlightenment.

11 From the explanation of *bodhisatta* in Spk it appears that the Pāli commentarial tradition recognizes alternative etymologies of the word, as equivalent either to Skt *bodhisattva* ("an enlightenment being") or to **bodhisakta* ("one devoted to enlightenment"); see PED, s.v. *satta* (1).

Spk: *Bodhi* is knowledge; a being endowed with *bodhi* is a bodhisatta, a knowing one, a wise one, a sagely one. For from the time he forms his aspiration at the feet of former Buddhas, that being is always wise, never a blind fool. Or else, just as a mature lotus that has risen up above the water and is due to blossom when touched by the sun's rays is called "an awakening lotus," so a being who has obtained the prediction (to future Buddhahood) from the Buddhas and who will inevitably fulfil the perfections (*pāramī*) and attain enlightenment is called an awakening being (*bujjhanasatta*); he is a bodhisatta. One who lives yearning for enlightenment—the knowledge of the four paths—is devoted to, attached to, enlightenment (*bodhiyaṃ satto āsatto*); he is a bodhisatta.

12 The Buddha Vipassī was the sixth Buddha of antiquity, counting back from the Buddha Gotama. A detailed account of his career is found at DN II 11–51. He arose in the world ninety-one aeons ago. Sikhī and Vessabhū arose thirty-one aeons ago; Kakusandha, Koṇāgamana, Kassapa, and Gotama all arose in this present "excellent aeon" (*bhaddakappa*). See DN II 2,15–28.

13 *Yoniso manasikārā ahu paññāya abhisamayo*. The commentaries consistently gloss *yoniso manasikāra* as *upāyamanasikāra, pathamanasikāra*, "attention that is the right means, attention on the (right) course."

There took place (*in me*) *a breakthrough by wisdom*. Spk: There was a breakthrough, a concurrence, a conjunction of the reason for aging-and-death *together with* wisdom (*paññāya saddhiṃ jarāmaraṇakāraṇassa abhisamayo samavāyo samāyogo*); the meaning is that it was seen by him, "Aging-and-death has birth as its condition." Or alternatively, the sense can be construed thus: Through careful attention *and* wisdom there took place a breakthrough (*yoniso manasikārena ca paññāya ca abhisamayo ahu*). The meaning is that the penetration of aging-and-death occurred thus, "When there is birth, aging-and-death comes to be."

The first of these explanations is improbable, and even the second is unsatisfactory in construing careful attention and wisdom as joint causes. In general sutta usage *yoniso manasikāra* is the forerunner of *paññā*, while *paññā* is the efficient cause of *abhisamaya*. As a technical term, *abhisamaya* appears in the Nikāyas in two main contexts: (i) As signifying the initial breakthrough to the Dhamma, *dhammābhisamaya*, it is identical with the obtaining of the vision of the Dhamma (*dhammacakkhupaṭilābha*), and thus with the attainment of stream-entry; see **13:1** (II 134,4–5). (ii) As signifying the complete breaking through of conceit (*sammā mānābhisamaya*) it is equivalent to the attainment of arahantship; see **36:5** (IV 207,14–15) and **I, v. 725**c. A third suttanta use is to denote the Buddha's discovery of the Dhamma, as here and in the verb form *abhisameti* at **12:20** below. In the commentaries *abhisamaya* is synonymous with *paṭivedha*, penetration, both terms being used interchangeably to characterize the four functions of the supramundane path; see Vism 689–91 (Ppn 22:92–97).

14 The two statements about the origination of aging-and-death from birth correspond respectively to the two forms of the abstract principle of conditionality. The abstract formula occurs at **12:21**, **22**, **49**, **50**, **61**, and **62**, with a variant at **12:41**. See below **n. 59**. From this it would evidently be a mistake to insist that the formulation in terms of existence (*sati ... hoti*) relates to synchronic conditionality while the formulation in terms of arising (*uppādā ... uppajjati*) relates to diachronic conditionality. Since both apply to every pair of factors, they seem to be alternative ways of expressing the conditioning relationship, either of which subsumes under itself all possible modes of conditionality in their wide variety.

15 In the account of his enlightenment at **12:65** (II 104,13 foll.) the Buddha traces the sequence of conditions back only as far as consciousness, which he then shows to arise in dependence on name-and-form. The same difference in treatment occurs in the corresponding passage on cessation (II 105,20 foll.).

16 The five Pāli words are *cakkhu*, *ñāṇa*, *paññā*, *vijjā*, and *āloka*. While *vijjā* is actually derived from *vindati*, Spk here glosses it as *paṭivedha*, penetration, as though it derived from *vijjhati*, to pierce.

17 *Bhūtānaṃ vā sattānaṃ ṭhitiyā sambhavesīnaṃ vā anuggahāya.* On *sambhavesin* as a future active participle formed from *-esi(n)*, see Geiger, *Pāli Grammar*, §193A, EV I, n. to 527, and CPD, s.v. *-esi(n)* (2). The commentators apparently were

not acquainted with this grammatical form (of which only very few instances exist in Pāli) and hence explain *sambhavesin* as if it was a *bahubbīhi* compound made up of the noun *sambhava* and the adjectival termination *-esin*. Thus Spk comments on the above line: "*Beings who have already come to be* are those who have been born, been produced. *Those about to come to be* (or, on Spk's interpretation, 'seekers of new existence') are those seeking, searching for, a new existence, birth, production (*sambhavesino ti ye sambhavaṃ jātiṃ nibbattiṃ esanti gavesanti*)."

18 Spk: The nutriments are conditions (*paccayā*), for conditions are called nutriments (*āhārā*) because they nourish (or bring forth, *āharanti*) their own effects. Although there are other conditions for beings, these four alone are called nutriments because they serve as *special conditions* for the personal life-continuity (*ajjhattikasantatiyā visesapaccayattā*). For edible food (*kabaliṅkāra āhāra*) is a special condition for the physical body of those beings who subsist on edible food. In the mental body, contact is the special condition for feeling, mental volition for consciousness, and consciousness for name-and-form. As to what they bring forth (or nourish): Edible food, as soon as it is placed in the mouth, brings forth the groups of form with nutritive essence as the eighth (*ojaṭṭhamakarūpāni*; an Abhidhamma term for the simplest cluster of material phenomena); the nutriment contact brings forth the three kinds of feeling; the nutriment mental volition brings forth the three kinds of existence; and the nutriment consciousness brings forth name-and-form on the occasion of rebirth.

In SN, nutriment is further discussed at **12:12**, **31**, **63**, and **64**. For general remarks on the four nutriments, see too Vism 341,7–18 (Ppn 11:1–3). Nyanaponika Thera, *The Four Nutriments of Life*, offers a collection of relevant suttas with commentaries. *Āhāra* is also used in a broader sense of "special condition," without reference to the four nutriments, at **46:51** and **55:31**.

19 *These four kinds of nutriment have craving as their source*. Spk: Beginning with the moment of rebirth, these kinds of nutriment comprised in the individual existence (*attabhāva*, the sentient organism) should be understood to originate by

way of prior craving (*purimataṇhā*; the craving of the previous life that generated rebirth). How? At the moment of rebirth, firstly, there exists nutritive essence (*ojā*) produced within the arisen (bodily) form; this is the kammically acquired edible food originating from prior craving. Then the contact and volition associated with the rebirth-consciousness, and that consciousness itself, are respectively the kammically acquired nutriments of contact, mental volition, and consciousness originating from (prior) craving. Thus at rebirth the nutriments have their source in prior craving. And as at rebirth, so those produced subsequently at the moment of the first *bhavaṅgacitta* should be similarly understood.

On the conditioning role of the nutriments, see CMA 8:23. The commentarial explanation of how craving is the cause of the four nutriments seems roundabout. A simpler explanation, more consonant with the spirit of the suttas, might be that it is craving which impels beings into the perpetual struggle to obtain physical and mental nutriment, both in the present life and in future lives.

20 Spk: The Blessed One stopped the teaching at this point because he knew that a theorist (*diṭṭhigatika*) was sitting in the assembly and he wanted to give him an opportunity to ask his questions.

21 Spk explains that the name "Moḷiya" was given to him in lay life because he wore his hair in a huge topknot (*moḷi*), and the nickname stuck with him after he went forth as a monk. At MN I 122–24 he is admonished by the Buddha for his excessively familiar relations with the bhikkhunīs; in **12:32** below it is announced that he has left the Order and returned to lay life.

22 Phagguna's question, "*Who* consumes...?" is "pregnant" with an implicit view of self. He sees *someone*—a self—standing behind consciousness in the role of a substantial subject. The Buddha must therefore reject as invalid the question itself, which is based on an illegitimate assumption. Spk: *"I do not say, 'One consumes'"*: "I do not say someone—a being or a person (*koci satto vā puggalo vā*)—consumes."

23 In the valid question, the Buddha replaces the personal pronoun *ko*, fraught with substantialist connotations, with

the impersonal form *kissa*, genitive singular of the stem *ki-* (see Geiger, *Pāli Grammar*, §111.1). Although all eds. read here *kissa nu kho bhante viññāṇāhāro*, the sense seems to require that we add *paccayo* at the end. Spk glosses: *Bhante ayaṃ viññāṇāhāro katamassa dhammassa paccayo*? *Paccayo* does in fact occur in the reply.

24 Spk: *The nutriment consciousness*: rebirth-consciousness (*paṭisandhicitta*). *The production of future renewed existence* (*āyatiṃ punabbhavābhinibbatti*): the name-and-form arisen along with that same consciousness.

At AN I 223–24 it is said: "Kamma is the field, consciousness the seed, and craving the moisture, for consciousness ... to become established in a low (middling, superior) realm; thus there is production of future renewed existence (*kammaṃ khettaṃ viññāṇaṃ bījaṃ taṇhā sineho ... hīnāya (majjhimāya, paṇitāya) dhātuyā viññāṇaṃ patiṭṭhitaṃ; evaṃ āyatiṃ punabbhavābhinibbatti hoti*)." This implies that it is the stream of consciousness coming from the preceding existence that functions as the nutriment consciousness by generating, at the moment of conception, the initial rebirth-consciousness, which in turn brings forth (or "nourishes") the concomitant name-and-form.

25 *Tasmiṃ bhūte sati saḷāyatanaṃ*. Spk: When that name-and-form called "the production of renewed existence" is generated, when it exists, the six sense bases come to be. The conjunction *bhūte sati* is unusual and the redundancy can only be avoided if the past participle *bhūte* is here understood to function as a noun denoting the being that has come to be.

26 Spk: Why didn't the theorist ask, "Who comes to be?"? Because he held the belief that it is a being that comes to be, and the Buddha's answer would directly contradict his belief. Further, after being contradicted so many times, he became convinced, and also the Teacher continued the discourse without pause in order to prevent him from asking any more pointless questions.

27 Spk: They do not understand aging-and-death by way of the truth of suffering; nor its origin by way of the truth of the origin, i.e., that aging-and-death arises from birth and craving; nor its cessation by way of the truth of cessation;

nor the way to its cessation by way of the truth of the path. Similarly, in all the following passages, the meaning should be understood by way of the four truths.

Ignorance is not mentioned in the sequence because it is already implied by reference to the origin of volitional formations.

28 *Sāmaññatthaṃ vā brahmaññatthaṃ vā.* Spk: Here the noble path is asceticism and brahminhood, and in both cases the goal should be understood as the noble fruit. See **45:35–38**.

29 *Dvayanissito khvāyaṃ Kaccāna loko yebhuyyena atthitañ c' eva natthitañ ca.* Spk: "For the most part" (*yebhuyyena*) means: for the great multitude, with the exception of the noble individuals (*ariyapuggala*). *The notion of existence* (*atthitā*) is eternalism (*sassata*); *the notion of nonexistence* (*natthitā*) is annihilationism (*uccheda*). Spk-pṭ: The notion of existence is eternalism because it maintains that the entire world (of personal existence) exists forever. The notion of nonexistence is annihilationism because it maintains that the entire world does not exist (forever) but is cut off.

In view of these explanations it would be misleading to translate the two terms, *atthitā* and *natthitā,* simply as "existence" and "nonexistence" and then to maintain (as is sometimes done) that the Buddha rejects all ontological notions as inherently invalid. The Buddha's utterances at **22:94**, for example, show that he did not hesitate to make pronouncements with a clear ontological import when they were called for. In the present passage *atthitā* and *natthitā* are abstract nouns formed from the verbs *atthi* and *natthi*. It is thus the metaphysical assumptions implicit in such abstractions that are at fault, not the ascriptions of existence and nonexistence themselves. I have tried to convey this sense of metaphysical abstraction, conveyed in Pāli by the terminal *-tā*, by rendering the two terms "*the notion* of existence" and "*the notion* of nonexistence," respectively. On the two extremes rejected by the Buddha, see **12:48**, and for the Buddha's teaching on the origin and passing away of the world, **12:44**.

Unfortunately, *atthitā* and *bhava* both had to be rendered by "existence," which obscures the fact that in Pāli they are derived from different roots. While *atthitā* is the notion of existence in the abstract, *bhava* is concrete individual existence in one or another of the three realms. For the sake of marking the difference, *bhava* might have been rendered by "being" (as was done in MLDB), but this English word, I feel, is too broad (suggestive of "Being," the absolute object of philosophical speculation) and does not sufficiently convey the sense of concreteness intrinsic to *bhava*.

30 Spk: *The origin of the world*: the production of the world of formations. *There is no notion of nonexistence in regard to the world*: there does not occur in him the annihilationist view that might arise in regard to phenomena produced and made manifest in the world of formations, holding "They do not exist." Spk-pṭ: The annihilationist view might arise in regard to the world of formations thus: "On account of the annihilation and perishing of beings right where they are, there is no persisting being or phenomenon." It also includes the wrong view, having those formations as its object, which holds: "There are no beings who are reborn." That view *does not occur in him*; for one seeing with right understanding the production and origination of the world of formations in dependence on such diverse conditions as kamma, ignorance, craving, etc., that annihilationist view does not occur, since one sees the uninterrupted production of formations.

Spk: *The cessation of the world*: the dissolution (*bhaṅga*) of formations. *There is no notion of existence in regard to the world*: There does not occur in him the eternalist view which might arise in regard to phenomena produced and made manifest in the world of formations, holding "They exist." Spk-pṭ: The eternalist view might arise in regard to the world of formations, taking it to exist at all times, owing to the apprehension of identity in the uninterrupted continuum occurring in a cause-effect relationship. But that view *does not occur in him*; because he sees the cessation of the successively arisen phenomena and the arising of successively new phenomena, the eternalist view does not occur.

Spk: Further, "the origin of the world" is direct-order conditionality (*anuloma-paccayākāra*); "the cessation of the world," reverse-order conditionality (*paṭiloma-paccayākāra*).

[Spk-pṭ: "Direct-order conditionality" is the conditioning efficiency of the conditions in relation to their own effects; "reverse-order conditionality" is the cessation of the effects through the cessation of their respective causes.] For in seeing the dependency of the world, when one sees the nontermination of the conditionally arisen phenomena owing to the nontermination of their conditions, the annihilationist view, which might otherwise arise, does not occur. And in seeing the cessation of conditions, when one sees the cessation of the conditionally arisen phenomena owing to the cessation of their conditions, the eternalist view, which might otherwise arise, does not occur.

31 The reading I prefer is a hybrid of Be and Se: *upayupādānābhinivesavinibaddho.* I take *upay-* from Be (Se and Ee: *upāy-*) and *-vinibaddho* from Se (Be and Ee: *-vinibandho*). The rendering at KS 2:13, "grasping after systems and imprisoned by dogmas," echoed by SN-Anth 2:17, is too narrow in emphasis. Spk explains that each of the three nouns—engagement, clinging, and adherence—occurs by way of craving and views (*taṇhā, diṭṭhi*), for it is through these that one engages, clings to, and adheres to the phenomena of the three planes as "I" and "mine."

32 *Tañ cāyaṃ upayupādānaṃ cetaso adhiṭṭhānaṃ abhinivesānusayaṃ na upeti na upādiyati nādhiṭṭhāti "attā me" ti.* I have unravelled the difficult syntax of this sentence with the aid of Spk, which glosses *ayaṃ* as "this noble disciple" (*ayaṃ ariyasāvako*). Spk says that craving and views are also called "mental standpoints" (*adhiṭṭhāna*) because they are the foundation for the (unwholesome) mind, and "adherences and underlying tendencies" (*abhinivesānusaya*) because they adhere to the mind and lie latent within it. Spk connects the verb *adhiṭṭhāti* to the following *"attā me,"* and I conform to this interpretation in the translation.

33 Spk explains *dukkha* here as "the mere five aggregates subject to clinging" (*pañcupādānakkhandhamattam eva*). Thus what the noble disciple sees, when he reflects upon his personal existence, is not a self or a substantially existent person but a mere assemblage of conditioned phenomena arising and passing away through the conditioning process governed by dependent origination. In this connection see the verses

of the bhikkhunī Vajirā, **I, vv. 553–55**. Spk: By just this much—the abandonment of the idea of a being (*satta-saññā*)—there is right seeing.

Aparappaccayā ñāṇaṃ, "knowledge independent of others," is glossed by Spk as "personal direct knowledge without dependence on another" (*aññassa apattiyāyetvā attapaccakkha-ñāṇaṃ*). This is said because the noble disciple, from the point of stream-entry on, has seen the essential truth of the Dhamma and thus is not dependent on anyone else, not even the Buddha, for his or her insight into the Dhamma. Until arahantship is attained, however, such a disciple might still approach the Buddha (or another enlightened teacher) for practical guidance in meditation.

34 *Dhammānudhammapaṭipanno*. Spk: *Lokuttarassa nibbāna-dhammassa anudhammabhūtaṃ paṭipadaṃ paṭipanno*; "one practising the way that is in accordance with the supramundane Nibbāna-dhamma." Spk-pṭ glosses *nibbāna-dhamma* as "the noble path bringing Nibbāna," and explains "(the way) that is in accordance with" it as meaning "(the way) whose nature is appropriate for the achievement of Nibbāna" (*nibbānādhigamassa anucchavikasabhāvabhūtaṃ*). This statement shows the *sekha*, the trainee. Cp. **III, n. 51**.

35 *Diṭṭhadhammanibbānappatto*. This statement shows the arahant, or *asekha*, who has completed the training.

36 Spk: Why does the Blessed One refuse three times? In order to inspire reverence; for if theorists are answered too quickly they do not show reverence, but they do so if they are refused two or three times. Then they wish to listen and develop faith. Also, the Master refused in order to create an opportunity for the ascetic's faculty of knowledge to ripen.

37 Of the four alternatives, the first and second, as will be shown, are respectively implicit formulations of eternalism and annihilationism. The third is a syncretic solution, perhaps a form of partial-eternalism (*ekaccasassatavāda*; see DN I 17–21). The fourth is the doctrine of fortuitous origination (*adhiccasamuppannavāda*; see DN I 28–29).

38 Spk points out that the change of address, from the familiar *bho Gotama* to the respectful *bhante bhagavā*, indicates that he has acquired reverence for the Teacher.

39 Spk glosses *ādito sato* as *ādimhi yeva*, and explains it as

meaning "(if) at the beginning (one thinks)...." It seems to me more likely that this phrase is part of the eternalist view itself and means "of one existing from the beginning," i.e., of a being that has always existed. This interpretation can marshal support from the fact that the phrase is omitted just below in the corresponding restatement of the annihilationist view, which is otherwise constructed according to the same logic and thus, if Spk were correct, should include *ādito sato*. Spk says "it should be brought in," but the fact that the text replaces it by another phrase is strong evidence that it does not belong there; see **n. 40**.

Spk: If at the beginning (one thinks), "The one who acts is the same as the one who experiences (the result)," in such a case the belief (*laddhi*) afterwards follows, "Suffering is created by oneself." And here, what is meant by suffering is the suffering of the round (*vaṭṭadukkha*). Asserting thus, from the beginning one declares eternalism, one grasps hold of eternalism. Why? Because that view of his amounts to this. Eternalism comes upon one who conceives the agent and the experiencer to be one and the same.

Spk-pṭ: Prior to the belief that suffering is created by oneself there are the distortions of perception and of mind (*saññācittavipallāsā*) in the notion, "The one who acts is the same as the one who experiences (the result)," and then a wrong adherence to these distortions develops, namely, the belief "Suffering is created by oneself" (a distortion of views, *diṭṭhivipallāsa*).

On the three levels of distortion with their four modes, see AN II 52.

40 In this passage the phrase *ādito sato* found in the preceding statement of eternalism is replaced by *vedanābhitunnassa sato*, which countermands Spk's proposal that *ādito sato* should be brought in here. Spk interprets the sentence as stating that the annihilationist view is held *by one* who experiences the feeling associated with the view, but I understand the point to be that the view is held *with reference to* one "stricken by feeling," perhaps by painful feeling.

Spk: If at the beginning (one thinks), "The one who acts is one, the one who experiences (the result) is another," in such a case afterwards there comes the belief, "Suffering is created by another," held by one stricken by—that is, pierced by—the feeling associated with the annihilationist view that arises thus: "The agent is annihilated right here, and someone else ('another') experiences (the results) of his deeds." Asserting thus, from the beginning one declares annihilationism, one grasps hold of annihilationism. Why? Because the view one holds amounts to this. Annihilationism comes upon him.

41 Spk: The Tathāgata teaches the Dhamma by the middle without veering to either of these extremes—eternalism and annihilationism—having abandoned them without reservation. He teaches while being established in the middle way. What is that Dhamma? By the formula of dependent origination, the effect is shown to occur through the cause and to cease with the cessation of the cause, but no agent or experiencer (*kāraka, vedaka*) is described.

42 The going forth (*pabbajjā*) is the initial ordination as a novice (*sāmaṇera*); the higher ordination (*upasampadā*) admits the novice to full membership in the Saṅgha as a bhikkhu.

43 For details on the ordination of a wanderer formerly belonging to another sect, see Vin I 69–71. Spk: The candidate is actually given the going forth and lives as a novice during the probationary period, after which the bhikkhus give him the higher ordination if they are satisfied with him. The Buddha, however, is entitled to waive the usual procedure when he recognizes that the candidate is sufficiently competent and need not be tested. In Kassapa's case he had the going forth given to him; then, immediately after, Kassapa was brought back to him and he called an assembly of bhikkhus and administered the higher ordination.

44 See **I, n. 376.**

45 Spk: In this sutta pleasure and pain as feeling (*vedanāsukhadukkha*) are being discussed; it is also acceptable to say the subject is resultant pleasure and pain (*vipākasukhadukkha*).

46 Spk: If at the beginning (one thinks), "The feeling and the one who feels it are the same," there then comes the belief, "Pleasure and pain are created by oneself." For in this case

feeling is created by feeling itself, and asserting thus one admits the existence of this feeling already in the past. One declares eternalism, grasps hold of eternalism.

47 Spk: If at the beginning (one thinks), "The feeling is one, the one who feels it is another," there then comes the belief, "Pleasure and pain are created by another," held by one stricken by the feeling associated with the annihilationist view that arises thus: "The feeling of the agent (*kāraka-vedanā*) in the past has been annihilated, and someone else ('another') experiences (the result) of his deeds." Asserting thus, one declares and grasps the annihilationist view that the agent is annihilated and rebirth is taken by someone else.

48 Spk: *This body has thereby originated* (*evam ayaṃ kāyo samudāgato*): This body has been produced thus because he has been hindered by ignorance and fettered by craving. *So there is this body*: one's own conscious body. *And external name-and-form* (*bahiddhā ca nāmarūpaṃ*): the conscious body of others externally. The meaning should be explained in terms of the five aggregates and six sense bases of oneself and others.

This interpretation of *bahiddhā nāmarūpa* seems dubious. We may have here, rather, a rare example of the term *nāmarūpa* being employed to represent the entire field of experience available to consciousness, "external name" being the concepts used to designate the objects cognized. See the common expression *imasmiṃ saviññāṇake kāye bahiddhā ca sabbanimittesu*, "in regard to this conscious body and all external signs," at **18:21**, **22**; **22:71**, **72**, etc., and explained below in **n. 340**. Spk interprets *this dyad* (*etaṃ dvayaṃ*) as the internal and external sense bases, which it calls "the great dyad" (*mahādvaya*). However, while the sense bases are usually shown to be the condition for contact (e.g., at **12:43**, **44**) and are also called a dyad (e.g., at **35:92**, **93**), it seems that here the text intends the term dyad to denote one's own conscious body and "external name-and-form." The six sense bases are introduced only in the next sentence, after contact has already been said to arise from a duality. At DN II 62,12–37 too the Buddha demonstrates that name-and-form can be a direct condition for contact without mention of the six sense bases.

49 *Bhagavantaṃ yeva paṭibhātu etassa bhāsitassa.* Lit. "Let the meaning of this statement occur to the Blessed One." I translate this Pāli idiom freely in accordance with the sense. See **I, n. 227**.

50 In this brief sutta we find clearly adumbrated the later exegetical scheme of "the four groups" (*catusaṅkhepa*) and "twenty modes" (*vīsatākāra*), explained at Paṭis I 51–52; Vism 579–81 (Ppn 17:288–98); and CMA 8:7. See Table 4, p. 519. The past causes are the ignorance and craving that brought both the fool and the wise man into the present existence; the present results—the conscious body, name-and-form, the six sense bases, contact, and feeling; the present causes—the ignorance and craving that the fool does not abandon; the future results—the birth, aging, and death to which the fool is subject in the next existence. This should also help establish the validity of the "three-life" interpretation of *paṭicca-samuppāda* and demonstrate that such an interpretation is not a commentarial innovation.

51 *Ṭhitā va sā dhātu dhammaṭṭhitatā dhammaniyāmatā idappaccayatā.* Spk: That element (*sā dhātu*), the intrinsic nature of the conditions (*paccayasabhāva*), still persists; never is it the case that birth is not a condition for aging-and-death. By the next two terms too he indicates just the condition. For the dependently arisen phenomena stand because of the condition (*paccayena hi paccayuppannā dhammā tiṭṭhanti*); therefore the condition itself is called *the stableness of the Dhamma* (*dhammaṭṭhitatā*). The condition fixes (or determines) the dependent phenomena (*paccayo dhamme niyameti*); thus it is called *the fixed course of the Dhamma* (*dhammaniyāmatā*). *Specific conditionality* (*idappaccayatā*) is the set of specific conditions for aging-and-death, etc.

Spk-pṭ: Whether it is unpenetrated before and after the arising of Tathāgatas, or penetrated when they have arisen, that element still persists; it is not created by the Tathāgatas, but aging-and-death always occurs through birth as its condition. A Tathāgata simply discovers and proclaims this, but he does not invent it.

At AN I 286,8–24 exactly the same statement is made about the three characteristics: "All formations are impermanent/suffering" and "All phenomena are nonself." The two expressions, *dhammaṭṭhitatā dhammaniyāmatā,* must thus have a meaning that is common to *both* dependent origination *and* the three characteristics, and it therefore seems unfitting to explain them here, as Spk does, in a way that is specifically tied to conditionality. Moreover, it is more likely that here *dhamma* means the principle or lawfulness that holds sway over phenomena, not the phenomena subject to that principle. See too below **n. 105, n. 211**.

52 *Abhisambujjhati abhisameti.* The former verb, which is reserved for the Buddha's enlightenment, is transitive. I thus render it "awakens to (with the object)," though otherwise I generally translate words derived from the verb *bujjhati* as expressing the sense of "enlightenment." *Abhisameti* is the verb corresponding to *abhisamaya,* on which see **n. 13**.

53 Se contains a footnote which explains that the statement below, "Thus, bhikkhus, the actuality in this ..." should be inserted at the end of each section on the conditioning relationships; and each following section should begin with the statement, "whether there is an arising of Tathāgatas...."

54 At **56:20, 27** the Four Noble Truths are said to be *tatha, avitatha, anaññatha*—the adjectives corresponding to the first three abstract nouns here. Spk gives a very specific interpretation (translated just below), though we might suspect the original sense was simply that the teaching of dependent origination is true, not false, and not other than real.

Spk: *Actuality* (*tathatā*) is said to indicate the occurrence of each particular phenomenon when its assemblage of appropriate conditions is present. *Inerrancy* (*avitathatā*) means that once its conditions have reached completeness there is no nonoccurrence, even for a moment, of the phenomenon due to be produced from those conditions. *Not-otherwiseness* (*anaññathatā*) means that there is no production of one phenomenon by another's conditions. The phrase *specific conditionality* is used to refer to the (individual) conditions for aging-and-death, etc., or to the conditions taken as a group (*paccayasamūhato*).

55 *Sammappaññāya.* Spk: With path wisdom together with insight (*savipassanāya maggapaññāya*).

56 The sixteen cases of doubt are also mentioned at MN I 8,4–15. For a discussion of their abandonment, see Vism 599 (Ppn 19:5–6) and 603–5 (Ppn 19:21–27). Spk explains that the basic division expressed in the doubts—between existing and not existing in the past, etc.—reflects the antinomy of eternalism and annihilationism. The other doubts pertaining to past existence arise within an eternalist framework. Similar distinctions apply among the doubts pertaining to the future and the present.

57 The ten powers, which are powers of knowledge (*ñāṇabala*), are expounded at MN I 69–71, where they are called Tathāgata powers (*tathāgatabala*). The ten types of knowledge are also claimed by the Venerable Anuruddha at **52:15–24**, but in part only, according to Spk. A detailed analysis is at Vibh 335–44. The four grounds of self-confidence (*vesārajja*) are explained at MN I 71–72. In brief, they are the confidence: (i) that no one can challenge his claim to be enlightened about all phenomena; (ii) that no one can challenge his claim to have eradicated all the taints; (iii) that no one can challenge him regarding the states he declares to be obstacles; and (iv) that no one can challenge his claim that his teaching leads the one who practises it to liberation from suffering.

Spk glosses *brahma* as *seṭṭha, uttama*, "the best, the highest," and explains the Brahma-wheel as the purified Wheel of the Dhamma (*visuddhadhammacakka*). This is twofold, the knowledge of penetration (*paṭivedhañāṇa*) and the knowledge of teaching (*desanāñāṇa*). The former originates from wisdom and brings the Buddha's own attainment of the noble fruits; the latter originates from compassion and enables him to teach in such a way that his disciples attain the fruits. The knowledge of penetration is supramundane (*lokuttara*), the knowledge of teaching mundane (*lokiya*). Both are self-begotten types of knowledge belonging exclusively to the Buddhas, not held in common with others.

58 This stock meditation formula on the five aggregates is also found in SN at **12:23, 22:78, 89, 101**. It occurs too in the two versions of the Satipaṭṭhāna Sutta at DN II 301,29–302,13 and MN I 61,3–8. The origin (*samudaya*) and the passing away (*atthaṅgama*) of the aggregates are explained from the

standpoint of diachronic conditionality at **22:5** and from the standpoint of synchronic conditionality at **22:56, 57**. See too **n. 123**.

59 This is the abstract formula of dependent origination: *imasmiṃ sati idaṃ hoti, imass' uppādā idaṃ uppajjati; imasmiṃ asati idaṃ na hoti, imassa nirodhā idaṃ nirujjhati*. Spk-pṭ explains that what is meant by existence in the first part of the formula is not actual presence as such but "the state of not having been brought to cessation by the path"; similarly, what is meant by nonexistence in the second part of the formula is not mere absence as such but "the state of having been brought to cessation by the path." A long, complex explanation of the formula (abridged in Spk-pṭ) is found at Ud-a 38–42 (translated in Masefield, *The Udāna Commentary*, 1:66–72). See too **n. 14** above. The use of the formula here, immediately following the statement on the aggregates, connects the origin and passing away of the five aggregates to dependent origination, indicating that the former should be understood in terms of the latter.

60 *Chinnapilotika*. Spk: Patchwork (*pilotika*) is an old cloth, cut up and torn, that has been sewn and stitched here and there. If one does not wear this, but is clothed in a sheet of uncut cloth, one is said to be "free of patchwork." This Dhamma is similar, for in no way is it sewn up and stitched together by deceitful means, etc.

This encomium of the Dhamma is also at MN I 141–42. At **16:11** (II 220,1 and 221,5 foll.) there occurs the expression *paṭapilotikānaṃ saṅghāti*, "an outer robe of patches."

61 Spk calls this four-factored energy (*caturaṅgasamannāgataṃ viriyaṃ*); the four factors are to be understood by way of skin, sinews, bones, and flesh-and-blood. The vow recurs below at **21:3** (II 276,12–16) and is also at MN I 481,1–5. At Ja I 71,24–27 the Bodhisatta makes the same resolve when he takes his seat at the foot of the Bodhi Tree.

62 Spk glosses *sadatthaṃ*: *sobhanaṃ vā atthaṃ sakaṃ vā atthaṃ*, "beautiful good or own good." The latter explanation is more likely. The common translation of the expression as "true good," taking *sad* to represent *sant*, does not seem to have the support of the commentaries.

63 Spk: It is not by inferior faith, energy, mindfulness, con-

centration, and wisdom that the supreme—namely, arahantship—is to be attained. The supreme must be attained by supreme faith and so forth.

64 Spk explains *maṇḍapeyya* as a compound of *maṇḍa* in the sense of clear (*pasanna*) and *peyya* in the sense of what is to be drunk (*pātabba*). It seems that *maṇḍa* originally meant the best part of milk or butter, i.e., the cream, and like the English word came to signify the essence or finest part of anything. At **34:1**, etc., we find *sappimaṇḍa*, "cream-of-ghee," the finest of dairy products.

Spk: There are three types of cream: (i) the cream of teachings (*desanāmaṇḍa*), i.e., the Four Noble Truths and the thirty-seven aids to enlightenment; (ii) the cream of recipients (*paṭiggahamaṇḍa*), i.e., disciples capable of understanding those teachings; and (iii) the cream of holy lives (*brahmacariyamaṇḍa*), i.e., the Noble Eightfold Path. The words "while the Teacher is present" (*satthā sammukhībhūto*) show the reason: since the Teacher is present, having made an energetic effort, you should drink this cream.

This sentence serves as the heading for an entire treatise of Paṭis (No. 10; II 86–91), which applies the metaphor of cream in detail to all the factors of the Buddhist training.

65 We should read, with Be and Se, *tesaṃ te kārā amhesu mahapphalā bhavissanti*, as against *tesaṃ vo kārā* in Ee. The sense of this line has been missed by C.Rh.D at KS 2:24, and Walshe follows her at SN-Anth 3:20. Cp. MN I 140,23–24, 31–32: *Yaṃ kho idaṃ pubbe pariññātaṃ tattha me (no) evarūpā kārā karīyanti*. PED recognizes *kāra* in the sense of "service, act of mercy or worship," but does not include these references.

66 *Alam eva appamādena sampādetuṃ*. These words anticipate the Buddha's final injunction at **6:15** (I 157,34–158,2).

67 For an essay based on this important sutta, see Bodhi, *Transcendental Dependent Arising*. The opening paragraph recurs at **22:101**, but with a different sequel; see too **n. 58**. Spk states that the destruction of the taints (*āsavakkhaya*) is arahantship, which gains this name because it arises at the end of the destruction of the taints (*āsavānaṃ khayante jātattā*).

68 Spk: Having set up the teaching with its climax in arahantship, the Buddha next shows the preliminary practice

along which the arahant has travelled. *The knowledge of destruction in regard to destruction* (*khayasmiṃ khaye ñāṇaṃ*) is the reviewing knowledge (*paccavekkhaṇañāṇa*) which occurs when the destruction of the taints—namely, arahantship—has been obtained (see **I, n. 376** and Vism 676; Ppn 22:19–21). *Liberation* is the liberation of the fruit of arahantship (*arahattaphalavimutti*), which is a condition for reviewing knowledge by way of decisive-support condition (*upanissayapaccaya*). First the fruit of arahantship arises, then the knowledge of destruction.

Spk glosses *sa-upanisā* as *sakāraṇa, sappacayya,* "with cause, with condition." Spk-pṭ adds: *upanisīdati phalaṃ etthā ti kāraṇaṃ upanisā;* "the cause is called the proximate cause because the effect rests upon it." Thus the commentators take *upanisā* to be the equivalent of Skt *upaniṣad,* not a contraction of *upanissaya.* Although, as CPD points out, "a semantic blend" with the latter takes place, the two words must be kept distinct because not everything that is an *upanisā* (proximate cause) for other things is an *upanissayapaccaya* (decisive support condition) for those things. The latter refers solely to something which plays a strong causal role.

69 Spk glosses the terms in the above sequence thus (starting from the end): *Suffering* is the suffering of the round (*vaṭṭadukkha*). *Faith* is repeatedly arising faith (*aparāparaṃ uppajjanasaddhā*; that is, tentative faith, not the unwavering faith of a noble disciple). *Gladness* (*pāmojja*) is weak rapture, while *rapture* proper (*pīti*) is strong rapture. *Tranquillity* (*passaddhi*) is the subsiding of distress, a condition for the happiness preliminary to absorption. *Happiness* is the happiness in the preliminary phase of meditative absorption, *concentration* the jhāna used as a basis (for insight; *pādakajjhānasamādhi*). *Knowledge and vision of things as they really are* (*yathābhūtañāṇadassana*) is weak insight, namely, the knowledges of the discernment of formations, of the overcoming of doubt, of exploration, and of what is and what is not the path (see Vism chaps. 18–20). *Revulsion* (*nibbidā*) is strong insight, namely, knowledge of appearance as fearful, of contemplation of danger, of reflection, and of equanimity about formations (Vism 645–57; Ppn 21:29–66).

Dispassion (*virāga*) is the path, which arises expunging defilements.

Note that in the next paragraph suffering replaces aging-and-death of the usual formula.

70 The simile also occurs at **55:38**, AN I 243,27–32, and AN V 114,6–14.

71 On the identity of the four views see above **n. 37**.

72 A stock passage in the Nikāyas, recurring in SN in slightly different forms determined by the context, at **12:25**, **12:26**, **22:2**, **22:86**, **35:81**, **42:13**, **44:2**, and **45:5**. The readings alternate, even within the same volume, between *vādānuvādo* and *vādānupāto*, and it is uncertain which of the two is more original. The passage has stumped previous translators, mainly because of the phrase *koci sahadhammiko vādānupāto*, which at KS 2:28 is rendered "one who is of his doctrine, a follower of his views." To avoid such errors two meanings of *sahadhammika* must be distinguished: (i) a noun meaning a follower of the same doctrine (unambiguously so at MN I 64,13); and (ii) an adjective meaning legitimate, reasonable (unambiguously so at **41:8**; IV 299,25 foll.). Here the second meaning is applicable.

Spk explains: "How (should we answer) so that not the slightest consequence or implication (*vādānupāto vādappavatti*) of the ascetic Gotama's assertion—(a consequence) which is reasonable because of the reason stated (*vuttakāraṇena sakāraṇo hutvā*)—might give ground for criticism?" This is meant: "How can there be no ground for criticism in any way of the ascetic Gotama's assertion?" I dissent from Spk on what is to be safeguarded against criticism: Spk takes it to be the Buddha's assertion, while I understand it to be the *inquirer's account* of the Buddha's assertion. In other words, the inquirer wants to be sure he is representing the Buddha's position correctly, whether or not he agrees with it.

At AN III 4,10, 19 *sahadhammikā vādānuvādā gārayhā ṭhānā āgacchanti* occurs in a context where it means simply "reasonable rebukes, grounds for criticism, come up," and is contrasted with *sahadhammikā pāsaṃsā ṭhānā āgacchanti*, "reasonable grounds for praise come up."

73 On the expression *tadapi phassapaccayā*, "that (too) is condi-

tioned by contact," Spk says that this may be known from the fact that there is no experience of suffering without contact. It seems to me, however, that the point being made here is not that suffering does not arise without contact (though this is true), but that the adoption of a view does not occur without contact. The Brahmajāla Sutta states the same point in relation to the sixty-two speculative views—that the proclamation of each of these views is conditioned by contact and the views cannot be experienced without contact. See DN I 41–43, translated in Bodhi, *All-Embracing Net of Views*, pp. 85–87, with the commentary at pp. 197–98.

74 *Gambhīro c' eva assa gambhīrāvabhāso ca*. The same two terms are used at **12:60** and at DN II 55,9–10 to describe *paṭicca-samuppāda*. For the explanation of Sv, see Bodhi, *The Great Discourse on Causation*, pp. 64–67. Spk explains "that same meaning" (*es' ev' attho*) to be the meaning of dependent origination implicit in the proposition, "Suffering is dependent on contact."

75 He gives his name to the Bhūmija Sutta (MN No. 126), where he answers some questions of Prince Jayasena and then engages in conversation with the Buddha. The first part of the present sutta repeats the first part of the preceding one except that it is phrased in terms of "pleasure and pain."

76 It is difficult to understand how these ascetics could be "proponents of kamma" (*kammavādā*) when they hold that pleasure and pain arise fortuitously. Neither Spk nor Spk-pṭ offers any clarification.

77 This passage is also at AN II 157–59. Spk says that the Buddha added this section to show that pleasure and pain do not arise with contact alone as condition, but with other conditions as well. In this case the bodily, verbal, and mental volitions (*kāya-, vacī-, manosañcetanā*) are the kammically effective volitions that function as conditions for the resultant pleasure and pain (*vipākasukhadukkha*). I follow Be and Se in reading *avijjāpaccayā ca* and in taking this clause to belong to the end of the present paragraph. This has the support of Spk, which explains that this is said to show that these volitions are conditioned by ignorance. Ee reads *va* for *ca* and places the clause at the beginning of the next paragraph.

78 Spk identifies the three volitional formations—*kāyasaṅkhāra, vacīsaṅkhāra, manosaṅkhāra*—with the three types of volition mentioned just above. One generates them "on one's own initiative" (*sāmaṁ*) when one acts without inducement by others, with an unprompted mind (*asaṅkhārikacitta*); one generates them "prompted by others" when one acts with a prompted mind (*sasaṅkhārikacitta*). One acts deliberately (*sampajāno*) when one acts with knowledge of kamma and its fruit; undeliberately (*asampajāno*), when one acts without such knowledge. This text may be the original basis for the Abhidhamma distinction between *sasaṅkhārikacitta* and *asaṅkhārikacitta*, on which see CMA 1:4.

79 The term used here is *manosaṅkhāra*, but from the context this is clearly synonymous with *cittasaṅkhāra* at **12:2**. There is no textual justification for identifying the latter with the *cittasaṅkhāra* at **41:6** (IV 293,17) and MN I 301,28–29, defined as *saññā* and *vedanā*.

80 I read with Be and Se, *imesu Ānanda dhammesu avijjā anupatitā*. The *chasu* in Ee appears superfluous.

Spk: Ignorance is included among these states under the heading of decisive support (*upanissaya*); for they are all comprehended under this phrase, "With ignorance as condition, volitional formations." (On the interpretation of *paṭicca-samuppāda* by way of the twenty-four conditional relations of the *Paṭṭhāna*, see Vism, chap. 17, concisely explained in Nyanatiloka Thera, *Guide through the Abhidhamma Piṭaka*, pp. 159–73.)

81 Spk: That body does not exist which, if it existed, would enable pleasure and pain to arise conditioned by bodily volition; the same method of explanation applies to speech and mind. (Query:) But an arahant acts, speaks, and thinks, so how is it that his body, etc., do not exist? (Reply:) In the sense that they do not generate kammic results. For the deeds done by an arahant are neither wholesome nor unwholesome kamma, but merely functional (*kiriyamatta*); thus for him it is said, "that body, etc., do not exist."

On the functional consciousness of the arahant, see CMA 1:15. An alternative explanation might be simply that with the elimination of ignorance there will be no further arising of the five aggregates, the basis of all experience, and thus no further experiencing of pleasure and pain.

82 Spk: There is no *field* (*khetta*) in the sense of a place of growth; no *site* (*vatthu*) in the sense of a support; no *base* (*āyatana*) in the sense of a condition; no *foundation* (*adhikaraṇa*) in the sense of a cause.

83 Upavāṇa is the Buddha's attendant at **7:13**. The present sutta is almost identical with the first part of **12:24** except that it omits the qualifying expression *kammavādā* in the description of the ascetics and brahmins.

84 Spk: He understands the condition by way of the truth of suffering, and the origin of the condition, etc., by way of the truth of the origin, etc.

85 This whole passage is repeated at **12:28**, **33**, **49**, and **50**. Spk: He is endowed with the view of the path (*maggadiṭṭhi*), the vision of the path, etc.

Sekha is used here as an adjective to qualify *ñāṇa* and *vijjā*. The *sekha* or trainee is one who has arrived at the supramundane path and is training in it but has not yet reached arahantship, i.e., a stream-enterer, once-returner, or nonreturner; on reaching arahantship he becomes an *asekha*, "one beyond training."

The rendering of *amatadvāraṃ āhacca tiṭṭhati* at KS 2:33 as "who stands knocking at the door of the Deathless," if intended literally, shows a misunderstanding of the idiom *āhacca tiṭṭhati*. In both canon and commentaries the expression is often used to mean "reaching right up to, standing up against," and does not imply knocking on a door, which in Pāli is expressed by the verb *ākoṭeti* (e.g., at Vin I 248,5). The idiom is also at **17:28**, **29** (II 238,5, 16–17). For other instances, see CPD, s.v. *āhacca*. The Deathless, of course, is Nibbāna. Spk identifies the door to the Deathless as the noble path.

86 This sutta is almost identical with **12:13**; the only difference is in the operative verb, there *pajānāti* and here *parijānāti*. Spk says this sutta was spoken in accordance with the inclination (*ajjhāsaya*) of the bhikkhus who recite the words, for they are able to penetrate (the sense) when the prefix *pari-* is used.

87 The *Pārāyana*, the "Going to the Far Shore," is the last chapter of Sn. It consists of sixteen sections (plus prologue and

epilogue), in each of which the Buddha replies to questions posed by one of sixteen brahmin students. "The Questions of Ajita" is the first of the sixteen sections.

88 Spk-pṭ: *Those who have comprehended the Dhamma* (*saṅkhāta-dhammā*) are the arahants, who have penetrated the (four) truths. *The trainees* (*sekhā*) are the seven types of persons—those on the four paths and the lower three fruits.

Saṅkhātadhammā could be understood to mean either "those who have comprehended the Dhamma," i.e., the teaching, or "those who have comprehended things," i.e., phenomena and their principles. Nidd II 34–35 (Be) glosses in both ways: as those who have known the Dhamma (*ñātadhammā*), by knowing all formations as impermanent, etc.; and as those who have comprehended the aggregates, elements, sense bases, etc. The trainees (*sekhā*) are so called because they train in the higher virtue, the higher mind (the jhānas), and the higher wisdom. Though Norman says that Pj II and Nidd II do not take *sekhā* and *puthū* as going together (GD, p. 367, n. to 1038), read correctly both these texts do place the two words in apposition. The trainees are manifold (*puthū*) because they fall into the seven types.

89 Spk: Why did he remain silent up to the third time? He was not puzzled by the question but by the Buddha's intention (*ajjhāsaya*). For it was possible to answer in many ways—by way of the aggregates, elements, sense bases, or conditionality—and he wanted to catch the Teacher's intention. Then the Teacher, aware of the reason for his silence, gave him the method with the words, "Do you see...?"

90 Spk: *This has come to be* (*bhūtam idaṃ*): this is said of the five aggregates. Thus the Teacher gave the elder the method, implying, "Answer my question by way of the five aggregates." Then, just as the great ocean appears as one open expanse to a man standing on the shore, so as soon as he was given the method the answer to the question appeared to the elder with a hundred and a thousand methods. *With correct wisdom* (*sammā paññāya*): one sees it with path-wisdom together with insight. *One is practising*: from the stage of virtue as far as the path of arahantship one is said to be practising for the purpose of revulsion, etc. This section shows the practice of the trainee.

91 *Tadāhārasambhavaṃ.* On nutriment see **12:11**, **12**, and **n. 18** above. No doubt it is the dependence of the five aggregates on nutriment that accounts for the inclusion of this sutta in the Nidānasaṃyutta. A similar treatment of nutriment, in catechism form, is at MN I 260,7–32.

Spk resolves *tadāhārasambhavaṃ* as *taṃ āhārasambhavaṃ*, apparently taking *tad* to represent the five aggregates. I see the whole expression as qualifying an implicit subject ("its") and take *tad* ("that") as a specification of *āhāra*. Such an interpretation seems required by the parallel statement on cessation. See too the use of the expression *tadāhāra* at SN II 85,6, 86,12, 87,6, etc., which supports this interpretation.

92 *Anupādā vimutto.* Spk: One is liberated by not grasping anything at all with the four kinds of clinging (*upādāna*). This section shows the arahant.

93 The bhikkhu Kaḷāra the Khattiya is met only here. Moḷiya-phagguna appears in **12:12**; see **n. 21**. "Returned to the lower life" (*hīnāyavatto*) means that he reverted to the state of a layman.

Spk and Spk-pṭ together help to illuminate this cryptic exchange thus: "He did not find solace (*assāsa*)" means that he had not attained the three (lower) paths; for if he had attained them he would not have reverted to the lower life since then he would not have been tempted by sensual pleasures (his reason for disrobing). Sāriputta says "I have no perplexity" (*na kaṅkhāmi*) about having attained solace since his support is the knowledge of a disciple's perfection (*sāvakapāramīñāṇa*). "As to the future" (*āyatiṃ*) refers to future rebirth; the question is an indirect way of asking if he has attained arahantship.

94 Spk remarks that Sāriputta did not declare final knowledge in such words, but the elder Kaḷāra Khattiya had ascribed this statement to him because he was happy and pleased. Final knowledge (*aññā*) is arahantship.

95 Spk: The Blessed One asked him this question to get him to declare final knowledge, thinking: "He will not declare final knowledge of his own accord, but he will do so when answering my question."

96 Spk: Here too (as in **12:31**) the elder was puzzled not by the question but by the Buddha's intention; he was unsure

how the Teacher wanted him to declare arahantship. But he started to speak in terms of conditionality, which was what the Teacher wanted. When he realized that he had grasped the Teacher's intention, the answer appeared to him with a hundred and a thousand methods.

I have translated the first part of Sāriputta's reply in accordance with the gloss of Spk thus: "With the destruction of the specific condition for birth, I have understood, 'As the condition for birth is destroyed, the effect, namely birth, is destroyed.'"

97 Spk: The Buddha asks this to get Sāriputta to roar a lion's roar in his own proper domain. For Sāriputta attained the knowledge of a disciple's perfection after he had discerned the three feelings while the Buddha taught the wanderer Dīghanakha "The Discourse on the Discernment of Feelings" and this became his own domain (*savisaya*).

Spk refers here to the Dīghanakha Sutta (MN No. 74; see esp. MN I 500,9–501,6), and seems to be using "Vedanā-pariggaha Sutta" as an alternative title for that text. Ee (S II 53,8–9, 12) should be amended to read *vedanāsu nandī*.

98 *Yaṃ kiñci vedayitaṃ taṃ dukkhasmiṃ*. See **36:11** (IV 216,20–217,3).

99 Spk: *Internal deliverance* (*ajjhattaṃ vimokkho*): he attained arahantship while comprehending the internal formations. Spk refers here to a fourfold distinction in how the path emerges, found also at Vism 661–62 (Ppn 21:84–85).

Spk: *The taints do not flow within me* (*āsavā nānussavanti*): The three taints, the taint of sensuality, etc., do not flow through the six sense doors towards the six sense objects, i.e., they do not arise in me. *And I do not despise myself* (*attānañ ca nāvajānāmi*): by this the abandoning of self-contempt (*omāna*) is indicated. C.Rh.D, at KS 2:40, has misunderstood this expression, rendering it "and I admit no (immutable) soul."

100 *Pubbe appaṭisaṃviditaṃ*. Spk: "I had not previously known or understood, 'He will ask me this.' His hesitancy was for the purpose of finding out the Teacher's intention."

The past participle *appaṭisaṃvidita* suggests the Skt noun *pratisaṃvid*, counterpart of Pāli *paṭisambhidā*, the analytical knowledges in which Sāriputta excelled.

101 Spk: *That element of the Dhamma* (*sā dhammadhātu*): Here, "element of the Dhamma" is the knowledge of a disciple's perfection, which is capable of seeing the principle of conditionality without obscuration (*paccayākārassa vivaṭabhāvadassanasamatthaṃ sāvakapāramīñāṇaṃ*).

102 *Dhamme ñāṇa*. Spk explains the Dhamma here as the Four Noble Truths (*catusaccadhamma*) or path knowledge (*maggañāṇadhamma*).

103 *Iminā dhammena diṭṭhena viditena akālikena pattena pariyogāḷhena*. Note that the string of participles here corresponds exactly to the terms used in the standard description of one who has gained "the vision of the Dhamma" (*dhammacakkhu*): *diṭṭhadhammo, pattadhammo, viditadhammo, pariyogāḷhadhammo* ("seen the Dhamma, attained the Dhamma, understood the Dhamma, fathomed the Dhamma," e.g., at DN I 110,14–15). This implies that the Dhamma which the stream-enterer has seen is dependent origination, an inference additionally confirmed by the closing passage of the present sutta.

Spk here treats *akālikena* as an independent adjective qualifying *dhammena* and explains it to mean that the path yields its fruit immediately after it is penetrated, without passage of time (*kiñci kālaṃ anatikkamitvā paṭivedhānantaraṃ yeva phaladāyakena*). However, in commenting on **42:11** (IV 328,21–22), where the same statement is found, Spk explains *akālikena* as an adverb of manner used in apposition to *pattena* (see **IV, n. 352**). I understand *akālikena* in the present passage in exactly the same way; otherwise it is difficult to see why it should be included amidst a string of past participles. Moreover, since the word here characterizes the relationship between temporal events like birth and aging, the common rendering of it as "timeless" is not entirely satisfactory. The desired sense in this context is "not involving the passage of time," i.e., immediate, which qualifies *the knowledge* of the conditional relationship between the factors, not the factors themselves. The point is that this knowledge is a matter of direct "ocular" experience rather than of reasoning and inference.

104 *Anvaye ñāṇa*. Spk: The knowledge (that follows) as a consequence of the knowledge of the principle; this is a name

for reviewing knowledge (see **n. 68**). It is not possible to apply the method to the past and future by means of the *dhamma* of the four truths or the *dhamma* of path knowledge, but when the four paths have been penetrated by path knowledge, reviewing knowledge subsequently occurs, and one applies the method by means of that.

This explanation is difficult to square with the account of reviewing knowledge at Vism 676 and elsewhere as knowledge of the path and fruit attained, the defilements abandoned, those remaining, and Nibbāna. What is meant here, rather, is an inference extended to past and future, based on the immediate discernment of the conditionality operative between any given pair of factors.

The following paragraph is also at **12:27**, **28**. Spk says that the arahant's (prior) plane of traineeship (*khīṇāsavassa sekhabhūmi*) is being discussed, on which Spk-pṭ remarks: the moment of the supreme path (*aggamaggakhaṇa*).

105 Spk: The *knowledge of the stability of the Dhamma* (*dhammaṭṭhitiñāṇa*) is the knowledge of the principle of conditionality. For the principle of conditionality is called "the stability of the Dhamma" because it is the cause for the continued occurrence of phenomena (*pavattiṭṭhitikāraṇattā*); the knowledge of it is "the knowledge of the stability of the Dhamma." This is a designation for just this sixfold knowledge.

I render *dhammaṭṭhitatā* (at **12:20**; **n. 51**) "*stableness* of the Dhamma" and *dhammaṭṭhiti* "*stability* of the Dhamma." The latter also occurs at **12:70** (II 124,10). The two seem to be effectively synonymous.

The knowledge *that* this knowledge too is subject to destruction is called by Spk "counter-insight into insight" (*vipassanā-paṭivipassanā*), i.e., insight into the dissolution of the very act of insight knowledge that had just cognized the dissolution of the primary object. See Vism 641–42 (Ppn 21:11–13), where, however, the expression *vipassanā-paṭivipassanā* does not occur.

106 *Kassa ca pan' idaṃ jarāmaraṇaṃ*. This question, and the following ones moulded on the same pattern, presuppose the reality of a self and thus, like the questions at **12:12**, must be rejected by the Buddha as invalid.

Spk: Even though the question, "What is aging-and-death?" is properly formulated, because it is combined with the question, "For whom is there aging-and-death?"—which implicitly affirms belief in a being (*sattūpaladdhi-vāda*)—the entire question becomes wrongly formulated. This is like a dish of delicious food served on a golden platter, on top of which a small lump of excrement is placed: all the food becomes inedible and must be discarded.

107 Spk: *The living of the holy life* (*brahmacariyavāsa*) is the living of the noble path. One who holds the view "the soul and the body are the same" (*taṃ jīvaṃ taṃ sarīraṃ*) holds that the soul and the body are annihilated together (at death). For one who holds this, the annihilationist view follows, for he holds that "a being is annihilated." Now this noble path arises to stop and eradicate the round of existence. But on the annihilationist view the round ceases even without the development of the path, and thus the development of the path becomes purposeless. In the second case, one holding the view "the soul is one thing, the body another" (*aññaṃ jīvaṃ aññaṃ sarīraṃ*) holds that the body alone is annihilated here, while the soul goes about freely like a bird released from a cage. This view is eternalism. But if there were even one formation that is permanent, stable, and eternal, the noble path would not be able to bring the round to an end; thus again the development of the path would be purposeless.

108 I read with Be: *yāni 'ssa tāni visūkāyikāni visevitāni vipphanditāni kānici kānici*. Se is almost the same, but the orthography in Ee is very unsatisfactory. Spk explains that the three nouns are all synonyms for wrong view. This is called a *contortion* (*visūkāyika*) because it is an obstruction to oneself, being like a spike (*visūkam iva*; Spk-pṭ: = *kaṇṭaka*, a thorn) in the sense that it punctures right view (*sammādiṭṭhiyā vinivijjhanaṭṭhena*). It is a *manoeuvre* (*visevita*) because it fails to conform to right view but instead runs contrary to it; and a *vacillation* (*vipphandita*) because of grasping now annihilationism, now eternalism.

Spk takes *visūkāyika* to be related to *sūci*, needle, but it would be difficult to justify this derivation by the actual use of the term. The three synonyms also occur at **4:24**

(I 123,30–31) and MN I 234,19–20; at MN I 446,12–13 they describe the behaviour of an untrained horse.

109 Spk glosses *tālāvatthukatāni* as *tālavatthu viya katāni*, "made like a palm-base," and explains: "Made like a palm with cut-off head (i.e., a palm stump) in the sense of never growing again; and made like a place for the support of a palm after it has been extricated along with its root" (*puna aviruhaṇaṭṭhena matthakacchinnatālo viya samūlaṃ tālaṃ uddharitvā tassa patiṭṭhitaṭṭhānaṃ viya ca katāni*). Spk-pṭ first accepts the original reading *tālāvatthu* (lit. "palm-non-base") as it stands and explains: "The palm itself is the 'palm-non-base' because it is not a base for leaves, flowers, fruit, and sprouts. But some read *tālavatthukatāni*, which means: 'made like a palm because of being without a base.'"

110 Spk: Since there actually is no self, there is nothing belonging to self; thus he says, "It is not yours" (*na tumhākaṃ*). And since there is no self of others, he says, "Neither does it belong to others" (*na pi aññesaṃ*). See too **22:33** and **35:101**.

111 Spk: *It is old kamma* (*purāṇam idaṃ kammaṃ*): This body is not actually old kamma, but because it is produced by old kamma it is spoken of in terms of its condition. It should be seen *as generated* (*abhisaṅkhata*), in that it is made by conditions; *as fashioned by volition* (*abhisañcetayita*), in that it is based on volition, rooted in volition; and *as something to be felt* (*vedaniya*), in that it is a basis for what is to be felt [Spk-pṭ: because it is a basis and object of feeling].

See too **35:146**, where the same idea is extended to the six internal sense bases. To reflect upon the body in terms of dependent origination, one considers that this body can be subsumed under "form" in the compound "name-and-form." One then reflects that name-and-form comes into being with consciousness, i.e., the rebirth-consciousness, as a conascent condition, and that both consciousness and name-and-form originate from the volitional formations, i.e., the kammic activities of the preceding existence. Thus the theme of this sutta ties up with the three that immediately follow.

112 Spk: Here, the phrase *one intends* (*ceteti*) includes all wholesome and unwholesome volition of the three planes; *one*

plans (*pakappeti*), the mental fabrications of craving and views (*taṇhādiṭṭhikappā*) in the eight cittas accompanied by greed [Spk-pṭ: the fabrications of views occur only in the four cittas associated with views]; and *whatever one has a tendency towards* (*anuseti*) implies the underlying tendencies (*anusaya*) under the headings of conascence and decisive-support conditions for the twelve (unwholesome) volitions. (On the twelve unwholesome cittas, see CMA 1:4–7.)

This becomes a basis (*ārammaṇam etaṃ hoti*): These various states such as volition become a condition; for here the word *ārammaṇa* is intended as condition (*paccaya*; that is, here *ārammaṇa* does *not* signify an object of consciousness, the usual meaning in the Abhidhamma). *For the maintenance of consciousness* (*viññāṇassa ṭhitiyā*): for the purpose of maintaining the kammic consciousness. When there is this condition, *there is a support for the establishing of consciousness* (*patiṭṭhā viññāṇassa hoti*), i.e., for the establishing of that kammic consciousness [Spk-pṭ: it has a capacity to yield fruit in one's mental continuum]. *When that (kammic) consciousness is established and has come to growth* (*tasmiṃ patiṭṭhite viññāṇe ... virūḷhe*): when, having impelled kamma, it has grown, produced roots, through its ability to precipitate rebirth, *there is the production of future renewed existence,* i.e., production consisting in renewed existence.

Cp. **12:64** and **22:53–54** below. AN I 223–24 explains the process of renewed existence in similar terms (see **n. 24**). I see the verbs *ceteti* and *pakappeti* as allusions to *saṅkhārā* (which, as kammic activities, are expressive of *cetanā*—see AN III 415,7–8). *Anuseti* clearly refers to the *anusaya* or underlying tendencies, which include *avijjānusaya,* the underlying tendency to ignorance (= ignorance in the usual formula of dependent origination) and *rāgānusaya,* the underlying tendency to lust (= craving in the usual formula). The way they maintain consciousness is thus no different from the way the volitional formations, fueled by ignorance and craving, serve as the condition for consciousness: together, they underlie the flow of consciousness, infuse it with kammic potentials for renewed existence, and project it into a new existence, thereby initiating the process that will culminate in birth. I am not in full agreement with Spk in taking the *viññāṇa* that is "maintained" and "established" as the kammic consciousness. I interpret it simply as the ongoing process of consciousness, including both the kammically active and resultant phases. At **22:53–54** the other four aggregates are spoken of as the *ārammaṇa* and *patiṭṭhā* of *viññāṇa*, but I am doubtful that this application will work here. To use the categories of the Abhidhamma, it seems that in this sutta the terms *ārammaṇa* and *patiṭṭhā* denote the decisive-support condition (*upanissayapaccaya*) for consciousness, while in the two suttas in the Khandhasaṃyutta they denote the conascence and support conditions (*sahajātapaccaya, nissayapaccaya*).

I use "volition" as a rendering for *cetanā* but "intends" for the corresponding verb *ceteti*; I use "intention" for the unrelated noun *saṅkappa*. I justify this apparent inconsistency on the ground that in Pāli the verb *saṅkappeti* (corresponding to *saṅkappa*) occurs very rarely (if at all), while English lacks a simple verb corresponding to "volition." "A support for the establishing of consciousness" renders *patiṭṭhā viññāṇassa*. I find that "established" works consistently better as a rendering for the participle *patiṭṭhita*, but "support" for the noun *patiṭṭhā*, so to bridge the participle and the noun in the present passage (and at **22:53, 54**) I have coined this compound expression.

113 Spk: This refers to a moment when there is no occurrence of [wholesome and unwholesome] volition of the three planes, and no occurrence of the mental fabrications of craving and views. *But one still has a tendency*: by this the underlying tendencies are included because they have not been abandoned here in the resultants of the three planes, in the limited functional states (the five-door adverting and mind-door adverting cittas), and in form. As long as the underlying tendencies exist, they become a condition for the kammic consciousness, for there is no way to prevent its arising.

Spk-pṭ: This second section is stated to show that wholesome and unwholesome kamma capable of producing rebirth is accumulated in the preliminary portion (of the path of practice), and that even without planning (through craving and views), the volitions of insight meditation in a meditator who has seen the dangers in existence are still conditioned by the underlying tendencies and are capable of generating rebirth. It is also stated to show that even when wholesome and unwholesome states are not occurring there is still an establishing of kammic consciousness with underlying defilements as condition; for so long as these have not been abandoned they lie latent in the existing resultants of the three planes, etc.

114 Spk: *When one does not intend,* etc.: By the first phrase ("does not intend") he shows that the wholesome and unwholesome volitions pertaining to the three planes have ceased; by the second ("does not plan"), that the craving and views in the eight cittas (accompanied by greed) have ceased; by the third ("does not have a tendency"), that the underlying tendencies lying latent in the aforesaid states have ceased. What is being discussed here? The function of the path of arahantship (*arahattamaggassa kiccaṃ*). It can also be interpreted as the arahant's doing of his task (*khīṇāsavassa kiccakaraṇaṃ*) and the nine supramundane states (*navalokuttaradhammā*; i.e., the four paths, their fruits, and Nibbāna).

Spk-pṭ: In this third section the function of the path of arahantship is discussed because that path completely stops the production of the underlying tendencies. The "arahant's doing of his task" can be said because of the exclusion of feeling, etc. (meaning unclear). The nine supramundane states can be said because the underlying tendencies are extirpated by the series of paths, and the fruits follow immediately upon the paths, and Nibbāna is the object of both.

I understand the "unestablished consciousness" (*appatiṭṭhita viññāṇa*) here to mean a consciousness without the prospect of a future rebirth through the propulsive power of ignorance, craving, and the volitional formations. The arahant is said to expire with consciousness "unestablished," as at **4:23** and **22:87**.

115 *Nāmarūpassa avakkanti*. See **12:12**, where the production of future renewed existence is placed between consciousness and the six sense bases. Taken in conjunction, the two suttas imply that the "descent of name-and-form" and the "pro-

duction of future renewed existence" are interchangeable (this in spite of the commentarial predilection for always seeing the latter as kammically active existence). Spk states that there is a "link" (*sandhi*) between consciousness and name-and-form; thus on this interpretation consciousness denotes the kammically generative consciousness of the previous existence, name-and-form the beginning of the present existence. It seems to me, however, more likely that *viññāṇa* straddles both the past life and the present life, as the principle of personal continuity.

116 Spk: *Inclination* (*nati*) is craving, called "inclination" in the sense of inclining (*namanaṭṭhena*) towards pleasant forms, etc. *There is coming and going* (*āgatigati*): there is a going of consciousness by way of rebirth towards what has come up (at death), presenting itself as kamma or the sign of kamma or the sign of future destiny. (The allusion is to the three objects of the last conscious process preceding death; see CMA 5:35–37.) *There is passing away*, passing from here, *and being reborn*, rebirth there.

117 Cp. the "teaching of the Blessed One" recited by Mahācunda at **35:87** (IV 59,10–14).

118 The sutta is also at **55:28** and at AN V 182–84. Spk glosses *bhayāni verāni* as volitions (bringing) fear and enmity (*bhayaveracetanāyo*). Spk-pṭ: The destruction of life and so forth are fearful and dreadful both for the perpetrator and for the victim; they are productive of fear and enmity, which are to be feared.

The self-assured declaration of stream-entry is also at **55:8–10**. The stream-enterer is exempt from the prospect of rebirth in the lower realms; he is *fixed in destiny* (*niyata*), as he cannot take more than seven rebirths, all in the human or celestial realms; and he *has enlightenment as his destination* (*sambodhiparāyaṇa*), as he will necessarily attain the enlightenment of arahantship.

119 The version at AN V 183 includes another line here: "But one who abstains from the destruction of life (etc.) does not engender fearful animosity pertaining to the present life and fearful animosity pertaining to the future life, and he does not experience mental pain and displeasure" (*pāṇātipātā paṭivirato n' eva diṭṭhadhammikaṃ bhayaṃ veraṃ*

pasavati, na samparāyikaṃ bhayaṃ veraṃ pasavati, na cetasikaṃ dukkhaṃ domanassaṃ paṭisaṃvedeti). It seems that the logic of the discourse requires this addition; its omission from the present text could be an early scribal error.

120 Spk: The factors of stream-entry (*sotāpattiyaṅga*) are of two kinds: (i) the factors *for* stream-entry, the preliminary practices that lead to the attainment of stream-entry, namely, associating with superior persons, hearing the true Dhamma, careful attention, and practice in accordance with the Dhamma (see **55:55**); (ii) the factors *of* one who abides having attained stream-entry. The latter are intended here. *Confirmed confidence* is unshakable confidence (gained) through what has been achieved [Spk-pṭ: namely, the path] (*aveccappasādenā ti adhigatena* [*maggena*] *acalappasādena*).

Aveccappasāda is a syntactical compound (see **I, n. 68**), with *avecca* (Skt *avetya*) absolutive of **aveti*, to undergo, to know, to experience. The formulas for recollection of the Buddha, the Dhamma, and the Saṅgha are analysed in detail at Vism 197–221 (Ppn 7:1–100).

121 Spk: The *virtues dear to the noble ones* (*ariyakantāni sīlāni*) are the five precepts, which the noble ones do not forsake even when they pass on to a new existence.

The terms are explained at Vism 222 (Ppn 7:104). These virtues are "ungrasped" (*aparāmaṭṭha*) in the sense that they are not adhered to with craving and wrong view.

122 Spk: *The method* (*ñāya*) is both dependent origination and the stable knowledge after one has known the dependently arisen. As he says: "It is dependent origination that is called the method; the method is also the Noble Eightfold Path" (untraced). *Wisdom* here is repeatedly arisen insight-wisdom (*aparāparaṃ uppannā vipassanāpaññā*).

Spk-pṭ: Dependent origination is called "the method" because, with the application of the right means, it is what is known (*ñāyati*) as it actually is in the dependently arisen. But knowledge (*ñāṇa*) is called "the method" because it is *by this* that the latter is known.

Despite the commentators, *ñāya* has no relation to *ñāṇa* but is derived from *ni + i*.

123 Spk: Suffering here is the suffering of the round (*vaṭṭadukkha*). There are two kinds of *origin*, momentary origin

(*khaṇikasamudaya*) and origin through conditions (*paccaya-samudaya*). A bhikkhu who sees the one sees the other. *Passing away* is also twofold, final passing away (*accantatthaṅgama;* Spk-pṭ: nonoccurrence, cessation, Nibbāna) and dissolutional passing away (*bhedatthaṅgama;* Spk-pṭ: the momentary cessation of formations). One who sees the one sees the other.

124 Spk: *The world* here is the world of formations (*saṅkhāra-loka*). On the nature of the world in the Buddha's teaching, see **I, n. 182**.

125 *Dhammapariyāya,* a method of presenting the teaching. This sutta recurs at **35:113**, where it is called Upassuti, "Listening In." On Ñātika, see **V, n. 330**.

126 See **12:17, 18**, and **n. 39, n. 40**.

127 A brahmin Jāṇussoṇi is mentioned at **45:4** and elsewhere in the Nikāyas. Spk says that he was a great chaplain (*mahāpurohita*) of much wealth who had gained his name by reason of his position. On the theme of this sutta see **12:15**.

128 *Lokāyatika*. Spk says that he was versed in *lokāyata,* the science of debate (*vitaṇḍasatthe lokāyate kataparicayo*). Spk-pṭ explains the etymology of the word thus: "*Lokāyata* is so called because by means of this the world does not strive for, does not advance towards, future welfare (*āyatiṃ hitaṃ tena loko na yatati na īhatī ti lokāyataṃ*). For on account of this belief, beings do not arouse even the thought of doing deeds of merit, much less do they make the effort."

Spk-pṭ's explanation seems to reflect the understanding of *lokāyata* held at the time of the commentaries, as seen in MW's definition of the word as "materialism, the system of atheistical philosophy (taught by Cārvāka)." There is cogent evidence, however, that the word acquired these connotations only in a later period. As Rhys Davids points out in a detailed discussion (at *Dialogues of the Buddha,* 1:166–72), *lokāyata* is used in the Nikāyas in a complimentary sense to designate a branch of brahmanical learning (as at DN I 88,7, 114,3, etc.). He suggests that the word originally meant nature-lore and only gradually acquired the negative meaning of sophistry and materialism. Jayatilleke has proposed that since the word is always used with reference to *loka,* the world, or *sabba,* the all, it originally signified, not nature-lore in general, but cosmology, and that the arrangement of *lokāyata* theses in opposing pairs indicates that the brahmins used the rival cosmological theories as topics of debate (*Early Buddhist Theory of Knowledge*, pp. 48–57).

129 *Jeṭṭhaṃ etaṃ lokāyataṃ*. Spk glosses *jeṭṭhaṃ* with *paṭhamaṃ* and explains: "*Lokāyata* is an inferior, tainted speculative view that appears great and deep" (*mahantaṃ gambhīran ti upaṭṭhitaṃ parittaṃ sāsavaṃ diṭṭhigataṃ*; reading as in Se, which seems more reliable here than Be).

130 *Ekattaṃ*. Spk: He asks whether it has a permanent nature (*niccasabhāva*); the first and third views are forms of the eternalist view (*sassatadiṭṭhi*).

131 *Puthuttaṃ*. Spk: This means a nature different from the previous nature; the second and fourth views are forms of the annihilationist view (*ucchedadiṭṭhi*).

132 The bracketed passages here and below are enclosed in brackets in all three eds., with notes to the effect that they are not found in certain eds. (Se says they are not found in the Thai ed. or in Sinhalese mss). It is really necessary to exclude them, for if they are included nothing would distinguish this sutta from the following one. Spk confirms this with its comment on **12:50** that this sutta differs from the preceding one only by stating the two methods together (*dve nayā ekato vuttā*), on which Spk-pṭ remarks: "This is said because the method stated in the ninth sutta, beginning 'When there is consciousness, name-and-form comes to be,' is included by the method stated in the tenth sutta, beginning 'When there is ignorance, volitional formations come to be.'"

133 This vagga is entitled Dukkhavagga in Be and Se, but Rukkhavagga in Ee.

134 *Kittāvatā ... bhikkhu parivīmaṃsamāno parivīmaṃseyya sabbaso sammā dukkhakkhayāya*. Spk glosses *parivīmaṃsamāno* with *upaparikkhamāno*.

135 *Jarāmaraṇanirodhasāruppagāminī paṭipadā*. Spk: *The way leading on that is in conformity with the cessation of aging-and-death* means the way leading on by its conformation with the cessation of aging-and-death, being similar (to cessation) by reason of its undefiled nature, its purity.

In the repetition series just below, Ee omits *jāti panāyaṃ kinnidānā*, no doubt an editorial oversight.

136 Spk: *A meritorious volitional formation* (*puññaṃ saṅkhāraṃ*) is the thirteen kinds of volition (i.e., the volitions of the eight wholesome sense-sphere cittas and the five wholesome cittas of the form sphere; see **n.** 7). *Consciousness fares on to the meritorious* (*puññūpagaṃ hoti viññāṇaṃ*): the kammic consciousness becomes associated with a meritorious kamma, the resultant consciousness with the fruits of merit. *A demeritorious volitional formation* (*apuññaṃ saṅkhāraṃ*) is the twelve kinds of volition (i.e., in the twelve unwholesome cittas; see **n.** 7). *An imperturbable volitional formation* (*āneñjaṃ saṅkhāraṃ*): the four kinds of volition (i.e., in the four wholesome cittas of the formless sphere). And here by mentioning the three kinds of kammic formations, the twelve-factored principle of conditionality is implied. To this extent the round of existence is shown.

An analysis of these three types of volitional formations is at Vibh 135. At MN II 262–63 the Buddha explains in detail how *viññāṇa* becomes *āneñjūpaga*.

137 *Paritassati* clearly represents Skt *paritṛṣyati*, "to crave, to thirst for," and is connected etymologically with *taṇhā*. However, in Pāli (and perhaps in MIA dialects generally) the verbal stem has become conflated with *tasati* = to fear, to tremble, and thus its noun derivatives such as *paritassanā* and *paritasita* acquire the sense of nouns derived from *tasati*. This convergence of meanings, already evident in the Nikāyas, is made explicit in the commentaries. I have tried to capture both nuances by rendering the verb "to be agitated" and the noun "agitation."

Here Spk glosses *na paritassati*: "He is not agitated with the agitation of craving (*taṇhāparitassanā*) or the agitation of fear (*bhayaparitassanā*); the meaning is, he does not crave and does not fear." Neither Spk nor Spk-pṭ comment on *parinibbāyati*, but what is meant is obviously the attainment of *kilesaparinibbāna*, the full quenching of defilements, on which see the General Introduction, pp. 49–50. On the arahant's reviewing knowledge, see **I, n. 376**.

138 Spk: After the arahant's reviewing knowledge has been shown, this passage is stated to show his constant dwelling (*satatavihāra*). The passage recurs, but with a different simile, at **22:88**, **36:7**, **8**, and **54:8**.

139 Spk: *A feeling terminating with the body* (*kāyapariyantikaṃ vedanaṃ*) is one delimited by the body (*kāyaparicchinnaṃ*); *a feeling terminating with life* (*jīvitapariyantikaṃ vedanaṃ*) is one delimited by life. As long as the body with its five sense doors continues, the feelings occurring at the five sense doors continue; as long as life continues, the feelings occurring at the mind door continue.

140 Spk: *Will become cool right here* (*idh' eva ... sītibhavissanti*): Right here, without having gone elsewhere by way of rebirth, they *will become cool*, subject to no further occurrence, devoid of the palpitation and disturbance of their occurrence.

141 The unusual use of the plural *sarīrāni* here mirrors the unusual use of the plural *kapillāni* to mean potsherds. Spk glosses *sarīrāni* as *dhātusarīrāni*, bodily elements, which Spk-pṭ identifies as the bones (*aṭṭhikakaṅkala*). *Kapilla* usually means a pot or a bowl, but Spk says the plural here denotes potsherds bound together along with the rim.

Spk elaborates the simile: The blazing potter's oven represents the three realms of existence, the potter the meditator, and his rod the knowledge of the path of arahantship. The smooth piece of ground represents Nibbāna. The time when the potter removes the hot clay pot from the oven and places it on the ground is like the time when the meditator, having attained the supreme fruit of arahantship, removes his individual form from the four realms of misery and places it on the surface of Nibbāna by way of fruition attainment. Just as the hot clay pot (does not break up at once), so the arahant does not attain parinibbāna on the same day he reaches arahantship. He lives on for fifty or sixty years, striving to sustain the Buddha's dispensation. When he reaches his last thought-moment, with the breakup of the aggregates he attains parinibbāna by the Nibbāna element without residue. Then, as with the potsherds of the pot, only inanimate bodily remains are left behind.

142 Spk: "Would a rebirth-consciousness (*paṭisandhiviññāṇa*) be discerned?"

143 Spk: "Just this is the end of the suffering of the round, its termination, that is, Nibbāna."

144 *Upādāniyesu dhammesu*. Spk: In the phenomena of the three planes, which are the conditions for the four kinds of clinging. On *upādāniyā dhammā*, see **22:121**, **35:110**, **123**, where clinging (*upādāna*) is explained simply as desire and lust (*chandarāga*) for the things that can be clung to.

145 Spk: The great bonfire represents the three realms of existence; the man tending the fire, the blind worldling attached to the round. His casting of fuel into the fire is like the worldling who contemplates gratification, creating wholesome and unwholesome kamma through the six sense doors on account of craving. The increase of the bonfire is like the blind worldling's repeated production of the suffering of the round by the accumulation of kamma.

146 Spk: A benefactor might come along and teach the man how to extinguish the fire, and the man would follow his advice. The benefactor represents the Buddha; his advice, the explanation of a meditation subject and an exhortation to gain release from suffering. The time the man follows the instructions is like the time the meditator is sitting in an empty hut applying insight to the phenomena of the three planes. The time when the man has bathed and adorned himself and is sitting tranquil and happy represents the time when the meditator, having cleansed himself of defilements by the noble path, sits absorbed in the attainment of fruition having Nibbāna as object. The time when the great bonfire is extinguished represents the time when the arahant's aggregates break up and he passes away into the Nibbāna element without residue.

147 *Saṃyojaniyesu dhammesu*. Spk: The conditions for the ten fetters. On "things that can fetter," see **22:120**, **35:109**, **122**. Here too "the fetter" is explained simply as desire and lust.

148 Spk: The great tree represents the round of existence with its three planes; the roots, the sense bases; the sending up of the sap through the roots, the building up of kamma through the six sense doors; the stability of the tree, the blind worldling's long continuation in saṃsāra as he repeatedly sustains the round by building up kamma.

149 Spk: The man wishing to destroy the great tree represents the meditator, his shovel (or axe) knowledge, the basket concentration. The time the tree is cut down at its root is

like the occasion when wisdom arises in the meditator as he attends to his meditation subject. The cutting of the tree into pieces is like attending to the body in brief by way of the four great elements; the splitting of the pieces is like attending to the body in detail in forty-two aspects (Vism 348–51; Ppn 11:31–38); reducing the pieces to slivers is like the discernment of name-and-form by way of derived form and consciousness; cutting up the roots is like the search for the conditions of name-and-form. The time of burning the slivers is like the time when the meditator attains the supreme fruit (of arahantship). The collecting of the ashes is like the arahant's life up to the time of his parinibbāna. The winnowing of the ashes, or their being carried away by the river, is like the stilling of the round when the arahant attains parinibbāna by the Nibbāna element without residue.

150 *Nāmarūpassa avakkanti.* Spk does not comment, but in the light of other suttas we might assume the statement to mean that the craving that underlies "contemplating gratification in things that can fetter" is the principal sustaining cause for the process of rebirth, which begins with "the descent of name-and-form." See in this connection **12:39**, **12:64**, and **n. 115**.

151 *Viññāṇassa avakkanti.* At DN II 63,2–4 it is said that if consciousness were not to descend into the mother's womb, name-and-form would not take shape in the womb. The "descent of the embryo" (*gabbhassāvakkanti*)—spoken of at MN I 265,35–266,6, II 156,29–157,3, and AN I 176,31—presumably refers to the descent of the consciousness that initiates conception.

152 The opening of this sutta as far as "the nether world, saṃsāra" is nearly identical with the opening of the Mahānidāna Suttanta (DN No. 15), which differs only in including the aorist *avaca*. The present sutta is a composite, made up of the opening of the Mahānidāna grafted on to the body of **12:55**. Spk here incorporates the long opening of the commentary to the Mahānidāna, for which see Bodhi, *The Great Discourse on Causation*, pp. 58–73. Spk, however, does not attempt to explain how the same opening could have such a different sequel.

153 Spk: *Uninstructed* (*assutavā*): devoid of learning, interrogation, and discrimination regarding the aggregates, elements, sense bases, conditionality, the establishments of mindfulness, etc. *Worldling* (*puthujjana*) is a "many-being," so called because of generating many diverse defilements, etc. (*puthūnaṃ nānappakārānaṃ kilesādīnaṃ jananādikāraṇehi puthujjano*); and also because he is included among the many people (*puthūnaṃ janānaṃ antogadhattā*), in number beyond reckoning, who are engaged in a low Dhamma contrary to the Dhamma of the noble ones. Or else *puthu* means "reckoned as separate"; the worldling is a person separated from the noble ones, who possess such qualities as virtue, learning, etc. (*puthu vā ayaṃ visuṃ yeva saṅkhaṃ gato; visaṃsaṭṭho sīlasutādiguṇayuttehi ariyehi jano ti puthujjano*).

This twofold etymology stems from a twofold understanding of Pāli *puthu*: as representing either Vedic *pṛthu* = numerous, many; or *pṛthak* = separate, distinct. The BHS form *pṛthagjana* indicates a preference for the latter derivation, though the Pāli commentators tend to take the former as primary.

154 *Cittaṃ iti pi mano iti pi viññāṇaṃ iti pi*. Cp. DN I 21,21: *Yaṃ ... idaṃ vuccati cittan ti vā mano ti vā viññāṇan ti vā*. Spk says these are all names for the mind base (*manāyatana*). Normally I render both *citta* and *mano* as "mind," but since English has only two words of common usage to denote the faculty of cognition—"mind" and "consciousness"—here I am compelled to use "mentality" as a makeshift for *mano*. While technically the three terms have the same denotation, in the Nikāyas they are generally used in distinct contexts. As a rough generalization, *viññāṇa* signifies the particularizing awareness through a sense faculty (as in the standard sixfold division of *viññāṇa* into eye-consciousness, etc.) as well as the underlying stream of consciousness, which sustains personal continuity through a single life and threads together successive lives (emphasized at **12:38–40**). *Mano* serves as the third door of action (along with body and speech) and as the sixth internal sense base (along with the five physical sense bases); as the mind base it coordinates the data of the other five senses and also cognizes mental phenomena (*dhammā*), its own

special class of objects. *Citta* signifies mind as the centre of personal experience, as the subject of thought, volition, and emotion. It is *citta* that needs to be understood, trained, and liberated. For a more detailed discussion, see Hamilton, *Identity and Experience*, chap. 5.

155 Spk: It is *held to* (*ajjhosita*) by being swallowed up by craving; *appropriated* (*mamāyita*) by being appropriated by craving; and *grasped* (*parāmaṭṭha*) by being grasped through views. *"This is mine"* (*etaṃ mama*): the grip of craving (*taṇhāgāha*); by this the 108 thoughts of craving are included (see AN II 212,31–213,2). *"This I am"* (*eso 'ham asmi*): the grip of conceit (*mānagāha*); by this the nine kinds of conceit are included (see **I, n. 37**). *"This is my self"* (*eso me attā*): the grip of views (*diṭṭhigāha*); by this the sixty-two views are included (see DN I 12–38).

156 *Because this body ... is seen standing for a hundred years, or even longer*. Spk: (Query:) Why does the Blessed One say this? Isn't it true that the physical form present in the first period of life does not last through to the middle period, and the form present in the middle period does not last through to the last period?... Isn't it true that formations break up right on the spot, stage by stage, section by section, just as sesamum seeds pop when thrown on a hot pan? (Reply:) This is true, but the body is said to endure for a long time in continuous sequence (*paveṇivasena*), just as a lamp is said to burn all night as a connected continuity (*paveṇisambandhavasena*) even though the flame ceases right where it burns without passing over to the next section of the wick.

157 Spk: *By day and by night* (*rattiyā ca divasassa ca*): This is a genitive in the locative sense, i.e., during the night and during the day. *Arises as one thing and ceases as another* (*aññadeva uppajjati, aññaṃ nirujjhati*): The meaning is that (the mind) that arises and ceases during the day is other than (the mind) that arises and ceases during the night. The statement should not be taken to mean that one thing arises and something altogether different, which had not arisen, ceases. "Day and night" is said by way of continuity, taking a continuity of lesser duration than the previous one (i.e., the one stated for the body). But one citta is not

able to endure for a whole day or a whole night. Even in the time of a fingersnap many hundred thousand of *koṭis* of cittas arise and cease (1 *koṭi* = 10 million). The simile of the monkey should be understood thus: The "grove of objects" is like the forest grove. The mind arising in the grove of objects is like the monkey wandering in the forest grove. The mind's taking hold of an object is like the monkey grabbing hold of a branch. Just as the monkey, roaming through the forest, leaves behind one branch and grabs hold of another, so the mind, roaming through the grove of objects, arises sometimes grasping hold of a visible object, sometimes a sound, sometimes the past, sometimes the present or future, sometimes an internal object, sometimes an external object. When the monkey does not find a (new) branch it does not descend and sit on the ground, but sits holding to a single leafy branch. So too, when the mind is roaming through the grove of objects, it cannot be said that it arises without holding to an object; rather, it arises holding to an object of a single kind.

It should be noted that neither the sutta nor the commentary interprets the monkey simile here as saying that the untrained mind is as restless as a monkey; the point, rather, is that the mind is always dependent on an object.

158 Spk explains the order of this discourse thus: First, because these bhikkhus were excessively obsessed with form, the Buddha spoke as if it were improper to grasp form (because its growth and decline are seen) but not improper to grasp mind. Next (in the passage beginning, "It would be better to take as self the body") he speaks as if it were proper to grasp the body but improper to grasp the mind (because of its incessant change). Now, in the present passage, he speaks with the aim of removing their obsession with both body and mind.

159 I read with Se and Ee *nānābhāvā vinikkhepā*, as against Be *nānākatavinibbhogā*. The simile recurs at **36:10** (IV 215,22–25) and **48:39** (V 212,21–24); in both places Be has the same reading as Se and Ee here. Spk: The sense base is like the lower firestick, the object is like the upper firestick, contact is like the friction of the two, and feeling is like the heat element.

160 A translation of the long commentary to this sutta is

included in Nyanaponika, *The Four Nutriments of Life*. Spk explains that the Buddha spoke this discourse because the Bhikkhu Saṅgha was receiving abundant almsfood and other requisites, and the Buddha wanted to place before the bhikkhus "a mirror of the Dhamma for their self-control and restraint, so that, contemplating on it again and again, the bhikkhus of the future will make use of the four requisites only after due reflection." The opening paragraph is identical with that of **12:11**.

161 Spk: Edible food should be considered as similar to son's flesh by way of the ninefold repulsiveness: the repulsiveness of having to go out for it, of having to seek it, of eating it, of the bodily secretions, of the receptacle for the food (i.e., the stomach), of digestion and indigestion, of smearing, and of excretion. (For details see Vism 342–46; Ppn 11:5–26; there ten aspects are mentioned, the additional one being "fruit," i.e., the repulsive parts of the body produced by food.) A bhikkhu should use his almsfood in the way the couple eat their son's flesh: without greed and desire, without pickiness, without gorging themselves, without selfishness, without delusion about what they are eating, without longing to eat such food again, without hoarding, without pride, without disdain, and without quarreling.

162 Spk: *When the nutriment edible food is fully understood*: It is fully understood by these three kinds of full understanding: (i) the full understanding of the known (*ñātapariññā*); (ii) the full understanding by scrutinization (*tīraṇapariññā*); and (iii) the full understanding as abandonment (*pahāna-pariññā*). Therein, (i) a bhikkhu understands: "This nutriment edible food is 'form with nutritive essence as the eighth' (see **n. 18**) together with its base. This impinges on the tongue-sensitivity, which is dependent on the four great elements. Thus nutriment, tongue-sensitivity, and the four elements—these things are the form aggregate. The contact pentad (contact, feeling, perception, volition, consciousness) arisen in one who discerns this—these are the four mental aggregates. All these five aggregates are, in brief, name-and-form." Next he searches out the conditions for these phenomena and sees dependent origination

in direct and reverse order. By thus seeing name-and-form with its conditions as it actually is, the nutriment of edible food is fully understood by *the full understanding of the known*. (ii) Next he ascribes the three characteristics to that same name-and-form and explores it by way of the seven contemplations (of impermanence, suffering, nonself, revulsion, dispassion, cessation, and relinquishment—see Vism 607; Ppn 20:4). Thus it is fully understood by *the full understanding by scrutinization*. (iii) It is fully understood by *the full understanding as abandonment* when it is fully understood by the path of nonreturning, which cuts off desire and lust for that same name-and-form.

Lust for the five cords of sensual pleasure is fully understood: It is fully understood by (i) *the singlefold full understanding* (*ekapariññā*), namely, that the craving for tastes arisen at the tongue door is the same craving that arises at all five sense doors; (ii) *the comprehensive full understanding* (*sabbapariññā*), namely, that lust for all five cords of sensual pleasure arises even in regard to a single morsel of food placed in the bowl (for food stimulates desire in all five senses); (iii) *the root full understanding* (*mūlapariññā*), namely, that nutriment is the root for all five types of sensual lust, since sensual desire thrives when people are well fed.

163 Spk: *There is no fetter bound by which*: This teaching is taken only as far as the path of nonreturning; but if one develops insight into the five aggregates by way of these same forms, etc., it is possible to explain it as far as arahantship.

164 Spk: Just as a cow, seeing the danger of being eaten by the creatures living in the places she might be exposed to, would not wish to be honoured and venerated, or to be massaged, rubbed, given hot baths, etc., so a bhikkhu, seeing the danger of being eaten by the defilement-creatures rooted in the nutriment contact, becomes desireless towards contact in the three planes of existence.

165 Spk explains the full understanding of contact in the same way as for edible food, except that contact is taken as the starting point for the discernment of the five aggregates. When contact is fully understood *the three feelings are fully understood* because they are rooted in contact and associated

with it. The teaching by way of the nutriment contact is carried as far as arahantship.

166 Spk: The charcoal pit represents the round of existence with its three planes; the man wanting to live, the foolish worldling attached to the round; the two strong men, wholesome and unwholesome kamma. When they grab the man by both arms and drag him towards the pit, this is like the worldling's accumulation of kamma; for the accumulated kamma drags along a rebirth. The pain from falling into the charcoal pit is like the suffering of the round.

167 Spk: *The three kinds of craving are fully understood*: The three kinds of craving are craving for sensual pleasures, craving for existence, and craving for extermination. They are fully understood because craving is the root of mental volition. Here too the teaching is carried as far as arahantship by way of mental volition.

168 Spk: The king represents kamma; the criminal, the worldling; the three hundred spears, the rebirth-consciousness. The time the king gives his command is like the time the worldling is driven towards rebirth by King Kamma. The pain from being struck by the spears is like the resultant suffering in the course of existence once rebirth has taken place.

169 Spk: *Name-and-form* is fully understood when consciousness is fully understood because it is rooted in consciousness and arises along with it. By way of consciousness too the teaching is carried as far as arahantship.

170 Spk explains lust (*rāga*), delight (*nandī*), and craving (*taṇhā*) as synonyms for greed (*lobha*). *Consciousness becomes established there and comes to growth* (*patiṭṭhitaṃ tattha viññāṇaṃ virūḷhaṃ*): having impelled a kamma, it "becomes established and comes to growth" through its ability to drag along a rebirth. On the establishing of consciousness, see **12:38** and **n. 112**, and on the descent of name-and-form, **12:39** and **n. 115**.

171 Spk: *Wherever* (*yattha*) is a locative referring to the round of existence with its three planes. Or else, in all instances, this locative is used with reference to the correlative term in the preceding phrase. [Spk-pṭ: This locative expression *yattha ... tattha* is used with reference to each preceding phrase, which is its sphere of application.]

172 *Atthi tattha saṅkhārānaṃ vuddhi.* Spk: This is said with reference to the volitional formations that are the cause of a future round of existence for one abiding in the present round of results.

The variation here on the usual sequence is very interesting. When "the growth of volitional formations" is placed *between* name-and-form and future existence, this implies that the expression corresponds to three critical terms of the standard formula—craving, clinging, and (kamma-)existence—with *āyatiṃ punabbhavābhinibbatti* signifying the process of entering the new existence.

173 Spk: The painter represents kamma with its adjuncts [Spk-pṭ: craving and ignorance, and time and destination, etc.]; the panel, wall, or canvas represents the round with its three realms. As the painter creates a figure on the panel, so kamma with its adjuncts creates a form in the realms of existence. As the figure created by an unskilled painter is ugly, deformed, and disagreeable, so the kamma performed with a mind dissociated from knowledge gives rise to an ugly, deformed, disagreeable figure. But as the figure created by a skilled painter is beautiful and well shaped, so the kamma performed with a mind associated with knowledge gives rise to a beautiful and comely figure.

174 Spk: The kamma of the arahant is similar to the sunbeam. However, the sunbeam does exist, but because there is no place for it to settle it is said to be unestablished (*appatiṭṭhitā*). But the arahant's kamma is said to be unestablished because it is nonexistent. Although he has a body, etc., no wholesome or unwholesome kamma is thereby created. His deeds are merely functional, not productive of results (*kiriyamatte ṭhatvā avipākaṃ hoti*). In this connection, see **12:25** and **n. 81**.

It should be noted that Spk explains the statement that the arahant's *consciousness* is unestablished to mean that his kamma is unestablished. This seems too free an interpretation. Nevertheless, I think it would be wrong to interpret the sutta as saying that after his parinibbāna the arahant's consciousness persists in some mode that can only be described as unestablished. The present passage is clearly speaking of the arahant's consciousness *while he is alive*. Its purport is not that an "unestablished consciousness" remains after the arahant's parinibbāna, but that his consciousness, being devoid of lust, does not "become established in" the four nutriments in any way that might generate a future existence.

175 Opening as at **12:10**.

176 Dependent origination is formulated in identical terms in the account of the Buddha Vipassī's enlightenment at DN II 32,22–30. For the Buddha's explanation of the mutual dependency of consciousness and name-and-form, see DN II 62,38–63,26. A translation of the detailed explanation at Sv II 501–3 with excerpts from Sv-pṭ can be found in Bodhi, *The Great Discourse on Causation*, pp. 84–89. See too below **12:67**.

Spk: *When there is name-and-form, consciousness comes to be*: Here it should be said, "When there are volitional formations, consciousness comes to be," and "When there is ignorance, volitional formations come to be." But neither is mentioned. Why not? Because ignorance and volitional formations belong to a third existence and this insight is not connected with them (*avijjāsaṅkhārā hi tatiyo bhavo, tehi saddhiṃ ayaṃ vipassanā na ghaṭīyati*). For the Great Man (the Bodhisatta) undertakes insight by way of the present five-constituent existence (*pañcavokārabhava*, i.e., existence where all five aggregates are present).

(Query:) Isn't it true that one cannot become enlightened as long as ignorance and volitional formations are unseen? (Reply:) True, one cannot. But these are seen by way of craving, clinging, and existence. If a man pursuing a lizard has seen it enter a pit, he would descend, dig up the place where it entered, catch it, and depart; he wouldn't dig up some other place where the lizard can't be found. Similarly, when the Great Man was sitting on the seat of enlightenment, he searched for the conditions beginning with aging-and-death. Having traced the conditions for the phenomena back to name-and-form, he searched for its condition too and saw it to be consciousness. Then, realizing "So much is the range of exploration by way of five-constituent existence," he reversed his insight (*vipassanaṃ paṭinivattesi*). Beyond this there is still the pair, ignorance and volitional formations, which are like the unbroken region of the empty pit. But because they have been included by insight earlier (under craving, etc.?), they do not undergo exploration separately; hence he does not mention them.

177 *This consciousness turns back* (*paccudāvattati kho idaṃ viññāṇāṃ*). Spk: What is the consciousness that turns back here? The rebirth-consciousness and the insight-consciousness. Rebirth-consciousness turns back from its condition, insight-consciousness from its object. Neither overcomes name-and-form, goes further than name-and-form.

Spk-pṭ: *From its condition*: Rebirth-consciousness turns back from volitional formations—the special cause for consciousness—which has not been mentioned; it does not turn back from all conditions, as name-and-form is stated as the condition for consciousness. *From its object*: from ignorance and volitional formations as object, or from the past existence as object.

It is possible the Bodhisatta had been seeking a self of the Upaniṣadic type, a self-subsistent subject consisting of pure consciousness that requires nothing but itself in order to exist. His discovery that consciousness is invariably dependent on name-and-form would have disclosed to him the futility of such a quest and thereby shown that even consciousness, the subtlest basis for the sense of self (see **12:61**), is conditioned and thus marked by impermanence, suffering, and selflessness.

178 Spk: *To this extent one may be born* (*ettāvatā jāyetha vā*), *etc.*: With consciousness as a condition for name-and-form, and with name-and-form as a condition for consciousness, to this extent one may be born and undergo rebirth. What is there beyond this that can be born or undergo rebirth? Isn't it just this that is born and undergoes rebirth?

Spk-pṭ: *To this extent*: that is, by the occurrence of consciousness and name-and-form mutually supporting one another. *One may be born and undergo rebirth*: Though the expression "A being is born and undergoes rebirth" is used, there is nothing that serves as the referent of the designation "a being" apart from consciousness and name-and-form. Hence the commentator says, "What is there beyond this?" *Just this* (*etadeva*): namely, the pair consciousness and name-and-form.

It might be noted that *jāyetha, jīyetha*, etc., are middle-voice optatives in the third person singular. At KS 2:73, C.Rh.D seems to have mistaken them for second person plural optatives in the active voice, while at LDB, pp. 211, 226, Walshe has used a roundabout rendering, presumably to avoid having to identify the forms. For a detailed discussion of the mutual conditionality of consciousness and name-and-form, see Bodhi, *The Great Discourse on Causation*, pp. 18–22.

179 The mutual cessation of consciousness and name-and-form is also found in the version at DN II 34,21–35,13. Spk does not comment on the expression "I have discovered the path to enlightenment" (*adhigato kho myāyaṃ maggo bodhāya*), but the corresponding passage of DN is commented upon at Sv II 461,5–8 thus: "*Path*: the path of insight. *To enlightenment*: for the awakening to the Four Noble Truths, or for the awakening to Nibbāna. Further, enlightenment is so called because it becomes enlightened (*bujjhatī ti bodhi*); this is a name for the noble path. What is meant is (that he has discovered the path) for the sake of that. For the noble path is rooted in the path of insight. Now, making that path explicit, he says, 'With the cessation of name-and-form,' and so forth."

This explanation hinges upon the distinction (only implicit in the Nikāyas) between the mundane preliminary portion of the path (*pubbabhāgapaṭipadā*), which is the "path of insight," and the noble supramundane path (*lokuttaramagga*), which directly realizes Nibbāna. Since the supramundane path is identical with enlightenment, the commentary holds that "the path *to* enlightenment" the Bodhisatta discovered must be the mundane path of insight. In the DN version, having discovered the path to enlightenment, the Bodhisatta Vipassī continues to contemplate the rise and fall of the five aggregates, as a result of which "his mind was liberated from the taints by not clinging."

180 Spk elaborates minutely upon the parable of the ancient city and then draws extensive correspondences between the elements of the parable and their counterparts in the Dhamma.

181 At this point *saṅkhārā*, omitted earlier, are finally introduced,

and *avijjā*, their condition, is implied by the mention of "their origin."

182 This passage is also at **51:10** (V 262,9–14). I follow Spk in its explanation of *yāva devamanussehi suppakāsitaṃ*. The point is that, despite the use of the instrumental form *-ehi*, the Dhamma is not proclaimed *by* devas and humans, but "throughout the region (inhabited) by devas and humans in the ten-thousandfold galaxy, within this extent it is well proclaimed, well taught, *by the Tathāgata*" (*yāva dasasahassa-cakkavāḷe devamanussehi paricchedo atthi, etasmiṃ antare sup-pakāsitaṃ sudesitaṃ tathāgatena*). It is possible *-ehi* here is a vestigial Eastern locative plural; see Geiger, *Pāli Grammar*, §80.3.

183 Spk: Why did he address the bhikkhus? Because a subtle Dhamma discourse, one stamped with the three characteristics, had presented itself to him. In this country (the Kuru country), it is said, the people had good roots [Spk-pṭ: supporting conditions for achievement of the noble Dhamma] and were wise [Spk-pṭ: with the wisdom of a three-rooted rebirth-consciousness and pragmatic wisdom]. They were capable of penetrating a deep Dhamma talk stamped with the three characteristics. Therefore the Buddha taught here the two Satipaṭṭhāna Suttas (DN No. 22, MN No. 10), the Mahānidāna Sutta (DN No. 15), the Āneñjasappāya Sutta (MN No. 106), the Cūḷanidāna Sutta (**12:60**), and other deep suttas.

184 *Sammasatha no tumhe bhikkhave antaraṃ sammasan ti*. Spk explains "inward exploration" as internal exploration of conditions (*abbhantaraṃ paccayasammasanaṃ*). In the exegetical literature, *sammasana-ñāṇa* is a technical term for the comprehension of the five aggregates by way of the three characteristics (see Paṭis I 53–54, quoted at Vism 607–8; Ppn 20:6–20). Here, however, *sammasana* is used in a sense that comes closer to the exegetical notion of *paccaya-pariggaha*, "discernment of conditions," as at Vism 598–600; Ppn 19:1–13.

185 Spk: The Blessed One wanted him to answer by way of conditionality, but he could not grasp the Master's intention and answered by way of the thirty-two aspects (of bodily foulness).

186 As at **12:51**, but with a different sequel. I read with Be *idaṃ kho dukkhaṃ kiṃnidānaṃ*. Ee here is unsatisfactory.

187 *Idaṃ kho dukkhaṃ upadhinidānaṃ,* etc. Spk: It has its source in "acquisition as the aggregates" (*khandhupadhinidānaṃ*); for here the five aggregates are intended by "acquisition." On *upadhi,* see **I, n. 21**. The standard exegetical analysis of *upadhi* is fourfold: as defilements, aggregates, sensual pleasures, and volitional formations. As *upadhi* is conditioned by *taṇhā,* one might contend that here *upadhi* is synonymous with *upādāna*. Spk, however, does not endorse this interpretation, and the fact that *upadhi* is declared the basis for aging-and-death and the other types of suffering supports Spk's gloss *khandhupadhi*. Possibly a double meaning is intended: *upadhi* as the aggregates is the immediate condition for aging-and-death, while *upadhi* as equivalent to *upādāna* is the remote condition for existence and birth, which in turn is the remote condition for aging-and-death. On *upadhi* as the origin of suffering, see Sn p. 141,7–8: *yaṃ kiñci dukkhaṃ sambhoti sabbaṃ upadhipaccayā*.

188 *Upadhinirodhasāruppagāminī paṭipadā*. As at **12:51**; see **n. 135**.

189 For a more elaborate treatment, see the Mahāsatipaṭṭhāna Sutta, DN II 308,6–309,11.

190 The same simile, but with slight differences in wording, is at MN I 316,10–23.

191 Spk: The bronze cup of beverage represents worldly objects of a pleasant and agreeable nature. The man oppressed by the heat represents the worldling attached to the round; the man who invites him to drink, the people who invite the worldling to enjoy objects in the world with a pleasant and agreeable nature. The man in charge of the drink, who explains its virtues and dangers, is like a spiritual friend, one's preceptor, teacher, etc., who explains the gratification and danger in the five cords of sensual pleasure. Just as the man in the simile suddenly, without reflection, drinks the beverage and meets death or deadly suffering, so the worldling, eager to enjoy sensual pleasures, spurns the advice of his preceptor and teacher, gives up the training, and reverts to the lower life. There he commits a crime and is punished by the king, and in the next life he experiences great suffering in the four realms of misery.

192 Spk: In the counterpart, the man oppressed by the heat represents the meditator at the time he is still attached to the round. When he reflects, rejects the beverage, and dispels his thirst with some other drink, this is like the bhikkhu's abiding by the advice of his preceptor and teacher, guarding the sense doors, gradually developing insight, and attaining the fruit of arahantship. The other four beverages are like the four paths. As the man dispels his thirst with the other four beverages and goes happily wherever he wants, so the arahant, having drunk of the four paths, dispels craving and goes to the region of Nibbāna.

193 Mahākoṭṭhita was the foremost disciple in the analytical knowledges (*paṭisambhidā*). He often appears in dialogue with Sāriputta. As C.Rh.D remarks (KS 2:79, n. 1), since both elders were arahants it is likely these dialogues were intended as "lessons" for their students rather than as genuine inquiries.

194 The underlying presuppositions of the four alternatives are eternalism, annihilationism, partial-eternalism, and fortuitous origination; see **n. 37**.

195 On the reciprocal conditionality of consciousness and name-and-form, see **12:65**.

196 Cp. **12:16**. Spk: *On thirty-six grounds*: for thirty-six reasons, obtained by taking three cases in relation to each of the twelve terms. The first is the quality of being a speaker on the Dhamma, the second the practice, the third the fruit of the practice. By the first method the excellence of the teaching is discussed, by the second the plane of the trainee (*sekha*), by the third the plane of the arahant (*asekha*, one beyond training).

197 Spk does not identify these elders. Saviṭṭha appears at AN I 118–19, Nārada at AN III 57–62.

198 These five grounds for the acceptance of a thesis recur at **35:153** and are examined critically by the Buddha at MN II 170,26–171,25; see too MN II 218,15–21. Here they are being contrasted with personal knowledge (*paccattameva ñāṇa*). For a detailed discussion, see Jayatilleke, *Early Buddhist Theory of Knowledge*, pp. 182–88, 274–76.

Spk: One person accepts something through *faith* (*saddhā*) by placing faith in another and accepting what he says as true. Another accepts something through *personal preference* (*ruci*) when he approves of some thesis by reflecting on it and then takes it to be true. One accepts a thesis by *oral tradition* (*anussava*) when one thinks: "This has come down from ancient times by oral tradition, so it must be true." For another, as he thinks, a certain thesis appears valid, and he concludes, "So it is": he accepts it by *reasoned reflection* (*ākāraparivitakka*). (Jayatilleke discusses *ākāra* as meaning "reason" at p. 274.) In the fifth case, as one reflects, a view arises by pondering some hypothesis; this is *acceptance of a view after pondering it* (*diṭṭhinijjhānakkhanti*).

199 *Bhavanirodho nibbānaṃ*. Spk: Nibbāna is the cessation of the five aggregates.

200 Spk: The elder Musīla was an arahant, but without saying whether or not it was so he just kept silent.

201 Spk: Why did he speak up? It is said that he reflected thus: "This proposition—'Nibbāna is the cessation of existence'—can be understood even by trainees. But this elder (Saviṭṭha) places that one (Musīla) on the plane of the arahant. I will make him understand this matter correctly."

202 Spk: *Clearly seen ... with correct wisdom*: clearly seen with path wisdom together with insight. *I am not an arahant*: he indicates this because he stands on the path of nonreturning. But his knowledge that "Nibbāna is the cessation of existence" is a type of reviewing knowledge (*paccavekkhaṇañāṇa*) apart from the nineteen (regular) types of reviewing knowledge (see Vism 676; Ppn 22:19–21).

203 *Na ca kāyena phusitvā vihareyya*, lit. "but he would not dwell having contacted it with the body." Spk glosses: "He would not be able to draw out the water."

204 Spk: The seeing of water in the well represents the seeing of Nibbāna by the nonreturner. The man afflicted by heat represents the nonreturner; the water bucket, the path of arahantship. As the man oppressed by heat sees water in the well, the nonreturner knows by reviewing knowledge, "There exists a breakthrough to the path of arahantship" (reading with Se *arahattaphalābhisamaya*). But as the man lacking the bucket cannot draw out the water and touch it with the body, so the nonreturner, lacking the path of arahantship, cannot sit down and become absorbed in the

attainment of the fruit of arahantship, which has Nibbāna as its object.

It would be a misunderstanding of Nārada's reply to take it as a rejoinder to Musīla's tacit claim that he is an arahant (the interpretation adopted by Gombrich, *How Buddhism Began*, pp. 128–29). The point is not that Musīla was unjustified in consenting to that title, but that Saviṭṭha drew an incorrect inference, for he held the wrong belief that the defining mark of an arahant is the understanding of dependent origination and the nature of Nibbāna. This understanding, rather, is common property of the trainee and the arahant. What distinguishes the arahant from the trainee is not his insight into dependent origination (and other principles of the Dhamma) but the fact that he has used this insight to eradicate all defilements and has thereby gained access to a unique meditative state (called in the commentaries *arahattaphalasamāpatti*, the fruition attainment of arahantship) in which he can dwell "touching the deathless element with his body." At **48:53**, too, the expression *kāyena phusitvā viharati* highlights the essential difference between the *sekha* and the *asekha*; see **V, n. 238**. For parallel texts on the difference between the stream-enterer and the arahant, see **22:109–110** (stated in terms of the five aggregates) and **48:2–5, 26–27, 32–33** (in terms of the faculties).

205 In all three eds. the question begins with *evaṃvādī tvaṃ* and the reply with *evaṃvādāhaṃ*. However, since it was Nārada who just spoke, it seems we should read the question portion as *evaṃvādiṃ tvaṃ* and resolve *evaṃvādāhaṃ* in the reply into *evaṃvādiṃ ahaṃ*. Neither Spk nor Spk-pṭ offers any help here, but a note in Be of the text suggests this amendation. The Ee reading of a parallel passage at **55:23** (V 374,24–27) has the reading I prefer, though there Be and Se have the same reading as here. At MN II 214,14 foll. we find *evaṃvādāhaṃ* in a context where it would have to be resolved as an accusative plural, *evaṃvādino* (*nigaṇṭhe*) *ahaṃ*, which further supports my proposal regarding the present passage.

206 This sutta is discussed in relation to its Chinese counterpart by Gombrich, *How Buddhism Began*, pp. 123–27.

Spk: Susīma had approached the Venerable Ānanda,

thinking, "He is the most learned disciple, and also the Teacher frequently reports to him the Dhamma he has spoken on various occasions; under him I will be able to learn the Dhamma quickly." Ānanda brought him to the Buddha because he knew that Susīma had been a teacher in his own right and he was apprehensive that after going forth he might try to bring discredit to the Dispensation. The Buddha understood that Susīma's motive in taking ordination was "theft of the Dhamma," which made his entry into the Dispensation impure, but he foresaw that Susīma would shortly undergo a change of heart and attain arahantship. Hence he instructed Ānanda to give him the going forth.

It is puzzling that here, when it was most necessary to do so, the Buddha makes no mention of the probationary period normally imposed on wanderers of other sects who wish to enter the Buddhist order; perhaps the Buddha had foreseen that Susīma would have been discouraged by such a stipulation and would not have applied for admission, thus losing the chance to gain liberation.

207 Spk: Those bhikkhus, having received a meditation subject from the Teacher, entered upon the three-month rains residence, and during the rains, striving and struggling, they attained arahantship. At the end of the rains they went to the Teacher and informed him of their attainment. When Susīma heard about this he thought: "Final knowledge (*aññā*) must be the supreme standard in this Dispensation, the essential personal transmission of the teacher (*paramappamāṇaṃ sārabhūtā ācariyamuṭṭhi*, lit. 'teacher's fist'). Let me inquire and find out about it." Therefore he approached those bhikkhus.

The stock description of the five *abhiññās* that follows is commented upon in detail in Vism, chaps. 12 and 13.

208 Spk-pṭ: The formless jhānas and deliverance from perception (*āruppajjhāna-saññāvimokkhā*).

209 The text enclosed in brackets in Ee should be deleted and the question read as in Be and Se thus: *Ettha dāni āyasmanto idañ ca veyyākaraṇaṃ imesañ ca dhammānaṃ asamāpatti, idaṃ no āvuso kathan ti*. I take the *no* to be merely an interrogative particle (= *nu*).

210 *Paññāvimuttā kho mayaṃ āvuso Susīma.* Spk: He shows: "Friend, we are without jhāna, dry-insighters, liberated simply by wisdom" (*āvuso mayaṃ nijjhānakā sukkhavipassakā paññāmatten' eva vimuttā*). Spk-pṭ: *Liberated simply by wisdom*: not both-ways-liberated (*na ubhatobhāgavimuttā*).

While Spk seems to be saying that those bhikkhus did not have any jhānas, the sutta itself establishes only that they lacked the *abhiññās* and *āruppas*; nothing is said about whether or not they had achieved the four jhānas. It is significant that Susīma's questions do not extend to the jhānas, and it is even possible (though contrary to the commentaries) that *nijjhānaka* should be understood, not as the deprivative "without jhāna," but as an agent noun from *nijjhāna*, pondering, hence "ponderers." In any case, the sutta goes no further than to distinguish the *paññāvimutta* arahant from other arahants who have the six *abhiññās* and the formless attainments, and thus it offers nothing radically different from the Nikāyas as a whole.

The commentaries explain the *paññāvimutta* arahant to be of five kinds: those who attain one or another of the four jhānas, and the "dry-insighter" (*sukkhavipassaka*) who lacks mundane jhāna but still has the supramundane jhāna inseparable from the noble path (see Sv II 512,19–28). On the contrast between *paññāvimutta* and *ubhatobhāgavimutta* arahants, see MN I 477–78; Pp 14, 190–91.

211 *Pubbe kho Susīma dhammaṭṭhitiñāṇaṃ, pacchā nibbāne ñāṇaṃ.* Spk: Insight knowledge is "knowledge of the stability of the Dhamma," which arises first. At the end of the course of insight, path knowledge arises; that is "knowledge of Nibbāna," which arises later. Spk-pṭ: The "stability of the Dhamma" is the stableness of phenomena, their intrinsic nature (*dhammānaṃ ṭhitatā taṃsabhāvatā*): namely, impermanence, suffering, nonself. Knowledge of that is "knowledge of the stability of the Dhamma." See too **n. 51, n. 105**. A chapter on *dhammaṭṭhitiñāṇa* is at Paṭis I 50–52, where it is explained as the knowledge of the relations between each pair of factors in *paṭicca-samuppāda*.

212 Spk: Why is this said? For the purpose of showing the arising of knowledge thus even without concentration. This is what is meant: "Susīma, the path and fruit are not the issue

of concentration (*samādhinissanda*), nor the advantage brought about by concentration (*samādhi-ānisaṃsā*), nor the outcome of concentration (*samādhinipphatti*). They are the issue of insight (*vipassanā*), the advantage brought about by insight, the outcome of insight. Therefore, whether you understand or not, first comes knowledge of the stability of the Dhamma, afterwards knowledge of Nibbāna."

Spk-pṭ: *Even without concentration* (*vinā pi samādhiṃ*): even without previously established (concentration) that has acquired the characteristic of serenity (*samatha-lakkhaṇappattaṃ*); this is said referring to one who takes the vehicle of insight (*vipassanāyānika*).

If understood on its own terms, the text establishes only that arahantship can be attained without the supernormal powers and the formless attainments. Read in the light of Spk and Spk-pṭ, it may be seen to affirm the existence of a "vehicle of bare insight" which begins directly with mindful contemplation of mental and physical phenomena, without depending on a base of concentration by means of the jhānas or access concentration (*upacārasamādhi*). Though the suttas themselves say nothing about a system of bare insight meditation, some contemporary teachers regard the Satipaṭṭhāna Sutta as propounding such a method and appeal to Spk and Spk-pṭ for additional support.

213 Spk: Having known him to be capable of penetration, the Buddha speaks thus giving a Dhamma teaching with three turns, at the conclusion of which the elder attained arahantship. Spk-pṭ: The "three turns" (*teparivaṭṭaṃ*) are by way of the turning over of the three characteristics in relation to the five aggregates.

The catechism on the three characteristics recurs throughout the Khandha-saṃyutta, as at **22:49**, **59**, **79**, **80**, **82**, etc.

214 Spk: This query is started in order to make it evident that those bhikkhus were dry-insighters without jhāna (or: "dry-insight ponderers"). This is the purport here: "You are not the only dry-insighter without jhāna; those bhikkhus were also such."

215 *Dhammatthenaka*. The formula for confession and pardon is also at **16:6** (II 205,10–16).

216 *Antarapeyyāla.* As the preceding section contains eleven suttas, so each sutta to follow can be divided into eleven by taking separately each term and its condition. Spk says these were all spoken by way of the inclinations of the persons to be guided and enlightened according to their different inclinations (*sabbe pi tathā tathā bujjhanakānaṃ veneyyapuggalānaṃ ajjhāsayavasena vuttā*).

217 Spk: Whether it be the Buddha or a disciple, the one in dependence upon whom one gains path knowledge is called a teacher (*satthā,* a word usually reserved for the Buddha); he should be sought for.

13. Abhisamayasaṃyutta

218 The expression *diṭṭhisampanna* denotes one who has seen the truth of the Dhamma, beginning with the *sotāpanna*. See the closing paragraph of **12:27**, etc. MN III 64,16–65,12, and AN III 438–40 list various qualities of the *diṭṭhisampanna,* e.g., being incapable of regarding any formation as permanent, etc., being incapable of parricide and matricide, etc. Spk glosses *abhisametāvino*: "for one who abides having made the breakthrough to the noble truths by means of wisdom" (*paññāya ariyasaccāni abhisametvā ṭhitassa*). On *abhisamaya*, see **n. 13**.

Spk: What is the suffering that has been destroyed? That which might have arisen if the first path had not been developed. The suffering that might have arisen in the plane of misery during the next seven existences, and that which might have arisen anywhere at all beginning with the eighth rebirth—all that has been destroyed.

219 Both *dhammābhisamaya* and *dhammacakkhupaṭilābha* signify the attainment of stream-entry. On the benefit of stream-entry, see Dhp 178.

220 The *yojana* is a measure of distance roughly equal to ten kilometers. Spk explains *kākapeyya* (lit. "crow-drinkable") thus: "So that it is possible for a crow, standing on the bank, to drink from it naturally by inserting its beak."

221 According to early Buddhist cosmology, Sineru is the mountain at the centre of our world-sphere; the word is the Pāli counterpart of the better known Skt Meru. For a fuller

picture of Buddhist cosmology, see Vism 205–7 (Ppn 7:40–44), and Ppn 7: n. 15.

222 Note that the ending here is different from the stock ending in the preceding suttas.

14. Dhātusaṃyutta

223 Spk: *Diversity of elements*: the diversified intrinsic nature of phenomena, which gain the name "elements" in the sense that they have an intrinsic nature consisting in their emptiness and absence of a being (*nissattaṭṭha-suññataṭṭha-saṅkhātena sabhāvaṭṭhena dhātū ti laddhanāmānaṃ dhammānaṃ nānāsabhāvo dhātunānattaṃ*).

224 Spk: The *eye element* is eye-sensitivity (*cakkhupasāda*), the *form element* is the form object; the *eye-consciousness element* is the mind based on eye-sensitivity (*cakkhupasāda-vatthukaṃ cittaṃ*). The other four sense elements, their objects, and states of consciousness are explained in the same way, with the appropriate changes. The *mind element* (*manodhātu*) is the threefold mind element [Spk-pṭ: the two receiving (*sampaṭicchana*) mind elements and the functional mind element [= the five-door adverting citta]. The *mental-phenomena element* (*dhammadhātu*) is the three aggregates—feeling, (perception, and volitional formations)—subtle form, and Nibbāna. The *mind-consciousness element* is all mind-consciousness [Spk-pṭ: of seventy-six types].

Precise formal definitions of the elements are not to be found in the Nikāyas. Perhaps the oldest canonical source for the definitions of the eighteen elements is Vibh 87–90. This comes in the Abhidhamma-bhājaniya only, which implies that the compilers of Vibh considered the eighteen elements a proper Abhidhamma category rather than one pertaining to the suttas. Discussion from the commentarial standpoint is at Vism 484–90 (Ppn 15:17–43) and Vibh-a 76–82.

The "sensitivities" (*pasāda*) are types of material phenomena, located in the gross sense organs, that are especially receptive to the appropriate types of sense objects. Both Vibh-a and Vism frame their explanations on the basis of the Abhidhamma theory of the cognitive process, which, though articulated as such only in the commentaries, already seems to underlie the classification of cittas in the Abhidhamma Piṭaka. This scheme, however, is clearly later than the Nikāyas, and Spk's attempts to reconcile the two standpoints sometimes seems contrived.

The five types of sense consciousness are the cittas that exercise the rudimentary function of bare cognition of the sense object. Of the three mind elements, the "functional" (*kiriya*) is the first citta in the process, which merely adverts to the object, and hence is called the five-door adverting consciousness (*pañcadvārāvajjana-citta*). This is followed by the appropriate sense consciousness (eye-consciousness, etc.), a kammically resultant citta which may be either wholesome-resultant or unwholesome-resultant; hence the fivefold sense consciousness becomes tenfold. Next comes the receiving consciousness (*sampaṭicchana-citta*), which "picks up" the object for further scrutiny; this is a "mind element" and is either wholesome-resultant or unwholesome-resultant. Following this, an investigating consciousness (*santīraṇa-citta*) arises, a wholesome-resultant or unwholesome-resultant citta which investigates the object; then a determining consciousness (*votthapana-citta*), a functional citta which defines the object; and then comes a string of cittas called *javana*, which constitute either a wholesome or an unwholesome response to the object (or, in the case of the arahant, a merely "functional" response). This may be followed by a registration consciousness (*tadārammaṇa*), a resultant citta which records the impression of the object on the mental continuum. All the cittas from the investigating consciousness onwards are mind-consciousness element, which is of seventy-six types. In the mind door the process is somewhat different: it begins with a mind-door adverting consciousness (*manodvārāvajjana-citta*), followed immediately by the string of *javanas*. For details, see CMA 1:8–10, 4:1–23.

The mental-phenomena element (*dhammadhātu*) is not necessarily the object of mind-consciousness element, as one might suppose it to be by analogy with the other senses. Along with the object of mind-consciousness it includes all feeling, perception, and volitional factors that accompany consciousness in the process of cognition. Thus it belongs as much to the subjective pole of the cognitive act as to the objective pole. See particularly CMA, Table 7.4.

225 Spk: Eye-contact, etc., are associated with eye-consciousness, etc. Mind-contact is that associated with the first *javana* in the mind door; therefore when it is said, *in dependence on the mind element there arises mind contact,* this means that the contact of the first *javana* arises in dependence on the functional mind-consciousness element, i.e., the mind-door adverting citta.

On *javana,* see CMA 3:9, 4:12–16, and on the mind-door adverting citta, see CMA 1:10, 3:9.

226 Since, according to the Abhidhamma scheme of conditional relations, the mind element and its concomitant contact are mutually dependent, Spk is compelled to explain these terms in a way that does not place the sutta in contradiction with the Abhidhamma. Hence Spk says: "The functional mind-consciousness element with the function of adverting (i.e., the mind-door adverting citta) does not arise in dependence on the contact associated with the first *javana* in the mind door (which occurs subsequent to it)."

227 Spk: *Perception of form* (*rūpasaññā*): the perception associated with eye-consciousness. *Intention regarding form* (*rūpasaṅkappa*): the intention associated with three cittas—the receiving, (investigating, and determining cittas). *Desire for form* (*rūpacchanda*): desire in the sense of desirousness for form. *Passion for form* (*rūpapariḷāha*): passion (lit. "fever") in the sense of a burning in regard to form [Spk-pṭ: for the fire of lust, etc., has the function of "burning up" its own support]. *The quest for form* (*rūpapariyesanā*): searching in order to obtain that form, having taken along one's friends and comrades. Passion and the quest are found in different *javana* processes (so that passion can become an antecedent condition for the quest).

228 Ee should be corrected to read: *no saṅkappanānattaṃ paṭicca uppajjati saññānānattaṃ; no saññānānattaṃ paṭicca uppajjati dhātunānattaṃ.*

229 Text enclosed in brackets is found in Ee and Se, but without the elision. Se further develops the pattern for the sound element, while Be proceeds directly from *rūpadhātuṃ*

bhikkhave paṭicca uppajjati rūpasaññā to *dhammadhātuṃ paṭicca uppajjati dhammasaññā* and develops the pattern for the mental-phenomena element alone.

230 This attempt to combine into one series the discrete sequences beginning with contact and perception leads to some strange incongruities, which become even more bizarre among the negations of the following sutta. Elsewhere contact is said to be the condition for the manifestation of the aggregates of feeling, perception, and volitional formations (e.g., at **22:82** (III 101,33–102,2), and see **35:93** (IV 68,15–16)); yet here contact and feeling are said to be dependent on perception and intention. Neither Spk nor Spk-pṭ shows any signs of uneasiness over the discrepancies nor tries to justify them.

At MN I 111,35–112,13 a sequence of mental phenomena is given as follows: contact > perception > thought > conceptual proliferation > obsession by perceptions and notions arisen from proliferation. The texts often treat thought (*vitakka*) as identical with intention (*saṅkappa*); proliferation (*papañca*) includes craving (*taṇhā*), which is synonymous with desire (*chanda*); and obsession (*samudācāra*) may comprise passions and quests, etc. This would then give us a more cogent version of the series. Spk does in fact refer to one elder, Uruvelāyavāsī Cūḷatissa Thera, who said: "Although the Blessed One inserted contact and feeling in the middle of the text, having turned the text back (*pāḷiṃ pana parivaṭṭetvā*) we get: perception, intention, desire, passion, quest, and gain in regard to the stated object (form, etc.), 'gain of form' being the object gained together with craving; then there is contact as the (mental) contact with the object gained and feeling as the experiencing of the object. In such a way this pair—contact with form and feeling—is found."

Spk continues on its own: "And here, perception, intention, contact, feeling, and desire are found both in the same *javana* process and in different *javana* processes, while passion, quest, and gain are found only in different *javana* processes."

231 Spk: The *light element* (*ābhādhātu*) is a name for the jhāna together with its object, that is, light (*āloka*) and the jhāna

arisen after doing the preparatory work on the light-*kasiṇa*. The *beauty element* (*subhadhātu*) is just the jhāna together with its object, namely, the jhāna arisen on the basis of a beautiful *kasiṇa*. The others are self-explanatory.

232 Spk: *The light element is discerned in dependence on darkness*: for darkness is delimited by (contrasted with) light, and light by darkness. Similarly, foulness is delimited by (contrasted with) beauty, and beauty by foulness. *In dependence on form*: in dependence on a form-sphere meditative attainment. For when one has a form-sphere attainment one can overcome form or attain the base of the infinity of space. *In dependence on cessation* (*nirodhaṃ paṭicca*): in dependence on the reflectively induced nonoccurrence (*paṭisaṅkhā-appavatti*) of the four (mental) aggregates. For the attainment of cessation is discerned in dependence on the cessation of the aggregates, not on their occurrence. And here it is just the cessation of the four aggregates that should be understood as "the attainment of cessation."

233 Spk: *An attainment with a residue of formations* (*saṅkhārā-vasesasamāpatti*): because of a residue of subtle formations. According to Vism 337–38 (Ppn 10:47–54), in this attainment perception and the other mental factors are present merely in a subtle residual mode and thus cannot perform their decisive functions; hence the ambivalence in the name.

234 Spk: The *sensuality element* (*kāmadhātu*) is sensual thought, all sense-sphere phenomena in general, and in particular everything unwholesome except the ill-will element and the harmfulness element, which are mentioned separately here. Sensual perception arises in dependence on the sensuality element either by taking it as an object or by way of association (i.e., when sensual perception is associated with sensual thought in the same citta).

All these elements are defined at Vibh 86–87, quoted by Spk. Vibh-a 74 correlates sensual thought with sensuality as defilement (*kilesakāma*) and sense-sphere phenomena with sensuality as sensual objects (*vatthukāma*). Sensual intention arises in dependence on sensual perception by way either of association or decisive support. (Association condition (*sampayutta-paccaya*) is a relation between simultaneous mental phenomena; decisive-support condition (*upanissaya-paccaya*) is a relation between a cause and effect separated in time.)

235 Spk: The *ill will element* (*byāpādadhātu*) is thought of ill will or ill will itself [Spk-pṭ: i.e., hatred (*dosa*)]. Note that the commentaries, following the Abhidhamma's systematic treatment of the Buddha's teaching, differentiate between ill will and thought of ill will. The two are distinct mental constituents (*cetasikā dhammā*), the former being a mode of the unwholesome mental factor hatred (*dosa*), the latter the thought (*vitakka*) associated with that mental factor. Similarly with harmfulness, etc.

236 Spk: The *harmfulness element* (*vihiṃsādhātu*) is thought of harmfulness and harmfulness itself. Vibh 86 explains the harmfulness element as injuring beings in various ways.

237 Spk: The *renunciation element* (*nekkhammadhātu*) is thought of renunciation and all wholesome states except the other two elements, which are to be explained separately. Perception of renunciation arises in dependence on the renunciation element by way of such conditions as conascence (*sahajātapaccaya*), etc.

238 Spk: The *non-ill will element* (*abyāpādadhātu*) is thought of non-ill will and non-ill will itself, i.e., lovingkindness towards beings.

239 Spk: The *harmlessness element* (*avihiṃsādhātu*) is thought of harmlessness and compassion.

240 Spk: From this point on the word "element" means inclination (*ajjhāsaya*).

241 The name of the bhikkhu is given as in Ee. Be and Se cite it simply as Kaccāna, and Se notes a v.l., Sandha Kaccāyana. At **44:11** a Sabhiya Kaccāna is mentioned, also at the Brick Hall in Ñātika, and the two may be the same person.

Spk explains his question in two ways: (i) "Why does the view arise in the six (rival) teachers who are not perfectly enlightened, 'We are Perfectly Enlightened Ones'?" (ii) "Why does the view arise in their disciples in regard to (their teachers) who are not perfectly enlightened, 'They are Perfectly Enlightened Ones'?" Ee *sammāsambuddho ti* should be amended to *sammāsambuddhā ti*.

242 The contrast is between *hīnādhimuttikā* and *kalyāṇādhimuttikā*. Spk glosses *adhimuttikā* with *ajjhāsayā*, "inclination."

243 Sāriputta, as the bhikkhu disciple foremost in wisdom, attracted bhikkhus who were likewise of great wisdom. All the other disciples mentioned below attract pupils who share their specialty.

244 This sutta, including the verses, is at It 70–71. The verses alone, excluding the first two pādas, are at Th 147–48.

245 *Saṃsaggā vanatho jāto.* On *vanatha*, see **I, n. 474**. Spk: *From association*—from craving and affection based upon association through seeing and hearing—*the woods is born*, the woods of the defilements is born. *By nonassociation it is cut*: it is cut by nonassociation, by not-seeing, by avoiding standing and sitting privately (with a person of the opposite sex).

246 Spk: *Those of wrong knowledge*: those endowed with wrong reviewing (*micchāpaccavekkhaṇena samannāgatā*). *Those of wrong liberation*: those who abide in an unemancipating liberation, which they assume to be wholesome liberation. *Those of right knowledge*: those with right reviewing. *Those of right liberation*: those endowed with the emancipating liberation of the fruit.

Right knowledge and right liberation supplement the eight factors of the Noble Eightfold Path. They are said to be factors of the arahant (e.g., at MN III 76,8), but at **55:26** (V 384,1–12) they are also ascribed to Anāthapiṇḍika, a stream-enterer. Spk's gloss of right knowledge as right reviewing knowledge is difficult to accept. More likely the expression refers to the full knowledge of the Four Noble Truths by means of which arahantship is gained.

247 Spk interprets each element by way of its physical characteristic or function: the earth element is the foundational element (*patiṭṭhādhātu*); the water element, the cohesive element (*ābandhanadhātu*); the fire element, the maturing element (*paripācanadhātu*); and the air element, the distensive element (*vitthambhanadhātu*). For a more detailed treatment according to the commentarial method, see Vism 364–70 (Ppn 11:85–117).

248 Spk: Since it is contingent upon Nibbāna (*nibbānaṃ āgamma*) that desire and lust are removed and abandoned, Nibbāna is the escape from it.

249 Spk: In this sutta the Four Noble Truths are discussed. The

gratification (*assāda*) in the four elements is the truth of the origin; the *danger* (*ādīnava*) is the truth of suffering; the *escape* (*nissaraṇa*) is the truth of cessation; the *path that understands* the escape is the truth of the path.

250 Throughout I read with Se and Ee *cetovimutti* as against Be *vimutti*. Spk: The knowledge arose, "This liberation of mine by the fruit of arahantship is unshakable." Its unshakableness can be understood through the cause and through the object. It is unshakable through the cause because there can be no return of the defilements eradicated by the four paths. It is unshakable through the object because it occurs taking the unshakable state, Nibbāna, as object.

251 *Vimariyādikatena cetasā*. Spk: The barriers (*mariyādā*) are twofold: the barriers of defilements and the barriers of the round of existence. Here, because of the abandoning of both, it is said that they dwell with a mind rid of barriers.

252 Spk: It is pleasurable in that it is a condition for pleasant feeling.

253 There is a lack of symmetry between the two clauses in this statement: the first strings together four terms: *uppādo ṭhiti abhinibbatti pātubhāvo*, but the sequel exemplifies only three, omitting *abhinibbatti*. This is done consistently whenever this "template" is applied, as at **22:30** and **35:21–22**.

15. *Anamataggasaṃyutta*

254 *Anamataggo 'yaṃ bhikkhave saṃsāro*. Spk resolves *anamatagga* into *anu amatagga*, explaining: "Even if it should be pursued by knowledge for a hundred or a thousand years, it would be with unthought-of beginning, with unknown beginning (*vassasataṃ vassasahassaṃ ñāṇena* ***anu****gantvā pi* ***amataggo*** *aviditaggo*). It wouldn't be possible to know its beginning from here or from there; the meaning is that it is without a delimiting first or last point. *Saṃsāra* is the uninterruptedly occurring succession of the aggregates, etc. (*khandhādīnaṃ avicchinnappavattā paṭipāṭi*)."

The BHS equivalent of *anamatagga* is *anavarāgra* (e.g., at Mvu I 34,7), "without lower or upper limit." For various explanations, see CPD, s.v. *an-amat'-agga*.

255 Spk: The four great oceans delimited by the rays of Mount

Sineru. For Sineru's eastern slope is made of silver, its southern slope of jewels, its western slope of crystal, and its northern slope of gold. From the eastern and southern slopes rays of silver and jewels come forth, merge, traverse the surface of the ocean, and reach right up to the mountains that encircle the world-sphere; and so too with the rays coming forth from the other slopes. The four great oceans are situated between those rays.

256 *Kappa*. Apparently a *mahākappa* is intended, the length of time needed for a world system to arise, develop, and perish. Each *mahākappa* consists of four *asaṅkheyyakappas*, periods of expansion, stabilization, contraction, and dissolution: see AN II 142,15–28.

257 *Kāsikena vatthena*. Although this is often understood to be silk, Spk explains it to be an extremely delicate cloth made of thread spun from three fibres of cotton.

258 Reading, with Be and Se, *ananussaritā va*. Ee *anussaritā va* should be amended.

259 The simile is also at **56:33**.

260 The sutta, including the verses, is also at It 17–18.

261 Spk: For these beings, the times when they are born as invertebrates is greater than the times when they are born as vertebrates; for when they become creatures such as worms, etc., they have no bones. But when they become fish and tortoises, etc., their bones are numerous. Therefore, skipping over the time when they are invertebrates and the time when they have extremely numerous bones, only the time when they have a moderate number of bones (*samaṭṭhikakālo va*) should be taken.

262 The same group of bhikkhus provided the occasion for the Buddha to institute the offering of the *kaṭhina* robe at the end of the Vassa, the annual rains residence; see Vin I 253–54. Forest dwelling, etc., are four of the ascetic practices (*dhutaṅga*). Spk: *Yet all were still with fetters* (*sabbe sasaṃyojanā*): Some were stream-enterers, some once-returners, some nonreturners, but among them there were no worldlings or arahants.

263 On the variations in the human life span during the epochs of the different Buddhas, see DN II 3,28–4,5. DN III 68–76 explains how the life span of humans will

decline still further as a result of moral degeneration until it reaches a low of ten years, after which it will increase until it reaches 80,000 years in the time of the future Buddha Metteyya.

264 Spk says that the text should not be interpreted to mean that the life span gradually decreased from Kakusandha's age directly to that of Koṇāgamana's. Rather, the life span after Kakusandha's parinibbāna continually decreased until it reached the minimum of ten years, then it increased to an incalculable (*asaṅkheyya*), and then decreased again until it reached 30,000 years, at which time Koṇāgamana arose in the world. The same pattern applies to the subsequent cases, including that of Metteya (see **n. 263**).

265 Also at **6:15 (I, v. 609)**. See too **v. 21** and **I, n. 20**.

16. Kassapasaṃyutta

266 Spk discusses a threefold typology of contentment (*santosa*): (i) contentment that accords with one's gains (*yathālābhasantosa*), i.e., remaining content with any gains, whether fine or coarse; (ii) contentment that accords with one's ability (*yathābalasantosa*), i.e., remaining content with whatever one needs to sustain one's health; and (iii) contentment that accords with suitability (*yathāsāruppasantosa*), i.e., disposing of any luxury items received and retaining only the simplest and most basic requisites. A translation of the full passage—from the parallel commentary to the Sāmaññaphala Sutta (Sv I 206–8)—may be found in Bodhi, *Discourse on the Fruits of Recluseship*, pp. 134–37. Various types of wrong search (*anesanā*) are discussed at Vism 22–30 (Ppn 1:60–84).

267 Spk: *If he does not get a robe*: If he does not get a robe he does not become agitated (*na paritassati*) like one who, failing to get a robe, becomes frightened and agitated and associates with meritorious bhikkhus, thinking "How can I get a robe?" *Seeing the danger* (*ādīnavadassāvī*): the danger of an offence in improper search and of use while being tied to it. *Understanding the escape* (*nissaraṇapañña*): he uses it knowing the escape stated in the formula, "Only for warding off cold," etc. (On the formulas for the four requisites,

see MN I 10,4–20, with detailed analysis at Vism 30–35; Ppn 1:85–97) This passage (and the parallels in regard to the other requisites excluding medicines) is found in the Ariyavaṃsa Sutta in a description of the ideal ascetic monk (AN II 27–29).

268 *Kassapena vā hi vo bhikkhave ovadissāmi yo vā pan' assa Kassapasadiso*. Spk makes it clear that *yo … Kassapasadiso* should be construed as instrumental in force, parallel to *Kassapena*: "He exhorts by the example of Kassapa when he says, 'As the Elder Mahākassapa is content with the four requisites, so too should you be.' He exhorts by one who is similar to Kassapa when he says, 'If there should be anyone else here who is similar to Kassapa—that is, like the Elder Mahākassapa—in being content with the four requisites, you should be so too.'"

269 *Tathattāya paṭipajjitabbaṃ*. Spk: (He says:) "'In this sutta on contentment the Perfectly Enlightened One's responsibility (*bhāra*) is explaining the practice of effacement (*sallekhācāra*), while our responsibility is to fulfil it by the fulfilment of the practice. Let us accept the responsibility entrusted to us'—having reflected thus, you should practise accordingly, as explained by me."

270 Spk explains *not ardent* (*anātāpī*) as devoid of the energy that burns up (*ātapati*) defilements, and *unafraid of wrongdoing* (*anottappī*) as devoid of fear over the arising of defilements and the nonarising of wholesome qualities. Both words are derived from the same root, *tap*, to burn. Spk explains *anuttara yogakkhema* as arahantship, so called because it is secure from the four bonds (*yoga*; see **45:172**). See too **I, n. 463**.

271 The four parts of this reflection correspond to the four aspects of right effort (see **45:8**) or the four right kinds of striving (see **49:1–12**).

272 Spk: "As the moon, gliding across the sky, does not form intimacy, affection, or attachment with anyone, nor give rise to fondness, longing, and obsession, yet remains dear and agreeable to the multitude, so you too should not form intimacy, etc., with anyone; then, by doing so, you will approach families like the moon, dear and agreeable to the multitude. Further, as the moon dispels darkness and

emits light, so you will dispel the darkness of defilements and emit the light of knowledge."

Spk explains *apakassa* as an absolutive, equivalent to *apakassitvā* and glossed *apanetvā*, "having pulled away." A bhikkhu draws back the body when he lives in a forest abode (rather than a village temple) and draws back the mind when he refrains from sensual thoughts and other harmful mental states.

273 Spk: This is a unique phrase (*asambhinnapada*) in the Word of the Buddha preserved in the Tipiṭaka. Spk-pṭ: For nowhere else has this phrase, "The Blessed One waved his hand in space," been recorded.

274 This is a self-serving thought. The bhikkhu wants to see the bhikkhus receive offerings and the lay followers "make merit" by offering gifts to them. The bhikkhu who is elated over the gains of others has the virtue of altruistic joy (*muditā*); he does not become envious when others are chosen to receive gifts rather than himself.

275 *Pasannākāraṃ kareyyuṃ*. This idiom also occurs below at **20:9** (II 269,24, 33) and at MN III 131,30–31 and III 144,18–19. A *pasannākāraṃ* (lit. "a mode of the confident") is a gift given as an expression of appreciation. The hiatus in Ee should be closed up. Spk: "May they give the requisites, a robe and so forth!"

276 *Kāruññaṃ paṭicca anudayaṃ paṭicca anukampaṃ upādāya*. I generally translate both *karuṇā* (of which *kāruññaṃ* is a cognate) and *anukampā* as "compassion." This is usually successful as the two seldom occur together, but the present passage is a rare exception; thus I use "tender concern" as a makeshift for *anukampā*. Spk glosses *anudaya* with *rakkhaṇabhāva* (the protective state) and *anukampā* with *muducittatā* (tender-heartedness), and says that both terms are synonymous with *kāruññaṃ*. In the next paragraph, where the same statement is applied to Kassapa, Ee has omitted a line (at II 200,3), apparently by oversight: … *paresaṃ dhammaṃ deseti; kāruññaṃ paṭicca.…*

277 *Kulūpaka*. Spk: One who goes to the homes of families. As will be seen at **20:9, 10**, this could be dangerous for monks who were not inwardly strong enough to resist the temptations posed by intimate association with lay people.

278 Spk: Kassapa's robes are said to be worn-out (*nibbasana*) because the Blessed One, having worn them, had discarded them. (See below **16:11**; II 221,15–25.)

The Buddha is apparently requesting Mahākassapa to abandon three of the ascetic practices—wearing rag-robes, eating only food collected on alms round, and living in the forest. The Buddha himself wore robes offered by householders, accepted invitations to meals, and dwelt in town monasteries; see MN II 7–8. According to Spk, the Buddha did not really intend to make Kassapa give up his ascetic practices, but rather "just as a drum does not give off a sound unless it is struck, so such persons do not roar their lion's roar unless they are 'struck.' Thus he spoke to him in this way intending to make him roar his lion's roar."

279 This is Mahākassapa's lion's roar; see too MN I 214,1–17, where Kassapa describes the ideal monk in the same terms. The first four items are ascetic practices; the second four, virtues nurtured by observance of these practices. At AN I 23,20 the Buddha declares Mahākassapa the foremost among his bhikkhu disciples who are proponents of the ascetic practices, as is clear too from **14:15** above.

280 Reading with Se: *App' eva nāma pacchimā janatā diṭṭhānugatiṃ āpajjeyya*. Be and Ee have the plural *āpajjeyyuṃ*. At KS 2:136 this is rendered: "For surely these [those who will come after us] may fall into error." The translator here evidently understands *diṭṭhānugati* as resolvable into *diṭṭhi* + *anugati*, with *diṭṭhi* meaning wrong view. Spk and Spk-pṭ are silent, but I find it more plausible to take the first part of the compound as the past participle *diṭṭha*, "the seen" in the sense of an example or role model. This interpretation can claim support from the use of the idiom at AN I 126,19–20, 127,22–23; III 108,5–6, 251,8, and 422,10, 19. See too MLDB, n. 57.

281 Spk: He says this in order to appoint Mahākassapa to his own position. But weren't Sāriputta and Mahāmoggallāna around? They were, but he thought: "They will not live much longer, but Kassapa will live until the age of 120. After my parinibbāna he will hold a recital of the Dhamma and the Vinaya in the Sattapaṇṇi Cave, and he will enable my Dispensation to endure for a full 5,000 years. Let me

appoint him to my own position; then the bhikkhus will think he should be heeded." Despite this remark of Spk, it should be noted that the Buddha expressly refused to appoint a personal successor; instead he instructed the Saṅgha that the Dhamma and the Vinaya should represent him after his passing (DN II 154,4–8).

282 *Dovacassakaraṇehi dhammehi samannāgatā*: for a list of such qualities, see MN I 95,18–96,16.

283 The following, slightly expanded and including the simile of the moon, is also at AN V 123,10–124,19, ascribed to Sāriputta. There too the Buddha approves of the disciple's statement and repeats it in full.

284 I read with Ee: *evaṃ hi taṃ Kassapa sammā vadamāno vadeyya upaddutā brahmacārī brahmacārūpaddavena abhibhavanā brahmacārī brahmacārabhibhavanenā ti*. Se differs only in reading *vadanto* for *vadamāno*. Be, however, has *etarahi taṃ Kassapa sammā vadamāno vadeyya upaddutā brahmacārī brahmacārūpaddavena abhipatthanā brahmacārī brahmacāri-abhipatthanenā ti*. This version, I suspect, arose by substituting the commentarial gloss for the original. It seems that in Se and Ee the sense requires, in place of the first *abhibhavanā*, the past participle *abhibhūtā* (or *adhibhūta*), though no edition available to me has this reading. On how gain and honour ruin those who live the holy life, see MN III 116,22–117,13.

Spk (Se): They are ruined by the *ruination of those who lead the holy life*, namely, excessive desire and lust for the four requisites. *Vanquishment* is excessive longing (*abhibhavanā ti adhimattapatthanā*). *By the vanquishing of those who lead the holy life*: by the state of the four requisites that consists in the excessive longing of those who lead the holy life (*brahmacārabhibhavanenā ti brahmacārīnaṃ adhimattapatthanāsaṅkhātena catupaccayabhāvena*). Se has a note here to the gloss: *Evaṃ sabbattha. Catupaccayābhibhavena iti bhavitabbaṃ*.

285 In MLDB *cetovimutti paññāvimutti* is translated "deliverance of mind and deliverance by wisdom," as if the two terms were separate items standing in conjunction. I now think it better to omit the conjunctive particle (which is not in the Pāli) and to treat the two terms as a dual designation for what is essentially the same state. Spk explains

cetovimutti as the concentration of the fruit of arahantship (*arahattaphalasamādhi*), *paññāvimutti* as the wisdom of the fruit of arahantship (*arahattaphalapaññā*).

286 From the absence of any reference to the Blessed One in the introduction it is likely that this sutta takes place after his parinibbāna. Spk supports this supposition (see following note), as does Ānanda's use of the vocative *bhante* when addressing Mahākassapa. Before the Buddha expired the monks used to address one another as *āvuso*, "friend" (see DN II 154,9–15).

Spk: Ānanda asked him to come to the bhikkhunīs' quarters in order to inspire them and to explain a meditation subject, thinking they would place faith in the talk of the disciple who was the Buddha's counterpart (*buddha-paṭibhāga-sāvaka*).

287 Spk: He was not involved with building work, etc., but the four assemblies would come to the Elder Ānanda lamenting over the Buddha's demise and he would be obliged to console them (see **9:5** and **I, n. 541**).

288 Her name means "Fat Tissā." Spk glosses *vedehimuni* with *paṇḍitamuni*, "wise sage," explaining: "A wise person endeavours with erudition consisting in knowledge—that is, he does all his tasks—therefore he is called Videhan (*paṇḍito hi ñāṇasaṅkhā-tena vedena īhati … tasmā vedeho ti vuccati*). He was Videhan and a sage, hence 'the Videhan sage.'" Ap-a 128,12, however, offers a more plausible explanation: "Ānanda was called *vedehimuni* because he was a sage and the son of a mother from the Vedeha country [= Videha] (*Vedeharaṭṭhe jātattā Vedehiyā putto*)." See **I, n. 233**.

289 *Khamatha bhante Kassapa bālo mātugāmo.* I have translated this sentence with complete fidelity to the text, aware that some readers might find the rendering provocative. One consultant told me, "You've just lost half your readership," and suggested I avoid drawing criticism to the translation by rendering *bālo mātugāmo* as "she is a foolish woman." To my mind, this would distort the meaning of the Pāli in subservience to current views of gender. I do not see how the sentence could be construed in any other way than I have rendered it. I leave it to the reader to decide whether Ānanda himself could actually have made such a statement or

whether it was put into his mouth by the compilers of the canon.

290 Spk: This is what is meant: "Do not let the Saṅgha think, 'Ānanda restrained the disciple who was the Buddha's counterpart, but he did not restrain the bhikkhunī. Could there be some intimacy or affection between them?'" He utters the following passage (on his meditative attainments) to demonstrate how he is the Buddha's counterpart.

291 Spk glosses *sattaratana* (seven cubits) as *sattahatthappamāṇa* (the measurement of seven hands); a *hattha* (lit. "hand"), which extends from the elbow to the fingertip, is approximately two feet. This is one of the rare texts in the Nikāyas where the word *abhiññā* is used collectively to designate the six higher knowledges.

292 Spk: After she had censured the disciple who was the Buddha's counterpart, even while Mahākassapa was roaring his lion's roar about the six *abhiññās,* her saffron robes began to irritate her body like thorny branches or a prickly plant. As soon as she removed them and put on the white clothes (of a lay woman) she felt at ease.

293 A BHS parallel of this sutta is at Mvu III 47–56. Spk: Dakkhiṇāgiri was a country in the southern region of the hills surrounding Rājagaha. After the Buddha's parinibbāna Ānanda had gone to Sāvatthī to inform the multitude; then he left for Rājagaha and along the way was walking on tour in Dakkhiṇāgiri.

294 This is said with reference to Pācittiya 32. See Vin IV 71–75.

295 See Vin II 196, which relates the original background story to the rule, namely, Devadatta's attempt to create a schism in the Saṅgha (also at Vin IV 71). Spk alludes to this in its gloss of the expression *mā pāpicchā pakkhaṃ nissāya saṅghaṃ bhindeyyuṃ*: "It was laid down for this reason: 'As Devadatta along with his retinue ate after informing families and, by relying on those of evil wishes, divided the Saṅgha, so let it not come to pass that others of evil wishes—by collecting a group, eating among families after informing them, and enlarging their group—divide the Saṅgha in reliance on their faction.'"

Spk seems to interpret *dummaṅkūnaṃ puggalānaṃ niggahāya* and *pesalānaṃ bhikkhūnaṃ phāsuvihārāya* as complementary sides of a single reason, a view explicitly endorsed by Spk-pṭ: *dummaṅkūnaṃ niggaho eva pesalānaṃ phāsuvihāro ti idaṃ ekaṃ aṅgaṃ*. Thus on this interpretation "*mā pāpicchā* ..." would become a second, independent reason. But I follow Horner (at BD 5:275) and C.Rh.D (at KS 2:147), both of whom take the restraint of ill-behaved persons and the comforting of well-behaved bhikkhus as two distinct reasons, to which "*mā pāpicchā* ..." is subordinate. This seems to be corroborated by the list of ten reasons for the laying down of the training rules (at Vin III 21, etc.), where these two factors are counted as separate reasons. As to the third reason, "out of sympathy for families" (*kulānuddayatāya*), Spk says: "When the Bhikkhu Saṅgha is living in harmony and performing the Uposatha and Pavāraṇā, people who give ticket-meals, etc., become destined for heaven." A more plausible explanation is that families are spared the burden of having to support too many bhikkhus at one time. In the Mvu version (at III 48) only two reasons are mentioned, "the protection, safeguarding, and comfort of families" and "the breaking up of cliques of wicked men."

296 *Kumārakavādā na muccāma*. Commentarial tradition holds that Ānanda was born on the same day as the Bodhisatta (see Sv II 425, Ap-a 58, 358, Ja I 63 (Be, but not in the Se or Ee versions)). If this were true, however, he would now be over eighty years of age and thus would hardly have to point to a few grey hairs to prove he is no longer a youngster. Other facts recorded in the canon suggest that Ānanda must have been considerably younger than the Buddha, perhaps by as much as thirty years. On the different opinions about his age held by the early Buddhist schools, see C. Witanachchi's article "Ānanda," in the *Encyclopaedia of Buddhism*, Vol. I, fasc. 4, p. 529.

Spk paraphrases in a way that supports the traditional view: "Since you wander around with newly ordained bhikkhus devoid of sense restraint, you wander around with youngsters and thus you yourself deserve to be called a youngster."

297 The name means "Fat Nandā." She is frequently mentioned in the Bhikkhunī Vibhaṅga as a troublemaker in the

Bhikkhunī Saṅgha; see e.g. Vin IV 216, 218, 223–24, etc. KS 2:148 mistakenly calls this nun "Fat Tissā," confusing her with the petulant nun of the preceding sutta.

298 *Aññatitthiyapubbo samāno*. Spk: Since the elder was not known to have any teacher or preceptor in this Dispensation, and he had put on the saffron robes himself when he renounced the world, out of indignation she depicts him as having been formerly a member of another sect. On Ānanda as the "Videhan sage" see above **n. 288**.

299 *Paṭapilotikānaṃ*. See **n. 60** above.

300 Spk relates here the entire biographical background of Mahākassapa, including several past lives, culminating in his meeting with the Buddha. For a paraphrase, see Hecker, "Mahākassapa: Father of the Saṅgha," in Nyanaponika and Hecker, *Great Disciples of the Buddha*, pp. 109–19.

301 I translate Kassapa's thought just above following Spk, which paraphrases each sentence as a conditional: "'If I should see the Teacher, it is just the Blessed One that I would see; there cannot be any other Teacher than him. If I should see the Fortunate One—called *sugata* because he has gone well by the right practice—it is just this Blessed One that I would see; there cannot be any other Fortunate One than him. If I should see the Perfectly Enlightened One—so called because he awakened fully to the truths by himself—it is just the Blessed One that I would see; there cannot be any other Perfectly Enlightened One than him.' By this he shows, 'Merely by seeing him, I had no doubt that this is the Teacher, this is the Fortunate One, this is the Perfectly Enlightened One.'"

The repetition of Kassapa's declaration of discipleship is in Be and Se though not in Ee. Spk confirms the repetition, explaining that although the utterance is recorded twice we should understand that it was actually spoken three times.

302 Spk: If a disciple so single-minded (*evaṃ sabbacetasā samannāgato*)—so confident in mind (*pasannacitto*)—should perform such an act of supreme humility towards an outside teacher who, without knowing, claims to know (i.e., to be enlightened), that teacher's head would fall off from the neck like a palm fruit broken at the stalk; the meaning is, it

would split into seven pieces. But when such an act of humility is done at the Master's golden feet, it cannot stir even a hair on his body. The following "Therefore" implies: "Since knowing, I say 'I know,' therefore you should train thus."

303 Here Spk explains *sabbacetasā* differently than above: "attending with a completely attentive mind (*sabbena samannāhāracittena*), without allowing the mind to stray even a little."

304 *Sātasahagatā ca me kāyagatā sati.* Spk: This is mindfulness of the body associated with pleasure by way of the first jhāna in the foulness meditation and mindfulness of breathing. This threefold exhortation was itself the elder's going forth and higher ordination.

305 Spk (Se): *Sāṇo ti sakileso sa-iṇo hutvā.* Be (text and Spk) reads *saraṇo* instead of *sāṇo*, which is less satisfactory. The line is also at MN III 127, 7–8, with *sāṇo*.

Spk: There are four modes of using the requisites: (i) by theft (*theyyaparibhoga*), the use made by a morally depraved monk; (ii) as a debtor (*iṇaparibhoga*), the unreflective use made by a virtuous monk; (iii) as an heir (*dāyajjaparibhoga*), the use made by the seven trainees; (iv) as an owner (*sāmiparibhoga*), the use made by an arahant. Thus only an arahant uses the requisites as an owner, without debt. The elder speaks of his use of the requisites when he was still a worldling as use by a debtor.

306 Spk: This took place on the day of their first meeting. The attainment of arahantship was mentioned beforehand because of the sequence of the teaching, but it actually took place afterwards. The Buddha descended from the road with the intention of making Kassapa a forest dweller, a rag-robe wearer, and a one-meal eater from his very birth (as a monk).

307 Spk: The Blessed One wanted to exchange robes with Kassapa because he wished to appoint the elder to his own position (*theraṃ attano ṭhāne ṭhapetukāmatāya*). When he asked whether the elder could wear his rag-robes he was not referring to his bodily strength but to the fulfilment of the practice (*paṭipattipūraṇa*). The Buddha had made this robe from a shroud that had covered a slave woman

named Puṇṇā, which had been cast away in a cremation ground. When he picked it up, brushed away the creatures crawling over it, and established himself in the great lineage of the nobles ones, the earth quaked and sounded a roar and the devas applauded. In offering the robe, the Buddha implied: "This robe should be worn by a bhikkhu who is from birth an observer of the ascetic practices. Will you be able to make proper use of it?" And Kassapa's assent signifies, "I will fulfil this practice." At the moment they exchanged robes the great earth resounded and shook to its ocean boundaries.

308 Cp. the Buddha's praise of Sāriputta at MN III 29,8–13. Spk: By this statement the elder has absolved his going forth from the charge of Thullanandā. This is the purport: "Does one without teacher or preceptor, who takes the saffron robe himself, and who leaves another sect, receive the honour of having the Buddha go out to welcome him, or take ordination by a triple exhortation, or get to exchange robes with the Buddha in person? See how offensive the bhikkhunī Thullanandā's utterance was!"

309 As at **16:10**.

310 Spk glosses "Tathāgata" here as *satta,* a being, on which Spk-pṭ comments: "As in past aeons, in past births, one has come into being by way of kamma and defilements, so one has also come now (***tathā*** *etarahi pi* ***āgato***); hence it is said '*tathāgata.*' Or else, according to the kamma one has done and accumulated, just so has one come, arrived, been reborn in this or that form of individual existence (***tathā*** *taṃ taṃ attabhāvaṃ* ***āgato*** *upagato upapanno*)."

This explanation seems implausible, especially when other texts clearly show that the philosophical problem over the Tathāgata's post-mortem state concerns "the Tathāgata, the highest type of person, the supreme person, the one who has attained the supreme attainment (*tathāgato uttamapuriso paramapuriso paramapattipatto*)" (**22:86** (III 116,13–14) = **44:2** (IV 380,14–15)).

311 The same question, but with a different reply, is at MN I 444,36–445,25. Possibly Mahākassapa's concern with the preservation of the true Dhamma, demonstrated in this sutta, presages his role as the convener of the First

Buddhist Council soon after the Buddha's parinibbāna (described at Vin II 284–85). There we see, in the ebullient reaction of the old bhikkhu Subhadda to the report of the Buddha's death, the first stirring towards the emergence of a "counterfeit" Dhamma. Mahākassapa convenes the First Council precisely to ensure that the true Dhamma and Discipline will endure long and will not be driven out by counterfeit versions devised by unscrupulous monks.

312 Spk: There are two counterfeits of the true Dhamma (*saddhammapaṭirūpaka*): one with respect to attainment (*adhigama*), the other with respect to learning (*pariyatti*). The former is the ten corruptions of insight knowledge (see Vism 633–38; Ppn 20:105–28). The latter consists of texts other than the authentic Word of the Buddha authorized at the three Buddhist councils, exception made of these five topics of discussion (*kathāvatthu*): discussion of elements, discussion of objects, discussion of foulness, discussion of the bases of knowledge, the casket of true knowledge. [The counterfeit texts include] the Secret Vinaya (*guḷhavinaya*), the Secret Vessantara, the Secret Mahosadha, the Vaṇṇa Piṭaka, the Aṅgulimāla Piṭaka, the Raṭṭhapāla-gajjita, the Āḷavaka-gajjita, and the Vedalla Piṭaka.

Spk-pṭ: The "Vedalla Piṭaka" is the Vetulla Piṭaka, which they say had been brought from the abode of the nāgas; others say it consists of what was spoken in debates (*vādabhāsita*). "Other than the authentic Word of the Buddha" (*abuddhavacana*), because of contradicting the Word of the Buddha; for the Enlightened One does not speak anything internally inconsistent (*pubbāparaviruddha*). They apply a dart to it; the removal of defilements is not seen there, so it is inevitably a condition for the arising of defilements.

An attempt to identify the texts cited by Spk is made in the fourteenth century work, *Nikāyasaṅgraha*, discussed by Adikaram, *Early History of Buddhism in Ceylon*, pp. 99–100. The *Nikāyasaṅgraha* assigns each text to a different non-Theravādin school. The late date of this work casts doubt on its reliability, and its method of identification is just too neat to be convincing. Spk-pṭ's comment on the Vedalla Piṭaka suggests it may be a collection of Mahāyāna sūtras.

The Mahāyāna is referred to in the Sri Lankan chronicles as the Vetullavāda (Skt Vaitulyavāda); see Rahula, *History of Buddhism in Ceylon*, pp. 87–90. Spk-pṭ is apparently alluding to the belief that Nāgārjuna had brought the Prajñāpāramitā Sūtras from the nāga realm. The five types of "topics of discussion" (*kathāvatthu*), accepted by the Theravādins though not authorized as canonical, were probably philosophical treatises recording the opinions of famous teachers on important points of doctrine. Spk describes at length the gradual disappearance of the Buddha's Dispensation as a threefold disappearance of achievement, practice, and learning (*adhigama-, paṭipatti-, pariyatti-saddhamma*).

313 Spk glosses: *ādikenā ti ādānena gahaṇena; opilavatī ti nimujjati*. Spk-pṭ: *ādānaṃ ādi, ādi eva ādikaṃ*. Spk explains the simile thus: "Unlike a ship crossing the water, which sinks when receiving goods, there is no disappearance of the true Dhamma by being filled up with learning, etc. For when learning declines the practice declines, and when the practice declines achievement declines. But when learning becomes full, persons rich in learning fill up the practice, and those filling up the practice fill up achievement. Thus when learning, etc., are increasing, my Dispensation increases, just like the new moon."

C.Rh.D, following this explanation, renders the line: "Take the sinking of a ship, Kassapa, by overloading" (KS 2:152). I find dubious, however, Spk's understanding of *ādikena* as meaning "taking, grasping." Elsewhere *ādikena* has the sense of "all at once, suddenly," contrasted with *anupubbena*, "gradually" (see MN I 395,4, 479,35; II 213,4; Ja VI 567,6, 14). This is clearly the meaning required here.

314 *Pañca okkamaniyā dhammā*. Spk glosses: *okkamaniyā ti heṭṭhāgamanīya*, "leading downwards." A parallel passage at AN III 247 repeats the first four causes but replaces the fifth by "lack of mutual respect and deference."

315 Spk: One dwells without reverence for concentration when one does not attain the eight attainments (*aṭṭha samāpattiyo*) or make any effort to attain them.

17. Lābhasakkārasaṃyutta

316 Spk: *Gain* (*lābha*) is the gain of the four requisites; *honour* (*sakkāra*), the gain of (requisites) that are well made and well produced; *praise* (*siloka*), acclamation (*vaṇṇaghosa*).

317 Pāli indiscriminately uses two words, *kumma* and *kacchapa*, for both turtle and tortoise. Here *kumma* refers to the lake-dwelling variety, but at **35:240** *kumma kacchapa* jointly denote what seems to be a land-dwelling creature, while at **56:47** *kacchapa* alone refers to the sea-dwelling variety. Spk glosses *mahākummakula* with *mahantaṃ aṭṭhikacchapakula*, which further confirms the interchangeability of the two words. I have rendered both terms "turtle" when they denote a predominantly aquatic creature (here and at **56:47**), "tortoise" when they refer to a land-dwelling creature.

318 *Papatā*. Spk explains this as an iron spear shaped like a hooked dart, kept in an iron case. When it is dropped on its target with a certain force, the spear comes out from the case and the rope follows along, still attached to it.

319 Although all three eds. read *giddho papatāya*, it seems we should read *viddho papatāya*, proposed by a note in Be.

320 In all three eds. the text as it stands is unintelligible and is likely to be corrupt. Spk does not offer enough help to reconstruct an original reading, while Be appends a long note with a circuitous explanation intended to resolve the difficulties. I would prefer to amend the final verb in Be and Se (and SS) from *anupāpuṇātu* to *anupāpuṇāti* so that we read: *Kaṃ bhikkhave asanivicakkaṃ āgacchatu? Sekhaṃ appattamānasaṃ lābhasakkārasiloko anupāpuṇāti*. Ee does have *anupāpuṇāti*, and it is possible *anupāpuṇātu* entered the other eds. under the influence of the preceding *āgacchatu* and the corresponding sentences in **17:23, 24**.

Spk paraphrases the question: "Which person should a bright thunderbolt strike, hitting him on the head and crushing him?" and comments on the reply: "The Blessed One does not speak thus because he desires suffering for beings, but in order to show the danger. For a lightning bolt, striking one on the head, destroys only a single individual existence, but one with a mind obsessed by gain, honour, and praise experiences endless suffering in hell, etc." *Who has not yet reached his mind's ideal* (*appattamānasa*): who has not achieved arahantship.

321 Be and Se read: *Kaṃ bhikkhave diddhagatena visallena sallena vijjhatu?* The reading in Ee is less satisfactory. Spk: *Diddhagatenā ti gatadiddhena* [Spk-pṭ: *acchavisayuttā ti vā diddhe gatena*]; *visallenā ti visamakkhitena; sallenā ti sattiyā.*

The rhetorical construction parallels that in the preceding sutta. *Visallena* is problematic, and we might accept C.Rh.D's suggestion *visa-sallena,* though *diddha* (= Skt *digdha*) already conveys the idea of poisoned. See Ja IV 435,26: *Saro diddho kalāpaṃ va/Alittaṃ upalimpati.*

322 *Ukkaṇṭaka* (so Be and Se; Ee: *ukkaṇṇaka*). Spk: This is the name of a disease, said to arise in the cold season. The hairs fall off from the entire body, and the entire body, fully exposed, breaks open all over. Struck by the wind, the wounds ooze. Just as a man, bitten by a rabid dog, runs around in circles, so does the jackal when it has contracted this disease, and there is no place where it finds safety.

323 *Verambhavātā*. Spk: A strong type of wind, discerned at a height from which the four continents appear the size of lotus leaves.

324 This verse and the next are at Th 1011–12 and It 74,22–75,3. Here I read with Be and Se *appamāṇavihārino,* as against Ee *appamādavihārino*. The latter, however, is found in all three eds. of Th 1011d; readings of It 74,25 are divided. Spk supports *appamāṇa-* with its gloss: *appamāṇena phalasamādhinā viharantassa*; "as he is dwelling in the measureless fruition concentration." Th-a does not comment on the pāda at Th 1011, and the comment in It-a reads *appamāda-* in Be and *appamāṇa-* in Se.

325 We should read pāda b with Se *sukhumadiṭṭhivipassakaṃ* as against *sukhumaṃ diṭṭhivipassakaṃ* in Be and Ee. The former is also the reading at Th 1012b and It 75,1. Spk: It is a *subtle view* because (it is reached) through the view of the path of arahantship, and he is an *insight-seer* (*vipassaka*) because he has arrived there after having set up insight for the sake of fruition attainment. *Delighting in the destruction of clinging*: Delighted with Nibbāna, called the destruction of clinging.

326 The *suvaṇṇanikkha* and the *siṅginikkha* seem to be two different types of golden coin, the latter presumably of greater

value than the former, or made from a superior species of gold. Spk glosses *suvaṇṇanikkhassa* as *ekassa kañcana-nikkhassa*, and *siṅginikkhassa* as *siṅgisuvaṇṇanikkhassa*.

327 *Janapadakalyāṇī*. See below **17:22** and **47:20**, and the famous simile at MN II 33,6–22.

328 Cp. AN I 88,13–89,3. This sutta and the next seem to be quoting from AN II 164,4–22, where the Buddha names the "standards and criteria" for the four classes of his followers. Citta the householder was the foremost male lay disciple among the speakers on the Dhamma; see the Cittasaṃyutta (**41:1–10**). Hatthaka Āḷavaka was the foremost of those who propitiate an assembly with the four means of beneficence; see AN I 26,5–9 and AN IV 217–20, and **I, n. 604**.

329 Khujjuttarā was the foremost female lay disciple among those who have learned much, Veḷukaṇḍakiyā (or Uttarā) Nandamātā the foremost of the meditators; see AN I 26,19, 21. Khemā and Uppalavaṇṇā, mentioned just below, were the foremost bhikkhunīs in regard to wisdom and spiritual power, respectively. Uppalavaṇṇā has appeared at **5:5**, and Khemā gives a discourse at **44:1**.

330 See above **n. 249**.

331 Spk: *Its origin* (*samudaya*): an individual form of existence together with past kamma, status as a son of good family, beauty of complexion, eloquence as a speaker, the display of ascetic virtues, the wearing of the robe, possession of a retinue, etc., are called the origin of gain and honour. They do not understand this by way of the truth of the origin, and so cessation and the path should be understood by way of the truths of cessation and the path.

332 Spk: The *pleasant dwellings in this very life* (*diṭṭhadhamma-sukhavihārā*) are the pleasant dwellings in fruition attainment. For when a meritorious arahant receives conjee, sweets, etc., he must give thanks to those who come, teach them the Dhamma, answer questions, etc., and thus he does not get a chance to sit down and enter fruition attainment.

Spk's identification of the "pleasant dwellings" with fruition attainment is certainly too narrow. The term usually means the jhānas, as at II 278,10–11.

333 The three wholesome roots are nongreed, nonhatred, and

nondelusion. Spk explains this to mean that the wholesome roots have been cut off to such an extent that Devadatta is incapable of taking rebirth in heaven or of achieving the path and fruit; it does not mean that his wholesome roots have been permanently eradicated. The next two suttas state the same meaning using different terms.

334 This sutta and the following one also occur at Vin II 187–88 in inverted order, without the homily on gains, honour, and fame, and with the verse at the end. See too AN II 73. The verse = **I, v. 597**, also spoken with reference to Devadatta. On the simile of the mule just below, Spk says that they mate her with a horse. If she becomes pregnant, when her time for delivery arrives she is unable to give birth. She stands striking the ground with her feet. Then they tie her feet to four stakes, split open her belly, and remove the foal. She dies right there.

335 *Pittaṃ bhindeyyuṃ*. PED, s.v. *pittaṃ*, says the passage is unclear and refers to an alternative interpretation proposed by Morris, JPTS 1893, 4. My rendering accords with Spk's comment: "They throw (*pakhippeyyuṃ*) bear bile or fish bile over its nostrils." Spk-pṭ glosses *pakhippeyyuṃ* here with *osiñceyyuṃ*, "they sprinkle." Horner renders "as if they were to throw a bladder at a fierce dog's nose" (BD 5:263).

336 Spk: When bandits grab hold of his mother in the wilderness and say they will release her only if he tells a deliberate lie, even then he won't tell a deliberate lie. The same method in the other cases.

18. Rāhulasaṃyutta

337 Rāhula was the Buddha's son. He became a novice (*sāmaṇera*) at the age of seven, during the Buddha's first visit to his native city of Kapilavatthu after his enlightenment. Other discourses spoken to him are: MN Nos. 61, 62, and 147 (the latter = **35:121**) and Sn II, 11 (pp. 58–59).

338 Spk explains the three "grips" (*gāha*) of "mine, I, and my self" exactly as in **n. 155**. It takes dispassion (*virāga*) to denote the four paths, liberation (*vimutti*) the four fruits. Spk does not comment on *nibbindati*, "experiences revul-

sion," but the commentaries consistently identify the corresponding noun *nibbidā* with strong insight knowledge (see above **n. 69**).

339 To the four primary elements of the form aggregate (*cattāro mahābhūtā*) the suttas sometimes add the space element (*ākāsadhātu*)—which (according to the commentaries) represents derived form (*upādāya rūpa*)—and the consciousness element (*viññāṇadhātu*), which represents the entire mental side of existence. For a detailed analysis of all six elements, see MN III 240,17–243,10.

340 Spk: *In regard to this body with consciousness* (*imasmiṃ saviññāṇake kāye*): he shows his own conscious body. *And in regard to all external signs* (*bahiddhā ca sabbanimittesu*): the conscious body of others and insentient objects. Or alternatively: by the former expression he shows his own sentient organism and that of others (reading with Se *attano ca parassa ca saviññāṇakam eva*); by the latter, external form not bound up with sense faculties (*bahiddhā anindriyabaddharūpaṃ*). (The compound) *ahaṅkāramamaṅkāramānānusayā* is to be resolved thus: *I-making* (*ahaṅkāra*), *mine-making* (*mamaṅkāra*), and *the underlying tendency to conceit* (*mānānusayā*). (So the text in Be and Se, but if, as seems likely, the plural termination derives from the *asamāhāra* compound, after resolution the last member should be *mānānusayo*.)

"I-making" is regarded as the function of wrong view (the view of self), "mine-making" of craving. The root conceit is the conceit "I am" (*asmimāna*), so conceit is also responsible for "I-making."

341 This elevenfold classification of each of the five aggregates is analysed in detail at Vibh 1–12.

342 Spk: *Has transcended discrimination* (*vidhā samatikkantaṃ*): has fully gone beyond the different kinds of conceit; *is peaceful* (*santaṃ*): by the appeasement of defilements; *and well liberated* (*suvimuttaṃ*): fully liberated from defilements.

19. Lakkhaṇasaṃyutta

343 The series of suttas included in this saṃyutta also occurs at Vin III 104–8. Spk: The Venerable Lakkhaṇa, a great disciple,

had been one of the thousand jaṭila ascetics who received higher ordination by the "Come, bhikkhu" utterance (see Vin I 32–34). He attained arahantship at the end of the Discourse on Burning (**35:28**). Since he possessed a Brahmā-like body that was endowed with auspicious marks (*lakkhaṇasampanna*), perfect in all respects, he was called "Lakkhaṇa."

344 Spk: The reason for Moggallāna's smile, as is mentioned in the text below, is that he saw a being reborn in the world of ghosts whose body was a skeleton. Having seen such a form of individual existence, he should have felt compassion, so why did he display a smile? Because he recollected his own success in gaining release from the prospect of such forms of rebirth and the success of the Buddha-knowledge; for the Buddhas teach such things through their own direct cognition (*paccakkhaṃ katvā*) and have thoroughly penetrated the element of phenomena (*suppaṭividdhā buddhānaṃ dhammadhātu*).

345 I follow Be: *vitudenti vitacchenti virājenti*. Se reads *vitudanti* only, while Ee has *vitacchenti vibhajenti*. Spk comments only on *vitudenti*: "They ran and moved here and there, piercing him again and again with their metal beaks as sharp as sword blades." According to Spk, the vultures, etc., were actually yakkhas (*yakkhagijjhā, yakkhakākā, yakkhakulalā*); for such a form does not come into the visual range of natural vultures, etc.

346 *Evarūpo pi nāma satto bhavissati evarūpo pi nāma yakkho bhavissati evarūpo pi nāma attabhāvapaṭilābho bhavissati*. Spk: In saying this Moggallāna shows his sense of urgency in the Dhamma, arisen out of compassion for such beings.

The expression *attabhāvapaṭilābho*, which literally means "acquisition of selfhood," is used idiomatically to denote a concrete form of individual identity. *Attabhāva* sometimes occurs in a more restricted sense with reference to the physical body, for instance at Ud 54,17–19.

347 Spk: *As a residual result of that same kamma* (*tass' eva kammassa vipākāvasesena*): of that "kamma (to be experienced) in subsequent lives" (*aparāpariyakamma*) accumulated by different volitions. For the rebirth in hell is produced by a certain volition, and when its result is exhausted rebirth is

produced among the ghosts, etc., having as its object the residue of that kamma or the sign of the kamma (see CMA 5:35–38). Therefore, because that rebirth comes about through correspondence of kamma or correspondence of object (*kammasabhāgatāya ārammaṇasabhāgatāya vā*), it is called "a residual result of that same kamma." It is said that at the time he passed away from hell, a heap of fleshless cows' bones became the sign (i.e., the object of the last conscious process, which then becomes the object of the rebirth-consciousness). Thus he became a ghost (in the form of) a skeleton, as if making manifest to the wise the hidden kamma.

348 Spk: He had earned his living for many years as a cattle butcher who seasoned pieces of beef, dried them, and sold the dried meat. When he passed away from hell, a piece of meat became the sign and he became a ghost (in the form of) a piece of meat.

349 Spk: He was an executioner who inflicted many punishments on state criminals and then finally shot them with arrows. After arising in hell, when he was subsequently reborn through the residual result of that kamma the state of being pierced by an arrow became the sign and therefore he became a ghost with body-hairs of arrows.

350 In Be and Se, this sutta is entitled Sūciloma and the following sutta Dutiya-sūciloma, while in Ee the former is entitled Sūci-sārathi and the latter Sūcako. In Be and Se, the miserable spirit in the former sutta is said to have been a *sūta*, glossed by Spk as *assadamaka*, a horse trainer, while in Ee he is said to have been a *sūcaka*. In all three eds., the spirit in the following sutta is said to have been a *sūcaka*, glossed by Spk as *pesuññakāraka*, a slanderer. I follow Be and Se both with respect to the titles of the two suttas and the former identities of the tormented spirits.

351 Spk: He was a slanderer who divided people from each other and brought them to ruin and misery by his insinuations. Therefore, as people were divided by him through his insinuations (*tena sūcetvā manussā bhinnā*), to experience the pain of being pierced by needles (*sūcīhi bhedanadukkhaṃ paccanubhotuṃ*), he took that kamma itself as the sign and became a needle-haired ghost (*sūcilomapeta*). (The aptness

of the retribution is established by the similarity between the Pāli word *sūci*, needle, and the verb *sūceti*, to insinuate, to indicate.)

352 *Gāmakūṭa*, lit. "village cheat." Spk: He secretly accepted bribes and, committing an evident wrong by his skewed judgements, misallocated the belongings of others. Hence his private parts were exposed. Since he caused an unbearable burden for others by imposing harsh penalties, his private parts became an unbearable burden for him. And since he was unrighteous (*visama*) when he should have been righteous, his private parts became uneven (*visama*) and he had to sit on them.

Interestingly, Ee (apparently based on SS) here reads *dhaṅkā* for crows in place of *kākā* in the other eds. See **I, v. 808**d and **I, n. 566**.

353 Spk: Having experienced contact with another man's wife, having enjoyed vile pleasure, sensual pleasure, he has been reborn in circumstances where, as a counterpart of that kamma, he experiences contact with filth and undergoes pain.

354 I read the first word of this sentence with Se and SS as *ato*, as against the exclamation *aho* in Be and Ee.

355 Spk: She cheated on her husband and enjoyed contact with other men. Thus she fell away from pleasant contact and, as a counterpart of that kamma, was reborn as a flayed woman to experience painful contact.

356 *Maṅgulitthi*. Spk glosses: *maṅgulin ti virūpaṃ duddasikaṃ bībhacchaṃ*. She deceived people, accepting scents and flowers, telling them they could become rich by performing certain rites. She caused the multitude to accept a bad view, a wrong view. Thus she herself became foul-smelling because of taking scents and flowers, and ugly because of making them accept a bad view.

357 Spk explains *uppakkaṃ okiliniṃ okirinaṃ* thus: She was lying on a bed of coals, trembling and turning around as she was cooked, therefore she was *roasting* (*uppakkā*), i.e., with body cooked by the hot fire. She was *sweltering* (*okilinī*), with a sweating body; and *sooty* (*okirinī*), completely covered with soot.

358 Spk: While using the four requisites provided by the people

out of faith, being unrestrained in bodily and verbal conduct and corrupt in his means of livelihood, he went about playfully to his heart's content. The same method of explanation applies in the following cases too.

20. Opammasaṃyutta

359 The simile of the peaked house, common in the Nikāyas, recurs in SN at **22:102** (III 156,3–5), **45:141**, **46:7**, **48:52**. Spk glosses "diligent" as "constantly yoked with mindfulness" (*appamattā ti satiyā avippavāse ṭhitā hutvā*).

360 This theme is treated in greater detail at **56:102–31**. Spk says that the devas are included here along with humans, so that the statement should be understood to mean that few are reborn among humans and devas.

361 The simile is also at Vin II 256,16–18 and AN IV 278,22–25, but with a different application. *Corehi kumbhatthenakehi* is lit. "pot-thief bandits." Spk explains: Having entered the houses of others, having surveyed the scene by the light of a lamp, desiring to steal the belongings of others, they make a lamp in a jar (*ghaṭe*) and enter. Even mud-sprites (*paṃsupisācakā*) assail those devoid of development of lovingkindness, how much more then powerful nonhumans?

Amanussa, lit. "nonhuman," usually denotes a malevolent spirit or demon.

362 Be and Se: *okkhāsataṃ*; Ee: *ukkhāsataṃ*. Spk: = *mahāmukha-ukkhalīnaṃ sataṃ*. Spk-pṭ: = *mahāmukhānaṃ mahantakoḷumbānaṃ sataṃ*. The reference is to large pots used to boil a great quantity of rice. AN IV 394–96 makes the same point somewhat differently, and adds that developing the perception of impermanence even for a fingersnap is still more fruitful than developing a mind of lovingkindness.

363 Spk: *Gadduhanamattan ti goduhanamattaṃ* (lit. "the extent of a cow's milking"), that is, the extent of time needed to take one pull on a cow's teat. Or else (*gadduhanamattaṃ* =) *gandha-ūhanamattaṃ* (lit. "the extent of a scent-sniff"), that is, the extent of time needed to take a single sniff of a piece of incense picked up with two fingers. If, for even such a short time, one is able to develop a mind of loving-kindness, pervading all beings in immeasurable world

systems with a wish for their welfare, this is more fruitful even than that alms given three times in a single day.

364 Spk explains the three verbs thus: *paṭileṇeti,* having struck the top, bending it like a cotton wick, one makes it fuse together as if it were a strand of resin; *paṭikoṭṭeti,* having struck it in the middle and bent it back, or having struck it along the blade, one makes the two blades fuse together; *paṭivaṭṭeti,* turning it around as if making a cotton wick (?), one twirls it around for a long time, unravels it, and again twirls it around.

365 This sutta also appears in the introduction to Ja No. 476, which turns upon the same theme. In this story the Bodhisatta, in his incarnation as the swift goose Javanahaṃsa, performs the remarkable feat to be described just below.

Spk explains the stock description of the archers thus: *Firm-bowed archers* (*daḷhadhammā dhanuggahā*): archers with firm bows (*daḷhadhanuno issāsā*). A "firm bow" is called the strength of two thousand. "The strength of two thousand" means that a weight of metal, such as bronze or lead, etc. (used for the arrowhead), bound to the string when the bow is lifted (for the shot), is released from the earth when the bow is grasped by its handle and drawn back the full length of the arrow. *Trained* (Se and Ee: *sikkhitā;* Be: *susikkhitā,* "well trained"): they have studied the craft in their teacher's circle for ten or twelve years. *Dexterous* (*katahatthā*): one who has simply studied a craft is not yet dexterous, but these are dexterous, having achieved mastery over it. *Experienced* (*katūpāsanā*): they have displayed their craft in the king's court, etc.

366 *Āyusaṅkhārā.* Spk: This is said with reference to the physical life faculty (*rūpajīvitindriya*); for this perishes even faster than that. But it is not possible to describe the breakup of formless phenomena (i.e., of mental states, because according to the Abhidhamma they break up sixteen times faster than material phenomena).

367 Spk: The Dasārahas were a khattiya clan, so called because they took a tenth portion from a hundred (*satato dasabhāgaṃ gaṇhiṃsu*—reference not clear). The Summoner (*ānaka*) was the name of a drum, made from the claw of a

giant crab. It gave off a sound that could be heard for twelve *yojanas* all around and was therefore used to summon the people to assembly on festival days.

368 Spk: *Deep* (*gambhīra*) by way of the text (*pāḷivasena*), like the Salla Sutta (Sn III, 8; Se: Sallekha Sutta = MN No. 8); *deep in meaning* (*gambhīrattha*), like the Mahāvedalla Sutta (MN No. 43); *supramundane* (*lokuttara*), i.e., pointing to the supramundane goal; *dealing with emptiness* (*suññatā-paṭisaṃyutta*), explaining mere phenomena devoid of a being (*sattasuññata-dhammamattam eva pakāsakā*), like the Saṅkhittasaṃyutta (?).

This passage recurs at **55:53**, in commenting on which Spk cites as examples texts that sometimes differ from those cited here. See **V, n. 366**.

369 Spk glosses *sāvakabhāsitā* as *tesaṃ tesaṃ sāvakehi bhāsitā*, referring back to the outsiders (*bāhiraka*). Spk-pṭ clarifies: "By the disciples of any of those who were not known as the Buddha's disciples."

370 "Block of wood" is *kaliṅgara*. Spk: In the first period of the Buddha's ministry the bhikkhus would practise meditation from the time they finished their meal (before noon) through the first watch of the night. They would sleep in the middle watch, resting their heads on pieces of wood (*kaṭṭhakaṇḍa*, a gloss on *kaliṅgara*); then they would rise early and resume their walking meditation.

The mood of this sutta is similar to the "fears of the future" suttas, AN III 105–10.

371 The elephant simile is also at Vin II 120, used in relation to Devadatta.

372 *Pasannākāraṃ karonti*. Spk: They give the four requisites. See **n. 275**.

373 See the following sutta for an explanation.

374 *Sandhisamalasaṅkaṭīre*. Spk explains *sandhi* as an alley between two detached houses; *samala* as a channel for the discharge of waste from a house; and *saṅkaṭīra* as a rubbish bin; see too Ps III 418,16 (commenting on MN I 334,27). At MLDB p. 433 the compound was translated, "by a door-post or a dust-bin or a drain," but it seems these last two nouns should be inverted.

375 *Aññataraṃ saṅkiliṭṭhaṃ āpattiṃ āpajjati yathārūpāya āpattiyā*

vuṭṭhānaṃ paññāyati. An offence motivated by a defilement (in this case lust) but of a kind that can be expiated by undergoing the appropriate penalty (as opposed to an offence of the *pārājikā* class, which does not allow for expiation but requires permanent expulsion from the Saṅgha).

376 See **17:8** and **n. 322** above. Spk identifies the "certain person" as Devadatta. I understand *Sakyaputtiya* to be an adjective meaning "following the Sakyan son," not a noun meaning "Sakyan son." The Sakyan son is the Buddha himself, who went forth from the Sakyan clan (see **55:7**, V 352,18). Thus a *samaṇa sakyaputtiya* (see **28:10** (III 240,3-4) and **42:10** (IV 325,19–21)) is an ascetic following the Sakyan son, i.e., a Buddhist monk.

377 Spk: This too is said with reference to the behaviour of Devadatta. Spk relates an anecdote about a jackal who had been rescued from a python by a farmer. When the python grabbed the farmer, the jackal, out of gratitude, went to the farmer's brothers and led them to the scene, thereby enabling them to rescue the farmer.

21. *Bhikkhusaṃyutta*

378 Kolita was Mahāmoggallāna's personal name, Moggallāna being derived from his clan name. The present sutta is nearly identical with **40:2** and must be simply a variant on the latter, formulated in terms of noble silence rather than the second jhāna. As Spk makes clear, the sutta refers back to Moggallāna's week of striving for arahantship.

379 Spk explains that the second jhāna is called noble silence (*ariya tuṇhībhāva*) because within it thought and examination (*vitakka-vicārā*) cease, and with their cessation speech cannot occur. At **41:6** (IV 293,24–26) thought and examination are called the verbal formation (*vacīsaṅkhāra*), the mental factors responsible for articulation of speech. But, Spk adds, when the Buddha says "either speak on the Dhamma or observe noble silence" (e.g., at MN I 161,32–33), even attention to a meditation subject can be considered noble silence.

380 Spk: It is said that by this means, over seven days, the Teacher helped the elder to develop concentration on occasions

when it was tending to decline (*hānabhāgiya*) and thus led him to "greatness of direct knowledge" (*mahābhiññatā*), i.e., to the six direct knowledges.

381 Upatissa was Sāriputta's personal name.

382 We should read simply *āvuso* with Be and Se, as against Ee *āvuso Sāriputta*.

383 Spk: *For a long time*: he says this referring to the time that had passed since the Buddha taught the wanderer Dīghanakha "The Discourse on the Discernment of Feelings" at the door of the Boar's Cave. For it was on that day that these defilements inherent in the round of existence were uprooted in the elder. See **n. 97** above.

384 Spk: The dwelling is called gross on account of its object. For he dwelt in the exercise of the divine eye and divine ear element, which take gross objects, namely, the form base and the sound base.

385 I translate the peculiar Pāli idiom here a little freely to bring out the meaning. My rendering follows Spk's paraphrase: "The elder wondered, 'Where is the Blessed One now dwelling?' Having extended light, he saw him with the divine eye sitting in his Fragrant Cottage in Jeta's Grove; then he heard his voice with the divine ear element. The Teacher did the same, and thus they could see each other and hear each other's voices."

386 As at **12:22** (II 28,24–28).

387 See **51:10** (V 259,18–20). Spk glosses *kappa* here as *āyukappa*, meaning the full human life span of 120 years. However, there seems to be no textual basis for taking *kappa* in this passage as meaning anything other than a cosmic aeon, the full extent of time required for a world system to evolve and dissolve. See V, **n. 249**.

388 The word "nāga" here is used in the sense of arahant.

389 *Jetvā Māraṃ savāhanaṃ*. Spk does not comment on the "mount," but other commentaries explain it as either the elephant Girimekha (Pj II 392,3 to Sn 442) or Māra's army (Mp III 18,26 to AN II 15,29). At Ja I 72, Māra is shown mounting his elephant Girimekha before going to attack the future Buddha under the Bodhi Tree.

390 His name means "Bhaddiya the Dwarf." The prose portion is at Ud 76; see too Ud 74,20–75,6. Spk notes that it was the

monks of the "gang of six" (*chabbhagiyā bhikkhū*, the mischief-makers of the Saṅgha often mentioned in the Vinaya Piṭaka) who had been ridiculing him. Bhaddiya's ugliness, according to Spk, was the kammic result of his behaviour in a previous life when he was a king who mocked and harassed old people. Though ugly in appearance, he had a lovely voice, which resulted from another past life when he was a cuckoo who offered a sweet mango to the Buddha Vipassī. The Buddha declared him the foremost of bhikkhus having a sweet voice (*mañjussara*; AN I 23,24). His verses at Th 466–72 do not include the verses here.

391 His verses are at Th 209–10. The same description is given of Sāriputta's talk at **8:6**. This entire sutta is at AN II 51.

392 We should read with Be (and Ee at AN II 51,29): *nābhāsamānaṃ jānanti*. The readings *no bhāsamānaṃ* (Ee) and *na bhāsamānaṃ* (Se) give a meaning opposite to the one required. The BHS parallel of the verse at Uv 29:43–44 supports Be: *nābhāṣamānā jñāyante.*

393 He was the son of the Buddha's father Suddhodana and his aunt and foster mother, Mahāpajāpatī Gotamī. Hence, though he was also the Buddha's half-brother through their common father, the text refers to him as *mātucchāputta*, "maternal cousin." His story is at Ud 21–24 and, more elaborately, at Dhp-a I 115–22; see BL 1:217–23.

Spk: Why did the elder behave thus? To find out what the Teacher thought about it, thinking: "If the Teacher says, 'My half-brother is beautiful like this,' I'll conduct myself in this way all my life. But if he points out a fault here, I'll give this up, wear a rag-robe, and dwell in a remote lodging."

394 *Aññātuñchena yāpentaṃ*. Spk: Scraps gained by one seeking delicious, well-seasoned food at the homes of affluent and powerful people are called "scraps of known people" (*ñātuncha*, lit. "known scraps"). But the mixed food obtained by standing at the doors of houses is called "scraps of strangers" (lit. "unknown scraps").

395 He was the Buddha's *pitucchāputta*, son of the Buddha's paternal aunt, Amitā (DPPN, s.v. Tissa Thera (14)).

396 Spk explains that while he was still a novice, when elders arrived at the monastery from distant regions to see the Buddha he remained seated and did not perform any

services to them or show them due respect. This was all because of his khattiya pride and his pride of being the Buddha's cousin. The other bhikkhus had surrounded him and censured him sharply for his lack of courtesy. A variant of this incident is recorded at Dhp-a I 37–39; see BL 1:166–67.

397 *Aññataro bhikkhu theranāmako.* Spk does not explain this peculiar name or further identify the monk.

398 Spk: The past is said to be abandoned (*pahīnaṃ*) by the abandoning of desire and lust for the five aggregates of the past; the future is relinquished (*paṭinissaṭṭhaṃ*) by the relinquishing of desire and lust for the five aggregates of the future. Cp. MN III 188–89, 195–98. The plural *attabhāvapaṭilābhesu* is hard to account for; perhaps it means the five aggregates taken individually, though this would be an unusual use of the expression. See **n. 346**.

399 The first three pādas are at Sn 211 and, with a variation, at Dhp 353. Spk: *All-conqueror* (*sabbābhibhuṃ*): one who abides having overcome all aggregates, sense bases, and elements, and the three kinds of existence. *Unsullied* (*anupalittaṃ*, or "unstuck") among those very things by the paste (*lepa*) of craving and views. *Liberated in the destruction of craving* (*taṇhakkhaye vimuttaṃ*): liberated in Nibbāna, called the destruction of craving by way of the liberation that takes this as its object.

400 He was the foremost bhikkhu disciple among those who exhort bhikkhus (*bhikkhu-ovādaka;* AN I 25,13). His verses are at Th 547–56, and he is commended by the Buddha at **54:7**. Spk: He had been a king who ruled over the city of Kukkuṭavatī. As soon as he heard about the Buddha, the Dhamma, and the Saṅgha from a group of travelling merchants he left his kingdom for Sāvatthī together with his thousand ministers, intending to go forth. His queen Anojā followed him, accompanied by the ministers' wives, all with the same intention. The Buddha came out to meet both parties. He first ordained the men as bhikkhus with the "Come, bhikkhu" ordination, and then he had the women ordained as bhikkhunīs by the elder nun Uppalavaṇṇā.

401 Spk: It is said that they had been companions in five hundred past births.

Part III
The Book of the Aggregates
(*Khandhavagga*)

Contents

Chapter II
23. *Rādhasaṃyutta*
Connected Discourses with Rādha

Chapter III
24. *Diṭṭhisaṃyutta*
Connected Discourses on Views

Chapter IV
25. *Okkantisaṃyutta*
Connected Discourses on Entering

Chapter V
26. *Uppādasaṃyutta*
Connected Discourses on Arising

Chapter VI
27. *Kilesasaṃyutta*
Connected Discourses on Defilements

Chapter VII
28. *Sāriputtasaṃyutta*
Connected Discourses with Sāriputta

Chapter VIII
29. *Nāgasaṃyutta*
Connected Discourses on Nāgas

Chapter IX
30. *Supaṇṇasaṃyutta*
Connected Discourses on Supaṇṇas

Chapter X
31. *Gandhabbakāyasaṃyutta*
Connected Discourses on Orders of Gandhabbas

Chapter XI
32. *Valāhakasaṃyutta*
Connected Discourses on Cloud Devas

Chapter XII
33. *Vacchagottasaṃyutta*
Connected Discourses with Vacchagotta

Chapter XIII
34. *Jhānasaṃyutta*
Connected Discourses on Meditation

Introduction

The *Khandhavagga*, The Book of the Aggregates, continues along the trail of philosophical exposition opened up by The Book of Causation, but this time breaking into another major area of early Buddhist discourse, the five aggregates. Like its predecessor, the Khandhavagga is named after its opening saṃyutta, which dominates the entire collection. Though the Vagga contains thirteen saṃyuttas, none of the minor ones even approaches the length of the Khandhasaṃyutta, which in the PTS edition takes up 188 of the 278 pages in this volume. But even more, within this Vagga three minor saṃyuttas—SN 23, 24, and 33—focus on the aggregates as their point of interest. These chapters seem to be offshoots from the original Khandhasaṃyutta which at some point were broken off and made into autonomous saṃyuttas. Thus the theme of the five aggregates leaves its stamp throughout this whole collection.

22. *Khandhasaṃyutta*

The Khandhasaṃyutta contains 159 suttas arranged into three divisions called *paññāsakas*, "sets of fifty." Each *paññāsaka* is made up of five vaggas consisting of approximately ten suttas each, though several vaggas have slightly more than ten. The length and character of the suttas vary widely, ranging from texts several pages long with a unique flavour of their own to extremely terse suttas that merely instantiate a common template.

The topic of this saṃyutta is the five aggregates (*pañcakkhandha*), the primary scheme of categories the Buddha draws upon to analyse sentient existence. Whereas the teaching on dependent origination is intended to disclose the dynamic pattern running through everyday experience that propels the round of birth and death forward from life to life, the teaching on the five aggregates concentrates on experience in its lived immediacy in the continuum from birth to death.

Examination of the five aggregates plays a critical role in the Buddha's teaching for at least four reasons. First, because the five aggregates are the ultimate referent of the first noble truth, the noble truth of suffering (see **56:13**), and since all four truths revolve around suffering, understanding the aggregates is essential for understanding the Four Noble Truths as a whole. Second, because the five aggregates are the objective domain of clinging and as such contribute to the causal origination of future suffering. Third, because the removal of clinging is necessary for the attainment of release, and clinging must be removed from the objects around which its tentacles are wrapped, namely, the five aggregates. And fourth, because the removal of clinging is achieved by wisdom, and the kind of wisdom needed is precisely clear insight into the real nature of the aggregates.

The five aggregates are at once the constituents of sentient existence and the operative factors of lived experience, for within the thought world of the Nikāyas existence is of concern only to the extent that it is implicated in experience. Thus the five aggregates simultaneously serve the Buddha as a scheme of categories for analysing human identity and for explicating the structure of experience. However, the analysis into the aggregates undertaken in the Nikāyas is not pursued with the aim of reaching an objective, scientific understanding of the human being along the lines pursued by physiology and psychology; thus comparisons of the Buddhist analysis with those advanced by modern scientific disciplines can easily lead to spurious conclusions. For the Buddha, investigation into the nature of personal existence always remains subordinate to the liberative thrust of the Dhamma, and for this reason only those aspects of human existence that contribute to the realization of this purpose receive the spotlight of his attention.

The word *khandha* (Skt *skandha*) means, among other things, a heap or mass (*rāsi*). The five aggregates are so called because they each unite under one label a multiplicity of phenomena that share the same defining characteristic. Thus whatever form there is, "past, future, or present, internal or external, gross or subtle, inferior or superior, far or near," is incorporated into the form aggregate, and so for each of the other aggregates (**22:48**). Two suttas in the Khandhasaṃyutta (**22:56, 57**) spell out the constituents of each aggregate, doing so in much simpler terms than the later, more elaborate analyses found in the *Visuddhimagga* and the commentaries. The breakdown of the aggregates according to the suttas is shown in Table 5. Another sutta (**22:79**) explains why each aggregate is called by its assigned name, and it is revealing that these explanations are phrased in terms of functions rather than fixed essences. This treatment of the aggregates as dynamic functions rather than substantial entities already pulls the ground away from the urge to grasp upon them as containing a permanent essence that can be considered the ultimate ground of being.

TABLE 5

The Five Aggregates according to the Suttas
(based on SN 22:56 and 57)

Aggregate	Contents	Condition
form	4 great elements and form derived from them	nutriment
feeling	6 classes of feeling: feeling born of contact through eye, ear, nose, tongue, body, and mind	contact
perception	6 classes of perception: perception of forms, sounds, odours, tastes, tactiles, and mental phenomena	contact
volitional formations	6 classes of volition: volition regarding forms, sounds, odours, tastes, tactiles, and mental phenomena	contact
consciousness	6 classes of consciousness: eye-consciousness, ear-, nose-, tongue-, body-, and mind-consciousness	name-and-form

The Khandhasaṃyutta stresses in various ways that the five aggregates are *dukkha*, suffering, a point clearly articulated by the Buddha already in his first sermon when he states, "In brief, the five aggregates subject to clinging are suffering" (**56:11**). The aggregates are suffering because they tend to affliction and cannot be made to conform with our desires (**22:59**); because attachment to them leads to sorrow, lamentation, pain, displeasure, and despair (**22:1**); because their change induces fear, distress, and anxiety (**22:7**). Even more pointedly, the five aggregates are already suffering simply because they are impermanent (**22:15**) and thus can never fulfil our hopes for perfect happiness and security. While they give pleasure and joy, which is the gratification (*assāda*) in them, eventually they must change and pass away, and this instability is the danger (*ādīnava*) perpetually concealed within them (**22:26**). Though we habitually assume that we are in control of the aggregates, in truth they are perpetually devouring *us*, making us their hapless victims (**22:79**). To identify with the aggregates and seek fulfilment in them is to be like a man who employs as his servant a vicious murderer out to take his life (**22:85**).

The five aggregates are the objective domain of the defilements that bind living beings to the round of existence, particularly the taints (*āsava*) and clinging (*upādāna*). Whatever in the world one might cling to, it is only form, feeling, perception, volitional formations, and consciousness that one clings to (**22:79**). For this reason the aggregates that make up our mundane experience are commonly called the five aggregates subject to clinging (*pañcupādānakkhandha*). Clinging, it will be recalled, is one of the links in the chain of dependent origination, the link that leads into the production of a new existence in the future. In **22:5**, the five aggregates are spliced into the second half of the formula for dependent origination, thereby revealing how clinging to the five aggregates in this existence brings forth a new birth and thus the reappearance of the five aggregates in the next existence. Sutta **22:54** states that because of attachment to the five aggregates, consciousness grows and thrives from life to life; but with the destruction of lust, consciousness becomes unsupported and is then peaceful and liberated. This sutta assigns to consciousness a special place among the five aggregates, since consciousness stands supported by the other aggregates and passes away and undergoes rebirth in dependence on them. This dictum accords with the suttas on dependent origination (such as **12:12**, **38**, and **64**) that treat consciousness as the channel or vehicle of the rebirth process.

Clinging to the five aggregates occurs in two principal modes, which we might call appropriation and identification. In clinging to the aggregates, one either grasps them with desire and lust (*chandarāga*) and assumes possession of them, or one identifies with them, taking them as the basis for conceit or for views about one's real self. In a phrase often met with in the Khandhasaṃyutta, we are prone to think of the aggregates, "This is mine, this I am, this is my self" (*etaṃ mama, eso 'ham asmi, eso me attā*). Here, the notion "This is mine" represents the act of appropriation, a function of craving (*taṇhā*). The notions "This I am" and "This is my self" represent two types of identification, the former expressive of conceit (*māna*), the latter of views (*diṭṭhi*).

To break our appropriation of the aggregates, the Buddha often enjoins us to abandon desire and lust for them (**22:137–45**). Sometimes he tells us to abandon the aggregates themselves, for they are as completely alien to us as the twigs and foliage in Jeta's Grove (**22:33–34**). But to give up clinging is difficult because clinging is reinforced by views, which rationalize our identification with the aggregates and thus equip clinging with a protective shield.

The type of view that lies at the bottom of all affirmation of selfhood is called identity view (*sakkāyadiṭṭhi*). All views of self are formulated with reference to the five aggregates either collectively or individually (**22:47**). The suttas often mention twenty types of identity view, obtained by considering one's self to stand in any of four relations to each of the five aggregates: either as identical with it, as possessing it, as containing it, or as contained within it (**22:1**, **7**, **47**, **81**, **82**, etc.). The Buddha describes identity view as the leash that keeps the worldling bound to the round of rebirths, revolving in circles like a dog going around a post (**22:99**, **117**). He also makes identity view the first of the ten fetters to be eradicated on the path to liberation. The most common way the suttas distinguish between "the uninstructed worldling" (*assutavā puthujjana*) and "the instructed noble disciple" (*sutavā ariyasāvaka*) is precisely by way of identity view: the worldling perpetually regards the aggregates as a self or a self's accessories;

the noble disciple never does so, for such a disciple has seen with wisdom the selfless nature of the aggregates (**22:1**, etc.).

As the formula for dependent origination demonstrates, clinging to the five aggregates is ultimately sustained by ignorance (*avijjā*). In relation to the aggregates, ignorance weaves a net of three delusions that nurture desire and lust. These delusions, which infiltrate cognition at a variety of levels, are the notions that the five aggregates are permanent, a true source of happiness, and a self or the accessories of a self. The antidote needed to break the spell of this delusion is wisdom (*paññā*) or knowledge (*vijjā*), which means knowing and seeing the five aggregates as they really are: as impermanent (*anicca*), as suffering (*dukkha*), and as nonself (*anattā*). These are known in the Buddhist tradition as the three characteristics (*tilakkhaṇa*), and in the Khandhasaṃyutta they are extensively applied to the five aggregates in a variety of patterns. The suttas devoted to this theme can be highly repetitive, but the repetition is designed to serve a vital purpose: to strip away the delusions of permanence, pleasure, and selfhood that envelop the five aggregates and keep us trapped in the chain of dependent origination.

Perhaps the original nucleus of the Khandhasaṃyutta consisted of the template suttas at **22:9–20**, along with the auxiliary template suttas prevalent in The Final Fifty. These suttas were never intended to be read merely to gather information, but to offer concise instructions on the development of insight (*vipassanābhāvanā*). Behind the repetitive utterances, occasionally irksome on first acquaintance, the attentive eye can discern subtle variations attuned to the diversity in the proclivities and intellectual capacities of the people to be guided. Some suttas seem to make the contemplation of one or another of the three characteristics alone sufficient for reaching the goal, though the exegetical texts insist that all must be contemplated to some degree. As the three characteristics are closely intertwined, the most common formula throughout the Nikāyas is the one that discloses their internal relationship. This formula, first enunciated in the Buddha's second discourse at Bārāṇasī (**22:59**), uses the characteristic of impermanence to reveal the characteristic of suffering, and both conjointly to reveal the characteristic of nonself. But whatever approach is taken, all the different expositions of the three characteristics eventually converge on the eradication of clinging by showing, with regard to each aggregate, "This is not mine, this I am not, this is not my self." The lesson this maxim teaches is that there is no point in appropriating anything, no point in identifying with anything, because the subject of appropriation and identification, the "self," is merely a fabrication of conceptual thought woven in the darkness of ignorance.

Different suttas within the Khandhasaṃyutta speak of the three characteristics under various synonyms, and to navigate one's way through this chapter it is important to recognize which characteristic is being indicated. Thus the statement that the five aggregates are "impermanent, conditioned, dependently arisen, subject to destruction, to vanishing, to fading away, to cessation" (**22:21**) is obviously using different terms to point out the characteristic of impermanence. Less obviously, the sutta on the fragile (**22:32**) and the two on arising, vanishing, and alteration (**22:37, 38**) are doing the same thing. The suttas that speak of knowing the aggregates as subject to arising and vanishing are also commending contemplation of impermanence (**22:126–28**). Such suttas as the one on the burden (**22:22**), on misery (**22:31**), and on being devoured (**22:79**), emphasize the contemplation of suffering. Among the many suttas that directly expound nonself, one that deserves special attention is the discourse on the lump of foam (**22:95**), with its striking similes for the empty, insubstantial nature of the aggregates.

Besides the three characteristics, the Khandhasaṃyutta makes use of other patterns as guidelines for contemplation and understanding. The "gratification triad" is often applied to the aggregates (**22:26, 107, 130**), sometimes expanded into a pentad by the addition of "origin and passing away" (**22:108, 132**). Another is the four-truth pattern: understanding each aggregate, its origin, its cessation, and the way to its cessation (**22:56, 114**). A sevenfold hybrid is obtained by merging the four-truth pattern with the gratification triad (**22:57**). In two suttas (**22:122, 123**) the Venerable Sāriputta recommends a scheme of eleven ways of attending to the aggregates, obtained by differentiating various aspects of the three characteristics. This method of contemplation, he says, leads all the way from the first steps on the path of meditation to the final stage of arahantship and can even be recommended to the arahant.

According to a stock formula attached to most of the suttas on the three characteristics, the insight into the five aggregates as impermanent, suffering, and nonself induces revulsion (*nibbidā*), dispassion (*virāga*), and liberation (*vimutti*). Revulsion is explained by the commentaries as a profound inward turning away from conditioned existence that comes with the higher stages of insight. Dispassion is the supramundane path, particularly the path of arahantship, which eliminates the last traces of craving. Dispassion culminates in liberation, the release of the mind from clinging and the taints, and liberation is in turn ascertained by the subsequent "knowledge and vision of liberation," a reviewing knowledge that gives the assurance that the round of rebirths has been stopped and nothing further remains to be done.

The Khandhasaṃyutta shows that the elimination of clinging occurs in two distinct stages. The first is the elimination of the conceptual types of clinging expressed by wrong views, above all by identity view. This stage of release comes with the breakthrough to the Dhamma, the attainment of stream-entry. At this point the disciple sees the selfless nature of the aggregates and thus overcomes all views of self. For this reason the defining mark of the "instructed noble disciple," the one who has made the breakthrough, is the elimination of every kind of identity view. However, disciples in training (*sekha*), even those at the penultimate stage of nonreturner, still retain a subtle notion of "I am" that continues to linger over the five aggregates like the scent of soap over newly washed clothes. This is spoken of as "a residual conceit 'I am,' a desire 'I am,' an underlying tendency 'I am'" (**22:89**). However, as the noble disciple continues to contemplate the rise and fall of the aggregates, in time even this residual notion of "I am" disappears. It is only the arahant who has fully understood the five aggregates down to the root and thus eradicated the subtlest tendencies to self-affirmation.

Elsewhere in the Khandhasaṃyutta the distinction between the trainee and the arahant is drawn in other terms, based on the same principle but differently expressed. Sutta **22:56** explains that trainees have directly known the five aggregates by way of the four-truth pattern and are practising for their fading away and cessation; thereby they "have gained a foothold in this Dhamma and Discipline." Arahants have also directly known the five aggregates by way of the four-truth pattern, but they have extirpated all attachment to the aggregates and are liberated by nonclinging; thus they are called consummate ones for whom "there is no round for describing them" (see too **22:57**, which expands the sphere of direct knowledge into a sevenfold pattern). While direct knowledge (*abhiññā*) of the aggregates is ascribed to both trainees and arahants, only arahants are said to have full understanding (*pariññā*) of the aggregates, for full understanding implies the destruction of lust, hatred, and delusion (**22:106**; see too **22:23**). At **22:79** the trainee is described as one who is abandoning the five aggregates and does not cling to them. The arahant, in contrast, is one who neither abandons nor clings, but "abides having abandoned." And at **22:109–10**, the stream-enterer is defined as one who understands the five aggregates by way of their origin, passing away, gratification, danger, and escape, while the arahant is one who, having understood the aggregates thus, is liberated by nonclinging. Thus these passages indicate the essential difference between the trainee and the arahant to consist in the extent to which they have developed liberating knowledge. The trainee has arrived at this knowledge and thereby eliminated the conceptually explicit types of ignorance crystallized in wrong views, but he has not yet fully utilized it to eradicate the emotively tinged types of ignorance manifest as clinging. The arahant has mastered this knowledge and fully developed it, so that in his mind all the defilements along with the subtlest shades of ignorance have been abolished. The trainee might be compared to a person walking along a mountain path who catches a distant glimpse of a splendid city but must still walk across several more mountains to reach his destination. The arahant is like one who has arrived at the city and now dwells comfortably within its bounds.

Beneath its repetitiveness and copious use of template formulas, the Khandhasaṃyutta is a rich compilation of texts, and no brief introduction can do justice to all its suggestive themes. Special mention, however, might be made of the Theravagga, the fourth vagga, on the elder monks. Here we find Ānanda's firsthand account of his breakthrough to the Dhamma while listening to a discourse on the aggregates (**22:83**); Sāriputta's refutation of the annihilationist interpretation of Nibbāna (**22:85**); Anurādha's puzzlement about the Tathāgata's status after death (**22:86**); the story of Vakkali, who attained final Nibbāna while dying at his own hand (**22:87**); the Khemaka Sutta, on the distinction between the trainee and the arahant (**22:89**); and the story of the refractory monk Channa whose change of heart proved abundantly fruitful (**22:90**).

23. Rādhasaṃyutta

This saṃyutta is virtually an appendix to the Khandhasaṃyutta as it revolves entirely around the five aggregates, but it has a distinct internal unity in that all its suttas are addressed to a single bhikkhu named Rādha. According to the commentary, the Buddha liked to speak to this monk on deep and subtle matters, and thus a large number of texts have come down through him. The saṃyutta consists of four vaggas with a total of forty-six suttas, all relating to the aggregates. Suttas **23:4–10** have exact counterparts in the Khandhasaṃyutta. The contents of the second and third vagga largely overlap, while the third and fourth vaggas are identical except for the circumstances of their delivery.

24. Diṭṭhisaṃyutta

This saṃyutta, too, is an extension of the Khandhasaṃyutta, an outgrowth of its last vagga, called Diṭṭhivagga and dealing with views. However, while the Diṭṭhivagga focuses only on a few basic views, here an attempt is made to cover a much wider range. The aim of the chapter is to show, from various angles, how all these views originate from clinging to the five aggregates.

The views fall into several distinct classes: first comes a strange philosophy, not encountered elsewhere in the Nikāyas, but apparently a species of eternalism; then come several familiar views—the view "this is mine," etc., eternalism, and annihilationism (**24:2–4**). This is followed by four philosophical theories advocated by the Buddha's contemporaries, all of which he condemned as morally pernicious (**24:5–8**); and next come the ten speculative views that the Buddha consistently rejected as invalid (**24:9–18**). Beginning with the second vagga, eighteen additional views are introduced, all concerning the nature of the self after death (**24:19–36**). It is unclear why these views are not included in the first vagga, as they would have fit in there without any difficulty.

The saṃyutta contains four vaggas, which centre upon the same collection of views, except that the first vagga lacks the eighteen views of self. Each mode of treatment in the four vaggas is called a "trip" (*gamana*), though the word appears only from the second vagga on. The suttas of the first trip define the mark of the stream-enterer as the overcoming of perplexity (*kaṅkhā*) regarding six things—namely, the arising of views from clinging to the five aggregates and the four types of sense objects (the four counted as one), which are impermanent, suffering, and subject to change—and the overcoming of perplexity about the Four Noble Truths. The second shows that since the five aggregates are impermanent, suffering, and subject to change, views arise by clinging and adhering to suffering. The third includes the refrain that the views arise by clinging to the five aggregates, which are suffering because they are impermanent. The fourth applies the catechism, "Is form permanent or impermanent?" to the five aggregates to expose their nature as nonself, showing how liberation arises through realizing the selflessness of the aggregates.

25. *Okkantisaṃyutta*
26. *Uppādasaṃyutta*
27. *Kilesasaṃyutta*

These three saṃyuttas can be treated together, as they are each built upon a common foundation, differing only in the way they use this material to articulate their distinctive themes. The foundation on which they are built is a tenfold scheme for classifying the factors of experience already encountered in the Rāhulasaṃyutta (18): the six internal sense bases; the six external sense bases; the six classes each of consciousness, contact, feeling, perception, volition, and craving; the six elements; and the five aggregates. Thus each saṃyutta contains ten suttas, one devoted to each group of items.

In relation to these ten groups, the Okkantisaṃyutta makes a distinction between two types of individuals who enter upon "the fixed course of rightness" (*sammattaniyāma*), i.e., the transcendental Noble Eightfold Path, the path of stream-entry. The difference between them is determined by their dominant faculty. The one who emphasizes faith resolves (*adhimuccati*) on the impermanence of the factors in the ten groups; this type of person is called a faith-follower (*saddhānusārī*). The one who emphasizes wisdom gains understanding of the impermanence of the factors in the ten groups; this type of person is called a Dhamma-follower (*dhammānusārī*). Of both it is said that they cannot pass away without having realized the fruit of stream-entry. Regardless of this distinction in means of entering the path, when they know and see the truth of the teaching for themselves, they become stream-enterers. This saṃyutta does not distinguish between their character as stream-enterers, but elsewhere (MN I 478) it is indicated that the stream-enterer who gives prominence to faith is called "liberated by faith" (*saddhāvimutta*) while one who gives prominence to wisdom is called "attained by view" (*diṭṭhippatta*). A third class, without counterpart among path-attainers, consists of one who gains the formless meditations; this type is known as a "body-witness" (*kāyasakkhī*).

28. Sāriputtasaṃyutta

The Venerable Sāriputta was the Buddha's foremost disciple with respect to wisdom, but here he is depicted as an adept in meditation as well. The first nine suttas of the saṃyutta are composed from a stereotyped formula in which Sāriputta explains how he enters and emerges from the nine meditative attainments without giving rise to ego-affirming thoughts. Each time his reply is applauded by Ānanda. In the tenth sutta Sāriputta replies to some provocative questions from a female wanderer and his answers win her approval.

29. Nāgasaṃyutta
30. Supaṇṇasaṃyutta
31. Gandhabbakāyasaṃyutta
32. Valāhakasaṃyutta

These four saṃyuttas can be discussed together, as they all deal with certain classes of sentient beings that, from a modern perspective, would be considered mythological. In each the Buddha enumerates the different species into which the class can be divided and the courses of kamma that lead to rebirth into that particular mode of existence. By counting separately each type of gift given by the aspirant for rebirth into those destinies, and connecting them with the subdivisions among the beings, a large number of very short suttas are generated.

The *nāgas* are dragons, serpent-like beings, powerful and mysterious, believed to reside in the Himalayas, beneath the earth, and in the depths of the ocean. They are often thought to have access to hidden treasures and the ability to grant favours to their human benefactors. They also appear on earth and can assume human form, though only temporarily. The Vinaya Piṭaka even relates the story of a nāga who obtained ordination as a bhikkhu but was forced to relinquish his monastic status; as a result, every candidate for ordination must affirm, before the Saṅgha, that he is a human being (and not a nāga in disguise; see Vin I 86–87). The *supaṇṇas*, identical with the *garuḍas*, are their arch-enemies: fierce birds of prey that pounce on unwary nāgas, carry them away, and devour them. The *gandhabbas* are more benign: though sometimes depicted as celestial musicians, here they are obviously plant deities. They are identified as the spirits of fragrant plants because *gandha* means fragrance. The identity of the *valāhakas* or cloud-dwelling devas is evident from the explanation given in the texts.

These beings do not fit neatly into the scheme of cosmology outlined in the Introduction to Part I. The nāgas and gandhabbas are said to be ruled over by two of the Four Great Kings presiding over the heaven of that name, though as depicted here they can hardly be described as dwelling in heavenly worlds themselves. Rather, all these beings seem to belong to an intermediate zone between the human world and the lowest heaven, twilight creatures described with striking uniformity in the mythologies of many different cultures.

33. *Vacchagottasaṃyutta*

Vacchagotta was a wanderer who often approached the Buddha to ask questions, almost always of a philosophical hue. Finally convinced, he became a bhikkhu and attained arahantship (see MN Nos. 71–73).

This saṃyutta shows him during his phase as an inquirer. The saṃyutta has fifty-five chapters, undivided into vaggas, created by a process of permutation. In the first five suttas, in response to Vaccha's questions, the Buddha explains why the ten speculative views arise in the world, namely, from not knowing the five aggregates. Each sutta deals with a separate aggregate, treated by way of the four-truth pattern; hence five suttas. The remaining fifty suttas are created by taking ten synonyms for not knowing—e.g., not seeing, etc.—and relating them individually to the five aggregates in exactly the same way.

34. Jhānasaṃyutta

This saṃyutta is concerned with the types of skills required for success in attaining concentration (*samādhi*). Despite the title, it does not deal explicitly with the jhānas as states of meditation but with the process of meditation. A proper Jhānasaṃyutta, concerned with the jhānas, is found in Part V. Perhaps at one point this chapter was called the Jhāyanasaṃyutta, which seems more appropriate. The saṃyutta explores, in pairwise combinations, ten meditative skills. Each pair is related to four types of meditators: one who possesses one skill but not the other, one who has neither, and one who has both. In each case the last in the tetrad is extolled as the best. In this way fifty-five suttas are generated covering all possible permutations.

[1] PART III: The Book of the Aggregates (*Khandhavagga*)

Homage to the Blessed One,
the Arahant, the Perfectly Enlightened One

Chapter I

22 *Khandhasaṃyutta* Connected Discourses on the Aggregates

Division I
THE ROOT FIFTY

I. NAKULAPITĀ

1 (1) Nakulapitā

Thus have I heard. On one occasion the Blessed One was dwelling among the Bhaggas at Suṃsumāragira in the Bhesakaḷā Grove, the Deer Park. Then the householder Nakulapitā approached the Blessed One, paid homage to him, sat down to one side, and said to him:[1]

"I am old, venerable sir, aged, burdened with years, advanced in life, come to the last stage, afflicted in body, often ill. I rarely get to see the Blessed One and the bhikkhus worthy of esteem.[2] Let the Blessed One exhort me, venerable sir, let him instruct me, since that would lead to my welfare and happiness for a long time."

"So it is, householder, so it is! This body of yours is afflicted, weighed down, encumbered.[3] If anyone carrying around this body were to claim to be healthy even for a moment, what is that due to other than foolishness? Therefore, householder, you should train yourself thus: 'Even though I am afflicted in body, my mind will be unafflicted.' Thus should you train yourself."

Then the householder Nakulapitā, having delighted and rejoiced in the Blessed One's statement, [2] rose from his seat and, having paid homage to the Blessed One, keeping him on his right, he approached the Venerable Sāriputta. Having paid homage to the Venerable Sāriputta, he sat down to one side, and the Venerable Sāriputta then said to him:

"Householder, your faculties are serene, your facial complexion is pure and bright. Did you get to hear a Dhamma talk today in the presence of the Blessed One?"

"Why not, venerable sir? Just now I was anointed by the Blessed One with the ambrosia of a Dhamma talk."

"With what kind of ambrosia of a Dhamma talk did the Blessed One anoint you, householder?"

"Here, venerable sir, I approached the Blessed One....

(*The householder Nakulapitā repeats his entire conversation with the Buddha.*)

"It was with the ambrosia of such a Dhamma talk, venerable sir, that the Blessed One anointed me."

"Didn't it occur to you, householder, to question the Blessed One further as to how one is afflicted in body and afflicted in mind, and how one is afflicted in body but not afflicted in mind?" [3]

"We would come from far away, venerable sir, to learn the meaning of this statement from the Venerable Sāriputta. It would be good indeed if the Venerable Sāriputta would clear up the meaning of this statement."

"Then listen and attend closely, householder, I will speak."

"Yes, venerable sir," the householder Nakulapitā replied. The Venerable Sāriputta said this:

"How, householder, is one afflicted in body and afflicted in mind? Here, householder, the uninstructed worldling,[4] who is not a seer of the noble ones and is unskilled and undisciplined in their Dhamma, who is not a seer of superior persons and is unskilled and undisciplined in their Dhamma, regards form as self, or self as possessing form, or form as in self, or self as in form. He lives obsessed by the notions: 'I am form, form is mine.'[5] As he lives obsessed by these notions, that form of his changes and alters. With the change and alteration of form, there arise in him sorrow, lamentation, pain, displeasure, and despair.

"He regards feeling as self, or self as possessing feeling, or feeling as in self, or self as in feeling. He lives obsessed by the notions: 'I am feeling, feeling is mine.' As he lives obsessed by these notions, that feeling of his changes and alters. With the change and alteration of feeling, there arise in him sorrow, lamentation, pain, displeasure, and despair.

"He regards perception as self, or self as possessing perception, or perception as in self, or self as in perception. He lives obsessed by the notions: 'I am perception, perception is mine.' As he lives obsessed by these notions, that perception of his changes and alters. With the change and alteration of perception, there arise in him sorrow, lamentation, pain, displeasure, and despair.

"He regards volitional formations as self, or self as possessing volitional formations, or volitional formations as in self, or self as in volitional formations. He lives obsessed by the notions: 'I am volitional formations, volitional formations are mine.' As he lives obsessed by these notions, those volitional formations of his change and alter. [4] With the change and alteration of volitional formations, there arise in him sorrow, lamentation, pain, displeasure, and despair.

"He regards consciousness as self, or self as possessing consciousness, or consciousness as in self, or self as in consciousness. He lives obsessed by the notions: 'I am consciousness, consciousness is mine.' As he lives obsessed by these notions, that consciousness of his changes and alters. With the change and alteration of consciousness, there arise in him sorrow, lamentation, pain, displeasure, and despair.

"It is in such a way, householder, that one is afflicted in body and afflicted in mind.[6]

"And how, householder, is one afflicted in body but not afflicted in mind? Here, householder, the instructed noble disciple, who is a seer of the noble ones and is skilled and disciplined in their Dhamma, who is a seer of superior persons and is skilled and disciplined in their Dhamma, does not regard form as self, or self as possessing form, or form as in self, or self as in form.[7] He does not live obsessed by the notions: 'I am form, form is mine.' As he lives unobsessed by these notions, that form of his changes and alters. With the change and alteration of form, there do not arise in him sorrow, lamentation, pain, displeasure, and despair.

"He does not regard feeling as self, or self as possessing feeling, or feeling as in self, or self as in feeling. He does not live obsessed by the notions: 'I am feeling, feeling is mine.' As he lives unobsessed by these notions, that feeling of his changes and alters. With the change and alteration of feeling, there do not arise in him sorrow, lamentation, pain, displeasure, and despair.

"He does not regard perception as self, or self as possessing perception, or perception as in self, or self as in perception. He does not live obsessed by the notions: 'I am perception, perception is mine.' As he lives unobsessed by these notions, that perception of his changes and alters. With the change and alteration of perception, there do not arise in him sorrow, lamentation, pain, displeasure, and despair. [5]

"He does not regard volitional formations as self, or self as possessing volitional formations, or volitional formations as in self, or self as in volitional formations. He does not live obsessed by the notions: 'I am volitional formations, volitional formations are mine.' As he lives unobsessed by these notions, those volitional formations of his change and alter. With the change and alteration of volitional formations, there do not arise in him sorrow, lamentation, pain, displeasure, and despair.

"He does not regard consciousness as self, or self as possessing consciousness, or consciousness as in self, or self as in consciousness. He does not live obsessed by the notions: 'I am consciousness, consciousness is mine.' As he lives unobsessed by these notions, that consciousness of his changes and alters. With the change and alteration of consciousness, there do not arise in him sorrow, lamentation, pain, displeasure, and despair.

"It is in such a way, householder, that one is afflicted in body but not afflicted in mind."[8]

This is what the Venerable Sāriputta said. Elated, the householder Nakulapitā delighted in the Venerable Sāriputta's statement.

2 (2) At Devadaha

Thus have I heard. On one occasion the Blessed One was dwelling among the Sakyans where there was a town of the Sakyans named Devadaha. Then a number of westward-bound bhikkhus approached the Blessed One, paid homage to him, sat down to one side, and said to him:

"Venerable sir, we wish to go to the western province in order to take up residence there."[9]

"Have you taken leave of Sāriputta, bhikkhus?"

"No, venerable sir."

"Then take leave of Sāriputta, bhikkhus. Sāriputta is wise, he is one who helps his brothers in the holy life."[10] [6]

"Yes, venerable sir," those bhikkhus replied. Now on that occasion the Venerable Sāriputta was sitting not far from the Blessed One in a cassia bush.[11] Then those bhikkhus, having delighted and rejoiced in the Blessed One's statement, rose from their seats and paid homage to the Blessed One. Then, keeping him on their right, they approached the Venerable Sāriputta. They exchanged greetings with the Venerable Sāriputta and, when they had concluded their greetings and cordial talk, they sat down to one side and said to him:

"Friend Sāriputta, we wish to go to the western province in order to take up residence there. We have taken leave of the Teacher."

"Friends, there are wise khattiyas, wise brahmins, wise householders, and wise ascetics who question a bhikkhu when he has gone abroad[12]—for wise people, friends, are inquisitive: 'What does your teacher say, what does he teach?' I hope that you venerable ones have learned the teachings well, grasped them well, attended to them well, reflected on them well, and penetrated them well with wisdom, so that when you answer you will state what has been said by the Blessed One and will not misrepresent him with what is contrary to fact; so that you will explain in accordance with the Dhamma, and no reasonable consequence of your assertion would give ground for criticism."[13]

"We would come from far away, friend, to learn the meaning of this statement from the Venerable Sāriputta. It would be good indeed if the Venerable Sāriputta would clear up the meaning of this statement."

"Then listen and attend closely, friends, I will speak."

"Yes, friend," those bhikkhus replied. The Venerable Sāriputta said this: [7]

"There are, friends, wise khattiyas, wise brahmins, wise householders, and wise ascetics who question a bhikkhu when he has gone abroad—for wise people, friends, are inquisitive: 'What does your teacher say, what does he teach?' Being asked thus, friends, you should answer: 'Our teacher, friends, teaches the removal of desire and lust.'

"When you have answered thus, friends, there may be wise khattiyas ... wise ascetics who will question you further—for wise people, friends, are inquisitive: 'In regard to what does your teacher teach the removal of desire and lust?' Being asked thus, friends, you should answer: 'Our teacher, friends, teaches the removal of desire and lust for form, the removal of desire and lust for feeling ... perception ... volitional formations ... consciousness.'

"When you have answered thus, friends, there may be wise khattiyas ... wise ascetics who will question you further—for wise people, friends, are inquisitive: 'Having seen what danger does your teacher teach the removal of desire and lust for form, the removal of desire and lust for feeling ... perception ... volitional formations ... consciousness?' Being asked thus, friends, you should answer thus: 'If, friends, one is not devoid of lust, desire, affection, thirst, passion, and craving in regard to form,[14] then with the change and alteration of form there arise in one sorrow, lamentation, pain, displeasure, and despair. If, friends, one is not devoid of lust, desire, affection, thirst, passion, and craving in regard to feeling ... perception ... volitional formations ... consciousness, then with the change and alteration of consciousness there arise in one sorrow, lamentation, pain, displeasure, and despair. Having seen this danger, our teacher teaches the removal of desire and lust for form, the removal of desire and lust for feeling ... perception ... volitional formations ... consciousness.' [8]

"When you have answered thus, friends, there may be wise khattiyas ... wise ascetics who will question you further—for wise people, friends, are inquisitive: 'Having seen what benefit does your teacher teach the removal of desire and lust for form, the removal of desire and lust for feeling ... perception ... volitional formations ... consciousness?' Being asked thus, friends, you should answer thus: 'If, friends, one is devoid of lust, desire, affection, thirst, passion, and craving in regard to form, then with the change and alteration of form sorrow, lamentation, pain, displeasure, and despair do not arise in one. If one is devoid of lust, desire, affection, thirst, passion, and craving in regard to feeling ... perception ... volitional formations ... consciousness, then with the change and alteration of consciousness sorrow, lamentation, pain, displeasure, and despair do not arise in one. Having seen this benefit, our teacher teaches the removal of desire and lust for form, the removal of desire and lust for feeling ... perception ... volitional formations ... consciousness.'

"If, friends,[15] one who enters and dwells amidst unwholesome states could dwell happily in this very life, without vexation, despair, and fever, and if, with the breakup of the body, after death, he could expect a good destination, then the Blessed One would not praise the abandoning of unwholesome states. But because one who enters and dwells amidst unwholesome states dwells in suffering in this very life, with vexation, despair, and fever, and because he can expect a bad destination with the breakup of the body, after death, the Blessed One praises the abandoning of unwholesome states.

"If, friends, one who enters and dwells amidst wholesome states would dwell in suffering in this very life, with vexation, [9] despair, and fever, and if, with the breakup of the body, after death, he could expect a bad destination, then the Blessed One would not praise the acquisition of wholesome states. But because one who enters and dwells amidst wholesome states dwells happily in this very life, without vexation, despair, and fever, and because he can expect a good destination with the breakup of the body, after death, the Blessed One praises the acquisition of wholesome states."

This is what the Venerable Sāriputta said. Elated, those bhikkhus delighted in the Venerable Sāriputta's statement.

3 (3) Hāliddakāni (1)

Thus have I heard. On one occasion the Venerable Mahākaccāna was dwelling among the people of Avanti on Mount Papāta at Kuraraghara.[16] Then the householder Hāliddakāni approached the Venerable Mahākaccāna, paid homage to him, sat down to one side, and said to him:

"Venerable sir, this was said by the Blessed One in 'The Questions of Māgandiya' of the Aṭṭhakavagga:[17]

'Having left home to roam without abode,
In the village the sage is intimate with none;

> Rid of sensual pleasures, without expectations,
> He would not engage people in dispute.'

How, venerable sir, should the meaning of this, stated by the Blessed One in brief, be understood in detail?"

"The form element, householder, is the home of consciousness; one whose consciousness is shackled by lust for the form element is called one who roams about in a home.[18] The feeling element is the home of consciousness … [10] The perception element is the home of consciousness … The volitional formations element is the home of consciousness; one whose consciousness is shackled by lust for the volitional formations element is called one who roams about in a home. It is in such a way that one roams about in a home.[19]

"And how, householder, does one roam about homeless? The desire, lust, delight, and craving, the engagement and clinging, the mental standpoints, adherences, and underlying tendencies regarding the form element: these have been abandoned by the Tathāgata, cut off at the root, made like a palm stump, obliterated so that they are no more subject to future arising.[20] Therefore the Tathāgata is called one who roams about homeless. The desire, lust, delight, and craving, the engagement and clinging, the mental standpoints, adherences, and underlying tendencies regarding the feeling element … the perception element … the volitional formations element … the consciousness element:[21] these have been abandoned by the Tathāgata, cut off at the root, made like a palm stump, obliterated so that they are no more subject to future arising. Therefore the Tathāgata is called one who roams about homeless. It is in such a way that one roams about homeless.

"And how, householder, does one roam about in an abode? By diffusion and confinement in the abode [consisting in] the sign of forms, one is called one who roams about in an abode.[22] By diffusion and confinement in the abode [consisting in] the sign of sounds … the sign of odours … the sign of tastes … the sign of tactile objects … the sign of mental phenomena, one is called one who roams about in an abode.

"And how, householder, does one roam about without abode? Diffusion and confinement in the abode [consisting in] the sign of forms: these have been abandoned by the Tathāgata, cut off at the root, made like a palm stump, obliterated so that they are no more subject to future arising. Therefore the Tathāgata is called one who roams about without abode. Diffusion and confinement in the abode [consisting in] the sign of sounds ... the sign of odours ... the sign of tastes ... the sign of tactile objects ... the sign of mental phenomena: these have been abandoned by the Tathāgata, cut off at the root, made like a palm stump, [11] obliterated so that they are no more subject to future arising. Therefore the Tathāgata is called one who roams about without abode. It is in such a way that one roams about without abode.[23]

"And how, householder, is one intimate in the village? Here, householder, someone lives in association with laypeople: he rejoices with them and sorrows with them, he is happy when they are happy and sad when they are sad, and he involves himself in their affairs and duties.[24] It is in such a way that one is intimate in the village.

"And how, householder, is one intimate with none in the village? Here, householder, a bhikkhu does not live in association with laypeople. He does not rejoice with them or sorrow with them, he is not happy when they are happy and sad when they are sad, and he does not involve himself in their affairs and duties. It is in such a way that one is intimate with none in the village.

"And how, householder, is one not rid of sensual pleasures? Here, householder, someone is not devoid of lust, desire, affection, thirst, passion, and craving in regard to sensual pleasures. It is in such a way that one is not rid of sensual pleasures.

"And how, householder, is one rid of sensual pleasures? Here, householder, someone is devoid of lust, desire, affection, thirst, passion, and craving in regard to sensual pleasures. It is in such a way that one is rid of sensual pleasures.

"And how, householder, does one entertain expectations?[25] Here, householder, someone thinks: 'May I have such form in the future! May I have such feeling in the future! May I have such perception in the future! May I have such volitional formations in the future! May I have such consciousness in the future!' It is in such a way that one entertains expectations.

"And how, householder, is one without expectations? Here, householder, someone does not think: 'May I have such form in the future!... [12] May I have such consciousness in the future!' It is in such a way that one is without expectations.

"And how, householder, does one engage people in dispute? Here, householder, someone engages in such talk as this:[26] 'You don't understand this Dhamma and Discipline. I understand this Dhamma and Discipline. What, you understand this Dhamma and Discipline! You're practising wrongly, I'm practising rightly. What should have been said before you said after; what should have been said after you said before. I'm consistent, you're inconsistent. What you took so long to think out has been overturned. Your thesis has been refuted. Go off to rescue your thesis, for you're defeated, or disentangle yourself if you can.' It is in such a way that one engages people in dispute.

"And how, householder, does one not engage people in dispute? Here, householder, someone does not engage in such talk as this: 'You don't understand this Dhamma and Discipline.... ' It is in such a way that one does not engage people in dispute.

"Thus, householder, when it was said by the Blessed One in 'The Questions of Māgandiya' of the Aṭṭhakavagga:

> 'Having left home to roam without abode,
> In the village the sage is intimate with none;
> Rid of sensual pleasures, without expectations,
> He would not engage people in dispute'—

it is in such a way that the meaning of this, stated in brief by the Blessed One, should be understood in detail."

4 (4) Hāliddakāni (2)

Thus have I heard. On one occasion the Venerable Mahākaccāna was dwelling among the people of Avantī on Mount Papāta at Kuraraghara. [13] Then the householder Hāliddakāni approached the Venerable Mahākaccāna, paid homage to him, sat down to one side, and said to him:

"Venerable sir, this was said by the Blessed One in 'The Questions of Sakka':[27] 'Those ascetics and brahmins who are liberated in the extinction of craving are those who have reached the ultimate end, the ultimate security from bondage, the ultimate holy life, the ultimate goal, and are best among devas and humans.'[28] How, venerable sir, should the meaning of this, stated in brief by the Blessed One, be understood in detail?"

"Householder, through the destruction, fading away, cessation, giving up, and relinquishment of desire, lust, delight, craving, engagement and clinging, mental standpoints, adherences, and underlying tendencies towards the form element, the mind is said to be well liberated.

"Through the destruction, fading away, cessation, giving up, and relinquishment of desire, lust, delight, craving, engagement and clinging, mental standpoints, adherences, and underlying tendencies towards the feeling element ... the perception element ... the volitional formations element ... the consciousness element, the mind is said to be well liberated.

"Thus, householder, when it was said by the Blessed One in 'The Questions of Sakka': 'Those ascetics and brahmins who are liberated in the extinction of craving are those who have reached the ultimate end, the ultimate security from bondage, the ultimate holy life, the ultimate goal, and are best among devas and humans'—it is in such a way that the meaning of this, stated in brief by the Blessed One, should be understood in detail."

5 (5) Concentration

Thus have I heard. At Sāvatthī.... There the Blessed One said this:

"Bhikkhus, develop concentration. A bhikkhu who is concentrated understands things as they really are.

"And what does he understand as it really is? The origin and passing away of form; the origin and passing away of feeling; [14] the origin and passing away of perception; the origin and passing away of volitional formations; the origin and passing away of consciousness.[29]

"And what, bhikkhus, is the origin of form? What is the origin of feeling? What is the origin of perception? What is the origin of volitional formations? What is the origin of consciousness?

"Here, bhikkhus, one seeks delight, one welcomes, one remains holding. And what is it that one seeks delight in, what does one welcome, to what does one remain holding? One seeks delight in form, welcomes it, and remains holding to it. As a consequence of this, delight arises. Delight in form is clinging. With one's clinging as condition, existence [comes to be]; with existence as condition, birth; with birth as condition, aging-and-death, sorrow, lamentation, pain, displeasure, and despair come to be. Such is the origin of this whole mass of suffering.

"One seeks delight in feeling ... in perception ... in volitional formations ... in consciousness, welcomes it, and remains holding to it. As a consequence of this, delight arises.... Such is the origin of this whole mass of suffering.

"This, bhikkhus, is the origin of form; this is the origin of feeling; this is the origin of perception; this is the origin of volitional formations; this is the origin of consciousness.[30]

"And what, bhikkhus, is the passing away of form? What is the passing away of feeling? What is the passing away of perception? What is the passing away of volitional formations? What is the passing away of consciousness?

"Here, bhikkhus, one does not seek delight, one does not welcome, one does not remain holding. And what is it that one does not seek delight in? What doesn't one welcome? To what doesn't one remain holding? One does not seek delight in form, does not welcome it, does not remain holding to it. As a consequence of this, delight in form ceases. With the cessation of delight comes cessation of clinging; with cessation of clinging, cessation of existence.... Such is the cessation of this whole mass of suffering.

"One does not seek delight in feeling ... [15] ... in perception ... in volitional formations ... in consciousness, does not welcome it, does not remain holding to it. As a consequence of this, delight in consciousness ceases.... Such is the cessation of this whole mass of suffering.

"This, bhikkhus, is the passing away of form; this is the passing away of feeling; this is the passing away of perception; this is the passing away of volitional formations; this is the passing away of consciousness."

6 (6) Seclusion

At Sāvatthī. "Bhikkhus, make an exertion in seclusion.[31] A bhikkhu who is secluded understands things as they really are.

"And what does he understand as it really is? The origin and passing away of form; the origin and passing away of feeling; the origin and passing away of perception; the origin and passing away of volitional formations; the origin and passing away of consciousness.

"And what, bhikkhus, is the origin of form?..."

(*The rest of this sutta is identical with the preceding one.*)

7 (7) Agitation through Clinging (1)

At Sāvatthī. "Bhikkhus, I will teach you agitation through clinging and nonagitation through nonclinging.[32] Listen to that and attend closely, I will speak." [16]

"Yes, venerable sir," those bhikkhus replied. The Blessed One said this:

"And how, bhikkhus, is there agitation through clinging? Here, bhikkhus, the uninstructed worldling, who is not a seer of the noble ones and is unskilled and undisciplined in their Dhamma, who is not a seer of superior persons and is unskilled and undisciplined in their Dhamma, regards form as self, or self as possessing form, or form as in self, or self as in form. That form of his changes and alters. With the change and alteration of form, his consciousness becomes preoccupied with the change of form. Agitation and a constellation of mental states born of preoccupation with the change of form remain obsessing his mind.[33] Because his mind is obsessed, he is frightened, distressed, and anxious, and through clinging he becomes agitated.

"He regards feeling as self ... perception as self ... volitional formations as self ... consciousness as self, or self as possessing consciousness, or consciousness as in self, or self as in consciousness. That consciousness of his changes and alters. [17] With the change and alteration of consciousness, his consciousness becomes preoccupied with the change of consciousness. Agitation and a constellation of mental states born of preoccupation with the change of consciousness remain obsessing his mind. Because his mind is obsessed, he is frightened, distressed, and anxious, and through clinging he becomes agitated.

"It is in such a way, bhikkhus, that there is agitation through clinging.

"And how, bhikkhus, is there nonagitation through nonclinging? Here, bhikkhus, the instructed noble disciple, who is a seer of the noble ones and is skilled and disciplined in their Dhamma, who is a seer of superior persons and is skilled and disciplined in their Dhamma, does not regard form as self, or self as possessing form, or form as in self, or self as in form. That form of his changes and alters. Despite the change and alteration of form, his consciousness does not become preoccupied with the change of form. No agitation and constellation of mental states born of preoccupation with the change of form remain obsessing his mind. Because his mind is not obsessed, he is not frightened, distressed, or anxious, and through nonclinging he does not become agitated.

"He does not regard feeling as self … perception as self … volitional formations as self … [18] … consciousness as self, or self as possessing consciousness, or consciousness as in self, or self as in consciousness. That consciousness of his changes and alters. Despite the change and alteration of consciousness, his consciousness does not become preoccupied with the change of consciousness. No agitation and constellation of mental states born of preoccupation with the change of consciousness remain obsessing his mind. Because his mind is not obsessed, he is not frightened, distressed, or anxious, and through nonclinging he does not become agitated.

"It is in such a way, bhikkhus, that there is nonagitation through nonclinging."

8 (8) Agitation through Clinging (2)

At Sāvatthī. "Bhikkhus, I will teach you agitation through clinging and nonagitation through nonclinging. Listen to that and attend closely….

"And how, bhikkhus, is there agitation through clinging? Here, bhikkhus, the uninstructed worldling regards form thus: 'This is mine, this I am, this is my self.'[34] That form of his changes and alters. With the change and alteration of form, there arise in him sorrow, lamentation, pain, displeasure, and despair.

"He regards feeling thus … perception thus … volitional formations thus … consciousness thus: 'This is mine, this I am, this is my self.' That consciousness of his changes and alters. With the change and alteration of consciousness, there arise in him sorrow, lamentation, pain, displeasure, and despair.

"It is in such a way, bhikkhus, that there is agitation through clinging.

"And how, bhikkhus, is there nonagitation through nonclinging? [19] Here, bhikkhus, the instructed noble disciple does not regard form thus: 'This is mine, this I am, this is my self.' That form of his changes and alters. With the change and alteration of form, there do not arise in him sorrow, lamentation, pain, displeasure, and despair.

"He does not regard feeling thus ... perception thus ... volitional formations thus ... consciousness thus: 'This is mine, this I am, this is my self.' That consciousness of his changes and alters. With the change and alteration of consciousness, there do not arise in him sorrow, lamentation, pain, displeasure, and despair.

"It is in such a way, bhikkhus, that there is nonagitation through nonclinging."

9 (9) Impermanent in the Three Times

At Sāvatthī. "Bhikkhus, form is impermanent, both of the past and the future, not to speak of the present. Seeing thus, bhikkhus, the instructed noble disciple is indifferent towards form of the past; he does not seek delight in form of the future; and he is practising for revulsion towards form of the present, for its fading away and cessation.

"Feeling is impermanent ... Perception is impermanent ... Volitional formations are impermanent ... Consciousness is impermanent, both of the past and the future, not to speak of the present. Seeing thus, bhikkhus, the instructed noble disciple is indifferent towards consciousness of the past; he does not seek delight in consciousness of the future; and he is practising for revulsion towards consciousness of the present, for its fading away and cessation."

10 (10) Suffering in the Three Times

At Sāvatthī. "Bhikkhus, form is suffering, both of the past and the future, not to speak of the present. [20] Seeing thus, bhikkhus, the instructed noble disciple is indifferent towards form of the past; he does not seek delight in form of the future; and he is practising for revulsion towards form of the present, for its fading away and cessation.

"Feeling is suffering ... Perception is suffering ... Volitional formations are suffering ... Consciousness is suffering, both of the past and the future, not to speak of the present. Seeing thus, bhikkhus, the instructed noble disciple is indifferent towards consciousness of the past; he does not seek delight in consciousness of the future; and he is practising for revulsion towards consciousness of the present, for its fading away and cessation."

11 (11) Nonself in the Three Times

At Sāvatthī. "Bhikkhus, form is nonself, both of the past and the future, not to speak of the present. Seeing thus, bhikkhus, the instructed noble disciple is indifferent towards form of the past; he does not seek delight in form of the future; and he is practising for revulsion towards form of the present, for its fading away and cessation.

"Feeling is nonself ... Perception is nonself ... Volitional formations are nonself ... Consciousness is nonself, both of the past and the future, not to speak of the present. Seeing thus, bhikkhus, the instructed noble disciple is indifferent towards consciousness of the past; he does not seek delight in consciousness of the future; and he is practising for revulsion towards consciousness of the present, for its fading away and cessation."

[21] II. Impermanent

12 (1) Impermanent

Thus have I heard. At Sāvatthī.... There the Blessed One said this:

"Bhikkhus, form is impermanent, feeling is impermanent, perception is impermanent, volitional formations are impermanent, consciousness is impermanent. Seeing thus, bhikkhus, the instructed noble disciple experiences revulsion towards form, revulsion towards feeling, revulsion towards perception, revulsion towards volitional formations, revulsion towards consciousness. Experiencing revulsion, he becomes dispassionate. Through dispassion [his mind] is liberated. When it is liberated there comes the knowledge: 'It's liberated.' He understands: 'Destroyed is birth, the holy life has been lived, what had to be done has been done, there is no more for this state of being.'"

13 (2) Suffering

At Sāvatthī. "Bhikkhus, form is suffering, feeling is suffering, perception is suffering, volitional formations are suffering, consciousness is suffering. Seeing thus … He understands: '… there is no more for this state of being.'"

14 (3) Nonself

At Sāvatthī. "Bhikkhus, form is nonself, feeling is nonself, perception is nonself, volitional formations are nonself, consciousness is nonself. Seeing thus … He understands: '… there is no more for this state of being.'" [22]

15 (4) What is Impermanent

At Sāvatthī. "Bhikkhus, form is impermanent. What is impermanent is suffering. What is suffering is nonself. What is nonself should be seen as it really is with correct wisdom thus: 'This is not mine, this I am not, this is not my self.'

"Feeling is impermanent…. Perception is impermanent…. Volitional formations are impermanent…. Consciousness is impermanent. What is impermanent is suffering. What is suffering is nonself. What is nonself should be seen as it really is with correct wisdom thus: 'This is not mine, this I am not, this is not my self.'

"Seeing thus … He understands: '… there is no more for this state of being.'"

16 (5) What is Suffering

At Sāvatthī. "Bhikkhus, form is suffering. What is suffering is nonself. What is nonself should be seen as it really is with correct wisdom thus: 'This is not mine, this I am not, this is not my self.'

"Feeling is suffering…. Perception is suffering…. Volitional formations are suffering…. Consciousness is suffering. What is suffering is nonself. What is nonself should be seen as it really is with correct wisdom thus: 'This is not mine, this I am not, this is not my self.'

"Seeing thus … He understands: '… there is no more for this state of being.'"

17 (6) What is Nonself

At Sāvatthī. "Bhikkhus, form is nonself. What is nonself [23] should be seen as it really is with correct wisdom thus: 'This is not mine, this I am not, this is not my self.'

"Feeling is nonself.... Perception is nonself.... Volitional formations are nonself.... Consciousness is nonself. What is nonself should be seen as it really is with correct wisdom thus: 'This is not mine, this I am not, this is not my self.'

"Seeing thus ... He understands: '... there is no more for this state of being.'"

18 (7) Impermanent with Cause

At Sāvatthī. "Bhikkhus, form is impermanent. The cause and condition for the arising of form is also impermanent. As form has originated from what is impermanent, how could it be permanent?

"Feeling is impermanent.... Perception is impermanent.... Volitional formations are impermanent.... Consciousness is impermanent. The cause and condition for the arising of consciousness is also impermanent. As consciousness has originated from what is impermanent, how could it be permanent?

"Seeing thus ... He understands: '... there is no more for this state of being.'"

19 (8) Suffering with Cause

At Sāvatthī. "Bhikkhus, form is suffering. The cause and condition for the arising of form is also suffering. As form has originated from what is suffering, how could it be happiness?

"Feeling is suffering.... Perception is suffering.... Volitional formations are suffering.... [24] Consciousness is suffering. The cause and condition for the arising of consciousness is also suffering. As consciousness has originated from what is suffering, how could it be happiness?

"Seeing thus ... He understands: '... there is no more for this state of being.'"

20 (9) Nonself with Cause

At Sāvatthī. "Bhikkhus, form is nonself. The cause and condition for the arising of form is also nonself. As form has originated from what is nonself, how could it be self?

"Feeling is nonself.... Perception is nonself.... Volitional formations are nonself.... Consciousness is nonself. The cause and condition for the arising of consciousness is also nonself. As consciousness has originated from what is nonself, how could it be self?

"Seeing thus ... He understands: '... there is no more for this state of being.'"

21 (10) Ānanda

At Sāvatthī. Then the Venerable Ānanda approached the Blessed One, paid homage to him, sat down to one side, and said to him:

"Venerable sir, it is said, 'cessation, cessation.' Through the cessation of what things is cessation spoken of?"

"Form, Ānanda, is impermanent, conditioned, dependently arisen, subject to destruction, to vanishing, to fading away, to cessation. Through its cessation, cessation is spoken of.

"Feeling is impermanent ... Perception is impermanent ... Volitional formations are impermanent ... [25] ... Consciousness is impermanent, conditioned, dependently arisen, subject to destruction, to vanishing, to fading away, to cessation. Through its cessation, cessation is spoken of.

"It is through the cessation of these things, Ānanda, that cessation is spoken of."

III. The Burden

22 (1) The Burden

At Sāvatthī.... There the Blessed One said this:

"Bhikkhus, I will teach you the burden, the carrier of the burden,[35] the taking up of the burden, and the laying down of the burden. Listen to that....

"And what, bhikkhus, is the burden? It should be said: the five aggregates subject to clinging. What five? The form aggregate subject to clinging, the feeling aggregate subject to clinging, the perception aggregate subject to clinging, the volitional formations aggregate subject to clinging, the consciousness aggregate subject to clinging. This is called the burden.[36]

"And what, bhikkhus, is the carrier of the burden? It should be said: the person, this venerable one of such a name and clan. This is called the carrier of the burden.[37] [26]

"And what, bhikkhus, is the taking up of the burden? It is this craving that leads to renewed existence, accompanied by delight and lust, seeking delight here and there; that is, craving for sensual pleasures, craving for existence, craving for extermination. This is called the taking up of the burden.[38]

"And what, bhikkhus, is the laying down of the burden? It is the remainderless fading away and cessation of that same craving, the giving up and relinquishing of it, freedom from it, nonreliance on it. This is called the laying down of the burden."[39]

This is what the Blessed One said. Having said this, the Fortunate One, the Teacher, further said this:

"The five aggregates are truly burdens,
The burden-carrier is the person.
Taking up the burden is suffering in the world,
Laying the burden down is blissful.

Having laid the heavy burden down
Without taking up another burden,
Having drawn out craving with its root,
One is free from hunger, fully quenched."[40]

23 (2) Full Understanding

At Sāvatthī. [27] "Bhikkhus, I will teach you things that should be fully understood and also full understanding. Listen to that....

"And what, bhikkhus, are the things that should be fully understood? Form, bhikkhus, is something that should be fully understood; feeling ... perception ... volitional formations ... consciousness is something that should be fully understood. These are called the things that should be fully understood.

"And what, bhikkhus, is full understanding? The destruction of lust, the destruction of hatred, the destruction of delusion. This is called full understanding."[41]

24 (3) Directly Knowing

At Sāvatthī. "Bhikkhus, without directly knowing and fully understanding form, without becoming dispassionate towards it and abandoning it, one is incapable of destroying suffering. Without directly knowing and fully understanding feeling ... perception ... volitional formations ... consciousness, without becoming dispassionate towards it and abandoning it, one is incapable of destroying suffering.

"Bhikkhus, by directly knowing and fully understanding form, by becoming dispassionate towards it and abandoning it, one is capable of destroying suffering. By directly knowing and fully understanding feeling ... perception ... volitional formations ... consciousness, by becoming dispassionate towards it and abandoning it, one is capable of destroying suffering."[42]

25 (4) Desire and Lust

At Sāvatthī. "Bhikkhus, abandon desire and lust for form. Thus that form will be abandoned, cut off at the root, made like a palm stump, obliterated so that it is no more subject to future arising.

"Abandon desire and lust for feeling ... for perception ... for volitional formations ... for consciousness. Thus that consciousness will be abandoned, cut off at the root, made like a palm stump, obliterated so that it is no more subject to future arising."

26 (5) Gratification (1)

At Sāvatthī. "Bhikkhus, before my enlightenment, while I was still a bodhisatta, not yet fully enlightened, it occurred to me: 'What is the gratification, what is the danger, what is the escape in the case of form? What is the gratification, what is the danger, what is the escape in the case of feeling ... perception ... volitional formations ... consciousness?'[43] [28]

"Then, bhikkhus, it occurred to me: 'The pleasure and joy that arise in dependence on form: this is the gratification in form. That form is impermanent, suffering, and subject to change: this is the danger in form. The removal and abandonment of desire and lust for form: this is the escape from form.

"'The pleasure and joy that arise in dependence on feeling ...

in dependence on perception ... in dependence on volitional formations ... in dependence on consciousness: this is the gratification in consciousness. That consciousness is impermanent, suffering, and subject to change: this is the danger in consciousness. The removal and abandonment of desire and lust for consciousness: this is the escape from consciousness.'

"So long, bhikkhus, as I did not directly know as they really are the gratification as gratification, the danger as danger, and the escape as escape in the case of these five aggregates subject to clinging, I did not claim to have awakened to the unsurpassed perfect enlightenment in this world with its devas, Māra, and Brahmā, in this generation with its ascetics and brahmins, its devas and humans. But when I directly knew all this as it really is, then I claimed to have awakened to the unsurpassed perfect enlightenment in this world with ... its devas and humans.

"The knowledge and vision arose in me: 'Unshakable is my liberation of mind; this is my last birth; now there is no more renewed existence.'" [29]

27 (6) Gratification (2)

At Sāvatthī. "Bhikkhus, I set out seeking the gratification in form. Whatever gratification there is in form—that I discovered. I have clearly seen with wisdom just how far the gratification in form extends.

"Bhikkhus, I set out seeking the danger in form. Whatever danger there is in form—that I discovered. I have clearly seen with wisdom just how far the danger in form extends.

"Bhikkhus, I set out seeking the escape from form. Whatever escape there is from form—that I discovered. I have clearly seen with wisdom just how far the escape from form extends.

"Bhikkhus, I set out seeking the gratification in ... the danger in ... the escape from feeling ... from perception ... from volitional formations ... from consciousness. Whatever escape there is from consciousness—that I discovered. I have clearly seen with wisdom just how far the escape from consciousness extends.

"So long, bhikkhus, as I did not directly know as they really are the gratification as gratification, the danger as danger, and the escape as escape in the case of these five aggregates subject to clinging, I did not claim to have awakened to the unsurpassed perfect enlightenment in this world with its devas, Māra, and Brahmā, in this generation with its ascetics and brahmins, its devas and humans. But when I directly knew all this as it really is, then I claimed to have awakened to the unsurpassed perfect enlightenment in this world with ... its devas and humans.

"The knowledge and vision arose in me: 'Unshakable is my liberation of mind; this is my last birth; now there is no more renewed existence.'"

28 (7) Gratification (3)

At Sāvatthī. "Bhikkhus, if there were no gratification in form, [30] beings would not become enamoured with it; but because there is gratification in form, beings become enamoured with it. If there were no danger in form, beings would not experience revulsion towards it; but because there is danger in form, beings experience revulsion towards it. If there were no escape from form, beings would not escape from it; but because there is an escape from form, beings escape from it.

"Bhikkhus, if there were no gratification in feeling ... in perception ... in volitional formations ... in consciousness, beings would not become enamoured with it ... but because there is an escape from consciousness, beings escape from it.

"So long, bhikkhus, as beings have not directly known as they really are the gratification as gratification, the danger as danger, and the escape as escape in the case of these five aggregates subject to clinging, they have not escaped from this world with its devas, Māra, [31] and Brahmā, from this generation with its ascetics and brahmins, its devas and humans; they have not become detached from it, released from it, nor do they dwell with a mind rid of barriers. But when beings have directly known all this as it really is, then they have escaped from this world with ... its devas and humans; they have become detached from it, released from it, and they dwell with a mind rid of barriers."

29 (8) Delight

At Sāvatthī. "Bhikkhus, one who seeks delight in form seeks delight in suffering. One who seeks delight in suffering, I say, is not freed from suffering. One who seeks delight in feeling ... in perception ... in volitional formations ... in consciousness seeks delight in suffering. One who seeks delight in suffering, I say, is not freed from suffering.

"One who does not seek delight in form ... in consciousness does not seek delight in suffering. One who does not seek delight in suffering, I say, is freed from suffering."

30 (9) Arising

At Sāvatthī. "Bhikkhus, the arising, continuation, production, [32] and manifestation of form is the arising of suffering, the continuation of disease, the manifestation of aging-and-death. The arising of feeling ... of perception ... of volitional formations ... of consciousness is the arising of suffering, the continuation of disease, the manifestation of aging-and-death.

"The cessation, subsiding, and passing away of form ... of consciousness is the cessation of suffering, the subsiding of disease, the passing away of aging-and-death."

31 (10) The Root of Misery

At Sāvatthī. "Bhikkhus, I will teach you misery[44] and the root of misery. Listen to that....

"And what, bhikkhus, is misery? Form is misery; feeling is misery; perception is misery; volitional formations are misery; consciousness is misery. This is called misery.

"And what, bhikkhus, is the root of misery? It is this craving that leads to renewed existence, accompanied by delight and lust, seeking delight here and there; that is, craving for sensual pleasures, craving for existence, craving for extermination. This is called the root of misery."

32 (11) The Fragile

At Sāvatthī. "Bhikkhus, I will teach you the fragile[45] and the unfragile. Listen to that....

"And what, bhikkhus, is the fragile, and what the unfragile? [33] Form is the fragile; its cessation, subsiding, passing away is the unfragile. Feeling is the fragile ... Perception is the fragile ...

Volitional formations are the fragile ... Consciousness is the fragile; its cessation, subsiding, passing away is the unfragile."

IV. Not Yours

33 (1) Not Yours (1)

At Sāvatthī. "Bhikkhus, whatever is not yours, abandon it. When you have abandoned it, that will lead to your welfare and happiness.[46] And what is it, bhikkhus, that is not yours? Form is not yours: abandon it. When you have abandoned it, that will lead to your welfare and happiness. Feeling is not yours ... Perception is not yours ... [34] Volitional formations are not yours ... Consciousness is not yours: abandon it. When you have abandoned it, that will lead to your welfare and happiness.

"Suppose, bhikkhus, people were to carry off the grass, sticks, branches, and foliage in this Jeta's Grove, or to burn them, or to do with them as they wish. Would you think: 'People are carrying us off, or burning us, or doing with us as they wish'?"

"No, venerable sir. For what reason? Because, venerable sir, that is neither our self nor what belongs to our self."

"So too, bhikkhus, form is not yours ... consciousness is not yours: abandon it. When you have abandoned it, that will lead to your welfare and happiness."

34 (2) Not Yours (2)

(This sutta is identical with the preceding one except that it omits the simile.)

35 (3) A Certain Bhikkhu (1)

At Sāvatthī. [35] Then a certain bhikkhu approached the Blessed One, paid homage to him, sat down to one side, and said to him: "Venerable sir, it would be good if the Blessed One would teach me the Dhamma in brief, so that, having heard the Dhamma from the Blessed One, I might dwell alone, withdrawn, diligent, ardent, and resolute."

"Bhikkhu, if one has an underlying tendency towards something, then one is reckoned in terms of it.[47] If one does not have an underlying tendency towards something, then one is not reckoned in terms of it."

"Understood, Blessed One! Understood, Fortunate One!"

"In what way, bhikkhu, do you understand in detail the meaning of what was stated by me in brief?"

"If, venerable sir, one has an underlying tendency towards form, then one is reckoned in terms of it. If one has an underlying tendency towards feeling, then one is reckoned in terms of it. If one has an underlying tendency towards perception, then one is reckoned in terms of it. If one has an underlying tendency towards volitional formations, then one is reckoned in terms of them. If one has an underlying tendency towards consciousness, then one is reckoned in terms of it.

"If, venerable sir, one does not have an underlying tendency towards form, then one is not reckoned in terms of it. If one does not have an underlying tendency towards feeling … towards perception … towards volitional formations … towards consciousness, then one is not reckoned in terms of it.

"It is in such a way, venerable sir, that I understand in detail the meaning of what was stated by the Blessed One in brief."

"Good, good, bhikkhu! It is good that you understand in detail the meaning of what was stated by me in brief. If, bhikkhu, one has an underlying tendency towards form … (*as above in full*) … then one is not reckoned in terms of it. It is in such a way that the meaning of what was stated by me in brief should be understood in detail."

Then that bhikkhu, having delighted and rejoiced in the Blessed One's statement, [36] rose from his seat, and, after paying homage to the Blessed One, keeping him on his right, he departed.

Then, dwelling alone, withdrawn, diligent, ardent, and resolute, that bhikkhu, by realizing it for himself with direct knowledge, in this very life entered and dwelt in that unsurpassed goal of the holy life for the sake of which clansmen rightly go forth from the household life into homelessness. He directly knew: "Destroyed is birth, the holy life has been lived, what had to be done has been done, there is no more for this state of being." And that bhikkhu became one of the arahants.[48]

36 (4) A Certain Bhikkhu (2)

At Sāvatthī. Then a certain bhikkhu approached the Blessed One, paid homage to him, sat down to one side, and said to him: "Venerable sir, it would be good if the Blessed One would teach me the Dhamma in brief, so that, having heard the Dhamma from the Blessed One, I might dwell alone, withdrawn, diligent, ardent, and resolute."

"Bhikkhu, if one has an underlying tendency towards something, then one is measured in accordance with it;[49] if one is measured in accordance with something, then one is reckoned in terms of it. If one does not have an underlying tendency towards something, then one is not measured in accordance with it; if one is not measured in accordance with something, then one is not reckoned in terms of it."

"Understood, Blessed One! Understood, Fortunate One!"

"In what way, bhikkhu, do you understand in detail the meaning of what was stated by me in brief?"

"If, venerable sir, one has an underlying tendency towards form, then one is measured in accordance with it; if one is measured in accordance with it, then one is reckoned in terms of it. If one has an underlying tendency towards feeling ... towards perception ... towards volitional formations ... towards consciousness, then one is measured in accordance with it; if one is measured in accordance with it, then one is reckoned in terms of it.

"If, venerable sir, one does not have an underlying tendency towards form, then one is not measured in accordance with it; [37] if one is not measured in accordance with it, then one is not reckoned in terms of it. If one does not have an underlying tendency towards feeling ... towards perception ... towards volitional formations ... towards consciousness, then one is not measured in accordance with it; if one is not measured in accordance with it, then one is not reckoned in terms of it.

"It is in such a way, venerable sir, that I understand in detail the meaning of what was stated by the Blessed One in brief."

"Good, good, bhikkhu! It is good that you understand in detail the meaning of what was stated by me in brief. If, bhikkhu, one has an underlying tendency towards form ... (*as above in full*) ... then one is not reckoned in terms of it. It is in such a way that the meaning of what was stated by me in brief should be understood in detail."

Then that bhikkhu, having delighted and rejoiced in the Blessed One's words, rose from his seat ... And that bhikkhu became one of the arahants.

37 (5) Ānanda (1)

At Sāvatthī. Then the Venerable Ānanda approached the Blessed One.... The Blessed One then said to the Venerable Ānanda as he was sitting to one side:

"If, Ānanda, they were to ask you: 'Friend Ānanda, what are the things of which an arising is discerned, a vanishing is discerned, an alteration of that which stands is discerned?'—being asked thus, how would you answer?"[50] [38]

"Venerable sir, if they were to ask me this, I would answer thus: 'Friends, with form an arising is discerned, a vanishing is discerned, an alteration of that which stands is discerned. With feeling ... perception ... volitional formations ... consciousness an arising is discerned, a vanishing is discerned, an alteration of that which stands is discerned. These, friends, are the things of which an arising is discerned, a vanishing is discerned, an alteration of that which stands is discerned.' Being asked thus, venerable sir, I would answer in such a way."

"Good, good, Ānanda! With form, Ānanda, an arising is discerned, a vanishing is discerned, an alteration of that which stands is discerned. With feeling ... perception ... volitional formations ... consciousness an arising is discerned, a vanishing is discerned, an alteration of that which stands is discerned. These, Ānanda, are the things of which an arising is discerned, a vanishing is discerned, an alteration of that which stands is discerned. Being asked thus, Ānanda, you should answer in such a way."

38 (6) Ānanda (2)

At Sāvatthī.... The Blessed One then said to the Venerable Ānanda as he was sitting to one side:

"If, Ānanda, they were to ask you: 'Friend Ānanda, what are the things of which an arising was discerned, a vanishing was discerned, an alteration of that which stands was discerned?

What are the things of which an arising will be discerned, a vanishing will be discerned, an alteration of that which stands will be discerned? What are the things of which an arising is discerned, a vanishing is discerned, an alteration of that which stands is discerned?'—being asked thus, Ānanda, how would you answer?"

"Venerable sir, if they were to ask me this, [39] I would answer thus: 'Friends, with form that has passed, ceased, changed, an arising was discerned, a vanishing was discerned, an alteration of that which stands was discerned. With feeling … perception … volitional formations … consciousness that has passed, ceased, changed, an arising was discerned, a vanishing was discerned, an alteration of that which stands was discerned. It is of these things, friends, that an arising was discerned, that a vanishing was discerned, that an alteration of that which stands was discerned.

"'Friends, with form that has not been born, not become manifest, an arising will be discerned, a vanishing will be discerned, an alteration of that which stands will be discerned. With feeling … perception … volitional formations … consciousness that has not been born, not become manifest, an arising will be discerned, a vanishing will be discerned, an alteration of that which stands will be discerned. It is of these things, friends, that an arising will be discerned, that a vanishing will be discerned, that an alteration of that which stands will be discerned.

"'Friends, with form that has been born, that has become manifest, an arising is discerned, a vanishing is discerned, an alteration of that which stands is discerned. With feeling … perception … volitional formations … consciousness that has been born, that has become manifest, an arising is discerned, a vanishing is discerned, an alteration of that which stands is discerned. It is of these things, friends, that an arising is discerned, that a vanishing is discerned, that an alteration of that which stands is discerned.'

"Being asked thus, venerable sir, I would answer in such a way."

"Good, good, Ānanda!"

(*The Buddha here repeats the entire answer of the Venerable Ānanda, concluding*:) [40]

"Being asked thus, Ānanda, you should answer in such a way."

39 (7) In Accordance with the Dhamma (1)

At Sāvatthī. "Bhikkhus, when a bhikkhu is practising in accordance with the Dhamma,[51] this is what accords with the Dhamma: he should dwell engrossed in revulsion towards form, feeling, perception, volitional formations, and consciousness.[52] One who dwells engrossed in revulsion towards form … and consciousness, fully understands form, feeling, perception, volitional formations, and consciousness. One who fully understands form … and consciousness is freed from form, [41] feeling, perception, volitional formations, and consciousness. He is freed from birth, aging, and death; freed from sorrow, lamentation, pain, displeasure, and despair; freed from suffering, I say."

40 (8) In Accordance with the Dhamma (2)

At Sāvatthī. "Bhikkhus, when a bhikkhu is practising in accordance with the Dhamma, this is what accords with the Dhamma: he should dwell contemplating impermanence in form … (*as above*) … he is freed from suffering, I say."

41 (9) In Accordance with the Dhamma (3)

… "he should dwell contemplating suffering in form … (*as above*) … he is freed from suffering, I say."

42 (10) In Accordance with the Dhamma (4)

… "he should dwell contemplating nonself in form … (*as above*) … he is freed from suffering, I say."

[42] V. WITH YOURSELVES AS AN ISLAND

43 (1) With Yourselves as an Island

At Sāvatthī. "Bhikkhus, dwell with yourselves as an island, with yourselves as a refuge, with no other refuge; with the Dhamma as an island, with the Dhamma as a refuge, with no other refuge.[53] When you dwell with yourselves as an island, with yourselves as a refuge, with no other refuge; with the Dhamma as an island, with the Dhamma as a refuge, with no other refuge, the basis itself should be investigated thus:[54] 'From what are sorrow, lamentation, pain, displeasure, and despair born? How are they produced?'

"And, bhikkhus, from what are sorrow, lamentation, pain, displeasure, and despair born? How are they produced? Here, bhikkhus, the uninstructed worldling, who is not a seer of the noble ones and is unskilled and undisciplined in their Dhamma, who is not a seer of superior persons and is unskilled and undisciplined in their Dhamma, regards form as self, or self as possessing form, or form as in self, or self as in form. That form of his changes and alters. With the change and alteration of form, there arise in him sorrow, lamentation, pain, displeasure, and despair.

"He regards feeling as self ... perception as self ... volitional formations as self ... consciousness as self, or self as possessing consciousness, or consciousness as in self, or self as in consciousness. [43] That consciousness of his changes and alters. With the change and alteration of consciousness, there arise in him sorrow, lamentation, pain, displeasure, and despair.

"But, bhikkhus, when one has understood the impermanence of form, its change, fading away, and cessation, and when one sees as it really is with correct wisdom thus: 'In the past and also now all form is impermanent, suffering, and subject to change,' then sorrow, lamentation, pain, displeasure, and despair are abandoned. With their abandonment, one does not become agitated.[55] Being unagitated, one dwells happily. A bhikkhu who dwells happily is said to be quenched in that respect.[56]

"When one has understood the impermanence of feeling ... of perception ... of volitional formations ... of consciousness, its change, fading away, and cessation, and when one sees as it really is with correct wisdom thus: 'In the past and also now all consciousness is impermanent, suffering, and subject to change,' then sorrow, lamentation, pain, displeasure, and despair are abandoned. With their abandonment, one does not become agitated. Being unagitated, one dwells happily. A bhikkhu who dwells happily is said to be quenched in that respect."

44 (2) The Way

At Sāvatthī. [44] "Bhikkhus, I will teach you the way leading to the origination of identity and the way leading to the cessation of identity. Listen to that....

"And what, bhikkhus, is the way leading to the origination of identity? Here, bhikkhus, the uninstructed worldling ... regards form as self ... feeling as self ... perception as self ... volitional formations as self ... consciousness as self ... or self as in consciousness. This, bhikkhus, is called the way leading to the origination of identity. When it is said, 'The way leading to the origination of identity,' the meaning here is this: a way of regarding things that leads to the origination of suffering.[57]

"And what, bhikkhus, is the way leading to the cessation of identity? Here, bhikkhus, the instructed noble disciple ... does not regard form as self ... nor feeling as self ... nor perception as self ... nor volitional formations as self ... nor consciousness as self ... nor self as in consciousness. This, bhikkhus, is called the way leading to the cessation of identity. When it is said, 'The way leading to the cessation of identity,' the meaning here is this: a way of regarding things that leads to the cessation of suffering."

45 (3) Impermanent (1)

At Sāvatthī. "Bhikkhus, form is impermanent. What is impermanent is suffering. [45] What is suffering is nonself. What is nonself should be seen as it really is with correct wisdom thus: 'This is not mine, this I am not, this is not my self.' When one sees this thus as it really is with correct wisdom, the mind becomes dispassionate and is liberated from the taints by nonclinging.[58]

"Feeling is impermanent.... Perception is impermanent.... Volitional formations are impermanent.... Consciousness is impermanent. What is impermanent is suffering. What is suffering is nonself. What is nonself should be seen as it really is with correct wisdom thus: 'This is not mine, this I am not, this is not my self.' When one sees this thus as it really is with correct wisdom, the mind becomes dispassionate and is liberated from the taints by nonclinging.

"If, bhikkhus, a bhikkhu's mind has become dispassionate towards the form element, it is liberated from the taints by nonclinging. If his mind has become dispassionate towards the feeling element ... towards the perception element ... towards the volitional formations element ... towards the consciousness element, it is liberated from the taints by nonclinging.

"By being liberated, it is steady; by being steady, it is content; by being content, he is not agitated. Being unagitated, he personally attains Nibbāna. He understands: 'Destroyed is birth, the holy life has been lived, what had to be done has been done, there is no more for this state of being.'"[59]

46 (4) Impermanent (2)

At Sāvatthī. "Bhikkhus, form is impermanent.... Feeling is impermanent.... Perception is impermanent.... Volitional formations are impermanent.... Consciousness is impermanent. What is impermanent is suffering. What is suffering is nonself. What is nonself should be seen as it really is with correct wisdom thus: 'This is not mine, this I am not, this is not my self.'

"When one sees this thus as it really is with correct wisdom, one holds no more views concerning the past. When one holds no more views concerning the past, [46] one holds no more views concerning the future. When one holds no more views concerning the future, one has no more obstinate grasping.[60] When one has no more obstinate grasping, the mind becomes dispassionate towards form, feeling, perception, volitional formations, and consciousness, and is liberated from the taints by nonclinging.

"By being liberated, it is steady; by being steady, it is content; by being content, one is not agitated. Being unagitated, one personally attains Nibbāna. One understands: 'Destroyed is birth, the holy life has been lived, what had to be done has been done, there is no more for this state of being.'"

47 (5) Ways of Regarding Things

At Sāvatthī. "Bhikkhus, those ascetics and brahmins who regard [anything as] self in various ways all regard [as self] the five aggregates subject to clinging, or a certain one among them. What five?

"Here, bhikkhus, the uninstructed worldling, who is not a seer of the noble ones and is unskilled and undisciplined in their Dhamma, who is not a seer of superior persons and is unskilled and undisciplined in their Dhamma, regards form as self, or self as possessing form, or form as in self, or self as in form. He regards feeling as self ... perception as self ... volitional formations as self ... consciousness as self, or self as possessing consciousness, or consciousness as in self, or self as in consciousness.

"Thus this way of regarding things and [the notion] 'I am' have not vanished in him.[61] As 'I am' has not vanished, there takes place a descent of the five faculties—of the eye faculty, the ear faculty, the nose faculty, the tongue faculty, the body faculty.[62] There is, bhikkhus, the mind, there are mental phenomena, there is the element of ignorance. When the uninstructed worldling is contacted by a feeling born of ignorance-contact, 'I am' occurs to him; 'I am this' occurs to him; 'I will be' and 'I will not be,' and 'I will consist of form' and 'I will be formless,' and 'I will be percipient' and 'I will be nonpercipient' and 'I will be neither percipient nor nonpercipient'—these occur to him.[63] [47]

"The five faculties remain right there, bhikkhus, but in regard to them the instructed noble disciple abandons ignorance and arouses true knowledge. With the fading away of ignorance and the arising of true knowledge, 'I am' does not occur to him; 'I am this' does not occur to him; 'I will be' and 'I will not be,' and 'I will consist of form' and 'I will be formless,' and 'I will be percipient' and 'I will be nonpercipient' and 'I will be neither percipient nor nonpercipient'—these do not occur to him."

48 (6) Aggregates

At Sāvatthī. "Bhikkhus, I will teach you the five aggregates and the five aggregates subject to clinging. Listen to that....

"And what, bhikkhus, are the five aggregates? Whatever kind of form there is, whether past, future, or present, internal or external, gross or subtle, inferior or superior, far or near: this is called the form aggregate.[64] Whatever kind of feeling there is ... this is called the feeling aggregate. Whatever kind of perception there is ... this is called the perception aggregate. Whatever kind of volitional formations there are ... these are called the volitional formations aggregate. Whatever kind of consciousness there is, whether past, future, or present, internal or external, gross or subtle, inferior or superior, far or near: this is called the consciousness aggregate. These, bhikkhus, are called the five aggregates.

"And what, bhikkhus, are the five aggregates subject to clinging? Whatever kind of form there is, whether past, future, or present ... far or near, that is tainted, that can be clung to: this is called the form aggregate subject to clinging. Whatever kind of feeling there is ... that is tainted, that can be clung to: this is called the feeling aggregate subject to clinging. Whatever kind of perception there is ... that is tainted, that can be clung to: this is called the perception aggregate subject to clinging. Whatever kind of volitional formations there are ... that are tainted, that can be clung to: these are called the volitional formations aggregate subject to clinging. [48] Whatever kind of consciousness there is, whether past, future, or present, internal or external, gross or subtle, inferior or superior, far or near, that is tainted, that can be clung to: this is called the consciousness aggregate subject to clinging. These, bhikkhus, are called the five aggregates subject to clinging."[65]

49 (7) Soṇa (1)

Thus have I heard. On one occasion the Blessed One was dwelling at Rājagaha in the Bamboo Grove, the Squirrel Sanctuary. Then Soṇa the householder's son approached the Blessed One.... The Blessed One then said to Soṇa the householder's son:

"Soṇa, when any ascetics and brahmins, on the basis of form—which is impermanent, suffering, and subject to change—regard themselves thus: 'I am superior,' or 'I am equal,' or 'I am inferior,' what is that due to apart from not seeing things as they really are?[66]

"When any ascetics and brahmins, on the basis of feeling ... on the basis of perception ... on the basis of volitional formations ... on the basis of consciousness—which is impermanent, suffering, and subject to change—regard themselves thus: 'I am superior,' or 'I am equal,' or 'I am inferior,' what is that due to apart from not seeing things as they really are?

"Soṇa, when any ascetics and brahmins do not, on the basis of form—which is impermanent, suffering, and subject to change—regard themselves thus: 'I am superior,' or 'I am equal,' [49] or 'I am inferior,' what is that due to apart from seeing things as they really are?

"When any ascetics and brahmins do not, on the basis of feeling ... on the basis of perception ... on the basis of volitional formations ... on the basis of consciousness—which is impermanent, suffering, and subject to change—regard themselves thus: 'I am superior,' or 'I am equal,' or 'I am inferior,' what is that due to apart from seeing things as they really are?

"What do you think, Soṇa, is form permanent or impermanent?" – "Impermanent, venerable sir." – "Is what is impermanent suffering or happiness?" – "Suffering, venerable sir." – "Is what is impermanent, suffering, and subject to change fit to be regarded thus: 'This is mine, this I am, this is my self'?" – "No, venerable sir."

"Is feeling permanent or impermanent?... Is perception permanent or impermanent?... Are volitional formations permanent or impermanent?... Is consciousness permanent or impermanent?" – "Impermanent, venerable sir." – "Is what is impermanent suffering or happiness?" – "Suffering, venerable sir." – "Is what is impermanent, suffering, and subject to change fit to be regarded thus: 'This is mine, this I am, this is my self'?" – "No, venerable sir."

"Therefore, Soṇa, any kind of form whatsoever, whether past, future, or present, internal or external, gross or subtle, inferior or superior, far or near, all form should be seen as it really is with correct wisdom thus: 'This is not mine, this I am not, this is not my self.'

"Any kind of feeling whatsoever ... Any kind of perception whatsoever ... Any kind of volitional formations whatsoever ... Any kind of consciousness whatsoever, whether past, future, or present, [50] internal or external, gross or subtle, inferior or superior, far or near, all consciousness should be seen as it really is with correct wisdom thus: 'This is not mine, this I am not, this is not my self.'

"Seeing thus, Soṇa, the instructed noble disciple experiences revulsion towards form, revulsion towards feeling, revulsion towards perception, revulsion towards volitional formations, revulsion towards consciousness. Experiencing revulsion, he becomes dispassionate. Through dispassion [his mind] is liberated. When it is liberated there comes the knowledge: 'It's liberated.' He understands: 'Destroyed is birth, the holy life has been lived, what had to be done has been done, there is no more for this state of being.'"

50 (8) Soṇa (2)

Thus have I heard. On one occasion the Blessed One was dwelling at Rājagaha in the Bamboo Grove, the Squirrel Sanctuary. Then Soṇa the householder's son approached the Blessed One.... The Blessed One then said to Soṇa the householder's son:

"Soṇa, those ascetics or brahmins who do not understand form, its origin, its cessation, and the way leading to its cessation; who do not understand feeling ... perception ... volitional formations ... consciousness, its origin, its cessation, and the way leading to its cessation: these I do not consider to be ascetics among ascetics or brahmins among brahmins, and these venerable ones do not, by realizing it for themselves with direct knowledge, in this very life enter and dwell in the goal of asceticism or the goal of brahminhood.[67]

"But, Soṇa, those ascetics and brahmins who understand form, [51] its origin, its cessation, and the way leading to its cessation; who understand feeling ... perception ... volitional formations ... consciousness, its origin, its cessation, and the way leading to its cessation: these I consider to be ascetics among ascetics and brahmins among brahmins, and these venerable ones, by realizing it for themselves with direct knowledge, in this very life enter and dwell in the goal of asceticism and the goal of brahminhood."

51 (9) Destruction of Delight (1)

At Sāvatthī. "Bhikkhus, a bhikkhu sees as impermanent form which is actually impermanent: that is his right view. Seeing rightly, he experiences revulsion. With the destruction of delight comes the destruction of lust; with the destruction of lust comes the destruction of delight. With the destruction of delight and lust the mind is liberated and is said to be well liberated.[68]

"A bhikkhu sees as impermanent feeling which is actually impermanent ... perception which is actually impermanent ... volitional formations which are actually impermanent ... consciousness which is actually impermanent: that is his right view.... With the destruction of delight and lust the mind is liberated and is said to be well liberated."

52 (10) Destruction of Delight (2)

At Sāvatthī. [52] "Bhikkhus, attend carefully to form. Recognize the impermanence of form as it really is. When a bhikkhu attends carefully to form and recognizes the impermanence of form as it really is, he experiences revulsion towards form. With the destruction of delight comes the destruction of lust; with the destruction of lust comes the destruction of delight. With the destruction of delight and lust the mind is liberated and is said to be well liberated.

"Bhikkhus, attend carefully to feeling ... to perception ... to volitional formations ... to consciousness.... With the destruction of delight and lust the mind is liberated and is said to be well liberated."

[53]

Division II
The Middle Fifty

I. Engagement

53 (1) Engagement

At Sāvatthī. "Bhikkhus, one who is engaged is unliberated;[69] one who is disengaged is liberated. Consciousness, bhikkhus, while standing, might stand engaged with form; based upon form, established upon form, with a sprinkling of delight, it might come to growth, increase, and expansion. Or consciousness, while standing, might stand [engaged with feeling ... engaged with perception ...] engaged with volitional formations; based upon volitional formations, established upon volitional formations, with a sprinkling of delight, it might come to growth, increase, and expansion.[70]

"Bhikkhus, though someone might say: 'Apart from form, apart from feeling, apart from perception, apart from volitional formations, I will make known the coming and going of consciousness, its passing away and rebirth, its growth, increase, and expansion'—that is impossible.

"Bhikkhus, if a bhikkhu has abandoned lust for the form element, with the abandoning of lust the basis is cut off: there is no support for the establishing of consciousness.[71] If he has abandoned lust for the feeling element … for the perception element … for the volitional formations element … for the consciousness element, with the abandoning of lust the basis is cut off: there is no support for the establishing of consciousness.

"When that consciousness is unestablished, not coming to growth, nongenerative, [54] it is liberated.[72] By being liberated, it is steady; by being steady, it is content; by being content, he is not agitated. Being unagitated, he personally attains Nibbāna. He understands: 'Destroyed is birth, the holy life has been lived, what had to be done has been done, there is no more for this state of being.'"

54 (2) Seeds

At Sāvatthī. "Bhikkhus, there are these five kinds of seeds. What five? Root-seeds, stem-seeds, joint-seeds, cutting-seeds, and germ-seeds as the fifth.[73] If these five kinds of seeds are unbroken, unspoilt, undamaged by wind and sun, fertile, securely planted, but there is no earth or water, would these five kinds of seeds come to growth, increase, and expansion?"

"No, venerable sir."

"If these five kinds of seeds are broken, spoilt, damaged by wind and sun, unfertile, not securely planted, but there is earth and water, would these five kinds of seeds come to growth, increase, and expansion?"

"No, venerable sir."

"If these five kinds of seeds are unbroken, unspoilt, undamaged by wind and sun, fertile, securely planted, and there is earth and water, would these five kinds of seeds come to growth, increase, and expansion?"

"Yes, venerable sir."

"Bhikkhus, the four stations of consciousness should be seen as like the earth element. Delight and lust should be seen as like the water element. Consciousness together with its nutriment should be seen as like the five kinds of seeds.[74]

"Consciousness, bhikkhus, while standing, might stand engaged with form; [55] based upon form, established upon form, with a sprinkling of delight, it might come to growth, increase, and expansion. Or consciousness, while standing, might stand engaged with feeling … engaged with perception … engaged with volitional formations; based upon volitional formations, established upon volitional formations, with a sprinkling of delight, it might come to growth, increase, and expansion.

"Bhikkhus, though someone might say: 'Apart from form, apart from feeling, apart from perception, apart from volitional formations, I will make known the coming and going of consciousness, its passing away and rebirth, its growth, increase, and expansion'—that is impossible.

"Bhikkhus, if a bhikkhu has abandoned lust for the form element, with the abandoning of lust the basis is cut off: there is no support for the establishing of consciousness. If he has abandoned lust for the feeling element ... for the perception element ... for the volitional formations element ... for the consciousness element, with the abandoning of lust the basis is cut off: there is no support for the establishing of consciousness.

"When that consciousness is unestablished, not coming to growth, nongenerative, it is liberated. By being liberated, it is steady; by being steady, it is content; by being content, he is not agitated. Being unagitated, he personally attains Nibbāna. He understands: 'Destroyed is birth, the holy life has been lived, what had to be done has been done, there is no more for this state of being.'"

55 (3) Inspired Utterance

At Sāvatthī. There the Blessed One uttered this inspired utterance: "'It might not be, and it might not be for me; it will not be, [and] it will not be for me': [56] resolving thus, a bhikkhu can cut off the lower fetters."[75]

When this was said, a certain bhikkhu said to the Blessed One: "But how, venerable sir, can a bhikkhu, resolving thus: 'It might not be, and it might not be for me; it will not be, [and] it will not be for me,' cut off the lower fetters?"

"Here, bhikkhu, the uninstructed worldling, who is not a seer of the noble ones ... regards form as self ... or self as in consciousness.

"He does not understand as it really is impermanent form as 'impermanent form' ... impermanent feeling as 'impermanent feeling' ... impermanent perception as 'impermanent perception' ... impermanent volitional formations as 'impermanent volitional formations' ... impermanent consciousness as 'impermanent consciousness.'

"He does not understand as it really is painful form as 'painful form' ... painful feeling as 'painful feeling' ... painful perception as 'painful perception' ... painful volitional formations as 'painful volitional formations' ... painful consciousness as 'painful consciousness.'

"He does not understand as it really is selfless form as 'selfless form' ... selfless feeling as 'selfless feeling' ... selfless perception as 'selfless perception' ... selfless volitional formations as 'selfless volitional formations' ... selfless consciousness as 'selfless consciousness.'

"He does not understand as it really is conditioned form as 'conditioned form' ... conditioned feeling as 'conditioned feeling' ... conditioned perception as 'conditioned perception' ... conditioned volitional formations as 'conditioned volitional formations' ... conditioned consciousness as 'conditioned consciousness.'

"He does not understand as it really is: 'Form will be exterminated' ... 'Feeling will be exterminated' ... 'Perception will be exterminated' ... 'Volitional formations will be exterminated' ... 'Consciousness will be exterminated.'[76] [57]

"The instructed noble disciple, bhikkhu, who is a seer of the noble ones ... does not regard form as self ... or self as in consciousness.

"He understands as it really is impermanent form as 'impermanent form' ... impermanent consciousness as 'impermanent consciousness.'

"He understands as it really is painful form as 'painful form' ... painful consciousness as 'painful consciousness.'

"He understands as it really is selfless form as 'selfless form' ... selfless consciousness as 'selfless consciousness.'

"He understands as it really is conditioned form as 'conditioned form' ... conditioned consciousness as 'conditioned consciousness.'

"He understands as it really is: 'Form will be exterminated' ... 'Feeling will be exterminated' ... 'Perception will be exterminated' ... 'Volitional formations will be exterminated' ... 'Consciousness will be exterminated.'

"With the extermination of form, feeling, perception, volitional formations, and consciousness, that bhikkhu, resolving thus: 'It might not be, and it might not be for me; it will not be, [and] it will not be for me,' can cut off the lower fetters."[77]

"Resolving thus, venerable sir, a bhikkhu can cut off the lower fetters. But how should one know, how should one see, for the immediate destruction of the taints to occur?"[78]

"Here, bhikkhu, the uninstructed worldling becomes frightened over an unfrightening matter. For this is frightening to the uninstructed worldling: 'It might not be, and it might not be for me; it will not be, [and] it will not be for me.' But the instructed noble disciple does not become frightened over an unfrightening matter. For this is not frightening to the noble disciple: 'It might not be, and it might not be for me; it will not be, [and] it will not be for me.'[79] [58]

"Consciousness, bhikkhu, while standing, might stand engaged with form ... engaged with feeling ... engaged with perception ... engaged with volitional formations; based upon volitional formations, established upon volitional formations, with a sprinkling of delight, it might come to growth, increase, and expansion.

"Bhikkhu, though someone might say: 'Apart from form, apart from feeling, apart from perception, apart from volitional formations, I will make known the coming and going of consciousness, its passing away and rebirth, its growth, increase, and expansion'—that is impossible.

"Bhikkhu, if a bhikkhu has abandoned lust for the form element, with the abandoning of lust the basis is cut off: there is no support for the establishing of consciousness. If he has abandoned lust for the feeling element ... for the perception element ... for the volitional formations element ... for the consciousness element, with the abandoning of lust the basis is cut off: there is no support for the establishing of consciousness.

"When that consciousness is unestablished, not coming to growth, nongenerative, it is liberated. By being liberated, it is steady; by being steady, it is content; by being content, he is not agitated. Being unagitated, he personally attains Nibbāna. He understands: 'Destroyed is birth, the holy life has been lived, what had to be done has been done, there is no more for this state of being.'

"It is, bhikkhu, for one who knows thus, for one who sees thus, that the immediate destruction of the taints occurs."

56 (4) Phases of the Clinging Aggregates

At Sāvatthī. "Bhikkhus, there are these five aggregates subject to clinging. What five? The form aggregate subject to clinging, [59] the feeling aggregate subject to clinging, the perception aggregate subject to clinging, the volitional formations aggregate subject to clinging, the consciousness aggregate subject to clinging.

"So long as I did not directly know as they really are the five aggregates subject to clinging in four phases,[80] I did not claim to have awakened to the unsurpassed perfect enlightenment in this world with its devas, Māra, and Brahmā, in this generation with its ascetics and brahmins, its devas and humans. But when I directly knew all this as it really is, then I claimed to have awakened to the unsurpassed perfect enlightenment in this world with … its devas and humans.

"And how, bhikkhus, are there four phases? I directly knew form, its origin, its cessation, and the way leading to its cessation. I directly knew feeling … perception … volitional formations … consciousness, its origin, its cessation, and the way leading to its cessation.

"And what, bhikkhus, is form? The four great elements and the form derived from the four great elements: this is called form. With the arising of nutriment there is the arising of form. With the cessation of nutriment there is the cessation of form. This Noble Eightfold Path is the way leading to the cessation of form; that is, right view … right concentration.[81]

"Whatever ascetics and brahmins, having thus directly known form, its origin, its cessation, and the way leading to its cessation, are practising for the purpose of revulsion towards form, for its fading away and cessation, they are practising well. Those who are practising well have gained a foothold in this Dhamma and Discipline.[82]

"And whatever ascetics and brahmins, having thus directly known form, its origin, its cessation, and the way leading to its cessation, through revulsion towards form, through its fading away and cessation, are liberated by nonclinging, they are well liberated. Those who are well liberated are consummate ones. As to those consummate ones, there is no round for describing them.[83]

"And what, bhikkhus, is feeling? [60] There are these six classes of feeling: feeling born of eye-contact, feeling born of ear-contact, feeling born of nose-contact, feeling born of tongue-contact, feeling born of body-contact, feeling born of mind-contact. This is called feeling. With the arising of contact there is the arising of feeling.[84] With the cessation of contact there is the cessation of feeling. This Noble Eightfold Path is the way leading to the cessation of feeling; that is, right view ... right concentration.

"Whatever ascetics and brahmins, having thus directly known feeling, its origin, its cessation, and the way leading to its cessation, are practising for the purpose of revulsion towards feeling, for its fading away and cessation, they are practising well. Those who are practising well have gained a foothold in this Dhamma and Discipline.

"And whatever ascetics and brahmins, having thus directly known feeling ... and the way leading to its cessation ... As to those consummate ones, there is no round for describing them.

"And what, bhikkhus, is perception? There are these six classes of perception: perception of forms, perception of sounds, perception of odours, perception of tastes, perception of tactile objects, perception of mental phenomena. This is called perception. With the arising of contact there is the arising of perception. With the cessation of contact there is the cessation of perception. This Noble Eightfold Path is the way leading to the cessation of perception; that is, right view ... right concentration.

"Whatever ascetics and brahmins ... As to those consummate ones, there is no round for describing them.

"And what, bhikkhus, are volitional formations? There are these six classes of volition:[85] volition regarding forms, volition regarding sounds, volition regarding odours, volition regarding tastes, volition regarding tactile objects, volition regarding mental phenomena. This is called volitional formations. With the arising of contact there is the arising of volitional formations. With the cessation of contact there is the cessation of volitional formations. This Noble Eightfold Path is the way leading to the cessation of volitional formations; that is, right view ... right concentration.

"Whatever ascetics and brahmins ... [61] ... As to those consummate ones, there is no round for describing them.

"And what, bhikkhus, is consciousness? There are these six classes of consciousness: eye-consciousness, ear-consciousness, nose-consciousness, tongue-consciousness, body-consciousness, mind-consciousness. This is called consciousness. With the arising of name-and-form there is the arising of consciousness. With the cessation of name-and-form there is the cessation of consciousness. This Noble Eightfold Path is the way leading to the cessation of consciousness; that is, right view ... right concentration.[86]

"Whatever ascetics and brahmins, having thus directly known consciousness, its origin, its cessation, and the way leading to its cessation, are practising for the purpose of revulsion towards consciousness, for its fading away and cessation, they are practising well. Those who are practising well have gained a foothold in this Dhamma and Discipline.

"And whatever ascetics and brahmins, having thus directly known consciousness, its origin, its cessation, and the way leading to its cessation, through revulsion towards consciousness, through its fading away and cessation, are liberated by nonclinging, they are well liberated. Those who are well liberated are consummate ones. As to those consummate ones, there is no round for describing them."

57 (5) The Seven Cases

At Sāvatthī. "Bhikkhus, a bhikkhu who is skilled in seven cases and a triple investigator is called, in this Dhamma and Discipline, a consummate one, one who has fully lived the holy life, the highest kind of person.[87]

"And how, bhikkhus, is a bhikkhu skilled in seven cases? [62] Here, bhikkhus, a bhikkhu understands form, its origin, its cessation, and the way leading to its cessation; he understands the gratification, the danger, and the escape in the case of form.

"He understands feeling ... perception ... volitional formations ... consciousness, its origin, its cessation, and the way leading to its cessation; he understands the gratification, the danger, and the escape in the case of consciousness.

"And what, bhikkhus, is form? The four great elements and the form derived from the four great elements: this is called form. With the arising of nutriment there is the arising of form. With the cessation of nutriment there is the cessation of form. This Noble Eightfold Path is the way leading to the cessation of form; that is, right view ... right concentration.

"The pleasure and joy that arise in dependence on form: this is the gratification in form. That form is impermanent, suffering, and subject to change: this is the danger in form. The removal and abandonment of desire and lust for form: this is the escape from form.

"Whatever ascetics and brahmins, having thus directly known form, its origin, its cessation, and the way leading to its cessation, having thus directly known the gratification, the danger, and [63] the escape in the case of form, are practising for the purpose of revulsion towards form, for its fading away and cessation, they are practising well. Those who are practising well have gained a foothold in this Dhamma and Discipline.

"And whatever ascetics and brahmins, having thus directly known form, its origin, its cessation, and the way leading to its cessation, having thus directly known the gratification, the danger, and the escape in the case of form, through revulsion towards form, through its fading away and cessation, are liberated by nonclinging, they are well liberated. Those who are well liberated are consummate ones. As to those consummate ones, there is no round for describing them.

"And what, bhikkhus, is feeling? There are these six classes of feeling: feeling born of eye-contact ... (*as in preceding sutta*) ... feeling born of mind-contact. This is called feeling. With the arising of contact there is the arising of feeling. With the cessation of contact there is the cessation of feeling. This Noble Eightfold Path is the way leading to the cessation of feeling; that is, right view ... right concentration.

"The pleasure and joy that arise in dependence on feeling: this is the gratification in feeling. That feeling is impermanent, suffering, and subject to change: this is the danger in feeling. The removal and abandonment of desire and lust for feeling: this is the escape from feeling.

"Whatever ascetics and brahmins, having thus directly known feeling, its origin, its cessation, and the way leading to its cessation, having thus directly known the gratification, the danger, and the escape in the case of feeling, are practising for the purpose of revulsion towards feeling, for its fading away and cessation, they are practising well. Those who are practising well have gained a foothold in this Dhamma and Discipline.

"And whatever ascetics and brahmins, having thus directly

known feeling ... and the escape in the case of feeling ... As to those consummate ones, there is no round for describing them.

"And what, bhikkhus, is perception? There are these six classes of perception: perception of forms ... perception of mental phenomena. This is called perception. With the arising of contact there is the arising of perception. With the cessation of contact there is the cessation of perception. This Noble Eightfold Path is the way leading to the cessation of perception; that is, right view ... right concentration.

"The pleasure and joy that arise in dependence on perception: this is the gratification in perception. That perception is impermanent, suffering, and subject to change: this is the danger in perception. The removal and abandonment of desire and lust for perception: this is the escape from perception.

"Whatever ascetics and brahmins ... As to those consummate ones, there is no round for describing them.

"And what, bhikkhus, are volitional formations? There are these six classes of volition: volition regarding forms ... volition regarding mental phenomena. This is called volitional formations. With the arising of contact there is the arising of volitional formations. With the cessation of contact there is the cessation of volitional formations. [64] This Noble Eightfold Path is the way leading to the cessation of volitional formations; that is, right view ... right concentration.

"The pleasure and joy that arise in dependence on volitional formations: this is the gratification in volitional formations. That volitional formations are impermanent, suffering, and subject to change: this is the danger in volitional formations. The removal and abandonment of desire and lust for volitional formations: this is the escape from volitional formations.

"Whatever ascetics and brahmins ... As to those consummate ones, there is no round for describing them.

"And what, bhikkhus, is consciousness? There are these six classes of consciousness: eye-consciousness ... mind-consciousness. This is called consciousness. With the arising of name-and-form there is the arising of consciousness. With the cessation of name-and-form there is the cessation of consciousness. This Noble Eightfold Path is the way leading to the cessation of consciousness; that is, right view ... right concentration.

"The pleasure and joy that arise in dependence on consciousness:

this is the gratification in consciousness. That consciousness is impermanent, suffering, and subject to change: this is the danger in consciousness. The removal and abandonment of desire and lust for consciousness: this is the escape from consciousness.

"Whatever ascetics and brahmins, having thus directly known consciousness, its origin, its cessation, and the way leading to its cessation, having thus directly known the gratification, the danger, and the escape in the case of consciousness, are practising for the purpose of revulsion towards consciousness, for its fading away and cessation, they are practising well. Those who are practising well have gained a foothold in this Dhamma and Discipline. [65]

"And whatever ascetics and brahmins, having thus directly known consciousness, its origin, its cessation, and the way leading to its cessation, having thus directly known the gratification, the danger, and the escape in the case of consciousness, through revulsion towards consciousness, through its fading away and cessation, are liberated by nonclinging, they are well liberated. Those who are well liberated are consummate ones. As to those consummate ones, there is no round for describing them.

"It is in such a way, bhikkhus, that a bhikkhu is skilled in seven cases.

"And how, bhikkhus, is a bhikkhu a triple investigator? Here, bhikkhus, a bhikkhu investigates by way of the elements, by way of the sense bases, and by way of dependent origination. It is in such a way that a bhikkhu is a triple investigator.[88]

"Bhikkhus, a bhikkhu who is skilled in these seven cases and a triple investigator is called, in this Dhamma and Discipline, a consummate one, one who has fully lived the holy life, the highest kind of person."

58 (6) The Perfectly Enlightened One

At Sāvatthī. "Bhikkhus, the Tathāgata, the Arahant, the Perfectly Enlightened One, liberated by nonclinging through revulsion towards form, through its fading away and cessation, is called a Perfectly Enlightened One. A bhikkhu liberated by wisdom, liberated by nonclinging through revulsion towards form, through its fading away and cessation, is called one liberated by wisdom.[89]

"The Tathāgata, the Arahant, the Perfectly Enlightened One,

liberated by nonclinging through revulsion towards feeling ... perception ... volitional formations ... consciousness, through its fading away [66] and cessation, is called a Perfectly Enlightened One. A bhikkhu liberated by wisdom, liberated by nonclinging through revulsion towards feeling ... perception ... volitional formations ... consciousness, through its fading away and cessation, is called one liberated by wisdom.

"Therein, bhikkhus, what is the distinction, what is the disparity, what is the difference between the Tathāgata, the Arahant, the Perfectly Enlightened One, and a bhikkhu liberated by wisdom?"

"Venerable sir, our teachings are rooted in the Blessed One, guided by the Blessed One, take recourse in the Blessed One. It would be good if the Blessed One would clear up the meaning of this statement. Having heard it from him, the bhikkhus will remember it."

"Then listen and attend closely, bhikkhus, I will speak."

"Yes, venerable sir," the bhikkhus replied. The Blessed One said this:

"The Tathāgata, bhikkhus, the Arahant, the Perfectly Enlightened One, is the originator of the path unarisen before, the producer of the path unproduced before, the declarer of the path undeclared before. He is the knower of the path, the discoverer of the path, the one skilled in the path. And his disciples now dwell following that path and become possessed of it afterwards.

"This, bhikkhus, is the distinction, the disparity, the difference between the Tathāgata, the Arahant, the Perfectly Enlightened One, and a bhikkhu liberated by wisdom."

59 (7) The Characteristic of Nonself

Thus have I heard. On one occasion the Blessed One was dwelling at Bārāṇasī in the Deer Park at Isipatana.[90] There the Blessed One addressed the bhikkhus of the group of five thus: "Bhikkhus!"

"Venerable sir!" those bhikkhus replied. The Blessed One said this:

"Bhikkhus, form is nonself. For if, bhikkhus, form were self, this form would not lead to affliction, and it would be possible to have it of form: 'Let my form be thus; let my form not be thus.'

But because form is nonself, form leads to affliction, and it is not possible to have it of form: 'Let my form be thus; let my form not be thus.'[91]

"Feeling is nonself.... [67] ... Perception is nonself.... Volitional formations are nonself.... Consciousness is nonself. For if, bhikkhus, consciousness were self, this consciousness would not lead to affliction, and it would be possible to have it of consciousness: 'Let my consciousness be thus; let my consciousness not be thus.' But because consciousness is nonself, consciousness leads to affliction, and it is not possible to have it of consciousness: 'Let my consciousness be thus; let my consciousness not be thus.'

"What do you think, bhikkhus, is form permanent or impermanent?" – "Impermanent, venerable sir." – "Is what is impermanent suffering or happiness?" – "Suffering, venerable sir." – "Is what is impermanent, suffering, and subject to change fit to be regarded thus: 'This is mine, this I am, this is my self'?" – "No, venerable sir."

"Is feeling permanent or impermanent?... Is perception permanent or impermanent?... Are volitional formations permanent or impermanent?... Is consciousness permanent or impermanent?" – "Impermanent, venerable sir." – "Is what is impermanent suffering or happiness?" – [68] "Suffering, venerable sir." – "Is what is impermanent, suffering, and subject to change fit to be regarded thus: 'This is mine, this I am, this is my self'?" – "No, venerable sir."

"Therefore, bhikkhus, any kind of form whatsoever, whether past, future, or present, internal or external, gross or subtle, inferior or superior, far or near, all form should be seen as it really is with correct wisdom thus: 'This is not mine, this I am not, this is not my self.'

"Any kind of feeling whatsoever ... Any kind of perception whatsoever ... Any kind of volitional formations whatsoever ... Any kind of consciousness whatsoever, whether past, future, or present, internal or external, gross or subtle, inferior or superior, far or near, all consciousness should be seen as it really is with correct wisdom thus: 'This is not mine, this I am not, this is not my self.'

"Seeing thus, bhikkhus, the instructed noble disciple experiences revulsion towards form, revulsion towards feeling, revulsion towards perception, revulsion towards volitional formations, revulsion towards consciousness. Experiencing revulsion, he becomes dispassionate. Through dispassion [his mind] is liberated. When it is liberated there comes the knowledge: 'It's liberated.' He understands: 'Destroyed is birth, the holy life has been lived, what had to be done has been done, there is no more for this state of being.'"

That is what the Blessed One said. Elated, those bhikkhus delighted in the Blessed One's statement. And while this discourse was being spoken, the minds of the bhikkhus of the group of five were liberated from the taints by nonclinging.

60 (8) Mahāli

Thus have I heard. On one occasion the Blessed One was dwelling at Vesālī in the Great Wood in the Hall with the Peaked Roof. Then Mahāli the Licchavi approached the Blessed One [69] … and said to him:

"Venerable sir, Pūraṇa Kassapa speaks thus: 'There is no cause or condition for the defilement of beings; beings are defiled without cause or condition. There is no cause or condition for the purification of beings; beings are purified without cause or condition.' What does the Blessed One say about this?"[92]

"There is, Mahāli, a cause and condition for the defilement of beings; beings are defiled with cause and condition. There is a cause and condition for the purification of beings; beings are purified with cause and condition."

"But, venerable sir, what is the cause and condition for the defilement of beings? How is it that beings are defiled with cause and condition?"

"If, Mahāli, this form were exclusively suffering, immersed in suffering, steeped in suffering, and if it were not [also] steeped in pleasure, beings would not become enamoured with it. But because form is pleasurable, immersed in pleasure, steeped in pleasure, and is not steeped [only] in suffering, beings become enamoured with it.[93] By being enamoured with it, they are captivated by it, and by being captivated by it they are defiled. This, Mahāli, is a cause and condition for the defilement of beings; it is thus that beings are defiled with cause and condition.

"If, Mahāli, this feeling were exclusively suffering … If this perception ... these volitional formations ... [70] ... this consciousness were exclusively suffering ... beings would not become enamoured with it. But because consciousness is pleasurable ... beings become enamoured with it. By being enamoured with it, they are captivated by it, and by being captivated by it they are defiled. This too, Mahāli, is a cause and condition for the defilement of beings; it is thus that beings are defiled with cause and condition."

"But, venerable sir, what is the cause and condition for the purification of beings? How is it that beings are purified with cause and condition?"

"If, Mahāli, this form were exclusively pleasurable, immersed in pleasure, steeped in pleasure, and if it were not [also] steeped in suffering, beings would not experience revulsion towards it. But because form is suffering, immersed in suffering, steeped in suffering, and is not steeped [only] in pleasure, beings experience revulsion towards it. Experiencing revulsion, they become dispassionate, and through dispassion they are purified. This, Mahāli, is a cause and condition for the purification of beings; it is thus that beings are purified with cause and condition.

"If, Mahāli, this feeling were exclusively pleasurable ... If this perception ... these volitional formations ... this consciousness were exclusively pleasurable ... beings would not experience revulsion towards it. But because consciousness is suffering ... beings experience revulsion towards it. Experiencing revulsion, they become dispassionate, and through dispassion they are purified. [71] This too, Mahāli, is a cause and condition for the purification of beings; it is thus that beings are purified with cause and condition."

61 (9) Burning

At Sāvatthī. "Bhikkhus, form is burning, feeling is burning, perception is burning, volitional formations are burning, consciousness is burning.[94] Seeing thus, bhikkhus, the instructed noble disciple experiences revulsion towards form, revulsion towards feeling, revulsion towards perception, revulsion towards volitional formations, revulsion towards consciousness. Experiencing revulsion, he becomes dispassionate. Through dispassion [his mind] is liberated. When it is liberated there comes the knowledge: 'It's liberated.' He understands: 'Destroyed is birth, the holy life has been lived, what had to be done has been done, there is no more for this state of being.'"

62 (10) Pathways of Language

At Sāvatthī. "Bhikkhus, there are these three pathways of language, pathways of designation, pathways of description,[95] that are unmixed, that were never mixed, that are not being mixed, that will not be mixed, that are not rejected by wise ascetics and brahmins. What three?

"Whatever form, bhikkhus, has passed, ceased, changed: the term, label, and description 'was' applies to it, not the term 'is' or the term 'will be.'

"Whatever feeling ... Whatever perception ... Whatever volitional formations ... [72] Whatever consciousness has passed, ceased, changed: the term, label, and description 'was' applies to it, not the term 'is' or the term 'will be.'

"Whatever form, bhikkhus, has not been born, has not become manifest: the term, label, and description 'will be' applies to it, not the term 'is' or the term 'was.'

"Whatever feeling ... Whatever perception ... Whatever volitional formations ... Whatever consciousness has not been born, has not become manifest: the term, label, and description 'will be' applies to it, not the term 'is' or the term 'was.'

"Whatever form, bhikkhus, has been born, has become manifest: the term, label, and description 'is' applies to it, not the term 'was' or the term 'will be.'

"Whatever feeling ... Whatever perception ... Whatever volitional formations ... Whatever consciousness has been born, has become manifest: the term, label, and description 'is' applies to it, not the term 'was' or the term 'will be.'

"These, bhikkhus, are the three pathways of language, pathways of designation, pathways of description, that are unmixed, that were never mixed, that are not being mixed, [73] that will not be mixed, that are not rejected by wise ascetics and brahmins.

"Bhikkhus, even Vassa and Bañña of Ukkalā, proponents of noncausality, of the inefficacy of action, and of nihilism, did not think that these three pathways of language, pathways of designation, pathways of description should be criticized or scorned.

For what reason? Because they fear blame, attack, and condemnation."[96]

II. Arahants

63 (1) In Clinging

Thus have I heard. On one occasion the Blessed One was dwelling at Sāvatthī, in Jeta's Grove, Anāthapiṇḍika's Park. Then a certain bhikkhu approached the Blessed One, paid homage to him, sat down to one side, and said to him:

"Venerable sir, it would be good if the Blessed One would teach me the Dhamma in brief, so that, having heard the Dhamma from the Blessed One, I might dwell alone, withdrawn, diligent, ardent, and resolute."

"Bhikkhu, in clinging one is bound by Māra; by not clinging one is freed from the Evil One."[97] [74]

"Understood, Blessed One! Understood, Fortunate One!"

"In what way, bhikkhu, do you understand in detail the meaning of what was stated by me in brief?"

"In clinging to form, venerable sir, one is bound by Māra; by not clinging to it one is freed from the Evil One. In clinging to feeling ... to perception ... to volitional formations ... to consciousness one is bound by Māra; by not clinging to it one is freed from the Evil One.

"It is in such a way, venerable sir, that I understand in detail the meaning of what was stated by the Blessed One in brief."

"Good, good, bhikkhu! It is good that you understand in detail the meaning of what was stated by me in brief. In clinging to form, bhikkhu, one is bound by Māra ... (*as above in full*) ... by not clinging to it one is freed from the Evil One. It is in such a way that the meaning of what was stated by me in brief should be understood in detail."

Then that bhikkhu, having delighted and rejoiced in the Blessed One's words, rose from his seat, and, after paying homage to the Blessed One, keeping him on his right, he departed.

Then, dwelling alone, withdrawn, diligent, ardent, and resolute, that bhikkhu, by realizing it for himself with direct knowledge, in this very life entered and dwelt in that unsurpassed goal of the holy life for the sake of which clansmen rightly go forth from the household life into homelessness. He directly knew: "Destroyed is birth, the holy life has been lived, what had to be done has been done, there is no more for this state of being." And that bhikkhu became one of the arahants.

64 (2) In Conceiving

At Sāvatthī. Then a certain bhikkhu approached the Blessed One ... and said to him: [75]

"Venerable sir, it would be good if the Blessed One would teach me the Dhamma in brief...."

"Bhikkhu, in conceiving one is bound by Māra; by not conceiving one is freed from the Evil One."

"Understood, Blessed One! Understood, Fortunate One!"

"In what way, bhikkhu, do you understand in detail the meaning of what was stated by me in brief?"

"In conceiving form, venerable sir, one is bound by Māra; by not conceiving it one is freed from the Evil One. In conceiving feeling ... perception ... volitional formations ... consciousness one is bound by Māra; by not conceiving it one is freed from the Evil One.

"It is in such a way, venerable sir, that I understand in detail the meaning of what was stated by the Blessed One in brief."

"Good, good, bhikkhu! It is good that you understand in detail the meaning of what was stated by me in brief. In conceiving form, bhikkhu, one is bound by Māra ... (*as above in full*) ... by not conceiving it one is freed from the Evil One. It is in such a way that the meaning of what was stated by me in brief should be understood in detail."

... And that bhikkhu became one of the arahants.

65 (3) In Seeking Delight

At Sāvatthī. Then a certain bhikkhu approached the Blessed One ... and said to him:

"Venerable sir, it would be good if the Blessed One would teach me the Dhamma in brief...."

"Bhikkhu, in seeking delight one is bound by Māra; by not seeking delight one is freed from the Evil One."

"Understood, Blessed One! Understood, Fortunate One!"

"In what way, bhikkhu, do you understand in detail the meaning of what was stated by me in brief?"

"In seeking delight in form, venerable sir, one is bound by Māra; by not seeking delight in it one is freed from the Evil One. In seeking delight in feeling ... in perception ... in volitional formations ... in consciousness one is bound by Māra; by not seeking delight in it one is freed from the Evil One. [76]

"It is in such a way, venerable sir, that I understand in detail the meaning of what was stated by the Blessed One in brief."

"Good, good, bhikkhu! It is good that you understand in detail the meaning of what was stated by me in brief. In seeking delight in form, bhikkhu, one is bound by Māra ... (*as above in full*) ... by not seeking delight in it one is freed from the Evil One. It is in such a way that the meaning of what was stated by me in brief should be understood in detail."

... And that bhikkhu became one of the arahants.

66 (4) Impermanent

At Sāvatthī. Then a certain bhikkhu approached the Blessed One ... and said to him:

"Venerable sir, it would be good if the Blessed One would teach me the Dhamma in brief...."

"Bhikkhu, you should abandon desire for whatever is impermanent."

"Understood, Blessed One! Understood, Fortunate One!"

"In what way, bhikkhu, do you understand in detail the meaning of what was stated by me in brief?"

"Form, venerable sir, is impermanent; I should abandon desire for it. Feeling is impermanent ... Perception is impermanent ... Volitional formations are impermanent ... Consciousness is impermanent; I should abandon desire for it.

"It is in such a way, venerable sir, that I understand in detail the meaning of what was stated by the Blessed One in brief."

"Good, good, bhikkhu! It is good that you understand in detail the meaning of what was stated by me in brief. Form is impermanent ... Consciousness is impermanent; you should abandon desire for it. It is in such a way that the meaning of what was stated by me in brief should be understood in detail." [77]

... And that bhikkhu became one of the arahants.

67 (5) Suffering

(*Opening as in preceding sutta*:)

… "Bhikkhu, you should abandon desire for whatever is suffering."…

68 (6) Nonself

… "Bhikkhu, you should abandon desire for whatever is nonself."… [78]

69 (7) What Does Not Belong to Self

… "Bhikkhu, you should abandon desire for whatever does not belong to self."… [79]

70 (8) Whatever Appears Tantalizing

… "Bhikkhu, you should abandon desire for whatever appears tantalizing."…

71 (9) Rādha

At Sāvatthī. Then the Venerable Rādha approached the Blessed One, [80] paid homage to him, sat down to one side, and said to him:[98]

"Venerable sir, how should one know, how should one see so that, in regard to this body with consciousness and in regard to all external signs, I-making, mine-making, and the underlying tendency to conceit no longer occur within?"

"Any kind of form whatsoever, Rādha, whether past, future, or present, internal or external, gross or subtle, inferior or superior, far or near—one sees all form as it really is with correct wisdom thus: 'This is not mine, this I am not, this is not my self.'

"Any kind of feeling whatsoever … Any kind of perception whatsoever … Any kind of volitional formations whatsoever … Any kind of consciousness whatsoever, whether past, future, or present, internal or external, gross or subtle, inferior or superior, far or near—one sees all consciousness as it really is with correct wisdom thus: 'This is not mine, this I am not, this is not my self.'

"When one knows and sees thus, Rādha, then in regard to this body with consciousness and in regard to all external signs, I-making, mine-making, and the underlying tendency to conceit no longer occur within."

Then the Venerable Rādha ... became one of the arahants.

72 (10) Surādha

At Sāvatthī. Then the Venerable Surādha approached the Blessed One ... and said to him:

"Venerable sir, how should one know, how should one see so that, in regard to this body with consciousness and in regard to all external signs, the mind is rid of I-making, mine-making, and conceit, has transcended discrimination, and is peaceful and well liberated?"

"Any kind of form whatsoever, Surādha, whether past, future, or present ... far or near—having seen all form as it really is with correct wisdom thus: 'This is not mine, this I am not, this is not my self,' one is liberated by nonclinging.

"Any kind of feeling whatsoever ... Any kind of perception whatsoever ... Any kind of volitional formations whatsoever ... [81] Any kind of consciousness whatsoever, whether past, future, or present, internal or external, gross or subtle, inferior or superior, far or near—having seen all consciousness as it really is with correct wisdom thus: 'This is not mine, this I am not, this is not my self,' one is liberated by nonclinging.

"When one knows and sees thus, Surādha, then in regard to this body with consciousness and in regard to all external signs, the mind is rid of I-making, mine-making, and conceit, has transcended discrimination, and is peaceful and well liberated."

Then the Venerable Surādha ... became one of the arahants.

III. Being Devoured

73 (1) Gratification

At Sāvatthī. "Bhikkhus, the uninstructed worldling does not understand as it really is the gratification, the danger, and the escape in the case of form, feeling, perception, volitional formations, and consciousness.

"But, bhikkhus, the instructed noble disciple [82] understands as it really is the gratification, the danger, and the escape in the case of form, feeling, perception, volitional formations, and consciousness."

74 (2) Origin (1)

At Sāvatthī. "Bhikkhus, the uninstructed worldling does not understand as it really is the origin and the passing away, the gratification, the danger, and the escape in the case of form, feeling, perception, volitional formations, and consciousness.

"But, bhikkhus, the instructed noble disciple understands as it really is the origin and the passing away, the gratification, the danger, and the escape in the case of form, feeling, perception, volitional formations, and consciousness."

75 (3) Origin (2)

At Sāvatthī. "Bhikkhus, the instructed noble disciple understands as it really is the origin and the passing away, the gratification, the danger, and the escape in the case of form, feeling, perception, volitional formations, and consciousness."

76 (4) Arahants (1)

At Sāvatthī. "Bhikkhus, form is impermanent. What is impermanent is suffering. What is suffering is nonself. What is nonself [83] should be seen as it really is with correct wisdom thus: 'This is not mine, this I am not, this is not my self.'

"Feeling is impermanent.... Perception is impermanent.... Volitional formations are impermanent.... Consciousness is impermanent. What is impermanent is suffering. What is suffering is nonself. What is nonself should be seen as it really is with correct wisdom thus: 'This is not mine, this I am not, this is not my self.'

"Seeing thus, bhikkhus, the instructed noble disciple experiences revulsion towards form, revulsion towards feeling, revulsion towards perception, revulsion towards volitional formations, revulsion towards consciousness. Experiencing revulsion, he becomes dispassionate. Through dispassion [his mind] is liberated.

When it is liberated there comes the knowledge: 'It's liberated.' He understands: 'Destroyed is birth, the holy life has been lived, what had to be done has been done, there is no more for this state of being.'

"To whatever extent, bhikkhus, there are abodes of beings, even up to the pinnacle of existence,[99] these are the foremost in the world, these are the best, that is, the arahants."

This is what the Blessed One said. Having said this, the Fortunate One, the Teacher, further said this:

"Happy indeed are the arahants!
No craving can be found in them.
Cut off is the conceit 'I am,'
Burst asunder is delusion's net.

"They have reached the unstirred state,[100]
Limpid are their minds;
They are unsullied in the world—
The holy ones, without taints.

"Having fully understood the five aggregates,
Ranging in the seven good qualities,[101]
Those praiseworthy superior men
Are the Buddha's bosom sons.

"Endowed with the seven gems,
Trained in the threefold training,[102]
Those great heroes wander about
With fear and trembling abandoned.

"Endowed with the ten factors,
Those great nāgas, concentrated,
Are the best beings in the world:
No craving can be found in them.[103]

"The adepts' knowledge has arisen in them:
'This body is the last I bear.'
In regard to the core of the holy life
They no longer depend on others. [84]

"They do not waver in discrimination,[104]
They are released from renewed existence.
Having reached the stage of the tamed,
They are the victors in the world.

"Above, across, and below,
Delight is no more found in them.
They boldly sound their lion's roar:
'The enlightened are supreme in the world.'"

77 (5) Arahants (2)

(*This sutta is identical with the preceding one except that the verses are omitted.*)

78 (6) The Lion

At Sāvatthī. "Bhikkhus, in the evening the lion, the king of beasts, comes out from his lair. Having come out, he stretches himself, surveys the four quarters all around, and roars his lion's roar three times. Then he sets out in search of game. [85]

"When the lion, the king of beasts, roars, whatever animals hear the sound are for the most part filled with fear, a sense of urgency, and terror. Those who live in holes enter their holes; those who live in the water enter the water; those who live in the woods enter the woods; and the birds fly up into the air. Even those royal bull elephants, bound by strong thongs in the villages, towns, and capital cities, burst and break their bonds asunder; frightened, they urinate and defecate and flee here and there. So powerful, bhikkhus, is the lion, the king of beasts, among the animals, so majestic and mighty.

"So too, bhikkhus,[105] when the Tathāgata arises in the world, an arahant, perfectly enlightened, accomplished in true knowledge and conduct, fortunate, knower of the world, unsurpassed leader of persons to be tamed, teacher of devas and humans, the Enlightened One, the Blessed One, he teaches the Dhamma thus: 'Such is form, such its origin, such its passing away; such is feeling ... such is perception ... such are volitional formations ... such is consciousness, such its origin, such its passing away.'[106]

"Then, bhikkhus, when those devas who are long-lived, beautiful, abounding in happiness, dwelling for a long time in lofty palaces, hear the Tathāgata's teaching of the Dhamma, they are for the most part filled with fear, a sense of urgency, and terror, [saying]: 'It seems, sir, that we are impermanent, though we thought ourselves permanent; it seems, sir, that we are unstable, though we thought ourselves stable; it seems, sir, that we are noneternal, though we thought ourselves eternal. It seems, sir, that we are impermanent, unstable, noneternal, included within identity.'[107] So powerful, bhikkhus, is the Tathāgata over this world together with its devas, so majestic and mighty."

This is what the Blessed One said. Having said this, the Fortunate One, the Teacher, further said this: [86]

"When the Buddha, through direct knowledge,
Sets in motion the Wheel of Dhamma,
The peerless Teacher in this world
With its devas [makes this known]:

"The cessation of identity
And the origin of identity,
Also the Noble Eightfold Path
That leads to suffering's appeasement.

"Then those devas with long life spans,
Beautiful, ablaze with glory,
Are struck with fear, filled with terror,
Like beasts who hear the lion's roar.

"'We've not transcended identity;
It seems, sir, we're impermanent,'
[So they say] having heard the utterance
Of the Arahant, the released Stable One."

79 (7) Being Devoured

At Sāvatthī. "Bhikkhus, those ascetics and brahmins who recollect their manifold past abodes all recollect the five aggregates subject to clinging or a certain one among them.[108] What five?

"When recollecting thus, bhikkhus: 'I had such form in the past,' it is just form that one recollects. When recollecting: 'I had such a feeling in the past,' it is just feeling that one recollects. When recollecting: 'I had such a perception in the past,' it is just perception that one recollects. When recollecting: 'I had such volitional formations in the past,' it is just volitional formations that one recollects. When recollecting: 'I had such consciousness in the past,' it is just consciousness that one recollects.

"And why, bhikkhus, do you call it form?[109] 'It is deformed,' bhikkhus, therefore it is called form.[110] Deformed by what? Deformed by cold, deformed by heat, deformed by hunger, deformed by thirst, deformed by contact with flies, mosquitoes, wind, sun, and serpents. 'It is deformed,' bhikkhus, therefore it is called form.

"And why, bhikkhus, do you call it feeling? 'It feels,' bhikkhus, therefore it is called feeling.[111] And what does it feel? It feels pleasure, it feels pain, [87] it feels neither-pain-nor-pleasure. 'It feels,' bhikkhus, therefore it is called feeling.

"And why, bhikkhus, do you call it perception? 'It perceives,' bhikkhus, therefore it is called perception. And what does it perceive? It perceives blue, it perceives yellow, it perceives red, it perceives white. 'It perceives,' bhikkhus, therefore it is called perception.

"And why, bhikkhus, do you call them volitional formations? 'They construct the conditioned,' bhikkhus, therefore they are called volitional formations.[112] And what is the conditioned that they construct? They construct conditioned form as form;[113] they construct conditioned feeling as feeling; they construct conditioned perception as perception; they construct conditioned volitional formations as volitional formations; they construct conditioned consciousness as consciousness. 'They construct the conditioned,' bhikkhus, therefore they are called volitional formations.

"And why, bhikkhus, do you call it consciousness? 'It cognizes,' bhikkhus, therefore it is called consciousness. And what does it cognize? It cognizes sour, it cognizes bitter, it cognizes pungent, it cognizes sweet, it cognizes sharp, it cognizes mild, it cognizes salty, it cognizes bland. 'It cognizes,' bhikkhus, therefore it is called consciousness.[114]

"Therein, bhikkhus, the instructed noble disciple reflects thus: 'I am now being devoured by form.[115] In the past too I was devoured by form in the very same way that I am now being devoured by present form. If I were to seek delight in future form, then in the future too I shall be devoured by form in the very same way that I am now being devoured by present form.' Having reflected thus, he becomes indifferent towards past form, he does not seek delight in future form, and he is practising for revulsion towards present form, for its fading away and cessation.

"[He reflects thus:] 'I am now being devoured by feeling.' ... [88] ... 'I am now being devoured by perception.' ... 'I am now being devoured by volitional formations.' ... 'I am now being devoured by consciousness. In the past too I was devoured by consciousness in the very same way that I am now being devoured by present consciousness. If I were to seek delight in future consciousness, then in the future too I shall be devoured by consciousness in the very same way that I am now being devoured by present consciousness.' Having reflected thus, he becomes indifferent towards past consciousness, he does not seek delight in future consciousness, and he is practising for revulsion towards present consciousness, for its fading away and cessation.

"What do you think, bhikkhus, is form permanent or impermanent?... Is feeling ... perception ... volitional formations ... [89] consciousness permanent or impermanent?"[116] – "Impermanent, venerable sir." – "Is what is impermanent suffering or happiness?" – "Suffering, venerable sir." – "Is what is impermanent, suffering, and subject to change fit to be regarded thus: 'This is mine, this I am, this is my self'?" – "No, venerable sir."

"Therefore, bhikkhus, any kind of form whatsoever ... Any kind of feeling whatsoever ... Any kind of perception whatsoever ... Any kind of volitional formations whatsoever ... Any kind of consciousness whatsoever, whether past, future, or present, internal or external, gross or subtle, inferior or superior, far or near, all consciousness should be seen as it really is with correct wisdom thus: 'This is not mine, this I am not, this is not my self.'

"This is called, bhikkhus, a noble disciple who dismantles and does not build up; who abandons and does not cling; who scatters and does not amass; who extinguishes and does not kindle.[117]

"And what is it that he dismantles and does not build up? He dismantles form and does not build it up. He dismantles feeling

... perception ... volitional formations ... consciousness and does not build it up.

"And what is it that he abandons and does not cling to? He abandons form and does not cling to it. He abandons feeling ... perception ... volitional formations ... consciousness and does not cling to it.

"And what is it that he scatters and does not amass? He scatters form and does not amass it. He scatters feeling ... perception ... volitional formations ... consciousness and does not amass it. [90]

"And what is it that he extinguishes and does not kindle? He extinguishes form and does not kindle it. He extinguishes feeling ... perception ... volitional formations ... consciousness and does not kindle it.

"Seeing thus, bhikkhus, the instructed noble disciple experiences revulsion towards form, revulsion towards feeling, revulsion towards perception, revulsion towards volitional formations, revulsion towards consciousness. Experiencing revulsion, he becomes dispassionate. Through dispassion [his mind] is liberated. When it is liberated there comes the knowledge: 'It's liberated.' He understands: 'Destroyed is birth, the holy life has been lived, what had to be done has been done, there is no more for this state of being.'

"This is called, bhikkhus, a noble disciple who neither builds up nor dismantles, but who abides having dismantled; who neither abandons nor clings, but who abides having abandoned; who neither scatters nor amasses, but who abides having scattered; who neither extinguishes nor kindles, but who abides having extinguished.[118]

"And what is it, bhikkhus, that he neither builds up nor dismantles, but abides having dismantled? He neither builds up nor dismantles form, but abides having dismantled it. He neither builds up nor dismantles feeling ... perception ... volitional formations ... consciousness, but abides having dismantled it.

"And what is it that he neither abandons nor clings to, but abides having abandoned? He neither abandons nor clings to form, but abides having abandoned it. He neither abandons nor clings to feeling ... perception ... volitional formations ... consciousness, but abides having abandoned it.

"And what is it that he neither scatters nor amasses, but abides having scattered? He neither scatters nor amasses form, but abides having scattered it. He neither scatters nor amasses feeling … perception … volitional formations … consciousness, but abides having scattered it.

"And what is it that he neither extinguishes nor kindles, but abides having extinguished? He neither extinguishes nor kindles form, but abides having extinguished it. He neither extinguishes nor kindles feeling … perception … volitional formations … consciousness, but abides having extinguished it.

"When, bhikkhus, a bhikkhu is thus liberated in mind, the devas together with Indra, Brahmā, and Pajāpati pay homage to him from afar: [91]

"'Homage to you, O thoroughbred man!
Homage to you, O highest among men!
We ourselves do not directly know
Dependent upon what you meditate.'"[119]

80 (8) Alms-Gatherer

On one occasion the Blessed One was dwelling among the Sakyans at Kapilavatthu in Nigrodha's Park.

Then the Blessed One, having dismissed the bhikkhus for a particular reason,[120] dressed in the morning and, taking bowl and robe, entered Kapilavatthu for alms. When he had walked for alms in Kapilavatthu and had returned from the alms round, after his meal he went to the Great Wood for the day's abiding. Having plunged into the Great Wood, he sat down at the foot of a *beluva* sapling for the day's abiding.

Then, while the Blessed One was alone in seclusion, a reflection arose in his mind thus:[121] "The Saṅgha of bhikkhus has been dismissed by me. There are bhikkhus here who are newly ordained, not long gone forth, recently come to this Dhamma and Discipline. If they do not see me there may take place in them some alteration or change. Just as when a young calf does not see its mother there may take place in it some alteration or change, so too there are bhikkhus here who are newly ordained, not long gone forth, recently come to this Dhamma and Discipline. If they do not see me there may take place in them some alteration or change. Just as when young seedlings do not get water there may take place in them some alteration or change, so too there are bhikkhus here who are newly ordained, not long gone forth, recently come to this Dhamma and Discipline. If they do not see me there may take place in them some alteration or change. Let me assist the Saṅgha of bhikkhus now just as I have assisted it in the past."

Then Brahmā Sahampati, having known with his own mind the reflection in the Blessed One's mind, just as quickly as a strong man might extend his drawn-in arm or draw in his extended arm, disappeared from the brahmā world and reappeared before the Blessed One. [92] He arranged his upper robe over one shoulder, raised his joined hands in reverential salutation towards the Blessed One, and said to him: "So it is, Blessed One! So it is, Fortunate One! The Saṅgha of bhikkhus has been dismissed by the Blessed One. There are bhikkhus here who are newly ordained ... (*as above, including the similes*) ... If they do not see the Blessed One there may take place in them some alteration or change. Venerable sir, let the Blessed One take delight in the Saṅgha of bhikkhus! Let the Blessed One welcome the Saṅgha of bhikkhus! Let the Blessed One assist the Saṅgha of bhikkhus now just as he has assisted it in the past."

The Blessed One consented by silence. Then Brahmā Sahampati, having understood the Blessed One's consent, paid homage to the Blessed One and, keeping him on his right, he disappeared right there.

Then in the evening the Blessed One emerged from seclusion and went to Nigrodha's Park. He sat down in the appointed seat and performed such a feat of spiritual power that the bhikkhus would come to him, alone and in pairs, in a timid manner.[122] Then those bhikkhus approached the Blessed One, alone and in pairs, in a timid manner. [93] Having approached, they paid homage to the Blessed One and sat down to one side. The Blessed One then said to them:

"Bhikkhus, this is the lowest form of livelihood, that is, gathering alms. In the world this is a term of abuse:[123] 'You almsgatherer; you roam about with a begging bowl in your hand!' And yet, bhikkhus, clansmen intent on the good take up that way of life for a valid reason. It is not because they have been driven to it by kings that they do so, nor because they have been driven to it by thieves, nor owing to debt, nor from fear, nor to earn a livelihood. But they do so with the thought: 'I am immersed in birth, aging, and death; in sorrow, lamentation, pain, displeasure, and despair. I am immersed in suffering, oppressed by suffering. Perhaps an ending of this entire mass of suffering might be discerned!'

"It is in such a way, bhikkhus, that this clansman has gone forth. Yet he is covetous, inflamed by lust for sensual pleasures, with a mind full of ill will, with intentions corrupted by hate, muddle-minded, lacking clear comprehension, unconcentrated, scatter-brained, loose in his sense faculties. Just as a brand from a funeral pyre, burning at both ends and smeared with excrement in the middle, cannot be used as timber either in the village or in the forest, in just such a way do I speak about this person: he has missed out on the enjoyments of a householder, yet he does not fulfil the goal of asceticism.

"There are, bhikkhus, these three kinds of unwholesome thoughts: sensual thought, thought of ill will, thought of harming.[124] And where, bhikkhus, do these three unwholesome thoughts cease without remainder? For one who dwells with a mind well established in the four establishments of mindfulness, or for one who develops the signless concentration. This is reason enough, bhikkhus, to develop the signless concentration. When the signless concentration is developed and cultivated, bhikkhus, it is of great fruit and benefit.

"There are, bhikkhus, these two views: the view of existence and the view of extermination.[125] [94] Therein, bhikkhus, the instructed noble disciple reflects thus: 'Is there anything in the world that I could cling to without being blameworthy?' He understand thus: 'There is nothing in the world that I could cling to without being blameworthy. For if I should cling, it is only form that I would be clinging to, only feeling ... only perception ... only volitional formations ... only consciousness that I would be clinging to. With that clinging of mine as condition, there would be existence; with existence as condition, birth; with birth as condition, aging-and-death, sorrow, lamentation, pain, displeasure, and despair would come to be. Such would be the origin of this whole mass of suffering.'[126]

"What do you think, bhikkhus, is form permanent or impermanent?... Is feeling ... perception ... volitional formations ... consciousness permanent or impermanent?" – "Impermanent, venerable sir." – "Is what is impermanent suffering or happiness?"

– "Suffering, venerable sir." – "Is what is impermanent, suffering, and subject to change fit to be regarded thus: 'This is mine, this I am, this is my self'?" – "No, venerable sir."

"Seeing thus ... He understands: '... there is no more for this state of being.'"[127]

81 (9) Pārileyya

On one occasion the Blessed One was dwelling at Kosambī in Ghosita's Park.

Then, in the morning, the Blessed One dressed and, taking bowl and robe, entered Kosambī for alms. When he had walked for alms in Kosambī and had returned from the alms round, after his meal [95] he set his lodging in order himself, took his bowl and robe, and without informing his personal attendants, without taking leave of the Bhikkhu Saṅgha, he set out on tour alone, without a companion.[128]

Then, not long after the Blessed One had departed, a certain bhikkhu approached the Venerable Ānanda and told him: "Friend Ānanda, the Blessed One has set his lodging in order himself, taken his bowl and robe, and without informing his personal attendants, without taking leave of the Bhikkhu Saṅgha, he has set out on tour alone, without a companion."

"Friend, whenever the Blessed One sets out like that he wishes to dwell alone. On such an occasion the Blessed One should not be followed by anyone."

Then the Blessed One, wandering by stages, arrived at Pārileyyaka. There at Pārileyyaka the Blessed One dwelt at the foot of an auspicious sal tree.[129]

Then a number of bhikkhus approached the Venerable Ānanda and exchanged greetings with him.[130] When they had concluded their greetings and cordial talk, they sat down to one side and said to the Venerable Ānanda: "Friend Ānanda, it has been a long time since we heard a Dhamma talk in the presence of the Blessed One. We should like to hear such a talk, friend Ānanda."

Then the Venerable Ānanda together with those bhikkhus approached the Blessed One at Pārileyyaka, at the foot of the auspicious sal tree. Having approached, they paid homage to the Blessed One and sat down to one side. The Blessed One then instructed, exhorted, inspired, and gladdened those bhikkhus with a Dhamma talk. [96] Now on that occasion a reflection arose in the mind of a certain bhikkhu thus: "How should one know, how should one see, for the immediate destruction of the taints to occur?"[131]

The Blessed One, having known with his own mind the reflection in that bhikkhu's mind, addressed the bhikkhus thus:

"Bhikkhus, this Dhamma has been taught by me discriminately.[132] The four establishments of mindfulness have been taught by me discriminately. The four right strivings … The four bases for spiritual power … The five spiritual faculties … The five powers … The seven factors of enlightenment … The Noble Eightfold Path has been taught by me discriminately. Bhikkhus, in regard to the Dhamma that has been thus taught by me discriminately, a reflection arose in the mind of a certain bhikkhu thus: 'How should one know, how should one see, for the immediate destruction of the taints to occur?'

"And how, bhikkhus, should one know, how should one see, for the immediate destruction of the taints to occur? Here, bhikkhus, the uninstructed worldling, who is not a seer of the noble ones and is unskilled and undisciplined in their Dhamma, who is not a seer of superior persons and is unskilled and undisciplined in their Dhamma, regards form as self. That regarding, bhikkhus, is a formation.[133] That formation—what is its source, what is its origin, from what is it born and produced? When the uninstructed worldling is contacted by a feeling born of ignorance-contact, craving arises: thence that formation is born.

"Thus, bhikkhus, that formation is impermanent, conditioned, dependently arisen; that craving is impermanent, conditioned, dependently arisen; that feeling is impermanent, conditioned, dependently arisen; that contact is impermanent, conditioned, dependently arisen; that ignorance is impermanent, conditioned, dependently arisen. [97] When one knows and sees thus, bhikkhus, the immediate destruction of the taints occurs.

"He may not regard form as self, but he regards self as possessing form. That regarding is a formation … (*all as above*) … When one knows and sees thus, bhikkhus, the immediate destruction of the taints occurs.

"He may not regard form as self or self as possessing form, but he regards form as in self. That regarding is a formation….

"He may not regard form as self or self as possessing form or form as in self, but he regards self as in form. That regarding is a formation.... [98]

"He may not regard form as self ... or self as in form, but he regards feeling as self ... perception as self ... volitional formations as self ... consciousness as self ... self as in consciousness. That regarding is a formation.... When one knows and sees thus, bhikkhus, the immediate destruction of the taints occurs.

"He may not regard form as self ... [99] ... or self as in consciousness, but he holds such a view as this: 'That which is the self is the world; having passed away, that I shall be—permanent, stable, eternal, not subject to change.'[134] That eternalist view is a formation.... When one knows and sees thus, bhikkhus, the immediate destruction of the taints occurs.

"He may not regard form as self ... or hold such an [eternalist] view, but he holds such a view as this: 'I might not be, and it might not be for me; I will not be, [and] it will not be for me.'[135] That annihilationist view is a formation....

"He may not regard form as self ... or hold such an [annihilationist] view, but he is perplexed, doubtful, indecisive in regard to the true Dhamma. That perplexity, doubtfulness, indecisiveness in regard to the true Dhamma is a formation. That formation—what is its source, what is its origin, from what is it born and produced? When the uninstructed worldling is contacted by a feeling born of ignorance-contact, craving arises: thence that formation is born.[136]

"So that formation, bhikkhus, is impermanent, conditioned, dependently arisen; that craving is impermanent, conditioned, dependently arisen; that feeling is impermanent, conditioned, dependently arisen; that contact is impermanent, conditioned, dependently arisen; that ignorance is impermanent, conditioned, dependently arisen. When one knows and sees thus, bhikkhus, the immediate destruction of the taints occurs."[137] [100]

82 (10) The Full-Moon Night

On one occasion the Blessed One was dwelling at Sāvatthī in the Eastern Park, in the Mansion of Migāra's Mother, together with a great Saṅgha of bhikkhus.[138] Now on that occasion—the Uposatha day of the fifteenth, a full-moon night—the Blessed One was sitting out in the open surrounded by the Saṅgha of bhikkhus.

Then a certain bhikkhu rose from his seat, arranged his upper robe over one shoulder, raised his joined hands in reverential salutation towards the Blessed One, and said to him: "Venerable sir, I would ask the Blessed One about a certain point, if the Blessed One would grant me the favour of answering my question."

"Well then, bhikkhu, sit down in your own seat and ask whatever you wish."

"Yes, venerable sir," that bhikkhu replied. Then he sat down in his own seat and said to the Blessed One:

"Aren't these the five aggregates subject to clinging, venerable sir: that is, the form aggregate subject to clinging, the feeling aggregate subject to clinging, the perception aggregate subject to clinging, the volitional formations aggregate subject to clinging, the consciousness aggregate subject to clinging?"

"Those are the five aggregates subject to clinging, bhikkhu: that is, the form aggregate subject to clinging, the feeling aggregate subject to clinging, the perception aggregate subject to clinging, the volitional formations aggregate subject to clinging, the consciousness aggregate subject to clinging."

Saying, "Good, venerable sir," that bhikkhu delighted and rejoiced in the Blessed One's statement. Then he asked the Blessed One a further question:

"But, venerable sir, in what are these five aggregates subject to clinging rooted?"

"These five aggregates subject to clinging, bhikkhu, are rooted in desire."[139]

"Venerable sir, is that clinging the same as these five aggregates subject to clinging, or is the clinging something apart from the five aggregates subject to clinging?"

"Bhikkhus, that clinging is neither the same as these five aggregates subject to clinging, [101] nor is the clinging something apart from the five aggregates subject to clinging. But rather, the desire and lust for them, that is the clinging there."[140]

Saying, "Good, venerable sir," that bhikkhu ... asked the Blessed One a further question:

"But, venerable sir, can there be diversity in the desire and lust for the five aggregates subject to clinging?"

"There can be, bhikkhu," the Blessed One said. "Here, bhikkhu, it occurs to someone: 'May I have such form in the future! May I have such feeling in the future! May I have such perception in the future! May I have such volitional formations in the future! May I have such consciousness in the future!' Thus, bhikkhu, there can be diversity in the desire and lust for the five aggregates subject to clinging."

Saying, "Good, venerable sir," that bhikkhu ... asked the Blessed One a further question:

"In what way, venerable sir, does the designation 'aggregates' apply to the aggregates?"

"Whatever kind of form there is, bhikkhu, whether past, future, or present, internal or external, gross or subtle, inferior or superior, far or near: this is called the form aggregate. Whatever kind of feeling there is, whether past, future, or present, internal or external, gross or subtle, inferior or superior, far or near: this is called the feeling aggregate. Whatever kind of perception there is, whether past, future, or present, internal or external, gross or subtle, inferior or superior, far or near: this is called the perception aggregate. Whatever kind of volitional formations there are, whether past, future, or present, internal or external, gross or subtle, inferior or superior, far or near: this is called the volitional formations aggregate. Whatever kind of consciousness there is, whether past, future, or present, internal or external, gross or subtle, inferior or superior, far or near: this is called the consciousness aggregate. It is in this way, bhikkhu, that the designation 'aggregates' applies to the aggregates."

Saying, "Good, venerable sir," that bhikkhu ... asked the Blessed One a further question:

"What is the cause and condition, venerable sir, for the manifestation of the form aggregate?[141] What is the cause and condition for the manifestation of the feeling aggregate?... for the manifestation of the perception aggregate?... for the manifestation of the volitional formations aggregate?... for the manifestation of the consciousness aggregate?"

"The four great elements, bhikkhu, are the cause and condition for the manifestation of the form aggregate. Contact is the cause and condition for the manifestation of the feeling aggregate. Contact is the cause and condition for the manifestation of the perception aggregate. [102] Contact is the cause and condition for the manifestation of the volitional formations aggregate. Name-and-form is the cause and condition for the manifestation of the consciousness aggregate."

"Venerable sir, how does identity view come to be?"

"Here, bhikkhu, the uninstructed worldling, who is not a seer of the noble ones and is unskilled and undisciplined in their Dhamma, who is not a seer of superior persons and is unskilled and undisciplined in their Dhamma, regards form as self, or self as possessing form, or form as in self, or self as in form. He regards feeling as self ... perception as self ... volitional formations as self ... consciousness as self, or self as possessing consciousness, or consciousness as in self, or self as in consciousness. That is how identity view comes to be."

"But, venerable sir, how does identity view not come to be?"

"Here, bhikkhu, the instructed noble disciple, who is a seer of the noble ones and is skilled and disciplined in their Dhamma, who is a seer of superior persons and is skilled and disciplined in their Dhamma, does not regard form as self, or self as possessing form, or form as in self, or self as in form. He does not regard feeling as self ... perception as self ... volitional formations as self ... consciousness as self, or self as possessing consciousness, or consciousness as in self, or self as in consciousness. That is how identity view does not come to be."

"What, venerable sir, is the gratification, the danger, and the escape in the case of form? What is the gratification, the danger, and the escape in the case of feeling?... in the case of perception?... in the case of volitional formations?... in the case of consciousness?"

"The pleasure and joy, bhikkhu, that arise in dependence on form: this is the gratification in form. That form is impermanent, suffering, and subject to change: this is the danger in form. The removal and abandonment of desire and lust for form: this is the escape from form. The pleasure and joy that arise in dependence on feeling ... [103] in dependence on perception ... in dependence on volitional formations ... in dependence on consciousness: this is the gratification in consciousness. That consciousness is impermanent, suffering, and subject to change: this is the danger in consciousness. The removal and abandonment of desire and lust for consciousness: this is the escape from consciousness."

Saying, "Good, venerable sir," that bhikkhu delighted and rejoiced in the Blessed One's statement. Then he asked the Blessed One a further question:

"Venerable sir, how should one know, how should one see so

that, in regard to this body with consciousness and in regard to all external signs, I-making, mine-making, and the underlying tendency to conceit no longer occur within?"

"Any kind of form whatsoever, bhikkhu, whether past, future, or present, internal or external, gross or subtle, inferior or superior, far or near—one sees all form as it really is with correct wisdom thus: 'This is not mine, this I am not, this is not my self.'

"Any kind of feeling whatsoever ... Any kind of perception whatsoever ... Any kind of volitional formations whatsoever ... Any kind of consciousness whatsoever, whether past, future, or present, internal or external, gross or subtle, inferior or superior, far or near—one sees all consciousness as it really is with correct wisdom thus: 'This is not mine, this I am not, this is not my self.'

"When one knows and sees thus, bhikkhu, then in regard to this body with consciousness and in regard to all external signs, I-making, mine-making, and the underlying tendency to conceit no longer occur within."

Now on that occasion the following reflection arose in the mind of a certain bhikkhu: "So it seems that form is nonself, feeling is nonself, perception is nonself, volitional formations are nonself, consciousness is nonself. What self, then, will deeds done by what is nonself affect?"[142]

Then the Blessed One, knowing with his own mind the reflection in the mind of that bhikkhu, addressed the bhikkhus thus: "It is possible, bhikkhus, that some senseless man here, obtuse and ignorant, with his mind dominated by craving, might think that he can outstrip the Teacher's Teaching thus: 'So it seems that form is nonself ... consciousness is nonself. [104] What self, then, will deeds done by what is nonself affect?' Now, bhikkhus, you have been trained by me through interrogation here and there in regard to diverse teachings.[143]

"What do you think, bhikkhu, is form permanent or impermanent?" – "Impermanent, venerable sir."... – "Is feeling permanent or impermanent?... Is perception permanent or impermanent?... Are volitional formations permanent or impermanent?... Is consciousness permanent or impermanent?" – "Impermanent, venerable sir." – "Is what is impermanent suffering or happiness?" – "Suffering, venerable sir." – "Is what is impermanent, suffering, and subject to change fit to be regarded thus: 'This is mine, this I am, this is my self'?" – "No, venerable sir."

"Therefore ... Seeing thus ... He understands: '... there is no more for this state of being.'"[144]

These are the ten questions
The bhikkhu came to ask:
Two about the aggregates,
Whether the same, can there be,
Designation and the cause,
Two about identity,
[One each on] gratification
And [this body] with consciousness.

[105] IV. The Elders

83 (1) Ānanda

At Sāvatthī. There the Venerable Ānanda addressed the bhikkhus thus: "Friends, bhikkhus!"

"Friend!" those bhikkhus replied. The Venerable Ānanda said this:

"Friends, the Venerable Puṇṇa Mantāniputta was very helpful to us when we were newly ordained.[145] He exhorted us with the following exhortation:

> "It is by clinging, Ānanda, that [the notion] 'I am' occurs, not without clinging. And by clinging to what does 'I am' occur, not without clinging?[146] It is by clinging to form that 'I am' occurs, not without clinging. It is by clinging to feeling ... to perception ... to volitional formations ... to consciousness that 'I am' occurs, not without clinging.
>
> "Suppose, friend Ānanda, a young woman—or a man—youthful and fond of ornaments, would examine her own facial image in a mirror or in a bowl filled with pure, clear, clean water: she would look at it with clinging, not without clinging. So too, it is by clinging to form that 'I am' occurs, not without clinging. It is by clinging to feeling ... to perception ... to volitional formations ... to consciousness that 'I am' occurs, not without clinging.
>
> "What do you think, friend Ānanda, is form permanent

> or impermanent?"... (*as in preceding sutta*) ... "Seeing thus ... He understands: '... there is no more for this state of being.'"

"Friends, the Venerable Puṇṇa Mantāniputta [106] was very helpful to us when we were newly ordained. He exhorted us with that exhortation. And when I heard his Dhamma teaching I made the breakthrough to the Dhamma."[147]

84 (2) Tissa

At Sāvatthī. Now on that occasion the Venerable Tissa, the Blessed One's paternal cousin,[148] informed a number of bhikkhus: "Friends, my body seems as if it has been drugged, I have become disoriented, the teachings are no longer clear to me.[149] Sloth and torpor persist obsessing my mind. I am leading the holy life dissatisfied, and I have doubt about the teachings."

Then a number of bhikkhus approached the Blessed One, paid homage to him, sat down to one side, and reported this matter to him. The Blessed One then addressed a certain bhikkhu thus: "Come, bhikkhu, tell the bhikkhu Tissa in my name that the Teacher calls him."

"Yes, venerable sir," that bhikkhu replied, and he went to the Venerable Tissa and told him: "The Teacher calls you, friend Tissa."

"Yes, friend," the Venerable Tissa replied, and he approached the Blessed One, paid homage to him, and sat down to one side. The Blessed One then said to him: "Is it true, Tissa, [107] that you informed a number of bhikkhus thus: 'Friends, my body seems as if it were drugged ... and I have doubt about the teachings'?"

"Yes, venerable sir."

"What do you think, Tissa, if one is not devoid of lust for form, not devoid of desire, affection, thirst, passion, and craving for it, then with the change and alteration of that form, do sorrow, lamentation, pain, displeasure, and despair arise within?"

"Yes, venerable sir."

"Good, good, Tissa! So it is, Tissa, with one who is not devoid of lust for form. If one is not devoid of lust for feeling ... for perception ... for volitional formations ... for consciousness, not devoid of desire, [108] affection, thirst, passion, and craving for it, then with the change and alteration of that consciousness, do sorrow, lamentation, pain, displeasure, and despair arise within?"

"Yes, venerable sir."

"Good, good, Tissa! So it is, Tissa, with one who is not devoid of lust for consciousness. If one is devoid of lust for form, devoid of desire, affection, thirst, passion, and craving for it, then with the change and alteration of that form, do sorrow, lamentation, pain, displeasure, and despair arise within?"

"No, venerable sir."

"Good, good, Tissa! So it is, Tissa, with one who is devoid of lust for form. If one is devoid of lust for feeling ... for perception ... for volitional formations ... for consciousness, devoid of desire, affection, thirst, passion, and craving for it, then with the change and alteration of that consciousness, do sorrow, lamentation, pain, displeasure, and despair arise within?"

"No, venerable sir."

"Good, good, Tissa! So it is, Tissa, with one who is devoid of lust for consciousness. What do you think, Tissa, is form permanent or impermanent?" – "Impermanent, venerable sir."... – "Therefore ... Seeing thus ... He understands: '... there is no more for this state of being.'

"Suppose, Tissa, there were two men: one unskilled in the path, the other skilled in the path. The man unskilled in the path would ask the skilled man a question about the path, and the latter would say: 'Come, good man, this is the path. Go along it a little way and you will see a fork in the road. Avoid the left-hand branch and take the right-hand branch. Go a little further and you will see a dense thicket. Go a little further and you will see a vast marshy swamp. Go a little further and you will see a steep precipice. Go a little further and you will see a delightful expanse of level ground.'

"I have made up this simile, Tissa, in order to convey a meaning. This here is the meaning: 'The man unskilled in the path': this is a designation for the worldling. 'The man skilled in the path': this is a designation for the Tathāgata, the Arahant, the Perfectly Enlightened One. 'The forked road': this is a designation for doubt. [109] 'The left-hand branch': this is a designation for the wrong eightfold path; that is, wrong view ... wrong concentration. 'The right-hand branch': this is a designation for the Noble Eightfold Path; that is, right view ... right concentration.

'The dense thicket': this is a designation for ignorance. 'The vast marshy swamp': this is a designation for sensual pleasures. 'The steep precipice': this is a designation for despair due to anger. 'The delightful expanse of level ground': this is a designation for Nibbāna.

"Rejoice, Tissa! Rejoice, Tissa! I am here to exhort, I am here to assist, I am here to instruct!"

This is what the Blessed One said. Elated, the Venerable Tissa delighted in the Blessed One's statement.[150]

85 (3) Yamaka

On one occasion the Venerable Sāriputta was dwelling at Sāvatthī in Jeta's Grove, Anāthapiṇḍika's Park. Now on that occasion the following pernicious view had arisen in a bhikkhu named Yamaka: "As I understand the Dhamma taught by the Blessed One, a bhikkhu whose taints are destroyed is annihilated and perishes with the breakup of the body and does not exist after death."[151]

A number of bhikkhus heard that such a pernicious view had arisen in the bhikkhu Yamaka. Then they approached the Venerable Yamaka and exchanged greetings with him, after which they sat down to one side and said to him: "Is it true, friend Yamaka, that such a pernicious view as this has arisen in you: [110] 'As I understand the Dhamma taught by the Blessed One, a bhikkhu whose taints are destroyed is annihilated and perishes with the breakup of the body and does not exist after death'?"

"Exactly so, friends. As I understand the Dhamma taught by the Blessed One, a bhikkhu whose taints are destroyed is annihilated and perishes with the breakup of the body and does not exist after death."

"Friend Yamaka, do not speak thus. Do not misrepresent the Blessed One. It is not good to misrepresent the Blessed One. The Blessed One would not speak thus: 'A bhikkhu whose taints are destroyed is annihilated and perishes with the breakup of the body and does not exist after death.'"

Yet, although he was admonished by the bhikkhus in this way, the Venerable Yamaka still obstinately grasped that pernicious view, adhered to it, and declared: "As I understand the Dhamma taught by the Blessed One, a bhikkhu whose taints are destroyed is annihilated and perishes with the breakup of the body and does not exist after death."

Since those bhikkhus were unable to detach the Venerable Yamaka from that pernicious view, they rose from their seats, approached the Venerable Sāriputta, and told him all that had occurred, adding: "It would be good if the Venerable Sāriputta would approach the bhikkhu Yamaka out of compassion for him." The Venerable Sāriputta consented by silence.

Then, in the evening, the Venerable Sāriputta emerged from seclusion. He approached the Venerable Yamaka and exchanged greetings with him, after which he sat down to one side and said to him: "Is it true, friend Yamaka, that such a pernicious view as this has arisen in you: 'As I understand the Dhamma taught by the Blessed One, [111] a bhikkhu whose taints are destroyed is annihilated and perishes with the breakup of the body and does not exist after death'?"

"Exactly so, friend."

"What do you think, friend Yamaka, is form permanent or impermanent?" – "Impermanent, friend."... – "Therefore ... Seeing thus ... He understands: '... there is no more for this state of being.'[152]

"What do you think, friend Yamaka, do you regard form as the Tathāgata?" – "No, friend." – "Do you regard feeling ... perception ... volitional formations ... consciousness as the Tathāgata?" – "No, friend."

"What do you think, friend Yamaka, do you regard the Tathāgata as in form?" – "No, friend." – "Do you regard the Tathāgata as apart from form?" – "No, friend." – "Do you regard the Tathāgata as in feeling? As apart from feeling? As in perception? As apart from perception? As in volitional formations? As apart from volitional formations? As in consciousness? As apart from consciousness?" – "No, friend."

"What do you think, friend Yamaka, do you regard form, feeling, perception, volitional formations, and consciousness [taken together] as the Tathāgata?" – "No, friend." [112]

"What do you think, friend Yamaka, do you regard the Tathāgata as one who is without form, without feeling, without perception, without volitional formations, without consciousness?" – "No, friend."[153]

"But, friend, when the Tathāgata is not apprehended by you as real and actual here in this very life,[154] is it fitting for you to declare: 'As I understand the Dhamma taught by the Blessed One, a bhikkhu whose taints are destroyed is annihilated and perishes with the breakup of the body and does not exist after death'?"

"Formerly, friend Sāriputta, when I was ignorant, I did hold that pernicious view, but now that I have heard this Dhamma teaching of the Venerable Sāriputta I have abandoned that pernicious view and have made the breakthrough to the Dhamma."[155]

"If, friend Yamaka, they were to ask you: 'Friend Yamaka, when a bhikkhu is an arahant, one whose taints are destroyed, what happens to him with the breakup of the body, after death?'—being asked thus, what would you answer?"

"If they were to ask me this, friend, I would answer thus: 'Friends, form is impermanent; what is impermanent is suffering; what is suffering has ceased and passed away. Feeling ... Perception ... Volitional formations ... Consciousness is impermanent; what is impermanent is suffering; what is suffering has ceased and passed away.' Being asked thus, friend, I would answer in such a way."[156]

"Good, good, friend Yamaka! Now, friend Yamaka, I will make up a simile for you in order to convey this same meaning even more clearly. Suppose, friend Yamaka, there was a householder or a householder's son, a rich man, with much wealth and property, protected by a bodyguard. Then some man would appear who wanted to ruin him, to harm him, to endanger him, to take his life. [113] It would occur to that man: 'This householder or householder's son is a rich man, with much wealth and property, protected by a bodyguard. It won't be easy to take his life by force. Let me get close to him and then take his life.'

"Then he would approach that householder or householder's son and say to him: 'I would serve you, sir.' Then the householder or householder's son would appoint him as a servant. The man would serve him, rising up before him, retiring after him, doing whatever he wants, agreeable in his conduct, endearing in his speech. The householder or householder's son would consider him a friend,[157] a bosom friend, and he would place trust in him. But when the man becomes aware that the householder or householder's son has placed trust in him, then, finding him alone, he would take his life with a sharp knife.

"What do you think, friend Yamaka, when that man had approached that householder or householder's son and said to him: 'I would serve you, sir,' wasn't he a murderer even then, though the other did not recognize him as 'my murderer'? And when the man was serving him, rising up before him, retiring after him, doing whatever he wants, agreeable in his conduct, endearing in his speech, wasn't he a murderer then too, though the other did not recognize him as 'my murderer'? And when the man came upon him while he was alone and took his life with a sharp knife, wasn't he a murderer then too, though the other did not recognize him as 'my murderer'?"

"Yes, friend."

"So too, friend Yamaka,[158] the uninstructed worldling, who is not a seer of the noble ones and is unskilled and undisciplined in their Dhamma, who is not a seer of superior persons and is unskilled and undisciplined in their Dhamma, regards form as self, or self as possessing form, or form as in self, or self as in form.

"He regards feeling as self ... perception as self ... volitional formations as self ... consciousness as self, [114] or self as possessing consciousness, or consciousness as in self, or self as in consciousness.

"He does not understand as it really is impermanent form as 'impermanent form'[159] ... impermanent feeling as 'impermanent feeling' ... impermanent perception as 'impermanent perception' ... impermanent volitional formations as 'impermanent volitional formations' ... impermanent consciousness as 'impermanent consciousness.'

"He does not understand as it really is painful form as 'painful form' ... painful feeling as 'painful feeling' ... painful perception as 'painful perception' ... painful volitional formations as 'painful volitional formations' ... painful consciousness as 'painful consciousness.'

"He does not understand as it really is selfless form as 'selfless form' ... selfless feeling as 'selfless feeling' ... selfless perception as 'selfless perception' ... selfless volitional formations as 'selfless volitional formations' ... selfless consciousness as 'selfless consciousness.'

"He does not understand as it really is conditioned form as 'conditioned form' ... conditioned feeling as 'conditioned feeling'

... conditioned perception as 'conditioned perception' ... conditioned volitional formations as 'conditioned volitional formations' ... conditioned consciousness as 'conditioned consciousness.'

"He does not understand as it really is murderous form as 'murderous form' ... murderous feeling as 'murderous feeling' ... murderous perception as 'murderous perception' ... murderous volitional formations as 'murderous volitional formations' ... murderous consciousness as 'murderous consciousness.'

"He becomes engaged with form, clings to it, and takes a stand upon it as 'my self.'[160] He becomes engaged with feeling ... with perception ... with volitional formations ... with consciousness, clings to it, and takes a stand upon it as 'my self.' These same five aggregates of clinging, to which he becomes engaged and to which he clings, lead to his harm and suffering for a long time.

"But, friend, the instructed noble disciple, who is a seer of the noble ones ... does not regard form as self, or self as possessing form, or form as in self, or self as in form.

"He does not regard feeling as self ... perception as self ... volitional formations as self ... consciousness as self, or self as possessing consciousness, or consciousness as in self, or self as in consciousness. [115]

"He understands as it really is impermanent form as 'impermanent form' ... impermanent consciousness as 'impermanent consciousness.'

"He understands as it really is painful form as 'painful form' ... painful consciousness as 'painful consciousness.'

"He understands as it really is selfless form as 'selfless form' ... selfless consciousness as 'selfless consciousness.'

"He understands as it really is conditioned form as 'conditioned form' ... conditioned consciousness as 'conditioned consciousness.'

"He understands as it really is murderous form as 'murderous form' ... murderous consciousness as 'murderous consciousness.'

"He does not become engaged with form, cling to it, and take a stand upon it as 'my self.' He does not become engaged with feeling ... with perception ... with volitional formations ... with consciousness, cling to it, and take a stand upon it as 'my self.' These same five aggregates of clinging, to which he does not become engaged and to which he does not cling, lead to his welfare and happiness for a long time."

"So it is, friend Sāriputta, for those venerable ones who have such compassionate and benevolent brothers in the holy life to admonish and instruct them. And now that I have heard this Dhamma teaching of the Venerable Sāriputta, my mind is liberated from the taints by nonclinging." [116]

This is what the Venerable Sāriputta said. Elated, the Venerable Yamaka delighted in the Venerable Sāriputta's statement.[161]

86 (4) Anurādha

On one occasion the Blessed One was dwelling at Vesālī in the Great Wood in the Hall with the Peaked Roof.[162] Now on that occasion the Venerable Anurādha was dwelling in a forest hut not far from the Blessed One. Then a number of wanderers of other sects approached the Venerable Anurādha and exchanged greetings with him. When they had concluded their greetings and cordial talk, they sat down to one side and said to him:

"Friend Anurādha, when a Tathāgata is describing a Tathāgata—the highest type of person, the supreme person, the attainer of the supreme attainment[163]—he describes him in terms of these four cases: 'The Tathāgata exists after death,' or 'The Tathāgata does not exist after death,' or 'The Tathāgata both exists and does not exist after death,' or 'The Tathāgata neither exists nor does not exist after death.'"

When this was said, the Venerable Anurādha said to those wanderers: 'Friends, when a Tathāgata is describing a Tathāgata—the highest type of person, the supreme person, the attainer of the supreme attainment—he describes him apart from these four cases: 'The Tathāgata exists after death,' or 'The Tathāgata does not exist after death,' or 'The Tathāgata both exists and does not exist after death,' or 'The Tathāgata neither exists nor does not exist after death.'"[164]

When this was said, those wanderers said to the Venerable Anurādha: 'This bhikkhu must be newly ordained, not long gone forth; or, if he is an elder, he must be an incompetent fool."

Then those wanderers of other sects, having denigrated the Venerable Anurādha with the terms "newly ordained" and "fool," rose from their seats and departed. [117]

Then, not long after those wanderers had left, it occurred to the Venerable Anurādha: "If those wanderers of other sects should question me further, how should I answer if I am to state what has been said by the Blessed One and not misrepresent him with what is contrary to fact? And how should I explain in accordance with the Dhamma, so that no reasonable consequence of my assertion would give ground for criticism?"

Then the Venerable Anurādha approached the Blessed One, paid homage to him, sat down to one side, and reported to the Blessed One everything that had happened, [118] asking: "If those wanderers of other sects should question me further, how should I answer ... so that no reasonable consequence of my assertion would give ground for criticism?"

"What do you think, Anurādha, is form permanent or impermanent?" – "Impermanent, venerable sir."... – "Therefore ... Seeing thus ... He understands: '... there is no more for this state of being.'

"What do you think, Anurādha, do you regard form as the Tathāgata?" – "No, venerable sir." – "Do you regard feeling ... perception ... volitional formations ... consciousness as the Tathāgata?" – "No, venerable sir."

"What do you think, Anurādha, do you regard the Tathāgata as in form?" – "No, venerable sir." – "Do you regard the Tathāgata as apart from form?" – "No, venerable sir." – "Do you regard the Tathāgata as in feeling? As apart from feeling? As in perception? As apart from perception? As in volitional formations? As apart from volitional formations? As in consciousness? As apart from consciousness?" – "No, venerable sir."

"What do you think, Anurādha, do you regard form, feeling, perception, volitional formations, and consciousness [taken together] as the Tathāgata?" – "No, venerable sir."

"What do you think, Anurādha, do you regard the Tathāgata as one who is without form, without feeling, without perception, without volitional formations, without consciousness?" – "No, venerable sir."

"But, Anurādha, when the Tathāgata is not apprehended by you as real and actual here in this very life, is it fitting for you to declare: 'Friends, when a Tathāgata is describing a Tathāgata—the highest type of person, the supreme person, the attainer of the supreme attainment—he describes him apart from these four cases: [119] 'The Tathāgata exists after death,' or ... 'The Tathāgata neither exists nor does not exist after death'?"

"No, venerable sir."

"Good, good, Anurādha! Formerly, Anurādha, and also now, I make known just suffering and the cessation of suffering."[165]

87 (5) Vakkali

Thus have I heard. On one occasion the Blessed One was dwelling at Rājagaha in the Bamboo Grove, the Squirrel Sanctuary. Now on that occasion the Venerable Vakkali was dwelling in a potter's shed, sick, afflicted, gravely ill.[166] Then the Venerable Vakkali addressed his attendants:

"Come, friends, approach the Blessed One, pay homage to him in my name with your head at his feet, and say: 'Venerable sir, the bhikkhu Vakkali is sick, afflicted, gravely ill; he pays homage to the Blessed One with his head at his feet.' Then say: 'It would be good, venerable sir, if the Blessed One would approach the bhikkhu Vakkali out of compassion.'"

"Yes, friend," those bhikkhus replied, and they approached the Blessed One, paid homage to him, sat down to one side, and delivered their message. The Blessed One consented by silence.

Then the Blessed One dressed and, taking bowl and robe, approached the Venerable Vakkali. [120] The Venerable Vakkali saw the Blessed One coming in the distance and stirred on his bed.[167] The Blessed One said to him: "Enough, Vakkali, do not stir on your bed. There are these seats ready, I will sit down there."

The Blessed One then sat down on the appointed seat and said to the Venerable Vakkali: "I hope you are bearing up, Vakkali, I hope you are getting better. I hope that your painful feelings are subsiding and not increasing, and that their subsiding, not their increase, is to be discerned."

"Venerable sir, I am not bearing up, I am not getting better. Strong painful feelings are increasing in me, not subsiding, and their increase, not their subsiding, is to be discerned."

"I hope then, Vakkali, that you are not troubled by remorse and regret."

"Indeed, venerable sir, I have quite a lot of remorse and regret."

"I hope, Vakkali, that you have nothing for which to reproach yourself in regard to virtue."

"I have nothing, venerable sir, for which to reproach myself in regard to virtue."

"Then, Vakkali, if you have nothing for which to reproach yourself in regard to virtue, why are you troubled by remorse and regret?"

"For a long time, venerable sir, I have wanted to come to see the Blessed One, but I haven't been fit enough to do so."

"Enough, Vakkali! Why do you want to see this foul body? One who sees the Dhamma sees me; one who sees me sees the Dhamma.[168] For in seeing the Dhamma, Vakkali, one sees me; and in seeing me, one sees the Dhamma.

"What do you think, Vakkali, is form permanent or impermanent?" – [121] "Impermanent, venerable sir."... – "Therefore ... Seeing thus ... He understands: '... there is no more for this state of being.'"

Then the Blessed One, having given this exhortation to the Venerable Vakkali, rose from his seat and departed for Mount Vulture Peak.

Then, not long after the Blessed One had left, the Venerable Vakkali addressed his attendants thus: "Come, friends, lift me up on this bed and carry me to the Black Rock on the Isigili Slope.[169] How can one like me think of dying among the houses?"

"Yes, friend," those bhikkhus replied and, having lifted up the Venerable Vakkali on the bed, they carried him to the Black Rock on the Isigili Slope.

The Blessed One spent the rest of that day and night on Mount Vulture Peak. Then, when the night was well advanced, two devatās of stunning beauty approached the Blessed One, illuminating the whole of Mount Vulture Peak.... Standing to one side, one devatā said to the Blessed One: "Venerable sir, the bhikkhu Vakkali is intent on deliverance."[170] The other devatā said: "Surely, venerable sir, he will be liberated as one well liberated."[171] This is what those devatās said. Having said this, they paid homage to the Blessed One and, keeping him on their right, they disappeared right there.

Then, when the night had passed, the Blessed One addressed the bhikkhus thus: "Come, bhikkhus, approach the bhikkhu Vakkali and say to him: 'Friend Vakkali, listen to the word of the Blessed One [122] and two devatās. Last night, friend, when the night was well advanced, two devatās of stunning beauty approached the Blessed One. One devatā said to the Blessed One: "Venerable sir, the bhikkhu Vakkali is intent on deliverance." The other devatā said: "Surely, venerable sir, he will be liberated as one well liberated." And the Blessed One says to you, friend Vakkali: "Do not be afraid, Vakkali, do not be afraid! Your death will not be a bad one. Your demise will not be a bad one."'"

"Yes, venerable sir," those bhikkhus replied, and they approached the Venerable Vakkali and said to him: "Friend Vakkali, listen to the word of the Blessed One and two devatās."

Then the Venerable Vakkali addressed his attendants: "Come, friends, lower me from the bed. How can one like me think of listening to the Blessed One's teaching while seated on a high seat."

"Yes, friend," those bhikkhus replied, and they lowered the Venerable Vakkali from the bed.

"Last night, friend, two devatās of stunning beauty approached the Blessed One. One devatā said to the Blessed One: 'Venerable sir, the bhikkhu Vakkali is intent on deliverance.' The other devatā said: 'Surely, venerable sir, he will be liberated as one well liberated.' And the Blessed One says to you, friend Vakkali: 'Do not be afraid, Vakkali, do not be afraid! Your death will not be a bad one. Your demise will not be a bad one.'"

"Well then, friends, pay homage to the Blessed One in my name with your head at his feet and say: 'Venerable sir, the bhikkhu Vakkali is sick, afflicted, gravely ill; he pays homage to the Blessed One with his head at his feet.' Then say: 'Form is impermanent: I have no perplexity about this, venerable sir, I do not doubt that whatever is impermanent is suffering. I do not doubt that in regard to what is impermanent, suffering, and subject to change, I have no more desire, lust, or affection. [123] Feeling is impermanent ... Perception is impermanent ... Volitional formations are impermanent ... Consciousness is impermanent: I have no perplexity about this, venerable sir, I do not doubt that whatever is impermanent is suffering. I do not doubt that in regard to what is impermanent, suffering, and subject to change, I have no more desire, lust, or affection.'"

"Yes, friend," those bhikkhus replied, and then they departed. Then, not long after those bhikkhus had left, the Venerable Vakkali used the knife.[172]

Then those bhikkhus approached the Blessed One ... and delivered their message. The Blessed One then addressed the bhikkhus thus: "Come, bhikkhus, let us go to the Black Rock on the Isigili Slope, where the clansman Vakkali has used the knife."

"Yes, venerable sir," those bhikkhus replied. Then the Blessed

One, together with a number of bhikkhus, went to the Black Rock on the Isigili Slope. The Blessed One saw in the distance the Venerable Vakkali lying on the bed with his shoulder turned. [124]

Now on that occasion a cloud of smoke, a swirl of darkness, was moving to the east, then to the west, to the north, to the south, upwards, downwards, and to the intermediate quarters. The Blessed One then addressed the bhikkhus thus: "Do you see, bhikkhus, that cloud of smoke, that swirl of darkness, moving to the east, then to the west, to the north, to the south, upwards, downwards, and to the intermediate quarters?"

"Yes, venerable sir."

"That, bhikkhus, is Māra the Evil One searching for the consciousness of the clansman Vakkali, wondering: 'Where now has the consciousness of the clansman Vakkali been established?' However, bhikkhus, with consciousness unestablished, the clansman Vakkali has attained final Nibbāna."

88 (6) Assaji

On one occasion the Blessed One was dwelling at Rājagaha in the Bamboo Grove, the Squirrel Sanctuary. Now on that occasion the Venerable Assaji was dwelling at Kassapaka's Park, sick, afflicted, gravely ill.

(*As in preceding sutta, down to*:) [125]

"Then if you have nothing for which to reproach yourself in regard to virtue, Assaji, why are you troubled by remorse and regret?"

"Formerly, venerable sir, when I was ill I kept on tranquillizing the bodily formations, but [now] I do not obtain concentration.[173] As I do not obtain concentration, it occurs to me: 'Let me not fall away!'"

"Those ascetics and brahmins, Assaji, who regard concentration as the essence and identify concentration with asceticism,[174] failing to obtain concentration, might think, 'Let us not fall away!'

"What do you think, Assaji, is form permanent or impermanent?" – "Impermanent, venerable sir."... [126] – "Therefore ... Seeing thus ... He understands: '... there is no more for this state of being.'[175]

"If he feels a pleasant feeling, he understands: 'It is impermanent'; he understands: 'It is not held to'; he understands: 'It is not delighted in.' If he feels a painful feeling, he understands: 'It is impermanent'; he understands: 'It is not held to'; he understands: 'It is not delighted in.' If he feels a neither-painful-nor-pleasant feeling, he understands: 'It is impermanent'; he understands: 'It is not held to'; he understands: 'It is not delighted in.'

"If he feels a pleasant feeling, he feels it detached; if he feels a painful feeling, he feels it detached; if he feels a neither-painful-nor-pleasant feeling, he feels it detached.

"When he feels a feeling terminating with the body, he understands: 'I feel a feeling terminating with the body.' When he feels a feeling terminating with life, he understands: 'I feel a feeling terminating with life.' He understands: 'With the breakup of the body, following the exhaustion of life, all that is felt, not being delighted in, will become cool right here.'

"Just as, Assaji, an oil lamp burns in dependence on the oil and the wick, and with the exhaustion of the oil and the wick it is extinguished through lack of fuel, so too, Assaji, when a bhikkhu feels a feeling terminating with the body ... terminating with life ... He understands: 'With the breakup of the body, following the exhaustion of life, all that is felt, not being delighted in, will become cool right here.'"

89 (7) Khemaka

On one occasion a number of elder bhikkhus were dwelling at Kosambī in Ghosita's Park. Now on that occasion the Venerable Khemaka was living at Jujube Tree Park, sick, afflicted, gravely ill. [127]

Then, in the evening, those elder bhikkhus emerged from seclusion and addressed the Venerable Dāsaka thus: "Come, friend Dāsaka, approach the bhikkhu Khemaka and say to him: 'The elders say to you, friend Khemaka: We hope that you are bearing up, friend, we hope that you are getting better. We hope that your painful feelings are subsiding and not increasing, and that their subsiding, not their increase, is to be discerned.'"

"Yes, friends," the Venerable Dāsaka replied, and he approached the Venerable Khemaka and delivered his message.

[The Venerable Khemaka answered:] "I am not bearing up, friend, I am not getting better. Strong painful feelings are increasing in me, not subsiding, and their increase, not their subsiding, is to be discerned."

Then the Venerable Dāsaka approached the elder bhikkhus and reported what the Venerable Khemaka had said. They told him: "Come, friend Dāsaka, approach the bhikkhu Khemaka and say to him: 'The elders say to you, friend Khemaka: These five aggregates subject to clinging, friend, have been spoken of by the Blessed One; that is, the form aggregate subject to clinging, the feeling aggregate subject to clinging, the perception aggregate subject to clinging, the volitional formations aggregate subject to clinging, the consciousness aggregate subject to clinging. Does the Venerable Khemaka regard anything as self or as belonging to self among these five aggregates subject to clinging?'"

"Yes, friends," the Venerable Dāsaka replied, and he approached the Venerable Khemaka and delivered his message.

[The Venerable Khemaka replied:] [128] "These five aggregates subject to clinging have been spoken of by the Blessed One; that is, the form aggregate subject to clinging ... the consciousness aggregate subject to clinging. Among these five aggregates subject to clinging, I do not regard anything as self or as belonging to self."

Then the Venerable Dāsaka approached the elder bhikkhus and reported what the Venerable Khemaka had said. They replied: "Come, friend Dāsaka, approach the bhikkhu Khemaka and say to him: 'The elders say to you, friend Khemaka: These five aggregates subject to clinging, friend, have been spoken of by the Blessed One; that is, the form aggregate subject to clinging ... the consciousness aggregate subject to clinging. If the Venerable Khemaka does not regard anything among these five aggregates subject to clinging as self or as belonging to self, then he is an arahant, one whose taints are destroyed.'"

"Yes, friends," the Venerable Dāsaka replied, and he approached the Venerable Khemaka and delivered his message.

[The Venerable Khemaka replied:] "These five aggregates subject to clinging have been spoken of by the Blessed One; that is, the form aggregate subject to clinging ... the consciousness aggregate subject to clinging. I do not regard anything among these five aggregates subject to clinging as self or as belonging to self, yet I am not an arahant, one whose taints are destroyed. Friends, [the notion] 'I am' has not yet vanished in me in relation to these five aggregates subject to clinging, but I do not regard [anything among them] as 'This I am.'"[176] [129]

Then the Venerable Dāsaka approached the elder bhikkhus and reported what the Venerable Khemaka had said. They replied: "Come, friend Dāsaka, approach the bhikkhu Khemaka and say to him: 'The elders say to you, friend Khemaka: Friend Khemaka, when you speak of this "I am"—what is it that you speak of as "I am"? Do you speak of form as "I am," or do you speak of "I am" apart from form? Do you speak of feeling … of perception … of volitional formations … of consciousness as "I am," or do you speak of "I am" apart from consciousness? When you speak of this "I am," friend Khemaka, what is it that you speak of as "I am"?'"

"Yes, friends," the Venerable Dāsaka replied, and he approached the Venerable Khemaka and delivered his message.

"Enough, friend Dāsaka! Why keep running back and forth? Bring me my staff, friend. I'll go to the elder bhikkhus myself."

Then the Venerable Khemaka, leaning on his staff, approached the elder bhikkhus, exchanged greetings with them, and sat down to one side. [130] The elder bhikkhus then said to him: "Friend Khemaka, when you speak of this 'I am' … what is it that you speak of as 'I am'?"

"Friends, I do not speak of form as 'I am,' nor do I speak of 'I am' apart from form. I do not speak of feeling as 'I am' … nor of perception as 'I am' … nor of volitional formations as 'I am' … nor of consciousness as 'I am,' nor do I speak of 'I am' apart from consciousness. Friends, although [the notion] 'I am' has not yet vanished in me in relation to these five aggregates subject to clinging, still I do not regard [anything among them] as 'This I am.'

"Suppose, friends, there is the scent of a blue, red, or white lotus. Would one be speaking rightly if one would say, 'The scent belongs to the petals,' or 'The scent belongs to the stalk,'[177] or 'The scent belongs to the pistils'?"

"No, friend."

"And how, friends, should one answer if one is to answer rightly?"

"Answering rightly, friend, one should answer: 'The scent belongs to the flower.'"

"So too, friends, I do not speak of form as 'I am,' nor do I speak of 'I am' apart from form. I do not speak of feeling as 'I am' … nor of perception as 'I am' … nor of volitional formations as 'I am' … nor of consciousness as 'I am,' nor do I speak of 'I am' apart from consciousness. Friends, although [the notion] 'I am' has not yet vanished in me in relation to these five aggregates subject to clinging, still I do not regard [anything among them] as 'This I am.'

"Friends, even though a noble disciple has abandoned the five lower fetters, still, in relation to the five aggregates subject to clinging, there lingers in him a residual conceit 'I am,' a desire 'I am,' an underlying tendency 'I am' that has not yet been uprooted. Sometime later he dwells contemplating rise and fall in the five aggregates subject to clinging: 'Such is form, such its origin, [131] such its passing away; such is feeling ... such is perception ... such are volitional formations ... such is consciousness, such its origin, such its passing away.' As he dwells thus contemplating rise and fall in the five aggregates subject to clinging, the residual conceit 'I am,' the desire 'I am,' the underlying tendency 'I am' that had not yet been uprooted—this comes to be uprooted.

"Suppose, friends, a cloth has become soiled and stained, and its owners give it to a laundryman. The laundryman would scour it evenly with cleaning salt, lye, or cowdung, and rinse it in clean water. Even though that cloth would become pure and clean, it would still retain a residual smell of cleaning salt, lye, or cowdung that had not yet vanished. The laundryman would then give it back to the owners. The owners would put it in a sweet-scented casket, and the residual smell of cleaning salt, lye, or cowdung that had not yet vanished would vanish.[178]

"So too, friends, even though a noble disciple has abandoned the five lower fetters, still, in relation to the five aggregates subject to clinging, there lingers in him a residual conceit 'I am,' a desire 'I am,' an underlying tendency 'I am' that has not yet been uprooted.... As he dwells thus contemplating rise and fall in the five aggregates subject to clinging, the residual conceit 'I am,' the desire 'I am,' the underlying tendency 'I am' that had not yet been uprooted—this comes to be uprooted."

When this was said, the elder bhikkhus said to the Venerable Khemaka: "We did not ask our questions in order to trouble the Venerable Khemaka, [132] but we thought that the Venerable Khemaka would be capable of explaining, teaching, proclaiming, establishing, disclosing, analysing, and elucidating the Blessed One's teaching in detail. And the Venerable Khemaka has explained, taught, proclaimed, established, disclosed, analysed, and elucidated the Blessed One's teaching in detail."

This is what the Venerable Khemaka said. Elated, the elder bhikkhus delighted in the Venerable Khemaka's statement. And while this discourse was being spoken, the minds of sixty elder bhikkhus and of the Venerable Khemaka were liberated from the taints by nonclinging.

90 (8) Channa

On one occasion a number of bhikkhus were dwelling at Bārāṇasī in the Deer Park at Isipatana. Then, in the evening, the Venerable Channa emerged from seclusion and, taking his key, went from dwelling to dwelling saying to the elder bhikkhus: "Let the elder venerable ones exhort me, let them instruct me, let them give me a Dhamma talk in such a way that I might see the Dhamma."[179]

When this was said, the elder bhikkhus said to the Venerable Channa: "Form, friend Channa, is impermanent, feeling is impermanent, perception is impermanent, volitional formations are impermanent, consciousness is impermanent. Form is nonself, [133] feeling is nonself, perception is nonself, volitional formations are nonself, consciousness is nonself. All formations are impermanent; all phenomena are nonself."[180]

Then it occurred to the Venerable Channa: "I too think in this way: 'Form is impermanent … consciousness is impermanent. Form is nonself … consciousness is nonself. All formations are impermanent; all phenomena are nonself.' But my mind does not launch out upon the stilling of all formations, the relinquishing of all acquisitions, the destruction of craving, dispassion, cessation, Nibbāna; nor does it acquire confidence, settle down, and resolve on it. Instead, agitation and clinging arise and the mind turns back, thinking: 'But who is my self?'[181] But such does not happen to one who sees the Dhamma. So who can teach me the Dhamma in such a way that I might see the Dhamma?"

Then it occurred to the Venerable Channa: "This Venerable Ānanda is dwelling at Kosambī in Ghosita's Park, and he has been praised by the Teacher and is esteemed by his wise brothers in the holy life. The Venerable Ānanda is capable of teaching me the Dhamma in such a way that I might see the Dhamma. Since I have so much trust in the Venerable Ānanda, let me approach him."

Then the Venerable Channa set his lodging in order, took his bowl and robe, and went to Ghosita's Park in Kosambī, where he approached the Venerable Ānanda and exchanged greetings with him. When they had concluded their greetings and cordial talk, he sat down to one side and told the Venerable Ānanda everything that had happened, adding: [134] "Let the Venerable Ānanda exhort me, let him instruct me, let him give me a Dhamma talk in such a way that I might see the Dhamma."

"Even by this much am I pleased with the Venerable Channa. Perhaps the Venerable Channa has opened himself up and broken through his barrenness.[182] Lend your ear, friend Channa, you are capable of understanding the Dhamma."

Then at once a lofty rapture and gladness arose in the Venerable Channa as he thought: "It seems that I am capable of understanding the Dhamma."

[The Venerable Ānanda then said:] "In the presence of the Blessed One I have heard this, friend Channa, in his presence I have received the exhortation he spoke to the bhikkhu Kaccānagotta:[183]

> "This world, Kaccāna, for the most part relies upon a duality … [135] (*the entire sutta 12:15 is cited here*) … Such is the cessation of this whole mass of suffering."

"So it is, friend Ānanda, for those venerable ones who have such compassionate and benevolent brothers in the holy life to admonish and instruct them. And now that I have heard this Dhamma teaching of the Venerable Ānanda, I have made the breakthrough to the Dhamma."

91 (9) Rāhula (1)

At Sāvatthī.[184] Then the Venerable Rāhula approached the Blessed One, paid homage to him, sat down to one side, [136] and said to him:

"Venerable sir, how should one know, how should one see so that, in regard to this body with consciousness and in regard to all external signs, I-making, mine-making, and the underlying tendency to conceit no longer occur within?"

"Any kind of form whatsoever, Rāhula, whether past, future,

or present, internal or external, gross or subtle, inferior or superior, far or near—one sees all form as it really is with correct wisdom thus: 'This is not mine, this I am not, this is not my self.'

"Any kind of feeling whatsoever ... Any kind of perception whatsoever ... Any kind of volitional formations whatsoever ... Any kind of consciousness whatsoever, whether past, future, or present, internal or external, gross or subtle, inferior or superior, far or near—one sees all consciousness as it really is with correct wisdom thus: 'This is not mine, this I am not, this is not my self.'

"When one knows and sees thus, Rāhula, then in regard to this body with consciousness and in regard to all external signs, I-making, mine-making, and the underlying tendency to conceit no longer occur within."

92 (10) Rāhula (2)

At Sāvatthī. Then the Venerable Rāhula ... said to the Blessed One:

"Venerable sir, how should one know, how should one see so that, in regard to this body with consciousness and in regard to all external signs, the mind is rid of I-making, mine-making, and conceit, has transcended discrimination, and is peaceful and well liberated?"

"Any kind of form whatsoever, Rāhula, whether past, future, or present ... far or near—having seen all form as it really is with correct wisdom thus: 'This is not mine, this I am not, this is not my self,' one is liberated by nonclinging.

"Any kind of feeling whatsoever ... Any kind of perception whatsoever ... Any kind of volitional formations whatsoever ... Any kind of consciousness whatsoever, whether past, future, or present, internal or external, gross or subtle, inferior or superior, far or near—[137] having seen all consciousness as it really is with correct wisdom thus: 'This is not mine, this I am not, this is not my self,' one is liberated by nonclinging.

"When one knows and sees thus, Rāhula, then in regard to this body with consciousness and in regard to all external signs, the mind is rid of I-making, mine-making, and conceit, has transcended discrimination, and is peaceful and well liberated."

V. Flowers

93 (1) *The River*

At Sāvatthī. "Bhikkhus, suppose there was a mountain river sweeping downwards, flowing into the distance with a swift current. If on either bank of the river *kāsa* grass or *kusa* grass were to grow, it would overhang it; if rushes, reeds, or trees were to grow, they would overhang it. If a man being carried along by the current should grasp the *kāsa* grass, it would break off and he would thereby meet with calamity and disaster; if he should grasp the *kusa* grass, it would break off and he would thereby meet with calamity and disaster; if he should grasp the rushes, reeds, or trees, [138] they would break off and he would thereby meet with calamity and disaster.

"So too, bhikkhus, the uninstructed worldling … regards form as self, or self as possessing form, or form as in self, or self as in form. That form of his disintegrates and he thereby meets with calamity and disaster. He regards feeling as self … perception as self … volitional formations as self … consciousness as self, or self as possessing consciousness, or consciousness as in self, or self as in consciousness. That consciousness of his disintegrates and he thereby meets with calamity and disaster.

"What do you think, bhikkhus, is form permanent or impermanent?" – "Impermanent, venerable sir."… – "Therefore … Seeing thus … He understands: '… there is no more for this state of being.'"

94 (2) *Flowers*

At Sāvatthī. "Bhikkhus, I do not dispute with the world; rather, it is the world that disputes with me. A proponent of the Dhamma does not dispute with anyone in the world. Of that which the wise in the world agree upon as not existing, I too say that it does not exist. And of that which the wise in the world agree upon as existing, I too say that it exists.[185]

"And what is it, bhikkhus, that the wise in the world agree upon as not existing, of which I too say that it does not exist? [139] Form that is permanent, stable, eternal, not subject to change: this the wise in the world agree upon as not existing, and I too say that it does not exist. Feeling … Perception … Volitional formations … Consciousness that is permanent, stable, eternal, not subject to change: this the wise in the world agree upon as not existing, and I too say that it does not exist.

"That, bhikkhus, is what the wise in the world agree upon as not existing, of which I too say that it does not exist.

"And what is it, bhikkhus, that the wise in the world agree upon as existing, of which I too say that it exists? Form that is impermanent, suffering, and subject to change: this the wise in the world agree upon as existing, and I too say that it exists. Feeling … Perception … Volitional formations … Consciousness that is impermanent, suffering, and subject to change: this the wise in the world agree upon as existing, and I too say that it exists.

"That, bhikkhus, is what the wise in the world agree upon as existing, of which I too say that it exists.

"There is, bhikkhus, a world-phenomenon[186] in the world to which the Tathāgata has awakened and broken through. Having done so, he explains it, teaches it, proclaims it, establishes it, discloses it, analyses it, elucidates it.

"And what is that world-phenomenon in the world to which the Tathāgata has awakened and broken through? Form, bhikkhus, is a world-phenomenon in the world to which the Tathāgata has awakened and broken through. Having done so, he explains it, teaches it, proclaims it, establishes it, discloses it, analyses it, elucidates it. When it is being thus explained … [140] … and elucidated by the Tathāgata, if anyone does not know and see, how can I do anything with that foolish worldling, blind and sightless, who does not know and does not see?

"Feeling … Perception … Volitional formations … Consciousness is a world-phenomenon in the world to which the Tathāgata has awakened and broken through. Having done so, he explains it, teaches it, proclaims it, establishes it, discloses it, analyses it, elucidates it. When it is being thus explained … and elucidated by the Tathāgata, if anyone does not know and see, how can I do anything with that foolish worldling, blind and sightless, who does not know and does not see?

"Bhikkhus, just as a blue, red, or white lotus is born in the water and grows up in the water, but having risen up above the water, it stands unsullied by the water, so too the Tathāgata was born in the world and grew up in the world, but having overcome the world, he dwells unsullied by the world."[187]

95 (3) A Lump of Foam

On one occasion the Blessed One was dwelling at Ayojjhā on the bank of the river Ganges. There the Blessed One addressed the bhikkhus thus:[188]

"Bhikkhus, suppose that this river Ganges was carrying along a great lump of foam. A man with good sight would inspect it, ponder it, and carefully investigate it, and it would appear to him to be void, hollow, insubstantial. For what substance could there be in a lump of foam? So too, bhikkhus, whatever kind of form there is, whether past, future, or present, internal or external, gross or subtle, inferior or superior, far or near: [141] a bhikkhu inspects it, ponders it, and carefully investigates it, and it would appear to him to be void, hollow, insubstantial. For what substance could there be in form?[189]

"Suppose, bhikkhus, that in the autumn, when it is raining and big rain drops are falling, a water bubble arises and bursts on the surface of the water. A man with good sight would inspect it, ponder it, and carefully investigate it, and it would appear to him to be void, hollow, insubstantial. For what substance could there be in a water bubble? So too, bhikkhus, whatever kind of feeling there is, whether past, future, or present, internal or external, gross or subtle, inferior or superior, far or near: a bhikkhu inspects it, ponders it, and carefully investigates it, and it would appear to him to be void, hollow, insubstantial. For what substance could there be in feeling?[190]

"Suppose, bhikkhus, that in the last month of the hot season, at high noon, a shimmering mirage appears. A man with good sight would inspect it, ponder it, and carefully investigate it, and it would appear to him to be void, hollow, insubstantial. For what substance could there be in a mirage? So too, bhikkhus, whatever kind of perception there is, whether past, future, or present, internal or external, gross or subtle, inferior or superior, far or near: a bhikkhu inspects it, ponders it, and carefully investigates it, and it would appear to him to be void, hollow, insubstantial. For what substance could there be in perception?[191]

"Suppose, bhikkhus, that a man needing heartwood, seeking heartwood, wandering in search of heartwood, would take a sharp axe and enter a forest. There he would see the trunk of a large plantain tree, straight, fresh, without a fruit-bud core.[192] He would cut it down at the root, cut off the crown, and unroll the coil. As he unrolls the coil, he would not find even softwood, let alone heartwood. A man with good sight would inspect it, ponder it, and carefully investigate it, [142] and it would appear to him to be void, hollow, insubstantial. For what substance could there be in the trunk of a plantain tree? So too, bhikkhus, whatever kind of volitional formations there are, whether past, future, or present, internal or external, gross or subtle, inferior or superior, far or near: a bhikkhu inspects them, ponders them, and carefully investigates them. As he investigates them, they appear to him to be void, hollow, insubstantial. For what substance could there be in volitional formations?[193]

"Suppose, bhikkhus, that a magician or a magician's apprentice would display a magical illusion at a crossroads. A man with good sight would inspect it, ponder it, and carefully investigate it, and it would appear to him to be void, hollow, insubstantial. For what substance could there be in a magical illusion? So too, bhikkhus, whatever kind of consciousness there is, whether past, future, or present, internal or external, gross or subtle, inferior or superior, far or near: a bhikkhu inspects it, ponders it, and carefully investigates it, and it would appear to him to be void, hollow, insubstantial. For what substance could there be in consciousness?[194]

"Seeing thus, bhikkhus, the instructed noble disciple experiences revulsion towards form, revulsion towards feeling, revulsion towards perception, revulsion towards volitional formations, revulsion towards consciousness. Experiencing revulsion, he becomes dispassionate. Through dispassion [his mind] is liberated. When it is liberated there comes the knowledge: 'It's liberated.' He understands: 'Destroyed is birth, the holy life has been lived, what had to be done has been done, there is no more for this state of being.'"

This is what the Blessed One said. Having said this, the Fortunate One, the Teacher, further said this:

"Form is like a lump of foam,
Feeling like a water bubble;
Perception is like a mirage,
Volitions like a plantain trunk,

And consciousness like an illusion,
So explained the Kinsman of the Sun.

"However one may ponder it
And carefully investigate it,
It appears but hollow and void
When one views it carefully. [143]

"With reference to this body
The One of Broad Wisdom has taught
That with the abandoning of three things
One sees this form discarded.

"When vitality, heat, and consciousness
Depart from this physical body,
Then it lies there cast away:
Food for others, without volition.[195]

"Such is this continuum,
This illusion, beguiler of fools.
It is taught to be a murderer;
Here no substance can be found.[196]

"A bhikkhu with energy aroused
Should look upon the aggregates thus,
Whether by day or at night,[197]
Comprehending, ever mindful.

"He should discard all the fetters
And make a refuge for himself;
Let him fare as with head ablaze,
Yearning for the imperishable state."

96 (4) A Lump of Cowdung

At Sāvatthī. Then a certain bhikkhu ... Sitting to one side, that bhikkhu said to the Blessed One:

"Venerable sir, is there any form that is permanent, stable, eternal, not subject to change, and that will remain the same just like eternity itself? Is there, venerable sir, any feeling ... any perception ... any volitional formations ... any consciousness [144] that is permanent, stable, eternal, not subject to change, and that will remain the same just like eternity itself?"

"Bhikkhu, there is no form that is permanent, stable, eternal, not subject to change, and that will remain the same just like eternity itself. There is no feeling ... no perception ... no volitional formations ... no consciousness that is permanent, stable, eternal, not subject to change, and that will remain the same just like eternity itself."

Then the Blessed One took up a little lump of cowdung in his hand and said to that bhikkhu: "Bhikkhu, there is not even this much individual existence that is permanent, stable, eternal, not subject to change, and that will remain the same just like eternity itself. If there was this much individual existence that was permanent, stable, eternal, not subject to change, this living of the holy life for the complete destruction of suffering could not be discerned.[198] But because there is not even this much individual existence that is permanent, stable, eternal, not subject to change, this living of the holy life for the complete destruction of suffering is discerned.

"In the past, bhikkhu, I was a head-anointed khattiya king.[199] I had 84,000 cities, the chief of which was the capital Kusāvatī. I had 84,000 palaces, the chief of which was the palace [named] Dhamma. I had 84,000 halls with peaked roofs, the chief of which was the hall [named] the Great Array. I had 84,000 couches made of ivory, of heartwood, of gold and silver, decked with long-haired coverlets, embroidered with flowers, with choice spreads made of antelope hides, [145] with red awnings overhead and red cushions at both ends.

"I had 84,000 bull elephants with golden ornaments and golden banners, covered with nets of golden thread, the chief of which was the royal bull elephant [named] Uposatha.[200] I had 84,000 steeds with golden ornaments and golden banners, covered with nets of golden thread, the chief of which was the royal steed [named] Valāhaka. I had 84,000 chariots with golden ornaments and golden banners, covered with nets of golden thread, the chief of which was the chariot [named] Vejayanta.

"I had 84,000 jewels, the chief of which was the jewel-gem. I had 84,000 women, the chief of whom was Queen Subhaddā. I had 84,000 vassals of the khattiya caste, the chief of whom was the commander-gem. I had 84,000 cows with tethers of fine jute and milk pails of bronze. I had 84,000 *koṭis* of garments made of fine linen, of fine silk, of fine wool, of fine cotton. I had 84,000 plates on which my meals were served both in the morning and in the evening.

"Of those 84,000 cities,[201] bhikkhu, there was only one city in which I resided at that time: the capital Kusāvatī. Of those 84,000 palaces, [146] there was only one palace in which I resided at that time: the palace [named] Dhamma. Of those 84,000 halls with peaked roof, there was only one hall with peaked roof in which I resided at that time: the hall [named] the Great Array. Of those 84,000 couches, there was only one couch that I used at that time, one made either of ivory or of heartwood or of gold or of silver.

"Of those 84,000 elephants, there was only one elephant that I rode at that time, the royal bull elephant [named] Uposatha. Of those 84,000 steeds, there was only one steed that I rode at that time, the royal steed [named] Valāhaka. Of those 84,000 chariots, there was only one chariot that I rode in at that time, the chariot [named] Vejayanta.

"Of those 84,000 women, there was only one woman who waited on me at that time, either a khattiya maiden or a *velāmika* maiden.[202] Of those 84,000 *koṭis* of garments, there was only one pair of garments that I wore at that time, one made either of fine linen or of fine silk or of fine wool or of fine cotton. Of those 84,000 plates, there was only one plate from which I ate at most a measure of rice with a suitable curry.

"Thus, bhikkhu, all those formations have passed, ceased, changed. So impermanent are formations, bhikkhu, so unstable, so unreliable. [147] It is enough, bhikkhu, to feel revulsion towards all formations, enough to become dispassionate towards them, enough to be liberated from them."

97 (5) The Fingernail

At Sāvatthī. Sitting to one side, that bhikkhu said to the Blessed One: "Is there, venerable sir, any form that is permanent, stable, eternal, not subject to change, and that will remain the same just like eternity itself? Is there any feeling ... any perception ... any volitional formations ... any consciousness that is permanent, stable, eternal, not subject to change, and that will remain the same just like eternity itself?"

"Bhikkhu, there is no form … no feeling … no perception … no volitional formations … no consciousness that is permanent, stable, eternal, not subject to change, and that will remain the same just like eternity itself."

Then the Blessed One took up a little bit of soil in his fingernail and said to that bhikkhu: "Bhikkhu, there is not even this much form that is permanent, stable, eternal, not subject to change, and that will remain the same just like eternity itself. If there was this much form that was permanent, stable, eternal, not subject to change, this living of the holy life for the complete destruction of suffering could not be discerned. But because there is not even this much form that is permanent, stable, eternal, not subject to change, this living of the holy life for the complete destruction of suffering is discerned. [148]

"There is not even this much feeling … perception … volitional formations … consciousness that is permanent, stable, eternal, not subject to change, and that will remain the same just like eternity itself. If there was this much consciousness … But because there is not even this much consciousness that is permanent, stable, eternal, not subject to change, this living of the holy life for the complete destruction of suffering is discerned.

"What do you think, bhikkhu, is form permanent or impermanent?" – "Impermanent, venerable sir."… [149] … – "Therefore … Seeing thus … He understands: '… there is no more for this state of being.'"

98 (6) Simple Version

At Sāvatthī. Sitting to one side, that bhikkhu said to the Blessed One: "Is there, venerable sir, any form, any feeling, any perception, any volitional formations, any consciousness that is permanent, stable, eternal, not subject to change, and that will remain the same just like eternity itself?"

"Bhikkhu, there is no form, no feeling, no perception, no volitional formations, no consciousness that is permanent, stable, eternal, not subject to change, and that will remain the same just like eternity itself."

99 (7) The Leash (1)

At Sāvatthī. "Bhikkhus, this saṃsāra is without discoverable beginning. A first point is not discerned of beings roaming and wandering on hindered by ignorance and fettered by craving.[203]

"There comes a time, bhikkhus, when the great ocean dries up and evaporates and no longer exists,[204] but still, I say, there is no making an end of suffering for those beings roaming and wandering on hindered by ignorance and fettered by craving.

"There comes a time, bhikkhus, when Sineru, the king of mountains, burns up and perishes and no longer exists, but still, I say, [150] there is no making an end of suffering for those beings roaming and wandering on hindered by ignorance and fettered by craving.

"There comes a time, bhikkhus, when the great earth burns up and perishes and no longer exists, but still, I say, there is no making an end of suffering for those beings roaming and wandering on hindered by ignorance and fettered by craving.

"Suppose, bhikkhus, a dog tied up on a leash was bound to a strong post or pillar: it would just keep on running and revolving around that same post or pillar. So too, the uninstructed worldling … regards form as self … feeling as self … perception as self … volitional formations as self … consciousness as self…. He just keeps running and revolving around form, around feeling, around perception, around volitional formations, around consciousness.[205] As he keeps on running and revolving around them, he is not freed from form, not freed from feeling, not freed from perception, not freed from volitional formations, not freed from consciousness. He is not freed from birth, aging, and death; not freed from sorrow, lamentation, pain, displeasure, and despair; not freed from suffering, I say.

"But the instructed noble disciple … does not regard form as self … nor feeling as self … nor perception as self … nor volitional formations as self … nor consciousness as self…. He no longer keeps running and revolving around form, around feeling, around perception, around volitional formations, around consciousness. As he no longer keeps running and revolving around them, he is freed from form, freed from feeling, freed from perception, freed from volitional formations, freed from consciousness. He is freed from birth, aging, and death; freed from sorrow, lamentation, pain, displeasure, and despair; freed from suffering, I say." [151]

100 (8) The Leash (2)

"Bhikkhus, this saṃsāra is without discoverable beginning. A first point is not discerned of beings roaming and wandering on hindered by ignorance and fettered by craving....

"Suppose, bhikkhus, a dog tied up on a leash was bound to a strong post or pillar. If it walks, it walks close to that post or pillar. If it stands, it stands close to that post or pillar. If it sits down, it sits down close to that post or pillar. If it lies down, it lies down close to that post or pillar.

"So too, bhikkhus, the uninstructed worldling regards form thus: 'This is mine, this I am, this is my self.' He regards feeling ... perception ... volitional formations ... consciousness thus: 'This is mine, this I am, this is my self.' If he walks, he walks close to those five aggregates subject to clinging. If he stands, he stands close to those five aggregates subject to clinging. If he sits down, he sits down close to those five aggregates subject to clinging. If he lies down, he lies down close to those five aggregates subject to clinging.

"Therefore, bhikkhus, one should often reflect upon one's own mind thus: 'For a long time this mind has been defiled by lust, hatred, and delusion.' Through the defilements of the mind beings are defiled; with the cleansing of the mind beings are purified.

"Bhikkhus, have you seen the picture called 'Faring On'?"[206]

"Yes, venerable sir."

"Even that picture called 'Faring On' has been designed in its diversity by the mind, yet the mind is even more diverse than that picture called 'Faring On.'[207]

"Therefore, bhikkhus, one should often reflect upon one's own mind thus: 'For a long time this mind has been defiled by lust, hatred, and delusion.' Through the defilements of the mind beings are defiled; with the cleansing of the mind beings are purified. [152]

"Bhikkhus, I do not see any other order of living beings so diversified as those in the animal realm. Even those beings in the animal realm have been diversified by the mind,[208] yet the mind is even more diverse than those beings in the animal realm.

"Therefore, bhikkhus, one should often reflect upon one's own mind thus: 'For a long time this mind has been defiled by lust, hatred, and delusion.' Through the defilements of the mind beings are defiled; with the cleansing of the mind beings are purified.

"Suppose, bhikkhus, an artist or a painter, using dye or lac or turmeric or indigo or crimson, would create the figure of a man or a woman complete in all its features on a well-polished plank or wall or canvas.[209] So too, when the uninstructed worldling produces anything, it is only form that he produces; only feeling that he produces; only perception that he produces; only volitional formations that he produces; only consciousness that he produces.

"What do you think, bhikkhus, is form permanent or impermanent?" – "Impermanent, venerable sir."... – "Therefore ... Seeing thus ... He understands: '... there is no more for this state of being.'"

101 (9) The Adze Handle (or The Ship)

At Sāvatthī. "Bhikkhus, I say that the destruction of the taints is for one who knows and sees, not for one who does not know and does not see. For one who knows what, who sees what, does the destruction of the taints come about? 'Such is form, such its origin, such its passing away; such is feeling ... such is perception ... such are volitional formations ... such is consciousness, such its origin, [153] such its passing away': it is for one who knows thus, for one who sees thus, that the destruction of the taints comes about.[210]

"Bhikkhus, when a bhikkhu does not dwell devoted to development, even though such a wish as this might arise in him: 'Oh, that my mind might be liberated from the taints by nonclinging!' yet his mind is not liberated from the taints by nonclinging. For what reason? It should be said: because of nondevelopment. Because of not developing what? Because of not developing the four establishments of mindfulness ... the four right strivings ... the four bases for spiritual power ... the five spiritual faculties ... the five powers ... the seven factors of enlightenment ... the Noble Eightfold Path.[211]

"Suppose, bhikkhus there was a hen with eight, ten, or twelve eggs that she had not covered, incubated, and nurtured properly.

Even though such a wish as this might arise in her: 'Oh, that my chicks might pierce their shells with the points of their claws and beaks and hatch safely!' yet the chicks are incapable of piercing their shells with the points of their claws and beaks and hatching safely. For what reason? Because that hen with eight, ten, or twelve eggs had not covered, incubated, and nurtured them properly.

"So too, bhikkhus, when a bhikkhu does not dwell devoted to development, even though such a wish as this might arise in him: 'Oh, that my mind might be liberated from the taints by nonclinging!' yet his mind is not liberated from the taints by nonclinging. For what reason? It should be said: because of nondevelopment. Because of not developing what? Because of not developing ... the Noble Eightfold Path.

"Bhikkhus, when a bhikkhu dwells devoted to development, [154] even though no such wish as this might arise in him: 'Oh, that my mind might be liberated from the taints by nonclinging!' yet his mind is liberated from the taints by nonclinging. For what reason? It should be said: because of development. Because of developing what? Because of developing the four establishments of mindfulness ... the four right strivings ... the four bases for spiritual power ... the five spiritual faculties ... the five powers ... the seven factors of enlightenment ... the Noble Eightfold Path.

"Suppose, bhikkhus, there was a hen with eight, ten, or twelve eggs that she had covered, incubated, and nurtured properly. Even though no such wish as this might arise in her: 'Oh, that my chicks might pierce their shells with the points of their claws and beaks and hatch safely!' yet the chicks are capable of piercing their shells with the points of their claws and beaks and of hatching safely. For what reason? Because that hen with eight, ten, or twelve eggs had covered, incubated, and nurtured them properly.

"So too, bhikkhus,[212] when a bhikkhu dwells devoted to development, even though no such wish as this might arise in him: 'Oh, that my mind might be liberated from the taints by nonclinging!' yet his mind is liberated from the taints by nonclinging. For what reason? It should be said: because of development. Because of developing what? Because of developing ... the Noble Eightfold Path.

"When, bhikkhus, a carpenter[213] or a carpenter's apprentice looks at the handle of his adze, he sees the impressions of his fingers and his thumb, but he does not know: 'So much of the adze handle has been worn away today, so much yesterday, so much earlier.' But when it has worn away, the knowledge occurs to him that it has worn away.

"So too, bhikkhus, when a bhikkhu dwells devoted to development, [155] even though no such knowledge occurs to him: 'So much of my taints has been worn away today, so much yesterday, so much earlier,' yet when they are worn away, the knowledge occurs to him that they have been worn away.

"Suppose, bhikkhus, there was a seafaring ship bound with rigging that had been worn away in the water for six months.[214] It would be hauled up on dry land during the cold season and its rigging would be further attacked by wind and sun. Inundated by rain from a rain cloud, the rigging would easily collapse and rot away. So too, bhikkhus, when a bhikkhu dwells devoted to development, his fetters easily collapse and rot away."

102 (10) Perception of Impermanence

At Sāvatthī. "Bhikkhus, when the perception of impermanence is developed and cultivated, it eliminates all sensual lust, it eliminates all lust for existence, it eliminates all ignorance, it uproots all conceit 'I am.'[215]

"Just as, bhikkhus, in the autumn a ploughman ploughing with a great ploughshare cuts through all the rootlets as he ploughs, so too, when the perception of impermanence is developed and cultivated, it eliminates all sensual lust ... it uproots all conceit 'I am.'

"Just as, bhikkhus, a rush-cutter would cut down a rush, grab it by the top, and shake it down and shake it out and thump it about, so too, when the perception of impermanence is developed and cultivated, it eliminates all sensual lust ... it uproots all conceit 'I am.'

"Just as, bhikkhus, when the stalk of a bunch of mangoes has been cut, [156] all the mangoes attached to the stalk follow along with it, so too, when the perception of impermanence is developed ... it uproots all conceit 'I am.'

"Just as, bhikkhus, all the rafters of a house with a peaked roof lead to the roof peak, slope towards the roof peak, and converge upon the roof peak, and the roof peak is declared to be their chief, so too, when the perception of impermanence is developed … it uproots all conceit 'I am.'[216]

"Just as, bhikkhus, among fragrant roots, black orris is declared to be their chief, so too, when the perception of impermanence is developed … it uproots all conceit 'I am.'

"Just as, bhikkhus, among fragrant heartwoods, red sandalwood is declared to be their chief, so too, when the perception of impermanence is developed … it uproots all conceit 'I am.'

"Just as, bhikkhus, among fragrant flowers, jasmine is declared to be their chief, so too, when the perception of impermanence is developed … it uproots all conceit 'I am.'

"Just as, bhikkhus, all petty princes are the vassals of a wheel-turning monarch, and the wheel-turning monarch is declared to be their chief, so too, when the perception of impermanence is developed … it uproots all conceit 'I am.'

"Just as, bhikkhus, the radiance of all the stars does not amount to a sixteenth part of the radiance of the moon, and the radiance of the moon is declared to be their chief, so too, when the perception of impermanence is developed … it uproots all conceit 'I am.'

"Just as, bhikkhus, in the autumn, when the sky is clear and cloudless, the sun, ascending in the sky, dispels all darkness from space as it shines and beams and radiates, so too, when the perception of impermanence is developed and cultivated, it eliminates all sensual lust, it eliminates all lust for existence, it eliminates all ignorance, it uproots all conceit 'I am.'

"And how, bhikkhus, is the perception of impermanence developed [157] and cultivated so that it eliminates all sensual lust, eliminates all lust for existence, eliminates all ignorance, and uproots all conceit 'I am'? 'Such is form, such its origin, such its passing away; such is feeling … such is perception … such are volitional formations … such is consciousness, such its origin, such its passing away': that is how the perception of impermanence is developed and cultivated so that it eliminates all sensual lust, eliminates all lust for existence, eliminates all ignorance, and uproots all conceit 'I am.'"

Division III
The Final Fifty

I. Portions

103 (1) Portions

At Sāvatthī. "Bhikkhus, there are these four portions.[217] What four? [158] The portion of identity, the portion of the origin of identity, the portion of the cessation of identity, the portion of the way leading to the cessation of identity.

"And what, bhikkhus, is the portion of identity? It should be said: the five aggregates subject to clinging. What five? The form aggregate subject to clinging, the feeling aggregate subject to clinging, the perception aggregate subject to clinging, the volitional formations aggregate subject to clinging, the consciousness aggregate subject to clinging. This is called the portion of identity.

"And what, bhikkhus, is the portion of the origin of identity? It is this craving that leads to renewed existence, accompanied by delight and lust, seeking delight here and there; that is, craving for sensual pleasures, craving for existence, craving for extermination. This is called the portion of the origin of identity.

"And what, bhikkhus, is the portion of the cessation of identity? It is the remainderless fading away and cessation of that same craving, the giving up and relinquishing of it, freedom from it, nonreliance on it. This is called the portion of the cessation of identity.

"And what, bhikkhus, is the portion of the way leading to the cessation of identity? It is this Noble Eightfold Path; that is, right view ... right concentration. This is called the portion of the way leading to the cessation of identity.

"These, bhikkhus, are the four portions."

104 (2) Suffering

At Sāvatthī. "Bhikkhus, I will teach you suffering, the origin of suffering, the cessation of suffering, and the way leading to the cessation of suffering.

"And what, bhikkhus, is suffering? It should be said: the five aggregates subject to clinging. What five?... (*as above*) ... This is called suffering.

"And what, bhikkhus, is the origin of suffering? It is this craving that leads to renewed existence.... This is called the origin of suffering.

"And what, bhikkhus, is the cessation of suffering? It is the remainderless fading away and cessation of that same craving.... This is called the cessation of suffering. [159]

"And what, bhikkhus, is the way leading to the cessation of suffering? It is this Noble Eightfold Path; that is, right view ... right concentration. This is called the way leading to the cessation of suffering."

105 (3) Identity

At Sāvatthī. "Bhikkhus, I will teach you identity, the origin of identity, the cessation of identity, and the way leading to the cessation of identity."

(*The remainder of this sutta is identical with the preceding one, with appropriate substitutions.*)

106 (4) To Be Fully Understood

At Sāvatthī. "Bhikkhus, I will teach you things that should be fully understood, full understanding, and the person that has fully understood.[218] Listen to that....

"And what, bhikkhus, are the things that should be fully understood? Form, bhikkhus, is something that should be fully understood. Feeling ... Perception ... Volitional formations ... Consciousness is something that should be fully understood. These are called the things that should be fully understood. [160]

"And what, bhikkhus, is full understanding? The destruction of lust, the destruction of hatred, the destruction of delusion: this is called full understanding.[219]

"And who, bhikkhus, is the person that has fully understood? It should be said: the arahant, the venerable one of such a name and clan. This is called the person that has fully understood."

107 (5) Ascetics (1)

At Sāvatthī. "Bhikkhus, there are these five aggregates subject to clinging. What five? The form aggregate subject to clinging ... the consciousness aggregate subject to clinging.

"Bhikkhus, those ascetics and brahmins who do not understand as they really are the gratification, the danger, and the escape in the case of these five aggregates subject to clinging: these I do not consider to be ascetics among ascetics or brahmins among brahmins, and these venerable ones do not, by realizing it for themselves with direct knowledge, in this very life enter and dwell in the goal of asceticism or the goal of brahminhood.

"But, bhikkhus, those ascetics and brahmins who understand these things as they really are: these I consider to be ascetics among ascetics and brahmins among brahmins, and these venerable ones, by realizing it for themselves with direct knowledge, in this very life enter and dwell in the goal of asceticism and the goal of brahminhood."

108 (6) Ascetics (2)

At Sāvatthī.[220] "Bhikkhus, there are these five aggregates subject to clinging. What five? The form aggregate subject to clinging ... the consciousness aggregate subject to clinging.

"Bhikkhus, those ascetics and brahmins who do not understand as they really are the origin and the passing away, the gratification, the danger, and the escape in the case of these five aggregates subject to clinging: these I do not consider to be ascetics among ascetics or brahmins among brahmins....

"But, bhikkhus, those ascetics and brahmins who understand these things as they really are ... in this very life enter and dwell in the goal of asceticism and the goal of brahminhood."

109 (7) Stream-Enterer

At Sāvatthī. "Bhikkhus, there are these five aggregates subject to clinging. What five? The form aggregate subject to clinging ... the consciousness aggregate subject to clinging.

"When, bhikkhus, a noble disciple understands as they really are the origin and the passing away, [161] the gratification, the danger, and the escape in the case of these five aggregates subject to clinging, then he is called a noble disciple who is a stream-enterer, no longer bound to the nether world, fixed in destiny, with enlightenment as his destination."

110 (8) Arahant

... "When, bhikkhus, having understood as they really are the origin and the passing away, the gratification, the danger, and the escape in the case of these five aggregates subject to clinging, a bhikkhu is liberated by nonclinging,[221] then he is called a bhikkhu who is an arahant, one whose taints are destroyed, who has lived the holy life, done what had to be done, laid down the burden, reached his own goal, utterly destroyed the fetters of existence, one completely liberated through final knowledge."

111 (9) Abandoning Desire (1)

At Sāvatthī. "Bhikkhus, whatever desire there is for form, whatever lust, delight, craving—abandon it. Thus that form will be abandoned, cut off at the root, made like a palm stump, obliterated so that it is no more subject to future arising. So too in the case of feeling, perception, volitional formations, and consciousness."

112 (10) Abandoning Desire (2)

At Sāvatthī. "Bhikkhus, whatever desire there is for form, whatever lust, delight, craving, whatever engagement and clinging, mental standpoints, adherences, and underlying tendencies—[162] abandon them. Thus that form will be abandoned, cut off at the root, made like a palm stump, obliterated so that it is no more subject to future arising. So too in the case of feeling, perception, volitional formations, and consciousness."

II. A Speaker on the Dhamma

113 (1) Ignorance

At Sāvatthī. Then a certain bhikkhu approached the Blessed One, paid homage to him, sat down to one side, and said to him:

"Venerable sir, it is said, 'ignorance, ignorance.' What now, venerable sir, is ignorance, and in what way is one immersed in ignorance?"

"Here, bhikkhu, the uninstructed worldling does not understand form, its origin, its cessation, and the way leading to its cessation.

He does not understand feeling ... perception ... volitional formations ... consciousness, its origin, its cessation, and the way leading to its cessation. [163] This is called ignorance, and in this way one is immersed in ignorance."

114 (2) True Knowledge

At Sāvatthī.... Sitting to one side, that bhikkhu said to the Blessed One:

"Venerable sir, it is said, 'true knowledge, true knowledge.' What now, venerable sir, is true knowledge, and in what way has one arrived at true knowledge?"

"Here, bhikkhu, the instructed noble disciple understands form, its origin, its cessation, and the way leading to its cessation. He understands feeling ... perception ... volitional formations ... consciousness, its origin, its cessation, and the way leading to its cessation. This is called true knowledge, and in this way one has arrived at true knowledge."

115 (3) A Speaker on the Dhamma (1)

At Sāvatthī.... Sitting to one side, that bhikkhu said to the Blessed One:

"Venerable, sir, it is said, 'a speaker on the Dhamma, a speaker on the Dhamma.' In what way, venerable sir, is one a speaker on the Dhamma?"[222]

"Bhikkhu, if one teaches the Dhamma for the purpose of revulsion towards form, for its fading away and cessation, one can be called a bhikkhu who is a speaker on the Dhamma. If one is practising for the purpose of revulsion towards form, for its fading away and cessation, one can be called a bhikkhu who is practising in accordance with the Dhamma. If, through revulsion towards form, through its fading away and cessation, one is liberated by nonclinging, one can be called a bhikkhu who has attained Nibbāna in this very life.

"Bhikkhu, if one teaches the Dhamma for the purpose of revulsion towards feeling ... perception ... volitional formations ... consciousness, for its fading away and cessation, one can be called a bhikkhu who is a speaker on the Dhamma. If one is practising for the purpose of revulsion towards consciousness, for its fading away and cessation, one can be called a bhikkhu who is practising in accordance with the Dhamma. If, through revulsion towards consciousness, [164] through its fading away and cessation, one is liberated by nonclinging, one can be called a bhikkhu who has attained Nibbāna in this very life."

116 (4) A Speaker on the Dhamma (2)

At Sāvatthī.... Sitting to one side, that bhikkhu said to the Blessed One:

"Venerable, sir, it is said, 'a speaker on the Dhamma, a speaker on the Dhamma.' In what way, venerable sir, is one a speaker on the Dhamma? In what way is one practising in accordance with the Dhamma? In what way has one attained Nibbāna in this very life?"

(*The rest of this sutta is identical with the preceding one.*)

117 (5) Bondage

At Sāvatthī. "Here, bhikkhus, the uninstructed worldling ... regards form as self, or self as possessing form, or form as in self, or self as in form. This is called, bhikkhus, an uninstructed worldling who is bound by bondage to form, who is bound by inner and outer bondage, who does not see the near shore and the far shore, who grows old in bondage,[223] who dies in bondage, who in bondage goes from this world to the other world. [165]

"He regards feeling as self ... perception as self ... volitional formations as self ... consciousness as self, or self as possessing consciousness, or consciousness as in self, or self as in consciousness. This is called, bhikkhus, an uninstructed worldling who is bound by bondage to consciousness ... who in bondage goes from this world to the other world.

"But, bhikkhus, the instructed noble disciple ... does not regard form as self, or self as possessing form, or form as in self, or self as in form. This is called, bhikkhus, an instructed noble disciple who is not bound by bondage to form, who is not bound by inner and outer bondage, who sees the near shore and the far shore. He is freed from suffering, I say.

"He does not regard feeling as self ... perception as self ... volitional formations as self ... consciousness as self ... or self as in consciousness. This is called, bhikkhus, an instructed noble disciple who is not bound by bondage to consciousness.... He is freed from suffering, I say."

118 (6) Interrogation (1)[224]

At Sāvatthī. "Bhikkhus, what do you think, do you regard form thus: 'This is mine, this I am, this is my self'?"

"No, venerable sir."

"Good, bhikkhus! Form should be seen as it really is with correct wisdom thus: 'This is not mine, this I am not, this is not my self.'

"Do you regard feeling ... perception ... volitional formations ... [166] consciousness thus: 'This is mine, this I am, this is my self'?"

"No, venerable sir."

"Good, bhikkhus! Consciousness should be seen as it really is with correct wisdom thus: 'This is not mine, this I am not, this is not my self.'

"Seeing thus ... He understands: '... there is no more for this state of being.'"

119 (7) Interrogation (2)

At Sāvatthī. "Bhikkhus, what do you think, do you regard form thus: 'This is not mine, this I am not, this is not my self'?"

"Yes, venerable sir."

"Good, bhikkhus! Form should be seen as it really is with correct wisdom thus: 'This is not mine, this I am not, this is not my self.'

"Do you regard feeling ... perception ... volitional formations ... consciousness thus: 'This is not mine, this I am not, this is not my self'?"

"Yes, venerable sir."

"Good, bhikkhus! Consciousness should be seen as it really is with correct wisdom thus: 'This is not mine, this I am not, this is not my self.'

"Seeing thus ... He understands: '... there is no more for this state of being.'"

120 (8) Things That Fetter

At Sāvatthī. "Bhikkhus, I will teach you the things that fetter and the fetter. Listen to that....

"And what, bhikkhus, are the things that fetter, and what is the fetter? Form, bhikkhus, is a thing that fetters; the desire and lust for it is the fetter there. Feeling ... Perception ... Volitional formations ... [167] Consciousness is a thing that fetters; the desire and lust for it is the fetter there. These are called the things that fetter, and this the fetter."

121 (9) Things That Can Be Clung To

"Bhikkhus, I will teach you the things that can be clung to and the clinging. Listen to that....

"And what, bhikkhus, are the things that can be clung to, and what is the clinging? Form, bhikkhus, is a thing that can be clung to; the desire and lust for it is the clinging there. Feeling ... Perception ... Volitional formations ... Consciousness is a thing that can be clung to; the desire and lust for it is the clinging there. These are called the things that can be clung to, and this the clinging."

122 (10) Virtuous

On one occasion the Venerable Sāriputta and the Venerable Mahākoṭṭhita were dwelling at Bārāṇasī in the Deer Park at Isipatana. Then, in the evening, the Venerable Mahākoṭṭhita emerged from seclusion, approached the Venerable Sāriputta, exchanged greetings, and said to him: "Friend Sāriputta, what are the things that a virtuous bhikkhu should carefully attend to?"

"Friend Koṭṭhita, a virtuous bhikkhu should carefully attend to the five aggregates subject to clinging as impermanent, as suffering, as a disease, as a tumour, as a dart, as misery, as an affliction, as alien, as disintegrating, as empty, as nonself.[225] What five? The form aggregate subject to clinging, the feeling aggregate subject to clinging, the perception aggregate subject to clinging, the volitional formations aggregate subject to clinging, the consciousness aggregate subject to clinging. A virtuous bhikkhu should carefully attend to these five aggregates subject to clinging as impermanent ... as nonself. [168] When, friend, a virtuous bhikkhu carefully attends thus to these five aggregates subject to clinging, it is possible that he may realize the fruit of stream-entry."

"But, friend Sāriputta, what are the things that a bhikkhu who is a stream-enterer should carefully attend to?"

"Friend Koṭṭhita, a bhikkhu who is a stream-enterer should carefully attend to these five aggregates subject to clinging as impermanent ... as nonself. When, friend, a bhikkhu who is a stream-enterer carefully attends thus to these five aggregates subject to clinging, it is possible that he may realize the fruit of once-returning."

"But, friend Sāriputta, what are the things that a bhikkhu who is a once-returner should carefully attend to?"

"Friend Koṭṭhita, a bhikkhu who is a once-returner should carefully attend to these five aggregates subject to clinging as impermanent ... as nonself. When, friend, a bhikkhu who is a once-returner carefully attends thus to these five aggregates subject to clinging, it is possible that he may realize the fruit of nonreturning."

"But, friend Sāriputta, what are the things that a bhikkhu who is a nonreturner should carefully attend to?"

"Friend Koṭṭhita, a bhikkhu who is a nonreturner should carefully attend to these five aggregates subject to clinging as impermanent ... as nonself. When, friend, a bhikkhu who is a nonreturner carefully attends thus to these five aggregates subject to clinging, it is possible that he may realize the fruit of arahantship."

"But, friend Sāriputta, what are the things that a bhikkhu who is an arahant should carefully attend to?"

"Friend Koṭṭhita, a bhikkhu who is an arahant should carefully attend to these five aggregates subject to clinging as impermanent, as suffering, as a disease, as a tumour, as a dart, as misery, as an affliction, as alien, as disintegrating, as empty, as nonself. For the arahant, friend, there is nothing further that has to be done and no repetition of what he has already done.[226] [169] However, when these things are developed and cultivated, they lead to a pleasant dwelling in this very life and to mindfulness and clear comprehension."

123 (11) Instructed

(*This sutta is identical with the preceding one except that the opening question and reply are phrased in terms of "an instructed bhikkhu."*)

124 (12) Kappa (1)

At Sāvatthī. Then the Venerable Kappa approached the Blessed One, paid homage to him, sat down to one side, and said to him:

"Venerable sir, how should one know, how should one see so that, in regard to this body with consciousness and in regard to all external signs, I-making, mine-making, and the underlying tendency to conceit no longer occur within?"

(*Remainder identical with §71, but addressed to Kappa.*) [170]

125 (13) Kappa (2)

At Sāvatthī. Then the Venerable Kappa approached the Blessed One ... and said to him:

"Venerable sir, how should one know, how should one see so that, in regard to this body with consciousness and in regard to all external signs, the mind is rid of I-making, mine-making, and conceit, has transcended discrimination, and is peaceful and well liberated?"

(*Remainder identical with §72, but addressed to Kappa.*)

III. Ignorance

126 (1) Subject to Arising (1)

At Sāvatthī. [171] Then a certain bhikkhu approached the Blessed One ... and said to him: "Venerable sir, it is said, 'ignorance, ignorance.' What now, venerable sir, is ignorance, and in what way is one immersed in ignorance?"

"Here, bhikkhu, the uninstructed worldling does not understand form subject to arising as it really is thus: 'Form is subject to arising.' He does not understand form subject to vanishing as it really is thus: 'Form is subject to vanishing.' He does not understand form subject to arising and vanishing as it really is thus: 'Form is subject to arising and vanishing.' He does not understand feeling ... perception ... volitional formations ... consciousness subject to arising ... subject to vanishing ... subject to arising and vanishing as it really is thus: 'Consciousness is subject to arising and vanishing.'

"This is called ignorance, bhikkhu, and in this way one is immersed in ignorance."

When this was said, that bhikkhu said to the Blessed One: "Venerable sir, it is said, 'true knowledge, true knowledge.' What now, venerable sir, is true knowledge, and in what way has one arrived at true knowledge?"

"Here, bhikkhu, the instructed noble disciple understands form subject to arising as it really is thus: 'Form is subject to arising.' He understands form subject to vanishing as it really is thus: 'Form is subject to vanishing.' [172] He understands form subject to arising and vanishing as it really is thus: 'Form is subject to arising and vanishing.' He understands feeling ... perception ... volitional formations ... consciousness subject to arising ... subject to vanishing ... subject to arising and vanishing as it really is thus: 'Consciousness is subject to arising and vanishing.'

"This is called true knowledge, bhikkhu, and in this way one has arrived at true knowledge."

127 (2) Subject to Arising (2)

On one occasion the Venerable Sāriputta and the Venerable Mahākoṭṭhita were dwelling at Bārāṇasī in the Deer Park at Isipatana. Then, in the evening, the Venerable Mahākoṭṭhita emerged from seclusion, approached the Venerable Sāriputta, ... and said to him: "Friend Sāriputta, it is said, 'ignorance, ignorance.' What now, friend, is ignorance, and in what way is one immersed in ignorance?"

(*The rest of this sutta is identical with the exchange on ignorance in the preceding sutta.*) [173]

128 (3) Subject to Arising (3)

At Bārāṇasī in the Deer Park at Isipatana. Sitting to one side, the Venerable Mahākoṭṭhita said to the Venerable Sāriputta: "Friend Sāriputta, it is said, 'true knowledge, true knowledge.' What now, friend, is true knowledge, and in what way has one arrived at true knowledge?"

(*The rest of this sutta is identical with the exchange on true knowledge in §126.*)

129 (4) Gratification (1)

At Bārāṇasī in the Deer Park at Isipatana. Sitting to one side, the Venerable Mahākoṭṭhita said to the Venerable Sāriputta: "Friend Sāriputta, it is said, 'ignorance, ignorance.' What now, friend, is ignorance, and in what way is one immersed in ignorance?"

"Here, friend, the uninstructed worldling does not understand as it really is the gratification, the danger, and the escape in the case of form, feeling, perception, volitional formations, and consciousness. This, friend, is called ignorance, and in this way one is immersed in ignorance."

130 (5) Gratification (2)

At Bārāṇasī in the Deer Park at Isipatana.... [174] "Friend Sāriputta, it is said, 'true knowledge, true knowledge.' What now, friend, is true knowledge, and in what way has one arrived at true knowledge?"

"Here, friend, the instructed noble disciple understands as it really is the gratification, the danger, and the escape in the case of form, feeling, perception, volitional formations, and consciousness. This, friend, is called true knowledge, and in this way one has arrived at true knowledge."

131 (6) Origin (1)

At Bārāṇasī in the Deer Park at Isipatana.... "Friend Sāriputta, it is said, 'ignorance, ignorance.' What now, friend, is ignorance, and in what way is one immersed in ignorance?"

"Here, friend, the uninstructed worldling does not understand as it really is the origin and the passing away, the gratification, the danger, and the escape in the case of form, feeling, perception, volitional formations, and consciousness. This, friend, is called ignorance, and in this way one is immersed in ignorance."

132 (7) Origin (2)

At Bārāṇasī in the Deer Park at Isipatana.... "Friend Sāriputta, it is said, 'true knowledge, true knowledge.' What now, friend, is true knowledge, and in what way has one arrived at true knowledge?"

"Here, friend, the instructed noble disciple understands as it really is the origin and the passing away, the gratification, the danger, and the escape in the case of form, feeling, perception, volitional formations, and consciousness. This, friend, is called true knowledge, and in this way one has arrived at true knowledge." [175]

133 (8) Koṭṭhita (1)

(*Identical with §129 and §130 combined, except here Sāriputta asks the questions and Mahākoṭṭhita replies.*)

134 (9) Koṭṭhita (2)

(*Identical with §131 and §132 combined, except here Sāriputta asks the questions and Mahākoṭṭhita replies.*) [176]

135 (10) Koṭṭhita (3)

The same setting. Sitting to one side, the Venerable Sāriputta said to the Venerable Mahākoṭṭhita: "Friend Koṭṭhita, it is said, 'ignorance, ignorance.' What now, friend, is ignorance, and in what way is one immersed in ignorance?"

"Here, friend, the uninstructed worldling does not understand form, its origin, its cessation, and the way leading to its cessation. He does not understand feeling ... perception ... volitional formations ... consciousness, its origin, its cessation, and the way leading to its cessation. This, friend, is called ignorance, and in this way one is immersed in ignorance."

When this was said, the Venerable Sāriputta said to the Venerable Mahākoṭṭhita: "Friend Koṭṭhita, it is said, 'true knowledge, true knowledge.' What now, friend, is true knowledge, and in what way has one arrived at true knowledge?"

"Here, friend, the instructed noble disciple understands form,

[177] its origin, its cessation, and the way leading to its cessation. He understands feeling ... perception ... volitional formations ... consciousness, its origin, its cessation, and the way leading to its cessation. This, friend, is called true knowledge, and in this way one has arrived at true knowledge."

IV. Hot Embers

136 (1) Hot Embers

At Sāvatthī. "Bhikkhus, form is hot embers,[227] feeling is hot embers, perception is hot embers, volitional formations are hot embers, consciousness is hot embers. Seeing thus, bhikkhus, the instructed noble disciple experiences revulsion towards form ... revulsion towards consciousness. Experiencing revulsion, he becomes dispassionate.... He understands: '... there is no more for this state of being.'"

137 (2) Impermanent (1)

At Sāvatthī. "Bhikkhus, you should abandon desire for whatever is impermanent. And what is impermanent? [178] Form is impermanent; you should abandon desire for it. Feeling ... Perception ... Volitional formations ... Consciousness is impermanent; you should abandon desire for it. Bhikkhus, you should abandon desire for whatever is impermanent."

138 (3) Impermanent (2)

... "Bhikkhus, you should abandon lust for whatever is impermanent."...

(*Complete as in the preceding sutta, with "lust" instead of "desire."*)

139 (4) Impermanent (3)

... "Bhikkhus, you should abandon desire and lust for whatever is impermanent."...

(*Complete as in §137, with "desire and lust" instead of "desire."*)

140 (5) Suffering (1)

... "Bhikkhus, you should abandon desire for whatever is suffering."...

141 (6) Suffering (2)

... "Bhikkhus, you should abandon lust for whatever is suffering."...

142 (7) Suffering (3)

... "Bhikkhus, you should abandon desire and lust for whatever is suffering."...

143 (8) Nonself (1)

... "Bhikkhus, you should abandon desire for whatever is nonself."... [179]

144 (9) Nonself (2)

... "Bhikkhus, you should abandon lust for whatever is nonself."...

145 (10) Nonself (3)

... "Bhikkhus, you should abandon desire and lust for whatever is nonself."...

146 (11) Engrossed in Revulsion

At Sāvatthī. "Bhikkhus, for a clansman who has gone forth out of faith, this is what accords with the Dhamma: he should dwell engrossed in revulsion towards form, feeling, perception, volitional formations, and consciousness.[228] One who dwells engrossed in revulsion towards form ... towards consciousness, fully understands form, feeling, perception, volitional formations, and consciousness. One who fully understands form ... consciousness is freed from form, feeling, perception, volitional formations, and consciousness. He is freed from birth, aging, and death; freed from sorrow, lamentation, pain, displeasure, and despair; freed from suffering, I say."

147 (12) Contemplating Impermanence

At Sāvatthī.[229] "Bhikkhus, for a clansman who has gone forth out of faith, this is what accords with the Dhamma: he should dwell contemplating impermanence in form ... (*as above*) ... [180] he is freed from suffering, I say."

148 (13) Contemplating Suffering

... "he should dwell contemplating suffering in form ... he is freed from suffering, I say."

149 (14) Contemplating Nonself

... "he should dwell contemplating nonself in form ... he is freed from suffering, I say."

V. Views

150 (1) Internally

At Sāvatthī. "Bhikkhus, when what exists, by clinging to what, do pleasure and pain arise internally?"[230] [181]

"Venerable sir, our teachings are rooted in the Blessed One...."

"When there is form, bhikkhus, by clinging to form, pleasure and pain arise internally. When there is feeling ... perception ... volitional formations ... consciousness, by clinging to consciousness, pleasure and pain arise internally.

"What do you think, bhikkhus, is form permanent or impermanent?"

"Impermanent, venerable sir."

"Is what is impermanent suffering or happiness?"

"Suffering, venerable sir."

"But without clinging to what is impermanent, suffering, and subject to change, could pleasure and pain arise internally?"

"No, venerable sir."

"Is feeling ... perception ... volitional formations ... consciousness permanent or impermanent?... But without clinging to what is impermanent, suffering, and subject to change, could pleasure and pain arise internally?"

"No, venerable sir."

"Seeing thus ... He understands: '... there is no more for this state of being.'"

151 (2) This Is Mine

At Sāvatthī. "Bhikkhus, when what exists, by clinging to what, by adhering to what,[231] does one regard things thus: 'This is mine, this I am, this is my self'?"

"Venerable sir, our teachings are rooted in the Blessed One...."

"When there is form, bhikkhus, by clinging to form, by adhering to form, [182] one regards things thus: 'This is mine, this I am, this is my self.' When there is feeling ... perception ... volitional formations ... consciousness, by clinging to consciousness, by adhering to consciousness, one regards things thus: 'This is mine, this I am, this is my self.'

"What do you think, bhikkhus, is form ... consciousness permanent or impermanent?"

"Impermanent, venerable sir."...

"But without clinging to what is impermanent, suffering, and subject to change, could one regard anything thus: 'This is mine, this I am, this is my self'?"

"No, venerable sir."

"Seeing thus ... He understands: '... there is no more for this state of being.'"

152 (3) The Self

At Sāvatthī. "Bhikkhus, when what exists, by clinging to what, by adhering to what, does such a view as this arise: 'That which is the self is the world; having passed away, that I shall be—permanent, stable, eternal, not subject to change'?"[232]

"Venerable sir, our teachings are rooted in the Blessed One...."

"When there is form, bhikkhus, by clinging to form, by adhering to form, such a view as this arises: 'That which is the self is the world; having passed away, that I shall be—permanent, stable, eternal, not subject to change.' When there is feeling ... perception ... volitional formations ... consciousness, by clinging to consciousness, by adhering to consciousness, such a view as this [183] arises: 'That which is the self is the world ... not subject to change.'

"What do you think, bhikkhus, is form ... consciousness permanent or impermanent?"

"Impermanent, venerable sir."...

"But without clinging to what is impermanent, suffering, and subject to change, could such a view as that arise?"

"No, venerable sir."

"Seeing thus ... He understands: '... there is no more for this state of being.'"

153 (4) It Might Not Be For Me

At Sāvatthī. "Bhikkhus, when what exists, by clinging to what, by adhering to what, does such a view as this arise: 'I might not be, and it might not be for me; I will not be, [and] it will not be for me'?"[233]

"Venerable sir, our teachings are rooted in the Blessed One...."

"When there is form, bhikkhus, by clinging to form, by adhering to form, such a view as this arises: 'I might not be, and it might not be for me; I will not be, [and] it will not be for me.' When there is feeling ... perception ... volitional formations ... [184] consciousness, by clinging to consciousness, by adhering to consciousness, such a view as this arises: 'I might not be ... and it will not be for me.'

"What do you think, bhikkhus, is form ... consciousness permanent or impermanent?"

"Impermanent, venerable sir."...

"But without clinging to what is impermanent, suffering, and subject to change, could such a view as that arise?"

"No, venerable sir."

"Seeing thus ... He understands: '... there is no more for this state of being.'"

154 (5) Wrong View

At Sāvatthī. "Bhikkhus, when what exists, by clinging to what, by adhering to what, does wrong view arise?"[234]

"Venerable sir, our teachings are rooted in the Blessed One...."

"When there is form, bhikkhus, by clinging to form, by adhering to form, wrong view arises. When there is feeling ... perception ... volitional formations ... consciousness, by clinging to consciousness, by adhering to consciousness, wrong view arises.

"What do you think, bhikkhus, is form ... consciousness permanent or impermanent?" [185]

"Impermanent, venerable sir."...

"But without clinging to what is impermanent, suffering, and subject to change, could wrong view arise."

"No, venerable sir."

"Seeing thus ... He understands: '... there is no more for this state of being.'"

155 (6) Identity View

At Sāvatthī. "Bhikkhus, when what exists, by clinging to what, by adhering to what, does identity view arise?"[235]

"Venerable sir, our teachings are rooted in the Blessed One...."

"When there is form, bhikkhus, by clinging to form, by adhering to form, identity view arises. When there is feeling ... perception ... volitional formations ... consciousness, by clinging to consciousness, by adhering to consciousness, identity view arises."...

"Seeing thus ... He understands: '... there is no more for this state of being.'"

156 (7) View of Self

At Sāvatthī. "Bhikkhus, when what exists, by clinging to what, by adhering to what, does view of self arise?"[236]

"Venerable sir, our teachings are rooted in the Blessed One...."

"When there is form, bhikkhus, by clinging to form, by adhering to form, view of self arises. [186] When there is feeling ... perception ... volitional formations ... consciousness, by clinging to consciousness, by adhering to consciousness, view of self arises."...

"Seeing thus ... He understands: '... there is no more for this state of being.'"

157 (8) Adherence (1)

At Sāvatthī. "Bhikkhus, when what exists, by clinging to what, by adhering to what, do the fetters, adherences, and shackles arise?"[237]

"Venerable sir, our teachings are rooted in the Blessed One…."

"When there is form, bhikkhus, by clinging to form, by adhering to form, the fetters, adherences, and shackles arise. When there is feeling … perception … volitional formations … consciousness, by clinging to consciousness, by adhering to consciousness, the fetters, adherences, and shackles arise."…

"Seeing thus … He understands: '… there is no more for this state of being.'" [187]

158 (9) Adherence (2)

At Sāvatthī. "Bhikkhus, when what exists, by clinging to what, by adhering to what, do the fetters, adherences, shackles, and holding arise?"

"Venerable sir, our teachings are rooted in the Blessed One…." (*Complete as above.*)

159 (10) Ānanda

At Sāvatthī. Then the Venerable Ānanda approached the Blessed One … and said to him: "Venerable sir, it would be good if the Blessed One would teach me the Dhamma in brief, so that having heard the Dhamma from the Blessed One, I might dwell alone, withdrawn, diligent, ardent, and resolute."[238]

"What do you think, Ānanda, is form permanent or impermanent?" – "Impermanent, venerable sir." – "Is what is impermanent suffering or happiness?" – "Suffering, venerable sir." – "Is what is impermanent, suffering, and subject to change fit to be regarded thus: 'This is mine, this I am, this is my self'?" – "No, venerable sir."

"Is feeling permanent or impermanent?… Is perception permanent or impermanent?… Are volitional formations permanent or impermanent?… Is consciousness permanent or impermanent?" – "Impermanent, venerable sir." – "Is what is impermanent suffering or happiness?" – "Suffering, venerable sir." – "Is what is impermanent, suffering, and subject to change fit to be regarded thus: 'This is mine, this I am, this is my self'?" – "No, venerable sir."

"Therefore, Ānanda, any kind of form whatsoever, whether past, future, or present.... [188]

"Seeing thus ... He understands: '... there is no more for this state of being.'"

Chapter II

23 *Rādhasaṃyutta*
Connected Discourses with Rādha

I. The First Māra Subchapter

1 (1) Māra

At Sāvatthī. Then the Venerable Rādha approached the Blessed One,[239] [189] paid homage to him, sat down to one side, and said to him: "Venerable sir, it is said, 'Māra, Māra.' In what way, venerable sir, might Māra be?"[240]

"When there is form, Rādha, there might be Māra, or the killer, or the one who is killed.[241] Therefore, Rādha, see form as Māra, see it as the killer, see it as the one who is killed. See it as a disease, as a tumour, as a dart, as misery, as real misery. Those who see it thus see rightly.

"When there is feeling ... When there is perception ... When there are volitional formations ... When there is consciousness, Rādha, there might be Māra, or the killer, or the one who is killed. Therefore, Rādha, see consciousness as Māra, see it as the killer, see it as the one who is killed. See it as a disease, as a tumour, as a dart, as misery, as real misery. Those who see it thus see rightly."

"What, venerable sir, is the purpose of seeing rightly?"

"The purpose of seeing rightly, Rādha, is revulsion."

"And what, venerable sir, is the purpose of revulsion?"

"The purpose of revulsion is dispassion."

"And what, venerable sir, is the purpose of dispassion?"

"The purpose of dispassion is liberation."

"And what, venerable sir, is the purpose of liberation?"

"The purpose of liberation is Nibbāna."[242]

"And what, venerable sir, is the purpose of Nibbāna?"

"You have gone beyond the range of questioning, Rādha.[243]

You weren't able to grasp the limit to questioning. For, Rādha, the holy life is lived with Nibbāna as its ground, Nibbāna as its destination, Nibbāna as its final goal."[244]

2 (2) A Being

At Sāvatthī. Sitting to one side, the Venerable Rādha said to the Blessed One: [190] "Venerable sir, it is said, 'a being, a being.' In what way, venerable sir, is one called a being?"

"One is stuck, Rādha, tightly stuck, in desire, lust, delight, and craving for form; therefore one is called a being.[244] One is stuck, tightly stuck, in desire, lust, delight, and craving for feeling … for perception … for volitional formations … for consciousness; therefore one is called a being.

"Suppose, Rādha, some little boys or girls are playing with sand castles. So long as they are not devoid of lust, desire, affection, thirst, passion, and craving for those sand castles, they cherish them, play with them, treasure them,[245] and treat them possessively. But when those little boys or girls lose their lust, desire, affection, thirst, passion, and craving for those sand castles, then they scatter them with their hands and feet, demolish them, shatter them, and put them out of play.

"So too, Rādha, scatter form, demolish it, shatter it, put it out of play; practise for the destruction of craving. Scatter feeling … Scatter perception … Scatter volitional formations … Scatter consciousness, demolish it, shatter it, put it out of play; practise for the destruction of craving. For the destruction of craving, Rādha, is Nibbāna."

3 (3) The Conduit to Existence

At Sāvatthī. Sitting to one side, the Venerable Rādha said to the Blessed One: "Venerable sir, it is said, 'the conduit to existence, the conduit to existence.'[246] What, venerable sir, is the conduit to existence, and what is the cessation of the conduit to existence?" [191]

"Rādha, the desire, lust, delight, craving, engagement and clinging, mental standpoints, adherences, and underlying tendencies regarding form:[247] this is called the conduit to existence. Their cessation is the cessation of the conduit to existence.

"The desire, lust, delight, craving, engagement and clinging, mental standpoints, adherences, and underlying tendencies regarding feeling ... perception ... volitional formations ... consciousness: this is called the conduit to existence. Their cessation is the cessation of the conduit to existence."

4 (4)–10 (10) To Be Fully Understood, Etc.

(*These seven suttas are identical with 22:106–12, but addressed to Rādha.*) [192–94]

[195] II. THE SECOND MĀRA SUBCHAPTER

11 (1) Māra

At Sāvatthī. Sitting to one side, the Venerable Rādha said to the Blessed One: "Venerable sir, it is said, 'Māra, Māra.' What now, venerable sir, is Māra?"

"Form, Rādha, is Māra. Feeling ... Perception ... Volitional formations ... Consciousness is Māra. Seeing thus ... He understands: '... there is no more for this state of being.'"

12 (2) Subject to Māra

At Sāvatthī. Sitting to one side, the Venerable Rādha said to the Blessed One: "Venerable sir, it is said, 'subject to Māra, subject to Māra.'[248] What now, venerable sir, is subject to Māra?"

"Form, Rādha, is subject to Māra. Feeling ... Perception ... Volitional formations ... Consciousness is subject to Māra. Seeing thus ... He understands: '... there is no more for this state of being.'"

13 (3) Impermanent

At Sāvatthī. Sitting to one side, the Venerable Rādha said to the Blessed One: "Venerable sir, it is said, 'impermanent, impermanent.' What now, venerable sir, is impermanent?"

"Form, Rādha, is impermanent. Feeling ... Perception ... Volitional formations ... Consciousness is impermanent. Seeing thus ... He understands: '... there is no more for this state of being.'"

14 (4) Of Impermanent Nature

At Sāvatthī. Sitting to one side, the Venerable Rādha said to the Blessed One: "Venerable sir, it is said, 'of an impermanent nature, of an impermanent nature.' What now, venerable sir, is of an impermanent nature?"

"Form, Rādha, is of an impermanent nature. Feeling ... [196] Perception ... Volitional formations ... Consciousness is of an impermanent nature. Seeing thus ... He understands: '... there is no more for this state of being.'"

15 (5) Suffering

At Sāvatthī. Sitting to one side, the Venerable Rādha said to the Blessed One: "Venerable sir, it is said, 'suffering, suffering.' What now, venerable sir, is suffering?"

"Form, Rādha, is suffering, feeling is suffering, perception is suffering, volitional formations are suffering, consciousness is suffering. Seeing thus ... He understands: '... there is no more for this state of being.'"

16 (6) Of Painful Nature

At Sāvatthī. Sitting to one side, the Venerable Rādha said to the Blessed One: "Venerable sir, it is said, 'of a painful nature, of a painful nature.' What now, venerable sir, is of a painful nature?"

"Form, Rādha, is of a painful nature. Feeling ... Perception ... Volitional formations ... Consciousness is of a painful nature. Seeing thus ... He understands: '... there is no more for this state of being.'"

17 (7) Nonself

At Sāvatthī. Sitting to one side, the Venerable Rādha said to the Blessed One: "Venerable sir, it is said, 'nonself, nonself.' What now, venerable sir, is nonself?"

"Form, Rādha, is nonself, feeling is nonself, perception is nonself, volitional formations are nonself, consciousness is nonself. Seeing thus ... He understands: '... there is no more for this state of being.'"

18 (8) Of Selfless Nature

At Sāvatthī. Sitting to one side, the Venerable Rādha said to the Blessed One: "Venerable sir, it is said, 'of a selfless nature, of a selfless nature.' What now, venerable sir, is of a selfless nature?"

"Form, Rādha, is of a selfless nature. Feeling ... [197] Perception ... Volitional formations ... Consciousness is of a selfless nature. Seeing thus ... He understands: '... there is no more for this state of being.'"

19 (9) Subject to Destruction

At Sāvatthī. Sitting to one side, the Venerable Rādha said to the Blessed One: "Venerable sir, it is said, 'subject to destruction, subject to destruction.' What now, venerable sir, is subject to destruction?"

"Form, Rādha, is subject to destruction. Feeling ... Perception ... Volitional formations ... Consciousness is subject to destruction. Seeing thus ... He understands: '... there is no more for this state of being.'"

20 (10) Subject to Vanishing

At Sāvatthī. Sitting to one side, the Venerable Rādha said to the Blessed One: "Venerable sir, it is said, 'subject to vanishing, subject to vanishing.' What now, venerable sir, is subject to vanishing?"

"Form, Rādha, is subject to vanishing. Feeling ... Perception ... Volitional formations ... Consciousness is subject to vanishing. Seeing thus ... He understands: '... there is no more for this state of being.'"

21 (11) Subject to Arising

At Sāvatthī. Sitting to one side, the Venerable Rādha said to the Blessed One: "Venerable sir, it is said, 'subject to arising, subject to arising.' What now, venerable sir, is subject to arising?"

"Form, Rādha, is subject to arising. Feeling ... Perception ... Volitional formations ... Consciousness is subject to arising. Seeing thus ... He understands: '... there is no more for this state of being.'"

22 (12) *Subject to Cessation*

At Sāvatthī. Sitting to one side, the Venerable Rādha said to the Blessed One: "Venerable sir, it is said, 'subject to cessation, [198] subject to cessation.' What now, venerable sir, is subject to cessation?"

"Form, Rādha, is subject to cessation. Feeling … Perception … Volitional formations … Consciousness is subject to cessation. Seeing thus … He understands: '… there is no more for this state of being.'"

III. Request

23 (1) *Māra*

At Sāvatthī. Sitting to one side, the Venerable Rādha said to the Blessed One: "Venerable sir, it would be good if the Blessed One would teach me the Dhamma in brief, so that, having heard the Dhamma from the Blessed One, I might dwell alone, withdrawn, diligent, ardent, and resolute."

"Rādha, you should abandon desire, you should abandon lust, you should abandon desire and lust, for whatever is Māra. And what, Rādha, is Māra? Form is Māra. Feeling … Perception … Volitional formations … Consciousness is Māra. Seeing thus … He understands: '… there is no more for this state of being.'"

24 (2)–34 (12) *Subject to Māra, Etc.*

… "Rādha, you should abandon desire, you should abandon lust, you should abandon desire and lust, for whatever is subject to Māra … [199] … for whatever is impermanent … for whatever is of an impermanent nature … for whatever is suffering … for whatever is of a painful nature … for whatever is nonself … for whatever is of a selfless nature … for whatever is subject to destruction … for whatever is subject to vanishing … for whatever is subject to arising … for whatever is subject to cessation. And what, Rādha, is subject to cessation? Form is subject to cessation. Feeling … Perception … Volitional formations … Consciousness is subject to cessation. Seeing thus … He understands: '… there is no more for this state of being.'"

[200] IV. Sitting Nearby

35 (1) Māra

At Sāvatthī. The Blessed One said to the Venerable Rādha as he was sitting to one side: "Rādha, you should abandon desire, you should abandon lust, you should abandon desire and lust, for whatever is Māra. And what, Rādha, is Māra?"... (*Complete as in* §23.)

36 (2)–46 (12) Subject to Māra, Etc.

(*Identical with* §§*24–34, but opening as in the preceding sutta.*) [201]

[202] Chapter III

24 *Diṭṭhisaṃyutta*
Connected Discourses on Views

I. Stream-Entry

1 (1) Winds

At Sāvatthī. "Bhikkhus, when what exists, by clinging to what, by adhering to what, does such a view as this arise: 'The winds do not blow, the rivers do not flow, pregnant women do not give birth, the moon and sun do not rise and set but stand as steady as a pillar'?"[249]

"Venerable sir, our teachings are rooted in the Blessed One…."

"When there is form, bhikkhus, by clinging to form, by adhering to form, such a view as this arises: 'The winds do not blow … but stand as steady as a pillar.' When there is feeling … perception … volitional formations … consciousness, by clinging to consciousness, by adhering to consciousness, such a view as this arises: 'The winds do not blow … but stand as steady as a pillar.'

"What do you think, bhikkhus, is form permanent or impermanent?… [203] … Is consciousness permanent or impermanent?"

"Impermanent, venerable sir."…

"But without clinging to what is impermanent, suffering, and subject to change, could such a view as that arise?"

"No, venerable sir."

"That which is seen, heard, sensed, cognized, attained, sought after, and ranged over by the mind:[250] is that permanent or impermanent?"

"Impermanent, venerable sir."

"Is what is impermanent suffering or happiness?"

"Suffering, venerable sir."

"But without clinging to what is impermanent, suffering, and subject to change, could such a view as that arise?"

"No, venerable sir."

"When, bhikkhus, a noble disciple has abandoned perplexity in these six cases,[251] and when, further, he has abandoned perplexity about suffering, the origin of suffering, the cessation of suffering, and the way leading to the cessation of suffering, he is then called a noble disciple who is a stream-enterer, no longer bound to the nether world, fixed in destiny, with enlightenment as his destination."

2 (2) This Is Mine

At Sāvatthī. "Bhikkhus, when what exists, by clinging to what, by adhering to what, does such a view as this arise: 'This is mine, this I am, this is my self'?"

"Venerable sir, our teachings are rooted in the Blessed One...." [204]

"When there is form, bhikkhus, by clinging to form, by adhering to form, such a view as this arises: 'This is mine, this I am, this is my self.' When there is feeling ... perception ... volitional formations ... consciousness, by clinging to consciousness, by adhering to consciousness, such a view as this arises: 'This is mine, this I am, this is my self.'...

"When, bhikkhus, a noble disciple has abandoned perplexity in these six cases ... he is then called a noble disciple who is a stream-enterer ... with enlightenment as his destination."

3 (3) The Self

At Sāvatthī. "Bhikkhus, when what exists, by clinging to what, by adhering to what, does such a view as this arise: 'That which is the self is the world; having passed away, that I shall be—permanent, stable, eternal, not subject to change'?"[252] [205]

"Venerable sir, our teachings are rooted in the Blessed One...."

"When there is form, bhikkhus, by clinging to form, by adhering to form, such a view as this arises: 'That which is the self is the world; having passed away, that I shall be—permanent, stable, eternal, not subject to change' When there is feeling ... perception ... volitional formations ... consciousness, by clinging to consciousness, by adhering to consciousness, such a view as this arises: 'That which is the self is the world ... not subject to change.' ...

"When, bhikkhus, a noble disciple has abandoned perplexity in these six cases ... he is then called a noble disciple who is a stream-enterer ... with enlightenment as his destination."

4 (4) It Might Not Be For Me

At Sāvatthī. "Bhikkhus, when what exists, by clinging to what, by adhering to what, does such a view as this arise: 'I might not be, and it might not be for me; I will not be, [and] it will not be for me'?"[253]

"Venerable sir, our teachings are rooted in the Blessed One...."

"When there is form, bhikkhus, by clinging to form, by adhering to form, [206] such a view as this arises: 'I might not be, and it might not be for me; I will not be, [and] it will not be for me.' When there is feeling ... perception ... volitional formations ... consciousness, by clinging to consciousness, by adhering to consciousness, such a view as this arises: 'I might not be ... it will not be for me.'...

"When, bhikkhus, a noble disciple has abandoned perplexity in these six cases ... he is then called a noble disciple who is a stream-enterer ... with enlightenment as his destination."

5 (5) There Is Not

At Sāvatthī. "Bhikkhus, when what exists, by clinging to what, by adhering to what, does such a view as this arise:[254] 'There is nothing given, nothing offered, nothing presented in charity; no fruit or result of good and bad actions; no this world, no other world; no mother, no father; no beings who are reborn spontaneously; no ascetics and brahmins faring and practising rightly in the world who, having realized this world and the other world for themselves by direct knowledge, make them known to others. This person consists of the four great elements. [207] When one dies, earth returns to and merges with the earth-body; water returns to and merges with the water-body; fire returns to and merges with the fire-body; air returns to and merges with the air-body; the faculties are transferred to space. [Four] men with the bier as fifth carry away the corpse. The funeral orations last as far as the charnel ground; the bones whiten; burnt offerings end with ashes. Giving is a doctrine of fools. When anyone asserts the doctrine that there is [giving and the like], it is empty, false prattle. Fools and the wise are alike cut off and perish with the breakup of the body; after death they do not exist'?"

"Venerable sir, our teachings are rooted in the Blessed One...."

"When there is form, bhikkhus, when there is feeling ... perception ... volitional formations ... consciousness, by clinging to consciousness, by adhering to consciousness, such a view as this arises: 'There is nothing given ... [208] ... after death they do not exist.'...

"When, bhikkhus, a noble disciple has abandoned perplexity in these six cases ... he is then called a noble disciple who is a stream-enterer ... with enlightenment as his destination."

6 (6) Acting

At Sāvatthī. "Bhikkhus, when what exists, by clinging to what, by adhering to what, does such a view as this arise:[255] 'When one acts or makes others act, when one mutilates or makes others mutilate, when one tortures or makes others inflict torture, when one inflicts sorrow or makes others inflict sorrow, when one oppresses or makes others inflict oppression, when one intimidates or makes others inflict intimidation, when one destroys life, takes what is not given, breaks into houses, plunders wealth, commits burglary, ambushes highways, seduces another's wife, utters falsehood—no evil is done by the doer. If, with a razor-rimmed wheel, one were to make the living beings of this earth into one mass of flesh, into one heap of flesh, because of this there would be no evil and no outcome of evil. If one where to go along the south bank of the Ganges [209] killing and slaughtering, mutilating and making others mutilate, torturing and making others inflict torture, because of this there would be no evil and no outcome of evil. If one where to go along the north bank of the Ganges giving gifts and making others give gifts, making offerings and making others make offerings, because of this there would be no merit and no outcome of merit. By giving, by taming oneself, by self-control, by speaking truth, there is no merit and no outcome of merit'?"

"Venerable sir, our teachings are rooted in the Blessed One...."

"When there is form, bhikkhus, when there is feeling ... perception ... volitional formations ... consciousness, by clinging to consciousness, by adhering to consciousness, such a view as this arises: 'When one acts or makes others act ... there is no merit and no outcome of merit.'...

"When, bhikkhus, a noble disciple has abandoned perplexity in these six cases ... he is then called a noble disciple who is a stream-enterer ... with enlightenment as his destination." [210]

7 (7) Cause

At Sāvatthī. "Bhikkhus, when what exists, by clinging to what, by adhering to what, does such a view as this arise:[256] 'There is no cause or condition for the defilement of beings; beings are defiled without cause or condition. There is no cause or condition for the purification of beings; beings are purified without cause or condition. [There is no action by self, no action by others, no manly action.] There is no power, no energy, no manly strength, no manly exertion. All beings, all living beings, all creatures, all souls are without mastery, power, and energy; moulded by destiny, circumstance, and nature, they experience pleasure and pain in the six classes'?"[257]

"Venerable sir, our teachings are rooted in the Blessed One...."

"When there is form, bhikkhus, when there is feeling ... perception ... volitional formations ... consciousness, by clinging to consciousness, by adhering to consciousness, such a view as this arises: 'There is no cause or condition for the defilement of beings ... they experience pleasure and pain in the six classes.'...

"When, bhikkhus, a noble disciple has abandoned perplexity in these six cases ... [211] ... he is then called a noble disciple who is a stream-enterer ... with enlightenment as his destination."

8 (8) The Great View

At Sāvatthī. "Bhikkhus, when what exists, by clinging to what, by adhering to what, does such a view as this arise:[258] 'There are these seven bodies that are unmade, not brought forth, uncreated, without a creator, barren, steady as mountain peaks, steady as pillars. They do not move or change or obstruct each other.

None is able to cause pleasure or pain or pleasure-and-pain to others. What are the seven? They are: the earth-body, the water-body, the fire-body, the air-body, pleasure, pain, and the soul as the seventh. These seven bodies are unmade.... [Herein, there is no killer, no slaughterer, no hearer, no speaker, no knower, no intimater.][259] Even one who cuts off another's head with a sharp sword does not deprive anyone of life; the sword merely passes through the space between the seven bodies. There are fourteen hundred thousand principal modes of generation,[260] and six thousand, and six hundred; there are five hundred kinds of kamma, and five kinds of kamma, and three kinds of kamma, and full kamma, and half-kamma; there are sixty-two pathways, sixty-two sub-aeons, six classes, eight stages in the life of man, forty-nine hundred kinds of Ājīvakas,[261] forty-nine hundred kinds of wanderers, forty-nine hundred abodes of nāgas, twenty hundred faculties, thirty hundred hells, thirty-six realms of dust, seven spheres of percipient beings, seven spheres of nonpercipient beings, seven spheres of knotless ones, seven [212] kinds of devas, seven kinds of human beings, seven kinds of demons, seven great lakes, seven kinds of knots, seven hundred [other] kinds of knots, seven precipices, seven hundred [other] precipices, seven kinds of dreams, seven hundred [other] kinds of dreams, eighty-four hundred thousand great aeons through which the foolish and the wise roam and wander, after which they will alike make an end to suffering. There is none of this: "By this virtue or vow or austerity or holy life I will make unripened kamma ripen or eradicate ripened kamma by repeatedly experiencing it"—not so! Pleasure and pain are meted out; saṃsāra's limits are fixed; there is no shortening it or extending it, no advancing forward or falling back. Just as, when a ball of string is thrown, it runs away unwinding, so too the foolish and the wise, by unwinding, flee from pleasure and pain'?"[262]

"Venerable sir, our teachings are rooted in the Blessed One...."

"When there is form, bhikkhus, when there is feeling ... perception ... volitional formations ... consciousness, by clinging to consciousness, by adhering to consciousness, such a view as this arises: 'There are these seven bodies that are unmade ... the foolish and the wise, by unwinding, flee from pleasure and pain.'... [213] ...

"When, bhikkhus, a noble disciple has abandoned perplexity

in these six cases … he is then called a noble disciple who is a stream-enterer … with enlightenment as his destination."

9 (9) The World Is Eternal

At Sāvatthī. "Bhikkhus, when what exists, by clinging to what, by adhering to what, does such a view as this arise: 'The world is eternal'?"[263]

"Venerable sir, our teachings are rooted in the Blessed One…."

"When there is form, bhikkhus, when there is feeling … perception … volitional formations … consciousness, by clinging to consciousness, by adhering to consciousness, such a view as this arises: 'The world is eternal.'… [214] …

"When, bhikkhus, a noble disciple has abandoned perplexity in these six cases … he is then called a noble disciple who is a stream-enterer … with enlightenment as his destination."

10 (10) The World Is Not Eternal

At Sāvatthī. "Bhikkhus, when what exists, by clinging to what, by adhering to what, does such a view as this arise: 'The world is not eternal'?"

"Venerable sir, our teachings are rooted in the Blessed One…."

"When, bhikkhus, a noble disciple … with enlightenment as his destination."

11 (11) The World is Finite

At Sāvatthī. "Bhikkhus, when what exists, by clinging to what, by adhering to what, does such a view as this arise: 'The world is finite'?"

"Venerable sir, our teachings are rooted in the Blessed One…."

"When, bhikkhus, a noble disciple … with enlightenment as his destination." [215]

12 (12) The World Is Infinite

At Sāvatthī. "Bhikkhus, when what exists, by clinging to what, by adhering to what, does such a view as this arise: 'The world is infinite'?"

"Venerable sir, our teachings are rooted in the Blessed One...."

"When, bhikkhus, a noble disciple ... with enlightenment as his destination."

13 (13) Soul and Body Are the Same

At Sāvatthī. "Bhikkhus, when what exists, by clinging to what, by adhering to what, does such a view as this arise: 'The soul and the body are the same'?"

"Venerable sir, our teachings are rooted in the Blessed One...."

"When, bhikkhus, a noble disciple ... with enlightenment as his destination."

14 (14) Soul and Body Are Different

At Sāvatthī. "Bhikkhus, when what exists, by clinging to what, by adhering to what, does such a view as this arise: 'The soul is one thing, the body another'?"

"Venerable sir, our teachings are rooted in the Blessed One...."

"When, bhikkhus, a noble disciple ... with enlightenment as his destination."

15 (15) The Tathāgata Exists

At Sāvatthī. "Bhikkhus, when what exists, by clinging to what, by adhering to what, does such a view as this arise: 'The Tathāgata exists after death'?"

"Venerable sir, our teachings are rooted in the Blessed One...."

"When, bhikkhus, a noble disciple ... with enlightenment as his destination."

16 (16) The Tathāgata Does Not Exist

At Sāvatthī. "Bhikkhus, when what exists, by clinging to what, by adhering to what, does such a view as this arise: 'The Tathāgata does not exist after death'?"

"Venerable sir, our teachings are rooted in the Blessed One...."

"When, bhikkhus, a noble disciple ... with enlightenment as his destination."

17 (17) The Tathāgata Both Exists and Does Not Exist

At Sāvatthī. "Bhikkhus, when what exists, [216] by clinging to what, by adhering to what, does such a view as this arise: 'The Tathāgata both exists and does not exist after death'?"

"Venerable sir, our teachings are rooted in the Blessed One...."

"When, bhikkhus, a noble disciple ... with enlightenment as his destination."

18 (18) The Tathāgata Neither Exists Nor Does Not Exist

At Sāvatthī. "Bhikkhus, when what exists, by clinging to what, by adhering to what, does such a view as this arise: 'The Tathāgata neither exists nor does not exist after death'?"

"Venerable sir, our teachings are rooted in the Blessed One...."

"When there is form, bhikkhus, by clinging to form, by adhering to form, such a view as this arises: 'The Tathāgata neither exists nor does not exist after death.' When there is feeling ... perception ... volitional formations ... consciousness, by clinging to consciousness, by adhering to consciousness, such a view as this arises: 'The Tathāgata neither exists nor does not exist after death.'

"What do you think, bhikkhus, is form ... consciousness permanent or impermanent?"

"Impermanent, venerable sir."...

"But without clinging to what is impermanent, suffering, and subject to change, could such a view as that arise?"

"No, venerable sir."

"That which is seen, heard, sensed, cognized, attained, sought after, and ranged over by the mind: is that permanent or impermanent?"

"Impermanent, venerable sir."

"Is what is impermanent suffering or happiness?"

"Suffering, venerable sir."

"But without clinging to what is impermanent, suffering, and subject to change, could such a view as that arise?"

"No, venerable sir."

"When, bhikkhus, a noble disciple has abandoned perplexity in these six cases, and when, further, he has abandoned perplexity about suffering, the origin of suffering, the cessation of suffering, and the way leading to the cessation of suffering, he is then called a noble disciple who is a stream-enterer, no longer bound to the nether world, fixed in destiny, with enlightenment as his destination." [217]

II. The Second Trip[264]

19 (1) Winds

At Sāvatthī. "Bhikkhus, when what exists, by clinging to what, by adhering to what, does such a view as this arise: 'The winds do not blow, the rivers do not flow, pregnant women do not give birth, the moon and sun do not rise and set but stand as steady as a pillar'?"

"Venerable sir, our teachings are rooted in the Blessed One...."

"When there is form, bhikkhus, by clinging to form, by adhering to form, such a view as this arises: 'The winds do not blow ... but stand as steady as a pillar.' When there is feeling ... perception ... volitional formations ... consciousness, by clinging to consciousness, by adhering to consciousness, such a view as this arises: 'The winds do not blow ... but stand as steady as a pillar.'

"What do you think, bhikkhus, is form ... [218] ... consciousness permanent or impermanent?"

"Impermanent, venerable sir."...

"But without clinging to what is impermanent, suffering, and subject to change, could such a view as that arise?"

"No, venerable sir."

"Thus, bhikkhus, when there is suffering, it is by clinging to suffering, by adhering to suffering,[265] that such a view as this arises: 'The winds do not blow ... but stand as steady as a pillar.'"

20 (2)–36 (18) This Is Mine, Etc.

(These suttas repeat the views of 24:2–18, but modelled on the above paradigm.)

37 (19) A Self Consisting of Form

At Sāvatthī. "Bhikkhus, when what is present ... [219] ... does such a view as this arise: 'The self consists of form and is unimpaired after death'?"...[266]

38 (20) *A Formless Self*

At Sāvatthī. "Bhikkhus, when what is present … does such a view as this arise: 'The self is formless and is unimpaired after death'?"…

39 (21) *A Self Both Consisting of Form and Formless*

At Sāvatthī. "Bhikkhus, when what is present … does such a view as this arise: 'The self both consists of form and is formless, and is unimpaired after death'?"…

40 (22) *A Self Neither Consisting of Form nor Formless*

At Sāvatthī. "Bhikkhus, when what is present … does such a view as this arise: 'The self neither consists of form nor is formless, and is unimpaired after death'?"…

41 (23) *Exclusively Happy*

At Sāvatthī. "Bhikkhus, when what is present … does such a view as this arise: 'The self is exclusively happy and is unimpaired after death'?"… [220]

42 (24) *Exclusively Miserable*

At Sāvatthī. "Bhikkhus, when what is present … does such a view as this arise: 'The self is exclusively miserable and is unimpaired after death'?"…

43 (25) *Both Happy and Miserable*

At Sāvatthī. "Bhikkhus, when what is present … does such a view as this arise: 'The self is both happy and miserable and is unimpaired after death'?"…

44 (26) *Neither Happy nor Miserable*

At Sāvatthī. "Bhikkhus, when what is present … does such a view as this arise: 'The self is neither happy nor miserable and is unimpaired after death'?"…

III. The Third Trip

45 (1) Winds

[221] At Sāvatthī. "Bhikkhus, when what exists, by clinging to what, by adhering to what, does such a view as this arise: 'The winds do not blow, the rivers do not flow, pregnant women do not give birth, the moon and sun do not rise and set but stand as steady as a pillar'?"

"Venerable sir, our teachings are rooted in the Blessed One...."

"When there is form, bhikkhus, by clinging to form, by adhering to form, such a view as this arises: 'The winds do not blow ... but stand as steady as a pillar.' When there is feeling ... perception ... volitional formations ... consciousness, by clinging to consciousness, by adhering to consciousness, such a view as this arises: 'The winds do not blow ... but stand as steady as a pillar.'

"What do you think, bhikkhus, is form ... consciousness permanent or impermanent?"

"Impermanent, venerable sir."...

"But without clinging to what is impermanent, suffering, and subject to change, could such a view as that arise?"

"No, venerable sir."

"Thus, bhikkhus, whatever is impermanent is suffering. When that is present, it is by clinging to that, that such a view as this arises:[267] 'The winds do not blow ... but stand as steady as a pillar.'"

46 (2)–70 (26) This Is Mine, Etc.

(*These suttas repeat the views of The Second Trip, but are modelled on the above paradigm.*) [222]

IV. The Fourth Trip

71 (1) Winds

At Sāvatthī. "Bhikkhus, when what exists, by clinging to what, by adhering to what, does such a view as this arise: 'The winds do not blow, the rivers do not [223] flow, pregnant women do not give birth, the moon and sun do not rise and set but stand as steady as a pillar'?"

"Venerable sir, our teachings are rooted in the Blessed One…."

"When there is form, bhikkhus, by clinging to form, by adhering to form, such a view as this arises: 'The winds do not blow … but stand as steady as a pillar.' When there is feeling … perception … volitional formations … consciousness, by clinging to consciousness, by adhering to consciousness, such a view as this arises: 'The winds do not blow … but stand as steady as a pillar.'

"What do you think, bhikkhus, is form … feeling … perception … volitional formations … consciousness permanent or impermanent?" – "Impermanent, venerable sir." – "Is what is impermanent suffering or happiness?" – "Suffering, venerable sir." – "Is what is impermanent, suffering, and subject to change fit to be regarded thus: 'This is mine, this I am, this is my self'?" – "No, venerable sir."

"Therefore, bhikkhus, any kind of form whatsoever … Any kind of feeling whatsoever … Any kind of perception whatsoever … Any kind of volitional formations whatsoever … Any kind of consciousness whatsoever, whether past, future, or present, internal or external, gross or subtle, inferior or superior, far or near—all consciousness should be seen as it really is with correct wisdom thus: 'This is not mine, this I am not, this is not my self.'

"Seeing thus, bhikkhus, the instructed noble disciple experiences revulsion towards form, revulsion towards feeling, revulsion towards perception, revulsion towards volitional formations, revulsion towards consciousness. Experiencing revulsion, he becomes dispassionate. Through dispassion [his mind] is liberated. When it is liberated there comes the knowledge: 'It's liberated.' He understands: 'Destroyed is birth, the holy life has been lived, what had to be done has been done, there is no more for this state of being.'"

72 (2)–96 (26) This Is Mine, Etc.

(*These suttas repeat the views of The Second Trip, but are modelled on the above paradigm.*) [224]

[225] Chapter IV

25 *Okkantisaṃyutta*
Connected Discourses on Entering

1 The Eye

At Sāvatthī. "Bhikkhus, the eye is impermanent, changing, becoming otherwise. The ear ... The nose ... The tongue ... The body ... The mind is impermanent, changing, becoming otherwise. One who places faith in these teachings and resolves on them thus is called a faith-follower, one who has entered the fixed course of rightness, entered the plane of superior persons, transcended the plane of the worldlings. He is incapable of doing any deed by reason of which he might be reborn in hell, in the animal realm, or in the domain of ghosts; he is incapable of passing away without having realized the fruit of stream-entry.[268]

"One for whom these teachings are accepted thus after being pondered to a sufficient degree with wisdom is called a Dhamma-follower,[269] one who has entered the fixed course of rightness, entered the plane of superior persons, transcended the plane of the worldlings. He is incapable of doing any deed by reason of which he might be reborn in hell, in the animal realm, or in the domain of ghosts; he is incapable of passing away without having realized the fruit of stream-entry.

"One who knows and sees these teachings thus is called a stream-enterer, no longer bound to the nether world, fixed in destiny, with enlightenment as his destination."[270]

2 Forms

At Sāvatthī. "Bhikkhus, forms are impermanent, changing, becoming otherwise. Sounds ... Odours ... Tastes ... Tactile objects ... Mental phenomena are impermanent, changing, becoming otherwise. [226] One who places faith in these teachings and resolves on them thus is called a faith-follower, one who has entered the fixed course of rightness...; he is incapable of passing away without having realized the fruit of stream-entry.

"One for whom these teachings are accepted thus after being pondered to a sufficient degree with wisdom is called a Dhamma-follower, one who has entered the fixed course of rightness...; he is incapable of passing away without having realized the fruit of stream-entry.

"One who knows and sees these teachings thus is called a stream-enterer, no longer bound to the nether world, fixed in destiny, with enlightenment as his destination."

3 Consciousness

At Sāvatthī. "Bhikkhus, eye-consciousness is impermanent, changing, becoming otherwise. Ear-consciousness ... Nose-consciousness ... Tongue-consciousness ... Body-consciousness ... Mind-consciousness is impermanent, changing, becoming otherwise. One who ... with enlightenment as his destination."

4 Contact

At Sāvatthī. "Bhikkhus, eye-contact is impermanent, changing, becoming otherwise. Ear-contact ... Nose-contact ... Tongue-contact ... Body-contact ... Mind-contact is impermanent, changing, becoming otherwise. One who ... with enlightenment as his destination."

5 Feeling

At Sāvatthī. "Bhikkhus, feeling born of eye-contact is impermanent, changing, becoming otherwise. Feeling born of ear-contact ... Feeling born of nose-contact ... Feeling born of tongue-contact ... Feeling born of body-contact ... Feeling born of mind-contact is impermanent, changing, becoming otherwise. One who ... with enlightenment as his destination." [227]

6 Perception

At Sāvatthī. "Bhikkhus, perception of forms is impermanent, changing, becoming otherwise. Perception of sounds ... Perception of odours ... Perception of tastes ... Perception of tactile objects ... Perception of mental phenomena is impermanent, changing, becoming otherwise. One who ... with enlightenment as his destination."

7 Volition

At Sāvatthī. "Bhikkhus, volition regarding forms is impermanent, changing, becoming otherwise. Volition regarding sounds ... Volition regarding odours ... Volition regarding tastes ... Volition regarding tactile objects ... Volition regarding mental phenomena is impermanent, changing, becoming otherwise. One who ... with enlightenment as his destination."

8 Craving

At Sāvatthī. "Bhikkhus, craving for forms is impermanent, changing, becoming otherwise. Craving for sounds ... Craving for odours ... Craving for tastes ... Craving for tactile objects ... Craving for mental phenomena is impermanent, changing, becoming otherwise. One who ... with enlightenment as his destination."

9 Elements

At Sāvatthī. "Bhikkhus, the earth element is impermanent, changing, becoming otherwise. The water element ... The heat element ... The air element ... The space element ... The consciousness element is impermanent, changing, becoming otherwise.[271] One who ... with enlightenment as his destination."

10 Aggregates

At Sāvatthī. "Bhikkhus, form is impermanent, changing, becoming otherwise. Feeling ... Perception ... Volitional formations ... Consciousness is impermanent, changing, becoming otherwise.

One who places faith in these teachings and resolves on them thus is called a faith-follower, one who has entered the fixed course of rightness, [228] entered the plane of superior persons, transcended the plane of the worldlings. He is incapable of doing any deed by reason of which he might be reborn in hell, in the animal realm, or in the domain of ghosts; he is incapable of passing away without having realized the fruit of stream-entry.

"One for whom these teachings are accepted thus after being pondered to a sufficient degree with wisdom is called a Dhamma-follower, one who has entered the fixed course of rightness, entered the plane of superior persons, transcended the plane of the worldlings. He is incapable of doing any deed by reason of which he might be reborn in hell, in the animal realm, or in the domain of ghosts; he is incapable of passing away without having realized the fruit of stream-entry.

"One who knows and sees these teachings thus is called a stream-enterer, no longer bound to the nether world, fixed in destiny, with enlightenment as his destination."

Chapter V

26 *Uppādasaṃyutta*
Connected Discourses on Arising

1 The Eye

At Sāvatthī. "Bhikkhus, the arising, continuation, production, and manifestation of the eye is the arising of suffering, the continuation of disease, the manifestation of aging-and-death.[272] The arising, continuation, production, and manifestation of the ear ... of the nose ... of the tongue ... of the body ... of the mind [229] is the arising of suffering, the continuation of disease, the manifestation of aging-and-death.

"The cessation, subsiding, and passing away of the eye ... the mind is the cessation of suffering, the subsiding of disease, the passing away of aging-and-death."

2 Forms

At Sāvatthī. "Bhikkhus, the arising, continuation, production, and manifestation of forms ... of sounds ... of odours ... of tastes ... of tactile objects ... of mental phenomena is the arising of suffering, the continuation of disease, the manifestation of aging-and-death.

"The cessation, subsiding, and passing away of forms ... of mental phenomena is the cessation of suffering, the subsiding of disease, the passing away of aging-and-death."

3 Consciousness

At Sāvatthī. "Bhikkhus, the arising, continuation, production, and manifestation of eye-consciousness ... of mind-consciousness is the arising of suffering, the continuation of disease, the manifestation of aging-and-death.

"The cessation, subsiding, and passing away of eye-consciousness ... of mind-consciousness is the cessation of suffering, the subsiding of disease, the passing away of aging-and-death." [230]

4 Contact

At Sāvatthī. "Bhikkhus, the arising, continuation, production, and manifestation of eye-contact ... of mind-contact is the arising of suffering, the continuation of disease, the manifestation of aging-and-death.

"The cessation, subsiding, and passing away of eye-contact ... of mind-contact is the cessation of suffering, the subsiding of disease, the passing away of aging-and-death."

5 Feeling

At Sāvatthī. "Bhikkhus, the arising, continuation, production, and manifestation of feeling born of eye-contact ... of feeling born of mind-contact is the arising of suffering, the continuation of disease, the manifestation of aging-and-death.

"The cessation, subsiding, and passing away of feeling born of eye-contact ... of feeling born of mind-contact is the cessation of suffering, the subsiding of disease, the passing away of aging-and-death."

6 Perception

At Sāvatthī. "Bhikkhus, the arising, continuation, production, and manifestation of perception of forms ... of perception of mental phenomena is the arising of suffering, the continuation of disease, the manifestation of aging-and-death.

"The cessation, subsiding, and passing away of perception of forms ... of perception of mental phenomena is the cessation of suffering, the subsiding of disease, the passing away of aging-and-death."

7 Volition

At Sāvatthī. "Bhikkhus, the arising, continuation, production, and manifestation of volition regarding forms ... of volition regarding mental phenomena is the arising of suffering, the continuation of disease, the manifestation of aging-and-death.

"The cessation, subsiding, and passing away of volition regarding forms ... of volition regarding mental phenomena is the cessation of suffering, the subsiding of disease, the passing away of aging-and-death."

8 Craving

At Sāvatthī. "Bhikkhus, the arising, continuation, production, and manifestation of craving for forms ... of craving for mental phenomena is the arising of suffering, the continuation of disease, the manifestation of aging-and-death. [231]

"The cessation, subsiding, and passing away of craving for forms ... of craving for mental phenomena is the cessation of suffering, the subsiding of disease, the passing away of aging-and-death."

9 Elements

At Sāvatthī. "Bhikkhus, the arising, continuation, production, and manifestation of the earth element ... of the water element ... of the heat element ... of the air element ... of the space element ... of the consciousness element is the arising of suffering, the continuation of disease, the manifestation of aging-and-death.

"The cessation, subsiding, and passing away of the earth element ... of the consciousness element is the cessation of suffering, the subsiding of disease, the passing away of aging-and-death."

10 Aggregates

At Sāvatthī. "Bhikkhus, the arising, continuation, production, and manifestation of form ... of feeling ... of perception ... of volitional formations ... of consciousness is the arising of suffering, the continuation of disease, the manifestation of aging-and-death.

"The cessation, subsiding, and passing away of form ... of consciousness is the cessation of suffering, the subsiding of disease, the passing away of aging-and-death."

[232] Chapter VI

27 *Kilesasaṃyutta*
Connected Discourses on Defilements

1 The Eye

At Sāvatthī. "Bhikkhus, desire and lust for the eye is a corruption of the mind.[273] Desire and lust for the ear ... for the nose ... for the tongue ... for the body ... for the mind is a corruption of the mind. When a bhikkhu has abandoned the mental corruption in these six cases, his mind inclines to renunciation. A mind fortified by renunciation becomes wieldy in regard to those things that are to be realized by direct knowledge."[274]

2 Forms

At Sāvatthī. "Bhikkhus, desire and lust for forms is a corruption of the mind. Desire and lust for sounds ... for odours ... for tastes ... for tactile objects ... for mental phenomena is a corruption of the mind. When a bhikkhu has abandoned the mental corruption in these six cases, his mind inclines to renunciation. A mind fortified by renunciation becomes wieldy in regard to those things that are to be realized by direct knowledge."

3 Consciousness

"Bhikkhus, desire and lust for eye-consciousness ... for mind-consciousness is a corruption of the mind. When a bhikkhu has abandoned the mental corruption in these six cases ... [233] ... [his mind] becomes wieldy in regard to those things that are to be realized by direct knowledge."

4 Contact

"Bhikkhus, desire and lust for eye-contact ... for mind-contact is a corruption of the mind. When a bhikkhu has abandoned the mental corruption in these six cases ... [his mind] becomes wieldy in regard to those things that are to be realized by direct knowledge."

5 Feeling

"Bhikkhus, desire and lust for feeling born of eye-contact ... for feeling born of mind-contact is a corruption of the mind. When a bhikkhu has abandoned the mental corruption in these six cases ... [his mind] becomes wieldy in regard to those things that are to be realized by direct knowledge."

6 Perception

"Bhikkhus, desire and lust for perception of forms ... for perception of mental phenomena is a corruption of the mind. When a bhikkhu has abandoned the mental corruption in these six cases ... [his mind] becomes wieldy in regard to those things that are to be realized by direct knowledge."

7 Volition

"Bhikkhus, desire and lust for volition regarding forms ... [234] ... for volition regarding mental phenomena is a corruption of the mind. When a bhikkhu has abandoned the mental corruption in these six cases ... [his mind] becomes wieldy in regard to those things that are to be realized by direct knowledge."

8 Craving

"Bhikkhus, desire and lust for craving for forms ... for craving for mental phenomena is a corruption of the mind. When a bhikkhu has abandoned the mental corruption in these six cases ... [his mind] becomes wieldy in regard to those things that are to be realized by direct knowledge."

9 Elements

"Bhikkhus, desire and lust for the earth element ... for the water element ... for the heat element ... for the air element ... for the space element ... for the consciousness element is a corruption of the mind. When a bhikkhu has abandoned the mental corruption in these six cases ... [his mind] becomes wieldy in regard to those things that are to be realized by direct knowledge."

10 Aggregates

"Bhikkhus, desire and lust for form ... for feeling ... for perception ... for volitional formations ... for consciousness is a corruption of the mind. When a bhikkhu has abandoned the mental corruption in these five cases, his mind inclines to renunciation. A mind fortified by renunciation becomes wieldy in regard to those things that are to be realized by direct knowledge."

[235] Chapter VII

28 *Sāriputtasaṃyutta*

Connected Discourses with Sāriputta

1 Born of Seclusion

On one occasion the Venerable Sāriputta was dwelling at Sāvatthī in Jeta's Grove, Anāthapiṇḍika's Park.

Then, in the morning, the Venerable Sāriputta dressed and, taking bowl and robe, entered Sāvatthī for alms. Then, when he had walked for alms in Sāvatthī and had returned from the alms round, after his meal he went to the Blind Men's Grove for the day's abiding. Having plunged into the Blind Men's Grove, he sat down at the foot of a tree for the day's abiding.

Then, in the evening, the Venerable Sāriputta emerged from seclusion and went to Jeta's Grove, Anāthapiṇḍika's Park. The Venerable Ānanda saw the Venerable Sāriputta coming in the distance and said to him: "Friend Sāriputta, your faculties are serene, your facial complexion is pure and bright. In what dwelling has the Venerable Sāriputta spent the day?"[275]

"Here, friend, secluded from sensual pleasures, secluded from unwholesome states, I entered and dwelt in the first jhāna, which is accompanied by thought and examination, with rapture and happiness born of seclusion. Yet, friend, it did not occur to me, 'I am attaining the first jhāna,' or 'I have attained the first jhāna,' or 'I have emerged from the first jhāna.'" [236]

"It must be because I-making, mine-making, and the underlying tendency to conceit have been thoroughly uprooted in the Venerable Sāriputta for a long time that such thoughts did not occur to him."[276]

2 *Without Thought*

At Sāvatthī.... (*as above*) ... The Venerable Ānanda saw the Venerable Sāriputta coming in the distance and said to him: "Friend Sāriputta, your faculties are serene, your complexion is pure and bright. In what dwelling has the Venerable Sāriputta spent the day?"

"Here, friend, with the subsiding of thought and examination, I entered and dwelt in the second jhāna, which has internal confidence and unification of mind, is without thought and examination, and has rapture and happiness born of concentration. Yet, friend, it did not occur to me, 'I am attaining the second jhāna,' or 'I have attained the second jhāna,' or 'I have emerged from the second jhāna.'"

"It must be because I-making, mine-making, and the underlying tendency to conceit have been thoroughly uprooted in the Venerable Sāriputta for a long time that such thoughts did not occur to him."

3 *Rapture*

At Sāvatthī.... The Venerable Ānanda saw the Venerable Sāriputta coming in the distance....

"Here, friend, with the fading away as well of rapture, I dwelt equanimous and, mindful and clearly comprehending, I experienced happiness with the body; I entered and dwelt in the third jhāna of which the noble ones declare: 'He is equanimous, mindful, one who dwells happily.' [237] Yet, friend, it did not occur to me, 'I am attaining the third jhāna....'" (*Complete as in preceding sutta.*)

4 *Equanimity*

At Sāvatthī.... The Venerable Ānanda saw the Venerable Sāriputta coming in the distance....

"Here, friend, with the abandoning of pleasure and pain, and with the previous passing away of joy and displeasure, I entered and dwelt in the fourth jhāna, which is neither painful nor pleasant and includes the purification of mindfulness by equanimity. Yet, friend, it did not occur to me, 'I am attaining the fourth jhāna....'"

5 The Base of the Infinity of Space

At Sāvatthī.... The Venerable Ānanda saw the Venerable Sāriputta coming in the distance....

"Here, friend, with the complete transcendence of perceptions of forms, with the passing away of perceptions of sensory impingement, with nonattention to perceptions of diversity, aware that 'space is infinite,' I entered and dwelt in the base of the infinity of space. Yet, friend, it did not occur to me, 'I am attaining the base of the infinity of space....'"

6 The Base of the Infinity of Consciousness

At Sāvatthī.... The Venerable Ānanda saw the Venerable Sāriputta coming in the distance....

"Here, friend, by completely transcending the base of the infinity of space, aware that 'consciousness is infinite,' I entered and dwelt in the base of the infinity of consciousness. Yet, friend, it did not occur to me, 'I am attaining the base of the infinity of consciousness....'"

7 The Base of Nothingness

At Sāvatthī.... The Venerable Ānanda saw the Venerable Sāriputta coming in the distance....

"Here, friend, by completely transcending the base of the infinity of consciousness, aware that 'there is nothing,' I entered and dwelt in the base of nothingness. Yet, friend, it did not occur to me, 'I am attaining the base of nothingness....'" [238]

8 The Base of Neither-Perception-Nor-Nonperception

At Sāvatthī.... The Venerable Ānanda saw the Venerable Sāriputta coming in the distance....

"Here, friend, by completely transcending the base of nothingness, I entered and dwelt in the base of neither-perception-nor-nonperception. Yet, friend, it did not occur to me, 'I am attaining the base of neither-perception-nor-nonperception....'"

9 The Attainment of Cessation

At Sāvatthī.... The Venerable Ānanda saw the Venerable Sāriputta coming in the distance....

"Here, friend, by completely transcending the base of neither-perception-nor-nonperception, I entered and dwelt in the cessation of perception and feeling. Yet, friend, it did not occur to me, 'I am attaining the cessation of perception and feeling,' or 'I have attained the cessation of perception and feeling,' or 'I have emerged from the cessation of perception and feeling.'"

"It must be because I-making, mine-making, and the underlying tendency to conceit have been thoroughly uprooted in the Venerable Sāriputta for a long time that such thoughts did not occur to him."

10 Sucimukhī

On one occasion the Venerable Sāriputta was dwelling at Rājagaha in the Bamboo Grove, the Squirrel Sanctuary. Then, in the morning, the Venerable Sāriputta dressed and, taking bowl and robe, entered Rājagaha for alms. Then, when he had walked for alms on continuous alms round in Rājagaha,[277] he ate that almsfood leaning against a certain wall.

Then the female wanderer Sucimukhī approached the Venerable Sāriputta and said to him: "Ascetic, do you eat facing downwards?"[278]

"I don't eat facing downwards, sister."

"Then, ascetic, do you eat facing upwards?"

"I don't eat facing upwards, sister." [239]

"Then, ascetic, do you eat facing the [four] quarters?"[279]

"I don't eat facing the [four] quarters, sister."

"Then, ascetic, do you eat facing the intermediate directions?"

"I don't eat facing the intermediate directions, sister."

"When you are asked, 'Ascetic, do you eat facing downwards?'... 'Do you eat facing the intermediate directions?' you reply, 'I don't eat thus, sister.' How then do you eat, ascetic?"

"Sister, those ascetics and brahmins who earn their living by the debased art of geomancy[280]—a wrong means of livelihood—these are called ascetics and brahmins who eat facing downwards. Those ascetics and brahmins who earn their living by the debased art of astrology[281]—a wrong means of livelihood—these are called ascetics and brahmins who eat facing upwards. Those ascetics and brahmins who earn their living by undertaking to go on errands and run messages[282]—a wrong means of livelihood—these are called ascetics and brahmins who eat facing the [four] quarters. Those ascetics and brahmins who earn their living by the debased art of palmistry[283]—a wrong means of livelihood—these are called ascetics and brahmins who eat facing the intermediate directions.

"Sister, I do not earn my living by such wrong means of livelihood as the debased art of geomancy, or the debased art of astrology, or by undertaking to go on errands and run messages, or by the debased art of palmistry. I seek almsfood righteously and, having sought it, I eat my almsfood righteously." [240]

Then the female wanderer Sucimukhī went from street to street and from square to square in Rājagaha announcing: "The ascetics following the Sakyan son eat righteous food; they eat blameless food. Give almsfood to the ascetics following the Sakyan son."

Chapter VIII

29 *Nāgasaṃyutta*

Connected Discourses on Nāgas

1 Simple Version

At Sāvatthī. "Bhikkhus, there are these four modes of generation of nāgas.[284] What four? Nāgas born from eggs, nāgas born from the womb, nāgas born from moisture, nāgas of spontaneous birth. These are the four modes of generation of nāgas."

2 Superior

At Sāvatthī. "Bhikkhus, there are these four modes of generation of nāgas.... [241]

"Therein, bhikkhus, nāgas born from the womb, from moisture, and born spontaneously are superior to nāgas born from eggs. Nāgas born from moisture and born spontaneously are superior to nāgas born from eggs and from the womb. Nāgas born spontaneously are superior to nāgas born from eggs, from the womb, and from moisture.

"These, bhikkhus, are the four modes of generation of nāgas."

3 The Uposatha (1)

At Sāvatthī. Then a certain bhikkhu approached the Blessed One, paid homage to him, sat down to one side, and said to him: "Venerable sir, what is the cause and reason why some egg-born nāgas here observe the Uposatha and relinquish [concern for] their bodies?"[285]

"Here, bhikkhus, some egg-born nāgas think thus: 'In the past we acted ambivalently in body, speech, and mind.[286] Having done so, with the breakup of the body, after death, we were reborn in the company of egg-born nāgas. If today we practise good conduct of body, speech, and mind, then with the breakup of the body, after death, we shall be reborn in a happy destination, in a heavenly world. Come now, let us practise good conduct of body, speech, and mind.'

"This, bhikkhu, is the cause and reason why some egg-born nāgas here observe the Uposatha and relinquish [concern for] their bodies." [242]

4–6 The Uposatha (2–4)

(*The same is repeated for the other three types of nāgas.*) [243]

7 He Has Heard (1)

At Sāvatthī.... Sitting to one side, that bhikkhu said to the Blessed One: "Venerable sir, what is the cause and reason why someone here, with the breakup of the body, after death, is reborn in the company of egg-born nāgas?"

"Here, bhikkhu, someone acts ambivalently in body, speech, and mind. He has heard: 'Egg-born nāgas are long-lived, beautiful, and abound in happiness.' He thinks: 'Oh, with the breakup of the body, after death, may I be reborn in the company of egg-born nāgas!' Then, with the breakup of the body, after death, he is reborn in the company of egg-born nāgas.

"This, bhikkhu, is the cause and reason why someone here, with the breakup of the body, after death, is reborn in the company of egg-born nāgas."

8–10 He Has Heard (2–4)

(*These three suttas repeat the same for the other three types of nāgas.*) [244]

11–20 With the Support of Giving (1)

Sitting to one side, that bhikkhu said to the Blessed One: "Venerable sir, what is the cause and reason why [245] someone here, with the breakup of the body, after death, is reborn in the company of egg-born nāgas?"

"Here, bhikkhu, someone acts ambivalently in body, speech, and mind. He has heard: 'Egg-born nāgas are long-lived, beautiful, and abound in happiness.' He thinks: 'Oh, with the breakup of the body, after death, may I be reborn in the company of egg-born nāgas!' He gives food.... He gives drink.... He gives clothing.... He gives a vehicle.... He gives a garland.... He gives a fragrance.... He gives an unguent.... He gives a bed.... He gives a dwelling.... He gives a lamp.[287] Then, with the breakup of the body, after death, he is reborn in the company of egg-born nāgas.

"This, bhikkhu, is the cause and reason why someone here, with the breakup of the body, after death, is reborn in the company of egg-born nāgas."

21–50 With the Support of Giving (2–4)

(*These three decads each repeat the preceding decad for the other three types of nāgas.*) [246]

Chapter IX

30 *Supaṇṇasaṃyutta*
Connected Discourses on Supaṇṇas

1 Simple Version

At Sāvatthī. "Bhikkhus, there are these four modes of generation of supaṇṇas. What four? Supaṇṇas born from eggs, supaṇṇas born from the womb, supaṇṇas born from moisture, supaṇṇas of spontaneous birth. These are the four modes of generation of supaṇṇas." [247]

2 They Carry Off

At Sāvatthī. "Bhikkhus, there are these four modes of generation of supaṇṇas....

"Therein, bhikkhus, egg-born supaṇṇas carry off only nāgas that are egg-born, not those that are womb-born, moisture-born, or spontaneously born.[288] Womb-born supaṇṇas carry off nāgas that are egg-born and womb-born, but not those that are moisture-born or spontaneously born. Moisture-born supaṇṇas carry off nāgas that are egg-born, womb-born, and moisture-born, but not those that are spontaneously born. Spontaneously born supaṇṇas carry off nāgas that are egg-born, womb-born, moisture-born, and spontaneously born.

"These, bhikkhus, are the four modes of generation of supaṇṇas."

3 Ambivalent (1)

At Sāvatthī.... Sitting to one side, that bhikkhu said to the Blessed One: "Venerable sir, what is the cause and reason why someone here, with the breakup of the body, after death, is reborn in the company of egg-born supaṇṇas?"

"Here, bhikkhu, someone acts ambivalently in body, speech, and mind. He has heard: 'Egg-born supaṇṇas are long-lived, beautiful, and abound in happiness.' He thinks: 'Oh, with the breakup of the body, after death, may I be reborn in the company of egg-born supaṇṇas!' Then, with the breakup of the body, after death, he is reborn in the company of egg-born supaṇṇas.

"This, bhikkhu, is the cause and reason why someone here, with the breakup of the body, after death, is reborn in the company of egg-born supaṇṇas."

4–6 Ambivalent (2–4)

(*The same is repeated for the other three types of supaṇṇas.*) [248]

7–16 With the Support of Giving (1)

Sitting to one side, that bhikkhu said to the Blessed One: "Venerable sir, what is the cause and reason why someone here, with the breakup of the body, after death, is reborn in the company of egg-born supaṇṇas?"

"Here, bhikkhu, someone acts ambivalently in body, speech, and mind. He has heard: 'Egg-born supaṇṇas are long-lived, beautiful, and abound in happiness.' He thinks: 'Oh, with the breakup of the body, after death, may I be reborn in the company of egg-born supaṇṇas!' He gives food.... He gives drink.... He gives clothing.... He gives a vehicle.... He gives a garland.... He gives a fragrance.... He gives an unguent.... He gives a bed.... He gives a dwelling.... He gives a lamp. Then, with the breakup of the body, after death, he is reborn in the company of egg-born supaṇṇas.

"This, bhikkhu, is the cause and reason why someone here, with the breakup of the body, after death, is reborn in the company of egg-born supaṇṇas."

17–46 With the Support of Giving (2–4)

(*These three decads each repeat the preceding decad for the other three types of supaṇṇas.*) [249]

Chapter X

31 *Gandhabbakāyasaṃyutta*

Connected Discourses on Orders of Gandhabbas

1 Simple Version

At Sāvatthī. [250] "Bhikkhus, I will teach you about the devas of the gandhabba order. Listen to that....

"And what, bhikkhus, are the devas of the gandhabba order? There are, bhikkhus, devas dwelling in fragrant roots,[289] devas dwelling in fragrant heartwood, devas dwelling in fragrant softwood, devas dwelling in fragrant bark, devas dwelling in fragrant shoots, devas dwelling in fragrant leaves, devas dwelling in fragrant flowers, devas dwelling in fragrant fruits, devas dwelling in fragrant sap, and devas dwelling in fragrant scents.

"These, bhikkhus, are called the devas of the gandhabba order."

2 Good Conduct

At Sāvatthī.... Sitting to one side, that bhikkhu said to the Blessed One: "Venerable sir, what is the cause and reason why someone here, with the breakup of the body, after death, is reborn in the company of the devas of the gandhabba order?"

"Here, bhikkhu, someone practises good conduct of body, speech, and mind.[290] He has heard: 'The devas of the gandhabba order are long-lived, beautiful, and abound in happiness.' He thinks: 'Oh, with the breakup of the body, after death, may I be reborn in the company of the devas of the gandhabba order!' Then, with the breakup of the body, after death, he is reborn in the company of the devas of the gandhabba order.

"This, bhikkhu, is the cause and reason why someone here,

with the breakup of the body, after death, is reborn in the company of the devas of the gandhabba order."

3 Giver (1)

At Sāvatthī.... Sitting to one side, that bhikkhu [251] said to the Blessed One: "Venerable sir, what is the cause and reason why someone here, with the breakup of the body, after death, is reborn in the company of the devas who dwell in fragrant roots?"

"Here, bhikkhu, someone practises good conduct of body, speech, and mind. He has heard: 'The devas who dwell in fragrant roots are long-lived, beautiful, and abound in happiness.' He thinks: 'Oh, with the breakup of the body, after death, may I be reborn in the company of the devas who dwell in fragrant roots!' He becomes a giver of fragrant roots. Then, with the breakup of the body, after death, he is reborn in the company of the devas who dwell in fragrant roots.

"This, bhikkhu, is the cause and reason why someone here, with the breakup of the body, after death, is reborn in the company of the devas who dwell in fragrant roots."

4–12 Giver (2–10)

(*The same paradigm is repeated for each of the other groups of gandhabbas—those who dwell in fragrant heartwood, etc.—as enumerated in §1, each the giver of the corresponding type of gift.*) [252]

13–22 With the Support of Giving (1)

At Sāvatthī.... Sitting to one side, that bhikkhu said to the Blessed One: "Venerable sir, what is the cause and reason why someone here, with the breakup of the body, after death, is reborn in the company of the devas who dwell in fragrant roots?"

"Here, bhikkhu, someone practises good conduct of body, speech, and mind. He has heard: 'The devas who dwell in fragrant roots are long-lived, beautiful, and abound in happiness.'

"He thinks: 'Oh, with the breakup of the body, after death, may I be reborn in the company of the devas who dwell in fragrant roots!' He gives food.... He gives drink.... He gives clothing.... He gives a vehicle.... He gives a garland.... He gives a fragrance.... He gives an unguent.... He gives a bed.... He gives a dwelling.... He gives a lamp. Then, with the breakup of the body, after death, he is reborn in the company of the devas who dwell in fragrant roots.

"This, bhikkhu, is the cause and reason why someone here, with the breakup of the body, after death, is reborn in the company of the devas who dwell in fragrant roots." [253]

23–112 With the Support of Giving (2)

(Repeat the paradigm of §§13–22 for each of the other types of gandhabbas, those who dwell in fragrant heartwood, etc.)

[254] Chapter XI

32 *Valāhakasaṃyutta*

Connected Discourses on Cloud Devas

1 Simple Version

At Sāvatthī. "Bhikkhus, I will teach you about the devas of the cloud-dwelling order. Listen to that....

"And what, bhikkhus, are the devas of the cloud-dwelling order?[291] There are, bhikkhus, cool-cloud devas, warm-cloud devas, storm-cloud devas, wind-cloud devas, and rain-cloud devas.

"These, bhikkhus, are called the devas of the cloud-dwelling order."

2 Good Conduct

(Identical with 31:2, but concerning rebirth in the company of the devas of the cloud-dwelling order.)

3–12 With the Support of Giving (1)

(These suttas are modelled on 31:13–22, but concerning rebirth in the company of the cool-cloud devas.)[292] [255]

13–52 With the Support of Giving (2)

(These suttas repeat the paradigm in regard to rebirth among the other types of cloud-dwelling devas.) [256]

53 Cool-Cloud Devas

At Sāvatthī.... Sitting to one side, that bhikkhu said to the Blessed

One: "Venerable sir, what is the cause and reason why it sometimes becomes cool?"

"There are, bhikkhu, what are called cool-cloud devas. When it occurs to them, 'Let us revel in our own kind of delight,'[293] then, in accordance with their wish, it becomes cool. This, bhikkhu, is the cause and reason why it sometimes becomes cool."

54 Warm-Cloud Devas

... "Venerable sir, what is the cause and reason why it sometimes becomes warm?"

"There are, bhikkhu, what are called warm-cloud devas. When it occurs to them, 'Let us revel in our own kind of delight,' then, in accordance with their wish, it becomes warm. This, bhikkhu, is the cause and reason why it sometimes becomes warm."

55 Storm-Cloud Devas

... "Venerable sir, what is the cause and reason why it sometimes becomes stormy?"

"There are, bhikkhu, what are called storm-cloud devas. When it occurs to them, 'Let us revel in our own kind of delight,' then, in accordance with their wish, it becomes stormy. This, bhikkhu, is the cause and reason why it sometimes becomes stormy."

56 Wind-Cloud Devas

... "Venerable sir, what is the cause and reason why it sometimes becomes windy?"

"There are, bhikkhu, what are called wind-cloud devas. [257] When it occurs to them, 'Let us revel in our own kind of delight,' then, in accordance with their wish, it becomes windy. This, bhikkhu, is the cause and reason why it sometimes becomes windy."

57 Rain-Cloud Devas

... "Venerable sir, what is the cause and reason why it sometimes rains?"

"There are, bhikkhu, what are called rain-cloud devas. When it occurs to them, 'Let us revel in our own kind of delight,' then, in accordance with their wish, it rains. This, bhikkhu, is the cause and reason why it sometimes rains."

Chapter XII

33 *Vacchagottasaṃyutta*

Connected Discourses with Vacchagotta

1 Because of Not Knowing (1)

At Sāvatthī. Then the wanderer Vacchagotta approached the Blessed One and exchanged greetings with him.[294] When they had concluded their greetings and cordial talk, he sat down to one side and said to him: [258]

"Master Gotama, what is the cause and reason why these various speculative views arise in the world: 'The world is eternal' or 'The world is not eternal'; or 'The world is finite' or 'The world is infinite'; or 'The soul and the body are the same' or 'The soul is one thing, the body is another'; or 'The Tathāgata exists after death,' or 'The Tathāgata does not exist after death,' or 'The Tathāgata both exists and does not exist after death,' or 'The Tathāgata neither exists nor does not exist after death'?"

"It is, Vaccha, because of not knowing form, its origin, its cessation, and the way leading to its cessation that those various speculative views arise in the world: 'The world is eternal' ... or 'The Tathāgata neither exists nor does not exist after death.' This, Vaccha, is the cause and reason why those various speculative views arise in the world."[295]

2 Because of Not Knowing (2)

At Sāvatthī....

"It is, Vaccha, because of not knowing feeling, its origin, its cessation, and the way leading to its cessation that those various speculative views arise in the world: 'The world is eternal' ... or 'The Tathāgata neither exists nor does not exist after death.' This,

Vaccha, is the cause and reason why those various speculative views arise in the world."

3 Because of Not Knowing (3)

[259] … "It is, Vaccha, because of not knowing perception, its origin, its cessation, and the way leading to its cessation that those various speculative views arise in the world…."

4 Because of Not Knowing (4)

… "It is, Vaccha, because of not knowing volitional formations, their origin, their cessation, and the way leading to their cessation that those various speculative views arise in the world…."

5 Because of Not Knowing (5)

[260] … "It is, Vaccha, because of not knowing consciousness, its origin, its cessation, and the way leading to its cessation that those various speculative views arise in the world…."

6–10 Because of Not Seeing

… "It is, Vaccha, because of not seeing form … feeling … perception … volitional formations … consciousness, its origin, its cessation, and the way leading to its cessation that those various speculative views arise in the world…."[296]

11–15 Because of Not Breaking Through

… "It is, Vaccha, because of not breaking through to form … feeling … perception … volitional formations … consciousness, its origin, its cessation, and the way leading to its cessation that those various speculative views arise in the world…." [261]

16–20 Because of Not Comprehending

(The same, but read "not comprehending form," etc.)

21–25 Because of Not Penetrating

26–30 Because of Not Discerning

31–35 Because of Not Discriminating

36–40 Because of Not Differentiating

41–45 Because of Not Examining

[262]

46–50 Because of Not Closely Examining

51–55 Because of Not Directly Cognizing

... "It is, Vaccha, because of not directly cognizing form ... feeling ... perception ... volitional formations ... consciousness, its origin, its cessation, and the way leading to its cessation that those various speculative views arise in the world: [263] 'The world is eternal' ... or 'The Tathāgata neither exists nor does not exist after death.' This, Vaccha, is the cause and reason why those various speculative views arise in the world: 'The world is eternal' or 'The world is not eternal'; or 'The world is finite' or 'The world is infinite'; or 'The soul and the body are the same' or 'The soul is one thing, the body is another'; or 'The Tathāgata exists after death,' or 'The Tathāgata does not exist after death,' or 'The Tathāgata both exists and does not exist after death,' or 'The Tathāgata neither exists nor does not exist after death.'"

Chapter XIII

34 *Jhānasaṃyutta*[297]

Connected Discourses on Meditation

1 Attainment in relation to Concentration

At Sāvatthī. "Bhikkhus, there are these four kinds of meditators. What four? [264]

"Here, bhikkhus, a meditator is skilled in concentration regarding concentration but not skilled in attainment regarding concentration.[298]

"Here a meditator is skilled in attainment regarding concentration but not skilled in concentration regarding concentration.

"Here a meditator is skilled neither in concentration regarding concentration nor in attainment regarding concentration.

"Here a meditator is skilled both in concentration regarding concentration and in attainment regarding concentration.

"Therein, bhikkhus, the meditator who is skilled both in concentration regarding concentration and in attainment regarding concentration is the chief, the best, the foremost, the highest, the most excellent of these four kinds of meditators.

"Just as, bhikkhus, from a cow comes milk, from milk comes cream, from cream comes butter, from butter comes ghee, and from ghee comes cream-of-ghee,[299] which is reckoned the best of all these, so too the meditator who is skilled both in concentration regarding concentration and in attainment regarding concentration is the chief, the best, the foremost, the highest, the most excellent of these four kinds of meditators."

2 Maintenance in relation to Concentration

At Sāvatthī. "Bhikkhus, there are these four kinds of meditators. What four?

"Here, bhikkhus, a meditator is skilled in concentration regarding concentration but not skilled in maintenance regarding concentration.[300]

"Here a meditator is skilled in maintenance regarding concentration but not skilled in concentration regarding concentration.

"Here a meditator is skilled neither in concentration nor in maintenance regarding concentration.

"Here a meditator is skilled both in concentration and in maintenance regarding concentration.

"Therein, bhikkhus, the meditator who is skilled both in concentration and in maintenance regarding concentration [265] is the chief, the best, the foremost, the supreme, the most excellent of these four kinds of meditators.

"Just as, bhikkhus, from a cow comes milk ... and from ghee comes cream-of-ghee, which is reckoned the best of all these, so too the meditator who is skilled both in concentration and in maintenance regarding concentration ... is the most excellent of these four kinds of meditators."

3 Emergence in relation to Concentration

(The same, but for "skilled in maintenance" read "skilled in emergence.")[301]

4 Pliancy in relation to Concentration

(The same, but read "skilled in pliancy.")[302] [266]

5 The Object in relation to Concentration

(The same, but read "skilled in the object.")[303]

6 The Range in relation to Concentration

(The same, but read "skilled in the range.")[304] [267]

7 Resolution in relation to Concentration

(The same, but read "skilled in resolution.")[305]

8 Thoroughness in relation to Concentration

(*The same, but read "a thorough worker regarding concentration."*)[306] [268]

9 Persistence in relation to Concentration

(*The same, but read "a persistent worker regarding concentration."*)[307]

10 Suitability in relation to Concentration

(*The same, but read "one who does what is suitable regarding concentration."*)[308] [269]

11 Maintenance in relation to Attainment

At Sāvatthī. "Bhikkhus, there are these four kinds of meditators. What four?

"Here, bhikkhus, a meditator is skilled in attainment regarding concentration but not skilled in maintenance regarding concentration.

"Here a meditator is skilled in maintenance regarding concentration but not skilled in attainment regarding concentration.

"Here a meditator is skilled neither in attainment nor in maintenance regarding concentration.

"Here a meditator is skilled both in attainment and in maintenance regarding concentration.

"Therein, bhikkhus, the meditator who is skilled both in attainment and in maintenance regarding concentration is the chief, the best, the foremost, the highest, the most excellent of these four kinds of meditators.

"Just as, bhikkhus, from a cow comes milk ... and from ghee comes cream-of-ghee, which is reckoned the best of all these, so too the meditator who is skilled both in attainment and in maintenance regarding concentration ... is the most excellent of these four kinds of meditators."

12 Emergence in relation to Attainment

(*The same, but for "skilled in maintenance regarding concentration" read "skilled in emergence regarding concentration."*) [270]

13 Pliancy in relation to Attainment

(The same, but read "skilled in pliancy.")

14 The Object in relation to Attainment

(The same, but read "skilled in the object.")

15 The Range in relation to Attainment

(The same, but read "skilled in the range.") [271]

16 Resolution in relation to Attainment

(The same, but read "skilled in resolution.")

17 Thoroughness in relation to Attainment

(The same, but read "a thorough worker regarding concentration.")

18 Persistence in relation to Attainment

(The same, but read "a persistent worker regarding concentration.")

19 Suitability in relation to Attainment

(The same, but read "one who does what is suitable regarding concentration.") [272]

20 Emergence in relation to Maintenance

At Sāvatthī. "Bhikkhus, there are these four kinds of meditators. What four?

"Here, bhikkhus, a meditator is skilled in maintenance regarding concentration but not skilled in emergence regarding concentration.

"Here a meditator is skilled in emergence regarding concentration but not skilled in maintenance regarding concentration.

"Here a meditator is skilled neither in maintenance nor in emergence regarding concentration.

"Here a meditator is skilled both in maintenance and in emergence regarding concentration.

"Therein, bhikkhus, the meditator who is skilled both in maintenance and in emergence regarding concentration is the chief ... the most excellent of these four kinds of meditators." [273]

21–27 Pliancy in relation to Maintenance, Etc.

(These seven suttas are modelled on the preceding one, but "emergence" is replaced by the seven terms from "pliancy" through "one who does what is suitable," as in §§13–19.)

28 Pliancy in relation to Emergence

At Sāvatthī. "Bhikkhus, there are these four kinds of meditators. What four?

"Here, bhikkhus, a meditator is skilled in emergence but not in pliancy ... [274] ... skilled in pliancy but not in emergence ... skilled neither in emergence nor in pliancy ... skilled both in emergence and in pliancy regarding concentration.

"Therein, bhikkhus, the meditator who is skilled both in emergence and in pliancy regarding concentration is the chief ... the most excellent of these four kinds of meditators."

29–34 The Object in relation to Emergence, Etc.

(These six suttas are modelled on the preceding one, but "pliancy" is replaced by the six terms from "the object" through "one who does what is suitable.") [275]

35 The Object in relation to Pliancy

At Sāvatthī. "Bhikkhus, there are these four kinds of meditators. What four?

"Here, bhikkhus, a meditator is skilled in pliancy but not in the object ... skilled in the object but not in pliancy ... skilled neither in pliancy nor in the object ... skilled both in pliancy and in the object regarding concentration.

"Therein, bhikkhus, the meditator who is skilled both in pliancy and in the object regarding concentration is the chief ... the most excellent of these four kinds of meditators."

36–40 The Range in relation to Pliancy, Etc.

(These five suttas are modelled on the preceding one, but "the object" is replaced by the five terms from "the range" through "one who does what is suitable.")

41 The Range in relation to the Object

At Sāvatthī. "Bhikkhus, there are these four kinds of meditators. What four?

"Here, bhikkhus, a meditator is skilled in the object but not in the range ... skilled in the range but not in the object ... skilled neither in the object nor in the range ... skilled both in the object and in the range regarding concentration.

"Therein, bhikkhus, the meditator who is skilled both in the object and in the range regarding concentration is the chief ... the most excellent of these four kinds of meditators." [276]

42–45 Resolution in relation to the Object, Etc.

(These four suttas are modelled on the preceding one, but "the range" is replaced by the four terms from "resolution" through "one who does what is suitable.")

46 Resolution in relation to the Range

At Sāvatthī. "Bhikkhus, there are these four kinds of meditators. What four?

"Here, bhikkhus, a meditator is skilled in the range but not in resolution ... skilled in resolution but not in the range ... skilled neither in the range nor in resolution ... skilled both in the range and in resolution regarding concentration.

"Therein, bhikkhus, the meditator who is skilled both in the range and in resolution regarding concentration is the chief ... the most excellent of these four kinds of meditators."

47–49 Thoroughness in relation to the Range, Etc.

(These three suttas are modelled on the preceding one, but "resolution" is replaced by the three terms: "a thorough worker," "a persistent worker," and "one who does what is suitable.")

50 Thoroughness in relation to Resolution

At Sāvatthī. "Bhikkhus, there are these four kinds of meditators. What four?

"Here, bhikkhus, a meditator is skilled in resolution [277] but not a thorough worker ... a thorough worker but not skilled in resolution ... neither skilled in resolution nor a thorough worker ... both skilled in resolution and a thorough worker regarding concentration.

"Therein, bhikkhus, the meditator who is both skilled in resolution and a thorough worker regarding concentration is the chief ... the most excellent of these four kinds of meditators."

51–52 Thoroughness in relation to the Range, Etc.

(These two suttas are modelled on the preceding one, but "a thorough worker" is replaced by the two terms: "a persistent worker" and "one who does what is suitable.")

53 Persistence in relation to Thoroughness

At Sāvatthī. "Bhikkhus, there are these four kinds of meditators. What four?

"Here, bhikkhus, a meditator is a thorough worker but not a persistent worker ... a persistent worker but not a thorough worker ... neither a thorough worker nor a persistent worker ... both a thorough worker and a persistent worker regarding concentration.

"Therein, bhikkhus, the meditator who is both a thorough worker and a persistent worker regarding concentration is the chief ... the most excellent of these four kinds of meditators."

54 Suitability in relation to Thoroughness

At Sāvatthī. "Bhikkhus, there are these four kinds of meditators. What four?

"Here, bhikkhus, a meditator is a thorough worker but not one who does what is suitable regarding concentration...."

55 Suitability in relation to Persistence

At Sāvatthī. "Bhikkhus, there are these four kinds of meditators. What four?

"Here, bhikkhus, a meditator is a persistent worker but not one who does what is suitable ... one who does what is suitable but not a persistent worker ... neither a persistent worker nor one who does what is suitable ... [278] both a persistent worker and one who does what is suitable regarding concentration.

"Therein, bhikkhus, the meditator who is both a persistent worker and one who does what is suitable regarding concentration is the chief, the best, the foremost, the highest, the most excellent of these four kinds of meditators.

"Just as, bhikkhus, from a cow comes milk, from milk comes cream, from cream comes butter, from butter comes ghee, and from ghee comes cream-of-ghee, which is reckoned the best of all these, so too the meditator who is both a persistent worker and one who does what is suitable regarding concentration is the chief, the best, the foremost, the highest, the most excellent of these four kinds of meditators."

The Book of the Aggregates is finished.

Notes

22. *Khandhasaṃyutta*

1 The name means "Nakula's father." His wife is called Nakulamātā, "Nakula's mother," though the texts never disclose the identity of Nakula. The Buddha pronounced him and his wife the most trusting (*etadaggaṃ vissāsakānaṃ*) of his lay disciples (AN I 26). According to Spk, they had been the Blessed One's parents in five hundred past lives and his close relations in many more past lives. For additional references see DPPN 2:3 and Hecker, "Shorter Lives of the Disciples," in Nyanaponika and Hecker, *Great Disciples of the Buddha*, pp. 375–78.

2 All three eds. of SN, and both eds. of Spk, read *aniccadassāvī*, "not always a seer," but the SS reading *adhiccadassāvī*, "a chance seer," may be more original; CPD also prefers the latter. Spk: "Because of my affliction I am unable to come whenever I want; I get to see (him) only sometimes, not constantly."

Manobhāvanīyā, used in apposition to *bhikkhū*, has often been misinterpreted by translators to mean "with developed mind." However, the expression is a gerundive meaning literally "who should be brought to mind," i.e., who are worthy of esteem. Spk: "Those great elders such as Sāriputta and Moggallāna are called 'worthy of esteem' ('to be brought to mind') because the mind (*citta*) grows in wholesome qualities whenever they are seen."

3 Be and Se read the second descriptive term as *aṇḍabhūto*, lit. "egg-become," and Spk endorses this with its explanation:

"*Aṇḍabhūto*: become weak (*dubbala*) like an egg. For just as one cannot play with an egg by throwing it around or hitting it—since it breaks apart at once—so this body has 'become like an egg' because it breaks apart even if one stumbles on a thorn or a stump." Despite the texts and Spk, Ee *addhabhūto* may be preferable; see **35:29** and **IV, n. 14**.

4 On the commentarial etymology of *puthujjana*, see **II, n. 153**. Spk gives a long analysis of this passage; for a translation of the parallel at Ps I 20–25, see Bodhi, *Discourse on the Root of Existence*, pp. 33–38. The commentaries distinguish between the "uninstructed worldling" (*assutavā puthujjana*) and the "good worldling" (*kalyāṇa puthujjana*). While both are worldlings in the technical sense that they have not reached the path of stream-entry, the former has neither theoretical knowledge of the Dhamma nor training in the practice, while the latter has both and is striving to reach the path.

5 Text here enumerates the twenty types of identity view (*sakkāyadiṭṭhi*), obtained by positing a self in the four given ways in relation to the five aggregates that constitute personal identity (*sakkāya*; see **22:105**). Identity view is one of the three fetters to be eradicated by the attainment of the path of stream-entry.

Spk: He *regards form as self* (*rūpaṃ attato samanupassati*), by regarding form and the self as indistinguishable, just as the flame of an oil lamp and its colour are indistinguishable. He regards *self as possessing form* (*rūpavantaṃ attānaṃ*), when he takes the formless (i.e., the mind or mental factors) as a self that possesses form, in the way a tree possesses a shadow; *form as in self* (*attani rūpaṃ*), when he takes the formless (mind) as a self within which form is situated, as the scent is in a flower; *self as in form* (*rūpasmiṃ attānaṃ*), when he takes the formless (mind) as a self situated in form, as a jewel is in a casket. *He is obsessed by the notions, "I am form, form is mine"*: he swallows these ideas with craving and views, takes his stand upon them, and grasps hold of them.

Spk states that the identification of each aggregate individually with the self is the annihilationist view (*uccheda-diṭṭhi*), while the other views are variants of eternalism (*sas-*

satadiṭṭhi); thus there are five types of annihilationism and fifteen of eternalism. To my mind this is unacceptable, for eternalist views can clearly be formulated by taking the individual mental aggregates as the self. It also seems to me questionable that a view of self must implicitly posit one (or more) of the aggregates as self; for a view of self to have any meaning or content, it need only posit a relationship between a supposed self and the aggregates, but it need not identify one of the aggregates as self. According to the Buddha, all such positions collapse under analysis. See the "considerations of self" section of the Mahānidāna Sutta (DN II 66–68), translated with commentary in Bodhi, *The Great Discourse on Causation*, pp. 53–55, 92–98.

6 Spk: Even for the Buddhas the body is afflicted, but the mind is afflicted when it is accompanied by lust, hatred, and delusion.

7 This is a common formula describing a disciple whose minimal attainment is stream-entry (*sotāpatti*). The path of stream-entry eradicates the lower three fetters: identity view, doubt, and grasping of rules and vows.

8 Spk: Here, nonaffliction of mind is shown by the absence of defilements. Thus in this sutta the worldly multitude is shown to be afflicted in both body and mind, the arahant to be afflicted in body but unafflicted in mind. The seven trainees (*sekha*: the four on the path and three at the fruition stages) are neither [entirely] afflicted in mind nor [entirely] unafflicted in mind, but they are pursuing nonaffliction of mind (*anāturacittataṃ yeva bhajanti*).

9 Spk: They wanted to spend the three months of the rains residence there.

10 Spk here gives a long account of how Sāriputta assists his fellow monks with both their material needs (*āmisānuggaha*) and with the Dhamma (*dhammānuggaha*). For a translation, see Nyanaponika Thera, "Sāriputta: The Marshal of the Dhamma," in Nyanaponika and Hecker, *Great Disciples of the Buddha*, pp. 21–22.

11 *Eḷagalāgumbha*. PED identifies *eḷagalā* as the plant *Cassia tora*. Spk: This bush grows where there is a constant supply of flowing water. People made a bower with four posts, over which they let the bush grow, forming a pavilion.

Below this they made a seat by placing bricks down and strewing sand over them. It was a cool place during the day, with a fresh breeze blowing from the water.

12 Spk: *Gone abroad* (*nānāverajjagataṃ*): Gone to a realm different from the realm of one king. A foreign realm (*virajja*) is another realm; for as a region different from one's own is called a foreign region (*videsa*), so a realm different from the one where one normally resides is called a foreign realm. That is what is meant by "abroad."

13 See **II, n. 72**.

14 Spk says that all these terms should be understood as synonyms of craving (*taṇhā*). I deliberately translate *pariḷāha* in two ways: as "passion" when it is used as a synonym for craving (as here), and as "fever" (just below) when it is used to signify a severe degree of suffering.

15 Spk: This passage is introduced to show the danger facing one who is not devoid of lust for the five aggregates, and the benefits won by one who is devoid of lust.

16 Mahākaccāna was the Buddha's foremost disciple in the detailed exposition of brief sayings, a skill he displays in this sutta and the next, and elsewhere in SN at **35:130, 132**. For a concise account of his life and teachings, see Bodhi, "Mahākaccāna: The Master of Doctrinal Exposition," in Nyanaponika and Hecker, *Great Disciples of the Buddha*, pp. 213–44. Avantī, his native region, was to the far southwest of the Ganges basin. This entire sutta is quoted verbatim at Nidd I 197–200 in place of a commentary on the verse below.

17 Sn 844. In analysing the first line of the verse, Mahākaccāna does not simply explain the literal meaning of the words, which taken literally make perfectly good sense. Instead he treats the terms as metaphors bearing figurative meanings, and then draws out these meanings by plotting the terms on to a technical system of exegesis not evident in the verse itself. This approach to interpretation was to become characteristic of the later commentaries.

18 The first line of the verse reads: *okaṃ pahāya aniketasārī*. No mention is made of *okasārī* or *anokasārī*, "one who roams in a home" and "one who roams about homeless," but Mahākaccāna introduces these terms as implicit in the absolutive construction *okaṃ pahāya*. The use of *dhātu* as a synonym

for *khandha* is unusual; more often the two are treated as headings for different schemes of classification. But see **22:45**, **53**, **54**, etc., where we also meet this usage.

I follow the reading of the text in Se and Ee, *rūpadhātu-rāgavinibaddhaṃ*, also supported by Spk (Be), as against Be *-vinibandhaṃ*. Spk resolves the compound, *rūpadhātumhi rāgena vinibaddhaṃ*, and explains this consciousness as the kammic consciousness (*kammaviññāṇa*). The passage confirms the privileged status of consciousness among the five aggregates. While all the aggregates are conditioned phenomena marked by the three characteristics, consciousness serves as the connecting thread of personal continuity through the sequence of rebirths. This ties up with the idea expressed at **12:38–40** that consciousness is the persisting element in experience that links together the old existence with the new one. The other four aggregates serve as the "stations for consciousness" (*viññāṇaṭṭhitiyo;* see **22:53–54**). Even consciousness, however, is not a self-identical entity but a sequence of dependently arisen occasions of cognizing; see MN I 256–60.

19 Spk: Why isn't the consciousness element mentioned here (as a "home for consciousness")? To avoid confusion, for "home" is here spoken of in the sense of a condition (*paccaya*). An earlier kammic consciousness is a condition for both a later kammic consciousness and a resultant consciousness, and an (earlier) resultant consciousness for both a (later) resultant consciousness and a (later) kammic consciousness. Therefore the confusion could arise: "What kind of consciousness is intended here?" To avoid such confusion, consciousness is not included, and the teaching is expressed without disorder. Further, the other four aggregates, as objects (or bases: *ārammaṇavasena*), are said to be "stations for the kammically generative consciousness" (*abhisaṅkhāraviññāṇaṭṭhitiyo*), and to show them thus consciousness is not mentioned here.

20 *Engagement and clinging* (*upay' upādāna*), etc. See **12:15** and **II, n. 31**. Spk explains that although all arahants abandon these, the Tathāgata, the Perfectly Enlightened One, is mentioned as the supreme example because his status as an arahant is most evident to all the world.

21 Spk: Why is consciousness mentioned here? To show the abandoning of defilements. For defilements are not fully abandoned in relation to the other four aggregates only, but in relation to all five.

22 I read the long compound with Be and Se *rūpanimittaniketavisāravinibandha*. Ee has *-sāra-* in place of *-visāra-*. The interpretation is as difficult as it looks. I have unravelled it with the aid of Spk, which explains: "Form itself is the 'sign' (*nimitta*) in the sense that it is a condition for defilements, and it is also the abode (consisting in) the 'sign of forms,' being an abode in the sense of a dwelling place, namely, for the act of objectification. By the two terms 'diffusion and confinement' (*visāra-vinibandha*) what is meant is the expansion of defilements and their confining (or binding) nature. (Thus the full compound should be resolved:) 'diffusion and confinement in the abode (consisting in) the sign of forms.' Hence the meaning is: 'by the diffusion of defilements, and by the bondage of defilements arisen in the abode (consisting in) the sign of forms.' *One is called 'one who roams about in an abode'*: one is called 'one who roams about in a dwelling place' by making (forms) an object."

23 Spk: Why are the five aggregates here called "home" (*oka*), while the six objects are called "an abode" (*niketa*)? Because of the relative strength and weakness of desire and lust, respectively. For though they are similar in being places of residence, "home" means one's house, a permanent dwelling place, while "abode" is a place where one dwells for a special purpose, such as a park, etc. As desire and lust are strong in relation to one's home, which is inhabited by one's wife, children, wealth, and possessions, so too they are strong in regard to the internal aggregates. But as lust and desire are weaker in regard to such places as parks, etc., so too in relation to external objects.

Spk-pṭ: Because desire and lust are strong in relation to the internal five aggregates, the latter are called "home," and because desire and lust are weaker in relation to the six external objects, the latter are called "an abode."

24 Such intimacy with lay people in the affairs of lay life is considered unsuitable for a monk; see **9:7** and **35:241**

(IV 180,17–21).

25 Se: *purekkharāno*; Be and Ee: *purakkharāno*. Sn reads as in Se. The word usually means "honouring, revering," but the text here plays on the literal meaning "putting in front," interpreted as projecting into the future through desire. Spk glosses it with *vaṭṭaṃ purato kurumāno*, "putting the round of existence in front." The negative *apurekkharāno* is here glossed *vaṭṭaṃ purato akurumāno*, and at Pj II 547,6–7 *āyatiṃ attabhāvaṃ anabhinibbattento*, "not producing individual existence in the future." Mahākaccāna's explanation echoes the Buddha's exegesis of the Bhaddekaratta verses at MN III 188,15–26.

26 This passage is also found at **56:9**, also at DN I 8,9–16 and elsewhere. The expressions used are probably taken from the arsenal of rhetoric used in the heated philosophical debates that took place between the wanderers of different sects. The mood of these debates, and the Buddha's evaluation of them, is effectively conveyed by a number of suttas in the Aṭṭhakavagga; see Sn IV, 8, 12, 13.

27 The quote is from DN II 283,9–13, but the words *seṭṭhā devamanussānaṃ* are not found there. They are, however, attached to the partly parallel statement, also addressed to Sakka, at MN I 252,3–5.

28 Spk: "*Liberated in the extinction of craving* (*taṇhāsaṅkhayavimuttā*): Liberated *in* Nibbāna, the extinction of craving, *by* the liberation of the fruit, which takes Nibbāna as object." This explanation, it seems, is supported by the texts. While simple *khaya*, in relation to *vimutta*, usually occurs in the ablative (see e.g. MN III 31,1–2 foll.), *saṅkhaya* is in the locative (e.g., at **4:25**: *anuttare upadhisaṅkhaye vimutto*).

29 See **II, n. 58**.

30 Here the text speaks of the diachronic or distal origination of the five aggregates, in contrast to the synchronic or proximal origination shown below at **22:56**, **57**. The concluding portion of the passage shows that we have here a compressed statement of dependent origination. To "seek delight, welcome, and remain holding" is the work of craving (*taṇhā*). The delight (*nandi*) obtained is clinging (*upādāna*), from which the remaining links of the series flow. The passage thus demonstrates how craving for the

present five aggregates is the efficient cause for the arising of a fresh batch of five aggregates in the next existence. The section on passing away should be understood in the converse manner: when craving for the present five aggregates ceases, one has eliminated the efficient cause for the arising of the five aggregates in a future existence.

31 *Paṭisallāna.* Spk: The Blessed One saw those bhikkhus falling away from physical seclusion (*kāyaviveka*) and spoke to them thus because he knew that their meditation would succeed if they would obtain physical seclusion.

32 A nearly identical passage is incorporated into MN No. 138 (III 227,25–229,9). The reading here shows that *anupādā paritassanā* and *anupādāya paritassati* there are ancient errors which had crept into the texts even before the age of the commentators, who were beguiled into devising bad explanations of the bad reading. The MN text should be corrected on the basis of SN.

33 Spk explains *paritassanādhammasamuppādā* as a *dvanda* compound: *taṇhāparitassanā ca akusaladhammasamuppādā ca*; "the agitation of craving *and* a constellation of unwholesome states." The long compound might also have been construed as a *tappurisa*: "a constellation of states (arisen from, associated with) agitation." While both Spk and Spk-pṭ understand *paritassanā* in the sense of craving, it seems to me that the text emphasizes *bhaya-paritassanā*, "agitation through fear." On how *paritassanā* has come to bear two meanings, see **II, n. 137**.

34 While the preceding sutta is framed solely in terms of identity view, this one is framed in terms of the "three grips" (*gāha*): "this is mine" (*etaṃ mama*) is the grip of craving; "this I am" (*eso 'ham asmi*), the grip of conceit; and "this is my self" (*eso me attā*), the grip of views. A shift also occurs in the implications of *paritassanā*, from craving and fear to sorrow and grief.

35 Collins translates *bhārahāra* as "the bearing of the burden," contending that *hāra* must here be understood as an action noun rather than as an agent noun (*Selfless Persons*, p. 165). MW, however, lists "a carrier, a porter" as meanings of *hāra*, and it seems clear that this is the sense required here.

36 Spk: In what sense are these "five aggregates subject to clinging" called the burden? In the sense of having to be borne through maintenance. For their maintenance—by being lifted up, moved about, seated, laid to rest, bathed, adorned, fed and nourished, etc.—is something to be borne; thus they are called a burden in the sense of having to be borne through maintenance.

37 The *puggalavāda* or "personalist" schools of Buddhism appealed to this passage as proof for the existence of the person (*puggala*) as a real entity, neither identical with the five aggregates nor different from them. It is the *puggala*, they claimed, that persists through change, undergoes rebirth, and eventually attains Nibbāna. This tenet was bluntly rejected by the other Buddhist schools, who saw in it a camouflaged version of the *ātman*, the self of the non-Buddhist systems. For an overview of the arguments, see Dutt, *Buddhist Sects in India*, pp. 184–206. The mainstream Buddhist schools held that the person was a mere convention (*vohāra*) or concept (*paññatti*) derivative upon (*upādāya*) the five aggregates, not a substantial reality in its own right. For the Theravāda response, see the first part of Kvu, a lengthy refutation of the "personalist" thesis.

Spk: Thus, by the expression "the carrier of the burden," he shows the person to be a mere convention. For the person is called the carrier of the burden because it "picks up" the burden of the aggregates at the moment of rebirth, maintains the burden by bathing, feeding, seating, and laying them down during the course of life, and then discards them at the moment of death, only to take up another burden of aggregates at the moment of rebirth.

38 *Bhārādāna*. This formula is identical with the definition of the second noble truth (see **56:11**). So too, the explanation of the laying down of the burden (*bhāranikkhepa*) is identical with the definition of the third truth.

Spk: *Seeking delight here and there* (*tatratatrābhinandinī*): having the habit of seeking delight in the place of rebirth or among the various objects such as forms. Lust for the five cords of sensual pleasure is *craving for sensual pleasures* (*kāmataṇhā*). Lust for form-sphere or formless-sphere existence, attachment to jhāna, and lust accompanied by the eternalist view: this is called craving for existence (*bhavataṇhā*). Lust accompanied by the annihilationist view is craving for extermination (*vibhavataṇhā*).

This explanation of the last two kinds of craving seems to me too narrow. More likely, craving for existence should be understood as the primal desire to continue in existence (whether supported by a view or not), craving for extermination as the desire for a complete end to existence, based on the underlying assumption (not necessarily formulated as a view) that such extermination brings an end to a real "I."

39 Spk: All these terms are designations for Nibbāna. For it is contingent upon this (*taṃ hi āgamma*) that craving fades away without remainder, ceases, is given up, is relinquished, and released; and here there is no reliance on sensual pleasures or views. For such a reason Nibbāna gains these names.

40 Spk: The root of craving is ignorance. One draws out craving along with its root by the path of arahantship.

41 The explanation of *pariññā*, full understanding, in terms of the destruction of lust (*rāgakkhaya*), etc., initially seems puzzling, but see MN I 66–67, where *pariññā* is used as a virtual synonym for *pahāna*. Spk specifies *pariññā* here as *accantapariññā*, ultimate abandonment, which it glosses as *samatikkama*, transcendence, and identifies with Nibbāna. Apparently *accantapariññā* is distinct from the usual three kinds of *pariññā*, on which see the following note.

42 *Anabhijānaṃ*, etc., are present participles, glossed *anabhijānanto*, etc. Spk: By "directly knowing" (*abhijānaṃ*), the full understanding of the known (*ñātapariññā*) is indicated; by "fully understanding" (*parijānaṃ*), full understanding by scrutinization (*tīraṇapariññā*); by "becoming dispassionate" and "abandoning," the full understanding as abandonment (*pahānapariññā*).

On the three kinds of full understanding, see **I, n. 36**. In sutta usage, the distinction between *abhijānāti* and *parijānāti* is drawn more sharply than in the commentaries. In the suttas, *abhijānāti* (and its cognates) indicates direct knowledge of phenomena in accordance with the pattern established by the Four Noble Truths. This knowledge is shared by both the *sekha* and the arahant. In contrast, *parijānāti* (and its cognates) is generally used only in relation to the arahant, and signifies the consummation of the knowledge initiated by *abhijānāti*. The Mūlapariyāya Sutta, for example (at MN I 4,7–34), stresses that the *sekha* "has directly known" (*abhiññāya*) each of the twenty-four bases of "conceiving," but must still train further in order to fully understand them (*pariññeyyaṃ tassa*). Only of the arahant is it said "he has fully understood" (*pariññātaṃ tassa*).

43 The next three suttas are composed on the pattern of **14:31–33**. Just below, **22:29–30** correspond to **14:35–36**. Spk explains that in the former three texts, the Four Noble Truths are discussed (see **II, n. 249**); in the latter two, the round of existence and its cessation. The parallel of **14:34** in embedded in **22:60**.

44 *Agha*, glossed *dukkha* by Spk.

45 *Pabhaṅga*, glossed *pabhijjanasabhāva*, "subject to breaking apart." Spk: Here the characteristic of impermanence is discussed.

46 The parallel at MN I 140,33–141,19 includes *dīgharattaṃ*, "for a long time"; **35:101** also omits this. Spk says that form and the other aggregates are abandoned by the abandoning of desire and lust, confirmed by **22:25** and **22:111**.

47 *Yaṃ kho bhikkhu anuseti tena saṅkhaṃ gacchati*. The verb *anuseti* implies *anusaya*, the seven underlying tendencies (see **45:175**), or, more simply, the three underlying tendencies of lust, aversion, and ignorance (see **36:3**). Spk: If one has an underlying tendency towards form by way of sensual lust, etc., then one is described in terms of that same underlying tendency as "lustful, hating, deluded." But when that underlying tendency is absent, one is not reckoned thus.

Additionally, we might suppose, one is reckoned not only by way of the defilements, but even more prominently by way of the aggregate with which one principally identifies. One who inclines to form is reckoned a "physical" person, one who inclines to feeling a "hedonist," one who inclines to perception an "aesthete" (or fact-gatherer?), one who inclines to volition a "man of action," one who inclines to consciousness a thinker, etc.

48 See **I, n. 376**.

49 Spk explains *anumīyati* as if it were equivalent to Skt *anumṛyate*, "to die along with": "When the underlying tendency is dying, the form to which it tends dies along with it (*anumarati*!); for when the object is breaking up, the mental factors that take it as object cannot persist." This of course is ludicrous, for *anumīyati* is doubtlessly from *anu* + *mā*; CPD defines the verb as meaning "to be measured after," which I follow here. This statement then sheds light on the famous passage at **44:1** (IV 376–77 = MN I 487–88) declaring that the Tathāgata, freed from reckoning in terms of form, etc. (*rūpasaṅkhāvimutto*), is immeasurable (*appameyyo*) like the great ocean.

50 *Uppāda, vaya, ṭhitassa aññathattaṃ*. At AN I 152,6–10 these are called the three conditioned characteristics of the conditioned (*tīṇi saṅkhatassa saṅkhatalakkhaṇāni*). The commentaries identify them with the three sub-moments in the momentary life span of a *dhamma*: arising (*uppāda*), persistence or presence (*ṭhiti*), and dissolution (*bhaṅga*). (For more on this, see CMA 4:6.) Spk explains *ṭhitassa aññathatta* as the aging (or decay) of the persisting living entity (*dharamānassa jīvamānassa jarā*), namely, of the life faculty. The commentator mentions the opinion held by some teachers that it is not possible to posit a moment of decay in the case of the mental phenomena (feeling, etc.) [Spk-pṭ: because of the extreme brevity of the moment, decay being quickly overtaken by dissolution], but he rejects this view on the basis of the sutta itself. Spk-pṭ proposes a logical argument for the sub-moment of presence: "Just as a stage of dissolution distinct from the stage of arising is admitted, for otherwise it would follow that an entity dissolves in the very act of arising, so we must admit, as distinct from the stage of dissolution, a stage when an entity 'confronts its own dissolution' (*bhaṅgābhimukhāvatthā*); for something cannot break up unless it has confronted its own dissolution."

51 *Dhammānudhammapaṭipanna*. Spk: *Navannaṃ lokuttaradhammānaṃ anulomadhammaṃ pubbabhāgapaṭipadaṃ paṭipannassa*; "when he is practising the preliminary portion of the practice that is in conformity with the ninefold supramundane Dhamma (the four paths, their fruits, and Nibbāna)." Cp. **II, n. 34**.

52 *Rūpe nibbidābahulaṃ vihareyya. Nibbidā,* "revulsion," is usually taken to refer to an advanced level of insight, which follows knowledge and vision of things as they really are (see **12:23** and **II, n. 69**). Spk explains "fully understands" by way of the three kinds of full understanding (see **n. 42**), and "is freed" (*parimuccati*) as meaning "freed through the full understanding of abandonment arisen at the moment of the path." Alternatively, we might take the former as the arahant's full knowledge of the first noble truth, the latter as the liberation from future rebirth ensured by the eradication of the taints.

53 These words are identical with the Buddha's famous injunction to Ānanda in the Mahāparinibbāna Sutta (at DN II 100,20–22), also below at **47:9, 13, 14** (V 154,5–6, 163,10–11, 164,28–29). In explaining the expression *attadīpa,* "with self as island," Spk says: "What is meant by 'self'? The mundane and supramundane Dhamma (*ko pan' ettha attā nāma? lokiyalokuttaro dhammo*). Therefore he says next, 'with the Dhamma as an island,' etc." This comment overlooks the obvious point that the Buddha is inculcating self-reliance.

54 The Se reading seems best: *yoni yeva upaparikkhitabbā*. Be omits *yeva* and Ee treats *yoni* as a masculine noun. Spk glosses *yoni* with *kāraṇa,* "cause," and refers to MN III 142,23–24: *yoni h' esā Bhūmija phalassa adhigamāya;* "For this, Bhūmija, is the basis for the achievement of the fruit." See too **35:239** (IV 175,27–28) and AN II 76,24–25. Spk-pṭ offers an etymology: *yavati etasmā phalaṃ pasavatī ti yoni.* At **22:95** we repeatedly find the phrase *yoniso upaparikkhati,* "carefully investigates," and it is quite possible that here too *yoniso* was the original reading. A Burmese v.l. cited by Ee actually has *yoniso va.*

55 *Na paritassati.* See **n. 33** above and **II, n. 137**.

56 *Tadaṅganibbuto ti vuccati.* Though *nibbuto* is the past participle generally used to describe one who has attained Nibbāna, the prefix *tadaṅga-* qualifies that sense, suggesting he has not actually attained Nibbāna but has only approximated its attainment. One might have rendered this expression "one who has attained Nibbāna in that respect," i.e., only in respect of a particular freedom. Spk: He is "quenched in

that respect" because of the quenching of the defilements with respect to (or: through the factor of) insight. In this sutta it is just insight (*vipassanā va*) that is discussed.

57 *Dukkhasamudayagāminī samanupassanā*. Identity view (*sakkāyadiṭṭhi*) is so called because the five aggregates of clinging, which constitute personal identity (*sakkāya*), are also the most basic manifestation of suffering (*dukkha*), as declared in the first noble truth: *saṅkhittena pañc' upādānakkhandhā dukkhā* (see **56:11**). According to Spk, *samanupassanā* is here equivalent to views (*diṭṭhi*), while in the following passage on the cessation of suffering it denotes the knowledge of the four paths along with insight.

58 Spk: Seeing with correct wisdom (*sammappaññāya*) is the wisdom of the path together with insight. The mind becomes dispassionate (*virajjati*) at the moment of the path, and is liberated (*vimuccati*) at the moment of the fruit.

59 Spk: It is *steady* (*ṭhitaṃ*) because there is no further work to be done; and *content* (*santussitaṃ*) because what was to be attained has been attained.

It is noteworthy that the passage makes an unexpected transition from impersonal neuter nominatives (describing the bhikkhu's mind, *cittaṃ*) to verbs that imply a personal subject (*na paritassati, parinibbāyati, pajānāti*).

60 The two expressions, "views concerning the past" (*pubbantānudiṭṭhiyo*) and "views concerning the future" (*aparantānudiṭṭhiyo*), clearly allude to the Brahmajāla Sutta (DN No. 1), which describes the famous sixty-two speculative views, eighteen about the past and forty-four about the future. Spk confirms this, and explains that at this point the first path has been shown [Spk-pṭ: by showing the complete abandonment of views]. The following passage shows the three higher paths and fruits; or, alternatively, the former passage shows the abandoning of views by way of mere insight, the sequel the four paths along with insight.

For "obstinate grasping," Se *thāmasā parāmāso* seems superior to Be *thāmaso parāmāso* and Ee *thāmaso parāmaso*; that is the reading at MN I 130,34, 257,4, etc. Spk glosses "obstinate grasping" as the obstinacy of views (*diṭṭhithāmaso*) and the grasping of views (*diṭṭhiparāmāso*), apparently construing *thāmasā*, an instrumental used adverbially, as if it were an independent noun.

61 I read with Be and Se: *asmī ti c' assa avigataṃ hoti*. Ee, and many mss, read *adhigataṃ* for *avigataṃ*. That the latter reading must be correct is proved by AN III 292,16–17, where the affirmative occurs, *asmī ti kho me vigataṃ*. This same argument applies to the reading at **22:89** below (III 128,34 foll.), despite the prevalence of *adhigataṃ* there.

Spk explains "this way of regarding things" as regarding with views (*diṭṭhisamanupassanā*), and "the notion 'I am'" as the "triple proliferation" (*papañcattaya*) of craving, conceit, and views. The two differ in that "regarding" is a conceptually formulated view, the notion "I am" a subtler manifestation of ignorance expressive of desire and conceit; see the important discussion at **22:89**. The view of self is eliminated by the path of stream-entry; the notion "I am" is fully eradicated only by the path of arahantship.

62 I take this terse sentence to be describing the rebirth process contingent upon the persistence of the delusion of personal selfhood. Elsewhere "descent" (*avakkanti*)—of consciousness, or of name-and-form—indicates the commencement of a new existence (as at **12:39, 58, 59**). Spk: When there is this group of defilements, there is the production of the five faculties conditioned by defilements and kamma.

63 I interpret this whole passage as a demonstration of how the new kammically active phase of existence commences through the renewal of conceiving in terms of the notion "I am" and speculative views of selfhood. Spk identifies "mind" (*mano*) with the kamma-mind (*kammamano*) and "mental phenomena" (*dhammā*) with its objects, or the former as the *bhavaṅga* and adverting consciousness. *Ignorance-contact* (*avijjāsamphassa*) is the contact associated with ignorance (*avijjāsampayuttaphassa*).

Ignorance is the most fundamental condition underlying this process, and when this is activated by feeling it gives rise to the notion "I am" (a manifestation of craving and conceit). The idea "I am *this*" arises subsequently, when the vacuous "I" is given a content by being identified with one or another of the five aggregates. Finally, full eternalist and annihilationist views originate when the imagined self is held either to survive death or to undergo destruction at death. This passage thus presents us with an alternative version of dependent origination, where the "way of regarding things" and the notion "I am" belong to the causally active side of the past existence; the five faculties to the resultant side of the present existence; and the recurrence of the notion "I am" to the causal side of the present existence. This will in turn generate renewed existence in the future.

64 The word *khandha*, aggregate, is glossed in the commentaries with *rāsi*, "group." Each aggregate includes all instances of the particular phenomenological type that share its defining characteristic. The eleven categories into which each aggregate is classified are analysed at Vibh 1–12.

65 This sutta is quoted and discussed at Vism 477–78 (Ppn 14:214–15), in relation to the difference between the aggregates and the aggregates subject to clinging. The key terms distinguishing the *pañc' upādānakkhandhā* from the *pañcakkhandhā* are *sāsava upādāniya*, "with taints and subject to clinging." The *pañc' upādānakkhandhā* are included within the *pañcakkhandhā*, for all members of the former set must also be members of the latter set. However, the fact that a distinction is drawn between them implies that there are *khandha* which are *anāsava anupādāniya*, "untainted and not subject to clinging." On first consideration it would seem that the "bare aggregates" are those of the arahant, who has eliminated the *āsava* and *upādāna*. However, in the Abhidhamma all *rūpa* is classified as *sāsava* and *upādāniya*, and so too the resultant (*vipāka*) and functional (*kiriya*) mental aggregates of the arahant (see Dhs §§1103, 1219). The only aggregates classed as *anāsava* and *anupādāniya* are the four mental aggregates occurring on the cognitive occasions of the four supramundane paths and fruits (see Dhs §§1104, 1220). The reason for this is that *sāsava* and *upādāniya* do not mean "accompanied by taints and by clinging," but "capable of being taken as the objects of the taints and of clinging," and the arahant's mundane aggregates can be taken as objects of the taints and clinging *by others* (see As 347). For a detailed study of this problem, see

Bodhi, "Aggregates and Clinging Aggregates."

Spk: Among the five aggregates the form aggregate is of the sense sphere, the other four aggregates are of the four planes (sense sphere, form sphere, formless sphere, supramundane). *With taints* (*sāsava*) means: what becomes a condition for the taints by way of object; so too *that can be clung to* (*upādāniya*) means what becomes a condition for clinging [Spk-pṭ: by being made its object]. Among the aggregates subject to clinging, stated by way of the practice of insight, the form aggregate is sense sphere, the others pertain to the three planes (i.e., excluding only the supramundane).

66 This is the threefold conceit: superiority, equality, and inferiority.

67 This passage applies the formula for the Four Noble Truths to each of the five aggregates, in accordance with the Buddha's statement, "the five aggregates subject to clinging are suffering" (**56:11**). See **12:13** and **II, n. 27**.

68 Spk: The mutual destruction of delight (*nandi*) and lust (*rāga*) is stated to show that in denotation there is actually no difference between them. Or, alternatively, one abandons delight by experiencing revulsion, (which occurs) through the contemplation of revulsion (*nibbidānupassanā*); one abandons lust by becoming dispassionate, (which occurs) through the contemplation of dispassion (*virāgānupassanā*). To this extent, having set up insight [Spk-pṭ: with the phrase, "with the destruction of delight comes the destruction of lust," which consummates the function of insight], by the phrase "with the destruction of lust comes the destruction of delight" he shows the path; and by the phrase "with the destruction of delight and lust the mind is liberated" the fruit is shown.

69 I read *upayo* with Be and Se, as against Ee *upāyo*. Here it seems the noun is being used as a virtual present participle. Spk: *Engaged*: one who has approached (*upagato*) the five aggregates by way of craving, conceit, and views.

70 I translate in accordance with Se. Be and Ee have omitted the clauses on *vedanā* and *saññā*, apparently an old scribal error. I also read *nandūpasecana*, with Be and Se, as against Ee *nandupasevana*. Though Spk does not offer a gloss, the Be–Se reading can claim support from the underlying

metaphor of vegetation, which is made explicit in the simile in the next sutta. In the simile *nandirāga* is compared to the water element, and it is thus appropriate that it be "sprinkled."

The passage is quoted at DN III 228,6–13 in explanation of the "four stations of consciousness" (*catasso viññaṇaṭṭhitiyo*); see too Nidd II 1. We find here still another indication of how consciousness grows and evolves in dependence on the other four aggregates. This sutta and the next should be compared with **12:38–40**, **12:64**, and **22:3**. As to why consciousness is not "engaged" with itself, see above **n. 19**, which makes essentially the same point.

71 Spk: *The basis is cut off* (*vocchijjatārammaṇaṃ*): the basis (or object) is cut off through the lack of any ability to precipitate rebirth. Spk-pṭ: The basis (or object), which is the condition for rebirth by way of the sign of kamma, etc., is "cut off" by way of (the cutting off of) the kamma that generates rebirth.

Spk-pṭ thus takes *ārammaṇa* here in the sense dominant in the Abhidhamma, i.e., as the object of rebirth-consciousness (see CMA 3:17). However, I understand the word in the older sense of "basis," elsewhere glossed simply as *paccaya*; see **II, n. 112**. Spk's explanation need not entail the interpretation proposed by Spk-pṭ.

72 Be, Se: *Anabhisaṅkhacca vimuttaṃ* (Ee: *anabhisaṅkhārañca vimuttaṃ*). The "nongenerative consciousness" is the consciousness that does not generate volitional formations (*saṅkhāra*). Spk says it is "liberated" because it does not generate rebirth.

73 The five kinds of "seeds" (*bīja*) are actually five means of propagation. Spk gives examples of the five kinds drawn from Vin IV 35.

74 For a poetic version of the vegetation simile, see **5:9**; for an elaboration of the comparison of consciousness to a seed, see AN I 223–24.

75 Spk: The Blessed One uttered this inspired utterance because he was aroused by powerful joy while reviewing the emancipating nature (*niyyānikabhāva*) of the Teaching. The five lower fetters (*pañc' orambhāgiyāni saṃyojanāni*) are: identity view, doubt, distorted grasp of rules and vows,

sensual lust, and ill will.

The formula for resolution recommended by the Buddha occurs in the suttas in two versions, one used by the annihilationists, the other the Buddha's adaptation of this; as the two versions differ only with respect to two verb forms, they are sometimes confounded in the various recensions. From the commentarial glosses, it appears that the confusion had already set in before the age of the commentaries. Readings also differ among several editions of the same text. Generally I prefer the readings in Se, though in relation to the present sutta Se follows the lemma and gloss of Spk, which has adopted the first phrase in its annihilationist variant (though not interpreted as such). This corruption was probably already present in the text available to the commentators.

The annihilationist version—explicitly identified as *ucchedadiṭṭhi* at **22:81** and classed among the wrong views at **22:152** and **24:4**—reads: *no c' assaṃ no ca me siyā, na bhavissāmi na me bhavissati.* At AN V 63,28–64,2 the Buddha describes this creed as the highest of outside speculative views (*etadaggaṃ bāhirakānaṃ diṭṭhigatānaṃ*), the reason being that one who accepts such a view will not be attracted to existence nor averse to the cessation of existence. It is problematic how the optative clause in the annihilationist version should be interpreted; perhaps it can be read as an assertion that personal existence, along with its experienced world, is utterly fortuitous ("I might not have been and it might not have been mine"). The clause in the future tense clearly asserts that personal existence and its world will terminate at death.

The Buddha transformed this formula into a theme for contemplation consonant with his own teaching by replacing the first person verbs with their third person counterparts: *No c' assa no ca me siyā, na bhavissati na me bhavissati.* The change of person shifts the stress from the view of self implicit in the annihilationist version ("I will be annihilated") to an impersonal perspective that harmonizes with the *anattā* doctrine. In the present sutta, resolving (*adhimuccamāno*) on the formula is said to culminate in the destruction of the five lower fetters, that is, in the stage of nonreturning (*anāgāmitā*). Elsewhere the formula includes a rider, *yad atthi yaṃ bhūtaṃ taṃ pajahāmi*, "what exists, what has come to be, that I am abandoning." Contemplation of this is said to lead to equanimity. At MN II 264,29–265,20 practice guided by the full formula, with the rider, culminates in rebirth in the base of neither-perception-nor-nonperception (if the meditator clings to the equanimity) or in Nibbāna (if there is no clinging to the equanimity). At AN IV 70–74, resolution guided by the formula, again with the rider, leads to one of the five levels of nonreturning or to arahantship. At Ud 78,2–3 the shorter formula is applied to mindfulness of the body; one who dwells thus gradually crosses attachment, i.e., wins arahantship.

It may be significant that in the Nikāyas the precise meaning of the formula is never explicated, which suggests it may have functioned as an open-ended guide to reflection to be filled in by the meditator through personal intuition. As to the actual word meaning, the commentaries take the opening particle *c'* to represent *ce*, "if," glossed *sace* by Spk and *yadi* by Spk-pṭ. On this basis they interpret each part of the formula as a conditional. Spk explains the formula in the present sutta on the basis of the questionable reading *c' assaṃ*, though its second alternative conforms to the superior reading *c' assa*. I translate here from Spk very literally, rendering the lemma in the way favoured by the explanation: "*If I were not, it would not be for me*: If I were not (*sace ahaṃ na bhaveyyaṃ*), neither would there be my belongings (*mama parikkhāro*). Or else: If in my past there had not been kammic formation (*kammābhi-saṅkhāro*), now there would not be for me these five aggregates. *I will not be, (and) it will not be for me*: I will now so strive that there will not be any kammic formation of mine producing the aggregates in the future; when that is absent, there will be for me no future rebirth."

I part with the commentaries on the meaning of *c'*, which I take to represent *ca*; the syntax of the phrase as a whole clearly requires this. The Skt parallels actually contain *ca* (e.g., at Uv 15:4, parallel to Ud 78). If we accept this reading, then (in the present sutta) the first "it" can be taken to refer to the personal five aggregates, the second to the world apprehended through the aggregates. For the worldling this dyad is misconstrued as the duality of self and world; for the noble disciple it is simply the duality of internal and external phenomena. On this basis I would interpret the formula thus: "The five aggregates can be terminated, and the world presented by them can be terminated. I will so strive that the five aggregates will be terminated, (and) so that the world presented by them will be terminated." Alternatively, the first "it" might be taken to refer to craving, and the second to the five aggregates arisen through craving. In the additional rider, "what exists, what has come to be" denotes the presently existent set of five aggregates, which are being abandoned through the abandonment of the cause for their continued re-manifestation, namely, craving or desire-and-lust.

My understanding of this passage has been largely influenced by discussions with VĀT and Bhikkhu Ñāṇatusita. I am also indebted to Peter Skilling for information on the Skt and Tibetan versions of the formula.

76 *Rūpaṃ vibhavissati*, etc. Spk glosses: *rūpaṃ bhijjissati*, "form will break up," and Spk-pṭ: *rūpaṃ vinasissati*, "form will perish." The commentators seem to understand "extermination" here as the incessant momentary cessation of the aggregates, but I believe the verb refers to the final cessation of the aggregates with the attainment of the *anupādisesa-nibbānadhātu*. This meaning harmonizes better with the opening formula, and also seems supported by Th 715cd: *saṅkhārā vibhavissanti, tattha kā paridevanā*, "formations (only) will be exterminated, so what lamentation can there be over that."

77 Spk: *With the extermination of form* (*rūpassa vibhavā*): by the seeing of extermination, together with insight [Spk-pṭ: for the word "extermination" in the text is stated by elision of the word "seeing"]. For the four paths together with insight are called "the seeing of the extermination of form, etc." This is said with reference to that.

On the interpretation that I prefer (as stated in the preceding note), "the extermination of form," etc., refers to the ultimate cessation of the aggregates in Nibbāna, and thus the realization that such cessation takes place functions as the spur implicit in the meditation formula that inspires the bhikkhu to break the five fetters.

78 *Anantarā āsavānaṃ khayo.* Here "the destruction of the taints" refers to arahantship, and it seems the bhikkhu is asking how one can attain arahantship directly, without being detained at the stage of nonreturner. Spk explains that there are two types of immediacy (*anantara*), proximate and distant. Insight is the proximate immediate cause for the path (since the supramundane path arises when insight has reached its peak), and the distant immediate cause for the fruit (since the fruit directly follows the path). Thus the bhikkhu is asking: "How should one know and see, with insight as the immediate cause, to attain the fruit of arahantship called 'the destruction of the taints'?"

79 Spk: The worldling becomes frightened with the arising of weak insight (*dubbalavipassanā*); for he cannot overcome self-love and thus he becomes afraid, thinking, "Now I will be annihilated and won't exist any more." He sees himself falling into an abyss (see MN I 136,30–37,4 and **n. 181** below). But when strong insight occurs to the instructed noble disciple, he doesn't become frightened but thinks, "It is formations only that arise, formations only that cease." Spk-pṭ: When the good worldling sees, with the knowledge of appearance as fearful, that formations are fearful, he doesn't become afraid.

"Knowledge of appearance as fearful" (*bhayat' upaṭṭhānañāṇa*) is an advanced stage of insight knowledge which lays bare the fearful nature of formations in all three periods of time; see Vism 645–47; Ppn 21:29–34.

80 *Catuparivaṭṭa*, lit. "four turnings." Spk-pṭ: By way of turning round the Four Noble Truths with respect to each of the five aggregates.

81 Strangely, the Nikāyas do not offer an analysis of the form derived from the four great elements (*catunnaṃ mahābhūtānaṃ upādāya rūpaṃ*). This analysis first appears only in the Abhidhamma Piṭaka, according to which such form includes the five sense faculties, four sense objects (the tactile object being assigned to three of the great elements, excluding the water element), the space element, sexual determination, physical nutriment (= edible food), etc.; see CMA 6:2–5. On nutriment as a condition for the physical

body, see **II, n. 18**. In this sutta the proximate condition for the origination of each of the five aggregates is shown, in contrast with **22:5**, which shows the collective distal or remote condition for all five aggregates. For the distinction of the two types of conditions, see **II, n. 58**.

82 This paragraph shows trainees (*sekha*), who have directly known the Four Noble Truths and are practising for attainment of Nibbāna, the ultimate cessation of the five aggregates. For this reason the trainees are said to have "gained a foothold (*gādhanti*) in this Dhamma and Discipline," in contrast to the arahants, who have completed their work.

83 This paragraph shows those beyond training (*asekha*), the arahants. Spk: They are *well liberated* (*suvimuttā*) by the liberation of the fruit of arahantship; *consummate ones* (*kevalino*), complete, having done all their duties. *There is no round for describing them* (*vaṭṭaṃ tesaṃ natthi paññāpanāya*): there is no remaining round (of rebirths) for the description of them. Or else "round" means basis (*kāraṇa*), so there is no basis for description. At this point the plane of the one beyond training (*asekhabhūmi*, i.e., of the arahant) has been discussed.

On "consummate one," see **I, n. 446**. On the idea of the arahant as beyond description or free from reckoning, see **22:35** and **n. 47** above. The expression *vaṭṭaṃ tesaṃ natthi paññāpanāya* recurs at **44:6** (IV 391,10); see too DN II 63,30–64,1. The phrase might also have been translated, "There is no round for their manifestation."

84 Contact (*phassa*) is the coming together of sense object and consciousness via a sense faculty. When this occurs, the other mental factors arise, most notably feeling, perception, and volition.

85 The fact that there is a difference between the name of the aggregate (*saṅkhārakkhandha*) and the term of definition (*sañcetanā*) suggests that this aggregate has a wider compass than the others. In the Abhidhamma Piṭaka and the commentaries, the *saṅkhārakkhandha* is treated as an "umbrella category" for classifying all mental factors other than feeling and perception. Volition is mentioned only as the most important factor in this aggregate, not as its exclusive constituent.

86 It is significant that while contact is the proximate condition for feeling, perception, and volitional formations, name-and-form in its entirety is the proximate condition for consciousness. This ties up with the idea, as stated in **22:3**, that the other four aggregates are the "home" of consciousness. See too in this connection **12:65** and **12:67**.

87 The seven cases (*sattaṭṭhānā*) are obtained by merging the tetrad of the preceding sutta with the triad of **22:26**. Spk: This sutta is a statement of both congratulations (*ussadanandiya*) and enticement (*palobhanīya*). For just as a king who has won a battle rewards and honours his victorious warriors in order to inspire the other soldiers to become heroes, so the Blessed One extols and praises the arahants in order to inspire the others to attain the fruit of arahantship.

88 *A triple investigator* (*tividhūpaparikkhī*). This may be understood by way of the Dhātusaṃyutta (SN 14), the Saḷāyatanasaṃyutta (SN 35), and the Nidānasaṃyutta (SN 12). See too MN No. 115, where skill in the elements, sense bases, and dependent origination is explained in detail, augmented by the skill of knowing the possible and the impossible.

89 It seems that here *bhikkhu paññāvimutto* should be understood as any arahant disciple, not specifically as the *paññāvimutta* contrasted with the *ubhatobhāgavimutta* type, as in MN I 477–78. See **II, n. 210**.

90 This is the second discourse of the Buddha, recorded at Vin I 13–14. The five bhikkhus are the first five disciples, who at this point are still trainees (*sekha*). They attain arahantship by the end of the discourse. Spk: Following the Dhammacakkappavattana Sutta (the first sermon), given on the full-moon day of Āsaḷha (July), the five were gradually established in the fruit of stream-entry. On the fifth of the following fortnight, he addressed them, thinking, "Now I will teach them the Dhamma for the destruction of the taints."

91 The sutta offers two "arguments" for the *anattā* thesis. The first demonstrates the selfless nature of the five aggregates on the ground that they are insusceptible to the exercise of mastery (*avasavattitā*). If anything is to count as our "self"

it must be subject to our volitional control; since, however, we cannot bend the five aggregates to our will, they are all subject to affliction and therefore cannot be our self. For a fuller presentation of this argument, see MN I 230–33. The second argument for *anattā* is introduced just below, beginning with the words "What do you think?..." This argument demonstrates the characteristic of nonself on the basis of the other two characteristics, impermanence and suffering, taken conjointly.

92 In the Sāmaññaphala Sutta this view is ascribed to the Ājīvika teacher Makkhali Gosāla (DN I 53,24–28). The same source ascribes to Pūraṇa Kassapa the theory of the inefficacy of action (*akiriyavāda*; DN I 52,21–53,2), stated at **24:6** but without ascription. At **46:56** a different noncausality doctrine (*ahetukavāda*) is ascribed to Pūraṇa Kassapa.

93 See **14:34**.

94 This is a compressed version of the fuller Āditta Sutta at **35:28**, which applies the metaphor of burning to the twelve sense bases. Perhaps the present sutta was composed by simply replacing the sense bases with the aggregates, and was then compressed so that it would not "steal the show" from the more famous sutta, popularly known as the Fire Sermon, regarded by the Pāli tradition as the third formal discourse of the Buddha's ministry.

95 *Niruttipathā adhivacanapathā paññattipathā*. Spk: Language (*nirutti*, linguistic expression) is itself the pathway of language; or alternatively, language is called the pathway of language because it is the pathway for the communication of meanings to be understood through language. The other two terms should be understood in the same way; the three are synonyms.

Dhs §§1306–8 distinguishes between *nirutti, adhivacana,* and *paññatti* on the one hand, and their respective *patha* on the other. There *nirutti* and the other two are treated as synonymous, but their respective *patha* are said to comprise *all phenomena* (*sabb' eva dhammā*). At DN II 63,28–64,2, name-and-form together with consciousness is said to be *adhivacanapatha, niruttipatha, paññattipatha*. On the basis of these texts it seems that Spk has gone astray here, and we should understand that the three pathways of language, etc., are the five aggregates pertaining to the three time periods, and the corresponding temporal "term, label, description" applied to them is "language, designation, description."

The sutta is quoted at Kv 150 as support for the Theravādin argument against the Sarvāstivādins, who held that past and future phenomena exist in some way.

96 Spk explains *ukkalā* as residents of the country of Ukkala (also called Okkala, according to CPD corresponding to modern Orissa). Spk treats *vasabhaññā* as a *dvanda*, *vasso ca bhañño ca*, and explains that the two held the three wrong views found at **24:5–7**. I read the last expression with Se and Ee, *nindabyārosa-uparambhabhayā*. Be includes an additional term in the second place, *ghaṭṭana*, not found in the other eds. See the parallel at MN III 78,12–16, which reads as Se and Ee do here. In Spk, *ghaṭṭana* is the gloss on *byārosa*, which Be apparently has absorbed into the text.

97 Spk: *Clinging* (*upādiyamāno*): seizing by way of craving, conceit, and views. In the next two suttas, *conceiving* (*maññamāno*) and *seeking delight* (*abhinandamāno*) are explained in the same way.

98 This sutta is identical with **18:21** (and **22:91**), the next with **18:22** (and **22:92**). A whole saṃyutta (SN 23) consists of suttas spoken to the Venerable Rādha.

99 Nine abodes of beings (*sattāvāsa*) are enumerated at AN IV 401 (= DN III 263). The "pinnacle of existence" (*bhavagga*) is presumably the sphere of neither-perception-nor-nonperception, the highest realm of sentient existence. The term is used in this sense at Vibh 426,8 and regularly in the commentaries.

100 We should read with Be and Se: *anejaṃ te anuppattā*. Spk: This is arahantship, the abandoning of craving, which is known as "the stirring" (*ejā*). See **35:90, 91**.

101 *Sattasaddhammagocarā*. The seven good qualities: faith, moral shame, fear of wrongdoing, learning, energy, mindfulness, and wisdom; see MN I 356,1–21; DN III 252,10–12.

102 The seven gems (*sattaratana*) are the seven factors of enlightenment (*satta bojjhaṅgā*); see **46:42**. The threefold training (*tisikkhā*) is the training in the higher virtue, the higher mind, and the higher wisdom; see AN I 235–36.

103 The ten factors (*dasaṅga*): the eight perfected factors of the Noble Eightfold Path, augmented by right knowledge and right liberation. They are known more specifically as the ten factors of the one beyond training (*asekha*); see MN I 446,29–447,6, II 29,2–12, etc. On *nāga*, see **I, n. 84**.

104 *Vidhāsu na vikampati*. Spk: This refers to the three modes of conceit (superior, equal, inferior).

105 Spk elaborates point-by-point on the comparison between the lion's emerging from his lair and roaring, and the Buddha's arising in the world and teaching the Dhamma. The lion's sounding his roar is like the Buddha's "setting in motion" the Wheel of the Dhamma in the Deer Park, and the terror of the smaller animals like the "arising of the terror of knowledge" (*ñāṇasantāsassa uppatti*) in the long-lived deities when they hear the Buddha expound the Four Noble Truths.

106 Also at **12:21**, etc.; see **II, n. 58**. Spk refers to **22:56** for an explanation of the origin and passing away of the five aggregates.

107 Spk: "For the most part" (*yebhuyyena*) is said to make an exception of those devas who are noble disciples. For no fear at all arises in the arahants, though they experience "urgency of knowledge" (*ñāṇasaṃvega*) because they have attained what should be attained through careful striving by one stirred by a sense of urgency. The other devas, as they attend to impermanence, experience both fear as mental fright (*cittutrāsabhaya*) and, at the time of strong insight, the fear of knowledge (*ñāṇabhaya*: probably the advanced stage of insight called *bhayat' upaṭṭhānañāṇa*, "knowledge of appearance as fearful"; see **n. 79**). *Included within identity* (*sakkāyapariyāpannā*): included in the five aggregates. Thus, when the Buddha teaches them the Dhamma stamped with the three characteristics, exposing the faults in the round of existence, the fear of knowledge enters them.

108 Spk says that this does not refer to recollection by direct knowledge (i.e., by retrocognition of the past) but to the recollection of one's past abodes by way of insight. Spk seems to understand the purport of the Buddha's statement to be that they *deliberately* recollect the past in terms of the aggregates. I take the point differently, i.e., that

though these ascetics imagine they are recalling the past experience of a permanent self, they are only recollecting past configurations of the five aggregates. This interpretation seems to be confirmed by the next paragraph, which reduces first-person memories (*evaṃrūpo ahosiṃ*) to experiences framed solely in terms of the aggregates (*rūpaṃ yeva*). It can also draw support from the parallel paragraph opening **22:47**. Spk entitles this passage "the emptiness section" (*suññatāpabba*). A parallel commentary on the passage, slightly more elaborate, is at Vibh-a 3–6.

109 Spk: Even though emptiness has been discussed, the discussion is not yet definitive because the characteristic of emptiness (*suññatālakkhaṇa*) has not been discussed. The present passage is introduced to show the characteristic of emptiness. Spk-pṭ: Since form, etc., are neither a self nor the belongings of a self, but are insubstantial and ownerless, they are empty of that (self). Their nature is emptiness, their characteristic is "being deformed," etc.

110 *Ruppatī ti kho bhikkhave tasmā rūpan ti vuccati.* I have tried, though clumsily, to capture the subtle word play of the Pāli, which capitalizes on the apparent correspondence between the verb *ruppati* and the noun *rūpa*. Etymologically, the two are not related. *Ruppati* is a passive verb from the root *rup* (= Skt *lup*), "to break, injure, spoil." MW lists *rupyate* (s.v. *rup*), "to suffer violent or racking pain." See too PED, s.v. *ruppati*. Spk glosses: *Ruppatī ti kuppati ghaṭṭīyati pīḷiyati, bhijjatī ti attho; "It is deformed*: it is disturbed, stricken, oppressed, meaning 'it is broken.'"

At KS 2:73, n. 1, Woodward has misunderstood the point of the commentary. It is not the case that Buddhaghosa misconstrues "these various contacts not as referring to this life, but as 'informing' creatures in other spheres." Rather, he merely cites the cold hells, hot hells, etc., as the realms where the different types of "deformation" are most evident (*pākaṭa*). Spk adds that being "deformed" is the specific characteristic (*paccattalakkhaṇa*) of form, which distinguishes it from feeling and the other aggregates; but the general characteristics (*sāmaññalakkhaṇa*) are what they have in common, namely, impermanence, suffering, and nonself.

111 Spk: It is feeling itself that feels, not another—a being or a person.

112 *Saṅkhataṃ abhisaṅkharontī ti bhikkhave tasmā saṅkhārā ti vuccanti.* Unfortunately English is a poor medium for capturing the interconnections of this sentence in the Pāli, with the object (*saṅkhataṃ*), the verb (*abhisaṅkharonti*), and the subject (*saṅkhārā*) all derived from the same stem. See my discussion of *saṅkhārā* in the General Introduction, pp. 44–47. To replicate the Pāli we might have rendered it, "They construct the constructed, therefore they are called volitional constructions," though this would bear certain connotations quite alien to the original. It is also an unfortunate coincidence that "volitional formations," my rendering for *saṅkhārā*, is related to "form," my rendering for *rūpa*. In Pāli there is no etymological tie between *rūpa* and *saṅkhārā*. To capture the several nuances of the verb *abhisaṅkharoti* we might have taken the liberty of rendering it, in this passage, by two verbs: "to generate," which conveys the idea that the volitional formations actually produce the other aggregates (see the following note); and "to form," which makes apparent the correspondence with the noun "formations."

This passage shows the active role of *cetanā*, volition, in constructing experienced reality. Not only does volition influence the objective content of the experience, but it also shapes the psychophysical organism within which it has arisen and, via its role as kamma, shapes the future configurations of the five aggregates to be produced by kamma. In this connection see **35:146**, on the six sense bases as "old kamma."

113 All three printed eds. of SN read, *rūpaṃ rūpattāya saṅkhataṃ abhisaṅkharonti*, and so for the other aggregates, except *viññāṇa*, where Ee reads, *viññāṇatthāya*; however, since Ee has no note on vv.ll., this is almost certainly an editorial inconsistency rather than a meaningful variant. Spk (Se and Ee) reads *rūpatthāya* in its lemma, implying that the termination *-atthāya* should apply to every aggregate, and apparently old Sinhalese mss of SN had this reading. Spk (Be), however, has *rūpattāya*. The explanation in Spk is equally intelligible on either reading of SN.

I follow Be here: "As one is said to cook conjee as conjee, to bake a cake as a cake, so it [Spk-pṭ: the collection of states headed by volition] constructs, builds up, amasses (*abhisaṅkharoti āyūhati sampiṇḍati*) form itself—called 'the conditioned' because it is made by a combination of conditions—so that it becomes 'conditioned form' in accordance with its nature, for its formness (*tathattāya rūpabhāvāya*); the meaning is that it produces it (*nipphādetī ti attho*). This is the sense in brief: It constructs, produces the form arising along with itself and the associated feeling, etc. Here, too, the Blessed One shows just the specific characteristic of volitional formations, whose characteristic is volition. [Spk-pṭ: This is said because volition is the chief of the states belonging to the aggregate of volitional formations.]"

114 The eight flavours are: *ambila, tittaka, kaṭuka, madhuka, khārika, akhārika, loṇaka, aloṇaka*; see too **47:8**. The explanation of *viññāṇa* here is very similar to that of *saññā*, the difference being only in the type of sense object they cognize. Spk explains that the difference in object highlights a difference in their cognitive functions: "Perception is analysed by way of the eye door because it is evident in grasping the appearance and shape of the object; consciousness is analysed by way of the tongue door because it can grasp particular distinctions in an object even when there is no appearance and shape." Spk continues with an explanation (also found at Vism 437; Ppn 14:3–5) according to which *saññā, viññāṇa,* and *paññā* are cognitive functions of increasing depth, discriminative acumen, and power of comprehension; this, however, is difficult to reconcile with the account of these factors found in the Nikāyas. Usually in the suttas *viññāṇa* is presented simply as the basic awareness of an object through one of the sense bases, i.e., as bare "consciousness of" rather than as a discriminative capacity. A parallel treatment of *viññāṇa* at MN I 292,26–29 defines it through its ability to cognize the three types of feelings (pleasant, painful, neutral); this just shifts the problem to that of distinguishing between *viññāṇa* and *vedanā*. Hamilton discusses the problem posed by these passages (*Identity and Experience*, pp. 53–55, 92–93). She offers the helpful suggestion that although *viññāṇa* is here

defined in a way that encroaches upon the domain of *saññā*, we should understand that *saññā* does the actual discrimination (of objects at all five senses) while *viññāṇa* "is the awareness by which we experience every stage of the cognitive process, including the process of discriminating" (p. 92). From the commentarial standpoint, *saññā* is discussed more fully at As 110–11 and *viññāṇa* (under the name *citta*) at As 63–64.

115 Spk: The first two sections—the emptiness section and the section on the characteristic of emptiness—have discussed the characteristic of nonself. Now he will discuss the characteristic of suffering. Therein, form does not devour one as a dog does a piece of meat, by tearing one apart, but rather in the way a soiled garment might cause discomfort, as when one says, "This shirt is devouring me." The lines following the reflection incorporate the conclusion of **22:9–11**.

116 Spk: This passage is stated to show the characteristic of impermanence, and to do so by bringing the three characteristics together.

117 I render this passage with the aid of Spk, which glosses the last two pairs of terms thus: *Visineti na ussinetī ti vikirati na sampiṇḍeti; vidhūpeti na sandhūpetī ti nibbāpeti na jālāpeti* (some texts read *viseneti, usseneti*); cp. AN II 214–16. The present passage describes the *sekha*, who is still in the process of dismantling the round.

118 Spk: This shows the arahant, who abides having dismantled the round.

119 Pādas cd should be read: *yassa te nābhijānāma, yampi nissāya jhāyati*. See AN V 324–26 and MN I 140,3–6. Spk states that at the end of this discourse five hundred bhikkhus were established in arahantship.

120 Spk: After spending the rains residence at Sāvatthī, the Buddha had set out for Kapilavatthu together with a large company of bhikkhus. When they arrived, the Sakyans came to see him, bringing many gifts for the Saṅgha. A noisy quarrel broke out among the bhikkhus over the distribution of the gifts, and it was for this reason that the Teacher dismissed them. He wanted to teach them, "It isn't for the sake of such things as robes, etc., that you have gone

forth into homelessness, but for the sake of arahantship."

121 A similar passage is at MN I 457–59, but there the Sakyans first request the Buddha to pardon the bhikkhus, followed by Brahmā Sahampati, who makes the same appeal. In the MN version the sequence of the two similes is inverted.

122 I follow Se here, which reads: *Tathārūpaṃ iddhābhisaṅkhāraṃ abhisaṅkhāsi yathā te bhikkhū ekadvīhikāya sārajjamānarūpā yena bhagavā ten' upasaṅkameyyuṃ*. Be and Ee read *yenāhaṃ* in place of *yena bhagavā*; it seems the whole phrase is missing in SS. Spk glosses: *Ekadvīhikāyā ti ek' eko c' eva dve dve ca hutvā. Sārajjamānarūpā ti ottappamānasabhāvā bhāyamānā.*

Spk: Why did the Buddha perform such a feat? From a desire for their welfare. For if they had come to him in groups they would not have shown reverence towards the Buddha nor would they have been able to receive a Dhamma teaching. But when they come timidly, ashamed, alone and in pairs, they show reverence and can receive a teaching.

123 *Abhisāpa*, glossed *akkosa* by Spk, which explains: "For when people get angry they abuse their antagonist by saying, 'You should put on a monk's robe, get yourself a begging bowl, and roam about seeking alms!'" *Kapāla*, rendered here "begging bowl," is not the usual word for a monk's almsbowl (= *patta*), but refers to the kind of bowl used by non-Buddhist ascetics (sometimes made from a skull); the use of the word seems pejorative. This paragraph and the next are also at It 89–90. Some of the terms describing the deviant monk just below are commented on in **I, n. 176**.

124 Spk says this passage is introduced to show that this person has become like a brand from a funeral pyre because of his evil thoughts. The "signless concentration" (*animitta-samādhi*) is insight concentration (*vipassanā-samādhi*), called "signless" because it removes the signs of permanence, etc. For more on the signless concentration, see **IV, nn. 280, 312, 368**.

125 Spk: The view of existence (*bhavadiṭṭhi*) is eternalism (*sassatadiṭṭhi*); the view of extermination (*vibhavadiṭṭhi*) is annihilationism (*ucchedadiṭṭhi*). This passage is introduced to show that the signless concentration removes not only the three wrong thoughts but also eternalism and annihilationism.

126 Here the Buddha connects clinging, which arises on the basis of the mere five aggregates mistakenly held to as a self, with the last portion of the formula on dependent origination, thus showing present clinging to be the sustaining cause for the continuation of the round of existence. For a parallel, see MN I 511,30–512,2.

127 Spk: At the end of the discourse five hundred bhikkhus attained arahantship together with the analytical knowledges (*paṭisambhidā*).

128 Spk assigns this sutta to the time of the famous quarrel at Kosambī. After he had failed in three attempts to reconcile the factious parties, the Buddha decided to set out alone. For a full account, see Vin I 337–57 and Ñāṇamoli, *Life of the Buddha*, pp. 109–19.

129 Spk: The residents of Pārileyyaka built a leaf hall for the Blessed One in a protected grove near their town. An auspicious (*bhadda*) sal tree grew there. While living in dependence on the town, the Blessed One dwelt at the foot of the tree near the leaf hut in the grove. Spk relates here the story of the bull elephant who came to wait upon the Buddha; see Ud 41–42 and Vin I 352–53.

130 Spk: These were not the factious bhikkhus, but five hundred other monks who had come from various quarters after the rains.

131 See **22:55** and **n. 78** above. Spk explains this as referring to "the fruit of arahantship immediately following the path" (*maggānantaraṃ arahattaphalaṃ*). However, as in the commentarial system the fruit inevitably occurs in immediate succession to the path, I think the monk is really asking how to attain arahantship swiftly and directly, without being detained at any lower stage of awakening.

132 *Vicayaso*. Spk glosses with *vicayena* and explains: "Having delimited with knowledge that is capable of discriminating the real nature of the various phenomena." What follows are the thirty-seven aids to enlightenment (*bodhipakkhiyā dhammā*); see pp. 1485–87.

133 Spk glosses "that regarding" (*sā sasamanupassanā*) as a "view-formation" (*diṭṭhi-saṅkhāra*). I understand *saṅkhāra* here as meaning what is conditioned rather than the active power of generation, i.e., as the *saṅkhata-saṅkhāra* of the commentaries

rather than as *abhisaṅkharaṇa-saṅkhāra*, the act of volitional formation. The point, it seems, is that by calling the act of regarding a "formation," the Buddha underlines its conditioned origination. This in turn highlights its impermanence, recognition of which knocks away the adherence to the very notion "I am," thus culminating in arahantship. On "ignorance-contact" (*avijjāsamphassa*), see **n. 63**.

134 This view, which posits the identity of the self and the world (*so attā so loko*), seems to be derived from the Upaniṣads. Strangely, Spk passes over this view in silence, and Ps (commenting on MN I 135,37) offers only an unilluminating word gloss. For a discussion, see Wijesekera, "An Aspect of Upaniṣadic Ātman and Buddhist 'Anattā,'" *Buddhist and Vedic Studies*, pp. 261–63.

135 Here I read with Se and Ee: *no c' assaṃ no ca me siyā, na bhavissāmi na me bhavissati*. Be reads the third negated verb as *nābhavissaṃ*. Spk: "If I were not, neither would there be my belongings; if I will not be in the future, neither will there be my belongings." For a fuller discussion, see **n. 75**.

136 Spk: Even though doubt (*vicikicchā*) does not exist in the cittas associated with craving, the doubt-formation arises from it because craving has not been abandoned. For doubt arises in one who has not abandoned craving.

137 Spk: In this sutta, in twenty-three cases, insight culminating in arahantship has been explained.

138 This entire sutta is at MN No. 109.

139 *Ime ... pañcupādānakkhandhā chandamūlakā*. Spk: *Taṇhā-chandamūlakā*. On how the five aggregates originate from craving, see **22:5** and **n. 30**.

140 This exchange is also at MN I 299,33–300,3; see too **22:121** below.

Spk: "Clinging is neither the same as the five aggregates subject to clinging" because the aggregates are not reducible simply to desire and lust; "nor is the clinging something apart from the five aggregates subject to clinging" because there is no clinging apart from the aggregates either as conascent factors or as object. For when a citta associated with craving occurs, the form produced by that citta belongs to the form aggregate, and the remaining mental states except craving belong to the other four aggregates: thus there is no clinging apart from the aggregates as conascent factors. (Craving is excepted because craving is what clings to the aggregates, and a mental factor cannot cling to itself.) Then, too, there is no clinging apart from the aggregates as object, because when clinging arises it takes as object one of the aggregates such as form.

141 *Rūpakkhandhassa paññāpanāya.* This might have been rendered "for the *description* of the form aggregate." *Paññāpana* is literally "making known," and something is "made known" either by becoming manifest or by being described.

142 I prefer the reading of the parallel at MN III 19,12–13, *anattakatāni kammāni kam attānaṃ phusissanti.* In the SN text, Be and Se read *katham attānaṃ,* and Ee *katam attānaṃ,* which perhaps should be amended to *kam attānaṃ.* Spk is silent, but MA explains that this monk had slipped into an eternalist view.

143 *Paṭipucchā-vinītā kho me tumhe bhikkhave tatra tatra tesu tesu dhammesu.* The readings in Ee and MN (Ee) should be amended accordingly. Neither MA nor Spk offers any explanation, but it is clear enough that the "training through interrogation" is the catechistic method to be applied in the following paragraph.

144 MN No. 109 concludes by stating that while this discourse was being spoken the minds of sixty bhikkhus were liberated from the taints. Spk states that at the conclusion of each sutta in this vagga five hundred bhikkhus attained arahantship! The verse that follows is in Be and Ee, but not in Se or MN. Pāda c should be read with Be: *sakkāyena duve vuttā.*

145 Puṇṇa Mantāniputta was declared by the Buddha the foremost among the bhikkhus who were speakers on the Dhamma (AN I 23,26). See **14:15**.

146 *Upādāya* has a double meaning that is difficult to capture in translation. As absolutive of *upādiyati* it means "having clung to," but it also has an idiomatic sense, "derived from, dependent on," as in the expression *catunnañ ca mahābhūtānaṃ upādāya rūpaṃ,* "the form derived from the four great elements." I have translated it here "by clinging to," on the supposition that the literal meaning is primary, but the

gloss of Spk emphasizes the idiomatic sense: *Upādāyā ti āgamma ārabbha sandhāya paṭicca*; "*upādāya*: contingent on, referring to, on the basis of, in dependence on." The mirror simile can support either meaning, and both are probably intended: The youth looks at his or her image with concern for his or her personal appearance ("with clinging"), and the image becomes manifest in dependence on the mirror. Similarly, a person conceives "I am" *by clinging to* the five aggregates, and it is *in dependence on* the five aggregates, i.e., with the aggregates as objective referents, that the notion "I am" arises. See **22:151**, which again plays upon this dual meaning of *upādāya*.

147 *Dhammo me abhisameto*. Spk: He penetrated the Four Noble Truths with wisdom and became a stream-enterer. On *abhisamaya*, see **II, n. 13**.

148 See **21:9**.

149 This passage occurs elsewhere, e.g., in SN at **47:9** (V 153,11–12) and **47:13** (V 162,15–16). Spk does not explain the etymology of *madhurakajāto* but paraphrases, "It has become unwieldy, as if heavy." *Madhuraka* means "sweet, pleasant, charming," but I follow PED's explanation, "full of sweet drink, intoxicated." See *madhupītā* in **I, v. 842** and **I, n. 590**. In explaining *dhammā pi maṃ na paṭibhanti*, Spk takes *dhammā* as "the teachings": "Even the doctrinal teachings are not clear to me; what I learned and studied does not appear." Possibly *dhammā* here bears the more general sense of "things."

150 Spk: He not only delighted in it, but having gained this consolation from the Teacher, struggling and striving, after some time he was established in arahantship.

151 His position is not quite the same as that of the common annihilationist, since he does not hold that all beings are annihilated at death. He seems to hold an eternalist view in regard to unenlightened beings (since they have a lasting self which transmigrates) and annihilationism in regard to the arahant (since he utterly perishes at death).

Spk: If he had thought, "Formations arise and cease; a simple process of formations reaches nonoccurrence," this would not be a view (*diṭṭhigata*) but knowledge in accordance with the Teaching. But since he thought, "A being is annihilated and destroyed," this becomes a view. What follows is paralleled by MN I 130–31 and I 256–57.

152 Spk: At the end of this teaching on the three characteristics Yamaka became a stream-enterer. Sāriputta asks the following questions to examine him and to get him to show that he has given up his wrong view.

Spk glosses *tathāgata* here as "a being" (*satta*), which I think does not quite hit the mark. I take the subject of the discussion to be, not a being in general, but the arahant *conceived as a being*, as a substantial self. Thus the catechism will show that Yamaka has abandoned his identity view (*sakkāyadiṭṭhi*) regarding the arahant, and therewith his view of the arahant as a self that undergoes annihilation. We find a similar transition from the arahant (*vimuttacitta bhikkhu*) to the Tathāgata at MN I 140,3–7 and I 486–88.

153 The first three alternatives—conceiving the aggregates individually as the Tathāgata, the Tathāgata as within the aggregates, and the Tathāgata as apart from the aggregates—correspond to the first three modes of conceiving in the Mūlapariyāya Sutta (MN I 1), which are set in relation to the sense bases at **35:30, 31**. The fourth position conceives the aggregates collectively as the Tathāgata (perhaps a view of supervenience); the fifth conceives the Tathāgata as entirely transcendent, without any essential relation to the aggregates. These modes of conceiving can also be correlated with the twenty types of identity view.

154 *Diṭṭh' eva dhamme saccato thetato tathāgato anupalabbhiyamāno.* Cp. MN I 138,5–6: *Attani ca bhikkhave attaniye ca saccato thetato anupalabbhamāne.* MN I 140,6–7: *Diṭṭh' evāhaṃ bhikkhave dhamme tathāgataṃ ananuvejjo ti vadāmi.*

155 See **n. 147**.

156 This passage can be read as a gloss on the Buddha's famous dictum, "I make known just suffering and the cessation of suffering" (see end of **22:86**).

157 Ee *daheyya* may be better than *saddaheyya*, in Be and Se.

158 Spk: The uninstructed worldling attached to the round is like the gullible householder, the five fragile aggregates like the murderous enemy. When the enemy comes up to the householder and offers to serve him, that is like the time the aggregates are acquired at the moment of rebirth.

When the householder takes the enemy to be his friend, that is like the time the worldling grasps the aggregates, thinking, "They are mine." The honour the householder bestows on the enemy, thinking, "He is my friend," is like the honour the worldling bestows on the aggregates by bathing them, feeding them, etc. The murder of the householder by the enemy is like the destruction of the worldling's life when the aggregates break up.

159 The next four paragraphs are also at **22:55**.

160 As in **12:15**; see **II, n. 31**, **n. 32**.

161 This last sentence is not in Be.

162 This sutta also occurs at **44:2**, with the questionnaire given in full (though abridged in this translation).

163 *Tathāgato uttamapuriso paramapuriso paramapattipatto.* This should establish that "the Tathāgata" here is not just "a being," but a Buddha or an arahant; the expression recurs at **44:9**. The four theses are all rooted in a conception of the Tathāgata as a self. The commentaries explain the first as eternalism, the second as annihilationism, the third as a syncretic view (partial-eternalism), the fourth as evasive scepticism. Two whole chapters in SN deal with these issues, the Vacchagottasaṃyutta (SN 33) and the Abyākatasaṃyutta (SN 44). See too **16:12**.

164 Spk: It is said that he thought, "These are hostile enemies of the Teaching. The Teacher would not describe (the Tathāgata) as they say. He must have described him in some other way."

165 This oft-quoted dictum can be interpreted at two levels. At the more superficial level the Buddha can be read as saying that he does not make any declaration about such metaphysical questions as an afterlife but teaches only a practical path for reaching the end of suffering here and now. This interpretation, however, does not connect the dictum with the Buddha's previous statement that the Tathāgata is not apprehended in this very life. To make this connection we have to bring in the second interpretation, according to which the "Tathāgata" is a mere term of conventional usage referring to a compound of impermanent formations, which are "suffering" because they contain no permanent essence. It is just these that stand while

the Tathāgata lives, and just these that cease with his passing away. The context in which the dictum occurs at MN I 140,14–15 also supports this interpretation.

166 Vakkali was declared by the Buddha the foremost bhikkhu of those resolved through faith (*etadaggaṃ saddhādhimuttānaṃ*; AN I 24,15).

Spk: After completing the rains residence, the elder was on his way to see the Blessed One when he fell ill in the middle of the city. He could not walk, so they put him on a stretcher and carried him to a potter's shed.

167 *Samadhosi*. Spk: He showed his respect by making a movement; for, it is said, even a patient is obliged to show respect to a superior by making a gesture of rising.

168 *Yo kho Vakkali dhammaṃ passati, so maṃ passati. Yo maṃ passati, so dhammaṃ passati*. Spk: Here the Blessed One shows (himself as) the Dhamma-body, as stated in the passage, "The Tathāgata, great king, is the Dhamma-body." For the ninefold supramundane Dhamma is called the Tathāgata's body.

I cannot trace a statement that corresponds exactly to the one cited by Spk. Spk may be misquoting DN III 84,23–24, which actually reads: "For this, Vāseṭṭha, is a designation of the Tathāgata, that is, the Dhamma-body ..." (*tathāgatassa h' etaṃ Vāseṭṭha adhivacanaṃ dhammakāyo iti pi* ...). On the ninefold supramundane Dhamma, see **n. 51**. Though the second clause seems to be saying that simply by seeing the Buddha's body one sees the Dhamma, the meaning is surely that in order to *really* see the Buddha one should see the Dhamma, the truth to which he awakened. Hence the following catechism, intended to guide Vakkali towards that realization.

169 It was here too that the Venerable Godhika expired by his own hand; see **4:23**.

170 *Vimokkhāya ceteti*. Spk: For the sake of the deliverance of the path (*magga-vimokkhatthāya*). Although *vimokkha* and *vimutti* are derived from the same prefixed root (*vi* + *muc*), they usually appear in different contexts. To avoid confusion I have rendered the former as "deliverance," the latter as "liberation." Here they are synonymous.

171 *Suvimutto vimuccissati*. Spk: He will be liberated as one liberated by the liberation of the fruit of arahantship. Those

devas spoke thus because they knew, "By whatever method he arouses insight, he will attain arahantship immediately."

172 Vakkali's message to the Buddha implies that he already considered himself an arahant. Spk, however, explains: "The elder, it is said, overestimated himself. As he had suppressed the defilements by concentration and insight, he did not see himself assailed by them and thus thought he was an arahant. Disgusted with his miserable life, he cut his jugular vein with a sharp knife. Just then, painful feelings arose in him. Realizing he was still a worldling, he took up his main meditation subject, explored it with knowledge, and attained arahantship just as he died." On the basis of the sutta alone it is impossible to tell whether the commentary is right. For another account of a monk who took his life while thinking he was an arahant, see **35:87**. Godhika (in **4:23**) did not have this conviction, but took his life from despair due to his illness. He too, however, attained arahantship at the time of death. The sequel is as at **4:23**; see **I, nn. 313, 314**.

173 I read with Be: *gelaññe passambhetvā passambhetvā kāysaṅkhāre viharāmi, so 'haṃ samādhiṃ nappaṭilabhāmi*. The "bodily formations" are in-breathing and out-breathing (*assāsa-passāsa*); see MN I 56,20–22 and MN I 301,20–21 (= **41:6**; IV 293,16).

Spk: He kept tranquillizing in-and-out breathing when he dwelt in the fourth jhāna, where breathing ceases (**36:11**; IV 217,8–9). Because he had fallen away from all the meditative absorptions that he had previously attained, he thought, "Let me not fall away from the Teaching."

174 Spk: *Samādhisārakā samādhisāmaññā ti samādhiṃ yeva sārañ ca sāmaññañ ca maññanti*. "In my Teaching that is not the essence; the essence is insight, path, and fruit."

175 Spk says that at the end of the Buddha's exposition of the three characteristics, Assaji attained arahantship. Spk explains that the Buddha introduces the following passage to show the arahant's constant abiding. See too **12:51**, where the same text is coupled with a different simile. The present version is also at **36:7**, **36:8**, and **54:8**.

176 Although all three eds. of SN and both eds. of Spk read

asmī ti adhigataṃ, this is probably an old corruption. I propose reading *asmī ti avigataṃ*; see my argument in support of this amendation at **n. 61**. Spk: Craving and conceit are found occurring in the mode "I am."

This passage clarifies the essential difference between the *sekha* and the arahant. While the *sekha* has eliminated identity view and thus no longer identifies any of the five aggregates as a self, he has not yet eradicated ignorance, which sustains a residual conceit and desire "I am" (*anusahagato asmī ti māno asmī ti chando*) in relation to the five aggregates. The arahant, in contrast, has eradicated ignorance, the root of all misconceptions, and thus no longer entertains any ideas of "I" and "mine." The other elders apparently had not yet attained any stage of awakening and thus did not understand this difference, but the Venerable Khemaka must have been at least a stream-enterer [Spk-pṭ: some hold he was a nonreturner, others a once-returner] and thus knew that the elimination of identity view does not completely remove the sense of personal identity. Even for the nonreturner, an "odour of subjectivity" based on the five aggregates still lingers over his experience.

177 I prefer *vaṇṭassa*, found in SS, over *vaṇṇassa* in all three printed eds.

178 Spk: The worldling's mental process is like the soiled cloth. The three contemplations (of impermanence, suffering, and nonself) are like the three cleansers. The mental process of the nonreturner is like the cloth that has been washed with the three cleansers. The defilements to be eradicated by the path of arahantship are like the residual smell of the cleansers. The knowledge of the path of arahantship is like the sweetly scented casket, and the destruction of all defilements by that path is like the vanishing of the residual smell of the cleansers from the cloth after it has been placed in the casket.

179 Spk identifies this Channa with the Bodhisatta's charioteer who led him out of the palace on the night of his great renunciation. He had received ordination as a monk but, because of his former close relationship with the Buddha, he became proud and domineering and spoke harshly to the other bhikkhus. Shortly before his parinibbāna the

Buddha had instructed the Saṅgha to impose on him the *brahmadaṇḍa*, "the silence treatment" (DN II 154,18–23). When Channa realized he was being treated as a pariah by the Saṅgha, he was shaken by a sense of urgency (*saṃvega*). It is at this point that the sutta opens.

180 Spk: All formations of the three planes (*sabbe tebhūmakā saṅkhārā*) are impermanent; all phenomena of the four planes (*sabbe catubhūmakā dhammā*) are nonself. Why didn't those bhikkhus mention the characteristic of suffering? Because they thought, "This bhikkhu is argumentative. If we mention suffering he will quarrel with us, saying, 'If form, etc., are suffering, the path and fruit too are suffering, so you monks have attained nothing but suffering.'" Thus they answered in a way that could not be faulted.

See too MN I 228,10–14, 230,5–8, where only impermanence and nonself are mentioned in the explicit context of debate. The commentary to this passage gives a similar explanation of the omission of suffering.

181 *Atha ko carahi me attā*. Spk: It is said that this elder had started to practise insight meditation without having done discernment of conditions. His weak insight could not eliminate the grip of self (*attagāha*), and thus when formations appeared to him as empty, agitation arose in him along with the annihilationist view, "I will be annihilated, I will be destroyed." He saw himself falling into an abyss. [Spk-pṭ: Agitation through fear (*bhayaparitassanā*) and clinging to views (*diṭṭh' upādāna*) arose in him over the thought, "If phenomena are nonself, then what self can deeds done by what is nonself affect?" (see **22:82** (III 104,1) and **n. 142**)].

Discernment of conditions (*paccayapariggaha*) is a stage in the development of insight in which the meditator explores the conditions for the five aggregates (see Vism, chap. 19). In the proper sequence of development this stage should *precede* investigation of the aggregates as impermanent, suffering, and nonself.

182 *Khilaṃ pabhindi*. MN I 101,9–27 mentions five types of mental barrenness (*cetokhila*). Channa's problem seems to have been the fifth, anger and contemptuousness towards his fellow monks.

183 Ānanda's choice of the Kaccānagotta Sutta is especially

apt, as this sutta teaches how dependent origination counters the two extreme views of eternalism and annihilationism and replaces the view of self with the realization that it is only *dukkha* that arises and ceases.

184 This sutta and the next are identical with **18:21–22** and **22:71–72**.

185 This portion of the sutta offers an important counterpoint to the message of the Kaccānagotta Sutta (**12:15**). Here the Buddha emphasizes that he does not reject all ontological propositions, but only those that transcend the bounds of possible experience. While the Kaccānagotta Sutta shows that the "middle teaching" excludes static, substantialist conceptions of existence and nonexistence, the present text shows that the same "middle teaching" can accommodate definite pronouncements about these ontological issues. The affirmation of the existence of the five aggregates, as impermanent processes, serves as a rejoinder to illusionist theories, which hold that the world lacks real being.

186 *Lokadhamma*. Spk: The five aggregates are called thus because it is their nature to disintegrate (*lujjanasabhāvattā*). *Loka* is derived from *lujjati* at **35:82**. The etymology cannot be accepted literally but serves a pedagogic purpose.

187 Spk: In this sutta three types of world are spoken of. When it is said, "I do not dispute with the world," it is the world of beings (*sattaloka*). "A world-phenomenon in the world": here, the world of formations (*saṅkhāraloka*). "The Tathāgata was born in the world": here, the geographic world (*okāsaloka*). Ee has omitted *loke jāto*, no doubt by oversight. The simile is also at AN II 38,30–39,3; see too AN V 152,12–16.

188 Spk: One evening, while dwelling in that abode, the Blessed One came out from his fragrant cottage and sat down by the bank of the Ganges. He saw a great lump of foam coming downstream and thought, "I will give a Dhamma talk relating to the five aggregates." Then he addressed the bhikkhus sitting around him.

The sutta is one of the most radical discourses on the empty nature of conditioned phenomena; its imagery (especially the similes of the mirage and the magical illusion) has been taken up by later Buddhist thinkers, most persistently by the Mādhyamikas. Some of the images are found elsewhere in the Pāli Canon, e.g., at Dhp 46, 170. In the context of early Buddhist thought these similes have to be handled with care. They are not intended to suggest an illusionist view of the world but to show that our conceptions of the world, and of our own existence, are largely distorted by the process of cognition. Just as the mirage and magical illusion are based on real existents—the sand of the desert, the magician's appurtenances—so these false conceptions arise from a base that objectively exists, namely, the five aggregates; but when seen through a mind subject to conceptual distortion, the aggregates appear in a way that deviates from their actual nature. Instead of being seen as transient and selfless, they appear as substantial and as a self.

189 Spk explains at length how form (i.e., the body) is like a lump of foam (*pheṇapiṇḍa*). I give merely the highlights: as a lump of foam lacks any substance (*sāra*), so form lacks any substance that is permanent, stable, a self; as the lump of foam is full of holes and fissures and the abode of many creatures, so too form; as the lump of foam, after expanding, breaks up, so does form, which is pulverized in the mouth of death. Spk's commentary is also at Vibh-a 32–35.

190 Spk: A bubble (*bubbuḷa*) is feeble and cannot be grasped, for it breaks up as soon as it is seized; so too feeling is feeble and cannot be grasped as permanent and stable. As a bubble arises and ceases in a drop of water and does not last long, so too with feeling: 100,000 *koṭis* of feelings arise and cease in the time of a fingersnap (one *koṭi* = 10 million). As a bubble arises in dependence on conditions, so feeling arises in dependence on a sense base, an object, the defilements, and contact.

191 Spk: Perception is like a mirage (*marīcikā*) in the sense that it is insubstantial, for one cannot grasp a mirage to drink or bathe or fill a pitcher. As a mirage deceives the multitude, so does perception, which entices people with the idea that the colourful object is beautiful, pleasurable, and permanent.

192 *Akukkukajātaṃ*. Spk: There is no pith growing inside (*anto asañjātaghanadaṇḍakaṃ*).

193 The simile is used for a different purpose at MN I 233,15–23.

Spk: As a plantain trunk (*kadalikkhandha*) is an assemblage of many sheaths, each with its own characteristic, so the aggregate of volitional formations is an assemblage of many phenomena, each with its own characteristic.

194 Spk: Consciousness is like a magical illusion (*māyā*) in the sense that it is insubstantial and cannot be grasped. Consciousness is even more transient and fleeting than a magical illusion. For it gives the impression that a person comes and goes, stands and sits, with the same mind, but the mind is different in each of these activities. Consciousness deceives the multitude like a magical illusion.

For a modern parable illustrating the deceptive nature of consciousness, based on this simile, see Ñāṇananda, *The Magic of the Mind*, pp. 5–7.

195 See MN I 296,9–11, spoken by Sāriputta. I cannot trace a parallel spoken by the Buddha himself, but see Dhp 41.

196 Spk explains that *māyāyaṃ bālalāpinī*, in pāda b, refers specifically to the aggregate of consciousness. The aggregate-mass is a murderer in two ways: (i) because the aggregates slay each other; and (ii) because murder appears in dependence on the aggregates. As to (i), when the earth element breaks up it takes along the other elements, and when the form aggregate breaks up it takes along the mental aggregates. As to (ii), when the aggregates exist such things as murder, bondage, injury, etc., come into being. On the comparison of the aggregates to murderers, see too **22:85** (III 114,20–24).

197 Read: *divā vā yadi vā rattiṃ.*

198 Spk: The holy life of the path arises stilling the formations of the three planes. If even this much individual existence were permanent, though the path might arise it would not be able to still the round of formations. Thus the holy life would not be discerned.

199 Spk: This is said to show: "If any formations were permanent, then the success I enjoyed as King Mahāsudassana would have been permanent." On King Mahāsudassana, a past incarnation of the Buddha, see the eponymic sutta, DN No. 17.

200 The elephant, the steed, the jewel-gem, the beautiful queen, and the commander-gem are five of the seven gems

of the wheel-turning monarch (*rājā cakkavatti*). The other two, which Mahāsudassana also possessed, are the wheel-gem and the steward-gem; for details, see DN II 172–77. The seven gems are mentioned at **46:42**.

201 The passage beginning "Of those 84,000 cities" to the end is also at DN II 197–98, but the latter includes an additional closing paragraph. The homily on impermanence is at **15:20** (II 193,3–6).

Spk: Having shown his success at the time when he was King Mahāsudassana, he now shows its impermanence. Just as a man might place a ladder against a *campaka* tree, climb up, take a *campaka* flower, and then descend, so the Blessed One has climbed up the story of King Mahāsudassana's success, taken the characteristic of impermanence at the top, and descended.

202 I read with Se, *khattiyā vā velāmikā vā*. Spk explains a *velāmika* as one born from a khattiya father and a brahmin mother, or a brahmin father and a khattiya mother.

203 As at **15:1**, etc. See **II, n. 254**.

204 On the destruction of the world by fire, see Vism 414–17 (Ppn 13:32–41).

205 The simile of the dog is also at MN II 232,24–233,4. Spk: The foolish worldling is like the dog, his view is like the leash, his personal identity (*sakkāya*) is like the post. Like the dog's running around the post is the worldling's running around his personal identity bound to it by craving and views.

206 *Caraṇaṃ nāma cittaṃ. Citta* here is the equivalent of Skt *citra*, picture. The exact meaning of the picture's title is obscure. Spk glosses *vicaraṇacitta*, "the wandering picture" [Spk-pṭ: because they take it and wander about with it], but *caraṇa* here possibly means conduct, as in other contexts.

Spk: The Saṅkha were a sect of heretical brahmins. Having taken a canvas, they had various pictures painted on it of the good and bad destinations to illustrate success and failure, and then they took it around on their wanderings. They would show it to the people, explaining, "If one does this deed, one gets this result; if one does that, one gets that."

207 *Tam pi … caraṇaṃ nāma cittaṃ citten' eva cittitaṃ, tena pi …*

caraṇena cittena cittaññeva cittataraṃ. There are several puns here that cannot be successfully conveyed in translation (nor even in Skt for that matter). *Citta* is both mind (as in Skt) and picture (= Skt *citra*). *Cittita* (Ee: *cintita*) is "thought out" (related to *citta*, mind) and "diversified" (related to *citra*, picture). I have used "designed in its diversity" to capture both nuances. As 64–65 quotes this passage in its discussion of how mind designs the world.

208 *Te pi ... tiracchānagatā pāṇā citten' eva cittitā, tehi pi ... tiracchānagatehi pāṇehi cittaññeva cittataraṃ*. Another series of puns. The point is that the diversity of the creatures in the animal realm reflects the diversity of the past kamma that causes rebirth as an animal, and this diversity of kamma in turn stems from the diversity of volition (*cetanā*), a mental factor. As 64–65 discusses this passage at length.

Spk: Quails and partridges, etc., do not accumulate diverse kamma, thinking, "We will become diversified in such and such a way," but the kamma arrives at the appropriate species (*yoni*), and the diversity is rooted in the species. For beings that arise in a particular species become diversified in the way appropriate to that species. Thus the diversity is achieved through the species, and the species reflect kamma.

209 The simile is also at **12:64**. See **II, n. 173**.

210 Also at **12:23**. The following, through to the end, is also at AN IV 125–27.

211 Again, these are the thirty-seven aids to enlightenment. The theme of this sutta might be compared with MN No. 126, which deals with the question whether, in living the holy life, it is necessary to make a wish (*āsañ ce pi karitvā*) in order to achieve the fruit (*phalassa adhigamāya*). Here the word rendered "wish" is *icchā*.

212 The simile of the chicks is applied differently at MN I 104,3–13 and MN I 357,6–358,2. See too Vin III 3–5. Spk elaborates on the comparison of the bhikkhu's enlightenment to the hatching of chicks: The hen's preparatory work is like the bhikkhu's devotion to development. The nonrotting of the eggs is like the bhikkhu's not falling away from insight knowledge; the drying up of the moisture in the eggs is like the drying up of attachment to the three realms of

existence; the thinning of the egg shells is like the thinning of ignorance; the maturation of the chicks is like the maturation of insight knowledge. The time when the chicks break the shells and emerge safely is like the time when the bhikkhu breaks the shell of ignorance and attains arahantship. And as the chicks go about adorning the village field, so the great arahant enters into fruition attainment which takes Nibbāna as its object, and thus adorns his monastery.

213 Reading *palagaṇḍassa* with Be and Se. Spk glosses *vaḍḍhakissa*.

214 The simile is also at **45:158**. I read it as in Se and Ee. Spk develops this simile even more minutely than the simile of the chicks. In brief: Like the wearing away of the rigging by the ocean water is the wearing away of the bhikkhu's fetters by his going forth (into homelessness), study, and questioning. Like the time the ship is hauled onto dry land is the time the bhikkhu takes up a meditation subject and dwells in the forest. Like the drying up of the rigging by wind and sun during the day is the drying up of craving by insight knowledge. Like the wetting by snow at night is the wetting of the mind by gladness and joy arisen from meditation. Like the rain cloud pouring down is the knowledge of the path of arahantship. Like the decay of the rigging is the attainment of the fruit of arahantship. Like the persistence of the rigging in a decrepit state is the persistence of the arahant as he lives on benefitting the multitude. Like the collapse of the decrepit rigging is the arahant's attainment of the Nibbāna element without residue.

215 Sensual lust is eliminated by the path of nonreturning; lust for existence, ignorance, and the conceit "I am" by the path of arahantship.

216 This simile, and the six to follow, are applied differently at **45:141–47**. The simile of the ascending sun is also at **2:29**.

217 Spk glosses *antā*, lit. "ends," with *koṭṭhāsā*, and explains that this sutta interprets the five aggregates by way of the Four Noble Truths.

218 Spk glosses *pariññeyya* with *samatikkamitabba* and *pariññā*

with *samatikkama;* see **n. 41**. The "person who has fully understood" (*pariññātāvī*) is a conventional expression; see **n. 37**.

219 Spk: By this, Nibbāna is shown.

220 Woodward, at KS 3:136, says that this sutta is the same as the preceding one, but that is not the case; this one adds *samudayañ ca atthaṅgamañ ca.*

221 The stream-enterer (in the preceding sutta) and the arahant share the same understanding of the five aggregates. They differ in that the arahant has used this understanding to extricate all defilements, while the stream-enterer (and higher trainees) have yet to complete this task. Note too that whereas the stream-enterer is explained in terms of a noble disciple, the arahant is always defined as a bhikkhu.

222 As at **12:16**. See **II, nn. 34**, **35**.

223 I follow Be, which reads *baddho jīyati,* as against Se and Ee, which have *baddho jāyati,* "who is born in bondage."

224 The Ee title, *Parimucchita,* should be amended to *Paripucchita.*

225 This list is found elsewhere in the Nikāyas (e.g., at MN I 435,33–35, MN I 500,3–5, AN II 128,16–18, AN IV 422,25–423,1). The eleven terms are expanded to forty at Paṭis II 238, and commented on at Vism 611–13 (Ppn 20:19–20). Spk reduces them to the three contemplations: "impermanence" and "disintegration" represent contemplation of impermanence; "empty" and "nonself," contemplation of nonself; and the others, contemplation of suffering. Vism 613 and Ps III 146,13, however, assign "as alien" (*parato*) to the contemplation of nonself, which seems more plausible.

226 *Natthi ... arahato uttarikaraṇīyaṃ katassa vā paṭicayo.* Spk does not comment on this, but Mp IV 165,3–5 (commenting on AN IV 355,24–25) explains: "*There is nothing further to be done,* because he has done the four tasks imposed by the Four Noble Truths (see **56:11**). *And no repetition of what he has already done,* for the developed path need not be developed again and the abandoned defilements need not be abandoned again."

On "a pleasant dwelling in this very life," just below, see **II, n. 332**.

227 *Kukkuḷa.* See **I, v. 824**. Spk: A great conflagration, hot and

blazing. In this sutta the characteristic of suffering is discussed.

228 See **22:39** and **n. 52**.

229 The next three suttas correspond to **22:40–42**. Ee has omitted the text of **22:148**, apparently by oversight as the title is correct while the text is that of **22:149**. Accordingly, in this saṃyutta all the following sutta numbers in Ee are short by one.

230 Spk glosses *kiṃ upādāya* with *kiṃ paṭicca*, but a word play is probably involved; see **n. 146**. The double sense would then be that pleasure and pain arise because one clings to the five aggregates with desire and lust, and they arise in dependence on the five aggregates as their support and object.

231 *Kiṃ abhinivissa*. Spk: *Kiṃ abhinivisitvā; paccayaṃ katvā ti attho*. Spk, it seems, does not see *abhinivissa* as contributing anything more to the meaning than a synonym for *upādāya*, but the question then arises why it should be added in the case of views but not in the case of pleasure and pain. *Abhinivissa* is an absolutive related to the noun *abhinivesa*, "adherence," which implies an element of interpretation, namely, interpretation of experience through the lens of a wrong view. When this is acknowledged, we can then see that *abhinivissa* suggests the imposition of a cognitive interpretation on the aggregates, which goes beyond the bare conative clinging implied by *upādāya*.

232 This is the full eternalist view; see **22:81** and **n. 134**.

233 The annihilationist view; see **22:81**, and **nn. 75, 135**.

234 *Micchādiṭṭhi*. In the Nikāyas usually explained as the nihilist view, e.g., at MN I 287,12–18. For text, see **24:5**.

235 *Sakkāyadiṭṭhi*. See **n. 5**.

236 *Attānudiṭṭhi*. At Paṭis I 143 defined by the formula for the twenty kinds of *sakkāyadiṭṭhi*.

237 Spk-pṭ explains *adherences* (*abhinivesa*) as craving, conceit, and views, and *shackles* (*vinibandha*) as the mental shackles of not being devoid of lust for form, etc. (see MN I 101,28–102,16). *Holding* (*ajjhosāna*), in the next sutta, is defined by Spk-pṭ as craving and views.

238 Spk: Ānanda had seen other bhikkhus receive from the Buddha a meditation subject based on the five aggregates,

attain arahantship, and declare final knowledge in the Teacher's presence. He thus approached thinking to do the same. The Buddha knew he would not attain the three higher paths during his own lifetime, but he gave him instructions to satisfy him. Ānanda would attend to his meditation subject for one or two turns before going to serve the Teacher, and it became one of the factors that matured in his liberation.

23. Rādhasaṃyutta

239 DPPN 2:730 explains that he was a brahmin of Rājagaha who had become a monk in his old age. The Buddha declared him the foremost of those who could inspire ingenuity in others (*etadaggaṃ paṭibhāṇakeyyānaṃ;* AN I 25,15). He has two verses at Th 133–34 (= Dhp 13–14).

Spk: Whenever the Tathāgata saw this elder, a subtle topic occurred to him. Thus the Blessed One taught him the Dhamma in various ways. In this saṃyutta, two vaggas have come down by way of questions, a third by way of request, and a fourth by way of intimate discourse (*upanisinnakakathā,* lit. "sitting nearby talk").

240 Spk: Here "Māra" is a metaphor for death and the aggregates (*maraṇa-māra, khandha-māra*).

241 *Māro vā assa māretā vā yo vā pana mīyati.* Spk glosses *māretā* with *māretabbo,* but the word is clearly an agent noun with an active sense.

242 *Vimutti kho Rādha nibbānatthā.* Spk: This "liberation of the fruit" is for the purpose of Nibbāna without clinging (*phalavimutti nām' esā anupādānibbānatthā*).

243 This paragraph is also at **48:42** (V 218,19–21) and MN I 304,20–22. Be consistently reads the verb as *accayāsi* (aorist of *atiyāti*), Se as *accasarā* (aorist of *atisarati*). Ee's *assa* here and *ajjhaparam* below must stem from faulty manuscripts.

The last sentence is: *Nibbānogadhaṃ hi Rādha brahmacariyaṃ vussati nibbānaparāyanaṃ nibbānapariyosānaṃ.* Many translators take *nibbānogadha* to mean "the plunge into Nibbāna" or "merging with Nibbāna," which the commentaries encourage by connecting *ogadha* with *ogāha,* a plunge (from the verb *ogāhati,* to plunge into). But *ogadha* is actually a by-form of *ogādha*, from the verb *ogādhati*, which the commentaries treat as synonymous with *patiṭṭhahati*, "to be established." They confirm this link by consistently glossing *ogadha* with *patiṭṭhā*, support; hence my rendering "ground." For the references, see CPD, s.v. *ogadha, ogādhati, ogāha*, and the use of the word *gādha*, both literal and metaphorical, in **I, v. 263**. MW defines *gādha* (from the root *gādh*, to stand firmly) as a ground for standing on in water, a shallow place, a ford.

244 This reply hinges on a pun between *satta* as the Pāli equivalent of Skt *sattva*, "a being," and as the past participle of *sajjati* (= Skt *sakta*), "attached."

245 I read *dhanāyanti* with Be and Se, glossed *dhanaṃ viya maññanti* by Spk.

246 I follow Se. Be reads *bhavanetti-nirodho* twice, Ee *bhavanetti bhavanetti-nirodho. Bhavanetti*, lit. "what leads to existence," is glossed *bhavarajju*, "rope of existence," by Spk. The expression is a synonym of *bhavataṇhā*, craving for existence, and often occurs in verse.

247 A partly similar series of terms is met at **12:15**. See **II, nn. 31, 32**.

248 *Māradhamma*. Spk glosses with *maraṇadhamma*, "subject to death." In some of the suttas that follow (namely, in relation to impermanence, suffering, and nonself), I translate the suffix *-dhamma* as "nature" rather than "subject to."

24. *Diṭṭhisaṃyutta*

249 This strange view seems to be a poetic statement of the illusory nature of change. The compound *esikaṭṭhāyiṭṭhita*, "stands as steady as a pillar," occurs in the statement of the eternalist views at DN I 14–16 and in the doctrine of the seven bodies just below (**24:8**; III 211,8). A doctrine holding time and change to be illusory (*avicalita-nityatva*) emerged later in the history of the Ājīvika school and may have been brought into the system from the school of Pakudha Kaccāyana, the propounder of the "doctrine of the seven bodies." See Basham, *History and Doctrines of the Ājīvikas*, p. 236. At Mvu III 317 a similar view, stated in nearly identical terms, is cited as an example of the "wicked and

wrong beliefs" that were circulating in Magadha before the Buddha arrived on the scene; see Jones 3:306.

Spk: This, it is said, was their view: "Although winds blow breaking the branches of trees, etc., these are not (really) winds; they are facsimiles of wind (*vātalesā*; Spk-pṭ: *vātalesā ti vātasadisā*). The wind stands as steady as a pillar and a mountain peak. [Spk-pṭ: The phrase 'as a pillar' shows its immobility (*niccalabhāva*); 'a mountain peak,' its eternality (*sassatisama*).] Similarly with water. Though it is said that pregnant women give birth, the fetuses do not (really) emerge; those are facsimiles of fetuses. Though the sun and moon rise and set, they do not (really) do so; those are facsimiles of the sun and moon, which stand as steady as a pillar and a mountain peak."

250 This is a fourfold classification of all objects. According to Spk, *the seen* (*diṭṭha*) is the visible-form base; *the heard* (*suta*), the sound base; *the sensed* (*muta*), the objects of smell, taste, and touch; and *the cognized* (*viññāta*), the other seven bases (i.e., the six internal sense bases and the mental-phenomena base). The words "attained, sought after, and ranged over by the mind" (*pattaṃ pariyesitaṃ anuvicaritaṃ manasā*) are just an elaboration of the fourth. In the following suttas of this vagga, this portion has been elided in the abridgement, but it should be understood in all.

251 I read *imesu chasu ṭhānesu*, with Se and Ee, as against Be *imesu ca ṭhānesu*. Spk is silent, but it seems the six cases are the five aggregates and the tetrad of sense objects taken collectively as one. Cp. MN I 135,34–36, where the tetrad of sense objects actually replaces *viññāṇa* as a basis for wrong views (*diṭṭhiṭṭhāna*).

252 As at **22:81**; see **n. 134**.

253 As at **22:81**; see **n. 135**.

254 This is the full nihilist doctrine (*natthikavāda*). At DN I 55,15–31, it is called annihilationism (*ucchedavāda*) and ascribed to Ajita Kesakambalī. For the commentarial explanation, see Bodhi, *Discourse on the Fruits of Recluseship*, pp. 77–83.

255 The doctrine of the inefficacy of action (*akiriyavāda*), at DN I 52,22–53,2 ascribed to Pūraṇa Kassapa. See *Fruits of Recluseship*, pp. 69–70.

256 The doctrine of noncausality (*ahetukavāda*) is ascribed to Makkhali Gosāla at DN I 53,25–33, but at **22:60** a portion of it is attributed to Pūraṇa Kassapa; see above **n. 92**. For the commentary, see *Fruits of Recluseship*, pp. 70–72. Strict determinism (*niyativāda*) is known to have been the main plank of Makkhali's Ājīvika philosophy, discussed in detail by Basham, *History and Doctrines of the Ājīvikas*, pp. 224–39. The sentence in brackets is brought in from DN I 53,28–29, but is not in the SN text or in the version at MN I 516,33–517,3.

257 The six classes (*chaḷabhijātiyo*)—the black, the blue, the red, the yellow, the white, and the ultimate white—represent stages along the Ājīvika road to perfection; see *Fruits of Recluseship*, pp. 73–75. At AN III 383,18–84,7 this scheme is ascribed to Pūraṇa Kassapa, which again shows the connection between the two systems (a point noted by Basham, pp. 23–24).

258 At DN I 56,21–34 this doctrine of the seven bodies (*sattakāyavāda*) is ascribed to Pakudha Kaccāyana.

259 I have imported the sentence in brackets from the DN and MN versions of this view; it seems to have been lost in the SN transmission.

260 In the DN version, this fantastic cosmology is connected to the doctrine of noncausality and subsumed under the teaching of Makkhali Gosāla, where the whole system is called the doctrine of purity by wandering on (*saṃsārasuddhi*). At MN I 517,31–518,15 however, as here, the cosmology is attached to the doctrine of the seven bodies. This dual ascription suggests that the cosmological scheme may have been shared by both systems, and in fact the schools of Makkhali and Pakudha later coalesced to form the southern branch of the Ājīvika school. Basham discusses the different ascriptions at pp. 18–23, but treats the cosmology as an integral feature of Makkhali's system at pp. 240–54.

The passage contains a number of anomalous grammatical forms, such as nominatives both singular and plural terminating in *-e*, which are probably vestiges of ancient Māgadhī. Variant readings are common. I have generally translated the passage with the aid of Spk, but we must bear in mind that the commentaries are explaining the obscure terms at double remove: first, from the outside perspective of the Buddhist community (which may already have been acquainted with a distorted version of the doctrine), and then from the additional distance of the centuries that separated the commentators from the period when the views were current. Often the commentary is obviously engaging in conjecture, and sometimes is clearly wrong. For a translation of the full commentary, see *Fruits of Recluseship*, pp. 72–77, and for a critical assessment, see Basham's discussion of the passage at pp. 240–54.

261 Here I part with Spk, which glosses *ājīvaka* with *ājivavutti*, "means of livelihood."

262 *Bāle ca paṇḍite ca nibbeṭhiyamānā sukhadukkhaṃ paleti.* Spk: Starting from a mountain top or a tree top, a ball of thread goes along unwinding for the length of the thread; then, when the thread is finished, it stops right there and goes no farther. Just so, fools and the wise flee from pleasure and pain, "unwinding" by way of time. They do not exceed the aforesaid time.

The versions at DN I 54,20–21 and MN I 518,13–15 read: *bāle ca paṇḍite ca sandhāvitvā saṃsaritvā dukkhass' antaṃ karissanti*; "the foolish and the wise, having roamed and wandered on, will make an end of suffering." Note in both versions the nominative plurals terminating in *-e*.

263 The next ten suttas are each devoted to one of the ten "undeclared points," also dealt with from still different angles in SN 33 and SN 44.

264 I translate the titles of the next three vaggas as in Be: *Dutiyagamanavagga, Tatiyagamanavagga, Catutthagamanavagga*. In Se, the third and fourth vaggas are similarly named, but the second is called *Gamanavagga*. Ee includes all the suttas after the first eighteen in a single chapter (Chapter II) subdivided into four sections called *gamana*. Ee applies the title *Purimagamana* to the first eighteen suttas of this chapter, and *Dutiyagamana* to the second eighteen; the third and fourth chapters are named as in the other eds., but without *-vagga*. In his introduction to this part (p. ix) Feer proposes to count the eighteen suttas of the *Sotāpattivagga* twice, and thus maintains that the whole

saṃyutta consists of 114 suttas (18 + 18 + (3 x 26)). This, however, involves an unnecessary duplication (which Feer admits, to his puzzlement). It is thus best to follow the arrangement of this saṃyutta in Be and Se.

265 This is said because the five aggregates are *dukkha*.

266 The next eight views are varieties of eternalism with regard to the after-death condition of the self. They are also mentioned at DN I 31,6–15. For a translation of the commentary, see Bodhi, *All-Embacing Net of Views*, pp. 176–82.

Spk: The view of a *self consisting of form* arises from taking the object alone [Spk-pṭ: the *kasiṇa*] as self; a *formless self*, from taking the jhāna as self; the syncretic view, from taking both object and jhāna as self; the double negation, from mere reasoning (*takkamattena*). The view of the self as *exclusively happy* arises in the meditator, the rationalist, and those who remember past births. The same for those who view the self as exclusively miserable, etc.

267 This paragraph distinguishes the suttas of this "trip" (*gamana*) from those of the preceding trips. Similarly, the fourth trip is distinguished simply by the concluding argument.

25. *Okkantisaṃyutta*

268 The faith-follower (*saddhānusārī*) and the Dhamma-follower (*dhammānusārī*), described just below, are the two classes of disciples who are practising for realization of the fruit of stream-entry. The two are the lowest ranking members of a comprehensive sevenfold typology of noble disciples found, with formal definitions, at MN I 477–79. The seven types are also defined, somewhat differently, at Pp 14–15 (§§30–36) and at Vism 659–60 (Ppn 21:74–78). The faith-follower and the Dhamma-follower are also distinguished at **55:24** (V 377,8–24) and **55:25** (V 379,10–21), though the terms themselves are not used there. At **48:12–17** they come at the end of the more usual list of noble persons, in place of the one practising for the realization of the fruit of stream-entry, and here the faith-follower is placed below the Dhamma-follower for the reason that his faculties are weaker.

Briefly, the faith-follower and the Dhamma-follower differ with regard to their dominant faculty: the former relies on faith as the vehicle of progress, the latter on wisdom. When they attain the fruit of stream-entry, the former becomes "one liberated by faith" (*saddhāvimutta;* see MN I 478,29–34), the latter "one attained by view" (*diṭṭhippatta;* see MN I 478,18–23).

According to the Abhidhamma system, with its conception of the supramundane path as lasting for only a single mind-moment, both the faith-follower and the Dhamma-follower should be such for only the one mind-moment of the path. This interpretation, however, though advocated by the commentaries, is difficult to reconcile with the Nikāyas. For an interesting discussion of the two models, see Gethin, *The Buddhist Path to Awakening,* pp. 129–33.

Spk explains "the fixed course of rightness" (*sammattaniyāma*) as the noble path (*ariyamagga*). On the clause, "he is incapable of passing away without having realized the fruit of stream-entry," Spk says that once the path has arisen there can be no obstruction to the fruit. It quotes Pp 13 (§20): "Should this person be one practising for the realization of the fruit of stream-entry, and should it be the time when the aeon is to burn up, the aeon will not burn up until that person realizes the fruit of stream-entry."

269 On the Dhamma-follower, see **n. 268**. The commentaries do not clarify the syntax of the expression *ime dhammā evaṃ paññāya mattaso nijjhānaṃ khamanti*. Though *nijjhānam* is accusative, in English idiom it is more naturally rendered with an ablative sense.

Spk: *Mattaso nijjhānaṃ khamantī ti pamāṇato olokanaṃ khamanti;* "Accepted after being pondered to a sufficient degree": accepted in measure (through) examination. Spk-pṭ: *Olokanan ti saccābhisamayasaṅkhātaṃ dassanaṃ; khamanti sahanti, ñayantī ti attho;* "Examination": vision consisting in the breakthrough to the truths. "Accepted": consented to, meaning "are known."

Spk-pṭ is trying to identify the Dhamma-follower's "examination" or "pondering" of the teachings with the breakthrough to the truths achieved on the occasion of stream-entry, but the sutta itself distinguishes them, the former being merely preliminary to the latter.

270 This statement makes it clear how the stream-enterer dif-

fers from those on the way to stream-entry. The faith-follower accepts the teachings on trust (with a limited degree of understanding), the Dhamma-follower through investigation; but the stream-enterer has *known and seen* the teachings directly. I read with Se: *evaṃ jānāti evaṃ passati.*

271 *Viññāṇadhātu* is missing in Ee, but found in Be and Se.

26. Uppādasaṃyutta

272 This is a template, to be filled in with the same content as in the preceding chapter. **26:9** is almost identical with **14:36**, but includes as well the space element and the consciousness element. **26:10** is fully identical with **22:30**. See **II, n. 253**.

27. Kilesasaṃyutta

273 *Cittass' eso upakkileso.* Spk: A corruption of what mind? The mind of the four planes. Admittedly, it is so for the mind of the three (mundane) planes, but how is it a corruption of the supramundane mind? By obstructing its arising. For it is a corruption because it does not allow that mind to arise.

Although the title of the chapter has *kilesa,* which I render "defilement," the body of the text uses *upakkilesa,* which I render "corruption." MN I 36–37 enumerates sixteen "corruptions of mind," while **46:33** applies this designation to the five hindrances.

274 Spk: *His mind inclines to renunciation* (*nekkhammaninnaṃ c' assa cittaṃ hoti*): The mind of serenity and insight inclines to the nine supramundane states. *Those things to be realized by direct knowledge* (*abhiññā sacchikaraṇīyesu dhammesu*): the things pertaining to the six direct knowledges. Spk does not gloss the verb *khāyati,* lit. "appears."

28. Sāriputtasaṃyutta

275 As at **21:3**. See **I, n. 18**.

276 See **II, n. 340.**

277 See **I, n. 377**.

278 Her name means "Pure Face." Spk explains that she

approached the elder intending to mock him with her questions and to instigate a debate. Each question and reply has an implicit meaning, which is elicited just below.

279 *Disāmukha*. Spk: *Catasso disā olokento ti attho.*

280 *Vatthuvijjā*, the science of sites, included among the types of wrong livelihood for ascetics at DN I 9,7. Spk explains it as the means of determining whether a site will be suitable for agricultural cultivation, but Sv I 93,14–17 as the science of determining the virtues and faults of sites selected for homes and monasteries, etc., including the protective charms to be recited over them.

281 *Nakkhattavijjā*. See DN I 10,10–31 for more detailed treatment.

282 *Dūteyya-pahiṇagamanānuyoga*. See DN I 8,20–25. This is considered unfitting for a bhikkhu because it reduces his role to that of a messenger for others.

283 *Aṅgavijjā*, mentioned also at DN I 9,7. Spk explains as the science of determining a person's future from his or her bodily features. "Palmistry" is certainly too narrow, but there is no other simple English word that quite captures the sense.

29. *Nāgasaṃyutta*

284 On the nāgas and the beings featured in the next three saṃyuttas, see Introduction to Part III, pp. 850–51. The four modes of generation (*yoni*) are intended to comprise all sentient beings; see MN I 73,3–15. According to Spk, the Buddha spoke this sutta in order to rescue these bhikkhus from the nāga modes of generation (*nāgayonīhi uddharaṇatthaṃ*; or Se: *ukkaṇṭhanatthaṃ*, to make them fed up with the nāga modes of generation).

285 *Uposathaṃ upavasanti vossaṭṭhakāyā ca bhavanti.* According to Buddhist folklore, the nāgas can undertake the precepts of virtue on the Uposatha days (see **I, n. 513**), and may even resolve to uphold the precepts at the cost of their lives. The classic illustration is the Campeyya Jātaka (No. 506), in which the Bodhisatta, reborn as a nāga-king, maintains the Uposatha precepts even when cruelly tormented by a snake-charmer.

Spk-pṭ: "Relinquish their bodies": as they are determined

to maintain the precepts, they have given up their bodies with a mind of unconcern, thinking, "Let those who have need of my skin, blood, or bones take them all."

286 Spk glosses *dvayakārino* with *duvidhakārino,* and explains that they do both wholesome and unwholesome deeds.

287 Each gift item is the subject of a separate sutta.

30. Supaṇṇasaṃyutta

288 Spk: Supaṇṇas of a given class are able to carry off only nāgas that are of an inferior or equal class but not their superiors.

31. Gandhabbakāyasaṃyutta

289 The gandhabbas are associated with fragrant substances, no doubt because the word is based on the stem *gandha,* meaning scent. Spk: Those dwelling in fragrant roots are born with the support of a tree whose roots are fragrant, but the entire tree is available to them as a dwelling place. The same for the other types.

On the Vedic origins of the Buddhist conception of the gandhabbas, see Wijesekera, "Vedic Gandharva and Pāli Gandhabba," in *Buddhist and Vedic Studies,* esp. pp. 191–93.

290 Rebirth as a gandhabba is considered favourable and is thus the direct result of good conduct, unlike rebirth as a nāga or supaṇṇa, which is of mixed status and thus the result of ambivalent kamma.

32. Valāhakasaṃyutta

291 Spk: These are devas living in space who have arisen in the company of the devas called the cloud dwellers.

292 The numbering of suttas in Ee has gone awry here, both in text and translation.

293 I follow Se and Ee: *Yaṃ nūna mayaṃ sakāya ratiyā rameyyāma.* Be reads the verb as *vaseyyāma.* Spk explains that cool weather during the rainy season or winter is a natural coolness caused by the change of seasons, but when it becomes extremely cold during the cool season, or

cold during the summer, that is caused by the power of these devas. Similar explanations are given for the other cases.

33. Vacchagottasaṃyutta

294 Vacchagotta appears as the inquirer in three suttas in MN, Nos. 71, 72, and 73. In the third he becomes a monk and attains arahantship. In SN he reappears in **44:7–11**, again with questions about the undeclared points.

295 This sutta, and those to follow, apply the framework of the Four Noble Truths to each of the five aggregates. Since not knowing the Four Noble Truths (*dukkhe aññāṇaṃ*, etc.) is ignorance (*avijjā;* see **12:2**; II 4,11–14), these suttas collectively establish that ignorance (i.e., lack of knowledge) is the underlying cause of the ten speculative views. Spk says that this saṃyutta contains eleven suttas with a total of fifty-five explanations, but I have followed the printed editions, which count each explanation as a separate sutta.

296 Spk explains each of the causes as a synonym of not knowing. The Pāli ablatives are: *adassanā, anabhisamayā, ananubodhā, appaṭivedhā, asallakkhaṇā, anupalakkhaṇā, apaccupalakkhaṇā, asamapekkhaṇā, appaccupekkhaṇā, apaccakkhakammā.*

34. Jhānasaṃyutta

297 Jhānasaṃyutta is also the title of SN 53, which concerns the four jhānas as meditative attainments. Since the present saṃyutta focuses on *the process* of meditation rather than on the results, I have translated the title accordingly. The saṃyutta is constructed as a "wheel" (*cakka*) showing all the possible dyadic permutations of eleven skills related to meditation practice. Each pair is further considered by way of the four possibilities: possession of one but not the other, possession of neither, and possession of both. The last is always the best. Spk states that this entire Jhānasaṃyutta is discussed by way of mundane jhāna.

Several of the skills are mentioned elsewhere: six at AN III 311,27–30; a partly overlapping six at AN III 427,25–428,4; and seven at AN IV 34,5–9. Between them these other sources cover all the skills dealt with here except "skill in the object" (*ārammaṇakusala*), which seems to be unique to this saṃyutta. The explanations at Mp III 354–55 correspond closely to those of Spk, but a few minor differences will be noted below.

298 Spk: *Skilled in concentration* (*samādhikusala*): skilled in determining the factors thus, "The first jhāna has five factors, the second three factors," etc. *But not skilled in attainment regarding concentration* (*na samādhismiṃ samāpattikusala*): though he makes the mind pliant by gladdening it [Spk-pṭ: by removing the opposed states and collecting the cooperative causes], he is unable to attain the jhāna.

Mp III 354, on *samāpattikusala*: "Having collected suitable food and climate, he is skilled in attaining concentration—adroit, capable, and adept at it."

I doubt these explanations capture the intended meaning and think it more likely skill in attainment is synonymous with the "mastery in attainment" (*samāpattivasī*) described at Paṭis I 100 thus: "He attains the first jhāna (etc.) where, when, and for as long as he wishes; he has no difficulty in attaining."

299 *Sappimaṇḍa*. See **II, n. 64**.

300 *Na samādhismiṃ ṭhitikusalo*. Spk: Not skilled in steadying the jhāna, unable to steady the jhāna for a mere seven or eight fingersnaps.

This skill may correspond to the "mastery in determination" (*adhiṭṭhānavasī*) described at Paṭis I 100: "He determines (the duration of) the first jhāna (etc.) where, when, and for as long as he wishes; he has no difficulty in determining (the duration)."

301 *Na vuṭṭhānakusalo*. Spk: Unable to emerge from the jhāna at the predetermined time. See the definition of "mastery in emergence" (*vuṭṭhānavasī*) at Paṭis I 100, parallel to the definitions of the previous two masteries.

302 *Na kallitakusalo*. Spk: Unskilled in making the mind pliant by gladdening it.

303 *Na ārammaṇakusalo*. Spk: Unskilled in the *kasiṇa* object. The objects of the various meditation subjects used for gaining concentration are discussed at Vism 113 (Ppn 3:117).

304 *Na gocarakusalo*. Spk: Unskilled in the range of the medita-

tion subject [Spk-pṭ: in the range of the concentration to be produced, in the place of its occurrence known as the meditation subject], and unskilled in the range of the alms round [Spk-pṭ: owing to lack of mindfulness and clear comprehension].

Mp III 354 comments somewhat differently: "Having avoided the unsuitable things that are unhelpful and pursued the suitable things that are helpful, he is skilled in the range when he knows, 'This concentration has a sign (*nimitta,* a mental image) as object, this one the characteristics (impermanence, etc.) as object.'" This last sentence refers to the distinction between *samatha* (serenity meditation) and *vipassanā* (insight meditation).

305 *Na abhinīhārakusalo*. Spk has nothing helpful, but Spk-pṭ says: "Unskilled in resolving to elevate the meditation subject so that it partakes of distinction (*kammaṭṭhānaṃ visesabhāgiyatāya abhinīharituṃ akusalo*). This means being unable to raise it from the first jhāna to the second, from the second to the third, etc."

Mp III 354–55: "He is said to be skilled in resolution in regard to concentration when he is able to resolve on the concentration of the first jhāna, etc., for the sake of attaining the successively higher attainments."

306 *Na sakkaccakārī*. Spk: He does not act carefully enough to enter jhāna.

307 *Na sātaccakārī*.

308 *Na sappāyakārī*. Spk: He is unable to fulfil the qualities that are helpful, suitable, for concentration.

Part IV

The Book of the Six Sense Bases

(*Saḷāyatanavagga*)

Contents

DIVISION III. THE THIRD FIFTY

Chapter VI
40. *Moggallānasaṃyutta*
Connected Discourses with Moggallāna

Chapter VII
41. *Cittasaṃyutta*
Connected Discourses with Citta

Chapter VIII
42. *Gāmaṇisaṃyutta*
Connected Discourses to Headmen

Chapter IX
43. *Asaṅkhatasaṃyutta*
Connected Discourses on the Unconditioned

Chapter X
44. *Abyākatasaṃyutta*
Connected Discourses on the Undeclared

Introduction

The *Saḷāyatanavagga*, The Book of the Six Sense Bases, is the third great collection of connected discourses with a philosophical orientation. Like its two predecessors, the Vagga is dominated by its first chapter, the Saḷāyatanasaṃyutta, which takes up 208 of the 403 pages in the PTS edition of this volume. Its junior partner is the Vedanāsaṃyutta, which deals with another closely related theme of the Buddha's teaching, feeling. Feeling assumes special importance because it serves as the main condition, in the doctrine of dependent origination, for the arising of craving. Feeling also finds a place among the four establishments of mindfulness, to be explored in Part V, and thus links theory with practice. The other saṃyuttas in this book do not have any intimate connection with the two major themes, but cover a wide variety of topics ranging from the weaknesses and strengths of women to the nature of the unconditioned.

35. Saḷāyatanasaṃyutta

The Saḷāyatanasaṃyutta draws together a vast assortment of texts dealing with the six internal and external sense bases. Though most of these are very short, a few, especially towards the end, tend to approach the size of the shorter discourses in the Majjhima Nikāya. To organize such a large number of suttas into a convenient format, the saṃyutta is divided into four *paññāsakas*, sets of fifty. While the first three sets of fifty actually contain roughly fifty suttas each, the fourth has ninety-three, including a single vagga (among four) with a full sixty suttas! This is the "Sixtyfold Repetition Series," a compilation of sixty extremely brief suttas grouped into batches of three. If each of the triplets were to be compressed into a single sutta, as Feer has done in Ee, we would then get a vagga of twenty suttas, the number counted by Feer. But Be and Se, followed here, count the triplets as three individual suttas, thus yielding sixty suttas, a total supported by the title of the vagga. Principally on account of this difference in the treatment of the repetition series, Ee has a total of 207 suttas while the present translation has 248; the additional difference of one obtains because Feer has combined two suttas which clearly should have been kept distinct.

On first consideration, it would seem that the six internal and external sense bases should be understood simply as the six sense faculties and their objects, with the term *āyatana*, base, having the sense of origin or source. Though many suttas lend support to this supposition, the Theravāda exegetical tradition, beginning already from the Abhidhamma period, understands the six pairs of bases as a complete scheme of classification capable of accommodating all the factors of existence mentioned in the Nikāyas. This conception of the six bases probably originated from the Sabba Sutta (**35:23**), in which the Buddha says that the six pairs of bases are "the all" apart from which nothing at all exists. To make the six bases capable of literally incorporating everything, the *Vibhaṅga* of the Abhidhamma Piṭaka defines the mind base (*manāyatana*) as including all classes of consciousness, and the mental phenomena base (*dhammāyatana*) as including the other three mental aggregates, subtle nonsensuous types of form, and even the unconditioned element, Nibbāna (see Vibh 70–73).

Seen from this angle, the six internal and external sense bases offer an alternative to the five aggregates as a scheme of phenomenological classification. The relationship between the two schemes might be seen as roughly analogous to that between horizontal and vertical cross-sections of an organ, with the analysis by way of the aggregates corresponding to the horizontal slice, the analysis by way of the six sense bases to the vertical slice (see Table 6). Thus, we are told, on an occasion of visual cognition, eye-consciousness arises in dependence on the eye and forms; the meeting of the three is contact; and with contact as condition there arise feeling, perception, and volition. Viewing this experience "vertically" by way of the sense bases, the eye and visible forms are each a separate base, respectively the eye base and the form base; eye-consciousness belongs to the mind base; and eye-contact, feeling, perception, and volition are all assigned to the mental phenomena base. Then, using the scalpel of thought to cut "horizontally" across the occasion of visual cognition, we can ask what is present from the form aggregate? The eye and a visible form (and the body as the physical basis of consciousness). What from the feeling aggregate? A feeling born of eye-contact. What from the perception aggregate? A perception of a visible form. What from the aggregate of volitional formations? A volition regarding a form. And what from the consciousness aggregate? An act of eye-consciousness.

TABLE 6

An Occasion of Visual Cognition in Terms of the Aggregates and Sense Bases

Aggregates	Visual Cognition	Sense Bases
form	*eye* *form*	eye base form base
consciousness	*eye-consciousness*	mind base
(volitional formations)	*eye-contact*	mental phenomena base
feeling	*feeling born of eye-contact*	mental phenomena base
perception	*perception of form*	mental phenomena base
volitional formations	*volition regarding form*	mental phenomena base

Note: Contact (*phassa*) is classified in the aggregate of volitional formations in the Abhidhamma and the commentaries, though in the Nikāyas it is not explicitly assigned a place among the five aggregates.

Strangely, though some connection between the aggregates and sense bases, as just sketched, is already suggested in at least two suttas (**35:93**, **121**), the Nikāyas do not explicitly correlate the two schemes. Conscious correlation begins only with the Abhidhamma Piṭaka, especially in the opening sections of the *Dhātukathā*, which reflects the attempt of the early Buddhist community to merge the more pragmatic schemes of the suttas into a single all-inclusive system that assigned to every element a precisely defined place.

Nevertheless, though this treatment of the sense bases stems from an early period, the Nikāyas themselves usually present the six pairs of sense bases not as a complete phenomenological scheme but as starting points for the genesis of cognition. Often, because of their role in mediating between consciousness and its objects, the internal bases are spoken of as the "bases for contact" (*phassāyatana*). If this interpretation is adopted, then mind (*mano*), the base for the arising of mind-consciousness (*manoviññāṇa*), probably denotes the passive flow of mind from which active cognition emerges, and *dhammā* the nonsensuous objects of consciousness apprehended by introspection, imagination, and reflection.

As with the aggregates, so with the sense bases, concern with their classification and interactions is governed not by an interest in theoretical completeness but by the practical exigencies of the Buddha's path aimed at liberation from suffering. The sense bases are critically important because it is through them that suffering arises (**35:106**). Even more, it is said that the holy life is lived under the Buddha for the full understanding of suffering, and if others should ask what is the suffering that should be fully understood, the correct answer is that the eye and forms, the ear and sounds, etc., and all phenomena derived from them, are the suffering that should be fully understood (**35:81, 152**).

The main pragmatic concern with the sense bases is the eradication of clinging, for like the aggregates the sense bases serve as the soil where clinging takes root and thrives. Because clinging originates from ignorance and craving, and because ignorance sustains clinging by weaving its web of the triple delusion—permanence, happiness, and self—we find in the Saḷāyatanasaṃyutta almost all the familiar templates used in the Khandhasaṃyutta; often, in fact, these templates are here applied twice to generate parallel suttas for the internal and external sense bases. Thus, to dispel ignorance and generate true knowledge, we repeatedly hear the same melodies, in a slightly different key, reminding us that the sense bases and their derivatives are impermanent, suffering, and nonself; that we must discern the gratification, danger, and escape in regard to the sense bases; that we should abandon desire and lust for the sense bases.

However, despite large areas of convergence between the two saṃyuttas, the Saḷāyatanasaṃyutta introduces several new perspectives that bear on the sense bases but have no exact parallels in relation to the aggregates. Thus the saṃyutta includes a long chain of twenty suttas which expose the flaws in conditioned existence, summed up under the caption "the all." All, it is said, is subject to birth, aging, sickness, death, and so forth, and the all is nothing other than the sense bases and the mental processes arising from them (**35:33–42**). Several suttas in this chapter identify the six sense bases with the world, because the world (*loka*) is whatever disintegrates (*lujjati*), and because in the Noble One's Discipline the world is understood as "that in the world by which one is a perceiver and conceiver of the world" (**35:82, 84, 116**). In one sutta the question is raised why the world is said to be empty (*suñña*), and the answer given is because the six bases are empty of a self and of what belongs to self (**35:85**). No parallels to these discourses are found in the Khandhasaṃyutta. This saṃyutta also describes the six internal sense bases as "old kamma" (**35:146**), which could not be said so plainly about the aggregates, for they comprise both kammically active and resultant phases of experience. We further find here that greater stress is placed on "conceiving" (*maññita*), the distorted cognitions influenced by craving, conceit, and views, with several discourses devoted to the methods of contemplation for uprooting all conceivings (**35:30–32, 90–91**). The entire saṃyutta ends with a masterly discourse in which the Buddha urges the monks to uproot conceiving in all its guises (**35:248**).

Although the aggregates and sense bases jointly serve as the domain of craving and wrong views, a difference in emphasis can be discerned in the way the two saṃyuttas connect these two defilements to their respective domains. The Khandhasaṃyutta consistently treats the aggregates as the objective referent of identity view (*sakkāyadiṭṭhi*), the views that seek to give substance to the idea of a self. When the *puthujjana* or "worldling" fashions a view about his or her identity, he or she always does so in relation to the five aggregates. We do not find any parallel text expressing identity view in terms of the sense bases. This difference in emphasis is understandable when we realize that the scheme of the aggregates spans a wider spectrum of categories than the sense bases themselves and therefore offers the worldling more variety to choose from when attempting to give substance to the notion of "my self." This, it must be stressed, indicates a difference in emphasis, not a fundamental doctrinal difference, for the sense bases can be grasped upon with the notions "This is mine, this I am, this is my self" just as tenaciously as the aggregates can. Thus we even find a series of three suttas which state that contemplating the sense bases as impermanent, suffering, and nonself leads respectively to the abandoning of wrong view, identity view, and view of self (**35:165–67**). However, as a general rule, the sense bases are not taken up for a thematic exposition of identity view in the way the five aggregates are, which is certainly significant. We see too that the entire Diṭṭhisaṃyutta, on the diversity of views, traces all these views to a misapprehension of the aggregates, not of the sense bases.

In relation to the sense bases the interest in views recedes into the background, and a new theme takes centre stage: the need to control and master the senses. It is the sense faculties that give us access to the agreeable and disagreeable phenomena of the world, and it is our spontaneous, impulsive responses to these phenomena that sow the seeds of so much suffering. Within the untrained mind lust, hatred, and delusion, the three roots of evil, are always lying latent, and with delusion obscuring the true nature of things, agreeable objects are bound to provoke lust and greed, disagreeable objects hatred and aversion. These spontaneous reactions flood the mind and bid for our consent. If we are not careful we may rush ahead in pursuit of immediate gratification, oblivious to the fact that the fruit of sensual enjoyment is misery (see **35:94–98**).

To inculcate sense restraint, the Saḷāyatanasaṃyutta makes constant use of two formulas. One is the stock description of sense restraint (*indriyasaṃvara*) usually embedded in the sequence on the gradual training, common in the Dīgha Nikāya (e.g., at I 70) and the Majjhima Nikāya (e.g., at I 180–81). This formula enjoins the practice of sense restraint to keep the "evil unwholesome states of covetousness and displeasure" from invading the mind. In the present chapter it occurs at **35:120**, **127**, **239**, **240**, and elsewhere. The second formula posits a contrast between one who is "intent upon a pleasing form and repelled by a displeasing form" and one who is not swayed by these pairs of opposites. The latter has set up mindfulness of the body, dwells with a measureless mind, and understands the "liberation of mind, liberation by wisdom" where the evil states of lust and aversion cease without remainder. This formula is found at **35:132, 243, 244**, and **247**. Though no explicit doctrinal allocations are made for these two formulas, it seems the first is prescribed in general for a bhikkhu in the initial stages of training, while the second describes the sense restraint of the trainee (*sekha*), one at a minimal level of stream-enterer, perhaps too the natural sense restraint of the arahant.

The practice of sense restraint is necessary in the Buddhist training, not only to avoid the mental distress provoked here and now by attachment and aversion, but for a reason more deeply connected to the ultimate aim of the Dhamma. The doctrine of dependent origination reveals that craving is the propelling cause of suffering, and craving springs up with feeling as its proximate cause. Feeling occurs in the six sense bases, as pleasant, painful, and neutral feeling, and through our unwholesome responses to these feelings we nourish the craving that holds us in bondage. To gain full deliverance from suffering, craving must be contained and eradicated, and thus the restraint of the senses becomes an integral part of the discipline aimed at the removal of craving.

There is also a cognitive side to the teaching on sense restraint. Craving and other defilements arise and flourish because the mind seizes upon the "signs" (*nimitta*) and "features" (*anubyañjana*) of sensory objects and uses them as raw material for creating imaginative constructs, to which it clings as a basis for security. This process, called mental proliferation (*papañca*), is effectively synonymous with conceiving (*maññanā*). These constructs, created under the influence of the defilements, serve in turn as springboards for still stronger and more tenacious defilements, thus sustaining a vicious cycle. To break this cycle, what is needed as a preliminary step is to restrain the senses, which involves stopping at the bare sensum, without plastering it over with layers of meaning whose origins are purely subjective. Hence the Buddha's instructions to the bhikkhu Māluṅkyaputta, "In the seen there will be merely the seen," and the beautiful poem the bhikkhu composes to convey his understanding of this maxim (**35:95**; see too **35:94**).

This aspect of sense restraint receives special emphasis in the last two vaggas of the Saḷāyatanasaṃyutta, which stand out by reason of their startling imagery and extended similes. Here the six sense faculties are spoken of as an ocean, the sense objects as their current, and the faring along the spiritual path as a voyage in which we are exposed to dangers that we can only surmount by sense restraint (**35:228**). Again, agreeable sense objects are like baited hooks cast out by Māra; one who swallows them comes under Māra's control; one who resists them escapes unharmed (**35:230**). It is better, we are told, to have our sense faculties lacerated by sharp instruments, hot and glowing, than to become infatuated with attractive sense objects; for such infatuation can lead to rebirth in the lower realms (**35:235**). Our existential condition is depicted by the parable of a man pursued by four vipers, five murderous enemies, and an assassin, his only means to safety a handmade raft (**35:238**). A bhikkhu in training should draw his senses inward as a tortoise draws its limbs into its shell, for Māra is like a hungry jackal trying to get a grip on him (**35:240**). The six senses are like six animals each drawn to their natural habitat, which must be tied by the rope of sense restraint and bound to the strong post of body-directed mindfulness (**35:247**). The saṃyutta ends with a parable about the magical bonds of the asura-king Vepacitti and sounds a decisive call to eliminate all modes of conceiving rooted in craving and wrong views (**35:248**).

36. Vedanāsaṃyutta

Although feeling has often been mentioned as a product of contact at the six sense bases, since it is a potent force in the activation of the defilements it receives separate treatment in a saṃyutta of its own, with three vaggas containing thirty-one suttas. The Sinhala-script editions of SN include this chapter in the Saḷāyatanasaṃyutta, presumably because feeling arises through the six sense bases. In the present collection of suttas, however, feeling is seldom correlated with the sense bases but is far more often expounded by way of its threefold division into the pleasant, painful, and neutral (i.e., neither-painful-nor-pleasant feeling). Thus it seems better to follow the Burmese textual tradition, which treats this chapter as a separate saṃyutta.

Feeling is a key link in the chain of dependent origination, the immediate precursor of craving, and thus to break the chain requires that our defiled responses to feeling be overcome. For this reason the Buddha has made feeling one of the four "establishments of mindfulness" (*satipaṭṭhāna*) and here he assigns it a saṃyutta of its own. Several suttas in the first vagga explain that the three types of feelings serve as stimuli for the "underlying tendencies" (*anusaya*). Each feeling is correlated with a different tendency: pleasant feeling with lust, painful feeling with aversion, and neutral feeling with ignorance. The Buddha's system of mental training aims at controlling our reactions to these feelings at the very point where they arise, without allowing them to proliferate and call their corresponding tendencies into play (**36:3**, **4**). The noble disciple, of course, continues to experience feeling as long as he lives, but by eradicating the underlying tendencies he cannot be inwardly perturbed by feelings (**36:6**). In two suttas we see the Buddha visit the sick ward and give profound discourses on the contemplation of feelings to ailing monks (**36:7**, **8**). These suttas culminate in a description of the arahant and his inner detachment from feelings.

A long sutta in the second vagga (**36:19**) describes the calibration in types of happiness that human beings can experience, ranging from sensual happiness to the bliss of the cessation of feeling and perception. In the third vagga we find a classification of illnesses (**36:21**) commonly used in traditional Indian medicine, and also a detailed numerical classification of the different types of feelings along the lines that became prominent in the Abhidhamma (**36:22**). The final sutta offers an interesting gradation of rapture, happiness, equanimity, and deliverance into three levels each—as carnal, spiritual, and "more spiritual than the spiritual" (**36:31**).

37. Mātugāmasaṃyutta

This saṃyutta brings together thirty-four short suttas on women. The Buddha explains what makes a woman attractive to a man, the kinds of suffering peculiar to women, and the moral qualities that lead a woman to either a bad rebirth or a good one. In this saṃyutta the Venerable Anuruddha plays a major role, since his skill in the divine eye led him to make inquiries about such matters from the Master. The Buddha also explains how a woman wins the goodwill of her husband and his parents, the most important qualification being a virtuous character.

38. Jambukhādakasaṃyutta
39. Sāmaṇḍakasaṃyutta

These two saṃyuttas, with sixteen suttas each, have identical contents and differ only with respect to the interlocutors, two wanderers who lend their names to the two collections. The second is almost totally abridged. The suttas take the form of questions addressed to Sāriputta on such topics as Nibbāna, arahantship, the taints, the realms of existence, etc. Each ends with words of praise for the Noble Eightfold Path. The last sutta, which differs from this format, displays a gentle touch of humour.

40. Moggallānasaṃyutta

Mahāmoggallāna was the Buddha's second chief disciple. In the first nine suttas here he describes his struggle for enlightenment, which was beset with difficulties in meditation. On each occasion he could overcome his difficulty only with the aid of the Buddha, who used his psychic powers to give the disciple "long-distance" guidance. In the last two suttas Moggallāna visits the heavens and preaches to the devas on the going for refuge to the Triple Gem. The first of these texts is extensive, the second (identical except for the audience) drastically abridged.

41. Cittasaṃyutta

Citta was a householder who was named by the Buddha the foremost male lay disciple among the speakers on the Dhamma (AN I 26,5). The present saṃyutta collects ten suttas that corroborate this designation. Even when Citta assumes the role of questioner rather than respondent, we are given to understand that he already knows the answers and is posing his questions as a way of starting a Dhamma discussion with the monks. Several times we see him teaching the Dhamma to bhikkhus, and the bhikkhus applaud him as one who has "the eye of wisdom that ranges over the deep Word of the Buddha" (**41:1**, **5**, **7**). The portrait of Citta we find in this chapter evinces a genuine historical personality, a layman with wide knowledge of the teaching, deep experience in meditation, sharp wisdom, and a mischievous sense of humour. The humour surfaces in his meeting with the Jain teacher Nigaṇṭha Nātaputta, whom he leads into an embarrassing verbal trap (**41:8**). On meeting an old friend of his, who had been a naked ascetic for thirty years but had gained nothing from his asceticism but nakedness and a shaved head, he claims to have gained such high attainments as the four jhānas and the fruit of nonreturning even while living as a householder (**41:9**). Even his deathbed scene conveys a sense of humour: when his relatives think he is babbling to himself, he is actually teaching the devas a lesson in impermanence (**41:10**).

42. Gāmaṇisaṃyutta

This collection of thirteen suttas is united by the fact that all the inquirers are described as *gāmaṇis*, headmen of various sorts. With a few exceptions, the inquirers are initially not followers of the Buddha and are sometimes hostile to him, but in each case the Buddha wins them over with his reasoned arguments and careful analyses of the problems they pose.

Among the headmen we meet Talapuṭa, a theatre director who was so moved by his conversation with the Buddha that he became a bhikkhu and attained arahantship (**42:2**). His verses (at Th 1091–1145) are masterly expressions of deep spiritual yearning. We also see a follower of the Jains come to the Buddha with the intention of tripping him up in debate, only to be stopped in his tracks and led to correct understanding (**42:9**). The long discourse to Rāsiya (**42:12**) distinguishes householders along a finely graded scale of excellence, and also evaluates different types of ascetics. In the final sutta the Buddha responds to the charge, apparently devised by envious rivals, that he is a magician (**42:13**).

43. Asaṅkhatasaṃyutta

This saṃyutta functions as a compendium of the different designations of Nibbāna and the various modes of practice that lead to Nibbāna. The first vagga, which speaks of Nibbāna as the unconditioned, offers eleven presentations of the path to the unconditioned (**43:1–11**). The second vagga begins again with the unconditioned, and in one vast sutta (**43:12**) enumerates under forty-five headings the various path factors that constitute the way to the unconditioned, including those of **43:2–11** divided into their components. Thereafter, in **43:13–44**, Nibbāna is expounded by way of another thirty-two epithets; the presentation of the path here is drastically condensed, but the text implies that all the factors of the first twelve suttas should be connected with each epithet. If **43:12** were to be broken up into separate suttas by way of the path factors, and these added to the first eleven suttas, we would then have fifty-six suttas on the unconditioned alone. And if this method were then to be applied to each epithet, the number of suttas in this saṃyutta would total 1,848.

44. Abyākatasaṃyutta

The suttas in this saṃyutta all respond to the question why the Buddha has not adopted any of the metaphysical tenets advocated and hotly debated by his contemporaries. Of particular concern is the problem whether the Tathāgata exists after death. The first sutta features a discussion on this topic between King Pasenadi of Kosala and the bhikkhunī Khemā, the nun foremost in wisdom, whose profound reply to the king is later affirmed by the Master (**44:1**). The suttas in this chapter are enough to dispose of the common assumption that the Buddha refrained from adopting any of these metaphysical standpoints merely on pragmatic grounds, i.e., because they are irrelevant to the quest for deliverance from suffering. The answers given to the queries show that the metaphysical tenets are rejected primarily because, at the fundamental level, they all rest upon the implicit assumption of a self, an assumption which in turn springs from ignorance about the real nature of the five aggregates and the six sense bases. For one who has fathomed the real nature of these phenomena, all these speculative views turn out to be untenable.

[1] Part IV: The Book of the Six Sense Bases (*Saḷāyatanavagga*)

Homage to the Blessed One,
the Arahant, the Perfectly Enlightened One

Chapter I

35 *Saḷāyatanasaṃyutta*
Connected Discourses on the Six Sense Bases

Division I
The Root Fifty

I. The Impermanent

1 (1) The Internal as Impermanent[1]

Thus have I heard.[2] On one occasion the Blessed One was dwelling at Sāvatthī in Jeta's Grove, Anāthapiṇḍika's Park. There the Blessed One addressed the bhikkhus thus: "Bhikkhus!"

"Venerable sir!" those bhikkhus replied. The Blessed One said this:

"Bhikkhus, the eye is impermanent.[3] What is impermanent is suffering. What is suffering is nonself. What is nonself should be seen as it really is with correct wisdom thus: 'This is not mine, this I am not, this is not my self.'

"The ear is impermanent.... The nose is impermanent.... The tongue is impermanent.... The body is impermanent.... The mind is impermanent. What is impermanent is suffering. What is suffering is nonself. What is nonself should be seen as it really is with correct wisdom thus: 'This is not mine, this I am not, this is not my self.' [2]

"Seeing thus, bhikkhus, the instructed noble disciple experiences revulsion towards the eye, revulsion towards the ear, revulsion towards the nose, revulsion towards the tongue, revulsion towards the body, revulsion towards the mind. Experiencing revulsion, he becomes dispassionate. Through dispassion [his mind] is liberated. When it is liberated there comes the knowledge: 'It's liberated.' He understands: 'Destroyed is birth, the holy life has been lived, what had to be done has been done, there is no more for this state of being.'"

2 (2) The Internal as Suffering

"Bhikkhus, the eye is suffering. What is suffering is nonself. What is nonself should be seen as it really is with correct wisdom thus: 'This is not mine, this I am not, this is not my self.'

"The ear is suffering.... The nose is suffering.... The tongue is suffering.... The body is suffering.... The mind is suffering. What is suffering is nonself. What is nonself should be seen as it really is with correct wisdom thus: 'This is not mine, this I am not, this is not my self.'

"Seeing thus ... He understands: '... there is no more for this state of being.'"

3 (3) The Internal as Nonself

"Bhikkhus, the eye is nonself. What is nonself should be seen as it really is with correct wisdom thus: 'This is not mine, this I am not, this is not my self.'

"The ear is nonself.... The nose is nonself.... The tongue is nonself.... The body is nonself.... The mind is nonself. What is nonself should be seen as it really is with correct wisdom thus: 'This is not mine, this I am not, this is not my self.'

"Seeing thus ... He understands: '... there is no more for this state of being.'"

4 (4) The External as Impermanent

"Bhikkhus, forms are impermanent. What is impermanent is suffering. What is suffering is nonself. What is nonself should be seen as it really is with correct wisdom thus: 'This is not mine, [3] this I am not, this is not my self.'

"Sounds ... Odours ... Tastes ... Tactile objects ... Mental phenomena are impermanent.[4] What is impermanent is suffering. What is suffering is nonself. What is nonself should be seen as it really is with correct wisdom thus: 'This is not mine, this I am not, this is not my self.'

"Seeing thus, bhikkhus, the instructed noble disciple experiences revulsion towards forms, revulsion towards sounds, revulsion towards odours, revulsion towards tastes, revulsion towards tactile objects, revulsion towards mental phenomena. Experiencing revulsion, he becomes dispassionate. Through dispassion [his mind] is liberated. When it is liberated there comes the knowledge: 'It's liberated.' He understands: 'Destroyed is birth, the holy life has been lived, what had to be done has been done, there is no more for this state of being.'"

5 (5) The External as Suffering

"Bhikkhus, forms are suffering. What is suffering is nonself. What is nonself should be seen as it really is with correct wisdom thus: 'This is not mine, this I am not, this is not my self.'

"Sounds ... Odours ... Tastes ... Tactile objects ... Mental phenomena are suffering. What is suffering is nonself. What is nonself should be seen as it really is with correct wisdom thus: 'This is not mine, this I am not, this is not my self.'

"Seeing thus ... He understands: '... there is no more for this state of being.'"

6 (6) The External as Nonself

"Bhikkhus, forms are nonself. What is nonself should be seen as it really is with correct wisdom thus: 'This is not mine, this I am not, this is not my self.'

"Sounds ... Odours ... Tastes ... Tactile objects ... Mental phenomena are nonself. What is nonself should be seen as it really is with correct wisdom thus: 'This is not mine, this I am not, this is not my self.'

"Seeing thus ... He understands: '... there is no more for this state of being.'" [4]

7 (7) The Internal as Impermanent in the Three Times

At Sāvatthī. "Bhikkhus, the eye is impermanent, both of the past and the future, not to speak of the present. Seeing thus, bhikkhus, the instructed noble disciple is indifferent towards the eye of the past; he does not seek delight in the eye of the future; and he is practising for revulsion towards the eye of the present, for its fading away and cessation.

"The ear is impermanent ... The nose is impermanent ... The tongue is impermanent ... The body is impermanent ... The mind is impermanent, both of the past and the future, not to speak of the present. Seeing thus, bhikkhus, the instructed noble disciple is indifferent towards the mind of the past ... for its fading away and cessation."

8 (8) The Internal as Suffering in the Three Times

At Sāvatthī. "Bhikkhus, the eye is suffering, both of the past and the future, not to speak of the present. Seeing thus ... The mind is suffering ... for its fading away and cessation."

9 (9) The Internal as Nonself in the Three Times

At Sāvatthī. "Bhikkhus, the eye is nonself, both of the past and the future, not to speak of the present. Seeing thus ... [5] ... The mind is nonself ... for its fading away and cessation."

10 (10)–12 (12) The External as Impermanent in the Three Times, Etc.

(*These three suttas are identical with §§7–9, but by way of the six external sense bases.*) [6]

II. The Pairs

13 (1) Before My Enlightenment (1)

At Sāvatthī. "Bhikkhus, before my enlightenment, [7] while I was still a bodhisatta, not yet fully enlightened, it occurred to me: 'What is the gratification, what is the danger, what is the escape in the case of the eye? What is the gratification, what is the danger, what is the escape in the case of the ear ... the nose ... the tongue ... the body ... the mind?'

"Then, bhikkhus, it occurred to me: 'The pleasure and joy that arise in dependence on the eye: this is the gratification in the eye. That the eye is impermanent, suffering, and subject to change: this is the danger in the eye. The removal and abandonment of desire and lust for the eye: this is the escape from the eye.

"'The pleasure and joy that arise in dependence on the ear ... the nose ... the tongue ... the body ... the mind: this is the gratification in the mind. That the mind is impermanent, suffering, and subject to change: this is the danger in the mind. The removal and abandonment of desire and lust for the mind: this is the escape from the mind.'

"So long, bhikkhus, as I did not directly know as they really are the gratification as gratification, the danger as danger, and the escape as escape in the case of these six internal sense bases, I did not claim to have awakened to the unsurpassed perfect enlightenment in this world with its devas, Māra, and Brahmā, in this generation with its ascetics and brahmins, its devas and humans. But when I directly knew all this as it really is, then I claimed to have awakened to the unsurpassed perfect enlightenment in this world with ... its devas and humans.[5] [8]

"The knowledge and vision arose in me: 'Unshakable is my liberation of mind; this is my last birth; now there is no more renewed existence.'"

14 (2) Before My Enlightenment (2)

(*The same is repeated for the six external sense bases.*)

15 (3) Seeking Gratification (1)

"Bhikkhus, I set out seeking the gratification in the eye. Whatever gratification there is in the eye—that I discovered. I have clearly seen with wisdom just how far the gratification in the eye extends. [9]

"Bhikkhus, I set out seeking the danger in the eye. Whatever danger there is in the eye—that I discovered. I have clearly seen with wisdom just how far the danger in the eye extends.

"Bhikkhus, I set out seeking the escape from the eye. Whatever escape there is from the eye—that I discovered. I have clearly seen with wisdom just how far the escape from the eye extends.

"Bhikkhus, I set out seeking the gratification in ... the danger in ... the escape from the ear ... the nose ... the tongue ... the body ... the mind. Whatever escape there is from the mind—that I discovered. I have clearly seen with wisdom just how far the escape from the mind extends.

"So long, bhikkhus, as I did not directly know as they really are the gratification as gratification, the danger as danger, and the escape as escape in the case of these six internal sense bases, I did not claim to have awakened to the unsurpassed perfect enlightenment in this world with its devas, Māra, and Brahmā, in this generation with its ascetics and brahmins, its devas and humans. But when I directly knew all this as it really is, then I claimed to have awakened to the unsurpassed perfect enlightenment in this world with ... its devas and humans.

"The knowledge and vision arose in me: 'Unshakable is my liberation of mind; this is my last birth; now there is no more renewed existence.'"

16 (4) Seeking Gratification (2)

(*The same for the six external sense bases.*) [10]

17 (5) If There Were No (1)

"Bhikkhus, if there were no gratification in the eye, beings would not become enamoured with it; but because there is gratification in the eye, beings become enamoured with it. If there were no danger in the eye, beings would not experience revulsion towards it; but because there is danger in the eye, beings experience revulsion towards it. If there were no escape from the eye, beings would not escape from it; but because there is an escape from the eye, beings escape from it.

"Bhikkhus, if there were no gratification in the ear ... [11] ... in the nose ... in the tongue ... in the body ... in the mind, beings would not become enamoured with it ... but because there is an escape from the mind, beings escape from it.

"So long, bhikkhus, as beings have not directly known as they really are the gratification as gratification, the danger as danger, and the escape as escape in the case of these six internal sense bases, they have not escaped from this world with its devas, Māra, and Brahmā, from this generation with its ascetics and brahmins, its devas and humans; they have not become detached from it, released from it, nor do they dwell with a mind rid of barriers. But when beings have directly known all this as it really is, [12] then they have escaped from this world with its devas and humans … they have become detached from it, released from it, and they dwell with a mind rid of barriers."

18 (6) If There Were No (2)

(*The same for the six external sense bases.*) [13]

19 (7) Delight (1)

"Bhikkhus, one who seeks delight in the eye seeks delight in suffering. One who seeks delight in suffering, I say, is not freed from suffering. One who seeks delight in the ear … in the nose … in the tongue … in the body … in the mind seeks delight in suffering. One who seeks delight in suffering, I say, is not freed from suffering.

"One who does not seek delight in the eye … in the mind does not seek delight in suffering. One who does not seek delight in suffering, I say, is freed from suffering."

20 (8) Delight (2)

(*The same for the six external sense bases.*) [14]

21 (9) Arising of Suffering (1)

"Bhikkhus, the arising, continuation, production, and manifestation of the eye is the arising of suffering, the continuation of disease, the manifestation of aging-and-death. The arising of the ear … the nose … the tongue … the body … the mind is the arising of suffering, the continuation of disease, the manifestation of aging-and-death.

"The cessation, subsiding, and passing away of the eye … the mind is the cessation of suffering, the subsiding of disease, the passing away of aging-and-death."

22 (10) Arising of Suffering (2)

(*The same for the six external sense bases.*) [15]

III. The All

23 (1) The All

At Sāvatthī. "Bhikkhus, I will teach you the all.[6] Listen to that....

"And what, bhikkhus, is the all? The eye and forms, the ear and sounds, the nose and odours, the tongue and tastes, the body and tactile objects, the mind and mental phenomena. This is called the all.

"If anyone, bhikkhus, should speak thus: 'Having rejected this all, I shall make known another all'—that would be a mere empty boast on his part.[7] If he were questioned he would not be able to reply and, further, he would meet with vexation. For what reason? Because, bhikkhus, that would not be within his domain."[8]

24 (2) Abandonment (1)

"Bhikkhus, I will teach you the Dhamma for abandoning all. Listen to that....

"And what, bhikkhus, is the Dhamma for abandoning all? The eye is to be abandoned, forms are to be abandoned, eye-consciousness is to be abandoned, eye-contact is to be abandoned, [16] and whatever feeling arises with eye-contact as condition—whether pleasant or painful or neither-painful-nor-pleasant—that too is to be abandoned.[9]

"The ear is to be abandoned ... The mind is to be abandoned, mental phenomena are to be abandoned, mind-consciousness is to be abandoned, mind-contact is to be abandoned, and whatever feeling arises with mind-contact as condition—whether pleasant or painful or neither-painful-nor-pleasant—that too is to be abandoned.

"This, bhikkhus, is the Dhamma for abandoning all."

25 (3) Abandonment (2)

"Bhikkhus, I will teach you the Dhamma for abandoning all through direct knowledge and full understanding.[10] Listen to that....

"And what, bhikkhus, is the Dhamma for abandoning all through direct knowledge and full understanding? The eye is to be abandoned through direct knowledge and full understanding, forms are to be so abandoned, eye-consciousness is to be so abandoned, eye-contact is to be so abandoned, and whatever feeling arises with eye-contact as condition—whether pleasant or painful or neither-painful-nor-pleasant—that too is to be abandoned through direct knowledge and full understanding.

"The ear is to be abandoned through direct knowledge and full understanding ... The mind is to be abandoned through direct knowledge and full understanding, mental phenomena [17] are to be so abandoned, mind-consciousness is to be so abandoned, mind-contact is to be so abandoned, and whatever feeling arises with mind-contact as condition—whether pleasant or painful or neither-painful-nor-pleasant—that too is to be abandoned through direct knowledge and full understanding.

"This, bhikkhus, is the Dhamma for abandoning all through direct knowledge and full understanding."

26 (4) Full Understanding (1)

At Sāvatthī. "Bhikkhus, without directly knowing and fully understanding the all, without developing dispassion towards it and abandoning it, one is incapable of destroying suffering.[11]

"And what, bhikkhus, is that all without directly knowing and fully understanding which, without developing dispassion towards which and abandoning which, one is incapable of destroying suffering?

"Without directly knowing and fully understanding the eye, without developing dispassion towards it and abandoning it, one is incapable of destroying suffering. Without directly knowing and fully understanding forms ... eye-consciousness ... eye-contact ... and whatever feeling arises with eye-contact as condition ... without developing dispassion towards it and abandoning it, one is incapable of destroying suffering.

"Without directly knowing and fully understanding the ear … the mind … and whatever feeling arises with mind-contact as condition … without developing dispassion towards it and abandoning it, one is incapable of destroying suffering.

"This, bhikkhus, is the all without directly knowing and fully understanding which … one is incapable of destroying suffering.

"Bhikkhus, by directly knowing and fully understanding the all, by developing dispassion towards it and abandoning it, one is capable of destroying suffering. [18]

"And what, bhikkhus, is that all by directly knowing and fully understanding which, by developing dispassion towards which and abandoning which, one is capable of destroying suffering?

"By directly knowing and fully understanding the eye … the mind … and whatever feeling arises with mind-contact as condition … by developing dispassion towards it and abandoning it, one is capable of destroying suffering.

"This, bhikkhus, is the all by directly knowing and fully understanding which … one is capable of destroying suffering."

27 (5) Full Understanding (2)

"Bhikkhus, without directly knowing and fully understanding the all, without developing dispassion towards it and abandoning it, one is incapable of destroying suffering.

"And what, bhikkhus, is the all…?

"The eye and forms and eye-consciousness and things to be cognized by eye-consciousness.[12] [19] The ear and sounds and ear-consciousness and things to be cognized by ear-consciousness…. The mind and mental phenomena and mind-consciousness and things to be cognized by mind-consciousness.

"This, bhikkhus, is the all without directly knowing and fully understanding which, without developing dispassion towards which and abandoning which, one is incapable of destroying suffering.

"But, bhikkhus, by directly knowing and fully understanding the all, by developing dispassion towards it and abandoning it, one is capable of destroying suffering.

"And what, bhikkhus, is the all…? (*as above*)

"This, bhikkhus, is the all by directly knowing and fully

understanding which, by developing dispassion towards which and abandoning which, one is capable of destroying suffering."

28 (6) Burning

On one occasion the Blessed One was dwelling at Gayā, at Gayā's Head, together with a thousand bhikkhus. There the Blessed One addressed the bhikkhus thus:[13]

"Bhikkhus, all is burning. And what, bhikkhus, is the all that is burning? The eye is burning, forms are burning, eye-consciousness is burning, eye-contact is burning, and whatever feeling arises with eye-contact as condition—whether pleasant or painful or neither-painful-nor-pleasant—that too is burning. Burning with what? Burning with the fire of lust, with the fire of hatred, with the fire of delusion; burning with birth, aging, and death; with sorrow, lamentation, pain, displeasure, and despair, I say.

"The ear is burning ... [20] ... The mind is burning ... and whatever feeling arises with mind-contact as condition—whether pleasant or painful or neither-painful-nor-pleasant—that too is burning. Burning with what? Burning with the fire of lust, with the fire of hatred, with the fire of delusion; burning with birth, aging, and death; with sorrow, lamentation, pain, displeasure, and despair, I say.

"Seeing thus, bhikkhus, the instructed noble disciple experiences revulsion towards the eye, towards forms, towards eye-consciousness, towards eye-contact, towards whatever feeling arises with eye-contact as condition—whether pleasant or painful or neither-painful-nor-pleasant; experiences revulsion towards the ear ... towards the mind ... towards whatever feeling arises with mind-contact as condition.... Experiencing revulsion, he becomes dispassionate. Through dispassion [his mind] is liberated. When it is liberated there comes the knowledge: 'It's liberated.' He understands: 'Destroyed is birth, the holy life has been lived, what had to be done has been done, there is no more for this state of being.'"

This is what the Blessed One said. Elated, those bhikkhus delighted in the Blessed One's statement. And while this discourse was being spoken, the minds of the thousand bhikkhus were liberated from the taints by nonclinging.

29 (7) Weighed Down

Thus have I heard. On one occasion the Blessed One was dwelling at Rājagaha in the Bamboo Grove, the Squirrel Sanctuary. There the Blessed One addressed the bhikkhus thus:

"Bhikkhus, all is weighed down.[14] [21] And what, bhikkhus, is the all that is weighed down? The eye is weighed down, forms are weighed down, eye-consciousness is weighed down, eye-contact is weighed down, and whatever feeling arises with eye-contact as condition—whether pleasant or painful or neither-painful-nor-pleasant—that too is weighed down. Weighed down by what? Weighed down by birth, aging, and death; by sorrow, lamentation, pain, displeasure, and despair, I say.

"The ear is weighed down ... The mind is weighed down ... Weighed down by what? Weighed down by birth ... by despair, I say.

"Seeing thus ... He understands: '... there is no more for this state of being.'"

30 (8) Appropriate for Uprooting

"Bhikkhus, I will teach you the way that is appropriate for uprooting all conceivings. [22] Listen to that and attend closely, I will speak....

"And what, bhikkhus, is the way that is appropriate for uprooting all conceivings?[15] Here, bhikkhus, a bhikkhu does not conceive the eye, does not conceive in the eye, does not conceive from the eye, does not conceive, 'The eye is mine.'[16] He does not conceive forms ... eye-consciousness ... eye-contact ... and as to whatever feeling arises with eye-contact as condition—whether pleasant or painful or neither-painful-nor-pleasant—he does not conceive that, does not conceive in that, does not conceive from that, does not conceive, 'That is mine.'

"He does not conceive the ear ... He does not conceive the mind ... mental phenomena ... mind-consciousness ... mind-contact ... [23] and as to whatever feeling arises with mind-contact as condition ... he does not conceive that, does not conceive in that, does not conceive from that, does not conceive, 'That is mine.'

"He does not conceive all, does not conceive in all, does not conceive from all, does not conceive, 'All is mine.'

"Since he does not conceive anything thus, he does not cling to anything in the world. Not clinging, he is not agitated. Being unagitated, he personally attains Nibbāna. He understands: 'Destroyed is birth, the holy life has been lived, what had to be done has been done, there is no more for this state of being.'[17]

"This, bhikkhus, is the way that is appropriate for uprooting all conceivings."

31 (9) Suitable for Uprooting (1)

"Bhikkhus, I will teach you the way that is suitable for uprooting all conceivings.[18] Listen to that....

"And what, bhikkhus, is the way that is suitable for uprooting all conceivings? Here, bhikkhus, a bhikkhu does not conceive the eye, does not conceive in the eye, does not conceive from the eye, does not conceive, 'The eye is mine.' He does not conceive forms ... eye-consciousness ... eye-contact ... and as to whatever feeling arises with eye-contact as condition—whether pleasant or painful or neither-painful-nor-pleasant—he does not conceive that, does not conceive in that, does not conceive from that, does not conceive, 'That is mine.' For, bhikkhus, whatever one conceives, whatever one conceives in, whatever one conceives from, whatever one conceives as 'mine'—that is otherwise. The world, becoming otherwise, attached to becoming, seeks delight only in becoming.[19]

"He does not conceive the ear ... [24] ... He does not conceive the mind ... and as to whatever feeling arises with mind-contact as condition ... he does not conceive that, does not conceive in that, does not conceive from that, does not conceive, 'That is mine.' For, bhikkhus, whatever one conceives, whatever one conceives in, whatever one conceives from, whatever one conceives as 'mine'—that is otherwise. The world, becoming otherwise, attached to becoming, seeks delight only in becoming.

"Whatever, bhikkhus, is the extent of the aggregates, the elements, and the sense bases, he does not conceive that, does not conceive in that, does not conceive from that, does not conceive, 'That is mine.'

"Since he does not conceive anything thus, he does not cling to anything in the world. Not clinging, he is not agitated. Being unagitated, he personally attains Nibbāna. He understands: 'Destroyed is birth, the holy life has been lived, what had to be done has been done, there is no more for this state of being.'

"This, bhikkhus, is the way that is suitable for uprooting all conceivings."[20]

32 (10) Suitable for Uprooting (2)

"Bhikkhus, I will teach you the way that is suitable for uprooting all conceivings. Listen to that....

"And what, bhikkhus, is the way that is suitable for uprooting all conceivings? What do you think, bhikkhus, is the eye permanent or impermanent?" – "Impermanent, venerable sir." – "Is what is impermanent suffering or happiness?" – [25] "Suffering, venerable sir." – "Is what is impermanent, suffering, and subject to change fit to be regarded thus: 'This is mine, this I am, this is my self'?" – "No, venerable sir."

"Are forms permanent or impermanent?... Is eye-consciousness ... Is eye-contact ... Is any feeling that arises with eye-contact as condition—whether pleasant or painful or neither-painful-nor-pleasant—permanent or impermanent?...

"Is the ear permanent or impermanent?... Is the mind ... Is any feeling that arises with mind-contact as condition permanent or impermanent?" – "Impermanent, venerable sir." – "Is what is impermanent suffering or happiness?" – "Suffering, venerable sir." – "Is what is impermanent, suffering, and subject to change fit to be regarded thus: 'This is mine, this I am, this is my self'?" – "No, venerable sir." [26]

"Seeing thus, bhikkhus, the instructed noble disciple experiences revulsion towards the eye, towards forms, towards eye-consciousness, towards eye-contact, towards whatever feeling arises with eye-contact as condition—whether pleasant or painful or neither-painful-nor-pleasant. He experiences revulsion towards the ear ... towards the mind ... towards whatever feeling arises with mind-contact as condition.... Experiencing revulsion, he becomes dispassionate. Through dispassion [his mind] is liberated. When it is liberated there comes the knowledge: 'It's liberated.' He understands: 'Destroyed is birth, the holy life has been lived, what had to be done has been done, there is no more for this state of being.'

"This, bhikkhus, is the way that is suitable for uprooting all conceivings."

IV. Subject to Birth

33 (1) Subject to Birth

At Sāvatthī. "Bhikkhus, all is subject to birth. And what, bhikkhus, is the all that is subject to birth? [27] The eye is subject to birth. Forms ... Eye-consciousness ... Eye-contact ... Whatever feeling arises with eye-contact as condition ... that too is subject to birth.

"The ear ... The tongue ... The body ... The mind ... Whatever feeling arises with mind-contact as condition ... that too is subject to birth.

"Seeing thus, bhikkhus, the instructed noble disciple experiences revulsion towards the eye, towards forms, towards eye-consciousness, towards eye-contact ... He understands: '... there is no more for this state of being.'"

34 (2)–42 (10) Subject to Aging, Etc.

"Bhikkhus, all is subject to aging.... All is subject to sickness.... All is subject to death.... All is subject to sorrow.... All is subject to defilement.... [28] All is subject to destruction.... All is subject to vanishing.... All is subject to origination.... All is subject to cessation...." (*Each is to be completed as above.*)

V. Impermanent

43 (1)–52 (10) Impermanent, Etc.

At Sāvatthī. "Bhikkhus, all is impermanent.... All is suffering.... All is nonself.... [29] All is to be directly known.... All is to be fully understood.... All is to be abandoned.... All is to be realized.... All is to be fully understood through direct knowledge.... All is oppressed.... All is stricken...." (*Each to be completed as in* §33.) [30]

Division II
The Second Fifty

I. Ignorance

53 (1) Abandoning Ignorance

At Sāvatthī. Then a certain bhikkhu approached the Blessed One, paid homage to him, sat down to one side, [31] and said to him:

"Venerable sir, how should one know, how should one see, for ignorance to be abandoned and true knowledge to arise?"

"Bhikkhu, when one knows and sees the eye as impermanent, ignorance is abandoned and true knowledge arises.[21] When one knows and sees forms as impermanent … When one knows and sees as impermanent whatever feeling arises with mind-contact as condition—whether pleasant or painful or neither-painful-nor-pleasant—ignorance is abandoned and true knowledge arises. When one knows and sees thus, bhikkhu, ignorance is abandoned and true knowledge arises."

54 (2) Abandoning the Fetters

… "Venerable sir, how should one know, how should one see, for the fetters to be abandoned?"[22]

(*The Buddha's reply is as above.*)

55 (3) Uprooting the Fetters

… "Venerable sir, how should one know, how should one see, for the fetters to be uprooted?"

"Bhikkhu, when one knows and sees the eye as nonself, [32] the fetters are uprooted. When one knows and sees forms as nonself … (*all as above*) … When one knows and sees thus, bhikkhu, the fetters are uprooted."

56 (4)–59 (7) Abandoning the Taints, Etc.

… "Venerable sir, how should one know, how should one see, for the taints to be abandoned?… for the taints to be uprooted?… for the underlying tendencies to be abandoned?... for the underlying tendencies to be uprooted?"[23]

"Bhikkhu, when one knows and sees the eye as nonself, the underlying tendencies are uprooted. When one knows and sees forms as nonself ... (*all as above*) ... When one knows and sees thus, bhikkhu, the underlying tendencies are uprooted."

60 (8) The Full Understanding of All Clinging

"Bhikkhus, I will teach you the Dhamma for the full understanding of all clinging.[24] Listen to that....

"And what, bhikkhus, is the Dhamma for the full understanding of all clinging? In dependence on the eye and forms, eye-consciousness arises. The meeting of the three is contact. With contact as condition, feeling [comes to be]. [33] Seeing thus, the instructed noble disciple experiences revulsion towards the eye, towards forms, towards eye-consciousness, towards eye-contact, towards feeling. Experiencing revulsion, he becomes dispassionate. Through dispassion [the mind] is liberated. With its deliverance[25] he understands: 'Clinging has been fully understood by me.'

"In dependence on the ear and sounds ... In dependence on the mind and mental phenomena, mind-consciousness arises. The meeting of the three is contact. With contact as condition, feeling [comes to be]. Seeing thus, the instructed noble disciple experiences revulsion towards the mind, towards mental phenomena, towards mind-consciousness, towards mind-contact, towards feeling. Experiencing revulsion, he becomes dispassionate. Through dispassion [the mind] is liberated. With its deliverance he understands: 'Clinging has been fully understood by me.'

"This, bhikkhus, is the Dhamma for the full understanding of all clinging."

61 (9) The Exhaustion of All Clinging (1)

"Bhikkhus, I will teach you the Dhamma for the exhaustion of all clinging. Listen to that....

"And what, bhikkhus, is the Dhamma for the exhaustion of all clinging? In dependence on the eye and forms, eye-consciousness arises.... (*as above*) ... With its deliverance he understands: 'Clinging has been exhausted by me.'

"In dependence on the ear and sounds ... the mind and mental phenomena, mind-consciousness arises.... [34] ... With its deliverance he understands: 'Clinging has been exhausted by me.'

"This, bhikkhus, is the Dhamma for the exhaustion of all clinging."

62 (10) The Exhaustion of All Clinging (2)

"Bhikkhus, I will teach you the Dhamma for the exhaustion of all clinging. Listen to that...."

"And what, bhikkhus, is the Dhamma for the exhaustion of all clinging? What do you think, bhikkhus, is the eye permanent or impermanent?"

... (*To be completed as in §32*) ... [35]

"This, bhikkhus, is the Dhamma for the exhaustion of all clinging."

II. Migajāla

63 (1) Migajāla (1)

At Sāvatthī. Then the Venerable Migajāla approached the Blessed One, paid homage to him, sat down to one side, and said to him:[26]

"Venerable sir, it is said, 'a lone dweller, a lone dweller.'[27] [36] In what way, venerable sir, is one a lone dweller, and in what way is one dwelling with a partner?"[28]

"There are, Migajāla, forms cognizable by the eye that are desirable, lovely, agreeable, pleasing, sensually enticing, tantalizing. If a bhikkhu seeks delight in them, welcomes them, and remains holding to them, delight arises. When there is delight, there is infatuation. When there is infatuation, there is bondage. Bound by the fetter of delight, Migajāla, a bhikkhu is called one dwelling with a partner.

"There are, Migajāla, sounds cognizable by the ear ... odours cognizable by the nose ... tastes cognizable by the tongue ... tactile objects cognizable by the body ... mental phenomena cognizable by the mind that are desirable, lovely, agreeable, pleasing, sensually enticing, tantalizing. If a bhikkhu seeks delight in them ... he is called one dwelling with a partner.

"Migajāla, even though a bhikkhu who dwells thus resorts to forests and groves, to remote lodgings where there are few sounds and little noise, desolate, hidden from people, appropriate for seclusion, he is still called one dwelling with a partner. For what reason? Because craving is his partner, and he has not abandoned it; therefore he is called one dwelling with a partner.

"There are, Migajāla, forms cognizable by the eye that are desirable, lovely, agreeable, pleasing, sensually enticing, tantalizing. If a bhikkhu does not seek delight in them, does not welcome them, and does not remain holding to them, delight ceases. When there is no delight, there is no infatuation. When there is no infatuation, [37] there is no bondage. Released from the fetter of delight, Migajāla, a bhikkhu is called a lone dweller.

"There are, Migajāla, sounds cognizable by the ear ... odours cognizable by the nose ... tastes cognizable by the tongue ... tactile objects cognizable by the body ... mental phenomena cognizable by the mind that are desirable, lovely, agreeable, pleasing, sensually enticing, tantalizing. If a bhikkhu does not seek delight in them ... he is called a lone dweller.

"Migajāla, even though a bhikkhu who dwells thus lives in the vicinity of a village, associating with bhikkhus and bhikkhunīs, with male and female lay followers, with kings and royal ministers, with sectarian teachers and their disciples, he is still called a lone dweller. For what reason? Because craving is his partner, and he has abandoned it; therefore he is called a lone dweller."

64 (2) Migajāla (2)

Then the Venerable Migajāla approached the Blessed One, paid homage to him, sat down to one side, and said to him: "Venerable sir, it would be good if the Blessed One would teach me the Dhamma in brief, so that, having heard the Dhamma from the Blessed One, I might dwell alone, withdrawn, diligent, ardent, and resolute."

"There are, Migajāla, forms cognizable by the eye that are desirable, lovely, agreeable, pleasing, sensually enticing, tantalizing. If a bhikkhu seeks delight in them, welcomes them, and remains holding to them, delight arises. With the arising of delight, I say, Migajāla, there is the arising of suffering.

"There are, Migajāla, sounds cognizable by the ear ... odours cognizable by the nose ... tastes cognizable by the tongue ... tactile objects cognizable by the body ... mental phenomena cognizable by the mind that are desirable, lovely, agreeable, pleasing, sensually enticing, tantalizing. If a bhikkhu seeks delight in them, ... delight arises. [38] With the arising of delight, I say, Migajāla, there is the arising of suffering.

"There are, Migajāla, forms cognizable by the eye that are desirable, lovely, agreeable, pleasing, sensually enticing, tantalizing. If a bhikkhu does not seek delight in them, does not welcome them, and does not remain holding to them, delight ceases. With the cessation of delight, I say, Migajāla, comes the cessation of suffering.

"There are, Migajāla, sounds cognizable by the ear ... odours cognizable by the nose ... tastes cognizable by the tongue ... tactile objects cognizable by the body ... mental phenomena cognizable by the mind that are desirable, lovely, agreeable, pleasing, sensually enticing, tantalizing. If a bhikkhu does not seek delight in them ... delight ceases. With the cessation of delight, I say, Migajāla, comes the cessation of suffering."

Then the Venerable Migajāla, having delighted and rejoiced in the Blessed One's words, rose from his seat, and, after paying homage to the Blessed One, keeping him on his right, he departed.

Then, dwelling alone, withdrawn, diligent, ardent, and resolute, the Venerable Migajāla, by realizing it for himself with direct knowledge, in this very life entered and dwelt in that unsurpassed goal of the holy life for the sake of which clansmen rightly go forth from the household life into homelessness. He directly knew: "Destroyed is birth, the holy life has been lived, what had to be done has been done, there is no more for this state of being." And the Venerable Migajāla became one of the arahants.

65 (3) Samiddhi (1)

On one occasion the Blessed One was dwelling at Rājagaha in the Bamboo Grove, the Squirrel Sanctuary. Then the Venerable Samiddhi approached the Blessed One ... and said to him:[29] "Venerable sir, it is said, 'Māra, Māra.' In what way, venerable sir, might there be Māra or the description of Māra?"[30]

"Where there is the eye, Samiddhi, where there are forms, [39] eye-consciousness, things to be cognized by eye-consciousness, there Māra exists or the description of Māra.

"Where there is the ear ... the mind, where there are mental phenomena, mind-consciousness, things to be cognized by mind-consciousness, there Māra exists or the description of Māra.

"Where there is no eye, Samiddhi, no forms, no eye-consciousness, no things to be cognized by eye-consciousness, there Māra does not exist nor any description of Māra.

"Where there is no ear ... no mind, no mental phenomena, no mind-consciousness, no things to be cognized by mind-consciousness, there Māra does not exist nor any description of Māra."

66 (4) Samiddhi (2)

"Venerable sir, it is said, 'a being, a being.' In what way, venerable sir, might there be a being or the description of a being?"

(*The reply is as in the preceding sutta.*)

67 (5) Samiddhi (3)

"Venerable sir, it is said, 'suffering, suffering.' In what way, venerable sir, might there be suffering or the description of suffering?"...

68 (6) Samiddhi (4)

"Venerable sir, it is said, 'the world, the world.' In what way, venerable sir, might there be the world or the description of the world?"

"Where there is the eye, Samiddhi, where there are forms, eye-consciousness, things to be cognized by eye-consciousness, there the world exists or the description of the world.

"Where there is the ear ... [40] the mind, where there are mental phenomena, mind-consciousness, things to be cognized by mind-consciousness, there the world exists or the description of the world.

"Where there is no eye, Samiddhi, no forms, no eye-consciousness, no things to be cognized by eye-consciousness, there the world does not exist nor any description of the world.

"Where there is no ear ... no mind, no mental phenomena, no mind-consciousness, no things to be cognized by mind-consciousness, there the world does not exist nor any description of the world."

69 (7) Upasena

On one occasion the Venerable Sāriputta and the Venerable Upasena were dwelling at Rājagaha in the Cool Grove, in the Snake's Hood Grotto.[31] Now on that occasion a viper had fallen on the Venerable Upasena's body. Then the Venerable Upasena addressed the bhikkhus thus: "Come, friends, lift this body of mine on to the bed and carry it outside before it is scattered right here like a handful of chaff."[32]

When this was said, the Venerable Sāriputta said to the Venerable Upasena: "We do not see any alteration in the Venerable Upasena's body nor any change in his faculties; yet the Venerable Upasena says: 'Come, friends, lift this body of mine on to the bed and carry it outside before it is scattered right here like a handful of chaff.'"

"Friend Sāriputta, for one who thinks, 'I am the eye' or 'The eye is mine'; 'I am the ear' or 'The ear is mine' ... 'I am the mind' or 'The mind is mine,' there might be alteration of the body or a change of the faculties. But, friend Sāriputta, [41] it does not occur to me, 'I am the eye' or 'The eye is mine'; 'I am the ear' or 'The ear is mine' ... 'I am the mind' or 'The mind is mine,' so why should there be any alteration in my body or any change in my faculties?"[33]

"It must be because I-making, mine-making, and the underlying tendency to conceit have been thoroughly uprooted in the Venerable Upasena for a long time that it does not occur to him, 'I am the eye' or 'The eye is mine'; 'I am the ear' or 'The ear is mine' ... 'I am the mind' or 'The mind is mine.'"

Then those bhikkhus lifted the Venerable Upasena's body on to the bed and carried it outside. Then the Venerable Upasena's body was scattered right there just like a handful of chaff.

70 (8) Upavāṇa

Then the Venerable Upavāṇa approached the Blessed One ... and said to him: "Venerable sir, it is said, 'the directly visible Dhamma, the directly visible Dhamma.'[34] In what way, venerable sir, is the Dhamma directly visible, immediate, inviting one to come and see, applicable, to be personally experienced by the wise?"

"Here, Upavāṇa, having seen a form with the eye, a bhikkhu experiences the form as well as lust for the form. He understands that lust for forms exists internally thus: 'There is in me lust for forms internally.' Since that is so, Upavāṇa, the Dhamma is directly visible, immediate, inviting one to come and see, applicable, to be personally experienced by the wise. [42]

"Further, Upavāṇa, having heard a sound with the ear ... having cognized a mental phenomenon with the mind, a bhikkhu experiences the mental phenomenon as well as lust for the mental phenomenon. He understands that lust for mental phenomena exists internally thus: 'There is in me lust for mental phenomena internally.' Since that is so, Upavāṇa, the Dhamma is directly visible, immediate, inviting one to come and see, applicable, to be personally experienced by the wise.

"But here, Upavāṇa, having seen a form with the eye, a bhikkhu experiences the form without experiencing lust for the form. He understands that lust for forms does not exist internally thus: 'There is in me no lust for forms internally.' Since that is so, Upavāṇa, the Dhamma is directly visible, immediate, inviting one to come and see, applicable, to be personally experienced by the wise.

"Further, Upavāṇa, having heard a sound with the ear ... [43] ... having cognized a mental phenomenon with the mind, a bhikkhu experiences the mental phenomenon without experiencing lust for the mental phenomenon. He understands that lust for mental phenomena does not exist internally thus: 'There is in me no lust for mental phenomena internally.' Since that is so, Upavāṇa, the Dhamma is directly visible, immediate, inviting one to come and see, applicable, to be personally experienced by the wise."[35]

71 (9) The Six Bases for Contact (1)

"Bhikkhus, if a bhikkhu does not understand as they really are the origin and the passing away, the gratification, the danger, and the escape, in the case of these six bases for contact, then he has not lived the holy life; he is far away from this Dhamma and Discipline."

When this was said, a certain bhikkhu said to the Blessed One: "Here, venerable sir, I am lost,[36] for I do not understand as they really are the origin and the passing away, the gratification, the danger, and the escape, in the case of these six bases for contact."

"What do you think, bhikkhu, do you regard the eye thus: 'This is mine, this I am, this is my self'?"

"No, venerable sir."

"Good, bhikkhu! And here, bhikkhu, you should clearly see the eye as it really is with correct wisdom thus: 'This is not mine, this I am not, this is not my self.' This itself is the end of suffering.

"Do you regard the ear thus…? Do you regard the mind thus: 'This is mine, this I am, this is my self'?"

"No, venerable sir."

"Good, bhikkhu! And here, bhikkhu, you should clearly see the mind as it really is with correct wisdom thus: 'This is not mine, this I am not, this is not my self.' This itself is the end of suffering." [44]

72 (10) The Six Bases for Contact (2)

(*The first two paragraphs as in the preceding sutta.*)

"What do you think, bhikkhu, do you regard the eye thus: 'This is not mine, this I am not, this is not my self'?"

"Yes, venerable sir."

"Good, bhikkhu! And here, bhikkhu, you should clearly see the eye as it really is with correct wisdom thus: 'This is not mine, this I am not, this is not my self.' Thus this first base for contact will be abandoned by you for no future renewed existence.[37]

"Do you regard the ear thus…? Thus this second base for contact will be abandoned by you for no future renewed existence….

"Do you regard the mind thus: 'This is not mine, this I am not, this is not my self'?"

"Yes, venerable sir."

"Good, bhikkhu! And here, bhikkhu, you should clearly see the mind as it really is with correct wisdom thus: 'This is not mine, this I am not, this is not my self.' Thus this sixth base for contact will be abandoned by you for no future renewed existence."

73 (11) The Six Bases for Contact (3)

(*The first two paragraphs as in §71.*) [45]

"What do you think, bhikkhu, is the eye permanent or impermanent?" – "Impermanent, venerable sir." – "Is what is impermanent suffering or happiness?" – "Suffering, venerable sir." – "Is what is impermanent, suffering, and subject to change fit to be regarded thus: 'This is mine, this I am, this is my self'?" – "No, venerable sir."

"Is the ear ... the mind permanent or impermanent?" – "Impermanent, venerable sir." – "Is what is impermanent suffering or happiness?" – "Suffering, venerable sir." – "Is what is impermanent, suffering, and subject to change fit to be regarded thus: 'This is mine, this I am, this is my self'?" – "No, venerable sir."

"Seeing thus, bhikkhu, the instructed noble disciple experiences revulsion towards the eye ... revulsion towards the mind. Experiencing revulsion, he becomes dispassionate. Through dispassion [his mind] is liberated. When it is liberated there comes the knowledge: 'It's liberated.' He understands: 'Destroyed is birth, the holy life has been lived, what had to be done has been done, there is no more for this state of being.'"

[46]

III. Sick

74 (1) Sick (1)

At Sāvatthī. Then a certain bhikkhu approached the Blessed One, paid homage to him, sat down to one side, and said to him: "Venerable sir, in such and such a dwelling there is a certain newly ordained bhikkhu, not well known, who is sick, afflicted, gravely ill. It would be good, venerable sir, if the Blessed One would approach that bhikkhu out of compassion."

Then, when the Blessed One heard the words "newly ordained" and "sick," and understood that he was not a well-known bhikkhu, he went to him. That bhikkhu saw the Blessed One coming in the distance and stirred on his bed.[38] The Blessed One said to him: "Enough, bhikkhu, do not stir on your bed. There are these seats ready, I will sit down there."

The Blessed One then sat down on the appointed seat and said to that bhikkhu: "I hope you are bearing up, bhikkhu, I hope you are getting better. I hope that your painful feelings are subsiding and not increasing, and that their subsiding, not their increase, is to be discerned."

"Venerable sir, I am not bearing up, I am not getting better. Strong painful feelings are increasing in me, not subsiding, and their increase, not their subsiding, is to be discerned."

"I hope then, bhikkhu, that you are not troubled by remorse and regret."

"Indeed, venerable sir, I have quite a lot of remorse and regret." [47]

"I hope, bhikkhu, that you have nothing for which to reproach yourself in regard to virtue."

"I have nothing, venerable sir, for which to reproach myself in regard to virtue."

"Then, bhikkhu, if you have nothing for which to reproach yourself in regard to virtue, why are you troubled by remorse and regret?"

"I understand, venerable sir, that it is not for the sake of purification of virtue that the Dhamma has been taught by the Blessed One."

"If, bhikkhu, you understand that the Dhamma has not been taught by me for the sake of purification of virtue, then for what purpose do you understand the Dhamma to have been taught by me?"

"Venerable sir, I understand the Dhamma to have been taught by the Blessed One for the sake of the fading away of lust."[39]

"Good, good, bhikkhu! It is good that you understand the Dhamma to have been taught by me for the sake of the fading away of lust. For the Dhamma is taught by me for the sake of the fading away of lust.

"What do you think, bhikkhu, is the eye permanent or impermanent?" – "Impermanent, venerable sir."... "Is the ear ... the mind permanent or impermanent?" – "Impermanent, venerable sir." – "Is what is impermanent suffering or happiness?" – "Suffering, venerable sir." – "Is what is impermanent, suffering, and subject to change fit to be regarded thus: 'This is mine, this I am, this is my self'?" – "No, venerable sir."

"Seeing thus ... He understands: '... there is no more for this state of being.'"

This is what the Blessed One said. Elated, that bhikkhu delighted in the Blessed One's statement. And while this discourse was being spoken, there arose in that bhikkhu the dust-free, stainless vision of the Dhamma: "Whatever is subject to origination is all subject to cessation."[40]

75 (2) Sick (2)

(*As above down to:*) [48]

"If, bhikkhu you understand that the Dhamma has not been taught by me for the sake of purification of virtue, then for what purpose do you understand the Dhamma to have been taught by me?"

"Venerable sir, I understand the Dhamma to have been taught by the Blessed One for the sake of final Nibbāna without clinging."

"Good, good, bhikkhu! It is good that you understand the Dhamma to have been taught by me for the sake of final Nibbāna without clinging. For the Dhamma is taught by me for the sake of final Nibbāna without clinging.[41]

"What do you think, bhikkhu, is the eye permanent or impermanent?" – "Impermanent, venerable sir."... "Is the ear ... the nose ... the tongue ... the body ... the mind ... mind-consciousness ... mind-contact ... whatever feeling arises with mind-contact as condition—whether pleasant or painful or neither-painful-nor-pleasant—permanent or impermanent?" – "Impermanent, venerable sir." – "Is what is impermanent suffering or happiness?" – "Suffering, venerable sir." – "Is what is impermanent, suffering, and subject to change fit to be regarded thus: 'This is mine, this I am, this is my self'?" – "No, venerable sir."

"Seeing thus ... He understands: '... there is no more for this state of being.'"

This is what the Blessed One said. Elated, that bhikkhu delighted in the Blessed One's statement. And while this discourse was being spoken, that bhikkhu's mind was liberated from the taints by nonclinging.

76 (3) Rādha (1)

Then the Venerable Rādha approached the Blessed One ... and said to him: "Venerable sir, it would be good if the Blessed One would teach me the Dhamma in brief, so that, having heard the Dhamma from the Blessed One, I might dwell alone, withdrawn, diligent, ardent, and resolute."

"Rādha, you should abandon desire for whatever is impermanent. And what is impermanent? The eye is impermanent; you should abandon desire for it. Forms are impermanent ... Eye-consciousness is impermanent ... Eye-contact is impermanent ... Whatever feeling arises with eye-contact as condition—whether pleasant or painful or neither-painful-nor-pleasant—that too is impermanent; you should abandon desire for it.

"The ear ... The mind is impermanent ... Whatever feeling arises with mind-contact as condition ... that too is impermanent; you should abandon desire for it. [49] Rādha, you should abandon desire for whatever is impermanent."

77 (4) Rādha (2)

... "Rādha, you should abandon desire for whatever is suffering."...

78 (5) Rādha (3)

... "Rādha, you should abandon desire for whatever is nonself."...

79 (6) Abandoning Ignorance (1)

Then a certain bhikkhu approached the Blessed One ... and said to him: "Venerable sir, is there one thing through the abandoning of which ignorance is abandoned by a bhikkhu and true knowledge arises?"

"There is one thing, bhikkhu, through the abandoning of which ignorance is abandoned by a bhikkhu and true knowledge arises."

"And what is that one thing, venerable sir?" [50]

"Ignorance, bhikkhu, is that one thing through the abandoning of which ignorance is abandoned by a bhikkhu and true knowledge arises."[42]

"But, venerable sir, how should a bhikkhu know, how should he see, for ignorance to be abandoned by him and true knowledge to arise?"

"Bhikkhu, when a bhikkhu knows and sees the eye as impermanent, ignorance is abandoned by him and true knowledge arises. When he knows and sees forms as impermanent ... When he knows and sees as impermanent whatever feeling arises with mind-contact as condition ... ignorance is abandoned by him and true knowledge arises.

"When, bhikkhu, a bhikkhu knows and sees thus, ignorance is abandoned by him and true knowledge arises."

80 (7) Abandoning Ignorance (2)

(*As above down to:*)

"But, venerable sir, how should a bhikkhu know, how should he see, for ignorance to be abandoned by him and true knowledge to arise?"

"Here, bhikkhu, a bhikkhu has heard, 'Nothing is worth adhering to.' When a bhikkhu has heard, 'Nothing is worth adhering to,' he directly knows everything. Having directly known everything, he fully understands everything. Having fully understood everything, he sees all signs differently.[43] He sees the eye differently, he sees forms differently ... whatever feeling arises with mind-contact as condition ... that too he sees differently.

"When, bhikkhu, a bhikkhu knows and sees thus, ignorance is abandoned by him and true knowledge arises."

81 (8) A Number of Bhikkhus

Then a number of bhikkhus approached the Blessed One ... and said to him: [51] "Here, venerable sir, wanderers of other sects ask us: 'For what purpose, friends, is the holy life lived under the ascetic Gotama?' When we are asked thus, venerable sir, we answer those wanderers thus: 'It is, friends, for the full understanding of suffering that the holy life is lived under the Blessed One.' We hope, venerable sir, that when we answer thus we state what has been said by the Blessed One and do not misrepresent him with what is contrary to fact; that we explain in accordance with the Dhamma, and that no reasonable consequence of our assertion gives ground for criticism."[44]

"For sure, bhikkhus, when you answer thus you state what has been said by me and do not misrepresent me with what is contrary to fact; you explain in accordance with the Dhamma, and no reasonable consequence of your assertion gives ground for criticism. For, bhikkhus, it is for the full understanding of suffering that the holy life is lived under me.

"But, bhikkhus, if wanderers of other sects ask you: 'What, friends, is that suffering for the full understanding of which the holy life is lived under the ascetic Gotama?'—being asked thus, you should answer them thus: 'The eye, friends, is suffering: it is for the full understanding of this that the holy life is lived under the Blessed One. Forms are suffering ... Whatever feeling arises with eye-contact as condition ... that too is suffering ... The mind is suffering ... Whatever feeling arises with mind-contact as condition ... that too is suffering: it is for the full understanding of this that the holy life is lived under the Blessed One. This, friends, is that suffering for the full understanding of which the holy life is lived under the Blessed One.' [52]

"Being asked thus, bhikkhus, you should answer those wanderers of other sects in such a way."

82 (9) The World

Then a certain bhikkhu approached the Blessed One ... and said to him: "Venerable sir, it is said, 'the world, the world.' In what way, venerable sir, is it said 'the world'?"

"It is disintegrating, bhikkhu, therefore it is called the world.[45] And what is disintegrating? The eye, bhikkhu, is disintegrating, forms are disintegrating, eye-consciousness is disintegrating, eye-contact is disintegrating, and whatever feeling arises with eye-contact as condition ... that too is disintegrating. The ear is disintegrating ... The mind is disintegrating ... Whatever feeling arises with mind-contact as condition ... that too is disintegrating. It is disintegrating, bhikkhu, therefore it is called the world."

83 (10) Phagguna

Then the Venerable Phagguna approached the Blessed One ... and said to him: "Venerable sir, is there any eye by means of which one describing the Buddhas of the past could describe them—those who have attained final Nibbāna, cut through proliferation, cut through the rut, exhausted the round, and transcended all suffering?[46] Is there any ear by way of which one describing the Buddhas of the past could describe them?... Is there any mind by way of which one describing the Buddhas of the past could describe them—those who have attained final

Nibbāna, cut through proliferation, cut through the rut, exhausted the round, and transcended all suffering?"

"There is no eye, Phagguna, by means of which one describing the Buddhas of the past could describe them—those who have attained final Nibbāna, cut through proliferation, cut through the rut, exhausted the round, and transcended all suffering. There is no ear by means of which one describing the Buddhas of the past could describe them.... [53] There is no mind by means of which one describing the Buddhas of the past could describe them—those who have attained final Nibbāna, cut through proliferation, cut through the rut, exhausted the round, and transcended all suffering."

IV. Channa

84 (1) Subject to Disintegration

At Sāvatthī. Then the Venerable Ānanda approached the Blessed One ... and said to him: "Venerable sir, it is said, 'the world, the world.' In what way, venerable sir, is it said 'the world'?"

"Whatever is subject to disintegration, Ānanda, is called the world in the Noble One's Discipline.[47] And what is subject to disintegration? The eye, Ānanda, is subject to disintegration, forms ... eye-consciousness ... eye-contact ... whatever feeling arises with eye-contact as condition ... that too is subject to disintegration. The ear is subject to disintegration ... The mind is subject to disintegration ... Whatever feeling arises with mind-contact as condition ... that too is subject to disintegration. Whatever is subject to disintegration, Ānanda, is called the world in the Noble One's Discipline." [54]

85 (2) Empty Is the World

Then the Venerable Ānanda approached the Blessed One ... and said to him: "Venerable sir, it is said, 'Empty is the world, empty is the world.' In what way, venerable sir, is it said, 'Empty is the world'?"

"It is, Ānanda, because it is empty of self and of what belongs to self that it is said, 'Empty is the world.' And what is empty of self and of what belongs to self? The eye, Ānanda, is empty of self and of what belongs to self. Forms are empty of self and of what belongs to self. Eye-consciousness is empty of self and of what belongs to self. Eye-contact is empty of self and of what belongs to self.... Whatever feeling arises with mind-contact as condition—whether pleasant or painful or neither-painful-nor-pleasant—that too is empty of self and of what belongs to self.

"It is, Ānanda, because it is empty of self and of what belongs to self that it is said, 'Empty is the world.'"

86 (3) The Dhamma in Brief

Sitting to one side, the Venerable Ānanda said to the Blessed One: "Venerable sir, it would be good if the Blessed One would teach me the Dhamma in brief, so that, having heard the Dhamma from the Blessed One, I might dwell alone, withdrawn, diligent, ardent, and resolute."

"What do you think, Ānanda, is the eye permanent or impermanent?" – "Impermanent, venerable sir."

(Complete as in §32, down to "there is no more for this state of being.") [55]

87 (4) Channa

On one occasion the Blessed One was dwelling at Rājagaha in the Bamboo Grove, the Squirrel Sanctuary.[48] Now on that occasion the Venerable Sāriputta, the Venerable Mahācunda, and the Venerable Channa were dwelling on Mount Vulture Peak, and the Venerable Channa was sick, afflicted, gravely ill. Then, in the evening, the Venerable Sāriputta [56] emerged from seclusion, approached the Venerable Mahācunda, and said to him: "Come, friend Cunda, let us approach the Venerable Channa and ask about his illness."

"Yes, friend," the Venerable Mahācunda replied.

Then the Venerable Sāriputta and the Venerable Mahācunda approached the Venerable Channa and exchanged greetings with him, after which they sat down in the appointed seats. The Venerable Sāriputta then said to the Venerable Channa: "I hope you are bearing up, friend Channa, I hope you are getting better. I hope that your painful feelings are subsiding and not increasing, and that their subsiding, not their increase, is to be discerned."

"Friend Sāriputta, I am not bearing up, I am not getting better.[49] Strong painful feelings are increasing in me, not subsiding, and their increase, not their subsiding, is to be discerned. Just as if a strong man were to split my head open with a sharp sword, so too violent winds cut through my head. I am not bearing up.... Just as if a strong man were to tighten a tough leather strap around my head as a headband, so too there are violent pains in my head. I am not bearing up.... Just as if a skilled butcher or his apprentice were to carve up an ox's belly with a sharp butcher's knife, so too violent winds are carving up my belly. I am not bearing up.... Just as if two strong men were to seize a weaker man by both arms and roast him over a pit of hot coals, [57] so too there is a violent burning in my body. I am not bearing up, I am not getting better. Strong painful feelings are increasing in me, not subsiding, and their increase, not their subsiding, is to be discerned. I will use the knife,[50] friend Sāriputta, I have no desire to live."

"Let the Venerable Channa not use the knife. Let the Venerable Channa live. We want the Venerable Channa to live. If the Venerable Channa lacks suitable food, I will go in search of suitable food for him; if he lacks suitable medicine, I will go in search of suitable medicine for him; if he lacks a proper attendant, I will attend on him. Let the Venerable Channa not use the knife. Let the Venerable Channa live. We want the Venerable Channa to live."

"Friend Sāriputta, it is not that I lack suitable food; I have suitable food. It is not that I lack suitable medicine; I have suitable medicine. It is not that I lack proper attendants; I have proper attendants. Moreover, friend, for a long time the Teacher has been served by me in an agreeable way, not in a disagreeable way; for it is proper for a disciple to serve the Teacher in an agreeable way, not in a disagreeable way. Remember this, friend Sāriputta: the bhikkhu Channa will use the knife blamelessly."[51]

"We would ask the Venerable Channa about a certain point, if he would grant us the favour of answering our question." [58]

"Ask, friend Sāriputta. When I have heard I shall know."

"Friend Channa, do you regard the eye, eye-consciousness, and things cognizable with eye-consciousness thus: 'This is mine, this I am, this is my self'? Do you regard the ear, ear-consciousness, and things cognizable with ear-consciousness thus...? Do you regard the mind, mind-consciousness, and things cognizable with mind-consciousness thus: 'This is mine, this I am, this is my self'?

"Friend Sāriputta, I regard the eye, eye-consciousness, and things cognizable with eye-consciousness thus: 'This is not mine, this I am not, this is not my self.' I regard the ear, ear-consciousness, and things cognizable with ear-consciousness thus … I regard the mind, mind-consciousness, and things cognizable with mind-consciousness thus: 'This is not mine, this I am not, this is not my self.'"

"Friend Channa, what have you seen and directly known in the eye, in eye-consciousness, and in things cognizable with eye-consciousness, that you regard them thus: 'This is not mine, this I am not, this is not my self'? What have you seen and directly known in the ear … in the mind, in mind-consciousness, and in things cognizable with mind-consciousness, that you regard them thus: 'This is not mine, this I am not, this is not my self'?"

"Friend Sāriputta, it is because I have seen and directly known cessation in the eye, in eye-consciousness, and in things cognizable with eye-consciousness, that I regard them thus: 'This is not mine, this I am not, this is not my self.' It is because I have seen and directly known cessation in the ear … [59] … in the mind, in mind-consciousness, and in things cognizable with mind-consciousness, that I regard them thus: 'This is not mine, this I am not, this is not my self.'"[52]

When this was said, the Venerable Mahācunda said to the Venerable Channa: "Therefore, friend Channa, this teaching of the Blessed One is to be constantly given close attention: 'For one who is dependent there is wavering; for one who is independent there is no wavering. When there is no wavering, there is tranquillity; when there is tranquillity, there is no inclination; when there is no inclination, there is no coming and going; when there is no coming and going, there is no passing away and being reborn; when there is no passing away and being reborn, there is neither here nor beyond nor in between the two. This itself is the end of suffering.'"[53]

Then, when the Venerable Sāriputta and the Venerable Mahācunda had given the Venerable Channa this exhortation, they rose from their seats and departed. Then, soon after they had left, the Venerable Channa used the knife.[54]

Then the Venerable Sāriputta approached the Blessed One, paid homage to him, sat down to one side, and said to him: "Venerable sir, the Venerable Channa has used the knife. What is his destination, what is his future bourn?"

"Sāriputta, didn't the bhikkhu Channa declare his blamelessness right in your presence?"[55]

"Venerable sir, there is a Vajjian village named Pubbavijjhana. There the Venerable Channa had friendly families, intimate families, hospitable families."[56]

"The Venerable Channa did indeed have these friendly families, Sāriputta, intimate families, hospitable families; but I do not [60] say that to this extent one is blameworthy. Sāriputta, when one lays down this body and takes up another body, then I say one is blameworthy. This did not happen in the case of the bhikkhu Channa. The bhikkhu Channa used the knife blamelessly. Thus, Sāriputta, should you remember it."[57]

88 (5) Puṇṇa

Then the Venerable Puṇṇa approached the Blessed One ... and said to him:[58] "Venerable sir, it would be good if the Blessed One would teach me the Dhamma in brief, so that, having heard the Dhamma from the Blessed One, I might dwell alone, withdrawn, diligent, ardent, and resolute."

"Puṇṇa, there are forms cognizable by the eye that are desirable, lovely, agreeable, pleasing, sensually enticing, tantalizing. If a bhikkhu seeks delight in them, welcomes them, and remains holding to them, delight arises in him. With the arising of delight, Puṇṇa, there is the arising of suffering, I say. There are, Puṇṇa, sounds cognizable by the ear ... mental phenomena cognizable by the mind that are desirable, lovely, agreeable, pleasing, sensually enticing, tantalizing. If a bhikkhu seeks delight in them, welcomes them, and remains holding to them, delight arises in him. With the arising of delight, Puṇṇa, there is the arising of suffering, I say.

"Puṇṇa, there are forms cognizable by the eye ... mental phenomena cognizable by the mind that are desirable, lovely, agreeable, pleasing, sensually enticing, tantalizing. [61] If a bhikkhu does not seek delight in them, does not welcome them, and does not remain holding to them, delight ceases in him.

With the cessation of delight, Puṇṇa, there is the cessation of suffering, I say.

"Now that you have received this brief exhortation from me, Puṇṇa, in which country will you dwell?"

"There is, venerable sir, a country named Sunāparanta. I will dwell there."

"Puṇṇa, the people of Sunāparanta are wild and rough. If they abuse and revile you, what will you think about that?"

"Venerable sir, if the people of Sunāparanta abuse and revile me, then I will think: 'These people of Sunāparanta are excellent, truly excellent, in that they do not give me a blow with the fist.' Then I will think thus, Blessed One; then I will think thus, Fortunate One."

"But, Puṇṇa, if the people of Sunāparanta do give you a blow with the fist, what will you think about that?"

"Venerable sir, if the people of Sunāparanta give me a blow with the fist, then I will think: 'These people of Sunāparanta are excellent, truly excellent, in that they do not give me a blow with a clod.' Then I will think thus, Blessed One; then I will think thus, Fortunate One."

"But, Puṇṇa, if the people of Sunāparanta do give you a blow with a clod, what will you think about that?"

"Venerable sir, if the people of Sunāparanta give me a blow with a clod, then I will think: 'These people of Sunāparanta are excellent, truly excellent, in that they do not give me a blow with a rod.' [62] Then I will think thus, Blessed One; then I will think thus, Fortunate One."

"But, Puṇṇa, if the people of Sunāparanta do give you a blow with a rod, what will you think about that?"

"Venerable sir, if the people of Sunāparanta give me a blow with a rod, then I will think: 'These people of Sunāparanta are excellent, truly excellent, in that they do not stab me with a knife.' Then I will think thus, Blessed One; then I will think thus, Fortunate One."

"But, Puṇṇa, if the people of Sunāparanta do stab you with a knife, what will you think about that?"

"Venerable sir, if the people of Sunāparanta stab me with a knife, then I will think: 'These people of Sunāparanta are excellent, truly excellent, in that they do not take my life with a sharp knife.' Then I will think thus, Blessed One; then I will think thus, Fortunate One."

"But, Puṇṇa, if the people of Sunāparanta do take your life with a sharp knife, what will you think about that?"

"Venerable sir, if the people of Sunāparanta take my life with a sharp knife, then I will think: 'There have been disciples of the Blessed One who, being repelled, humiliated, and disgusted by the body and by life, sought for an assailant.[59] But I have come upon this assailant even without a search.' Then I will think thus, Blessed One; then I will think thus, Fortunate One."

"Good, good, Puṇṇa! Endowed with such self-control and peacefulness, you will be able to dwell in the Sunāparanta country. Now, Puṇṇa, you may go at your own convenience."[60]

Then, having delighted and rejoiced in the Blessed One's statement, the Venerable Puṇṇa rose from his seat, paid homage to the Blessed One, [63] and departed, keeping him on his right. He then set his lodging in order, took his bowl and outer robe, and set out to wander towards the Sunāparanta country. Wandering by stages, he eventually arrived in the Sunāparanta country, where he dwelt. Then, during that rains, the Venerable Puṇṇa established five hundred male lay followers and five hundred female lay followers in the practice, and he himself, during that same rains, realized the three true knowledges. And during that same rains he attained final Nibbāna.[61]

Then a number of bhikkhus approached the Blessed One ... and said to him: "Venerable sir, the clansman named Puṇṇa, who was given a brief exhortation by the Blessed One, has died. What is his destination? What is his future bourn?"

"Bhikkhus, the clansman Puṇṇa was wise. He practised in accordance with the Dhamma and did not trouble me on account of the Dhamma. The clansman Puṇṇa has attained final Nibbāna."

89 (6) Bāhiya

Then the Venerable Bāhiya approached the Blessed One ... and said to him: "Venerable sir, it would be good if the Blessed One would teach me the Dhamma in brief, so that, having heard the Dhamma from the Blessed One, I might dwell alone, withdrawn, diligent, ardent, and resolute."

"What do you think, Bāhiya, is the eye permanent or impermanent?" – "Impermanent, venerable sir." ... (*as in §32 down to:*)

[64] ... "He understands: 'Destroyed is birth, the holy life has been lived, what had to be done has been done, there is no more for this state of being.'"

Then the Venerable Bāhiya, having delighted and rejoiced in the Blessed One's words, rose from his seat, and, after paying homage to the Blessed One, keeping him on his right, he departed. Then, dwelling alone, withdrawn, diligent, ardent, and resolute, the Venerable Bāhiya, by realizing it for himself with direct knowledge, in this very life entered and dwelt in that unsurpassed goal of the holy life for the sake of which clansmen rightly go forth from the household life into homelessness. He directly knew: "Destroyed is birth, the holy life has been lived, what had to be done has been done, there is no more for this state of being." And the Venerable Bāhiya became one of the arahants.

90 (7) Being Stirred (1)

"Bhikkhus, being stirred is a disease, being stirred is a tumour, being stirred is a dart.[62] Therefore, bhikkhus, the Tathāgata dwells unstirred, with the dart removed. [65] Therefore, bhikkhus, if a bhikkhu should wish, 'May I dwell unstirred, with the dart removed!' he should not conceive the eye, should not conceive in the eye, should not conceive from the eye, should not conceive, 'The eye is mine.'[63]

"He should not conceive forms ... eye-consciousness ... eye-contact ... and as to whatever feeling arises with eye-contact as condition ... he should not conceive that, should not conceive in that, should not conceive from that, should not conceive, 'That is mine.'

"He should not conceive the ear ... He should not conceive the mind ... mental phenomena ... mind-consciousness ... mind-contact ... and as to whatever feeling arises with mind-contact as condition ... he should not conceive that, should not conceive in that, should not conceive from that, should not conceive, 'That is mine.'

"He should not conceive all, should not conceive in all, should not conceive from all, should not conceive, 'All is mine.'

"Since he does not conceive anything thus, he does not cling to anything in the world. Not clinging, he is not agitated. Being unagitated, he personally attains Nibbāna. [66] He understands:

'Destroyed is birth, the holy life has been lived, what had to be done has been done, there is no more for this state of being.'"

91 (8) Being Stirred (2)

"Bhikkhus, being stirred is a disease, being stirred is a tumour, being stirred is a dart. Therefore, bhikkhus, the Tathāgata dwells unstirred, with the dart removed. Therefore, bhikkhus, if a bhikkhu should wish, 'May I dwell unstirred, with the dart removed!' he should not conceive the eye ... forms ... eye-consciousness ... eye-contact ... and as to whatever feeling arises with eye-contact as condition ... he should not conceive that, should not conceive in that, should not conceive from that, should not conceive, 'That is mine.' For whatever one conceives, bhikkhus, whatever one conceives in, whatever one conceives from, whatever one conceives as 'mine'—that is otherwise. The world, becoming otherwise, attached to existence, seeks delight only in existence.[64]

"He should not conceive the ear ... He should not conceive the mind ... mental phenomena ... mind-consciousness ... mind-contact ... and as to whatever feeling arises with mind-contact as condition ... he should not conceive that, should not conceive in that, should not conceive from that, should not conceive, 'That is mine.' For whatever one conceives, bhikkhus, whatever one conceives in, [67] whatever one conceives from, whatever one conceives as 'mine'—that is otherwise. The world, becoming otherwise, attached to existence, seeks delight only in existence.

"Whatever, bhikkhus, is the extent of the aggregates, the elements, and the sense bases, he does not conceive that, does not conceive in that, does not conceive from that, does not conceive, 'That is mine.'

"Since he does not conceive anything thus, he does not cling to anything in the world. Not clinging, he is not agitated. Being unagitated, he personally attains Nibbāna. He understands: 'Destroyed is birth, the holy life has been lived, what had to be done has been done, there is no more for this state of being.'"

92 (9) The Dyad (1)

"Bhikkhus, I will teach you the dyad. Listen to that...."

"And what, bhikkhus, is the dyad? The eye and forms, the ear and sounds, the nose and odours, the tongue and tastes, the body and tactile objects, the mind and mental phenomena. This is called the dyad.

"If anyone, bhikkhus, should speak thus: 'Having rejected this dyad, I shall make known another dyad'—that would be a mere empty boast on his part. If he was questioned he would not be able to reply and, further, he would meet with vexation. For what reason? Because, bhikkhus, that would not be within his domain."[65]

93 (10) The Dyad (2)

"Bhikkhus, consciousness comes to be in dependence on a dyad. And how, bhikkhus, does consciousness come to be in dependence on a dyad? In dependence on the eye and forms there arises eye-consciousness. The eye is impermanent, changing, becoming otherwise; [68] forms are impermanent, changing, becoming otherwise. Thus this dyad is moving and tottering,[66] impermanent, changing, becoming otherwise.

"Eye-consciousness is impermanent, changing, becoming otherwise. The cause and condition for the arising of eye-consciousness is also impermanent, changing, becoming otherwise. When, bhikkhus, eye-consciousness has arisen in dependence on a condition that is impermanent, how could it be permanent?

"The meeting, the encounter, the concurrence of these three things is called eye-contact. Eye-contact too is impermanent, changing, becoming otherwise. The cause and condition for the arising of eye-contact is also impermanent, changing, becoming otherwise. When, bhikkhus, eye-contact has arisen in dependence on a condition that is impermanent, how could it be permanent?

"Contacted, bhikkhus, one feels, contacted one intends, contacted one perceives.[67] Thus these things too are moving and tottering, impermanent, changing, becoming otherwise.

"In dependence on the ear and sounds there arises ear-consciousness ... [69] ... In dependence on the mind and mental phenomena there arises mind-consciousness. The mind is impermanent, changing, becoming otherwise; mental phenomena are impermanent, changing, becoming otherwise. Thus this dyad is moving and tottering, impermanent, changing, becoming otherwise.

"Mind-consciousness is impermanent, changing, becoming

otherwise. The cause and condition for the arising of mind-consciousness is also impermanent, changing, becoming otherwise. When, bhikkhus, mind-consciousness has arisen in dependence on a condition that is impermanent, how could it be permanent?

"The meeting, the encounter, the concurrence of these three things is called mind-contact. Mind-contact too is impermanent, changing, becoming otherwise. The cause and condition for the arising of mind-contact is also impermanent, changing, becoming otherwise. When, bhikkhus, mind-contact has arisen in dependence on a condition that is impermanent, how could it be permanent?

"Contacted, bhikkhus, one feels, contacted one intends, contacted one perceives. Thus these things too are moving and tottering, impermanent, changing, becoming otherwise.

"It is in such a way, bhikkhus, that consciousness comes to be in dependence on a dyad."

[70] V. The Sixes

94 (1) Untamed, Unguarded[68]

At Sāvatthī. "Bhikkhus, these six bases for contact—if untamed, unguarded, unprotected, unrestrained—are bringers of suffering.[69] What six?

"The eye, bhikkhus, as a base for contact—if untamed, unguarded, unprotected, unrestrained—is a bringer of suffering. The ear as a base for contact … The mind as a base for contact … is a bringer of suffering. These six bases for contact—if untamed, unguarded, unprotected, unrestrained—are bringers of suffering.

"Bhikkhus, these six bases for contact—if well tamed, well guarded, well protected, well restrained—are bringers of happiness.[70] What six?

"The eye, bhikkhus, as a base for contact—if well tamed, well guarded, well protected, well restrained—is a bringer of happiness. The ear as a base for contact … The mind as a base for contact … is a bringer of happiness. These six bases for contact—if well tamed, well guarded, well protected, well restrained—are bringers of happiness."

This is what the Blessed One said. Having said this, the Fortunate One, the Teacher, further said this:

"Just six, O bhikkhus, are the bases for contact,
Where one unrestrained meets with suffering.
Those who know how to restrain them
Dwell uncorrupted, with faith their partner.

"Having seen forms that delight the mind
And having seen those that give no delight,
Dispel the path of lust towards the delightful
And do not soil the mind by thinking,
'[The other] is displeasing to me.' [71]

"Having heard sounds both pleasant and raucous,
Do not be enthralled with pleasant sound.
Dispel the course of hate towards the raucous,
And do not soil the mind by thinking,
'[This one] is displeasing to me.'

"Having smelt a fragrant, delightful scent,
And having smelt a putrid stench,
Dispel aversion towards the stench
And do not yield to desire for the lovely.

"Having enjoyed a sweet delicious taste,
And having sometimes tasted what is bitter,
Do not greedily enjoy the sweet taste,
Do not feel aversion towards the bitter.

"When touched by pleasant contact do not be enthralled,
Do not tremble when touched by pain.
Look evenly on both the pleasant and painful,
Not drawn or repelled by anything.

"When common people of proliferated perception
Perceive and proliferate they become engaged.
Having dispelled every mind-state bound to the home life,
One travels on the road of renunciation.[71]

"When the mind is thus well developed in six,
If touched, one's mind never flutters anywhere.

Having vanquished both lust and hate, O bhikkhus,
Go to the far shore beyond birth and death!" [72]

95 (2) Māluṅkyaputta

Then the Venerable Māluṅkyaputta approached the Blessed One ... and said to him:[72] "Venerable sir, it would be good if the Blessed One would teach me the Dhamma in brief, so that, having heard the Dhamma from the Blessed One, I might dwell alone, withdrawn, diligent, ardent, and resolute."

"Here now, Māluṅkyaputta, what should I say to the young bhikkhus when a bhikkhu like you—old, aged, burdened with years, advanced in life, come to the last stage—asks me for an exhortation in brief?"[73]

"Although, venerable sir, I am old, aged, burdened with years, advanced in life, come to the last stage, let the Blessed One teach me the Dhamma in brief, let the Fortunate One teach me the Dhamma in brief. Perhaps I may understand the meaning of the Blessed One's statement, perhaps I may become an heir to the Blessed One's statement."

"What do you think, Māluṅkyaputta, do you have any desire, lust, or affection for those forms cognizable by the eye that you have not seen and never saw before, that you do not see and would not think might be seen?"[74]

"No, venerable sir."

"Do you have any desire, lust, or affection for those sounds cognizable by the ear ... for those odours cognizable by the nose ... for those tastes cognizable by the tongue ... for those tactile objects cognizable by the body ... [73] for those mental phenomena cognizable by the mind that you have not cognized and never cognized before, that you do not cognize and would not think might be cognized?"

"No, venerable sir."

"Here, Māluṅkyaputta, regarding things seen, heard, sensed, and cognized by you: in the seen there will be merely the seen; in the heard there will be merely the heard; in the sensed there will be merely the sensed; in the cognized there will be merely the cognized.

"When, Māluṅkyaputta, regarding things seen, heard, sensed, and cognized by you, in the seen there will be merely the seen, in the heard there will be merely the heard, in the sensed there will be merely the sensed, in the cognized there will be merely the cognized, then, Māluṅkyaputta, you will not be 'by that.' When, Māluṅkyaputta, you are not 'by that,' then you will not be 'therein.' When, Māluṅkyaputta, you are not 'therein,' then you will be neither here nor beyond nor in between the two. This itself is the end of suffering."[75]

"I understand in detail, venerable sir, the meaning of what was stated by the Blessed One in brief:

"Having seen a form with mindfulness muddled,
Attending to the pleasing sign,
One experiences it with infatuated mind
And remains tightly holding to it.

"Many feelings flourish within,
Originating from the visible form,
Covetousness and annoyance as well
By which one's mind becomes disturbed.[76]
For one who accumulates suffering thus
Nibbāna is said to be far away.

"Having heard a sound with mindfulness muddled ... [74]

"Having smelt an odour with mindfulness muddled ...

"Having enjoyed a taste with mindfulness muddled ...

"Having felt a contact with mindfulness muddled ...

"Having known an object with mindfulness muddled ...
For one who accumulates suffering thus
Nibbāna is said to be far away.

"When, firmly mindful, one sees a form,
One is not inflamed by lust for forms;
One experiences it with dispassionate mind
And does not remain holding it tightly.

"One fares mindfully in such a way
That even as one sees the form,
And while one undergoes a feeling,
[Suffering] is exhausted, not built up.[77]
For one dismantling suffering thus,
Nibbāna is said to be close by.

"When, firmly mindful, one hears a sound,
One is not inflamed by lust for sounds; ... [75]

"When, firmly mindful, one smells an odour,
One is not inflamed by lust for odours; ...

"When, firmly mindful, one enjoys a taste,
One is not inflamed by lust for tastes; ...

"When, firmly mindful, one feels a contact,
One is not inflamed by lust for contacts; ...

"When, firmly mindful, one knows an object,
One is not inflamed by lust for objects; ...
For one diminishing suffering thus
Nibbāna is said to be close by.

"It is in such a way, venerable sir, that I understand in detail the meaning of what was stated by the Blessed One in brief."

"Good, good, Māluṅkyaputta! It is good that you understand in detail the meaning of what was stated by me in brief.

(*The Buddha here repeats the above verses in full.*) [76]

"It is in such a way, Māluṅkyaputta, that the meaning of what was stated by me in brief should be understood in detail."

Then the Venerable Māluṅkyaputta, having delighted and rejoiced in the Blessed One's words, rose from his seat, and, after paying homage to the Blessed One, keeping him on his right, he departed.

Then, dwelling alone, withdrawn, diligent, ardent, and resolute, the Venerable Māluṅkyaputta, by realizing it for himself with direct knowledge, in this very life entered and dwelt in that unsurpassed goal of the holy life for the sake of which clansmen rightly go forth from the household life into homelessness. He directly knew: "Destroyed is birth, the holy life has been lived, what had to be done has been done, there is no more for this state of being." And the Venerable Māluṅkyaputta became one of the arahants.

96 (3) Decline

"Bhikkhus, I will teach you about one who is subject to decline, about one who is not subject to decline, and about the six mastered bases. Listen to that....

"And how, bhikkhus, is one subject to decline?[78] Here, bhikkhus, when a bhikkhu has seen a form with the eye, there arise in him evil unwholesome states, memories and intentions connected with the fetters.[79] If the bhikkhu tolerates them and does not abandon them, dispel them, put an end to them, and obliterate them, he should understand this thus: 'I am declining away from wholesome states. For this has been called decline by the Blessed One.'

"Further, bhikkhus, when a bhikkhu has heard a sound with the ear ... cognized a mental phenomenon with the mind, [77] there arise in him evil unwholesome states, memories and intentions connected with the fetters. If the bhikkhu tolerates them and does not abandon them, dispel them, put an end to them, and obliterate them, he should understand this thus: 'I am declining away from wholesome states. For this has been called decline by the Blessed One.'

"It is in such a way, bhikkhus, that one is subject to decline.

"And how, bhikkhus, is one not subject to decline? Here, bhikkhus, when a bhikkhu has seen a form with the eye, there arise in him evil unwholesome states, memories and intentions connected with the fetters. If the bhikkhu does not tolerate them, but abandons them, dispels them, puts on end to them, and obliterates them, he should understand this thus: 'I am not declining away from wholesome states. For this has been called nondecline by the Blessed One.'

"Further, bhikkhus, when a bhikkhu has heard a sound with the ear ... cognized a mental phenomenon with the mind, there arise in him evil unwholesome states, memories and intentions connected with the fetters. If the bhikkhu does not tolerate them, but abandons them, dispels them, puts an end to them, and obliterates them, he should understand this thus: 'I am not declining away from wholesome states. For this has been called nondecline by the Blessed One.'

"It is in such a way, bhikkhus, that one is not subject to decline.

"And what, bhikkhus, are the six mastered bases?[80] Here, bhikkhus, when a bhikkhu has seen a form with the eye, there do not arise in him evil unwholesome states, nor any memories and intentions connected with the fetters. The bhikkhu should understand this thus: 'This base has been mastered. For this has been called a mastered base by the Blessed One.'

"Further, bhikkhus, when a bhikkhu has heard a sound with the ear ... cognized a mental phenomenon with the mind, there do not arise in him evil unwholesome states, nor any memories and intentions connected with the fetters. The bhikkhu should understand this thus: 'This base has been mastered. For this has been called a mastered base by the Blessed One.' These, bhikkhus, are called the six mastered bases." [78]

97 (4) Dwelling Negligently

"Bhikkhus, I will teach you about one who dwells negligently, and about one who dwells diligently. Listen to that....

"And how, bhikkhus, does one dwell negligently? If one dwells without restraint over the eye faculty, the mind is soiled[81] among forms cognizable by the eye. If the mind is soiled, there is no gladness. When there is no gladness, there is no rapture. When there is no rapture, there is no tranquillity. When there is no tranquillity, one dwells in suffering.[82] The mind of one who suffers does not become concentrated. When the mind is not concentrated, phenomena do not become manifest.[83] Because phenomena do not become manifest, one is reckoned as 'one who dwells negligently.'

"If one dwells without restraint over the ear faculty, the mind is soiled among sounds cognizable by the ear.... If one dwells without restraint over the mind faculty, the mind is soiled among mental phenomena cognizable by the mind.... Because phenomena do not become manifest, one is reckoned as 'one who dwells negligently.'

"It is in such a way, bhikkhus, that one dwells negligently.

"And how, bhikkhus, does one dwell diligently? If one dwells with restraint over the eye faculty, the mind is not soiled among forms cognizable by the eye. If the mind is not soiled, gladness is born. When one is gladdened, rapture is born. When the mind is uplifted by rapture, the body becomes tranquil. One tranquil in body experiences happiness. The mind of one who is happy becomes concentrated. When the mind is concentrated, [79] phenomena become manifest. Because phenomena become manifest, one is reckoned as 'one who dwells diligently.'

"If one dwells with restraint over the ear faculty, the mind is not soiled among sounds cognizable by the ear.... If one dwells with restraint over the mind faculty, the mind is not soiled among mental phenomena cognizable by the mind.... Because phenomena become manifest, one is reckoned as 'one who dwells diligently.'

"It is in such a way, bhikkhus, that one dwells diligently."

98 (5) Restraint

"Bhikkhus, I will teach you restraint and nonrestraint. Listen to that....

"And how, bhikkhus, is there nonrestraint? There are, bhikkhus, forms cognizable by the eye that are desirable, lovely, agreeable, pleasing, sensually enticing, tantalizing. If a bhikkhu seeks delight in them, welcomes them, and remains holding to them, he should understand this thus: 'I am declining away from wholesome states. For this has been called decline by the Blessed One.'

"There are, bhikkhus, sounds cognizable by the ear ... mental phenomena cognizable by the mind that are desirable, lovely, agreeable, pleasing, sensually enticing, tantalizing. If a bhikkhu seeks delight in them, welcomes them, and remains holding to them, he should understand this thus: 'I am declining away from wholesome states. For this has been called decline by the Blessed One.'

"Such, bhikkhus, is nonrestraint.

"And how, bhikkhus, is there restraint? There are, bhikkhus, forms cognizable by the eye that are desirable, lovely, agreeable, pleasing, sensually enticing, tantalizing. If a bhikkhu does not seek delight in them, does not welcome them, and does not remain holding to them, he should understand this thus: [80] 'I am not declining away from wholesome states. For this has been called nondecline by the Blessed One.'

"There are, bhikkhus, sounds cognizable by the ear ... mental phenomena cognizable by the mind that are desirable, lovely, agreeable, pleasing, sensually enticing, tantalizing. If a bhikkhu does not seek delight in them, does not welcome them, and does not remain holding to them, he should understand this thus: 'I am not declining away from wholesome states. For this has been called nondecline by the Blessed One.'

"Such, bhikkhus, is restraint."

99 (6) Concentration

"Bhikkhus, develop concentration. A bhikkhu who is concentrated understands things as they really are.[84]

"And what does he understand as they really are? He understands as it really is: 'The eye is impermanent.' He understands as it really is: 'Forms are impermanent.'... 'Eye-consciousness is impermanent.'... 'Eye-contact is impermanent.'... 'Whatever feeling arises with eye-contact as condition—whether pleasant or painful or neither-painful-nor-pleasant—that too is impermanent.'...

"He understand as it really is: 'The mind is impermanent.'... He understand as it really is: 'Whatever feeling arises with mind-contact as condition ... that too is impermanent.'

"Bhikkhus, develop concentration. A bhikkhu who is concentrated understands things as they really are."

100 (7) Seclusion

"Bhikkhus, make an exertion in seclusion. A secluded bhikkhu understands things as they really are."

(*The rest is identical with the preceding sutta.*) [81]

101 (8) Not Yours (1)

"Bhikkhus, whatever is not yours, abandon it.[85] When you have abandoned it, that will lead to your welfare and happiness. And what is it, bhikkhus, that is not yours? The eye is not yours: abandon it. When you have abandoned it, that will lead to your welfare and happiness. Forms are not yours ... Eye-consciousness is not yours ... Eye-contact is not yours ... Whatever feeling arises with eye-contact as condition—whether pleasant or painful or neither-painful-nor-pleasant—that too is not yours: abandon it. When you have abandoned it, that will lead to your welfare and happiness.

"The ear is not yours ... [82] ... The mind is not yours ... Whatever feeling arises with mind-contact as condition ... that too is not yours: abandon it. When you have abandoned it, that will lead to your welfare and happiness.

"Suppose, bhikkhus, people were to carry off the grass, sticks, branches, and foliage in this Jeta's Grove, or to burn them, or to do with them as they wish. Would you think: 'People are carrying us off, or burning us, or doing with us as they wish'?"

"No, venerable sir. For what reason? Because, venerable sir, that is neither our self nor what belongs to our self."

"So too, bhikkhus, the eye is not yours ... Whatever feeling arises with mind-contact as condition ... that too is not yours: abandon it. When you have abandoned it, that will lead to your welfare and happiness."

102 (9) Not Yours (2)

(*This sutta is identical with the preceding one except that it omits the simile.*) [83]

103 (10) Uddaka

"Bhikkhus, Uddaka Rāmaputta used to make this declaration:

"'This, surely a knowledge-master—
This, surely a universal conqueror—
This, surely he has excised
The tumour's root not excised before!'[86]

"Bhikkhus, though Uddaka Rāmaputta was not himself a knowledge-master, he declared: 'I am a knowledge-master.' Though he was not himself a universal conqueror, he declared: 'I am a universal conqueror.' Though he had not excised the tumour's root, he declared: 'I have excised the tumour's root.' But here, bhikkhus, a bhikkhu speaking rightly might say:

"'This, surely a knowledge-master—
This, surely a universal conqueror—
This, surely he has excised
The tumour's root not excised before!'

"And how, bhikkhus, is one a knowledge-master? When a bhikkhu understands as they really are the origin, the passing away, the gratification, the danger, and the escape in regard to the six bases for contact, such a bhikkhu is a knowledge-master.

"And how, bhikkhus, is a bhikkhu a universal conqueror? When, having understood as they really are the origin, the passing away, the gratification, the danger, and the escape in regard to the six bases for contact, a bhikkhu is liberated by nonclinging, such a bhikkhu is a universal conqueror.

"And how, bhikkhus, does a bhikkhu excise the tumour's root not excised before? 'The tumour,' bhikkhus: this is a designation for this body consisting of the four great elements, originating from mother and father, built up out of rice and gruel, subject to impermanence, to rubbing and pressing, to breaking apart and dispersal.[87] 'The tumour's root': this is a designation for craving. When craving has been abandoned by a bhikkhu, cut off at the root, [84] made like a palm stump, obliterated so that it is no more subject to future arising, in such a case the bhikkhu has excised the tumour's root not excised before.

"Bhikkhus, though Uddaka Rāmaputta was not himself a knowledge-master, he declared: 'I am a knowledge-master.'... But here, bhikkhus, a bhikkhu speaking rightly might say:

"'This, surely a knowledge-master—
This, surely a universal conqueror—
This, surely he has excised
The tumour's root not excised before!'"

[85]

Division III
The Third Fifty

I. Secure from Bondage

104 (1) Secure from Bondage

At Sāvatthī. "Bhikkhus, I will teach you a Dhamma exposition on the theme of the one who declares the exertion to become secure from bondage.[88] Listen to that....

"And what, bhikkhus, is the Dhamma exposition on the theme of the one who declares the exertion to become secure from bondage? There are, bhikkhus, forms cognizable by the eye that are desirable, lovely, agreeable, pleasing, sensually enticing, tantalizing. These have been abandoned by the Tathāgata, cut off at the root, made like a palm stump, obliterated so that they are no more subject to future arising. He declares an exertion [should be made] for their abandoning. Therefore the Tathāgata is called one who declares the exertion to become secure from bondage.[89]

"There are, bhikkhus, sounds cognizable by the ear ... mental phenomena cognizable by the mind that are desirable, lovely, agreeable, pleasing, sensually enticing, tantalizing. These have been abandoned by the Tathāgata, cut off at the root, made like a palm stump, obliterated so that they are no more subject to future arising. He declares an exertion [should be made] for their abandoning. Therefore the Tathāgata is called one who declares the exertion to become secure from bondage.

"This, bhikkhus, is the Dhamma exposition on the theme of the one who declares the exertion to become secure from bondage."

105 (2) By Clinging

"Bhikkhus, when what exists, by clinging to what, do pleasure and pain arise internally?"[90]

"Venerable sir, our teachings are rooted in the Blessed One...."

"When there is the eye, bhikkhus, by clinging to the eye, pleasure and pain arise internally. When there is the ear ... the mind, by clinging to the mind, pleasure and pain arise internally.

"What do you think, bhikkhus, is the eye permanent or impermanent?"

"Impermanent, venerable sir."

"Is what is impermanent suffering or happiness?"

"Suffering, venerable sir."

"But without clinging to what is impermanent, suffering, and subject to change, could pleasure and pain arise internally?"

"No, venerable sir." [86]

"Is the ear ... the mind permanent or impermanent?... But without clinging to what is impermanent, suffering, and subject to change, could pleasure and pain arise internally?"

"No, venerable sir."

"Seeing thus, bhikkhus, the instructed noble disciple experiences revulsion towards the eye ... the mind. Experiencing revulsion, he becomes dispassionate. Through dispassion [his mind] is liberated. When it is liberated there comes the knowledge: 'It's liberated.' He understands: 'Destroyed is birth, the holy life has been lived, what had to be done has been done, there is no more for this state of being.'"

106 (3) The Origin of Suffering

(*Identical with 12:43.*) [87]

107 (4) The Origin of the World

(*Identical with 12:44.*) [88]

108 (5) I Am Superior

"Bhikkhus, when what exists, by clinging to what, by adhering to what, does the thought occur: 'I am superior' or 'I am equal' or 'I am inferior'?"[91]

"Venerable sir, our teachings are rooted in the Blessed One...."

"When there is the eye, bhikkhus, by clinging to the eye, by adhering to the eye, the thought occurs: 'I am superior' or 'I am equal' or 'I am inferior.' When there is the ear ... When there is the mind, by clinging to the mind, by adhering to the mind, the thought occurs: 'I am superior' or 'I am equal' or 'I am inferior.'

"What do you think, bhikkhus, is the eye ... the mind permanent or impermanent?"

"Impermanent, venerable sir."...

"But without clinging to what is impermanent, suffering, and subject to change, could the thought occur: 'I am superior' or 'I am equal' or 'I am inferior'?"

"No, venerable sir."

"Seeing thus … He understands: '… there is no more for this state of being.'" [89]

109 (6) Things That Fetter

"Bhikkhus, I will teach you the things that fetter and the fetter. Listen to that….[92]

"And what, bhikkhus, are the things that fetter, and what is the fetter? The eye, bhikkhus, is a thing that fetters; the desire and lust for it is the fetter there. The ear is a thing that fetters … The mind is a thing that fetters; the desire and lust for it is the fetter there. These are called the things that fetter, and this the fetter."

110 (7) Things That Can Be Clung To

"Bhikkhus, I will teach you the things that can be clung to and the clinging. Listen to that….

"And what, bhikkhus, are the things that can be clung to, and what is the clinging? The eye, bhikkhus, is a thing that can be clung to; the desire and lust for it is the clinging there. The ear is a thing that can be clung to … The mind is a thing that can be clung to; the desire and lust for it is the clinging there. These are called the things that can be clung to, and this the clinging."

111 (8) Fully Understanding (1)

"Bhikkhus, without directly knowing and fully understanding the eye,[93] without developing dispassion towards it and abandoning it, one is incapable of destroying suffering. Without directly knowing and fully understanding the ear … the mind, without developing dispassion towards it and abandoning it, one is incapable of destroying suffering. But by directly knowing and fully understanding the eye … the mind, by developing dispassion towards it and abandoning it, one is capable of destroying suffering." [90]

112 (9) Fully Understanding (2)

(*Identical with §111, but stated by way of the six external sense bases.*)

113 (10) Listening In

(*Identical with 12:45.*) [91]

II. The World and Cords of Sensual Pleasure

114 (1) Māra's Snare (1)

"Bhikkhus, there are forms cognizable by the eye that are desirable, lovely, agreeable, pleasing, sensually enticing, tantalizing. If a bhikkhu seeks delight in them, welcomes them, and remains holding to them, he is called a bhikkhu who has entered Māra's lair, who has come under Māra's control; Māra's snare has been fastened to him[94] so that he is bound by the bondage of Māra and the Evil One can do with him as he wishes.

"There are, bhikkhus, sounds cognizable by the ear ... mental phenomena cognizable by the mind that are desirable, lovely, agreeable, pleasing, sensually enticing, tantalizing. If a bhikkhu seeks delight in them ... [92] ... the Evil One can do with him as he wishes.

"There are, bhikkhus, forms cognizable by the eye that are desirable, lovely, agreeable, pleasing, sensually enticing, tantalizing. If a bhikkhu does not seek delight in them, does not welcome them, and does not remain holding to them, he is called a bhikkhu who has not entered Māra's lair, who has not come under Māra's control; Māra's snare has been unfastened from him so that he is not bound by the bondage of Māra and the Evil One cannot do with him as he wishes.

"There are, bhikkhus, sounds cognizable by the ear ... mental phenomena cognizable by the mind that are desirable, lovely, agreeable, pleasing, sensually enticing, tantalizing. [93] If a bhikkhu does not seek delight in them ... the Evil One cannot do with him as he wishes."

115 (2) Māra's Snare (2)

"Bhikkhus, there are forms cognizable by the eye that are desirable, lovely, agreeable, pleasing, sensually enticing, tantalizing. If a bhikkhu seeks delight in them, welcomes them, and remains holding to them, he is called a bhikkhu who is bound among forms cognizable by the eye, who has entered Māra's lair, who has come under Māra's control; [Māra's snare has been fastened to him so that he is bound by the bondage of Māra][95] and the Evil One can do with him as he wishes.

"There are, bhikkhus, sounds cognizable by the ear … mental phenomena cognizable by the mind that are desirable, lovely, agreeable, pleasing, sensually enticing, tantalizing. If a bhikkhu seeks delight in them … the Evil One can do with him as he wishes.

"There are, bhikkhus, forms cognizable by the eye that are desirable, lovely, agreeable, pleasing, sensually enticing, tantalizing. If a bhikkhu does not seek delight in them, does not welcome them, and does not remain holding to them, he is called a bhikkhu who is free among forms cognizable by the eye, who has not entered Māra's lair, who has not come under Māra's control; [Māra's snare has been unfastened from him so that he is not bound by the bondage of Māra] and the Evil One cannot do with him as he wishes.

"There are, bhikkhus, sounds cognizable by the ear … mental phenomena cognizable by the mind that are desirable, lovely, agreeable, pleasing, sensually enticing, tantalizing. If a bhikkhu does not seek delight in them … the Evil One cannot do with him as he wishes."

116 (3) Going to the End of the World

"Bhikkhus, I say that the end of the world cannot be known, seen, or reached by travelling. Yet, bhikkhus, I also say that without reaching the end of the world there is no making an end to suffering."[96]

Having said this, the Blessed One rose from his seat and entered his dwelling.[97] Then, soon after the Blessed One had left, the bhikkhus considered: "Now, friends, the Blessed One has risen from his seat and entered his dwelling after reciting a synopsis in brief without expounding the meaning in detail. Now who will expound in detail the meaning of the synopsis that the Blessed One recited in brief?" Then they considered: "The Venerable Ānanda is praised by the Teacher and esteemed by his wise brothers in the holy life; the Venerable Ānanda is capable of expounding in detail the meaning of this synopsis recited in brief by the Blessed One without expounding the meaning in detail. Let us approach him and ask him the meaning of this."

Then those bhikkhus approached the Venerable Ānanda and exchanged greetings with him, after which they sat down to one side and told him what had taken place, [94] adding: "Let the Venerable Ānanda expound it to us."

[The Venerable Ānanda replied:] "Friends, it is as though a man needing heartwood, seeking heartwood, wandering in search of heartwood, would pass over the root and trunk of a great tree standing possessed of heartwood, thinking that heartwood should be sought among the branches and foliage. And so it is with you venerable ones: when you were face to face with the Teacher you passed by the Blessed One, thinking that I should be asked about the meaning. For, friends, knowing, the Blessed One knows; seeing, he sees; he has become vision, he has become knowledge, he has become the Dhamma, he has become the holy one; he is the expounder, the proclaimer, the elucidator of meaning, the giver of the Deathless, the lord of the Dhamma, the Tathāgata. That was the time when you should have asked the Blessed One the meaning. [95] As he explained it to you, so you should have remembered it."

"Surely, friend Ānanda, knowing, the Blessed One knows; seeing, he sees; he has become vision ... the Tathāgata. That was the time when we should have asked the Blessed One the meaning, and as he explained it to us, so we should have remembered it. Yet the Venerable Ānanda is praised by the Teacher and esteemed by his wise brothers in the holy life; the Venerable Ānanda is capable of expounding the detailed meaning of this synopsis recited in brief by the Blessed One without expounding the meaning in detail. Let the Venerable Ānanda expound it without finding it troublesome."

"Then listen, friends, and attend closely to what I shall say."

"Yes, friend," the bhikkhus replied. The Venerable Ānanda said this:

"Friends, when the Blessed One rose from his seat and entered his dwelling after reciting a synopsis in brief without expounding the meaning in detail, that is: 'Bhikkhus, I say that the end of the world cannot be known, seen, or reached by travelling. Yet, bhikkhus, I also say that without reaching the end of the world there is no making an end to suffering,' I understand the detailed meaning of this synopsis as follows: That in the world by which one is a perceiver of the world, a conceiver of the world—this is called the world in the Noble One's Discipline.[98] And what, friends, is that in the world by which one is a perceiver of the world, a conceiver of the world? The eye is that in the world by which one is a perceiver of the world, a conceiver of the world.[99] The ear ... The nose ... The tongue ... The body ... The mind is that in the world by which one is a perceiver of the world, a conceiver of the world. That in the world by which one is a perceiver of the world, a conceiver of the world—this is called the world in the Noble One's Discipline. [96]

"Friends, when the Blessed One rose from his seat and entered his dwelling after reciting a synopsis in brief without expounding the meaning in detail, that is: 'Bhikkhus, I say that the end of the world cannot be known, seen, or reached by travelling. Yet, bhikkhus, I also say that without reaching the end of the world there is no making an end to suffering,' I understand the meaning of this synopsis in detail to be thus. Now, friends, if you wish, go to the Blessed One and ask him about the meaning of this. As the Blessed One explains it to you, so you should remember it."

"Yes, friends," those bhikkhus replied, and having risen from their seats, they went to the Blessed One. After paying homage to him, they sat down to one side and told the Blessed One all that had taken place after he had left, adding: [97] "Then, venerable sir, we approached the Venerable Ānanda and asked him about the meaning. The Venerable Ānanda expounded the meaning to us in these ways, with these terms, with these phrases."

"Ānanda is wise, bhikkhus, Ānanda has great wisdom. If you had asked me the meaning of this, I would have explained it to you in the same way that it has been explained by Ānanda. Such is the meaning of this, and so you should remember it."

117 (4) Cords of Sensual Pleasure

"Bhikkhus, before my enlightenment, while I was still a bodhisatta, not yet fully enlightened, the thought occurred to me: 'My mind may often stray towards those five cords of sensual pleasure that have already left their impression on the heart[100] but which have passed, ceased, and changed, or towards those that are present, or slightly towards those in the future.' Then it occurred to me: 'Being set on my own welfare,[101] I should practise diligence, mindfulness, and guarding of the mind in regard to those five cords of sensual pleasure that have already left their impression on the heart, which have passed, ceased, and changed.'

"Therefore, bhikkhus, in your case too your minds may often stray towards those five cords of sensual pleasure that have already left their impression on the heart but which have passed, ceased, and changed, or towards those that are present, or slightly towards those in the future. Therefore, bhikkhus, [98] being set on your own welfare, you should practise diligence, mindfulness, and guarding of the mind in regard to those five cords of sensual pleasure that have already left their impression on the heart but which have passed, ceased, and changed.

"Therefore, bhikkhus, that base should be understood,[102] where the eye ceases and perception of forms fades away.[103] That base should be understood, where the ear ceases and perception of sounds fades away.... That base should be understood, where the mind ceases and perception of mental phenomena fades away. That base should be understood."

Having said this, the Blessed One rose from his seat and entered his dwelling. Then, soon after the Blessed One had left, the bhikkhus considered ... (*all as in preceding sutta down to:*) [99–100] ... The Venerable Ānanda said this:

"Friends, when the Blessed One rose from his seat and entered his dwelling after reciting a synopsis in brief without expounding the meaning in detail—that is: 'Therefore, bhikkhus, that base should be understood, where the eye ceases and perception of forms fades away.... That base should be understood, where the mind ceases and perception of mental phenomena fades away. That base should be understood'—I understand the detailed meaning of this synopsis as follows: This was stated by the Blessed One, friends, with reference to the cessation of the six sense bases.[104]

"Friends, when the Blessed One rose from his seat and entered his dwelling after reciting a synopsis in brief without expounding the meaning in detail ... I understand the meaning of this synopsis in detail to be thus. Now, friends, if you wish, go to the Blessed One and ask him about the meaning of this. As the Blessed One explains it to you, so you should remember it."

"Yes, friends," those bhikkhus replied, and having risen from their seats, they went to the Blessed One. After paying homage to him, they sat down to one side and told the Blessed One all that had taken place after he had left, adding: [101] "Then, venerable sir, we approached the Venerable Ānanda and asked him about the meaning. The Venerable Ānanda expounded the meaning to us in these ways, with these terms, with these phrases."

"Ānanda is wise, bhikkhus, Ānanda has great wisdom. If you had asked me the meaning of this, I would have explained it to you in the same way that it has been explained by Ānanda. Such is the meaning of this, and so you should remember it."

118 (5) Sakka's Question

On one occasion the Blessed One was dwelling at Rājagaha on Mount Vulture Peak. Then Sakka, lord of the devas, approached the Blessed One, paid homage to him, stood to one side, and said to him:

"Venerable sir, what is the cause and reason [102] why some beings here do not attain Nibbāna in this very life? And what is the cause and reason why some beings here attain Nibbāna in this very life?"

"There are, lord of the devas, forms cognizable by the eye that are desirable, lovely, agreeable, pleasing, sensually enticing, tantalizing. If a bhikkhu seeks delight in them, welcomes them, and remains holding to them, his consciousness becomes dependent upon them and clings to them. A bhikkhu with clinging does not attain Nibbāna.[105]

"There are, lord of the devas, sounds cognizable by the ear ... mental phenomena cognizable by the mind that are desirable, lovely, agreeable, pleasing, sensually enticing, tantalizing. If a bhikkhu seeks delight in them, welcomes them, and remains holding to them, his consciousness becomes dependent upon them and clings to them. A bhikkhu with clinging does not attain Nibbāna.

"This is the cause and reason, lord of the devas, why some beings here do not attain Nibbāna in this very life.

"There are, lord of the devas, forms cognizable by the eye ... mental phenomena cognizable by the mind that are desirable, lovely, agreeable, pleasing, sensually enticing, tantalizing. If a bhikkhu does not seek delight in them, does not welcome them, and does not remain holding to them, his consciousness does not become dependent upon them or cling to them. A bhikkhu without clinging attains Nibbāna.

"This is the cause and reason, lord of the devas, why some beings here attain Nibbāna in this very life." [103]

119 (6) Pañcasikha

(*The same except that the interlocutor is Pañcasikha, son of the gandhabbas.*)[106]

120 (7) Sāriputta

On one occasion the Venerable Sāriputta was dwelling at Sāvatthī in Jeta's Grove, Anāthapiṇḍika's Park. Then a certain bhikkhu approached the Venerable Sāriputta and exchanged greetings with him. When they had concluded their greetings and cordial talk, he sat down to one side and said to the Venerable Sāriputta:

"Friend Sāriputta, a bhikkhu who was my co-resident has given up the training and returned to the lower life."

"So it is, friend, when one does not guard the doors of the sense faculties, is immoderate in eating, and is not devoted to wakefulness. That a bhikkhu who does not guard the doors of the sense faculties, who is immoderate in eating, [104] and who is not devoted to wakefulness will maintain all his life the complete and pure holy life—this is impossible. But, friend, that a bhikkhu who guards the doors of the sense faculties, who is moderate in eating, and who is devoted to wakefulness will maintain all his life the complete and pure holy life—this is possible.

"And how, friend, does one guard the doors of the sense faculties? Here, having seen a form with the eye, a bhikkhu does not grasp its signs and features.[107] Since, if he left the eye faculty unrestrained, evil unwholesome states of covetousness and displeasure might invade him, he practises the way of its restraint, he guards the eye faculty, he undertakes the restraint of the eye faculty. Having heard a sound with the ear ... Having smelt an odour with the nose ... Having savoured a taste with the tongue ... Having felt a tactile object with the body ... Having cognized a mental phenomenon with the mind, a bhikkhu does not grasp its signs and features. Since, if he left the mind faculty unrestrained, evil unwholesome states of covetousness and displeasure might invade him, he practises the way of its restraint, he guards the mind faculty, he undertakes the restraint of the mind faculty. It is in this way, friend, that one guards the doors of the sense faculties.

"And how, friend, is one moderate in eating? Here, reflecting carefully, a bhikkhu takes food neither for amusement nor for intoxication nor for the sake of physical beauty and attractiveness, but only for the support and maintenance of this body, for ending discomfort, and for assisting the holy life, considering: 'Thus I shall terminate the old feeling and not arouse a new feeling, and I shall be healthy and blameless and live in comfort.'[108] It is in this way, friend, that one is moderate in eating.

"And how, friend, is one devoted to wakefulness? Here, during the day, while walking back and forth and sitting, a bhikkhu purifies his mind of obstructive states. In the first watch of the night, while walking back and forth and sitting, he purifies his mind of obstructive states. [105] In the middle watch of the night he lies down on his right side in the lion's posture with one foot overlapping the other, mindful and clearly comprehending, after noting in his mind the idea of rising. After rising, in the last watch of the night, while walking back and forth and sitting, he purifies his mind of obstructive states. It is in this way, friend, that one is devoted to wakefulness.

"Therefore, friend, you should train yourself thus: 'We will guard the doors of the sense faculties; we will be moderate in eating; we will be devoted to wakefulness.' Thus, friend, should you train yourself."

121 (8) Exhortation to Rāhula

On one occasion the Blessed One was dwelling at Sāvatthī in Jeta's Grove, Anāthapiṇḍika's Park.[109] Then, while the Blessed

One was alone in seclusion, a reflection arose in his mind thus: "The states that ripen in liberation have come to maturity in Rāhula. Let me lead him on further to the destruction of the taints."[110]

Then, in the morning, the Blessed One dressed and, taking bowl and robe, walked for alms in Sāvatthī. When he had returned from the alms round, after his meal he addressed the Venerable Rāhula thus: "Take a sitting cloth, Rāhula. Let us go to the Blind Men's Grove for the day's abiding."

"Yes, venerable sir," the Venerable Rāhula replied and, having taken a sitting cloth, he followed close behind the Blessed One.

Now on that occasion many thousands of devatās followed the Blessed One, thinking: "Today the Blessed One will lead the Venerable Rāhula on further to the destruction of the taints."[111] Then the Blessed One plunged into the Blind Men's Grove and sat down at the foot of a certain tree on a seat that was prepared for him. The Venerable Rāhula paid homage to the Blessed One and sat down to one side. [106] The Blessed One then said to him:

"What do you think, Rāhula, is the eye permanent or impermanent?" – "Impermanent, venerable sir." – "Is what is impermanent suffering or happiness?" – "Suffering, venerable sir." – "Is what is impermanent, suffering, and subject to change fit to be regarded thus: 'This is mine, this I am, this is my self'?" – "No, venerable sir."

"Are forms permanent or impermanent?… Is eye-consciousness … Is eye-contact … Is anything included in feeling, perception, volitional formations, and consciousness arisen with eye-contact as condition permanent or impermanent?" – "Impermanent, venerable sir." (*The rest as in the preceding paragraph.*)

"Is the ear … the mind permanent or impermanent?… [107] … Are mental phenomena … Is mind-consciousness … Is mind-contact … Is anything included in feeling, perception, volitional formations, and consciousness arisen with mind-contact as condition permanent or impermanent?" – "Impermanent, venerable sir." – "Is what is impermanent suffering or happiness?" – "Suffering, venerable sir." – "Is what is impermanent, suffering, and subject to change fit to be regarded thus: 'This is mine, this I am, this is my self'?" – "No, venerable sir."

"Seeing thus, Rāhula, the instructed noble disciple experiences revulsion towards the eye, revulsion towards forms, revulsion towards eye-consciousness, revulsion towards eye-contact; revulsion towards anything included in feeling, perception, volitional formations, and consciousness arisen with eye-contact as condition. He experiences revulsion towards the ear ... towards the mind ... towards anything included in feeling, perception, volitional formations, and consciousness arisen with mind-contact as condition.

"Experiencing revulsion, he becomes dispassionate. Through dispassion [his mind] is liberated. When it is liberated there comes the knowledge: 'It's liberated.' He understands: 'Destroyed is birth, the holy life has been lived, what had to be done has been done, there is no more for this state of being.'"

This is what the Blessed One said. Elated, the Venerable Rāhula delighted in the Blessed One's statement. And while this discourse was being spoken, the Venerable Rāhula's mind was liberated from the taints by nonclinging, and in those many thousands of devatās there arose the dust-free, stainless vision of the Dhamma: "Whatever is subject to origination is all subject to cessation."[112]

122 (9) Things That Fetter

(*Identical with §109, but by way of the six external sense bases.*) [108]

123 (10) Things That Can Be Clung To

(*Identical with §110, but by way of the six external sense bases.*)

[109]

III. The Householder

124 (1) At Vesālī

On one occasion the Blessed One was dwelling at Vesālī in the Great Wood in the Hall with the Peaked Roof. Then the householder Ugga of Vesālī approached the Blessed One ... and said to him....[113]

(*The question and the reply are exactly the same as in §118.*)

125 (2) Among the Vajjians

On one occasion the Blessed One was dwelling among the Vajjians at Hatthigāma. Then the householder Ugga of Hatthigāma approached the Blessed One … and said to him.…[114]

(*As in §118.*) [110]

126 (3) At Nālandā

On one occasion the Blessed One was dwelling at Nālandā in Pāvārika's Mango Grove. Then the householder Upāli approached the Blessed One … and said to him.…[115]

(*As in §118.*)

127 (4) Bhāradvāja

On one occasion the Venerable Piṇḍola Bhāradvāja was dwelling at Kosambī in Ghosita's Park.[116] Then King Udena approached the Venerable Piṇḍola Bhāradvāja and exchanged greetings with him.[117] When they had concluded their greetings and cordial talk, he sat down to one side and said to him:

"Master Bhāradvāja, what is the cause and reason why these young bhikkhus, lads with black hair, endowed with the blessing of youth, in the prime of life, who have not dallied with sensual pleasures, lead the complete and pure holy life all their lives and maintain it continuously?"[118]

"Great king, this was said by the Blessed One who knows and sees, the Arahant, the Fully Enlightened One: 'Come, bhikkhus, towards women old enough to be your mother set up the idea that they are your mother;[119] [111] towards those of an age to be your sisters set up the idea that they are your sisters; towards those young enough to be your daughters set up the idea that they are your daughters.' This is a cause and reason, great king, why these young bhikkhus … lead the complete and pure holy life all their lives and maintain it continuously."

"The mind is wanton, Master Bhāradvāja. Sometimes states of lust arise even towards women old enough to be one's mother; sometimes they arise towards women of an age to be one's sister; sometimes they arise towards women young enough to be one's daughter. Is there any other cause and reason why these young bhikkhus ... lead the complete and pure holy life all their lives and maintain it continuously?"

"Great king, this was said by the Blessed One who knows and sees, the Arahant, the Fully Enlightened One: 'Come, bhikkhus, review this very body upwards from the soles of the feet, downwards from the tips of the hairs, enclosed in skin, as full of many kinds of impurities:[120] "There are in this body head-hairs, body-hairs, nails, teeth, skin, flesh, sinews, bones, bone-marrow, kidneys, heart, liver, pleura, spleen, lungs, intestines, mesentery, contents of the stomach, excrement, bile, phlegm, pus, blood, sweat, fat, tears, grease, saliva, snot, fluid of the joints, urine."' This too, great king, is a cause and reason why these young bhikkhus ... lead the complete and pure holy life all their lives and maintain it continuously."

"That is easy, Master Bhāradvāja, for those bhikkhus who are developed in body, developed in virtue, developed in mind, developed in wisdom. But it is difficult for those bhikkhus who are undeveloped in body,[121] undeveloped in virtue, undeveloped in mind, undeveloped in wisdom. Sometimes, though one thinks, 'I will attend to the body as foul,' one beholds it as beautiful. [112] Is there any other cause and reason why these young bhikkhus ... lead the complete and pure holy life all their lives and maintain it continuously?"

"Great king, this was said by the Blessed One who knows and sees, the Arahant, the Fully Enlightened One: 'Come, bhikkhus, dwell guarding the doors of the sense faculties. Having seen a form with the eye, do not grasp its signs and features. Since, if you leave the eye faculty unguarded, evil unwholesome states of covetousness and displeasure might invade you, practise the way of its restraint, guard the eye faculty, undertake the restraint of the eye faculty. Having heard a sound with the ear ... Having smelt an odour with the nose ... Having savoured a taste with the tongue ... Having felt a tactile object with the body ... Having cognized a mental phenomenon with the mind, do not grasp its signs and features. Since, if you leave the mind faculty unguarded, evil unwholesome states of covetousness and displeasure might invade you, practise the way of its restraint, guard the mind faculty, undertake the restraint of the mind faculty.' This too, great king, is a cause and reason why these young bhikkhus

... lead the complete and pure holy life all their lives and maintain it continuously."

"It is wonderful, Master Bhāradvāja! It is amazing, Master Bhāradvāja! How well this has been stated by the Blessed One who knows and sees, the Arahant, the Fully Enlightened One. So this is the cause and reason why these young bhikkhus, lads with black hair, endowed with the blessing of youth, in the prime of life, who have not dallied with sensual pleasures, lead the complete and pure holy life all their lives and maintain it continuously. In my case too, when I enter my harem unguarded in body, speech, and mind, without setting up mindfulness, unrestrained in the sense faculties, on that occasion states of lust assail me forcefully. But when I enter my harem guarded in body, speech, and mind, [113] with mindfulness set up, restrained in the sense faculties, on that occasion states of lust do not assail me in such a way.

"Magnificent, Master Bhāradvāja! Magnificent, Master Bhāradvāja! The Dhamma has been made clear in many ways by Master Bhāradvāja, as though he were turning upright what had been turned upside down, revealing what was hidden, showing the way to one who was lost, or holding up a lamp in the dark for those with eyesight to see forms. Master Bhāradvāja, I go for refuge to the Blessed One, and to the Dhamma, and to the Bhikkhu Saṅgha. From today let Master Bhāradvāja remember me as a lay follower who has gone for refuge for life."

128 (5) Soṇa

On one occasion the Blessed One was dwelling at Rājagaha in the Bamboo Grove, the Squirrel Sanctuary. Then the householder's son Soṇa approached the Blessed One ... and said to him.....

(*As in §118.*)

129 (6) Ghosita

On one occasion the Venerable Ānanda was dwelling at Kosambī in Ghosita's Park. Then the householder Ghosita approached the Venerable Ānanda ... and said to him: [114] "Venerable Ānanda, it is said, 'diversity of elements, diversity of elements.'[122] In what way, venerable sir, has the diversity of elements been spoken of by the Blessed One?"

"Householder, there exists the eye element, and forms that are agreeable, and eye-consciousness: in dependence on a contact to be experienced as pleasant, a pleasant feeling arises.[123] There exists the eye element, and forms that are disagreeable, and eye-consciousness: in dependence on a contact to be experienced as painful, a painful feeling arises. There exists the eye element, and forms that are a basis for equanimity, and eye-consciousness: in dependence on a contact to be experienced as neither-painful-nor-pleasant, a neither-painful-nor-pleasant feeling arises.

"Householder, there exists the ear element … the nose element … the tongue element … the body element … the mind element, and mental phenomena that are agreeable, and mind-consciousness: in dependence on a contact to be experienced as pleasant, a pleasant feeling arises. There exists the mind element, and mental phenomena that are disagreeable, and mind-consciousness: in dependence on a contact to be experienced as painful, a painful feeling arises. There exists the mind element, and mental phenomena that are a basis for equanimity, and mind-consciousness: in dependence on a contact to be experienced as neither-painful-nor-pleasant, a neither-painful-nor-pleasant feeling arises.

"It is in this way, householder, that the diversity of elements has been spoken of by the Blessed One." [115]

130 (7) Hāliddakāni

Thus have I heard. On one occasion the Venerable Mahākaccāna was dwelling among the people of Avantī on Mount Papāta at Kuraraghara. Then the householder Hāliddakāni approached the Venerable Mahākaccāna … and said to him:[124]

"Venerable sir, it was said by the Blessed One: 'It is in dependence on the diversity of elements that there arises the diversity of contacts; in dependence on the diversity of contacts that there arises the diversity of feelings.'[125] How is this so, venerable sir?"

"Here, householder, having seen a form with the eye, a bhikkhu understands an agreeable one thus: 'Such it is!'[126] There is eye-consciousness, and in dependence on a contact to be experienced as pleasant there arises a pleasant feeling.[127] Then, having seen a form with the eye, a bhikkhu understands a disagreeable one thus: 'Such it is!' There is eye-consciousness, and in dependence on a contact to be experienced as painful there arises a painful feeling. Then, having seen a form with the eye, a bhikkhu understands one that is a basis for equanimity thus: 'Such it is!' There is eye-consciousness, and in dependence on a contact to be experienced as neither-painful-nor-pleasant there arises a neither-painful-nor-pleasant feeling.

"Further, householder, having heard a sound with the ear … having smelt an odour with the nose … having savoured a taste with the tongue … having felt a tactile object with the body … having cognized a mental phenomenon with the mind, a bhikkhu understands an agreeable one thus … [116] … a disagreeable one thus … one that is a basis for equanimity thus: 'Such it is!' There is mind-consciousness, and in dependence on a contact to be experienced as neither-painful-nor-pleasant there arises a neither-painful-nor-pleasant feeling.

"It is in this way, householder, that in dependence on the diversity of elements there arises the diversity of contacts, and in dependence on the diversity of contacts there arises the diversity of feelings."

131 (8) Nakulapitā

On one occasion the Blessed One was dwelling among the Bhaggas at Suṃsumāragira in the Bhesakaḷā Grove, the Deer Park. Then the householder Nakulapitā approached the Blessed One … and said to him….[128]

(*As in §118.*)

132 (9) Lohicca

On one occasion the Venerable Mahākaccāna was dwelling among the people of Avantī in a forest hut at Makkarakaṭa. [117] Then a number of brahmin youths, students of the brahmin Lohicca, while collecting firewood, approached the Venerable Mahākaccāna's forest hut. Having approached, they stomped and trampled all around the hut, and in a boisterous and noisy manner they played various pranks,[129] saying: "These shaveling ascetics, menials, swarthy offspring of the Lord's feet, are honoured, respected, esteemed, worshipped, and venerated by their servile devotees."[130]

Then the Venerable Mahākaccāna came out of his dwelling and said to those brahmin youths: "Don't make any noise, boys. I will speak to you on the Dhamma." When this was said, those youths became silent. Then the Venerable Mahākaccāna addressed those youths with verses:

"Those men of old who excelled in virtue,
Those brahmins who recalled the ancient rules,
Their sense doors guarded, well protected,
Dwelt having vanquished wrath within.
They took delight in Dhamma and meditation,[131]
Those brahmins who recalled the ancient rules.

"But these have fallen, claiming 'We recite.'
Puffed up by clan, faring unrighteously,
Overcome by anger, armed with diverse weapons,
They molest both frail and firm.

"For one with sense doors unguarded
[All the vows he undertakes] are vain
Just like the wealth a man gains in a dream: [118]
Fasting and sleeping on the ground,
Bathing at dawn, [study of] the three Vedas,
Rough hides, matted locks, and dirt;
Hymns, rules and vows, austerities,
Hypocrisy, bent staffs, ablutions:
These emblems of the brahmins
Are used to increase their worldly gains.[132]

"A mind that is well concentrated,
Clear and free from blemish,
Tender towards all sentient beings—
That is the path for attaining Brahmā."

Then those brahmin youths, angry and displeased, approached the brahmin Lohicca and told him: "See now, sir, you should know that the ascetic Mahākaccāna categorically denigrates and scorns the hymns of the brahmins."

When this was said, the brahmin Lohicca was angry and displeased. But then it occurred to him: "It is not proper for me to abuse and revile the ascetic Mahākaccāna solely on the basis of what I have heard from these youths. Let me approach him and inquire."

Then the brahmin Lohicca, together with those brahmin youths, approached the Venerable Mahākaccāna. [119] He exchanged greetings with the Venerable Mahākaccāna and, when they had concluded their greetings and cordial talk, he sat down to one side and said to him: "Master Kaccāna, did a number of brahmin youths, my students, come this way while collecting firewood?"

"They did, brahmin."

"Did Master Kaccāna have any conversation with them?"

"I did have a conversation with them, brahmin."

"What kind of conversation did you have with them, Master Kaccāna?"

"The conversation I had with those youths was like this:

"'Those men of old who excelled in virtue,
Those brahmins who recalled the ancient rules, …
Tender towards all sentient beings—
That is the path for attaining Brahmā.'

Such was the conversation that I had with those youths."

"Master Kaccāna said 'with sense doors unguarded.' In what way, Master Kaccāna, is one 'with sense doors unguarded'?"

"Here, brahmin, having seen a form with the eye, someone is intent upon a pleasing form and repelled by a displeasing form.[133] He dwells without having set up mindfulness of the body, with a limited mind, [120] and he does not understand as it really is that liberation of mind, liberation by wisdom, wherein those evil unwholesome states cease without remainder. Having heard a sound with the ear … Having cognized a mental phenomenon with the mind, someone is intent upon a pleasing mental phenomenon and repelled by a displeasing mental phenomenon. He dwells without having set up mindfulness of the body … cease without remainder. It is in such a way, brahmin, that one is 'with sense doors unguarded.'"

"It is wonderful, Master Kaccāna! It is amazing, Master Kaccāna! How Master Kaccāna has declared one whose sense doors are actually unguarded to be one 'with sense doors unguarded'! But Master Kaccāna said 'with sense doors guarded.' In what way, Master Kaccāna, is one 'with sense doors guarded'?"

"Here, brahmin, having seen a form with the eye, someone is not intent upon a pleasing form and not repelled by a displeasing form. He dwells having set up mindfulness of the body, with a measureless mind, and he understands as it really is that liberation of mind, liberation by wisdom, wherein those evil unwholesome states cease without remainder. Having heard a sound with the ear ... Having cognized a mental phenomenon with the mind, someone is not intent upon a pleasing mental phenomenon and not repelled by a displeasing mental phenomenon. He dwells having set up mindfulness of the body ... cease without remainder. It is in such a way, brahmin, that one is 'with sense doors guarded.'"

"It is wonderful, Master Kaccāna! It is amazing, Master Kaccāna! [121] How Master Kaccāna has declared one whose sense doors are actually guarded to be one 'with sense doors guarded'! Magnificent, Master Kaccāna! Magnificent, Master Kaccāna! The Dhamma has been made clear in many ways by Master Kaccāna ... (*as in §127*) ... From today let Master Kaccāna remember me as a lay follower who has gone for refuge for life.

"Let Master Kaccāna approach the Lohicca family just as he approaches the families of the lay followers in Makkarakaṭa. The brahmin youths and maidens there will pay homage to Master Kaccāna, they will stand up for him out of respect, they will offer him a seat and water, and that will lead to their welfare and happiness for a long time."

133 (10) Verahaccāni

On one occasion the Venerable Udāyī was living at Kāmaṇḍā in the brahmin Todeyya's Mango Grove. Then a brahmin youth, a student of the brahmin lady of the Verahaccāni clan, approached the Venerable Udāyī and greeted him. When they had concluded their greetings and cordial talk, he sat down to one side, and the Venerable Udāyī instructed, exhorted, inspired, and gladdened him with a Dhamma talk. Having been instructed, exhorted, inspired, and gladdened by the Dhamma talk, the brahmin youth rose from his seat, approached the brahmin lady of the Verahaccāni clan, and said to her: "See now, madam, you should know that the ascetic Udāyī teaches a Dhamma that is good in the beginning, good in the middle, and good in the end, [122] with the right meaning and phrasing; he reveals a holy life that is perfectly complete and pure."

"In that case, young man, invite the ascetic Udāyī in my name for tomorrow's meal."

"Yes, madam," the youth replied. Then he went to the Venerable Udāyī and said to him: "Let Master Udāyī consent to accept tomorrow's meal from our revered teacher,[134] the brahmin lady of the Verahaccāni clan."

The Venerable Udāyī consented by silence. Then, when the night had passed, in the morning the Venerable Udāyī dressed, took his bowl and outer robe, and went to the residence of the brahmin lady of the Verahaccāni clan. There he sat down in the appointed seat. Then, with her own hands, the brahmin lady served and satisfied the Venerable Udāyī with various kinds of delicious food. When the Venerable Udāyī had finished eating and had put away his bowl,[135] the brahmin lady put on her sandals, sat down on a high seat, covered her head, and told him: "Preach the Dhamma, ascetic." Having said, "There will be an occasion for that, sister," he rose from his seat and departed.[136]

A second time that brahmin youth approached the Venerable Udāyī ... (*as above down to:*) ... "See now, madam, you should know that the ascetic Udāyī teaches a Dhamma that is good in the beginning, good in the middle, [123] and good in the end, with the right meaning and phrasing; he reveals a holy life that is perfectly complete and pure."

"In such a way, young man, you keep on praising the ascetic Udāyī, but when I told him, 'Preach the Dhamma, ascetic,' he said, 'There will be an occasion for that, sister,' and he rose from his seat and departed."

"That, madam, was because you put on your sandals, sat down on a high seat, covered your head, and told him: 'Preach the Dhamma, ascetic.' For these worthies respect and revere the Dhamma."

"In that case, young man, invite the ascetic Udāyī in my name for tomorrow's meal."

"Yes, madam," he replied. Then he went to the Venerable Udāyī ... (*all as above*) ... When the Venerable Udāyī had finished eating and had put away his bowl, the brahmin lady removed her sandals, sat down on a low seat, uncovered her head, and said to him: "Venerable sir, what do the arahants maintain must exist for there to be pleasure and pain? And what is it that the arahants maintain must cease to exist for there to be no pleasure and pain?"

"Sister, the arahants maintain that when the eye exists there is pleasure and pain, and when the eye does not exist there is no pleasure and pain. [124] The arahants maintain that when the ear exists there is pleasure and pain, and when the ear does not exist there is no pleasure and pain.... The arahants maintain that when the mind exists there is pleasure and pain, and when the mind does not exist there is no pleasure and pain."

When this was said, the brahmin lady of the Verahaccāni clan said to the Venerable Udāyī: "Magnificent, venerable sir! Magnificent, venerable sir! The Dhamma has been made clear in many ways by Master Udāyī ... (*as in §127*) ... From today let Master Udāyī remember me as a lay follower who has gone for refuge for life."

IV. Devadaha

134 (1) At Devadaha[137]

On one occasion the Blessed One was dwelling among the Sakyans where there was a town of the Sakyans named Devadaha. There the Blessed One addressed the bhikkhus thus:

"Bhikkhus, I do not say of all bhikkhus that they still have work to do with diligence in regard to the six bases for contact, [125] nor do I say of all bhikkhus that they do not have work to do with diligence in regard to the six bases for contact.

"I do not say of those bhikkhus who are arahants, whose taints are destroyed, who have lived the holy life, done what had to be done, laid down the burden, reached their own goal, utterly destroyed the fetters of existence, and are completely liberated through final knowledge, that they still have work to do with diligence in regard to the six bases for contact. Why is that? They have done their work with diligence; they are incapable of being negligent.

"But I say of those bhikkhus who are trainees, who have not attained their mind's ideal, who dwell aspiring for the unsurpassed security from bondage, that they still have work to do with diligence in regard to the six bases for contact. Why is that? There are, bhikkhus, forms cognizable by the eye that are agreeable and those that are disagreeable. [One should train so that] these do not persist obsessing one's mind even when they are repeatedly experienced. When the mind is not obsessed, tireless energy is aroused, unmuddled mindfulness is set up, the body becomes tranquil and untroubled, the mind becomes concentrated and one-pointed. Seeing this fruit of diligence, bhikkhus, I say that those bhikkhus still have work to do with diligence in regard to the six bases for contact.

"There are, bhikkhus, sounds cognizable by the ear … mental phenomena cognizable by the mind that are agreeable and those that are disagreeable. [One should train so that] these do not persist obsessing one's mind even when they are repeatedly experienced. When the mind is not obsessed, tireless energy is aroused, unmuddled mindfulness is set up, the body becomes tranquil and untroubled, the mind becomes concentrated and one-pointed. Seeing this fruit of diligence, bhikkhus, I say that those bhikkhus still have work to do with diligence in regard to the six bases for contact." [126]

135 (2) The Opportunity

"Bhikkhus, it is a gain for you, it is well gained by you, that you have obtained the opportunity for living the holy life. I have seen, bhikkhus, the hell named 'Contact's Sixfold Base.'[138] There whatever form one sees with the eye is undesirable, never desirable; unlovely, never lovely; disagreeable, never agreeable. Whatever sound one hears with the ear … Whatever odour one smells with the nose … Whatever taste one savours with the tongue … Whatever tactile object one feels with the body … Whatever mental phenomenon one cognizes with the mind is undesirable, never desirable; unlovely, never lovely; disagreeable, never agreeable.

"It is a gain for you, bhikkhus, it is well gained by you, that you have obtained the opportunity for living the holy life. I have seen, bhikkhus, the heaven named 'Contact's Sixfold Base.'[139] There whatever form one sees with the eye is desirable, never undesirable; lovely, never unlovely; agreeable, never disagreeable.

Whatever sound one hears with the ear ... Whatever odour one smells with the nose ... Whatever taste one savours with the tongue ... Whatever tactile object one feels with the body ... Whatever mental phenomenon one cognizes with the mind is desirable, never undesirable; lovely, never unlovely; agreeable, never disagreeable.

"It is a gain for you, bhikkhus, it is well gained by you, that you have obtained the opportunity for living the holy life."

136 (3) Delight in Forms (1)[140]

"Bhikkhus, devas and humans delight in forms, take delight in forms, rejoice in forms. With the change, fading away, and cessation of forms, devas and humans dwell in suffering. Devas and humans delight in sounds ... delight in odours ... delight in tastes ... delight in tactile objects ... delight in mental phenomena, [127] take delight in mental phenomena, rejoice in mental phenomena. With the change, fading away, and cessation of mental phenomena, devas and humans dwell in suffering.

"But, bhikkhus, the Tathāgata, the Arahant, the Fully Enlightened One, has understood as they really are the origin and the passing away, the gratification, the danger, and the escape in the case of forms. He does not delight in forms, does not take delight in forms, does not rejoice in forms. With the change, fading away, and cessation of forms, the Tathāgata dwells happily.

"He has understood as they really are the origin and the passing away, the gratification, the danger, and the escape in the case of sounds ... odours ... tastes ... tactile objects ... mental phenomena. He does not delight in mental phenomena, does not take delight in mental phenomena, does not rejoice in mental phenomena. With the change, fading away, and cessation of mental phenomena, the Tathāgata dwells happily."

This is what the Blessed One said. Having said this, the Fortunate One, the Teacher, further said this:[141]

"Forms, sounds, odours, tastes,
Tactiles and all objects of mind—
Desirable, lovely, agreeable,
So long as it's said: 'They are.'

"These are considered happiness
By the world with its devas;
But where these cease,
That they consider suffering.

"The noble ones have seen as happiness
The ceasing of identity.
This [view] of those who clearly see
Runs counter to the entire world.[142]

"What others speak of as happiness,
That the noble ones say is suffering;
What others speak of as suffering,
That the noble ones know as bliss.

"Behold this Dhamma hard to comprehend:
Here the foolish are bewildered.
For those with blocked minds it is obscure,
Sheer darkness for those who do not see. [128]

"But for the good it is disclosed,
It is light here for those who see.
The dullards unskilled in the Dhamma
Don't understand it in its presence.

"This Dhamma isn't easily understood
By those afflicted with lust for existence,
Who flow along in the stream of existence,
Deeply mired in Māra's realm.

"Who else apart from the noble ones
Are able to understand this state?
When they have rightly known that state,
The taintless ones are fully quenched."[143]

137 (4) Delight in Forms (2)

(*Identical with the preceding sutta, but without the verses.*)

138 (5) Not Yours (1)[144]

"Bhikkhus, whatever is not yours, abandon it. When you have abandoned it, that will lead to your welfare and happiness. And what is it, bhikkhus, that is not yours? The eye is not yours: abandon it. When you have abandoned it, that will lead to your welfare and happiness. The ear is not yours … [129] … The mind is not yours: abandon it. When you have abandoned it, that will lead to your welfare and happiness.

"Suppose, bhikkhus, people were to carry off the grass, sticks, branches, and foliage in this Jeta's Grove, or to burn them, or to do with them as they wish. Would you think: 'People are carrying us off, or burning us, or doing with us as they wish'?"

"No, venerable sir. For what reason? Because, venerable sir, that is neither our self nor what belongs to our self."

"So too, bhikkhus, the eye is not yours … The ear … The mind is not yours … When you have abandoned it, that will lead to your welfare and happiness."

139 (6) Not Yours (2)

(Identical with the preceding sutta, but stated by way of the six external bases.)

140 (7) Impermanent with Cause (Internal)

"Bhikkhus, the eye is impermanent.[145] The cause and condition for the arising of the eye is also impermanent. As the eye has originated from what is impermanent, how could it be permanent? [130]

"The ear is impermanent.… The mind is impermanent. The cause and condition for the arising of the mind is also impermanent. As the mind has originated from what is impermanent, how could it be permanent?

"Seeing thus, bhikkhus, the instructed noble disciple experiences revulsion towards the eye … towards the mind. Experiencing revulsion, he becomes dispassionate. Through dispassion [his mind] is liberated. When it is liberated there comes the knowledge: 'It's liberated.' He understands: 'Destroyed is birth, the holy life has been lived, what had to be done has been done, there is no more for this state of being.'"

141 (8) Suffering with Cause (Internal)

"Bhikkhus, the eye is suffering. The cause and condition for the arising of the eye is also suffering. As the eye has originated from what is suffering, how could it be happiness?

"The ear is suffering.... The mind is suffering. The cause and condition for the arising of the mind is also suffering. As the mind has originated from what is suffering, how could it be happiness?

"Seeing thus ... He understands: '... there is no more for this state of being.'"

142 (9) Nonself with Cause (Internal)

"Bhikkhus, the eye is nonself. The cause and condition for the arising of the eye is also nonself. As the eye has originated from what is nonself, how could it be self?

"The ear is nonself.... The mind is nonself. The cause and condition for the arising of the mind [131] is also nonself. As the mind has originated from what is nonself, how could it be self?

"Seeing thus ... He understands: '... there is no more for this state of being.'"

143 (10)–145 (12) Impermanent with Cause, Etc. (External)

(These three suttas are identical with §§140–42, but are stated by way of the six external sense bases.)

[132] V. New and Old

146 (1) Kamma

"Bhikkhus, I will teach you new and old kamma, the cessation of kamma, and the way leading to the cessation of kamma. Listen to that and attend closely, I will speak....

"And what, bhikkhus, is old kamma? The eye is old kamma, to be seen as generated and fashioned by volition, as something to be felt.[146] The ear is old kamma ... The mind is old kamma, to be seen as generated and fashioned by volition, as something to be felt. This is called old kamma.

"And what, bhikkhus is new kamma? Whatever action one

does now by body, speech, or mind. This is called new kamma.

"And what, bhikkhus, is the cessation of kamma? When one reaches liberation through the cessation of bodily action, verbal action, and mental action, [133] this is called the cessation of kamma.

"And what, bhikkhus, is the way leading to the cessation of kamma? It is this Noble Eightfold Path; that is, right view, right intention, right speech, right action, right livelihood, right effort, right mindfulness, right concentration.

"Thus, bhikkhus, I have taught old kamma, I have taught new kamma, I have taught the cessation of kamma, I have taught the way leading to the cessation of kamma. Whatever should be done, bhikkhus, by a compassionate teacher out of compassion for his disciples, desiring their welfare, that I have done for you. These are the feet of trees, bhikkhus, these are empty huts. Meditate, bhikkhus, do not be negligent, lest you regret it later. This is our instruction to you."

147 (2) Suitable for Attaining Nibbāna (1)

"Bhikkhus, I will teach you the way that is suitable for attaining Nibbāna.[147] Listen to that....

"And what, bhikkhus, is the way that is suitable for attaining Nibbāna? Here, a bhikkhu sees the eye as impermanent, he sees forms as impermanent, he sees eye-consciousness as impermanent, he sees eye-contact as impermanent, he sees as impermanent whatever feeling arises with eye-contact as condition, whether pleasant or painful or neither-painful-nor-pleasant.

"He sees the ear as impermanent ... [134] ... He sees the mind as impermanent, he sees mental phenomena as impermanent, he sees mind-consciousness as impermanent, he sees mind-contact as impermanent, he sees as impermanent whatever feeling arises with mind-contact as condition, whether pleasant or painful or neither-painful-nor-pleasant.

"This, bhikkhus, is the way that is suitable for attaining Nibbāna."

148 (3)–149 (4) Suitable for Attaining Nibbāna (2–3)

(*Same as preceding sutta, with "suffering" and "nonself" substituted for "impermanent."*) [135]

150 (5) Suitable for Attaining Nibbāna (4)

"Bhikkhus, I will teach the way that is suitable for attaining Nibbāna. Listen to that….

"What do you think, bhikkhus, is the eye permanent or impermanent?"… (*all as in* §32) …

"Seeing thus … [136] He understands: '… there is no more for this state of being.'

"This, bhikkhus, is the way that is suitable for attaining Nibbāna."

151 (6) A Student

"Bhikkhus, this holy life is lived without students and without a teacher.[148] A bhikkhu who has students and a teacher dwells in suffering, not in comfort. A bhikkhu who has no students and no teacher dwells happily, in comfort.

"And how, bhikkhus, does a bhikkhu who has students and a teacher dwell in suffering, not in comfort? Here, bhikkhus, when a bhikkhu has seen a form with the eye, there arise in him evil unwholesome states, memories and intentions connected with the fetters.[149] *They dwell within him.* Since those evil unwholesome states dwell within him, he is called 'one who has students.' *They assail him.* Since evil unwholesome states assail him, he is called 'one who has a teacher.'

"Further, when a bhikkhu has heard a sound with the ear … cognized a mental phenomenon with the mind … [137] he is called 'one who has a teacher.'

"It is in this way that a bhikkhu who has students and a teacher dwells in suffering, not in comfort.

"And how, bhikkhus, does a bhikkhu who has no students and no teacher dwell happily, in comfort? Here, bhikkhus, when a bhikkhu has seen a form with the eye, there do not arise in him evil unwholesome states, memories and intentions connected with the fetters. *They do not dwell within him.* Since those evil unwholesome states do not dwell within him, he is called 'one who has no students.' *They do not assail him.* Since evil unwholesome states do not assail him, he is called 'one who has no teacher.'

"Further, when a bhikkhu has heard a sound with the ear …

cognized a mental phenomenon with the mind ... he is called 'one who has no teacher.'

"It is in this way, bhikkhus, that a bhikkhu who has no students and no teacher dwells happily, in comfort.

"Bhikkhus, this holy life is lived without students and without a teacher. [138] A bhikkhu who has students and a teacher dwells in suffering, not in comfort. A bhikkhu who has no students and no teacher dwells happily, in comfort."

152 (7) For What Purpose the Holy Life?

"Bhikkhus, if wanderers of other sects ask you: 'For what purpose, friends, is the holy life lived under the ascetic Gotama?'—being asked thus, you should answer those wanderers thus: 'It is, friends, for the full understanding of suffering that the holy life is lived under the Blessed One.' Then, bhikkhus, if those wanderers ask you: 'What, friends, is that suffering for the full understanding of which the holy life is lived under the ascetic Gotama?'—being asked thus, you should answer those wanderers thus:

"'The eye, friends, is suffering: it is for the full understanding of this that the holy life is lived under the Blessed One. Forms are suffering: it is for the full understanding of them that the holy life is lived under the Blessed One. Eye-consciousness is suffering ... Eye-contact is suffering ... Whatever feeling arises with eye-contact as condition—whether pleasant or painful or neither-painful-nor-pleasant—that too is suffering: it is for the full understanding of this that the holy life is lived under the Blessed One. The ear is suffering ... The mind is suffering ... Whatever feeling arises with mind-contact as condition ... that too is suffering: it is for the full understanding of this that the holy life is lived under the Blessed One. This, friends, is the suffering for the full understanding of which the holy life is lived under the Blessed One.'

"Being asked thus, bhikkhus, you should answer those wanderers of other sects in such a way."

153 (8) Is There a Method?

"Is there a method of exposition, bhikkhus, by means of which a bhikkhu—apart from faith, apart from personal preference, apart from oral tradition, apart from reasoned reflection, apart from acceptance of a view after pondering it[150]—[139] can declare final knowledge thus: 'Destroyed is birth, the holy life has been lived, what had to be done has been done, there is no more for this state of being'?"

"Venerable sir, our teachings are rooted in the Blessed One, guided by the Blessed One, take recourse in the Blessed One. It would be good if the Blessed One would clear up the meaning of this statement. Having heard it from him, the bhikkhus will remember it."

"Then listen and attend closely, bhikkhus, I will speak."

"Yes, venerable sir," the bhikkhus replied. The Blessed One said this:

"There is a method of exposition by means of which a bhikkhu—apart from faith ... apart from acceptance of a view after pondering it—can declare final knowledge thus: 'Destroyed is birth ... there is no more for this state of being.' And what is that method of exposition? Here, bhikkhus, having seen a form with the eye, if there is lust, hatred, or delusion internally, a bhikkhu understands: 'There is lust, hatred, or delusion internally'; or, if there is no lust, hatred, or delusion internally, he understands: 'There is no lust, hatred, or delusion internally.'[151] Since this is so, are these things to be understood by faith, or by personal preference, or by oral tradition, or by reasoned reflection, or by acceptance of a view after pondering it?"

"No, venerable sir."

"Aren't these things to be understood by seeing them with wisdom?"

"Yes, venerable sir."

"This, bhikkhus, is the method of exposition by means of which a bhikkhu can declare final knowledge thus: 'Destroyed is birth ... there is no more for this state of being.'

"Further, bhikkhus, having heard a sound with the ear ... [140] ... Having cognized a mental phenomenon with the mind, if there is lust, hatred, or delusion internally, a bhikkhu understands: 'There is lust, hatred, or delusion internally'; or, if there is no lust, hatred, or delusion internally, he understands: 'There is no lust, hatred, or delusion internally.' Since this is so, are these things to be understood by faith, or by personal preference, or by oral tradition, or by reasoned reflection, or by acceptance of a view after pondering it?"

"No, venerable sir."

"Aren't these things to be understood by seeing them with wisdom?"

"Yes, venerable sir."

"This, bhikkhus, is the method of exposition by means of which a bhikkhu—apart from faith, apart from personal preference, apart from oral tradition, apart from reasoned reflection, apart from acceptance of a view after pondering it—can declare final knowledge thus: 'Destroyed is birth, the holy life has been lived, what had to be done has been done, there is no more for this state of being.'"

154 (9) Equipped with Faculties

Then a certain bhikkhu approached the Blessed One ... and said to him: "Venerable sir, it is said, 'equipped with faculties, equipped with faculties.'[152] In what way, venerable sir, is one equipped with faculties?"

"If, bhikkhu, while one dwells contemplating rise and fall in the eye faculty, one experiences revulsion towards the eye faculty; if, while one dwells contemplating rise and fall in the ear faculty, one experiences revulsion towards the ear faculty; ... if, while one dwells contemplating rise and fall in the mind faculty, one experiences revulsion towards the mind faculty, then, experiencing revulsion, one becomes dispassionate.... When [the mind] is liberated, there comes the knowledge: 'It's liberated.' One understands: 'Destroyed is birth, the holy life has been lived, what had to be done has been done, there is no more for this state of being.' It is in this way, bhikkhu, that one is equipped with faculties." [141]

155 (10) A Speaker on the Dhamma

Then a certain bhikkhu approached the Blessed One ... and said to him: "Venerable sir, it is said, 'a speaker on the Dhamma, a speaker on the Dhamma.' In what way, venerable sir, is one a speaker on the Dhamma?"[153]

"Bhikkhu, if one teaches the Dhamma for the purpose of revulsion towards the eye, for its fading away and cessation, one can be called a bhikkhu who is a speaker on the Dhamma. If one is practising for the purpose of revulsion towards the eye, for its fading away and cessation, one can be called a bhikkhu who is practising in accordance with the Dhamma. If, through revulsion towards the eye, through its fading away and cessation, one is liberated by nonclinging, one can be called a bhikkhu who has attained Nibbāna in this very life.

"Bhikkhu, if one teaches the Dhamma for the purpose of revulsion towards the ear ... for the purpose of revulsion towards the mind, for its fading away and cessation, one can be called a bhikkhu who is a speaker on the Dhamma. If one is practising for the purpose of revulsion towards the mind, for its fading away and cessation, one can be called a bhikkhu who is practising in accordance with the Dhamma. If, through revulsion towards the mind, through its fading away and cessation, one is liberated by nonclinging, one can be called a bhikkhu who has attained Nibbāna in this very life."

[142]

Division IV
The Fourth Fifty

I. The Destruction of Delight

156 (1) The Destruction of Delight (1)

"Bhikkhus, a bhikkhu sees as impermanent the eye which is actually impermanent: that is his right view.[154] Seeing rightly, he experiences revulsion. With the destruction of delight comes destruction of lust; with the destruction of lust comes destruction of delight. With the destruction of delight and lust the mind is said to be well liberated.

"Bhikkhus, a bhikkhu sees as impermanent the ear which is actually impermanent... the mind which is actually impermanent: that is his right view.... With the destruction of delight and lust the mind is said to be well liberated."

157 (2) The Destruction of Delight (2)

(*The same for the external sense bases.*)

158 (3) The Destruction of Delight (3)

"Bhikkhus, attend carefully to the eye.[155] Recognize the impermanence of the eye as it really is. When a bhikkhu, attending carefully to the eye, recognizes the impermanence of the eye as it really is, he feels revulsion towards the eye. With the destruction of delight comes destruction of lust; with the destruction of lust comes destruction of delight. With the destruction of delight and lust the mind is said to be well liberated. [143]

"Bhikkhus, attend carefully to the ear ... to the mind. Recognize the impermanence of the mind as it really is.... With the destruction of delight and lust the mind is said to be well liberated."

159 (4) The Destruction of Delight (4)

(*The same for the external sense bases.*)

160 (5) Jīvaka's Mango Grove (1)

On one occasion the Blessed One was dwelling at Rājagaha in Jīvaka's Mango Grove. There he addressed the bhikkhus thus:[156]

"Bhikkhus, develop concentration. [144] When a bhikkhu is concentrated, things become manifest[157] to him as they really are. And what becomes manifest to him as it really is? The eye becomes manifest to him as it really is—as impermanent. Forms become manifest to him as they really are—as impermanent. Eye-consciousness ... Eye-contact ... Whatever feeling arises with eye-contact as condition—whether pleasant or painful or neither-painful-nor-pleasant—becomes manifest to him as it really is—as impermanent.

"The ear becomes manifest to him as it really is ... The mind becomes manifest to him as it really is ... Whatever feeling arises with mind-contact as condition ... becomes manifest to him as it really is—as impermanent.

"Develop concentration, bhikkhus. When a bhikkhu is concentrated, things become manifest to him as they really are."

161 (6) Jīvaka's Mango Grove (2)

On one occasion the Blessed One was dwelling at Rājagaha in Jīvaka's Mango Grove. There he addressed the bhikkhus thus:

"Bhikkhus, make an exertion in seclusion. When a bhikkhu is secluded, things become manifest to him as they really are. And what becomes manifest to him as it really is?"

(*All as in preceding sutta.*) [145]

162 (7) Koṭṭhita (1)

Then the Venerable Mahākoṭṭhita approached the Blessed One ... and said to him:[158] "Venerable sir, it would be good if the Blessed One would teach me the Dhamma in brief, so that, having heard the Dhamma from the Blessed One, I might dwell alone, withdrawn, diligent, ardent, and resolute."

"Koṭṭhita, you should abandon desire for whatever is impermanent. And what is impermanent? The eye is impermanent; you should abandon desire for it. Forms are impermanent ... Eye-consciousness is impermanent ... Eye-contact is impermanent ... Whatever feeling arises with eye-contact as condition ... that too is impermanent; you should abandon desire for it.

"The ear is impermanent ... The mind is impermanent ... Whatever feeling arises with mind-contact as condition ... that too is impermanent; you should abandon desire for it.

"Koṭṭhita, you should abandon desire for whatever is impermanent." [146]

163 (8) Koṭṭhita (2)

... "Koṭṭhita, you should abandon desire for whatever is suffering."... (*Complete as in preceding sutta.*)

164 (9) Koṭṭhita (3)

... "Koṭṭhita, you should abandon desire for whatever is nonself."... [147]

165 (10) Abandoning Wrong View

Then a certain bhikkhu approached the Blessed One ... and said to him: "Venerable sir, how should one know, how should one see, for wrong view to be abandoned?"[159]

"Bhikkhu, when one knows and sees the eye as impermanent, wrong view is abandoned. When one knows and sees forms as impermanent ... eye-consciousness as impermanent ... eye-contact as impermanent ... whatever feeling arises with mind-contact as condition ... as impermanent, wrong view is abandoned. It is when one knows and sees thus that wrong view is abandoned."

166 (11) Abandoning Identity View

... "Venerable sir, how should one know, how should one see, for identity view to be abandoned?"

"Bhikkhu, when one knows and sees the eye as impermanent, identity view is abandoned."... (*Complete as above.*) [148]

167 (12) Abandoning the View of Self

... "Venerable sir, how should one know, how should one see, for the view of self to be abandoned?"

"Bhikkhu, when one knows and sees the eye as impermanent, the view of self is abandoned."... (*Complete as above.*)

II. The Sixtyfold Repetition Series[160]

168 (1) Desire for the Impermanent (Internal)

"Bhikkhus, you should abandon desire for whatever is impermanent. And what is impermanent? [149] The eye is impermanent ... The mind is impermanent; you should abandon desire for it. Bhikkhus, you should abandon desire for whatever is impermanent."

169 (2) Lust for the Impermanent (Internal)

"Bhikkhus, you should abandon lust for whatever is impermanent. And what is impermanent? The eye is impermanent ... The mind is impermanent; you should abandon lust for it. Bhikkhus, you should abandon lust for whatever is impermanent."

170 (3) Desire and Lust for the Impermanent (Internal)

"Bhikkhus, you should abandon desire and lust for whatever is impermanent. And what is impermanent? The eye is impermanent ... The mind is impermanent; you should abandon desire and lust for it. Bhikkhus, you should abandon desire and lust for whatever is impermanent."

171 (4)–173 (6) Desire for Suffering (Internal), Etc.

"Bhikkhus, you should abandon desire for whatever is suffering.... You should abandon lust for whatever is suffering.... You should abandon desire and lust for whatever is suffering. And what is suffering? The eye is suffering ... The mind is suffering; you should abandon desire and lust for it. [150] Bhikkhus, you should abandon desire and lust for whatever is suffering."

174 (7)–176 (9) Desire for Nonself (Internal), Etc.

"Bhikkhus, you should abandon desire for whatever is nonself.... You should abandon lust for whatever is nonself.... You should abandon desire and lust for whatever is nonself. And what is nonself? The eye is nonself ... The mind is nonself; you should abandon desire for it. Bhikkhus, you should abandon desire and lust for whatever is nonself."

177 (10)–179 (12) Desire for the Impermanent (External), Etc.

"Bhikkhus, you should abandon desire for whatever is impermanent.... You should abandon lust for whatever is impermanent.... You should abandon desire and lust for whatever is impermanent. And what is impermanent? Forms are impermanent ... Mental phenomena are impermanent; you should abandon desire and lust for them. Bhikkhus, you should abandon desire and lust for whatever is impermanent."

180 (13)–182 (15) Desire for Suffering (External), Etc.

"Bhikkhus, you should abandon desire for whatever is suffering.... You should abandon lust for whatever is suffering.... You should abandon desire and lust for whatever is suffering. And what is suffering? Forms are suffering... Mental phenomena are suffering; you should abandon desire and lust for them. Bhikkhus, you should abandon desire and lust for whatever is suffering." [151]

183 (16)–185 (18) Desire for Nonself (External), Etc.

"Bhikkhus, you should abandon desire for whatever is nonself.... You should abandon lust for whatever is nonself.... You should abandon desire and lust for whatever is nonself. And what is nonself? Forms are nonself ... Mental phenomena are nonself; you should abandon desire and lust for them. Bhikkhus, you should abandon desire and lust for whatever is nonself."

186 (19) The Past as Impermanent (Internal)

"Bhikkhus, the eye ... the mind of the past was impermanent. Seeing thus, the instructed noble disciple experiences revulsion towards the eye ... towards the mind. Experiencing revulsion, he becomes dispassionate. Through dispassion [his mind] is liberated. When it is liberated there comes the knowledge: 'It's liberated.' He understands: 'Destroyed is birth, the holy life has been lived, what had to be done has been done, there is no more for this state of being.'"

187 (20) The Future as Impermanent (Internal)

"Bhikkhus, the eye ... the mind of the future will be impermanent. Seeing thus, the instructed noble disciple experiences revulsion towards the eye ... towards the mind. He understands: '... there is no more for this state of being.'"

188 (21) The Present as Impermanent (Internal)

"Bhikkhus, the eye ... the mind of the present is impermanent.

Seeing thus, the instructed noble disciple experiences revulsion towards the eye ... towards the mind. He understands: '... there is no more for this state of being.'" [152]

189 (22)–191 (24) The Past, Etc., as Suffering (Internal)

"Bhikkhus, the eye ... the mind of the past ... of the future ... of the present is suffering. Seeing thus ... He understands: '... there is no more for this state of being.'"

192 (25)–194 (27) The Past, Etc., as Nonself (Internal)

"Bhikkhus, the eye ... the mind of the past ... of the future ... of the present is nonself. Seeing thus ... He understands: '... there is no more for this state of being.'"

195 (28)–197 (30) The Past, Etc., as Impermanent (External)

"Bhikkhus, forms ... mental phenomena of the past ... of the future ... of the present are impermanent. Seeing thus ... He understands: '... there is no more for this state of being.'"

198 (31)–200 (33) The Past, Etc., as Suffering (External)

"Bhikkhus, forms ... mental phenomena of the past ... of the future ... of the present are suffering. Seeing thus ... He understands: '... there is no more for this state of being.'"

201 (34)–203 (36) The Past, Etc., as Nonself (External)

"Bhikkhus, forms ... mental phenomena of the past ... of the future ... of the present are nonself. Seeing thus ... He understands: '... there is no more for this state of being.'"

204 (37) What Is Impermanent of the Past (Internal)

"Bhikkhus, the eye ... [153] ... the mind of the past was impermanent. What is impermanent is suffering. What is suffering is nonself. What is nonself should be seen as it really is with correct wisdom thus: 'This is not mine, this I am not, this is not my self.'

Seeing thus ... He understands: '... there is no more for this state of being.'"

205 (38) What Is Impermanent of the Future (Internal)

"Bhikkhus, the eye ... the mind of the future will be impermanent. What is impermanent is suffering. What is suffering is nonself. What is nonself should be seen as it really is with correct wisdom thus: 'This is not mine, this I am not, this is not my self.' Seeing thus ... He understands: '... there is no more for this state of being.'"

206 (39) What Is Impermanent of the Present (Internal)

"Bhikkhus, the eye ... the mind of the present is impermanent. What is impermanent is suffering. What is suffering is nonself. What is nonself should be seen as it really is with correct wisdom thus: 'This is not mine, this I am not, this is not my self.' Seeing thus ... He understands: '... there is no more for this state of being.'" [154]

207 (40)–209 (42) What Is Suffering of the Past, Etc. (Internal)

"Bhikkhus, the eye ... the mind of the past ... of the future ... of the present is suffering. What is suffering is nonself. What is nonself should be seen as it really is with correct wisdom thus: 'This is not mine, this I am not, this is not my self.' Seeing thus ... He understands: '... there is no more for this state of being.'"

210 (43)–212 (45) What Is Nonself of the Past, Etc. (Internal)

"Bhikkhus, the eye ... the mind of the past ... of the future ... of the present is nonself. What is nonself should be seen as it really is with correct wisdom thus: 'This is not mine, this I am not, this is not my self.' Seeing thus ... He understands: '... there is no more for this state of being.'"

213 (46)–215 (48) What Is Impermanent of the Past, Etc. (External)

"Bhikkhus, forms ... mental phenomena of the past ... of the future … of the present are impermanent. What is impermanent is suffering. What is suffering is nonself. What is nonself should be seen as it really is with correct wisdom thus: 'This is not mine, this I am not, this is not my self.' Seeing thus … He understands: '… there is no more for this state of being.'" [155]

216 (49)–218 (51) What Is Suffering of the Past, Etc. (External)

"Bhikkhus, forms … mental phenomena of the past … of the future … of the present are suffering. What is suffering is nonself. What is nonself should be seen as it really is with correct wisdom thus: 'This is not mine, this I am not, this is not my self.' Seeing thus … He understands: '… there is no more for this state of being.'"

219 (52)–221 (54) What Is Nonself of the Past, Etc. (External)

"Bhikkhus, forms … mental phenomena of the past … of the future … of the present are nonself. What is nonself should be seen as it really is with correct wisdom thus: 'This is not mine, this I am not, this is not my self.' Seeing thus … He understands: '… there is no more for this state of being.'"

222 (55) The Bases as Impermanent (Internal)

"Bhikkhus, the eye is impermanent … the mind is impermanent. Seeing thus … He understands: '… there is no more for this state of being.'"

223 (56) The Bases as Suffering (Internal)

"Bhikkhus, the eye is suffering … the mind is suffering. Seeing thus … He understands: '… there is no more for this state of being.'" [156]

224 (57) The Bases as Nonself (Internal)

"Bhikkhus, the eye is nonself … the mind is nonself. Seeing thus … He understands: '… there is no more for this state of being.'"

225 (58) The Bases as Impermanent (External)

"Bhikkhus, forms are impermanent... mental phenomena are impermanent. Seeing thus ... He understands: '... there is no more for this state of being.'"

226 (59) The Bases as Suffering (External)

"Bhikkhus, forms are suffering ... mental phenomena are suffering. Seeing thus ... He understands: '... there is no more for this state of being.'"

227 (60) The Bases as Nonself (External)

"Bhikkhus, forms are nonself ... mental phenomena are nonself. Seeing thus ... He understands: '... there is no more for this state of being.'"

[157] III. THE OCEAN

228 (1) The Ocean (1)

"Bhikkhus, the uninstructed worldling speaks of 'the ocean, the ocean.' But that is not the ocean in the Noble One's Discipline; that is only a great mass of water, a great expanse of water.

"The eye, bhikkhus, is the ocean for a person; its current consists of forms.[161] One who withstands that current consisting of forms is said to have crossed the ocean of the eye with its waves, whirlpools, sharks, and demons.[162] Crossed over, gone beyond, the brahmin stands on high ground.

"The ear, bhikkhus, is the ocean for a person.... The mind is the ocean for a person; its current consists of mental phenomena. One who withstands that current consisting of mental phenomena is said to have crossed the ocean of the mind with its waves, whirlpools, sharks, and demons. Crossed over, gone beyond, the brahmin stands on high ground."

This is what the Blessed One said. Having said this, the Fortunate One, the Teacher, further said this:

"One who has crossed this ocean so hard to cross,
With its dangers of sharks, demons, waves,
The knowledge-master who has lived the holy life,
Reached the world's end, is called one gone beyond."

229 (2) The Ocean (2)

"Bhikkhus, the uninstructed worldling speaks of 'the ocean, the ocean.' [158] But that is not the ocean in the Noble One's Discipline; that is only a great mass of water, a great body of water.

"There are, bhikkhus, forms cognizable by the eye that are desirable, lovely, agreeable, pleasing, sensually enticing, tantalizing. This is called the ocean in the Noble One's Discipline. Here this world with its devas, Māra, and Brahmā, this generation with its ascetics and brahmins, its devas and humans, for the most part is submerged,[163] become like a tangled skein, like a knotted ball of thread, like matted reeds and rushes, and cannot pass beyond the plane of misery, the bad destinations, the nether world, saṃsāra.

"There are sounds cognizable by the ear ... mental phenomena cognizable by the mind that are desirable, lovely, agreeable, pleasing, sensually enticing, tantalizing. Here this world with its devas, Māra, and Brahmā, this generation with its ascetics and brahmins, its devas and humans, for the most part is submerged, become like a tangled skein, like a knotted ball of thread, like matted reeds and rushes, and cannot pass beyond the plane of misery, the bad destinations, the nether world, saṃsāra.[164]

"One who has expunged lust and hate
Along with [the taint of] ignorance,
Has crossed this ocean so hard to cross
With its dangers of sharks, demons, waves.

"The tie-surmounter, death-forsaker, without acquisitions,
Has abandoned suffering[165] for no renewed existence.
Passed away, he cannot be measured, I say:
He has bewildered the King of Death."

230 (3) The Fisherman Simile

"Bhikkhus, suppose a fisherman would cast a baited hook into a deep lake, [159] and a fish on the lookout for food would swallow it. That fish who has thus swallowed the fisherman's hook would meet with calamity and disaster, and the fisherman could do with it as he wishes. So too, bhikkhus, there are these six hooks in the world for the calamity of beings, for the slaughter[166] of living beings.

"There are, bhikkhus, forms cognizable by the eye that are desirable, lovely, agreeable, pleasing, sensually enticing, tantalizing. If a bhikkhu seeks delight in them, welcomes them, and remains holding to them, he is called a bhikkhu who has swallowed Māra's hook. He has met with calamity and disaster, and the Evil One can do with him as he wishes.

"There are, bhikkhus, sounds cognizable by the ear ... mental phenomena cognizable by the mind that are desirable ... tantalizing. If a bhikkhu seeks delight in them ... the Evil One can do with him as he wishes.

"There are, bhikkhus, forms cognizable by the eye that are desirable, lovely, agreeable, pleasing, sensually enticing, tantalizing. If a bhikkhu does not seek delight in them, does not welcome them, and does not remain holding to them, he is called a bhikkhu who has not swallowed Māra's hook, who has broken the hook, demolished the hook. He has not met with calamity and disaster, and the Evil One cannot do with him as he wishes.

"There are, bhikkhus, sounds cognizable by the ear ... mental phenomena cognizable by the mind that are desirable ... tantalizing. If a bhikkhu does not seek delight in them ... the Evil One cannot do with him as he wishes."

231 (4) The Milk-Sap Tree

"Bhikkhus, in regard to forms cognizable by the eye, if in any bhikkhu or bhikkhunī [160] lust still exists and has not been abandoned, if hatred still exists and has not been abandoned, if delusion still exists and has not been abandoned, then even trifling forms that enter into range of the eye obsess the mind, not to speak of those that are prominent. For what reason? Because lust still exists and has not been abandoned, hatred still exists and has not been abandoned, delusion still exists and has not been abandoned. The same in regard to sounds cognizable by the ear … mental phenomena cognizable by the mind.

"Suppose, bhikkhus, there was a milk-sap tree[167]—an *assattha* or a banyan or a *pilakkha* or an *udumbara*—fresh, young, tender. If a man breaks it here and there with a sharp axe, would sap come out?"

"Yes, venerable sir. For what reason? Because there is sap."

"So too, bhikkhus, in regard to forms cognizable by the eye … even trifling forms that enter into range of the eye obsess the mind, not to speak of those that are prominent. For what reason? Because lust still exists and has not been abandoned, hatred still [161] exists and has not been abandoned, delusion still exists and has not been abandoned. The same in regard to sounds cognizable by the ear … mental phenomena cognizable by the mind.

"Bhikkhus, in regard to forms cognizable by the eye, if in any bhikkhu or bhikkhunī lust does not exist and has been abandoned, if hatred does not exist and has been abandoned, if delusion does not exist and has been abandoned, then even prominent forms that enter into range of the eye do not obsess the mind, not to speak of those that are trifling. For what reason? Because lust does not exist and has been abandoned, hatred does not exist and has been abandoned, delusion does not exist and has been abandoned. The same in regard to sounds cognizable by the ear … mental phenomena cognizable by the mind.

"Suppose, bhikkhus, there was a milk-sap tree—an *assattha* or a banyan or a *pilakkha* or an *udumbara*—dried up, desiccated, past its prime. If a man breaks it here and there with a sharp axe, would sap come out?" [162]

"No, venerable sir. For what reason? Because there is no sap."

"So too, bhikkhus, in regard to forms cognizable by the eye … even prominent forms that enter into range of the eye do not obsess the mind, not to speak of those that are trifling. For what reason? Because lust does not exist and has been abandoned, hatred does not exist and has been abandoned, delusion does not exist and has been abandoned. The same in regard to sounds cognizable by the ear … mental phenomena cognizable by the mind."

232 (5) Koṭṭhita

On one occasion the Venerable Sāriputta and the Venerable Mahākoṭṭhita were dwelling at Bārāṇasī in the Deer Park at Isipatana. Then, in the evening, the Venerable Mahākoṭṭhita emerged from seclusion and approached the Venerable Sāriputta. He exchanged greetings with the Venerable Sāriputta and, when they had concluded their greetings and cordial talk, he sat down to one side and said to him:

"How is it, friend Sariputta, is the eye the fetter of forms or are forms the fetter of the eye? Is the ear the fetter of sounds or are sounds the fetter of the ear?… [163] Is the mind the fetter of mental phenomena or are mental phenomena the fetter of the mind?"

"Friend Koṭṭhita, the eye is not the fetter of forms nor are forms the fetter of the eye, but rather the desire and lust that arise there in dependence on both: that is the fetter there. The ear is not the fetter of sounds nor are sounds the fetter of the ear, but rather the desire and lust that arise there in dependence on both: that is the fetter there…. The mind is not the fetter of mental phenomena nor are mental phenomena the fetter of the mind, but rather the desire and lust that arise there in dependence on both: that is the fetter there.

"Suppose, friend, a black ox and a white ox were yoked together by a single harness or yoke. Would one be speaking rightly if one were to say: 'The black ox is the fetter of the white ox; the white ox is the fetter of the black ox'?"

"No, friend. The black ox is not the fetter of the white ox nor is the white ox the fetter of the black ox, but rather the single harness or yoke by which the two are yoked together: that is the fetter there."

"So too, friend, the eye is not the fetter of forms … nor are mental phenomena the fetter of the mind, but rather the desire and lust that arise there in dependence on both: that is the fetter there.

"If, friend, the eye were the fetter of forms or if forms were the fetter of the eye, this living of the holy life could not be discerned for the complete destruction of suffering.[168] But since the eye is not the fetter of forms nor are forms the fetter of the eye [164]—but rather the desire and lust that arise there in dependence on both is the fetter there—the living of the holy life is discerned for the complete destruction of suffering.

"If, friend, the ear were the fetter of sounds or if sounds were the fetter of the ear … If the mind were the fetter of mental phenomena or if mental phenomena were the fetter of the mind, this living of the holy life could not be discerned for the complete destruction of suffering. But since the mind is not the fetter of mental phenomena nor are mental phenomena the fetter of the mind—but rather the desire and lust that arise there in dependence on both is the fetter there—the living of the holy life is discerned for the complete destruction of suffering.

"In this way too, friend, it may be understood how that is so: There exists in the Blessed One the eye, the Blessed One sees a form with the eye, yet there is no desire and lust in the Blessed One; the Blessed One is well liberated in mind. There exists in the Blessed One the ear, the Blessed One hears a sound with the ear … There exists in the Blessed One the nose, the Blessed One smells an odour with the nose … There exists in the Blessed One the tongue, the Blessed One savours a taste with the tongue … There exists in the Blessed One the body, the Blessed One feels a tactile object with the body … There exists in the Blessed One the mind, the Blessed One cognizes [165] a mental phenomenon with the mind, yet there is no desire and lust in the Blessed One; the Blessed One is well liberated in mind.

"In this way, friend, it can be understood how the eye is not the fetter of forms nor forms the fetter of the eye, but rather the desire and lust that arise there in dependence on both is the fetter there; how the ear is not the fetter of sounds nor sounds the fetter of the ear…; how the mind is not the fetter of mental phenomena nor mental phenomena the fetter of the mind, but rather the desire and lust that arise there in dependence on both is the fetter there."

233 (6) Kāmabhū

On one occasion the Venerable Ānanda and the Venerable Kāmabhū were dwelling at Kosambī in Ghosita's Park. Then, in the evening, the Venerable Kāmabhū emerged from seclusion and approached the Venerable Ānanda. He exchanged greetings with the Venerable Ānanda and, when they had concluded their greetings and cordial talk, he sat down to one side and said to him:

"How is it, friend Ānanda, is the eye the fetter of forms or are forms the fetter of the eye?... Is the mind the fetter of mental phenomena or are mental phenomena the fetter of the mind?"

"Friend Kāmabhū, the eye is not the fetter of forms nor are forms the fetter of the eye ... The mind is not the fetter of mental phenomena nor are mental phenomena the fetter of the mind, but rather the desire and lust that arise there in dependence on both: that is the fetter there. [166]

"Suppose, friend, a black ox and a white ox were yoked together by a single harness or yoke. Would one be speaking rightly if one were to say: 'The black ox is the fetter of the white ox; the white ox is the fetter of the black ox'?"

"No, friend. The black ox is not the fetter of the white ox nor is the white ox the fetter of the black ox, but rather the single harness or yoke by which the two are yoked together: that is the fetter there."

"So too, friend, the eye is not the fetter of forms ... nor are mental phenomena the fetter of the mind, but rather the desire and lust that arise there in dependence on both: that is the fetter there."

234 (7) Udāyī

On one occasion the Venerable Ānanda and the Venerable Udāyī were dwelling at Kosambī in Ghosita's Park. Then, in the evening, the Venerable Udāyī emerged from seclusion and approached the Venerable Ānanda. He exchanged greetings with the Venerable Ānanda and, when they had concluded their greetings and cordial talk, he sat down to one side and said to him:

"Friend Ānanda, in many ways [the nature of] this body has been declared, disclosed, and revealed by the Blessed One thus: 'For such a reason this body is nonself.' Is it possible to explain [the nature of] this consciousness in a similar way—to teach, proclaim, establish, disclose, analyse, and elucidate it thus: 'For such a reason this consciousness is nonself'?"

"It is possible, friend Udāyī. Doesn't eye-consciousness arise in dependence on the eye and forms?" [167]

"Yes, friend."

"If the cause and condition for the arising of eye-consciousness would cease completely and totally without remainder, could eye-consciousness be discerned?"

"No, friend."

"In this way, friend, this has been declared, disclosed, and revealed by the Blessed One thus: 'For such a reason this consciousness is nonself.'

"Doesn't ear-consciousness arise in dependence on the ear and sounds?... Doesn't mind-consciousness arise in dependence on the mind and mental phenomena?"

"Yes, friend."

"If the cause and condition for the arising of mind-consciousness would cease completely and totally without remainder, could mind-consciousness be discerned?"

"No, friend."

"In this way too, friend, this has been declared, disclosed, and revealed by the Blessed One thus: 'For such a reason this consciousness is nonself.'

"Suppose, friend, a man needing heartwood, seeking heartwood, wandering in search of heartwood, would take a sharp axe and enter a forest.[169] There he would see the trunk of a large plantain tree, straight, fresh, without a fruit-bud core. [168] He would cut it down at the root, cut off the crown, and unroll the coil. As he unrolls the coil, he would not find even softwood, let alone heartwood.

"So too, a bhikkhu does not recognize either a self or anything belonging to a self in these six bases for contact. Since he does not recognize anything thus, he does not cling to anything in the world. Not clinging, he is not agitated. Being unagitated, he personally attains Nibbāna. He understands: 'Destroyed is birth, the holy life has been lived, what had to be done has been done, there is no more for this state of being.'"

235 (8) The Exposition on Burning

"Bhikkhus, I will teach you a Dhamma exposition on the theme of burning. Listen to that....

"And what, bhikkhus, is the Dhamma exposition on the theme of burning? It would be better, bhikkhus, for the eye faculty to be lacerated by a red-hot iron pin burning, blazing, and glowing, than for one to grasp the sign through the features in a form cognizable by the eye.[170] For if consciousness should stand tied to gratification in the sign or in the features, and if one should die on that occasion, it is possible that one will go to one of two destinations: hell or the animal realm. Having seen this danger, I speak thus.

"It would be better, bhikkhus, for the ear faculty to be lacerated by a sharp iron stake burning, blazing, and glowing, than for one to grasp the sign through the features in a sound cognizable by the ear. For if consciousness should stand tied to gratification in the sign or in the features, and if one should die on that occasion, it is possible that one will go to one of two destinations: hell or the animal realm. Having seen this danger, I speak thus. [169]

"It would be better, bhikkhus, for the nose faculty to be lacerated by a sharp nail cutter burning, blazing, and glowing, than for one to grasp the sign through the features in an odour cognizable by the nose. For if consciousness should stand tied to gratification in the sign or in the features, and if one should die on that occasion, it is possible that one will go to one of two destinations: hell or the animal realm. Having seen this danger, I speak thus.

"It would be better, bhikkhus, for the tongue faculty to be lacerated by a sharp razor burning, blazing, and glowing, than for one to grasp the sign through the features in a taste cognizable by the tongue. For if consciousness should stand tied to gratification in the sign or in the features, and if one should die on that occasion, it is possible that one will go to one of two destinations: hell or the animal realm. Having seen this danger, I speak thus.

"It would be better, bhikkhus, for the body faculty to be lacerated by a sharp spear burning, blazing, and glowing, than for one to grasp the sign through the features in a tactile object cognizable by the body. For if consciousness should stand tied to gratification in the sign or in the features, and if one should die on that occasion, it is possible that one will go to one of two destinations: hell or the animal realm. Having seen this danger, I speak thus.

"It would be better, bhikkhus, to sleep—for sleep, I say, is barren for the living, fruitless for the living, insensibility for the living—than to think such thoughts as would induce one who has come under their control to bring about a schism in the Saṅgha. [170] Having seen this danger, I speak thus.[171]

"In regard to this, bhikkhus, the instructed noble disciple reflects thus: 'Leave off lacerating the eye faculty with a red-hot iron pin burning, blazing, and glowing. Let me attend only to this: So the eye is impermanent, forms are impermanent, eye-consciousness is impermanent, eye-contact is impermanent, whatever feeling arises with eye-contact as condition—whether pleasant or painful or neither-painful-nor-pleasant—that too is impermanent.

"'Leave off lacerating the ear faculty with a sharp iron stake burning, blazing, and glowing. Let me attend only to this: So the ear is impermanent, sounds are impermanent, ear-consciousness is impermanent, ear-contact is impermanent, whatever feeling arises with ear-contact as condition ... that too is impermanent.

"'Leave off lacerating the nose faculty with a sharp nail cutter burning, blazing, and glowing. Let me attend only to this: So the nose is impermanent, odours are impermanent, nose-consciousness is impermanent, nose-contact is impermanent, whatever feeling arises with nose-contact as condition ... that too is impermanent.

"'Leave off lacerating the tongue faculty with a sharp razor burning, blazing, and glowing. Let me attend only to this: So the tongue is impermanent, tastes are impermanent, tongue-consciousness is impermanent, tongue-contact is impermanent, whatever feeling arises with tongue-contact as condition ... that too is impermanent.

"'Leave off lacerating the body faculty with a sharp spear burning, blazing, and glowing. Let me attend only to this: So the body is impermanent, [171] tactile objects are impermanent, body-consciousness is impermanent, body-contact is impermanent, whatever feeling arises with body-contact as condition ... that too is impermanent.

"'Leave off sleeping. Let me attend only to this: So the mind is impermanent, mental phenomena are impermanent, mind-consciousness is impermanent, mind-contact is impermanent, whatever feeling arises with mind-contact as condition ... that too is impermanent.'

"Seeing thus, bhikkhus, the instructed noble disciple experiences revulsion towards the eye, forms, eye-consciousness, eye-contact, and whatever feeling arises with eye-contact as condition—whether pleasant or painful or neither-painful-nor-pleasant ... towards the mind, mental phenomena, mind-consciousness, mind-contact, and whatever feeling arises with mind-contact as condition.... Experiencing revulsion, he becomes dispassionate.

Through dispassion [his mind] is liberated. When it is liberated there comes the knowledge: 'It's liberated.' He understands: 'Destroyed is birth, the holy life has been lived, what had to be done has been done, there is no more for this state of being.'

"This, bhikkhus, is the Dhamma exposition on the theme of burning."

236 (9) The Simile of Hands and Feet (1)

"Bhikkhus, when there are hands, picking up and putting down are discerned. When there are feet, coming and going are discerned. When there are limbs, bending and stretching are discerned. When there is the belly, hunger and thirst are discerned.

"So too, bhikkhus, when there is the eye, pleasure and pain arise internally with eye-contact as condition.[172] When there is the ear, pleasure and pain arise internally with ear-contact as condition.... When there is the mind, pleasure and pain arise internally with mind-contact as condition.

"When, bhikkhus, there are no hands, picking up and putting down are not discerned. When there are no feet, coming and going are not discerned. When there are no limbs, bending and stretching are not discerned. When there is no belly, hunger and thirst are not discerned.

"So too, bhikkhus, when there is no eye, [172] no pleasure and pain arise internally with eye-contact as condition. When there is no ear, no pleasure and pain arise internally with ear-contact as condition.... When there is no mind, no pleasure and pain arise internally with mind-contact as condition."

237 (10) The Simile of Hands and Feet (2)

"Bhikkhus, when there are hands, there is picking up and putting down....

"So too, bhikkhus, when there is the eye, pleasure and pain arise internally with eye-contact as condition.... When there is the mind, pleasure and pain arise internally with mind-contact as condition.

"When, bhikkhus, there are no hands, there is no picking up and putting down....

"So too, bhikkhus, when there is no eye ... no mind, no pleasure and pain arise internally with mind-contact as condition."

IV. The Vipers

238 (1) The Simile of the Vipers

"Bhikkhus, suppose there were four vipers of fierce heat and deadly venom.[173] Then a man would come along wanting to live, not wanting to die, desiring happiness and averse to suffering. They would tell him: 'Good man, these four vipers are of fierce heat and deadly venom. [173] From time to time they must be lifted up; from time to time they must be bathed; from time to time they must be fed; from time to time they must be laid to rest.[174] But if one or another of these vipers ever becomes angry with you, then, good man, you will meet death or deadly suffering. Do whatever has to be done, good man!'

"Then, bhikkhus, afraid of the four vipers of fierce heat and deadly venom, that man would flee in one direction or another. They would tell him: 'Good man, five murderous enemies are pursuing you, thinking, "Wherever we see him, we will take his life right on the spot." Do whatever has to be done, good man!'

"Then, bhikkhus, afraid of the four vipers of fierce heat and deadly venom, and of the five murderous enemies, that man would flee in one direction or another. They would tell him: 'Good man, a sixth murderer, an intimate companion,[175] is pursuing you with drawn sword, thinking, "Wherever I see him I will cut off his head right on the spot." Do whatever has to be done, good man!'

"Then, bhikkhus, afraid of the four vipers of fierce heat and deadly venom, and of the five murderous enemies, and of the sixth murderer, the intimate companion with drawn sword, that man would flee in one direction or another. He would see an empty village. Whatever house he enters is void, deserted, empty. Whatever pot he takes hold of is void, hollow, empty. They would tell him: 'Good man, just now village-attacking dacoits will raid[176] this empty village. Do whatever has to be done, good man!' [174]

"Then, bhikkhus, afraid of the four vipers of fierce heat and deadly venom, and of the five murderous enemies, and of the sixth murderer—the intimate companion with drawn sword—and of the village-attacking dacoits, that man would flee in one direction or another. He would see a great expanse of water whose near shore was dangerous and fearful, and whose further shore was safe and free from danger, but there would be no ferryboat or bridge for crossing over from the near shore to the far shore.[177]

"Then the man would think: 'There is this great expanse of water whose near shore is dangerous and fearful, and whose further shore is safe and free from danger, but there is no ferryboat or bridge for crossing over. Let me collect grass, twigs, branches, and foliage, and bind them together into a raft, so that by means of that raft, making an effort with my hands and feet, I can get safely across to the far shore.'

"Then the man would collect grass, twigs, branches, and foliage, and bind them together into a raft, so that by means of that raft, making an effort with his hands and feet, he would get safely across to the far shore. Crossed over, gone beyond, the brahmin stands on high ground.[178]

"I have made up this simile, bhikkhus, in order to convey a meaning. This is the meaning here: 'The four vipers of fierce heat and deadly venom': this is a designation for the four great elements—the earth element, the water element, the heat element, the air element.[179]

"'The five murderous enemies': this is a designation for the five aggregates subject to clinging; that is, the material form aggregate subject to clinging, the feeling aggregate subject to clinging, the perception aggregate subject to clinging, the volitional formations aggregate subject to clinging, the consciousness aggregate subject to clinging.[180]

"'The sixth murderer, the intimate companion with drawn sword': this is a designation for delight and lust.[181]

"'The empty village': this is a designation for the six internal sense bases. If, bhikkhus, a wise, competent, intelligent person examines them by way of the eye, they appear to be void, hollow, [175] empty. If he examines them by way of the ear ... by way of the mind, they appear to be void, hollow, empty.

"'Village-attacking dacoits': this is a designation for the six external sense bases. The eye, bhikkhus, is attacked by agreeable and disagreeable forms. The ear ... The nose ... The tongue ...

The body … The mind is attacked by agreeable and disagreeable mental phenomena.

"'The great expanse of water': this is a designation for the four floods: the flood of sensuality, the flood of existence, the flood of views, and the flood of ignorance.

"'The near shore, which is dangerous and fearful': this is a designation for identity.[182]

"'The further shore, which is safe and free from danger': this is a designation for Nibbāna.

"'The raft': this is a designation for the Noble Eightfold Path; that is, right view … right concentration.

"'Making effort with hands and feet': this is a designation for the arousing of energy.

"'Crossed over, gone beyond, the brahmin stands on high ground': this is a designation for the arahant."

239 (2) The Simile of the Chariot

"Bhikkhus, by possessing three qualities, a bhikkhu lives full of happiness and joy in this very life, and he has laid a foundation[183] for the destruction of the taints. What are the three? He is one who guards the doors of the sense faculties, who is moderate in eating, and who is devoted to wakefulness. [176]

"And how, bhikkhus, is a bhikkhu one who guards the doors of the sense faculties? Here, having seen a form with the eye, a bhikkhu does not grasp its signs and features. Since, if he left the eye faculty unrestrained, evil unwholesome states of covetousness and displeasure might invade him, he practises the way of its restraint, he guards the eye faculty, he undertakes the restraint of the eye faculty. Having heard a sound with the ear … Having smelt an odour with the nose … Having tasted a taste with the tongue … Having felt a tactile object with the body … Having cognized a mental phenomenon with the mind, a bhikkhu does not grasp its signs and its features. Since, if he left the mind faculty unrestrained, evil unwholesome states of covetousness and displeasure might invade him, he practises the way of its restraint, he guards the mind faculty, he undertakes the restraint of the mind faculty.

"Suppose, bhikkhus, a chariot harnessed to thoroughbreds was standing ready on even ground at a crossroads, with a goad on hand. Then a skilful trainer, a charioteer of horses to be tamed, would mount it and, taking the reins in his left hand and the goad in his right, would drive away and return by any route he wants, whenever he wants. So too, a bhikkhu trains in protecting these six sense faculties, trains in controlling them, trains in taming them, trains in pacifying them. It is in this way, bhikkhus, that a bhikkhu guards the doors of the sense faculties.

"And how, bhikkhus, is a bhikkhu moderate in eating? Here, reflecting wisely, a bhikkhu takes food neither for amusement nor for intoxication nor for the sake of physical beauty and attractiveness, but only for the support and maintenance of this body, for ending discomfort, and for assisting the holy life, considering: 'Thus I shall terminate the old feeling and not arouse a new feeling, and I shall be healthy and blameless and live in comfort.' [177] Just as a person anoints a wound only for the purpose of enabling it to heal, or just as one greases an axle only for the sake of transporting a load, so a bhikkhu, reflecting wisely, takes food ... for assisting the holy life. It is in this way, bhikkhus, that a bhikkhu is moderate in eating.

"And how, bhikkhus, is a bhikkhu devoted to wakefulness? Here, during the day, while walking back and forth and sitting, a bhikkhu purifies his mind of obstructive states. In the first watch of the night, while walking back and forth and sitting, he purifies his mind of obstructive states. In the middle watch of the night he lies down on the right side in the lion's posture with one foot overlapping the other, mindful and clearly comprehending, after noting in his mind the idea of rising. After rising, in the last watch of the night, while walking back and forth and sitting, he purifies his mind of obstructive states. It is in this way, bhikkhus, that a bhikkhu is devoted to wakefulness.

"Bhikkhus, it is by possessing these three qualities that a bhikkhu lives full of happiness and joy in this very life, and he has laid the foundation for the destruction of the taints."

240 (3) The Simile of the Tortoise

"Bhikkhus, in the past a tortoise[184] was searching for food along the bank of a river one evening. On that same evening a jackal was also searching for food along the bank of that same river. When the tortoise saw the jackal in the distance searching for food, [178] it drew its limbs and neck inside its shell and passed the time keeping still and silent.[185]

"The jackal had also seen the tortoise in the distance searching for food, so he approached and waited close by, thinking, 'When this tortoise extends one or another of its limbs or its neck, I will grab it right on the spot, pull it out, and eat it.' But because the tortoise did not extend any of its limbs or its neck, the jackal, failing to gain access to it, lost interest in it and departed.

"So too, bhikkhus, Māra the Evil One is constantly and continually waiting close by you, thinking, 'Perhaps I will gain access to him through the eye or through the ear ... or through the mind.' Therefore, bhikkhus, dwell guarding the doors of the sense faculties. Having seen a form with the eye, do not grasp its signs and features. Since, if you leave the eye faculty unguarded, evil unwholesome states of covetousness and displeasure might invade you, practise the way of its restraint, guard the eye faculty, undertake the restraint of the eye faculty. Having heard a sound with the ear ... Having smelt an odour with the nose ... Having savoured a taste with the tongue ... Having felt a tactile object with the body ... Having cognized a mental phenomenon with the mind, do not grasp its signs and features. Since, if you leave the mind faculty unguarded, evil unwholesome states of covetousness and displeasure might invade you, practise the way of its restraint, guard the mind faculty, undertake the restraint of the mind faculty.

"When, bhikkhus, you dwell guarding the doors of the sense faculties, Māra the Evil One, failing to gain access to you, will lose interest in you and depart, just as the jackal departed from the tortoise." [179]

> Drawing in the mind's thoughts
> As a tortoise draws its limbs into its shell,
> Independent, not harassing others, fully quenched,
> A bhikkhu would not blame anyone.[186]

241 (4) The Simile of the Great Log (1)

On one occasion the Blessed One was dwelling at Kosambī on the bank of the river Ganges. The Blessed One saw a great log being carried along by the current of the river Ganges, and he addressed the bhikkhus thus: "Do you see, bhikkhus, that great log being carried along by the current of the river Ganges?"

"Yes, venerable sir."

"If, bhikkhus, that log does not veer towards the near shore, does not veer towards the far shore, does not sink in mid-stream, does not get cast up on high ground, does not get caught by human beings, does not get caught by nonhuman beings, does not get caught in a whirlpool, and does not become inwardly rotten, it will slant, slope, and incline towards the ocean. For what reason? Because the current of the river Ganges slants, slopes, and inclines towards the ocean.

"So too, bhikkhus, if you do not veer towards the near shore, do not veer towards the far shore, do not sink in mid-stream, do not get cast up on high ground, do not get caught by human beings, do not get caught by nonhuman beings, do not get caught in a whirlpool, and do not become inwardly rotten, [180] you will slant, slope, and incline towards Nibbāna. For what reason? Because right view slants, slopes, and inclines towards Nibbāna."

When this was said, a certain bhikkhu asked the Blessed One: "What, venerable sir, is the near shore? What is the far shore? What is sinking in mid-stream? What is getting cast up on high ground? What is getting caught by human beings, what is getting caught by nonhuman beings, what is getting caught in a whirlpool? What is inward rottenness?"

"'The near shore,' bhikkhu: this is a designation for the six internal sense bases. 'The far shore': this is a designation for the six external sense bases. 'Sinking in mid-stream': this is a designation for delight and lust. 'Getting cast up on high ground': this is a designation for the conceit 'I am.'

"And what, bhikkhu, is getting caught by human beings? Here, someone lives in association with laypeople; he rejoices with them and sorrows with them, he is happy when they are happy and sad when they are sad, and he involves himself in their affairs and duties.[187] This is called getting caught by human beings.

"And what, bhikkhu, is getting caught by nonhuman beings? Here, someone lives the holy life with the aspiration [to be reborn] into a certain order of devas, thinking: 'By this virtue or vow or austerity or holy life I will become a deva or one among the devas.' This is called getting caught by nonhuman beings.

"'Getting caught in a whirlpool': this, bhikkhu, is a designation for the five cords of sensual pleasure.

"And what, bhikkhu, is inward rottenness? Here someone is immoral, one of evil character, of impure and suspect behaviour, secretive in his acts, no ascetic though claiming to be one, [181] not a celibate though claiming to be one, inwardly rotten, corrupt, depraved.[188] This is called inward rottenness."

Now on that occasion the cowherd Nanda was standing near the Blessed One. He then said to the Blessed One: "Venerable sir, I will not veer[189] towards the near shore, I will not veer towards the far shore, I will not sink in mid-stream, I will not get cast up on high ground, I will not get caught by human beings, I will not get caught by nonhuman beings, I will not get caught in a whirlpool, I will not become inwardly rotten. May I receive the going forth under the Blessed One, may I receive the higher ordination?"

"In that case, Nanda, return the cows to their owners."

"The cows will go back of their own accord, venerable sir, out of attachment to the calves."

"Return the cows to their owners, Nanda."

Then the cowherd Nanda returned the cows to their owners, came back to the Blessed One, and said: "The cows have been returned to their owners, venerable sir. May I receive the going forth under the Blessed One, may I receive the higher ordination?"

Then the cowherd Nanda received the going forth under the Blessed One, and he received the higher ordination. And soon, not long after his higher ordination, dwelling alone, withdrawn, diligent, ardent, and resolute ... the Venerable Nanda became one of the arahants."

242 (5) The Simile of the Great Log (2)

On one occasion the Blessed One was dwelling at Kimbilā on the bank of the river Ganges. The Blessed One saw a great log being carried along by the current of the river Ganges, and he addressed the bhikkhus thus: "Do you see, bhikkhus, [182] that great log being carried along by the current of the river Ganges?"

"Yes, venerable sir."... (*as above*) ...

When this was said, the Venerable Kimbila asked the Blessed One: "What, venerable sir, is the near shore ... what is inward rottenness?"

(Replies as above except the following:)

"And what, Kimbila, is inward rottenness? Here, Kimbila, a bhikkhu commits a certain defiled offence, an offence of a kind that does not allow for rehabilitation.[190] This is called inward rottenness."

243 (6) Exposition on the Corrupted

On one occasion the Blessed One was dwelling among the Sakyans at Kapilavatthu in Nigrodha's Park. Now on that occasion a new assembly hall had just been built for the Sakyans of Kapilavatthu and it had not yet been inhabited by any ascetic or brahmin or by any human being at all. Then the Sakyans of Kapilavatthu approached the Blessed One, paid homage to him, sat down to one side, and said to him:

"Venerable sir, a new council hall has just been built for the Sakyans of Kapilavatthu and it has not yet been inhabited by any ascetic or brahmin or by any human being at all. [183] Venerable sir, let the Blessed One be the first to use it. When the Blessed One has used it first, then the Sakyans of Kapilavatthu will use it afterwards. That will lead to their welfare and happiness for a long time."[191]

The Blessed One consented by silence. Then, when the Sakyans understood that the Blessed One had consented, they rose from their seats and, after paying homage to the Blessed One, keeping him on their right, they went to the new assembly hall. They covered it thoroughly with mats, prepared seats, put out a large water jug, and hung up an oil lamp. Then they approached the Blessed One and informed him of this, adding: "Let the Blessed One come at his own convenience."

Then the Blessed One dressed and, taking bowl and robe, went together with the Saṅgha of bhikkhus to the new assembly hall. After washing his feet, he entered the hall and sat down against the central pillar facing east. The bhikkhus too, after washing their feet, entered the hall and sat down against the western wall facing east, with the Blessed One in front of them. The Sakyans of Kapilavatthu too, after washing their feet, entered the hall and sat down against the eastern wall facing west, with the Blessed One in front of them.

The Blessed One then instructed, exhorted, inspired, and gladdened the Sakyans with a Dhamma talk through much of the night, after which he dismissed them, saying: "The night has passed, Gotamas.[192] You may go at your own convenience." [184]

"Yes, venerable sir," they replied. Then they rose from their seats and, after paying homage to the Blessed One, keeping him on their right, they departed. Then, not long after the Sakyans of Kapilavatthu had left, the Blessed One addressed the Venerable Mahāmoggallāna thus: "The Saṅgha of bhikkhus is free from sloth and torpor, Moggallāna. Give a Dhamma talk to the bhikkhus. My back is aching, so I will stretch it."[193]

"Yes, venerable sir," the Venerable Mahāmoggallāna replied.

Then the Blessed One prepared his outer robe folded in four and lay down on his right side in the lion's posture, with one foot overlapping the other, mindful and clearly comprehending, after noting in his mind the idea of rising. Thereupon the Venerable Mahāmoggallāna addressed the bhikkhus thus: "Friends, bhikkhus!"

"Friend!" those bhikkhus replied. The Venerable Mahāmoggallāna said this:

"I will teach you, friends, an exposition on the corrupted and the uncorrupted.[194] Listen to it and attend closely, I will speak."

"Yes, friend," those bhikkhus replied. The Venerable Mahāmoggallāna said this:

"How, friends, is one corrupted? Here, having seen a form with the eye, a bhikkhu is intent upon a pleasing form and repelled by a displeasing form.[195] He dwells without having set up mindfulness of the body, with a limited mind, and he does not understand as it really is that liberation of mind, liberation by wisdom, wherein those evil unwholesome states cease without remainder. [185] Having heard a sound with the ear ... Having cognized a mental phenomenon with the mind, he is intent upon a pleasing mental phenomenon and repelled by a displeasing mental phenomenon. He dwells without having set up mindfulness of the body, with a limited mind, and he does not understand as it really is that liberation of mind, liberation by wisdom, wherein those evil unwholesome states cease without remainder.

"This is called, friends, a bhikkhu who is corrupted amidst forms cognizable by the eye, corrupted amidst sounds cognizable by the ear, corrupted amidst odours cognizable by the nose, corrupted amidst tastes cognizable by the tongue, corrupted amidst tactile objects cognizable by the body, corrupted amidst mental phenomena cognizable by the mind. When a bhikkhu dwells thus, if Māra approaches him through the eye, Māra gains access to him, Māra gets a hold on him. If Māra approaches him through the ear ... through the mind, Māra gains access to him, Māra gets a hold on him.

"Suppose, friends, there is a shed made of reeds or of grass, dried up, desiccated, past its prime. If a man approaches it from the east with a blazing grass torch, or from the west, from the north, from the south, from below, or from above, whichever way he approaches it the fire gains access to it, the fire gets a hold on it. So too, friends, when a bhikkhu dwells thus, if Māra approaches him through the eye ... through the mind, Māra gains access to him, Māra gets a hold on him.

"When a bhikkhu dwells thus, forms overwhelm him; he does not overwhelm forms. Sounds overwhelm him; [186] he does not overwhelm sounds. Odours overwhelm him; he does not overwhelm odours. Tastes overwhelm him; he does not overwhelm tastes. Tactile objects overwhelm him; he does not overwhelm tactile objects. Mental phenomena overwhelm him; he does not overwhelm mental phenomena. This is called, friends, a bhikkhu who is overwhelmed by forms, overwhelmed by sounds, overwhelmed by odours, overwhelmed by tastes, overwhelmed by tactile objects, overwhelmed by mental phenomena—one who is overwhelmed and who does not overwhelm. Evil unwholesome states have overwhelmed him, states that defile, that lead to renewed existence, that bring trouble, that result in suffering, and that lead to future birth, aging, and death.

"It is in this way, friends, that one is corrupted.

"And how, friends, is one uncorrupted? Here, having seen a form with the eye, a bhikkhu is not intent upon a pleasing form and not repelled by a displeasing form. He dwells having set up mindfulness of the body, with a measureless mind, and he understands as it really is that liberation of mind, liberation by wisdom, wherein those evil unwholesome states cease without remainder. Having heard a sound with the ear ... Having cognized a mental phenomenon with the mind, he is not intent upon a pleasing mental phenomenon and not repelled by a displeasing mental phenomenon. He dwells having set up mindfulness of the body, with a measureless mind, and he understands as it really is that liberation of mind, liberation by wisdom, wherein those evil unwholesome states cease without remainder.

"This is called, friends, a bhikkhu who is uncorrupted amidst forms cognizable by the eye, uncorrupted amidst sounds cognizable by the ear, uncorrupted amidst odours cognizable by the nose, uncorrupted amidst tastes cognizable by the tongue, uncorrupted amidst tactile objects cognizable by the body, uncorrupted amidst mental phenomena cognizable by the mind. When a bhikkhu dwells thus, if Māra approaches him through the eye, Māra fails to gain access to him, Māra fails to get a hold on him. If Māra approaches him through the ear … through the mind, Māra fails to gain access to him, Māra fails to get a hold on him.

"Suppose, friends, there is a peaked house or a hall [187] built of thickly packed clay and freshly plastered. If a man approaches it from the east with a blazing grass torch, or from the west, from the north, from the south, from below, or from above, whichever way he approaches it the fire fails to gain access to it, the fire fails to get a hold on it. So too, friends, when a bhikkhu dwells thus, if Māra approaches him through the eye … through the mind, Māra fails to gain access to him, Māra fails to get a hold on him.

"When a bhikkhu dwells thus, he overwhelms forms; forms do not overwhelm him. He overwhelms sounds; sounds do not overwhelm him. He overwhelms odours; odours do not overwhelm him. He overwhelms tastes; tastes do not overwhelm him. He overwhelms tactile objects; tactile objects do not overwhelm him. He overwhelms mental phenomena; mental phenomena do not overwhelm him. This is called, friends, a bhikkhu who overwhelms forms, who overwhelms sounds, who overwhelms odours, who overwhelms tastes, who overwhelms tactile objects, who overwhelms mental phenomena—one who overwhelms and who is not overwhelmed. He has overwhelmed those evil unwholesome states that defile, that lead to renewed existence, that bring trouble, that result in suffering, and that lead to future birth, aging, and death.

"It is in this way, friends, that one is uncorrupted."

Then the Blessed One got up and addressed the Venerable Mahāmoggallāna thus: "Good, good, Moggallāna! You have spoken well to the bhikkhus the exposition on the corrupted and the uncorrupted."

This is what the Venerable Mahāmoggallāna said. [188] The Teacher approved. Elated, those bhikkhus delighted in the Venerable Mahāmoggallāna's statement.

244 (7) States That Entail Suffering

"Bhikkhus, when a bhikkhu understands as they really are the origin and the passing away of all states whatsoever that entail suffering, then sensual pleasures have been seen by him in such a way that as he looks at them sensual desire, sensual affection, sensual infatuation, and sensual passion do not lie latent within him in regard to sensual pleasures; then he has comprehended a mode of conduct and manner of dwelling in such a way that as he conducts himself thus and as he dwells thus, evil unwholesome states of covetousness and displeasure do not flow in upon him.[196]

"And how, bhikkhus, does a bhikkhu understand as they really are the origin and the passing away of all states whatsoever that entail suffering?[197] 'Such is form, such its origin, such its passing away; such is feeling ... such is perception ... such are volitional formations ... such is consciousness, such its origin, such its passing away': it is in such a way that a bhikkhu understands as they really are the origin and the passing away of all states whatsoever that entail suffering.

"And how, bhikkhus, are sensual pleasures seen by a bhikkhu in such a way that as he looks at them sensual desire, sensual affection, sensual infatuation, and sensual passion do not lie latent within him in regard to sensual pleasures? Suppose there is a charcoal pit deeper than a man's height, filled with glowing coals without flame or smoke.[198] A man would come along wanting to live, not wanting to die, desiring happiness and averse to suffering. Then two strong men would grab him by both arms and drag him towards the charcoal pit. The man would wriggle his body this way and that. For what reason? Because he knows: [189] 'I will fall into this charcoal pit and I will thereby meet death or deadly suffering.' So too, bhikkhus, when a bhikkhu has seen sensual pleasures as similar to a charcoal pit, sensual desire, sensual affection, sensual infatuation, and sensual passion do not lie latent within him in regard to sensual pleasures.

"And how, bhikkhus, has a bhikkhu comprehended a mode of conduct and manner of dwelling in such a way that as he conducts himself thus and as he dwells thus, evil unwholesome states of covetousness and displeasure do not flow in upon him? Suppose a man would enter a thorny forest. There would be thorns in front of him, thorns behind him, thorns to his left, thorns to his right, thorns below him, thorns above him. He would go forward mindfully,[199] he would go back mindfully, thinking, 'May no thorn prick me!' So too, bhikkhus, whatever in the world has a pleasing and agreeable nature is called a thorn in the Noble One's Discipline. Having understood this thus as 'a thorn,'[200] one should understand restraint and nonrestraint.

"And how, bhikkhus, is there nonrestraint? Here, having seen a form with the eye, a bhikkhu is intent upon a pleasing form and repelled by a displeasing form. He dwells without having set up mindfulness of the body, with a limited mind, and he does not understand as it really is that liberation of mind, liberation by wisdom, wherein those evil unwholesome states cease without remainder. Having heard a sound with the ear ... Having cognized a mental phenomenon with the mind, he is intent upon a pleasing mental phenomenon and repelled by a displeasing mental phenomenon. He dwells without having set up mindfulness of the body, with a limited mind, and he does not understand as it really is that liberation of mind, liberation by wisdom, wherein those evil unwholesome states cease without remainder. It is in such a way that there is nonrestraint.

"And how, bhikkhus, is there restraint? Here, having seen a form with the eye, a bhikkhu is not intent upon a pleasing form and not repelled by a displeasing form. He dwells having set up mindfulness of the body, with a measureless mind, and he understands as it really is that liberation of mind, liberation by wisdom, [190] wherein those evil unwholesome states cease without remainder. Having heard a sound with the ear ... Having cognized a mental phenomenon with the mind, he is not intent upon a pleasing mental phenomenon and not repelled by a displeasing mental phenomenon. He dwells having set up mindfulness of the body, with a measureless mind, and he understands as it really is that liberation of mind, liberation by wisdom, wherein those evil unwholesome states cease without remainder. It is in such a way that there is restraint.

"When, bhikkhus, a bhikkhu is conducting himself and dwelling in such a way, if occasionally, due to a lapse of mindfulness, evil unwholesome memories and intentions connected with the fetters arise in him, slow might be the arising of his mindfulness, but then he quickly abandons them, dispels them, puts an end to them, obliterates them.[201] Suppose a man let two or three drops of water fall onto an iron plate heated for a whole day. Slow might be the falling of the water drops, but then they would quickly vaporize and vanish. So too, when a bhikkhu is conducting himself and dwelling in such a way … slow might be the arising of his mindfulness, but then he quickly abandons them, dispels them, puts an end to them, obliterates them.

"Thus a bhikkhu has comprehended a mode of conduct and manner of dwelling in such a way that as he conducts himself and as he dwells thus, evil unwholesome states of covetousness and displeasure do not flow in upon him.

"When a bhikkhu is conducting himself thus and dwelling thus, kings or royal ministers, friends or colleagues, relatives or kinsmen, might invite him to accept wealth, saying: 'Come, good man, why let these saffron robes weigh you down? Why roam around with a shaven head and a begging bowl? Come, having returned to the lower life, enjoy wealth and do meritorious deeds.' Indeed, bhikkhus, when that bhikkhu is conducting himself thus and dwelling thus, it is impossible that he will give up the training and return to the lower life. [191]

"Suppose, bhikkhus, that when the river Ganges slants, slopes, and inclines towards the east, a great crowd of people would come along bringing a shovel and basket, thinking: 'We will make this river Ganges slant, slope, and incline towards the west.' What do you think, bhikkhus, would that great crowd of people be able to make the river Ganges slant, slope, and incline towards the west?"

"No, venerable sir. For what reason? Because the river Ganges slants, slopes, and inclines towards the east, and it is not easy to make it slant, slope, and incline towards the west. That great crowd of people would only reap fatigue and vexation."

"So too, bhikkhus, when a bhikkhu is conducting himself thus and dwelling thus, kings or royal ministers, friends or colleagues, relatives or kinsmen, might invite him to accept wealth … [but] it is impossible that he will give up the training and return to the lower life. For what reason? Because for a long time his mind has slanted, sloped, and inclined towards seclusion. Thus it is impossible that he will give up the training and return to the lower life."

245 (8) The Kiṃsuka *Tree*

One bhikkhu approached another and asked him: "In what way, friend, is a bhikkhu's vision well purified?"[202]

"When, friend, a bhikkhu understands as they really are the origin and the passing away of the six bases for contact, [192] in this way his vision is well purified."[203]

Then the first bhikkhu, dissatisfied with the other's answer, approached another bhikkhu and asked him: "In what way, friend, is a bhikkhu's vision well purified?"

"When, friend, a bhikkhu understands as they really are the origin and the passing away of the five aggregates subject to clinging, in this way his vision is well purified."

Again, the first bhikkhu, dissatisfied with the other's answer, approached still another bhikkhu and asked him: "In what way, friend, is a bhikkhu's vision well purified?"

"When, friend, a bhikkhu understands as they really are the origin and the passing away of the four great elements, in this way his vision is well purified."

Again, the first bhikkhu, dissatisfied with the other's answer, approached still another bhikkhu and asked him: "In what way, friend, is a bhikkhu's vision well purified?"

"When, friend, a bhikkhu understands as it really is: 'Whatever is subject to origination is all subject to cessation,' in this way his vision is well purified."

Then the first bhikkhu, dissatisfied with the other's answer, approached the Blessed One, reported everything that had happened, [193] and asked: "In what way, venerable sir, is a bhikkhu's vision well purified?"

"Bhikkhu, suppose there was a man who had never before seen a *kiṃsuka* tree.[204] He might approach a man who had seen a *kiṃsuka* tree and ask him: 'Sir, what is a *kiṃsuka* tree like?' The other might answer: 'Good man, a *kiṃsuka* tree is blackish, like a charred stump.' On that occasion a *kiṃsuka* tree might have been exactly as that man had seen it.

"Then that man, dissatisfied with the other's answer, might approach another man who had seen a *kiṃsuka* tree and ask him: 'Sir, what is a *kiṃsuka* tree like?' The other might answer: 'Good man, a *kiṃsuka* tree is reddish, like a piece of meat.' On that occasion a *kiṃsuka* tree might have been exactly as that man had seen it.

"Then that man, dissatisfied with the other's answer, might approach still another man who had seen a *kiṃsuka* tree and ask him: 'Sir, what is a *kiṃsuka* tree like?' The other might answer: 'Good man, a *kiṃsuka* tree has strips of bark hanging down and burst pods, like an acacia tree.'[205] On that occasion a *kiṃsuka* tree might have been exactly as that man had seen it.

"Then that man, dissatisfied with the other's answer, [194] might approach still another man who had seen a *kiṃsuka* tree and ask him: 'Sir, what is a *kiṃsuka* tree like?' The other might answer: 'Good man, a *kiṃsuka* tree has plenty of leaves and foliage and gives abundant shade, like a banyan tree.' On that occasion a *kiṃsuka* tree might have been exactly as that man had seen it.

"So too, bhikkhu, those superior men answered as they were disposed in just the way their own vision had been well purified.[206]

"Suppose, bhikkhu, a king had a frontier city with strong ramparts, walls, and arches, and with six gates.[207] The gatekeeper posted there would be wise, competent, and intelligent; one who keeps out strangers and admits acquaintances. A swift pair of messengers would come from the east and ask the gatekeeper: 'Where, good man, is the lord of this city?' He would reply: 'He is sitting in the central square.' Then the swift pair of messengers would deliver a message of reality to the lord of the city and leave by the route by which they had arrived. Similarly, messengers would come from the west, from the north, from the south, deliver their message, and leave by the route by which they had arrived.

"I have made up this simile, bhikkhu, in order to convey a meaning. This is the meaning here: 'The city': this is a designation for this body consisting of the four great elements, originating from mother and father, built up out of boiled rice and gruel, subject to impermanence, to being worn and rubbed away, to breaking apart and dispersal.[208] 'The six gates': this is a designation for the six internal sense bases. 'The gatekeeper': this is a designation for mindfulness. [195] 'The swift pair of messengers': this is a designation for serenity and insight. 'The lord of the city': this is designation for consciousness.[209] 'The central square': this is a designation for the four great elements—the earth element, the water element, the heat element, the air element. 'A message of reality': this is a designation for Nibbāna.[210] 'The route by which they had arrived': this is a designation for the Noble Eightfold Path; that is, right view ... right concentration."

246 (9) The Simile of the Lute

"Bhikkhus, if in any bhikkhu or bhikkhunī desire or lust or hatred or delusion or aversion of mind should arise in regard to forms cognizable by the eye, such a one should rein in the mind from them thus:[211] 'This path is fearful, dangerous, strewn with thorns, covered by jungle, a deviant path, an evil path, a way beset by scarcity.[212] This is a path followed by inferior people; it is not the path followed by superior people. This is not for you.' In this way the mind should be reined in from these states regarding forms cognizable by the eye. So too regarding sounds cognizable by the ear ... regarding mental phenomena cognizable by the mind.

"Suppose, bhikkhus, that the barley has ripened and the watchman is negligent. If a bull fond of barley enters the barley field, he might indulge himself as much as he likes. [196] So too, bhikkhus, the uninstructed worldling who does not exercise restraint over the six bases for contact indulges himself as much as he likes in the five cords of sensual pleasure.[213]

"Suppose, bhikkhus, that the barley has ripened and the watchman is vigilant. If a bull fond of barley enters the barley field, the watchman would catch hold of him firmly by the muzzle. While holding him firmly by the muzzle, he would get a secure grip on the locks between his horns and, keeping him in check there, would give him a sound beating with his staff. After giving him that beating, he would drive the bull away. This might happen a second time and a third time. Thus that bull fond of barley, whether he has gone to the village or the forest, whether he is accustomed to standing or to sitting, remembering the previous beating he got from the staff, would not enter that barley field again.

"So too, bhikkhus, when a bhikkhu's mind has been subdued, well subdued,[214] regarding the six bases for contact, it then becomes inwardly steady, settled, unified, and concentrated.

"Suppose, bhikkhus, there was a king or a royal minister who had never before heard the sound of a lute. He might hear the sound of a lute and say: 'Good man, what is making this sound—so tantalizing, so lovely, so intoxicating, [197] so entrancing, so enthralling?' They would say to him: 'Sire, it is a lute that is making this sound—so tantalizing, so lovely, so intoxicating, so entrancing, so enthralling.' He would reply: 'Go, man, bring me that lute.'

"They would bring him the lute and tell him: 'Sire, this is that lute, the sound of which was so tantalizing, so lovely, so intoxicating, so entrancing, so enthralling.' The king would say: 'I've had enough with this lute, man. Bring me just that sound.' The men would reply: 'This lute, sire, consists of numerous components, of a great many components, and it gives off a sound when it is played upon with its numerous components; that is, in dependence on the parchment sounding board, the belly, the arm, the head, the strings, the plectrum, and the appropriate effort of the musician.[215] So it is, sire, that this lute consisting of numerous components, of a great many components, gives off a sound when it is played upon with its numerous components.'

"The king would split the lute into ten or a hundred pieces, then he would reduce these to splinters. Having reduced them to splinters, he would burn them in a fire and reduce them to ashes, and he would winnow the ashes in a strong wind or let them be carried away by the swift current of a river. Then he would say: 'A poor thing, indeed sir, is this so-called lute, as well as anything else called a lute. How the multitude are utterly heedless about it, utterly taken in by it!'[216]

"So too, bhikkhus, a bhikkhu investigates form to the extent that there is a range for form, he investigates feeling to the extent that there is a range for feeling, he investigates perception to the extent that there is a range for perception, he investigates volitional formations to the extent that there is a range for volitional formations, he investigates consciousness to the extent that there is a range for consciousness. [198] As he investigates form to the extent that there is a range for form ... consciousness to the extent that there is a range for consciousness, whatever notions of 'I' or 'mine' or 'I am' had occurred to him before no longer occur to him."[217]

247 (10) The Simile of the Six Animals

"Bhikkhus, suppose a man with limbs wounded and festering would enter a wood of thorny reeds,[218] and the *kusa* thorns would prick his feet and the reed blades would slash his limbs. Thus that man would thereby experience even more pain and displeasure. So too, bhikkhus, some bhikkhu here, gone to the village or the forest, meets someone who reproaches him thus: 'This venerable one, acting in such a way, behaving in such a way, is a foul village thorn.' Having understood him thus as a 'thorn,' one should understand restraint and nonrestraint.[219]

"And how, bhikkhus is there nonrestraint? Here, having seen a form with the eye, a bhikkhu is intent upon a pleasing form and repelled by a displeasing form. He dwells without having set up mindfulness of the body, with a limited mind, and he does not understand as it really is that liberation of mind, liberation by wisdom, wherein those evil unwholesome states cease without remainder. Having heard a sound with the ear ... Having cognized a mental phenomenon with the mind, he is intent upon a pleasing mental phenomenon and repelled by a displeasing mental phenomenon. He dwells without having set up mindfulness of the body, with a limited mind, and he does not understand as it really is that liberation of mind, liberation by wisdom, wherein those evil unwholesome states cease without remainder.

"Suppose, bhikkhus, a man would catch six animals—with different domains and different feeding grounds—and tie them by a strong rope. He would catch a snake, a crocodile, a bird, a dog, [199] a jackal, and a monkey, and tie each by a strong rope. Having done so, he would tie the ropes together with a knot in the middle and release them. Then those six animals with different domains and different feeding grounds would each pull in the direction of its own feeding ground and domain. The snake would pull one way, thinking, 'Let me enter an anthill.' The crocodile would pull another way, thinking, 'Let me enter the water.' The bird would pull another way, thinking, 'Let me fly up into the sky.' The dog would pull another way, thinking, 'Let me enter a village.' The jackal would pull another way, thinking, 'Let me enter a charnel ground.' The monkey would pull another way, thinking, 'Let me enter a forest.'

"Now when these six animals become worn out and fatigued, they would be dominated by the one among them that was strongest; they would submit to it and come under its control. So too, bhikkhus, when a bhikkhu has not developed and cultivated mindfulness directed to the body, the eye pulls in the direction of agreeable forms and disagreeable forms are repulsive; the ear pulls in the direction of agreeable sounds and disagreeable sounds are repulsive; the nose pulls in the direction of agreeable odours and disagreeable odours are repulsive; the tongue pulls in the direction of agreeable tastes and disagreeable tastes are repulsive; the body pulls in the direction of agreeable tactile objects and disagreeable tactile objects are repulsive; the mind pulls in the direction of agreeable mental phenomena and disagreeable mental phenomena are repulsive.

"It is in such a way that there is nonrestraint.

"And how, bhikkhus, is there restraint? Here, having seen a form with the eye, a bhikkhu is not intent upon a pleasing form and not repelled by a displeasing form. He dwells having set up mindfulness of the body, with a measureless mind, and he understands as it really is that liberation of mind, liberation by wisdom, wherein those evil unwholesome states cease without remainder. Having heard a sound with the ear ... Having cognized a mental phenomenon with the mind, he is not intent upon a pleasing mental phenomenon and not repelled by a displeasing mental phenomenon. [200] He dwells having set up mindfulness of the body, with a measureless mind, and he understands as it really is that liberation of mind, liberation by wisdom, wherein those evil unwholesome states cease without remainder. It is in such a way that there is restraint.

"Suppose, bhikkhus, a man would catch six animals—with different domains and different feeding grounds—and tie them by a strong rope. He would catch a snake, a crocodile, a bird, a dog, a jackal, and a monkey, and tie each by a strong rope. Having done so, he would bind them to a strong post or pillar. Then those six animals with different domains and different feeding grounds would each pull in the direction of its own feeding ground and domain. The snake would pull one way, thinking,

'Let me enter an anthill' ... (*as above*) ... The monkey would pull another way, thinking, 'Let me enter a forest.'

"Now when these six animals become worn out and fatigued, they would stand close to that post or pillar, they would sit down there, they would lie down there. So too, bhikkhus, when a bhikkhu has developed and cultivated mindfulness directed to the body, the eye does not pull in the direction of agreeable forms nor are disagreeable forms repulsive; the ear does not pull in the direction of agreeable sounds nor are disagreeable sounds repulsive; the nose does not pull in the direction of agreeable odours nor are disagreeable odours repulsive; the tongue does not pull in the direction of agreeable tastes nor are disagreeable tastes repulsive; the body does not pull in the direction of agreeable tactile objects nor are disagreeable tactile objects repulsive; the mind does not pull in the direction of agreeable mental phenomena nor are disagreeable mental phenomena repulsive.

"It is in such a way that there is restraint.

"'A strong post or pillar': this, bhikkhus, is a designation for mindfulness directed to the body. Therefore, bhikkhus, you should train yourselves thus: 'We will develop and cultivate mindfulness directed to the body, make it our vehicle, make it our basis, stabilize it, exercise ourselves in it, and fully perfect it.' Thus should you train yourselves." [201]

248 (11) The Sheaf of Barley

"Bhikkhus, suppose a sheaf of barley were set down at a crossroads. Then six men would come along with flails in their hands[220] and they would strike that sheaf of barley with the six flails. Thus that sheaf of barley would be well struck, having been struck by the six flails. Then a seventh man would come along with a flail in his hand and he would strike that sheaf of barley with the seventh flail. Thus that sheaf of barley would be struck even still more thoroughly, having been struck by the seventh flail.

"So too, bhikkhus, the uninstructed worldling is struck in the eye by agreeable and disagreeable forms; struck in the ear by agreeable and disagreeable sounds; struck in the nose by agreeable and disagreeable odours; struck in the tongue by agreeable and disagreeable tastes; struck in the body by agreeable and disagreeable tactile objects; struck in the mind by agreeable and disagreeable mental phenomena. If that uninstructed worldling sets his mind upon future renewed existence,[221] then that senseless man is struck even still more thoroughly, just like the sheaf of barley struck by the seventh flail.

"Once in the past, bhikkhus, the devas and the asuras were arrayed for battle.[222] Then Vepacitti, lord of the asuras, addressed the asuras thus: 'Good sirs, if in this impending battle the asuras win and the devas are defeated, bind Sakka, lord of the devas, by his four limbs and neck and bring him to me in the city of the asuras.' And Sakka, lord of the devas, addressed the Tāvatiṃsa devas: 'Good sirs, if in this impending battle the devas win and the asuras are defeated, bind Vepacitti, lord of the asuras, by his four limbs and neck and bring him to me in Sudhamma, the assembly hall of the devas.'

"In that battle the devas won and the asuras were defeated. [202] Then the Tāvatiṃsa devas bound Vepacitti by his four limbs and neck and brought him to Sakka in Sudhamma, the assembly hall of the devas. And there Vepacitti, lord of the asuras, was bound by his four limbs and neck.

"When it occurred to Vepacitti: 'The devas are righteous, the asuras are unrighteous; now right here I have gone to the city of the devas,' he then saw himself freed from the bonds around his limbs and neck and he enjoyed himself furnished and endowed with the five cords of divine sensual pleasure. But when it occurred to him: 'The asuras are righteous, the devas are unrighteous; now I will go there to the city of the asuras,' then he saw himself bound by his four limbs and neck and he was deprived of the five cords of divine sensual pleasure.

"So subtle, bhikkhus, was the bondage of Vepacitti, but even subtler than that is the bondage of Māra. In conceiving, one is bound by Māra; by not conceiving, one is freed from the Evil One.[223]

"Bhikkhus, 'I am' is a conceiving; 'I am this' is a conceiving; 'I shall be' is a conceiving; 'I shall not be' is a conceiving; 'I shall consist of form' is a conceiving; 'I shall be formless' is a conceiving; 'I shall be percipient' is a conceiving; 'I shall be nonpercipient' is a conceiving; 'I shall be neither percipient nor nonpercipient' is a conceiving.[224] Conceiving is a disease, conceiving is a tumour, conceiving is a dart. Therefore, bhikkhus, you should train yourselves thus: 'We will dwell with a mind devoid of conceiving.'

"Bhikkhus, 'I am' is a perturbation;[225] 'I am this' is a perturbation; 'I shall be' is a perturbation … 'I shall be neither percipient nor nonpercipient' is a perturbation. Perturbation [203] is a disease, perturbation is a tumour, perturbation is a dart. Therefore, bhikkhus, you should train yourselves thus: 'We will dwell with an imperturbable mind.'

"Bhikkhus, 'I am' is a palpitation; 'I am this' is a palpitation; 'I shall be' is a palpitation … 'I shall be neither percipient nor nonpercipient' is a palpitation. Palpitation is a disease, palpitation is a tumour, palpitation is a dart. Therefore, bhikkhus, you should train yourselves thus: 'We will dwell with a mind devoid of palpitation.'

"Bhikkhus, 'I am' is a proliferation; 'I am this' is a proliferation; 'I shall be' is a proliferation … 'I shall be neither percipient nor nonpercipient' is a proliferation. Proliferation is a disease, proliferation is a tumour, proliferation is a dart. Therefore, bhikkhus, you should train yourselves thus: 'We will dwell with a mind devoid of proliferation.'

"Bhikkhus, 'I am' is an involvement with conceit;[226] 'I am this' is an involvement with conceit; 'I shall be' is an involvement with conceit; 'I shall not be' is an involvement with conceit; 'I shall consist of form' is an involvement with conceit; 'I shall be formless' is an involvement with conceit ; 'I shall be percipient' is an involvement with conceit; 'I shall be nonpercipient' is an involvement with conceit; 'I shall be neither percipient nor nonpercipient' is an involvement with conceit. Involvement with conceit is a disease, involvement with conceit is a tumour, involvement with conceit is a dart. Therefore, bhikkhus, you should train yourselves thus: 'We will dwell with a mind in which conceit has been struck down.' Thus should you train yourselves."

[204] Chapter II

36 *Vedanāsaṃyutta*

Connected Discourses on Feeling

I. With Verses

1 (1) Concentration

"Bhikkhus, there are these three feelings. What three? Pleasant feeling, painful feeling, neither-painful-nor-pleasant feeling. These are the three feelings."

> A disciple of the Buddha, mindful,
> Concentrated, comprehending clearly,
> Understands feelings
> And the origin of feelings,
> Where they finally cease,
> And the path leading to their destruction.
> With the destruction of feelings
> A bhikkhu is hungerless and fully quenched.[227]

2 (2) Pleasure

"Bhikkhus, there are these three feelings. What three? Pleasant feeling, painful feeling, neither-painful-nor-pleasant feeling. These are the three feelings." [205]

> Whether it be pleasant or painful
> Along with the neither-painful-nor-pleasant,
> Both the internal and the external,
> Whatever kind of feeling there is:
> Having known, "This is suffering,
> Perishable, disintegrating,"

Having touched and touched them, seeing their fall,
Thus one loses one's passion for them.[228]

3 (3) Abandonment

"Bhikkhus, there are these three feelings. What three? Pleasant feeling, painful feeling, neither-painful-nor-pleasant feeling. The underlying tendency to lust should be abandoned in regard to pleasant feeling. The underlying tendency to aversion should be abandoned in regard to painful feeling. The underlying tendency to ignorance should be abandoned in regard to neither-painful-nor-pleasant feeling.[229]

"When, bhikkhus, a bhikkhu has abandoned the underlying tendency to lust in regard to pleasant feeling, the underlying tendency to aversion in regard to painful feeling, and the underlying tendency to ignorance in regard to neither-painful-nor-pleasant feeling, then he is called a bhikkhu without underlying tendencies,[230] one who sees rightly. He has cut off craving, severed the fetters, and by completely breaking through conceit,[231] he has made an end to suffering."

When one experiences pleasure,
If one does not understand feeling
The tendency to lust is present
For one not seeing the escape from it.

When one experiences pain,
If one does not understand feeling
The tendency to aversion is present
For one not seeing the escape from it.

The One of Broad Wisdom has taught
With reference to that peaceful feeling,
Neither-painful-nor-pleasant:
If one seeks delight even in this,
One is still not released from suffering. [206]

But when a bhikkhu who is ardent
Does not neglect clear comprehension,
Then that wise man fully understands
Feelings in their entirety.

Having fully understood feelings,
He is taintless in this very life.
Standing in Dhamma, with the body's breakup
The knowledge-master cannot be reckoned.

4 (4) The Bottomless Abyss

"Bhikkhus, when the uninstructed worldling makes the statement, 'In the great ocean there is a bottomless abyss,'[232] he makes such a statement about something that is nonexistent and unreal. This, bhikkhus, is rather a designation for painful bodily feelings, that is, 'bottomless abyss.'

"When the uninstructed worldling is contacted by a painful bodily feeling, he sorrows, grieves, and laments; he weeps and beats his breast and becomes distraught. This is called an uninstructed worldling who has not risen up in the bottomless abyss, one who has not gained a foothold.

"But, bhikkhus, when the instructed noble disciple is contacted by a painful bodily feeling, he does not sorrow, grieve, or lament; he does not weep and beat his breast and become distraught. This is called an instructed noble disciple who has risen up in the bottomless abyss, one who has gained a foothold."

One who cannot endure
The arisen painful feelings,
Bodily feelings that sap one's life,
Who trembles when they touch him,
A weakling of little strength
Who weeps out loud and wails:
He has not risen up in the bottomless abyss,
Nor has he even gained a foothold. [207]

But one who is able to endure them—
The arisen painful feelings,
Bodily feelings that sap one's life—
Who trembles not when they touch him:
He has risen up in the bottomless abyss,
And he has also gained a foothold.

5 (5) Should Be Seen

"Bhikkhus, there are these three feelings. What three? Pleasant feeling, painful feeling, neither-painful-nor-pleasant feeling. Pleasant feeling, bhikkhus, should be seen as painful;[233] painful feeling should be seen as a dart; neither-painful-nor-pleasant feeling should be seen as impermanent.

"When, bhikkhus, a bhikkhu has seen pleasant feeling as painful, painful feeling as a dart, and neither-painful-nor-pleasant feeling as impermanent, he is called a bhikkhu who sees rightly. He has cut off craving, severed the fetters, and by completely breaking through conceit, he has made an end to suffering."

One who has seen the pleasant as painful
And the painful as a dart,
Seen as impermanent the peaceful feeling
Neither painful nor pleasant:
He is a bhikkhu who sees rightly,
One who fully understands feelings.

Having fully understood feelings,
He is taintless in this very life.
Standing in Dhamma, with the body's breakup
The knowledge-master cannot be reckoned.

6 (6) The Dart

"Bhikkhus, the uninstructed worldling feels a pleasant feeling, a painful feeling, and a neither-painful-nor-pleasant feeling. The instructed noble disciple too feels a pleasant feeling, [208] a painful feeling, and a neither-painful-nor-pleasant feeling. Therein, bhikkhus, what is the distinction, the disparity, the difference between the instructed noble disciple and the uninstructed worldling?"

"Venerable sir, our teachings are rooted in the Blessed One, guided by the Blessed One, take recourse in the Blessed One. It would be good if the Blessed One would clear up the meaning of this statement. Having heard it from him, the bhikkhus will remember it."

"Then listen and attend closely, bhikkhus, I will speak."

"Yes, venerable sir," the bhikkhus replied. The Blessed One said this:

"Bhikkhus, when the uninstructed worldling is being contacted by a painful feeling, he sorrows, grieves, and laments; he weeps beating his breast and becomes distraught. He feels two feelings—a bodily one and a mental one. Suppose they were to strike a man with a dart, and then they would strike him immediately afterwards with a second dart,[234] so that the man would feel a feeling caused by two darts. So too, when the uninstructed worldling is being contacted by a painful feeling ... he feels two feelings—a bodily one and a mental one.

"Being contacted by that same painful feeling, he harbours aversion towards it. When he harbours aversion towards painful feeling, the underlying tendency to aversion towards painful feeling lies behind this. Being contacted by painful feeling, he seeks delight in sensual pleasure. For what reason? Because the uninstructed worldling does not know of any escape from painful feeling other than sensual pleasure.[235] When he seeks delight in sensual pleasure, the underlying tendency to lust for pleasant feeling lies behind this. He does not understand as it really is the origin and the passing away, the gratification, the danger, and the escape in the case of these feelings. When he does not understand these things, the underlying tendency to ignorance in regard to neither-painful-nor-pleasant feeling lies behind this.

"If he feels a pleasant feeling, he feels it attached. If he feels a painful feeling, he feels it attached. [209] If he feels a neither-painful-nor-pleasant feeling, he feels it attached. This, bhikkhus, is called an uninstructed worldling who is attached to birth, aging, and death; who is attached to sorrow, lamentation, pain, displeasure, and despair; who is attached to suffering, I say.

"Bhikkhus, when the instructed noble disciple is contacted by a painful feeling, he does not sorrow, grieve, or lament; he does not weep beating his breast and become distraught.[236] He feels one feeling—a bodily one, not a mental one. Suppose they were to strike a man with a dart, but they would not strike him immediately afterwards with a second dart, so that the man would feel a feeling caused by one dart only. So too, when the instructed noble disciple is contacted by a painful feeling ... he feels one feeling—a bodily one, not a mental one.

"Being contacted by that same painful feeling, he harbours no aversion towards it. Since he harbours no aversion towards painful feeling, the underlying tendency to aversion towards painful feeling does not lie behind this. Being contacted by painful feeling, he does not seek delight in sensual pleasure. For what reason? Because the instructed noble disciple knows of an escape from painful feeling other than sensual pleasure. Since he does not seek delight in sensual pleasure, the underlying tendency to lust for pleasant feeling does not lie behind this. He understands as it really is the origin and the passing away, the gratification, the danger, and the escape in the case of these feelings. Since he understands these things, the underlying tendency to ignorance in regard to neither-painful-nor-pleasant feeling does not lie behind this.

"If he feels a pleasant feeling, he feels it detached. If he feels a painful feeling, [210] he feels it detached. If he feels a neither-painful-nor-pleasant feeling, he feels it detached. This, bhikkhus, is called a noble disciple who is detached from birth, aging, and death; who is detached from sorrow, lamentation, pain, displeasure, and despair; who is detached from suffering, I say.

"This, bhikkhus, is the distinction, the disparity, the difference between the instructed noble disciple and the uninstructed worldling."

> The wise one, learned, does not feel
> The pleasant and painful [mental] feeling.
> This is the great difference between
> The wise one and the worldling.
>
> For the learned one who has comprehended Dhamma,
> Who clearly sees this world and the next,
> Desirable things do not provoke his mind,
> Towards the undesired he has no aversion.
>
> For him attraction and repulsion no more exist;
> Both have been extinguished, brought to an end.
> Having known the dust-free, sorrowless state,
> The transcender of existence rightly understands.

7 (7) The Sick Ward (1)

On one occasion the Blessed One was dwelling at Vesālī in the Great Wood in the Hall with the Peaked Roof. Then, in the evening, the Blessed One emerged from seclusion and went to the sick ward,[237] where he sat down in the appointed seat and addressed the bhikkhus thus: [211]

"Bhikkhus, a bhikkhu should await his time mindful and clearly comprehending. This is our instruction to you.

"And how, bhikkhus, is a bhikkhu mindful? Here, bhikkhus, a bhikkhu dwells contemplating the body in the body, ardent, clearly comprehending, mindful, having put away covetousness and displeasure in regard to the world. He dwells contemplating feelings in feelings ... mind in mind ... phenomena in phenomena, ardent, clearly comprehending, mindful, having put away covetousness and displeasure in regard to the world. It is in such a way that a bhikkhu is mindful.

"And how, bhikkhus, does a bhikkhu exercise clear comprehension? Here, bhikkhus, a bhikkhu is one who acts with clear comprehension when going forward and returning; when looking ahead and looking aside; when drawing in and extending the limbs; when wearing his robes and carrying his outer robe and bowl; when eating, drinking, chewing his food, and tasting; when defecating and urinating; when walking, standing, sitting, falling asleep, waking up, speaking, and keeping silent. It is in such a way that a bhikkhu exercises clear comprehension.

"A bhikkhu should await his time mindful and clearly comprehending. This is our instruction to you.

"Bhikkhus, while a bhikkhu dwells thus, mindful and clearly comprehending, diligent, ardent, and resolute, if there arises in him a pleasant feeling, he understands thus: 'There has arisen in me a pleasant feeling. Now that is dependent, not independent. Dependent on what? Dependent on this very body. But this body is impermanent, conditioned, dependently arisen. So when the pleasant feeling has arisen in dependence on a body that is impermanent, conditioned, dependently arisen, how could it be permanent?' He dwells contemplating impermanence in the body and in pleasant feeling, he dwells contemplating vanishing, contemplating fading away, contemplating cessation, contemplating relinquishment.[238] As he dwells thus, [212] the underlying tendency to lust in regard to the body and in regard to pleasant feeling is abandoned by him.

"Bhikkhus, while a bhikkhu dwells thus, mindful and clearly comprehending, diligent, ardent, and resolute, if there arises in him a painful feeling, he understands thus: 'There has arisen in me a painful feeling. Now that is dependent, not independent. Dependent on what? Dependent on just this body. But this body is impermanent, conditioned, dependently arisen. So when the painful feeling has arisen in dependence on a body that is impermanent, conditioned, dependently arisen, how could it be permanent?' He dwells contemplating impermanence in the body and in painful feeling, he dwells contemplating vanishing, contemplating fading away, contemplating cessation, contemplating relinquishment. As he dwells thus, the underlying tendency to aversion in regard to the body and in regard to painful feeling is abandoned by him.

"Bhikkhus, while a bhikkhu dwells thus, mindful and clearly comprehending, diligent, ardent, and resolute, if there arises in him a neither-painful-nor-pleasant feeling, he understands thus: 'There has arisen in me a neither-painful-nor-pleasant feeling. Now that is dependent, not independent. Dependent on what? Dependent on just this body. But this body is impermanent, conditioned, dependently arisen. So when the neither-painful-nor-pleasant feeling has arisen in dependence on a body that is impermanent, conditioned, dependently arisen, how could it be permanent?' He dwells contemplating impermanence in the body and in neither-painful-nor-pleasant feeling, he dwells contemplating vanishing, contemplating fading away, contemplating cessation, contemplating relinquishment. As he dwells thus, the underlying tendency to ignorance in regard to the body and in regard to neither-painful-nor-pleasant feeling is abandoned by him. [213]

"If he feels a pleasant feeling,[239] he understands: 'It is impermanent'; he understands: 'It is not held to'; he understands: 'It is not delighted in.' If he feels a painful feeling, he understands: 'It is impermanent'; he understands: 'It is not held to'; he understands: 'It is not delighted in.' If he feels a neither-painful-nor-pleasant feeling, he understands: 'It is impermanent'; he understands: 'It is not held to'; he understands: 'It is not delighted in.'

"If he feels a pleasant feeling, he feels it detached; if he feels a painful feeling, he feels it detached; if he feels a neither-painful-nor-pleasant feeling, he feels it detached.

"When he feels a feeling terminating with the body, he understands: 'I feel a feeling terminating with the body.' When he feels a feeling terminating with life, he understands: 'I feel a feeling terminating with life.' He understands: 'With the breakup of the body, following the exhaustion of life, all that is felt, not being delighted in, will become cool right here.'

"Just as, bhikkhus, an oil lamp burns in dependence on the oil and the wick, and with the exhaustion of the oil and the wick it is extinguished through lack of fuel, so too, bhikkhus, when a bhikkhu feels a feeling terminating with the body … terminating with life … He understands: 'With the breakup of the body, following the exhaustion of life, all that is felt, not being delighted in, will become cool right here.'"

8 (8) The Sick Ward (2)

(*As in preceding sutta down to the second injunction:*) [214]

"A bhikkhu should await his time mindful and clearly comprehending. This is our instruction to you.

"Bhikkhus, while a bhikkhu dwells thus, mindful and clearly comprehending, diligent, ardent, and resolute, if there arises in him a pleasant feeling, he understands thus: 'There has arisen in me a pleasant feeling. Now that is dependent, not independent. Dependent on what? Dependent on just this contact. But this contact is impermanent, conditioned, dependently arisen. So when the pleasant feeling has arisen in dependence on a contact that is impermanent, conditioned, dependently arisen, how could it be permanent?' He dwells contemplating impermanence in contact and in pleasant feeling, he dwells contemplating vanishing, contemplating fading away, contemplating cessation, contemplating relinquishment. As he dwells thus, the underlying tendency to lust in regard to contact and in regard to pleasant feeling is abandoned by him.

"Bhikkhus, while a bhikkhu dwells thus, mindful and clearly comprehending, diligent, ardent, and resolute, if there arises in him a painful feeling, he understands thus: 'There has arisen in me a painful feeling. Now that is dependent, not independent. Dependent on what? Dependent on just this contact. But this contact is impermanent, conditioned, dependently arisen. So when the painful feeling has arisen in dependence on a contact that is impermanent, conditioned, dependently arisen, how could it be permanent?' He dwells contemplating impermanence in contact and in painful feeling, he dwells contemplating vanishing, contemplating fading away, contemplating cessation, contemplating relinquishment. As he dwells thus, the underlying tendency to aversion in regard to contact and in regard to painful feeling is abandoned by him.

"Bhikkhus, while a bhikkhu dwells thus, mindful and clearly comprehending, diligent, ardent, and resolute, if there arises in him a neither-painful-nor-pleasant feeling, he understands thus: 'There has arisen in me a neither-painful-nor-pleasant feeling. Now that is dependent, not independent. Dependent on what? Dependent on just this contact. But this contact is impermanent, conditioned, dependently arisen. So when the neither-painful-nor-pleasant feeling has arisen in dependence on a contact that is impermanent, conditioned, dependently arisen, how could it be permanent?' He dwells contemplating impermanence in contact and in neither-painful-nor-pleasant feeling, he dwells contemplating vanishing, contemplating fading away, contemplating cessation, contemplating relinquishment. As he dwells thus, the underlying tendency to ignorance in regard to contact and in regard to neither-painful-nor-pleasant feeling is abandoned by him.

"If he feels a pleasant feeling ... (*all as in preceding sutta*) ... He understands: 'With the breakup of the body, following the exhaustion of life, all that is felt, not being delighted in, will become cool right here.'"

9 (9) Impermanent

"Bhikkhus, these three feelings are impermanent, conditioned, dependently arisen, subject to destruction, subject to vanishing, subject to fading away, subject to cessation. What three? Pleasant feeling, painful feeling, neither-painful-nor-pleasant feeling. These three feelings are impermanent, conditioned, dependently arisen, subject to destruction, subject to vanishing, subject to fading away, subject to cessation." [215]

10 (10) Rooted in Contact

"Bhikkhus, these three feelings are born of contact, rooted in contact, with contact as their source and condition. What three? Pleasant feeling, painful feeling, neither-painful-nor-pleasant feeling.

"In dependence on a contact to be experienced as pleasant, bhikkhus, a pleasant feeling arises. With the cessation of that contact to be experienced as pleasant, the corresponding feeling—the pleasant feeling that arose in dependence on that contact to be experienced as pleasant—ceases and subsides.

"In dependence on a contact to be experienced as painful, a painful feeling arises. With the cessation of that contact to be experienced as painful, the corresponding feeling—the painful feeling that arose in dependence on that contact to be experienced as painful—ceases and subsides.

"In dependence on a contact to be experienced as neither-painful-nor-pleasant, a neither-painful-nor-pleasant feeling arises. With the cessation of that contact to be experienced as neither-painful-nor-pleasant, the corresponding feeling—the neither-painful-nor-pleasant feeling that arose in dependence on that contact to be experienced as neither-painful-nor-pleasant—ceases and subsides.

"Bhikkhus, just as heat is generated and fire is produced from the conjunction and friction of two fire-sticks, but when the sticks are separated and laid aside the resultant heat ceases and subsides;[240] so too, these three feelings are born of contact, rooted in contact, with contact as their source and condition. In dependence on the appropriate contacts the corresponding feelings arise; with the cessation of the appropriate contacts the corresponding feelings cease."

[216] II. ALONE

11 (1) Alone

Then a certain bhikkhu approached the Blessed One, paid homage to him, sat down to one side, and said to him: "Here, venerable sir, while I was alone in seclusion, a reflection arose in my mind thus: 'Three feeling have been spoken of by the Blessed One: pleasant feeling, painful feeling, neither-painful-nor-pleasant feeling. These three feelings have been spoken of by the Blessed One. But the Blessed One has said: "Whatever is felt is included in suffering." Now with reference to what was this stated by the Blessed One?'"

"Good, good, bhikkhu! These three feelings have been spoken of by me: pleasant feeling, painful feeling, neither-painful-nor-pleasant feeling. These three feelings have been spoken of by me. And I have also said: 'Whatever is felt is included in suffering.' That has been stated by me with reference to the impermanence of formations. That has been stated by me with reference to formations being subject to destruction ... to formations being subject to vanishing ... to formations being subject to fading away [217] ... to formations being subject to cessation ... to formations being subject to change.[241]

"Then, bhikkhu, I have also taught the successive cessation of formations.[242] For one who has attained the first jhāna, speech has ceased. For one who has attained the second jhāna, thought and examination have ceased. For one who has attained the third jhāna, rapture has ceased. For one who has attained the fourth jhāna, in-breathing and out-breathing have ceased. For one who has attained the base of the infinity of space, the perception of form has ceased. For one who has attained the base of the infinity of consciousness, the perception pertaining to the base of the infinity of space has ceased. For one who has attained the base of nothingness, the perception pertaining to the base of the infinity of consciousness has ceased. For one who has attained the base of neither-perception-nor-nonperception, the perception pertaining to the base of nothingness has ceased. For one who has attained the cessation of perception and feeling, perception and feeling have ceased. For a bhikkhu whose taints are destroyed, lust has ceased, hatred has ceased, delusion has ceased.

"Then, bhikkhu, I have also taught the successive subsiding of formations. For one who has attained the first jhāna speech has subsided.... For one who has attained the cessation of perception and feeling, perception and feeling have subsided. For a bhikkhu whose taints are destroyed, lust has subsided, hatred has subsided, delusion has subsided.

"There are, bhikkhu, these six kinds of tranquillization. For one who has attained the first jhāna, speech has been tranquillized. For one who has attained the second jhāna, thought and examination have been tranquillized. For one who has attained the third jhāna, rapture has been tranquillized. For one who has attained the fourth jhāna, in-breathing and out-breathing have been tranquillized. [218] For one who has attained the cessation of perception and feeling, perception and feeling have been tranquillized. For a bhikkhu whose taints are destroyed, lust has been tranquillized, hatred has been tranquillized, delusion has been tranquillized."

12 (2) The Sky (1)

"Bhikkhus, just as various winds blow in the sky: winds from the east, winds from the west, winds from the north, winds from the south, dusty winds and dustless winds, cold winds and hot winds, mild winds and strong winds; so too, various feelings arise in this body: pleasant feeling arises, painful feeling arises, neither-painful-nor-pleasant feeling arises."

Just as many diverse winds
Blow back and forth across the sky,
Easterly winds and westerly winds,
Northerly winds and southerly winds,
Dusty winds and dustless winds,
Sometimes cold, sometimes hot,
Those that are strong and others mild—
Winds of many kinds that blow;

So in this very body here
Various kinds of feelings arise,
Pleasant ones and painful ones,
And those neither painful nor pleasant.

But when a bhikkhu who is ardent[243]
Does not neglect clear comprehension,
Then that wise man fully understands
Feelings in their entirety.

Having fully understood feelings,
He is taintless in this very life.
Standing in Dhamma, with the body's breakup,
The knowledge-master cannot be reckoned. [219]

13 (3) The Sky (2)

(*Same as the preceding, but without the verses.*)

14 (4) The Guest House

"Bhikkhus, suppose there is a guest house. People come from the east, west, north, and south and lodge there; khattiyas, brahmins, vessas, and suddas come and lodge there. So too, bhikkhus, various feelings arise in this body: pleasant feeling arises, painful feeling arises, neither-painful-nor-pleasant feeling arises; carnal pleasant feeling arises; carnal painful feeling arises; carnal neither-painful-nor-pleasant feeling arises; spiritual pleasant feeling arises; spiritual painful feeling arises; spiritual neither-painful-nor-pleasant feeling arises."[244]

15 (5) Ānanda (1)

Then the Venerable Ānanda approached the Blessed One, paid homage to him, sat down to one side, and said to him: "Venerable sir, what now is feeling? What is the origin of feeling? What is the cessation of feeling? [220] What is the way leading to the cessation of feeling? What is the gratification in feeling? What is the danger? What is the escape?"

"Ānanda, these three feelings—pleasant feeling, painful feeling, neither-painful-nor-pleasant feeling—are called feeling. With the arising of contact there is the arising of feeling. With the cessation of contact there is the cessation of feeling. This Noble Eightfold Path is the way leading to the cessation of feeling; that is, right view ... right concentration. The pleasure and joy that arise in dependence on feeling: this is the gratification in feeling. That feeling is impermanent, suffering, and subject to change: this is the danger in feeling. The removal and abandonment of desire and lust for feeling: this is the escape from feeling.

"Then, Ānanda, I have also taught the successive cessation of formations ... (*as in §11*).... [221] For a bhikkhu whose taints are destroyed, lust has been tranquillized, hatred has been tranquillized, delusion has been tranquillized."

16 (6) Ānanda (2)

Then the Venerable Ānanda approached the Blessed One, paid homage to him, and sat down to one side. The Blessed One then said to the Venerable Ānanda as he was sitting to one side: "Ānanda, what now is feeling? What is the origin of feeling? What is the cessation of feeling? What is the way leading to the cessation of feeling? What is the gratification in feeling? What is the danger? What is the escape?"

"Venerable sir, our teachings are rooted in the Blessed One, guided by the Blessed One, take recourse in the Blessed One. It would be good if the Blessed One would clear up the meaning of this statement. Having heard it from him, the bhikkhus will remember it."

"Then listen and attend closely, Ānanda. I will speak."

"Yes, venerable sir," the Venerable Ānanda replied. The Blessed One said this:

"Ānanda, these three feelings—pleasant feeling, painful feeling, neither-painful-nor-pleasant feeling—are called feeling…."

(*All as in the preceding sutta.*)

17 (7)–18 (8) A Number of Bhikkhus

(*These two suttas are identical with §§15–16 except that in each "a number of bhikkhus" is the interlocutor in place of Ānanda.*) [222–23]

19 (9) Pañcakaṅga

Then the carpenter Pañcakaṅga approached the Venerable Udāyī, paid homage to him, sat down to one side, and asked him: "Venerable Udāyī, how many kinds of feelings have been spoken of by the Blessed One?"[245]

"Three kinds of feelings, carpenter, have been spoken of by the Blessed One: pleasant feeling, painful feeling, neither-painful-nor-pleasant feeling. These are the three kinds of feelings that have been spoken of by the Blessed One."

When this was said, the carpenter Pañcakaṅga said to the Venerable Udāyī: "The Blessed One did not speak of three kinds of feelings, Venerable Udāyī. He spoke of two kinds of feelings: pleasant feeling and painful feeling. As to this neither-painful-nor-pleasant feeling, venerable sir, the Blessed One has said that this is included in the peaceful and sublime pleasure."

A second time [224] and a third time the Venerable Udāyī stated his position, and a second time and a third time the carpenter Pañcakaṅga stated his, but the Venerable Udāyī could not convince the carpenter Pañcakaṅga nor could the carpenter Pañcakaṅga convince the Venerable Udāyī.

The Venerable Ānanda heard this conversation between the Venerable Udāyī and the carpenter Pañcakaṅga. Then he approached the Blessed One, paid homage to him, sat down to one side, and reported to the Blessed One the entire conversation. [The Blessed One said:]

"Ānanda, it was a true method of exposition that the carpenter Pañcakaṅga would not approve of from the bhikkhu Udāyī, and it was a true method of exposition that the bhikkhu Udāyī would not approve of from the carpenter Pañcakaṅga. I have spoken of two kinds of feelings by [one] method of exposition; I have spoken of three kinds of feelings by [another] method of exposition; I have spoken of five kinds of feelings ... six kinds of feelings ... eighteen kinds of feelings ... thirty-six kinds of feelings by [another] method of exposition; [225] and I have spoken of one hundred and eight kinds of feelings by [still another] method of exposition. Thus, Ānanda, the Dhamma has been taught by me through [different] methods of exposition.[246]

"When the Dhamma has been taught by me in such a way through [different] methods of exposition, it may be expected of those who will not concede, allow, and approve of what is well stated and well spoken by others that they will become contentious and quarrelsome and engage in disputes, and that they will dwell stabbing each other with verbal daggers. But when the Dhamma has been taught by me in such a way through [different] methods of exposition, it may be expected of those who will concede, allow, and approve of what is well stated and well spoken by others that they will live in concord, with mutual appreciation, without disputing, blending like milk and water, viewing each other with kindly eyes.

"Ānanda, there are these five cords of sensual pleasure. What five? Forms cognizable by the eye that are desirable, lovely, agreeable, pleasing, sensually enticing, tantalizing. Sounds cognizable by the ear ... Odours cognizable by the nose ... Tastes cognizable by the tongue ... Tactile objects cognizable by the body that are desirable, lovely, agreeable, pleasing, sensually enticing, tantalizing. These are the five cords of sensual pleasure. The pleasure and joy that arise in dependence on these five cords of sensual pleasure: this is called sensual pleasure.

"Though some may say, 'This is the supreme pleasure and joy that beings experience,' I would not concede this to them. Why is that? Because there is another kind of happiness more excellent and sublime than that happiness. And what is that other kind of happiness? Here, Ānanda, secluded from sensual pleasures, secluded from unwholesome states, a bhikkhu enters and dwells in the first jhāna, which is accompanied by thought and examination, with rapture and happiness born of seclusion. This is that other kind of happiness more excellent and sublime than the previous kind of happiness. [226]

"Though some may say, 'This is the supreme pleasure and joy that beings experience,' I would not concede this to them. Why is that? Because there is another kind of happiness more excellent and sublime than that happiness. And what is that other kind of happiness? Here, Ānanda, with the subsiding of thought and examination, a bhikkhu enters and dwells in the second jhāna, which has internal confidence and unification of mind, is without thought and examination, and has rapture and happiness born of concentration. This is that other kind of happiness more excellent and sublime than the previous kind of happiness.

"Though some may say, 'This is the supreme pleasure and joy that beings experience,' I would not concede this to them. Why is that? Because there is another kind of happiness more excellent and sublime than that happiness. And what is that other kind of happiness? Here, Ānanda, with the fading away as well of rapture, a bhikkhu dwells equanimous and, mindful and clearly comprehending, he experiences happiness with the body; he enters and dwells in the third jhāna of which the noble ones declare: 'He is equanimous, mindful, one who dwells happily.' This is that other kind of happiness more excellent and sublime than the previous kind of happiness.

"Though some may say, 'This is the supreme pleasure and joy that beings experience,' I would not concede this to them. Why is that? Because there is another kind of happiness more excellent and sublime than that happiness. And what is that other kind of happiness? Here, Ānanda, with the abandoning of pleasure and pain, and with the previous passing away of joy and displeasure, a bhikkhu enters and dwells in the fourth jhāna, which is neither painful nor pleasant and includes the purification of mindfulness by equanimity. This is that other kind of happiness more excellent and sublime than the previous kind of happiness.[247]

"Though some may say, 'This is the supreme pleasure and joy that beings experience,' I would not concede this to them. [227] Why is that? Because there is another kind of happiness more excellent and sublime than that happiness. And what is that other kind of happiness? Here, Ānanda, with the complete transcendence of perceptions of forms, with the passing away of perceptions of sensory impingement, with nonattention to perceptions of diversity, aware that 'space is infinite,' a bhikkhu enters and dwells in the base of the infinity of space. This is that other kind of happiness more excellent and sublime than the previous kind of happiness.

"Though some may say, 'This is the supreme pleasure and joy that beings experience,' I would not concede this to them. Why is that? Because there is another kind of happiness more excellent and sublime than that happiness. And what is that other kind of happiness? Here, Ānanda, by completely transcending the base of the infinity of space, aware that 'consciousness is infinite,' a bhikkhu enters and dwells in the base of the infinity of consciousness. This is that other kind of happiness more excellent and sublime than the previous kind of happiness.

"Though some may say, 'This is the supreme pleasure and joy that beings experience,' I would not concede this to them. Why is that? Because there is another kind of happiness more excellent and sublime than that happiness. And what is that other kind of happiness? Here, Ānanda, by completely transcending the base of the infinity of consciousness, aware that 'there is nothing,' a bhikkhu enters and dwells in the base of nothingness. This [228] is that other kind of happiness more excellent and sublime than the previous kind of happiness.

"Though some may say, 'This is the supreme pleasure and joy that beings experience,' I would not concede this to them. Why is that? Because there is another kind of happiness more excellent and sublime than that happiness. And what is that other kind of happiness? Here, Ānanda, by completely transcending the base of nothingness, a bhikkhu enters and dwells in the base of neither-perception-nor-nonperception. This is that other kind of happiness more excellent and sublime than the previous kind of happiness.

"Though some may say, 'This is the supreme pleasure and joy that beings experience,' I would not concede this to them. Why is that? Because there is another kind of happiness more excellent and sublime than that happiness. And what is that other kind of happiness? Here, Ānanda, by completely transcending the base of neither-perception-nor-nonperception, a bhikkhu enters and dwells in the cessation of perception and feeling. This is that other kind of happiness more excellent and sublime than the previous kind of happiness.[248]

"Now it is possible, Ānanda, that wanderers of other sects might speak thus: 'The ascetic Gotama speaks of the cessation of perception and feeling, and he maintains that it is included in happiness. What is that? How is that?' When wanderers of other sects speak thus, Ānanda, they should be told: 'The Blessed One, friends, does not describe a state as included in happiness only with reference to pleasant feeling. But rather, friends, wherever happiness is found and in whatever way, the Tathāgata describes that as included in happiness.'"[249]

20 (10) Bhikkhus

"Bhikkhus, I have spoken of two kinds of feelings by [one] method of exposition.... Thus, bhikkhus, the Dhamma has been taught by me through [different] methods of exposition...."

(*Complete as in the preceding sutta.*) [229]

[230] III. The Theme of the Hundred and Eight

21 (1) Sīvaka

On one occasion the Blessed One was dwelling at Rājagaha in the Bamboo Grove, the Squirrel Sanctuary. Then the wanderer Moḷiyasīvaka approached the Blessed One and exchanged greetings with him.[250] When they had concluded their greetings and cordial talk, he sat down to one side and said to the Blessed One:

"Master Gotama, there are some ascetics and brahmins who

hold such a doctrine and view as this: 'Whatever a person experiences, whether it be pleasant or painful or neither-painful-nor-pleasant, all that is caused by what was done in the past.'[251] What does Master Gotama say about this?"

"Some feelings, Sīvaka, arise here originating from bile disorders: that some feelings arise here originating from bile disorders one can know for oneself, and that is considered to be true in the world. Now when those ascetics and brahmins hold such a doctrine and view as this, 'Whatever a person experiences, whether it be pleasant or painful or neither-painful-nor-pleasant, all that is caused by what was done in the past,' they overshoot what one knows by oneself and they overshoot what is considered to be true in the world. Therefore I say that this is wrong on the part of those ascetics and brahmins.[252]

"Some feelings, Sīvaka, arise here originating from phlegm disorders … originating from wind disorders … originating from an imbalance [of the three] … produced by change of climate … produced by careless behaviour … caused by assault … [231] produced as the result of kamma: that some feelings arise here produced as the result of kamma one can know for oneself, and that is considered to be true in the world.[253] Now when those ascetics and brahmins hold such a doctrine and view as this, 'Whatever a person experiences, whether it be pleasant or painful or neither-painful-nor-pleasant, all that is caused by what was done in the past,' they overshoot what one knows by oneself and they overshoot what is considered to be true in the world. Therefore I say that this is wrong on the part of those ascetics and brahmins."

When this was said, the wanderer Moḷiyasivaka said to the Blessed One: "Magnificent, Master Gotama! Magnificent, Master Gotama!… From today let Master Gotama remember me as a lay follower who has gone for refuge for life."

Bile, phlegm, and also wind,
Imbalance and climate too,
Carelessness and assault,
With kamma result as the eighth.

22 (2) The Theme of the Hundred and Eight

"Bhikkhus, I will teach you a Dhamma exposition on the theme of the hundred and eight. Listen to that....

"And what, bhikkhus, is the Dhamma exposition on the theme of the hundred and eight? I have spoken of two kinds of feelings by [one] method of exposition; I have spoken of three kinds of feelings by [another] method of exposition; I have spoken of five kinds of feelings ... six kinds of feelings ... eighteen kinds of feelings ... thirty-six kinds of feelings by [another] method of exposition; and I have spoken of one hundred and eight kinds of feelings by [still another] method of exposition.

"And what, bhikkhus, are the two kinds of feelings? Bodily and mental. These are called the two kinds of feelings. [232]

"And what, bhikkhus, are the three kinds of feelings? Pleasant feeling, painful feeling, neither-painful-nor-pleasant feeling. These are called the three kinds of feelings.

"And what, bhikkhus, are the five kinds of feelings? The pleasure faculty, the pain faculty, the joy faculty, the displeasure faculty, the equanimity faculty. These are called the five kinds of feelings.[254]

"And what, bhikkhus, are the six kinds of feelings? Feeling born of eye-contact ... feeling born of mind-contact. These are called the six kinds of feeling.

"And what, bhikkhus, are the eighteen kinds of feelings? Six examinations accompanied by joy, six examinations accompanied by displeasure, six examinations accompanied by equanimity. These are called the eighteen kinds of feelings.[255]

"And what, bhikkhus, are the thirty-six kinds of feelings? Six types of joy based on the household life, six types of joy based on renunciation; six types of displeasure based on the household life, six types of displeasure based on renunciation; six types of equanimity based on the household life, six types of equanimity based on renunciation. These are called the thirty-six kinds of feelings.[256]

"And what, bhikkhus, are the hundred and eight kinds of feelings? The [above] thirty-six feelings in the past, the [above] thirty-six feelings in the future, the [above] thirty-six feelings at present. These are called the hundred and eight kinds of feelings.

"This, bhikkhus, is the Dhamma exposition on the theme of the hundred and eight."

23 (3) *A Certain Bhikkhu*

Then a certain bhikkhu approached the Blessed One, paid homage to him, sat down to one side, and said to him: "Venerable sir, what now is feeling? What is the origin of feeling? What is the way leading to the origination of feeling? What is the cessation of feeling? What is the way leading to the cessation of feeling? What is the gratification in feeling? What is the danger? What is the escape?" [233]

"There are, bhikkhu, these three feelings: pleasant feeling, painful feeling, neither-painful-nor-pleasant feeling. This is called feeling. With the arising of contact there is the arising of feeling. Craving is the way leading to the origination of feeling. With the cessation of contact there is the cessation of feeling. This Noble Eightfold Path is the way leading to the cessation of feeling; that is, right view … right concentration.

"The pleasure and joy that arise in dependence on feeling: this is the gratification in feeling. That feeling is impermanent, suffering, and subject to change: this is the danger in feeling. The removal and abandonment of desire and lust for feeling: this is the escape from feeling."

24 (4) *Before*

"Bhikkhus, before my enlightenment, while I was still a bodhisatta, not yet fully enlightened, it occurred to me: "What now is feeling? What is the origin of feeling? What is the way leading to the origination of feeling? What is the cessation of feeling? What is the way leading to the cessation of feeling? What is the gratification in feeling? What is the danger? What is the escape?"

"Then, bhikkhus, it occurred to me: 'There are these three feelings … (*all as in preceding sutta*) … this is the escape from feeling.'"

25 (5) *Knowledge*[257]

"'These are feelings': thus, bhikkhus, in regard to things unheard before, there arose in me vision, knowledge, wisdom, true knowledge, and light.

"'This is the origin of feeling': thus, bhikkhus, in regard to things unheard before, there arose in me vision … and light.

"'This is the way leading to the origination of feeling': thus, bhikkhus, in regard to things unheard before, there arose in me vision ... and light.

"'This is the cessation of feeling': thus, bhikkhus, in regard to things unheard before, there arose in me vision ... and light. [234]

"'This is the way leading to the cessation of feeling': thus, bhikkhus, in regard to things unheard before, there arose in me vision ... and light.

"'This is the gratification in feeling' ... 'This is the danger in feeling' ... 'This is the escape from feeling': thus, bhikkhus, in regard to things unheard before, there arose in me vision, knowledge, wisdom, true knowledge, and light."

26 (6) A Number of Bhikkhus

(*Identical with §23 except that "a number of bhikkhus" are the interlocutors rather than "a certain bhikkhu."*)

27 (7) Ascetics and Brahmins (1)

"Bhikkhus, there are these three feelings. What three? Pleasant feeling, painful feeling, neither-painful-nor-pleasant feeling.

"Those ascetics or brahmins, bhikkhus, who do not understand as they really are the gratification, the danger, and the escape in the case of these three feelings:[258] these I do not consider to be ascetics among ascetics or brahmins among brahmins, and these venerable ones do not, by realizing it for themselves with direct knowledge, in this very life enter and dwell in the goal of asceticism or the goal of brahminhood.

"But, bhikkhus, those ascetics and brahmins who understand these things as they really are: these I consider to be ascetics among ascetics and brahmins among brahmins, and these venerable ones, by realizing it for themselves with direct knowledge, in this very life enter and dwell in the goal of asceticism and the goal of brahminhood." [235]

28 (8) Ascetics and Brahmins (2)

"Those ascetics or brahmins, bhikkhus, who do not understand as they really are the origination and the passing away, the gratification, the danger, and the escape in the case of these three feelings: these I do not consider to be ascetics among ascetics or brahmins among brahmins, and these venerable ones do not, by realizing it for themselves with direct knowledge, in this very life enter and dwell in the goal of asceticism or the goal of brahminhood.

"But, bhikkhus, those ascetics and brahmins who understand these things as they really are: these I consider to be ascetics among ascetics and brahmins among brahmins, and these venerable ones, by realizing it for themselves with direct knowledge, in this very life enter and dwell in the goal of asceticism and the goal of brahminhood."

29 (9) Ascetics and Brahmins (3)

"Those ascetics or brahmins, bhikkhus, who do not understand feeling, its origin, its cessation, and the way leading to its cessation: these I do not consider to be ascetics among ascetics … nor do they enter and dwell in the goal of asceticism or the goal of brahminhood.

"But, bhikkhus, those ascetics and brahmins who understand feeling, its origin, its cessation, and the way leading to its cessation: these I consider to be ascetics among ascetics … and they enter and dwell in the goal of asceticism and the goal of brahminhood."

30 (10) Simple Version

"Bhikkhus, there are these three feelings. What three? Pleasant feeling, painful feeling, neither-painful-nor-pleasant feeling."[259]

31 (11) Spiritual

"Bhikkhus, there is carnal rapture, there is spiritual rapture, there is rapture more spiritual than the spiritual. There is carnal happiness, there is spiritual happiness, there is happiness more spiritual than the spiritual. There is carnal equanimity, there is spiritual equanimity, there is equanimity more spiritual than the spiritual. There is carnal deliverance, there is spiritual deliverance, there is deliverance more spiritual than the spiritual.

"And what, bhikkhus, is carnal rapture? There are, bhikkhus, these five cords of sensual pleasure. What five? Forms cognizable by the eye … tactile objects cognizable by the body that are desirable, lovely, agreeable, pleasing, sensually enticing, tantalizing. These are the five cords of sensual pleasure. The rapture that arises in dependence on these five cords of sensual pleasure: this is called carnal rapture. [236]

"And what, bhikkhus, is spiritual rapture? Here, secluded from sensual pleasures, secluded from unwholesome states, a bhikkhu enters and dwells in the first jhāna, which is accompanied by thought and examination, with rapture and happiness born of seclusion. With the subsiding of thought and examination, he enters and dwells in the second jhāna, which has internal confidence and unification of mind, is without thought and examination, and has rapture and happiness born of concentration. This is called spiritual rapture.

"And what, bhikkhus, is rapture more spiritual than the spiritual? When a bhikkhu whose taints are destroyed reviews his mind liberated from lust, liberated from hatred, liberated from delusion, there arises rapture. This is called rapture more spiritual than the spiritual.[260]

"And what, bhikkhus, is carnal happiness? There are, bhikkhus, these five cords of sensual pleasure. What five? Forms cognizable by the eye … tactile objects cognizable by the body that are desirable, lovely, agreeable, pleasing, sensually enticing, tantalizing. These are the five cords of sensual pleasure. The happiness that arises in dependence on these five cords of sensual pleasure: this is called carnal happiness.

"And what, bhikkhus, is spiritual happiness? Here, bhikkhus, secluded from sensual pleasures … a bhikkhu enters and dwells in the first jhāna … the second jhāna…. With the fading away as well of rapture, he dwells equanimous and, mindful and clearly comprehending, he experiences happiness with the body; he enters and dwells in the third jhāna of which the noble ones declare: 'He is equanimous, mindful, one who dwells happily.' This is called spiritual happiness.

"And what, bhikkhus, is happiness more spiritual than the spiritual? When a bhikkhu whose taints are destroyed reviews his mind liberated from lust, liberated from hatred, [237] liberated from delusion, there arises happiness. This is called happiness more spiritual than the spiritual.

"And what, bhikkhus, is carnal equanimity? There are, bhikkhus, these five cords of sensual pleasure. What five? Forms cognizable by the eye ... tactile objects cognizable by the body that are desirable, lovely, agreeable, pleasing, sensually enticing, tantalizing. These are the five cords of sensual pleasure. The equanimity that arises in dependence on these five cords of sensual pleasure: this is called carnal equanimity.

"And what, bhikkhus, is spiritual equanimity? With the abandoning of pleasure and pain, and with the previous passing away of joy and displeasure, a bhikkhu enters and dwells in the fourth jhāna, which is neither painful nor pleasant and includes the purification of mindfulness by equanimity.

"And what, bhikkhus, is equanimity more spiritual than the spiritual? When a bhikkhu whose taints are destroyed reviews his mind liberated from lust, liberated from hatred, liberated from delusion, there arises equanimity. This is called equanimity more spiritual than the spiritual.

"And what, bhikkhus, is carnal deliverance? Deliverance connected with the form sphere is carnal deliverance.

"And what, bhikkhus, is spiritual deliverance? Deliverance connected with the formless sphere is spiritual deliverance.[261]

"And what, bhikkhus, is deliverance more spiritual than the spiritual? When a bhikkhu whose taints are destroyed reviews his mind liberated from lust, liberated from hatred, liberated from delusion, there arises deliverance. This is called deliverance more spiritual than the spiritual."

[238] Chapter III

37 *Mātugāmasaṃyutta*

Connected Discourses on Women

I. First Repetition Series
(Women)

1 (1) Agreeable and Disagreeable (1)

"Bhikkhus, when a woman possesses five factors she is extremely disagreeable to a man. What five? She is not beautiful, not wealthy, not virtuous; she is lethargic; and she does not beget children. When a woman possesses these five factors she is extremely disagreeable to a man.

"Bhikkhus, when a woman possesses five factors she is extremely agreeable to a man. What five? She is beautiful, wealthy, and virtuous; she is clever and industrious; and she begets children. When a woman possesses these five factors she is extremely agreeable to a man."

2 (2) Agreeable and Disagreeable (2)

"Bhikkhus, when a man possesses five factors he is extremely disagreeable to a woman. What five? He is not handsome, not wealthy, not virtuous; he is lethargic; and he does not beget children. [239] When a man possesses these five factors he is extremely disagreeable to a woman.

"Bhikkhus, when a man possesses five factors he is extremely agreeable to a woman. What five? He is handsome, wealthy, and virtuous; he is clever and industrious; and he begets children. When a man possesses these five factors he is extremely agreeable to a woman."

(*The same as the above.*)

3 (3) Peculiar

"Bhikkhus, there are five kinds of suffering peculiar to women,[262] which women experience but not men. What five?

"Here, bhikkhus, even when young, a woman goes to live with her husband's family and is separated from her relatives. This is the first kind of suffering peculiar to women....

"Again, a woman is subject to menstruation. This is the second kind of suffering peculiar to women....

"Again, a woman becomes pregnant. This is the third kind of suffering peculiar to women....

"Again, a woman gives birth. This is the fourth kind of suffering peculiar to women....

"Again, a woman is made to serve a man. This is the fifth kind of suffering peculiar to women....

"These, bhikkhus, are the five kinds of suffering peculiar to women, which women experience but not men." [240]

4 (4) Three Qualities

"Bhikkhus, when a woman possesses three qualities, with the breakup of the body, after death, she is generally reborn in a state of misery, in a bad destination, in the nether world, in hell. What are the three? Here, bhikkhus, in the morning a woman dwells at home with her heart obsessed by the taint of selfishness; at noon she dwells at home with her heart obsessed by envy; in the evening she dwells at home with her heart obsessed by sensual lust. When a woman possesses these three qualities ... she is generally reborn in a state of misery ... in hell."

(Anuruddha: (i) The Dark Side)

5 (5) Angry

Then the Venerable Anuruddha approached the Blessed One ... and said to him:[263] "Here, venerable sir, with the divine eye, which is purified and surpasses the human, I see women, with the breakup of the body, after death, being reborn in a state of misery, in a bad destination, in the nether world, in hell. When a woman possesses how many qualities, venerable sir, is she reborn thus?"

"When, Anuruddha, a woman possesses five qualities, with the breakup of the body, after death, she is reborn in a state of misery, in a bad destination, in the nether world, in hell. What five?

"She is without faith, shameless, unafraid of wrongdoing, angry, unwise. When a woman possesses these five qualities [241] she is reborn in a state of misery … in hell."

6 (6)–13 (13) Malicious, Etc.

"When, Anuruddha, a woman possesses five qualities, with the breakup of the body, after death, she is reborn in a state of misery, in a bad destination, in the nether world, in hell. What five?

"She is without faith, shameless, unafraid of wrongdoing, malicious, [envious … stingy … of loose conduct … immoral … unlearned … lazy … muddle-minded,][264] unwise. When a woman possesses these five qualities she is reborn in a state of misery … in hell." [242–43]

14 (14) The Five

"When, Anuruddha, a woman possesses five qualities, with the breakup of the body, after death, she is reborn in a state of misery, in a bad destination, in the nether world, in hell. What are the five?

"She destroys life, takes what is not given, engages in sexual misconduct, speaks falsehood, and indulges in wine, liquor, and intoxicants that cause negligence. When a woman possesses these five qualities she is reborn in a state of misery … in hell."

II. Second Repetition Series
(Anuruddha)

(Anuruddha: (ii) The Bright Side)

15 (1) Without Anger

Then the Venerable Anuruddha approached the Blessed One … and said to him: "Here, venerable sir, with the divine eye, which is purified and surpasses the human, I see women, with the breakup of the body, after death, being reborn in a good destination, in a heavenly world. When a woman possesses how many qualities, venerable sir, is she reborn thus?"

"When, Anuruddha, a woman possesses five qualities, with the breakup of the body, after death, she is reborn in a good destination, in a heavenly world. What are the five?

"She has faith, she has a sense of shame, she is afraid of wrongdoing, she is without anger, she is wise. When a woman possesses these five qualities [244] she is reborn in a good destination, in a heavenly world."

16 (2)–23 (9) Without Malice, Etc.

"When, Anuruddha, a woman possesses five qualities, with the breakup of the body, after death, she is reborn in a good destination, in a heavenly world. What are the five?

"She has faith, she has a sense of shame, she is afraid of wrongdoing, she is without malice, [without envy … not stingy … not of loose conduct … virtuous … learned … energetic … mindful,][265] wise. When a woman possesses these five qualities she is reborn in a good destination, in a heavenly world." [245]

24 (10) The Five Precepts

"When, Anuruddha, a woman possesses five qualities, with the breakup of the body, after death, she is reborn in a good destination, in a heavenly world. What are the five?

"She abstains from the destruction of life, abstains from taking what is not given, abstains from sexual misconduct, abstains from false speech, abstains from wine, liquor, and intoxicants that cause negligence. When a woman possesses these five qualities, with the breakup of the body, after death, she is reborn in a good destination, in a heavenly world."

[246] III. Powers

25 (1) Confident

"Bhikkhus, there are five powers of a woman. What are the five? The power of beauty, the power of wealth, the power of relatives, the power of sons, the power of virtue. These are the five powers of a woman. When a woman possesses these five powers, she dwells confident at home."

26 (2) Having Won Over

"Bhikkhus, there are five powers of a woman.... (*as above*) ... When a woman possesses these five powers, she dwells at home having won over her husband."[266]

27 (3) Under Her Control

"Bhikkhus, there are five powers of a woman.... (*as above*) ... When a woman possesses these five powers, she abides with her husband under her control."

28 (4) One

"Bhikkhus, when a man possesses one power, he abides with a woman under his control. What is that one power? The power of authority. When a woman has been overcome by the power of authority, neither the power of beauty can rescue her, nor the power of wealth, nor the power of relatives, nor the power of sons, nor the power of virtue." [247]

29 (5) In That Respect

"Bhikkhus, there are these five powers of a woman. What are the five? The power of beauty, the power of wealth, the power of relatives, the power of sons, the power of virtue.

"If, bhikkhus, a woman possesses the power of beauty but not the power of wealth, then she is deficient in that respect. But if she possesses the power of beauty and the power of wealth too, then she is complete in that respect.

"If, bhikkhus, a woman possesses the powers of beauty and wealth, but not the power of relatives, then she is deficient in that respect. But if she possesses the powers of beauty and wealth, and the power of relatives too, then she is complete in that respect.

"If, bhikkhus, a woman possesses the powers of beauty,

wealth, and relatives, but not the power of sons, then she is deficient in that respect. But if she possesses the powers of beauty, wealth, and relatives, and the power of sons too, then she is complete in that respect.

"If, bhikkhus, a woman possesses the powers of beauty, wealth, relatives, and sons, but not the power of virtue, then she is deficient in that respect. But if she possesses the powers of beauty, wealth, relatives, and sons, and the power of virtue too, then she is complete in that respect.

"These are the five powers of a woman."

30 (6) They Expel

"Bhikkhus, there are these five powers of a woman … [248] … the power of virtue.

"If, bhikkhus, a woman possesses the power of beauty but not the power of virtue, they expel her; they do not accommodate her in the family.[267]

"If, bhikkhus, a woman possesses the powers of beauty and wealth, but not the power of virtue, they expel her; they do not accommodate her in the family.

"If, bhikkhus, a woman possesses the powers of beauty, wealth, and relatives, but not the power of virtue, they expel her; they do not accommodate her in the family.

"If, bhikkhus, a woman possesses the powers of beauty, wealth, relatives, and sons, but not the power of virtue, they expel her; they do not accommodate her in the family.

"If, bhikkhus, a woman possesses the power of virtue but not the power of beauty, they accommodate her in the family; they do not expel her.[268]

"If, bhikkhus, a woman possesses the power of virtue but not the power of wealth, they accommodate her in the family; they do not expel her.

"If, bhikkhus, a woman possesses the power of virtue but not the power of relatives, they accommodate her in the family; they do not expel her.

"If, bhikkhus, a woman possesses the power of virtue but not the power of sons, they accommodate her in the family; they do not expel her.

"These are the five powers of a woman."

31 (7) The Cause

"Bhikkhus, there are these five powers of a woman ... the power of virtue.

"Bhikkhus, it is not because of the power of beauty, or the power of wealth, or the power of relatives, or the power of sons, that with the breakup of the body, after death, a woman is reborn in a good destination, in a heavenly world. It is because of the power of virtue that a woman is reborn in a good destination, in a heavenly world.

"These are the five powers of a woman." [249]

32 (8) Situations

"Bhikkhus, there are five situations that are difficult to obtain for a woman who has not done merit. What are the five?

"She may wish: 'May I be born into a suitable family!' This is the first situation that is difficult to obtain for a woman who has not done merit.

"She may wish: 'Having been born into a suitable family, may I marry into a suitable family!' This is the second situation....

"She may wish: 'Having been born into a suitable family and having married into a suitable family, may I dwell at home without a rival!'[269] This is the third situation....

"She may wish: 'Having been born into a suitable family ... dwelling at home without a rival, may I bear sons!' This is the fourth situation.... [250]

"She may wish: 'Having been born into a suitable family ... having borne sons, may I abide with my husband under my control!' This is the fifth situation....

"These are the five situations that are difficult to obtain for a woman who has not done merit.

"Bhikkhus, there are five situations that are easy to obtain for a woman who has done merit. What are the five?

"She may wish: 'May I be born into a suitable family!' This is the first situation....

"She may wish: 'Having been born into a suitable family ... having borne sons, may I abide with my husband under my control!' This is the fifth situation....

"These are the five situations that are easy to obtain for a woman who has done merit."

33 (9) Confident

"Bhikkhus, when a woman possesses five qualities she dwells confident at home. What are the five? She abstains from the destruction of life, abstains from taking what is not given, abstains from sexual misconduct, abstains from false speech, abstains from wine, liquor, and intoxicants that cause negligence. When a woman possesses these five qualities she dwells confident at home."

34 (10) Growth

"Bhikkhus, growing in five areas of growth, a woman noble disciple grows with a noble growth, and she acquires the essence, acquires the best, of this bodily existence. What are the five? She grows in faith, in virtue, in learning, in generosity, and in wisdom. Growing in these five areas of growth, a woman noble disciple grows with a noble growth, and she acquires the essence, acquires the best, of this bodily existence.

"When she grows here in faith and virtue,
In wisdom, generosity, and learning,
The virtuous woman lay disciple
Acquires right here the essence for herself."

[251] Chapter IV

38 *Jambukhādakasaṃyutta*
Connected Discourses with Jambukhādaka

1 A Question on Nibbāna

On one occasion the Venerable Sāriputta was dwelling in Magadha at Nālakagāma. Then the wanderer Jambukhādaka[270] approached the Venerable Sāriputta and exchanged greetings with him. When they had concluded their greetings and cordial talk, he sat down to one side and said to the Venerable Sāriputta:

"Friend Sāriputta, it is said, 'Nibbāna, Nibbāna.' What now is Nibbāna?"

"The destruction of lust, the destruction of hatred, the destruction of delusion: this, friend, is called Nibbāna."[271]

"But, friend, is there a path, is there a way for the realization of this Nibbāna?"

"There is a path, friend, there is a way for the realization of this Nibbāna." [252]

"And what, friend, is that path, what is that way for the realization of this Nibbāna?"

"It is, friend, this Noble Eightfold Path; that is, right view, right intention, right speech, right action, right livelihood, right effort, right mindfulness, right concentration. This is the path, friend, this is the way for the realization of this Nibbāna."

"Excellent is the path, friend, excellent is the way for the realization of this Nibbāna. And it is enough, friend Sāriputta, for diligence."

2 *Arahantship*

"Friend Sāriputta, it is said, 'arahantship, arahantship.' What now is arahantship?"

"The destruction of lust, the destruction of hatred, the destruction of delusion: this, friend, is called arahantship."

"But, friend, is there a path, is there a way for the realization of this arahantship?"

"There is a path, friend, there is a way for the realization of this arahantship."

"And what, friend, is that path, what is that way for the realization of this arahantship?"

"It is, friend, this Noble Eightfold Path; that is, right view ... right concentration. This is the path, friend, this is the way for the realization of this arahantship."

"Excellent is the path, friend, excellent is the way for the realization of this arahantship. And it is enough, friend Sāriputta, for diligence."

3 *Proponents of Dhamma*

"Friend Sāriputta, who are the proponents of Dhamma in the world? Who are practising well in the world? Who are the fortunate ones in the world?"

"Those, friend, who teach the Dhamma for the abandonment of lust, [253] for the abandonment of hatred, for the abandonment of delusion: they are the proponents of Dhamma in the world. Those who are practising for the abandonment of lust, for the abandonment of hatred, for the abandonment of delusion: they are practising well in the world. Those for whom lust, hatred, and delusion have been abandoned, cut off at the root, made like palm stumps, obliterated so that they are no more subject to future arising: they are the fortunate ones in the world."[272]

"But, friend, is there a path, is there a way for the abandonment of this lust, hatred, and delusion?"

"There is a path, friend, there is a way for the abandonment of this lust, hatred, and delusion."

"And what, friend, is that path...?"

"It is, friend, this Noble Eightfold Path...."

"Excellent is the path, friend, excellent is the way for the abandonment of this lust, hatred, and delusion. And it is enough, friend Sāriputta, for diligence."

4 For What Purpose?

"For what purpose, friend Sāriputta, is the holy life lived under the ascetic Gotama?"

"It is, friend, for the full understanding of suffering that the holy life is lived under the Blessed One."

"But, friend, is there a path, is there a way for the full understanding of this suffering?"

"There is a path, friend, there is a way ... [254] this Noble Eightfold Path...."

5 Consolation

"Friend Sāriputta, it is said, 'one who has attained consolation, one who has attained consolation.' In what way, friend, has one attained consolation?"[273]

"When, friend, a bhikkhu understands as it really is the origin and the passing away, the gratification, the danger, and the escape in the case of the six bases for contact, in this way he has attained consolation."

"But, friend, is there a path, is there a way for the realization of this consolation?"

"There is a path, friend, there is a way ... this Noble Eightfold Path...."

6 Supreme Consolation

"Friend Sāriputta, it is said, 'one who has attained supreme consolation, one who has attained supreme consolation.' In what way, friend, has one attained supreme consolation?"

"When, friend, [255] having understood as it really is the origin and the passing away, the gratification, the danger, and the escape in the case of the six bases for contact, a bhikkhu is liberated by nonclinging, in this way he has attained supreme consolation."

"But, friend, is there a path, is there a way for the realization of this supreme consolation?"

"There is a path, friend, there is a way … this Noble Eightfold Path…."

7 Feeling

"Friend Sāriputta, it is said, 'feeling, feeling.' What now is feeling?"

"There are, friend, these three feelings: pleasant feeling, painful feeling, neither-painful-nor-pleasant feeling. These are the three feelings."

"But, friend, is there a path, is there a way for the full understanding of these three feelings?"

"There is a path, friend, there is a way … this Noble Eightfold Path…." [256]

8 Taints

"Friend Sāriputta, it is said, 'taint, taint.' What now is a taint?"

"There are, friend, these three taints: the taint of sensuality, the taint of existence, the taint of ignorance. These are the three taints."

"But, friend, is there a path, is there a way for the abandonment of these three taints?"

"There is a path, friend, there is a way … this Noble Eightfold Path…."

9 Ignorance

"Friend Sāriputta, it is said, 'ignorance, ignorance.' What now is ignorance?"

"Not knowing suffering, not knowing the origin of suffering, not knowing the cessation of suffering, not knowing the way leading to the cessation of suffering. This is called ignorance."

"But, friend, is there a path, is there a way for the abandonment of this ignorance?"

"There is a path, friend, there is a way … this Noble Eightfold Path…." [257]

10 Craving

"Friend Sāriputta, it is said, 'craving, craving.' What now is craving?"

"There are, friend, these three kinds of craving: craving for sensual pleasures, craving for existence, craving for extermination. These are the three kinds of craving."

"But, friend, is there a path, is there a way for the abandonment of this craving?"

"There is a path, friend, there is a way ... this Noble Eightfold Path...."

11 Floods

"Friend Sāriputta, it is said, 'flood, flood.' What now is a flood?"

"There are, friend, these four floods: the flood of sensuality, the flood of existence, the flood of views, the flood of ignorance. These are the four floods."

"But, friend, is there a path, is there a way for the abandonment of these four floods?"

"There is a path, friend, there is a way ... this Noble Eightfold Path...." [258]

12 Clinging

"Friend Sāriputta, it is said, 'clinging, clinging.' What now is clinging?"

"There are, friend, these four kinds of clinging: clinging to sensual pleasures, clinging to views, clinging to rules and vows, clinging to a doctrine of self. These are the four kinds of clinging."

"But, friend, is there a path, is there a way for the abandonment of these four kinds of clinging?"

"There is a path, friend, there is a way ... this Noble Eightfold Path...."

13 Existence

"Friend Sāriputta, it is said, 'existence, existence.' What now is existence?"

"There are, friend, these three kinds of existence: sense-sphere existence, form-sphere existence, formless-sphere existence. These are the three kinds of existence."

"But, friend, is there a path, is there a way for the full understanding of these three kinds of existence?" [259]

"There is a path, friend, there is a way … this Noble Eightfold Path…."

14 Suffering

"Friend Sāriputta, it is said, 'suffering, suffering.' What now is suffering?"

"There are, friend, these three kinds of suffering: the suffering due to pain, the suffering due to formations, the suffering due to change. These are the three kinds of suffering."[274]

"But, friend, is there a path, is there a way for the full understanding of these three kinds of suffering?"

"There is a path, friend, there is a way … this Noble Eightfold Path…."

15 Identity

"Friend Sāriputta, it is said, 'identity, identity.' What now is identity?"

"These five aggregates subject to clinging, friend, have been called identity by the Blessed One; that is, the form aggregate subject to clinging, the feeling aggregate subject to clinging, the perception aggregate subject to clinging, the volitional formations aggregate subject to clinging, [260] the consciousness aggregate subject to clinging. These five aggregates subject to clinging have been called identity by the Blessed One."

"But, friend, is there a path, is there a way for the full understanding of this identity?"

"There is a path, friend, there is a way for the full understanding of this identity."

"And what, friend, is that path, what is that way for the full understanding of this identity."

"It is, friend, this Noble Eightfold Path; that is, right view … right concentration. This is the path, friend, this is the way for the full understanding of this identity."

"Excellent is the path, friend, excellent is the way for the full understanding of this identity. And it is enough, friend Sāriputta, for diligence."

16 Difficult to Do

"Friend Sāriputta, what is difficult to do in this Dhamma and Discipline?"

"Going forth, friend, is difficult to do in this Dhamma and Discipline."

"What, friend, is difficult to do by one who has gone forth?"

"To find delight, friend, is difficult to do by one who has gone forth."

"What, friend, is difficult to do by one who has found delight?"

"Practice in accordance with the Dhamma, friend, is difficult to do by one who has found delight."

"But, friend, if a bhikkhu is practising in accordance with the Dhamma, would it take him long to become an arahant?"

"Not long, friend."[275]

[261] Chapter V

39 *Sāmaṇḍakasaṃyutta*

Connected Discourses with Sāmaṇḍaka

1–16 A Question on Nibbāna, Etc.

On one occasion the Venerable Sāriputta was dwelling among the Vajjians at Ukkacelā. Then the wanderer Sāmaṇḍaka approached the Venerable Sāriputta and exchanged greetings with him. When they had concluded their greetings and cordial talk, he sat down to one side and said to the Venerable Sāriputta:

"Friend Sāriputta, it is said, 'Nibbāna, Nibbāna.' What now is Nibbāna?"…

(*The remainder of this saṃyutta is identical with the preceding one except for the identity of the interlocutor.*) [262]

"But, friend, if a bhikkhu is practising in accordance with the Dhamma, would it take him long to become an arahant?"

"Not long, friend."

Chapter VI

40 *Moggallānasaṃyutta*
Connected Discourses with Moggallāna

1 The First Jhāna

On one occasion the Venerable Mahāmoggallāna was dwelling at Sāvatthī in Jeta's Grove, Anāthapiṇḍika's Park. [263] There the Venerable Mahāmoggallāna addressed the bhikkhus thus: "Friends, bhikkhus!"[276]

"Friend!" those bhikkhus replied. The Venerable Mahāmoggallāna said this:

"Here, friends, while I was alone in seclusion, a reflection arose in my mind thus: 'It is said, "the first jhāna, the first jhāna." What now is the first jhāna?'

"Then, friends, it occurred to me: 'Here, secluded from sensual pleasures, secluded from unwholesome states, a bhikkhu enters and dwells in the first jhāna, which is accompanied by thought and examination, with rapture and happiness born of seclusion. This is called the first jhāna.'

"Then, friends, secluded from sensual pleasures, secluded from unwholesome states, I entered and dwelt in the first jhāna.... While I dwelt therein perception and attention accompanied by sensuality assailed me.[277]

"Then, friends, the Blessed One came to me by means of spiritual power and said this: 'Moggallāna, Moggallāna, do not be negligent, brahmin, regarding the first jhāna. Steady your mind in the first jhāna, unify your mind in the first jhāna, concentrate your mind in the first jhāna.' Then, friends, on a later occasion, secluded from sensual pleasures, secluded from unwholesome states, I entered and dwelt in the first jhāna, which is accompanied by thought and examination, with rapture and happiness born of seclusion.

"If, friends, one speaking rightly could say of anyone: 'He is a disciple who attained to greatness of direct knowledge[278] with the assistance of the Teacher,' it is of me that one could rightly say this."

2 The Second Jhāna

... "Here, friends, while I was alone in seclusion, a reflection arose in my mind thus: 'It is said, "the second jhāna, the second jhāna." What now is the second jhāna?'[279]

"Then, friends, it occurred to me: 'Here, [264] with the subsiding of thought and examination, a bhikkhu enters and dwells in the second jhāna, which has internal confidence and unification of mind, is without thought and examination, and has rapture and happiness born of concentration. This is called the second jhāna.'

"Then, friends, with the subsiding of thought and examination, I entered and dwelt in the second jhāna.... While I dwelt therein perception and attention accompanied by thought and examination assailed me.

"Then, friends, the Blessed One came to me by means of spiritual power and said this: 'Moggallāna, Moggallāna, do not be negligent, brahmin, regarding the second jhāna. Steady your mind in the second jhāna, unify your mind in the second jhāna, concentrate your mind in the second jhāna.' Then, on a later occasion, with the subsiding of thought and examination, I entered and dwelt in the second jhāna, which has internal confidence and unification of mind, is without thought and examination, and has rapture and happiness born of concentration.

"If, friends, one speaking rightly could say of anyone: 'He is a disciple who attained to greatness of direct knowledge with the assistance of the Teacher,' it is of me that one could rightly say this."

3 The Third Jhāna

... "Here, friends, while I was alone in seclusion, a reflection arose in my mind thus: 'It is said, "the third jhāna, the third jhāna." What now is the third jhāna?'

"Then, friends, it occurred to me: 'Here, with the fading away as well of rapture, a bhikkhu dwells equanimous and, mindful and clearly comprehending, he experiences happiness with the body; he enters and dwells in the third jhāna of which the noble ones declare: "He is equanimous, mindful, one who dwells happily." This is called the third jhāna.'

"Then, friends, with the fading away as well of rapture ... I entered and dwelt in the third jhāna.... While I dwelt therein perception and attention accompanied by rapture assailed me. [265]

"Then, friends, the Blessed One came to me by means of spiritual power and said this: 'Moggallāna, Moggallāna, do not be negligent, brahmin, regarding the third jhāna. Steady your mind in the third jhāna, unify your mind in the third jhāna, concentrate your mind in the third jhāna.' Then, on a later occasion, with the fading away as well of rapture, I dwelt equanimous and, mindful and clearly comprehending, I experienced happiness with the body; I entered and dwelt in the third jhāna of which the noble ones declare: 'He is equanimous, mindful, one who dwells happily.'

"If, friends, one speaking rightly could say of anyone: 'He is a disciple who attained to greatness of direct knowledge with the assistance of the Teacher,' it is of me that one could rightly say this."

4 The Fourth Jhāna

... "Here, friends, while I was alone in seclusion, a reflection arose in my mind thus: 'It is said, "the fourth jhāna, the fourth jhāna." What now is the fourth jhāna?'

"Then, friends, it occurred to me: 'Here, with the abandoning of pleasure and pain, and with the previous passing away of joy and displeasure, a bhikkhu enters and dwells in the fourth jhāna, which is neither painful nor pleasant and includes the purification of mindfulness by equanimity. This is called the fourth jhāna.'

"Then, friends, with the abandoning of pleasure and pain ... I entered and dwelt in the fourth jhāna.... While I dwelt therein perception and attention accompanied by happiness assailed me.

"Then, friends, the Blessed One came to me by means of spiritual power and said this: 'Moggallāna, Moggallāna, do not be negligent, brahmin, regarding the fourth jhāna. Steady your mind in the fourth jhāna, unify your mind in the fourth jhāna, concentrate your mind in the fourth jhāna.' Then, on a later occasion, with the abandoning of pleasure and pain, and with the previous passing away of joy and displeasure, [266] I entered and dwelt in the fourth jhāna, which is neither painful nor pleasant and includes the purification of mindfulness by equanimity.

"If, friends, one speaking rightly could say of anyone: 'He is a disciple who attained to greatness of direct knowledge with the assistance of the Teacher,' it is of me that one could rightly say this."

5 The Base of the Infinity of Space

... "Here, friends, while I was alone in seclusion, a reflection arose in my mind thus: 'It is said, "the base of the infinity of space, the base of the infinity of space." What now is the base of the infinity of space?'

"Then, friends, it occurred to me: 'Here, with the complete transcendence of perceptions of forms, with the passing away of perceptions of sensory impingement, with nonattention to perceptions of diversity, aware that "space is infinite," a bhikkhu enters and dwells in the base of the infinity of space. This is called the base of the infinity of space.'

"Then, friends, with the complete transcendence of perceptions of forms ... I entered and dwelt in the base of the infinity of space. While I dwelt therein perception and attention accompanied by forms assailed me.

"Then, friends, the Blessed One came to me by means of spiritual power and said this: 'Moggallāna, Moggallāna, do not be negligent, brahmin, regarding the base of the infinity of space. Steady your mind in the base of the infinity of space, unify your mind in the base of the infinity of space, concentrate your mind in the base of the infinity of space.' Then, on a later occasion, with the complete transcendence of perceptions of forms, with the passing away of perceptions of sensory impingement, with nonattention to perceptions of diversity, aware that 'space is infinite,' I entered and dwelt in the base of the infinity of space.

"If, friends, one speaking rightly could say of anyone: 'He is a disciple who attained to greatness of direct knowledge with the assistance of the Teacher,' it is of me that one could rightly say this."

6 The Base of the Infinity of Consciousness

… "Here, friends, while I was alone in seclusion, a reflection arose in my mind thus: 'It is said, "the base of the infinity of consciousness, the base of the infinity of consciousness." What now is the base of the infinity of consciousness?' [267]

"Then, friends, it occurred to me: 'Here, by completely transcending the base of the infinity of space, aware that "consciousness is infinite," a bhikkhu enters and dwells in the base of the infinity of consciousness. This is called the base of the infinity of consciousness.'

"Then, friends, by completely transcending the base of the infinity of space, aware that 'consciousness is infinite,' I entered and dwelt in the base of the infinity of consciousness. While I dwelt therein perception and attention accompanied by the base of the infinity of space assailed me.

"Then, friends, the Blessed One came to me by means of spiritual power and said this: 'Moggallāna, Moggallāna, do not be negligent, brahmin, regarding the base of the infinity of consciousness. Steady your mind in the base of the infinity of consciousness, unify your mind in the base of the infinity of consciousness, concentrate your mind in the base of the infinity of consciousness.' Then, on a later occasion, by completely transcending the base of the infinity of space, aware that 'consciousness is infinite,' I entered and dwelt in the base of the infinity of consciousness.

"If, friends, one speaking rightly could say of anyone: 'He is a disciple who attained to greatness of direct knowledge with the assistance of the Teacher,' it is of me that one could rightly say this."

7 The Base of Nothingness

… "Here, friends, while I was alone in seclusion, a reflection arose in my mind thus: 'It is said, "the base of nothingness, the base of nothingness." What now is the base of nothingness?'

"Then, friends, it occurred to me: 'Here, by completely transcending the base of the infinity of consciousness, aware that "there is nothing," a bhikkhu enters and dwells in the base of nothingness. This is called the base of nothingness.'

"Then, friends, by completely transcending the base of the infinity of consciousness, aware that 'there is nothing,' I entered and dwelt in the base of nothingness. While I dwelt therein perception and attention accompanied by the base of the infinity of consciousness assailed me.

"Then, friends, the Blessed One came to me by means of spiritual power and said this: 'Moggallāna, Moggallāna, do not be negligent, brahmin, regarding the base of nothingness. Steady your mind in the base of nothingness, [268] unify your mind in the base of nothingness, concentrate your mind in the base of nothingness.' Then, on a later occasion, by completely transcending the base of the infinity of consciousness, aware that 'there is nothing,' I entered and dwelt in the base of nothingness.

"If, friends, one speaking rightly could say of anyone: 'He is a disciple who attained to greatness of direct knowledge with the assistance of the Teacher,' it is of me that one could rightly say this."

8 The Base of Neither-Perception-Nor-Nonperception

... "Here, friends, while I was alone in seclusion, a reflection arose in my mind thus: 'It is said, "the base of neither-perception-nor-nonperception, the base of neither-perception-nor-nonperception." What now is the base of neither-perception-nor-nonperception?'

"Then, friends, it occurred to me: 'Here, by completely transcending the base of nothingness, a bhikkhu enters and dwells in the base of neither-perception-nor-nonperception. This is called the base of neither-perception-nor-nonperception.'

"Then, friends, by completely transcending the base of nothingness, I entered and dwelt in the base of neither-perception-nor-nonperception. While I dwelt therein perception and attention accompanied by the base of nothingness assailed me.

"Then, friends, the Blessed One came to me by means of spiritual power and said this: 'Moggallāna, Moggallāna, do not be negligent, brahmin, regarding the base of neither-perception-nor-nonperception. Steady your mind in the base of neither-perception-nor-nonperception, unify your mind in the base of neither-perception-nor-nonperception, concentrate your mind in the base of neither-perception-nor-nonperception.' Then, on a later occasion, by completely transcending the base of nothingness, I entered and dwelt in the base of neither-perception-nor-nonperception.

"If, friends, one speaking rightly could say of anyone: 'He is a disciple who attained to greatness of direct knowledge with the assistance of the Teacher,' it is of me that one could rightly say this."

9 The Signless

... "Here, friends, while I was alone in seclusion, a reflection arose in my mind thus: 'It is said, "the signless concentration of mind, the signless concentration of mind." What now is the signless concentration of mind?'[280]

"Then, friends, it occurred to me: 'Here, [269] by nonattention to all signs, a bhikkhu enters and dwells in the signless concentration of mind. This is called the signless concentration of mind.'

"Then, friends, by nonattention to all signs, I entered and dwelt in the signless concentration of mind. While I dwelt therein my consciousness followed along with signs.[281]

"Then, friends, the Blessed One came to me by means of spiritual power and said this: 'Moggallāna, Moggallāna, do not be negligent, brahmin, regarding the signless concentration of mind. Steady your mind in the signless concentration of mind, unify your mind in the signless concentration of mind, concentrate your mind in the signless concentration of mind.' Then, on a later occasion, by nonattention to all signs, I entered and dwelt in the signless concentration of mind.

"If, friends, one speaking rightly could say of anyone: 'He is a disciple who attained to greatness of direct knowledge with the assistance of the Teacher,' it is of me that one could rightly say this."

10 Sakka

I

On one occasion the Venerable Mahāmoggallāna was dwelling at Sāvatthī in Jeta's Grove, Anāthapiṇḍika's Park. Then, just as quickly as a strong man might extend his drawn-in arm or draw in his extended arm, the Venerable Mahāmoggallāna disappeared from Jeta's Grove and reappeared among the Tāvatiṃsa devas. Then Sakka, lord of the devas, approached the Venerable Mahāmoggallāna together with five hundred devatās. [270] Having approached, he paid homage to the Venerable Mahāmoggallāna and stood to one side. The Venerable Mahāmoggallāna then said to him:

"Good, lord of the devas, is the going for refuge to the Buddha. Because of going for refuge to the Buddha, some beings here, with the breakup of the body, after death, are reborn in a good destination, in a heavenly world. Good, lord of the devas, is the going for refuge to the Dhamma. Because of going for refuge to the Dhamma, some beings here, with the breakup of the body, after death, are reborn in a good destination, in a heavenly world. Good, lord of the devas, is the going for refuge to the Saṅgha. Because of going for refuge to the Saṅgha, some beings here, with the breakup of the body, after death, are reborn in a good destination, in a heavenly world."

"Good, Sir Moggallāna, is the going for refuge to the Buddha ... to the Dhamma ... to the Saṅgha. Because of going for refuge to the Saṅgha, some beings here, with the breakup of the body, after death, are reborn in a good destination, in a heavenly world."

Then Sakka, lord of the devas, approached the Venerable Mahāmoggallāna together with six hundred devatās ... seven hundred devatās ... eight hundred devatās ... eighty thousand devatās.[282] Having approached, he paid homage to the Venerable Mahāmoggallāna and stood to one side. The Venerable Mahāmoggallāna then said to him:

(*The conversation is exactly the same as above.*) [271]

II

Then Sakka, lord of the devas, approached the Venerable Mahāmoggallāna together with five hundred devatās. Having approached, he paid homage to the Venerable Mahāmoggallāna and stood to one side. The Venerable Mahāmoggallāna then said to him:

"Good, lord of the devas, is the possession of confirmed confidence in the Buddha thus:[283] 'The Blessed One is an arahant, fully enlightened, accomplished in true knowledge and conduct, fortunate, knower of the world, unsurpassed leader of persons to be tamed, teacher of devas and humans, the Enlightened One, the Blessed One.' Because of possessing confirmed confidence in the Buddha, some beings here, with the breakup of the body, after death, are reborn in a good destination, in a heavenly world.

"Good, lord of the devas, is the possession of confirmed confidence in the Dhamma thus: [272] 'The Dhamma is well expounded by the Blessed One, directly visible, immediate, inviting one to come and see, applicable, to be personally experienced by the wise.' Because of possessing confirmed confidence in the Dhamma, some beings here, with the breakup of the body, after death, are reborn in a good destination, in a heavenly world.

"Good, lord of the devas, is the possession of confirmed confidence in the Saṅgha thus: 'The Saṅgha of the Blessed One's disciples is practising the good way, practising the straight way, practising the true way, practising the proper way; that is, the four pairs of persons, the eight types of individuals—this Saṅgha of the Blessed One's disciples is worthy of gifts, worthy of hospitality, worthy of offerings, worthy of reverential salutation, the unsurpassed field of merit for the world.' Because of possessing confirmed confidence in the Saṅgha, some beings here, with the breakup of the body, after death, are reborn in a good destination, in a heavenly world.

"Good, lord of the devas, is the possession of the virtues dear to the noble ones, unbroken, untorn, unblemished, unmottled, freeing, praised by the wise, ungrasped, leading to concentration. Because of possessing the virtues dear to the noble ones, some beings here, with the breakup of the body, after death, are reborn in a good destination, in a heavenly world."

"Good, Sir Moggallāna, is the possession of confirmed confidence in the Buddha ... the possession of confirmed confidence in the Dhamma ... the possession of confirmed confidence in the Saṅgha ... [273] ... the possession of the virtues dear to the noble ones, unbroken ... leading to concentration. Because of possessing the virtues dear to the noble ones, some beings here, with the breakup of the body, after death, are reborn in a good destination, in a heavenly world."

Then Sakka, lord of the devas, approached the Venerable Mahāmoggallāna together with six hundred devatās ... seven hundred devatās ... eight hundred devatās ... eighty thousand devatās. Having approached, he paid homage to the Venerable Mahāmoggallāna and stood to one side. The Venerable Mahāmoggallāna then said to him:

(*As above.*) [274]

III

Then Sakka, lord of the devas, approached the Venerable Mahāmoggallāna together with five hundred devatās. Having approached, he paid homage to the Venerable Mahāmoggallāna and stood to one side. The Venerable Mahāmoggallāna then said to him:

"Good, lord of the devas, is the going for refuge to the Buddha. Because of going for refuge to the Buddha, some beings here, [275] with the breakup of the body, after death, are reborn in a good destination, in a heavenly world. They surpass other devas in ten respects: in celestial life span, in celestial beauty, in celestial happiness, in celestial fame, in celestial sovereignty, and in celestial forms, sounds, odours, tastes, and tactile objects.

"Good, lord of the devas, is the going for refuge to the Dhamma … the going for refuge to the Saṅgha. Because of going for refuge to the Saṅgha … and in celestial forms, sounds, odours, tastes, and tactile objects."

"Good, Sir Moggallāna, is the going for refuge to the Buddha … to the Dhamma … to the Saṅgha. Because of going for refuge to the Saṅgha … and in celestial forms, sounds, odours, tastes, and tactile objects."

Then Sakka, lord of the devas, approached the Venerable Mahāmoggallāna together with six hundred devatās … seven hundred devatās… [276] … eight hundred devatās … eighty thousand devatās. Having approached, he paid homage to the Venerable Mahāmoggallāna and stood to one side. The Venerable Mahāmoggallāna then said to him:

(*As above.*)

IV

Then Sakka, lord of the devas, approached the Venerable Mahāmoggallāna together with five hundred devatās. Having approached, he paid homage to the Venerable Mahāmoggallāna and stood to one side. [277] The Venerable Mahāmoggallāna then said to him:

"Good, lord of the devas, is the possession of confirmed confidence in the Buddha thus: 'The Blessed One is ... teacher of devas and humans, the Enlightened One, the Blessed One.' Because of possessing confirmed confidence in the Buddha, some beings here, with the breakup of the body, after death, are reborn in a good destination, in a heavenly world. They surpass other devas in ten respects: in celestial life span, in celestial beauty, in celestial happiness, in celestial fame, in celestial sovereignty, and in celestial forms, sounds, odours, tastes, and tactile objects.

"Good, lord of the devas, is the possession of confirmed confidence in the Dhamma thus ... the possession of confirmed confidence in the Saṅgha thus ... Good, lord of the devas, is the possession of the virtues dear to the noble ones, unbroken ... leading to concentration. Because of possessing the virtues dear to the noble ones ... and in celestial forms, sounds, odours, tastes, and tactile objects."

"Good, Sir Moggallāna, is the possession of confirmed confidence in the Buddha ... the possession of confirmed confidence in the Dhamma ... the possession of confirmed confidence in the Saṅgha ... [278] ... the possession of the virtues dear to the noble ones, unbroken ... leading to concentration. Because of possessing the virtues dear to the noble ones some beings here, with the breakup of the body, after death, are reborn in a good destination, in a heavenly world. They surpass other devas in ten respects: in celestial life span, in celestial beauty, in celestial happiness, in celestial fame, in celestial sovereignty, and in celestial forms, sounds, odours, tastes, and tactile objects."

Then Sakka, lord of the devas, approached the Venerable Mahāmoggallāna together with six hundred devatās ... seven hundred devatās ... eight hundred devatās ... eighty thousand devatās. Having approached, he paid homage to the Venerable Mahāmoggallāna and stood to one side. The Venerable Mahāmoggallāna then said to him:

(*As above.*) [279–80]

11 Candana

Then Candana, a young deva....
Then Suyāma, a young deva....
Then Santusita, a young deva....
Then Sunimmita, a young deva....
Then Vasavatti, a young deva....
(*To be elaborated in full exactly as in §10.*)[284]

[281] Chapter VII

41 *Cittasaṃyutta*
Connected Discourses with Citta

1 The Fetter

On one occasion a number of elder bhikkhus were dwelling at Macchikāsaṇḍa in the Wild Mango Grove.

Now on that occasion, when the elder bhikkhus had returned from their alms round, after their meal they assembled in the pavilion and were sitting together when this conversation arose: "Friends, 'the fetter' and 'the things that fetter': are these things different in meaning and also different in phrasing, or are they one in meaning and different only in phrasing?"

Some elder bhikkhus answered thus: "Friends, 'the fetter' and 'the things that fetter' are different in meaning and also different in phrasing." But some [other] elder bhikkhus answered thus: "Friends, 'the fetter' and 'the things that fetter' are one in meaning and different only in phrasing."

Now on that occasion Citta the householder had arrived in Migapathaka on some business.[285] [282] Then Citta the householder heard: "A number of elder bhikkhus, it is said, on returning from their alms round, had assembled in the pavilion after their meal and were sitting together when this conversation arose...." Then Citta the householder approached those elder bhikkhus, paid homage to them, sat down to one side, and said to them: "I have heard, venerable sirs, that when a number of elder bhikkhus were sitting together this conversation arose: 'Friends, "the fetter" and "the things that fetter": are these things different in meaning and also different in phrasing, or are they one in meaning and different only in phrasing?'"

"That is so, householder."

"Venerable sirs, 'the fetter' and 'the things that fetter' are different in meaning and also different in phrasing. I will give you a simile for this, since some wise people here understand the meaning of a statement by means of a simile.

"Suppose, venerable sirs, a black ox and a white ox were yoked together by a single harness or yoke.[286] Would one be speaking rightly if one were to say: 'The black ox is the fetter of the white ox; the white ox is the fetter of the black ox'?" [283]

"No, householder. The black ox is not the fetter of the white ox nor is the white ox the fetter of the black ox, but rather the single harness or yoke by which the two are yoked together: that is the fetter there."

"So too, friend, the eye is not the fetter of forms nor are forms the fetter of the eye, but rather the desire and lust that arise there in dependence on both: that is the fetter there. The ear is not the fetter of sounds ... The nose is not the fetter of odours ... The tongue is not the fetter of tastes ... The body is not the fetter of tactile objects ... The mind is not the fetter of mental phenomena nor are mental phenomena the fetter of the mind, but rather the desire and lust that arises there in dependence on both: that is the fetter there."

"It is a gain for you, householder, it is well gained by you, householder, in that you have the eye of wisdom that ranges over the deep Word of the Buddha."

2 Isidatta (1)

On one occasion a number of elder bhikkhus were dwelling at Macchikāsaṇḍa in the Wild Mango Grove. Then Citta the householder approached those elder bhikkhus, paid homage to them, sat down to one side, and said to them: "Venerable sirs, let the elders consent to accept tomorrow's meal from me."

The elder bhikkhus consented by silence. [284] Then Citta the householder, having understood that the elders had consented, rose from his seat, paid homage to them, and departed, keeping them on his right.

When the night had passed, in the morning the elder bhikkhus dressed, took their bowls and outer robes, and went to the residence of Citta the householder. There they sat down on the appointed seats. Then Citta the householder approached the elder bhikkhus, paid homage to them, sat down to one side, and said to the venerable chief elder:

"Venerable Elder, it is said, 'diversity of elements, diversity of elements.' In what way, venerable sir, has the diversity of elements been spoken of by the Blessed One?"[287]

When this was said, the venerable chief elder was silent. A second time and a third time Citta the householder asked the same question, and a second time and a third time the venerable chief elder was silent.[288]

Now on that occasion the Venerable Isidatta was the most junior bhikkhu in that Saṅgha.[289] Then the Venerable Isidatta said to the venerable chief elder: "Allow me, venerable elder, to answer Citta the householder's question."

"Answer it, friend Isidatta."

"Now, householder, are you asking thus: 'Venerable elder, it is said, "diversity of elements, diversity of elements." In what way, venerable sir, has the diversity of elements been spoken of by the Blessed One?'" [285]

"Yes, venerable sir."

"This diversity of elements, householder, has been spoken of by the Blessed One thus: the eye element, form element, eye-consciousness element ... the mind element, mental-phenomena element, mind-consciousness element. It is in this way, householder, that the diversity of elements has been spoken of by the Blessed One."

Then Citta the householder, having delighted and rejoiced in the Venerable Isidatta's words, with his own hand served and satisfied the elder bhikkhus with the various kinds of delicious food. When the elder bhikkhus had finished eating and had put away their bowls,[290] they rose from their seats and departed.

Then the venerable chief elder said to the Venerable Isidatta: "It is good, friend Isidatta, that the answer to this question occurred to you. The answer did not occur to me. Therefore, friend Isidatta, whenever a similar question comes up at some other time, you should clear it up."[291]

3 Isidatta (2)

(*Opening as in the preceding sutta down to:*) [286]

Then Citta the householder approached the elder bhikkhus,

paid homage to them, sat down to one side, and said to the venerable chief elder:

"Venerable Elder, there are various views that arise in the world: 'The world is eternal' or 'The world is not eternal'; or 'The world is finite' or 'The world is infinite'; or 'The soul and the body are the same' or 'The soul is one thing, the body is another'; or 'The Tathāgata exists after death,' or 'The Tathāgata does not exist after death,' or 'The Tathāgata both exists and does not exist after death,' or 'The Tathāgata neither exists nor does not exist after death'—these as well as the sixty-two views mentioned in the Brahmajāla.[292] Now when what exists do these views come to be? When what is nonexistent do these views not come to be?"

When this was said, the venerable chief elder was silent. A second time and a third time Citta the householder asked the same question, and a second time and a third time the venerable chief elder was silent.

Now on that occasion the Venerable Isidatta was the most junior bhikkhu in that Saṅgha. Then the Venerable Isidatta said to the venerable chief elder: "Allow me, venerable elder, to answer Citta the householder's question."

"Answer it, friend Isidatta." [287]

"Now, householder, are you asking thus: 'Venerable elder, there are various views that arise in the world: "The world is eternal" ... —these as well as the sixty-two speculative views mentioned in the Brahmajāla. Now when what exists do these views come to be? When what is nonexistent do these views not come to be?'"

"Yes, venerable sir."

"As to the various views that arise in the world, householder, 'The world is eternal' ... —these as well as the sixty-two speculative views mentioned in the Brahmajāla: when there is identity view, these views come to be; when there is no identity view, these views do not come to be."

"But, venerable sir, how does identity view come to be?"

"Here, householder, the uninstructed worldling, who has no regard for the noble ones and is unskilled and undisciplined in their Dhamma, who has no regard for the good persons and is unskilled and undisciplined in their Dhamma, regards form as self, or self as possessing form, or form as in self, or self as in form. He regards feeling as self ... perception as self ... volitional formations as self ... consciousness as self, or self as possessing consciousness, or consciousness as in self, or self as in consciousness. It is in such a way that identity view comes to be."

"And, venerable sir, how does identity view not come to be?"

"Here, householder, the instructed noble disciple, who has regard for the noble ones and is skilled and disciplined in their Dhamma, who has regard for the good persons and is skilled and disciplined in their Dhamma, does not regard form as self, or self as possessing form, or form as in self, or self as in form. He does not regard feeling as self ... or perception as self ... or volitional formations as self ... or consciousness as self ... or self as in consciousness. It is in such a way that identity view does not come to be." [288]

"Venerable sir, where does Master Isidatta come from?"

"I come from Avantī, householder."

"There is, venerable sir, a clansman from Avantī named Isidatta, an unseen friend of ours, who has gone forth. Has the venerable one ever met him?"

"Yes, householder."

"Where is that venerable one now dwelling, venerable sir?"

When this was said, the Venerable Isidatta was silent.

"Is the master Isidatta?"

"Yes, householder."

"Then let Master Isidatta delight in the delightful Wild Mango Grove at Macchikāsaṇḍa. I will be zealous in providing Master Isidatta with robes, almsfood, lodgings, and medicinal requisites."

"That is kindly said, householder."

Then Citta the householder, having delighted and rejoiced in the Venerable Isidatta's words, with his own hand served and satisfied the elder bhikkhus with the various kinds of delicious food. When the elder bhikkhus had finished eating and had put away their bowls, they rose from their seats and departed.

Then the venerable chief elder said to the Venerable Isidatta: "It is good, friend Isidatta, that the answer to this question occurred to you. The answer did not occur to me. Therefore, friend Isidatta, whenever a similar question comes up at some other time, you should clear it up."

Then the Venerable Isidatta set his lodging in order and, taking bowl and robe, he left Macchikāsaṇḍa. When he left Macchikāsaṇḍa, he left for good and he never returned.[293]

4 Mahaka's Miracle

On one occasion a number of elder bhikkhus were dwelling at Macchikāsaṇḍa in the Wild Mango Grove. [289] Then Citta the householder approached those elder bhikkhus, paid homage to them, sat down to one side, and said to them: "Venerable sirs, let the elders consent to accept tomorrow's meal from me in my cowshed."

The elder bhikkhus consented by silence. Then Citta the householder, having understood that the elders had consented, rose from his seat, paid homage to them, and departed, keeping them on his right.

When the night had passed, in the morning the elder bhikkhus dressed, took their bowls and outer robes, and went to the cowshed of Citta the householder. There they sat down on the appointed seats.

Then Citta the householder, with his own hand, served and satisfied the elder bhikkhus with delicious milk-rice made with ghee. When the elder bhikkhus had finished eating and had put away their bowls, they rose from their seats and departed.

Then Citta the householder, having said, "Give away the remainder," followed close behind the elder bhikkhus. Now on that occasion the heat was sweltering,[294] and the elders went along as if their bodies were melting because of the food they had eaten.

Now on that occasion the Venerable Mahaka was the most junior bhikkhu in that Saṅgha. Then the Venerable Mahaka said to the venerable chief elder: "It would be good, venerable elder, if a cool wind would blow, and a canopy of clouds would form, and the sky would drizzle."

"That would be good, friend."

Then the Venerable Mahaka performed such a feat of spiritual power [290] that a cool wind blew, and a canopy of clouds formed, and the sky drizzled.

Then it occurred to Citta the householder: "Such is the spiritual power and might possessed by the most junior bhikkhu in this Saṅgha!"

Then, when the Venerable Mahaka arrived at the monastery, he said to the venerable chief elder: "Is this much enough, Venerable Elder?"

"That's enough, friend Mahaka. What's been done is sufficient, friend Mahaka, what's been offered is sufficient."

Then the elder bhikkhus went to their dwellings and the Venerable Mahaka went to his own dwelling.

Then Citta the householder approached the Venerable Mahaka, paid homage to him, sat down to one side, and said to him: "It would be good, venerable sir, if Master Mahaka would show me a superhuman miracle of spiritual power."

"Then, householder, spread your cloak upon the verandah and scatter a bundle of grass upon it."

"Yes, venerable sir," Citta the householder replied, and he spread his cloak upon the verandah and scattered a bundle of grass upon it.

Then, when he had entered his dwelling and shut the bolt, the Venerable Mahaka performed a feat of spiritual power such that a flame shot through the keyhole and the chink of the door and burnt the grass but not the cloak.[295] Citta the householder shook out his cloak and stood to one side, shocked and terrified.

Then the Venerable Mahaka came out of his dwelling and said to Citta the householder: "Is this much enough, householder?" [291]

"That's enough, Venerable Mahaka. What's been done is sufficient, Venerable Mahaka, what's been offered is sufficient. Let Master Mahaka delight in the delightful Wild Mango Grove at Macchikāsaṇḍa. I will be zealous in providing Master Mahaka with robes, almsfood, lodgings, and medicinal requisites."

"That is kindly said, householder."

Then the Venerable Mahaka set his lodging in order and, taking bowl and robe, he left Macchikāsaṇḍa. When he left Macchikāsaṇḍa, he left for good and he never returned.

5 Kāmabhū (1)

On one occasion the Venerable Kāmabhū was dwelling at Macchikāsaṇḍa in the Wild Mango Grove. Then Citta the householder approached the Venerable Kāmabhū, paid homage to him, and sat down to one side. The Venerable Kāmabhū then said to him:

"This has been said, householder:

> "'With faultless wheel and a white awning,
> The one-spoked chariot rolls.
> See it coming, trouble-free,
> The stream cut, without bondage.'[296]

How, householder, should the meaning of this brief statement be understood in detail?"

"Was this stated by the Blessed One, venerable sir?"

"Yes, householder."

"Then wait a moment, venerable sir, while I consider its meaning."

Then, after a moment's silence, Citta the householder said to the Venerable Kāmabhū: [292]

"'Faultless': this, venerable sir, is a designation for the virtues. 'White awning': this is a designation for liberation. 'One spoke': this is a designation for mindfulness. 'Rolls': this is a designation for going forward and returning. 'Chariot': this is a designation for this body consisting of the four great elements, originating from mother and father, built up out of rice and gruel, subject to impermanence, to being worn and rubbed away, to breaking apart and dispersal.

"Lust, venerable sir, is trouble; hatred is trouble; delusion is trouble. For a bhikkhu whose taints are destroyed, these have been abandoned, cut off at the root, made like palm stumps, obliterated so that they are no more subject to future arising. Therefore the bhikkhu whose taints are destroyed is called 'trouble-free.' The 'one who is coming' is a designation for the arahant.

"'The stream': this, venerable sir, is a designation for craving. For a bhikkhu whose taints are destroyed, this has been abandoned, cut off at the root, made like a palm stump, obliterated so that it is no more subject to future arising. Therefore the bhikkhu whose taints are destroyed is called 'one with the stream cut.'

"Lust, venerable sir, is bondage; hatred is bondage; delusion is bondage. For a bhikkhu whose taints are destroyed, these have been abandoned, cut off at the root, made like palm stumps, obliterated so that they are no more subject to future arising. Therefore the bhikkhu whose taints are destroyed is called 'one no more in bondage.'

"Thus, venerable sir, when it was said by the the Blessed One:

"'With faultless wheel and a white awning,
The one-spoked chariot rolls.
See it coming, trouble-free,
The stream cut, without bondage'—

it is in such a way that I understand in detail the meaning of what was stated by the Blessed One in brief."

"It is a gain for you, householder, it is well gained by you, householder, in that you have the eye of wisdom that ranges over the deep Word of the Buddha." [293]

6 Kāmabhū (2)

On one occasion the Venerable Kāmabhū was dwelling at Macchikāsaṇḍa in the Wild Mango Grove. Then Citta the householder approached the Venerable Kāmabhū, paid homage to him, sat down to one side, and said to him: "Venerable sir, how many kinds of formations are there?"[297]

"There are, householder, three kinds of formations: the bodily formation, the verbal formation, and the mental formation."[298]

"Good, venerable sir," Citta the householder said. Then, having delighted and rejoiced in the Venerable Kāmabhū's statement, he asked him a further question: "But, venerable sir, what is the bodily formation? What is the verbal formation? What is the mental formation?"

"In-breathing and out-breathing, householder, are the bodily formation; thought and examination are the verbal formation; perception and feeling are the mental formation."

"Good, venerable sir," Citta the householder said. Then ... he asked him a further question: "But, venerable sir, why are in-breathing and out-breathing the bodily formation? Why are thought and examination the verbal formation? Why are perception and feeling the mental formation?"

"Householder, in-breathing and out-breathing are bodily, these things are dependent upon the body; that is why in-breathing and out-breathing are the bodily formation. First one thinks and examines, then afterwards one breaks into speech; that is why thought and examination are the verbal formation. Perception and feeling are mental, these things are dependent upon the mind; that is why perception and feeling are the mental formation."

Saying, "Good, venerable sir,"… he then asked him a further question: "Venerable sir, how does the attainment of the cessation of perception and feeling come about?"[299]

"Householder, when a bhikkhu is attaining the cessation of perception and feeling, it does not occur to him: 'I will attain the cessation of perception and feeling,' or 'I am attaining the cessation of perception and feeling,' or 'I have attained the cessation of perception and feeling'; [294] but rather his mind has previously been developed in such a way that it leads him to such a state."[300]

Saying, "Good, venerable sir,"… he then asked him a further question: "Venerable sir, when a bhikkhu is attaining the cessation of perception and feeling, which of these things ceases first in him: the bodily formation, the verbal formation, or the mental formation?"

"Householder, when a bhikkhu is attaining the cessation of perception and feeling, first the verbal formation ceases, after that the bodily formation, and after that the mental formation."[301]

Saying, "Good, venerable sir,"… he then asked him a further question: "Venerable sir, what is the difference between one who is dead and gone, and a bhikkhu who has attained the cessation of perception and feeling?"

"Householder, in the case of one who is dead and gone, the bodily formation has ceased and subsided, the verbal formation has ceased and subsided, the mental formation has ceased and subsided; his vitality is extinguished, his physical heat has been dissipated, and his faculties are fully broken up. In the case of a bhikkhu who has attained the cessation of perception and feeling, the bodily formation has ceased and subsided, the verbal formation has ceased and subsided, the mental formation has ceased and subsided; but his vitality is not extinguished, his physical heat has not been dissipated, and his faculties are serene.[302] This is the difference between one who is dead and gone, and a bhikkhu who has attained the cessation of perception and feeling."

Saying, "Good, venerable sir,"… he then asked him a further question: "Venerable sir, how does emergence from the cessation of perception and feeling come about?"

"Householder, when a bhikkhu is emerging from the attainment of the cessation of perception and feeling, it does not occur to him: 'I will emerge from the attainment of the cessation of perception and feeling,' or 'I am emerging from the attainment of the cessation of perception and feeling,' or 'I have emerged from the attainment of the cessation of perception and feeling'; but rather his mind has previously been developed in such a way that it leads him to such a state."[303] [295]

Saying, "Good, venerable sir,"... he then asked him a further question: "Venerable sir, when a bhikkhu is emerging from the attainment of the cessation of perception and feeling, which of these things arises first in him: the bodily formation, the verbal formation, or the mental formation?"

"Householder, when a bhikkhu is emerging from the attainment of the cessation of perception and feeling, first the mental formation arises, after that the bodily formation, and after that the verbal formation."[304]

Saying, "Good, venerable sir,"... he then asked him a further question: "Venerable sir, when a bhikkhu has emerged from the attainment of the cessation of perception and feeling, how many kinds of contact touch him?"

"Householder, when a bhikkhu has emerged from the attainment of the cessation of perception and feeling, three kinds of contact touch him: emptiness-contact, signless-contact, undirected-contact."[305]

Saying, "Good, venerable sir,"... he then asked him a further question: "Venerable sir, when a bhikkhu has emerged from the attainment of the cessation of perception and feeling, towards what does his mind slant, slope, and incline?"

"Householder, when a bhikkhu has emerged from the attainment of the cessation of perception and feeling, his mind slants, slopes, and inclines towards seclusion."[306]

"Good, venerable sir," Citta the householder said. Then, having delighted and rejoiced in the Venerable Kāmabhū's statement, he asked him a further question: "Venerable sir, how many things are helpful for the attainment of the cessation of perception and feeling?"

"Indeed, householder, you are asking last what should have been asked first; but still I will answer you. For the attainment of the cessation of perception and feeling, two things are helpful: serenity and insight."[307]

7 Godatta

On one occasion the Venerable Godatta was dwelling at Macchikāsaṇḍa in the Wild Mango Grove. [296] Then Citta the householder approached the Venerable Godatta, paid homage to him, and sat down to one side. The Venerable Godatta then said to him as he was sitting to one side:[308]

"Householder, the measureless liberation of mind, the liberation of mind by nothingness, the liberation of mind by emptiness, and the signless liberation of mind: are these things different in meaning and also different in phrasing, or are they one in meaning and different only in phrasing?"

"There is a method, venerable sir, by which these things are different in meaning and also different in phrasing, and there is a method by which they are one in meaning and different only in phrasing.

"And what, venerable sir, is the method by which these things are different in meaning and also different in phrasing? Here a bhikkhu dwells pervading one quarter with a mind imbued with lovingkindness, likewise the second quarter, the third quarter, and the fourth quarter. Thus above, below, across, and everywhere, and to all as to himself, he dwells pervading the entire world with a mind imbued with lovingkindness, vast, exalted, measureless, without hostility, without ill will. He dwells pervading one quarter with a mind imbued with compassion … with a mind imbued with altruistic joy … with a mind imbued with equanimity, likewise the second quarter, the third quarter, and the fourth quarter. Thus above, below, across, and everywhere, and to all as to himself, he dwells pervading the entire world with a mind imbued with equanimity, vast, exalted, measureless, without hostility, without ill will. This is called the measureless liberation of mind.[309]

"And what, venerable sir, is the liberation of mind by nothingness? Here, by completely transcending the base of the infinity of consciousness, aware that 'there is nothing,' a bhikkhu enters and dwells in the base of nothingness. This is called the liberation of mind by nothingness.[310]

"And what, venerable sir, is the liberation of mind by emptiness? Here a bhikkhu, gone to the forest or to the foot of a tree or to an empty hut, reflects thus: 'Empty is this of self [297] or of what belongs to self.' This is called the liberation of mind by emptiness.[311]

"And what, venerable sir, is the signless liberation of mind? Here, with nonattention to all signs, a bhikkhu enters and dwells in the signless concentration of mind. This is called the signless liberation of mind.[312]

"This, venerable sir, is the method by which these things are different in meaning and also different in phrasing.[313] And what, venerable sir, is the method by which these things are one in meaning and different only in phrasing?

"Lust, venerable sir, is a maker of measurement, hatred is a maker of measurement, delusion is a maker of measurement. For a bhikkhu whose taints are destroyed, these have been abandoned, cut off at the root, made like palm stumps, obliterated so that they are no more subject to future arising. To whatever extent there are measureless liberations of mind, the unshakable liberation of mind is declared the chief among them.[314] Now that unshakable liberation of mind is empty of lust, empty of hatred, empty of delusion.

"Lust, venerable sir, is a something, hatred is a something, delusion is a something.[315] For a bhikkhu whose taints are destroyed, these have been abandoned, cut off at the root, made like palm stumps, obliterated so that they are no more subject to future arising. To whatever extent there are liberations of mind by nothingness, the unshakable liberation of mind is declared the chief among them. Now that unshakable liberation of mind is empty of lust, empty of hatred, empty of delusion.

"Lust, venerable sir, is a maker of signs, hatred is a maker of signs, delusion is a maker of signs.[316] For a bhikkhu whose taints are destroyed, these have been abandoned, cut off at the root, made like palm stumps, obliterated so that they are no more subject to future arising. To whatever extent there are signless liberations of mind, the unshakable liberation of mind is declared the chief among them. Now that unshakable liberation of mind is empty of lust, empty of hatred, empty of delusion.

"This, venerable sir, is the method by which these things are one in meaning and different only in phrasing."[317]

"It is a gain for you, householder, it is well gained by you, householder, in that you have the eye of wisdom that ranges over the deep Word of the Buddha."

8 Nigaṇṭha Nātaputta

Now on that occasion Nigaṇṭha Nātaputa had arrived at Macchikāsaṇḍa [298] together with a large retinue of nigaṇṭhas.[318] Citta the householder heard about this and, together with a number of lay followers, approached Nigaṇṭha Nātaputta.[319] He exchanged greetings with Nigaṇṭha Nātaputta and, when they had concluded their greetings and cordial talk, sat down to one side. Nigaṇṭha Nātaputta then said to him: "Householder, do you have faith in the ascetic Gotama when he says: 'There is a concentration without thought and examination, there is a cessation of thought and examination'?"[320]

"In this matter, venerable sir, I do not go by faith in the Blessed One[321] when he says: 'There is a concentration without thought and examination, there is a cessation of thought and examination.'"

When this was said, Nigaṇṭha Nātaputta looked up proudly[322] towards his own retinue and said: "See this, sirs! How straightforward is this Citta the householder! How honest and open! One who thinks that thought and examination can be stopped might imagine he could catch the wind in a net or arrest the current of the river Ganges with his own fist."

"What do you think, venerable sir, which is superior: knowledge or faith?"

"Knowledge, householder, is superior to faith."

"Well, venerable sir, to whatever extent I wish, secluded from sensual pleasures, secluded from unwholesome states, I enter and dwell in the first jhāna, which is accompanied by thought and examination, with rapture and happiness born of seclusion. [299] Then, to whatever extent I wish, with the subsiding of thought and examination, I enter and dwell in the second jhāna.... Then, to whatever extent I wish, with the fading away as well of rapture ... I enter and dwell in the third jhāna.... Then, to whatever extent I wish, with the abandoning of pleasure and pain ... I enter and dwell in the fourth jhāna.

"Since I know and see thus, venerable sir, in what other ascetic or brahmin need I place faith regarding the claim that there is a concentration without thought and examination, a cessation of thought and examination?"

When this was said, Nigaṇṭha Nātaputta looked askance at his own retinue and said: "See this, sirs! How crooked is this Citta the householder! How fraudulent and deceptive!"

"Just now, venerable sir, we understood you to say: 'See this, sirs! How straightforward is this Citta the householder! How honest and open!'—yet now we understand you to say: 'See this, sirs! How crooked is this Citta the householder! How fraudulent and deceptive!' If your former statement is true, venerable sir, then your latter statement is false, while if your former statement is false, then your latter statement is true.

"Further, venerable sir, these ten reasonable questions come up. When you understand their meaning, then you might respond to me along with your retinue.[323] One question, one synopsis, one answer. Two questions, two synopses, two answers. Three ... four ... five ... six ... seven ... [300] eight ... nine ... ten questions, ten synopses, ten answers."

Then Citta the householder rose from his seat and departed without having asked Nigaṇṭha Nātaputta these ten reasonable questions.[324]

9 The Naked Ascetic Kassapa

Now on that occasion the naked ascetic Kassapa, who in lay life had been an old friend of Citta the householder, had arrived in Macchikāsaṇḍa. Citta the householder heard about this and approached the naked ascetic Kassapa. He exchanged greetings with him and, when they had concluded their greetings and cordial talk, he sat down to one side and said to him:

"How long has it been, Venerable Kassapa, since you went forth?"

"It has been thirty years, householder, since I went forth."

"In these thirty years, venerable sir, have you attained any superhuman distinction in knowledge and vision worthy of the noble ones,[325] any dwelling in comfort?"

"In these thirty years since I went forth, householder, I have not attained any superhuman distinction in knowledge and vision worthy of the noble ones, no dwelling in comfort, but only nakedness, and the shaven head, and the brush for cleaning my seat."[326]

When this was said, Citta the householder said to him: "It is wonderful indeed, sir! It is amazing indeed, sir! How well expounded is the Dhamma[327] in that, after thirty years, [301] you have not attained any superhuman distinction in knowledge and vision worthy of the noble ones, no dwelling in comfort, but only nakedness, and the shaven head, and the brush for cleaning your seat."

"But, householder, how long has it been it since you became a lay follower?"

"In my case too, venerable sir, it has been thirty years."

"In these thirty years, householder, have you attained any superhuman distinction in knowledge and vision worthy of the noble ones, any dwelling in comfort?"

"How could I not, venerable sir?[328] For to whatever extent I wish, secluded from sensual pleasures, secluded from unwholesome states, I enter and dwell in the first jhāna, which is accompanied by thought and examination, with rapture and happiness born of seclusion. Then, to whatever extent I wish, with the subsiding of thought and examination, I enter and dwell in the second jhāna.... Then, to whatever extent I wish, with the fading away as well of rapture ... I enter and dwell in the third jhāna.... Then, to whatever extent I wish, with the abandoning of pleasure and pain ... I enter and dwell in the fourth jhāna. Further, if I were to die before the Blessed One does, it would not be surprising if the Blessed One were to declare of me: 'There is no fetter bound by which Citta the householder could return to this world.'"[329]

When this was said, the naked ascetic Kassapa said to Citta the householder: "It is wonderful indeed, sir! It is amazing indeed, sir! How well expounded is the Dhamma, in that a layman clothed in white can attain a superhuman distinction in knowledge and vision worthy of the noble ones, a dwelling in comfort. [302] May I receive the going forth in this Dhamma and Discipline, may I receive the higher ordination?"

Then Citta the householder took the naked ascetic Kassapa to the elder bhikkhus and said to them: "Venerable sirs, this naked ascetic Kassapa is an old friend of ours from lay life. Let the elders give him the going forth, let them give him the higher ordination. I will be zealous in providing him with robes, almsfood, lodging, and medicinal requisites."

Then the naked ascetic Kassapa received the going forth in this Dhamma and Discipline, he received the higher ordination. And soon, not long after his higher ordination, dwelling alone, withdrawn, diligent, ardent, and resolute, the Venerable Kassapa, by realizing it for himself with direct knowledge, in this very life entered and dwelt in that unsurpassed goal of the holy life for the sake of which clansmen rightly go forth from the household life into homelessness. He directly knew: "Destroyed is birth, the holy life has been lived, what had to be done has been done, there is no more for this state of being." And the Venerable Kassapa became one of the arahants.

10 Seeing the Sick

Now on that occasion Citta the householder was sick, afflicted, gravely ill. Then a number of park devatās, grove devatās, tree devatās, and devatās dwelling in medicinal herbs and forest giants assembled and said to Citta the householder: "Make a wish, householder, thus: 'May I become a wheel-turning monarch in the future!'"

When this was said, Citta the householder said to those devatās: "That too is impermanent; that too is unstable; one must abandon that too and pass on."

When this was said, Citta the householder's friends and companions, relatives and kinsmen, said to him: [303] "Set up mindfulness, master. Don't babble."

"What did I say that makes you speak to me thus."

"You said to us: 'That too is impermanent; that too is unstable; one must abandon that too and pass on.'"

"That was because park devatās, grove devatās, tree devatās, and devatās dwelling in medicinal herbs and forest giants assembled and said to me: 'Make a wish, householder, thus: "May I become a wheel-turning monarch in the future!"' And I said to them: 'That too is impermanent; that too is unstable; one must abandon that too and pass on.'"

"What advantage do those devatās see, master, that they speak to you thus?"

"It occurs to those devatās: 'This Citta the householder is virtuous, of good character. If he should wish: "May I become a wheel-turning monarch in the future!"—as he is virtuous, this wish of his would succeed because of its purity. The righteous king of righteousness will provide righteous offerings.'[330] Seeing this advantage, those devatās assembled and said: 'Make a wish, householder, thus: "May I become a wheel-turning monarch in the future!"' And I said to them: 'That too is impermanent; that too is unstable; one must abandon that too and pass on.'"

"Then exhort us too, householder."

"Therefore, you should train yourselves thus: [304] 'We will be possessed of confirmed confidence in the Buddha thus: "The Blessed One is an arahant, perfectly enlightened, accomplished in true knowledge and conduct, fortunate, knower of the world, unsurpassed leader of persons to be tamed, teacher of devas and humans, the Enlightened One, the Blessed One."

"'We will be possessed of confirmed confidence in the Dhamma thus: "The Dhamma is well expounded by the Blessed One, directly visible, immediate, inviting one to come and see, applicable, to be personally experienced by the wise."

"'We will be possessed of confirmed confidence in the Saṅgha thus: "The Saṅgha of the Blessed One's disciples is practising the good way, practising the straight way, practising the true way, practising the proper way; that is, the four pairs of persons, the eight types of individuals—this Saṅgha of the Blessed One's disciples is worthy of gifts, worthy of hospitality, worthy of offerings, worthy of reverential salutation, the unsurpassed field of merit for the world."

"'Whatever there may be in our family that can be given away, all that we will share unreservedly with the virtuous ones who are of good character.' It is in such a way that you should train yourselves."

Then, having inspired confidence in the Buddha, the Dhamma, and the Saṅgha among his friends and colleagues, his relatives and kinsmen, and having exhorted them in generosity,[331] Citta the householder passed away.

[305] Chapter VIII

42 *Gāmaṇisaṃyutta*

Connected Discourses to Headmen

1 Caṇḍa

At Sāvatthī. Then the headman Caṇḍa the Wrathful[332] approached the Blessed One, paid homage to him, sat down to one side, and said to him: "Venerable sir, what is the cause and reason why someone here is reckoned as wrathful? And what is the cause and reason why someone here is reckoned as gentle?"[333]

"Here, headman, someone has not abandoned lust. Because he has not abandoned lust, other people irritate him. Being irritated by others, he manifests irritation: he is reckoned as wrathful. He has not abandoned hatred. Because he has not abandoned hatred, other people irritate him. Being irritated by others, he manifests irritation: he is reckoned as wrathful. He has not abandoned delusion. Because he has not abandoned delusion, other people irritate him. Being irritated by others, he manifests irritation: he is reckoned as wrathful.

"This, headman, is the cause and reason why someone here is reckoned as wrathful.

"Here, headman, someone has abandoned lust. Because he has abandoned lust, other people do not irritate him. Not being irritated by others, he does not manifest irritation: he is reckoned as gentle. He has abandoned hatred. Because he has abandoned hatred, other people do not irritate him. Not being irritated by others, he does not manifest irritation: he is reckoned as gentle. He has abandoned delusion. Because he has abandoned delusion, other people do not irritate him. Not being irritated by others, he does not manifest irritation: he is reckoned as gentle.

"This, headman, is the cause and reason why someone here is reckoned as gentle." [306]

When this was said, Caṇḍa the headman said to the Blessed One: "Magnificent, venerable sir! Magnificent, venerable sir! The Dhamma has been made clear in many ways by the Blessed One, as though he were turning upright what had been turned upside down, revealing what was hidden, showing the way to one who was lost, or holding up a lamp in the dark for those with eyesight to see forms. I go for refuge to the Blessed One, and to the Dhamma, and to the Bhikkhu Saṅgha. From today let the Blessed One remember me as a lay follower who has gone for refuge for life."

2 *Talapuṭa*

On one occasion the Blessed One was dwelling at Rājagaha in the Bamboo Grove, the Squirrel Sanctuary. Then Talapuṭa the troupe headman[334] approached the Blessed One, paid homage to him, sat down to one side, and said to him: "Venerable sir, I have heard it said among actors of old in the lineage of teachers: 'If an actor, in the theatre or the arena, entertains and amuses people by truth and lies,[335] then with the breakup of the body, after death, he is reborn in the company of the laughing devas.' What does the Blessed One say about that?"

"Enough, headman, let it be! Don't ask me that!"

A second time and a third time Talapuṭa the troupe headman said: "Venerable sir, I have heard it said among actors of old in the lineage of teachers: ... [307] ... What does the Blessed One say about that?"

"Surely, headman, I am not getting through to you[336] when I say, 'Enough, headman, let it be! Don't ask me that!' But still, I will answer you. In the theatre or arena, among beings who are not yet free from lust, who are bound by the bondage of lust, an actor entertains them with titillating things that excite them even more strongly to lust. In the theatre or arena, among beings who are not yet free from hatred, who are bound by the bondage of hatred, an actor entertains them with infuriating things that excite them even more strongly to hatred. In the theatre or arena, among beings who are not yet free from delusion, who are bound by the bondage of delusion, an actor entertains them with bewildering things that excite them even more strongly to delusion.

"Thus, being intoxicated and negligent himself, having made

others intoxicated and negligent, with the breakup of the body, after death, he is reborn in the 'Hell of Laughter.'[337] But should he hold such a view as this: 'If an actor, in the theatre or the arena, entertains and amuses people by truth and lies, then with the breakup of the body, after death, he is reborn in the company of the laughing devas'—that is a wrong view on his part. For a person with wrong view, I say, there is one of two destinations: either hell or the animal realm."[338]

When this was said, Talapuṭa the troupe headman cried out and burst into tears. [The Blessed One said:] "So I did not get through to you when I said, 'Enough, headman, let it be! Don't ask me that!'"

"I am not crying, venerable sir, because of what the Blessed One said to me, but because I have been tricked, cheated, and deceived for a long time by those actors of old in the lineage of teachers who said: 'If an actor, [308] in the theatre or the arena, entertains and amuses people by truth and lies, then with the breakup of the body, after death, he is reborn in the company of the laughing devas.'

"Magnificent, venerable sir! Magnificent, venerable sir! The Dhamma has been made clear in many ways by the Blessed One, as though he were turning upright what had been turned upside down, revealing what was hidden, showing the way to one who was lost, or holding up a lamp in the dark for those with eyesight to see forms. I go for refuge to the Blessed One, and to the Dhamma, and to the Bhikkhu Saṅgha. May I receive the going forth under the Blessed One, venerable sir, may I receive the higher ordination?"

Then Talapuṭa the troupe headman received the going forth under the Blessed One, he received the higher ordination. And soon, not long after his higher ordination … the Venerable Talapuṭa became one of the arahants.

3 Yodhājīva

Then the headman Yodhājīva the Mercenary[339] approached the Blessed One, paid homage to him, sat down to one side, and said to him: "Venerable sir, I have heard it said by mercenaries of old in the lineage of teachers: 'When a mercenary is one who strives and exerts himself in battle, if others slay him and finish him off while he is striving and exerting himself in battle, then with the breakup of the body, after death, he is reborn in the company of the battle-slain devas.'[340] What does the Blessed One say about that?"

"Enough, headman, let it be! Don't ask me that!"

A second time and a third time Yodhājīva the headman said: "Venerable sir, I have heard it said by mercenaries of old in the lineage of teachers: ... What does the Blessed One say about that?" [309]

"Surely, headman, I am not getting through to you when I say, 'Enough, headman, let it be! Don't ask me that!' But still, I will answer you. When, headman, a mercenary is one who strives and exerts himself in battle, his mind is already low, depraved, misdirected by the thought: 'Let these beings be slain, slaughtered, annihilated, destroyed, or exterminated.' If others then slay him and finish him off while he is striving and exerting himself in battle, then with the breakup of the body, after death, he is reborn in the 'Battle-Slain Hell.'[341] But should he hold such a view as this: 'When a mercenary strives and exerts himself in battle, if others slay him and finish him off while he is striving and exerting himself in battle, then with the breakup of the body, after death, he is reborn in the company of the battle-slain devas'—that is a wrong view on his part. For a person with wrong view, I say, there is one of two destinations: either hell or the animal realm."

When this was said, Yodhājīva the headman cried out and burst into tears. [The Blessed One said:] "So I did not get through to you when I said, 'Enough, headman, let it be! Don't ask me that!'"

"I am not crying, venerable sir, because of what the Blessed One said to me, but because I have been tricked, cheated, and deceived for a long time by those mercenaries of old in the lineage of teachers who said: 'When a mercenary is one who strives and exerts himself in battle, if others slay him and finish him off while he is striving and exerting himself in battle, then with the breakup of the body, after death, he is reborn in the company of the battle-slain devas.'

"Magnificent, venerable sir!... From today let the Blessed One remember me as a lay follower who has gone for refuge for life." [310]

4 Hatthāroha

Then the headman Hatthāroha the Elephant Warrior approached the Blessed One ... (*text is elided, ending:*) "... who has gone for refuge for life."

5 Assāroha

Then the headman Assāroha the Cavalry Warrior approached the Blessed One ... and said to him:

(*All as in §3 except phrased in terms of the cavalry warrior* (assāroha) *who strives and exerts himself in battle.*) [311]

6 Asibandhakaputta

On one occasion the Blessed One was dwelling at Nālandā in Pāvārika's Mango Grove. [312] Then Asibandhakaputta the headman approached the Blessed One, paid homage to him, sat down to one side, and said to him: "Venerable sir, the brahmins of the western region—those who carry around waterpots, wear garlands of water plants, immerse themselves in water, and tend the sacred fire—are said to direct a dead person upwards, to guide him along, and conduct him to heaven.[342] But the Blessed One, the Arahant, the Perfectly Enlightened One, is able to bring it about that with the breakup of the body, after death, the entire world might be reborn in a good destination, in a heavenly world."

"Well then, headman, I will question you about this. Answer as you see fit. What do you think, headman? Suppose there is a person here who destroys life, takes what is not given, engages in sexual misconduct, speaks falsely, speaks divisively, speaks harshly, chatters idly, one who is covetous, full of ill will, and holds wrong view. Then a great crowd of people would come together and assemble around him, and they would send up prayers and recite praise and circumambulate him making reverential salutations, saying: 'With the breakup of the body, after death, may this person be reborn in a good destination, in a heavenly world.' What do you think, headman? Because of the prayers of the great crowd of people, because of their praise, because they circumambulate him making reverential salutations, would that person, with the breakup of the body, after death, be reborn in a good destination, in a heavenly world?"

"No, venerable sir."

"Suppose, headman, a person would hurl a huge boulder into a deep pool of water. Then a great crowd of people would come together and assemble around it, and they would send up prayers and recite praise and circumambulate it making reverential salutations, saying: 'Emerge, good boulder! Rise up, [313] good boulder! Come up on to high ground, good boulder!' What do you think, headman? Because of the prayers of the great crowd of people, because of their praise, because they circumambulate it making reverential salutations, would that boulder emerge, rise up, and come up on to high ground?"

"No, venerable sir."

"So, too, headman, if a person is one who destroys life … and holds wrong view, even though a great crowd of people would come together and assemble around him … still, with the breakup of the body, after death, that person will be reborn in a state of misery, in a bad destination, in the nether world, in hell.

"What do you think, headman? Suppose there is a person here who abstains from the destruction of life, from taking what is not given, from sexual misconduct, from false speech, from divisive speech, from harsh speech, from idle chatter, one who is not covetous, without ill will, who holds right view. Then a great crowd of people would come together and assemble around him, and they would send up prayers and recite praise and circumambulate him making reverential salutations, saying: 'With the breakup of the body, after death, may this person be reborn in a state of misery, in a bad destination, in the nether world, in hell.' What do you think, headman? Because of the prayers of the great crowd of people, because of their praise, because they circumambulate him making reverential salutations, would that person, with the breakup of the body, after death, be reborn in a state of misery … in hell?"

"No, venerable sir."

"Suppose, headman, a man submerges a pot of ghee or a pot of oil in a deep pool of water and breaks it. Any of its shards or fragments there would sink downwards, but the ghee or oil would rise upwards. [314] Then a great crowd of people would come together and assemble around it, and they would send up prayers and recite praise and circumambulate it making reverential salutations, saying: 'Sink down, good ghee or oil! Settle, good ghee or oil! Go downwards, good ghee or oil!' What do you think, headman? Because of the prayers of the great crowd of people, because of their praise, because they circumambulate it making reverential salutations, would that ghee or oil sink down or settle or go downwards?"

"No, venerable sir."

"So, too, headman, if a person is one who abstains from the destruction of life ... who holds right view, even though a great crowd of people would come together and assemble around him ... still, with the breakup of the body, after death, that person will be reborn in a good destination, in a heavenly world."

When this was said, Asibandhakaputta the headman said to the Blessed One: "Magnificent, venerable sir!... From today let the Blessed One remember me as a lay follower who has gone for refuge for life."

7 The Simile of the Field

On one occasion the Blessed One was dwelling at Nālandā in Pāvārika's Mango Grove. Then Asibandhakaputta the headman approached the Blessed One, paid homage to him, sat down to one side, and said to him: "Venerable sir, doesn't the Blessed One dwell compassionate towards all living beings?"

"Yes, headman, the Tathāgata dwells compassionate towards all living beings."

"Then why is it, venerable sir, that the Blessed One teaches the Dhamma thoroughly to some, yet not so thoroughly to others?" [315]

"Well then, headman, I will question you about this. Answer as you see fit. What do you think, headman? Suppose a farmer here had three fields: one excellent, one of middling quality, and one inferior—rough, salty, with bad ground. What do you think, headman? If that farmer wishes to sow seed, where would he sow it first: in the excellent field, in the field of middling quality, or in the field that was inferior, the one that was rough, salty, with bad ground?"

"If, venerable sir, that farmer wishes to sow seed, he would sow it in the excellent field. Having sown seed there, he would next sow seed in the field of middling quality. Having sown seed there, he might or might not sow seed in the field that was inferior, the one that was rough, salty, with bad ground. For what reason? Because at least it can be used as fodder for the cattle."

"Headman, just like the field that is excellent are the bhikkhus and bhikkhunis to me. I teach them the Dhamma that is good in the beginning, good in the middle, and good in the end, with the right meaning and phrasing; I reveal the holy life that is perfectly complete and pure. For what reason? Because they dwell with me as their island, with me as their shelter, with me as their protector, with me as their refuge.

"Then, headman, just like the field of middling quality are the male and female lay followers to me. To them too I teach the Dhamma that is good in the beginning, good in the middle, and good in the end, with the right meaning and phrasing; I reveal the holy life that is perfectly complete and pure. For what reason? Because they dwell with me as their island, with me as their shelter, with me as their protector, with me as their refuge.

"Then, headman, just like that field that is inferior—[316] rough, salty, with bad ground—are the ascetics, brahmins, and wanderers of other sects to me. Yet to them too I teach the Dhamma that is good in the beginning, good in the middle, and good in the end, with the right meaning and phrasing; I reveal the holy life that is perfectly complete and pure. For what reason? Because if they understand even a single sentence, that will lead to their welfare and happiness for a long time.

"Suppose, headman, a man had three waterpots: one without cracks, which does not let water seep through and escape; one without cracks, but which lets water seep through and escape; and one with cracks, which lets water seep through and escape. What do you think, headman? If that man wants to store water, where would he store it first: in the waterpot that is without cracks, which does not let water seep through and escape; or in the waterpot that is without cracks, but which lets water seep through and escape; or in the waterpot that has cracks, which lets water seep through and escape?"

"If, venerable sir, that man wants to store water, he would store it in the waterpot that is without cracks, which does not let water seep through and escape. Having stored water there, he would next store it in the waterpot that is without cracks, but which lets water seep through and escape. Having stored it there, he might or might not store it in the waterpot that has cracks, which lets water seep through and escape. For what reason? Because it can at least be used for washing dishes."

"Headman, just like the waterpot that is without cracks, which does not let water seep through and escape, are the bhikkhus and bhikkhunīs to me. I teach them the Dhamma that is good in the beginning, good in the middle, and good in the end, with the right meaning and phrasing; I reveal the holy life that is perfectly complete and pure. For what reason? Because they dwell with me as their island, with me as their shelter, with me as their protector, with me as their refuge.

"Then, headman, just like the waterpot that is without cracks, but which lets water seep through and escape, are the male and female lay followers to me. To them [317] too I teach the Dhamma that is good in the beginning, good in the middle, and good in the end, with the right meaning and phrasing; I reveal the holy life that is perfectly complete and pure. For what reason? Because they dwell with me as their island, with me as their shelter, with me as their protector, with me as their refuge.

"Then, headman, just like the waterpot that has cracks, which lets water seep through and escape, are the ascetics, brahmins, and wanderers of other sects to me. Yet to them too I teach the Dhamma that is good in the beginning, good in the middle, and good in the end, with the right meaning and phrasing; I reveal the holy life that is perfectly complete and pure. For what reason? Because if they understand even a single sentence, that will lead to their welfare and happiness for a long time."

When this was said, Asibandhakaputta the headman said to the Blessed One: "Magnificent, venerable sir!... From today let the Blessed One remember me as a lay follower who has gone for refuge for life."

8 The Conch Blower

On one occasion the Blessed One was dwelling at Nālandā in Pāvārika's Mango Grove. Then Asibandhakaputta the headman, a lay disciple of the nigaṇṭhas,[343] approached the Blessed One.... The Blessed One then said to him as he was sitting to one side:

"In what way, headman, does Nigaṇṭha Nātaputta teach the Dhamma to his disciples?"

"Venerable sir, Nigaṇṭha Nātaputta teaches the Dhamma to his disciples thus: 'Anyone at all who destroys life is bound for a state of misery, bound for hell. Anyone at all who takes what is not given is bound for a state of misery, bound for hell. Anyone at all who engages in sexual misconduct is bound for a state of misery, bound for hell. Anyone at all who speaks falsehood is bound for a state of misery, bound for hell. One is led on [to rebirth] by the manner in which one usually dwells.' It is in such a way, venerable sir, that Nigaṇṭha Nātaputta teaches the Dhamma to his disciples."

"If, headman, it were the case that one is led on [to rebirth] by the manner in which one usually dwells, [318] then according to Nigaṇṭha Nātaputta's word, no one at all would be bound for a state of misery, bound for hell. What do you think, headman? In the case of a person who destroys life, if one compares one occasion with another, whether by day or by night, which is more frequent: the occasions when he is destroying life or those when he is not doing so?"

"In the case of a person who destroys life, venerable sir, if one compares one occasion with another, whether by day or by night, the occasions when he is destroying life are infrequent while those when he is not doing so are frequent."

"So, headman, if it were the case that one is led on [to rebirth] by the manner in which one usually dwells, then according to Nigaṇṭha Nātaputta's word no one at all would be bound for a state of misery, bound for hell.

"What do you think, headman? In the case of a person who takes what is not given … who engages in sexual misconduct … [319] who speaks falsehood, if one compares one occasion with another, whether by day or by night, which is more frequent: the occasions when he is speaking falsehood or those when he is not speaking falsehood?"

"In the case of a person who speaks falsehood, venerable sir, if one compares one occasion with another, whether by day or by night, the occasions when he is speaking falsehood are infrequent while those when he is not speaking falsehood are frequent."

"So, headman, if it were the case that one is led on [to rebirth] by the manner in which one usually dwells, then according to

Nigaṇṭha Nātaputta's word no one at all would be bound for a state of misery, bound for hell.

"Here, headman, some teacher holds such a doctrine and view as this: 'Anyone at all who destroys life ... who takes what is not given ... who engages in sexual misconduct ... who speaks falsehood is bound for a state of misery, is bound for hell.' Then a disciple has full confidence in that teacher. It occurs to him: 'My teacher holds such a doctrine and view as this: "Anyone at all who destroys life is bound for a state of misery, bound for hell." Now I have destroyed life, so I too am bound for a state of misery, bound for hell.' Thus he acquires such a view. If he does not abandon that assertion and that state of mind, and if he does not relinquish that view, then according to his deserts he will be, as it were, dropped off in hell.[344]

"It occurs to him: 'My teacher holds such a doctrine and view as this: "Anyone at all who takes what is not given is bound for a state of misery, bound for hell." Now I have taken what is not given, so I too am bound for a state of misery, bound for hell.' Thus he acquires such a view. If he does not abandon that assertion ... he will be, as it were, dropped off in hell.

"It occurs to him: 'My teacher holds such a doctrine and view as this: "Anyone at all who engages in sexual misconduct [320] is bound for a state of misery, bound for hell." Now I have engaged in sexual misconduct, so I too am bound for a state of misery, bound for hell.' Thus he acquires such a view. If he does not abandon that assertion ... he will be, as it were, dropped off in hell.

"It occurs to him: 'My teacher holds such a doctrine and view as this: "Anyone at all who speaks falsehood is bound for a state of misery, bound for hell." Now I have spoken falsehood, so I too am bound for a state of misery, bound for hell.' Thus he acquires such a view. If he does not abandon that assertion ... he will be, as it were, dropped off in hell.

"But here, headman, a Tathāgata arises in the world, an arahant, perfectly enlightened, accomplished in true knowledge and conduct, fortunate, knower of the world, unsurpassed leader of persons to be tamed, teacher of devas and humans, the Enlightened One, the Blessed One. In many ways he criticizes and censures the destruction of life, and he says: 'Abstain from the destruction of life.' He criticizes and censures the taking of what is not given, and he says: 'Abstain from taking what is not given.' He criticizes and censures sexual misconduct, and he says: 'Abstain from sexual misconduct.' He criticizes and censures false speech, and he says: 'Abstain from false speech.'

"Then a disciple has full confidence in that teacher. He reflects thus: 'In many ways the Blessed One criticizes and censures the destruction of life, and he says: "Abstain from the destruction of life." Now I have destroyed life to such and such an extent. That wasn't proper; that wasn't good. But though I feel regret over this, that evil deed of mine cannot be undone.' Having reflected thus, he abandons the destruction of life and he abstains from the destruction of life in the future. Thus there comes about the abandoning of that evil deed;[345] thus there comes about the transcending of that evil deed.

"He reflects thus: 'In many ways the Blessed One criticizes and censures the taking of what is not given, and he says: "Abstain from taking what is not given." Now I have taken what is not given to such and such an extent. That wasn't proper; that wasn't good. But though I feel regret over this, that evil deed of mine cannot be undone.' Having reflected thus, [321] he abandons the taking of what is not given and he abstains from taking what is not given in the future. Thus there comes about the abandoning of that evil deed; thus there comes about the transcending of that evil deed.

"He reflects thus: 'In many ways the Blessed One criticizes and censures sexual misconduct, and he says: "Abstain from sexual misconduct." Now I have engaged in sexual misconduct to such and such an extent. That wasn't proper; that wasn't good. But though I feel regret over this, that evil deed of mine cannot be undone.' Having reflected thus, he abandons sexual misconduct and he abstains from sexual misconduct in the future. Thus there comes about the abandoning of that evil deed; thus there comes about the transcending of that evil deed.

"He reflects thus: 'In many ways the Blessed One criticizes and censures false speech, and he says: "Abstain from false speech." Now I have spoken falsehood to such and such an extent. That wasn't proper; that wasn't good. But though I feel regret over this, that evil deed of mine cannot be undone.' Having reflected thus, he abandons false speech and he abstains from false speech in the future. Thus there comes about the abandoning of that evil deed; thus there comes about the transcending of that evil deed.

"Having abandoned the destruction of life, he abstains from the destruction of life. Having abandoned the taking of what is not given, he abstains from taking what is not given. Having abandoned sexual misconduct, he abstains from sexual misconduct. Having abandoned false speech, he abstains from false speech. Having abandoned divisive speech, he abstains from divisive speech. Having abandoned harsh speech, he abstains from harsh speech. Having abandoned idle chatter, he abstains from idle chatter. Having abandoned covetousness, he is uncovetous. [322] Having abandoned ill will and hatred, he has a mind without ill will. Having abandoned wrong view, he is one of right view.

"Then, headman, that noble disciple—who is thus devoid of covetousness, devoid of ill will, unconfused, clearly comprehending, ever mindful—dwells pervading one quarter with a mind imbued with lovingkindness, likewise the second quarter, the third quarter, and the fourth quarter. Thus above, below, across, and everywhere, and to all as to himself, he dwells pervading the entire world with a mind imbued with lovingkindness, vast, exalted, measureless, without hostility, without ill will. Just as a strong conch blower can easily send his signal to the four quarters, so too, when the liberation of mind by lovingkindness is developed and cultivated in this way, any limited kamma that was done does not remain there, does not persist there.[346]

"He dwells pervading one quarter with a mind imbued with compassion ... with a mind imbued with altruistic joy ... with a mind imbued with equanimity, likewise the second quarter, the third quarter, and the fourth quarter. Thus above, below, across, and everywhere, and to all as to himself, he dwells pervading the entire world with a mind imbued with equanimity, vast, exalted, measureless, without hostility, without ill will. Just as a strong conch blower can easily send his signal to the four quarters, so too, when the liberation of mind by equanimity is developed and cultivated in this way, any limited kamma that was done does not remain there, does not persist there."

When this was said, Asibandhakaputta the headman said to the Blessed One: "Magnificent, venerable sir!... From today let the Blessed One remember me as a lay follower who has gone for refuge for life."

9 Families

On one occasion the Blessed One, while wandering on tour among the Kosalans together with a large Saṅgha of bhikkhus, arrived at Nālandā. [323] He stayed there at Nālandā in Pāvārika's Mango Grove.

Now on that occasion Nālandā was in the grip of famine, a time of scarcity, with crops blighted and turned to straw.[347] On that occasion Nigaṇṭha Nātaputta was residing at Nālandā together with a large retinue of nigaṇṭhas. Then Asibandhakaputta the headman, a lay disciple of the nigaṇṭhas, approached Nigaṇṭha Nātaputta, paid homage to him, and sat down to one side. Nigaṇṭha Nātaputta then said to him: "Come, headman, refute the doctrine of the ascetic Gotama. Then a good report concerning you will be spread about thus: 'Asibandhakaputta the headman has refuted the doctrine of the ascetic Gotama, who is so powerful and mighty.'"

"But how, venerable sir, shall I refute the doctrine of the ascetic Gotama, who is so powerful and mighty?"

"Go, headman, approach the ascetic Gotama and ask him: 'Venerable sir, doesn't the Blessed One in many ways praise sympathy towards families, the protection of families, compassion towards families?' If, when he is questioned by you thus, the ascetic Gotama answers, 'Yes, headman, the Tathāgata in many ways praises sympathy for families, the protection of families, compassion for families,' then you should say to him: 'Then why, venerable sir, is the Blessed One wandering on tour with a large Saṅgha of bhikkhus at a time of famine, a time of scarcity, when crops are blighted and have turned to straw? The Blessed One is practising for the annihilation of families, for the calamity of families, for the destruction of families.' When the ascetic Gotama is posed this dilemma by you, he will neither be able to throw it up nor to gulp it down." [324]

"Yes, venerable sir," Asibandhakaputta the headman replied. Then he rose from his seat and, after paying homage to Nigaṇṭha Nātaputta, keeping him on his right, he departed and went to the Blessed One. After paying homage to the Blessed One, he sat down to one side and said to him: "Venerable sir, doesn't the Blessed One in many ways praise sympathy for families, the protection of families, compassion for families?"

"Yes, headman, the Tathāgata in many ways praises sympathy for families, the protection of families, compassion for families."

"Then why, venerable sir, is the Blessed One wandering on tour with a large Saṅgha of bhikkhus at a time of famine, a time of scarcity, when crops are blighted and have turned to straw? The Blessed One is practising for the annihilation of families, for the calamity of families, for the destruction of families."

"I recollect ninety-one aeons back, headman, but I do not recall any family that has ever been destroyed merely by offering cooked almsfood. Rather, whatever families there are that are rich, with much wealth and property, with abundant gold and silver, with abundant possessions and means of subsistence, with abundant wealth and grain, they have all become so from giving, from truthfulness, and from self-control.[348]

"There are, headman, eight causes and conditions for the destruction of families. Families come to destruction on account of the king, or on account of thieves, or on account of fire, or on account of water; or they do not find what they have put away;[349] or mismanaged undertakings fail; or there arises within a family a wastrel who squanders, dissipates, and fritters away its wealth; [325] and impermanence is the eighth. These are the eight causes and conditions for the destruction of families. But while these eight causes and conditions for the destruction of families exist, if anyone speaks thus of me: 'The Blessed One is practising for the annihilation of families, for the calamity of families, for the destruction of families,' if he does not abandon that assertion and that state of mind, and if he does not relinquish that view, then according to his deserts he will be, as it were, dropped off in hell."

When this was said, Asibandhakaputta the headman said to the Blessed One: "Magnificent, venerable sir!... From today let the Blessed One remember me as a lay follower who has gone for refuge for life."

10 Maṇicūḷaka

On one occasion the Blessed One was dwelling at Rājagaha in the Bamboo Grove, the Squirrel Sanctuary. Now on that occasion the members of the king's retinue had assembled in the royal palace and were sitting together when the following conversation arose: "Gold and silver are allowable for the ascetics following the

Sakyan son; the ascetics following the Sakyan son consent to gold and silver; the ascetics following the Sakyan son accept gold and silver."

Now on that occasion Maṇicūḷaka the headman was sitting in that assembly. Then Maṇicūḷaka the headman said to that assembly: "Do not speak thus, masters. Gold and silver are not allowable for the ascetics following the Sakyan son; the ascetics following the Sakyan son do not consent to gold and silver; the ascetics following the Sakyan son do not accept gold and silver. They have renounced jewellery and gold; they have given up the use of gold and silver."[350] And Maṇicūḷaka was able to convince that assembly.

Then Maṇicūḷaka approached the Blessed One, paid homage to him, and sat down to one side. [326] Sitting to one side, he reported to the Blessed One all that had happened, adding: "I hope, venerable sir, that when I answered thus I stated what has been said by the Blessed One and did not misrepresent him with what is contrary to fact; that I explained in accordance with the Dhamma, and that no reasonable consequence of my statement gives ground for criticism."

"For sure, headman, when you answered thus you stated what has been said by me and did not misrepresent me with what is contrary to fact; you explained in accordance with the Dhamma, and no reasonable consequence of your statement gives ground for criticism. For, headman, gold and silver are not allowable for the ascetics following the Sakyan son; the ascetics following the Sakyan son do not consent to gold and silver; the ascetics following the Sakyan son do not accept gold and silver. They have renounced jewellery and gold; they have given up the use of gold and silver. If gold and silver are allowable for anyone, the five cords of sensual pleasure are allowable for him. If the five cords of sensual pleasure are allowable for anyone, you can definitely consider him to be one who does not have the character of an ascetic or of a follower of the Sakyan son.

"Further, headman, I say this: 'Straw may be sought by one needing straw; timber may be sought by one needing timber; a cart may be sought by one needing a cart; a workman may be sought by one needing a workman.' [327] But I do not say that there is any method by which gold and silver may be consented to or sought."

11 Bhadraka

On one occasion the Blessed One was dwelling at a town of the Mallans named Uruvelakappa. Then Bhadraka the headman approached the Blessed One, paid homage to him, sat down to one side, and said to him: "It would be good, venerable sir, if the Blessed One would teach me about the origin and the passing away of suffering."

"If, headman, I were to teach you about the origin and the passing away of suffering with reference to the past, saying, 'So it was in the past,' perplexity and uncertainty about that might arise in you. And if I were to teach you about the origin and the passing away of suffering with reference to the future, saying, 'So it will be in the future,' perplexity and uncertainty about that might arise in you. Instead, headman, while I am sitting right here, and you are sitting right there, I will teach you about the origin and the passing away of suffering. Listen to that and attend closely, I will speak."

"Yes, venerable sir," Bhadraka the headman replied. The Blessed One said this:

"What do you think, headman? Are there any people in Uruvelakappa on whose account sorrow, lamentation, pain, displeasure, and despair would arise in you if they were to be executed, imprisoned, fined, or censured?"[351]

"There are such people, venerable sir."

"But are there any people in Uruvelakappa on whose account [328] sorrow, lamentation, pain, displeasure, and despair would not arise in you in such an event?"

"There are such people, venerable sir."

"What, headman, is the cause and reason why in relation to some people in Uruvelakappa sorrow, lamentation, pain, displeasure, and despair would arise in you if they were to be executed, imprisoned, fined, or censured, while in regard to others no such sorrow, lamentation, pain, displeasure, and despair would arise in you?"

"Those people in Uruvelakappa, venerable sir, in relation to whom sorrow, lamentation, pain, displeasure, and despair would arise in me if they were to be executed, imprisoned, fined, or censured—these are the ones for whom I have desire and attachment. But those people in Uruvelakappa in relation to whom no sorrow, lamentation, pain, displeasure, and despair would arise in me—these are the ones for whom I have no desire and attachment."

"Headman, by means of this principle that is seen, understood, immediately attained, fathomed, apply the method to the past and to the future thus:[352] 'Whatever suffering arose in the past, all that arose rooted in desire, with desire as its source; for desire is the root of suffering. Whatever suffering will arise in the future, all that will arise rooted in desire, with desire as its source; for desire is the root of suffering.'"

"It is wonderful, venerable sir! It is amazing, venerable sir! How well that has been stated by the Blessed One: 'Whatever suffering arises, [329] all that is rooted in desire, has desire as its source; for desire is the root of suffering.'[353] Venerable sir, I have a boy named Ciravāsī, who stays at an outside residence. I rise early and send a man, saying, 'Go, man, and find out how Ciravāsī is.' Until that man returns, venerable sir, I am upset, thinking, 'I hope Ciravāsī has not met with any affliction!'"

"What do you think, headman? If Ciravāsī were to be executed, imprisoned, fined, or censured, would sorrow, lamentation, pain, displeasure, and despair arise in you?"

"Venerable sir, if Ciravāsī were to be executed, imprisoned, fined, or censured, even my life would be upset, so how could sorrow, lamentation, pain, displeasure, and despair not arise in me?"

"In this way too, headman, it can be understood: 'Whatever suffering arises, all that arises rooted in desire, with desire as its source; for desire is the root of suffering.'

"What do you think, headman? Before you saw Ciravāsī's mother or heard about her, did you have any desire, attachment, or affection for her?"

"No, venerable sir."

"Then was it, headman, because of seeing her or hearing about her that this desire, attachment, and affection arose in you?"

"Yes, venerable sir."

"What do you think, headman? If Ciravāsī's mother were to be executed, imprisoned, fined, or censured, would sorrow, lamentation, pain, displeasure, and despair arise in you?" [330]

"Venerable sir, if Ciravāsī's mother were to be executed, imprisoned, fined, or censured, even my life would be upset, so how could sorrow, lamentation, pain, displeasure, and despair not arise in me?"

"In this way too, headman, it can be understood: 'Whatever suffering arises, all that arises rooted in desire, with desire as its source; for desire is the root of suffering.'"

12 Rāsiya

Then Rāsiya the headman approached the Blessed One, paid homage to him, sat down to one side, and said to him: "Venerable sir, I have heard: 'The ascetic Gotama criticizes all austerity. He categorically blames and reviles any ascetic who leads a rough life.' Do those who speak thus, venerable sir, state what has been said by the Blessed One and not misrepresent him with what is contrary to fact? Do they explain in accordance with the Dhamma so that no reasonable consequence of their assertion would be open to criticism?"

"Those who speak thus, headman, do not state what has been said by me but misrepresent me with untruth and falsehood.

I

"There are, headman, these two extremes which should not be cultivated by one who has gone forth into homelessness: the pursuit of sensual happiness in sensual pleasures, which is low, vulgar, the way of worldlings, ignoble, unbeneficial; and the pursuit of self-mortification, which is painful, ignoble, unbeneficial. Without veering towards either of these extremes, the Tathāgata has awakened to the middle way, [331] which gives rise to vision, which gives rise to knowledge, which leads to peace, to direct knowledge, to enlightenment, to Nibbāna. And what is that middle way awakened to by the Tathāgata, which gives rise to vision ... leads to Nibbāna? It is this Noble Eightfold Path; that is, right view ... right concentration. This is that middle way awakened to by the Tathāgata, which gives rise to vision, which gives rise to knowledge, which leads to peace, to direct knowledge, to enlightenment, to Nibbāna.[354]

II

"There are, headman, these three persons who enjoy sensual pleasures existing in the world. What three?[355]

(i)

"Here, headman, someone who enjoys sensual pleasures seeks wealth unlawfully, by violence. Having done so, he does not make himself happy and pleased, nor does he share it and do meritorious deeds.

(ii)

"Then, headman, someone here who enjoys sensual pleasures seeks wealth unlawfully, by violence. Having done so, he makes himself happy and pleased, but he does not share it and do meritorious deeds.

(iii)

"Then, headman, someone here who enjoys sensual pleasures seeks wealth unlawfully, by violence. Having done so, he makes himself happy and pleased, and he shares it and does meritorious deeds.

(iv)

"Then, headman, someone here who enjoys sensual pleasures seeks wealth both lawfully and unlawfully, both by violence and without violence. Having done so, [332] he does not make himself happy and pleased, nor does he share it and do meritorious deeds.

(v)

"Then, headman, someone here who enjoys sensual pleasures seeks wealth both lawfully and unlawfully, both by violence and without violence. Having done so, he makes himself happy and pleased, but he does not share it and do meritorious deeds.

(vi)

"Then, headman, someone here who enjoys sensual pleasures seeks wealth both lawfully and unlawfully, both by violence and without violence. Having done so, he makes himself happy and pleased, and he shares it and does meritorious deeds.

(vii)

"Then, headman, someone here who enjoys sensual pleasures seeks wealth lawfully, without violence. Having done so, he does not make himself happy and pleased, nor does he share it and do meritorious deeds.

(viii)

"Then, headman, someone here who enjoys sensual pleasures seeks wealth lawfully, without violence. Having done so, he makes himself happy and pleased, but he does not share it and do meritorious deeds.

(ix)

"Then, headman, someone here who enjoys sensual pleasures seeks wealth lawfully, without violence. Having done so, he makes himself happy and pleased, and he shares it and does meritorious deeds. But he uses his wealth while being tied to it, infatuated with it, blindly absorbed in it, not seeing the danger in it, not understanding the escape.

(x)

"Then, headman, someone here who enjoys sensual pleasures seeks wealth lawfully, without violence. Having done so, [333] he makes himself happy and pleased, and he shares it and does meritorious deeds. And he uses his wealth without being tied to it, uninfatuated with it, not blindly absorbed in it, seeing the danger in it, understanding the escape.

III

(i)

"Therein, headman, the one enjoying sensual pleasures who seeks wealth unlawfully, by violence, and who does not make himself happy and pleased nor share it and do meritorious deeds, may be criticized on three grounds. On what three grounds may he be criticized? 'He seeks wealth unlawfully, by violence'—this is the first ground on which he may be criticized. 'He does not make himself happy and pleased'—this is the second ground on which he may be criticized. 'He does not share it and do meritorious deeds'—this is the third ground on which he may be criticized. This one enjoying sensual pleasures may be criticized on these three grounds.

(ii)

"Therein, headman, the one enjoying sensual pleasures who seeks wealth unlawfully, by violence, and who makes himself happy and pleased but does not share it and do meritorious deeds, may be criticized on two grounds and praised on one ground. On what two grounds may he be criticized? 'He seeks wealth unlawfully, by violence'—this is the first ground on which he may be criticized. 'He does not share it and do meritorious deeds'—this is the second ground on which he may be criticized. And on what one ground may he be praised? 'He makes himself happy and pleased'—this is the one ground on which he may be praised. This one enjoying sensual pleasures may be criticized on these two grounds and praised on this one ground.

(iii)

"Therein, headman, the one enjoying sensual pleasures who seeks wealth unlawfully, by violence, and [334] makes himself happy and pleased, and shares it and does meritorious deeds, may be criticized on one ground and praised on two grounds. On what one ground may he be criticized? 'He seeks wealth unlawfully, by violence'—this is the one ground on which he may be criticized. And on what two grounds may he be praised? 'He makes himself happy and pleased'—this is the first ground on which he may be praised. 'He shares it and does meritorious deeds'—this is the second ground on which he may be praised. This one enjoying sensual pleasures may be criticized on this one ground and praised on these two grounds.

(iv)

"Therein, headman, the one enjoying sensual pleasures who seeks wealth both lawfully and unlawfully, both by violence and without violence, and who does not make himself happy and pleased nor share it and do meritorious deeds, may be praised on one ground and criticized on three grounds. On what one ground may he be praised? 'He seeks wealth lawfully, without violence'—this is the one ground on which he may be praised. On what three grounds may he be criticized? 'He seeks wealth unlawfully, by violence'—this is the first ground on which he may be criticized. 'He does not make himself happy and pleased'—this is the second ground on which he may be criticized. 'He does not share it and do meritorious deeds'—this is the third ground on which he may be criticized. This one enjoying sensual pleasures may be praised on this one ground and criticized on these three grounds.

(v)

"Therein, headman, the one enjoying sensual pleasures who seeks wealth both lawfully and unlawfully, both by violence and without violence, and who makes himself happy and pleased but does not share it and do meritorious deeds, may be praised on two grounds and criticized on two grounds. On what two grounds may he be praised? 'He seeks wealth lawfully, without violence'—this is the first ground on which he may be praised. 'He makes himself happy and pleased'—this is the second ground on which he may be praised. [335] On what two grounds may he be criticized? 'He seeks wealth unlawfully, by violence'—this is the first ground on which he may be criticized. 'He does not share it and do meritorious deeds'—this is the second ground on which he may be criticized. This one enjoying sensual pleasures may be praised on these two grounds and criticized on these two grounds.

(vi)

"Therein, headman, the one enjoying sensual pleasures who seeks wealth both lawfully and unlawfully, both by violence and without violence, and who makes himself happy and pleased and shares it and does meritorious deeds, may be praised on three grounds and criticized on one ground. On what three grounds may he be praised? 'He seeks wealth lawfully, without violence'—this is the first ground on which he may be praised. 'He makes himself happy and pleased'—this is the second ground on which he may be praised. 'He shares it and does meritorious deeds'—this is the third ground on which he may be praised. On what one ground may he be criticized? 'He seeks wealth unlawfully, by violence'—this is the one ground on which he may be criticized. This one enjoying sensual pleasures may be praised on these three grounds and criticized on this one ground.

(vii)

"Therein, headman, the one enjoying sensual pleasures who

seeks wealth lawfully, without violence, and who does not make himself happy and pleased nor share it and do meritorious deeds, may be praised on one ground and criticized on two grounds. On what one ground may he be praised? 'He seeks wealth lawfully, without violence'—this is the one ground on which he may be praised. On what two grounds may he be criticized? 'He does not make himself happy and pleased'—this is the first ground on which he may be criticized. 'He does not share it and do meritorious deeds'—this is the second ground on which he may be criticized. This one enjoying sensual pleasures may be praised on this one ground and criticized on these two grounds. [336]

(viii)

"Therein, headman, the one enjoying sensual pleasures who seeks wealth lawfully, without violence, and who makes himself happy and pleased but does not share it and do meritorious deeds, may be praised on two grounds and criticized on one ground. On what two grounds may he be praised? 'He seeks wealth lawfully, without violence'—this is the first ground on which he may be praised. 'He makes himself happy and pleased'—this is the second ground on which he may be praised. On what one ground may he be criticized? 'He does not share it and do meritorious deeds'—this is the one ground on which he may be criticized. This one enjoying sensual pleasures may be praised on these two grounds and criticized on this one ground.

(ix)

"Therein, headman, the one enjoying sensual pleasures who seeks wealth lawfully, without violence, and makes himself happy and pleased, and shares it and does meritorious deeds, but who uses that wealth while being tied to it, infatuated with it, blindly absorbed in it, not seeing the danger in it, not understanding the escape—he may be praised on three grounds and criticized on one ground. On what three grounds may he be praised? 'He seeks wealth lawfully, without violence'—this is the first ground on which he may be praised. 'He makes himself happy and pleased'—this is the second ground on which he may be praised. 'He shares it and does meritorious deeds'—this is the third ground on which he may be praised. On what one ground may he be criticized? 'He uses that wealth while being tied to it, infatuated with it, blindly absorbed in it, not seeing the danger in it, not understanding the escape'—this is the one ground on which he may be criticized. This one enjoying sensual pleasures may be praised on these three grounds and criticized on this one ground.

(x)

"Therein, headman, the one enjoying sensual pleasures who seeks wealth lawfully, without violence, and makes himself happy and pleased, and shares it and does meritorious deeds, [337] and who uses that wealth without being tied to it, uninfatuated with it, not blindly absorbed in it, seeing the danger in it, understanding the escape—he may be praised on four grounds. On what four grounds may he be praised? 'He seeks wealth lawfully, without violence'—this is the first ground on which he may be praised. 'He makes himself happy and pleased'—this is the second ground on which he may be praised. 'He shares it and does meritorious deeds'—this is the third ground on which he may be praised. 'He uses that wealth without being tied to it, uninfatuated with it, not blindly absorbed in it, seeing the danger in it, understanding the escape'—this is the fourth ground on which he may be praised. This one enjoying sensual pleasures may be praised on these four grounds.

IV

"There are, headman, these three kinds of ascetics of rough life existing in the world. What three?

(i)

"Here, headman, some ascetic of rough life has gone forth out of faith from the household life into homelessness with the thought: 'Perhaps I may achieve a wholesome state; perhaps I may realize a superhuman distinction in knowledge and vision worthy of the noble ones.'[356] He afflicts and torments himself, yet he does not achieve a wholesome state or realize a superhuman distinction in knowledge and vision worthy of the noble ones.

(ii)

"Then, headman, some ascetic of rough life has gone forth out of faith.... He afflicts and torments himself, and achieves a wholesome state, yet he does not realize a superhuman distinction in knowledge and vision worthy of the noble ones. [338]

(iii)

"Then, headman, some ascetic of rough life has gone forth out of faith.... He afflicts and torments himself, achieves a wholesome state, and realizes a superhuman distinction in knowledge and vision worthy of the noble ones.

V

(i)

"Therein, headman, the ascetic of rough life who afflicts and torments himself, yet does not achieve a wholesome state or realize a superhuman distinction in knowledge and vision worthy of the noble ones, may be criticized on three grounds. On what three grounds may he be criticized? 'He afflicts and torments himself'—this is the first ground on which he may be criticized. 'He does not achieve a wholesome state'—this is the second ground on which he may be criticized. 'He does not realize a superhuman distinction in knowledge and vision worthy of the noble ones'—this is the third ground on which he may be criticized. This ascetic of rough life may be criticized on these three grounds.

(ii)

"Therein, headman, the ascetic of rough life who afflicts and torments himself, and achieves a wholesome state, yet does not realize a superhuman distinction in knowledge and vision worthy of the noble ones, may be criticized on two grounds and praised on one ground. On what two grounds may he be criticized? 'He afflicts and torments himself'—this is the first ground on which he may be criticized. 'He does not realize a superhuman distinction in knowledge and vision worthy of the noble ones'—this is the second ground on which he may be criticized. On what one ground may he be praised? 'He achieves a wholesome state'—this is the one ground on which he may be praised. This ascetic of rough life may be criticized on these two grounds and praised on this one ground. [339]

(iii)

"Therein, headman, the ascetic of rough life who afflicts and torments himself, achieves a wholesome state, and realizes a superhuman distinction in knowledge and vision worthy of the noble ones, may be criticized on one ground and praised on two grounds. On what one ground may he be criticized? 'He afflicts and torments himself'—this is the one ground on which he may be criticized. On what two grounds may he be praised? 'He achieves a wholesome state'—this is the first ground on which he may be praised. 'He realizes a superhuman distinction in knowledge and vision worthy of the noble ones'—this is the second ground on which he may be praised. This ascetic of rough life may be criticized on this one ground and praised on these two grounds.

VI

"There are, headman, these three kinds of wearing away that are directly visible,[357] immediate, inviting one to come and see, applicable, to be personally experienced by the wise. What three?

(i)

"Someone is lustful, and on account of lust he intends for his own affliction, for the affliction of others, for the affliction of both. When lust is abandoned, he does not intend for his own affliction, or for the affliction of others, or for the affliction of both. The wearing away is directly visible, immediate, inviting one to come and see, applicable, to be personally experienced by the wise.

(ii)

"Someone is full of hatred, and on account of hatred he intends for his own affliction, for the affliction of others, for the affliction of both. When hatred is abandoned, he does not intend for his own affliction, or for the affliction of others, or for the affliction of both. [340] The wearing away is directly visible, immediate, inviting one to come and see, applicable, to be personally experienced by the wise.

(iii)

"Someone is deluded, and on account of delusion he intends for his own affliction, for the affliction of others, for the affliction of both. When delusion is abandoned, he does not intend for his own affliction, or for the affliction of others, or for the affliction of both. The wearing away is directly visible, immediate, inviting one to come and see, applicable, to be personally experienced by the wise.

"These, headman, are the three kinds of wearing away that are directly visible, immediate, inviting one to come and see, applicable, to be personally experienced by the wise."

When this was said, Rāsiya the headman said to the Blessed One: "Magnificent, venerable sir!... From today let the Blessed One remember me as a lay follower who has gone for refuge for life."

13 Pāṭaliya

On one occasion the Blessed One was dwelling among the Koliyans where there was a town of the Koliyans named Uttara. Then Pāṭaliya the headman approached the Blessed One, paid homage to him, sat down to one side, and said to him:

"I have heard, venerable sir: 'The ascetic Gotama knows magic.'[358] I hope, venerable sir, that those who say, 'The ascetic Gotama knows magic,' state what has been said by the Blessed One and do not misrepresent him with what is contrary to fact; that they explain in accordance with the Dhamma, and that no reasonable consequence of their assertion gives ground for criticism. For we would not wish to misrepresent the Blessed One, venerable sir."

"Those, headman, who say, 'The ascetic Gotama knows magic,' state what has been said by me and do not misrepresent me with what is contrary to fact; they explain in accordance with the Dhamma, and no reasonable consequence of their assertion gives ground for criticism." [341]

"Then, sir, we did not believe the plain truth asserted by those ascetics and brahmins who said, 'The ascetic Gotama knows magic.' Indeed, sir, the ascetic Gotama is a magician!"[359]

"Headman, does one who asserts, 'I know magic,' also assert, 'I am a magician'?"

"So it is, Blessed One! So it is, Fortunate One!"

"Well then, headman, I will question you about this same matter. Answer as you see fit.

I

(i)

"What do you think, headman? Do you know the Koliyans' hirelings with drooping head-dresses?"[360]

"I do, venerable sir."

"What do you think, headman? What is the job of the Koliyans' hirelings with drooping head-dresses?"

"Their job, venerable sir, is to arrest thieves for the Koliyans and to carry the Koliyans' messages."

"What do you think, headman? Do you know whether the Koliyans' hirelings with drooping head-dresses are virtuous or immoral?"

"I know, venerable sir, that they are immoral, of bad character. They are to be included among those in the world who are immoral, of bad character."

"Would one be speaking rightly, headman, if one were to say: 'Pāṭaliya the headman knows the Koliyans' hirelings with drooping head-dresses, who are immoral, of bad character. Pāṭaliya the headman too is immoral, of bad character'?"

"No, venerable sir. I am quite different from the Koliyans' hirelings with drooping head-dresses. My character is quite different from theirs." [342]

"If, headman, it can be said about you, 'Pāṭaliya the headman knows the Koliyans' hirelings with drooping head-dresses, who are immoral, of bad character, but Pāṭaliya the headman is not immoral, of bad character,' then why can't it be said about the Tathāgata: 'The Tathāgata knows magic, but the Tathāgata is not a magician'? I understand magic, headman, and the result of magic, and I understand how a magician, faring along, with the breakup of the body, after death, is reborn in a state of misery, in a bad destination, in the nether world, in hell.

(ii)

"I understand, headman, the destruction of life, and the result of the destruction of life, and I understand how one who destroys life, faring along, with the breakup of the body, after death, is reborn in a state of misery, in a bad destination, in the nether world, in hell.

"I understand, headman, the taking of what is not given … sexual misconduct … false speech … divisive speech … harsh speech … [343] … idle chatter … covetousness … ill will and hatred … wrong view, and the result of wrong view, and I understand how one who holds wrong view, faring along, with the breakup of the body, after death, is reborn in a state of misery, in a bad destination, in the nether world, in hell.

II

"There are, headman, some ascetics and brahmins who hold such a doctrine and view as this: 'Anyone at all who destroys life experiences pain and grief in this very life. Anyone at all who takes what is not given … who engages in sexual misconduct … who speaks falsely experiences pain and grief in this very life.'

(i)

"Someone here, headman, is seen garlanded and adorned, freshly bathed and groomed, with hair and beard trimmed, enjoying sensual pleasures with women as if he were a king. They ask someone about him: 'Sir, what has this man done, that he has been garlanded and adorned … enjoying sensual pleasures with women as if he were a king?' [344] They answer: 'Sir, this man attacked the king's enemy and took his life. The king was pleased with him and bestowed a reward upon him. That is why this man is garlanded and adorned … enjoying sensual pleasures with women as if he were a king.'

(ii)

"Then, headman, someone here is seen with his arms tightly bound behind him with a strong rope, his head shaven, being led around from street to street, from square to square, to the ominous beating of a drum, and then taken out through the south gate and beheaded to the south of the city. They ask someone about him: 'Sir, what has this man done, that with his arms tightly tied behind his back … he is beheaded to the south of the city?' They answer: 'Sir, this man, an enemy of the king, has taken the life of a man or a woman. That is why the rulers, having had him arrested, imposed such a punishment upon him.'

"What do you think, headman, have you ever seen or heard of such a case?"

"I have seen this, venerable sir, and I have heard of it, and I will hear of it [still again]."

"Therein, headman, when those ascetics and brahmins who hold such a doctrine and view as this say: 'Anyone at all who destroys life experiences pain and grief here and now,' do they speak truthfully or falsely?"

"Falsely, venerable sir."

"Are those who prattle empty falsehood virtuous or immoral?" [345]

"Immoral, venerable sir."

"Are those who are immoral and of bad character practising wrongly or rightly?"

"Practising wrongly, venerable sir."

"Do those who are practising wrongly hold wrong view or right view?"

"Wrong view, venerable sir."

"Is it proper to place confidence in those who hold wrong view?"

"No, venerable sir."

(iii)

"Then, headman, someone here is seen garlanded and adorned, freshly bathed and groomed, with hair and beard trimmed, enjoying sensual pleasures with women as if he were a king. They ask someone about him: 'Sir, what has this man done, that he has been garlanded and adorned ... enjoying sensual pleasures with women as if he were a king?' They answer: 'Sir, this man attacked the king's enemy and stole a gem. The king was pleased with him and bestowed a reward upon him. That is why this man is garlanded and adorned ... enjoying sensual pleasures with women as if he were a king.'

(iv)

"Then, headman, someone here is seen with his arms tightly bound behind him with a strong rope, his head shaven, being led around from street to street, from square to square, to the ominous beating of a drum, and then taken out through the south gate and beheaded to the south of the city. They ask someone about him: 'Sir, what has this man done, that with his arms tightly bound behind him … he is beheaded to the south of the city?' They answer: 'Sir, this man, an enemy of the king, stole something from a village or a forest, he committed theft. That is why the rulers, having had him arrested, imposed such a punishment on him.'

"What do you think, headman, have you ever seen or heard of such a case?"

"I have seen this, venerable sir, and I have heard of it, and I will hear of it [still again]." [346]

"Therein, headman, when those ascetics and brahmins who hold such a doctrine and view as this say: 'Anyone at all who takes what is not given experiences pain and grief here and now,' do they speak truthfully or falsely?… Is it proper to place confidence in those who hold wrong view?"

"No, venerable sir."

(v)

"Then, headman, someone here is seen garlanded and adorned, freshly bathed and groomed, with hair and beard trimmed, enjoying sensual pleasures with women as if he were a king. They ask someone about him: 'Sir, what has this man done, that he has been garlanded and adorned … enjoying sensual pleasures with women as if he were a king?' They answer: 'Sir, this man seduced the wives of the king's enemy. The king was pleased with him and bestowed a reward upon him. That is why this man is garlanded and adorned … enjoying sensual pleasures with women as if he were a king.'

(vi)

"Then, headman, someone here is seen with his arms tightly bound behind him with a strong rope, his head shaven, being led around from street to street, from square to square, to the ominous beating of a drum, and then taken out through the south gate and beheaded to the south of the city. They ask someone about him: 'Sir, what has this man done, that with his arms tightly bound behind him … he is beheaded to the south of the city?' They answer: 'Sir, this man seduced women and girls of good families. That is why the rulers, having had him arrested, imposed such a punishment upon him.'

"What do you think, headman, have you ever seen or heard of such a case?"

"I have seen this, venerable sir, and I have heard of it, and I will hear of it [still again]."

"Therein, headman, when those ascetics and brahmins who hold such a doctrine and view as this say: 'Anyone at all who engages in sexual misconduct experiences pain and grief here and now,' do they speak truthfully or falsely?... Is it proper to place confidence in those who hold wrong view?"

"No, venerable sir." [347]

(vii)

"Then, headman, someone here is seen garlanded and adorned, freshly bathed and groomed, with hair and beard trimmed, enjoying sensual pleasures with women as if he were a king. They ask someone about him: 'Sir, what has this man done, that he has been garlanded and adorned ... enjoying sensual pleasures with women as if he were a king?' They answer: 'Sir, this man amused the king with false speech. The king was pleased with him and bestowed a reward upon him. That is why this man is garlanded and adorned ... enjoying sensual pleasures with women as if he were a king.'

(viii)

"Then, headman, someone here is with his arms tightly bound behind him with a strong rope, his head shaven, being led around from street to street, from square to square, to the ominous beating of a drum, and then taken out through the south gate and beheaded to the south of the city. They ask someone about him: 'Sir, what has this man done, that with his arms tightly bound behind him ... he is beheaded to the south of the city?' They answer: 'Sir, this man has brought to ruin a householder or a householder's son with false speech. That is why the rulers, having had him arrested, imposed such a punishment upon him.'

"What do you think, headman, have you ever seen or heard of such a case?"

"I have seen this, venerable sir, and I have heard of it, and I will hear of it [still again]."

"Therein, headman, when those ascetics and brahmins who hold such a doctrine and view as this say: 'Anyone at all who speaks falsely experiences pain and grief here and now,' [348] do they speak truthfully or falsely?... Is it proper to place confidence in those who hold wrong view?"

"No, venerable sir.

III

"It is wonderful, venerable sir! It is amazing, venerable sir! I have a rest house in which there are beds, seats, a waterpot, and an oil lamp. When any ascetic or brahmin comes to reside there, then I share it with him to the best of my means and ability. In the past, venerable sir, four teachers—holding different views, with different convictions, different preferences—came to dwell in that rest house.

(i)

"One teacher held such a doctrine and view as this:[361] 'There is nothing given, nothing offered, nothing presented in charity; no fruit or result of good and bad actions; no this world, no other world; no mother, no father; no beings who are reborn spontaneously; no ascetics and brahmins faring and practising rightly in the world who, having realized this world and the other world for themselves by direct knowledge, make them known to others.'

(ii)

"One teacher held such a doctrine and view as this: 'There is what is given, [349] what is offered, what is presented in charity; there is fruit and result of good and bad actions; there is this world and the other world; there is mother and father; there are beings who are reborn spontaneously; there are ascetics and brahmins faring and practising rightly in the world who, having realized this world and the other world for themselves by direct knowledge, make them known to others.'

(iii)

"One teacher held such a doctrine and view as this:[362] 'When one acts or makes others act, when one mutilates or makes others mutilate, when one tortures or makes others inflict torture, when one inflicts sorrow or makes others inflict sorrow, when one oppresses or makes others inflict oppression, when one intimidates or makes others inflict intimidation, when one destroys life, takes what is not given, breaks into houses, plunders wealth, commits burglary, ambushes highways, seduces another's wife, utters falsehood—no evil is done by the doer. If, with a razor-rimmed wheel, one were to make the living beings of this earth into one mass of flesh, into one heap of flesh, because of this there would be no evil and no outcome of evil. If one were to go along the south bank of the Ganges killing and slaughtering, mutilating and making others mutilate, torturing and making others inflict torture, because of this there would be no evil and no outcome of evil. If one were to go along the north bank of the Ganges giving gifts and making others give gifts, making offerings and making others make offerings, because of this there would be no merit and no outcome of merit. By giving, by taming oneself, by self-control, by speaking truth, there is no merit and no outcome of merit.'

(iv)

"One teacher held such a doctrine and view as this: 'When one acts or makes others act, when one mutilates or makes others mutilate ... [350] ... evil is done by the doer. If, with a razor-rimmed wheel, one were to make the living beings of this earth into one mass of flesh, into one heap of flesh, because of this there would be evil and an outcome of evil. If one were to go along the south bank of the Ganges killing and slaughtering, mutilating and making others mutilate, torturing and making others inflict torture, because of this there would be evil and an outcome of evil. If one were to go along the north bank of the Ganges giving gifts and making others give gifts, making offerings and making others make offerings, because of this there would be merit and an outcome of merit. By giving, by taming oneself, by self-control, by speaking truth, there is merit and an outcome of merit.'

"There arose in me, venerable sir, the perplexity and doubt: 'Which of these honourable ascetics and brahmins speak truth and which speak falsehood?'"

"It is fitting for you to be perplexed, headman, fitting for you to doubt. Doubt has arisen in you about a perplexing matter."

"I have confidence in the Blessed One thus: 'The Blessed One is capable of teaching me the Dhamma in such a way that I might abandon this state of perplexity.'"

IV

"There is, headman, concentration of the Dhamma. If you were to obtain concentration of mind in that, you might abandon this state of perplexity.[363] And what, headman, is concentration of the Dhamma?

(i)

"Herein, headman, having abandoned the destruction of life, the noble disciple abstains from the destruction of life. Having abandoned the taking of what is not given, he abstains from taking what is not given. Having abandoned sexual misconduct, he abstains from sexual misconduct. Having abandoned false speech, he abstains from false speech. [351] Having abandoned divisive speech, he abstains from divisive speech. Having abandoned harsh speech, he abstains from harsh speech. Having abandoned idle chatter, he abstains from idle chatter. Having abandoned covetousness, he is uncovetous. Having abandoned ill will and hatred, he has a mind without ill will. Having abandoned wrong view, he is one of right view.

"Then, headman, that noble disciple—who is thus devoid of covetousness, devoid of ill will, unconfused, clearly comprehending, ever mindful—dwells pervading one quarter with a mind imbued with lovingkindness, likewise the second quarter, the third quarter, and the fourth quarter. Thus above, below, across, and everywhere, and to all as to himself, he dwells pervading the entire world with a mind imbued with lovingkindness, vast, exalted, measureless, without hostility, without ill will.

"He reflects thus: 'This teacher holds such a doctrine and view as this: "There is nothing given, nothing offered … no ascetics and brahmins faring and practising rightly in the world who, having realized this world and the other world for themselves by direct knowledge, make them known to others." If the word of this good teacher is true, for me it yet counts as incontrovertible[364] that I do not oppress anyone whether frail or firm. In both respects I have made a lucky throw:[365] since I am restrained in body, speech, and mind, and since, with the breakup of the body, after death, I shall be reborn in a good destination, in a heavenly world.' [As he reflects thus] gladness is born. When one is gladdened, rapture is born. When the mind is elated by rapture the body becomes tranquil. One tranquil in body experiences happiness. The mind of one who is happy becomes concentrated.

"This, headman, is concentration of the Dhamma. [352] If you were to obtain concentration of mind in that, you might abandon that state of perplexity.

(ii)

"Then, headman, that noble disciple—who is thus devoid of covetousness, devoid of ill will, unconfused, clearly comprehending, ever mindful—dwells pervading one quarter with a mind imbued with lovingkindness … without ill will.

"He reflects thus: 'This teacher holds such a doctrine and view as this: "There is what is given, there is what is offered … there are ascetics and brahmins faring and practising rightly in the world who, having realized this world and the other world for themselves by direct knowledge, make them known to others." If the word of this good teacher is true, for me it yet counts as incontrovertible that I do not oppress anyone whether frail or firm. In both respects I have made a lucky throw: since I am restrained in body, speech, and mind, and since, with the breakup of the body, after death, I shall be reborn in a good destination, in a heavenly world.' [As he reflects thus] gladness is born. When one is gladdened, rapture is born. When the mind is elated by rapture the body becomes tranquil. One tranquil in body experiences happiness. The mind of one who is happy becomes concentrated.

"This, headman, is concentration of the Dhamma. If you were to obtain concentration of mind in that, you might abandon that state of perplexity.

(iii)

"Then, headman, that noble disciple—who is thus devoid of covetousness, devoid of ill will, unconfused, clearly comprehending, ever mindful—dwells pervading one quarter with a mind imbued with lovingkindness … [353] without ill will.

"He reflects thus: 'This teacher holds such a doctrine and view as this: "When one acts or makes others act … By giving, by taming oneself, by self-control, by speaking truth, there is no merit and no outcome of merit." If the word of this good teacher is true, for me it yet counts as incontrovertible that I do not oppress anyone whether frail or firm. In both respects I have made a lucky throw: since I am restrained in body, speech, and mind, and since, with the breakup of the body, after death, I shall be reborn in a good destination, in a heavenly world.' [As he reflects thus] gladness is born. When one is gladdened, rapture is born. When the mind is elated by rapture the body becomes tranquil. One tranquil in body experiences happiness. The mind of one who is happy becomes concentrated.

"This, headman, is concentration of the Dhamma. If you were to obtain concentration of mind in that, you might abandon that state of perplexity.

(iv)

"Then, headman, that noble disciple—who is thus devoid of covetousness, devoid of ill will, unconfused, clearly comprehending, ever mindful—dwells pervading one quarter with a mind imbued with lovingkindness … [354] … without ill will.

"He reflects thus: 'This teacher holds such a doctrine and view as this: "When one acts or makes others act … By giving, by taming oneself, by self-control, by speaking truth, there is merit and an outcome of merit." If the word of this good teacher is true, for me it yet counts as incontrovertible that I do not oppress anyone whether frail or firm. In both respects I have made a lucky throw: since I am restrained in body, speech, and mind, and since, with the breakup of the body, after death, I shall be reborn in a good destination, in a heavenly world.' [As he reflects thus] gladness is born. When one is gladdened, rapture is born. When the mind is elated by rapture the body becomes tranquil. One tranquil in body experiences happiness. The mind of one who is happy becomes concentrated.

"This, headman, is concentration of the Dhamma. If you were to obtain concentration of mind in that, you might abandon that state of perplexity.

V

(i)

"Then, headman, that noble disciple—who is thus devoid of covetousness, devoid of ill will, unconfused, clearly comprehending, ever mindful—dwells pervading one quarter with a mind imbued with compassion ... [355] ... with a mind imbued with altruistic joy ... with a mind imbued with equanimity, likewise the second quarter, the third quarter, and the fourth quarter. Thus above, below, across, and everywhere, and to all as to himself, he dwells pervading the entire world with a mind imbued with equanimity, vast, exalted, measureless, without hostility, without ill will.

"He reflects thus: 'This teacher holds such a doctrine and view as this: "There is nothing given, nothing offered ... no ascetics and brahmins faring and practising rightly in the world who, having realized this world and the other world for themselves by direct knowledge, make them known to others."' ... This, headman, is concentration of the Dhamma. If you were to obtain concentration of mind in that, you might abandon that state of perplexity.

(ii)–(iv)

"Then, headman, that noble disciple—who is thus devoid of covetousness, devoid of ill will, unconfused, clearly comprehending, ever mindful—dwells pervading one quarter with a mind imbued with compassion ... with a mind imbued with altruistic joy ... with a mind imbued with equanimity ... [356] ... without ill will.

"He reflects thus: 'This teacher holds such a doctrine and view as this: "There is what is given, there is what is offered ... there are ascetics and brahmins faring and practising rightly in the world who, having realized this world and the other world for themselves by direct knowledge, make them known to others."' ... This, headman, is concentration of the Dhamma. If you were to obtain concentration of mind in that, you might abandon that state of perplexity.

"He reflects thus: 'This teacher holds such a doctrine and view as this: "When one acts or makes others act ... [357] ... By giving, by taming oneself, by self-control, by speaking truth, there is no merit and no outcome of merit."' ... This, headman, is concentration of the Dhamma. If you were to obtain concentration of mind in that, you might abandon that state of perplexity.

"He reflects thus: 'This teacher holds such a doctrine and view as this: "When one acts or makes others act, when one mutilates or makes others mutilate ... [358] ... By giving, by taming oneself, by self-control, by speaking truth, there is merit and an outcome of merit." If the word of this good teacher is true, for me it yet counts as incontrovertible that I do not oppress anyone whether frail or firm. In both respects I have made a lucky throw: since I am restrained in body, speech, and mind, and since, with the breakup of the body, after death, I shall be reborn in a good destination, in a heavenly world.' [As he reflects thus] gladness is born. When one is gladdened, rapture is born. When the mind is elated by rapture the body becomes tranquil. One tranquil in body experiences happiness. The mind of one who is happy becomes concentrated.

"This, headman, is concentration based upon the Dhamma. If you were to obtain concentration of mind in that, then you might abandon that state of perplexity."

When this was said, Pāṭaliya the headman said to the Blessed One: "Magnificent, venerable sir!... From today let the Blessed One remember me as a lay follower who has gone for refuge for life."

[359] Chapter IX

43 *Asaṅkhatasaṃyutta*
Connected Discourses on the Unconditioned

I. The First Subchapter

1 (1) Mindfulness Directed to the Body

At Sāvatthī. "Bhikkhus, I will teach you the unconditioned and the path leading to the unconditioned. Listen to that....

"And what, bhikkhus, is the unconditioned? The destruction of lust, the destruction of hatred, the destruction of delusion: this is called the unconditioned.

"And what, bhikkhus, is the path leading to the unconditioned? Mindfulness directed to the body:[366] this is called the path leading to the unconditioned.

"Thus, bhikkhus, I have taught you the unconditioned and the path leading to the unconditioned. Whatever should be done, bhikkhus, by a compassionate teacher out of compassion for his disciples, desiring their welfare, that I have done for you. These are the feet of trees, bhikkhus, these are empty huts. Meditate, bhikkhus, do not be negligent, lest you regret it later. This is our instruction to you." [360]

2 (2) Serenity and Insight

"Bhikkhus, I will teach you the unconditioned and the path leading to the unconditioned. Listen to that....

"And what, bhikkhus, is the unconditioned? The destruction of lust, the destruction of hatred, the destruction of delusion: this is called the unconditioned.

"And what, bhikkhus, is the path leading to the unconditioned? Serenity and insight: this is called the path leading to the unconditioned…."

3 (3) With Thought and Examination

… "And what, bhikkhus, is the path leading to the unconditioned? Concentration with thought and examination; concentration without thought, with examination only; concentration without thought and examination:[367] this is called the path leading to the unconditioned…."

4 (4) Emptiness Concentration

… "And what, bhikkhus, is the path leading to the unconditioned? The emptiness concentration, the signless concentration, the undirected concentration:[368] this is called the path leading to the unconditioned…."

5 (5) Establishments of Mindfulness[369]

… "And what, bhikkhus, is the path leading to the unconditioned? The four establishments of mindfulness…."

6 (6) Right Strivings

… "And what, bhikkhus, is the path leading to the unconditioned? The four right strivings…."

7 (7) Bases for Spiritual Power

… "And what, bhikkhus, is the path leading to the unconditioned? The four bases for spiritual power…." [361]

8 (8) Spiritual Faculties

… "And what, bhikkhus, is the path leading to the unconditioned? The five spiritual faculties…."

9 (9) Powers

... "And what, bhikkhus, is the path leading to the unconditioned? The five powers...."

10 (10) Factors of Enlightenment

... "And what, bhikkhus, is the path leading to the unconditioned? The seven factors of enlightenment...."

11 (11) The Eightfold Path

... "And what, bhikkhus, is the path leading to the unconditioned? The Noble Eightfold Path: this is called the path leading to the unconditioned.

"Thus, bhikkhus, I have taught you the unconditioned and the path leading to the unconditioned.... This is our instruction to you."

[362] II. The Second Subchapter

12 (1) The Unconditioned

(i. Serenity)

"Bhikkhus, I will teach you the unconditioned and the path leading to the unconditioned. Listen to that....

"And what, bhikkhus, is the unconditioned? The destruction of lust, the destruction of hatred, the destruction of delusion: this is called the unconditioned.

"And what, bhikkhus, is the path leading to the unconditioned? Serenity: this is called the path leading to the unconditioned....

"Thus, bhikkhus, I have taught you the unconditioned and the path leading to the unconditioned.... This is our instruction to you."

(ii. Insight)

... "And what, bhikkhus, is the path leading to the unconditioned? Insight: this is called the path leading to the unconditioned...."

(iii–viii. Concentration)

(iii) … "And what, bhikkhus, is the path leading to the unconditioned? [363] Concentration with thought and examination: this is called the path leading to the unconditioned…."

(iv) … "And what, bhikkhus, is the path leading to the unconditioned? Concentration without thought, with examination only…."

(v) … "And what, bhikkhus, is the path leading to the unconditioned? Concentration without thought and examination…."

(vi) … "And what, bhikkhus, is the path leading to the unconditioned? Emptiness concentration…."

(vii) … "And what, bhikkhus, is the path leading to the unconditioned? Signless concentration…."

(viii) … "And what, bhikkhus, is the path leading to the unconditioned? Undirected concentration: this is called the path leading to the unconditioned…."

(ix–xii. The four establishments of mindfulness)

(ix) … "And what, bhikkhus, is the path leading to the unconditioned? Here, bhikkhus, a bhikkhu dwells contemplating the body in the body, ardent, clearly comprehending, mindful, having removed covetousness and displeasure in regard to the world: this is called the path leading to the unconditioned…."

(x) … "And what, bhikkhus, is the path leading to the unconditioned? Here, bhikkhus, a bhikkhu dwells contemplating feelings in feelings, ardent, clearly comprehending, mindful, having removed covetousness and displeasure in regard to the world…." [364]

(xi) … "And what, bhikkhus, is the path leading to the unconditioned? Here, bhikkhus, a bhikkhu dwells contemplating mind in mind, ardent, clearly comprehending, mindful, having removed covetousness and displeasure in regard to the world…."

(xii) … "And what, bhikkhus is the path leading to the unconditioned? Here, bhikkhus, a bhikkhu dwells contemplating phenomena in phenomena, ardent, clearly comprehending, mindful, having removed covetousness and displeasure in regard to the world: this is called the path leading to the unconditioned…."

(xiii–xvi. The four right strivings)

(xiii) ... "And what, bhikkhus, is the path leading to the unconditioned? Here, bhikkhus, a bhikkhu generates desire for the nonarising of unarisen evil unwholesome states; he makes an effort, arouses energy, applies his mind, and strives: this is called the path leading to the unconditioned...."

(xiv) ... "And what, bhikkhus, is the path leading to the unconditioned? Here, bhikkhus, a bhikkhu generates desire for the abandoning of arisen evil unwholesome states; he makes an effort, arouses energy, applies his mind, and strives...."

(xv) ... "And what, bhikkhus, is the path leading to the unconditioned? Here, bhikkhus, a bhikkhu generates desire for the arising of unarisen wholesome states; he makes an effort, arouses energy, applies his mind, and strives...."

(xvi) ... "And what, bhikkhus, is the path leading to the unconditioned? Here, bhikkhus, a bhikkhu generates desire for the continuance of arisen wholesome states, [365] for their nondecay, increase, expansion, and fulfilment by development; he makes an effort, arouses energy, applies his mind, and strives: this is called the path leading to the unconditioned...."

(xvii–xx. The four bases for spiritual power)

(xvii) ... "And what, bhikkhus, is the path leading to the unconditioned? Here, bhikkhus, a bhikkhu develops the basis for spiritual power that possesses concentration due to desire and volitional formations of striving: this is called the path leading to the unconditioned...."

(xviii) ... "And what, bhikkhus, is the path leading to the unconditioned? Here, bhikkhus, a bhikkhu develops the basis for spiritual power that possesses concentration due to energy and volitional formations of striving...."

(xix) ... "And what, bhikkhus, is the path leading to the unconditioned? Here, bhikkhus, a bhikkhu develops the basis for spiritual power that possesses concentration due to mind and volitional formations of striving...."

(xx) ... "And what, bhikkhus, is the path leading to the unconditioned? Here, bhikkhus, a bhikkhu develops the basis for spiritual power that possesses concentration due to investigation and volitional formations of striving: this is called the path leading to the unconditioned...."

(xxi–xxv. The five spiritual faculties)

(xxi) … "And what, bhikkhus, is the path leading to the unconditioned? Here, bhikkhus, a bhikkhu develops the faculty of faith, which is based upon seclusion, dispassion, and cessation, maturing in release: this is called the path leading to the unconditioned…." [366]

(xxii–xxv) … "And what, bhikkhus, is the path leading to the unconditioned? Here, bhikkhus, a bhikkhu develops the faculty of energy … the faculty of mindfulness … the faculty of concentration … the faculty of wisdom, which is based upon seclusion, dispassion, and cessation, maturing in release: this is called the path leading to the unconditioned…."

(xxvi–xxx. The five powers)

(xxvi) … "And what, bhikkhus, is the path leading to the unconditioned? Here, bhikkhus, a bhikkhu develops the power of faith, which is based upon seclusion, dispassion, and cessation, maturing in release: this is called the path leading to the unconditioned…."

(xxvii–xxx) … "And what, bhikkhus, is the path leading to the unconditioned? Here, bhikkhus, a bhikkhu develops the power of energy … the power of mindfulness … [367] … the power of concentration … the power of wisdom, which is based upon seclusion, dispassion, and cessation, maturing in release: this is called the path leading to the unconditioned…."

(xxxi–xxxvii. The seven factors of enlightenment)

(xxxi) … "And what, bhikkhus, is the path leading to the unconditioned? Here, bhikkhus, a bhikkhu develops the enlightenment factor of mindfulness, which is based upon seclusion, dispassion, and cessation, maturing in release: this is called the path leading to the unconditioned…."

(xxxii–xxxvii) … "And what, bhikkhus, is the path leading to the unconditioned? Here, bhikkhus, a bhikkhu develops the enlightenment factor of discrimination of states … the enlightenment factor of energy … the enlightenment factor of rapture … the enlightenment factor of tranquillity … the enlightenment factor of concentration … the enlightenment factor of equanimity, which is based upon seclusion, dispassion, and cessation, maturing in release: this is called the path leading to the unconditioned…."

(xxxviii–xlv. The Noble Eightfold Path)

(xxxviii) … "And what, bhikkhus, is the path leading to the unconditioned? Here, bhikkhus, a bhikkhu develops right view, which is based upon seclusion, dispassion, and cessation, maturing in release: this is called the path leading to the unconditioned…." [368]

(xxxix–xlv) … "And what, bhikkhus, is the path leading to the unconditioned? Here, bhikkhus, a bhikkhu develops right intention … right speech … right action … right livelihood … right effort … right mindfulness … right concentration, which is based upon seclusion, dispassion, and cessation, maturing in release: this is called the path leading to the unconditioned.

"Thus, bhikkhus, I have taught you the unconditioned and the path leading to the unconditioned. Whatever should be done, bhikkhus, by a compassionate teacher out of compassion for his disciples, desiring their welfare, that I have done for you. These are the feet of trees, bhikkhus, these are empty huts. Meditate, bhikkhus, do not be negligent, lest you regret it later. This is our instruction to you."

13 (2) The Uninclined[370]

"Bhikkhus, I will teach you the uninclined and the path leading to the uninclined. Listen to that….

"And what, bhikkhus, is the uninclined?…"

(*To be elaborated in full as in §§1–12.*)[371] [369]

14 (3)–43 (32) The Taintless, Etc.

"Bhikkhus, I will teach you the taintless and the path leading to the taintless. Listen to that….

"Bhikkhus, I will teach you the truth and the path leading to the truth…. I will teach you the far shore … the subtle … the very difficult to see … the unaging … [370] … the stable … the undisintegrating … the unmanifest … the unproliferated[372] … the peaceful … the deathless … the sublime … the auspicious … [371] … the secure …. the destruction of craving … the wonderful … the amazing … the unailing … the unailing state … Nibbāna … the unafflicted … dispassion … [372] … purity … freedom …

the unadhesive … the island … the shelter … the asylum … the refuge … [373] …"

44 (33) The Destination

"Bhikkhus, I will teach you the destination and the path leading to the destination. Listen to that….

"And what, bhikkhus, is the destination? The destruction of lust, the destruction of hatred, the destruction of delusion: this is called the destination.

"And what, bhikkhus, is the path leading to the destination? Mindfulness directed to the body: this is called the path leading to the destination.

"Thus, bhikkhus, I have taught you the destination and the path leading to the destination. Whatever should be done, bhikkhus, by a compassionate teacher out of compassion for his disciples, desiring their welfare, that I have done for you. These are the feet of trees, bhikkhus, these are empty huts. Meditate, bhikkhus, do not be negligent, lest you regret it later. This is our instruction to you."

(*Each to be elaborated in full as in §§1–12.*)

[374] Chapter X

44 *Abyākatasaṃyutta* Connected Discourses on the Undeclared

1 Khemā

On one occasion the Blessed One was dwelling at Sāvatthī in Jeta's Grove, Anāthapiṇḍika's Park. Now on that occasion the bhikkhunī Khemā,[373] while wandering on tour among the Kosalans, had taken up residence in Toraṇavatthu between Sāvatthī and Sāketa. Then King Pasenadi of Kosala, while travelling from Sāketa to Sāvatthī, took up residence for one night in Toraṇavatthu between Sāketa and Sāvatthī. Then King Pasenadi of Kosala addressed a man thus: "Go, good man, and find out whether there is any ascetic or brahmin in Toraṇavatthu whom I could visit today."

"Yes, sire," the man replied, but though he traversed the whole of Toraṇavatthu he did not see any ascetic or brahmin there whom King Pasenadi could visit. The man did see, however, the bhikkhunī Khemā resident in Toraṇavatthu, so he approached King Pasenadi and said to him:

"Sire, there is no ascetic or brahmin in Toraṇavatthu whom your majesty could visit. But, sire, there is the bhikkhunī named Khemā, a disciple of the Blessed One, the Arahant, the Perfectly Enlightened One. Now a good report concerning this revered lady has spread about thus: [375] 'She is wise, competent, intelligent, learned, a splendid speaker, ingenious.' Let your majesty visit her."

Then King Pasenadi of Kosala approached the bhikkhunī Khemā, paid homage to her, sat down to one side, and said to her:

"How is it, revered lady, does the Tathāgata exist after death?"[374]

"Great king, the Blessed One has not declared this: 'The Tathāgata exists after death.'"

"Then, revered lady, does the Tathāgata not exist after death?"

"Great king, the Blessed One has not declared this either: 'The Tathāgata does not exist after death.'"

"How is it then, revered lady, does the Tathāgata both exist and not exist after death?"

"Great king, the Blessed One has not declared this: 'The Tathāgata both exists and does not exist after death.'"

"Then, revered lady, does the Tathāgata neither exist nor not exist after death?"

"Great king, the Blessed One has not declared this either: 'The Tathāgata neither exists nor does not exist after death.'"

"How is this, revered lady? When asked, 'How is it, revered lady, does the Tathāgata exist after death?' ... And when asked, 'Then, revered lady, does the Tathāgata neither exist nor not exist after death?'—in each case you say: 'Great king, the Blessed One has not declared this.' What now, [376] revered lady, is the cause and reason why this has not been declared by the Blessed One?"

"Well then, great king, I will question you about this same matter. Answer as you see fit. What do you think, great king? Do you have an accountant or calculator or mathematician who can count the grains of sand in the river Ganges thus: 'There are so many grains of sand,' or 'There are so many hundreds of grains of sand,' or 'There are so many thousands of grains of sand,' or 'There are so many hundreds of thousands of grains of sand'?"

"No, revered lady."

"Then, great king, do you have an accountant or calculator or mathematician who can count the water in the great ocean thus: 'There are so many gallons of water,' or 'There are so many hundreds of gallons of water,' or 'There are so many thousands of gallons of water,' or 'There are so many hundreds of thousands of gallons of water'?"

"No, revered lady. For what reason? Because the great ocean is deep, immeasurable, hard to fathom."

"So too,[375] great king, that form by which one describing the Tathāgata might describe him has been abandoned by the Tathāgata, cut off at the root, made like a palm stump, obliterated so that it is no more subject to future arising. The Tathāgata, great king, is liberated from reckoning in terms of form; he is deep, immeasurable, hard to fathom like the great ocean.[376] 'The Tathāgata exists after death' does not apply; 'the Tathāgata does not exist after death' does not apply; 'the Tathāgata both exists and does not exist after death' does not apply; 'the Tathāgata neither exists nor does not exist after death' does not apply.

"That feeling by which one describing the Tathāgata might describe him [377] ... That perception by which one describing the Tathāgata might describe him ... Those volitional formations by which one describing the Tathāgata might describe him ... That consciousness by which one describing the Tathāgata might describe him has been abandoned by the Tathāgata, cut off at the root, made like a palm stump, obliterated so that it is no more subject to future arising. The Tathāgata, great king, is liberated from reckoning in terms of consciousness; he is deep, immeasurable, hard to fathom like the great ocean. 'The Tathāgata exists after death' does not apply; 'the Tathāgata does not exist after death' does not apply; 'the Tathāgata both exists and does not exist after death' does not apply; 'the Tathāgata neither exists nor does not exist after death' does not apply."

Then King Pasenadi of Kosala, having delighted and rejoiced in the bhikkhunī Khemā's statement, rose from his seat, paid homage to her, and departed, keeping her on his right.

Then, on a later occasion, King Pasenadi of Kosala approached the Blessed One. Having approached, he paid homage to the Blessed One, sat down to one side, and said to him:

"How is it, venerable sir, does the Tathāgata exist after death?" [378]

"Great king, I have not declared this: 'The Tathāgata exists after death.'"

(*All as above down to:*)

"Great king, I have not declared this either: 'The Tathāgata neither exists nor does not exist after death.'"

"How is this, venerable sir? When asked, 'How is it, venerable sir, does the Tathāgata exist after death?' ... And when asked, 'Then, venerable sir, does the Tathāgata neither exist nor not exist after death?'—in each case you say: 'Great king, I have not declared this.' What now, venerable sir, is the cause and reason why this has not been declared by the Blessed One?"

"Well then, great king, I will question you about this same matter. Answer as you see fit. What do you think, great king? Do you have an accountant or calculator or mathematician ... (*all as above down to:*) [379] ... The Tathāgata, great king, is liberated from reckoning in terms of consciousness: he is deep, immeasurable, hard to fathom like the great ocean. 'The Tathāgata exists after death' does not apply; 'the Tathāgata does not exist after death' does not apply; 'the Tathāgata both exists and does not exist after death' does not apply; 'the Tathāgata neither exists nor does not exist after death' does not apply."

"It is wonderful, venerable sir! It is amazing, venerable sir! How the meaning and the phrasing of both teacher and disciple coincide and agree with each other and do not diverge, that is, in regard to the chief matter.[377] On one occasion, venerable sir, I approached the bhikkhunī Khemā and asked her about this matter. The revered lady explained this matter to me in exactly the same terms and phrases that the Blessed One used. It is wonderful, venerable sir! It is amazing, venerable sir! How the meaning and the phrasing of both teacher and disciple coincide and agree with each other and do not diverge, that is, in regard to the chief matter. Now, venerable sir, we must go. We are busy and have much to do."

"Then, great king, you may go at your own convenience."

Then King Pasenadi of Kosala, having delighted and rejoiced in the Blessed One's statement, [380] rose from his seat, paid homage to him, and departed, keeping him on his right.

2 Anurādha

(*Identical with 22:86.*) [381–84]

3 Sāriputta and Koṭṭhita (1)

On one occasion the Venerable Sāriputta and the Venerable Mahākoṭṭhita were dwelling at Bārāṇasī in the Deer Park at Isipatana. Then, in the evening, the Venerable Mahākoṭṭhita emerged from seclusion and approached the Venerable Sāriputta. He exchanged greetings with the Venerable Sāriputta and, when they had concluded their greetings and cordial talk, he sat down to one side and said to him:

"How is it, friend Sāriputta, does the Tathāgata exist after death?"

"Friend, the Blessed One has not declared this: 'The Tathāgata exists after death.'"

(*As in the preceding sutta down to:*) [385]

"Friend, the Blessed One has not declared this either: 'The Tathāgata neither exists nor does not exist after death.'"

"How is this, friend? When asked, 'How is it, friend, does the Tathāgata exist after death?' ... And when asked, 'Then, friend, does the Tathāgata neither exist nor not exist after death?'—in each case you say: 'Friend, the Blessed One has not declared this.' What now, friend, is the cause and reason why this has not been declared by the Blessed One?"

"'The Tathāgata exists after death': this, friend, is an involvement with form.[378] 'The Tathāgata does not exist after death': this is an involvement with form. 'The Tathāgata both exists and does not exist after death': this is an involvement with form. 'The Tathāgata neither exists nor does not exist after death': this is an involvement with form.

"'The Tathāgata exists after death': this, friend, is an involvement with feeling ... an involvement with perception ... an involvement with volitional formations [386] ... an involvement with consciousness. 'The Tathāgata does not exist after death': this is an involvement with consciousness. 'The Tathāgata both exists and does not exist after death': this is an involvement with consciousness. 'The Tathāgata neither exists nor does not exist after death': this is an involvement with consciousness.

"This, friend, is the cause and reason why this has not been declared by the Blessed One."

4 Sāriputta and Koṭṭhita (2)

(*As above down to:*)

"What now, friend, is the cause and reason why this has not been declared by the Blessed One?"

"Friend, it is one who does not know and see form as it really is, who does not know and see its origin, its cessation, and the way leading to its cessation, that thinks: 'The Tathāgata exists after death,' or 'The Tathāgata does not exist after death,' or 'The Tathāgata both exists and does not exist after death,' or 'The

Tathāgata neither exists nor does not exist after death.' It is one who does not know and see feeling as it really is ... who does not know and see perception as it really is ... who does not know and see volitional formations as they really are ... who does not know and see consciousness as it really is, who does not know and see its origin, its cessation, and the way leading to its cessation, that thinks: 'The Tathāgata exists after death' ... [387] ... or 'The Tathāgata neither exists nor does not exist after death.'

"But, friend, one who knows and sees form ... feeling ... perception ... volitional formations ... consciousness as it really is, who knows and sees its origin, its cessation, and the way leading to its cessation, does not think: 'The Tathāgata exists after death' ... or 'The Tathāgata neither exists nor does not exist after death.'

"This, friend, is the cause and reason why this has not been declared by the Blessed One."

5 Sāriputta and Koṭṭhita (3)

(*As above down to:*)

"What now, friend, is the cause and reason why this has not been declared by the Blessed One?"

"Friend, it is one who is not devoid of lust for form, who is not devoid of desire, affection, thirst, passion, and craving for form, that thinks: 'The Tathāgata exists after death,' or 'The Tathāgata does not exist after death,' or 'The Tathāgata both exists and does not exist after death,' or 'The Tathāgata neither exists nor does not exist after death.' It is one who is not devoid of lust for feeling ... who is not devoid of lust for perception ... who is not devoid of lust for volitional formations ... who is not devoid of lust for consciousness, who is not devoid of desire, affection, thirst, passion, and craving for consciousness, that thinks: 'The Tathāgata exists after death' ... [388] or 'The Tathāgata neither exists nor does not exist after death.'

"But, friend, one who is devoid of lust for form ... who is devoid of lust for feeling ... who is devoid of lust for perception ... who is devoid of lust for volitional formations ... who is devoid of lust for consciousness, who is devoid of desire, affection, thirst, passion, and craving for consciousness, does not think: 'The Tathāgata exists after death' ... or 'The Tathāgata neither exists nor does not exist after death.'

"This, friend, is the cause and reason why this has not been declared by the Blessed One."

6 Sāriputta and Koṭṭhita (4)

On one occasion the Venerable Sāriputta and the Venerable Mahākoṭṭhita were dwelling at Bārāṇasī in the Deer Park at Isipatana. Then, in the evening, the Venerable Sāriputta emerged from seclusion and approached the Venerable Mahākoṭṭhita. He exchanged greetings with the Venerable Mahākoṭṭhita and, when they had concluded their greetings and cordial talk, he sat down to one side and said to him:

"How is it, friend Koṭṭhita, does the Tathāgata exist after death?"

(*All as above down to:*)

"What now, friend, is the cause and reason why this has not been declared by the Blessed One?"

(i. Delight in the aggregates)

"Friend, it is one who delights in form, who takes delight in form, who rejoices in form, and who does not know and see the cessation of form as it really is, that thinks: [389] 'The Tathāgata exists after death' ... or 'The Tathāgata neither exists nor does not exist after death.' It is one who delights in feeling ... who delights in perception ... who delights in volitional formations ... who delights in consciousness, who takes delight in consciousness, who rejoices in consciousness, and who does not know and see the cessation of consciousness as it really is, that thinks: 'The Tathāgata exists after death' ... or 'The Tathāgata neither exists nor does not exist after death.'

"But, friend, one who does not delight in form ... who does not delight in feeling ... who does not delight in perception ... who does not delight in volitional formations ... who does not delight in consciousness, who does not take delight in consciousness, who does not rejoice in consciousness, and who knows and sees the cessation of consciousness as it really is, does not think: 'The Tathāgata exists after death' ... or 'The Tathāgata neither exists nor does not exist after death.'

"This, friend, is the cause and reason why this has not been declared by the Blessed One."

(ii. Delight in existence)

"But, friend, could there be another method of explaining why this has not been declared by the Blessed One?"

"There could be, friend. It is one who delights in existence, who takes delight in existence, who rejoices in existence, and who does not know and see the cessation of existence as it really is, that thinks: 'The Tathāgata exists after death' ... or 'The Tathāgata neither exists nor does not exist after death.' [390]

"But, friend, one who does not delight in existence, who does not take delight in existence, who does not rejoice in existence, and who knows and sees the cessation of existence as it really is, does not think: 'The Tathāgata exists after death' ... or 'The Tathāgata neither exists nor does not exist after death.'

"This, friend, is the cause and reason why this has not been declared by the Blessed One."

(iii. Delight in clinging)

"But, friend, could there be another method of explaining why this has not been declared by the Blessed One?"

"There could be, friend. It is one who delights in clinging, who takes delight in clinging, who rejoices in clinging, and who does not know and see the cessation of clinging as it really is, that thinks: 'The Tathāgata exists after death' ... or 'The Tathāgata neither exists nor does not exist after death.'

"But, friend, one who does not delight in clinging, who does not take delight in clinging, who does not rejoice in clinging, and who knows and sees the cessation of clinging as it really is, does not think: 'The Tathāgata exists after death' ... or 'The Tathāgata neither exists nor does not exist after death.'

"This, friend, is the cause and reason why this has not been declared by the Blessed One."

(iv. Delight in craving)

"But, friend, could there be another method of explaining why this has not been declared by the Blessed One?"

"There could be, friend. It is one who delights in craving, who takes delight in craving, who rejoices in craving, and who does not know and see the cessation of craving as it really is, that thinks: 'The Tathāgata exists after death' ... [391] or 'The Tathāgata neither exists nor does not exist after death.'

"But, friend, one who does not delight in craving, who does not take delight in craving, who does not rejoice in craving, and who knows and sees the cessation of craving as it really is, does not think: 'The Tathāgata exists after death' ... or 'The Tathāgata neither exists nor does not exist after death.'

"This, friend, is the cause and reason why this has not been declared by the Blessed One."

(v. Another method?)

"But, friend, could there be another method of explaining why this has not been declared by the Blessed One?"

"Here now, friend Sāriputta, why should you want anything additional to this? Friend Sāriputta, when a bhikkhu is liberated by the destruction of craving, there is no round for describing him."[379]

7 Moggallāna

Then the wanderer Vacchagotta approached the Venerable Mahāmoggallāna and exchanged greetings with him. When they had concluded their greetings and cordial talk, he sat down to one side and said to the Venerable Mahāmoggallāna:

"How is it, Master Moggallāna, is the world eternal?"

"Vaccha, the Blessed One has not declared this: 'The world is eternal.'"

"Then, Master Moggallāna, is the world not eternal?"

"Vaccha, the Blessed One has not declared this either: 'The world is not eternal.'"

"How is it then, Master Moggallāna, is the world finite?"

"Vaccha, the Blessed One has not declared this: 'The world is finite.'"

"Then, Master Moggallāna, is the world infinite?"

"Vaccha, the Blessed One has not declared this either: 'The world is infinite.'" [392]

"How is it then, Master Moggallāna, are the soul and the body the same?"

"Vaccha, the Blessed One has not declared this: 'The soul and the body are the same.'"

"Then, Master Moggallāna, is the soul one thing, the body another?"

"Vaccha, the Blessed One has not declared this either: 'The soul is one thing, the body is another.'"

"How is it, Master Moggallāna, does the Tathāgata exist after death?"

"Vaccha, the Blessed One has not declared this: 'The Tathāgata exists after death.'"

"Then, Master Moggallāna, does the Tathāgata not exist after death?"

"Vaccha, the Blessed One has not declared this either: 'The Tathāgata does not exist after death.'"

"How is it, then, Master Moggallāna, does the Tathāgata both exist and not exist after death?"

"Vaccha, the Blessed One has not declared this either: 'The Tathāgata both exists and does not exist after death.'"

"Then, Master Moggallāna, does the Tathāgata neither exist nor not exist after death?"

"Vaccha, the Blessed One has not declared this either: 'The Tathāgata neither exists nor does not exist after death.'"

"What, Master Moggallāna, is the cause and reason why, when wanderers of other sects are asked such questions, they give such answers as: 'The world is eternal' or 'The world is not eternal'; or 'The world is finite' or 'The world is infinite'; or 'The soul and the body are the same' or 'The soul is one thing, the body is another'; or 'The Tathāgata exists after death,' or 'The Tathāgata does not exist after death,' or 'The Tathāgata both exists and does not exist after death,' or 'The Tathāgata neither exists nor does not exist after death'? [393] And what is the cause and reason why, when the ascetic Gotama is asked such questions, he does not give such answers?"

"Vaccha, wanderers of other sects regard the eye thus: 'This is mine, this I am, this is my self.' They regard the ear … the nose … the tongue … the body … the mind thus: 'This is mine, this I am, this is my self.' Therefore, when the wanderers of other sects are asked such questions, they give such answers as: 'The world is eternal' … or 'The Tathāgata neither exists nor does not exist after death.' But, Vaccha, the Tathāgata, the Arahant, the Perfectly Enlightened One, regards the eye thus: 'This is not mine, this I am not, this is not my self.' He regards the ear … the mind thus: 'This is not mine, this I am not, this is not my self.' Therefore, when the Tathāgata is asked such questions, he does not give such answers."

Then the wanderer Vacchagotta rose from his seat and approached the Blessed One. He exchanged greetings with the Blessed One ... and said to him:

"How is it, good Gotama, is the world eternal?"

(*All as above down to:*)

"Vaccha, I have not declared this either: 'The Tathāgata neither exists nor does not exist after death.'" [394]

"What, Master Gotama, is the cause and reason why, when wanderers of other sects are asked such questions, they give such answers as: 'The world is eternal' ... or 'The Tathāgata neither exists nor does not exist after death'? And what is the cause and reason why, when the ascetic Gotama is asked such questions, he does not give such answers?"

"Vaccha, wanderers of other sects regard the eye ... the mind thus: 'This is mine, this I am, this is my self.' Therefore, when the wanderers of other sects are asked such questions, they give such answers as: 'The world is eternal' ... or 'The Tathāgata neither exists nor does not exist after death.' But, Vaccha, the Tathāgata, the Arahant, the Perfectly Enlightened One, regards the eye ... the mind thus: 'This is not mine, this I am not, this is not my self.' Therefore, when the Tathāgata is asked such questions, he does not give such answers."

"It is wonderful, Master Gotama! It is amazing, Master Gotama! How the meaning and the phrasing of both teacher and disciple coincide and agree with each other and do not diverge, that is, in regard to the chief matter. Just now, Master Gotama, I approached the ascetic Moggallāna [395] and asked him about this matter. The ascetic Moggallāna explained this matter to me in exactly the same terms and phrases that Master Gotama used. It is wonderful, Master Gotama! It is amazing, Master Gotama! How the meaning and the phrasing of both teacher and disciple coincide and agree with each other and do not diverge, that is, in regard to the chief matter."

8 Vacchagotta

Then the wanderer Vacchagotta approached the Blessed One and exchanged greetings with him. When they had concluded their greetings and cordial talk, he sat down to one side and said to him:

"How is it, Master Gotama, is the world eternal?"... (*as above*) ...

"What, Master Gotama, is the cause and reason why, when wanderers of other sects are asked such questions, they give such answers as: 'The world is eternal' ... or 'The Tathāgata neither exists nor does not exist after death.' And what is the cause and reason why, when Master Gotama is asked such questions, he does not give such answers?"

"Vaccha, wanderers of other sects regard form as self, or self as possessing form, or form as in self, or self as in form. They regard feeling as self ... perception as self ... volitional formations as self ... consciousness as self, or self as possessing consciousness, or consciousness as in self, or self as in consciousness. Therefore, [396] when the wanderers of other sects are asked such questions, they give such answers as: 'The world is eternal' ... or 'The Tathāgata neither exists nor does not exist after death.' But, Vaccha, the Tathāgata, the Arahant, the Perfectly Enlightened One, does not regard form as self ... or self as in consciousness. Therefore, when the Tathāgata is asked such questions, he does not give such answers."

Then the wanderer Vacchagotta rose from his seat and approached the Venerable Mahāmoggallāna. He exchanged greetings with the Venerable Mahāmoggallāna ... and said to him:

"How is it, Master Moggallāna, is the world eternal?"

(*All as above down to:*)

"Vaccha, the Blessed One has not declared this either: 'The Tathāgata neither exists nor does not exist after death.'"

"What, Master Moggallāna, is the cause and reason why, when wanderers of other sects are asked such questions, they give such answers as: 'The world is eternal' ... or 'The Tathāgata neither exists nor does not exist after death'? And what is the cause and reason why when the ascetic Gotama is asked such questions, he does not give such answers?" [397]

"Vaccha, wanderers of other sects regard form as self ... or self as in consciousness. Therefore, when the wanderers of other sects are asked such questions, they give such answers as: 'The world is eternal' ... or 'The Tathāgata neither exists nor does not exist after death.' But, Vaccha, the Tathāgata, the Arahant, the Perfectly Enlightened One, does not regard form as self ... or self as in consciousness. Therefore, when the Tathāgata is asked such questions, he does not give such answers."

"It is wonderful, Master Moggallāna! It is amazing, Master Moggallāna! How the meaning and the phrasing of both teacher and disciple coincide and agree with each other and do not diverge, that is, in regard to the chief matter. Just now, Master Moggallāna, I approached the ascetic Gotama and asked him about this matter. The ascetic Gotama explained this matter to me in exactly the same terms and phrases that Master Moggallāna used. It is wonderful, Master Moggallāna! It is amazing, Master Moggallāna! How the meaning and the phrasing of both teacher and disciple coincide and agree with each other and do not diverge, that is, in regard to the chief matter." [398]

9 The Debating Hall

Then the wanderer Vacchagotta approached the Blessed One and exchanged greetings with him. When they had concluded their greetings and cordial talk, he sat down to one side and said to the Blessed One:

"In recent days, Master Gotama, a number of ascetics, brahmins, and wanderers of various sects had assembled in the debating hall and were sitting together when this conversation arose among them:[380] 'This Pūraṇa Kassapa—the leader of an order, the leader of a group, the teacher of a group, the well known and famous spiritual guide considered holy by many people—declares the rebirth of a disciple who has passed away and died thus: "That one was reborn there, that one was reborn there." And in the case of a disciple who was a person of the highest kind, a supreme person, one who had attained the supreme attainment, when that disciple has passed away and died he also declares his rebirth thus: "That one was reborn there, that one was reborn there." This Makkhali Gosāla ... This Nigaṇṭha Nātaputta ... This Sañjaya Belaṭṭhiputta ... This Pakudha Kaccāyana ... This Ajita Kesakambalī ... when that disciple has passed away [399] and died he also declares his rebirth thus: "That one was reborn there, that one was reborn there." This ascetic Gotama—the leader of an order, the leader of a group, the teacher of a group, the well known and famous spiritual guide considered holy by many people—declares the rebirth of a disciple who has passed away and died thus: "That one was reborn there, that one was reborn there." But in the case of a disciple who was a person of the highest kind, a supreme person, one who had attained the supreme attainment, when that disciple has passed away and died he does not declare his rebirth thus: "That one was reborn there, that one was reborn there." Rather, he declares of him: "He cut off craving, severed the fetter, and, by completely breaking through conceit, he has made an end to suffering."'

"There was perplexity in me, Master Gotama, there was doubt: 'How is the Dhamma of the ascetic Gotama to be understood?'"

"It is fitting for you to be perplexed, Vaccha, it is fitting for you to doubt. Doubt has arisen in you about a perplexing matter. I declare, Vaccha, rebirth for one with fuel, not for one without fuel. Just as a fire burns with fuel, but not without fuel, so, Vaccha, I declare rebirth for one with fuel, not for one without fuel."[381]

"Master Gotama, when a flame is flung by the wind and goes some distance, what does Master Gotama declare to be its fuel on that occasion?"

"When, Vaccha, a flame is flung by the wind and goes some distance, I declare that it is fuelled by the wind. For on that occasion the wind is its fuel." [400]

"And, Master Gotama, when a being has laid down this body but has not yet been reborn in another body, what does Master Gotama declare to be its fuel on that occasion?"

"When, Vaccha, a being has laid down this body but has not yet been reborn in another body, I declare that it is fuelled by craving.[382] For on that occasion craving is its fuel."

10 Ānanda (Is There a Self?)

Then the wanderer Vacchagotta approached the Blessed One ... and said to him:

"How is it now, Master Gotama, is there a self?"

When this was said, the Blessed One was silent.

"Then, Master Gotama, is there no self?"

A second time the Blessed One was silent.

Then the wanderer Vacchagotta rose from his seat and departed.

Then, not long after the wanderer Vacchagotta had left, the

Venerable Ānanda said to the Blessed One: "Why is it, venerable sir, that when the Blessed One was questioned by the wanderer Vacchagotta, he did not answer?"

"If, Ānanda, when I was asked by the wanderer Vacchagotta, 'Is there a self?' I had answered, 'There is a self,' this would have been siding with[383] those ascetics and brahmins who are eternalists. And if, when I was asked by him, 'Is there no self?' I had answered, 'There is no self,' [401] this would have been siding with those ascetics and brahmins who are annihilationists.

"If, Ānanda, when I was asked by the wanderer Vacchagotta, 'Is there a self?' I had answered, 'There is a self,' would this have been consistent on my part with the arising of the knowledge that 'all phenomena are nonself'?"[384]

"No, venerable sir."

"And if, when I was asked by him, 'Is there no self?' I had answered, 'There is no self,' the wanderer Vacchagotta, already confused, would have fallen into even greater confusion, thinking, 'It seems that the self I formerly had does not exist now.'"[385]

11 Sabhiya Kaccāna

On one occasion the Venerable Sabhiya Kaccāna was dwelling at Ñātika in the Brick Hall. Then the wanderer Vacchagotta approached the Venerable Sabhiya Kaccāna and exchanged greetings with him. When they had concluded their greetings and cordial talk, he sat down to one side and said to him:

"How is it, Master Kaccāna, does the Tathāgata exist after death?"

(*All as in §1 down to:*) [402]

"What then, Master Kaccāna, is the cause and reason why this has not been declared by the Blessed One?"

"Vaccha, as to the cause and condition for describing him as 'consisting of form' or as 'formless' or as 'percipient' or as 'nonpercipient' or as 'neither percipient nor nonpercipient': if that cause and condition were to cease completely and totally without remainder, in what way could one describe him as 'consisting of form' or as 'formless' or as 'percipient' or as 'nonpercipient' or as 'neither percipient nor nonpercipient'?"

"How long has it been since you went forth, Master Kaccāna?"

"Not long, friend. Three years."

"One, friend, who has gotten so much in such a time has indeed gotten much,[386] not to speak of one who has surpassed this!" [403]

The Book of the Six Sense Bases is finished.

Notes

35. Saḷāyatanasaṃyutta

1 The "internal" (*ajjhattika = adhi + atta + ika*) exclusively denotes the six sense faculties, and is contrasted with "external" (*bāhira*), which exclusively denotes the six sense objects (though according to the Abhidhamma, *dhammāyatana* denotes the objects of *manoviññāṇa* and the mental concomitants of all *viññāṇa*). Despite the similarity, the dyad *ajjhattika–bāhira* is *not* synonymous with the dyad *ajjhatta–bahiddhā;* the latter marks the distinction between what pertains to oneself and what is external to oneself. The sense faculties of other beings are *ajjhattika* but *bahiddhā,* while one's own pigmentation, voice, scent, etc., are *ajjhatta* but *bāhira.*

2 **35:1–22** are composed in accordance with templates met with earlier; see Concordance 3 for the correlations. In this saṃyutta, each template is instantiated twice, first with the internal bases, then with the external ones.

3 Spk distinguishes the different types of "eyes" referred to in the canon. These are first divided into two general classes: the eye of knowledge (*ñāṇacakkhu*) and the physical eye (*maṃsacakkhu*). The former is fivefold: (i) the *Buddha eye* (*buddhacakkhu*), the knowledge of the inclinations and underlying tendencies of beings, and the knowledge of the degree of maturity of their spiritual faculties; (ii) the *Dhamma eye* (*dhammacakkhu*), the knowledge of the three lower paths and fruits; (iii) the universal eye (*samantacakkhu*), the Buddha's knowledge of omniscience; (iv) the divine eye (*dibbacakkhu*), the knowledge arisen by suf-

fusion of light (which sees the passing away and rebirth of beings); and (v) the wisdom eye (*paññācakkhu*), the discernment of the Four Noble Truths. The physical eye is twofold: (i) the composite eye (*sasambhāracakkhu*), the physical eyeball; and (ii) the sensitive eye (*pasādacakkhu*), i.e., the sensitive substance in the visual apparatus that responds to forms (perhaps the retina and optic nerve). Here the Blessed One speaks of the sensitive eye as the "eye base." The ear, etc., should be similarly understood. Mind (*mano*) is the mind of the three planes, which is the domain of exploration with insight (*tebhūmakasammasanacāracitta*).

For the commentarial treatment of the sense bases, see Vism 444–46 (Ppn 14:36–53). Hamilton challenges the commentarial classification of the first five sense bases under the *rūpakkhandha*, arguing from the fact that the standard definition of the form aggregate in the suttas does not include them. In her view, the sense faculties are powers of perception partaking of both material and mental characteristics and thus unclassifiable exclusively under *rūpa* (*Identity and Experience*, pp. 14–22). By the same logic, however, it might be argued that the five external sense bases should not be assigned to the *rūpakkhandha*, for again the suttas do not place them there. The plain fact is that the correlations between the *khandhas*, *āyatanas*, and *dhātus* are not made explicit in the Nikāyas at all, but only in the Abhidhamma Piṭaka, which classifies both the first five internal and external sense bases under *rūpa*. The five faculties and four sense objects (excluding the tactile object) are categorized as "derivative form" (*upādā rūpa*), i.e., form derived from the four primary elements; the tactile object is classified under three of the primary elements: earth (hardness or softness), heat (hotness or coolness), and air (pressure and motion). The suttas themselves do not enumerate the types of derivative form, and the Abhidhamma texts seem to be filling in this lacuna.

4 Spk: *Mental phenomena*: the mental-phenomena object of the three planes (*dhammā ti tebhūmakadhammārammaṇaṃ*).

I render *dhammā* here as "mental phenomena" rather than as "mental object"—the standard rendering—in compliance with the idea, stressed in the Abhidhamma and the commentaries, that the *dhammāyatana* comprises not only the types of objects peculiar to the mind base (*manāyatana*), but also all the mental phenomena associated with consciousness of any type, that is, as including the associated feeling, perception, and volitional formations. See the definition of the *dhammāyatana* at Vibh 72, and the explanation at Vism 484 (Ppn 15:14). The three planes are the sensuous plane, the form plane, and the formless plane.

5 Spk: The "internalness" of the sense faculties should be understood as stemming from the strength of desire and lust for them. For people regard the six internal bases like the interior of a house, the six external bases like the house's vicinity. Just as the desire and lust of people are extremely strong in relation to what is inside the house and they don't let anyone unknown enter, so is it in relation to the six internal bases. But as people's desire and lust are not so strong in relation to the house's vicinity, and they don't forcibly prevent others from walking by, so is it in relation to the external sense bases.

6 Spk: The all (*sabba*) is fourfold: (i) the all-inclusive all (*sabbasabba*), i.e., everything knowable, all of which comes into range of the Buddha's knowledge of omniscience; (ii) the all of the sense bases (*āyatanasabba*), i.e., the phenomena of the four planes; (iii) the all of personal identity (*sakkāyasabba*), i.e., the phenomena of the three planes; and (iv) the partial all (*padesasabba*), i.e., the five physical sense objects. Each of these, from (i) to (iv), has a successively narrower range than its predecessor. In this sutta the all of the sense bases is intended.

The four planes are the three mundane planes (see **n. 4**) and the supramundane plane (the four paths, their fruits, and Nibbāna).

7 *Tassa vācāvatthur ev' assa*. Spk: It would be just a mere utterance. But if one passes over the twelve sense bases, one cannot point out any real phenomenon.

8 *Yathā taṃ bhikkhave avisayasmiṃ*. Spk: People become vexed when they go outside their domain. Just as it is outside one's domain to cross a deep body of water while carrying a stone palace on one's head, or to drag the sun and moon

off their course, and one would only meet with vexation if one makes the attempt, so too in this case.

9 It might seem that in adding factors of experience not enumerated among the twelve sense bases—namely, consciousness, contact, and feeling—the Buddha has just now violated his own decree that the "all" comprises everything. However, according to the Abhidhamma system, the factors mentioned here (and below) can be classified among the twelve bases. The six types of consciousness are included in the mind base (*manāyatana*). Mind (*mano*) as a separate factor, the supporting condition for mind-consciousness, then becomes narrower in scope than the mind base; according to the commentarial system it denotes the *bhavaṅgacitta* or subliminal life-continuum. Among the bases, contact and feeling are included in the base of mental phenomena (*dhammāyatana*), along with other mental concomitants and certain objects of mind-consciousness. Mind-consciousness itself, according to Spk, comprises the mind-door adverting consciousness (*manodvārāvajjanacitta*) and the javanas. On these technical terms from the Abhidhamma, see CMA 3:8–11.

10 *Sabbaṃ abhiññā pariññā pahānāya*. Spk glosses: *sabbaṃ abhijānitvā parijānitvā pajahanatthāya*. On the distinction between *abhiññā* and *pariññā*, see **III, n. 42**.

11 Spk: In this sutta the three kinds of full understanding are discussed: full understanding of the known, full understanding by scrutinization, and full understanding as abandonment. See **I, n. 36, III, n. 42**.

12 *Cakkhuviññāṇaviññātabbā dhammā*. Spk gives several alternative explanations to show how these might differ from *rūpā*: "He shows this, taking into account the same form taken in above (by the word *rūpā*); or else *rūpa* takes into account form that actually comes into range (of consciousness), while this denotes form that does not come into range. This is the decision here: Above (all form) is included, whether or not it comes into range, but here the three aggregates associated with consciousness are included, because they are to be cognized *along with* eye-consciousness. The same method applies to the remaining terms." This explanation seems to me contrived.

13 This sutta, often called "The Fire Sermon," is the third discourse of the Buddha as recorded in the narrative of his ministry at Vin I 34–35. According to this source, the thousand bhikkhus were former jaṭila (matted-hair) ascetics under the leadership of the three Kassapa brothers. The Buddha had converted them by a series of miracles, after which he preached the present sermon. The sermon gains special meaning from the fact that before their conversion these ascetics had been devoted to the fire sacrifice. The full account is at Vin I 24–34; see Ñāṇamoli, *Life of the Buddha*, pp. 54–60, 64–69.

Spk: Having led the thousand bhikkhus to Gayā's Head, the Blessed One reflected, "What kind of Dhamma talk would be suitable for them?" He then realized, "In the past they worshipped the fire morning and evening. I will teach them that the twelve sense bases are burning and blazing. In this way they will be able to attain arahantship." In this sutta the characteristic of suffering is discussed.

14 Se and Ee read *andhabhūtaṃ*, but I prefer Be *addhabhūtaṃ*, which Spk supports with its gloss: *Addhabhūtan ti adhibhūtaṃ ajjhotthaṭaṃ, upaddutan ti attho*; "*weighed down*: overcome, overloaded, meaning oppressed." See **I, v. 203** and **I, n. 121**; **22:1** (III 1,20) and **III, n. 3**. Norman explains that *addhabhūta* might have developed from the aorist *addhabhavi* = *ajjhabhavi* (< **adhy-a-bhavi*). Once the origin of the aorist was no longer understood, the verb was assumed to be *addhabhavati* with a past participle *addhabhūta*; see GD, p. 356, n. 968.

15 *Sabbamaññitasamugghātasāruppaṃ paṭipadaṃ*. "Conceiving" (*maññanā*) is the distortional thought process governed by craving, conceit, and views; the notions that arise from such modes of thought are also called conceivings (with the past participle *maññita*). They include the ideas "I am," "I am this," and all other notions derived from these root errors; see **35:248** (IV 202,18–27). The most extensive survey of conceiving is the Mūlapariyāya Sutta (MN No. 1); see Bodhi, *Discourse on the Root of Existence*, for a translation of the sutta and its commentary.

16 This fourfold pattern of conceiving also underlies the Mūlapariyāya Sutta, though the latter does not apply the pattern explicitly to the sense bases.

Spk: *He does not conceive the eye* (*cakkhuṃ na maññati*): He does not conceive the eye as "I" or "mine," or as "another" or "another's." *He does not conceive in the eye* (*cakkhusmiṃ na maññati*): He does not conceive, "I am in the eye, my appurtenances are in the eye; another is in the eye, another's appurtenances are in the eye." *He does not conceive from the eye* (*cakkhuto na maññati*): He does not conceive, "I have emerged from the eye, my appurtenances have emerged from the eye; another has emerged from the eye, another's appurtenances have emerged from the eye." He does not arouse even one of the conceivings of craving, conceit, or views.

17 See **I, n. 376** and **II, n. 137**. Spk: In this sutta, insight culminating in arahantship is discussed in forty-four cases. Spk-pṭ: In the eye door there are seven items: eye, forms, eye-consciousness, eye-contact, and pleasant, painful, and neutral feeling. So too in the other five doors, making forty-two. The passage on "not conceiving the all" makes forty-three, and the phrase "he does not cling to anything in the world" brings the total to forty-four.

18 *Sabbamaññitasamugghātasappāyapaṭipadā.*

19 *Tato taṃ hoti aññathā; aññathābhāvī bhavasatto loko bhavam ev' ābhinandati.* There seems to be a word play here revolving around the two ideas of "being/becoming otherwise." According to Spk, the first sentence asserts that the object exists in a different mode (*aññen' ākārena hoti*) from that in which it is conceived [Spk-pṭ: the object conceived in the mode of permanence actually exists in the mode of impermanence, etc.]. In the second sentence, I take *aññathābhāvī* to mean "undergoing alteration," i.e., becoming other than it was before. As Spk explains, "It is becoming otherwise by arriving at alteration, at change" (*aññathābhāvaṃ vipariṇāmaṃ upagamanena aññathābhāvī hutvā*). In the expression *bhavasatto, satto* is the past participle of *sajjati,* glossed *laggo, laggito, paḷibuddho*. See in this connection Ud 32,29–32 (where the text should be corrected to *bhavasatto*), Sn 756–57, and MN III 42,28–29. Here "world" (*loko*) is obviously intended in the sense of *sattaloka,* "the world of beings."

20 Spk: In this sutta, insight culminating in arahantship is dis-

cussed in forty-eight cases. Spk-pṭ: The "that is otherwise" passage should be added to each section, making eight items per section. Thus there are forty-eight cases. (Spk-pṭ does not explain why the combined passage on the aggregates, etc., and the phrase "he does not cling ..." could not be counted separately to give a total of fifty cases, which would correspond to the method adopted in the preceding sutta.)

21 Spk: It is also abandoned for one who knows and sees by way of suffering and nonself, but impermanence is stated out of consideration for the inclination of the person being instructed.

22 On the ten fetters (*saṃyojana*), see **45:179–80**.

23 On the three taints (*āsava*), see **38:8**, **45:163**; for the seven underlying tendencies (*anusaya*), see **45:175**.

24 For the four kinds of clinging (*upādāna*), see **12:2**, **45:173**; for the three kinds of full understanding (*pariññā*), see **n. 11** above. Spk paraphrases: "For the full understanding of all four kinds of clinging by the three kinds of full understanding."

25 *Vimokkhā*. An unusual construction. One would have expected *vimuttiyā,* the noun more directly related to *vimuccati*.

26 He was the son of Visākhā, the chief patroness of the Saṅgha. His verses are at Th 417–22.

27 *Ekavihārī ekavihārī*. Cp. **21:10**.

28 *Sadutiyavihārī*. *Dutiya,* lit. "a second," often signifies a spouse.

29 See **1:20**, **4:22**.

30 *Māro vā assa mārapaññatti vā*. Spk: By "Māra" he asks about death (*maraṇa*); "the description of Māra" is the description, name, appellation "Māra." Cp. **23:11–12**.

31 Upasena was Sāriputta's younger brother. His verses are at Th 577–86. Spk explains that the grotto was called "Snake's Hood Grotto" (*sappasoṇḍikapabbhāra*) because of its shape.

32 Spk: After his meal the elder had taken his large robe and was sitting in the shade of the cave doing some sewing. At that moment two young vipers were playing in the thatch over the cave; one fell and landed on the elder's shoulder. Its mere touch was poisonous, and the poison spread over

the elder's body. He addressed the bhikkhus thus so that his body would not perish inside the cave.

33 There is a word play in the exchange between Sāriputta and Upasena. The expression *indriyānaṃ aññathatta,* "alteration of the faculties," is sometimes used as a euphemism meaning "profoundly distressed," "not in one's right mind" (see MN II 106,12). Here the text reads *kāyassa vā aññathattaṃ indriyānaṃ vā vipariṇāmaṃ,* but I think the implications are very similar. Sāriputta, then, is speaking literally while Upasena intends his words to be taken figuratively, as meaning that for one free from the notions of "I" and "mine" there is no distress even in the face of death. On being free from "I-making," etc., see **21:2** (II 275,1–5) and **II, n. 340**.

34 *Sandiṭṭhiko dhammo.* What follows is the standard formula for reflection on the Dhamma, minus only the first term, *svākkhāto;* see **I, n. 33**. Upavāṇa was the Buddha's attendant when he was suffering from a wind ailment; see **7:13**.

35 Spk says that this sutta discusses the reflections of the trainee (in the first part) and of the arahant (in the second part).

36 Be: *anassasaṃ;* Se and Ee: *anassāsiṃ.* This is the first person aorist of *nassati.* Spk glosses: *naṭṭho nāma ahaṃ.*

37 *Āyatiṃ apunabbhavāya.* Spk: Here, "no future renewed existence" is Nibbāna. The meaning is, "It will be abandoned by you for the sake of Nibbāna."

38 See **III, n. 167**. The sequel is also at **22:87**.

39 *Rāgavirāgatthaṃ.* The sense of the expression is almost reiterative, since *virāga* itself means the absence of *rāga* or lust. But *virāga* originally meant the removal of colour, and thus the whole expression could be taken to mean the "fading away" of the "colour" spread by lust.

40 The arising of the vision of the Dhamma (*dhammacakkhu*) means the attainment of one of the three lower stages of awakening, usually stream-entry.

41 *Anupādāparinibbānatthaṃ.* Here there is a double entendre, for the Pāli *upādā* (or *upādāna*) means both clinging and fuel, so the goal of the Dhamma can also be understood as "the quenching (of a fire) through lack of fuel." The fire, of course, is the threefold fire of lust, hatred, and delusion (see

35:28). Ee omits the next paragraph on the assumption that it is identical with the corresponding section of the preceding sutta, and Woodward follows suit at KS 4:25. This is not the case, however, in Be and Se. The preceding sutta mentions only the six internal bases, but this one enumerates all the phenomena that originate through each sense base. This may explain (at least in part) why the bhikkhu here attained arahantship, while the bhikkhu in the preceding sutta gained only the vision of the Dhamma.

42 Though it may sound redundant to say that ignorance must be abandoned in order to abandon ignorance, this statement underscores the fact that ignorance is the most fundamental cause of bondage, which must be eliminated to eliminate all the other bonds.

43 The first part of this instruction, as far as "he fully understands everything," is included in the "brief advice on liberation through the extinction of craving" at MN I 251,21–25 and AN IV 88,11–15; the sequel is different. Spk: "He sees all signs differently" (*sabbanimittāni aññato passati*): He sees all the signs of formations (*saṅkhāranimittāni*) in a way different from that of people who have not fully understood the adherences. For such people see all signs as self, but one who has fully understood the adherences sees them as nonself, not as self. Thus in this sutta the characteristic of nonself is discussed.

44 See **II, n. 72**.

45 *Lujjatī ti kho bhikkhu tasmā loko ti vuccati.* On the playful didactic attempt to derive *loka* from *lujjati*, see **III, n. 186**. On the six sense bases as "the world," see **35:116**.

46 Spk explains *chinnapapañca*, "cut through proliferation," as referring to "the proliferation of craving," and *chinnavaṭuma*, "cut through the rut," as referring to "the rut of craving." The meaning of the question seems to be: Do the Buddhas of the past, on attaining the Nibbāna element without residue, still retain the six sense faculties?

47 *Yaṃ kho Ānanda palokadhammaṃ ayaṃ vuccati ariyassa vinaye loko. Paloka* is from *palujjati*, "to disintegrate," an augmented form of *lujjati*, and has no etymological connection with *loka*, world; see **35:82** just above.

48 The sutta is also at MN No. 144, entitled the Channovāda

Sutta. Obviously, this Channa is different from the one who appears at **22:90**.

49 What follows is the stock description of unbearable pain.

50 *Satthaṃ āharissāmi*. An expression for committing suicide.

51 *Anupavajjaṃ Channo bhikkhu satthaṃ āharissati*. By this he seems to be insinuating that he is an arahant. Spk glosses "blamelessly" (*anupavajjaṃ*) with "without continued existence, without rebirth (*appavattikaṃ appaṭisandhikaṃ*)."

52 Spk: Channa replied to Sāriputta's questions by ascribing arahantship to himself, but Sāriputta, while knowing that he was still a worldling, just kept quiet. Mahācunda, however, gave him an exhortation to convince him of this.

53 This "teaching of the Blessed One" is at Ud 81,6–10. Spk explains the connection between the teaching and the present situation thus: *For one who is dependent* (*nissitassa*): "dependent" on account of craving, conceit, and views; *there is wavering* (*calitaṃ*): palpitation. As Channa is unable to endure the arisen pain, there is now the palpitation of one who isn't free from the grip of such thoughts as "I am in pain, the pain is mine." By this, he is telling him, "You're still a worldling." *No inclination* (*nati*): no inclination of craving. *No coming* by way of rebirth, *no going* by way of death. *This itself is the end of suffering*: this itself is the end, the termination, the limit, of the suffering of defilements and of the suffering of the round. As to those who argue that the phrase "in between the two" (*ubhayamantarena*) implies an intermediate state (*antarābhava*), their statement is nonsense, for the existence of an intermediate state is rejected in the Abhidhamma. Therefore the meaning is: "Neither here, nor there, nor both—the other alternative."

Though the Theravāda Abhidhamma (see Kvu 362–66) and the commentaries argue against the existence of an *antarābhava*, a number of canonical texts seem to support this notion. See below **n. 382**, and **V, n. 65**.

54 Spk: He cut his jugular vein and just then the fear of death entered him. As the sign of his rebirth destiny appeared, he realized he was still a worldling and his mind became agitated. He set up insight, discerned the formations, and reaching arahantship, he attained final Nibbāna as a "same-header" (*samasīsī*; see **I, n. 312**).

55 Spk: Although this declaration (of blamelessness) was made while Channa was still a worldling, as his attainment of final Nibbāna followed immediately, the Buddha answered by referring to that very declaration.

It should be noted that this commentarial interpretation is imposed on the text from the outside, as it were. If one sticks to the actual wording of the text it seems that Channa was already an arahant when he made his declaration, the dramatic punch being delivered by the failure of his two brother-monks to recognize this. The implication, of course, is that excruciating pain might motivate even an arahant to take his own life—not from aversion but simply from a wish to be free from unbearable pain.

56 The name of the village differs slightly among the various eds.; I follow Ee here. I take *mittakulāni suhajjakulāni upavajjakulāni*—the terms used to describe the lay families that supported the Venerable Channa—to be synonyms. The third term gives the opportunity for a word play. Spk glosses it as *upasaṅkamitabbakulāni*, "families to be approached" (that is, for his requisites). According to CPD, *upavajja* here represents Skt *upavrajya*; the word in this sense is not in PED, though this may be the only instance where it bears such a meaning. The word is homonymous with another word meaning "blameworthy," representing Skt *upavadya*, thus linking up with Channa's earlier avowal that he would kill himself blamelessly (*anupavajja*). See the following note.

57 When the Buddha speaks about the conditions under which one is blameworthy (*sa-upavajja*), *upavajja* represents *upavadya*. Though earlier Spk explained the correct sense of *upavajjakulāni*, here the commentator seems oblivious to the pun and comments as if Channa had actually been at fault for associating too closely with lay people: "The Elder Sāriputta, showing the fault of intimacy with families (*kulasaṃsaggadosa*) in the preliminary stage of practice, asks: 'When that bhikkhu had such supporters, could he have attained final Nibbāna?' The Blessed One answers showing that he was not intimate with families." For intimacy with families as a fault in monks, see **9:7**, **16:3**, **16:4**, **20:9**, **20:10**.

58 Also at MN No. 145, entitled Puṇṇovāda Sutta; the opening and closing paragraphs of the two versions are slightly different. According to Spk, Puṇṇa had been a merchant from the Sunāparanta country who came to Sāvatthī on business. Hearing the Buddha preach, he decided to become a bhikkhu. After his ordination he found the area around Sāvatthī uncongenial to his meditation and wished to return to his home country to continue his practice. He approached the Buddha to obtain guidance before departing. For biographical details, see DPPN 2:220–21. Sunāparanta was on the west coast of India. Its capital was Suppāraka, modern Sopāra in the district of Thāna near modern Mumbai.

59 See **54:9**.

60 See **I, n. 650**.

61 Ee omits *ten' ev' antaravassena pañcamattāni upāsikāsatāni paṭipādesi*, found in Be and Se (but in the latter with the verb *paṭivedesi*). At MN III 269,28–29 it is said that he attained final Nibbāna "at a later time" (*aparena samayena*), without specifying that this occurred during the same rains.

62 Spk: *Stirring* (*ejā*) is craving, so called in the sense of moving (*calanaṭṭhena*). *Anejā*, "unstirred," is a common description of an arahant.

63 As at **35:30**; see **n. 16**.

64 As at **35:31**; see **n. 19**.

65 As at **35:23**; see **n. 8**.

66 I read with Be *calañ c' eva byathañ ca*. Se and Ee read *vyayañ* in place of *byathañ*, but Be seems to have the support of Spk and Spk-pṭ. Spk (Be): *Calañ c' eva byathañ cā ti attano sabhāvena asaṇṭhahanato calati c' eva byathati ca*; "*Moving and tottering*: it moves and totters because it does not remain stable in its own nature." (Spk (Se) is the same, but with the v.l. *asaṃvahanato*.) Spk-pṭ: *Byathatī ti jarāya maraṇena ca pavedhati*; "[*It*] *totters*: it trembles because of aging and death." See too MW, s.v. *vyath*, to tremble, waver, come to naught, fail.

67 *Phuṭṭho bhikkhave vedeti phuṭṭho ceteti phuṭṭho sañjānāti*. This shows the three aggregates of feeling, volitional formations, and perception respectively. Thus in regard to each

physical sense base, all five aggregates are introduced: the sense base and its object belong to the aggregate of form; the corresponding consciousness to the aggregate of consciousness; and the other three aggregates arise from contact. In the case of the mind base, the physical basis of mind (*vatthurūpa*) and, in certain cases, the object are the form aggregate.

68 The title follows Be. In Se this sutta is called *Cha phassāyatana*, "The Six Bases for Contact," and in Ee this sutta and the next are called *Saṅgayha*, "Including," i.e., including verses.

69 *Dukkhādhivāhā*. Spk: They are bringers (*āvahanakā*) of extreme suffering (*adhidukkha*), classified as infernal, etc.

70 *Sukhādhivāhā*. Spk: They are bringers of extreme happiness, classified as jhāna, path, and fruit.

71 Pāda a reads, *papañcasaññā itarītarā narā*, on which Spk comments: "Common beings become 'of proliferated perception' on account of defiled perception (*kilesasaññāya*)." On how "perceptions and notions affected by proliferation" arise and obsess a person, see MN I 111,35–112,13. *Papañca* is explained by the commentaries as of threefold origin: through craving, conceit, and views (*taṇhā, māna, diṭṭhi*) in their capacity to cause mental distortion and obsession. "Proliferated perception" might be interpreted as the distorted perception of permanence, pleasure, self, and beauty in relation to what is really impermanent, suffering, nonself, and foul (see the treatment of *saññāvipallāsa* at AN II 52). Such distorted perception is caused by the proliferating defilements.

"Mind-state" renders *manomaya*, an adjective meaning "mind-made," with the qualified noun left implicit. Spk glosses the second couplet thus: "Having dispelled every mind-made thought (*manomayaṃ vitakkaṃ*) connected to the 'home life' of the five cords of sensual pleasure, a competent bhikkhu travels on [the way] bound up with renunciation." The contrast between worldly pleasure and the pleasure of renunciation is developed at MN III 217,13–218,6.

72 Māluṅkyaputta appears at MN Nos. 63 and 64. His verses here are also at Th 794–817. See too AN II 248–49, where he again requests a teaching in his old age. Spk explains that

in his youth he had been negligent and had dallied with sensual pleasures; now in his old age he wanted to dwell in the forest and practise meditation.

73 Spk: The Blessed One speaks thus both to reproach him and to extol him. He reproaches him for putting off the work of an ascetic until old age, and extols him in order to set an example for the younger monks.

74 Spk explains *adiṭṭhā adiṭṭhapubbā* as respectively "not seen in this existence" and "never seen before" in the past. An illustration can be found at **42:11** (IV 329,20–22).

75 The same advice is given to the ascetic Bāhiya Dārucīriya at Ud 8,5–12. The meaning is extremely compressed and in places the passage seems to defy standard grammar (e.g., by treating *na tena* and *na tattha* as nominative predicates). Spk gives a long explanation, which I translate here partly abridged:

In the form base, i.e., in what is seen by eye-consciousness, "there will be merely the seen." For eye-consciousness sees only form in form, not some essence that is permanent, etc. So too for the remaining types of consciousness [Spk-pṭ: i.e., for the *javanas*], there will be here merely the seen. Or alternatively: What is called "the seen in the seen" is eye-consciousness, which means the cognizing of form in form. "Merely" indicates the limit (*mattā ti pamāṇaṃ*). It has merely the seen; thus "merely the seen," (an attribute of) the mind. The meaning is: "My mind will be just a mere eye-consciousness." This is what is meant: As eye-consciousness is not affected by lust, hatred, or delusion in relation to a form that has come into range, so the *javana* will be just like a mere eye-consciousness by being destitute of lust, etc. I will set up the *javana* with just eye-consciousness as the limit. I will not go beyond the limit and allow the mind to arise by way of lust, etc. So too for the heard and the sensed. The "cognized" is the object cognized by mind-door adverting (*manodvārāvajjana*). In that cognized, "merely the cognized" is the adverting (consciousness) as the limit. As one does not become lustful, etc., by adverting, so I will set up my mind with adverting as the limit, not allowing it to arise by way of lust, etc. *You will not be "by that" (na tena)*: you will not be aroused *by that* lust, or irritated *by that* hatred, or deluded *by that* delusion. *Then you will not be "therein" (na tattha)*: When you are not aroused by that lust, etc., then "you will not be therein"—bound, attached, established in what is seen, heard, sensed, and cognized.

Spk's explanation of "neither here nor beyond nor in between the two" is the same as that summed up in **n. 53** above, again proposed to avoid having to admit an intermediate state.

The verses that follow are intended to explicate the Buddha's brief dictum. From these, it seems that to go beyond "merely the seen" is to ascribe a pleasing sign (*piyanimitta*)—an attractive attribute—to the objects seen, heard, etc., and from this such defilements as attraction and annoyance result.

76 We should read: *cittam ass' ūpahaññati.*

77 *Khīyati no pacīyati.* No subject is provided, but Spk suggests both suffering and the various defilements would be appropriate.

78 *Parihānadhamma.*

79 *Sarasaṅkappā saṃyojaniyā.* Spk derives *sara* from *saranti*, to run (glossed *dhavanti*), but I take it to be from the homonym meaning "to remember" (which is also the basis of the noun *sati*, meaning both memory and mindfulness).

80 *Cha abhibhāyatanāni.* Spk glosses with *abhibhavitāni āyatanāni.* These are altogether different from the *aṭṭha abhibhāyatanāni*, the eight bases of mastery (mentioned at DN II 110–11, MN II 13–14, etc.).

81 *Byāsiñcati*, lit. "sprinkled with." Spk: It occurs tinted by defilements (*kilesatintaṃ hutvā vattati*).

82 Reading *dukkhaṃ viharati* with Se and Ee, as against Be *dukkhaṃ hoti.*

83 *Dhammā na pātubhavanti.* Spk takes this to mean that the states of serenity and insight (*samatha-vipassanā dhammā*) do not become manifest, but I think the point is that the internal and external sense bases (the *dhammā*) do not appear as impermanent, suffering, and nonself; see **35:99** just below.

84 This sutta and the next parallel **22:5–6**. See **III, n. 31**.

85 This sutta and the next parallel **22:33–34**. See **III, n. 46**.

86 Uddaka Rāmaputta was the Buddha's second teacher when he was engaged in his quest for enlightenment; see MN I 165–66. In the declaration the reference of the pronoun *idaṃ*, "this," occurring thrice, is unclear. Spk says it is a mere indeclinable (*nipātamatta*), but adds that it might represent "this statement" (*idaṃ vacanaṃ*). Perhaps it should be connected with *gaṇḍamūlaṃ*, though this is uncertain. *Vedagū* is a common brahmanical epithet adopted by the Buddha as a description of the arahant. *Sabbajī*, "all-conqueror," is glossed as "one who has definitely conquered and overcome the entire round." Ee *palikhataṃ* should be corrected to *apalikhataṃ*, as in Be and Se.

87 A stock description of the body, in SN found also at **35:245** and **41:5**. Spk explains rubbing (*ucchādana*) as the application of scents and ointments to remove its bad smell, and pressing (*parimaddana*) as massaging with water to dispel affliction in the limbs. The entire description shows, in stages, the origination, growth, decline, and destruction of the body.

88 *Yogakkhemīpariyāyaṃ*. My verbose rendering of the expression is intended to capture the word play hidden in the expository section (see following note). *Yogakkhema* is often a synonym for arahantship or Nibbāna, explained by the commentators as security or release from the four bonds (*yoga*) of sensual desire, existence, ignorance, and views.

89 There is a pun here, impossible to replicate, based on a twofold derivation of *yogakkhemī*. Properly, the latter is a personalized form of the abstract *yogakkhema*, meaning one secure from bondage. Besides meaning bond, however, *yoga* can also mean effort or exertion, a meaning relevant to the preceding sentence: *tesañ ca pahānāya akkhāsi yogaṃ*. Phonetically, this seems to connect the verb *akkhāsi* (via the root *khā*) to *khemī*, though they have no etymological relation at all. Thus *yogakkhemī* can mean either "one secure from bondage" (the true meaning) or "the declarer of effort" (the contrived meaning conveyed by the pun). Spk says that one is called *yogakkhemī*, not merely because one declares (the effort), but because one has abandoned (desire and lust).

90 Cp. **22:150**, and see **III, n. 146**.

91 These are the three modes of conceit; see **22:49**.

92 This sutta and the next parallel **22:120–21**.

93 This sutta and the next closely resemble **35:26**.

94 Be's orthography is preferable here: *paṭimukk' assa mārapāso* (and just below, *ummukk' assa mārapāso*). Spk: Māra's snare is fastened to, wound around, his neck. Cp. It 56,15–21.

95 The bracketed words here and below are in Be only.

96 See **2:26** (= AN II 47–49), to which this sutta might be taken as a commentary.

97 What follows is stock, found also at MN I 110–11, MN III 223–25, and elsewhere. Spk explains that the Buddha retired to his dwelling because he had foreseen that the bhikkhus would approach Ānanda, and that Ānanda would give a proper answer that would win praise from himself. The bhikkhus would then esteem Ānanda and this would promote their welfare and happiness for a long time.

98 *Yena kho āvuso lokasmiṃ lokasaññī hoti lokamānī ayaṃ vuccati ariyassa vinaye loko.* On the implications of this, see **2:26** and **I, n. 182**.

99 On the six sense bases as "the world" in the sense of disintegrating, see **35:82**. Here they are called the world because they are the conditions for being a perceiver and a conceiver of the world. We might conjecture that the five physical sense bases are prominent in making one a "perceiver of the world," the mind base in making one a "conceiver of the world." No such distinction, however, is made in the text. The six sense bases are at once part of the world ("that in the world") and the media for the manifestation of a world ("that by which"). The "end of the world" that must be reached to make an end to suffering is Nibbāna, which is called (among other things) the cessation of the six sense bases.

100 *Cetaso samphuṭṭhapubbā*, glossed by Spk with *cittena anubhūtapubbā*, "experienced before by the mind."

Spk: *My mind may often stray* (*tatra me cittaṃ bahulaṃ gaccheyya*): He shows, "On many occasions it would move towards the five cords of sensual pleasure previously experienced when I was enjoying prosperity in the three palaces with their three kinds of dancing girls, etc." *Or towards those that are present* (*paccuppannesu vā*): He shows, "During my years of striving it would often arise having taken, as cords of sensual pleasure, such beautiful sense objects as the flowering groves and flocks of birds, etc." *Or slightly towards those in the future* (*appaṃ vā anāgatesu*): He shows, "It might arise even slightly towards the future, when he thinks, 'Metteyya will be the Buddha, Saṅkha the king, Ketumatī the capital.'" Apparently Spk cannot conceive of beautiful future sense objects apart from a future Buddha.

101 *Attarūpena.* Spk: *Attano hitakāmajātikena,* "by one who desires his own welfare." The expression also occurs at AN II 120,7 foll. Spk explains that diligence and mindfulness are to be practised *for the purpose of* guarding the mind in regard to the five cords of sensual pleasures.

102 Be and Se read *se āyatane veditabbe*—supported by Spk (Be and Se)—as against *ye āyatane veditabbe* in Ee. This is apparently an old Eastern form of the neuter nominative that for some reason escaped transposition into standard Pāli.

Spk: "Since diligence and mindfulness are to be practised for the sake of guarding the mind, and since, when that base is understood, there is nothing to be done by diligence and mindfulness, therefore 'that base is to be understood'; the meaning is, 'that cause is to be known' (*taṃ kāraṇaṃ jānitabbaṃ*)." At Ud 80,10–16, Nibbāna is described as an *āyatana.*

103 I read with Se and Ee: *yattha cakkhuñ ca nirujjhati rūpasaññā ca virajjati.* Be consistently has the second verb too as *nirujjhati,* but the variant in Se and Ee is more likely to be original.

104 *Saḷāyatananirodhaṃ … sandhāya bhāsitaṃ.* Spk: "It is Nibbāna that is called the cessation of the six sense bases, for in Nibbāna the eye, etc., cease and perceptions of forms, etc., fade away." We might note that Ānanda's answer, though called an account of the "detailed meaning," is actually shorter than the Buddha's original statement.

105 *Sa-upādāno … bhikkhu no parinibbāyati.* To bring out the implicit metaphor, the line might also have been rendered, "A bhikkhu with fuel is not fully quenched."

106 Pañcasikha appears in DN No. 21 as a celestial musician and poet.

107 For a detailed analysis, see Vism 20–22 (Ppn 1:53–59).

108 See Vism 31–33 (Ppn 1:89–94).

109 Identical with MN No. 147.

110 *Vimuttiparipācaniyā dhammā*. Spk interprets these as the fifteen qualities that purify the five faculties (faith, energy, mindfulness, concentration, and wisdom), namely, in regard to each faculty: avoiding people who lack the faculty, associating with those endowed with it, and reflecting on suttas that inspire its maturation. Spk expands on this with another fifteen qualities: the five faculties again; the five perceptions partaking of penetration, namely, perception of impermanence, suffering, nonself, abandoning, and dispassion (on the last two, see AN V 110,13–20); and the five qualities taught to Meghiya, namely, noble friendship, the virtue of the monastic rules, suitable conversation, energy, and wisdom (see AN IV 357,5–30; Ud 36,3–28).

111 Spk: These devas had made their aspiration (for enlightenment) along with Rāhula when the latter made his aspiration (to become the son of a Buddha) at the feet of the Buddha Padumuttara. They had been reborn in various heavenly worlds but on this day they all assembled in the Blind Men's Grove.

112 Spk: In this sutta "the vision of the Dhamma" denotes the four paths and their fruits. For some devas became stream-enterers, some once-returners, some nonreturners, and some arahants. The devas were innumerable.

113 At AN I 26,11 he is declared the foremost male lay disciple among those who offer agreeable things (*etadaggaṃ manāpadāyakānaṃ*); see too AN IV 208–12.

114 At AN I 26,12 he is declared the foremost of those who attend on the Saṅgha (*etadaggaṃ saṅgh' upaṭṭhākānaṃ*); see too AN IV 212–16.

115 For the story of his conversion, see MN No. 56.

116 At AN I 23,25 he is declared the foremost of those who sound a lion's roar (*etadaggaṃ sīhanādikānaṃ*). His declaration of arahantship is at **48:49**; see too Vin II 111–12.

117 He was the king of Kosambī; for details of his story, see Dhp-a I 161–227; BL 1:247–93. Spk: One day the king had gone to his park and was lying down while some of his concubines massaged his feet and others entertained him

with music and song. When he dozed off the women left him to take a walk around the park. They saw the Venerable Bhāradvāja meditating under a tree and approached him to pay their respects. Meanwhile the king awoke and, seeing his concubines sitting around the ascetic, he became furious and tried to attack the elder with a nest of biting ants. His plan backfired and the ants fell over him and bit him all over. The women reproached him for his rude conduct and he became repentant. On the next occasion when the elder came to the park, the king approached him and asked his questions.

118 *Addhānaṃ āpādenti.* Spk glosses: *paveṇiṃ paṭipādenti; dīgharattaṃ anubandhāpenti;* "they extend it continuously; they pursue it for a long time."

119 *Mātumattīsu mātucittaṃ upaṭṭhapetha.* Lit. "Set up a mother-mind towards those of a mother-measure," and similarly with the other two. Spk says that one's mother, sisters, and daughters are the three "respected objects" (*garukārammaṇa*) who are not to be transgressed against. Interestingly, this saying, though ascribed to the Buddha as if it were a common piece of advice, is not found elsewhere in the Nikāyas.

120 This is the meditation subject called *asubhasaññā*, perception of foulness (e.g., at AN V 109,18–27), or *kāyagatāsati*, explained in detail at Vism 239–66 (Ppn 8:42–144).

121 *Abhāvitakāyā.* Spk: Undeveloped in the "body" of the five (sense) doors (*abhāvitapañcadvārikakāyā*), i.e., lacking in sense restraint.

122 *Dhātunānatta.* See **14:1–10**. For each sense modality there are three elements—sense faculty, object, and consciousness—hence a total of eighteen.

123 Spk: *In dependence on a contact to be experienced as pleasant*: that is, a contact associated with eye-consciousness that functions as a condition, by way of decisive support (*upanissaya*), for a pleasant feeling in the *javana* phase. The pleasant feeling arises in the *javana* phase in dependence on a single contact. The same method in the following passages.

124 As at **22:3–4**.

125 The quote is from **14:4**.

126 *Manāpaṃ itth' etan ti pajānāti.* Spk: He understands the agreeable form seen by him thus, "Such it is," that is, "This is just an agreeable one."

127 I read with Be and Se, *Cakkhuviññāṇaṃ sukhavedanīyañ ca phassaṃ paṭicca...*, which seems preferable to Ee, *Cakkhuviññāṇaṃ sukhavedaniyaṃ. Sukhavedaniyaṃ phassaṃ paṭicca....* It is unclear whether *cakkhuviññāṇaṃ* is being listed as an additional element or is intended merely as a condition for the feeling. I follow Spk in taking it in the former sense: "(There is) eye-consciousness, and a contact which is a condition for pleasant feeling under the heading of decisive support, proximity, contiguity, or association (see Vism 532–41; Ppn 17:66–100). In dependence on that contact to be experienced as pleasant, there arises a pleasant feeling."

128 See **22:1** and **III, n. 1**.

129 Be: *Seleyyakāni karonti;* Se: *selissakāni karontā;* Ee: *selissakāni karonti.* Spk's explanation suggests the games were like our "leapfrog," i.e., one boy jumping over the back of another.

130 The first four terms are a stock brahmanical denigration of ascetics. *Bandhupādāpaccā* alludes to the brahmin idea that Brahmā created ascetics from the soles of his feet (below even the suddas, who were created from his knees, while the brahmins were created from his mouth). Spk glosses *bharataka* as *kuṭumbikā*, "landholders," though I think it is a derogatory term for the Buddhist lay supporters.

131 Spk: They took delight in Dhamma, namely, in the ten courses of wholesome action, and in meditation (*jhāna*), i.e., in the meditations of the eight attainments.

132 *Katā kiñcikkhabhāvanā.* The exact meaning is obscure, but I translate in accordance with the gloss of Spk: *āmisakiñcikkhassa vaḍḍhanatthāya katan ti attho,* "done for the sake of an increase in their material possessions."

133 One is intent upon (*adhimuccati*) an object by way of greed, repelled by it (*byāpajjati*) by way of ill will or aversion.

134 *Amhākaṃ ācariyabhariyāya.* This might have been taken to mean "our teacher's wife" (a widow), but CPD, s.v. *ācariyabhariyā*, says with reference to this text: "dealing with a female teacher, the meaning becomes: our mistress the teacher." Above, the youth was described as a student

(*antevāsī*) of this brahmin lady. Waldschmidt has published a Skt version of this sutta (see Bibliography).

135 Be and Se read *onītapattapāṇiṃ*, but Ee has *oṇitapattapāṇiṃ* here and *oṇitapattapāṇiṃ* just below; at **41:2–4**, where the nominative plural occurs, all three read *onītapattapāṇino* (see **n. 290**), though vv.ll. *oṇīta-* and even *oṇitta-* are found. Norman, who discusses the expression at length (GD, pp. 257–58, and *Collected Papers* 2:123–24), explains the construction here as an accusative absolute. He maintains that the form of the compound requires that the initial past participle should apply to both the hand and the bowl and suggests that *onīta-* is from Skt *ava-nī*, "to put or bring (into water)." Thus in his view the compound means "having put hands and bowl into water" in order to wash them. At an alms offering, however, the Buddhist monk does not immerse his bowl in water; rather, when the meal is finished, water is poured into his empty bowl, and he uses his soiled right hand to clean the bowl, so that bowl and hand are washed simultaneously. Further, Norman seems to have overlooked the phrase *bhagavantaṃ dhotahatthaṃ onītapattapāṇiṃ* (at Vin I 221,20, 245,35, 249,4), where the washing of the hand is already covered by *dhotahatthaṃ*. Therefore I accept the usual commentarial gloss: *onītapattapāṇin ti pattato onītapāṇiṃ apanītahatthan ti vuttaṃ hoti*, "one with hand removed from the bowl," or more idiomatically, "one who has put away (or aside) the bowl."

The commentaries make mention of the interesting v.l. *oṇitta-* (at Sv I 277,18), glossed *āmisāpanayanena sucikata* (at Sv-pṭ I 405,9–10). *Oṇitta* (or *onitta*) probably corresponds to Skt *avanikta*; see MW, s.v. *ava-nij* and PED, s.v. *oṇojana, oṇojeti*. The meaning would then be "one who has washed bowl and hand."

136 For a bhikkhu to teach the Dhamma to one wearing sandals who is not ill is a violation of the Vinaya rule Sekhiya 61; to teach to one sitting on a high seat, a violation of Sekhiya 69; to teach to one with the head covered, a violation of Sekhiya 67. All such actions indicate disrespect on the part of the listener.

137 Due to a misreading of the summary verse at IV 132, Ee wrongly entitles this sutta "Devadahakhaṇo" and the next

"Saṅgayha." Correctly, as in Be and Se, this sutta is "Devadaha," the next "Khaṇa," and the third "Saṅgayha."

138 *Chaphassāyatanikā*. Spk: There is no separate hell named "Contact's Sixfold Base," for this designation applies to all thirty-one great hells; but this is said here with reference to the great hell Avīci. At **56:43**, a hell so described is referred to as *mahāpariḷāha niraya,* the Hell of the Great Conflagration.

139 Spk: Here the Tāvatiṃsa city is intended. What does he show by this? "It isn't possible to live the holy life of the path either in hell, because of extreme suffering, or in heaven, because of extreme pleasure, on account of which negligence arises through continuous amusements and delights. But the human world is a combination of pleasure and pain, so this is the field of action for the holy life of the path. The human state gained by you is the opportunity, the occasion, for living the holy life."

140 Ee wrongly entitles this sutta *Agayha,* and runs it together with the next (beginning at IV 128,8). Thus from **35:137** on my count exceeds Ee's by one. Be entitles **35:136** *Paṭhama-rūpārāma* and **35:137** *Dutiya-rūpārāma,* while in Se they are called *Sagayha* and *Gayha* respectively. The latter, it seems, should be amended to *Agayha,* as the distinction between them is the inclusion of verses in the former and their absence in the latter.

141 The verses = Sn 759–65. The following corrections should be made in Ee (at IV 127–28): v. 5a read: *Passa dhammaṃ durājānaṃ;* 6cd: *santike na vijānanti, magā dhammass' akovidā;* 8b: *buddhuṃ*. At 3b, Be and Ee have *sakkāyassa nirodhanaṃ,* Se *sakkāyass' uparodhanaṃ;* the meaning is the same. I read 3d with Be and Se as *passataṃ,* though Ee *dassanaṃ* is supported by some mss, and Spk can be read as leaning towards either alternative (see following note).

142 Spk: This view of the wise who see (*idaṃ passantānaṃ paṇḍitānaṃ dassanaṃ*) runs counter (*paccanīkaṃ*), contrary, to the entire world. For the world conceives the five aggregates as permanent, happiness, self, and beautiful, while to the wise they are impermanent, suffering, nonself, and foul.

143 Spk: Who else except the noble ones are able to know that state of Nibbāna (*nibbānapadaṃ*)? Having known it rightly

by the wisdom of arahantship, they immediately become taintless and are fully quenched by the quenching of the defilements (*kilesaparinibbānena parinibbanti*). Or else, having become taintless by rightly knowing, in the end they are fully quenched by the quenching of the aggregates (*khandhaparinibbānena parinibbanti*).

144 This sutta and the next are parallel to **22:33–34**, and are more concise variants on **35:101–2**. My title here follows Be; Se entitles them *Palāsa,* Ee *Palāsinā,* both meaning "foliage."

145 **35:140–45** are parallel to **22:18–20**.

146 Cp. **12:37**. Spk here offers essentially the same explanation as that included in **II, n. 111**, adding that in this sutta the preliminary stage of insight (*pubbabhāgavipassanā*) is discussed.

147 *Nibbānasappāyaṃ paṭipadaṃ*. Spk: The practice that is helpful (*upakārapaṭipadā*), suitable, for Nibbāna.

148 *Antevāsikam idaṃ bhikkhave brahmacariyaṃ vussati anācariyakaṃ*. This is a riddle which turns upon two puns difficult to replicate in English. A "student" (*antevāsī*) is literally "one who dwells within," and thus (as the text explains below) one for whom defilements do not dwell within (*na antovasanti*) is said to be "without students." The word "teacher" (*ācariya*) is here playfully connected with the verb "to assail" (*samudācarati*); thus one unassailed by defilements is said to be "without a teacher." Spk glosses *anantevāsikaṃ* with *anto vasanakilesavirahitaṃ* ("devoid of defilements dwelling within"), and *anācariyakaṃ* with *ācaraṇakilesavirahitaṃ* ("devoid of the 'assailing' defilements").

149 See **n. 79** above.

150 As at **12:68**. See **II, n. 198**.

151 Cp. **35:70**. Spk says that in this sutta the reviewing (*paccavekkhaṇā*) of the *sekha* and the arahant is discussed.

152 *Indriyasampanno*. Spk: Complete in faculties (*paripuṇṇindriyo*). One who has attained arahantship by exploring with insight the six (sense) faculties is said to be "complete in faculties" because he possesses tamed faculties, or because he possesses the (spiritual) faculties of faith, etc., arisen by exploring with insight the six (sense) faculties,

the eye, etc. For another interpretation of "equipped with faculties," see **48:19**.

153 Parallel to **12:16** and **22:115**.

154 This sutta and the next are parallel to **22:51**, but while the last sentence of the latter reads *cittaṃ vimuttaṃ suvimuttan ti vuccati*, the present one has simply *cittaṃ suvimuttan ti vuccati*.

155 This sutta and the next are parallel to **22:52**.

156 This sutta and the next are partly parallel to **22:5–6**.

157 *Okkhāyati*. Spk glosses with *paññāyati pākaṭaṃ hoti*, "is discerned, becomes clear."

158 This sutta and the next two correspond to **22:137**, **140**, and **143**.

159 This sutta and the next two correspond to **22:154–56**.

160 In Pāli, "Saṭṭhipeyyāla." Ee groups each triad of suttas under one sutta number, but Be and Se, which I follow, count each sutta separately. Thus by the end of this series our numbering schemes end respectively at 186 and 227.

Spk: These sixty suttas were spoken differently on account of the inclinations of those to be enlightened; thus they are all expounded separately by way of the person's inclination (*puggala-ajjhāsayavasena*). At the end of each sutta sixty bhikkhus attained arahantship.

161 Spk: *The eye is the ocean for a person*: both in the sense of being hard to fill and in the sense of submerging (*samuddanaṭṭhena*). It is an ocean in the sense of being hard to fill because it is impossible to fill it (satisfy it) with visible objects converging on it from the earth up to the highest brahmā world. And the eye is an ocean in the sense of submerging because it submerges (one) among various objects, that is, when it becomes unrestrained, flowing down, it goes in a faulty way by being a cause for the arising of defilements. *Its current consists of forms*: As the ocean has countless waves, so the "ocean of the eye" has countless waves consisting of the various visible objects converging on it.

162 At It 114,15–18 the following explanation of these dangers is given: "waves" (*ūmi*) are anger and despair (*kodhūpāyāsa*); "whirlpools" (*āvaṭṭa*) are the five cords of sensual pleasure; "sharks and demons" (*gāharakkhasa*) are women. A similar

explanation is at MN I 460–62, with *susukā* in place of *gāharakkhasa*. Cp. It 57,8–16. For the image of the brahmin standing on high ground, see **2:5** and AN II 5,29–6,5.

163 *Samunna*, glossed by Spk with *kilinna tinta nimugga*, "defiled, tainted, submerged." In Skt *samunna* is the past participle of the verb *samunatti*, from which the noun *samudra* (Pāli: *samudda*), ocean, is also derived; see MW, s.v. *samud*. Spk says that "for the most part" (*yebhuyyena*) is said making an exception of the noble disciples. The sequel is also at **12:60**.

164 Ee wrongly takes the first verse below to be prose and makes it the first paragraph of the next sutta. Woodward, at KS 4:99, has been misled by this division. The verses are also at It 57–58.

165 I read with Be and Se *pahāsi dukkhaṃ*, as against Ee *pahāya dukkhaṃ*. It 58 also has *pahāsi*.

166 I read *vadhāya* with Be, as against *vyābādhāya* in Se and Ee. See **I, v. 371**d, which supports *vadhāya*.

167 *Khīrarukkha*: a tree that exudes a milky sap. The four are types of fig trees; see too **46:39**.

168 Because, as long as one has the six sense bases, one would always be fettered to the six sense objects and thus liberation would be impossible.

169 As at **22:95** (III 141,25–31).

170 This passage is quoted at Vism 36,24–27 (Ppn 1:100). Spk: One "grasps the sign through the features" (*anubyañjanaso nimittaggāho*) thinking: "The hands are beautiful, so too the feet, etc." The grasp of the sign is the composite grasping, the grasp of the features occurs by separation. The grasp of the sign grasps everything at once, like a crocodile; the grasp of the features takes up the individual aspects like the hands and feet separately, like a leech. These two grasps are found even in a single *javana* process, not to speak of different *javana* processes.

171 Maliciously creating a schism in the Saṅgha is one of the five crimes with immediate retribution (*ānantarikakamma*) said to bring about rebirth in hell in the next existence; see It 10–11 and Vin II 198, 204–5.

I read the last sentence with Se: *imaṃ khvāhaṃ bhikkhave ādīnavaṃ disvā evaṃ vadāmi*. Be and Ee (following a Burmese ms) read *imaṃ khvāhaṃ bhikkhave vañjaṃ jīvitānaṃ ādīnavaṃ disvā*, which seems unintelligible.

172 Spk: In this sutta and the next, the round of existence and its cessation are discussed by showing kammically resultant pleasure and pain.

173 Spk says this sutta was addressed to bhikkhus who practised meditation using the characteristic of suffering as their meditation subject. Spk takes the "four vipers" (*cattāro āsīvisā*) as referring to the four *families* of vipers, not four individual serpents. The four are: (i) the wooden-mouthed (*kaṭṭhamukha*), whose bite causes the victim's entire body to stiffen like dry wood; (ii) the putrid-mouthed (*pūtimukha*), whose bite makes the victim's body decay and ooze like a decaying fruit; (iii) the fiery-mouthed (*aggimukha*), whose bite causes its victim's body to burn up and scatter like ashes or chaff (see **35:69**); and (iv) the dagger-mouthed (*satthamukha*), whose bite causes the victim's body to break apart like a pole struck by lightning.

The etymology of *āsīvisa* is uncertain. Spk offers three alternatives, none especially persuasive: (i) *āsittavisa*, "with besprinkled poison," because their poison is stored as if it were sprinkling (*āsiñcitvā viya*) their whole body; (ii) *asitavisa*, "with eaten poison," because whatever they eat becomes poison; and (iii) *asisadisavisa*, "with swordlike poison," because their poison is sharp like a sword. Sp I 220,13 offers: *āsu sīghaṃ etassa visaṃ āgacchatī ti āsīviso*; "it is a viper because its poison comes on quick and fast." Four types of *āsīvisa* are mentioned at AN II 110–11.

174 Be and Se: *saṃvesetabbā* (Ee: *pavesetabbā*). Spk glosses with *nipajjāpetabbā*, "to be made to lie down." Spk provides an elaborate background story, making this a punishment imposed on the man by the king.

175 *Chaṭṭho antaracaro vadhako*. Spk: The king spoke to his ministers thus: "First, when he was pursued by the vipers, he fled here and there, tricking them. Now, when pursued by five enemies, he flees even more swiftly. We can't catch him, but by trickery we can. Therefore send as a murderer an intimate companion from his youth, one who used to eat and drink with him." The ministers then sought out such a companion and sent him as a murderer.

176 Be: *pivisanti*; Se and Ee: *vadhissanti*.

177 See the better known simile of the raft at MN I 134–35.

178 As at **35:228** above.

179 Spk correlates each element with a particular family of vipers: the earth element with the wooden-mouthed; the water element with the putrid-mouthed; the fire element with the fiery-mouthed; and the air element with the dagger-mouthed. See too Vism 367–68 (Ppn 11:102). Spk devotes three pages to elaborating on the comparison.

180 See the simile of the murderous servant at **22:85** (III 112–14). The explanation Spk gives here is almost identical with the explanation it gives of the word *vadhako* in **22:95**, v. 5c, summarized in **III, n. 196**.

181 *Nandirāga*. Spk: Delight and lust is like a murderer with drawn sword in two respects: (i) because when greed arises for a specific object it fells one's head, namely, the head of wisdom; and (ii) because it sends one off to rebirth in the womb, and all fears and punishments are rooted in rebirth.

182 *Sakkāya*. Spk: "Identity" (personal identity) is the five aggregates pertaining to the three planes. Like the near shore with its vipers, etc., "identity" is dangerous and fearful because of the four great elements and so forth.

183 *Yoni c' assa āraddhā hoti*. Spk: *Kāraṇañ c' assa paripuṇṇaṃ hoti*; "and the cause for it is complete." See **III, n. 54**. Cp. AN I 113–14. The simile of the charioteer is also at MN III 97,6–10.

184 Text uses both words, *kummo kacchapo*. See **II, n. 317**.

185 *Apposukko tuṇhībhūto saṅkasāyati*. As at **21:4**. See too **I, n. 54**.

186 The verse = **I, v. 34**. As the verse is not preceded by the usual sentence stating that the Buddha spoke it on this occasion, it seems the redactors of the canon have tacked it on by reason of the tortoise simile.

187 Also at **22:3** (III 11,5–7).

188 Also at AN II 239,29–240,1, IV 128,23–26, 201,20–23; Ud 52,13–16, 55,10–13. On *saṅkassarasamācāro*, "of suspect behaviour," Spk says: "His conduct is to be recalled with suspicion (*saṅkāya saritabbasamācāro*) by others thus, 'It seems he did this and that'; or else he recalls the conduct of others with suspicion (*saṅkāya paresaṃ samācāraṃ sarati*), thinking, when he sees a few people talking among them-

selves, 'They must be discussing my faults.'" Spk glosses *kasambujāto* thus: *rāgādīhi kilesehi kacavarajāto*, "rubbish-like because of such defilements as lust, etc."

189 I understand *upagacchāmi* here to be a true future form, in conformity with the futures that follow.

190 *Aññataraṃ saṅkiliṭṭhaṃ āpattiṃ āpanno hoti.* Spk says there is no offence (i.e., an infraction of the monastic rules) that is not "defiled" from the time it is "concealed" (i.e., not confessed to a fellow monk to obtain absolution). However, I take the expression here to refer to a serious offence, one belonging to either the Pārājika or Saṅghādisesa class; the former entails expulsion from the Saṅgha, the latter a special process of rehabilitation.

The next phrase is read differently in the various eds. of both text and commentary. Be, which I follow, reads: *yathārūpāya āpattiyā na vuṭṭhānaṃ paññāyati*, on which Spk says: "Rehabilitation is not seen (*na dissati*) by means of *parivāsa, mānatta,* and *abbhāna*"—these being the three stages of rehabilitation from a Saṅghādisesa offence. Se and Ee do not include the negative *na* in either text or commentary. Thus, on the testimony of Be, the monk is guilty of Pārājika, while on that of Se and Ee, of Saṅghādisesa. I side with Be on the assumption that this "inward rottenness" must have the same implications as the corresponding passage of the preceding sutta, according to which the monk is not a genuine bhikkhu. At **20:10** (II 271,15–16) *saṅkiliṭṭhā āpatti* clearly refers to a Saṅghādisesa, since this offence is described as "deadly suffering" in contrast to "spiritual death" (the consequence of a Pārājika).

191 This invitation reflects the widespread belief in South Asian religion that it is auspicious to invite a holy man to spend the first night in a new residence before the lay owners move in to occupy it. This honour would have been especially cherished by the Sakyans, who were the Buddha's own kinsmen. Similar ceremonies are reported at MN I 353–54 and DN II 84–85 (= Ud 85–86).

192 He refers to them as Gotamas because they were members of the Gotama clan, to which he himself belonged.

193 Spk: During his six years of ascetic practice the Blessed One had experienced great bodily pain. Therefore, in his

old age, he suffered from back winds (*piṭṭhivāta*, rheumatism?). Or else he lay down because he wanted to use the council hall in all four postures, having already used it by way of walking, standing, and sitting.

194 *Avassutapariyāya, anavassutapariyāya. Avassuta* means literally "flown into," or leaky, implying a mind permeated by defilements. The substantives *avassuta* and *āsava*, and the verbs *anvāssavati* and *anu(s)savati*, are all based on the same root *su*, "to flow." Waldschmidt has published a Skt version of Moggallāna's discourse (see Bibliography).

195 As at **35:132** (IV 119,27–120,11).

196 This sentence, as inordinately complex in the Pāli as in my translation, introduces three themes that will be taken up for detailed explanation just below. The syntax seems to be irregular, since the initial relative *yato* is not completed by its corresponding demonstrative *tato*. I read the last word with Se and Ee as *nānu(s)savanti*, as against Be *nānusenti*.

197 Spk explains *dukkhadhammā* as *dukkhasambhavadhammā*, "states from which suffering originates"; "for when the five aggregates exist, suffering of various kinds, such as being wounded, slain, and imprisoned, originates."

198 The simile is at **12:63** (II 99,27–100,4), but here the phrasing is a little different.

199 Wherever Ee has *yato ca*, I read with Be and Se *sato va*.

200 I follow Se here: … *ayaṃ vuccati ariyassa vinaye kaṇṭako. Taṃ kaṇṭako ti iti viditvā saṃvaro ca asaṃvaro ca veditabbo.* **35:247** (IV 198,11–12) supports this reading; see **n. 219** below.

201 The simile is also at MN I 453,26–29 and MN III 300,19–23. Spk: Just the arising of mindfulness is slow, but as soon as it has arisen the defilements are suppressed and cannot persist. For when lust, etc., have arisen in the eye door, with the second *javana* process one knows that the defilements have arisen and the third *javana* process occurs with restraint. It is not surprising that an insight meditator can suppress defilements by the third *javana* process; for when a desirable object comes into range and a defiled *javana* process is about to occur, an insight meditator can stop it and arouse a wholesome *javana* process. This is the advantage for insight meditators of being well established in meditation and reflection.

202 The purification of vision (*dassana*) usually means the attainment of stream-entry, the gaining of "the vision of the Dhamma" (*dhammacakkhu*). Here, however, the qualification "well purified" (*suvisuddhaṃ*) seems to imply that the question concerns the path to arahantship. It is so taken by Spk.

203 Spk says that all the bhikkhus who replied were arahants; they answered in accordance with their own method of practice. The inquirer was dissatisfied with the reply of the first because it mentioned the formations only partly (*padesasaṅkhāresu ṭhatvā*); he was dissatisfied with the other replies because they seemed to contradict one another.

204 *Kiṃsuka* means literally "what's it?" The name may have originated from an ancient Indian folk riddle. *Kiṃśuka* is also known in Skt literature (see MW, s.v. *kiṃ*). Both PED and MW identify it as the tree *Butea frondosa*. Liyanaratne lists two kinds of *kiṃsuka* ("South Asian flora as reflected in the Abhidhanappadīpikā," §§43–44.). One, also called the *pāḷibadda*, is identified as *Erythrina variegata*; the English equivalent is the coral tree (elsewhere used to render the *pāricchattaka* tree—see **48:68**). The other, also called the *palāsa*, is identified as *Butea monosperma*; its English name is the Bengal kino tree or the dhak tree. Woodward translates it as "Judas tree," but this is unlikely as the Judas tree is of the genus *Sercis*.

The Kiṃsukopama Jātaka (No. 248; Ja II 265–66) begins with an incident similar to the one with which the present sutta starts, but employs a somewhat different story about the *kiṃsuka* to make the same point. In the Jātaka version the *kiṃsuka* appears like a charred stump at the time the buds are sprouting; like a banyan tree, when the leaves turn green; like a piece of meat, at the time of blossoming; like an acacia, when bearing fruit. According to Spk, the *kiṃsuka* is like a charred stump when the leaves have been shed; like a piece of meat, when blossoming; with strips of bark hanging down and burst pods, when bearing fruit; and giving abundant shade, when covered with leaves. The similarity of its flowers to meat is the theme of a humorous poem at Vism 196,5–15 (Ppn 6:91–92), about a jackal who chanced upon a *kiṃsuka* and rejoiced at finding "a meat-bearing tree."

205 *Sirīsa.* This was the Bodhi Tree of the Buddha Kakusandha (see DN II 4,12).

206 Spk: Just as the four men who described the *kiṃsuka* described it just as they had seen it, so these four bhikkhus, having attained arahantship by purifying their vision, described Nibbāna, the purifier of vision, in accordance with the path by which they themselves had attained it. Spk draws parallels between the four modes of appearance of the tree and the four different approaches to meditation by which the monks attained arahantship.

207 Spk: Why is this introduced? If that bhikkhu understood (the meaning being conveyed by the *kiṃsuka* simile), then it is introduced to teach him the Dhamma. If he did not understand, this simile of the city is introduced to explain and clarify the meaning.

Again, Spk gives a much more elaborate version of the simile and its application. In brief: The lord of the city is a prince, son of a virtuous world monarch, who had been appointed by his father to administer one of the outlying provinces. Under the influence of bad friends the prince had become dissolute and passed his time drinking liquor and enjoying music and dance. The king sent the two messengers to admonish the prince to abandon his heedless ways and resume his duties. One messenger is a brave warrior (representing the *samatha* meditation subject), the other a wise minister (representing the *vipassanā* meditation subject). The brave warrior grabs hold of the wayward prince by the head and threatens to decapitate him if he doesn't change his ways: this is like the time the mind has been grabbed and made motionless by the concentration arisen through the first jhāna. The fleeing of the prince's dissolute friends is like the disappearance of the five hindrances when the first jhāna has arisen. When the prince agrees to follow the king's command, this is like the time the meditator has emerged from jhāna. When the minister delivers the king's command, this is like the time when the meditator, with his mind made pliable through concentration, develops insight meditation. When the two messengers raise up the white canopy over the prince after he has been coronated, this is like the time the white canopy of liberation is raised over the meditator after he has attained arahantship by means of serenity and insight.

208 Also at **35:103**; see above **n. 87**.

209 Spk identifies this as the insight-mind (*vipassanācitta*), which is the prince to be coronated with the coronation of arahantship by the two messengers, serenity and insight. This interpretation strikes me as too narrow. I see the point to be simply that consciousness is the functional centre of personal experience.

210 Spk: Nibbāna is called the "message of reality" (*yathābhūtaṃ vacanaṃ*) because in its real nature it is unshakable and immutable (*yathābhūtasabhāvaṃ akuppaṃ avikāri*).

211 Apart from SN 5, references to bhikkhunīs are rare in SN, but see **35:231** above. The five defilements are also at MN III 294–95. Spk: Desire (*chanda*) is freshly arisen weak craving (*taṇhā*), lust (*rāga*) is repeatedly arisen strong craving. Similarly, hatred (*dosa*) is freshly arisen weak anger (*kodha*), aversion (*paṭigha*) is repeatedly arisen strong anger. The five terms incorporate the three unwholesome roots, and when these are included, all the subsidiary defilements are included. The five terms also imply the twelve unwholesome cittas (of the Abhidhamma—see CMA 1:4–7).

212 *Duhitika*. Spk analyses this word as *du-ihiti-ka*, *ihiti* being synonymous with *iriyanā*, "moving, faring": *Ettha ihitī ti iriyanā; dukkhā ihiti etthā ti duhitiko* (verbal analysis). Along whatever path there is no food or refreshments such as roots and fruits, the faring there is difficult; one cannot fare on it to reach one's destination. Similarly, one cannot reach success by faring along the path of defilements, thus the path of defilements is *duhitika*.

The correct derivation of *duhitika*, apparently lost by the time of the commentators, is from *du-hita*. See the discussion below at **n. 347**, and see too MW, s.v. *dur-hita*, and its antonym, *su-hita*.

213 I follow Se and Ee, which do not include *pamādaṃ āpajjeyya/āpajjati*, found in Be. Spk: Just as the owner of the crops fails to gain the fruits of the harvest when, due to the watchman's negligence, the bull eats the barley, so when

the mind is separated from the mindfulness that guards the six sense doors, it enjoys the five cords of sensual pleasure; then, because his wholesome qualities are destroyed, the bhikkhu fails to attain the fruits of asceticism.

214 Be: *udujitaṃ hoti sudujitaṃ*; Se: *udujjitaṃ hoti sudujjitaṃ*; Ee: *ujujātaṃ hoti sammujujātaṃ*. Spk glosses with *tajjitaṃ, sutajjitaṃ*, and says the meaning is *sujitaṃ*, "well conquered," *udu* and *sudu* being mere indeclinables (*nipātamatta*). Possibly all texts are corrupted here. Spk says that at this point the Buddha has discussed the guarding of serenity and the virtue of restraint of the sense faculties (*samathānurakkhaṇa-indriyasaṃvarasīla*).

215 The Pāli terms for the parts of the lute (*viṇā*) are: *camma, doṇi, daṇḍa, upavīṇā, tanti, koṇa*. The simile occurs at Mil 53, inclusive of the list of terms (preceded by *patta*, sling). In translating the names of the parts I follow Horner, at *Milinda's Questions*, 1:74, who bases her renderings on A.K. Coomaraswamy, "The Parts of a Vīṇā" (*Journal of the American Oriental Society*, 50:3).

216 I read with Be: *Asatī kir' āyaṃ bho vīṇā nāma, yath' evaṃ yaṃ kiñci vīṇā nāma, ettha ca pan' āyaṃ jano ativelaṃ pamatto palaḷito*. Se differs only in the v.l. *palāḷito*, but Ee differs more widely. The exact meaning is obscure. Spk glosses *asatī* with *lāmikā* and paraphrases: "It is not only the lute that is a poor thing, but like this so-called lute, whatever else is bound with strings—all that is just a poor thing."

217 Spk: The five aggregates are like the lute, the meditator is like the king. As the king did not find any sound in the lute even after splitting it up and searching, and therefore lost interest in the lute, so the meditator, exploring the five aggregates, does not see any graspable "I" or "mine" and therefore loses interest in the aggregates. By the terms "I" or "mine" or "I am" in regard to form, etc., the three "grips" of views, craving, and conceit are respectively described. These do not exist in the arahant.

There is an important difference between the king and the meditator, not conveyed either by sutta or commentary: In the parable the king, looking for the sound of the lute by taking the instrument apart, seems foolish, while the meditator, dissecting the aggregates to dispel the delusion of a self, becomes wise.

Spk ends its commentary on the sutta with a quotation from the Great Commentary (*Mahā-aṭṭhakathā*, no longer extant):

"In the beginning virtue is discussed,
In the middle, development of concentration,
And at the end, Nibbāna:
The Simile of the Lute is thus composed."

218 *Saravanaṃ*. Spk (Se) glosses with *kaṇṭakavanaṃ*. *Sara*, according to PED, is the reed *Saccharum sara*, used to make arrows.

219 Here Be and Se both read: ... *asucigāmakaṇṭako ti. Taṃ kaṇṭako ti iti viditvā saṃvaro ca asaṃvaro ca veditabbo*. Ee is the same except for the omission of *iti*. See **n. 200**. Spk: He is *a foul village thorn*: "foul" in the sense of impure, a "village thorn" in the sense of wounding the villagers [Spk-pṭ: that is, oppressing them by accepting their services while being unworthy of them].

220 *Byābhaṅgihatthā*. Spk glosses *kājahatthā*, Spk-pṭ *daṇḍahatthā*.

221 *Āyatiṃ punabbhavāya ceteti*. Spk: Thus beings, thoroughly struck by the defilements (rooted in) the longing for existence, experience the suffering rooted in existence (*bhavamūlakaṃ dukkhaṃ*).

222 On the enmity between the devas and the asuras, see **11:1–6**. The following is parallel to **11:4** (I 221,3–17).

223 As at **22:64** (III 75,3–4). Spk says: "In conceiving the aggregates by way of craving, conceit, and views."

224 *Maññita*. Spk: "I am" (*asmi*) is a conceiving through craving; "I am this" (*ayam aham asmi*), a conceiving through views; "I shall be," a conceiving through the eternalist view; "I shall not be," a conceiving through the annihilationist view. The rest are specific types of eternalism.

The connection Spk makes between "I am" and craving is unusual, as the notion "I am" (*asmi*) is typically ascribed to conceit; however, **22:89** (III 130,31) has *asmī ti chando*, and possibly the commentator had this in mind. "I am this" is the seminal type of identity view, whereby a person establishes a personal identity by identifying one or another of the five aggregates as a self. The ninefold conceiving is mentioned at **22:47**; see too MN III 246,11–17.

225 The key terms of the next three paragraphs are *iñjita*, *phandita*, and *papañcita*. Spk: "This is to show that on account of these defilements (craving, etc.), beings are perturbed, vacillate, and procrastinate." *Papañca* is often explained in the commentaries as *pamādakarā dhammā*, the factors responsible for heedlessness or procrastination.

226 *Mānagata*. Spk: Conceit itself is an involvement with conceit. In this passage, "I am" is stated by way of the conceit associated with craving; "I am this," by way of view. Although conceit does not arise in immediate conjunction with views (according to the Abhidhamma analysis of mind-moments, they are mutually exclusive), views occur because conceit has not been abandoned. So this is said with reference to views rooted in conceit.

36. Vedanāsaṃyutta

227 Since these verses (and those in the suttas to follow) are not expressly ascribed to the Buddha, I do not enclose them in quotation marks. Though several have parallels in other texts, where they *are* ascribed to the Buddha, here they seem to have been added by the redactors, perhaps quoting from these other sources.

The verse alludes to the Four Noble Truths, with feeling in the place of suffering (on the ground that "whatever is felt is included in suffering" and because feeling is one of the five aggregates mentioned in the formula for the first truth). Spk points out that two terms respectively signify serenity and insight (Spk-pṭ: *samāhito* and *sampajāno*); the rest, the Four Noble Truths. "Hungerless" (*nicchāto*) means without craving, and "fully quenched" (*parinibbuto*) implies the full quenching of defilements (*kilesaparinibbāna*). Thus the verses are all-inclusive, comprising all states of the four planes (see **n. 6**).

228 I render *mosadhammaṃ* in pāda c in accordance with the gloss of Spk, *nassanadhammaṃ*, "subject to destruction," on

which Spk-pṭ remarks: "There is nothing to be seen after its dissolution owing to its momentariness." The word may also be related to *musā*, from the same verbal root but with the acquired meaning "false." Thus *mosadhamma* could have been rendered "of false nature" or "deceitful." This meaning seems to be conveyed at MN III 245,16–18, and perhaps at Sn 757d, though it is also possible both nuances are intended in every case. Spk glosses *phussa phussa vayaṃ passaṃ* with *ñāṇena phusitvā phusitvā vayaṃ passanto*, "seeing its fall, having repeatedly contacted it (touched it) with knowledge." Spk-pṭ takes *virajjati* to be an allusion to the path (*maggavirāgena virajjati*).

229 In Pāli the three underlying tendencies are *rāgānusaya, paṭighānusaya, avijjānusaya*. Among the seven *anusaya* (see **45:175**), these three are specially correlated with feelings; see too MN I 303,6–11.

230 I read *niranusayo* with Be, as against *pahīnarāgānusayo* in Se and Ee.

231 *Mānābhisamayā*. Spk: Breaking through conceit by seeing it (*dassanābhisamayā*) and by abandoning it (*pahānābhisamayā*). See **II, n. 13**.

232 *Pātālo*. Also at **I, v. 147**d, **v. 517**b, **v. 759**c. Here Spk derives the word from *pātassa alaṃ pariyatto*, "enough, a sufficiency of falling," and says the word denotes a place without bottom (*natthi ettha patiṭṭhā*). "Painful bodily feeling" here renders *sārīrikā dukkhā vedanā*.

233 Spk: Because it undergoes change.

234 I prefer the reading in Se: *tam enaṃ dutiyena sallena anuvedhaṃ vijjheyyuṃ*. Be differs only in having a singular verb. Spk: The second wound (*anugatavedhaṃ*) would be only one or two inches away from the opening of the first. For one wounded thus, the subsequent feeling would be worse than the first.

235 Spk: The escape is concentration, path, and fruit. This he does not know; the only escape of which he knows is sensual pleasure.

236 Spk says that among the noble disciples, here the stress is on the arahant, though the nonreturner would also be appropriate. According to the commentarial system, both have abandoned *paṭigha* or *dosa* and thus are no longer sub-

ject to displeasure (*domanassa*), painful mental feeling. Everyone with a body, including the Buddhas, is subject to bodily painful feeling (here, *kāyikā dukkhā vedanā*).

237 Spk: He went so that the bhikkhus, seeing the Tathāgata, the foremost person in the world, attending on the sick, would think, "We too should attend on the sick." He also went to explain a meditation subject to those who needed one.

238 Spk: At this point, what has been shown? This bhikkhu's way of arrival [Spk-pṭ: the preliminary practice (*pubbabhāgapaṭipadā*) that is the cause for arrival at the noble path]. For the establishments of mindfulness are only preliminary, and in regard to clear comprehension the contemplations of impermanence, vanishing, and fading away are also only preliminary. These two—contemplation of cessation and of relinquishment—are mixed [Spk-pṭ: mundane and supramundane]. At this point, the time of the bhikkhu's development (in meditation) is shown.

239 From here to the end also at **12:51** (but with a different simile) and also at **22:88** and **54:8** (with the same simile).

240 The simile is also at **12:62**. Here, and below at **48:39**, all three eds. read *nānābhāvā vinikkhepā* (see **II, n. 159**).

241 Spk: The impermanence of formations is itself the impermanence of feelings, and this impermanence is death. There is no suffering worse than death: with this intention it is said, "All feeling is suffering."

On this maxim, see too **12:32** (II 53,20–21) and MN III 208,27. Spk's explanation is not very cogent. The real reason all feeling is suffering is because all feeling is impermanent and thus cannot provide stable happiness and security.

242 *Anupubbasaṅkhārānaṃ nirodho*. Spk: This is introduced to show, "I describe not only the cessation of feelings, but also the cessation of these (other) states." Below, "subsiding" (*vūpasama*) and "tranquillization" (*passaddhi*) are spoken of in conformity with the inclinations of those to be enlightened by the teaching.

243 In Be and Se, this verse and the next are the same as at **36:3**, but Ee reads pāda b *sampajāno nirūpadhi* rather than *sampajaññaṃ no riñcati*.

244 Spk: Carnal (*sāmisā*) pleasant feeling is the feeling connected with carnal sensuality; spiritual (*nirāmisā*) pleasant feeling is the feeling arisen in the first jhāna, etc., or by way of insight, or by way of recollection (of the Buddha, etc.). Carnal painful feeling is the carnal feeling arisen through carnal sensuality [Spk-pṭ: the painful feeling of those who undergo suffering because of sensuality]; spiritual painful feeling, the feeling of displeasure (*domanassa*) arisen through yearning for the unsurpassed deliverances [Spk-pṭ: namely, the fruit of arahantship]. Carnal neutral feeling is the carnal feeling arisen through carnal sensuality; spiritual neutral feeling, the neutral feeling arisen by way of the fourth jhāna. See too **36:31**.

245 This sutta is also at MN No. 59, entitled the Bahuvedanīya Sutta.

246 All are explained at **36:22**.

247 Spk: From the fourth jhāna up, there is neither-painful-nor-pleasant feeling, called pleasure (or happiness) in the sense that it is peaceful and sublime.

248 Spk: Cessation is called happiness in the sense that it is unfelt happiness (*avedayitasukha*, the happiness of nonfeeling). Thus felt happiness (*vedayitasukha*) arises by way of the cords of sensual pleasure and the eight meditative attainments, while cessation is called unfelt happiness. Whether it is felt or not, it is exclusively happiness in that happiness consists in the absence of suffering (*niddukkhabhāva*).

249 I read: *Yattha yattha āvuso sukhaṃ upalabbhati yamhi yamhi, taṃ taṃ tathāgato sukhasmiṃ paññāpeti*. Spk: Whether felt happiness or unfelt happiness is found, the Tathāgata describes whatever is without suffering as happiness.

250 Spk: His name was Sīvaka, but because he had a topknot (*cūḷā*) he was called Moḷiyasīvaka (*moḷi* or *moli* being another word for topknot).

251 This view is often referred to as *pubbakatahetuvāda*. At MN II 214–23, where it is ascribed to the Jains, the Buddha criticizes it from one angle, and at AN I 173,27–174,15 from still another angle.

252 In the argument, *vedanā* is being used in the narrower sense of painful feeling. Bile (*pitta*), phlegm (*semha*), and wind

(*vāta*) are the three bodily humours (*dosa*) of Indian Ayurveda medicine. It should be noted that the Buddha's appeal to personal experience and common sense as the two criteria for rejecting the view that all feeling is caused by past kamma implies that the view against which he is arguing is the claim that past kamma is the *sole and sufficient cause* of all present feeling. However, the Buddha's line of argument also implies that he is not denying kamma may induce the illnesses, etc., that serve as the immediate causes of the painful feelings; for this level of causality is not immediately perceptible to those who lack supernormal cognitive faculties. Thus kamma can still be an indirect cause for the painful feeling directly induced by the first seven causes. It is the sufficient cause only in the eighth case, though even then it must operate in conjunction with various other conditions.

253 I have translated *sannipātikāni, visamaparihārajāni,* and *opakkamikāni* in accordance with the explanations given by Spk. On *kammavipākajāni vedayitāni,* Spk says that these are produced solely (*kevalaṃ*) as a result of kamma. Feelings arisen directly from the other seven causes are not "feelings produced by kamma," even though kamma may function as an underlying cause of the illness, etc., responsible for the painful feelings. According to the Abhidhamma, all bodily painful feeling is the result of kamma (*kammavipāka*), but it is not necessarily produced exclusively by kamma; kamma usually operates through more tangible networks of causality to yield its result.

Spk says that this sutta is spoken from the standpoint of worldly convention (*lokavohāra*), on which Spk-pṭ comments: "Because it is generally accepted in the world that (feelings) originate from bile and so forth. Granted, feelings based on the physical body are actually produced by kamma, but this worldly convention is arrived at by way of the present condition (*paccuppannapaccayavasena*). Accepting what is said, the opponent's doctrine is refuted."

254 Elaborated at **48:31–40**.

255 See MN III 216,29–217,4. Each type becomes sixfold by arising in relation to the six sense objects—forms, sounds, etc.

256 See MN III 217–19. Again, each type becomes sixfold in relation to the six sense objects.

257 In Ee, this sutta is not counted separately but is printed as though it were a continuation of the preceding one. Be and Se, which I follow, treat it as a separate sutta.

258 In all three eds., the text of this sutta includes the words *samudayañ ca atthaṅgamañ ca* ("the origination and the passing away"), and the wording of the next sutta is the same. Since this would obviate the need for its separate existence, we can be sure that **36:27** originally had only the three terms *assāda, ādinava, nissaraṇa,* and **36:28** all five. I have translated on the basis of this hypothesis, which can claim support from the parallels: **14:37–38**, **22:107–8**, and **22:129–34**.

259 In Ee, this sutta is considered the opening paragraph of the following sutta, but in Be and Se (which I follow) it is counted separately.

260 *Nirāmisā nirāmisatarā pīti.* Spk: More spiritual than the spiritual rapture of the jhānas.

261 Having called the rapture, etc., of the jhānas spiritual (lit. "noncarnal") rapture, etc., it seems contradictory for the text to say that the form-sphere deliverance is carnal. Spk explains that form-sphere deliverance is called carnal because its object is a carnal form (*rūpāmisavasen' eva sāmiso nāma*).

37. Mātugāmasaṃyutta

262 *Mātugāmassa āveṇikāni dukkhāni.* Spk: Particular (to women); not shared by men.

263 I follow the arrangement of Be, which includes the opening paragraph under the fifth sutta of this vagga and records **37:5–24** as addressed solely to Anuruddha. Ee places the introductory paragraph here (and in "The Bright Side") *before* the first sutta of each series. In this respect Se corresponds with Be. In Se, however, only the first sutta in each series, dark and bright, is addressed to Anuruddha. Se then repeats the same sutta but addressed to the bhikkhus, and then records the following suttas in each series as addressed solely to the bhikkhus. For this reason Se winds

up with two suttas more than Be and Ee, namely, the two addressed only to Anuruddha. These suttas lack *yebhuyyena,* "generally (reborn)," found in the preceding sutta.

Anuruddha excelled in the exercise of the divine eye, which discerns the passing away and rebirth of beings, and also seems to have had frequent encounters with women, both human and celestial (see **9:6**). For a biographical sketch, see Hecker, "Anuruddha: Master of the Divine Eye," in Nyanaponika and Hecker, *Great Disciples of the Buddha,* pp. 185–210.

264 In **37:7–13**, the terms in square brackets successively replace "malicious" as the fourth item in the list.

265 In **37:17–23**, the terms in square brackets successively replace "without malice" as the fourth item in the list.

266 *Sāmikaṃ pasayha agāraṃ ajjhāvasati.* Spk glosses *pasayha* with *abhibhavitvā,* and in the next sutta *abhibhuyya vattati* with *abhibhavati ajjhottharati.* In this way the two become simply verbal variants on the same idea.

267 *Nāsent' eva naṃ, kule na vāsenti.* Spk gives us a glimpse of the social mores of the period: "Saying, 'You immoral, unchaste adulteress,' they take her by the neck and eject her; they do not accommodate her in that family."

268 *Vāsent' eva naṃ kule, na nāsenti.* Spk: "Reflecting, 'What does beauty or wealth, etc., matter when she is virtuous and upright?' the relatives accommodate her in that family; they do not expel her."

269 *Asapattī.* That is, without another wife of her husband. It was not unusual at the time for affluent men to take a second wife or concubine, especially if the first wife turned out to be barren. See Singh, *Life in North-Eastern India,* pp. 38–41.

38. Jambukhādakasaṃyutta

270 Spk: He was Sāriputta's nephew. The name means "Rose-apple-eater."

271 Spk argues against the idea that Nibbāna is the mere destruction of the defilements (*kilesakkhayamattaṃ nibbānaṃ*), holding that Nibbāna is called the destruction of lust, etc., in the sense that lust, etc., are destroyed contin-

gent upon Nibbāna (*yaṃ āgamma rāgādayo khīyanti, taṃ nibbānaṃ*). For a fuller version of the argument, see Vism 507–9 (Ppn 16:67–74). The key point in the commentarial position is that Nibbāna is the unconditioned element apprehended with the attainment of the supramundane path. Because this experience of the unconditioned effects the destruction of the defilements, Nibbāna comes to be called the destruction of lust, hatred, and delusion, but it is not reducible to their mere destruction.

272 Cp. AN I 217–19. *Sugata* is usually an epithet of the Buddha but here, in the plural, it denotes all arahants.

273 *Assāsapatta*. The answer is a coded formula for the *sekha*. The next sutta, on *paramassāsapatta*, concerns the arahant.

274 The three types are explained at Vism 499,14–21 (Ppn 16:34–35). Briefly, suffering due to pain (*dukkhadukkhatā*) is painful bodily and mental feeling; suffering due to the formations (*saṅkhāradukkhatā*) is all conditioned phenomena of the three planes, because they are oppressed by rise and fall; and suffering due to change (*vipariṇāmadukkhatā*) is pleasant feeling, which brings suffering when it comes to an end.

275 Spk quotes MN II 96,19–20: "Instructed in the evening, by the morning he will attain distinction (enlightenment); instructed in the morning, by the evening he will attain distinction."

40. *Moggallānasaṃyutta*

276 The first nine suttas of this saṃyutta report Moggallāna's experiences during his week-long struggle for arahantship immediately after his ordination as a bhikkhu. For another account of his development, see AN IV 85–88, and for a connected narrative, see Hecker, "Mahāmoggallāna: Master of Psychic Powers," in Nyanaponika and Hecker, *Great Disciples of the Buddha*, pp. 78–83.

277 *Kāmasahagatā saññā manasikārā samudācaranti*. Spk glosses: accompanied by the five hindrances.

278 *Mahābhiññataṃ patto*. Moggallāna excelled in the supernormal powers (*iddhividha*); see **51:14**, **51:31**.

279 Cp. **21:1**, where the same experience is discussed in terms

of "noble silence" (*ariya tuṇhībhāva*), a technical code term for the second jhāna.

280 *Animitta cetosamādhi.* Spk: This refers to insight concentration (*vipassanāsamādhi*), which occurs when one has abandoned the sign of permanence, etc.

The "signless concentration of mind" is not defined further in the Nikāyas, but its placement after the eighth formless attainment suggests it is a *samādhi* qualitatively different from those attained in *samatha* meditation. Below, it occurs in the explanation of the "signless liberation of mind" (*animittā cetovimutti*, at **41:7**; IV 297,3–6). At **43:4**, the signless concentration (*animitta samādhi*) is called the path leading to the unconditioned. For a wide-ranging overview of the signless meditation, see Harvey, "Signless Meditation in Pāli Buddhism." See too below **nn. 312, 368**.

281 *Nimittānusāri viññāṇaṃ hoti.* Spk: This occurred while his insight knowledge was flowing along sharply and strongly as he dwelt in insight concentration. Just as, when a man is cutting down a tree with a sharp axe, if he constantly inspects the blade he doesn't accomplish the function of cutting down the tree, so the elder developed a liking (*nikanti*) for insight and thus did not accomplish its function.

282 Reading with Be and Se *asītiyā devatāsahassehi saddhiṃ*, as against Ee *asītiyā devatāsatehi saddhiṃ*, "eighty hundred."

283 *Buddhe aveccappasāda.* This is the faith of a noble disciple at the minimal level of stream-enterer; see **II, n. 120**. The four qualities to be extolled here are called the four factors of stream-entry (*sotāpattiyaṅga*); see **12:41**. Sakka is shown attaining stream-entry at DN II 288,20–23.

284 The above suttas are abridged in all three eds. Candana is at **2:5**; the other devas are the reigning deities of the four sense-sphere heavens above Tāvatiṃsa.

41. Cittasaṃyutta

285 At AN I 26,5 Citta is declared the chief male lay disciple among the speakers on the Dhamma (*etadaggaṃ dhammakathikānaṃ*); see too **17:23**. For a biographical sketch, see Hecker, "Shorter Lives of the Disciples," in Nyanaponika

and Hecker, *Great Disciples of the Buddha,* pp. 365–72. Migapathaka, according to Spk, was his own tributary village (*bhogagāma*), situated just behind the Wild Mango Grove.

286 The simile and its application are also at **35:232**.

287 The problem is also posed at **35:129**, but the reply given below draws on **14:1**.

288 Spk says that he knew the answer but was not a confident speaker. This explanation is not very convincing in view of the elder's confession below.

289 Th 120 is ascribed to Isidatta. According to Th-a I 248, while Isidatta was still a layman, his "unseen friend" Citta (see next sutta) sent him a letter in which he praised the virtues of the Buddha, Dhamma, and Saṅgha. Isidatta gained confidence in the Triple Gem, went forth as a monk under the Venerable Mahākaccāna, and quickly attained arahantship with the six direct knowledges.

290 *Onītapattapāṇino.* Here Spk expands: "Having removed their bowls from their hands and washed them (*pāṇito apanītapattā dhovitvā*), having deposited them into their bags, (they left) with the bowls hanging from their shoulders." This explanation goes further than the more typical commentarial gloss, which interprets the expression to mean simply that the monk has put the bowl aside; see **n. 135**. On *osāpeti,* "to deposit," see **I, n. 223**.

291 I translate the awkward idiom freely in accordance with the natural sense.

292 DN No. 1. This is translated, along with the commentary and excerpts from the sub-commentary, in Bodhi, *The All-Embracing Net of Views.*

293 Neither Spk nor Spk-pṭ gives an explanation for his sudden departure. He may have seen the danger in fame and honour and preferred to dwell in complete anonymity.

294 In Se and Ee the reading is *kuṭṭhitaṃ,* glossed *kuthitaṃ* by Spk (Se); Be has *kuthitaṃ,* glossed *kudhitaṃ*. SS have *kikitaṃ* or *kikiṭaṃ,* preferred by Woodward. Spk, calling this a term of unique occurrence in the Word of the Buddha preserved in the Tipiṭaka (*tepiṭike buddhavacane asambhinnapadaṃ*), glosses it as "extremely sharp" (*atitikhiṇaṃ*), because of the hot sand underfoot and the hot sun above.

295 The passage is quoted at Vism 393–94 (Ppn 12:85).

296 At Ud 76,26–27, spoken with reference to the arahant Lakuṇṭaka Bhaddiya (see **21:6**). All the terms refer literally to a chariot and figuratively to an arahant. The key to the riddle is given just below in the text, with fuller explanations at Ud-a 370–71; see the translation in Masefield, *The Udāna Commentary*, 2:959–61. The following is a summary: *ela* is a fault (*dosa*); one without faults is *nela*, faultless. The chariot is described as *nelaṅga* because its wheel (*aṅga*, I follow Masefield, and see MW, s.v. *rathāṅga*)—its most essential part—is faultless. In the application of the simile this represents the virtue associated with the fruit of arahantship. "Awning" is the woollen cloth spread on top of the chariot; the white awning (*setapachāda*) signifies the liberation associated with the fruit of arahantship, which is by nature thoroughly and completely pure. "Trouble-free" (*anīgha*) means without the agitation (*parikhobha*) of the defilements, as with a vehicle in which jolting (*khobha*) is absent. "The stream cut" (*chinnasota*): an ordinary chariot has an uninterrupted stream of oil smeared on the axle-heads and nave, but this one has "the stream cut" because the thirty-six streams (of craving) have been fully abandoned. "Without bondage" (*abandhana*): an ordinary chariot has an abundance of bonds to prevent the platform from being shaken by the axle, etc., but in this one all the bonds—that is, the fetters—have been completely destroyed; thus it is "without bondage."

297 In this discussion, IV 293,7–294,10 corresponds to MN I 301,17–302,5; IV 294,11–24 to MN I 296,11–23; and IV 294,26–295,21 to MN I 302,6–27. The last question and answer, however, are not found in either MN No. 43 or 44. Spk explains that Citta used to abide in cessation [Spk-pṭ: as a nonreturner] and thus he raised the question to ask about the formations that are the basis for cessation (see **n. 299**).

298 The three terms—*kāyasaṅkhāra, vacīsaṅkhāra, cittasaṅkhāra*—are in Pāli identical with those that make up the *saṅkhāra* factor of dependent origination (as at **12:2**; see **II, n. 7**), but in this context the purport is different, as the following discussion will show. Here, in the compounds *kāyasaṅkhāra*

and *cittasaṅkhāra*, *saṅkhāra* clearly has a passive sense: what is formed or generated (*saṅkharīyati*) in dependence on the body or the mind. In the case of *vacīsaṅkhāra* the sense is active: what generates (*saṅkharoti*) speech.

299 The question refers to *saññāvedayitanirodha,* also called *nirodhasamāpatti*, the attainment of cessation, a meditative state in which mind and all mental functions stop. It is said to be accessible only to arahants and nonreturners who have mastered the eight attainments of *samādhi.* For a detailed treatment according to the commentarial method, see Vism 702–9 (Ppn 23:16–52). Spk says Citta had asked this question to find out if the monk was familiar with the attainment.

300 Spk: This means that before attaining cessation he has delimited the duration of the attainment, resolving, "I will be mindless (*acittaka*) for such a time."

301 The verbal formation (thought and examination) ceases in the second jhāna; the bodily formation (in-and-out breathing) ceases in the fourth jhāna; the mental formation (perception and feeling) ceases on entering the attainment of cessation.

302 *Indriyāni vippasannāni*. Spk: The sense faculties are fatigued when activity occurs and external objects impinge on the senses. They are afflicted, soiled as it were, like a mirror set up at a crossroads hit by dust carried by the wind. But as a mirror placed in a casket and deposited in a case shines within, so the five senses of a bhikkhu who has attained cessation shine brightly within cessation.

303 Spk: Before attaining cessation, at the time of delimiting the duration, he resolves, "I will be mindless for such a time and afterwards will again become mindful."

304 Spk: When one emerges from cessation the mind of fruition attainment is the first to arise. It is with reference to the perception and feeling associated with that mind that it is said, "First the mental formation arises." Afterwards, at the time of *bhavaṅga*, the bodily formation (breathing) arises, and still later, at the time of regular activity, the verbal formation resumes, namely, thought and examination able to originate speech.

305 *Suññataphassa, animittaphassa, appaṇihitaphassa.* Spk: These

can be explained by way of their own quality (*saguṇa*) or by way of their object (*ārammaṇa*). By way of quality: the attainment of fruition (*phalasamāpatti*) is called emptiness, and the accompanying contact is called emptiness-contact; the same method in the other two cases. By way of object: Nibbāna is called emptiness because it is empty of lust, etc.; signless, because the signs of lust, etc., are absent; and undirected, because it is not directed towards lust, hatred, or delusion. The contact of the arisen fruition attainment, which takes emptiness-Nibbāna as object, is called emptiness-contact; the same method in the other two cases.

Fruition attainment is a special meditative attainment in which the mind directly experiences the bliss of Nibbāna. It is said to be of four levels, corresponding to the four levels of awakening (the fruition attainment of stream-entry, etc.). See Vism 698–702 (Ppn 23:3–15).

306 Spk: It is Nibbāna that is called seclusion (*viveka*). His mind slants, slopes, and inclines towards that seclusion.

307 This is said because cessation is attained by first entering each jhāna and formless attainment and then contemplating it with insight by way of the three characteristics. The procedure is explained at Vism 705–7 (Ppn 23:31–43).

308 Godatta's verses are at Th 659–72. The conversation that follows is also at MN I 297,9–298,27, with Sāriputta and Mahākoṭṭhita as the speakers.

309 Spk: There are twelve kinds of measureless liberation of mind (*appamāṇā cetovimutti*): the four divine abodes, the four paths, and the four fruits. The divine abodes are called "measureless" because of their measureless radiation (towards countless beings), the paths and fruits because they remove the defilements, the causes of measurement.

310 Spk: There are nine kinds of liberation of mind by nothingness (*ākiñcaññā cetovimutti*): the base of nothingness, and the four paths and fruits. The first is called "nothingness" because it does not have any "something" (impediment; see **n. 315** just below) as object, the paths and fruits because of the nonexistence in them of the excruciating and obstructive defilements.

311 Spk does not gloss this, but it seems the expression "liberation of mind by emptiness" (*suññatā cetovimutti*) is used to

signify concentration based on insight into the selfless nature of phenomena and also the supramundane paths and fruits.

312 Spk: There are thirteen kinds of signless liberation of mind (*animittā cetovimutti*): insight—because it removes the "signs" of permanence, happiness, and self; the four formless attainments—because the sign of form is absent in them; and the four paths and fruits—because the defilements, the "makers of signs," are absent in them.

313 On this interpretation, the measureless liberation of mind is the four divine abodes; the liberation of mind by nothingness, the third formless attainment; and the liberation of mind by emptiness, concentration based on insight into the selfless nature of phenomena. The signless liberation of mind is hard to pinpoint in terms of a familiar doctrinal category. Spk takes it here as supramundane with Nibbāna as object.

314 *Akuppā cetovimutti*. Spk: The liberation of mind consisting in the fruition of arahantship.

315 Spk explains *kiñcana* as if it were derived from a verb *kiñcati* glossed *maddati palibundhati* ("crushes, impedes"), thus as meaning obstruction or impediment. The true derivation, however, is from *kiṃ* + *cana*—meaning simply "something"; see MW, s.v. (2) *ka, kas, ka, kim*. The word is used idiomatically in Pāli to mean a possession considered as an impediment; see MN II 263,34–264,1. This acquired meaning seems to have been devised for a didactic purpose. See PED for other references where this sense is evident.

316 Spk explains that lust, etc., are called sign-makers (*nimittakaraṇa*) because they mark a person as lustful, hating, or deluded. Perhaps, though, the statement means that lust causes the "sign of beauty" (*subhanimitta*) to appear, hatred the "sign of the repulsive" (*paṭighanimitta*), and delusion the signs of permanence, pleasure, and self.

317 Spk: Though the emptiness liberation of mind is not mentioned separately, it is included throughout by the phrase "empty of lust," etc.

318 Nigaṇṭha Nātaputta is identical with Mahāvīra, the historical progenitor of Jainism. Though he makes several personal appearances in the Pāli Canon (see particularly MN

No. 56), there is no report of him meeting the Buddha. His followers were called nigaṇṭhas, "knotless ones."

319 Spk: Why did this noble disciple, a nonreturner, approach a wretched, misguided, naked ascetic? To free (the Buddhists) from blame and to refute his doctrine. For the nigaṇṭhas held that the Buddha's followers do not show hospitality to anyone else, and he wanted to free his co-religionists from this criticism. He also approached with the idea of refuting Nātaputta's doctrine.

320 *Atthi avitakko avicāro samādhi, atthi vitakkavicārānaṃ nirodho.* As will be shown, this refers to the second jhāna.

321 *Na khvāhaṃ ettha bhante bhagavato saddhāya gacchāmi.* Citta is here laying a verbal trap, which will be sprung just below. While he appears to be disclaiming allegiance to the Buddha, he is actually asserting that he has realized the truth of the Buddha's statement by personal experience and thus need not rely on mere faith in his word. The pun recurs at **48:44**.

322 All three eds. read *ulloketvā* here, though SS read *apaloketvā* and Spk (Se) *oloketvā*. The explanation in Spk supports *ulloketvā*: "He swelled his chest, drew in his belly, stretched forth his neck, surveyed all directions, and then looked up." Below I follow Be and Ee in reading *apaloketvā* (Se repeats *ulloketvā*), which provides a meaningful contrast: he looks askance because he is too embarrassed to look his followers in the eye.

323 *Atha maṃ paṭihareyyāsi saddhiṃ nigaṇṭhaparisāya.* Spk paraphrases: "When the meaning of these (questions) is known, then you might come up to me (*abhigaccheyyāsi*) along with your retinue of nigaṇṭhas; having come into my doorkeeper's presence (*patīhārassa me santikaṃ āgantvā*), you might inform me of your arrival." Spk thus glosses the verb *paṭiharati* with *abhigacchati* and connects it with *patīhāra* as doorkeeper (a sense confirmed by MW, s.v. *prati-hṛ* > *pratihāra*). At MN II 220,8, however, we find the expression *sahadhammikaṃ vādapaṭihāraṃ*, which in context seems to mean "a reasonable defense of (their) doctrine." Thus here *paṭiharati* could mean "to respond, to offer a rejoinder," a meaning that appears more relevant than the one proposed by Spk.

The exact import of the following sentences is obscure in the Pāli. Spk identifies the ten questions with the catechism at AN V 50–54 (see too Khp 2). The questions begin, "What is one?" with the answer, "All beings subsist on nutriment," "What is two?"—"Name and form," etc. According to Spk-pṭ the "question" (*pañha*) means the inquiry (*vīmaṃsā*); the synopsis (*uddesa*), a brief statement of the meaning; and the answer (*veyyākaraṇa*), a detailed explanation of the meaning. One might have translated, "The question about one ... the question about ten," but the numbers are clearly distributive and the expressions *dve pañhā* and so forth are plurals. It is unclear whether Citta actually posed the questions (which were then abbreviated by the redactors) or merely indicated the format of the questions without filling it in. See the following note.

324 I follow Ee here in reading *pañhe apucchitvā*. Both Be and Se read *pañhe āpucchitvā*, which is problematic, as the latter verb generally means "to take leave" and is not typically used in relation to asking questions. The point seems to be that because Nātaputta did not accept Citta's challenge, Citta left without actually posing his ten questions.

325 Reading with Be and Se, *koci uttari manussadhammā alamariyañāṇadassanaviseso*. Ee should be amended accordingly. The expression occurs often in the suttas as an umbrella term for all the higher meditative attainments and stages of realization. The analysis at Vin III 91 bifurcates the the two main components of the compound and treats *uttari manussadhammā* as an independent plural compound, but the singular *koci* here (and just below, the *evarūpaṃ* before *-visesaṃ*) indicates that in sutta usage *uttari manussadhammā* functions as an adjectival ablative in relation to *alamariyañāṇadassanavisesa*. Spk explains *manussadhamma*, "the human norm," as the ten courses of wholesome action. What is beyond that (*tato manussadhammato uttari*) is "superhuman." *Alamariyañāṇadassanavisesa* is explained as "distinction of knowledge and vision capable of engendering the state of a noble one."

326 *Pāvaḷanipphoṭanā*. According to Spk, this is a brush made from peacock's feathers, used to sweep the ground of grit and dust before sitting down.

327 *Dhammassa svākkhātatā*. It is not clear to me whether Citta's exclamation is intended as a straightforward praise of the Buddha's teaching or as an ironic putdown of the ascetic's teaching.

328 I read with Se: *kiṃ hi no siyā bhante.*

329 This means he is a nonreturner, having eradicated the five lower fetters binding beings to the sense-sphere realm.

330 Se alone has the correct reading here: *dhammiko dhammarājā dhammikaṃ baliṃ anuppadassati.* The devatās want him to become a universal monarch so they will be assured of receiving the offerings due to them. I translate *dhammarājā* as "king of righteousness" rather than "king of the Dhamma," since the latter is properly an epithet only of the Buddha.

331 Ee seems to have the best reading: *saṅghe ca pasādetvā cāge ca samādapetvā.*

42. Gāmaṇisaṃyutta

332 According to Spk, *caṇḍa* ("wrathful") is a sobriquet assigned to this headman by the redactors of the Dhamma. I give the name both in Pāli and English, also at **42:3–5**.

333 *Sorata* (Ee: *sūrata*). See **I, nn. 256**, **462**.

334 His name means "palmyra box." Spk says he was called thus because his facial complexion was the colour of a ripe palmyra fruit just fallen from its stalk. He was the director of a large troupe of actors and had become famous throughout India. His verses, which stand out by their moral earnestness, are at Th 1091–1145.

335 *Saccālikena*. Woodward renders "by his counterfeiting of the truth" (KS 4:214), but I follow Spk, which glosses this as a *dvanda* compound: *saccena ca alikena ca.*

336 Here, where the present is required, we should read with Be and Se *na labhāmi*, and below, where the aorist is appropriate, *nālatthaṃ*. Ee has the latter reading in both places.

337 *Pahāso nāma nirayo*. Spk: There is no separate hell with this name. This is actually one part of the Avīci hell where the denizens are tortured in the guise of actors dancing and singing.

338 See MN I 387–89, partly parallel to this passage, though concerned with a different wrong view about rebirth.

339 Spk explains the name as meaning "one who earns his living by warfare" (*yuddhena jīvikaṃ kappanako*); this name, too, was assigned by the redactors of the Dhamma. I take the occupation to be that of a mercenary or professional soldier.

340 This free rendering of the name was suggested by VĀT. Se and Ee read *sarañjitānaṃ*, but Be *parajitānaṃ*, "conquered by others," makes better sense.

341 Again, Spk says this is not a separate hell but a section of Avīci where beings appear as soldiers conquered in battle.

342 The three verbs are *uyyāpenti* (glossed *upari yāpenti*), *saññāpenti* (glossed *sammā ñāpenti*), and *saggaṃ okkāmenti*, on which Spk says: "They stand around him saying, 'Go, sir, to the brahmā world; go, sir, to the brahmā world,' and thus make him enter (*pavesenti*) heaven."

343 The Jains. On Nigaṇṭha Nātaputta, see **41:8**.

344 *Yathābhataṃ* (Ee: *yathā hataṃ*) *nikkhitto evaṃ niraye*. The idiom is obscure and the rendering here conjectural. The phrase also occurs at MN I 71,31, rendered at MLDB p. 167: "then as [surely as if he had been] carried off and put there he will wind up in hell." This rendering, which follows Ps II 32 (*yathā nirayapālehi ābharitvā niraye ṭhapito*), is problematic, for *yathābhataṃ* is an indeclinable with an adverbal function, not a substantive set in apposition to the subject. The function of *evaṃ*, too, is obscure. See the inconclusive discussion in PED, s.v. *yathā*.

345 Ee here omits *evam etassa pāpassa kammassa pahānaṃ hoti*.

346 Cp. AN V 299-301. Spk: When (simple) "lovingkindness" is said, this can be interpreted either as access concentration or absorption, but when it is qualified as "liberation of mind" (*cetovimutti*) it definitely means absorption. It is sense-sphere kamma that is called limited kamma (*pamāṇakataṃ kammaṃ*); form-sphere kamma is called limitless (or measureless, *appamāṇakataṃ*) kamma. This is called limitless because it is done by transcending the limit, for it is developed by way of specified, unspecified, and directional pervasion (see Vism 309–11; Ppn 9:49–58).

Does not remain there, does not persist there (*na taṃ tatrāvasissati, na taṃ tatrāvatiṭṭhati*). Spk: That sense-sphere kamma does not linger on, does not stay on, in that form-sphere or formless-sphere kamma. What is meant? That sense-sphere kamma is unable to overpower the form-sphere or formless-sphere kamma or to persist and gain the opportunity (to yield its own results); rather, as a great flood might inundate a little stream, the form-sphere or formless-sphere kamma overpowers the sense-sphere kamma and remains after having made an opportunity (for its own results). The superior kamma, having prevented the sense-sphere kamma from producing its result, on its own leads to rebirth in the brahmā world.

347 I follow von Hinüber's proposals regarding the correct reading and interpretation of these terms in his paper, "The Ghost Word *Dvīhitikā* and the Description of Famines in Early Buddhist Literature." The reading, firstly, should be: *Nālandā dubbhikkhā hoti duhitikā setaṭṭikā salākāvuttā*. All extant mss, it seems, have been contaminated by *dvīhitikā* and *setaṭṭhikā*, though Spk recognizes *duhitikā* as a v.l. here and other texts on crop failure preserve *setaṭṭikā* (Vin II 256,21–23 = AN IV 278,28–279,2). While Spk explains both *dvīhitikā* and *duhitikā* as derived from *du-īhiti* (or *du-ihiti*, "difficult faring"), the correct derivation is from *du-hita* (see **n. 212** above). The corrupt reading *setaṭṭhikā* is explained by Spk as meaning "white with bones," i.e., with the bones of people who have perished in the famine, but other commentaries identify *setaṭṭikā* as a crop disease (*rogajāti*) caused by insects that devour the pith of the grain stalks. The word is analysed *seta-aṭṭi-kā*, "the white disease," because the afflicted crops turn white and do not yield grain (see Sp VI 1291,5–7 = Mp IV 136,16–18; Sp I 175,4–8).

348 I read *saññamasambhūtāni*, as in Se and Ee, as against Be *sāmaññasambhūtāni*. Spk merely glosses with *sesasīlaṃ*.

349 I read *nihitaṃ vā nādhigacchati*, again with Se and Ee, as against Be *nihitaṃ vā ṭhānā vigacchati*.

350 The rule is Nissaggiya-pācittiya No. 18; see Vin III 236–39 and Vin I 245,2–7. The sutta is cited at Vin II 296–97 as testimony for the prohibition against the acceptance of gold and silver by bhikkhus. At Vin III 238, "silver" is more broadly defined as including coins made of silver, copper, wood, or lac, or whatever serves as a medium of exchange.

Its commentary (Sp III 690) extends this to include bone, hide, fruit, seeds, etc., whether imprinted with a figure or not. Thus in effect the expression "gold and silver" signifies money. On *samaṇa sakyaputtiya*, see **II, n. 376**.

351 Be omits the second question, apparently by editorial oversight, as it is in Se and Ee.

352 Cp. **12:33** (II 58,3–5). Spk's treatment of the line here indicates that it takes *akālikena pattena* as a single expression, with *akālikena* functioning as an adverbial instrumental in apposition to *pattena*: *Akālikena pattenā ti na kālantarena pattena; kālaṃ anatikkamitvā va pattenā ti attho*; "*Immediately attained*: not attained after an interval of time; the meaning is that it is attained even without any time having elapsed." For more on *akālikena*, see **I, n. 33, II, n. 103**. The opening of this paragraph in Ee seems garbled.

353 Note that the headman here ascribes to the Buddha, as a direct quotation, a general statement of the causal tie between desire and suffering (*yaṃ kiñci dukkhaṃ uppajjamānaṃ uppajjati ...*). As this statement is not found in the Buddha's words above but is clearly needed as the referent of "this principle" (*iminā dhammena*), it seems likely that the statement had been in the original text but at some point had been elided. Just below the Buddha does make the generalization himself.

354 These are the words with which the Buddha opened his first sermon; see **56:11**. Spk: The pursuit of sensual happiness is mentioned to show the types who enjoy sensual pleasure (II–III); the pursuit of self-mortification to show the ascetics (IV–V); the middle way to show the three types of wearing away (VI). What is the purpose in showing all this? The Tathāgata, who attained perfect enlightenment by abandoning the two extremes and by following the middle way, does not criticize or praise all enjoyers of sensual pleasures or all ascetics. He criticizes those who deserve criticism and praises those who deserve praise.

355 The three coordinates of the pattern to be expanded upon are: (i) how wealth is acquired, whether unlawfully, lawfully, or both; (ii) whether or not it is used for one's own benefit; and (iii) whether or not it is used to benefit others. Those who rank positive on all three counts will be further

divided into those who remain attached to their wealth and those who are unattached to it. This same tenfold analysis of the *kāmabhogī* is at AN V 177–82.

356 See **n. 325**. Here a wholesome state (*kusala dhamma*) must rank lower than a "superhuman distinction," since the attainment of the former does not necessarily entail the latter. The former can include simple moral conduct and ordinary wholesome states of mind, while the latter includes only the jhānas, formless attainments, direct knowledges, and supramundane paths and fruits.

357 *Tisso sandiṭṭhikā nijjarā. Nijjarā,* "wearing away," was a Jain term adopted by the Buddha. The Jains held that ascetic practice was the means to "wear away" all suffering (*sabbaṃ dukkhaṃ nijjiṇṇaṃ bhavissati*); see their position at MN I 93,2–11 and II 214,7–13, and the Buddha's alternative approach to "wearing away" at MN II 223–25. Three other kinds of *sandiṭṭhikā nijjarā* are described at AN I 221,5–30 (i.e., virtue, the jhānas, the destruction of the taints) and a twentyfold *nijjarā* is at MN III 76,12–77,23. Spk says that one path is described as three kinds of wearing away because of the wearing away of the three defilements.

358 *Samaṇo Gotamo māyaṃ jānāti.* At MN I 375,12–14 the Jains proclaim, "The ascetic Gotama is a magician (*māyāvī*); he knows a converting magic (*āvaṭṭaniṃ māyaṃ jānāti*) by which he converts the disciples of other teachers." The same charge comes up for discussion at AN II 190–94.

359 *Samaṇo khalu bho Gotamo māyāvī.*

360 *Lambacūḷakā bhaṭā.* Spk gives no help, but Rhys Davids interprets the passage thus in his *Buddhist India* (p. 21): "The Koliyan central authorities were served by a special body of *peons*, or police, distinguished, as by a kind of uniform, from which they took their name, by a special head-dress. These particular men had a bad reputation for extortion and violence."

361 See **24:5, III, n. 254**.

362 See **24:6, III, n. 255**.

363 Spk proposes alternative interpretations of *dhammasamādhi* and *cittasamādhi*: (i) *dhammasamādhi* is the *dhamma* of the ten wholesome courses of action, *cittasamādhi* the four paths along with insight; (ii) the five *dhammā* (mentioned

below)—namely, gladness, rapture, tranquillity, happiness, and concentration—are called *dhammasamādhi,* while *cittasamādhi* is again the four paths along with insight; (iii) the ten wholesome courses of action and the four divine abodes are *dhammasamādhi,* the one-pointedness of mind arisen for one who fulfils this *dhammasamādhi* is *cittasamādhi.*

364 *Apaṇṇakatāya mayhaṃ.* Spk: "This practice leads to what is incontrovertible for me, to absence of wrongness (*anaparādhakatāya*)." At Ps III 116,21 *apaṇṇaka* is glossed *aviruddho advejjhagāmī ekaṃsagāhiko;* "uncontradicted, unambiguous, definitive."

365 *Kaṭaggaha.* The allusion is to the lucky throw at dice, glossed *jayaggaha,* "the victorious throw." The opposite is *kaliggaha,* the dark throw or losing throw. The style of reasoning here is reminiscent of that used at MN I 402–11 (which also includes the metaphor of dice) and at AN I 192–93.

43. *Asaṅkhatasaṃyutta*

366 *Kāyagatā sati.* In sutta usage this includes all the practices comprised under "contemplation of the body" (*kāyānupassanā*) in the Satipaṭṭhāna Sutta (DN No. 22, MN No. 10). They are treated separately under this heading in the Kāyagatāsati Sutta (MN No. 119). The commentaries generally confine the term to the meditation on the thirty-two aspects of the body, as at Vism 240 (Ppn 8:44).

367 This triad of concentrations occurs elsewhere in the Nikāyas, e.g., at DN III 219,19–20, MN III 162,14–15, and AN IV 300,28–301,1. A concentration without thought but with examination (*avitakka vicāramatta samādhi*) does not fit into the familiar sequence of the four jhānas, in which the first jhāna includes both thought and examination and the second excludes both. To reconcile the two schemes, the Abhidhamma supplements the fourfold sequence of jhānas with a fivefold sequence in which the second jhāna is the *avitakka vicāramatta samādhi.* The second jhāna of the tetrad then becomes the third jhāna of the pentad. See As 179–80, which explains the reasons for the two sets.

368 *Suññata samādhi, animitta samādhi, appaṇihita samādhi.* Spk gives no explanation of these terms. The three are mentioned as a set at DN III 219,21–22, again without explanation, but Sv III 1003–4 comments on them thus: One who, at the stage of advanced insight, contemplates things as nonself, acquires the emptiness concentration on arriving at the path and fruit (because he has seen things as empty of self); one who contemplates things as impermanent acquires the signless concentration (because he has seen through the "sign of permanence"); one who contemplates things as suffering acquires the undirected concentration (because he has no leaning to things seen as painful). See too the discussion of the "triple gateway to liberation" at Vism 657–59 (Ppn 21:66–73). On *animitta cetosamādhi*, see **n. 280** above.

369 This sutta and the next six cover the "thirty-seven aids to enlightenment," elaborated at **43:12** (ix–xlv). More detailed explanations are given in the Introduction to Part V and in the notes to SN 45–51.

370 I follow the numbering in Ee. Though Woodward says "the sections are wrongly numbered in the text" (KS 4:261, n. 1), in fact it is the text that is correct and Woodward's numbering that is off. For this sutta I prefer the Be reading *anataṃ* and the gloss in Spk (Be): *taṇhānatiyā abhāvena anataṃ*; "uninclined due to the absence of inclination through craving." This seems more original than the Se and Ee reading *antaṃ*, "the end," with Spk (Se) explaining: *taṇhāratiyā abhāvena antaṃ*; "the end due to the absence of delight through craving."

371 Under each of the epithets for Nibbāna, Ee has "I–XLV" as if the elaboration is to be developed only as in §12. In the last sutta, however, "the path leading to the destination" begins with "mindfulness directed to the body," which means that each elaboration is to be developed in full as in §§1–12. This means that each epithet should be conjoined with fifty-six versions of the path.

372 *Nippapañcaṃ*. Spk: Through the absence of proliferation by craving, conceit, and views.

44. Abyākatasaṃyutta

373 At AN I 25,19 she is declared the foremost bhikkhunī among those with great wisdom (*etadaggaṃ mahāpaññānaṃ*), and at **17:24** she is extolled as a model for the other bhikkhunīs. For a biographical sketch, see Hecker, "Great Woman Disciples of the Buddha," in Nyanaponika and Hecker, *Great Disciples of the Buddha*, pp. 263–66, and Pruitt, *Commentary on the Verses of the Therīs*, pp. 164–74.

374 As at **16:12, 24:15–18, 33:1–55.**

375 The reply here is identical with the Buddha's famous reply to Vacchagotta at MN I 487–88. Though worded in terms of the Tathāgata, the questions refer to any arahant misconceived as a "being" or a self.

376 Spk: "The form by which one might describe the Tathāgata" considered as a being (*sattasaṅkhātaṃ tathāgataṃ*)—as tall or short, dark or light, etc.—has been abandoned by the omniscient Tathāgata through the abandoning of its origin. He is "liberated from reckoning in terms of form" (*rūpasaṅkhāya vimutto*), that is, because there will be no arising of form in the future for him, even the statement, "He will be such and such" through his physical form and mental qualities, loses its validity; thus he is liberated even from description by way of form. He is deep (*gambhīra*) through the depth of his inclination (*ajjhāsayagambhīratā*) and through the depth of his qualities (*guṇagambhīratā*). As to the description that might be used in relation to the omniscient Tathāgata with such deep qualities, considering him as a being, when one sees the nonexistence (invalidity) of this description [Spk-pṭ: "a being"] owing to the nonexistence [Spk-pṭ: of the five aggregates], then the statement "The Tathāgata—considered as a being—exists after death" does not apply, i.e., it is not valid.

377 Be and Ee read the last verb as *virodhayissati*, Se *vihāyissati*. Spk glosses *na viruddhaṃ padaṃ* (Se: *viruddhasaddaṃ*) *bhavissati*; "there will be no contradictory term." Spk glosses *aggapadasmiṃ* simply as "in the teaching" (*desanāya*). *Aggapadasmiṃ* occurs also at AN V 320,32, glossed by Mp with *nibbāne*.

378 *Rūpagatam etaṃ*. Spk: This is mere form. He shows: "No other being is found here apart from form, but when there is form there is merely this name." Spk-pṭ: What is being rejected here? The self posited by the outside thinkers, spoken of here as "Tathāgata."

379 See **III, n. 83**.

380 Spk explains *kutūhalasālā* (lit. "commotion hall") as a place where ascetics and brahmins of other sects engage in various discussions. It is so named because commotion arises as they say, "What does this one say? What does that one say?"

The teachers mentioned are the famous "six heretics," the rivals of Gotama (see **I, n. 200**). It is strange that predictions about rebirth are ascribed to Ajita, since elsewhere he is reported to have taught materialism and to have denied an afterlife. Even Sañjaya is reported to have been a sceptic about such issues.

381 *Sa-upādānassa khvāhaṃ Vaccha upapattiṃ paññāpemi no anupādānassa*. There is a double meaning here, with *upādāna* meaning both "fuel" and subjective "clinging," but I have translated the sentence in consonance with the following simile. It was also in a discourse to Vacchagotta that the Buddha used his famous simile of the fire that goes out from lack of fuel to illustrate the status of one who has attained Nibbāna; see MN I 487,11–30.

382. *Tam ahaṃ taṇhūpādānaṃ vadāmi*. The Buddha's statement seems to imply that a temporal gap can intervene between the death moment and reconception. Since this contradicts Theravāda orthodoxy, Spk contends that at the death moment itself the being is said to be "not yet reborn" because the rebirth-consciousness has not yet arisen.

383 Here and below I read *saddhiṃ*, with Be and Ee, as against *laddhi* in Se. Spk glosses: *tesaṃ laddhiyā saddhiṃ etaṃ abhavissa*. To my knowledge *laddhi*, in the sense of belief, is a term of later usage, and it may have been incorporated into Se via a misunderstanding of the commentary.

384 I read *ñāṇassa uppādāya*, with Be and Se, as against *ñāṇassa upādāya* in Ee. Spk: "As to the insight knowledge that arises thus, 'All phenomena are nonself,' would I have been consistent with that?"

385 Probably this means that Vacchagotta would have interpreted the Buddha's denial as a rejection of his empirical personality, which (on account of his inclination towards views of self) he would have been identifying as a self. We should carefully heed the two reasons the Buddha does not declare, "There is no self": not because he recognizes a transcendent self of some kind (as some interpreters allege), or because he is concerned only with delineating "a strategy of perception" devoid of ontological implications (as others hold), but (i) because such a mode of expression was used by the annihilationists, and the Buddha wanted to avoid aligning his teaching with theirs; and (ii) because he wished to avoid causing confusion in those already attached to the idea of self. The Buddha declares that "all phenomena are nonself" (*sabbe dhammā anattā*), which means that if one seeks a self anywhere one will not find one. Since "all phenomena" includes both the conditioned and the unconditioned, this precludes an utterly transcendent, ineffable self.

386 *Yassa p' assa āvuso etam ettakena ettakam eva, tam p' assa bahuṃ*. I translate this obscure exclamation with the aid of Spk.

Part V
The Great Book
(*Mahāvagga*)

Contents

Chapter II
46. *Bojjhaṅgasaṃyutta*
Connected Discourses on the Factors of Enlightenment

Chapter III
47. *Satipaṭṭhānasaṃyutta*
Connected Discourses on the Establishments of Mindfulness

Chapter IV
48. *Indriyasaṃyutta*
Connected Discourses on the Faculties

Chapter VI
50. *Balasaṃyutta*
Connected Discourses on the Powers

Chapter VII
51. *Iddhipādasaṃyutta*
Connected Discourses on the Bases for Spiritual Power

Chapter VIII
52. *Anuruddhasaṃyutta*
Connected Discourses with Anuruddha

Introduction

The fifth and final part of the Saṃyutta Nikāya is the *Mahāvagga*, The Great Book. There are at least three explanations that might be given for this title. First, it is the largest division of SN, and could become exponentially larger if the abbreviated repetition series, at the end of many chapters, were to be expanded in full. Second, we find here, not one giant saṃyutta towering over a retinue of lesser peaks, but a veritable Himalayan range of saṃyuttas, with at least eight major chapters among a total of twelve. And third, almost all the saṃyuttas in this book deal with different formulations of the Buddha's path to liberation, the most precious part of his legacy to the world.

A glance at the contents of the Mahāvagga shows that its first seven chapters are devoted to seven sets of training factors which occur elsewhere in the Pāli Canon, though in a different sequence. In the standard sequence these are:

the four establishments of mindfulness (*cattāro satipaṭṭhānā*)
the four right strivings (*cattāro sammappadhānā*)
the four bases for spiritual power (*cattāro iddhipādā*)
the five spiritual faculties (*pañc' indriyāni*)
the five powers (*pañca balāni*)
the seven factors of enlightenment (*satta bojjhaṅgā*)
the Noble Eightfold Path (*ariya aṭṭhaṅgika magga*).

In SN we have already met these sets several times: at **22:81**, when the Buddha explains how the Dhamma has been taught discriminately; at **22:101**, as the things to be developed for the mind to be liberated from the taints; at **43:12**, as different aspects of the path leading to the unconditioned. In the Buddhist exegetical tradition, beginning very soon after the age of the canon, these seven sets are known as the thirty-seven aids to enlightenment (*sattatiṃsa bodhipakkhiyā dhammā*). Although this term is not used in the Nikāyas themselves as a collective appellation for the seven sets, the sets themselves frequently appear in the Nikāyas as a compendium of the practice leading to enlightenment. On several occasions the Buddha himself underlined their critical importance, referring to them, in his talks to the bhikkhus, as "the things I have taught you through direct knowledge" (*ye vo mayā dhammā abhiññā desitā*). In the prelude to his parinibbāna he urged the bhikkhus to learn, pursue, develop, and cultivate them so that the holy life would endure long in the world, out of compassion for the world, for the good, welfare, and happiness of devas and humans (DN II 119–20). He requested the bhikkhus to meet often and recite the seven sets "meaning for meaning, phrase for phrase," without disputes, again so that the holy life would endure long (DN III 127–28). He made unity in the Sangha contingent upon concord regarding the seven sets (MN II 245) and urged the disciples to train in them "united, in concord, not disputing" (MN II 238). It is because he teaches these seven sets that his disciples venerate him, and by developing them many of these disciples have attained consummation and perfection in direct knowledge (MN II 11–12).

The presentation of the seven sets in a graded sequence might convey the impression that they constitute seven successive stages of practice. This, however, would be a misinterpretation. Close consideration of the series would show that the seven sets are ranked in a numerically ascending order, from four to eight, which means that their arrangement is purely pedagogic and implies nothing about a later set being more advanced than the earlier sets. Even more decisively, when we examine the contents of the seven sets as formally defined and explained in the suttas, we would see that their contents are inextricably interwoven. Often factors in one set are identical with those in another; sometimes one set reorders the constituents of another; sometimes one set subdivides a factor treated synoptically in another. What emerges from a close study of the seven sets, as presented in the Mahāvagga, is an array of overlapping, intersecting, mutually illuminating portraits of a single course of practice aimed at a single goal, deliverance from suffering. By presenting the course of practice from different angles, in different keys, and with different degrees of detail, the texts are able to finely modulate the practice of the path to suit the diverse needs of the people to be trained. This accounts for the versatility of the Buddha's teaching, its ability to assume variable expressions in accordance with the different aptitudes, preferences, and propensities of different human beings.

The need for a path is bound up with the whole structure of the Dhamma, girded from below by the abstract principle of conditionality, "When this arises, that arises; when this ceases, that ceases." Bondage and suffering arise from ignorance, from a failure to see and understand the subjects treated in the earlier saṃyuttas: the five aggregates, the six sense bases, and the eighteen elements as the constituent factors of sentient existence; dependent origination as the inherent dynamism by which saṃsāra again and again renews itself from within, bringing along the suffering of repeated birth, aging, and death. To gain irreversible release from suffering we have to cut through the tangle of craving and clinging, and for this "disentanglement" to be final and complete, we must extricate the most deeply buried root of all, namely, ignorance.

The direct antidote to ignorance is knowledge—not mere conceptual knowledge, but direct insight into things as they really are—and it was one of the Buddha's key discoveries that the knowledge needed for liberation can be developed. Such knowledge does not depend on divine grace or arise as a mystical intuition, but emerges out of a matrix of persistent spiritual practice governed by a precisely articulated groundplan. This course of practice is a process of self-cultivation sustained by the unvarying laws of conditionality. The different factors embedded in the seven sets are the qualities that need to be developed. They are the conditions which, when methodically generated and fortified, directly conduce to the arising of the liberating knowledge.

The major saṃyuttas of the Mahāvagga can be seen as offering a conception of the path that is the converse of the Asaṅkhatasaṃyutta (43). The latter begins with the goal, the unconditioned, and then asks, "What is the path leading to this goal?" The answer given is framed in terms of the seven sets, and thus here the texts extract the path from the goal. The Mahāvagga takes the complementary approach. Here we begin with the seven sets and by following their course of movement we are brought to see that they "slant, slope, and incline towards Nibbāna" just as surely as the waters in the great Indian rivers flow towards the ocean. Thus, from the perspective offered by the Mahāvagga, the seven sets become the constellation of training factors that bring the realization of a goal towards which they inherently incline. We might even speak of the path factors as being "pregnant" with the goal, though we must qualify this by noting that the development of the path does not bring Nibbāna itself into being, but rather promotes the attainment of a goal which, as unconditioned, is not locked into the process of causality.

I said just above that the seven sets overlap and intersect. How this is so becomes clearer when we recognize that the terms used to designate different items among the thirty-seven aids to enlightenment are often synonyms representing the same mental factor. The different names merely serve to illuminate different functions of these mental factors while the arrangement into seven sets shows how the factors can collaborate in diverse patterns of mutual support.

This aspect of the aids to enlightenment becomes more evident through the analytical treatment of the Abhidhamma, which collates the synonymous terms used to represent a single mental factor. A concise statement of the results obtained is found at Vism 680 (Ppn 22:41–43). Applied to the seven sets, we see, firstly, that one mental factor, energy (*viriya*), occurs in nine roles: as the four right strivings; as the basis for spiritual power headed by energy; as a faculty, power, and enlightenment factor; and as the path factor of right effort. Mindfulness (*sati*) takes on eight roles: as the four establishments of mindfulness; as a faculty, power, and enlightenment factor; and as the path factor of right mindfulness. Wisdom (*paññā*) serves in five capacities: as the basis for spiritual power headed by investigation; as a faculty and power; as the enlightenment factor of discrimination; and as the path factor of right view. Concentration (*samādhi*) occurs four times under its own name: as a faculty, power, enlightenment factor, and path factor; it also participates in all four bases for spiritual power. Faith (*saddhā*) occurs twice, as a faculty and power. The other nine aids to enlightenment occur only once each. Table 7 represents this correlation visually.

TABLE 7

The Aids to Enlightenment by Way of Mental Factors
(based on Vism 680 and CMA 7:32–33)

MENTAL FACTORS		AIDS TO ENLIGHTENMENT: 4 establ. mindfulness	4 right strivings	4 bases for power	5 faculties	5 powers	7 enlightenment factors	8 noble path factors	Total
1	Energy		4	1	1	1	1	1	9
2	Mindfulness	4			1	1	1	1	8
3	Wisdom			1	1	1	1	1	5
4	Concentration				1	1	1	1	4
5	Faith				1	1			2
6	Intention							1	1
7	Tranquillity						1		1
8	Rapture						1		1
9	Equanimity						1		1
10	Desire			1					1
11	Mind			1					1
12	Right speech							1	1
13	Right action							1	1
14	Right livelihood							1	1

From this we can see that four factors permeate the practice in a variety of guises: energy, mindfulness, concentration, and wisdom. These factors, it must be noted, are not different from mental qualities that arise periodically in the ordinary, undeveloped mind. In the untrained mind, however, their occurrence is sporadic and random. The intention behind the Buddha's presentation of the practice is to train the disciple to arouse these factors deliberately, through the exercise of the will, and then to strengthen them and unify their functions so that they can work together as members of an indomitable team. Hence the stress laid, over and over, on the idea that one "develops and cultivates" (*bhāveti bahulīkaroti*) the aids to enlightenment. When they are developed and cultivated in unison, under the dominion of an overarching purpose, their inherent potentials can be actualized and gradually raised to the pitch of intensity needed to snap the fetters that, since beginningless time, have kept us in bondage to suffering.

When the factors in the seven sets are said to be "aids to enlightenment" (or, literally, "states on the side of enlightenment"), this raises the question of their relationship to the experience of enlightenment itself. In the Nikāyas the word enlightenment (*bodhi, sambodhi*) seems always to be used to denote the cognition issuing directly in arahantship, hence as equivalent to the knowledge of the destruction of the taints (*āsavakkhaya-ñāṇa*). In these oldest sources, the thirty-seven factors constitute the practice *leading to* enlightenment. When they are fulfilled, enlightenment naturally follows.

The Pāli commentaries, however, offer a more complex answer to our question, based on the more minute and technical analysis of experience undertaken in the Abhidhamma treatises. Their more recent provenance should not be a reason for rejecting them out of hand, for the Abhidhamma and the commentaries often make explicit principles derivable from the older texts but not yet worked out in them. The commentaries understand enlightenment as consisting in four discrete momentary attainments, called the four supramundane paths (*lokuttaramagga*), each of which eliminates or attenuates a particular group of defilements and is followed immediately by its fruit (*phala*). Attainment of the path and fruit transforms the disciple into a "noble person" (*ariyapuggala*) at the corresponding level of sanctity: a stream-enterer, a once-returner, a nonreturner, or an arahant. The path of stream-entry eradicates the lowest three fetters—identity view, doubt, and wrong grasp of rules and vows; the path of once-returning does not eradicate any fetters but attenuates lust, hatred, and delusion; the path of nonreturning eradicates sensual desire and ill will; and the path of arahantship eradicates the five higher fetters—lust for form, lust for the formless, conceit, restlessness, and ignorance. The alignment of stages of liberation with the elimination of defilements is already found in the Nikāyas. What is innovative in the Abhidhamma is the conception of the supramundane path as a momentary breakthrough, though even this can claim precedents in the canon (see just below).

On the basis of this picture of the spiritual path, the commentaries hold that the development of the aids to enlightenment takes place in two stages or at two levels. The first is called the preliminary portion of practice (*pubbabhāga-paṭipadā*), during which the practitioner develops and cultivates the aids to enlightenment for the purpose of attaining the supramundane path (see Vism 679–80; Ppn 22:39–40). The virtuous worldling does so with the aim of reaching the path of stream-entry; those established in the lower three fruits do so with the aim of reaching the next higher path. In the preliminary portion of practice the aids to enlightenment are developed because *they lead to enlightenment*. And while a number of factors will naturally occur simultaneously, some degree of progression will be inevitable as more powerful and deeper forces gradually gain ascendency. With the arising of the supramundane path, however, all thirty-seven aids to enlightenment occur simultaneously. At this point the thirty-seven factors no longer lead to enlightenment. Rather, *they are enlightenment*; they constitute the constellation of mental factors, raised to supramundane stature, that make the cognitive event in which they occur a distinctive experience of awakening (see Vism 670; Ppn 21:130–33; and Vism 679–80; Ppn 22:39–40). Refined and strengthened by the power of prior development, they collectively contribute to the total experience by which the aspirant attains freedom from suffering. In terms of a classical paradigm, they each participate in the process of fully understanding the noble truth of suffering; of abandoning craving, the cause of suffering; of realizing Nibbāna, the cessation of suffering; and of developing the path, the way to the cessation of suffering.

In the Mahāvagga itself the idea of a supramundane path, understood as a momentary peak experience, is not explicit, though precedents for this idea may be located in the canonical model of the breakthrough to the Dhamma (i.e., the attainment of stream-entry; see **22:83**, **90**; **35:74**, **46:30**, etc.) and the liberation from the taints (i.e., the attainment of arahantship; see **15:13**; **22:59**; **35:28**, **75**, **121**) as sudden transformative events that usually follow a period of prior gradual preparation. But whether or not the notion of a momentary path attainment has a basis in the suttas, the Mahāvagga (read in conjunction with other parts of the Nikāyas) implies that the path has a dual character. The first phase is the practice taken up by one who is technically still a worldling (*puthujjana*) training to make the breakthrough to the Dhamma. Such a person will develop the thirty-seven aids to enlightenment for the purpose of making the breakthrough. At a certain point, when the practice has ripened, this person will enter upon "the fixed course of rightness" (*sammatta-niyāma*), either as a faith-follower or a Dhamma-follower (see **25:1**). At this point the attainment of stream-entry is certain within that life itself. Now the thirty-seven factors acquire a truly transcendental dimension, since they are "pregnant" with the realization of Nibbāna and will give birth to this realization when the due time arrives. As the practitioner continues to "develop and cultivate" them, even over several more lifetimes, the various defilements are eliminated and the path yields the successive fruits of the holy life, culminating in true knowledge and liberation (*vijjāvimutti*), which marks the end of the journey.

In the Mahāvagga, as I said earlier, the seven sets appear in a different order from the simple numerical one in which they are usually presented. The chapter on the Noble Eightfold Path was probably placed first for the sake of emphasis: to show this most ancient formulation of the practice as the quintessential expression of the Buddha's way to liberation. The seven factors of enlightenment may have been placed next, again out of turn, because they have the widest compass after the eightfold path. The arrangement of the following chapters does not appear to conform to a deliberate pattern. The Anuruddhasaṃyutta seems to be an appendix to the Satipaṭṭhānasaṃyutta and may have evolved from that collection. The last four chapters of the Mahāvagga do not deal explicitly with topics that fall under the seven sets, but even these tie up with them, as we shall see below when we examine the individual chapters.

In the General Introduction I discussed the use of templates to generate suttas that cut across the different saṃyuttas, arranging their subject matter into distinctive and revealing patterns. In the Mahāvagga a new cluster of templates appears, apart from the "repetition series," which I will touch on in the survey of the Maggasaṃyutta. The allotment of templates to subjects is as follows (see Concordance 3 for sutta references):

> Several practices "lead to going beyond from the near shore to the far shore": said of the eightfold path, the enlightenment factors, the establishments of mindfulness, and the bases for spiritual power.
>
> "Those who have neglected them have neglected the noble path leading to the complete destruction of suffering, while those who have undertaken them have undertaken the noble path": said of the same four groups.
>
> "They are noble and emancipating and lead to the complete destruction of suffering": said of the enlightenment factors, the establishments of mindfulness, and the bases for spiritual power—but not of the eightfold path.
>
> "They lead to utter revulsion, dispassion, cessation, peace, direct knowledge, enlightenment, and Nibbāna": again, said of the same three groups.
>
> "They do not arise, developed and cultivated, apart from the appearance of a Buddha or outside his Discipline": said of the eightfold path, the enlightenment factors, and the faculties.
>
> "They yield one of two fruits, final knowledge (i.e., arahantship) or nonreturning": said of the enlightenment factors, the establishments of mindfulness, the faculties, the bases for spiritual power, and mindfulness of breathing.
>
> "They yield seven fruits and benefits" (obtained by a finer differentiation of the above two fruits): said of the enlightenment factors, the faculties, the bases for spiritual power, and mindfulness of breathing—but not of the establishments of mindfulness.

It is a matter for conjecture why some templates are applied to certain sets of practices but not to others. However, as all the above templates seem fully applicable to all the sets, this may be due to sheer chance (or to the loss of certain suttas in the line of transmission) and not to a policy of deliberate exclusion.

45. Maggasaṃyutta

The best known of the seven sets is, of course, the Noble Eightfold Path, announced already by the Buddha in his first sermon at Bārāṇasī and repeatedly referred to throughout his discourses. The Noble Eightfold Path is given such prominence not only because it has an honoured place as the fourth of the Four Noble Truths, and is thus comprised within the chief doctrine of early Buddhism, but because it is the most comprehensive of the seven sets. Its eight factors have a wider scope than the others, making the practice of the Dhamma a complete way of life. The eightfold path spans the three trainings in virtue, concentration, and wisdom; it guides action of body, speech, and mind; and it transforms our ordinary conduct, thought, and view into the conduct, thought, and view of the noble ones. The other sets, though oriented towards the same goal, are more restricted in scope, pertaining almost exclusively to the meditative phase of the eightfold path.

The Noble Eightfold Path is also the most inclusive in relation to the other six sets, capable of accommodating within itself most, though not all, of their components. Thus right view, as a synonym for wisdom, includes the basis for spiritual power headed by investigation; the faculty and power of wisdom; and the enlightenment factor of discrimination of states. Right effort includes the four right strivings; the basis for spiritual power headed by energy; the faculty, power, and enlightenment factor of energy. Right mindfulness includes the four establishments of mindfulness, and the faculty, power, and enlightenment factor of mindfulness. Right concentration explicitly includes the faculty, power, and enlightenment factor of concentration, and implicitly all four bases for spiritual power. Thus, when the other six sets are correlated with the Noble Eightfold Path, we can see that of their twenty-nine constituents, twenty-four have counterparts among the path factors.

The eightfold path is described by the Buddha as *ariya*, noble, and this qualification is important. It would be too restrictive to maintain, as some interpreters of early Buddhism have done, that the eightfold path can be practised only by those who are technically *ariyapuggalas*, noble individuals beginning with the faith-follower (*saddhānusārī*). Certainly the Buddha offered the eightfold path to all his disciples who aspired to release from the suffering of saṃsāra, and for this reason he called it the way leading to the cessation of suffering. We might understand the adjective *ariya* in a broader sense as indicating not only that this is the path followed by the ariyans, but also that this is the path to be practised to arrive at the ariyan state, the state of inward spiritual nobility. To reach the truly ariyan Noble Eightfold Path that leads infallibly to Nibbāna, one has to start somewhere, and the most reasonable place to start is with the development of the eight path factors in their humbler, more immediately accessible manifestations.

The eight path factors are formally defined at **45:8**, using stock definitions found elsewhere in the Pāli Canon (e.g., at DN II 311 and MN III 251–52). But these definitions scarcely indicate how the path is to be developed as a whole. On this question we do not find detailed instructions made explicit anywhere in the Mahāvagga, and thus a "how-to manual" of the practice has to be pieced together from various sources. We can start with the Buddha's statement that each path factor emerges from its predecessor (**45:1**) and use this as a key for sketching a picture of how the path unfolds in actual experience. On gaining faith in the Buddha in his role as the Tathāgata, the supreme guide to deliverance, the disciple must first arrive at a clear conceptual understanding of the teaching, particularly with respect to the principle of kamma and its fruit and the Four Noble Truths. This is *right view* (*sammādiṭṭhi*) in its embryonic stage. Right view alters the disciple's motives and purposes, steering him or her away from sensuality, ill will, and cruelty, towards renunciation, benevolence, and compassion: this is *right intention* (*sammāsaṅkappa*). Guided by right intention, the disciple undertakes the three ethical factors of the path: *right speech*, *right action*, and *right livelihood* (*sammāvācā, sammākammanta, sammā-ājīva*). Standing on this foundation of virtue (see **45:149**), the disciple trains the mind by diligently and energetically developing the four establishments of mindfulness: this is *right effort* (*sammāvāyāmā*) applied to the practice of *right mindfulness* (*sammāsati*). When the effort bears fruit, the disciple enters and dwells in the four jhānas (or, according to the commentaries, a lower degree of concentration bordering on the first jhāna): this is *right concentration* (*sammāsamādhi*).

Right concentration, however, is not the end of the path. Now the disciple must use the concentrated mind to explore the nature of experience. Again, the method is right mindfulness, but this time with emphasis on the fourth establishment, mindful contemplation of phenomena. The disciple contemplates the phenomena comprised in the five aggregates and the six sense bases to discern their marks of impermanence, suffering, and nonself. This is right view at a higher plane, the plane of insight (*vipassanā*). At a certain point in the course of contemplation, when insight becomes sharp and penetrative, the disciple enters upon the fixed course of rightness (*sammatta-niyāma*), the supramundane path, either as a faith-follower or a Dhamma-follower, and thereby becomes bound to win the fruit of stream-entry within this life itself. Now he or she is described as one practising for the realization of the fruit of stream-entry (*sotāpattiphalasacchikiriyāya paṭipanna*). When the practice of the path is fully ripe, all eight factors converge and join forces, setting off the "breakthrough to the Dhamma" by which the disciple directly sees the Four Noble Truths and cuts off the three lower fetters.

Now the disciple has truly plunged into the stream of the Dhamma, the transcendental eightfold path, which will bear him or her onwards towards the great ocean of Nibbāna. But the disciple must continue to cultivate the eight path factors until the remaining fetters are eradicated and the underlying tendencies uprooted. This occurs in the three successive stages of once-returner (*sakadāgāmī*), nonreturner (*anāgāmī*), and arahantship, each with its twin phases of path and fruition. With the attainment of arahantship, the development of the path comes to an end. The arahant remains endowed with the eight qualities that constitute the path, completed by right knowledge and right liberation (see the person "better than the superior person," **45:26**), but for the arahant there is nothing further to develop, for the aim of developing the path has been reached.

It is within the process of perfecting the path that all the other aids to enlightenment are simultaneously perfected. Thus we can describe the way to deliverance alternatively as the development of the Noble Eightfold Path, or of the seven factors of enlightenment, or of the four establishments of mindfulness. Each one implicitly contains the others, and thus selecting one system as a basis for practice naturally brings the others to completion.

Because of its liberal use of repetition series, the exact structure of the Maggasaṃyutta is hard to discern, and even different Oriental editions divide the chapter up in different ways. There is general agreement that the total number of suttas is 180; the problem concerns the arrangement of the later vaggas. The first five vaggas, with forty-eight suttas, are simple enough. These vaggas extol the Noble Eightfold Path as the supreme expression of the way to Nibbāna, the removal and destruction of lust, hatred, and delusion. The eightfold path is the holy life in its broadest extent (**45:6**, **19**, **20**), a holy life which yields the four fruits of liberation and culminates in the destruction of the three root defilements (**45:39–40**). The path is also the essence of asceticism and brahminhood (**45:35–38**), and thus by implication the way that all genuine ascetics and brahmins should be following. But the path is not exclusively for renunciants. It can be commended to both laypersons and monastics, for what matters is not the outward way of life but engagement in the right practice (**45:23–24**). These suttas also stress the importance of good friendship for following the eightfold path, giving a communal dimension to spiritual practice. Indeed, in one text the Buddha declares that good friendship is the entire holy life (**45:2**). Vagga V enumerates the purposes for which the holy life is lived under the Blessed One—the fading away of lust, the abandoning of the fetters, etc.—and in each case the Noble Eightfold Path is prescribed as the means for fulfilling that purpose.

With vagga VI the *peyyāla* or repetition series begin. The first three vaggas of this type mention seven prerequisites and aids for the arising of the Noble Eightfold Path, presumably in its transcendental dimension. The seven conditions are: (1) good friendship (*kalyāṇamittatā*); (2) virtue (*sīla*); (3) desire (*chanda*), wholesome desire for the goal; (4) self (*attā*), perhaps meaning self-possession; (5) view (*diṭṭhi*), the conceptual right view of kamma and its fruit and of the Four Noble Truths; (6) diligence (*appamāda*), heedfulness in the practice; and (7) careful attention (*yoniso manasikāra*), thorough consideration of things in ways conducive to spiritual growth. Elsewhere the Buddha singles out good friendship as the chief external aid in the practice of his teaching, with careful attention as the chief internal aid (see **46:48, 49**).

The seven conditions are presented under three different aspects, each of which features in one of the three vaggas: as the "forerunner and precursor" for the arising of the Noble Eightfold Path; as the "one thing very helpful" for the arising and fulfilment of the path; and as the "one thing that is most effective" for the arising of the path. Each vagga runs through the seven conditions twice, according to two different descriptions of the eight path factors. The first of these characterizes each path factor as "based upon seclusion, dispassion, and cessation, maturing in release," the second as having "as its final goal the removal of lust, the removal of hatred, the removal of delusion." The significance of these epithets is explained by the commentary (see **V, nn. 7, 15**).

Next come four repetition series rooted in a simile comparing the orientation of the path towards Nibbāna to the sloping of India's five great rivers first towards the east, and then (what amounts to the same thing) towards the ocean. As the five rivers are treated first individually and then collectively, each half-vagga contains six suttas, for a total of twelve. Each string of twelve suttas is expounded in four versions, but rather than subsume the different versions under one vagga (as was done in vaggas VI, VII, and VIII), the text makes each version a vagga in its own right, so that the four versions extend over vaggas IX–XII. The two new versions, in vaggas XI and XII, respectively describe each path factor as "having the Deathless as its ground, destination, and final goal," and as "slanting, sloping, and inclining towards Nibbāna."

In vaggas XIII and XIV, the method of assignment is inverted. In these two vaggas, with twenty-two suttas between them, the same four versions are used, but now the sutta is taken as the unit of enumeration and the four versions are incorporated within each sutta, without separate numbering. The suttas bring forth a dazzling series of similes, and the effect of reading them all at a single sitting can be exhilarating, like watching the waves of the ocean break upon the shore on a full-moon night.

The last two vaggas, XV and XVI, list various groups of defilements (such as the *āsavas* or taints) and aspects of existence (such as the three *bhavas* or types of existence). Of each group it is said that the Noble Eightfold Path is to be developed for four purposes: for direct knowledge of it (*abhiññā*), for full understanding of it (*pariññā*), for its utter destruction (*parikkhaya*), and for its abandonment (*pahāna*). Taken together, these two vaggas show unambiguously that the Noble Eightfold Path is aimed at the destruction of suffering and its causes. The fourfold treatment is given in full only for **45:161**, but it can be applied to the subject of every sutta, of which there are twenty, ten per vagga. If each mode of treatment were to be counted as a separate sutta, the number of suttas in the two vaggas would be increased fourfold, and with four different versions taken into account, sixteenfold.

46. Bojjhaṅgasaṃyutta

The word *bojjhaṅga* is a compound of *bodhi*, enlightenment, and *aṅga*, limb or factor. The commentaries tend to interpret the word on the analogy of *jhānaṅga*, the jhāna factors, taking it to mean the factors constitutive of enlightenment. In the Abhidhamma Piṭaka this interpretation becomes so prominent that in texts applying the strict Abhidhamma method (as opposed to those making use of the Suttanta method) the *bojjhaṅgas* are assigned only to supramundane states of consciousness, those pertaining to the paths of liberation, not to wholesome states of mundane consciousness. In the Bojjhaṅgasaṃyutta, however, the factors of enlightenment are given this designation primarily because they lead to enlightenment (**46:5**, **21**). They are thus the constellation of mental factors that function as causes and conditions for arriving at enlightenment, the liberating knowledge and vision (**46:56**).

The seven factors of enlightenment are, for a Buddha, like the seven precious gems of a wheel-turning monarch (**46:42**). The factors initially emerge in sequence, with each serving as the condition for the next (**46:3**). They arise within the practice of the last three factors of the Noble Eightfold Path, guided by right view; but they represent this segment of the path in finer detail, with recognition of the contrasting qualities that must be brought into delicate balance for the path to yield its fruits. First one attends mindfully to an object of meditation, generally selected from among the four objective bases of mindfulness (body, feelings, mind, phenomena): this is the enlightenment factor of mindfulness (*sati-sambojjhaṅga*). As mindfulness becomes steady, one learns to discern the object's features more clearly, and can also distinguish between the wholesome and unwholesome states of mind that arise within the process of contemplation: the enlightenment factor of discrimination of states (*dhammavicaya-sambojjhaṅga*). This fires one's efforts: the enlightenment factor of energy (*viriya-sambojjhaṅga*). From energy applied to the work of mental purification joy arises and escalates: the enlightenment factor of rapture (*pīti-sambojjhaṅga*). With the refinement of rapture the body and mind calm down: the enlightenment factor of tranquillity (*passaddhi-sambojjhaṅga*). The tranquil mind is easily unified: the enlightenment factor of concentration (*samādhi-sambojjhaṅga*). One looks on evenly at the concentrated mind: the enlightenment factor of equanimity (*upekkhā-sambojjhaṅga*). As each subsequent factor arises, those already arisen do not disappear but remain alongside it as its adjuncts (though rapture inevitably subsides as concentration deepens). Thus, at the mature stage of development, all seven factors are present simultaneously, each making its own distinctive contribution.

The suttas of the Bojjhaṅgasaṃyutta commonly describe the enlightenment factors by the stock formula "based upon seclusion, dispassion, and cessation, maturing in release." Since in the Nikāyas, outside the Mahāvagga, this phrase occurs only in apposition to the enlightenment factors, it is possible this was its original provenance and its application to the other sets among the aids to enlightenment is derivative. As the commentarial explanation of the terms suggests, this description best fits the *bojjhaṅgas* only in the advanced stages of insight and at the level of the supramundane path, when the *bojjhaṅgas* are actively eliminating the defilements and leaning towards the realization of Nibbāna. It is only then that they can actually be described as leading to enlightenment. Earlier their function is merely preparatory.

The supramundane dimension of the *bojjhaṅgas* seems to be signalled by a phrase occasionally appended to the familiar formula: "vast, exalted, measureless, without ill will" (*vipulaṃ mahaggataṃ appamāṇaṃ abyāpajjhaṃ*). So described, the enlightenment factors are said to enable a bhikkhu to abandon craving (**46:26**) and to penetrate and sunder the mass of greed, hatred, and delusion not penetrated before (**46:28**). With the breakthrough to the Dhamma the *bojjhaṅgas* become inalienable possessions, and the noble disciple who has acquired them has "obtained the path" (*maggo paṭiladdho*) that leads infallibly to liberation from the taints (**46:30**). It is significant that in this passage the seven enlightenment factors assume the function usually ascribed to the Noble Eightfold Path. Even arahants continue to arouse the *bojjhaṅgas*, not for some ulterior goal, but simply as a way of noble dwelling in the present (**46:4**).

The seven enlightenment factors fall into two classes, the activating and the restraining. The former arise first: discrimination of states, energy, and rapture. The latter emerge later: tranquillity, concentration, and equanimity. The activating factors are to be cultivated when the mind is sluggish, as one feeds a small fire with fuel to make it blaze up. The restraining factors are to be cultivated when the mind is excited, as one sprinkles a bonfire with water and wet grass to reduce it. Mindfulness does not belong to either class, for it is useful everywhere, particularly in ensuring that the activating and restraining factors are kept in balance (**46:53**).

Repeatedly, the Bojjhaṅgasaṃyutta establishes an antithesis between the seven enlightenment factors and the five hindrances (*pañca nīvaraṇa*): sensual desire, ill will, sloth and torpor, restlessness and remorse, and doubt. The latter are the main obstacles to meditative progress in both concentration and insight. The abandoning of the hindrances is often described in the texts on the disciple's gradual training (e.g., at DN I 71–73 and MN I 181). Here the five hindrances are called obstructions of the mind that weaken wisdom, while the enlightenment factors are assets that lead to true knowledge and liberation (**46:37**). The hindrances are comparable to corruptions of gold, to parasitic forest trees, to impurities in water which obscure the reflection of one's face (**46:33, 39, 55**). They are makers of blindness, destructive to wisdom, distractions from the path to Nibbāna; the enlightenment factors are makers of vision and knowledge, promoters of wisdom, aids along the path to Nibbāna (**46:40, 56**).

In the Bojjhaṅgasaṃyutta the Buddha describes in detail the conditions responsible for the arising and growth of both the hindrances and the enlightenment factors. He thereby shows how the general principle of conditionality can also be applied to the specific psychological causes of bondage and liberation. The conditions of both sorts are spoken of as nutriments (*āhāra*), a word which underlines the gradual, assimilative aspect of conditionality in relation to mental degeneration and development. At **46:2** the role of the nutriments in relation to the hindrances and enlightenment factors is compared to the sustenance of the body. Here only the active side of nutrition is in evidence. A later sutta (**46:51**) goes further and shows as well the "denourishment" of the hindrances and enlightenment factors, that is, the measures that prevent them from arising and developing. Prominent among the nutriments for all five hindrances is careless attention (*ayoniso manasikāra*), and prominent among the nutriments for all seven enlightenment factors is careful attention (*yoniso manasikāra*). The role of attention in relation to the hindrances and enlightenment factors is also emphasized at **46:23**, **24**, and **35**.

While the Bojjhaṅgasaṃyutta does not include parallels to the vaggas of the Maggasaṃyutta that identify the conditions for the path, we can put together a picture of the conditions for the enlightenment factors by collating suttas scattered across this collection. Careful attention is the forerunner of the enlightenment factors and also the chief internal condition for their arising (**46:13**, **49**). But good friendship is equally efficacious as a forerunner and is the chief external condition for their arising (**46:48**, **50**). Other conditions mentioned are virtue (**46:11**) and diligence (**46:31**). In a discussion with a wanderer, the Buddha holds up true knowledge and liberation as the goal of the holy life. This is achieved by developing the seven enlightenment factors, which are in turn fulfilled by the four establishments of mindfulness, which depend on the three kinds of good conduct (of body, speech, and mind), which in turn depend on sense restraint (**46:6**). Thus we see traces here of another version of "transcendental dependent origination" running parallel to the series described at **12:23**.

Two suttas show eminent monks recovering from illness when the Buddha recites the enlightenment factors in their presence, and a third shows the Buddha himself recovering when a monk recites them to him (**46:14–16**). Thus these suttas seem to ascribe a mystical healing power to the recitation of the enlightenment factors. Of course, the healing power does not reside in the words of the text alone, but requires the concentrated attention of the listener. In Sri Lanka these three suttas are included in the *Maha*

Pirit Pota, "The Great Book of Protection," a collection of *paritta* or protective discourses, and monks commonly recite them to patients afflicted with serious illness.

In **46:54**, the Buddha links the development of the enlightenment factors to the four divine abodes (*brahmavihāra*): boundless lovingkindness, compassion, altruistic joy, and equanimity. Although the text says that the bhikkhu develops the factors of enlightenment *accompanied by* lovingkindness (*mettāsahagataṃ satisambojjhaṅgaṃ bhāveti*), etc., the commentary explains that one actually uses the divine abodes to develop concentration, and then, *based on this concentration,* one develops the seven enlightenment factors in the mode of insight. In view of the fact that the divine abodes and enlightenment factors, taken in themselves, have different orientations, this explanation sounds reasonable. The text further states that accomplishment in this practice of combining the divine abodes and the enlightenment factors enables the meditator to exercise a fivefold mastery over perception, the ability to alter one's perceptual framework by a simple act of will.

Vaggas VII and VIII continue to connect the development of the seven enlightenment factors with other meditation subjects, detailing six benefits in each case. Possibly the seven benefits mentioned at **46:3** should also be inserted here. Among the meditation subjects, in vagga VII the first five are cemetery contemplations, then come the four divine abodes and mindfulness of breathing; in vagga VIII, we find ten kinds of perception pertaining both to serenity and insight.

Finally, vaggas IX–XVIII elaborate the repetition series by way of the enlightenment factors, but this time they are reduced to little more than mnemonic verses. Two versions are recorded in full, though abridged in form: the "based upon seclusion" version and the "removal of lust" version. But the last sutta (**46:184**) adds the key phrases of the third and fourth versions (those with "having the Deathless as ground" and "slants towards Nibbāna" as their refrains). This inconspicuous addition implies that the whole series should be run through twice more, in these two versions, a task which the assiduous student would no doubt take up with relish.

47. Satipaṭṭhānasaṃyutta

The phrase *cattāro satipaṭṭhānā* is commonly translated "the four foundations of mindfulness," a rendering which takes the compound to represent *sati + paṭṭhāna* and emphasizes the objective bases of the practice: the body, feelings, mind, and phenomena. It seems more likely, however, that *satipaṭṭhāna* should actually be resolved into *sati + upaṭṭhāna*, and thus translated "the establishment of mindfulness." Such an interpretation, which puts the spotlight on the subjective qualities marshalled in the development of mindfulness, is implied by the adjective *upaṭṭhitasati* used to describe one who has set up mindfulness (see **V, n. 122** for other reasons). Occasionally in the texts the objective bases of mindfulness are doubtlessly intended as the meaning of *satipaṭṭhāna*, as at **47:42**, but this is the exception rather than the rule.

Within the Satipaṭṭhānasaṃyutta we do not find a detailed explanation of the fourfold contemplation undertaken in this practice. For that we have to turn to the Satipaṭṭhāna Sutta in either of its two versions, the longer one at DN No. 22 or the middle-length one at MN No. 10 (which differs only in lacking the detailed analysis of the Four Noble Truths). The sutta explains contemplation of the body (*kāyānupassanā*) in terms of fourteen exercises: mindfulness of breathing, attention to the postures, mindfulness and clear comprehension in all activities, investigation of the thirty-one parts of the body (as illustrative of foulness; see **51:20**), analysis into the four elements, and nine cemetery contemplations. Contemplation of feeling (*vedanānupassanā*) is singlefold but considers feelings in terms of their affective quality—as either pleasant, painful, or neutral—with each being viewed again as either carnal or spiritual. Contemplation of mind (*cittānupassanā*) is also singlefold but examines sixteen states of mind coloured by their concomitants (as in **51:11**). Contemplation of phenomena (*dhammānupassanā*) is the most diversified exercise. The exact meaning of *dhammā* here has been subject to dispute. The word is often rendered "mind-objects" or "mental objects," as if it denoted the sixth external sense base, but this seems too narrow and specific. More likely *dhammā* here signifies all phenomena, which for purposes of insight are grouped into fixed modes of classification determined by the Dhamma itself—the doctrine or teaching—and culminating in the realization of the ultimate Dhamma comprised within the Four Noble Truths. There are five such schemes: the five hindrances, the five aggregates, the six pairs of internal and external sense bases, the seven factors of enlightenment, and the Four Noble Truths.

The importance of *satipaṭṭhāna* is emphasized in the Satipaṭṭhānasaṃyutta right from the start by describing it as the *ekāyana magga* for the overcoming of suffering and the realization of Nibbāna (**47:1**). Though the Pāli expression is often rendered "the sole way" or "the only way," this translation has little support either from the suttas or the commentaries. The probable meaning, derived from its usage in a nondoctrinal context, is "the one-way path," so called because it goes in one direction: towards the purification of beings, freedom from suffering, and the realization of Nibbāna. The Buddha is shown reflecting on the four *satipaṭṭhānas* as "the one-way path" soon after his enlightenment, and Brahmā Sahampati appears before him and sings its praises in verse (**47:18, 43**).

The Buddha recommends the four *satipaṭṭhānas* to novices, trainees, and even arahants, each for a different purpose. Novices are to practise them to know body, feelings, mind, and phenomena as they really are, that is, to arouse the insight needed to reach the transcendental path. Trainees, who have attained the path, are to practise them to fully understand these things and thereby reach arahantship. Arahants practise them detached from body, feelings, mind, and phenomena (**47:4**). The four *satipaṭṭhānas* are the proper resort and domain of a bhikkhu. Those bhikkhus who stray from them into the "cords of sensual pleasure" become vulnerable to Māra; those who remain within them are inaccessible to the Evil One (**47:6, 7**).

To emphasize further the importance of *satipaṭṭhāna*, three suttas connect the practice with the longevity of the Buddha's dispensation (**47:22, 23, 25**). Towards the end of his life, when his health was failing, the Buddha instructed the bhikkhus to dwell "with yourselves as your own island, with yourselves as your own refuge." The way this is to be done, he explained, is by developing the four establishments of mindfulness (**47:9**). He gave the Saṅgha the same advice after the deaths of Sāriputta and Mahāmoggallāna (**47:13, 14**), which must have been stirring reminders for all of the law of impermanence.

The practice of *satipaṭṭhāna* centres upon the cultivation of *sati*, mindfulness, which may be understood as focused awareness applied to immediate experience in both its subjective and objective sectors. The heart of the practice is succinctly stated in the formula found in almost every sutta in this chapter. The formula shows that the exercise of *sati* has a reflexive character: one is to contemplate the body *in the body*, feelings *in feelings*, mind *in mind*, phenomena *in phenomena*. The reiteration signals that the contemplative act must isolate each domain of mindfulness from the others and attend to it as it is in itself. This means the given object has to be laid bare, stripped of the layers of mental proliferation which usually clutter our perception and prevent us from seeing the true characteristics of phenomena. The meditator must see the body in the act of breathing as simply a breathing body, not a person or self who is breathing; feelings as simply feelings, not as episodes in a long biography; states of mind as simply states of mind, not as scenes in a personal drama; phenomena as mere phenomena, not as personal achievements or liabilities.

The full formula makes it clear that mindfulness does not work alone but in company. The term "ardent" (*ātāpī*) implies energy, "clearly comprehending" (*sampajāno*) implies incipient wisdom, and the occasional addition, "concentrated, with one-pointed mind (*samāhitā ekaggacittā*)" (**47:4**), points to the presence of concentration. Thus the practice of *satipaṭṭhāna* spreads over the last three factors of the Noble Eightfold Path. And since virtue and straightened view are said to be its prerequisites (**47:3**, **15**), the former comprising the three ethical path factors of right speech, right action, and right livelihood, and the latter synonymous with right view, this implies that the development of the entire Noble Eightfold Path can be encapsulated within the practice of *satipaṭṭhāna*. This much is suggested when the eightfold path is called "the way leading to the development of the establishments of mindfulness" (**47:30**).

In the Satipaṭṭhāna Sutta each exercise in mindfulness is followed by two further extensions of the practice, expressed in two paragraphs attached to the basic instructions. These are also found in the Satipaṭṭhānasaṃyutta, though mentioned separately. Thus at **47:3** the Buddha instructs a bhikkhu to contemplate each base of mindfulness "internally" (i.e., within himself), and "externally" (i.e., in other people), and then both "internally and externally" (in himself and others in rapid succession). At **47:40** he explains "the development of the establishment of mindfulness" to mean contemplating each base as having the nature of origination, the nature of vanishing, and the nature of both origination and vanishing. These two extensions deepen and broaden the practice, spreading it outwards from a narrow fixation on one's immediate experience towards a discernment of its wider expanse and intrinsic patterning.

The practice of mindfulness is often coupled with another quality, clear comprehension (*sampajañña*), which is mentioned within the basic formula and also separately. At **47:2** clear comprehension is explained with reference to the bodily postures and routine activities of everyday life, at **47:35** with reference to the arising and passing away of feelings, thoughts, and perceptions. The commentaries explain clear comprehension to have a fourfold application: as full awareness of the purpose of one's actions; as prudence in the choice of means; as engagement of the mind with the meditation subject; and as discernment of things in their true nature, free from delusion.

It is interesting to note that the Satipaṭṭhānasaṃyutta pits the four establishments of mindfulness against the five hindrances; the hindrances are a "heap of the unwholesome," the *satipaṭṭhānas* a "heap of the wholesome" (**47:5**). That the five hindrances should be counteracted by both the seven enlightenment factors and the four establishments of mindfulness is perfectly comprehensible when we realize that the first enlightenment factor is mindfulness itself, which is activated by the development of the four establishments of mindfulness. One summary of the practice adopted by all the Buddhas of the past, present, and future describes the path in three steps: the abandoning of the five hindrances, the settling of the mind in the four establishments of mindfulness, and the correct development of the seven enlightenment factors (**47:12**). The practice of *satipaṭṭhāna* is precisely the method for abandoning the hindrances, and it is within the womb of this practice, again, that the seven enlightenment factors are conceived and grow towards their immanent aim, true knowledge and liberation (*vijjāvimutti*; see **46:6**). Thus, while they claim only one place among the seven sets making up the aids to enlightenment, the four establishments of mindfulness can be seen as the trunk from which all the other sets branch out and bring forth their fruits.

Lest engagement in mindfulness meditation be branded a narcissistic indulgence, the Buddha makes it clear that it is by protecting oneself through the development of mindfulness that one can most effectively protect others. Conversely, the practice of introspective meditation must be balanced by the cultivation of such social virtues as patience, harmlessness, lovingkindness, and sympathy (**47:19**). The Buddha also urges his disciples to share the benefits of their practice with others by establishing their relatives, friends, and colleagues in the fourfold development of mindfulness (**47:48**). The Master especially commends this practice to the sick, probably because mindfulness and clear comprehension directed to body, feelings, mind, and phenomena are the best aids in dealing with the bodily affliction, physical pain, and mental distress brought on by illness.

At the end of the saṃyutta come the inevitable repetition series. Since the four establishments of mindfulness are accompanied by their own formula—"he dwells contemplating the body in the body," etc.—there is only one version of each sutta, stated by way of this formula. These again, with the exception of the first and last suttas, are reduced to mnemonic verses.

48. Indriyasaṃyutta

Unlike the preceding saṃyuttas, the Indriyasaṃyutta is made up of heterogeneous material. It deals not only with the five spiritual faculties, a set included among the thirty-seven aids to enlightenment, but also with a variety of other items united under the rubric *indriya*. Possibly the most ancient recension of this saṃyutta consisted solely of texts centred around the spiritual faculties, but since the word *indriya* has a wider compass, at some point the compilers of the canon may have felt obliged to include in this collection texts concerned with the other types of faculties. This hypothesis, though unverifiable, may account for the somewhat haphazard organization of this saṃyutta.

By the early Abhidhamma period the Buddhist doctrinal specialists had drawn up a list of twenty-two faculties proposed as a compendium of phenomenological categories on a par with the five aggregates, twelve sense bases, and eighteen elements. As such, the faculties are collected and analysed in the *Vibhaṅga* of the Abhidhamma Piṭaka (chap. 5). Significantly, even though all the faculties were drawn from the suttas, the Indriyavibhaṅga has only an Abhidhamma analysis, not a Suttanta analysis, implying that the ancient compilers of the *Vibhaṅga* did not consider the complete assemblage of faculties to constitute a unified scheme within the framework of the Sutta Piṭaka.

The twenty-two *indriyas* fall into five distinct groups as follows:

five spiritual faculties
six sense faculties
five affective faculties
three faculties related to final knowledge
a triad made up of the femininity faculty, the masculinity faculty, and the life faculty.

All these faculties, treated at least briefly in the Indriyasaṃyutta, are called *indriyas* in the sense that they exercise dominion in a particular sphere of activity or experience, just as Indra (after whom they are named) exercises dominion over the devas.

The saṃyutta begins with two vaggas devoted to the five spiritual faculties, the faculties of faith (*saddhā*), energy (*viriya*), mindfulness (*sati*), concentration (*samādhi*), and wisdom (*paññā*). The opening suttas treat these faculties by way of templates we have met several times already: the gratification triad, the origin pentad, and the ascetics and brahmins templates. In the second ascetics and brahmins sutta we find the spiritual faculties assigned to the place occupied by suffering in the pattern of the Four Noble Truths. This move initially seems odd, at striking variance with the unqualified accolades accorded to the other sets among the aids to enlightenment. It becomes intelligible when we realize that the faculties are here being considered, not simply as factors conducive to enlightenment, but as members of a broader scheme of phenomenological categories parallel to the aggregates, sense bases, and elements.

Four suttas in the first vagga draw a distinction between the stream-enterer and the arahant. The stream-enterer is defined as one who has understood the faculties by way of the given templates; the arahant, having acquired this knowledge, has developed it to the point where his mind has been freed from clinging (**48:2–5**; cp. **22:109–10**). In **48:8–11** the Buddha explains the domains and practical implementation of the faculties, and then in **48:12–18** he shows how the relative strength of the faculties determines the gradation among the different classes of noble disciples (**48:24**, apparently out of place, also belongs to this set).

In the third vagga we find mention made of the femininity triad (**48:22**) and the final knowledge triad (**48:23**), but without explanations. Formal definitions are found only in the Abhidhamma Piṭaka and the commentaries (see **V, nn. 205, 206** for the references). In **48:26–30** the focus falls on the six sense faculties, almost identical with the six internal sense bases. These are treated merely by way of the template patterns, with nothing new of special interest.

Vagga IV is devoted to the five affective faculties, finer divisions of the three feelings: the pleasure and joy faculties are respectively bodily and mental pleasant feeling; the pain and displeasure faculties are bodily and mental painful feeling; and the equanimity faculty is neutral feeling (**48:36–38**). The last sutta in this series deals with the stage at which the faculties completely cease; the text is difficult to interpret without the aid of the commentary (paraphrased in the notes).

In vagga V we return to the spiritual faculties, this time to a phalanx of suttas that shed a brighter light on their place in the Buddhist path. These suttas show that the five faculties constitute a complete structure capable of leading all the way to the destruction of the taints (**48:43**, end). In **48:50**, Sāriputta explains that the faculties unfold in a progressive series, faith leading to the arousal of energy, energy to mindfulness, mindfulness to concentration, and concentration to wisdom. Among the five faculties, wisdom is repeatedly given the highest valuation; it is called the chief among the states conducive to enlightenment and extolled with lovely similes (**48:51, 54, 55, 68–70**). Indeed, wisdom is said to be the faculty that stabilizes the other four faculties, making them faculties in the proper sense (**48:45, 52**).

Both the five faculties and the five powers draw upon the same selection of spiritual qualities, and this raises the question of their relationship. It may seem that the faculties represent these five qualities at an earlier phase, and the powers at a later, more advanced phase, but the texts do not countenance this view. The Buddha declares the two sets to be identical, with the designations "faculties" and "powers" being used simply to highlight different aspects of the same set of qualities; they are like the two streams of the same river flowing around a midstream island (**48:43**). The commentary explains that the five factors become faculties when considered as exercising control in their respective domains, and powers when considered as unshaken by their opposites.

One relationship among the faculties, not mentioned in the suttas but discussed in the commentaries, is worth noting. This is their arrangement into mutually complementary pairs. Faith is paired with wisdom, ensuring that the emotional and intellectual sides of the spiritual life are kept in balance; energy is paired with concentration, ensuring that the activating and restraining sides of mental development are kept in balance. Mindfulness belongs to neither side but oversees the others, holding them together in a mutually enriching tension.

The Indriyasaṃyutta ends with the repetition series, this time in two versions, the "based upon seclusion" version and the "removal of lust" version.

49. Sammappadhānasaṃyutta
50. Balasaṃyutta

These two saṃyuttas do not contain any original suttas but merely instantiate the repetition series. Since the four right strivings are described by their own stock formula, the repetition series in the Sammappadhānasaṃyutta is stated only once, accompanied by this formula. The five powers are parallel to the five faculties, and therefore the Balasaṃyutta is to be elaborated with the repetition series filled out in the two versions.

51. Iddhipādasaṃyutta

The term *iddhipāda,* rendered "basis for spiritual power," is a compound of *iddhi* and *pāda*. *Iddhi* (Skt *ṛddhi*) originally meant success, growth, or prosperity, but early on in the Indian yogic tradition the word had come to mean a special kind of success obtained through meditation, namely, the ability to perform wondrous feats that defy the normal order of events. Such feats, for Indian spirituality, are not to be regarded as miracles proving the divine stature of the person who performs them. They are understood, rather, as extensions of natural causality which become accessible to the meditator through accomplishment in concentration (*samādhi*). The mind trained in concentration is able to discern subtle interconnections between bands of mental and material energy invisible to ordinary sensory consciousness. Such perception enables the accomplished yogi to tap into the deep undercurrents of natural causality and use them to perform feats which, to the uninitiated, appear mystical or miraculous.

While early Buddhism is often depicted as a rationalistic system of ethics or a path of purely ascetic meditation, the Nikāyas themselves are replete with texts in which the Buddha is shown performing feats of psychic power and extolling disciples who excel in these skills. What the Buddha rejected was not the acquisition of such powers per se but their misuse for irresponsible ends. He prohibited his monks and nuns from displaying these powers to impress the laity and convert unbelievers, and he emphasized that these powers themselves are no proof that their bearer has genuine wisdom. In his system the real miracle was the "miracle of instruction" (*anusāsani-pāṭihāriya*), the ability to transform a person through teachings on how to overcome evil and fulfil the good.

Nevertheless, the Buddha incorporated the *iddhis* into his path of training with an eightfold scheme often encountered in the texts. The scheme is called simply "the various kinds of spiritual power" (*anekavihitaṃ iddhividhaṃ*), and is mentioned close to a dozen times in the present saṃyutta, most notably in the formal definition of *iddhi* (at **51:19**). He also offers an expanded interpretation of the types of spiritual success obtainable through meditation, one which subsumes the *iddhis* under a broader category of six types of higher knowledge commonly known as the *chaḷabhiññā* or six direct knowledges. These are: the eight kinds of spiritual powers; the divine ear; the ability to know the minds of other beings; the recollection of one's past lives; the knowledge of the passing away and rebirth of beings according to their kamma; and the knowledge of the destruction of the taints (**51:11**, etc.). The first five are mundane, desirable as ornaments of an accomplished meditator but not essential for liberation (see **12:70**). The last is supramundane and the culmination of the step-by-step training. By adopting this wider and more profound conception of spiritual success, the Buddha could include within his system the various spiritual powers esteemed so highly in the

Indian yogic culture while giving pride of place to the achievement peculiar to his own discipline: the liberation of mind attainable only through the destruction of the defilements.

The four *iddhipādas* are the means to attainment of the spiritual powers, whether of the mundane or the transcendental kind. Thus, though included among the thirty-seven aids to enlightenment, this set of factors has a somewhat different flavour than the others. While the others are all expounded solely for the contribution they make to enlightenment and the realization of Nibbāna, the *iddhipādas* can be used to achieve both the wonder-working *iddhis* and the supreme spiritual power of arahantship.

The Iddhipādasaṃyutta sets the *iddhipādas* in a universal context by declaring that all ascetics and brahmins—past, present, and future—who generate spiritual power do so by their means (**51:6–7**). Again, it is by developing the four *iddhipādas* that all ascetics and brahmins of the three times become mighty and powerful (**51:16**), or acquire the six direct knowledges (**51:17**). Indeed, it is by developing the *iddhipādas* that the Buddha has become a Perfectly Enlightened One (**51:8**).

The four *iddhipādas* are defined by a formula cited in almost every sutta of this collection. The formula can be analysed into three portions, two common to all four bases, the third differentiating them as fourfold. The two common components are concentration (*samādhi*) and "volitional formations of striving" (*padhānasaṅkhārā*). The latter is defined by the formula for the four right strivings (*sammappadhānā*), so that the *iddhipādas*, the third set of the aids to enlightenment, implicitly contain the second set.

The components unique to each *iddhipāda* are the factors that take the lead in generating concentration: desire (*chanda*), energy (*viriya*), mind (*citta*), and investigation (*vīmaṃsā*). The commentary interprets desire here as "desire to act" (*kattukaṃyatā*) and "investigation" (*vīmaṃsā*) as wisdom. Energy and mind are not given any special definitions apart from the general synonyms for these factors. Presumably, while all four qualities coexist in every state of concentration, on any given occasion only one of the four will assume the dominant role in generating concentration and this gives its name to the *iddhipāda*. It is interesting to observe that the formula for right striving, included in the *iddhipāda* formula as noted above, mentions three factors that function as *iddhipādas*, namely, desire, energy, and mind; and since right striving presupposes discrimination between wholesome and unwholesome states, some degree of investigation is also involved. Thus once again we can see the interwoven character of the seven sets.

The standard formula for the *iddhipādas* is sometimes embedded in a longer, more complex statement which shows that they are to be cultivated in conjunction with a number of other meditative skills necessary to ensure balance, thoroughness, and breadth to their development. The passage is stated baldly at **51:11**, as a discovery the Buddha made while still a bodhisatta striving for enlightenment; they recur at **51:12**, as describing how a bhikkhu achieves the six direct knowledges. Read alone, the passage is far from self-explanatory, but **51:20** provides an internal commentary on each term, almost in the manner of an Abhidhamma treatise. Another text, recurring five times with variations only in the auditors, gives individual definitions of spiritual power, the bases for spiritual power, the development of the bases for spiritual power, and the way to the development of the bases (**51:19**, **27–30**). The last definition connects the four *iddhipādas* with the Noble Eightfold Path, again drawing our attention to the interdependence of the seven sets.

In sum, the *iddhis* or spiritual powers to be acquired by meditation are: most narrowly, the eight kinds of spiritual powers, wondrous feats of psychic power; more broadly, the six direct knowledges; and consummately, the taintless liberation of mind. The means of achieving these powers, their bases or "feet" (the literal meaning of *pāda*), are the four *iddhipādas*. These employ the four kinds of right striving and a particular dominant mental factor to generate concentration, and this concentration, in conjunction with the effort and the dominant factor, enables the meditator to exercise spiritual powers. To show that while the *iddhipādas* can lead to all three kinds of *iddhi*, the last is sufficient in itself, the suttas sometimes state simply that the four *iddhipādas*, when developed and cultivated, lead to the taintless liberation of mind (**51:18**, **23**).

In several texts, from the Iddhipādasaṃyutta and elsewhere, other marvellous potencies are ascribed to the four *iddhipādas*. One who has mastered them, it is said, can extend his life span even as long as a *kappa*, a term whose meaning here has been a subject of controversy but which seems to signify a full cosmic aeon. The Buddha ascribes this ability to himself in the famous dialogue with Ānanda at the Cāpāla Shrine near Vesālī, related in the Mahāparinibbāna Sutta and reported here as well (**51:10**). Sāriputta ascribes the same ability to Moggallāna (at **21:3**), who ironically is reported to have been killed by assassins. By developing the *iddhipādas*, Moggallāna can set off a minor earthquake with his toe (**51:14**), and the Buddha can use his physical body to travel to the brahmā world (**51:22**). The saṃyutta closes with the repetition series, which is run through in one round using the stock description of the *iddhipādas*.

52. *Anuruddhasaṃyutta*

This saṃyutta features the Venerable Anuruddha as an exponent of the four establishments of mindfulness, which figure in every sutta in the chapter. The saṃyutta may have originally belonged to the Satipaṭṭhānasaṃyutta, later to be detached and given independent status. The Satipaṭṭhānasaṃyutta preserves three suttas spoken by Anuruddha (**47:26–28**), which are consonant in character with those found here, and it is unclear why they were not taken out and brought into this collection.

The first sutta of the Anuruddhasaṃyutta is of special interest, for it merges into one complex pattern the two extensions of the *satipaṭṭhāna* formula concerned with insight, one dealing with the contemplation of the four bases as internal and external, the other with contemplation of the four bases as having the nature of origination and vanishing. Also of interest is the long series of texts in the second vagga which show Anuruddha claiming it was by the practice of the four establishments of mindfulness that he developed various spiritual powers. Among these are the six direct knowledges (divided into two segments, **52:12–14, 22–24**), which are usually ascribed to the practice of the four *iddhipādas*. The assertion that they result from the practice of *satipaṭṭhāna* means that the latter method need not be understood as exclusively a system of insight meditation (a widespread view) but can also be seen as a path conducive to the fulfilment of all the jhānas. We also find here (at **52:15–24**) the ten knowledges elsewhere called the ten powers of the Tathāgata (MN I 69–71). As the tradition regards these as unique endowments of a

Perfectly Enlightened One, the commentary explains that Anuruddha possessed them only in part.

53. *Jhānasaṃyutta*

This saṃyutta contains only the standard jhāna formula integrated with the repetition series in a single round.

54. *Ānāpānasaṃyutta*

Mindfulness of breathing (*ānāpānasati*) is generally regarded as the most important meditation subject taught in the Nikāyas. The Pāli exegetical tradition holds that it was mindfulness of breathing that the Buddha practised on the night of his enlightenment, prior to attaining the four jhānas and the three true knowledges, and during his teaching career he occasionally would go off into seclusion to devote himself to this meditation. He calls it "the Tathāgata's dwelling," a lofty honour, and often recommends it to both trainees and arahants. For those in training it leads to the destruction of the taints; for arahants it leads to a pleasant dwelling here and now and to mindfulness and clear comprehension (**54:11**).

The practice of mindfulness of breathing is defined by a sixteen-step formula first introduced in **54:1** and repeated throughout the Ānāpānasaṃyutta. The sixteen steps are not necessarily sequential but to some extent overlap; thus they might be called phases rather than steps. The first four are also mentioned in the Satipaṭṭhāna Sutta, in the section on mindfulness of the body, but the sixteenfold formula gives the practice a wider range. The sixteen aspects are divided into four tetrads, each of which is correlated with one of the four establishments of mindfulness. The correlations are first explained in **54:10** and recur in several later suttas.

The first six suttas of the Ānāpānasaṃyutta are framed in terms simply of mindfulness of breathing (*ānāpānasati*). From **54:7** onwards, a shift takes place, and the suttas are phrased in terms of *concentration by* mindfulness of breathing (*ānāpānasati-samādhi*). This is the concentration obtained by being mindful of the breath. Here again, as with the path factors, enlightenment factors, and faculties, mindfulness is a condition for concentration. In **54:8** the Buddha enumerates the benefits that come from concentration gained by mindfulness of breathing: it is physically easeful, removes worldly memories and thoughts, and leads to many exalted attainments including the four jhānas, the formless states, the attainment of cessation, and even liberation from the taints. Sutta **54:9** records the curious occasion when a large number of monks, after hearing the Buddha preach on the foulness of the body, committed suicide. Subsequently the Buddha taught the bhikkhus *ānāpānasati-samādhi* as a "peaceful and sublime" dwelling.

The most important sutta in the Ānāpānasaṃyutta is **54:13**, the substance of which is repeated at **54:14–16**. Here the Buddha explains how concentration by mindfulness of breathing fulfils the four establishments of mindfulness; these in turn fulfil the seven factors of enlightenment; and these in turn fulfil true knowledge and liberation. This method of exposition shows mindfulness of breathing as a complete subject of meditation that begins with simple attention to the breath and culminates in the highest deliverance of the mind. This theme is reconfirmed by the last string of suttas in the chapter, which declare that concentration by mindfulness of breathing leads to the abandoning of the fetters and the eradication of all defilements (**54:17–20**).

55. Sotāpattisaṃyutta

This chapter might have been more accurately entitled Sotāpattiyaṅgasaṃyutta, for it is not concerned with stream-entry in a general way but with a specific group of factors that define a person as a stream-enterer (*sotāpanna*). The stream (*sota*) is the Noble Eightfold Path, and the stream-enterer is so called because he or she, by directly penetrating the truth of the Dhamma, has become possessed of the eight factors of the path (**55:5**).

The four qualities that define a person as a stream-enterer are called the four *sotāpattiyaṅga*, factors of stream-entry. The Pāli term is actually used with reference to two different tetrads. The more frequently mentioned tetrad is the set of four qualities possessed by a stream-enterer, and in this context the term is properly rendered "factors *of* stream-entry," or even "factors of the stream-enterer." But alongside this tetrad we find another one, less often mentioned, consisting of the qualities that must be actualized to attain stream-entry. I translate *sotāpattiyaṅga* in this sense as "factors *for* stream-entry."

The four factors possessed by the stream-enterer are confirmed confidence in the Buddha, the Dhamma, and the Sangha (confidence in each being reckoned a separate factor), and "the virtues dear to the noble ones" (*ariyakantāni sīlāni*). Confirmed confidence (*aveccappasāda*) is faith rooted in personal validation of the truth of the Dhamma. The decisive event that marks the transition from the stage of one "practising for the realization of the fruit of stream-entry" to that of a full-fledged stream-enterer is the "breakthrough to the Dhamma," also called the obtaining of the vision of the Dhamma (see **13:1**). This consists in the direct seeing of the Four Noble Truths, or (more concisely) of the principle that "whatever has the nature of arising, all that has the nature of cessation." On seeing the truth of the Dhamma, the disciple eradicates the three lower fetters—identity view, doubt, and distorted grasp of rules and vows—and thus acquires confidence grounded upon this experiential confirmation. Such confidence is placed in the "Three Jewels" of Buddhism: in the Buddha as the supreme teacher of the path to Nibbāna; in the Dhamma as the map and goal of the path; and in the Saṅgha as the community of noble ones who share in the realization of the Dhamma. The attainment of stream-entry also issues in profound reverence for morality, particularly for the basic moral virtues comprised in the five precepts: abstinence from the destruction of life, taking what is not given, sexual misconduct, false speech, and the use of intoxicants.

The stream-enterer is characterized by a stock formula repeated many times in the Sotāpattisaṃyutta and elsewhere in the Nikāyas. He or she is "no longer bound to the nether world (*avinipātadhamma*)," incapable of taking rebirth in any of the lower realms of existence—the hells, the animal realm, or the domain of ghosts; "fixed in destiny" (*niyata*), bound to reach liberation without regression after seven lives at most, all lived either in the human world or in a celestial realm; and "with enlightenment as destination" (*sambodhiparāyana*), bound to attain full knowledge of the Four Noble Truths culminating in the destruction of the taints.

The Buddha calls the four factors of stream-entry "the mirror of the Dhamma," for reflection on them can enable the disciple to determine whether he or she is a stream-enterer (**55:8**). He also calls them "streams of merit, streams of the wholesome, nutriments of happiness" (**55:31, 41**) and "divine tracks of the devas for the purification of beings" (**55:34, 35**). The four factors of stream-entry lead to a celestial rebirth (**55:18, 36**), but whether the disciple is reborn in heaven or in the human world, the factors bring long life, beauty, happiness, and dominion (**55:30**). They also still the fear of death, for a noble disciple who possesses these four factors has escaped the prospect of rebirth into a bad destination (**55:14, 15**). Thus, when ill, a stream-enterer can be consoled by being reminded that he or she possesses the four factors, as Ānanda comforts the householder Anāthapiṇḍika (**55:27**). The controversial discourse on Sarakāni (in two versions, **55:24, 25**) tells the story of a Sakyan noble who had been fond of drinking yet was declared by the Buddha a stream-enterer after his death. When this announcement drew a storm of protest from the Sakyans, the Buddha explained that Sarakāni had completed the training before his death and thus had died a stream-enterer.

Several suttas in this saṃyutta present alternatives to the fourth item in the list. On two occasions, in place of "the virtues dear to the noble ones," generosity is cited as the fourth factor of stream-entry (**55:6, 39**); twice it is cited as the fourth stream of merit (**55:32, 42**). Two texts cite "wisdom directed to arising and passing away," i.e., the wisdom of insight into impermanence, as the fourth stream of merit (**55:33, 43**). Thus, by collating the lists and taking the common core of the first three items to exemplify faith, we arrive at four central qualities of a stream-enterer: faith, virtue, generosity, and wisdom (*saddhā, sīla, cāga, paññā*), elsewhere mentioned together as the marks of a *sappurisa*, a superior person.

Possessing the four factors of stream-entry is not the end of the road for the noble disciple, but only a way station towards the final goal. They "lead to the destruction of the taints" (**55:38**), and one endowed with them "slants, slopes, and inclines to Nibbāna" (**55:22**). However, though the stream-enterer is bound to win final realization, the Buddha urges such disciples not to become complacent but to hasten their progress by diligence (**55:20**). To a critically ill youth who has already reached stream-entry, he teaches six contemplations that "partake of true knowledge" by practising which the youth dies as a nonreturner (**55:3**). He even instructs one lay follower how to guide another on his deathbed so as to lead him all the way to arahantship (**55:54**).

The other tetrad consists of the four factors *for* stream-entry, that is, for attainment of stream-entry. These are: association with superior persons, hearing the true Dhamma, careful attention, and practice in accordance with the Dhamma (**55:5**, **50**). These qualities lead not only to stream-entry but to all the fruits of the path. They also bring to fulfilment the various potentialities of wisdom (**55:55–74**).

56. Saccasaṃyutta

The final saṃyutta of the Mahāvagga is devoted to the truths discovered by the Buddha on the night of his enlightenment and placed by him at the core of his teaching. These, of course, are the Four Noble Truths, and thus this chapter on the truths makes a fitting conclusion to the entire Saṃyutta Nikāya. The Four Noble Truths were first announced in the Dhammacakkappavattana Sutta, the first discourse at Bārāṇasī. Accordingly we find this sutta in the midst of this collection, tucked away almost inconspicuously (**56:11**), but with its importance signalled by the applause of the devas resounding throughout the ten thousandfold world system.

To highlight their significance, the Saccasaṃyutta casts the Four Noble Truths against a universal background. They are not merely particular pronouncements of doctrine peculiar to one historical spiritual teacher known as the Buddha, but the content of realization for all who arrive at liberating truth, whether past, present, or future (**56:3**, **4**). The Buddha is called the Perfectly Enlightened One just because he has awakened to these truths (**56:23**); even more, all the Buddhas of the past, present, and future become fully enlightened by awakening to these truths (**56:24**). The truths are described as noble (*ariya*) because they are actual, unerring, not otherwise (**56:27**), and because they are taught by the supreme noble one, the Buddha (**56:28**). They might also be called noble because they are the truths understood by the noble ones, from the stream-enterer upwards, and because their realization confers noble stature.

The reason sentient beings roam and wander in saṃsāra is because they have not understood and penetrated the Four

Noble Truths (**56:21**). Ignorant of the truths, they go from one existence to the next like a stick thrown into the air, falling now on its tip, now on its butt (**56:33**). At the base of the causal genesis of suffering is ignorance (*avijjā*), as is shown by the chain of dependent origination, and ignorance consists just in unawareness of the Four Noble Truths (**56:17**). Its antidote is knowledge (*vijjā*), which accordingly is just knowledge of the four truths (**56:18**). But the world cannot find the way to liberation on its own. Before the arising of a Buddha the world is enveloped in thick spiritual darkness, as the cosmos is enveloped in physical darkness before the sun and moon are formed. The task of a Buddha is to discover the Four Noble Truths and teach them to the world. His doing so is "the manifestation of great light and radiance" (**56:38**).

The things the Buddha knows but does not disclose are many, like the leaves in a *siṃsapā* forest; the things he discloses are few, like the leaves in his hand. These few things are all comprised in the Four Noble Truths. They are taught because they are beneficial, pertain to the fundamentals of the holy life, and lead to enlightenment and Nibbāna (**56:31**). For the same reason the monks are to think thoughts connected with the truths and confine their conversation to talk about the truths (**56:8–10**).

The first penetration of the Four Noble Truths occurs with the breakthrough to the Dhamma, which marks the attainment of stream-entry. To make this breakthrough is extremely difficult, more so even than piercing with an arrow the tip of a hair split into seven strands (**56:45**). But this achievement is a matter of the utmost urgency, for without making the breakthrough it is impossible to put an end to suffering (**56:44**). Hence the Buddha again and again urges his disciples to "arouse extraordinary desire" and "make an extraordinary effort" to make the breakthrough to the truths (**56:34**).

Once the disciple makes the breakthrough and sees the truths, more work still lies ahead, for each of the truths imposes a task (*kicca*), and after entering the path the disciple must fulfil these tasks in order to win the final fruit. The Buddha discovered these tasks along with his enlightenment and announced them already in the first sermon (**56:11**). They are also discovered and declared by all Tathāgatas (**56:12**). The truth of suffering, which ultimately consists of the five aggregates and the six internal sense bases

(**56:13, 14**), should be fully understood (*pariññeyya*). The truth of its origin, craving, should be abandoned (*pahātabba*). The truth of cessation, Nibbāna, should be realized (*sacchikātabba*). And the truth of the way, the Noble Eightfold Path, should be developed (*bhāvetabba*). Developing the path brings to completion all four tasks, at which point the disciple becomes an arahant who can sound the lion's roar of liberation, "What had to be done has been done." What had to be done is precisely the fulfilment of these four tasks.

The Saccasaṃyutta ends with several long repetition series. In vagga VI, **56:49–60** illustrate, with twelve similes, the magnitude of what has been achieved by one who has made the break-through to the truths. Vaggas VII–X pile up sutta upon sutta to illustrate the dire consequences of not seeing the truths. Vaggas XI–XII show how sentient beings migrate among the five destinations, going mostly from the higher realms to the lower ones, because they have not seen the truths. Thus the Saṃyutta Nikāya ends with this stark revelation of the pernicious nature of saṃsāra, and with an urgent call to make an end to suffering by understanding, with direct vision, the Four Noble Truths which the Buddha himself discovered on the night of his enlightenment and left as his message to the world.

[1] PART V: The Great Book (*Mahāvagga*)

Homage to the Blessed One,
the Arahant, the Perfectly Enlightened One

Chapter I

45 *Maggasaṃyutta*
Connected Discourses on the Path

I. IGNORANCE

1 (1) Ignorance

Thus have I heard. On one occasion the Blessed One was dwelling at Sāvatthī in Jeta's Grove, Anāthapiṇḍika's Park. There the Blessed One addressed the bhikkhus thus: "Bhikkhus!"

"Venerable sir!" those bhikkhus replied. The Blessed One said this:

"Bhikkhus, ignorance is the forerunner in the entry upon unwholesome states, with shamelessness and fearlessness of wrongdoing following along.[1] For an unwise person immersed in ignorance, wrong view springs up. For one of wrong view, wrong intention springs up. For one of wrong intention, wrong speech springs up. For one of wrong speech, wrong action springs up. For one of wrong action, wrong livelihood springs up. For one of wrong livelihood, wrong effort springs up. For one of wrong effort, wrong mindfulness springs up. For one of wrong mindfulness, wrong concentration springs up.

"Bhikkhus, true knowledge is the forerunner in the entry upon wholesome states, with a sense of shame and fear of wrongdoing following along.[2] [2] For a wise person who has arrived at true knowledge, right view springs up. For one of right view, right intention springs up. For one of right intention, right speech springs up. For one of right speech, right action springs up. For one of right action, right livelihood springs up. For one of right livelihood, right effort springs up. For one of right effort, right mindfulness springs up. For one of right mindfulness, right concentration springs up."[3]

2 (2) Half the Holy Life

Thus have I heard. On one occasion the Blessed One was dwelling among the Sakyans where there was a town of the Sakyans named Nāgaraka.[4] Then the Venerable Ānanda approached the Blessed One. Having approached, he paid homage to the Blessed One, sat down to one side, and said to him:

"Venerable sir, this is half of the holy life, that is, good friendship, good companionship, good comradeship."[5]

"Not so, Ānanda! Not so, Ānanda! This is the entire holy life, Ānanda, that is, good friendship, good companionship, good comradeship. When a bhikkhu has a good friend, a good companion, a good comrade, it is to be expected that he will develop and cultivate the Noble Eightfold Path.[6]

"And how, Ānanda, does a bhikkhu who has a good friend, a good companion, a good comrade, develop and cultivate the Noble Eightfold Path? Here, Ānanda, a bhikkhu develops right view, which is based upon seclusion, dispassion, and cessation, maturing in release.[7] He develops right intention ... right speech ... right action ... right livelihood ... right effort ... right mindfulness ... right concentration, which is based upon seclusion, dispassion, and cessation, maturing in release. It is in this way, Ānanda, that a bhikkhu who has a good friend, a good companion, a good comrade, develops and cultivates the Noble Eightfold Path. [3]

"By the following method too, Ānanda, it may be understood how the entire holy life is good friendship, good companionship, good comradeship: by relying upon me as a good friend, Ānanda, beings subject to birth are freed from birth; beings subject to aging are freed from aging; beings subject to death are freed from death; beings subject to sorrow, lamentation, pain, displeasure, and despair are freed from sorrow, lamentation, pain, displeasure, and despair. By this method, Ānanda, it may be understood how the entire holy life is good friendship, good companionship, good comradeship."

3 (3) Sāriputta

At Sāvatthī. Then the Venerable Sāriputta approached the Blessed One ... and said to him:

"Venerable sir, this is the entire holy life, that is, good friendship, good companionship, good comradeship."[8]

"Good, good, Sāriputta! This is the entire holy life, Sāriputta, that is, good friendship, good companionship, good comradeship. When a bhikkhu has a good friend, a good companion, a good comrade, it is to be expected that he will develop and cultivate the Noble Eightfold Path.

"And how, Sāriputta, does a bhikkhu who has a good friend, a good companion, a good comrade, develop and cultivate the Noble Eightfold Path?"

(*The rest as in the preceding sutta.*) [4]

4 (4) The Brahmin

At Sāvatthī. Then, in the morning, the Venerable Ānanda dressed and, taking bowl and robe, entered Sāvatthī for alms. The Venerable Ānanda saw the brahmin Jāṇussoṇi departing from Sāvatthī in an all-white chariot drawn by mares.[9] The horses yoked to it were white, its ornaments were white, the chariot was white, its upholstery was white, the reins, goad, and canopy were white, his turban, clothes, and sandals were white, and he was being fanned by a white chowry. People, having seen this, said: "Divine indeed, sir, is the vehicle! It appears to be a divine vehicle indeed, sir!"[10]

Then, when the Venerable Ānanda had walked for alms in Sāvatthī and returned from his alms round, after his meal he approached the Blessed One, [5] paid homage to him, sat down to one side, and said to him:

"Here, venerable sir, in the morning I dressed and, taking bowl and robe, entered Sāvatthī for alms. I saw the brahmin Jāṇussoṇi departing from Sāvatthī in an all-white chariot drawn by mares.... People, having seen this, said: 'Divine indeed, sir, is the vehicle! It appears to be a divine vehicle indeed, sir!' Is it possible, venerable sir, to point out a divine vehicle in this Dhamma and Discipline?"

"It is possible, Ānanda," the Blessed One said. "This is a designation for this Noble Eightfold Path: 'the divine vehicle' and 'the vehicle of Dhamma' and 'the unsurpassed victory in battle.'

"Right view, Ānanda, when developed and cultivated, has as its final goal the removal of lust, the removal of hatred, the removal of delusion. Right intention ... Right concentration, when developed and cultivated, [6] has as its final goal the removal of lust, the removal of hatred, the removal of delusion.

"In this way, Ānanda, it may be understood how this is a designation for this Noble Eightfold Path: 'the divine vehicle' and 'the vehicle of Dhamma' and 'the unsurpassed victory in battle.'"

This is what the Blessed One said. Having said this, the Fortunate One, the Teacher, further said this:

"Its qualities of faith and wisdom
Are always yoked evenly together.[11]
Shame is its pole, mind its yoke-tie,
Mindfulness the watchful charioteer.

"The chariot's ornament is virtue,
Its axle jhāna,[12] energy its wheels;
Equanimity keeps the burden balanced,
Desirelessness serves as upholstery.

"Good will, harmlessness, and seclusion:
These are the chariot's weaponry,
Forbearance its armour and shield,[13]
As it rolls towards security from bondage.

"This divine vehicle unsurpassed
Originates from within oneself.[14]
The wise depart from the world in it,
Inevitably winning the victory."

5 (5) For What Purpose?

At Sāvatthī. Then a number of bhikkhus approached the Blessed One.... Sitting to one side, those bhikkhus said to the Blessed One:

"Here, venerable sir, wanderers of other sects ask us: 'For what purpose, friends, is the holy life lived under the ascetic Gotama?' When we are asked thus, venerable sir, we answer those wanderers thus: 'It is, friends, for the full understanding of suffering that the holy life is lived under the Blessed One.' We hope, venerable sir, that when we answer thus we state what has been said by the Blessed One and do not misrepresent him with what is contrary to fact; [7] that we explain in accordance with the Dhamma, and that no reasonable consequence of our assertion gives ground for criticism."

"Surely, bhikkhus, when you answer thus you state what has been said by me and do not misrepresent me with what is contrary to fact; you explain in accordance with the Dhamma, and no reasonable consequence of your assertion gives ground for criticism. For, bhikkhus, it is for the full understanding of suffering that the holy life is lived under me.

"If, bhikkhus, wanderers of other sects ask you: 'But, friends, is there a path, is there a way for the full understanding of this suffering?'—being asked thus, you should answer them thus: 'There is a path, friends, there is a way for the full understanding of this suffering.'

"And what, bhikkhus, is that path, what is that way for the full understanding of this suffering? It is this Noble Eightfold Path; that is, right view ... right concentration. This is the path, this is the way for the full understanding of this suffering.

"Being asked thus, bhikkhus, you should answer those wanderers of other sects in such a way."

6 (6) A Certain Bhikkhu (1)

At Sāvatthī. Then a certain bhikkhu approached the Blessed One.... Sitting to one side, that bhikkhu said to the Blessed One:

"Venerable sir, it is said, 'the holy life, the holy life.' What, venerable sir, is the holy life? What is the final goal of the holy life?"

"This Noble Eightfold Path, bhikkhu, is the holy life; that is, right view ... right concentration. [8] The destruction of lust, the destruction of hatred, the destruction of delusion: this is the final goal of the holy life."

7 (7) A Certain Bhikkhu (2)

"Venerable sir, it is said, 'the removal of lust, the removal of hatred, the removal of delusion.' Of what now, venerable sir, is this the designation?"

"This, bhikkhu, is a designation for the element of Nibbāna: the removal of lust, the removal of hatred, the removal of delusion. The destruction of the taints is spoken of in that way."[15]

When this was said, that bhikkhu said to the Blessed One: "Venerable sir, it is said, 'the Deathless, the Deathless.' What now, venerable sir, is the Deathless? What is the path leading to the Deathless?"

"The destruction of lust, the destruction of hatred, the destruction of delusion: this is called the Deathless. This Noble Eightfold Path is the path leading to the Deathless; that is, right view ... right concentration."

8 (8) Analysis

At Sāvatthī. "Bhikkhus, I will teach you the Noble Eightfold Path and I will analyse it for you. Listen to that and attend closely, I will speak."

"Yes, venerable sir," those bhikkhus replied. The Blessed One said this:

"And what, bhikkhus, is the Noble Eightfold Path? Right view ... right concentration.[16]

"And what, bhikkhus, is right view? Knowledge of suffering, knowledge of the origin of suffering, [9] knowledge of the cessation of suffering, knowledge of the way leading to the cessation of suffering: this is called right view.

"And what, bhikkhus, is right intention? Intention of renunciation, intention of non-ill will, intention of harmlessness: this is called right intention.

"And what, bhikkhus, is right speech? Abstinence from false speech, abstinence from divisive speech, abstinence from harsh speech, abstinence from idle chatter: this is called right speech.

"And what, bhikkhus, is right action? Abstinence from the destruction of life, abstinence from taking what is not given, abstinence from sexual misconduct:[17] this is called right action.

"And what, bhikkhus, is right livelihood? Here a noble disciple, having abandoned a wrong mode of livelihood, earns his living by a right livelihood: this is called right livelihood.

"And what, bhikkhus, is right effort? Here, bhikkhus, a bhikkhu generates desire for the nonarising of unarisen evil unwholesome states; he makes an effort, arouses energy, applies his mind, and strives. He generates desire for the abandoning of arisen evil unwholesome states.... He generates desire for the arising of unarisen wholesome states.... He generates desire for the maintenance of arisen wholesome states, for their nondecay, increase, expansion, and fulfilment by development; he makes an effort, arouses energy, applies his mind, and strives. This is called right effort.

"And what, bhikkhus is right mindfulness? Here, bhikkhus, a bhikkhu dwells contemplating the body in the body, ardent, clearly comprehending, mindful, having removed covetousness and displeasure in regard to the world. He dwells contemplating feelings in feelings, ardent, clearly comprehending, mindful, having removed covetousness and displeasure in regard to the world. He dwells contemplating mind in mind, ardent, [10] clearly comprehending, mindful, having removed covetousness and displeasure in regard to the world. He dwells contemplating phenomena in phenomena, ardent, clearly comprehending, mindful, having removed covetousness and displeasure in regard to the world. This is called right mindfulness.

"And what, bhikkhus, is right concentration? Here, bhikkhus, secluded from sensual pleasures, secluded from unwholesome states, a bhikkhu enters and dwells in the first jhāna, which is accompanied by thought and examination, with rapture and happiness born of seclusion. With the subsiding of thought and examination, he enters and dwells in the second jhāna, which has internal confidence and unification of mind, is without thought and examination, and has rapture and happiness born of concentration. With the fading away as well of rapture, he dwells equanimous and, mindful and clearly comprehending, he experiences happiness with the body; he enters and dwells in the third jhāna of which the noble ones declare: 'He is equanimous, mindful, one who dwells happily.' With the abandoning of pleasure and pain, and with the previous passing away of joy and displeasure, he enters and dwells in the fourth jhāna, which is neither painful nor pleasant and includes the purification of mindfulness by equanimity. This is called right concentration."

9 (9) The Spike

At Sāvatthī. "Bhikkhus, suppose a spike of rice or a spike of barley were wrongly directed and were pressed upon by the hand or the foot. That it could pierce the hand or the foot and draw blood: this is impossible. For what reason? Because the spike is wrongly directed. So too, bhikkhus, that a bhikkhu with a wrongly directed view, with a wrongly directed development of the path, could pierce ignorance, arouse true knowledge, and realize Nibbāna: this is impossible. For what reason? Because his view is wrongly directed.

"Bhikkhus, suppose a spike of rice or a spike of barley were rightly directed and were pressed upon by the hand or the foot. That it could pierce the hand or the foot and draw blood: this is possible. For what reason? Because the spike is rightly directed. [11] So too, bhikkhus, that a bhikkhu with a rightly directed view, with a rightly directed development of the path, could pierce ignorance, arouse true knowledge, and realize Nibbāna: this is possible. For what reason? Because his view is rightly directed.

"And how does a bhikkhu do so? Here, bhikkhus, a bhikkhu develops right view, which is based upon seclusion, dispassion, and cessation, maturing in release. He develops ... right concentration, which is based upon seclusion, dispassion, and cessation, maturing in release.

"It is in this way, bhikkhus, that a bhikkhu with a rightly directed view, with a rightly directed development of the path, pierces ignorance, arouses true knowledge, and realizes Nibbāna."

10 (10) Nandiya

At Sāvatthī. Then the wanderer Nandiya approached the Blessed One and exchanged greetings with him. When they had concluded their greetings and cordial talk, he sat down to one side and said to the Blessed One: "How many things, Master Gotama, when developed and cultivated, lead to Nibbāna, have Nibbāna as their destination, Nibbāna as their final goal?"

"These eight things, Nandiya, when developed and cultivated, lead to Nibbāna, have Nibbāna as their destination, Nibbāna as their final goal. What eight? Right view ... right concentration. These eight things, when developed and cultivated, lead to Nibbāna, have Nibbāna as their destination, Nibbāna as their final goal."

When this was said, the wanderer Nandiya said to the Blessed One: "Magnificent, Master Gotama! Magnificent, Master [12] Gotama!... From today let Master Gotama remember me as a lay follower who has gone for refuge for life."

II. Dwelling

11 (1) Dwelling (1)

At Sāvatthī. "Bhikkhus, I wish to go into seclusion for half a month. I should not be approached by anyone except the one who brings me almsfood."[18]

"Yes, venerable sir," those bhikkhus replied, and no one approached the Blessed One except the one who brought him almsfood.

Then, when that half-month had passed, the Blessed One emerged from seclusion and addressed the bhikkhus thus:

"Bhikkhus, I have been dwelling in part of the abode in which I dwelt just after I became fully enlightened.[19] I have understood thus: 'There is feeling with wrong view as condition, also feeling with right view as condition.... There is feeling with wrong concentration as condition, also feeling with right concentration as condition. There is feeling with desire as condition, also feeling with thought as condition, also feeling with perception as condition.[20]

"'When desire has not subsided, and thought has not subsided, and perception has not subsided, there is feeling with that as condition. [When desire has subsided, and thoughts have not subsided, [13] and perceptions have not subsided, there is also feeling with that as condition. When desire has subsided, and thoughts have subsided, and perceptions have not subsided, there is also feeling with that as condition.] When desire has subsided, and thought has subsided, and perception has subsided, there is also feeling with that as condition. There is effort for the attainment of the as-yet-unattained. When that stage has been reached, there is also feeling with that as condition.'"[21]

12 (2) Dwelling (2)

At Sāvatthī. "Bhikkhus, I wish to go into seclusion for three months. I should not be approached by anyone except the one who brings me almsfood."

"Yes, venerable sir," those bhikkhus replied, and no one approached the Blessed One except the one who brought him almsfood.

Then, when those three months had passed, the Blessed One emerged from seclusion and addressed the bhikkhus thus:

"Bhikkhus, I have been dwelling in part of the abode in which I dwelt just after I became fully enlightened. I have understood thus: 'There is feeling with wrong view as condition, also feeling with the subsiding of wrong view as condition.[22] There is feeling with right view as condition, also feeling with the subsiding of right view as condition.... There is feeling with wrong concentration as condition, also feeling with the subsiding of wrong concentration as condition. There is feeling with right concentration as condition, also feeling with the subsiding of right concentration as condition. There is feeling with desire as condition, also feeling with the subsiding of desire as condition. There is feeling with thought as condition, also feeling with the subsiding of thought as condition. There is feeling with perception as condition, also feeling with the subsiding of perception as condition.

"'When desire has not subsided, and thought has not subsided, and perception has not subsided, there is feeling with that as condition. [When desire has subsided, and thoughts have not subsided, and perceptions have not subsided, there is also feeling with that as condition. When desire has subsided, and thoughts have subsided, and perceptions have not subsided, there is also feeling with that as condition]. [14] When desire has subsided, and thought has subsided, and perception has subsided, there is also feeling with that as condition. There is effort for the attainment of the as-yet-unattained. When that stage has been reached, there is also feeling with that as condition.'"

13 (3) A Trainee

At Sāvatthī. Then a certain bhikkhu approached the Blessed One.... Sitting to one side, that bhikkhu said to the Blessed One:

"Venerable sir, it is said, 'a trainee, a trainee.' In what way is one a trainee?"

"Here, bhikkhu, one possesses a trainee's right view ... a trainee's right concentration. It is in this way that one is a trainee."

14 (4) Arising (1)

At Sāvatthī. "Bhikkhus, these eight things, developed and cultivated, if unarisen do not arise apart from the appearance of a Tathāgata, an Arahant, a Perfectly Enlightened One. What eight? Right view ... right concentration. These eight things...."

15 (5) Arising (2)

At Sāvatthī. "Bhikkhus, these eight things, developed and cultivated, if unarisen do not arise apart from the Discipline of a Fortunate One. What eight? Right view ... [15] right concentration. These eight things...."

16 (6) Purified (1)

At Sāvatthī. "Bhikkhus, these eight things, purified, cleansed, flawless, free from corruptions, if unarisen do not arise apart from the appearance of a Tathāgata, an Arahant, a Perfectly Enlightened One. What eight? Right view ... right concentration. These eight things...."

17 (7) Purified (2)

At Sāvatthī. "Bhikkhus, these eight things, purified, cleansed, flawless, free from corruptions, if unarisen do not arise apart from the Discipline of a Fortunate One. What eight? Right view ... right concentration. These eight things...."

18 (8) The Cock's Park (1)

Thus have I heard. On one occasion the Venerable Ānanda and the Venerable Bhadda were dwelling at Pāṭaliputta in the Cock's Park. Then, in the evening, the Venerable Bhadda emerged from seclusion, approached the Venerable Ānanda, and exchanged greetings with him. When they had concluded their greetings and cordial talk, he sat down to one side and said to the Venerable Ānanda:

"Friend Ānanda, it is said, 'the unholy life, the unholy life.' What now, friend, is the unholy life?" [16]

"Good, good, friend Bhadda! Your intelligence is excellent,[23] friend Bhadda, your ingenuity is excellent, your inquiry is a good one. For you have asked me: 'Friend Ānanda, it is said, "the unholy life, the unholy life." What now, friend, is the unholy life?'"

"Yes, friend."

"This eightfold wrong path, friend, is the unholy life; that is, wrong view ... wrong concentration."

19 (9) The Cock's Park (2)

At Pāṭaliputta. "Friend Ānanda, it is said, 'the holy life, the holy life.' What now, friend, is the holy life and what is the final goal of the holy life?"

"Good, good, friend Bhadda! Your intelligence is excellent, friend Bhadda, your ingenuity is excellent, your inquiry is a good one. For you have asked me: 'Friend Ānanda, it is said, "the holy life, the holy life." What now, friend, is the holy life and what is the final goal of the holy life?'"

"Yes, friend."

"This Noble Eightfold Path, friend, is the holy life; that is, right view ... right concentration. The destruction of lust, the destruction of hatred, the destruction of delusion: this, friend, is the final goal of the holy life."

20 (10) The Cock's Park (3)

At Pāṭaliputta. "Friend Ānanda, it is said, 'the holy life, the holy life.' What now, friend, is the holy life, and who is a follower of the holy life, and what is the final goal of the holy life?" [17]

"Good, good, friend Bhadda! Your intelligence is excellent, friend Bhadda, your ingenuity is excellent, your inquiry is a good one. For you have asked me: 'Friend Ānanda, it is said, "the holy life, the holy life." What now, friend, is the holy life, and who is a follower of the holy life, and what is the final goal of the holy life?'"

"Yes, friend."

"This Noble Eightfold Path, friend, is the holy life; that is, right view ... right concentration. One who possesses this Noble Eightfold Path is called a liver of the holy life. The destruction of lust, the destruction of hatred, the destruction of delusion: this, friend, is the final goal of the holy life."

III. Wrongness

21 (1) Wrongness

At Sāvatthī. "Bhikkhus, I will teach you wrongness and rightness. Listen to that…. [18]

"And what, bhikkhus, is wrongness? It is: wrong view ... wrong concentration. This is called wrongness.

"And what, bhikkhus, is rightness? It is: right view ... right concentration. This is called rightness."

22 (2) Unwholesome States

At Sāvatthī. "Bhikkhus, I will teach you unwholesome states and wholesome states. Listen to that….

"And what, bhikkhus, are unwholesome states? They are: wrong view ... wrong concentration. These are called unwholesome states.

"And what, bhikkhus, are wholesome states? They are: right view ... right concentration. These are called wholesome states."

23 (3) The Way (1)

At Sāvatthī. "Bhikkhus, I will teach you the wrong way and the right way. Listen to that….

"And what, bhikkhus, is the wrong way? It is: wrong view ... wrong concentration. This is called the wrong way.

"And what, bhikkhus, is the right way? It is: right view ... right concentration. This is called the right way."

24 (4) The Way (2)

At Sāvatthī. "Bhikkhus, whether for a layperson or one gone forth, I do not praise the wrong way. Whether it is a layperson or one gone forth who is practising wrongly, [19] because of undertaking the wrong way of practice he does not attain the method, the Dhamma that is wholesome.[24] And what, bhikkhus, is the wrong way? It is: wrong view … wrong concentration. This is called the wrong way. Whether it is a layperson or one gone forth who is practising wrongly, because of undertaking the wrong way of practice he does not attain the method, the Dhamma that is wholesome.

"Bhikkhus, whether for a layperson or one gone forth, I praise the right way. Whether it is a layperson or one gone forth who is practising rightly, because of undertaking the right way of practice he attains the method, the Dhamma that is wholesome. And what, bhikkhus, is the right way? It is: right view … right concentration. This is called the right way. Whether it is a layperson or one gone forth who is practising rightly, because of undertaking the right way of practice he attains the method, the Dhamma that is wholesome."

25 (5) The Inferior Person (1)

At Sāvatthī. "Bhikkhus, I will teach you the inferior person and the superior person. Listen to that….

"And what, bhikkhus, is the inferior person? Here someone is of wrong view, wrong intention, wrong speech, wrong action, wrong livelihood, wrong effort, wrong mindfulness, wrong concentration. This is called the inferior person.

"And what, bhikkhus, is the superior person? Here someone is of right view, right intention, right speech, [20] right action, right livelihood, right effort, right mindfulness, right concentration. This is called the superior person."

26 (6) The Inferior Person (2)

At Sāvatthī. "Bhikkhus, I will teach you the inferior person and the one who is worse than the inferior person. I will teach you the superior person and the one who is better than the superior person. Listen to that….

"And what, bhikkhus, is the inferior person? Here someone is of wrong view … wrong concentration. This is called the inferior person.

"And what, bhikkhus, is the one who is worse than the inferior person? Here someone is of wrong view ... wrong concentration, wrong knowledge, wrong liberation.[25] This is called the one who is worse than the inferior person.

"And what, bhikkhus, is the superior person? Here someone is of right view ... right concentration. This is called the superior person.

"And what, bhikkhus, is the one who is better than the superior person? Here someone is of right view ... right concentration, right knowledge, right liberation. This is called the one who is better than the superior person."

27 (7) The Pot

At Sāvatthī. "Bhikkhus, just as a pot without a stand is easily knocked over, while one with a stand is difficult to knock over, so the mind without a stand is easily knocked over, while the mind with a stand is difficult to knock over. [21]

"And what, bhikkhus, is the stand of the mind? It is this Noble Eightfold Path; that is, right view ... right concentration. This is the stand of the mind.

"Bhikkhus, just as a pot ... so the mind without a stand is easily knocked over, while the mind with a stand is difficult to knock over."

28 (8) Concentration

At Sāvatthī. "Bhikkhus, I will teach you noble right concentration with its supports and its accessories.[26] Listen to that....

"And what, bhikkhus, is noble right concentration with its supports and its accessories? There are: right view ... right mindfulness. The one-pointedness of mind equipped with these seven factors is called noble right concentration 'with its supports,' and also 'with its accessories.'"

29 (9) Feeling

At Sāvatthī. "Bhikkhus, there are these three feelings. What three? Pleasant feeling, painful feeling, neither-painful-nor-pleasant feeling. These are the three feelings.

"The Noble Eightfold Path, bhikkhus, is to be developed for the full understanding of these three feelings. What is the Noble Eightfold Path? It is: right view ... right concentration. [22] The Noble Eightfold Path is to be developed for the full understanding of these three feelings."

30 (10) Uttiya

At Sāvatthī. Then the Venerable Uttiya approached the Blessed One ... and said to him:

"Here, venerable sir, when I was alone in seclusion a reflection arose in my mind thus: 'Five cords of sensual pleasure have been spoken of by the Blessed One. But what now are those five cords of sensual pleasure?'"

"Good, good, Uttiya! These five cords of sensual pleasure have been spoken of by me. What five? Forms cognizable by the eye that are desirable, lovely, agreeable, pleasing, sensually enticing, tantalizing. Sounds cognizable by the ear ... Odours cognizable by the nose ... Tastes cognizable by the tongue ... Tactile objects cognizable by the body that are desirable, lovely, agreeable, pleasing, sensually enticing, tantalizing. These are the five cords of sensual pleasure spoken of by me.

"The Noble Eightfold Path, Uttiya, is to be developed for the abandoning of these five cords of sensual pleasure. And what is the Noble Eightfold Path? It is: right view ... right concentration. This Noble Eightfold Path is to be developed for the abandoning of these five cords of sensual pleasure."

[23] IV. Practice

31 (1) Practice (1)

At Sāvatthī. "Bhikkhus, I will teach you wrong practice and right practice. Listen to that....

"And what, bhikkhus, is wrong practice? It is: wrong view ... wrong concentration. This is called wrong practice.

"And what, bhikkhus, is right practice? It is: right view ... right concentration. This is called right practice."

32 (2) Practice (2)

At Sāvatthī. "Bhikkhus, I will teach you the one practising wrongly and the one practising rightly. Listen to that….

"And what, bhikkhus, is the one practising wrongly? Here someone is of wrong view … wrong concentration. This is called the one practising wrongly.

"And what, bhikkhus, is the one practising rightly? Here someone is of right view … right concentration. This is called the one practising rightly."[27]

33 (3) Neglected

At Sāvatthī. "Bhikkhus, those who have neglected the Noble Eightfold Path have neglected the noble path[28] leading to the complete destruction of suffering. Those who have undertaken the Noble Eightfold Path have undertaken the noble path leading to the complete destruction of suffering. [24]

"And what, bhikkhus, is the Noble Eightfold Path? It is: right view … right concentration. Those who have neglected this Noble Eightfold Path … Those who have undertaken this Noble Eightfold Path have undertaken the noble path leading to the complete destruction of suffering."

34 (4) Going Beyond

At Sāvatthī. "Bhikkhus, these eight things, when developed and cultivated, lead to going beyond from the near shore to the far shore. What eight? Right view … right concentration. These eight things, when developed and cultivated, lead to going beyond from the near shore to the far shore."[29]

This is what the Blessed One said. Having said this, the Fortunate One, the Teacher, further said this:

"Few are those among humankind
Who go beyond to the far shore.
The rest of the people merely run
Up and down along the bank.

"When the Dhamma is rightly expounded
Those who practise in accord with the Dhamma
Are the people who will go beyond
The realm of Death so hard to cross.

"Having left behind the dark qualities,
The wise man should develop the bright ones.
Having come from home into homelessness,
Where it is hard to take delight—

"There in seclusion he should seek delight,
Having left behind sensual pleasures.
Owning nothing, the wise man
Should cleanse himself of mental defilements.

"Those whose minds are well developed
In the factors of enlightenment,
Who through nonclinging find delight
In the relinquishment of grasping:
Those luminous ones with taints destroyed
Are fully quenched in the world." [25]

35 (5) Asceticism (1)

At Sāvatthī. "Bhikkhus, I will teach you asceticism and the fruits of asceticism. Listen to that....

"And what, bhikkhus, is asceticism? It is this Noble Eightfold Path; that is, right view ... right concentration. This is called asceticism.

"And what, bhikkhus, are the fruits of asceticism? The fruit of stream-entry, the fruit of once-returning, the fruit of nonreturning, the fruit of arahantship. These are called the fruits of asceticism."

36 (6) Asceticism (2)

At Sāvatthī. "Bhikkhus, I will teach you asceticism and the goal of asceticism. Listen to that....

"And what, bhikkhus, is asceticism? It is this Noble Eightfold Path; that is, right view ... right concentration. This is called asceticism.

"And what, bhikkhus, is the goal of asceticism? The destruction of lust, the destruction of hatred, the destruction of delusion. This is called the goal of asceticism."

37 (7) Brahminhood (1)

At Sāvatthī. "Bhikkhus, I will teach you brahminhood and the fruits of brahminhood. Listen to that….

"And what, bhikkhus, is brahminhood? It is this Noble Eightfold Path; that is, right view … right concentration. This is called brahminhood.

"And what, bhikkhus, are the fruits of brahminhood? [26] The fruit of stream-entry, the fruit of once-returning, the fruit of non-returning, the fruit of arahantship. These are called the fruits of brahminhood."

38 (8) Brahminhood (2)

At Sāvatthī. "Bhikkhus, I will teach you brahminhood and the goal of brahminhood. Listen to that….

"And what, bhikkhus, is brahminhood? It is this Noble Eightfold Path; that is, right view … right concentration. This is called brahminhood.

"And what, bhikkhus, is the goal of brahminhood? The destruction of lust, the destruction of hatred, the destruction of delusion. This is called the goal of brahminhood."

39 (9) The Holy Life (1)

At Sāvatthī. "Bhikkhus, I will teach you the holy life and the fruits of the holy life. Listen to that….

"And what, bhikkhus, is the holy life? It is this Noble Eightfold Path; that is, right view … right concentration. This is called the holy life.

"And what, bhikkhus, are the fruits of the holy life? The fruit of stream-entry, the fruit of once-returning, the fruit of non-returning, the fruit of arahantship. These are called the fruits of the holy life."

40 (10) The Holy Life (2)

At Sāvatthī. "Bhikkhus, I will teach you the holy life and the goal of the holy life. Listen to that….

"And what, bhikkhus, is the holy life? It is this Noble Eightfold Path; that is, right view … right concentration. This is called the holy life. [27]

"And what, bhikkhus, is the goal of the holy life? The destruction of lust, the destruction of hatred, the destruction of delusion. This is called the goal of the holy life."

V. Wanderers of Other Sects[30]

41 (1) The Fading Away of Lust

At Sāvatthī. "Bhikkhus, if wanderers of other sects ask you: 'For what purpose, friends, is the holy life lived under the ascetic Gotama?'—being asked thus, you should answer them thus: 'It is, friends, for the fading away of lust that the holy life is lived under the Blessed One.'

"Then, bhikkhus, if the wanderers of other sects ask you: 'But, friends, is there a path, is there a way for the fading away of lust?'—being asked thus, you should answer them thus: 'There is a path, friends, there is a way for the fading away of lust.'

"And what, bhikkhus, is that path, what is that way [28] for the fading away of lust? It is this Noble Eightfold Path; that is, right view … right concentration. This is the path, this is the way for the fading away of lust.

"Being asked thus, bhikkhus, you should answer those wanderers of other sects in such a way."

42 (2)–48 (8) The Abandoning of the Fetters, Etc.

"Bhikkhus, if wanderers of other sects ask you: 'For what purpose, friends, is the holy life lived under the ascetic Gotama?'—being asked thus, you should answer them thus: 'It is, friends, for the abandoning of the fetters … for the uprooting of the underlying tendencies … for the full understanding of the course[31] … for the destruction of the taints … for the realization of the fruit of true knowledge and liberation … for the sake of knowledge and vision ... [29] ... for the sake of final Nibbāna without clinging that the holy life is lived under the Blessed One.'

"Then, bhikkhus, if the wanderers of other sects ask you: 'But, friends, is there a path, is there a way for attaining final Nibbāna without clinging?'—being asked thus, you should answer them thus: 'There is a path, friends, there is a way for attaining final Nibbāna without clinging.'

"And what, bhikkhus, is that path, what is that way for attaining final Nibbāna without clinging? It is this Noble Eightfold Path; that is, right view ... right concentration. This is the path, this is the way for attaining final Nibbāna without clinging.

"Being asked thus, bhikkhus, you should answer those wanderers of other sects in such a way."

VI. The Sun Repetition Series

(i) Based upon Seclusion Version

49 (1) Good Friend

At Sāvatthī. "Bhikkhus, this is the forerunner and precursor of the rising of the sun, that is, the dawn. So too, bhikkhus, [30] for a bhikkhu this is the forerunner and precursor for the arising of the Noble Eightfold Path, that is, good friendship.[32] When a bhikkhu has a good friend, it is to be expected that he will develop and cultivate this Noble Eightfold Path.

"And how does a bhikkhu who has a good friend develop and cultivate the Noble Eightfold Path? Here, bhikkhus, a bhikkhu develops right view, which is based upon seclusion, dispassion, and cessation, maturing in release.... He develops right concentration, which is based upon seclusion, dispassion, and cessation, maturing in release. It is in this way, bhikkhus, that a bhikkhu who has a good friend develops and cultivates the Noble Eightfold Path."

50 (2)–55 (7) Accomplishment in Virtue, Etc.

"Bhikkhus, this is the forerunner and precursor of the rising of the sun, that is, the dawn. So too, bhikkhus, for a bhikkhu this is the forerunner and precursor for the arising of the Noble Eightfold Path, that is, accomplishment in virtue ... accomplishment in desire ... accomplishment in self ... accomplishment in view ... accomplishment in diligence ... [31] ... accomplishment in careful attention.[33] When a bhikkhu is accomplished in careful attention, it is to be expected that he will develop and cultivate this Noble Eightfold Path.

"And how does a bhikkhu who is accomplished in careful attention develop and cultivate the Noble Eightfold Path? Here, bhikkhus, a bhikkhu develops right view, which is based upon seclusion, dispassion, and cessation, maturing in release.... He develops right concentration, which is based upon seclusion, dispassion, and cessation, maturing in release. It is in this way, bhikkhus, that a bhikkhu who is accomplished in careful attention develops and cultivates the Noble Eightfold Path."

(ii) REMOVAL OF LUST VERSION

56 (1) Good Friend

"Bhikkhus, this is the forerunner and precursor of the rising of the sun, that is, the dawn. So too, bhikkhus, for a bhikkhu this is the forerunner and precursor for the arising of the Noble Eightfold Path, that is, good friendship. When a bhikkhu has a good friend, it is to be expected that he will develop and cultivate this Noble Eightfold Path.

"And how does a bhikkhu who has a good friend develop and cultivate the Noble Eightfold Path? Here, bhikkhus, a bhikkhu develops right view, which has as its final goal the removal of lust, the removal of hatred, the removal of delusion.... He develops right concentration, which has as its final goal the removal of lust, the removal of hatred, the removal of delusion. It is in this way, bhikkhus, that a bhikkhu who has a good friend develops and cultivates the Noble Eightfold Path."

57 (2)–62 (7) Accomplishment in Virtue, Etc.

"Bhikkhus, this is the forerunner and precursor of the rising of the sun, that is, the dawn. So too, bhikkhus, for a bhikkhu this is the forerunner and precursor for the arising of the Noble Eightfold Path, that is, accomplishment in virtue ... [32] ... accomplishment in desire ... accomplishment in self ... accomplishment in view ... accomplishment in diligence ... accomplishment in careful attention. When a bhikkhu is accomplished in careful attention, it is to be expected that he will develop and cultivate this Noble Eightfold Path.

"And how does a bhikkhu who is accomplished in careful attention develop and cultivate the Noble Eightfold Path? Here, bhikkhus, a bhikkhu develops right view, which has as its final goal the removal of lust, the removal of hatred, the removal of delusion.... He develops right concentration, which has as its final goal the removal of lust, the removal of hatred, the removal of delusion. It is in this way, bhikkhus, that a bhikkhu who is accomplished in careful attention develops and cultivates the Noble Eightfold Path."

VII. One Thing Repetition Series (1)

(i) based upon seclusion version

63 (1) Good Friend

At Sāvatthī. "Bhikkhus, one thing is very helpful for the arising of the Noble Eightfold Path. What one thing? Good friendship. [33] When a bhikkhu has a good friend, it is to be expected that he will develop and cultivate the Noble Eightfold Path.

"And how does a bhikkhu who has a good friend develop and cultivate the Noble Eightfold Path? Here, bhikkhus, a bhikkhu develops right view, which is based upon seclusion, dispassion, and cessation, maturing in release.... He develops right concentration, which is based upon seclusion, dispassion, and cessation, maturing in release. It is in this way, bhikkhus, that a bhikkhu who has a good friend develops and cultivates the Noble Eightfold Path."

64 (2)–69 (7) Accomplishment in Virtue, Etc.

"Bhikkhus, one thing is very helpful for the arising of the Noble Eightfold Path. What one thing? Accomplishment in virtue ... Accomplishment in desire ... Accomplishment in self ... Accomplishment in view ... Accomplishment in diligence ... Accomplishment in careful attention ... (*complete as in* §63) [34] ... He develops right concentration, which is based upon seclusion, dispassion, and cessation, maturing in release. It is in this way, bhikkhus, that a bhikkhu who is accomplished in careful attention develops and cultivates the Noble Eightfold Path."

(ii) REMOVAL OF LUST VERSION

70 (1) Good Friend

At Sāvatthī. "Bhikkhus, one thing is very helpful for the arising of the Noble Eightfold Path. What one thing? Good friendship. When a bhikkhu has a good friend, it is to be expected that he will develop and cultivate the Noble Eightfold Path.

"And how does a bhikkhu who has a good friend develop and cultivate the Noble Eightfold Path? Here, bhikkhus, a bhikkhu develops right view, which has as its final goal the removal of lust, the removal of hatred, the removal of delusion.... He develops right concentration, which has as its final goal the removal of lust, the removal of hatred, the removal of delusion. It is in this way, bhikkhus, that a bhikkhu who has a good friend develops and cultivates the Noble Eightfold Path."

71 (2)–76 (7) Accomplishment in Virtue, Etc.

"Bhikkhus, one thing is very helpful for the arising of the Noble Eightfold Path. What one thing? Accomplishment in virtue ... Accomplishment in desire ... Accomplishment in self ... Accomplishment in view ... [35] Accomplishment in diligence ... Accomplishment in careful attention ... (*complete as in §70*) ... He develops right concentration, which has as its final goal the removal of lust, the removal of hatred, the removal of delusion. It is in this way, bhikkhus, that a bhikkhu who is accomplished in careful attention develops and cultivates the Noble Eightfold Path."

VIII. ONE THING REPETITION SERIES (2)

(i) BASED UPON SECLUSION VERSION

77 (1) Good Friend

"Bhikkhus, I do not see even one other thing by means of which the unarisen Noble Eightfold Path arises and the arisen Noble Eightfold Path goes to fulfilment by development so effectively as by this: good friendship. When a bhikkhu has a good friend, it is to be expected that he will develop and cultivate the Noble Eightfold Path.

"And how does a bhikkhu who has a good friend develop and cultivate the Noble Eightfold Path? [36] Here, bhikkhus, a bhikkhu develops right view, which is based upon seclusion, dispassion, and cessation, maturing in release.... He develops right concentration, which is based upon seclusion, dispassion, and cessation, maturing in release. It is in this way, bhikkhus, that a bhikkhu who has a good friend develops and cultivates the Noble Eightfold Path."

78 (2)–83 (7) Accomplishment in Virtue, Etc.

"Bhikkhus, I do not see even one other thing by means of which the unarisen Noble Eightfold Path arises and the arisen Noble Eightfold Path goes to fulfilment by development so effectively as by this: accomplishment in virtue ... accomplishment in desire ... accomplishment in self ... accomplishment in view ... accomplishment in diligence ... accomplishment in careful attention ... (*complete as in* §77) ... He develops right concentration, which is based upon seclusion, dispassion, and cessation, maturing in release. It is in this way, bhikkhus, that a bhikkhu who is accomplished in careful attention develops and cultivates the Noble Eightfold Path." [37]

(ii) REMOVAL OF LUST VERSION

84 (1) Good Friend

"Bhikkhus, I do not see even one other thing by means of which the unarisen Noble Eightfold Path arises and the arisen Noble Eightfold Path goes to fulfilment by development so effectively as by this: good friendship. When a bhikkhu has a good friend, it is to be expected that he will develop and cultivate the Noble Eightfold Path.

"And how does a bhikkhu who has a good friend develop and cultivate the Noble Eightfold Path? Here, bhikkhus, a bhikkhu develops right view, which has as its final goal the removal of lust, the removal of hatred, the removal of delusion.... He develops right concentration, which has as its final goal the removal of lust, the removal of hatred, the removal of delusion. It is in this way, bhikkhus, that a bhikkhu who has a good friend develops and cultivates the Noble Eightfold Path."

85 (2)–90 (7) Accomplishment in Virtue, Etc.

"Bhikkhus, I do not see even one other thing by means of which the unarisen Noble Eightfold Path arises and the arisen Noble Eightfold Path goes to fulfilment by development so effectively as by this: accomplishment in virtue ... accomplishment in desire ... accomplishment in self ... accomplishment in view ... accomplishment in diligence ... accomplishment in careful attention ... (*complete as in §84*) [38] ... He develops right concentration, which has as its final goal the removal of lust, the removal of hatred, the removal of delusion. It is in this way, bhikkhus, that a bhikkhu who is accomplished in careful attention develops and cultivates the Noble Eightfold Path."

IX. First Ganges Repetition Series[34]

(i) Based upon Seclusion Version

91 (1) Slanting to the East (1)

At Sāvatthī. "Bhikkhus, just as the river Ganges slants, slopes, and inclines towards the east, so too a bhikkhu who develops and cultivates the Noble Eightfold Path slants, slopes, and inclines towards Nibbāna.

"And how, bhikkhus, does a bhikkhu develop and cultivate the Noble Eightfold Path so that he slants, slopes, and inclines towards Nibbāna? Here, bhikkhus, a bhikkhu develops right view, which is based upon seclusion, dispassion, and cessation, maturing in release.... He develops right concentration, which is based upon seclusion, dispassion, and cessation, maturing in release. It is in this way, bhikkhus, that a bhikkhu develops and cultivates the Noble Eightfold Path so that he slants, slopes, and inclines towards Nibbāna."

92 (2)–96 (6) Slanting to the East (2–6)

"Bhikkhus, just as the river Yamunā ... [39] ... the river Aciravatī ... the river Sarabhū ... the river Mahī ... whatever great rivers there are—that is, the Ganges, the Yamunā, the Aciravatī, the Sarabhū, the Mahī—all slant, slope, and incline towards the east, so too a bhikkhu who develops and cultivates the Noble Eightfold Path slants, slopes, and inclines towards Nibbāna."

(*Complete as in §91.*)

97 (7)–102 (12) The Ocean

"Bhikkhus, just as the river Ganges ... [40] ... whatever great rivers there are ... all slant, slope, and incline towards the ocean, so too a bhikkhu who develops and cultivates the Noble Eightfold Path slants, slopes, and inclines towards Nibbāna."

(*Complete as in §§91–96.*)

X. Second Ganges Repetition Series
(ii) removal of lust version

103 (1)–108 (6) Slanting to the East
109 (7)–114 (12) The Ocean

(*In this version §§103–108 are identical with §§91–96, and §§109–114 with §§97–102, except for the following change:*)

"Here, bhikkhus, a bhikkhu develops and cultivates right view ... right concentration, which has as its final goal the removal of lust, the removal of hatred, the removal of delusion."

[41]

XI. Third Ganges Repetition Series
(iii) the deathless as its ground version

115 (1)–120 (6) Slanting to the East
121 (7)–126 (12) The Ocean

(*In this version §§115–120 are identical with §§91–96, and §§121–126 with §§97–102, except for the following change:*)

"Here, bhikkhus, a bhikkhu develops and cultivates right view

… right concentration, which has the Deathless as its ground, the Deathless as its destination, the Deathless as its final goal."[35]

XII. Fourth Ganges Repetition Series
(iv) Slants towards Nibbāna Version

127 (1)–132 (6) Slanting to the East
133 (7)–138 (12) The Ocean

(*In this version §§127–132 are identical with §§91–96, and §§133–138 with §§97–102, except for the following change:*)

"Here, bhikkhus, a bhikkhu develops and cultivates right view … right concentration, which slants, slopes, and inclines towards Nibbāna."

XIII. Diligence[36]

139 (1) The Tathāgata

(i) Based upon Seclusion Version

At Sāvatthī. "Bhikkhus, whatever beings there are—whether those without feet or those with two feet or those with four feet or those with many feet, whether consisting of form or formless, whether percipient, [42] nonpercipient, or neither percipient nor nonpercipient—the Tathāgata, the Arahant, the Perfectly Enlightened One, is declared to be the chief among them. So too, whatever wholesome states there are, they are all rooted in diligence, converge upon diligence, and diligence is declared to be the chief among them.[37] When a bhikkhu is diligent, it is to be expected that he will develop and cultivate the Noble Eightfold Path.

"And how, bhikkhus, does a bhikkhu who is diligent develop and cultivate the Noble Eightfold Path? Here, bhikkhus, a bhikkhu develops right view … right concentration, which is based upon seclusion, dispassion, and cessation, maturing in release. It is in this way, bhikkhus, that a bhikkhu who is diligent develops and cultivates the Noble Eightfold Path."

(ii) REMOVAL OF LUST VERSION

... "Here, bhikkhus, a bhikkhu develops right view ... right concentration, which has as its final goal the removal of lust, the removal of hatred, the removal of delusion...." [43]

(iii) THE DEATHLESS AS ITS GROUND VERSION

... "Here, bhikkhus, a bhikkhu develops right view ... right concentration, which has the Deathless as its ground, the Deathless as its destination, the Deathless as its final goal...."

(iv) SLANTS TOWARDS NIBBĀNA VERSION

... "Here, bhikkhus, a bhikkhu develops right view ... right concentration, which slants, slopes, and inclines towards Nibbāna...."

(Each of the following suttas, §§140–148, is to be elaborated in accordance with the fourfold method of §139.)

140 (2) The Footprint

"Bhikkhus, just as the footprints of all living beings that walk fit into the footprint of the elephant, and the elephant's footprint is declared to be the chief among them, that is, with respect to size, so too whatever wholesome states there are, they are all rooted in diligence, converge upon diligence, and diligence is declared to be the chief among them. When a bhikkhu is diligent, it is to be expected that he will develop and cultivate the Noble Eightfold Path...."

141 (3) The Roof Peak

"Bhikkhus, just as all the rafters of a peaked house lean towards the roof peak, slope towards the roof peak, converge upon the roof peak, and the roof peak is declared to be their chief, so too ..."[38] [44]

142 (4) Roots

"Bhikkhus, just as, of all fragrant roots, black orris is declared to be their chief, so too ..."

143 (5) Heartwood

"Bhikkhus, just as, of all fragrant heartwoods, red sandalwood is declared to be their chief, so too ..."

144 (6) Jasmine

"Bhikkhus, just as, of all fragrant flowers, the jasmine is declared to be their chief, so too ..."

145 (7) Monarch

"Bhikkhus, just as all petty princes are the vassals of a wheel-turning monarch, and the wheel-turning monarch is declared to be their chief, so too ..."

146 (8) The Moon

"Bhikkhus, just as the radiance of all the stars does not amount to a sixteenth part of the radiance of the moon, and the radiance of the moon is declared to be their chief, so too ..."

147 (9) The Sun

"Bhikkhus, just as in the autumn, when the sky is clear and cloudless, the sun, ascending in the sky, dispels all darkness from space as it shines and beams and radiates, so too ..." [45]

148 (10) The Cloth

"Bhikkhus, just as, of all woven cloths, Kāsian cloth is declared to be their chief, so too whatever wholesome states there are, they are all rooted in diligence, converge upon diligence, and diligence is declared to be the chief among them. When a bhikkhu is diligent, it is to be expected that he will develop and cultivate the Noble Eightfold Path.

"And how, bhikkhus, does a bhikkhu who is diligent develop and cultivate the Noble Eightfold Path? Here, bhikkhus, a bhikkhu develops right view ... right concentration, which is based upon seclusion, dispassion, and cessation, maturing in release. It is in this way, bhikkhus, that a bhikkhu who is diligent develops and cultivates the Noble Eightfold Path."

XIV. Strenuous Deeds

(*Each sutta is to be elaborated in accordance with the same fourfold method.*)

149 (1) Strenuous

At Sāvatthī. "Bhikkhus, just as whatever strenuous deeds are done, are all done based upon the earth, established upon the earth, [46] so too, based upon virtue, established upon virtue, a bhikkhu develops and cultivates the Noble Eightfold Path.

"And how, bhikkhus, does a bhikkhu, based upon virtue, established upon virtue, develop and cultivate the Noble Eightfold Path? Here, bhikkhus, a bhikkhu develops right view ... right concentration, which is based upon seclusion, dispassion, and cessation, maturing in release. It is in this way, bhikkhus, that a bhikkhu, based upon virtue, established upon virtue, develops and cultivates the Noble Eightfold Path."

150 (2) Seeds

"Bhikkhus, just as whatever kinds of seed and plant life attain to growth, increase, and expansion, all do so based upon the earth, established upon the earth, so too, based upon virtue, established upon virtue, a bhikkhu develops and cultivates the Noble Eightfold Path, and thereby he attains to growth, increase, and expansion in [wholesome] states.

"And how does a bhikkhu do so? Here, bhikkhus, a bhikkhu develops right view ... right concentration, which is based upon seclusion, dispassion, [47] and cessation, maturing in release. It is in this way, bhikkhus, that a bhikkhu, based upon virtue, established upon virtue, develops and cultivates the Noble Eightfold Path, and thereby attains to growth, increase, and expansion in [wholesome] states."

151 (3) Nāgas

"Bhikkhus, based upon the Himalayas, the king of mountains, the nāgas nurture their bodies and acquire strength.[39] When they have nurtured their bodies and acquired strength, they then enter the pools. From the pools they enter the lakes, then the streams, then the rivers, and finally they enter the ocean. There they achieve greatness and expansiveness of body. So too, bhikkhus, based upon virtue, established upon virtue, a bhikkhu develops and cultivates the Noble Eightfold Path, and thereby he achieves greatness and expansiveness in [wholesome] states.

"And how does a bhikkhu do so? Here, bhikkhus, a bhikkhu develops right view … right concentration, which is based upon seclusion, dispassion, and cessation, maturing in release. It is in this way, bhikkhus, that a bhikkhu, based upon virtue, established upon virtue, develops and cultivates the Noble Eightfold Path, and thereby achieves greatness and expansiveness in [wholesome] states."

152 (4) The Tree

"Bhikkhus, suppose a tree were slanting, sloping, and inclining towards the east. If it were cut at its foot, in what direction would it fall?" [48]

"In whatever direction it was slanting, sloping, and inclining, venerable sir."

"So too, bhikkhus, a bhikkhu who develops and cultivates the Noble Eightfold Path slants, slopes, and inclines towards Nibbāna.

"And how does a bhikkhu do so? Here, bhikkhus, a bhikkhu develops right view … right concentration, which is based upon seclusion, dispassion, and cessation, maturing in release. It is in this way, bhikkhus, that a bhikkhu develops and cultivates the Noble Eightfold Path so that he slants, slopes, and inclines towards Nibbāna."

153 (5) The Pot

"Bhikkhus, just as a pot that has been turned upside down gives up its water and does not take it back, so a bhikkhu who develops and cultivates the Noble Eightfold Path gives up evil unwholesome states and does not take them back.

"And how does a bhikkhu do so? Here, bhikkhus, a bhikkhu develops right view … right concentration, which is based upon seclusion, dispassion, and cessation, maturing in release. It is in this way, bhikkhus, that a bhikkhu develops and cultivates the Noble Eightfold Path so that he gives up evil unwholesome states and does not take them back."

154 (6) The Spike

"Bhikkhus, suppose a spike of rice or a spike of barley were rightly directed and were pressed upon by the hand or the foot. That it could pierce the hand or the foot and draw blood: this is possible. For what reason? Because the spike is rightly directed. [49] So too, bhikkhus, that a bhikkhu with a rightly directed view, with a rightly directed development of the path, could pierce ignorance, arouse true knowledge, and realize Nibbāna: this is possible. For what reason? Because his view is rightly directed.

"And how does a bhikkhu do so? Here, bhikkhus, a bhikkhu develops right view … right concentration, which is based upon seclusion, dispassion, and cessation, maturing in release.

"It is in this way, bhikkhus, that a bhikkhu with a rightly directed view, with a rightly directed development of the path, pierces ignorance, arouses true knowledge, and realizes Nibbāna."

155 (7) The Sky

"Bhikkhus, just as various winds blow in the sky—easterly winds, westerly winds, northerly winds, southerly winds, dusty winds and dustless winds, cold winds and hot winds, gentle winds and strong winds[40]—so too, when a bhikkhu develops and cultivates the Noble Eightfold Path, then for him the four establishments of mindfulness go to fulfilment by development; the four right strivings go to fulfilment by development; the four bases for spiritual power go to fulfilment by development; the five spiritual faculties go to fulfilment by development; the five powers go to fulfilment by development; the seven factors of enlightenment go to fulfilment by development.

"And how is this so? Here, bhikkhus, a bhikkhu develops right view ... right concentration, which is based upon seclusion, dispassion, and cessation, maturing in release. It is in this way, bhikkhus, that when a bhikkhu [50] develops and cultivates the Noble Eightfold Path, then for him the four establishments of mindfulness ... the seven factors of enlightenment go to fulfilment by development."

156 (8) The Rain Cloud (1)

"Bhikkhus, just as, in the last month of the hot season, when a mass of dust and dirt has swirled up, a great rain cloud out of season disperses it and quells it on the spot; so too, when a bhikkhu develops and cultivates the Noble Eightfold Path, whenever evil unwholesome states arise, he disperses them and quells them on the spot.

"And how is this so? Here, bhikkhus, a bhikkhu develops right view ... right concentration, which is based upon seclusion, dispassion, and cessation, maturing in release. [51] It is in this way, bhikkhus, that a bhikkhu develops and cultivates the Noble Eightfold Path so that whenever evil unwholesome states arise, he disperses them and quells them on the spot."

157 (9) The Rain Cloud (2)

"Bhikkhus, just as, when a great rain cloud has arisen, a strong wind intercedes to disperse and quell it; so too, when a bhikkhu develops and cultivates the Noble Eightfold Path, whenever evil unwholesome states have arisen, he intercedes to disperse and quell them.

"And how is this so? Here, bhikkhus, a bhikkhu develops right view ... right concentration, which is based upon seclusion, dispassion, and cessation, maturing in release. It is in this way, bhikkhus, that a bhikkhu develops and cultivates the Noble Eightfold Path so that whenever evil unwholesome states have arisen, he intercedes to disperse and quell them."

158 (10) The Ship

"Bhikkhus, suppose there were a seafaring ship bound with rigging that had been worn out in the water for six months.[41] It would be hauled up on dry land during the cold season and its rigging would be further attacked by wind and sun. Inundated by rain from a rain cloud, the rigging would easily collapse and rot away. So too, when a bhikkhu develops and cultivates the Noble Eightfold Path, his fetters easily collapse and rot away.

"And how is this so? Here, bhikkhus, a bhikkhu develops right view ... right concentration, which is based upon seclusion, dispassion, and cessation, maturing in release. It is in this way, bhikkhus, that a bhikkhu develops and cultivates the Noble Eightfold Path so that his fetters easily collapse and rot away."

159 (11) The Guest House

"Bhikkhus, suppose there is a guest house.[42] People come from the east, west, north, and south and lodge there; khattiyas, brahmins, [52] vessas, and suddas come and lodge there. So too, when a bhikkhu develops and cultivates the Noble Eightfold Path, he fully understands by direct knowledge those things that are to be fully understood by direct knowledge; he abandons by direct knowledge those things that are to be abandoned by direct knowledge; he realizes by direct knowledge those things that are to be realized by direct knowledge; he develops by direct knowledge those things that are to be developed by direct knowledge.

"And what, bhikkhus, are the things to be fully understood by direct knowledge? It should be said: the five aggregates subject to clinging. What five? The form aggregate subject to clinging ... the consciousness aggregate subject to clinging. These are the things to be fully understood by direct knowledge.

"And what, bhikkhus, are the things to be abandoned by direct knowledge? Ignorance and craving for existence. These are the things to be abandoned by direct knowledge.

"And what, bhikkhus, are the things to be realized by direct knowledge? True knowledge and liberation. These are the things to be realized by direct knowledge.

"And what, bhikkhus, are the things to be developed by direct knowledge? Serenity and insight. These are the things to be developed by direct knowledge.

"And how is it, bhikkhus, that when a bhikkhu develops and cultivates the Noble Eightfold Path, he fully understands by direct knowledge those things that are to be fully understood by direct knowledge ... [53] ... he develops by direct knowledge those things that are to be developed by direct knowledge? Here, bhikkhus, a bhikkhu develops right view ... right concentration, which is based upon seclusion, dispassion, and cessation, maturing in release. It is in this way, bhikkhus, that a bhikkhu develops and cultivates the Noble Eightfold Path so that he fully understands by direct knowledge those things that are to be fully understood by direct knowledge ... he develops by direct knowledge those things that are to be developed by direct knowledge."

160 (12) The River

"Suppose, bhikkhus, that when the river Ganges slants, slopes, and inclines towards the east, a great crowd of people would come along bringing a shovel and a basket, thinking: 'We will make this river Ganges slant, slope, and incline towards the west.'[43] What do you think, bhikkhus, would that great crowd of people be able to make the river Ganges slant, slope, and incline towards the west?"

"No, venerable sir. For what reason? Because the river Ganges slants, slopes, and inclines towards the east, and it is not easy to make it slant, slope, and incline towards the west. That great crowd of people would only reap fatigue and vexation."

"So too, bhikkhus, when a bhikkhu is developing and cultivating the Noble Eightfold Path, kings or royal ministers, friends or colleagues, relatives or kinsmen, might invite him to accept wealth, saying: 'Come, good man, why let these saffron robes weigh you down? Why roam around with a shaven head and a begging bowl? Come, having returned to the lower life, enjoy wealth and do meritorious deeds.' Indeed, bhikkhus, when that bhikkhu is developing and cultivating the Noble Eightfold Path, it is impossible that he will give up the training and return to the lower life. For what reason? Because for a long time his mind has slanted, sloped, and inclined towards seclusion. Thus it is impossible that he will return to the lower life.

"And how, bhikkhus, does a bhikkhu develop and cultivate the Noble Eightfold Path? [54] Here, bhikkhus, a bhikkhu develops right view … right concentration, which is based upon seclusion, dispassion, and cessation, maturing in release. It is in this way, bhikkhus, that a bhikkhu develops and cultivates the Noble Eightfold Path."

XV. Searches

161 (1) Searches

At Sāvatthī.

(i. Direct knowledge)

"Bhikkhus, there are these three searches. What three? The search for sensual pleasure, the search for existence, the search for a holy life.[44] These are the three searches. The Noble Eightfold Path is to be developed for direct knowledge of these three searches.

"What Noble Eightfold Path? Here, bhikkhus, a bhikkhu develops right view … right concentration, which is based upon seclusion, dispassion, and cessation, maturing in release. This Noble Eightfold Path is to be developed for direct knowledge of these three searches."

… "What Noble Eightfold Path? Here, bhikkhus, a bhikkhu develops right view … right concentration, which has as its final goal the removal of lust, the removal of hatred, the removal of delusion."…

… "What Noble Eightfold Path? Here, bhikkhus, a bhikkhu develops right view … right concentration, which has the Deathless as its ground, the Deathless as its destination, the Deathless as its final goal."… [55]

… "What Noble Eightfold Path? Here, bhikkhus, a bhikkhu develops right view … right concentration, which slants, slopes, and inclines towards Nibbāna. This Noble Eightfold Path is to be developed for direct knowledge of these three searches."

Each of the following sub-sections (ii–iv) is to be elaborated in accordance with the method employed in the sub-section on direct knowledge.

(ii. Full understanding)

"Bhikkhus, there are these three searches. What three? The search for sensual pleasure, the search for existence, the search for a holy life. These are the three searches. The Noble Eightfold Path is to be developed for full understanding of these three searches."…

(iii. Utter destruction)

"Bhikkhus, there are these three searches. What three? The search for sensual pleasure, the search for existence, the search for a holy life. These are the three searches. The Noble Eightfold Path is to be developed for the utter destruction of these three searches."…

(iv. Abandoning)

"Bhikkhus, there are these three searches. What three? The search for sensual pleasure, the search for existence, the search for a holy life. These are the three searches. The Noble Eightfold Path is to be developed for the abandoning of these three searches."… [56]

Each of the following suttas is to be elaborated in accordance with the fourfold method employed in §161.

162 (2) Discriminations

"Bhikkhus, there are these three discriminations. What three? The discrimination 'I am superior,' the discrimination 'I am equal,' the discrimination 'I am inferior.' These are the three discriminations. The Noble Eightfold Path is to be developed for direct knowledge of these three discriminations, for the full understanding of them, for their utter destruction, for their abandoning.

"What Noble Eightfold Path? Here, bhikkhus, a bhikkhu develops right view … right concentration, which is based upon seclusion, dispassion, and cessation, maturing in release. This Noble Eightfold Path is to be developed for the direct knowledge of these three discriminations … for their abandoning."

163 (3) Taints

"Bhikkhus, there are these three taints. What three? The taint of sensuality, the taint of existence, the taint of ignorance. These are the three taints. The Noble Eightfold Path is to be developed for direct knowledge of these three taints, for the full understanding of them, for their utter destruction, for their abandoning."

164 (4) Existence

"Bhikkhus, there are these three kinds of existence. What three? Sense-sphere existence, form-sphere existence, formless-sphere existence. These are the three kinds of existence. The Noble Eightfold Path is to be developed for direct knowledge of these three kinds of existence, for the full understanding of them, for their utter destruction, for their abandoning."

165 (5) Suffering

"Bhikkhus, there are these three kinds of suffering. What three? Suffering due to pain, suffering due to formations, suffering due to change.[45] These are the three kinds of suffering. The Noble Eightfold Path is to be developed for direct knowledge of these three kinds of suffering, for the full understanding of them, for their utter destruction, for their abandoning." [57]

166 (6) Barrenness

"Bhikkhus, there are these three kinds of barrenness. What three? The barrenness of lust, the barrenness of hatred, the barrenness of delusion. These are the three kinds of barrenness. The Noble Eightfold Path is to be developed for direct knowledge of these three kinds of barrenness, for the full understanding of them, for their utter destruction, for their abandoning."

167 (7) Stains

"Bhikkhus, there are these three stains. What three? The stain of lust, the stain of hatred, the stain of delusion. These are the three stains. The Noble Eightfold Path is to be developed for direct knowledge of these three stains, for the full understanding of them, for their utter destruction, for their abandoning."

168 (8) Troubles

"Bhikkhus, there are these three kinds of trouble. What three? The trouble of lust, the trouble of hatred, the trouble of delusion. These are the three kinds of trouble. The Noble Eightfold Path is to be developed for direct knowledge of these three kinds of trouble, for the full understanding of them, for their utter destruction, for their abandoning."

169 (9) Feelings

"Bhikkhus, there are these three feelings. What three? Pleasant feeling, painful feeling, neither-painful-nor-pleasant feeling. These are the three feelings. The Noble Eightfold Path is to be developed for direct knowledge of these three feelings, for the full understanding of them, for their utter destruction, for their abandoning."

170 (10) Cravings

[58] "Bhikkhus, there are these three kinds of craving. What three? Craving for sensual pleasures, craving for existence, craving for extermination. These are the three kinds of craving. The Noble Eightfold Path is to be developed for direct knowledge of these three kinds of craving, for the full understanding of them, for their utter destruction, for their abandoning.

"What Noble Eightfold Path? Here, bhikkhus, a bhikkhu develops right view … right concentration, which is based upon seclusion, dispassion, and cessation, maturing in release. This Noble Eightfold Path is to be developed for direct knowledge of these three kinds of craving, for the full understanding of them, for their utter destruction, for their abandoning."

170 (11) Thirst[46]

"Bhikkhus, there are these three kinds of thirst. What three? Thirst for sensual pleasures, thirst for existence, thirst for extermination. These are the three kinds of thirst. The Noble Eightfold Path is to be developed for direct knowledge of these three kinds of thirst, for the full understanding of them, for their utter destruction, for their abandoning.

"What Noble Eightfold Path? Here, bhikkhus, a bhikkhu develops right view … right concentration, which is based upon seclusion, dispassion, and cessation, maturing in release. This Noble Eightfold Path is to be developed for direct knowledge of these three kinds of thirst, for the full understanding of them, for their utter destruction, for their abandoning."

[59] XVI. Floods

At Sāvatthī.

171 (1) Floods

"Bhikkhus, there are these four floods. What four? The flood of sensuality, the flood of existence, the flood of views, the flood of ignorance. These are the four floods. This Noble Eightfold Path is to be developed for direct knowledge of these four floods, for the full understanding of them, for their utter destruction, for their abandoning."

172 (2) Bonds

"Bhikkhus, there are these four bonds. What four? The bond of sensuality, the bond of existence, the bond of views, the bond of ignorance. These are the four bonds. This Noble Eightfold Path is to be developed for direct knowledge of these four bonds, for the full understanding of them, for their utter destruction, for their abandoning."

173 (3) Clinging

"Bhikkhus, there are these four kinds of clinging. What four? Clinging to sensual pleasure, clinging to views, clinging to rules and vows, clinging to a doctrine of self. These are the four kinds of clinging. This Noble Eightfold Path is to be developed for direct knowledge of these four kinds of clinging, for the full understanding of them, for their utter destruction, for their abandoning."

174 (4) Knots

"Bhikkhus, there are these four knots. What four? The bodily knot of covetousness, the bodily knot of ill will, the bodily knot of distorted grasp of rules and vows, the bodily knot of adherence to dogmatic assertion of truth.[47] [60] These are the four knots. This Noble Eightfold Path is to be developed for direct knowledge of these four knots, for the full understanding of them, for their utter destruction, for their abandoning."

175 (5) Underlying Tendencies

"Bhikkhus, there are these seven underlying tendencies. What seven? The underlying tendency to sensual lust,[48] the underlying tendency to aversion, the underlying tendency to views, the underlying tendency to doubt, the underlying tendency to conceit, the underlying tendency to lust for existence, the underlying tendency to ignorance. These are the seven underlying tendencies. This Noble Eightfold Path is to be developed for direct knowledge of these seven underlying tendencies, for the full understanding of them, for their utter destruction, for their abandoning."

176 (6) Cords of Sensual Pleasure

"Bhikkhus, there are these five cords of sensual pleasure. What five? Forms cognizable by the eye that are desirable, lovely, agreeable, pleasing, sensually enticing, tantalizing. Sounds cognizable by the ear ... Odours cognizable by the nose ... Tastes cognizable by the tongue ... Tactile objects cognizable by the body that are desirable, lovely, agreeable, pleasing, sensually enticing, tantalizing. These are the five cords of sensual pleasure. This Noble Eightfold Path is to be developed for direct knowledge of these five cords of sensual pleasure, for the full understanding of them, for their utter destruction, for their abandoning."

177 (7) Hindrances

"Bhikkhus, there are these five hindrances. What five? The hindrance of sensual desire, the hindrance of ill will, the hindrance of sloth and torpor, the hindrance of restlessness and remorse, the hindrance of doubt. These are the five hindrances. This Noble Eightfold Path is to be developed for direct knowledge of these five hindrances, for the full understanding of them, for their utter destruction, for their abandoning."

178 (8) Aggregates Subject to Clinging

"Bhikkhus, there are these five aggregates subject to clinging. What five? The form aggregate subject to clinging, the feeling aggregate subject to clinging, [61] the perception aggregate subject to clinging, the volitional formations aggregate subject to clinging, the consciousness aggregate subject to clinging. These are the five aggregates subject to clinging. This Noble Eightfold Path is to be developed for direct knowledge of these five aggregates subject to clinging, for the full understanding of them, for their utter destruction, for their abandoning."

179 (9) Lower Fetters

"Bhikkhus, there are these five lower fetters.[49] What five? Identity view, doubt, the distorted grasp of rules and vows, sensual desire, ill will. These are the five lower fetters. This Noble Eightfold Path is to be developed for direct knowledge of these five lower fetters, for the full understanding of them, for their utter destruction, for their abandoning."

180 (10) Higher Fetters

"Bhikkhus, there are these five higher fetters.[50] What five? Lust for form, lust for the formless, conceit, restlessness, ignorance. These are the five higher fetters. The Noble Eightfold Path is to be developed for direct knowledge of these five higher fetters, for the full understanding of them, for their utter destruction, for their abandoning.

"What Noble Eightfold Path? Here, bhikkhus, a bhikkhu develops right view … right concentration, which is based upon seclusion, dispassion, and cessation, maturing in release. This Noble Eightfold Path is to be developed for direct knowledge of these five higher fetters, for the full understanding of them, for their utter destruction, for their abandoning.

"Bhikkhus, there are these five higher fetters. What five?… [62] … The Noble Eightfold Path is to be developed for direct knowledge of these five higher fetters, for the full understanding of them, for their utter destruction, for their abandoning.

"What Noble Eightfold Path? Here, bhikkhus, a bhikkhu develops right view … right concentration, which has as its final goal the removal of lust, the removal of hatred, the removal of delusion … which has the Deathless as its ground, the Deathless as its destination, the Deathless as its final goal … which slants, slopes, and inclines towards Nibbāna. This Noble Eightfold Path is to be developed for direct knowledge of these five higher fetters, for the full understanding of them, for their utter destruction, for their abandoning."

[63] Chapter II

46 *Bojjhaṅgasaṃyutta* Connected Discourses on the Factors of Enlightenment

I. The Mountain

1 (1) The Himalayas

At Sāvatthī. "Bhikkhus, based upon the Himalayas, the king of mountains, the nāgas nurture their bodies and acquire strength.[51] When they have nurtured their bodies and acquired strength, they then enter the pools. From the pools they enter the lakes, then the streams, then the rivers, and finally they enter the ocean. There they achieve greatness and expansiveness of body. So too, bhikkhus, based upon virtue, established upon virtue, a bhikkhu develops and cultivates the seven factors of enlightenment, and thereby he achieves greatness and expansiveness in [wholesome] states.[52]

"And how does a bhikkhu, based upon virtue, established upon virtue, develop the seven factors of enlightenment? Here, bhikkhus, a bhikkhu develops the enlightenment factor of mindfulness, which is based upon seclusion, dispassion, and cessation, maturing in release. [64] He develops the enlightenment factor of discrimination of states ... the enlightenment factor of energy ... the enlightenment factor of rapture ... the enlightenment factor of tranquillity ... the enlightenment factor of concentration ... the enlightenment factor of equanimity, which is based upon seclusion, dispassion, and cessation, maturing in release. It is in this way, bhikkhus, that a bhikkhu, based upon virtue, established upon virtue, develops the seven factors of enlightenment, and thereby achieves greatness and expansiveness in [wholesome] states."

2 (2) The Body

(i. The nutriments for the hindrances)

At Sāvatthī. "Bhikkhus, just as this body, sustained by nutriment, subsists in dependence on nutriment and does not subsist without nutriment, so too the five hindrances, sustained by nutriment, subsist in dependence on nutriment and do not subsist without nutriment.[53]

"And what, bhikkhus, is the nutriment for the arising of unarisen sensual desire and for the increase and expansion of arisen sensual desire? There is, bhikkhus, the sign of the beautiful:[54] frequently giving careless attention to it is the nutriment for the arising of unarisen sensual desire and for the increase and expansion of arisen sensual desire.

"And what, bhikkhus, is the nutriment for the arising of unarisen ill will and for the increase and expansion of arisen ill will? There is, bhikkhus, the sign of the repulsive:[55] frequently giving careless attention to it is the nutriment for the arising of unarisen ill will and for the increase and expansion of arisen ill will.

"And what, bhikkhus, is the nutriment for the arising of unarisen sloth and torpor and for the increase and expansion of arisen sloth and torpor? There are, bhikkhus, discontent, lethargy, lazy stretching, drowsiness after meals, sluggishness of mind:[56] [65] frequently giving careless attention to them is the nutriment for the arising of unarisen sloth and torpor and for the increase and expansion of arisen sloth and torpor.

"And what, bhikkhus, is the nutriment for the arising of unarisen restlessness and remorse and for the increase and expansion of arisen restlessness and remorse? There is, bhikkhus, unsettledness of mind:[57] frequently giving careless attention to it is the nutriment for the arising of unarisen restlessness and remorse and for the increase and expansion of arisen restlessness and remorse.

"And what, bhikkhus, is the nutriment for the arising of unarisen doubt and for the increase and expansion of arisen doubt? There are, bhikkhus, things that are the basis for doubt: frequently giving careless attention to them is the nutriment for the arising of unarisen doubt and for the increase and expansion of arisen doubt.

"Just as this body, bhikkhus, sustained by nutriment, subsists in dependence on nutriment and does not subsist without nutriment, so too the five hindrances, sustained by nutriment, subsist in dependence on nutriment and do not subsist without nutriment.

(ii. The nutriments for the enlightenment factors)

"Bhikkhus, just as this body, sustained by nutriment, subsists in dependence on nutriment and does not subsist without nutriment, so too the seven factors of enlightenment, sustained by nutriment, subsist in dependence on nutriment and do not subsist without nutriment.

"And what, bhikkhus, is the nutriment for the arising of the unarisen enlightenment factor of mindfulness and for the fulfilment by development of the arisen enlightenment factor of mindfulness? There are, bhikkhus, things that are the basis for the enlightenment factor of mindfulness:[58] frequently giving careful attention to them is the nutriment for the arising of the unarisen enlightenment factor of mindfulness and for the fulfilment by development of the arisen enlightenment factor of mindfulness. [66]

"And what, bhikkhus, is the nutriment for the arising of the unarisen enlightenment factor of discrimination of states and for the fulfilment by development of the arisen enlightenment factor of discrimination of states? There are, bhikkhus, wholesome and unwholesome states, blameable and blameless states, inferior and superior states, dark and bright states with their counterparts:[59] frequently giving careful attention to them is the nutriment for the arising of the unarisen enlightenment factor of discrimination of states and for the fulfilment by development of the arisen enlightenment factor of discrimination of states.

"And what, bhikkhus, is the nutriment for the arising of the unarisen enlightenment factor of energy and for the fulfilment by development of the arisen enlightenment factor of energy? There are, bhikkhus, the element of arousal, the element of endeavour, the element of exertion:[60] frequently giving careful attention to them is the nutriment for the arising of the unarisen enlightenment factor of energy and for the fulfilment by development of the arisen enlightenment factor of energy.

"And what, bhikkhus, is the nutriment for the arising of the unarisen enlightenment factor of rapture and for the fulfilment by development of the arisen enlightenment factor of rapture? There are, bhikkhus, things that are the basis for the enlightenment factor of rapture: frequently giving careful attention to them is the nutriment for the arising of the unarisen enlightenment factor of rapture and for the fulfilment by development of the arisen enlightenment factor of rapture.

"And what, bhikkhus, is the nutriment for the arising of the unarisen enlightenment factor of tranquillity and for the fulfilment by development of the arisen enlightenment factor of tranquillity? There are, bhikkhus, tranquillity of body, tranquillity of mind:[61] frequently giving careful attention to them is the nutriment for the arising of the unarisen enlightenment factor of tranquillity and for the fulfilment by development of the arisen enlightenment factor of tranquillity.

"And what, bhikkhus, is the nutriment for the arising of the unarisen enlightenment factor of concentration and for the fulfilment by development of the arisen enlightenment factor of concentration? There are, bhikkhus, the sign of serenity, the sign of nondispersal:[62] frequently giving careful attention to them is the nutriment for the arising of the unarisen enlightenment factor of concentration and for the fulfilment by development of the arisen enlightenment factor of concentration. [67]

"And what, bhikkhus, is the nutriment for the arising of the unarisen enlightenment factor of equanimity and for the fulfilment by development of the arisen enlightenment factor of equanimity? There are, bhikkhus, things that are the basis for the enlightenment factor of equanimity: frequently giving careful attention to them is the nutriment for the arising of the unarisen enlightenment factor of equanimity and for the fulfilment by development of the arisen enlightenment factor of equanimity.

"Just as this body, bhikkhus, sustained by nutriment, subsists in dependence on nutriment and does not subsist without nutriment, so too these seven factors of enlightenment, sustained by nutriment, subsist in dependence on nutriment and do not subsist without nutriment."

3 (3) Virtue

"Bhikkhus, those bhikkhus who are accomplished in virtue,

accomplished in concentration, accomplished in wisdom, accomplished in liberation, accomplished in the knowledge and vision of liberation: even the sight of those bhikkhus is helpful, I say; even listening to them … even approaching them … even attending on them … even recollecting them … even going forth after them is helpful, I say. For what reason? Because when one has heard the Dhamma from such bhikkhus one dwells withdrawn by way of two kinds of withdrawal—withdrawal of body and withdrawal of mind.

"Dwelling thus withdrawn, one recollects that Dhamma and thinks it over. Whenever, bhikkhus, a bhikkhu dwelling thus withdrawn recollects that Dhamma and thinks it over, [68] on that occasion the enlightenment factor of mindfulness is aroused by the bhikkhu; on that occasion the bhikkhu develops the enlightenment factor of mindfulness; on that occasion the enlightenment factor of mindfulness comes to fulfilment by development in the bhikkhu.[63]

"Dwelling thus mindfully, he discriminates that Dhamma with wisdom, examines it, makes an investigation of it. Whenever, bhikkhus, a bhikkhu dwelling thus mindfully discriminates that Dhamma with wisdom, examines it, makes an investigation of it, on that occasion the enlightenment factor of discrimination of states is aroused by the bhikkhu; on that occasion the bhikkhu develops the enlightenment factor of discrimination of states; on that occasion the enlightenment factor of discrimination of states comes to fulfilment by development in the bhikkhu.

"While he discriminates that Dhamma with wisdom, examines it, makes an investigation of it, his energy is aroused without slackening. Whenever, bhikkhus, a bhikkhu's energy is aroused without slackening as he discriminates that Dhamma with wisdom, examines it, makes an investigation of it, on that occasion the enlightenment factor of energy is aroused by the bhikkhu; on that occasion the bhikkhu develops the enlightenment factor of energy; on that occasion the enlightenment factor of energy comes to fulfilment by development in the bhikkhu.

"When his energy is aroused, there arises in him spiritual rapture. Whenever, bhikkhus, spiritual rapture arises in a bhikkhu whose energy is aroused, on that occasion the enlightenment factor of rapture is aroused by the bhikkhu; on that occasion the bhikkhu develops the enlightenment factor of rapture; on that occasion the enlightenment factor of rapture comes to fulfilment by development in the bhikkhu.

"For one whose mind is uplifted by rapture the body becomes tranquil and the mind becomes tranquil. Whenever, bhikkhus, the body becomes tranquil and the mind becomes tranquil in a bhikkhu whose mind is uplifted by rapture, on that occasion the enlightenment factor of tranquillity is aroused by the bhikkhu; on that occasion the bhikkhu develops the enlightenment factor of tranquillity; on that occasion the enlightenment factor of tranquillity comes to fulfilment by development in the bhikkhu. [69]

"For one whose body is tranquil and who is happy the mind becomes concentrated.[64] Whenever, bhikkhus, the mind becomes concentrated in a bhikkhu whose body is tranquil and who is happy, on that occasion the enlightenment factor of concentration is aroused by the bhikkhu; on that occasion the bhikkhu develops the enlightenment factor of concentration; on that occasion the enlightenment factor of concentration comes to fulfilment by development in the bhikkhu.

"He closely looks on with equanimity at the mind thus concentrated. Whenever, bhikkhus, a bhikkhu closely looks on with equanimity at the mind thus concentrated, on that occasion the enlightenment factor of equanimity is aroused by the bhikkhu; on that occasion the bhikkhu develops the enlightenment factor of equanimity; on that occasion the enlightenment factor of equanimity comes to fulfilment by development in the bhikkhu.

"Bhikkhus, when these seven factors of enlightenment have been developed and cultivated in this way, seven fruits and benefits may be expected. What are the seven fruits and benefits?

"One attains final knowledge early in this very life.

"If one does not attain final knowledge early in this very life, then one attains final knowledge at the time of death.

"If one does not attain final knowledge early in this very life or at the time of death, then with the utter destruction of the five lower fetters one becomes an attainer of Nibbāna in the interval.[65]

"If one does not attain final knowledge early in this very life … or become an attainer of Nibbāna in the interval, then with the utter destruction of the five lower fetters one becomes an attainer of Nibbāna upon landing.

"If one does not attain final knowledge early in this very life … [70] … or become an attainer of Nibbāna upon landing, then with the utter destruction of the five lower fetters one becomes an attainer of Nibbāna without exertion.

"If one does not attain final knowledge early in this very life ... or become an attainer of Nibbāna without exertion, then with the utter destruction of the five lower fetters one becomes an attainer of Nibbāna with exertion.

"If one does not attain final knowledge early in this very life ... or become an attainer of Nibbāna with exertion, then with the utter destruction of the five lower fetters one becomes one bound upstream, heading towards the Akaniṭṭha realm.

"When, bhikkhus, the seven factors of enlightenment have been developed and cultivated in this way, these seven fruits and benefits may be expected."

4 (4) Clothes

On one occasion the Venerable Sāriputta was dwelling at Sāvatthī in Jeta's Grove, Anāthapiṇḍika's Park. There the Venerable Sāriputta addressed the bhikkhus thus: "Friends, bhikkhus!" [71]

"Friend," they replied. The Venerable Sāriputta said this:

"Friends, there are these seven factors of enlightenment. What seven? The enlightenment factor of mindfulness, the enlightenment factor of discrimination of states, the enlightenment factor of energy, the enlightenment factor of rapture, the enlightenment factor of tranquillity, the enlightenment factor of concentration, the enlightenment factor of equanimity. These are the seven factors of enlightenment.[66]

"Whichever of these seven factors of enlightenment I want to dwell in during the morning, I dwell in that factor of enlightenment during the morning. Whichever I want to dwell in during the middle of the day, I dwell in that factor of enlightenment during the middle of the day. Whichever I want to dwell in during the evening, I dwell in that factor of enlightenment during the evening.

"If, friends, it occurs to me, '[Let it be] the enlightenment factor of mindfulness,' it occurs to me, 'It's measureless'; it occurs to me, 'It's fully perfected.' While it persists, I understand, 'It persists.' If it abates in me, I understand, 'It has abated in me for a particular reason.' ...

"If, friends, it occurs to me, '[Let it be] the enlightenment factor of equanimity,' it occurs to me, 'It's measureless'; it occurs to me, 'It's fully perfected.' While it persists, I understand, 'It persists.' But if it abates in me, I understand, 'It has abated in me for a particular reason.'

"Suppose, friends, a king or a royal minister had a wardrobe full of differently coloured clothes. Whatever suit he might want to wear in the morning he would wear in the morning. Whatever suit he might want to wear during the middle of the day he would wear during the middle of the day. Whatever suit he might want to wear in the evening he would wear in the evening. [72] So too, friends, whichever of these seven factors of enlightenment I want to dwell in during the morning ... during the middle of the day ... during the evening, I dwell in that factor of enlightenment during the evening.

"If, friends, it occurs to me, '[Let it be] the enlightenment factor of mindfulness' ... (*all as above*) ... I understand, 'It has abated in me for a particular reason.'"

5 (5) A Bhikkhu

At Sāvatthī. Then a certain bhikkhu approached the Blessed One ... and said to him: "Venerable sir, it is said, 'factors of enlightenment, factors of enlightenment.' In what sense are they called factors of enlightenment?"

"They lead to enlightenment, bhikkhu, therefore they are called factors of enlightenment. Here, bhikkhu, one develops the enlightenment factor of mindfulness, which is based upon seclusion, dispassion, and cessation, maturing in release.... One develops the enlightenment factor of equanimity, which is based upon seclusion, dispassion, and cessation, maturing in release. While one is developing these seven factors of enlightenment, one's mind is liberated from the taint of sensuality, from the taint of existence, from the taint of ignorance. When it is liberated there comes the knowledge: 'It's liberated.' One understands: 'Destroyed is birth, the holy life has been lived, what had to be done has been done, there is no more for this state of being.' They lead to enlightenment, bhikkhu, therefore they are called factors of enlightenment." [73]

6 (6) Kuṇḍaliya

On one occasion the Blessed One was dwelling at Sāketa in the Deer Park at the Añjana Grove. Then the wanderer Kuṇḍaliya approached the Blessed One and exchanged greetings with him. When they had concluded their greetings and cordial talk, he sat down to one side and said to the Blessed One:

"Master Gotama, I am one who stays around monastic parks and frequents assemblies. After the meal, when I have finished my breakfast, it is my custom to roam and wander from park to park, from garden to garden. There I see some ascetics and brahmins engaged in discussion for the benefits of rescuing their own theses in debate and condemning [the theses of others].[67] But what is the benefit that Master Gotama lives for?"

"Kuṇḍaliya, the Tathāgata lives for the benefit and fruit of true knowledge and liberation."[68]

"But, Master Gotama, what things, when developed and cultivated, fulfil true knowledge and liberation?"

"The seven factors of enlightenment, Kuṇḍaliya, when developed and cultivated, fulfil true knowledge and liberation."

"But, Master Gotama, what things, when developed and cultivated, fulfil the seven factors of enlightenment?"

"The four establishments of mindfulness, Kuṇḍaliya, when developed and cultivated, fulfil the seven factors of enlightenment."

"But, Master Gotama, what things, when developed and cultivated, fulfil the four establishments of mindfulness?"

"The three kinds of good conduct, Kuṇḍaliya, when developed and cultivated, fulfil the four establishments of mindfulness."

"But, Master Gotama, what things, when developed and cultivated, fulfil the three kinds of good conduct?" [74]

"Restraint of the sense faculties, Kuṇḍaliya, when developed and cultivated, fulfils the three kinds of good conduct.

"And how, Kuṇḍaliya, is restraint of the sense faculties developed and cultivated so that it fulfils the three kinds of good conduct? Here, Kuṇḍaliya, having seen an agreeable form with the eye, a bhikkhu does not long for it, or become excited by it, or generate lust for it. His body is steady and his mind is steady, inwardly well composed and well liberated. But having seen a disagreeable form with the eye, he is not dismayed by it, not daunted, not dejected, without ill will.[69] His body is steady and his mind is steady, inwardly well composed and well liberated.

"Further, Kuṇḍaliya, having heard an agreeable sound with the ear ... having smelt an agreeable odour with the nose ... having savoured an agreeable taste with the tongue ... having felt an agreeable tactile object with the body ... having cognized an agreeable mental phenomenon with the mind, a bhikkhu does not long for it, or become excited by it, or generate lust for it. But having cognized a disagreeable mental phenomenon with the mind, he is not dismayed by it, not daunted, not dejected, without ill will. His body is steady and his mind is steady, inwardly well composed and well liberated.

"When, Kuṇḍaliya, after he has seen a form with the eye, a bhikkhu's body is steady and his mind is steady, inwardly well composed and well liberated in regard to both agreeable and disagreeable forms; when, after he has heard a sound with the ear ... smelt an odour with the nose ... savoured a taste with the tongue ... felt a tactile object with the body ... cognized a mental phenomenon with the mind, a bhikkhu's body is steady and his mind is steady, inwardly well composed and well liberated in regard to both agreeable and disagreeable mental phenomena, [75] then his restraint of the sense faculties has been developed and cultivated in such a way that it fulfils the three kinds of good conduct.

"And how, Kuṇḍaliya, are the three kinds of good conduct developed and cultivated so that they fulfil the four establishments of mindfulness? Here, Kuṇḍaliya, having abandoned bodily misconduct, a bhikkhu develops good bodily conduct; having abandoned verbal misconduct, he develops good verbal conduct; having abandoned mental misconduct, he develops good mental conduct. It is in this way that the three kinds of good conduct are developed and cultivated so that they fulfil the four establishments of mindfulness.

"And how, Kuṇḍaliya, are the four establishments of mindfulness developed and cultivated so that they fulfil the seven factors of enlightenment? Here, Kuṇḍaliya, a bhikkhu dwells contemplating the body in the body, ardent, clearly comprehending and mindful, having removed covetousness and displeasure in regard to the world. He dwells contemplating feelings in feelings ... mind in mind ... phenomena in phenomena, ardent, clearly comprehending and mindful, having removed covetousness and displeasure in regard to the world. It is in this way that the four establishments of mindfulness are developed and cultivated so that they fulfil the seven factors of enlightenment.

"And how, Kuṇḍaliya, are the seven factors of enlightenment developed and cultivated so that they fulfil true knowledge and liberation? Here, Kuṇḍaliya, a bhikkhu develops the enlightenment factor of mindfulness, which is based upon seclusion, dispassion, and cessation, maturing in release.... He develops the enlightenment factor of equanimity, which is based upon seclusion, dispassion, and cessation, maturing in release. It is in this way that the seven factors of enlightenment are developed and cultivated so that they fulfil true knowledge and liberation."

When this was said, the wanderer Kuṇḍaliya said to the Blessed One: "Magnificent, Master Gotama! Magnificent, Master Gotama! The Dhamma has been made clear in many ways by Master Gotama, as though he were turning upright what had been turned upside down, revealing what was hidden, showing the way to one who was lost, or holding up a lamp in the dark for those with eyesight to see forms. I go for refuge to Master Gotama, and to the Dhamma, and to the Bhikkhu Saṅgha. From today let Master Gotama remember me as a lay follower who has gone for refuge for life."

7 (7) The Peaked House

"Bhikkhus, just as all the rafters of a peaked house slant, slope, and incline towards the roof peak, so too, when a bhikkhu develops and cultivates the seven factors of enlightenment, he slants, slopes, and inclines towards Nibbāna. [76]

"And how is this so? Here, bhikkhus, a bhikkhu develops the enlightenment factor of mindfulness, which is based upon seclusion, dispassion, and cessation, maturing in release.... He develops the enlightenment factor of equanimity, which is based upon seclusion, dispassion, and cessation, maturing in release. It is in this way that a bhikkhu develops and cultivates the seven factors of enlightenment so that he slants, slopes, and inclines towards Nibbāna."

8 (8) Upavāṇa

On one occasion the Venerable Upavāṇa and the Venerable Sāriputta were dwelling at Kosambī in Ghosita's Park. Then, in the evening, the Venerable Sāriputta emerged from seclusion and approached the Venerable Upavāṇa. He exchanged greetings with the Venerable Upavāṇa and, when they had concluded their greetings and cordial talk, he sat down to one side and said to him:

"Friend Upavāṇa, can a bhikkhu know for himself: 'By careful attention the seven factors of enlightenment have been fully perfected by me in such a way that they lead to dwelling in comfort'?"

"A bhikkhu can know this for himself, friend Sāriputta. When arousing the enlightenment factor of mindfulness, friend, a bhikkhu understands: 'My mind is well liberated; I have uprooted sloth and torpor and thoroughly removed restlessness and remorse. My energy has been aroused. I attend as a matter of vital concern, not sluggishly.'... When arousing the enlightenment factor of equanimity, he understands: [77] 'My mind is well liberated; I have uprooted sloth and torpor and thoroughly removed restlessness and remorse. My energy has been aroused. I attend as a matter of vital concern, not sluggishly.'

"It is in this way, friend, that a bhikkhu can know for himself: 'By careful attention the seven factors of enlightenment have been fully perfected by me in such a way that they lead to dwelling in comfort.'"

9 (9) Arisen (or Arising) (1)

"Bhikkhus, these seven factors of enlightenment, developed and cultivated, if unarisen do not arise apart from the appearance of a Tathāgata, an Arahant, a Perfectly Enlightened One. What seven? The enlightenment factor of mindfulness ... the enlightenment factor of equanimity. These seven factors of enlightenment, developed and cultivated, if unarisen do not arise apart from the appearance of a Tathāgata, an Arahant, a Perfectly Enlightened One."

10 (10) Arisen (or Arising) (2)

"Bhikkhus, these seven factors of enlightenment, developed and cultivated, if unarisen do not arise apart from the Discipline of a Fortunate One. What seven? The enlightenment factor of mindfulness ... the enlightenment factor of equanimity. These seven factors of enlightenment, developed and cultivated, if unarisen do not arise apart from the Discipline of a Fortunate One."

[78] II. ILL

11 (1) Living Beings

"Bhikkhus, whatever living beings there are which assume the four postures—sometimes walking, sometimes standing, sometimes sitting, sometimes lying down—all assume the four postures based upon the earth, established upon the earth. So too, based upon virtue, established upon virtue, a bhikkhu develops and cultivates the seven factors of enlightenment.

"And how does he do so? Here, bhikkhus, a bhikkhu develops the enlightenment factor of mindfulness, which is based upon seclusion, dispassion, and cessation, maturing in release.... He develops the enlightenment factor of equanimity, which is based upon seclusion, dispassion, and cessation, maturing in release. It is in this way, bhikkhus, that a bhikkhu, based upon virtue, established upon virtue, develops and cultivates the seven factors of enlightenment."

12 (2) The Simile of the Sun (1)

"Bhikkhus, this is the forerunner and precursor of the rising of the sun, that is, the dawn. So too, bhikkhus, for a bhikkhu this is the forerunner and precursor of the arising of the seven factors of enlightenment, that is, good friendship. When a bhikkhu has a good friend, it is to be expected that he will develop and cultivate the seven factors of enlightenment.

"And how does a bhikkhu who has a good friend develop and cultivate the seven factors of enlightenment? Here, bhikkhus, a bhikkhu develops the enlightenment factor of mindfulness, which is based upon seclusion, dispassion, and cessation, maturing in release.... He develops the enlightenment factor of equanimity, which is based upon seclusion, dispassion, and cessation, maturing in release. It is in this way, bhikkhus, [79] that a bhikkhu who has a good friend develops and cultivates the seven factors of enlightenment."

13 (3) The Simile of the Sun (2)

"Bhikkhus, this is the forerunner and precursor of the rising of the sun, that is, the dawn. So too, bhikkhus, for a bhikkhu this is the forerunner and precursor of the arising of the seven factors of enlightenment, that is, careful attention. When a bhikkhu is accomplished in careful attention, it is to be expected that he will develop and cultivate the seven factors of enlightenment.

"And how does a bhikkhu who is accomplished in careful attention develop and cultivate the seven factors of enlightenment? Here, bhikkhus, a bhikkhu develops the enlightenment factor of mindfulness, which is based upon seclusion, dispassion, and cessation, maturing in release.... He develops the enlightenment factor of equanimity, which is based upon seclusion, dispassion, and cessation, maturing in release. It is in this way, bhikkhus, that a bhikkhu who is accomplished in careful attention develops and cultivates the seven factors of enlightenment."

14 (4) Ill (1)

On one occasion the Blessed One was dwelling at Rājagaha in the Bamboo Grove, the Squirrel Sanctuary.[70] Now on that occasion the Venerable Mahākassapa was dwelling in the Pipphali Cave—sick, afflicted, gravely ill. Then, in the evening, the Blessed One emerged from seclusion and approached the Venerable Mahākassapa. He sat down in the appointed seat and said to the Venerable Mahākassapa:

"I hope you are bearing up, Kassapa, I hope you are getting better. I hope that your painful feelings are subsiding and not increasing, and that their subsiding, not their increase, is to be discerned." [80]

"Venerable sir, I am not bearing up, I am not getting better. Strong painful feelings are increasing in me, not subsiding, and their increase, not their subsiding, is to be discerned."

"These seven factors of enlightenment, Kassapa, have been rightly expounded by me; when developed and cultivated, they lead to direct knowledge, to enlightenment, to Nibbāna. What seven? The enlightenment factor of mindfulness has been rightly expounded by me; when developed and cultivated, it leads to direct knowledge, to enlightenment, to Nibbāna.... The enlightenment factor of equanimity has been rightly expounded by me; when developed and cultivated, it leads to direct knowledge, to enlightenment, to Nibbāna. These seven factors of enlightenment, Kassapa, have been rightly expounded by me; when developed and cultivated, they lead to direct knowledge, to enlightenment, to Nibbāna."

"Surely, Blessed One, they are factors of enlightenment! Surely, Fortunate One, they are factors of enlightenment!"

This is what the Blessed One said. Elated, the Venerable Mahākassapa delighted in the Blessed One's statement. And the Venerable Mahākassapa recovered from that illness.[71] In such a way the Venerable Mahākassapa was cured of his illness.

15 (5) Ill (2)

On one occasion the Blessed One was dwelling at Rājagaha in the Bamboo Grove, the Squirrel Sanctuary. Now on that occasion the Venerable Mahāmoggallāna was dwelling on Mount Vulture Peak—sick, afflicted, gravely ill. Then, in the evening, the Blessed One emerged from seclusion and approached the Venerable Mahāmoggallāna ... (*all as above, with the change of names being the only difference*) ... In such a way the Venerable Mahāmoggallāna was cured of his illness. [81]

16 (6) Ill (3)

On one occasion the Blessed One was dwelling at Rājagaha in the Bamboo Grove, the Squirrel Sanctuary. Now on that occasion the Blessed One was sick, afflicted, gravely ill. Then the Venerable Mahācunda approached the Blessed One, paid homage to him, and sat down to one side. The Blessed One then said to the Venerable Mahācunda:

"Recite the factors of enlightenment, Cunda."

"These seven factors of enlightenment, venerable sir, have

been rightly expounded by the Blessed One; when developed and cultivated, they lead to direct knowledge, to enlightenment, to Nibbāna. What seven? The enlightenment factor of mindfulness has been rightly expounded by the Blessed One; when developed and cultivated, it leads to direct knowledge, to enlightenment, to Nibbāna.... The enlightenment factor of equanimity has been rightly expounded by the Blessed One; when developed and cultivated, it leads to direct knowledge, to enlightenment, to Nibbāna. These seven factors of enlightenment, venerable sir, have been rightly expounded by the Blessed One; when developed and cultivated, they lead to direct knowledge, to enlightenment, to Nibbāna."

"Surely, Cunda, they are factors of enlightenment! Surely, Cunda, they are factors of enlightenment!"

This is what the Venerable Mahācunda said. The Teacher approved. And the Blessed One recovered from that illness. In such a way the Blessed One was cured of his illness.

17 (7) Going Beyond

"Bhikkhus, these seven factors of enlightenment, when developed and cultivated, lead to going beyond from the near shore to the far shore. What seven? The enlightenment factor of mindfulness ... the enlightenment factor of equanimity. These seven factors of enlightenment, when developed and cultivated, lead to going beyond from the near shore to the far shore." [82]

(*The verses attached to this sutta are identical with those at 45:34 above.*)

18 (8) Neglected

"Bhikkhus, those who have neglected the seven factors of enlightenment have neglected the noble path leading to the complete destruction of suffering. Those who have undertaken the seven factors of enlightenment have undertaken the noble path leading to the complete destruction of suffering.

"What seven? The enlightenment factor of mindfulness ... the enlightenment factor of equanimity.

"Bhikkhus, those who have neglected ... who have undertaken

these seven factors of enlightenment have undertaken the noble path leading to the complete destruction of suffering."

19 (9) Noble

"Bhikkhus, these seven factors of enlightenment, when developed and cultivated, are noble and emancipating; they lead the one who acts upon them out to the complete destruction of suffering. What seven? The enlightenment factor of mindfulness … the enlightenment factor of equanimity. These seven factors of enlightenment … lead the one who acts upon them out to the complete destruction of suffering."

20 (10) Revulsion

"Bhikkhus, these seven factors of enlightenment, when developed and cultivated, lead to utter revulsion, to dispassion, to cessation, to peace, to direct knowledge, to enlightenment, to Nibbāna. What seven? The enlightenment factor of mindfulness … the enlightenment factor of equanimity. These seven factors of enlightenment … lead to Nibbāna."

[83] III. UDĀYĪ

21 (1) To Enlightenment

Then a certain bhikkhu approached the Blessed One…. Sitting to one side, that bhikkhu said to the Blessed One: "Venerable sir, it is said, 'factors of enlightenment, factors of enlightenment.' In what sense are they called factors of enlightenment?"

"They lead to enlightenment, bhikkhu, therefore they are called factors of enlightenment. Here, bhikkhu, one develops the enlightenment factor of mindfulness, which is based upon seclusion, dispassion, and cessation, maturing in release…. One develops the enlightenment factor of equanimity, which is based upon seclusion, dispassion, and cessation, maturing in release. They lead to enlightenment, bhikkhu, therefore they are called factors of enlightenment."

22 (2) *A Teaching*

"Bhikkhus, I will teach you the seven factors of enlightenment. Listen to that....

"And what, bhikkhus, are the seven factors of enlightenment? The enlightenment factor of mindfulness ... the enlightenment factor of equanimity. These are the seven factors of enlightenment." [84]

23 (3) *A Basis*

"Bhikkhus, by frequently giving attention to things that are a basis for sensual lust, unarisen sensual desire arises and arisen sensual desire increases and expands. By frequently giving attention to things that are a basis for ill will, unarisen ill will arises and arisen ill will increases and expands. By frequently giving attention to things that are a basis for sloth and torpor, unarisen sloth and torpor arise and arisen sloth and torpor increase and expand. By frequently giving attention to things that are a basis for restlessness and remorse, unarisen restlessness and remorse arise and arisen restlessness and remorse increase and expand. By frequently giving attention to things that are a basis for doubt, unarisen doubt arises and arisen doubt increases and expands.

"Bhikkhus, by frequently giving attention to things that are a basis for the enlightenment factor of mindfulness, the unarisen enlightenment factor of mindfulness arises and the arisen enlightenment factor of mindfulness comes to fulfilment by development.... By frequently giving attention to things that are a basis for the enlightenment factor of equanimity, the unarisen enlightenment factor of equanimity arises and the arisen enlightenment factor of equanimity comes to fulfilment by development."

24 (4) *Careless Attention*

"Bhikkhus, when one attends carelessly, unarisen sensual desire arises and arisen sensual desire increases and expands; [85] when one attends carelessly, unarisen ill will arises and arisen ill will increases and expands; when one attends carelessly, unarisen sloth and torpor arise and arisen sloth and torpor increase and expand; when one attends carelessly, unarisen restlessness and remorse arise and arisen restlessness and remorse increase and expand; when one attends carelessly, unarisen doubt arises and arisen doubt increases and expands. Also, the unarisen enlightenment factor of mindfulness does not arise and the arisen enlightenment factor of mindfulness ceases ... the unarisen enlightenment factor of equanimity does not arise and the arisen enlightenment factor of equanimity ceases.

"When one attends carefully, bhikkhus, unarisen sensual desire does not arise and arisen sensual desire is abandoned. When one attends carefully, unarisen ill will ... sloth and torpor ... restlessness and remorse ... doubt does not arise and arisen doubt is abandoned. Also, the unarisen enlightenment factor of mindfulness arises and the arisen enlightenment factor of mindfulness comes to fulfilment by development ... the unarisen enlightenment factor of equanimity arises and the arisen enlightenment factor of equanimity comes to fulfilment by development."

25 (5) Nondecline

"Bhikkhus, I will teach you seven things that lead to nondecline.[72] Listen to that.... [86]

"And what, bhikkhus, are the seven things that lead to nondecline? They are: the seven factors of enlightenment. What seven? The enlightenment factor of mindfulness ... the enlightenment factor of equanimity. These are the seven things that lead to nondecline."

26 (6) The Destruction of Craving

"Bhikkhus, develop the path and the way that leads to the destruction of craving. And what is the path and the way that leads to the destruction of craving? It is: the seven factors of enlightenment. What seven? The enlightenment factor of mindfulness ... the enlightenment factor of equanimity."

When this was said, the Venerable Udāyī asked the Blessed One: "Venerable sir, how are the seven factors of enlightenment developed and cultivated so that they lead to the destruction of craving?"

"Here, Udāyī, a bhikkhu develops the enlightenment factor of mindfulness, which is based upon seclusion, dispassion, and cessation, maturing in release; which is vast, exalted, measureless, without ill will. When he develops the enlightenment factor of mindfulness, which is based upon seclusion ... without ill will, craving is abandoned. With the abandoning of craving, kamma is abandoned. With the abandoning of kamma, suffering is abandoned....

"He develops the enlightenment factor of equanimity, which is based upon seclusion, dispassion, and cessation, maturing in release; which is vast, exalted, measureless, without ill will. When he develops the enlightenment factor of equanimity, which is based upon seclusion ... without ill will, craving is abandoned. [87] With the abandoning of craving, kamma is abandoned. With the abandoning of kamma, suffering is abandoned.

"Thus, Udāyī, with the destruction of craving comes the destruction of kamma; with the destruction of kamma comes the destruction of suffering."

27 (7) The Cessation of Craving

"Bhikkhus, develop the path and the way that leads to the cessation of craving. And what is the path and the way that leads to the cessation of craving? It is: the seven factors of enlightenment. What seven? The enlightenment factor of mindfulness ... the enlightenment factor of equanimity.

"And how is it, bhikkhus, that the seven factors of enlightenment, when developed and cultivated, lead to the cessation of craving?

"Here, bhikkhus, a bhikkhu develops the enlightenment factor of mindfulness ... the enlightenment factor of equanimity, which is based upon seclusion, dispassion, and cessation, maturing in release. It is when the seven factors of enlightenment are developed and cultivated in this way that they lead to the cessation of craving."

28 (8) Partaking of Penetration

"Bhikkhus, I will teach you the path that partakes of penetration.[73] Listen to that...."

"And what, bhikkhus, is the path that partakes of penetration? It is: the seven factors of enlightenment. What seven? The enlightenment factor of mindfulness … the enlightenment factor of equanimity."

When this was said, the Venerable Udāyī asked the Blessed One: "Venerable sir, how are the seven factors of enlightenment developed and cultivated so that they lead to penetration?"

"Here, Udāyī, a bhikkhu develops the enlightenment factor of mindfulness, which is based upon seclusion, dispassion, and cessation, maturing in release; which is vast, exalted, [88] measureless, without ill will. With a mind that has developed the enlightenment factor of mindfulness, he penetrates and sunders the mass of greed that he has never before penetrated and sundered; he penetrates and sunders the mass of hatred that he has never before penetrated and sundered; he penetrates and sunders the mass of delusion that he has never before penetrated and sundered….

"He develops the enlightenment factor of equanimity, which is based upon seclusion, dispassion, and cessation, maturing in release; which is vast, exalted, measureless, without ill will. With a mind that has developed the enlightenment factor of equanimity, he penetrates and sunders the mass of greed … the mass of hatred … the mass of delusion that he has never before penetrated and sundered.

"It is, Udāyī, when the seven factors of enlightenment are developed and cultivated in this way that they lead to penetration."

29 (9) One Thing

"Bhikkhus, I do not see even one other thing that, when developed and cultivated, leads to the abandoning of the things that fetter so effectively as this: the seven factors of enlightenment. What seven? The enlightenment factor of mindfulness … the enlightenment factor of equanimity.

"And how, bhikkhus, are the seven factors of enlightenment developed and cultivated so that they lead to the abandoning of the things that fetter? Here, bhikkhus, a bhikkhu develops the enlightenment factor of mindfulness, which is based upon seclusion, dispassion, and cessation, maturing in release…. He develops the enlightenment factor of equanimity, which is based upon seclusion, dispassion, and cessation, maturing in release. It is when the seven factors of enlightenment are developed and cultivated in this way that they lead to the abandoning of the things that fetter. [89]

"And what, bhikkhus, are the things that fetter? The eye is a thing that fetters; it is here that these fetters, shackles, and clamps arise. The ear is a thing that fetters … The mind is a thing that fetters; it is here that these fetters, shackles, and clamps arise. These are called the things that fetter."

30 (10) Udāyī

On one occasion the Blessed One was dwelling among the Sumbhas, where there was a town of the Sumbhas named Sedaka. Then the Venerable Udāyī approached the Blessed One … and said to him:

"It is wonderful, venerable sir! It is amazing, venerable sir, how helpful has been my devotion and reverence for the Blessed One, my sense of shame and fear of wrongdoing. For in the past, venerable sir, when I was still a householder, I did not have much concern for the Dhamma or the Saṅgha.[74] But when I considered my devotion and reverence for the Blessed One, and my sense of shame and fear of wrongdoing, I went forth from the household life into homelessness. The Blessed One taught me the Dhamma thus: 'Such is form, such its origin, such its passing away; such is feeling … such is perception … such are volitional formations … such is consciousness, such its origin, such its passing away.'

"Then, venerable sir, while I was staying in an empty hut following along with the surge and decline[75] of the five aggregates subject to clinging, I directly knew as it really is: 'This is suffering'; [90] I directly knew as it really is: 'This is the origin of suffering'; I directly knew as it really is: 'This is the cessation of suffering'; I directly knew as it really is: 'This is the way leading to the cessation of suffering.' I have made the breakthrough to the Dhamma, venerable sir, and have obtained the path[76] which, when I have developed and cultivated it, will lead me on, while I am dwelling in the appropriate way, to such a state that I shall understand: 'Destroyed is birth, the holy life has been lived, what had to be done has been done, there is no more for this state of being.'

"I have obtained the enlightenment factor of mindfulness which, when I have developed and cultivated it, will lead me on, while I am dwelling in the appropriate way, to such a state that I shall understand: 'Destroyed is birth … there is no more for this state of being.'… I have obtained the enlightenment factor of equanimity which, when I have developed and cultivated it, will lead me on, while I am dwelling in the appropriate way, to such a state that I shall understand: 'Destroyed is birth … there is no more for this state of being.'

"This, venerable sir, is the path that I have obtained, which … will lead me on … to such a state that I shall understand: 'Destroyed is birth … there is no more for this state of being.'"

"Good, good, Udāyi! Indeed, Udāyi, this is the path that you have obtained, and when you have developed and cultivated it, it will lead you on, while you are dwelling in the appropriate way, to such a state that you will understand: 'Destroyed is birth, the holy life has been lived, what had to be done has been done, there is no more for this state of being.'"

[91] IV. The Hindrances

31 (1) Wholesome (1)

"Bhikkhus, whatever states there are that are wholesome, partaking of the wholesome,[77] pertaining to the wholesome, they are all rooted in diligence, converge upon diligence, and diligence is declared to be the chief among them. When a bhikkhu is diligent, it is to be expected that he will develop and cultivate the seven factors of enlightenment.

"And how, bhikkhus, does a bhikkhu who is diligent develop and cultivate the seven factors of enlightenment? Here, bhikkhus, a bhikkhu develops the enlightenment factor of mindfulness … the enlightenment factor of equanimity, which is based upon seclusion, dispassion, and cessation, maturing in release. It is in this way, bhikkhus, that a bhikkhu who is diligent develops and cultivates the seven factors of enlightenment."

32 (2) Wholesome (2)

"Bhikkhus, whatever states there are that are wholesome, partaking of the wholesome, pertaining to the wholesome, they are all rooted in careful attention, converge upon careful attention, and careful attention is declared to be the chief among them. When a bhikkhu is accomplished in careful attention, it is to be expected that he will develop and cultivate the seven factors of enlightenment.

"And how, bhikkhus, does a bhikkhu who is accomplished in careful attention develop and cultivate the seven factors of enlightenment?..." (*All as above.*) [92]

33 (3) Corruptions

"Bhikkhus, there are these five corruptions of gold, corrupted by which gold is neither malleable nor wieldy nor radiant but brittle and not properly fit for work. What five? Iron is a corruption of gold, corrupted by which gold is neither malleable nor wieldy nor radiant but brittle and not properly fit for work. Copper is a corruption of gold ... Tin is a corruption of gold ... Lead is a corruption of gold ... Silver is a corruption of gold.... These are the five corruptions of gold, corrupted by which gold is neither malleable nor wieldy nor radiant but brittle and not properly fit for work.

"So too, bhikkhus, there are these five corruptions of the mind, corrupted by which the mind is neither malleable nor wieldy nor radiant but brittle and not rightly concentrated for the destruction of the taints. What five? Sensual desire is a corruption of the mind, corrupted by which the mind is neither malleable nor wieldy nor radiant but brittle and not rightly concentrated for the destruction of the taints. [Ill will is a corruption of the mind ... Sloth and torpor are a corruption of the mind ... Restlessness and remorse are a corruption of the mind ... Doubt is a corruption of the mind....][78] [93] These are the five corruptions of the mind, corrupted by which the mind is neither malleable nor wieldy nor radiant but brittle and not rightly concentrated for the destruction of the taints."

34 (4) Noncorruptions

"Bhikkhus, these seven factors of enlightenment are nonobstructions, nonhindrances, noncorruptions of the mind; when developed and cultivated they lead to the realization of the fruit of true knowledge and liberation. What seven? The enlightenment factor of mindfulness, bhikkhus, is a nonobstruction … The enlightenment factor of equanimity is a nonobstruction, a nonhindrance, a noncorruption of the mind; when developed and cultivated it leads to the realization of the fruit of true knowledge and liberation. These seven factors of enlightenment are nonobstructions, nonhindrances, noncorruptions of the mind; when developed and cultivated they lead to the realization of the fruit of true knowledge and liberation."

35 (5) Careful Attention[79]

"Bhikkhus, when one attends carelessly, unarisen sensual desire arises and arisen sensual desire increases and expands; unarisen ill will arises and arisen ill will increases and expands; unarisen sloth and torpor arise and arisen sloth and torpor increase and expand; unarisen restlessness and remorse arise and arisen restlessness and remorse increase and expand; [94] unarisen doubt arises and arisen doubt increases and expands.

"Bhikkhus, when one attends carefully, the unarisen enlightenment factor of mindfulness arises and the arisen enlightenment factor of mindfulness goes to fulfilment by development … the unarisen enlightenment factor of equanimity arises and the arisen enlightenment factor of equanimity goes to fulfilment by development."

36 (6) Growth

"Bhikkhus, these seven factors of enlightenment, when developed and cultivated, lead to growth, to nondecline. What seven? The enlightenment factor of mindfulness … the enlightenment factor of equanimity. These seven factors of enlightenment, when developed and cultivated, lead to growth, to nondecline."

37 (7) Obstructions

"Bhikkhus, there are these five obstructions, hindrances, corruptions of the mind, weakeners of wisdom. What five? Sensual desire is an obstruction, a hindrance, a corruption of the mind, a weakener of wisdom. Ill will is an obstruction … Sloth and torpor are an obstruction ... [95] Restlessness and remorse are an obstruction ... Doubt is an obstruction ... a weakener of wisdom. These are the five obstructions, hindrances, corruptions of the mind, weakeners of wisdom.

"There are, bhikkhus, these seven factors of enlightenment, which are nonobstructions, nonhindrances, noncorruptions of the mind; when developed and cultivated they lead to the realization of the fruit of true knowledge and liberation. What seven? The enlightenment factor of mindfulness is a nonobstruction ... The enlightenment factor of equanimity is a nonobstruction.... These are the seven factors of enlightenment that are nonobstructions, nonhindrances, noncorruptions of the mind; when developed and cultivated they lead to the realization of the fruit of true knowledge and liberation."

38 (8) Without Hindrances[80]

"When, bhikkhus, a noble disciple listens to the Dhamma with eager ears, attending to it as a matter of vital concern, directing his whole mind to it, on that occasion the five hindrances are not present in him; on that occasion the seven factors of enlightenment go to fulfilment by development.

"And what are the five hindrances that are not present on that occasion? The hindrance of sensual desire is not present on that occasion; the hindrance of ill will ... the hindrance of sloth and torpor ... the hindrance of restlessness and remorse ... the hindrance of doubt is not present on that occasion. These are the five hindrances that are not present on that occasion.

"And what are the seven factors of enlightenment that go to fulfilment by development on that occasion? The enlightenment factor of mindfulness goes to fulfilment by development on that occasion.... The enlightenment factor of equanimity goes to fulfilment by development on that occasion. [96] These are the seven factors of enlightenment that go to fulfilment by development on that occasion.

"When, bhikkhus, a noble disciple listens to the Dhamma with eager ears, attending to it as a matter of vital concern, directing his whole mind to it, on that occasion these five hindrances are not present in him; on that occasion these seven factors of enlightenment go to fulfilment by development."

39 (9) Trees

"Bhikkhus, there are huge trees with tiny seeds and huge bodies, encirclers of other trees, and the trees which they encircle become bent, twisted, and split. And what are those huge trees with tiny seeds and huge bodies? The *assattha*, the banyan, the *pilakkha*, the *udumbara*, the *kacchaka*, and the *kapitthana*: these are those huge trees with tiny seeds and huge bodies, encirclers of other trees, and the trees which they encircle become bent, twisted, and split.[81] So too, bhikkhus, when some clansman here has left behind sensual pleasures and gone forth from the household life into homelessness, he becomes bent, twisted, and split because of those same sensual pleasures, or because of others worse than them.

"These five, bhikkhus, are obstructions, hindrances, encirclers of the mind, weakeners of wisdom. What five? Sensual desire is an obstruction, a hindrance encircling the mind, a weakener of wisdom. Ill will ... Sloth and torpor ... Restlessness and remorse ... Doubt is an obstruction ... a weakener of wisdom. [97] These are the five obstructions, hindrances, encirclers of the mind, weakeners of wisdom.

"These seven factors of enlightenment, bhikkhus, are nonobstructions, nonhindrances, nonencirclers of the mind; when developed and cultivated they lead to the realization of the fruit of true knowledge and liberation. What seven? The enlightenment factor of mindfulness is a nonobstruction ... The enlightenment factor of equanimity is a nonobstruction.... These seven factors of enlightenment are nonobstructions, nonhindrances, nonencirclers of the mind; when developed and cultivated they lead to the realization of the fruit of true knowledge and liberation."

40 (10) Hindrances

"Bhikkhus, these five hindrances are makers of blindness, causing lack of vision, causing lack of knowledge, detrimental to wisdom, tending to vexation, leading away from Nibbāna. What five? The hindrance of sensual desire is a maker of blindness ... The hindrance of ill will ... The hindrance of sloth and torpor ... The hindrance of restlessness and remorse ... The hindrance of doubt is a maker of blindness ... leading away from Nibbāna. These five hindrances are makers of blindness, causing lack of vision, causing lack of knowledge, detrimental to wisdom, tending to vexation, leading away from Nibbāna.

"These seven factors of enlightenment, bhikkhus, are makers of vision, makers of knowledge, promoting the growth of wisdom, free from vexation, leading towards Nibbāna. What seven? The enlightenment factor of mindfulness is a maker of vision ... The enlightenment factor of equanimity is a maker of vision ... leading towards Nibbāna. [98] These seven factors of enlightenment are makers of vision, makers of knowledge, promoting the growth of wisdom, free from vexation, leading towards Nibbāna."

V. Wheel-Turning Monarch

41 (1) Discriminations

At Sāvatthī. "Bhikkhus, whatever ascetics or brahmins in the past abandoned the three discriminations,[82] all did so because they had developed and cultivated the seven factors of enlightenment. Whatever ascetics or brahmins in the future will abandon the three discriminations, all will do so because they will have developed and cultivated the seven factors of enlightenment. Whatever ascetics or brahmins at present abandon the three discriminations, all do so because they have developed and cultivated the seven factors of enlightenment. What seven? The enlightenment factor of mindfulness ... the enlightenment factor of equanimity. Whatever ascetics or brahmins in the past ... in the future ... at present abandon the three discriminations, all do so because they have developed and cultivated these seven factors of enlightenment." [99]

42 (2) Wheel-Turning Monarch

"Bhikkhus, with the manifestation of a wheel-turning monarch comes the manifestation of seven gems. What seven? There comes the manifestation of the wheel-gem, the elephant-gem, the horse-gem, the jewel-gem, the woman-gem, the steward-gem, and the commander-gem.[83]

"With the manifestation of a Tathāgata, bhikkhus, an Arahant, a Perfectly Enlightened One, comes the manifestation of the seven gems of the factors of enlightenment. What seven? There comes the manifestation of the gem of the enlightenment factor of mindfulness ... the gem of the enlightenment factor of equanimity. With the manifestation of a Tathāgata, an Arahant, a Perfectly Enlightened One, comes the manifestation of these seven gems of the factors of enlightenment."

43 (3) Māra

"Bhikkhus, I will teach you the path crushing the army of Māra. Listen to that....

"And what, bhikkhus, is the path crushing the army of Māra? It is the seven factors of enlightenment. What seven? The enlightenment factor of mindfulness ... the enlightenment factor of equanimity. This is the path crushing the army of Māra."

44 (4) Unwise

Then a certain bhikkhu approached the Blessed One ... and said to him:

"Venerable sir, it is said, 'an unwise dolt, an unwise dolt.' In what way, venerable sir, is one called 'an unwise dolt'?"

"Bhikkhus, it is because one has not developed and cultivated the seven factors of enlightenment that one is called 'an unwise dolt.' [100] What seven? The enlightenment factor of mindfulness ... the enlightenment factor of equanimity. It is because one has not developed and cultivated these seven factors of enlightenment that one is called 'an unwise dolt.'"

45 (5) Wise

"Venerable sir, it is said, 'wise and alert, wise and alert.' In what way, venerable sir, is one called 'wise and alert'?"

"Bhikkhus, it is because one has developed and cultivated the seven factors of enlightenment that one is called 'wise and alert.' What seven?" (*As above.*)

46 (6) Poor

"Venerable sir, it is said, 'poor, poor.' In what way, venerable sir, is one called 'poor'?"

"Bhikkhus, it is because one has not developed and cultivated the seven factors of enlightenment that one is called 'poor.' What seven?" (*As above.*)

47 (7) Prosperous

"Venerable sir, it is said, 'prosperous, prosperous.' In what way, venerable sir, is one called 'prosperous'?"

"Bhikkhus, it is because one has developed and cultivated the seven factors of enlightenment that one is called 'prosperous.' What seven?" (*As above.*) [101]

48 (8) The Sun

"Bhikkhus, this is the forerunner and precursor of the rising of the sun, that is, the dawn. So too, for a bhikkhu this is the forerunner and precursor of the arising of the seven factors of enlightenment, that is, good friendship. When a bhikkhu has a good friend, it is to be expected that he will develop and cultivate the seven factors of enlightenment.

"And how does a bhikkhu who has a good friend develop and cultivate the seven factors of enlightenment? Here, bhikkhus, a bhikkhu develops the enlightenment factor of mindfulness ... he develops the enlightenment factor of equanimity, which is based upon seclusion, dispassion, and cessation, maturing in release. It is in this way that a bhikkhu who has a good friend develops and cultivates the seven factors of enlightenment."

49 (9) Internal Factor

"Bhikkhus, as to internal factors, I do not see any other factor that is so helpful for the arising of the seven factors of enlightenment as this: careful attention. When a bhikkhu is accomplished in careful attention, it is to be expected that he will develop and cultivate the seven factors of enlightenment." (*The rest as in §13.*) [102]

50 (10) External Factor

"Bhikkhus, as to external factors, I do not see any other factor that is so helpful for the arising of the seven factors of enlightenment as this: good friendship. When a bhikkhu has a good friend, it is to be expected that he will develop and cultivate the seven factors of enlightenment." (*The rest as in §12.*)

VI. Discussions

51 (1) Nutriment

At Sāvatthī. "Bhikkhus, I will teach you the nutriment and the denourishment in regard to the five hindrances and the seven factors of enlightenment. Listen to that....

(i. The nutriments for the hindrances)[84]

"And what, bhikkhus, is the nutriment for the arising of unarisen sensual desire and for the increase and expansion of arisen sensual desire? [103] There is, bhikkhus, the sign of the beautiful: frequently giving careless attention to it is the nutriment for the arising of unarisen sensual desire and for the increase and expansion of arisen sensual desire.

"And what, bhikkhus, is the nutriment for the arising of unarisen ill will and for the increase and expansion of arisen ill will? There is, bhikkhus, the sign of the repulsive: frequently giving careless attention to it is the nutriment for the arising of unarisen ill will and for the increase and expansion of arisen ill will.

"And what, bhikkhus, is the nutriment for the arising of unarisen sloth and torpor and for the increase and expansion of arisen sloth and torpor? There are, bhikkhus, discontent, lethargy, lazy stretching, drowsiness after meals, sluggishness of mind: frequently giving careless attention to them is the nutriment for the arising of unarisen sloth and torpor and for the increase and expansion of arisen sloth and torpor.

"And what, bhikkhus, is the nutriment for the arising of unarisen restlessness and remorse and for the increase and expansion of arisen restlessness and remorse? There is, bhikkhus, unsettledness of mind: frequently giving careless attention to it is the nutriment for the arising of unarisen restlessness and remorse and for the increase and expansion of arisen restlessness and remorse.

"And what, bhikkhus, is the nutriment for the arising of unarisen doubt and for the increase and expansion of arisen doubt? There are, bhikkhus, things that are the basis for doubt: frequently giving careless attention to them is the nutriment for the arising of unarisen doubt and for the increase and expansion of arisen doubt.

(ii. The nutriments for the enlightenment factors)

"And what, bhikkhus, is the nutriment for the arising of the unarisen enlightenment factor of mindfulness and for the fulfilment by development of the arisen enlightenment factor of mindfulness? There are, bhikkhus, things that are the basis for the enlightenment factor of mindfulness: [104] frequently giving careful attention to them is the nutriment for the arising of the unarisen enlightenment factor of mindfulness and for the fulfilment by development of the arisen enlightenment factor of mindfulness.[85]

"And what, bhikkhus, is the nutriment for the arising of the unarisen enlightenment factor of discrimination of states and for the fulfilment by development of the arisen enlightenment factor of discrimination of states? There are, bhikkhus, wholesome and unwholesome states, blameable and blameless states, inferior and superior states, dark and bright states with their counterparts: frequently giving careful attention to them is the nutriment for the arising of the unarisen enlightenment factor of discrimination of states and for the fulfilment by development of the arisen enlightenment factor of discrimination of states.[86]

"And what, bhikkhus, is the nutriment for the arising of the unarisen enlightenment factor of energy and for the fulfilment by development of the arisen enlightenment factor of energy? There are, bhikkhus, the element of arousal, the element of endeavour, the element of exertion: frequently giving careful attention to them is the nutriment for the arising of the unarisen enlightenment factor of energy and for the fulfilment by development of the arisen enlightenment factor of energy.[87]

"And what, bhikkhus, is the nutriment for the arising of the unarisen enlightenment factor of rapture and for the fulfilment by development of the arisen enlightenment factor of rapture? There are, bhikkhus, things that are the basis for the enlightenment factor of rapture: frequently giving careful attention to them is the nutriment for the arising of the unarisen enlightenment factor of rapture and for the fulfilment by development of the arisen enlightenment factor of rapture.[88]

"And what, bhikkhus, is the nutriment for the arising of the unarisen enlightenment factor of tranquillity and for the fulfilment by development of the arisen enlightenment factor of tranquillity? There are, bhikkhus, tranquillity of body, tranquillity of mind: frequently giving careful attention to them is the nutriment for the arising of the unarisen enlightenment factor of tranquillity and for the fulfilment by development of the arisen enlightenment factor of tranquillity.[89] [105]

"And what, bhikkhus, is the nutriment for the arising of the unarisen enlightenment factor of concentration and for the fulfilment by development of the arisen enlightenment factor of concentration? There are, bhikkhus, the sign of serenity, the sign of nondispersal: frequently giving careful attention to them is the nutriment for the arising of the unarisen enlightenment factor of concentration and for the fulfilment by development of the arisen enlightenment factor of concentration.[90]

"And what, bhikkhus, is the nutriment for the arising of the unarisen enlightenment factor of equanimity and for the fulfilment by development of the arisen enlightenment factor of equanimity? There are, bhikkhus, things that are the basis for the enlightenment factor of equanimity: frequently giving careful attention to them is the nutriment for the arising of the unarisen enlightenment factor of equanimity and for the fulfilment by development of the arisen enlightenment factor of equanimity.[91]

(iii. The denourishment of the hindrances)[92]

"And what, bhikkhus, is the denourishment that prevents unarisen sensual desire from arising and arisen sensual desire from increasing and expanding? There is, bhikkhus, the sign of foulness: frequently giving careful attention to it is the denourishment that prevents unarisen sensual desire from arising and arisen sensual desire from increasing and expanding.[93]

"And what, bhikkhus, is the denourishment that prevents unarisen ill will from arising and arisen ill will from increasing and expanding? There is, bhikkhus, the liberation of mind through lovingkindness: frequently giving careful attention to it is the denourishment that prevents unarisen ill will from arising and arisen ill will from increasing and expanding.[94]

"And what, bhikkhus, is the denourishment that prevents unarisen sloth and torpor from arising and arisen sloth and torpor from increasing and expanding? There are, bhikkhus, the element of arousal, the element of endeavour, the element of exertion: frequently giving careful attention to them is the denourishment that prevents unarisen sloth and torpor [106] from arising and arisen sloth and torpor from increasing and expanding.[95]

"And what, bhikkhus, is the denourishment that prevents unarisen restlessness and remorse from arising and arisen restlessness and remorse from increasing and expanding? There is, bhikkhus, peacefulness of mind: frequently giving careful attention to it is the denourishment that prevents unarisen restlessness and remorse from arising and arisen restlessness and remorse from increasing and expanding.[96]

"And what, bhikkhus, is the denourishment that prevents unarisen doubt from arising and arisen doubt from increasing and expanding? There are, bhikkhus, wholesome and unwholesome states, blameable and blameless states, inferior and superior states, dark and bright states with their counterparts: frequently giving careful attention to them is the denourishment that prevents unarisen doubt from arising and arisen doubt from increasing and expanding.[97]

(iv. The denourishment of the enlightenment factors)

"And what, bhikkhus, is the denourishment that prevents the unarisen enlightenment factor of mindfulness from arising and the arisen enlightenment factor of mindfulness from reaching fulfilment by development? There are, bhikkhus, things that are the basis for the enlightenment factor of mindfulness: not frequently giving attention to them is the denourishment that prevents the unarisen enlightenment factor of mindfulness from arising and the arisen enlightenment factor of mindfulness from reaching fulfilment by development.

"And what, bhikkhus, is the denourishment that prevents the unarisen enlightenment factor of discrimination of states from arising and the arisen enlightenment factor of discrimination of states from reaching fulfilment by development? There are, bhikkhus, wholesome and unwholesome states, blameable and blameless states, inferior and superior states, dark and bright states with their counterparts: not frequently giving attention to them is the denourishment that prevents the unarisen enlightenment factor of discrimination of states from arising and the arisen enlightenment factor of discrimination of states from reaching fulfilment by development.

"And what, bhikkhus, is the denourishment that prevents the unarisen enlightenment factor of energy from arising and the arisen enlightenment factor of energy from reaching fulfilment by development? [107] There are, bhikkhus, the element of arousal, the element of endeavour, the element of exertion: not frequently giving attention to them is the denourishment that prevents the unarisen enlightenment factor of energy from arising and the arisen enlightenment factor of energy from reaching fulfilment by development.

"And what, bhikkhus, is the denourishment that prevents the unarisen enlightenment factor of rapture from arising and the arisen enlightenment factor of rapture from reaching fulfilment by development? There are, bhikkhus, things that are the basis for the enlightenment factor of rapture: not frequently giving attention to them is the denourishment that prevents the unarisen enlightenment factor of rapture from arising and the arisen enlightenment factor of rapture from reaching fulfilment by development.

"And what, bhikkhus, is the denourishment that prevents the unarisen enlightenment factor of tranquillity from arising and the arisen enlightenment factor of tranquillity from reaching fulfilment by development? There are, bhikkhus, tranquillity of body, tranquillity of mind: not frequently giving attention to them is the denourishment that prevents the unarisen enlightenment factor of tranquillity from arising and the arisen enlightenment factor of tranquillity from reaching fulfilment by development.

"And what, bhikkhus, is the denourishment that prevents the unarisen enlightenment factor of concentration from arising and the arisen enlightenment factor of concentration from reaching fulfilment by development? There are, bhikkhus, the sign of serenity, the sign of nondispersal: not frequently giving attention to them is the denourishment that prevents the unarisen enlightenment factor of concentration from arising and the arisen enlightenment factor of concentration from reaching fulfilment by development.

"And what, bhikkhus, is the denourishment that prevents the unarisen enlightenment factor of equanimity from arising and the arisen enlightenment factor of equanimity from reaching fulfilment by development. There are, bhikkhus, things that are the basis for the enlightenment factor of equanimity: not frequently giving attention to them is the denourishment that prevents the unarisen enlightenment factor of equanimity from arising and the arisen enlightenment factor of equanimity from reaching fulfilment by development." [108]

52 (2) A Method of Exposition

Then, in the morning, a number of bhikkhus dressed and, taking their bowls and robes, entered Sāvatthī for alms. Then it occurred to them: "It is still too early to walk for alms in Sāvatthī. Let us go to the park of the wanderers of other sects."

Then those bhikkhus went to the park of the wanderers of other sects. They exchanged greetings with those wanderers and, when they had concluded their greetings and cordial talk, sat down to one side. The wanderers then said to them: "Friends, the ascetic Gotama teaches the Dhamma to his disciples thus: 'Come, bhikkhus, abandon the five hindrances, the corruptions of the mind that weaken wisdom, and develop correctly the seven factors of enlightenment.' We too teach the Dhamma to our disciples thus: 'Come, friends, abandon the five hindrances, the corruptions of the mind that weaken wisdom, and develop correctly the seven factors of enlightenment.' So, friends, what here is the distinction, the disparity, the difference between the ascetic Gotama and us, that is, regarding the one Dhamma teaching and the other, regarding the one manner of instruction and the other?"[98]

Then those bhikkhus neither delighted in nor rejected the statement of those wanderers. Without delighting in it, without rejecting it, they rose from their seats and left, thinking, "We shall learn the meaning of this statement in the presence of the Blessed One."

Then, when those bhikkhus had walked for alms in Sāvatthī and had returned from the alms round, after their meal they approached the Blessed One. Having paid homage to him, they sat down to one side [109] and reported to him the entire discussion between those wanderers and themselves. [The Blessed One said:]

"Bhikkhus, when wanderers of other sects speak thus, they should be asked: 'Friends, is there a method of exposition by means of which the five hindrances become ten, and the seven factors of enlightenment become fourteen?' Being asked thus, those wanderers would not be able to reply and, further, they would meet with vexation. For what reason? Because that would not be within their domain. I do not see anyone, bhikkhus, in this world with its devas, Māra, and Brahmā, in this generation with its ascetics and brahmins, its devas and humans, who could satisfy the mind with an answer to these questions except the Tathāgata or a disciple of the Tathāgata or one who has heard it from them. [110]

(i. The five become ten)

"And what, bhikkhus, is the method of exposition by means of which the five hindrances become ten?

"Whatever sensual desire there is for the internal is a hindrance; whatever sensual desire there is for the external is also a hindrance.[99] Thus what is spoken of concisely as the hindrance of sensual desire becomes, by this method of exposition, twofold.

"Whatever ill will there is towards the internal is a hindrance; whatever ill will there is towards the external is also a hindrance. Thus what is spoken of concisely as the hindrance of ill will becomes, by this method of exposition, twofold.

"Whatever sloth there is, is a hindrance; whatever torpor there is, is also a hindrance. Thus what is spoken of concisely as the hindrance of sloth and torpor becomes, by this method of exposition, twofold.

"Whatever restlessness there is, is a hindrance; whatever remorse there is, is also a hindrance. Thus what is spoken of concisely as the hindrance of restlessness and remorse becomes, by this method of exposition, twofold.

"Whatever doubt there is about the internal is a hindrance; whatever doubt there is about the external is also a hindrance. Thus what is spoken of concisely as the hindrance of doubt becomes, by this method of exposition, twofold.

(ii. The seven become fourteen)

"And what, bhikkhus, is the method of exposition by means of which the seven factors of enlightenment become fourteen?[100]

"Whatever mindfulness there is of things internal is the enlightenment factor of mindfulness; whatever mindfulness there is of things external is also the enlightenment factor of mindfulness. Thus what is spoken of concisely as the enlightenment factor of mindfulness becomes, by this method of exposition, twofold. [111]

"Whenever one discriminates things internally with wisdom, examines them, makes an investigation of them, that is the enlightenment factor of discrimination of states; whenever one discriminates things externally with wisdom, examines them, makes an investigation of them, that is also the enlightenment factor of discrimination of states. Thus what is spoken of concisely as the enlightenment factor of discrimination of states becomes, by this method of exposition, twofold.

"Whatever bodily energy there is, is the enlightenment factor of energy; whatever mental energy there is, is also the enlightenment factor of energy. Thus what is spoken of concisely as the enlightenment factor of energy becomes, by this method of exposition, twofold.

"Whatever rapture there is accompanied by thought and examination is the enlightenment factor of rapture; whatever rapture there is without thought and examination is also the enlightenment factor of rapture.[101] Thus what is spoken of concisely as the enlightenment factor of rapture becomes, by this method of exposition, twofold.

"Whatever tranquillity of body there is, is the enlightenment factor of tranquillity; whatever tranquillity of mind there is, is also the enlightenment factor of tranquillity.[102] Thus what is spoken of concisely as the enlightenment factor of tranquillity becomes, by this method of exposition, twofold.

"Whatever concentration there is accompanied by thought and examination is the enlightenment factor of concentration; whatever concentration there is without thought and examination is also the enlightenment factor of concentration.[103] Thus what is spoken of concisely as the enlightenment factor of concentration becomes, by this method of exposition, twofold.

"Whatever equanimity there is regarding things internal is the enlightenment factor of equanimity; whatever equanimity there is regarding things external is also the enlightenment factor of equanimity. Thus what is spoken of concisely as the enlightenment factor of equanimity becomes, by this method of exposition, twofold.

"This, bhikkhus, is the method of exposition by means of which the seven factors of enlightenment become fourteen." [112]

53 (3) Fire

Then, in the morning, a number of bhikkhus dressed and, taking their bowls and robes, entered Sāvatthī for alms … (*as in* §52 *down to:*) …[104] [The Blessed One said:]

"Bhikkhus, when wanderers of other sects speak thus, they should be asked: 'Friends, when the mind becomes sluggish, which factors of enlightenment is it untimely to develop on that occasion, and which factors of enlightenment is it timely to develop on that occasion? Then, friends, when the mind becomes excited, which factors of enlightenment is it untimely to develop on that occasion, and which factors of enlightenment is it timely to develop on that occasion?' Being asked thus, those wanderers would not be able to reply and, further, they would meet with vexation. For what reason? Because that would not be within their domain. I do not see anyone, bhikkhus, in this world with its devas, Māra, and Brahmā, in this generation with its ascetics and brahmins, its devas and humans, who could satisfy the mind with an answer to these questions except the Tathāgata or a disciple of the Tathāgata or one who has heard it from them.

(i. The sluggish mind: untimely)

"On an occasion, bhikkhus, when the mind becomes sluggish, it is untimely to develop the enlightenment factor of tranquillity, the enlightenment factor of concentration, and the enlightenment factor of equanimity. For what reason? Because the mind is sluggish, bhikkhus, and it is difficult to arouse it with those things.

"Suppose, bhikkhus, a man wants to make a small fire flare up. If he throws wet grass, wet cowdung, and wet timber into it, [113] sprays it with water, and scatters soil over it, would he be able to make that small fire flare up?"

"No, venerable sir."

"So too, bhikkhus, on an occasion when the mind becomes sluggish, it is untimely to develop the enlightenment factor of tranquillity, the enlightenment factor of concentration, and the enlightenment factor of equanimity. For what reason? Because the mind is sluggish, bhikkhus, and it is difficult to arouse it with those things.

(ii. The sluggish mind: timely)

"On an occasion, bhikkhus, when the mind becomes sluggish, it is timely to develop the enlightenment factor of discrimination of states, the enlightenment factor of energy, and the enlightenment factor of rapture. For what reason? Because the mind is sluggish, bhikkhus, and it is easy to arouse it with those things.

"Suppose, bhikkhus, a man wants to make a small fire flare up. If he throws dry grass, dry cowdung, and dry timber into it, blows on it, and does not scatter soil over it, would he be able to make that small fire flare up?"

"Yes, venerable sir."

"So too, bhikkhus, on an occasion when the mind becomes sluggish, it is timely to develop the enlightenment factor of discrimination of states, the enlightenment factor of energy, and the enlightenment factor of rapture. For what reason? Because the mind is sluggish, bhikkhus, and it is easy to arouse it with those things.

(iii. The excited mind: untimely)

"On an occasion, bhikkhus, when the mind becomes excited, it is untimely to develop the enlightenment factor of discrimination of states, the enlightenment factor of energy, [114] and the enlightenment factor of rapture. For what reason? Because the mind is excited, bhikkhus, and it is difficult to calm it down with those things.

"Suppose, bhikkhus, a man wants to extinguish a great bonfire. If he throws dry grass, dry cowdung, and dry timber into it, blows on it, and does not scatter soil over it, would he be able to extinguish that great bonfire?"

"No, venerable sir."

"So too, bhikkhus, on an occasion when the mind becomes excited, it is untimely to develop the enlightenment factor of discrimination of states, the enlightenment factor of energy, and the enlightenment factor of rapture. For what reason? Because the mind is excited, bhikkhus, and it is difficult to calm it down with those things.

(iv. The excited mind: timely)

"On an occasion, bhikkhus, when the mind becomes excited, it is timely to develop the enlightenment factor of tranquillity, the enlightenment factor of concentration, and the enlightenment factor of equanimity. For what reason? Because the mind is excited, bhikkhus, and it is easy to calm it down with those things.

"Suppose, bhikkhus, a man wants to extinguish a great bonfire. If he throws wet grass, wet cowdung, and wet timber into it, sprays it with water, and scatters soil over it, would he be able to extinguish that great bonfire?"

"Yes, venerable sir."

"So too, bhikkhus, on an occasion when the mind becomes excited, [115] it is timely to develop the enlightenment factor of tranquillity, the enlightenment factor of concentration, and the enlightenment factor of equanimity. For what reason? Because the mind is excited, bhikkhus, and it is easy to calm it down with those things.

"But mindfulness, bhikkhus, I say is always useful."[105]

54 (4) Accompanied by Lovingkindness

On one occasion the Blessed One was dwelling among the Koliyans, where there was a town of the Koliyans named Haliddavasana.[106] Then, in the morning, a number of bhikkhus dressed and, taking their bowls and robes, entered Haliddavasana for alms. Then it occurred to them: "It is still too early to walk for alms in Haliddavasana. Let us go to the park of the wanderers of other sects."

Then those bhikkhus went to the park of the wanderers of other sects. They exchanged greetings with those wanderers and, when they had concluded their greetings and cordial talk, sat down to one side. The wanderers then said to them: "Friends, the ascetic Gotama teaches the Dhamma to his disciples thus: 'Come, bhikkhus, abandon the five hindrances, the corruptions of the mind that weaken wisdom, and dwell pervading one quarter with a mind imbued with lovingkindness, likewise the second quarter, the third quarter, and the fourth quarter. Thus above, below, across, and everywhere, and to all as to oneself, dwell pervading the entire world with a mind imbued with lovingkindness, [116] vast, exalted, measureless, without hostility, without ill will. Dwell pervading one quarter with a mind imbued with compassion, likewise the second quarter, the third quarter, and the fourth quarter. Thus above, below, across, and everywhere, and to all as to oneself, dwell pervading the entire world with a mind imbued with compassion, vast, exalted, measureless, without hostility, without ill will. Dwell pervading one quarter with a mind imbued with altruistic joy, likewise the second quarter, the third quarter, and the fourth quarter. Thus above, below, across, and everywhere, and to all as to oneself, dwell pervading the entire world with a mind imbued with altruistic joy, vast, exalted, measureless, without hostility, without ill will. Dwell pervading one quarter with a mind imbued with equanimity, likewise the second quarter, the third quarter, and the fourth quarter. Thus above, below, across, and everywhere, and to all as to oneself, dwell pervading the entire world with a mind imbued with equanimity, vast, exalted, measureless, without hostility, without ill will.'

"We too, friends, teach the Dhamma to our disciples thus: 'Come, friends, abandon the five hindrances … (*all as above*) … dwell pervading the entire world with a mind imbued with lovingkindness … compassion … altruistic joy … equanimity … without ill will.' So, friends, what here is the distinction, the disparity, the difference between the ascetic Gotama and us, that is, [117] regarding the one Dhamma teaching and the other, regarding the one manner of instruction and the other?"[107]

Then those bhikkhus neither delighted in nor rejected the statement of those wanderers. Without delighting in it, without rejecting it, they rose from their seats and left, thinking, "We shall learn the meaning of this statement in the presence of the Blessed One."

Then, when those bhikkhus had walked for alms in Haliddavasana and had returned from the alms round, after their meal they approached the Blessed One. Having paid homage to him, they sat down to one side and reported to him the entire discussion between those wanderers and themselves. [118] [The Blessed One said:]

"Bhikkhus, when wanderers of other sects speak thus, they should be asked: 'Friends, how is the liberation of the mind by lovingkindness developed? What does it have as its destination, its culmination, its fruit, its final goal?[108] How is the liberation of the mind by compassion developed? What does it have as its destination, its culmination, its fruit, its final goal? How is the liberation of the mind by altruistic joy developed? What does it have as its destination, its culmination, its fruit, its final goal? How is the liberation of the mind by equanimity developed? What does it have as its destination, its culmination, its fruit, its final goal?' Being asked thus, those wanderers would not be able to reply and, further, they would meet with vexation. For what reason? Because that would not be within their domain. I do not see anyone, bhikkhus, in this world with its devas, Māra, and Brahmā, in this generation with its ascetics and brahmins, its devas and humans, who could satisfy the mind with an answer to these questions except the Tathāgata or a disciple of the Tathāgata or one who has heard it from them. [119]

"And how, bhikkhus, is the liberation of the mind by lovingkindness developed? What does it have as its destination, its culmination, its fruit, its final goal? Here, bhikkhus, a bhikkhu develops the enlightenment factor of mindfulness accompanied by lovingkindness … the enlightenment factor of equanimity accompanied by lovingkindness, based upon seclusion, dispassion, and cessation, maturing in release.[109] If he wishes: 'May I dwell perceiving the repulsive in the unrepulsive,' he dwells perceiving the repulsive therein. If he wishes: 'May I dwell perceiving the unrepulsive in the repulsive,' he dwells perceiving the unrepulsive therein. If he wishes: 'May I dwell perceiving the repulsive in the unrepulsive and in the repulsive,' he dwells perceiving the repulsive therein. If he wishes: 'May I dwell perceiving the unrepulsive in the repulsive and in the unrepulsive,' he dwells perceiving the unrepulsive therein. If he wishes: 'Avoiding both the unrepulsive and the repulsive, may I dwell equanimously, mindful and clearly comprehending,' then he dwells therein equanimously, mindful and clearly comprehending.[110] Or else he enters and dwells in the deliverance of the beautiful. Bhikkhus, the liberation of mind by lovingkindness has the beautiful as its culmination, I say, for a wise bhikkhu here who has not penetrated to a superior liberation.[111]

"And how, bhikkhus, is the liberation of the mind by compassion developed? What does it have as its destination, its culmination, its fruit, its final goal? Here, bhikkhus, a bhikkhu develops the enlightenment factor of mindfulness accompanied by compassion ... the enlightenment factor of equanimity accompanied by compassion, based upon seclusion, dispassion, and cessation, maturing in release. If he wishes: 'May I dwell perceiving the repulsive in the unrepulsive,' he dwells perceiving the repulsive therein.... If he wishes: 'Avoiding both the unrepulsive and the repulsive, may I dwell equanimously, mindful and clearly comprehending,' then he dwells therein equanimously, mindful and clearly comprehending. Or else, with the complete transcendence of perceptions of forms, with the passing away of perceptions of sensory impingement, with nonattention to perceptions of diversity, aware that 'space is infinite,' he enters and dwells in the base of the infinity of space. [120] Bhikkhus, the liberation of mind by compassion has the base of the infinity of space as its culmination, I say, for a wise bhikkhu here who has not penetrated to a superior liberation.

"And how, bhikkhus, is the liberation of the mind by altruistic joy developed? What does it have as its destination, its culmination, its fruit, its final goal? Here, bhikkhus, a bhikkhu develops the enlightenment factor of mindfulness accompanied by altruistic joy ... the enlightenment factor of equanimity accompanied by altruistic joy, based upon seclusion, dispassion, and cessation, maturing in release. If he wishes: 'May I dwell perceiving the repulsive in the unrepulsive,' he dwells perceiving the repulsive therein.... If he wishes: 'Avoiding both the unrepulsive and the repulsive, may I dwell equanimously, mindful and clearly comprehending,' then he dwells therein equanimously, mindful and clearly comprehending. Or else, by completely transcending the base of the infinity of space, aware that 'consciousness is infinite,' he enters and dwells in the base of the infinity of consciousness. Bhikkhus, the liberation of mind by altruistic joy has the base of the infinity of consciousness as its culmination, I say, for a wise bhikkhu here who has not penetrated to a superior liberation.

"And how, bhikkhus, is the liberation of the mind by equanimity developed? What does it have as its destination, its culmination, its fruit, its final goal? Here, bhikkhus, a bhikkhu develops the enlightenment factor of mindfulness accompanied by equanimity ... the enlightenment factor of equanimity accompanied by equanimity, based upon seclusion, dispassion, and cessation, maturing in release. If he wishes: 'May I dwell perceiving the repulsive in the unrepulsive,' he dwells perceiving the repulsive therein.... If he wishes: 'Avoiding both the unrepulsive and the repulsive, may I dwell equanimously, mindful and clearly comprehending,' then he dwells therein equanimously, mindful and clearly comprehending. [121] Or else, by completely transcending the base of the infinity of consciousness, aware that 'there is nothing,' he enters and dwells in the base of nothingness. Bhikkhus, the liberation of mind by equanimity has the base of nothingness as its culmination, I say, for a wise bhikkhu here who has not penetrated to a superior liberation."

55 (5) Saṅgārava

At Sāvatthī.[112] Then the brahmin Saṅgārava approached the Blessed One and exchanged greetings with him. When they had concluded their greetings and cordial talk, he sat down to one side and said to the Blessed One:

"Master Gotama, what is the cause and reason why sometimes even those hymns that have been recited over a long period do not recur to the mind, let alone those that have not been recited? What is the cause and reason why sometimes those hymns that have not been recited over a long period recur to the mind, let alone those that have been recited?"

(i. Why the hymns do not recur to the mind)

"Brahmin, when one dwells with a mind obsessed by sensual lust, overwhelmed by sensual lust, and one does not understand as it really is the escape from arisen sensual lust,[113] on that occasion one neither knows nor sees as it really is one's own good, or the good of others, or the good of both. Then even those hymns that have been recited over a long period do not recur to the mind, let alone those that have not been recited.

"Suppose, brahmin, there is a bowl of water mixed with lac, turmeric, blue dye, or crimson dye. If a man with good sight were to examine his own facial reflection in it, he would neither know nor see it as it really is. So too, brahmin, when one dwells with a mind obsessed by sensual lust ... [122] ... on that occasion even those hymns that have been recited over a long period do not recur to the mind, let alone those that have not been recited.

"Again, brahmin, when one dwells with a mind obsessed by ill will, overwhelmed by ill will, and one does not understand as it really is the escape from arisen ill will, on that occasion one neither knows nor sees as it really is one's own good, or the good of others, or the good of both. Then even those hymns that have been recited over a long period do not recur to the mind, let alone those that have not been recited.

"Suppose, brahmin, there is a bowl of water being heated over a fire, bubbling and boiling. If a man with good sight were to examine his own facial reflection in it, he would neither know nor see it as it really is. So too, brahmin, when one dwells with a mind obsessed by ill will ... on that occasion even those hymns that have been recited over a long period do not recur to the mind, let alone those that have not been recited.

"Again, brahmin, when one dwells with a mind obsessed by sloth and torpor, overwhelmed by sloth and torpor, and one does not understand as it really is the escape from arisen sloth and torpor, on that occasion one neither knows nor sees as it really is one's own good, or the good of others, or the good of both. Then even those hymns that have been recited over a long period do not recur to the mind, let alone those that have not been recited.

"Suppose, brahmin, there is a bowl of water covered over with water plants and algae. If a man with good sight were to examine his own facial reflection in it, [123] he would neither know nor see it as it really is. So too, brahmin, when one dwells with a mind obsessed by sloth and torpor ... on that occasion even those hymns that have been recited over a long period do not recur to the mind, let alone those that have not been recited.

"Again, brahmin, when one dwells with a mind obsessed by restlessness and remorse, overwhelmed by restlessness and remorse, and one does not understand as it really is the escape from arisen restlessness and remorse, on that occasion one neither knows nor sees as it really is one's own good, or the good of others, or the good of both. Then even those hymns that have been recited over a long period do not recur to the mind, let alone those that have not been recited.

"Suppose, brahmin, there is a bowl of water stirred by the wind, rippling, swirling, churned into wavelets. If a man with good sight were to examine his own facial reflection in it, he would neither know nor see it as it really is. So too, brahmin, when one dwells with a mind obsessed by restlessness and remorse ... on that occasion even those hymns that have been recited over a long period do not recur to the mind, let alone those that have not been recited.

"Again, brahmin, when one dwells with a mind obsessed by doubt, overwhelmed by doubt, and one does not understand as it really is the escape from arisen doubt, on that occasion one neither knows nor sees as it really is one's own good, or the good of others, or the good of both. Then even those hymns that have been recited over a long period do not recur to the mind, let alone those that have not been recited.

"Suppose, brahmin, there is a bowl of water that is turbid, unsettled, muddy, placed in the dark. If a man with good sight were to examine his own facial reflection in it, he would neither know nor see it as it really is. [124] So too, brahmin, when one dwells with a mind obsessed by doubt ... on that occasion even those hymns that have been recited over a long period do not recur to the mind, let alone those that have not been recited.

"This, brahmin, is the cause and reason why even those hymns that have been recited over a long period do not recur to the mind, let alone those that have not been recited.

(ii. Why the hymns recur to the mind)

"Brahmin, when one dwells with a mind that is not obsessed by sensual lust, not overwhelmed by sensual lust, and one understands as it really is the escape from arisen sensual lust, on that occasion one knows and sees as it really is one's own good, and the good of others, and the good of both. Then even those hymns that have not been recited over a long period recur to the mind, let alone those that have been recited.

"Suppose, brahmin, there is a bowl of water not mixed with lac, turmeric, blue dye, or crimson dye. If a man with good sight were to examine his own facial reflection in it, he would know and see it as it really is. So too, brahmin, when one dwells with a mind that is not obsessed by sensual lust ... on that occasion even those hymns that have not been recited over a long period recur to the mind, let alone those that have been recited.

"Again, brahmin, when one dwells with a mind that is not

obsessed by ill will … on that occasion even those hymns that have not been recited over a long period recur to the mind, let alone those that have been recited.

"Suppose, brahmin, there is a bowl of water not heated over a fire, not bubbling, not boiling. If a man with good sight were to examine his own facial reflection in it, he would know and see it as it really is. [125] So too, brahmin, when one dwells with a mind that is not obsessed by ill will … on that occasion even those hymns that have not been recited over a long period recur to the mind, let alone those that have been recited.

"Again, brahmin, when one dwells with a mind that is not obsessed by sloth and torpor … on that occasion even those hymns that have not been recited over a long period recur to the mind, let alone those that have been recited.

"Suppose, brahmin, there is a bowl of water not covered over with water plants and algae. If a man with good sight were to examine his own facial reflection in it, he would know and see it as it really is. So too, brahmin, when one dwells with a mind that is not obsessed by sloth and torpor … on that occasion even those hymns that have not been recited over a long period recur to the mind, let alone those that have been recited.

"Again, brahmin, when one dwells with a mind that is not obsessed by restlessness and remorse … on that occasion even those hymns that have not been recited over a long period recur to the mind, let alone those that have been recited.

"Suppose, brahmin, there is a bowl of water not stirred by the wind, without ripples, without swirls, not churned into wavelets. If a man with good sight were to examine his own facial reflection in it, he would know and see it as it really is. So too, brahmin, when one dwells with a mind that is not obsessed by restlessness and remorse … on that occasion even those hymns that have not been recited over a long period recur to the mind, let alone those that have been recited.

"Again, brahmin, when one dwells with a mind that is not obsessed by doubt … on that occasion even those hymns that have not been recited over a long period recur to the mind, let alone those that have been recited.

"Suppose, brahmin, there is a bowl of water that is clear, serene, limpid, set out in the light. If a man with good sight were to examine his own facial reflection in it, he would know and see it as it really is. So too, brahmin, when one dwells with a mind that is not obsessed by doubt ... on that occasion even those hymns that have not been recited over a long period recur to the mind, let alone those that have been recited. [126]

"This, brahmin, is the cause and reason why even those hymns that have not been recited over a long period recur to the mind, let alone those that have been recited.

"These seven factors of enlightenment, brahmin, are nonobstructions, nonhindrances, noncorruptions of the mind; when developed and cultivated they lead to the realization of the fruit of true knowledge and liberation. What seven? The enlightenment factor of mindfulness is a nonobstruction ... The enlightenment factor of equanimity is a nonobstruction.... These seven factors of enlightenment are nonobstructions, nonhindrances, noncorruptions of the mind; when developed and cultivated they lead to the realization of the fruit of true knowledge and liberation."

When this was said, the brahmin Saṅgārava said to the Blessed One: "Magnificent, Master Gotama!... From today let Master Gotama remember me as a lay follower who has gone for refuge for life."

56 (6) Abhaya

Thus have I heard. On one occasion the Blessed One was dwelling at Rājagaha on Mount Vulture Peak. Then Prince Abhaya approached the Blessed One, paid homage to him, sat down to one side, and said to him:[114]

"Venerable sir, Pūraṇa Kassapa says: 'There is no cause or condition for lack of knowledge and vision; lack of knowledge and vision is without cause or condition. There is no cause or condition for knowledge and vision; knowledge and vision are without cause or condition.'[115] What does the Blessed One say about this?"

"There is, prince, a cause and condition for lack of knowledge and vision; lack of knowledge and vision is with cause and condition. [127] There is a cause and condition for knowledge and vision; knowledge and vision are with cause and condition."

(i. The cause for lack of knowledge and vision)

"But, venerable sir, what is the cause and condition for lack of knowledge and vision? How is it that lack of knowledge and vision is with cause and condition?"

"On an occasion, prince, when one dwells with a mind obsessed by sensual lust, overwhelmed by sensual lust, and one neither knows nor sees as it really is the escape from arisen sensual lust: this is a cause and condition for lack of knowledge and vision; it is in this way that lack of knowledge and vision is with cause and condition.

"Again, prince, on an occasion when one dwells with a mind obsessed by ill will ... obsessed by sloth and torpor ... obsessed by restlessness and remorse ... obsessed by doubt, overwhelmed by doubt, and one neither knows nor sees as it really is the escape from arisen doubt: this too is a cause and condition for lack of knowledge and vision; it is in this way too that lack of knowledge and vision is with cause and condition."

"What is this Dhamma exposition called, venerable sir?"

"These are called the hindrances, prince."

"Surely they are hindrances, Blessed One! Surely they are hindrances, Fortunate One! One overcome by even a single hindrance would not know and see things as they really are, not to speak of one overcome by the five hindrances.

(ii. The cause of knowledge and vision)

"But, venerable sir, what is the cause and condition for knowledge and vision? How is it that knowledge and vision are with cause and condition?" [128]

"Here, prince, a bhikkhu develops the enlightenment factor of mindfulness, which is based upon seclusion, dispassion, and cessation, maturing in release. With a mind that has developed the enlightenment factor of mindfulness he knows and sees things as they really are. This is a cause for knowledge and vision; it is in this way that knowledge and vision are with cause and condition....

"Again, prince, a bhikkhu develops the enlightenment factor of equanimity, which is based upon seclusion, dispassion, and cessation, maturing in release. With a mind that has developed the enlightenment factor of equanimity he knows and sees things as they really are. This too is a cause for knowledge and vision;

it is in this way that knowledge and vision are with cause and condition."

"What is this Dhamma exposition called, venerable sir?"

"These are called the factors of enlightenment, prince."

"Surely they are factors of enlightenment, Blessed One! Surely they are factors of enlightenment, Fortunate One! One who possesses even a single factor of enlightenment would know and see things as they really are, not to speak of one who possesses the seven factors of enlightenment. The bodily fatigue and the mental fatigue that I experienced from climbing Mount Vulture Peak have subsided. I have made the breakthrough to the Dhamma."[116]

[129] VII. In-and-Out Breathing

57 (1) The Skeleton

(i. Of great fruit)

At Sāvatthī. "Bhikkhus, when the perception of a skeleton is developed and cultivated, it is of great fruit and benefit.[117]

"And how, bhikkhus, is the perception of a skeleton developed and cultivated so that it is of great fruit and benefit? Here, bhikkhus, a bhikkhu develops the enlightenment factor of mindfulness accompanied by the perception of a skeleton ... he develops the enlightenment factor of equanimity accompanied by the perception of a skeleton, based upon seclusion, dispassion, and cessation, maturing in release. It is in this way that the perception of a skeleton is developed and cultivated so that it is of great fruit and benefit."

(ii. One of two fruits)

"Bhikkhus, when the perception of a skeleton is developed and cultivated, one of two fruits is to be expected: either final knowledge in this very life or, if there is a residue of clinging,[118] the state of nonreturning.

"And how, bhikkhus, is the perception of a skeleton developed and cultivated so that one of two fruits is to be expected: either final knowledge in this very life or, if there is a residue of clinging, the state of nonreturning? Here, bhikkhus, a bhikkhu develops the enlightenment factor of mindfulness accompanied by the perception of a skeleton ... he develops the enlightenment factor of equanimity accompanied by the perception of a skeleton, based upon seclusion, dispassion, and cessation, maturing in release. It is in this way that the perception of a skeleton is developed and cultivated so that one of two fruits is to be expected: either final knowledge in this very life or, if there is a residue of clinging, the state of nonreturning." [130]

(iii. Great good)

"Bhikkhus, when the perception of a skeleton is developed and cultivated, it leads to great good.

"And how, bhikkhus, is the perception of a skeleton developed and cultivated so that it leads to great good? Here, bhikkhus, a bhikkhu develops the enlightenment factor of mindfulness accompanied by the perception of a skeleton ... he develops the enlightenment factor of equanimity accompanied by the perception of a skeleton, based upon seclusion, dispassion, and cessation, maturing in release. It is in this way that the perception of a skeleton is developed and cultivated so that it leads to great good."

(iv. Security from bondage)

"Bhikkhus, when the perception of a skeleton is developed and cultivated, it leads to great security from bondage.

"And how, bhikkhus, is the perception of a skeleton developed and cultivated so that it leads to great security from bondage?..." (*All as above.*)

(v. Sense of urgency)

"Bhikkhus, when the perception of a skeleton is developed and cultivated, it leads to a great sense of urgency.

"And how, bhikkhus, is the perception of a skeleton developed and cultivated so that it leads to a great sense of urgency?..." (*All as above.*) [131]

(vi. Dwelling in comfort)

"Bhikkhus, when the perception of a skeleton is developed and cultivated, it leads to dwelling in great comfort.

"And how, bhikkhus, is the perception of a skeleton developed and cultivated so that it leads to dwelling in great comfort?..." (*All as above.*)

(Each of the following suttas, §§58–76, is to be elaborated in accordance with the sixfold method of §57.)

58 (2) The Worm-Infested

"Bhikkhus, when the perception of a worm-infested corpse is developed ..."

59 (3) The Livid

"Bhikkhus, when the perception of a livid corpse is developed ..."

60 (4) The Fissured

"Bhikkhus, when the perception of a fissured corpse is developed ..."

61 (5) The Bloated

"Bhikkhus, when the perception of a bloated corpse is developed ..."

62 (6) Lovingkindness

"Bhikkhus, when lovingkindness is developed ..."

63 (7) Compassion

"Bhikkhus, when compassion is developed ..."

64 (8) Altruistic Joy

"Bhikkhus, when altruistic joy is developed ..."

65 (9) Equanimity

"Bhikkhus, when equanimity is developed ..." [132]

66 (10) Breathing

"Bhikkhus, when mindfulness of breathing is developed ..."

VIII. Cessation[119]

67 (1) Foulness

"Bhikkhus, when the perception of foulness ..."

68 (2) Death

"Bhikkhus, when the perception of death ..."

69 (3) Repulsiveness of Food

"Bhikkhus, when the perception of the repulsiveness of food ..."

70 (4) Nondelight

"Bhikkhus, when the perception of nondelight in the entire world ..."

71 (5) Impermanence

"Bhikkhus, when the perception of impermanence ..."

72 (6) Suffering

"Bhikkhus, when the perception of suffering in the impermanent ..." [133]

73 (7) Nonself

"Bhikkhus, when the perception of nonself in what is suffering ..."

74 (8) Abandonment

"Bhikkhus, when the perception of abandonment ..."

75 (9) Dispassion

"Bhikkhus, when the perception of dispassion ..."

76 (10) Cessation

(i. Of great fruit)

"Bhikkhus, when the perception of cessation is developed and cultivated, it is of great fruit and benefit.

"And how, bhikkhus, is the perception of cessation developed and cultivated so that it is of great fruit and benefit? Here, bhikkhus, a bhikkhu develops the enlightenment factor of mindfulness accompanied by the perception of cessation ... he develops the enlightenment factor of equanimity accompanied by the perception of cessation, based upon seclusion, dispassion, and cessation, maturing in release. It is in this way that the perception of cessation is developed and cultivated so that it is of great fruit and benefit."

(ii. One of two fruits)

"Bhikkhus, when the perception of cessation is developed and cultivated, one of two fruits is to be expected: either final knowledge in this very life or, if there is a residue of clinging, the state of nonreturning.

"And how, bhikkhus, is the perception of cessation developed...?"

(iii–vi. Great good, etc.)

"Bhikkhus, when the perception of cessation is developed and cultivated, it leads to great good ... to great security from bondage ... to a great sense of urgency ... to dwelling in great comfort. [134]

"And how does it do so? Here, bhikkhus, a bhikkhu develops the enlightenment factor of mindfulness accompanied by the perception of cessation ... he develops the enlightenment factor of equanimity accompanied by the perception of cessation, based upon seclusion, dispassion, and cessation, maturing in release. It is in this way that the perception of cessation is developed and cultivated so that it leads to great good ... to great security from bondage ... to a great sense of urgency ... to dwelling in great comfort."

IX. Ganges Repetition Series

77 (1)–88 (12) The River Ganges—Eastward, Etc.

"Bhikkhus, just as the river Ganges slants, slopes, and inclines towards the east, so too a bhikkhu who develops and cultivates the seven factors of enlightenment slants, slopes, and inclines towards Nibbāna.

"And how, bhikkhus, does a bhikkhu develop and cultivate the seven factors of enlightenment so that he slants, slopes, and inclines towards Nibbāna? Here, bhikkhus, a bhikkhu develops the enlightenment factor of mindfulness ... he develops the enlightenment factor of equanimity, which is based upon seclusion, dispassion, and cessation, maturing in release. It is in this way, bhikkhus, that a bhikkhu develops and cultivates the seven factors of enlightenment so that he slants, slopes, and inclines towards Nibbāna."

(*The remaining suttas of this vagga are to be similarly elaborated parallel to 45:92–102.*) [135]

Six about slanting to the east
And six about slanting to the ocean.
These two sixes make up twelve:
Thus the subchapter is recited.

X. Diligence

89 (1)–98 (10) The Tathāgata, Etc.

"Bhikkhus, whatever beings there are—whether those without feet or those with two feet or those with four feet or those with many feet—..."

(*To be elaborated by way of the factors of enlightenment parallel to 45:139–48.*)

Tathāgata, footprint, roof peak,
Roots, heartwood, jasmine,
Monarch, the moon and sun,
Together with the cloth as tenth.

XI. Strenuous Deeds

99 (1)–110 (12) Strenuous, Etc.[120]

"Bhikkhus, just as whatever strenuous deeds are done ..."
(*To be elaborated parallel to 45:149–60.*) [136]

Strenuous, seeds, and nāgas,
The tree, the pot, the spike,
The sky, and two on clouds,
The ship, guest house, and river.

XII. Searches

111 (1)–120 (10) Searches, Etc.

"Bhikkhus, there are these three searches. What three? The search for sensual pleasures, the search for existence, the search for a holy life...."
(*To be elaborated parallel to 45:161–70.*)

Searches, discriminations, taints,
Kinds of existence, threefold suffering,
Barrenness, stains, and troubles,
Feelings, craving, and thirst.

XIII. Floods

121 (1)–129 (9) Floods, Etc.

"Bhikkhus, there are these four floods. What four? The flood of sensuality, the flood of existence, the flood of views, the flood of ignorance...."
(*To be elaborated parallel to 45:171–79.*)

130 (10) Higher Fetters

"Bhikkhus, there are these five higher fetters. What five? Lust for form, lust for the formless, conceit, restlessness, [137] ignorance. These are the five higher fetters. The seven factors of enlightenment are to be developed for direct knowledge of these five higher fetters, for the full understanding of them, for their utter destruction, for their abandoning.

"What seven? Here, bhikkhus, a bhikkhu develops the enlightenment factor of mindfulness ... he develops the enlightenment factor of equanimity, which is based upon seclusion, dispassion, and cessation, maturing in release. These seven factors of enlightenment are to be developed for direct knowledge of these five higher fetters, for the full understanding of them, for their utter destruction, for their abandoning."

Floods, bonds, kinds of clinging,
Knots, and underlying tendencies,
Cords of sensual pleasure, hindrances,
Aggregates, fetters lower and higher.

XIV. Ganges Repetition Series (Removal of Lust Version)

131 (1) The River Ganges—Eastward

"Bhikkhus, just as the river Ganges slants ... towards the east, so too a bhikkhu ... inclines towards Nibbāna.

"And how does he do so? Here, bhikkhus, a bhikkhu develops the enlightenment factor of mindfulness ... he develops the enlightenment factor of equanimity, which has as its final goal the removal of lust, the removal of hatred, the removal of delusion. It is in this way that a bhikkhu ... inclines towards Nibbāna." [138]

132 (2)–142 (12) Slanting to the East, Etc.

(To be elaborated by way of the enlightenment factors having as their final goal the removal of lust, etc.)

Six about slanting to the east
And six about slanting to the ocean.
These two sixes make up twelve:
Thus the subchapter is recited.

XV. Diligence
(Removal of Lust Version)

143 (1)–152 (10) The Tathāgata, Etc.

(To be elaborated by way of the enlightenment factors having as their final goal the removal of lust, etc.)

Tathāgata, footprint, roof peak,
Roots, heartwood, jasmine,
Monarch, the moon and sun,
Together with the cloth as tenth.

XVI. Strenuous Deeds
(Removal of Lust Version)

153 (1)–164 (12) Strenuous, Etc.

(To be elaborated by way of the enlightenment factors having as their final goal the removal of lust, etc.)

Strenuous, seeds, and nāgas,
The tree, the pot, the spike,
The sky, and two on clouds,
The ship, guest house, and river.

[139]

XVII. Searches
(Removal of Lust Version)

165 (1)–174 (10) Searches, Etc.

(To be elaborated by way of the enlightenment factors having as their final goal the removal of lust, etc.)

Searches, discriminations, taints,
Kinds of existence, threefold suffering,
Barrenness, stains, and troubles,
Feelings, craving, and thirst.

XVIII. Floods
(Removal of Lust Version)

175 (1)–183 (9) Floods, Etc.

(To be elaborated by way of the enlightenment factors having as their final goal the removal of lust, etc.)

184 (10) Higher Fetters

"Bhikkhus, there are these five higher fetters. What five? Lust for form, lust for the formless, conceit, restlessness, ignorance. These are the five higher fetters. The seven factors of enlightenment are to be developed for direct knowledge of these five higher fetters, for the full understanding of them, for their utter destruction, for their abandoning.

"What seven? Here, bhikkhus, a bhikkhu develops the enlightenment factor of mindfulness ... he develops the enlightenment factor of equanimity, which has as its final goal the removal of lust, the removal of hatred, the removal of delusion ... which has the Deathless as its ground, the Deathless as its destination, the Deathless as its final goal ... which slants, slopes, and inclines towards Nibbāna. These seven factors of enlightenment, bhikkhus, are to be developed for direct knowledge of these five higher fetters, for the full understanding of them, for their utter destruction, for their abandoning."[121] [140]

Floods, bonds, kinds of clinging,
Knots, and underlying tendencies,
Cords of sensual pleasure, hindrances,
Aggregates, fetters lower and higher.

[141] Chapter III

47 *Satipaṭṭhānasaṃyutta*
Connected Discourses on the Establishments of Mindfulness

I. Ambapālī

1 (1) Ambapālī

Thus have I heard. On one occasion the Blessed One was dwelling at Vesālī in Ambapālī's Grove. There the Blessed One addressed the bhikkhus thus: "Bhikkhus!"[122]

"Venerable sir!" the bhikkhus replied. The Blessed One said this:

"Bhikkhus, this is the one-way path for the purification of beings, for the overcoming of sorrow and lamentation, for the passing away of pain and displeasure, for the achievement of the method, for the realization of Nibbāna, that is, the four establishments of mindfulness.[123] What four?

"Here, bhikkhus, a bhikkhu dwells contemplating the body in the body, ardent, clearly comprehending, mindful, having removed covetousness and displeasure in regard to the world.[124] He dwells contemplating feelings in feelings, ardent, clearly comprehending, mindful, having removed covetousness and displeasure in regard to the world. He dwells contemplating mind in mind, ardent, clearly comprehending, mindful, having removed covetousness and displeasure in regard to the world. He dwells contemplating phenomena in phenomena, ardent, clearly comprehending, mindful, having removed covetousness and displeasure in regard to the world.

"This, bhikkhus, is the one-way path for the purification of beings, for the overcoming of sorrow and lamentation, for the passing away of pain and displeasure, for the achievement of the method, for the realization of Nibbāna, that is, the four establishments of mindfulness."

This is what the Blessed One said. Elated, those bhikkhus delighted in the Blessed One's statement. [142]

2 (2) Mindful

On one occasion the Blessed One was dwelling at Vesālī in Ambapālī's Grove. There the Blessed One addressed the bhikkhus thus: "Bhikkhus!"

"Venerable sir!" the bhikkhus replied. The Blessed One said this:

"Bhikkhus, a bhikkhu should dwell mindful and clearly comprehending: this is our instruction to you.[125]

"And how, bhikkhus, is a bhikkhu mindful? Here, bhikkhus, a bhikkhu dwells contemplating the body in the body, ardent, clearly comprehending, mindful, having removed covetousness and displeasure in regard to the world. He dwells contemplating feelings in feelings ... mind in mind ... phenomena in phenomena, ardent, clearly comprehending, mindful, having removed covetousness and displeasure in regard to the world. It is in this way, bhikkhus, that a bhikkhu is mindful.

"And how, bhikkhus, does a bhikkhu exercise clear comprehension? Here, bhikkhus, a bhikkhu is one who acts with clear comprehension when going forward and returning; when looking ahead and looking aside; when drawing in and extending the limbs; when wearing his robes and carrying his outer robe and bowl; when eating, drinking, chewing his food, and tasting; when defecating and urinating; when walking, standing, sitting, falling asleep, waking up, speaking, and keeping silent. It is in such a way that a bhikkhu exercises clear comprehension.

"Bhikkhus, a bhikkhu should dwell mindful and clearly comprehending. This is our instruction to you."

3 (3) A Bhikkhu

On one occasion the Blessed One was dwelling at Sāvatthī in Jeta's Grove, Anāthapiṇḍika's Park. Then a certain bhikkhu approached the Blessed One, paid homage to him, sat down to one side, and said to him:

"Venerable sir, it would be good if the Blessed One would teach me the Dhamma in brief, so that, having heard the Dhamma from the Blessed One, [143] I might dwell alone, withdrawn, diligent, ardent, and resolute."

"It is in just such a way that some foolish persons here make requests of me, but when the Dhamma has been spoken to them, they think only of following me around."[126]

"Let the Blessed One teach me the Dhamma in brief! Let the Fortunate One teach me the Dhamma in brief! Perhaps I may understand the meaning of the Blessed One's statement; perhaps I may become an heir of the Blessed One's statement."

"Well then, bhikkhu, purify the very starting point of wholesome states. And what is the starting point of wholesome states? Virtue that is well purified and view that is straight.[127] Then, bhikkhu, when your virtue is well purified and your view straight, based upon virtue, established upon virtue, you should develop the four establishments of mindfulness in a threefold way.

"What four? Here, bhikkhu, dwell contemplating the body in the body internally, ardent, clearly comprehending, mindful, having removed covetousness and displeasure in regard to the world. Dwell contemplating the body in the body externally, ardent, clearly comprehending, mindful, having removed covetousness and displeasure in regard to the world. Dwell contemplating the body in the body internally and externally, ardent, clearly comprehending, mindful, having removed covetousness and displeasure in regard to the world.[128]

"Dwell contemplating feelings in feelings internally ... externally ... internally and externally, ardent, clearly comprehending, mindful, having removed covetousness and displeasure in regard to the world. Dwell contemplating mind in mind internally ... externally ... internally and externally, ardent, clearly comprehending, mindful, having removed covetousness and displeasure in regard to the world. Dwell contemplating phenomena in phenomena, internally ... externally ... internally and externally, ardent, clearly comprehending, mindful, having removed covetousness and displeasure in regard to the world.

"When, bhikkhu, based upon virtue, established upon virtue, you develop these four establishments of mindfulness thus in a threefold way, then, whether night or day comes, you may expect only growth in wholesome states, not decline."

Then that bhikkhu, having delighted and rejoiced in the Blessed One's statement, [144] rose from his seat and, after paying homage to the Blessed One, he departed keeping him on his right.

Then, dwelling alone, withdrawn, diligent, ardent, and resolute, that bhikkhu, by realizing it for himself with direct knowledge, in this very life entered and dwelt in that unsurpassed goal of the holy life for the sake of which clansmen rightly go forth from the household life into homelessness. He directly knew: "Destroyed is birth, the holy life has been lived, what had to be done has been done, there is no more for this state of being." And that bhikkhu became one of the arahants.

4 (4) At Sālā

On one occasion the Blessed One was dwelling among the Kosalans at the brahmin village of Sālā. There the Blessed One addressed the bhikkhus thus:

"Bhikkhus, those bhikkhus who are newly ordained, not long gone forth, recently come to this Dhamma and Discipline, should be exhorted, settled, and established by you in the development of the four establishments of mindfulness. What four?

"'Come, friends, dwell contemplating the body in the body, ardent, clearly comprehending, unified, with limpid mind, concentrated, with one-pointed mind, in order to know the body as it really is. Dwell contemplating feelings in feelings ... in order to know feelings as they really are. Dwell contemplating mind in mind ... in order to know mind as it really is. Dwell contemplating phenomena in phenomena ... in order to know phenomena as they really are.' [145]

"Bhikkhus, those bhikkhus who are trainees, who have not attained their mind's ideal, who dwell aspiring for the unsurpassed security from bondage: they too dwell contemplating the body in the body, ardent, clearly comprehending, unified, with limpid mind, concentrated, with one-pointed mind, in order to fully understand the body as it really is. They too dwell contemplating feelings in feelings ... in order to fully understand feelings as they really are. They too dwell contemplating mind in mind ... in order to fully understand mind as it really is. They too dwell contemplating phenomena in phenomena ... in order to fully understand phenomena as they really are.

"Bhikkhus, those bhikkhus who are arahants, whose taints are destroyed, who have lived the holy life, done what had to be done, laid down the burden, reached their own goal, utterly destroyed the fetters of existence, and are completely liberated through final knowledge: they too dwell contemplating the body in the body, ardent, clearly comprehending, unified, with limpid mind, concentrated, with one-pointed mind, detached from the body. They too dwell contemplating feelings in feelings ... detached from feelings. They too dwell contemplating mind in mind ... detached from mind. They too dwell contemplating phenomena in phenomena ... detached from phenomena.

"Bhikkhus, those bhikkhus who are newly ordained, not long gone forth, recently come to this Dhamma and Discipline, should be exhorted, settled, and established by you in the development of these four establishments of mindfulness."

5 (5) A Heap of the Wholesome

At Sāvatthī. There the Blessed One said this: "Bhikkhus, if one were to say of anything 'a heap of the unwholesome,' it is about the five hindrances that one could rightly say this. For this is a complete heap of the unwholesome, that is, the five hindrances. What five? [146] The hindrance of sensual desire, the hindrance of ill will, the hindrance of sloth and torpor, the hindrance of restlessness and remorse, the hindrance of doubt. If one were to say of anything 'a heap of the unwholesome,' it is about these five hindrances that one could rightly say this. For this is a complete heap of the unwholesome, that is, the five hindrances.

"If, bhikkhus, one were to say of anything 'a heap of the wholesome,' it is about the four establishments of mindfulness that one could rightly say this. For this is a complete heap of the wholesome, that is, the four establishments of mindfulness. What four? Here, bhikkhus, a bhikkhu dwells contemplating the body in the body, ardent, clearly comprehending, mindful, having removed covetousness and displeasure in regard to the world. He dwells contemplating feelings in feelings ... mind in mind ... phenomena in phenomena, ardent, clearly comprehending, mindful, having removed covetousness and displeasure in regard to the world.[129] If one were to say of anything 'a heap of the wholesome,' it is about these four establishments of mindfulness that one could rightly say this. For this is a complete heap of the wholesome, that is, the four establishments of mindfulness."

6 (6) The Hawk

"Bhikkhus, once in the past a hawk suddenly swooped down and seized a quail.[130] Then, while the quail was being carried off by the hawk, he lamented: 'We were so unlucky, of so little merit! We strayed out of our own resort into the domain of others. If we had stayed in our own resort today, in our own ancestral domain, this hawk wouldn't have stood a chance against me in a fight.' – 'But what is your own resort, quail, what is your own ancestral domain?' – 'The freshly ploughed field covered with clods of soil.' [147]

"Then the hawk, confident of her own strength, not boasting of her own strength,[131] released the quail, saying: 'Go now, quail, but even there you won't escape me.'

"Then, bhikkhus, the quail went to a freshly ploughed field covered with clods of soil. Having climbed up on a large clod, he stood there and addressed the hawk: 'Come get me now, hawk! Come get me now, hawk!'

"Then the hawk, confident of her own strength, not boasting of her own strength, folded up both her wings and suddenly swooped down on the quail. But when the quail knew, 'That hawk has come close,' he slipped inside that clod, and the hawk shattered her breast right on the spot. So it is, bhikkhus, when one strays outside one's own resort into the domain of others.

"Therefore, bhikkhus, do not stray outside your own resort into the domain of others. Māra will gain access to those who stray outside their own resort into the domain of others; Māra will get a hold on them.[132] [148]

"And what is not a bhikkhu's own resort but the domain of others? It is the five cords of sensual pleasure. What five? Forms cognizable by the eye that are desirable, lovely, agreeable, pleasing, sensually enticing, tantalizing. Sounds cognizable by the ear ... Odours cognizable by the nose ... Tastes cognizable by the tongue ... Tactile objects cognizable by the body that are desirable, lovely, agreeable, pleasing, sensually enticing, tantalizing. These are the five cords of sensual pleasure. This is what is not a bhikkhu's own resort but the domain of others.

"Move in your own resort, bhikkhus, in your own ancestral domain. Māra will not gain access to those who move in their own resort, in their own ancestral domain; Māra will not get a hold on them.

"And what is a bhikkhu's resort, his own ancestral domain? It is the four establishments of mindfulness. What four? Here, bhikkhus, a bhikkhu dwells contemplating the body in the body, ardent, clearly comprehending, mindful, having removed covetousness and displeasure in regard to the world. He dwells contemplating feelings in feelings ... mind in mind ... phenomena in phenomena, ardent, clearly comprehending, mindful, having removed covetousness and displeasure in regard to the world. This is a bhikkhu's resort, his own ancestral domain."

7 (7) The Monkey

"Bhikkhus, in the Himalayas, the king of mountains, there are rugged and uneven zones where neither monkeys nor human beings can go; there are rugged and uneven zones where monkeys can go but not human beings; there are even and delightful regions where both monkeys and human beings can go. There, along the monkey trails, hunters set out traps of pitch for catching monkeys.

"Those monkeys who are not foolish and frivolous, when they see the pitch, avoid it from afar. But a monkey who is foolish and frivolous approaches the pitch and seizes it with his hand; he gets caught there. Thinking, 'I will free my hand,' he seizes it with his other hand; he gets caught there. Thinking, 'I will free both hands,' he seizes it with his foot; he gets caught there. Thinking, 'I will free both hands and my foot,' he seizes it with his other foot; he gets caught there.' Thinking, 'I will free both hands and feet,' he applies his muzzle to it; he gets caught there.

"Thus, bhikkhus, that monkey, trapped at five points, lies there screeching. He has met with calamity and disaster and the hunter can do with him as he wishes. [149] The hunter spears him, fastens him to that same block of wood,[133] and goes off where he wants. So it is, bhikkhus, when one strays outside one's own resort into the domain of others.

"Therefore, bhikkhus, do not stray outside your own resort into the domain of others. Māra will gain access to those who stray outside their own resort into the domain of others; Māra will get a hold on them.

"And what is not a bhikkhu's own resort but the domain of others? It is the five cords of sensual pleasure.... (*as above*) ... This is what is not a bhikkhu's own resort but the domain of others.

"Move in your own resort, bhikkhus, in your own ancestral domain. Māra will not gain access to those who move in their own resort, in their own ancestral domain; Māra will not get a hold on them.

"And what is a bhikkhu's resort, his own ancestral domain? It is the four establishments of mindfulness. What four? Here, bhikkhus, a bhikkhu dwells contemplating the body in the body, ardent, clearly comprehending, mindful, having removed covetousness and displeasure in regard to the world. He dwells contemplating feelings in feelings ... mind in mind ... phenomena in phenomena, ardent, clearly comprehending, mindful, having removed covetousness and displeasure in regard to the world. This is a bhikkhu's resort, his own ancestral domain."

8 (8) The Cook

(i. The incompetent cook)

"Bhikkhus, suppose a foolish, incompetent, unskilful cook were to present a king or a royal minister with various kinds of curries: sour, bitter, pungent, sweet, sharp, mild, salty, bland. [150]

"That foolish, incompetent, unskilful cook does not pick up the sign of his own master's preference:[134] 'Today this curry pleased my master, or he reached for this one, or he took a lot of this one, or he spoke in praise of this one; or the sour curry pleased my master today, or he reached for the sour one, or he took a lot of the sour one, or he spoke in praise of the sour one; or the bitter curry ... or the pungent curry ... or the sweet curry ... or the sharp curry ... or the mild curry ... or the salty curry ... or the bland curry pleased my master ... or he spoke in praise of the bland one.'

"That foolish, incompetent, unskilful cook does not gain [gifts of] clothing, wages, and bonuses. For what reason? Because that foolish, incompetent, unskilful cook does not pick up the sign of his own master's preference.

"So too, bhikkhus, here some foolish, incompetent, unskilful bhikkhu dwells contemplating the body in the body, ardent, clearly comprehending, mindful, having removed covetousness and displeasure in regard to the world. While he dwells contemplating the body in the body, his mind does not become concentrated, his corruptions are not abandoned, he does not pick up that sign.[135] He dwells contemplating feelings in feelings ... mind in mind ... phenomena in phenomena, ardent, clearly comprehending, mindful, having removed covetousness and displeasure in regard to the world. While he dwells contemplating phenomena in phenomena, his mind does not become concentrated, his corruptions are not abandoned, he does not pick up that sign.

"That foolish, incompetent, unskilful bhikkhu does not gain pleasant dwellings in this very life, nor does he gain [151] mindfulness and clear comprehension. For what reason? Because, bhikkhus, that foolish, incompetent, unskilful bhikkhu does not pick up the sign of his own mind.

(ii. The competent cook)

"Suppose, bhikkhus, a wise, competent, skilful cook were to present a king or a royal minister with various kinds of curries: sour, bitter, pungent, sweet, sharp, mild, salty, bland.[136]

"That wise, competent, skilful cook picks up the sign of his own master's preference: 'Today this curry pleased my master ... or he spoke in praise of the bland one.'

"That wise, competent, skilful cook gains [gifts of] clothing, wages, and bonuses. For what reason? Because that wise, competent, skilful cook picks up the sign of his own master's preference.

"So too, bhikkhus, here some wise, competent, skilful bhikkhu dwells contemplating the body in the body, ardent, clearly comprehending, mindful, having removed covetousness and displeasure in regard to the world. While he dwells contemplating the body in the body, his mind becomes concentrated, his corruptions [152] are abandoned, he picks up that sign. He dwells contemplating feelings in feelings ... mind in mind ... phenomena in phenomena, ardent, clearly comprehending, mindful, having removed covetousness and displeasure in regard to the world. While he dwells contemplating phenomena in phenomena, his mind becomes concentrated, his corruptions are abandoned, he picks up that sign.

"That wise, competent, skilful bhikkhu gains pleasant dwellings in this very life, and he gains mindfulness and clear comprehension. For what reason? Because, bhikkhus, that wise, competent, skilful bhikkhu picks up the sign of his own mind."

9 (9) Ill

Thus have I heard.[137] On one occasion the Blessed One was dwelling at Vesālī in Beluvagāmaka. There the Blessed One addressed the bhikkhus thus:

"Come, bhikkhus, enter upon the rains wherever you have friends, acquaintances, and intimates in the vicinity of Vesālī. I myself will enter upon the rains right here in Beluvagāmaka."

"Yes, venerable sir," those bhikkhus replied, and they entered upon the rains wherever they had friends, acquaintances, and intimates in the vicinity of Vesālī, while the Blessed One entered upon the rains right there in Beluvagāmaka.

Then, when the Blessed One had entered upon the rains, a severe illness arose in him and terrible pains bordering on death assailed him. But the Blessed One endured them, mindful and clearly comprehending, without becoming distressed. Then the thought occurred to the Blessed One: "It is not proper for me to attain final Nibbāna without having addressed my attendants and taken leave of the Bhikkhu Saṅgha. Let me then suppress this illness by means of energy and live on, having resolved upon the life formation."[138] [153] Then the Blessed One suppressed that illness by means of energy and lived on, having resolved upon the life formation.

The Blessed One then recovered from that illness. Soon after he had recovered, he came out from his dwelling and sat down in the seat that had been prepared in the shade behind the dwelling. The Venerable Ānanda then approached the Blessed One, paid homage to him, sat down to one side, and said to him: "It's splendid, venerable sir, that the Blessed One is bearing up, splendid that he has recovered![139] But, venerable sir, when the Blessed One was ill my body seemed as if it were drugged, I had become disoriented, the teachings were not clear to me. Nevertheless, I had this much consolation: that the Blessed One would not attain final Nibbāna without having made some pronouncement concerning the Bhikkhu Saṅgha."

"What does the Bhikkhu Saṅgha now expect from me, Ānanda? I have taught the Dhamma, Ānanda, without making a distinction between inside and outside.[140] The Tathāgata has no closed fist of a teacher in regard to the teachings. If, Ānanda, anyone thinks, 'I will take charge of the Bhikkhu Saṅgha,' or 'The Bhikkhu Saṅgha is under my direction,' it is he who should make some pronouncement concerning the Bhikkhu Saṅgha. But, Ānanda, it does not occur to the Tathāgata, 'I will take charge of the Bhikkhu Saṅgha,' or 'The Bhikkhu Saṅgha is under my direction,' so why should the Tathāgata make some pronouncement concerning the Bhikkhu Saṅgha? Now I am old, Ānanda, aged, burdened with years, advanced in life, come to the last stage. My age is now turning eighty. Just as an old cart keeps going by a combination of straps,[141] so it seems the body of the Tathāgata keeps going by a combination of straps. [154]

"Whenever, Ānanda, by nonattention to all signs and by the cessation of certain feelings, the Tathāgata enters and dwells in the signless concentration of mind, on that occasion, Ānanda, the body of the Tathāgata is more comfortable.[142] Therefore, Ānanda, dwell with yourselves as your own island, with yourselves as your own refuge, with no other refuge; dwell with the Dhamma as your island, with the Dhamma as your refuge, with no other refuge. And how, Ānanda, does a bhikkhu dwell with himself as his own island, with himself as his own refuge, with no other refuge; with the Dhamma as his island, with the Dhamma as his refuge, with no other refuge? Here, Ānanda, a bhikkhu dwells contemplating the body in the body, ardent, clearly comprehending, mindful, having removed covetousness and displeasure in regard to the world. He dwells contemplating feelings in feelings … mind in mind … phenomena in phenomena, ardent, clearly comprehending, mindful, having removed covetousness and displeasure in regard to the world.

"Those bhikkhus, Ānanda, either now or after I am gone, who dwell with themselves as their own island, with themselves as their own refuge, with no other refuge; with the Dhamma as their island, with the Dhamma as their refuge, with no other refuge—it is these bhikkhus, Ānanda, who will be for me topmost of those keen on the training."[143]

10 (10) The Bhikkhunīs' Quarter

Then in the morning the Venerable Ānanda dressed and, taking bowl and robe, he approached the bhikkhunīs' quarters and sat down in the appointed seat. Then a number of bhikkhunīs approached the Venerable Ānanda, paid homage to him, sat down to one side, and said to him:

"Here, Venerable Ānanda, a number of bhikkhunīs, dwelling with their minds well established in the four establishments of mindfulness, perceive successively loftier stages of distinction."[144] [155]

"So it is, sisters, so it is! It may be expected of anyone, sisters—whether bhikkhu or bhikkhunī—who dwells with a mind well established in the four establishments of mindfulness, that such a one will perceive successively loftier stages of distinction."

Then the Venerable Ānanda instructed, exhorted, inspired, and gladdened those bhikkhunīs with a Dhamma talk, after which he rose from his seat and left. Then the Venerable Ānanda walked for alms in Sāvatthī. When he had returned from the alms round, after his meal he approached the Blessed One, paid homage to him, sat down to one side, and reported all that had happened. [The Blessed One said:]

"So it is, Ānanda, so it is! It may be expected of anyone, Ānanda—whether bhikkhu or bhikkhunī—who dwells with a mind well established in the four establishments of mindfulness, that such a one will perceive successively loftier stages of distinction.

"What four? Here, Ānanda, a bhikkhu dwells contemplating the body in the body, ardent, clearly comprehending, mindful, having removed covetousness and displeasure in regard to the world. [156] While he is contemplating the body in the body, there arises in him, based on the body, either a fever in the body or sluggishness of mind, or the mind is distracted outwardly. That bhikkhu should then direct his mind towards some inspiring sign.[145] When he directs his mind towards some inspiring sign, gladness is born. When he is gladdened, rapture is born. When the mind is uplifted by rapture, the body becomes tranquil. One tranquil in body experiences happiness. The mind of one who is happy becomes concentrated. He reflects thus: 'The purpose for the sake of which I directed my mind has been achieved. Let me now withdraw it.'[146] So he withdraws the mind and does not think or examine. He understands: 'Without thought and examination, internally mindful, I am happy.'[147]

"Again, a bhikkhu dwells contemplating feelings in feelings ... mind in mind ... phenomena in phenomena, ardent, clearly comprehending, mindful, having removed covetousness and displeasure in regard to the world. While he is contemplating phenomena in phenomena, there arises in him, based on phenomena, either a fever in the body or sluggishness of mind, or the mind is distracted outwardly. That bhikkhu should then direct his mind towards some inspiring sign. When he directs his mind towards some inspiring sign ... He understands: 'Without thought and examination, internally mindful, I am happy.'

"It is in such a way, Ānanda, that there is development by direction.[148] [157]

"And how, Ānanda, is there development without direction? Not directing his mind outwardly, a bhikkhu understands: 'My mind is not directed outwardly.' Then he understands: 'It is unconstricted after and before, liberated, undirected.'[149] Then he further understands: 'I dwell contemplating the body in the body, ardent, clearly comprehending, mindful; I am happy.'

"Not directing his mind outwardly, a bhikkhu understands: 'My mind is not directed outwardly.' Then he understands: 'It is unconstricted after and before, liberated, undirected.' Then he further understands: 'I dwell contemplating feelings in feelings, ardent, clearly comprehending, mindful; I am happy.'

"Not directing his mind outwardly, a bhikkhu understands: 'My mind is not directed outwardly.' Then he understands: 'It is unconstricted after and before, liberated, undirected.' Then he further understands: 'I dwell contemplating mind in mind, ardent, clearly comprehending, mindful; I am happy.'

"Not directing his mind outwardly, a bhikkhu understands: 'My mind is not directed outwardly.' Then he understands: 'It is unconstricted after and before, liberated, undirected.' Then he further understands: 'I dwell contemplating phenomena in phenomena, ardent, clearly comprehending, mindful; I am happy.'

"It is in this way, Ānanda, that there is development without direction.

"Thus, Ānanda, I have taught development by direction, I have taught development without direction. Whatever should be done, Ānanda, by a compassionate teacher out of compassion for his disciples, desiring their welfare, that I have done for you. These are the feet of trees, Ānanda, these are empty huts. Meditate, Ānanda, do not be negligent, lest you regret it later. This is our instruction to you."

This is what the Blessed One said. Elated, the Venerable Ānanda delighted in the Blessed One's statement.

[158] II. Nālandā

11 (1) A Great Man

At Sāvatthī. Then the Venerable Sāriputta approached the Blessed One, paid homage to him, sat down to one side, and said to him:

"Venerable sir, it is said, 'a great man, a great man.'[150] In what way, venerable sir, is one a great man?"

"With a liberated mind, I say, Sāriputta, one is a great man. Without a liberated mind, I say, one is not a great man.

"And how, Sāriputta, does one have a liberated mind? Here, Sāriputta, a bhikkhu dwells contemplating the body in the body, ardent, clearly comprehending, mindful, having removed covetousness and displeasure in regard to the world. As he dwells contemplating the body in the body, the mind becomes dispassionate, and by nonclinging it is liberated from the taints.

"He dwells contemplating feelings in feelings ... mind in mind ... phenomena in phenomena, ardent, clearly comprehending, mindful, having removed covetousness and displeasure in regard to the world. As he dwells contemplating phenomena in phenomena, the mind becomes dispassionate, and by nonclinging it is liberated from the taints.

"It is in such a way, Sāriputta, that one has a liberated mind. With a liberated mind, I say, Sāriputta, one is a great man. Without a liberated mind, I say, one is not a great man." [159]

12 (2) Nālandā

On one occasion the Blessed One was dwelling at Nālandā in Pāvārika's Mango Grove.[151] Then the Venerable Sāriputta approached the Blessed One, paid homage to him, sat down to one side, and said to him:

"Venerable sir, I have such confidence in the Blessed One that I believe there has not been nor ever will be nor exists at present another ascetic or brahmin more knowledgeable than the Blessed One with respect to enlightenment."

"Lofty indeed is this bellowing utterance of yours, Sāriputta, you have roared a definitive, categorical lion's roar:[152] 'Venerable sir, I have such confidence in the Blessed One that I believe there has not been nor ever will be nor exists at present another ascetic or brahmin more knowledgeable than the Blessed One with respect to enlightenment.' Have you now, Sāriputta, encompassed with your mind the minds of all the Arahants, the Perfectly Enlightened Ones, arisen in the past and known thus: 'Those Blessed Ones were of such virtue, or of such qualities, or of such wisdom, or of such dwellings, or of such liberation'?"[153]

"No, venerable sir."

"Then, Sāriputta, have you encompassed with your mind the minds of all the Arahants, the Perfectly Enlightened Ones, who will arise in the future and known thus: 'Those Blessed Ones will be of such virtue, or of such qualities, or of such wisdom, or of such dwellings, or of such liberation'?" [160]

"No, venerable sir."

"Then, Sāriputta, have you encompassed with your mind my own mind—I being at present the Arahant, the Perfectly Enlightened One—and known thus: 'The Blessed One is of such virtue, or of such qualities, or of such wisdom, or of such dwellings, or of such liberation'?"

"No, venerable sir."

"Sāriputta, when you do not have any knowledge encompassing the minds of the Arahants, the Perfectly Enlightened Ones of the past, the future, and the present, why do you utter this lofty, bellowing utterance and roar this definitive, categorical lion's roar: 'Venerable sir, I have such confidence in the Blessed One that I believe there has not been nor ever will be nor exists at present another ascetic or brahmin more knowledgeable than the Blessed One with respect to enlightenment'?"

"I do not have, venerable sir, any knowledge encompassing the minds of the Arahants, the Perfectly Enlightened Ones of the past, the future, and the present, but still I have understood this by inference from the Dhamma.[154] Suppose, venerable sir, a king had a frontier city with strong ramparts, walls, and arches, and with a single gate. The gatekeeper posted there would be wise, competent, and intelligent; one who keeps out strangers and admits acquaintances. While he is walking along the path that encircles the city he would not see a cleft or an opening in the walls even big enough for a cat to slip through. He might think: 'Whatever large creatures enter or leave this city, all enter and leave through this one gate.'

"So too, venerable sir, I have understood this by inference from the Dhamma: Whatever Arahants, Perfectly Enlightened Ones arose in the past, all those Blessed Ones had first abandoned the five hindrances, corruptions of the mind and weakeners of wisdom; and then, with their minds well established in the four establishments of mindfulness, [161] they had developed correctly the seven factors of enlightenment; and thereby they had awakened to the unsurpassed perfect enlightenment.[155] And, venerable sir, whatever Arahants, Perfectly Enlightened Ones will arise in the future, all those Blessed Ones will first abandon the five hindrances, corruptions of the mind and weakeners of wisdom; and then, with their minds well established in the four establishments of mindfulness, they will develop correctly the seven factors of enlightenment; and thereby they will awaken to the unsurpassed perfect enlightenment. And, venerable sir, the Blessed One, who is at present the Arahant, the Perfectly Enlightened One, first abandoned the five hindrances, corruptions of the mind and weakeners of wisdom; and then, with his mind well established in the four establishments of mindfulness, he developed correctly the seven factors of enlightenment; and thereby he has awakened to the unsurpassed perfect enlightenment."

"Good, good, Sāriputta! Therefore, Sāriputta, you should repeat this Dhamma exposition frequently to the bhikkhus and the bhikkhunīs, to the male lay followers and the female lay followers. Even though some foolish people may have perplexity or uncertainty regarding the Tathāgata, when they hear this Dhamma exposition their perplexity or uncertainty regarding the Tathāgata will be abandoned."[156]

13 (3) Cunda

On one occasion the Blessed One was dwelling at Sāvatthī in

Jeta's Grove, Anāthapiṇḍika's Park.[157] Now on that occasion the Venerable Sāriputta was dwelling among the Magadhans at Nālakagāma—sick, afflicted, gravely ill—and the novice Cunda was his attendant.[158] Then, because of that illness, the Venerable Sāriputta attained final Nibbāna.

The novice Cunda, taking the Venerable Sāriputta's bowl and robe, went to Sāvatthī, to Jeta's Grove, Anāthapiṇḍika's Park. There he approached the Venerable Ānanda, paid homage to him, sat down to one side, and said to him: [162] "Venerable sir, the Venerable Sāriputta has attained final Nibbāna. This is his bowl and robe."

"Friend Cunda, we should see the Blessed One about this piece of news. Come, friend Cunda, let us go to the Blessed One and report this matter to him."

"Yes, venerable sir," the novice Cunda replied.

Then the Venerable Ānanda and the novice Cunda approached the Blessed One, paid homage to him, and sat down to one side. The Venerable Ānanda then said to the Blessed One: "This novice Cunda, venerable sir, says that the Venerable Sāriputta has attained final Nibbāna, and this is his bowl and robe. Venerable sir, since I heard that the Venerable Sāriputta has attained final Nibbāna, my body seems as if it has been drugged, I have become disoriented, the teachings are no longer clear to me."[159]

"Why, Ānanda, when Sāriputta attained final Nibbāna, did he take away your aggregate of virtue, or your aggregate of concentration, or your aggregate of wisdom, or your aggregate of liberation, or your aggregate of the knowledge and vision of liberation?"[160]

"No, he did not, venerable sir. But for me the Venerable Sāriputta was an advisor and counsellor, one who instructed, exhorted, inspired, and gladdened me.[161] He was unwearying in teaching the Dhamma; he was helpful to his brothers in the holy life. We recollect the nourishment of Dhamma, the wealth of Dhamma, the help of Dhamma given by the Venerable Sāriputta."

"But have I not already declared, Ānanda, that we must be parted, separated, and severed from all who are dear and agreeable to us? [163] How, Ānanda, is it to be obtained here: 'May what is born, come to be, conditioned, and subject to disintegration not disintegrate!'? That is impossible. It is just as if the largest branch would break off a great tree standing possessed of heartwood: so too, Ānanda, in the great Bhikkhu Saṅgha standing possessed of heartwood, Sāriputta has attained final Nibbāna. How, Ānanda, is it to be obtained here: 'May what is born, come to be, conditioned, and subject to disintegration not disintegrate!'? That is impossible.

"Therefore, Ānanda, dwell with yourselves as your own island, with yourselves as your own refuge, with no other refuge; dwell with the Dhamma as your island, with the Dhamma as your refuge, with no other refuge ... (*as in* §9) ... Those bhikkhus, Ānanda, either now or after I am gone, who dwell with themselves as their own island, with themselves as their own refuge, with no other refuge; who dwell with the Dhamma as their island, with the Dhamma as their refuge, with no other refuge—it is these bhikkhus, Ānanda, who will be for me topmost of those keen on the training."

14 (4) Ukkacelā

On one occasion the Blessed One was dwelling among the Vajjians at Ukkacelā on the bank of the river Ganges, together with a great Bhikkhu Saṅgha, not long after Sāriputta and Moggallāna had attained final Nibbāna.[162] Now on that occasion the Blessed One was sitting in the open air in the midst of the Bhikkhu Saṅgha.

Then the Blessed One, having surveyed the silent Bhikkhu Saṅgha, addressed the bhikkhus thus: [164]

"Bhikkhus, this assembly appears to me empty now that Sāriputta and Moggallāna have attained final Nibbāna. This assembly was not empty for me [earlier],[163] and I had no concern for whatever quarter Sāriputta and Moggallāna were dwelling in.

"The Arahants, the Perfectly Enlightened Ones, who arose in the past also had just such a supreme pair of disciples as I had in Sāriputta and Moggallāna. The Arahants, the Perfectly Enlightened Ones, who will arise in the future will also have just such a supreme pair of disciples as I had in Sāriputta and Moggallāna.

"It is wonderful, bhikkhus, on the part of the disciples, it is amazing on the part of the disciples, that they will act in accordance with the Teacher's instructions and comply with his admonitions, that they will be dear and agreeable to the four assemblies, that they will be revered and esteemed by them.[164] It is wonderful, bhikkhus, on the part of the Tathāgata, it is amazing on the part of the Tathāgata, that when such a pair of disciples has attained final Nibbāna, there is no sorrow or lamentation in the Tathāgata.

"How, bhikkhus, is it to be obtained here: 'May what is born, come to be, conditioned, and subject to disintegration not disintegrate!'? That is impossible. It is just as if the largest branches would break off a great tree standing possessed of heartwood: so too, bhikkhus, in the great Bhikkhu Saṅgha standing possessed of heartwood, Sāriputta and Moggallāna have attained final Nibbāna. How, bhikkhus, is it to be obtained here: 'May what is born, come to be, conditioned, and subject to disintegration not disintegrate!'? That is impossible.

"Therefore, bhikkhus, dwell with yourselves as your own island, with yourselves as your own refuge, with no other refuge; dwell with the Dhamma as your island, with the Dhamma as your refuge, with no other refuge ... (*as in §9*) ... [165] Those bhikkhus, either now or after I am gone, who dwell with themselves as their own island, with themselves as their own refuge, with no other refuge; with the Dhamma as their island, with the Dhamma as their refuge, with no other refuge—it is these bhikkhus who will be for me topmost of those keen on the training."

15 (5) Bāhiya

At Sāvatthī. Then the Venerable Bāhiya approached the Blessed One, paid homage to him, sat down to one side, and said to him:

"Venerable sir, it would be good if the Blessed One would teach me the Dhamma in brief, so that, having heard the Dhamma from the Blessed One, I might dwell alone, withdrawn, diligent, ardent, and resolute."

"Well then, Bāhiya, purify the very starting point of wholesome states.[165] And what is the starting point of wholesome states? Virtue that is well purified and view that is straight. Then, Bāhiya, when your virtue is well purified and your view is straight, based upon virtue, established upon virtue, you should develop the four establishments of mindfulness.

"What four? Here, Bāhiya, dwell contemplating the body in the body, ardent, clearly comprehending, mindful, having removed covetousness and displeasure in regard to the world. Dwell contemplating feelings in feelings … mind in mind … phenomena in phenomena, ardent, clearly comprehending, mindful, having removed covetousness and displeasure in regard to the world.

"When, Bāhiya, based upon virtue, established upon virtue, you develop these four establishments of mindfulness in such a way, then whether night or day comes, you may expect only growth in wholesome states, not decline." [166]

Then the Venerable Bāhiya, having delighted and rejoiced in the Blessed One's words, rose from his seat, and, after paying homage to the Blessed One, keeping him on his right, he departed. Then, dwelling alone, withdrawn, diligent, ardent, and resolute, the Venerable Bāhiya, by realizing it for himself with direct knowledge, in this very life entered and dwelt in that unsurpassed goal of the holy life for the sake of which clansmen rightly go forth from the household life into homelessness. He directly knew: "Destroyed is birth, the holy life has been lived, what had to be done has been done, there is no more for this state of being." And the Venerable Bāhiya became one of the arahants.

16 (6) Uttiya

At Sāvatthī. Then the Venerable Uttiya approached the Blessed One … (*all as in preceding sutta down to:*) …

"When, Uttiya, based upon virtue, established upon virtue, you develop these four establishments of mindfulness in such a way, you will go beyond the realm of Death."

Then the Venerable Uttiya, having delighted and rejoiced in the Blessed One's words, rose from his seat … (*as in preceding sutta*) … And the Venerable Uttiya became one of the arahants.

17 (7) Noble

"Bhikkhus, these four establishments of mindfulness, when developed and cultivated, are noble and emancipating; they lead the one who acts upon them out to the complete destruction of suffering. What four? Here, bhikkhus, a bhikkhu dwells contemplating the body in the body, ardent, clearly comprehending, mindful, having removed covetousness and displeasure in regard to the world. He dwells contemplating feelings in feelings

... mind in mind ... phenomena in phenomena, ardent, clearly comprehending, mindful, having removed covetousness and displeasure in regard to the world. [167]

"These four establishments of mindfulness, bhikkhus, when developed and cultivated, are noble and emancipating; they lead the one who acts upon them out to the complete destruction of suffering."

18 (8) Brahmā

On one occasion the Blessed One was dwelling at Uruvelā on the bank of the river Nerañjarā at the foot of the Goatherd's Banyan Tree just after he had become fully enlightened. Then, while the Blessed One was alone in seclusion, a reflection arose in his mind thus: "This is the one-way path for the purification of beings, for the overcoming of sorrow and lamentation, for the passing away of pain and displeasure, for the achievement of the method, for the realization of Nibbāna, that is, the four establishments of mindfulness. What four? Here a bhikkhu dwells contemplating the body in the body, ardent, clearly comprehending, mindful, having removed covetousness and displeasure in regard to the world. He dwells contemplating feelings in feelings ... mind in mind ... phenomena in phenomena, ardent, clearly comprehending, mindful, having removed covetousness and displeasure in regard to the world. This is the one-way path for the purification of beings ... that is, the four establishments of mindfulness."

Then Brahmā Sahampati, having known with his own mind the reflection in the Blessed One's mind, just as quickly as a strong man might extend his drawn-in arm or draw in his extended arm, disappeared from the brahmā world and reappeared before the Blessed One.[166] He arranged his upper robe over one shoulder, raised his joined hands in reverential salutation towards the Blessed One, and said to him: "So it is, Blessed One! So it is, Fortunate One! Venerable sir, this is the one-way path for the purification of beings ... (*all as above*) [168] ... that is, the four establishments of mindfulness."

This is what Brahmā Sahampati said. Having said this, he further said this:

"The seer of the destruction of birth,
Compassionate, knows the one-way path
By which in the past they crossed the flood,
By which they will cross and cross over now."

19 (9) Sedaka

On one occasion the Blessed One was dwelling among the Sumbhas, where there was a town of the Sumbhas named Sedaka. There the Blessed One addressed the bhikkhus thus:

"Bhikkhus, once in the past an acrobat set up his bamboo pole and addressed his apprentice Medakathālikā thus:[167] 'Come, dear Medakathālikā, climb the bamboo pole and stand on my shoulders.' Having replied, 'Yes, teacher,' the apprentice Medakathālikā climbed up the bamboo pole and stood on the teacher's shoulders. The acrobat then said to the apprentice Medakathālikā: 'You protect me, dear Medakathālikā, and I'll protect you. Thus [169] guarded by one another, protected by one another, we'll display our skills, collect our fee, and get down safely from the bamboo pole.' When this was said, the apprentice Medakathālikā replied: 'That's not the way to do it, teacher. You protect yourself, teacher, and I'll protect myself. Thus, each self-guarded and self-protected, we'll display our skills, collect our fee, and get down safely from the bamboo pole.'[168]

"That's the method there," the Blessed One said. "It's just as the apprentice Medakathālikā said to the teacher. 'I will protect myself,' bhikkhus: thus should the establishments of mindfulness be practised. 'I will protect others,' bhikkhus: thus should the establishments of mindfulness be practised. Protecting oneself, bhikkhus, one protects others; protecting others, one protects oneself.

"And how is it, bhikkhus, that by protecting oneself one protects others? By the pursuit, development, and cultivation [of the four establishments of mindfulness]. It is in such a way that by protecting oneself one protects others.[169]

"And how is it, bhikkhus, that by protecting others one protects oneself? By patience, harmlessness, lovingkindness, and sympathy. It is in such a way that by protecting others one protects oneself.[170]

"'I will protect myself,' bhikkhus: thus should the establishments of mindfulness be practised. 'I will protect others,' bhikkhus: thus should the establishments of mindfulness be practised. Protecting oneself, bhikkhus, one protects others; protecting others, one protects oneself."

20 (10) The Most Beautiful Girl of the Land

Thus have I heard. On one occasion the Blessed One was living among the Sumbhas, where there was a town of the Sumbhas named Sedaka. [170] There the Blessed One addressed the bhikkhus thus: "Bhikkhus!"

"Venerable sir!" the bhikkhus replied. The Blessed One said this:[171]

"Bhikkhus, suppose that on hearing, 'The most beautiful girl of the land! The most beautiful girl of the land!' a great crowd of people would assemble. Now that most beautiful girl of the land would dance exquisitely and sing exquisitely. On hearing, 'The most beautiful girl of the land is dancing! The most beautiful girl of the land is singing!' an even larger crowd of people would assemble.[172] Then a man would come along, wishing to live, not wishing to die, wishing for happiness, averse to suffering. Someone would say to him: 'Good man, you must carry around this bowl of oil filled to the brim between the crowd and the most beautiful girl of the land. A man with a drawn sword will be following right behind you, and wherever you spill even a little of it, right there he will fell your head.'

"What do you think, bhikkhus, would that man stop attending to that bowl of oil and out of negligence turn his attention outwards?"

"No, venerable sir."

"I have made up this simile, bhikkhus, in order to convey a meaning. This here is the meaning: 'The bowl of oil filled to the brim': this is a designation for mindfulness directed to the body. Therefore, bhikkhus, you should train yourselves thus: 'We will develop and cultivate mindfulness directed to the body, make it our vehicle, make it our basis, stabilize it, exercise ourselves in it, and fully perfect it.' Thus, bhikkhus, should you train yourselves."

[171] III. Virtue and Duration

21 (1) Virtue

Thus have I heard. On one occasion the Venerable Ānanda and the Venerable Bhadda were dwelling at Pāṭaliputta in the Cock's Park. Then, in the evening, the Venerable Bhadda emerged from seclusion, approached the Venerable Ānanda, and exchanged greetings with him. When they had concluded their greetings and cordial talk, he sat down to one side and said to the Venerable Ānanda:[173]

"Friend Ānanda, as to the wholesome virtues spoken of by the Blessed One, what is the purpose for which they were spoken of by him?"

"Good, good, friend Bhadda! Your intelligence is excellent, your ingenuity is excellent, your inquiry is a good one. For you have asked me: 'Friend Ānanda, as to the wholesome virtues spoken of by the Blessed One, what is the purpose for which they were spoken of by him?'"

"Yes, friend."

"Those wholesome virtues spoken of by the Blessed One were spoken of by him for the purpose of developing the four establishments of mindfulness. What four? Here, friend, a bhikkhu dwells contemplating the body in the body … feelings in feelings … mind in mind … phenomena in phenomena, ardent, clearly comprehending, mindful, having removed covetousness and displeasure in regard to the world. [172]

"Those virtues spoken of by the Blessed One were spoken of by him for the sake of developing these four establishments of mindfulness."

22 (2) Duration

The same setting. Sitting to one side the Venerable Bhadda said to the Venerable Ānanda:

"Friend Ānanda, what is the cause and reason why the true Dhamma does not endure long after a Tathāgata has attained final Nibbāna? And what is the cause and reason why the true Dhamma endures long after a Tathāgata has attained final Nibbāna?"

"Good, good, friend Bhadda! Your intelligence is excellent, your acumen is excellent, your inquiry is a good one. For you have asked me: 'Friend Ānanda, what is the cause and reason why the true Dhamma does not endure long after a Tathāgata has attained final Nibbāna? And what is the cause and reason why the true Dhamma endures long after a Tathāgata has attained final Nibbāna?'"

"Yes, friend."

"It is, friend, because the four establishments of mindfulness are not developed and cultivated that the true Dhamma does not endure long after a Tathāgata has attained final Nibbāna. And it is because the four establishments of mindfulness are developed and cultivated that the true Dhamma endures long after a Tathāgata has attained final Nibbāna. What four? Here, friend, a bhikkhu dwells contemplating the body in the body ... feelings in feelings ... mind in mind ... phenomena in phenomena, ardent, clearly comprehending, mindful, having removed covetousness and displeasure in regard to the world.

"It is because these four establishments of mindfulness are not developed and cultivated that the true Dhamma does not endure long after a Tathāgata has attained final Nibbāna. And it is because these four establishments of mindfulness are developed and cultivated that the true Dhamma endures long after a Tathāgata has attained final Nibbāna." [173]

23 (3) Decline

(*As above down to:*)

"Friend Ānanda, what is the cause and reason for the decline of the true Dhamma? And what is the cause and reason for the nondecline of the true Dhamma?"...

"It is, friend, when these four establishments of mindfulness are not developed and cultivated that the true Dhamma declines. And it is when these four establishments of mindfulness are developed and cultivated that the true Dhamma does not decline."

24 (4) Simple Version

At Sāvatthī. "Bhikkhus, there are these four establishments of mindfulness. What four? Here, bhikkhus, a bhikkhu dwells contemplating the body in the body, ardent, clearly comprehending, mindful, having removed covetousness and displeasure in regard to the world. [174] He dwells contemplating feelings in feelings … mind in mind … phenomena in phenomena, ardent, clearly comprehending, mindful, having removed covetousness and displeasure in regard to the world. These are the four establishments of mindfulness."

25 (5) A Certain Brahmin

Thus have I heard. On one occasion the Blessed One was dwelling at Sāvatthī, in Jeta's Grove, Anāthapiṇḍika's Park. Then a certain brahmin approached the Blessed One and exchanged greetings with him. When they had concluded their greetings and cordial talk, he sat down to one side and said to the Blessed One:

"Master Gotama, what is the cause and reason why the true Dhamma does not endure long after a Tathāgata has attained final Nibbāna? And what is the cause and reason why the true Dhamma endures long after a Tathāgata has attained final Nibbāna?"

"It is, brahmin, because the four establishments of mindfulness are not developed and cultivated that the true Dhamma does not endure long after a Tathāgata has attained final Nibbāna. And it is because the four establishments of mindfulness are developed and cultivated that the true Dhamma endures long after a Tathāgata has attained final Nibbāna. What four? … (*as in* §22) … It is because these four establishments of mindfulness are not developed and cultivated … are developed and cultivated that the true Dhamma endures long after a Tathāgata has attained final Nibbāna."

When this was said, that brahmin said to the Blessed One: 'Magnificent, Master Gotama!… From today let Master Gotama remember me as a lay follower who has gone for refuge for life."

26 (6) Partly

On one occasion the Venerable Sāriputta and the Venerable Mahāmoggallāna and the Venerable Anuruddha were dwelling at Sāketa in the Thornbush Grove. Then, in the evening, the

Venerable Sāriputta and the Venerable Mahāmoggallāna emerged from seclusion, approached the Venerable Anuruddha, and exchanged greetings with him. When they had concluded their greetings and cordial talk, [175] they sat down to one side, and the Venerable Sāriputta said to the Venerable Anuruddha:

"Friend Anuruddha, it is said, 'A trainee, a trainee.' In what way, friend, is one a trainee?"

"It is, friend, because one has partly developed the four establishments of mindfulness that one is a trainee. What four? Here, friends, a bhikkhu dwells contemplating the body in the body ... feelings in feelings ... mind in mind ... phenomena in phenomena, ardent, clearly comprehending, mindful, having removed covetousness and displeasure in regard to the world. It is because one has partly developed these four establishments of mindfulness that one is a trainee."

27 (7) Completely

The same setting. Sitting to one side, the Venerable Sāriputta said to the Venerable Anuruddha:

"Friend Anuruddha, it is said, 'One beyond training, one beyond training.' In what way, friend, is one beyond training?"

"It is, friend, because one has completely developed the four establishments of mindfulness that one is beyond training. What four?... (*as above*) ... It is because one has completely developed these four establishments of mindfulness that one is beyond training."

28 (8) The World

The same setting. Sitting to one side, the Venerable Sāriputta said to the Venerable Anuruddha:

"By having developed and cultivated what things has the Venerable Anuruddha attained to greatness of direct knowledge?" [176]

"It is, friend, because I have developed and cultivated the four establishments of mindfulness that I have attained to greatness of direct knowledge. What four? Here, friend, I dwell contemplating the body in the body ... feelings in feelings ... mind in mind ... phenomena in phenomena, ardent, clearly comprehending, mindful, having removed covetousness and displeasure in regard to the world. It is, friend, because I have developed and cultivated these four establishments of mindfulness that I directly know this thousandfold world."[174]

29 (9) Sirivaḍḍha

On one occasion the Venerable Ānanda was dwelling at Rājagaha, in the Bamboo Grove, the Squirrel Sanctuary. Now on that occasion the householder Sirivaḍḍha was sick, afflicted, gravely ill. Then the householder Sirivaḍḍha addressed a man thus:

"Come, good man, approach the Venerable Ānanda, pay homage to him in my name with your head at his feet, and say: 'Venerable sir, the householder Sirivaḍḍha is sick, afflicted, gravely ill; he pays homage to the Venerable Ānanda with his head at his feet.' Then say: 'It would be good, venerable sir, if the Venerable Ānanda would come to the residence of the householder Sirivaḍḍha out of compassion.'"

"Yes, master," that man replied, and he approached the Venerable Ānanda, paid homage to him, sat down to one side, and delivered his message. [177] The Venerable Ānanda consented by silence.

Then, in the morning, the Venerable Ānanda dressed and, taking bowl and robe, went to the residence of the householder Sirivaḍḍha. He then sat down in the appointed seat and said to the householder Sirivaḍḍha: "I hope you are bearing up, householder, I hope you are getting better. I hope your painful feelings are subsiding and not increasing, and that their subsiding, not their increase, is to be discerned."

"I am not bearing up, venerable sir, I am not getting better. Strong painful feelings are increasing in me, not subsiding, and their increase, not their subsiding, is to be discerned."

"Well then, householder, you should train thus: 'I will dwell contemplating the body in the body, ardent, clearly comprehending, mindful, having removed covetousness and displeasure in regard to the world. I will dwell contemplating feelings in feelings … mind in mind … phenomena in phenomena, ardent, clearly comprehending, mindful, having removed covetousness and displeasure in regard to the world.' It is in such a way that you should train."

"Venerable sir, as to these four establishments of mindfulness taught by the Blessed One—these things exist in me, and I live in conformity with those things. I dwell, venerable sir, contemplating the body in the body … feelings in feelings … mind in mind … phenomena in phenomena, ardent, clearly comprehending, mindful, having removed covetousness and displeasure in regard to the world. And as to these five lower fetters taught by the Blessed One, I do not see any of these unabandoned in myself."

"It is a gain for you, householder! It is well gained by you, householder! You have declared, householder, the fruit of nonreturning." [178]

30 (10) Mānadinna

The same setting. Now on that occasion the householder Mānadinna was sick, afflicted, gravely ill. Then the householder Mānadinna addressed a man thus:

"Come, good man" … (*as above*) …

"I am not bearing up, venerable sir, I am not getting better. Strong painful feelings are increasing in me, not subsiding, and their increase, not their subsiding, is to be discerned. But, venerable sir, when I am being touched by such painful feeling, I dwell contemplating the body in the body … feelings in feelings … mind in mind … phenomena in phenomena, ardent, clearly comprehending, mindful, having removed covetousness and displeasure in regard to the world. And as to these five lower fetters taught by the Blessed One, I do not see any of these unabandoned in myself."

"It is a gain for you, householder! It is well gained by you, householder! You have declared, householder, the fruit of nonreturning."

IV. Unheard Before

31 (1) Unheard Before

At Sāvatthī. "'This is the contemplation of the body in the body'—thus, bhikkhus, [179] in regard to things unheard before, there arose in me vision, knowledge, wisdom, true knowledge, and light.[175]

"'That contemplation of the body in the body is to be developed' … 'That contemplation of the body in the body has been developed'—thus, bhikkhus, in regard to things unheard before, there arose in me vision, knowledge, wisdom, true knowledge, and light.

"'This is the contemplation of feelings in feelings' …

"'This is the contemplation of mind in mind' …

"'This is the contemplation of phenomena in phenomena'—thus, bhikkhus, in regard to things unheard before, there arose in me vision, knowledge, wisdom, true knowledge, and light.

"'That contemplation of phenomena in phenomena is to be developed' … 'That contemplation of phenomena in phenomena has been developed'—thus, bhikkhus, in regard to things unheard before, there arose in me vision, knowledge, wisdom, true knowledge, and light."

32 (2) Dispassion

"Bhikkhus, these four establishments of mindfulness, when developed and cultivated, lead to utter revulsion, to dispassion, to cessation, to peace, to direct knowledge, to enlightenment, to Nibbāna.

"What four? Here, bhikkhus, a bhikkhu dwells contemplating the body in the body … feelings in feelings … mind in mind … phenomena in phenomena, ardent, clearly comprehending, mindful, having removed covetousness and displeasure in regard to the world.

"These four establishments of mindfulness, bhikkhus, when developed and cultivated, lead to utter revulsion, to dispassion, to cessation, to peace, to direct knowledge, to enlightenment, to Nibbāna."

33 (3) Neglected

"Bhikkhus, those who have neglected these four establishments of mindfulness have neglected the noble path leading to the complete destruction of suffering. [180] Those who have undertaken these four establishments of mindfulness have undertaken the noble path leading to the complete destruction of suffering.

"What four?... (*as above*) ... Those who have neglected ... Those who have undertaken these four establishments of mindfulness have undertaken the noble path leading to the complete destruction of suffering."

34 (4) Development

"Bhikkhus, these four establishments of mindfulness, when developed and cultivated, lead to going beyond from the near shore to the far shore. What four? ... (*as above*) ... These four establishments of mindfulness, when developed and cultivated, lead to going beyond from the near shore to the far shore."

35 (5) Mindful

At Sāvatthī. "Bhikkhus, a bhikkhu should dwell mindful and clearly comprehending. This is our instruction to you.

"And how, bhikkhus, is a bhikkhu mindful? Here, bhikkhus, a bhikkhu dwells contemplating the body in the body ... feelings in feelings ... mind in mind ... phenomena in phenomena, ardent, clearly comprehending, mindful, having removed covetousness and displeasure in regard to the world. It is in this way, bhikkhus, that a bhikkhu is mindful.

"And how, bhikkhus, does a bhikkhu exercise clear comprehension? Here, bhikkhus, for a bhikkhu feelings are understood as they arise, understood [181] as they remain present, understood as they pass away. Thoughts are understood as they arise, understood as they remain present, understood as they pass away. Perceptions are understood as they arise, understood as they remain present, understood as they pass away. It is in this way, bhikkhus, that a bhikkhu exercises clear comprehension.[176]

"Bhikkhus, a bhikkhu should dwell mindful and clearly comprehending. This is our instruction to you."

36 (6) Final Knowledge

"Bhikkhus, there are these four establishments of mindfulness. What four? Here, bhikkhus, a bhikkhu dwells contemplating the body in the body ... feelings in feelings ... mind in mind ... phenomena in phenomena, ardent, clearly comprehending, mindful, having removed covetousness and displeasure in regard to the world.

"When, bhikkhus, these four establishments of mindfulness have been developed and cultivated, one of two fruits may be expected: either final knowledge in this very life or, if there is a residue of clinging, the state of nonreturning."

37 (7) Desire

"Bhikkhus, there are these four establishments of mindfulness. What four? Here, bhikkhus, a bhikkhu dwells contemplating the body in the body, ardent, clearly comprehending, mindful, having removed covetousness and displeasure in regard to the world. As he dwells thus contemplating the body in the body, whatever desire he has for the body is abandoned. With the abandoning of desire, the Deathless is realized.

"He dwells contemplating feelings in feelings ... [182] ... mind in mind ... phenomena in phenomena ... having removed covetousness and displeasure in regard to the world. As he dwells thus contemplating phenomena in phenomena, whatever desire he has for phenomena is abandoned. With the abandoning of desire, the Deathless is realized."

38 (8) Full Understanding

"Bhikkhus, there are these four establishments of mindfulness. What four? Here, bhikkhus, a bhikkhu dwells contemplating the body in the body, ardent, clearly comprehending, mindful, having removed covetousness and displeasure in regard to the world. As he dwells thus contemplating the body in the body, the body is fully understood. Because the body has been fully understood, the Deathless is realized.

"He dwells contemplating feelings in feelings ... mind in mind ... phenomena in phenomena ... having removed covetousness and displeasure in regard to the world. As he dwells thus contemplating phenomena in phenomena, the phenomena are fully understood. Because the phenomena have been fully understood, the Deathless is realized."

39 (9) Development

"Bhikkhus, I will teach you the development of the four establishments of mindfulness. Listen to that....

"What, bhikkhus, is the development of the four establishments of mindfulness? Here, bhikkhus, a bhikkhu dwells contemplating the body in the body, ardent, clearly comprehending, mindful, having removed covetousness and displeasure in regard to the world. He dwells contemplating feelings in feelings ... mind in mind ... phenomena in phenomena, [183] ardent, clearly comprehending, mindful, having removed covetousness and displeasure in regard to the world. This, bhikkhus, is the development of the four establishments of mindfulness."

40 (10) Analysis

"Bhikkhus, I will teach you the establishment of mindfulness,[177] and the development of the establishment of mindfulness, and the way leading to the development of the establishment of mindfulness. Listen to that....

"And what, bhikkhus, is the establishment of mindfulness? Here, bhikkhus, a bhikkhu dwells contemplating the body in the body, ardent, clearly comprehending, mindful, having removed covetousness and displeasure in regard to the world. He dwells contemplating feelings in feelings ... mind in mind ... phenomena in phenomena, ardent, clearly comprehending, mindful, having removed covetousness and displeasure in regard to the world. This is called the establishment of mindfulness.

"And what, bhikkhus, is the development of the establishment of mindfulness? Here, bhikkhus, a bhikkhu dwells contemplating the nature of origination in the body; he dwells contemplating the nature of vanishing in the body; he dwells contemplating the nature of origination and vanishing in the body—ardent, clearly comprehending, mindful, having removed covetousness and displeasure in regard to the world.[178] He dwells contemplating the nature of origination in feelings ... He dwells contemplating the nature of origination in mind ... He dwells contemplating the nature of origination in phenomena; he dwells contemplating the nature of vanishing in phenomena; he dwells contemplating the nature of origination and vanishing in phenomena—ardent, clearly comprehending, mindful, having removed covetousness and displeasure in regard to the world. This is called the development of the establishment of mindfulness.

"And what, bhikkhus, is the way leading to the development of the establishment of mindfulness? It is this Noble Eightfold Path; that is, right view … right concentration. This is called the way leading to the development of the establishment of mindfulness."

[184] V. The Deathless

41 (1) The Deathless

At Sāvatthī. "Bhikkhus, dwell with your minds well established in the four establishments of mindfulness. Do not let the Deathless be lost on you.[179]

"In what four? Here, bhikkhus, a bhikkhu dwells contemplating the body in the body … feelings in feelings … mind in mind … phenomena in phenomena, ardent, clearly comprehending, mindful, having removed covetousness and displeasure in regard to the world. Dwell, bhikkhus, with your minds well established in these four establishments of mindfulness. Do not let the Deathless be lost on you."

42 (2) Origination

"Bhikkhus, I will teach you the origination and the passing away of the four establishments of mindfulness.[180] Listen to that.

"And what, bhikkhus, is the origination of the body? With the origination of nutriment there is the origination of the body. With the cessation of nutriment there is the passing away of the body.

"With the origination of contact there is the origination of feeling. With the cessation of contact there is the passing away of feeling.

"With the origination of name-and-form there is the origination of mind. With the cessation of name-and-form there is the passing away of mind.[181]

"With the origination of attention there is the origination of phenomena. With the cessation of attention there is the passing away of phenomena."[182] [185]

43 (3) The Path

At Sāvatthī. There the Blessed One addressed the bhikkhus thus:[183]

"Bhikkhus, on one occasion I was dwelling at Uruvelā on the bank of the river Nerañjarā under the Goatherd's Banyan Tree just after I became fully enlightened. Then, while I was alone in seclusion, a reflection arose in my mind thus: 'This is the one-way path for the purification of beings, for the overcoming of sorrow and lamentation … (*as in §18*) … that is, the four establishments of mindfulness.'

"Then, bhikkhus, Brahmā Sahampati, having known with his own mind the reflection in my mind, just as quickly as a strong man might extend his drawn-in arm or draw in his extended arm, disappeared from the brahmā world and reappeared before me. He arranged his upper robe over one shoulder, extended his joined hands towards me in reverential salutation, and said to me: 'So it is, Blessed One! So it is, Fortunate One! Venerable sir, this is the one-way path for the purification of beings … [186] … that is, the four establishments of mindfulness.'

"This, bhikkhus, is what Brahmā Sahampati said. Having said this, he further said this:

"'The seer of the destruction of birth,
Compassionate, knows the one-way path
By which in the past they crossed the flood,
By which they will cross and cross over now.'"

44 (4) Mindful

"Bhikkhus, a bhikkhu should dwell mindful. This is our instruction to you.

"And how, bhikkhus, is a bhikkhu mindful? Here, bhikkhus, a bhikkhu dwells contemplating the body in the body, ardent, clearly comprehending, mindful, having removed covetousness and displeasure in regard to the world. He dwells contemplating feelings in feelings … mind in mind … phenomena in phenomena, ardent, clearly comprehending, mindful, having removed covetousness and displeasure in regard to the world. It is in this way, bhikkhus, that a bhikkhu is mindful.

"Bhikkhus, a bhikkhu should dwell mindful. This is our instruction to you."

45 (5) A Heap of the Wholesome

"Bhikkhus, if one were to say of anything 'a heap of the wholesome,' it is about the four establishments of mindfulness that one could rightly say this. For this is a complete heap of the wholesome, that is, the four establishments of mindfulness. What four? [187]

"Here, bhikkhus, a bhikkhu dwells contemplating the body in the body ... feelings in feelings ... mind in mind ... phenomena in phenomena, ardent, clearly comprehending, mindful, having removed covetousness and displeasure in regard to the world.

"If, bhikkhus, one were to say of anything 'a heap of the wholesome,' it is about these four establishments of mindfulness that one could rightly say this. For this is a complete heap of the wholesome, that is, the four establishments of mindfulness."

46 (6) The Restraint of the Pātimokkha

Then a certain bhikkhu approached the Blessed One, paid homage to him, sat down to one side, and said to him: "Venerable sir, it would be good if the Blessed One would teach me the Dhamma in brief, so that, having heard the Dhamma from the Blessed One, I might dwell alone, withdrawn, diligent, ardent, and resolute."

"In that case, bhikkhu, purify the very beginning of wholesome states. And what is the beginning of wholesome states? Here, bhikkhu, dwell restrained by the restraint of the Pātimokkha, accomplished in good conduct and proper resort, seeing danger in the slightest faults. Having undertaken the training rules, train in them. When, bhikkhu, you dwell restrained by the restraint of the Pātimokkha ... seeing danger in the slightest faults, then, based upon virtue, established upon virtue, you should develop the four establishments of mindfulness.

"What four? Here, bhikkhu, a bhikkhu dwells contemplating the body in the body ... feelings in feelings ... mind in mind ... phenomena in phenomena, ardent, clearly comprehending, mindful, having removed covetousness and displeasure in regard to the world.

"When, bhikkhu, based upon virtue, established upon virtue, you develop these four establishments of mindfulness in such a way, then, whether night or day comes, you may expect only growth in wholesome states, not decline."

Then that bhikkhu, having delighted and rejoiced in the Blessed One's statement, rose from his seat.... [188] And that bhikkhu became one of the arahants.

47 (7) Misconduct

Then a certain bhikkhu approached the Blessed One, paid homage to him, sat down to one side, and said to him: "Venerable sir, it would be good if the Blessed One would teach me the Dhamma in brief, so that, having heard the Dhamma from the Blessed One, I might dwell alone, withdrawn, diligent, ardent, and resolute."

"In that case, bhikkhu, purify the very beginning of wholesome states. And what is the beginning of wholesome states? Here, bhikkhu, having abandoned bodily misconduct, you should develop good bodily conduct. Having abandoned verbal misconduct, you should develop good verbal conduct. Having abandoned mental misconduct, you should develop good mental conduct. When, bhikkhu, having abandoned bodily misconduct ... you have developed good mental conduct, then, based upon virtue, established upon virtue, you should develop the four establishments of mindfulness.

"What four? Here, bhikkhu, a bhikkhu dwells contemplating the body in the body ... feelings in feelings ... mind in mind ... phenomena in phenomena, ardent, clearly comprehending, mindful, having removed covetousness and displeasure in regard to the world.

"When, bhikkhu, based upon virtue, established upon virtue, you develop these four establishments of mindfulness in such a way, then, whether night or day comes, you may expect only growth in wholesome states, not decline."

Then that bhikkhu ... became one of the arahants. [189]

48 (8) Friends

"Bhikkhus, those for whom you have compassion and who think you should be heeded—whether friends or colleagues, relatives or kinsmen—these you should exhort, settle, and establish in the development of the four establishments of mindfulness.

"What four? Here, bhikkhu, a bhikkhu dwells contemplating the body in the body ... feelings in feelings ... mind in mind ... phenomena in phenomena, ardent, clearly comprehending, mindful, having removed covetousness and displeasure in regard to the world.

"Bhikkhus, those for whom you have compassion ... these you should exhort, settle, and establish in the development of these four establishments of mindfulness."

49 (9) Feelings

"Bhikkhus, there are these three feelings. What three? Pleasant feeling, painful feeling, neither-painful-nor-pleasant feeling. These are the three feelings. The four establishments of mindfulness are to be developed for the full understanding of these three feelings.

"What four? Here, bhikkhus, a bhikkhu dwells contemplating the body in the body ... feelings in feelings ... mind in mind ... phenomena in phenomena, ardent, clearly comprehending, mindful, having removed covetousness and displeasure in regard to the world.

"These four establishments of mindfulness, bhikkhus, are to be developed for the full understanding of these three feelings."

50 (10) Taints

"Bhikkhus, there are these three taints. What three? The taint of sensuality, the taint of existence, the taint of ignorance. [190] These are the three taints. The four establishments of mindfulness are to be developed for the full understanding of these three taints.

"What four? Here, bhikkhus, a bhikkhu dwells contemplating the body in the body ... feelings in feelings ... mind in mind ... phenomena in phenomena, ardent, clearly comprehending, mindful, having removed covetousness and displeasure in regard to the world.

"These four establishments of mindfulness, bhikkhus, are to be developed for the full understanding of these three taints."

VI. Ganges Repetition Series

51 (1)–62 (12) The River Ganges—Eastward, Etc.

"Bhikkhus, just as the river Ganges slants, slopes, and inclines towards the east, so too a bhikkhu who develops and cultivates the four establishments of mindfulness slants, slopes, and inclines towards Nibbāna.

"And how, bhikkhus, does a bhikkhu develop and cultivate the four establishments of mindfulness so that he slants, slopes, and inclines towards Nibbāna? Here, bhikkhus, a bhikkhu dwells contemplating the body in the body ... feelings in feelings ... mind in mind ... phenomena in phenomena, ardent, clearly comprehending, mindful, having removed covetousness and displeasure in regard to the world. It is in this way, bhikkhus, that a bhikkhu develops and cultivates the four establishments of mindfulness so that he slants, slopes, and inclines towards Nibbāna."

(*The remaining suttas of this vagga are to be similarly elaborated parallel to 45:92–102.*)

Six about slanting to the east
And six about slanting to the ocean.
These two sixes make up twelve:
Thus the subchapter is recited.

[191]

VII. Diligence

63 (1)–72 (10) The Tathāgata, Etc.

(*To be elaborated by way of the establishments of mindfulness parallel to 45:139–48.*)

Tathāgata, footprint, roof peak,
Roots, heartwood, jasmine,
Monarch, the moon and sun,
Together with the cloth as tenth.

VIII. Strenuous Deeds

73 (1)–84 (12) Strenuous, Etc.[184]

(*To be elaborated parallel to 45:149–60.*)

Strenuous, seeds, and nāgas,
The tree, the pot, the spike,
The sky, and two on clouds,
The ship, guest house, and river.

IX. Searches

85 (1)–94 (10) Searches, Etc.

(*To be elaborated parallel to 45:161–70.*)

Searches, discriminations, taints,
Kinds of existence, threefold suffering,
Barrenness, stains, and troubles,
Feelings, craving, and thirst.[185]

X. Floods

95 (1)–103 (9) Floods, Etc.

(*To be elaborated parallel to 45:171–79.*)

104 (10) Higher Fetters

"Bhikkhus, there are these five higher fetters. What five? Lust for form, lust for the formless, conceit, restlessness, [192] ignorance. These are the five higher fetters. The four establishments of mindfulness are to be developed for direct knowledge of these five higher fetters, for the full understanding of them, for their utter destruction, for their abandoning.

"What four? Here, bhikkhus, a bhikkhu dwells contemplating the body in the body, ardent, clearly comprehending, mindful, having removed covetousness and displeasure in regard to the world. He dwells contemplating feelings in feelings ... mind in mind ... phenomena in phenomena, ardent, clearly comprehending, mindful, having removed covetousness and displeasure in regard to the world. These four establishments of mindfulness are to be developed for direct knowledge of these five higher fetters, for the full understanding of them, for their utter destruction, for their abandoning."

Floods, bonds, kinds of clinging,
Knots, and underlying tendencies,
Cords of sensual pleasure, hindrances,
Aggregates, fetters lower and higher.

The Connected Discourses on the Establishments of Mindfulness is to be elaborated in the same way as the Connected Discourses on the Path.[186]

[193] Chapter IV

48 *Indriyasaṃyutta*

Connected Discourses on the Faculties

I. Simple Version

1 (1) Simple Version

At Sāvatthī. There the Blessed One addressed the bhikkhus thus:

"Bhikkhus, there are these five faculties. What five? The faculty of faith, the faculty of energy, the faculty of mindfulness, the faculty of concentration, the faculty of wisdom. These are the five faculties."[187]

2 (2) Stream-Enterer (1)

"Bhikkhus, there are these five faculties. What five? The faculty of faith, the faculty of energy, the faculty of mindfulness, the faculty of concentration, the faculty of wisdom.

"When, bhikkhus, a noble disciple understands as they really are the gratification, the danger, and the escape in the case of these five faculties, then he is called a noble disciple who is a stream-enterer, no longer bound to the nether world, fixed in destiny, with enlightenment as his destination."[188]

3 (3) Stream-Enterer (2)

"Bhikkhus, there are these five faculties. What five? The faculty of faith ... the faculty of wisdom.

"When, bhikkhus, a noble disciple understands as they really are the origin and the passing away, the gratification, the danger, [194] and the escape in the case of these five faculties, then he is called a noble disciple who is a stream-enterer, no longer bound to the nether world, fixed in destiny, with enlightenment as his destination."

4 (4) Arahant (1)

"Bhikkhus, there are these five faculties. What five? The faculty of faith ... the faculty of wisdom.

"When, bhikkhus, having understood as they really are the gratification, the danger, and the escape in the case of these five faculties, a bhikkhu is liberated by nonclinging, then he is called a bhikkhu who is an arahant, one whose taints are destroyed, who has lived the holy life, done what had to be done, laid down the burden, reached his own goal, utterly destroyed the fetters of existence, one completely liberated through final knowledge."[189]

5 (5) Arahant (2)

"Bhikkhus, there are these five faculties. What five? The faculty of faith ... the faculty of wisdom.

"When, bhikkhus, having understood as they really are the origin and the passing away, the gratification, the danger, and the escape in the case of these five faculties, a bhikkhu is liberated by nonclinging, then he is called a bhikkhu who is an arahant ... one completely liberated through final knowledge."

6 (6) Ascetics and Brahmins (1)

"Bhikkhus, there are these five faculties. What five? The faculty of faith ... the faculty of wisdom.

"Those ascetics or brahmins, bhikkhus, who do not understand as they really are the gratification, the danger, and the escape in the case of these five faculties: these I do not consider to be ascetics among ascetics or brahmins among brahmins, [195] and these venerable ones do not, by realizing it for themselves with direct knowledge, in this very life enter and dwell in the goal of asceticism or the goal of brahminhood.

"But, bhikkhus, those ascetics and brahmins who understand these things: these I consider to be ascetics among ascetics and brahmins among brahmins, and these venerable ones, by realizing it for themselves with direct knowledge, in this very life enter and dwell in the goal of asceticism and the goal of brahminhood."

7 (7) Ascetics and Brahmins (2)

"Those ascetics or brahmins, bhikkhus, who do not understand the faculty of faith, its origin, its cessation, and the way leading to its cessation;[190] who do not understand the faculty of energy ... the faculty of mindfulness ... the faculty of concentration ... the faculty of wisdom, its origin, its cessation, and the way leading to its cessation: these I do not consider to be ascetics among ascetics or brahmins among brahmins, and these venerable ones do not, by realizing it for themselves with direct knowledge, in this very life enter and dwell in the goal of asceticism or the goal of brahminhood.

"But, bhikkhus, those ascetics and brahmins who understand [196] these things ... in this very life enter and dwell in the goal of asceticism and the goal of brahminhood."

8 (8) To Be Seen

"Bhikkhus, there are these five faculties. What five? The faculty of faith ... the faculty of wisdom.

"And where, bhikkhus, is the faculty of faith to be seen? The faculty of faith is to be seen here in the four factors of stream-entry.[191]

"And where, bhikkhus, is the faculty of energy to be seen? The faculty of energy is to be seen here in the four right strivings.[192]

"And where, bhikkhus, is the faculty of mindfulness to be seen? The faculty of mindfulness is to be seen here in the four establishments of mindfulness.

"And where, bhikkhus, is the faculty of concentration to be seen? The faculty of concentration is to be seen here in the four jhānas.

"And where, bhikkhus, is the faculty of wisdom to be seen? The faculty of wisdom is to be seen here in the Four Noble Truths.

"These, bhikkhus, are the five faculties."

9 (9) Analysis (1)

"Bhikkhus, there are these five faculties. What five? The faculty of faith ... the faculty of wisdom.

"And what, bhikkhus, is the faculty of faith? Here, bhikkhus, the noble disciple is a person of faith, one who places faith in the enlightenment of the Tathāgata thus: [197] 'The Blessed One is an arahant, perfectly enlightened, accomplished in knowledge and conduct, fortunate, knower of the world, unsurpassed leader of persons to be tamed, teacher of devas and humans, the Enlightened One, the Blessed One.'

"And what, bhikkhus, is the faculty of energy? Here, bhikkhus, the noble disciple dwells with energy aroused for the abandoning of unwholesome states and the acquisition of wholesome states; he is strong, firm in exertion, not shirking the responsibility of cultivating wholesome states. This is called the faculty of energy.

"And what, bhikkhus, is the faculty of mindfulness? Here, bhikkhus, the noble disciple is mindful, possessing supreme mindfulness and discretion, one who remembers and recollects what was done and said long ago. This is called the faculty of mindfulness.[193]

"And what, bhikkhus, is the faculty of concentration? Here, bhikkhus, the noble disciple gains concentration, gains one-pointedness of mind, having made release the object.[194] This is called the faculty of concentration.

"And what, bhikkhus, is the faculty of wisdom? Here, bhikkhus, the noble disciple is wise; he possesses wisdom directed to arising and passing away, which is noble and penetrative, leading to the complete destruction of suffering.[195] This is called the faculty of wisdom.

"These, bhikkhus, are the five faculties."[196]

10 (10) Analysis (2)

"Bhikkhus, there are these five faculties. What five? The faculty of faith … the faculty of wisdom.

"And what, bhikkhus, is the faculty of faith? Here, bhikkhus, the noble disciple is a person of faith, one who places faith in the enlightenment of the Tathāgata thus: 'The Blessed One is … teacher of devas and humans, the Enlightened One, the Blessed One.' [198]

"And what, bhikkhus, is the faculty of energy? Here, bhikkhus, the noble disciple dwells with energy aroused for the abandoning of unwholesome states and the acquisition of wholesome states; he is strong, firm in exertion, not shirking the responsibility of cultivating wholesome states. He generates desire for the non-arising of unarisen evil unwholesome states; he makes an effort, arouses energy, applies his mind, and strives. He generates desire for the abandoning of arisen evil unwholesome states; he makes an effort, arouses energy, applies his mind, and strives. He generates desire for the arising of unarisen wholesome states; he makes an effort, arouses energy, applies his mind, and strives. He generates desire for the maintenance of arisen wholesome states, for their nondecay, increase, expansion, and fulfilment by development; he makes an effort, arouses energy, applies his mind, and strives. This is called the faculty of energy.

"And what, bhikkhus, is the faculty of mindfulness? Here, bhikkhus, the noble disciple is mindful, possessing supreme mindfulness and discretion, one who remembers and recollects what was done and said long ago. He dwells contemplating the body in the body … feelings in feelings … mind in mind … phenomena in phenomena, ardent, clearly comprehending, mindful, having removed covetousness and displeasure in regard to the world. This is called the faculty of mindfulness.

"And what, bhikkhus, is the faculty of concentration? Here, bhikkhus, the noble disciple gains concentration, gains one-pointedness of mind, having made release the object. Secluded from sensual pleasures, secluded from unwholesome states, he enters and dwells in the first jhāna, which is accompanied by thought and examination, with rapture and happiness born of seclusion. With the subsiding of thought and examination, he enters and dwells in the second jhāna, which has internal confidence and unification of mind, is without thought and examination, and has rapture and happiness born of concentration. With the fading away as well of rapture, he dwells equanimous and, mindful and clearly comprehending, he experiences happiness with the body; he enters and dwells in the third jhāna of which the noble ones declare: 'He is equanimous, mindful, one who dwells happily.' With the abandoning of pleasure and pain, and with the previous passing away of joy and displeasure, he enters and dwells in the fourth jhāna, which is neither painful nor pleasant and includes the purification of mindfulness by equanimity. This is called the faculty of concentration. [199]

"And what, bhikkhus, is the faculty of wisdom? Here, bhikkhus, the noble disciple is wise; he possesses wisdom directed to arising and passing away, which is noble and penetrative, leading to the complete destruction of suffering. He understands as it really is: 'This is suffering.' He understands as it really is: 'This is the origin of suffering.' He understands as it really is: 'This is the cessation of suffering.' He understands as it really is: 'This is the way leading to the cessation of suffering.' This is called the faculty of wisdom.

"These, bhikkhus, are the five faculties."

II. Weaker Than That

11 (1) Obtainment

"Bhikkhus, there are these five faculties. What five? The faculty of faith … the faculty of wisdom.

"And what, bhikkhus, is the faculty of faith? Here, bhikkhus, the noble disciple is a person of faith, one who places faith in the enlightenment of the Tathāgata thus: 'The Blessed One is … teacher of devas and humans, the Enlightened One, the Blessed One.' This is called the faculty of faith.

"And what, bhikkhus, is the faculty of energy? The energy that one obtains on the basis of[197] the four right strivings. This is called the faculty of energy. [200]

"And what, bhikkhus, is the faculty of mindfulness? The mindfulness that one obtains on the basis of the four establishments of mindfulness. This is called the faculty of mindfulness.

"And what, bhikkhus, is the faculty of concentration? Here, bhikkhus, the noble disciple gains concentration, gains one-pointedness of mind, having made release the object. This is called the faculty of concentration.

"And what, bhikkhus, is the faculty of wisdom? Here, bhikkhus, the noble disciple is wise; he possesses wisdom directed to arising and passing away, which is noble and penetrative, leading to the complete destruction of suffering. This is called the faculty of wisdom.

"These, bhikkhus, are the five faculties."

12 (2) In Brief (1)

"Bhikkhus, there are these five faculties. What five? The faculty of faith ... the faculty of wisdom. These are the five faculties.

"One who has completed and fulfilled these five faculties is an arahant. If they are weaker than that, one is a nonreturner; if still weaker, a once-returner; if still weaker, a stream-enterer; if still weaker, a Dhamma-follower; if still weaker, a faith-follower."[198]

13 (3) In Brief (2)

"Bhikkhus, there are these five faculties. What five? The faculty of faith ... the faculty of wisdom. These are the five faculties.

"One who has completed and fulfilled these five faculties is an arahant. If they are weaker than that, one is a nonreturner ... a once-returner ... a stream-enterer ... a Dhamma-follower ... a faith-follower.

"Thus, bhikkhus, due to a difference in the faculties there is a difference in the fruits; due to a difference in the fruits[199] there is a difference among persons." [201]

14 (4) In Brief (3)

"Bhikkhus, there are these five faculties. What five? The faculty of faith ... the faculty of wisdom. These are the five faculties.

"One who has completed and fulfilled these five faculties is an arahant. If they are weaker than that, one is ... a faith-follower.

"Thus, bhikkhus, one who activates them fully succeeds fully; one who activates them partly succeeds partly. The five faculties, bhikkhus, are not barren, so I say."[200]

15 (5) In Detail (1)

"Bhikkhus, there are these five faculties. What five? The faculty of faith ... the faculty of wisdom. These are the five faculties.

"One who has completed and fulfilled these five faculties is an arahant. If they are weaker than that, one is an attainer of Nibbāna in the interval; if still weaker, an attainer of Nibbāna upon landing; if still weaker, an attainer of Nibbāna without exertion; if still weaker, an attainer of Nibbāna with exertion; if still weaker, one who is bound upstream, heading towards the Akaniṭṭha realm; if still weaker, a once-returner; if still weaker, a stream-enterer; if still weaker, a Dhamma-follower; if still weaker, a faith-follower."[201]

16 (6) In Detail (2)

"Bhikkhus, there are these five faculties. What five? The faculty of faith ... the faculty of wisdom. These are the five faculties.

"One who has completed and fulfilled these five faculties is an arahant. If they are weaker than that, one is an attainer of Nibbāna in the interval ... (*as in §15*) ... if still weaker, a faith-follower.

"Thus, bhikkhus, due to a difference in the faculties there is a difference in the fruits; due to a difference in the fruits there is a difference among persons." [202]

17 (7) In Detail (3)

"Bhikkhus, there are these five faculties. What five? The faculty of faith ... the faculty of wisdom. These are the five faculties.

"One who has completed and fulfilled these five faculties is an arahant. If they are weaker than that, one is an attainer of Nibbāna in the interval ... (*as in §15*) ... if still weaker, a faith-follower.

"Thus, bhikkhus, one who activates them fully succeeds fully; one who activates them partly succeeds partly. The five faculties, bhikkhus, are not barren, so I say."

18 (8) Practising

"Bhikkhus, there are these five faculties. What five? The faculty of faith ... the faculty of wisdom. These are the five faculties.

"One who has completed and fulfilled these five faculties is an arahant. If they are weaker than that, one is practising for the realization of the fruit of arahantship; if still weaker, one is a nonreturner; if still weaker, one is practising for the realization of the fruit of nonreturning; if still weaker, one is a once-returner; if still weaker, one is practising for the realization of the fruit of once-returning; if still weaker, one is a stream-enterer; if still weaker, one is practising for the realization of the fruit of stream-entry.

"But, bhikkhus, I say that one in whom these five faculties are completely and totally absent is 'an outsider, one who stands in the faction of worldlings.'" [202]

19 (9) Equipped

Then a certain bhikkhu approached the Blessed One, paid homage to him, sat down to one side, and said to him:

"Venerable sir, it is said, 'one equipped with faculties, one equipped with faculties.'[203] In what way, venerable sir, is one equipped with faculties?" [203]

"Here, bhikkhu, a bhikkhu develops the faculty of faith, which leads to peace, leads to enlightenment. He develops the faculty of energy … the faculty of mindfulness … the faculty of concentration … the faculty of wisdom, which leads to peace, leads to enlightenment.

"It is in this way, bhikkhu, that one is equipped with faculties."

20 (10) Destruction of the Taints

"Bhikkhus, there are these five faculties. What five? The faculty of faith … the faculty of wisdom. These are the five faculties.

"It is, bhikkhus, because he has developed and cultivated these five faculties that a bhikkhu, by the destruction of the taints, in this very life enters and dwells in the taintless liberation of mind, liberation by wisdom, realizing it for himself with direct knowledge."

III. The Six Faculties

21 (1) Renewed Existence[204]

"Bhikkhus, there are these five faculties. What five? The faculty of faith … the faculty of wisdom.

"So long, bhikkhus, as I did not directly know as they really are the origin and the passing away, the gratification, the danger, and the escape in the case of these five faculties, [204] I did not claim to have awakened to the unsurpassed perfect enlightenment in this world with its devas, Māra, and Brahmā, in this generation with its ascetics and brahmins, its devas and humans. But when I directly knew all this as it really is, then I claimed to have awakened to the unsurpassed perfect enlightenment in this world with ... its devas and humans.

"The knowledge and vision arose in me: 'Unshakable is my liberation of mind; this is my last birth; now there is no more renewed existence.'"

22 (2) *The Life Faculty*

"Bhikkhus, there are these three faculties. What three? The femininity faculty, the masculinity faculty, the life faculty. These are the three faculties."[205]

23 (3) *The Faculty of Final Knowledge*

"Bhikkhus, there are these three faculties. What three? The faculty 'I shall know the as-yet-unknown,' the faculty of final knowledge, the faculty of one endowed with final knowledge. These are the three faculties."[206]

24 (4) *One-Seeder*

"Bhikkhus, there are these five faculties. What five? The faculty of faith ... the faculty of wisdom. These are the five faculties.

"One, bhikkhus, who has completed and fulfilled these five faculties is an arahant. If they are weaker than that, one is an attainer of Nibbāna in the interval; if still weaker, an attainer of Nibbāna upon landing; if still weaker, an attainer of Nibbāna without exertion; [205] if still weaker, an attainer of Nibbāna with exertion; if still weaker, one who is bound upstream, heading towards the Akaniṭṭha realm; if still weaker, a once-returner; if still weaker, a one-seeder; if still weaker, a clan-to-clanner; if still weaker, a seven-lives-at-moster; if still weaker, a Dhamma-follower; if still weaker, a faith-follower."[207]

25 (5) *Simple Version*

"Bhikkhus, there are these six faculties. What six? The eye faculty, the ear faculty, the nose faculty, the tongue faculty, the body faculty, the mind faculty. These are the six faculties."[208]

26 (6) Stream-Enterer

"Bhikkhus, there are these six faculties. What six? The eye faculty ... the mind faculty.

"When, bhikkhus, a noble disciple understands as they really are the gratification, the danger, and the escape in the case of these six faculties, then he is called a noble disciple who is a stream-enterer, no longer bound to the nether world, fixed in destiny, with enlightenment as his destination."

27 (7) Arahant

"Bhikkhus, there are these six faculties. What six? The eye faculty ... the mind faculty.

"When, bhikkhus, having understood as they really are the gratification, the danger, and the escape in the case of these six faculties, a bhikkhu is liberated by nonclinging,[209] then he is called a bhikkhu who is an arahant, one whose taints are destroyed, who has lived the holy life, done what had to be done, laid down the burden, reached his own goal, utterly destroyed the fetters of existence, one completely liberated through final knowledge."

28 (8) Buddha

"Bhikkhus, there are these six faculties. What six? The eye faculty ... the mind faculty. [206]

"So long, bhikkhus, as I did not directly know as they really are the origin and the passing away, the gratification, the danger, and the escape in the case of these six faculties, I did not claim to have awakened to the unsurpassed perfect enlightenment in this world with ... its devas and humans. But when I directly knew all this as it really is, then I claimed to have awakened to the unsurpassed perfect enlightenment in this world with ... its devas and humans.

"The knowledge and vision arose in me: 'Unshakable is my liberation of mind; this is my last birth; now there is no more renewed existence.'"

29 (9) Ascetics and Brahmins (1)

"Bhikkhus, there are these six faculties. What six? The eye faculty ... the mind faculty.

"Those ascetics or brahmins, bhikkhus, who do not understand as they really are the gratification, the danger, and the escape in the case of these six faculties: these I do not consider to be ascetics among ascetics or brahmins among brahmins, and these venerable ones do not, by realizing it for themselves with direct knowledge, in this very life enter and dwell in the goal of asceticism or the goal of brahminhood.

"But, bhikkhus, those ascetics and brahmins who understand these things: these I consider to be ascetics among ascetics and brahmins among brahmins, and these venerable ones, by realizing it for themselves with direct knowledge, in this very life enter and dwell in the goal of asceticism and the goal of brahminhood."

30 (10) Ascetics and Brahmins (2)

"Those ascetics or brahmins, bhikkhus, who do not understand the eye faculty, its origin, its cessation, and the way leading to its cessation; who do not understand the ear faculty ... the mind faculty, its origin, its cessation, and the way leading to its cessation: these I do not consider to be ascetics among ascetics or brahmins among brahmins, and these venerable ones do not, by realizing it for themselves with direct knowledge, in this very life enter and dwell in the goal of asceticism or the goal of brahminhood. [207]

"But, bhikkhus, those ascetics and brahmins who understand these things ... in this very life enter and dwell in the goal of asceticism and the goal of brahminhood."

IV. The Pleasure Faculty

31 (1) Simple Version

"Bhikkhus, there are these five faculties. What five? The pleasure faculty, the pain faculty, the joy faculty, the displeasure faculty, the equanimity faculty. These are the five faculties."[210]

32 (2) Stream-Enterer

"Bhikkhus, there are these five faculties. What five? The pleasure faculty ... the equanimity faculty.

"When, bhikkhus, a noble disciple understands as they really are the gratification, the danger, and the escape in the case of these five faculties, then he is called a noble disciple who is a stream-enterer, no longer bound to the nether world, fixed in destiny, with enlightenment as his destination." [208]

33 (3) Arahant

"Bhikkhus, there are these five faculties. What five? The pleasure faculty ... the equanimity faculty.

"When, bhikkhus, having understood as they really are the gratification, the danger, and the escape in the case of these five faculties, a bhikkhu is liberated by nonclinging, then he is called a bhikkhu who is an arahant, one whose taints are destroyed, who has lived the holy life, done what had to be done, laid down the burden, reached his own goal, utterly destroyed the fetters of existence, one completely liberated through final knowledge."

34 (4) Ascetics and Brahmins (1)

"Bhikkhus, there are these five faculties. What five? The pleasure faculty ... the equanimity faculty.

"Those ascetics or brahmins, bhikkhus, who do not understand as they really are the gratification, the danger, and the escape in the case of these five faculties ... do not in this very life enter and dwell in the goal of asceticism or the goal of brahminhood.

"But, bhikkhus, those ascetics and brahmins who understand these things ... in this very life enter and dwell in the goal of asceticism and the goal of brahminhood."

35 (5) Ascetics and Brahmins (2)

"Those ascetics or brahmins, bhikkhus, who do not understand the pleasure faculty, its origin, its cessation, and the way leading to its cessation; who do not understand the joy faculty ... the pain faculty ... the displeasure faculty ... the equanimity faculty, its origin, its cessation, [209] and the way leading to its cessation … do not in this very life enter and dwell in the goal of asceticism or the goal of brahminhood.

"But, bhikkhus, those ascetics and brahmins who understand these things … in this very life enter and dwell in the goal of asceticism and the goal of brahminhood."

36 (6) Analysis (1)

"Bhikkhus, there are these five faculties. What five? The pleasure faculty … the equanimity faculty.

"And what, bhikkhus, is the pleasure faculty? Whatever bodily pleasure there is, whatever bodily comfort,[211] the pleasant comfortable feeling born of body-contact: this, bhikkhus, is called the pleasure faculty.

"And what, bhikkhus, is the pain faculty? Whatever bodily pain there is, whatever bodily discomfort, the painful uncomfortable feeling born of body-contact: this, bhikkhus, is called the pain faculty.

"And what, bhikkhus, is the joy faculty? Whatever mental pleasure there is, whatever mental comfort, the pleasant comfortable feeling born of mind-contact: this, bhikkhus, is called the joy faculty.

"And what, bhikkhus, is the displeasure faculty? Whatever mental pain there is, whatever mental discomfort, the painful uncomfortable feeling born of mind-contact: this, bhikkhus, is called the displeasure faculty.

"And what, bhikkhus, is the equanimity faculty? Whatever feeling there is, whether bodily or mental, that is neither comfortable nor uncomfortable: this, bhikkhus, is called the equanimity faculty.[212]

"These, bhikkhus, are the five faculties."

37 (7) Analysis (2)

(*All as in the preceding sutta, omitting the last sentence and with the following addition:*) [210]

"Therein, bhikkhus, the pleasure faculty and the joy faculty should be seen to be pleasant feeling. The pain faculty and the displeasure faculty should be seen to be painful feeling. The equanimity faculty should be seen to be neither-painful-nor-pleasant feeling.

"These, bhikkhus, are the five faculties."

38 (8) Analysis (3)

(*All as in the preceding sutta, but with the last two paragraphs as follows:*) [211]

"Therein, bhikkhus, the pleasure faculty and the joy faculty should be seen to be pleasant feeling. The pain faculty and the displeasure faculty should be seen to be painful feeling. The equanimity faculty should be seen to be neither-painful-nor-pleasant feeling.

"Thus, bhikkhus, according to the method of exposition, these five faculties, having been five, become three; and having been three, become five."

39 (9) The Simile of the Fire-Sticks

"Bhikkhus, there are these five faculties. What five? The pleasure faculty … the equanimity faculty.

"In dependence on a contact to be experienced as pleasant, bhikkhus, the pleasure faculty arises.[213] Being in a state of pleasure, one understands: 'I am in a state of pleasure.' One understands: 'With the cessation of that contact to be experienced as pleasant, the corresponding feeling—the pleasure faculty that arose in dependence on that contact to be experienced as pleasant—ceases and subsides.'

"In dependence on a contact to be experienced as painful, bhikkhus, the pain faculty arises. Being in a state of pain, one understands: 'I am in a state of pain.' One understands: 'With the cessation of that contact to be experienced as painful, the corresponding feeling—the pain faculty that arose in dependence on that [212] contact to be experienced as painful—ceases and subsides.'

"In dependence on a contact to be experienced joyously, bhikkhus, the joy faculty arises. Being in a state of joy, one understands: 'I am in a state of joy.' One understands: 'With the cessation of that contact to be experienced joyously, the corresponding feeling—the joy faculty that arose in dependence on that contact to be experienced joyously—ceases and subsides.'

"In dependence on a contact to be experienced with displeasure, bhikkhus, the displeasure faculty arises. Being in a state of displeasure, one understands: 'I am in a state of displeasure.' One understands: 'With the cessation of that contact to be experienced with displeasure, the corresponding feeling—the displeasure faculty that arose in dependence on that contact to be experienced with displeasure—ceases and subsides.'

"In dependence on a contact to be experienced with equanimity, bhikkhus, the equanimity faculty arises. Being in a state of equanimity, one understands: 'I am in a state of equanimity.' One understands: 'With the cessation of that contact to be experienced with equanimity, the corresponding feeling—the equanimity faculty that arose in dependence on that contact to be experienced with equanimity—ceases and subsides.'

"Bhikkhus, just as heat is generated and fire is produced from the conjunction and friction of two fire-sticks, but when the sticks are separated and laid aside the resultant heat ceases and subsides; so too, in dependence on a contact to be experienced as pleasant ... [213] ... a contact to be experienced as painful ... a contact to be experienced joyously ... a contact to be experienced with displeasure ... a contact to be experienced with equanimity, the equanimity faculty arises.... One understands: 'With the cessation of that contact to be experienced with equanimity, the corresponding feeling ... ceases and subsides.'"

40 (10) Irregular Order[214]

"Bhikkhus, there are these five faculties. What five? The pleasure faculty ... the equanimity faculty.

(i. The pain faculty)

"Here, bhikkhus, while a bhikkhu is dwelling diligent, ardent, and resolute, there arises in him the pain faculty. He understands thus: 'There has arisen in me this pain faculty. That has a basis, a source, a causal formation, a condition.[215] It is impossible for that pain faculty to arise without a basis, without a source, without a causal formation, without a condition.' He understands the pain faculty; he understands the origin of the pain faculty; he understands the cessation of the pain faculty; and he understands where the arisen pain faculty ceases without remainder.

"And where does the arisen pain faculty cease without remainder?[216] Here, bhikkhus, secluded from sensual pleasures, secluded from unwholesome states, a bhikkhu enters and dwells in the first jhāna, which is accompanied by thought and examination, with rapture and happiness born of seclusion. And it is here that the arisen pain faculty ceases without remainder.[217]

"This, bhikkhus, is called a bhikkhu who has understood the cessation of the pain faculty. He directs his mind accordingly.[218]

(ii. The displeasure faculty)

"Here, bhikkhus, while a bhikkhu is dwelling diligent, ardent, and resolute, there arises in him the displeasure faculty. [214] He understands thus: 'There has arisen in me this displeasure faculty. That has a basis, a source, a causal formation, a condition. It is impossible for that displeasure faculty to arise without a basis, without a source, without a causal formation, without a condition.' He understands the displeasure faculty; he understands the origin of the displeasure faculty; he understands the cessation of the displeasure faculty; and he understands where the arisen displeasure faculty ceases without remainder.

"And where does the arisen displeasure faculty cease without remainder? With the subsiding of thought and examination, a bhikkhu enters and dwells in the second jhāna, which has internal confidence and unification of mind, is without thought and examination, and has rapture and happiness born of concentration. And it is here that the arisen displeasure faculty ceases without remainder.[219]

"This, bhikkhus, is called a bhikkhu who has understood the cessation of the displeasure faculty. He directs his mind accordingly.

(iii. The pleasure faculty)

"Here, bhikkhus, while a bhikkhu is dwelling diligent, ardent, and resolute, there arises in him the pleasure faculty. He understands thus: 'There has arisen in me this pleasure faculty. That has a basis, a source, a causal formation, a condition. It is impossible for that pleasure faculty to arise without a basis, without a source, without a causal formation, without a condition.' He understands the pleasure faculty; he understands the origin of the pleasure faculty; he understands the cessation of the pleasure faculty; and he understands where the arisen pleasure faculty ceases without remainder.

"And where does the arisen pleasure faculty cease without remainder? With the fading away as well of rapture, a bhikkhu dwells equanimous and, mindful and clearly comprehending, experiences happiness with the body; he enters and dwells in the third jhāna of which the noble ones declare: 'He is equanimous, mindful, one who dwells happily.' And it is here that the arisen pleasure faculty ceases without remainder.[220]

"This, bhikkhus, is called a bhikkhu who has understood the cessation of the pleasure faculty. He directs his mind accordingly. [215]

(iv. The joy faculty)

"Here, bhikkhus, while a bhikkhu is dwelling diligent, ardent, and resolute, there arises in him the joy faculty. He understands thus: 'There has arisen in me this joy faculty. That has a basis, a source, a causal formation, a condition. It is impossible for that joy faculty to arise without a basis, without a source, without a causal formation, without a condition.' He understands the joy faculty; he understands the origin of the joy faculty; he understands the cessation of the joy faculty; and he understands where the arisen joy faculty ceases without remainder.

"And where does the arisen joy faculty cease without remainder? With the abandoning of pleasure and pain, and with the previous passing away of joy and displeasure, a bhikkhu enters and dwells in the fourth jhāna, which is neither painful nor pleasant and includes the purification of mindfulness by equanimity. And it is here that the arisen joy faculty ceases without remainder.[221]

"This, bhikkhus, is called a bhikkhu who has understood the cessation of the joy faculty. He directs his mind accordingly.

(v. The equanimity faculty)

"Here, bhikkhus, while a bhikkhu is dwelling diligent, ardent, and resolute, there arises in him the equanimity faculty. He understands thus: 'There has arisen in me this equanimity faculty. That has a basis, a source, a causal formation, a condition. It is impossible for that equanimity faculty to arise without a basis, without a source, without a causal formation, without a condition.' He understands the equanimity faculty; he understands the origin of the equanimity faculty; he understands the cessation of the equanimity faculty; and he understands where the arisen equanimity faculty ceases without remainder.

"And where does the arisen equanimity faculty cease without remainder? Here, bhikkhus, having completely transcended the base of neither-perception-nor-nonperception, a bhikkhu enters and dwells in the cessation of perception and feeling. And it is here that the arisen equanimity faculty ceases without remainder.

"This, bhikkhus, is called a bhikkhu [216] who has understood the cessation of the equanimity faculty. He directs his mind accordingly."

V. Aging

41 (1) Subject to Aging

Thus have I heard. On one occasion the Blessed One was dwelling at Sāvatthī in the Eastern Park in the Mansion of Migāra's Mother. Now on that occasion the Blessed One had emerged from seclusion in the evening and was sitting warming his back in the last rays of the sun.

Then the Venerable Ānanda approached the Blessed One. Having approached and paid homage, while massaging the Blessed One's limbs, he said to him: "It is wonderful, venerable sir! It is amazing, venerable sir! The Blessed One's complexion is no longer pure and bright, his limbs are all flaccid and wrinkled, his body is stooped, and some alteration is seen in his faculties—in the eye faculty, the ear faculty, the nose faculty, the tongue faculty, the body faculty."[222] [217]

"So it is, Ānanda! In youth one is subject to aging; in health one is subject to illness; while alive one is subject to death. The complexion is no longer pure and bright, the limbs are all flaccid and wrinkled, the body is stooped, and some alteration is seen in the faculties—in the eye faculty … the body faculty."

This is what the Blessed One said. Having said this, the Fortunate One, the Teacher, further said this:

"Fie on you, wretched aging,
Aging which makes beauty fade!
So much has the charming puppet[223]
Been crushed beneath advancing age.

One who might live a hundred years
Also has death as destination.
Death spares none along the way
But comes crushing everything."[224]

42 (2) The Brahmin Uṇṇābha

At Sāvatthī. Then the brahmin Uṇṇābha approached the Blessed One and exchanged greetings with him. When they had concluded their greetings and cordial talk, he sat down to one side and said to the Blessed One:

"Master Gotama, these five faculties have different domains, different resorts; they do not experience each others' resort and domain. What five? The eye faculty, the ear faculty, the nose faculty, the tongue faculty, the body faculty.[225] [218] Now, Master Gotama, as these five faculties have different domains, different resorts, and do not experience each others' resort and domain, what is it that they take recourse in? And what is it that experiences their resort and domain?"

"Brahmin, these five faculties have different domains, different resorts; they do not experience each others' resort and domain. What five? The eye faculty, the ear faculty, the nose faculty, the tongue faculty, the body faculty. Now, brahmin, these five faculties having different domains, different resorts, not experiencing each others' resort and domain—they take recourse in the mind, and the mind experiences their resort and domain."[226]

"But, Master Gotama, what is it that the mind takes recourse in?"

"The mind, brahmin, takes recourse in mindfulness."

"But, Master Gotama, what is it that mindfulness takes recourse in?"

"Mindfulness, brahmin, takes recourse in liberation."[227]

"But, Master Gotama, what is it that liberation takes recourse in?"

"Liberation, brahmin, takes recourse in Nibbāna."

"But, Master Gotama, what is it that Nibbāna takes recourse in?"

"You have gone beyond the range of questioning, brahmin. You weren't able to grasp the limit to questioning. For, brahmin, the holy life is lived with Nibbāna as its ground, Nibbāna as its destination, Nibbāna as its final goal."[228]

Then the brahmin Uṇṇābha, having delighted and rejoiced in the Blessed One's statement, rose from his seat and paid homage to the Blessed One, after which he departed keeping him on his right.

Then, not long after the brahmin Uṇṇābha had departed, the Blessed One addressed the bhikkhus thus:

"Bhikkhus, suppose in a house or hall with a peaked roof, opposite a window facing east, the sun was rising. When its rays enter through the window, where would they settle?"

"On the western wall, venerable sir." [219]

"So too, bhikkhus, the brahmin Uṇṇābha has gained faith in the Tathāgata that is settled, deeply rooted, established, firm. It cannot be removed by any ascetic or brahmin or deva or Māra or Brahmā or by anyone in the world. If, bhikkhus, the brahmin Uṇṇābha were to die at this time, there is no fetter bound by which he might again come to this world."[229]

43 (3) Sāketa

Thus have I heard. On one occasion the Blessed One was dwelling at Sāketa in the Añjana Grove, in the Deer Park. There the Blessed One addressed the bhikkhus thus:

"Bhikkhus, is there a method of exposition by means of which the five faculties become the five powers and the five powers become the five faculties?"

"Venerable sir, our teachings are rooted in the Blessed One, guided by the Blessed One, take recourse in the Blessed One. It would be good if the Blessed One would clear up the meaning of this statement. Having heard it from him, the bhikkhus will remember it."...

"There is a method of exposition, bhikkhus, by means of which the five faculties become the five powers and the five powers become the five faculties. And what is that method of exposition? That which is the faculty of faith is the power of faith; that which is the power of faith is the faculty of faith.[230] That which is the faculty of energy is the power of energy; that which is the power of energy is the faculty of energy. That which is the faculty of mindfulness is the power of mindfulness; that which is the power of mindfulness is the faculty of mindfulness. That which is the faculty of concentration is the power of concentration; that which is the power of concentration is the faculty of concentration. That which is the faculty of wisdom is the power of wisdom; that which is the power of wisdom is the faculty of wisdom.

"Suppose, bhikkhus, there is a river which slants, slopes, and inclines towards the east, with an island in the middle. There is a method of exposition by means of which that river could be considered to have one stream, but there is a method of exposition by means of which it could be considered to have two streams. [220]

"And what is the method of exposition by means of which that river could be considered to have one stream? Taking into account the water to the east of the island and the water to its west—this is the method of exposition by means of which that river could be considered to have one stream.

"And what is the method of exposition by means of which that river could be considered to have two streams? Taking into account the water to the north of the island and the water to the south—this is the method of exposition by means of which that river could be considered to have two streams.

"So too, bhikkhus, that which is the faculty of faith is the power of faith … that which is the power of wisdom is the faculty of wisdom.

"It is, bhikkhus, because he has developed and cultivated these five faculties that a bhikkhu, by the destruction of the taints, in this very life enters and dwells in the taintless liberation of mind, liberation by wisdom, realizing it for himself with direct knowledge."

44 (4) The Eastern Gatehouse

Thus have I heard. On one occasion the Blessed One was dwelling at Sāvatthī in the Eastern Gatehouse. There the Blessed One addressed the Venerable Sāriputta thus:

"Sāriputta, do you have faith that the faculty of faith, when developed and cultivated, has the Deathless as its ground, the Deathless as its destination, the Deathless as its final goal?... That the faculty of wisdom, when developed and cultivated, has the Deathless as its ground, the Deathless as its destination, the Deathless as its final goal." [221]

"Venerable sir, I do not go by faith in the Blessed One about this:[231] that the faculty of faith ... the faculty of wisdom, when developed and cultivated, has the Deathless as its ground, the Deathless as its destination, the Deathless as its final goal. Those by whom this has not been known, seen, understood, realized, and contacted with wisdom—they would have to go by faith in others about this: that the faculty of faith ... the faculty of wisdom, when developed and cultivated, has the Deathless as its ground, the Deathless as its destination, the Deathless as its final goal. But those by whom this has been known, seen, understood, realized, and contacted with wisdom—they would be without perplexity or doubt about this: that the faculty of faith ... the faculty of wisdom, when developed and cultivated, has the Deathless as its ground, the Deathless as its destination, the Deathless as its final goal.

"I am one, venerable sir, by whom this has been known, seen, understood, realized, and contacted with wisdom. I am without perplexity or doubt about this: that the faculty of faith ... the faculty of wisdom, when developed and cultivated, has the Deathless as its ground, the Deathless as its destination, the Deathless as its final goal."

"Good, good Sāriputta! Those by whom this has not been known ... they would have to go by faith in others about this.... But those by whom this has been known ... they would be without perplexity or doubt about this: that the faculty of faith ... [222] ... the faculty of wisdom, when developed and cultivated, has the Deathless as its ground, the Deathless as its destination, the Deathless as its final goal."

45 (5) The Eastern Park (1)

Thus have I heard. On one occasion the Blessed One was dwelling at Sāvatthī in the Eastern Park, in the Mansion of Migāra's Mother. There the Blessed One addressed the bhikkhus thus:

"Bhikkhus, by having developed and cultivated how many faculties does a bhikkhu who has destroyed the taints declare final knowledge thus: 'I understand: Destroyed is birth, the holy life has been lived, what had to be done has been done, there is no more for this state of being'?"

"Venerable sir, our teachings are rooted in the Blessed One...."

"It is, bhikkhus, because he has developed and cultivated one faculty that a bhikkhu who has destroyed the taints declares final knowledge thus. What is that one faculty? The faculty of wisdom. For a noble disciple who possesses wisdom, the faith that follows from it becomes stabilized, the energy that follows from it becomes stabilized, the mindfulness that follows from it becomes stabilized, the concentration that follows from it becomes stabilized.[232]

"It is, bhikkhus, because this one faculty has been developed and cultivated that a bhikkhu who has destroyed the taints declares final knowledge thus: 'I understand: Destroyed is birth, the holy life has been lived, what had to be done has been done, there is no more for this state of being.'"

46 (6) The Eastern Park (2)

The same setting. "Bhikkhus, by having developed and cultivated how many faculties does a bhikkhu who has destroyed the taints declare final knowledge thus: 'I understand: Destroyed is birth, the holy life has been lived, what had to be done has been done, there is no more for this state of being'?"

"Venerable sir, our teachings are rooted in the Blessed One...." [223]

"It is, bhikkhus, because he has developed and cultivated two faculties that a bhikkhu who has destroyed the taints declares final knowledge thus. What two? Noble wisdom and noble liberation. For his noble wisdom is his faculty of wisdom; his noble liberation is his faculty of concentration.

"It is, bhikkhus, because these two faculties have been developed and cultivated that a bhikkhu who has destroyed the taints declares final knowledge thus: 'I understand: Destroyed is birth ... there is no more for this state of being.'"

47 (7) The Eastern Park (3)

The same setting. "Bhikkhus, by having developed and cultivated how many faculties does a bhikkhu who has destroyed the taints declare final knowledge thus: 'I understand: Destroyed is birth, the holy life has been lived, what had to be done has been done, there is no more for this state of being'?"

"Venerable sir, our teachings are rooted in the Blessed One...."

"It is, bhikkhus, because he has developed and cultivated four faculties that a bhikkhu who has destroyed the taints declares final knowledge thus. What four? The faculty of energy, the faculty of mindfulness, the faculty of concentration, the faculty of wisdom.

"It is, bhikkhus, because these four faculties have been developed and cultivated that a bhikkhu who has destroyed the taints declares final knowledge thus: 'I understand: Destroyed is birth ... there is no more for this state of being.'"

48 (8) The Eastern Park (4)

The same setting. "Bhikkhus, by having developed and cultivated how many faculties does a bhikkhu who has destroyed the taints declare final knowledge thus: 'I understand: Destroyed is birth, the holy life has been lived, what had to be done has been done, there is no more for this state of being'?"

"Venerable sir, our teachings are rooted in the Blessed One...."

"It is, bhikkhus, because he has developed and cultivated five faculties that a bhikkhu who has destroyed the taints declares final knowledge thus. What five? [224] The faculty of faith, the faculty of energy, the faculty of mindfulness, the faculty of concentration, the faculty of wisdom.

"It is, bhikkhus, because these five faculties have been developed and cultivated that a bhikkhu who has destroyed the taints declares final knowledge thus: 'I understand: Destroyed is birth ... there is no more for this state of being.'"

49 (9) Piṇḍola

Thus have I heard. On one occasion the Blessed One was dwelling at Kosambī in Ghosita's Park. Now on that occasion the

Venerable Piṇḍola Bhāradvāja had declared final knowledge thus: "I understand: Destroyed is birth, the holy life has been lived, what had to be done has been done, there is no more for this state of being."

Then a number of bhikkhus approached the Blessed One, paid homage to him, sat down to one side, and said to him:

"Venerable sir, the Venerable Piṇḍola Bhāradvāja has declared final knowledge thus: 'I understand: Destroyed is birth....' Considering what reason has the Venerable Piṇḍola Bhāradvāja declared final knowledge thus?"

"It is, bhikkhus, because he has developed and cultivated three faculties that the bhikkhu Piṇḍola Bhāradvāja has declared final knowledge thus. What are those three? The faculty of mindfulness, the faculty of concentration, the faculty of wisdom. It is because he has developed and cultivated these three faculties that the bhikkhu Piṇḍola Bhāradvāja has declared final knowledge thus.

"In what, bhikkhus, do these three faculties end? They end in destruction. End in the destruction of what? Of birth, aging, and death. Considering that they end in the destruction of birth, aging, and death,[233] [225] the bhikkhu Piṇḍola Bhāradvāja has declared final knowledge thus: 'I understand: Destroyed is birth, the holy life has been lived, what had to be done has been done, there is no more for this state of being.'"

50 (10) At Āpaṇa

Thus have I heard. On one occasion the Blessed One was dwelling among the Aṅgans, where there was a town of the Aṅgans named Āpaṇa. There the Blessed One addressed the Venerable Sāriputta thus:

"Sāriputta, does the noble disciple who is completely dedicated to the Tathāgata and has full confidence in him entertain any perplexity or doubt about the Tathāgata or the Tathāgata's teaching?"

"Venerable sir, the noble disciple who is completely dedicated to the Tathāgata and has full confidence in him does not entertain any perplexity or doubt about the Tathāgata or the Tathāgata's teaching. It is indeed to be expected, venerable sir, that a noble disciple who has faith will dwell with energy aroused for the abandoning of unwholesome states and the acquisition of wholesome states; that he will be strong, firm in exertion, not shirking the responsibility of cultivating wholesome states. That energy of his, venerable sir, is his faculty of energy.

"It is indeed to be expected, venerable sir, that a noble disciple who has faith and whose energy is aroused will be mindful, possessing supreme mindfulness and discretion, one who remembers and recollects what was done and said long ago. That mindfulness of his, venerable sir, is his faculty of mindfulness.

"It is indeed to be expected, venerable sir, that a noble disciple who has faith, whose energy is aroused, and whose mindfulness is established, will gain concentration, will gain one-pointedness of mind, having made release the object. That concentration of his, venerable sir, is his faculty of concentration.

"It is indeed to be expected, venerable sir, that a noble disciple who has faith, whose energy is aroused, whose mindfulness is established, [226] and whose mind is concentrated, will understand thus: 'This saṃsāra is without discoverable beginning. A first point is not discerned of beings roaming and wandering on, hindered by ignorance and fettered by craving. But the remainderless fading away and cessation of ignorance, the mass of darkness: this is the peaceful state, this is the sublime state, that is, the stilling of all formations, the relinquishment of all acquisitions, the destruction of craving, dispassion, cessation, Nibbāna.' That wisdom of his, venerable sir, is his faculty of wisdom.

"And, venerable sir, when he has again and again strived in such a way, again and again recollected in such a way, again and again concentrated his mind in such a way, again and again understood with wisdom in such a way, that noble disciple gains complete faith thus: 'As to these things that previously I had only heard about, now I dwell having contacted them with the body and, having pierced them through with wisdom, I see.' That faith of his, venerable sir, is his faculty of faith."[234]

"Good, good, Sāriputta! Sāriputta, the noble disciple who is completely dedicated to the Tathāgata and has full confidence in him does not entertain any perplexity or doubt about the Tathāgata or the Tathāgata's teaching."

(*The Buddha then repeats verbatim Sāriputta's entire statement regarding the noble disciple's faculties.*) [227]

VI. The Boar's Cave

51 (1) Sālā

Thus have I heard. On one occasion the Blessed One was dwelling among the Kosalans at Sālā, a brahmin village. There the Blessed One addressed the bhikkhus thus:

"Bhikkhus, just as among animals the lion, the king of beasts, is declared to be their chief, that is, with respect to strength, speed, and courage, so too, among the states conducive to enlightenment[235] the faculty of wisdom is declared to be their chief, that is, for the attainment of enlightenment.

"And what, bhikkhus, are the states conducive to enlightenment? The faculty of faith, bhikkhus, is a state conducive to enlightenment; it leads to enlightenment. The faculty of energy is a state conducive to enlightenment; it leads to enlightenment. The faculty of mindfulness is a state conducive to enlightenment; it leads to enlightenment. The faculty of concentration is a state conducive to enlightenment; it leads to enlightenment. The faculty of wisdom is a state conducive to enlightenment; it leads to enlightenment. [228]

"Just as, bhikkhus, among animals the lion is declared to be their chief, so too, among the states conducive to enlightenment the faculty of wisdom is declared to be their chief, that is, for the attainment of enlightenment."

52 (2) Mallikas

Thus have I heard. On one occasion the Blessed One was dwelling among the Mallikas, where there was a town of the Mallikas named Uruvelakappa. There the Blessed One addressed the bhikkhus thus:

"Bhikkhus, so long as noble knowledge has not arisen in the noble disciple, there is as yet no stability of the [other] four faculties, no steadiness of the [other] four faculties.[236] But when noble knowledge has arisen in the noble disciple, then there is stability of the [other] four faculties, then there is steadiness of the [other] four faculties.

"It is, bhikkhus, just as in a house with a peaked roof: so long as the roof peak has not been set in place, there is as yet no stability of the rafters, there is as yet no steadiness of the rafters; but when the roof peak has been set in place, then there is stability of the rafters, then there is steadiness of the rafters. So too, bhikkhus, so long as noble knowledge has not arisen in the noble disciple, there is as yet no stability of the [other] four faculties, no steadiness of the [other] four faculties. But when noble knowledge has arisen in the noble disciple, then there is stability of the [other] four faculties, then there is steadiness of the [other] four faculties.

"What four? [229] The faculty of faith, the faculty of energy, the faculty of mindfulness, the faculty of concentration. In the case of a noble disciple who possesses wisdom, the faith that follows from it becomes stable; the energy that follows from it becomes stable; the mindfulness that follows from it becomes stable; the concentration that follows from it becomes stable."

53 (3) A Trainee

Thus have I heard. On one occasion the Blessed One was dwelling at Kosambī in Ghosita's Park. There the Blessed One addressed the bhikkhus thus:

"Bhikkhus, is there a method by means of which a bhikkhu who is a trainee, standing on the plane of a trainee, might understand: 'I am a trainee,' while a bhikkhu who is one beyond training, standing on the plane of one beyond training, might understand: 'I am one beyond training'?"

"Venerable sir, our teachings are rooted in the Blessed One...."

"There is a method, bhikkhus, by means of which a bhikkhu who is a trainee ... might understand: 'I am a trainee,' while a bhikkhu who is one beyond training ... might understand: 'I am one beyond training.'

"And what, bhikkhus, is the method by means of which a bhikkhu who is a trainee, standing on the plane of a trainee, understands: 'I am a trainee'?

"Here, bhikkhus, a bhikkhu who is a trainee understands as it really is: 'This is suffering'; he understands as it really is: 'This is the origin of suffering'; he understands as it really is: 'This is the cessation of suffering'; he understands as it really is: 'This is the way leading to the cessation of suffering.' This is a method by means of which a bhikkhu who is a trainee, standing on the plane of a trainee, understands: 'I am a trainee.'

"Again, bhikkhus, a bhikkhu who is a trainee considers thus: 'Is there outside here[237] another ascetic or brahmin who teaches a Dhamma so real, true, actual [230] as the Blessed One does?' He understands thus: 'There is no other ascetic or brahmin outside here who teaches a Dhamma so real, true, actual as the Blessed One does.' This too is a method by means of which a bhikkhu who is a trainee, standing on the plane of a trainee, understands: 'I am a trainee.'

"Again, bhikkhus, a bhikkhu who is a trainee understands the five spiritual faculties—the faculty of faith, the faculty of energy, the faculty of mindfulness, the faculty of concentration, the faculty of wisdom. He does not yet dwell having contacted with the body their destination, their culmination, their fruit, their final goal; but having pierced it through with wisdom, he sees.[238] This too is a method by means of which a bhikkhu who is a trainee, standing on the plane of a trainee, understands: 'I am a trainee.'

"And what, bhikkhus, is the method by means of which a bhikkhu who is one beyond training, standing on the plane of one beyond training, understands: 'I am one beyond training'? Here, bhikkhus, a bhikkhu who is one beyond training understands the five spiritual faculties—the faculty of faith … the faculty of wisdom. He dwells having contacted with the body their destination, their culmination, their fruit, their final goal; and having pierced it through with wisdom, he sees. This is a method by means of which a bhikkhu who is one beyond training, standing on the plane of one beyond training, understands: 'I am one beyond training.'

"Again, bhikkhus, a bhikkhu who is one beyond training understands the six faculties—the eye faculty, the ear faculty, the nose faculty, the tongue faculty, the body faculty, the mind faculty. He understands: 'These six faculties will cease completely and totally without remainder, and no other six faculties will arise anywhere in any way.' This too is a method by means of which a bhikkhu who is one beyond training, standing on the plane of one beyond training, understands: 'I am one beyond training.'" [231]

54 (4) Footprints

"Bhikkhus, just as the footprints of all living beings that walk fit into the footprint of the elephant, and the elephant's footprint is declared to be their chief by reason of its size, so too, among the steps that lead to enlightenment,[239] the faculty of wisdom is declared to be their chief, that is, for the attainment of enlightenment.

"And what, bhikkhus, are the steps that lead to enlightenment? The faculty of faith, bhikkhus, is a step that leads to enlightenment. The faculty of energy is a step that leads to enlightenment. The faculty of mindfulness is a step that leads to enlightenment. The faculty of concentration is a step that leads to enlightenment. The faculty of wisdom is a step that leads to enlightenment.

"Just as, bhikkhus, the footprints of all living beings that walk fit into the footprint of the elephant, ... so too, among the steps that lead to enlightenment, the faculty of wisdom is declared to be their chief, that is, for the attainment of enlightenment."

55 (5) Heartwood

"Bhikkhus, just as among fragrant heartwoods red sandalwood is declared to be their chief, so too, among the states conducive to enlightenment the faculty of wisdom is declared to be their chief, that is, for the attainment of enlightenment.

"And what, bhikkhus, are the states conducive to enlightenment? The faculty of faith ... the faculty of wisdom...." [232]

56 (6) Established

"Bhikkhus, when a bhikkhu is established in one thing, the five faculties are developed, well developed in him. In what one thing? In diligence.

"And what, bhikkhus, is diligence? Here, bhikkhus, a bhikkhu guards the mind against the taints and against tainted states.[240] While he is guarding the mind thus, the faculty of faith goes to fulfilment by development; the faculty of energy ... the faculty of mindfulness ... the faculty of concentration ... the faculty of wisdom goes to fulfilment by development.

"It is in this way, bhikkhus, that when a bhikkhu is established in one thing, the five faculties are developed, well developed in him."

57 (7) Brahmā Sahampati

On one occasion the Blessed One was dwelling at Uruvelā on the bank of the river Nerañjarā at the foot of the Goatherd's Banyan Tree just after he had become fully enlightened. Then, while the Blessed One was alone in seclusion, a reflection arose in his mind thus: "The five faculties, when developed and cultivated, have the Deathless as their ground, the Deathless as their destination, the Deathless as their final goal. What five? The faculty of faith, the faculty of energy, the faculty of mindfulness, the faculty of concentration, the faculty of wisdom. These five faculties, when developed and cultivated, have the Deathless as their ground, the Deathless as their destination, the Deathless as their final goal." [233]

Then Brahmā Sahampati, having known with his own mind the reflection in the Blessed One's mind, just as quickly as a strong man might extend his drawn-in arm or draw in his extended arm, disappeared from the brahmā world and reappeared before the Blessed One. He arranged his upper robe over one shoulder, extended his joined hands in reverential salutation towards the Blessed One, and said to him: "So it is, Blessed One! So it is, Fortunate One! Venerable sir, the five faculties ... (*all as above*) ... have the Deathless as their final goal.

"Once in the past, venerable sir, I lived the holy life under the Perfectly Enlightened One Kassapa. There they knew me as the bhikkhu Sahaka. By having developed and cultivated these same five faculties, venerable sir, I eliminated desire for sensual pleasures and thus, with the breakup of the body, after death, I was reborn in a good destination, in the brahmā world. There they know me as Brahmā Sahampati. So it is, Blessed One! So it is, Fortunate One! I know this, I see this: how these five faculties, when developed and cultivated, have the Deathless as their ground, the Deathless as their destination, the Deathless as their final goal."

58 (8) The Boar's Cave

On one occasion the Blessed One was dwelling at Rājagaha on Mount Vulture Peak, in the Boar's Cave. There the Blessed One addressed the Venerable Sāriputta thus:

"Considering what benefit, Sāriputta, does a bhikkhu whose taints are destroyed conduct himself in a way that shows supreme honour towards the Tathāgata and the Tathāgata's teaching?"[241] [234]

"It is, venerable sir, considering as benefit the unsurpassed security from bondage that a bhikkhu whose taints are destroyed conducts himself in a way that shows supreme honour towards the Tathāgata and the Tathāgata's teaching."

"Good, good, Sāriputta! For, Sāriputta, it is considering as benefit the unsurpassed security from bondage that a bhikkhu whose taints are destroyed conducts himself in a way that shows supreme honour towards the Tathāgata and the Tathāgata's teaching.

"And what, Sāriputta, is the unsurpassed security from bondage that a bhikkhu whose taints are destroyed considers as the benefit when he conducts himself in a way that shows supreme honour towards the Tathāgata and the Tathāgata's teaching?"

"Here, venerable sir, a bhikkhu whose taints are destroyed develops the faculty of faith, which leads to peace, leads to enlightenment. He develops the faculty of energy ... the faculty of mindfulness ... the faculty of concentration ... the faculty of wisdom, which leads to peace, leads to enlightenment. This, venerable sir, is the unsurpassed security from bondage that a bhikkhu whose taints are destroyed considers as the benefit when he conducts himself in a way that shows supreme honour towards the Tathāgata and the Tathāgata's teaching."

"Good, good, Sāriputta! For that, Sāriputta, is the unsurpassed security from bondage that a bhikkhu whose taints are destroyed considers as the benefit when he conducts himself in a way that shows supreme honour towards the Tathāgata and the Tathāgata's teaching.

"And what, Sāriputta, is the supreme honour with which a bhikkhu whose taints are destroyed conducts himself towards the Tathāgata and the Tathāgata's teaching?"

"Here, venerable sir, a bhikkhu whose taints are destroyed dwells reverential and deferential towards the Teacher, the Dhamma, the Saṅgha, the training, and concentration.[242] This, venerable sir, is that supreme honour with which a bhikkhu whose taints are destroyed conducts himself towards the Tathāgata and the Tathāgata's teaching." [235]

"Good, good, Sāriputta! For that, Sāriputta, is the supreme honour with which a bhikkhu whose taints are destroyed conducts himself towards the Tathāgata and the Tathāgata's teaching."

59 (9) Arising (1)

At Sāvatthī. "Bhikkhus, these five faculties, developed and cultivated, if unarisen do not arise apart from the appearance of a Tathāgata, an Arahant, a Perfectly Enlightened One. What five? The faculty of faith, the faculty of energy, the faculty of mindfulness, the faculty of concentration, the faculty of wisdom. These five faculties, developed and cultivated, if unarisen do not arise apart from the appearance of a Tathāgata, an Arahant, a Perfectly Enlightened One."

60 (10) Arising (2)

At Sāvatthī. "Bhikkhus, these five faculties, developed and cultivated, if unarisen do not arise apart from the Discipline of a Fortunate One. What five? The faculty of faith, the faculty of energy, the faculty of mindfulness, the faculty of concentration, the faculty of wisdom. These five faculties, developed and cultivated, if unarisen do not arise apart from the Discipline of a Fortunate One."

[236] VII. Conducive to Enlightenment

61 (1) Fetters

At Sāvatthī. "Bhikkhus, these five faculties, when developed and cultivated, lead to the abandoning of the fetters. What five? The faculty of faith … the faculty of wisdom. These five faculties…."

62 (2) Underlying Tendencies

"Bhikkhus, these five faculties, when developed and cultivated, lead to the uprooting of the underlying tendencies. What five? The faculty of faith … the faculty of wisdom. These five faculties…."

63 (3) Full Understanding

"Bhikkhus, these five faculties, when developed and cultivated, lead to the full understanding of the course. What five? The faculty of faith … the faculty of wisdom. These five faculties…."

64 (4) The Destruction of the Taints

"Bhikkhus, these five faculties, when developed and cultivated, lead to the destruction of the taints. What five? The faculty of faith … the faculty of wisdom.

"These five faculties, when developed and cultivated, lead to the abandoning of the fetters, to the uprooting of the underlying tendencies, to the full understanding of the course, to the destruction of the taints. What five? The faculty of faith … the faculty of wisdom….."

65 (5) Two Fruits

"Bhikkhus, there are these five faculties. What five? The faculty of faith … the faculty of wisdom. These are the five faculties.

"When, bhikkhus, these five faculties have been developed and cultivated, one of two fruits may be expected: either final knowledge in this very life or, if there is a residue of clinging, the state of nonreturning." [237]

66 (6) Seven Benefits

"Bhikkhus, there are these five faculties. What five? The faculty of faith … the faculty of wisdom. These are the five faculties.

"When, bhikkhus, these five faculties have been developed and cultivated, seven fruits and benefits may be expected. What are the seven fruits and benefits?

"One attains final knowledge early in this very life. If one does not attain final knowledge early in this very life, then one attains final knowledge at the time of death. If one does not attain final knowledge early in this very life, or at the time of death, then with the utter destruction of the five lower fetters one becomes an attainer of Nibbāna within the interval … an attainer of

Nibbāna upon landing ... an attainer of Nibbāna without exertion ... an attainer of Nibbāna with exertion ... one bound upstream, heading towards the Akaniṭṭha realm.

"When, bhikkhus, these five faculties have been developed and cultivated, these seven fruits and benefits may be expected."

67 (7) The Tree (1)

"Bhikkhus, just as, among the trees of Jambudīpa the rose-apple tree is declared to be their chief, so too, among the states conducive to enlightenment the faculty of wisdom is declared to be their chief, that is, for the attainment of enlightenment.

"And what, bhikkhus, are the states conducive to enlightenment? The faculty of faith, bhikkhus, is a state conducive to enlightenment; it leads to enlightenment.... The faculty of wisdom is a state conducive to enlightenment; it leads to enlightenment.

"Just as, bhikkhus, among the trees of Jambudīpa the rose-apple tree is declared to be their chief, so too, among the states conducive to enlightenment the faculty of wisdom is declared to be their chief, that is, for the attainment of enlightenment." [238]

68 (8) The Tree (2)

"Bhikkhus, just as, among the trees of the Tāvatiṃsa devas the coral tree[243] is declared to be their chief, so too, among the states conducive to enlightenment the faculty of wisdom is declared to be their chief, that is, for the attainment of enlightenment.

"And what, bhikkhus, are the states conducive to enlightenment? The faculty of faith ... The faculty of wisdom ... that is, for the attainment of enlightenment."

69 (9) The Tree (3)

"Bhikkhus, just as, among the trees of the asuras the trumpet-flower tree[244] is declared to be their chief, so too, among the states conducive to enlightenment the faculty of wisdom is declared to be their chief ... (*all as above*) ... that is, for the attainment of enlightenment."

70 (10) The Tree (4)

"Bhikkhus, just as, among the trees of the supaṇṇas the silk-cotton tree is declared to be their chief, so too, among the states conducive to enlightenment the faculty of wisdom is declared to be their chief ... (*all as above*) [239] ... that is, for the attainment of enlightenment."

VIII. Ganges Repetition Series

71 (1)–82 (12) The River Ganges—Eastward, Etc.

"Bhikkhus, just as the river Ganges slants, slopes, and inclines towards the east, so too a bhikkhu who develops and cultivates the five spiritual faculties slants, slopes, and inclines towards Nibbāna.

"And how, bhikkhus, does a bhikkhu develop and cultivate the five spiritual faculties so that he slants, slopes, and inclines towards Nibbāna? Here, bhikkhus, a bhikkhu develops the faculty of faith, which is based upon seclusion, dispassion, and cessation, maturing in release. He develops the faculty of energy ... the faculty of mindfulness ... the faculty of concentration ... the faculty of wisdom, which is based upon seclusion, dispassion, and cessation, maturing in release.

"It is in this way, bhikkhus, that a bhikkhu develops and cultivates the five spiritual faculties so that he slants, slopes, and inclines towards Nibbāna." [240]

(The remaining suttas of this vagga are to be similarly elaborated parallel to 45:92–102.)

Six about slanting to the east
And six about slanting to the ocean.
These two sixes make up twelve:
Thus the subchapter is recited.

IX. Diligence

83 (1)–92 (10) The Tathāgata, Etc.

(*To be elaborated by way of the faculties parallel to 45:139–48.*)

Tathāgata, footprint, roof peak,
Roots, heartwood, jasmine,
Monarch, the moon and sun,
Together with the cloth as tenth.

X. Strenuous Deeds

93 (1)–104 (12) Strenuous, Etc.

(*To be elaborated parallel to 45:149–60.*)

Strenuous, seeds, and nāgas,
The tree, the pot, the spike,
The sky, and two on clouds,
The ship, guest house, and river.

XI. Searches

105 (1)–114 (10) Searches, Etc.

(*To be elaborated parallel to 45:161–70.*)

Searches, discriminations, taints,
Kinds of existence, threefold suffering,
Barrenness, stains, and troubles,
Feelings, craving, and thirst.

[241]

XII. Floods

115 (1)–123 (9) Floods, Etc.

(*To be elaborated parallel to 45:171–79.*)

124 (10) Higher Fetters

"Bhikkhus, there are these five higher fetters. What five? Lust for form, lust for the formless, conceit, restlessness, ignorance. These are the five higher fetters. The five spiritual faculties are to be developed for direct knowledge of these five higher fetters, for the full understanding of them, for their utter destruction, for their abandoning.

"What five? Here, bhikkhus, a bhikkhu develops the faculty of faith ... the faculty of wisdom, which is based upon seclusion, dispassion, and cessation, maturing in release.

"These five spiritual faculties are to be developed for direct knowledge of these five higher fetters, for the full understanding of them, for their utter destruction, for their abandoning."

Floods, bonds, kinds of clinging,
Knots, and underlying tendencies,
Cords of sensual pleasure, hindrances,
Aggregates, fetters lower and higher.

XIII. Ganges Repetition Series (Removal of Lust Version)

125 (1)–136 (12) The River Ganges—Eastward, Etc.

"Bhikkhus, just as the river Ganges slants, slopes, and inclines towards the east, so too a bhikkhu who develops and cultivates the five spiritual faculties slants, slopes, and inclines towards Nibbāna.

"And how, bhikkhus, does a bhikkhu develop and cultivate the five spiritual faculties so that he slants, slopes, and inclines towards Nibbāna? Here, bhikkhus, a bhikkhu develops the faculty of faith ... the faculty of wisdom, which has as its final goal the removal of lust, the removal of hatred, the removal of delusion.

"It is in this way, bhikkhus, that a bhikkhu develops and cultivates the five spiritual faculties so that he slants, slopes, and inclines towards Nibbāna." [242]

XIV. Diligence
(Removal of Lust Version)

137 (1)–146 (10) The Tathāgata, Etc.

XV. Strenuous Deeds
(Removal of Lust Version)

147 (1)–158 (12) Strenuous, Etc.

XVI. Searches
(Removal of Lust Version)

159 (1)–168 (10) Searches, Etc.

XVII. Floods
(Removal of Lust Version)

169 (1)–177 (9) Floods, Etc.
178 (10) Higher Fetters

"Bhikkhus, there are these five higher fetters. What five? Lust for form, lust for the formless, conceit, restlessness, ignorance. These are the five higher fetters. The five spiritual faculties are to be developed for direct knowledge of these five higher fetters, for the full understanding of them, for their utter destruction, for their abandoning.

"What five? Here, bhikkhus, a bhikkhu develops the faculty of faith ... [243] ... the faculty of wisdom, which has as its final goal the removal of lust, the removal of hatred, the removal of delusion.

"These five spiritual faculties are to be developed for direct knowledge of these five higher fetters, for the full understanding of them, for their utter destruction, for their abandoning."

Floods, bonds, kinds of clinging,
Knots, and underlying tendencies,

Cords of sensual pleasure, hindrances,
Aggregates, fetters lower and higher.

(All to be elaborated by way of the five faculties having as their final goal the removal of lust, the removal of hatred, the removal of delusion.)

[244] Chapter V

49 *Sammappadhānasaṃyutta* Connected Discourses on the Right Strivings

I. Ganges Repetition Series

1 (1)–12 (12) The River Ganges—Eastward, Etc.

At Sāvatthī. There the Blessed One said this: "Bhikkhus, there are these four right strivings. What four? Here, bhikkhus, a bhikkhu generates desire for the nonarising of unarisen evil unwholesome states; he makes an effort, arouses energy, applies his mind, and strives. He generates desire for the abandoning of arisen evil unwholesome states; he makes an effort, arouses energy, applies his mind, and strives. He generates desire for the arising of unarisen wholesome states; he makes an effort, arouses energy, applies his mind, and strives. He generates desire for the maintenance of arisen wholesome states, for their nondecay, increase, expansion, and fulfilment by development; he makes an effort, arouses energy, applies his mind, and strives. These are the four right strivings.[245]

"Bhikkhus, just as the river Ganges slants, slopes, and inclines towards the east, so too a bhikkhu who develops and cultivates the four right strivings slants, slopes, and inclines towards Nibbāna.

"And how, bhikkhus, does a bhikkhu develop and cultivate the four right strivings so that he slants, slopes, and inclines towards Nibbāna? [245] Here, bhikkhus, a bhikkhu generates desire for the nonarising of unarisen evil unwholesome states; he makes an effort, arouses energy, applies his mind, and strives. He generates desire for the abandoning of arisen evil unwholesome states....

He generates desire for the arising of unarisen wholesome states.... He generates desire for the maintenance of arisen wholesome states, for their nondecay, increase, expansion, and fulfilment by development; he makes an effort, arouses energy, applies his mind, and strives. These are the four right strivings.

"It is in this way, bhikkhus, that a bhikkhu develops and cultivates the four right strivings so that he slants, slopes, and inclines towards Nibbāna."

(The remaining suttas of this vagga are to be similarly elaborated parallel to 45:92–102.)

Six about slanting to the east
And six about slanting to the ocean.
These two sixes make up twelve:
Thus the subchapter is recited.

II. Diligence

13 (1)–22 (10) The Tathāgata, Etc.

(*To be elaborated by way of the four right strivings parallel to 45:139–48.*)

Tathāgata, footprint, roof peak,
Roots, heartwood, jasmine,
Monarch, the moon and sun,
Together with the cloth as tenth.

[246]

III. Strenuous Deeds

23 (1)–34 (12) Strenuous, Etc.

"Bhikkhus, just as whatever strenuous deeds are done, are all done based upon the earth, established upon the earth, so too, based upon virtue, established upon virtue, a bhikkhu develops and cultivates the four right strivings.

"And how, bhikkhus, does a bhikkhu, based upon virtue, established upon virtue, develop and cultivate the four right strivings? Here, bhikkhus, a bhikkhu generates desire for the nonarising of unarisen evil unwholesome states; he makes an effort, arouses energy, applies his mind, and strives. He generates desire for the abandoning of arisen evil unwholesome states.... He generates desire for the arising of unarisen wholesome states.... He generates desire for the maintenance of arisen wholesome states, for their nondecay, increase, expansion, and fulfilment by development; he makes an effort, arouses energy, applies his mind, and strives. These are the four right strivings.

"It is in this way, bhikkhus, that a bhikkhu, based upon virtue, established upon virtue, develops and cultivates the four right strivings."

(*To be elaborated parallel to 45:149–60.*)

Strenuous, seeds, and nāgas,
The tree, the pot, the spike,
The sky, and two on clouds,
The ship, guest house, and river.

IV. Searches

35 (1)–44 (10) Searches, Etc.

"Bhikkhus, there are these three searches. What three? The search for sensual pleasure, the search for existence, the search for a holy life. These are the three searches. [247] The four right strivings are to be developed for direct knowledge of these three searches, for the full understanding of them, for their utter destruction, for their abandoning.

"What four? Here, bhikkhus, a bhikkhu generates desire for the nonarising of unarisen evil unwholesome states ... for the maintenance of arisen wholesome states, for their nondecay, increase, expansion, and fulfilment by development; he makes an effort, arouses energy, applies his mind, and strives.

"These four right strivings are to be developed for the direct knowledge of these three searches, for the full understanding of them, for their utter destruction, for their abandoning."

(*To be elaborated parallel to 45:161–70.*)

Searches, discriminations, taints,
Kinds of existence, threefold suffering,
Barrenness, stains, and troubles,
Feelings, craving, and thirst.

V. Floods

45 (1)–53 (9) Floods, Etc.

(*To be elaborated parallel to 45:171–79.*)

54 (10) Higher Fetters

"Bhikkhus, there are these five higher fetters. What five? Lust for form, lust for the formless, conceit, restlessness, ignorance. These are the five higher fetters. The four right strivings are to be developed for direct knowledge of these five higher fetters, for the full understanding of them, for their utter destruction, for their abandoning.

"What four? Here, bhikkhus, a bhikkhu generates desire for the nonarising of unarisen evil unwholesome states … for the maintenance of arisen wholesome states, for their nondecay, increase, expansion, and fulfilment by development; [248] he makes an effort, arouses energy, applies his mind, and strives.

"These four right strivings are to be developed for the direct knowledge of these five higher fetters, for the full understanding of them, for their utter destruction, for their abandoning."

Floods, bonds, kinds of clinging,
Knots, and underlying tendencies,
Cords of sensual pleasure, hindrances,
Aggregates, fetters lower and higher.

[249] Chapter VI

50 *Balasaṃyutta*

Connected Discourses on the Powers

I. Ganges Repetition Series

1 (1)–12 (12) The River Ganges—Eastward, Etc.

"Bhikkhus, there are these five powers. What five? The power of faith, the power of energy, the power of mindfulness, the power of concentration, the power of wisdom. These are the five powers.

"Bhikkhus, just as the river Ganges slants, slopes, and inclines towards the east, so too a bhikkhu who develops and cultivates the five powers slants, slopes, and inclines towards Nibbāna.

"And how, bhikkhus, does a bhikkhu develop and cultivate the five powers so that he slants, slopes, and inclines towards Nibbāna? Here, bhikkhus, a bhikkhu develops the power of faith, which is based upon seclusion, dispassion, and cessation, maturing in release. He develops the power of energy ... the power of mindfulness ... the power of concentration ... the power of wisdom, which is based upon seclusion, dispassion, and cessation, maturing in release.

"It is in this way, bhikkhus, that a bhikkhu develops and cultivates the five powers so that he slants, slopes, and inclines towards Nibbāna."

(*The remaining suttas of this vagga are to be similarly elaborated parallel to 45:92–102.*) [250]

Six about slanting to the east
And six about slanting to the ocean.
These two sixes make up twelve:
Thus the subchapter is recited.

II. Diligence

13 (1)–22 (10) The Tathāgata, Etc.

(*To be elaborated by way of the powers parallel to 45:139–48.*)

Tathāgata, footprint, roof peak,
Roots, heartwood, jasmine,
Monarch, the moon and sun,
Together with the cloth as tenth.

III. Strenuous Deeds

23 (1)–34 (12) Strenuous, Etc.

(*To be elaborated parallel to 45:149–60.*)

Strenuous, seeds, and nāgas,
The tree, the pot, the spike,
The sky, and two on clouds,
The ship, guest house, and river.

IV. Searches

35 (1)–44 (10) Searches, Etc.

(*To be elaborated parallel to 45:161–70.*)

Searches, discriminations, taints,
Kinds of existence, threefold suffering,
Barrenness, stains, and troubles,
Feelings, craving, and thirst.

[251]

V. Floods

45 (1)–53 (9) Floods, Etc.

(*To be elaborated parallel to 45:171–79.*)

54 (10) Higher Fetters

"Bhikkhus, there are these five higher fetters. What five? Lust for form, lust for the formless, conceit, restlessness, ignorance. These are the five higher fetters. The five powers are to be developed for direct knowledge of these five higher fetters, for the full understanding of them, for their utter destruction, for their abandoning.

"What five? Here, bhikkhus, a bhikkhu develops the power of faith ... the power of wisdom, which is based upon seclusion, dispassion, and cessation, maturing in release.

"These five powers are to be developed for direct knowledge of these five higher fetters, for the full understanding of them, for their utter destruction, for their abandoning."

Floods, bonds, kinds of clinging,
Knots, and underlying tendencies,
Cords of sensual pleasure, hindrances,
Aggregates, fetters lower and higher.

VI. Ganges Repetition Series
(Removal of Lust Version)

55 (1)–66 (12) The River Ganges—Eastward, Etc.

"Bhikkhus, just as the river Ganges slants, slopes, and inclines towards the east, [252] so too a bhikkhu who develops and cultivates the five powers slants, slopes, and inclines towards Nibbāna.

"And how, bhikkhus, does a bhikkhu develop and cultivate the five powers so that he slants, slopes, and inclines towards Nibbāna? Here, bhikkhus, a bhikkhu develops the power of faith ... the power of wisdom, which has as its final goal the removal of lust, the removal of hatred, the removal of delusion.

"It is in this way, bhikkhus, that a bhikkhu develops and cultivates the five powers so that he slants, slopes, and inclines towards Nibbāna."

VII. Diligence
(Removal of Lust Version)

67 (1)–76 (10) The Tathāgata, Etc.

VIII. Strenuous Deeds
(Removal of Lust Version)

77 (1)–88 (12) Strenuous, Etc.

IX. Searches
(Removal of Lust Version)

89 (1)–98 (10) Searches, Etc.

[253]

X. Floods
(Removal of Lust Version)

99 (1)–107 (9) Floods, Etc.
108 (10) Higher Fetters

"Bhikkhus, there are these five higher fetters. What five? Lust for form, lust for the formless, conceit, restlessness, ignorance. These are the five higher fetters. The five powers are to be developed for direct knowledge of these five higher fetters, for the full understanding of them, for their utter destruction, for their abandoning.

"What five? Here, bhikkhus, a bhikkhu develops the power of faith ... the power of wisdom, which has as its final goal the removal of lust, the removal of hatred, the removal of delusion.

"These five powers are to be developed for direct knowledge of these five higher fetters, for the full understanding of them, for their utter destruction, for their abandoning."

Floods, bonds, kinds of clinging,
Knots, and underlying tendencies,

Cords of sensual pleasure, hindrances,
Aggregates, fetters lower and higher.

(*All to be elaborated by way of the five powers having as their final goal the removal of lust, the removal of hatred, the removal of delusion.*)

[254]

Chapter VII

51. *Iddhipādasaṃyutta*
Connected Discourses on the Bases for Spiritual Power

I. Cāpāla

1 (1) From the Near Shore

"Bhikkhus, these four bases for spiritual power, when developed and cultivated, lead to going beyond from the near shore to the far shore. What four? Here, bhikkhus, a bhikkhu develops the basis for spiritual power that possesses concentration due to desire and volitional formations of striving.[246] He develops the basis for spiritual power that possesses concentration due to energy and volitional formations of striving. He develops the basis for spiritual power that possesses concentration due to mind and volitional formations of striving. He develops the basis for spiritual power that possesses concentration due to investigation and volitional formations of striving. These four bases for spiritual power, when developed and cultivated, lead to going beyond from the near shore to the far shore."

2 (2) Neglected

"Bhikkhus, those who have neglected the four bases for spiritual power have neglected the noble path leading to the complete destruction of suffering. Those who have undertaken the four bases for spiritual power have undertaken the noble path leading to the complete destruction of suffering.

"What four? Here, bhikkhus, a bhikkhu develops the basis for spiritual power that possesses concentration due to desire and volitional formations of striving. He develops the basis for spiritual power that possesses concentration due to energy … concentration due to mind … concentration due to investigation and volitional formations of striving. [255]

"Bhikkhus, those who have neglected … who have undertaken these four bases for spiritual power have undertaken the noble path leading to the complete destruction of suffering."

3 (3) Noble

"Bhikkhus, these four bases for spiritual power, when developed and cultivated, are noble and emancipating; they lead the one who acts upon them out to the complete destruction of suffering.

"What four? Here, bhikkhus, a bhikkhu develops the basis for spiritual power that possesses concentration due to desire and volitional formations of striving. He develops the basis for spiritual power that possesses concentration due to energy … concentration due to mind … concentration due to investigation and volitional formations of striving. These four bases for spiritual power … lead the one who acts upon them out to the complete destruction of suffering."

4 (4) Revulsion

"Bhikkhus, these four bases for spiritual power, when developed and cultivated, lead to utter revulsion, to dispassion, to cessation, to peace, to direct knowledge, to enlightenment, to Nibbāna.

"What four? Here, bhikkhus, a bhikkhu develops the basis for spiritual power that possesses concentration due to desire and volitional formations of striving. He develops the basis for spiritual power that possesses concentration due to energy … concentration due to mind … concentration due to investigation and volitional formations of striving. These four bases for spiritual power … lead to Nibbāna."

5 (5) In Part

"Bhikkhus, whatever ascetics or brahmins in the past generated spiritual power in part, all did so because they had developed and cultivated the four bases for spiritual power. [256] Whatever ascetics or brahmins in the future will generate spiritual power in part, all will do so because they will have developed and cultivated the four bases for spiritual power. Whatever ascetics or brahmins at present generate spiritual power in part, all do so because they have developed and cultivated the four bases for spiritual power.

"What four? Here, bhikkhus, a bhikkhu develops the basis for spiritual power that possesses concentration due to desire and volitional formations of striving. He develops the basis for spiritual power that possesses concentration due to energy ... concentration due to mind ... concentration due to investigation and volitional formations of striving.

"Bhikkhus, whatever ascetics or brahmins in the past ... in the future ... at present generate spiritual power in part, all do so because they have developed and cultivated these four bases for spiritual power."

6 (6) Completely

"Bhikkhus, whatever ascetics or brahmins in the past generated spiritual power completely, all did so because they had developed and cultivated the four bases for spiritual power. Whatever ascetics or brahmins in the future will generate spiritual power completely, all will do so because they will have developed and cultivated the four bases for spiritual power. Whatever ascetics or brahmins at present generate spiritual power completely, all do so because they have developed and cultivated the four bases for spiritual power.

"What four? Here, bhikkhus, a bhikkhu develops the basis for spiritual power that possesses concentration due to desire and volitional formations of striving. He develops the basis for spiritual power that possesses concentration due to energy ... concentration due to mind ... concentration due to investigation and volitional formations of striving.

"Bhikkhus, whatever ascetics or brahmins in the past ... in the future ... at present generate spiritual power completely, all do so because they have developed and cultivated these four bases for spiritual power." [257]

7 (7) Bhikkhus

"Bhikkhus, whatever bhikkhus in the past, by the destruction of the taints, in this very life entered and dwelt in the taintless liberation of mind, liberation by wisdom, realizing it for themselves with direct knowledge, all did so because they had developed and cultivated the four bases for spiritual power. Whatever bhikkhus in the future, by the destruction of the taints, in this very life will enter and dwell in the taintless liberation of mind, liberation by wisdom, realizing it for themselves with direct knowledge, all will do so because they will have developed and cultivated the four bases for spiritual power. Whatever bhikkhus at present, by the destruction of the taints, in this very life enter and dwell in the taintless liberation of mind, liberation by wisdom, realizing it for themselves with direct knowledge, all do so because they have developed and cultivated the four bases for spiritual power.

"What four? Here, bhikkhus, a bhikkhu develops the basis for spiritual power that possesses concentration due to desire and volitional formations of striving. He develops the basis for spiritual power that possesses concentration due to energy … concentration due to mind … concentration due to investigation and volitional formations of striving.

"Bhikkhus, whatever bhikkhus in the past … in the future … at present … enter and dwell in the taintless liberation of mind, liberation by wisdom, … all do so because they have developed and cultivated these four bases for spiritual power."

8 (8) Buddha

"Bhikkhus, there are these four bases for spiritual power. What four? Here, bhikkhus, a bhikkhu develops the basis for spiritual power that possesses concentration due to desire and volitional formations of striving. He develops the basis for spiritual power that possesses concentration due to energy … concentration due to mind … concentration due to investigation and volitional formations of striving. These are the four bases for spiritual power. It is because he has developed and cultivated these four bases for spiritual power that the Tathāgata is called the Arahant, the Perfectly Enlightened One." [258]

9 (9) Knowledge

"'This is the basis for spiritual power that possesses concentration due to desire and volitional formations of striving'—thus, bhikkhus, in regard to things unheard before, there arose in me vision, knowledge, wisdom, true knowledge, and light.[247]

"'That basis for spiritual power possessing concentration due to desire and volitional formations of striving is to be developed'—thus, bhikkhus, in regard to things unheard before, there arose in me vision, knowledge, wisdom, true knowledge, and light.

"'That basis for spiritual power possessing concentration due to desire and volitional formations of striving has been developed'—thus, bhikkhus, in regard to things unheard before, there arose in me vision, knowledge, wisdom, true knowledge, and light.

"'This is the basis for spiritual power that possesses concentration due to energy and volitional formations of striving'—thus, bhikkhus, in regard to things unheard before, there arose in me vision, knowledge, wisdom, true knowledge, and light.

"'That basis for spiritual power possessing concentration due to energy and volitional formations of striving is to be developed ... has been developed'—thus, bhikkhus, in regard to things unheard before, there arose in me vision, knowledge, wisdom, true knowledge, and light.

"'This is the basis for spiritual power that possesses concentration due to mind and volitional formations of striving'—thus, bhikkhus, in regard to things unheard before, there arose in me vision, knowledge, wisdom, true knowledge, and light.

"'That basis for spiritual power possessing concentration due to mind and volitional formations of striving is to be developed ... has been developed'—thus, bhikkhus, in regard to things unheard before, there arose in me vision, knowledge, wisdom, true knowledge, and light.

"'This is the basis for spiritual power possessing concentration due to investigation and volitional formations of striving'—thus, bhikkhus, in regard to things unheard before, there arose in me vision, knowledge, wisdom, true knowledge, and light.

"'That basis for spiritual power possessing concentration due to investigation and volitional formations of striving is to be developed ... has been developed'—thus, bhikkhus, in regard to things unheard before, there arose in me vision, knowledge, wisdom, true knowledge, and light."

10 (10) The Shrine

Thus have I heard.[248] On one occasion the Blessed One was dwelling at Vesālī in the Great Wood in the Hall with the Peaked Roof. [259] Then, in the morning, the Blessed One dressed and, taking bowl and robe, entered Vesālī for alms. When he had walked for alms in Vesālī and had returned from the alms round, after his meal he addressed the Venerable Ānanda thus:

"Take a sitting cloth, Ānanda. Let us go to the Cāpāla Shrine for the day's abiding."

"Yes, venerable sir," the Venerable Ānanda replied and, having taken a sitting cloth, he followed closely behind the Blessed One. The Blessed One then went to the Cāpāla Shrine and sat down on a seat that was prepared. The Venerable Ānanda, having paid homage to the Blessed One, also sat down to one side. The Blessed One then said to the Venerable Ānanda:

"Delightful is Vesālī, Ānanda. Delightful is the Udena Shrine, delightful the Gotamaka Shrine, delightful the Sattamba Shrine, delightful the Bahuputta Shrine, delightful the Sārandada Shrine, delightful the Cāpāla Shrine. Whoever, Ānanda, has developed and cultivated the four bases for spiritual power, made them a vehicle, made them a basis, stabilized them, exercised himself in them, and fully perfected them could, if he so wished, live on for the aeon or for the remainder of the aeon. The Tathāgata, Ānanda, has developed and cultivated the four bases for spiritual power, made them a vehicle, made them a basis, stabilized them, exercised himself in them, and fully perfected them. If he so wished, the Tathāgata could live on for the aeon or for the remainder of the aeon."[249]

But though the Venerable Ānanda was given such an obvious signal by the Blessed One, though he was given such an obvious hint, he was unable to penetrate it. He did not implore the Blessed One: "Venerable sir, let the Blessed One live on for the aeon! Let the Fortunate One live on for the aeon, for the welfare of the multitude, for the happiness of the multitude, out of compassion for the world, for the good, welfare, and happiness of devas and humans." To such an extent was his mind obsessed by Māra.[250]

A second time ... [260] A third time the Blessed One addressed the Venerable Ānanda: "Delightful is Vesālī, Ānanda.... Whoever, Ānanda, has developed and cultivated the four bases for spiritual power ... could, if he so wished, live on for the aeon or for the remainder of the aeon.... If he so wished, the Tathāgata could live on for the aeon or for the remainder of the aeon."

But again, though the Venerable Ānanda was given such an obvious signal by the Blessed One, though he was given such an obvious hint, he was unable to penetrate it.... To such an extent was his mind obsessed by Māra.

Then the Blessed One addressed the Venerable Ānanda: "You may go, Ānanda, at your own convenience."

"Yes, venerable sir," the Venerable Ānanda replied, and he rose from his seat, paid homage to the Blessed One, and, keeping his right side towards him, sat down nearby at the foot of a tree.

Then, not long after the Venerable Ānanda had left, Māra the Evil One approached the Blessed One and said to him: "Venerable sir, let the Blessed One now attain final Nibbāna! Let the Fortunate One now attain final Nibbāna! Now is the time for the Blessed One's final Nibbāna! This statement was made, venerable sir, by the Blessed One:[251] [261] 'I will not attain final Nibbāna, Evil One, until I have bhikkhu disciples who are wise, disciplined, confident, secure from bondage, learned, upholders of the Dhamma, practising in accordance with the Dhamma, practising in the proper way, conducting themselves accordingly; who have learned their own teacher's doctrine and can explain it, teach it, proclaim it, establish it, disclose it, analyse it, and elucidate it; who can refute thoroughly with reasons the prevalent tenets of others and can teach the efficacious Dhamma.'[252] But at present, venerable sir, the Blessed One has bhikkhu disciples who are wise ... and who can teach the efficacious Dhamma. Venerable sir, let the Blessed One now attain final Nibbāna! Let the Fortunate One now attain final Nibbāna! Now is the time for the Blessed One's final Nibbāna!

"And this statement was made, venerable sir, by the Blessed One: 'I will not attain final Nibbāna, Evil One, until I have bhikkhunī disciples ... until I have male lay disciples ... until I have female lay disciples who are wise ... and who can teach the efficacious Dhamma.' But at present, venerable sir, the Blessed One has female lay disciples who are wise, disciplined, confident, secure from bondage, learned, upholders of the Dhamma, practising in accordance with the Dhamma, [262] practising in the proper way, conducting themselves accordingly; who have learned their own teacher's doctrine and can explain it, teach it, proclaim it, establish it, disclose it, analyse it, and elucidate it; who can refute thoroughly with reasons the prevalent tenets of others and can teach the efficacious Dhamma. Venerable sir, let the Blessed One now attain final Nibbāna! Let the Fortunate One now attain final Nibbāna! Now is the time for the Blessed One's final Nibbāna!

"And this statement was made, venerable sir, by the Blessed One: 'I will not attain final Nibbāna, Evil One, until this holy life of mine has become successful and prosperous, extensive, popular, widespread, well proclaimed among devas and humans.' That holy life of the Blessed One, venerable sir, has become successful and prosperous, extensive, popular, widespread, well proclaimed among devas and humans.[253] Venerable sir, let the Blessed One now attain final Nibbāna! Let the Fortunate One now attain final Nibbāna! Now is the time for the Blessed One's final Nibbāna!"

When this was said, the Blessed One said to Māra the Evil One: "Be at ease, Evil One. It will not be long before the Tathāgata's final Nibbāna takes place. Three months from now the Tathāgata will attain final Nibbāna."

Then the Blessed One, at the Cāpāla Shrine, mindfully and with clear comprehension relinquished his vital formation.[254] And when the Blessed One had relinquished his vital formation, a great earthquake occurred, frightening and terrifying, and peals of thunder shook the sky.

Then, having understood the meaning of this, the Blessed One on that occasion uttered this inspired utterance: [263]

> "Comparing the incomparable and continued existence,
> The sage relinquished the formation of existence.
> Rejoicing within, concentrated, he broke
> Continued self-existence like a coat of armour."[255]

II. The Shaking of the Mansion

11 (1) Before

At Sāvatthī. "Bhikkhus, before my enlightenment, while I was still a bodhisatta, not yet fully enlightened, it occurred to me: 'What now is the cause and condition for the development of the bases for spiritual power?' It occurred to me: 'Here, a bhikkhu develops the basis for spiritual power that possesses concentration due to desire and volitional formations of striving, thinking: "Thus my desire will be neither too slack nor too tense; and it will be neither constricted internally nor distracted externally." And he dwells perceiving after and before: "As before, so after; as after, so before; as below, so above; as above, so below; as by day, so at night; as at night, so by day." Thus, with a mind that is open and unenveloped, he develops the mind imbued with luminosity.[256] [264]

"'He develops the basis for spiritual power that possesses concentration due to energy and volitional formations of striving, thinking: "Thus my energy will be neither too slack nor too tense; and it will be neither constricted internally nor distracted externally." And he dwells perceiving after and before: "As before, so after; as after, so before; as below, so above; as above, so below; as by day, so at night; as at night, so by day." Thus, with a mind that is open and unenveloped, he develops the mind imbued with luminosity.

"'He develops the basis for spiritual power that possesses concentration due to mind and volitional formations of striving, thinking: "Thus my mind will be neither too slack nor too tense; and it will be neither constricted internally nor distracted externally." And he dwells perceiving after and before: "As before, so after; as after, so before; as below, so above; as above, so below; as by day, so at night; as at night, so by day." Thus, with a mind that is open and unenveloped, he develops the mind imbued with luminosity.

"'He develops the basis for spiritual power that possesses concentration due to investigation and volitional formations of striving, thinking: "Thus my investigation will be neither too slack nor too tense; and it will be neither constricted internally nor distracted externally." And he dwells perceiving after and before:

"As before, so after; as after, so before; as below, so above; as above, so below; as by day, so at night; as at night, so by day." Thus, with a mind that is open and unenveloped, he develops the mind imbued with luminosity.

"'When the four bases for spiritual power have been developed and cultivated in this way, a bhikkhu wields the various kinds of spiritual power:[257] having been one, he becomes many; having been many, he becomes one; he appears and vanishes; he goes unhindered through a wall, through a rampart, through a mountain as though through space; he dives in and out of the earth as though it were water; he walks on water without sinking as though it were earth; [265] seated cross-legged, he travels in space like a bird; with his hand he touches and strokes the moon and sun so powerful and mighty; he exercises mastery with the body as far as the brahmā world.

"'When the four bases for spiritual power have been developed and cultivated in this way, a bhikkhu, with the divine ear element, which is purified and surpasses the human, hears both kinds of sounds, the divine and human, those that are far as well as near.

"'When the four bases for spiritual power have been developed and cultivated in this way, a bhikkhu understands the minds of other beings and persons, having encompassed them with his own mind. He understands a mind with lust as a mind with lust; a mind without lust as a mind without lust; a mind with hatred as a mind with hatred; a mind without hatred as a mind without hatred; a mind with delusion as a mind with delusion; a mind without delusion as a mind without delusion; a contracted mind as contracted and a distracted mind as distracted; an exalted mind as exalted and an unexalted mind as unexalted; a surpassable mind as surpassable and an unsurpassable mind as unsurpassable; a concentrated mind as concentrated and an unconcentrated mind as unconcentrated; a liberated mind as liberated and an unliberated mind as unliberated.

"'When the four bases for spiritual power have been developed and cultivated in this way, a bhikkhu recollects his manifold past abodes, that is, one birth, two births, three births, four births, five births, ten births, twenty births, thirty births, forty births, fifty [266] births, a hundred births, a thousand births, a hundred thousand births, many aeons of world-contraction, many aeons of world-expansion, many aeons of world-contraction and expansion thus: "There I was so named, of such a clan, with such an appearance, such was my food, such my experience of pleasure and pain, such my life span; passing away from there, I was reborn elsewhere, and there too I was so named, of such a clan, with such an appearance, such was my food, such my experience of pleasure and pain, such my life span; passing away from there, I was reborn here." Thus he recollects his manifold past abodes with their modes and details.

"'When the four bases for spiritual power have been developed and cultivated in this way, a bhikkhu, with the divine eye, which is purified and surpasses the human, sees beings passing away and being reborn, inferior and superior, beautiful and ugly, fortunate and unfortunate, and he understands how beings fare on in accordance with their kamma thus: "These beings who engaged in misconduct of body, speech, and mind, who reviled the noble ones, held wrong view, and undertook actions based on wrong view, with the breakup of the body, after death, have been reborn in a state of misery, in a bad destination, in the nether world, in hell; but these beings who engaged in good conduct of body, speech, and mind, who did not revile the noble ones, who held right view, and undertook action based on right view, with the breakup of the body, after death, have been reborn in a good destination, in the heavenly world." Thus with the divine eye, which is purified and surpasses the human, he sees beings passing away and being reborn, inferior and superior, beautiful and ugly, fortunate and unfortunate, and he understands how beings fare on in accordance with their kamma.

"'When the four bases for spiritual power have been developed and cultivated in this way, a bhikkhu, by the destruction of the taints, in this very life enters and dwells in the taintless liberation of mind, liberation by wisdom, realizing it for himself with direct knowledge.'" [267]

12 (2) Of Great Fruit

"Bhikkhus, these four bases for spiritual power, when developed and cultivated, are of great fruit and benefit. And how is it, bhikkhus, that the four bases for spiritual power, when developed and cultivated, are of great fruit and benefit?

"Here, bhikkhus, a bhikkhu develops the basis for spiritual power that possesses concentration due to desire and volitional formations of striving, thinking: 'Thus my desire will be neither too slack nor too tense; and it will be neither constricted internally nor distracted externally.' And he dwells perceiving after and before: 'As before, so after; as after, so before; as below, so above; as above, so below; as by day, so at night; as at night, so by day.' Thus, with a mind that is open and unenveloped, he develops the mind imbued with luminosity.

"He develops the basis for spiritual power that possesses concentration due to energy ... concentration due to mind ... concentration due to investigation ... he develops the mind imbued with luminosity.

"When, bhikkhus, the four bases for spiritual power have been developed and cultivated in this way, a bhikkhu wields the various kinds of spiritual power: having been one, he becomes many ... he exercises mastery with the body as far as the brahmā world.... [268]

"When, bhikkhus, the four bases for spiritual power have been developed and cultivated in this way, a bhikkhu, by the destruction of the taints, in this very life enters and dwells in the taintless liberation of mind, liberation by wisdom, realizing it for himself with direct knowledge."

13 (3) Concentration due to Desire

"Bhikkhus, if a bhikkhu gains concentration, gains one-pointedness of mind based upon desire,[258] this is called concentration due to desire. He generates desire for the nonarising of unarisen evil unwholesome states; he makes an effort, arouses energy, applies his mind, and strives. He generates desire for the abandoning of arisen evil unwholesome states; he makes an effort, arouses energy, applies his mind, and strives. He generates desire for the arising of unarisen wholesome states; he makes an effort, arouses energy, applies his mind, and strives. He generates desire for the maintenance of arisen wholesome states, for their nondecay, increase, expansion, and fulfilment by development; he makes an effort, arouses energy, applies his mind, and strives. These are called volitional formations of striving.[259] Thus this desire and this concentration due to desire and these volitional formations of striving: this is called the basis for spiritual power that possesses concentration due to desire and volitional formations of striving.

"If, bhikkhus, a bhikkhu gains concentration, gains one-pointedness of mind based upon energy, this is called concentration due to energy. He generates desire for the nonarising of unarisen evil unwholesome states ... for the maintenance of arisen wholesome states, for their nondecay, increase, expansion, and fulfilment by development; he makes an effort, arouses energy, applies his mind, and strives. These are called volitional formations of striving. Thus this energy and this concentration due to energy and these volitional formations of striving: this is called the basis for spiritual power that possesses concentration due to energy and volitional formations of striving. [269]

"If, bhikkhus, a bhikkhu gains concentration, gains one-pointedness of mind, based upon mind, this is called concentration due to mind.[260] He generates desire for the nonarising of unarisen evil unwholesome states ... for the maintenance of arisen wholesome states, for their nondecay, increase, expansion, and fulfilment by development; he makes an effort, arouses energy, applies his mind, and strives. These are called volitional formations of striving. Thus this mind and this concentration due to mind and these volitional formations of striving: this is called the basis for spiritual power that possesses concentration due to mind and volitional formations of striving.

"If, bhikkhus, a bhikkhu gains concentration, gains one-pointedness of mind based upon investigation, this is called concentration due to investigation.[261] He generates desire for the nonarising of unarisen evil unwholesome states ... for the maintenance of arisen wholesome states, for their nondecay, increase, expansion, and fulfilment by development; he makes an effort, arouses energy, applies his mind, and strives. These are called volitional formations of striving. Thus this investigation and this concentration due to investigation and these volitional formations of striving: this is called the basis for spiritual power that possesses concentration due to investigation and volitional formations of striving."

14 (4) Moggallāna

Thus have I heard. On one occasion the Blessed One was dwelling at Sāvatthī in the Eastern Park in the Mansion of Migāra's Mother. Now on that occasion a number of bhikkhus who dwelt on the ground floor of the mansion were restless, puffed up, personally vain, rough-tongued, rambling in their talk, muddle-minded, without clear comprehension, unconcentrated, scatter-brained, loose in their faculties.[262]

Then the Blessed One addressed the Venerable Mahāmoggallāna thus: "Moggallāna, your brothers in the holy life, [270] dwelling on the ground floor of the Mansion of Migāra's Mother, are restless ... loose in their faculties. Go, Moggallāna, stir up a sense of urgency in those bhikkhus."

"Yes, venerable sir," the Venerable Mahāmoggallāna replied. Then he performed a feat of spiritual power such that he made the Mansion of Migāra's Mother shake, quake, and tremble with his toe.[263] Then those bhikkhus, shocked and terrified, stood to one side and said: "It is wonderful indeed, sir! It is amazing indeed, sir! There is no wind, and this Mansion of Migāra's Mother has a deep base and is securely planted, immobile, unshaking; yet it shook, quaked, and trembled."

Then the Blessed One approached those bhikkhus and said to them: "Why, bhikkhus, are you standing to one side, shocked and terrified?"

"It is wonderful, venerable sir! It is amazing, venerable sir! There is no wind, and this Mansion of Migāra's Mother has a deep base and is securely planted, immobile, unshaking; yet it shook, it quaked, it trembled."

"Bhikkhus, the bhikkhu Moggallāna, desiring to stir up a sense of urgency in you, made the Mansion of Migāra's Mother shake, quake, and tremble with his toe. What do you think, bhikkhus, by having developed and cultivated what things has the bhikkhu Moggallāna become so powerful and mighty?"

"Venerable sir, our teachings are rooted in the Blessed One, guided by the Blessed One, take recourse in the Blessed One. It would be good if the Blessed One would clear up the meaning of this statement. Having heard it from him, the bhikkhus will remember it." [271]

"Then listen, bhikkhus.... It is because he has developed and cultivated the four bases for spiritual power that the bhikkhu Moggallāna has become so powerful and mighty. What four? Here, bhikkhus, the bhikkhu Moggallāna has developed the basis for spiritual power that possesses concentration due to desire and volitional formations of striving. He has developed the basis for spiritual power that possesses concentration due to energy ... concentration due to mind ... concentration due to investigation and volitional formations of striving, thinking: 'Thus my investigation will be neither too slack nor too tense; and it will be neither constricted internally nor distracted externally.'... Thus, with a mind that is open and unenveloped, he has developed the mind imbued with luminosity.

"It is, bhikkhus, because he has developed and cultivated these four bases for spiritual power that the bhikkhu Moggallāna has become so powerful and mighty.

"It is, bhikkhus, because the bhikkhu Moggallāna has developed and cultivated these four bases for spiritual power that he wields the various kinds of spiritual power ... he exercises mastery with the body as far as the brahmā world....[264]

"It is, bhikkhus, because the bhikkhu Moggallāna has developed and cultivated these four bases for spiritual power that by the destruction of the taints, in this very life he enters and dwells in the taintless liberation of mind, liberation by wisdom, realizing it for himself with direct knowledge."

15 (5) The Brahmin Uṇṇābha

Thus have I heard. On one occasion the Venerable Ānanda was dwelling at Kosambī in Ghosita's Park. [272] Then the brahmin Uṇṇābha approached the Venerable Ānanda and exchanged greetings with him.[265] When they had concluded their greetings and cordial talk, he sat down to one side and said to the Venerable Ānanda: "For what purpose, Master Ānanda, is the holy life lived under the ascetic Gotama?"

"It is for the sake of abandoning desire, brahmin, that the holy life is lived under the Blessed One."

"But, Master Ānanda, is there a path, is there a way for the abandoning of this desire?"

"There is a path, brahmin, there is a way for the abandoning of this desire."

"But, Master Ānanda, what is the path, what is the way for the abandoning of this desire?"

"Here, brahmin, a bhikkhu develops the basis for spiritual power that possesses concentration due to desire and volitional formations of striving. He develops the basis for spiritual power that possesses concentration due to energy ... concentration due to mind ... concentration due to investigation and volitional formations of striving. This, brahmin, is the path, this is the way for the abandoning of this desire."

"Such being the case, Master Ānanda, the situation is interminable, not terminable.[266] It is impossible that one can abandon desire by means of desire itself."

"Well then, brahmin, I will question you about this matter. Answer as you see fit. What do you think, brahmin, did you earlier have the desire, 'I will go to the park,' and after you went to the park, did the corresponding desire subside?"

"Yes, sir."

"Did you earlier arouse energy, thinking, 'I will go to the park,' and after you went to the park, did the corresponding energy subside?" [273]

"Yes, sir."

"Did you earlier make up your mind, 'I will go to the park,' and after you went to the park, did the corresponding resolution[267] subside?"

"Yes, sir."

"Did you earlier make an investigation, 'Shall I go to the park?' and after you went to the park, did the corresponding investigation subside?"

"Yes, sir."

"It is exactly the same, brahmin, with a bhikkhu who is an arahant, one whose taints are destroyed, who has lived the holy life, done what had to be done, laid down the burden, reached his own goal, utterly destroyed the fetters of existence, and is completely liberated through final knowledge. He earlier had the desire for the attainment of arahantship, and when he attained arahantship, the corresponding desire subsided. He earlier had aroused energy for the attainment of arahantship, and when he attained arahantship, the corresponding energy subsided. He earlier had made up his mind to attain arahantship, and when he attained arahantship, the corresponding resolution subsided. He earlier made an investigation for the attainment of arahantship, and when he attained arahantship, the corresponding investigation subsided.[268]

"What do you think, brahmin, such being the case, is the situation terminable or interminable?"

"Surely, Master Ānanda, such being the case, the situation is terminable, not interminable.[269] Magnificent, Master Ānanda!... From today let Master Ānanda remember me as a lay follower who has gone for refuge for life."

16 (6) Ascetics and Brahmins (1)

"Bhikkhus, whatever ascetics or brahmins in the past were of great spiritual power and might, all were so because they had developed and cultivated the four bases for spiritual power. Whatever ascetics or brahmins in the future will be of great spiritual power and might, all will be so because they will have developed and cultivated the four bases for spiritual power. Whatever ascetics or brahmins at present are of great spiritual power and might, all are so because they have developed and cultivated the four bases for spiritual power.

"What four? [274] Here, bhikkhus, a bhikkhu develops the basis for spiritual power that possesses concentration due to desire and volitional formations of striving. He develops the basis for spiritual power that possesses concentration due to energy ... concentration due to mind ... concentration due to investigation and volitional formations of striving.

"Bhikkhus, whatever ascetics or brahmins in the past ... in the future ... at present are of great spiritual power and might, all are so because they have developed and cultivated these four bases for spiritual power."

17 (7) Ascetics and Brahmins (2)

"Bhikkhus, whatever ascetics or brahmins in the past wielded the various kinds of spiritual power, such that: having been one, they became many ... they exercised mastery with the body as far as the brahmā world—all did so because they had developed and cultivated the four bases for spiritual power.

"Whatever ascetics or brahmins in the future will wield the various kinds of spiritual power, such that: having been one, they will become many … [275] … they will exercise mastery with the body as far as the brahmā world—all will do so because they will have developed and cultivated the four bases for spiritual power.

"Whatever ascetics or brahmins at present wield the various kinds of spiritual power, such that: having been one, they become many … they exercise mastery with the body as far as the brahmā world—all do so because they have developed and cultivated the four bases for spiritual power.

"What four? Here, bhikkhus, a bhikkhu develops the basis for spiritual power that possesses concentration due to desire and volitional formations of striving. He develops the basis for spiritual power that possesses concentration due to energy … concentration due to mind … concentration due to investigation and volitional formations of striving.

"Bhikkhus, whatever ascetics or brahmins in the past … in the future … at present wield the various kinds of spiritual power … all do so because they have developed and cultivated these four bases for spiritual power."

18 (8) A Bhikkhu

"Bhikkhus, it is because he has developed and cultivated the four bases for spiritual power that a bhikkhu, by the destruction of the taints, in this very life enters and dwells in the taintless liberation of mind, liberation by wisdom, realizing it for himself with direct knowledge.

"What four? Here, bhikkhus, a bhikkhu develops the basis for spiritual power that possesses concentration due to desire and volitional formations of striving. He develops the basis for spiritual power that possesses concentration due to energy … concentration due to mind … concentration due to investigation and volitional formations of striving.

"It is, bhikkhus, because he has developed and cultivated these four bases for spiritual power that a bhikkhu, [276] by the destruction of the taints, in this very life enters and dwells in the taintless liberation of mind, liberation by wisdom, realizing it for himself with direct knowledge."

19 (9) A Teaching

"Bhikkhus, I will teach you spiritual power, the basis for spiritual power, the development of the bases for spiritual power, and the way leading to the development of the bases for spiritual power.

"And what, bhikkhus, is spiritual power? Here, bhikkhus, a bhikkhu wields the various kinds of spiritual power: having been one, he becomes many ... he exercises mastery with the body as far as the brahmā world. This is called spiritual power.

"And what, bhikkhus, is the basis for spiritual power? It is the path and practice that leads to gaining spiritual power, to obtaining spiritual power.[270] This is called the basis for spiritual power.

"And what, bhikkhus, is the development of the bases for spiritual power? Here, bhikkhus, a bhikkhu develops the basis for spiritual power that possesses concentration due to desire and volitional formations of striving. He develops the basis for spiritual power that possesses concentration due to energy ... concentration due to mind ... concentration due to investigation and volitional formations of striving. This is called the development of the bases for spiritual power.

"And what, bhikkhus, is the way leading to the development of the bases for spiritual power? It is this Noble Eightfold Path; that is, right view, right intention, right speech, right action, right livelihood, right effort, right mindfulness, right concentration. This is called the way leading to the development of the bases for spiritual power."

20 (10) Analysis

"Bhikkhus, these four bases for spiritual power, when developed and cultivated, are of great fruit and benefit.

"And how, bhikkhus, are the four bases for spiritual power developed and cultivated so that they are of great fruit and benefit?

"Here, bhikkhus, a bhikkhu develops the basis for spiritual power that possesses concentration due to desire and volitional formations of striving, thinking: 'Thus my desire [277] will be neither too slack nor too tense; and it will be neither constricted internally nor distracted externally.' And he dwells perceiving after and before: 'As before, so after; as after, so before; as below, so above; as above, so below; as by day, so at night; as at night, so by day.' Thus, with a mind that is open and unenveloped, he develops the mind imbued with luminosity.

"He develops the basis for spiritual power that possesses concentration due to energy ... concentration due to mind ... concentration due to investigation ... he develops the mind imbued with luminosity.

(i. Analysis of desire as a basis)

"And what, bhikkhus, is desire that is too slack? It is desire that is accompanied by lassitude, associated with lassitude.[271] This is called desire that is too slack.

"And what, bhikkhus, is desire that is too tense? It is desire that is accompanied by restlessness, associated with restlessness. This is called desire that is too tense.

"And what, bhikkhus, is desire that is constricted internally? It is desire that is accompanied by sloth and torpor, associated with sloth and torpor. This is called desire that is constricted internally.

"And what, bhikkhus, is desire that is distracted externally? It is desire that is repeatedly distracted externally, repeatedly disturbed, on account of the five cords of sensual pleasure. This is called desire that is distracted externally.

"And how, bhikkhus, does a bhikkhu dwell perceiving after and before: 'As before, so after; as after, so before'? [278] Here, bhikkhus, the perception of after and before is well grasped by a bhikkhu, well attended to, well considered, well penetrated by wisdom. It is in this way, bhikkhus, that a bhikkhu dwells perceiving after and before: 'As before, so after; as after, so before.'[272]

"And how, bhikkhus, does a bhikkhu dwell 'as below, so above; as above, so below'? Here, bhikkhus, a bhikkhu reviews this very body upwards from the soles of the feet, downwards from the tips of the hairs, enclosed in skin, as full of many kinds of impurities: 'There are in this body head-hairs, body-hairs, nails, teeth, skin, flesh, sinews, bones, bone-marrow, kidneys, heart, liver, pleura, spleen, lungs, intestines, mesentery, contents of the stomach, excrement, bile, phlegm, pus, blood, sweat, fat, tears, grease, saliva, snot, fluid of the joints, urine.' It is in this way, bhikkhus, that a bhikkhu dwells 'as below, so above; as above, so below.'

"And how, bhikkhus, does a bhikkhu dwell 'as by day, so at night; as at night, so by day'? Here, bhikkhus, at night a bhikkhu develops the basis for spiritual power that possesses concentration due to desire and volitional formations of striving by way of the same qualities, the same features, the same aspects, as he develops that basis for spiritual power by day. Or else by day he develops the basis for spiritual power that possesses concentration due to desire and volitional formations of striving by way of the same qualities, the same features, the same aspects, as he develops that basis for spiritual power at night. It is in this way, bhikkhus, that a bhikkhu dwells 'as by day, so at night; as at night, so by day.'

"And how, bhikkhus, does a bhikkhu, with a mind that is open and unenveloped, develop the mind imbued with luminosity? Here, bhikkhus, the perception of light is well grasped by a bhikkhu; the perception of day is well resolved upon.[273] It is in this way, bhikkhus, that a bhikkhu, with a mind that is open and unenveloped, develops the mind imbued with luminosity. [279]

(ii. Analysis of energy as a basis)

"And what, bhikkhus, is energy that it too slack? It is energy that is accompanied by lassitude, associated with lassitude. This is called energy that is too slack.

"And what, bhikkhus, is energy that is too tense? It is energy that is accompanied by restlessness, associated with restlessness. This is called energy that is too tense.

"And what, bhikkhus, is energy that is constricted internally? It is energy that is accompanied by sloth and torpor, associated with sloth and torpor. This is called energy that is constricted internally.

"And what, bhikkhus, is energy that is distracted externally? It is energy that is repeatedly distracted externally, repeatedly disturbed, on account of the five cords of sensual pleasure. This is called energy that is distracted externally ... (*all as above*) ...

"It is in this way, bhikkhus, that a bhikkhu, with a mind that is open and unenveloped, develops the mind imbued with luminosity.

(iii. Analysis of mind as a basis)

"And what, bhikkhus, is mind that is too slack? It is mind that is accompanied by lassitude, associated with lassitude. This is called mind that is too slack.

"And what, bhikkhus, is mind that is too tense? It is mind that is accompanied by restlessness, associated with restlessness. This is called mind that is too tense.

"And what, bhikkhus, is mind that is constricted internally? It is mind that is accompanied by sloth and torpor, associated with sloth and torpor. This is called mind that is constricted internally. [280]

"And what, bhikkhus, is mind that is distracted externally? It is mind that is repeatedly distracted externally, repeatedly disturbed, on account of the five cords of sensual pleasure. This is called mind that is distracted externally … (*all as above*) …

"It is in this way, bhikkhus, that a bhikkhu, with a mind that is open and unenveloped, develops the mind imbued with luminosity.

(iv. Analysis of investigation as a basis)

"And what, bhikkhus, is investigation that is too slack? It is investigation that is accompanied by lassitude, associated with lassitude. This is called investigation that is too slack.

"And what, bhikkhus, is investigation that is too tense? It is investigation that is accompanied by restlessness, associated with restlessness. This is called investigation that is too tense.

"And what, bhikkhus, is investigation that is constricted internally? It is investigation that is accompanied by sloth and torpor, associated with sloth and torpor. This is called investigation that is constricted internally.

"And what, bhikkhus, is investigation that is distracted externally? It is investigation that is repeatedly distracted externally, repeatedly disturbed, on account of the five cords of sensual pleasure. This is called investigation that is distracted externally … (*all as above*) …

"It is in this way, bhikkhus, that a bhikkhu, with a mind that is open and unenveloped, develops the mind imbued with luminosity.

"When, bhikkhus, the four bases for spiritual power have been developed and cultivated in this way, they are of great fruit and benefit.

"When, bhikkhus, the four bases for spiritual power have been developed and cultivated in this way, a bhikkhu wields the various kinds of spiritual power: having been one, he becomes many; having been many, he becomes one … he exercises mastery with the body as far as the brahmā world….

"When, bhikkhus, the four bases for spiritual power have been developed and cultivated in this way, a bhikkhu, by the destruction of the taints, [281] in this very life enters and dwells in the taintless liberation of mind, liberation by wisdom, realizing it for himself with direct knowledge."

(*The six direct knowledges should be elaborated.*)

III. The Iron Ball

21 (1) The Path

At Sāvatthī. "Bhikkhus, before my enlightenment, while I was still a bodhisatta, not yet fully enlightened, the thought occurred to me: 'What is the path and practice for the development of the bases for spiritual power?' It occurred to me: 'Here, a bhikkhu develops the basis for spiritual power that possesses concentration due to desire and volitional formations of striving … (*as in §11 in full*) … that possesses concentration due to investigation and volitional formations of striving…. Thus, with a mind that is open and unenveloped, he develops the mind imbued with luminosity. [282]

"'When the four bases for spiritual power have been developed and cultivated in this way, a bhikkhu wields the various kinds of spiritual power: having been one, he becomes many; having been many, he becomes one … he exercises mastery with the body as far as the brahmā world….

"'When, bhikkhus, the four bases for spiritual power have been developed and cultivated in this way, a bhikkhu, by the destruction of the taints, in this very life enters and dwells in the taintless liberation of mind, liberation by wisdom, realizing it for himself with direct knowledge.'"

(*The six direct knowledges should be elaborated.*)

22 (2) The Iron Ball

At Sāvatthī. Then the Venerable Ānanda approached the Blessed

One, paid homage to him, sat down to one side, and said to him: "Venerable sir, does the Blessed One recall ever having gone to the brahmā world by spiritual power with a mind-made body?"[274]

"I recall, Ānanda, having gone to the brahmā world by spiritual power with a mind-made body."

"But, venerable sir, does the Blessed One recall ever having gone to the brahmā world by spiritual power with this body composed of the four great elements?"[275]

"I recall, Ānanda, having gone to the brahmā world by spiritual power with this body composed of the four great elements."

"That the Blessed One is able[276] to go to the brahmā world by spiritual power with a mind-made body, and that [283] he recalls having gone to the brahmā world by spiritual power with this body composed of the four great elements: that is wonderful and amazing, venerable sir, on the part of the Blessed One."

"The Tathāgatas, Ānanda, are wonderful and possess wonderful qualities; the Tathāgatas are amazing and possess amazing qualities.

"When, Ānanda, the Tathāgata immerses the body in the mind and the mind in the body,[277] and when he dwells having entered upon a blissful perception and a buoyant perception in regard to the body, on that occasion the body of the Tathāgata becomes more buoyant, malleable, wieldy, and luminous.

"Just as an iron ball, Ānanda, heated all day, becomes more buoyant, malleable, wieldy, and luminous, so too, when the Tathāgata immerses the body in the mind and the mind in the body, and when he dwells having entered upon a blissful perception and a buoyant perception in regard to the body, on that occasion the body of the Tathāgata becomes more buoyant, malleable, wieldy, and luminous.

"When, Ānanda, the Tathāgata immerses the body in the mind and the mind in the body, and when he dwells having entered upon a blissful perception and a buoyant perception in regard to the body, on that occasion the body of the Tathāgata rises up without difficulty from the earth into the air. He wields the various kinds of spiritual power: having been one, he becomes many; having been many, he becomes one; ... he exercises mastery with the body as far as the brahmā world. [284]

"Just as, Ānanda, a tuft of cotton wool or kapok, being light, sustained by the wind, rises up without difficulty from the earth into the air, so too, when the Tathāgata immerses the body in the mind and the mind in the body, and when he dwells having entered upon a blissful perception and a buoyant perception in regard to the body, on that occasion the body of the Tathāgata rises up without difficulty from the earth into the air. He wields the various kinds of spiritual power: having been one, he becomes many; having been many, he becomes one; ... he exercises mastery with the body as far as the brahmā world."

23 (3) A Bhikkhu

"Bhikkhus, there are these four bases for spiritual power. What four? Here, bhikkhus, a bhikkhu develops the basis for spiritual power that possesses concentration due to desire and volitional formations of striving. He develops the basis for spiritual power that possesses concentration due to energy ... concentration due to mind ... concentration due to investigation and volitional formations of striving. These are the four bases for spiritual power.

"It is, bhikkhus, because he has developed and cultivated these four bases for spiritual power that a bhikkhu, by the destruction of the taints, in this very life enters and dwells in the taintless liberation of mind, liberation by wisdom, realizing it for himself with direct knowledge."[278]

24 (4) Simple Version

"Bhikkhus, there are these four bases for spiritual power. What four? Here, bhikkhus, a bhikkhu develops the basis for spiritual power that possesses concentration due to desire and volitional formations of striving. He develops the basis for spiritual power that possesses concentration due to energy ... concentration due to mind ... concentration due to investigation and volitional formations of striving. These are the four bases for spiritual power." [285]

25 (5) Fruits (1)

"Bhikkhus, there are these four bases for spiritual power. What four? Here, bhikkhus, a bhikkhu develops the basis for spiritual power that possesses concentration due to desire and volitional formations of striving. He develops the basis for spiritual power that possesses concentration due to energy … concentration due to mind … concentration due to investigation and volitional formations of striving. These are the four bases for spiritual power.

"When, bhikkhus, these four bases for spiritual power have been developed and cultivated, one of two fruits may be expected: either final knowledge in this very life or, if there is a residue of clinging, the state of nonreturning."

26 (6) Fruits (2)

"Bhikkhus, there are these four bases for spiritual power. What four? Here, bhikkhus, a bhikkhu develops the basis for spiritual power that possesses concentration due to desire and volitional formations of striving. He develops the basis for spiritual power that possesses concentration due to energy … concentration due to mind … concentration due to investigation and volitional formations of striving. These are the four bases for spiritual power.

"When, bhikkhus, these four bases for spiritual power have been developed and cultivated, seven fruits and benefits may be expected. What are the seven fruits and benefits?

"One attains final knowledge early in this very life. If one does not attain final knowledge early in this very life, then one attains final knowledge at the time of death. If one does not attain final knowledge early in this very life, or at the time of death, then with the utter destruction of the five lower fetters one becomes an attainer of Nibbāna in the interval … an attainer of Nibbāna upon landing … an attainer of Nibbāna without exertion … an attainer of Nibbāna with exertion … one bound upstream, heading towards the Akaniṭṭha realm.

"When, bhikkhus, these four bases for spiritual power have been developed and cultivated, these seven fruits and benefits may be expected."

27 (7) Ānanda (1)

At Sāvatthī. Then the Venerable Ānanda approached the Blessed One, paid homage to him, sat down to one side, and said to him: "Venerable sir, what now [286] is spiritual power? What is the basis for spiritual power? What is the development of the bases for spiritual power? What is the way leading to the development of the bases for spiritual power?"

(*The Buddha's answers are exactly the same as in §19.*)

28 (8) *Ānanda (2)*

The Blessed One then said to the Venerable Ānanda: "Ānanda, what now is spiritual power? What is the basis for spiritual power? What is the development of the bases for spiritual power? What is the way leading to the development of the bases for spiritual power?"

(*The Buddha answers his own questions exactly as in §19.*) [287]

29 (9) *A Number of Bhikkhus (1)*

Then a number of bhikkhus approached the Blessed One, paid homage to him, sat down to one side, and said to him: "Venerable sir, what now is spiritual power? What is the basis for spiritual power? What is the development of the bases for spiritual power? What is the way leading to the development of the bases for spiritual power?"

(*The Buddha's answers are exactly the same as in §19.*) [288]

30 (10) *A Number of Bhikkhus (2)*

Then a number of bhikkhus approached the Blessed One.... The Blessed One then said to them: "Bhikkhus, what now is spiritual power? What is the basis for spiritual power? What is the development of the bases for spiritual power? What is the way leading to the development of the bases for spiritual power?"

(*The Buddha answers his own questions exactly as in §19.*)

31 (11) *Moggallāna*

There the Blessed One addressed the bhikkhus thus: "What do you think, bhikkhus, by having developed and cultivated what things has the bhikkhu Moggallāna become so powerful and mighty?"

"Venerable sir, our teachings are rooted in the Blessed One...."

"It is because he has developed and cultivated the four bases for spiritual power that the bhikkhu Moggallāna has become so powerful and mighty. What four? Here, bhikkhus, the bhikkhu Moggallāna has developed the basis for spiritual power that possesses concentration due to desire and volitional formations of striving, thinking: 'Thus my desire will be neither too slack nor too tense; and it will be neither constricted internally nor distracted externally.' And he has dwelt perceiving after and before: 'As before, so after; as after, so before; as below, so above; as above, so below; as by day, so at night; as at night, so by day.' Thus, with a mind that is open and unenveloped, he has developed the mind imbued with luminosity. He has developed the basis for spiritual power that possesses concentration due to energy ... concentration due to mind ... concentration due to investigation and volitional formations of striving, thinking: 'Thus my investigation will be neither too slack nor too tense; and it will be neither constricted internally nor distracted externally.'... Thus, with a mind that is open and unenveloped, he has developed the mind imbued with luminosity.

"It is, bhikkhus, because he has developed and cultivated these four bases for spiritual power that the bhikkhu Moggallāna has become so powerful and mighty.

"It is, bhikkhus, because the bhikkhu Moggallāna has developed and cultivated these four bases for spiritual power that he wields the various kinds of spiritual power, such that: having been one, he becomes many; having been many, he becomes one ... he exercises mastery with the body as far as the brahmā world.... [289]

"It is, bhikkhus, because the bhikkhu Moggallāna has developed and cultivated these four bases for spiritual power that by the destruction of the taints, in this very life he enters and dwells in the taintless liberation of mind, liberation by wisdom, realizing it for himself with direct knowledge."[279]

32 (12) The Tathāgata

There the Blessed One addressed the bhikkhus thus: "What do you think, bhikkhus, by having developed and cultivated what things has the Tathāgata become so powerful and mighty?"

"Venerable sir, our teachings are rooted in the Blessed One...."

"It is because he has developed and cultivated the four bases for spiritual power that the Tathāgata has become so powerful and mighty. What four? Here, bhikkhus, the Tathāgata has developed the basis for spiritual power that possesses concentration due to desire and volitional formations of striving, thinking: 'Thus my desire will be neither too slack nor too tense; and it will be neither constricted internally nor distracted externally.' And he has dwelt perceiving after and before: 'As before, so after; as after, so before; as below, so above; as above, so below; as by day, so at night; as at night, so by day.' Thus, with a mind that is open and unenveloped, he has developed the mind imbued with luminosity. He has developed the basis for spiritual power that possesses concentration due to energy ... concentration due to mind ... concentration due to investigation and volitional formations of striving, thinking: 'Thus my investigation will be neither too slack nor too tense; and it will be neither constricted internally nor distracted externally.'... Thus, with a mind that is open and unenveloped, he has developed the mind imbued with luminosity.

"It is, bhikkhus, because he has developed and cultivated these four bases for spiritual power that the Tathāgata has become so powerful and mighty.

"It is, bhikkhus, because the Tathāgata has developed and cultivated these four bases for spiritual power that he wields the various kinds of spiritual power, such that: having been one, he becomes many; having been many, he becomes one ... [290] he exercises mastery with the body as far as the brahmā world....

"It is, bhikkhus, because the Tathāgata has developed and cultivated these four bases for spiritual power that by the destruction of the taints, in this very life he enters and dwells in the taintless liberation of mind, liberation by wisdom, realizing it for himself with direct knowledge."

IV. Ganges Repetition Series

33 (1)–44 (12) The River Ganges—Eastward, Etc.

"Bhikkhus, just as the river Ganges slants, slopes, and inclines towards the east, so too a bhikkhu who develops and cultivates the four bases for spiritual power slants, slopes, and inclines towards Nibbāna.

"And how, bhikkhus, does a bhikkhu develop and cultivate the four bases for spiritual power so that he slants, slopes, and inclines towards Nibbāna? Here, bhikkhus, a bhikkhu develops the basis for spiritual power that possesses concentration due to desire and volitional formations of striving. He develops the basis for spiritual power that possesses concentration due to energy ... concentration due to mind ... concentration due to investigation and volitional formations of striving.

"It is in this way, bhikkhus, that a bhikkhu [291] develops and cultivates the four bases for spiritual power so that he slants, slopes, and inclines towards Nibbāna."

(*The remaining suttas of this vagga are to be similarly elaborated parallel to 45:92–102.*)

Six about slanting to the east
And six about slanting to the ocean.
These two sixes make up twelve:
Thus the subchapter is recited.

V. Diligence

45 (1)–54 (10) The Tathāgata, Etc.

(*To be elaborated by way of the bases for spiritual power parallel to 45:139–48.*)

Tathāgata, footprint, roof peak,
Roots, heartwood, jasmine,
Monarch, the moon and sun,
Together with the cloth as tenth.

VI. Strenuous Deeds

55 (1)–66 (12) Strenuous, Etc.

(*To be elaborated parallel to 45:149–60.*)

Strenuous, seeds, and nāgas,
The tree, the pot, the spike,

The sky, and two on clouds,
The ship, guest house, and river.

VII. Searches

67 (1)–76 (10) Searches, Etc.

(*To be elaborated parallel to 45:161–70.*) [292]

Searches, discriminations, taints,
Kinds of existence, threefold suffering,
Barrenness, stains, and troubles,
Feelings, craving, and thirst.

VIII. Floods

77 (1)–85 (9) Floods, Etc.

(*To be elaborated parallel to 45:171–79.*)

86 (10) Higher Fetters

"Bhikkhus, there are these five higher fetters. What five? Lust for form, lust for the formless, conceit, restlessness, ignorance. These are the five higher fetters. The four bases for spiritual power are to be developed for direct knowledge of these five higher fetters, for the full understanding of them, for their utter destruction, for their abandoning.

"What four? Here, bhikkhus, a bhikkhu develops the basis for spiritual power that possesses concentration due to desire and volitional formations of striving. He develops the basis for spiritual power that possesses concentration due to energy … concentration due to mind … concentration due to investigation and volitional formations of striving.

"These four bases for spiritual power are to be developed for direct knowledge of these five higher fetters, for the full understanding of them, for their utter destruction, for their abandoning." [293]

Floods, bonds, kinds of clinging,
Knots, and underlying tendencies,
Cords of sensual pleasure, hindrances,
Aggregates, fetters lower and higher.

[294]

Chapter VIII

52 *Anuruddhasaṃyutta*

Connected Discourses with Anuruddha

I. Alone

1 (1) Alone (1)

Thus have I heard. On one occasion the Venerable Anuruddha was dwelling at Sāvatthī in Jeta's Grove, Anāthapiṇḍika's Park.[280] Then, while the Venerable Anuruddha was alone in seclusion, a reflection arose in his mind thus: "Those who have neglected these four establishments of mindfulness have neglected the noble path leading to the complete destruction of suffering. Those who have undertaken these four establishments of mindfulness have undertaken the noble path leading to the complete destruction of suffering."

Then the Venerable Mahāmoggallāna, having known with his own mind the reflection in the Venerable Anuruddha's mind, just as quickly as a strong man might extend his drawn-in arm or draw in his extended arm, appeared in the presence of the Venerable Anuruddha and said to him:

"To what extent, friend Anuruddha, have these four establishments of mindfulness been undertaken by a bhikkhu?"

"Here, friend, a bhikkhu dwells contemplating the nature of origination in the body internally;[281] he dwells contemplating the nature of vanishing in the body internally; he dwells contemplating the nature of origination and vanishing in the body internally—[295] ardent, clearly comprehending, mindful, having removed covetousness and displeasure in regard to the world.

"He dwells contemplating the nature of origination in the body externally; he dwells contemplating the nature of vanishing in the body externally; he dwells contemplating the nature of origination and vanishing in the body externally—ardent, clearly comprehending, mindful, having removed covetousness and displeasure in regard to the world.

"He dwells contemplating the nature of origination in the body internally and externally; he dwells contemplating the nature of vanishing in the body internally and externally; he dwells contemplating the nature of origination and vanishing in the body internally and externally—ardent, clearly comprehending, mindful, having removed covetousness and displeasure in regard to the world.

"If he wishes:[282] 'May I dwell perceiving the repulsive in the unrepulsive,' he dwells perceiving the repulsive therein. If he wishes: 'May I dwell perceiving the unrepulsive in the repulsive,' he dwells perceiving the unrepulsive therein. If he wishes: 'May I dwell perceiving the repulsive in the unrepulsive and in the repulsive,' he dwells perceiving the repulsive therein. If he wishes: 'May I dwell perceiving the unrepulsive in the repulsive and in the unrepulsive,' he dwells perceiving the unrepulsive therein. If he wishes: 'Avoiding both the unrepulsive and the repulsive, may I dwell equanimously, mindful and clearly comprehending,' then he dwells therein equanimously, mindful and clearly comprehending.

"He dwells contemplating the nature of origination … the nature of vanishing … the nature of origination and vanishing in feelings internally … in feelings externally … in feelings internally and externally—[296] ardent, clearly comprehending, mindful, having removed covetousness and displeasure in regard to the world.

"If he wishes: 'May I dwell perceiving the repulsive in the unrepulsive,' he dwells perceiving the repulsive therein…. If he wishes: 'Avoiding both the unrepulsive and the repulsive, may I dwell equanimously, mindful and clearly comprehending,' then he dwells therein equanimously, mindful and clearly comprehending.

"He dwells contemplating the nature of origination … the nature of vanishing … the nature of origination and vanishing in mind internally … in mind externally … in mind internally and externally—ardent, clearly comprehending, mindful, having removed covetousness and displeasure in regard to the world.

"If he wishes: 'May I dwell perceiving the repulsive in the

unrepulsive,' he dwells perceiving the repulsive therein.... If he wishes: 'Avoiding both the unrepulsive and the repulsive, may I dwell equanimously, mindful and clearly comprehending,' then he dwells therein equanimously, mindful and clearly comprehending.

"He dwells contemplating the nature of origination ... the nature of vanishing ... the nature of origination and vanishing in phenomena internally ... in phenomena externally ... in phenomena internally and externally—ardent, clearly comprehending, mindful, having removed covetousness and displeasure in regard to the world.

"If he wishes: 'May I dwell perceiving the repulsive in the unrepulsive,' he dwells perceiving the repulsive therein.... If he wishes: 'Avoiding both the unrepulsive and the repulsive, may I dwell equanimously, mindful and clearly comprehending,' then he dwells therein equanimously, mindful and clearly comprehending.

"It is in this way, friend, that these four establishments of mindfulness have been undertaken by a bhikkhu."

2 (2) Alone (2)

At Sāvatthī. Then, while the Venerable Anuruddha was alone in seclusion, a reflection arose in his mind thus: "Those who have neglected these four establishments of mindfulness have neglected the noble path leading to the complete destruction of suffering. Those who have undertaken these four establishments of mindfulness have undertaken the noble path leading to the complete destruction of suffering."

Then the Venerable Mahāmoggallāna, having known with his own mind the reflection in the Venerable Anuruddha's mind, just as [297] quickly as a strong man might extend his drawn-in arm or draw in his extended arm, appeared in the presence of the Venerable Anuruddha and said to him:

"To what extent, friend Anuruddha, have these four establishments of mindfulness been undertaken by a bhikkhu?"

"Here, friend, a bhikkhu dwells contemplating the body in the body internally, ardent, clearly comprehending, mindful, having removed covetousness and displeasure in regard to the world. He dwells contemplating the body in the body externally, ardent, clearly comprehending, mindful, having removed covetousness and displeasure in regard to the world. He dwells contemplating the body in the body internally and externally, ardent, clearly comprehending, mindful, having removed covetousness and displeasure in regard to the world.

"He dwells contemplating feelings in feelings internally ... contemplating feelings in feelings externally ... contemplating feelings in feelings internally and externally, ardent, clearly comprehending, mindful, having removed covetousness and displeasure in regard to the world.

"He dwells contemplating mind in mind internally ... contemplating mind in mind externally ... contemplating mind in mind internally and externally, ardent, clearly comprehending, mindful, having removed covetousness and displeasure in regard to the world.

"He dwells contemplating phenomena in phenomena internally ... contemplating phenomena in phenomena externally ... contemplating phenomena in phenomena internally and externally, ardent, clearly comprehending, mindful, having removed covetousness and displeasure in regard to the world.

"It is in this way, friend, that these four establishments of mindfulness have been undertaken by a bhikkhu."

3 (3) Sutanu

On one occasion the Venerable Anuruddha was dwelling at Sāvatthī on the bank of the Sutanu. Then a number of bhikkhus approached the Venerable Anuruddha and exchanged greetings with him. When they had concluded their greetings and cordial talk, they sat down to one side [298] and said to the Venerable Anuruddha:

"By having developed and cultivated what things has the Venerable Anuruddha attained to greatness of direct knowledge?"

"It is, friends, because I have developed and cultivated the four establishments of mindfulness that I have attained to greatness of direct knowledge. What four? Here, friends, I dwell contemplating the body in the body, ardent, clearly comprehending, mindful, having removed covetousness and displeasure in regard to the world.

"I dwell contemplating feelings in feelings ... mind in mind ...

phenomena in phenomena, ardent, clearly comprehending, mindful, having removed covetousness and displeasure in regard to the world.

"It is, friends, because I have developed and cultivated these four establishments of mindfulness that I have attained to greatness of direct knowledge. Further, friends, it is because I have developed and cultivated these four establishments of mindfulness that I directly knew the inferior state as inferior; that I directly knew the middling state as middling; that I directly knew the sublime state as sublime."[283]

4 (4) The Thornbush Grove (1)

On one occasion the Venerable Anuruddha, the Venerable Sāriputta, and the Venerable Mahāmoggallāna were dwelling at Sāketa in the Thornbush Grove.[284] Then, in the evening, the Venerable Sāriputta and the Venerable Mahāmoggallāna emerged from seclusion, approached the Venerable Anuruddha, and exchanged greetings with him. When they had concluded their greetings and cordial talk, they sat down to one side, and the Venerable Sāriputta said to the Venerable Anuruddha:

"Friend Anuruddha, what are the things that a bhikkhu who is a trainee should enter and dwell in?"

"Friend, Sāriputta, a bhikkhu who is a trainee should enter and dwell in the four establishments of mindfulness. What four? Here, friend, a bhikkhu dwells contemplating the body in the body ... [299] ... feelings in feelings ... mind in mind ... phenomena in phenomena, ardent, clearly comprehending, mindful, having removed covetousness and displeasure in regard to the world. A bhikkhu who is a trainee should enter and dwell in these four establishments of mindfulness."

5 (5) The Thornbush Grove (2)

At Sāketa. Sitting to one side the Venerable Sāriputta said to the Venerable Anuruddha:

"Friend Anuruddha, what are the things that a bhikkhu who is beyond training should enter and dwell in?"

"Friend, Sāriputta, a bhikkhu who is beyond training should enter and dwell in the four establishments of mindfulness. What four? Here, friend, a bhikkhu dwells contemplating the body in the body … feelings in feelings … mind in mind … phenomena in phenomena, ardent, clearly comprehending, mindful, having removed covetousness and displeasure in regard to the world. A bhikkhu who is beyond training should enter and dwell in these four establishments of mindfulness."

6 (6) The Thornbush Grove (3)

At Sāketa. Sitting to one side, the Venerable Sāriputta said to the Venerable Anuruddha:

"By having developed and cultivated what things has the Venerable Aruruddha attained to greatness of direct knowledge?"

"It is, friend, because I have developed and cultivated the four establishments of mindfulness that I have attained to greatness of direct knowledge. What four? Here, friend, I dwell contemplating the body in the body … feelings in feelings … mind in mind … phenomena in phenomena, ardent, clearly comprehending, mindful, having removed covetousness and displeasure in regard to the world.

"It is, friend, because I have developed and cultivated these four establishments of mindfulness that I have attained to greatness of direct knowledge. Further, friend, it is because I have developed and cultivated these four establishments of mindfulness that I directly know the thousandfold world."[285] [300]

7 (7) The Destruction of Craving

At Sāvatthī. There the Venerable Anuruddha addressed the bhikkhus thus: "Friends, bhikkhus!"

"Friend!" those bhikkhus replied. The Venerable Anuruddha said this:

"Friends, these four establishments of mindfulness, when developed and cultivated, lead to the destruction of craving. What four? Here, friends, a bhikkhu dwells contemplating the body in the body … feelings in feelings … mind in mind … phenomena in phenomena, ardent, clearly comprehending, mindful, having removed covetousness and displeasure in regard to the world. These four establishments of mindfulness, when developed and cultivated, lead to the destruction of craving."

8 (8) *The* Salaḷa-*Tree Hut*

On one occasion the Venerable Anuruddha was living at Sāvatthī in a *salaḷa*-tree hut. There the Venerable Anuruddha addressed the bhikkhus thus....

"Friends, the river Ganges slants, slopes, and inclines towards the east. Now suppose a great crowd of people would come along bringing a shovel and basket, thinking: 'We will make this river Ganges slant, slope, and incline towards the west.'[286] What do you think, friends, would that great crowd of people be able to make the river Ganges slant, slope, and incline towards the west?"

"No, friend. For what reason? Because the river Ganges slants, slopes, and inclines towards the east, and it is not easy to make it slant, slope, and incline towards the west. That great crowd of people would only reap fatigue and vexation."

"So too, friends, when a bhikkhu is developing and cultivating the four establishments of mindfulness, kings or royal ministers, friends or colleagues, relatives or kinsmen, [301] might invite him to accept wealth, saying: 'Come, good man, why let these saffron robes weigh you down? Why roam around with a shaven head and begging bowl? Come, having returned to the lower life, enjoy wealth and do meritorious deeds.' Indeed, friends, when that bhikkhu is developing and cultivating the four establishments of mindfulness, it is impossible that he will give up the training and return to the lower life. For what reason? Because for a long time his mind has slanted, sloped, and inclined towards seclusion. Thus it is impossible that he will give up the training and return to the lower life.

"And how, friends, does a bhikkhu develop and cultivate the four establishments of mindfulness? Here, friends, a bhikkhu dwells contemplating the body in the body ... feelings in feelings ... mind in mind ... phenomena in phenomena, ardent, clearly comprehending, mindful, having removed covetousness and displeasure in regard to the world.

"It is in this way, friends, that a bhikkhu develops and cultivates the four establishments of mindfulness."

9 (9) All, or Ambapālī's Grove

On one occasion the Venerable Anuruddha and the Venerable Sāriputta were dwelling at Vesālī in Ambapālī's Grove. Then, in the evening, the Venerable Sāriputta emerged from seclusion.... Sitting to one side, the Venerable Sāriputta said to the Venerable Anuruddha:

"Friend Anuruddha, your faculties are serene, your complexion is pure and bright. In what dwelling does the Venerable Anuruddha now usually dwell?"

"Now, friend, I usually dwell with a mind well established in the four establishments of mindfulness. What four? Here, friend, I dwell contemplating the body in the body ... feelings in feelings ... mind in mind ... phenomena in phenomena, ardent, [302] clearly comprehending, mindful, having removed covetousness and displeasure in regard to the world.

"The bhikkhu, friend, who is an arahant, one whose taints are destroyed, who has lived the holy life, done what had to be done, laid down the burden, reached his own goal, utterly destroyed the fetters of existence, one completely liberated through final knowledge, usually dwells with a mind well established in these four establishments of mindfulness."

"It is a gain for us, friend, it is well gained by us, friend, that we were in the very presence of the Venerable Anuruddha when he made such a bellowing utterance."

10 (10) Gravely Ill

On one occasion the Venerable Anuruddha was dwelling at Sāvatthī in the Blind Men's Grove, sick, afflicted, gravely ill. Then a number of bhikkhus approached the Venerable Anuruddha and said to him:

"In what dwelling does the Venerable Anuruddha usually dwell so that the arisen bodily painful feelings do not persist obsessing his mind?"

"It is, friends, because I dwell with a mind well established in the four establishments of mindfulness that the arisen bodily feelings do not persist obsessing my mind. What four? Here, friend, I dwell contemplating the body in the body ... feelings in feelings ... mind in mind ... phenomena in phenomena, ardent, clearly comprehending, mindful, having removed covetousness and displeasure in regard to the world.

"It is, friends, because I dwell with a mind well established in these four establishments of mindfulness that the arisen bodily painful feelings do not persist obsessing my mind."

[303]

II. The Second Subchapter
(A Thousand)

11 (1) A Thousand Aeons

On one occasion the Venerable Anuruddha was dwelling at Sāvatthī in Jeta's Grove, Anāthapiṇḍika's Park. Then a number of bhikkhus approached the Venerable Anuruddha and exchanged greetings with him. When they had concluded their greetings and cordial talk, they sat down to one side and said to the Venerable Anuruddha:

"By having developed and cultivated what things has the Venerable Anuruddha attained to greatness of direct knowledge?"

"It is, friends, because I have developed and cultivated the four establishments of mindfulness that I have attained to greatness of direct knowledge. What four? Here, friends, I dwell contemplating the body in the body ... feelings in feelings ... mind in mind ... phenomena in phenomena, ardent, clearly comprehending, mindful, having removed covetousness and displeasure in regard to the world.

"It is, friends, because I have developed and cultivated these four establishments of mindfulness that I have attained to greatness of direct knowledge. Further, friends, it is because I have developed and cultivated these four establishments of mindfulness that I recollect a thousand aeons."

12 (2) Spiritual Power

... "Further, friends, it is because I have developed and cultivated these four establishments of mindfulness that I wield the various kinds of spiritual power: having been one I become many; having been many I become one ... I exercise mastery with the body as far as the brahmā world." [304]

13 (3) The Divine Ear

… "Further, friends, it is because I have developed and cultivated these four establishments of mindfulness that with the divine ear element, which is purified and surpasses the human, I hear both kinds of sound, the divine and the human, those that are far as well as near."

14 (4) Encompassing the Mind

… "Further, friends, it is because I have developed and cultivated these four establishments of mindfulness that I understand the minds of other beings and persons, having encompassed them with my own mind. I understand a mind with lust as a mind with lust … an unliberated mind as an unliberated mind."

15 (5) The Possible

… "Further, friends, it is because I have developed and cultivated these four establishments of mindfulness that I understand the possible as possible and the impossible as impossible."[287]

16 (6) The Undertaking of Kamma

… "Further, friends, it is because I have developed and cultivated these four establishments of mindfulness that I understand as it really is the result of past, future, and present kamma by way of potential and by way of cause."

17 (7) Leading Everywhere

… "Further, friends, it is because I have developed and cultivated these four establishments of mindfulness that I understand as it really is the way leading everywhere."

18 (8) Diverse Elements

… "Further, friends, it is because I have developed and cultivated these four establishments of mindfulness that I understand as it really is the world with its manifold and diverse elements." [305]

19 (9) Diverse Dispositions

... "Further, friends, it is because I have developed and cultivated these four establishments of mindfulness that I understand as it really is the diversity in the dispositions of beings."

20 (10) Degrees of the Faculties

... "Further, friends, it is because I have developed and cultivated these four establishments of mindfulness that I understand as it really is the degrees of maturity in the spiritual faculties of other beings and persons."

21 (11) The Jhānas, Etc.

... "Further, friends, it is because I have developed and cultivated these four establishments of mindfulness that I understand as it really is the defilement, the cleansing, and the emergence in regard to the jhānas, deliverances, concentrations, and attainments."

22 (12) Past Abodes

... "Further, friends, it is because I have developed and cultivated these four establishments of mindfulness that I recollect my manifold past abodes, that is, one birth, two births ... many aeons of world-contraction and expansion.... Thus I recollect my manifold past abodes with their modes and details."

23 (13) The Divine Eye

... "Further, friends, it is because I have developed and cultivated these four establishments of mindfulness that with the divine eye, which is purified and surpasses the human, I see beings passing away and being reborn ... and I understand how beings fare on in accordance with their kamma."

24 (14) The Destruction of the Taints

... "Further, friends, it is because I have developed and cultivated these four establishments of mindfulness that [306] by the destruction of the taints, in this very life I enter and dwell in the taintless liberation of mind, liberation by wisdom, realizing it for myself with direct knowledge."

[307] Chapter IX

53 *Jhānasaṃyutta*

Connected Discourses on the Jhānas

I. Ganges Repetition Series

1 (1)–12 (12) The River Ganges—Eastward, Etc.

At Sāvatthī. There the Blessed One said this:

"Bhikkhus, there are these four jhānas. What four? Here, bhikkhus, secluded from sensual pleasures, secluded from unwholesome states, a bhikkhu enters and dwells in the first jhāna, which is accompanied by thought and examination, with rapture and happiness born of seclusion. With the subsiding of thought and examination, he enters and dwells in the second jhāna, which has internal confidence and unification of mind, is without thought and examination, and has rapture and happiness born of concentration. With the fading away as well of rapture, he dwells equanimous and, mindful and clearly comprehending, he experiences happiness with the body; he enters and dwells in the third jhāna of which the noble ones declare: 'He is equanimous, mindful, one who dwells happily.' With the abandoning of pleasure and pain, and with the previous passing away of joy and displeasure, he enters and dwells in the fourth jhāna, which is neither painful nor pleasant and includes the purification of mindfulness by equanimity. These are the four jhānas.[288]

"Bhikkhus, just as the river Ganges slants, slopes, and inclines towards the east, so too a bhikkhu [308] who develops and cultivates the four jhānas slants, slopes, and inclines towards Nibbāna.

"And how, bhikkhus, does a bhikkhu who develops and cultivates the four jhānas slant, slope, and incline towards Nibbāna? Here, bhikkhus, secluded from sensual pleasures, secluded from unwholesome states, a bhikkhu enters and dwells in the first jhāna … the second jhāna … the third jhāna … the fourth jhāna.

"It is in this way, bhikkhus, that a bhikkhu who develops and cultivates the four jhānas slants, slopes, and inclines towards Nibbāna."

(*The remaining suttas of this vagga are to be similarly elaborated parallel to 45:92–102.*)

Six about slanting to the east
And six about slanting to the ocean.
These two sixes make up twelve:
Thus the subchapter is recited.

II. Diligence

13 (1)–22 (10) The Tathāgata, Etc.

(*To be elaborated by way of the jhānas parallel to 45:139–48.*)

Tathāgata, footprint, roof peak,
Roots, heartwood, jasmine,
Monarch, the moon and sun,
Together with the cloth as tenth.

III. Strenuous Deeds

23 (1)–34 (12) Strenuous, Etc.

(*To be elaborated parallel to 45:149–60.*) [309]

Strenuous, seeds, and nāgas,
The tree, the pot, the spike,
The sky, and two on clouds,
The ship, guest house, and river.

IV. Searches

35 (1)–44 (10) Searches, Etc.

(To be elaborated parallel to 45:161–70.)

Searches, discriminations, taints,
Kinds of existence, threefold suffering,
Barrenness, stains, and troubles,
Feelings, craving, and thirst.

V. Floods

45 (1)–53 (9) Floods, Etc.

(To be elaborated parallel to 45:171–79.)

54 (10) Higher Fetters

"Bhikkhus, there are these five higher fetters. What five? Lust for form, lust for the formless, conceit, restlessness, ignorance. These are the five higher fetters. The four jhānas are to be developed for direct knowledge of these five higher fetters, for the full understanding of them, for their utter destruction, for their abandoning.

"What four? Here, bhikkhus, secluded from sensual pleasures, secluded from unwholesome states, a bhikkhu enters and dwells in the first jhāna ... the second jhāna ... the third jhāna ... the fourth jhāna. [310]

"These four jhānas are to be developed for direct knowledge of these five higher fetters, for the full understanding of them, for their utter destruction, for their abandoning."

Floods, bonds, kinds of clinging,
Knots, and underlying tendencies,
Cords of sensual pleasure, hindrances,
Aggregates, fetters lower and higher.

[311] Chapter X

54 *Ānāpānasaṃyutta*
Connected Discourses on Breathing

I. One Thing

1 (1) One Thing

At Sāvatthī. There the Blessed One said this:

"Bhikkhus, one thing, when developed and cultivated, is of great fruit and benefit. What one thing? Mindfulness of breathing. And how, bhikkhus, is mindfulness of breathing developed and cultivated so that it is of great fruit and benefit?

"Here, bhikkhus, a bhikkhu, having gone to the forest, to the foot of a tree, or to an empty hut, sits down. Having folded his legs crosswise, straightened his body, and set up mindfulness in front of him, just mindful he breathes in, mindful he breathes out.[289]

"Breathing in long, he knows: 'I breathe in long'; or breathing out long, he knows: 'I breathe out long.' Breathing in short, he knows: 'I breathe in short'; or breathing out short, he knows: 'I breathe out short.' He trains thus: 'Experiencing the whole body, I will breathe in'; he trains thus: 'Experiencing the whole body, I will breathe out.' He trains thus: 'Tranquillizing the bodily formation, I will breathe in'; he trains thus: 'Tranquillizing the bodily formation, I will breathe out.'[290] [312]

"He trains thus: 'Experiencing rapture, I will breathe in'; he trains thus: 'Experiencing rapture, I will breathe out.' He trains thus: 'Experiencing happiness, I will breathe in'; he trains thus: 'Experiencing happiness, I will breathe out.' He trains thus: 'Experiencing the mental formation, I will breathe in'; he trains thus: 'Experiencing the mental formation, I will breathe out.' He trains thus: 'Tranquillizing the mental formation, I will breathe in'; he trains thus: 'Tranquillizing the mental formation, I will breathe out.'[291]

"He trains thus: 'Experiencing the mind, I will breathe in'; he trains thus: 'Experiencing the mind, I will breathe out.' He trains thus: 'Gladdening the mind, I will breathe in'; he trains thus: 'Gladdening the mind, I will breathe out.' He trains thus: 'Concentrating the mind, I will breathe in'; he trains thus: 'Concentrating the mind, I will breathe out.' He trains thus: 'Liberating the mind, I will breathe in'; he trains thus: 'Liberating the mind, I will breathe out.'[292]

"He trains thus: 'Contemplating impermanence, I will breathe in'; he trains thus: 'Contemplating impermanence, I will breathe out.' He trains thus: 'Contemplating fading away, I will breathe in'; he trains thus: 'Contemplating fading away, I will breathe out.' He trains thus: 'Contemplating cessation, I will breathe in'; he trains thus: 'Contemplating cessation, I will breathe out.' He trains thus: 'Contemplating relinquishment, I will breathe in'; he trains thus: 'Contemplating relinquishment, I will breathe out.'[293]

"It is, bhikkhus, when mindfulness of breathing is developed and cultivated in this way that it is of great fruit and benefit."

2 (2) Factors of Enlightenment

"Bhikkhus, mindfulness of breathing, when developed and cultivated, is of great fruit and benefit. And how, bhikkhus, is mindfulness of breathing developed and cultivated so that it is of great fruit and benefit?

"Here, bhikkhus, a bhikkhu develops the enlightenment factor of mindfulness accompanied by mindfulness of breathing, based upon seclusion, dispassion, and cessation, maturing in release. He develops the enlightenment factor of discrimination of states ... [313] ... the enlightenment factor of equanimity accompanied by mindfulness of breathing, based upon seclusion, dispassion, and cessation, maturing in release.

"It is in this way, bhikkhus, that mindfulness of breathing is developed and cultivated so that it is of great fruit and benefit."

3 (3) Simple Version

"Bhikkhus, mindfulness of breathing, when developed and cultivated, is of great fruit and benefit. And how, bhikkhus, is mindfulness of breathing developed and cultivated so that it is of great fruit and benefit?

"Here, bhikkhus, a bhikkhu, having gone to the forest, to the foot of a tree, or to an empty hut, sits down. Having folded his legs crosswise, straightened his body, and set up mindfulness in front of him, just mindful he breathes in, mindful he breathes out.... (*all as in §1*) ... He trains thus: 'Contemplating relinquishment, I will breathe in'; he trains thus: 'Contemplating relinquishment, I will breathe out.'

"It is in this way, bhikkhus, that mindfulness of breathing is developed and cultivated so that it is of great fruit and benefit."

4 (4) Fruits (1)

(*All as in preceding sutta, with the following addition:*)

[314] "When, bhikkhus, mindfulness of breathing has been developed and cultivated in this way, one of two fruits may be expected: either final knowledge in this very life or, if there is a residue of clinging, the state of nonreturning."

5 (5) Fruits (2)

(*All as in §3, with the following addition:*)

"When, bhikkhus, mindfulness of breathing has been developed and cultivated in this way, seven fruits and benefits may be expected. What are the seven fruits and benefits?

"One attains final knowledge early in this very life.

"If one does not attain final knowledge early in this very life, then one attains final knowledge at the time of death.

"If one does not attain final knowledge early in this very life or at the time of death, then with the utter destruction of the five lower fetters one becomes an attainer of Nibbāna in the interval.

"If one does not attain final knowledge early in this very life ... or become an attainer of Nibbāna in the interval, then with the utter destruction of the five lower fetters one becomes an attainer of Nibbāna upon landing.

"If one does not attain final knowledge early in this very life … or become an attainer of Nibbāna upon landing, then with the utter destruction of the five lower fetters one becomes an attainer of Nibbāna without exertion.

"If one does not attain final knowledge early in this very life … or become an attainer of Nibbāna without exertion, then with the utter destruction of the five lower fetters one becomes an attainer of Nibbāna with exertion.

"If one does not attain final knowledge early in this very life … or become an attainer of Nibbāna with exertion, then with the utter destruction of the five lower fetters one becomes one bound upstream, heading towards the Akaniṭṭha realm.

"When, bhikkhus, mindfulness of breathing has been developed and cultivated in this way, these seven fruits and benefits may be expected."

6 (6) Ariṭṭha

At Sāvatthī. There the Blessed One said this:

"Bhikkhus, do you develop mindfulness of breathing?"

When this was said, the Venerable Ariṭṭha said to the Blessed One: "Venerable sir, I develop mindfulness of breathing." [315]

"But in what way, Ariṭṭha, do you develop mindfulness of breathing?"

"I have abandoned sensual desire for past sensual pleasures, venerable sir, I have gotten rid of sensual desire for future sensual pleasures, and I have thoroughly dispelled perceptions of aversion towards things internally and externally. Just mindful I breathe in, mindful I breathe out. It is in this way, venerable sir, that I develop mindfulness of breathing."

"That is mindfulness of breathing, Ariṭṭha, I do not say that it is not. But as to how mindfulness of breathing is fulfilled in detail, Ariṭṭha, listen and attend closely, I will speak."[294]

"Yes, venerable sir," the Venerable Ariṭṭha replied. The Blessed One said this:

"And how, Ariṭṭha, is mindfulness of breathing fulfilled in detail? Here, Ariṭṭha, a bhikkhu, having gone to the forest, to the foot of a tree, or to an empty hut, sits down. Having folded his legs crosswise, straightened his body, and set up mindfulness in front of him, just mindful he breathes in, mindful he breathes out.... He trains thus: 'Contemplating relinquishment, I will breathe in'; he trains thus: 'Contemplating relinquishment, I will breathe out.'

"It is in this way, Ariṭṭha, that mindfulness of breathing is fulfilled in detail."

7 (7) Mahākappina

At Sāvatthī. Now on that occasion the Venerable Mahākappina was sitting not far from the Blessed One, with his legs folded crosswise, holding his body straight, having set up mindfulness in front of him. The Blessed One saw him sitting nearby, with his legs folded crosswise, his body straight, having set up mindfulness in front of him. Having seen him, he addressed the bhikkhus thus:

"Bhikkhus, do you see any shaking or trembling in this bhikkhu's body?"

"Venerable sir, whenever we see that venerable one, whether he is sitting in the midst of the Saṅgha or sitting alone in private, [316] we never see any shaking or trembling in that venerable one's body."

"Bhikkhus, that bhikkhu gains at will, without trouble or difficulty, that concentration through the development and cultivation of which no shaking or trembling occurs in the body, and no shaking or trembling occurs in the mind. And what concentration is it through the development and cultivation of which no shaking or trembling occurs in the body, and no shaking or trembling occurs in the mind?

"It is, bhikkhus, when concentration by mindfulness of breathing[295] has been developed and cultivated that no shaking or trembling occurs in the body, and no shaking or trembling occurs in the mind. And how, bhikkhus, is concentration by mindfulness of breathing developed and cultivated so that no shaking or trembling occurs in the body, and no shaking or trembling occurs in the mind?

"Here, bhikkhus, a bhikkhu, having gone to the forest, to the foot of a tree, or to an empty hut, sits down. Having folded his legs crosswise, straightened his body, and set up mindfulness in front of him, just mindful he breathes in, mindful he breathes out.... He trains thus: 'Contemplating relinquishment, I will breathe in'; he trains thus: 'Contemplating relinquishment, I will breathe out.'

"It is, bhikkhus, when concentration by mindfulness of breathing has been developed and cultivated in this way that no shaking or trembling occurs in the body, and no shaking or trembling occurs in the mind."

8 (8) The Simile of the Lamp

"Bhikkhus, concentration by mindfulness of breathing, when developed and cultivated, is of great fruit and benefit. And how, bhikkhus, is concentration by mindfulness of breathing developed and cultivated so that it is of great fruit and benefit? [317]

"Here, bhikkhus, a bhikkhu, having gone to the forest, to the foot of a tree, or to an empty hut, sits down. Having folded his legs crosswise, straightened his body, and set up mindfulness in front of him, just mindful he breathes in, mindful he breathes out.... He trains thus: 'Contemplating relinquishment, I will breathe in'; he trains thus: 'Contemplating relinquishment, I will breathe out.'

"It is in this way, bhikkhus, that concentration by mindfulness of breathing is developed and cultivated so that it is of great fruit and benefit.

"I too, bhikkhus, before my enlightenment, while I was still a bodhisatta, not yet fully enlightened, generally dwelt in this dwelling. While I generally dwelt in this dwelling, neither my body nor my eyes became fatigued and my mind, by not clinging, was liberated from the taints.

"Therefore, bhikkhus, if a bhikkhu wishes: 'May neither my body nor my eyes become fatigued and may my mind, by not clinging, be liberated from the taints,' this same concentration by mindfulness of breathing should be closely attended to.[296]

"Therefore, bhikkhus, if a bhikkhu wishes: 'May the memories and intentions connected with the household life be abandoned by me,' this same concentration by mindfulness of breathing should be closely attended to.

"Therefore, bhikkhus, if a bhikkhu wishes:[297] 'May I dwell perceiving the repulsive in the unrepulsive,' this same concentration by mindfulness of breathing should be closely attended to. If a bhikkhu wishes: 'May I dwell perceiving the unrepulsive in the repulsive,' this same concentration by mindfulness of breathing should be closely attended to. If a bhikkhu wishes: 'May I dwell perceiving the repulsive in the unrepulsive and the repulsive,' this same concentration by mindfulness of breathing should be closely attended to. If a bhikkhu wishes: [318] 'May I dwell perceiving the unrepulsive in the repulsive and the unrepulsive,' this same concentration by mindfulness of breathing should be closely attended to. If a bhikkhu wishes: 'Avoiding both the unrepulsive and the repulsive, may I dwell equanimous, mindful and clearly comprehending,' this same concentration by mindfulness of breathing should be closely attended to.

"Therefore, bhikkhus, if a bhikkhu wishes: 'May I, secluded from sensual pleasures, secluded from unwholesome states, enter and dwell in the first jhāna, which is accompanied by thought and examination, with rapture and happiness born of seclusion,' this same concentration by mindfulness of breathing should be closely attended to.

"Therefore, bhikkhus, if a bhikkhu wishes: 'May I, with the subsiding of thought and examination, enter and dwell in the second jhāna, which has internal confidence and unification of mind, is without thought and examination, and has rapture and happiness born of concentration,' this same concentration by mindfulness of breathing should be closely attended to.

"Therefore, bhikkhus, if a bhikkhu wishes: 'May I, with the fading away as well of rapture, dwell equanimous and, mindful and clearly comprehending, may I experience happiness with the body; may I enter and dwell in the third jhāna of which the noble ones declare: "He is equanimous, mindful, one who dwells happily,"' this same concentration by mindfulness of breathing should be closely attended to.

"Therefore, bhikkhus, if a bhikkhu wishes: 'May I, with the abandoning of pleasure and pain, and with the previous passing away of joy and displeasure, enter and dwell in the fourth jhāna, which is neither painful nor pleasant and includes the purification of mindfulness by equanimity,' this same concentration by mindfulness of breathing should be closely attended to.

"Therefore, bhikkhus, if a bhikkhu wishes: 'May I, with the complete transcendence of perceptions of forms, with the passing away of perceptions of sensory impingement, with nonattention to perceptions of diversity, aware that "space is infinite," enter and dwell in the base of the infinity of space,' this same concentration by mindfulness of breathing should be closely attended to.

"Therefore, bhikkhus, if a bhikkhu wishes: 'May I, by completely transcending the base of the infinity of space, [319] aware that "consciousness is infinite," enter and dwell in the base of the infinity of consciousness,' this same concentration by mindfulness of breathing should be closely attended to.

"Therefore, bhikkhus, if a bhikkhu wishes: 'May I, by completely transcending the base of the infinity of consciousness, aware that "there is nothing," enter and dwell in the base of nothingness,' this same concentration by mindfulness of breathing should be closely attended to.

"Therefore, bhikkhus, if a bhikkhu wishes: 'May I, by completely transcending the base of nothingness, enter and dwell in the base of neither-perception-nor-nonperception,' this same concentration by mindfulness of breathing should be closely attended to.

"Therefore, bhikkhus, if a bhikkhu wishes: 'May I, by completely transcending the base of neither-perception-nor-nonperception, enter and dwell in the cessation of perception and feeling,' this same concentration by mindfulness of breathing should be closely attended to.

"When, bhikkhus, the concentration by mindfulness of breathing has been developed and cultivated in this way, if he feels a pleasant feeling, he understands: 'It is impermanent'; he understands: 'It is not held to'; he understands: 'It is not delighted in.'[298] If he feels a painful feeling, he understands: 'It is impermanent'; he understands: 'It is not held to'; he understands: 'It is not delighted in.' If he feels a neither-painful-nor-pleasant feeling, he understands: 'It is impermanent'; he understands: 'It is not held to'; he understands: 'It is not delighted in.'

"If he feels a pleasant feeling, he feels it detached; if he feels a painful feeling, he feels it detached; if he feels a neither-painful-nor-pleasant feeling, he feels it detached.

"When he feels a feeling terminating with the body, he understands: 'I feel a feeling terminating with the body.' When he feels a feeling terminating with life, he understands: 'I feel a feeling terminating with life.' He understands: 'With the breakup of the body, following the exhaustion of life, all that is felt, not being delighted in, will become cool right here.'

"Just as, bhikkhus, an oil lamp burns in dependence on the oil and the wick, and with the exhaustion of the oil and the wick it is extinguished through lack of fuel, so too, bhikkhus, when a bhikkhu [320] feels a feeling terminating with the body … terminating with life … He understands: 'With the breakup of the body, following the exhaustion of life, all that is felt, not being delighted in, will become cool right here.'"

9 (9) At Vesālī

Thus have I heard. On one occasion the Blessed One was dwelling at Vesālī in the Great Wood in the Hall with the Peaked Roof.[299] Now on that occasion the Blessed One was giving the bhikkhus a talk on foulness in many ways, was speaking in praise of foulness, was speaking in praise of the development of foulness meditation.[300]

Then the Blessed One addressed the bhikkhus thus: "Bhikkhus, I wish to go into seclusion for half a month. I should not be approached by anyone except the one who brings me almsfood."[301]

"Yes, venerable sir," those bhikkhus replied, and no one approached the Blessed One except the one who brought him almsfood.

Then those bhikkhus, thinking: "The Blessed One was giving a talk on foulness in many ways, was speaking in praise of foulness, was speaking in praise of the development of foulness meditation," dwelt devoted to the development of foulness meditation in its many aspects and factors. Being repelled, humiliated, and disgusted with this body, they sought for an assailant. In one day ten bhikkhus used the knife, or in one day twenty or thirty bhikkhus used the knife.[302]

Then, when that half-month had passed, the Blessed One emerged from seclusion and addressed the Venerable Ānanda: "Why, Ānanda, does the Bhikkhu Saṅgha look so diminished?"[303]

"Venerable sir, that is because [the Blessed One had given a talk on foulness in many ways, had spoken in praise of foulness, [321] had spoken in praise of the development of foulness meditation, and those bhikkhus,][304] thinking: 'The Blessed One was giving a talk on foulness in many ways, was speaking in praise of foulness, was speaking in praise of the development of foulness meditation,' dwelt devoted to the development of foulness meditation in its many aspects and factors. Being repelled, humiliated, and disgusted with this body, they sought for an assailant. In one day ten bhikkhus used the knife, or in one day twenty or thirty bhikkhus used the knife. It would be good, venerable sir, if the Blessed One would explain another method so that this Bhikkhu Saṅgha may be established in final knowledge."

"Well then, Ānanda, assemble in the attendance hall all the bhikkhus who are living in dependence on Vesālī."

"Yes, venerable sir," the Venerable Ānanda replied, and he assembled in the attendance hall all the bhikkhus who were living in dependence on Vesālī, as many as there were. Then he approached the Blessed One and said to him: "The Bhikkhu Saṅgha has assembled, venerable sir. Let the Blessed One come at his own convenience."

Then the Blessed One went to the attendance hall, sat down in the appointed seat, and addressed the bhikkhus thus:

"Bhikkhus, this concentration by mindfulness of breathing, when developed and cultivated, is peaceful and sublime, an ambrosial pleasant dwelling, and it disperses and quells right on the spot evil unwholesome states whenever they arise.[305]

"Just as, bhikkhus, in the last month of the hot season, when a mass of dust and dirt has swirled up, a great rain cloud out of season disperses it and quells it on the spot,[306] so too concentration by mindfulness of breathing, when developed and cultivated, is peaceful and sublime, [322] an ambrosial pleasant dwelling, and it disperses and quells on the spot evil unwholesome states whenever they arise. And how is this so?

"Here, bhikkhus, a bhikkhu, having gone to the forest, to the foot of a tree, or to an empty hut, sits down. Having folded his legs crosswise, straightened his body, and set up mindfulness in front of him, just mindful he breathes in, mindful he breathes out.... He trains thus: 'Contemplating relinquishment, I will breathe in'; he trains thus: 'Contemplating relinquishment, I will breathe out.'

"It is in this way, bhikkhus, that concentration by mindfulness of breathing is developed and cultivated so that it is peaceful and sublime, an ambrosial pleasant dwelling, and it disperses and quells on the spot evil unwholesome states whenever they arise."

10 (10) Kimbila

Thus have I heard. On one occasion the Blessed One was dwelling at Kimbilā in the Bamboo Grove. There the Blessed One addressed the Venerable Kimbila thus: "How is it now, Kimbila, that concentration by mindfulness of breathing is developed and cultivated so that it is of great fruit and benefit?"

When this was said, the Venerable Kimbila was silent. A second time ... A third time the Blessed One addressed the Venerable Kimbila: "How is it now, Kimbila, that concentration by mindfulness of breathing is developed and cultivated so that it is of great fruit and benefit?" A third time the Venerable Kimbila was silent. [323]

When this happened, the Venerable Ānanda said to the Blessed One: "Now is the time for this, Blessed One! Now is the time for this, Fortunate One! The Blessed One should speak on concentration by mindfulness of breathing. Having heard it from the Blessed One, the bhikkhus will remember it."

"Well then, Ānanda, listen and attend closely, I will speak."

"Yes, venerable sir," the Venerable Ānanda replied. The Blessed One said this:

"And how, Ānanda, is concentration by mindfulness of breathing developed and cultivated so that it is of great fruit and benefit? Here, Ānanda, a bhikkhu, having gone to the forest, to the foot of a tree, or to an empty hut, sits down. Having folded his legs crosswise, straightened his body, and set up mindfulness in front of him, just mindful he breathes in, mindful he breathes out.... He trains thus: 'Contemplating relinquishment, I will breathe in'; he trains thus: 'Contemplating relinquishment, I will breathe out.'

(i. Contemplation of the body)

"Whenever,[307] Ānanda, a bhikkhu, when breathing in long, knows: 'I breathe in long'; or, when breathing out long, knows: 'I breathe out long'; when breathing in short, knows: 'I breathe in short'; or, when breathing out short, knows: 'I breathe out short'; when he trains thus: 'Experiencing the whole body, I will breathe in'; when he trains thus: 'Experiencing the whole body, I will breathe out'; when he trains thus: 'Tranquillizing the bodily formation, I will breathe in'; when he trains thus: 'Tranquillizing the bodily formation, I will breathe out'—on that occasion the bhikkhu dwells contemplating the body in the body, ardent, clearly comprehending, mindful, having removed covetousness and displeasure in regard to the world. For what reason? I call this a certain kind of body, Ānanda, that is, breathing in and breathing out.[308] Therefore, Ānanda, on that occasion the bhikkhu dwells contemplating the body in the body, ardent, clearly comprehending, mindful, having removed covetousness and displeasure in regard to the world.

(ii. Contemplation of feelings)

"Whenever, Ānanda, a bhikkhu trains thus: 'Experiencing rapture, I will breathe in'; when he trains thus: 'Experiencing rapture, I will breathe out'; when he trains thus: 'Experiencing happiness, I will breathe in'; when he trains thus: 'Experiencing happiness, I will breathe out'; when he trains thus: 'Experiencing the mental formation, [324] I will breathe in'; when he trains thus: 'Experiencing the mental formation, I will breathe out'; when he trains thus: 'Tranquillizing the mental formation, I will breathe in'; when he trains thus: 'Tranquillizing the mental formation, I will breathe out'—on that occasion the bhikkhu dwells contemplating feelings in feelings, ardent, clearly comprehending, mindful, having removed covetousness and displeasure in regard to the world. For what reason? I call this a certain kind of feeling, Ānanda, that is, close attention to breathing in and breathing out.[309] Therefore, Ānanda, on that occasion the bhikkhu dwells contemplating feelings in feelings, ardent, clearly comprehending, mindful, having removed covetousness and displeasure in regard to the world.

(iii. Contemplation of mind)

"Whenever, Ānanda, a bhikkhu trains thus: 'Experiencing the mind, I will breathe in'; when he trains thus: 'Experiencing the mind, I will breathe out'; when he trains thus: 'Gladdening the mind, I will breathe in'; when he trains thus: 'Gladdening the mind, I will breathe out'; when he trains thus: 'Concentrating the mind, I will breathe in'; when he trains thus: 'Concentrating the mind, I will breathe out'; when he trains thus: 'Liberating the mind, I will breathe in'; when he trains thus: 'Liberating the mind, I will breathe out'—on that occasion the bhikkhu dwells contemplating mind in mind, ardent, clearly comprehending, mindful, having removed covetousness and displeasure in regard to the world. For what reason? I say, Ānanda, that there is no development of concentration by mindfulness of breathing for one who is muddled and who lacks clear comprehension. Therefore, Ānanda, on that occasion the bhikkhu dwells contemplating mind in mind, ardent, clearly comprehending, mindful, having removed covetousness and displeasure in regard to the world.

(iv. Contemplation of phenomena)

"Whenever, Ānanda, a bhikkhu trains thus: 'Contemplating impermanence, I will breathe in'; when he trains thus: 'Contemplating impermanence, I will breathe out'; when he trains thus: 'Contemplating fading away, I will breathe in'; when he trains thus: 'Contemplating fading away, I will breathe out'; when he trains thus: 'Contemplating cessation, I will breathe in'; when he trains thus: 'Contemplating cessation, I will breathe out'; when he trains thus: 'Contemplating relinquishment, I will breathe in'; when he trains thus: 'Contemplating relinquishment, I will breathe out'—on that occasion the bhikkhu dwells contemplating phenomena in phenomena, ardent, clearly comprehending, mindful, having removed covetousness and displeasure in regard to the world. Having seen with wisdom the abandoning of covetousness and displeasure, he is one who looks on closely with equanimity.[310] Therefore, Ānanda, on that occasion the bhikkhu dwells contemplating phenomena in phenomena, ardent, clearly comprehending, mindful, having removed covetousness and displeasure in regard to the world. [325]

"Suppose, Ānanda, at a crossroads there is a great mound of soil. If a cart or chariot comes from the east, west, north, or south, it would flatten that mound of soil.[311] So too, Ānanda, when a bhikkhu dwells contemplating the body in the body, feelings in feelings, mind in mind, phenomena in phenomena, he flattens evil unwholesome states."

II. The Second Subchapter
(Ānanda)

11 (1) At Icchānaṅgala

On one occasion the Blessed One was dwelling at Icchānaṅgala in the Icchānaṅgala Wood. There the Blessed One addressed the bhikkhus thus:

"Bhikkhus, I wish to go into seclusion for three months. I should not be approached by anyone except the one who brings me almsfood."

"Yes, venerable sir," those bhikkhus replied, and no one approached the Blessed One except the one who brought him almsfood. [326]

Then, when those three months had passed, the Blessed One emerged from seclusion and addressed the bhikkhus thus:

"Bhikkhus, if wanderers of other sects ask you: 'In what dwelling, friends, did the Blessed One generally dwell during the rains residence?'—being asked thus, you should answer those wanderers thus: 'During the rains residence, friends, the Blessed One generally dwelt in the concentration by mindfulness of breathing.'

"Here, bhikkhus, mindful I breathe in, mindful I breathe out. When breathing in long I know: 'I breathe in long'; when breathing out long I know: 'I breathe out long.' When breathing in short I know: 'I breathe in short'; when breathing out short I know: 'I breathe out short.' I know: 'Experiencing the whole body I will breathe in.'... I know: 'Contemplating relinquishment, I will breathe out.'[312]

"If anyone, bhikkhus, speaking rightly could say of anything: 'It is a noble dwelling, a divine dwelling, the Tathāgata's dwelling,' it is of concentration by mindfulness of breathing that one could rightly say this.

"Bhikkhus, those bhikkhus who are trainees, who have not attained their mind's ideal, who dwell aspiring for the unsurpassed security from bondage: for them concentration by mindfulness of breathing, when developed and cultivated, leads to the destruction of the taints. Those bhikkhus who are arahants, whose taints are destroyed, who have lived the holy life, done what had to be done, laid down the burden, reached their own goal, utterly destroyed the fetters of existence, those completely liberated through final knowledge: for them concentration by mindfulness of breathing, when developed and cultivated, leads to a pleasant dwelling in this very life and to mindfulness and clear comprehension.[313]

"If anyone, bhikkhus, speaking rightly could say of anything: 'It is a noble dwelling, a divine dwelling, the Tathāgata's dwelling,' it is of concentration by mindfulness of breathing that one could rightly say this." [327]

12 (2) In Perplexity

On one occasion the Venerable Lomasavaṅgīsa was dwelling among the Sakyans at Kapilavatthu in Nigrodha's Park. Then Mahānāma the Sakyan approached the Venerable Lomasavaṅgisa, paid homage to him, sat down to one side, and said to him:

"Is it the case, venerable sir, that the dwelling of a trainee is itself the same as the Tathāgata's dwelling, or is it rather that the dwelling of a trainee is one thing and the Tathāgata's dwelling is another?"

"It is not the case, friend Mahānāma, that the dwelling of a trainee is itself the same as the Tathāgata's dwelling; rather, the dwelling of a trainee is one thing and the Tathāgata's dwelling is another.

"Friend Mahānāma, those bhikkhus who are trainees, who have not attained their mind's ideal, who dwell aspiring for the unsurpassed security from bondage, dwell having abandoned the five hindrances.[314] What five? The hindrances of sensual desire, ill will, sloth and torpor, restlessness and remorse, and doubt. Those bhikkhus who are trainees ... dwell having abandoned these five hindrances.

"But, friend Mahānāma, for those bhikkhus who are arahants, whose taints are destroyed, who have lived the holy life, done what had to be done, laid down the burden, reached their own goal, utterly destroyed the fetters of existence, become completely liberated through final knowledge, the five hindrances have been abandoned, cut off at the root, made like palm stumps, obliterated so that they are no more subject to future arising.[315] What five? The hindrances of sensual desire, ill will, sloth and torpor, restlessness and remorse, and doubt. [328] For those bhikkhus who are arahants ... these five hindrances have been abandoned, cut off at the root, made like palm stumps, obliterated so that they are no more subject to future arising.

"By the following method too, friend Mahānāma, it can be understood how the dwelling of a trainee is one thing and the Tathāgata's dwelling is another.

"On this one occasion, friend Mahānāma, the Blessed One was dwelling at Icchānaṅgala in the Icchānaṅgala Wood. There the Blessed One addressed the bhikkhus thus: 'Bhikkhus, I wish to go into seclusion for three months. I should not be approached by anyone except the one who brings me almsfood.'

(*He here repeats the entire contents of the preceding sutta, down to:*)

"'If anyone, bhikkhus, speaking rightly could say of anything: "It is a noble dwelling, a divine dwelling, the Tathāgata's dwelling," it is of concentration by mindfulness of breathing that one could rightly say this.'

"By this method, friend Mahānāma, it can be understood how the dwelling of a trainee is one thing and the Tathāgata's dwelling is another."

13 (3) Ānanda (1)

At Sāvatthī. Then the Venerable Ānanda approached the Blessed One, paid homage to him, sat down to one side, and said to him: [329]

"Venerable sir, is there one thing which, when developed and cultivated, fulfils four things? And four things which, when developed and cultivated, fulfil seven things? And seven things which, when developed and cultivated, fulfil two things?"

"There is, Ānanda, one thing which, when developed and cultivated, fulfils four things; and four things which, when developed and cultivated, fulfil seven things; and seven things which, when developed and cultivated, fulfil two things."

"But, venerable sir, what is the one thing which, when developed and cultivated, fulfils four things; and the four things which, when developed and cultivated, fulfil seven things; and the seven things which, when developed and cultivated, fulfil two things?"

"Concentration by mindfulness of breathing, Ānanda, is the

one thing which, when developed and cultivated, fulfils the four establishments of mindfulness. The four establishments of mindfulness, when developed and cultivated, fulfil the seven factors of enlightenment. The seven factors of enlightenment, when developed and cultivated, fulfil true knowledge and liberation.

(i. Fulfilling the four establishments of mindfulness)

"How, Ānanda, is concentration by mindfulness of breathing developed and cultivated so that it fulfils the four establishments of mindfulness? Here, Ānanda, a bhikkhu, having gone to the forest, to the foot of a tree, or to an empty hut, sits down. Having folded his legs crosswise, straightened his body, and set up mindfulness in front of him, just mindful he breathes in, mindful he breathes out.... He trains thus: 'Contemplating relinquishment, I will breathe in'; he trains thus: 'Contemplating relinquishment, I will breathe out.'

"Whenever, Ānanda, a bhikkhu, when breathing in long, knows: 'I breathe in long' ... (*as in §10*) ... when he trains thus: 'Tranquillizing the bodily formation, I will breathe out'—on that occasion the bhikkhu dwells contemplating the body in the body, ardent, clearly comprehending, mindful, having removed covetousness and displeasure in regard to the world. For what reason? I call this a certain kind of body, Ānanda, that is, [330] breathing in and breathing out. Therefore, Ānanda, on that occasion the bhikkhu dwells contemplating the body in the body, ardent, clearly comprehending, mindful, having removed covetousness and displeasure in regard to the world.

"Whenever, Ānanda, a bhikkhu trains thus: 'Experiencing rapture, I will breathe in' ... when he trains thus: 'Tranquillizing the mental formation, I will breathe out'—on that occasion the bhikkhu dwells contemplating feelings in feelings, ardent, clearly comprehending, mindful, having removed covetousness and displeasure in regard to the world. For what reason? I call this a certain kind of feeling, Ānanda, that is, close attention to breathing in and breathing out. Therefore, Ānanda, on that occasion the bhikkhu dwells contemplating feelings in feelings, ardent, clearly comprehending, mindful, having removed covetousness and displeasure in regard to the world.

"Whenever, Ānanda, a bhikkhu trains thus: 'Experiencing the mind, I will breathe in' ... when he trains thus: 'Liberating the mind, I will breathe out'—on that occasion the bhikkhu dwells contemplating mind in mind, ardent, clearly comprehending, mindful, having removed covetousness and displeasure in regard to the world. For what reason? I say, Ānanda, that there is no development of concentration by mindfulness of breathing for one who is muddled and who lacks clear comprehension. Therefore, Ānanda, on that occasion the bhikkhu dwells contemplating mind in mind, ardent, clearly comprehending, mindful, having removed covetousness and displeasure in regard to the world.

"Whenever, Ānanda, a bhikkhu trains thus: 'Contemplating impermanence, I will breathe in' ... when he trains thus: 'Contemplating relinquishment, I will breathe out'—on that occasion the bhikkhu dwells contemplating phenomena in phenomena, ardent, clearly comprehending, mindful, having removed covetousness and displeasure in regard to the world. Having seen with wisdom what is the abandoning of covetousness and displeasure, [331] he is one who looks on closely with equanimity. Therefore, Ānanda, on that occasion the bhikkhu dwells contemplating phenomena in phenomena, ardent, clearly comprehending, mindful, having removed covetousness and displeasure in regard to the world.

"It is, Ānanda, when concentration by mindfulness of breathing is developed and cultivated in this way that it fulfils the four establishments of mindfulness.

(ii. Fulfilling the seven factors of enlightenment)

"And how, Ānanda, are the four establishments of mindfulness developed and cultivated so that they fulfil the seven factors of enlightenment?

"Whenever, Ānanda, a bhikkhu dwells contemplating the body in the body, on that occasion unmuddled mindfulness is established in that bhikkhu.[316] Whenever, Ānanda, unmuddled mindfulness has been established in a bhikkhu, on that occasion the enlightenment factor of mindfulness is aroused by the bhikkhu; on that occasion the bhikkhu develops the enlightenment factor of mindfulness; on that occasion the enlightenment factor of mindfulness goes to fulfilment by development in the bhikkhu.

"Dwelling thus mindfully, he discriminates that Dhamma with

wisdom, examines it, makes an investigation of it. Whenever, Ānanda, a bhikkhu dwelling thus mindfully discriminates that Dhamma with wisdom, examines it, makes an investigation of it, on that occasion the enlightenment factor of discrimination of states is aroused by the bhikkhu; on that occasion the bhikkhu develops the enlightenment factor of discrimination of states; on that occasion the enlightenment factor of discrimination of states goes to fulfilment by development in the bhikkhu.

"While he discriminates that Dhamma with wisdom, examines it, makes an investigation of it, [332] his energy is aroused without slackening. Whenever, Ānanda, a bhikkhu's energy is aroused without slackening as he discriminates that Dhamma with wisdom, examines it, makes an investigation of it, on that occasion the enlightenment factor of energy is aroused by the bhikkhu; on that occasion the bhikkhu develops the enlightenment factor of energy; on that occasion the enlightenment factor of energy goes to fulfilment by development in the bhikkhu.

"When his energy is aroused, there arises in him spiritual rapture. Whenever, Ānanda, spiritual rapture arises in a bhikkhu whose energy is aroused, on that occasion the enlightenment factor of rapture is aroused by the bhikkhu; on that occasion the bhikkhu develops the enlightenment factor of rapture; on that occasion the enlightenment factor of rapture goes to fulfilment by development in the bhikkhu.

"For one whose mind is uplifted by rapture the body becomes tranquil and the mind becomes tranquil. Whenever, Ānanda, the body becomes tranquil and the mind becomes tranquil in a bhikkhu whose mind is uplifted by rapture, on that occasion the enlightenment factor of tranquillity is aroused by the bhikkhu; on that occasion the bhikkhu develops the enlightenment factor of tranquillity; on that occasion the enlightenment factor of tranquillity goes to fulfilment by development in the bhikkhu.

"For one whose body is tranquil and who is happy the mind becomes concentrated. Whenever, Ānanda, the mind becomes concentrated in a bhikkhu whose body is tranquil and who is happy, on that occasion the enlightenment factor of concentration is aroused by the bhikkhu; on that occasion the bhikkhu develops the enlightenment factor of concentration; on that occasion the enlightenment factor of concentration goes to fulfilment by development in the bhikkhu.

"He becomes one who closely looks on with equanimity at the mind thus concentrated. Whenever, Ānanda, a bhikkhu becomes one who closely looks on with equanimity at the mind thus concentrated, on that occasion the enlightenment factor of equanimity is aroused by the bhikkhu; on that occasion the bhikkhu develops the enlightenment factor of equanimity; on that occasion the enlightenment factor of equanimity goes to fulfilment by development in the bhikkhu.

"Whenever, Ānanda, a bhikkhu dwells contemplating feelings in feelings ... mind in mind ... phenomena in phenomena, on that occasion unmuddled mindfulness is established in that bhikkhu. [333] Whenever, Ānanda, unmuddled mindfulness has been established in a bhikkhu, on that occasion the enlightenment factor of mindfulness is aroused by the bhikkhu; on that occasion the bhikkhu develops the enlightenment factor of mindfulness; on that occasion the enlightenment factor of mindfulness goes to fulfilment by development in the bhikkhu.

(*All should be elaborated as in the case of the first establishment of mindfulness.*)

"He becomes one who closely looks on with equanimity at the mind thus concentrated. Whenever, Ānanda, a bhikkhu becomes one who closely looks on with equanimity at the mind thus concentrated, on that occasion the enlightenment factor of equanimity is aroused by the bhikkhu; on that occasion the bhikkhu develops the enlightenment factor of equanimity; on that occasion the enlightenment factor of equanimity goes to fulfilment by development in the bhikkhu.

"It is, Ānanda, when the four establishments of mindfulness are developed and cultivated in this way that they fulfil the seven factors of enlightenment.

(iii. Fulfilling true knowledge and liberation)

"How, Ānanda, are the seven factors of enlightenment developed and cultivated so that they fulfil true knowledge and liberation?

"Here, Ānanda, a bhikkhu develops the enlightenment factor of mindfulness, which is based upon seclusion, dispassion, and cessation, maturing in release. He develops the enlightenment factor of discrimination of states ... the enlightenment factor of energy ... the enlightenment factor of rapture ... the enlightenment factor of tranquillity ... the enlightenment factor of concentration … the enlightenment factor of equanimity, which is based upon seclusion, dispassion, and cessation, maturing in release.

"It is, Ānanda, when the seven factors of enlightenment are developed and cultivated in this way that they fulfil true knowledge and liberation."

14 (4) Ānanda (2)

Then the Venerable Ānanda approached the Blessed One, paid homage to him, and sat down to one side. The Blessed One then said to the Venerable Ānanda:

"Ānanda, is there one thing which, when developed and cultivated, fulfils four things? And four things which, when developed and cultivated, fulfil seven things? And seven things which, when developed and cultivated, fulfil two things?"

"Venerable sir, our teachings are rooted in the Blessed One…."

"There is, Ānanda, one thing which, when developed and cultivated, [334] fulfils four things; and four things which, when developed and cultivated, fulfil seven things; and seven things which, when developed and cultivated, fulfil two things.

"And what, Ānanda, is the one thing which, when developed and cultivated, fulfils four things; and the four things which, when developed and cultivated, fulfil seven things; and the seven things which, when developed and cultivated, fulfil two things? Concentration by mindfulness of breathing, Ānanda, is the one thing which, when developed and cultivated, fulfils the four establishments of mindfulness. The four establishments of mindfulness, when developed and cultivated, fulfil the seven factors of enlightenment. The seven factors of enlightenment, when developed and cultivated, fulfil true knowledge and liberation.

"And how, Ānanda, is concentration by mindfulness of breathing developed and cultivated so that it fulfils the four establishments of mindfulness?

"Here, Ānanda, a bhikkhu, having gone to the forest … (*all as in the preceding sutta down to:*) … It is, Ānanda, when the seven factors of enlightenment are developed and cultivated in this way that they fulfil true knowledge and liberation."

15 (5) Bhikkhus (1)

(Identical with §13 except that "a number of bhikkhus" are the interlocutors in place of Ānanda.) [335]

16 (6) Bhikkhus (2)

(Identical with §14 except that "a number of bhikkhus" are the interlocutors in place of Ānanda.) [336–40]

17 (7) The Fetters

"Bhikkhus, concentration by mindfulness of breathing, when developed and cultivated, leads to the abandoning of the fetters."

18 (8) The Underlying Tendencies

"... leads to the uprooting of the underlying tendencies."

19 (9) The Course

"... leads to the full understanding of the course."

20 (10) The Destruction of the Taints

"... leads to the destruction of the taints.

"And how, bhikkhus, is concentration by mindfulness of breathing developed and cultivated so that it leads to the abandoning of the fetters, to the uprooting of the underlying tendencies, to the full understanding of the course, to the destruction of the taints?

"Here, bhikkhus, a bhikkhu, having gone to the forest, to the foot of a tree, or to an empty hut, sits down. Having folded his legs crosswise, straightened his body, and set up mindfulness in front of him, just mindful he breathes in, mindful he breathes out.... [341] He trains thus: 'Contemplating relinquishment, I will breathe in'; he trains thus: 'Contemplating relinquishment, I will breathe out.'

"It is in this way, bhikkhus, that concentration by mindfulness of breathing is developed and cultivated so that it leads to the abandoning of the fetters, to the uprooting of the underlying tendencies, to the full understanding of the course, to the destruction of the taints."

[342] Chapter XI

55 *Sotāpattisaṃyutta*

Connected Discourses on Stream-Entry

I. Bamboo Gate

1 (1) Wheel-Turning Monarch

At Sāvatthī. There the Blessed One said this:

"Bhikkhus, although a wheel-turning monarch, having exercised supreme sovereign rulership over the four continents,[317] with the breakup of the body, after death, is reborn in a good destination, in a heavenly world, in the company of the devas of the Tāvatiṃsa realm, and there in the Nandana Grove, accompanied by a retinue of celestial nymphs, he enjoys himself supplied and endowed with the five cords of celestial sensual pleasure, still, as he does not possess four things, he is not freed from hell, the animal realm, and the domain of ghosts, not freed from the plane of misery, the bad destinations, the nether world.[318] Although, bhikkhus, a noble disciple maintains himself by lumps of almsfood and wears rag-robes, still, as he possesses four things, he is freed from hell, the animal realm, and the domain of ghosts, freed from the plane of misery, the bad destinations, the nether world.

"What are the four? [343] Here, bhikkhus, the noble disciple possesses confirmed confidence in the Buddha thus:[319] 'The Blessed One is an arahant, perfectly enlightened, accomplished in true knowledge and conduct, fortunate, knower of the world, unsurpassed leader of persons to be tamed, teacher of devas and humans, the Enlightened One, the Blessed One.'

"He possesses confirmed confidence in the Dhamma thus: 'The Dhamma is well expounded by the Blessed One, directly visible, immediate, inviting one to come and see, applicable, to be personally experienced by the wise.'

"He possesses confirmed confidence in the Saṅgha thus: 'The Saṅgha of the Blessed One's disciples is practising the good way, practising the straight way, practising the true way, practising the proper way; that is, the four pairs of persons, the eight types of individuals—this Saṅgha of the Blessed One's disciples is worthy of gifts, worthy of hospitality, worthy of offerings, worthy of reverential salutation, the unsurpassed field of merit for the world.'

"He possesses the virtues dear to the noble ones—unbroken, untorn, unblemished, unmottled, freeing, praised by the wise, ungrasped, leading to concentration.[320]

"He possesses these four things. And, bhikkhus, between the obtaining of sovereignty over the four continents and the obtaining of the four things, the obtaining of sovereignty over the four continents is not worth a sixteenth part of the obtaining of the four things."[321]

2 (2) *Grounded*

"Bhikkhus, a noble disciple who possesses four things is a stream-enterer, no longer bound to the nether world, fixed in destiny, with enlightenment as his destination.[322]

"What four? Here, bhikkhus, a noble disciple possesses confirmed confidence in the Buddha thus: 'The Blessed One is ... teacher of devas and humans, the Enlightened One, the Blessed One.' He possesses confirmed confidence in the Dhamma ... in the Saṅgha.... He possesses the virtues dear to the noble ones, unbroken ... leading to concentration. [344]

"A noble disciple, bhikkhus, who possesses these four things is a stream-enterer, no longer bound to the nether world, fixed in destiny, with enlightenment as his destination."

This is what the Blessed One said. Having said this, the Fortunate One, the Teacher, further said this:

"Those who possess faith and virtue,
Confidence and vision of the Dhamma,
In time arrive at the happiness
Grounded upon the holy life."[323]

3 (3) Dīghāvu

On one occasion the Blessed One was dwelling at Rājagaha in the Bamboo Grove, the Squirrel Sanctuary. Now on that occasion the lay follower Dīghāvu was sick, afflicted, gravely ill. Then the lay follower Dīghāvu addressed his father, the householder Jotika, thus: "Come, householder, approach the Blessed One, pay homage to him in my name with your head at his feet, and say: 'Venerable sir, the lay follower Dīghāvu is sick, afflicted, gravely ill; he pays homage to the Blessed One with his head at the Blessed One's feet.' Then say: 'It would be good, venerable sir, if the Blessed One would come to the residence of the lay follower Dīghāvu out of compassion.'"

"Yes, dear," the householder Jotika replied, and he approached the Blessed One, paid homage to him, sat down to one side, and delivered his message. The Blessed One consented by silence.

Then the Blessed One dressed and, taking bowl and robe, went to the residence of the lay follower Dīghāvu. [345] He then sat down in the appointed seat and said to the lay follower Dīghāvu: "I hope you are bearing up, Dīghāvu, I hope you are getting better. I hope your painful feelings are subsiding and not increasing, and that their subsiding, not their increase, is to be discerned."

"Venerable sir, I am not bearing up, I am not getting better. Strong painful feelings are increasing in me, not subsiding, and their increase, not their subsiding, is to be discerned."

"Therefore, Dīghāvu, you should train yourself thus: 'I will be one who possesses confirmed confidence in the Buddha thus: "The Blessed One is … teacher of devas and humans, the Enlightened One, the Blessed One." I will be one who possesses confirmed confidence in the Dhamma … in the Saṅgha.… I will be one who possesses the virtues dear to the noble ones, unbroken … leading to concentration.' It is in such a way that you should train yourself."

"Venerable sir, as to these four factors of stream-entry that have been taught by the Blessed One, these things exist in me, and I live in conformity with those things. For, venerable sir, I possess confirmed confidence in the Buddha … in the Dhamma … in the Saṅgha.… I possess the virtues dear to the noble ones, unbroken … leading to concentration."

"Therefore, Dīghāvu, established upon these four factors of

stream-entry, you should develop further six things that partake of true knowledge. Here, Dīghāvu, dwell contemplating impermanence in all formations, perceiving suffering in what is impermanent, perceiving nonself in what is suffering, perceiving abandonment, perceiving fading away, perceiving cessation.[324] It is in such a way that you should train yourself."

"Venerable sir, as to these six things that partake of true knowledge that have been taught by the Blessed One, these things exist in me, and I live in conformity with those things. For, venerable sir, I dwell contemplating impermanence in all formations, perceiving suffering in what is impermanent, perceiving nonself in what is suffering, perceiving abandonment, perceiving fading away, perceiving cessation. However, venerable sir, the thought occurs to me: 'After I am gone, may this householder Jotika not fall into distress.'" [346]

"Don't be concerned about this, dear Dīghāvu. Come now, dear Dīghāvu, pay close attention to what the Blessed One is saying to you."

Then the Blessed One, having given this exhortation to the lay follower Dīghāvu, rose from his seat and departed. Then, not long after the Blessed One had left, the lay follower Dīghāvu died.

Then a number of bhikkhus approached the Blessed One, paid homage to him, sat down to one side, and said to the Blessed One: "Venerable sir, that lay follower named Dīghāvu to whom the Blessed One gave a brief exhortation has died. What is his destination, what is his future bourn?"

"Bhikkhus, the lay follower Dīghāvu was wise. He practised in accordance with the Dhamma and did not trouble me on account of the Dhamma. Bhikkhus, with the utter destruction of the five lower fetters the lay follower Dīghāvu has become one of spontaneous birth, due to attain Nibbāna there without returning from that world."

4 (4) Sāriputta (1)

On one occasion the Venerable Sāriputta and the Venerable Ānanda were dwelling at Sāvatthī in Jeta's Grove, Anāthapiṇḍika's Park. Then, in the evening, the Venerable Ānanda emerged from seclusion.... Sitting to one side, the Venerable Ānanda said to the Venerable Sāriputta:

"Friend Sāriputta, on account of possessing how many things are people declared by the Blessed One to be stream-enterers, no longer bound to the nether world, fixed in destiny, with enlightenment as their destination?" [347]

"It is on account of possessing four things, friend Ānanda, that people are declared by the Blessed One to be stream-enterers, no longer bound to the nether world, fixed in destiny, with enlightenment as their destination. What four? Here, friend, a noble disciple possesses confirmed confidence in the Buddha thus: 'The Blessed One is ... teacher of devas and humans, the Enlightened One, the Blessed One.' He possesses confirmed confidence in the Dhamma ... in the Saṅgha.... He possesses the virtues dear to the noble ones, unbroken ... leading to concentration.

"It is, friend, on account of possessing these four things that people are declared by the Blessed One to be stream-enterers, no longer bound to the nether world, fixed in destiny, with enlightenment as their destination."

5 (5) Sāriputta (2)

Then the Venerable Sāriputta approached the Blessed One, paid homage to him, and sat down to one side. The Blessed One then said to him:

"Sāriputta, this is said: 'A factor for stream-entry, a factor for stream-entry.' What now, Sāriputta, is a factor for stream-entry?"

"Association with superior persons, venerable sir, is a factor for stream-entry. Hearing the true Dhamma is a factor for stream-entry. Careful attention is a factor for stream-entry. Practice in accordance with the Dhamma is a factor for stream-entry."[325]

"Good, good, Sāriputta! Association with superior persons, Sāriputta, is a factor for stream-entry. Hearing the true Dhamma is a factor for stream-entry. Careful attention is a factor for stream-entry. Practice in accordance with the Dhamma is a factor for stream-entry.

"Sāriputta, this is said: 'The stream, the stream.' What now, Sāriputta, is the stream?"

"This Noble Eightfold Path, venerable sir, is the stream; that is, right view, right intention, right speech, right action, right livelihood, right effort, right mindfulness, right concentration."

"Good, good, Sāriputta! This Noble Eightfold Path is the stream; that is, right view ... right concentration. [348]

"Sāriputta, this is said: 'A stream-enterer, a stream-enterer.' What now, Sāriputta, is a stream-enterer?"

"One who possesses this Noble Eightfold Path, venerable sir, is called a stream-enterer: this venerable one of such a name and clan."

"Good, good, Sāriputta! One who possesses this Noble Eightfold Path is a stream-enterer: this venerable one of such a name and clan."

6 (6) The Chamberlains

At Sāvatthī. Now on that occasion a number of bhikkhus were making a robe for the Blessed One, thinking: "After the three months, with his robe completed, the Blessed One will set out on tour."

Now on that occasion the chamberlains[326] Isidatta and Purāṇa were residing in Sādhuka on some business. They heard: "A number of bhikkhus, it is said, are making a robe for the Blessed One, thinking that after the three months, with his robe completed, the Blessed One will set out on tour."

Then the chamberlains Isidatta and Purāṇa posted a man on the road, telling him: "Good man, when you see the Blessed One coming, the Arahant, the Perfectly Enlightened One, then you should inform us." After standing for two or three days that man saw the Blessed One coming in the distance. Having seen him, the man approached the chamberlains Isidatta and Purāṇa and told them: "Sirs, this Blessed One is coming, the Arahant, the Perfectly Enlightened One. You may come at your own convenience."

Then the chamberlains Isidatta and Purāṇa approached the Blessed One, paid homage to him, and followed closely behind him. Then the Blessed One left the road, went to the foot of a tree, and sat down on a seat that was prepared for him. [349] The chamberlains Isidatta and Purāṇa paid homage to the Blessed One, sat down to one side, and said to him:

"Venerable sir, when we hear that the Blessed One will set out from Sāvatthī on tour among the Kosalans, on that occasion there arises in us distress and displeasure at the thought: 'The Blessed

One will be far away from us.' Then when we hear that the Blessed One has set out from Sāvatthī on tour among the Kosalans, on that occasion there arises in us distress and displeasure at the thought: 'The Blessed One is far away from us.'

"Further, venerable sir, when we hear that the Blessed One will set out from among the Kosalans on tour in the Mallan country ... that he has set out from among the Kosalans on tour in the Mallan country ... that he will set out from among the Mallans on tour in the Vajjian country ... that he has set out from among the Mallans on tour in the Vajjian country ... that he will set out from among the Vajjians on tour in the Kāsian country ... that he has set out from among the Vajjians on tour in the Kāsian country ... that he will set out from among the Kāsians on tour in Magadha, on that occasion there arises in us [350] distress and displeasure at the thought: 'The Blessed One will be far away from us.' Then when we hear that the Blessed One has set out from among the Kāsians on tour in Magadha, on that occasion there arises in us great distress and displeasure at the thought: 'The Blessed One is far away from us.'

"But, venerable sir, when we hear that the Blessed One will set out from among the Magadhans on tour in the Kāsian country, on that occasion there arises in us elation and joy at the thought: 'The Blessed One will be near to us.' Then when we hear that the Blessed One has set out from among the Magadhans on tour in the Kāsian country, on that occasion there arises in us elation and joy at the thought: 'The Blessed One is near to us.'

"Further, venerable sir, when we hear that the Blessed One will set out from among the Kāsians on tour in the Vajjian country ... that he has set out from among the Kāsians on tour in the Vajjian country ... that he will set out from among the Vajjians on tour in the Mallan country ... that he has set out from among the Vajjians on tour in the Mallan country ... that he will set out from among the Mallans on tour in Kosala ... that he has set out from among the Mallans on tour in Kosala ... that he will set out from among the Kosalans on tour to Sāvatthī, on that occasion there arises in us elation and joy at the thought: 'The Blessed One will be near to us.' Then, venerable sir, when we hear that the Blessed One is dwelling at Sāvatthī, in Jeta's Grove, Anāthapiṇḍika's Park, on that occasion there arises in us great elation and joy at the thought: 'The Blessed One is near to us.'"

"Therefore, chamberlains, the household life is confinement, a path of dust. The going forth is like the open air. It is enough for you, chamberlains, to be diligent."

"Venerable sir, we are subject to another confinement even more confining and considered more confining than the former one." [351]

"But what, chamberlains, is that other confinement to which you are subject, which is even more confining and considered more confining than the former one?"

"Here, venerable sir, when King Pasenadi of Kosala wants to make an excursion to his pleasure garden, after we have prepared his riding elephants we have to place the king's dear and beloved wives on their seats, one in front and one behind. Now, venerable sir, the scent of those ladies is just like that of a perfumed casket briefly opened; so it is with the royal ladies wearing scent. Also, venerable sir, the bodily touch of those ladies is just like that of a tuft of cotton wool or kapok; so it is with the royal ladies so delicately nurtured. Now on that occasion, venerable sir, the elephants must be guarded, and those ladies must be guarded, and we ourselves must be guarded, yet we do not recall giving rise to an evil state of mind in regard to those ladies. This, venerable sir, is that other confinement to which we are subject, which is even more confining and considered more confining than the former one."

"Therefore, chamberlains, the household life is confinement, a path of dust. The going forth is like the open air. It is enough for you, chamberlains, to be diligent. The noble disciple, chamberlains, who possesses four things is a stream-enterer, no longer bound to the nether world, fixed in destiny, with enlightenment as his destination.

"What four? Here, chamberlains, a noble disciple possesses confirmed confidence in the Buddha thus: 'The Blessed One is ... teacher of devas and humans, the Enlightened One, the Blessed One.' He possesses confirmed confidence in the Dhamma ... in the Saṅgha.... He dwells at home with a mind devoid of the stain of stinginess, freely generous, open-handed, delighting in relinquishment, one devoted to charity, delighting in giving and sharing.[327] A noble disciple who possesses these four things [352] is a stream-enterer, no longer bound to the nether world, fixed in destiny, with enlightenment as his destination.

"Chamberlains, you possess confirmed confidence in the Buddha … in the Dhamma … in the Saṅgha.… Moreover, whatever there is in your family that is suitable for giving, all that you share unreservedly among those who are virtuous and of good character. What do you think, carpenters, how many people are there among the Kosalans who are your equals, that is, in regard to giving and sharing?"

"It is a gain for us, venerable sir, it is well gained by us, venerable sir, that the Blessed One understands us so well."

7 (7) The People of Bamboo Gate

Thus have I heard. On one occasion the Blessed One was walking on tour among the Kosalans together with a great Saṅgha of bhikkhus when he reached the brahmin village of the Kosalans named Bamboo Gate. Then the brahmin householders of Bamboo Gate heard: "It is said, sirs, that the ascetic Gotama, the son of the Sakyans who went forth from a Sakyan family, has been walking on tour among the Kosalans together with a great Saṅgha of bhikkhus and has arrived at Bamboo Gate. Now a good report concerning that Master Gotama has spread about thus: 'That Blessed One is an arahant, perfectly enlightened, accomplished in true knowledge and conduct, fortunate, knower of the world, unsurpassed leader of persons to be tamed, teacher of devas and humans, the Enlightened One, the Blessed One. Having realized by his own direct knowledge this world with its devas, Māra, and Brahmā, this generation with its ascetics and brahmins, its devas and humans, he makes it known to others. He teaches a Dhamma that is good in the beginning, good in the middle, good in the end, with the right meaning and phrasing; he reveals a holy life that is perfectly complete and pure.' It is good to see such arahants." [353]

Then those brahmin householders of Bamboo Gate approached the Blessed One. Having approached, some paid homage to the Blessed One and sat down to one side. Some greeted the Blessed One and, having exchanged greetings and cordial talk, sat down to one side. Some extended their joined hands in reverential salutation towards the Blessed One and sat down to one side. Some announced their name and clan to the Blessed One and sat down to one side. Some remained silent and sat down to one side.

Sitting to one side, those brahmin householders of Bamboo Gate said to the Blessed One:

"Master Gotama, we have such wishes, desires, and hopes as these: 'May we dwell in a home crowded with children! May we enjoy Kāsian sandalwood! May we wear garlands, scents, and unguents! May we receive gold and silver! With the breakup of the body, after death, may we be reborn in a good destination, in a heavenly world!' As we have such wishes, desires, and hopes, let Master Gotama teach us the Dhamma in such a way that we might dwell in a home crowded with children ... and with the breakup of the body, after death, we might be reborn in a good destination, in a heavenly world."

"I will teach you, householders, a Dhamma exposition applicable to oneself.[328] Listen to that and attend closely, I will speak."

"Yes, sir," those brahmin householders of Bamboo Gate replied. The Blessed One said this:

"What, householders, is the Dhamma exposition applicable to oneself? Here, householders, a noble disciple reflects thus: 'I am one who wishes to live, who does not wish to die; I desire happiness and am averse to suffering. Since I am one who wishes to live ... and am averse to suffering, if someone were to take my life, that would not be pleasing and agreeable to me. Now if I were to take the life of another—of one who wishes to live, who does not wish to die, who desires happiness and is averse to suffering—that would not be pleasing and agreeable to the other either. What is displeasing and disagreeable to me [354] is displeasing and disagreeable to the other too. How can I inflict upon another what is displeasing and disagreeable to me?' Having reflected thus, he himself abstains from the destruction of life, exhorts others to abstain from the destruction of life, and speaks in praise of abstinence from the destruction of life. Thus this bodily conduct of his is purified in three respects.[329]

"Again, householders, a noble disciple reflects thus: 'If someone were to take from me what I have not given, that is, to commit theft, that would not be pleasing and agreeable to me. Now if I were to take from another what he has not given, that is, to commit theft, that would not be pleasing and agreeable to the other either. What is displeasing and disagreeable to me is displeasing and disagreeable to the other too. How can I inflict upon another what is displeasing and disagreeable to me?' Having reflected thus, he himself abstains from taking what is not given, exhorts others to abstain from taking what is not given, and speaks in praise of abstinence from taking what is not given. Thus this bodily conduct of his is purified in three respects.

"Again, householders, a noble disciple reflects thus: 'If someone were to commit adultery with my wives, that would not be pleasing and agreeable to me. Now if I were to commit adultery with the wives of another, that would not be pleasing and agreeable to the other either. What is displeasing and disagreeable to me is displeasing and disagreeable to the other too. How can I inflict upon another what is displeasing and disagreeable to me?' Having reflected thus, he himself abstains from sexual misconduct, exhorts others to abstain from sexual misconduct, and speaks in praise of abstinence from sexual misconduct. Thus this bodily conduct of his is purified in three respects.

"Again, householders, a noble disciple reflects thus: 'If someone were to damage my welfare with false speech, that would not be pleasing and agreeable to me. Now if I were to damage the welfare of another with false speech, that would not be pleasing and agreeable to the other either. [355] What is displeasing and disagreeable to me is displeasing and disagreeable to the other too. How can I inflict upon another what is displeasing and disagreeable to me?' Having reflected thus, he himself abstains from false speech, exhorts others to abstain from false speech, and speaks in praise of abstinence from false speech. Thus this verbal conduct of his is purified in three respects.

"Again, householders, a noble disciple reflects thus: 'If someone were to divide me from my friends by divisive speech, that would not be pleasing and agreeable to me. Now if I were to divide another from his friends by divisive speech, that would not be pleasing and agreeable to the other either....' Thus this verbal conduct of his is purified in three respects.

"Again, householders, a noble disciple reflects thus: 'If someone were to address me with harsh speech, that would not be pleasing and agreeable to me. Now if I were to address another with harsh speech, that would not be pleasing and agreeable to the other either....' Thus this verbal conduct of his is purified in three respects.

"Again, householders, a noble disciple reflects thus: 'If someone were to address me with frivolous speech and idle chatter, that would not be pleasing and agreeable to me. Now if I were to address another with frivolous speech and idle chatter, that would not be pleasing and agreeable to the other either. What is displeasing and disagreeable to me is displeasing and disagreeable to the other too. How can I inflict upon another what is displeasing and disagreeable to me?' Having reflected thus, he himself abstains from idle chatter, exhorts others to abstain from idle chatter, and speaks in praise of abstinence from idle chatter. Thus this verbal conduct of his is purified in three respects.

"He possesses confirmed confidence in the Buddha thus: 'The Blessed One is … teacher of devas and humans, the Enlightened One, the Blessed One.' [356] He possesses confirmed confidence in the Dhamma … in the Saṅgha.… He possesses the virtues dear to the noble ones, unbroken … leading to concentration.

"When, householders, the noble disciple possesses these seven good qualities and these four desirable states, if he wishes he could by himself declare of himself: 'I am one finished with hell, finished with the animal realm, finished with the domain of ghosts, finished with the plane of misery, the bad destinations, the nether world. I am a stream-enterer, no longer bound to the nether world, fixed in destiny, with enlightenment as my destination.'"

When this was said, the brahmin householders of Bamboo Gate said: "Magnificent, Master Gotama!… We go for refuge to Master Gotama, and to the Dhamma, and to the Bhikkhu Saṅgha. From today let the Blessed One remember us as lay followers who have gone for refuge for life."

8 (8) The Brick Hall (1)

Thus have I heard.[330] On one occasion the Blessed One was dwelling at Ñātika in the Brick Hall. Then the Venerable Ānanda approached the Blessed One, paid homage to him, sat down to one side, and said to him:

"Venerable sir, the bhikkhu named Sāḷha has died. What is his destination, what is his future bourn? The bhikkhunī named Nandā has died. What is her destination, what is her future bourn? The male lay follower named Sudatta has died. What is his destination, what is his future bourn? The female lay follower named Sujātā has died. What is her destination, what is her future bourn?"

"Ānanda, the bhikkhu Sāḷha who has died, by the destruction of the taints, in this very life had entered and dwelt in the taintless liberation of mind, liberation by wisdom, realizing it for himself with direct knowledge. The bhikkhunī Nandā who has died had, with the utter destruction of the five lower fetters, [357] become one of spontaneous birth, due to attain Nibbāna there without returning from that world. The male lay follower Sudatta who has died had, with the utter destruction of three fetters and with the diminishing of greed, hatred, and delusion, become a once-returner who, after coming back to this world only one more time, will make an end to suffering.[331] The female lay follower Sujātā who has died had, with the utter destruction of three fetters, become a stream-enterer, no longer bound to the nether world, fixed in destiny, with enlightenment as her destination.

"It is not surprising, Ānanda, that a human being should die. But if each time someone has died you approach and question me about this matter, that would be troublesome for the Tathāgata. Therefore, Ānanda, I will teach you a Dhamma exposition called the mirror of the Dhamma, equipped with which a noble disciple, if he wishes, could by himself declare of himself: 'I am one finished with hell, finished with the animal realm, finished with the domain of ghosts, finished with the plane of misery, the bad destinations, the nether world. I am a stream-enterer, no longer bound to the nether world, fixed in destiny, with enlightenment as my destination.'

"And what, Ānanda, is that Dhamma exposition, the mirror of the Dhamma, equipped with which a noble disciple, if he wishes, could by himself declare thus of himself? Here, Ānanda, a noble disciple possesses confirmed confidence in the Buddha thus: 'The Blessed One is ... teacher of devas and humans, the Enlightened One, the Blessed One.' He possesses confirmed confidence in the Dhamma ... in the Saṅgha.... He possesses the virtues dear to the noble ones, unbroken ... leading to concentration.

"This, Ānanda, is that Dhamma exposition, the mirror of the Dhamma, equipped with which a noble disciple, if he wishes, could by himself declare of himself: 'I am one finished with hell.... I am a stream-enterer, no longer bound to the nether world, fixed in destiny, with enlightenment as my destination.'" [358]

9 (9) The Brick Hall (2)

Sitting to one side, the Venerable Ānanda said to the Blessed One:
"Venerable sir, the bhikkhu named Asoka has died. What is his destination, what is his future bourn? The bhikkhunī named Asokā has died. What is her destination, what is her future bourn? The male lay follower named Asoka has died. What is his destination, what is his future bourn? The female lay follower named Asokā has died. What is her destination, what is her future bourn?"

"Ānanda, the bhikkhu Asoka who has died, by the destruction of the taints, in this very life had entered and dwelt in the taintless liberation of mind, liberation by wisdom, realizing it for himself with direct knowledge.... (*all the rest as in the preceding sutta*) ...

"This, Ānanda, is that Dhamma exposition, the mirror of the Dhamma, equipped with which a noble disciple, if he wishes, could by himself declare of himself: 'I am one finished with hell.... I am a stream-enterer, no longer bound to the nether world, fixed in destiny, with enlightenment as my destination.'"

10 (10) The Brick Hall (3)

Sitting to one side, the Venerable Ānanda said to the Blessed One:
"Venerable sir, the male lay follower named Kakkaṭa has died in Ñātika. What is his destination, what is his future bourn? The male lay follower named Kāḷiṅga ... Nikata ... Kaṭissaha ... Tuṭṭha ... Santuṭṭha ... Bhadda ... Subhadda has died in Ñātika. What is his destination, what is his future bourn?"

"Ānanda, the male lay follower Kakkaṭa who has died had, with the utter destruction of the five lower fetters, become one of spontaneous birth, due to attain Nibbāna there without returning from that world. So too the male lay followers Kāḷiṅga, [359] Nikata, Kaṭissaha, Tuṭṭha, Santuṭṭha, Bhadda, and Subhadda.

"The more than fifty male lay followers who have died in Ñātika had, with the utter destruction of the five lower fetters, become of spontaneous birth, due to attain Nibbāna there without returning from that world. The male lay followers exceeding ninety who have died in Ñātika had, with the utter destruction of three fetters and with the diminishing of greed, hatred, and delusion, become once-returners who, after coming back to this world only one more time, will make an end to suffering. The five hundred and six male lay followers who have died in Ñātika had, with the utter destruction of three fetters, become stream-enterers, no more bound to the nether world, fixed in destiny, with enlightenment as their destination.[332]

"It is not surprising, Ānanda, that a human being should die. But if each time someone has died you approach and question me about this matter, that would be troublesome for the Tathāgata. Therefore, Ānanda, I will teach you a Dhamma exposition called the mirror of the Dhamma....

"And what, Ānanda, is that Dhamma exposition, the mirror of the Dhamma...?" [360]

(*The remainder of the sutta as in §8.*)

II. The Thousandfold, or Royal Park

11 (1) The Thousand

On one occasion the Blessed One was dwelling at Sāvatthī in the Royal Park. Then a Saṅgha of a thousand bhikkhunīs approached the Blessed One, paid homage to him, and stood to one side. The Blessed One said to those bhikkhunīs:

"Bhikkhunīs, a noble disciple who possesses four things is a stream-enterer, no longer bound to the nether world, fixed in destiny, with enlightenment as his destination. What four? Here, bhikkhunīs, a noble disciple possesses confirmed confidence in the Buddha thus: 'The Blessed One is ... teacher of devas and humans, the Enlightened One, the Blessed One.' [361] He possesses confirmed confidence in the Dhamma ... in the Saṅgha.... He possesses the virtues dear to the noble ones, unbroken ... leading to concentration.

"A noble disciple, bhikkhunīs, who possesses these four things is a stream-enterer, no longer bound to the nether world, fixed in destiny, with enlightenment as his destination."

12 (2) The Brahmins

At Sāvatthī. "Bhikkhus, the brahmins proclaim a way called 'going upwards.' They enjoin a disciple thus: 'Come, good man, get up early and walk facing east. Do not avoid a pit, or a precipice, or a stump, or a thorny place, or a village pool, or a cesspool. You should expect death[333] wherever you fall. Thus, good man, with the breakup of the body, after death, you will be reborn in a good destination, in a heavenly world.'

"Now this practice of the brahmins, bhikkhus, is a foolish course, a stupid course; it does not lead to revulsion, to dispassion, to cessation, to peace, to direct knowledge, to enlightenment, to Nibbāna. But I, bhikkhus, proclaim the way going upwards in the Noble One's Discipline, the way which leads to utter revulsion, to dispassion, to cessation, to peace, to direct knowledge, to enlightenment, to Nibbāna.

"And what, bhikkhus, is that way going upwards, which leads to utter revulsion ... to Nibbāna. [362] Here, bhikkhus, a noble disciple possesses confirmed confidence in the Buddha thus: 'The Blessed One is ... teacher of devas and humans, the Enlightened One, the Blessed One.' He possesses confirmed confidence in the Dhamma ... in the Saṅgha.... He possesses the virtues dear to the noble ones, unbroken ... leading to concentration.

"This, bhikkhus, is that way going upwards, which leads to utter revulsion, to dispassion, to cessation, to peace, to direct knowledge, to enlightenment, to Nibbāna."

13 (3) Ānanda

On one occasion the Venerable Ānanda and the Venerable Sāriputta were dwelling at Sāvatthī in Jeta's Grove, Anāthapiṇḍika's Park. Then, in the evening, the Venerable Sāriputta emerged from seclusion, approached the Venerable Ānanda, and exchanged greetings with him. When they had concluded their greetings and cordial talk, he sat down to one side and said to the Venerable Ānanda:

"Friend Ānanda, by the abandoning of how many things and because of possessing how many things are people declared by the Blessed One thus: 'This one is a stream-enterer, no longer bound to the nether world, fixed in destiny, with enlightenment as his destination'?"

"It is, friend, by the abandoning of four things and because of possessing four things that people are declared thus by the Blessed One. What four?

"One does not have, friend, that distrust regarding the Buddha which the uninstructed worldling possesses, because of which the latter, with the breakup of the body, after death, is reborn in the plane of misery, in a bad destination, in the nether world, in hell. [363] And one has that confirmed confidence in the Buddha which the instructed noble disciple possesses, because of which the latter, with the breakup of the body, after death, is reborn in a good destination, in a heavenly world: 'The Blessed One is ... teacher of devas and humans, the Enlightened One, the Blessed One.'

"One does not have, friend, that distrust regarding the Dhamma which the uninstructed worldling possesses, because of which the latter, with the breakup of the body, after death, is reborn in the plane of misery, in a bad destination, in the nether world, in hell. And one has that confirmed confidence in the Dhamma which the instructed noble disciple possesses, because of which the latter, with the breakup of the body, after death, is reborn in a good destination, in a heavenly world: 'The Dhamma is well expounded by the Blessed One ... to be personally experienced by the wise.'

"One does not have, friend, that distrust regarding the Saṅgha which the uninstructed worldling possesses, because of which the latter, with the breakup of the body, after death, is reborn in the plane of misery, in a bad destination, in the nether world, in hell. And one has that confirmed confidence in the Saṅgha which the instructed noble disciple possesses, because of which the latter, with the breakup of the body, after death, is reborn in a good destination, in a heavenly world: 'The Saṅgha of the Blessed One's disciples is practising the good way ... the unsurpassed field of merit for the world.'

"One does not have, friend, that immorality which the uninstructed worldling possesses, because of which the latter, with the breakup of the body, after death, is reborn in the plane of misery, in a bad destination, in the nether world, in hell. And one has those virtues dear to the noble ones which the instructed noble disciple possesses, because of which the latter, with the breakup of the body, after death, is reborn in a good destination, in a heavenly world: virtues dear to the noble ones ... leading to concentration. [364]

"It is, friend, by the abandoning of these four things and because of possessing these four things that people are declared by the Blessed One thus: 'This one is a stream-enterer, no longer bound to the nether world, fixed in destiny, with enlightenment as his destination.'"

14 (4) Bad Destination (1)

"Bhikkhus, a noble disciple who possesses four things has transcended all fear of a bad destination. What four? Here, bhikkhus, a noble disciple possesses confirmed confidence in the Buddha thus: 'The Blessed One is ... teacher of devas and humans, the Enlightened One, the Blessed One.' He possesses confirmed confidence in the Dhamma ... in the Saṅgha.... He possesses the virtues dear to the noble ones, unbroken ... leading to concentration. A noble disciple who possesses these four things has transcended all fear of a bad destination."

15 (5) Bad Destination (2)

"Bhikkhus, a noble disciple who possesses four things has transcended all fear of a bad destination, of the nether world. What four?"

(*Complete as in the preceding sutta.*)

16 (6) Friends and Colleagues (1)

"Bhikkhus, those for whom you have compassion and who think you should be heeded—whether friends or colleagues, relatives or kinsmen—these you[334] should exhort, settle, and establish in the four factors of stream-entry.

"What four? [365] You should exhort, settle, and establish them in confirmed confidence in the Buddha thus: 'The Blessed One is ... teacher of devas and humans, the Enlightened One, the Blessed One.' You should exhort, settle, and establish them in confirmed confidence in the Dhamma ... in the Saṅgha ... in the virtues dear to the noble ones, unbroken ... leading to concentration.

"Those for whom you have compassion ... these you should exhort, settle, and establish in these four factors of stream-entry."

17 (7) Friends and Colleagues (2)

"Bhikkhus, those for whom you have compassion and who think you should be heeded—whether friends or colleagues, relatives or kinsmen—these you should exhort, settle, and establish in the four factors of stream-entry.

"What four? You should exhort, settle, and establish them in confirmed confidence in the Buddha thus: 'The Blessed One is ... teacher of devas and humans, the Enlightened One, the Blessed One.'...

"Bhikkhus, there may be alteration in the four great elements—in the earth element, the water element, the heat element, the air element—but there cannot be alteration in the noble disciple who possesses confirmed confidence in the Buddha. Therein this is alteration: that the noble disciple who possesses confirmed confidence in the Buddha might be reborn in hell, in the animal realm, or in the domain of ghosts. This is impossible.

"You should exhort, settle, and establish them in confirmed confidence in the Dhamma ... in the Saṅgha ... in the virtues dear to the noble ones ... leading to concentration.

"Bhikkhus, there may be alteration in the four great elements ... but there cannot be [366] alteration in the noble disciple who possesses the virtues dear to the noble ones. Therein this is alteration: that the noble disciple who possesses the virtues dear to the noble ones might be reborn in hell, in the animal realm, or in the domain of ghosts. This is impossible.

"Those for whom you have compassion ... these you should exhort, settle, and establish in these four factors of stream-entry."

18 (8) Visiting the Devas (1)

At Sāvatthī.[335] Then, just as quickly as a strong man might extend his drawn-in arm or draw in his extended arm, the Venerable Mahāmoggallāna disappeared from Jeta's Grove and reappeared among the Tāvatiṃsa devas. Then a number of devatās belonging to the Tāvatiṃsa host approached the Venerable Mahāmoggallāna, paid homage to him, and stood to one side. The Venerable Mahāmoggallāna then said to those devatās:

"It is good, friends, to possess confirmed confidence in the Buddha thus: 'The Blessed One is ... teacher of devas and humans, the Enlightened One, the Blessed One.' Because of possessing confirmed confidence in the Buddha, some beings here, with the breakup of the body, after death, are reborn in a good destination, in a heavenly world.

"It is good, friends, to possess confirmed confidence in the Dhamma ... in the Saṅgha ... to possess the virtues dear to the noble ones ... leading to concentration. [367] Because of possessing the virtues dear to the noble ones, some beings here, with the breakup of the body, after death, are reborn in a good destination, in a heavenly world."

"It is good, sir Moggallāna, to possess confirmed confidence in the Buddha ... in the Dhamma ... in the Saṅgha ... to possess the virtues dear to the nobles ones ... leading to concentration. Because of possessing the virtues dear to the noble ones, some beings here, with the breakup of the body, after death, are reborn in a good destination, in a heavenly world."

19 (9) Visiting the Devas (2)

(*This sutta is identical with the preceding one, except that wherever §18 reads "are reborn in a good destination," the present sutta reads "have been reborn in a good destination."*)

20 (10) Visiting the Devas (3)

Then, just as quickly as a strong man might extend his drawn-in arm or draw in his extended arm, the Blessed One disappeared from Jeta's Grove and reappeared among the Tāvatiṃsa devas. Then a number of devatās belonging to the Tāvatiṃsa host approached the Blessed One, paid homage to him, [368] and stood to one side. The Blessed One then said to those devatās:

"It is good, friends, to possess confirmed confidence in the Buddha thus: 'The Blessed One is ... teacher of devas and humans, the Enlightened One, the Blessed One.' Because of possessing confirmed confidence in the Buddha, some beings here are stream-enterers, no longer bound to the nether world, fixed in destiny, with enlightenment as their destination.

"It is good, friends, to possess confirmed confidence in the Dhamma ... in the Saṅgha ... to possess the virtues dear to the noble ones ... leading to concentration. Because of possessing the virtues dear to the noble ones, some beings here are stream-enterers, no longer bound to the nether world, fixed in destiny, with enlightenment as their destination."

"It is good, dear sir, to possess confirmed confidence in the Buddha ... in the Dhamma ... in the Saṅgha ... to possess the virtues dear to the nobles ones ... leading to concentration. Because of possessing the virtues dear to the noble ones, some beings here are stream-enterers, no longer bound to the nether world, fixed in destiny, with enlightenment as their destination."

[369] III. Sarakāni

21 (1) Mahānāma (1)

Thus have I heard. On one occasion the Blessed One was dwelling among the Sakyans at Kapilavatthu in Nigrodha's Park. Then Mahānāma the Sakyan approached the Blessed One, paid homage to him, sat down to one side, and said to him:

"Venerable sir, this Kapilavatthu is rich and prosperous, populous, crowded, with congested thoroughfares.[336] In the evening, when I am entering Kapilavatthu after visiting the Blessed One or the bhikkhus worthy of esteem, I come across a stray elephant, a stray horse, a stray chariot, a stray cart, a stray man.[337] On that occasion, venerable sir, my mindfulness regarding the Blessed One becomes muddled, my mindfulness regarding the Dhamma becomes muddled, my mindfulness regarding the Saṅgha becomes muddled. The thought then occurs to me: 'If at this moment I should die, what would be my destination, what would be my future bourn?'"

"Don't be afraid, Mahānāma! Don't be afraid, Mahānāma! Your death will not be a bad one, your demise will not be a bad one.[338] When a person's mind has been fortified over a long time by faith, virtue, learning, generosity, and wisdom, right here crows, vultures, hawks, dogs, jackals, or various creatures eat his body, consisting of form, composed of the four great elements, [370] originating from mother and father, built up out of rice and gruel, subject to impermanence, to being worn and rubbed away, to breaking apart and dispersal. But his mind, which has been fortified over a long time by faith, virtue, learning, generosity, and wisdom—that goes upwards, goes to distinction.[339]

"Suppose, Mahānāma, a man submerges a pot of ghee or a pot of oil in a deep pool of water and breaks it. All of its shards and fragments would sink downwards, but the ghee or oil there would rise upwards. So too, Mahānāma, when a person's mind has been fortified over a long time by faith, virtue, learning, generosity, and wisdom, right here crows ... or various creatures eat his body.... But his mind, which has been fortified over a long time by faith, virtue, learning, generosity, and wisdom—that goes upwards, goes to distinction. [371]

"Don't be afraid, Mahānāma! Don't be afraid, Mahānāma! Your death will not be a bad one, your demise will not be a bad one."

22 (2) Mahānāma (2)

(*As above down to:*)

"Don't be afraid, Mahānāma! Don't be afraid, Mahānāma! Your death will not be a bad one, your demise will not be a bad one. A noble disciple who possesses four things slants, slopes, and inclines towards Nibbāna. What four? Here, Mahānāma, a noble disciple possesses confirmed confidence in the Buddha ... in the Dhamma ... in the Saṅgha.... He possesses the virtues dear to the noble ones, unbroken ... leading to concentration.

"Suppose, Mahānāma, a tree was slanting, sloping, and inclining towards the east. If it was cut down at its foot, in what direction would it fall?"

"In whatever direction it was slanting, sloping, and inclining, venerable sir."

"So too, Mahānāma, a noble disciple who possesses these four things slants, slopes, and inclines towards Nibbāna."

23 (3) Godhā

At Kapilavatthu. Then Mahānāma the Sakyan approached Godhā the Sakyan and said to him: [372] "How many things, Godhā, must an individual possess for you to recognize him as a stream-enterer, one no longer bound to the nether world, fixed in destiny, with enlightenment as his destination?"

"When an individual possesses three things, Mahānāma, I recognize him as a stream-enterer, one no longer bound to the nether world, fixed in destiny, with enlightenment as his destination.

What three? Here, Mahānāma, a noble disciple possesses confirmed confidence in the Buddha ... in the Dhamma ... in the Saṅgha.... When an individual possesses these three things, I recognize him as a stream-enterer ... with enlightenment as his destination. But, Mahānāma, how many things must an individual possess for you to recognize him as a stream-enterer ... with enlightenment as his destination?"

"When an individual possesses four things, Godhā, I recognize him as a stream-enterer ... with enlightenment as his destination. What four? Here, Godhā, a noble disciple possesses confirmed confidence in the Buddha ... in the Dhamma ... in the Saṅgha.... He possesses the virtues dear to the noble ones, unbroken ... leading to concentration. When an individual possesses these four things, I recognize him as a stream-enterer ... with enlightenment as his destination."

"Wait, Mahānāma! Wait, Mahānāma! The Blessed One alone would know whether or not he possesses these things."

"Come, Godhā, we should approach the Blessed One. Having approached, we will report this matter to him." [373]

Then Mahānāma the Sakyan and Godhā the Sakyan approached the Blessed One, paid homage to him, and sat down to one side. Mahānāma the Sakyan then reported their conversation, [continuing thus]: [374]

"Here, venerable sir, some issue concerning the Dhamma may arise. The Blessed One might take one side and the Bhikkhu Saṅgha might take the other side. Whatever side the Blessed One would take, I would take that same side. Let the Blessed One remember me as one who has such confidence.[340]

"Here, venerable sir, some issue concerning the Dhamma may arise. The Blessed One might take one side, and the Bhikkhu Saṅgha and the Bhikkhunī Saṅgha might take the other side.... The Blessed One might take one side, and the Bhikkhu Saṅgha, the Bhikkhunī Saṅgha, and the male lay followers might take the other side.... The Blessed One might take one side, and the Bhikkhu Saṅgha, the Bhikkhunī Saṅgha, the male lay followers, and the female lay followers might take the other side. Whatever side the Blessed One would take, I would take that same side. Let the Blessed One remember me as one who has such confidence.

"Here, venerable sir, some issue concerning the Dhamma may arise. The Blessed One might take one side, and the Bhikkhu

Saṅgha, the Bhikkhunī Saṅgha, the male lay followers, the female lay followers, and the world with its devas, Māra, and Brahmā, this generation with its ascetics and brahmins, its devas and humans, might take the other side. Whatever side the Blessed One would take, I would take that same side. Let the Blessed One remember me as one who has such confidence."

[The Blessed One said:] "When he speaks like that,[341] Godhā, what would you say about Mahānāma the Sakyan?"

"When he speaks in such a way, venerable sir, I would not say anything about Mahānāma the Sakyan except what is good and favourable."[342] [375]

24 (4) Sarakāni (1)

At Kapilavatthu. Now on that occasion Sarakāni[343] the Sakyan had died, and the Blessed One had declared him to be a stream-enterer, no longer bound to the nether world, fixed in destiny, with enlightenment as his destination. Thereupon a number of Sakyans, having met and assembled, deplored this, grumbled, and complained about it, saying: "It is wonderful indeed, sir! It is amazing indeed, sir! Now who here won't be a stream-enterer when the Blessed One has declared Sarakāni the Sakyan after he died to be a stream-enterer … with enlightenment as his destination? Sarakāni the Sakyan was too weak for the training; he drank intoxicating drink!"[344]

Then Mahānāma the Sakyan approached the Blessed One, paid homage to him, sat down to one side, and reported this matter to him. [The Blessed One said:]

"Mahānāma, when a lay follower has gone for refuge over a long time to the Buddha, the Dhamma, and the Saṅgha, how could he go to the nether world? For if one speaking rightly were to say of anyone: 'He was a lay follower who had gone for refuge over a long time to the Buddha, the Dhamma, and the Saṅgha,' it is of Sarakāni the Sakyan that one could rightly say this. [376] Mahānāma, Sarakāni the Sakyan had gone for refuge over a long time to the Buddha, the Dhamma, and the Saṅgha, so how could he go to the nether world?

"Here, Mahānāma, some person possesses confirmed confidence in the Buddha thus: 'The Blessed One is … teacher of devas and humans, the Enlightened One, the Blessed One.' And so in the Dhamma and the Saṅgha. He is one of joyous wisdom, of swift wisdom, and he has attained liberation. By the destruction of the taints, in this very life he enters and dwells in the taintless liberation of mind, liberation by wisdom, realizing it for himself with direct knowledge. This person, Mahānāma, is freed from hell, the animal realm, and the domain of ghosts, freed from the plane of misery, the bad destinations, the nether world.[345]

"Here, Mahānāma, some person possesses confirmed confidence in the Buddha, the Dhamma, and the Saṅgha. He is one of joyous wisdom, of swift wisdom, yet he has not attained liberation. With the utter destruction of the five lower fetters he has become one of spontaneous birth, due to attain Nibbāna there without returning from that world. This person too, Mahānāma, is freed from hell, the animal realm, and the domain of ghosts, freed from the plane of misery, the bad destinations, the nether world.

"Here, Mahānāma, some person possesses confirmed confidence in the Buddha, the Dhamma, and the Saṅgha. He is not one of joyous wisdom, nor of swift wisdom, and he has not attained liberation. With the utter destruction of three fetters and with the diminishing of greed, hatred, and delusion, he is a once-returner who, after coming back to this world only one more time, will make an end to suffering. This person too, Mahānāma, is freed from hell, the animal realm, and the domain of ghosts, freed from the plane of misery, the bad destinations, the nether world. [377]

"Here, Mahānāma, some person possesses confirmed confidence in the Buddha, the Dhamma, and the Saṅgha. He is not one of joyous wisdom, nor of swift wisdom, and he has not attained liberation. With the utter destruction of three fetters he is a stream-enterer, no longer bound to the nether world, fixed in destiny, with enlightenment as his destination. This person too, Mahānāma, is freed from hell, the animal realm, and the domain of ghosts, freed from the plane of misery, the bad destinations, the nether world.

"Here, Mahānāma, some person does not possess confirmed confidence in the Buddha, the Dhamma, and the Saṅgha. He is not one of joyous wisdom, nor of swift wisdom, and he has not attained liberation. However, he has these five things: the faculty of faith, the faculty of energy, the faculty of mindfulness, the faculty of concentration, the faculty of wisdom. And the teachings proclaimed by the Tathāgata are accepted by him after being pondered to a sufficient degree with wisdom. This person too, Mahānāma, is one who does not go to hell, the animal realm, or the domain of ghosts, to the plane of misery, the bad destinations, the nether world.[346]

"Here, Mahānāma, some person does not possess confirmed confidence in the Buddha, the Dhamma, and the Saṅgha. He is not one of joyous wisdom, nor of swift wisdom, and he has not attained liberation. However, he has these five things: the faculty of faith … the faculty of wisdom. And he has sufficient faith in the Tathāgata, sufficient devotion to him. This person too, Mahānāma, is one who does not go to hell, the animal realm, or the domain of ghosts, to the plane of misery, the bad destinations, the nether world.

"Even if these great sal trees, Mahānāma, could understand what is well spoken and what is badly spoken, then I would declare these great sal trees to be stream-enterers, no longer bound to the nether world, fixed in destiny, with enlightenment as their destination. How much more, then, Sarakāni the Sakyan? Mahānāma, Sarakāni the Sakyan undertook the training at the time of his death."[347] [378]

25 (5) Sarakāni (2)

At Kapilavatthu. Now on that occasion Sarakāni the Sakyan had died, and the Blessed One had declared him to be a stream-enterer, no longer bound to the nether world, fixed in destiny, with enlightenment as his destination. Thereupon a number of Sakyans, having met and assembled, deplored this, grumbled, and complained about it, saying: "It is wonderful indeed, sir! It is amazing indeed, sir! Now who here won't be a stream-enterer when the Blessed One has declared Sarakāni the Sakyan after he died to be a stream-enterer … with enlightenment as his destination? Sarakāni the Sakyan was one who had failed to fulfil the training!"[348]

Then Mahānāma the Sakyan approached the Blessed One, paid homage to him, sat down to one side, and reported this matter to him. [The Blessed One said:]

"Mahānāma, when, over a long time, a lay follower has gone for refuge to the Buddha, the Dhamma, and the Saṅgha, how could he go to the nether world?... Mahānāma, over a long time Sarakāni the Sakyan had gone for refuge to the Buddha, the Dhamma, and the Saṅgha, so how could he go to the nether world?

"Here, Mahānāma, some person is completely dedicated to the Buddha and has full confidence in him thus:[349] 'The Blessed One is ... teacher of devas and humans, the Enlightened One, the Blessed One.' And so in regard to the Dhamma and the Saṅgha. He is one of joyous wisdom, of swift wisdom, and he has attained liberation. By the destruction of the taints, in this very life he enters and dwells in the taintless liberation of mind, liberation by wisdom, realizing it for himself with direct knowledge. This person, Mahānāma, is freed from hell, the animal realm, and the domain of ghosts, freed from the plane of misery, the bad destinations, the nether world.

"Here, Mahānāma, some person is completely dedicated to the Buddha and has full confidence in him.... And so in regard to the Dhamma and the Saṅgha. He is one of joyous wisdom, of swift wisdom, yet he has not attained liberation. With the utter destruction of the five lower fetters he has become an attainer of Nibbāna in the interval, or an attainer of Nibbāna upon landing, or an attainer of Nibbāna without exertion, or an attainer of Nibbāna with exertion, or one bound upstream, heading towards the Akaniṭṭha realm.[350] This person too, Mahānāma, is freed from hell, the animal realm, and the domain of ghosts, freed from the plane of misery, the bad destinations, the nether world.

"Here, Mahānāma, some person is completely dedicated to the Buddha and has full confidence in him.... And so in regard to the Dhamma and the Saṅgha. He is not one of joyous wisdom, nor of swift wisdom, and he has not attained liberation. With the utter destruction of three fetters and with the diminishing of greed, hatred, and delusion, he is a once-returner who, after coming back to this world only one more time, will make an end to suffering. This person too, Mahānāma, [379] is freed from hell, the animal realm, and the domain of ghosts, freed from the plane of misery, the bad destinations, the nether world.

"Here, Mahānāma, some person is completely dedicated to the Buddha and has full confidence in him.... And so in regard to the

Dhamma and the Saṅgha. He is not one of joyous wisdom, nor of swift wisdom, and he has not attained liberation. With the utter destruction of three fetters he is a stream-enterer, no longer bound to the nether world, fixed in destiny, with enlightenment as his destination. This person too, Mahānāma, is freed from hell, the animal realm, and the domain of ghosts, freed from the plane of misery, the bad destinations, the nether world.

"Here, Mahānāma, some person is not completely dedicated to the Buddha and does not have full confidence in him thus: 'The Blessed One is ... teacher of devas and humans, the Enlightened One, the Blessed One.' And so in regard to the Dhamma and the Saṅgha. He is not one of joyous wisdom, nor of swift wisdom, and he has not attained liberation. However, he has these five things: the faculty of faith ... the faculty of wisdom. And the teachings proclaimed by the Tathāgata are accepted by him after being pondered to a sufficient degree with wisdom. This person too, Mahānāma, is one who does not go to hell, the animal realm, or the domain of ghosts, to the plane of misery, the bad destinations, the nether world.

"Here, Mahānāma, some person is not completely dedicated to the Buddha and does not have full confidence in him.... And so in regard to the Dhamma and the Saṅgha. He is not one of joyous wisdom, nor of swift wisdom, and he has not attained liberation. However, he has these five things: the faculty of faith ... the faculty of wisdom. And he has sufficient faith in the Tathāgata, sufficient devotion to him. This person too, Mahānāma, is one who does not go to hell, the animal realm, or the domain of ghosts, to the plane of misery, the bad destinations, the nether world.

"Suppose, Mahānāma, there is a bad field, a bad piece of ground, with stumps not cleared, and the seeds sown there would be broken, spoilt, damaged by wind and sun, unfertile, not planted securely, and the sky would not send down a proper rainfall. Would those seeds come to growth, increase, and expansion?"

"No, venerable sir."

"So too, Mahānāma, here a Dhamma is badly expounded, badly proclaimed, unemancipating, not conducive to peace, proclaimed by one who is not perfectly enlightened. This, I say, is like the bad field. [380] And the disciple dwells in that Dhamma practising in accordance with it, practising it properly, conducting himself accordingly. This, I say, is like the bad seed.

"Suppose, Mahānāma, there is a good field, a good piece of ground, well cleared of stumps, and the seeds sown there would be unbroken, unspoilt, undamaged by wind and sun, fertile, planted securely, and the sky would send down a proper rainfall. Would those seeds come to growth, increase, and expansion?"

"Yes, venerable sir."

"So too, Mahānāma, here a Dhamma is well expounded, well proclaimed, emancipating, conducive to peace, proclaimed by one who is perfectly enlightened. This, I say, is like the good field. And the disciple dwells in that Dhamma practising in accordance with it, practising it properly, conducting himself accordingly. This, I say, is like the good seed. How much more, then, Sarakāni the Sakyan? Mahānāma, Sarakāni the Sakyan was one who fulfilled the training at the time of death."

26 (6) Anāthapiṇḍika (1)

At Sāvatthī. Now on that occasion the householder Anāthapiṇḍika was sick, afflicted, gravely ill. Then the householder Anāthapiṇḍika addressed a man thus:

"Come, good man, approach the Venerable Sāriputta, pay homage to him in my name with your head at his feet, and say: 'Venerable sir, the householder Anāthapiṇḍika is sick, afflicted, gravely ill; he pays homage to the Venerable Sāriputta with his head at his feet.' Then say: 'It would be good, venerable sir, if the Venerable Sāriputta would come to the residence of the householder Anāthapiṇḍika out of compassion.'" [381]

"Yes, master," that man replied, and he approached the Venerable Sāriputta, paid homage to him, sat down to one side, and delivered his message. The Venerable Sāriputta consented by silence.

Then, in the morning, the Venerable Sāriputta dressed and, taking bowl and robe, went to the residence of the householder Anāthapiṇḍika with the Venerable Ānanda as his companion. He then sat down in the appointed seat and said to the householder Anāthapiṇḍika: "I hope you are bearing up, householder, I hope you are getting better. I hope your painful feelings are subsiding and not increasing, and that their subsiding, not their increase, is to be discerned."

"I am not bearing up, venerable sir, I am not getting better.

Strong painful feelings are increasing in me, not subsiding, and their increase, not their subsiding, is to be discerned."

"You, householder, do not have that distrust towards the Buddha which the uninstructed worldling possesses because of which the latter, with the breakup of the body, after death, is reborn in the plane of misery, in a bad destination, in the nether world, in hell. And you have confirmed confidence in the Buddha thus: 'The Blessed One is … teacher of devas and humans, the Enlightened One, the Blessed One.' As you consider within yourself that confirmed confidence in the Buddha, your pains may subside on the spot.

"You, householder, do not have that distrust towards the Dhamma which the uninstructed worldling possesses because of which the latter [382] … is reborn in the plane of misery … in hell. And you have confirmed confidence in the Dhamma thus: 'The Dhamma is well expounded by the Blessed One … to be personally experienced by the wise.' As you consider within yourself that confirmed confidence in the Dhamma, your pains may subside on the spot.

"You, householder, do not have that distrust towards the Saṅgha which the uninstructed worldling possesses because of which the latter … is reborn in the plane of misery … in hell. And you have confirmed confidence in the Saṅgha thus: 'The Saṅgha of the Blessed One's disciples is practising the good way … the unsurpassed field of merit for the world.' As you consider within yourself that confirmed confidence in the Saṅgha, your pains may subside on the spot.

"You, householder, do not have that immorality which the uninstructed worldling possesses because of which the latter … is reborn in the plane of misery … in hell. And you have those virtues dear to the noble ones, unbroken … leading to concentration. As you consider within yourself those virtues dear to the noble ones, your pains may subside on the spot.

"You, householder, do not have that wrong view which the uninstructed worldling possesses because of which the latter … is reborn in the plane of misery … in hell. And you have right view. As you consider within yourself that right view, your pains may subside on the spot.

"You, householder, do not have that wrong intention … [383] … wrong speech … wrong action … wrong livelihood … wrong effort ... wrong mindfulness ... wrong concentration ... wrong knowledge ... wrong liberation which the uninstructed worldling possesses because of which the latter ... is reborn in the plane of misery ... in hell. And you have right intention ... right speech ... right action ... right livelihood ... right effort ... right mindfulness ... right concentration ... [384] ... right knowledge ... right liberation.[351] As you consider within yourself that right liberation, your pains may subside on the spot."

Then the pains of the householder Anāthapiṇḍika subsided on the spot.

Then the householder Anāthapiṇḍika served the Venerable Sāriputta and the Venerable Ānanda from his own dish. When the Venerable Sāriputta had finished his meal and had put away his bowl, the householder Anāthapiṇḍika took a low seat and sat down to one side, and the Venerable Sāriputta thanked him with these verses:

"When one has faith in the Tathāgata,
Unshakable and well established,
And good conduct built on virtue,
Dear to the noble ones and praised;

"When one has confidence in the Saṅgha
And view that has been rectified,
They say that one is not poor,
That one's life is not vain.

"Therefore the person of intelligence,
Remembering the Buddha's Teaching,
Should be devoted to faith and virtue,
To confidence and vision of the Dhamma."

Then the Venerable Sāriputta, having thanked the householder Anāthapiṇḍika with these verses, rose from his seat and departed. [385]

Then the Venerable Ānanda approached the Blessed One, paid homage to him, and sat down to one side. The Blessed One then said to him: "Now, Ānanda, where are you coming from in the middle of the day?"

"The householder Anāthapiṇḍika, venerable sir, has been

exhorted by the Venerable Sāriputta with such and such an exhortation."

"Sāriputta is wise, Ānanda, Sāriputta has great wisdom, in so far as he can analyse the four factors of stream-entry in ten modes."

27 (7) *Anāthapiṇḍika (2)*

(*The opening of this sutta as in the preceding one, except that Anāthapiṇḍika calls for Ānanda, down to:*)

"I am not bearing up, venerable sir, I am not getting better. Strong painful feelings are increasing in me, not subsiding, and their increase, not their subsiding, is to be discerned." [386]

"Householder, for the uninstructed worldling who possesses four things there is fright, there is trepidation, there is fear of imminent death.[352] What four?

"Here, householder, the uninstructed worldling has distrust towards the Buddha, and when he considers within himself that distrust towards the Buddha, there is fright, trepidation, and fear of imminent death.

"Again, householder, the uninstructed worldling has distrust towards the Dhamma, and when he considers within himself that distrust towards the Dhamma, there is fright, trepidation, and fear of imminent death.

"Again, householder, the uninstructed worldling has distrust towards the Saṅgha, and when he considers within himself that distrust towards the Saṅgha, there is fright, trepidation, and fear of imminent death.

"Again, householder, the uninstructed worldling is immoral, and when he considers within himself that immorality, there is fright, trepidation, and fear of imminent death.

"For the uninstructed worldling who possesses these four things there is fright, trepidation, and fear of imminent death.

"Householder, for the instructed noble disciple who possesses four things there is no fright, no trepidation, no fear of imminent death. What four?

"Here, householder, the instructed noble disciple possesses confirmed confidence in the Buddha thus: 'The Blessed One is … teacher of devas and humans, the Enlightened One, the Blessed One.' When he considers within himself that confirmed confidence in the Buddha, there is no fright, trepidation, or fear of imminent death.

"Again, householder, the instructed noble disciple possesses confirmed confidence in the Dhamma thus: 'The Dhamma is well expounded by the Blessed One … to be personally experienced by the wise.' When he considers within himself that confirmed confidence in the Dhamma, there is no fright, trepidation, or fear of imminent death.

"Again, householder, the instructed noble disciple possesses confirmed confidence in the Saṅgha thus: 'The Saṅgha of the Blessed One's disciples is practising the good way … the unsurpassed field of merit for the world.' When he considers within himself that confirmed confidence in the Saṅgha, there is no fright, trepidation, or fear of imminent death.

"Again, householder, the instructed noble disciple possesses the virtues dear to the noble ones, unbroken … leading to concentration. When he considers within himself those virtues dear to the noble ones, [387] there is no fright, trepidation, or fear of imminent death.

"For the instructed noble disciple who possesses these four things there is no fright, trepidation, or fear of imminent death."

"I am not afraid, Venerable Ānanda. Why should I be afraid? For, venerable sir, I possess confirmed confidence in the Buddha … in the Dhamma … in the Saṅgha. And as to these training rules for the laity taught by the Blessed One, I do not see within myself any that has been broken."

"It is a gain for you, householder! It is well gained by you, householder! You have declared, householder, the fruit of stream-entry."

28 (8) Fearful Animosities (1) [or Anāthapiṇḍika (3)]

(*This sutta is identical with 12:41.*) [388–89]

29 (9) Fearful Animosities (2)

At Sāvatthī. Then a number of bhikkhus approached the Blessed One … and sat down to one side. The Blessed One then said to them as they were sitting to one side:

(*All as in the preceding sutta; identical with 12:42.*)

30 (10) The Licchavi

On one occasion the Blessed One was dwelling at Vesālī in the Great Wood in the Hall with the Peaked Roof. Then Nandaka, the minister of the Licchavis, approached the Blessed One, paid homage to him, and sat down to one side. The Blessed One then said to him:

"Nandaka, a noble disciple who possesses four things is a stream-enterer, [390] no longer bound to the nether world, fixed in destiny, with enlightenment as his destination. What four? Here, Nandaka, a noble disciple possesses confirmed confidence in the Buddha thus: 'The Blessed One is … teacher of devas and humans, the Enlightened One, the Blessed One.' He possesses confirmed confidence in the Dhamma … in the Saṅgha.… He possesses the virtues dear to the noble ones, unbroken … leading to concentration. A noble disciple who possesses these four things is a stream-enterer, no longer bound to the nether world, fixed in destiny, with enlightenment as his destination.

"Further, Nandaka, a noble disciple who possesses these four things becomes endowed with a long life span, whether celestial or human; he becomes endowed with beauty, whether celestial or human; he becomes endowed with happiness, whether celestial or human; he becomes endowed with fame, whether celestial or human; he becomes endowed with sovereignty, whether celestial or human. Now I say this, Nandaka, without having heard it from another ascetic or brahmin; rather, I say just what I have known, seen, and understood by myself."

When this was said, a man said to Nandaka, the minister of the Licchavis: "It is time for your bath, sir."

"Enough now, I say, with that external bath. This internal bath will suffice, namely, confidence in the Blessed One."

[391] IV. Streams of Merit

31 (1) Streams of Merit (1)

At Sāvatthī. "Bhikkhus, there are these four streams of merit, streams of the wholesome, nutriments of happiness. What four?

"Here, bhikkhus, a noble disciple possesses confirmed confidence in the Buddha thus: 'The Blessed One is … teacher of devas and humans, the Enlightened One, the Blessed One.' This is the first stream of merit, stream of the wholesome, nutriment of happiness.

"Again, bhikkhus, a noble disciple possesses confirmed confidence in the Dhamma thus: 'The Dhamma is well expounded by the Blessed One ... to be personally experienced by the wise.' This is the second stream of merit....

"Again, bhikkhus, a noble disciple possesses confirmed confidence in the Saṅgha thus: 'The Saṅgha of the Blessed One's disciples is practising the good way ... the unsurpassed field of merit for the world.' This is the third stream of merit....

"Again, householder, the instructed noble disciple possesses the virtues dear to the noble ones, unbroken ... leading to concentration. This is the fourth stream of merit....

"These are the four streams of merit, streams of the wholesome, nutriments of happiness."

32 (2) Streams of Merit (2)

"Bhikkhus, there are these four streams of merit, streams of the wholesome, nutriments of happiness. What four?

(*As above for the first three, the fourth as follows:*) [392]

"Again, bhikkhus, a noble disciple dwells at home with a mind devoid of the stain of stinginess, freely generous, open-handed, delighting in relinquishment, one devoted to charity, delighting in giving and sharing. This is the fourth stream of merit.

"These are the four streams of merit, streams of the wholesome, nutriments of happiness."

33 (3) Streams of Merit (3)

"Bhikkhus, there are these four streams of merit, streams of the wholesome, nutriments of happiness. What four?

(*As in §31, with the fourth as follows:*)

"Again, bhikkhus, a noble disciple is wise, he possesses wisdom directed to arising and passing away, which is noble and penetrative, leading to the complete destruction of suffering. This is the fourth stream of merit....

"These are the four streams of merit, streams of the wholesome, nutriments of happiness."

34 (4) Divine Tracks (1)

At Sāvatthī. "Bhikkhus, there are these four divine tracks of the devas for the purification of beings who have not been purified, for the cleansing of beings who have not been cleansed.[353] What four?

"Here, bhikkhus, a noble disciple possesses confirmed confidence in the Buddha thus: 'The Blessed One is … teacher of devas and humans, the Enlightened One, the Blessed One.' This is the first divine track of the devas.… [393]

"Again, bhikkhus, a noble disciple possesses confirmed confidence in the Dhamma … in the Saṅgha.… He possesses the virtues dear to the noble ones, unbroken … leading to concentration. This is the fourth divine track of the devas.…

"These are the four divine tracks of the devas, for the purification of beings who have not been purified, for the cleansing of beings who have not been cleansed."

35 (5) Divine Tracks (2)

"Bhikkhus, there are these four divine tracks of the devas for the purification of beings who have not been purified, for the cleansing of beings who have not been cleansed. What four?[354]

"Here, bhikkhus, a noble disciple possesses confirmed confidence in the Buddha thus … He reflects thus: 'What now is the divine track of the devas?' He understands thus: 'I have heard that at present the devas hold nonoppression as supreme, and I do not oppress anyone, frail or firm. Surely I dwell possessing one of the divine tracks.' This is the first divine track of the devas.…

"Again, bhikkhus, a noble disciple possesses confirmed confidence in the Dhamma … in the Saṅgha.…

"Again, bhikkhus, a noble disciple possesses the virtues dear to the noble ones, unbroken … leading to concentration. He reflects thus: 'What now is the divine track of the devas?' He understands thus: 'I have heard that at present the devas hold nonoppression as supreme, and I do not oppress anyone, frail or firm. Surely I dwell possessing one of the divine tracks.' This [394] is the fourth divine track of the devas.…

"These are the four divine tracks of the devas for the purification of beings who have not been purified, for the cleansing of beings who have not been cleansed."

36 (6) Similar to the Devas

"Bhikkhus, when a noble disciple possesses four things, the devas are elated and speak of his similarity [to themselves].[355] What four?

"Here, bhikkhus, a noble disciple possesses confirmed confidence in the Buddha thus: 'The Blessed One is ... teacher of devas and humans, the Enlightened One, the Blessed One.' To those devatās who passed away here [in the human world] and were reborn there [in a heavenly world] possessing confirmed confidence in the Buddha, the thought occurs: 'As the noble disciple possesses the same confirmed confidence in the Buddha that we possessed when we passed away there and were reborn here, he will come[356] into the presence of the devas.'

"Again, bhikkhus, a noble disciple possesses confirmed confidence in the Dhamma ... in the Saṅgha.... He possesses the virtues dear to the noble ones, unbroken ... conducive to concentration. To those devatās who passed away here [in the human world] and were reborn there [in a heavenly world] possessing the virtues dear to the noble ones, the thought occurs: 'As the noble disciple possesses the same kind of virtues dear to the noble ones that we possessed when we passed away there and were reborn here, he will come into the presence of the devas.'

"When, bhikkhus, a noble disciple possesses these four things, the devas are elated and speak of his similarity [to themselves]." [395]

37 (7) Mahānāma

On one occasion the Blessed One was dwelling among the Sakyans at Kapilavatthu in Nigrodha's Park. Then Mahānāma the Sakyan approached the Blessed One, paid homage to him, sat down to one side, and said to him:

"Venerable sir, in what way is one a lay follower?"

"When, Mahānāma, one has gone for refuge to the Buddha, the Dhamma, and the Saṅgha, one is then a lay follower."

"In what way, venerable sir, is a lay follower accomplished in virtue?"

"When, Mahānāma, a lay follower abstains from the destruction of life, from taking what is not given, from sexual misconduct, from false speech, and from wines, liquor, and intoxicants that are a basis for negligence, the lay follower is accomplished in virtue."

"In what way, venerable sir, is a lay follower accomplished in faith?"

"Here, Mahānāma, a lay follower is a person of faith. He places faith in the enlightenment of the Tathāgata thus: 'The Blessed One is … teacher of devas and humans, the Enlightened One, the Blessed One.' In that way a lay follower is accomplished in faith."

"In what way, venerable sir, is a lay follower accomplished in generosity?"

"Here, Mahānāma, a lay follower dwells at home with a mind devoid of the stain of stinginess, freely generous, open-handed, delighting in relinquishment, one devoted to charity, delighting in giving and sharing. In that way a lay follower is accomplished in generosity."

"In what way, venerable sir, is a lay follower accomplished in wisdom?"

"Here, Mahānāma, a lay follower is wise, he possesses wisdom directed to arising and passing away, which is noble and penetrative, leading to the complete destruction of suffering. In that way a lay follower is accomplished in wisdom." [396]

38 (8) Rain

"Bhikkhus, just as, when rain pours down in thick droplets on a mountain top, the water flows down along the slope and fills the cleft, gullies, and creeks; these being filled fill up the pools; these being filled fill up the lakes; these being filled fill up the streams; these being filled fill up the rivers; and these being filled fill up the great ocean; so too, for a noble disciple, these things—confirmed confidence in the Buddha, the Dhamma, and the Saṅgha, and the virtues dear to the noble ones—flow onwards and, having gone beyond, they lead to the destruction of the taints."[357]

39 (9) Kāḷigodhā

On one occasion the Blessed One was dwelling among the Sakyans at Kapilavatthu in Nigrodha's Park. Then, in the morning, the Blessed One dressed and, taking bowl and robe, went to the residence of Kāḷigodhā the Sakyan lady, where he sat down in the appointed seat. Then Kāḷigodhā the Sakyan lady approached the Blessed One, paid homage to him, and sat down to one side. The Blessed One then said to her:

"Godhā, a noble woman disciple who possesses four things is a stream-enterer, no longer bound to the nether world, fixed in destiny, with enlightenment as her destination. What four?

"Here, Godhā, a noble woman disciple possesses confirmed confidence in the Buddha thus: 'The Blessed One is ... teacher of devas and humans, the Enlightened One, the Blessed One.' She possesses confirmed confidence in the Dhamma ... in the Saṅgha.... [397] She dwells at home with a mind devoid of the stain of stinginess, freely generous, open-handed, delighting in relinquishment, one devoted to charity, delighting in giving and sharing.

"A noble woman disciple, Godhā, who possesses these four things is a stream-enterer, no longer bound to the nether world, fixed in destiny, with enlightenment as her destination."

"Venerable sir, as to these four factors of stream-entry taught by the Blessed One, these things exist in me, and I live in conformity with those things. For, venerable sir, I possess confirmed confidence in the Buddha, the Dhamma, and the Saṅgha. Moreover, whatever there is in my family that is suitable for giving, all that I share unreservedly among those who are virtuous and of good character."

"It is a gain for you, Godhā! It is well gained by you, Godhā! You have declared the fruit of stream-entry."

40 (10) Nandiya

On one occasion the Blessed One was dwelling among the Sakyans at Kapilavatthu in Nigrodha's Park. Then Nandiya the Sakyan approached the Blessed One, paid homage to him, sat down to one side, and said to him:

"Venerable sir, when the four factors of stream-entry are completely and totally nonexistent in a noble disciple, would that noble disciple be one who dwells negligently?"

"Nandiya, I say that one in whom the four factors of stream-entry are completely and totally absent is 'an outsider, one who stands in the faction of worldlings.'[358] But, Nandiya, as to how a noble disciple is one who dwells negligently and one who dwells diligently, listen to that and attend closely, I will speak." [398]

"Yes, venerable sir," Nandiya the Sakyan replied. The Blessed One said this:

"And how, Nandiya, is a noble disciple one who dwells negligently? Here, Nandiya, a noble disciple possesses confirmed confidence in the Buddha thus: 'The Blessed One is ... teacher of devas and humans, the Enlightened One, the Blessed One.' Content with that confirmed confidence in the Buddha, he does not make further effort for solitude by day nor for seclusion at night. When he thus dwells negligently, there is no gladness.[359] When there is no gladness, there is no rapture. When there is no rapture, there is no tranquillity. When there is no tranquillity, he dwells in suffering. The mind of one who suffers does not become concentrated. When the mind is not concentrated, phenomena do not become manifest. Because phenomena do not become manifest, he is reckoned as 'one who dwells negligently.'

"Again, Nandiya, a noble disciple possesses confirmed confidence in the Dhamma ... in the Saṅgha.... He possesses the virtues dear to the noble ones, unbroken ... leading to concentration. Content with those virtues dear to the noble ones, he does not make further effort for solitude by day nor for seclusion at night. When he thus dwells negligently, there is no gladness.... Because phenomena do not become manifest, he is reckoned as 'one who dwells negligently.'

"It is in this way, Nandiya, that a noble disciple is one who dwells negligently.

"And how, Nandiya, is a noble disciple one who dwells diligently? Here, Nandiya, a noble disciple possesses confirmed confidence in the Buddha thus: 'The Blessed One is ... teacher of devas and humans, the Enlightened One, the Blessed One.' Not content with that confirmed confidence in the Buddha, he makes further effort for solitude by day and for seclusion at night. When he thus dwells diligently, gladness is born. When he is gladdened, rapture is born. When the mind is uplifted by rapture, the body becomes tranquil. One tranquil in body experiences happiness. The mind of one who is happy becomes concentrated. When the mind is concentrated, phenomena become manifest. Because phenomena become manifest, he is reckoned as 'one who dwells diligently.' [399]

"Again, Nandiya, a noble disciple possesses confirmed confidence in the Dhamma ... in the Saṅgha.... He possesses the virtues dear to the noble ones, unbroken ... leading to concentration. Not content with those virtues dear to the noble ones, he makes further effort for solitude by day and for seclusion at night. When he thus dwells diligently, gladness is born.... Because phenomena become manifest, he is reckoned as 'one who dwells diligently.'

"It is in this way, Nandiya, that a noble disciple is one who dwells diligently."

V. Streams of Merit with Verses

41 (1) Streams (1)

(*The opening is identical with §31, continuing thus:*) [400]

"When, bhikkhus, a noble disciple possesses these four streams of merit, streams of the wholesome, it is not easy to take the measure of his merit thus: 'Just so much is his stream of merit, stream of the wholesome, nutriment of happiness'; rather, it is reckoned as an incalculable, immeasurable, great mass of merit.

"Bhikkhus, just as it is not easy to take the measure of the water in the great ocean thus: 'There are so many gallons of water,' or 'There are so many hundreds of gallons of water,' or 'There are so many thousands of gallons of water,' or 'There are so many hundreds of thousands of gallons of water,' but rather it is reckoned as an incalculable, immeasurable, great mass of water; so too, when a noble disciple possesses these four streams of merit ... it is reckoned as an incalculable, immeasurable, great mass of merit."

This is what the Blessed One said. Having said this, the Fortunate One, the Teacher, further said this:

"Just as the many rivers used by the hosts of people,
Flowing downstream, finally reach the ocean,

The great mass of water, the boundless sea,
The fearsome receptacle of heaps of gems;

"So the streams of merit reach the wise man—
Giver of food, drink, and clothes,
Provider of beds, seats, and coverlets[360]—
As the rivers carry their waters to the sea." [401]

42 (2) Streams (2)

"Bhikkhus, there are these four streams of merit.… What four?

"Here, bhikkhus, a noble disciple possesses confirmed confidence in the Buddha … in the Dhamma … in the Saṅgha.…

"Again, bhikkhus, a noble disciple dwells at home with a mind devoid of the stain of stinginess, freely generous, open-handed, delighting in relinquishment, one devoted to charity, delighting in giving and sharing.

"These are the four streams of merit.…

"When, bhikkhus, a noble disciple possesses these four streams of merit, streams of the wholesome, it is not easy to take the measure of his merit thus: 'Just so much is his stream of merit, stream of the wholesome, nutriment of happiness'; rather, it is reckoned as an incalculable, immeasurable, great mass of merit.

"Bhikkhus, just as in the place where these great rivers meet and converge—namely, the Ganges, the Yamunā, the Aciravatī, the Sarabhū, and the Mahī—it is not easy to take the measure of the water there thus: 'There are so many gallons of water' … but rather it is reckoned as an incalculable, immeasurable, great mass of water; so too, when a noble disciple possesses these four streams of merit … it is reckoned as an incalculable, immeasurable, great mass of merit."

This is what the Blessed One said. Having said this, the Fortunate One, the Teacher, further said this:

"Just as the many rivers used by the hosts of people,
… (*verses as in §41*) …
As the rivers carry their waters to the sea."

43 (3) Streams (3)

"Bhikkhus, there are these four streams of merit.... What four?

"Here, bhikkhus, a noble disciple possesses confirmed confidence in the Buddha ... in the Dhamma ... in the Saṅgha....

"Again, bhikkhus, a noble disciple is wise, he possesses wisdom directed to arising and passing away, [402] which is noble and penetrative, leading to the complete destruction of suffering. This is the fourth stream of merit....

"These are the four streams of merit....

"When, bhikkhus, a noble disciple possesses these four streams of merit, streams of the wholesome, it is not easy to take the measure of his merit thus: 'Just so much is his stream of merit, stream of the wholesome, nutriment of happiness'; rather, it is reckoned as an incalculable, immeasurable, great mass of merit."

This is what the Blessed One said. Having said this, the Fortunate One, the Teacher, further said this:

"One who desires merit, established in the wholesome,
Develops the path to attain the Deathless;
He who has reached the Dhamma's core,
Delighting in destruction,
Does not tremble thinking,
'The King of Death will come.'"[361]

44 (4) Rich (1)

"Bhikkhus, a noble disciple who possesses four things is said to be rich, with much wealth and property.[362] What four?

"Here, bhikkhus, a noble disciple possesses confirmed confidence in the Buddha ... in the Dhamma ... in the Saṅgha.... He possesses the virtues dear to the noble ones, unbroken ... leading to concentration.

"A noble disciple who possesses these four things is said to be rich, with much wealth and property."

45 (5) Rich (2)

"Bhikkhus, a noble disciple who possesses four things is said to be rich, with much wealth and property, of great fame. What four?"

(*The rest as in §44.*) [403]

46 (6) Simple Version

"Bhikkhus, a noble disciple who possesses four things is a stream-enterer, no longer bound to the nether world, fixed in destiny, with enlightenment as his destination. What four?

"Here, bhikkhus, a noble disciple possesses confirmed confidence in the Buddha thus: 'The Blessed One is … teacher of devas and humans, the Enlightened One, the Blessed One.' He possesses confirmed confidence in the Dhamma … in the Saṅgha.… He possesses the virtues dear to the noble ones, unbroken … leading to concentration.

"A noble disciple, bhikkhus, who possesses these four things is a stream-enterer … with enlightenment as his destination."

47 (7) Nandiya

At Kapilavatthu. The Blessed One then said to Nandiya the Sakyan as he was sitting to one side:

(*The rest as in §46.*)

48 (8) Bhaddiya

(*The same, addressed to Bhaddiya the Sakyan.*) [404]

49 (9) Mahānāma

(*The same, addressed to Mahānāma the Sakyan.*)

50 (10) Factors

"Bhikkhus, there are these four factors for stream-entry. What four? Association with superior persons, hearing the true Dhamma, careful attention, practice in accordance with the Dhamma. These are the four factors for stream-entry."[363]

VI. The Wise One

51 (1) With Verses

(*The prose portion is the same as §46.*) [405]

This is what the Blessed One said. Having said this, the Fortunate One, the Teacher, further said this:[364]

"When one has faith in the Tathāgata,
Unshakable and well established,
And good conduct built on virtue,
Dear to the noble ones and praised;

"When one has confidence in the Saṅgha
And view that has been rectified,
They say that one is not poor,
That one's life is not vain.

"Therefore the person of intelligence,
Remembering the Buddha's Teaching,
Should be devoted to faith and virtue,
To confidence and vision of the Dhamma."

52 (2) One Who Spent the Rains

On one occasion the Blessed One was dwelling at Sāvatthī in Jeta's Grove, Anāthapiṇḍika's Park. Now on that occasion a certain bhikkhu who had spent the rains in Sāvatthī had arrived in Kapilavatthu on some business. The Sakyans of Kapilavatthu heard: "A certain bhikkhu, it is said, who spent the rains in Sāvatthī has arrived in Kapilavatthu."

Then the Sakyans of Kapilavatthu approached that bhikkhu and paid homage to him, after which they sat down to one side and said to him:

"We hope, venerable sir, that the Blessed One is healthy and robust."

"The Blessed One, friends, is healthy and robust." [406]

"We hope, venerable sir, that Sāriputta and Moggallāna are healthy and robust."

"Sāriputta and Moggallāna, friends, are healthy and robust."

"We hope, venerable sir, that the bhikkhus of the Saṅgha are healthy and robust."

"The bhikkhus of the Saṅgha, friends, are healthy and robust."

"Did you hear and learn anything, venerable sir, in the presence of the Blessed One during this rains?"

"In the presence of the Blessed One, friends, I heard and learnt this: 'Bhikkhus, those bhikkhus are few who, by the destruction of the taints, in this very life enter and dwell in the taintless liberation of mind, liberation by wisdom, realizing it for themselves with direct knowledge. Those bhikkhus are more numerous who, with the utter destruction of the five lower fetters, have become of spontaneous birth, due to attain Nibbāna there without returning from that world.'

"Further, friends, in the presence of the Blessed One I heard and learnt this: 'Bhikkhus, those bhikkhus are few who ... have become of spontaneous birth.... Those bhikkhus are more numerous who, with the utter destruction of three fetters and with the diminishing of greed, hatred, and delusion, have become once-returners who, after coming back to this world only one more time, will make an end to suffering.'

"Further, friends, in the presence of the Blessed One I heard and learnt this: 'Those bhikkhus are few who ... have become once-returners.... Those bhikkhus are more numerous who, with the utter destruction of three fetters, have become stream-enterers, no longer bound to the nether world, fixed in destiny, with enlightenment as their destination.'"

53 (3) Dhammadinna

On one occasion the Blessed One was dwelling at Bārāṇasī in the Deer Park at Isipatana. [407] Then the lay follower Dhammadinna, together with five hundred lay followers, approached the Blessed One, paid homage to him, and sat down to one side.[365] Sitting to one side, the lay follower Dhammadinna then said to the Blessed One: "Let the Blessed One, venerable sir, exhort us and instruct us in a way that may lead to our welfare and happiness for a long time."

"Therefore, Dhammadinna, you should train yourselves thus: 'From time to time we will enter and dwell upon those discourses spoken by the Tathāgata that are deep, deep in meaning, supramundane, dealing with emptiness.' It is in such a way that you should train yourselves."[366]

"Venerable sir, it is not easy for us—dwelling in a home crowded with children, enjoying Kāsian sandalwood, wearing garlands, scents, and unguents, receiving gold and silver—from time to time to enter and dwell upon those discourses spoken by the Tathāgata that are deep, deep in meaning, supramundane, dealing with emptiness. As we are established in the five training rules, let the Blessed One teach us the Dhamma further."

"Therefore, Dhammadinna, you should train yourselves thus: 'We will possess confirmed confidence in the Buddha ... in the Dhamma ... in the Saṅgha.... We will possess the virtues dear to the noble ones, unbroken ... leading to concentration.' It is in such a way that you should train yourselves."

"Venerable sir, as to these four factors of stream-entry taught by the Blessed One, these things exist in us, and we live in conformity with those things. For, venerable sir, we possess confirmed confidence in the Buddha, [408] the Dhamma, and the Saṅgha. We possess the virtues dear to the noble ones, unbroken ... leading to concentration."

"It is a gain for you, Dhammadinna! It is well gained by you, Dhammadinna! You have declared the fruit of stream-entry."

54 (4) Ill

On one occasion the Blessed One was dwelling among the Sakyans at Kapilavatthu in Nigrodha's Park. Now on that occasion a number of bhikkhus were making a robe for the Blessed One, thinking: "After the three months, with his robe completed, the Blessed One will set out on tour."

Mahānāma the Sakyan heard: "A number of bhikkhus, it is said, are making a robe for the Blessed One, thinking that after the three months, with his robe completed, the Blessed One will set out on tour."

Then Mahānāma the Sakyan approached the Blessed One, paid homage to him, sat down to one side, and said to him: "Venerable sir, I heard that a number of bhikkhus are making a robe for the Blessed One.... Now I have not heard and learnt in the presence of the Blessed One how a wise lay follower who is sick, afflicted, and gravely ill should be exhorted by another wise lay follower."

"A wise lay follower,[367] Mahānāma, who is sick, afflicted, and gravely ill should be consoled by another wise lay follower with four consolations: 'Let the venerable one[368] be consoled. You have confirmed confidence in the Buddha thus: "The Blessed One is … teacher of devas and humans, the Enlightened One, the Blessed One." You have confirmed confidence in the Dhamma … in the Saṅgha.… You have the virtues dear to the noble ones, unbroken … leading to concentration.' [409]

"After a wise lay follower, who is sick, afflicted, and gravely ill has been consoled by a wise lay follower with these four consolations, he should be asked: 'Are you anxious about your mother and father?' If he says: 'I am,' he should be told: 'But, good sir, you are subject to death. Whether you are anxious about your mother and father or not, you will die anyway. So please abandon your anxiety over your mother and father.'

"If he says: 'I have abandoned my anxiety over my mother and father,' he should be asked: 'Are you anxious about your wife and children?' If he says: 'I am,' he should be told: 'But, good sir, you are subject to death. Whether you are anxious about your wife and children or not, you will die anyway. So please abandon your anxiety over your wife and children.'

"If he says: 'I have abandoned my anxiety over my wife and children,' he should be asked: 'Are you anxious about the five cords of human sensual pleasure?' If he says: 'I am,' he should be told: 'Celestial sensual pleasures, friend, are more excellent and sublime than human sensual pleasures. So please withdraw your mind from human sensual pleasures and resolve on the devas of the realm of the Four Great Kings.'

"If he says: 'My mind has been withdrawn from human sensual pleasures and resolved on the devas of the realm of the Four Great Kings,' he should be told: [410] 'The Tāvatiṃsa devas, friend, are more excellent and sublime than the devas of the realm of the Four Great Kings. So please withdraw your mind from the devas of the realm of the Four Great Kings and resolve on the Tāvatiṃsa devas.'

"If he says: 'My mind has been withdrawn from the devas of the realm of the Four Great Kings and resolved on the Tāvatiṃsa devas,' he should be told: 'More excellent and sublime, friend, than the Tāvatiṃsa devas are the Yāma devas … the Tusita devas … the Nimmānarati devas … the Paranimmitavasavattī devas.…

The brahmā world, friend, is more excellent and sublime than the Paranimmitavasavattī devas. So please withdraw your mind from the Paranimmitavasavattī devas and resolve on the brahmā world.'[369]

"If he says: 'My mind has been withdrawn from the Paranimmitavasavattī devas and resolved on the brahmā world,' he should be told: 'Even the brahmā world, friend, is impermanent, unstable, included in identity. So please withdraw your mind from the brahmā world and direct it to the cessation of identity.'[370]

"If he says: 'My mind has been withdrawn from the brahmā world; I have directed my mind to the cessation of identity,' then, Mahānāma, I say there is no difference between a lay follower who is thus liberated in mind and a bhikkhu who has been liberated in mind for a hundred years,[371] that is, between one liberation and the other."[372]

55 (5) The Fruit of Stream-Entry

"Bhikkhus, these four things, when developed and cultivated, lead to the realization of the fruit of stream-entry. What four? [411] Association with superior persons, hearing the true Dhamma, careful attention, practice in accordance with the Dhamma. These four things, when developed and cultivated, lead to the realization of the fruit of stream-entry."

56 (6) The Fruit of Once-Returning

"Bhikkhus, these four things, when developed and cultivated, lead to the realization of the fruit of once-returning. What four?..." (*as above*).

57 (7) The Fruit of Nonreturning

" ... lead to the realization of the fruit of nonreturning...."

58 (8) The Fruit of Arahantship

" ... lead to the realization of the fruit of arahantship...."

59 (9) The Obtaining of Wisdom

" … lead to the obtaining of wisdom…."

60 (10) The Growth of Wisdom

" … lead to the growth of wisdom…."

61 (11) The Expansion of Wisdom

" … lead to the expansion of wisdom…."

[412] VII. GREAT WISDOM

62 (1) Greatness of Wisdom

"Bhikkhus, these four things, when developed and cultivated, lead to greatness of wisdom. What four? Association with superior persons, hearing the true Dhamma, careful attention, practice in accordance with the Dhamma. These four things, when developed and cultivated, lead to greatness of wisdom."

63 (2)–74 (13) Extensiveness of Wisdom, Etc.

"Bhikkhus, these four things, when developed and cultivated, lead to extensiveness of wisdom … to vastness of wisdom … to depth of wisdom … to the state of unequalled wisdom[373] … to breadth of wisdom … to abundance of wisdom … to quickness of wisdom … to buoyancy of wisdom … to joyousness of wisdom … [413] … to swiftness of wisdom … to sharpness of wisdom … to penetrativeness of wisdom.[374] What four? Association with superior persons, hearing the true Dhamma, careful attention, practice in accordance with the Dhamma. These four things, when developed and cultivated, lead to penetrativeness of wisdom."

[414] Chapter XII

56 *Saccasaṃyutta*

Connected Discourses on the Truths

I. Concentration

1 (1) Concentration

At Sāvatthī. "Bhikkhus, develop concentration. A bhikkhu who is concentrated understands things as they really are.[375]

"And what does he understand as it really is? He understands as it really is: 'This is suffering.' He understands as it really is: 'This is the origin of suffering.' He understands as it really is: 'This is the cessation of suffering.' He understands as it really is: 'This is the way leading to the cessation of suffering.'

"Bhikkhus, develop concentration. A bhikkhu who is concentrated understands things as they really are.

"Therefore, bhikkhus, an exertion should be made to understand: 'This is suffering.'[376] An exertion should be made to understand: 'This is the origin of suffering.' An exertion should be made to understand: 'This is the cessation of suffering.' An exertion should be made to understand: 'This is the way leading to the cessation of suffering.'"

2 (2) Seclusion

"Bhikkhus, make an exertion in seclusion. A bhikkhu who is secluded understands things as they really are.

"And what does he understand as it really is? He understands as it really is: 'This is suffering.'... 'This is the origin of suffering.'... 'This is the cessation of suffering.'... 'This is the way leading to the cessation of suffering.' [415]

"Bhikkhus, make an exertion in seclusion. A bhikkhu who is secluded understands things as they really are.

"Therefore, bhikkhus, an exertion should be made to understand: 'This is suffering.'… An exertion should be made to understand: 'This is the way leading to the cessation of suffering.'"

3 (3) Clansmen (1)

"Bhikkhus, whatever clansmen in the past rightly went forth from the household life into homelessness, all did so in order to make the breakthrough to the Four Noble Truths as they really are. Whatever clansmen in the future will rightly go forth from the household life into homelessness, all will do so in order to make the breakthrough to the Four Noble Truths as they really are. Whatever clansmen at present have rightly gone forth from the household life into homelessness, all have done so in order to make the breakthrough to the Four Noble Truths as they really are.

"What four? The noble truth of suffering, the noble truth of the origin of suffering, the noble truth of the cessation of suffering, the noble truth of the way leading to the cessation of suffering. Whatever clansmen rightly went forth … will rightly go forth … have rightly gone forth from household life into homelessness, all have done so in order to make the breakthrough to these Four Noble Truths as they really are.

"Therefore, bhikkhus, an exertion should be made to understand: 'This is suffering.'… An exertion should be made to understand: 'This is the way leading to the cessation of suffering.'"

4 (4) Clansmen (2)

"Bhikkhus, whatever clansmen in the past rightly went forth from the household life into homelessness and made the breakthrough to things as they really are, all made the breakthrough to the Four Noble Truths as they really are. Whatever clansmen in the future will rightly go forth from the household life into homelessness and make the breakthrough to things as they really are, [416] all will make the breakthrough to the Four Noble Truths as they really are. Whatever clansmen at present have rightly gone forth from the household life into homelessness and make the breakthrough to things as they really are, all make the breakthrough to the Four Noble Truths as they really are.

"What four? The noble truth of suffering, the noble truth of the origin of suffering, the noble truth of the cessation of suffering, the noble truth of the way leading to the cessation of suffering. Whatever clansmen made the breakthrough ... will make the breakthrough ... make the breakthrough to things as they really are, all make the breakthrough to these Four Noble Truths as they really are.

"Therefore, bhikkhus, an exertion should be made to understand: 'This is suffering.'... An exertion should be made to understand: 'This is the way leading to the cessation of suffering.'"

5 (5) Ascetics and Brahmins (1)

"Bhikkhus, whatever ascetics or brahmins in the past fully awakened to things as they really are, all fully awakened to the Four Noble Truths as they really are. Whatever ascetics or brahmins in the future will fully awaken to things as they really are, all will fully awaken to the Four Noble Truths as they really are. Whatever ascetics or brahmins at present have fully awakened to things as they really are, all have fully awakened to the Four Noble Truths as they really are.

"What four? The noble truth of suffering ... the noble truth of the way leading to the cessation of suffering. Whatever ascetics or brahmins fully awakened ... will fully awaken ... have fully awakened to things as they really are, all have fully awakened to these Four Noble Truths as they really are. [417]

"Therefore, bhikkhus, an exertion should be made to understand: 'This is suffering.'... An exertion should be made to understand: 'This is the way leading to the cessation of suffering.'"

6 (6) Ascetics and Brahmins (2)

"Bhikkhus, whatever ascetics or brahmins in the past revealed themselves as having fully awakened to things as they really are, all revealed themselves as having fully awakened to the Four Noble Truths as they really are. Whatever ascetics or brahmins in the future will reveal themselves as having fully awakened to things as they really are, all will reveal themselves as having fully awakened to the Four Noble Truths as they really are. Whatever ascetics or brahmins at present reveal themselves as having fully awakened to things as they really are, all reveal themselves as having fully awakened to the Four Noble Truths as they really are.

"What four? The noble truth of suffering ... the noble truth of the way leading to the cessation of suffering. Whatever ascetics or brahmins revealed themselves ... will reveal themselves ... reveal themselves as having fully awakened to things as they really are, all reveal themselves as having fully awakened to these Four Noble Truths as they really are.

"Therefore, bhikkhus, an exertion should be made to understand: 'This is suffering.'... An exertion should be made to understand: 'This is the way leading to the cessation of suffering.'"

7 (7) Thoughts

"Bhikkhus, do not think evil unwholesome thoughts; that is, sensual thought, thought of ill will, thought of harming. For what reason? These thoughts, bhikkhus, are unbeneficial, irrelevant to the fundamentals of the holy life, [418] and do not lead to revulsion, to dispassion, to cessation, to peace, to direct knowledge, to enlightenment, to Nibbāna.

"When you think, bhikkhus, you should think: 'This is suffering'; you should think: 'This is the origin of suffering'; you should think: 'This is the cessation of suffering'; you should think: 'This is the way leading to the cessation of suffering.' For what reason? These thoughts, bhikkhus, are beneficial, relevant to the fundamentals of the holy life, and lead to revulsion, to dispassion, to cessation, to peace, to direct knowledge, to enlightenment, to Nibbāna.

"Therefore, bhikkhus, an exertion should be made to understand: 'This is suffering.'... An exertion should be made to understand: 'This is the way leading to the cessation of suffering.'"

8 (8) Reflection

"Bhikkhus, do not reflect in an evil unwholesome way:[377] 'The world is eternal' or 'The world is not eternal'; or 'The world is finite' or 'The world is infinite'; or 'The soul and the body are the same' or 'The soul is one thing, the body is another'; or 'The Tathāgata exists after death,' or 'The Tathāgata does not exist after death,' or 'The Tathāgata both exists and does not exist after death,' or 'The Tathāgata neither exists nor does not exist after death.' For what reason? Because, bhikkhus, this reflection is unbeneficial, irrelevant to the fundamentals of the holy life, and does not lead to revulsion, to dispassion, to cessation, to peace, to direct knowledge, to enlightenment, to Nibbāna.

"When you reflect, bhikkhus, you should reflect: 'This is suffering'; you should reflect: 'This is the origin of suffering'; you should reflect: 'This is the cessation of suffering'; you should reflect: 'This is the way leading to the cessation of suffering.' For what reason? Because, bhikkhus, this reflection is beneficial, relevant to the fundamentals of the holy life, and leads to revulsion, to dispassion, to cessation, to peace, to direct knowledge, [419] to enlightenment, to Nibbāna.

"Therefore, bhikkhus, an exertion should be made to understand: 'This is suffering.'... An exertion should be made to understand: 'This is the way leading to the cessation of suffering.'"

9 (9) Disputatious Talk

"Bhikkhus, do not engage in disputatious talk,[378] saying: 'You don't understand this Dhamma and Discipline. I understand this Dhamma and Discipline. What, you understand this Dhamma and Discipline! You're practising wrongly, I'm practising rightly. What should have been said before you said after; what should have been said after you said before. I'm consistent, you're inconsistent. What you took so long to think out has been overturned. Your thesis has been refuted. Go off to rescue your thesis, for you're defeated, or disentangle yourself if you can.' For what reason? Because, bhikkhus, this talk is unbeneficial, irrelevant to the fundamentals of the holy life, and does not lead to revulsion, to dispassion, to cessation, to peace, to direct knowledge, to enlightenment, to Nibbāna.

"When you talk, bhikkhus, you should talk about: 'This is suffering'; you should talk about: 'This is the origin of suffering'; you should talk about: 'This is the cessation of suffering'; you should talk about: 'This is the way leading to the cessation of suffering.' For what reason? Because, bhikkhus, this talk is beneficial, relevant to the fundamentals of the holy life, and leads to revulsion, to dispassion, to cessation, to peace, to direct knowledge, to enlightenment, to Nibbāna.

"Therefore, bhikkhus, an exertion should be made to understand: 'This is suffering.'... An exertion should be made to understand: 'This is the way leading to the cessation of suffering.'"

10 (10) Pointless Talk

"Bhikkhus, do not engage in the various kinds of pointless talk,[379] that is, talk about kings, thieves, and ministers of state; talk about armies, dangers, and wars; talk about food, drink, garments, and beds; talk about garlands and scents; talk about relations, vehicles, villages, towns, cities, and countries; talk about women and talk about heroes; [420] street talk and talk by the well; talk about those departed in days gone by; rambling chitchat; speculation about the world and about the sea; talk about becoming this or that. For what reason? Because, bhikkhus, this talk is unbeneficial, irrelevant to the fundamentals of the holy life, and does not lead to revulsion, to dispassion, to cessation, to peace, to direct knowledge, to enlightenment, to Nibbāna.

"When you talk, bhikkhus, you should talk about: 'This is suffering'; you should talk about: 'This is the origin of suffering'; you should talk about: 'This is the cessation of suffering'; you should talk about: 'This is the way leading to the cessation of suffering.' For what reason? Because, bhikkhus, this talk is beneficial, relevant to the fundamentals of the holy life, and leads to revulsion, to dispassion, to cessation, to peace, to direct knowledge, to enlightenment, to Nibbāna.

"Therefore, bhikkhus, an exertion should be made to understand: 'This is suffering.'... An exertion should be made to understand: 'This is the way leading to the cessation of suffering.'"

II. Setting in Motion the Wheel of the Dhamma

11 (1) Setting in Motion the Wheel of the Dhamma

Thus have I heard. On one occasion the Blessed One was dwelling at Bārāṇasī in the Deer Park at Isipatana. [421] There the

Blessed One addressed the bhikkhus of the group of five thus:[380]

"Bhikkhus, these two extremes should not be followed by one who has gone forth into homelessness. What two? The pursuit of sensual happiness in sensual pleasures, which is low, vulgar, the way of worldlings, ignoble, unbeneficial; and the pursuit of self-mortification, which is painful, ignoble, unbeneficial. Without veering towards either of these extremes, the Tathāgata has awakened to the middle way, which gives rise to vision, which gives rise to knowledge, which leads to peace, to direct knowledge, to enlightenment, to Nibbāna.

"And what, bhikkhus, is that middle way awakened to by the Tathāgata, which gives rise to vision ... which leads to Nibbāna? It is this Noble Eightfold Path; that is, right view, right intention, right speech, right action, right livelihood, right effort, right mindfulness, right concentration. This, bhikkhus, is that middle way awakened to by the Tathāgata, which gives rise to vision, which gives rise to knowledge, which leads to peace, to direct knowledge, to enlightenment, to Nibbāna.

"Now this, bhikkhus, is the noble truth of suffering: birth is suffering, aging is suffering, illness is suffering, death is suffering;[381] union with what is displeasing is suffering; separation from what is pleasing is suffering; not to get what one wants is suffering; in brief, the five aggregates subject to clinging are suffering.

"Now this, bhikkhus, is the noble truth of the origin of suffering: it is this craving which leads to renewed existence, accompanied by delight and lust, seeking delight here and there; that is, craving for sensual pleasures, craving for existence, craving for extermination.

"Now this, bhikkhus, is the noble truth of the cessation of suffering: it is the remainderless fading away and cessation of that same craving, the giving up and relinquishing of it, freedom from it, nonreliance on it.

"Now this, bhikkhus, is the noble truth of the way leading to the cessation of suffering: [422] it is this Noble Eightfold Path; that is, right view ... right concentration.

"'This is the noble truth of suffering': thus, bhikkhus, in regard to things unheard before, there arose in me vision, knowledge, wisdom, true knowledge, and light.

"'This noble truth of suffering is to be fully understood': thus, bhikkhus, in regard to things unheard before, there arose in me vision, knowledge, wisdom, true knowledge, and light.

"'This noble truth of suffering has been fully understood': thus, bhikkhus, in regard to things unheard before, there arose in me vision, knowledge, wisdom, true knowledge, and light.

"'This is the noble truth of the origin of suffering': thus, bhikkhus, in regard to things unheard before, there arose in me vision, knowledge, wisdom, true knowledge, and light.

"'This noble truth of the origin of suffering is to be abandoned': thus, bhikkhus, in regard to things unheard before, there arose in me vision, knowledge, wisdom, true knowledge, and light.

"'This noble truth of the origin of suffering has been abandoned': thus, bhikkhus, in regard to things unheard before, there arose in me vision, knowledge, wisdom, true knowledge, and light.

"'This is the noble truth of the cessation of suffering': thus, bhikkhus, in regard to things unheard before, there arose in me vision, knowledge, wisdom, true knowledge, and light.

"'This noble truth of the cessation of suffering is to be realized': thus, bhikkhus, in regard to things unheard before, there arose in me vision, knowledge, wisdom, true knowledge, and light.

"'This noble truth of the cessation of suffering has been realized': thus, bhikkhus, in regard to things unheard before, there arose in me vision, knowledge, wisdom, true knowledge, and light.

"'This is the noble truth of the way leading to the cessation of suffering': thus, bhikkhus, in regard to things unheard before, there arose in me vision, knowledge, wisdom, true knowledge, and light.

"'This noble truth of the way leading to the cessation of suffering is to be developed': thus, bhikkhus, in regard to things unheard before, there arose in me vision, knowledge, wisdom, true knowledge, and light.

"'This noble truth of the way leading to the cessation of suffering has been developed': thus, bhikkhus, in regard to things unheard before, there arose in me vision, knowledge, wisdom, true knowledge, and light.

"So long, bhikkhus, as my knowledge and vision, in three phases and twelve aspects, was not thoroughly purified in this way regarding these Four Noble Truths,[382] [423] I did not claim to have awakened to the unsurpassed perfect enlightenment in this world with its devas, Māra, and Brahmā, in this generation with its ascetics and brahmins, its devas and humans. But when my knowledge and vision, in three phases and twelve aspects, was thoroughly purified in this way regarding these Four Noble Truths, then I claimed to have awakened to the unsurpassed perfect enlightenment in this world with its devas, Māra, and Brahmā, in this generation with its ascetics and brahmins, its devas and humans. The knowledge and vision arose in me: 'Unshakable is the liberation of my mind. This is my last birth. Now there is no more renewed existence.'"

This is what the Blessed One said. Elated, the bhikkhus of the group of five delighted in the Blessed One's statement. And while this discourse was being spoken, there arose in the Venerable Kondañña the dust-free, stainless vision of the Dhamma: "Whatever is subject to origination is all subject to cessation."

And when the Wheel of the Dhamma had been set in motion by the Blessed One,[383] the earth-dwelling devas raised a cry: "At Bārāṇasī, in the Deer Park at Isipatana, this unsurpassed Wheel of the Dhamma has been set in motion by the Blessed One, which cannot be stopped by any ascetic or brahmin or deva or Māra or Brahmā or by anyone in the world." Having heard the cry of the earth-dwelling devas, the devas of the realm of the Four Great Kings raised a cry: "At Bārāṇasī ... this unsurpassed Wheel of the Dhamma has been set in motion by the Blessed One, which cannot be stopped ... by anyone in the world." Having heard the cry of the devas of the realm of the Four Great Kings, the Tāvatiṃsa devas ... the Yāma devas ... the Tusita devas ... the Nimmānaratī devas ... the Paranimmitavasavattī devas ... the devas of Brahmā's company raised a cry: "At Bārāṇasī, in the Deer Park at Isipatana, this unsurpassed Wheel of the Dhamma has been set in motion by the Blessed One, [424] which cannot be stopped by any ascetic or brahmin or deva or Māra or Brahmā or by anyone in the world."

Thus at that moment, at that instant, at that second, the cry spread as far as the brahmā world, and this ten thousandfold world system shook, quaked, and trembled, and an immeasurable glorious radiance appeared in the world surpassing the divine majesty of the devas.

Then the Blessed One uttered this inspired utterance: "Koṇḍañña has indeed understood! Koṇḍañña has indeed understood!" In this way the Venerable Koṇḍañña acquired the name "Aññā Koṇḍañña—Koṇḍañña Who Has Understood."

12 (2) Tathāgatas

"'This is the noble truth of suffering': thus, bhikkhus, in regard to things unheard before, there arose in the Tathāgatas vision, knowledge, wisdom, true knowledge, and light.

"'This noble truth of suffering is to be fully understood': thus, bhikkhus, in regard to things unheard before, there arose in the Tathāgatas vision … and light.

"'This noble truth of suffering has been fully understood': thus, bhikkhus, in regard to things unheard before, there arose in the Tathāgatas vision … and light.

"'This is the noble truth of the origin of suffering' … 'This noble truth of the origin of suffering is to be abandoned' … 'This noble truth of the origin of suffering has been abandoned': thus, bhikkhus, in regard to things unheard before, there arose in the Tathāgatas vision … and light.

"'This is the noble truth of the cessation of suffering' … 'This noble truth of the cessation of suffering is to be realized' … [425] 'This noble truth of the cessation of suffering has been realized': thus, bhikkhus, in regard to things unheard before, there arose in the Tathāgatas vision … and light.

"'This is the noble truth of the way leading to the cessation of suffering' … 'This noble truth of the way leading to the cessation of suffering is to be developed' … 'This noble truth of the way leading to the cessation of suffering has been developed': thus, bhikkhus, in regard to things unheard before, there arose in the Tathāgatas vision, knowledge, wisdom, true knowledge, and light."

13 (3) Aggregates

"Bhikkhus, there are these Four Noble Truths. What four? The noble truth of suffering, the noble truth of the origin of suffering, the noble truth of the cessation of suffering, the noble truth of the way leading to the cessation of suffering.

"And what, bhikkhus, is the noble truth of suffering? It should be said: the five aggregates subject to clinging; that is, the form aggregate subject to clinging ... the consciousness aggregate subject to clinging. This is called the noble truth of suffering.

"And what, bhikkhus, is the noble truth of the origin of suffering? It is this craving which leads to renewed existence, accompanied by delight and lust, seeking delight here and there; that is, craving for sensual pleasures, craving for existence, craving for extermination. This is called the noble truth of the origin of suffering.

"And what, bhikkhus, is the noble truth of the cessation of suffering? It is the remainderless fading away and cessation of that same craving, the giving up and relinquishing of it, freedom from it, nonreliance on it. This is called the noble truth of the cessation of suffering.

"And what, bhikkhus, is the noble truth of the way leading to the cessation of suffering? It is this Noble Eightfold Path; that is, right view ... right concentration. This is called the noble truth of the way leading to the cessation of suffering. [426]

"These, bhikkhus, are the Four Noble Truths.

"Therefore, bhikkhus, an exertion should be made to understand: 'This is suffering.'... An exertion should be made to understand: 'This is the way leading to the cessation of suffering.'"

14 (4) Internal Sense Bases

"Bhikkhus, there are these Four Noble Truths. What four? The noble truth of suffering, the noble truth of the origin of suffering, the noble truth of the cessation of suffering, the noble truth of the way leading to the cessation of suffering.

"And what, bhikkhus, is the noble truth of suffering? It should be said: the six internal sense bases. What six? The eye base ... the mind base. This is called the noble truth of suffering."

(*The rest of the sutta is identical with §13.*)

15 (5) Remembrance (1)

"Bhikkhus, do you remember the Four Noble Truths taught by me?"

When this was said, a certain bhikkhu said to the Blessed One:

[427] "Venerable sir, I remember the Four Noble Truths taught by the Blessed One."

"But how, bhikkhu, do you remember the Four Noble Truths taught by me?"

"I remember suffering, venerable sir, as the first noble truth taught by the Blessed One. I remember the origin of suffering as the second noble truth taught by the Blessed One. I remember the cessation of suffering as the third noble truth taught by the Blessed One. I remember the way leading to the cessation of suffering as the fourth noble truth taught by the Blessed One. It is in this way, venerable sir, that I remember the Four Noble Truths taught by the Blessed One."

"Good, good, bhikkhu! It is good that you remember the Four Noble Truths taught by me. Suffering, bhikkhu, is the first noble truth taught by me: remember it thus. The origin of suffering is the second noble truth taught by me: remember it thus. The cessation of suffering is the third noble truth taught by me: remember it thus. The way leading to the cessation of suffering is the fourth noble truth taught by me: remember it thus. In this way, bhikkhu, remember the Four Noble Truths taught by me.

"Therefore, bhikkhu, an exertion should be made to understand: 'This is suffering.'... An exertion should be made to understand: 'This is the way leading to the cessation of suffering.'"

16 (6) Remembrance (2)

"Bhikkhus, do you remember the Four Noble Truths taught by me?" [428]

When this was said, a certain bhikkhu said to the Blessed One: "Venerable sir, I remember the Four Noble Truths taught by the Blessed One."

"But how, bhikkhu, do you remember the Four Noble Truths taught by me?"

"I remember suffering, venerable sir, as the first noble truth taught by the Blessed One. For if any ascetic or brahmin should speak thus: 'This is not the first noble truth of suffering taught by the ascetic Gotama; having rejected this first noble truth of suffering, I will make known another first noble truth of suffering'—this is impossible.

"I remember the origin of suffering as the second noble truth taught by the Blessed One.... I remember the cessation of suffering as the third noble truth taught by the Blessed One.... I remember the way leading to the cessation of suffering as the fourth noble truth taught by the Blessed One. For if any ascetic or brahmin should speak thus: 'This is not the fourth noble truth of the way leading to the cessation of suffering taught by the ascetic Gotama; having rejected this fourth noble truth of the way leading to the cessation of suffering, I will make known another fourth noble truth of the way leading to the cessation of suffering'—this is impossible.

"It is in this way, venerable sir, that I remember the Four Noble Truths taught by the Blessed One."

"Good, good, bhikkhu! It is good that you remember the Four Noble Truths taught by me. Suffering, bhikkhu, is the first noble truth taught by me: remember it thus. For if any ascetic or brahmin should speak thus ... (*as above*) ... [429] 'This is not the fourth noble truth of the way leading to the cessation of suffering taught by the ascetic Gotama; having rejected this fourth noble truth of the way leading to the cessation of suffering, I will make known another fourth noble truth of the way leading to the cessation of suffering'—this is impossible.

"In this way, bhikkhu, remember the Four Noble Truths taught by me.

"Therefore, bhikkhu, an exertion should be made to understand: 'This is suffering.'... An exertion should be made to understand: 'This is the way leading to the cessation of suffering.'"

17 (7) Ignorance

Sitting to one side, that bhikkhu said to the Blessed One: "Venerable sir, it is said, 'ignorance, ignorance.' What is ignorance, venerable sir, and in what way is one immersed in ignorance?"

"Bhikkhu, not knowing suffering, not knowing the origin of suffering, not knowing the cessation of suffering, not knowing the way leading to the cessation of suffering: this is called ignorance, bhikkhu, and it is in this way that one is immersed in ignorance.

"Therefore, bhikkhu, an exertion should be made to understand: 'This is suffering.'... An exertion should be made to understand: 'This is the way leading to the cessation of suffering.'"

18 (8) True Knowledge

Then a certain bhikkhu approached the Blessed One, paid homage to him, sat down to one side, and said to him: "Venerable sir, it is said, 'true knowledge, true knowledge.' What is true knowledge, venerable sir, and in what way has one arrived at true knowledge?" [430]

"Bhikkhu, knowledge of suffering, knowledge of the origin of suffering, knowledge of the cessation of suffering, knowledge of the way leading to the cessation of suffering: this is called true knowledge, bhikkhu, and it is in this way that one has arrived at true knowledge.

"Therefore, bhikkhu, an exertion should be made to understand: 'This is suffering.'… An exertion should be made to understand: 'This is the way leading to the cessation of suffering.'"

19 (9) Implications

"'This is the noble truth of suffering': such has been made known by me. In this statement, 'This is the noble truth of suffering,' there are innumerable nuances, innumerable details, innumerable implications.[384]

"'This is the noble truth of the origin of suffering' … 'This is the noble truth of the cessation of suffering' … 'This is the noble truth of the way leading to the cessation of suffering': such has been made known by me. In this statement, 'This is the noble truth of the way leading to the cessation of suffering,' there are innumerable nuances, innumerable details, innumerable implications.

"Therefore, bhikkhus, an exertion should be made to understand: 'This is suffering.'… An exertion should be made to understand: 'This is the way leading to the cessation of suffering.'"

20 (10) Actual

"Bhikkhus, these four things are actual, unerring, not otherwise.[385] What four?

"'This is suffering': this, bhikkhus, is actual, unerring, not otherwise. 'This is the origin of suffering': this is actual, unerring, not otherwise. 'This is the cessation of suffering': this is actual, unerring, not otherwise. [431] 'This is the way leading to the cessation of suffering': this is actual, unerring, not otherwise.

"These four things, bhikkhus, are actual, unerring, not otherwise.

"Therefore, bhikkhu, an exertion should be made to understand: 'This is suffering.'... An exertion should be made to understand: 'This is the way leading to the cessation of suffering.'"

III. Koṭigāma

21 (1) Koṭigāma (1)[386]

On one occasion the Blessed One was dwelling among the Vajjians at Koṭigāma. There the Blessed One addressed the bhikkhus thus: "Bhikkhus, it is because of not understanding and not penetrating the Four Noble Truths that you and I have roamed and wandered through this long course of saṃsāra. What four?

"It is, bhikkhus, because of not understanding and not penetrating the noble truth of suffering that you and I have roamed and wandered through this long course of saṃsāra. It is because of not understanding and not penetrating the noble truth of the origin of suffering ... the noble truth of the cessation of suffering ... the noble truth of the way leading to the cessation of suffering [432] that you and I have roamed and wandered through this long course of saṃsāra.

"That noble truth of suffering, bhikkhus, has been understood and penetrated. That noble truth of the origin of suffering has been understood and penetrated. That noble truth of the cessation of suffering has been understood and penetrated. That noble truth of the way leading to the cessation of suffering has been understood and penetrated. Craving for existence has been cut off; the conduit to existence has been destroyed; now there is no more renewed existence."

This is what the Blessed One said. Having said this, the Fortunate One, the Teacher, further said this:

"Because of not seeing as they are
The Four Noble Truths,

We have wandered through the long course
In the various kinds of births.

"Now these truths have been seen;
The conduit to existence is severed;
Cut off is the root of suffering:
Now there is no more renewed existence."

22 (2) *Koṭigāma (2)*[387]

"Bhikkhus, those ascetics or brahmins who do not understand as it really is: 'This is suffering'; who do not understand as it really is: 'This is the origin of suffering'; who do not understand as it really is: 'This is the cessation of suffering'; who do not understand as it really is: 'This is the way leading to the cessation of suffering': these I do not consider to be ascetics among ascetics or brahmins among brahmins, and these venerable ones do not, by realizing it for themselves with direct knowledge, enter and dwell, in this very life, in the goal of asceticism or the goal of brahminhood.

"But, bhikkhus, those ascetics or brahmins who understand these things: these I consider to be ascetics among ascetics and brahmins among brahmins, [433] and these venerable ones, by realizing it for themselves with direct knowledge, enter and dwell, in this very life, in the goal of asceticism and the goal of brahminhood."

This is what the Blessed One said. Having said this, the Fortunate One, the Teacher, further said this:

"Those who do not understand suffering,
Who do not know suffering's origin,
Nor where suffering completely stops,
Where it ceases without remainder;
Who do not know that path
Which leads to suffering's appeasement:
They are devoid of mind's liberation
And also of liberation by wisdom;
Incapable of making an end,
They fare on to birth and aging.

"But those who understand suffering,
Who know too suffering's origin,
And where suffering completely stops,
Where it ceases without remainder;
Who understand that path
Which leads to suffering's appeasement:
They are endowed with mind's liberation
And also with liberation by wisdom;
Being capable of making an end,
They fare no more in birth and aging."

23 (3) The Perfectly Enlightened One

At Sāvatthī. "Bhikkhus, there are these Four Noble Truths. What four? The noble truth of suffering ... the noble truth of the way leading to the cessation of suffering. It is because he has fully awakened to these Four Noble Truths as they really are that the Tathāgata is called the Arahant, the Perfectly Enlightened One.

"Therefore, bhikkhus, an exertion should be made to understand: 'This is suffering.'... An exertion should be made to understand: 'This is the way leading to the cessation of suffering.'"

24 (4) Arahants

At Sāvatthī. "Bhikkhus, whatever Arahants, Perfectly Enlightened Ones, in the past fully awakened to things as they really are, all fully awakened to the Four Noble Truths as they really are. [434] Whatever Arahants, Perfectly Enlightened Ones, in the future will fully awaken to things as they really are, all will fully awaken to the Four Noble Truths as they really are. Whatever Arahants, Perfectly Enlightened Ones, at present have fully awakened to things as they really are, all have fully awakened to the Four Noble Truths as they really are.

"What four? The noble truth of suffering, the noble truth of the origin of suffering, the noble truth of the cessation of suffering, the noble truth of the way leading to the cessation of suffering. Whatever Arahants, Perfectly Enlightened Ones, fully awakened ... will fully awaken ... have fully awakened to things as they really are, all have fully awakened to these Four Noble Truths as they really are.

"Therefore, bhikkhus, an exertion should be made to understand: 'This is suffering.'... An exertion should be made to understand: 'This is the way leading to the cessation of suffering.'"

25 (5) The Destruction of the Taints

"Bhikkhus, I say that the destruction of the taints is for one who knows and sees, not for one who does not know and does not see.[388] For one who knows what, for one who sees what, does the destruction of the taints come about? The destruction of the taints comes about for one who knows and sees: 'This is suffering'; for one who knows and sees: 'This is the origin of suffering'; for one who knows and sees: 'This is the cessation of suffering'; for one who knows and sees: 'This is the way leading to the cessation of suffering.' It is for one who knows thus, for one who sees thus, that the destruction of the taints comes about.

"Therefore, bhikkhus, an exertion should be made to understand: 'This is suffering.'... An exertion should be made to understand: 'This is the way leading to the cessation of suffering.'"

26 (6) Friends

"Bhikkhus, those for whom you have compassion and who think you should be heeded—whether friends or colleagues, relatives or kinsmen—[435] these you should exhort, settle, and establish for making the breakthrough to the Four Noble Truths as they really are.

"What four? The noble truth of suffering, the noble truth of the origin of suffering, the noble truth of the cessation of suffering, the noble truth of the way leading to the cessation of suffering.

"Those for whom you have compassion ... these you should exhort, settle, and establish for making the breakthrough to these Four Noble Truths as they really are.

"Therefore, bhikkhus, an exertion should be made to understand: 'This is suffering.'... An exertion should be made to understand: 'This is the way leading to the cessation of suffering.'"

27 (7) Actual

"Bhikkhus, there are these Four Noble Truths. What four? The noble truth of suffering, the noble truth of the origin of suffering, the noble truth of the cessation of suffering, the noble truth of the way leading to the cessation of suffering. These Four Noble Truths, bhikkhus, are actual, unerring, not otherwise. Therefore they are called noble truths.[389]

"Therefore, bhikkhus, an exertion should be made to understand: 'This is suffering.'... An exertion should be made to understand: 'This is the way leading to the cessation of suffering.'"

28 (8) The World

"Bhikkhus, there are these Four Noble Truths. What four? The noble truth of suffering, the noble truth of the origin of suffering, the noble truth of the cessation of suffering, the noble truth of the way leading to the cessation of suffering. In this world, with its devas, Marā, and Brahmā, in this generation with its ascetics and brahmins, its devas and humans, the Tathāgata is the noble one. Therefore they are called noble truths.

"Therefore, bhikkhus, an exertion should be made to understand: 'This is suffering.'... An exertion should be made to understand: 'This is the way leading to the cessation of suffering.'" [436]

29 (9) To Be Fully Understood

"Bhikkhus, there are these Four Noble Truths. What four? The noble truth of suffering, the noble truth of the origin of suffering, the noble truth of the cessation of suffering, the noble truth of the way leading to the cessation of suffering. These are the Four Noble Truths.

"Of these Four Noble Truths, bhikkhus, there is a noble truth that is to be fully understood; there is a noble truth that is to be abandoned; there is a noble truth that is to be realized; there is a noble truth that is to be developed.

"And what, bhikkhus, is the noble truth that is to be fully understood? The noble truth of suffering is to be fully understood; the noble truth of the origin of suffering is to be abandoned; the noble truth of the cessation of suffering is to be realized; the noble truth of the way leading to the cessation of suffering is to be developed.

"Therefore, bhikkhus, an exertion should be made to understand: 'This is suffering.'… An exertion should be made to understand: 'This is the way leading to the cessation of suffering.'"

30 (10) Gavampati

On one occasion a number of elder bhikkhus were dwelling among the Cetiyans at Sahajāti. Now on that occasion when the elder bhikkhus had returned from their alms round, after their meal they had assembled in the pavilion and were sitting together when this conversation arose: "Friend, does one who sees suffering also see the origin of suffering, also see the cessation of suffering, also see the way leading to the cessation of suffering?"

When this was said, the Venerable Gavampati said to the elder bhikkhus: "Friends, in the presence of the Blessed One I have heard and learnt this: [437] 'Bhikkhus, one who sees suffering also sees the origin of suffering, also sees the cessation of suffering, also sees the way leading to the cessation of suffering. One who sees the origin of suffering also sees suffering, also sees the cessation of suffering, also sees the way leading to the cessation of suffering. One who sees the cessation of suffering also sees suffering, also sees the origin of suffering, also sees the way leading to the cessation of suffering. One who sees the way leading to the cessation of suffering also sees suffering, also sees the origin of suffering, also sees the cessation of suffering.'"[390]

IV. The *Siṃsapā* Grove

31 (1) The Siṃsapā *Grove*

On one occasion the Blessed One was dwelling at Kosambī in a *siṃsapā* grove. Then the Blessed One took up a few *siṃsapā* leaves in his hand and addressed the bhikkhus thus: "What do you think, bhikkhus, which is more numerous: these few *siṃsapā* leaves that I have taken up in my hand or those in the *siṃsapā* grove overhead?" [438]

"Venerable sir, the *siṃsapā* leaves that the Blessed One has taken up in his hand are few, but those in the *siṃsapā* grove overhead are numerous."

"So too, bhikkhus, the things I have directly known but have not taught you are numerous, while the things I have taught you are few. And why, bhikkhus, have I not taught those many things? Because they are unbeneficial, irrelevant to the fundamentals of the holy life, and do not lead to revulsion, to dispassion, to cessation, to peace, to direct knowledge, to enlightenment, to Nibbāna. Therefore I have not taught them.

"And what, bhikkhus, have I taught? I have taught: 'This is suffering'; I have taught: 'This is the origin of suffering'; I have taught: 'This is the cessation of suffering'; I have taught: 'This is the way leading to the cessation of suffering.' And why, bhikkhus, have I taught this? Because this is beneficial, relevant to the fundamentals of the holy life, and leads to revulsion, to dispassion, to cessation, to peace, to direct knowledge, to enlightenment, to Nibbāna. Therefore I have taught this.

"Therefore, bhikkhus, an exertion should be made to understand: 'This is suffering.'... An exertion should be made to understand: 'This is the way leading to the cessation of suffering.'"

32 (2) Acacia

"Bhikkhus, if anyone should speak thus: 'Without having made the breakthrough to the noble truth of suffering as it really is, without having made the breakthrough to the noble truth of the origin of suffering as it really is, without having made the breakthrough to the noble truth of the cessation of suffering as it really is, without having made the breakthrough to the noble truth of the way leading to the cessation of suffering as it really is, I will completely make an end to suffering'—this is impossible.

"Just as, bhikkhus, if someone should speak thus: 'Having made a basket of acacia leaves or of pine needles or of myrobalan leaves,[391] [439] I will bring water or a palm fruit,'[392] this would be impossible; so too, if anyone should speak thus: 'Without having made the breakthrough to the noble truth of suffering as it really is ... I will completely make an end to suffering'—this is impossible.

"But, bhikkhus, if anyone should speak thus: 'Having made the breakthrough to the noble truth of suffering as it really is, having made the breakthrough to the noble truth of the origin of suffering as it really is, having made the breakthrough to the noble truth of the cessation of suffering as it really is, having made the breakthrough to the noble truth of the way leading to the cessation of suffering as it really is, I will completely make an end to suffering'—this is possible.

"Just as, bhikkhus, if someone should speak thus: 'Having made a basket of lotus leaves or of kino leaves or of *māluva* leaves,[393] I will bring water or a palm fruit,' this would be possible; so too, if anyone should speak thus: 'Having made the breakthrough to the noble truth of suffering as it really is … I will completely make an end to suffering'—this is possible.

"Therefore, bhikkhus, an exertion should be made to understand: 'This is suffering.'… An exertion should be made to understand: 'This is the way leading to the cessation of suffering.'"

33 (3) Stick

"Bhikkhus, just as a stick thrown up into the air falls now on its bottom, now on its top, so too as beings roam and wander on, hindered by ignorance and fettered by craving, now they go from this world to the other world, now they come from the other world to this world.[394] For what reason? Because they have not seen the Four Noble Truths. What four? The noble truth of suffering … the noble truth of the way leading to the cessation of suffering. [440]

"Therefore, bhikkhus, an exertion should be made to understand: 'This is suffering.'… An exertion should be made to understand: 'This is the way leading to the cessation of suffering.'"

34 (4) Clothes

"Bhikkhus, if one's clothes or head were ablaze, what should be done about it?"

"Venerable sir, if one's clothes or head were ablaze, to extinguish one's blazing clothes or head one should arouse extraordinary desire, make an extraordinary effort, stir up zeal and enthusiasm, be unremitting, and exercise mindfulness and clear comprehension."[395]

"Bhikkhus, one might look on equanimously at one's blazing clothes or head, paying no attention to them, but so long as one has not made the breakthrough to the Four Noble Truths as they really are, in order to make the breakthrough one should arouse extraordinary desire, make an extraordinary effort, stir up zeal and enthusiasm, be unremitting, and exercise mindfulness and clear comprehension. What four? The noble truth of suffering … the noble truth of the way leading to the cessation of suffering.

"Therefore, bhikkhus, an exertion should be made to understand: 'This is suffering.'… An exertion should be made to understand: 'This is the way leading to the cessation of suffering.'"

35 (5) A Hundred Spears

"Bhikkhus, suppose there were a man with a life span of a hundred years, who could live a hundred years. Someone would say to him: 'Come, good man, in the morning they will strike you with a hundred spears; at noon they will strike you with a hundred spears; in the evening they will strike you with a hundred spears.[396] And you, good man, being struck day after day by three hundred spears will have a life span of a hundred years, will live a hundred years; and then, after a hundred years have passed, you will make the breakthrough to the Four Noble Truths, to which you had not broken through earlier.' [441]

"It is fitting, bhikkhus, for a clansman intent on his good to accept the offer. For what reason? Because this saṃsāra is without discoverable beginning; a first point cannot be discerned of blows by spears, blows by swords, blows by axes. And even though this may be so, bhikkhus, I do not say that the breakthrough to the Four Noble Truths is accompanied by suffering or displeasure. Rather, the breakthrough to the Four Noble Truths is accompanied only by happiness and joy. What four? The noble truth of suffering … the noble truth of the way leading to the cessation of suffering.

"Therefore, bhikkhus, an exertion should be made to understand: 'This is suffering.'… An exertion should be made to understand: 'This is the way leading to the cessation of suffering.'"

36 (6) Creatures

"Bhikkhus, suppose a man were to cut up whatever grass, sticks, branches, and foliage there is in this Jambudipa and collect them into a single heap. Having done so, he would impale the large creatures in the ocean on the large stakes, the middle-sized creatures on the middle-sized stakes, and the small creatures on the small stakes. Still, bhikkhus, the gross creatures in the ocean would not be exhausted even after all the grass, sticks, branches, and foliage in Jambudīpa had been used up and exhausted. The small creatures in the ocean that could not easily be impaled on stakes would be even more numerous than this. For what reason? [442] Because of the minuteness of their bodies.

"So vast, bhikkhus, is the plane of misery. The person who is accomplished in view, freed from that vast plane of misery, understands as it really is: 'This is suffering.'... 'This is the way leading to the cessation of suffering.'

"Therefore, bhikkhus, an exertion should be made to understand: 'This is suffering.'... An exertion should be made to understand: 'This is the way leading to the cessation of suffering.'"

37 (7) The Sun (1)

"Bhikkhus, this is the forerunner and precursor of the rising of the sun, that is, the dawn. So too, bhikkhus, for a bhikkhu this is the forerunner and precursor of the breakthrough to the Four Noble Truths as they really are, that is, right view. It is to be expected that a bhikkhu with right view[397] will understand as it really is: 'This is suffering.'... 'This is the way leading to the cessation of suffering.'

"Therefore, bhikkhus, an exertion should be made to understand: 'This is suffering.'... An exertion should be made to understand: 'This is the way leading to the cessation of suffering.'"

38 (8) The Sun (2)

"Bhikkhus, so long as the sun and moon have not arisen in the world, for just so long there is no manifestation of great light and radiance, but then blinding darkness prevails, a dense mass of darkness; for just so long day and night are not discerned, the month and fortnight are not discerned, the seasons and the year are not discerned.

"But, bhikkhus, when the sun and moon arise in the world, then there is the manifestation of great light and radiance; [443]

then there is no blinding darkness, no dense mass of darkness; then day and night are discerned, the month and fortnight are discerned, the seasons and year are discerned.

"So too, bhikkhus, so long as a Tathāgata has not arisen in the world, an Arahant, a Perfectly Enlightened One, for just so long there is no manifestation of great light and radiance, but then blinding darkness prevails, a dense mass of darkness; for just so long there is no explaining, teaching, proclaiming, establishing, disclosing, analysing, or elucidating of the Four Noble Truths.

"But, bhikkhus, when a Tathāgata arises in the world, an Arahant, a Perfectly Enlightened One, then there is the manifestation of great light and radiance; then no blinding darkness prevails, no dense mass of darkness; then there is the explaining, teaching, proclaiming, establishing, disclosing, analysing, and elucidating of the Four Noble Truths. What four? The noble truth of suffering ... the noble truth of the way leading to the cessation of suffering.

"Therefore, bhikkhus, an exertion should be made to understand: 'This is suffering.'... An exertion should be made to understand: 'This is the way leading to the cessation of suffering.'"

39 (9) Indra's Pillar

"Bhikkhus, those ascetics or brahmins who do not understand as it really is 'This is suffering' ... 'This is the way leading to the cessation of suffering'—they look up at the face of another ascetic or brahmin, thinking: 'This worthy is surely one who really knows, who really sees.'

"Suppose, bhikkhus, a tuft of cotton wool or kapok, light, wafted by the wind, had settled on an even piece of ground. [444] An easterly wind would drive it westward; a westerly wind would drive it eastward; a northerly wind would drive it southward; a southerly wind would drive it northward. For what reason? Because of the lightness of the tuft.

"So too, bhikkhus, those ascetics or brahmins who do not understand as it really is 'This is suffering' ... 'This is the way leading to the cessation of suffering'—they look up at the face of another ascetic or brahmin, thinking: 'This worthy is surely one who really knows, who really sees.' For what reason? Because they have not seen the Four Noble Truths.

"But, bhikkhus, those ascetics or brahmins who understand as it really is 'This is suffering' … 'This is the way leading to the cessation of suffering'—they do not look up at the face of another ascetic or brahmin, thinking: 'This worthy is surely one who really knows, who really sees.'

"Suppose, bhikkhus, there was an iron pillar or an Indra's pillar[398] with a deep base, securely planted, immobile, unshaking. Even if a forceful blast of wind comes—whether from the east, the west, the north, or the south—that pillar would not shake, quake, or tremble. For what reason? Because the pillar has a deep base and is securely planted.

"So too, bhikkhus, those ascetics or brahmins who understand as it really is 'This is suffering' … 'This is the way leading to the cessation of suffering'—they do not look up at the face of another ascetic or brahmin, thinking: 'This worthy is surely one who really knows, who really sees.' For what reason? Because, bhikkhus, they have clearly seen the Four Noble Truths. What four? [445] The noble truth of suffering … the noble truth of the way leading to the cessation of suffering.

"Therefore, bhikkhus, an exertion should be made to understand: 'This is suffering.'… An exertion should be made to understand: 'This is the way leading to the cessation of suffering.'"

40 (10) Seeking an Argument

"Bhikkhus, if any bhikkhu understands as it really is: 'This is suffering' … 'This is the way leading to the cessation of suffering,' and then an ascetic or brahmin comes along—whether from the east, the west, the north, or the south—seeking an argument, searching for an argument, thinking: 'I will refute his thesis,' it is impossible that he could make that bhikkhu shake, quake, or tremble.

"Suppose, bhikkhus,[399] there was a stone column sixteen yards long: an eight yards' portion of it would be sunk in the ground, an eight yards' portion above ground. Even if a forceful blast of wind comes along—whether from the east, the west, the north, or the south—the column would not shake, quake, or tremble. For what reason? Because it has a deep base and is securely planted.

"So too, bhikkhus, if any bhikkhu understands as it really is

'This is suffering' ... 'This is the way leading to the cessation of suffering,' [446] and then an ascetic or a brahmin comes along ... it is impossible that he could make that bhikkhu shake, quake, or tremble. For what reason? Because he has clearly seen the Four Noble Truths. What four? The noble truth of suffering ... the noble truth of the way leading to the cessation of suffering.

"Therefore, bhikkhus, an exertion should be made to understand: 'This is suffering.'... An exertion should be made to understand: 'This is the way leading to the cessation of suffering.'"

V. The Precipice

41 (1) Reflection about the World

On one occasion the Blessed One was dwelling at Rājagaha in the Bamboo Grove, the Squirrel Sanctuary. There the Blessed One addressed the bhikkhus thus:

"Bhikkhus, once in the past a certain man set out from Rājagaha and went to the Sumāgadhā Lotus Pond, thinking: 'I will reflect about the world.'[400] [447] He then sat down on the bank of the Sumāgadhā Lotus Pond reflecting about the world. Then, bhikkhus, the man saw a four-division army entering a lotus stalk on the bank of the pond. Having seen this, he thought: 'I must be mad! I must be insane! I've seen something that doesn't exist in the world.' The man returned to the city and informed a great crowd of people: 'I must be mad, sirs! I must be insane! I've seen something that doesn't exist in the world.'

"[They said to him:] 'But how is it, good man, that you are mad? How are you insane? And what have you seen that doesn't exist in the world?'

"'Here, sirs, I left Rājagaha and approached the Sumāgadhā Lotus Pond ... (*as above*) ... I saw a four-division army entering a lotus stalk on the bank of the pond. That's why I'm mad, that's why I'm insane, and that's what I've seen that doesn't exist in the world.'

"'Surely you're mad, good man! Surely you're insane! And what you have seen doesn't exist in the world.'

"Nevertheless, bhikkhus, what that man saw was actually real, not unreal.[401] Once in the past the devas and the asuras were arrayed for battle. In that battle the devas won and the asuras were defeated. In their defeat, [448] the asuras were frightened and entered the asura city through the lotus stalk, to the bewilderment of the devas.

"Therefore, bhikkhus, do not reflect about the world, thinking: 'The world is eternal' or 'The world is not eternal'; or 'The world is finite' or 'The world is infinite'; or 'The soul and the body are the same' or 'The soul is one thing, the body is another'; or 'The Tathāgata exists after death,' or 'The Tathāgata does not exist after death,' or 'The Tathāgata both exists and does not exist after death,' or 'The Tathāgata neither exists nor does not exist after death.' For what reason? Because, bhikkhus, this reflection is unbeneficial, irrelevant to the fundamentals of the holy life, and does not lead to revulsion, to dispassion, to cessation, to peace, to direct knowledge, to enlightenment, to Nibbāna.

"When you reflect, bhikkhus, you should reflect: 'This is suffering'; you should reflect: 'This is the origin of suffering'; you should reflect: 'This is the cessation of suffering'; you should reflect: 'This is the way leading to the cessation of suffering.' For what reason? Because, bhikkhus, this reflection is beneficial, relevant to the fundamentals of the holy life, and leads to revulsion, to dispassion, to cessation, to peace, to direct knowledge, to enlightenment, to Nibbāna.

"Therefore, bhikkhus, an exertion should be made to understand: 'This is suffering.'... An exertion should be made to understand: 'This is the way leading to the cessation of suffering.'"

42 (2) The Precipice

On one occasion the Blessed One was dwelling at Rājagaha on Mount Vulture Peak. Then the Blessed One addressed the bhikkhus thus: "Come, bhikkhus, let us go to Paṭibhāna Peak for the day's abiding."

"Yes, venerable sir," those bhikkhus replied. [449] Then the Blessed One, together with a number of bhikkhus, went to Paṭibhāna Peak. A certain bhikkhu saw the steep precipice off Paṭibhāna Peak and said to the Blessed One: "That precipice is indeed steep, venerable sir; that precipice is extremely frightful. But is there, venerable sir, any other precipice steeper and more frightful than that one?"

"There is, bhikkhu."

"But what, venerable sir, is that precipice steeper and more frightful than that one?"

"Those ascetics and brahmins, bhikkhu, who do not understand as it really is: 'This is suffering'; who do not understand as it really is: 'This is the origin of suffering'; who do not understand as it really is: 'This is the cessation of suffering'; who do not understand as it really is: 'This is the way leading to the cessation of suffering'—they delight in volitional formations that lead to birth, in volitional formations that lead to aging, in volitional formations that lead to death, in volitional formations that lead to sorrow, lamentation, pain, displeasure, and despair. Delighting in such volitional formations, they generate volitional formations that lead to birth, generate volitional formations that lead to aging, generate volitional formations that lead to death, generate volitional formations that lead to sorrow, lamentation, pain, displeasure, and despair. Having generated such volitional formations, they tumble down the precipice of birth, tumble down the precipice of aging, tumble down the precipice of death, tumble down the precipice of sorrow, lamentation, pain, displeasure, and despair. They are not freed from birth, aging, and death; not freed from sorrow, lamentation, pain, displeasure, and despair; not freed from suffering, I say.[402] [450]

"But, bhikkhu, those ascetics and brahmins who understand as it really is: 'This is suffering' ... 'This is the way leading to the cessation of suffering'—they do not delight in volitional formations that lead to birth, nor in volitional formations that lead to aging, nor in volitional formations that lead to death, nor in volitional formations that lead to sorrow, lamentation, pain, displeasure, and despair. Not delighting in such volitional formations, they do not generate volitional formations that lead to birth, nor generate volitional formations that lead to aging, nor generate volitional formations that lead to death, nor generate volitional formations that lead to sorrow, lamentation, pain, displeasure, and despair. Not having generated such volitional formations, they do not tumble down the precipice of birth, nor tumble down the precipice of aging, nor tumble down the precipice of death, nor tumble down the precipice of sorrow, lamentation, pain, displeasure, and despair. They are freed from birth, aging, and death; freed from sorrow, lamentation, pain, displeasure, and despair; freed from suffering, I say.

"Therefore, bhikkhus, an exertion should be made to understand: 'This is suffering.'... An exertion should be made to understand: 'This is the way leading to the cessation of suffering.'"

43 (3) The Great Conflagration

"Bhikkhus, there exists a hell named the Great Conflagration. There, whatever form one sees with the eye is undesirable, [451] never desirable; unlovely, never lovely; disagreeable, never agreeable.[403] Whatever sound one hears with the ear ... Whatever odour one smells with the nose ... Whatever taste one savours with the tongue ... Whatever tactile object one feels with the body ... Whatever mental phenomenon one cognizes with the mind is undesirable, never desirable; unlovely, never lovely; disagreeable, never agreeable."

When this was said, a certain bhikkhu said to the Blessed One: "That conflagration, venerable sir, is indeed terrible; that conflagration is indeed very terrible. But is there, venerable sir, any other conflagration more terrible and frightful than that one?"

"There is, bhikkhu."

"But what, venerable sir, is that conflagration more terrible and frightful than that one?"

"Those ascetics or brahmins, bhikkhu, who do not understand as it really is: 'This is suffering' ... 'This is the way leading to the cessation of suffering'—they delight in volitional formations that lead to birth, in volitional formations that lead to aging, in volitional formations that lead to death, in volitional formations that lead to sorrow, lamentation, pain, displeasure, and despair. Delighting in such volitional formations, they generate volitional formations that lead to birth, generate volitional formations that lead to aging, generate volitional formations that lead to death, generate volitional formations that lead to sorrow, lamentation, pain, displeasure, and despair. Having generated such volitional formations, they are burnt by the conflagration of birth, burnt by the conflagration of aging, burnt by the conflagration of death, burnt by the conflagration of sorrow, lamentation, pain, displeasure, and despair. They are not freed from birth, aging, and death; not freed from sorrow, lamentation, pain, displeasure, and despair; not freed from suffering, I say.

"But, bhikkhu, those ascetics and brahmins who understand as it really is: 'This is suffering' ... 'This is the way leading to the cessation of suffering'—they do not delight in volitional formations that lead to birth, nor in volitional formations that lead to aging, nor in volitional formations that lead to death, nor in volitional formations that lead to sorrow, lamentation, pain, displeasure, and despair. Not delighting in such volitional formations, they do not generate volitional formations that lead to birth, nor generate volitional formations that lead to aging, nor generate volitional formations that lead to death, nor generate volitional formations that lead to sorrow, lamentation, pain, displeasure, and despair. Not having generated such volitional formations, they are not burnt by the conflagration of birth, nor burnt by the conflagration of aging, nor burnt by the conflagration of death, nor burnt by the conflagration of sorrow, lamentation, pain, displeasure, and despair. They are freed from birth, [452] aging, and death; freed from sorrow, lamentation, pain, displeasure, and despair; freed from suffering, I say.

"Therefore, bhikkhus, an exertion should be made to understand: 'This is suffering.'... An exertion should be made to understand: 'This is the way leading to the cessation of suffering.'"

44 (4) Peaked House

"Bhikkhus, if anyone should speak thus: 'Without having made the breakthrough to the noble truth of suffering as it really is, without having made the breakthrough to the noble truth of the origin of suffering as it really is, without having made the breakthrough to the noble truth of the cessation of suffering as it really is, without having made the breakthrough to the noble truth of the way leading to the cessation of suffering as it really is, I will completely make an end to suffering'—this is impossible.

"Just as, bhikkhus, if anyone should speak thus, 'Without having built the lower storey of a peaked house, I will erect the upper storey,' this would be impossible; so too, if anyone should speak thus: 'Without having made the breakthrough to the noble truth of suffering as it really is ... I will completely make an end to suffering'—this is impossible.

"But, bhikkhus, if anyone should speak thus: 'Having made the breakthrough to the noble truth of suffering as it really is, having made the breakthrough to the noble truth of the origin of suffering as it really is, having made the breakthrough to the noble truth of the cessation of suffering as it really is, having made the breakthrough to the noble truth of the way leading to the cessation of suffering as it really is, I will completely make an end to suffering'—this is possible.

"Just as, bhikkhus, if anyone should speak thus: 'Having built the lower storey of a peaked house, I will erect the upper storey,' this would be possible; so too, if anyone should speak thus: 'Having made the breakthrough to the noble truth of suffering as it really is ... I will completely make an end to suffering'—this is possible. [453]

"Therefore, bhikkhus, an exertion should be made to understand: 'This is suffering.'... An exertion should be made to understand: 'This is the way leading to the cessation of suffering.'"

45 (5) The Hair[404]

On one occasion the Blessed One was dwelling at Vesālī in the Great Wood in the Hall with the Peaked Roof. Then, in the morning, the Venerable Ānanda dressed and, taking bowl and robe, entered Vesālī for alms. The Venerable Ānanda saw a number of Licchavi youths practising archery in the training hall, shooting arrows from a distance through a very small keyhole, head through butt,[405] without missing. When he saw this, the thought occurred to him: "These Licchavi youths are indeed trained! These Licchavi youths are indeed well trained, in that they shoot arrows from a distance through a very small keyhole, head through butt, without missing."

Then, when the Venerable Ānanda had walked for alms in Vesālī and had returned from his alms round, after his meal he approached the Blessed One, paid homage to him, sat down to one side, and reported what he had seen. [454]

[The Blessed One said:] "What do you think, Ānanda, which is more difficult and challenging: to shoot arrows from a distance through a very small keyhole, head through butt, without missing, or to pierce with the arrowhead the tip of a hair split into seven strands?"[406]

"It is more difficult and challenging, venerable sir, to pierce with the arrowhead the tip of a hair split into seven strands."

"But, Ānanda, they pierce something even more difficult to

pierce who pierce as it really is: 'This is suffering' ...; who pierce as it really is: 'This is the way leading to the cessation of suffering.'

"Therefore, Ānanda, an exertion should be made to understand: 'This is suffering.'... An exertion should be made to understand: 'This is the way leading to the cessation of suffering.'"

46 (6) Darkness

"Bhikkhus, there are world interstices, vacant and abysmal[407] regions of blinding darkness and gloom, where the light of the sun and moon, so powerful and mighty, does not reach."

When this was said, a certain bhikkhu said to the Blessed One: "That darkness, venerable sir, is indeed great; that darkness is indeed very great. But is there, venerable sir, any other darkness greater and more frightful than that one?"

"There is, bhikkhu."

"But what, venerable sir, is that darkness greater and more frightful than that one?"

"Those ascetics and brahmins, bhikkhu, who do not understand as it really is: 'This is suffering'; [455] who do not understand as it really is: 'This is the origin of suffering'; who do not understand as it really is: 'This is the cessation of suffering'; who do not understand as it really is: 'This is the way leading to the cessation of suffering'—they delight in volitional formations that lead to birth, in volitional formations that lead to aging, in volitional formations that lead to death, in volitional formations that lead to sorrow, lamentation, pain, displeasure, and despair. Delighting in such volitional formations, they generate volitional formations that lead to birth, generate volitional formations that lead to aging, generate volitional formations that lead to death, generate volitional formations that lead to sorrow, lamentation, pain, displeasure, and despair. Having generated such volitional formations, they tumble into the darkness of birth, tumble into the darkness of aging, tumble into the darkness of death, tumble into the darkness of sorrow, lamentation, pain, displeasure, and despair. They are not freed from birth, aging, and death; not freed from sorrow, lamentation, pain, displeasure, and despair; not freed from suffering, I say.

"But, bhikkhu, those ascetics and brahmins who understand as it really is: 'This is suffering' ... 'This is the way leading to the cessation of suffering'—they do not delight in volitional formations that lead to birth, nor in volitional formations that lead to aging, nor in volitional formations that lead to death, nor in volitional formations that lead to sorrow, lamentation, pain, displeasure, and despair. Not delighting in such volitional formations, they do not generate volitional formations that lead to birth, nor generate volitional formations that lead to aging, nor generate volitional formations that lead to death, nor generate volitional formations that lead to sorrow, lamentation, pain, displeasure, and despair. Not having generated such volitional formations, they do not tumble into the darkness of birth, nor tumble into the darkness of aging, nor tumble into the darkness of death, nor tumble into the darkness of sorrow, lamentation, pain, displeasure, and despair. They are freed from birth, aging, and death; freed from sorrow, lamentation, pain, displeasure, and despair; freed from suffering, I say.

"Therefore, bhikkhus, an exertion should be made to understand: 'This is suffering.'... An exertion should be made to understand: 'This is the way leading to the cessation of suffering.'"

47 (7) Yoke with a Hole (1) [408]

"Bhikkhus, suppose a man would throw a yoke with a single hole into the great ocean, and there was a blind turtle which would come to the surface once every hundred years. What do you think, bhikkhus, would that blind turtle, coming to the surface once every hundred years, insert its neck into that yoke with a single hole?" [456]

"If it would ever do so, venerable sir, it would be only after a very long time."

"Sooner, I say, would that blind turtle, coming to the surface once every hundred years, insert its neck into that yoke with a single hole than the fool who has gone once to the nether world [would regain] the human state. For what reason? Because here, bhikkhus, there is no conduct guided by the Dhamma, no righteous conduct, no wholesome activity, no meritorious activity. Here there prevails mutual devouring, the devouring of the weak. For what reason? Because, bhikkhus, they have not seen the Four Noble Truths. What four? The noble truth of suffering ... the noble truth of the way leading to the cessation of suffering.

"Therefore, bhikkhus, an exertion should be made to understand: 'This is suffering.'... An exertion should be made to understand: 'This is the way leading to the cessation of suffering.'"

48 (8) Yoke with a Hole (2)

"Bhikkhus, suppose that this great earth had become one mass of water, and a man would throw a yoke with a single hole upon it. An easterly wind would drive it westward; a westerly wind would drive it eastward; a northerly wind would drive it southward; a southerly wind would drive it northward. There was a blind turtle which would come to the surface once every hundred years. What do you think, bhikkhus, would that blind turtle, coming to the surface once every hundred years, [457] insert its neck into that yoke with a single hole?"

"It would be by chance, venerable sir, that that blind turtle, coming to the surface once every hundred years, would insert its neck into that yoke with a single hole."

"So too, bhikkhus, it is by chance[409] that one obtains the human state; by chance that a Tathāgata, an Arahant, a Perfectly Enlightened One arises in the world; by chance that the Dhamma and Discipline proclaimed by the Tathāgata shines in the world.

"You have obtained that human state, bhikkhus; a Tathāgata, an Arahant, a Perfectly Enlightened One has arisen in the world; the Dhamma and Discipline proclaimed by the Tathāgata shines in the world.

"Therefore, bhikkhus, an exertion should be made to understand: 'This is suffering.'... An exertion should be made to understand: 'This is the way leading to the cessation of suffering.'"

49 (9) Sineru (1)

"Bhikkhus, suppose that a man would place on Sineru, the king of mountains, seven grains of gravel the size of mung beans.[410] What do you think, bhikkhus, which is more: the seven grains of gravel the size of mung beans that have been placed there or Sineru, the king of mountains?"

"Venerable sir, Sineru, the king of mountains, is more. The seven grains of gravel the size of mung beans are trifling. Compared to Sineru, the king of mountains, the seven grains of gravel the size of mung beans are not calculable, do not bear comparison, do not amount even to a fraction." [458]

"So too, bhikkhus, for a noble disciple, a person accomplished in view who has made the breakthrough, the suffering that has been utterly destroyed and eliminated is more, while that which remains is trifling. Compared to the former mass of suffering that has been destroyed and eliminated, the latter is not calculable, does not bear comparison, does not amount even to a fraction, as there is a maximum of seven more lives. He is one who understands as it really is: 'This is suffering' ... 'This is the way leading to the cessation of suffering.'

"Therefore, bhikkhus, an exertion should be made to understand: 'This is suffering.'... An exertion should be made to understand: 'This is the way leading to the cessation of suffering.'"

50 (10) Sineru (2)

"Bhikkhus, suppose that Sineru, the king of mountains, would be destroyed and eliminated except for seven grains of gravel the size of mung beans.[411] What do you think, bhikkhus, which is more: the portion of Sineru, the king of mountains, that has been destroyed and eliminated or the seven grains of gravel the size of mung beans that remain?"

"Venerable sir, the portion of Sineru, the king of mountains, that has been destroyed and eliminated is more. The seven grains of gravel the size of mung beans that remain are trifling. Compared to the portion of Sineru that would be destroyed and eliminated, the seven grains of gravel the size of mung beans that remain are not calculable, do not bear comparison, do not amount even to a fraction."

"So too, bhikkhus, for a noble disciple, a person accomplished in view who has made the breakthrough, [459] the suffering that has been utterly destroyed and eliminated is more, while that which remains is trifling. Compared to the former mass of suffering that has been destroyed and eliminated, the latter is not calculable, does not bear comparison, does not amount even to a fraction, as there is a maximum of seven more lives. He is one who understands as it really is: 'This is suffering' ... 'This is the way leading to the cessation of suffering.'

"Therefore, bhikkhus, an exertion should be made to understand: 'This is suffering.'... An exertion should be made to understand: 'This is the way leading to the cessation of suffering.'"

VI. The Breakthrough

51 (1) The Fingernail[412]

Then the Blessed One took up a little bit of soil in his fingernail and addressed the bhikkhus thus:

"Bhikkhus, what do you think which is more: the little bit of soil that I have taken up in my fingernail or this great earth?"

"Venerable sir, the great earth is more. The little bit of soil that the Blessed One has taken up in his fingernail is trifling. Compared to the great earth, that little bit of soil is not calculable, does not bear comparison, does not amount even to a fraction." [460]

"So too, bhikkhus, for a noble disciple, a person accomplished in view who has made the breakthrough, the suffering that has been destroyed and eliminated is more, while that which remains is trifling. Compared to the former mass of suffering that has been destroyed and eliminated, the latter is not calculable, does not bear comparison, does not amount even to a fraction, as there is a maximum of seven more lives. He is one who understands as it really is: 'This is suffering' ... 'This is the way leading to the cessation of suffering.'

"Therefore, bhikkhus, an exertion should be made to understand: 'This is suffering.'... An exertion should be made to understand: 'This is the way leading to the cessation of suffering.'"

52 (2) The Pond

"Bhikkhus, suppose there were a pond fifty *yojanas* long, fifty *yojanas* wide, and fifty *yojanas* deep, full of water, overflowing so that a crow could drink from it, and a man would draw out some water from it on the tip of a blade of *kusa* grass. What do you think, bhikkhus, which is more: the water drawn out on the tip of the blade of *kusa* grass or the water in the pond?"

"Venerable sir, the water in the pond is more. The water drawn out on the tip of the blade of *kusa* grass is trifling. Compared to the water in the pond, the water drawn out on the tip of the blade of *kusa* grass is not calculable, does not bear comparison, does not amount even to a fraction."

"So too, bhikkhus, for a noble disciple ... Therefore an exertion should be made...."

53 (3) *Water at the Confluence (1)*

"Bhikkhus, suppose that in the place where these great rivers meet and converge—that is, the Ganges, the Yamunā, the Aciravatī, the Sarabhū, and the Mahī—a man would draw out two or three drops of water. [461] What do you think, bhikkhus, which is more: these two or three drops of water that have been drawn out or the water at the confluence?"

"Venerable sir, the water at the confluence is more. The two or three drops of water that have been drawn out are trifling. Compared to the water at the confluence, the two or three drops of water that have been drawn out are not calculable, do not bear comparison, do not amount even to a fraction."

"So too, bhikkhus, for a noble disciple ... Therefore an exertion should be made...."

54 (4) *Water at the Confluence (2)*

"Bhikkhus, suppose that in the place where these great rivers meet and converge—that is, the Ganges, the Yamunā, the Aciravatī, the Sarabhū, and the Mahī—their water would be destroyed and eliminated except for two or three drops. What do you think, bhikkhus, which is more: the water at the confluence that has been destroyed and eliminated or the two or three drops of water that remain?"

"Venerable sir, the water at the confluence that has been destroyed and eliminated is more; the two or three drops of water that remain are trifling. Compared to the water at the confluence that has been destroyed and eliminated, the two or three drops of water that remain are trifling; they are not calculable, do not bear comparison, do not amount even to a fraction."

"So too, bhikkhus, for a noble disciple ... Therefore an exertion should be made...." [462]

55 (5) The Earth (1)

"Bhikkhus, suppose that a man would place seven little balls of clay the size of jujube kernels on the great earth. What do you think, bhikkhus, which is more: those seven little balls of clay the size of jujube kernels that have been placed there or the great earth?"

"Venerable sir, the great earth is more. The seven little balls of clay the size of jujube kernels are trifling. Compared to the great earth, those seven little balls of clay the size of jujube kernals are trifling; they are not calculable, do not bear comparison, do not amount even to a fraction."

"So too, bhikkhus, for a noble disciple ... Therefore an exertion should be made...."

56 (6) The Earth (2)

"Bhikkhus, suppose that the great earth would be destroyed and eliminated except for seven little balls of clay the size of jujube kernels. What do you think, bhikkhus, which is more: the great earth that has been destroyed and eliminated or the seven little balls of clay the size of jujube kernels that remain?"

"Venerable sir, the great earth that has been destroyed and eliminated is more. The seven little balls of clay the size of jujube kernels that remain are trifling. Compared to the great earth that has been destroyed and eliminated, the seven little balls of clay the size of jujube kernels that remain are not calculable, do not bear comparison, do not amount even to a fraction."

"So too, bhikkhus, for a noble disciple ... Therefore an exertion should be made...." [463]

57 (7) The Ocean (1)

"Bhikkhus, suppose that a man would draw out two or three drops of water from the great ocean. What do you think, bhikkhus, which is more: the two or three drops of water that have been drawn out or the water in the great ocean?"

"Venerable sir, the water in the great ocean is more. The two or three drops of water that have been drawn out are trifling. Compared to the water in the great ocean, the two or three drops of water that have been drawn out are not calculable, do not bear comparison, do not amount even to a fraction."

"So too, bhikkhus, for a noble disciple ... Therefore an exertion should be made...."

58 (8) The Ocean (2)

"Bhikkhus, suppose that the great ocean would be destroyed and eliminated except for two or three drops of water. What do you think, bhikkhus, which is more: the water in the great ocean that has been destroyed and eliminated or the two or three drops of water that remain?"

"Venerable sir, the water in the great ocean that has been destroyed and eliminated is more. The two or three drops of water that remain are trifling. Compared to the water that has been destroyed and eliminated, the two or three drops of water that remain are not calculable, do not bear comparison, do not amount even to a fraction."

"So too, bhikkhus, for a noble disciple ... Therefore an exertion should be made...." [464]

59 (9) The Mountain (1)

"Bhikkhus, suppose that a man would place on the Himalayas, the king of mountains, seven grains of gravel the size of mustard seeds. What do you think, bhikkhus, which is more: the seven grains of gravel the size of mustard seeds that have been placed there or the Himalayas, the king of mountains?"

"Venerable sir, the Himalayas, the king of mountains, is more. The seven grains of gravel the size of mustard seeds are trifling. Compared to the Himalayas, the king of mountains, the seven grains of gravel the size of mustard seeds are not calculable, do not bear comparison, do not amount even to a fraction."

"So too, bhikkhus, for a noble disciple ... Therefore an exertion should be made...."

60 (10) The Mountain (2)

"Bhikkhus, suppose that the Himalayas, the king of mountains, would be destroyed and eliminated except for seven grains of gravel the size of mustard seeds. What do you think, bhikkhus, which is more: the portion of the Himalayas, the king of mountains, that has been destroyed and eliminated or the seven grains of gravel the size of mustard seeds that remain?"

"Venerable sir, the portion of the Himalayas, the king of mountains, that has been destroyed and eliminated is more. The seven grains of gravel the size of mustard seeds that remain are trifling. Compared to the portion of the Himalayas, the king of mountains, that has been destroyed and eliminated, the seven grains of gravel the size of mustard seeds that remain are not calculable, do not bear comparison, do not amount even to a fraction."

"So too, bhikkhus, for a noble disciple, a person accomplished in view who has made the breakthrough, [465] the suffering that has been destroyed and eliminated is more, while that which remains is trifling. Compared to the former mass of suffering that has been destroyed and eliminated, the latter is not calculable, does not bear comparison, does not amount even to a fraction, as there is a maximum of seven more lives. He is one who understands as it really is: 'This is suffering' … 'This is the way leading to the cessation of suffering.'

"Therefore, bhikkhus, an exertion should be made to understand: 'This is suffering.'… An exertion should be made to understand: 'This is the way leading to the cessation of suffering.'"

VII. First Raw Grain Repetition Series[413]

61 (1) Elsewhere

Then the Blessed One took up a little bit of soil in his fingernail and addressed the bhikkhus thus:

"What do you think, bhikkhus, which is more: the little bit of soil in my fingernail or the great earth?" [466]

"Venerable sir, the great earth is more. The little bit of soil that the Blessed One has taken up in his fingernail is trifling. Compared to the great earth, that little bit of soil is not calculable, does not bear comparison, does not amount even to a fraction."

"So too, bhikkhus, those beings are few who are reborn among human beings. But those beings are more numerous who are reborn elsewhere than among human beings.[414] For what reason? Because, bhikkhus, they have not seen the Four Noble Truths.

What four? The noble truth of suffering, the noble truth of the origin of suffering, the noble truth of the cessation of suffering, the noble truth of the way leading to the cessation of suffering.

"Therefore, bhikkhus, an exertion should be made to understand: 'This is suffering.'… An exertion should be made to understand: 'This is the way leading to the cessation of suffering.'"

62 (2) Outlying Countries

Then the Blessed One took up a little bit of soil in his fingernail and addressed the bhikkhus thus.…

"So too, bhikkhus, those beings are few who are reborn in the middle countries. But those beings are more numerous who are reborn in the outlying countries among the uncultured barbarians.…" [467]

63 (3) Wisdom

… "So too, bhikkhus, those beings are few who possess the noble eye of wisdom. But these beings are more numerous, who are immersed in ignorance and confused.…"

64 (4) Wines and Liquors

… "So too, bhikkhus, those beings are few who abstain from wine, liquors, and intoxicants that are a basis for negligence. But these beings are more numerous who do not abstain from wines, liquors, and intoxicants that are a basis for negligence.…"

65 (5) Water-Born

… "So too, bhikkhus, those beings are few who are born on high ground. But these beings are more numerous who are born in water.…"

66 (6) Who Honour Mother

… "So too, bhikkhus, those beings are few who honour their mother. But these beings are more numerous who do not honour their mother.…"

67 (7) Who Honour Father

… "So too, bhikkhus, those beings are few who honour their father. But these beings are more numerous who do not honour their father…." [468]

68 (8) Who Honour Ascetics

… "So too, bhikkhus, those beings are few who honour ascetics. But these beings are more numerous who do not honour ascetics…."

69 (9) Who Honour Brahmins

… "So too, bhikkhus, those beings are few who honour brahmins. But these beings are more numerous who do not honour brahmins…."

70 (10) Who Respect Elders

… "So too, bhikkhus, those beings are few who respect their elders in the family. But these beings are more numerous who do not respect their elders in the family…."

VIII. Second Raw Grain Repetition Series

71 (1) Killing Living Beings[415]

… "So too, bhikkhus, those beings are few who abstain from the destruction of life. But these beings are more numerous who do not abstain from the destruction of life…." [469]

72 (2) Taking What Is Not Given

… "So too, bhikkhus, those beings are few who abstain from taking what is not given. But these beings are more numerous who do not abstain from taking what is not given…."

73 (3) Sexual Misconduct

… "So too, bhikkhus, those beings are few who abstain from sexual misconduct. But these beings are more numerous who do not abstain from sexual misconduct…."

74 (4) False Speech

… "So too, bhikkhus, those beings are few who abstain from false speech. But these beings are more numerous who do not abstain from false speech…."

75 (5) Divisive Speech

… "So too, bhikkhus, those beings are few who abstain from divisive speech. But these beings are more numerous who do not abstain from divisive speech…."

76 (6) Harsh Speech

… "So too, bhikkhus, those beings are few who abstain from harsh speech. But these beings are more numerous who do not abstain from harsh speech…."

77 (7) Idle Chatter

… "So too, bhikkhus, those beings are few who abstain from idle chatter. But these beings are more numerous who do not abstain from idle chatter…." [470]

78 (8) Seed Life[416]

… "So too, bhikkhus, those beings are few who abstain from damaging seed and plant life. But these beings are more numerous who do not abstain from damaging seed and plant life…."

79 (9) Improper Times

… "So too, bhikkhus, those beings are few who abstain from

eating at improper times. But these beings are more numerous who do not abstain from eating at improper times...."

80 (10) Scents and Unguents

... "So too, bhikkhus, those beings are few who abstain from wearing garlands, embellishing themselves with scents, and beautifying themselves with unguents. But these beings are more numerous who do not so abstain...."

IX. Third Raw Grain Repetition Series

81 (1) Dancing and Singing

... "So too, bhikkhus, those beings are few who abstain from dancing, singing, instrumental music, and unsuitable shows. [471] But these beings are more numerous who do not so abstain...."

82 (2) High Beds

... "So too, bhikkhus, those beings are few who abstain from high and luxurious beds and seats. But these beings are more numerous who do not so abstain...."

83 (3) Gold and Silver

... "So too, bhikkhus, those beings are few who abstain from accepting gold and silver. But these beings are more numerous who do not so abstain...."

84 (4) Raw Grain

... "So too, bhikkhus, those beings are few who abstain from accepting raw grain. But these beings are more numerous who do not so abstain...."

85 (5) Raw Meat

... "So too, bhikkhus, those beings are few who abstain from accepting raw meat. But these beings are more numerous who do not so abstain…."

86 (6) Girls

… "So too, bhikkhus, those beings are few who abstain from accepting women and girls. But these beings are more numerous who do not so abstain…." [472]

87 (7) Slaves

… "So too, bhikkhus, those beings are few who abstain from accepting male and female slaves. But these beings are more numerous who do not so abstain…."

88 (8) Goats and Sheep

… "So too, bhikkhus, those beings are few who abstain from accepting goats and sheep. But these beings are more numerous who do not so abstain…."

89 (9) Fowl and Swine

… "So too, bhikkhus, those beings are few who abstain from accepting fowl and swine. But these beings are more numerous who do not so abstain…."

90 (10) Elephants

… "So too, bhikkhus, those beings are few who abstain from accepting elephants, cattle, horses, and mares. But these beings are more numerous who do not so abstain…."

[473] X. Fourth Raw Grain Repetition Series

91 (1) Fields

… "So too, bhikkhus, those beings are few who abstain from accepting fields and land. But these beings are more numerous who do not so abstain…."

92 (2) Buying and Selling

... "So too, bhikkhus, those beings are few who abstain from buying and selling. But these beings are more numerous who do not so abstain...."

93 (3) Messages

... "So too, bhikkhus, those beings are few who abstain from running messages and errands. But these beings are more numerous who do not so abstain...."

94 (4) False Weights

... "So too, bhikkhus, those beings are few who abstain from false weights, false metals, and false measures. But these beings are more numerous who do not so abstain...."

95 (5) Bribery

... "So too, bhikkhus, those beings are few who abstain from the crooked ways of bribery, deception, and fraud. But these beings are more numerous who do not so abstain...."

96 (6)–101 (11) Mutilating, Etc.

... "So too, bhikkhus, those beings are few who abstain from mutilating, murder, binding, robbery, plunder, and violence. [474] But these beings are more numerous who do not so abstain. For what reason? Because, bhikkhus, they have not seen the Four Noble Truths. What four? The noble truth of suffering, the noble truth of the origin of suffering, the noble truth of the cessation of suffering, the noble truth of the way leading to the cessation of suffering.

"Therefore, bhikkhus, an exertion should be made to understand: 'This is suffering.'... An exertion should be made to understand: 'This is the way leading to the cessation of suffering.'"

XI. The Five Destinations Repetition Series

102 (1) Passing Away as Humans (1)

Then the Blessed One took up a little bit of soil in his fingernail and addressed the bhikkhus thus:

"What do you think, bhikkhus, which is more: the little bit of soil in my fingernail or the great earth?"

"Venerable sir, the great earth is more. The little bit of soil that the Blessed One has taken up in his fingernail is trifling. Compared to the great earth, the little bit of soil that the Blessed One has taken up in his fingernail is not calculable, does not bear comparison, does not amount even to a fraction."

"So too, bhikkhus, those beings are few who, when they pass away as human beings, are reborn among human beings. But those beings are more numerous who, when they pass away as human beings, are reborn in hell. For what reason? Because, bhikkhus, they have not seen the Four Noble Truths. What four? The noble truth of suffering, the noble truth of the origin of suffering, the noble truth of the cessation of suffering, the noble truth of the way leading to the cessation of suffering.

"Therefore, bhikkhus, an exertion should be made to understand: 'This is suffering.'... An exertion should be made to understand: 'This is the way leading to the cessation of suffering.'"

103 (2) Passing Away as Humans (2)

... "So too, bhikkhus, those beings are few who, when they pass away as human beings, are reborn among human beings. But those beings are more numerous who, when they pass away as human beings, are reborn in the animal realm...." [475]

104 (3) Passing Away as Humans (3)

... "So too, bhikkhus, those beings are few who, when they pass away as human beings, are reborn among human beings. But those beings are more numerous who, when they pass away as human beings, are reborn in the domain of ghosts...."

105 (4)–107 (6) Passing Away as Humans (4–6)

... "So too, bhikkhus, those beings are few who, when they pass away as human beings, are reborn among the devas. But those beings are more numerous who, when they pass away as human beings, are reborn in hell ... in the animal realm ... in the domain of ghosts...."

108 (7)–110 (9) Passing Away as Devas (1–3)

... "So too, bhikkhus, those beings are few who, when they pass away as devas, are reborn among the devas. But those beings are more numerous who, when they pass away as devas, are reborn in hell ... in the animal realm ... in the domain of ghosts...."

111 (10)–113 (12) Passing Away as Devas (4–6)

... "So too, bhikkhus, those beings are few who, when they pass away as devas, are reborn among human beings. But those beings are more numerous who, when they pass away as devas, are reborn in hell ... in the animal realm ... in the domain of ghosts...."

114 (13)–116 (15) Passing Away from Hell (1–3)

... "So too, bhikkhus, those beings are few who, when they pass away from hell, are reborn among human beings. But those beings are more numerous who, when they pass away from hell, are reborn in hell ... in the animal realm ... in the domain of ghosts...." [476]

117 (16)–119 (18) Passing Away from Hell (4–6)

... "So too, bhikkhus, those beings are few who, when they pass away from hell, are reborn among the devas. But those beings are more numerous who, when they pass away from hell, are reborn in hell ... in the animal realm ... in the domain of ghosts...."

120 (19)–122 (21) Passing Away from the Animal Realm (1–3)

... "So too, bhikkhus, those beings are few who, when they pass away from the animal realm, are reborn among human beings. But those beings are more numerous who, when they pass away from the animal realm, are reborn in hell ... in the animal realm ... in the domain of ghosts...."

123 (22)–125 (24) Passing Away from the Animal Realm (4–6)

... "So too, bhikkhus, those beings are few who, when they pass away from the animal realm, are reborn among the devas. But those beings are more numerous who, when they pass away from the animal realm, are reborn in hell ... in the animal realm ... in the domain of ghosts...."

126 (25)–128 (27) Passing Away from the Domain of Ghosts (1 –3)

... "So too, bhikkhus, those beings are few who, when they pass away from the domain of ghosts, are reborn among human beings. But those beings are more numerous who, when they pass away from the domain of ghosts, are reborn in hell ... in the animal realm ... in the domain of ghosts...."

129 (28) Passing Away from the Domain of Ghosts (4)

... "So too, bhikkhus, those beings are few who, when they pass away from the domain of ghosts, are reborn among the devas. But those beings are more numerous who, when they pass away from the domain of ghosts, are reborn in hell." [477]

130 (29) Passing Away from the Domain of Ghosts (5)

... "So too, bhikkhus, those beings are few who, when they pass away from the domain of ghosts, are reborn among the devas. But those beings are more numerous who, when they pass away from the domain of ghosts, are reborn in the animal realm."

131 (30) Passing Away from the Domain of Ghosts (6)

… "So too, bhikkhus, those beings are few who, when they pass away from the domain of ghosts, are reborn among the devas. But those beings are more numerous who, when they pass away from the domain of ghosts, are reborn in the domain of ghosts. For what reason? Because they have not seen the Four Noble Truths. What four? The noble truth of suffering, the noble truth of the origin of suffering, the noble truth of the cessation of suffering, the noble truth of the way leading to the cessation of suffering.

"Therefore, bhikkhus, an exertion should be made to understand: 'This is suffering.' An exertion should be made to understand: 'This is the origin of suffering.' An exertion should be made to understand: 'This is the cessation of suffering.' An exertion should be made to understand: 'This is the way leading to the cessation of suffering.'"

This is what the Blessed One said. Elated, those bhikkhus delighted in the Blessed One's statement. [478]

The Great Book is finished.

Notes

45. Maggasaṃyutta

1 Also at AN V 214, but with *micchāñāṇa* and *micchāvimutti* added to the "dark side," and *sammāñāṇa* and *sammāvimutti* added to the "bright side." The opening statements about ignorance and (just below) true knowledge are at It 34,6–10. See too MN III 76,1–9.

Spk: Ignorance is the forerunner (*pubbaṅgama*) in two modes, as a conascent condition (*sahajātavasena*, a condition for simultaneously arisen states) and as a decisive-support condition (*upanissayavasena*, a strong causal condition for subsequently arisen states). Spk-pṭ: It is a forerunner by way of conascence when it makes associated states conform to its own mode of confusion about the object, so that they grasp impermanent phenomena as permanent, etc.; it is a forerunner by way of both conascence and decisive support when a person overcome by delusion engages in immoral actions. *Shamelessness* (*ahirika*) has the characteristic of lack of shame (*alajjanā*, or lack of conscience regarding evil); *fearlessness of wrongdoing* (*anottappa*), the characteristic of lack of fear (*abhāyanā*, regarding evil conduct).

Spk glosses *anudeva* (or *anvadeva* in Be): *sah' eva ekato' va, na vinā tena uppajjati*; "it arises along with it, in unison, not without it."

2 Spk: *True knowledge* (*vijjā*) is knowledge of one's responsibility for one's own action (*kammassakatāñāṇa*). Here, too, it is a forerunner by way of both conascence and decisive support.

Shame (*hiri*) and fear of wrongdoing (*ottappa*) are called "the guardians of the world" (AN I 51,19–28). For a detailed discussion of *hiri* and *ottappa*, see As 124–27, presented more concisely at Vism 464–65 (Ppn 14:142).

3 Spk says that at the moment of the mundane path these are not all found together, but they are found together at the moment of the supramundane path. Even in the development of the mundane path it would be a mistake to see the eight factors as following in direct sequence. Right view is the guide for all the other path factors and the direct condition for right intention. Right view and right intention jointly condition the next three factors, which make up the virtue group. These in turn serve as the foundation for right effort and right mindfulness, the effort being the application of energy to the practice of the four establishments of mindfulness. The fruit of right effort and right mindfulness is right concentration.

4 This entire sutta is quoted by the Buddha at **3:18**, in a conversation with King Pasenadi. Spk has commented on the text there and thus passes over it here. I draw the excerpts below from Spk's exegesis of the earlier text. In Be and Ee the name of the town is Sakkara.

5 *Kalyāṇamittatā kalyāṇasahāyatā kalyāṇasampavaṅkatā.* The three are synonymous. Spk: When he was in seclusion Ānanda thought, "This practice of an ascetic succeeds for one who relies on good friends and on his own manly effort, so half of it depends on good friends and half on one's own manly effort."

6 C.Rh.D renders *kalyāṇamitto bhikkhu* "a bhikkhu who is a friend of righteousness" (KS 1:113); Woodward, "a monk who is a friend of what is lovely" (KS 5:2); Ireland, "a bhikkhu who is a friend of the good" (SN-Anth 1:75). These renderings all rest on a misunderstanding of the grammatical form of the expression. As an independent substantive, *kalyāṇamitta* means a good friend, i.e., a spiritual friend who gives advice, guidance, and encouragement. When used in apposition to *bhikkhu*, however, *kalyāṇamitta* becomes a *bahubbbīhi* compound, and the whole expression means "a bhikkhu *who has* a good friend." To represent this formally: *yassa bhikkhuno*

kalyāṇamittaṃ hoti (not *yo bhikkhu kalyāṇassa mittaṃ hoti*), *so kalyāṇamitto bhikkhū ti vuccati* (my own etymology). On the importance of the good friend, see below **45:49**, **63**, **77**, and also AN IV 351–53 (= Ud 34–37).

Spk: With children, it isn't possible to say, "So much comes from the mother, so much from the father"; the same is true in this case too. One cannot say, "So much of right view, etc., comes from good friends, so much from one's own manly effort." The Blessed One says in effect: "The four paths, the four fruits, etc., are all rooted in the good friend."

7 The *vivekanissita* formula is affixed to the path factors at Vibh 236. Spk explains seclusion (*viveka*) in the light of the commentarial notion of the fivefold seclusion: (i) "in a particular respect" (*tadaṅga*, temporarily, by the practice of insight); (ii) by suppression (*vikkhambhana*, temporarily, by attainment of jhāna); (iii) by eradication (*samuccheda*, permanently, by the supramundane path); (iv) by subsiding (*paṭippassaddhi*, permanently, in fruition); and (v) by escape (*nissaraṇa*, permanently, in Nibbāna). In the next two paragraphs I translate from Spk.

"*He develops right view dependent on seclusion* (*vivekanissitaṃ*): dependent on seclusion in a particular respect, dependent on seclusion by eradication, dependent on seclusion by escape. For at the moment of insight this meditator, devoted to the development of the noble path, develops right view dependent on seclusion in a particular respect by way of function and dependent on seclusion by escape as inclination (since he inclines to Nibbāna); at the time of the path, he develops it dependent on seclusion by eradication as function and dependent on seclusion by escape as object (since the path takes Nibbāna as object). The same method of explanation is also extended to the terms 'dependent on dispassion' (*virāganissita*) and 'dependent on cessation' (*nirodhanissita*).

"*Release* (*vossagga*) is twofold, release as giving up (*pariccāga*) and release as entering into (*pakkhandana*). 'Release as giving up' is the abandoning (*pahāna*) of defilements: in a particular respect (*tadaṅgavasena*) on the occasion of insight, by eradication (*samucchedavasena*) at the moment of the supramundane path. 'Release as entering into' is the entering into Nibbāna: by way of inclination towards that (*tadninnabhāvena*) on the occasion of insight, and by making it the object (*ārammaṇakaraṇena*) at the moment of the path. Both methods are suitable in this exposition, which combines the mundane (insight) and the supramundane (the path). The path is *maturing in release* (*vossaggapariṇāmi*) because it is maturing towards or has matured in release, meaning that it is ripening towards or has ripened (in release). The bhikkhu engaged in developing the path is 'ripening' the path for the sake of giving up defilements and entering into Nibbāna, and he develops it so that it has 'ripened' thus."

When I translate *vossagga* as "release," this should be understood as the act of releasing or the state of having released rather than as the experience of being released. *Vossagga* and *paṭinissagga* are closely related, both etymologically and in meaning, but as used in the Nikāyas a subtle difference seems to separate them. *Paṭinissagga,* here translated "relinquishment," pertains primarily to the phase of insight and thus might be understood as the active elimination of defilements through insight into the impermanence of all conditioned things. *Vossagga,* as that in which the path matures, probably signifies the final state in which all attachment is utterly given up, and thus comes close in meaning to Nibbāna as the goal of the path. *Paṭinissagga* occurs as a distinct contemplation, the last, in the sixteen steps in the development of mindfulness of breathing (see **54:1**). Though Spk glosses it in the same way as it does *vossagga* (see **n. 293** below), in the suttas themselves the two terms are used with different nuances.

8 Spk: Because Ānanda had not reached the peak in the knowledge of a disciple's perfections he did not know that the entire holy life of the path depends on a good friend, but since the General of the Dhamma (Sāriputta) had reached the peak in the knowledge of a disciple's perfections he knew this; therefore he spoke thus and the Blessed One applauded him.

9 The brahmin Jāṇussoṇi was a chaplain of King Pasenadi. He departs from Sāvatthī in a white chariot also at

MN I 175,15–17 and MN II 208,24–25. According to Spk, once every six months he rode around the city in his chariot "as if strewing the city with the excellence of his glory and prosperity."

10 *Brahmaṃ vata bho yānaṃ, brahmayānarūpaṃ vata hoti.* Here, *brahma* has the sense of best (*seṭṭha*).

11 The relative pronoun *yassa* with which the verses begin is completed only by the demonstrative *etad* in the last verse. Since English does not lend itself to such complex syntax, I am compelled to break up the passage into shorter sentences. I rely on Spk in interpreting the verses. See the other chariot simile at **1:46**.

12 *Jhānakkho.* Spk: "The axle made of jhāna by way of the five jhāna factors accompanying insight." The five jhāna factors are thought, examination, rapture, happiness, and one-pointedness of mind. Though when fully mature they bring the mind to the first jhāna, these factors are also present, though less prominently, in the concentration that accompanies insight meditation.

13 I read *vammasannāho* with Se, as against Be *camma-* and Ee *dhamma-*.

14 Spk: This vehicle of the path (*maggayāna*) is said to "originate within oneself" (*attani sambhūtaṃ*) because it is gained in dependence on one's own manly effort.

15 Spk: The removal of lust, etc., is a designation for the unconditioned, deathless Nibbāna element. The destruction of the taints is arahantship. The removal of lust, etc., is a name for arahantship too.

16 The definitions of the path factors to follow are also at DN II 311–13 and MN III 251–52. In the Abhidhamma Piṭaka, they are incorporated into the formal treatment of the path according to the sutta method in the Suttanta-bhājaniya at Vibh 235–36 (but see the following note). In the Abhidhamma-bhājaniya the path factors are considered as exclusively supramundane.

17 All eds. of SN have here *abrahmacariyā veramaṇī*, but elsewhere the reading is *kāmesu micchācārā veramaṇī*, "abstinence from sexual misconduct" (see DN II 312,12–13; MN III 74,22, III 251,24–25; Vibh 235,18–19). The former phrase is found in the precept observed by monks and

nuns, the latter in the precept undertaken by the laity. Spk does not comment, which suggests that the SN reading is the result of a scribal error, probably introduced after the age of the commentary; otherwise Spk surely would have explained the variant. I have therefore translated on the assumption that the correct reading should be *kāmesu micchācārā veramaṇī*.

18 Spk: Why does he speak thus? During that half-month, it is said, he had no one to guide. Then he thought, "I will pass this half-month in the bliss of fruition attainment. Thus I will enjoy a pleasant abiding and set an example for future generations."

19 Spk takes this to refer to the Buddha's forty-nine days of meditation in the vicinity of the Bodhi Tree just after his enlightenment. During that period (according to Spk) he contemplated the aggregates, sense bases, elements, Four Noble Truths, etc., in full (*nippadesa*); but now he contemplated them only partly (*padesena*), namely, in relation to feeling. Spk gives examples of how feelings arise conditioned by wrong view and by right view. The sutta is referred to at As 30–31 as "proof" that the Buddha taught the Abhidhamma. Vism 519 (Ppn 17:9) also cites the sutta in arguing against the view that dependent origination is a "simple arising."

20 Spk: *Feeling with desire* (chanda) *as condition* is the feeling associated with the eight cittas accompanied by greed (see CMA 1:4); that conditioned by thought is the feeling in the first jhāna; that conditioned by perception is the feeling in the six meditative attainments from the second jhāna through the base of nothingness.

21 The passage in brackets is not in Be and may have been imported into the Sinhalese tradition from Spk. Spk explains the feeling when none of the three have subsided as the feeling associated with the eight cittas accompanied by greed. The feeling when desire alone has subsided is that of the first jhāna; the feeling when perception alone remains is that of the second and higher jhānas. The feeling when all three have subsided is that of the base of neither-perception-nor-nonperception. The "as-yet-unattained" is the fruit of arahantship. The last expression includes the

supramundane feeling accompanying the four paths. The word rendered "effort" here is *āyāma*, effectively synonymous with *vāyāma*, the actual reading in some mss. Spk glosses with *viriya*.

22 Spk: The subsiding of wrong view means right view; therefore the feeling said to be conditioned by right view is the same as the feeling conditioned by the subsiding of wrong view. But in this sutta they (the ancients) do not include resultant feeling (*vipākavedanā*), thinking it is too remote. For whenever a feeling is said to be conditioned by the subsiding of a particular state, we should understand that it is conditioned by the quality opposed to that state. Feeling conditioned by the subsiding of desire is the feeling of the first jhāna; by the subsiding of thought, the feeling of the second jhāna; by the subsiding of perception, the feeling of the base of neither-perception-nor-nonperception.

23 Se and Ee: *Bhaddako te āvuso Bhadda ummaggo.* Be has *ummaṅgo. Bhaddako* almost surely involves a word play on the elder's name. Spk (Se): *Ummaggo ti pañha-ummaggo; pañhavīmaṃsanaṃ pañhagavesanan ti attho*; "'Intelligence': intelligence (in forming) a question; the meaning is, investigating a question, seeking out a question." (Here Se *pañha-* is preferable to Be *paññā-*.)

24 I translate *ñāyaṃ dhammaṃ* following Spk's gloss of the term as *ariyamaggadhammaṃ*. The sutta is the basis for a "dilemma" at Mil 242–43.

25 The two additional qualities are *micchāñāṇi* and *micchāvimutti*. Spk glosses the former as *micchāpaccavekkhaṇa*, "wrong reviewing," on which Spk-pṭ says: "When one has done something evil, one reviews it with the idea that it was good." Spk explains *micchāvimutti* as a false liberation (*ayāthāvavimutti*), a nonemancipating liberation (*aniyyānikavimutti*).

26 *Sa-upanisaṃ saparikkhāraṃ*. For a fuller analysis, see MN No. 117. The definition of noble right concentration just below rests on the conception of the mind as a constellation of mental factors each performing its own distinct function in coordination with the others. On the treatment of the path from this angle, see Introduction to Part V, pp. 1488–90.

27 Spk: While the former sutta is explained in terms of qualities (*dhammavasena*), this one is explained in terms of persons (*puggalavasena*).

28 Though all three eds. have *aṭṭhaṅgiko* here, I suggest deleting it to bring the wording into conformity with **46:18**, **47:33**, and **51:2**.

29 Read: *apārā pāraṃ gamanāya saṃvattanti*. Spk: "To going from the round of existence to Nibbāna." Woodward has mistranslated as "conduce to that state in which no further shore and no higher shore exist." The verses just below are also at Dhp 85–89.

30 At this point Ee stops numbering these groups of suttas and designates them merely as *peyyāla*, "repetitions," not as *vagga*; Se also calls them *peyyāla* but numbers them; Be numbers them and calls them *peyyālavagga*, "repetition groups." My scheme for numbering the vaggas corresponds closest to Se, but my numbering of the suttas agrees with Ee straight through to the end.

31 *Addhānapariññatthaṃ*. Spk: When one has reached Nibbāna, the course of saṃsāra is fully understood. Therefore Nibbāna is called the full understanding of the course.

32 Spk: Good friendship is like the dawn; the noble path along with insight, arisen by relying on good friendship, is like the appearance of the sun.

33 Spk: "Accomplishment in virtue" (*sīlasampadā*) is the fourfold purification of virtue (i.e., compliance with the Pātimokkha, restraint of the senses, proper use of the requisites, and right livelihood; see Vism 15–16; Ppn 1:42). "Accomplishment in desire" (*chandasampadā*) is desire as the wish to accomplish the wholesome (i.e., not desire as craving, another connotation of *chanda*). "Accomplishment in self" (*attasampadā*) is completeness of mind (*sampannacittatā*). All these suttas were spoken separately by way of the personal inclinations (of those to be taught).

34 In Ee this vagga does not have a separate number. Be numbers it "1," as if starting again from scratch, but then assigns each of the four "versions" within this repetition series a separate number. Se keeps the numbering of the vagga continuous, beginning here with "9." I here follow

Se, which seems more logical; I use upper case roman numbers for the sequential vaggas, and lower case roman numbers for the versions corresponding to the vaggas. The four versions are distinguished only by the phrases used to describe the path factors. In Pāli these are: (i) *vivekanissitaṃ virāganissitaṃ nirodhanissitaṃ vossaggapariṇāmiṃ*; (ii) *rāgavinayapariyosānaṃ dosavinayapariyosānaṃ mohavinayapariyosānaṃ*; (iii) *amatogadhaṃ amataparāyanaṃ amatapariyosānaṃ*; and (iv) *nibbānaninnaṃ nibbānapoṇaṃ nibbānapabbhāraṃ*. Spk explains that the different versions of the same sutta were spoken by the Buddha in response to the individual inclinations of the persons to be enlightened.

35 On *nibbānogadha*, see **III, n. 243**.

36 Ee calls this vagga "Chapter V," as if all the suttas from 31 to 138 fall under Chapter IV. Be also numbers this "5," following on the four sections of the Ganges Repetition Series. Since in Be the remaining vaggas of this saṃyutta are numbered 6–8, this means that in Be the saṃyutta includes two series of vaggas numbered 5–8, without any other basis for differentiating them. In Se this vagga is numbered 13 and the numbering continues in unbroken sequence, ending in 16. As this has greater cogency I follow it here. It is inconsistent and illogical, though, for the Ganges Repetition Series to make each repetition cycle a separate vagga, thus creating four vaggas, while the following vaggas, starting with the Appamādavagga, subsume the four repetitions under each individual sutta.

37 Spk: Diligence is called the chief of all wholesome states because it is by diligence that one acquires all the other wholesome states.

38 The similes of **45:141–47** are also at **22:102**.

39 Spk: When the female nāgas become pregnant they realize that if they gave birth in the ocean their offspring could be attacked by the supaṇṇas or swept away by a strong current. Thus they ascend the rivers to the Himalayas and give birth there. They then train their young in the mountain ponds until they have mastered the art of swimming.

40 As at **36:12**.

41 As at **22:101** (III 155,5–9). See **III, n. 214**.

42 As at **36:14**.

43 The simile and its application here parallel **35:244** (IV 191,1–24).

44 Spk explains *brahmacariyesanā* as the search for a holy life consisting in a wrong view [Spk-pṭ: because the wrong view is the basis for the holy life devised by the theorist].

45 See **IV, n. 274**.

46 This sutta is not found in Se or in SS. Be numbers it separately, Ee does not. I here follow the latter. Both connect the "based upon seclusion" refrain with §170 (10) and the other three refrains with §170 (11). This suggests the two are actually one sutta elaborated by way of alternative forms of the same word, both *taṇhā* and *tasinā* being Pāli equivalents of Skt *tṛṣṇā*.

47 Spk explains "bodily knot" (*kāyagantha*) as a knot in the name-body (*nāmakāya*), a defilement which knots and connects (*ganthanaghaṭanakilesa*). Spk-pṭ: A defilement which produces connection, bondage, known as the binding to suffering through the connection of cause with effect, of the round of kamma with the round of results. The fourth knot, *idaṃsaccābhinivesa kāyagantha*, is literally "the bodily knot of adherence to (the view) 'This (alone) is truth.'"

48 Spk: The "underlying tendency to sensual lust" (*kāmānusaya*) is sensual lust itself, which is an "underlying tendency" in the sense that it has gained strength (*thāmagataṭṭhena*). Spk-pṭ: "Gained strength" by being firmly implanted in a being's mental continuum.

49 These are the fetters that bind beings to the sense-sphere realm (*kāmadhātu*). The first three are eradicated by the stream-enterer and the once-returner, all five by the non-returner.

50 These are the fetters that bind beings to the form realm (*rūpadhātu*) and the formless realm (*arūpadhātu*), which are reached respectively through the jhānas and the formless attainments. Only the arahant has eradicated these fetters.

46. Bojjhaṅgasaṃyutta

51 As at **45:151**.

52 *Bojjhaṅga* is a compound of *bodhi* + *aṅga*. Spk offers a twofold definition: "Enlightenment factors are factors of

enlightenment or (factors) of the one being enlightened (*bodhiyā bodhissa vā aṅgā ti bojjhaṅgā*). What is meant? It is through the assemblage of states consisting in mindfulness ... equanimity, arisen at the moment of the mundane and supramundane paths (*lokiyalokuttaramaggakkhaṇe*) ... that the noble disciple is enlightened; therefore (that assemblage of states) is called enlightenment. 'He is enlightened' means that he rises up from the sleep of the continuum of defilements; what is meant is that he penetrates the Four Noble Truths or realizes Nibbāna. The enlightenment factors are the factors of the enlightenment consisting in that assemblage of states. Also, the noble disciple who becomes enlightened through the aforesaid assemblage of states is called 'one being enlightened' (*bodhī*). The factors of the one being enlightened are enlightenment factors."

In the Abhidhamma Piṭaka, the Bojjhaṅga-vibhaṅga (Vibh 227–29) first explains the enlightenment factors by the sutta method in three ways modelled on **46:3**, **46:52** (ii), and the bare *vivekanissita* formula, respectively. Then it analyses them according to the Abhidhamma method, which treats them solely as factors of the supramundane path (Vibh 229–32). For this reason the definitions in the Abhidhamma commentaries (As 217, Vibh-a 310), parallel to the passage cited from Spk above, omit "mundane" (*lokiya*) in relation to the path.

The Buddha's own definition of *bojjhaṅga*, at **46:5** below, implies they were originally conceived not as factors that *constitute* enlightenment (the position taken by the commentaries), but as factors that *lead to* enlightenment. This is further supported by the sequential account of their origination at **46:3**. Hence comparison of the different strata of early Pāli literature shows the usage of the term to have undergone some degree of evolution, from the more general and pragmatic to the more specific and technical.

53 Nutriment (*āhāra*) here has the meaning of condition (*paccaya*). This portion of the sutta is repeated below at **46:51**, to which Spk gives a detailed explanation of the nutriments for the individual enlightenment factors. See below, **nn. 85–91**. Cp. AN I 3–5.

54 The sign of the beautiful (*subhanimitta*) is a sensually attrac-

tive object, particularly an object that arouses sexual desire. The word *nimitta* is difficult to render in a way that fits all the major contexts where it occurs. I returned to "sign" only after several experiments with alternatives—"aspect," "feature," and "appearance"—proved unsatisfactory. Elsewhere it clearly means basis, cause, condition (e.g., at **48:40**; V 213,16, etc.).

Spk glosses careless attention (*ayoniso manasikāra*) with "unmethodical attention, offtrack attention" (*anupāyamanasikāra, uppathamanasikāra*; Spk-pṭ: because it is not the right method for gaining welfare and happiness). The commentaries consistently explain it as attention directed to the impermanent as permanent, to suffering as happiness, to the selfless as self, and to the foul as beautiful. This explanation is found already at Vibh 373.

55 *Paṭighanimitta*. Spk: The sign of the repulsive is aversion (*paṭigha*) or a repulsive object (*paṭighārammaṇa*).

56 The terms are defined, mostly by chains of synonyms, at Vibh 352. Spk cites the passage here. They are also mentioned at **I, vv. 30–31**.

57 *Cetaso avūpasama*. Spk: Unsettledness of mind is, in denotation, restlessness and remorse themselves.

58 *Satisambojjhaṅgaṭṭhāniyā dhammā*. Spk: The things that become objects of mindfulness [Spk-pṭ: the four establishments of mindfulness], the thirty-seven aids to enlightenment, and the nine supramundane states.

59 *Kaṇhasukkasappaṭibhāga*. Spk: Dark states are "with counterparts" because they yield dark results, and bright states because they yield bright results; the meaning is "having similar results." Or "with counterparts" means "with opposites": the dark states have the bright as their opposites, the bright the dark. Or "with counterparts" means "with exclusion": the unwholesome excludes the wholesome and yields its own results, and conversely.

An extended example of the opposition between good and bad states is found in MN No. 8, where the Buddha enumerates forty-four pairs of wholesome and unwholesome opposites. The explanation of this enlightenment factor suggests that while "discrimination of states" may be technically identified with *paññā*, the initial function of *paññā* as an enlightenment factor is not to discern the three characteristics, etc., but simply to discriminate between the good and bad mental states that become apparent with the deepening of mindfulness.

60 Spk: The element of arousal (*ārambhadhātu*) is the initial phase of energy, the element of endeavour (*nikkamadhātu*) intermediate energy, the element of exertion (*parakkamadhātu*) energy at full intensity.

61 Spk: Tranquillity of body (*kāyappassaddhi*) is the tranquillizing of distress in the three mental aggregates (feeling, perception, volitional formations), tranquillity of mind (*cittappassaddhi*) the tranquillizing of distress in the aggregate of consciousness.

The commentaries frequently interpret the pair, body and mind, mentioned in the texts in the light of the Abhidhamma, which draws a contrast between mind (*citta*), the chief factor in cognition, and its accompanying "body" of mental factors (*cetasika*), which perform secondary cognitive functions. It seems, however, that in such passages as the present one, "body" was intended quite literally as meaning the physical body, considered as actively contributing to the qualitative tone of an experience.

62 Spk: The sign of serenity (*samathanimitta*) is serenity itself as well as its object (Spk-pṭ: the *paṭibhāganimitta* or counterpart sign); the sign of nondispersal (*abyagganimitta*) is synonymous with it.

63 In stating that the *satisambojjhaṅga* arises by recollecting the Dhamma taught by accomplished monks, the text draws upon the etymological connection between *sati* as act of remembrance and the verb *anussarati*, to recollect. Though it has been overshadowed by *sati*'s more technical sense of awareness of the present, this nuance of the word is still occasionally preserved in Pāli (e.g., in the definition of the faculty of mindfulness at **48:9**).

The three phrases used to describe the cultivation of each enlightenment factor can be understood to depict three successive stages of development: initial arousal, maturation, and culmination. Spk says that in this sutta the enlightenment factors are to be understood as pertaining to insight in the preliminary stage of the path of arahantship.

They occur together in one mind-moment, though with different characteristics. The whole pattern is also at **54:13**, but beginning with the four establishments of mindfulness as the means of arousing the *satisambojjhaṅga*.

64 I follow Be here, which reads simply *passaddhakāyassa sukhino cittaṃ samādhiyati*. Se and Ee have *passaddhakāyassa sukhaṃ hoti, sukhino cittaṃ samādhiyati*, "for one whose body is tranquil there is happiness, for one who is happy the mind becomes concentrated." I suspect this reading has arisen from confusion with such texts as **47:10** and AN V 3,3–8, where *sukha* is a distinct stage in the sequence of development. Be is supported here by the Se and Ee reading of the exact parallel at **54:13**.

65 This fivefold typology of nonreturners recurs at **48:15**, **24**, **66**; **51:26**; **54:5**; and **55:25**. Spk explains the *antarāparinibbāyī* ("attainer of Nibbāna in the interval") as one reborn in the Pure Abodes who attains arahantship during the first half of the life span. This type is subdivided into three, depending on whether arahantship is reached: (i) on the very day of rebirth; (ii) after one or two hundred aeons have elapsed; or (iii) after four hundred aeons have elapsed. The *upahaccaparinibbāyī* ("attainer of Nibbāna upon landing") is explained as one who attains arahantship after passing the first half of the life span. For Spk, the *asaṅkhāraparinibbāyī* ("attainer without exertion") and the *sasaṅkhāraparinibbāyī* ("attainer with exertion") then become two modes in which the first two types of nonreturners attain the goal. This explanation originates from Pp 16–17 (commented on at Pp-a 198–201). However, not only does this account of the first two types disregard the literal meaning of their names, but it also overrides the sequential and mutually exclusive nature of the five types as delineated elsewhere in the suttas (see below).

If we understand the term *antarāparinibbāyī* literally, as it seems we should, it then means one who attains Nibbāna *in the interval between two lives*, perhaps while existing in a subtle body in the intermediate state. The *upahacca-parinibbāyī* then becomes one who attains Nibbāna "upon landing" or "striking ground" in the new existence, i.e., almost immediately after taking rebirth. The next two terms designate two types who attain arahantship in the course of the next life, distinguished by the amount of effort they must make to win the goal. The last, the *uddhaṃsota akaniṭṭhagāmī*, is one who takes rebirth in successive Pure Abodes, completes the full life span in each, and finally attains arahantship in the Akaniṭṭha realm, the highest Pure Abode.

This interpretation, adopted by several non-Theravāda schools of early Buddhism, seems to be confirmed by the Purisagati Sutta (AN IV 70–74), in which the simile of the flaming chip suggests that the seven types (including the three kinds of *antarāparinibbāyī*) are mutually exclusive and have been graded according to the sharpness of their faculties. Additional support comes from AN II 134,25–29, which explains the *antarāparinibbāyī* as one who has abandoned the fetter of rebirth (*upapattisaṃyojana*) without yet having abandoned the fetter of existence (*bhavasaṃyojana*). Though the Theravādin proponents argue against this interpretation of *antarāparinibbāyī* (e.g., at Kv 366), the evidence from the suttas leans strongly in its favour. For a detailed discussion, see Harvey, *The Selfless Mind*, pp. 98–108.

AN II 155–56 draws an alternative distinction between the *sasaṅkhāraparinibbāyī* and the *asaṅkhāraparinibbāyī*: the former reaches arahantship through meditation on the "austere" meditation subjects such as the foulness of the body, the perception of the repulsiveness of food, discontent with the whole world, the perception of impermanence in all formations, and mindfulness of death; the latter, through the four jhānas.

66 Spk: In this sutta the elder's fruition enlightenment factors (*phalabojjhaṅga*) are discussed. For when he enters fruition attainment after making the enlightenment factor of mindfulness the key, the other six enlightenment factors follow along; and so for the others. Thus the elder spoke this sutta to show his own mastery over fruition attainment. The simile of the wardrobe just below is also at MN I 215,6–15, again spoken by Sāriputta.

67 *Itivādappamokkhānisaṃsañ c' eva kathaṃ kathente upārambhānisaṃsañ ca*. Woodward translates "debating on the profit

of freedom from controversy and the profit of wrangling" (KS 5:60). Spk's explanation of the phrase here is not completely clear to me, but at MN I 133,28–30 the Buddha uses the same terms to reproach certain monks who master the Dhamma *upārambhānisaṃsā itivādappamokkhānisaṃsā*. Ps II 106,35–107,4 explains: "They master the Dhamma (intent on) the benefit of ascribing errors to their opponents' theses and on rescuing their own theses when their opponents ascribe errors to them." The stock Nikāya description of debates provides a clear illustration of what is meant; see, e.g., **22:3** (III 12,5–13) and **56:9** (V 419,5–12).

68 *Vijjāvimuttiphalānisaṃso ... Tathāgato viharati.* Woodward translates *vijjāvimutti* as "release by knowledge," assuming the compound is a subordinate *tappurisa*, but the expression *vijjā ca vimutti ca* (at V 52,19) implies it is actually a subordinate *dvanda*. See too V 329,9–16, where the seven enlightenment factors are said to fulfil *two* things, namely, *vijjāvimutti*.

69 The best reading is the one given by the lemmas of Spk (Se): *na maṅku hoti apatitthīnacitto adīnamānaso abyāpannacetaso*. Be and Ee misread the second term as *appatiṭṭhitacitto*, whose meaning ("an unestablished mind") is exactly the opposite of what is required. *Ap(p)atitthīna* is the negative past participle of *patitthīyati* (< Skt **prati-styai*). Spk glosses: *kilesavasena atthīnacitto*, "with a mind not stiffened by defilements." At AN I 124,6, II 203,17, and III 181,24 we find a series of terms that brings out the meaning well: *abhisajjati kuppati vyāpajjati patitthīyati kopañ ca dosañ ca appaccayañ ca pātukaroti*; "he becomes annoyed, irritated, bears ill will, is daunted, and shows irritation, hate, and animosity."

70 This sutta and the next two are included as protective discourses in the Sinhalese *Maha Pirit Pota*. Monks often recite them to patients.

71 Spk: As the elder listened closely to this teaching on the development of the enlightenment factors, it is said, the thought occurred to him: "When I penetrated the truths on the seventh day of my going forth, these enlightenment factors became manifest" (see **16:11**). Thinking, "The Master's teaching is indeed emancipating!" his blood

became clear, his bodily humours were purified, and the disease departed from his body like a drop of water fallen on a lotus leaf.

72 They are recommended to the bhikkhus as "factors of non-decline" at DN II 79,8–23.

73 *Nibbedhabhāgiyaṃ ... maggaṃ desessāmi.* The reason the path is so described is given just below in the text.

74 I have translated this passage according to its apparent sense, but it is hard to see how *bahukataṃ* in the previous sentence, used as an abstract noun, can have the same meaning as it does, in negative form, in *abahukato* here, an adjective set in apposition to *ahaṃ*. Spk glosses *abahukato* with *akatabahumāno*, "(I) was without much esteem," but passes over *bahukataṃ* just above.

75 *Ukkujjāvakujjaṃ samparivattento.* Spk says that arising is called surge (*ukkujja*) and fall is decline (*avakujja*). Thus he was exploring the aggregates by way of rise and fall (*udayabbayavasena*). His realization of the Four Noble Truths while contemplating rise and fall marks his attainment of the supramundane path.

76 *Dhammo ca me bhante abhisamito, maggo ca paṭiladdho.* The regular past participle of *abhisameti* is *abhisameta*. Spk says that he has arrived at the Dhamma of insight (*vipassanā-dhamma*) and gained the path of insight (*vipassanāmagga*), but these expressions invariably indicate the realization of the supramundane Dhamma and the gaining of the supramundane path. The text does not specify his level of attainment, but it would be at least that of stream-enterer, implied by making "the breakthrough to the Dhamma." As he must still develop the path further, he could not be an arahant.

77 We should read *kusalā kusalabhāgiyā.* The confused orthography in Ee has misled Woodward.

78 The bracketed passage is in Se only, but is clearly necessary. Cp. AN I 253–56, III 16–19. Curiously, the sutta makes no mention of the seven factors of enlightenment. This silence suggests that this sutta and the following one originally formed a single textual unit. See **46:35** and the following two notes for a similar case in which certain textual traditions have preserved the unity.

79 I follow Se. In Be and Ee, the next paragraph is counted as a separate sutta, but it is clear enough that the two are counterparts within a single text.

80 Again I follow Se here, which introduces a break and counts this as a separate sutta, titled Anīvaraṇa Sutta. In Be and Ee, the following is treated as a continuation of the preceding sutta, despite the fact that their themes are completely distinct.

81 These trees are all of the type known as strangling figs. On their behaviour I cannot do better than to quote from E.J.H. Corner's *Wayside Trees of Malaya*, cited by Emeneau, "The Strangling Figs in Sanskrit Literature," pp. 347–49:

> Fig-trees whose trunks are composed of a basket-work of interlacing and anastomosing roots are called strangling figs because normally they begin life on other trees and gradually squeeze them to death. Birds, squirrels, and monkeys, which eat the fruits, drop the seeds on the branches of the forest-trees, where they grow into epiphytic bushes that hold on by strong roots encircling the branches. From thence their roots spread down the trunk of the supporting tree to the ground, where they grow vigorously. Side-roots encircle the trunk, joining up with other side-roots where they touch, and aerial roots grow down into the soil from various heights.... [T]he supporting trunk becomes enveloped in a basket of fig-roots and the branches of the fig-bush begin to spread widely through the crown of its support. As the fig-roots and their supporting trunk increase in thickness they press upon each other, but the fig-roots, being the stronger, slowly crush the bark of the support against its wood, with the effect that the supporting trunk is gradually ringed, and its limbs begin to die back, its crown becoming stag-headed and uneven. A long struggle ensues between parasite and host, but if the fig-plant is vigorous it surely kills its support and finally stands in its place on a massive basket of roots.

Two Jātaka stories (Nos. 370 and 412) use the strangling fig to drive home the lesson that one should never tolerate the slightest evil, for while evil may appear innocuous in its origins it eventually proves fatal.

82 *Tisso vidhā*. See **45:162**.

83 The *rājā cakkavattī*, the ideal monarch of Buddhist literature; for details, see DN II 172–77, MN III 172–76.

84 Sections (i) and (ii) here are identical with **46:2**, but Spk, in commenting on the present sutta, adds a fresh passage on the additional conditions for the fulfilment of the seven enlightenment factors. Below I give merely the headings. The full passage is translated by Soma Thera in *The Way of Mindfulness*, pp. 174–90. The headings, with brief explanations, are also at Vism 132–34 (Ppn 4:54–62).

85 Spk: Besides this, there are *four* other conditions for the arising of the mindfulness enlightenment factor: (i) mindfulness and clear comprehension in all activities; (ii) avoiding unmindful people; (iii) associating with mindful people; and (iv) right resolution (i.e., a mind that "slants, slopes, and inclines" towards the establishing of mindfulness).

86 Spk: There are *seven* other conditions for its arising: (i) interrogation (about the meaning of the aggregates, elements, sense bases, etc.); (ii) personal cleanliness; (iii) balancing the faculties (see Vism 129–30; Ppn 4:45–49); (iv) reflecting on the sphere of deep knowledge; (v–vii) avoiding unwise people, associating with wise people, and right resolution.

87 Spk: *Eleven* other conditions are: (i) reflecting on the fearfulness of the plane of misery; (ii) seeing the benefits in arousal of energy; (iii) reflecting that one is following the path taken by all the Buddhas, etc.; (iv) reflecting on the need to honour the gifts of alms; (v–viii) reflecting on the greatness of the heritage, of the Master, of the lineage, and of one's fellow monks; (ix–xi) avoiding lazy people, associating with energetic people, and right resolution.

88 Spk: *Eleven* other conditions are: (i–vii) recollection of the Buddha, the Dhamma, the Saṅgha, virtue, generosity, the devas, and peace; (viii) avoiding coarse people; (ix) associating with refined people; (x) reflecting on inspiring suttas; and (xi) right resolution.

89 Spk: *Seven* other conditions are: (i) nutritious food; (ii) a congenial climate; (iii) the right posture; (iv) effort at neutrality;

(v–vii) avoiding restless people, associating with calm people, and right resolution.

90 Spk: *Ten* other conditions are: (i) personal cleanliness; (ii) balancing the faculties; (iii) skill in the sign (i.e., the meditation object); (iv–vi) exerting, restraining, and gladdening the mind at the right time for each; (vii) looking on with equanimity at the right time; (viii–x) avoiding unconcentrated people, associating with concentrated people, and right resolution. (The commentaries to the Satipaṭṭhāna Sutta add, as an eleventh factor, reflecting on the jhānas and the deliverances.)

91 Spk: *Five* other conditions are: (i) a detached attitude towards beings; (ii) a detached attitude towards formations (i.e., inanimate objects); (iii–v) avoiding possessive people, associating with equanimous people, and right resolution.

All the enlightenment factors, after arising, reach "fulfilment by development" (*bhāvanāya pāripūri*) through the path of arahantship.

92 *Anāhāro nīvaraṇānaṃ*. Spk gives an elaborate explanation of how to debilitate each hindrance. Again, I give merely the headings below. The full passage is translated in Soma, *The Way of Mindfulness*, pp. 155–67; see too Nyanaponika, *The Five Mental Hindrances*.

93 The sign of foulness (*asubhanimitta*), according to Spk, is one or another of the "ten foul objects," i.e., a corpse in one of the ten stages of decomposition (see Vism 178–79; Ppn 6:1–11). In sutta usage, however, the perception of foulness (*asubhasaññā*) is explained as the contemplation of the thirty-one parts of the body (as at AN V 109,19–27, increased to thirty-two in Paṭis and the commentaries by the addition of the brain).

Spk: *Six* things lead to the abandoning of sensual desire: (i) learning the foulness object, (ii) devotion to meditation on foulness; (iii) guarding the sense faculties; (iv) moderation in food; (v) good friendship; and (vi) suitable talk. Sensual desire, (temporarily) abandoned in these six ways, is fully abandoned by the path of arahantship. Spk-pṭ: This is said by taking sensual desire, according to the Abhidhamma method, to represent all greed (i.e., greed for existence as well as greed for sensual pleasures).

94 Spk: The liberation of the mind through lovingkindness (*mettācetovimutti*) is absorption (= jhāna). *Six things* lead to abandoning ill will: (i) learning the lovingkindness object; (ii) devotion to meditation on lovingkindness; (iii) reflecting on one's responsibility for one's own actions; (iv) frequent consideration; (v) good friendship; and (vi) suitable talk. Ill will is fully abandoned by the path of nonreturning.

95 On the three elements of energy, see **n. 60**. Spk: *Six things* lead to the abandoning of sloth and torpor: (i) avoidance of overeating; (ii) change of postures; (iii) attending to the perception of light (see **51:20**; V 278,29–32); (iv) dwelling out in the open; (v) good friendship; and (vi) suitable talk. Sloth and torpor are fully abandoned by the path of arahantship.

96 Spk: *Six things* lead to the abandoning of restlessness and remorse: (i) much learning; (ii) investigation; (iii) familiarity with the Vinaya; (iv) association with mature people; (v) good friendship; and (vi) suitable talk. Restlessness is abandoned by the path of arahantship, remorse by the path of nonreturning.

97 Spk: *Six things* lead to the abandoning of doubt: (i) much learning; (ii) investigation; (iii) familiarity with the Vinaya; (iv) resoluteness; (v) good friendship; and (vi) suitable talk. Doubt is fully abandoned by the path of stream-entry.

98 Spk says that the teachers of other sects do not have any original teachings on the five hindrances and the seven enlightenment factors. When they teach their own disciples they plagiarize the Buddha's teachings on these topics. Gethin points out, however, that the sutta itself does not go as far as the commentary but only stresses the differences between the two modes of teaching (*Buddhist Path to Awakening*, p. 180).

99 Spk: Sensual desire "for the internal" is desire for one's own five aggregates; "for the external," desire for the aggregates of others (and also, no doubt, for inanimate objects).

Similarly below, ill will towards the internal might be understood as anger directed towards oneself, ill will towards the external as anger directed to other beings and to external conditions. The distinction between sloth and torpor is drawn at Vism 469 (Ppn 14:167): Sloth (*thina*) has the characteristic of "lack of driving power," the function of removing energy, and manifestation as "sinking of the mind." Torpor (*middha*) has the characteristic of unwieldiness, the function of smothering, and manifestation as nodding and sleep. Sloth can thus be understood as mental dullness, torpor as drowsiness. Restlessness (*uddhacca*) is disquietude or agitation, remorse (*kukkucca*) regret over faults of commission and omission. Doubt about the internal, according to Spk, is uncertainty regarding one's own five aggregates (whether they are truly impermanent, etc.); doubt about the external is the "great doubt" (*mahāvicikicchā*) about eight matters (the Buddha, the Dhamma, the Saṅgha, and the training; the past, present, and future; and dependent origination).

100 The bifurcation of each enlightenment factor is also found at Vibh 228, modelled on the present sutta.

101 The former is the rapture of the first jhāna, the latter the rapture of the second jhāna.

102 Spk explains tranquillity of body (*kāyappassaddhi*) as the tranquillizing of distress in the three aggregates (feeling, perception, volitional formations), tranquillity of mind (*cittappassaddhi*) as the tranquillizing of distress in the aggregate of consciousness. But see **n. 61** above.

103 The former is the concentration of the first jhāna and the access to it; the latter, the concentration of the second jhāna and higher stages.

104 Quoted at Vism 130–31, 133 (Ppn 4:51, 57). Cp. AN III 375,18–22, which compares the balancing of the faculties to the tuning of a lute: for the pitch to be right the strings must be neither too tight nor too loose.

105 Spk: It is desirable everywhere, like salt and a versatile prime minister. Just as salt enhances the flavour of all curries, and just as a versatile prime minister accomplishes all the tasks of state, so the restraining of the excited mind and the exerting of the sluggish mind are all achieved by mindfulness, and without mindfulness this could not be done. See too Vism 130,15–20 (Ppn 4:49).

106 Quoted at Vism 324,9–15 (Ppn 9:119), which calls it the Haliddavasana Sutta.

107 Spk refers back to its comment recorded in **n. 98**. The other sects, according to Spk, do not have any original teachings on the abandonment of the five hindrances or the development of the divine abodes but plagiarize them from the Buddha.

108 *Kiṃgatikā kiṃparamā kiṃphalā kiṃpariyosānā.*

109 This conjunction of the enlightenment factors with the four divine abodes is unusual. On their own momentum the divine abodes lead to rebirth in the brahmā world rather than to Nibbāna (see MN II 82,24–27, II 207–8, AN II 128–29). When integrated into the structure of the Buddha's path, however, they can be used to generate concentration of sufficient strength to serve as a basis for insight, which in turn brings enlightenment. A striking instance is at MN I 351,18–352,2. Spk: The monk develops the three jhānas based on lovingkindness, then takes this as a basis for developing insight and attains arahantship. The enlightenment factors are developed by insight and the path.

110 At AN III 169–170, this practice is discussed more fully, with reference to the benefits of each contemplation. At DN III 112,25–13,10 it is called a "spiritual power which is taintless, acquisitionless, and noble" (*ayaṃ iddhi anāsavā anupadhikā ariyā*), and Paṭis II 212–13 calls it "the noble ones' spiritual power" (*ariyiddhi*); further explanation is given at Vism 381–82 (Ppn 12:36–38). The following is condensed from Spk: (i) to perceive the repulsive in the unrepulsive (*appaṭikkūle paṭikkūlasaññī*) one pervades an unrepulsive object (e.g., a sensually attractive person) with the idea of foulness or attends to it as impermanent; (ii) to perceive the unrepulsive in the repulsive (*paṭikkūle appaṭikkūlasaññī*) one pervades a repulsive object (e.g., a hostile person) with lovingkindness or attends to it as elements; (iii) and (iv) simply extend the first two modes of perception to both types of objects conjointly; and (v) is self-explanatory.

111 Spk: This teaching is brought in for one who is unable to reach arahantship after exploring formations based on jhāna through lovingkindness.

Spk explains *idhapaññassa* as if it were a *bahubbīhi* compound meaning "one of mundane wisdom" (*lokiyapaññassa*);

the expression also occurs at Dhp 375b and AN V 300,14. Mp V 78,10–11 explains it as "wisdom in regard to this teaching" (*imasmiṃ sāsane paññā*), which sounds more convincing than Spk's gloss.

In the commentaries the four divine abodes are regarded as practices that lead to form-sphere jhāna (see Vism 111,15–16; Ppn 3:107). While the Nikāyas do not draw explicit connections between the divine abodes and levels of jhāna, in several places they describe the divine abodes as means to rebirth in the brahmā world or the form realm (see **n. 109**). Thus Spk is compelled to give a laboured explanation of the puzzling stipulations made here about the "upper limit" of each meditation subject, particularly in regard to the formless attainments; the passage is also at Vism 324–25 (Ppn 9:120–23). In brief: (i) one who abides in lovingkindness can easily apply his mind to a beautiful colour *kasiṇa* and quickly attain the beautiful liberation (i.e., jhāna based on a colour *kasiṇa*); (ii) one who abides in compassion recognizes the danger in form and thus develops the base of the infinity of space, which is the escape from form; (iii) one who abides in altruistic joy apprehends the joyful consciousness of beings and thus easily enters the base of the infinity of consciousness; and (iv) one who abides in equanimity is skilled in diverting his mind from pleasure and pain, and thus can easily divert it to the absence of any concrete entity in the base of nothingness.

112 The sutta is also at AN III 230–36, but without the last paragraph on the enlightenment factors. See too Ja No. 185 (II 99–101).

113 Spk applies the idea of the threefold escape (*nissaraṇa*) to each hindrance: by suppression (*vikkhambhananissaraṇa*) through jhāna; in a particular respect (*tadaṅga-*) through insight; and by eradication (*samuccheda-*) through the path. Thus: (i) *sensual desire* is suppressed by the first jhāna based on foulness and eradicated by the path of arahantship (since *kāmacchanda* is here interpreted widely enough to include desire for any object, not only for sensual pleasures); (ii) *ill will* is suppressed by the first jhāna based on lovingkindness and eradicated by the path of nonreturning; (iii) *sloth and torpor* are suppressed by the perception of

light (i.e., visualization of a bright light, like the disc of the sun or the full moon) and eradicated by the path of arahantship; (iv) *restlessness and remorse* are suppressed by serenity, *remorse* is eradicated by the path of nonreturning and *restlessness* by the path of arahantship; and (v) *doubt* is suppressed by the defining of phenomena (*dhammavavatthāna;* see Vism 587–89; Ppn 18:3–8) and eradicated by the path of stream-entry.

114 Prince Abhaya was a son of King Bimbisāra, though not the crown prince.

115 See **III, n. 92**.

116 This, in effect, is a declaration that he has attained stream-entry.

117 The skeleton (*aṭṭhika*) is one of the ten meditation subjects on foulness (*asubhakammaṭṭhāna*) mentioned at Vism 178–79 (Ppn 6:1–11). So too the corpses listed below at **46:58–61**: the worm-infested (*puḷuvaka*), the livid (*vinīlaka*), the fissured (*vicchiddaka*), and the bloated (*uddhumātaka*). Each becomes associated with the enlightenment factors when the concentration it induces is made a basis for developing insight and arriving at the supramundane path.

118 *Sati vā upādisese.* Spk glosses: *gahaṇasese upādānasese vijjamānamhi;* "(if there is) a remainder of grasping, a remainder of clinging, existing." *Upādisesa* is found in two technical senses: (i) when contrasted with *aññā,* final knowledge, it means a residue of defilements, the minimum residue that the nonreturner must eliminate to attain arahantship; and (ii) in relation to Nibbāna, it denotes the five aggregates, which persist until the arahant expires. Nibbāna as experienced by the arahant during life is called the *sa-upādisesanibbānadhātu,* "the Nibbāna element with a residue (= the five aggregates) remaining"; as attained at his death it is the *anupādisesanibbānadhātu,* "the Nibbāna element without residue remaining." The commentaries take *upādi* in this context to mean what is clung to (*upādiyati*).

Although I translate *upādisesa* in the present passage as "residue of clinging," I do so simply for the sake of clarity, not because I am convinced that *upādi* actually stands for *upādāna.* The whole expression may simply be an idiom meaning "an (unspecified) residue." At MN II 257,1 foll., *sa-upādisesa* and *anupādisesa* are used in relation to the noxious matter left behind in a wound, and in that context "clinging" in any sense is irrelevant. It is possible the expression was a current medical idiom to which the Buddha simply ascribed a new meaning.

119 Of the meditation subjects mentioned below: (**67**) the perception of foulness (*asubhasaññā*) is the contemplation of the thirty-one (or thirty-two) parts of the body, dealt with at AN V 109,19–27, elaborated at Vism 239–66 (Ppn 8:42–144); (**68**) the perception of death (*maraṇasaññā*), usually called mindfulness of death, is at AN III 304–8, elaborated at Vism 229–39 (Ppn 8:1–41); (**69**) the perception of the repulsiveness of food (*āhāre paṭikkūlasaññā*) is occasionally mentioned in the suttas but explained in detail at Vism 341–47 (Ppn 11:1–26); (**70**) the perception of non-delight in the entire world (*sabbaloke anabhiratasaññā*) is defined at AN V 111,3–8 as the removal of all clinging, etc., to the world; (**74**) the perception of abandonment (*pahāna-saññā*) is defined at AN V 110,13–20 as reflection leading to the removal of defiled thoughts; and (**75–76**) the perception of dispassion (*virāgasaññā*) and the perception of cessation (*nirodhasaññā*) are defined at AN V 110,22–111,3 as discursive contemplations on Nibbāna, though elsewhere *virāgānupassanā* and *nirodhānupassanā* are treated as advanced contemplations of insight (e.g., at Paṭis II 67; Vism 629,3–5; Ppn 20:90).

120 Ee wrongly numbers these suttas "99–100," which throws off the subsequent numbers. (Feer has corrected this error in his introduction to Part V, p. v.) The following errors in Ee's numbering scheme should also be noted: Ee's block "100–110 (1–12)"—corresponding to my "111 (1)–120 (10)"—counts twelve suttas though there are only ten. (The summary verse in Be includes *taṇhā-tasināya*, but as the two are merged only ten suttas are counted.) Ee's block "154–164 (1–10)"—corresponding to my block "165 (1)–174 (10)"—has the right number of suttas but numbers them as if there were eleven.

121 I follow the method of Ee, which ends with 175. Apparently three repetitions of the entire series should be

understood for each of the three ways of describing the enlightenment factors. Here the other two methods—"the Deathless as its ground" series and the "slants towards Nibbāna" series—are mentioned only in the last sutta.

47. Satipaṭṭhānasaṃyutta

122 What follows is the *uddesa* (condensed statement) of the Satipaṭṭhāna Sutta (DN No. 22; MN No. 10) without the *niddesa* (elaboration). Full-length commentaries on the text are at Sv III 741–61 and Ps II 244–66; the commentary in Spk is much abridged. The relevant passages, with excerpts from the subcommentary, are translated in Soma, *The Way of Mindfulness*, pp. 35–64.

The commentaries offer two derivations of *satipaṭṭhāna*: one from *sati* + *upaṭṭhāna*, "the establishment of mindfulness"; the other from *sati* + *paṭṭhāna*, "the foundation of mindfulness." The former emphasizes the *act* of setting up mindfulness, the latter the *objects* to which mindfulness is applied. While the commentaries lean towards the derivation from *sati* + *paṭṭhāna*, the former is certainly more original and is supported by the Skt *smṛtyupasthāna*. See too the common expressions, *upaṭṭhitasati*, "with mindfulness established" (e.g., at **54:13**; V 331,10, etc.) and *parimukhaṃ satiṃ upaṭṭhapetvā*, "having established mindfulness in front of him" (e.g., at **54:1**; V 311,13, etc.). Paṭis, by consistently glossing *sati* with *upaṭṭhāna*, also shows a preference for this derivation. For a brief explanation of the expression according to the commentarial method, see Vism 678–79 (Ppn 22:34).

123 *Ekāyano ayaṃ maggo* is often translated "This is the only way" (Soma) or "This is the sole way" (Nyanaponika), implying that the Buddha's way of mindfulness is an exclusive path. The commentary to the Satipaṭṭhāna Sutta, however, gives five explanations of the phrase, of which only one suggests exclusivity (see Sv III 743–44; Ps I 229–30; translated in Soma, *The Way of Mindfulness*, pp. 36–39). Spk here mentions only the first: *ekamaggo ayaṃ bhikkhave maggo, na dvedhāpathabhūto*; "a single path, bhikkhus, is this path, not a forked path." *Ekāyana magga*

occurs elsewhere in the Nikāyas only at MN I 74,14–15 foll., where it clearly means a path leading straight to its destination. I thus understand the metaphorical use of the phrase to be a way of indicating that *satipaṭṭhāna* leads straight to "the purification of beings," etc.; perhaps the way of mindfulness is being contrasted with other types of meditation that do not always lead straight to the goal. For a fuller discussion, see Gethin, *The Buddhist Path to Awakening*, pp. 59–66. The word should not be confused with *ekayāna*, "one vehicle," the central theme of the Saddharma Puṇḍarīka Sūtra.

Spk explains the "method" (*ñāya*) as the Noble Eightfold Path. Thus, by developing the path of *satipaṭṭhāna*, which is mundane in the preliminary phase, one eventually achieves the supramundane path. On *ñāya*, see **II, n. 122**.

124 For a translation of the commentarial passage on this basic formula, see Soma, *The Way of Mindfulness*, pp. 51–64. An early word gloss is at Vibh 194–95. Gethin discusses the basic formula, *Buddhist Path to Awakening*, pp. 47–53.

A few key points: The repetitive phrase "contemplating the body in the body" (*kāye kāyānupassī*) serves "to determine the object (the body) by isolating it" from other things such as feeling, mind, etc., and to show that one contemplates only the body as such, not as permanent, pleasurable, a self, or beautiful. Similarly in regard to the other three establishments. "Ardent" (*ātāpī*) connotes energy, "clearly comprehending" (*sampajāno*) implies wisdom. "Covetousness and displeasure" (*abhijjhā-domanassa*) are code words for the first two hindrances, and thus their removal may be understood to imply some success in concentration. Thus altogether four of the five spiritual faculties (*indriya*) are indicated here, and while faith is not mentioned it is clearly a prerequisite for taking up the practice in the first place.

Spk glosses *vineyya*: *tadaṅgavinayena vā vikkhambhanavinayena vā vinayitvā*, "*having removed*: having removed by removal in a particular respect or by removal through suppression." "Removal in a particular respect" signifies temporary removal by deliberate restraint or by insight, "removal through suppression" temporary removal by the attainment of jhāna. The phrase need not be understood to mean that one must first abandon the hindrances before one starts to develop the four establishments of mindfulness. It would be sufficient to have temporarily suspended "covetousness and displeasure" through dedication to the practice itself.

125 The same advice is at **36:7** (IV 211,1–19). Spk comments at length on the practice of clear comprehension. For a translation see Soma, *The Way of Mindfulness*, pp. 83–132, and Bodhi, *Discourse on the Fruits of Recluseship*, pp. 96–134. Briefly, the four are: (1) clear comprehension of purposefulness (*sātthaka-sampajañña*), discerning a worthy purpose in one's intended action; (2) clear comprehension of suitability (*sappāya-sampajañña*), discerning a suitable means of achieving one's aim; (3) clear comprehension of the resort (*gocara-sampajañña*), maintaining awareness of one's meditation subject when engaged in various activities; and (4) clear comprehension as nondelusion (*asammoha-sampajañña*), discerning one's actions as conditioned processes devoid of a substantial self. For a good contemporary explanation, see Nyanaponika, *The Heart of Buddhist Meditation*, pp. 46–57.

126 Spk: This bhikkhu, it is said, after asking the Buddha to explain a meditation subject, had just roamed here and there and did not devote himself to solitude. Therefore the Buddha spoke thus to restrain him.

127 Spk: The view is that of one's responsibility for one's own action (*kammassakatādiṭṭhi*), i.e., belief in kamma and its fruits, which implies as well belief in rebirth.

The Buddha's statement here establishes that right view (the first factor of the Noble Eightfold Path) and right conduct (factors 3–5) are the basis for the successful practice of mindfulness meditation.

128 Spk says nothing, but Sv III 765,15–18 and Ps I 249,24–27 explain in regard to mindfulness of breathing: "At one time in his own and at another in another's respiration-body, he dwells in contemplation of the body. By this there is reference to the time when the yogi's mind moves repeatedly back and forth (internally and externally by way of object) without laying aside the familiar subject of

meditation" (*The Way of Mindfulness*, p. 74). In relation to the other three establishments, the commentaries give basically the same explanation, without addressing the problem of how one without psychic abilities can contemplate another person's feelings and states of mind.

129 Interestingly, the first section of the contemplation of phenomena deals with the five hindrances, showing how the application of mindfulness can turn even defilements into the raw material for the development of the practice.

130 The parable of the hawk and the quail is also related in the Sakuṇagghi Jātaka (No. 168; Jā II 58–59), with the Bodhisatta as the quail and Devadatta as the hawk. For additional references, see KS 5:125, n. 1. Though *sakuṇagghi* is a feminine, this need not imply the hawk is female. *Ajjhapattā* is a reduplicated aorist which, in the Pāli tradition, became transformed into a past participle; see von Hinüber, "Traces of the Reduplicated Aorist in Pāli," in *Selected Papers*, pp. 52–61. The conjunction of two finite verbs here seems hard to account for, as normally an absolutive would precede a finite verb.

131 PED does not list *apatthaddhā*, but CPD explains it as a past participle < Skt *apa-stambh*. Ja II 59,17,20 reads *atthaddhā/thaddhā*. Be and Ee have *sake bale asaṃvadamānā*, Se *sake bale avacamānā*; Spk explains it as though it were not a negation: *saṃvadamānā ti sammā vadamānā, attano balassa suṭṭhu vaṇṇaṃ vadamānā*; "*boasting*: speaking fully, thoroughly praising her own strength."

132 Cp. **35:243** (IV 185,7–15; 186,23–30).

133 Be reads *tasmiṃ yeva kaṭṭhakataṅgāre avassajjetvā*, followed by Ee (which differs only in having *avasajjetvā*); Se has *tasmiṃ yeva makkaṭaṃ uddharitvā avissajjetvā*, an obvious rewording of the received text to make it more intelligible. Neither Spk nor Spk-pṭ offers any help. CPD calls *kaṭṭhakataṅgāre* a "problematic reading of uncertain meaning" and supposes the sentence to be corrupt. However, in a recent review of *Sanskrit-Wörterbuch der buddhistischen Texte aus den Turfan-Funden*, Bhikkhu Pāsādiko points out that the *Wörterbuch* has an entry *kāṣṭha-kaḍambara* corresponding to *kaṭṭhakataṅgāra* of the Pāli; on this basis he suggests amending our text to read *kaṭṭhakaliṅgare āvajjetvā*, which he renders

"having fastened [the monkey] just to that wooden staff [of his]." Pāsādiko translates the Chinese version of the Saṃyuktāgama text thus: "Hardly has the hunter arrived when he takes the staff, fastens [the monkey] to it and goes away, carrying [the load] on his shoulder" (pp. 191–92). I accept the amendation of *kataṅgāre* to *kaliṅgare*, though I think it likely that the latter refers, not to the hunter's staff, but to the same (*tasmiṃ yeva*) block of wood on which the monkey was trapped by the pitch. Elsewhere *kaliṅgara* means log or block (see **20:8**, Dhp 41), though I know of no instance where it means a staff. I also do not see how *āvajjetvā* could mean "having fastened," and prefer to retain the verb given in the text. The sense then is that the hunter secures the monkey to the block of wood to which it is stuck and then goes off with the block, bringing the monkey along.

134 Reading with Se, *sakassa bhattu nimittaṃ na uggaṇhāti.* Be and Ee have *bhattassa*, but *bhattu* is genitive of *bhattar*, the relevant noun here (not *bhatta*). I translate literally, even at the cost of awkwardness, to preserve the parallel with the meditating monk.

135 Spk: He does not know, "This meditation subject of mine has reached up to conformity or change-of-lineage." He isn't able to grasp the sign of his own mind.

The terms "conformity" (*anuloma*) and "change-of-lineage" (*gotrabhū*) denote the final occasions of sense-sphere consciousness before one attains either jhāna or the supramundane path and fruit; presumably the preliminary to jhāna is intended. The phrase *cittassa nimittaṃ gahessati* is at AN III 423,13, glossed by Mp: *cittassa nimittan ti samādhivipassanācittassa nimittaṃ, samādhivipassanākāraṃ*; "sign of the mind: sign of the mind of concentration or insight, the mode of concentration or insight."

136 This portion of the sutta is quoted at Vism 150–51 (Ppn 4:122). Spk says that *satipaṭṭhāna* is treated as insight of the preliminary stage.

137 This incident is recorded in the Mahāparinibbāna Sutta, at DN II 98–101. Spk assigns the incident to the tenth month before the Master's demise.

138 *Jīvitasaṅkhāraṃ adhiṭṭhāya*. Spk: The life formation is life

itself [Spk-pṭ: because of revitalizing the body without letting it fail] as well as fruition attainment, by which life is vitalized, sustained, prolonged. The latter is intended here. The concise meaning is, "I will attain fruition attainment, which is capable of prolonging life." He entered the attainment with the determination, "Let the pain not arise for another ten months," and the pain, suppressed by the attainment, did not arise for another ten months.

139 I follow Se and Ee, which do not include the initial exclamation found in Be, *diṭṭho me bhante bhagavato phāsu*; the latter, however, is at DN II 99,21. I think Ee is correct in retaining *diṭṭhā*; in Se and Be the word is taken as a past participle and is represented as neuter *diṭṭhaṃ*, but here it seems to function idiomatically with the meaning "lucky" or "splendid." See DN III 73,18: *diṭṭhā bho satta jīvasi*, "It's splendid, sir being, that you're alive." The lines that follow are at **22:84** (III 106,19–21); see **III, n. 149**. Here Spk explains *dhammā pi nappaṭibhanti* as meaning, "The teachings on the establishments of mindfulness (*satipaṭṭhānadhammā*) are not clear to me." Possibly the expression means simply, "Things (in general) aren't clear to me."

140 *Anantaraṃ abāhiraṃ*. Spk: Without making a distinction of inside and outside with respect either to Dhamma or persons. One makes the distinction with respect to Dhamma when one thinks, "I will teach so much Dhamma to others but this much I won't teach." One does so with respect to persons when one thinks, "I'll teach this person but not that one." The Master did not teach in this way. The "teacher's closed fist" (*ācariyamuṭṭhi*) is found among outsiders, who reserve certain teachings for their favourite pupils only when they are lying on their deathbed; but the Tathāgata does not have this.

In connection with these two ideas, see Mil 144–45, 159–60.

141 Readings of this obscure compound vary. Be has *vekhamissakena*, Se *veghamissakena* (the reading at Ee DN II 100,14–15), Ee *vedhamissakena*. In a note Be proposes *veṭhamissakena*, the actual reading in the gloss given by Spk (both Be and Se). A similar expression occurs at Th 143a, in Ee *veghamissena*. At EV I, n. to 143, Norman presents the

case for *veṭha* (= Skt *veṣṭa*, "band, noose"). Gombrich discusses the problem in "Old Bodies Like Carts," arguing for the reading *vedha*, "trembling," but it is hard to see how this sits comfortably in a compound with *missakena*. Hence I follow Spk and Norman in reading *veṭhamissakena*.

Spk: *By a combination of straps*: by a combination of straps through being repaired with bands for the arms, bands for the wheels, etc. (*bāhābandhacakkabandhādinā paṭisaṅkharaṇena veṭhamissakena*). *So it seems … keeps going* (*maññe yāpeti*): He shows, "Like an old cart, it seems it is by a combination of straps, i.e., by being strapped with the fruition of arahantship (*arahattaphalaveṭhanena*), that the body of the Tathāgata assumes the four modes of deportment."

It should be noted that this passage would hardly make sense if the commentaries were right in holding that Ānanda was born on the same day as the Bodhisatta, for the Buddha would not need to insist on the frailties of old age if Ānanda too was an old man. See **II, n. 296**.

142 The expression used here is *animitta cetosamādhi*, but this concentration must be different from the one with the same name mentioned at **40:9**. Spk explains the latter as deep insight concentration, the present one as fruition attainment (*phalasamāpatti*). This would then make it identical with the *animitta cetovimutti* of **41:7** (IV 297,4–6).

143 The *attadīpa* exhortation is also at **22:43**. Spk explains *dhamma* in *dhammadīpa, dhammasaraṇa* as the ninefold supramundane Dhamma (the four paths, four fruits, and Nibbāna). *Tamatagge* has been much puzzled over in the scholarly literature on the Mahāparinibbāna Sutta. Spk (which parallels Sv II 548–49) takes the term as equivalent to *tama-agge*, with *-t-* inserted as a euphonic conjunct (*padasandhi*). It is possible that *tamatagge* should be understood as equivalent to *tamato agge*, on the analogy of *ajjatagge* or *daharatagge*, but this would still leave the problem of meaning unsolved; "from the darkness on" hardly makes good sense here. Spk is evidently perplexed about the meaning and, without quite admitting uncertainty, wavers between taking *tama* as the superlative suffix (transposed by metathesis) and as "darkness": "These are topmost (*aggatamā*), hence *tamataggā*. Thus, 'having cut the

entire stream of darkness (*tamasotaṃ* in both Be and Se, but *tamayogaṃ*, bond of darkness, in the parallel passage at Sv II 549,1), these bhikkhus of mine will be at the extreme top, in the highest place. They will be at the top of them. Among all those keen on the training, just those whose range is the four *satipaṭṭhānas* will be at the top.' Thus he brings the teaching to its culmination in arahantship." Spk-pṭ explains *tama-agge*: "In the absence of the bond of darkness (*tamayoga*!), (they will be) at the top of the world with its gods."

The words are not preserved in the fragments of the Turfan Skt version, but the Tibetan and Chinese parallels, probably based on Skt texts, point to a meaning as "the highest." I have followed suit with "topmost," though I cannot account for the exact meaning of the original or for the use of the locative. I have also gone along with the commentaries in taking *ye keci sikkhākāmā* as an implicit genitive.

144 I read with Be and Se, *uḷāraṃ pubbenāparaṃ visesaṃ sañjānanti*. Ee reads *sampajānanti*. Spk explains "successively loftier stages of distinction" by way of the successive stages of wisdom, from the comprehension of the four primary elements through the ascription of the three characteristics to all formations.

145 Spk: A fever of defilement (*kilesapariḷāha*) arises having made the body its basis (*ārammaṇa*). When this happens, one should not let oneself become excited by the defilement but "should then direct the mind to some inspiring sign" (*kismiñcideva pasādaniye nimitte cittaṃ paṇidahitabbaṃ*), that is, one should place the meditating mind on some object that inspires confidence, such as the Buddha, etc.

146 Spk: "Let me withdraw it from the inspiring object and redirect it towards the original meditation object."

147 Spk explains this to mean that he is "without defiled thought, without defiled examination," but the absence of *vitakka* and *vicāra* seems to imply he has reached the second jhāna. See too MN III 136,20–29, where the four *satipaṭṭhānas* do service for the first jhāna, and the Buddha also enjoins the practice of the four without thought and examination, hence in the mode of the second jhāna.

148 *Paṇidhāya bhāvanā*. Spk glosses *ṭhapetvā bhāvanā*, "development having put aside." Development by this method comes about by directing the mind away from its main object towards some other object. Spk compares this to a man carrying a load of sugar to a refinery who pauses from time to time, puts down the load, eats a sugar cane, and then continues on his way.

149 Spk gives various explanations of "unconstricted after and before" (*pacchā pure asaṅkhittaṃ*). See **51:20** (V 277,29–278,4) and **n. 272** below.

150 *Mahāpurisa*. See AN IV 228–35 for the eight thoughts of a great man (*aṭṭha mahāpurisavitakkā*).

151 This sutta is included in the Mahāparinibbāna Sutta at DN II 81–83 but without the last paragraph; a much more elaborate version makes up DN No. 28. In the former its chronological position seems questionable; see **n. 157**.

152 Spk: *A bellowing utterance* (*āsabhī vācā*): like (the bellowing) of a chief bull (*usabha*), unshaking, unwavering. *Definitive, categorical* (*ekaṃso gahito*): Not spoken in compliance with oral tradition, etc., but as if it had been penetrated by personal knowledge, thus it is "definitive, categorical." The meaning is that it is stated as a firm conclusion (*sanniṭṭhānakathā va*).

153 Spk explains *evaṃdhammā* as *samādhipakkhā dhammā*, "the states pertaining to concentration," and says *evaṃvihārino* is added in order to include the attainment of cessation.

154 *Api ca dhammanvayo vidito*. Spk: Inferential knowledge (*anumānañāṇa*) has arisen in accordance with the implications of his personal knowledge of the Dhamma; the methodology (*nayaggāha*) has been understood. He says, "Standing just upon the knowledge of a disciple's perfections, I know from this angle, O Blessed One."

155 Spk: Here the establishments of mindfulness are insight, the enlightenment factors are the path, and unsurpassed perfect enlightenment is arahantship. Or else the enlightenment factors are mixed (both insight and the path).

156 This conclusion also comes at the end of DN No. 28, at DN III 116, following the much more effusive praise of the Buddha found there.

157 The event related in this sutta poses a problem for the

traditional chronology of the Buddha's life. In the Mahāparinibbāna Sutta, Sāriputta's lion's roar (just above) takes place during what appears to be the Buddha's final journey along the route from Rājagaha to Vesālī. From Vesālī the Buddha heads towards Kusinārā without ever returning to Sāvatthī, some 200 km to the west. Yet the present sutta shows the Buddha residing at Sāvatthī when he receives the news of Sāriputta's death. To preserve the traditional chronology, the commentaries (Spk here, and Sv II 550) have the Buddha make an additional side trip to Sāvatthī following his rains retreat at Beluvagāmaka (see DN II 98–99), an excursion not mentioned in the Mahāparinibbāna Sutta. Sāriputta accompanies him on this trip to Sāvatthī, later takes his leave, and returns to his native village Nālakagāma, where he falls ill and dies. For the commentarial story of Sāriputta's death, see Nyanaponika, "Sāriputta: The Marshal of the Dhamma," in Nyanaponika and Hecker, *Great Disciples of the Buddha*, pp. 47–59.

158 Spk identifies this Cunda as Sāriputta's younger brother and says, improbably, that because the bhikkhus used to address him as "novice Cunda" before his higher ordination they continued to address him thus even when he was an elder.

159 Spk says that here *dhammā* signifies the condensed and catechistic teachings (*uddesaparipucchā dhammā*). The expression also occurs at **22:84** and **47:9**; see **n. 139** above and **III, n. 149**.

160 These are the five "aggregates of Dhamma" (*dhammakkhandha*) possessed in full only by arahants; see **6:2**. The ascription to Ānanda of the last two aggregates (liberation, and the knowledge and vision of liberation) seems puzzling, as he is still a trainee and thus not yet fully liberated. Such anomalies, however, do occasionally occur in the texts, as at **55:26** (V 384,1–12) where right knowledge and right liberation, usually unique attributes of the arahant, are ascribed to the stream-enterer Anāthapiṇḍika.

161 Be and Ee include *otiṇṇo* between *ovādako* and *viññāpako*. The word is not in Se or SS.

162 The commentaries assign the death of Moggallāna to a

fortnight after that of Sāriputta. Sāriputta expired on the full-moon day of the month Kattika (October–November), Moggallāna on the following new-moon day. For an account of his death, see Hecker, "Moggallāna: Master of Psychic Power," in Nyanaponika and Hecker, *Great Disciples of the Buddha*, pp. 100–5.

163 I translate on the basis of the Se reading: *asuññā me sā bhikkhave parisā hoti*. Be differs only in omitting *sā*, but Ee brings *parinibbutesu Sāriputta-Moggallānesu* into this sentence and then reads *suññā me bhikkhave parisā hoti*, "Now that Sāriputta and Moggallāna have attained final Nibbāna, this assembly, bhikkhus, has become empty." Spk gives no help in resolving the ambiguity.

164 The "four assemblies" are bhikkhus, bhikkhunīs, male lay followers, and female lay followers.

165 As at **47:3**.

166 As at **6:1**, **6:2**.

167 The name is a feminine (meaning "frying pan"), but Spk says the name is given in the feminine gender (*itthiliṅga-vasena laddhanāmaṃ*), presumably to a boy. The passage contains no pronouns that might establish the gender.

168 From Spk's description, it seems that the master places the lower end of the bamboo pole over the base of his throat or forehead (*galavāṭake vā nalāṭe*), and the pupil then climbs via his shoulders to the top of the pole. Though in the sutta the master speaks as if they both descend from the pole, this may be only a figure of speech. Spk: The master protects himself when he holds the pole firmly, moves with his apprentice, and looks constantly at the top of the pole. The apprentice protects himself when he keeps his body straight, balances himself against the wind, sets up steady mindfulness, and sits down motionless.

169 Spk: The bhikkhu who gives up frivolous activity and pursues, develops, and cultivates his basic meditation subject day and night attains arahantship. Then, when others see him and gain confidence in him, they become destined for heaven. This one protects others by protecting himself.

170 The four terms are *khantiyā avihiṃsāya mettatāya anudayatāya*. Spk takes the last three as respectively compassion, lovingkindness, and altruistic joy, and explains this maxim

from a narrowly monastic perspective thus: "The bhikkhu develops the jhānas based on the *brahmavihāra*, then uses the jhāna as a basis for insight and attains arahantship. This one protects himself by protecting others." For a broader and profounder treatment of this maxim, see Nyanaponika, *Protection through Satipaṭṭhāna*.

171 This sutta is related in the introduction to Ja No. 96 (I 393–401), which concludes with a verse that alludes back to the sutta:

Samatittikaṃ anavasesakaṃ
telapattaṃ yathā parihareyya
evaṃ sacittam anurakkhe
patthayāno disaṃ agatapubbaṃ.

As one might carry a bowl of oil
Full to the brim without spilling a drop,
So should one protect one's own mind,
Yearning for the quarter not reached
before (i.e., Nibbāna).

172 From the Pāli it cannot be determined whether the crowd gathers because they have *heard* "The most beautiful girl of the land!" being announced or gathers *exclaiming* "The most beautiful girl of the land!" I take it in the former way. Spk says such a girl is devoid of six physical defects (too tall or too short, too thin or too stout, too dark or too fair) and endowed with five kinds of beauty (of skin, flesh, sinews, bones, and age). The expression *paramapāsāvinī nacce, paramapāsāvinī gīte* seems to be unique to this text. PED explains *pāsāvin* as "bringing forth," but see MW, s.v. *pra-sava* (2) > *pra-savin*, derived from *pra-sūti* (1) and meaning "impelling, exciting." Spk: "In dancing and singing her presentation is supreme, her performance is the best; she dances and sings supremely well."

173 Modelled on **45:18**. "Wholesome virtues" (*kusalāni sīlāni*), just below, are identified by Spk with the fourfold purification of virtue. See **n. 33**.

174 *Sahassaṃ lokaṃ abhijānāmi*. Spk: This is stated by way of his constant dwelling. For after rising in the morning and

washing his face, the elder sits in his dwelling and recollects a thousand aeons in the past and a thousand aeons in the future (sic; no comment from Spk-pṭ). In regard to the thousandfold world system in the present, he follows its course just by adverting to it. Thus with the divine eye he directly knows the thousandfold world.

175 This passage extends to each of the four establishments of mindfulness the general formula for reviewing the truth of the path in the Dhammacakkappavattana Sutta (see **56:11**; V 422,23–30).

176 This practice is described at MN III 124,10–20 (as a wonderful quality of the Buddha); at AN II 45,15–20 (as a development of concentration, also at DN III 223,9–17); at AN IV 32,24–33,2 (as a factor leading to the four *paṭisambhidās*); and at AN IV 168,12–15 (as a practice of mindfulness and clear comprehension). Paṭis I 178–80 treats this practice in relation to mindfulness of breathing. Spk explains the feelings, thoughts, and perceptions as those that occur in relation to the sense bases and objects comprehended in developing insight.

177 Here the singular is used and the preferred sense would be "the establishing of mindfulness."

178 This practice is called *satipaṭṭhānabhāvanā* presumably because it carries the practice of contemplation to a deeper level than the basic exercise. In the basic exercise the task set for the meditator is to contemplate the particular establishment chosen according to the prescribed pattern. At this stage, however, one gains insight into the arising and vanishing of the object, which prepares the way for the deeper insight knowledges to emerge.

The expression *samudayadhammānupassī kāyasmiṃ viharati* is usually translated "he abides contemplating in the body its arising factors" (as at MLDB, p. 149), on the assumption that the compound contains a plural, *samudayadhammā*. A plural sense, however, is not mandatory, and it is more consistent with the use of the suffix *-dhamma* elsewhere to take it as meaning "subject to" or "having the nature of" here as well. At **22:126** (III 171–72) *samudayadhamma*, *vayadhamma*, and *samudayavayadhamma* serve as *bahubbīhi* (adjectival) compounds in apposition to each of the five aggregates, and it seems that in this passage too the terms should be understood in the same sense, as singulars meaning "subject to origination," etc.

179 *Mā vo amataṃ panassa*. Spk offers no help, but I take *panassa* to be an aorist of *panassati*. Woodward has apparently understood it as *pan' assa* and translates, "But let not that be to you the Deathless" (KS 5:161). But *pana* here would be syntactically out of place.

180 Here *satipaṭṭhāna* obviously refers to the four objects of mindfulness.

181 In this passage *citta* is taken to be synonymous with *viññāṇā*; *nāmarūpa*, being the condition for the latter, is the condition for the former as well. For *citta* always arises based on the physical organism (*rūpa*) and in conjunction with contact, feeling, perception, volition, and attention, the constituents of *nāma*.

182 *Manasikārasamudayā dhammānaṃ samudayo*. Spk: The phenomena of the enlightenment factors originate through careful attention; the phenomena of the hindrances through careless attention. Cp. AN V 107,6–7: *Manasikāra-sambhavā sabbe dhammā, phassasamudayā sabbe dhammā*; "All phenomena come into being through attention; all phenomena originate from contact."

183 This sutta differs from **47:18** only in being a reminiscence of the events narrated there.

184 Ee wrongly reads here "73–82 (1–10)," though there are twelve suttas. Also, in the Searches Chapter (*Esanavagga*, IX), Ee reads "83–93 (1–11)" instead of "85–94 (1–10)." Apparently Ee counts the "craving" suttas as two, though in the previous chapters it reckoned the two together.

185 The verse varies between the different eds. I translate from Be.

186 Be puts the summary verse after the note, but I follow Ee, whose arrangement is more logical.

48. Indriyasaṃyutta

187 As I point out in the Introduction to Part V (pp. 1508–9), while the other saṃyuttas of this Vagga each deal with a single closed group made up of a fixed number of items,

the Indriyasaṃyutta deals with a variety of sets collected under the general rubric of *indriya*. The most important is the group called the five spiritual faculties, which probably formed the original core of the saṃyutta. With the expanding interest in classification, the compilers of the canon probably felt obliged to include in this saṃyutta the other sets of faculties, thus imparting to it a heterogeneous character. The complete list of twenty-two faculties is at Vibh 122, commented on at Vibh-a 125–28; see too Vism 491–93 (Ppn 16:1–12). Interestingly, this list belongs to the Abhidhamma analysis; the Indriya-vibhaṅga does not include a Suttanta analysis, which suggests that the idea of *indriya* as a general category belongs to the Abhidhamma proper rather than to the suttas.

188 The faculties alone, among the various "aids to enlightenment," are treated in terms of the "gratification triad" (here), the "origin pentad," and "the noble-truth tetrad" (just below). The explanation for this probably lies in the fact that the five faculties are included in the wider list of twenty-two faculties intended as a "catalogue of phenomenal reality," and thus had to be expounded in terms of the wider categories used to analyse the constituents of reality. Gethin discusses this point more fully in *The Buddhist Path to Awakening*, pp. 123–25.

189 The difference drawn here between the arahant and the stream-enterer parallels that mentioned at **22:109–10**; see **III, n. 221**. Be and Ee read *ariyasāvaka* in the definition of the arahant too, but I follow Se, which reads *bhikkhu*.

190 Spk: They do not understand them by way of the Four Noble Truths. The faith faculty originates from adverting by way of resolution (*adhimokkha*); the energy faculty, from adverting by way of application (*paggaha*); the mindfulness faculty, from adverting by way of establishing (*upaṭṭhāna*); the concentration faculty, from adverting by way of nondistraction (*avikkhepa*); the wisdom faculty, from adverting by way of seeing (*dassana*). So too, all the faculties originate from adverting by way of desire (*chanda*; Spk-pṭ: wholesome desire to act, occurring in the mode of wanting to arouse the faculties) and from adverting by way of attention (*manasikāra*; Spk-pṭ: careful attention pro-

ductive of adverting when it occurs weakly by way of the faculties).

191 See **55:2**, etc. A parallel treatment of the five powers (*pañca bala*) is at AN III 11–12.

192 See **48:10** just below. Parallel definitions of the five powers are at AN III 10–11, but with the *samādhibala* defined solely by the jhāna formula.

193 Here the *satindriya* is explained with *sati* meaning memory rather than mindful awareness; see **n. 63**. Spk: Discretion (*nepakkha*) is a term for wisdom. But why is wisdom mentioned in the explanation of mindfulness? To show the strength of mindfulness; for here strong mindfulness is intended, and that is strong only when associated with wisdom, not when dissociated from it. Thus that is said to show mindfulness associated with wisdom.

194 *Vossaggārammaṇaṃ karitvā*. It is not clear whether the absolutive should be taken in apposition to the noble disciple or the concentration, but I understand it in the latter sense. Spk glosses: "having made Nibbāna the object."

At AN I 36,20–24 it is said that few beings gain the concentration that makes release its object, compared to the greater number who do not gain it. Not much else is said in the Nikāyas about *vossaggārammaṇa samādhi*, but the expression occurs in Paṭis, and this text and its commentary shed light on how the Pāli exegetical tradition interprets it. Paṭis II 96–97 uses the expression in explicating the phrase, "[one] develops serenity preceded by insight" (*vipassanāpubbaṅgamaṃ samathaṃ bhāveti*; AN II 157,10–11): "Insight has the sense of contemplation as impermanent, as suffering, as nonself. Concentration is nondistraction, one-pointedness of mind having as object release of the phenomena produced therein (*tattha jātānaṃ dhammānañ ca vossaggārammaṇatā cittassa ekaggatā avikkhepo samādhi*). Thus first comes insight, afterwards serenity."

On this Paṭis-a III 586–87 comments: "*The phenomena produced therein*: the phenomena of mind and mental factors produced by that insight. *Having as object release*: here release is Nibbāna, for Nibbāna is called release because it is the releasing of the conditioned, its relinquishment. Insight and the phenomena associated with it have

Nibbāna as object, Nibbāna as support, because they are established on Nibbāna as their support in the sense of slanting towards it by way of inclination.... *Concentration* is nondistraction distinguished into access and absorption (*upacārappanābhedo avikkhepo*), consisting in the one-pointedness of mind aroused by being established on Nibbāna, with that as cause by taking as object release of the phenomena produced therein. Concentration partaking of penetration (*nibbedhabhāgiyo samādhi*), aroused subsequent to insight, is described."

195 Spk resolves *udayatthagāmiyā* as *udayañ ca atthañ ca gacchantiyā* and glosses it with *udayabbayapariggahikāya* ("discerning rise and fall"). This is clearly identical with the wisdom that observes the origination (*samudaya*) and passing away (*atthagama*) of the five aggregates, as described in the stock formula at **12:21**, **22:5**, etc.

196 Spk: In this sutta the faculties of faith, mindfulness, and wisdom are preliminary (*pubbabhāga*, i.e., forerunners of the supramundane path); the faculty of energy is mixed (preliminary and supramundane); the faculty of concentration is exclusively supramundane.

197 *Sammappadhāne ārabbha*. Spk: *Sammappadhāne paṭicca, sammappadhāne bhāvento ti attho*; "in dependence on the right strivings; the meaning is, 'by developing the right strivings.'"

198 For the distinction between the *dhammānusārī* and the *saddhānusārī*, see **25:1**. Spk: The path of the *dhammānusārī* is sharp, his knowledge occurs valiantly. He cuts off the defilements effortlessly, like one cutting a plantain trunk with a sharp knife. The path of the *saddhānusārī* is not so sharp, nor does his knowledge occur so valiantly. He cuts off the defilements with effort, like one cutting a plantain trunk with a dull knife.

199 Ee has passed over the correct reading, *phalavemattatā*, in favour of the faulty *balavemattatā*. Spk glosses this as an instrumental, *phalanānattena*.

200 Spk: One who "activates them fully" (*paripūrakārī*), who practises fully the path of arahantship, "succeeds fully" (*paripūraṃ ārādheti*), i.e., achieves the fruit of arahantship. One who "activates them partly" (*padesakārī*), who practises

the lower three paths, "succeeds partly" (*padesaṃ ārādheti*), i.e., achieves only the lower three fruits. Cp. AN I 232,30–32, 235,11–13.

201 On the five types of nonreturner, see **n. 65**.

202 Spk: In this sutta the faculties are exclusively supramundane. Despite the statement here restricting the faculties to those at the minimum level of path-attainer, the Pāli tradition, beginning with the Abhidhamma, regards the faculties as general wholesome capacities also possessed by worldlings. Some of the other early Buddhist schools were more stringent. See the discussion in Gethin, *The Buddhist Path to Awakening*, pp. 126–38.

203 See **35:154** and **IV, n. 152**.

204 The title should be Punabbhava Sutta, as in Be and Se. The assimilation of the five faculties here to the elements, aggregates, and sense bases should be understood by way of the explanation in **n. 188** above.

205 The femininity faculty (*itthindriya*) and the masculinity faculty (*purisindriya*) are rarely mentioned in the Nikāyas, but play an important role in a sutta at AN IV 57–59. The two are included among the types of derivative form (*upādā rūpa*) in the Abhidhamma; they are defined at Dhs §§633–34 and Vibh 122–23, and commented on at As 321–23 and Vism 447 (Ppn 14:58). Spk says the femininity faculty exercises control over femininity (i.e., determines the distinctive feminine features of a female); the masculinity faculty exercises control over masculinity. The life faculty (*jīvitindriya*) is another type of derivative form, responsible for maintaining conascent physical phenomena. It is defined at Dhs §635 and Vibh 123 and commented on at As 323 and Vism 447 (Ppn 14:59).

206 This sutta is also at It 53, with the addition of verses that partly help to clarify the meaning. The three faculties are formally defined at Vibh 124, but more concisely than in Spk, which explains: The faculty "I shall know the as-yet-unknown" (*anaññātaññassāmītindriya*) is the faculty arising at the moment of the path of stream-entry in one practising with the thought, "I will know the Dhamma I have not known before in beginningless saṃsāra." The faculty of final knowledge (*aññindriya*) is the faculty arisen on the six

occasions from the fruit of stream-entry on (through the path of arahantship); it occurs in the mode of knowing more deeply those same things known (by the first path). The faculty of one endowed with final knowledge (*aññātāvindriya*) is the faculty arisen in regard to those things fully known at the fruit of arahantship.

207 This sutta, reverting to the five spiritual faculties, seems out of place here. On the five kinds of nonreturner, see above **n. 65**. Spk: A one-seeder (*ekabījī*) is a stream-enterer who attains arahantship after only one more existence; a clan-to-clanner (*kolaṅkola*), one who fares on in saṃsāra for two or three existences and then makes an end to suffering; a seven-lives-at-moster (*sattakhattuparama*), one who is reborn seven times at most, without taking an eighth existence. The three are defined at Pp 15–16, with elaboration at Pp-a 195–97.

208 Spk: It is the eye and a faculty in the sense of controlling or dominating the phenomena arisen in the eye door, thus the "eye faculty." The same method in regard to the ear, etc.

209 Here Be also reads *bhikkhu* in the definition, and so too below at **48:33**, in contrast to *ariyasāvaka* in the parallel texts **48:4–5**.

210 The distinctions among these faculties will be explained just below at **48:36**. Spk: It is pleasure and a faculty in the sense of controlling or dominating the conascent states: thus the "pleasure faculty," etc. Here, the pleasure, pain, and displeasure faculties are of the sense sphere only; the joy faculty is of three planes, excluding the formless sphere; the equanimity faculty is of four planes.

The allocation by way of planes is made on the basis of the Abhidhamma system, according to which physical *pleasure* and *pain* occur only in body-consciousness, a sense-sphere citta; *displeasure*, only in the cittas accompanied by aversion, likewise sense-sphere cittas; *joy*, in sense-sphere cittas, cittas of the lower three jhānas, and certain supramundane cittas; *equanimity*, in sense-sphere cittas, the fourth-jhāna citta of the form sphere, all formless-sphere cittas, and certain supramundane cittas. See CMA 3:2–4.

211 *Kāyikaṃ sātaṃ*. Spk: "Bodily" means based on bodily sensitivity (*kāyappasādavatthuka*); "comfort" is synonymous with pleasure and means sweet (*madhura*).

212 According to the Abhidhamma, all bodily feeling, that is, feeling arisen through bodily sensitivity (*kāyappasāda*), is either pleasant or painful; there is no neutral feeling based on bodily sensitivity. Hence Spk explains the bodily equanimity as feeling arisen based on the other four senses, the eye, etc. The word *upekkhā*, translated as equanimity, has two main denotations. In relation to feeling it denotes neutral feeling, *adukkhamasukhā vedanā*, feeling which is neither painful nor pleasant. As a mental quality, however, it denotes mental neutrality, impartiality, or balance of mind (called *tatramajjhattatā* in the Abhidhamma, which assigns it to the *saṅkhārakkhandha*). In this sense it occurs as the fourth divine abode (impartiality towards beings), as the seventh factor of enlightenment (mental equipoise), and as a quality of the meditative mind mentioned in the formulas for the third and fourth jhānas. For a fuller discussion of the different types of *upekkhā*, see Vism 160–62 (Ppn 4:156–70).

213 Cp. **12:62** and **36:10**, which both include the simile of the fire-sticks.

214 *Uppaṭipātika*. Spk: Though taught in the order that accords with the taste of the Dhamma (following Be: *yathādhamma-rasena*; Se has *yathādhammārammaṇavasena*), it is named "Irregular Order" because it is not taught like the other suttas in this Analysis of Faculties. Spk-pṭ: What is meant is that it is taught in the sequence of things to be abandoned, not like the other suttas which proceed in the regular sequence beginning with the pleasure faculty.

215 *Sanimittaṃ sanidānaṃ sasaṅkhāraṃ sappaccayaṃ*. All these terms are synonymous.

216 From this point on the sutta is quoted extensively at Vism 165–66. Spk's explanations correspond to Vism 166 (Ppn 4:186–89). In the following notes I select only the chief points.

217 Spk: The pain faculty actually ceases and is abandoned at the moment of the access to the first jhāna; displeasure, etc., (at the access) to the second jhāna, etc. Nevertheless, their cessation is said to take place in the jhānas themselves because their reinforced cessation (*atisayanirodha*) occurs there. Simple cessation occurs at the access, reinforced ces-

sation in the jhānas. Thus, for instance, though the pain faculty has ceased in the access to the first jhāna, it may arise again through contact with flies and mosquitoes or because of an uncomfortable seat; but not in absorption. (Within the absorption), when his whole body is suffused with rapture and engulfed in happiness, the pain faculty has thoroughly ceased because it is beaten away by opposition.

218 I read with Se and Ee *tathatthāya cittaṃ upasaṃharati*; Be has *tadatthāya*. Spk: The nonattainer directs his mind for the purpose of arousing it; the attainer, for the purpose of entering it.

219 This seems difficult to square with the usual jhāna formula, which indicates that the first jhāna is already free from all unwholesome states, including *domanassa*. Spk: The faculty of displeasure is abandoned in the access to the second jhāna but arises again when there is bodily fatigue and mental strain on account of thought and examination. But in the second jhāna, which is devoid of thought and examination, it does not arise at all.

220 The pleasure faculty (*sukhindriya*) here is bodily pleasant feeling, not the happiness (also called *sukha*) the meditator is said to "experience with the body" in the third jhāna. The latter *sukha* is actually mental happiness, identical with *somanassa*. Spk: The pleasure faculty is abandoned already in the access to the third jhāna, but it may arise when the body is touched by the sublime physical phenomena originating from rapture; but it does not arise in the third jhāna itself, for there the rapture that is a condition for bodily pleasure has entirely ceased.

221 Here the explanation in the sutta corresponds perfectly with the usual jhāna formula. Spk: Though the joy faculty has been abandoned even in the access to the fourth jhāna, because it is still close by it may arise again, for in the absence of equanimity that has reached the level of absorption (such joy) has not been fully overcome. But it does not arise in the fourth jhāna.

222 Spk seems reluctant to admit that the Buddha's body can show real signs of aging and repeatedly remarks that all these changes were not evident to others but only to Ānan-

da, who constantly dwelt in the Master's presence. Spk adds that the sense faculties themselves, being invisible, cannot be seen to have undergone deterioration, but Ānanda inferred this on the basis of the visible changes he had observed in the Blessed One.

223 *Manoramaṃ bimbaṃ*. The body.

224 This couplet is also at **I, v. 442**.

225 The same conversation is recorded at MN I 295,5–17. Though the five faculties are usually identified with the physical sense organs, here they seem to correspond to the five kinds of sense consciousness, for the physical sense faculties cannot properly be said to experience (*paccanubhoti*) an objective domain (*visaya*) or resort (*gocara*). Their function is only to serve as the media through which consciousness cognizes objects.

226 *Manopaṭisaraṇaṃ mano ca nesaṃ gocaravisayaṃ paccanubhoti*. Spk explains *mano* here as the mind-door *javana*, which experiences the object by way of lust, hatred, or delusion. In my view, this introduces an unnecessary ethical slant on the passage, which I take to be primarily epistemic in import. I interpret the sentence simply to mean that mind-consciousness has access to the data provided by the five types of sense consciousness, which it collates, categorizes, and interprets with its own stock-in-trade, namely, concepts.

227 Spk: Mindfulness is the path, liberation the fruit.

228 Also at **23:1**. See **III, n. 243**. Ee *ajjhaparaṃ* should be amended. Be has *accayāsi*, Se *accasarā*, either of which is acceptable.

229 This is the usual way of declaring him to be a nonreturner. Strangely, however, Spk says this was stated to indicate that he stood in the position of a "jhāna nonreturner," meaning that he was a stream-enterer who had abandoned the five hindrances by the first jhāna. If he were to die without having fallen away from jhāna he would be reborn in a higher world and attain final Nibbāna there, while if he were to lose the jhāna his destiny would be undetermined. However, he did not lose it, so his destiny was determined; thus the Buddha made this declaration to indicate he was a "jhāna nonreturner."

230 The statement as such seems to maintain that there is no essential difference between the faculties and the powers,

that they are the same five factors viewed from two different angles. Though it is tempting to see the powers (*bala*) as a more highly developed stage than the faculties, nothing in the canon or the commentaries supports this idea. Spk says that one factor is the faculty of faith "in the sense of exercising control in the characteristic of resolution" (*adhimokkhalakkhaṇe indaṭṭhena saddhindriyaṃ*), and the power of faith "in the sense of not being shaken by lack of faith" (*assaddhiye akampanena saddhābalaṃ*). Similarly, the other four are faculties exercising control respectively in regard to application, establishment, nondistraction, and seeing (*paggaha, upaṭṭhāna, avikkhepa, dassana*); they are powers in that they are unshaken by laziness, forgetfulness, distraction, and ignorance.

231 *Na khvāhaṃ ettha bhante bhagavato saddhāya gacchāmi*. On the idiom, see **IV, n. 321**.

232 Spk: In this sutta and the next five, the faculties of the fruit alone (*phalindriyān' eva*) are discussed. Spk-pṭ: Because the teaching has come down by way of the supreme fruit.

233 Be and Ee read *jātijarāmaraṇaṃ khayan ti kho*; Se has *jātijarāmaraṇaṃ khayantaṃ kho*. The line would make better sense if we read *jātijarāmaraṇassa khayantāni kho*.

234 Spk calls this "reviewing faith" (*paccavekkhaṇasaddhā*). Since the disciple has "pierced with wisdom" the things "previously heard," the precise role of faith here is unclear.

235 In Be and Se, *bodhipakkhiyā dhammā*, though Ee has *bodhapakkhikā*. In the commentaries *bodhipakkhiyā dhammā* is the umbrella term for the seven sets of training factors repeatedly taught by the Buddha, but in the suttas the expression has a more flexible, less technical meaning. See the discussion by Gethin, *Buddhist Path to Awakening*, pp. 289–98.

236 Noble knowledge (*ariyañāṇa*) obviously represents the wisdom faculty. Spk says that the other four faculties are mixed (mundane and supramundane), while noble knowledge is supramundane [Spk-pṭ: the knowledge of the path]; but it is possible to consider it as mixed too if it is understood to be based on the other four faculties.

237 *Ito bahiddhā*. That is, outside the Buddha's dispensation. See DN II 151,10–152,4; MN I 63,29–64,2; Dhp 254–55.

238 *Yaṃgatikāni yamparamāni yamphalāni yampariyosānāni na h' eva kho kāyena phusitvā viharati paññāya ca ativijjha passati.* A similar construction is at **46:54** (V 118,22–27 foll.). Woodward translates the above as if the negative *na* applies to both phrases: "he dwells not in personal experience thereof, nor does he pierce through and through by insight and see them plain" (KS 5:205). This rendering, however, misses the essential difference between the trainee and the arahant: the trainee *sees* Nibbāna, the final goal in which the five faculties culminate (see **48:57**), but cannot enter upon the full experience of it; the arahant both sees the goal and can experience it here and now. The conjunction *ca* should be understood in the disjunctive sense, as Spk confirms with its paraphrase: "He does not dwell having contacted that, having obtained that, with the name-body (*nāmakāya*, the corpus of mental factors); but (*pana* as a gloss on *ca*) he understands by reviewing wisdom, 'Beyond there is a faculty—the fruit of arahantship.' On the plane of the arahant he dwells having obtained this, and he understands by reviewing wisdom, 'There is a faculty—the fruit of arahantship.'"

239 *Yāni kānici padāni bodhāya saṃvattanti.* Spk: Whatever Dhamma-steps (*dhammapadāni*), sections of Dhamma (*dhammakoṭṭhāsā*), lead to enlightenment.

240 *Cittaṃ rakkhati āsavesu ca sāsavesu ca dhammesu.* Spk: He does this by preventing the arising of the taints in regard to the phenomena of the three planes.

241 *Tathāgate vā Tathāgatasāsane vā paramanipaccākāraṃ pavattamāno pavatteti.* Spk offers no help, but the expression *paramanipaccākāra* occurs in **7:15** (I 178,16); see **I, n. 472**. We find another example at MN II 120,6 foll., in relation to King Pasenadi's show of humble devotion towards the Buddha. It is puzzling that the text says a bhikkhu with taints destroyed, i.e., an arahant, should consider some benefit (*atthavasaṃ sampassamāno*) when he honours the Tathāgata, and the text adds to our puzzlement when just below it explains that the bhikkhu develops (*bhāveti*) the five faculties, as though he still had work to do to attain the final goal.

242 At **16:13** (II 225,8–12) these are said to be the five things that

lead to the nondecay and nondisappearance of the true Dhamma.

243 *Pārichattaka*. I follow PED, though Liyanaratne explains the *kiṃsuka* as the coral tree ("South Asian Flora as Reflected in the Abhidhānappadīpikā," §43). According to PED, the *pārichattaka* is *Erythmia indica,* but it is questionable whether the celestial trees mentioned here and in the next two suttas correspond to actual botanical species. See PED for references.

244 The trumpet-flower tree here = *cittapāṭali;* the silk-cotton tree of the asuras (in the following sutta) = *kūṭasimbali.*

49. Sammappadhānasaṃyutta

245 The terms of the formula are explained according to the sutta method at Vibh 208–10, commented on at Vibh-a 289–96; see too Vism 679 (Ppn 22:35). Briefly: The evil unwholesome states are greed, hatred, delusion, and the defilements associated with them; desire (*chanda*) is wholesome wish-to-do, wholesome righteous desire; effort, energy, and striving are all terms for energy (*viriya*); mind is defined by the standard register of terms for *citta*. The wholesome states are nongreed, nonhatred, nondelusion, and their concomitants. The Abhidhamma analysis, at Vibh 211–14, treats right striving as the energy factor in the supramundane paths, which accomplishes all four functions simultaneously.

51. Iddhipādasaṃyutta

246 The formula is analysed below at **51:13**. The terms are explained more elaborately, according to the sutta method, at Vibh 216–20. As usual, the Abhidhamma analysis, at Vibh 220–24, treats the *iddhipāda* as factors of the supramundane paths. Additional explanation is found at Vism 385 (Ppn 12:50–53) and Vibh-a 303–8.

Spk resolves *iddhipāda* into both *iddhiyā pādaṃ,* "base *for* spiritual power," and *iddhibhūtaṃ pādaṃ,* "base which is spiritual power." *Iddhi,* from the verb *ijjhati*—to prosper, to succeed, to flourish—originally meant success, but by the time of the Buddha it had already acquired the special nuance of spiritual success or, even more to the point, spiritual power. This can be of two kinds: success in the exercise of the *iddhividha*, the supernormal powers (as at **51:11, 14, 17**), and success in the endeavour to win liberation. The two converge in arahantship, which is both the sixth *abhiññā* (in continuity with the supernormal powers) and the final fruit of the Noble Eightfold Path. A full treatise on the various kinds of *iddhi* mentioned in the canon is at Paṭis 205–14.

The analysis at **51:13** makes it clear that an *iddhipāda* contains three main components: concentration (*samādhi*), the four volitional formations of striving (*padhānasaṅkhārā*), and the particular factor responsible for generating concentration—desire (*chanda*), energy (*viriya*), mind (*citta*), and investigation (*vīmaṃsā*). While concentration and striving are common to all four *iddhipāda*, it is the last-named factors that differentiate them as fourfold.

247 See **n. 175**.

248 The incident is included in the Mahāparinibbāna Sutta at DN II 102–7, with Spk here parallel to Sv II 554–58. The passage also occurs at Ud 62–64, commented on at Ud-a 322–30.

249 *Kappaṃ vā tiṭṭheyya kappāvasesaṃ vā*. Spk glosses *kappa*, "aeon," as *āyukappa*, "the life aeon," explained as the full normal life span of human beings at a particular time, presently a hundred years. *Kappāvasesaṃ*, "the remainder of the aeon," is explained as a little more than the normal life span of a hundred years. Spk mentions the view of one Mahāsīva Thera, who held that the Buddha could live on for the rest of this *bhaddakappa*, "excellent cosmic aeon," only to reject this proposition on the basis of the ancient commentaries. Mil 141 also interprets *kappa* here as *āyukappa*, perhaps drawing from the same source as the commentaries. Nevertheless, nowhere else in the Nikāyas is *kappa* used in the sense of a normal human life span, and there seems to be no valid reason to ascribe to *kappa* here a different meaning from the usual one, i.e., a cosmic aeon. Whether the present passage is genuine or an interpolation, and whether meditative success can confer such

extraordinary powers, are different questions about which conflicting opinions have been voiced.

250 *Yathā taṃ Mārena pariyuṭṭhitacitto.* Spk: Māra is able to obsess the mind of anyone who has not entirely abandoned all cognitive distortions (*vipallāsa*), and Ānanda had not done so (being still a stream-enterer, he was still subject to distortions of mind and perception, though not of views). Māra obsessed his mind by displaying a frightful sight, and when he saw it the elder failed to catch the hint given him by the Buddha.

251 Interestingly, no such earlier conversation between the Buddha and Māra is recorded elsewhere in the Nikāyas. Among the terms describing the disciples, *pattayogakkhemā*, "secure from bondage," is not found in Be nor mentioned in Spk (though all the other terms are glossed), but it does come in Se and Ee. The parallel DN II 104–5 excludes it, but DN III 125,19 has it.

252 *Sappāṭihāriyaṃ dhammaṃ desenti.* Spk does not explain the derivation of *sappāṭihāriya* but paraphrases: "They will teach the Dhamma, having made it emancipating." Spk-pṭ expands on this: "They will explain the Dhamma with reasons and examples so that it conveys the intended meaning; they will convey the ninefold supramundane Dhamma."

253 See **12:65** (II 107,2–4) and **II, n. 182.**

254 *Āyusaṅkhāraṃ ossaji.* Spk: The Blessed One did not relinquish his vital formation in the way one drops a clod of earth with one's hand, but he made a determination, "I will enter fruition attainment for only three months more, but not beyond that." Spk does not comment on *āyusaṅkhāra*, but it is probably identical with *jīvitindriya*, the life faculty, and with *jīvitasaṅkhāra* (at **47:9**, V 152,29) in its role of maintaining the future continuity of life. *Āyusaṅkhārā* (plural) occurs at **20:6** (II 266,19), and there is a discussion about the term at MN I 295,36–296,6.

255 The verse is difficult, especially the first couplet. It is commented on identically by Spk, Sv II 557–58, Mp IV 153–54, and Ud-a 329–30. These commentaries offer two alternative modes of interpretation, one taking *tulaṃ* and *atulaṃ* as contrasted opposites, the other taking *tulaṃ* as a present

participle and *atulaṃ* and *sambhavaṃ* as the contrasted opposites. I translate from Spk:

"(1) *Tulaṃ* is *tulitaṃ*, measured, that is delimited (*paricchinnaṃ*), because it is directly apparent even to dogs and jackals, etc.; this is sense-sphere kamma. *Atulaṃ* is what is not measurable (not comparable), because there is no other mundane kamma like it; this is exalted kamma (*mahaggatakamma*, the kamma of the jhānas and formless attainments). Or else: *tulaṃ* is sense-sphere and form-sphere kamma, *atulaṃ* formless-sphere kamma. Or *tulaṃ* is (kamma) with few results, *atulaṃ* kamma with many results. 'Continued existence' (*sambhavaṃ*) is the cause of continued existence, meaning the amassment or heaping up (of kamma). 'The formation of existence' (*bhavasaṅkhāraṃ*) is the formation (which engenders) renewed existence.... This is meant: He rejected mundane kamma consisting of the comparable and incomparable (measurable and measureless), which (kamma) is called 'continued existence' in the sense that it produces results and 'the formation of existence' in the sense that it engenders (future) existence. 'The sage' is the Buddha-sage (*buddhamuni*); 'self-existence' (*attasambhavaṃ*) is the defilements produced within oneself. Like a great warrior at the head of battle, rejoicing within and concentrated, he broke, like a coat of armour, self-existence and the defilements.

"(2) Or alternatively: *Tulaṃ* is (the present participle) *tulento*, 'comparing' = *tīrento*, 'scrutinizing.' 'The incomparable' and 'continued existence' are, respectively, Nibbāna and existence; 'the formation of existence' is kamma leading to existence. 'The sage relinquished': comparing the five aggregates as impermanent with Nibbāna, their cessation, as permanent, and having seen the danger in existence and the advantage in Nibbāna, the Buddha-sage relinquished the 'formation of existence,' which is the root-cause of the aggregates, by means of the noble path, which effects the destruction of kamma; as it is said, 'It leads to the destruction of kamma.'"

So the commentary. Initially it seemed to me very unlikely that *tulaṃ* and *atulaṃ* should function in grammatically distinct ways, and I therefore inclined to the former interpretation, in principle if not in details. On reflection, however, I now believe that the verse is deliberately playing upon *tulaṃ* and *atulaṃ* as different grammatical forms rather than as a pair of opposites. *Atulaṃ* (or its cognates) occurs elsewhere in the texts: at Sn 85b *atulyo* describes a teacher of the path (reading *maggakkhāyī* with Be), probably the Buddha; at Sn 683a, it is used in apposition to the Bodhisatta, the future Buddha; at Thī 201a *atuliyaṃ* describes the *akampitaṃ dhammaṃ*, "the unshaken state," presumably Nibbāna. Nevertheless, though I believe the commentary's second explanation is correct grammatically, I disagree with its interpretation.

In my understanding, *sambhavaṃ* here does not mean continued existence in saṃsāra, the cause of which the Buddha had already ended with his attainment of enlightenment forty-five years earlier. Here the word means, rather, the continuation of his *present* life until the end of the *kappa*. *Bhavasaṅkhāra* is not "kamma leading to new existence," but the vital formation (*āyusaṅkhāra*) that the Buddha has just rejected. On this interpretation, the meaning that emerges from the verse is perfectly consonant with the preceding prose passage: Having compared the prospect of continuing on until the end of the aeon with the prospect of attaining final Nibbāna, "the incomparable," the Buddha opted for the latter; and he did so by mindfully relinquishing his vital formation, the same life formation (as *jīvitasaṅkhāra*) that earlier, during his illness, he had resolved to maintain (see **47:9**). Thus by rejecting the *bhavasaṅkhāra* that might have sustained him until the end of the aeon, the Buddha renounced the extension of his life.

On the second couplet Spk says: "He *rejoiced within* by way of insight, and was *concentrated* by way of serenity. Thus, from the preliminary stage onwards, by the power of serenity and insight he broke the entire mass of defilements that had enveloped his whole individual existence like a coat of armour and that was called 'self-existence' (*attasambhavaṃ*) because it originates within oneself. When there are no more defilements, in the absence of rebirth kamma is said to be relinquished; thus he cast off kamma by the abandoning of defilements. Since there is no fear for one who has abandoned defilements, he relinquished his vital formation fearlessly. The Buddha 'uttered this inspired utterance' to show his freedom from fear."

There is also an ancient commentary on this verse at Nett 61. This commentary takes *tulaṃ* as the *saṅkhāradhātu*, the totality of conditioned things, and *atulaṃ* as the *nibbānadhātu*. Apparently here *tulaṃ* and *atulaṃ* are taken as by-forms of *tullaṃ* and *atullaṃ* respectively.

256 A detailed analysis of the terms is found below at **51:20**.

257 *Anekavihitaṃ iddhividhaṃ paccanubhoti.* This passage shows the exercise of the supernormal powers to be the fruit of developing the four *iddhipādas*. The six direct knowledges appear above at **12:70** and **16:9**. The mundane modes of supernormal power are analysed in detail in Vism chaps. 12 and 13.

258 Spk glosses desire (*chanda*) as the "wish-to-do" (*kattukaṃyatāchanda*). See too Vibh 216,27–29.

259 Spk: The "volitional formations of striving" (*padhānasaṅkhārā*) is a designation for energy which accomplishes the fourfold function of right striving.

260 Vibh 218,29–31 defines *citta* only with the stock register of terms but does not specify how it becomes a basis for power.

261 Vibh 219,23–25 defines *vīmaṃsā* with the register of terms for *paññā*.

Spk says that the elder Raṭṭhapāla (MN No. 82) produced the supramundane state (*lokuttara dhamma*) by putting emphasis on desire; the elder Soṇa (AN III 374–79; Vin I 179–85), by putting emphasis on energy; the elder Sambhūta (Th 291–94), by putting emphasis on mind; and the elder Mogharāja (Sn 1116–19), by putting emphasis on investigation. Spk illustrates these with the case of four royal ministers aspiring to high appointment. One who gains his position by waiting upon the king day and night, seeking to satisfy his wishes and preferences, is comparable to one who produces a supramundane state by emphasizing desire. One who gains the position by his valour, as in crushing a border rebellion, is like one who produces a supramundane state by emphasizing energy. One who gains the position by offering the king counsel in statecraft is like one who produces a supramundane state by emphasizing mind. And one who gains the position solely by reason of his birth (or class, *jāti*) is like one who produces a supramundane state by emphasizing investigation.

The same explanation is at Sv II 642–43, but a variant at Vibh-a 305–6 inverts the illustrations for mind and investigation, with birth representing mind and counsel representing investigation. This seems more cogent, since investigation (*vīmaṃsā*) and counsel (*manta*) are both from the root *man*, to think, and mind is often classified according to its class (*jāti*) as wholesome, unwholesome, or indeterminate. Gethin discusses the two versions of the simile, *The Buddhist Path to Awakening*, pp. 90–91.

262 As at **2:5**, **9:13**.

263 Spk: He entered into meditation on the water-*kasiṇa*, emerged, and determined that the ground on which the mansion stood should become water. Then he rose up into the air and struck it with his toe.

264 Be puts a *pe* here, implying that the other four mundane *abhiññās* should be filled in. This seems confirmed too by Spk's comment on **51:31**; see **n. 279** below.

265 A brahmin of this name appears at **48:42**. It is uncertain whether the two are the same person.

266 All three eds. read here *santakaṃ hoti no asantakaṃ*. This, however, is exactly the wording we find at the end of the sutta, when the brahmin has been won over by Ānanda's argument. Spk offers no help, but as Woodward realized, the reading required is found in SS: *anantakaṃ hoti no santakaṃ*, "it is without an end (i.e., an infinite regress), not with an end." *Santaka* is *sa* + *antaka*.

267 The Pāli has *citta*, but "mind" would not work here.

268 Cp. AN II 145,35–146,21, where Ānanda shows how craving is abandoned in reliance upon craving, conceit in reliance upon conceit.

269 Here again all three eds. read *santakaṃ hoti no asantakaṃ*. And again, the most intelligible reading is buried in SS: *santakaṃ hoti no anantakaṃ*.

270 Spk: The fourth jhāna used as a basis for *abhiññā*.

271 *Kosajjasahagata*. I usually translate *kosajja* as laziness, but that seems too strong here. What is intended is a slight dullness or feebleness in the force of desire.

272 *Yathā pure tathā pacchā, yathā pacchā tathā pure.* Spk: This should be understood: (i) by way of the meditation subject; and (ii) by way of the teaching. (i) The interpretation (*abhinivesa*, or "introduction") of the meditation subject is "before" and arahantship is "after." A bhikkhu who, after interpreting the root meditation subject, does not allow the mind to fall into the four undesirable conditions (overly lax, etc.) goes on to attain arahantship; he is called one who dwells "as before, so after." (ii) By way of teaching, the head-hairs are "before" and the brain is "after" (among the solid parts in the contemplation of the body). A bhikkhu who develops his meditation from beginning to end without sliding into the four undesirable conditions is called one who dwells "as before, so after."

The explanation sounds strained. The phrase refers simply to maintaining consistency in attending to the meditation subject in all its aspects throughout the session, from start to finish. See too the use of the phrase in the sentence *pacchāpure saññī caṅkamaṃ adhiṭṭheyyāsi* (AN IV 87,2–3), where it seems to have a spatial meaning: "Percipient of what is behind and in front, you should determine on walking back and forth."

273 Spk: A bhikkhu sits on the terrace attending to the perception of light, sometimes shutting his eyes, sometimes opening them. When (the light) appears to him the same whether his eyes are open or shut, then the perception of light has arisen. Whether it be day or night, if one dispels sloth and torpor with light and attends to one's meditation subject, the perception arisen in regard to the light has been well grasped.

274 The mind-made body (*manomayakāya*) is a subtle body created from the physical body by a meditator who has mastered the fourth jhāna. It is described as "consisting of form, mind-made, complete in all its parts, not lacking faculties (*rūpiṃ manomayaṃ sabbaṅgapaccaṅgiṃ ahīndriyaṃ*)." See DN I 77,6–26; MN II 17,23–18,7; Paṭis II 210–11, quoted and expanded upon at Vism 406 (Ppn 12:139). For a contemporary discussion, see Hamilton, *Identity and Experience*, pp. 155–64.

On *upasaṅkamitā* as a misconstrued absolutive, not a true

agent noun, see von Hinüber, "Pāli as an Artificial Language," pp. 135–37.

275 This is the natural physical body.

276 Be: *Yañ ca kho omāti bhante*; Se: *Opātiha bhante*; Ee: *Yaṃ ca kho opapāti ha bhante*. The verb is not encountered elsewhere. Spk (Be) glosses, *omātī ti pahoti sakkoti*, and remarks: "This is a term of unique occurrence in the Word of the Buddha preserved in the Tipiṭaka (*idaṃ tepiṭake buddhavacane asambhinnapadaṃ*)." Spk (Se) omits "*omātī ti*," or anything corresponding to it, and highlights *pahoti* as if it were the lemma.

277 In both cases I read the verb with Be as *samodahati*, over *samādahati* in Se and Ee. Both Be and Se of Spk have *samodahati*, which is strongly supported by the explanation: "*(He) immerses the body in the mind*: having taken the body, he mounts it on the mind; he makes it dependent on the mind; he sends it along the course of the mind. The mind is an exalted mind. Movement along the course of the mind is buoyant (quick). *(He) immerses the mind in the body*: having taken the mind, he mounts it on the body; he makes it dependent on the body; he sends it along the course of the body. The body is the coarse physical body. Movement along the course of the body is sluggish (slow). *A blissful perception, a buoyant perception* (*sukhasaññañ ca lahusaññañ ca*): this is the perception associated with the mind of direct knowledge; for it is a blissful perception because it accompanies the peaceful bliss (of this mind), and a buoyant perception because there is no inhibition by the defilements."

A more detailed account of this supernormal power is at Paṭis II 209, quoted and expanded on at Vism 401–5 (Ppn 12:119–36).

278 Spk: In this sutta and the next, *iddhi* is discussed as a basis for the ending of the round.

279 Spk: In this sutta and the next, the six direct knowledges are discussed.

52. *Anuruddhasaṃyutta*

280 The Venerable Anuruddha already appears as a proponent of *satipaṭṭhāna* at **47:26–28**. The present saṃyutta is virtually an appendix to the Satipaṭṭhānasaṃyutta.

281 This paragraph and the two that follow merge the two supplementary sections to each exercise in the Satipaṭṭhāna Sutta; in the latter they follow in sequence but are kept distinct. I explain my reason for translating *samudayadhamma*, etc., as "the nature of origination," etc., in **n. 178**.

282 What follows is at **46:54** (V 119,6–16); see **n. 110**.

283 On the three levels, Spk quotes Dhs §§1025–27, which defines inferior phenomena (*hīnā dhammā*) as the twelve unwholesome classes of consciousness; middling phenomena (*majjhimā dhammā*) as mundane wholesome states, resultants, functionals (*kiriya*), and form; and sublime phenomena (*paṇītā dhammā*) as the four paths, their fruits, and Nibbāna. See, however, AN I 223–24, where the three terms are correlated with the three realms of rebirth—the sensuous realm, the form realm, and the formless realm.

284 This sutta and the next closely correspond to **47:26–27**.

285 See **47:28** and **n. 174**.

286 As at **35:244** (IV 190–91) and **45:160**.

287 The ten kinds of knowledge to follow are usually called the ten powers of a Tathāgata (*dasa tathāgatabala*); see MN I 69–71, elaborated at Vibh 335–44. Spk says that a disciple may possess them in part (*ekadesena*), but in their fullness they are possessed in all modes only by omniscient Buddhas.

53. *Jhānasaṃyutta*

288 The formula for the four jhānas is analysed at Vibh 244–61 and in Vism chap. 4.

54. *Ānāpānasaṃyutta*

289 What follows are the sixteen steps or aspects in the practice of mindfulness of breathing, which form the core of the Ānāpānasati Sutta (MN No. 118). The sixteen steps are explained in detail at Vism 267–91 (Ppn 8:146–237), to which Spk refers the reader. A collection of important texts on this meditation subject, translated by Ñāṇamoli and entitled *Mindfulness of Breathing*, includes the Ānāpānasati Sutta, the passage from Vism, a treatise from Paṭis, and selected suttas.

As will be shown at **54:10**, the sixteen aspects fall into four tetrads, which are correlated with the four establishments of mindfulness. Thus, while mindfulness of breathing begins in the domain of "contemplation of the body" (*kāyānupassanā*), it eventually comprehends all four contemplations.

On the phrase "having set up mindfulness in front of him" (*parimukhaṃ satiṃ upaṭṭhapetvā*), Vibh 252,14–16 says: "This mindfulness is set up, well set up at the tip of the nose or at the centre of the upper lip."

290 Vism 273–74 (Ppn 8:171–73) explains the third step of this tetrad to mean "making known, making plain, the beginning, middle, and end of the entire in-breath body ... of the entire out-breath body." The "bodily formation" (*kāyasaṅkhāra*), in the fourth step, is the in-and-out breathing itself, which becomes progressively calmer and more subtle as mindfulness of the breath develops. See SN IV 293,16: *Assāsapassāsā kho gahapati kāyasaṅkhāro*, "In-breathing and out-breathing, householder, are the bodily formation."

291 This note and the two to follow are based on Vism 287–91 (Ppn 8:226–37).

Rapture (*pīti*) is experienced when he has entered upon the lower two jhānas and when, after entering upon and emerging from one of those jhānas, he comprehends with insight the rapture associated with the jhāna as subject to destruction and vanishing. Happiness (*sukha*) is experienced when he has entered upon the lower three jhānas and when, after entering upon and emerging from one of those jhānas, he comprehends with insight the happiness associated with the jhāna as subject to destruction and vanishing. The mental formation (*cittasaṅkhāra*) is feeling and perception, which are experienced in all four jhānas.

292 "Experiencing the mind" is to be understood by way of the four jhānas. The mind is "gladdened" by the attainment of the two jhānas accompanied by rapture or by the penetration of these with insight as subject to destruction and vanishing. "Concentrating the mind" refers either to the concentration of the jhāna or to the momentary concentration that arises along with insight. "Liberating the mind" means liberating it from the hindrances and grosser jhāna

factors by attaining successively higher levels of concentration, and from the distortions of cognition by way of insight knowledge.

293 "Contemplating impermanence" (*aniccānupassī*) is contemplation of the five aggregates as impermanent because they undergo rise and fall and change, or because they undergo momentary dissolution. This tetrad deals entirely with insight, unlike the other three, which can be interpreted by way of both serenity and insight. "Contemplating fading away" (*virāgānupassī*) and "contemplating cessation" (*nirodhānupassī*) can be understood both as the insight into the momentary destruction and cessation of phenomena and as the supramundane path, which realizes Nibbāna as the fading away of lust (*virāga*, dispassion) and the cessation of formations. "Contemplating relinquishment" (*paṭinissaggānupassī*) is the giving up (*pariccāga*) or abandoning (*pahāna*) of defilements through insight and the entering into (*pakkhandana*) Nibbāna by attainment of the path. See **n. 7**.

294 Spk: Ariṭṭha had explained his own (attainment of) the nonreturner's path [Spk-pṭ: because he spoke obliquely of the eradication of the five lower fetters], but the Buddha explained the insight practice to gain the path of arahantship.

295 At this point a shift is introduced in the text from simple *ānāpānasati* to *ānāpānasatisamādhi*. This change continues through the following suttas.

296 Spk: When one works on other meditation subjects the body becomes fatigued and the eyes are strained. For example, when one works on the meditation subject of the (four) elements, the body becomes fatigued and reaches a stage of oppression such that one feels as if one has been thrown into a mill. When one works on a *kasiṇa*, the eyes throb and become fatigued and when one emerges one feels as if one is tumbling. But when one works on this meditation subject the body is not fatigued and the eyes do not become strained.

297 See **n. 110**. Spk: This passage on the "noble one's spiritual power" (*ariyiddhi*) is included to show the advantage (in developing mindfulness of breathing). For if a bhikkhu

wishes for the noble one's spiritual power, or the four jhānas, or the four formless attainments, or the attainment of cessation, he should attend closely to this concentration by mindfulness of breathing. Just as, when a city is captured, all the merchandise in the four quarters that enters the city through the four gates and the country is captured as well—this being the advantage of a city—so all the attainments listed in the text are achieved by a meditator when this concentration by mindfulness of breathing has been fully developed.

298 From here down as at **12:51**, **22:88**, and **36:7**.

299 A more elaborate version of the strange background story to this sutta is at Vin III 68–70. I summarize the commentarial version just below at **n. 301**. The problems raised by the story are discussed in Mills, "The Case of the Murdered Monks."

300 That is, he was explaining the meditation on the thirty-one parts of the body (increased to thirty-two in the commentaries) and the stages of decomposition of a corpse.

301 Spk: Why did he speak thus? In the past, it is said, five hundred men earned their living together as hunters. They were reborn in hell, but later, through some good kamma, they took rebirth as human beings and went forth as monks under the Blessed One. However, a portion of their original bad kamma had gained the opportunity to ripen during this fortnight and was due to bring on their deaths both by suicide and homicide. The Blessed One foresaw this and realized he could do nothing about it. Among those monks, some were worldlings, some stream-enterers, some once-returners, some nonreturners, some arahants. The arahants would not take rebirth, the other noble disciples were bound for a happy rebirth, but the worldlings were of uncertain destiny. The Buddha spoke of foulness to remove their attachment to the body so that they would lose their fear of death and could thus be reborn in heaven. Therefore he spoke on foulness in order to help them, not with the intention of extolling death. Realizing he could not turn back the course of events, he went into seclusion to avoid being present when destiny took its toll.

So the commentary, but the idea of a kammically predetermined suicide seems difficult to reconcile with the conception of suicide as a volitionally induced act.

302 In the Vinaya account (repeated by Spk) they take their own lives, and deprive one another of life, and request the "sham ascetic" Migalaṇḍika to kill them. Spk adds that the noble ones did not kill anyone, or enjoin others to kill, or consent to killing; it was only the worldlings who did so.

303 Spk's paraphrase is poignant: "Earlier, Ānanda, many bhikkhus gathered in the assembly, and the park seemed ablaze with them. But now, after only half a month, the Saṅgha has become diminished, thin, scanty, like sparse foliage. What is the cause? Where have the bhikkhus gone?"

304 Bracketed phrase is not in Be.

305 Commented on at Vism 267–68 (Ppn 8:146–50). On *asecanaka*, see **I, n. 591**.

306 The simile is also at **45:156**.

307 What follows is also in the Ānāpānasati Sutta (at MN III 83,20–85,6), brought in to show how mindfulness of breathing fulfils the four foundations of mindfulness (see **54:13** below). The commentary on this passage is translated in Ñāṇamoli, *Mindfulness of Breathing*, pp. 49–52.

308 Spk: "I call it the wind body (*vāyokāya*) among the 'bodies' of the four elements. Or else it is 'a certain kind of body' because it is included in the tactile base among the various components of the form body."

309 Spk: Attention is not actually pleasant feeling, but this is a heading of the teaching. In this tetrad, in the first portion feeling is spoken of (obliquely) under the heading of rapture, in the second portion directly as happiness. In the third and fourth portions feeling is included in the mental formation (*saññā ca vedanā ca cittasaṅkhāro*, SN IV 293,17).

310 Spk: *Having seen with wisdom, etc.* Here, "covetousness" is just the hindrance of sensual desire; by "displeasure" the hindrance of ill will is shown. This tetrad is stated by way of insight only. These two hindrances are the first among the five hindrances, the first section in the contemplation of mental phenomena. Thus he says this to show the beginning of the contemplation of mental phenomena. By "abandoning" is meant the knowledge which effects aban-

doning, e.g., one abandons the perception of permanence by contemplation of impermanence. By the words "having seen with wisdom" he shows the succession of insights thus: "With one insight knowledge (he sees) the knowledge of abandonment consisting in the knowledges of impermanence, dispassion, cessation, and relinquishment; and that too (he sees) by still another." *He is one who looks on closely with equanimity*: one is said to look on with equanimity (at the mind) that has fared along the path [Spk-pṭ: by neither exerting nor restraining the mind of meditative development that has properly fared along the middle way], and by the presentation as a unity [since there is nothing further to be done in that respect when the mind has reached one-pointedness]. "Looking on with equanimity" can apply either to the conascent mental states (in the meditative mind) or to the object; here the looking on at the object is intended.

311 Spk: The six sense bases are like the crossroads; the defilements arising in the six sense bases are like the mound of soil there. The four establishments of mindfulness, occurring with respect to their four objects, are like the four carts or chariots. The "flattening" of the evil unwholesome states is like the flattening of the mound of soil by the cart or chariot.

312 In the Buddha's description of his own practice of mindfulness of breathing, *sato va* ("*just* mindful") is replaced by simple *sato*, and *sikkhati* ("he trains") is entirely dropped. Spk explains that *va* is omitted to show the exceptional peacefulness of his practice, since the in-breaths and out-breaths are always clear to him; *sikkhati* is omitted because he has no need to train himself.

313 Cp. **22:122** (III 169,1–3) and **II, n. 332**.

314 *Te ime pañca nīvaraṇe pahāya viharanti*. All trainees have completely abandoned the hindrance of doubt; nonreturners have, in addition, eradicated ill will and remorse (as well as sensual desire in its more restricted sense). Trainees abandon the other hindrances only temporarily through jhāna and insight; see **n. 7** on the five kinds of seclusion. The absolutive *pahāya* here should be construed in the light of these qualifications.

315 *Tesaṃ pañca nīvaraṇā pahīnā ucchinnamūlā tālāvatthukatā anabhāvakatā āyatiṃ anuppādadhammā*. This emphasizes the final and complete abandonment of the five hindrances.

316 The sequel as in **46:3**. This passage is also included in the Ānāpānasati Sutta, at MN III 85,7–87,37. Section (iii), on true knowledge and liberation, is at MN III 88,1–11.

55. Sotāpattisaṃyutta

317 On the wheel-turning monarch, the ideal ruler of Buddhist legend, see **22:96** and **46:42**, and for details DN II 172–77 and MN III 172–76. The four continents are Jambudīpa, Aparagoyāna, Uttarakuru, and Pubbavideha, respectively to the south, west, north, and east of Mount Sineru, the world axis. See AN I 227,28–228,8 for a fuller cosmological picture. The "four things" are explained just below.

318 The hells, animal realm, and domain of ghosts are themselves the plane of misery, the bad destinations, and the nether world.

319 The formulas of homage to the Buddha, the Dhamma, and the Saṅgha are explicated at Vism 198–221 (Ppn 7:2–100). On *aveccappasāda*, "confirmed confidence," see **II, n. 120**.

320 The terms describing the noble one's virtue are explicated at Vism 221–22 (Ppn 7:101–6). Spk says that noble ones do not violate (*na kopenti*) the Five Precepts even when they pass on to a new existence; hence these virtues are dear to them.

321 Cp. Dhp 178.

322 This is the stock definition of a stream-enterer. "Fixed in destiny" (*niyata*) means that the stream-enterer is bound to reach final liberation in a maximum of seven more lives passed either in the human world or the celestial realms. Enlightenment (*sambodhi*) is the final knowledge of arahantship.

323 *Brahmacariyogadhaṃ sukhaṃ*. On *ogadha* see **III, n. 243**. Spk: This is the happiness associated with the higher three paths. The confidence mentioned in the verse can be interpreted either as the confidence concomitant with the path (*maggappasāda*) or as the reviewing confidence of one who has reached the path (*āgatamaggassa paccavekkhaṇappasāda*).

324 These six perceptions are found along with others at **46:71–76**; see **n. 119**. As a group, the six things that partake of true knowledge (*cha vijjābhāgiyā dhammā*) are mentioned at AN III 334,5–9, but without elaboration. The text uses the suffix *-anupassī* for the first contemplation and *-saññī* for the others. Their meanings are the same.

325 These are the preliminary factors for attaining stream-entry, also called *sotāpattiyaṅga* but distinct from the other four, which are the factors that define a person as a stream-enterer. See below **55:55–74**, where they are said to be instrumental in obtaining all the fruits of the spiritual life. Though the Pāli is the same, to avoid confusion I have rendered the first "factors *for* stream-entry." This can be justified by appeal to DN III 227, where the four factors for attaining stream-entry are alone called *sotāpattiyaṅga* (§13), while the other four are called *sotāpannassa aṅgāni*, the factors of a stream-enterer (§14).

326 Though elsewhere *thapati* evidently means a carpenter, from the description of their duties below it seems these two were royal chamberlains. In Skt literature *sthāpatya* are often keepers of the women's apartments, and that seems to be their function here. The two are also mentioned as employed in the service of King Pasenadi at MN II 124,1–10. According to Spk, at the time Isidatta was a once-returner, Purāṇa a stream-enterer content with his own wife (i.e., not celibate). At AN III 348,1–5, it is said that after their deaths the Buddha declared them both once-returners reborn in the Tusita heaven; Purāṇa was then celibate, Isidatta content with his own wife.

327 Here the usual fourth factor of stream-entry, the virtues dear to the noble ones, is replaced by generosity. The terms are commented on at Vism 223–24 (Ppn 7:107–14). On my preference for the reading *yājayoga*, see **I, n. 635**.

328 *Attūpanāyikaṃ dhammapariyāyaṃ*. Spk-pṭ: Having related it to oneself, it is to be applied to others (*attani netvā parasmiṃ upanetabbaṃ*). As it is said: "What is displeasing and disagreeable to me is displeasing and disagreeable to the other too."

What follows are the first seven of the ten courses of wholesome action, each practised in three ways: by observing them oneself, by enjoining others to observe them, and by speaking in their praise.

329 Ee *ti koṭiparisuddho* should be corrected to *tikoṭiparisuddho* (without the hiatus). The "three respects" are: personally abstaining from killing, exhorting others to abstain, and speaking in praise of abstinence from killing.

330 Along with **55:10** (but *not* **55:9**), this text is included in the Mahāparinibbāna Sutta at DN II 91–94. The latter calls the town Nādikā, but both Sv and Spk explain the name in a way that supports Ñātika: "There were two villages close by the same pond, inhabited by the sons of two brothers; thus one of these was called Ñātika ('of the relatives')."

331 Spk: The diminishing (of lust, etc.) should be understood in two ways: as arising infrequently and as lacking obsessive force. For in once-returners lust, etc., do not arise often as they do in worldlings, but only occasionally; and when they do arise they are not thick, as in worldlings, but thin like a fly's wings. "This world" (*imaṃ lokaṃ*) is the sense-sphere world. If one who attains the fruit of once-returning as a human being is reborn among the devas and realizes arahantship, that is good. But if one cannot do so, having come back to the human world one definitely realizes it. Conversely, if one who attains the fruit of once-returning as a deva is reborn among human beings and realizes arahantship, that is good. But if one cannot do so, having come back to the deva world one definitely realizes it.

332 The number seems inflated, but Spk explains that while the village was not very large, the noble disciples there were said to be many. On account of a plague, 24,000 creatures died at one stroke, among whom were many noble disciples.

333 Be: *maraṇaṃ āgameyyāsi*; Se and Ee read *āgaccheyyāsi*. Spk glosses: *maraṇaṃ iccheyyāsi, pattheyyāsi vā*; "one should wish for or long for death."

334 Here and in all parallel passages I read *te vo*, which is consonant with **47:48** (V 189,4–5).

335 Cp. **40:10** (ii).

336 *Sambādhabyūhaṃ*. The explanation in Spk suggests that *byūhā* are major traffic routes. They are said to be "congested" (*sambādha*) to show the crowded living conditions in the city.

337 On *manobhāvanīya*, "worthy of esteem," see **III, n. 2**. Ee *bhante na* should be changed globally to *bhantena*, instrumental past participle of *bhamati*. Spk glosses with "wandering about here and there, roaming excitedly" (*ito c' ito ca paribbhamantena uddhatacārinā*).

338 At the time Mahānāma was at least a stream-enterer, possibly a once-returner; hence he was assured of a good rebirth and had no reason to fear death.

339 *Taṃ uddhaṅgāmi hoti visesagāmi*. The passage shows *citta* as the principle of personal continuity which survives the death of the body and reaps the fruits of kamma. In the case of a noble disciple it "goes to distinction" by way of a higher rebirth and by evolving onwards to Nibbāna. The following simile of the pot is at **42:6** (IV 313,27–30), differently applied.

340 Spk: He thought: "The Bhikkhu Saṅgha might speak without knowing, as it lacks omniscient knowledge, but there is no lack of knowledge in the Teacher." *Kocideva dhammasamuppādo*, "issue concerning the Dhamma," is glossed by Spk *kiñcideva kāraṇam*. At **22:7** the same compound *dhammasamuppāda* has quite a different meaning, rendered "a constellation of mental states."

341 Here Ee alone has the reading required, *evaṃvādiṃ*. Be and Se have *evaṃvādī*. See **II, n. 205**.

342 Though the argument has not been explicitly settled, the matter seems to be clinched through Mahānāma's testimony to his faith. By expressing so intensely his confidence in the Buddha, Mahānāma confirms his status as a noble disciple, and thus his viewpoint must be correct. Spk-pṭ says that while one endowed with any one of these four qualities is a stream-enterer, one should explain in terms of possessing all four.

343 I transcribe the name as in Se. Be and Ee have Saraṇāni.

344 *Sikkhādubbalyaṃ āpādi majjapānaṃ apāyi*. This would be a breach of the fifth precept. The Sakyans thought that if Sarakāni violated a precept he would lack the fourth factor of stream-entry and thus could not be a stream-enterer.

345 This is the arahant, who is actually free from all future rebirth; freedom from the nether world is mentioned only as the "thread" tying the sutta together. On "joyous wis-

dom, swift wisdom" (*hāsapañña, javanapañña*), see **I, n. 184**.

346 This is the *dhammānusārī*, the Dhamma-follower; the next paragraph describes the *saddhānusārī*, the faith-follower. Though the terms themselves are not used here, their descriptions match their formal definitions at MN I 479. According to **25:1**, these two types have reached the plane of the noble ones but have not yet realized the fruit of stream-entry; they are bound to do so before they die. See **III, n. 268**.

It should be noted that while they have faith (one of the five faculties), they do not yet have "confirmed confidence" (*aveccappasāda*) in the Triple Gem. And though it is said that they "do not go to hell" (*agantā nirayaṃ*), etc., it cannot be said that they are "*freed* from hell" (*parimutto nirayā*), etc., for actual release from the bad destinations comes only with the attainment of the fruit.

347 Spk says that at the time of his death he was a fulfiller of the three trainings (in virtue, concentration, and wisdom). This implies that while he might have indulged in strong drink earlier, before his death he undertook strict observance of the precepts and thereafter attained stream-entry.

348 *Sikkhāya aparipūrakārī ahosi*. The wording is slightly different from that in the preceding sutta but the purport is the same.

349 As at **48:50**. The expression, *ekantagato abhippasanno*, is effectively synonymous with *aveccappasādena samannāgato*.

350 A fivefold elaboration on the nonreturner; see **n. 65**.

351 At MN III 76,7–9, it is said that the trainee in the practice has eight factors, the arahant ten. Yet here, strangely, the last two factors, *sammāñāṇa* and *sammāvimutti*, which are supposed to be unique to the arahant, are ascribed to the stream-enterer Anāthapiṇḍika. The last line of the sutta confirms that this was not a mere editorial oversight. For another example of such anomalies, see **47:13** (and **n. 160**), where two factors of an arahant—liberation, and knowledge and vision of liberation—are ascribed to the trainee Ānanda.

352 *Samparāyikaṃ maraṇabhayaṃ*. Spk: *samparāyahetukaṃ maraṇabhayaṃ*, which might mean "fear of death caused (by expectations for) the next life."

353 Spk: They are tracks of the devas (*devapadāni*) as tracks tread upon by the knowledge of the devas, or with the knowledge of a deva. In this sutta the four persons established in the fruits are called devas in the sense of purity.

354 Woodward mistakenly assumes that this sutta is identical with the previous one and thus does not translate the sequel.

355 Woodward understands *sabhāgataṃ* to be resolvable into *sabhā* + *gataṃ*, "joined the company," but it is actually the accusative singular of the abstract noun *sabhāgatā*, "similarity."

356 Be and Ee have *ehī ti*, presumably understood as an imperative, while Se has *etīti*, which seems hard to explain. I suggest reading the singular future *ehiti*.

357 The simile of the water flowing down the slope is at **12:23** (II 32,3–10). Spk: "*Having gone beyond*: the beyond is Nibbāna; the meaning is, 'having reached that.' *They lead to the destruction of the taints*: it is not that they first go to Nibbāna and later lead (to the destruction of the taints); rather, they lead there as they go to Nibbāna."

358 As at **48:18**.

359 From here on as at **35:97**, and conversely for the passage on dwelling diligently.

360 Reading with Se and Ee *seyyā-nissajja-ttharaṇassa*, as against Be *seyyāni-paccattharaṇassa*.

361 Spk glosses "the Dhamma's core" (*dhammasāra*) as the noble fruit, and "destruction" (*khaya*) as the destruction of defilements. I suggest reading the last line: *Na vedhati maccurāj' āgamissatī ti*.

362 I follow Be and Se in not inserting *mahāyaso* here. If this is inserted, as in Ee, there is no difference between this sutta and the next one.

363 See **n. 325**.

364 Verses as in **55:26**.

365 Spk: He was one of the seven people in the Buddha's time who had a retinue of five hundred; the others were the lay follower Visākha, the householder Ugga, the householder Citta, Hatthaka Āḷavaka, Anāthapiṇḍika the Lesser, and Anāthapiṇḍika the Great.

366 Cp. **20:7**. It is unusual for the Buddha to give such an

injunction to householders, but Spk gives a bizarre explanation, which I reproduce just below. Dhammadinna's words of protest echo **55:7** (V 353,11–15). In addressing Dhammadinna, the Buddha consistently uses the plural, implying that his statements refer to the entire group.

Spk: "*Deep* (*gambhīra*), like the Salla Sutta (Sn III, 8); *deep in meaning* (*gambhīrattha*), like the Cetanā Sutta (**12:38–40**?); *supramundane* (*lokuttara*), like the Asaṅkhatasaṃyutta (SN 43); *dealing with emptiness* (*suññatāpaṭisaṃyutta*), that is, explaining the emptiness of beings, like the Khajjaniya Sutta (**22:79**). *It is in such a way that you should train yourselves*: 'You should train by fulfilling the practice of the moon simile (**16:3**), the practice of the relay of chariots (MN No. 24), the practice of sagehood (*moneyyapaṭipadā*, Sn I, 12), the practice of the great noble lineage (*mahā-ariyavaṃsa*, AN II 27–29).' (These all allude to suttas that advocate a strict ascetic life; the identity of some of the allusions is uncertain.) Thus the Teacher charged these lay followers with an unbearable task. Why? Because, it is said, they had asked for an exhortation without taking a stand on their own plane (*na attano bhūmiyaṃ ṭhatvā*), but had asked as if they could take up any task indiscriminately. Hence the Teacher charged them with an unbearable task. But when they asked for an exhortation after taking a stand on their own plane (with the words 'as we are established …'), the Master complied by saying, 'Therefore ….'" It is difficult to reconcile this explanation with the principle that the Buddha always adjusts his teaching to the mental proclivities of his audience.

Spk had commented on the terms describing the deep suttas earlier, in relation to **20:7**. Some of the suttas referred to there are different from those referred to here. See **II, n. 368**.

367 *Sapañño upāsako*. Spk: A stream-enterer is intended.

368 *Āyasmā*, usually an address for monks, but occasionally used for lay followers. In what follows I have translated using idiomatic English second-person constructions where the Pāli uses indirect, third-person forms, e.g., "The venerable one has confirmed confidence in the Buddha…."

369 At MN II 194–95, Sāriputta guides a dying brahmin

through a similar sequence of reflections, but stops after directing him to the brahmā world. For stopping there he is later reproached by the Buddha.

370 *Sakkāyanirodha*, i.e., Nibbāna. This injunction is intended to turn the mind of the dying lay follower away from a rebirth in the brahmā world and direct it towards the attainment of Nibbāna.

371 I read with Be *evaṃvimuttacittassa*, as against Se *evaṃvimucittattassa* (probably a typographical error) and Ee *evaṃvuttassa*. But with Se I read *vassasatavimuttacittena*, as against Be and Ee *āsavā vimuttacittena*.

372 I read with Se and Ee *vimuttiyā vimuttin ti*, as against Be *vimuttiyā vimuttan ti*. The phrase *vimuttiyā vimuttiṃ* is also at AN III 34,6–7, again referring to arahantship. Spk: When one liberation is compared to the other, there is no difference to be described. When the path or fruit is penetrated, there is no difference between lay followers and bhikkhus.

The Buddha's statement thus indicates that the lay follower has become an arahant. Apart from the few instances of lay people who attained arahantship just before renouncing the household life (like Yasa at Vin I 17,1–3), this may be the only mention of a lay arahant in the Nikāyas, and in his case the attainment occurs on the verge of death. Mil 264–66 lays down the thesis that a lay person who attains arahantship either goes forth that day (i.e., becomes a monk or nun) or passes away into final Nibbāna.

373 Reading with Se *asāmantapaññatāya*, as against *appamatta-* in Be and Ee.

374 Paṭis II 189–202 quotes the passage in full and defines all the terms with the aid of the full conceptual apparatus of early Theravāda scholasticism.

56. Saccasaṃyutta

375 As at **22:5**; the next sutta as at **22:6**.

376 *Tasmātiha bhikkhave idaṃ dukkhan ti yogo karaṇīyo*. Spk: Since a concentrated bhikkhu understands the Four Noble Truths as they really are, therefore you should make an exertion to become concentrated in order to understand the four truths as they really are. And since the round of

existence increases for those who do not penetrate them, but stops increasing from the time they are penetrated, therefore you should make an exertion to understand them, thinking, "Let the round not increase for us."

377 Reading with Se and Ee: *Mā bhikkhave pāpakaṃ akusalaṃ cintaṃ cinteyyātha*. Be has *cittaṃ*.

378 *Mā bhikkhave viggāhikakathaṃ katheyyātha*. As at **22:3** (III 12,6–12).

379 *Mā bhikkhave anekavihitaṃ tiracchānakathaṃ katheyyātha. Tiracchānakathā* is literally "animal talk," but Spk explains it as talk that "runs horizontal" (*tiracchānabhūtaṃ*) to the paths leading to heaven and liberation.

380 What follows is the Buddha's first sermon, recorded in the narration of his ministry at Vin I 10–12. The sutta is analysed at MN No. 141 and Vibh 99–105, and commented upon at Vism 498–510 (Ppn 16:32–83) and Vibh-a 93–122. For a detailed explanation according to the method of the commentaries, see Rewata Dhamma, *The First Discourse of the Buddha*.

381 I follow Be and Se here. Ee includes *sokaparidevadukkha-domanass' upāyāsā*, which is found elsewhere in formal definitions of the first truth but lacking in most versions of the first sermon.

382 The three phases (*tiparivaṭṭa*) are: (i) the knowledge of each truth (*saccañāṇa*), e.g., "This is the noble truth of suffering"; (ii) the knowledge of the task to be accomplished regarding each truth (*kiccañāṇa*), e.g., "This noble truth of suffering is to be fully understood"; and (iii) the knowledge of accomplishment regarding each truth (*katañāṇa*), e.g., "This noble truth of suffering has been fully understood." The twelve aspects (*dvādasākāra*) are obtained by applying the three phases to the four truths.

383 Spk explains *dhammacakka* by way of the knowledge of penetration (*paṭivedhañāṇa*) and the knowledge of teaching (*desanāñāṇa*); see **II, n. 57**. Until Koṇḍañña and the eighteen *koṭis* of brahmās were established in the fruit of stream-entry the Blessed One was still *setting in motion* (*pavatteti nāma*) the Wheel of the Dhamma; but when they were established in the fruit, then the Wheel *had been set in motion* (*pavattitaṃ nāma*).

384 *Aparimāṇā vaṇṇā aparimāṇā byañjanā aparimāṇā saṅkāsanā.* Spk says the three terms are synonyms, all meaning *akkharā*, but I think their connotations are slightly different.

385 *Tathāni avitathāni anaññathāni.* See **12:20** and **II, n. 54**. Spk: "*Actual* in the sense of not departing from the real nature of things; for suffering is stated to be just suffering. *Unerring,* because of the nonfalsification of its real nature; for suffering does not become nonsuffering. *Not otherwise,* because of not arriving at a different nature; for suffering does not arrive at the nature of the origin (of suffering), etc. The same method for the other truths." I understand *anaññatha* in the simpler and more straightforward sense that the truths are "not otherwise" than the way things really are.

386 I use the title of Be and Se. The Ee title should be changed from Vijjā to Vajji (also for the next sutta). This sutta too is included in the Mahāparinibbāna Sutta, at DN II 90–91, and is also at Vin I 230,25–231,10.

387 The entire sutta with the verses is at It 104–6, the verses alone at Sn 724–27.

388 Cp. **12:23** (II 29,24–25) and **22:101** (III 152,26–27).

389 Spk: "Since they are actual, unerring, not otherwise, they are called the truths of the noble ones (*ariyānaṃ saccāni*); for the noble ones do not penetrate errors as noble truths." An explanation of the expression "noble truths" (*ariyasacca*) at Vism 495 (Ppn 16:20–22) quotes **56:27** and **28**, as well as **56:23**.

390 The passage quoted is not found elsewhere in the Nikāyas but is cited at Vism 690,10–13 (Ppn 22:93) to prove that path knowledge performs four functions at a single moment. See Kv 220.

391 All these leaves are small and delicate. I follow Be for the name of the second type of leaf, *saralapatta*, which Liyanaratne ("South Asian Flora," §170) renders as the long-leaved Indian pine.

392 I read with Se *tālapakkaṃ*. All the other texts, including SS, read *tālapattaṃ*, "a palm leaf," which does not make good sense. *Tālapakkaṃ* is also at It 84,20.

393 Though *palāsa* usually means foliage, here it denotes a specific tree. Liyanaratne (§44) identifies this as a kind of *kiṃsuka*, but different, it seems, from the *kiṃsuka* men-

tioned at **35:245** (listed by Liyanaratne at §43). The English name for the *palāsa* is the Bengal kino tree or Dhak tree. The *māluvā* is a broad-leaved creeper, mentioned also at **I, v. 810**; see too **I, n. 568**.

394 Cp. **15:9**, which says the stick might also fall on its middle.

395 Many of these expressions are also at **12:85–92**.

396 Cp. **12:63** (II 100,10–25).

397 Reading with Se and Ee, *sammādiṭṭhikass' etaṃ*. Be has *tass' etaṃ*.

398 *Indakhīla*. PED defines this as a post or stake set at or before the city gate; also as a large slab of stone let into the ground at the entrance of a house.

399 As at AN IV 404,21–405,5.

400 *Lokacintaṃ cintessāmi*. Spk gives as an example: "Who created the sun and moon? The great earth? The ocean? Who begot beings? The mountains? Mangoes, palms, and coconuts?"

401 Spk: It is said that the asuras had applied the Sambari magic (see **11:23**) and resolved that the man would see them mounted on their elephants and horses entering through slits in the lotus stalks. At AN II 80,22–24 it is said that speculating about the world leads to madness, yet here, strangely, it turns out that the man is not really mad after all.

402 This passage offers an interesting condensed version of dependent origination (*paṭicca-samuppāda*). Not understanding the Four Noble Truths is ignorance (*avijjā*; see **56:17**). The phrase "they delight in (*abhiramanti*) volitional formations that lead to birth" implies craving, which gives rise to delight (*rati, abhirati*) when one's craving is fulfilled. The phrase "they generate volitional formations that lead to birth (*jātisaṃvattanike saṅkhāre abhisaṅkharonti*)" clearly points to the volitional formations. And falling into "the precipice of birth, aging, and death" obviously corresponds to the last two links in the series. So we here find ignorance and craving, in conjunction with volitional formations, bringing new birth, aging, and death (undergone by consciousness together with name-and-form).

403 *Mahāpariḷāho nāma nirayo*. The description is also at **35:135**.

404 The title in Be and Se is Vāla, but Ee titles it Chiggaḷa 1.

405 *Poṅkhānupoṅkhaṃ*. Spk: He saw them shoot one arrow, then shoot another—called the "afterbutt" (*anupoṅkhaṃ*)—in such a way that the butt of the first arrow's shaft was split, then shoot still another through the butt of the second arrow.

406 Spk glosses *durabhisambhavataraṃ* with *dukkarataraṃ*. On the splitting of the hair, I follow Be, which reads *sattadhā*, supported by Spk (both Be and Se). Se and Ee of text have *satadhā*, "a hundred strands."

Spk: Having split one hair into seven strands, they fix one strand to an eggplant and another to the tip of the arrowhead; then, standing at a distance of an *usabha* (about 200 feet), they pierce the strand fixed to the arrowhead through the strand fixed to the eggplant.

407 *Lokantarikā aghā asaṃvutā andhakārakā andhakāratiṃsā*. The expression occurs at DN II 12,11, MN III 120,9, and AN II 130,26–27. Spk does not comment, but Sv, Ps, and Mp to the above consistently explain: "Between every three spiral world-spheres (*cakkavāḷa*) there is one world-interstice, like the space between three cart wheels set down so that they touch. That is a 'world-interstice hell,' measuring 8,000 *yojanas* (= appx. 80,000 kilometres). It is 'vacant' (*agha*), i.e., always open (*niccavivaṭa*); and 'abysmal' (*asaṃvutā*), i.e., without an underlying support, and so dark even eye-consciousness cannot arise."

408 Ee titles this sutta Chiggaḷa 2, but in Se it is simply called Chiggala (and the next, Chiggala 2); in Be, the two are respectively called the Paṭhama- and Dutiya-chiggaḷayuga Sutta. The simile of the blind turtle and the yoke is also at MN III 169,9–22, which is partly elaborated as in the following sutta.

409 *Adhiccam idaṃ*. The statement has to be taken as rhetorical rather than philosophical in intent. At the doctrinal level, all three occurrences mentioned here come about through precise causes and conditions, not by chance.

410 Cp. **13:11**.

411 Cp. **13:10**.

412 **56:51–60** are parallel to **13:1–10**, but wherever the earlier series reads *n' eva satimaṃ kalaṃ upeti na sahassimaṃ kalaṃ upeti na satasahassimaṃ kalaṃ upeti … upanidhāya*, the pres-

ent one reads *saṅkham pi na upeti upanidham pi na upeti kalabhāgam pi na upeti … upanidhāya.*

413 The titles are as in Be and Se, though raw grain itself (*āmakadhañña*) is mentioned only at **56:84**.

414 This is also at AN I 35,12–14, but without the connection to the Four Noble Truths. Similarly, the theme of **56:62** is at AN I 35,15–18; of **56:63,** at AN I 35,24–26; and of **56:65,** at AN I 35,10–11.

415 In **56:71–77**, the comparisons are based on the first seven courses of wholesome action (*kusalakammapatha*). With celibacy replacing abstention from sexual misconduct (in the third sutta), these are also the first seven guidelines to conduct in the Nikāya account of the bhikkhu's discipline (see, e.g., DN I 63,20–64,14).

416 In **56:78–101**, the minor training rules of the bhikkhu's discipline are the basis of comparison (see, e.g., DN I 64,16–32).

Concordances

1. Verse Parallels

A. Internal

For Part I, the left-hand column gives the sutta number; the middle column, the verse numbers of this translation (following Ee2); the right-hand column, the verse numbers for parallels in Part I, and the volume, page, and line numbers for parallels in the other parts. For Parts II–V, the left-hand column gives the sutta number; the middle column, the volume, page, and line numbers; the right-hand column, the verse numbers for parallels in Part I, and the volume, page, and line numbers for parallels in the other parts. When a sutta has been abridged to the exclusion of the verses, in the right-hand column the verse numbers or sutta numbers are followed by an asterisk. Brackets around a number indicate that the parallelism is only approximate. Verses repeated within the same sutta have not been collated.

Part I: Sagāthāvagga

Sutta	Verse	Parallel
1:3	3–4	310–11
1:4	5–6	359–60
1:9	15–16	127–28
1:11	20–21	775–76
	21c–f	[609]
1:12	22–23	461–62
1:15	28–29	789–90
1:17	34	IV 179,1–4

Sutta	Verse	Parallel
1:20	49	105
	50	135
1:21	51–52	301–2
1:22	54	623
1:23	55–58	625–28
	58ab	175ab
1:26	65–67	259–61
1:29	74–75	361–62
1:31	78–84	320–26
1:32	85	95
	87	146, 335
1:33	95	85
1:34	104	[118]
	105	49
1:36	118	[104]
1:38	127–28	15–16
1:40	135	50
1:43	144–46	333–35
	146	87
1:48	156–59	312–15
	159	II 277,3–4
1:50	170–82	340–52*
	175ab	58ab
1:58	198	236c, 237
1:71	223–24	257–58, 613–14, 939–40
1:73	227–28	846–47
1:76	237	198b–f
2:2	256	294
2:3	257–58	223–24, 613–14, 939–40
2:4	259–61	65–67
2:13	294	256
2:16	301–2	51–52
2:19	310–11	3–4
2:20	312–15	156–59
2:21	320–26	78–84
2:23	333–35	144–46
2:25	353–56	791–94
2:27	359–60	5–6
2:28	361–62	74–75

SUTTA	VERSE	PARALLEL
3:2	383	433
3:4	387	[417]
	388	418, 432
3:6	390	[391]
3:7	391	[390]
3:17	411	413
3:18	413	311
3:20	417	[387]
	418	388, 432
3:23	433	383
3:25	442cd	V 217,15–16
4:2	449	450
4:3	450	449
4:8	461–62	22–23
4:19	484–85	500–1
4:20	487	488
4:21	488	487
4:24	498	509
	500–1	484–85
4:25	509	498
6:1	560	919
6:9	588–91	592–595*
6:11	596	II 284,26–27
6:12	597	II 241,30–33
6:15	609	[21c–f, 776c–f]; II 193,13–16
7:1	613–14	223–24, 257–58, 939–40
7:2	616–618	620–22*, 880–82, 889–91*
7:4	623	54
7:6	625–628	55–58
7:8	634	677
	636–37	641–42*, 667–68*
7:9	646	705
7:13	677	634
7:21	705	646
9:6	775–76	20–21
9:12	789–90	28–29
9:13	791–94	353–56
10:12	846–47	227–28
11:1	858–62	863–67*

Sutta	Verse	Parallel
11:4	874–82	883–91
	880–82	616–618, 620–22*, 889–91*
11:5	883–91	874–82
11:11	904–5	906–7*, 908–9*
11:14	910–12	V 384,23–28, 405,9–14
11:17	919	560
11:18	924–25	[930–31], [937–38]
11:19	930–31	[924–25], [937–38]
11:20	937–38	[924–25], [930–31]
11:21	939–40	223–24, 257–58, 613–14

Part II: Nidānavagga

Sutta	Text	Parallel
15:20	II 193,13–16	609
17:35	241,30–33	597
21:3	277,3–4	159
21:11	284,26–27	596

Part IV: Saḷāyatanavagga

Sutta	Text	Parallel
35:240	IV 179,1–4	34
36:3	206,1–5	IV 218,21–25
	206,3–5	IV 207,20–22
36:5	207,20–22	IV 206,3–5
36:12	218,21–25	IV 206,1–5

Part V: Mahāvagga

Sutta	Text	Parallel
45:34	V 24,17–27	V 82,1–2*
47:18	168,12–15	V 186,11–14
47:43	186,11–14	V 168,12–15
48:41	217,15–16	442cd
55:26	384,23–28	910–12; V 405,9–14
55:41	400,20–27	V 401,16–23
55:51	405,9–14	910–12; V 384,23–28

B. External

This concordance makes no claim to completeness as the only non-canonical Pāli texts that have been collated are Nett, Peṭ, Mil, and Vism, while only a few texts in Skt and BHS have been drawn upon. No attempt has been made to trace parallels to individual pādas. Parallels from Pāli sources which only approximate to the corresponding verses of SN are set in brackets; parallels from non-Pāli sources almost always differ from the Pāli and thus have not been bracketed. When a string of SN verses is indexed, the complete string is given first followed by individual verses and subordinate strings for which the parallels do not correspond in all respects to those for the complete string. SN verses that repeat verses indexed earlier have not been indexed separately, but their external parallels can be determined by first consulting the concordance of internal parallels and then tracing the relevant verse numbers in the present table. Parallels taken from Enomoto's *Comprehensive Study of the Chinese Saṃyuktāgama* are signalled by an asterisk (see Bibliography).

Part I: Sagāthāvagga

Sutta	Verse	Parallel
1:1	1	Nidd I 437
1:3	3	AN I 155
	3ab, 4ab	Ja IV 398
1:4	5ab, 6ab	Ja IV 487
1:5	8	Dhp 370; Th 15, 633; Nett 170; G-Dhp 78
1:6	9ab	Ja III 404
1:11	21c–f	see 609
1:12	22–23	Sn 33–34; Nett 34; Peṭ 55; Mvu III 417–18
1:13	24–25	Nett 185
	24	Peṭ 54
1:16	30ab, 31ab	Ja VI 57
1:17	32–33	Uv 11:6–7
	32	Nett 132
	34	Mil 371; Uv 26:1; Ybhūś 27*; SHT 6, no. 1293*

Sutta	Verse	Parallel
1:18	35	Dhp 143; Uv 19:5
1:20	42–43	Ja II 57–58
	46–49	Ybhūś 2:1–4*
	46–47ab	It 53–54
	48	Sn 842
	50	Ybhūś 1*; Divy pp.489, 494*
1:21	51–52	Th 39–[40], 1162–[63]; Nett 146
	51	Peṭ 48
1:22	54	Dhp 125; Sn 662; Pv 24; Ja III 203; Vism 301–2; Uv 28:9
1:23	55–56	Vism 1
	56	Peṭ 44 (or 45?); Mil 34; Uv 6:8
	57a–c	G-Dhp 26a–c
1:26	66cd	Uv 33:74ab
1:27	68–69	Ybhūś 8:1–3*; SHT 4, no. 50a, 25–27*
	69ab	Ud 9; Uv 26:26
	69ef	DN I 223
1:28	73a–d	Thī 18a–d
1:29	75a–c	Uv 33:59
1:30	76a–e	Sn 165ab & 166abc
	77	Sn 171; Kv 367
1:31	78	Ja V 483, 494
	84	G-Dhp 250
1:32	85–87	Ja IV 64
	89	Ja IV 65
	90–91	Ja II 86, IV 65, VI 571
	91	Uv 5:27; P-Dhp 208
	92–94	Ja IV 66–67
1:33	97	Ja III 472; Uv 30:8
	98	Ja III 472
	99	Pv 28; Ja III 472
	100, 101	Ja III 472
1:34	102	Uv 2:8
	103	AN III 411; Uv 2:7; G-Dhp 96
	104	Dhp 221; Uv 20:1; P-Dhp 238; G-Dhp 274
1:35	108	Vin III 90
	109	Th 226; G-Dhp 338

SUTTA	VERSE	PARALLEL
1:36	117	P-Dhp 332
	118	[Dhp 221]; see 105
	119–20	MN II 105; Dhp 26–[27]; Th 883–84
	119	Uv 4:10; P-Dhp 17; G-Dhp 117
	120	Uv 4:12; G-Dhp 129
1:37	121–24	DN II 254–55; MSjSū 1–3*; Divy pp.195–96*
	124	Ja I 97
1:41	136–37	AN I 156; Ja III 471
	139–40	Nidd I 5
1:43	146cd	Uv 5:22cd
1:45	148	Sn 177
1:46	150–52	G-Dhp 97–99
1:47	154–55	Kv 345, 440
	155ab	AN II 65
1:48	156–59	MN III 262; Nett 148
	157	Vism 3
	159	Th 1182
1:51	184	Uv 6:4
1:59	200	Uv 10:6
1:60	202cd	Abhidh-k-bh p.81*
1:62	205–6	AN II 177
	206	Abhidh-k-vy 1, p.95*
1:64	209–10	Sn 1108–9
1:66	213–14	Nett 22
	214	Th 448; Nidd I 411
	214ab	Ja VI 26
1:70	221–22	Sn 168–69
1:71	223–24	Nett 145; G-Dhp 288–89
	224	Uv 20:3
1:72	226	Nidd II 221
1:73	227–28	Sn 181–82
	228	Uv 10:3
1:75	232–33	[Ja IV 110]; Nett 186
1:77	242	Uv 10:11
2:1	255	Th 239; Uv 23:1
2:4	260cd	Uv 33:74ab
2:5	262–64	Ybhūś 12:1–4*; Śrāv-bh p.341*

Sutta	Verse	Parallel
2:6	265–68	Nett 148
2:7	269	AN IV 449
2:8	271	Uv 11:1; G-Dhp 9
	271ab	Dhp 383ab
	272	Dhp 313; Uv 11:2
	273	Dhp 314; Uv 29:41ab, 42ab; G-Dhp 337
	274	Dhp 311; Uv 11:4; P-Dhp 296; G-Dhp 215
	275	Dhp 312; Th 277; Uv 11:3
2:9	281–84	Chandra Sū*
2:15	298–300	[Sn 173–75]; Ybhūś 10:1–3*
	299	Vism 3
	299c–300	[Nett 146]
2:17	303–4	Ybhūś 5:1–2*
2:18	309	Nidd I 437
2:22	327–29	Dhp 66–68; Uv 9:13–15; P-Dhp 174–76
	327–28	Nett 131–32
	330–32	Mil 66–67; P-Dhp 110–12
2:26	357–58	AN II 49–50; Vism 204
2:30	372–73	Mil 242
3:1	374–82	Saṅghabh 1, pp.181–83*
3:2	383	It 45; Nidd I 16, 364, 471; Nidd II 201
3:3	384	Dhp 151; Ja V 483, 494; Uv 1:28; G-Dhp 160
3:4	385–88	Nett 175
	385	Uv 5:13
	386–87	Nett 178
	388	Uv 5:22
3:5	389	Mil 399
	389a–d	Dhp 361; Peṭ 57; Mil 167; Uv 7:11; P-Dhp 51; G-Dhp 52; Mvu III 423; Abhidh-k-bh p.208*
3:6	390ef	Th 146cd
3:8	392	Ud 47; Nett 164; Vism 297; Uv 5:18

Sutta	Verse	Parallel
3:9	393–96	AN II 42–43
3:10	397–98	Dhp 345–46; Ja II 140; Nett 35, 153; Peṭ 26; Uv 2:5–6; P-Dhp 143–44; G-Dhp 169–70
3:11	399–400	Uv 29:11–12
	400	Nidd I 448
3:12	401	AN III 239; Ja I 116; Vism 388
3:13	402	Ja II 294; Uv 29:14; P-Dhp 78
3:14	404	Dhp 201; Uv 30:1; P-Dhp 81; G-Dhp 180; Avś 1, p.57*
3:15	405	Ja II 239; Uv 9:9
	406	[Dhp 69]
3:17	410–11	AN III 48–49
	410ef–11	It 16–17; Uv 4:25–26
3:21	422cd	AN I 130
3:22	431	Nett 94; [Peṭ 9]; Uv 1:23–24
3:24	438a,c–39ef	It 66
3:25	441–45	MSV 2, pp.74–77*
	441–43	Vism 232;
4:4	452–53	Vin I 22
4:5	454–55	Vin I 21; Mvu III 416; CPS 21:4–5*; Saṅghabh 1, p.149*
4:6	458	Nett 35
4:7	460ab	Dhp 180ab; P-Dhp 277ab; Uv 29:53ab; Mvu III 92
4:9	464	Nidd I 44, 119; Vism 237
4:10	466	Th 145; Nidd I 44, 119; Vism 231; Uv 1:18
4:11	467	Nett 35
4:15	476–77	Vin I 21; Mvu III 416–17
4:17	480–81	Nidd I 360
	481cd	Uv 6:12cd
4:18	482	MN I 338
	483	Dhp 200; Ja VI 55; Uv 30:49
4:20	486–87	Uv 2:19–20; MSV 1, p.96*; Divy p.224*
	487	[Nett 61]; [Peṭ 15]
4:22	489	Th 46
4:23	497	Sn 449

Sutta	Verse	Parallel
4:25	506–7	Mvu III 281–82
	509–10	Mvu III 284–85; Ybhūś 14:1–2*
	510	AN V 46–48
	511–13	Mvu III 283–84; Ybhūś 4:1–3*
	515	Vin I 43; Uv 21:8; G-Dhp 267; Mvu III 90
	516–18	Mvu III 285–86
5:1	519	Thī 57
	521	Thī 58, 234
5:2	522–23	Thī 60–61
5:3	527ab	Thī 59ab, 142ab, 188ab, 195ab, etc.
5:4	528	[Thī 139]
	530	[Thī 140]
	530ab	Uv 1:37ab
5:5	532–35	[Thī 230–33]
5:6	537	[Thī 191]
	539	Sn 754; It 62
5:7	540–43	[Thī 197, 198, 200, 201]
	542	Nidd I 411; Mvu I 33
5:8	544–45	Thī 183–[84]
	546ab	Thī 185ab
	547ab	AN II 24; It 123
5:10	553–55	Nidd I 439; Kvu 66
	553–54	Abhidh-k-bh pp.465–66*
	554	Mil 28
	554–55	Vism 593
6:1	556–61	Vin I 5–7; MN I 168–69; Mvu III 314–19
	556–57, 559–61	DN II 38–39
	559	It 33; Nidd I 360, 453–54; Nidd II 138; Uv 21:18
6:2	562–64	AN II 21; Uv 21:11–13; Abhidh-k-bh p.467*
6:4	572–79	Ja III 359–63
6:5	580–81	MN I 338; Th 1198–1200
6:7	585	Nidd I 411
6:8	587	Nett 132

Sutta	Verse	Parallel
6:9	588–91	AN V 171, 174; Sn 657–60; Nett 132–33; Uv 8:2–5; P-Dhp 299–302; Āps 40*
	589–91	AN II 3–4
6:11	596	DN I 99, III 97; MN I 358; AN V 327–28
6:12	597	Vin II 188; AN II 73; Nett 130; Uv 13:1; Saṅghabh 2, p.73*
6:13	598	Th 142; Mil 402
	603	DN II 218
6:14	604–5	Kvu 203; Divy pp.68, 138, 162, etc.
	604	Th 256; Nett 40; Peṭ 71; Mil 245; Uv 4:37; G-Dhp 123
	605	DN II 121; Th 257; Uv 4:38; G-Dhp 125
6:15	608–12	DN II 157; Avś 2, pp.198–99*; MPS 44:4–11*
	609	DN II 199; Th 1159; Ja I 392; Uv 1:3
	610	Th 1046
	611	[DN II 157]
	611–12	Th 905–6
7:2	615–18	Th 441–44
	616–17	Vism 298
7:3	619	Uv 20:13; P-Dhp 182
7:8	634–35ab	AN I 165, 167–68; It 100–1; Thī 63cd–64; G-Dhp 5–6
	634	MN II 144; Dhp 423a–d; [Sn 647]; Uv 33:47a–d
	636–37	Sn 81–82, 480–81
	636	Mil 228
7:9	638	Sn 462
	639ab	Sn 463ab
	645	Nidd II 247
	646	Saṅghabh 1, p.193*
7:11	662–68	Sn 76–82
7:12	669–70	Th 531–32; Mvu III 108–9
7:13	674–75	Th 185–86

Sutta	Verse	Parallel
7:18	700	[Nett 24, 53]; [Peṭ 17]
7:19	702	[Ja VI 94]
	702c–f	AN II 70
7:20	703–4	Dhp 266–67; Uv 32:18–19; G-Dhp 67–68; Mvu III 422
8:1	707–11	Th 1209–13
8:2	712–16	Th 1214–18; SHT 5, no.1140*
8:3	717–20	Th 1219–22
8:4	721–25	Ybhūś 3:1–5*; SHT 5, no.1140*; Abhidh-k-bh p.284*; Abhidh-k-vy 2, p.455*
	721–22	Th 1223–24
	721–23	[Vism 38]
	722cd	Sn 341ab
	724–25	Sn 341cd, 340cd, 342; Th 1225–26
	724ab, 725	Thī 19cd–20
8:5	726–30	Sn 450–54; Uv 8:11–15; Ybhūś 20*
	727–30	Th 1227–30
8:6	731–33	Th 1231–33
	731ab	Mil 22; Uv 33:33ab
8:7	734–37	Th 1234–37; MR pp.38–39*; SHT 6, no.1598*
8:8	738–41	Th 1238–41
	742–45	Th 1242–45
8:9	746–48	Th 1246–48
	746ab	Th 679ab
8:10	749–51	Th 1249–51
	749	Nidd II 105
8:11	752	Th 1252
8:12	753	[Th 1253]
	754	[Th 1254–55]
	755	[Th 1256–57]
	756	[Th 1261]
	757	[Th 1262]
9:2	761	[Sn 331]
9:3	769	Peṭ 79

Sutta	Verse	Parallel
9:4	770–71	Mvu III 420–21
	771	Nidd I 494
9:5	772	Th 119
9:6	777	Th 908
	777cd	[Ud 46]; Uv 32:41, 43, 45, 47cd
9:9	784	Th 62
9:14	795–801	Ja III 308–9
	799	Th 652, 1001
10:1	803–4	Ja IV 496; Kvu 494; Abhidh-k-bh p.130*; Abhidh-sam-bh p.55*
	803ab	Vism 476
10:2	805–7	Nett 147
10:3	808–11	Sn 270–73; Nett 147; Ybhūś 11:1, 2, 4*
	808	Nidd I 16, 364, 471; Nidd II 201
	811cd	Uv 27:28cd
10:4	812	[Peṭ 71]
	814	P-Dhp 249
	814cd	AN IV 151; It 22; Ja IV 71; P-Dhp 248–52cd; G-Dhp 198cd
10:5	816a–d	Thī 31a–d
	816a–e	AN I 144; Ja IV 320, VI 118, 120–23; Vv 17:19, etc.
	820cd–821	Thī 247c–248b; Ud 51; Pv 21; Nett 131; Peṭ 44; Uv 9:4
	822	Th 44
10:8	837–41	Vin II 156; Saṅghabh 1, pp.168–69*
	840–41	AN I 138; Uv 30:28–29
10:9	842	[Thī 54]
	843	Thī 55
10:11	845	[Thī 111]
10:12	846–57	Sn 181–92
	847	Uv 10:3
	848–49	Ybhūś 9:1–2*
	849	Mil 36; Uv 10:5
	850, 852	Ybhūś 7:1–2*; SHT 5, no.1250*
	851	Uv 10:4
	851–52	Nett 146–47

SUTTA	VERSE	PARALLEL
11:4	874ab	Ja II 386
	878	Uv 20:7
	879	Uv 20:6; P-Dhp 183
	880	Uv 20:18
	881–82	Uv 20:11–12
11:5	883–91	Nett 172–73
11:6	892	Ja I 203
11:8	896cd	Ja IV 127
11:9	898–99	Ja V 138–39; Mvu III 367
11:10	903	Ja II 202; Nett 184; [Peṭ 46]
11:11	904–5	Ja I 202
11:14	910–12	AN II 57, III 54; Th 507–9; P-Dhp 339–41
	910–11	Peṭ 71
	911cd–912	AN IV 5
	912	Th 204
11:15	914	Dhp 98; Th 991; Uv 29:18; P-Dhp 245
11:16	915–17	Vv 32 & 41; Kv 554
	916	Pv 61
	916–17	AN IV 292–93
11:20	934–35	[Thī 282–83]
	935	Ja V 252; Mvu III 453
	936c–e	Dhp 406a–c; Sn 630a–c; G-Dhp 29a–c
11:25	945c–f	Uv 20:21

Part II: Nidānavagga

SUTTA	TEXT	PARALLEL
12:31	II 47,13–14	Sn 1038
14:16	158,26–31	It 70–71
	158,27–31	Th 147–48
	158,30–31	Mil 409
15:10	185,18–186,1	It 17–18
	185,23–24	Dhp 191; Th 1259; Thī 186, 193, 310, 321
15:20	193,13–16	see 609
17:10	232,17–24	It 74–75; Th 1011–12

Sutta	Text	Parallel
17:35	241,30–33	see 597
21:4	278,18–21	Th 1165–66; Nett 151–52
21:6	279,28–31	Ja II 144
21:7	280,28–31	AN II 51; Uv 29:43–44; G-Dhp 235–36
21:8	281,18–21	Nett 145
21:9	282,18–21	Nett 145
21:10	284,3–5	[Vin I 8]; [MN I 171]; [Dhp 353]; Sn 211; Uv 21:1a–c
21:11	284,28–30	Dhp 387; Uv 33:74; P-Dhp 39; G-Dhp 50
21:12	285,19–22	Nett 151

Part III: Khandhavagga

Sutta	Text	Parallel
22:3	III 9,20–23	Sn 844
22:22	26,12–15	Uv 30:32
22:78	86,1–8	AN II 34
22:79	91,1–2	AN V 325, 326; Th 1084; Nett 151

Part IV: Saḷāyatanavagga

Sutta	Text	Parallel
35:95	IV 73,18–76,6	Th 794–817
	73,18–20	Th 98a–d
	73,24–25	Th 99a–d
35:136	127,16–128,7	Sn 759–65
35:228	157,22–25	Nett 155
35:229	158,19–25	It 57–58
36:1	204,15–18	It 46
36:2	205,1–6	Sn 738–39d
36:5	207,16–19	It 47
36:6	210,9–20	AN IV 157
37:34	250,25–28	[AN III 80]
41:5	291,20–23	Ud 76; Peṭ 50

Part V: Mahāvagga

Sutta	Text	Parallel
45:34	V 24,17–28	AN V 232–33, 253–54; Dhp 85–89; P-Dhp 261–65
	24,17–20	Uv 29:33–34
	24,21–25	Uv 16:14
	24,26–28	Uv 31:39
47:18	168,12–15	Nidd I 456, II 114; Uv 12:13
48:41	217,9–16	Uv 1:29–30; G-Dhp 140–41
51:10	263,1–4	DN II 107; AN IV 312; Ud 64; Nett 60; Peṭ 68; Uv 26:30
51:26	384,23–28	see 910–12
55:41	400,20–27	AN II 55–56
55:51	405,9–14	see 910–12
56:21	432,10–13	Vin I 231; DN II 91; Nett 166
56:22	433,5–14	Sn 724–27; It 106

2. Exact Sutta Parallels

A. Internal

Whole suttas which appear elsewhere in the Saṃyutta Nikāya.

Sutta	Parallel
3:18	see 45:2
12:15	22:90 (III 134,30–135,19)
12:41	55:28
12:42	55:29
12:43	35:106
12:44	35:107
12:45	35:113
18:21	22:91
18:22	22:92
22:86	44:2
22:90	see 12:15
22:91	18:21
22:92	18:22
35:106	12:43
35:107	12:44
35:113	12:45
44:2	22:86
45:2	3:18 (I 87,22–88,29)
46:2	46:51 (i–ii)
46:12	46:48
47:2	36:7 (IV 211,1–19)
47:45	47:5 (V 146,6–16)
55:18	40:10 (IV 271,26–273,9)
55:28	12:41
55:29	12:42

B. External

Whole suttas, or substantial portions of suttas, which appear elsewhere in the Pāli Canon.

Sutta	Parallel
2:26	AN II 47–49
3:8	Ud 47
3:11	Ud 64–66
3:21	AN II 85–86
4:4	Vin I 22,24–36
4:5	Vin I 20,36–21,16
6:1	Vin I 4,32–7,10; MN I 167,30–169,30
6:2	AN II 20–21
6:4	Ja No. 405 (III 358–63)
6:9–10	AN V 170–74
6:10	Sn pp.123–27,15
6:15	DN II 155,31–157,19
7:11	Sn pp.12–16
10:8	Vin II 154–56
11:5	Nett 172–73
12:11	MN I 261,5–31, 263,8–16
12:25	II 39,34–41,4 = AN II 157,33–159,3
12:41	AN V 182–84
17:35	Vin II 187–88
19:1–21	Vin III 104–8
22:7	MN III 227,25–228,31
22:59	Vin I 13–14
22:78	AN II 33–34
22:80	III 93,4–20 = It 89–90
22:82	MN No. 109 (III 15–20)
22:101	III 153,3–155,12 = AN IV 125–27
35:28	Vin I 34,16–35,12
35:87	MN No. 144 (III 263–66)
35:88	MN No. 145 (III 267–70)
35:121	MN No. 147 (III 277–80)
36:19	MN No. 59 (I 396–400)
41:6	IV 293,7–294,9 = MN I 301,17–302,5
	IV 294,11–24 = MN I 296,11–23
	IV 294,26–295,21 = MN I 302,6–27

Sutta	Parallel
41:7	MN I 297,9–298,27
42:12	IV 331,11–337,11 = AN V 177,1–181,29
45:1	AN V 214,10–28
45:8	DN II 311,30–313,25; MN III 251,8–252,17
46:55	AN III 230,9–236,24
47:1	DN II 290,8–19; MN I 55,32–56,10
47:2	DN II 94,29–95,14
47:5	AN III 65,2–10
47:9	DN II 99,3–101,4
47:12	DN II 81,35–83,32
48:23	It 53,2–4
51:10	DN II 102,2–107,6
54:13	MN III 82,17–88,11
55:8, 10	DN II 91,22–94,14
56:11	Vin I 10,10–12,18
56:21	Vin I 230,25–231,10; DN II 90,8–91,5
56:22	It 104–6

3. Template Parallels

The notion of "template parallels" is explained in the General Introduction (pp. 36–39). This concordance includes only suttas in *different* saṃyuttas that fully, or substantially, exemplify a given template. It does not include suttas within the same saṃyutta that exhibit variations on a pattern peculiar to that saṃyutta, or the repetition series at the end of saṃyuttas 45–51 and 54. While the latter are molded upon templates, their schematic character and uniform position make it unnecessary to include them. As the dividing line between template parallels and suttas constructed from stock formulas is imprecise, this concordance might have been either expanded or contracted by shifting the dividing line forward or back.

abandon desire (and lust) (*tatra vo chando (rāgo) pahātabbo*) 22:137–45; 35:76–78, 162–64, 168–85

abandoning of the fetters, etc. (*saṃyojanappahānādi*) 48:61–64; 54:17–20

analysis, a teaching through (*vibhaṅga*) 12:2; 45:8; 47:40; 48:9–10, 36–38; 51:20

arises dependent on contact (*phassaṃ paṭicca uppajjati*) 12:62 (II 96,26–97,29); 36:10; 48:39

the arising of suffering (*dukkhass' eso uppādo*) 14:36; 22:30; 26:1–10; 35:21–22

ascetics and brahmins (*samaṇā vā brāhmaṇā vā*):
 (1) gratification triad 14:37; 17:25; 22:107; 23:5; 36:27; 48:6, 29, 34
 (2) origin–&–passing pentad 14:38; 17:26; 22:108; 23:6; 36:28
 (3) four truth pattern 12:13, 14, 29, 30, 71–80; 14:39; 17:27; 22:50; 36:29; 48:7, 30, 35; 56:22
 (4) past, future, present 51:5, 6, 16, 17; 56:5, 6

burning (*āditta*) 22:61; 35:28

by clinging to what? (*kiṃ upādāya*) 22:150–58; 24:1–96; 35:105, 108

clinging and the clung to (*upādāna, upādāniyā dhammā*) 22:121; 35:110, 123

delight in suffering (*dukkhaṃ so abhinandati*) 14:35; 22:29; 35:19–20

destruction of delight (*nandikkhaya*) 22:51–52; 35:156–57, 158–59

destruction of the taints (*āsavakkhaya*) 48:20; 51:23

develop concentration (*samādhiṃ bhāvetha*) 22:5; 35:99; 35:160; 56:1
development, a teaching on (*bhāvanā-desanā*) 47:40; 51:19
directly knowing, without/by (*anabhijānaṃ, abhijānaṃ*) 22:24; 35:111–12
exhort, settle, and establish them (*samādapetabba nivesetabba patiṭṭhāpetabba*) 47:48; 55:16–17; 56:26
the fetter and things that fetter (*saṃyojana, saṃyojaniyā dhammā*) 22:120; 35:109, 122
the fingernail similes, etc. (*nakhasikhādi-upamā*) 13:1–10; 56:51–60
fruits (*phala*):
  (1) one of two fruits 46:57 (ii); 47:36; 48:65; 51:25; 54:4
  (2) seven fruits and benefits 46:3 (V 69,16–70,27); 48:66; 51:26; 54:5
the Ganges can't be made to slant westwards (*gaṅgā nadī na sukarā pacchāninnaṃ kātuṃ*) 35:244 (IV 190,23–191,23); 45:160; 52:8
going beyond (*apārā pāraṃ gamanāya*) 45:34; 46:17; 47:34; 51:1
gratification, danger, escape (*assāda, ādīnava, nissaraṇa*):
  (1) what is the gratification, etc.? 14:31; 22:26; 35:13–14
  (2) I set out seeking, etc. 14:32; 22:27; 35:15–16
  (3) if there was no gratification, etc. 14:33; 22:28; 35:17–18
the holy life, for what purpose? (*kimatthi brahmacariyaṃ*) 35:81, 152; 38:4; 45:5, 41–48
ignorance and knowledge (*avijjā, vijjā*) 22:113–14; 56:17–18
impermanent, suffering, non-self (*anicca, dukkha, anattā*):
  (1) what is impermanent is suffering 22:15–17; 35:1–3, 4–6
  (2) past, future, present 22:9–11; 35:7–9, 10–12
  (3) revulsion, dispassion, liberation 22:12–14; 35:222–24, 225–27
  (4) the cause and condition for 22:18–20; 35:140–42; 143–45
make an exertion in seclusion (*paṭisallāne yogaṃ āpajjatha*) 22:6; 35:100, 161; 56:2
neglected/undertaken the noble path (*viraddha/āraddha ariyaṃ maggaṃ*) 45:33; 46:18; 47:33; 51:2
noble and emancipating (*ariya niyyānika*) 46:19; 47:17; 51:3
not apart from a Buddha (*nāññatra tathāgatassa pātubhāvā*) 45:14–15; 46:9–10; 48:59–60
not yours (*na tumhākaṃ*) 22:33–34; 35:101–2, 138–39
rebirth, causes for (*ko hetu upapajjanti*) 29:7–10; 30:3–6; 31:2–12; 32:2–12

4. Auditor–Setting Variants

The suttas collated here are almost identical in content but differ only in regard to the person to whom they are addressed, the protagonist, and/or the circumstances under which they are spoken.

11:1, 2: Sakka's advice on exertion
11:12, 13: Sakka's names
12:4–10: the Buddhas discover dependent origination
12:35–36: with ignorance as condition
12:41–42: ten qualities of a stream-enterer
18:21, 22:71, 22:124: ending "I-making" and conceit
18:22, 22:72, 22:125: transcending discrimination
22:106–12, 23:4–10: discourses on the aggregates
22:115–16: a speaker on the Dhamma
22:126, 127–28: ignorance and knowledge (subject to arising pattern)
22:133, 22:131–32: ignorance and knowledge (gratification triad)
23:23–34, 23:35–46: the nature of the aggregates
35:76–78, 162–64, 168, 171, 174: abandon desire and lust
35:81, 152: for what purpose the holy life?
35:118, 119, 124, 125, 126, 128, 131: how a bhikkhu attains/fails to attain Nibbāna
36:15–18: analysis of feeling
36:19–20: gradations of happiness
36:23, 24, 26: more analysis of feeling
38:1–16; 39:1–16: questions on Nibbāna, etc.
40:10, 11: to the devas, on going for refuge to the Buddha, etc.
46:14, 15: the enlightenment factors and illness
47:18, 43: the Buddha's reflections on mindfulness
47:22, 25: how the true Dhamma endures long
51:19, 27–30: on developing the bases for spiritual power
54:13–16: on developing mindfulness of breathing
55:18, 20: to the devas, on the factors of stream-entry
55:28, 29: ten qualities of a stream-enterer
55:46–49: the four factors of stream-entry

Bibliography

I. Primary Pāli Texts

A. Saṃyutta Nikāya

Roman script: edited by Léon Feer, 5 vols. London: PTS, 1884–98.

New Roman-script edition of Part I: Sagāthāvagga, with critical apparatus by G.A. Somaratne. Oxford: PTS, 1998.

Burmese script: Chaṭṭhasaṅgāyana (Sixth Buddhist Council) edition, 3 vols. Rangoon: Buddhasāsana Samiti, 1954.

Sinhala script: Buddha Jayanti Tripiṭaka Series, 5 vols. Colombo: Government of Sri Lanka, 1960–83. Pāli with Sinhala translation on facing pages.

B. Saṃyutta Nikāya Commentary

Burmese script: Saṃyutta Nikāya-aṭṭhakathā (= Sāratthappakāsinī). Chaṭṭhasaṅgāyana edition, 3 vols. Rangoon: Buddhasāsana Samiti, 1957.

Sinhala script: Saṃyutta Nikāya-aṭṭhakathā (= Sāratthappakāsinī). Simon Hewavitarne Bequest edition, ed. by Ven. Pandit Widurupola Piyatissa Mahāthera, 3 vols. Colombo 1924–30. Reprint, 1990.

C. Saṃyutta Nikāya Subcommentary

Burmese script: Saṃyutta-ṭīkā (Sāratthappakāsinī-purāṇa-ṭīkā = Līnatthappakāsanā). Chaṭṭhasaṅgāyana edition, 2 vols. Rangoon: Buddhasāsana Samiti, 1961.

II. Translations and Secondary Works

Adikaram, E. W. *Early History of Buddhism in Ceylon*. 1946. Reprint, Dehiwala, Sri Lanka: Buddhist Cultural Centre, 1994.

Alsdorf, Ludwig. *Die Āryā-Strophen des Pāli-Kanons*. Mainz: Akademie der Wissenschaften und der Literatur, 1968.

Basham, A.L. *History and Doctrines of the Ājīvikas*. 1951. Reprint, Delhi: Motilal Banarsidass, 1981.

Bechert, Heinz, ed. *Buddhism in Ceylon and Studies in Religious Syncretism in Buddhist Countries*. Göttingen: Vandenhoeck and Ruprecht, 1978.

——, ed. *The Language of the Earliest Buddhist Tradition*. Göttingen: Vandenhoeck and Ruprecht, 1980.

Bernhard, Franz, ed. *Udānavarga* (Sanskrittexte aus den Turfanfunden, 10; Abhandlungen der Akademie der Wissenschaften in Göttingen, 54). 2 vols. Göttingen: Vandenhoeck and Ruprecht, 1965–68.

Bodhi, Bhikkhu. "Aggregates and Clinging Aggregates." *Pāli Buddhist Review* 1 (1976): 91–102.

——, ed. *A Comprehensive Manual of Abhidhamma* (trans. of Abhidhammattha-saṅgaha with explanatory guide). Kandy: BPS, 1993.

——. *The Discourse on the All-Embracing Net of Views: The Brahmajāla Sutta and its Commentaries* (trans. of DN No. 1). 1978. 2nd ed. Kandy: BPS, 1992.

——. *The Discourse on the Fruits of Recluseship: The Sāmaññaphala Sutta and its Commentaries* (trans. of DN No. 2). Kandy: BPS, 1989.

——. *The Discourse on the Root of Existence: The Mūlapariyāya Sutta and its Commentaries* (trans. of MN No. 1). 1980. 2nd ed. Kandy: BPS, 1992.

——. *The Great Discourse on Causation: The Mahānidāna Sutta and its Commentaries* (trans. of DN No. 15). 1984. 2nd ed. Kandy: BPS, 1995.

——. *Transcendental Dependent Arising: An Exposition of the Upanisā Sutta* (Wheel No. 277/278). Kandy: BPS, 1980.

Brough, John. *The Gāndhārī Dharmapada*. London: Oxford University Press, 1962.

Burlingame, E.W. *Buddhist Legends* (trans. of Dhp-a). 1921. Reprint, 3 vols. London: PTS, 1969.

Collins, Steven. *Nirvana and Other Buddhist Felicities: Utopias of the Pali Imaginaire*. Cambridge: Cambridge University Press, 1998.

——. *Selfless Persons: Imagery and Thought in Theravāda Buddhism.* Cambridge: Cambridge University Press, 1982.

Cone, Margaret. "Patna Dharmapada." *Journal of the Pali Text Society* 13 (1989): 101–217.

Cowell, E.B., ed. *The Jātakas or Stories of the Buddha's Former Births*. 6 vols., 1895–1907. Reprint, 3 vols. London: PTS, 1969.

Cowell, E.B., and R.A. Neil, eds. *Divyāvadāna*. Cambridge 1886.

Deussen, Paul. *Sixty Upaniṣads of the Veda*. Trans. from the German by V.M. Bedeker and G.B. Palsule. Delhi: Motilal Banarsidass, 1980.

Dutt, Nalinaksha. *Buddhist Sects in India*. 2nd ed. Delhi: Motilal Banarsidass, 1978.

——, ed. *Mūla-sarvāstivāda-vinayavastu*, Part III of *Gilgit Manuscripts*. Calcutta, Srinagar 1939–59.

Emeneau, M.B. "The Strangling Figs in Sanskrit Literature." *University of California Publications in Classical Philology*, 13:10 (1949): 345–70.

Enomoto, Fumio. *A Comprehensive Study of the Chinese Saṃyuktāgama. Part 1: *Saṃgītanipāta*. Kyoto 1994.

——. Śarīrārthagāthā of the *Yogācārabhūmi*, in F. Enomoto, J-U Hartmann, and H. Matsumura, *Sanskrit-Texte aus dem buddhistischen Kanon: Neuentdeckungen und Neueditionen, 1*. Göttingen 1989.

Geiger, Wilhelm. *A Pāli Grammar*. Rev. ed. by K.R. Norman. Oxford: PTS, 1994.

——. *Saṃyutta-Nikāya*, Part I (German trans. of SN). Munich-Neubiberg: Benares-Verlag, 1930.

Gethin, R.M.L. *The Buddhist Path to Awakening: A Study of the Bodhi-Pakkhiyā Dhammā*. Leiden: Brill, 1992.

Gnoli, R. *The Gilgit Manuscript of the Saṅghabhedavastu* (Serie Orientale Roma, 49). 2 parts. Rome 1977–78.

Gombrich, Richard F. *How Buddhism Began: The Conditioned Genesis of the Early Teachings*. London & Atlantic Highlands, N.J.: Athlone, 1996.

——. "Old Bodies Like Carts." *Journal of the Pali Text Society* 11 (1987): 1–3.

Hamilton, Sue. *Identity and Experience: The Constitution of the Human Being according to Early Buddhism*. London: Luzac, 1996.

Harvey, Peter. *The Selfless Mind: Personality, Consciousness, and Nirvāṇa in Early Buddhism*. Richmond, Surrey: Curzon, 1995.

——. "Signless Meditation in Pāli Buddhism." *Journal of the International Association of Buddhist Studies* 9 (1986): 28–51.

Hinüber, Oskar von. "The Ghost Word *Dvīhitikā* and the Description of Famines in Early Buddhist Literature." *Journal of the Pali Text Society* 9 (1981): 74–85.

——. *A Handbook of Pāli Literature*. Berlin, New York: Walter de Gruyter, 1996.

——. "On the Tradition of Pāli Texts in India, Ceylon, and Burma." In Bechert 1978.

——. "Pāli as an Artificial Language." *Indologica Taurinensia* 10 (1982): 133–40.

——. *Selected Papers on Pāli Studies*. Oxford: PTS, 1994.

Hoernle, A.F.R. *Manuscript Remains of Buddhist Literature Found in Eastern Turkestan*. Oxford 1916.

Horner, I.B. *The Book of the Discipline* (trans. of Vin). 6 vols. London: PTS, 1938–66.

——. *Milinda's Questions* (trans. of Mil). 2 vols. London: PTS, 1963–64.

Ireland, John D. *Saṃyutta Nikāya: An Anthology*, Part I (Wheel No. 107/109). Kandy: BPS, 1967.

----. *Vaṅgīsa: An Early Buddhist Poet* (Wheel No. 417/418). Kandy: BPS, 1997.

Jayatilleke, K.N. *Early Buddhist Theory of Knowledge*. London: George Allen & Unwin, 1963.

Jones, J.J., trans. *The Mahāvastu*. 3 vols. London: Luzac, 1949–56.

Liyanaratne, Jinadasa. "South Asian Flora as reflected in the Twelfth-Century Pāli Lexicon *Abhidhānappadīpikā*." *Journal of the Pali Text Society* 20 (1994): 43–161.

Lokuliyana, Lionel, trans. *The Great Book of Protections, Sinhala Maha Pirit Pota*. Colombo: Mrs. H.M. Gunasekera Trust, n.d.

Macdonell, A.A., and A.B. Keith. *Vedic Index of Names and Subjects*. 2 vols., 1912. Reprint, Delhi: Motilal Banarsidass, 1958.

Malalasekera, G.P. *Dictionary of Pāli Proper Names*. 2 vols., 1937–38. Reprint, London: PTS, 1960.

Manné, Joy. "Categories of Sutta in the Pāli Nikāyas and Their Implications for Our Appreciation of the Buddhist Teaching and Literature." *Journal of the Pali Text Society* 15 (1990): 29–87.

——. "On a Departure Formula and its Translation." *Buddhist Studies Review* 10 (1993): 27–43.

Masefield, Peter. *The Udāna Commentary* (trans. of Ud-a). 2 vols. Oxford: PTS, 1994–95.

Matsumura, H., ed. *Āyuṃparyantasūtra*, in F. Enomoto, J-U. Hartmann, and H. Matsumura, *Sanskrit-Texte aus dem buddhistischen Kanon: Neuentdeckungen und Neueditionen, 1*. Göttingen 1989.

Mills, Laurence C.R. "The Case of the Murdered Monks." *Journal of the Pali Text Society* 16 (1992): 71–75.

Müller, F. Max. *The Upanishads*. 2 vols. Reprint, Delhi: AVF Books, 1987.

Ñāṇamoli, Bhikkhu. *The Guide* (trans. of Nett). London: PTS, 1962.

——. *The Life of the Buddha according to the Pāli Canon*. 1972. 3rd ed. Kandy: BPS, 1992.

——. *The Middle Length Discourses of the Buddha* (trans. of MN, ed. and rev. by Bhikkhu Bodhi). Boston: Wisdom Publications; Kandy: BPS, 1995.

——. *Mindfulness of Breathing (Ānāpānasati)*. Kandy: BPS, 1964.

——. *Minor Readings and the Illustrator of Ultimate Meaning* (trans. of Khp and Khp-a). London: PTS, 1962.

——. *The Path of Purification* (trans. of Vism). 1956. 5th ed. Kandy: BPS, 1991.

Ñāṇananda, Bhikkhu. *The Magic of the Mind: An Exposition of the Kālakārāma Sutta*. Kandy: BPS, 1974.

——. *Saṃyutta Nikāya: An Anthology*, Part II (Wheel No. 183/185). Kandy: BPS, 1972.

Norman, K.R. *Collected Papers*, I–VI. Oxford: PTS, 1990–95.

——. *Elders' Verses I* (trans. of Th). London: PTS, 1969.

——. *Elders' Verses II* (trans. of Thī). London: PTS, 1971.

——. *The Group of Discourses II* (trans. of Sn). Oxford: PTS, 1992.

——. *Pāli Literature, including the Canonical Literature in Prakrit and Sanskrit of All the Hīnayāna Schools of Buddhism*. Wiesbaden: Otto Harrassowitz, 1983.

Nyanaponika Thera. *The Five Mental Hindrances* (Wheel No. 26). Kandy: BPS, 1961.

——. *The Four Nutriments of Life* (Wheel No. 105/106). Kandy: BPS, 1967.

——. *Protection through Satipaṭṭhāna* (Bodhi Leaves No. 34). Kandy: BPS, 1967.

Nyanaponika Thera and Hellmuth Hecker. *Great Disciples of the Buddha: Their Lives, Their Works, Their Legacy*. Boston: Wisdom Publications; Kandy: BPS, 1997.

Nyanatiloka Thera. *Guide through the Abhidhamma Piṭaka*. Kandy: BPS, 1971.

Palihawadana, Mahinda. "From Gambler to Camouflage: The Strange Semantic Metamorphosis of Pāli *Kitavā*." *Sri Lanka Journal of Buddhist Studies* 3 (1991): 17–25.

Pāsādiko, Bhikkhu. "Review of *Sanskrit-Wörterbuch der buddhistischen Texte aus den Turfan-Funden*." *Buddhist Studies Review* 14 (1997): 190–92.

Pradhan, P. ed.; rev. 2nd ed. Aruna Haldar. Vasubandhu: *Abhidharmakośabhāṣya* (Tibetan Sanskrit Works Series, 8). Patna 1975.

Pruitt, William. *Commentary on the Verses of the Therīs* (trans. of Thī-a). Oxford: PTS, 1998.

Rahula, Walpola. *History of Buddhism in Ceylon: The Anuradhapura Period*. 1956. Reprint, Dehiwala, Sri Lanka: Buddhist Cultural Centre, 1993.

Rewata Dhamma. *The First Discourse of the Buddha: Turning the Wheel of the Dhamma*. Boston: Wisdom Publications, 1997.

Rhys Davids, C.A.F., and F.L. Woodward. *The Book of the Kindred Sayings* (trans. of SN). 5 vols. London: PTS, 1917–30. Rhys Davids trans. 1 (1917), 2 (1922); Woodward trans. 3 (1925), 4 (1927), 5 (1930).

Rhys Davids, T.W. *Buddhist India*. 1903. Reprint, Delhi: Motilal Banarsidass, 1997.

Rhys Davids, T.W. and C.A.F. *Dialogues of the Buddha* (trans. of DN). 3 vols. London: PTS, 1899–1921.

Roth, Gustav. "Particular Features of the Language of the Ārya-Mahāsāṅghika-Lokottaravādins and their Importance for Early Buddhist Tradition" (includes text of Patna Dharmapada). In Bechert 1980.

Senart, E., ed. *The Mahāvastu*. 3 parts. Paris 1882–97.

Shukla, K., ed. *Śrāvakabhūmi* (Tibetan Sanskrit Works Series, 14). Patna 1973.

Singh, Madan Mohan. *Life in North-Eastern India in Pre-Mauryan Times*. Delhi: Motilal Banarsidass, 1967.

Soma Thera. *The Way of Mindfulness: The Satipaṭṭhāna Sutta and its Commentary*. 1941. 4th ed. Kandy: BPS, 1975.

Speyer, J.S., ed. *Avadānaśataka*. 2 vols. (Bibliotheca Buddhica 3). St. Petersburg 1902–9.

Skilling, Peter. *Mahā Sūtras* II, Parts 1 & 2. Oxford: PTS, 1997.

Tatia, N., ed. *Abhidharmasamuccayabhāṣya* (Tibetan Sanskrit Works Series, 17). Patna 1976.

Thanissaro Bhikkhu. *The Wings to Awakening: An Anthology from the Pāli Canon*. Barre, Mass.: Dhamma Dana Publications, 1996.

Thittila, Ashin. *The Book of Analysis* (trans. of Vibh). London: PTS, 1969.

Waldschmidt, E. "Buddha Frees the Disc of the Moon (*Chandrasūtra*)." *Bulletin of the School of Oriental and African Studies*. 33:1 (1970).

——. *Das Catuṣpariṣatsūtra* (Abhandlungen der Deutschen Akademie der Wissenschaften zu Berlin, Klasse für Sprachen, Literatur, und Kunst; 1952,2; 1956,1; 1960,1). Berlin 1952–62.

——. *Das Mahāparinirvāṇasūtra* (Abhandlungen der Deutschen Akademie der Wissenschaften zu Berlin, Klasse für Sprachen, Literatur, und Kunst; 1949,1; 1950,2,3). Berlin 1950–51.

——. "Mahāmaudgalyāyana's Sermon on the Letting-in and Not Letting-in (of Sensitive Influences)." *Journal of the International Association of Buddhist Studies*. 1:1 (1978).

——. *Mahāsamājasūtra*, included in "Central Asian Sūtra Fragments and their Relations to the Chinese Āgamas," in Bechert 1980.

——. *On a Sanskrit Version of the Verahaccāni Sutta of the Saṃyuttanikāya* (Nachrichten der Akademie der Wissenschaften in Göttingen Philologisch-Historische Klasse). Göttingen: Vandenhoeck and Ruprecht, 1980.

——, et al. *Sanskrithandschriften aus den Turfanfunden* (Verzeichnis der orientalischen Handschriften in Deutschland, 10). Wiesbaden, Stuttgart 1965ff.

Walshe, Maurice. *The Long Discourses of the Buddha* (trans. of DN). Boston: Wisdom Publications, 1987, 1995.

——. *Saṃyutta Nikāya: An Anthology*, Part III (Wheel No. 318/321). Kandy: BPS, 1985.

Wijesekera, O.H. de A. *Buddhist and Vedic Studies*. Delhi: Motilal Banarsidass, 1994.

Witanachchi, C. "Ānanda." *Encyclopaedia of Buddhism*, Vol. I, fasc. 4. Colombo: Government of Ceylon, 1965.

Wogihara, U., ed. Yaśomitra: *Sputārthā Abhidharmakośavyākhyā*. 2 parts. Tokyo 1932–36.

Abbreviations

I. Primary Works

Be	Burmese-script ed. of SN
Ee	Roman-script ed. of SN (for Part 1: Ee1 = 1884 ed.; Ee2 = 1998 ed.)
Se	Sinhala-script ed. of SN
SN	Saṃyutta Nikāya
Spk (Be)	Sāratthappakāsinī, Saṃyutta Nikāya-aṭṭhakathā (Burmese-script ed.)
Spk (Se)	Sāratthappakāsinī, Saṃyutta Nikāya-aṭṭhakathā (Sinhala-script ed.)
Spk-pṭ	Sāratthappakāsinī-purāṇa-ṭīkā, Saṃyutta-ṭīkā (Burmese-script ed.)
SS	Sinhala-script mss. of SN (referred to in notes of Ee)

Note: References to Spk without any additional qualification are to Be. Spk (Be) and Spk (Se) are distinguished only when discussing variant readings between the two eds.

II. Other Pāli Texts

AN	Aṅguttara Nikāya
As	Atthasālini (Dhammasaṅgaṇī-aṭṭhakathā)
Dhp	Dhammapada
Dhp-a	Dhammapada-aṭṭhakathā
Dhs	Dhammasaṅgaṇī
DN	Dīgha Nikāya
It	Itivuttaka

It-a	Itivuttaka-aṭṭhakathā
Ja	Jātaka
Khp	Khuddakapāṭha
Mil	Milindapañha
MN	Majjhima Nikāya
Mp	Manorathapūraṇī (Aṅguttara Nikāya-aṭṭhakathā)
Nett	Nettippakaraṇa
Nidd I	Mahāniddesa
Nidd II	Cūḷaniddesa
Paṭis	Paṭisambhidāmagga
Paṭis-a	Paṭisambhidāmagga-aṭṭhakathā
Peṭ	Peṭakopadesa
Pj II	Paramatthajotikā, Part II (Suttanipāta-aṭṭhakathā)
Pp	Puggalapaññatti
Pp-a	Puggalapaññatti-aṭṭhakathā
Ps	Papañcasūdanī (Majjhima Nikāya-aṭṭhakathā)
Pv	Petavatthu
Sn	Suttanipāta
Sp	Samantapāsādikā (Vinaya-aṭṭhakathā)
Sv	Sumaṅgalavilāsinī (Dīgha Nikāya-aṭṭhakathā)
Sv-pṭ	Sumaṅgalavilāsinī-purāṇa-ṭīkā (Dīgha Nikāya-ṭīkā) (Be)
Th	Theragāthā
Th-a	Theragāthā-aṭṭhakathā
Thī	Therīgāthā
Thī-a	Therīgāthā-aṭṭhakathā (1998 ed.)
Ud	Udāna
Ud-a	Udāna-aṭṭhakathā
Vibh	Vibhaṅga
Vibh-a	Vibhaṅga-aṭṭhakathā (Sammohavinodanī)
Vibh-mṭ	Vibhaṅga-mūlaṭīkā (Be)
Vin	Vinaya
Vism	Visuddhimagga

Note: References to Pāli texts, unless specified otherwise, are to volume and page number of the PTS ed., with line numbers in reduced type. References to DN and MN, followed by No., are to the whole sutta; references to Ja followed by No. are to the whole story. Though references to the commentaries give volume and page numbers of the PTS ed., as the PTS eds. were not in every case available to me, I have sometimes had to determine these by conversion from Be or Ce through the PTS's *Pāli Aṭṭhakathā Correspondence Tables*. Page references to Vism are followed by the chapter and paragraph number of Ppn (see IV below).

III. Non-Pāli Texts

(see Bibliography, under author's name)

Abhidh-k-bh	Abhidharmakośabhāṣya (Pradhan)
Abhidh-k-vy	Sphuṭārtha Abhidharmakośavyākhyā (Wogihara)
Abhidh-sam-bh	Abhidharmasamuccayabhāṣya (Tatia)
Āps	Āyuṃparyantasūtra (Matsumura)
Avś	Avadānaśataka (Speyer)
Chandra Sū	Chandra Sūtra (Waldschmidt 1970)
CPS	Catuṣpariṣatsūtra (Waldschmidt 1952–62)
Divy	Divyāvadāna (Cowell and Neil)
G-Dhp	Gāndhārī Dharmapada (Brough)
MPS	Mahāparinirvāṇasūtra (Waldschmidt 1950–51)
MR	Manuscript Remains (Hoernle)
MSjSū	Mahāsamājasūtra (Waldschmidt 1980)
MSV	Mūla-sarvāstivāda-vinayavastu (Dutt)
Mvu	Mahāvastu (Senart)
P-Dhp	Patna Dharmapada (Cone, Roth; numbers as in Cone)
Saṅghabh	Saṅghabhedavastu (Gnoli)
SHT	Sanskrithandschriften aus den Turfanfunden (Waldschmidt 1965ff.)
Śrāv-bh	Śrāvakabhūmi (Shukla)
Uv	Udānavarga (Bernhard)
Ybhūś	Yogācārabhūmi Śarīrārthagāthā (Enomoto 1989)

IV. Translations

(see Bibliography, under author's name)

BL	Buddhist Legends (Burlingame)
CMA	A Comprehensive Manual of Abhidhamma (Bodhi)

EV I	Elders' Verses I (Norman)
EV II	Elders' Verses II (Norman)
GD	Group of Discourses II (Norman)
GermTr	Saṃyutta Nikāya, German translation (Geiger)
KS	Kindred Sayings (Rhys Davids, Woodward)
LDB	Long Discourses of the Buddha (Walshe)
MLDB	Middle Length Discourses of the Buddha (Ñāṇamoli)
Ppn	Path of Purification (Ñāṇamoli)
SN-Anth	Saṃyutta Nikāya: An Anthology (Ireland, Ñāṇananda, Walshe)

V. Reference Works

CPD	Critical Pāli Dictionary (Royal Danish Academy of Sciences & Letters)
CSCS	A Comprehensive Study of the Chinese Saṃyuktāgama (Enomoto)
DPPN	Dictionary of Pāli Proper Names (Malalasekera)
MW	Monier-Williams' Sanskrit-English Dictionary
PED	Pāli-English Dictionary (Pali Text Society)

VI. Other Abbreviations

BHS	Buddhist Hybrid Sanskrit
BPS	Buddhist Publication Society
C.Rh.D	C.A.F. Rhys Davids
PTS	Pali Text Society
Skt	Sanskrit
VĀT	Vanarata Ānanda Thera
n.	note
v.	verse
v.l.	variant reading
>	develops into, leads to
<	is derived from, corresponds to
*	word not listed in dictionary
[ ]	encloses page number of Ee
< >	encloses page number of Ee2 (SN Part I, 1998 ed.)

In the Introductions and Notes, textual references in bold are to suttas within this translation, either by sutta number (e.g., **6:10**) or by verse number (**v. 146**). Note numbers in bold (**n. 432**) are to notes on the translation. When one note refers to a note in the same part there is no preceding part number; when the reference is to a note in another part, the note number is preceded by the part number, also in bold (**II, n. 53**).

Pāli-English Glossary

This glossary consists mainly of important doctrinal terms. When a listed term has both doctrinal and ordinary meanings, only the former is given. Preference is given to nouns over cognate adjectives and verbs. Compounds are included only when their meaning is not immediately derivable from their members. Distinct meanings of a single term are indicated by an enumeration, with semicolons as separation; different renderings intended to capture distinct nuances of a word are separated by commas, without enumeration.

PALI	ENGLISH
akālika	immediate
akiñcana	one who owns nothing
akiriyavāda	doctrine of the inefficacy of action
akuppa	unshakable
akusala	unwholesome
agha	misery
aṅga	factor
accaya	transgression
ajjhattaṃ	internally
ajjhattika	internal
ajjhosāna	clamp
ajjhosāya	holding
añjali	reverential salutation (with palms joined and extended)
aññatitthiya	belonging to other sects (i.e., wanderers outside the Buddhist fold)
aññathābhāva	alteration

PALI	ENGLISH
aññathābhāvī	becoming otherwise
aññā	final knowledge (of arahantship)
aññāṇa	not knowing
atīta	past (time)
attakilamatha	self-mortification
attaniya	belonging to self
attabhāva	individual existence
attā	self
attānudiṭṭhi	view of self
attha	(1) good, benefit; (2) purpose, goal; (3) meaning
atthaṅgama	passing away
adinnādāna	taking what is not given
adukkhamasukha	neither-painful-nor-pleasant (feeling)
addhāna	course (of saṃsāra)
addhuva	unstable
adhigama	achievement
adhiccasamuppanna	fortuitously arisen
adhiṭṭhāna	standpoint
adhippayāsa	disparity
adhimuccati	to resolve upon, to be intent on
adhimutti	disposition
adhivacana	designation
anaññatha	not otherwise
anattā	nonself
anattha	harm
anapekha	indifferent
anabhāva	obliteration
anamatagga	without discernible beginning
anaya	calamity
anāgata	future
anāgariya	homelessness
anāgāmī	nonreturner
anālaya	nonreliance
anicca	impermanent
animitta	signless
anukampā	compassion, tender concern
anuttara	unsurpassed, unsurpassable

PALI	ENGLISH
anudayā	sympathy
anupassī	contemplating
anubyañjana	feature
anuyoga	pursuit
anusaya	underlying tendency
anusāsanā, anusāsanī	instruction
anuseti	to tend towards, to lie latent within, to underlie
anussava	oral tradition
aneja	unstirred
anottappa	fearlessness of wrongdoing
antaradhāna	disappearance
antarāya	obstacle
anvaya	inference
apāya	plane of misery
apuñña	demerit, demeritorious
apekha	anxious, concerned
appaṭivānī	unremittingness
appaṇihita	undirected
appatiṭṭhita	unestablished
appamatta	diligent
appamāṇa	measureless
appamāda	diligence
appameyya	immeasurable
appicchatā	fewness of wishes
appossukka	living at ease
abyākata	undeclared
abyāpāda	non-ill will
abhijānāti	to directly know
abhijjhā	covetousness
abhiññā	direct knowledge
abhinandati	to seek delight
abhinibbatti	production
abhinivesa	adherence
abhinīhāra	resolution
abhivadati	to welcome
abhisaṅkhata	generated (by volition)

Pali	English
abhisaṅkharoti	to generate (a volitional formation), to construct
abhisaṅkhāra	volitional formation
abhisañcetayita	fashioned by volition
abhisamaya	breakthrough
abhisameti	to break through to, to make a breakthrough
abhisambujjhati	to awaken to
abhisambuddha	awakened
amata	the Deathless
amanāpa	disagreeable
ayoniso	careless, carelessly
arahant	untranslated: a "worthy one," one fully liberated from all defilements
ariya	noble, a noble one
arūpa	formless (meditation or realm of existence)
avakkanti	descent
avassuta	corrupted
avijjā	ignorance
avitatha	unerring
avihiṃsā	harmlessness
aveccappasāda	confirmed confidence
asaṃsagga	aloofness from society
asaṅkhata	unconditioned
asubha	foul, foulness
asura	untranslated: a class of titanic beings in perpetual conflict with the devas
asekha	one beyond training (i.e., an arahant)
asmimāna	the conceit "I am"
assāda	gratification
assāsa-passāsa	in-breathing and out-breathing
ahaṅkāra	I-making
ahirika	shamelessness
ahetukavāda	doctrine of noncausality
ākāra	aspect, quality, reason
ākāsa	space

PALI	ENGLISH
ākāsānañcāyatana	base of the infinity of space
ākiñcañña	nothingness
ākiñcaññāyatana	base of nothingness
ājīva	livelihood
ātāpī	ardent
ādīnava	danger
ānāpāna	breathing
ānisaṃsā	benefit, advantage
āneñja	imperturbable
āpatti	offence
āpo	water
ābādha	affliction
ābhā	light
āyatana	base, sense base
āyatiṃ	future
āyu	life, life span, vitality
ārambha	arousal
ārammaṇa	(1) basis; (2) object (of meditation)
āruppa	formless attainment
ārogya	health
āloka	light
āvaraṇa	obstruction
āsava	taint
āhāra	nutriment
icchā	wish
itthatta	this state of being (i.e., individual existence as such)
idappaccayatā	specific conditionality
iddhi	spiritual power
iddhipāda	base for spiritual power
indriya	faculty (primarily the five spiritual faculties or the six sense faculties)
issā	envy
uttāsa	fright
udāna	inspired utterance
uddesa	synopsis

PALI	ENGLISH
uddhacca	restlessness
upakkilesa	corruption
upadhi	acquisition (as act or as object)
upanisā	proximate cause
upapatti	rebirth
upaya	engagement
upavicāra	examination
upasama	peace
upasampadā	(1) acquisition; (2) higher ordination (i.e., admission into the monastic order)
upādāna	clinging
upādāya	(1) derived from; (2) clinging to
upādisesa	residue (of clinging)
upāyāsa	despair
upāsaka	male lay follower
upāsikā	female lay follower
upekkhā	equanimity
uppāda	arising
ussoḷhi	enthusiasm
ekaggatā	one-pointedness
ekāyana	one-way
ekodibhāva	unification (of mind)
eja	stirring
esanā	search
ehipassika	inviting to come and see
okkanti	descent, entering upon
ogadha	grounded upon (suffix)
ogha	flood
ottappa	fear of wrongdoing
opanayika	applicable
opapātika	spontaneously reborn
oḷārika	gross
ovāda	exhortation
kaṅkhā	perplexity

Pali	English
kappa	aeon
kabaliṅkāra	edible food
kamma	(1) untranslated: morally determinate action; (2) action, deed
kammanta	action
karuṇā	compassion
kalyāṇa	good
kalla	pliant, pliancy
kāma	(1) sensual pleasure, sensuality; (2) desire; (3) sense-sphere (existence)
kāmaguṇa	cord of sensual pleasure
kāmasukhallika	sensual happiness
kāmesu micchācāra	sexual misconduct
kāya	(1) body, bodily; (2) class (of items)
kāruñña	compassion
kukkucca	remorse
kulaputta	clansman
kusīta	lazy
kevalī	consummate one
kodha	anger
kovida	skilled
khattiya	untranslated: a member of the warrior-administrative class (among the four social classes of Indian society)
khanti	(1) patience; (2) acquiescence, acceptance (of a view)
khandha	aggregate, mass
khaya	destruction
khila	barrenness
khema	security
gati	destination
gantha	knot (of mind)
gandha	odour
gandhabba	untranslated: a type of deity dwelling in trees and plants

Pali	English
gilānapaccaya-bhesajja-parikkhāra	medicinal requisites
gocara	range
ghāna	nose
cakka	wheel
cakkavattī	wheel-turning (monarch)
cakkhu	eye, vision
caṇḍāla	untranslated: an outcast
caraṇa	conduct, esp. good conduct
cāga	(1) giving up; (2) generosity
citta	mind
cintā	reflection
cīvara	robe
cuti	passing away
cetanā	volition
cetasika	mental
cetiya	shrine
ceteti	to intend
cetovimutti	liberation of mind
chanda	desire
chambhitatta	trepidation
jambudīpa	untranslated: "Rose-Apple Land," the Indian subcontinent
jarā	aging
jāgariya	wakefulness
jāti	birth
jivhā	tongue
jīva	soul
jīvita	life
jhāna	untranslated: a state of deep meditative concentration
jhāyī	a meditator

PALI	ENGLISH
ñāṇa	knowledge
ñāya	method
ṭhiti	maintenance, stability, continuation
taṇhā	craving
tatha	actual
tathatā	actuality
tathāgata	untranslated: an epithet of the Buddha (or more generally of any arahant) meaning "thus come one" or "thus gone one"
tapa	austerity
tapassī	ascetic
tasiṇā	thirst
tiracchānayoni	animal realm
tuccha	hollow
tuṇhībhāva	silence
tejo	heat
thīna	sloth
thera	elder (bhikkhu)
dama	taming, self-control
dara	anguish
dassana	vision, sight
dāna	(1) act of giving; (2) gift
diṭṭha	seen
diṭṭhadhammika	pertaining to the present life
diṭṭhi	view
diṭṭhe 'va dhamme	in this very life
dukkha	(1) suffering; (2) pain, painful (feeling)
duggata	miserable, unfortunate
duggati	bad destination
duccarita	misconduct
deva	untranslated: a deity, celestial being
devatā	untranslated: synonymous with deva
devaputta	a young deva

Pali	English
desanā	teaching (of the Dhamma)
domanassa	displeasure
dosa	hatred
dvaya	dyad
dhamma	(1) untranslated: the Buddha's teaching; (2) things, phenomena; (3) mental phenomena, (mental) states; (4) qualities; (5) principle, law; (6) as suffix: subject to, having the nature of
dhammānusārī	Dhamma-follower
dhammika	righteous
dhātu	element
dhuva	stable
nati	inclination
natthikavāda	nihilism
nandī	delight
nāga	untranslated: (1) a dragon; (2) a bull elephant; (3) metaphoric term for an arahant
nānatta	diversity
nānākaraṇa	difference
nāma	name (both literally and as a collective term for the basic cognitive functions)
nāmarūpa	name-and-form
nikāya	order (of beings)
nikkama	endeavour
nigha	trouble
nicca	permanent
nijjarā	wearing away
nijjhāna	pondering
nidāna	source
ninna	slanting towards (suffix)
nibbāna	untranslated: the extinction of all defilements and emancipation from the round of rebirths
nibbidā	revulsion

Pali	English
nibbuta	quenched
nibbedha	penetration
nibbedhika	penetrative
nimitta	(1) sign; (2) basis
niyata	fixed in destiny
niyāma	fixed order
niraya	hell
nirāmisa	spiritual (lit. noncarnal)
nirutti	language
nirodha	cessation
nissaraṇa	escape
nissita	based upon (suffix)
nīvaraṇa	hindrance
nekkhamma	renunciation
nepakka	discretion
n'evasaññānāsaññāyatana	base of neither-perception-nor-nonperception
paṃsukūla	rag-robe
pakappeti	to plan
paccattaṃ	personally
paccaya	condition
paccānubhoti	to experience
paccuppanna	present (time)
paccekabuddha	untranslated: "privately enlightened one," who awakens to the Four Noble Truths but does not communicate them to others
pajahati	to abandon
pajā	generation (i.e., the total order of living beings)
pajānāti	to understand
paññatti	description
paññā	wisdom
paññāpana	(1) describing; (2) manifestation
paññāvimutta	liberated by wisdom
paññāvimutti	liberation by wisdom
paṭikkūla	repulsive

PALI	ENGLISH
paṭigha	(1) (sensory) impingement; (2) aversion
paṭicca-samuppanna	dependently arisen
paṭicca-samuppāda	dependent origination
paṭinissagga	relinquishment
paṭipatti	practice
paṭipadā	way (of practice)
paṭipanna	practising
paṭibhāna	ingenuity
paṭivedha	penetration
paṭisaṃvedeti	to experience
paṭisallāna	seclusion
paṇidhi	wish
paṇīta	sublime, superior
paṇḍita	wise person
patiṭṭhā	support
patiṭṭhita	established
patti	attainment
patthanā	longing
pathavī	earth
pada	(1) term, sentence, passage, stanza; (2) step, footprint, track; (3) state
padhāna	striving
papañca	proliferation (as act)
papañcita	proliferation (as product)
pabbajita	one who has gone forth into homelessness
pabbajjā	"going forth" into homelessness, the Buddhist novice ordination
pabbhāra	inclining (suffix)
pabhāsa	luminosity
pamāda	negligence
parakkama	exertion
parāmāsa	grasping
parāyana	destination
parikkhāra	requisite, accessory
parijānāti	to fully understand
pariññā	full understanding
pariṇāmī	maturing in (suffix)

PALI	ENGLISH
paritassati	to be agitated
paritassanā	agitation
parideva	lamentation
parinibbāna	final Nibbāna
parinibbāyati	to attain (final) Nibbāna
parinibbuta	attained final Nibbāna, quenched
paribbājaka	(non-Buddhist) wanderer
pariyādāna	exhaustion
pariyādāya	obsessing
pariyāya	exposition, method (of exposition)
pariyesanā	quest
pariyosāna	goal, final goal
pariḷāha	fever, passion
parivitakka	reflection
parisā	assembly
parihāna	decline
paloka	disintegration
palokita	disintegrating
paviveka	solitude
pasāda	confidence
passaddhi	tranquillity, tranquillization
pahāna	abandoning, abandonment
pahitatta	resolute
pāṇa	living being
pāṇātipāta	destruction of life
pātimokkha	untranslated: the code of monastic rules
pātubhāva	manifestation
pāmojja	gladness
pāra	the far shore, the beyond
pāripūri	fulfilment
pārisuddhi	purification
piṇḍapāta	almsfood
pipāsa	thirst
pisuṇavācā	divisive speech
pīti	rapture
puggala	individual, person
puñña	merit, meritorious
puthujjana	worldling

Pali	English
punabbhava	renewed existence
pubbaṅgama	forerunner
pubbanimitta	precursor
pubbenivāsa	past abode (i.e., previous life)
purisa	person
pettivisaya	domain of ghosts
pema	affection, devotion
poṇa	sloping towards (suffix)
pharusavācā	harsh speech
phala	fruit
phassa	contact
phāsuvihāra	dwelling in comfort
phoṭṭhabba	tactile object
bandha	bond
bandhana	bondage
bala	power
bahiddhā	external, externally
bahujana	multitude (of people)
bahulīkaroti	to cultivate
bahussuta	learned
bāla	fool, foolish
bāhira	(1) external (sense bases); (2) outsider
buddha	(1) untranslated: honorific for Gotama; (2) an Enlightened One, enlightened
bodha	enlightenment
bodhisatta	untranslated: an aspirant for Buddhahood
byañjana	phrase
byantikaroti	to put an end to
byasana	disaster
byāpajjati	to be repelled by
byāpāda	ill will
byābādha	affliction
brahmacariya	holy life
brahmā	untranslated: a sublime deity of the brahmā world

Pali	English
bhagavā	the Blessed One
bhaya	fear
bhava	existence
bhāvanā	development
bhāveti	to develop
bhikkhu	untranslated: fully ordained Buddhist monk
bhikkhunī	untranslated: fully ordained Buddhist nun
bhiyyobhāva	increase
bhūmi	plane
magga	path
macchariya, macchera	selfishness
majjhima	middle, middling
maññanā	conceiving (as act)
maññita	conceiving (as product)
manasikāra	attention
manāpa	agreeable
manussa	human being
mano	mind, mental
manomaya	mind-made
mamaṅkāra	mine-making
maraṇa	death
marīcikā	mirage
mala	stain
mahaggata	exalted
mahābhūta	great element
mātugāma	womankind, a woman
māna	conceit
māyā	magic, magical illusion
micchatta	wrongness
micchā	wrong
middha	torpor
muṭṭhasati	unmindful
mutti	freedom
muditā	altruistic joy
musāvāda	false speech

PALI	ENGLISH
mūla	root
mettā	lovingkindness
moha	delusion
yakkha	untranslated: a spirit (usually malevolent)
yathābhūtaṃ	as it really is
yasa	fame, glory
yoga	(1) exertion; (2) bond, bondage
yogakkhema	security from bondage
yojana	untranslated: a measure of distance (appx. ten kilometres)
yoni	mode of generation
yoniso	careful, carefully
rasa	taste
rāga	lust
rittaka	void
ruci	personal preference
rūpa	(1) form (i.e., materiality); (2) form (i.e., visible object); (3) form-sphere (existence)
lābha	gain
loka	world
lokuttara	supramundane
lomahaṃsa	terror
vacī	verbal
vaṭṭa	round (of existence)
vaṇṇa	(1) beauty; (2) praise
vata	vow (as vowed observance)
vaya	vanishing
vācā	speech
vāda	doctrine
vāyāma	effort
vāyo	air
vikkhitta	distracted

PALI	ENGLISH
vighāta	vexation
vicaya	discrimination
vicāra	examination
vicikicchā	doubt
vijānāti	to cognize
vijjā	true knowledge
viññāṇa	consciousness
viññāṇañcāyatana	base of the infinity of consciousness
viññū	wise person
vitakka	thought
vidhā	discrimination
vinaya	(1) discipline; (2) removal
vinipāta	nether world
vinibandha	shackle
vinīta	disciplined
vinodeti	to dispel
vipaṭisāra	regret
vipariṇāma	change
vipassanā	insight
vipāka	result (of kamma)
vibhava	extermination
vimati	uncertainty
vimutti	liberation
vimokkha	deliverance
virāga	(1) dispassion; (2) fading away
viriya	energy
virūḷhi	increase
vivaṭṭa	world-expansion
viveka	seclusion
visaya	domain
visuddhi	purification
visesa	distinction
vihāra	dwelling
vihiṃsā	harmfulness
vīmaṃsā	investigation
vuṭṭhāna	emergence
vuddhi	growth
vūpakaṭṭha	withdrawn

Pali	English
vūpasama	subsiding
vedanā	feeling
vedayita	feeling, what is felt
vepulla	expansion
vera	animosity
veramaṇī	abstinence
vesārajja	ground of self-confidence
vodāna	cleansing
vossagga	release
vy- = *by-*	
saṃyama	self-control
saṃyoga	bondage
saṃyojana	fetter
saṃvaṭṭa	world-contraction
saṃvara	restraint
saṃvega	sense of urgency
saṃsāra	untranslated: the beginningless round of rebirths
sakadāgāmī	once-returner
sakkāya	identity
sakkāra	honour
sagārava	reverential
sagga	heaven, heavenly
saṅkappa	intention
saṅkilesa	defilement
saṅkhaya	extinction
saṅkhā	term, reckoning
saṅkhāra	(1) volitional formation; (2) formation; (3) exertion
saṅkhitta	contracted (of mind)
saṅgha	untranslated: (1) as *bhikkhusaṅgha*, the Buddhist monastic order; (2) as *sāvakasaṅgha*, the community of noble disciples, i.e., those who have reached the four paths and fruits of awakening
sacchikiriya	realization
sañcetanā	volition

Pali	English
sañjānāti	to perceive
saññā	perception
sati	mindfulness
satipaṭṭhāna	establishment of mindfulness
satta	a being
satthā	teacher
sadda	sound
saddhamma	the true Dhamma
saddhā	faith
saddhānusārī	faith-follower
santuṭṭhi	contentment
sandiṭṭhika	directly visible
sappaṭissa	deferential
sappurisa	superior person
sabba	all
samaṇa	ascetic
samatikkama	transcendence
samatha	serenity
samanupassanā	way of regarding
samādhi	concentration
samāpatti	attainment
samāhita	concentrated
samugghāta	uprooting
samudaya	origin, origination, arising
sampajañña	clear comprehension
sampajāna	clearly comprehending
samparāyika	pertaining to the future life
sampasādana	confidence
samphappalāpa	idle chatter
samphassa	contact
sambuddha	enlightened
sambojjhaṅga	factor of enlightenment
sambodha, sambodhi	enlightenment
sambhava	origination
sammatta	rightness
sammasa	exploration
sammā	right, correct, perfectly
sammosa	decay

Pali	English
saraṇa	refuge
sarīra	body
saḷāyatana	six sense bases
sassata	eternal
sāta	comfort, comfortable
sātacca	perseverance
sāmisa	carnal
sāra	substance, core
sārāga	infatuation
sāvaka	disciple
sāsava	tainted
sikkhā	training
sikkhāpada	training rule
siloka	praise
sīla	(1) virtue; (2) precept, rule
sīlabbata	rules and vows
sīlavā	virtuous
sukha	(1) happiness; (2) pleasure, pleasant (feeling)
sukhuma	subtle
sugata	(1) fortunate; (2) the Fortunate One (epithet of the Buddha)
sugati	good destination
sucarita	good conduct
suñña	empty
suññatā	emptiness
suta	learning
suddhi	purity
supaṇṇa	untranslated: a supernatural bird of prey, arch-enemy of the nāgas
subha	beauty, beautiful
sekha	trainee
senāsana	lodging
soka	sorrow
sota	(1) ear; (2) stream (of the Dhamma)
sotāpatti	stream-entry
sotāpanna	stream-enterer
somanassa	joy

Pali	English
hita	welfare
hiri	sense of shame
hīna	low, inferior
hetu	cause; because of (as suffix)

Index of Subjects

This index lists significant references only. Italicized numbers refer to page numbers of an Introduction (general or part). References may be listed under an entry even when the term itself does not appear in the text, as long as the passage is pertinent to the term of entry; for example, passages expressed by way of form, feeling, perception, volitional formations, and consciousness are listed under "Aggregates," even though the word "aggregates" may not occur in them. When a stock formulation is applied to each term in a set of categories, the reference is given only under the name of the set, not under the individual members of that set; an exception is made when these items are singled out for special treatment. Pāli equivalents are provided for all key doctrinal terms. Usually the Pāli term is given in the singular, though the English equivalent may be a plural. When two Pāli technical terms are rendered by a single English word, the two are listed as separate entries. Thus "Desire" is listed twice, corresponding to *chanda* and *icchā*.

Index of Proper Names

Index of Similes

Index of Pāli Terms Discussed in the Introduction and Notes

Substantives are given in the stem form unless the inflected form is idiomatic or otherwise essential to the instance discussed in the relevant note. When a note discusses a term for which there are several variants, the term is usually indexed under the reading that seems most probable.

About Wisdom Publications

Wisdom Publications is dedicated to offering works relating to and inspired by Buddhist traditions.

To learn more about us or to explore our other books, please visit our website at www.wisdompubs.org. You can subscribe to our e-newsletter or request our print catalog online, or by writing to:

Wisdom Publications
199 Elm Street
Somerville, Massachusetts 02144 USA

You can also contact us at 617-776-7416, or info@wisdompub.org.

Wisdom is a nonprofit, charitable 501(c)(3) organization, and donations in support of our mission are tax deductible.

Wisdom Publications is affiliated with the Foundation for the Preservation of the Mahayana Tradition (FPMT).